October 15–19, 2016
Amsterdam, The Netherlands

Association for Computing Machinery

Advancing Computing as a Science & Profession

MM'16

Proceedings of the 2016 ACM Multimedia Conference

Sponsored by:

ACM SIGMM

Supported by:

Qualcomm Research, FXPal, COMMIT, IBM, Facebook, Microsoft Research, Google, Unified Streaming Platform, & ViSENZE

Association for
Computing Machinery

Advancing Computing as a Science & Profession

The Association for Computing Machinery
2 Penn Plaza, Suite 701
New York, New York 10121-0701

ISBN: 978-1-4503-3603-1 (Digital)

ISBN: 978-1-4503-4684-9 (Print)

Additional copies may be ordered prepaid from:

ACM Order Department
PO Box 30777
New York, NY 10087-0777, USA

Phone: 1-800-342-6626 (USA and Canada)
+1-212-626-0500 (Global)
Fax: +1-212-944-1318
E-mail: acmhelp@acm.org
Hours of Operation: 8:30 am – 4:30 pm ET

Printed in the USA

ACM Multimedia 2016 Chairs' Welcome

We warmheartedly welcome you to the 24th ACM Multimedia conference, which is hosted for the first time in the Netherlands, in the wonderful city of Amsterdam. ACM Multimedia 2016 brings an extensive program consisting of technical sessions covering all aspects of the multimedia field in the form of oral and poster presentations, tutorials, panels, exhibits, demonstrations and workshops, bringing into focus the principal subjects of investigation, competitions of research teams on challenging problems, and an interactive art program stimulating artists and computer scientists to meet and discover together the frontiers of artistic communication. The call for contributions attracted submissions from all over the world, which were all thoroughly reviewed for their merit in terms of scientific quality, innovation, and match to the conference. In summary, the various dedicated program committees reviewed and accepted the following:

Track	*Reviewed*	*Accepted*	
Long papers	237	52	22%
Short papers	413	127	31%
Brave new idea papers	14	4	29%
Demos	54	31	57%
Doctoral symposium papers	14	9	64%
Multimedia grand challenge submissions	20	12	60%
Video demonstrations	3	3	100%
Open source competition submissions	22	16	73%
Interactive art papers	23	10	43%

In addition to these, the main program has two exciting keynote presentations, by **Dirk Helbing** from ETH Zurich, Switzerland, titled "A digital world to thrive in – How the Internet of Things can make the ‚invisible hand' work" and by **Jack van Wijk** from Eindhoven University of Technology, the Netherlands, titled "Visual Analytics for Multimedia: Challenges and Opportunities". Furthermore, a visionary presentation will be given by the winner of the SIGMM Award for Outstanding Technical Contributions to Multimedia Computing, Communications and Applications 2016, **Alberto del Bimbo**, from the University of Florence, Italy. The main program will conclude with the SIGMM Rising Stars Symposium, highlighting the scientific results and vision of the invited young researchers, who demonstrated great potential in multimedia research and who are considered to become future leaders in the multimedia field.

The main program is accompanied by eight workshops to discuss challenging topics and six tutorials to bring you up to speed on important foundations of our multimedia field. The unique co-location of ACM Multimedia 2016 with the European Conference on Computer Vision (ECCV 2016) has brought the opportunity to have additional twelve invited tutorials from world leaders covering both multimedia and computer vision.

Putting together a conference like ACM Multimedia is a team effort with many people volunteering their precious time. We would like to thank all who contributed to making this year's conference a success: the authors for submitting their latest work, the chairs and reviewers of the various tracks and activities for realizing a high quality program, and all others who assured smooth organization and realization of the conference. Finally, we would like to thank our sponsors and supporters, SIGMM, University of Amsterdam, Delft University of Technology, Qualcomm Research, FxPal, COMMIT, Facebook, Microsoft, Google, Unified Streaming, IBM and ViSenze for allowing us to bring you more than just the scientific program.

ACM Multimedia 2016 General Chairs

Alan Hanjalic
Delft University of Technology

Cees Snoek
Qualcomm Research & University of Amsterdam

Marcel Worring
University of Amsterdam

Message from the Program Coordinator

I am very happy to welcome you to Amsterdam for Multimedia 2016. This is the 24th edition of what can be considered as the premier academic conference on multimedia systems, content and applications.

The conference general and technical program chairs have given a wealth of information on the nature, structure and process used to assemble the program that will unfold this week. I, too, would like to add a few comments to help participants better understand the nature of the sessions and the combination of program elements that we hope will serve as the basis of an inspiring visit.

There are always two broad audiences for the collections of papers presented as part of the ACM Multimedia series. First are researchers who access individual papers via the ACM Digital Library. Over the coming years, this is where the greatest impact of the contributions presented here is likely to manifest itself. The Technical Program Committee has done an excellent job in providing a corpus of research that reflects the current state of the various sub-disciplines covered at the conference. As a Program Coordinator, I have little influence on the selection of these papers: this is the work of the reviewers, various area chairs and the technical program committee chairs.

The second audience for this year's papers, posters and presentations are the attendees of the conference in Amsterdam. These people come to the conference not only to hear the latest individual research results – this is something that they can do more quickly and cheaply via the ACM DL! – but also to be inspired by work that is perhaps (just) outside their own areas of expertise. Here, the Program Coordinator has the responsibility to 'package' the papers at the conference in a way that makes new work available to as many people as possible while also maintaining the community bonds within our various historical and emerging interests groups.

This year, the conference program has been architected so that each session block contains a *Topics in Multimedia* session, along with three more specialized special-interest sessions. The *Topics* session contains a collection of papers from different disciplines but often on (somewhat) related topics. The specialized sessions allow members of particular groups to interact more directly. In this way, there should always be a session of interest (either in breadth or depth) to capture the imagination of the participant. We hope that you find this approach useful and inspiring.

Another responsibility of the Program Coordinator is to coordinate the selection of the best paper at the conference. This year, the program committee nominated eight candidate papers. A second committee was formed (using recommendations from the technical program chairs) that selected four of these papers as candidates for the award at the conference. This was a particularly difficult task, as the quality of each of the candidates was very high. Since ACM Multimedia is a generalist conference, we used this as a guide in the ultimate selection. I encourage you to attend the best paper session to see this broad sampling of first-class research in our community.

Coming to a conference is an expense and time-consuming venture, but I hope that the work of all of the members of our community who volunteered to put together ACM Multimedia 2016 will inspire your own research, allow you to make new contacts and help us all advance the quality of our fields.

Dick C.A. Bulterman, *CWI and Vrije Universiteit Amsterdam*

Message from the Technical Program Chairs

We are pleased to introduce to you to the Technical Program for the ACM International Conference on Multimedia (ACM Multimedia) 2016, which will take place in Amsterdam in October 2016. While adopting the best practices from previous ACM Multimedia conferences, this year we also introduced new approaches and guidelines in the review process to ensure an efficient and fair evaluation of all submissions in providing a high quality conference.

Following last year's structure, fifteen areas of interest were grouped into four research themes, including a System Theme (covering Multimedia Transport and Delivery, Multimedia Systems and Middleware, Multimedia Telepresence and Virtual/Augmented Reality, Multimedia Scalability and Management, Mobile Multimedia), an Experience Theme (covering Multimedia HCI and Quality of Experience, Music, Speech and Audio Processing in Multimedia, Multimedia Art, Entertainment and Culture, Multimedia for Collaboration in Education & Distributed Environments), an Understanding Theme (covering Deep Learning for Multimedia, Multimodal Analysis and Description, Multimedia and Vision), and an Engagement Theme (covering Emotional and Social Signals In Multimedia, Social Multimedia, Multimedia Search and Recommendation). Minor changes compared to last year's structure included moving the Multimedia Art area from the Engagement to the Experience theme and the addition of the Multimedia Scalability and Management area within the System's theme.

Among the noticeable changes for ACM Multimedia 2016 is the addition of a fifth page (reserved for citations) for the short papers, demos, grand challenge and open source software competitions, doctoral symposium, and interactive art submissions. Additionally, long paper submissions can range from 8 to 10 pages, with the minimum page length introduced this year.

Each research theme was overseen by one of this year's Technical Program Chairs. For each area of interest, a team of Area Chairs (ACs), ranging from one to eight members, was recruited to handle the paper review process. In total, 46 ACs were appointed. A new contribution this year was the preparation of detailed instructions for ACs and reviewers, describing each step of the process and an accompanying time schedule. Organizationally, we believe it helped ACs and reviewers with overall planning logistics and time management. It is suggested that this process should be updated and used as a standard practice in future conferences. The second innovation this year was the use of the Toronto Paper Matching System (TPMS) for paper-reviewer assignment. This system has gained adoption in both machine learning and computer vision conferences and is being used, for example by CVPR, ICCV and ECCV. The TPMS worked in conjunction with the conference management system (CMT), whereby invited reviewers uploaded their own papers for analysis as part of the automatic assignment process. Overall, the matching system provided reasonably reliable results in most cases, but required close supervision and tweaking by the technical program chairs, to avoid issues such as reviewers from one area being allocated papers from another. The conference ACs played an important role here also in

The paper review and submission is described in detail below:

- Submission of full (abstract pre-submission was allowed for better review planning) and short papers were separated from each other, with the short paper submission deadline one month later than the deadline for full paper submissions.
- Following the previous year's approach, a two-stage review process for full paper submissions was applied. Authors were invited to submit a rebuttal based on the first round of reviews. The reviewers were then asked to consider the rebuttal, to revise their reviews accordingly, and to enter discussion with other reviewers with the aim of improving review consensus on each paper. The results of the second round reviews and discussions were then summarized by the ACs into meta-reviews, which included tentative recommendations, to be discussed and finalized during the TPC meeting.
- In the second review stage, authors had the opportunity to communicate with the Author's Advocate if they believed there were issues or anomalies with the reviews. During this year's review cycle, the Author's Advocate was utilized in several cases to ensure a more equitable and satisfying review procedure.

- Submissions from any authors who also acted as ACs/TPCs were handled personally by non-conflicting Technical Program Chairs.
- Deadlines were predominantly adhered to, with minor delays on occasion.

In total, 248 full and 425 short paper submissions were received by their respective deadlines and entered into the regular review process.

The table below gives the exact submission numbers across the various research areas

Area	Full	Short
Emotional and Social Signals In Multimedia	7	26
Multimedia Search and Recommendation	41	52
Social Multimedia	16	19
Multimedia Art, Entertainment and Culture	9	7
Multimedia for Collaboration in Education & Distributed Environments	2	3
Multimedia HCI and Quality of Experience	12	21
Music, Speech and Audio Processing in Multimedia	8	17
Mobile Multimedia	6	12
Multimedia Scalability and Management	5	5
Multimedia Systems and Middleware	13	12
Multimedia Telepresence and Virtual/Augmented Reality	10	12
Multimedia Transport and Delivery	17	10
Deep Learning for Multimedia	20	57
Multimedia and Vision	45	125
Multimodal Analysis and Description	26	35

Decisions on full and short paper acceptances were made at the one-day TPC meeting held at Columbia University on June 10, 2016. All four Technical Program Chairs attended the meeting and handled their assigned themes in different allocated rooms. The emphasis of the TPC meeting was on high-score, borderline, and controversial paper submissions. The discussions were detailed and intensive, taking into account all the available data, including reviews, the authors' rebuttals, the post-rebuttal discussions, the initial recommendations by the ACs (in the form of a meta-review) and any subsequent reviews performed by other ACs during the meeting itself. For some papers that span across multiple themes, the TPC/AC Chairs collaborate across theme to reach a consensus on the decision. Technical Program Chairs and ACs were requested to leave the room when a conflicting submission was discussed.

After the separate meetings, a plenary session coordinated by the TPCs took place to make final decisions, where the overall quality and balance of different tracks was taken into consideration. By the end of the day, the participants accepted 52 full and 127 short papers, leading to acceptance rates of 22.2% and 30.3% for full and short papers, respectively. Five high quality full paper submissions were also recommended for acceptance as short papers.

The TPC meeting was organized in conjunction with a supporting workshop as per previous years. This years' workshop (http://acmmmtpcws16.eurecom.fr/) was integrated with the ICMR conference which also took place in New York in June. Workshop participants had the chance to listen to 13 enlightening talks about recent research developments from the entire spectrum of topics covered by ACM Multimedia.

The Technical Program Committee has worked diligently over the last year to ensure that the technical program of this year's conference is of the highest possible quality. We would like to recognize the great effort and hard work from the volunteer team of ACs and reviewers who helped shape an exciting technical program.

We look forward to seeing you this autumn, in Amsterdam, Netherlands for a compelling ACM Multimedia technical program.

Benoit Huet, *EURECOM (FR)*

Yiannis Kompatsiaris, *CERTH-ITI (GR)*

Aisling Kelliher, *Virginia Tech (USA)*

Jin Li, *Microsoft (USA)*

Table of Contents

Session: Video Program

Demonstrations

Session: Art Exhibition

Session: Topics in Multimedia I

Session: Analysis & Search

Session: Video Analysis & Streaming

Session: Topics in Multimedia II

Session: Brave News Topic

Session: Deep Learning

Session: Events and Context

Session: Multimedia Grand Challenge..........

Session: Keynote 2

Session: Topics in Multimedia III

Session: Open Source Software Competition

Session: Learning & Hashing

Session: Transport & Experience

Session: Tutorials

Session: Workshops

MM 2016 Conference Organization

General Chairs:	Alan Hanjalic *(Delft University of Technology)* Cees Snoek *(Qualcomm Research Netherlands / University of Amsterdam)* Marcel Worring *(University of Amsterdam)*
Honorary Chair:	Arnold Smeulders *(University of Amsterdam)*
Program Coordinator:	Dick Bulterman *(CWI / VU University Amsterdam)*
Program Chairs:	Benoit Huet *(EURECOM)* Aisling Kelliher *(Virginia Tech)* Yiannis Kompatsiaris *(CERTH-ITI)* Jin Li *(Microsoft)*
Local Arrangements Chairs:	Hayley Hung *(Delft University of Technology)* Cynthia Liem *(Delft University of Technology)*
Author's Advocate:	Shervin Shirmohammadi *(University of Ottawa)*
Workshop Chairs:	Lexing Xie *(Australian National University)* Alan Smeaton *(Dublin City University)*
Brave New Idea Chairs:	Martha Larson *(Delft University of Technology / Radboud University Nijmegen)* Hari Sundaram *(University of Illinois)*
Tutorial Chairs:	Rita Cucchiara *(University of Modena)* Susanne Boll *(University of Oldenburg)*
Doctoral Symposium Chairs:	Winston Hsu *(National Taiwan University & IBM TJ Watson)* Eckehard Steinbach *(Technische Universität München)*
Panel Chairs:	Alberto Del Bimbo *(University of Florence)* David Shamma *(Yahoo Labs)*
Multimedia Grand Challenge Chairs:	Xavier Anguera *(ELSA Corp.)* Shuicheng Yan *(Qihoo 360 & NUS)*
Demo Chairs:	Pablo Cesar *(CWI)* Max Mühlhäuser *(Technische Universität Darmstadt)*
Open Source Competition Chairs:	Tao Mei *(Microsoft Research Asia)* Christian Timmerer *(Alpen-Adria-Universität Klagenfurt)*

Travel Grant Chairs: Wessel Kraaij *(Radboud University Nijmegen / TNO)*
Remco Veltkamp *(Utrecht University)*

Video Chairs: Marco Bertini *(University of Florence)*
Shin'ichi Satoh *(University of Tokyo)*

Interactive Arts Chairs: Lucas Evers *(Waag Society)*
Frank Nack *(University of Amsterdam)*

Sponsor Chairs: Touradj Ebrahimi *(EPFL)*
Gerald Friedland *(ICSI)*

Publicity Chairs: Carsten Griwodz *(University of Oslo)*
Meng Wang *(Hefei University of Technology)*

Publication Chairs: Chong-Wah Ngo *(City University of Hong Kong)*
Balakrishnan Prabhakaran *(University of Texas at Dallas)*

Web Chairs: Stevan Rudinac *(University of Amsterdam)*
Pascal Mettes *(University of Amsterdam)*

History Preservation Chairs: Yong Rui *(Microsoft Research Asia)*
Heng Tao Shen *(University of Queensland)*

MM 2016 Area Chairs

Emotional and Social Signals in Multimedia:	Julien Epps *(University of New South Wales)* Mohammad Soleymani *(University of Geneva)* Jean-Marc Odobez *(IDIAP)*
Multimedia Search and Recommendation:	Joemon Jose *(Glasgow)* Stéphane Marchand-Maillet *(UNIGE)* Michele Merler *(IBM TJ Watson Research Center)* Muriel Visani *(University of La Rochelle)* Zheng-Jun Zha *(University of Science and Technology of China)*
Social Multimedia:	Luca Maria Aiello *(Yahoo Labs, London, UK)* Symeon Papadopoulos *(CERTH-ITI)* Jonathon Hare *(University of Southampton)*
Multimedia Art, Entertainment and Culture:	Jinsil Hwaryoung Seo *(Simon Fraser)* David Ayman Shamma *(Yahoo)*
Multimedia for Collaboration in Education & Distributed Environments:	Matt Cooper *(FXPAL)*
Multimedia HCI and Quality of Experience:	Teresa Chambel *(Lisbon University)* Judith Redi *(Delft)* Bart Thomee *(Yahoo)*
Music, Speech and Audio Processing in Multimedia:	Brian Pardo *(Northwestern)*
Mobile Multimedia:	Winston Hsu *(National Taiwan University, Taiwan)* Jochen Huber *(MIT Media Lab, USA)*
Multimedia Scalability and Management System:	Xiansheng Hua *(Alibaba, China)* Lei Zhang *(Microsoft, USA)*
Multimedia Systems and Middleware:	Jiangchuan Liu *(Simon Fraser University, Canada)* Wenwu Zhu *(Tsinghua University, China)* Roger Zimmerman *(NUS, Singapore)*
Multimedia Telepresence and Virtual/Augmented Reality:	Pablo Cesar *(CWI)* Zicheng Liu *(Microsoft, USA)*
Multimedia Transport and Delivery:	Ali Begen *(CISCO, USA)* Christian Timmerer *(Alpen-Adria-Universität Klagenfurt, Austria)*

Deep Learning for Multimedia: Ed Chang *(HTC)*
Guo-Jun Qi *(University of Central Florida)*
Elisa Ricci *(FBK Trento)*
Efstratios Gavves *(University of Amsterdam)*
Fiona Yan Liu *(Hong Kong Polytechnic University)*

Multimedia and Vision: Francois Bremond *(INRIA)*
Wen-Huang Cheng *(Academia Sinica)*
Xavier Giró-i-Nieto *(Universitat Politècnica de Catalunya)*
Yu-Gang Jiang *(Fudan)*
Noel O'Connor *(DCU)*
Maja Pantic *(Imperial College)*
Qi Tian *(University of Texas at San Antonio)*
Concetto Spampinato *(Uni Catania)*

Multimodal Analysis and Description: Guillaume Gravier *(IRISA)*
Alex Hauptmann *(CMU)*
Ichiro Ide *(Nagoya University)*
Sofia Tsekeridou *(Intrasoft International)*

MM 2016 Program Committee

Luca Maria Aiello
Ergun Akleman
Xavier Alameda Pineda
Kevin Almeroth
Jose M Alvarez
Joseph Antony
Ahsan Arefin
Grenville Armitage
Yannis Avrithis
Slawomir Bak
Saeideh Bakhshi
Prabhakaran Balakrishnan
Lamberto Ballan
Tadas Baltrusaitis
Jean-Charles Bazin
Alejandro Bellogin
Jenny Benois-Pineau
Marco Bertini
Laurent Besacier
Chidansh Bhatt
Piotr Bilinski
Arijit Biswas
Isabelle Bloch
Tom Blount
Giulia Boato
Marc Bolanos
Egor Bondarev
Fernando Boronat Seguí
Damian Borth
Alessandro Bozzon
Herve Bredin
Andrei Bursuc
Junjie Cai
Jianfei Cai
Simone Calderara
Cristian Canton
Liangliang Cao
Kristin Carlson
Mark Cartwright
Carlos Castellanos
Andrea Cavallaro
Shayok Chakraborty
Houssem Chatbri
Faouzi Cheikh
Huizhong Chen
Kuan-Ta Chen
KuanTing Chen
Shu-Ching Chen
Songqing Chen
Yung-Yao Chen
Gong Chen
Jia Chen
Jun-Cheng Chen
Yan-Ying Chen
Hsu-Yung Cheng
Jian Cheng
Mohamed Chetouani
Liang-Tien Chia
Jason Chou
Wei-Ta Chu
Yung-Yu Chuang
Adrian Clark
Cyril Concolato
Greg Corness
Nuno Correia
Marco Cristani
Peng Cui
Yong Cui
Dubravko Culibrk
Ricardo da Silva Torres
Petros Daras
Claire-Helene Demarty
Cheng Deng
Om Deshmukh
Niloo Dezfuli
Mariella Dimiccoli
Keisuke Doman
Jean-Philippe Domenger
Zhiyao Duan
Carlos Duarte
Stefan Duffner
Jean-Claude Dufourd
Pinar Duygulu-Sahin
Sebastian Egger
Peter Eisert
Tahra Eissa
Abdulmotaleb El Saddik
Sebastian Ewert
Philipp Fechteler
Jie Feng
Wu-Chi Feng
Marcio Ferreira Moreno
Robert Fisher
Manuel Fonseca
Jason Freeman
Gerald Friedland
Pascal Frossard
Takuya Funatomi
Philip Galanter
Andrew Gallagher
Chuang Gan
Debasis Ganguly
Marie-Neige Garcia
Antonis Gasteratos
Kirill Gavrilyuk
George Ghinea
Andreas Girgensohn
Roland Goecke
Mar Gonzalez-Franco
Jordi Gonzàlez
Fabien Gouyon
Costantino Grana
Carsten Griwodz
Zhouye Gu
Ling Guan
Charlie Gullström
Yandong Guo

Michael Gurevich
Cathal Gurrin
Michael Gygli
Martin Halvey
Pal Halvorsen
Bill Hamilton
Yahong Han
Frank Hartung
Mohamed Hefeeda
Hermann Hellwagner
Niels Henze
Keita Higuchi
Keiichiro Hoashi
Richang Hong
Frank Hopfgartner
Ehsan Hoque
Timothy Hospedales
Tobias Hossfeld
Cheng-Hsin Hsu
Min-Chun Hu
Qinghua Hu
Kai-Lung Hua
Zixia Huang
LiangKang Huang
Noureldien Hussein
Wolfgang Hürst
James Ivory
Ebroul Izquierdo
Jack Jansen
Iveel Jargalsaikhan
Morgan Jenks
I-Hong Jhuo
Rongrong Ji
Lu Jiang
shuqiang Jiang
Cheng Jin
Alexis Joly
Dhiraj Joshi
Bhautik Joshi
Brendan Jou
Rene Kaiser
Yannis Kalantidis
Sebastian Kaltwang
Eunsu Kang
Li-Wei Kang
Rafal Kapela
Svebor Karaman
Marie Katsurai
Isaak Kavasidis
Ian Kegel
Christian Keimel
Aisling Kelliher
John Kender
Sara Kepplinger
Hua Kien
Ewa Kijak
Yelin Kim
Bongjun Kim
Akisato Kimura
Hill Kobayashi
Dorothea Kolossa
Stephan Kopf
Pavel Korshunov
Joke Kort
Dimitrios Kosmopoulos
Iaroslav Kryvyi
Fons Kuijk
Gauthier Lafruit
Rodrigo Laiola Guimaraes
Agata Lapedriza
Duy-Dinh Le
Thi-Lan Le
Jonathan Le Roux
Gwénolé Lecorvé
Hyun Jean Lee
Jin Ha Lee
Vincent Lemaire
Baochun Li
Xinchao Li
Zhu Li
Kai Li
Bochen Li
Haojie Li
Xi Li
Yen Liang
Miao Liao
Cynthia Liem
Weisi Lin
Georges Linares
Rhema Linder
Dimitris Liparas
Suzanne Little
Dong Liu
Fangming Liu
Xueliang Liu
Hantao Liu
Jing Liu
Si Liu
Xiang Liu
Zhen Liu
Xiaobai Liu
Antoine Liutkus
Josep Llados
Joan Llobera
Yijuan Lu
Jiwen Lu
Hanqing Lu
Jiebo Luo
Minnan Luo
Mathias Lux
Kevin Ma
Joao Magalhaes
Marwa Mahmoud
Diego Maranan
Mark Marsden
Jean Martinet
Maria Martini
Saverio Mascolo
Masoud Mazloom
Chris McCool
Philip McParlane
Andrew McPherson
Tao Mei

Britta Meixner
Rufael Mekuria
Angeliki Metallinou
Vasileios Mezaris
Eva Mohedano
Mario Montagud
Sean Moran
Francesc Moreno-Noguer
Vicki Moulder
Emily Mower Provost
Francesca Murabito
Niall Murray
Klara Nahrstedt
Yuta Nakashima
Ryohei Nakatsu
Manish Narwaria
Edith Ngai
Laurent Nguyen
Rongrong Ni
Eric Nichols
Liqiang Nie
Marcos Nieto
Nikolaos Nikolaidis
Kuo Nini
Masafumi Nishida
Naoko Nitta
Neil O'Hare
Jean-Marc Ogier
Hiroaki Ohshima
Wei Tsang Ooi
Jörg Ott
Simone Palazzo
Pan Pan
Ioannis Panagakis
Nikolaos Papamarkos
Frederic Parke
Omkar Parkhi
Jose Luis Patino Vilchis
Ioannis Patras
Amy Pavel
George Pavlidis
Yuxin Peng
Giorgos Petkos
Stavros Petridis
Julien Pinquier
Hamed Pirsiavash
Fatemeh Pishdadian
Adrian Popescu
Ronald Poppe
Gerasimos Potamianos
Ioannis Pratikakis
Nicholas Race
Zafar Rafii
Benjamin Rainer
Miriam Redi
Gael Richard
Fabien Ringeval
George Rizos
Edgar Roman-Rangel
Samuel Rota-Bulò
Ognjen Rudovic
Javier Ruiz
Enrico Rukzio
Tom Runia
Andreas Sackl
Diego Saez Trumper
Alan Said
Albert Salah
Amaia Salvador
Juan-Carlos SanMiguel
Nabil Sarhan
Shin'ichi Satoh
Peter Schelkens
Manos Schinas
Marwin Schmitt
Klaus Schoeffmann
Bjoern Schuller
Florence Sedes
Prem Seetharaman
Shiguang Shan
Ling Shao
James She
Koichi Shinoda
Frank Shipman
Shervin Shirmohammadi
Hong-Han Shuai
Behjat Siddiquie
Stefan Siersdorfer
Gwendal Simon
Vivek Singh
Sudipta Sinha
Mats Sjoberg
Malcolm Slaney
Nasim Souly
Eleftherios Spyromitros-Xioufis
Ryan Stables
Jacopo Staiano
Vladimir Stankovic
Eckehard Steinbach
Thomas Steiner
Ralf Steinmetz
Ramanathan Subramanian
Chen Sun
Lifeng Sun
Jinhui Tang
Anastasios Tefas
Jelena Tesic
Xinmei Tian
Yonghong Tian
Steve Tjoa
Michele Trevisiol
Remi Trichet
Andrew Tryba
Chun-Yu Tsai
Sam Tsai
Jeremy Turner
Rosario Uceda-Sosa
Jasper Uijlings
Luis Unzueta
Thierry Urruty
Yoshitaka Ushiku
Peter Vajda
Michel Valstar

Radu Vatavu
Vladan Velisavljevic
Carles Ventura
Tuomas Virtanen
Stefanos Vrochidis
Feng Wang
Meng Wang
Yang Wang
Yao Wang
Zhangyang Wang
Zhi Wang
Xialong Wang
Chen Wang
Ye Wang
Zhaowen Wang
Yonggang Wen
Bo Wu
Chuan Wu
Xiao Wu
Gangshan Wu
Hui Wu
Yue Wu
Zuxuan Wu
Tao Xiang
Lingxi Xie
Toshihiko Yamasaki
Junchi Yan
Yan Yan
Keiji Yanai
Kuiyuan Yang
Lu Yang
Ting Yao
Dengpan Ye
Guangnan Ye
Jun Ye
Mei-Chen Yeh
Lijun Yin
Felix Yu
Jun Yu
Yi Yu
Shoou-I Yu
Stefanos Zafeiriou
Maia Zaharieva
Markos Zampoglou
Gloria Zen
Matthias Zeppelzauer
Biqiao Zhang
Cha Zhang
Jian Zhang
Jing Zhang
Shiliang Zhang
Wei Zhang
Yimin Zhang
Luming Zhang
Weinan Zhang
Hanwang Zhang
Tianzhu Zhang
Yongdong Zhang
Liang Zheng
Changtao Zhong
Shenghua Zhong
Wengang Zhou
Ce Zhu
Shiai Zhu
Michael Zink
Marcos Zuniga
Wangmeng Zuo

MM 2016 Brave New Idea Committee

Chairs: Martha Larson *(Delft University of Technology / Radboud University Nijmegen)*
Hari Sundaram *(University of Illinois at Urbana-Champaign)*

Program Committee: Giulia Boato *(University of Trento)*
Ramesh Jain *(University of California, Irvine)*
Gareth Jones *(Dublin City University)*
Klara Nahrstedt *(University of Illinois)*
Jasminko Novak *(European Institute for Participatory Media e.V.)*

MM 2016 Doctoral Symposium Committee

Chairs: Winston Hsu *(National Taiwan University & IBM TJ Watson)*
Eckehard Steinbach *(Technische Universität München)*

Program Committee: Kiyoharu Aizawa *(University of Tokyo)*
Ali Begen *(Ozyegin University)*
Yan-Ying Chen *(FX Palo Alto Laboratory)*
Hermann Hellwagner *(Klagenfurt University)*
Cheng-Hsin Hsu *(National Tsing Hua University)*
Rainer Lienhart *(University of Augsburg)*
Hari Sundaram *(University of Illinois at Urbana-Champaign)*
Bart Thomee *(Yahoo Labs)*

MM 2016 Grand Challenge Committee

Chairs: Xavier Anguera *(ELSA Corp.)*
Shuicheng Yan *(Qihoo 360 & NUS)*

Program Committee: **MSR Image Recognition Challenge**
Yuxiao Hu *(Microsoft Research)*
Lei Zhang *(Microsoft Research)*
Shiguang Shan *(Chinese Academy of Sciences)*

Additional reviewers:
Cheng Cheng *(Chongqing Institute of Green and Intelligent Technology, Chinese Academy of Sciences)*
Jianshu Li *(National University of Singapore)*
Shilun Lin *(Beijing University of Posts and Telecommunications)*
Jie Shao *(Beijing University of Posts and Telecommunications)*
Yue Wu *(Northeastern University, Boston, US)*
Yingbin Zheng *(Shanghai Advanced Research Institute, Chinese Academy of Sciences)*
Xiang-Dong Zhou *(Chongqing Institute of Green and Intelligent Technology, Chinese Academy of Sciences)*

Flickr Grand Challenge on Tag and Caption Prediction
Bart Thomee *(Yahoo Labs)*
Pierre Guarrigues *(Yahoo Labs)*
Liangliang Cao *(Yahoo Labs)*
David A. Shamma *(Yahoo Labs)*

Additional reviewers:
Yuncheng Li *(University of Rochester)*
Stacey Svetlichnaya *(Flickr)*

MSR Video to Language Challenge
Tao Mei *(Microsoft Research Asia)*
Ting Yao *(Microsoft Research Asia)*
Yong Rui *(Microsoft Research Asia)*

Additional reviewers
Jianlong Fu *(Microsoft Research Asia)*
Yingwei Pan *(University of Science and Technology of China)*

Sky and the Social Eye: Enriching Remote-Sensed Events

Alan Woodley *(Queensland University of Technology)*
Shlomo Geva *(Queensland University of Technology)*

Additional reviewers
Timothy Chappell *(Queensland University of Technology)*
Lance De Vine *(Queensland University of Technology)*
Roman Fedorov *(Politecnico di Milano)*
Alan Woodley *(Queensland University of Technology)*

MM 2016 Demo Committee

Chairs: Pablo Cesar *(CWI)*
Max Mühlhäuser *(Technische Universität Darmstadt)*

Program Committee: Marco Bertini *(University of Florence)*
Dick Bulterman *(CWI / VU University Amsterdam)*
Teresa Chambel *(University of Lisbon)*
Raimund Dachselt *(Technische Universität Dresden)*
Niloo Dezfuli *(TU Darmstadt)*
Gerald Friedland *(ICSI)*
Andreas Girgensohn *(FX Palo Alto Laboratory)*
Mar Gonzalez Franco *(Microsoft Research)*
Wolfgang Hürst *(Utrecht University)*
Ichiro Ide *(Nagoya university)*
Rene Kaiser *(JOANNEUM RESEARCH)*
Ian Kegel *(BT)*
Joke Kort *(TNO)*
Rodrigo Laiola Guimaraes *(IBM Research)*
Cynthia Liem *(Delft University of Technology)*
Artur Lugmayr *(Curtin University)*
Kris Luyten *(Hasselt University)*
Britta Meixner *(FX Palo Alto Laboratory)*
Vasileios Mezaris *(Information Technologies Institute / Centre for Research and Technology Hellas (ITI/CERTH)*)
Mario Montagud *(Universitat Politècnica de València)*
Frank Nack *(University of Amsterdam)*
Suranga Nanayakkara *(Singapore University of Technology and Design)*
Shin'ichi Satoh *(University of Tokyo)*
Christian Timmerer *(Alpen-Adria-Universität Klagenfurt)*
Doug Williams *(BT)*
Roger Zimmermann *(National University of Singapore)*

MM 2016 Open Source Competition Committee

Chairs: Tao Mei *(Microsoft Research Asia)*
Christian Timmerer *(Alpen-Adria-Universität Klagenfurt)*

Program Committee: Marco Bertini *(University of Florence)*
Pablo Cesar *(CWI, The Netherlands)*
Kuan-Ta Chen *(Academia Sinica)*
Yan-Yin Chen *(FXPAL)*
Wen-Huang Cheng *(SINICA)*
Jianlong Fu *(Microsoft Research)*
Steven Hoi *(SMU)*
Yu-Gang Jiang *(Fudan University)*
Chia-Wen Lin *(National Tsing Hua University)*
Mathias Lux *(University of Klagenfurt)*
Michael Riegler *(Simula)*
Klaus Schoffmann *(University of Klagenfurt)*
Gwendal Simon *(Telecom Bretagne)*
Jingdong Wang *(Microsoft Research)*
Yonggang Wen *(Nanyang Technological University)*
Kuiyuan Yang *(Microsoft Reasearch)*
Yi Yang *(UTS)*
Ting Yao *(Microsoft Research)*
Lei Zhang *(Microsoft Research)*
Yimin Zhang *(Intel)*
H. Vicky Zhao *(Tsinghua University)*
Roger Zimmermann *(NUS)*

ACM Multimedia 2016 Sponsor & Supporters

Sponsor

Platinum Supporter

Silver Supporters

Bronze Supporters

facebook

Microsoft Research

Google

Unified Streaming Platform

ViSENZE™

A Digital World to Thrive In — How the Internet of Things Can Make the "Invisible Hand" Work

Dirk Helbing
Eidgenössische Technische Hochschule Zürich, Switzerland

Abstract
Managing data-rich societies wisely and reaching sustainable development are among the greatest challenges of the 21st century. We are faced with existential threats and huge opportunities. If we don't act now, large parts of our society will not be able to economically benefit from the digital revolution. This could lead to mass unemployment and social unrest. It is time to create the right framework for the digital society to come.

Author Keywords: Internet of Things, big data, data-rich societies

Short Bio

Dirk Helbing is Professor of Computational Social Science at the Department of Humanities, Social and Political Sciences and affiliate of the Computer Science Department at ETH Zurich. He earned a PhD in physics and was Managing Director of the Institute of Transport & Economics at Dresden University of Technology in Germany. He is internationally known for his work on pedestrian crowds, vehicle traffic, and agent-based models of social systems. His work is documented in hundreds of scientific articles, keynote lectures and media reports worldwide.

Prof. Helbing is a member of the Swiss Federal Committee on the Future of Data Processing and Data Security. Furthermore, he coordinates the FuturICT Initiative (http://www.futurict.eu), which focuses on the understanding of techno-socio-economic systems, using smart data. Prof. Helbing is an elected member of the prestigious German Academy of Sciences "Leopoldina" and a member of the Academy's "Digital Society" Committee. He also worked for the World Economic Forum's Global Agenda Council on Complex Systems and is co-founder of the Physics of Socio-Economic Systems Division of the German Physical Society and of ETH Zurich's Risk Center.

In January 2014 Prof. Helbing received a honorary PhD from Delft University of Technology (TU Delft). Since June 2016 he is affiliate professor at the faculty of Technology, Policy and Management at TU Delft, where he leads the PhD school in "Engineering Social Technologies for a Responsible Digital Future."

MM'16, October 15–19, 2016, Amsterdam, The Netherlands.
ACM ISBN 978-1-4503-3603-1/16/10.
DOI: http://dx.doi.org/10.1145/2964284.2984749

Multi-modal Multi-view Topic-opinion Mining for Social Event Analysis

Shengsheng Qian[1,2], Tianzhu Zhang[1,2], Changsheng Xu[1,2]
[1]National Lab of Pattern Recognition, Institute of Automation, CAS, Beijing 100190, China
[2]University of Chinese Academy of Sciences
{shengsheng.qian, tzzhang, csxu}@nlpr.ia.ac.cn

ABSTRACT

In this paper, we propose a novel multi-modal multi-view topic-opinion mining (MMTOM) model for social event analysis in multiple collection sources. Compared with existing topic-opinion mining methods, our proposed model has several advantages: (1) The proposed MMTOM can effectively take into account multi-modal and multi-view properties jointly in a unified and principled way for social event modeling. (2) Our model is general and can be applied to many other applications in multimedia, such as opinion mining and sentiment analysis, multi-view association visualization, and topic-opinion mining for movie review. (3) The proposed MMTOM is able to not only discover multi-modal common topics from all collections as well as summarize the similarities and differences of these collections along each specific topic, but also automatically mine multi-view opinions on the learned topics across different collections. (4) Our topic-opinion mining results can be effectively applied to many applications including multi-modal multi-view topic-opinion retrieval and visualization, which achieve much better performance than existing methods. To evaluate the proposed model, we collect a real-world dataset for research on multi-modal multi-view social event analysis, and will release it for academic use. We have conducted extensive experiments, and both qualitative and quantitative evaluation results have demonstrated the effectiveness of the proposed MMTOM.

Keywords

social media, topic-opinion mining, multi-modal, multi-view

1. INTRODUCTION

Topic-opinion mining is one of the most important tasks in multimedia due to its wide range of applications such as aspect-based opinion mining for product review [17], social event topic analysis across different news medias [23, 21, 25], political controversial opinion mining [9], and topic-opinion mining for movie review [15]. The goal of topic-opinion mining is to learn the representative topics and the corresponding opinions jointly by utilizing multiple cross-collection sources. Let's take topic-opinion mining

MM '16, October 15-19, 2016, Amsterdam, Netherlands
© 2016 ACM. ISBN 978-1-4503-3603-1/16/10...$15.00
DOI: http://dx.doi.org/10.1145/2964284.2964294

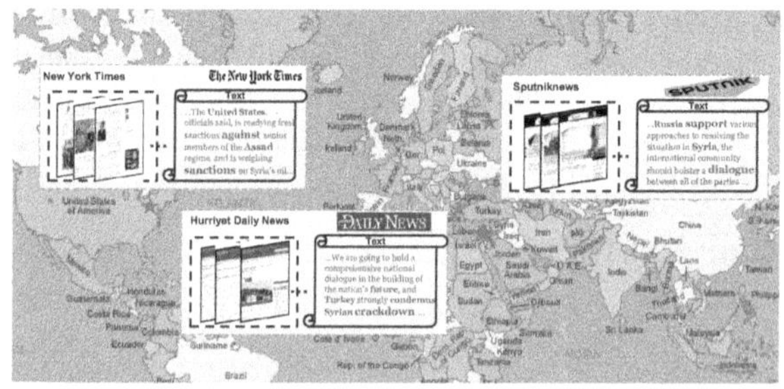

Figure 1: An example about multi-modal multi-view topic-opinion mining for social event analysis.

for social event analysis in multiple social news medias as an example. There are many political controversial social events in political debates, newspapers, and many social media sites (e.g., YouTube, Facebook, and Google News), which have the potential to affect tens of thousands of people, such as "The crises in Libya", "Syrian civil war", and "The war in Afghanistan". For these events, every news media over a controversial topic not only has many different aspects, but also has its own opinion tendencies, and there is no absolute true opinion for this topic. Therefore, joint topic-opinion mining is important to automatically understand the topics of the hot political controversial social events and the corresponding opinions in different news medias. Moreover, topic-opinion mining can discover collective and subjective information from the vast amounts of multiple cross-collection sources in social news medias, and the mining results can be helpful for many applications such as multiple views retrieval [9], opinion mining and sentiment analysis [18], and multi-view association visualization [13].

Topic learning for social event has multi-view and multi-modal property in multiple news medias. This is because different news medias may have similar reports about a hot event, while they also have cross-collection differences in the same topic. Generally, the report content information from different medias can be divided into two parts: common topics from all collections (news medias) and collection-specific topics from each collection. In Figure 1, we show an example about different reports of a hot topic "how to treat Assad regime at the beginning of Syria unrest" in multiple news medias. We can see that the common words, such as "Syria, rights, Assad", are the common topics among all collections, and the specific words, such as "States, revolution, Obama", appear frequently in the New York Times, while "Russian, proposals" appear frequently in the Sputniknews. This suggests that, instead of the general topic analysis from all collections regarding the hot event, a fine-grained topic analysis in multiple views across multiple news medias could help consume information in a more efficient and ef-

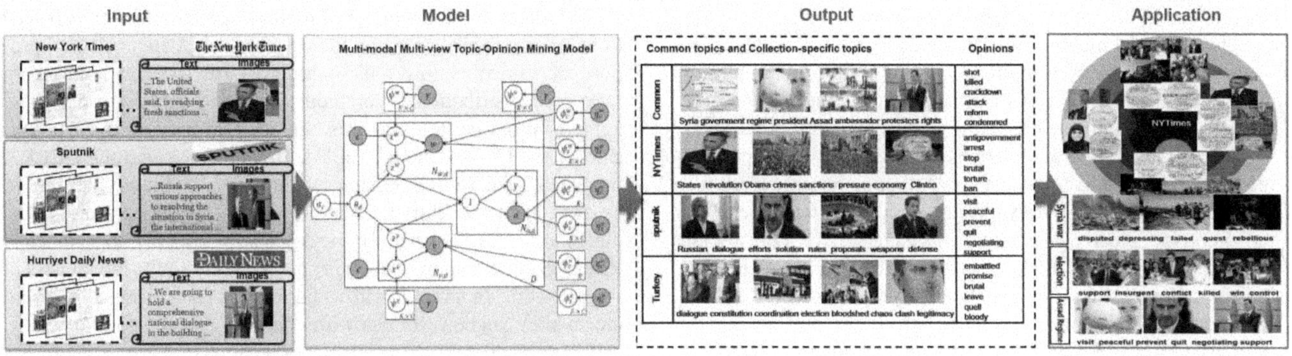

(a) Multi-modal Multi-view Topic-Opinion Mining (b) Visualization and Retrieval

Figure 2: The flowchart of the proposed multi-modal multi-view topic-opinion mining model for social event analysis. Given the input data with multi-modality from multiple collections, the proposed MMTOM can output textual topics, visual topics and opinions in multiple views, which can be applied to multi-modal multi-view topic-opinion retrieval and visualization.

fective way. Meanwhile, each document in social news media can be described with images and texts simultaneously, and the textual and visual information can complement and enhance each other. Therefore, given a set of social event documents from multiple collections, it is necessary and important to jointly analyze the multimodal topics and differentiate the common topics and collection-specific topics in multiple views across all collections.

Opinion mining for social event has multi-view property in real-world scenarios. A topic via the above topic learning not only contains the words that describe the topic, but also the words that express the opinions about the topic. In other words, we need to automatically identify the multi-view differences in opinion discovery on these learned multi-modal topics across different collections. As shown in Figure 1, we give an example and show different opinions across multiple views for a hot topic "how to treat Assad regime at the beginning of Syria unrest". Different news medias have different tendencies because of the stakeholders in their nations, such as the U.S., Russia, and Turkey. From the figure, we can see that U.S. empathizes on "sanctions" and "human rights", while Russia empathizes on "dialogue" and "support", and for Turkey, it criticizes Assad regime strongly, and its opinion words include "embattled, brutal". This example clearly shows that it is very helpful to know which nations or other stakeholders take which position when learning multi-view differences in opinion discovery. Moreover, for a user who is not closely familiar to an event topic, on one hand, it is very time-consuming for him/her to read such huge amounts of documents to understand what has happened recently across multiple news medias. On the other hand, the user cannot quickly capture the whole event overview and obtain the opinion in multiple views. Therefore, it is important to automatically mine multi-view opinions on the learned topics across different collections for social event analysis.

How to conduct topic-opinion mining in multiple views across different collections has attracted much research interest. Basically, there are two major research topics: (1) a fine-grained topic analysis at the cross-collections by adopting an extended cross-collections LDA to discover common topics across all collections as well as model their similarities and differences across multiple collections [19, 26]. For example, Paul et al. [19] propose a cross-collections topic mining algorithm to learn two topic distributions: common topics and specific topics, and apply to cross-cultural analysis. (2) The combination of topic and opinion mining by adopting the extended topic model methods or other latent variable models to learn the topic and the corresponding opinion simultaneously. For example, an aspect-based opinion mining method is proposed to be applied to product analysis from online customers reviews [17, 18, 23]. Qiu et al. propose a latent variable model for viewpoint discovery from threaded forum posts by jointly modeling three important factors: viewpoint specific topic preference, user identity and user interactions [23]. These two research topics focus on topic and opinion mining in textual content analysis by utilizing a latent model for cross-collections data modeling. However, these existing methods still cannot deal with the following challenges well: (1) *The topics in multiple collections have multi-view property.* There are various topic types across multiple collections. Generally, the topics across multiple collections have two parts: common topics from all collections and collection-specific topics. As shown in Figure 1, for the hot topic "how to treat Assad regime at the beginning of Syria unrest", the New York Times and the Sputniknews have both some common topics and their specific topics. These latent common topics and collection-specific topics in multiple views could help understand social event across all collections. (2) *The opinions in multiple collections have multi-view property.* For a hot political controversial topic, different news medias may have different opinions because the stakeholders have different nations, such as the U.S., Russia, and Turkey. (3) *The media data have multi-modal property.* As shown in Figure 1, each data instance in social media sites can be described with images and texts simultaneously, and the textual and visual information can enhance and complement each other for social event analysis. Based on the above discussion, for social event analysis, it is desirable to take into account the three properties for joint topic-opinion mining.

In this paper, we propose a novel multi-modal multi-view topic-opinion mining (MMTOM) model for social event analysis. The goal is to mine multi-modal common topics from all collections and multi-modal collection-specific topics as well as the corresponding opinions in multiple views by leveraging rich social event data in multiple collections. As shown in Figure 2, the input consists of social event data in multiple collections. Here, we collect news articles in different nations including New York Times, Sputniknews, and Hurriyet Daily News about the hot social event "Syrian civil war", and these articles consist of textual topics words and images as well as opinion words. Given the input, the proposed MMTOM is adopted to mine the topics and opinions of social event jointly to obtain the output, which captures three important factors: textual topics, visual topics and opinions in multiple views. In details, the output includes multi-modal common topics from all collections , multi-modal collection-specific topic among each collection, and multi-view opinions of the learned topics. With the derived multi-modal multi-view topics and the corresponding opinions, we can apply them to multi-modal multi-view topic-opinion retrieval and topic-opinion association visualization as shown in Figure 2(b). The multi-modal multi-view topic-opinion retrieval is to explore the derived associations among topics and opinions, and identify the multi-view differences in opinion discovery for cross-media and opinion retrieval tasks. Topic-opinion association visualization can clearly visualize the associations of a hot social event for different topics with the corresponding opinions for social event understanding. We evaluate the proposed MMTOM on a real-world dataset, which is collected from different news media sites.The extensive experimental results demonstrate the effectiveness of our MMTOM for multi-modal multi-view topic-opinion mining and topic-opinion based applications. Compared with existing methods, the contributions of this work are three-fold.

- We propose a novel multi-modal multi-view topic-opinion mining (MMTOM) model for social event analysis. The proposed MMTOM can effectively model multi-modal and multi-view properties jointly, and is general and can be applied to many other applications in multimedia, such as opinion mining and sentiment analysis, multi-view association visualization, and topic-opinion mining for movie review.
- The proposed MMTOM is able to not only discover multi-modal common topics from all collections as well as summarize the similarities and differences of these collections along each specific topic, but also automatically identify the multi-view differences in opinion discovery on these learned topics across different collections.
- The topic-opinion mining results can be effectively applied to many applications including multi-modal multi-view topic-opinion retrieval and visualization, which achieve much better performance than existing methods. Besides, we collect a real-world dataset for research on multi-modal multi-view social event analysis, and will release it for academic use.

The rest of the paper is organized as follows. In Section 2, the related work is reviewed. Section 3 introduces the formulation of the proposed MMTOM. Two multi-modal multi-view topic-opinion applications are presented in Section 4. In Section 5, we report and analyze extensive experimental results. Finally, we conclude the paper with future work in Section 6.

2. RELATED WORK

In this Section, we briefly review previous methods which are most related to our work including probabilistic topic models and opinion mining and sentiment analysis.

Probabilistic Topic Models: Topic models, such as latent Dirichlet allocation (LDA) [7] and probabilistic latent semantic analysis (PLSA) [12], have been widely applied to various applications and have many extensions, such as supervised latent Dirichlet allocation (SLDA) [4, 22], dynamic latent Dirichlet allocation and its variations [6, 16]. However, these traditional topic models are inadequate to obtain a fine-grained topic analysis for modeling data from different collections, and cannot discover common topics across all collections as well as model their similarities and differences across multiple collections. To overcome this issue, Zhai et al. [26] extend the PLSA model and propose a Cross-Collection Mixture Model (CCMix) by explicitly distinguishing common topics that characterize common information across all collections from special topics that characterize collection-specific information. Common topics and collection-specific topics are aligned under the same set of indices and the number of topics in each collection is forced to be the number of common topics. Similarly, Paul et al. [19] propose a cross-collections topic mining (CCLDA) algorithm to learn two topic distributions: common topics and specific topics, and apply to cross-cultural analysis, and it is actually a Bayesian version of the CCMix model. In [3], Bao et al. extend the CCLDA model to a supervised version which could be directly applied to cross-domain text classification. However, the above topic model methods [3, 19, 26] mainly focus on how to apply the model to textual corpora and may not be appropriate for multi-modal data in social media. In a real-world scenario, each data instance in social media sites can be described with images and texts simultaneously, and the textual and visual information can also enhance and complement each other. In order to extend the LDA model to learn the joint correlations among data of different modalities, such as texts and images, some variants of topic models are developed, such as Corr-LDA [5], mm-LDA [24]. In this work, we extend the CCLDA model to a multi-modal topic model based on the traditional mm-LDA model method to model multi-modal data. Though the above topic models are a powerful tool for topic modeling, they are not well suitable for opinion modeling. In other words, traditional topic models do not differentiate opinion words from topic words, which makes both opinions and topics obscure for opinion mining. To deal with the above issue, we propose a novel topic model, called multi-modal multi-view topic-opinion mining model for social event analysis. The proposed model is able to not only learn multi-modal topics including textual topics and visual topics, but also mine opinions of the learned topics in multiple views.

Opinion Mining and Sentiment Analysis: Opinion mining and sentiment analysis have attracted broad attentions in recent years. For a general survey, please refer to [15]. There are several studies conducted on opinion mining for product review data [17, 18], because of the wide availability of review data and their relatively obvious sentiment orientations such as good, bad and so on. In [17], the interdependent LDA model (ILDA) is proposed to learn latent topics and their ratings from online product reviews. Moghaddam et al. [18] comprehensively analyze the effectiveness of a series of LDA-based models for aspect-based opinion mining. There are also several studies conducted on multi-view opinion mining in social event analysis. In [23], a latent variable model was proposed for viewpoint discovery by jointly modeling three important factors: viewpoint specific topic preference, user identity and user interactions. Fang et al. [8] propose a multi-modal aspect-opinion model to enable extraction of the semantic-sensitive correlations between textual and visual modalities as well as the interdependency relationships between aspects and opinions by jointly modeling aspects and opinions. Fang et al. [9] propose a cross-perspective topic (CP-T) model which breaks up the terms in the vocabulary into topic terms and perspective terms with different generative processes, and differentiates between different collections of documents within the corpus. Gutierrez et al. [11] propose a multilingual topic model to simultaneously learn a set of common topics from multilingual, non-parallel data and automatically discover the differences in perspectives on these topics across linguistic communities, which is to understand multi-view cultural differences. In terms of multi-view opinion mining in social event analysis, our work is related to [9] and [11]. Different from [9, 11], our work focuses on multi-modal multi-view topic-opinion modeling by leveraging rich social event data in multiple collections, and learns multi-modal topics as well as their corresponding opinions in multiple views. Furthermore, we also apply the proposed MMTOM to the multi-modal multi-view topic-opinion retrieval and visualization.

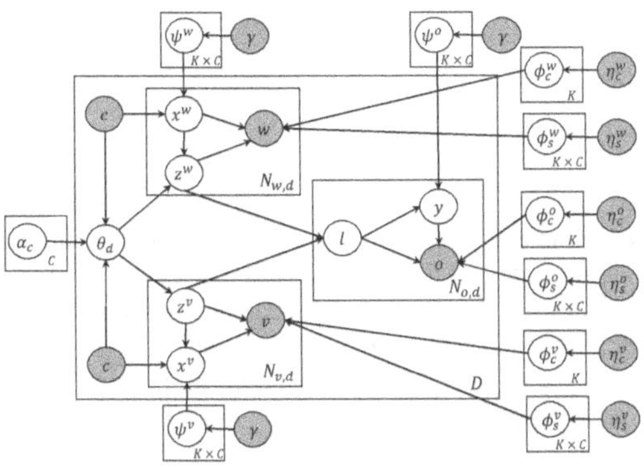

Figure 3: The graphical representation of the proposed multi-modal multi-view topic-opinion mining model (MMTOM).

Table 1: The key notations of the proposed MMTOM model.

Notations	Description
K, C	number of topics, number of collections
w, v, o	textual topic word, visual topic word, opinion word
α_c, γ, η	Dirichlet prior for hidden variables
θ	document-topic proportions
ϕ_c^w, ϕ_c^v	textual common topic-word distribution and visual common topic-word distribution
$\phi_{s,c}^w, \phi_{s,c}^v$	textual collection-specific topic-word distribution and visual collection-specific topic-word distribution
$\phi_c^o, \phi_{s,c}^o$	common opinion-word distribution and collection-specific opinion-word distribution
ψ^w, ψ^v, ψ^o	switching variable distribution
$\mathbf{w}_{-i}, \mathbf{z}_{-i}, \mathbf{v}_{-i}$	The vector values of $\mathbf{w}, \mathbf{z}, \mathbf{v}$ on all the other dimensions except i
$\mathbf{l}_{-i}, \mathbf{o}_{-i}$	The vector values of $\mathbf{l}, \mathbf{o}$ on all the other dimensions except i
x^w	binary variable denoting whether the textual topic word is generated from ϕ_c^w or $\phi_{s,c}^w$
x^v	binary variable denoting whether the visual topic word is generated from ϕ_c^v or $\phi_{s,c}^v$
y	binary variable denoting whether the opinion word is generated from ϕ_c^o or $\phi_{s,c}^o$

3. OUR APPROACH

In this Section, we will first show the problem statement, and then introduce the details of the proposed multi-modal multi-view topic-opinion mining model. Finally, we show the model inference.

3.1 Problem Statement

Our goal is to mine multi-modal multi-view topic-opinion for social event analysis from multiple cross-collection sources in social news media. Given social event multi-modal data, we not only learn multi-modal topics but also mine the corresponding opinions across multiple views. Suppose we are given multiple cross-collection documents $\mathcal{D} = \{D_1, \ldots, D_C\}$ from different social medias, where C denotes the number of collections. As in [9], we treat nouns as topic words in the documents and verbs and adjectives as opinion words. Each collection D_c has many documents, and each document $d_i = \{W_i, V_i, O_i\}$ consists of three components: textual component W_i, visual component V_i, and opinion component O_i. W_i and V_i describe textual and visual words respectively, and O_i describes the corresponding opinion words for $\{W_i, V_i\}$. Note that the opinion words O_i are not necessary to be contained, which means O_i may be empty. We construct three vocabularies $\{\mathcal{W}, \mathcal{V}, \mathcal{O}\}$ to represent documents in all collections containing textual aspect words, visual aspect words, and opinion words, respectively. Table 1 lists the key notations. Based on the above definitions, the model can be defined as follows:

DEFINITION 1. (MULTI-MODAL MULTI-VIEW TOPIC-OPINION MINING). *Given multiple cross-collection documents $\mathcal{D}$, each document d_i corresponds to a three-dimensional tuple $[W_i, V_i, O_i]$. The goal of multi-modal multi-view topic-opinion mining is to model and extract (1) multi-modal common topics from all collections including textual common topics $\{\phi_c^w \in \mathbb{R}^{K\times|\mathcal{W}|}\}$ and visual common topics $\phi_c^v \in \mathbb{R}^{K\times|\mathcal{V}|}$ (2) multi-modal collection-specific topic among each collection c including textual collection-specific topics $\{\phi_{s,c}^w \in \mathbb{R}^{K\times|\mathcal{W}|}\}$ and visual collection-specific topics $\phi_{s,c}^v \in \mathbb{R}^{K\times|\mathcal{V}|}$ (3) the corresponding multi-view opinion space including $\{\phi_c^o \in \mathbb{R}^{K\times|\mathcal{O}|}\}$ for $\{\phi_c^w, \phi_c^v\}$, and $\{\phi_{s,c}^o \in \mathbb{R}^{K\times|\mathcal{O}|}\}$ for $\{\phi_{s,c}^w, \phi_{s,c}^v\}$. (4) Document-topic distributions $\{\theta \in \mathbb{R}^{|\mathcal{D}|\times K}\}$.*

3.2 Multi-modal Multi-view Topic-Opinion Mining (MMTOM)

The graphical representation of the proposed MMTOM is shown in Figure 3. In our model, we assume that there are two kinds of topics in multiple collections: 1) multi-modal common topics including textual common topic space ϕ_c^w and visual common topic space ϕ_c^v, which are shared among all collections. 2) multi-modal collection-specific topics including textual collection-specific topic ϕ_s^w and visual collection-specific topic ϕ_s^v, which are unique to the collection. In addition, the corresponding multi-view opinions of topics including common opinion space ϕ_c^o and collection-specific opinion space ϕ_s^o can be obtained from each kind of topics. Therefore, in the document generative process, the topic words are drawn from the shared multi-modal common topic-word distribution or the multi-modal collection-specific topic-word distribution. The opinions from different views could be different, and the opinion words are drawn from the opinion-words distribution on the corresponding topics. In order to realize the above process, we use the binary variable x^w to control whether the topic word is generated from the textual common topic space ϕ_c^w or the textual collection-specific topic space ϕ_s^w. When $x^w = 0$, the topic textual word is generated from the textual common topic space ϕ_c^w. When $x^w = 1$, the topic textual word is generated from the textual collection-specific topic space ϕ_s^w. Similarly, the visual word is generated by using the binary variable x^v. Correspondingly, the binary variable y is used to indicate whether the opinion word is generated from the opinion distribution conditioned on the multi-modal common topics or the multi-modal collection-specific topics. The θ_d represents that the textual and visual information in a social media document shares the same document-topic distribution. Accordingly, the generative process of a document d in the proposed MMTOM model can be described as follows:

1. For each multi-modal common topic including textual common topic z^w and visual common topic z^v, draw a common multinomial distribution over topic words, $\phi_c^w \sim \text{Dir}(\eta_c^w)$ and $\phi_c^v \sim \text{Dir}(\eta_c^v)$.

2. For each multi-modal common topic z , draw a common multinomial distribution over opinion words, $\phi_c^o \sim \text{Dir}(\eta_c^o)$.

3. For each collection c,

   (a) For each multi-modal collection-specific topic including textual collection-specific topic z^w and visual collection-specific topic z^v, draw a collection-specific multinomial distribution over topic words, $\phi_{s,c,z}^w \sim \text{Dir}(\eta_s^w)$ and $\phi_{s,c,z}^v \sim \text{Dir}(\eta_s^v)$.

(b) For each multi-modal collection-specific topic including textual collection-specific topic z^w and visual collection-specific topic z^v, draw a Bernoulli distribution, $\psi^w_{c,z} \sim Beta(\gamma)$ and $\psi^v_{c,z} \sim Beta(\gamma)$.

(c) For each multi-modal collection-specific topic z, draw a collection-specific multinomial distribution over opinion words, $\phi^o_{s,c,z} \sim \mathrm{Dir}(\eta^o_s)$.

(d) For each collection-specific opinion l, draw a Bernoulli distribution $\psi^o_{c,z} \sim Beta(\gamma)$.

4. For each document d:

   (a) Draw a multinomial distribution over topics, $\theta_d \sim Dir(\alpha_c)$

   (b) For each textual word w_n in d:
   - Draw a topic assignment $z^w_n \sim Mult(\theta_d)$
   - Draw a binary switch $x^w_n \sim Bern(\psi^w_{c,z})$
   - if $x^w_n = 0$, draw a topic word $w_n \sim \mathrm{Mult}(\phi^w_c)$
   - if $x^w_n = 1$, draw a topic word $w_n \sim \mathrm{Mult}(\phi^w_{s,c,z})$

   (c) For each visual word v_n in d:
   - Draw a topic assignment $z^v_n \sim Mult(\theta_d)$
   - Draw a switch variable $x^v_n \sim Bern(\psi^v_{c,z})$
   - if $x^v_n = 0$, draw a topic word $v_n \sim \mathrm{Mult}(\phi^v_c)$
   - if $x^v_n = 1$, draw a topic word $v_n \sim \mathrm{Mult}(\phi^v_{s,c,z})$

   (d) For each opinion word o_n in d:
   - Draw a topic assignment l^o_n from $(z^w_1, z^w_2, ..., z^w_{N_{w,d}}, z^v_1, z^v_2, ..., z^v_{N_{v,d}})$
   - Draw a switch variable $y^o_n \sim Bern(\psi^o_{c,z})$
   - if $y^o_n = 0$, draw a topic word $o_n \sim \mathrm{Mult}(\phi^o_c)$
   - if $y^o_n = 1$, draw a topic word $o_n \sim \mathrm{Mult}(\phi^o_{s,c,z})$

During the model learning process, we assume that the priors $(\alpha_c, \gamma, \eta^w_c, \eta^w_s, \eta^v_c, \eta^v_s, \eta^o_c, \eta^o_s)$ follow symmetric Dirichlet, which are conjugate priors for multinomial (or Beta for Bernoulli).

3.3 Model Inference

Exact inference is often intractable in many topic models and appropriate methods must be used, such as variational inference [7] and Gibbs sampling [10]. Let hyper-parameters $\{\alpha_c, \gamma, \eta^w_c, \eta^w_s, \eta^v_c, \eta^v_s, \eta^o_c, \eta^o_s\}$ be denoted as Ψ, and hidden variables$\{\theta, \psi^w, \psi^v, \psi^o, \phi^w_c, \phi^w_s, \phi^v_c, \phi^v_s, \phi^o_c, \phi^o_s\}$ as Φ and we need to estimate the latent variables conditioned on the observed variables, namely $p(\mathbf{z}^w, \mathbf{z}^v, \mathbf{l}, \mathbf{x}^w, \mathbf{x}^v, \mathbf{y}|\mathbf{w}, \mathbf{v}, \mathbf{o}, c, \Psi)$, where $\mathbf{x}^w, \mathbf{x}^v, \mathbf{y}$ are binary switches, $\mathbf{z}^w$ and $\mathbf{z}^v$ are topic assignments, and $\mathbf{l}$ is opinion assignment. We employ collapsed Gibbs sampling method to obtain samples of latent variables and estimate unknown parameters $\{\theta, \psi^w, \psi^v, \psi^o, \phi^w_c, \phi^w_s, \phi^v_c, \phi^v_s, \phi^o_c, \phi^o_s\}$ in the proposed MMTOM.

In a Gibbs sampler, one iteratively samples new assignments of latent variables by drawing from the distributions conditioned on the previous state of the model. We list the update rules for latent variables z^w, x^w, z^v, x^v, l, y as follows. We first sample the variables z^w, x^w, and z^v, x^v for each text topic word and visual topic word. The conditional posterior distribution of latent topic indicators z^w, x^w in text document can be written as:

$$p(z^w_i = k|\mathbf{z}^w_{-i}, \mathbf{x}^w, \mathbf{w}, \mathbf{v}, \mathbf{o}, \Psi) = (n_{c,d,k,-i} + \alpha_{cd}) \times \begin{cases} \frac{n^w_{c,k,w',-i} + \eta^w_c}{\sum_{w'} (n^w_{c,k,w',-i} + \eta^w_c)}, x^w_i = 0 \\ \frac{n^w_{s,c,k,w',-i} + \eta^w_s}{\sum_{w'} (n^w_{s,c,k,w',-i} + \eta^w_s)}, x^w_i = 1 \end{cases} \tag{1}$$

$$p(x^w_i = j|\mathbf{x}^w_{-i}, \mathbf{z}^w, \mathbf{w}, \mathbf{v}, \mathbf{o}, \Psi) = \frac{n^{w,x}_{c,z,j,-i} + \gamma}{\sum_j (n^{w,x}_{c,z,j,-i} + \gamma)} \times \begin{cases} \frac{n^w_{c,k,w',-i} + \eta^w_c}{\sum_{w'} (n^w_{c,k,w',-i} + \eta^w_c)}, j = 0 \\ \frac{n^w_{s,c,k,w',-i} + \eta^w_s}{\sum_{w'} (n^w_{s,c,k,w',-i} + \eta^w_s)}, j = 1 \end{cases} \tag{2}$$

where the superscript $-i$ denotes a counting variable that excludes the i-th word index in the corpus. $n_{c,d,k,-i}$ denotes the times of textual words and visual words in document d assigned to topic k except the current assignment. $n^w_{c,z,w',-i}$, and $n^w_{s,c,z,w',-i}$ denote the times of textual word w' assigned to textual common topic ϕ^w_c and textual collection-specific topic $\phi^w_{s,c}$ except the current assignment, respectively. $n^{w,x}_{c,z,j,-i}$, and $n^{v,x}_{c,z,j,-i}$ denote the number of word tokens d in collection c which satisfies $z_{d_w} = z \& x_{d_w} = j$, and $z_{d_v} = z \& x_{d_v} = j$ except the current assignment, respectively.

The descriptions of parameters in visual words are similar, and the conditional posterior distribution of latent topic indicators z^v, x^v in text document can be written as:

$$p(z^v_i = k|\mathbf{z}^v_{-i}, \mathbf{x}^v, \mathbf{w}, \mathbf{v}, \mathbf{o}, \Psi) = (n_{c,d,k,-i} + \alpha_{cd}) \times \begin{cases} \frac{n^v_{c,k,v',-i} + \eta^v_c}{\sum_{v'} (n^v_{c,k,v',-i} + \eta^v_c)}, x^v_i = 0 \\ \frac{n^v_{s,c,k,v',-i} + \eta^v_s}{\sum_{v'} (n^v_{s,c,k,v',-i} + \eta^v_s)}, x^v_i = 1 \end{cases} \tag{3}$$

$$p(x^v_i = j|\mathbf{x}^v_{-i}, \mathbf{z}^v, \mathbf{w}, \mathbf{v}, \mathbf{o}, \Psi) = \frac{n^{v,x}_{c,z,j,-i} + \gamma}{\sum_j (n^{v,x}_{c,z,j,-i} + \gamma)} \times \begin{cases} \frac{n^v_{c,k,v',-i} + \eta^v_c}{\sum_{v'} (n^v_{c,k,v',-i} + \eta^v_c)}, j = 0 \\ \frac{n^v_{s,c,k,v',-i} + \eta^v_s}{\sum_{v'} (n^v_{s,c,k,v',-i} + \eta^v_s)}, j = 1 \end{cases} \tag{4}$$

Next, we sample the hidden variable l and switch variable y for the opinion word with the following formula:

$$p(l_i = k|\mathbf{l}_{-i}, \mathbf{y}, \mathbf{w}, \mathbf{v}, \mathbf{o}, \Psi) = \frac{n_{c,d,k}}{\sum_k n_{c,d,k}} \times \begin{cases} \frac{n^o_{c,k,o',-i} + \eta^o_c}{\sum_{o'} (n^o_{c,k,o',-i} + \eta^o_c)}, y_i = 0 \\ \frac{n^o_{s,c,k,o',-i} + \eta^o_s}{\sum_{o'} (n^o_{s,c,k,o',-i} + \eta^o_s)}, y_i = 1 \end{cases} \tag{5}$$

$$p(y_i = j|\mathbf{y}_{-i}, \mathbf{l}, \mathbf{w}, \mathbf{v}, \mathbf{o}, \Psi) = \frac{n^{o,y}_{c,z,j,-i} + \gamma}{\sum_j (n^{o,y}_{c,z,j,-i} + \gamma)} \times \begin{cases} \frac{n^o_{c,k,o',-i} + \eta^o_c}{\sum_{o'} (n^o_{c,k,o',-i} + \eta^o_c)}, j = 0 \\ \frac{n^o_{s,c,k,o',-i} + \eta^o_s}{\sum_{o'} (n^o_{s,c,k,o',-i} + \eta^o_s)}, j = 1 \end{cases} \tag{6}$$

After finishing the Gibbs sampling, we can estimate the parameters $\theta, \phi^w_c, \phi^w_s, \phi^v_c, \phi^v_s, \phi^o_c, \phi^o_s$ just like [10]. Therefore, we have:

$$\phi^w_{ckw'} = \frac{n^w_{c,k,w'} + \eta^w_c}{\sum_{w'} (n^w_{c,k,w'} + \eta^w_c)}, \phi^w_{sckw'} = \frac{n^w_{s,c,k,w'} + \eta^w_s}{\sum_{w'} (n^w_{s,c,k,w'} + \eta^w_s)}$$

$$\phi^v_{ckv'} = \frac{n^v_{c,k,v',-i} + \eta^v_c}{\sum_{v'} (n^v_{c,k,v',-i} + \eta^v_c)}, \phi^v_{sckv'} = \frac{n^v_{s,c,k,v'} + \eta^v_s}{\sum_{v'} (n^v_{s,c,k,v'} + \eta^v_s)}$$

$$\phi^o_{cko'} = \frac{n^o_{c,k,o'} + \eta^o_c}{\sum_{o'} (n^o_{c,k,o'} + \eta^o_c)}, \phi^o_{scko'} = \frac{n^o_{s,c,k,o'} + \eta^o_s}{\sum_{o'} (n^o_{s,c,k,o'} + \eta^o_s)}$$

$$\theta_{cdk} = \frac{n_{c,d,k} + \alpha_{cd}}{\sum_k (n_{c,d,k} + \alpha_{cd})} \tag{7}$$

4. APPLICATION

In this Section, we introduce how to leverage the topic-opinion mining results of our MMTOM for multi-modal multi-view topic-opinion retrieval and topic-opinion association visualization.

4.1 Topic-Opinion Retrieval

Multi-modal multi-view topic-opinion retrieval is to explore the derived associations among topics and opinions and identify the multiple-view differences in opinion discovery for cross-media and opinion retrieval tasks. The MMTOM model can learn soft associations between multi-modal topics and observed opinions in multiple views. Specifically, There are two classes of soft associations in different views: (1) dependency relationship between textual topics and visual topics. (2) interdependency between multi-modal topics and opinions. These useful soft associations can be integrated into a variety of topic-opinion tasks [8]. Multi-modal multi-view topic-opinion retrieval is important for many applications, such as finding some detailed annotation that best matches a given image, obtaining a set of images that best visually illustrate a given text query, or searching relevant opinion words by a set of combined document including textual and visual information.

In this subsection, we introduce how to apply the proposed MMTOM to multi-modal topic retrieval and multi-view opinion retrieval. (1) The multi-modal topic retrieval aims to find images or text documents (text words) that are most relevant to a given text (images) query, and includes text-based retrieval and image annotation. For text-based retrieval, denote the text query $\mathbf{w} = \{w_1, \ldots, w_N\}$, the score for each multi-modal document d is calculated by score $d_i = \prod_{n=1}^{N} p(w_n|d_i) = \prod_{n=1}^{N} \sum_{k=1}^{K} p(w_n|z = k)p(z = k|d_i)$. For image annotation, given a set of images $\{I_i\}_{i=1}^{D}$, the score for a textual word w is calculated as score(w)= $\sum_{i=1}^{D} \sum_{k=1}^{K} p(w|z = k)p(z = k|I_i)$, where k is the topic assignment, and we use the multi-modal common topics ϕ_c^w and ϕ_c^v as the relationship distribution between textual topics and visual topics for multi-modal topic retrieval. After computing the scores, we return a list of samples in descending order as the retrieved results. (2) The multi-view opinion retrieval aims to present the most relevant opinion words in multiple views to users with respect to a given query topic. The query $\mathbf{q} = \{q_1, \ldots, q_N\}$ can be represented by textual words, visual words, or both. We can tackle the task by calculating a predictive likelihood $p(o|q)$ that the opinion word o could be generated by the query as follows:

$$p(o = o'|q) = \sum_{k}^{K} p(o = o'|z = k)p(z = k|q) \tag{8}$$

Here, $p(z = k|q) = \frac{p(q|z=k|)p(z=k)}{p(q)}$. In our model, there are two kinds of multi-view opinions of topics including common opinion space ϕ_c^o and collection-specific opinion space ϕ_s^o from each kind of topics based on the estimated MMTOM model. Therefore, we can obtain the corresponding retrieval results for common opinion space and collection-specific opinion space. When given common topic space and common opinion space ϕ_c^o, we can obtain $p(o = o'|z = k) = \phi_{cko'}^o$, and the Eq.(8) can be written as:

$$p(o = o'|q, \phi_c^o) \propto \sum_{k}^{K} \phi_{cko'}^o \prod_{n=1}^{N} p(q_n|z = k)n_k \tag{9}$$

Similarly, when given collection-specific topic space and collection-specific opinion space ϕ_s^o, we can obtain $p(o = o'|z = k) = \phi_{scko'}^o$ for each collection c, and the Eq.(8) can be written as:

$$p(o = o'|q, \phi_s^o) \propto \sum_{k}^{K} \phi_{scko'}^o \prod_{n=1}^{N} p(q_n|z = k)n_k \tag{10}$$

Here, $\phi_{cko'}^o, \phi_{scko'}^o$ are the common topic-opinion distribution and collection-specific topic-opinion distribution, respectively. n_k denotes the total number of words associated with topic k. The opinion words are ranked by the descending order of $p(o|q)$ in response to the query q. Since $\phi_{cko'}^o, \phi_{scko'}^o$, and n_k are all computed offline, the Eq. (9) and Eq. (10) are a weighted inner product between two vectors, which make the search process very efficient.

4.2 Topic-Opinion Association Visualization

Topic-opinion association visualization is to exploit the output of our MMTOM to conduct association analysis among the learned topics and opinions for social event understanding. One type of topic-opinion association is the entity or product aspect-opinion association [13]. For example, the entity Apple may include its products or topics like ipod, ipad, iphone and its founder of Steve Jobs, and there are positive or negative opinion words towards Apple. For social event, topic-opinion association visualization can clearly visualize the associations of different topics with the corresponding opinions. As a result, users can have a quick capture about the whole evolutionary process of event over time and obtain its opinions. Furthermore, because the proposed MMTOM can learn two kinds of topic-opinion space including common topic space and collection-specific topic space, user also can understand what happens and the corresponding opinions in multiple views.

Inspired by the Nielsen mapping algorithm [2], we visualize the learned multi-modal topics and the corresponding opinions by a circular layout map. Specifically, we consider two fundamental requirements $(\mathbf{r}, \boldsymbol{\vartheta})$ which are the polar coordinates of all the mined topic-opinion clusters of a hot event to place the mined topics and the corresponding opinions.The radial distance r denotes that a significant topic-opinion cluster appears closer to the center of the map, and the angular distance ϑ denotes the closeness density between two topic-opinion clusters. The smaller ϑ between clusters is, the higher the closeness is. Specifically, we calculate the radial distance r by counting the topic assignment variables of textual and visual topic words in the documents for each leaned topic-opinion cluster (z_k, l_k), $\mathcal{S}(z_k, l_k) = \log(\sum_d(\sum_{i=1} \mathbb{1}(z_{di}^w = k) + \sum_{i=1} \mathbb{1}(z_{di}^v = k)) + 1)$. Here, z_{di}^w and z_{di}^v denote the topic assignments for the i-th textual topic word and visual topic word in the document d, $\mathbb{1}(\cdot)$ is a indicator function: $\mathbb{1}(true) = 1$ and $\mathbb{1}(false) = 0$. Then we normalize the score to interval $[0, 1]$ by calculating the radial coordinates $\mathbf{r}(z_k, l_k)$ of topic-opinion cluster (z_k, l_k) with logistic increasing function $\mathcal{F}(x) = \frac{1}{1+e^{-x}}$. To obtain the angular coordinates $\boldsymbol{\vartheta}$, we first compute all pairwise similarities $\mathbf{S} \in \mathbb{R}^{(K)\times(K)}$ between the topics, and apply the modified spherical Laplacian Eigenmap method [14] to project the aspect-opinion clusters into a circular manifold by optimizing the objective as $\boldsymbol{\vartheta} = \arg\min_{\{\vartheta_i\}} \sum_i \sum_j S_{ij}|\vartheta_i - \vartheta_j| - |\vartheta_i - \vartheta_j|^\gamma$. We then employ a gradient descent procedure to obtain the $\boldsymbol{\vartheta}$. Finally, by the obtained radial distance r and the angular distance ϑ, we can visualize each topic-opinion cluster on the map. To make visualization more visually pleasant and informative, we slightly refine the position of each topic-opinion cluster by separating the overlapped pairs and reducing the blank areas on the map.

5. EXPERIMENTS

In this Section, we firstly introduce our data collection and implementation details. Then, we show the evaluation of the proposed MMTOM. Finally, we give the results of two applications.

5.1 Data Collection

The evaluation dataset is constructed from online social media sources. We mainly focus on the hot social event "Syria civil war"

Table 2: The statistics of the collected dataset.

Hot social event	Syria civil war		
	New York Times	Sputnik	Hurriyet Daily News
Number of text documents	8,968	13,097	12,211
Number of photos	12,655	15,061	8,367
Number of topic words	2,541,868	1,946,555	2,400,790
Number of opinion words	415,586	230,765	325,283

which happens recently and is a very representative and controversial event. We crawled news published in the websites of New York Times[1], Sputnik[2], and Hurriyet Daily News[3], which are important news agencies in U.S., Russia, and Turkey, respectively. These websites are all in English and cover a long period. We attempt to mine these newspaper documents including text information and images to obtain the political topics and the corresponding opinions of the three countries. Totally, we collect 34,276 textual documents and 36,083 images from March 2011 to December 2015. Table 2 shows the detailed statistics of the dataset. Therefore, we can find a wide range of topics and compare the different opinions of the three countries in multiple views. Before using our topic models, we remove stop words using the standard list of stop words, and also remove words which have frequencies less than 5.

5.2 Implementation details

For visual description, the words are based on image patches, which are obtained by SLIC segmentation method [1]. To obtain the description for image patch, we densely sample SIFT points, and adopt the popular sparse coding based method [27, 28] to encode each SIFT point. Then, based on the feature codes of all SIFT points of each patch, we adopt max pooling to obtain its description. Once obtaining all image patch descriptions, we adopt K-means to build a codebook. By hard assignment coding of each patch, each image can be described as the counts of the words in the codebook. To obtain the textual topic words and opinion words from the collected dataset, we extract all the nouns in the documents as the topic words and the adjectives, verbs, and adverbs as the opinion words. To classify tokens into nouns, adjectives, verbs, and adverbs, we use the Part-of-Speech tagging function provided by Stanford NLP toolkits[4]. As for the hyper-parameters of the model, without any prior knowledge, we empirically set fixed values, i.e., $\alpha_c = 50/K, \gamma = 0.5, \eta = 0.01$.

5.3 Evaluation of the Proposed MMTOM

In this section, we show both qualitative and quantitative evaluations of the proposed MMTOM model. The results clearly demonstrate the effectiveness of our model in mining the multi-modal topics and the corresponding opinions in multiple views.

5.3.1 *Quantitative Evaluation*

Evaluation Metrics: To conduct quantitative evaluation of multi-modal multi-view topic-opinion mining, we resort to the perplexity as the metric, which is a standard quantitative measure in topic modeling literature to compare the performance of various topic models [7]. Moreover, to demonstrate the effectiveness of the proposed model to correctly model the relationships between the topic words and the opinion words, we adopt opinion prediction as a performance measure referred to [5, 20].

Baseline Methods: To demonstrate the effectiveness of the proposed MMTOM model, we compare it with five baseline methods: **(1)** LDA [7]. This is a LDA-based extension by concatenating the textual and visual features. **(2)** Correspondence LDA (Corr-LDA) [5]. This model assumes a one-to-one correspondence among the topics of different modalities, which capture the topic-level relations between images and text annotations. **(3)** mm-LDA [24]: This model extends LDA to represent the joint distribution of images and text by using textual and visual information jointly. **(4)** Topic-opinion Mining Model (TOM): This model only mines the topics and the corresponding opinions on text, and does not differentiate common topics and collection-specific topics across all collections. **(5)** Multi-view Topic-opinion Mining Model (MTOM): This model is a simplification of the proposed MMTOM without considering image information.

The Comparison of Joint Probability Perplexity: We firstly utilize the perplexity as our goodness-of-fit-measure to assess the generalization performance of our model. The joint probability perplexity reflects the ability of the model to predict the topic words and the corresponding opinion words for new unseen documents. More formally, the joint probability of a test set of documents D_{test} is calculated as in Eq. (11). Here, $p(\mathbf{w}_d, \mathbf{v}_d, \mathbf{o}_d) = p(\mathbf{w}_d) + p(\mathbf{v}_d) + p(\mathbf{o}_d|\mathbf{w}_d, \mathbf{v}_d), p(\mathbf{w}_d) = \prod_{i=1}^{N_{w,d}} \sum_{k\in K} p(w_i|z_i^w = k)p(z_i^w = k|d), p(\mathbf{v}_d) = \prod_{i=1}^{N_{v,d}} \sum_{k\in K} p(v_i|z_i^v = k)p(z_i^v = k|d)$, and $p(\mathbf{o}_d|\mathbf{w}_d, \mathbf{v}_d) = \prod_{i=1}^{N_{o,d}} \sum_{k\in K} p(o_i|l_i = k)p(l_i = k|d)$.

$$perplexity(D_{test}) = \exp\left\{-\frac{\sum_{d\in D_{test}} \log p(\mathbf{w}_d, \mathbf{v}_d, \mathbf{o}_d)}{\sum_{d\in D_{test}} (N_{w,d} + N_{v,d} + N_{o,d})}\right\} \tag{11}$$

The joint probability perplexity is calculated via Eq.(11) by using joint probability of a test data set. We randomly divide the dataset into two parts: the training set and the test set, and randomly select 10% of the documents as a held-out test data and train the model on the remaining documents. We compute the perplexity for each baseline method with different number of topics. In our experiments, we adapt LDA to model all documents by concatenating the topic words and opinion words. In Corr-LDA and mm-LDA, we model multi-modal topics and opinions jointly. Figure 4 shows the joint probability perplexity of all methods, and the proposed MMTOM achieves the best with different number of topics.

The Comparison of Opinion Prediction Perplexity: To measure the performance of opinion prediction, we compute the perplexity on the held-out test set. In this case, opinion prediction perplexity reflects the ability of a method to model the relationships between the topic words and the opinion words and predict opinion words for new unseen documents. The perplexity is calculated using Eq. (11) by replacing $p(\mathbf{w}_d, \mathbf{v}_d, \mathbf{o}_d)$ with $p(\mathbf{o}_d)$, $p(D_{test}) = \exp\{-\frac{\sum_{d\in D_{test}} \log p(\mathbf{o}_d)}{\sum_{d\in D_{test}} N_{o,d}}\}$, where $p(\mathbf{o}_d) = \prod_{i=1}^{N_{o,d}} \sum_{k\in K} p(o_i|l_i = k)p(l_i = k|d)$, $\mathbf{o}_\mathbf{d}$ is the set of opinion words appearing in the test document d. We compute the perplexity for each method with different number of topics. In our experiments, we train a LDA model only on the opinion words. The lower opinion prediction perplexity score shows better performance. The results for different models are shown in Figure 5.

[1] http://www.nytimes.com

[2] http://sputniknews.com

[3] www.hurriyetdailynews.com

[4] http://nlp.stanford.edu/software/index.shtml

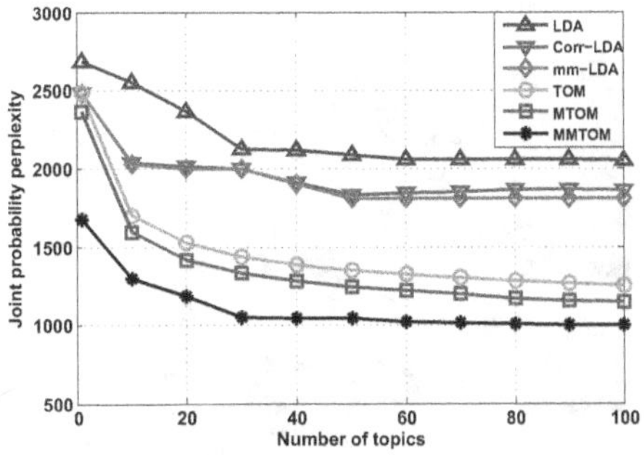

Figure 4: The joint probability perplexity scores for different topic models on our collected dataset.

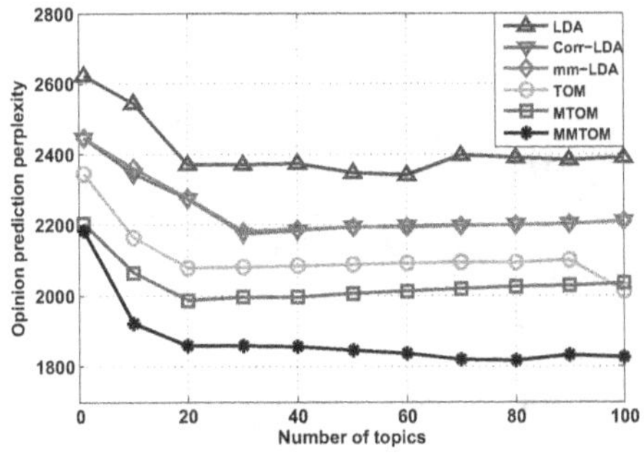

Figure 5: The opinion prediction perplexity scores for different topic models on our collected dataset.

Based on the results in Figure 4 and Figure 5, we can make the following conclusions: **(1)** The LDA shows inferior performance. This is due to the fact that LDA models textual, visual topic words and opinion words obscurely and cannot differentiate the associations between multi-modal topics and opinions. **(2)** The Corr-LDA, mm-LDA, and TOM achieve better results by leveraging the dependencies between topic words and opinion words. However, they do not differentiate common topics and collection-specific topics across all collections, and do not utilize extra information, such as document's collection and collection-specific topics, to assign a higher probability to words more likely to fit the data. **(3)** The MMTOM model achieves better performance than the MTOM, which shows that it is useful to model and exploit the multi-modal information. Moreover, the proposed MTOM and MMTOM consistently and significantly outperform other state-of-the-art topic models. The major reason is that our proposed method can reasonably model the correlations between multi-modal topics and opinions more accurately by separating the multi-modal common topics and collection-specific topics in multiple views without needing to introduce noise topics, which makes better document representations in the latent semantic space. It is clear that the perplexity is stable when K = 30. Therefore, we choose the desired topic number $K = 30$ for the proposed MMTOM in the following experiments.

5.3.2 Qualitative Evaluation

We qualitatively demonstrate the effectiveness of our MMTOM by illustrating the discovered topics and the corresponding opinions. Figure 6 presents a sample of topics and the corresponding opinions for "topic#11", "topic#16", "topic#22" and "topic#28" on the collected dataset, respectively. We present the top-ranked textual words and visual images for each common topic and collection-specific topic, and top-ranked opinion words for the corresponding opinion space, which can help interpret the property of social event. In topic and opinion visualization, textual topic words and opinion words are sorted from the distribution $p(w|z)$, and $p(o|z)$, while the images are sorted by counting the number of visual descriptions and textual topic words with the topic in different document $p(z|w, v)$. The coupling between $p(w|z)$ and $p(v|z)$ of each multi-modal topic in multiple views can indicate the correlations between the textual words and image patches. The coupling between $p(w|z)$, $(p(v|z))$ and $p(o|z)$ can illustrate each view's opinions on the topic z represented by multi-modal topic words w, v. Figure 6 shows four multi-modal topics and the corresponding opinions in multiple views from the dataset. From the figure, we can see that the words of each topic and the corresponding opinions reveal clear interpretations and identify the multi-view differences in opinion discovery. For example, Topic 11 is about topic "Assad regime at the beginning of Syria Unrest". In this topic, three countries have common topics and the corresponding opinions, such as "shot, killed, crackdown, reform". Meanwhile, the three countries have different biases. U.S. emphasizes on "human rights" and "sanction", and its opinion words include "antigovernment, stop, ban", Russia emphasizes on "dialogue" and "support", and its opinion words include "visit, peaceful, negotiating", while Turkey criticizes Assad regime strongly, and its opinion words include "embattled promise brutal leave quell bloody". In Topic 16, which is about the topic "Syrian presidential election", there are common opinion words like "support insurgent conflict killed win control". However, three countries have differences in their opinions. U.S. has negative opinions, and there are opinion words like "disputed, depressing, failed", Turkey also has negative opinions, and there are opinion words like "disputed depressing embarrassing", but Russia has positive opinions, and its opinion words are "stop, consolidated, achieve, positive, legal". The discovered topic words and opinion words with clear semantics can be treated as informative attributes of social event, which can be used for various applications. For the discovered opinion words, we can observe that the opinions reveal the collective views and multi-view differences towards the correlated topics.

5.4 Evaluation of the Applications

In this subsection, we evaluate the effectiveness of the proposed MMTOM on multi-modal multi-view topic-opinion retrieval and topic-opinion association visualization.

5.4.1 Multi-modal Multi-view Topic-Opinion Retrieval

In this subsection, we conduct quantitative experiments to evaluate the performance of retrieval functionality of our MMTOM including multi-modal topic retrieval and multi-view opinion retrieval as described in Section 4. For multi-modal topic retrieval, we have two retrieval tasks including text-based retrieval, and image annotation. For multi-view opinion retrieval, given each query topic, the model returns a ranked list of opinion words in multiple views. In our experiment, we manually build 20 queries for each kind of retrieval task. We choose these queries based on several knowledge sources, such as Wikipedia[5]. For each query, the model returns a ranked list of results for each view, and the retrieved results are judged by people who are familiar with the queries. We use a binary judgment (i.e., "relevant" or "not relevant") for each returned result against the query, and use Normalized Discounted Cumulative Gain (NDCG) as evaluation metric. Here, NDCG at position k is defined as NDCG@$k = \frac{1}{Z} \times \sum_{i=1}^{k} \frac{2^{r_i}-1}{\log_2(i+1)}$, where r_i is the relevance rating of result at rank i. Note that, r_i is 1 if the query is relevant to the returned result and 0 otherwise. Z is a normalization term. We compute the NDCG@k for each query, $k = \{5, 10, 15, 20\}$, and the final results of NDCG@k are averaged on all queries for each retrieval task.

[5]http://www.wikipedia.org/

Figure 6: Illustration of samples of discovered topics and the corresponding opinions (Common represents the common topic space. NYTimes, Sputnik, Hurriyet denote the collection-specific topic space in each collection, respectively.).

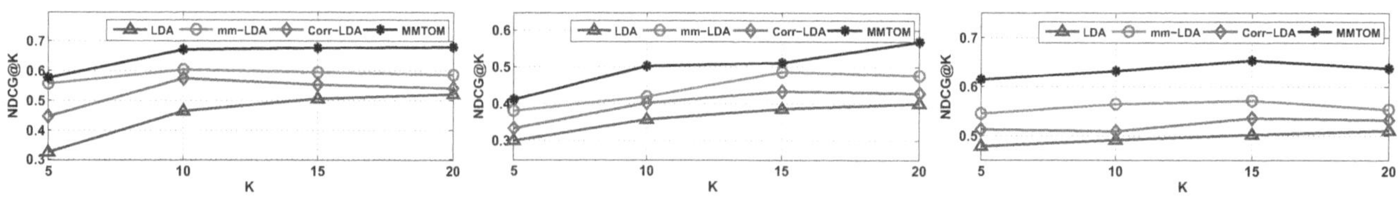

(a) Text-based retrieval (b) Image annotation (c) Multi-view opinion retrieval

Figure 7: Comparison of multi-modal multi-view topic-opinion retrieval averaged on all queries in terms of NDCG@5, 10, 15, 20.

In our experiments, the textual and visual words and opinion words are added into each model in a different setting way for different kinds of retrieval task. For the text-based retrieval, LDA, Corr-LDA, and mm-LDA are trained on the mixed textual and visual topic words. For the opinion retrieval task, we model multi-modal topics and opinions jointly for Corr-LDA and mm-LDA. The proposed MMTOM has two kinds of multi-view opinions of topics including common opinion space ϕ_c^o and collection-specific opinion space ϕ_s^o, and we can obtain the corresponding retrieval results in multiple views, and then rank the obtained retrieval results by scores. The settings of model training for all retrieval tasks are implemented in a standard way. The evaluation results of different methods for three kinds of retrieval tasks are shown in Figure 7. From the results, we have the following conclusions: **(1)** The LDA shows inferior performance. This is due to its incapability of learning the latent association relationships between multi-modal topics and opinions. **(2)** The Corr-LDA and mm-LDA achieve better results. This shows that it is useful to adopt multi-modal models to capture the intrinsic relationships between textual and visual information. **(3)** The proposed MMTOM outperforms the Corr-LDA and mm-LDA, and achieves the best retrieval performance for the three tasks under all values of K. This further demonstrates that the proposed model can effectively capture textual topic, visual topic and opinion in multiple views jointly, and learn multi-modal topics as well as corresponding opinions in multiple views.

5.4.2 Topic-opinion Association Visualization

Figure 8 shows the visualization process of topic-opinion association maps for each collection in multiple views about the hot controversial event "Syria civil war". Here, the map visualizes the top identified topic-opinion clusters which are placed according to the topic scores and angular values. For each topic, we generate a word cloud for the textual topic and opinion words using Tagxedo[6]. We use a circle plate to mark one topic, and the larger the size of mark is, the more significant the topic is. From the Figure 8, we make several interesting observations: **(1)** The topic-opinion association visualization can effectively discover different textual and visual topics with the corresponding opinions for a hot social event, and user also can understand what happens and the corresponding opinions in multiple views about the hot political controversial top-

[6]http://www.tagxedo.com/

Figure 8: Topic-opinion association maps in multiple views for event "Syria civil war". Please use high resolution for better view.

ics. **(2)** This map can concisely visualize important concepts of social event, and the top-ranked clusters correspond to certain popular and famous characteristics of the topics, such as "sanction" for "New York Times", "Russian" for "Sputnik", and "Turkey, crisis" for "Hurriyet Daily News". Based on the topic-opinion association visualization with multiple topics and opinions, it is easy for an intuitive topic exploration and a quick hot event understanding.

6. CONCLUSION

In this paper, we propose a novel multi-modal multi-view topic-opinion mining (MMTOM) model for social event analysis by utilizing multiple cross-collection sources in social news media. The proposed MMTOM can simultaneously model multi-modal topics as well as the corresponding opinions in multiple views in a unified and principled way. In experiments, the qualitative and quantitative results clearly demonstrate the effectiveness of the proposed model. Moreover, the proposed model is successfully applied to two applications. In the future, we will evaluate our model on more social events and investigate more applications, such as social event summarization and social event tracking and evolution.

7. ACKNOWLEDGMENT

This work was supported in part by National Basic Research Program of China (No. 2012CB316304), National Natural Science Foundation of China (No. 61225009, 61303173, 61432019, 61572498, 61532009, 61472379, 61572296, 61472115)

8. REFERENCES

[1] R. Achanta, A. Shaji, K. Smith, A. Lucchi, P. Fua, and S. Susstrunk. Slic superpixels, 2010. In Technical report, EPFL.

[2] N. Akiva, E. Greitzer, Y. Krichman, and J. Schler. Mining and visualizing online web content using bam: Brand association map. In *ICWSM*, 2008.

[3] Y. Bao, N. Collier, and A. Datta. A partially supervised cross-collection topic model for cross-domain text classification. In *CIKM*, pages 239–248, 2013.

[4] D. Blei and J. McAuliffe. Supervised topic models. In *NIPS*, pages 121–128. 2008.

[5] D. M. Blei and M. I. Jordan. Modeling annotated data. In *SIGIR*, pages 127–134, 2003.

[6] D. M. Blei and J. D. Lafferty. Dynamic topic models. In *ICML*, pages 113–120, 2006.

[7] D. M. Blei, A. Y. Ng, and M. I. Jordan. Latent dirichlet allocation. *JMLR*, 3:993–1022, 2003.

[8] Q. Fang, C. Xu, J. Sang, M. S. Hossain, and M. Ghulam. Word-of-mouth understanding: Entity-centric multimodal aspect-opinion mining in social media. *IEEE Trans. Multimedia*, 17(12):2281–2296, 2015.

[9] Y. Fang, L. Si, N. Somasundaram, and Z. Yu. Mining contrastive opinions on political texts using cross-perspective topic model. In *WSDM '12*, pages 63–72, 2012.

[10] T. L. Griffiths and M. Steyvers. Finding scientific topics. *Proceedings of the National Academy of Sciences*, 101:5228–5235, 2004.

[11] E. D. Gutiérrez, E. Shutova, P. Lichtenstein, G. de Melo, and L. Gilardi. Detecting cross-cultural differences using a multilingual topic model. *TACL*, 4:47–60, 2016.

[12] T. Hofmann. Probabilistic latent semantic analysis. In *UAI*, pages 289–296, 1999.

[13] K. L. Keller. Conceptualizing, measuring, and managing customer based brand equity. *Journal of Marketing*, pages 1–22, 1993.

[14] A. O. H. I. Kevin M. Carter, Raviv Raich. Spherical laplacian information maps (slim) for dimensionality reduction. In *SSP*, 2009.

[15] B. Liu and L. Zhang. A survey of opinion mining and sentiment analysis. In *Mining Text Data*, pages 415–463. 2012.

[16] W. Min, B. Bao, and C. Xu. Multimodal spatio-temporal theme modeling for landmark analysis. *IEEE MultiMedia*, 21(3):20–29, 2014.

[17] S. Moghaddam and M. Ester. Ilda: Interdependent lda model for learning latent aspects and their ratings from online product reviews. In *SIGIR '11*, pages 665–674, 2011.

[18] S. Moghaddam and M. Ester. On the design of lda models for aspect-based opinion mining. In *CIKM '12*, pages 803–812, 2012.

[19] M. Paul and R. Girju. Cross-cultural analysis of blogs and forums with mixed-collection topic models. In *EMNLP '09*, pages 1408–1417, 2009.

[20] D. Putthividhya, H. T. Attias, and S. S. Nagarajan. Topic regression multi-modal latent dirichlet allocation for image annotation. In *CVPR*, pages 3408–3415, 2010.

[21] S. Qian, T. Zhang, R. Hong, and C. Xu. Cross-domain collaborative learning in social multimedia. In *Proceedings of the 23rd Annual ACM Conference on Multimedia Conference, MM '15*, pages 99–108, 2015.

[22] S. Qian, T. Zhang, C. Xu, and M. S. Hossain. Social event classification via boosted multimodal supervised latent dirichlet allocation. *TOMCCAP*, 11(2):27:1–27:22, 2014.

[23] M. Qiu and J. Jiang. A latent variable model for viewpoint discovery from threaded forum posts. In *In Proceedings of the 2013 Conference of the North American Chapter of the Association for Computational Linguistics*, pages 1031–1040, 2013.

[24] D. Ramage, P. Heymann, C. D. Manning, and H. Garcia-Molina. Clustering the tagged web. In *WSDM*. ACM, 2009.

[25] X. Yang, T. Zhang, and C. Xu. Cross-domain feature learning in multimedia. *IEEE Trans. Multimedia*, 17(1):64–78, 2015.

[26] C. Zhai, A. Velivelli, and B. Yu. A cross-collection mixture model for comparative text mining. In *KDD '04*, pages 743–748, 2004.

[27] T. Zhang, B. Ghanem, S. Liu, C. Xu, and N. Ahuja. Low-rank sparse coding for image classification. In *ICCV*, pages 281–288, 2013.

[28] T. Zhang, S. Liu, N. Ahuja, and M.-H. Yang. Robust visual tracking via consistent low-rank sparse learning. *International Journal of Computer Vision*, 111(2):171–190, 2015.

Patterns of Free-form Curation: Visual Thinking with Web Content

Nic Lupfer, Andruid Kerne, Andrew M. Webb, Rhema Linder
Interface Ecology Lab, Department of Computer Science and Engineering, Texas A&M University
nic, andruid, andrew, rhema@ecologylab.net

ABSTRACT

Web curation involves choosing, organizing, and commenting on content. Popular web curation apps—e.g., Facebook, Twitter, and Pinterest—provide linear feeds that show people the latest content, but provide little support for articulating relationships among content elements. The new medium of *free-form web curation* enables multimedia elements to be spontaneously gathered from the web, written about, sketched amidst, manipulated, and visually assembled in a continuous space. Through free-form web curation, content is collected, interpreted, and arranged, creating context.

We conducted a field study of 1581 students in 6 courses, spanning diverse fields. We derive patterns of free-form curation through a visual grounded theory analysis of the resulting dataset of 4426 curations. From the observed range of invocations of the patterns in the performance of ideation tasks, we conclude that free-form is valuable as a new medium of web curation in how it supports creative visual thinking.

Keywords

curation; visual thinking; design; web media; education; pattern language

1. INTRODUCTION

Each day, on social media, hundreds of millions of people engage in *web curation*—they choose, comment on, and organize content. A limitation is that popular apps—e.g., Facebook, Twitter, and Pinterest—constrain organization of curated content to feeds and boards, using ranking algorithms based on parameters such as recency and popularity. Linear feeds are great for showing people the latest content, but provide limited support for free-form visual thinking that articulates relationships among content elements. Visual patterns, blends and combinations that express relationships are significant generative mechanisms of creative cognition [18].

We define curation in a broader cultural context by drawing from the arts *Curation* is the creative conceptualization and organization of an exhibition [36]. Works are collected, interpreted, and arranged, creating context, giving form to visual thinking, and producing cultural meaning.

MM '16, October 15 - 19, 2016, Amsterdam, Netherlands

ISBN 978-1-4503-3603-1/16/10... $15.00

DOI: http://dx.doi.org/10.1145/2964284.2964303

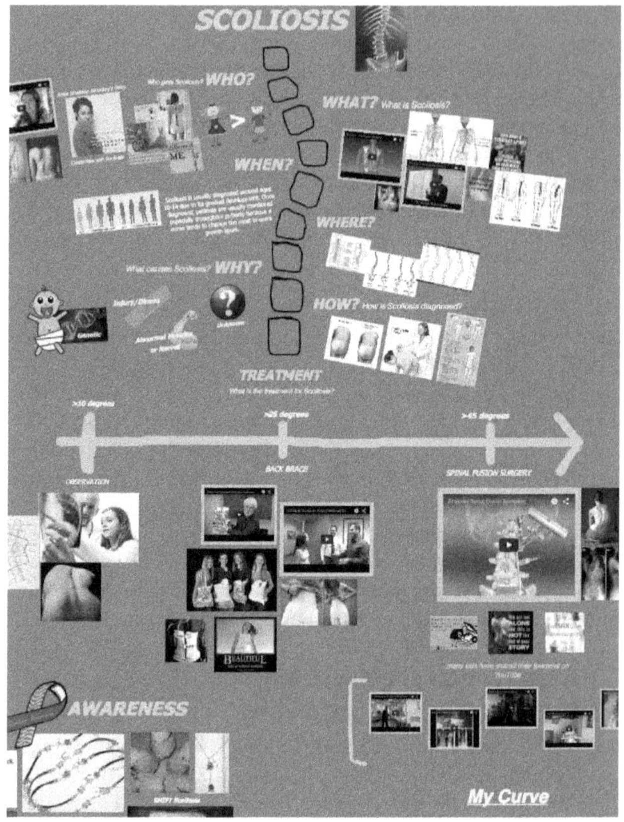

Figure 1: In *Scoliosis*, a personal health informatics free-form web curation, Katharine Kimmel manifests visual thinking by assembling her own sketches and writing with images from the web and YouTube videos [https://ideamache.ecologylab.net/v/bM6IaLoVvT/]. As a whole, the curation is educational and hopeful, conveying a sense of complexity and connectedness in dealing with a great challenge. $curation\_patterns = \{morphology|concrete,\ morphology|abstract,\ group|spatial\}$

We integrate trends in art and social media to create the new medium of free-form web curation. We draw from *free-form thinking*, a creative cognitive process of open exploration, association, improvisation, synthesis, emergence, and ideation [31]. *Free-form web curation* enables multimedia elements to be spontaneously gathered from the web, written about, sketched amidst, manipulated, and visually assembled in a continuous space (see example, Figure 1). The visual assemblage forms a digital abstract map, liberated from the confines of particular websites by a zoomable user interface. The goal of this holistic medium is to support creative cognition [18] of relationships and the emergence of new ideas.

Figure 2: Jordan Jump curated *Laundry Notifier* [`https://ideamache.ecologylab.net/v/teGYF8lbi5/`] in the ideation stage of designing an innovative product. Elements—a conceptual statement, potential devices and companies to partner with, and patents of prior products—are spatially organized over a washing machine. $curation\_patterns = \{overlap|compose,\ group|spatial,\ group|nested\}$

Our research question is: how does free-form curation support visual thinking with web content? *Visual thinking* is a creative process—understood by connecting the fields of art and psychology—in which perception becomes integrated with higher order cognitive operations, such as exploration, analysis, synthesis, and abstraction. In visual thinking, "Concepts take shape" [2].

We conducted a field study of 1581 students in 10 course offerings, in a variety of subjects. We formed a dataset of 4426 free-form web curations. Students used the *IdeaMâché* web app to perform free-form curation [`https://ideamache.ecologylab.net`] on ideation assignments addressing diverse intellectual activities: personal health informatics (Figure 1), entrepreneurial innovation (Figure 2), research paper inception (Figure 3), architectural design (Figures 4, 5), and lecture presentation (Figures 6, 7).

The study participants were everyday students, not professional designers or curators. Prominent creativity researchers recognize that people achieve significant ideation across a spectrum of levels of impact: mini-c (personal learning), little-c (involving friends or classmates), Pro-C (professsional), and Big-C (societal innovation) [24]. The curations in the dataset are mostly mini-c to little-c. This is appropriate because our objective is to investigate how free-form web curation functions as a medium for creative visual thinking by everyday students, in diverse fields. The range of curation forms we discover has implications for the potential engagement in visual thinking by millions of users of popular web curation apps.

Through a visual grounded theory analysis of the dataset, we derive patterns of free-form web curation: 1) *morphology* (concrete, abstract), 2) *overlap* (compose, composite, map), 3) *group* (spatial, nested), and 4) *path* (linear, non-linear).

A *pattern language* is a set of forms of spatial organization, each of which supports particular human activity [1]. A pattern language is generative. Patterns—like words, phrases, grammars, and other forms of written language—can be combined in an infinity of emergent systems of unforeseen relationships. We use the pattern language to demonstrate how free-form curation supports creative visual thinking. From our investigation, we derive implications for the design of web curation apps.

2. SENSITIZING CONCEPTS

We derive and connect sensitizing concepts from research in visual thinking, visual grounded theory, pattern languages, hypertext, information composition, found objects, assemblage, and curation.

2.1 Visual Thinking

Psychologist and art theorist, Rudolf Arnheim, introduced the term *visual thinking*, finding that perception, recognition, and reflection become intertwined in creative acts of forming and illustrating new meanings [2]. Psychologist Barbara Tversky provides empirical evidence of the abstract and concrete functions of forms of visual thinking, such as lines, arrows, maps and diagrams [45]. An ACM CHI workshop addressed how visual thinking and curation are es-

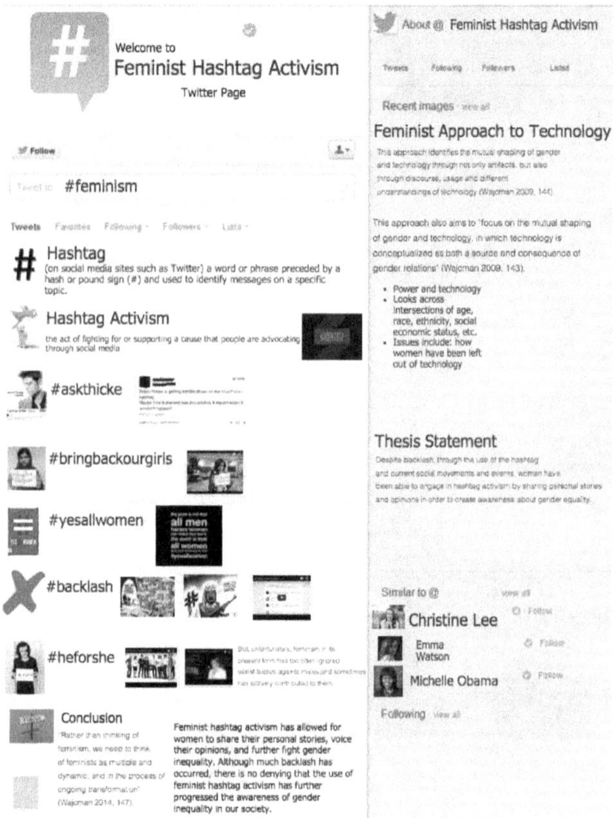

Figure 3: Christine Lee's final paper ideation, *Feminist Hashtag Activism* [`https://ideamache.ecologylab.net/v/NcH3CXW73n/`], conceptualizes Twitter as a site of feminist activism. *curation_patterns* = {*morphology*|*concrete*, *overlap*|*compose*, *group*|*spatial*, *group*|*nested*}

sential to human-computer interaction [7]. The present research supports visual thinking through curation, as a means of knowledge creation and ideation, using web multimedia content. *Pictorial*, a recent ACM publication format (non-interactive), uses images as primary material for creating and articulating knowledge about interactivity [8]. The present research uses visual data as the primary material for creating knowledge with grounded theory methods.

2.2 Visual Grounded Theory

Charmaz articulates an iterative empirical qualitative methodology for constructing grounded theory, involving: gathering rich data, initial coding, theoretical sampling, focused coding, categorization, the incorporation of sensitizing concepts, and conceptual refinement [13]. Much grounded theory uses field notes and transcriptions of interviews as the primary form of rich data [14, 13]. Konecki advances *visual grounded theory*, shifting the primary source of empirical material from textual to visual data, as motivated by a context of research [27].

To investigate visual thinking, we treat the collected free-form web curations as visual data. We invoke visual qualitative methods [3], following other researchers who use visual evidence as a primary form of data [21]. Studies investigated how visual objects, as material, are seen, watched, touched, and carried [39]. The materiality of visual data has been addressed in terms of physical characteristics of media, such as print [16]. We recontextualize visual ethnography to address multimedia digital objects in the web browser. We develop materiality in terms of how digital found objects become recontextualized as material through curation.

Free-form curations function as meta-indexical representations through assemblage of web content [22]. Meta-indexical visual representations are not self-contained. They reference multiple meanings, which manifest through the viewer's interpretation. In the present research, we investigate visual and conceptual means for the design of structures that extend the indexicality already inherent in the materiality of web content and its hypermedia links.

2.3 Pattern Languages

Alexander introduced the construct of *pattern language*, in architecture, for developing, "a solution to a problem in context," which accounts for situated physical and cultural variables [1]. Pattern languages have been used in human-computer interaction to focus contextualized design and discussion [17, 10]. They have been used in software engineering as a means for codifying recurrent problems, solutions, and consequences [19]. Observing how patterns are used in practice has been shown to serve as impetus for reflection, discussion, and the derivation of implications for design [15].

2.4 Hypertext / Hypermedia

Free-form web curation is a type of hypermedia. Digital humanities scholar Bolter recognizes that hypermedia enables an author to represent a set of ideas as a web, which connects verbal and visual elements in a conceptual space [9]. Writer Michael Joyce creates hypertext works that help readers recognize and manipulate connections [23]. Spatial hypertext has been shown to support representation of early stages of design [35].

2.5 Information Composition

Information composition is a holistic medium of curation, which extends spatial hypertext to support ideation by promoting creative cognition of relationships among curated clippings and annotations [25]. Composition visually and semantically juxtaposes and contextualizes elements. Studies have shown that information composition supports ideation [25]. In the present research, free-form web curation extends information composition with sketching, multimedia, a zoomable user interface, and contextualization on the web.

2.6 Assemblage of Found Objects ⇒ Curation

We situate free-form web curation amidst art practices in which context transforms the meanings of found objects and their assemblages. Marcel Duchamp developed the *found object* conceptual construct by taking an ordinary article, exhibiting it with a new title, in a new context, and so transforming its significance [33]. Paul D. Miller, aka DJ Spooky, identifies the internet as a source of found object *material*, to be recontextualized in remix and mashup [34]. Assemblage is means for making a work of art by fastening found object materials together. Assemblage showcases the duality and tension between the original and resulting contexts [40]. Curation serves as a means for framing and conceptualizing how creative work and its contexts are understood [36].

In the twentieth century, practices of art and curation converged. In art, Dada [33] and Surrealism [12] launched the wave of art works made by appropriating and assembling found objects. Meanwhile, curation evolved from caring for a collection, to active specification and assemblage of new art works for a particular exhibition; curators, such as Lucy Lippard and Harald Szeemann, took the role of art creators [36]. Curation emerged as a distinct mode of discourse and framework for interaction across disciplines. Christiane Paul observes that new media art curation requires a "Parallel, distributed, living information space, open to artistic inference—a space of exchange and presentation that is transparent and flexible" [37].

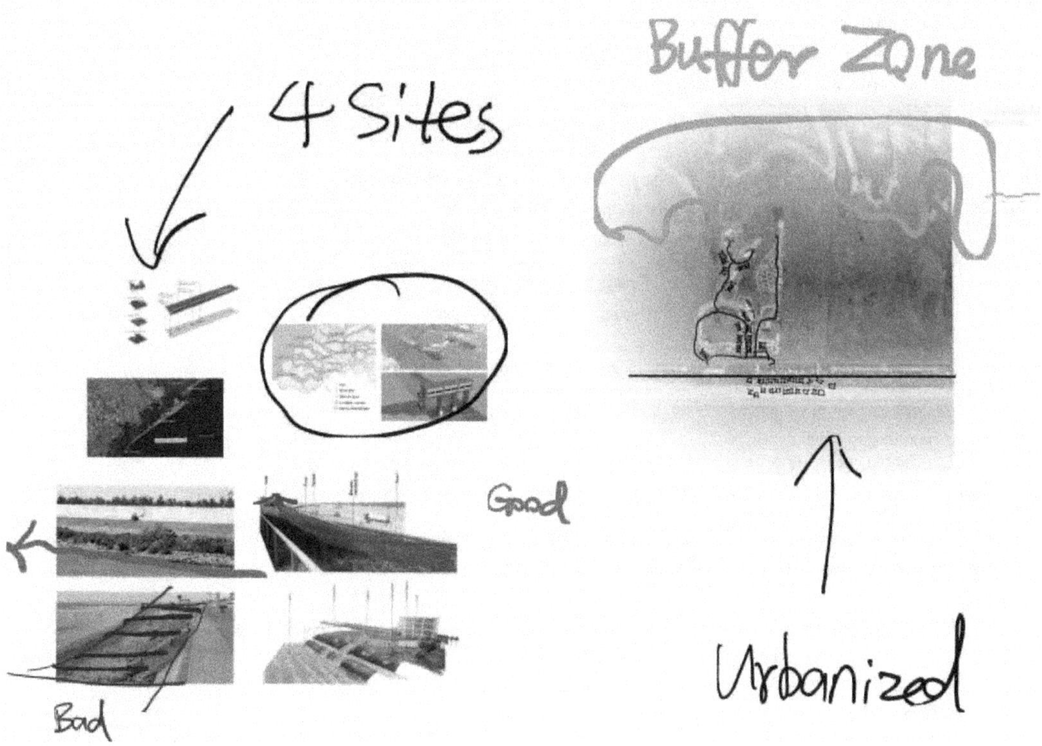

Figure 4: *buffer zone* (Professional Study) arranges beachfront and satellite coastal images in grids [`https://ideamache.ecologylab.net/v/6F7MNpHZ8K/`]. Visual thinking contrasts approaches to flood management in the Netherlands ("Good") and Texas ("Bad"). Sketches over images analyze and abstract visual forms. *curation_patterns* = {*overlap*|*map*, *group*|*spatial*}

3. METHODOLOGY

Our methodology for investigating expression through free-form web curation was to conduct a field study across six courses, form a visual dataset, and analyze it with grounded theory methods. Through the analysis, we identified codes. Incorporating sensitizing concepts, we used the codes as the basis for a pattern language of visual thinking in free-form web curation.

Participating students used the IdeaMâché web curation app to create free-form web curations on various ideation assignments. IdeaMâché is characterized by a zoomable user interface, which enables assembling large amounts of content across scales. It supports collecting multiple types of elements: text, image, video, and sound. The user collects content elements through drag and drop in the web browser. Users can perform visual transformations on elements, including scale, rotation, Z-order, and opacity. Users can annotate their curations through sketching and writing with text.

3.1 Study Protocol

In our ongoing field study, we work with university professors to incorporate free-form web curation into coursework. In each course, before students perform assignments, we present an introductory lecture about web curation and the IdeaMâché app. Students then author free-form web curations as part of mandatory or extra credit ideation assignments. Instructors decide the number of assignments to offer and the specifications. Course instructors collaborate with us to design situated ideation assignments involving free-form curation.

While Institutional Review Boards emphasize confidentiality, we recognize the rights of student study participants to be credited for their creative work. Thus, our study protocol gives students the right to opt out, participate confidentially, or be attributed for their work.

3.2 Study Contexts: Courses

The six courses contributing to the dataset span four university departments: Environmental Design (1 course, 1481 students), Landscape Architecture (3 courses, 63 students), Communication (1 course, 22 students), and Computer Science (1 course, 15 students). Students and instructors in the computer science course are among the authors of this paper. Authors of this paper were not students or instructors in the other courses.

We formed the free-form web curation dataset by aggregating works authored by consenting students using the IdeaMâché environment, over 5 semesters, from the Spring 2013 semester through Spring 2015. Through 10 offerings of the 6 courses, 1581 participating students created a total of 4426 curations.

An introductory undergraduate environmental design course, *The Design Process: Creativity and Entrepreneurship* (DPCE), participated in the study over all 5 semesters. Students work as inventors and proto-entrepreneurs, creating concepts and sketches for innovations. On an open-ended ideation assignment, students chose a curation topic, e.g., wedding planning, workout routines, or personal health informatics (*Scoliosis*, Figure 1). Students also curated free-form *prior work collections*, each addressing needs, resources, and precedents for an innovation (*Laundry Notifier*, Figure 2.).

Two undergraduate architecture courses participated in Spring 2015 and one graduate course in Fall 2014. In *History of Landscape Architecture I*, students curated to create ideas involving a historic landscape (Figure 5). In *Landscape Design IV*, student teams used curation for landscape design ideation. In *Professional Study*, a graduate studio, students gained experience designing for real-world sites incorporating photographs, satellite images, and geographic maps (*buffer zone*, Figure 4).

Pattern	Sub-pattern	Definition	Example Figures	Occurrences
morphology		The arrangement of elements corresponds to a recognizable form.		253
	concrete	The corresponding form is a physical or digital object or being.	1, 3, 5	
	abstract	The corresponding form is a map, shape, or plot.	1, 6	
overlap		The use of arrangement and transparency, such that elements coincide in the X-Y plane, and are stacked in Z.		385
	compose	The use of partial or complete overlap to strongly connect multiple elements.	2, 3, 5	
	composite	The use of alpha blending to visually synthesize multiple elements.		
	map	The underlying elements relate to a physical space or geographic area.	4	
group		Arrangement of elements to delineate distinct subsets.		830
	spatial	The use of positioning to create white space, which clearly separates one or more sets of elements.	1, 2, 3, 7, 6, 4	
	nested	The use of scale and arrangement to place some elements within the bounds of another.	2, 3, 5	
path		Arrangement of elements into one or more legible sequences. May involve connecting sketches.		537
	linear	A single, well-defined, ordered sequence.		
	non−linear	Branching, with subsequences that fork and junction, and / or with multiple connected components.	7	

Table 1: A visual thinking pattern language of free-form web curation, with examples. Occurrences denotes the number of times the pattern appeared among the 881 curations coded in the second round. In the text, we use the notation $major\_pattern \mid minor\_pattern$**.**

One upper level undergraduate communication course, *Cultural Studies of Communication Technology*, participated in Fall 2014. Each student created a free-form web curation in the ideation stage of the final paper (*Feminist Hashtag Activism*, Figure 3).

One graduate level computer science course, *Curation and Ideation meet Social Media*, participated in Fall 2014. Here, web curation served as a means of practice and as a subject of theory. Students used *IdeaMâché* for presentations on assigned readings and research projects (Figures 6, 7). Linder et al. studied how presentation with free-form web curation in this course stimulated open, free-form discussion in the classroom [31]; they did not analyze visual patterns.

3.3 Visual Grounded Theory Analysis

We took a visual grounded theory approach, performing initial and focused coding of the free-form web curation dataset. We formed an initial set of 44 curations by theoretically sampling the dataset through a situated, interpretive process conducted over time, in which teaching team members for the various courses and the IdeaMâché team identified best curations. Initial coding was performed by interpreting each free-form curation in terms of its visual and conceptual forms and writing down descriptors. These descriptors, or codes, could refer to the curation in part or as a whole.

We initially identified 13 unique codes. From these 13 initial codes, we formed a set of 9 focused codes by collapsing similar codes together. The process of deriving clear and distinct focused codes involved the researchers either choosing from the initial codes or synthesizing small subsets into combined codes. For example the two initial codes *design mimicry* and *shape nesting* were combined into the *morphology* focused code.

Using the focused codes, we performed a second round of coding of another 881 curations. These 881 curations were theoretically sampled from the dataset based on the Fluency ideation metric. Fluency, the quantity of elements, is an ideation metric [41, 25], which has been validated by creativity researchers as an indicator of creativity [20, 42]. We theorize that the Fluency metric tends to indicate significant design phenomena. The mean Fluency of the initial set of 44 curations was 79.8 elements ($\sigma = 70.6$). The mean Fluency of the second round subset was 79.1 elements ($\sigma = 38.6$).

We reached saturation and stopped coding. During the focused coding, we validated codes and organized them into distinct categories. We synthesized these categories into patterns of free-form web curation, which we describe in the next section.

> Every individual act of building is a process in which space gets differentiated [p 19].
>
> Each pattern is ... a bundle of relationships, capable of being different each time it occurs... A collection of these patterns, each one a fluid field... is capable of generating an entirely unpredictable system of new and unforeseen relationships [p. 223].
>
> By building our lives out of these patterns, we are people of our culture [p 71].
>
> –C. Alexander, *The Timeless Way of Building* [1]

4. PATTERNS OF FREE-FORM WEB CURATION

We use *pattern language* as a sensitizing concept to build on our visual grounded theory analysis of the dataset. A pattern language is a generative vocabulary for creative expression in some medium, be it physical architecture or free-form web curation. Patterns of spatial organization directly support patterns of human activity [1].

We sought to understand how typical students use free-form web curation as everyday designers [47] to engage in ideation [32] through visual thinking. We identified spatial patterns, in which students curate content in a manner distinct from practice with popular feed and board techniques. As in Dada, Surrealism, remix, mash-up, and everyday design, we expected to observe the appropriation of content as material. In contrast with Tufte [43, 44], we did not expect our investigation of everyday, mini-c visual thinking to identify groundbreaking techniques for the presentation of visual data.

We used our focused codes to derive a visual thinking pattern language of free-form web curation (Table 1). We identified major patterns and distinct categories within each. We define a notation for pattern types and sub-types: $major\_pattern \mid minor\_pattern$.

Like Alexander, we observe that patterns are combined in a great variety of ways in order to support human expression and activity as culture. Some patterns are complementary and often appear

Figure 5: *Christina Vaughn's World* features bridge and skyscraper sketches [https://ideamache.ecologylab.net/v/1MnMBuSkTs/]. Vaughn appropriates and tiles photographs of historic buildings to fill in the skyscraper sketch. The curation gives form to ideation involving the recycling of building designs and materials. $curation\_patterns = \{morphology|concrete,\ overlap|compose,\ group|nested\}$

together. For example, *group* is often used in conjunction with *path*; authors form sequences not just of individual elements, but of element sub-sets. Another complementary patterns example combines *morphology* and *overlap*; authors use Z-axis ordering to create larger shapes out of a set of elements.

As described above, we performed a second round of focused coding on 881 curations. Among these, we identified a mean of 2.69 patterns per curation ($\sigma = 1.14$). The distribution of occurrences of the patterns across the dataset is presented in Table 1.

4.1 Morphology

The *morphology* pattern visually arranges elements in a recognizable form, which may be concrete or abstract. A morphology conjoins visual structures to support gestalt reading of a curation [28]. The *morphology* pattern provides a basis for Tufte's micro / macro designs [43], in which a form mitigates complexity by providing detail in one level of reading and serving as a texture in another. This supports interleaved levels of contextual interpretation.

morphology | concrete sometimes uses mimicry to creatively integrate form and content. In *Feminist Hashtag Activism*, Christine Lee instantiates this pattern by organizing her curation to mimic the layout of a Twitter page (Figure 3). Appropriated materials include the Twitter layout and linked hashtags. Lee uses morphology of these appropriated materials to create a holistic, meta-indexical perspective on the role of Twitter in contemporary feminism.

Christina Vaughn's World exhibits *morphology | concrete* by tiling images of prior buildings within a sketched skyscraper (Figure 5). The new building is constructed by appropriating found objects. Her free-form curation develops and indexes a creative concept of creating new buildings, using old ones as material.

morphology | abstract enables authors to map a curation space to a mathematical or rhetorical space. Andrew Webb's *graphic sign system: analysis of information* invokes the *morphology | abstract* pattern by organizing elements as a 2D plot (Figure 6). The elements are material clipped from Bertin's Semiology of Graphics curriculum [6]. Along the *x* axis, labeled 'concepts', elements are positioned left to right, according to topic. Along the *y* axis, labeled 'specifics', elements are positioned according to level of detail. More general elements are at the bottom, with more specific elements placed toward the top of the graph.

The top half of *Scoliosis* (Figure 1) exhibits the *morphology | concrete* pattern. Top center, Kimmel sketches a curved spine. Sets of content elements, addressing aspects of the disease, are rotated to align with vertebrae. The next vertical segment is organized as a 1D plot, instantiating *morphology | abstract*. The axis is labeled according to the severity of spinal curve deformation. Exhibition forms below the axis correspond to associated treatment options.

4.2 Overlap

The *overlap* pattern assembles elements using X-Y positioning,

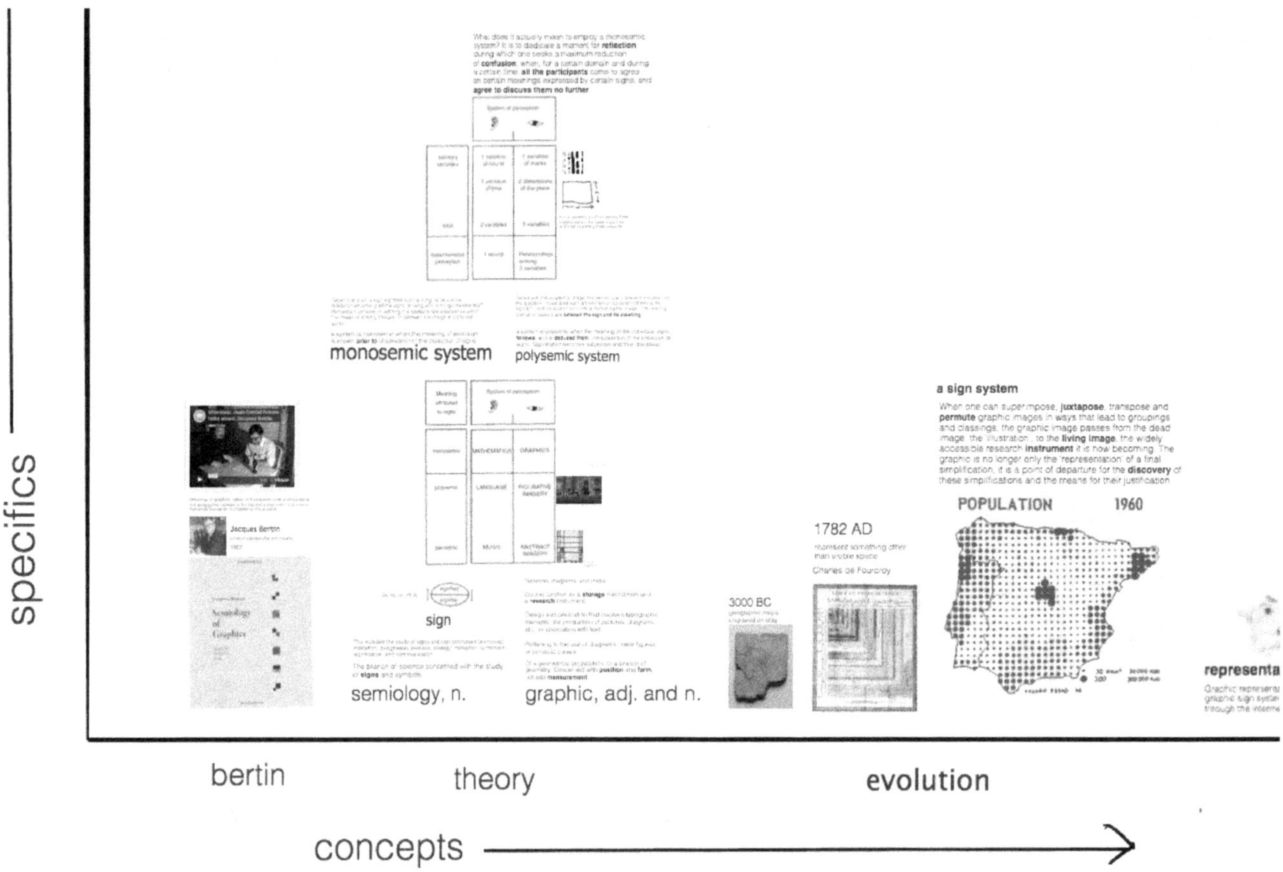

Figure 6: Andrew M. Webb curated *Graphic Sign System: Analysis of Information* as a visual aid for his presentation on Bertin's *Semiology of Graphics: Diagrams, Networks, Maps* [6], in the Curation and Ideation meet Social Media seminar [`https://ideamache.ecologylab.net/v/Hz9Ky6Uh6x/`]. Webb creates conceptual axes in order to visually and semantically organize Bertin's concepts for information presentation, while meta-indexically invoking these concepts. $curation\_patterns = \{morphology|abstract,\ group|spatial\}$

Z-ordering, and transparency. Using overlap in free-form web curation manifests Tufte's principle of layering information to express relationships and adds dimensionality in a visualization [43]. Arnheim shows how overlap intensifies formal relations by concentrating them within tightly integrated patterns [2].

Overlap sub-patterns address how layers give form and support abstraction. *overlap | compose* combines elements to create a coherent whole. Some elements function as background and others as foreground. Sketching over is a common technique here. *overlap | composite* invokes image translucence to create new visual syntheses. *overlap | map* places foreground elements over a geographic map or other image of a physical place, relating curation space to physical or geographic space.

Background elements provide a basis for the *overlap | compose* sub-pattern. Sometimes a single visual comprises the background. In the innovation curation, *Laundry Notifier*, Jump appropriates a washing machine image as thematic background (Figure 2). In *Feminist Hashtag Activism*, Lee assembles linked content elements mimicking tweets on a Twitter feed template background (Figure 3).

Other forms of *overlap* I *compose* assemble repeated found elements. *Christina Vaughn's World* (Figure 5) tiles images of a day and a night sky. With visible seams, the assemblage illustrates a world that is simultaneously natural and manufactured.

Another pattern subtype is *overlap* I *map*. Exhibition forms are placed over a representation of a physical space, such as a geography or blueprint. *buffer zone* (Figure 4) exhibits multiple instances of mapping. The author sketches texts and glyphs over photographs of beach fronts and satellite images.

Mapping through *overlap* differs from the *morphology* pattern, in that elements are arranged in correspondence to an inherently spatial representation. To differentiate between mapping and morphology, consider the following case. A curation that plans an Italian vacation by arranging elements in the shape of Italy exhibits *morphology*. A curation that places elements on a map or satellite image of Italy exhibits *overlap* I *map*. Mapping creates proportional relationships between exhibition space and physical space.

4.3 Group

The *group* pattern uses spatial arrangement to associate elements into distinct subsets. It is the most common pattern. Creating relations through proximity or visual similarity is a fundamental design practice [30]. *group | spatial* uses white space and rotation in the X-Y plane to separate a selection of elements. *group | nested* uses scale and the Z dimension as a means for group delineation.

The lower half of *Scoliosis* (Figure 1) uses the *group | spatial* pattern. Elements are organized with proximity. White space separates the sets. While the bottom left group addresses awareness, the bottom right assembles personal stories of scoliosis and treatment, ending with, 'My Curve', which links to Kimmel's personal blog. *Scoliosis* also invokes rotation as a *group | spatial* technique. In the top half, the author delimits groups of content elements by rotating them in alignment with vertebrae in her spinal curve sketch.

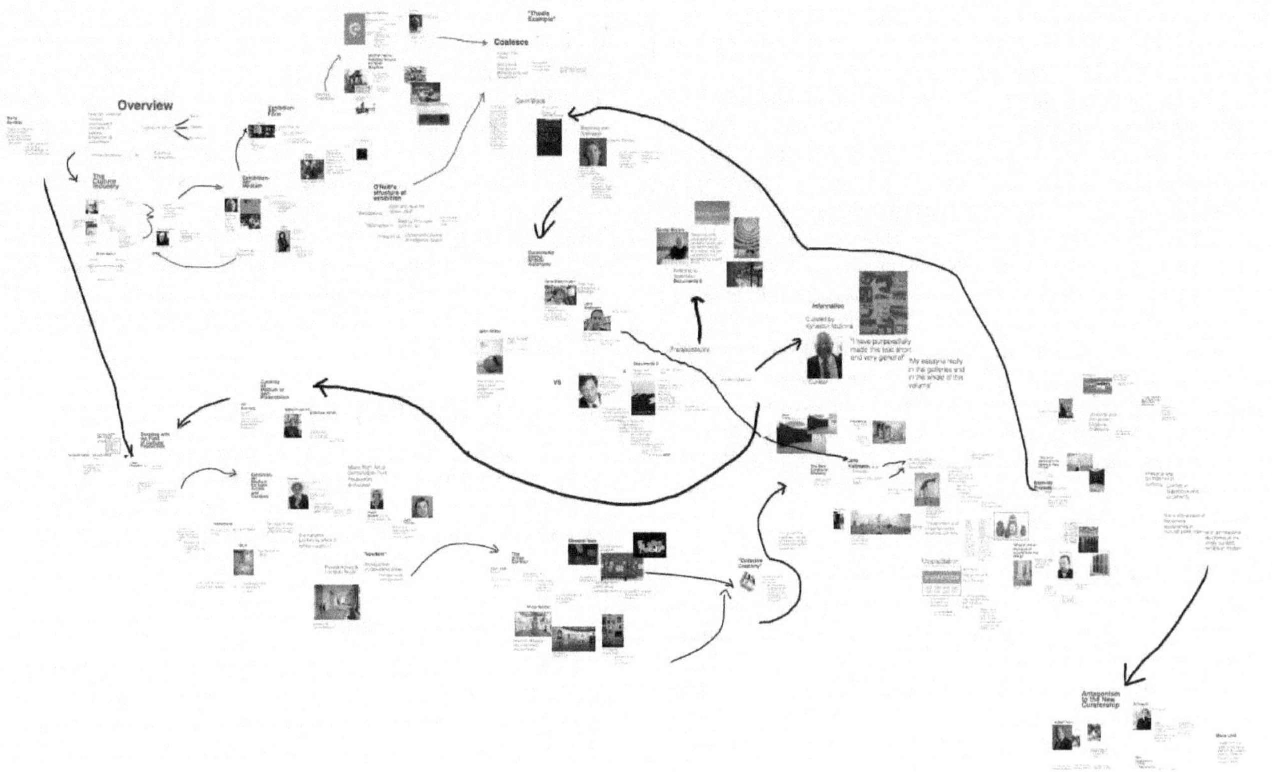

Figure 7: Trey Rhody's *curation 2*, a visual aid for his presentation on a chapter of O'Neil's book [36], in Curation and Ideation meet Social Media [`https://ideamache.ecologylab.net/v/WclWQvZdTT/`]. Rhody created an extensive non-linear path of exhibition form elements to illustrate and relate art curation practices. $curation\_patterns = \{group|spatial,\ path|non-linear\}$

Laundry Notifier (Figure 2) uses scale to exhibit the $group \mid nested$ pattern. The nested groups—addressing design ideas, existing patents, notification methods, and partnerships—can be read at the overview level. The elements within these groups are smaller, requiring zoom in for details to become legible. Through $group \mid nested$, a curation exhibits different amounts of information at different levels. This suggests the *semantic zooming* information visualization technique, in which the representation of information, as well as its size, changes in response to changes in visual scale [38].

Christina Vaughn's World (Figure 5) exhibits $group \mid nested$ in a different way. In overview, the curation presents a gray skyscraper with a sketched outline. Zooming in on the skyscraper, we find its walls are a texture of tiled image found objects. Each tile can be read individually as a photo of an old building. $group \mid nested$ is invoked with scaled, found images to convey a concept of reuse.

4.4 Path

The *path* pattern arranges found, sketched, and written elements to form one or more sequences, which may branch. Paths constitute a form of node-link diagram [48], reminiscent of Tufte's links and causal arrows, which are used to depict associations and relationships [44]. Curators use connecting glyphs, such as lines and arrows [45], to create paths that indicate relationships among elements. Connecting glyphs can be sketches drawn by the author or found digital images that the s/he has collected.

In addition to glyphs, authors use writing to create texts to describe a path's structure. Common examples include 'start here', 'read this first', or explanations of a path as a whole. A curation can incorporate a single $path \mid linear$ connected component or multiple connected components as the $path \mid non-linear$ pattern.

Rhody's *curation 2* (Figure 7) exhibits $path \mid non-linear$. Sketched arrows connect conceptual groups and sub-groups. The starting point of the non-linear path is in the top left, where he wrote 'Overview'. From this initial group, the path splits. The reader can choose to move down or to the right. We also see that Rhody has created multi-directional relationships among groups, illustrating a multiplicity of interconnections among his exhibition forms. Through *path*, curation authors articulate narratives that scaffold presentation and interpretation.

5. IMPLICATIONS FOR DESIGN

The present research investigates students' creative practices in a range of courses to discover a pattern language of visual thinking with in free-form curation. From the patterns, we derive implications for the design of web curation apps. First, by supporting free-form assemblage, enable authors to create design synthesis, visual thinking, and meta-indexical structures in online exhibits. Next, support authors in creating emergent ideas by constructing visual hypermedia narratives. Third, enable authors to create analogical mappings between representations of spaces with overlap and juxtaposition.

5.1 Free-form Assemblage

Kolko notes that designers visually explore quantities of seemingly unrelated material to discover hidden, relationships [26]. He explains how continuous rearrangement and work across scales facilitate design synthesis. This process of synthesis matches Arnheim's findings of the roles of exploration, analysis, and synthesis in visual thinking. Synthesis is a generative process of ideation [18].

Free-form assemblage serves as a means for authors to engage in continuous rearrangement, visual exploration, and discovery.

The four major free-form curation patterns—*morphology*, *overlap*, *groups*, and *paths*—function as ideation structures of design synthesis and visual thinking.

Web curations index concepts through the morphology pattern of assemblage of exhibition forms. For example, the morphology of *Feminist Hashtag Activism*, indexes the social medium of Twitter, the concept of hashtag, and specific hashtag instances (Figure 3). In Webb's *Graphic Sign System: Analysis of Information*, exhibition forms and writings are assembled into a 2D map. The assemblage connects form and content by manifesting graphic system principles described in its elements (Figure 6). The curation thus indexes semiotic graphical system concepts contained in its assemblage.

To support free-form assemblage, web curation environments must incorporate design tools for graphical manipulation of position, scale, and other visual characteristics of exhibition forms. Such free-form assemblage capabilities will enable authors to encode new meanings via structure and design. This will provide new opportunities for authors to develop emergent and meta-indexical syntheses and juxtapositions on the web.

5.2 Visual Hypermedia Narratives

Authors use free-form web curation to develop emergent ideas through visual hypermedia narratives. Through spatial arrangement, visual transformation, writing, and sketching, authors create linear and forking [11] paths within their curations. These visual hypermedia narrative pathways give form to what Landow [29] identifies as Barthes' "ideal textuality"—in which plural networks of elements extend, supporting multiple interpretations [4]. A visual hypermedia narrative uses storytelling to express relationships over time, while exhibiting a multiplicity of framings, uses, and outcomes.

curation 2 (Figure 7) uses a web of paths to construct a complex, interconnected narrative. Rhody groups exhibition forms and writings around "Documenta 9". He adds a label, "Predecessors", with two outgoing arrows, one pointing to Daniel Buren and the other to Kynaston McShine. This structure supports the reader in choosing her own progression through *curation 2*'s 392 exhibition forms.

The visual hypermedia narrative in Kimmel's *Scoliosis* is less explicit. Starting at the top, one is drawn downward, following a sketch of the spine. The reader learns about scoliosis through groups of exhibition forms and writings, placed alongside the spine, and rotated to index the spinal curve. At the base of the spine, the curation reads from left to right, along a single axis graph of spinal curve severity, with corresponding treatment options. Below, are two groups of exhibition forms. One is labeled "AWARENESS." The other is labeled "My Curve." It indexes Kimmel's personal blog, which details her own experiences with scoliosis. We interpret the overall narrative as conveying challenges and hope.

Free-form capabilities in web curation apps enable users to draw from navigational aids—such as writing, drawing, and positioning—to construct visual hypermedia narratives. These help authors to guide viewers through their curations. As the number of exhibition forms and their visual complexity increases, does the need to support narrative structure construction in web curation.

5.3 Mapping Spaces

Another design affordance of free-form curation is enable mapping and indexing spaces. Distance and proximity within a digital space of web curation can be designed to directly correspond to physical or geographic space represented within exhibition forms. These mappings can be abstract, such as placing exhibitions forms on graphs or plots, or they can be more concrete, such as placing forms on maps, satellite images, or blueprints.

For example, *buffer zone* (Figure 4) overlays sketches on exhibition forms representing particular physical spaces. The author arranges photographs of beach fronts and satellite images into two columns, representing specific regions: Texas and the Netherlands. In the top row, maps of the Texas and Netherlands coastlines are adjacent. The middle row overlaps sketches of forms on images of Netherlands beaches, with the label, "Good." The bottom row, a parallel structure, overlaps sketches on Texas beaches, with the label, "Bad" The curation juxtaposes alternative coastal designs. This visual analogy compares approaches to flood management, and their effects during natural disasters such as hurricanes. Visual analogies serve as valuable means for thinking about and developing emergent concepts and ideas. Free-form web curation supports visual thinking through the mapping of spaces.

6. ACKNOWLEDGEMENTS

This material is based upon work supported by the National Science Foundation under grants IIS-074742, IIS-1247126, and IIS-1528044. Any opinions, findings, and conclusions or recommendations expressed in this material are those of the authors and do not necessarily reflect the views of the NSF.

7. CONCLUSION

Free-form is valuable as a new medium of web curation for a broad range of intellectual work, because it supports ideation through visual thinking. We know this because of the observed range of patterns manifested in the visual dataset and the concomitant range of invocations of the patterns in the performance of ideation tasks. Their aggregation as a pattern language provides a basis for potential recombination in an infinity of emergent relationships.

The present research makes visual data and its analysis primary, because our focus is visual thinking and expression. We took an art-based approach, seeing and interpreting creative products as visual data. As Berger says, "Seeing comes before words... Every image embodies a way of seeing" [5]. Through the invocation of patterns of free-form curation, our study participants interweave seeing, collecting, organizing, and visual thinking to achieve ideation.

We investigated a dataset of thousands of free-form web curations, created by students in a variety of courses, to fulfill ideation assignments. We observed that ideas take shape through concrete and abstract morphology (253 instances), composed, composited and mapped forms of overlap (385 instances), spatial and nested groups (830 instances), and linear and non-linear paths (537 instances). The patterns capture visual, material and indexical characteristics of exhibition forms, and of their assemblages, as wholes.

A large population of students in a range of fields—e.g., humanities, science, and entrepreneurship—engaged in visual thinking and ideation with the patterns. We primarily identify their activity as mini-c and little-c creativity, that is, expression significant to themselves and their courses, rather than to society at large. These everyday students engaged in a form of curatorial practice akin to that in the arts, where curators design exhibits in which they choose and assemble objects created by others, and spatially organize them, along with their own interpretive writing and sketching.

These everyday visual thinking curatorial practices differ from curation in the most popular web apps—Facebook, Pinterest, and Twitter—whose feeds do not now support visual thinking through free-form curation. Our evidence motivates the incorporation of capabilities for free-form assemblage, visual hypermedia narratives, and mapping spaces in social media and productivity environments.

Gestalt psychologists, for over a century, have recognized grouping—through principles such as proximity, color, size, orientation, region, symmetry, continuity, and closure—as the fundamental means of visual organization [46]. We see these gestalt visual principles manifested in the present patterns of free-form web curation. Across the patterns and dataset, everyday users invoke gestalt principles to engage in visual thinking through free-form web curation.

Free-form web curation is in infancy. We make no claim that the present set of patterns of free-form web curation is complete. We hope and expect, with wider adoption and practice over time, that continuing research will discover a wider and deeper pattern language of free-form web curation, more closely resembling Alexander et al.'s in specificity, nuance, and extent.

Free-form web curation moves toward the flexible space of exchange and presentation that Christiane Paul, new media curator at New York's Whitney Museum, requires for new media art [37]. The growing pattern language of free-form web curation advances how humans draw on the incredible resources of the internet, as building blocks of visual thinking, and so promotes our fulfillment through expression, ideation, and innovation.

8. REFERENCES

[1] C. Alexander. *The timeless way of building*, volume 1. New York: Oxford University Press, 1979.

[2] R. Arnheim. *Visual Thinking*. Univ of California Press, 1969.

[3] M. Banks. *Using visual data in qualitative research*. Sage, 2008.

[4] R. Barthes. S/Z: An essay. *New York: Hill and Wang*, 1974.

[5] J. Berger. *Ways of Seeing*. Penguin Books, 2008.

[6] J. Bertin. Semiology of graphics: diagrams, networks, maps. 1983.

[7] E. Blevis, E. Churchill, W. Odom, J. Pierce, D. Roedl, and R. Wakkary. Visual thinking & digital imagery. In *Proc. CHI EA*, 2012.

[8] E. Blevis, S. Hauser, and W. Odom. Sharing the hidden treasure in pictorials. *interactions*, 22(3):32–43, Apr. 2015.

[9] J. D. Bolter. *Writing space: Computers, hypertext, and the remediation of print*. Routledge, 2001.

[10] J. O. Borchers. A pattern approach to interaction design. *Ai & Society*, 15(4):359–376, 2001.

[11] J. L. Borges. The aleph and other stories, 1933–1969, trans. *Thomas di Giovanni (London: Jonathan Cape, 1971)*, 1970.

[12] A. Breton. *Manifestos of surrealism*. U Michigan Press, 1969.

[13] K. Charmaz. *Constructing grounded theory*. Sage, 2014.

[14] J. Corbin and A. Strauss. *Basics of qualitative research: Techniques and procedures for developing grounded theory*. Sage, 2008.

[15] S. Denef and D. Keyson. Talking about implications for design in pattern language. In *Proc. CHI*, 2012.

[16] E. Edwards. Material beings: objecthood and ethnographic photographs. *Visual Studies*, 17(1):67–75, 2002.

[17] T. Erickson. Lingua francas for design: Sacred places and pattern languages. In *Proc. ACM DIS 2000.*

[18] R. A. Finke, T. B. Ward, and S. M. Smith. Creative cognition: Theory, research, and applications. 1992.

[19] E. Gamma et al. *Design patterns: Elements of reusable object-oriented software*. Pearson, 1995.

[20] J. Guilford. Creativity. *Am Psychologist*, 5:444–454, 1950.

[21] D. Harper. *Visual Sociology*. Taylor & Francis, 2012.

[22] K. Henderson. *On line and on paper: Visual representations, visual culture, and computer graphics in design engineering*. MIT Press, 1998.

[23] M. Joyce. *Of two minds: Hypertext pedagogy and poetics*. University of Michigan Press, 1996.

[24] J. C. Kaufman and R. A. Beghetto. Beyond big and little: The four c model of creativity. *Review Gen Psych*, 13(1):1, 2009.

[25] A. Kerne, A. M. Webb, S. M. Smith, R. Linder, N. Lupfer, Y. Qu, J. Moeller, and S. Damaraju. Using metrics of curation to evaluate information-based ideation. *ACM Transactions on Computer-Human Interaction*, 21(3):1–48, June 2014.

[26] J. Kolko. Information architecture and design strategy: The importance of synthesis during the process of design. In *Industrial Designers Society of America Conf 2007.*

[27] K. T. Konecki. Visual grounded theory: A methodological outline and examples from empirical work. *Revija za sociologiju*, 41(2):131–160, 2011.

[28] G. R. Kress and T. Van Leeuwen. *Reading images: The grammar of visual design*. Psychology Press, 1996.

[29] G. P. Landow. *Hypertext 3.0: Critical theory and new media in an era of globalization*. JHU Press, 2006.

[30] W. Lidwell, K. Holden, and J. Butler. *Universal Principles of Design, Revised and Updated: 125 Ways to Enhance Usability, Influence Perception, Increase Appeal, Make Better Design Decisions*. Rockport Publishers, 2010.

[31] R. Linder, N. Lupfer, A. Kerne, A. M. Webb, C. Hill, Y. Qu, K. Keith, M. Carrasco, and E. Kellogg. Beyond slideware: How a free-form presentation medium stimulates free-form thinking in the classroom. In *Proc. ACM C & C*, 2015.

[32] R. Linder, C. Snodgrass, and A. Kerne. Everyday ideation: All of my ideas are on pinterest. In *Proc. CHI*, 2014.

[33] L. Lippard. *Dadas on Art*. Spectrum. Prentice-Hall, 1971.

[34] P. D. Miller. *Rhythm science*. MIT Press, 2004.

[35] K. Nakakoji, Y. Yamamoto, S. Takada, and B. N. Reeves. Two-dimensional spatial positioning as a means for reflection in design. In *Proc DIS 2000.*

[36] P. O'Neill. *The Culture of Curating and the Curating of Culture (s)*. MIT Press, 2012.

[37] C. Paul. *New media in the white cube and beyond: Curatorial models for digital art*. Univ of California Press, 2008.

[38] K. Perlin and D. Fox. Pad: An alternative approach to the computer interface. In *In Proc. SIGGRAPH*, 1993.

[39] G. Rose. *Visual Methodologies: An Introduction to Researching with Visual Materials*. SAGE Publications, 2011.

[40] W. C. Seitz. *The Art of Assemblage*. Museum of Modern Art New York, 1961.

[41] J. Shah, S. Smith, and N. Vargas-Hernandez. Metrics for measuring ideation effectiveness. *Design Studies*, 24(2), 2002.

[42] D. K. Simonton. Creativity as blind variation and selective retention: Is the creative process darwinian? *Psychological Inquiry*, 10(4):pp. 309–328, 1999.

[43] E. R. Tufte. *Envisioning Information*. Graphics Press, 1990.

[44] E. R. Tufte. Beautiful evidence. *New York*, 2006.

[45] B. Tversky. Visualizing thought. *Topics in Cognitive Science*, 3(3):499–535, 2011.

[46] J. Wagemans, J. H. Elder, M. Kubovy, S. E. Palmer, M. A. Peterson, M. Singh, and R. von der Heydt. A century of gestalt psychology in visual perception: I. perceptual grouping and figure–ground organization. *Psychological bulletin*, 138(6):1172, 2012.

[47] R. Wakkary and L. Maestri. The resourcefulness of everyday design. In *Proc. ACM Creativity & Cognition*, 2007.

[48] C. Ware. *Information visualization: perception for design*. Elsevier, 2012.

DASH2M: Exploring HTTP/2 for Internet Streaming to Mobile Devices

Mengbai Xiao[1,2] Viswanathan Swaminathan[2] Sheng Wei[2,3] Songqing Chen[1]

[1]Dept. of CS
George Mason University
{mxiao3, sqchen}@gmu.edu

[2]Adobe Research
Adobe Systems Inc.
vishy@adobe.com

[3]Dept. of CSE
University of Nebraska-Lincoln
shengwei@unl.edu

ABSTRACT

Today HTTP/1.1 is the most popular vehicle for delivering Internet content, including streaming video. Standardized in 2015 with a few new features, HTTP/2 is gradually replacing HTTP 1.1 to improve user experience. Yet, how HTTP/2 can help improve the video streaming delivery has not been thoroughly investigated. In this work, we set to investigate how to utilize the new features offered by HTTP/2 for video streaming over the Internet, focusing on the streaming delivery to mobile devices as, today, more and more users watch video on their mobile devices. For this purpose, we design DASH2M, Dynamic Adaptive Streaming over HTTP/2 to Mobile Devices. DASH2M deliberately schedules the streaming content delivery by comprehensively considering the user's Quality of Experience (QoE), the dynamics of the network resources, and the power efficiency on the mobile devices. Experiments based on an implemented prototype show that DASH2M can outperform prior strategies for users' QoE while minimizing the battery power consumption on mobile devices.

Keywords

HTTP Streaming; HTTP/2; server push; video delivery;

1. INTRODUCTION

Recent years have witnessed the steady increase of video traffic on the Internet. According to Cisco, consumer Internet video traffic will be 80% of all consumer Internet traffic in 2019, up from 64% in 2014 [1].

In tandem, mobile devices are gaining increasing popularity, thanks to the technology advancement and the ever-decreasing prices. As a result, Internet streaming clients are also experiencing a steady shift from the traditional wired desktops to the wireless mobile devices. Today, mobile video traffic accounts for more than half (55%) of all mobile data traffic [1].

HTTP has been the most popular delivery vehicle for Internet video traffic, given its considerable market penetration and browser support. Video content providers, such as YouTube [9] and Netflix [7], mostly deliver their videos via HTTP. In HTTP based video streaming services, the video data are usually encoded into various bit rate levels, and are further segmented in terms of playback length, such as 1 second. These segments reside on HTTP servers and are delivered via HTTP responses. HTTP streaming and the ISO/MPEG standard is referred as to Dynamic Adaptive Streaming over HTTP (DASH) [28]. DASH is currently widely used on the Internet for delivering video streaming to both wired desktop users and wireless mobile users [25, 26, 18].

MM '16, October 15-19, 2016, Amsterdam, Netherlands

DOI: http://dx.doi.org/10.1145/2964284.2964313

Today the most widely used HTTP protocol is HTTP/1.1 [3]. DASH based on HTTP/1.1 can only switch the video quality at the video segment boundary. This demands accurate bandwidth prediction or a long playback buffer to deal with network jitter for achieving best streaming performance. Furthermore, HTTP/1.1 also imposes some unnecessary overhead. For example, a client needs to send a request for every video segment. This leads to increased delay as it takes at least a round-trip time (RTT) before the next segment is delivered.

The limitations of HTTP/1.1 not only impact Internet streaming delivery, but also Internet content delivery in general. They have motivated the development of HTTP/2, pioneered by Google SPDY [22]. As the successor of HTTP/1.1, HTTP/2 has been standardized in RFC 7540 [4] in February 2015. The new HTTP protocol inserts an interpreted layer, where the traditional HTTP requests and responses are dissembled into *frames*, above the transport layer. A typical HTTP session (a request and a response) is represented as a *stream* in this layer. In addition to the frames carrying the HTTP payload, control frames are used to implement new functions, such as *stream termination* and *server push*. More discussions of these new features are in Section 2.

Due to the improved web access performance, HTTP/2 has started to replace HTTP/1.1 and is expected to eventually fully replace its predecessor. This provides an unprecedented opportunity for utilizing HTTP/2 to further improve the Internet video streaming performance. For example, HTTP/2 enables the server to speculatively push HTTP responses to the client without receiving the corresponding requests. In this way, a server can push additional segments back when responding to the client's request for one segment. This potentially can eliminate the time overhead (one RTT) for every segment. Furthermore, HTTP/2 provides a termination mechanism. Thus, it can enable the client to conduct rate adaptation in the middle of a segment, offering better streaming experience to the client.

A few pioneering studies have investigated HTTP/2 for Internet streaming delivery [33, 31, 32, 16, 13]. For example, Mueller et al. [24] found that Secure Socket Layer (SSL) encryption, which is mandatory in SPDY, incurred noticeable overhead. Wei et al. studied the potential of the push mechanism in reducing the live latency [32], eliminating unnecessary requests [31], and saving power in cellular network [33]. In [16], the authors focused on improving the live experience of HTTP streaming by exploiting the HTTP/2 features. It adopts *full-push* while additional messages are used to control the video quality adaptation. Cherif et al. [13] also investigated the push mechanism for fast start in the DASH-compliant video streaming.

However, properly leveraging HTTP/2 for streaming delivery also poses some challenges. For example, while utilizing the push mechanism [16, 33, 31, 32, 13], it is critical to determine the push number (the number of segments to be pushed). A large number of segments to be pushed can greatly improve the streaming throughput. However the pushed contents are wasted if the user stops watching the video prematurely. Thus, a fixed number of segments for push, as in [33, 32, 31], risk network resource waste. In addition, setting the server push with the same bit rate until a switch request is sent from the client [16] is not a timely response for adapting to the frequent network fluctuations. Therefore, properly delivering video on HTTP/2 is not straightforward, and an inappropriate use can lead to network resource waste and degraded user experience.

The problem becomes more sophisticated if the client is a mobile device. Today over 40% of cellular traffic is reported as video streaming [14]. Mobile devices are inherently energy-constrained because of the limited battery capacity. As a result, in addition to the concerns that are often critical for streaming services on desktop computers, such as Quality-of-Experience (QoE), power efficiency is of high priority as well.

To address these challenges, in this work, we explore HTTP/2 to improve DASH for streaming to mobile devices and propose DASH2M (Dynamic Adaptive Streaming over HTTP/2 to Mobile Devices). DASH2M aims to optimize the mobile user's streaming experience while minimizing the resource consumption. Instead of a fixed number of segments to be pushed, in DASH2M, the number of segments for pushing is determined dynamically based on the predicted available network resources and the impact of the user's early termination. Compared to prior exploration, DASH2M also enables graceful quality degradation to deal with network fluctuations in the middle of a push cycle. Furthermore, once the prediction deviates from the reality, the HTTP/2 termination is utilized to start a new push cycle.

We design and implement a prototype of DASH2M. Experimental results show that DASH2M can maximize the streaming throughput, user's QoE, as well as the battery power efficiency.

While details are presented in the paper, some highlights of our contributions include the following:

- By exploring HTTP/2 new features, such as server push and stream termination, DASH2M can greatly improve the Internet streaming delivery to mobile users.
- DASH2M carefully schedules the segment delivery by comprehensively considering the QoE required by the user, the network fluctuations, the potential premature termination, and the mobile user's battery consumption.
- The evaluation results show that DASH2M can maximize the streaming throughput, optimize the user's QoE, and improve the power efficiency for mobile devices.

The rest of the paper is organized as follows. Section 2 discusses background and related work. Section 3 presents the design of DASH2M. Section 4 describes the prototype implementation. The results of evaluation is presented in Section 5, and Section 6 concludes the paper.

2. BACKGROUND AND RELATED WORK

In this section, we briefly introduce the most relevant features in HTTP/2. This is followed by a discussion on HTTP based video streaming over the Internet.

2.1 HTTP/2

HTTP/2 [4] originates from SPDY [22] developed by Google. Cardaci et al. [12] showed that the SPDY protocol slightly outperformed HTTP/1.1 over high latency satellite links. To the applications above the HTTP layer, HTTP/2 shares the same Application Programming Interfaces (APIs) as HTTP/1.1. The new protocol inserts an additional interpreted layer between the application layer and the transmission layer, which breaks the traditional HTTP requests and responses into *frames*. HTTP messages are associated to their own *streams*, which represent individual HTTP requests or responses. By manipulating the frames as well as the streams, HTTP/2 attains some prominent features like stream termination, server push, etc.

Server push: In HTTP/2, a server is able to speculatively push a response to the client prior to receiving a corresponding request. To make the client aware of what all are arriving, the server needs to send frames named *PUSH_PROMISE* in an active stream. The client can then hold the requests with same URLs if the pushed contents are still unavailable, or respond immediately with the pushed data from the cache. The server push is usually applied to push associated resources of an HTML page to effectively reduce page loading time.

Stream termination: Stream termination is achieved by sending a specific *RST_STREAM* frame, either from the sender or the receiver. When an endpoint receives a *RST_STREAM* frame, the active stream delivering that frame is then closed. Though this is an effective solution to cancel any undesired transmission, about half of a RTT is still required.

2.2 HTTP Streaming

One of the most significant characteristics of video streaming over HTTP is the capability of selecting suitable quality level based on various network conditions. Commonly the HTTP based streaming protocol, such as MPEG-DASH, only provides the mechanism supporting the segment-based designation of specific quality level, and the responsibility of choosing the proper bit rate of next segments is left to the client side (video player).

Many prior studies focused on the quality selection algorithms. QDASH [23] integrated a proxy-like bandwidth measurement component to accurately and promptly derive the network bandwidth. The authors also suggested a gradual quality switching algorithm to improve the subjective user-perceived quality. FESTIVE [17] identified three prominent metrics, namely efficiency, fairness, and stability, in HTTP streaming systems. A suite of techniques are developed to help make beneficial trade-offs among these metrics. Huang et al. [15] suggested that it is difficult to accurately estimate the underlying bandwidth above the HTTP layer according to the surveys done on popular video streaming services. In [11], the authors showed the instability problem when there are competing flows. The root cause is due to the ON-OFF activity pattern on the client-side, and a server-based traffic shaper is implemented to eliminate the quality oscillations. Zou et al. [34] investigated that accurate bandwidth prediction at short time scales of a cellular network is possible, and they proposed a scheme based on integer linear programming to maximize the quality of the downloaded segments.

With the emerging mobile platforms, power efficiency is also becoming a major concern for HTTP streaming. GreenTube [19] found the special power profile of cellular network interfaces, which is the special *TAIL* state in Radio Resource Control (RRC). It maintained a smart cache for reshaping the network traffic and helping the network interface greedily stay in the sleep state. Other studies [30, 33, 20] shared the same methodology but explored different contexts. These existing studies indicate that a prominent challenge is how to balance the trade-off between the magnitude in one download and the probability that the downloaded data are dropped.

3. DESIGN OF DASH2M

Ideally, while watching a video streamed over Internet, a user expects (1) continuous playback (subject to the buffer size constraint), and (2) smooth rate adaptations to the network fluctuations (graceful and timely bit rate switching according to the available network bandwidth). If the receiving device is a mobile device, the user additionally expects (3) a minimum consumption of the battery power, which depends on (a) how the streaming data is delivered, and (b) how much data is received but not watched due to the client's premature termination. To achieve these goals, the media player needs to have an accurate bandwidth prediction.

In this section, first we will present the design considerations of DASH2M followed by the detailed design.

3.1 Overview of DASH2M Design

To optimize the users' streaming experience, DASH2M addresses the above issues as follows.

[Data Delivery vs. Power Consumption] Our previous work [33] showed that the server push has the capability of reshaping network traffic, which is important to network interface power efficiency on mobile devices. Aggregating network transmissions, which can be easily accomplished via server push, helps the network interface (WiFi or 3G/4G) enter sleep mode more efficiently. While pushing all segments in one time saves the most energy, it may also lead to over-pushed contents. On mobile devices, these downloaded but not watched segments mean significant waste of battery power consumption (in addition to the bandwidth waste, which may also mean monetary loss for some mobile users.). Consequently, DASH2M aims to balance the push number for achieving power efficiency on mobile devices.

[Rate Adaptation vs. Network Fluctuations] With the push mechanism introduced in HTTP/2, some prior studies have suggested to eliminate the request overhead via only sending a leading request for a set of segments, which we call a *push cycle*. This is particularly helpful to live streaming that demands a low live latency. For example, k-push [33, 32, 31] suggests to push additional k segments in response to a leading HTTP request. Hence k-push is only capable of switching to a new quality after every k segments. Alternatively, full-push [16] keeps pushing segments at a constant bit rate level until special requests are sent to the server for switching current video quality. While potentially good for a low latency if the segment size is very small, neither k-push nor full-push can support graceful rate switching in the middle of a push cycle to quickly respond to network fluctuations. That is, in a push cycle, only one quality level (i.e., bit rate) can be used. Instead, DASH2M aims to enable fine quality control by allowing bit rate switching even in a push cycle, swiftly responding to the network fluctuations.

[Bandwidth Estimation vs. Prediction Inaccuracy] To enable rate adaptation, DASH2M requires a bandwidth prediction method. In DASH2M, this is done based on local measurement information to estimate the available network resources. Meanwhile, as the available throughput of a stream is also dependent on the server's outgoing bandwidth, the server information can improve the accuracy of bandwidth prediction. Thus, as an option, the server's information is also used to help estimate the future bandwidth whenever possible. Nevertheless, the bandwidth prediction can deviate from the reality, particularly when the prediction period is long. Therefore, DASH2M also utilizes the stream termination feature to cancel all upcoming pushed segments in a timely manner.

To accomplish these goals, DASH2M consists of the following four major components:

- Push Number Determination per Cycle (subsection 3.2): it quantitatively decides how many segments should be pushed in a push cycle.
- Bit Rate Selection per Segment (subsection 3.3): it determines the bit rate of each involved segment in a push cycle according to the bandwidth prediction.
- Bandwidth Prediction (subsection 3.4): it predicts the bandwidth availability in the next push cycle based on local information and optional server information.
- Push Cycle Termination (subsection 3.5): it is a complement method for correcting the inaccuracy of bandwidth prediction.

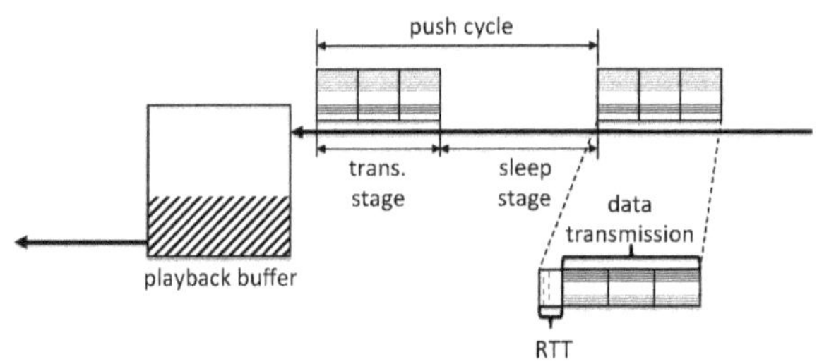

Figure 1: A DASH2M session with server push

DASH2M considers the design of these components based on a push cycle, illustrated by Figure 1. That is, the network activities of a DASH2M session consist of HTTP sessions interleaved with probable idle durations. According to the server push technique, several segment transmissions are bonded together and only one HTTP request overhead is incurred at the beginning of the transmission. As shown in Figure 1, a *playback buffer* stores video data received and relays the data to the display at a constant rate. The buffer accepts data from the network at a varying speed. The network activities are composed of *push cycles*, which can be further divided into *transmission stages* and *sleep stages*. To this end, DASH2M is to launch a push cycle with a push number K, denoting the number of segments involved, and the bit rate arrangement of these segments, represented by

$$\mathbf{b} = (b_1, \ldots, b_K).$$

Next, we present how DASH2M decides the push number K and the bit rates $\mathbf{b}$ in a cycle.

3.2 Push Number Determination per Cycle

Intuitively, a larger push number K can lead to less consumed battery energy. But the amount of pre-fetched segments may unnecessarily drain the battery energy due to potential user abandonment behaviors [27]. Furthermore, with a larger K, the bandwidth prediction period for this push cycle is also longer, which potentially introduces more prediction inaccuracy. Ultimately, K is also constrained by the playback buffer size. Therefore, K cannot be too large and is bound by K_{max}. At a high level, a streaming session always starts with a small K (e.g., 2) for the low startup latency. During the playback, if the predicted bandwidth increases,

Table 1: Variables of A Push Cycle

Symbol	Meaning
K	the segment number in the push cycle
b_i	the bit rate of the i-th segment
D	the segment duration
t_0	the start timestamp of the push cycle
$B(t)$	network throughput of time t
L_0	the buffer length at t_0
L_c	the critical buffer length
S_0	the buffer size at t_0
S_{max}	the maximum buffer size

K will increase accordingly, but not beyond the upper bound. If the predicted bandwidth decreases, K will decrease accordingly.

As K is closely related to the energy consumption, DASH2M dynamically determines K that can minimize the potential energy consumption on the mobile device. To characterize the energy efficiency, we first calculate the overall energy consumption of a push cycle. We characterize the time distribution, which includes T_{cyc} (the push cycle duration), T_{trans} (the transmission stage duration) and T_{sleep} (the sleep stage duration), and combine them with the power profile of network interfaces to calculate the energy consumption. The time distribution of the push cycle, given a K, is

$$\begin{cases} T_{cyc} = L_0 + K \cdot D - L_c \\ T_{trans} = RTT + \frac{\sum_{i=1}^{K} b_i \cdot D}{E[B_i]} \\ T_{sleep} = T_{cycle} - T_{trans} \end{cases} .$$

$E[B_i]$ represents the bandwidth expectation until the i-th segments are transmitted, and Table 1 lists the parameters we use. It is worth noting that during T_{sleep} the network interface may consume different levels of power. We will explain the details next.

With the corresponding power profile, which depends on device types, network types, network operators and etc., we can derive the overall energy consumption of a push cycle for a smartphone as follows:

$$Energy(K) = T_{trans} \cdot p_a + C \cdot p_t + (T_{cyc} - T_{trans} - C) \cdot P_i,$$

when using a 3G/4G network [19], where p_a, p_t and p_i are the power consumption when the network interface is in ACTIVE, TAIL and IDLE states, respectively. C is the duration of the TAIL state. For cellular network interfaces, usually the intermediate TAIL state with a constant duration is desired for promptly returning to the ACTIVE state. The power profiles of other network interfaces (e.g., WiFi) can be presented similarly with slight modifications.

Then the watching energy efficiency can be represented as $\frac{Energy(K)}{K_w}$, where K_w is the watched segment number in this push cycle before abandonment. We define $P\{t \geq T\}$ as the probability a user watches this video for at least T seconds. This probability can be obtained from a general distribution, such as the one suggested in [27], which is characterized by the session duration. We define $\mathscr{E}(\cdot)$ as the watching energy efficiency, and then we can calculate its expectation in a push cycle, for a specific K, as

$$E[\mathscr{E}(K)] = \sum_{i=1}^{K-1} \frac{P\{t_0 + (i-1)D \leq t < t_0 + iD\} \cdot Energy(K)}{i \cdot P\{t \geq t_0\}} + \frac{P\{t \geq t_0 + KD\} \cdot Energy(K)}{K \cdot P\{i \geq t_0\}}. \quad (1)$$

For every push number candidate, we can calculate a corresponding watching energy efficiency expectation from Eq. 1. By comparing these results, a best K leading to the lowest watching energy efficiency is selected as the pushed segment number in the next push cycle. So we have

$$\underset{K}{argmax}\ E[\mathscr{E}(K)] \quad \text{for} \quad K = 1, \ldots, K_{max},$$

where K_{max} is the upper bound of K. As mentioned before, K_{max} is constrained by a fixed duration, after which the bandwidth prediction is believed unreliable. In addition K_{max} also helps to limit the space of candidate Ks. A constant K_{max}^C is helpful in reducing complexity of searching optimal K at the beginning stage of a video session, where the probability of users stopping is high. The prior study by Shafiq et al. [27] shows that terrible network dynamics increase the user abandonment rate. So we scale down K_{max} if the quality level of the last segment in the last push cycle is not the highest one. We have

$$K_{max} = \max(\frac{K_{max}^C}{2^{|\mathbf{b}| - Index(b^*)}}, 1),$$

where b^* is last bit rate level, and $Index(\cdot)$ represents the index of target bit rate. K_{max} is also constrained by how many segments the remaining streaming session is composed of. So we have the maximum K as

$$\min(K_{max}, \lceil \frac{t_e - t_0}{D} \rceil),$$

where t_0 and t_e are the timestamps of now and the end of the video session, respectively.

Once the number of segments involved in next push cycle is determined, an efficient bit rate arrangement for these segments can be determined, as presented in the next subsection.

3.3 Bit Rate Selection per Segment

The goal of bit rate selection for each segment in a push cycle is to maximize the quality of the video for the user, along with several constraints fulfilled for the user's QoE requirements. A set of ideal bit rates should be the highest ones that the network can sustain. Meanwhile, with such bit rate selection, users should be able to watch the video without noticing stalling playback and abrupt quality switches.

As a result, given a K, and a bandwidth prediction function that predicts $B(t)$ (subsection 3.4), our bit rate selection problem is formulated as an *integer linear programming*. If the segment duration is consistent across the video session, we have the objective function as

$$\text{maximize:} \quad \sum_{i=1}^{K} b_i.$$

In practice, the bit rate b_i is usually selected from a discrete set.

During a streaming session, to maximize the QoE experienced by a user, we need to minimize the re-buffering events, abrupt quality degradation. In addition, the memory a mobile device provides for a streaming session is not unlimited [21]. Therefore the above objective function is subject to several constraints:

Continuous playback: To avoid playback stalls, the time used to transmit the next segment should be less than current buffer length. In a DASH session based on HTTP/1.1, we have

$$T_{req} + T_{resp} < L_0,$$

where T_{req} and T_{resp} are the transmission times of the request and the response, respectively. In a push cycle powered by HTTP/2, only one request is required for multiple responses. If the time to transmit the request payload is considered trivial and the buffer length is extended by a segment duration whenever a segment has been downloaded, the constraint now becomes

$$RTT + \frac{\sum_{i=1}^{n} b_i \cdot D}{E[B_i]} < L_0 + (n-1)D \quad \text{for} \quad n = 1, \ldots, K.$$

Smooth playback: Existing research [23] shows that gradual quality adaptation is more favored in improving subjective perception experience. Therefore we smooth the video quality adaptation in two dimensions, namely quality duration and quality variance. In a quality degradation process, if the duration of an individual video quality is too short, users can still perceive an abrupt quality degradation even when every intermediate bit rate is traversed. So every segment should be in a group of continuous segments at the same bit rate, and the group size, denoted as m, is sufficiently large before moving on to next higher or lower quality group.

To formalize such QoE requirements, a bit rate arrangement in a push cycle can be expressed a vector of J two-tuples, $\langle \hat{b}, n \rangle_1, \ldots, \langle \hat{b}, n \rangle_J$, where $J \leq K$. So the quality duration constraint can be expressed as

$$\begin{cases} n_1 + n^* \geq m & n^* < m \\ n_1 \geq m & n^* \geq m \\ n_j \geq m & 1 < j < J \end{cases},$$

where n^* and $\hat{b}^*$ are the group size and the bit rate inherited from the last group of last push cycle. To represent the quality variance constraint, we have

$$\begin{cases} \hat{b}_1 = \hat{b}^* & n^* < m \\ \hat{b}_1 \in \{N(\hat{b}^*), \hat{b}^*\} & n^* \geq m \\ \hat{b}_j \in \{N(\hat{b}_{j-1}), \hat{b}_{j-1}\} & j > 1 \end{cases},$$

where $N(\cdot)$ represents the neighboring bit rate levels.

Maximum buffer size: Usually the buffer size of a media player on a mobile device is bounded [21]. Every time a segment is downloaded and is put into the buffer, the total buffer size should not exceed the watermark upper bound. We denote the buffer size as S. Then the downloaded segments are subject to

$$S_0 - S_p + \sum_{i=1}^{n} b_i \cdot D < S_{max} \quad \text{for} \quad n = 1, \ldots, K,$$

where S_p is the data amount sent to the decoder.

By solving this integer linear programming problem, we can get the bit rate selection result for each segment in the cycle.

3.4 Bandwidth Prediction

To effectively utilize the network resources according to the bit rate selection algorithm, DASH2M demands a reliable and accurate bandwidth prediction. In DASH2M, the future bandwidth availability is predicted by two means, a short-term estimation based on local measurement and a long-term prediction by analyzing the population distribution of all users watching the video from the server. The latter is optional because the availability of a server's assistance is not guaranteed.

Local measurement: Previous study [29] shows that the simple prediction based on historical information has the best prediction accuracy. So we use the measured bandwidth information of previous segments to predict the future bandwidth. Specifically, We extract the measured information of last push cycles, and use the average value as the future bandwidth.

However, not all the measurement points are reliable. Only two measurement points, the one measured where the first segment is transmitted, and the one measured at the end of the whole push cycle are selected for a push cycle. The reason for not choosing other points is due to potential inaccurate information associated with them. For example, a segment may already be in the cache (in a web browser context), and it only takes around ten milliseconds to complete this operation.

If we assume that there is a historical time point only the newer information after that can be used, then there is a maximum effective measurement duration "D_{max}", ending at now. We then have a set of data points available: $B_m(t_1^*), \ldots, B_m(t_u^*)$, where $t_1^* > \ldots > t_u^*$ and $t_u^* > D_{max}$. Correspondingly, we have a weighted function $w(t)$ that $\int_0^{D_{max}} w(t)dt = 1$. Hence, we have

$$B = \sum_{i=1}^{u} B_m(t_i^*) \int_{t_0 - t_{i-1}^*}^{t_0 - t_i^*} w(t_0 - t_i^*)dt,$$

where $t_0^* = t_0$. The weighted function can be defined as

$$w(t) = \frac{2}{D_{max}^2} t.$$

(Optional) Server support: Note that the throughput of a streaming session is also dependent on the server's network bandwidth allocation. A population distribution of all users watching the video along time, combined with the network capacity of the server, is beneficial in predicting the trend of available bandwidth variation in the long term. The bandwidth function provided by the server is

$$B_s(t) = \frac{B^*}{A + \int_{t_0}^{t_0+t} (a(x) - b(x))dx},$$

where B^* is the overall outgoing bandwidth capacity of the server. A is the user number at time t_0. $a(x)$ and $b(x)$ are the user arrival rate and departure rate, respectively.

When the server support is available, we can combine the local measurement and the remote bandwidth information for more accurate prediction. We choose the lower value for a given t as the predicted bandwidth.

3.5 Push Cycle Termination

For a streaming session, a stable state where the video bit rate approximates the available bandwidth means that a relatively small playback buffer is adequate on the client player. So we always expect that the next scheduling operation starts as long as the buffer length is smaller than a critical value L_c, for example, two segments.

However, accurate bandwidth prediction is not always guaranteed. A bandwidth mismatch can be discovered by periodically comparing the measured bandwidth values to the predicted ones. If the real bandwidth is higher than the prediction, the expected video quality and power efficiency are guaranteed. Thus the risk of degrading current streaming session comes from the bandwidth decrease. When a bandwidth mismatch is found, a longer buffer length is helpful in scaling down the video quality gracefully. So a relaunch of the transmission stage to reschedule video quality is preferred when a large bandwidth mismatch is discovered. The bandwidth mismatch can be quantified as

$$Diff(t) = \int_{t_0}^{t} B_m(t)dt - \int_{t_0}^{t} B(t)dt,$$

where $B_m(t)$ is the measured bandwidth function. $\int_{t_0}^{t} B_m(t)dt$ shows the actual consumed network resources, and the second component represents the predicted consumed network resources. We can expect a push cycle to relaunch once $Diff(t)$ reaches a threshold.

To relaunch, DASH2M utilizes HTTP/2 stream termination. It works as follows. After the client sends a request with a push directive, it is expected to receive *PUSH_PROMISE* frames notifying the client what segments are being pushed. Corresponding URLs and stream IDs can be extracted from these *PUSH_PROMISE* frames and preserved at the client side. These pushed segments will be returned to the application level once the client receives all the content in the promised streams. If a bandwidth mismatch is found, the client can cancel the promised but not complete streams by sending *RST_STREAM* frames associated with the stream IDs.

Procedure 1 *DASH2M segment scheduling in a push cycle*

Input: $B_l(t)$, $B_s(t)$, $Energy[\cdot]$, RTT, m^*, b^*, $P\{\cdot\}$

Determine K_{max}
$E[\mathscr{E}]_{min} \leftarrow \infty$
$B(t) \leftarrow$ synthesizing $B_l(t)$ and $B_s(t)$

for K in $1 \dots K_{max}$ **do**
  Calculate **b** by integer linear programming
  Calculate $E[\mathscr{E}]$
  if $E[\mathscr{E}] < E[\mathscr{E}]_{min}$ **then**
    $K_{min} \leftarrow K$
    $\mathbf{b}_{min} \leftarrow \mathbf{b}$
    $E[\mathscr{E}]_{min} \leftarrow E[\mathscr{E}]$
  end if
end for

$b^* \leftarrow b[K]$
$m^{**} \leftarrow 1$
for K in $(K_{min}-1)\dots 1$ **do**
  if $b[K] = b[K_{min}]$ **then**
    $m^{**} \leftarrow m^{**}+1$
  else
    break
  end if
end for

if $m^{**} = K_{min}$ **then**
  $m^* \leftarrow m^* + m^{**}$
else
  $m^* \leftarrow m^{**}$
end if
return $(K_{min}, \mathbf{b}_{min})$

As shown in Procedure 1, the client first determines the range of push number candidates. Then for each possible K value, a set of bit rates are selected via linear programming. With such designs, the algorithm sketches the segment scheduling in a push cycle for DASH2M.

4. IMPLEMENTATION

To evaluate the performance of DASH2M, we have implemented a prototype. We present the implementation details in this section.

4.1 DASH2M Server Implementation

We build our DASH2M Server on the top of the Jetty Project [5], a Java based HTTP server that has implemented features of HTTP/2. The major functions implemented on the server side include the following.

Streaming Push: The core module of DASH2M is implemented as a *Filter* class. A HTTP header named *PushSegments* is used to indicate a new push cycle. All URLs of the remaining segments in this push cycle are passed in as the value of this field. Once this field is received as part of a request, 1) the server will then build a new stream to send the corresponding response, 2) *PUSH_PROMISE* frames of the pushed segments will also be sent over this stream, 3) the server will also open a stream within a newly launched thread for each pushed segment, 4) the server determines the dependencies of these pushed segments based on when they should be played. These segments are sequentially pushed without affecting the normal playback.

Stream Termination: While the HTTP/2 interfaces that manipulate frames are not exposed to an application level program, we implement a workaround to simulate the HTTP/2 stream termination feature as our client is implemented in javascript. To relaunch a push cycle, we attach a special HTTP header, named *ResetStreams* to request that. If the server receives such a request, before it launches a new push cycle, the server sends the *RST_FRAME* frames to all active streams to close them. The client can expect the failures of all other ongoing sessions when sending the stream termination directive.

4.2 DASH2M Client Implementation

We implement the video player based on the open source project *dash.js* [2], which is a DASH-compliant video player in JavaScript. The video player is packaged as a web-app and deployed on an HTTP server. Our player has three modules, which are the *push-cycle configuration*, the *bandwidth monitoring*, and the *bandwidth prediction* modules as described below.

push-cycle configuration: This module determines both the number and qualities of segments involved in the next push cycle. This component is normally triggered when the playback buffer reaches a critical level, and it is abnormally triggered by the *bandwidth monitoring* module when a bandwidth mismatch is found. This module takes the output of the *bandwidth prediction* module and follows Procedure 1 to generate the configuration of the next push cycle. Then, the player encodes this result in the header of the first request and sends that request to the server for launching a push cycle.

bandwidth monitoring: This module is triggered by the *onProgress* callback of the standard XMLHttpRequest API of the web browser. It is periodically invoked when the player receives the response content. It estimates the instantaneous bandwidth by checking how many bytes have been loaded, and further compares the result to the predicted value generated by the *bandwidth prediction* module. As long as a significant mismatch is found, it updates the prediction function and calls the *push-cycle configuration* module to relaunch a push cycle. The sent request carries the directive to terminate all ongoing streams on the server.

bandwidth prediction: This module outputs the predicted bandwidth. It keeps accepting local measurement results from the *bandwidth monitoring* module and the remote server (optionally) for updating its output. It follows the description in subsection 3.4 to estimate the bandwidth.

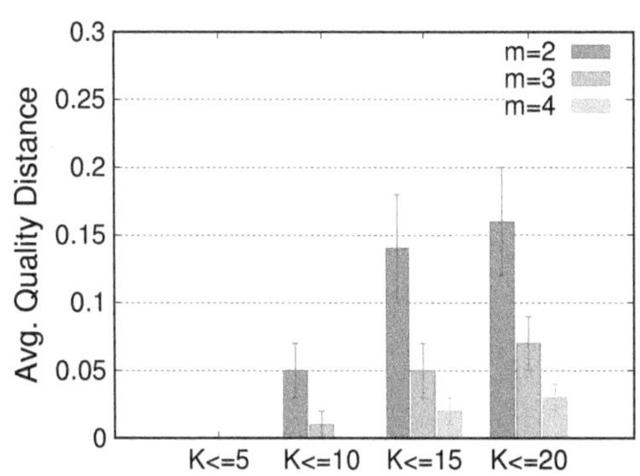

Figure 2: The average quality distance from the time-bound greedy solutions to the optimal solutions

4.3 Scheduling Algorithm Implementation

The core of DASH2M lies in the segment scheduling at the client side as described by Procedure 1. It uses linear programming and is implemented in the Push-cycle Configuration module. When the push number is large, the time used to search the optimal result is impractical because of the huge solution space. So we optimize the linear programming implementation with two heuristics. First, we impose a time constraint on the linear programming implementation. We think a few hundreds of milliseconds is reasonable while not impairing the streaming throughput. Thus, the result is locally optimal since only a part of the solution space is explored. Second, to improve the performance of linear programming, we take advantage of the objective function that is to seek the maximum sum of the bit rate sum. The search always starts from the highest bit rate level when constructing solutions by deepest first search. The greedy algorithm greatly helps find feasible solutions in the limited time with high probability.

5. EVALUATION

To evaluate DASH2M, we run experiments to compare with the standard HTTP/1.1 and the k-push scheme. We actively manipulate the network conditions to observe how the different schemes react to the network fluctuations.

5.1 Experiment Setup

We firstly conduct a series of experiments in a control environment for characterizing the basic features of our scheme. The HTTP server resides on a Linux machine with a 64-bit Intel Pentium CPU 2.8 GHz dual core, 6 GB memory, 2×32 KB L1 caches, 2×256 KB L2 caches and shared 3 MB L3 cache. The installed operating system is Ubuntu 12.04 with Linux kernel 3.13.0-66-generic.

The Jetty server supporting DASH2M and k-push is launched as a normal HTTP server, serving all requests to port 8444 in HTTP/2. It also supports HTTP/1.1 DASH based streaming. The available resources on the HTTP server includes the video player and the video segments, which are packaged by the tool *MP4Box* [6]. The Chrome browser is used to acquire and run the video player. The network shaping rules are imposed on this interface targeting the IP packets that have 8444 as either *dport* or *sport*. Such a setting is to eliminate the impact of other uncertain factors so that we can get a more accurate assessment of DASH2M functions.

5.2 Linear Programming Evaluation

We firstly evaluate the performance of our linear programming implementation. In the experiment, the video bit rate levels are set as 51 kbps, 195 kbps, 515 kbps and 771 kbps, respectively. The segment duration is 2 seconds and the RTT is 50 milliseconds. The buffer length is 10 seconds and we always start with $b^* = 195$ kbps and $n^* = 1$. We search the solutions for $K \leq 20$. We compare our time-bound greedy searching algorithm, which exits after 100 milliseconds, with the optimal algorithm. The bandwidth variation in the future 40 seconds is predictable and the value varies every 10 seconds as follows. The bandwidth candidates are selected from $\{60, 200, 600, 800\}$ kbps randomly so there are 256 combinations to traverse. We repeat the experiment with different m, which is $2, 3, 4$, to observe whether the result differentiates with the different scales of legal solution space.

We define the *quality distance* as the bit rate level difference from the scheduled bit rate to the optimal one. For example, if we schedule a segment with the bit rate of 51 kbps while the optimal one is 515 kbps, the quality distance is 2. We use the average quality distance for specific K to reflect the quality degradation of a solution from the optimal quality arrangement. If we can not get a solution for a specific K, the lowest bit rate level is selected for all segments. We exhaustively search the optimal solutions from the solution space of 4^{20}, and the average size of the solution space is 52425, 9033, and 2867, respectively, corresponding to the increasing m. The time to perform the search is on average 15.58, 2.51, and 0.8 seconds. For the time bound greedy algorithm, the average legal solution space is bound by the limited search times, which are 336, 341, and 343, respectively. We report the average quality distance statistics in Figure 2. The y-axis is the average quality distance with 95% confidence interval, and the x-axis represents different K ranges. The bars in a cluster shows how the quality distance varies when the legal solution space, i.e. m, changes. We can see that both the m and K increments lead to a higher average quality distance, which is reasonable since the m increment means a larger legal solution space and the K increment means a larger solution space. Ultimately, across all parameter sets, the video quality does not obviously degrade due to our time-bound greedy algorithm while the average quality distances are always less than 0.2.

5.3 Rate Adaptation Evaluation

We evaluate how different schemes react to the network dynamics. In particular, we want to assess whether DASH2M can bring in graceful rate adaptation. The video we used in this experiment is two-minute long, and is encoded into four different bit rate levels, which are 51 kbps, 195 kbps, 515 kbps, and 771 kbps, respectively. The segment duration is 2 seconds. We test different push numbers 2, 5, 10, 20 with the k-push schemes. In addition, we also repeat the experiments for regular DASH streaming based on HTTP/1.1, denoted as *DASH* in the figures.

In the regular DASH scheme, the client estimates current bandwidth according to the duration for receiving the last segment, and chooses the maximum bit rate level that are smaller than the measured bandwidth as the quality of next segment to request. The k-push schemes follow the similar rule but estimate the bandwidth by measuring across the entire last push cycle. Meanwhile the network variations are preset in DASH2M, in order to eliminate the impact of bandwidth prediction. We set the watch probability to 1 all the time since the experiment is conducted until the end of video. In this case, DASH2M prefers a large K for the power efficiency. The quality duration m is selected as 4 to smooth the quality variations in the video session.

In all schemes, the critical buffer is set as 20 seconds, which means a new push cycle is launched as long as there are no other active push cycles and the buffer length is below the critical value. We manually introduce the bandwidth drops to result in the bandwidth sequence of $\{1600, 800, 600, 400, 800, 600, 400\}$ kbps. The bandwidth varies every 15 seconds. The RTT is set as 20 ms all the time, and all schemes start from the lowest bit rate.

Figure 3 shows the request result of a playback session. The x-axis is the time when the requests are sent and the y-axis is bit rates of the requested segments. The bandwidth changes are also plotted as a solid line in the figure. *x-push* presents the k-push scheme with the push number set to x. As we can observe from the figure, the regular DASH scheme performs similar to the 2-push scheme and they can react the bandwidth variation in a timely manner. DASH2M scales up the requested bit rate with a little delay at the beginning because the bit rate switch is gradual in DASH2M. When the bandwidth drops at the 30th and the 90th second, DASH2M firstly exploits the current buffer data to maintain the maximum video quality for a while, and then gracefully decreases the requested bit rate. When the requested bit rate is low at around the 60th second, DASH2M reduces the push cycle and it promptly increases the requested bit rate since the higher bandwidth is discovered. For the other k-push schemes, 5-push and

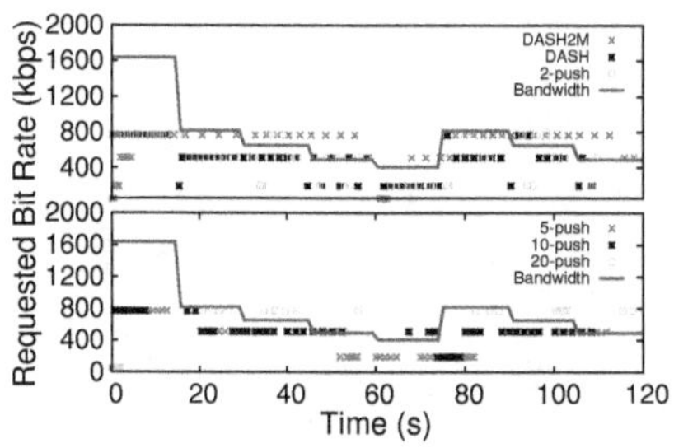

Figure 3: Requested segment bit rate

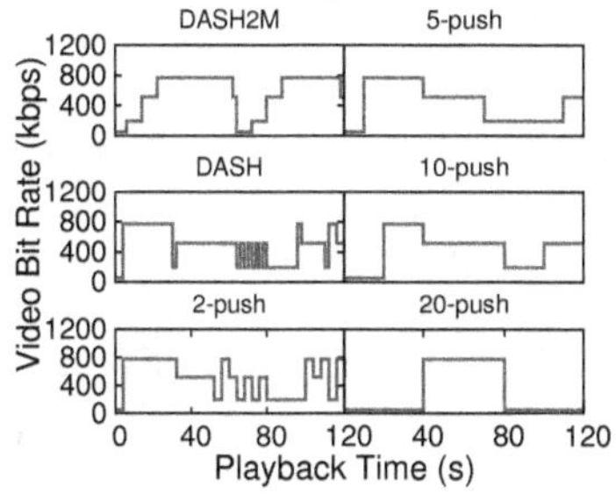

Figure 4: Perceived video quality variations

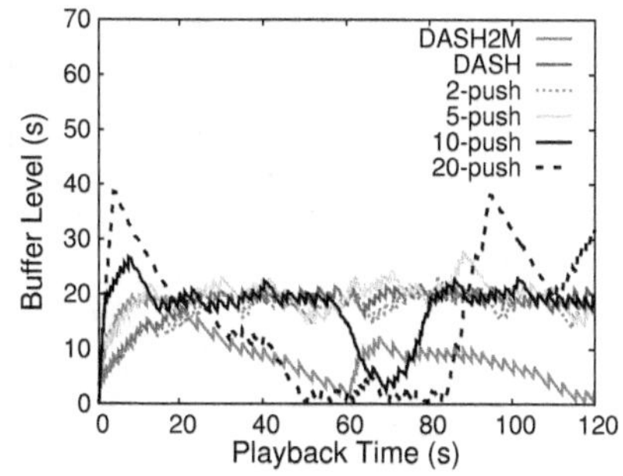

Figure 5: Buffer length variations

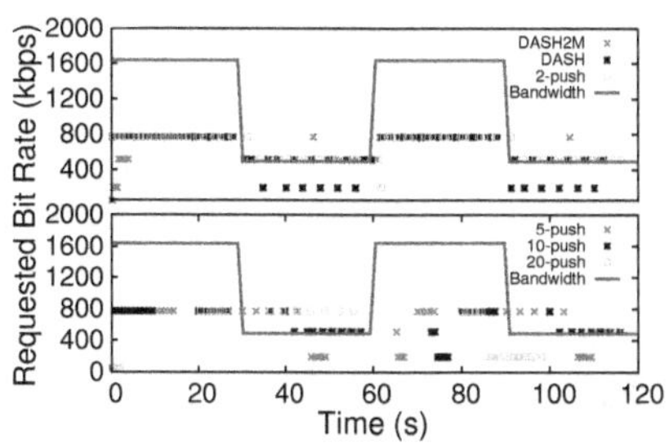

Figure 6: Requested segment bit rate

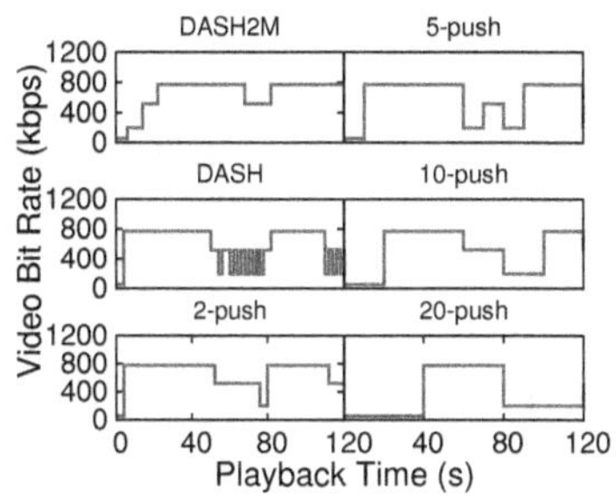

Figure 7: Perceived video quality variations

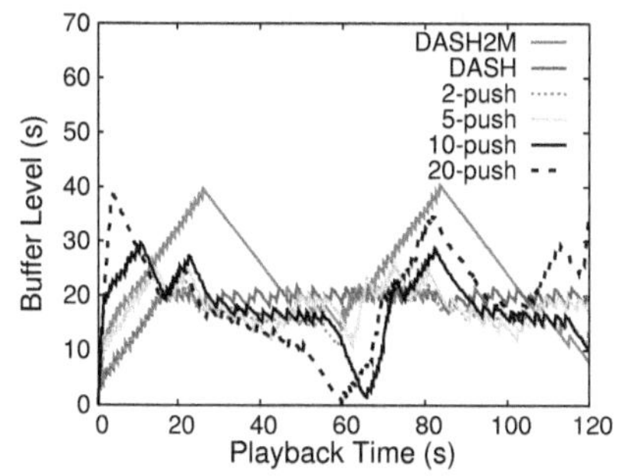

Figure 8: Buffer length variations

10-push fit the bandwidth variation well because their push cycles (10 and 20 seconds) approach the bandwidth variation period. 20-push fails to accommodate the network variations, which are more frequent than its push cycle.

Figure 4 shows how the user perceived quality changes for these schemes. In this figure, the x-axis is the playback time in seconds and the y-axis is the playback video bit rate in kbps. We can see from the figure that DASH2M introduces graceful quality degradation and improvement in response to the network dynamics. While for all other schemes, there are a lot of fluctuations and abrupt quality changes on the client side.

We further calculate the average quality of segments that played on the client. The regular DASH based on HTTP/1.1 has an average bit rate of 485 kbps. In the 2-, 5-, 10- and 20-push schemes, the client received the video at an average bit rates of 489 kbps, 440 kbps, 434 kbps and 293 kbps, respectively. While in DASH2M, the client received the highest average quality across all the schemes, which is 572 kbps.

Figure 5 further shows the buffer variation of all schemes in the above experiment. In this figure, the x-axis is the playback time in seconds, and the y-axis represents the buffer length in seconds. From the figure, we can observe that in the regular DASH scheme and the 2-push and 5-push schemes, the buffer can be maintained at a stable level, indicating that they can react to the network variations in a timely manner. There are large fluctuation when the push number increases. We can see that the 10-push and the 20-push significantly consume the buffer when there is an unpredictable network variation. In the worst case, 20-push triggers a re-buffering at around the 60th second when the bandwidth is the lowest.

On the other hand, with the accurate bandwidth information, Figure 5 shows that DASH2M can always maintain the playback buffer at a low level even when there are rate adaptations, since DASH2M always aims to serve the client with the highest possible bit rates to maximize the video quality.

5.4 Push Termination Evaluation

We have shown that DASH2M outperforms the push schemes with a fixed push number K with graceful quality changes in response to network dynamics. Next we test to see whether the stream termination can also assist DASH2M if the actual bandwidth deviates from the predicted one. That is, when prediction is not accurate. We use the configuration of last experiment except the network variations are set as the sequence of $\{1600, 600, 1600, 600\}$ kbps. The bandwidth drops occur every 30 seconds.

Figure 6 shows the requested segment bit rates distribution plotted against time. Two deviated points can be found for DASH2M when the bandwidth drops to a low value. This is the time when DASH2M has monitored a significant bandwidth mismatch, and DASH2M immediately sends a directive for terminating all active push streams to the server. DASH2M further decided to switch to a lower quality next to the current bit rate level. The other schemes perform similarly as in the previous experiment that a large K leads to the failure of adapting to the bandwidth fluctuations.

Figure 7 further shows the received video quality at the client. As we can see from the figure, the results are similar to what we have observed in the last experiment. DASH2M still introduces the highest average perceived quality, which is 647 kbps. The regular DASH scheme based on HTTP/1.1 streams the video at an average rate of 586 kbps. The k-push schemes have the average rates of 644 kbps, 561 kbps, 512 kbps and 357 kbps, respectively, following the increasing push number from 2 to 20.

Figure 8 shows the corresponding buffer level variations. Compared to the last experiment, DASH2M accumulates the buffer in a faster manner, which is similar to the k-push schemes with a high push number (e.g., 10 or 20) when the network resources are abundant. However when a bandwidth mismatch is found, DASH2M terminates the segment pushing, which helps the client promptly switch to an appropriate bit rate without consuming the entire buffer. While for 10-push and 20-push, there are re-buffering events due to the drainage of the playback buffer.

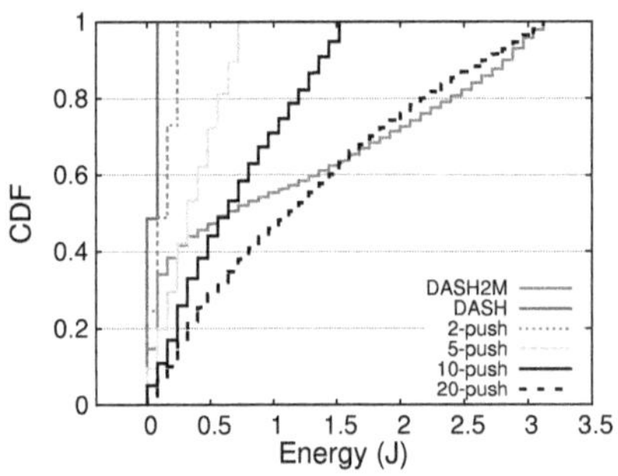

Figure 9: Cumulative Distribution Function (CDF) of energy wasted by over-pushed segments when the ratio of bandwidth to video quality is 10 : 1

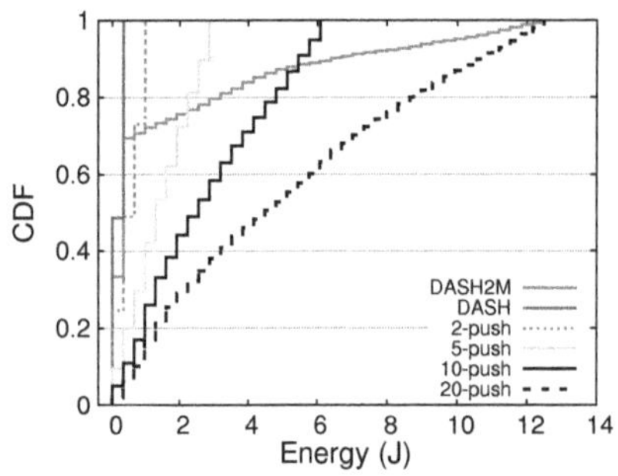

Figure 10: Cumulative Distribution Function (CDF) of energy wasted by over-pushed segments when the ratio of bandwidth to video quality is 10 : 4

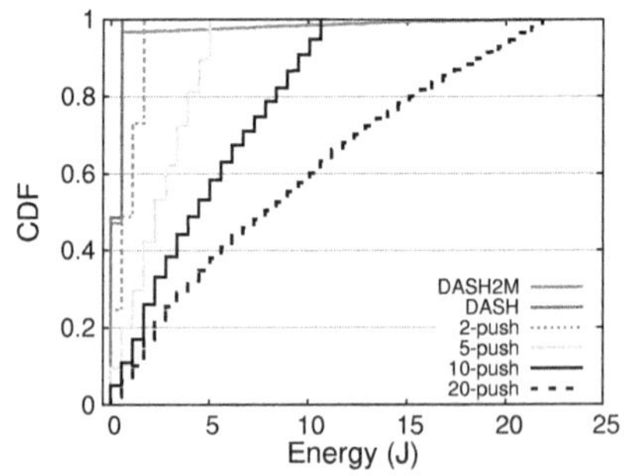

Figure 11: Cumulative Distribution Function (CDF) of energy wasted by over-pushed segments when the ratio of bandwidth to video quality is 10 : 7

Figure 12: Summarized user watching portion

5.5 Power Efficiency

We also conduct a simulation based on a large scale of HLS trace to evaluate the power efficiency of DASH2M. Our purpose is to find out how many segments are over-pushed and how much energy is wasted. This trace is measured on the mobile devices, which ranges from 07/15/2015 to 08/31/2015, and there are ~ 12 million records from the second largest mobile streaming service provider Vuclip [8]. To study the over-push result, we implement a simulator in perl following the same algorithm described in Procedure 1. In the simulator, we set the segment duration as 2 seconds. In order to retrieve a general distribution of the watching portion, we split the whole data set into two sub-traces with the equal size. One of them is summarized as a normalized distribution, which is represented in Figure 12. This distribution is further built into the simulator. The other sub-trace is fed to the simulator as the input. For evaluating the energy consumption of a push cycle in cellular network, several parameters are required. We set the timeout value between ACTIVE and TAIL as 5 seconds and the timeout value between TAIL and SLEEP as 12 seconds, which are the typical values from AT&T [10]. The average power consumed when transmitting data is set as 800 mW and the TAIL state consumes 400 mW on average, which is measured on ASUS ZenPad 10.

We vary the ratio of the video quality to the network bandwidth for observing how DASH performs under different network utilization. The time used to transmit a video segment is set as 10%, 40% and 70% of the segment duration. We present the simulation results in Figure 9, 10 and 11, respectively. The x-axis is the energy wasted by over-pushed segments and the y-axis is the cumulative distribution function. The k-push schemes and the regular DASH scheme perform almost the same whatever the bandwidth utilization is. The regular DASH scheme rarely downloads the segments that users do not watch, and the segments over-pushed by 20-push waste the most energy, whose value increases with the transmission time. DASH2M aggressively increases the push number when the network resources are abundant, because the transmission time is short and the over-push operations will not waste too much energy. However if the network resources are limited, DASH2M then carefully chooses a smaller push number and no more energy is wasted. Therefore DASH2M is aware of the power profile of current network interface and adopts an efficient transmission solution.

6. CONCLUSION AND FUTURE WORK

As the major delivery mechanism for Internet streaming delivery, HTTP is starting the transition from HTTP/1.1 to HTTP/2, which offers a set of new schemes for improving Internet content delivery. In this work, we systematically explore how to best utilize HTTP/2 to optimize the Internet streaming delivery to mobile devices. For this purpose, we have designed DASH2M, Dynamic and Adaptive Streaming over HTTP/2. DASH2M deliberately considers the network fluctuations and the resource consumption on the mobile devices to optimize the user's streaming experience. To evaluate DASH2M, we have implemented a prototype, and experiments have been conducted in a controlled local LAN environment. The experimental results show that DASH2M outperforms prior strategies by greatly enhancing the user's experience while preserving the energy consumption on the mobile device.

With HTTP/2 playing an increasingly critical role in HTTP streaming, the server-initiated push is a promising technique to effectively improve the streaming experience. While some previous studies have suggested continuous push and shorter segment duration for live streaming, we plan to investigate their effectiveness in practice. A designated short segment duration imposes a small playback buffer to a live stream, which is vulnerable to network fluctuations in Internet. In the future, we expect to practically improve the live streaming experience even with a complicated network conditions.

7. ACKNOWLEDGMENTS

We appreciate constructive comments from anonymous referees. The work is partially supported by NSF under grants CNS-1117300 and CNS-1524462.

8. REFERENCES

[1] Consumer internet traffic report. http://www.cisco.com/c/en/us/solutions/collateral/service-provider/ip-ngn-ip-next-generation-network/white_paper_c11-481360.html.

[2] dash.js. https://github.com/Dash-Industry-Forum/dash.js/wiki.

[3] Hypertext Transfer Protocol – HTTP/1.1. https://tools.ietf.org/html/rfc2068.

[4] Hypertext Transfer Protocol Version 2 (HTTP/2). https://tools.ietf.org/html/rfc7540.

[5] Jetty. http://www.eclipse.org/jetty/.

[6] MP4Box. https://gpac.wp.mines-telecom.fr/mp4box/.

[7] Netflix. https://www.netflix.com/.

[8] Vuclip. http://www.vuclip.com/index.html.

[9] YouTube. https://www.youtube.com/.

[10] A. Gerber et al. A call for more energy-efficient apps, available online. http://www.research.att.com.

[11] S. Akhshabi, L. Anantakrishnan, C. Dovrolis, and A. C. Begen. Server-based traffic shaping for stabilizing oscillating adaptive streaming players. In *Proceeding of the 23rd ACM Workshop on Network and Operating Systems Support for Digital Audio and Video*, pages 19–24. ACM, 2013.

[12] A. Cardaci, L. Caviglione, A. Gotta, and N. Tonellotto. Performance evaluation of SPDY over high latency satellite channel. In *Personal Satellite Services*, pages 123–134. Springer, 2013.

[13] W. Cherif, Y. Fablet, E. Nassor, J. Taquet, and Y. Fujimori. DASH fast start using HTTP/2. In *Proceedings of the 25th ACM Workshop on Network and Operating Systems Support for Digital Audio and Video*, pages 25–30. ACM, 2015.

[14] J. Erman, A. Gerber, K. Ramadrishnan, S. Sen, and O. Spatscheck. Over the top video: the gorilla in cellular networks. In *Proceedings of the 2011 ACM SIGCOMM conference on Internet measurement conference*, pages 127–136. ACM, 2011.

[15] T.-Y. Huang, N. Handigol, B. Heller, N. McKeown, and R. Johari. Confused, timid, and unstable: picking a video streaming rate is hard. In *Proceedings of the 2012 ACM conference on Internet measurement conference*, pages 225–238. ACM, 2012.

[16] R. Huysegems, T. Bostoen, P. Rondao Alface, J. van der Hooft, S. Petrangeli, T. Wauters, and F. De Turck. HTTP/2-based methods to improve the live experience of adaptive streaming. In *Proceedings of the 23rd International ACM Conference on Multimedia Conference*, pages 541–550. ACM, 2015.

[17] J. Jiang, V. Sekar, and H. Zhang. Improving fairness, efficiency, and stability in HTTP-based adaptive video streaming with festive. In *Proceedings of the 8th international conference on Emerging networking experiments and technologies*, pages 97–108. ACM, 2012.

[18] V. Krishnamoorthi, N. Carlsson, D. Eager, A. Mahanti, and N. Shahmehri. Quality-adaptive prefetching for interactive branched video using HTTP-based adaptive streaming. In *Proceedings of the 22nd ACM International Conference on Multimedia*, pages 317–326, New York, NY, USA, 2014. ACM.

[19] X. Li, M. Dong, Z. Ma, and F. C. Fernandes. Greentube: power optimization for mobile videostreaming via dynamic cache management. In *Proceedings of the 20th ACM international conference on Multimedia*, pages 279–288. ACM, 2012.

[20] Y. Liu, F. Li, L. Guo, Y. Guo, and S. Chen. Bluestreaming: towards power-efficient internet p2p streaming to mobile devices. In *Proceedings of the 19th ACM international conference on Multimedia*, pages 193–202. ACM, 2011.

[21] Y. Liu, F. Li, L. Guo, B. Shen, and S. Chen. A comparative study of Android and iOS for accessing internet streaming services. In *Passive and Active Measurement*, pages 104–114. Springer, 2013.

[22] M. Belshe et al. SPDY Protcol. https://tools.ietf.org/html/daft-ietf-httpbis-http2-00.

[23] R. K. Mok, X. Luo, E. W. Chan, and R. K. Chang. QDASH: a QoE-aware DASH system. In *Proceedings of the 3rd Multimedia Systems Conference*, pages 11–22. ACM, 2012.

[24] C. Mueller, S. Lederer, C. Timmerer, and H. Hellwagner. Dynamic adaptive streaming over HTTP/2.0. In *2013 IEEE International Conference on Multimedia and Expo*, pages 1–6. IEEE, 2013.

[25] B. Rainer and C. Timmerer. Self-organized inter-destination multimedia synchronization for adaptive media streaming. In *Proceedings of the 22nd ACM International Conference on Multimedia*, pages 327–336, New York, NY, USA, 2014. ACM.

[26] M. Ryu and U. Ramachandran. Flashstream: A multi-tiered storage architecture for adaptive HTTP streaming. In *Proceedings of the 21st ACM International Conference on Multimedia*, MM '13, pages 313–322, New York, NY, USA, 2013. ACM.

[27] M. Z. Shafiq, J. Erman, L. Ji, A. X. Liu, J. Pang, and J. Wang. Understanding the impact of network dynamics on mobile video user engagement. In *ACM SIGMETRICS Performance Evaluation Review*, volume 42, pages 367–379. ACM, 2014.

[28] T. Stockhammer. Dynamic adaptive streaming over HTTP–: standards and design principles. In *Proceedings of the second annual ACM conference on Multimedia systems*, pages 133–144. ACM, 2011.

[29] G. Tian and Y. Liu. Towards agile and smooth video adaptation in dynamic HTTP streaming. In *Proceedings of the 8th international conference on Emerging networking experiments and technologies*, pages 109–120. ACM, 2012.

[30] G. Tian and Y. Liu. On adaptive HTTP streaming to mobile devices. In *2013 20th International Packet Video Workshop*, pages 1–8. IEEE, 2013.

[31] S. Wei and V. Swaminathan. Cost effective video streaming using server push over HTTP 2.0. In *2014 IEEE 16th International Workshop on Multimedia Signal Processing*, pages 1–5. IEEE, 2014.

[32] S. Wei and V. Swaminathan. Low latency live video streaming over HTTP 2.0. In *Proceedings of Network and Operating System Support on Digital Audio and Video Workshop*, page 37. ACM, 2014.

[33] S. Wei, V. Swaminathan, and M. Xiao. Power efficient mobile video streaming using HTTP/2 server push. In *2015 IEEE 17th International Workshop on Multimedia Signal Processing*, pages 1–6. IEEE, 2015.

[34] X. K. Zou, J. Erman, V. Gopalakrishnan, E. Halepovic, R. Jana, X. Jin, J. Rexford, and R. K. Sinha. Can accurate predictions improve video streaming in cellular networks? In *Proceedings of the 16th International Workshop on Mobile Computing Systems and Applications*, pages 57–62. ACM, 2015.

Deep-based Ingredient Recognition for Cooking Recipe Retrieval

Jingjing Chen
City University of HongKong
Kowloon, HongKong
jingjchen9-c@my.city.edu.hk

Chong-Wah Ngo
City University of HongKong
Kowloon, HongKong
cscwngo@cityu.edu.hk

ABSTRACT

Retrieving recipes corresponding to given dish pictures facilitates the estimation of nutrition facts, which is crucial to various health relevant applications. The current approaches mostly focus on recognition of food category based on global dish appearance without explicit analysis of ingredient composition. Such approaches are incapable for retrieval of recipes with unknown food categories, a problem referred to as zero-shot retrieval. On the other hand, content-based retrieval without knowledge of food categories is also difficult to attain satisfactory performance due to large visual variations in food appearance and ingredient composition. As the number of ingredients is far less than food categories, understanding ingredients underlying dishes in principle is more scalable than recognizing every food category and thus is suitable for zero-shot retrieval. Nevertheless, ingredient recognition is a task far harder than food categorization, and this seriously challenges the feasibility of relying on them for retrieval. This paper proposes deep architectures for simultaneous learning of ingredient recognition and food categorization, by exploiting the mutual but also fuzzy relationship between them. The learnt deep features and semantic labels of ingredients are then innovatively applied for zero-shot retrieval of recipes. By experimenting on a large Chinese food dataset with images of highly complex dish appearance, this paper demonstrates the feasibility of ingredient recognition and sheds light on this zero-shot problem peculiar to cooking recipe retrieval.

Keywords

Food categorization; ingredient recognition; zero-shot retrieval; multitask deep learning

Figure 1: Variations in visual appearance and composition of ingredients show the challenges of predicting ingredients even for dishes within the same food category. The first row shows three examples of dishes for the category "fried green peppers", followed by "yuba salad" ad "steam egg custard" in second and third rows respectively.

1. INTRODUCTION

While there is a large number of cooking recipes posted on the Internet, finding a right recipe given a picture of dish remains a challenge yet to be fully explored. The major problem underlying this challenge is the recognition of food categories as well as their ingredients. Indeed, the problem is commonly shared among health-related applications. For example, food-log management [1], which records daily food intake for dietary habit monitoring, often requires manual input of food intake. In addition to time-consuming, the process is error-prone. As investigated in [11], self-reporting data obtained from unfriendly acquired process tends to underestimate the actual food intake. These concerns motivate the use of mobile devices as a convenient means in capturing pictures of food intake for automatic recognition [24] [14] [25] [3] [16].

This paper studies the recognition of ingredients for recipe retrieval in the domain of Chinese dishes. Different from food categorization, which is to identify the name of a dish (e.g., fried green pepper shown in Figure 1), ingredient recognition is to uncover the ingredients inside a dish (e.g., green pepper, black bean, chopped garlic). In the literature, associating food categories to their respective recipes is regarded as a general pipeline that facilitates the estimation of calories and nutrition facts [35] [14]. The pipeline is effective for recognizing restaurant dishes and the food categories with standardized cooking method (e.g., fast food) that often have similar visual appearance with the same ingredients. However, most dishes in Chinese food have no standardized cooking method, food presentation and ingredient composition. Direct mapping between dishes and recipes, by using the names of food categories, is not likely to attain satisfactory retrieval rate, not mentioning the imperfect performance in food recognition. The difficulty of this task is probably alleviated, nevertheless, with the presence of GPS and restaurant menus as utilized by Im2Calories [24] and Menu-

MM '16, October 15-19, 2016, Amsterdam, Netherlands

 ISBN 978-1-4503-3603-1/16/10...$15.00

DOI: http://dx.doi.org/10.1145/2964284.2964315

Match [2]. However, restaurant information are difficult to acquire as stated in [24] and such context-aware recognition is only limited to restaurant food. Therefore, this paper argues the need of ingredient recognition beyond food categorization for general recipe retrieval.

In the domain of Chinese food, two major obstacles in recognition are diverse appearances of dishes and wild composition of ingredients. Figure 1 shows some examples of Chinese dishes. Automatic recognition is challenged by the wildly different ways of mixing and placing ingredients even for the same food category. For the food category "steamed egg custard" (last row of Figure 1), there is even no overlap in ingredients except egg. Retrieving recipes without explicitly naming the underneath ingredients is expected to include false positives. Basically, ingredients can be treated as attributes of food categories. As the number of food categories is generally far larger than the number of ingredients, recognizing attributes is more feasible than food categories in terms of scale. Furthermore, ingredient recognition also gives light to the retrieval of recipes for unknown food categories during model training, a problem generally referred to as zero-shot recognition or retrieval [29].

Generally speaking, ingredient recognition is more difficult than food categorization. As observed in Figure 1, the size, shape and color of ingredients can exhibit large visual differences due to diverse ways of cutting and cooking, in addition to changes in viewpoints and lighting conditions. Recognizing ingredients alone without food category in mind is likely to result in unsatisfactory performance. This paper considers simultaneous recognition of food and ingredients, aiming to exploit the mutual relationship between them for enhancing the robustness of recognition. The key ingredients of a category remain similar despite composing with different auxiliary ingredients. Knowing food category basically eases the recognition of ingredients. On the other hand, the prediction of ingredients also helps food categorization, for example, the ingredient "fungus" has a higher chance than "pork" to appear in the food "yuba salad". Hence, learning food categories with the composition of ingredients in mind, and vice versa, in principle shall lead to better performance.

Figure 2 gives an overview of the proposed framework, which is composed of two modules: ingredient recognition and zero-shot recipe retrieval. The first module formulates the recognition of ingredients as a problem of multi-task learning using deep convolution neural network (DCNN). Given a picture of dish, the module outputs the name of dish along with a histogram of ingredients. The developed DCNN can recognize 172 Chinese food categories and 353 ingredients. To the best of our knowledge, there is no result published yet for ingredient recognition on such a large scale. The second module performs zero-shot retrieval, by matching the predicted ingredients against a large corpus containing more than 60,000 recipes. The corpus includes some food categories as well as ingredients unknown to the multi-task DCNN. To boost retrieval performance, a graph encoding the contextual relationship among ingredients is learnt from the recipe corpus. Using this graph, conditional random field (CRF) is employed to probabilistically tune the probability distribution of ingredients to reduce potential recognition error due to unseen food category.

To summary, this paper contributes by developing multi-task learning technique for ingredient recognition and demonstrates its application for zero-shot recipe retrieval. Our work differs from the existing works, which mostly focus on recognition of food categories and operate in domains such as western and Japanese food [4] [22]. To our knowledge, zero-shot recipe retrieval, which requires knowledge of ingredients, has not yet been considered in the literature. Along with this paper, we will release the collected Chinese food dataset, VIREO Food-172, which contains 172 food and 353 ingredient labels. The dataset is larger than the publicly available datasets such as Food-101 [4], UEC Food-100 [22] and PFID [6], each with around 100 western or Japanese food categories but without ingredient labels.

2. RELATED WORK

Variants of recognition-centric approaches have been investigated for different food-related applications. These efforts include food quantity estimation based on depth images [7], image segmentation for volume estimation [25], context-based recognition by GPS and restaurant menus [3], taste estimation [23], multi-food recognition [22], multi-modal fusion [13] and real-time recognition [14]. This section mainly reviews previous works on recognition of food and ingredients using deep and hand-crafted features.

The challenge of food recognition comes from visual variations in shape, color and texture layout. These variations are hard to be tackled by hand-crafted features such as SIFT [21], HOG [8] and color [30]. Instead, deep features extracted from DCNN [17], which is trained on ImageNet [9] and fine-tuned on food images, often exhibit impressive recognition performance [24] [36] [34]. Combination of multi-modal features sometimes also leads to better recognition performance, as reported in [15] [34]. One of best the performances on UEC Food-100 dataset is achieved by fusion of DCNN features with RootHOG and color moment [15], and similarly for UPMC Food-101 dataset by fusion of textual and deep features [34]. Different from these works which directly adopt DCNN for food recognition, this paper proposes new architectures based upon DCNN for simultaneous recognition of food categories and ingredients.

Compared to food categorization, recognition of ingredients receives fewer attentions. One early model is PFD (pairwise local feature distribution) [37], which leverages the result of ingredient recognition for food categorization. In PFD, based upon the appearance of image patches, pixels are softly labeled with ingredient categories. The spatial relationship between pixels is then modeled as a multi-dimensional histogram, characterized by label co-occurrence and their geometric properties such as distance and orientation. With this histogram representation, PFD shows impressive food recognition performance. PFD, nevertheless, is hardly scalable to the number of ingredients. Using only eight categories of ingredients as demonstrated in [37], the histogram already grows up to tens of thousands of dimensions, not mentioning 353 categories as in our paper where the number of dimensions could be as high as ten millions. Our work is more scalable and based on multi-task learning, in contrast to the two-step recognition in PFD without the feedback loop.

Few recent works explore spatial layout [12], feature mining [4] and image segmentation [24] for ingredient or food item recognition. In [12], ingredient regions are detected by shape and texture models, where the shape is based on DPM (deformable part-based model) while the texture is based on STF (semantic texton forest). Similar to PFD [37], the regions are encoded into a histogram modeling spatial relationship between them for food recognition. The spatial relationship is not statistically encoded as in [37], but rather explicit relationships such as "above", "below" and "overlapping" are modeled. Such relationships are helpful for recognizing food such as dessert and fast food, but difficult to be generalized such as for Chinese dishes. In [4], an interesting work which mines the composition of ingredients as discriminative patterns is proposed for food classification. A drawback of this approach is the requirement of image segmentation, which is sensitive to parameter setting

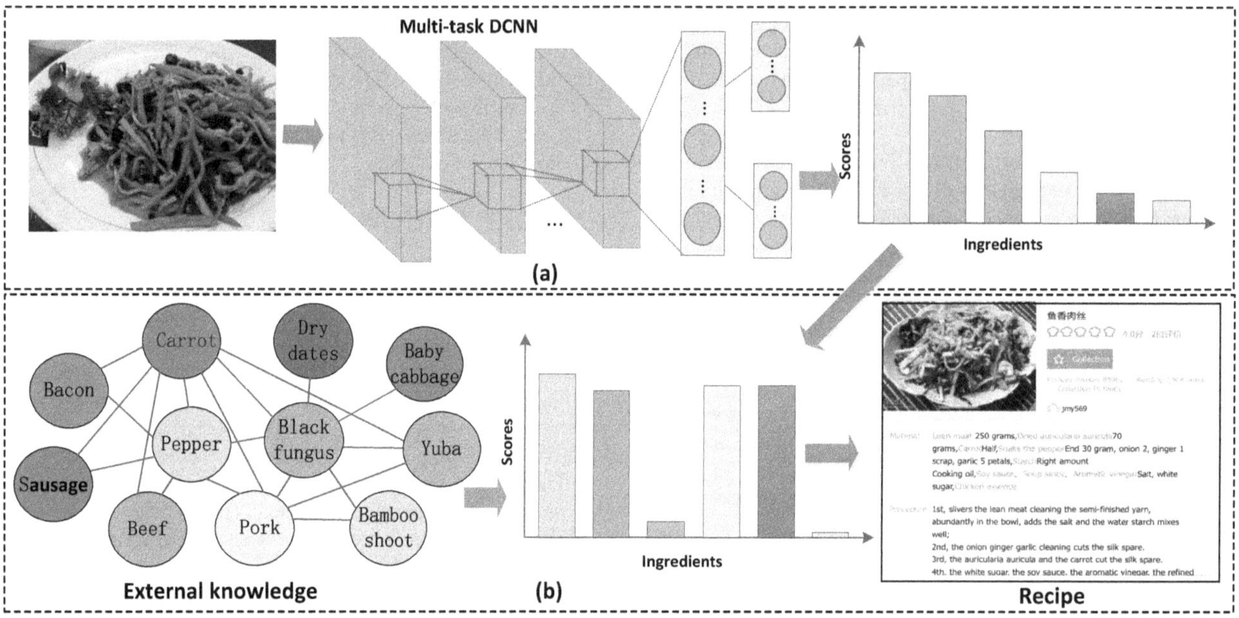

Figure 2: Framework overview: (a) ingredient recognition, (b) zero-shot recipe retrieval. Given a picture of dish with unknown food category, the framework retrieves a recipe for the dish. The recipe is originally in Chinese and Google translated to English.

and can impact recognition performance. As reported in [4], the performance is not better than of DCNN without image segmentation on Food-101 dataset. Similar to [25], image segmentation is employed in [24], but using a more advanced technique based on conditional random field (CRF) with unary potentials provided by DCNN [5]. The promising performance in segmentation for western food, nevertheless, comes from the price for requiring training labels that need manual segmentation of food items for model learning. For Chinese food, collecting such training labels is extremely difficult, given the fuzzy composition and placement of ingredients as shown in Figure 1.

Our work is also related to multi-task learning [10] [31] [32] and fine-grained classification [18] [20] [19]. In [10], multi-task DCNN models are proposed for simultaneous categorization and pose estimation of general objects (e.g., airplane, sofa, car). In [31], a deep network is designed for the tasks of face classification and verification. As concluded by [31], adding one more supervisory signals for feature learning greatly improves the performance of face verification. Similarly for cascade network [18] [20] and bilinear model [19] which couple multiple deep models for fine-grained classification. Nevertheless, these models mostly focus on localization, alignment and classification of object parts, which are not directly applicable to our problem. As ingredients can scatter around a dish and occlude each other (e.g., "yuba salad" in Figure 1), localization and alignment of ingredients are hardly applied for food domain. To the best of our knowledge, there is no multi-task learning model yet developed for food recognition.

3. MULTI-TASK DEEP LEARNING

The conventional DCNN is an end-to-end system with input as picture and output as the prediction scores of class labels. DCNN models such as AlexNet [17] and VGG [28] are trained under the single-label scenario, specifically, there is an assumption of exactly one label for each input picture. As ingredient recognition is a multi-label problem, i.e., more than one labels per image, a different loss function needs to be used for training DCNN. On the other hand, directly revising DCNN with appropriate loss function for ingredient recognition may not yield satisfactory performance, given the varying appearances of an ingredient in different dishes. To this end, we propose to couple food categorization problem, which is a single-label problem, together with ingredient recognition for simultaneous learning.

3.1 Architecture Design

We formulate food categorization and ingredient recognition as a multi-task deep learning problem and modify the architecture of DCNN for our purpose. The modification is not straightforward for involvement of two design issues. The first issue is about whether the prediction scores of both tasks should *directly* or *indirectly* influence each other. Direct influence means that the input of one task is connected as the output of another task. Indirect influence decouples the connection such that each task is on a different path of the network. Both tasks influence each other through updating the shared intermediate layers. The second issue is about the degree in which the intermediate layers should be shared. Ideally, each task should have its own private layer(s) given that the nature of both tasks, single versus multi-labeling, is different. In such a way, the updating of parameters can be done more freely for optimization of individual performance.

Based on the two design issues, we derive four different deep architectures as depicted in Figure 3, respectively name as Arch-A to Arch-D. The first design (Arch-A) considers stacked architecture by placing food categorization on top of ingredient recognition, and vice versa. As the composition of ingredients for different dishes under the same food category can be different, this architecture has the risk that model learning converges slowly as observed in the experiment. The second design (Arch-B) is similar except that indirect influence is adopted and both tasks are at different pathways. Both designs are relatively straightforward to implement by adding additional layers to DCNN. The next two architectures consider the decoupling of some intermediate layers. The third design (Arch-C) allows each task to privately own two intermediate layers on top of the convolutional layers for parameter learning. The last design

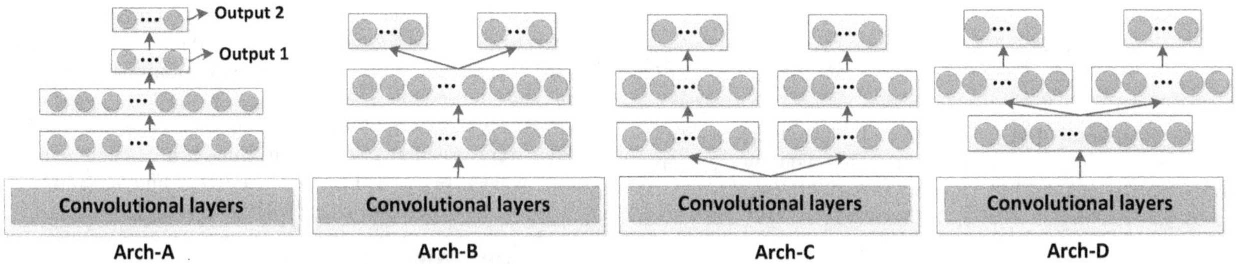

Figure 3: Four different deep architectures for multi-task learning of food category and ingredient recognition.

(Arch-D) is a compromise version between the second and third architectures, by having one shared and one private layer. Arch-D has the peculiarity that the shared layer can correspond to the high or mid-level features common between two tasks at the early stage of learning, while the private layer preserves the learning of specialized features useful for optimizing the performance of each task.

3.2 Implementation

The architectures are modified from VGG 16-layers network [28]. In terms of design, the major modification is made on the fully connected layers. For the private layers in Arch-D, there are 4,096 neurons for food categorization, and 1024 neurons for ingredient layers. Due to different natures of the tasks, we adopt multinomial logistic loss function L_1 for single-label food categorization, and cross-entropy as the loss function L_2 for multi-label ingredient recognition. Denote N as the total number of training images, the overall loss function L is as following:

$$L = -\frac{1}{N}\sum_{n=1}^{N}(L_1 + \lambda L_2) \quad (1)$$

where λ is a parameter trading off the loss terms. This loss function is also widely used in other works such as [31]. During training, the errors propagated from two branches are linearly combined and the weights of first 11 layers shared between two tasks will be updated accordingly. The updating will subsequently affect the last two layers simultaneously, adjustify the features separately owned by food and ingredient recognition. Let $\hat{q}_{n,y}$ as the predicted score of an image x_n for its ground-truth food label y, L_1 is defined as following:

$$L_1 = log(\hat{q}_{n,y}) \quad (2)$$

where $\hat{q}_{n,y}$ is obtained from softmax activation function. Furthermore, denote $p_n \in \{0,1\}^I$, represented as a vector in I dimensions, as the ground-truth ingredients for an image x_n. Basically p_n is a binary vector with entries of value 1 or 0 indicating the presence or absence of an ingredient. The loss function L_2 is defined as

$$L_2 = \sum_{c=1}^{I} p_{n,c}log(\hat{p}_{n,c}) + (1 - p_{n,c})log(1 - \hat{p}_{n,c}) \quad (3)$$

where $\hat{p}_{n,c}$ denotes the probability of having ingredient category c for x_n, obtained through sigmoid activation function.

4. ZERO-SHOT RETRIEVAL

Training a deep network for recognizing all available food categories is not feasible. In addition to the reality that there exist more than tens of thousands of categories, collecting training examples for each of the categories can be a daunting task. Hence, a practical problem is how to leverage the limited knowledge learnt in a network for recognizing dishes of previously unseen category. As the proposed architectures are capable of predicted ingredients, in principle the problem can be addressed by retrieving recipes through matching of ingredients. We refer this problem to as zero-shot retrieval, which is to find recipes for test pictures of unseen food categories. Two scenarios are considered here. Suppose each recipe is associated with a picture of the dish. The first scenario is to use the FC7 features, specifically the features extracted from the private layer(s) of Arch-C or Arch-D, to represent images for retrieval. In other words, the search of recipe is equivalent to image retrieval. The second scenario assumes absence of pictures in recipes, and uses the predicted scores of ingredients as the semantic labels for text-based retrieval of recipes. As the approach for the first scenario can be straightforwardly implemented, this section focuses on the presentation of the second scenario. The idea is to incorporate external knowledge to refine the predicted ingredient scores for more realistic way of zero-shot retrieval.

4.1 Ingredient Refinement with CRF

While the composition of ingredients is fuzzy in Chinese food, the mixing is not purely random. Intuitively, certain groups of ingredients co-occur more often (e.g., corn and carrot), while some ingredients are likely exclusive of each other (e.g., fish and beef). Such statistics can be mined from training data and utilized for adjusting the predicting scores of ingredients. Nevertheless, considering the zero-shot problem and potentially the limited knowledge in deep network, we mine the statistics from a large corpus composed of more than 60,000 Chinese cooking recipes. The major advantage of doing so is to learn a graph modeling ingredient relationships, where their correlations are more generalizable and not restricted by training data, and hence enhance the success rate of zero-shot retrieval.

We extract ingredients from recipes and construct a graph modeling their co-occurrences based on conditional random field (CRF). Denote $\mathcal{N} = \{c_1, ..., c_I\}$ as the set of available ingredients and I as its set cardinality. The graph G is composed of the elements of $\mathcal{N}$ as vertices and their pairwise relationships, denoted as $\phi_i(\cdot)$, as edges. Further let l_i as an indication function that signals the presence or absence of an ingredient c_i. The joint probability of ingredients given the graph is

$$p(l_1, ...l_I) = \frac{1}{Z(\phi)}exp(\sum_{i,j\in\mathcal{N}} l_i l_j \phi(i,j)) \quad (4)$$

where $Z(\cdot)$ is a partitioning function. To learn the graph, we employ Monte Carlo integration to approximate $Z(\cdot)$ and the gradient descent to estimate $\phi(\cdot)$ to optimize the data likelihood [26]. Given a test image, CRF inferences a label sequence $\mathbf{y}$ based on the graph G. The energy function for inference is composed of unary and pairwise potentials, defined as

$$E(\mathbf{y}) = \sum_{c \in \mathcal{N}} \psi_u(y_c) + \sum_{(c,v) \in \varepsilon} \psi_p(y_c, y_v) \tag{5}$$

where ε denotes the set of pairwise cliques. The unary term is set as $\psi_u(y_c) = -log(x_c)$, where x_c is the predicted score by the deep network for ingredient c. The pairwise potential is defined as

$$\psi(y_u, y_v) = \begin{cases} 0 & \text{if } y_u = y_v \\ \phi(y_u, y_v) & \text{if } y_c \neq y_v \end{cases} \tag{6}$$

where the value of $\phi(\cdot)$ is obtained from the graph G. Through inferencing, CRF searchs for the optimal label sequence of $\mathbf{y}$ that agrees with the predicted scores and the contextual relationship captured in the graph G. We employ off-the-shelf algorithm, loopy belief propagation [illegible], for minimize Eqn-5. The output label sequence $\mathbf{y}$ will indicate the presences or absences of ingredients and their probabilities.

4.2 Recipe Search

With the output sequence $\mathbf{y}$ by CRF, a query image is represented as a vector Q^i. Every element in Q^i corresponds to an ingredient and its value indicates the probability output by CRF. On the other hand, the ingredients extracted from a recipe is represented as a binary vector O. The matching score, s_i, between them is defined as

$$s_i = \sum_{c \in O \cap c \in Q^i} x_c \tag{7}$$

Note that the score is not normalized in order not to bias recipes with a small number of ingredients. As a result, Eqn-7 tends to give a higher score for the recipes with excessive number of ingredients. To prevent such cases, the matching between Q^i and O is performed only for the top-k predicted ingredients with higher probability scores. The value of k is empirically set to 10 as there are few recipes with more than 10 ingredients in our dataset.

5. DATASET COLLECTION

We construct a large food dataset specifically for Chinese dishes, namely VIREO Food-172[1], which is made publicly available. Different from other publicly available datasets [4] [22] [6], both food category and ingredient labels are included. In addition, a large corpus of recipes along with dish pictures is also collected.

5.1 VIREO Food-172

The food categories were compiled from "Go Cooking" [2] and "Meishi" [3], which are two websites for popular Chinese dishes. We combine the categories from both websites by removing duplication. All the images in the dataset were crawled from Baidu and Google image search. For each category, the name was issued as keywords in Chinese to search engines. Categories with no more than 100 images returned were removed from the list. For the remaining categories, we manually checked each crawled images up to the depth of 1,300, for excluding images with the resolution lower than 256×256 or suffer from blurring, images with more than one dishes, and false positives. This process ends up with 172 food categories in the dataset.

The 172 categories cover eight major groups of food, as shown in Figure 5. The group *meat* contains the most number of categories, with examples include "braised pork" and "sautéed shredded pork in sweet bean sauce". On the other hand, there are only eight categories under the group *bean product*, and examples include "Mapo tofu" and "braised tofu". All the images in the dataset were crawled from Baidu and Google image search. The names of food categories, were issued as keywords in Chinese to search engines, and 1,300 images are crawled per food category. Figure 4 shows some examples of food categories in VIREO Food-172.

5.2 Ingredient labeling

We compiled a list of more than 300 ingredients based on the recipes of 172 food categories. The ingredients range from popular items such as "shredded pork" and "shredded pepper" to rare items such as "codonopsis pilosula" and "radix astragali". Labeling over hundreds of ingredients for over hundred thousands of images could be extremely tedious, not mentioning the challenge of ingredient annotation. First, some ingredients are difficult to be recognized, for example, ingredients under soup or sauce. Second, some ingredients are invisible in flour-made food categories such as dumpling and noodle. Third, certain ingredients such as egg exhibit large visual variations (see Figure 6) due to different ways of cutting and cooking. Hence, the labeling considers only the annotation of visible ingredients. In addition, we create additional labels for ingredients with large visual appearance, for example, we have 13 different labels for "egg", such as "preserved egg slices" and "boiled egg".

We recruited 10 homemakers who have cooking experience for ingredient labeling. The homemakers were instructed to label only visible and recognizable ingredients. They were also allowed to annotate new ingredients not in the list, which would be explicitly checked by us. To guarantee the accuracy of labeling, we purposely awarded homemakers with cash bonus as incentives to provide quality annotation, in addition to regular payment. For this purpose, we checked a small subset of labels and provided immediate feedback to homemakers such that they were aware of their performance. The whole labeling process ended in two weeks. By excluding images with no ingredient labels, VIREO Food-172 contains a total of 353 ingredient labels and 110,241 images, with the average of 3 ingredients per image. Figure 7 shows the distribution of positive examples in food and ingredient categories. On average, there are 640 positive samples per food category, and 745 per ingredient.

5.3 Recipe Corpus

The corpus was compiled from a popular website "Xinshipu" [4]. The website offers ontology for 530 key ingredients in Chinese food. Using all of these ingredients as queries, a total of 65,284 Chinese cooking recipes were crawled from this website. Each recipe basically contains four sections, including brief introduction, ingredient list, cooking procedure, and a picture showing the appearance of the dish. The recipes were uploaded by Internet users, and thus there may be multiple recipes sharing the same name but with different ingredient lists. Conversely, there are also few recipes about the same dish but in different names.

6. EXPERIMENTS

We split the experiments into three parts, verifying the performances of multi-task learning (Section 6.1), the impact of CRF (Section 6.2) and the application for zero-shot retrieval (Section 6.3). The first part aims to evaluate different deep architectures for multi-task learning in comparison to single-task DCNN. The last

[1] http://vireo.cs.cityu.edu.hk/VireoFood172/

[2] https://www.xiachufang.com/category/

[3] http://www.meishij.net

[4] http://www.xinshipu.com

Figure 4: Examples of food categories in VIREO Food-172.

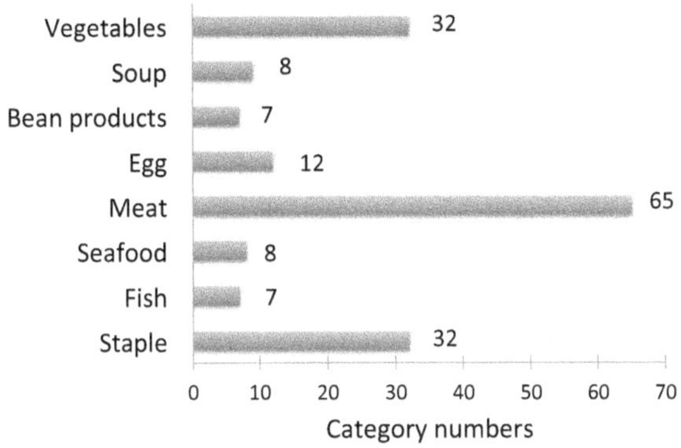

Figure 5: The distribution of food categories under eight major food groups in VIREO Food-172.

Figure 6: The ingredient "egg" shows large difference in visual appearance across different kinds of dishes.

part aims to demonstrate the merit of leveraging ingredient labels for novel recipe retrieval.

6.1 Deep Architectures

The experiments are conducted mainly on VIREO Food-172 dataset. In each food category, 60% of images are randomly picked for training, while 10% for validation and the remaining 30% of images for testing. For performance evaluation, the average top-1 and top-5 accuracies are adopted for food categorization, which are standard measures for the single-label task. For ingredient recognition which belongs to multi-label, micro-F1 and macro-F1 that take into account both precision and recall for each ingredient are employed.

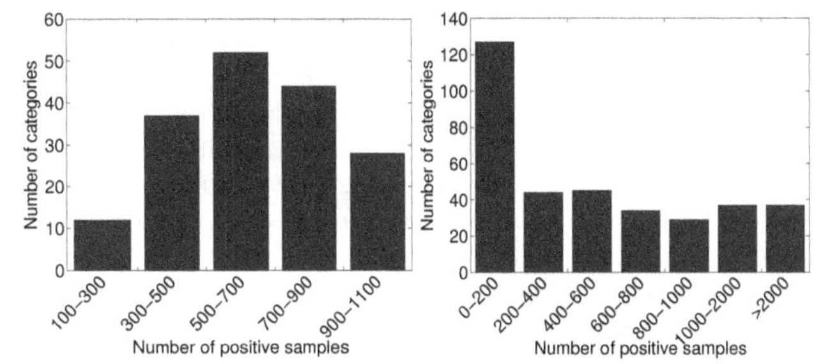

(a) Food category (b) Ingredient

Figure 7: The distribution of food categories (a) and ingredients (b).

The evaluation compares baseline, single and multi-task learnings. The baseline includes SVM classifiers trained using hand-crafted (Gist [27] and color moment [30]) and deep (FC7 of DCNN [17]) features. The single-task learning includes the AlexNet and VGG networks fine-tuned on training and validation sets. Note that for baseline and single-task, different classifiers and networks need to be trained separately for food categorization and ingredient recognition. Specifically, multi-label SVM (MSVM) is trained for baseline, and cross entropy loss function (Eqn-3) is used for single-task DNN. The multi-task learning includes the four deep architectures illustrated in Figure 3. Note that we experiment two variants of Arch-A, with the layer of food categorization on top of ingredient recognition (Arch-A1) and vice versa (Arch-A2).

Grid search of parameters is performed to find the best possible model settings for all the compared approaches, based on the training and verification sets. As ingredient recognition involves multiple labels, a threshold is required to gate the selection of labels. The threshold is set to be the value of 0.5 following the standard setting when sigmoid is used as the activation function. For multi-task deep architectures, the learning rate is set to 0.001 and the batch size to 50. The learning rate decays after every 8,000 iterations. Using Arch-D as example, Figure 8 shows the impact of λ parameter in Eqn-1. Basically, the Top-1 and Mirco-F1 measures fluctuate within the range of 0.06, when the value of λ varies from 0.1 to 1.0. The best performances attained for food categorization (Top-1) is when $\lambda = 0.1$, and for ingredient recognition (Micro-F1) when $\lambda = 0.3$. To balance the performances, we use F1 of Top-1 and Micro-F1 measures to pick the optimal value, where $\lambda = 0.2$ as shown in Figure 8.

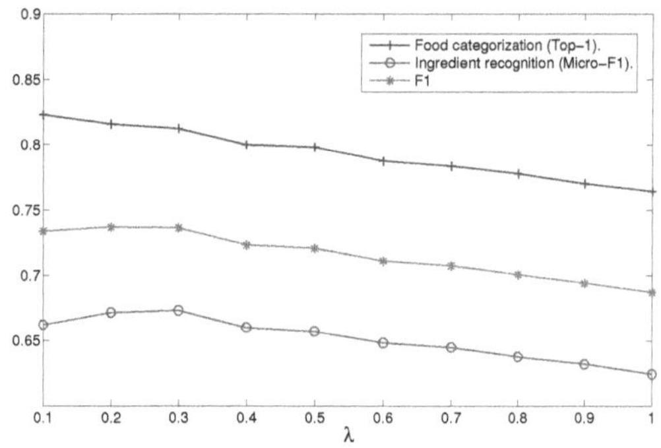

Figure 8: Sensitivity of λ parameter in Eqn-1 for multi-task deep architecture Arch-D.

Table 1 lists the performance for food categorization. The general trend is that deep architectures significantly outperform baselines with either deep or hand-crafted features, while large performance gap is also observed between the results of VGG network and AlexNet. Among the deep architectures for multi-task learning, the designs based on simple modification of DCNN, i.e., Arch-A and Arch-B, show slightly worse performance in Top-1 accuracy compared with single-task VGG. Since the recognition results for both food and ingredients are imperfect, layer stacking as in Arch-A actually could hurt each other's performance. Specifically, the inaccurate prediction in one task will directly affect the other task. On the other hand, while having separate paths as in Arch-B leads to better performance, the improvement is rather minor by the fact that both tasks share the same lower layers. Basically the performances of Arch-C and Arch-D show the merit of having separate paths and layers for both tasks. Arch-C, which only shares convolution layers, improves slightly over single-task VGG. We speculate that the design of Arch-C eventually trains two independent leaners and hence the advantage over single-task is not obvious. Arch-D, which shares one layer while also learning separate layers tailor-made for different tasks, attains the best performance among all the compared approach for both average Top-1 and Top-5 accuracies.

Table 2 shows the performance of ingredient recognition, and similar trends are observed as food categorization. For multi-task learning, all deep architectures but except Arch-A outperform single-task VGG, and with larger performance gaps compared with food categorization. The result basically verifies the merit of joint learning for both tasks. Different from food categorization, sharing layers appears to be a better design choice for ingredient recognition when comparing Arch-B and Arch-C. The best result is attained by Arch-D, which could be viewed as a compromised design between Arch-B and Arch-C. To verify that the improvement is not by chance, we conduct significance test to compare multi-task (Arch-D) and single-task (VGG) using the source code provided by TRECVID[5]. The test is performed by partial randomization with 100,000 numbers of iterations, with the null hypothesis that the improvement is due to chance. At a significance level of 0.05, Arch-D is significantly different from VGG in both food categorization and ingredient recognition by Top-1 accuracy and Macro-F1, respectively. The p-values are close to 0, which reject the null hypothesis.

To validate the proposed work on other food domain, we also conduct experiments on UEC Food-100 [22] dataset for Japanese dishes. The dataset contains 100 categories of food and totally 12,564 images. Each category has at least 100 positive examples. Nevertheless, ingredient labels are not provided. Similar to VIREO Food-172, we compiled a list of 190 ingredients for Japanese food and conducted manual labeling. A total of 1,997 images are excluded from experiments for no ingredient labels. The experiment is conducted based on 5-fold cross-validation, using the same data split and settings as [36]. In [36], DCNN based on AlexNet is first pre-trained with 2,000 categories in ImageNet, including 1,000 food-related categories. The network is then fine-tuned with training examples in the dataset. Table 3 lists the detailed performance. Note that, although not using 1,000 food categories for pre-training, Arch-D still manages to outperform [36] by 3.5% in terms of average top-1 accuracy for food categorization. Overall, similar to the performance on VIREO Food-172, Arch-D attains the best performances for both tasks.

[5]http://www-nlpir.nist.gov/projects/t01v/trecvid.tools/randomization.testing

	Method	Top-1 (%)	Top-5 (%)
Baseline	FC7	48.02	72.01
	Gist	15.39	31.85
	CM	16.54	39.76
Single-task	AlexNet	64.91	85.32
	VGG	80.41	94.59
Multi-task	Arch-A1	78.58	94.24
	Arch-A2	78.63	94.10
	Arch-B	79.05	94.70
	Arch-C	80.66	95.05
	Arch-D	**82.06**	**95.88**

Table 1: Average top-1 and top-5 accuracies for single-label food categorization on VIREO Food-172 dataset.

	Method	*Micro-F1 (%)*	*Macro-F1 (%)*
Baseline	FC7	42.94	32.22
	Gist	23.01	19.45
	CM	21.08	14.06
Single-task	AlexNet	47.63	34.81
	VGG	60.81	43.73
Multi-task	Arch-A1	55.17	43.75
	Arch-A2	59.69	43.48
	Arch-B	66.32	44.85
	Arch-C	63.44	44.26
	Arch-D	**67.17**	**47.18**

Table 2: Performance of multi-label ingredient recognition on VIREO Food-172 dataset.

Method	Categorization		Ingredient recognition	
	Top-1 (%)	Top-5 (%)	*Micro-F1 (%)*	*Macro-F1 (%)*
FC7	58.03	83.71	52.80	32.51
Gist	30.53	58.80	23.93	11.84
CM	24.11	46.42	16.01	7.830
AlexNet	75.62	92.43	55.62	35.63
VGG	81.31	96.72	57.38	38.62
[36]	78.77	95.15	–	–
Arch-D	**82.12**	**97.29**	**70.72**	**43.94**

Table 3: Performance comparision on UEC Food-100 dataset.

6.2 Effect of CRF

This section verifies the use of CRF in refining the predicted ingredients. All the 65,284 recipes are used for the construction of CRF. A special note is that most recipes do not include the fine-grained description of ingredients. For example, a recipe will simply list "egg" as ingredient, instead of explicitly stating whether the ingredient as either "sliced egg" or "boiled egg". Rather such

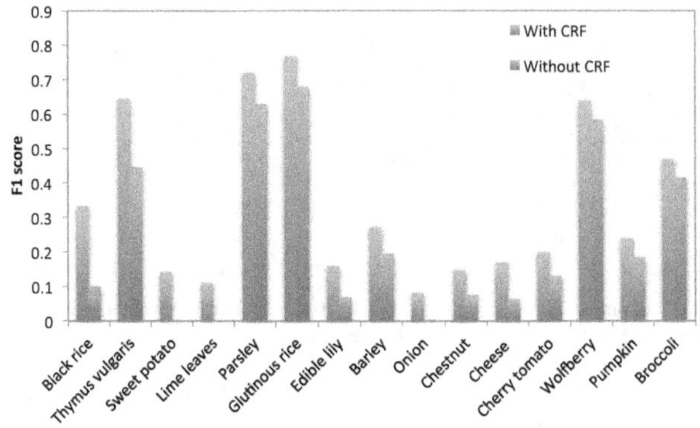

Figure 9: The F1 scores of 15 ingredients that achieve large margin of improvement after CRF.

information can only be inferred from cooking procedure, such as "leaving the eggs boil for 4 minutes". In this experiment, we do not perform natural language processing to obtain the fine-grained description of ingredients. As a consequence, some labels in VIREO Food-172 are merged and this ends up to 257 ingredient labels for experimentation. For the deep architectures, max pooling is adopted to merge the results of fine-grained ingredients. Specifically, if a network predicts "boiled egg" with the probability of 0.5 and "sliced egg" with 0.1, the probability for "egg" is set to be 0.5 in the CRF.

	Method	*Micro-F1 (%)*	*Macro-F1 (%)*
Baseline (recipe)	Food category	40.75	37.47
	Food ingredient	37.39	33.69
Single-task	Without CRF	63.94	46.81
	With CRF	66.23	48.25
Multi-task	Without CRF	68.84	49.98
	With CRF	**71.25**	**51.18**

Table 4: Ingredient recognition with contextual modeling using CRF.

In addition to assessing the effect of CRF for single and multi-task learnings, we also compare the results against the baseline that directly infers the ingredients from a retrieved recipe. More specifically, given a predicted food category by VGG network, the corresponding recipe is retrieved based on name matching. The predicted labels are then based on the ingredients listed in the recipes. This strategy is often used by some approaches [14] for estimation of nutrition facts. We compare to two baselines, based on the predicted names of food categories or ingredients. Note that as a few recipes have the same name despite using different ingredients, and hence multiple recipes could be retrieved. In this case, we only show the result for the recipe which obtains the highest F1 score.

Table 4 lists the performance of different approaches. Note that the performance of multi-task is based on Arch-D. Basically, CRF improves the performance of both single and multi-task learnings. All variants of baseline perform poorly in this experiment, far lower than directly using the ingredients predicted by deep architectures. The result is not surprising due to the fact that, for Chinese food, the composition of ingredients for dishes under the same category can vary depending on factors such as geographical regions, weather and culture.

A few ingredients record large improvement as shown in Figure 9. The examples include "black rice" (F1 score = 0.1 to 0.33), "sweet potatoes" (F1 score = 0 to 0.14), and "cherry tomato" (F1 score = 0.13 to 0.2). CRF successfully captures the knowledge that "black rice" often co-occurs with "rice" and "soybeans" for food categories involving "cereal porridge". Similarly for the co-occurrence among "cherry tomato", "corn" and "lettuce" for food categories related to "vegetable salad". Figure 10 shows a few of success and fail examples refined by CRF. While CRF successfully improves the F1 score and particularly the precision of detection, the recall for few labels is also dropped as noticed in Figure 10(e) and Figure 10(f). Overall, the average precision (micro) is boosted from 0.795 to 0.833, with 193 out of 257 ingredients show improvement. The average recall (micro) is also boosted from 0.607 to 0.623, with 91 ingredients show improvement and 88 ingredients dropped.

6.3 Zero-shot Recipe Retrieval

This section assesses the use of predicted ingredients for retrieving recipes for food categories unknown in VIREO Food-172 dataset. We compile a list of 20 food categories as shown in Table 6 for the experiment. Each category is associated with 1 to 20 recipes. For each category, we make sure that at least its key ingredients are known to VIREO Food-172. On average, there are 3 key ingredients per category. Among the 20 categories, 4 out of them include ingredients that are not seen in VIREO Food-172. For each category, a total of 50 images are crawled from Baidu for testing. The experiment is conducted by, given a test image, the system searches against 65,284 recipes in the corpus and returns top-10 recipes. The performance is measured by top-10 hit rate, which counts the percentage of test images where the ground-truth recipes is found in the top-10 rank list.

We compare three major groups of approaches: image retrieval, ingredient matching (Eqn-7) and their combination. For image retrieval, only the pictures associated with recipes are involved. We compare the effectiveness of different features for retrieval. For VGG, FC7 feature is extracted from the model trained for ingredient recognition. Similarly for Arch-D, where the deep feature is extracted from the private layer specialized for ingredient labels. For ingredient matching, we compare the performances of single (VGG) and multi-task (Arch-D) learnings, where the ingredient prediction scores are both adjusted by CRF. Finally, late fusion is performed for Arch-D and VGG by combining the scores obtained from image retrieval and ingredient matching. Min-max normalization is employed to convert the scores into the range of [0,1]. The fusion is based on joint probability, specifically $1-(1-p_i)\times(1-p_j)$, where p_i and p_j are scores from different approaches.

	Method	*Top-10 hit rate*
Image Retrival	Gist	0.039
	Color moment	0.035
	VGG	0.439
	Arch-D	0.523
Ingredient matching	VGG	0.447
	Arch-D (without CRF)	0.462
	Arch-D	0.554
Fusion	VGG	0.464
	Arch-D	**0.570**

Table 5: Performance of zero-shot recipe retrieval.

Table 5 lists the performance of different approaches. For image retrieval, deep features perform significantly better than hand-crafted features. Our proposed model Arch-D outperforms VGG, showing the superiority of multi-task learning not only in recognition but also feature learning. For text-based ingredient matching, Arch-D also shows better performance than VGG, attributed mainly to the lower recognition error made in ingredient predic-

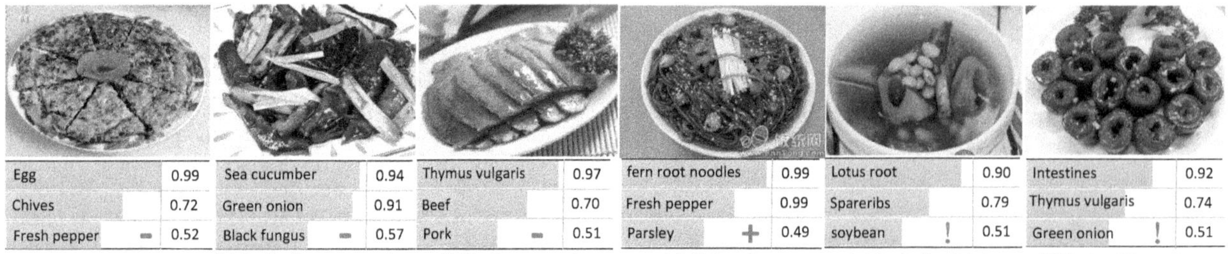

(a) Fried egg (b) Braised sea cucumber with scallion (c) Beef seasoned with soy sauce (d) Hot and sour fern root noodles (e) Pork ribs & lotus root soup (f) Braised intestines in brown source

Figure 10: Example of test images showing effect of CRF in refining ingredient labels. The "-" sign means the false positives that are successfully excluded after CRF, while the "+" sign means the false negatives that are recalled by CRF. The "!" sign indicates true positives that are erroneously removed by CRF.

tion, especially after CRF refinement. Further fusion of both results from Arch-D achieves the overall best performance among all the compared approaches.

Category	Image retrival	Ingredient matching	Fusion
Assorted corn (12)	**0.92**	0.84	0.86
Braised noodles with lentil (16)	0.44	0.42	**0.46**
Braised chicken & potato (8)	**0.42**	0.34	0.34
Cucum. & fungus with eggs (2)	**0.68**	0.34	0.56
Carrot & kelp (4)	**0.78**	0.64	0.72
Cabbage & vermicelli (5)	0.30	**0.54**	0.44
Corn, carrot & ribs soup (19)	0.62	0.64	**0.70**
Dried tofu & pepper(8)	0.48	**0.80**	0.68
Griddle cooked chicken*(7)	0.36	0.40	**0.44**
Loofah egg soup (15)	0.76	**0.98**	0.92
Mustard pork noodles (10)	0.34	**0.74**	0.70
Noodles with peas & meat*(4)	**0.30**	0.22	**0.30**
Pepper & bitter gourd (7)	**0.68**	0.60	**0.68**
Ribs claypot (5)	0.16	**0.50**	0.12
Sichuan cold noodles (12)	**0.86**	0.82	0.84
Soybeans & pork leg soup (12)	0.48	0.46	**0.54**
Sausage claypot (19)	0.30	**0.66**	0.60
Spicy crab*(20)	**0.82**	0.38	0.56
Shredded chicken & pea sprouts*(1)	**0.20**	0.08	0.08
Tomato & egg noodles (18)	0.56	**0.94**	0.86

Table 6: Recipe retrieval performance on 20 unknown food category. The parenthesis indicates the number of recipes for a category. The categories containing unseen ingredients in VIREO Food-172 are indicated by "*".

Table 6 shows the detailed performance of Arch-D on 20 unknown food categories. The performance of image retrieval is influenced by the quality of pictures associated with recipes, particularly for the pictures in low resolution, having different appearances or lighting conditions than the queries. Such examples include "mustard pork noodle" and "tomato & egg noodles". On the other hand, solely matching ingredient lists is limited by the fact that the same set of ingredients can be used for different food categories. One such example is "cucumber & fungus with eggs", where the ingredients are also found in several other food categories, despite different visual appearance due to different ways of cooking and cutting. Image retrieval using the deep features, which are trained to deal with these visual variations, generally shows better performance. Fusion basically compromises both performances and produces the overall best performance. There are four categories where fusion successfully boosts the performances of both approaches. In these cases, image retrieval helps by "disambiguating" the rank lists generated by ingredient matching.

The retrieval performance is also affected by occlusion of ingredients. For example, the "chicken" in "shredded chicken & pea sprouts" is hardly visible under "pea sprouts", which is an ingredient unseen in VIREO Food-172. In this case, ingredient matching performs poorly as seen in Table 6. Image retrieval also performs unsatisfactorily due to diverse dish appearances for test images under this category. Another example is "spicy crab", where crab is hidden under other ingredients. Image retrieval, however, performs surprisingly well for this category because of the unique color and texture of the dishes. Finally, there are four categories that have unseen ingredients. Except "spicy crab", the performance of these categories is below average, showing the challenges of retrieval for recipes with unknown ingredients.

7. CONCLUSIONS

We have presented two main pieces of our work: ingredient recognition and zero-shot recipe retrieval. The former is grounded on a deep architecture (Arch-D) that exploits the joint relationship between food and ingredient labels through multi-task learning. The latter extends the knowledge of Arch-D for the out-of-vocabulary scenario, by learning contextual relationships of ingredients from a large textual corpus of recipes. Experimental results on a challenging Chinese food dataset (VIREO Food-172) show that, while the performance of food categorization is enhanced slightly, the improvement in ingredient recognition is statistically significant compared to the best single-task VGG model. The superiority in performance is not only noticed in VIREO Food-172 but also UEC Food-100, a large-scale Japanese food dataset. More importantly, when extracting the deep features (FC7) from the specialized or private layer learnt for ingredient recognition, the features show highly favorable performance for zero-shot recipe retrieval, in comparison to hand-crafted features and single-task model. The performance of ingredient recognition is also successfully enhanced with the contextual relationship modeling of ingredients and CRF. The experiment also indicates that using our proposed architecture and CRF for ingredient prediction can produce better performance than directly inferring ingredients from recipes searched by VGG. When further using the predicted ingredients for matching recipes of unknown food categories, our model also demonstrates impressive performance, including when fusing with the deep features.

While encouraging, the current work is worth further investigation in two directions. First, cooking method (e.g., frying, steaming, grilling) is not explicitly considered in the developed deep architecture. In the experiment, we notice that some dishes have the same ingredients but appear visually different mainly due to different cooking methods. Our current approach basically cannot distinguish recipes for this kind of dishes. Similarly for ways of cutting ingredients (e.g., chop, slice, mince) which may demand hierarchical way of ingredient recognition in deep network. In addition, our multi-task model could not deal with ingredients (e.g., honey, soybean oil) that are not observable or visible from dishes. Secondly, while this paper considers the zero-shot problem of unknown food categories, how to couple this problem together with unseen ingredients remains unclear. Future work may include learning of embedded space that can capture the inherent "translation" between dish pictures and textual recipes, for dealing with the problem of unknown food and ingredient labels.

8. ACKNOWLEDGMENTS

This work was supported in part by the National Natural Science Foundation of China (No. 61272290), and the National Hi-Tech Research and Development Program (863 Program) of China under Grant 2014AA015102.

9. REFERENCES

[1] K. Aizawa and M. Ogawa. Foodlog: Multimedia tool for healthcare applications. *IEEE MultiMedia*, 22(2):4–8, 2015.

[2] O. Beijbom, N. Joshi, D. Morris, S. Saponas, and S. Khullar. Menu-match: Restaurant-specific food logging from images. In *Applications of Computer Vision (WACV), 2015 IEEE Winter Conference on*, pages 844–851. IEEE, 2015.

[3] V. Bettadapura, E. Thomaz, A. Parnami, G. D. Abowd, and I. Essa. Leveraging context to support automated food recognition in restaurants. In *Applications of Computer Vision (WACV), 2015 IEEE Winter Conference on*, pages 580–587. IEEE, 2015.

[4] L. Bossard, M. Guillaumin, and L. Van Gool. Food-101–mining discriminative components with random forests. In *Computer Vision–ECCV 2014*, pages 446–461. Springer, 2014.

[5] L.-C. Chen, G. Papandreou, I. Kokkinos, K. Murphy, and A. L. Yuille. Semantic image segmentation with deep convolutional nets and fully connected crfs. *arXiv preprint arXiv:1412.7062*, 2014.

[6] M. Chen, K. Dhingra, W. Wu, L. Yang, R. Sukthankar, and J. Yang. Pfid: Pittsburgh fast-food image dataset. In *Image Processing (ICIP), 2009 16th IEEE International Conference on*, pages 289–292. IEEE, 2009.

[7] M.-Y. Chen, Y.-H. Yang, C.-J. Ho, S.-H. Wang, S.-M. Liu, E. Chang, C.-H. Yeh, and M. Ouhyoung. Automatic chinese food identification and quantity estimation. In *SIGGRAPH Asia 2012 Technical Briefs*, page 29. ACM, 2012.

[8] N. Dalal and B. Triggs. Histograms of oriented gradients for human detection. *Computer Vision and Pattern Recognition*, pages 886–893, 2005.

[9] J. Deng, W. Dong, R. Socher, L.-J. Li, K. Li, and L. Fei-Fei. Imagenet: A large-scale hierarchical image database. In *Computer Vision and Pattern Recognition, 2009. CVPR 2009. IEEE Conference on*, pages 248–255. IEEE, 2009.

[10] M. Elhoseiny, T. El-Gaaly, A. Bakry, and A. Elgammal. Convolutional models for joint object categorization and pose estimation. *arXiv preprint arXiv:1511.05175*, 2015.

[11] A. H. Goris, M. S. Westerterp-Plantenga, and K. R. Westerterp. Undereating and underrecording of habitual food intake in obese men: selective underreporting of fat intake. *The American journal of clinical nutrition*, 71(1):130–134, 2000.

[12] H. He, F. Kong, and J. Tan. Dietcam: Multi-view food recognition using a multi-kernel svm. *Journal of Biomedical and Health Informatics*, 2015.

[13] H. Hoashi, T. Joutou, and K. Yanai. Image recognition of 85 food categories by feature fusion. In *Multimedia (ISM), 2010 IEEE International Symposium on*, pages 296–301. IEEE, 2010.

[14] Y. Kawano and K. Yanai. Real-time mobile food recognition system. In *Computer Vision and Pattern Recognition Workshop*, 2013.

[15] Y. Kawano and K. Yanai. Food image recognition with deep convolutional features. *Proc. of ACM UbiComp Workshop on Cooking and Eating Activities (CEA)*, 2014.

[16] K. Kitamura, T. Yamasaki, and K. Aizawa. Food log by analyzing food images. In *Proceedings of the 16th ACM international conference on Multimedia*, pages 999–1000. ACM, 2008.

[17] A. Krizhevsky, I. Sutskever, and G. E. Hinton. Imagenet classification with deep convolutional neural networks. *Advances in neural information processing systems*, pages 1097–1105, 2012.

[18] D. Lin, X. Shen, C. Lu, and J. Jia. Deep lac: Deep localization, alignment and classification for fine-grained recognition. In *Proceedings of the IEEE Conference on Computer Vision and Pattern Recognition*, pages 1666–1674, 2015.

[19] T.-Y. Lin, A. RoyChowdhury, and S. Maji. Bilinear cnn models for fine-grained visual recognition. In *Proceedings of the IEEE International Conference on Computer Vision*, pages 1449–1457, 2015.

[20] Z. Liu, P. Luo, X. Wang, and X. Tang. Deep learning face attributes in the wild. In *Proceedings of the IEEE International Conference on Computer Vision*, pages 3730–3738, 2015.

[21] D. G. Lowe. Object recognition from local scale-invariant features. *The proceedings of the seventh IEEE international conference on Computer Vision,*, pages 1150–1157, 1999.

[22] Y. Matsuda and K. Yanai. Multiple-food recognition considering co-occurrence employing manifold ranking. In *Pattern Recognition (ICPR), 2012 21st International Conference on*, pages 2017–2020. IEEE, 2012.

[23] H. Matsunaga, K. Doman, T. Hirayama, I. Ide, D. Deguchi, and H. Murase. Tastes and textures estimation of foods based on the analysis of its ingredients list and image. In *New Trends in Image Analysis and Processing–ICIAP 2015 Workshops*, pages 326–333. Springer, 2015.

[24] A. Meyers, N. Johnston, V. Rathod, A. Korattikara, A. Gorban, N. Silberman, S. Guadarrama, G. Papandreou, J. Huang, and K. P. Murphy. Im2calories: towards an automated mobile vision food diary. In *Proceedings of the IEEE International Conference on Computer Vision*, pages 1233–1241, 2015.

[25] M. Puri, Z. Zhu, Q. Yu, A. Divakaran, and H. Sawhney. Recognition and volume estimation of food intake using a mobile device, 2009.

[26] C. Robert and G. Casella. *Monte Carlo statistical methods*. Springer Science & Business Media, 2013.

[27] C. Siagian and L. Itti. Rapid biologically-inspired scene classification using features shared with visual attention. *Pattern Analysis and Machine Intelligence, IEEE Transactions on*, 29(2):300–312, 2007.

[28] K. Simonyan and A. Zisserman. Very deep convolutional networks for large-scale image recognition. *arXiv preprint arXiv:1409.1556*, 2014.

[29] R. Socher, M. Ganjoo, C. D. Manning, and A. Ng. Zero-shot learning through cross-modal transfer. In *Advances in neural information processing systems*, pages 935–943, 2013.

[30] M. A. Stricker and M. Orengo. Similarity of color images. In *IS&T/SPIE's Symposium on Electronic Imaging: Science & Technology*, pages 381–392. International Society for Optics and Photonics, 1995.

[31] Y. Sun, Y. Chen, X. Wang, and X. Tang. Deep learning face representation by joint identification-verification. In *Advances in Neural Information Processing Systems*, pages 1988–1996, 2014.

[32] Y. Sun, X. Wang, and X. Tang. Deep learning face representation from predicting 10,000 classes. In *Proceedings of the IEEE Conference on Computer Vision and Pattern Recognition*, pages 1891–1898, 2014.

[33] M. J. Wainwright and M. I. Jordan. Graphical models, exponential families, and variational inference. *Foundations and Trends® in Machine Learning*, 1(1-2):1–305, 2008.

[34] X. Wang, D. Kumar, N. Thome, M. Cord, and F. Precioso. Recipe recognition with large multimodal food dataset. In *Multimedia & Expo Workshops (ICMEW), 2015 IEEE International Conference on*, pages 1–6. IEEE, 2015.

[35] W. Wu and J. Yang. Fast food recognition from videos of eating for calorie estimation. In *Multimedia and Expo, 2009. ICME 2009. IEEE International Conference on*, pages 1210–1213. IEEE, 2009.

[36] K. Yanai and Y. Kawano. Food image recognition using deep convolutional network with pre-training and fine-tuning. In *Multimedia & Expo Workshops (ICMEW), 2015 IEEE International Conference on*, pages 1–6. IEEE, 2015.

[37] S. Yang, M. Chen, D. Pomerleau, and R. Sukthankar. Food recognition using statistics of pairwise local features. *Computer Vision and Pattern Recognition (CVPR)*, pages 2249–2256, 2010.

GeoTracks: Adaptive Music for Everyday Journeys

Chris Greenhalgh, Adrian Hazzard, Sean McGrath, Steve Benford

The University of Nottingham
School of Computer Science, Wollaton Road,
Nottingham NG8 1BB, UK
+44 115 9514251

chris.greenhalgh, adrian.hazzard, sean.mcgrath, steve.benford@nottingham.ac.uk

ABSTRACT

Listening to music on the move is an everyday activity for many people. This paper proposes *geotracks* and *geolists*, music tracks and playlists of existing music that are aligned and adapted to specific journeys. We describe how everyday walking journeys such as commutes to work and existing popular music tracks can each be analysed, decomposed and then brought together, using musical adaptations including skipping and repeating parts of tracks, dynamically remixing tracks and cross-fades. Using a naturalistic experiment we compared walking while listening to geotracks (dynamically adapted using GPS location information) to walking while listening to a fixed playlist. Overall, participants enjoyed the walk more when listening to the adaptive geotracks. However adapting the lengths of tracks appeared to detract from the experience of the music in some situations and for some participants, revealing trade-offs in achieving fine-grained alignment of music and walking journeys.

Keywords

Music; soundtrack; mobile; pedestrian; walk; commute; adaptive; experience; geotrack; geolist.

1. INTRODUCTION

Many of our everyday music listening experiences are concerned with accompanying our commonplace travelling and housework chores [19]. Mobile music listening, particularly in mundane settings such as a commute to work, can "*serve to alter perception of surroundings, not simply by enhancing awareness of particular features*" [13]. For example an individual's curated playlist can 'aestheticize' the urban environment, turning a journey into a personal narrative [5]. Over the last 15 years locative media experiences have sought to re-connect us to environments through bespoke soundtracks that adapt to our trajectory through a space [2]. But these are not everyday experiences and typically they do not engage with music of our own choice.

Our aim is to make people's own music and playlists more responsive and in-touch with their everyday journeys, so as to form a stronger connection between music and place that enhances the experience of both. Thus, we are not concerned with the creation of original music, but rather the adaptation of existing commercial music, situated within everyday listening such as urban pedestrian commuter journeys.

MM '16, October 15-19, 2016, Amsterdam, Netherlands
© 2016 ACM. ISBN 978-1-4503-3603-1/16/10...$15.00
DOI: http://dx.doi.org/10.1145/2964284.2967181

In this paper we present the "geotrack" concept, and a prototype geotrack music player application in which the structure of a song is rearranged, or re-worked, to match both the context and user activity, in this instance driven by GPS location sensing (section 3). We have developed a process and a set of methods for track adaptation, as undertaken by our composer (section 4). Finally, we have evaluated the created geotracks through a naturalistic study, comparing two similar journeys, one with a regular playlist of music and one with adaptive geotracks (section 5).

2. RELATED WORK

We begin by reviewing related works in locative media and clarify their relationships to the geotracks proposal. We then consider other precedents for re-arranging music, which is an essential component of geotracks, and emerging formats for interactive audio that might support geotracks in the future.

2.1 Mobile, Context-Aware and Locative Music Listening

There is a rich history of exploration in the field of context-aware mobile music applications and services. A number of context-aware mobile 'apps' have explored dynamic accompaniment to sports and exercise routines, such as *TripleBeat* [10] and *Spotify Running* [20], which utilize playlists tagged with tempo metadata to match or lead a user's chosen level of exertion or cadence.

Lifetrack [17] describes a 'context-sensitive music engine' for mobile devices that drew on the contextual data of *space*, *time*, *kinesis*, *entropy*, and *weather* to control song *selection*. The system required users to tag their music collection with a set of corresponding system-defined labels such as music for daytime/night-time or for specific locations (defined by zip-codes). In our work we bring complementary foci to changes *within* individual tracks and to musical choices in adaptation.

Locative sound and music experiences [4, 11, 12] use location as a novel stage for music-based experiences where the user's role is also partly one of composer, as their spatial interactions shape the arrangement of the resultant soundtrack. Behrendt [2] proposes a number of categories for these experiences, for instance *sonified mobility* [11] that can be experienced anywhere, and *placed sound* experiences [4, 12], which are site specific and typically use GPS for positioning. Hazzard et al. [12] present the design and evaluation of a placed sound musical soundtrack to be listened to while visiting a sculpture park. Like the work presented here, the music is tied specifically to the location and changes dynamically as listeners move based on GPS. However, in that case original music was composed specifically for the experience, and adaptations were limited to fading particular tracks and stems in and out. Their approach also aims to support free exploration within a large physical area, while our focus is on defined routes and journeys.

2.2 Re-arranging Music

Music practice is littered with examples of 'fixed' musical arrangements being re-arranged or adapted. For instance, conductors of classical music regularly ignore the instructions in Mozart's scores and omit repeats of sections of his symphonies [14]. An electronic dance music DJ's whole job of work is to turn separate fixed linear recordings into a blended sequence [6]. Rubin et al. [18] propose a tool and process to enable the re-sequencing of segmented music tracks to generate scores to accompany audio stories. Wenner et al. [23] note the challenge of the real-time rescaling of audio that accompanies dynamic visual images, such as might be found in the video editing process or computer games. Their work explored an approach based on the feature extraction of a music track's structural segments with an accompanying algorithm to find the "least costly path" through a reshuffling of segments. These examples set a precedent for some of the adaptations of existing music that we consider here.

2.3 Interactive Audio

Interactive audio is found in a number of settings and many approaches to interactivity are used. Typically, large-scale musical arrangements are formed from smaller inter-changeable fragments that can be presented in different combinations and sequences. A common example can be found in computer games, where non-linear interactive soundtracks typically respond to the duration of gameplay by extending or reducing the number of segments of music (i.e. cells) and the phases of gameplay (e.g. periods of action or respite) by the vertical remixing of instrument layers (i.e. stems) [16]. The Infinite Jukebox web app uses beat recognition and feature matching to jump between beats in the song that are deemed similar. *Stems* [21] is an 'open multi-track' MP4 container format, that plays as a single 'mix' on standard software audio players, but when played on associated hardware systems the format contains separate elements that can be individually controlled. *Weav* [22] provides a player that allows for the adaptation of tempo that dynamically blends between different treatments or variants within the track to suit its changing 'energy'. The broadcast industry is currently engaged in creating 'object-based audio' broadcasts. *Responsive Radio* by the British Broadcasting Corporation (BBC) presents multiple readings of an online radio documentary in response to a listener's desired listening duration [1]. Our work does not propose such a format, but might be realized as a particular application of a sufficiently flexible format - a dynamic digital music object that could facilitate the assembly and rendering of novel locative experiences.

3. GEOTRACKS AND GEOLISTS

We propose two related concepts: *geotracks* and *geolists*. A *geotrack* is essentially a normal song or track which can be assigned to part of a journey or route; a *geoplaylist* (or simply *geolist*) is a set of geotracks to be used together for a *particular* journey. Aspects of the geotrack's playback and transitions between geotracks can then be influenced by the listener's progress, activity and context. For example, a dynamically selected subset of a track may be played so that the music reaches a suitable ending point when the listener reaches the end of a particular part of the journey.

At the level of a complete geolist of geotracks, the basic concept associates the music with a particular journey or part of a journey. Figure 1 illustrates the relationship between geotracks and geolists as part of a journey. Geotracks are chosen because they are in some sense appropriate to where they will be heard. For example, a musically dense track might fit a walk by a busy road, while a quieter and more reflective track might fit a walk across a park. Tracks might also be chosen and placed to reflect elements of their lyrics or mood, for example Money, by Pink Floyd, in the financial district. Tracks might also be chosen to reflect personal associations or memories.

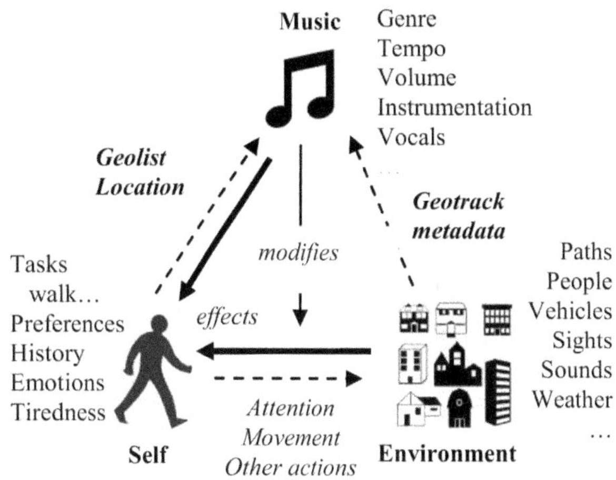

Figure 1. Geotrack experience framework

3.1 Prototype Player

We now briefly describe daoplayer[1], the prototype geotrack player application that we have developed. This is implemented as a native Android application as there are features which are not achievable with the Web Audio API. The current prototype loads and plays a single combined geolist file. This specifies all of the media (tracks and stems) for each geotrack, plus their associated metadata (e.g. specific locations to be associated with particular geotracks or adaptations) and dynamic behaviours, specified using JavaScript code fragments.

The geotrack player updates and adapts its playback once per second, as each new GPS location report is received. It uses the new GPS location to update its estimate of position and velocity. The *geolist* includes a specification of the intended route to be taken, which allows the player to estimate the user's position on the route, speed and time of arrival at waypoints. The scripts of the current geotrack can then be re-evaluated resulting in a new state for the audio engine, which specifies changes to the volume and exact playback point(s) of each audio track or stem over the next second or so. Scripts can also trigger a transition to a new part of the current geotrack or to a new geotrack.

4. EXAMPLE GEOLIST & GEOTRACKS

Having introduced the concept and technology of geotracks we now present an example of putting this approach to work in creating a walk, which also formed the basis of the user study we present in the next section.

The walk begins and ends at a building on an urban university campus. The outward journey of about 2.5km leaves the campus,

[1] https://github.com/cgreenhalgh/daoplayer

passes along and crosses a major road, continues along a quiet suburban street and enters the grounds of a stately home. Within the grounds the walk is along tree-lined pedestrian paths, and ends by climbing a small hill to the house itself. The return walk, also about 2.5km, descends the hill, follows a different set of tree-lined paths out of the grounds, re-crosses the major road, continues along a quiet suburban street to an alternative entrance into university campus, leading back to the starting point.

To accompany the walk we chose 6 tracks from *Medley DB* [3] and *The Open Multi-track Testbed* [9], which are open repositories of stereo mixes and multi-track stems held under Creative Commons licences. The tracks were chosen to deliberately offer a range of vocal 'pop / rock' styles at differing tempi and levels of intensity that were considered broadly accessible for most listeners.

4.1 Mapping the Music to the Walk

We view our selected playlist of tracks (geolist) as similar to film and computer game soundtracks, whose role is to support the narrative by setting context, regulating the mood and drawing attention to key visual events [8] via temporally congruent music [7]. In developing our methods of mapping track adaptations to the physical landscape we drew motivation from Hazzard et al.'s [12] work on soundtrack composition for a sculpture park. After study and reflection on the route to be walked along with previous pilot walks we identified 5 key considerations: (1) changes of course, such as a transition from one street to another represent the significant structural events in the walk; (2) the walker needs to negotiate junctions and other obstacles that may require attending to; (3) the walk contained a number of distinct environments (i.e. urban, residential, and parkland); (4) there are points of interest along the way that draw attention; (5) and finally that beginnings and endings, whilst on the surface appearing trivial, require careful planning.

We placed tracks along the route in relation to types of environment. We felt that upbeat music would be best suited for those urban busy areas, moderate intensity music for residential areas, and music of a lower intensity for the parkland. These choices aimed to match the character and the density of the built environment with the level of activity and density of orchestration within the music tracks. In response to our observations of the routes, we chose to introduce a new track at every significant *change of course* along the route. This dictated the number of tracks we used for the walk, as there were 6 of these key points along both the outward and return routes. For the *beginning* and *ending* of the walk we used two similar original pieces of instrumental music, a largely static musical texture with no melodic or rhythm content.

The brief gap typically found between songs on a playlist were removed wherever possible in favour of using cross-fades, so as to create a continuous, seamless soundtrack. This reflected our concept of geotracks being more like a soundtrack accompaniment for walks.

One of the main forms of adaptation employed was to dynamically extend or shorten the track depending on how soon the listener was likely to reach the end of the route assigned for that track. Sections (i.e. intro, verse, chorus) and subsections were semi-automatically determined. This deconstructed segmentation (cell) data could then be used by the dynamic scripts of the geotrack player. For instance cells could be looped, removed or sequentially re-arranged. Options to extend or shorten each track were specified in advance to the player, which can then select between them depending on the user's progress. For example, if a track required extending then it was deemed preferable to repeat an instrumental section, such as an 'intro' or failing that a chorus rather than a vocal verse. If a track required shortening then instrumental sections, verses and chorus, if multiple, were removed. Our approach shares some similarities to audio accompaniment for video [23] which explores methods of dynamically adjusting track length and re-ordering segments.

While most of the geotracks used a stereo mix, in two instances we used multi-track stems to enable dynamic remixing of the tracks. Typically the stems were sub-mixes (e.g. vocals, drums and guitars) produced from the larger number of individual tracks. The first of these multi-tracks treated the major road crossing, where all of the stems were reduced in volume but to differing amounts. This reduced intensity to allow the listener to focus on *negotiating the environment*, specifically traffic crossings. An adaptive mix of the second multi-tracks was used on transition from a residential area to a path in the park. Initially, only the vocal and piano stems can be heard while the path is tightly constrained. At the point where the fence-lined path opens up to reveal a view across the parkland, the remaining stems fade in (an example of adaptation to suit a scenic *point of interest*).

5. STUDY

We evaluated the geotracks prototype described above using a naturalistic experiment. Each participant undertook the same circular walk described above. While walking they listened on headphones to music from a smart phone, generated by the geotrack player. During one half of each participant's journey they heard geotracks, i.e., the music adapted dynamically. On the other half of the journey they heard a fixed playlist comprising the same songs. There were two conditions: adaptive music on the outward journey (fixed playlist on the return); and fixed playlist on the outward journey (adaptive music on the return). Participants were not informed about the two conditions or the adaptive functionality of geotracks. Rather, they were simply asked to walk the defined route whilst listening to some accompanying music. Participants were asked to complete a short questionnaire twice, first at the halfway point on arrival at the stately home, second on their return to campus at the end of the walk. The participants then had a semi-structured interview lasting around 15 minutes. Participants were recruited from the local area via e-mail, poster advertisements and snowballing. A total of 28 participants completed the walk, consisting of 12 males and 16 females. Participants were randomly allocated to conditions, balancing gender between conditions.

5.1 Results

Participants' subjective ratings in the questionnaires[2] at the end of each leg of the walk used a 7-point Likert scale (with associated ordinal values) ranging from *entirely agree* (1) through *neither agree nor disagree* (4) to *entirely disagree* (7). Results were analysed using the nparLD [15] package for nonparametric analysis (parametric tests being unsuitable for individual Likert items). Significance results are nparLD's non-parametric ANOVA-Type Statistics.

Considering statement 1, "I enjoyed the walk", all participants enjoyed both walks to some extent (median: 2, mostly agree).

[2] Anonymised data available: http://dx.doi.org/10.17639/nott.50

Overall participants enjoyed the adaptive leg of the walk more than the non-adaptive leg (p=0.044, statistic=4.04, df=1), which was largely due to differences in the return walk, with relative treatment effects of 0.39 (return, adaptive) and 0.67 (return, fixed) (for reference, an effect size of 0.2 is often considered to be "small" but significant). Participants also preferred the return-adaptive condition (p=0.024, statistic=5.06, df=1), with relative treatment effects of 0.58 (out adaptive) and 0.42 (return adaptive).

Considering statement 2, "I enjoyed the music", 26 out of 28 participants enjoyed the music to some extent (median, mostly agree (2)). Participants enjoyed the music more on the outward journey than on the return journey (p=0.046, statistic=4.00, df=1), relative treatment effects 0.45 (out) and 0.55 (return). Participants also enjoyed the music marginally more in the return-adaptive condition (p=0.073, statistic=3.21, df=1).

Considering statement 3, "The music enhanced the walk", most participants reported that the music enhanced the walk (median, mostly agree (2)). The music was reported to enhance the walk significantly more on the outward journey than on the return journey (p=0.0043, statistic=8.14, df=1), relative treatment effects 0.42 (out) and 0.58 (return). The different between conditions was not significant.

Considering statement 5, "Changes in the music complemented changes in the walk", the median response was somewhat agree (3). Overall, changes in the adaptive music complemented changes in the walk more than changes in the non-adaptive music (p=0.000036, Statistic=17.04, df=1).

5.2 Discussion

Based on feedback, all participants enjoyed the walk. Most enjoyed the music and most felt that it enhanced the walk irrespective of whether the music was adaptive or not.

Participants *enjoyed the walk* more on the leg with the adaptive music than with the non-adaptive music. Participants also report that *changes* in the music complement changes in the walk more with the adaptive music than with the non-adaptive music. This seems to match comments made by many participants about whether the music 'fitted', or was 'appropriate' for particular stages of the walk: *"If the music fitted the surroundings it really complemented the experience but had the opposite effect if not"*. The 'fit' of the music to the walking activity was also influenced by its tempo for some.

Participants *enjoyed the music* more on the outward leg than on the return leg (ignoring adaptation), and also report that the music *enhances* the walk more on the outward leg than on the return leg. In part this appears to be due to the novelty of the music on the outward leg; on the return leg the same songs were repeated (albeit in a different order) and this was largely noted with disappointment. At least for some people, the return leg also *"felt as though I was returning to normal life"*. A lack of 'fit' may account in part for people enjoying the music least on the non-adaptive return journey. Two participants highlighted the incongruence between the fixed playlist, which starts with two high intensity tracks, and that part of walk from the stately home along a tree-lined avenue. However some participants appreciated the higher-energy tracks within the park environment.

Considering only the return leg of the journey, participants *enjoyed the walk* more and *enjoyed the music* marginally more with the adaptive music than with the non-adaptive music. Considering only the outward leg, participants enjoyed the walk the same with or without adaptive music, enjoyed the adaptive music marginally less and felt that it did not complement the walk as much as the fixed playlist. While some participants commented positively about certain transitions, a small number of participants reported that some transitions were 'clunky' or otherwise disruptive, and two participants were disappointed when specific tracks were 'cut off' before the end as a result of passing a transition point. One participant reported hearing "glitches" in a track, which probably correspond to jumps between sections of a track, and two noted hearing repetitions within a track on the adaptive leg. These issues may help to explain why on the outward leg of the walk, participants felt that the adaptive music enhanced the walk less than the non-adaptive music, and why some enjoyed the non-adaptive music more.

As described, two tracks were remixed on the fly from multi-track versions. The first reduced the volume and cut out some stems on approach to the pedestrian crossing. Two participants specifically noticed and appreciated this adaptation while three participants commented negatively about negotiating the pedestrian crossing with the non-adaptive music, where the chosen track presented a loud and dense texture at this point.

6. CONCLUSIONS AND FUTURE WORK

We have found that the basic geotrack concept is sound, i.e. that geo-locating the playlist can enhance the walking journey. This seems to be primarily as a result of increasing the 'fit' or appropriateness of the music to particular stages of the journey. There is also evidence that the multi-track adaptations can yield practical and experiential value for at least some participants, e.g. easing the use of crossings or enhancing elements in the environment at particular points. However there are still challenges to the execution of sensitive and musical adaptations of existing musical arrangements that require further work. It would also be beneficial to test the generalisability of these results to other journeys and choices of music. For example, many participants had a strong preference for particular genres, artists or songs of their own selection. This in turn raises the question of how people would feel about the adaptation of songs they are familiar with: whether breaking their expectations of a track's arrangement would disrupt any benefit gained from 'fitting' with a journey segment.

More broadly, we would like to extend this work to include other triggers for adaptation in addition to location. For example, participants' reported that their experiences were affected by: the weather (sunshine, temperature, wind); the season; the time of day and day of week; ambient noise (traffic and people); road-works; other people and animals nearby. Considering a broader range of contextual factors would also combine naturally with automating the *choice* of tracks (e.g. as in [17]), in addition to adaptation within tracks and transitions. In turn, this would require more automated support for creating geotracks and geolists, whether as part of a human-led authoring process or perhaps even an entirely automatic process.

7. ACKNOWLEDGMENTS

This work was supported by the Engineering and Physical Sciences Research Council [grant numbers EP/L019981/1, EP/M000877/1]. Tracks used were *Stella* and *Boys* by Clara Berry and Wooldog; *Mitad Del Mundo* by Helado Negro; *Not Alone* by Freddy V; *Sister Cities* by Hop Along; and *Waiting for GA* by Faces on Film.

8. REFERENCES

[1] Armstrong, M., Brooks, M., Churnside, A., Evans, M., Melchior, F. and Shotton, M. 2014. Object-based broadcasting-curation, responsiveness and user experience. (2014). Retrieved September 7, 2015 from http://digital-library.theiet.org/content/conferences/10.1049/ib.2014.0038

[2] Behrendt, F. 2012. The sound of locative media. *Convergence: The International Journal of Research into New Media Technologies*. 18, 3 (Aug. 2012), 283–295. DOI=10.1177/1354856512441150 http://doi.org/10.1177/1354856512441150

[3] Bittner, R., Salamon, J., Tierney, M., Mauch, M., Cannam, C. and Bello, J. 2014. MedleyDB: a multitrack dataset for annotation-intensive MIR research. *15th International Society for Music Information Retrieval Conference (ISMIR 2014)* (2014), 155–160.

[4] Bluebrain: *http://bluebrainmusic.blogspot.co.uk*. Accessed: 2014-07-22.

[5] Bull, M. 2006. Investigating the culture of mobile listening: From Walkman to iPod. *Consuming music together*. Springer. 131–149. DOI=10.1007/1-4020-4097-0_7

[6] Cliff, D. 2000. Hang the DJ: Automatic sequencing and seamless mixing of dance-music tracks. *HP LABORATORIES TECHNICAL REPORT HPL*. 104 (2000). Retrieved August 29, 2015 from http://www.hpl.hp.com/techreports/2000/HPL-2000-104.pdf

[7] Cohen, A.J. 1993. Associationism and musical soundtrack phenomena. *Contemporary music review*. 9, 1-2 (1993), 163–178. DOI=10.1080/07494469300640421 http://dx.doi.org/10.1080/07494469300640421

[8] Collins, K. 2013. *Playing with sound: a theory of interacting with sound and music in video games*. MIT Press.

[9] De Man, B., Mora-Mcginity, M., Fazekas, G. and Reiss, J.D. 2014. The Open Multitrack Testbed. *Audio Engineering Society Convention 137* (2014).

[10] De Oliveira, R. and Oliver, N. 2008. TripleBeat: enhancing exercise performance with persuasion. *Proceedings of the 10th international conference on Human computer interaction with mobile devices and services* (2008), 255–264.

[11] Gaye, L., Mazé, R. and Holmquist, L.E. 2003. Sonic city: the urban environment as a musical interface. *Proceedings of the 2003 conference on New interfaces for musical expression* (2003), 109–115.

[12] Hazzard, A., Benford, S. and Burnett, G. 2015. Sculpting a Mobile Musical Soundtrack. *Proceedings of the 33rd annual ACM conference on Human factors in computing systems* (2015). DOI=10.1145/2702123.2702236 http://doi.acm.org/10.1145/2702123.2702236

[13] Herbert, R. 2013. An empirical study of normative dissociation in musical and non-musical everyday life experiences. *Psychology of Music*. 41, 3 (May 2013), 372–394. DOI=10.1177/0305735611430080 http://doi.org/10.1177/0305735611430080

[14] Macdonald, H. 1984. To Repeat or Not to Repeat? *Proceedings of the Royal Musical Association*. 111, 1 (Jan. 1984), 121–138. DOI=10.1093/jrma/111.1.121 http://doi.org/10.1093/jrma/111.1.121

[15] Kimihiro Noguchi, Yulia R. Gel, Edgar Brunner, Frank Konietschke. nparLD: An R Software Package for the Nonparametric Analysis of Longitudinal Data in Factorial Experiments. *Journal of Statistical Software*, 50(12), 1-23. 2012

[16] Phillips, W. 2014. *A Composer's Guide to Game Music*. MIT Press.

[17] Reddy, S. and Mascia, J. 2006. Lifetrak: music in tune with your life. *Proceedings of the 1st ACM international* DOI=10.1145/1178745.1178754 http://dx.doi.org/10.1145/1178745.1178754 *workshop on Human-centered multimedia* (2006), 25–34.

[18] Rubin, S. and Agrawala, M. 2014. Generating emotionally relevant musical scores for audio stories. (2014), 439–448.

[19] Sloboda, J.A., O'Neill, S.A. and Ivaldi, A. 2001. Functions of music in everyday life: An exploratory study using the experience sampling method. *Musicae scientiae*. 5, 1 (2001), 9–32.

[20] Spotify Running: 2015. *https://www.spotify.com/uk/running/*. Accessed: 2015-09-07.

[21] Stems: 2015. *http://www.stems-music.com/index.html*. Accessed: 2015-09-08.

[22] Weav: 2015. *http://weav.io/*. Accessed: 2015-09-08.

[23] Wenner, S., Bazin, J.-C., Sorkine-Hornung, A., Kim, C. and Gross, M. 2013. Scalable music: Automatic music retargeting and synthesis. *Computer Graphics Forum* (2013), 345–354. doi:10.1111/cgf.12054.

Abnormal Event Discovery in User Generated Photos

Xiaoshan Yang[1,2], Tianzhu Zhang[1,2], Changsheng Xu[1,2]
[1]National Lab of Pattern Recognition, Institute of Automation, Chinese Academy of Sciences, Beijing, China
[2]University of Chinese Academy of Sciences, Beijing, China
{xiaoshan.yang, tzzhang, csxu}@nlpr.ia.ac.cn

ABSTRACT

Vision based event analysis plays a very critical role in automatically organizing user generated photos. As one of the important tasks in event analysis, abnormal event discovery still does not obtain much attentions. It is difficult because only few samples can be used for event pattern learning. In this paper, by considering the photo taken time, we propose a novel one-class structured event modeling (OSEM) where we explore the temporal event patterns in negative photos of the event using the continuous conditional random field (CRF). With the estimated piecewise training of CRF, the proposed OSEM can be efficiently solved using stochastic gradients descent (SGD) in an end-to-end form. The results on a collected abnormal event dataset demonstrate the effectiveness of the proposed OSEM.

Keywords

Social Media; Event Analysis; Abnormal Event Discovery

1. INTRODUCTION

With the impressive progress of mobile Internet, more and more smart phones with digital cameras have been connected directly or indirectly to the Internet, which successfully facilitates the photo sharing and propagation. As a result, a huge number of photos have been uploaded by users on the Internet. Automatic event analysis from massive user generated photos is important and helpful to better browse, search and monitor events by users or governments. Many methods have been proposed [22, 17, 21, 16, 8, 28, 29, 25, 24, 3, 19, 6, 20, 13, 27, 18] for event analysis. As one of the important tasks in event analysis, abnormal event discovery still does not obtain much attentions. It is challenging because the abnormal events rarely occur in the daily life and have few related photos on the Internet. As a result, no enough samples can be used for event pattern learning. For example, as shown in Figure 1, when the accident event Paris attack happens, only few photos can be used to train the event model.

MM '16, October 15-19, 2016, Amsterdam, Netherlands

DOI: http://dx.doi.org/10.1145/2964284.2975215

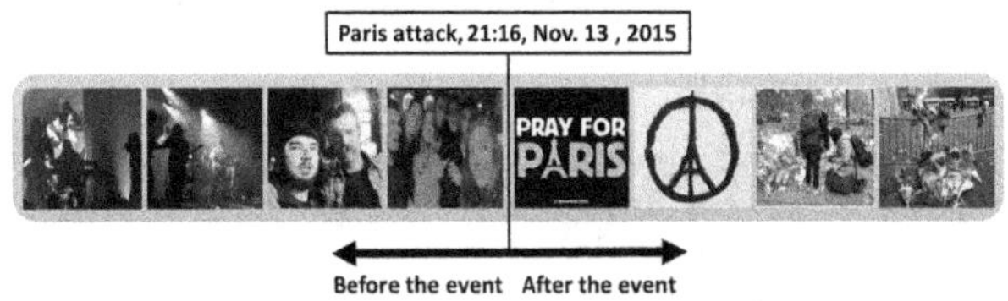

Figure 1: Abnormal event related photos over time at the location of Paris attack.

To deal with the above issue, we resort to the photo taken time, which can be easily obtained on the social sites (e.g., Flicker and Instagram), to cast the photos into a sequence for effective event analysis. To overcome the sample scarcity problem for abnormal events, we shift our attention to the negative samples (normal photos unrelated to the abnormal events) which consist of photos taken before the abnormal events. By learning the features of the negative samples, we can find the abnormal event related photos which have large discrepancies with the negative photos. This point can be more clearly illustrated in Figure 1. For the photos taken at the location of Paris attack, there is an apparent change of visual appearance when the event happens.

Motivated by the above observations, we propose a novel one-class structured event modeling (**OSEM**) method for abnormal event discovery by exploiting temporal information in the photo sequence. The visual features are learned via the convolutional neural networks (CNNs), and their temporal relationship is exploited via the recurrent neural networks (RNNs). The structured auto-encoders based on the continuous CRF are used on top of neural networks to learn the temporal patterns of the negative photo samples. Compared with existing methods, the major contributions of this work are three-fold:

1. By casting photos into a sequence and exploiting its temporal information, we propose a novel one-class structured event modeling (**OSEM**) for abnormal event discovery.

2. The proposed **OSEM** adopts the structured auto-encoders based on the continuous CRF on top of neural networks (RNNs and CNNs) for learning the temporal patterns of the negative photo samples and can effectively deal with the sample scarcity problem.

3. Extensive experimental results on an abnormal event dataset collected from Instagram demonstrate the effectiveness of the proposed **OSEM**.

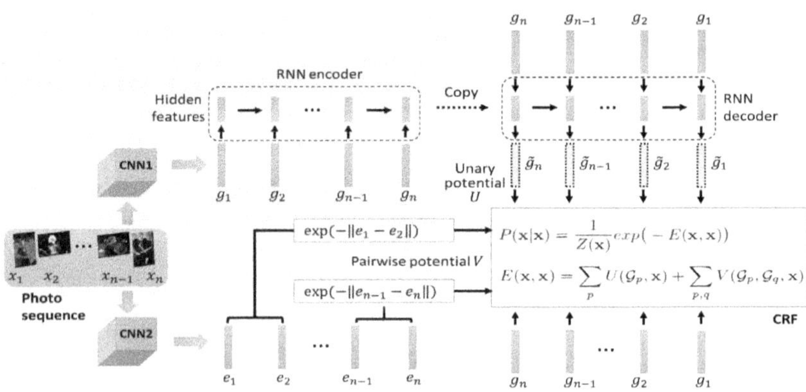

Figure 2: The proposed one-class structured event modeling (OSEM).

2. THE PROPOSED METHOD

In this section, we firstly introduce how to extract temporal features in a photo sequence. Then, we introduce the proposed OSEM in details.

2.1 Sequential features

As shown in Figure 2, we obtain the visual feature of individual photo using the shared CNNs. To capture the common objects or event patterns in the photo sequence, we adopt the RNNs with gated recurrent units (GRU) which have been shown to perform as well as LSTM [7] on sequence modelling tasks [5] while being conceptually simpler. If we use $\boldsymbol{x}$ to denote an image, the feature outputted by the CNNs with parameters $\boldsymbol{\Theta}_{cnn1}$ can be denoted as $\boldsymbol{g} = \mathbb{F}(\boldsymbol{x}; \boldsymbol{\Theta}_{cnn1}) \in \mathbb{R}^d$. $\boldsymbol{g}$ is further imported into RNNs to extract temporal event features. The details of the GRU based RNNs are illustrated as follows. The reset gate $\boldsymbol{r}$ is computed by

$$\boldsymbol{r} = \delta(\mathbf{W}_{xr}\boldsymbol{g} + \mathbf{W}_{hr}\boldsymbol{h}_{<t-1>}), \tag{1}$$

where δ is the element-wise logistic sigmoid function. $\boldsymbol{h}_{<t-1>}$ is the previous hidden state. Similarly, the update gate $\boldsymbol{z}$ is computed by

$$\boldsymbol{z} = \delta(\mathbf{W}_{xz}\boldsymbol{g} + \mathbf{W}_{hz}\boldsymbol{h}_{<t-1>}). \tag{2}$$

The actual activation $\boldsymbol{h}_{<t>}$, which is used as the extracted sequential feature for the photo $\boldsymbol{x}$, is then computed by

$$\boldsymbol{h}_{<t>} = \boldsymbol{z} \odot \boldsymbol{h}_{<t-1>} + (1-\boldsymbol{z}) \odot \phi\big(\mathbf{W}_{xh}\boldsymbol{g} + \mathbf{W}_{hh}(\boldsymbol{r} \odot \boldsymbol{h}_{<t-1>})\big), \tag{3}$$

where $\odot$ denotes element-wise multiplication and ϕ is an element-wise nonlinearity.

In this work, for all photos in the sequence $\mathbf{x} = \{\boldsymbol{x}_1, ..., \boldsymbol{x}_n\}$, the features generated by the CNNs with parameters $\boldsymbol{\Theta}_{cnn1}$ are denoted as $\mathbf{g} = \{\boldsymbol{g}_1, ..., \boldsymbol{g}_n\}$. We use $\mathbf{h} = \mathbb{F}(\mathbf{g}; \boldsymbol{\Theta}_{rnn})$ to denote the hidden feature sequence computed for the photo sequence $\mathbf{x}$ using the CNNs and the GRU based RNNs. Here, the hidden features in sequence $\mathbf{h} = \{\boldsymbol{h}_1, ..., \boldsymbol{h}_n\}$ correspond to photos in the sequence $\mathbf{x} = \{\boldsymbol{x}_1, ..., \boldsymbol{x}_n\}$. $\boldsymbol{\Theta}_{rnn}$ consists of weight matrices $\mathbf{W}_{xr}$, $\mathbf{W}_{hr}$, $\mathbf{W}_{xz}$, $\mathbf{W}_{hz}$, $\mathbf{W}_{xh}$ and $\mathbf{W}_{hh}$. The parameters $\boldsymbol{\Theta}_{cnn1}$ and $\boldsymbol{\Theta}_{rnn}$ will be learned in Section 2.2.

2.2 One-class structured event modeling

For the abnormal event discovery task, we only have the sequence of normal photos taken before the abnormal event, and no enough samples can be used to train the abnormal event model. Therefore, we adopt the structured reconstruction in an unsupervised form to learn patterns in the normal photos. The reconstruction aims to predict the continuous features of the photos other than the discrete class labels. Thus, we adopt the continuous CRF. The details of the proposed one-class structured event modeling (**OSEM**) are shown in Figure 2. The **OSEM** consists of two CNNs and two RNNs which are formulated in the continuous CRF. The variable-length photo sequence is firstly encoded into the fixed-length hidden vector representation by the RNNs encoder on top of the first CNN. Then, the fixed-length hidden representation is decoded back into the variable-length feature sequence by the RNNs decoder. Finally, the decoded features and the original photo features extracted from the first CNN are used to create unary potentials of the structured reconstruction in CRF where the pairwise potentials are computed from the image pair features obtained by the second CNN. The details are illustrated as follows.

2.2.1 Formulations

In order to discovery photos of abnormal events, we propose a structured auto-encoder to learn patterns in the normal photo sequence. Given a normal photo sequence $\mathbf{x} = \{\boldsymbol{x}_1, ..., \boldsymbol{x}_n\}$, we make use of the CRF to consider the relationship among photos in the sequence:

$$P(\mathbf{x}|\mathbf{x}) = \frac{1}{Z(\mathbf{x})} exp\big(-E(\mathbf{x}, \mathbf{x})\big). \tag{4}$$

Here, E is the energy function formulated by unary and pairwise potentials $E(\mathbf{x}, \mathbf{x}) = \sum_p U(\mathcal{G}_p, \mathbf{x}) + \sum_{p,q} V(\mathcal{G}_p, \mathcal{G}_q, \mathbf{x})$. Z is the partition function: $Z(\mathbf{x}) = \int_{\mathcal{G}} exp\big(-E(\mathbf{x}, \mathbf{x})\big) d\mathcal{G}$, where U is a unary potential function and V is a pairwise potential function.

The unary potential can be written as $U(\mathcal{G}_p, \mathbf{x}) = (\mathcal{G}_p - \tilde{\mathcal{G}}_p)^2$, where $\mathcal{G}$ is a nd dimensional column vector by concatenating all d dimensional features in $\mathbf{g} = \{\boldsymbol{g}_1, ..., \boldsymbol{g}_n\}$ which are computed using CNNs as introduced in Section 2.1, $\mathcal{G}_p$ denotes the pth element of the column vector $\mathcal{G}$. Similarly, $\tilde{\mathcal{G}}$ corresponds to the column vector of $\tilde{\mathbf{g}} = \{\tilde{\boldsymbol{g}}_1, ..., \tilde{\boldsymbol{g}}_n\}$ which is the reconstructed features from the decoded hidden feature sequence $\tilde{\mathbf{h}} = \{\tilde{\boldsymbol{h}}_1, ..., \tilde{\boldsymbol{h}}_n\}$. Specifically, $\tilde{\boldsymbol{g}} = \mathbf{W}_R\tilde{\boldsymbol{h}}$, where $\mathbf{W}_R$ denotes the transform matrix from the decode hidden feature to the reconstructed feature. The decode hidden feature sequence $\tilde{\mathbf{h}}$ is computed by $\mathbb{F}(\boldsymbol{h}_n, \mathbf{g}; \boldsymbol{\Theta}_{rnnd})$ with the last feature vector in the hidden feature sequence $\mathbf{h}$ and the feature sequence $\mathbf{g}$ obtained by CNNs as inputs. Here, $\mathbf{\Theta}_{rnnd}$ denote parameters of the RNNs decoder. As shown in Figure 2, the variable-length photo sequence is firstly encoded into a fixed-length hidden feature $\boldsymbol{h}_n$ by the RNNs encoder $\mathbb{F}(.;\mathbf{\Theta}_{rnn})$. Then, the fixed-length hidden feature is decoded back into feature sequence $\tilde{\mathbf{h}}$ by the RNNs decoder $\mathbb{F}(.;\mathbf{\Theta}_{rnnd})$.

The pairwise potential can be written as $V(\mathcal{G}_p, \mathcal{G}_q, \mathbf{x}) = \frac{1}{2}\mathbf{R}_{p,q}(\mathcal{G}_p - \mathcal{G}_q)^2$. If we use $l(p)$ to denote the position in the sequence of the photo where the hidden feature element $\mathcal{G}_p$ belongs to, $\mathbf{R}_{p,q}$ can be defined as follows.

$$\mathbf{R}_{p,q} = \begin{cases} \mathbf{S}(l(p), l(q)), & \text{if } l(p) \neq l(q) \\ 0, & \text{else}, \end{cases} \tag{5}$$

where $\mathbf{S}$ is the similarity matrix and $\mathbf{S}(l(p), l(q))$ is defined as $exp\big(-\|\boldsymbol{e}_{l(p)} - \boldsymbol{e}_{l(q)}\|\big)$. Here, $\boldsymbol{e}_{l(p)} = \mathbb{F}(\boldsymbol{x}_{l(p)}; \mathbf{\Theta}_{cnn2})$ and $\boldsymbol{e}_{l(q)} = \mathbb{F}(\boldsymbol{x}_{l(q)}; \mathbf{\Theta}_{cnn2})$ denote the features of photo $\boldsymbol{x}_{l(p)}$ and photo $\boldsymbol{x}_{l(q)}$ obtained by the second CNN with parameters $\mathbf{\Theta}_{cnn2}$. In this case, the probability distribution function can be written as [12]:

$$P(\mathbf{x}|\mathbf{x}) = \frac{|\mathbf{A}|^{\frac{1}{2}}}{(\pi)^{\frac{nd}{2}}} exp\Big(-\mathcal{G}^\top \mathbf{A}\mathcal{G} - \tilde{\mathcal{G}}^\top \mathbf{A}^{-1}\tilde{\mathcal{G}} + 2\tilde{\mathcal{G}}^\top \mathcal{G}\Big). \tag{6}$$

Here, $\mathbf{A} = \mathbf{I} + \mathbf{D} - \mathbf{R}$, $\mathbf{I}$ is an identity matrix, and $\mathbf{D}$ is a diagonal matrix with $\mathbf{D}_{pp} = \sum_q \mathbf{R}_{pq}$.

2.2.2 *Learning*

To minimize the negative conditional log-likelihood of the structured auto-encoders, the final optimization problem is:

$$\min_{\mathbf{\Theta}} \frac{\lambda}{2}\|\mathbf{\Theta}\|_2^2 - \log P(\mathbf{x}|\mathbf{x}), \tag{7}$$

where $\mathbf{\Theta}$ denotes all parameters including $\mathbf{\Theta}_{cnn1}$, $\mathbf{\Theta}_{cnn2}$, $\mathbf{\Theta}_{rnn}$, $\mathbf{\Theta}_{rnnd}$ and $\mathbf{W}_R$, the $-\log P(\mathbf{x}|\mathbf{x})$ can be written as

$$\mathcal{G}^\top \mathbf{A}\mathcal{G} + \tilde{\mathcal{G}}^\top \mathbf{A}^{-1}\tilde{\mathcal{G}} - 2\tilde{\mathcal{G}}^\top \mathcal{G} - \frac{1}{2}\log(|\mathbf{A}|) + \frac{nd}{2}\log(\pi). \tag{8}$$

It is slow to directly solve the above minimization problem. Instead, we adopt an approximated solution similar to the piecewise training estimation [23, 11]. The negative $\log P(\mathbf{x}|\mathbf{x})$ is simplified as:

$$\begin{aligned} -\log P(\mathbf{x}|\mathbf{x}) &= \sum_{j=1}^{d} -\log P(\mathbf{G}_j|\mathbf{G}_j) \\ &= Tr(\mathbf{G}^\top \mathbf{A}\mathbf{G}) + Tr(\tilde{\mathbf{G}}^\top \mathbf{A}^{-1}\tilde{\mathbf{G}}) - 2Tr(\tilde{\mathbf{G}}^\top \mathbf{G}) \\ &\quad - \frac{d}{2}\log(|\mathbf{A}|) + \frac{nd}{2}\log(\pi). \end{aligned} \tag{9}$$

where $\mathbf{G}_j$ is the jth column of the feature matrix $\mathbf{G} = [\boldsymbol{g}_1, ..., \boldsymbol{g}_n]^\top \in \mathcal{R}^{n \times d}$, which consists of features in $\mathbf{g}$. $\tilde{\mathbf{G}}$ is the matrix of the reconstructed features, and d is the feature dimension.

2.2.3 *Prediction*

To predict the reconstructed features of a new photo sequence $\mathbf{x}$, we need to solve the maximum a posteriori (MAP) inference:

$$\begin{aligned} \mathcal{G}^* &= argmax_{\mathcal{G}} P(\mathbf{x}|\mathbf{x}) \\ &= argmax_{\mathcal{G}}\Big(-\mathcal{G}^\top \mathbf{A}\mathcal{G} + 2\tilde{\mathcal{G}}^\top \mathcal{G}\Big) \quad = \mathbf{A}^{-1}\tilde{\mathcal{G}}. \end{aligned} \tag{10}$$

Specifically, this means the final reconstructed features of the new photo sequence can be obtained by multiplying the decoded features with the inverse matrix of $\mathbf{A}$. Then, we can predict the abnormal photos in the new photo sequence according to the reconstruction error: $\|\boldsymbol{g}^* - \boldsymbol{g}\|$.

3. EXPERIMENTS

In this section, we evaluate the proposed OSEM for abnormal event discovery in photos. We firstly introduce the implementation details. Then we introduce the adopted baselines and dataset. Finally we give the results and analysis.

3.1 Implementation details

We implement the OSEM using the Theano platform [2, 1]. In the CRF framework, to reduce the computational cost, we only consider the neighborhood structure in the sequence. Based on the piece-wise training, the gradients of the parameters in the CNNs and RNNs can be obtained by simple chain rule. Thus, the cost computed in the loss layer is back-propagated into the previous RNNs layers and the CNNs layers. The training is implemented using the stochastic gradient descent (SGD) in an end-to-end form. For the CNNs, we initialize the parameters of the convolutional layers using the reference CaffeNet model [9, 10]. Remaining parameters are initialized with uniform distribution in scale [-0.1, 0.1]. Dimension of the output feature vector in all the CNNs is 4096. Dimension of the hidden feature vector in the RNNs layer is set to 800. The learning rate is set to 0.01. The weight decay is set to 0.0005. The training process is stopped with 100 epochs. In the training phase, we set the batch size to 10 and each batch contains photo subsequences with fixed length 30.

3.2 Baselines

For abnormal event discovery, we have four baseline methods including: **(1) Random:** This baseline is to randomly assign abnormal labels to photos. Since the abnormal photos are always less than the normal ones, the performance using this simple baseline is not too bad. **(2) Sparse coding with gradient features (SC_grad):** This is the abnormal event detection method using sparse combination learning framework in video [14]. Here we revise it to learn sparse combination of the 3D gradient features of photos. **(3) Sparse coding with CNN features (SC_cnn):** This baseline uses the method [14] to learn sparse combinations of the CNN features extracted by the pretrained model in [26, 4]. **(4) RNN based auto-encoders (RNN):** The RNN based auto-encoders are similar to [15], where denoising auto-encoders are used to detect the acoustic abnormal signals. Here we revise it for abnormal event discovery in photos. The visual features extracted using the pre-trained CNN model are imported to the RNN based auto-encoders.

3.3 Dataset

To evaluate our OSEM method, we collect photos of four abnormal events in the Instagram including the Chattanooga, Tennessee (CTN) shooting, the Pairs attack, the United States blizzard and the Umpqua Community College shooting by fixed geographic coordinates where the events happened. For the photo collection, we firstly search the nearest 33 location IDs of the geographic coordinate where the abnormal event happens on the Instagram using

Table 1: **Examples of the abnormal event dataset.**

Events	Time	Normal photos	Abnormal photos
CTN shooting	July 16, 2015	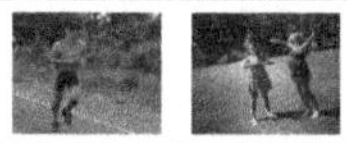	
Pairs attack	Nov. 13, 2015		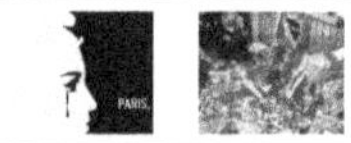
Times blizzard	Jan. 22, 2016		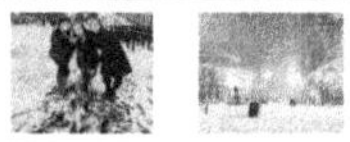
Umpqua shooting	Oct. 1, 2015		

the location search API [1]. For each location ID, we download photos created before and after the abnormal events using the location recent media API. To remove noisy photos, we get rid of location IDs which have fewer than 10 photos. After downloading photos, we manually label all photos as normal or abnormal according to wether they are relevant to the abnormal events. In Table 1, we show several exemplar photos. More details about the abnormal events and the collected photos are illustrated as follows.

Chattanooga, Tennessee (CTN) shooting: On July 16, 2015, a man opened fire on two military installations in Chattanooga, Tennessee. A Navy sailor, a Marine recruiter, and a police officer were wounded [2]. We collect photos uploaded by users from April, 2011 to February, 2016 at the location (geographic coordinate 35.095011, -85.253421) where the shooting occurred. Finally, we obtained 660 photos, and 326 of them uploaded before June 1, 2015 are used as the training set while the remaining are the test set.

Paris attack: In the evening of November 13, 2015, a series of coordinated terrorist attacks occurred in Paris and its northern suburb. The attackers killed 130 people, most of them at the Bataclan theatre [3]. We collect photos on the Instagram by fixed the location at the Batclan theatre. We obtain 18562 photos uploaded before January 15, 2016. We use the 8439 photos uploaded before November 1, 2015 as training set and the remaining as test set.

Times Square blizzard: From January 22 to 24, 2016, a major blizzard produced up to 91 cm of snow in parts of the Northeast United States. About 103 million people were affected by the storm [4]. We collect 11848 photos uploaded at the Times Square in New York city from January 9 to Feb 28, 2016. We use the 8137 photos uploaded before January 20, 2016 as training set and the remaining as test set.

Umpqua shooting: The umpqua community college shooting occurred on October 1, 2015, at the campus near Roseburg, Oregon, United States. A 26-year-old man enrolled at the school, fatally shot an assistant professor and eight students in a classroom [5]. For this event, we collect photos uploaded from January 9, 2012 to February 28, 2016 at the location (geographic coordinate 43.2888, -123.332) where the shooting occurred. We obtained 641 photos, and 288 of them uploaded before October 1, 2015 are used as the training set while the remaining are the test set.

[1] https://www.instagram.com/developer/

[2] https://en.wikipedia.org/wiki/2015_Chattanooga_shootings

[3] https://en.wikipedia.org/wiki/November_2015_Paris_attacks

[4] https://en.wikipedia.org/wiki/January_2016_United_States_blizzard

[5] https://en.wikipedia.org/wiki/Umpqua_Community_College_shooting

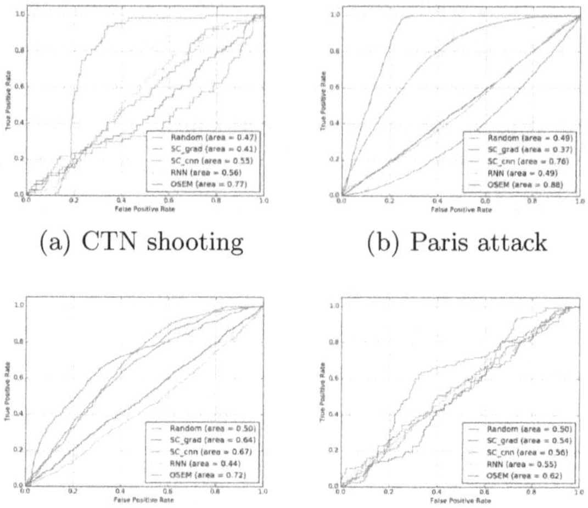

(a) CTN shooting (b) Paris attack

(c) Times blizzard (d) Umpqua shooting

Figure 3: The ROC curve on the abnormal photo dataset.

3.4 Results and analysis

In Figure 3, we show the receiver operating characteristic (ROC) curves which are created by plotting the true positive rate (TPR) against the false positive rate (FPR) at various discrimination thresholds. Here, we use true positive (TP) to denote the photo which is correctly predicted by the abnormal event discovery method. We can see that the proposed OSEM method performs better than all the baselines at most thresholds. The baseline SC_grad performs worse because it is designed in videos where the temporal continuous visual information of all frames can be captured. However, for the user generated photos, the visual information in most time stamps of the event may lost. Though the 3D gradient features are effective to capture event motion patterns in videos, they cannot capture the complex event features in photos due to the sparse sampling. For the SC_cnn method, by replacing the gradient motion feature with the CNN feature obtained by the pre-trained deep model, the performance can be improved. But it is still worse than the proposed OSEM method which can capture event temporal information in photo sequence. Compared with the RNN method, the proposed OSEM method has a large performance improvement, which demonstrates the effectiveness to capture the temporal patterns of the abnormal event in the photo sequence.

To further explore the effectiveness of the structured reconstruction model, in Figure 4(a) and Figure 4(b), we show the reconstruction errors calculated for the photo sequence of the Paris attack event using the RNN method and the proposed OSEM method. For the RNN method, we can see that some photos uploaded after the Paris attack have extremely large reconstructed errors compared with the ones before the attack. However, most of the photos still have similar reconstruction errors. For the proposed OSEM method, most photos have large reconstruction errors than the photos uploaded before the attack.

4. CONCLUSIONS

In this paper, we propose a novel structured event modeling method OSEM for abnormal event discovery

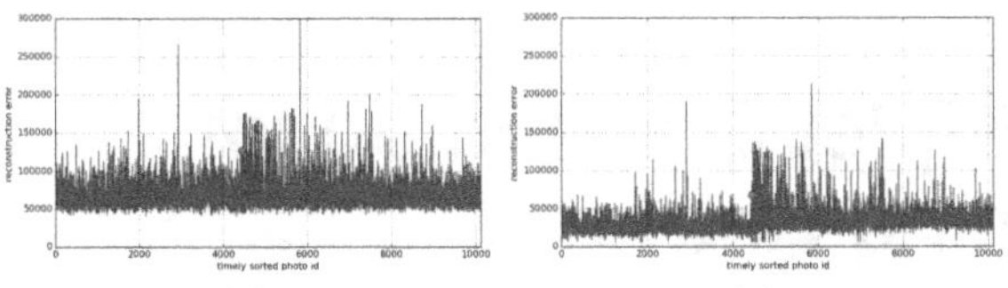

(a) (b)

Figure 4: (a) and (b) are the reconstruction errors using RNN and OSEM, respectively.

by exploiting temporal information in photo sequence. The experiment results on the abnormal event dataset collected from Instagram demonstrate the effectiveness of the proposed model. In the future, we will evaluate the proposed event modeling method on larger photo dataset.

5. ACKNOWLEDGMENTS

This work was supported in part by National Natural Science Foundation of China (No. 61225009, 61303173, 61432019, 61572498, 61532009, 61472379, 61572296, 61472115), and the Importation and Development of High-Caliber Talents Project of Beijing Municipal Institutions under Grant IDHT20140224.

6. REFERENCES

[1] F. Bastien, P. Lamblin, R. Pascanu, J. Bergstra, I. J. Goodfellow, A. Bergeron, N. Bouchard, and Y. Bengio. Theano: new features and speed improvements, 2012.

[2] J. Bergstra, O. Breuleux, F. Bastien, P. Lamblin, R. Pascanu, G. Desjardins, J. Turian, D. Warde-Farley, and Y. Bengio. Theano: a CPU and GPU math expression compiler. In *SciPy*, June 2010. Oral Presentation.

[3] L. Bossard, M. Guillaumin, and L. V. Gool. Event recognition in photo collections with a stopwatch HMM. In *ICCV*, pages 1193–1200, 2013.

[4] K. Chatfield, K. Simonyan, A. Vedaldi, and A. Zisserman. Return of the devil in the details: Delving deep into convolutional nets. In *BMVC*, 2014.

[5] J. Chung, Ç. Gülçehre, K. Cho, and Y. Bengio. Empirical evaluation of gated recurrent neural networks on sequence modeling. *CoRR*, abs/1412.3555, 2014.

[6] C. S. Firan, M. Georgescu, W. Nejdl, and R. Paiu. Bringing order to your photos: event-driven classification of flickr images based on social knowledge. In *CIKM*, pages 189–198, 2010.

[7] S. Hochreiter and J. Schmidhuber. Long short-term memory. *Neural Computation*, 9(8):1735–1780, 1997.

[8] N. Imran, J. Liu, J. Luo, and M. Shah. Event recognition from photo collections via pagerank. In *MM*, pages 621–624, 2009.

[9] Y. Jia, E. Shelhamer, J. Donahue, S. Karayev, J. Long, R. Girshick, S. Guadarrama, and T. Darrell. Caffe: Convolutional architecture for fast feature embedding. *arXiv preprint arXiv:1408.5093*, 2014.

[10] A. Krizhevsky, I. Sutskever, and G. E. Hinton. Imagenet classification with deep convolutional neural networks. In *NIPS*, pages 1106–1114, 2012.

[11] G. Lin, C. Shen, I. D. Reid, and A. van den Hengel. Efficient piecewise training of deep structured models for semantic segmentation. *CoRR*, abs/1504.01013, 2015.

[12] F. Liu, C. Shen, and G. Lin. Deep convolutional neural fields for depth estimation from a single image. In *CVPR*, pages 5162–5170, 2015.

[13] X. Liu and B. Huet. Heterogeneous features and model selection for event-based media classification. In *ICMR*, pages 151–158, New York, NY, USA, 2013. ACM.

[14] C. Lu, J. Shi, and J. Jia. Abnormal event detection at 150 FPS in MATLAB. In *ICCV*, pages 2720–2727, 2013.

[15] E. Marchi, F. Vesperini, F. Eyben, S. Squartini, and B. W. Schuller. A novel approach for automatic acoustic novelty detection using a denoising autoencoder with bidirectional LSTM neural networks. In *ICASSP*, pages 1996–2000, 2015.

[16] R. Mattivi, J. Uijlings, F. G. De Natale, and N. Sebe. Exploitation of time constraints for (sub-)event recognition. In *Proceedings of the 2011 Joint ACM Workshop on Modeling and Representing Events*, J-MRE '11, pages 7–12, 2011.

[17] G. Petkos, S. Papadopoulos, V. Mezaris, and Y. Kompatsiaris. Social event detection at mediaeval 2014: Challenges, datasets, and evaluation. In *MediaEval Workshop*, 2014.

[18] S. Qian, T. Zhang, R. Hong, and C. Xu. Cross-domain collaborative learning in social multimedia. In *MM*, pages 99–108, 2015.

[19] S. Qian, T. Zhang, C. Xu, and M. S. Hossain. Social event classification via boosted multimodal supervised latent dirichlet allocation. *TOMCCAP*, 11(2):27:1–27:22, 2014.

[20] T. Reuter and P. Cimiano. Event-based classification of social media streams. In *ICMR*, page 22, 2012.

[21] T. Reuter, S. Papadopoulos, G. Petkos, V. Mezaris, Y. Kompatsiaris, P. Cimiano, C. M. D. Vries, and S. Geva. Social event detection at mediaeval 2013: Challenges, datasets, and evaluation. In *MM Workshop*, 2013.

[22] A. Scherp, R. Jain, M. S. Kankanhalli, and V. Mezaris. Modeling, detecting, and processing events in multimedia. In *MM*, pages 1739–1740, 2010.

[23] C. A. Sutton and A. McCallum. Piecewise training for undirected models. In *UAI*, pages 568–575, 2005.

[24] S. Tsai, L. Cao, F. Tang, and T. S. Huang. Compositional object pattern: a new model for album event recognition. In *MM*, pages 1361–1364, 2011.

[25] S. Tsai, T. S. Huang, and F. Tang. Album-based object-centric event recognition. In *ICME*, pages 1–6, 2011.

[26] A. Vedaldi and K. Lenc. Matconvnet – convolutional neural networks for matlab.

[27] X. Yang, T. Zhang, and C. Xu. Cross-domain feature learning in multimedia. *TMM*, 17(1):64–78, 2015.

[28] J. Yuan, J. Luo, H. A. Kautz, and Y. Wu. Mining GPS traces and visual words for event classification. In *MIR*, pages 2–9, 2008.

[29] T. Zhang and C. Xu. Cross-domain multi-event tracking via co-pmht. *ACM TOMCCAP*, 10(4):31, 2014.

Deep Bi-directional Cross-triplet Embedding for Cross-Domain Clothing Retrieval

Shuhui Jiang[†], Yue Wu[†], Yun Fu[†‡]
[†]Department of Electrical & Computer Engineering, Northeastern University, Boston, USA
[‡]College of Computer & Information Science, Northeastern University, Boston, USA
{shjiang, yuewu, yunfu}@ece.neu.edu

ABSTRACT

In this paper, we address two practical problems when shopping online: 1) What will I look like when wearing this clothing on the street? 2) How to find the exact same or similar clothing that other people are wearing on the street or in a movie? In this paper, we jointly solve these two problems with one bi-directional shop-to-street street-to-shop clothing retrieval framework. There are three main challenges of cross-domain clothing retrieval task. First is to learn the discrepancy (e.g., background, pose, illumination) between street domain and shop domain clothing. Second, both intra-domain and cross-domain similarity need to be considered during feature embedding. Third, there is large bias between the number of matched and non-matched street and shop pairs. To solve these challenges, in this paper, we propose a deep bi-directional cross-triplet embedding algorithm by extending the start-of-the-art triplet embedding into cross-domain retrieval scenario. Extensive experiments demonstrate the effectiveness of the proposed algorithm.

Keywords

Clothing retrieval; Cross domain; Triplet embedding

1. INTRODUCTION

Studies such as clothing parsing (predicting pixel-wise labelings of garment items) [26, 22], fashion style classification [13, 11, 3], clothing recommendation [15, 9, 8, 21] and clothing retrieval [6, 5, 17, 12, 4] are receiving increasing attentions recently mainly due to the huge clothing market. Using AI technology to facilitate online clothing shopping has gradually become a research hotspot because of a growing e-commerce operation. When shopping online, people may ask two questions. How to find a specific item (e.g., dress, shirts, hats) which is very attractive when other people wearing on the street or in movie? Users may want to search an exact same or similar clothing with a photo captured in unconstrained environment (e.g., pose, illumination, background). Another question is how do I look when wearing this item on? Most online shopping websites only provide the pictures of goods, or better, show how the clothing wearing on skinny model on clean background taken by professional photographers. However, how will ordinary people look when wearing this item on the street?

Existing works mainly focus on street-to-shop scenario [17, 5, 12, 6] by assuming user would manually provide bounding box of the query item, and the retrieval shop items are in clear background with almost frontal view. However, in shop-to-street scenario, we need to search one item in street images with various poses and complex background. How to learn the discrepancy [18] (e.g., background, pose, illumination) between street domain and shop domain clothing remains a challenging problem. In this paper, we address street-to-shop and shop-to-street clothing retrieval with a jointly bi-directional clothing retrieval framework using deep cross-triplet embedding with convolutional network.

Deep feature embedding with convolutional neural networks receives a lot of attentions recently [1, 19, 20, 2, 16, 23]. Bell et al. [1] introduced contrastive embedding [7] for interior design search. FaceNet [19] applied triplet embedding [24] for face verification and recognition by learning deep feature embedding, and achieved state-of-the-art performance. However existing triplet embedding methods do not focus on cross-domain scenarios. Especially, in our cross-domain clothing retrieval task, we have three main challenges. First is to learn the discrepancy (e.g., background, pose, illumination) between street domain and shop domain clothing. Second, intra-domain and cross-domain similarity need to be considered simultaneously during feature embedding. The cross-domain similarity need to be placed in a higher priority due to the large discrepancy. Third, there is large bias between the number of matched and non-matched street and shop pairs. We have very less positive pairs (exact match) and far larger number of negative pairs (not match).

To solve these problems, we propose a deep cross-triplet embedding algorithm by extending the triplet embedding into cross-domain scenario. We fine-tune the AlexNet [14] with the cross-triplet embedding to model the item similarity. For both intra and cross domain, the training process enlarges the difference between points in matched pairs and narrows the difference between points in non-matched pairs. The cross-domain triplet sampling strategy is conducted for solving large unbalance of matched and non-matched pairs. The cross-domain triplets is assigned with higher weights than intra-domain triplets to better solve the discrepancy across domain. The extensive experiments well demonstrate the effectiveness of the proposed framework.

MM '16, October 15-19, 2016, Amsterdam, Netherlands

DOI: http://dx.doi.org/10.1145/2964284.2967182

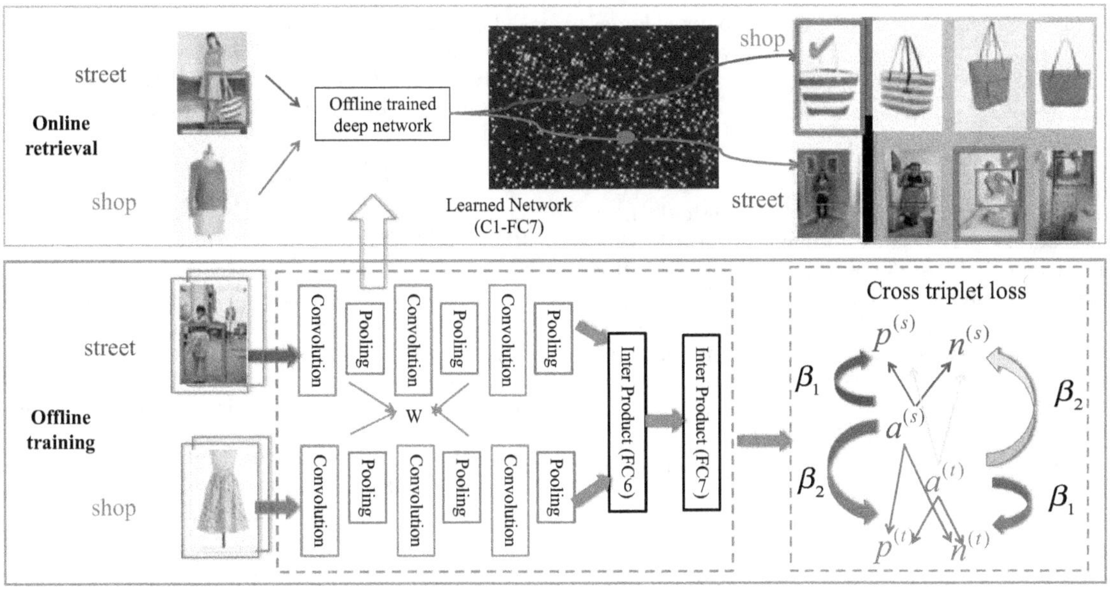

Figure 1: Bi-directional clothing retrieval framework. The inputs of offline training module are street images with bounding boxes and shop images. A cross-triplet embedding is used to train the deep convolutional network. The off-line learned network (C1-FC7) is used to embed the online query from either street or shop domain. In cross-triplet loss, $\{a^{(s)}, p^{(s)}, n^{(s)}\}$ and $\{a^{(t)}, p^{(t)}, n^{(t)}\}$ present the triplets in source and domain and β_1 and β_2 present the weight of intra-domain loss and cross-domain loss.

2. BI-DIRECTIONAL CLOTHING RETRIEVAL

In this section, we first introduce the framework of bi-directional clothing retrieval. Second, we introduce the cross-triplet embedding, and discuss the differences between cross-triplet embedding and existing deep embedding methods.

2.1 Framework

As shown in Figure 1, the framework of bi-directional clothing retrieval contains offline training and online retrieval modules. The offline trained deep network is applied for feature embedding in online retrieval modules.

The inputs of online training consist of both street and shop domain images. For the street domain images, the category of the item, and a bounding box around the item are provided manually by the user or detected by clothing parsing [25]. For the shop domain images, the entire image is used as input due to the large volume.

Although our clothing dataset contains more than 20,000 street images, and 200,000 shop images, it is still far less than the number used for training AlexNet on ImageNet dataset including 1,000 categories [14]. Thus, instead of fully relying on clothing data to newly train a deep network, we keep the pooling layers and convolution layers of AlexNet and fine-tune a three layer fully-connected network with a newly proposed cross-triplet embedding. More specifically, we fine-tune a category-specific model for each category (e.g., hat and pants) by modeling the similarity between a query feature descriptor and cross-domain feature descriptor with cross-triplet embedding.

The fine-tuning is based on the well-known Caffe[10] framework. The learning rate is initially set to 10^{-5} and decreases by factor of 10 every 70 epochs. The model is fine-tuned for about 140 epochs. The batch size is set as 512 images. The other setting of the network is the same with the original AlexNet [14]. The training is conducted on a single GTX Titan X with about 5 GB GPU memory.

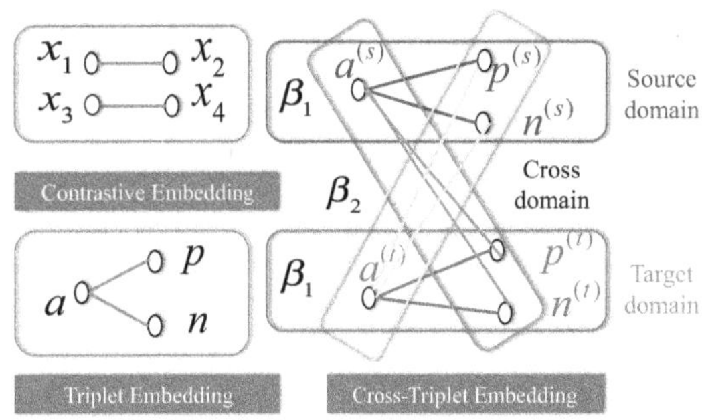

Figure 2: Illustration of contrastive embedding, triplet embedding and cross-triplet embedding. In contrastive embedding, $\{x_1, x_2\}$ and $\{x_3, x_4\}$ are two pairs could be either positive or negative pair. In cross-triplet embedding, similar as in Figure 2, $\{a^{(s)}, p^{(s)}, n^{(s)}\}$ and $\{a^{(t)}, p^{(t)}, n^{(t)}\}$ present the triplets in source and domain and β_1 and β_2 presents the weight of intra-domain loss and cross-domain loss.

In online retrieval, the input could be either a street or shop domain image. The off-line trained network is applied for feature extraction. Then we calculate the cosine similarity to rank the cross-domain items in this category.

2.2 Cross-Triplet Embedding

Triplet embedding [19, 24] is trained on the triplet data $\{(x_a^{(i)}, x_p^{(i)}, x_n^{(i)})\}$ where $(x_a^{(i)}, x_p^{(i)})$ have the same class labels and $(x_a^{(i)}, x_n^{(i)})$ have different class labels. The $x_a^{(i)}$ is denoted as an anchor of a triplet. The training encourages the network to find an embedding where the distance

$D_{ia,in} = ||f(x_i^a) - f(x_i^n)||_2$ between negative pairs is larger than distance $D_{ia,ap} = ||f(x_i^a) - f(x_i^p)||_2$ between matched pairs plus the margin parameter α:

$$J = \frac{3}{2m} \sum_i^{m/3} [D_{ia,ip}^2 - D_{ia,in}^2 + \alpha]_+^2. \quad (1)$$

Although the existing triplet embedding methods have achieved satisfactory performance in many fields [19], they do not well consider the cross-domain retrieval scenario. It is easy to think about still using the triplet embedding and neglecting the domain information. It means that we randomly sample a, p and n from two domains. However such strategy may cause some problems. First, existing triplet embedding assigns the same weight for all the triplets when calculating the total triplet loss. Thus, it may treat the intra-domain and cross-domain equally. However, when facing cross-domain scenario, the cross-domain triplet loss needs to be assigned higher weights due to the difficultly of learning large cross-domain discrepancy. Secondly, if we randomly sample a, p and n from two domains, we will have eight different situations including the four conditions shown in cross-triplet embedding in Figure 2, plus $\{(a^{(s)}, p^{(t)}, n^{(s)})\}$, $\{(a^{(s)}, p^{(s)}, n^{(t)})\}$, $\{(a^{(t)}, p^{(s)}, n^{(t)})\}$ and $\{(a^{(t)}, p^{(t)}, n^{(s)})\}$. It is difficult to decide the different margins α and weights for such complex situations. For example, it is hard to judge whether the loss of positive pair (e.g., $D(a^{(s)}, p^{(t)})$) across domain should be larger than the loss of negative pair intra domain (e.g., $D(a^{(s)}, n^{(s)})$)?

To address these concerns, we extend the existing tippet embedding into a cross-domain scenario. As shown in Figure 2, cross-triplet embedding is trained on both source domain and target domain data with domain information. Note that, in our bi-directional framework, in street-to-shop direction, street domain is denoted as source domain and shop domain is denoted as target domain, and vice-versa. The cross-domain triplet loss considers four conditions:

$$J = \underbrace{\beta_1 J^{s,s} + \beta_1 J^{t,t}}_{\text{intra domain}} + \underbrace{\beta_2 J^{s,t} + \beta_2 J^{t,s}}_{\text{cross domain}}, \quad (2)$$

where $J^{s,s}$ denotes the intra-domain lost function of triplet data in source domain $\{a^{(s)}, p^{(s)}, n^{(s)}\}$. $J^{t,t}$ denotes the in target domain $\{a^{(t)}, p^{(t)}, n^{(t)}\}$. $J^{s,t}$ denotes the cross domain triplet $\{a^{(s)}, p^{(t)}, n^{(t)}\}$ and similarly, $J^{t,s}$ denotes the cross domain triplet $\{a^{(t)}, p^{(s)}, n^{(s)}\}$. β_1 is used as the weight for intra-domain loss and β_2 is used as the weight for cross-domain loss. In order to emphasis more on the cross domain triplet, we set $\beta_2/\beta_1 > 1$. Within each condition, the triplet loss is calculation as Eq (1).

As we face the challenge that the number of exact match pairs is far less than the number of negative pairs, we propose a cross-triplet sampling algorithm. For each sample a, we extract the product id as the label and random sample an image with the same product id, either in the same domain or cross domain. Since the number of same exact item is very small, if there is no sample with same product id, we choose the sample itself as the positive pair. We compare the domain information of a and p. If a and p are from same domain we set the weight of this triplet as β_1. If a and p are from different domain, we set the weight of this triplet as β_2. Then we sample a negative sample with the same domain as p but with different label as a.

The objective function could be easily solved by Stochastic Gradient Descent (SGD). Each triplet could be optimized by applying standard triplet embedding optimization method with multiplying corresponding weight β_1 and β_2.

3. EXPERIMENT

3.1 Dataset

We use the Exact Steet2Shop dataset [6][1]. It contains 20,357 street photos and 204,795 shop photos in 11 categories. Street photos are captured in everyday uncontrolled environment (e.g., pose, background). Shop photos are from 25 different online clothing stores. The evaluation dataset is constructed by items appear in both street and shop domain.

3.2 Comparison Methods

AlexNet [14]: AlexNet [14] is one of the most widely used CNN model, which is also applied as baseline in [6]. The activation of the 4096-dimensional fully-connected layer FC6 is used as feature presentation.

Where to buy it (Where)[6]: Where to buy it paves the way of Exact Street to Shop. It learns the similarity between street and shop domain by minimizing the cross-entropy error.

Triplet embedding (Triplet) [19]: In order to show the effectiveness of our cross-triple embedding, we compare the existing cross-triple embedding [19] as shown in Eq (1). In this method, the triplets are sampled randomly from two domains without considering the domain information.

Cross-triple embedding(Ours): This method contains the whole framework of our deep bi-directional embedding with convolutional network.

3.3 Experimental results

The experimental settings are following [6]. For clothing retrieval task, since the category of item is pre-provided either by human label or clothing parsing, the retrieval experiments are conducted within-category. For each category, the exact matching pairs are split into training and test with ratio of 4:1. For street-to-shop task, the query is with bounding box and for shop-to-street task, the whole image is used as query with the category label. Top-k accuracy is to measure the performance.

Table 1 presents the exact matching performance for k=20. The left of Table 1 shows the top 20 accuracy in street-to-shop direction with AlexNet [6], Where [6], Triplet [19] and ours. We copy the results of Where shown in [6]. In the right of Table 1, since no previous methods mainly focused on shop-to-street clothing retrieval, we report the performance implemented using AlexNet [6] and Triplet embedding [19] to solve the shop-to-street retrieval task. We observe that:

(1) In street-to-shop direction, our proposed method performs the best (in bold fond) or the second best (in red color) except outerwear and tops. In street-to-shop direction, in all the categories our method achieves the best performance. Note that in Where [6], a selective search process is conducted for the shop domain images, which do not conducted in AlexNet [6], Triplet [19] and ours. In Where [6], 100 proposals are kept for each shop image. That results in the time complexity is 100 times larger than simply using the shop image itself. Also, in the shop-to-street scenario, it makes

[1]http://www.tamaraberg.com/street2shop.

Table 1: Top 20 accuracy for exact-street-to-shop task and exact shop-to-street retrieval tasks. The best and second best results in each domain is shown in bold fond and red color respectively.

	street-to-shop				shop-to-street		
Category	AlexNet[6]	Where[6]	Triplet[19]	Ours	AlexNet[6]	Triplet[19]	Ours
Bags	23.56	**37.4**	25.12	27.01	56.28	56.42	**59.13**
Belts	4.49	13.5	15.73	**16.85**	70.27	71.21	**72.97**
Dresses	18.10	**37.1**	19.91	21.18	31.26	28.42	**31.42**
Eyewear	3.62	**35.5**	20.41	25.36	62.16	65.21	**70.27**
Footwear	5.06	9.6	10.32	**14.25**	22.88	23.17	**26.36**
Hats	11.63	**38.4**	27.32	29.07	61.19	65.67	**73.13**
Leggings	9.48	**22.1**	11.42	14.51	37.85	39.23	**41.59**
Outerwear	6.31	**21.0**	16.12	15.71	33.23	36.11	**40.28**
Pants	15.38	29.2	30.02	**32.16**	52.24	53.15	**61.94**
Skirts	11.26	**54.6**	11.24	10.32	47.92	48.93	**56.04**
Tops	11.93	**38.1**	13.51	17.42	39.33	40.28	**42.73**

Figure 3: Visualization of bi-directional street-to-shop (upper) and shop-to-street (bottom) retrieval results. The exact correct retrieval result is shown with red frame and checkmark.

less sense to retrieval street images from 100 proposals instead of using the original shop image. Thus, we conduct experiments of the street-to-shop and the shop-to-street under the same condition with the original shop image. From results in the table, we can observe that even without using the proposals, our method can match or exceed the results in Where [6] in some cases. This demonstrates the superiority of our method.

(2) In both two directions, in all the categories our method achieves better performance than Triplet [19], except outerwear and tops in the street-to-shop direction. It indicates that by extending existing triplet embedding into cross-domain scenario, our cross-triplet embedding could better learn the discrepancy between two domains.

Figure 3 provides two visualization examples.

3.4 Discussion of Cross-triplet Embedding

In this section, we discuss the impact of different ratios of cross-domain weight and intra-domain weight, denoted as β_2/β_1 in Eq.(2). Figure 4 discusses the impact of ratio of $\beta_2/\beta_1 = 1, 2, 3, 4, 5$. We fix $\beta_1 = 1$ and show the top 20 accuracy when $\beta_2 = 1, 2, 3, 4, 5$. We fix the margin $\alpha = 0.5$. We could see that in Figure 4 (a), the performance under $\beta_2/\beta_1 = 2, 3, 4$ is higher than $\beta_2/\beta_1 = 1$. In figure 4 (b), we could see that the performance under $\beta_2/\beta_1 = 2, 3$ is higher than $\beta_2/\beta_1 = 1$. It indicates the effectiveness of assigning a relatively high weight of cross-domain triplet loss to accelerate learning the cross-domain discrepancy.

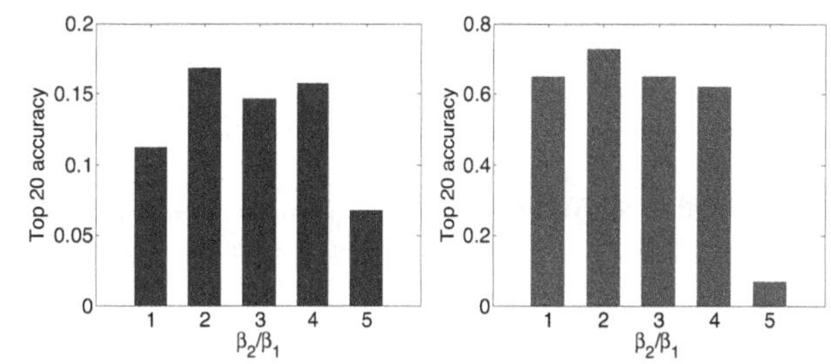

(a) Street2shop (b) Shop2street

Figure 4: Top 20 accuracy of street-to-shop and shop-to-street clothing retrieval of "belts" category, across different ratios of cross-domain weight and intra-domain weight in Eq.(2) denoted as β_2/β_1.

4. CONCLUSIONS

In this paper, we proposed a cross-triplet embedding with deep convolutional network to jointly solve the bi-directional shop-to-street and street-to-shop clothing retrieval problems. We fine-tuned AlexNet and applied the cross-triplet embedding to model the similarity between cross-domain photos. We extended existing triplet embedding into cross domain-scenario and discussed the ratio of weights in intra-domain loss and cross-domain loss. In the future, we plan to expand the dataset by adding run-way (e.g., New York fashion week) fashion data to provide users both trend-setting and everyday-esthetic styles.

5. ACKNOWLEDGEMENT

The research is supported in part by the MIT Lincoln Labs Grant G00004573, ONR award N00014-12-1-1028, ONR Young Investigator Award N00014-14-1-0484, and U.S. Army Research Office Young Investigator Award W911NF-14-1-0218.

6. REFERENCES

[1] S. Bell and K. Bala. Learning visual similarity for product design with convolutional neural networks. *ACM Transactions on Graphics*, 34(4):98, 2015.

[2] J. Bromley, J. W. Bentz, L. Bottou, I. Guyon, Y. LeCun, C. Moore, E. Säckinger, and R. Shah. Signature verification using a âĂIJsiameseâĂİ time delay neural network. *International Journal of Pattern Recognition and Artificial Intelligence*, 7(04):669–688, 1993.

[3] Q. Chen, J. Huang, R. Feris, L. M. Brown, J. Dong, and S. Yan. Deep domain adaptation for describing people based on fine-grained clothing attributes. In *Proceedings of the IEEE Conference on Computer Vision and Pattern Recognition*, pages 5315–5324, 2015.

[4] W. Di, C. Wah, A. Bhardwaj, R. Piramuthu, and N. Sundaresan. Style finder: Fine-grained clothing style detection and retrieval. In *Proceedings of the IEEE Conference on Computer Vision and Pattern Recognition Workshops*, pages 8–13, 2013.

[5] J. Fu, J. Wang, Z. Li, M. Xu, and H. Lu. Efficient clothing retrieval with semantic-preserving visual phrases. In *Proceedings of the Asian Conference on Computer Vision*, pages 420–431. Springer, 2012.

[6] M. Hadi Kiapour, X. Han, S. Lazebnik, A. C. Berg, and T. L. Berg. Where to buy it: Matching street clothing photos in online shops. In *Proceedings of the IEEE International Conference on Computer Vision*, pages 3343–3351, 2015.

[7] R. Hadsell, S. Chopra, and Y. LeCun. Dimensionality reduction by learning an invariant mapping. In *IEEE computer society conference on Computer vision and pattern recognition*, volume 2, pages 1735–1742. IEEE, 2006.

[8] T. Iwata, S. Wanatabe, and H. Sawada. Fashion coordinates recommender system using photographs from fashion magazines. In *International Joint Conference on Artificial Intelligence*, volume 22, page 2262. Citeseer, 2011.

[9] V. Jagadeesh, R. Piramuthu, A. Bhardwaj, W. Di, and N. Sundaresan. Large scale visual recommendations from street fashion images. In *Proceedings of the 20th ACM SIGKDD international conference on Knowledge discovery and data mining*, pages 1925–1934. ACM, 2014.

[10] Y. Jia, E. Shelhamer, J. Donahue, S. Karayev, J. Long, R. Girshick, S. Guadarrama, and T. Darrell. Caffe: Convolutional architecture for fast feature embedding. In *Proceedings of the ACM International Conference on Multimedia*, pages 675–678. ACM, 2014.

[11] S. Jiang, M. Shao, C. Jia, and Y. Fu. Consensus style centralizing auto-encoder for weak style classification. In *Proceedings of the Thirtieth AAAI Conference on Artificial Intelligence*. AAAI, 2016.

[12] Y. Kalantidis, L. Kennedy, and L.-J. Li. Getting the look: clothing recognition and segmentation for automatic product suggestions in everyday photos. In *Proceedings of the 3rd ACM conference on International conference on multimedia retrieval*, pages 105–112. ACM, 2013.

[13] M. H. Kiapour, K. Yamaguchi, A. C. Berg, and T. L. Berg. Hipster wars: Discovering elements of fashion styles. In *Proceedings of the European Conference on Computer Vision*, pages 472–488. Springer, 2014.

[14] A. Krizhevsky, I. Sutskever, and G. E. Hinton. Imagenet classification with deep convolutional neural networks. In *Advances in Neural Information Processing Systems*, pages 1097–1105, 2012.

[15] S. Liu, J. Feng, Z. Song, T. Zhang, H. Lu, C. Xu, and S. Yan. Hi, magic closet, tell me what to wear! In *Proceedings of the 20th ACM International Conference on Multimedia*, pages 619–628. ACM, 2012.

[16] S. Liu, X. Liang, L. Liu, X. Shen, J. Yang, C. Xu, L. Lin, X. Cao, and S. Yan. Matching-cnn meets knn: quasi-parametric human parsing. In *Proceedings of the IEEE Conference on Computer Vision and Pattern Recognition*, pages 1419–1427, 2015.

[17] S. Liu, Z. Song, G. Liu, C. Xu, H. Lu, and S. Yan. Street-to-shop: Cross-scenario clothing retrieval via parts alignment and auxiliary set. In *Proceedings of the IEEE Conference on Computer Vision and Pattern Recognition*, pages 3330–3337. IEEE, 2012.

[18] K. Saenko, B. Kulis, M. Fritz, and T. Darrell. Adapting visual category models to new domains. In *European conference on computer vision*, pages 213–226. Springer, 2010.

[19] F. Schroff, D. Kalenichenko, and J. Philbin. Facenet: A unified embedding for face recognition and clustering. In *Proceedings of the IEEE Conference on Computer Vision and Pattern Recognition*, pages 815–823, 2015.

[20] H. O. Song, Y. Xiang, S. Jegelka, and S. Savarese. Deep metric learning via lifted structured feature embedding. *arXiv preprint arXiv:1511.06452*, 2015.

[21] A. Veit, B. Kovacs, S. Bell, J. McAuley, K. Bala, and S. Belongie. Learning visual clothing style with heterogeneous dyadic co-occurrences. In *Proceedings of the IEEE International Conference on Computer Vision*, pages 4642–4650, 2015.

[22] S. Vittayakorn, K. Yamaguchi, A. C. Berg, and T. L. Berg. Runway to realway: Visual analysis of fashion. In *IEEE Winter Conference on Applications of Computer Vision*, pages 951–958. IEEE, 2015.

[23] J. Wang, Y. Song, T. Leung, C. Rosenberg, J. Wang, J. Philbin, B. Chen, and Y. Wu. Learning fine-grained image similarity with deep ranking. In *Proceedings of the IEEE Conference on Computer Vision and Pattern Recognition*, pages 1386–1393, 2014.

[24] K. Q. Weinberger and L. K. Saul. Distance metric learning for large margin nearest neighbor classification. *The Journal of Machine Learning Research*, 10:207–244, 2009.

[25] K. Yamaguchi, M. Kiapour, and T. Berg. Paper doll parsing: Retrieving similar styles to parse clothing items. In *Proceedings of the IEEE International Conference on Computer Vision*, pages 3519–3526, 2013.

[26] K. Yamaguchi, M. H. Kiapour, L. E. Ortiz, and T. L. Berg. Parsing clothing in fashion photographs. In *Proceedings of the IEEE Conference on Computer Vision and Pattern Recognition*, pages 3570–3577. IEEE, 2012.

A Discriminative and Compact Audio Representation for Event Detection

Liping Jing[1], Bo Liu[1], Jaeyoung Choi[2,3], Adam Janin[2], Julia Bernd[2], Michael W. Mahoney[2,4], and Gerald Friedland[2,4]

[1]Beijing Key Lab of Traffic Data Analysis and Mining, Beijing Jiaotong University, Beijing, China
[2]International Computer Science Institute, Berkeley, CA, USA
[3]Delft University of Technology, Delft, Netherlands
[4]University of California, Berkeley, CA, USA

{lpjing,12112082}@bjtu.edu.cn
{jaeyoung,janin,jbernd,mmahoney,fractor}@icsi.berkeley.edu

ABSTRACT

This paper presents a novel two-phase method for audio representation: Discriminative and Compact Audio Representation (DCAR). In the first phase, each audio track is modeled using a Gaussian mixture model (GMM) that includes several components to capture the variability within that track. The second phase takes into account both global structure and local structure. In this phase, the components are rendered more discriminative and compact by formulating an optimization problem on Grassmannian manifolds, which we found represents the structure of audio effectively. Experimental results on the YLI-MED dataset show that the proposed DCAR representation consistently outperforms state-of-the-art audio representations: i-vector, mv-vector, and GMM.

CCS Concepts

•Information systems → Multimedia and multimodal retrieval; •Computing methodologies → Machine learning;

Keywords

Event Detection; Audio Data; Discriminative and Compact Representation

1. INTRODUCTION

With the rapid increase in the number of user-generated videos shared on the Internet, it is becoming increasingly advantageous to explore new ways of retrieving them—for example, by automatically detecting events occurring in them.

Approaches to the event detection task have largely focused on visual-based methods—but audio content often provides complementary information. Multimodal approaches that use both visual and audio cues have recently gained traction. However, there has not been much in-depth exploration of how to best leverage audio information, especially unfiltered user-generated audio—though the focus is changing. For example, sound event detection was included in the 2013 DCASE challenge at IEEE AASP [18].

Major aspects of audio-based event detection include audio data representation and learning methodologies. In this work, we focus on the first aspect, audio data representation, which aims to extract specific features that can refine raw audio into higher-level information. These include low-level features (e.g., energy, cepstral, and harmonic features) and intermediate-level features [3]. The most popular low-level features are Mel-frequency cepstral coefficients (MFCCs) [7], as well as first-order statistics [9] and second-order statistics [15] (e.g., mv-vector [16]) derived from the MFCC features.

Another exciting recent approach is i-vectors, which use latent factor analysis to compensate for foreground and background variability [5, 6, 8]. Though these representation methods have shown promising performance, they have some limitations with regard to event detection. For example, most audio representations are derived unsupervised, i.e., they do not make use of existing label information—though label information is very useful in tasks such as image classification [11] and text classification [12]. In addition, these methods risk losing information about geometric structure within the data [17], and they do not capture signal variance within tracks, nor explicitly consider the local structure between Gaussian components, which may be useful for distinguishing events.

In this paper, we address these issues by introducing a Discriminative and Compact Audio Representation (DCAR) to model audio information. This method is implemented in two phases. First, each audio track is modeled using a Gaussian mixture model (GMM) with several components, to capture within-track variability and reduce storage space. Second, by integrating the labels for the audio tracks and the local structure among the Gaussian components, we identify an embedding to reduce the dimensionality of the mixture components and render them more discriminative. Consequently, the discriminative mixture components of the training data can be represented with low dimensionality.

MM '16, October 15-19, 2016, Amsterdam, Netherlands

DOI: http://dx.doi.org/10.1145/2964284.2970377

The DCAR model is presented in Sec. 2. Sec. 3 describes experiments with a real-world dataset, demonstrating that DCAR significantly improves event-detection performance. Conclusions and future work are discussed in Sec. 4.

2. DISCRIMINATIVE AND COMPACT AUDIO REPRESENTATION

2.1 Characterizing Per-Track Variability

Given a set of audio tracks, we first extract their low-level MFCC features. Let $\mathbf{X} = \{\mathbf{X}^i\}_{i=1}^n$ denote a set of n labeled audio files; each file is segmented into m_i frames. Each frame is modeled via a vector with d-dimension MFCC features ($d = 60$), i.e., $x_j^i \in \mathbb{R}^{60}$ (including the first 20 MFCC features and their first-order and second-order derivatives). Previous work has demonstrated that second-order statistics are much more appropriate for describing complicated multimedia data [5]. Therefore, we train a GMM with P components for each audio file (P can be tuned via cross-validation in experiments), and a set of components $G=\{g_i\}_{i=1}^N$ ($N=nP$) can be obtained from n training audio files. Each component has its weight w_i, mean μ_i, and covariance matrix Σ_i, i.e., $g_i = \{w_i, \mu_i, \Sigma_i\}$.

2.2 Identifying a Discriminative Embedding

The audio file can be represented using these mixture components, but this ignores the global structure of the data (e.g., label information) and the local structure among the components (e.g., nearest neighbors). Meanwhile, the original feature representation is usually large (since there are 60 MFCC features, each mean vector has 60 elements, and each covariance matrix contains 60×60 elements), which may be time-consuming in later processing. Therefore we propose a new method for generating a discriminative and compact representation from the high-dimensional mixture components. The DCAR method is summarized in Fig. 1.

Our main goal is to learn an embedding $\mathbf{W} \in \mathbb{R}^{d\times r}$ ($r < d$, here d is number MFCC features, r is embedding space size) based on N components generated from all labeled audio tracks, belonging to L event classes (i.e., $G = \{g_i, \ell_i\}_{i=1}^N$, where ℓ_i is the label for component g_i, based on the label of the corresponding audio file from which g_i was generated, and $L = |\{\ell_i\}_{i=1}^N|$). Therefore, the resulting low-dimensional GMM components should preserve the important structure of the original GMM components as much as possible. We introduce an embedding $\mathbf{W}$ and define new GMM components with mean

$$\hat{\mu} = \mathbf{W}^T \mu \tag{1}$$

and covariance matrix

$$\hat{\Sigma} = \mathbf{W}^T \Sigma \mathbf{W}. \tag{2}$$

The covariance matrix Σ can easily be transformed to a symmetric positive definite matrix by adding a small constant to its diagonal elements. To maintain this property, the embedding $\mathbf{W}$ is constrained to be full rank. A simple way of enforcing this requirement is to impose orthonormality constraints on $\mathbf{W}$ (i.e., $\mathbf{W}^T\mathbf{W} = \mathbf{I}_r$), so that the embedding can be identified by solving an optimization problem on the Grassmannian manifold.

For event detection, each training file has label information, which we also assign to its GMM components. This

Figure 1: Framework for generating the discriminative and compact audio representation (DCAR). The left side shows the original d-dim GMM components (i.e., $\mu \in \mathbb{R}^d$ and $\Sigma \in \mathbb{R}^{d\times d}$); the right side shows the DCAR representation with r-dim ($r < d$) mixture components (i.e., $\hat{\mu} \in \mathbb{R}^r$ and $\hat{\Sigma} \in \mathbb{R}^{r\times r}$).

valuable information can be interpreted as global structure for those components. There is also intrinsic internal structure among the components, such as the affinity between each pair. When reducing the dimensionality of GMM components, it is necessary to maintain these two types of structure. Motivated by the idea of linear discriminative analysis [14] and the Maximum Margin Criterion [13], DCAR aims to minimize intra-class distance while maximizing inter-class distance, by solving the optimization problem in (3):

$$\begin{aligned}\mathbf{F}(\mathbf{W}) = \min_{\mathbf{W}^T\mathbf{W}=I_r} \sum_{i,j} A_{ij} \Big(\lambda \|\mathbf{W}^T(\mu_i - \mu_j)\|_2^2 \\ + \|\log(\mathbf{W}^T\Sigma_i\mathbf{W}) - \log(\mathbf{W}^T\Sigma_j\mathbf{W})\|_F^2\Big)\end{aligned} \tag{3}$$

The first term indicates the euclidean distance between mean vectors, and the second term is the distance between two covariance matrices measured by the Log-Euclidean Metric (LEM) [2]. The tunable trade-off parameter λ balances the effects of the two terms. The affinity matrix $\mathbf{A}$ is defined by building an intra- (within)-class similarity graph and an inter- (between)-class similarity graph.

$$\mathbf{A}_{ij} = \mathbf{S}_w - \mathbf{S}_b \tag{4}$$

$\mathbf{S}_w$ and $\mathbf{S}_b$ are two binary matrices describing the intra-class and inter-class similarity graphs respectively, formulated as:

$$\mathbf{S}_w(g_i, g_j) = \begin{cases} 1 & \text{if } g_i \in \text{NN}_w(g_j) \text{ or } g_j \in \text{NN}_w(g_i) \\ 0 & \text{otherwise} \end{cases} \tag{5}$$

$$\mathbf{S}_b(g_i, g_j) = \begin{cases} 1 & \text{if } g_i \in \text{NN}_b(g_j) \text{ or } g_j \in \text{NN}_b(g_i) \\ 0 & \text{otherwise,} \end{cases} \tag{6}$$

where $\text{NN}_w(g_i)$ contains the n_w nearest neighbors of component g_i drawn from G that share the same label as ℓ_i, and $\text{NN}_b(g_i)$ is the set of n_b nearest neighbors of g_i that have different labels. Here, the nearest neighbors of each component can be identified via their similarity. We use heat kernel weight with a self-tuning technique (for parameters σ_μ and σ_Σ) to measure the similarity between components:

$$S(g_i, g_j) = \lambda \exp\Big(\frac{-\delta_\mu^2(\mu_i, \mu_j)}{2\sigma_\mu^2}\Big) + \exp\Big(\frac{-\delta_\Sigma^2(\Sigma_i, \Sigma_j)}{2\sigma_\Sigma^2}\Big) \tag{7}$$

where λ is a trade-off parameter, δ_μ is the euclidean metric and δ_Σ is the LEM metric. This matrix $\mathbf{A}$ serves to effectively combine local structure (nearest neighbors) and global structure (label information).

The problem in (3) is a typical optimization problem with orthogonality constraints; it can therefore be formulated as a unconstrained optimization problem on Grassmannian manifolds [1]. Given that the objective function $\mathbf{F}(\mathbf{W})$ has the property that for any rotation matrix $\mathbf{R} \in SO(r)$ (i.e., $\mathbf{R}\mathbf{R}^T = \mathbf{R}^T\mathbf{R} = \mathbf{I}_r$), $\mathbf{F}(\mathbf{W}) = \mathbf{F}(\mathbf{W}\mathbf{R})$, this optimization problem is most compatible with a Grassmannian manifold. In other words, we can model the embedding $\mathbf{W}$ as a point on a Grassmannian manifold $\mathcal{G}(r,d)$, which consists of the set of all linear r-dimensional subspaces of $\mathbb{R}^d$.

We employ the conjugate gradient (CG) technique [1] to solve (3). On a Grassmannian manifold, CG performs minimization along geodesics with specific search directions. Here, the geodesic is the shortest path between two points on the manifold. For each point on the manifold $\mathcal{G}$, its tangent space is a vector space that contains the tangent vectors of all possible curves passing through that point. On the manifold, the tangent vectors must parallel transport along the geodesics. Optimizing $\mathbf{F}(\mathbf{W})$ results in a situation where the low-dimensional components are close if their corresponding original high-dimensional components are event-aware neighbors; otherwise, they will be as far apart as possible.

2.3 Detecting Events Using DCAR

To make use of the manifold structure, we adopted the Kernel Ridge Regression (KRR) method [17] to build the event classifiers. Let $\hat{G}=\{\hat{g}_i\}_{i=1}^N$ and $\hat{g}_i=\{\hat{\mu}_i,\hat{\Sigma}_i\}$ be the learned low-dimensional components. $Y \in \mathbb{R}^{N\times L}$ is the label information (where $\mathbf{Y}_{ij}$=1 if $\hat{g}_i$ belongs to the jth event; otherwise $\mathbf{Y}_{ij}$=0). The KRR method aims to train a classifier by solving the following optimization problem:

$$\min_{\mathbf{H}} \mathbf{J}(\mathbf{H}) = \|\phi(\hat{G})^T\mathbf{H} - \mathbf{Y}\|_F^2 + \alpha\|\mathbf{H}\|_F^2 \tag{8}$$

where the kernel function can be written as $K = \phi(\hat{G})^T\phi(\hat{G})$. Since each component $\hat{g}_i$ has a mean $\hat{\mu}_i$ and a covariance matrix $\hat{\Sigma}_i$, we adopt the similarity (7) as the kernel function, i.e., $K(\hat{g}_i,\hat{g}_j) = S(\hat{g}_i,\hat{g}_j)$. The problem in (8), as a quadratic convex problem, can be optimized by setting its derivative with respect to H to zero, and then computing H in closed form:

$$\mathbf{H} = \phi(\hat{G})(K+\alpha\mathbf{I})^{-1}\mathbf{Y}$$

Given a new test audio track, the P mixture components $\{g_p\}_{p=1}^P = \{w_p,\mu_p,\Sigma_p\}_{p=1}^P$ can be obtained. Then the corresponding discriminative, low-dimension mixture components $\{\hat{g}_p\}_{p=1}^P$ can be generated, as in (1) for $\hat{\mu}_p = W^T\mu_p$, and as in (2) for $\hat{\Sigma}_p = W^T\Sigma_pW$, where the embedding $\mathbf{W}$ is learned from the training data. The class membership matrix $M = \{M_p\}_{p=1}^P$ (where $M_p \in \mathbb{R}^{1\times L}$ is the event membership of the p-th component) can be calculated:

$$M_p{=}\phi(\hat{g}_p)^T\mathbf{H}{=}\phi(\hat{g}_p)^T\phi(\hat{G})(K+\alpha\mathbf{I})^{-1}\mathbf{Y}{=}K_p(K+\alpha\mathbf{I})^{-1}\mathbf{Y}$$

Here $K_p = [K(\hat{g}_p,\hat{g}_i)]_{i=1}^N$, indicating the similarity between $\hat{g}_p$ and all of the training mixture components in $\hat{G}$. We can then make a final event prediction for the new audio track with P components using an average voting scheme

$$\ell = arg\max_j \sum_{p=1}^P w_pM_p(j)$$

where w_p is the weight of the pth component.

3. EXPERIMENTAL RESULTS

3.1 Dataset and Methodology

Our experiments used YLI-MED [4], a recently released public video corpus with ten events, based on the YFCC100M [19]. Table 1 describes YLI-MED; the variation in track length makes event detection more challenging.

We compared the proposed DCAR with the state-of-the-art audio representations used for event detection: mv-vector [16], i-vector [6], and GMM. By "GMM", we mean the base GMMs extracting the GMM components from each audio file, but without discriminative dimensional reduction. For each method, we tuned the parameters using cross-validation on the training data to obtain the best result.

We describe results using the same classification method, KRR, with all representations.[1] For the l-th event in t testing tracks, we compared the prediction result to the ground truth to determine the number of true positives (TP_l), false positives (FP_l), true negatives (TN_l), and false negatives (FN_l). We evaluated event detection performance using four common metrics, *Accuracy*, $FScore$, $FalseAlarmRate$ (FAR), and $MissRate$. Higher *Accuracy* and $FScore$ and lower FAR and $MissRate$ indicate better performance.

3.2 Results and Discussion

We evaluated DCAR and the three baseline representations on a ten-event detection task. Table 2 shows detection performance for each event and the average over the ten events, in terms of $FScore$ and $MissRate$. Combined *Accuracy* for mv-vector, i-vector, GMM, and DCAR is 0.3907, 0.4640, 0.4923, and **0.5321**, respectively (p=0.01 for DCAR vs. each baseline [McNemar's two-tailed]), and the average FAR scores are 0.0674, 0.0593, 0.0570, and **0.0523**.

For each individual event and on average, DCAR achieves superior or competitive performance. In particular, DCAR consistently performs best for all four metrics on the *average* or *combined* scores (an average of more than 8% gain on all metrics relative to the second-best representation).

To explore DCAR's performance under different difficulty levels, we extracted two subsets (based on results from other tasks). Events in EC5 ("EasyCase") (Ev101, Ev104, Ev105, Ev108, and Ev109) are easy to distinguish from (most of) the others; those in HC4 ("HardCase") (Ev103, Ev106, Ev107, and Ev110) are more difficult. For both subsets, DCAR achieved the best results on each evaluation metric, for example, $FScores$ of **0.7067** on EC5 and **0.5283** on HC4 for DCAR, as opposed to 0.4773, 0.6415, and 0.6670 on EC5 and 0.4278, 0.2795, and 0.4821 on HC4 for mv-vector, i-vector, and GMM respectively. Interestingly, i-vector performs better than mv-vector on EC5, but worse on HC4.

We can make a number of observations about these results. First, it seems that modeling GMM components for each audio track (as in GMM, mv-vector, and DCAR) is

[1]Using SVM, KNN, or PLDA for this step does not change the performance rankings between representations.

Table 1: Dataset Composition

Event ID	Event Name	Training Data		Testing Data	
		# of Videos	length (ms)	# of Videos	length (ms)
Ev101	Birthday Party	99	6850∼248950	131	8380∼328960
Ev102	Flash Mob	91	8290∼325630	49	11710∼152560
Ev103	Getting a Vehicle Unstuck	89	5590∼591670	39	11170∼157690
Ev104	Parade	95	7840∼303850	127	5770∼216460
Ev105	Person Attempting a Board Trick	99	5950∼391150	88	5500∼254980
Ev106	Person Grooming an Animal	97	5950∼574300	38	7210∼292870
Ev107	Person Hand-Feeding an Animal	95	6850∼174880	113	7840∼244450
Ev108	Person Landing a Fish	99	7930∼363610	41	7480∼250120
Ev109	Wedding Ceremony	90	9640∼631630	108	9820∼646300
Ev110	Working on a Woodworking Project	98	5590∼373690	44	6760∼281080

Table 2: Per-event comparison of detection performance (as FScore and MissRate) using four representations: mv-vector, i-vector, GMM, and DCAR. (Best results in boldface; second-best underlined.)

	FScore (↑)				MissRate (↓)			
	mv-vector	i-vector	GMM	DCAR	mv-vector	i-vector	GMM	DCAR
Ev101	0.7259	**0.7842**	0.7303	0.7835	0.2824	0.1679	0.1527	**0.1298**
Ev102	0.2837	0.3396	0.3651	**0.4603**	0.5918	0.6327	0.5306	**0.4082**
Ev103	0.2178	0.2569	0.2410	**0.3820**	0.7179	0.6410	0.7436	**0.5641**
Ev104	0.4274	0.6206	0.6000	**0.6207**	0.6063	0.4331	0.3622	**0.3621**
Ev105	0.3354	0.3899	**0.5714**	0.5178	0.6932	0.6477	**0.3864**	0.4205
Ev106	0.1964	0.1835	0.2963	**0.3750**	0.7105	0.7368	0.6842	**0.6053**
Ev107	0.3850	0.3298	0.3250	**0.4024**	**0.6814**	0.7257	0.7699	0.7080
Ev108	0.3191	0.3853	0.3878	**0.4231**	0.6341	0.4878	0.5366	**0.4634**
Ev109	0.4211	0.5028	0.4286	**0.5176**	0.6667	**0.5833**	0.6667	0.5926
Ev110	0.0833	0.2299	**0.2857**	0.2162	0.9091	0.7727	**0.7500**	0.8182
Average	0.3395	0.4023	0.4231	**0.4699**	0.6494	0.5829	0.5583	**0.5072**

more effective than modeling a GMM on all the training audio tracks together (as in i-vector) when the events are closely related, as in HC4. We believe this is because, in real-world applications (e.g., with user-generated content), each track may have a large variance. The set of strategies that model each track via GMM capture the hidden structure within each audio track, while the i-vector strategy may smooth away that structure (even between events), leading to a less useful representation.

Second, GMM and DCAR perform better than mv-vector on both subsets, which indicates that one mixture component (as in mv-vector) may not sufficiently capture the full structure of the audio; in addition, vectorizing the mean and variance inevitably distorts the intrinsic geometrical structure among the data. Third, DCAR outperforms the base GMM, because DCAR takes into account the label information and the intrinsic nearest neighbor structure among the audio files when modeling the training data, and outputs a mapping function to effectively represent the test data. This result confirms that discriminative dimensionality reduction is beneficial for characterizing the distinguishing information for each audio file, leading to a better representation and significantly improving event detection performance.

4. CONCLUSIONS AND FUTURE WORK

We have presented a new audio representation, DCAR, and demonstrated its use in event detection.[2] The DCAR method stands out in its ability to capture the variability within each audio file. In addition, it achieves better discriminativity by integrating label information and the graph of the components' nearest neighbors among the audio files. In experiments, representing audio using the proposed DCAR notably improves performance on event detection. In a nutshell, the novelty of DCAR lies in its being a *compact representation* of an audio signal that *captures variability* and has *better discriminative ability* than other representations.

Videos are of course *multi*modal; visual content, captions, and other metadata can provide valuable information. We therefore plan to use these to extend the current model, along with complex information about temporal evolution [3]. We may also explore modeling only the most information-rich audio segments. Within audio, we also hope to evaluate the use of DCAR for other related tasks, such as audio scene classification (for example, testing it with the DCASE acoustic scenes dataset [18]).

5. ACKNOWLEDGMENTS

This work was partially supported by the NSFC (61370129, 61375062), the PCSIRT (Grant IRT201206), and a collaborative LDRD led by Lawrence Livermore National Laboratory (U.S. Dept. of Energy contract DE-AC52-07NA27344). Any findings and conclusions are the authors', and do not necessarily reflect the views of the funders.

[2]Further details about how DCAR is built and additional experimental results can be found in Jing et al. 2016 [10].

6. REFERENCES

[1] P. Absil, R. Mahony, and R. Sepulcher, editors. *Optimization algorithms on matrix manifolds.* Princeton University Press, 2008.

[2] V. Arsigny, P. Fillard, X. Pennec, and N. Apache. Geometric means in a novel vector space structure on symmetric positive definite matrices. *SIAM on Matrix Analysis*, 29(1):328–347, 2007.

[3] D. Barchiesi, D. Giannoulis, D. Stowell, and M. Plumbley. Acoustic scene classification: classifying environments from the sounds they produce. *Signal Processing Magazine*, 32(3):16–34, 2015.

[4] J. Bernd, D. Borth, B. Elizalde, G. Friedland, H. Gallagher, L. Gottlieb, A. Janin, S. Karabashlieva, J. Takahashi, and J. Won. The YLI-MED corpus: Characteristics, procedures, and plans (TR-15-001). Technical report, ICSI, 2015. arXiv:1503.04250.

[5] N. Dehak, P. Kenny, R. Dehak, P. Dumouchefl, and P. Ouellet. Front-end factor analysis for speaker verification. *IEEE Transactions on Audio, Speech and Language Processing*, 19(4):788–798, 2011.

[6] B. Elizalde, H. Lei, and G. Friedland. An i-vector representation of acoustic environment for audio-based video event detection on user generated content. In *Proceedings of the IEEE International Symposium on Multimedia*, 2013.

[7] A. Eronen, J. Tuomi, A. Klapuri, and S. Fagerlund. Audio-based context awareness - acoustic modeling and perceptual evaluation. In *Proceedings of the IEEE International Conference on Acoustics, Speech and Signal Processing (ICASSP)*, pages 529–532, 2003.

[8] Z. Huang, Y. Cheng, K. Li, V. Hautamaki, and C. Lee. A blind segmentation approach to acoustic event detection asked on i-vector. In *Proceedings of INTERSPEECH*, 2013.

[9] Q. Jin, P. Schulman, S. Rabat, S. Burger, and D. Ding. Event-based video retrieval using audio. In *Proceedings of INTERSPEECH*, pages 2085–2088, 2012.

[10] L. Jing, B. Liu, J. Choi, A. Janin, J. Bernd, M. W. Mahoney, and G. Friedland. DCAR: A discriminative and compact audio representation to improve event detection. *http://arxiv.org/abs/1607.04378*, 2016.

[11] L. Jing, C. Zhang, and M. Ng. SNMFCA: Supervised NMF-based image classification and annotation. *IEEE Transactions on Image Processing*, 21(11):4508–4521, 2012.

[12] M. Lan, C. Tan, J. Su, and Y. Lu. Supervised and traditional term weighting methods for automatic text categorization. *IEEE Transactions on Pattern Analysis and Machine Intelligence*, 31(4):721–735, 2009.

[13] H. Li, T. Jiang, and K. Zhang. Efficient and robust feature extraction by maximum margin criterion. In *Proceedings of the Conference on Neural Information Processing Systems (NIPS)*, 2004.

[14] G. McLachlan, editor. *Discriminant analysis and statistical pattern recognition.* Wiley Interscience, 2004.

[15] R. Mertens, H. Lei, L. Gottlieb, G. Friedland, and A. Divakaran. Acoustic super models for large scale videos event detection. In *Proceedings of ACM Multimedia*, 2011.

[16] G. Roma, W. Nogueira, and P. Herrera. Recurrence quantification analysis features for auditory scene classification. In *Proceedings of IEEE AASP Challenge on DCASE*, 2013.

[17] B. Scholkopf and A. Smola, editors. *Learning with Kernels.* MIT Press, 2002.

[18] D. Stowell, D. Giannoulis, E. Benetos, M. Lagrange, and M. Plumbley. Detection and classification of audio scenes and events. *IEEE Transactions on Multimedia*, 17(10):1733–1746, 2015.

[19] B. Thomee, D. Shamma, G. Friedland, B. Elizalde, K. Ni, D. Poland, D. Borth, and L. Li. YFCC100M: The new data in multimedia research. *Communications of the ACM*, 59(2):64–73, 2016.

Jockey Time: Making Video Playback to Enhance Emotional Effect

Kyeong Ah Jeong
KAIST
291 Daehak-ro, Yuseong-gu
Daejeon 34141, Republic of Korea
+82-42-350-4563
kyeongah17@kaist.ac.kr

Hyeon-Jeong Suk
KAIST
291 Daehak-ro, Yuseong-gu
Daejeon 34141, Republic of Korea
+82-42-350-4523
color@kaist.ac.kr

ABSTRACT
In order to effectively and easily deliver the affective quality of a video, this study investigated the emotional manifests induced by the playback design of the video. In designing the playback, we articulated speed, direction, and continuity of the video and surveyed observers' responses. Based on the results, we propose seven categories of playback design, and each appeals cheerful, happy, relaxed, funny, urgent, angry, and sad emotion. For an easy use, we offer an online video editing service, "Jockey Time." A beta version was operated for a month for monitoring purpose, and finally, Jockey Time v.1.0 is now launched for anybody to easily enhance the emotional effect of one's video.

CCS Concepts
• Information systems→Information systems applications→Multimedia information systems→Multimedia content creation • Human-centered computing→Human computer interaction (HCI)→Empirical studies in HCI.

Keywords
Video editing; movement; temporal attributes of video; playback design; tool development

1. INTRODUCTION
Since social media such as YouTube® and Facebook® have been developed, there has been a rapidly growing interest in sharing videos about everyday life [2, 10]. Accordingly, not only experts but also many novice users are now attempting to make their videos more appealing.

Various types of desktop-based video editing software are now available, but even experts need a substantial amount of hands-on experience before they can use the tools with fluency. Fortunately, some mobile phone based editing applications are available, and these tools enable even naïve users to create reasonably satisfying videos easily. Using templates, these tools combine an uploaded video with background music, add some graphical elements, or modify the playback style. However, little studies have been done to share the method or to figure out the affective effect of them. For the systemized expansion and sustainable use of video template, this study approaches to a new way of creating video templates by addressing the relevant aspect of tempo. In particular, we investigated the temporal aspect of video and identified the affective effect induced by design of video playback. Also, we intended to launch a service to examine whether the empirical results make contributions to a practical use.

MM '16, October 15-19, 2016, Amsterdam, Netherlands
© 2016 ACM. ISBN 978-1-4503-3603-1/16/10…$15.00
DOI: http://dx.doi.org/10.1145/2964284.2967183

2. RELATED WORK
Concerning the elements of video, different points of view have been debated. [18] described media aesthetics in terms of five elements: light and color, two-dimensional space, three-dimensional space, time-motion, and sound. [3] considered six elements, including line, shape, tone, color, movement, and rhythm. The definitions varied mainly caused by different perspectives depending on disciplines.

After reviewing the studies on video elements in the field of human computer interaction, dance, and film, we identified overlap with the following three elements: layout, image, and tempo [3, 17, 18]. Firstly, layout refers to plans for the spatial composition of the video screen, which can include actor position, background space configuration, light position, and camera angle.

Secondly, the image indicates the visualization of the video contents, and this has been investigated under the name of imaging processing [4, 6, 9]. Studies include, for instance, investigating the effect of color changes on emotional reactions [8, 9].

Lastly, tempo has been considered important, as its adjustment could affect viewers' feelings significantly [13]. For instance, [8] and [16] demonstrated that the impact of video playback speed was greater than that of other attributes on the emotional judgement of the observer. Furthermore, despite of its impact, little has been done to reveal the effect of the temporal characteristics of video on viewer's response. Instead, from various disciplines the studies have introduced the attributes of the tempo as summarized in Table 1. For example, [17] does not define any attributes, while [12] distinguishes speed from smoothness. After having reviewed studies in various topics, we decided to consider the following four as the attributes of video playback: speed, direction, continuity, and acceleration. Accordingly, in this study, we defined "playback design" as an articulation of these four temporal attributes. However, among the four attributes, acceleration refers to the state of changing playback speed, and thus we considered acceleration as an articulation of speed. Therefore, excluding acceleration. we studied on the other three remaining attributes, speed, direction, and continuity.

Table 1. Temporal attributes considered in previous studies

Author	Attribute	Definition
Laban [17]	-	Time consumption of one movement expression
Nam et al. [12]	Speed	Speed of object movement
	Smoothness	Continuity of movement
Montepare et al. [11]	Speed	Speed of object movement
	Continuity	Smooth–rough movement
Zettl [18]	Speed	Movement speed based on frame density
Block [3]	Speed	Speed of object movement
	Time	Starting point of movement on a timeline
Andrienko et al. [1]	Speed	Speed of object movement
	Acceleration	The change of speed

3. SURVEY ABOUT THE EMOTIONAL EFFECTS OF VIDEO PLAYBACK DESIGN

In the survey, we attempted to identify what kind of affective effects would be induced through the playback design. For example, we assumed an identical video clip appeals differently when its playback is differently designed.

3.1 Material

3.1.1 Levels of Video Playback Design

In order to decide the levels for the playback speed attribute, we analyzed the playback speed of commercially available movies and advertisements. From the first to fourth weekly box office rankings in May and June 2015, four domestic movies and four foreign movies were selected for playback speed analysis. In addition, we collected ten popular domestic advertisements aired in 2015 in which playback speed control was dominantly applied. Adobe After Effects® was utilized to find the video segments in which the playback speed changed. The playback speeds were calculated by reversely editing those segments into cognitively normal playback speed (1× speed). Both movies and advertisements mostly used a playback speed of 0.25× or 0.5× for slower speeds, and 2× or 4× for faster speeds. As such, we defined the five levels of video playback speed as 0.25×, 0.5×, 1×, 2×, and 4× speed of the original video.

Secondly, with regard to the direction attribute, forward and backward levels were defined.

Lastly, two levels were defined for the continuity: continuous and discontinuous (rough). The continuous style had 30 fps. In order to make a discontinuous style, we played a video at 5 fps by sampling 1/6 of frames, because humans can distinguish the behavioral characteristics of a person in a video at 5–7 fps [15].

Table 2. Levels of video playback design attributes

Attributes	Levels
Speed	0.25 × – 0.5× – original – 2× – 4×
Direction	Forward – Backward
Continuity	Continuous (30 fps) – Discontinuous (5 fps)

Consequently, the levels of each temporal attribute were decided, as presented in Table 2. In total, twenty playback designs were created by combining five types of playback speed, two types of direction, and two types of continuity.

3.1.2 Video Stimuli

We recruited a 23-year-old amateur actress with experience and asked her to perform actions that express emotions. To characterize the target emotions, we used the emotion space whose axes are defined with the first two dimensions of the PAD theory [14], pleasure (horizontal axis) and arousal (vertical axis). In addition to the four quadrants, we included a neutral emotion; thus, a total of five types of target emotion were formed as illustrated in Figure 1. The actress's performance was taped with a video recorder, Sony RX10 II, which supported up to 120 fps and full-HD (1920 * 1080 pixels) quality.

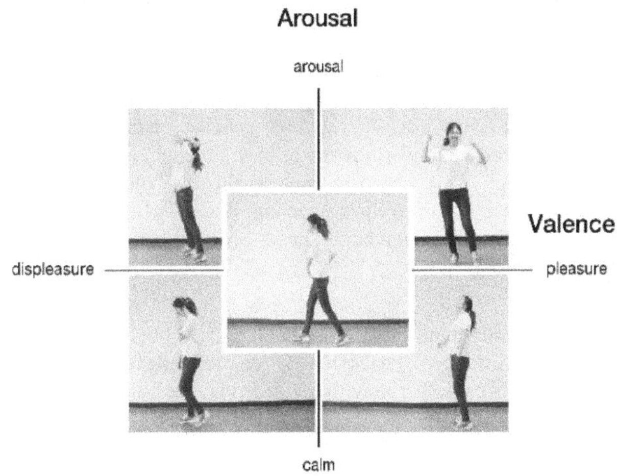

Figure 1. Five still cuts and each represents five video clips

3.2 Participants

Thirty Korean college students, sixteen males and fourteen females, participated in this study; on average, they were 22.23 years old, with a standard deviation of 3.21 years. All were paid volunteers and majoring in various disciplines.

3.3 Procedure

To investigate the difference in responses caused by the video playback articulation of the same emotional content, two videos were presented simultaneously to each participant. One was the video in original playback, whereas the other was a video whose playback was articulated. All video clips were played muted. In this way, the participants could compare the two videos at the same time and specify what emotional reactions were induced through the playback design.

We asked participants to describe the emotional responses induced by the playback design in a word. We encouraged participants to write as many words as possible to describe their emotional experiences by providing a monetary incentive as a reward. The sets of two video clips were displayed on a 42-inch TV, and the video stimuli were randomly given. The procedure took approximately one hour for each participant.

3.4 Results and Analyses

A total of 3,849 words were initially collected. The redundant words were removed, resulting in a total of 899 words for participants to describe their emotional experiences. Next, we referred to Wordnet® (www.wordnet.co.kr), the largest online thesaurus dictionary for the Korean language, to cluster the 899 words into a smaller number of categories. Through this procedure, redundant and synonymous words were merged, and finally, the 899 words were grouped into 52 term categories, which are available at http://jockeytime.kaist.ac.kr/Terms.html.

Then, we began by analyzing the frequency of term categories collected for the neutral video clip. The frequency of each term category was counted if used more than twice. For example, when the neutral video was played in a slow-forward-continuous playback design, *relaxed* category was expressed for eight times, indicating that a slow playback enhanced the relaxing feeling of the original video. Likewise, we continued the analyses with regard to the other four types of video introduced in Figure 1. The full frequency data for each of the five videos are available at http://jockeytime.kaist.ac.kr/FrequencyOfEmotionCategory.html. Subsequently, we identified the relationship between the attributes of video playback design and their affective effects, which led to three primary observations.

Firstly, the playback speed had a positive relationship with the magnitude of arousal. That is, the slower playback speed elicited emotions of low arousal, such as *relaxed*, while the faster playback speed elicited emotions of high arousal, such as *urgent*. This tendency was, however, not applicable when the video already contained an arousing feeling. For the highly arousing video contents, any playback speed articulation leveraged the arousing feeling.

Secondly, the playback direction was related to the hedonic quality. For example, forward playback elicited positive emotions, whereas backward playback mostly elicited negative emotions, especially when combined with a slower playback speed.

Lastly, the playback continuity had a relatively marginal effect. The continuity attribute affected the frequency of *reflective* feelings, which is related to the concept of time. In contrast to the emotional appraisal of an image, the emotional response to a video could be influenced by the time flow.

4. DEVELOPMENT OF PLAYBACK DESIGN TOOL

We continued to build a service that would allow users to choose a target emotion and to apply the proper playback design. For the development of such a service, we sorted the video playback designs according to the term categories. By doing so, users may efficiently find alternative video playback designs when they declare the emotion they wish to recreate in their video.

4.1 From Emotion Terms to Playback Types

Among the 52 term categories, in fact, eleven categories covered almost 77% of the participants' responses. They were *angry, cheerful, dynamic, frivolous, frustrated, funny, happy, painful, relaxed, sad,* and *urgent*. However, as the eleven categories were extracted in a descending order of frequency, each category might not be independent from each other. Thus, we integrated similar categories to make a set of independent emotion categories. For example, *happy* and *dynamic* were integrated into *cheerful* emotion. Similarly, *frustrated, frivolous,* and *painful* were integrated into *angry*, *funny*, and *sad* emotion, respectively. Thus, a total of six independent emotion categories–*cheerful, angry, funny, sad, relaxed,* and *urgent*–were selected for implementation of our tool, Jockey Time Beta.

Next, alternative video playback designs that best express each emotion category were suggested. The selection was based on the calculation of the frequency of six emotion categories in neutral emotion video. For instance, when the neutral video was played in a 'slow-forward-continuous' or a 'slow-forward-discontinuous' playback design, the *relaxed* emotion was most frequently expressed, and hence, two playback designs were selected for *relaxed* emotion. Similarly, four playback designs were suggested for *urgent*, and two for *sad* emotion. The same process was repeated for other four emotion videos. In total, four alternative video playback designs were selected for each of the six emotion categories. All the playback designs alternatives are available at http://jockeytime.kaist.ac.kr/PlaybackDesignAlternatives.html.

4.2 Jockey Time Beta

Using the six emotion categories and the four alternative playback designs of each category, we built a beta version of an online service. Called as Jockey Time Beta, the service consists of three parts: selection of an emotion, selection of a playback design among four alternatives, and then a short survey and download. The interface of Jockey Time Beta was implemented using HTML/CSS, JavaScript, PHP, and FFmpeg (a free software project mainly for handling multimedia data). In this section, we present details of the interface design of the tool.

4.2.1 Uploading a video and selection of emotion

On the first page, the user could upload a video and then select a desired emotion (Figure 2). The six emotions were positioned in a two-dimensional emotion space resembling Figure 1. The *cheerful, angry, sad,* and *relaxed* were placed in the corresponding quadrants. Besides, *urgent* and *funny* were positioned on the arousal axis. When a user moves the mouse cursor point over each of the six emotions, one of the examples of playback design is previewed within the circle to help users predict the results.

Figure 2. Start of the Jockey Time Beta: video uploading and emotion selection (http://jockeytime.kaist.ac.kr)

4.2.2 Selection of favorable playback design

Once the target emotion was selected, four alternatives were created and presented below the original video clip (see the right panel of Figure 3). The user could then download one out of the four alternatives. The download process would only begin after the user completed a short survey.

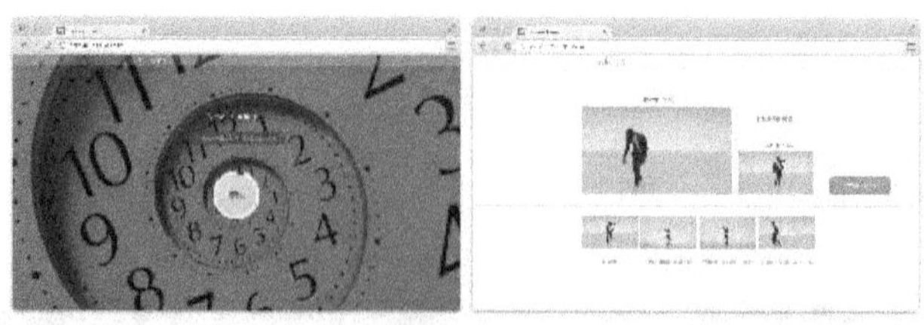

Figure 3. Four video playback designs were provided

4.2.3 Survey and download

The survey consisted of two questions, asking the user to name the new video file (left panel of Figure 4), and to assess his/her satisfaction level using a 5-point scale (right panel of Figure 4). Then, the user could download the new video file in mp4 format.

Figure 4. Survey and download

4.3 Jockey Time v.1.0

The beta version operated on a server computer for one month from 15 November to 15 December 2015. During this period, a total of 84 users accessed the website, and each experienced the application of video playback design upon his or her own video. Based on the 84 video clips and users' answers to the survey questionnaire, we could figure out some issues for improvement.

Firstly, users acquired positive emotions more, so we tried to add an in-between category between *cheerful* and *relaxed* to provide more diversified options for making videos more positive. The category of *happy* was additionally offered with *cheerful* and *relaxed*, creating a total of seven emotions.

Secondly, Jockey Time v.1.0 included clay animations to illustrate how each emotion category would be demonstrated. As shown in some recent studies, cartoon characters could be more effective to be recognized with particular emotions [5, 7] than verbal expressions. The clay animations are paused as default, and played for approximately two seconds when the user moves the mouse over each animation. Also, we added three words below each animation to describe the animated contents more clearly.

Moreover, we arrayed the seven categories of emotion by considering each as an independent substance. In the beta version, we placed the six emotions within pleasure–arousal plane, and the *funny* category did not properly fit as it could hold both positive and negative state simultaneously. Finally, the four positive emotions—*cheerful, happy, relaxed, and funny*—have been placed at the top, and the three negative emotions—*urgent*, *angry*, and *sad*—have been arrayed at the bottom (Figure 5).

After that, we launched Jockey Time v.1.0 in January 2016. The major improvements are described in the following.

5. DISCUSSION

We consider the contribution of this study from two aspects. One is to have provided empirical evidence regarding how the articulation of video playback might enhance, reduce, or change the emotional qualities of a video from its original state.

The other aspect is to have utilized empirical data to develop a tool that helps users to quickly create drafts for professionals designing videos. Jockey Time enables a novice user to easily make a video with articulated video playback designs adequate for the target emotion.

However, this study did not cover the temporal attribute of acceleration, which can significantly impact viewers' emotional responses to videos. In order to properly account for acceleration in the stimuli, the sequence design of the playback should also be considered as another factor. In this study, the sequence between different playback designs was not investigated. In order to provide more attractive and elaborative results, both acceleration and sequence design must be included in the articulation of a playback design. Furthermore, future research can reveal the compound effects of spatial and temporal attributes in video on viewers' emotional responses.

Nevertheless, unlike previous studies that have focused mainly on playback speed, this study expanded the temporal attributes by including direction and continuity. In particular, the results were summarized as alternative playback designs for each target emotion, to be used in developing an online video editing tool. Also, as we tested with the beta version, further studies could be conducted because the online service is now available for anyone, anywhere, anytime.

6. CONCLUSION

This study investigated the emotional responses elicited when a video playback was articulated in different ways. Called video playback design, we generated twenty kinds of playback designs for a video and asked participants what kinds of emotions were elicited when compared to the original video. From the survey of thirty participants, we collected 3,849 words, which were later reduced into eleven term categories. These categories were compressed again into seven since they were not emotionally independent. Based on that, we finally proposed seven categories of playback design: cheerful, happy, relaxed, funny, urgent, angry, and sad emotion. Moreover, we developed an online service tool in order to examine the practical aspects of our empirical result. The seven categories were adopted for the emotion categories of Jockey Time. Alternative video playback designs were selected for each of the categories as well. By doing so, the user interface was realized in Jockey Time, an online service tool that allows users to choose and apply a playback design to their own videos. A beta version was operated for a month to monitor usage, and finally, the improved version of Jockey Time v.1.0 was launched.

Figure 5. New interface in Jockey Time v.1.0. Clay animation is briefly played when the mouse is over. The animation demonstrates what emotion can be induced by playback designs.

7. REFERENCES

[1] Andrienko, N., Andrienko, G., Pelekis, N., and Spaccapietra, S. 2008. *Basic concepts of movement data.* Mobility, data mining and privacy. Springer. 15-38.

[2] Barker, M., Barker, D. I., Bormann, N., and Neher, K. 2012. *Social media marketing: A strategic approach.* Nelson Education.

[3] Block, B. 2013. *The visual story: creating the visual structure of film, TV and digital media.* CRC Press.

[4] Bonneel, N., Sunkavalli, K., Paris, S., and Pfister, H. 2013. Example-based video color grading. *ACM Trans. Graph.* 32, 4, 39.

[5] Desmet, P. 2005. *Measuring emotion: Development and application of an instrument to measure emotional responses to products.* Funology. Springer. 111-123.

[6] Detenber, B. H., Simons, R. F., and Reiss, J. E. 2000. The emotional significance of color in television presentations. *Media psychology.* 2, 4, 331-355.

[7] Huisman, G., and Van Hout, M. (2010. *The development of a graphical emotion measurement instrument using caricatured expressions: the LEMtool.* Paper presented at the Emotion in HCI-designing for people: proceedings of the 2008 international workshop, C. Peter, E. Crane, M. Fabri, H. Agius, and L. Axelrod, Eds., Fraunhofer.

[8] Jeong, K. A., Choi, K., and Suk, H. J. 2015. Affective Effect by Articulation of the Speed and Color Attributes of a Video. In *Korea Society of Color Studies Spring Conference 2015.* 43-46.

[9] Kim, B., Kim, Y., Kim, D., and Park, Y. 2014. Analysis of Sensibility based on Color Compensation in Movie and Drama. *Journal of Korea Society of Color Studies.* 28, 2, 37-48.

[10] Manovich, L. 2009. The practice of everyday (media) life: From mass consumption to mass cultural production? *Critical Inquiry.* 35, 2, 319-331.

[11] Montepare, J. M., Goldstein, S. B., and Clausen, A. 1987. The identification of emotions from gait information. *Journal of Nonverbal Behavior.* 11, 1, 33-42.

[12] Nam, T. J., Lee, J. H., Park, S., and Suk, H. J. 2014. Understanding the Relation between Emotion and Physical Movements. *International Journal of Affective Engineering.* 13, 3, 217-226.

[13] Pearlman, K. 2012. *Cutting rhythms: shaping the film edit.* CRC Press.

[14] Russell, J. A. 1980. A circumplex model of affect. *Journal of personality and social psychology.* 39, 6, 1161.

[15] Schindler, K., and Van Gool, L. 2008. Action snippets: How many frames does human action recognition require? In *Computer Vision and Pattern Recognition, 2008. CVPR 2008. IEEE Conference on.* 1-8.

[16] Visch, V., and Tan, E. 2007. Effect of film velocity on genre recognition. *Media Psychology.* 9, 1, 59-75.

[17] von Laban, R. 1975. *Modern educational dance.* Princeton Book Co Pub.

[18] Zettl, H. 2013. *Sight, sound, motion: Applied media aesthetics.* Cengage Learning.

Discriminative Paired Dictionary Learning for Visual Recognition

Hui-Hung Wang
National Chung Cheng University, Taiwan
huihung55@gmail.com

Yi-Ling Chen
National Taiwan University, Taiwan
yilingchenntu@ntu.edu.tw

Chen-Kuo Chiang
National Chung Cheng University, Taiwan
ckchiang@cs.ccu.edu.tw

ABSTRACT

A Paired Discriminative K-SVD (PD-KSVD) dictionary learning method is presented in this paper for visual recognition. To achieve high discrimination and low reconstruction errors simultaneously for sparse coding, we propose to learn class-specific sub-dictionaries from pairs of positive and negative classes to jointly reduce the reconstruction errors of positive classes while keeping the reconstruction errors of negative classes high. Then, multiple sub-dictionaries are concatenated with respect to the same negative class so that the non-zero sparse coefficients can be discriminatively distributed to improve classification accuracy. Compared to the current dictionary learning methods, the proposed PD-KSVD method achieves very competitive performance in a variety of visual recognition tasks on several publicly available datasets.

Keywords

Dictionary learning; sparse coding; visual recognition

1. INTRODUCTION

In recent years, sparse coding is applied to a variety of image processing and computer vision applications, such as image classification [28, 15, 22, 26, 27, 23], image de-noising [3], compression [2, 8], inpainting [3] and other applications. It recovers a sparse linear representation of a query datum with respect to a set of non-parametric basis set, known as *dictionary*. Originally, predefined dictionaries have been used based on various types of wavelets. Lately, learning the dictionary instead of using predefined bases has been shown to improve signal reconstruction significantly [2].

K-SVD [2] aims to learn the optimal dictionary that leads to the lowest reconstruction error with a set of sparse coefficients. The success of K-SVD method triggers the application in image classification tasks. Instead of learning one dictionary for the whole dataset, class-specific sub-dictionaries are learned to improve the discriminative capability of reconstruction residual [17, 20, 6]. Later, researchers attempts to promote discrimination among classes by enforcing the sparse coefficients to be discriminative[28, 15, 22, 26, 23, 27] by means of including the class labels and learning the classifier simultaneously with the dictionary. Recent dictionary learning methods achieve the discrimination by either enforcing structural constraints on the dictionary or imposing class separation criterion in the sparse coding formulation [27, 26, 23]. As a result, previous dictionary learning methods usually has very complex objective functions and require difficult optimization approaches to obtain the solutions.

MM '16, October 15–19, 2016, Amsterdam, Netherlands

DOI: http://dx.doi.org/10.1145/2964284.2967184

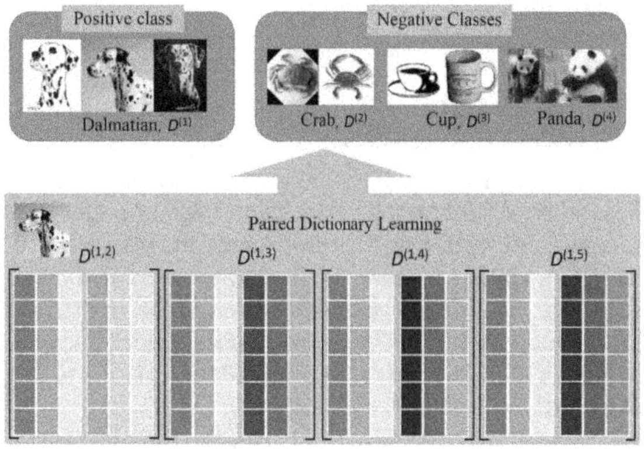

Figure 1: An example of positive and negative classes and the corresponding paired dictionaries of the class "Dalmatian".

To develop a simple yet effective dictionary learning method, we go back to the essence of sparse coding that uses the reconstruction error to achieve the discrimination. Motivated by the current machine learning methods, discriminative classifiers are usually trained by positive and negative data samples. Pair-wise relationships are utilized between data samples or datasets to further improve the discrimination. In [14], highly discriminative variables are selected from the high-dimensional data space according to the statistical analysis of paired samples for feature selection. In [16], a multilinear canonical correlation analysis method is proposed to extract features directly from tensors based on tensor-to-vector projection of paired tensor sets.

We argue that the discrimination of dictionary can be also achieved through learning from pairs of classes. To learn the class-specific sub-dictionaries, images can be divided into two kinds of classes: *Positive class* and *Negative class*. Positive class is the target class. Negative classes are all the rest of classes. For example, when training the sub-dictionary for class "Dalmatian", the training class "Dalmatian" is the positive class. The rest classes ("Crab", "Cup", "Panda") are negative classes in this case. Figure 1 depicts an example of using positive class and negative classes to learn sub-dictionaries for the class "Dalmatian".

In this paper, we propose a novel Paired Discriminative K-SVD (PD-KSVD) based on K-SVD [2] to learn sub-dictionaries from pairs of positive and negative classes. The idea is to learn such sub-dictionaries that can best reconstruct the positive class while reconstructing the negative class worse. With such capability of reconstruction, multiple sub-dictionaries are concatenated with respect to the same negative class to discriminatively distribute the non-zero coefficients. The sparse coefficients are then used to train multiple SVM classifiers [4].

2. PREVIOUS WORK

K-SVD [2] learns the dictionary by iteratively alternating between sparse coding the input data based on the current dictionary, and updating the dictionary atoms to better fit the training data. It aims to find the optimal dictionary that leads to the lowest reconstruction error with a set of sparse coefficients. Typical reconstructive dictionary learning methods include method of optimal direction (MOD) [9], K-SVD and analysis K-SVD [21].

The success of K-SVD method triggers the application in image classification tasks. Rather than learning one dictionary for all classes, one type of dictionary learning methods learn a sub-dictionary for each class and improving the discriminative capability of reconstruction residual [17, 20, 6]. In the class-specific dictionary learning, each dictionary atom is associated to a single class label. Mairal *et al.* [17] assumed a dictionary associated to the class should reconstruct this class better than the other classes. A penalty term is introduced in the cost function to re-weight the reconstruction error. Ramirez *et al.* [20], introduce a new term into sparse representation to promote the incoherence between dictionaries so that each sub-dictionary can represent the class optimally.

3. PROPOSED METHOD

3.1 Reconstruction Error of Inverted Signals

Following the nature of K-SVD that reduces the reconstruction errors of both positive and negative classes, our idea is to *invert* the negative signals. If the dictionary is learned from the inverted negative samples, the dictionary can reconstruct the the inverted negative samples well. In other words, using such dictionary to construct the original negative samples leads to larger reconstruction errors.

The Caltech101 dataset [10] was used to evaluate our assumption. we first set class 2 as our positive class. Then, sub-dictionary was trained by only using samples from class 2. We create a new class by applying the inversion operation to all samples in class 2. Using the trained sub-dictionary, we calculate the reconstruction errors for all 102 classes (101 objects and one background class) in Caltect101 and the inverted class. The results are presented in Figure 2.

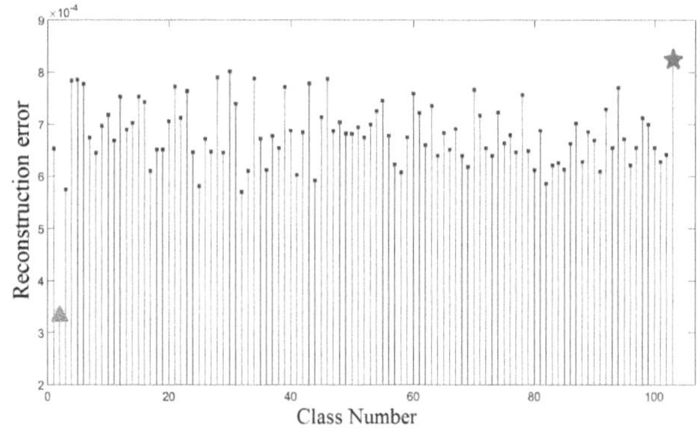

Figure 2: Reconstruction errors of 102 classes of Caltech101 dataset and the inverted class. The dictionary is trained by class 2. The green triangle presents the lowest reconstruction error of positive class 2. The red star sign depicts the highest reconstruction error of the inverted class among all the classes.

One can see that the reconstruction error of class 2 is the lowest (marked by the green triangle sign) since the sub-dictionary was trained from class 2. The inverted class (marked by red star sign) has the highest reconstruction error among all classes. Similar results can be obtained by choosing another class as positive class and repeat the experiment above.

We should note that the *signals* here are referred to as the image features. Each feature can be considered as a vector of signal. For example, one SIFT feature is a 128-dimensional vector of signal. Figure 3 depicts one possible operation of signal inversion. Signals can be inverted according to the data mean of minimum and maximum values in this class. The *max* value of class c can be calculated by: $\max^{(c)} = \max(\max(y_1^{(c)}, ..., y_n^{(c)}))$ which calculates a maximum vector from all feature vectors $y_1^{(c)}, ..., y_n^{(c)}$. Then, applying another *max* operation to extract the maximum value of class c. The signal mean can be defined by $mean^{(c)} = (1/2)(\max^{(c)} + \min^{(c)})$. Denote $y_{i,j}^{(c)}$ the j-th element of $y_i^{(c)}$, the inverted signal $\hat{y}_{i,j}^{(c)}$ can be obtained by $\hat{y}_{i,j}^{(c)} = 2 * mean^{(c)} - y_{i,j}^{(c)}$. Under this operation, signals are symmetry to class mean. The maximum value becomes the minimum and vice versa. The operation of inversion can be also conducted by finding the orthogonal vector of signal $y_i^{(c)}$, which means to find a $\hat{y}_i^{(c)}$ such that $y_i^{(c)} \cdot \hat{y}_i^{(c)} = 0$. In our experiments, the difference of classification accuracy is around 0.1%.

3.2 Paired Discriminative K-SVD

Denote $Y^{(c)}, c = 1, ..., C$ the positive training samples of class c. The inverted signals can be defined by $\hat{Y}^{(c)}$. Our goal of dictionary learning is to learn sub-dictionaries that can simultaneously increase the reconstruct error of negative classes while reducing the reconstruction error of the positive class. To this end, our dictionary learning is performed on a pair of one positive class and one inverted negative class. If the learned dictionary achieves low reconstruction errors of both the positive class and the inverted negative class in a K-SVD fashion, it introduces high reconstruction errors to the original negative class. This boosts the discrimination capability between the positive class and the negative class.

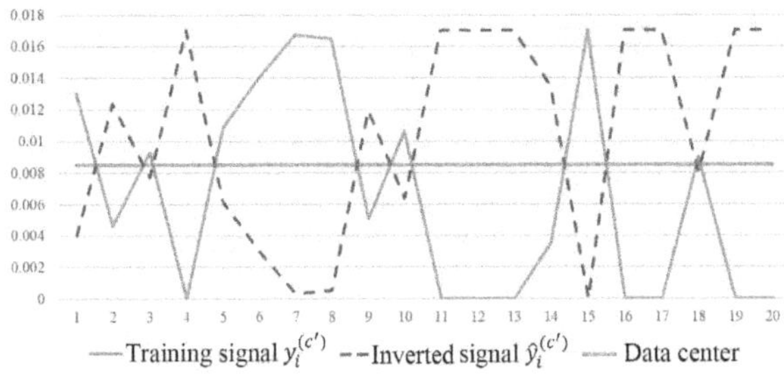

Figure 3: An example of one inverted signal.

To obtain the sub-dictionary of the positive class c, we choose one negative class c' with the minimal reconstruction error. Then we form the training set by joining $Y^{(c)}$ and the inverted negative class $\hat{Y}_i^{(c')}$. The objective function of paired discriminative dictionary learning can be written as:

$$min_{D^{(c,c')},X^{(c,c')}}||[Y^{(c)}\hat{Y}^{(c')}] - D^{(c,c')}X^{(c,c')}||_F^2, \quad s.t. \forall i, ||x_i^{(c,c')}||_1 \leq T_0 \tag{1}$$

where $D^{(c,c')}$ is the dictionary learned from the paired positive class c and the inverted negative class c'. $X^{(c,c')}$ is the sparse coefficients. Then, the reconstruction residual can be formulated as:

$$\begin{aligned} &||[Y^{(c)}\hat{Y}^{(c')}] - D^{(c,c')}X^{(c,c')}||_F^2 \\ &= ||[Y^{(c)}\hat{Y}^{(c')}] - \sum_{j=1}^{K} d_j^{(c,c')}x_T^{j(c,c')}||_F^2 \\ &= ||[Y^{(c)}\hat{Y}^{(c')}] - \sum_{j\neq k} d_j^{(c,c')}x_T^{j(c,c')} - d_k^{(c,c')}x_T^{k(c,c')}||_F^2 \\ &= ||e_k^{(c,c')} - d_k^{(c,c')}x_T^{k(c,c')}||_F^2 \end{aligned} \tag{2}$$

The reconstruction error when taking out the kth atom can be written as:

$$e_k^{(c,c')} = [Y^{(c)}\hat{Y}^{(c')}] - \sum_{j\neq k} d_j^{(c,c')}x_T^{j(c,c')} \tag{3}$$

To learn dictionary column $d_k^{(c,c')}$, SVD is applied to decompose $e_k^{(c,c')}$ to three matrices: $e_k^{(c,c')} = U\Delta V^T$. The first column of U is used to update dictionary column $d_k^{(c,c')}$ and first column of V multiplied by Δ $(1,1)$ is exploited to update the row $x_T^{k(c,c')}$ of the coefficient matrix. In PD-KSVD, a sub-dictionary is learned from the positive class c and one of its negative class c'.

3.3 Classification

To efficiently exploit all sub-dictionaries for classification, all sub-dictionaries with respect to the same negative class are combined. Denote the combined dictionary with respect to negative class c', $D_{com}^{(c')} = [D^{(1,c')}, D^{(2,c')}, ..., D^{(i,c')}], i = 1, ..., C, i \neq c'$. Therefore, $D_{com}^{(c')}$ can not reconstruct samples of class c' well. On the contrary, it can well construct class $c, c = 1, ..., C, c \neq c'$.

The reasons to combine such sub-dictionaries are two-fold. Firstly, for a test sample y_1 of class 1, using $D_{com}^{(2)} = [D^{(1,2)}, D^{(3,2)}, ..., D^{(6,2)}]$ to reconstruct y_1 makes the non-zero coefficients more concentrated on dictionary atoms of $D^{(1,2)}$, since $D^{(1,2)}$ is trained by positive samples of class 1 and inverted negative samples of class 2. To better reconstruct y_1, more dictionary atoms in $D^{(1,2)}$ which are trained from class 1 should be selected for reconstruction instead of using dictionary atoms trained from inverted negative samples of class 2. This makes the non-zero coefficients more concentrated to the dictionary atoms of the correct class. Secondly, after combining all sub-dictionaries with respect to the same negative class, it reduces the number of dictionaries which could have practical significance in terms of computational efficiency in real-world applications.

In the classification process, training signals are sparsely coded by dictionary $D = [D_{com}^{(1)}, D_{com}^{(2)}, ..., D_{com}^{(C)}]$. The corresponding sparse coefficients $SP_{train}^{(1)}$, $SP_{train}^{(2)}$,...,$SP_{train}^{(C)}$ are used to train multiple multi-class SVMs: $SVM^{(1)}$, $SVM^{(2)}$,...,$SVM^{(C)}$. After obtaining all the decisions from SVMs, a major voting mechanism is exploited to predict the class label. The process of classification is depicted in Figure 4.

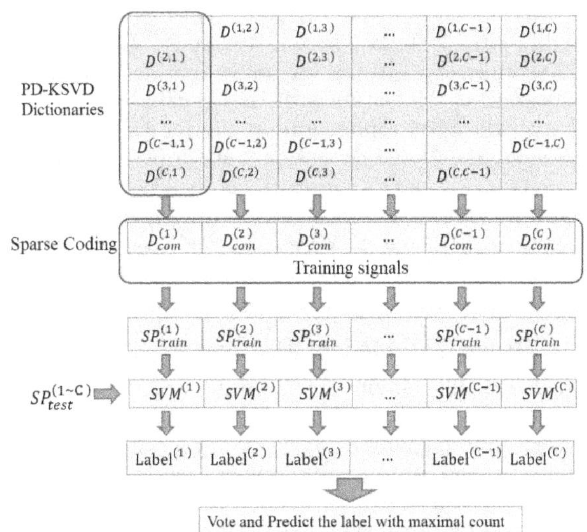

Figure 4: The classification process using combined sub-dictionaries.

4. EXPERIMENTAL RESULTS

We applied PD-KSVD to the tasks of object recognition, handwritten digits recognition and scene recognition in our experiments. Our method was evaluated on the following datasets: Caltech101 database [10], Caltech256 database [12], USPS database [1] and MIT Indoor Scene Database [19]. The parameter setting of PD-KSVD is easy. Our method is nearly parameter-free except for the sparsity factor when solving the sparse coefficients. Following the experimental settings in [15], the sparsity factor was set to 30 in our experiments and the maximum number of iterations was set to 80 following [2].

We compared PD-KSVD to SVM [7], K-SVD [2], Label Consistent K-SVD (LC-KSVD) [15], Dictionary Pair Learn-

Table 1: Recognition accuracy (%) on Caltech256 Dataset with dictionary size 7710 and 15420, respectively.

Dictionary Size	7710	15420
SVM [7]	18.5	24.5
K-SVD [2]	15.8	20.2
DPL [13]	15.9	21.8
SVGDL [5]	19.9	23.2
JDDLDR [11]	18.3	21.3
PD-KSVD	**22.2**	**29.3**

ing (DPL)[13], Support Vector Guided Dictionary Learning(SVGDL) [5], Joint Discriminative Dimensionality Reduction and Dictionary Learning(JDDLDR) [11]. We used OMP [18] for solving the optimization problem of sparse coding. SVM is used as the baseline method in our comparison. K-SVD and another K-SVD based method LC-KSVD were also included in our comparison. DLP and SVGDL which also explore the pair-wise relationship in dictionary learning achieve the state-of-the-art performance.

We use bag-of-words (BOW) of 200 vocabulary and spatial pyramid matching (SPM) as feature representation of each image. SIFT descriptors are extracted on three level spatial pyramid of sizes 1×1, 2×2 and 4×4 regions. Then, we obtain 4200-dimension features for image representation. We also extract LLC [24] feature with 1204 vocabulary in BOW model with the SPM representation of sizes 1×1, 2×2 and 4×4. Finally, the 21,504 dimensional feature is extracted.

The reference codes of the methods listed above are all available on authors' websites. We ran their reference codes with features extracted as aforementioned to compare the experimental results. Therefore, the accuracy might be different from those reported in the original papers.

4.1 Caltech 256 Object Dataset

Caltech 256 [12] contains 30607 images in 256 object categories and one background class. It is a very challenging dataset because the number of object categories is very high and contains more object variations in each category. Following the custom setup, 30 and 60 images per class are randomly selected for training, and all the rest for testing. SPM feature is used for performance evaluation.

The experiments are repeated three times and the average accuracy are reported. The results are summarized in Table 1. On this benchmark, the proposed PD-KSVD outperforms all these five methods by using 7710 and 15420 dictionary atoms. It achieves nearly 5% higher than the second best recognition accuracy with 15420 dictionary atoms.

4.2 USPS Handwritten Digit Dataset

We then perform handwritten digit recognition on the USPS dataset [1]. It contains images with contents from "0" to "9" in 8-bit grayscale format. The dataset is composed of 10 classes with 1100 images for each class. The images in the dataset are resized to 16×16. Then, features are extracted by the 256-dimensional histogram of the image intensity in grayscale.

In this experiment, we use 100 and 500 images per class for training, and the rest 1000 and 600 images for testing. The results are summarized in Table 2. From the table,

Table 2: Recognition accuracy (%) on USPS Dataset.

Dictionary Size	1000	5000
SVM [7]	85.3	87.8
SRC [25]	86.2	95.0
K-SVD [2]	84.7	88.8
LC-KSVD [15]	83.7	89.7
DPL [13]	**89.8**	**95.2**
SVGDL [5]	88.7	91.8
JDDLDR [11]	86.0	87.8
PD-KSVD	87.7	92.5

Table 3: Recognition accuracy (%) on MIT Indoor Scene Dataset with dictionary size 5360.

Method	Accuracy
SVM [7]	15.3
K-SVD [2]	14.8
LC-KSVD [15]	12.6
DPL [13]	13.3
SVGDL [5]	20.9
JDDLDR [11]	16.9
PD-KSVD	**21.4**

DPL [13] outperforms other methods. Our PD-KSVD also provide comparable recognition accuracy for handwritten digit recognition. It is worth pointing out that the recognition can achieve 93.5 when PD-KSVD trains dictionary of size 2500.

4.3 MIT Indoor Scene Dataset

MIT Indoor Scene dataset contains 67 Indoor categories. It is a very challenging dataset because of the large within-class variety and significant between-class confusion. Each category has at least 100 images. The dataset has 15620 images in total. We use 80 images per class for training, and all the rest for testing. SPM feature is used for performance evaluation.

Table 3 lists the recognition results of PD-KSVD and the competing methods. It can be seen that accuracy of PD-KSVD is superior to all the other methods.

5. CONCLUSIONS

In this paper, we propose PD-KSVD algorithm to learn class-specific sub-dictionaries by using pairs of positive and negative classes. The data samples from the negative class are inverted to train the sub-dictionary, making the reconstruction of samples from the original negative class worse by the learned dictionary. Overall, PD-KSVD is simple yet effective. It also holds a good property that better recognition results can be achieved by reducing the dictionary size. This makes it efficient for real applications. The experimental results show that the accuracy of PD-KSVD is very competitive to others methods in all recognition tasks. In the future, we would like to analyze the importance of each sub-dictionary. It will be interesting to weighted combine these sub-dictionaries based on the analysis of their importance to improve the discrimination of dictionary learning.

6. REFERENCES

[1] Usps handwritten digit database. http://www-i6. informatik.rwth-aachen.de/ keysers/usps.html.

[2] M. Aharon, M. Elad, and A. Bruckstein. k -svd: An algorithm for designing overcomplete dictionaries for sparse representation. *Signal Processing, IEEE Transactions on*, 54(11):4311–4322, Nov 2006.

[3] C. Bao, J.-F. Cai, and H. Ji. Fast sparsity-based orthogonal dictionary learning for image restoration. In *Computer Vision (ICCV), 2013 IEEE International Conference on*, pages 3384–3391, Dec 2013.

[4] C. J. C. Burges. A tutorial on support vector machines for pattern recognition. *Data Min. Knowl. Discov.*, 2(2):121–167, 1998.

[5] S. Cai, W. Zuo, L. Zhang, X. Feng, and P. Wang. Support vector guided dictionary learning. In *Computer Vision–ECCV 2014*, pages 624–639. Springer, 2014.

[6] A. Castrodad and G. Sapiro. Sparse modeling of human actions from motion imagery. *International Journal of Computer Vision*, 100(1):1–15, 2012.

[7] C.-C. Chang and C.-J. Lin. LIBSVM: A library for support vector machines. *ACM Transactions on Intelligent Systems and Technology*, 2:27:1–27:27, 2011. Software available at http://www.csie.ntu.edu.tw/~cjlin/libsvm.

[8] B. Deka, K. Gorain, N. Kalita, and B. Das. Single image super-resolution using compressive sensing with learned overcomplete dictionary. In *Computer Vision, Pattern Recognition, Image Processing and Graphics (NCVPRIPG), 2013 Fourth National Conference on*, pages 1–5, Dec 2013.

[9] K. Engan, S. O. Aase, and J. H. Husøy. Frame based signal compression using method of optimal directions (MOD). In *International Symposium on Circuits and Systems (ISCAS 1999), May 30 - June 2, 1999, Orlando, Florida, USA*, pages 1–4, 1999.

[10] L. Fei-Fei, R. Fergus, and P. Perona. Learning generative visual models from few training examples: An incremental bayesian approach tested on 101 object categories. *Computer Vision and Image Understanding*, 106(1):59–70, 2007.

[11] Z. Feng, M. Yang, L. Zhang, Y. Liu, and D. Zhang. Joint discriminative dimensionality reduction and dictionary learning for face recognition. *Pattern Recognition*, 46(8):2134–2143, 2013.

[12] G. Griffin, A. Holub, and P. Perona. Caltech-256 object category dataset. Technical Report 7694, California Institute of Technology, 2007.

[13] S. Gu, L. Zhang, W. Zuo, and X. Feng. Projective dictionary pair learning for pattern classification. In *Advances in Neural Information Processing Systems*, pages 793–801, 2014.

[14] S. Heng Toh, P. Prathipati, E. Motakis, K. Chee Keong, P. Yenamandra, and V. Kuznetsov. A robust tool for discriminative analysis and feature selection in paired samples impacts the identification of the genes essential for reprogramming lung tissue to adenocarcinoma. *BMC Genomics*, 12(3), 2011.

[15] Z. Jiang, Z. Lin, and L. Davis. Learning a discriminative dictionary for sparse coding via label consistent k-svd. pages 1697–1704, June 2011.

[16] H. Lu. Learning canonical correlations of paired tensor sets via tensor-to-vector projection. In *IJCAI 2013, Proceedings of the 23rd International Joint Conference on Artificial Intelligence, Beijing, China, August 3-9, 2013*, 2013.

[17] J. Mairal, F. R. Bach, J. Ponce, G. Sapiro, and A. Zisserman. Discriminative learned dictionaries for local image analysis. In *2008 IEEE Computer Society Conference on Computer Vision and Pattern Recognition (CVPR 2008), 24-26 June 2008, Anchorage, Alaska, USA*, 2008.

[18] Y. Pati, R. Rezaiifar, and P. Krishnaprasad. Orthogonal matching pursuit: recursive function approximation with applications to wavelet decomposition. pages 40–44 vol.1, Nov 1993.

[19] A. Quattoni and A. Torralba. Recognizing indoor scenes. In *2009 IEEE Computer Society Conference on Computer Vision and Pattern Recognition (CVPR 2009), 20-25 June 2009, Miami, Florida, USA*, pages 413–420, 2009.

[20] I. Ramírez, P. Sprechmann, and G. Sapiro. Classification and clustering via dictionary learning with structured incoherence and shared features. In *IEEE Conference on Computer Vision and Pattern Recognition, CVPR*, pages 3501–3508, 2010.

[21] R. Rubinstein, T. Peleg, and M. Elad. Analysis K-SVD: A dictionary-learning algorithm for the analysis sparse model. *IEEE Transactions on Signal Processing*, 61(3):661–677, 2013.

[22] L. Shen, S. Wang, G. Sun, S. Jiang, and Q. Huang. Multi-level discriminative dictionary learning towards hierarchical visual categorization. In *Computer Vision and Pattern Recognition (CVPR), 2013 IEEE Conference on*, pages 383–390, June 2013.

[23] Y. Sun, Q. Liu, J. Tang, and D. Tao. Learning discriminative dictionary for group sparse representation. *Image Processing, IEEE Transactions on*, 23(9):3816–3828, Sept 2014.

[24] J. Wang, J. Yang, K. Yu, F. Lv, T. S. Huang, and Y. Gong. Locality-constrained linear coding for image classification. In *The Twenty-Third IEEE Conference on Computer Vision and Pattern Recognition, CVPR 2010, San Francisco, CA, USA, 13-18 June 2010*, pages 3360–3367, 2010.

[25] J. Wright, A. Y. Yang, A. Ganesh, S. S. Sastry, and Y. Ma. Robust face recognition via sparse representation. *IEEE Trans. Pattern Anal. Mach. Intell.*, 31(2):210–227, 2009.

[26] M. Yang, D. Dai, L. Shen, and L. Van Gool. Latent dictionary learning for sparse representation based classification. In *Computer Vision and Pattern Recognition (CVPR), 2014 IEEE Conference on*, pages 4138–4145, June 2014.

[27] M. Yang, D. Zhang, X. Feng, and D. Zhang. Fisher discrimination dictionary learning for sparse representation. In *Computer Vision (ICCV), 2011 IEEE International Conference on*, pages 543–550, Nov 2011.

[28] Q. Zhang and B. Li. Discriminative k-svd for dictionary learning in face recognition. pages 2691–2698, June 2010.

From Seed Discovery to Deep Reconstruction: Predicting Saliency in Crowd via Deep Networks

Yanhao Zhang[1],Lei Qin[2],Qingming Huang[1,2],Kuiyuan Yang[3],Jun Zhang[4],Hongxun Yao[1]
[1]Harbin Institute of Technology, Harbin, China
[2]Key Lab of Intell. Info. Process., Inst. of Comput. Tech., CAS, China
[3]Microsoft Research Asia, Beijing, China, [4]Hefei University of Technology, Hefei, China
{yhzhang,h.yao}@hit.edu.cn,kuyang@microsoft.com,{lqin, qmhuang}@jdl.ac.cn

ABSTRACT

Although saliency prediction in crowd has been recently recognized as an essential task for video analysis, it is not comprehensively explored yet. The challenges lie in that eye fixations in crowded scenes are inherently "distinct" and "multi-modal", which differs from those in regular scenes. To this end, the existing saliency prediction schemes typically rely on hand designed features with shallow learning paradigm, which neglect the underlying characteristics of crowded scenes. In this paper, we propose a saliency prediction model dedicated for crowd videos with two novelties: 1) Distinct units are discovered using deep representation learned by a Stacked Denoising Auto-Encoder (SDAE), considering perceptual properties of crowd saliency; 2) Contrast-based saliency is measured through deep reconstruction errors in the second SDAE trained on all units excluding distinct units. A unified model is integrated for online processing crowd saliency. Extensive evaluations on two crowd video benchmark datasets demonstrate that our approach can effectively explore crowd saliency mechanism in two-stage SDAEs and achieve significantly better results than state-of-the-art methods, with robustness to parameters.

Keywords

Crowd Saliency; Deep AutoEncoders; Reconstruction Errors

1. INTRODUCTION

Crowd saliency essentially targets at identifying the potential regions in crowded scenes that most attract visual attention. Crowded scenes are prevalent in surveillance videos [20, 27, 28, 29], which are however more risky especially in salient regions [18, 3]. It is therefore emerging to design crowd saliency model for video surveillance.

The straightforward solutions directly apply conventional saliency approaches, which focus on detecting saliency regions in regular scenes. In principle, it is assumed that saliency regions can stand out from their neighbors with high contrast, which serves as the basis for various saliency detection models proposed in the image and video domain [8, 5, 1, 21, 2]. Recent advances in saliency detection mainly focus on detecting salient objects via bottom-up measurements, such as rareness [26, 19] and contrast variants [25, 11]. Besides, it is also shown that the context-dependent, top-down mechanisms incorporated with object/background prior are comparably accurate and effective [13]. Nevertheless, these approaches are inappropriate for saliency prediction in crowded scenes as they are with different underlying characteristics. As revealed by the psychological evidence on crowds [24], two important perceptual cues should be highlighted in crowd saliency: The "seed", i.e., an individual or small group attempting to engage with the crowd; The crowd engages with a seed to occur its flow motion. Hence, the salient crowd motion typically appears from the crowd seed where the crowd modifies the existing states to influent its neighbors. This inspires us to model the crowd seeds that are *distinct* to separate the common patterns from the crowds, as well as propagate the influence in *multi-modal* context. To this end, it is nontrivial to design handcraft features to differentiate the salient regions. Thus, we resort to learning such features via deep networks that encodes the hierarchical mechanisms underlying crowd saliency.

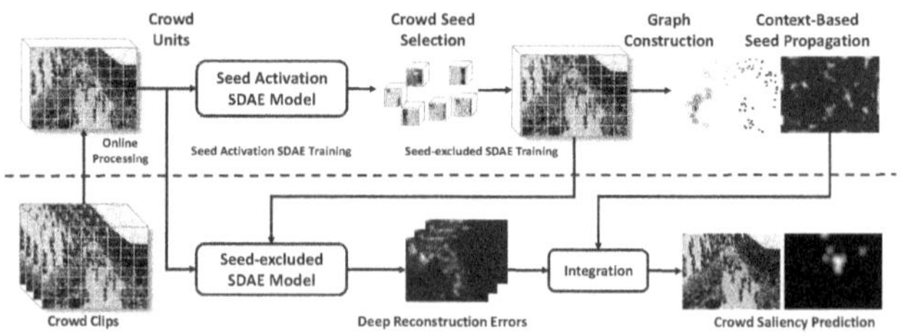

Figure 1: Overview of the framework for crowd saliency prediction based on deep networks.

Following this intuition, in this work, we propose a unified framework for crowd saliency prediction as shown in Figure 1. Firstly, we select crowd seeds from crowd units with a seed activation Stacked Denoising Auto-Encoder (SDAE). We further calculate deep reconstruction errors using a seed-excluded SDAE, which measure global contrast between the salient patterns and common patterns. Crowd seeds are subsequently leveraged to learn the propagation errors in a ranking function. The score of crowd saliency is finally refined by context-based seed propagation. The main contributions of this work are summarized as following three aspects: **(1)** We explore the characteristics of crowd units by training a seed activation SDAE, which introduces

MM '16, October 15-19, 2016, Amsterdam, Netherlands

 ISBN 978-1-4503-3603-1/16/10...$15.00
DOI: http://dx.doi.org/10.1145/2964284.2967185

activation metrics of deep representation to discover crowd seeds. **(2)** We make use of the reconstruction error by training a seed-excluded SDAE, which effectively measures the contrast-based saliency in crowds. **(3)** A unified model is assembled to predict crowd saliency, and verified on two crowd video datasets with significant performance gains.

2. CROWD SALIENCY DEEP NETWORKS

In this section, we present the proposed model for crowd saliency prediction in details.

2.1 Stacked Denoising Auto-Encoders (SDAE)

SDAE essentially builds a deep architecture by stacking multiple layers of Denoising Auto-Encoders (DAE) [22]. DAE basically consists of two components, i.e., encoder and decoder [22]. Both components attempt to learn two mapping functions, termed as $\mathbf{h}(\mathbf{W},\mathbf{b})$ and $\mathbf{g}(\hat{\mathbf{W}},\hat{\mathbf{b}})$, where $\mathbf{W}$, $\mathbf{b}$ denote the weights and bias parameters of the encoder and $\hat{\mathbf{W}}$, $\hat{\mathbf{b}}$ correspond to the terms of decoder. Before encoding, $\tilde{\mathbf{x}}$ is a noise-corrupted version of the clean input data $\mathbf{x}$ by stochastic mapping $\tilde{\mathbf{x}} = \mathbf{D}(\tilde{\mathbf{x}}|\mathbf{x})$. For a corrupted input $\tilde{\mathbf{x}}_i$, the hidden layer representation $\mathbf{z}_i$ can be obtained through $\mathbf{z}_i = \mathbf{h}(\tilde{\mathbf{x}}_i|\mathbf{W},\mathbf{b}) = s(\mathbf{W}\tilde{\mathbf{x}}_i + \mathbf{b})$, where $s(.)$ is the sigmoid activation function. The decoder tries to map the hidden representation $\mathbf{z}_i$ back to input $\mathbf{x}_i$ by computing $\hat{\mathbf{x}}_i = \mathbf{g}(\mathbf{z}_i|\hat{\mathbf{W}},\hat{\mathbf{b}}) = s(\hat{\mathbf{W}}\mathbf{z}_i + \hat{\mathbf{b}})$. Given the training set $\mathcal{C} = \{\mathbf{x}_i\}_{i=1}^N$, the parameters $\mathbf{W},\mathbf{b},\hat{\mathbf{W}},\hat{\mathbf{b}}$ can be optimized as a regularized least square optimization problem, i.e.,

$$\min_{\mathbf{W},\mathbf{b},\hat{\mathbf{W}},\hat{\mathbf{b}}} \sum_{i=1}^{N} ||\hat{\mathbf{x}}_i - \mathbf{x}_i||_2^2 + \gamma(||\mathbf{W}||_F^2 + ||\hat{\mathbf{W}}||_F^2), \quad (1)$$

where γ balances the reconstruction error and regularization. The non-linearity of activation function allows SDAE to learn complex mapping and capture the latent patterns that reflect the correlation shared among training data.

2.2 Two-stage SDAEs based Deep Structure

Our goal is to assign a saliency value $\text{Sal}(\mathbf{x}_i,\mathcal{C}) \in [0,1]$ to each crowd unit $\mathbf{x}_i$ which best fits the given crowd unit set $\mathcal{C} = \{\mathbf{x}_i\}_{i=1}^N$ in a time window t. Let $\mathcal{C}_s$ denote the set containing distinct crowd units as "crowd seeds". $\mathcal{C}_r = \mathcal{C}\backslash\mathcal{C}_s$ denotes the rest. The selection of crowd seeds will separate the distinct units from the common units. The contrast-based saliency are measured by deep reconstruction error between a given crowd unit $\mathbf{x}_i$ and the common units $\mathcal{C}_r$.

A two-stage SDAE model is presented to achieve this goal as shown in Figure 1, which contains two phases, i.e.,

- To distinguish crowd seeds, we design deep representation based metrics using neuron activations of the first SDAE trained on all crowd units.
- To calculate the global contrast, we leverage deep reconstruction errors of the second SDAE trained on crowd units without seed units.

Both of the SDAEs are with the same structure, including one input layer and three hidden layers, as shown in Figure 2. Inspired by [23], an over-complete set of filters is used to better capture the image/video structure in the first hidden layer, followed by two equal-sized hidden layers. In the training phases, SDAEs are layer-wise trained by optimizing Eq. 1 using gradient descent, and then fine-tuned globally. Therefore, the contrast-based saliency can be indicated by the reconstruction cost of the seed-excluded SDAE.

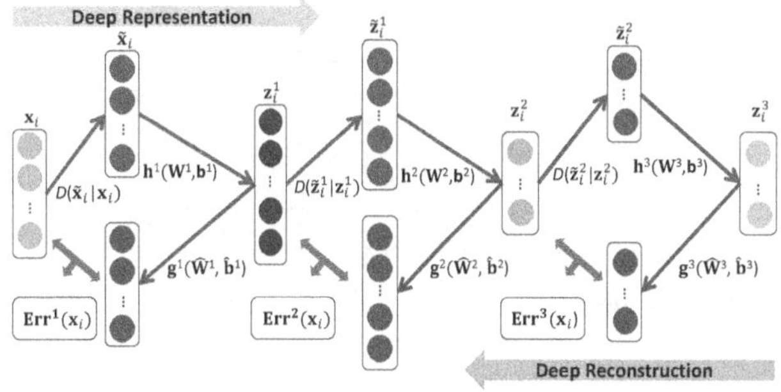

Figure 2: Schematic illustration of two-stage SDAE.

2.2.1 Seed Prediction via Deep Representation

The deep structured SDAE provides an effective means to characterize the crowd seed set $\mathcal{C}_s$, especially in virtue of its ability to learn latent patterns in an unsupervised manner.

Training Seed Activation SDAE: The first SDAE is trained on all crowd units $\mathcal{C}$ to select crowd seeds. The metrics of the output (hidden) representation should favor distinct crowd units as the seed set. In order to distinguish the crowd seeds $\mathcal{C}_s$, the units should be outstanding from the whole set $\mathcal{C}$ according to the activation value.

Crowd Firing Rate: In neural science, neuron's firing rate increases or decreases when certain patterns appear in receptive field [12]. The importance of input signal is reflected as how much energy the activity consumes. It is therefore reasonable to assume that the larger energy of crowd unit consumes, the more distinct it is. Accordingly, the crowd seed can be measured by energy consumption of all hidden units. Thus, we define Crowd Firing Rate (CFR) to describe the average activity of the j-th neuron in the last hidden layer:

$$\text{CFR}_j = \sum_{i=1}^{N} \mathcal{H}_j^3(\mathbf{x}_i)/N, \quad (2)$$

where $\mathcal{H}_j^3(\mathbf{x}_i)$ refers to the activation value of the j-th neuron of the last hidden layer $\mathbf{z}_i^3$ for the i-th input unit $\mathbf{x}_i$, N is the number of crowd units.

Seed Activation Rate: Next, we define Seed Activation Rate (SAR) to calculate how much energy will be consumed for a given crowd unit:

$$\text{SAR}_i = \sum_{j=1}^{r} ||\mathcal{H}_j^3(\mathbf{x}_i) - \text{CFR}_j||_2^2, \quad (3)$$

For each unit $\mathbf{x}_i$, SAR_i denotes the accumulation of energy cost according to CFR of all the neurons. We sort the SAR of all the units in a descending order and select the top n as crowd seeds $\mathcal{C}_s$. Given $\mathcal{C}_s$, we make a binary indicator as $\delta(\mathbf{x}_i) = 1, \text{if } \mathbf{x}_i \text{ is } s \in \mathcal{C}_s, \text{otherwise } \delta(\mathbf{x}_i) = 0$.

2.2.2 Contrast Inference via Deep Reconstruction

By hierarchically capturing latent patterns, SDAE helps to measure the contrast between the salient and the common units through deep reconstruction. We model the common crowd units with SDAE and indicate the contrast-based saliency of $\mathbf{x}_i$ with the deep reconstruction error.

Training Seed-excluded SDAE: We establish the second SDAE trained on $C_r = C\backslash C_s$ to model common crowd units. The principle is to measure the contrast via the differences between the input and the reconstructed patterns by SDAE. The deep reconstruction error is the cost that converts the input to hidden representations of common patterns through non-linear transformations. As in Figure 2, seed-excluded SDAE is comprised of 3 encoders and 3 decoders.

Methods	*AUC*	*SE*	*NSS*	*SE*	*CC*	*SE*
AWS [4]	0.790	0.0010	1.019	0.0057	0.343	0.0017
IS [8]	0.790	0.0010	0.999	0.0056	0.339	0.0017
SR [9]	0.788	0.0010	1.003	0.0058	0.340	0.0018
FT [1]	0.784	0.0009	1.018	0.0054	0.344	0.0016
GBVS [7]	0.791	0.0009	1.005	0.0051	0.341	0.0015
HBS [15]	0.794	0.0009	1.029	0.0055	0.346	0.0016
OB [15]	0.796	0.0009	1.039	0.0049	0.356	0.0014
Ours-NS	0.797	0.0011	1.042	0.0050	0.357	0.0017
Ours-NR	0.807	0.0011	1.052	0.0050	0.360	0.0017
Ours	**0.815**	0.0010	**1.064**	0.0048	**0.368**	0.0017

Table 1: Comparisons with image saliency methods on ASCMN-CROWD dataset.

Methods	*AUC*	*SE*	*NSS*	*SE*	*CC*	*SE*
RARE [19]	0.703	0.0060	1.253	0.0672	0.216	0.0098
SUN [26]	0.653	0.0089	1.160	0.0654	0.196	0.0109
SDSR [21]	0.673	0.0070	1.013	0.0734	0.166	0.0110
PQFT [6]	0.688	0.0065	1.234	0.0645	0.181	0.0089
CE [14]	0.638	0.0088	0.508	0.1228	0.125	0.0068
DC [30]	0.680	0.0025	0.721	0.0741	0.179	0.0035
SP [17]	0.739	0.0052	0.945	0.1787	0.238	0.0099
Ours-NS	0.772	0.0067	1.375	0.0890	0.271	0.0039
Ours-NR	0.782	0.0065	1.390	0.1120	0.302	0.0050
Ours	**0.785**	0.0022	**1.505**	0.1190	**0.306**	0.0037

Table 2: Comparisons with video saliency methods on ASCMN-CROWD dataset.

Deep Reconstruction Error: We calculate deep reconstruction error in Eq. 4 for $\mathbf{x}_i \in \mathcal{C}$ by seed-excluded SDAE, which globally reflects the contrast with the common crowd units. The reason is that common patterns are fitted better in the deeper layer, which is further verified in the experiment.

$$\mathrm{Err}^d(\mathbf{x}_i) = ||\mathbf{g}^3(\mathbf{h}^3(\mathbf{D}(\tilde{\mathbf{z}}_i^2|\mathbf{z}_i^2))) - \mathbf{z}_i^2||_2^2, \qquad (4)$$

The errors $\mathrm{Err}^d(\mathbf{x}_i)$ captures the difference between the unit $\mathbf{x}_i$ and common patterns, which generally leads to promising results in contrast-based saliency detection.

Context-based Seed Propagation: Considering that crowd seeds strongly affect the neighborhood in crowd flow, we intend to purify the salient foreground by the propagation of the seeds. Therefore, crowd seeds are set as queries and processed sequentially by propagating the relevances in a ranking manifold as [16]. We establish the graph $G=(V,E)$ with all units encoded in the affinity, where V represents crowd units, E denotes the edge weighted by $\mathbf{W}=[W_{ij}]_{N\times N}$ with W_{ij} is the difference between crowd units. The degree matrix is $\mathbf{S} = \mathrm{diag}(\mathbf{s}_{11},\ldots,\mathbf{s}_{NN})$, where $\mathbf{s}_{ii} = \Sigma_j \mathbf{W}_{ij}$. This ranking function assigns a ranking value f_i as to each unit $\mathbf{x}_i$, and $\mathbf{f}$ can be viewed as a vector $\mathbf{f} = [f_i|_{i=1}^N]$. Let $\mathbf{y}=[\delta(\mathbf{x}_i)|_{i=1}^N]$ denote a binary vector indicating crowd seed queries. The normalized Laplacian matrix is denoted as $\tilde{\mathbf{L}} = \mathbf{S}^{-1/2}\mathbf{W}\mathbf{S}^{-1/2}$. We get the close form solution as $\mathbf{f} = (\mathbf{I}-\alpha\tilde{\mathbf{L}})^{-1}\mathbf{y}$, where $\mathbf{I}$ is an identity matrix, $\alpha = 1/(1+\mu)$. For all queries indicated by $\mathbf{y}$, the rank score f_i gives the propagation errors of the seeds.

2.3 Online Processing Crowd Saliency

When crowd unit set $\mathcal{C}$ arrives, we first train the two SDAEs based on $\mathcal{C}$ and $\mathcal{C}_r$. We make a simple forward pass on $\mathbf{x}_i \in \mathcal{C}$ through seed-excluded SDAE to get the deep reconstruction error. The saliency score $\mathrm{Sal}(\mathbf{x}_i,\mathcal{C})$ is then determined based on Eq. 5 by integrating the refined propagation error and center bias [8] as,

$$\mathrm{Sal}(\mathbf{x}_i,\mathcal{C}) = (\mathrm{Err}^d(\mathbf{x}_i)+f_i)\cdot \exp\left\{-||\mathrm{Ctr}-\mathrm{Pos}(\mathbf{x}_i)||^2\right\} \quad (5)$$

where $\mathrm{Pos}(\mathbf{x}_i)$ defines the coordinates of the unit, Ctr is the center of the frame. We assign the saliency score to corresponding $\mathrm{Pos}(\mathbf{x}_i)$ in the frame to generate the saliency map with Gaussian smoothing for robustness.

3. EXPERIMENTS

We evaluate our method on two dynamic video datasets, i.e., ASCMN-CROWD dataset [20] and CRCNS-CROWD dataset [10]. We present results of applying our model in yielding saliency maps for predicting eye fixations in crowds.

Parameter Settings. For input videos, each frame is resized to 120×160 and uniformly partitioned into non-overlapping spatio-temporal cubes of size $5\times5\times5$. We compute 3D gradient of the cube as raw motion signals and 2-dim coordinates of the cube center to describe each cube as a *crowd unit.* Two SDAEs are both fixed as 3 hidden layers with 250, 100 and 100 hidden nodes, respectively. For each time window t containing 5 frames, we select top $n = 20\%$ as $\mathcal{C}_s$ according to Eq. 3. We set $\gamma = 0.002$, $\alpha = 0.99$ and the mini-batch size to 10. The corruption size in DAE is set to 0.2. These parameters are empirically chosen and fixed through all the following experiments. Three metrics are used to quantify the performance of saliency models for predicting eye fixations [17], including AUC, NSS and CC with corresponding Standard Error (SE).

3.1 Evaluations on ASCMN-CROWD Dataset

In order to evaluate the performance on the eye fixation prediction in the crowded scenes, we conduct experiments on CROWD subset of ASCMN dataset [20] containing 14 videos in 3 categories that are crowd-specific: 5 videos for Abnormal Crowd (Abn-Crd), 4 for Surveillance Crowd (Sur-Crd), 5 for Crowd Activity (Act-Crd).

(1) Image saliency approaches. We compare our model with the widely compared methods and accomplish an objective comparison with original fixation data as groundtruth. Table 1 shows the AUC, NSS and CC with SE for different models. Note that the metrics of these compared models are obviously surpassed by our model, which is attributed to meaningful deep representation. Our model explores the high-level correlation of crowd units for modeling crowd saliency, which achieves better performance than others with improvements 0.02-0.08 in all metrics.

(2) Video saliency approaches. To further validate our model on capturing dynamic crowded scenes, we compare our approach to video saliency methods. In this case, the evaluation measures are designed to use fixation heat maps as the groundtruth. The average measures are reported in Table 2, which shows Ours is superior to other studied methods. There is a consistent improvement in the performance of all metrics. Overall, our approach outperforms the other models under all metrics, which indicates that semantics of crowd perception encoded in deep networks is beneficial in cluttered foreground.

Validation of Model Components. We further evaluate the effectiveness of our approach with respect to model components. From Table 1 and 2, we note that, 1) Without the seed prediction (Ours-NS), the AUC score slightly drops, illustrating the significance of distinct crowd seed. 2) Without reconstruction component (Ours-NR), also performs worse than ours, which indicates that the effectiveness of the reconstruction stage for the contrast measurement. Besides, crowd seeds are helpful to eliminate the distraction and enhance the salient regions in crowd context. 3) Exploring contrast (Ours) by fusing seed prediction and

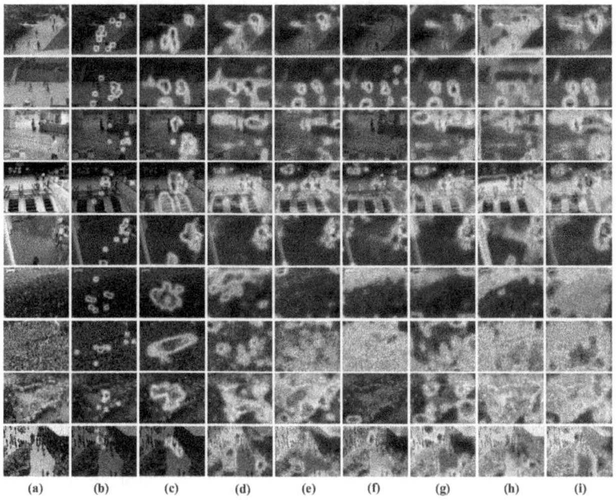

Figure 3: Visual comparisons of state-of-the-art saliency detection models. (a) Video frame, (b) Eye fixation, (c) Ours, (d) RARE, (e) PQFT, (f) SR, (g) AWS, (h) FT and (i) IS. Best viewed in color.

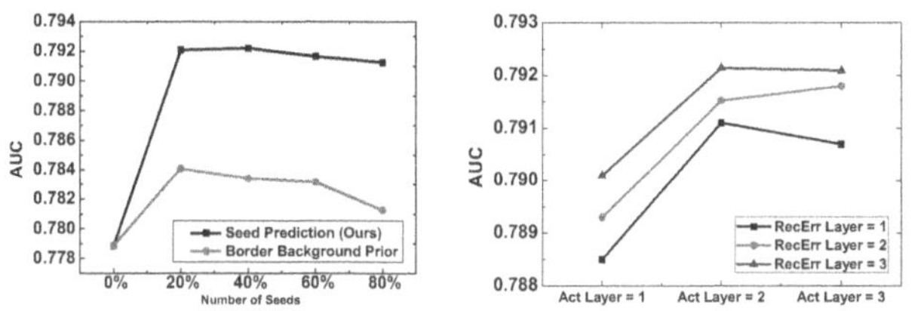

(a) (b)

Figure 4: (a) The effect of the number of seeds. (b) The effect of layers in SDAEs.

reconstruction yields the best results, demonstrating both components are complimentary to each other. Ours-NS and Ours-NR still outperform all existing methods show the advancement of the deep representation. Qualitative comparisons of the selected image and video saliency methods are shown in Figure 3. It is obvious that most approaches look like to be influenced significantly when the crowd is cluttered and similar appearances occupy the scenes. On the contrary, ours tends to be less distracted by the common foreground as well as the cluttered background, which still predicts desirable fixations in such crowded scenes.

Robustness to Parameters. Figure 4(a) shows how the main metric AUC score for Act-Crd Category is affected by the number of seeds ranging from 0% to 80%. We also compare with the alternative method with the seed selected from the border set using border background prior [13]. As we can see, AUC starts to increase dramatically and gradually decrease when the seed number is larger. It is not very sensitive within a range of values. It is superior to border background prior, indicating common patterns are falsely detected in border background set while ours not. Keeping seed number as 20%, we tune the layers of the two SDAEs (Figure 4(b)). Note that AUC generally increase with deeper layers of reconstruction (RecErr Layer) when crowd seeds are predicted from different activation layers (Act Layer = 1, 2, 3). Deeper activation and reconstruction layers help more to identify salient regions.

Methods	*AUC*	*SE*	*NSS*	*SE*	*CC*	*SE*
AWS [4]	0.596	0.0024	0.340	0.0386	0.028	0.0002
RARE [19]	0.727	0.0018	0.923	0.0554	0.078	0.0004
PQFT [6]	0.678	0.0082	0.772	0.1502	0.065	0.0011
IS [8]	0.710	0.0009	0.756	0.0157	0.062	0.0001
Ours	**0.844**	0.0036	**1.662**	0.0439	**0.141**	0.0005

Table 3: Comparisons of saliency models on crowd videos in CRCNS-CROWD dataset.

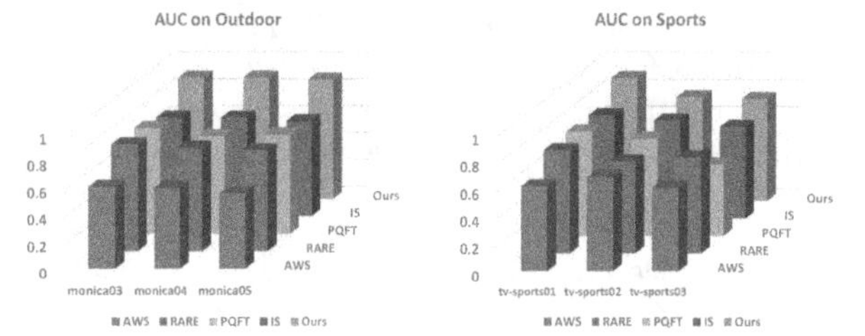

(a) (b)

Figure 5: AUC on (a) Outdoor, (b) Sports scenarios.

3.2 Evaluations on CRCNS-CROWD Dataset

We further evaluate our model on a more challenging CRCNS-CROWD dataset [10]. We select totally 10 crowd videos, including "Outdoor", "Sports" and "TV news", etc, which is provided together with eye traces of 8 subjects.

Together, we quantitatively compare our model with four saliency models that show superior performances on ASCMN-CROWD dataset, i.e., AWS, RARE, PQFT and IS. The AUC, NSS and CC values with SE on CRCNS-CROWD dataset are provided in Table 3. Consistent with the results on ASCMN-CROWD dataset, our model performs significant improvements compared with other models. To gain a deeper insight, AUC values for videos in "Outdoor" and 'Sports" are shown in Figure 5, suggesting our model's ability to adapt to diversified scenarios of crowds. Objective evaluation shows our model yields more correct and robust eye fixation prediction on various scenes. Our model tends to learn the scene-specific deep representation that is less distracted by the common crowd patterns than existing models. Moreover, it is capable of highlighting salient regions in crowd context through deep networks. The great improvement shows the scene adaptiveness and robustness of our model as well.

4. CONCLUSION

In this paper, we have proposed a deep-structured saliency model for predicting eye fixations in crowd videos, which benefits from the rich and discriminative properties of SDAE to discover crowd seeds and measure the contrast-based saliency. Our proposed model takes advantages of deep representation and reconstruction capability of deep networks, which simultaneously explores perceptual properties of both crowd and saliency. Comprehensive experiments are conducted on crowd videos of the publicly available benchmarks, which demonstrates superior results with comparisons to the state-of-the-art methods.

5. ACKNOWLEDGMENTS

This work was supported in part by National Basic Research Program of China (973 Program):2015CB351802 and 2012CB316400, in part by National Natural Science Foundation of China:61133003, 61332016, 61390510, 61572465. The authors also thank the suggestion and help from Rongrong Ji and Pengfei Xu.

6. REFERENCES

[1] R. Achanta, S. Hemami, F. Estrada, and S. Susstrunk. Frequency-tuned salient region detection. In *IEEE CVPR*, pages 1597–1604, 2009.

[2] D. Culibrk, M. Mirkovic, V. Zlokolica, M. Pokric, V. Crnojevic, and D. Kukolj. Salient motion features for video quality assessment. *IEEE TIP*, 20(4):948–958, 2011.

[3] J. K. Dutta and B. Banerjee. Online detection of abnormal events using incremental coding length. In *AAAI*, 2015.

[4] A. Garcia-Diaz, X. R. Fdez-Vidal, X. M. Pardo, and R. Dosil. Decorrelation and distinctiveness provide with human-like saliency. In *Advanced concepts for intelligent vision systems*, pages 343–354. Springer, 2009.

[5] S. Goferman, L. Zelnik-Manor, and A. Tal. Context-aware saliency detection. *IEEE TPAMI*, 34(10):1915–1926, 2012.

[6] C. Guo, Q. Ma, and L. Zhang. Spatio-temporal saliency detection using phase spectrum of quaternion fourier transform. In *IEEE CVPR*, pages 1–8, 2008.

[7] J. Harel, C. Koch, and P. Perona. Graph-based visual saliency. In *NIPS*, pages 545–552, 2006.

[8] X. Hou, J. Harel, and C. Koch. Image signature: Highlighting sparse salient regions. *IEEE TPAMI*, 34(1):194–201, 2012.

[9] X. Hou and L. Zhang. Saliency detection: A spectral residual approach. In *IEEE CVPR*, pages 1–8, 2007.

[10] L. Itti and P. Baldi. A principled approach to detecting surprising events in video. In *IEEE CVPR*, volume 1, pages 631–637, 2005.

[11] R. M. Jiang and D. Crookes. Visual saliency estimation through manifold learning. In *AAAI*, 2012.

[12] E. R. Kandel, J. H. Schwartz, T. M. Jessell, S. Mack, and J. Dodd. Principles of neural science. *McGraw-Hill.*, 50(6):823–839, 2000.

[13] X. Li, H. Lu, L. Zhang, X. Ruan, and M.-H. Yang. Saliency detection via dense and sparse reconstruction. In *IEEE ICCV*, pages 2976–2983, 2013.

[14] Y. Li, Y. Zhou, J. Yan, Z. Niu, and J. Yang. Visual saliency based on conditional entropy. In *ACCV 2009*, pages 246–257. Springer, 2010.

[15] M. Liang and X. Hu. Predicting eye fixations with higher-level visual features. *IEEE TIP*, 24(3):1178–1189, 2015.

[16] M. K. Lim, V. J. Kok, C. C. Loy, and C. S. Chan. Crowd saliency detection via global similarity structure. In *IEEE ICPR*, pages 3957–3962, 2014.

[17] Z. Liu, X. Zhang, S. Luo, and O. Le Meur. Superpixel-based spatiotemporal saliency detection. *IEEE TCSVT*, 24(9):1522–1540, 2014.

[18] C. C. Loy, T. Xiang, and S. Gong. Salient motion detection in crowded scenes. In *ISCCSP*, pages 1 – 4, 2012.

[19] M. Mancas, N. Riche, J. Leroy, and B. Gosselin. Abnormal motion selection in crowds using bottom-up saliency. In *IEEE ICIP*, pages 229–232, 2011.

[20] N. Riche, M. Mancas, D. Culibrk, V. Crnojevic, B. Gosselin, and T. Dutoit. Dynamic saliency models and human attention: a comparative study on videos. In *ACCV*, pages 586–598. Springer, 2012.

[21] H. J. Seo and P. Milanfar. Static and space-time visual saliency detection by self-resemblance. *Journal of vision*, 9(12):15, 2009.

[22] P. Vincent, H. Larochelle, I. Lajoie, Y. Bengio, and P.-A. Manzagol. Stacked denoising autoencoders: Learning useful representations in a deep network with a local denoising criterion. *JLMR*, 11:3371–3408, 2010.

[23] N. Wang and D.-Y. Yeung. Learning a deep compact image representation for visual tracking. In *NIPS*, pages 809–817, 2013.

[24] K. Zeitz, H. Tan, M. Grief, and C. Zeitz. Crowd behavior at mass gatherings: a literature review. *Prehospital and disaster medicine*, vol.24(1):pp.32, 2010.

[25] J. Zhang, M. Wang, J. Gao, Y. Wang, X. Zhang, and X. Wu. Saliency detection with a deeper investigation of light field. In *IJCAI*, 2015.

[26] L. Zhang, M. H. Tong, T. K. Marks, H. Shan, and G. W. Cottrell. Sun: A bayesian framework for saliency using natural statistics. *Journal of vision*, 8(7):32, 2008.

[27] Y. Zhang, L. Qin, R. Ji, H. Yao, and Q. Huang. Social attribute-aware force model: Exploiting richness of interaction for abnormal crowd detection. *IEEE TCSVT*, 25(7):1231–1245, 2015.

[28] Y. Zhang, L. Qin, S. Zhang, H. Yao, and Q. Huang. Formation period matters: Towards socially consistent group detection via dense subgraph seeking. In *ICMR*, 2015.

[29] Y. Zhang, L. Qin, S. Zhao, R. Ji, X. Lu, H. Yao, and Q. Huang. Crowd video retrieval via deep attribute-embedding graph ranking. In *ICME*, 2016.

[30] S.-h. Zhong, Y. Liu, F. Ren, J. Zhang, and T. Ren. Video saliency detection via dynamic consistent spatio-temporal attention modelling. In *AAAI*, 2013.

Facial Age Estimation Using Robust Label Distribution

Ke Chen and Joni-Kristian Kämäräinen
Department of Signal Processing
Tampere University of Technology
Tampere, Finland
firstname.lastname@tut.fi

Zhaoxiang Zhang
Institute of Automation
Chinese Academy of Sciences
Beijing, P.R. China

ABSTRACT

Facial age estimation, to predict the persons' exact ages given facial images, usually encounters the data sparsity problem due to the difficulties in data annotation. To mitigate the suffering from sparse data, a recent label distribution learning (LDL) algorithm attempts to embed label correlation into a classification based framework. However, the conventional label distribution learning framework only considers correlations across the neighbouring variables (ages), which omits the intrinsic complexity of age classes during different ageing periods (age groups). In the light of this, we introduce a novel concept of robust label distribution for scalar-valued labels, which is designed to encode the age scalars into label distribution matrices, i.e. two-dimensional Gaussian distributions along age classes and age groups respectively. Overcoming the limitations of conventional hard group boundaries in age grouping and capturing intrinsic inter-group dependency, our framework achieves robust and competitive performance over the conventional algorithms on two popular benchmarks for human age estimation.

Keywords

facial age estimation; hard group boundaries; robust label distribution learning (RLDL)

1. INTRODUCTION

Facial age estimation [5, 10, 11, 15, 22, 23, 28] is to predict persons' age given their facial images, which is a hot yet challenging topic in computer vision. This problem and other similar problems such as crowd counting [2, 5, 6, 7, 8] are aimed to learn a mapping function from imagery feature representation to scalar-valued targets. However, due to inherent ambiguities in age annotation, data sparsity problem is encountered with the lack of sufficient samples for covering the whole data distribution. For example, a large number of facial images can be readily found on the Internet, but reliable annotation of the exact age of images is usually lacking, which leads to sparsely distributed data [5] in the public benchmarks such as the FG-NET and MORPH datasets. Sparse data distribution can increase the difficulty in learning a robust mapping function, which thus leads to poor performance of the existing algorithms especially for those age classes without sufficient training data.

MM '16, October 15-19, 2016, Amsterdam, Netherlands
© 2016 ACM. ISBN 978-1-4503-3603-1/16/10...$15.00
DOI: http://dx.doi.org/10.1145/2964284.2967186

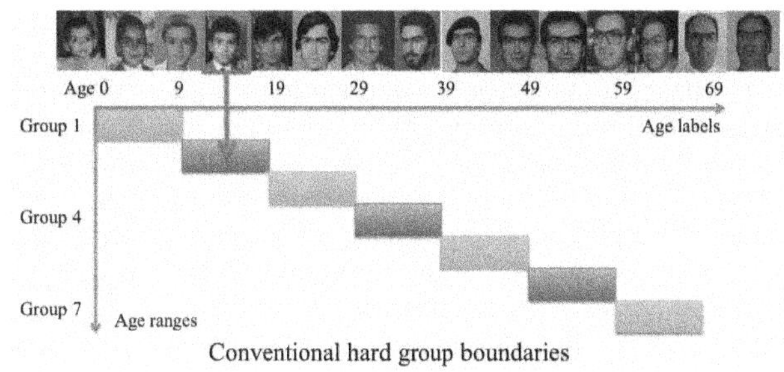

Figure 1: Conventional hard boundaries between age groups.

Human age estimation is usually formulated into a multi-class classification problem [16, 19] or a single-variate regression problem [5, 17, 18, 28]. Compared to classification based algorithms, regression frameworks are more favourable owing to the inherently cumulative and dependent characteristics of facial age estimation, i.e. the closer age labels of two facial images are, the more visual similarity they share. Recently, label distribution learning (LDL) was proposed by Geng *et al.* [14, 15] to represent each target scalar with a vector-formed label distribution which represents label correlation in classification frameworks in the fashion of multi-labels. Compared to 1-of-K target coding in the classic one-vs-all multi-class classification, label distribution vectors have positive values for neighbouring samples instead of zero, which can contribute to transferring the knowledge of neighbouring classes to those age classes without any training samples. For intuitive explanation, let us take one certain age (e.g. age 40) as an example, which can be learnt indirectly from the samples of neighbouring ages such as 39 and 41, even when age 40 has few or even no training samples, as element-wise difference of predicted and ground truth label distributions are designed to enforce to the minimal. In other words, the entry for age 40 class in label distribution can also be trained when training samples with the positive value on the element for age 40 class in LDL (e.g. 39 or 41). In the light of this, label distribution learning can mitigate the suffering from sparse data.

Assuming a fixed age label distribution, the conventional label distribution learning (LDL) framework [15] is limited by intrinsic complex relationship across age classes because of inconsistent ageing patterns as well as sensitiveness to personal identities and head poses. Adaptive label distribution learning [12] was proposed to model the inconsistent ageing patterns by iteratively updating dynamic label distribution for each age group, but it still adopted and thus suffered from hard boundaries between chronological age groups. We observe that facial images for age estimation have inter-group correlation during different ageing periods (age groups), which have not been exploited in label distribution learning. Specifically, inter-group correlation can be considered to reflect the *global* piecewise-like relationship of age labels in terms of localised chronological age groups corresponding to varying ageing periods. Moreover, conventional hard age group boundaries shown in Figure 1 were widely employed [12, 21, 22, 23], which relied heavily on the accuracy of age group classification. In other words, misclassification on coarse age groups can lead to significant performance reduction on the following fine age estimation. A naive solution [23] to improve the robustness led by age group misclassification is to employ the overlapping age ranges but such a strategy is data-specific sensitive to the size of the overlapped age ranges.

Motivated by the aforementioned observation, we introduce a novel concept of robust label distribution for single-variate scalar-valued problems, e.g. facial age estimation, which can simultaneously address both challenges in a unique framework. In the proposed framework, we attempt to jointly minimise the estimation errors along both age class and group distribution in order to improve the robustness of the conventional label distribution learning framework. Owing to the introduction of an additional group distribution dimension in our framework, both suffering of cross-group dependency and hard group boundaries are alleviated in addition to the capability to cope with data sparsity inherited from conventional LDL framework. Experiments on two popular age estimation benchmarks verify the effectiveness of our framework with superior performance over conventional algorithms.

2. RELATED WORK

The recent methods for estimating human age given facial images can be divided into three categories: classification based [16, 19], regression based [17, 18, 28], and ranking based [4, 24]. Facial age estimation was firstly formulated into a multi-class classification problem, but those classification based algorithms [16, 19] omitted the latent correlation across age labels, i.e. the closer age labels of facial images are, the more visually similar they are as well. Regression base frameworks [5, 17, 18, 28] are usually considered more suitable for age estimation owing to cumulative dependent nature of regression labels. Recently, a ranking based method, namely OHRank, was proposed [4] by utilising a series of ordinal hyperplane (i.e. binary classifiers) with all the data in the dataset in order to mitigate data sparsity problem, but it is extremely expensive to train such a model. Chen *et al.* [5] exploited the cumulative nature across age classes to achieve robust performance in a two-layer attribute learning framework. Geng *et al.* [15] designed a framework by learning from label distributions in the manner of multi-label learning. For each instance, a label distribution (e.g. Gaussian distribution) was first generated to give the degree that the neighbouring class labels describe the instance. Such a learning paradigm designed for data sparsity problem can improve the performance owing to the reduction of ambiguity in the label space by using multi-labels instead of a single label. However, learning with label distribution [15] (or termed, learning with soft labels) only considered increasing the global discrimination by incorporating consistent local label relations, which is not valid because of dynamic ageing procedure. An advanced attempt of label distribution learning with adaptively updating label distribution for each age group was introduced in [12], but hard group boundaries can still have a negative effect on performance. As a result, to capture complex relationship across ages, we propose a framework to learn with over-complete robust label distribution (RLD) for age estimation in the fashion of soft group boundaries to incorporate inter-dependency across groups and improve the robustness of age grouping. Our performance is superior to the conventional approaches on two public benchmarking datasets justifying the usage of robust label distributions.

3. METHODOLOGY

Given imagery feature representation $\boldsymbol{x}$ and its corresponding age label y, training samples consist of $\{\boldsymbol{x}_i, y_i\}^{i=1,2,\ldots,N}$, where N denotes the number of training samples. The pipeline of the proposed algorithm is given as follows:

- We first construct a two-dimensional robust label distribution $\boldsymbol{L}$ for each training sample according to its relative position y in a "chronological age map", which adopts different Gaussian distributions along age labels and groups (See Sec. 3.1).
- Learning the mapping between imagery feature representation $\boldsymbol{x}$ and a robust label distribution $\boldsymbol{L}$ is achieved by employing multivariate distribution learning in Sec. 3.2.

During testing, imagery features of an unseen image are fed into the trained model to estimate the person's age with the maximum predicted description degree along age classes in robust label distribution.

3.1 Robust Label Distribution

We first investigate the framework about one dimensional label distribution along age classes proposed by Geng *et al.* [15] to lay the basis for further discussion. Given a scalar-valued age label $y \in \mathbb{R}$, a label distribution vector $\boldsymbol{y} \in \mathbb{R}^K$ with the sum of description degree $d_{\boldsymbol{x}}$ (real values) of all the labels equal to one can be obtained, where K denotes the size of age range. The assumption of label distribution is two-fold: a) true labels have the highest description degree in $\boldsymbol{y}$; and b) the farther labels are away from true labels, the lower description degree they have. It is noted that non-zero description degree in a label distribution vector reflects ambiguity of feature-label relationship, which also indicates the importance of neighbouring labels contributing to the exact label y associated to instance $\boldsymbol{x}$. In this sense, even without sufficient training samples, label distribution learning can also achieve robust performance. Typical label distributions are Gaussian and triangle distributions [15], and Gaussian distribution can keep consistently superior performance to triangle distribution, which encourages us to employ Gaussian distribution in the experiments of this paper.

Aiming to incorporate inter-correlation across different ageing patterns and improve the robustness against hard age grouping, we propose an over-complete two-dimensional label distribution, namely robust label distribution, for a scalar-valued target. Conventional label distribution for human age estimation in [12, 15] is designed only along the chronological age dimension, but the proposed RLD extend an extra dimension along age groups. To construct a RLD $\boldsymbol{L} \in \mathbb{R}^{K\times D}$ for each instance $\boldsymbol{x}$ with D denoting the number of age groups, we first divide the whole age range into D subsets by their chronological ages via either manually-defined or clustering. Here we adopt manual definition as it is straightforward to define age groups $\mathcal{G} = \{G_1, G_2, \cdots, G_D\}$ (typically each $[-5, +5]$ interval forms a group). Consequently, the scalar label y have extended to a two-dimensional $\bar{\boldsymbol{y}}$ composed by its age label and group label. As mentioned before that Gaussian distribution is preferred in [15], we adopt a discretized bivariate Gaussian distribution [13] anchored at the extended label $\bar{\boldsymbol{y}}$ in RLD:

$$d_{\boldsymbol{x}}(\boldsymbol{z}) = \frac{1}{2\pi\sqrt{|\Sigma|}F}\exp(-\frac{1}{2}(\boldsymbol{z}-\bar{\boldsymbol{y}})^T\Sigma^{-1}(\boldsymbol{z}-\bar{\boldsymbol{y}})),$$

where the variable $\boldsymbol{z}$ is other labels in RLD besides $\bar{\boldsymbol{y}}$ and F is a normalisation factor to make the sum of $d_{\boldsymbol{x}}$ be one. Considering different characteristics of distribution along age classes and groups, we set the covariance matrix $\Sigma \in \mathbb{R}^{2\times 2}$ as a diagonal matrix with two finest granularity for age classes and groups respectively. Evidently, with the introduction of a group distribution in RLD, the following advantages are achieved: 1) utilise interdependency across age groups reflecting different ageing patterns with multi group labels instead of a single label; and 2) attempt to replace hard group boundaries with soft group distribution to improve robustness.

3.2 Learning with RLD

With the generated RLD for each image, the training set becomes $\{\boldsymbol{x}, \boldsymbol{L}\}_i, i = 1, 2, \cdots, N$. Element $\boldsymbol{L}_{jk}, j = 1, 2, \cdots, K, k = 1, 2, \cdots, D$ of $\boldsymbol{L} \in \mathbb{R}^{K\times D}$ consists of jth age class label and kth group label. The aim is to learn a conditional density function $p(\bar{\boldsymbol{y}}|\boldsymbol{x};\boldsymbol{\theta})$ to minimise the distance between the predicted $\hat{\boldsymbol{L}}$ generated by $\boldsymbol{\theta}$ and the ground truth $\boldsymbol{L}$, where $\boldsymbol{\theta}$ is the parameter vector to be optimised. It is evident that the learning with robust label distribution becomes a multi-variate distribution learning problem, which has been well presented in [13].

The object function for robust label distribution learning can be written as:

$$\min_{\theta} \quad \sum_i P(\boldsymbol{L}_i||p(\bar{\boldsymbol{y}}_i|\boldsymbol{x}_i;\boldsymbol{\theta})), \tag{1}$$

where weighted Jeffrey's divergence $P(\boldsymbol{L}_a||\boldsymbol{L}_b)$ is to measure the similarity between two distributions $\boldsymbol{L}_a$ and $\boldsymbol{L}_b$ with considering inter-element relationship, which can be formulated as the following:

$$P(\boldsymbol{L}_a||\boldsymbol{L}_b) = \sum_{w,h}\lambda_{w,h}(\boldsymbol{L}_a^w - \boldsymbol{L}_b^h)\ln\frac{\boldsymbol{L}_a^w}{\boldsymbol{L}_b^h}, \tag{2}$$

where $\boldsymbol{L}_a^w$ and $\boldsymbol{L}_b^h$ denote the wth and hth element in $\boldsymbol{L}_a$ and $\boldsymbol{L}_b$ respectively, and λ is used to weight the relationship across elements. Evidently λ is an important factor to model underlying correlation of neighbourhood among ages. In this paper, we adopt the same λ setting in [13] to reflect localised correlation of the nine neighbouring points in robust label distribution space as

$$\lambda_{jkmn} = \frac{1}{F}\exp(\frac{\|\bar{\boldsymbol{y}}_{jk} - \bar{\boldsymbol{y}}_{mn}\|^2}{-\delta}), \tag{3}$$

where F is normalised term, $\bar{\boldsymbol{y}}_{jk}$ and $\bar{\boldsymbol{y}}_{mn}$ are jkth corresponding label in the ground truth RLD $\boldsymbol{L}$ and mnth label in the predicted RLD $p(\bar{\boldsymbol{y}}_i|\boldsymbol{x}_i;\boldsymbol{\theta})$ respectively. δ is a parameter to adjust influence of the distance between $\bar{\boldsymbol{y}}_{jk}$ and $\bar{\boldsymbol{y}}_{mn}$.

Let us assume a maximum entropy model [1] as

$$p(\bar{\boldsymbol{y}}_{mn}|\boldsymbol{x}_i;\boldsymbol{\theta}) = \frac{\exp(\sum_r \boldsymbol{\theta}_{mn,r}\boldsymbol{x}_i^r)}{\sum_{m,n}\exp(\sum_r \boldsymbol{\theta}_{mn,r}\boldsymbol{x}_i^r)}, \tag{4}$$

where $\boldsymbol{x}_i^r$ denotes the rth entry of feature $\boldsymbol{x}_i$ and $\boldsymbol{\theta}_{mn,r}$ is the element of $\boldsymbol{\theta}$ associated to the label $\bar{\boldsymbol{y}}_{mn}$ and rth feature element. Substituting Equations (2) and (4) into (1) reformulates the object function as

$$\begin{aligned}\min_{\theta} \quad & \sum_i \ln(\sum_{m,n}\exp(\sum_r \boldsymbol{\theta}_{mn,r}\boldsymbol{x}_i^r)) + \\ & \sum_{i,j,k,m,n}\lambda_{jkmn}[\frac{\exp(\sum_r \boldsymbol{\theta}_{mn,r}\boldsymbol{x}_i^r)}{\sum_{m,n}\exp(\sum_r \boldsymbol{\theta}_{mn,r}\boldsymbol{x}_i^r)}\times \\ & (\sum_r \boldsymbol{\theta}_{mn,r}\boldsymbol{x}_i^r - \ln(\sum_{m,n}\exp(\sum_r \boldsymbol{\theta}_{mn,r}\boldsymbol{x}_i^r)) - \\ & \ln d_{\boldsymbol{x}_i}(\bar{\boldsymbol{y}}_{jk})) - d_{\boldsymbol{x}_i}(\bar{\boldsymbol{y}}_{jk})\sum_r \boldsymbol{\theta}_{mn,r}\boldsymbol{x}_i^r],\end{aligned}$$

which can be solved by using limited-memory quasi-Newton method L-BFGS introduced in [20]. The advantages of L-BFGS is to avoid the expensive Hessian matrix inversion but iteratively approximate its inverse.

4. EXPERIMENTS

Datasets and Settings – For evaluating the proposed framework, two public benchmarks, FG-NET [4, 5, 16, 17, 28] and MORPH [4, 5, 16], were used. Specifically, the FG-NET dataset contains 82 persons varying from age 0 to age 69 with 1002 images in total, while the MORPH dataset covers the range of age 16 to age 77 with 5475 images[1]. Active Appearance Model (AAM) feature [9] is adopted as low-level imagery features because of its popularity in the recent works [4, 5, 16, 17, 26, 27, 28]. We followed the same leave-one-person-out setting as in [4, 5, 17, 26, 27, 28] for FG-NET, while the MORPH dataset was randomly split into 80% data for training and the remaining 20% for testing and we repeated the experiments 30 times as in [4, 5]. We employed two evaluation metrics, namely *Mean Absolute Error* (MAE) and *Cumulative Score* (CS) with the error level 5 as in [4, 5, 16].

Comparison to State-of-the-Art – Comparative results on two benchmarks are given in Table 1. Among those algorithms, RUN [27], Ranking [26], LARR [17], LSLR [25], SVR [17], CA-SVR [5] are regression based and RED-SVM [3] and OHRank [4] are ranking based, while the rest are classification based. All comparative evaluation are using the identical AAM features except AGES [16]. Evidently, our robust label distribution learning can consistently achieve the best performance over state-of-the-arts especially label distribution learning based frameworks including IIS-LLD, CPNN,

[1]The size of MORPH has increased to 55,608 images (MORPH-II), but we use the original MORPH dataset for fair comparison with the existing algorithms [3, 4, 5, 16, 17, 28].

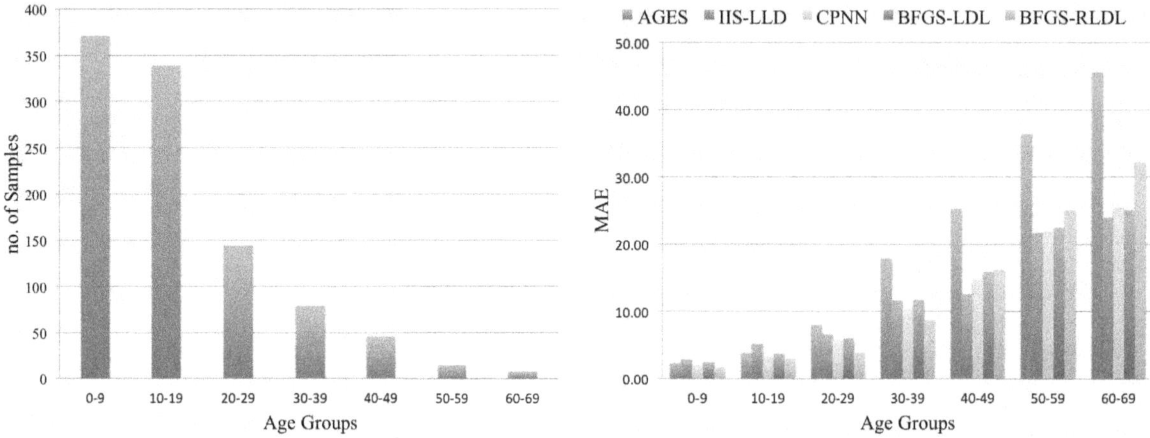

Figure 2: Data distribution (left plot) and comparative performance (right plot) on the FG-NET benchmark of the proposed BFGS-RLDL with AGES [16], IIS-LLD [14], CPNN [15], and BFGS-LDL [11] in different age range.

Table 1: Age estimation performance comparison.

Methods	FG-NET [16]		MORPH [4]	
	MAE	CS	MAE	CS
AGES [16]	6.77	–	8.83	–
RUN [27]	5.78	–	–	–
Ranking [26]	5.33	–	–	–
RED-SVM [3]	5.24	–	6.49	–
LARR [17]	5.07	–	–	–
MTWGP [28]	4.83	–	6.28	–
LSLR [25]	5.25	–	–	–
OHRank [4]	4.85	74.4%	**5.69**	56.3%
SVR [17]	5.66	68.0%	5.77	57.1%
CA-SVR [5]	4.67	74.5%	5.88	57.9%
IIS-LLD [14]	5.77	–	–	–
CPNN [15]	4.76	–	–	–
BFGS-LDL [11]	5.23	69.4%	5.94	56.5%
BFGS-RLDL	**4.27**	**76.2%**	**5.69**	**59.2%**

and BFGS-LDL on both benchmarks. The most direct effect of using robust label distribution can be observed by comparing between BFGS-LDL [11] and BFGS-RLDL, while BFGS-RLDL significantly beat BFGS-LDL. Since using the identical low-level AAM features and using the same optimisation algorithm BFGS, the performance improvement can only be explained by superior robust label distribution proposed in this paper.

Evaluation on Different Age Ranges – We visualise the data distribution and also comparative performance of a number of algorithms on the FG-NET benchmark in Figure 2. It can be observed that, compared to LDL based algorithms (IIS-LLD [14], CPNN [15], and BFGS-LDL [11]), the proposed RLDL can reduce errors when the size of training samples for a specific group is sufficient and yet achieve comparable performance for sparse data. The explanation for such a phenomenon is that soft group distribution for sparse data can be different from the dense data. With imbalanced data, our model is enforced to drift to the young ages during optimisation for the lower mean error over all samples. This observation inspired us to improve the design for age grouping to reflect the dynamic ageing patterns.

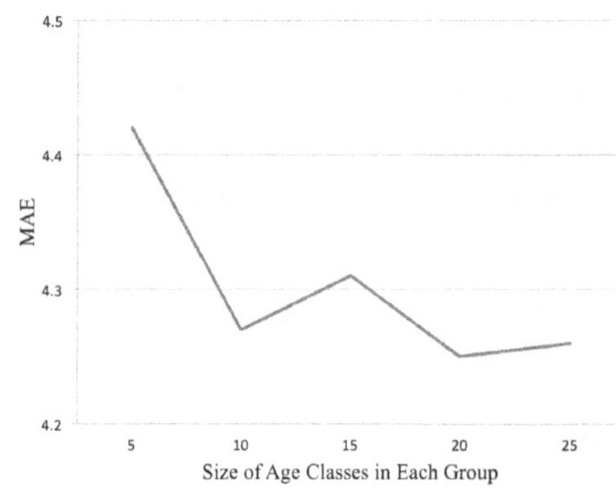

Figure 3: Effect with varying size of age classes in each group on the FG-NET dataset.

Effect with Varying Age Group Size – The size of age groups is an important parameter to decide the complexity of label distribution in view of the dimension of RLD linearly proportional to the size of age groups. Figure 3 illustrates the effect on the varying age group size. Figure 3 shows that the size of age groups plays an important role on the success of the algorithm. However, even the worst results of RLDL in Figure 3 are still superior to the existing algorithms, which further demonstrates its effectiveness.

5. CONCLUSIONS

This paper proposes a novel over-complete label distribution learning framework for visual regression. For facial age estimation our framework achieves superior accuracy as compared to conventional methods with hard age class and group boundaries. In our future work, unsupervised construction of the label distribution and more advanced design on incorporating group information into label distribution will be investigated.

6. ACKNOWLEDGMENTS

This work was funded by the Academy of Finland under Grant No. 267581.

7. REFERENCES

[1] A. L. Berger, V. J. D. Pietra, and S. A. D. Pietra. A maximum entropy approach to natural language processing. *Computational linguistics*, 1996.

[2] A. B. Chan and N. Vasconcelos. Counting people with low-level features and bayesian regression. *TIP*, 2012.

[3] K.-Y. Chang, C.-S. Chen, and Y.-P. Hung. A ranking approach for human ages estimation based on face images. In *ICPR*, 2010.

[4] K.-Y. Chang, C.-S. Chen, and Y.-P. Hung. Ordinal hyperplanes ranker with cost sensitivities for age estimation. In *CVPR*, 2011.

[5] K. Chen, S. Gong, T. Xiang, and C. C. Loy. Cumulative attribute space for age and crowd density estimation. In *CVPR*, 2013.

[6] K. Chen and J.-K. Kämäräinen. Learning to count with back-propagated information. In *ICPR*, 2014.

[7] K. Chen and J.-K. Kämäräinen. Pedestrian density analysis in public scenes with spatio-temporal tensor features. *TITS*, 2016.

[8] K. Chen, C. C. Loy, S. Gong, and T. Xiang. Feature mining for localised crowd counting. In *BMVC*, 2012.

[9] T. F. Cootes, G. J. Edwards, and C. J. Taylor. Active appearance models. *TPAMI*, 2001.

[10] Y. Fu, G. Guo, and T. S. Huang. Age synthesis and estimation via faces: a survey. *TPAMI*, 2010.

[11] X. Geng and R. Ji. Label distribution learning. In *ICDMW*, 2013.

[12] X. Geng, Q. Wang, and Y. Xia. Facial age estimation by adaptive label distribution learning. In *ICPR*, 2014.

[13] X. Geng and Y. Xia. Head pose estimation based on multivariate label distribution. In *CVPR*, 2014.

[14] X. Geng, C. Yin, and Z.-H. Zhou. Facial age estimation by learning from label distributions. In *AAAI*, 2010.

[15] X. Geng, C. Yin, and Z.-H. Zhou. Facial age estimation by learning from label distributions. *TPAMI*, 2014.

[16] X. Geng, Z.-H. Zhou, and K. Smith-Miles. Automatic age estimation based on facial aging patterns. *TPAMI*, 2007.

[17] G. Guo, Y. Fu, T. S. Huang, and C. R. Dyer. Image-based human age estimation by manifold learning and locally adjusted robust regression. *TIP*, 2008.

[18] G. Guo, G. Mu, Y. Fu, and T. S. Huang. Human age estimation using bio-inspired features. In *CVPR*, 2009.

[19] A. Lanitis, C. Draganova, and C. Christodoulou. Comparing different classifiers for automatic age estimation. *TSMC*, 2004.

[20] D. C. Liu and J. Nocedal. On the limited memory BFGS method for large scale optimization. *Mathematical programming*, 1989.

[21] K.-H. Liu, S. Yan, and C.-C. J. Kuo. Age estimation via grouping and decision fusion. *TIFS*, 2015.

[22] K. Luu, K. Ricanek Jr, T. D. Bui, and C. Y. Suen. Age estimation using Active Appearance Models and support vector machine regression. In *BTAS*, 2009.

[23] J. K. Pontes, A. S. Britto, C. Fookes, and A. L. Koerich. A flexible hierarchical approach for facial age estimation based on multiple features. *PR*, 2015.

[24] S. Wang, D. Tao, and J. Yang. Relative attribute SVM+ learning for age estimation. *TC*, 2015.

[25] C. Yan, C. Lang, and S. Feng. Facial age estimation based on structured low-rank representation. In *ACM MM*, 2015.

[26] S. Yan, H. Wang, T. S. Huang, Q. Yang, and X. Tang. Ranking with uncertain labels. In *ICME*, 2007.

[27] S. Yan, H. Wang, X. Tang, and T. S. Huang. Learning auto-structured regressor from uncertain nonnegative labels. In *ICCV*, 2007.

[28] Y. Zhang and D. Yeung. Multi-tasks warped Gaussian process for personalized age estimation. In *CVPR*, 2010.

What Makes a Good Movie Trailer? Interpretation from Simultaneous EEG and Eyetracker Recording

Sidi Liu[1]*, Jinglei Lv[1]*, Yimin Hou[2], Ting Shoemaker[1], Qinglin Dong[1], Kaiming Li[3], Tianming Liu[1].

[1]Cortical Architecture Imaging and Discovery Lab, Department of Computer Science and Bioimaging Research Center, The University of Georgia, GA, USA; [2]School of Automation Engineering, Northeast Dianli University, Jilin, China; [3]Huaxi MR Research Center, West China Hospital of Sichuan Univerity, Chengdu, China.

*Co-first Author.

{chrisliu8709, lvjinglei}@gmail.com, ymh7821@163.com, {workspacext, lynnqd2000, likaiming, tianming.liu}@gmail.com.

ABSTRACT
What makes a good movie trailer? It's a big challenge to answer this question because of the complexity of multimedia in both low level sensory features and high level semantic features. However, human perception and reactivity could be straightforward evidence for evaluation. Modern Electro-encephalography (EEG) technology provides measurement of consequential brain neural activity to external stimuli. Meanwhile, visual perception and attention could be captured and interpreted by Eye Tracking technology. Intuitively, simultaneous EEG and Eye Tracker recording of human audience with multimedia stimuli could bridge the gap between human comprehension and multimedia analysis, and provide a new way for movie trailer evaluation. In this paper, we propose a novel platform to simultaneously record EEG and eye movement for participants with video stimuli by integrating 256-channel EEG, Eye Tracker and video display device as a system. Based on the proposed system a novel experiment has been designed, in which independent and joint features of EEG and Eye tracking data were mined to evaluate the movie trailer. Our analysis has shown interesting features that are corresponding with trailer quality and video shoot changes.

Keywords
Electroencephalography; Eye-Tracker; Multimedia evaluation.

1. INTRODUCTION
In both the industry and academic fields, how to effectively and evaluate the quality of movie trailers is a challenge because of the rich information conveyed by videos and the complex low level perception features and high level semantic features of multimedia. Intuitively, human perception and reactivity under multimedia stimuli could be straightforward evidence and reference for multimedia analysis and evaluation. Recently, with the development of neuroimaging technology such as Electroencephalography(EEG) and fMRI, research studies have been devoted to bridge multimedia analysis with human neuroscience [1]. EEG is a well-established technology to record the electrical activity from the human brain by arranging electrodes on the scalp surface [2]. It reflects the neural activity of the brain at rest status or with stimuli. On the other hand, Eye Tracking is another important technology used in scientific study of human perception and vision. By recording human eye movement and position, eye tracker provides accurate and quantitative physiological information to study visual and attentional processes [5]. Continuous collaborative efforts have been made to decipher the neural semantics of multimedia comprehension with EEG [3, 4, 8], and a variety of works have also been reported about computer vision and multimedia research with eye tracking [6, 7,]. However, simultaneous EEG and eye tracking recording and joint analysis has been rarely explored for multimedia research.

In our opinion, human perception and brain reactivity are both important information sources for multimedia analysis, and merging EEG and Eye tracking data could potentially offer new clues for multimedia analysis. Bridging neural activity and visual perception with multimedia interpretation entails a new platform of hardware system and methods of joint analysis. Facing with this challenge, in this paper we designed a platform to simultaneously record EEG and eye movement data of participants with multimedia stimuli by integrating the 256-channel EGI EEG system and Tobii Eye Tracker device with a video display system. Further, an innovative method has been proposed to combine EEG and eye tracking data for analysis of the content of multimedia. An experiment has been designed for movie trailer evaluation. Participants are required to watch pre-scored and categorized movie trailers. Joint analysis of EEG and Eye tracking data could find features that are correlated with trailer quality and interesting features could also be found for video shot changes.

2. SYSTEM DESIGN
In the present study, we use the 256 channel EGI EEG system and Tobii Eye Tracker for neural electrical signal and eye movement recording, respectively. In order to integrate them into a platform, a double computer system is designed: one control computer running Eye Tracker software and displaying multimedia stimuli, and the other computer running EEG recording. The framework of the system is shown in Fig. 1. The Eye Tracker is connected to the control computer via Ethernet (by using the USB-Ethernet adapter provided by Tobii).

MM'16, October 15–19, 2016, Amsterdam, The Netherlands.

DOI: http://dx.doi.org/10.1145/2964284.2967187

Additionally, the EEG computer and the control computer are connected via USB Serial port.

One key issue of the system is time stamp alignment of EEG and Eye Tracking data. We realized this by binary signal communication of two computers through serial port. At the beginning of each recording, the Eye Tracker is firstly calibrated. Then the control computer begins to record the eye movement data, and meanwhile it sends information about the onset of the stimulus to the EEG computer through USB. Receiving the signal, EEG computer starts to record EEG data at the same time. This procedure makes sure that we can obtain two different data recordings with identical event related information.

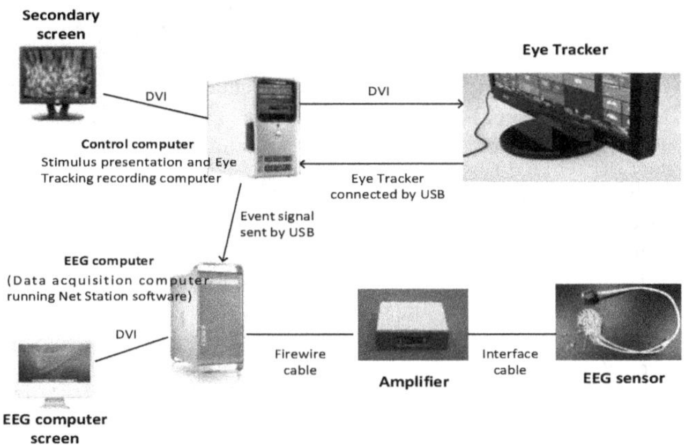

Fig. 1. Architecture of the system.

3. EXPERIMENTS AND METHODS

The experiment is conducted on 6 healthy volunteers of the University of Georgia. They were asked to wear the EEG caps and sit in a sound-attenuated room at 1.5 meter from the 17-inch monitor of the control computer with the eye tracker. Participants are required to watch 20 movie trailers in random order while their eye tracking and EEG data is recorded.

3.1 Video Stimulus

The 20 movie trailers, whose names are shown in Table.1, are downloaded from https://www.youtube.com with length between 2-3 minutes. All of the 20 trailers are selected from 725 trailers which are pre-evaluated by a group of professional researchers from the field of theatre and film studies and researchers from computer science at the University of Georgia. All the 725 trailers are categorized into two groups: 363 good movie trailers and 362 are bad ones. The categorization is based on the vote number of like or dislike of Youtube audiences and expert evaluation [9]. According to the research report in [9], the 20 movie trailers are selected from the 725 ones because that their low-level features, especially the mean values and variances of shot changing, are highly correlated with the audiences' evaluations. Thus, joint analysis of shot change features and eye tracking/EEG data is performed in this work.

3.2 EEG Data Processing and Analysis

EEG raw data often involves several kinds of artifacts, such as electrical noise, muscle activity, eye blinks, etc. To remove these artifacts, the raw data is first filtered with a 1 Hz high-pass filter and 80 Hz low-pass filter to eliminate electronic noise.

Table 1. 20 Movie Trailers presented to subjects.

No.	Movie Trailer Name (Bad)	Movie Trailer Name (Good)
1	Chairman of the Board	Watchman
2	The Double	Pirates of the Caribbean 3
3	Young Adult	TED
4	Zombie Nation	Seven Psychopaths
5	Sharknado	Hitchcock
6	Assault on Wall Street	The Bucket List
7	Cosmopolis	Jack the Giant Killer
8	The Wicked	Wrath of the Titans
9	The Room	Mud
10	Bounty Killer	Die Hard 5

Then a 60 Hz notch filter is applied to remove alternating current (AC) noise. We also use standard artifact detection and rejection procedures to remove channels containing jumps larger than 50μV/ms, segments with amplitude differences that exceeded 140μV/200ms, and segments with amplitude differences that did not exceed 0.5μV/200ms. The filtered data is then processed using Independent Component Analysis (ICA) to eliminate muscle activity and eye blinks. After the preprocessing of the above steps in our experiment, 76 reliable and common channel signals of all subjects are selected for joint analysis with eye tracking data and video features.

In the EEG signal analysis field, the dynamic interactions among channels are usually more explored. There are two major metrics about the interaction, which are Coherency and Synchronization Index (SI). Coherency measures synchronization in EEG signal which is defined as the squared absolute value of the cross-spectrum divided by the product of the power spectra of X and Y signals:

$$Coherence_{xy} = \frac{S_{XY}(f,t)^2}{S_{XX}S_{YY}} \tag{1}$$

Phase Synchronization Index (SI) measures the interaction of multiple frequency bands (Alpha, Beta, Theta, Gamma, Delta) of EEG signal. The SI of two signals X and Y is defined as:

$$r_{x,y}^2 = <\cos\phi_{x,y}(t)>^2 + <\sin\phi_{x,y}(t)>^2 \tag{2}$$

where ϕ denotes for Hilbert transform and the brackets denote the average over time. In our analysis, Coherency and SI are used to compare the functional interactions under good movie trailer stimulus and bad ones.

3.3 Joint Analysis of EEG and Eye Tracking

In this study, Eye Tracking data is collected as two dimensional screen coordinates with time stamps. The coordinates are collected at a rate of 40 Hz, while EEG signals have the sampling rate of 250 Hz, so that down-sampling of EEG data is necessary to joint analysis. In practice, we use the Kaiser Window resampling method implemented in MATLAB to realize the down-sampling.

One direct aim of joint analysis is to evaluate the relationship between EEG channels and eye movement data. Thus, measurements of signal synchrony act as key factors in our result analysis procedure. In order to achieve this goal, three measurements are used to investigate the temporal synchronization of the signal. One of the most widely used measurements of synchronization is the Pearson's correlation coefficient. It represents the linear dependence of two random variables, x and y. If each variable has N scalar observations, then the Pearson correlation coefficient is defined as:

$$r_{xy} = \frac{\sum_{i=1}^{N}(x_i - \bar{x})(y_i - \bar{y})}{N(\sigma_x)(\sigma_y)} \tag{3}$$

where $\bar{x}$ and σ_x are the mean and standard deviation of X, and $\bar{y}$ and σ_y are the mean and standard deviation of Y.

4. EXPERIMENT RESULTS

4.1 EEG Features

We selected 76 reliable and common EEG channels for all subjects using the noise elimination method described in section 3.2, and they are marked by red boxes in Fig. 2. The results in the following sections are based on these channels.

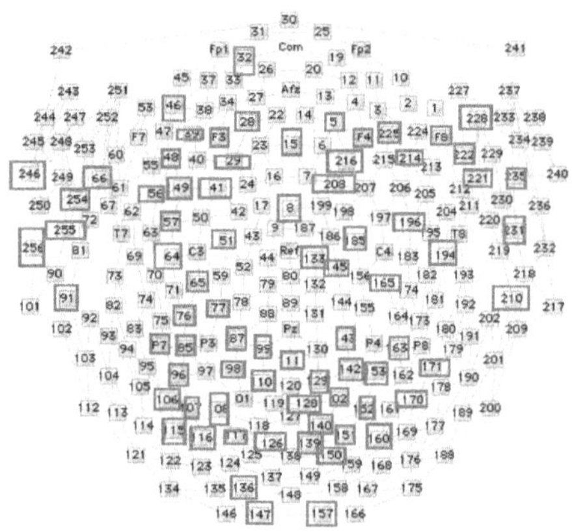

Fig. 2. Selected 76 reliable and common EEG channels (marked by red boxes) by applying noise elimination methods.

Coherency of EEG signals is calculated for each channel pair of the 76 to measure the phase synchronization under good movie trailer stimulus and bad ones. Thus, for each subject and each trailer, we will obtain a 76×76 semi matrix. We average the coherency matrix under all good trailers among all subjects, and after sorting all the channel pairs, we could identify the top 10 channel pair. Similarly, we could also select the top 10 channel pairs in coherency for bad trailers. These channels and their coherency values are shown and compared in Fig.3.

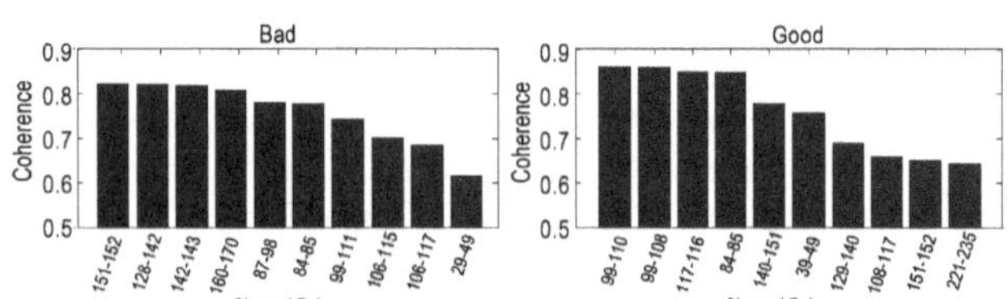

Fig. 3. The top 10 EEG channel pairs and the coherency values under bad movie trailer stimulus and good movie trailer stimulus.

Globally, the coherency values for good movie trailers are larger than bad ones (Fig.3). From Fig.2, it is noticeable that the most positions of top synchronized channels of both bad and good movie trailers are located at the frontal and occipital area. This indicates that these brain regions were highly interacting during perception and comprehension of video contents. Furthermore, we also observe that EEG channels are substantially more synchronized within the left brain regions for good trailers than bad ones. On the other hand, bad trailers are more coherent within the right hemisphere.

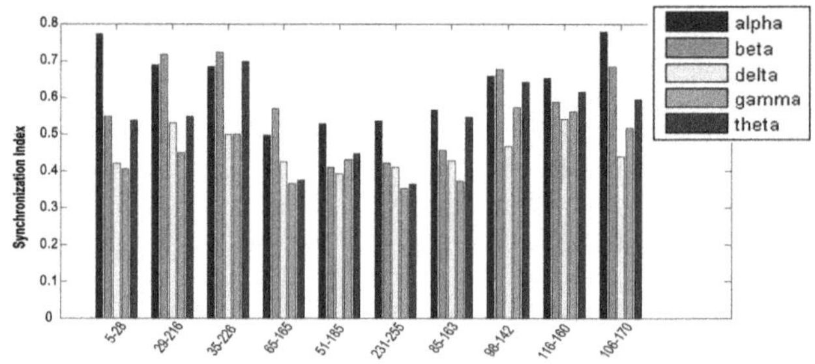

Fig. 4. SI values in Delta (1-3Hz), Theta (4-7Hz), Alpha (8-12Hz), beta (13-30Hz) and gamma (35-41Hz) bands of manually selected 10 example pairs of channels.

Multiple frequency bands are covered in the EEG signals, i.e., Delta (1-3Hz), Theta (4-7Hz), Alpha (8-12Hz), Beta (13-30Hz) and Gamma (35-41Hz). Within each band, we calculate the average Synchronization Index (SI) value of each pair of EEG channels across all trailers and subjects. The distributions of SI values across bands are quite similar. In Fig.4, we manually select 10 example pairs of symmetric channels to visualize, i.e., frontal (5-28, 29-216, 35-226), central (65-165, 51-185), temporal (231-255), posterior (85-163), occipital (98-142, 116-160, 106-170). A few highlights could be interpreted from Fig.4. First, channels on the frontal and occipital channels are the most synchronized channels compared to the others, which is consistent with the conclusion we mentioned in the previous coherency analysis. In addition, the result clearly indicates that the alpha, beta and theta bands reflect the highest SIs at the frontal and occipital regions, as well as on other regions. These two brain regions and the corresponding bands could be highly relevant to human preference towards multimedia stimuli.

4.2 EEG and Eye Tracker Features

Here for convenience, all the 76 selected channels are relabeled from 1 to 76, according to the ascending order of their original labels. First, along the time line of recording, for each two temporally adjacent eye fixing points, g1(x1, y1) and g2(x2, y2), we calculate the Euclidean distance of them. In this way, the absolute eye movement distance could be traced as a time series. Second, in order to align the EEG signal with the eye movement distance time series, we calculate the differential time series of each channel, which represents the dynamic change of amplitude in each channel. And finally, we calculate the correlation between two types of time series to analyze the synchronization between eye movement and each EEG channel. The results from 6 subjects under good movie trailers and bad movie trailers are shown in Fig. 5. For each subject, we take the average correlation values of 10 trailers in the "good" category and 10 trailers in "bad" category.

First of all, we find that on average, the good trailers have significantly higher correlation value than bad trailers (good: 0.164; bad: 0.085). There is high probability that participants are more likely to stare at the screen while they are watching the good trailers, so the coherence of their eye movements and brain's functional responses are relatively high. On contrast, they tend to lose concentration while watching bad trailers. As a result, their eye movement will be larger and disordered, which leads to less correlation with their EEG responses.

Moreover, we select the common top 10 EEG channels that have the highest correlation value with eye movement across all categories and subjects: 39, 91, 106, 128, 141, 32, 165, 116, 160, 5. Most of them are located in the frontal and occipital areas. In the neuroscience field, the frontal lobe is known to be associated with human's attention, the choice between good and bad actions and the distinction of similarities and differences [10]. Meanwhile the occipital lobe is the visual processing center of the brain. It is critical to low-level description of the local orientation, spatial-frequency and color properties [10]. Furthermore, the occipital response has been related to the encoding of visual stimuli in the literature [10]. These theories in neuroscience support our result that frontal and occipital areas are highly correlated to eye movements. From this, we can conclude that the eye-brain synchronization serves an important criterion to evaluate the movie trailer quality.

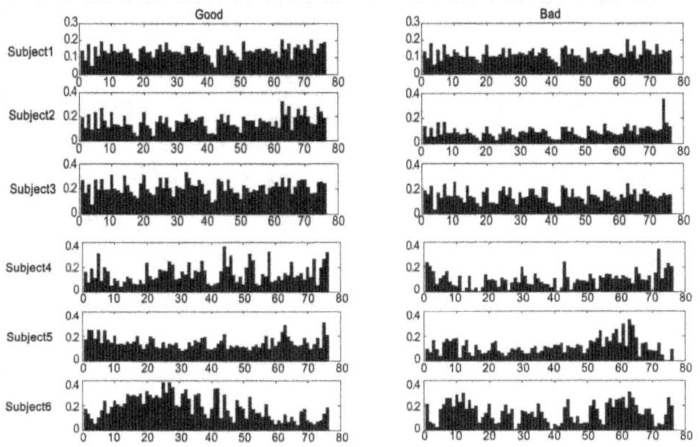

Fig. 5. Average correlation coefficient value between eye movement and each EEG channel for 6 subjects while watching good movie trailer and bad ones.

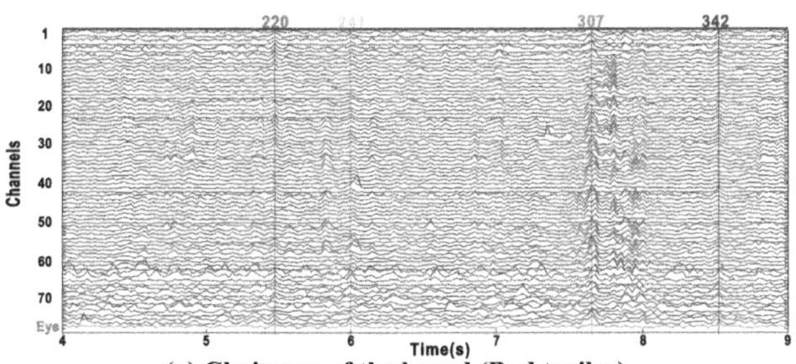

(a) Chairman of the board (Bad trailer)

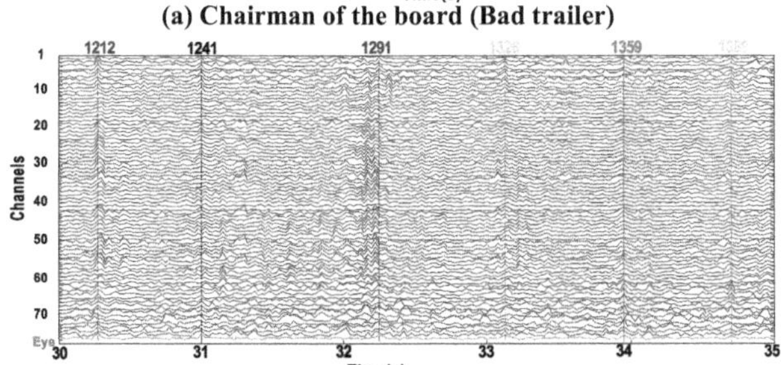

(b) Die Hard 5 (Good trailer)

Fig. 6. The 76 EEG signal and eye movement signals with 4 shot changes in a bad movie trailer and a good movie trailer from one subjects. The eye movement signals are marked with red at the bottom of each subfigure.

4.3 EEG and Eye Tracker Features for Shot Changes

In a continuous video shot, the characteristics of frames, such as intensity histogram, will not change too much between adjacent fames, whereas the difference increases significantly when the shot change occurs [9]. In this section, we will explore whether the shot change will cause consequential influence on the neural functional activity and eye gazing point, i.e., whether the abrupt characteristic change of visual stimuli could be captured or reflected by EEG signals and eye tracking recordings. We detected the shot change points by abrupt video transition detection [11].

In our experiment, we first apply the shot detection algorithm on all the 20 trailers, and obtain a set of key frames of each trailer. Here we take 2 trailers, one bad trailer and one good trailer, as examples. From each of them, we select 12 sequential key frames. Then, we visualize all the 76 EEG channels of time series, as well as the eye movement data (highlighted with red). Taking one subject as an example, we marked 4 and 6 example key frames using colored lines on the time lines where shot change occur in Fig.6. From Fig.6, we can observe that near the shot changing points, there are peaks in both eye movement data and most of the EEG channels data. The result indicates that when shot change occurs, EEG magnitude eye movement would also react with significant change.

5. CONCLUSION

In this study, we built a platform to simultaneously record 256-channel EEG and Eye Tracker data for movie trailer evaluation. First, our results support the theory that synchronization serves as a significant and useful feature for understanding the perception of brain regions when multimedia stimuli are presented, i.e., different synchronization patterns could be observed while watching good and bad movie trailers. Second, , by analyzing EEG and eye movement data together, we find that on average, the good trailers have substantially higher correlation value than bad trailers. At last, we found that when shot changing occurs, EEG signals and eye movement could also perform significant changes.

However, it should be noted limits exist in the present work. First of all, there is a small number of subjects in the study. But our ongoing/future data acquisition would significantly address this issue. In addition, the criterion about good and bad movie trailer in this study is limited. More comprehensive criteria should be considered in the future, and the rating from Youtube should also be validated from other perspectives. Moreover, additional experimental results are needed to establish the robustness of our findings. For instance, there are other methods to measure the neural signal synchrony, such as Mutual Information and Phase Locking Value. It is necessary to test them for reproducible results in the future.

In summary, introducing human perception and functional brain response to movie trailer evaluation is promising, though it still entails significant efforts by joint data mining of EEG and eye tracking signals. Our exploration of movie trailers with human interaction could inspire new features or help select existing features in multimedia analysis. And possibly, an automatic movie trailer evaluation system based on learning of both multimedia features and human interaction features, is supposed to designed for both industrial and academic use.

6. ACKNOWLEDGMENTS

This work was supported by NIH R01 DA033393, NIH R01 AG-042599, NSF CAREER Award IIS-1149260, NSF CBET-1302089 and NSF BCS-1439051.

7. REFERENCES

[1] Tianming Liu, Xintao Hu, Xiaojin Li, Mo Chen, Junwei Han, Lei Guo. Merging Neuroimaging and Multimedia: Methods, Opportunities and Challenges. *IEEE Transactions on Human-Machine Systems*. 2014.

[2] E. Niedermeyer, F. H. Lopes da Silva. Electroencephalography: Basic principles, clinical applications and related fields. 3rd edition, Lippincott, Williams & Wilkins, Philadelphia, 1993.

[3] S. Scholler, S. Bosse, M. S. Treder et al., "Toward a Direct Measure of Video Quality Perception Using EEG," *Image Processing, IEEE Transactions*, vol. 21, no. 5, pp. 2619-2629, 2012.

[4] J. Antons, R. Schleicher, S. Arndt et al., "Analyzing speech quality perception using electro-encephalography," *IEEE Journal of Selected Topics in Signal Processing*, vol. 6, no. 6, pp. 721-731, 2012.

[5] Vassiliki Filippakopoulou and Byron Nakos. "Eyemmv toolbox: An eye movement post-analysis tool based on a two-step spatial dispersion threshold for fixation identification". *Journal of Eye Movement Research*, 7(1):1–10, 2014.

[6] Salvucci, Dario D. "An interactive model-based environment for eye-movement protocol analysis and visualization." *Proceedings of the 2000 symposium on Eye tracking research & applications. ACM*, 2000.

[7] P. Sajda, E. Pohlmeyer, J. Wang et al., "In a blink of an eye and a switch of a transistor: cortically coupled computer vision," *Proceedings of the IEEE*, vol. 98, no. 3, pp. 462-478, 2010.

[8] S. Koelstra, C. Muhl, and I. Patras, "EEG analysis for implicit tagging of video data" in *Affective Computing and Intelligent Interaction and Workshops*, 2009. ACII 2009. 3rd International Conference on, 2009, pp. 1-6.

[9] Hou, Y., Xiao, T., Zhang, S., Jiang, X., Li, X., Hu, X., Han, J., Guo, L., Miller, L.S., Neupert, R. and Liu, T., 2016. Predicting Movie Trailer Viewer's "Like/Dislike" via Learned Shot Editing Patterns. IEEE Transactions on Affective Computing, 7(1), pp.29-44.

[10] Hald, L. A., Bastiaansen, M. C. M., & Hagoort, P. EEG theta and gamma responses to semantic violations in online sentence processing. *Brain and Language*, 96, 90–105. 2006.

[11] Patel, Nilesh V., and Ishwar K. Sethi. "Video shot detection and characterization for video databases." *Pattern Recognition* 30.4 (1997): 583-592.

LIME: A Method for Low-light IMage Enhancement

Xiaojie Guo
State Key Laboratory of Information Security, Institute of Information Engineering
Chinese Academy of Sciences, Beijing, 100093, China
xj.max.guo@gmail.com

ABSTRACT

When one captures images in low-light conditions, the images often suffer from low visibility. This poor quality may significantly degrade the performance of many computer vision and multimedia algorithms that are primarily designed for high-quality inputs. In this paper, we propose a very simple and effective method, named as LIME, to enhance low-light images. More concretely, the illumination of each pixel is first estimated individually by finding the maximum value in R, G and B channels. Further, we refine the initial illumination map by imposing a structure prior on it, as the final illumination map. Having the well-constructed illumination map, the enhancement can be achieved accordingly. Experiments on a number of challenging real-world low-light images are present to reveal the efficacy of our LIME and show its superiority over several state-of-the-arts.

Keywords

Illumination Estimation, Illumination (Light) Transmission, Low-light Image Enhancement

Figure 1: **Upper Row:** Three natural low-light images. **Lower Row:** The enhanced results by our method.

1. INTRODUCTION

High-visibility images reflect clear details of target scenes, which are critical to many vision-based techniques, such as object detection [16] and tracking [20]. But, images captured in low-light conditions are often of low visibility. Besides degrading the visual quality of images, it very likely hurts the performance of algorithms that are primarily designed for high-visibility inputs. Figure 1 provides three such examples, from which, we can see that many details, the paintings on the wall in the first case for example, have almost been "buried" in the dark. To make the buried information visible again, low-light image enhancement is demanded.

Directly amplifying the low-light image is probably the most intuitive and simplest way to recall the visibility of dark regions. But this operation gives birth to another problem, say relatively bright regions might be saturated and thus loss corresponding details. Histogram equalization strategies [17, 4, 1] can avoid the above problem by somehow forcing the output image to fall in the range $[0, 1]$. However, in nature, they focus on contrast enhancement instead of exploiting real illumination causes, having the risk of over- and under-enhancement. The method proposed in [18] tries to enhance contrast while preserving naturalness of illumination. Although it prevents the result from over-enhancement, in our test, its performance is not so attractive in terms of both efficiency and visual quality.

As noticed in [6], inverted low-light images look like hazy images, as shown in Fig. 2. Based on this observation, the authors of [6] alternatively resorted to dehaze the inverted low-light images. After dehazing, the obtained unrealistic images is inverted again as the final enhanced results. Recently, Li *et al.* followed this technical line and further improved the visual quality by first over-segmenting the input image and then adaptively denoising different segments [13]. Even though the above methods can provide reasonable results, the basic model they rely on is lacking in physical explanation. This paper will try to connect this un-rooted model to a more physically meaningful one that our method adopts.

This work intends to enhance a low-light image by estimating its illumination map. The illumination map is first constructed by finding the maximum intensity of each pixel

MM '16, October 15–19, 2016, Amsterdam, The Netherlands.
© 2016 ACM. ISBN 978-1-4503-3603-1/16/10...$15.00
DOI: http://dx.doi.org/10.1145/2964284.2967188

Figure 2: The inverted versions (unrealistic images) of those shown in the upper row of Fig. 1.

Figure 3: Comparison of (6) and (4) with the same illumination map. The atmospheric light a estimated by [10] is larger than 0.95. Even though, the difference is still noticeable.

in R, G and B channels. Then, we exploit the structure of the illumination and execute structure-aware smoothing to refine the illumination map. Experiments on a number of challenging images are conducted to demonstrate the advantages of our method in comparison with other state-of-the-art methods.

2. PROPOSED METHOD

Our method is built upon the following model, which explains the formation of a low-light image:

$$\mathbf{L} = \mathbf{I} \circ \mathbf{T}, \tag{1}$$

where $\mathbf{L}$ and $\mathbf{I}$ are the captured image and the desired recovery, respectively. In addition, $\mathbf{T}$ represents the illumination map, and the operator $\circ$ means element-wise multiplication. The model (1) is with clear physical meaning, say the observed image can be decomposed into the product of the desired scene and the illumination image. As can be seen, the estimation of $\mathbf{T}$ is key to the recovery of $\mathbf{I}$.

As mentioned, another widely used model is based on the observation that inverted low-light images $\mathbf{1}-\mathbf{L}$ look similar to haze images, which is thus expressed as [10, 15, 14]:

$$\mathbf{1} - \mathbf{L} = (\mathbf{1} - \mathbf{I}) \circ \tilde{\mathbf{T}} + a(\mathbf{1} - \tilde{\mathbf{T}}), \tag{2}$$

where a represents the global atmospheric light. Although the visual effect of inverted low-light images $\mathbf{1} - \mathbf{L}$ is intuitively similar to haze images, compared to the model (1), the physical meaning of the above is not easy to directly explain. We will show the relation between (2) and (1) later.

2.1 Initial Illumination Map Estimation

As one of the first color constancy methods, Max-RGB [12] tries to estimate the illumination by seeking the maximum value of three color channels, say R, G and B. But this estimation can only boost the global illumination. In this paper, to handle non-uniform illuminations, we alternatively adopt the following initial estimation:

$$\hat{\mathbf{T}}(x) \leftarrow \max_{c \in \{R,G,B\}} \mathbf{L}^c(x). \tag{3}$$

The obtained $\hat{\mathbf{T}(x)}$ guarantees that the recovery will not be saturated, because of

$$\mathbf{I}(x) = \mathbf{L}(x) / (\max_c \mathbf{L}^c(x) + \epsilon), \tag{4}$$

where ϵ is a very small constant to avoid the zero denominator. Let us here recall the dark channel prior, a commonly used prior to estimate the transmission map for dehazing [10], on $\mathbf{1} - \mathbf{L}$ as follows:

$$\tilde{\mathbf{T}}(x) \leftarrow 1 - \min_c \frac{1 - \mathbf{L}^c(x)}{a} = 1 - \frac{1}{a} + \max_c \frac{\mathbf{L}^c(x)}{a}. \tag{5}$$

Accordingly, substituting (5) into (2) yields:

$$\mathbf{I}(x) = \frac{\mathbf{L}(x) - 1 + a}{(1 - \frac{1}{a} + \max_c \frac{\mathbf{L}^c(x)}{a} + \epsilon)} + (1 - a). \tag{6}$$

We can see that when $a = 1$, both (4) and (6) reach the same result. But, if a gets away from 1, the equivalence between the model (6) [6] and (4) breaks (see Fig. 3 for difference).

In this work, we employ (3) to initially estimate illumination map $\hat{\mathbf{T}}$, due to its simplicity, although various approaches, like [7, 8, 11], have been developed to improve the accuracy in past decades. Most of these improvements essentially consider the local consistency of illumination by taking into account neighboring pixels within a small region around the target pixel. In the following, we provide a more powerful scheme to better achieve this goal.

2.2 Illumination Map Refinement

As aforementioned, the illumination estimation can benefit from local consistency. Two representative ways are:

$$\begin{aligned} \hat{\mathbf{T}}(x) &\leftarrow \max_{y \in \Omega(x)} \max_{c \in \{R,G,B\}} \mathbf{L}^c(y); \\ \hat{\mathbf{T}}(x) &\leftarrow \operatorname*{mean}_{y \in \Omega(x)} \max_{c \in \{R,G,B\}} \mathbf{L}^c(y), \end{aligned} \tag{7}$$

where $\Omega(x)$ is a region centered at pixel x, and y is the location index within the region. These strategies can somewhat enhance the local consistency, but they are structure-blind.

A "good" solution should simultaneously preserve the overall structure and smooth the textural details. To address this issue, based on the initial illumination map $\hat{\mathbf{T}}$, we propose to solve the following optimization problem:

$$\min_{\mathbf{T}} \|\hat{\mathbf{T}} - \mathbf{T}\|_F^2 + \alpha \|\mathbf{W} \circ \nabla \mathbf{T}\|_1, \tag{8}$$

where α (0.15 for all the experiments) is the coefficient to balance the involved two terms and, $\|\cdot\|_F$ and $\|\cdot\|_1$ designate the Frobenious and ℓ_1 norms, respectively. Further, $\mathbf{W}$ is the weight matrix, and ∇ that contains $\nabla_h \mathbf{T}$ (horizontal) and $\nabla_v \mathbf{T}$ (vertical), is the first order derivative filter. In the objective (8), the first term takes care of the fidelity between the initial map $\hat{\mathbf{T}}$ and the refined one $\mathbf{T}$, while the second term considers the (structure-aware) smoothness. It can be seen that setting the weight matrix to $\mathbf{1}$ (all entries being 1) leads (8) to a classic ℓ_2 loss total variation minimization

Figure 4: Comparison of different illumination maps and corresponding enhanced results. **From (a) to (f):** Illumination map estimated individually on each pixel (Initial), refined by local max (7) (Max), bilateral filtering (BF), ℓ_2 loss total variation minimization (TV), and our structure-aware smoothing, respectively.

problem (TV for short) [3], which is also short of ability to distinguish between strong structural edges and texture [19].

Hence, the key is the design of $\mathbf{W}$. Inspired by RTV [19], for each location, the weight (*e.g.* $\mathbf{W}_h(x)$) is set via:

$$\mathbf{W}_h(x) \leftarrow \sum_{y\in\Omega(x)} \frac{G_\sigma(x,y)}{|\sum_{y\in\Omega(x)} G_\sigma(x,y)\nabla_h\hat{\mathbf{T}}(y)|+\epsilon}, \tag{9}$$

where $G_\sigma(x,y)$ is produced by the Gaussian kernel with the standard deviation σ (we use 2 throughout this paper), and $|\cdot|$ is the absolute value operator. Please note that, different to RTV, our weight matrix is constructed based on the given $\hat{\mathbf{T}}$ instead of being iteratively updated according to $\mathbf{T}$. That means $\mathbf{W}$ only needs to be calculated once.

Traditionally, the problem (8) can be effectively solved via alternating direction minimization techniques. To speed up the calculation, we approximate (8) by the following:

$$\min_{\mathbf{T}} \|\hat{\mathbf{T}}-\mathbf{T}\|_F^2+\alpha\sum_x \frac{\mathbf{W}_h(x)(\nabla_h\mathbf{T}(x))^2}{|\nabla_h\hat{\mathbf{T}}(x)|+\epsilon}+\frac{\mathbf{W}_v(x)(\nabla_v\mathbf{T}(x))^2}{|\nabla_v\hat{\mathbf{T}}(x)|+\epsilon}. \tag{10}$$

As can be seen, the problem now only involves quadratic terms. Thus, the solution can be directly computed without requiring any iterations. Figure 4 shows a comparison of different methods on illumination map, from which, we can see the advance of our method.

2.3 Other Operations

Having the refined illumination map $\mathbf{T}$, we can recover $\mathbf{I}$ by following (4). One can also manipulate the illumination map through gamma transformation, say $\mathbf{T} \leftarrow \mathbf{T}^\gamma$. From the upper row of Fig. 6, we can see the difference between the results by setting γ to 0.5, 0.8 and 1. For the rest experiments, we adopt $\gamma = 0.8$. Moreover, possible noises previously hiding in the dark are also accordingly amplified, especially for the very low-light inputs (regions), as shown in Fig. 6. Denoising techniques are required to further improve the visual quality. Many off-the-shelf denosing tools, such

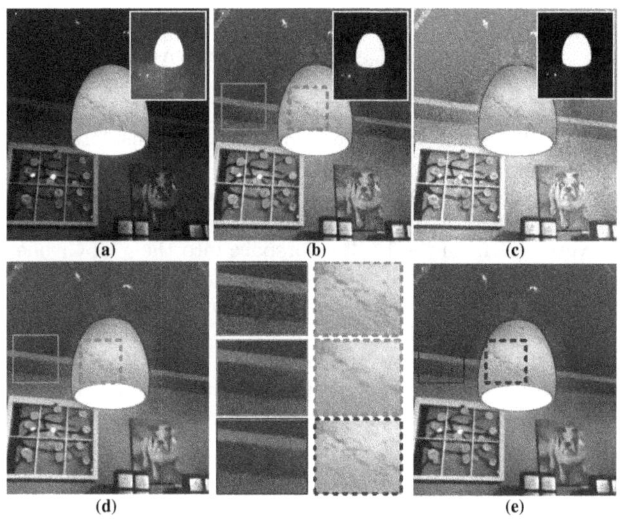

Figure 6: Gamma correction, denosing and recomposition. (a)-(c) are the recovered images using $\mathbf{T}^\gamma$ with $\gamma = 0.5$, $\gamma = 0.8$ and $\gamma = 1$, respectively. The corresponding illumination map is given in the up-right corner of each sub-picture. Noises appear in the enhanced images. (d) is the denoised version of (b) by BM3D, while (e) is the recomposed result of (b) and (e) by (11). It can be seen from the zoomed-in patches that the recomposition adaptively keeps the fine details of the bright region and suppresses the noises of the dark region.

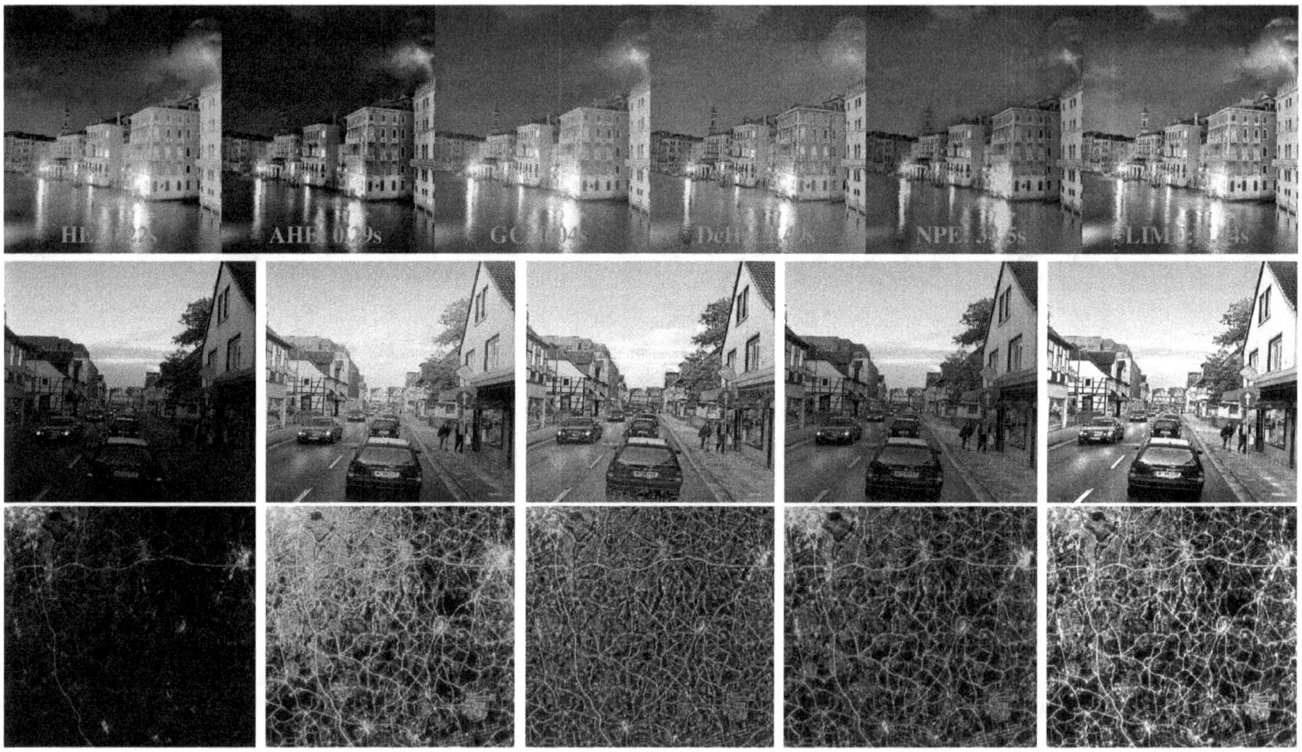

(a) Input (b) HE (c) DeHz (d) NPE (e) LIME

Figure 5: Comparison of different methods without denoising involved.

as [5, 2, 9], can be employed to do the job. Considering the comprehensive performance, BM3D [5] is the choice of this work. In our implementation, for further cutting the computational load, we only execute BM3D on the Y channel by converting $\mathbf{I}$ from the RGB colorspace into the YCbCr one. In addition, the magnitude of noises is not the same for different regions of the input, as the amplification is different. And BM3D treats different patches equally. Therefore, to avoid the unbalance of processing, *e.g.* some (dark) places are well-denoised while some (brighter) over-smoothed, we employ the following operation:

$$\mathbf{I}_f \leftarrow \mathbf{I} \circ \mathbf{T} + \mathbf{I}_d \circ (\mathbf{1} - \mathbf{T}), \tag{11}$$

where $\mathbf{I}_d$ and $\mathbf{I}_f$ are the results after denoising and recomposing, respectively. The merit of this operation can be viewed from Fig. 6 (e), compared with Fig. 6 (d). We would like to mention that the denoising, as a post-processing step, can be concatenated to any low-light image enhancing method.

3. EXPERIMENTAL RESULTS

In this section, we compare our LIME with several state-of-the-art methods, including histogram equalization (HE), adaptive histogram equalization (AHE), Gamma Correction (GC), Dehazing based method [6] (DeHz) and Naturalness Preserved Enhancement algorithm (NPE) [18]. All the codes are in Matlab[1], which ensures the fairness of time comparison. All the experiments are conducted on a machine running Windows 7 OS with 64G RAM and 2.4GHz CPU.

Figure 5 provides several comparisons. From the top row (the input is the second case of Fig. 1 with size 680x720), we can see that AHE can not effectively recall the information in dark regions while GC ($\gamma = 0.4$) changes the color of the whole image. These problems almost exist always, therefore we discard them for the rest comparisons. HE, DeHz and NPE outperform AHE and GC in this case, but are inferior to our method in terms of visual quality. In time cost, although LIME spends more than HE, AHE and GC, it is comparable to or even more efficient than DeHz, while much more efficient than NPE. Most cost of DeHz comes from the estimation of atmospheric light. Two more comparisons are given in Fig. 5, which are the additional evidence of the advantage of LIME, compared with HE, DeHz and NPE.

Figure 7 gives another test. The very low-light input hides intensive noises in the dark. After performing LIME, the details of the scene get enhanced, but the noises also come out, as shown in the middle of Fig. 7. This is an inevitable problem encountered by almost all of existing low-light enhancement algorithms. As we have discussed in Sec. 2.3, denoising is required. The right picture in Fig. 7 is the denoised result by executing BM3D on the middle of Fig. 7, from which we can see the improvement in terms of visual quality. To allow more experimental verification and comparisons, we provide our code at http://cs.tju.edu.cn/orgs/vision/%7exguo/homepage.htm.

[1]HE and AHE uses *histeq* and *adapthisteq* functions integrated in the Matlab toolbox. GC is achieved by $\mathbf{L}^{\gamma}$, while the code of NPE is downloaded from the authors' website.

The code of DeHz is not publicly available when this paper is prepared, but it is easy to be implemented based on [10].

(a) Input **(b) Illumination map** **(c) Without denoising** **(d) With denoising**

Figure 7: Comparison of results without and with denoising.

4. CONCLUSION

This paper has proposed an efficient and effective method to enhance low-light images for boosting the visual quality and offering contemporary vision applications with reliable inputs. The key to the enhancement is how well the illumination map is estimated. The structure-aware smoothing has been developed to improve the illumination consistency. The experimental results have revealed the advance of our method compared with several state-of-the-art alternatives.

Acknowledgment

This work was supported by the National Natural Science Foundation of China (Grant No. 11526215, 61402467, 61528204), the "Strategic Priority Research Program" of the Chinese Academy of Sciences (Grant No. XDA06010701), and the National Key Research and Development Plan (Grant No. 2016YFB1001200).

5. REFERENCES

[1] M. Abdullah-Al-Wadud, M. Kabir, M. Dewan, and O. Chae. A dynamic histograme equalization for image contrast enhancement. *IEEE Trans. on Consumer Electronics*, 53(2):593–600, 2007.

[2] H. Burger, C. Schuler, and S. Harmeling. Image denoising: Can plain neural networks compete with bm3d. In *Proceedings of IEEE Conference on Computer Vision and Pattern Recognition (CVPR)*, pages 2392–2399, 2012.

[3] S. Chan, R. Khoshabeh, K. Gibson, P. Gill, and T. Nguyen. An augmented lagrangian method for total variation video restoration. *IEEE Trans. on Image Processing (TIP)*, 20(11):3097–3111, 2011.

[4] H. Cheng and X. Shi. A simple and effective histogram equalization approach to image enhancement. *Digital Signal Processing*, 14(2):158–170, 2004.

[5] K. Dabov, A. Foi, V. Katkovnik, and K. Egiazarian. Image denoising by sparse 3d transform-domain collaborative filtering. *IEEE Trans. on Image Processing (TIP)*, 16(8):2080–2095, 2007.

[6] X. Dong, G. Wang, Y. Pang, W. Li, J. Wen, W. Meng, and Y. Lu. Fast efficient algorithm for enhancement of low lighting video. In *Proceedings of IEEE Conference on Multimedia & Expo (ICME)*, pages 1–6, 2011.

[7] D. Forsyth. A novel approach to color constancy. In *Proceedings of International Conference on Computer Vision*, pages 9–18, 1988.

[8] B. Funt and L. Shi. The rehabilitation of maxrgb. In *Proceedings of Color Imaging Conference*, pages 256–259, 2010.

[9] S. Gu, L. Zhang, W. Zuo, and X. Feng. Weighted nuclear norm minimization with applications to image denoising. In *Proceedings of IEEE Conference on Computer Vision and Pattern Recognition (CVPR)*, pages 2862–2869, 2014.

[10] K. He, J. Sun, and X. Tang. Single image haze removal using dark channel prior. *IEEE Trans. on Pattern Analysis and Machine Intelligence (TPAMI)*, 33(12):2341–2353, 2011.

[11] H. Joze, M. Drew, G. Finlayson, and P. Rey. The role of bright pixels in illumination estimation. In *Proceedings of European Conference on Colour in Graphics, Imaging and Vision*, 2012.

[12] E. Land. The retinex theory of color vision. *Scientific American*, 237(6):108–128, 1977.

[13] L. Li, R. Wang, W. Wang, and W. Gao. A low-light image enhancement method for both denoising and contrast enlarging. In *Proceedings of IEEE Conference on Image Processing (ICIP)*, pages 3730–3734, 2015.

[14] G. Meng, Y. Wang, J. Duan, S. Xiang, and C. Pan. Efficient image dehazing with boundary constraint and contextual regularization. In *Proceedings of International Conference on Computer Vision (ICCV)*, pages 617–624, 2013.

[15] S. Narasimhan and S. Nayar. Contrast restoration of weather degraded images. *IEEE Trans. on Pattern Analysis and Machine Intelligence (TPAMI)*, 25(6):713–724, 2003.

[16] D. Oneata, J. Revaud, J. Verbeek, and C. Schmid. Spatio-temporal object detection proposals. In *Proceedings of European Conference on Computer Vision (ECCV)*, pages 737–752, 2014.

[17] E. Pisano, S. Zong, B. Hemminger, M. DeLuce, J. Maria, E. Johnston, K. Muller, P. Braeuning, and S. Pizer. Contrast limited adaptive histogram equalization image processing to improve the detection of simulated spiculations in dense mammograms. *Journal of Digital Imaging*, 11(4):193–200, 1998.

[18] S. Wang, J. Zheng, H. Hu, and B. Li. Naturalness preserved enhancement algorithm for non-uniform illumination images. *IEEE Trans. on Image Processing (TIP)*, 22(9):3538–3578, 2013.

[19] L. Xu, Q. Yan, Y. Xia, and J. Jia. Strucutre extraction from texture via relative total variation. *ACM Trans. on Graphics (TOG)*, 31(6):139:1–139:10, 2013.

[20] K. Zhang, L. Zhang, and M. Yang. Real-time compressive tracking. In *Proceedings of European Conference on Computer Vision (ECCV)*, pages 866–879, 2014.

Multi-Protocol Video Delivery with Late Trans-Muxing

Rufael Mekuria
Unified Streaming B.V
Overtoom 60
1054 HK Amsterdam
rufael@unified-streaming.com

Jelte Fennema
Universiteit van Amsterdam
Science Park 904
1090 GE Amsterdam
me@jeltef.nl

Dirk Griffioen
Unified Streaming B.V
Overtoom 60
1054 HK Amsterdam
dirk@unified-streaming.com

ABSTRACT

In practice, video delivery using multiple protocols is needed to support the wide range of clients in the digital media ecosystem. Naive approaches increase backhaul traffic and cache storage requirements proportional to the number of protocols in use. To reduce this overhead, we present an efficient multi-protocol video delivery architecture. It exploits the fact that media segments in different protocols are often based on the same raw encoded media data. Instead of caching and distributing near duplicate media segments for each protocol throughout the content delivery network, we push their generation towards the edge. We call this Late Trans-Muxing (LTM). We implement LTM in a smart edge cache that can request and cache media byte ranges and generate protocol specific media segments on the fly. Experiments in an emulation testbed show that backhaul traffic and cache storage are reduced up to 85% and 50% respectively compared to CDN based approaches. This shows the benefit of LTM in multi-protocol DASH based video delivery.

Keywords

HTTP Streaming; Video Streaming; Caching; Trans-Multiplexing; Edge Computing; Cloud Computing

1. INTRODUCTION

Video Streaming in the Internet has converged to delivery using HTTP as the primary transport protocol. Video delivery using HTTP provides key benefits such as the re-use of the existing Internet infrastructure, e.g. cache and application servers. In addition, it poses a smaller number of connectivity problems related to firewalls and port numbering compared to legacy streaming solutions such as those based on RTP/RTCP [1]. Popular protocols include Apple's HTTP Live Streaming (HLS) [2], Microsoft's HTTP Smooth Streaming HSS [3] and Adobe's HTTP Dynamic Streaming HDS [4] and the international ISO standard MPEG-DASH [5]. These protocols generally work for subsets of devices and media players throughout the media ecosystem. A feature found in most HTTP based video streaming protocols is that they subdivide a longer source video in small media segments. These can then be downloaded and decoded independently by the client side players. This results in near instant play-out and less bandwidth wasted on parts of the video that are ultimately not watched by the user. Moreover, this approach allows quality/bit-rate switching at the client for each segment. This can be used to adapt video quality to viewer and/or network conditions.

MM '16, October 15-19, 2016, Amsterdam, Netherlands
© 2016 ACM. ISBN 978-1-4503-3603-1/16/10...$15.00
DOI: http://dx.doi.org/10.1145/2964284.2967189

However, for distributors of video content, the existence of multiple video streaming protocols introduces the need for *multi-protocol video delivery* to target **all end devices and video players**. These features make Adaptive Bit-Rate Streaming over HTTP a popular approach for video delivery in the Internet. Convergence to a single video streaming protocol could alleviate this need, but in practice *multi-protocol video delivery* is necessary when targeting a wide range of consumer devices.

A Naive approach for multi-protocol video delivery would be to deploy multiple solutions simultaneously. In this case, sets of media segments for each of the protocols would be prepared and stored independently. Subsequently, they will be distributed throughout a content delivery network (CDN) for delivery.

A drawback of this approach is that it ignores the fact that media segments for different protocols share a common media source. When streaming source content using N different protocols, this would result in roughly N times as many different media segment data to be requested and cached throughout the network. As each media segment is identified by its own URL, they are treated as independent entities throughout the CDN. As parts of the data in media segments overlap due to the common media source, this leads to redundant caching and transport of media information.

As video traffic is already the dominant source of data in the Internet today and expected to increase to over 80% in 2019 according to [6], such naïve approaches are clearly unsustainable. More efficient multi-protocol video streaming that exploits redundancy between media segments is needed. Therefore, we introduce a multi-protocol video delivery architecture based on Late Trans Muxing (LTM). In the LTM architecture, we move the generation of the actual media segments to the edge of the network, i.e. at the CDN or edge cache. This approach aims to reduce the transmission and caching storage required for multi-protocol video delivered over HTTP.

To prove the feasibility and benefits of the LTM architecture, we introduce a smart cache/edge node that can both store and request raw compressed media data byte ranges and generate protocol specific media segments on the fly. We achieve this by combining popular HTTP servers integrated with an on the fly trans-muxer. The developed solution is evaluated in a testbed using emulated network conditions and multi-protocol streaming scenarios. Results show that Late Trans-Muxing results in a reduction of backhaul traffic up to 85 % and cache storage up to 50% compared to the normal CDN approach when a video has been streamed previously using another protocol.

The paper is structured as follows. Section 2 presents the related work and motivation. In Section 3 we present research questions, the LTM architecture and edge node design and implementation. In Section 4 we present the experimental evaluation. Section 5 concludes the paper.

2. RELATED WORK

Dynamic Adaptive Streaming over HTTP (DASH) has evolved from proprietary [2] [3] [4] solutions towards adoption in an international ISO standard [5]. The possibility of per segment bit-rate selection has triggered research resulting in rate-adaptation algorithms. Some works focus on improving the reception at the client using rate adaptation based on network capacity and congestion monitoring [7] and prediction and monitoring of the user Quality of Experience (QoE) [8]. Other work investigates the server side deployment of DASH and an efficient use of network resources. For example, [9] focusses on resource efficient transcoding in the cloud and [10] on efficient and content aware caching and deployment. Most works focus on achieving performance using a single streaming protocol. However, in practice, the network and server load for delivery using multiple protocols is critical. Nevertheless, it has received much less attention from research. A technique for reducing the overhead of using multiple HTTP based protocols using trans-muxing has been presented in [11]. But so far little experimental implementation and performance evaluation has been presented. In addition, in this work we focus on Real-time trans-muxing on the *edge network cache* as far away as possible from the content source. As far as we know this the first experimental work on late trans-muxing.

3. MULTI PROTOCOL VIDEO DELIVERY USING LATE TRANSMUXING

3.1 Research Question & Contributions

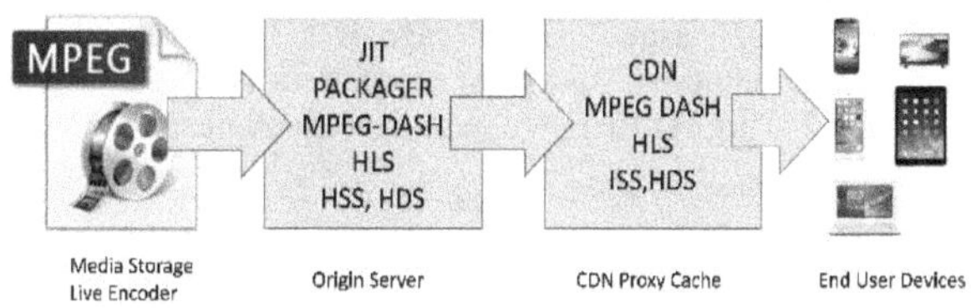

Figure 1 Multi-Protocol Video Packaging and Delivery

Figure 1 shows a typical setup for multi-protocol video delivery. Raw compressed media is retrieved from storage (in case of VoD) or a live encoder (in case of live broadcast). At the origin server, this media can be packaged just in time, generating protocol specific media segments and manifest files for different protocols on the fly. For example, the Unified Origin Server [12] supports just in time packaging for HDS, HLS, HSS and MPEG-DASH. The output is then pulled into the CDN to enable a large amount of end devices / users to retrieve the media segments for playback. This workflow enables massive distribution of media content, due to the scalability offered by CDN's. However, the distribution throughout the CDN's is independent of the preceding work flow. We believe that this can be improved and made more media aware. One possible way to achieve this would be to move the packaging operation to the edge of the network (i.e. the cache node). This would avoid redundant storage and transmission of media segments based on a common media source. This is the focus of this work leading to the following main **research question:**

Can we make multi-protocol video streaming more efficient by moving on the fly media segment generation to the edge of the network, i.e. late trans-muxing?

We address this research question in three **sub questions**:

1) How can we efficiently implement on-the-fly trans-muxing and caching on edge caches using existing HTTP infrastructures (i.e. web servers)?
2) Can on the fly edge trans-muxing reduce cache storage needed for multi-protocol video streaming compared to a CDN based approach?
3) Can on the fly edge trans-muxing reduce backhaul traffic in the network for multi-protocol video streaming when comparing to a CDN based approach?

To understand these research questions better, we present more details on the location and function of the components in Figure 1 in Table 1. The traditional deployment of the source/origin at the datacenter/core and the CDN at the edge has the following consequences.

Redundant Caching: media segments for each of the different protocols are stored independently in the edge caches. As caches are not aware of the similarities between media segments redundant caching occurs.

Redundant Backhaul Traffic: Media segments for different protocols are transported independently from the origin to the edge CDN caches. As the network is not aware of the similarity between segments redundant backhaul traffic occurs.

Origin Storage: The origin server stores all media segments for different protocols. This leads to redundant storage at the origin application server.

The last challenge of storage at the origin server can be addressed by generating segments from source media on the fly at the origin. This operation, based on trans-muxing, is light weight and does not increase the computational load on the server much. By doing this for each request, media segment storage at the server is reduced. To address the first two challenges, we will aim for deployment of trans-muxing on the edge cache instead. This avoids duplicate segment distribution throughout the CDN. This could potentially reduce both media backhaul traffic and caching storage. However, to best of our knowledge, the implications of practical implementation, deployment and evaluation of such a streaming architecture with *late trans-muxing* have not been presented in prior work. Therefore this paper presents the following **Contributions:**

1) The design and implementation of a highly scalable and robust smart edge cache with trans-muxing capabilities that is compatible with existing HTTP infrastructures
2) Media aware backhaul data exchange for multi-protocol video streaming using HTTP range requests
3) Evaluation of the prototype in a testbed with media streaming workloads. This shows up to 85 % reduced backhaul traffic and up to 50 % caching storage when the same video has been streamed in a different format.

We present the first and second contributions in the rest of this section. In section 4 we present the testbed evaluation.

Table 1 Components in Multi-Protocol Video Streaming

Component	Description/Function	Network Location
Media Source	Media File or Live Stream to deliver	Core / Remote edge
Origin Server	Creation of protocol specific media segments	Core / Datacenter
CDN	Cache segments	Edge

3.2 Design

In Figure 2 we present the LTM architecture with segment generation at the edge cache. The first design challenge is related to the implementation of the edge cache, presented in section 3.2.1. The second challenge is related to the exchange and caching of media byte ranges between the storage and LTM cache, presented in 3.2.2.

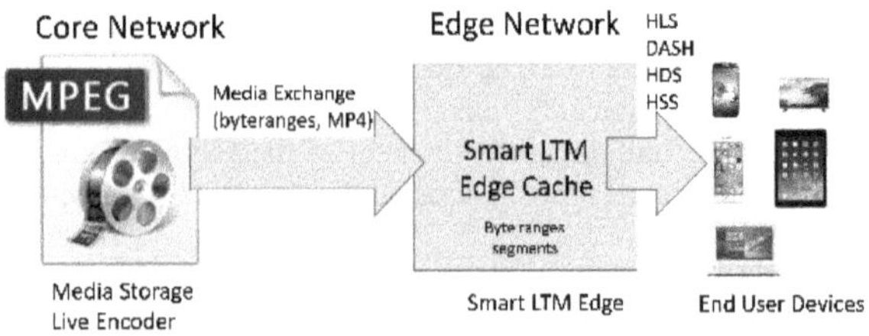

Figure 2 LTM Architecture

3.2.1 Web Server Design Considerations

We aim to implement the smart edge in existing web servers that are commonly used in the internet and have stood the test of time. The smart LTM edge needs to run on the fly trans-muxing and cache raw compressed media data. Trans-muxing is available for two commonly used HTTP webservers: Apache [13] and Nginx [14], based on the Unified Streaming Platform [12] (USP). Based on analyzing the differences between the two webservers, we decide to combine them as they have complementary strengths. Apache spawns a process for each request, while Nginx handles multiple requests in a single event loop. Because of this, Apache is better as an application server. On the other hand Nginx is better at supporting a large number of connections and has better support for caching. For example, Nginx 1.9.8 includes byte range caching, which we need to store the byte ranges retrieved from the origin. A second important feature in Nginx is cache locking. Cache locking blocks second duplicate requests that are still pending from forwarding to the upstream. On the upstream response the, both requests can then be handled simultaneously. Therefore, Cache locking reduces the load on the storage server in case many duplicate requests occur. For these reasons, we chose Nginx as the reverse proxy cache due to its better caching support, and Apache for the trans-muxing as it performs better as an application server.

3.2.2 Range Request and Range Caching

Our intention is to support the exchange of raw encoded media byte ranges from the storage / media source to the smart edge using HTTP byte range requests. Byte range request are a part of the HTTP specification [15] and enable ranges of bytes from files to be requested. This is useful for trans-muxing, as from media byte ranges of media files (fMP4), media segments can be generated. In addition, the smart edge could benefit from caching of byte ranges. Byte ranges can then be re-used at the cache to generate segments for other client requests. For byte-range caching we consider the following 3 options.

Ignore Range: This is the simplest option, the Nginx proxy cache will simply ignore the range request and request and cache the full file instead. This behavior is allowed by the current RFC specification [15] and the Nginx default.

Exact Byte Range: It is possible when using Nginx as a reverse proxy cache to force Nginx to forward the range request and store the exact range by adding the byte range to the Nginx cache key. This solution enables exact byte ranges to be requested and cached. The disadvantage is that when a request with a non-exact overlapping byte range comes, it will not be able to fetch it from the cache. In this approach, different byte ranges are treated as different/separate URL's.

Range Matching: This extends the previous solution. Every time a range request comes in, instead of forwarding it directly to the upstream server, it generates a set of range requests that together contain all bytes requested. These new range requests always have the same block size and they also start at the same byte positions. This way, even though the initial range request can be any range and can overlap with others, the requests sent to upstream will always match previously sent requests. This makes sure that cache hits occur every time when a subset of a range that was requested before is requested, even though it's not exactly the same. This approach has two drawbacks. Sometimes more data is requested from the upstream (origin) server than is actually needed, and range request for a large range of bytes may result in a large number of range request.

3.3 Implementation

The final implementation of the Late Trans-Muxing smart edge cache runs both Nginx and Apache at the same server. It is shown in Figure 3. Nginx is used for both traditional (CDN style) caching and for range requests caching. For range requests caching, the second method described in the previous section is used (exact byte range caching). An Apache server runs the trans-muxer based on the Unified Origin software in proxy pass mode [12]. Initially, we have also tried running the trans-muxing in an Nginx instance but this resulted in deadlock when a large amount of users connected. The usage of an Apache webserver instance circumvented this issue. The storage was implemented as an Apache server, but could also been any other service that supports data retrieval using HTTP range requests (e.g. Amazon S3 storage etc.).

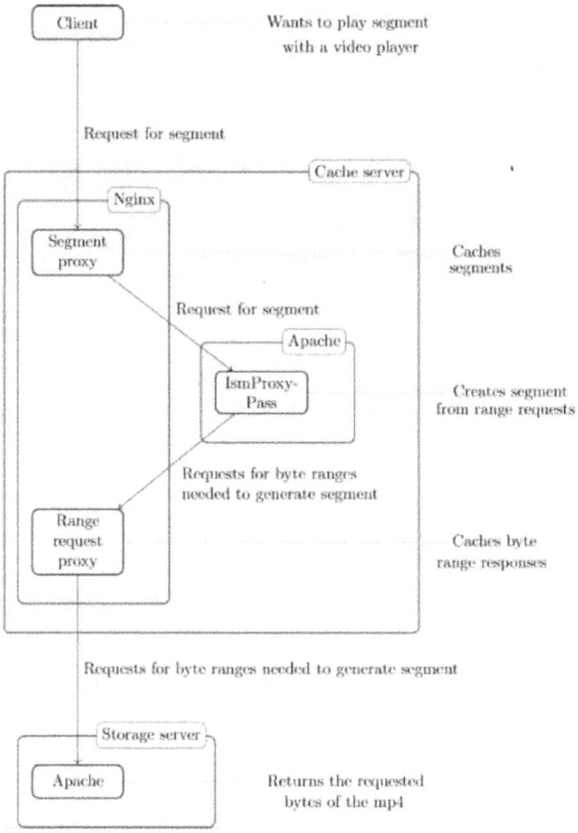

Figure 3 Final Implementation of smart LTM edge cache

4. EXPERIMENTAL EVALUATION

4.1 Experimental Setup

The server side running the storage and smart LTM edge nodes is emulated using two virtual machines (Linux 2GB, one CPU core). The bandwidth between the storage server) and edge node is throttled to 100 Mbit/s using Comcast [16]. The tests performed are with three different setups: the pure LT (LT-Single) that only caches byte ranges and uses Late Trans-Muxing, the LT-double that also caches the responded media segments and the CDN setup that caches each segment but not byte ranges. These setups have been created from enabling/disabling the Nginx cache functions in Figure 3. To generate workloads, a single client is running WRK [17] is used. It spawns 1-50 connections replaying URL requests previously recorded from a real video player. Three different cache conditions have been tested. First, when it is empty (cold cache). Second with the same format in the cache (warm). Third, with a different format (Shown in Figures 5-7). The original video was tears of steel stored in the fragmented MP4 (ismv) format [18].

The experimental tests focus on 6 Key Performance Indicators (KPI's). Three client side KPI indicators are: Received MB/s, (client throughput), average latency for a handled request, and the number of requests handled per second. The three server/network side KPI's are: average internal traffic between storage and the cache, the number of request between storage and the cache and the average cache usage (MB). To summarize, we are testing 3 setups for 6 KPI's for 3 cache conditions using 4 different protocols.

4.2 Experimental Results

The Client side KPI's latency and throughput are shown in Figure 4. For a cold cache scenario and a large number of connections (>10) the client side KPI's are similar for the CDN and LT-single/double setups. For the case when caches are filled with the same format the CDN setup outperforms the LT-Single in client side KPI's (latency, throughput, requests handled per second). However the double LT setup matches the performance of the CDN setup in this case, as the LT-Double also works as a CDN. For a cache filled with a different format the LT single and double setups outperform the CDN setup in each of the client side KPI's: latency, number of request handled and throughput. This effect is due to the Late Trans-Muxing and byte range caching that enable generation of media segments on the fly to serve client requests.

The server side KPI's when the cache is cold or filled with the same format are summarized as follows. In this case the cache usage and internally sent MB's (throughput) are similar for CDN/LT Single, but the LT-Single setup sends more internal requests. Figures 5 – 7 show the results for each of the server side KPI's with a different format in the cache. The cache usage is almost halved by using the single-LT setup instead of the CDN setup, and the amount of internally sent data is heavily reduced (up to 85 %). In addition, the number of internal requests between the cache and the storage server are reduced up to 85% and caching up to 50%. These results highlight the main benefits of the LTM architecture.

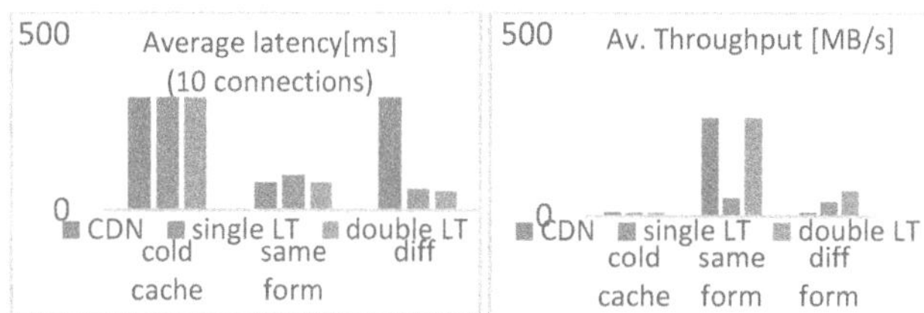

Figure 4 Client side performance indicators (latency, throughput)

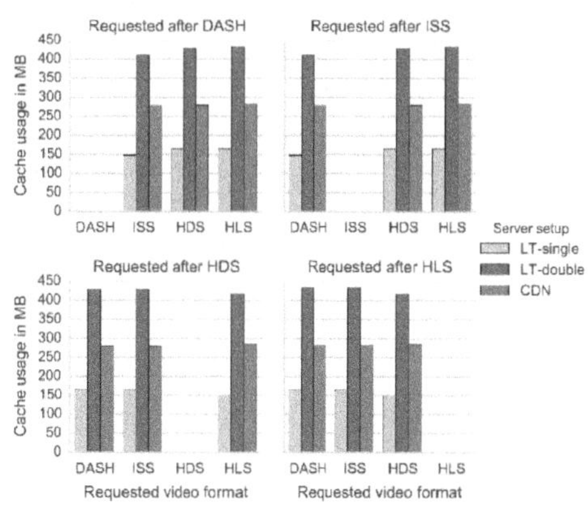

Figure 5 Cache usage MB's, cache filled with a different format

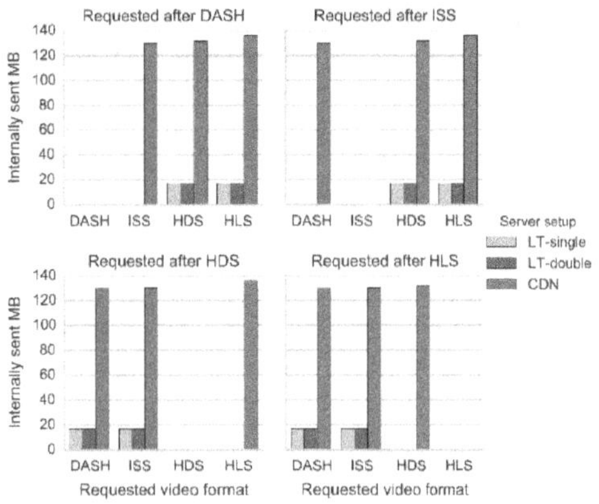

Figure 6 Internally sent data, cache filled with a different format

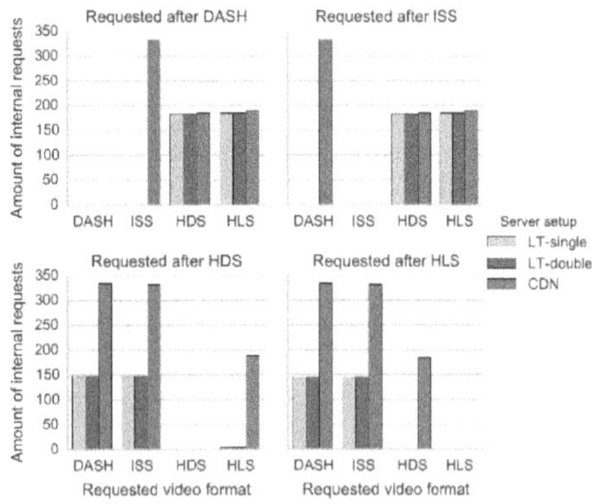

Figure 7 Internal requests, cache filled with a different format

DISCUSSION AND CONCLUSION

In this work we presented on the fly Late Trans-Muxing (LTM) for multi-protocol video streaming. The LTM edge was implemented using popular HTTP servers and a commercially available trans-muxer plugin. The results show comparable client side performance (KPI's) to traditional CDN setups in the different caching conditions. However, the approach shows much improved network/server performance (KPI's) when the cache is filled with a different format. Cache usage is reduced up to 50 %, and backhaul traffic between the cache and the storage server up to 85 %. Taking into account the large share of video traffic in the Internet, integration of Late Trans-Muxing is desirable in future streaming architectures. In future work, we will deploy LTM in realistic mobile edge computing (MEC) setups. This work is supported by the European Union (H2020 RIA, GA No. 671566).

5. REFERENCES

[1] H. Schulzrinne et al., "RFC 3550 RTP: A Transport Protocol for Real-Time Applications," IETF, 2003.

[2] Apple, "HTTP Live Streaming," 3 2016. [Online]. Available: https://developer.apple.com/streaming/.

[3] Microsoft, "Microsoft Smooth Streaming," [Online]. Available: http://www.iis.net/downloads/microsoft/smooth-streaming.

[4] Adobe, "HTTP Dynamic Streaming," 5 4 2016. [Online]. Available: http://www.adobe.com/products/hds-dynamic-streaming.html.

[5] ISO/IEC JCT1/SC29 MPEG, "ISO/IEC 23009-1:2014: Dynamic adaptive streaming over HTTP (DASH) -- Part 1: Media presentation description and segment formats," ISO, 2014.

[6] Cisco, "Cisco Visual Networking Index: Forecast and Methodology, 2014-2019 White Paper," 27 May 2015. [Online]. Available: http://www.cisco.com/c/en/us/solutions/collateral/service-provider/ip-ngn-ip-next-generation-network/white_paper_c11-481360.html. [Accessed 6 4 2016].

[7] Chenghao Liu et al., "Rate adaptation for dynamic adaptive streaming over HTTP in content distribution network," *Signal Processing: Image Communication,* vol. 4, no. 27, pp. 288-311, 2012.

[8] Ricky K. P. Mok et al, "QDASH: a QoE-aware DASH system," in *ACM Multimedia Systems'12*, Chapel Hill, North Carolina, 2012.

[9] He Ma et al., "Dynamic scheduling on video transcoding for MPEG DASH in the cloud environment," in *ACM Multimedia Systems*, Singapore, 2014.

[10] Danny H. Lee et al., "HTTP Adaptive Streaming Friend or Foe?.," in *ACM NOSSDAV*, Singapore, 2014.

[11] Robert Linwood Myers et al., "Methods and systems for real-time transmuxing of streaming media content". United States Patent US 20130275557 A1, april 2013.

[12] CodeShop B.V., "Unified Streaming," 5 4 2016. [Online]. Available: www.unified-streaming.com.

[13] Apache, "Apache Foundation," 1 5 2016. [Online]. Available: http://www.apache.org/.

[14] Nginx, "Nginx," 2016. [Online]. Available: http://nginx.org/.

[15] Fielding et al., "RFC 7233 Hypertext Transfer Protocol (HTTP/1.1): Range Requests," Internet Engineering Task Force, 2014.

[16] Comcast, "COMCAST network emulator," 6 4 2016. [Online]. Available: https://github.com/tylertreat/comcast. [Accessed 2016].

[17] W. Glozer, "WRK Modern HTTP benchmarking tool," 8 4 2016. [Online]. Available: https://github.com/wg/wrk.

[18] Mango Blender "Tears of Steel," Mango Blender foundation, 27 June 2016. [Online]. Available: https://mango.blender.org/production/tears-of-steel-download-watch/. [Accessed 2016].

Analyzing Structural Characteristics of Object Category Representations From Their Semantic-part Distributions

Ravi Kiran Sarvadevabhatla
ravikiran@grads.cds.iisc.ac.in

Venkatesh Babu R
venky@cds.iisc.ac.in

Video Analytics Lab
Department of Computational & Data Sciences
Indian Institute of Science
Bangalore, INDIA

ABSTRACT

Studies from neuroscience show that part-mapping computations are employed by human visual system in the process of object recognition. In this paper, we present an approach for analyzing semantic-part characteristics of object category representations. For our experiments, we use category-epitome, a recently proposed sketch-based spatial representation for objects. To enable part-importance analysis, we first obtain semantic-part annotations of hand-drawn sketches originally used to construct the epitomes. We then examine the extent to which the semantic-parts are present in the epitomes of a category and visualize the relative importance of parts as a word cloud. Finally, we show how such word cloud visualizations provide an intuitive understanding of category-level structural trends that exist in the category-epitome object representations. Our method is general in applicability and can also be used to analyze part-based visual object representations for other depiction methods such as photographic images.

Keywords

object category representation, semantic part, freehand sketch, visualization

1. INTRODUCTION

Studies from neuroscience show that structural part-mapping computations are employed by the human visual system in the process of recognition [5]. Put another way, the presence of certain parts seems to be anticipated by the visual system when it attempts to recognize an object. The knowledge of what these parts are and their relative importance for the overall task of recognition can lead to insights regarding the neuro-visual representation of objects.

In a recent work, Sarvadevabhatla and Radhakrishnan [7] describe the construction of sketch-based spatial representations for object categories termed *category-epitomes*. The epitomes are constructed to as sparse as possible while still being machine-recognizable (see Figure 2). To study these epitomes on a per-category basis, one possibility would be to visually examine them for structural similarities. However, if the number of such epitomes is large, visual examination can be ineffective. An alternate approach would be to examine the distribution of semantic-parts[1] in the epitomes of each category. As we show in this paper, such an approach can lead to an intuitive understanding of category-specific "signature" structural elements (parts) which persist in *category-epitomes* (see Figure 1). We are also encouraged by Rosalia et al. [8] who suggest that topological (part-based) representations enable robustness in analysis since such analysis is typically not affected by small stroke-level differences. Our method is general in applicability and can also be used to analyze part-based visual object representations for other depiction methods such as photographic images.

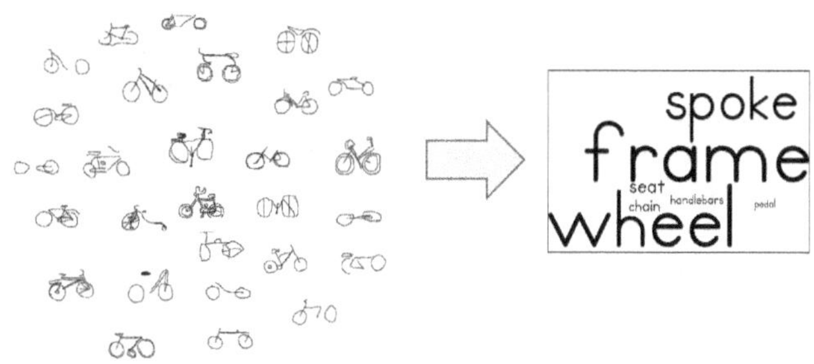

Figure 1: Sparsified yet recognizable freehand sketch representations of object category `bicycle` on the left. Examining such a large number of instances visually for structural similarities can be ineffective. Instead, the approach we propose captures the structurally significant parts as a semantic-part word cloud (on the right). The size of a part's name in the word cloud reflects its importance across the set of sparsified representations of the category.

2. RELATED WORK

Determining the relative importance of part-level structural primitives for object category understanding has been explored only to a limited extent. Rosalia et al. [8] suggest that topological (part-based) representations enable robustness in analysis since such analysis is typically not affected

[1]E.g. spokes, seat, wheel, handle etc. are the semantic parts of a bicycle.

MM '16, October 15-19, 2016, Amsterdam, Netherlands

DOI: http://dx.doi.org/10.1145/2964284.2967190

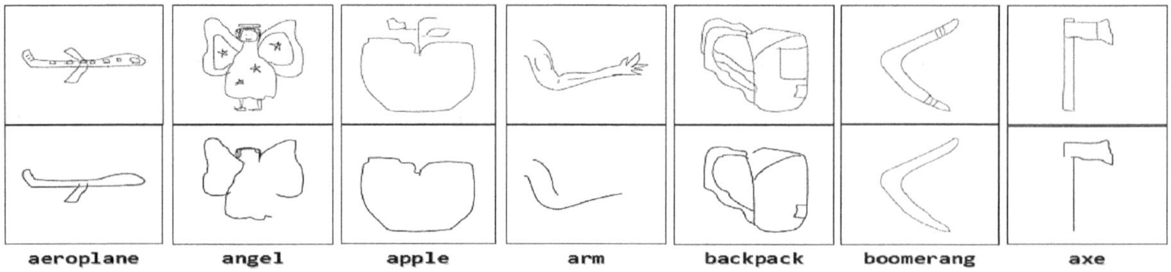

Figure 2: Original sketches (top row) and corresponding *category-epitomes* (bottom row) for various object categories. The figure is from the work of Sarvadevabhatla and Radhakrishnan [7].

by small stroke-level differences. Guo et al. [3] present an importance measure of shape parts based on their ability to reconstruct the whole object shape of 2-D silhouettes. However, the authors interpret parts to mean segments on the contour of the object and not semantic-parts. Ma et al. [6] propose a method based on human perception principles to segment a sketch into semantically meaningful parts. Interestingly, they demonstrate the effectiveness of utilizing semantic-parts rather than just consider parts as unnamed "regions" of the object. Our decision to utilize semantic parts is motivated by this finding. To the best of our knowledge, the relative importance of the semantic parts among images of an object category has not been studied. Because of this reason, it is difficult to compare previous approaches with the one presented in this paper.

3. A PART-ANNOTATED SKETCH DB

As the first step towards the semantic-part based understanding of *category-epitomes*, we manually performed part-level annotation hand-drawn sketches from 13 categories[2] from the sketch database of Eitz et al. [2] for our analysis. A direction of research we intend to pursue in future involves simultaneous analysis of image and sketch based categories (assuming part-level segmentations have been provided). With this in mind, the 13 categories we examine were chosen to overlap with PASCAL-parts [1] – an image dataset containing part-level segmentations of 20 object categories. From the 20 categories in PASCAL-parts, we retained only those containing at least two dominant labeled parts. For example, category `tv` had only one dominant labeled part (*screen*) and therefore was not admissible. Within the sketches of a category, we considered only the correctly classified sketches since *category-epitomes* (the sparsified sketch-based object depictions), by definition, cannot be constructed for misclassified sketches. Please refer to Section 4 of [7] for details regarding *category-epitome* construction.

In what follows, part contour refers to the a closed curve enclosing a region within the object sketch where the part is expected to present. The annotation of part contours in the sketches was performed by 10 annotators who used an annotation tool developed in-house. As an annotation guide, a prototypical image of the category, labeled with parts, was also provided alongside the sketch for annotation. At the end, we obtained semantic-part contour annotations for 283 sketches across 13 object categories for an average of 22 sketches per category. For each annotated sketch, the corresponding sparsified representation (*category-epitome*) was obtained [3].

4. OUR APPROACH

An overview of our approach can be seen in Figure 3. In the figure, locations with numbers circled in orange correspond to important processing stages which we shall refer to in the discussion that follows. We utilize an example from the category `bicycle` for the purpose of illustration. Let $\mathbb{S}$ be the original full-sketch image from category $\mathcal{C}$, $\mathbb{E}$ its *category-epitome* (the sparsified sketch representation) and $\mathbb{A}$, the set of 2-D contour points which correspond to user-annotated boundaries of semantic-parts in $\mathbb{S}$. Since the *category-epitome* is constructed from its full-sketch counterpart, we have $\mathbb{E} \subseteq \mathbb{S}$ (i.e. the set of sketch strokes in the epitome is a subset of the strokes in the corresponding full-sketch). Let us also suppose the cardinality of $\mathbb{A}$ is n_a and the number of semantic-parts in $\mathcal{C}$ is M.

4.1 Obtaining candidate part contours

In some instances, part contours may enclose an insignificant number of pixels from epitome $\mathbb{E}$. As the first step, we filter out such contours. For each part contour, we compute the number of stroke pixels n_{full} in $\mathbb{S}$ that lie within the part's boundary. We also compute the number of stroke pixels n_{epi} in $\mathbb{E}$ that lie within the part's boundary. If the ratio $\frac{n_{epi}}{n_{full}}$ is larger than a threshold, the contour is added to the candidate contour list. In Figure 3, the candidate contours are shown in bold (region labeled ①). Note that multiple occurrences of the same semantic-part type (e.g. spokes of the `bicycle`) which satisfy the threshold criterion are counted independently. To avoid undue importance to multiple occurrences of the same part type, we normalize by the corresponding part contour counts in full sketch to obtain a 'coarse' part-importance factor p_{im} for each semantic-part (see ② in Figure 3). We term it a 'coarse' importance factor since it implicitly takes raw pixel counts into account for determining part importance. Shortly, we shall see how the spatial structure of the stroke is also utilized in determining the final semantic-part importance.

4.2 Obtaining 'fine-grained' part-importance weights

The process of annotating a part typically results in a 2-D closed contour. Points on the contour tend to be in close

[2]`airplane, bicycle, bus, car (sedan), cat, cow, dog, flying bird, horse, person walking, potted plant, sheep, train`

[3]The sparsified representations are provided by [7] at http://val.serc.iisc.ernet.in/eotd/epitome_images/.

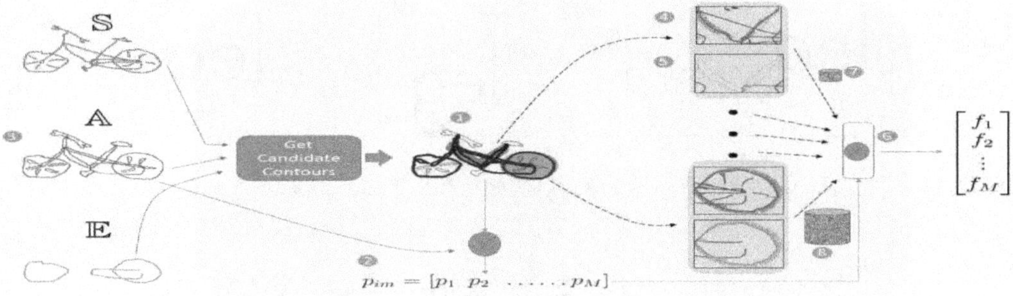

Figure 3: Determining part-importances given the full sketch $\mathbb{S}$, the corresponding *category-epitome* $\mathbb{E}$ and the set of user annotations $\mathbb{A}$ from the category `bicycle`. The output is a vector of semantic-part importances. Locations with numbered orange circles indicate key aspects of the pipeline. The sketches and annotation data have been color-coded for visualization purposes. This figure is best viewed in color.

proximity with the boundary pixels of the object. We exploit this observation to obtain a 'fine-grained' part importance factor for each part enclosed by a candidate contour.

Let

$$B^{(j)} = \{b_i^{(j)} = (x_i^{(j)}, y_i^{(j)})\}_{i=1}^{n_b}, j = 1 \dots n_a$$

be the sets of points comprising user-annotated boundary contours. Examples of such contours can be in the annotation image $\mathbb{A}$ in Figure 3 (region ③). For a given 'part contour set' $B^{(j)}$, let

$$S^{(j)} = \{s_k^{(j)} = (x_k^{(j)}, y_k^{(j)})\}_{k=1}^{n_s}, j = 1 \dots n_a$$

be the 'full-sketch point' set of 2-D locations of stroke pixels enclosed by the part contour in the full sketch $\mathbb{S}$. Similarly, let

$$E^{(j)} = \{e_l^{(j)} = (x_l^{(j)}, y_l^{(j)})\}_{l=1}^{n_e}, j = 1 \dots n_a$$

be the 'epitome point' set of 2-D locations of stroke pixels enclosed by the part contour in epitome $\mathbb{E}$.

For each member in the 'full-sketch point' set, $s_k^{(j)} = (x_k^{(j)}, y_k^{(j)}) \in S^{(j)}$, we find the closest-by-distance matching point $b_i^{(j)} = (x_i^{(j)}, y_i^{(j)})$ from $B^{(j)}$. i.e.

$$b_i^{(j)} = \arg\min_x d(s_k^{(j)}, b_x^{(j)})$$

We retain only those matches $s_k^{(j)}, b_i^{(j)}$ whose distance is less than a threshold. Intuitively, this procedure enables us to identify stroke pixels of the full sketch which "hug" the candidate contour's boundary. Let $n_{valid\_full}^{(j)}$ be the number of such stroke pixels $s_k^{(j)}$. Valid matches found using the above procedure are shown in red for a candidate part boundary in Figure 3 – refer to region ④. A similar procedure gives us $n_{valid\_epi}^{(j)}$ – the number of stroke pixels in the epitome which "hug" the candidate contour's boundary (See region ⑤ in Figure 3). Next, we compute

$$w_{part}^{(j)} = \frac{n_{valid\_epi}^{(j)}}{n_{valid\_full}^{(j)}}$$

The ratio $w_{part}^{(j)}$ provides a fine-grained importance for the part enclosed by the boundary – the higher the value of $w_{part}^{(j)}$, the more the number of pixels from both full sketch and the epitome which commonly "hug" the annotated part boundary. The part-importance is depicted in Figure 3 by the height of orange-colored cylinders adjoining numbered regions ⑦,⑧. Examination of epitome $\mathbb{E}$ shows that the 'wheel' is more prominently present compared to the 'bicycle frame' consequently according the former a larger part-importance ($w_{part}^{(j)}$) value.

4.3 Obtaining category-wise part weights

The above procedure of obtaining fine-grained importance weight $w_{part}^{(j)}$ is repeated for each part (indexed by $j = 1, 2 \dots n_a$) enclosed by a candidate contour boundary $B^{(j)}$ by utilizing pixel location sets $S^{(j)}$ and $E^{(j)}$. These weights are combined along with the coarse importance weights p_{im} obtained in Section 4.1 to obtain the image-level part-wise importance weights $f_i, i = 1, 2, \dots M$ (region labeled ⑥ in Figure 3). The part-wise aggregation of these weights over all the 'full sketch'-epitome pairs of a category is normalized to obtain a probability distribution $\hat{f}$ indicating the relative importance of each part. This distribution can then be visualized as a semantic-part word cloud (see Figure 1) to determine the "signature" structural elements (semantic-parts) which persist in the epitomes of a category[4].

5. ANALYZING SEMANTIC-PART WORD CLOUDS

Before we proceed, it is important to point out that the *category-epitome* of a full sketch implicitly depends upon the order in which individual strokes of the full sketch are considered. For example, the epitome can be constructed by considering the temporal order in which the sketches were originally added. Yet another epitome can be constructed if we consider strokes in decreasing order of stroke length. Essentially, for each full sketch, there can be as many *category-epitomes* as the number of stroke orderings. In our analysis that follows, we keep the stroke ordering fixed over the set of categories. Details on stroke orderings and their effect on *category-epitomes* that result can be found in Sections 4, 5 of [7].

As a preliminary step in our analysis, we sort the parts by

[4]The pseudo-code for the procedure mentioned above can be viewed at http://val.serc.iisc.ernet.in/eotd/epipartviz/#pc

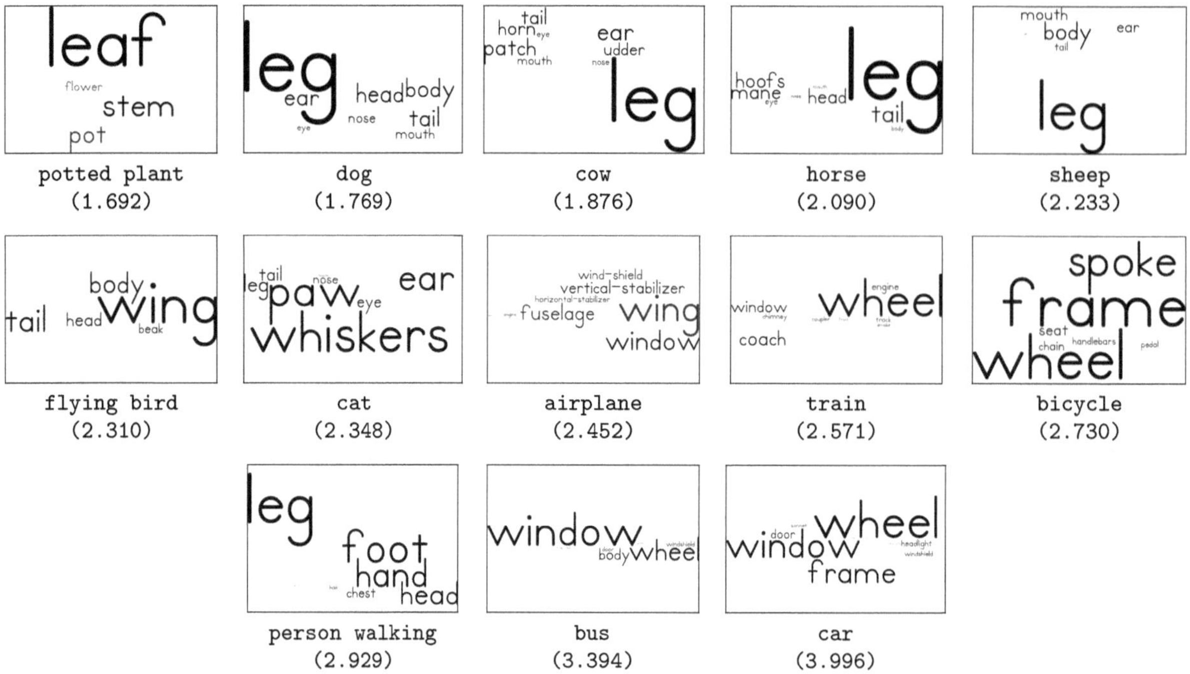

Figure 4: Importance of semantic structural parts for object categories : Each image shows a word cloud of parts for epitomes of each category. The number alongside the category name indicates the kurtosis of part-importance distribution (see Section 5). The size of the part name indicates its relative importance across epitomes of the category. The above depictions are for Length stroke sequence ordering.

their normalized part-importances weights $\hat{f}_i$ (Section 4.3) and construct their cumulative histogram $F_i = \sum_{j=1}^{i} \hat{f}_j, i = 1, 2, \dots M$.

If the category contains many dominant parts, their cumulative histograms would have a distinctly different "peakiness" structure compared to categories which contain one or two dominant parts. To quantify this "peakiness", we computed the unbiased kurtosis K of $\mathbb{F}$ as $K = \frac{(M-1)}{(M-2)(M-3)}((M+1)K_b - 3(M-1)) + 3$ where $K_b = \frac{\frac{1}{M}\sum_{i=1}^{M}(F_i - \bar{F})^4}{\left(\frac{1}{M}\sum_{i=1}^{M}(F_i - \bar{F})^2\right)^2}$ and $\bar{F} = \frac{\sum_{i=1}^{M} F_i}{M}$.

The values of kurtosis and the associated part-importance distribution for each category can be viewed in Figure 4. Instead of the depicting the distributions as traditional (part) histograms, we utilize a word-cloud method. The advantage of this representation is that it indicates at a glance, the dominant parts in the sparsified representations (*epitomes*) for a category – the larger the size of a semantic-part's name , the more its dominance.

As Figure 4 shows, categories with low kurtosis are usually the ones with one or two dominant parts (e.g. `horse, dog, potted plant`). This also indicates that such parts are consistently present in most of the *epitomes*. This, in turn, suggests a consistency in which sketches of the category are drawn. Word clouds of categories with more variety in depictions (e.g. `airplane, person walking`) have higher kurtosis and tend to contain many parts whose names are similar in size. Another interesting trend exists across semantically related categories. For instance, 'leg' is found to be the common defining dominant signature part for the animal categories (`cow, dog, horse, person walking, sheep`). Similarly, for the vehicular categories (`car, bus, bicycle, train`), 'wheel' is a dominant part and for the flying categories (`airplane, bird`), 'wing' is a dominant part.

The trends mentioned above are for epitomes arising out of LENGTH stroke ordering. However, almost identical trends have been observed for TEMPORAL and ALTERNATE stroke orderings as well. These results across the stroke ordering schemes suggest that the "signature" semantic parts live up to their name – they capture the discriminative structural elements of the category and are invariant to the manner in which sketch strokes are considered in the process of *epitome* construction.

6. DISCUSSION AND FUTURE WORK

In this paper, we have presented a novel framework for analyzing the structural characteristics of *category-epitomes*. We have shown that semantic-part annotations of sketches can be utilized to gain an intuitive understanding of category-level and sketch-stroke-ordering level structural trends in *category-epitomes*. The database of part-annotated sketches is another significant contribution to the community since it enables simultaneous analysis of sketches and photographic image counterparts at a semantic-part level for object categories[5]. The word cloud based analysis we have presented is quite general and can be applied to any spatial visual object representation wherein the part labelings have been provided. In additon, to examine the generalizability of our approach and results, it would be interesting to apply it to the part-segmented sketch database of Huang et al. [4].

[5]The database of part-annotated sketches is available at http://val.serc.iisc.ernet.in/eotd/epipartviz/#dataset

7. REFERENCES

[1] X. Chen, R. Mottaghi, X. Liu, S. Fidler, R. Urtasun, and A. Yuille. Detect what you can: Detecting and representing objects using holistic models and body parts. In *CVPR*, 2014.

[2] M. Eitz, J. Hays, and M. Alexa. How do humans sketch objects? *SIGGRAPH*, 2012.

[3] G. Guo, Y. Wang, T. Jiang, A. L. Yuille, F. Fang, and W. Gao. A shape reconstructability measure of object part importance with applications to object detection and localization. *IJCV*, 2014.

[4] Z. Huang, H. Fu, and R. W. H. Lau. Data-driven segmentation and labeling of freehand sketches. *SIGGRAPH Asia*, 2014.

[5] A. Lovett, D. Gentner, K. Forbus, and E. Sagi. Using analogical mapping to simulate time-course phenomena in perceptual similarity. *Cognitive Systems Research*, 2009.

[6] C. Ma, Z. Dong, T. Jiang, Y. Wang, and W. Gao. A method of perceptual-based shape decomposition. In *ICCV*, 2013.

[7] R. K. Sarvadevabhatla and V. B. Radhakrishnan. Eye of the dragon: Exploring discriminatively minimalist sketch-based abstractions for object categories. In *Proceedings of the 23rd ACM International Conference on Multimedia*, MM '15, pages 271–280, New York, NY, USA, 2015. ACM.

[8] R. G. Schneider and T. Tuytelaars. Sketch classification and classification-driven analysis using fisher vectors. *SIGGRAPH Asia*, 2014.

Action Recognition Based on Joint Trajectory Maps Using Convolutional Neural Networks

Pichao Wang[1]*, Zhaoyang Li[2]*, Yonghong Hou[2]† and Wanqing Li[1]
[1]Advanced Multimedia Research Lab, University of Wollongong, Australia
[2]School of Electronic Information Engineering, Tianjin University, China
pw212@uowmail.edu.au,lizhaoyang@tju.edu.cn, houroy@tju.edu.cn, wanqing@uow.edu.au

ABSTRACT

Recently, Convolutional Neural Networks (ConvNets) have shown promising performances in many computer vision tasks, especially image-based recognition. How to effectively use ConvNets for video-based recognition is still an open problem. In this paper, we propose a compact, effective yet simple method to encode spatio-temporal information carried in $3D$ skeleton sequences into multiple $2D$ images, referred to as Joint Trajectory Maps (JTM), and ConvNets are adopted to exploit the discriminative features for real-time human action recognition. The proposed method has been evaluated on three public benchmarks, i.e., MSRC-12 Kinect gesture dataset (MSRC-12), G3D dataset and UTD multimodal human action dataset (UTD-MHAD) and achieved the state-of-the-art results.

Keywords

Action Recognition, Convolutional Neural Networks, Skeleton, Trajectory

1. INTRODUCTION

Recognition of human actions from RGB-D (Red, Green, Blue and Depth) data has attracted increasing attention in multimedia signal processing in recent years due to the advantages of depth information over conventional RGB video, e.g. being insensitive to illumination changes. Since the first work of such a type [9] reported in 2010, many methods [17, 12, 23, 10] have been proposed based on specific hand-crafted feature descriptors extracted from depth. With the recent development of deep learning, a few methods [18, 19] have been developed based on Convolutional Neural Networks (ConvNets). A common and intuitive method to represent human motion is to use a sequence of skeletons. With the development of the cost-effective depth cameras and algorithms for real-time pose estimation [14], skeleton extraction has become more robust and many hand-designed skeleton features [22, 24, 5, 20, 16] for action recognition have been proposed. Recently, Recurrent Neural Networks (RNNs) [3, 15, 28, 13] have also been adopted for action recognition from skeleton data. The hand-crafted features are always shallow and dataset-dependent. RNNs tend to overemphasize the temporal information especially when the training data is not sufficient, leading to overfitting. In this paper, we present a compact, effective yet simple method that encodes the joint trajectories into texture images, referred to as Joint Trajectory Maps (JTM), as the input of ConvNets for action recognition. In this way, the capability of the ConvNets in learning discriminative features can be fully exploited [25].

One of the challenges in action recognition is how to properly model and use the spatio-temporal information. The commonly used bag-of-words model tends to overemphasize the spatial information. On the other hand, Hidden Markov Model (HMM) or RNN based methods are likely to overstress the temporal information. The proposed method addresses this challenge in a different way by encoding as much the spatio-temporal information as possible (without a need to decide which one is important and how important it is) into images and letting the CNNs to learn the discriminative one. This is the key reason that the proposed method outperformed previous ones. In addition, the proposed encoding method can be extended to online recognition due to the accumulative nature of the encoding process. Furthermore, such encoding of spatio-temporal information into images allows us to leverage the advanced methods developed for image recognition.

2. THE PROPOSED METHOD

The proposed method consists of two major components, as illustrated in Fig. 1, three ConvNets and the construction of three JTMs as the input of the ConvNets in three orthogonal planes from the skeleton sequences. Final classification of a given test skeleton sequence is obtained through a late fusion of the three ConvNets. The main contribution of this paper is on the construction of suitable JTMs for the ConvNets to learn discriminative features.

We argue that an effective JTM should have the following properties to keep sufficient spatial-temporal information of an action:

- The joints or group of joints should be distinct in the JTM such that the spatial information of the joints is well reserved.
- The JTM should encode effectively the temporal evolution, i.e. trajectories of the joints, including the direction and speed of joint motions.
- The JTM should be able to encode the difference in motion among the different joints or parts of the body to reflect how the joints are synchronized during the action.

*Both authors contributed equally to this work
†Corresponding author

MM '16, October 15-19, 2016, Amsterdam, Netherlands

DOI: http://dx.doi.org/10.1145/2964284.2967191

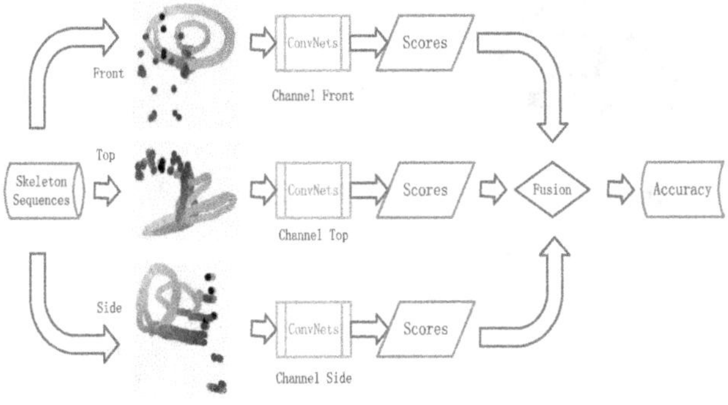

Figure 1: The framework of the proposed method.

Specifically, JTM can be recursively defined as follows

$$JTM_i = JTM_{i-1} + f(i) \tag{1}$$

where $f(i)$ is a function encoding the spatial-temporal information at frame or time-stamp i. Since JTM is accumulated over the period of an action, $f(i)$ has to be carefully defined such that the JTM for an action sample has the required properties and the accumulation over time has little adverse impact on the spatial-temporal information encoded in the JTM. We propose in this paper to use hue, saturation and brightness to encode the spatial-temporal motion patterns.

2.1 Joint Trajectory Maps

Assume an action H has n frames of skeletons and each skeleton consists of m joints. The skeleton sequence is denoted as $H = \{F_1, F_2, ..., F_n\}$, where $F_i = \{P_1^i, P_2^i, ..., P_m^i\}$ is a vector of the joint coordinates at frame i, and P_j^i is the $3D$ coordinates of the jth joint in frame i. The skeleton trajectory T for an action of n frames consists of the trajectories of all joints and is defined as:

$$T = \{T_1, T_2, \cdots, T_i, \cdots, T_{n-1}\} \tag{2}$$

where $T_i = \{t_1^i, t_2^i, ..., t_m^i\} = F_{i+1} - F_i$ and the kth joint trajectory is $t_k^i = P_k^{i+1} - P_k^i$. At this stage, the function $f(i)$ is the same as T_i, that is,

$$f(i) = T_i = \{t_1^i, t_2^i, ..., t_m^i\}. \tag{3}$$

The skeleton trajectory is projected to the three orthogonal planes, i.e. three Cartesian planes, to form three JTMs. Fig. 2 shows the three projected trajectories of the right hand joint for action "right hand draw circle (clockwise)" in the UTD-MHAD dataset. From these JTMs, it can be seen that the spatial information of this joint is preserved but the direction of the motion is lost.

2.2 Encoding Joint Motion Direction

To capture the motion information in the JTM, it is proposed to use hue to represent the motion direction. Different kinds of colormaps can be chosen. In this paper, the jet colormap, ranging from blue to red, and passing through the colors cyan, yellow, and orange, was adopted. Assume the color of a joint trajectory is C and the length of the trajectory L, and let $C_l, l \in (0, L)$ be the color at position l. For the qth trajectory T_q from 1 to $n-1$, a color C_l, where $l = \frac{q}{n-1} \times L$ is specified to the joint trajectory, making different trajectories have their own color corresponding to their temporal positions in the sequence as illustrated in Fig. 3. Herein, the trajectory with color is denoted as $C\_t_k^i$ and the function $f(i)$ is updated to:

$$f(i) = \{C\_t_1^i, C\_t_2^i, ..., C\_t_m^i\}. \tag{4}$$

This ensures that different actions are encoded to a same length colormap. The effects can be seen in Fig. 4, sub-figures (1) to (2). Even though the same actions with different number of cycles will be encoded into different color shapes, the direction can still be reflected in color variation and the differences between actions can still be captured due to the different spatial information.

(1) (2) (3)

Figure 2: The trajectories projected onto three Cartesian planes for action "right hand draw circle (clockwise)" in UTD-MHAD [2]: (1) the front plane; (2) the top plane; (3) the side plane.

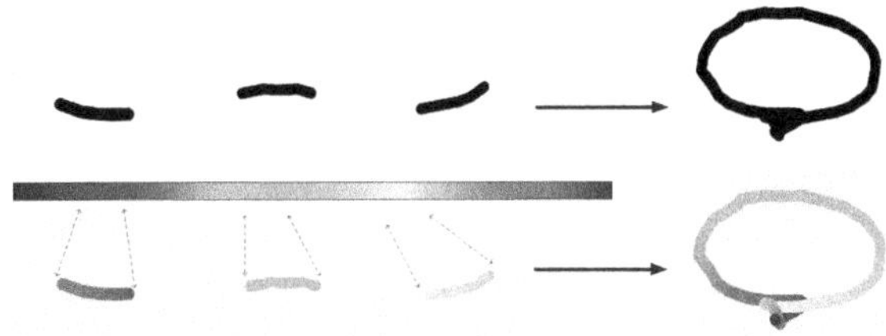

Figure 3: The trajectories of different body parts have their different colors reflecting the temporal orders.

2.3 Encoding Body Parts

To distinguish different body parts, multiple colormaps are employed. There are many ways to achieve this. For example, each joint is assigned to one colormap, or several groups of joints are assigned to different colormaps randomly. Considering arms and legs often have more motion than other body parts, we empirically generate three colormaps ($C1, C2, C3$) to encode three body parts. $C1$ is used for the left body part (consisting of left shoulder, left elbow, left wrist, left hand, left hip, left knee, left ankle and left foot), $C2$ for the right body part (consisting of right shoulder, right elbow, right wrist, right hand, right hip, right knee, right ankle and right foot), and $C3$ for the middle body part (consisting of head, neck, torso and hip center). $C1$ is the same as C, i.e. the jet colormap, $C2$ is a reversed colormap of $C1$, and $C3$ is a colormap ranging from light gray to black. Here, the trajectory encoded by multiple colormaps is denoted as $MC\_t_k^i$, and the function $f(i)$ is formulated as:

$$f(i) = \{MC\_t_1^i, MC\_t_2^i, ..., MC\_t_m^i\}. \tag{5}$$

The effects can be seen in Fig. 4, sub-figures (2) to (3).

2.4 Encoding Motion Magnitude

Motion magnitude is one of the most important factors in human motion. For one action, large magnitude of motion usually indicates more motion information. In this paper, it is proposed to encode the motion magnitude of joints into the saturation and brightness components, so that such encoding not only encodes the motion but also enriches the texture of trajectories which are expected to be beneficial for ConvNets to learn discriminative features. For joints with high motion magnitude or speed, high saturation will be assigned as high motion usually carries more discriminative information. Specifically, the saturation is set to range from s_{min} to s_{max}. Given a trajectory, its saturation S_j^i in HSV color space could be calculated as

$$S_j^i = \frac{v_j^i}{max\{v\}} \times (s_{max} - s_{min}) + s_{min} \tag{6}$$

where v_j^i is the jth joint speed at the ith frame.

$$v_j^i = \|P_j^{i+1} - P_j^i\|_2 \tag{7}$$

The trajectory adjusted by saturation is denoted as $MC_s\_t_k^i$ and the function $f(i)$ is refined as:

$$f(i) = \{MC_s\_t_1^i, MC_s\_t_2^i, ..., MC_s\_t_m^i\} \tag{8}$$

The encoding effect can be seen in Figure 4, sub-figures (3) to (4), where the slow motion becomes diluted (e.g. trajectory of knees and ankles) while the fast motion becomes saturated (e.g. the green part of the circle).

To further enhance the motion patterns in the JTM, the brightness is modulated by the speed of joints so that motion information is enhance in the JTM by rapidly changing the brightness according to the joint speed. In particular, the brightness is set to range from b_{min} to b_{max}. Given a trajectory t_j^i whose speed is v_j^i, its brightness B_j^i in the HSV color space is calculated as

$$B_j^i = \frac{v_j^i}{max\{v\}} \times (b_{max} - b_{min}) + b_{min} \tag{9}$$

The trajectory adjusted by brightness is denoted as $MC_b\_t_k^i$ and the function $f(i)$ is updated to:

$$f(i) = \{MC_b\_t_1^i, MC_b\_t_2^i, ..., MC_b\_t_m^i\}. \tag{10}$$

The effect can be seen in Fig 4, sub-figures (3) to (5), where texture becomes apparent (e.g. the yellow parts of the circle). Finally, motion magnitude is encoded with saturation and brightness together. The trajectory is denoted as $MC_{sb}\_t_k^i$ and the function $f(i)$ is refined as:

$$f(i) = \{MC_{sb}\_t_1^i, MC_{sb}\_t_2^i, ..., MC_{sb}\_t_m^i\}. \tag{11}$$

As illustrated in Fig. 4, sub-figures(3) to (6), it not only enriches the texture information but also highlights the faster motion.

2.5 Training and Recognition

In the experiments, the layer configuration of the three ConvNets was same as the one in [8]. The implementation was derived from the publicly available Caffe toolbox [7] based on one NVIDIA GeForce GTX TITAN X card and the pre-trained models over ImageNet [8] were used for initialization in training. The network weights are learned using the mini-batch stochastic gradient descent with the momentum being set to 0.9 and weight decay being set to 0.0005. At each iteration, a mini-batch of 256 samples is constructed by sampling 256 shuffled training JTMs. All JTMs are resized to 256 × 256. The learning rate is to 10^{-3} for

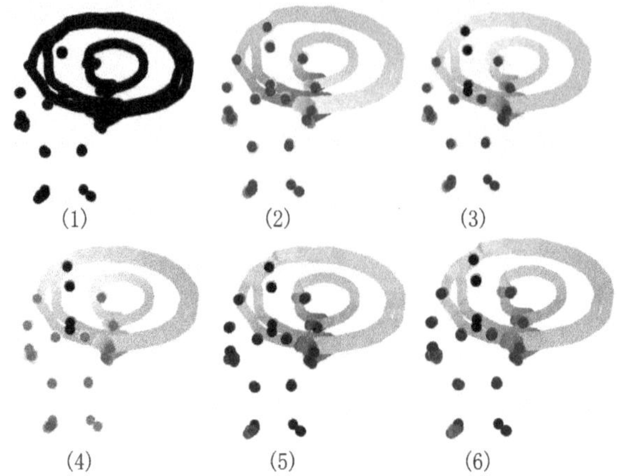

Figure 4: Illustration of visual differences for different techniques in JTM.

fine-tuning and then it is decreased according to a fixed schedule, which is kept the same for all training sets. For each ConvNet the training undergoes 100 cycles and the learning rate decreases every 20 cycles. For all experiments, the dropout regularisation ratio was set to 0.5 in order to reduce complex co-adaptations of neurons in nets. Three ConvNets are trained on the JTMs in the three Cartesian planes and the final score for a test sample are the averages of the outputs from the three ConvNets. The testing process can easily achieved real-time speed (average 0.36 seconds/sample).

3. EXPERIMENTAL RESULTS

The proposed method was evaluated on three public benchmark datasets: MSRC-12 Kinect Gesture Dataset [4], G3D [1] and UTD-MHAD [2]. These three datasets have different varieties of contexts [26]. Experiments were conducted to evaluate the effectiveness of each encoding scheme in the proposed method and the final results were compared with the state-of-the-art reported on the same datasets. In all experiments, the saturation and brightness covers the full range (from 0% $\sim$ 100% mapped to 0 $\sim$ 255) in HSV color space.

3.1 Evaluation of Different Encoding Schemes

The effectiveness of different encoding schemes (corresponding to the sub-figures in Fig. 4) was evaluated on the G3D dataset using the front JTM and the recognition accuracies are listed in Table 1.

Techniques	Accuracy (%)
Trajectory: t_1^i	63.64%
Trajectory: $C\_t_1^i$	74.24%
Trajectory: $MC\_t_1^i$	78.48%
Trajectory: $MC_s\_t_1^i$	81.82%
Trajectory: $MC_b\_t_1^i$	82.12%
Trajectory: $MC_{sb}\_t_1^i$	85.45%

Table 1: Comparisons of the different encoding schemes on the G3D dataset using the JTM projected to the front plane alone.

From this Table it can be seen that the proposed encoding techniques effectively captures the spatio-temporal information and the ConvNets are able to learn the discriminative features from the JTM for action recognition.

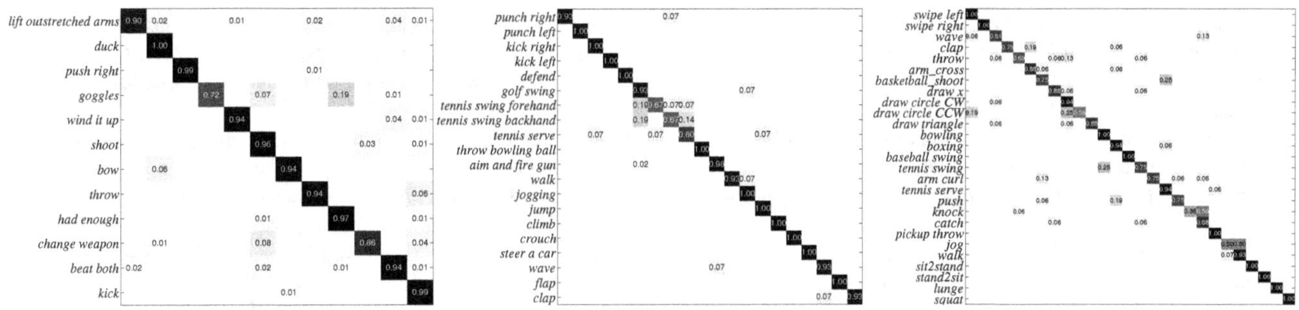

(a) MSRC-12 dataset (b) G3D dataset (c) UTD-MHAD dataset

Figure 5: The confusion matrices of proposed method for MSRC-12, G3D and UTD-MHAD datasets.

Table 2: Recognition accuracies of the exiting methods and proposed methods on the three datasets.

Methods	Datasets		
	MSRC-12	G3D	UTD-MHAD
HGM [21]	66.25%	-	-
ELC-KSVD [27]	90.22%	-	-
Cov3DJ [6]	91.70%	-	-
LRBM [11]	-	90.50%	-
Kinect & Inertial [2]	-	-	79.10%
Ours	**93.12%**	**94.24%**	**85.81%**

3.2 MSRC-12 Kinect Gesture Dataset

MSRC-12 [4] is a relatively large dataset for gesture/action recognition from 3D skeleton data captured by a Kinect sensor. The dataset has 594 sequences, containing 12 gestures by 30 subjects, 6244 gesture instances in total. For this dataset, cross-subjects protocol is adopted, that is odd subjects for training and even subjects for testing. Table 2 lists the performance of the proposed method and the results reported before.

The confusion matrix is shown in Fig. 5(a). From the confusion matrix we can see that the proposed method distinguishes most of actions very well, but it is not very effective to distinguish "goggles" and "had enough" which shares the similar appearance of JTM probably caused by 3D to 2D projection.

3.3 G3D Dataset

Gaming 3D Dataset (G3D) [1] focuses on real-time action recognition in gaming scenario. It contains 10 subjects performing 20 gaming actions. For this dataset, the first 4 subjects were used for training, the fifth for validation and the remaining 5 subjects for testing as configured in [11]. Table 2 compared the performance of the proposed method and that reported in [11].

The confusion matrix is shown in Fig. 5(b). From the confusion matrix we can see that the proposed method recognizes most of actions well. Compared with LRBM, our proposed method outperforms LRBM in spatial information mining. LRBM confused mostly the actions between "tennis swing forehand" and "bowling", "golf" and "tennis swing backhand", "aim and fire gun" and "wave", "jump" and "walk", however, these actions were quite well distinguished in our method because of the good spatial information exploitation in our method. As for "aim and fire gun" and "wave", our method could not distinguish them well before encoding the motion magnitude, which means the temporal information enhancement procedure is effective. However, in our method, "tennis swing forehand" and "tennis swing backhand" are confused. It's probably because the body shapes in the front and side projections of the two actions are too similar, and scores fusion is not very effective to improve the recognition.

3.4 UTD-MHAD

UTD-MHAD [2] is a multimodal action dataset, captured by one Microsoft Kinect camera and one wearable inertial sensor. This dataset contains 27 actions performed by 8 subjects (4 females and 4 males) with each subject perform each action 4 times. For this dataset, cross-subjects protocol is adopted as in [2], namely, the data from the subject numbers 1, 3, 5, 7 used for training while 2, 4, 6, 8 used for testing. Table 2 compared the performance of the proposed method and that reported in [2]. Please notice that the method used in [2] is based on Depth and Inertial sensor data, not skeleton data alone.

The confusion matrix is shown in Fig. 5(c). This dataset is much more challenging compared to previous two datasets. From the confusion matrix we can see that the proposed method can not distinguish some actions well, for example, "jog" and "walk". A probable reason is that the proposed encoding process is also a normalization process along temporal axis (Section 3.2). The actions "jog" and "walk" will be normalized to have a very similar JTM after the encoding.

4. CONCLUSION

This paper addressed the problem of human action recognition by applying ConvNets to skeleton sequences. We proposed a compact, effective yet simple method to encode the joints trajectories to JTM where the motion information is converted into texture patterns. ConvNets learn discriminative features from these maps for real-time human action recognition. The experimental results showed that the proposed method worked effectively. The proposed method can benefit from effective data augmentation process and be extended to online action recognition.

5. ACKNOWLEDGMENTS

This work was supported by the National Natural Science Foundation of China (grant 61571325) and Key Projects in the Tianjin Science & Technology Pillar Program (grant 15ZCZD GX001900).

6. REFERENCES

[1] V. Bloom, D. Makris, and V. Argyriou. G3D: A gaming action dataset and real time action recognition evaluation

framework. In *Proc. IEEE Computer Society Conference on Computer Vision and Pattern Recognition Workshops (CVPRW)*, pages 7–12, 2012.

[2] C. Chen, R. Jafari, and N. Kehtarnavaz. Utd-mhad: A multimodal dataset for human action recognition utilizing a depth camera and a wearable inertial sensor. In *Image Processing (ICIP), 2015 IEEE International Conference on*, pages 168–172, 2015.

[3] Y. Du, W. Wang, and L. Wang. Hierarchical recurrent neural network for skeleton based action recognition. In *Proc. IEEE Conference on Computer Vision and Pattern Recognition (CVPR)*, pages 1110–1118, 2015.

[4] S. Fothergill, H. M. Mentis, S. Nowozin, and P. Kohli. Instructing people for training gestural interactive systems. In *ACM Conference on Computer-Human Interaction (ACM HCI)*, 2012.

[5] M. A. Gowayyed, M. Torki, M. E. Hussein, and M. El-Saban. Histogram of oriented displacements (HOD): Describing trajectories of human joints for action recognition. In *Proc. International Joint Conference on Artificial Intelligence (IJCAI)*, pages 1351–1357, 2013.

[6] M. E. Hussein, M. Torki, M. A. Gowayyed, and M. El-Saban. Human action recognition using a temporal hierarchy of covariance descriptors on 3D joint locations. In *Proc. International Joint Conference on Artificial Intelligence (IJCAI)*, pages 2466–2472, 2013.

[7] Y. Jia, E. Shelhamer, J. Donahue, S. Karayev, J. Long, R. B. Girshick, S. Guadarrama, and T. Darrell. Caffe: Convolutional architecture for fast feature embedding. In *Proc. ACM international conference on Multimedia (ACM MM)*, pages 675–678, 2014.

[8] A. Krizhevsky, I. Sutskever, and G. E. Hinton. Imagenet classification with deep convolutional neural networks. In *Proc. Annual Conference on Neural Information Processing Systems (NIPS)*, pages 1106–1114, 2012.

[9] W. Li, Z. Zhang, and Z. Liu. Action recognition based on a bag of 3D points. In *Proc. IEEE Computer Society Conference on Computer Vision and Pattern Recognition Workshops (CVPRW)*, pages 9–14, 2010.

[10] C. Lu, J. Jia, and C.-K. Tang. Range-sample depth feature for action recognition. In *Proc. IEEE Conference on Computer Vision and Pattern Recognition (CVPR)*, pages 772–779, 2014.

[11] S. Nie, Z. Wang, and Q. Ji. A generative restricted boltzmann machine based method for high-dimensional motion data modeling. *Computer Vision and Image Understanding*, pages 14–22, 2015.

[12] O. Oreifej and Z. Liu. HON4D: Histogram of oriented 4D normals for activity recognition from depth sequences. In *Proc. IEEE Conference on Computer Vision and Pattern Recognition (CVPR)*, pages 716–723, 2013.

[13] A. Shahroudy, J. Liu, T.-T. Ng, and G. Wang. NTU RGB+ D: A large scale dataset for 3D human activity analysis. In *Proc. IEEE Conference on Computer Vision and Pattern Recognition (CVPR)*, 2016.

[14] J. Shotton, A. Fitzgibbon, M. Cook, T. Sharp, M. Finocchio, R. Moore, A. Kipman, and A. Blake. Real-time human pose recognition in parts from single depth images. In *Proc. IEEE Conference on Computer Vision and Pattern Recognition (CVPR)*, pages 1297–1304, 2011.

[15] V. Veeriah, N. Zhuang, and G.-J. Qi. Differential recurrent neural networks for action recognition. In *Proc. IEEE International Conference on Computer Vision (ICCV)*, pages 4041–4049, 2015.

[16] R. Vemulapalli, F. Arrate, and R. Chellappa. Human action recognition by representing 3D skeletons as points in a lie group. In *Proc. IEEE Conference on Computer Vision and Pattern Recognition (CVPR)*, pages 588–595, 2014.

[17] J. Wang, Z. Liu, Y. Wu, and J. Yuan. Mining actionlet ensemble for action recognition with depth cameras. In *Proc. IEEE Conference on Computer Vision and Pattern Recognition (CVPR)*, pages 1290–1297, 2012.

[18] P. Wang, W. Li, Z. Gao, C. Tang, J. Zhang, and P. O. Ogunbona. Convnets-based action recognition from depth maps through virtual cameras and pseudocoloring. In *Proc. ACM international conference on Multimedia (ACM MM)*, pages 1119–1122, 2015.

[19] P. Wang, W. Li, Z. Gao, J. Zhang, C. Tang, and P. Ogunbona. Action recognition from depth maps using deep convolutional neural networks. *Human-Machine Systems, IEEE Transactions on*, PP(99):1–12, 2015.

[20] P. Wang, W. Li, P. Ogunbona, Z. Gao, and H. Zhang. Mining mid-level features for action recognition based on effective skeleton representation. In *Proc. International Conference on Digital Image Computing: Techniques and Applications (DICTA)*, pages 1–8, 2014.

[21] S. Yang, C. Yuan, W. Hu, and X. Ding. A hierarchical model based on latent dirichlet allocation for action recognition. In *Pattern Recognition (ICPR), 2014 22nd International Conference on*, pages 2613–2618. IEEE, 2014.

[22] X. Yang and Y. Tian. Eigenjoints-based action recognition using Naive-Bayes-Nearest-Neighbor. In *Proc. International Workshop on Human Activity Understanding from 3D Data (HAU3D) (CVPRW)*, pages 14–19, 2012.

[23] X. Yang and Y. Tian. Super normal vector for activity recognition using depth sequences. In *Proc. IEEE International Conference on Computer Vision and Pattern Recognition (CVPR)*, pages 804–811, 2014.

[24] M. Zanfir, M. Leordeanu, and C. Sminchisescu. The moving pose: An efficient 3D kinematics descriptor for low-latency action recognition and detection. In *Proc. IEEE International Conference on Computer Vision (ICCV)*, pages 2752–2759, 2013.

[25] M. D. Zeiler and R. Fergus. Visualizing and understanding convolutional networks. In *Proc. European Conference on Computer Vision (ECCV)*, pages 818–833. 2014.

[26] J. Zhang, W. Li, P. O. Ogunbona, P. Wang, and C. Tang. RGB-D-based action recognition datasets: A survey. *Pattern Recognition*, 60:86–105, 2016.

[27] L. Zhou, W. Li, Y. Zhang, P. Ogunbona, D. T. Nguyen, and H. Zhang. Discriminative key pose extraction using extended lc-ksvd for action recognition. In *Proc. International Conference on Digital Image Computing: Techniques and Applications (DICTA)*, pages 1–8. IEEE, 2014.

[28] W. Zhu, C. Lan, J. Xing, W. Zeng, Y. Li, L. Shen, and X. Xie. Co-occurrence feature learning for skeleton based action recognition using regularized deep LSTM networks. In *The 30th AAAI Conference on Artificial Intelligence (AAAI)*, 2016.

Efficient Digital Holographic Image Reconstruction on Mobile Devices

Chung-Hua Chu
Department of Multimedia Design,
National Taichung University of Science and Technology
Taichung, Taiwan, ROC
chchu@gm.nutc.edu.tw

ABSTRACT

Advanced digital holography attracts a lot of attentions for 3D visualization nowadays. The representation of digital holographic images suffers from computational inefficiency on the mobile devices due to the limited hardware for digital holographic processing. In this paper, we point out that the above critical issue deteriorates the digital holographic image representation on the mobile devices. To reduce computational complexity in digital holographic image reconstruction, we propose an efficient and effective algorithm to simplify Fresnel transforms for the mobile devices. Our algorithm outperforms previous approaches in not only smaller running time but also the better quality of the digital holographic image representation for the mobile devices.

CCS Concepts

•Computing methodologies → Image representations;

Keywords

Digital Holographic Image Reconstruction, mobile devices.

1. INTRODUCTION

Digital holography [3] enables PC to record and represent the 3D information of real world objects by capturing their illuminated part and desired perspectives. The recorded 3D information of the object is called digital hologram. The digital holographic image can be constructed by propagating the wave field to the digital hologram with the theory of diffraction. Different from AR and VR, the digital holography can represent a more real 3D object with the recorded illuminated and perspective information of a real scene. In recent years, the digital holography has been a promising technology for various 3D visual applications. For example, Microsoft 10 has launched its own holographic headset HoloLens to interact with virtual objects appearing in your real world [1]. The digital holography is thereby becoming popular in the visual entertainments and video games. Since the optical diffraction on the digital hologram leads to large computational complexity, the digital holographic image reconstruction suffers from large burden on running time [13] [15] [16]. In addition to the high computational complexity for the digital holography reconstruction, Cheng et al. [5] pointed out that the cost for the representation of the digital holographic image is still expensive due to the need of extra hardware on the display devices such as a high-end GPU. Compared with the high-end digital holographic display devices, it is much more difficult for a user to view the high quality of the digital holography with a consumer mobile device because the current mobile devices lack dedicated digital holography imaging hardware. In addition, Kantabutra [10] indicated that the efficiency of the hardware-based methods [2] [5] [15] is limited for the digital holography imaging. This is because most hardware-based digital holography representations adopt iteration-based arithmetic algorithms to calculate exponential functions and trigonometric functions, but they result in large convergent time to reconstruct the holographic image. Therefore, we indeed require a scheme to efficiently represent the digital holography for the mobile devices.

We briefly introduce the procedure of the digital holographic reconstruction as follows. The digital hologram is an image plane photographically recording interference pattern between a wave field scattered from the real 3D object and the reference wave. Therefore, the digital hologram contains real scene information with the entire 3D wave field. We can reconstruct a digital holographic image by superimposing the bright reconstruction wave with the digital hologram. In contrast to the interference of the waves in the digital hologram, the digital holographic image reconstruction adopts the diffraction of the reconstruction wave. The diffraction of the light wave at the digital hologram is modeled as the Fresnel integral [12]. However, many prior works [13] [15] [16] showed that the Fresnel integral still suffers from high computational complexity due to recursive manners in the calculation for the exponential function. Additionally, Kim et al. [11] further demonstrated that most lookup-table-based methods for the digital holography required large memories. In this paper, we thereby aim to reduce the high complexity for calculating the Fresnel integral and large table sizes in the digital holographic reconstruction.

Given a digital hologram and a reference wave, our proposed method is to reduce the computational complexity and memory sizes for the digital holographic image reconstruction. The complexity of calculating the Fresnel integral

MM '16, October 15-19, 2016, Amsterdam, Netherlands

DOI: http://dx.doi.org/10.1145/2964284.2967192

in the digital holographic reconstruction can be seriously reduced by many factors such as reduction in the number of FFT (Fast Fourier Transformation) and the simplification of an exponential function. First, we propose a method called Efficient Digital Holographic Image Reconstruction (EDHIR). Specifically, EDHIR re-formulate the Fresnel integral in the digital holographic reconstruction to reduce two FFTs to one FFT. In addition, EDHIR fastens the exponential function used in the Fresnel integral. EDHIR minimizes the tables and speeds up the exponential function. More specifically, the domain of the argument x in the exponential function is equally divided into smaller subintervals. Next, EDHIR calculates the values of the exponential function for each subinterval boundary point, and stores them in a table. Then, EDHIR finds a close subinterval boundary point p to x. Finally, EDHIR adopt a polynomial approximation [14] to approximate the exponential function with the remaining argument r (i.e., $r = x - p$). Our main contributions focus on practical values and hardware cost to design our algorithm in the mobile devices. With our approach implemented into a practical mobile APP, the generic mobile devices are able to efficiently view the digital holographic image without expensive digital holographic imaging hardware and large memory sizes. The main contribution of EDHIR is that we propose an efficient process to reconstruct the digital holography on the current mobile devices. Our method not only needs fewer arithmetic costs and memory sizes allowed by the mobile devices but also achieves high precision in the digital holographic reconstruction.

The rest of this paper is organized as follows. In Section 2, we propose algorithm EDHIR. The experimental results are shown in Section 3. Finally, we conclude this paper in Section 4.

2. EFFICIENT DIGITAL HOLOGRAPHIC IMAGE RECONSTRUCTION

Digital holography image reconstruction is a critical problem for 3D visual applications on mobile devices. In view of this, we develop an Efficient Digital Holographic Image Reconstruction (EDHIR). Our algorithm includes two stages: the reduction of the number of FFT and the fast calculation of the exponential function in the Fresnel integral for the digital holography image reconstruction. We derive a formulation to mitigate the number of FFT in the Fresnel integral. In the fast calculation of the exponential function in the Fresnel integral, EDHIR equally separates the domain of the argument in the exponential function into several subintervals. EDHIR only uses a polynomial approximation to approximate the exponential function with the remaining argument belonging to a separated subinterval. The details are as follows.

2.1 Digital Holographic Image Reconstruction

Gabor [7] devised holography to record and reconstruct the amplitude and phase of a wave field in the real world. In this method, the reference wave (e.g., laser) interferes with the real object wave, and the interference patterns are recorded in the photographic plate. The recorded photography is called hologram that contains 3D information about the entire 3D wave field that shows the effects of perspective, illumination, and depth of focus. Lighting the hologram with the reference wave can reconstruct the object wave to represent a clear perception of the 3D scene for the human viewer. Therefore, the digital holographic image reconstruction is based on the diffraction of the light wave at the hologram, and such an optical diffraction is modeled as the Fresnel integral [12]. The Fresnel transformation gives high computational complexity such that it is difficult to reconstruct the digital holographic image in a mobile device with hardware restrictions.

2.2 Fast Fresnel Integral

We first model the diffraction of the reference wave over the digital hologram by using the Fresnel method [12]. Reference wave R is modeled as

$$R(x,y) = a_0 \frac{e^{-i\frac{2\pi}{\lambda}r+\theta_0}}{r}, \quad (1)$$

where λ is the wavelength of the reference wave, a_0 is the real-valued amplitude, r is the distance, and θ_0 is the initial phase. We can assume that a_0 is equal to 1 and θ_0 is equal to 0 for convenience. r can be obtained as

$$r = \sqrt{d^2 + (x-u)^2 + (y-v)^2}, \quad (2)$$

where (x, y) and (u, v) are defined as the spatial coordinates in the hologram and reconstructed plane respectively. d is the distance between the reconstructed virtual image appearing at the position of the original object and the real image. The diffraction of reference wave R over given digital hologram $H(x, y)$ is described by the Fresnel integral expressed as

$$D(u,v) = \frac{i}{\lambda} \int_{-\infty}^{\infty}\int_{-\infty}^{\infty} [H(x,y)R(x,y)]dxdy, \quad (3)$$

where $D(u, v)$ is reconstructed holographic image in spatial domain.

To reduce this high computational complexity, traditional works [8] [9] efficiently implemented Eq. 3 in Fourier domain. Specifically, the digital holographic reconstruction can be viewed as a linear system. Since Eq. 3 expresses the spatial convolution between the digital hologram and the reference wave [9], Eq. 3 can be computed as

$$D(u,v) = \frac{i}{\lambda} e^{-i\frac{2\pi}{\lambda}d} F^{-1}\{F[H(x,y)]F[R(x,y)]\}, \quad (4)$$

where F and F^{-1} are defined as Fourier transformation and its inverse respectively. However, such convolution methods take too many calculations in the Fourier transformation.

To reduce the number of the Fourier transformation, we have to deal with Eq. 3 in discreted domain. By substituting Eq. 1 and Eq. 2 into Eq. 3, we obtain

$$\begin{aligned} D(u,v) &= \frac{i}{\lambda} e^{-i\frac{2\pi}{\lambda}d} e^{-i\frac{\pi}{\lambda d}(u^2+v^2)} \times \\ & \int_{-\infty}^{\infty}\int_{-\infty}^{\infty} [H(x,y) e^{i\frac{\pi}{\lambda d}(x^2+y^2)} \times \\ & e^{-i\frac{2\pi}{\lambda d}(xu+yv)}]dxdy. \end{aligned} \quad (5)$$

For the digital hologram, $H(x, y)$ is discreted to $M \times N$ samples at periods $\triangle x$ and $\triangle y$ in the x and y directions respectively. Therefore, x is equal to $k\triangle x$, and y is equal to $l\triangle y$, where k and l are integer numbers. Similarly, we obtain digital reconstructed image $D(n\triangle u, m\triangle v)$ with size $N\times M$. In other words, $D(u,v)$ is discreted to $M\times N$ samples at periods $\triangle u$ and $\triangle v$ in the u and v directions respectively. Therefore, u is equal to $n\triangle u$, and v is equal to $m\triangle v$, where n and m are integer numbers. In Eq. 5, we replace the integral and the continuous coordinates with summations and discreted coordinates respectively. Therefore, we can obtain

$$\begin{aligned} D(n\triangle u, m\triangle v) &= \frac{i}{\lambda}e^{-i\frac{2\pi}{\lambda}d}e^{-i\frac{\pi}{\lambda d}(n^2\triangle u^2+m^2\triangle v^2)}\times \\ &\sum_{k=-\frac{N}{2}}^{\frac{N}{2}-1}\sum_{l=-\frac{M}{2}}^{\frac{M}{2}-1}[H(k\triangle x, l\triangle y)\times \\ &e^{i\frac{\pi}{\lambda d}(k^2\triangle x^2+l^2\triangle y^2)}\times \\ &e^{-i\frac{2\pi}{\lambda d}(k\triangle xn\triangle u+l\triangle ym\triangle v)}]. \end{aligned} \quad (6)$$

The direct computation of Eq. 6 is $O(MN)$. To reduce this high complexity, we further re-formulate Eq. 6 to

$$\begin{aligned} D(n\triangle u, m\triangle v) &= \frac{i}{\lambda}e^{-i\frac{2\pi}{\lambda}d}e^{-i\frac{\pi}{\lambda d}(n^2\triangle u^2+m^2\triangle v^2)}\times \\ &FFT[H(k\triangle x, l\triangle y)\times \\ &e^{i\frac{\pi}{\lambda d}(k^2\triangle x^2+l^2\triangle y^2)}]. \end{aligned} \quad (7)$$

Eq. 4 shows that the computational complexity of the digital holographic reconstruction can be reduced to $O(3MlogN)$ by using Fast Fourier Transform (FFT). Compared to the convolution methods [8] [9], Eq. 7 demonstrates that we merely take one FFT in $O(MlogN)$ complexity to reconstruct the digital holographic image.

2.3 Fast Exponential Function

To further speed up the exponential function in Eq. 7, EDHIR adopts a polynomial approximation [14] collaborating with a lookup table. Since the argument of the exponential function is a complex number, we transform e^{ix} into $cos(x) + isin(x)$, where i is equal to $\sqrt{-1}$. Therefore, we focus on fast sine and cosine functions with argument x. The approximation of the sine and cosine functions gives large domain by merely using polynomial or rational functions with large degrees. This leads to large computational complexity, and also makes the numerical error. We thereby split the argument domain into several smaller subintervals, and then store the solutions of the subinterval boundaries in a table. Such a way results in fewer memory sizes than the stored solutions in the whole argument domain. For each small subinterval, the coefficients of a low-degree polynomial approximation are sufficient for the high quality of digital holography image reconstruction. This can also dramatically reduce the expensive computation.

2.3.1 Argument Domain Separation

EDHIR accelerates sine and cosine functions by equally separating the domain of argument x into 2^n small subintervals, where n is a positive integer. Then, EDHIR finds a close subinterval boundary point p to x. Finally, remaining argument r is defined as $x-p$. In other words, EDHIR decomposes x to $p+r$ because p is a most significant argument to affect the solutions of the sine and cosine functions with argument x. On the other hand, remaining argument r is a least significant argument to affect those. The goal of the argument domain separation is to reduce the large argument to small one such that the polynomial approximation can fast converge. In contrast to traditional methods [6], such an argument domain separation is flexible and efficient since the subintervals can be dependent on precision for the sine and cosine functions.

2.3.2 Polynomial Approximation and Lookup Table

In light of trigonometric addition formulas, the $sin(p+r)$ and $cos(p+r)$ become $sin(p)cos(r) + cos(p)sin(r)$ and $cos(p)cos(r) - sin(p)sin(r)$ respectively. EDHIR stores $sin(p)$ and $cos(p)$ values in tables $TS(p)$ and $TC(p)$ with argument p respectively, and each table has 2^n entries. Next, EDHIR adopts a polynomial approximation to approximate the sine and cosine functions with the remaining argument r. That is, $S(r)$ approximates $sin(r)$ expressed as

$$S(r) = a_0 + a_1r + a_2r^2 + a_3r^3. \quad (8)$$

On the other hand, $C(r)$ approximates $cos(r)$ modeled as

$$C(r) = b_0 + b_1r + b_2r^2 + b_3r^3. \quad (9)$$

Coefficients a_i and b_i can be obtained from Remez's Algorithm [14], where $0 \le i \le 3$.

Although Taylor expansion is easy to use, it is much worse and less efficient than the other approximations [10]. This is because Taylor expansion only provides local approximations rather than global approximations. On the other hand, the computation of rational approximation [14] is more expensive than the polynomial approximation due to lots of dividers. Compared to these approximations, the polynomial approximation gives more accurate and efficient in the digital holography image reconstruction. We give an example for the above procedure.

Example: We approximate the sine function with argument $3\pi/16$ in $[0, \pi/4]$. EDHIR first equally separates the domain into two intervals $[0, \pi/8]$ and $[\pi/8, \pi/4]$, where n is 1. Since $3\pi/16$ is in $[\pi/8, \pi/4]$, we decompose $3\pi/16$ to $\pi/8 + \pi/16$ (i.e., $p = \pi/8$ and $r = \pi/16$). $sin(3\pi/16)$ can be rewritten as $sin(\pi/8 + \pi/16)$ that is equal to $sin(\pi/8) \times cos(\pi/16) + cos(\pi/8) \times sin(\pi/16)$. Next, EDHIR stores the solutions of the sine and cosine functions among the subinterval boundaries, i.e., $sin(0)$, $sin(\pi/8)$, $sin(\pi/4)$, $cos(0)$, $cos(\pi/8)$, and $cos(\pi/4)$, in tables TS and TC respectively. EDHIR then uses the polynomial approximation to approximate the solutions of the sine and cosine functions with the remaining argument $\pi/16$, i.e., $sin(\pi/16)$ and $cos(\pi/16)$. With the polynomial approximation, $sin(\pi/16)$, i.e., $S(\pi/16)$, is equal to $a_0+a_1(\pi/16)+a_2(\pi/16)^2+a_3(\pi/16)^3$, and $cos(\pi/16)$, i.e., $C(\pi/16)$ is equal to $b_0 + b_1(\pi/16) + b_2(\pi/16)^2 + b_3(\pi/16)^3$. Coefficients $\{a_i\}$ are $\{0, 1, -0.0001, -0.1658\}$, and $\{b_i\}$ are $\{1, 0.0001, -0.5020, 0.0163\}$ both obtained from Remez's Algorithm [14], where $0 \le i \le 3$. Finally, we can obtain $sin(3\pi/16)$ as $TS(\pi/8)\times S(\pi/16)+TC(\pi/8)\times C(\pi/16)$ that is equal to 0.5556, where $TS(\pi/8)$ is equal to 0.3827, and $TC(\pi/8)$ is equal to 0.9239. ■

3. EXPERIMENTAL RESULTS

3.1 Experimental Environment

In this section, we conduct several experiments to evaluate the performance of algorithm EDHIR. We compare our

Figure 1: Results of digital holographic image reconstruction under each algorithm (a) original object (b) hologram of (a) (c) reconstructed image from (b) under THIR (d) reconstructed image from (b) under HHIR (e) reconstructed image from (b) under EDHIR (f) original object (g) hologram of (f) (h) reconstructed image from (g) under THIR (i) reconstructed image from (g) under HHIR (j) reconstructed image from (g) under EDHIR

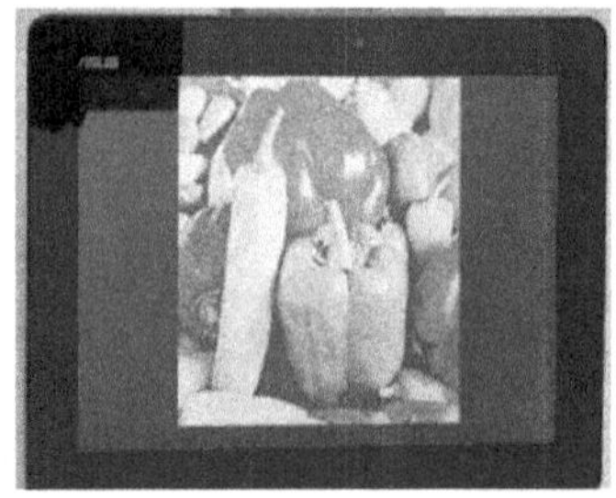

Figure 2: Digital holographic image reconstruction under EDHIR on ASUS Transformer Pad

algorithm with Hardware-based Holographic Image Reconstruction (HHIR) [13] and Traditional Holographic Image Reconstruction (THIR) [16]. HHIR proposes a hardware-based method to speed up the computation in Fast Fourier transform for the reconstruction of digital holographic images. For the GPU dependent components of HHIR, HHIR is implemented by using CUDA with AndroidWorks for Android Development [4] that is native to the NVidia GeForce hardware platform in the android devices. On the other hand, THIR is a convolution method to accelerate the reconstruction of digital holographic images.

We implement our algorithm on a ASUS Transformer Pad (TF701T) Android Pad with Quad-core 1.9 GHz Cortex-A15, Chipset Nvidia Tegra 4 T40X, 3GB RAM, ULP GeForce GPU processor, Android 4.2, 2560×1600 pixels Super IPS+L CD display, and 5M pixels camera. Fig. 2 shows an example of running EDHIR on the ASUS Transformer Android Pad. Note that our program can be installed and runs on any Android devices.

Before evaluating the performance of our algorithm, we describe our data set and set up parameters as follows. Experimental images are from the USC-SIPI and European research center databases at http://sipi.usc.edu/database/ and http://www.erc-interfere.eu/downloads.html respectivel y. We generate synthetic holograms with size 512×512 and their corresponding parameters. We follow traditional setting for each hologram where all samples can be used for holography reconstruction. We normalize the spatial-domain amplitude and phase values of each hologram to [0,1] and [0, π], respectively. The parameters for the hologram generation correspond to an off-axis configuration as $\lambda = 517\times10^{-9}$, $\triangle x = \triangle y = 6\times10^{-6}$, and d=63×10^{-2}. In the following, we compare the execution time of each algorithm and the quality for different algorithms with respect to different factors on the mobile device.

3.2 Performance Analysis

The performance of the proposed algorithm is evaluated using the two objects, 'Peppers' and 'Dice', whose reconstructed images are shown in Figs. 1. The distortion of the reconstructed image is measured by peak-signal-to-noise ratio (PSNR). The mean squared error (MSE) for reconstructed image $D(n,m)$ and original image $O(n,m)$ with size $N \times M$ is given as

$$MSE = \frac{1}{N \times M} \sum_n \sum_m [D(n,m) - O(n,m)]^2. \qquad (10)$$

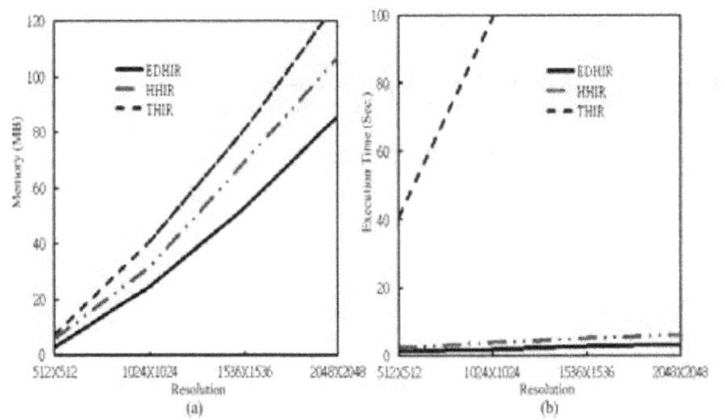

Figure 3: Comparisons of the hardware performance under each algorithm (a) memory consumption (b) execution time

The PSNR is expressed as

$$PSNR = 10log\frac{255^2}{MSE}. \quad (11)$$

Figs. 1 show that EDHIR with the average PSNR of 21.74dB is superior to THIR of 15.95dB and HHIR of 14.26dB. This is because EDHIR can achieve high accuracy for the numerical reconstruction of the holographic image in the exponential functions. Specifically, the accuracy of EDHIR overpasses that of HHIR and THIR by storing the high-precision results of the significant arguments. However, THIR and HHIR perform worse since they approximate these arithmetic results by merely using polynomial algorithms [17].

Fig. 3(a) shows that the memory sizes of EDHIR are smaller than HHIR and THIR since EDHIR effectively adopts the lookup table to store the solutions for more significant arguments rather than those of whole arguments. However, HHIR and THIR still cannot effectively save the memory since the 2D FFT is quite memory demanding. We observe that the 2D FFT allocates almost two times the hologram size of additional memory. Although EDHIR mainly stores the results of the significant arguments, EDHIR with one FFT can also conserve more memory sizes as compared to the traditional methods.

3.3 Efficiency Analysis

In this section, Fig. 3(b) shows that our algorithm is efficient and very feasible for the digital holographic image reconstruction on mobile devices. The computational time of the digital holographic image reconstruction on EDHIR is close to HHIR since EDHIR combines a lookup table and a polynomial approximation to fast calculate the exponential functions. Specifically, EDHIR needs fewer adders and multipliers accepted by a general-purpose CPU to execute the sum and product for the least significant arguments. GPU is very efficient for scientific computing since its high parallel structure is faster than the general-purpose CPU for FFTs and exponential functions. Although HHIR adopts GPU to speed up the Fresnel integral, it needs lots of dividers, multipliers, and memory sizes to burden the performance of HHIR. THIR performs worst since lots of FFTs yield heavy load in computation.

4. CONCLUSION

With the rapid advanced digital holographic visual technologies for mobile devices, the holographic image reconstruction in the mobile devices has become indispensable. However, the previous works are infeasible for the current mobile devices due to unacceptable computational complexity. In this paper, we have proposed an efficient and effective algorithm to reconstruct the digital holographic images. The experimental results have shown that our approach is not only of smaller running time but for higher quality of the digital holographic image reconstruction as compared to the existing works on the mobile devices.

5. REFERENCES

[1] Microsoft hololens. In https://www.microsoft.com/microsoft-hololens/en-us, 2015.

[2] A. H. B. M.-J. N. T. Ahrenberg, L.; Page. In Using Commodity Graphics Hardware for Real-Time Digital Hologram View-Reconstruction, volume 5 of 4. JOURNAL OF DISPLAY TECHNOLOGY, 2009.

[3] R. J. H. Alfred M. Bruckstein and A. N. Netravali. In Holographic Representations of Images, volume 7 of 11. IEEE TRANSACTIONS ON IMAGE PROCESSING, 1998.

[4] N. AndroidWorks. https://developer.nvidia.com/AndroidWorks, 2015.

[5] C.-T. C. Chau-Jern Cheng, Wen-Jyi Hwang and X.-J. Lai. In Efficient FPGA-Based Fresnel Transform Architecture for Digital Holography, volume 10 of 4. JOURNAL OF DISPLAY TECHNOLOGY, 2014.

[6] W. Cody and W. Waite. In Software Manual for the Elementary Functions. Prentice-Hall, 1980.

[7] G. D. In A new microscopic principle. Nature, 1948.

[8] J. W. Goodman. In Introduction to Fourier Optics 3rd edition. Greenwood Village CO Roberts and Company, 2005.

[9] D. T. H and M. R. In Digital and optical reconstruction of images from suboptical diffraction patterns. Applied Optical, 1974.

[10] V. Kantabutra. In On Hardware for Computing Exponential and Trigonometric functions, volume 45 of 3. IEEE Transactions on Computers, 1996.

[11] S.-C. Kim and E.-S. Kim. In Effective generation of digital holograms of three dimensional objects using a novel look-up table method, volume 47 of 19. Applied Optics, 2008.

[12] W. Lauterborn and T. Kurz. In Coherent Optics Fundamentals and Applications, pages 129–151. Springer, 2003.

[13] M. Z. I. Mohammad Shorif Uddin, Madeena Sultana. Microsoft hololens. In Fast Holographic Image Reconstruction using Graphics Processing Unit, volume 2, pages 35–42. JOURNAL OF SCIENCE AND ENGINEERING, 2011.

[14] J. Muller. In Elementary Functions Algorithms and Implementation. Birkhauser Boston, 1997.

[15] T. J. N. Nitesh Pandey, Damien P. Kelly and B. M. Hennelly. In Speed up of Fresnel transforms for digital holography using precomputed chirp and GPU processing, volume 7442. Proc. of SPIE, 2009.

[16] K. C. P.W.M. Tsang and T.-C. Poon. In Real-time relighting of digital holograms based on wavefront recording plane method, volume 20 of s2, pages 5962–5967. OPTICS EXPRESS, 2012.

[17] P. Z. Vincent Lefevre, Damien Stehle. Worst cases for the exponential function in the ieee 754r decimal64 format. In Reliable Implementation of Real Number Algorithms: Theory and Practice, volume 5045, pages 114–126. Springer, 2008.

Scene Image Synthesis from Natural Sentences Using Hierarchical Syntactic Analysis

Tetsuaki Mano
Graduate School of Information
Science and Technology
The University of Tokyo
mano@mi.t.u-tokyo.ac.jp

Hiroaki Yamane
Graduate School of Information
Science and Technology
The University of Tokyo
yamane@mi.t.u-tokyo.ac.jp

Tatsuya Harada
Graduate School of Information
Science and Technology
The University of Tokyo
harada@mi.t.u-tokyo.ac.jp

ABSTRACT

Synthesizing a new image from verbal information is a challenging task that has a number of applications. Most research on the issue has attempted to address this question by providing external clues, such as sketches. However, no study has been able to successfully handle various sentences for this purpose without any other information. We propose a system to synthesize scene images solely from sentences. Input sentences are expected to be complete sentences with visualizable objects. Our priorities are the analysis of sentences and the correlation of information between input sentences and visible image patches. A hierarchical syntactic parser is developed for sentence analysis, and a combination of lexical knowledge and corpus statistics is designed for word correlation. The entire system was applied to both a clip-art dataset and an actual image dataset. This application highlighted the capability of the proposed system to generate novel images as well as its ability to succinctly convey ideas.

CCS Concepts

•**Information systems → Multimedia content creation;**
•**Computing methodologies → Image processing;**

Keywords

Syntactic Abstraction, Word Mapping, Image Synthesis

1. INTRODUCTION

What if a visual expression can be successfully synthesized from linguistic information? The relevant technology would spark groundbreaking applications, such as the automatic generation of illustrated pictures, language translation with images as intermediaries, and so forth.

Our objective is to achieve image synthesis solely from natural language sentences. A natural language sentence is defined here as a complete sentence of a reasonable length to describe a scene with non-conceptual objects that can be visualized. The target of the outcome image is set as the image of a scene with the necessary and sufficient information derived from the input sentence.

MM '16, October 15-19, 2016, Amsterdam, Netherlands
© 2016 ACM. ISBN 978-1-4503-3603-1/16/10... $15.00
DOI: http://dx.doi.org/10.1145/2964284.2967193

Figure 1: Examples of synthesized images.

Most research on automatic image synthesis exploits powerful clues, such as sketches [2], in addition to from linguistic information. Only a few studies have addressed syntheses that can be obtained solely from verbal information. There are two state-of-the-art proposals, that have considered image synthesis. One study set out to add a word to an image [7] through the learning of spatial, scale-related, and appearance-based contexts; the other attempted to describe short sentences containing fewer than 10 words [16]. As far as we know, no work to date has been able to successfully generate images of scenes by only using sentences, without any other hints, due to the complexity of the representation of information in both sentences and images.

Three steps are needed to convert a sentence into an image: (I) analysis of the input sentence, (II) correlation between words in the sentence and image patch labels, and (III) allocation of image patches over a canvas. Since people can at least interpret the gist of the linguistic description of a given scene with appropriate objects in a sentence at suitable positions, even if the corresponding images have aberrant brightness or odd camera angles, we focus on the first two steps. Examples of synthesized images are shown in Figure 1. Our contributions are fourfold:

- Implementation of a system for scene image synthesis by only using natural language sentences.
- Development of a hierarchical syntactic parser for sentence analysis.

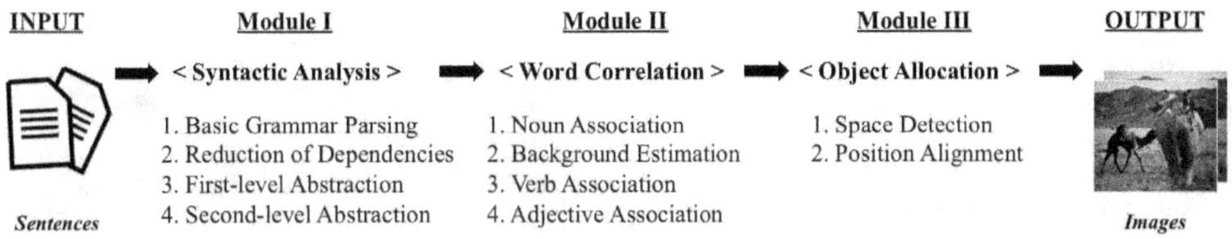

Figure 2: Overview of the proposed system.

- Design of an assignment algorithm for word correlation.
- Demonstration of the capability of our system to produce novel images and succinctly convey ideas.

2. SCENE IMAGE SYNTHESIS

An overview of our system is provided in Figure 2. A module is used to deal with each of the three steps stated in Section 1.

2.1 Syntactic Analysis (Module I)

The purpose of this module is to understand the syntactic structure of input sentences. In general, there is great variety in the patterns of grammars; thus, this module attempts to abstract fundamental grammatical structures from sentences. We assume that all essential information for constructing an interpretable image is summarized into three variables: objects, their states, and interactions among them. Furthermore, we assume that all objects are described by nouns, all states are expressed by either adjectives or verbs, and all interactions are either relative locations signified by prepositions, or interactions expressed through verbal actions.

An overview of this module is shown in Figure 3. Words in red represent objects, those in green express states of objects, and words in blue represent interactions among objects. In addition, words in pink describe body parts.

Fundamental Grammar Extraction. The input sentence is initially adjusted to eliminate ambiguity, and a parser [3] is applied to extract the fundamental grammar. At this stage, the input sentence is represented as a tree, where each node represents a word with order index within the sentence, and each edge is tagged by one of 50 possible dependencies.

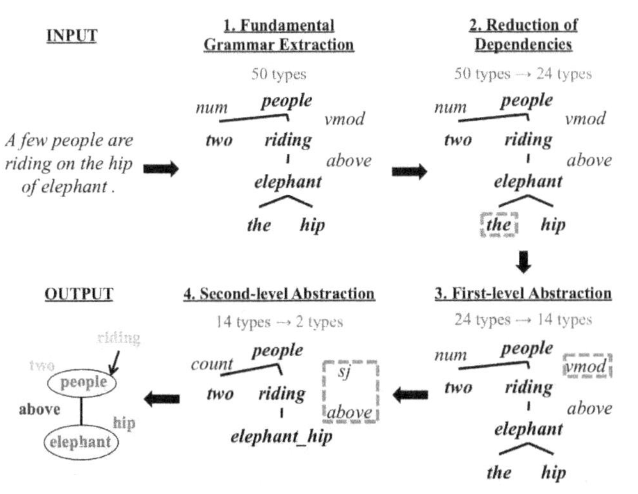

Figure 3: Overview of functions in Module I.

Reduction of Dependencies. Prior to abstraction, 26 dependencies are eliminated due to low occurrence rates (less than 1%) in a mixo-corpus [6, 14, 10], which explains the dispensable nature of rules and minor parts of speech.

First-level Abstraction. The remaining 24 types of dependencies G^{L0} are organized into the 14 varieties G^{L1} shown in Table 1. Here, G^{L0} represents a group of dependencies at hierarchical level 0. Types in G^{L1} can be bundled into three categories: subjective or objective G^{L1}_{sjoj}, and location G^{L1}_{loc} and modification G^{L1}_{mod}. This procedure is carried out by using the rules listed in Table 2, which depend on part of speech and scales of objects. In the tables, the † can take any form within the context of the grammatical pattern or word.

Second-level Abstraction. By leveraging the three categories, those in G^{L1} finally fall into two types of G^{L2}, that is, state M and interaction R. The possible operations are summarized in Table 3.

Table 1: 14 types in G^{L1}.

Group	Type
G^{L1}_{sjoj}	*subjective (sj), objective (oj)*
G^{L1}_{loc}	*inside (in), property (with), nearby (by), on (above)* *in front of (ifo), far away (away), below (below)* *back (behind), upward (over), downward (under)*
G^{L1}_{mod}	*adjective (adj), count (count)*

Table 2: Patterns of first-level abstraction.

Target	Operation	Example
Edge	shift to *sj*	$(agent, VP, N) \rightarrow (sj, VP, N)$
	shift to *oj*	$(acomp, V, J) \rightarrow (oj, V, J)$
	shift to *adj*	$(amod, N, J) \rightarrow (adj, N, J)$
	shift to parent's	$(conj\_and, J, J) \rightarrow (parent's, J, J)$
	shift to G^{L1}_{loc}	$(prep\_in, N_1, N_2) \rightarrow$ $\begin{cases}(in, N_1, N_2) & f_{size}(N_1) \leq f_{size}(N_2)\\(with, N_1, N_2) & f_{size}(N_1) > f_{size}(N_2)\end{cases}$
Node	integrate	$(nn, N_1, N_2), (\dagger, \dagger, N_2) \rightarrow (\dagger, \dagger, N_1\_N_2)$
	lift up	$(npadvmod, R, N) \rightarrow (\dagger, groundparent's, N)$

Table 3: Patterns of second-level abstraction.

Role	Operation: Target	Operation: Flow
State	$g \in G^{L1}_{mod}$	$(adj, N, \dagger) \Rightarrow$ $M_N = M_N \cup \dagger$
	words used to detect relations	$(sj, \dagger, N_1), (oj, \dagger, N_2) \Rightarrow$ $M_{N_1} = M_{N_1} \cup \dagger$
Relation	*sj* and *oj* sharing the same word	$(sj, \dagger, N_1), (oj, \dagger, N_2) \Rightarrow$ $R_{N_1,N_2} = \dagger$
	sj and $g \in G^{L1}_{loc}$ sharing the same word	$(sj, \dagger, N_1), (g, \dagger, N_2) \Rightarrow$ $R_{N_1,N_2} = g$
	$g \in G^{L1}_{loc}$ which connects two nouns	$(g, N_1, N_2) \Rightarrow$ $R_{N_1,N_2} = g$

Algorithm 1 Noun Association

Require: $w_1, w_2, ..., w_N, t$
  for $j = 1, 2, ..., N$ **do**
    Get a list of synsets $s_1, s_2, ...$ for w_j.
    for $i = 1$ **to** $\min(\text{listsize}, \theta_{\text{syn}})$ **do**
      Trace back from $\mathrm{s_i}$ to the nearest keystone $\mathrm{k_i}$.
      Get confidence $c^{\mathrm{k_i}} = q_{\text{all}}(\mathrm{s_i}, \mathrm{k_i}, t)$ via (1)~(4).
    end for
    • **Domain**
    Set domain $d_j = \underset{i}{\operatorname{argmax}}\, c^{k_i}$.
    • **Patch**
    Get a set of visualizable patches P_j that belongs to d_j.
    Set object patch $p_j \in P_j$.
    • **Scale**
    Trace back from p_j to the nearest keystone k_j with scale.
    Set object scale u_j to the scale of k_j.
  end for

2.2 Word Correlation (Module II)

The goal of this module is to associate nouns, verbs, and adjectives in the input sentence with those in the image dataset. The size of objects and the background images are estimated as well. As is often the case in synthesis, it is difficult to collect a wide variety of image patches. Therefore, we need to correlate a word in the sentences with a patch of the closest concept within a small number of choices. The mapping is based on three lexical pyramids for each sentence, where statistical measurements are used to make judgments. While nouns are explored within WordNet [5], verbs are used from VerbNet [12]. Adjectives are used only when they express emotions or sizes.

In this module, word similarity is measured by word2vec [11], and sentence similarity is obtained by a method proposed by Li et al. [9] with an alteration to use word2vec to calculate word similarity. $\text{sim}_{\text{syn-sent}}(\mathrm{s}, \mathrm{t})$, which is the similarity between synset s and sentence t, is given by computing the average of sentence similarities between synset's example and the given sentence, and synset's definition and the given sentence, respectively. Synset similarity $\text{sim}_{\text{syn-syn}}(\mathrm{s_1}, \mathrm{s_2})$ is the average of sentence similarities for computable pairs.

Noun Association. We specify a set of major nodes (keystones) that must contain at least one visualizable image class with a certain scale of object on their leaves. Keystones are collected by grouping words in WordNet until accumulated frequency in a certain subset exceeds 1% for general objects, humans, and backgrounds. Scales are only attached to leaf nodes in the keystones.

Given a synset s, its nearest keystone k, and system input sentence t, we define a score to evaluate the accuracy of assigning a proper synset as:

$$q_{\text{all}}(\mathrm{s}, \mathrm{k}, t) = q_{\text{path}} + q_{\text{sim}} + q_{\text{freq}}, \tag{1}$$

$$q_{\text{path}}(\mathrm{s}, \mathrm{k}) = \frac{1}{2}\Big(\frac{1}{\theta_{\text{path}} + r_{\text{rel}}(\mathrm{s}, \mathrm{k})} + \frac{r_{\text{abs}}(\mathrm{s})}{\max_{\mathrm{s} \in \mathrm{s}^{\text{all}}} r_{\text{abs}}(\mathrm{s})}\Big), \tag{2}$$

$$q_{\text{sim}}(s, t) = \text{sim}_{\text{syn-sent}}(s, t), \tag{3}$$

$$q_{\text{freq}}(s) = \frac{1}{\theta_{\text{syn}} + f_{\text{synind}}(s)}, \tag{4}$$

where r is a function that measures either absolute depth or relative depth, s^{all} represents all synsets available in WordNet, and function f_{synind} returns the order index of synsets.

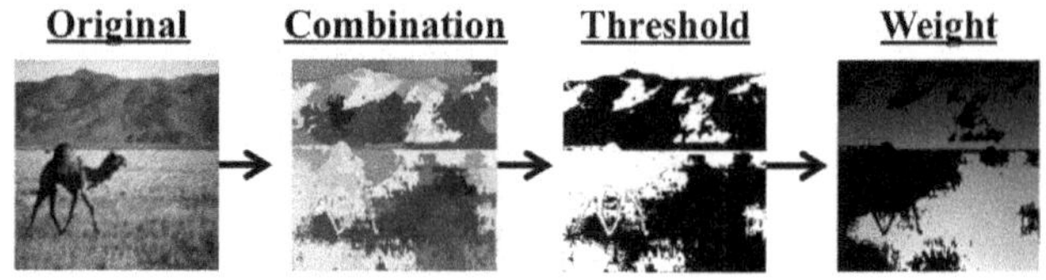

Figure 4: An example of spacious area computation.

θ_{path}, which adjusts the score weights of paths, is set to 3, and θ_{syn}, which is the maximum number of synsets to be considered as candidates, is set to 5. The entire process is described in Algorithm 1.

Background Estimation. A background is eventually estimated. We define the background through scene estimation, and domains are selected based on the nouns associated. That is, a set of these domains D is used to estimate a background among available scenes B as follows:

$$\underset{b \in B}{\operatorname{argmax}} \sum_{d_j \in D} \Big(\text{sim}_{\text{syn-syn}}(b, d_j) + \text{sim}_{\text{syn-sent}}(b, t)\Big). \tag{5}$$

Verb and Adjective Association. Compared with noun association, these operations are more straightforward, and are grounded on the appearance of images. All verbs are classified into six self-contained activities and four interactive activities spanning both sites of action. Adjectives are simply assigned to abstract classes with the closest meaning.

2.3 Object Allocation (Module III)

The role of this module is to synthesize image patches over the estimated background. Two things this function needs to do is detect spacious areas in the background and combine the result with knowledge from the Module II.

Spacious Area Computation. An example of this procedure is shown in Figure 4. A saliency map [8] (S) is first computed to find rough candidates for the spacious region. A segmentation map (L) based on SLIC [1] is then obtained to specify object boundaries. The outcomes are mingled by:

$$\forall i, \boldsymbol{C}[x, y] = \frac{1}{N_i} \sum_{\acute{x}, \acute{y} \in L_i} \boldsymbol{S}[\acute{x}, \acute{y}], \tag{6}$$

where x, y is the position of the image, $S[x, y], C[x, y]$ represents the value at that position, i is the index of segmentation, and N_i is the number of pixels belonging to the label group of L_i. A threshold $\delta * \mu$ is used to render the combined map C more sophisticated, where μ denotes the mean of the combined map. From this threshold map T, small areas the ratio of active pixels of which to the area are smaller than η are removed. The area size is 0.08% of the image size, and we set δ, η to 0.9, 0.6, respectively. Finally, a Gaussian filter is applied to reduce areas near the outer edge, and a linear filter weighs either the foreground or the background to yield the final weighted map W.

Position Adjustment. The system prepares a canvas and places the center of the main object at a point that can maximize the summation of values within the object area. All other objects are sequentially connected to it along the lines of rules in Figure 5, which assumes three patterns of relations: vertical links, horizontal links, and immediate surroundings. Following linkage, patches are considered to be a single chunk. In case the chunk expands to the top row

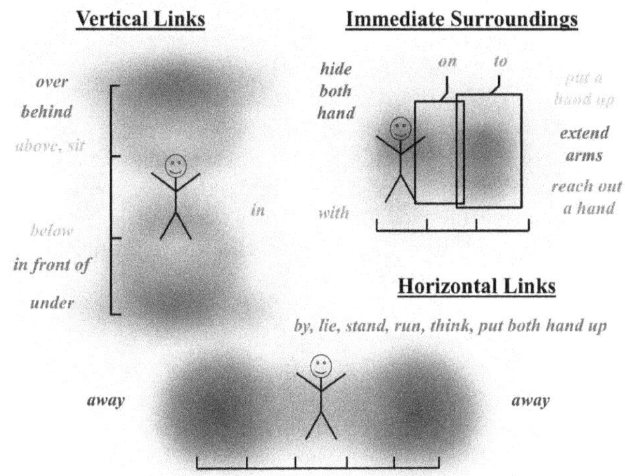

Figure 5: Positioning of all potential links.

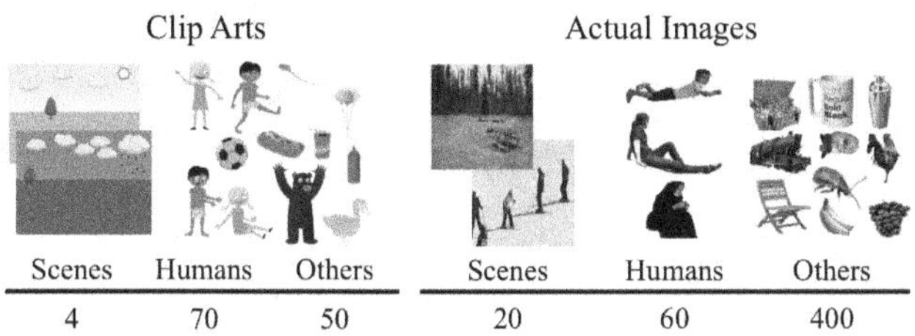

Figure 6: Examples of image patches.

Table 4: Experimental Tasks

Task	Method	# of subjects	# of sentences	Comparison				Time Limit
				ours	w/o M1	w/o M2	original	
1A	Scoring	100	20	✓	✓			-
1B	Scoring	100	15	✓		✓		-
1C	Scoring	100	20	✓		✓		-
2	Ranking	200	60	✓	✓	✓	✓	-
3	Q&A	100	20	✓			✓	4 sec.

of the canvas or the left, it is transferred or scaled as needed. The patches are finally synthesized over the background.

3. EXPERIMENT

We applied our system to the clip-art dataset [16] and an actual image dataset, which was a mixo-dataset of existing datasets. Scenes were sampled from Places205 [15] and general objects were excerpted from ImageNet [4]. Fifty images classified with the highest confidence scores in the VGG16 network [13] were chosen as candidates, and a few images were manually selected. Images of people in different poses were collected manually from the Internet. The examples are shown in Figure 6.

Input sentences are sampled from those datasets with images and corresponding sentences. Examples of the outcome are shown in Figure 1. The supplemental material provides more examples. Output images are evaluated through three tasks by crowd-sourced workers. Experimental setting is provided in Table 4. Results are shown in Figure 9 on the next page.

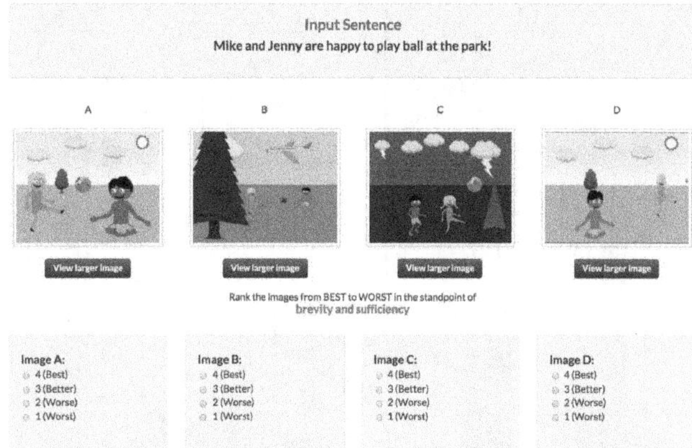

Figure 7: Experimental design of Task 2.

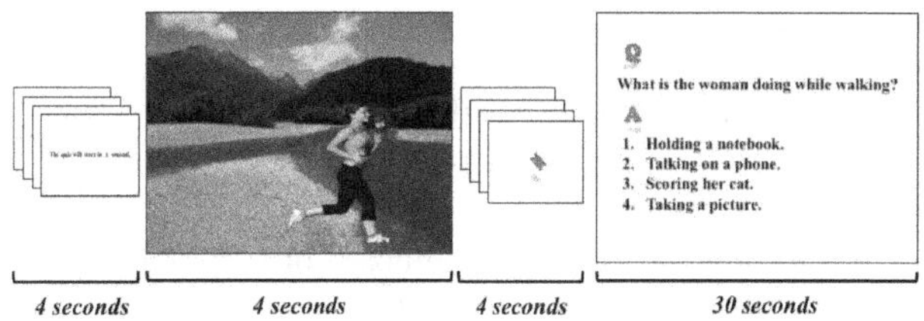

Figure 8: Experimental design of Task 3.

Task 1. The modules' effectiveness in terms of relation extraction (A), object correlation (B), and scale decision (C) were verified by absolute scoring. The synthesized images and their corresponding sentences, from either the entire system or partially deficient systems, were randomly ordered. Subjects were asked to score these using an integer from 4 (Very Good) to 1 (Very Poor) according to quality. The results indicated that all three aspects exerted a favorable influence on outcomes.

Task 2. Figure 7 depicts overall performance with relative ranking, obtained by comparing the performances with and without modules M1 and M2. Given a sentence and four images, including the original image, the contributors were asked to rank images from 4 (Best) to 1 (Worst). Three images were produced by the algorithm using both Modules I and II, using only Module II (without Module I), and using only Module I (without Module II). The other image is the original image taken from the dataset. These four images are randomly mixed in each session. The result showed that the original images were generally superior to the ones generated by our system. However, a few synthesized images were valued higher than the originals.

Task 3. The ability to convey the gist was measured by quickly asking questions of the subjects relating to parts of a scene. As shown in Figure 8, the subjects watched short videos that began with a blank screen for four seconds, was followed by an image that was shown for four seconds, another blank screen that lasted four seconds, and followed by a question related to the theme of the image. The respondents had four choices of answers to choose from, and these choices were formulated using the input sentences. There was a clear, significant difference in the average recall accuracy of the images, indicating that concise images without unnecessary depictions could more efficiently convey important ideas in sentences under the designated time limit.

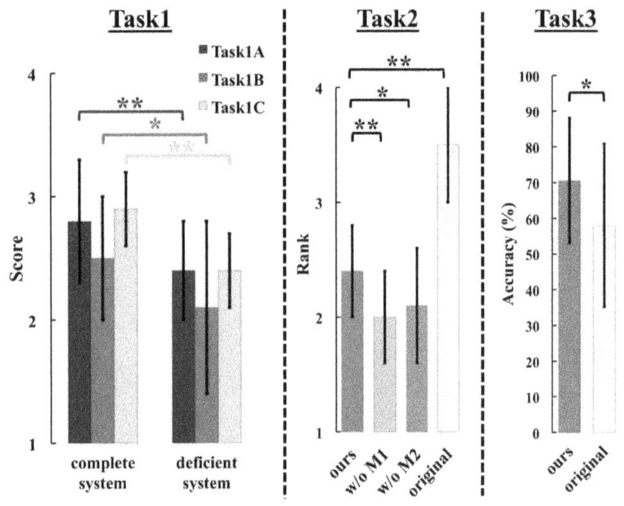

Figure 9: The result of experiments.

4. CONCLUSION

We implemented a system composed of three modules to achieve scene image synthesis using only natural language sentences. We focused on two modules.

Module I conducts syntactic analysis, for which a sentence parser using hierarchical syntactic analysis was developed. While it can handle common grammatical patterns, it is somewhat limited in dealing with collocations, time series, and words with various choices of parts of speech. Module II is responsible for word correlation, and we proposed a combination of lexical knowledge and corpus statistics to this end. This module solves an inherited problem of fewer image patches. Because its performance relies on a variety of elements, such as the chosen WordNet synsets, prepared word domains, and collected image patches, each image patch selection can fail when incorrect.

Through experiments, we showed that the two modules play an important role in image synthesis from natural language sentences. Another major insight of our experiments was the effectiveness of concise images as a means of delivering gists of scenes in a short time. Our future work will consist of the analysis of more complex grammars, collection of a greater number of image patches, and the comprehension of multiple sentences.

5. ACKNOWLEDGEMENT

This work was funded by the ImPACT Program of the Council for Science, Technology, and Innovation (Cabinet Office, Government of Japan).

6. REFERENCES

[1] R. Achanta, S. Appu, S. Kevin, L. Aurelien, F. Pascal, and S. Sabine. Slic superpixels compared to state-of-the-art superpixel methods. *PAMI*, 34(11):2274–2282, 2012.

[2] T. Chen, M.-M. Cheng, P. Tan, A. Shamir, and S.-M. Hu. Sketch2photo: internet image montage. *ACM TOG*, 28(5):124:1–10, 2009.

[3] M.-C. De Marneffe, B. MacCartney, C. D. Manning, et al. Generating typed dependency parses from phrase structure parses. In *ICLRE*, 2006.

[4] J. Deng, W. Dong, R. Socher, L.-J. Li, K. Li, and L. Fei-Fei. Imagenet: A large-scale hierarchical image database. In *CVPR*, pages 248–255, 2009.

[5] C. Fellbaum. *WordNet: An Electronic Lexical Database*. Bradford Books, 1998.

[6] M. Hodosh, P. Young, and J. Hockenmaier. Framing image description as a ranking task: Data, models and evaluation metrics. *JAIR*, 47:853–899, 2013.

[7] S. Inaba, A. Kanezaki, and T. Harada. Automatic image synthesis from keywords using scene context. In *ACMMM*, pages 1149–1152, 2014.

[8] L. Itti, C. Koch, and E. Niebur. A model of saliency-based visual attention for rapid scene analysis. *PAMI*, 20(11):1254–1259, 1998.

[9] Y. Li, D. McLean, Z. Bandar, J. D. O'shea, K. Crockett, et al. Sentence similarity based on semantic nets and corpus statistics. *TKDE*, 18(8):1138–1150, 2006.

[10] T.-Y. Lin, M. Maire, S. Belongie, J. Hays, P. Perona, D. Ramanan, P. Dollár, and C. L. Zitnick. Microsoft coco: Common objects in context. In *ECCV*, pages 740–755, 2014.

[11] T. Mikolov, I. Sutskever, K. Chen, G. S. Corrado, and J. Dean. Distributed representations of words and phrases and their compositionality. In *NIPS*, 2013.

[12] K. K. Schuler. *Verbnet: A Broad-coverage, Comprehensive Verb Lexicon*. PhD thesis, Philadelphia, PA, USA, 2005. AAI3179808.

[13] K. Simonyan and A. Zisserman. Very deep convolutional networks for large-scale image recognition. *arXiv preprint arXiv:1409.1556*, 2014.

[14] P. Young, A. Lai, M. Hodosh, and J. Hockenmaier. From image descriptions to visual denotations: New similarity metrics for semantic inference over event descriptions. *ACL*, 2:67–78, 2014.

[15] B. Zhou, A. Lapedriza, J. Xiao, A. Torralba, and A. Oliva. Learning deep features for scene recognition using places database. In *NIPS*, pages 487–495, 2014.

[16] C. L. Zitnick, D. Parikh, and L. Vanderwende. Learning the visual interpretation of sentences. In *ICCV*, 2013.

A Fast 3D Retrieval Algorithm via Class-Statistic and Pair-Constraint Model

Zan Gao[1,2,*], Deyu Wang[1,2], Hua Zhang[1,2,*], Yanbing Xue[1,2], Guangping Xu[1,2]
[1] Key Laboratory of Computer Vision and System, Tianjin University of Technology, Ministry of Education,Tianjin, 300384, China
[2]Tianjin Key Laboratory of Intelligence Computing and Novel Software Technology, Tianjin University of Technology, Tianjin, 300384, China
zangao@tjut.edu.cn, xzero3547w@163.com, hzhang62@126.com, yanbingxue@163.com, xugp2008@aliyun.com

ABSTRACT

With the development of 3D technologies and devices, 3D model retrieval becomes a hot research topic where multi-view matching algorithms have demonstrated satisfying performance. However, exciting works overlook the common factors among objects in a single class, and they are time consuming in retrieval processing. In this paper, a class-statistics and pair-constraint model (CSPC) method is originally proposed for 3D model retrieval, which is composed of supervised class-based statistics model and pair-constraint object retrieval model. In our CSPC model, we firstly convert view-based distance measure into object-based distance measure without falling in performance, which will advance 3D model retrieval speed. Secondly, the generality of the distribution of each feature dimension in each class is computed to judge category information, and then we further adopt this distribution information to build class models. Finally, an object-based pairwise constraint is introduced on the base of the class-statistic measure, which can remove a lot of false alarm samples in retrieval. Experimental results on ETH, NTU-60, MVRED and PSB 3D datasets show that our method is fast, and its performance is also comparable with the-state-of-the-art algorithms.

Keywords

3D model retrieval; Class-statistics; Pair-Constraint; Object-Based Distance Measure;

1. INTRODUCTION

With development of modeling tools and improvement of computer performance, there is an increasing number of 3D models in diverse domains, such as medical simulation model and architectural design model. Comparing with 2D graphic recognition or retrieval, 3D model recognition or retrieval is more realistic. Therefore, it is necessary to design a practical 3D model retrieval method for model matching. Recently, a lot of 3D model retrieval methods [1-6] have been proposed, where multi-view matching algorithms often be utilized due to good retrieval performance; For example, Lu et al. [2] mines the relevance of view-based and model-based in a graph-based model; Weighted Bipartite Graph Matching (WBGM) [3], Spectral Matching (SM) [4], Reweighted Random Walks Matching (RRWM) [5] belong to graph matching methods, where they select representative views from the query or candidate model, and then the representative view weights are initialized by calculating the proportion of each cluster and updated by literately calculating views matching degree. In these multi-view matching algorithms, WBGM builds the weighted bipartite graph based on 2D views; SM and RRWM utilize graphic unary and pairwise attribute to implement graph matching. WBGM, SM and RRWM analyze graph information and improve graph matching level. In above multi-view matching algorithms, although they have obtained satisfying performance, these algorithms are time-consuming because of view-based distance measure. In addition, for the basic Hausdorff distance (HAUS) and Nearest Neighbor (NN) graph matching distance algorithms, HAUS calculates the farthest distance of all the views between two objects to obtain the similarity of two objects, whereas NN calculates the similarity of two objects via finding the nearest distance of all the views. HAUS and NN don't require training model, but they have bad retrieval speed and precision. Such approaches generally convert 3D object matching to 2D multi-view matching and obtain the final retrieval results via calculating view similarity between two objects. But these view-based methods will reduce the retrieval speed so that they can't be utilized in real time system. Recently, Gao et al. [6] proposes CCVF algorithms, where it groups all query views to generate view clusters to represent each model in query. And then, the author proposes a view-based pairwise training method, where the distances between positive and positive samples, and the distances between positive and negative samples are calculated. After that, the Gaussian models are constructed based on these distance distributions.

Inspired by these, we originally propose a class-statistics and pair-constraint model (CSPC) method, which is composed of supervised class-based statistics model and pair-constraint object retrieval models. In CSPC model, we firstly convert view-based distance measure into object-based distance measure, which will advance 3D model retrieval speed. After that the generality of the distribution of each feature dimension in each class is computed to judge category information, and then we further adopt this distribution information to build class models. Finally, an object-based pairwise constraint is introduced on the base of the class-

MM '16, October 15 - 19, 2016, Amsterdam, Netherlands

ISBN 978-1-4503-3603-1/16/10...$15.00
DOI: http://dx.doi.org/10.1145/2964284.2967194

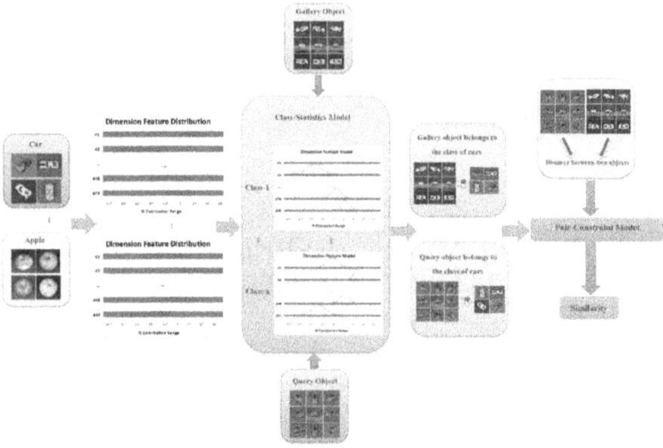

Figure 1: The architecture of proposed CSPC 3D model retrieval algorithm

statistic measure, which can remove a lot of false alarm samples in retrieval. The architecture of CSPC model is given in Fig.1. The proposed algorithm consists of the following procedures: First, the class models are trained by utilizing the distribution of each feature dimension. Then, we both calculate class information for query object and gallery object by using pre-training class models. Next, the object-based distance information is calculated for pairwise objects. Finally, we can obtain the similarity between two objects by CSPC model. The main contributions of our CSPC are summarized as follow:

- View-based distance measure is converted into object-based distance measure without falling in performance, which will speed up retrieval.
- A supervised class-based statistics model is proposed to obtain the distribution of each feature dimension in the class, and then, the probabilistic model is built for each feature dimension of all classes. Moreover, we analyze the impact factors for each feature dimension of all classes, and adaptively allocate weights for each feature dimension for the class based on impact factors.
- In the terms of retrieval, the object-based pairwise constraint model is proposed, which utilizes our pre-training class-based statistics model and object-based distance measure. By using pair-constraint model, we can reduce a lot of false alarm results.

The rest of this paper is organized as follows. CSPC model will be given in Section 2, and then extensive experimental results are introduced in Section 3 and Section 4 concludes this paper.

2. CLASS-STATISTICS AND PAIR-CONSTRAINT MODEL

In this section, we will first introduce class-statistics probabilistic model, and then object-based measure and pair-constraint model will be given, finally, CSPC model will be introduced in detail.

2.1 Class-Statistics Probabilistic Model

2.1.1 *Task Formulation*

Suppose there is a set of query objects, the retrieval task is to find the matched object from gallery objects. Let $C^Q = \{c_1^Q, ...c_n^Q, ..., c_m^Q\}$ denote the class set in query Q, where m is the number of classes. We denote $O^Q = \{o_1^Q, ...o_l^Q, ..., o_x^Q\} \in c_n^Q$ as the object set of class c_n^Q with x objects, where n is the sequence number of the class. Let $V^Q = \{v_1^Q, ..., v_y^Q\} \in o_l^Q$ denote the view set of object o_l^Q with y views, where l is the sequence number of the object. Similarly, the class set in gallery M is denoted by $C^M = \{c_1^M, ...c_n^M, ..., c_m^M\}$, and we denote $O^M = \{o_1^M, ...o_l^M, ..., o_x^M\} \in c_n^M$ as the object set of class c_N^M with x objects. Let $V^M = \{v_1^M, ..., v_y^M\} \in o_l^M$ denote the view set of object o_l^M with y views, where l is the sequence number of the object. The goal of 3D model retrieval is searching similar objects between Q and M.

2.1.2 *Class-Statistics Probabilistic Model*

Let $\{f_1^Q, f_2^Q, ..., f_m^Q\} \in R^K$ denote the feature set of the query object, and let $\{f_1^M, f_2^M, ..., f_m^M\} \in R^K$ denote the feature set of the gallery object, Where K is the number of feature dimensions. For object α in query objects and object β in gallery objects, we further employ $\{d_{\alpha 1}^Q, d_{\alpha 2}^Q, ..., d_{\alpha m}^Q\} \in f_{\alpha m}^Q$ and $\{d_{\beta 1}^M, d_{\beta 2}^M, ..., d_{\beta m}^M\} \in f_{\alpha n}^M$ to denote each feature dimension, where $f_{\alpha m}^Q$ and $f_{\beta n}^M$ are the features of one sample in query objects and gallery objects respectively. By experimental analysis and observation, we discover that the distributions of each feature dimension for different classes are very different. Therefore, we build the distribution probabilistic model of each feature dimension to describe the generality of class feature. Furthermore, we build the class-statistics model. The distribution probabilistic model can be define as:

$$g_i(x_i|\mu_i, \sigma_i^2) = \exp(-\frac{(x_i - \mu_i^{c_m^M})^2}{2(\sigma^{c_m^M})^2}) \tag{1}$$

Where c_m^M denotes class m in gallery objects, $\mu_i^{c_m^M}$ and $\sigma_i^{c_m^M}$ are the expectation and the variance of i-th dimension feature respectively. x_i denotes the i-th dimension feature of object x. We define $\mu_i^{c_m^M}$ and $\sigma_i^{c_m^M}$ as:

$$\mu_i^{c_m^M} = \frac{1}{D_m^M} \sum_{j=1}^{D_m^M} d_{ij}^M \tag{2}$$

$$(\sigma_i^{c_m^M})^2 = \frac{1}{D_m^M - 1} \sum_{j=1}^{D_m^M} (d_{ij}^M - \mu_i^{c_m^M})^2 \tag{3}$$

Where d_{ij}^M denotes the i-th dimension of the j-th view feature, and D_m^M denotes the total number of all views in m-th class of gallery. We further discover that, for each feature dimension in a single class, the degree of convergence and divergence can embody the representation of this dimension feature for this class. When a dimension feature is more convergent than other dimension features, it suggests that this dimension feature is more representative for this class. Therefore, we adaptively allocate weight to each dimension feature by considering the degree of convergence and divergence of each dimension. The proportion formulation is defined as follow:

$$r_i = \frac{\max_{j=1,...,d_m^M}(d_{ij}^M) - \min_{j=1,...,d_m^M}(d_{ij}^M)}{\sum_{i=1}^{K}\{\max_{j=1,...,d_m^M}(d_{ij}^M) - \min_{j=1,...,d_m^M}(d_{ij}^M)\}} \tag{4}$$

Where d_m^M denotes the total number of all views in m-th class. Thus, the weight factor can be formulated by considering proportion formulation:

$$w_i = \exp(-\lambda r_i^2) \tag{5}$$

Where λ indicates the impact of weights. Finally, the class-statistics model is defined as:

$$P_{class}^m(x) = \sum_{i=1}^{K} w_i g_i(x_i|\mu_i^{c_m^M}, (\sigma_i^{c_m^M})^2) \tag{6}$$

Where K is the number of feature dimensions, and x_i is the i-th dimension feature of object x. $P_{class}^{m}(x)$ denotes the possibility of object x belongs to class m.

2.2 Object-based Measure and Pair-Constraint Model

2.2.1 *Object-based Measure*

Since the most of multi-view matching algorithms are based on view distance measure, thus, these algorithms are time-consuming. In order to speed up the retrieval time, we convert view-based distance measure into object-based distance measure, where the average feature of all views in a class is calculated. Suppose there is a query object α, whose features set can be represented by $\{f_{\alpha 1}^{Q}, f_{\alpha 2}^{Q}, ..., f_{\alpha m}^{Q}\} \in R^K$ and we can utilize $d_{\alpha}^{Q} = \frac{1}{n_\alpha}\sum_{i=1}^{n_\alpha} f_{\alpha i}^{Q}$ to represent the feature of object α where n_α is the number of views of object α, and $f_{\alpha i}^{Q}$ is the i-th view in object α. Thus, the feature of query object α can be represented by $\{d_{\alpha 1}^{Q}, ..., d_{\alpha k}^{Q}\} \in R^K$, where K indicates the number of feature dimensions of object α. Similarly, for gallery object β, whose features set also can be represented by $\{f_{\beta 1}^{M}, f_{\beta 2}^{M}, ..., f_{\beta m}^{M}\} \in R^K$, and then the average results are obtained by $d_{\beta}^{M} = \frac{1}{n_\beta}\sum_{i=1}^{n_\beta} f_{\beta i}^{M}$, thus, its feature can be denoted by $\{d_{\beta 1}^{M}, ..., d_{\beta k}^{M}\} \in R^K$. In this way, we convert view-based matching to object-based matching which can significantly improve retrieval speed.

2.2.2 *Pair-Constraint Model*

First, we compute the category probabilities of query object α and gallery object β by utilizing Eq. (6) respectively, and then, the category labels can be formulated as follows:

$$label_\alpha = \arg \max_{m=1,...,\tau} \{\sum_{i=1}^{K} w_i \exp(-\frac{(d_{\alpha i}^{Q} - \mu_i^{c_m^Q})^2}{2(\sigma_i^{c_m^Q})^2})\} \quad (7)$$

$$label_\beta = \arg \max_{m=1,...,\varsigma} \{\sum_{i=1}^{K} w_i \exp(-\frac{(d_{\alpha i}^{M} - \mu_i^{c_m^M})^2}{2(\sigma_i^{c_m^M})^2})\} \quad (8)$$

Where τ is the number of categories in query, and ς is the number of classes in gallery. In our experiments, τ is equal to ς. The meanings of $\mu_i^{c_m^M}$ and $\sigma_i^{c_m^M}$ are same to Eq. (1). Moreover, we compute the Euclidian distance between object α and object β:

$$Dist(\alpha, \beta) = \sqrt{(d_\alpha^Q - d_\beta^M)(d_\alpha^Q - d_\beta^M)^T} \quad (9)$$

Here, we convert distance information to distance probability which will combine with class-statistics information as retrieval conditions. The distance probability model is calculated by:

$$P_{dist}(\alpha, \beta) = 1 - \frac{Dist(\alpha, \beta)}{\max_{i,j \in M} \sqrt{(d_i^M - d_j^M)(d_i^M - d_j^M)^T}} \quad (10)$$

Where d_i^M and d_j^M are features of two different objects in gallery objects.

2.3 CSPC Model

By analyzing the retrieval results of different 3D models, we observe that CS model can obtain the generality of each class, object-based measure can speed up the retrieval, and the pair-constraint can improve the accuracy of retrieval. Thus, class-statistics and pair-constraint model is defined as:

$$sim(\alpha, \beta) = \begin{cases} \lambda + \varphi P_{dist}(\alpha, \beta) + \psi P_{class}^{label_\alpha}(\alpha) P_{class}^{label_\beta}(\beta), \\ \qquad if \ \ label_\alpha = label_\beta \\ \varphi P_{dist}(\alpha, \beta) + \psi P_{class}^{label_\alpha}(\alpha) P_{class}^{label_\alpha}(\beta), \\ \qquad otherwise \end{cases} \quad (11)$$

$$s.t. \varphi + \psi = 1$$

Where φ and ψ are utilized to control the balance among object-based measure, pair-constraint and class-statistics. It is noted that we adopt respective class-statistics model to calculate probability for query object α and gallery object β. If the predictions in Eq. (7) and Eq. (8) are the same, the corresponding probabilities of Eq. (7) and Eq. (8) are utilized in Eq. (11), what's more, the rewarding mechanism is employed, λ is added into the probability computation. Otherwise, the corresponding query class-statistics model is used to calculate the probability of query object α and gallery object β respectively.

3. EXPERIMENTS AND DISCUSSIONS

In order to evaluate the performance of CSPC, we perform 3D model retrieval on four public 3D datasets. We initially study the influence of the parameters in our algorithm, and then, the performance of CSPC model is evaluated. After that, the computation time is analyzed, at the same time, it is also compared with state-of-the-art algorithms.

3.1 Datasets

In our experiments, four widely-used datasets are employed: ETH 3D object dataset [7], where it contains 80 objects belonging to 8 categories, and each object from ETH includes 41 different view images; NTU-60 3D model dataset [8], where it contains 549 objects belonging to 47 categories, and each object from NTU-60 includes 60 different view samples; MVRED 3D category dataset [9], where it contains 505 objects belonging to 61 categories, and each object from MVRED includes 73 different view images; PSB 3D object dataset [10], where it contains 1813 objects belonging to 161 categories, and each object from PSB includes 60 different view features. For each dataset, the leave-one-object-out scheme is employed, that is to say, one object in the 3D dataset is chosen as the query object, and others are utilized as the gallery object, and then we repeat 80, 549, 505 and 1813 times for ETH, NTU, MVRED and PSB datasets respectively, and finally the average results are computed. In addition, since Zernike moment has been demonstrated to be robust to image translation, scaling, and rotation, and generally applied in multi-view analysis task [2], [11], [12], the Zernike moment descriptor is extracted to describe each image in query and gallery set, whose dimension is 49-dims.

3.2 Parameters Setting

In CSPC model, there are the parameters λ , φ and ψ ($s.t. \varphi + \psi = 1$), which will affect the performance of retrieval. Thus, we study the performance of CSPC with the change of these parameters, and we obtain the average optimal result by setting $\lambda = 30$, $\varphi = 0.2$ and $\psi = 0.8$. The experimental results can be obtained in the supplemented material. In addition, the following evaluation criteria are employed to evaluate the retrieval performance. 1) Nearest Neighbor (NN), 2) First Tier (FT), 3) Second Tier (ST), 4) F-measure (F), 5) Discounted Cumulative Gain (DCG), 6)

Average Normalized Modified Retrieval Rank (ANMRR), 7) Precision-Recall Curve (PR-Curve). The detail information can be found in [9].

3.3 Performance Analysis

We firstly assess the performance of CSPC model on four 3D dataset, and we also compare it with the state-of-the-art algorithms, whose performances are obtained by running the codes offered by the authors with default settings. Their results are shown in Fig.2 and Fig.3. From them, we can observe that the proposed CSPC method always has excellent performance compared with exciting methods. For example, from Fig.2 (a) and Fig.2 (c), we can see that CSPC can consistently outperform all the others, and on ETH dataset, CSPC can achieve a gain of 5%-29%, 11%-30%, 12%-35%, 2%-22%, 9%-34% on NN, FT, ST, DCG, F and obtain a decline of 7%-28% on ANMRR. From Fig.2 (b), CSPC outperforms 3%-25%, 4%-20% and 3%-25% on FT, ST, F, and achieves a decline of 0.5%-20% on ANMRR. From Fig.2 (d), CSPC outperforms 5%-27%, 5%-31%, and 2%-30% on FT, ST and F. In addition, Fig.3 (a-d) shows the PR curve comparison of different 3D model retrieval algorithms on ETH, NTU-60, MVRED and PSB datasets. It also proves that CSPC is comparable with other the state-of-the-art algorithms. In other words, our CSPC model is efficient and effective.

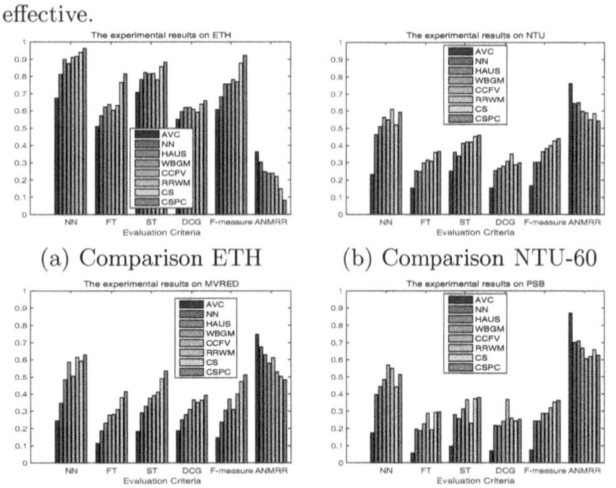

(a) Comparison ETH (b) Comparison NTU-60

(c) Comparison MVRED (d) Comparison PSB

Figure 2: Retrieval result comparison of different 3D model retrieval algorithms on ETH, NTU-60, MVRED and PSB 3D datasets

3.4 Computation Time Analysis

In this section, we will evaluate the computation time of all algorithms. To ensure fairness, all algorithms are implemented on the same laptop PC platform with a 2.10 GHz, Intel Core i3 CPU, 4GB RAM and 64bit OS. All of them are estimated by using MATLAB which has been published by the paper authors. The average retrieval time of each object in gallery is utilized as computation time of the corresponding algorithm. Table.1 list the retrieval time cost of six methods on four 3D datasets. From it, we can see that on ETH, our CSPC method ranks 1 among six algorithms, whose computation time is 20 milliseconds, and it speeds up 10-381 times than other methods. Similarly, CSPC also has significant improvement on other datasets. Our method speeds up 24-136 times, 26-156 times, 25-246 times on NTU-60, MVRED and PSB datasets respectively, which is very

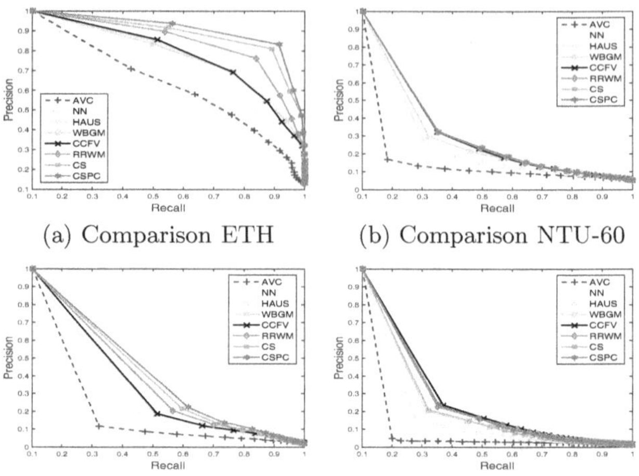

(a) Comparison ETH (b) Comparison NTU-60

(c) Comparison MVRED (d) Comparison PSB

Figure 3: PR Curve comparison of different 3D model retrieval algorithms on ETH, NTU-60, MVRED and PSB 3D datasets

Table 1: Average retrieval time on four datasets with six methods

Methods	Data Sets (sec)			
	ETH	NTU-60	MVRED	PSB
NN	0.17	2.73	3.10	8.90
HAUS	0.18	2.70	3.09	8.50
CCFV[6]	0.48	10.12	3.31	50.24
AVC[13]	6.05	15.26	18.34	82.86
WBGM[3]	0.51	3.32	5.18	10.44
CSPC	**0.02**	**0.11**	**0.12**	**0.34**

useful in real-time system. The reason why our algorithm can be so quick is that we have converted view-based distance measure into object-based distance measure without falling in performance. Accordingly, our CSPC model is fast, and whose performance is efficient and effective.

4. CONCLUSION

In this paper, a fast 3D model retrieval algorithm via a supervised class-statistics and pair-constraint model is proposed. In this model, we firstly convert view-based distance measure into object-based distance measure without falling in performance, which can advance 3D model retrieval speed. And then the generality of each dimension feature distribution of a single class is computed to judge category information. Finally, an object-based pairwise constraint is introduced on the base of the class-statistic measure, which can remove a lot of false alarm samples in retrieval. Experimental results on four public datasets show that our method is comparable with the state-of-the-art algorithms. More importantly, its fast property has great significance for our daily life.

5. ACKNOWLEDGMENTS

This work was supported in part by the National Natural Science Foundation of China (No.61572357, No.61202168); Tianjin Training plan of University Innovation Team (No.TD12-5016); Tianjin Research Program of Application Foundation and Advanced Technology (14JCZDJC31700 and 13JCQN-JC0040). Tianjin Municipal Natural Science Foundation (No.13JCQNJC0040).

6. REFERENCES

[1] Y. Gao, A. Liu, and W. Nie, 3d object retrieval with multimodal views, in Eurographics Workshop on 3D Object Retrieval, 2015, pp. 129-136.

[2] K. Lu, N. He, J. Xue, J. Dong, and L. Shao, Learning view-model joint relevance for 3d object retrieval, IEEE Transactions on Image Processing, vol. 24, no. 5, pp. 1449-1459, 2015.

[3] Y. Gao, Q. Dai, M. Wang, and N. Zhang, 3d model retrieval using weighted bipartite graph matching, Signal Processing: Image Communication, vol. 26, pp. 39-47, 2011.

[4] M. Leordeanu and M. Hebert, A spectral technique for correspondence problems using pairwise constraints, in 10th IEEE International Conference on Computer Vision (ICCV 2005), 17-20 October 2005, Beijing,China, 2005, pp. 1482-1489.

[5] M. Cho, J. Lee, and K. M. Lee, Reweighted random walks for graph matching, in ECCV, 2010, pp. 492-505.

[6] Y. Gao, J. Tang, R. Hong, S. Yan, Q. Dai, N. Zhang, and T.-S.Chua, Camera constraint-free view-based 3d object retrieval, IEEE Transactions on Image Processing, vol. 21, no. 4, pp. 2269-2281, 2012.

[7] A. Ess, B. Leibe, K. Schindler, and L. van Gool, A mobile vision system for robust multi-person tracking, in IEEE Conference on Computer Vision and Pattern Recognition (CVPR08). IEEE Press, June2008.

[8] D.-Y. Chen, X.-P. Tian, Y.-T. Shen, and M. Ouhyoung, On visual similarity based 3d model retrieval, in Computer graphics forum, vol. 22, no. 3. Wiley Online Library, 2003, pp. 223-232.

[9] A.Liu, W.Nie, Y.Gao, Y.Su, Multi-Modal Clique-Graph Matching for View-Based 3D Model Retrieval, in IEEE Transaction on Image Processing, vol. 25, no 5, pp. 2103-2116, 2016

[10] P. Shilane, P. Min, M. Kazhdan, and T. Funkhouser, The princeton shape benchmark, in Shape modeling applications, 2004. Proceedings. IEEE, 2004, pp. 167-178.

[11] B. Leng, J. Zeng, M. Yao, and Z. Xiong, 3d object retrieval with multi-topic model combining relevance feedback and lda model, IEEE Transactions on Image Processing, vol. 24, no. 1, pp. 94-105, 2015

[12] Y. Gao, M. Wang, D. Tao, R. Ji, and Q. Dai, 3d object retrieval and recognition with hypergraph analysis, IEEE Transactions on Image Processing, vol. 21, no. 9, pp. 4290-4303, 2012

[13] T. F. Ansary,M. Daoudi, and J. P. Vandeborre, A Bayesian 3-D search engine using adaptive views clustering, IEEE Trans. Multimedia, vol.9, no. 1, pp. 78-88, Jan. 2007.

Analyzing and Predicting GIF Interestingness

Michael Gygli*
Computer Vision Lab
ETH Zurich
Switzerland
gygli@vision.ee.ethz.ch

Mohammad Soleymani*
Swiss Center for Affective Sciences
University of Geneva
Switzerland
mohammad.soleymani@unige.ch

ABSTRACT

Animated GIFs have regained huge popularity. They are used in instant messaging, online journalism, social media, among others. In this paper, we present an in-depth study on the interestingness of GIFs. We create and annotate a dataset with a set of affective labels, which allows us to investigate the sources of interest. We show that GIFs of pets are considered more interesting that GIFs of people. Furthermore, we study the connection of interest to other features and factors such as popularity. Finally, we build a predictive model and show that it can estimate GIF interestingness with high accuracy. Our model outperforms the existing methods on GIF popularity, as well as a model based on still image interestingness, by a large margin. We envision that the insights and method developed can be used for automatic recognition and generation of interesting GIFs.

1. INTRODUCTION

Interest is related to curiosity and attention and as a result an important factor in driving multimedia users' online behavior [15]. It has various applications in multimedia such as video highlight detection [20] and media recommendation. Flickr, for example[1], highlights interesting photos shared on their website. Rather than analyzing the visual content, however, they rely on information such as the number of likes, comments, etc. [5]. Thus, they require users' feedback and social interactions in order to surface interesting content. However, social interactions and interestingness do not always co-exist [14], as we will show in our experiments.

The Graphics Interchange Format (GIF) is a graphical format that was introduced in 1987 by the Internet provider company CompuServe to depict moving pictures on the low-bandwidth Internet of that time. Recently, GIFs are making a comeback [22] and there are popular websites such as Tumblr[2] which is mainly used for posting and sharing GIFs.

*Equal contributions
[1]https://www.flickr.com/explore/interesting/
[2]https://www.tumblr.com/

MM '16, October 15 - 19, 2016, Amsterdam, Netherland

ISBN 978-1-4503-3603-1/16/10...$15.00

DOI: http://dx.doi.org/10.1145/2964284.2967195

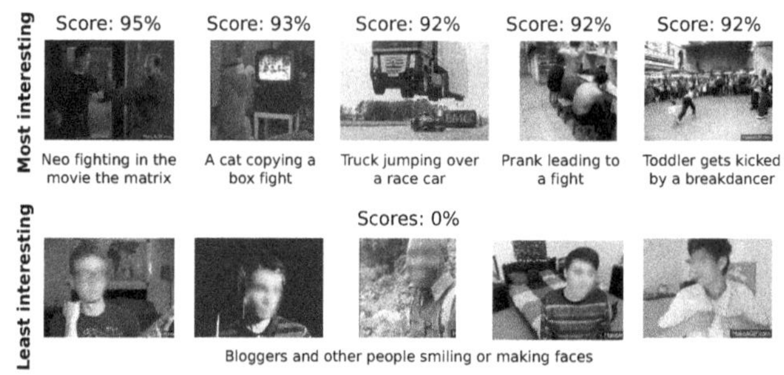

Figure 1: Most and least interesting GIFs from our dataset. GIFs of action scenes, pets and accidents are considered most interesting, while most boring GIFs are of people.

GIFs have become a very popular media, due to their unique properties. In contrast to images, animated GIFs have better capabilities to show dynamic content, tell stories and convey emotions. At the same time they remain short and without sound, which makes them more discreet and easily consumable compared to videos, which require higher time and bandwidth commitment [1].

In this paper, we conduct an in-depth study on what makes GIFs interesting. Towards this goal, we constructed a database of GIFs annotated with interest and other affective attributes. 2739 GIFs were selected from the previous studies on GIFs [9, 1] and labeled on Amazon Mechanical Turk. A content-based GIF interestingness method is developed and evaluated. We obtain a prediction performance that is comparable to the ones on still images [18, 8, 7]. The contributions of this work are as follows: (i) We analyze the effect of emotional attributes on GIF interestingness and provide an in-depth analysis into what makes a GIF interesting; (ii) We study the relationship between GIF interestingness to GIF popularity as well as image interestingness. (iii) We build a computational model for automatic prediction of GIF interestingness.

2. BACKGROUND

Interest is a state which is related to curiosity and drives our attention. Silvia among other psychologist posited that interest is an emotion which has consistent subjective feelings and expressions in adults [15]. Halonen *et al.* [10] identified a set of characteristics that are related to visual interestingness through a qualitative study. The characteristics which were deemed relevant were aesthetics, affect, colors, composition, genre and personal connection. Chu *et al.* [6] studied the effect of familiarity of faces and images context

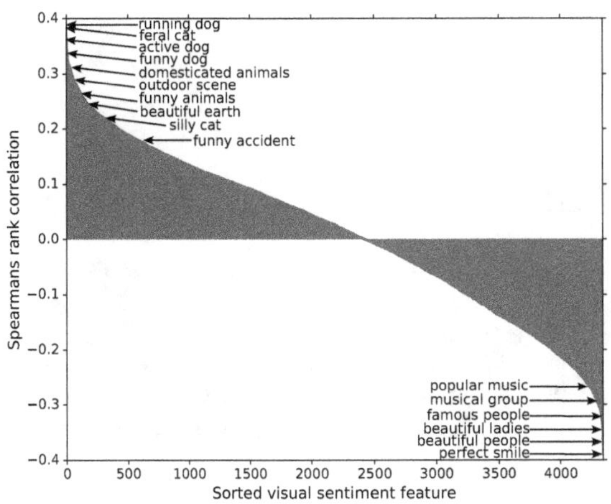

Figure 2: Correlations of visual sentiment attributes [13] with GIF interest. Some groups of contents stand out: pets, natural/aesthetic scenes and, on the negative side, music and people (see text).

on visual interestingness. They found that personally familiar faces and unfamiliar contexts are positively correlated with the interestingness in images.

In the light of the recent surge in the popularity of GIFs, Bakhshi *et al.* [1] studied the engaging factors in GIFs using a combination of interviews with GIF users and simple computational features. They found that animation, lack of sound, immediacy of consumption, low bandwidth and minimal time demands, the storytelling capabilities and utility for expressing emotions were the most important factors in making GIFs engaging. Jou *et al.* [12] built a tool for automatic prediction of perceived emotion in GIF viewers. Color histogram, facial expressions depicted in GIFs, visual features related to aesthetics and visual sentiment [2] were used as their content features. They found that facial expressions depicted in GIFs were the most effective features in determining perceived emotions in response to GIFs.

Gygli et al. and Grabner et al. [8, 7] showed that visual content features related to unusualness, aesthetics and general preference are effective in predicting visual interestingness. More recently, Soleymani [18] built a model for personalized interest prediction for images. He found that affective content, quality, coping potential and complexity have a significant effect on visual interest in images.

3. DATASET

We sampled 1729 GIFs from the Video2GIF dataset [9] and 1010 GIFs from the Tumblr dataset of [1]. We sampled randomly from Video2GIF, while for Tumblr, we undersampled GIFs with few likes, to have a more balanced distribution of likes and reblogs. We manually removed GIFs containing text and pornographic material. We deliberately removed the GIFs with subtitles to focus on visual interestingness of the content rather than language in the dialogues. In total, we selected 2739 GIFs to be labeled for our dataset, which is available online[3]. GIFs were in average 4.25 seconds long with the average frame rate of 11 frames/second.

[3]http://cvml.unige.ch/databases/gifInterest/

Scale	Kri. $\alpha \uparrow$
Interesting - Uninteresting	0.25
Boring - Exciting	0.32
Arousing - Soothing	0.31
Pleasant - Unpleasant	0.16
Appealing - Unappealing	0.13
Want full video - Don't want full video	0.17
Explicit - Non-explicit	0.30

Table 1: Krippendorff's alpha for different scales. All the scales were ordinal with the exception of explicitness which was nominal.

Scale	Arousal	Valence	Appeal	Curiosity
ρ	0.439	0.299	0.526	0.779

Table 2: Spearman's correlation coefficients (ρ) between the interestingness and emotional ratings.

GIFs were labeled through crowdsourcing on Amazon Mechanical Turk. Motivated by the affective dimension of interest and the previous findings on interestingness in images [18, 10], we labeled GIFs on interestingness, aesthetics, arousal and valence (pleasantness) on five point scales. We also labeled them on the presence of explicit or erotic content due to the strong effect of sexual arousal in emotional responses [3]. The scales were appealing-unappealing for aesthetics, arousing-soothing for arousal, pleasant-unpleasant for valence, interesting-uninteresting and boring-exciting for interest and "want to see full video"-"do not want to watch the full video" for curiosity. Each GIF received five labels on all these scales. 41 crowd-workers, 21 male, aged between 22 - 59 years old ($\mu = 35.0, \sigma = 9.6$) annotated the GIFs. They receive \$0.07 to annotate each GIF. Due to the culture specific references in the content of GIFs, we decided to restrict the tasks to the workers based in the USA. We calculated Krippendorff's alpha to measure the agreement of the labels adjusted to the chance agreement ($max(\alpha) = 1$). All the inter-rater agreements were in range of fair to moderate agreement similar to previous studies [18] (see Table 1).

Similar to [16], the interesting - uninteresting scale was combined with reverse boring - exciting to form the interestingness score which is used in the remaining of this paper.

4. ANALYSIS

While GIFs have gained immense popularity, they have not been analyzed from a computational perspective. One notable exception is the work of Baskshi *et al.* [1]. They however only analyze the relationship of low-level image features and GIF popularity. Instead, we use our new dataset to do an in-depth analysis of what makes a GIF interesting. Concerning the affective dimension of interest, the Spearman's rank correlation was calculated between interest and the emotional ratings (see Table 2). As expected, there is a strong correlation between interest and curiosity. All emotional ratings are significantly correlated with interest. Aesthetic appeal of GIFs has a higher correlation with interest compared to arousal or valence. In Figure 2, we relate visual sentiments, detected by [13], and interest, while Figure 3 shows a hierarchical clustering on the same features.

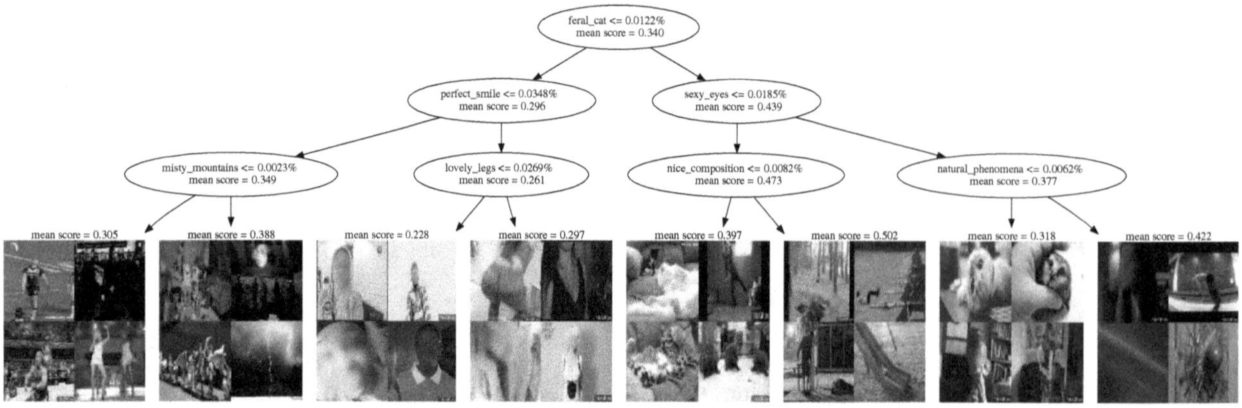

Figure 3: Hierarchical clustering of GIFs according to their interestingness scores by means of a CART tree [4] and visual sentiment features [13].

Thereby we observe several groups of attributes that are strongly correlated with interest. Namely GIFs of pets, lead by cats and dogs are typically considered of interest. Furthermore, beautiful and natural scenes, as well as funny content in general are deemed interesting. Negatively correlated attributes are mainly from two groups: music and people. Surprisingly, the presence of people has inverse correlation with GIF's interestingness, even though there are very popular memes of facial expressions. However, these are exceptions and the larger part of GIFs containing people are considered dull. This suggests that for finding interesting GIFs of people, a more fine-grained analysis of facial expressions is necessary. Thus, we extracted facial expressions for the subpart of GIFs containing a considerable amount of frames containing faces and correlated joyful, surprised, sad and angry expressions with interest. While joy remains negatively correlated (-0.129), the other emotions have a weak positive correlation with interest (surprise: 0.019, sorrow (sadness) 0.036, anger 0.096). Next, we put our annotated attributes in relation to the number of views and reblogs (Table 3). For this, we use the GIFs from Tumblr only, as it provides accurate social data [1]. In accordance with one's expectation, interest is related to the number of likes ($\rho = 0.279$). In fact, it is the most correlated among all the attributes we investigated. The number of times a GIF was re-blogged, however is not significantly correlated (p-value> 0.01) with any attribute, except the explicitness of content. Explicitness has a significant negative correlation, meaning that fewer Tumblr bloggers are re-sharing explicit GIFs compared to other content. While interest and the number of likes are related, their correlation is relatively weak. Popularity is not only influenced by the content but also by social factors such as uploaders' popularity. This effect was also observed and investigated by Schifanella *et al.* [14], who surface appealing photos among unpopular Flickr images.

	rank correlation ρ with	
Attribute	**# of likes**	**# of reblogs**
Interest	0.279	-0.039
Arousal	0.056	-0.015
Curiosity	0.251	-0.069
Appeal	0.224	0.018
Valence	0.152	0.010
Explicit	-0.035	-0.149

Table 3: The annotated attributes in relation to popularity (views and reblogs)

5. INTEREST PREDICTION

In order to predict the interestingness of GIFs, we learn a model using a support vector regression (SVR) with an RBF kernel. As feature representation, we use a range of visual features, as described in the next Section.

Baselines. We compare our model with two related work, namely, image interestingness [8] and Video2GIF [9].

For image interestingness, we follow [8] and train a SVR with RBF kernel on the dataset of [11] with their interestingness labels. Rather than using low-level features, however, we use the outputs from the fully connected layer 6 (fc6) of a deep convolutional neural network, i.e., VGGNet-19 [17]. For reference, we evaluated this model on the test set of [8] and obtained a performance of $\rho = 0.70$, thus outperforming the original work of [8] ($\rho = 0.60$).

Video2GIF is a method that learns to rank segments within a video according to their likelihood to be selected as GIFs. To this end, it uses pairs of video segments (positive vs. negative). A positive is a video segment that was selected to produce a GIF, while a negative segment is one that was never selected by users to produce a GIF. We compare two configurations: (i) A ranking learned from pairs (pos, neg) in the same video ("within") and (ii) a ranking learned from (pos, neg) in different videos ("across").

Implementation details. We report results on the full dataset, using cross-validation: We split the dataset into 5 parts, and train on four parts and test on the fifth, in turn. As performance metrics, we report Spearman's rank correlation ρ as well as root mean square error (RMSE). When training the SVRs, we optimize C after cross-validation for each training split. For the RBF-kernel we set $\gamma = 1/d$, where d is the dimensionality of the feature representation.

5.1 Visual features

We use a range of visual features at varying levels of abstraction. Based on [1], a set of simple low-level features is extracted from every frame of GIFs. These simple features are pooled at the frame level by mean, standard deviation

	Feature	Description	Dimensionality
Simple features	Visual features [1]	Entropy, exposure, balance, brightness, compression quality [21], contrast, sharpness, uniformity, face count, face region, image asymmetry, motion energy, Contrast balance (Euclidean distance between the original image and the contrast-equalized image)	33
	Meta-information [1]	GIF frame rate, number of pixels, duration and aspect-ratio	4
	Loopiness	Distance between last and first frame	1
Google API	Text and face area	Ratio between text and face area and the full GIF[4]	2
	Spoof likelihood	Likelihood that a modification was made to the GIF to make it appear funny or offensive[4]	1
	Violence likelihood	Likelihood that the GIF depicts violent content[4]	1
	Facial expressions	Degree of the emotions sorrow, anger, surprise and joy[4]	4
	Visual sentiments [13]	Probabilities of adjective noun pairs related to sentiments	4342
	C3D [19]	Features from a CNN with spatio-temporal convolutions trained for action recognition in videos. We use the first fully-connected layer	4096

Table 4: Visual features, their descriptions and dimensionality.

and skewness to form a feature vector for each GIF. Similar to [1], GIF characteristics such as frame rate, number of pixels, duration and aspect-ratio are also extracted. We further extract attributes related to the content of frames using Google Cloud Vision API[4], namely the area covering faces and text, spoof and violence likelihood, as well as facial expressions. Features by Google Cloud API are pooled by averaging their values at frame level. Furthermore, we use two types of CNN-based features. (i) Spatio-temporal CNN features that were trained for action recognition and (ii) Visual sentiment attributes, which consist of probabilities for adjective noun pairs. A comprehensive list of features and their dimensionality is given in Table 4.

5.2 Results

The results for prediction GIF interest are summarized in Figure 5. Results demonstrate that our approach is able to predict GIF interestingness with high accuracy, compared to the baselines. It is interesting to observe that the sentiment features, while lacking temporal information, perform better than C3D. This indicates that the types of objects and their associated sentiments are more important than motion information. Our best performing model has a rank correlation of 0.53 showing that GIF interest can be predicted well from visual information only. When comparing the models trained for predicting GIF interestingness with previous methods, they perform much better than the baselines. This is not surprising, given that the baselines were not trained for this task directly. Somewhat surprisingly, Video2GIF trained to rank segments from the same video is actually uncorrelated with GIF interest (Video2GIF within). However, Video2GIF trained with samples coming from different videos is correlated. Its correlation (0.21) is even higher than that of image interestingness (0.15), despite not being trained with interest labels.

	Method	rank corr $\rho \uparrow$	RMSE $\downarrow$
As is	Image Interest [8]	0.1544	-
	Video2GIF [9] within	-0.0082	-
	Video2GIF [9] across	0.2055	-
Retrained SVR	Simple features [1]	0.3870	0.1818
	C3D [19]	0.4809	0.1746
	Sentiment features [13]	0.5219	0.1695
	Google API features	0.3806	0.1817
	C3D+Sentiments	0.5222	0.1694
	Full	**0.5308**	**0.1685**

Table 5: Predicting mean interest in GIFs

6. CONCLUSIONS

In this work, we analyzed and predicted human interest in GIFs. Towards this goal, we have introduced a new GIF dataset with interestingness annotation. We found the adjective noun pairs or sentiment features to be the most informative features, even though they are extracted from still images. GIFs depicting pets were in average found to be more interesting than the ones showing people. We also found that interestingness is associated with likability, i.e., number of likes a GIF receives. However, interestingness was not correlated with reblogging behavior or social popularity. Finally, we used our dataset to build a predictive model and showed its effectiveness in predicting interestingness. In the future, we would like to extend this model to predict personalized interest.

7. ACKNOWLEDGMENT

The work of Gygli was supported by the ERC project VarCity (#273940). Soleymani received support from the Swiss National Science Foundation (Ambizione and NCCR Affective Sciences).

[4]https://cloud.google.com/vision/

8. REFERENCES

[1] S. Bakhshi, D. Shamma, L. Kennedy, Y. Song, P. de Juan, and J. Kaye. Fast, Cheap, and Good: Why Animated GIFs Engage Us. In *Proceedings of the 34rd Annual ACM Conference on Human Factors in Computing Systems (CHI)*, 2016.

[2] D. Borth, T. Chen, R. Ji, and S.-F. Chang. Sentibank: large-scale ontology and classifiers for detecting sentiment and emotions in visual content. In *Proceedings of the 21st ACM international conference on Multimedia*, pages 459–460. ACM, 2013.

[3] M. M. Bradley, M. Codispoti, D. Sabatinelli, and P. J. Lang. Emotion and motivation ii: sex differences in picture processing. *Emotion*, 1(3):300, 2001.

[4] L. Breiman, J. Friedman, C. J. Stone, and R. A. Olshen. *Classification and regression trees.* CRC press, 1984.

[5] D. S. Butterfield, C. Fake, C. J. Henderson-Begg, and S. Mourachov. Interestingness ranking of media objects, patent application 20060242139. (US 20060242139), 2006.

[6] S. L. Chu, E. Fedorovskaya, F. Quek, and J. Snyder. The effect of familiarity on perceived interestingness of images. In *Proc. SPIE 8651, Human Vision and Electronic Imaging XVIII*, 2013.

[7] H. Grabner, F. Nater, M. Druey, and L. Van Gool. Visual interestingness in image sequences. In *Proceedings of the 21st Annual ACM Conference on Multimedia*, 2013.

[8] M. Gygli, H. Grabner, H. Riemenschneider, F. Nater, and L. Van Gool. The Interestingness of Images. In *The IEEE International Conference on Computer Vision (ICCV)*, 2013.

[9] M. Gygli, Y. Song, and L. Cao. Video2GIF: Automatic Generation of Animated GIFs from Video. In *2016 IEEE Conference on Computer Vision and Pattern Recognition (CVPR)*, 2016.

[10] R. Halonen, S. Westman, and P. Oittinen. Naturalness and interestingness of test images for visual quality evaluation. In *IS&T/SPIE Electronic Imaging*, 2011.

[11] P. Isola, J. Xiao, A. Torralba, and A. Oliva. What makes an image memorable? In *Computer Vision and Pattern Recognition (CVPR), 2011 IEEE Conference on*, pages 145–152. IEEE, 2011.

[12] B. Jou, S. Bhattacharya, and S.-F. Chang. Predicting Viewer Perceived Emotions in Animated GIFs. In *Proceedings of the 22Nd ACM International Conference on Multimedia*, MM '14, pages 213–216, New York, NY, USA, 2014. ACM.

[13] B. Jou, T. Chen, N. Pappas, M. Redi, M. Topkara, and S.-F. Chang. Visual Affect Around the World: A Large-scale Multilingual Visual Sentiment Ontology. In *ACM International Conference on Multimedia*, number 1, 2015.

[14] R. Schifanella, M. Redi, and L. M. Aiello. An Image is Worth More than a Thousand Favorites : Surfacing the Hidden Beauty of Flickr Pictures. *International Conference on Web and Social Media (ICWSM)*, 2015.

[15] P. J. Silvia. *Exploring the psychology of interest.* Oxford University Press, 2006.

[16] P. J. Silvia, R. A. Henson, and J. L. Templin. Are the sources of interest the same for everyone? using multilevel mixture models to explore individual differences in appraisal structures. *Cognition and Emotion*, 23(7):1389–1406, 2009.

[17] K. Simonyan and A. Zisserman. Very deep convolutional networks for large-scale image recognition. *arXiv preprint arXiv:1409.1556*, 2014.

[18] M. Soleymani. The quest for visual interest. In *Proceedings of the 23rd Annual ACM Conference on Multimedia*, pages 919–922. ACM, 2015.

[19] D. Tran, L. Bourdev, R. Fergus, L. Torresani, and M. Paluri. Learning Spatiotemporal Features with 3D Convolutional Networks. In *The IEEE International Conference on Computer Vision (ICCV)*, 2015.

[20] B. T. Truong and S. Venkatesh. Video abstraction: A systematic review and classification. *ACM Transactions on Multimedia Computing, Communications, and Applications (TOMM)*, 3(1):3, 2007.

[21] Z. Wang, H. R. Sheikh, and A. C. Bovik. No-reference perceptual quality assessment of JPEG compressed images. In *International Conference on Image Processing*, volume 1, pages I–477. IEEE, 2002.

[22] A. Williams. Fresh From the Internet's Attic. New York Times, Feb 13, 2013.

Emotion in Context: Deep Semantic Feature Fusion for Video Emotion Recognition

Chen Chen, Zuxuan Wu, Yu-Gang Jiang
School of Computer Science, Shanghai Key Lab of Intelligent Information Processing,
Fudan University, Shanghai, China
{cchen14, zxwu, ygj}@fudan.edu.cn

ABSTRACT

Human emotions demonstrate high correlations with certain *events* that consist of the interaction of *objects*, and are usually constrained by particular *scenes*. In this paper, we exploit these abundant context clues for video emotion recognition. We first compute event, object and scene scores with state-of-the-art detectors based on deep neural networks. The extracted high-level features serve as effective contextual information demonstrating what is occurring in the video, and are further integrated in a context fusion network to generate a unified representation aiming to bridge the affective gap. The contribution of this paper is three-fold: (a) we are the first to incorporate event as context for emotion recognition, and we demonstrate its superiority for emotion understanding, (b) we utilize a context fusion network to exploit a comprehensive set of high-level semantics features as contextual clues and (c) the proposed framework can realize recognition in real-time and achieves state-of-the-art performance on two challenging emotion recognition benchmarks, 50.6% on VideoEmotion and 51.8% on Ekman.

Keywords

Emotion; Video; Object; Scene; Context.

1. INTRODUCTION

The ubiquity of use-generated videos nowadays has encouraged techniques that can recognize their semantic contents automatically. In addition to analyzing the visual contents, such as objects and scenes, the understanding of sentiment in videos has many practical applications such as video recommendation and smart advertising. Different from typical visual recognition focusing on the likelihood of a certain concept (*e.g.*, objects/actions) occurring in a video clip [8, 14, 23], emotion recognition is a higher-level abstraction concerning what affect the video conveys, which results in the huge affective gap [16] between low-level features and sentiment.

Compared with a large amount of works on text sentiment analysis, limited efforts have been conducted for emotion

Figure 1: Context provides valuable information to differentiate emotions. Reproduced from [2].

recognition in videos, most of which focus on commercial movies [13, 24] and animated gifs [12]. User-generated videos which usually consist of severe camera motion and cluttered background, have been much less explored. Jiang *et al.* proposed a computational system that leverages multiple features to capture emotions [11]. Recently, the resurgence of Convolutional Neural Networks (CNNs), which demonstrated effectiveness for various domains [8, 21], has encouraged a few pioneer works exploiting deep features for emotion analysis [27, 6]. For instance, Chen *et al.* proposed trained a CNN model to recognize emotions in images [6]. Xu *et al.* systematically evaluated the performance of different deep features for emotion recognition [26]. These deep features have achieved better performance than hand-crafted features (*e.g.*, SIFT [15]) and concepts (*e.g.*, SentiBank [4]), yet they are still low-level and fail to bridge the affective gap.

In this paper, we tackle the above problems by fully exploiting the semantic context to narrow down the affective gap for improved emotion recognition. Intuitively, an emotion is usually triggered by the interaction of multiple objects performing certain events under a particular scenario. Therefore, the recognition of a target emotion would benefit from its mutual contextual clues, including actions, objects and scenes. For instance, Fig 1 illustrates that a scowl could indicate anger or disgust, but it is more likely to demonstrate excitement when placed in the context by considering this is a *tennis player* with a *racket* in her hand *playing tennis* in a *sports field*, and is celebrating the victory.

Motivated by the above observations, we utilize a context fusion framework for emotion recognition that integrates high-level semantic features as context clues extracted from state-of-the-art deep models, as illustrated in Fig. 2. More specifically, we first train detectors to recognize human actions and complex events with two large-scale video bench-

MM '16, October 15-19, 2016, Amsterdam, Netherlands

DOI: http://dx.doi.org/10.1145/2964284.2967196

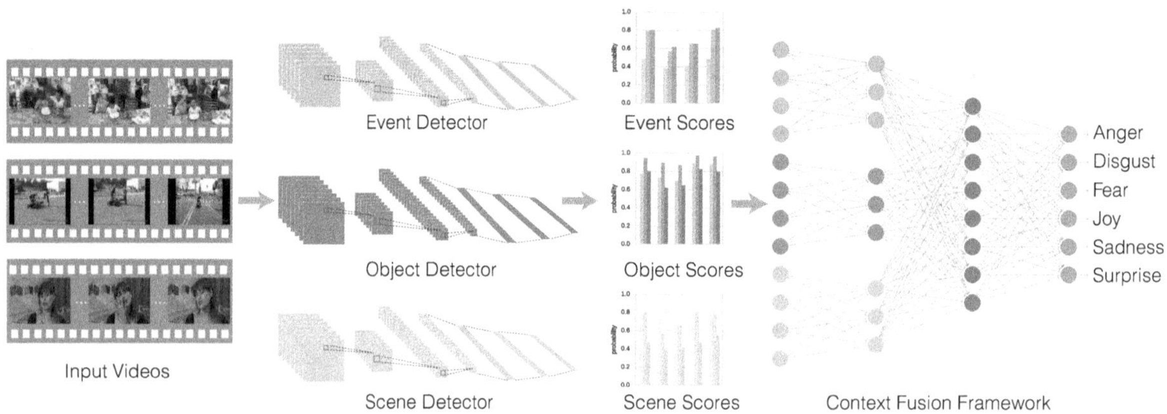

Figure 2: An overview of our framework. See text for discussion. We first apply state-of-the-art detectors based on deep neural networks to obtain the event, object and scene scores as contextual clues. These high-level semantic features are further integrated in a context fusion framework for improved emotion recognition performance.

marks, providing valuable information about what is occurring in the video. Then, we compute object features with large-scale object detectors trained to recognize 1K classes and we also leverage scene scores from a popular deep scene detector. Finally, we leverage a context fusion network to integrate these deep semantic features for emotion recognition. The main contributions of this paper are three-fold (i) to the best of our knowledge, we are the first to leverage event as context information for emotion understanding, which we empirically validated to be effective; (ii) we adopt a context fusion network to exploit a comprehensive set of contextual clues to bridge affective the gap; (iii) the proposed framework can recognize emotions in real-time and achieves state-of-the-art performance on two challenging benchmarks.

2. OUR APPROACH

In this section, we will first introduce the adopted high-level semantic features, and then describe the proposed context fusion network that integrates multiple sources of context information for emotion recognition.

2.1 High-level Semantic Features

Event Features. Human actions and events are highly associated with emotions. For instance, one often feels *happy* when celebrating a *birthday party* whereas *fighting* usually comes with *anger*. Therefore, to extract emotion labels from a video sequence, it is desirable to understand what events are taking place. To this end, we first train event detectors using two large-scale video benchmarks, Fudan-Columbia Video Dataset (FCVID) [10] and ActivityNet [5] respectively. FCVID contains 91,223 web videos labeled manually into 239 categories, covering a wide range of categories popularly seen in Web videos such as social events (*e.g.*, "tailgate party") and procedural events (*e.g.*, "making cake"). Since events can usually be decomposed into several actions, to capture more detailed action information, we also leverage ActivityNet, a newly released video benchmark focusing on human actions, which consists of 27,801 video clips annotated into 203 activity classes. The combination of these two large-scale benchmarks contains a broad spectrum of topics in our daily lives that could boost the understanding of emotions. More specifically, we compute features from the first fully-connected layer (fc_6) of the VGG19 network pre-trained on ImageNet [22] and then train linear SVM classifiers to recognize events on these two benchmarks respectively. Let $g_F(\cdot) \in \mathbb{R}^{239}$ and $g_A(\cdot) \in \mathbb{R}^{203}$ denote the trained models on FCVID and ActivityNet respectively, which map an input video to a set of concept scores. We then concatenate these two sets of scores into $P_x^E \in \mathbb{R}^{442}$ to represent the likelihood of a certain event occurring in video x.

Object Features. Objects also contain useful clues about the visual contents in a video that might be complementary with event features. In addition, psychologists also found objects themselves can reflect emotions to some extent. For example, flowers often brings positive emotions while blood might lead to negative feelings. Existing works usually hand-pick a small collection of objects for emotion analysis [11], in this work, we leverage a large-scale object detector pre-trained to recognize 1K classes on ImageNet [7]. The detector leverages the state-of-the-art VGG19 model [22], which consists of sixteen convolutional layers and three fully connected layers. More specifically, we calculate the probability of 1K object categories occurring in each frame of a video clip with the softmax layer in the VGG19 network, which results in a 1K dimensional vector of object scores. We then obtain the video-level representation by simply averaging all the score vectors across frames $P_x^O = \frac{1}{N}\sum P_{x_i}^O \in \mathbb{R}^{1000}$, where x_i denotes the object score for the i-th frame in video x and N is the number of frames for the video.

Scene Features. To extract scene information that could potentially help recognize emotions, we adopt a VGG16 model pre-trained on Places205 dataset [28], which consists of 2.5 million images annotated into 205 scene classes. Similar to object scores, we compute the output from the classification layer as our features $P_x^S = \frac{1}{N}\sum P_{x_i}^S \in \mathbb{R}^{205}$, which demonstrate the likelihood of the presence of the corresponding scene classes averaged across all frames.

Feature Normalization. To improve the generalization ability of these features, we adopt the RootSift technique [1], which performs element-wise square root for the feature vector after L_1 normalization.

2.2 Context Fusion Network

For a video clip x we now have three high-level semantic features (P_x^E, P_x^O, P_x^S) that demonstrate the probability of corresponding events, objects and scenes occurring in the video clip. Since these clues characterize the video from multiple perspectives, inspired by [25], we adopt a context fusion network that derives a unified feature representation and simultaneously performs categorization for improved emotion recognition, as illustrated in Figure 2.

More precisely, we first transform each of the input features to a high-level space (250 neurons for event and object features, and 50 neurons for scenes) independently before fusion, which could preserve their distinct properties and increase the discriminative ability. Since these features are extracted from the same video clip demonstrating the same sentiment in different forms, we then use a fusion layer with 250 neurons for absorbing all the information to obtain a shared representation, which is further topped by a softmax classifier to recognize emotions. The optimal parameter could be derived by using back-propagation with stochastic gradient descent [3]. We set the learning rate to be $1e-3$, and maximum iterations being 200. Such a network could be easily trained using GPU, and can achieve real-time prediction.

3. EXPERIMENTS

3.1 Experimental Setup

3.1.1 Datasets and Evaluation Metrics

We adopt two challenging video emotion recognition benchmarks to evaluate the proposed framework.

Video Emotion Dataset [11]. The Video Emotion dataset contains 1,101 videos from YouTube and Flickr with an average duration of 107 seconds. It is manfully annotated into 8 basic emotion categories according to the Plutchik's wheel of Emotions [19], including "anger", "anticipation", "disgust", "fear", "sadness", "joy", "surprise" and "trust". We conduct evaluations using 10 train/test splits provided by the dataset and report the mean accuracy over ten splits, following [11].

Ekman Emotion Dataset [26]. It consists of 1,637 videos labeled into Ekman's 6 basic emotions by 10 volunteers with a minimum number of 221 videos per category. We follow the convention defined in [26] to use a training set of 819 videos and a testing set of 818 videos. The performance is measured by classification accuracy.

3.1.2 Compared Approaches

To validate the effectiveness of our context fusion framework, we compare with the following fusion approaches:

- Early Fusion with Neural Networks (EF-NN). The three high-level semantic features are concatenated as inputs for a neural network for classification.
- Classifier Fusion with Neural Networks (CF-NN). Each feature is trained using a separate neural network, and then the scores of different models are averaged as final predictions.
- Early Fusion with SVM (EF-SVM). χ^2 kernel is computed for each of the features and then averaged as the inputs for the SVMs.
- Classifier Fusion with SVM (CF-SVM). A χ^2 SVM is trained for each feature and prediction results are then combined linearly.
- Fusion with Multiple Kernel Learning (MKL-SVM) [17]. We adopt MKL with χ^2 kernel to learn the fusion weights when integrating all these features.

3.2 Results and Analysis

In this section, we first report the performance of individual high-level semantic features for emotion recognition. After that, we analyze results of integrating multiple sources of context information with the proposed context fusion framework, and compare with recent state-of-the-art results.

3.2.1 Individual High-level Semantic Feature

The performance of each single high-level semantic feature for video emotion recognition is summarized in Table 1, which is divided into two groups. The results in the top group are from linear SVMs, while those in the bottom group are obtained using a 3-layer neural network to increase the discriminative power for each of the features. As we can see from the table, non-linear classifiers lead to significant improvements (about 5%–9% performance gain) compared with their linear counterparts. Scene detectors are usually sensitive to noises when applied to long videos with cluttered backgrounds, but still obtain decent performance on both datasets. We also incorporate the widely adopted low-level feature [20] extracted from the first fully connected layer (*i.e.*, fc_6) of a VGG19 model pre-trained on ImageNet for comparison, which achieves good performance on both datasets confirming the fact that fc_6 enjoys high generalization ability. In addition, results on VideoEmotion are slightly worse than those on Ekman due to two extra emotions "anticipation" and "trust" in VideoEmotion that incur difficulties for recognition.

	Features	VideoEmotion	Ekman
Linear	fc_6	39.95	41.59
	Event	41.10	42.45
	Object	34.11	36.43
	Scene	28.71	40.95
NN	fc_6	48.16	47.51
	Event	48.33	48.10
	Object	44.88	46.45
	Scene	33.97	46.33

Table 1: Performance of each individual high-level semantic feature using linear SVMs and NN as classifier.

Surprisingly, we observe that event features attain the best performance on both datasets: 48.33% on VideoEmotion and 48.10% on Ekman, outperforming fc_6 by 0.17% and 0.59% respectively. This is appealing since the dimension of the event feature (442) is about nine times smaller than that of fc_6 (4,096), which indicates high-level semantic features are more effective to bridge the affective gap. In addition, the superiority of event feature confirms emotions are tightly associated with events.

To further understand this relationship between events and emotions, we conduct a qualitative experiment using method from [9]. To compute the importance of the i-th event for

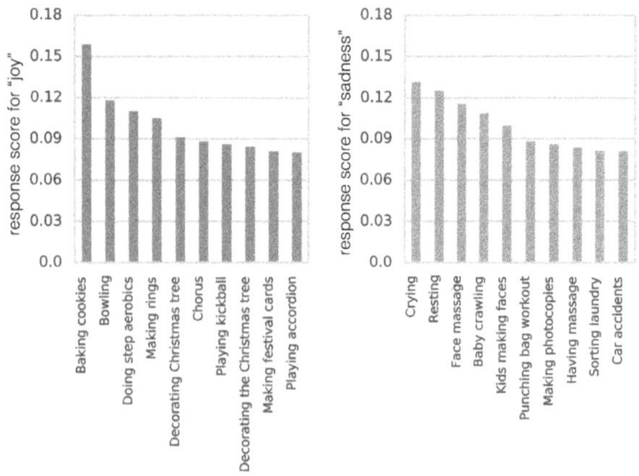

Figure 3: Top-10 related events for *joy* (left) and *sad* (right), and their response scored derived from Ekman.

the j-th emotion, we simply take all the videos belonging to the j-th class and average their event features: $w_j(i) = \sum_{x \in C_j} P_x^E(i)$. Figure 3 visualizes the results for the top-10 related events of *joy and* sadness on Ekman respectively. The events with high responses for the *joy* category are mostly related to leisure activities (*e.g.*, *Baking cookies* and *Making rings*), sports (*e.g.*, *Bowling* and *Playing kickball*), or music (*e.g.*, *chorus* and *Playing accordion*), and these events indeed could demonstrate pleasure and joy. For the *sadness* emotion, in addition to the *crying* event that naturally makes sense, *face massage* is discovered for it involves actions covering faces that might be considered as sad. Also, since the *sadness* category consists of a lot of baby crying videos, events related to kids and baby are also identified.

3.2.2 Context Fusion Network

We now assess the performance of the proposed context fusion network, which integrates a comprehensive set of context clues for emotion recognition and compare with alternative fusion baselines. The results are summarized in Table 2. Our context fusion network achieves 50.4% and 51.8% on VideoEmotion and Ekman respectively, outperforming alternative fusion methods by clear margins. Different from EF-NN that mixes multiple features before fusion, our framework first transforms the semantic features into high-level space to preserve their unique characteristics and then performs fusion exploiting their correlations, which offers about 2% performance gain on both datasets. In addition, the concatenation of features as inputs for fusion often generates high-dimensional feature representations, which could lead to over-fitting especially when training samples are limited. Classifier fusion combines prediction scores from separately trained models, which relies on the assumption that these models are all robust to noises and their scores are explicitly complementary. Comparing across different classifiers, it seems that neural networks perform on par with SVMs since the amount of videos in these two emotion benchmarks is limited. With sufficient training samples, we might observe better results of neural networks.

We also compare state-of-the-art results in recent literatures. Our context fusion network achieves 0.7% and 1.4% performance gain on VideoEmotion and Ekman respectively.

	VideoEmotion	Ekman
EF-NN	47.9	49.3
CF-NN	46.8	48.5
EF-SVM	47.1	48.9
CF-SVM	46.7	48.1
MKL-SVM [17]	47.8	50.1
Pang *et al.* [18]	49.9	–
Xu *et al.* [26]	46.7	50.4
Context Fusion Network	**50.6**	**51.8**

Table 2: Comparisons with alternative baselines on VideoEmotion and Ekman datasets.

Pang *et al.* [18] leveraged additional 156,219 YouTube videos to train Deep Boltzmann Machines. Xu *et al.* [26] utilized more advanced strategies to generate video-level representations instead of average pooling. In addition, both works [26, 18] incorporated audio clues to compensate visual information. Note that our work attains superior performance by only jointly exploiting the contextual information from events, objects and scenes features generated by off-the-shelf detectors. And the framework could easily be extended to combine audio clues for further improvements.

Computational Efficiency. Finally, we briefly discuss the computational efficiency of the proposed framework. Since each component in the proposed framework is based on neural network, the proposed framework could achieve emotion recognition in real-time once the networks are trained. For example, for a video clip in the VideoEmotion dataset with an average duration of 107 seconds, it takes less than 30 seconds to compute all the high-level semantic features and 0.01 seconds for classification on a sever with one NVIDIA K40 GPU card.

4. CONCLUSION

We have proposed a novel context fusion framework for emotion recognition in videos, which is able to jointly explore the benefits of rich context clues, including events, objects and scenes, for improved performance. In the framework, we first compute high-level semantic features using state-of-the-art event, object scene detectors based on deep neural networks. The extracted features, indicating the likelihood of presence of *objects* performing certain *events* under particular *scenes*, act as high-level semantic inputs for a context fusion network to derive a unified representation targeting at the understanding of emotions. Extensive experiments on two video emotion benchmarks have shown that events are critical for emotion understanding and our framework consistently outperforms the alternative baselines as well as the recent state-of-the-art works. In addition, the proposed framework can achieve real-time recognition which is appealing for real-world large-scale applications.

Acknowledgment

This work was supported by a China's National 863 Program (#2014AA015101), and two grants from National Natural Science Foundation of China (#61572134 and #U1509206).

5. REFERENCES

[1] R. Arandjelovic and A. Zisserman. Three things everyone should know to improve object retrieval. In *CVPR*, 2012.

[2] L. F. Barrett, B. Mesquita, and M. Gendron. Context in emotion perception. *Current Directions in Psychological Science*, 2011.

[3] Y. Bengio. Learning deep architectures for AI. *Foundations and trends in machine learning*, 2009.

[4] D. Borth, R. Ji, T. Chen, T. Breuel, and S.-F. Chang. Large-scale visual sentiment ontology and detectors using adjective noun pairs. In *ACM Multimedia*, 2013.

[5] F. Caba Heilbron, V. Escorcia, B. Ghanem, and J. Carlos Niebles. Activitynet: A large-scale video benchmark for human activity understanding. In *CVPR*, 2015.

[6] T. Chen, D. Borth, T. Darrell, and S.-F. Chang. Deepsentibank: Visual sentiment concept classification with deep convolutional neural networks. *CoRR*, 2014.

[7] J. Deng, W. Dong, R. Socher, L.-J. Li, K. Li, and L. Fei-Fei. ImageNet: A large-scale hierarchical image database. In *CVPR*, 2009.

[8] R. Girshick, J. Donahue, T. Darrell, and J. Malik. Rich feature hierarchies for accurate object detection and semantic segmentation. In *CVPR*, 2014.

[9] M. Jain, J. C. van Gemert, and C. G. Snoek. What do 15,000 object categories tell us about classifying and localizing actions? In *CVPR*, 2015.

[10] Y.-G. Jiang, Z. Wu, J. Wang, X. Xue, and S.-F. Chang. Exploiting feature and class relationships in video categorization with regularized deep neural networks. *arXiv preprint arXiv:1502.07209*, 2015.

[11] Y.-G. Jiang, B. Xu, and X. Xue. Predicting emotions in user-generated videos. In *AAAI*, 2014.

[12] B. Jou, S. Bhattacharya, and S.-F. Chang. Predicting viewer perceived emotions in animated gifs. In *ACM Multimedia*, 2014.

[13] H.-B. Kang. Affective content detection using hmms. In *ACM Multimedia*, 2003.

[14] A. Krizhevsky, I. Sutskever, and G. E. Hinton. Imagenet classification with deep convolutional neural networks. In *NIPS*, 2012.

[15] D. G. Lowe. Distinctive image features from scale-invariant keypoints. *IJCV*, 2004.

[16] J. Machajdik and A. Hanbury. Affective image classification using features inspired by psychology and art theory. In *ACM Multimedia*, 2010.

[17] P. Natarajan, S. Wu, S. Vitaladevuni, X. Zhuang, S. Tsakalidis, U. Park, and R. Prasad. Multimodal feature fusion for robust event detection in web videos. In *CVPR*, 2012.

[18] L. Pang and C.-W. Ngo. Mutlimodal learning with deep boltzmann machine for emotion prediction in user generated videos. In *ICMR*, 2015.

[19] R. Plutchik. The nature of emotions human emotions have deep evolutionary roots, a fact that may explain their complexity and provide tools for clinical practice. *American Scientist*, 2001.

[20] A. S. Razavian, H. Azizpour, J. Sullivan, and S. Carlsson. CNN features off-the-shelf: an astounding baseline for recognition. *CoRR*, 2014.

[21] K. Simonyan and A. Zisserman. Two-stream convolutional networks for action recognition in videos. In *NIPS*, 2014.

[22] K. Simonyan and A. Zisserman. Very deep convolutional networks for large-scale image recognition. In *ICLR*, 2015.

[23] H. Wang and C. Schmid. Action recognition with improved trajectories. In *ICCV*, 2013.

[24] H. L. Wang and L.-F. Cheong. Affective understanding in film. *IEEE TCSVT*, 2006.

[25] Z. Wu, Y. Fu, Y.-G. Jiang, and L. Sigal. Harnessing object and scene semantics for large-scale video understanding. In *CVPR*, 2016.

[26] B. Xu, Y. Fu, Y.-G. Jiang, B. Li, and L. Sigal. Video emotion recognition with transferred deep feature encodings. In *ICMR*, 2016.

[27] Q. You, J. Luo, H. Jin, and J. Yang. Robust image sentiment analysis using progressively trained and domain transferred deep networks. In *AAAI*, 2015.

[28] B. Zhou, A. Lapedriza, J. Xiao, A. Torralba, and A. Oliva. Learning deep features for scene recognition using places database. In *NIPS*, 2014.

Exploiting Hierarchical Activations of Neural Network for Image Retrieval

Ying Li[1], Xiangwei Kong[1], Liang Zheng[2], Qi Tian[2]
[1]Dalian University of Technology, China
[2]Dept. of Computer Science, University of Texas at San Antonio, Texas, TX 78249
liying08@mail.dlut.edu.cn, kongxw@dlut.edu.cn, liangzheng06@gmail.com, wywqtian@gmail.com

ABSTRACT

The Convolutional Neural Networks (CNNs) have achieved breakthroughs on several image retrieval benchmarks. Most previous works re-formulate CNNs as global feature extractors used for linear scan. This paper proposes a Multi-layer Orderless Fusion (MOF) approach to integrate the activations of CNN in the Bag-of-Words (BoW) framework. Specifically, through only one forward pass in the network, we extract multi-layer CNN activations of local patches. Activations from each layer are aggregated in one BoW model, and several BoW models are combined with late fusion. Experimental results on two benchmark datasets demonstrate the effectiveness of the proposed method.

CCS Concepts

•**Computing methodologies → Visual content-based indexing and retrieval;**

Keywords

Image retrieval; Bag-of-Words; Feature fusion

1. INTRODUCTION

Given a certain query image, image retrieval [11, 13, 23, 25, 24, 26] aims at returning similar images from the database. To reliably measure the pairwise similarity between images, low level handcrafted descriptors (*e.g.*, SIFT [15]) are usually plunged into Bag-of-Words (BoW) model. These low level descriptors capture the local patterns of images, making BoW pipeline robust to occlusion, truncation, and rotation.

Given a visual vocabulary learned off-line, BoW counts the frequency of local descriptors in an image. As a consequence, each image is encoded using a visual histogram, which is later compared under cosine distance [16] or Hellinger kernel [1]. To reduce the quantization loss, the "soft-assignment" strategy [19] is proposed, which assigns each local descriptor to more than one visual words. Simultaneously, larger efforts are also devoted to more advanced encoding methods [12, 20] and postprocessing algorithms [7, 22, 4].

In recent years, deep learning approaches have demonstrated superior performances in various applications in multimedia community, such as image categorization [6, 14], 3D shape recognition [5], object detection [8], *etc.* In [9, 3, 2, 21], Convolutional Neutral Network (CNN) is used as a generic feature extractor for image retrieval. The extracted features are usually activations of the high layers of CNN (*e.g.*, fully connected layers), taken as holistic representations which can reveal the high level semantics of images.

In this paper, we propose an effective Multi-layer Orderless Fusion (MOF) method to simultaneously capture the low-level patterns and high-level semantics of images by using a single deep neutral network. While previous works typically focus on the discriminative ability of activations from high layers, we observe that the activations from low layers (*e.g.*, convolution layers) of deep neutral network are effective as low-level cues for image retrieval.

In order to capture the local visual patterns of images, we extract these descriptors on densely sampled patches. This is the primary difference compared with previous works [3, 2, 21] which use the global images. To estimate the matching strength between two images, we use the conventional BoW model, accelerated by inverted index [16] to reduce the computational complexity and memory usage. By doing so, we are capable of achieving satisfactory retrieval performances with acceptable indexing cost.

Meanwhile, inspired by Hamming Embedding (HE) [10], these features are also binarized to improve the matching accuracy. Furthermore, to leverage the complementarity between the low level patterns and high level semantics, we fuse the activations from different layers in the score level. As opposed to Multi-scale Orderless Pooling (MOP) [9] that aggregates activations of images at different image scales, the aggregation in this paper is applied to activations of different layers of deep neutral network. As a result, the retrieval performance is improved further due to the integration of low level cues and high level semantics.

The rest of this paper is organized as follows. The proposed MOF framework is described in Section 2. In Section 3, the experimental results are presented and discussed. Finally, we conclude in Section 4.

2. PROPOSED APPROACH

In this section, we give a formal description of the proposed Multi-layer Orderless Fusion (MOF) based image retrieval pipeline. Figure 1 illustrates the framework of the proposed method.

MM '16, October 15-19, 2016, Amsterdam, Netherlands

DOI: http://dx.doi.org/10.1145/2964284.2967197

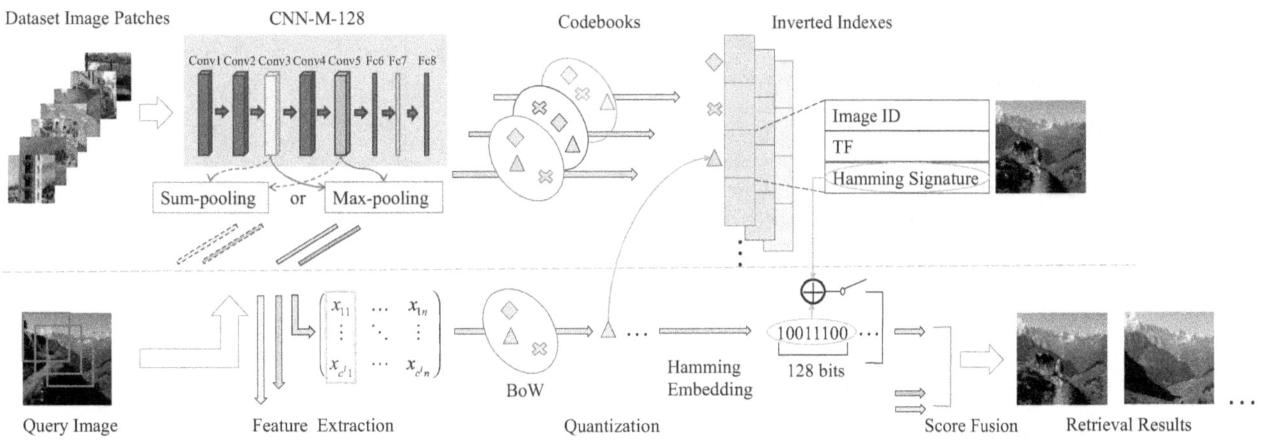

Figure 1: The pipeline of the proposed approach.

2.1 Multiple Deep Convolutional Description

Despite that several previous works [9, 3] claim that fully connected (Fc) layers give the best results compared with other layers when performing image retrieval, activations from convolutional layers should not be ignored since they preserve more instance-level details, which are especially meaningful for local area based image retrieval. In this paper, a fully connected layer, the last convolutional layer, and an intermediate convolutional layer of the CNN-M-128 [6] model are employed to construct the multiple deep convolutional description. The 7th layer (Fc7) activation of this model is compact with 128 dimensions and yields a competitive performance that will be discussed in the experiments.

For the convolutional layers, sum-pooling and max-pooling are applied separately to generate feature vectors. Given the pre-trained CNN-M model $\mathcal{C}$, deep convolutional feature maps f^l are obtained by passing image patches $\mathcal{P}$ through the network $\mathcal{C}$, with l presenting different layers. The size of f^l can be denoted as $w^l \times h^l \times c^l$, with w^l, h^l, and c^l denoting the width, height, and the number of channels of the layer l, respectively. Then sum-pooling is performed on f^l, aggregating each feature map into a single value, resulting in $p^l_{sum} \in \mathbb{R}^{1\times 1\times c^l}$. Denote the kth element of p^l_{sum} as $p_{sum}(k)$, then

$$p^l_{sum}(k) = \sum_{i=1}^{w^l} \sum_{j=1}^{h^l} f^l(i,j,k), \quad k = 1, 2, ..., c^l. \tag{1}$$

The max-pooling version also generates a $1 \times 1 \times c^l$ dimensional p^l_{max} as

$$p^l_{max}(k) = \max_{1 \leqslant i \leqslant w^l, 1 \leqslant j \leqslant h^l} f^l(i,j,k), \quad k = 1, 2, ..., c^l. \tag{2}$$

In this paper, the convolutional layers employed have 512 convolutional kernels, so the pooling result is a $1 \times 1 \times 512$ dimensional feature, which is then reshaped to a single column vector.

2.2 Two-step Quantization

In this section, we explore a feasible way to integrate deep features into the Bag-of-Words (BoW) structure, which is compatible with previous complementary techniques like Hamming Embedding (HE) in the hand-crafted low level feature based retrieval field at the same time. The procedures of assigning CNN features to visual words and generating binary signatures are two steps of quantization, with the Hamming codes acting as a finer division to boost the discriminative power of quantized features.

To get an adequate number of descriptors for constructing the BoW description of images, we densely sample image patches on a fixed size of 224×224 through a sliding window method with a stride size of 32 on the grid. We denote the set of image patches as $\mathcal{P}$ which is the input of the CNN-M-128 model $\mathcal{C}$, where $\mathcal{P} = \{P_1, P_2, ..., P_n\}$ includes n image patches in total. After the forward propagation through the pre-trained network $\mathcal{C}$, n features are obtained from each layer for a single image.

Considering activations from the three different layers separately, we train codebooks using Approximate K-Means (AKM) [18] clustering, followed by assigning features to the nearest visual word of the corresponding quantizer using the Approximate Nearest Neighbors (ANN) algorithm. Multiple Assignment (MA) [19] is applied in this quantization step to expand candidate visual centers for boosting recall. In this paper, the vocabulary size is set to be 20k and a feature is empirically assigned to three visual words.

Based on the built BoW structures, the inverted indexes are individually constructed, storing image IDs and Term Frequency (TF) scores aligned to the visual words. As complement for visual words, Hamming Embedding (HE) [10] is employed in this paper as a binary signature to refine the matching results by sub-splitting the quantized feature space. Assuming that the dimension of the original feature is c^l, and the code length after Hamming Embedding turns into h ($h \leqslant c^l$) which is set to be 128 in this paper, then a transition matrix P^l, with $P^l \in \mathbb{R}^{h*c^l}$, is trained to project both training data and target features from the c^l dimensional CNN description to another h dimensional space.

It should be paid attention to that the transition matrix P^l differs between layers. That may cause different information loss among the three layers, since convolutional layers obviously suffer more from the dimensional reduction. However, in our experiments, the two convolutional layers still gain comparable performance with the fully connected layer in this condition, proving the discriminative power of regional CNN descriptors.

2.3 Multi-layer Orderless Fusion (MOF)

Inspired by Multi-scale Orderless Pooling (MOP) [9], which extracts 4096-dimensional features from the fully connected layer at multiple scales, we proposed another Multi-layer Orderless Fusion (MOF) approach, where CNN features from convolutional layers are also taken into consideration with all the features extracted at the same single scale. Our work is different from MOP on three aspects, *i.e.*, features, quantization methods, and scales, though we both make efforts to explore local CNN based retrieval.

The two main advantages of the proposed MOF are: First, the convolutional layer activations can present low and mediate level cues apart from the high level semantics from the fully connected layer, so the fusion of them is complementary to each other. Second, all the activations can be obtained by passing a set of single scaled image patches through the deep neural network only once, without being extracted individually by several times. In addition, the activations employed in this paper are of much lower dimension than the 4096-dimensional ones utilized in previous works [9, 3] while the proposed approach still yields competitive performance.

Let x and y be two feature vectors in F_t, where $x, y \in \mathbb{R}^{c^l}$, the matching score between them is defined as

$$s = \begin{cases} idf^2_{q(x)}, & q(x) = q(y), \\ 0, & q(x) \neq q(y), \end{cases} \quad (3)$$

where $q(x)$ and $q(y)$ represent the visual words corresponding to x and y, respectively, and $idf_{q(x)}$ is the Inverse Document Frequency (IDF) of $q(x)$,

$$idf_{q(x)} = \log \frac{N}{n_{q(x)}}, \quad (4)$$

where N is the amount of images in total, and $n_{q(x)}$ counts for those ones containing $q(x)$.

Taking the binary signature into consideration, the matching results in Equation (3) are filtered as

$$s_h = \begin{cases} idf^2_{q(x)} \cdot w_h, & q(x) = q(y) \text{ and } d(b_x, b_y) < d_t, \\ 0, & \text{otherwise}, \end{cases} \quad (5)$$

with w_h added as a matching strength

$$w_h = \exp\left(-\frac{d^2(b_x, b_y)}{\sigma^2}\right). \quad (6)$$

b_x and b_y are Hamming codes of feature vectors x and y respectively, and $d(b_x, b_y)$ measures the distance between them as

$$d(b_x, b_y) = \sum_{i=1}^{h} b_x(i) \oplus b_y(i), \quad (7)$$

where $\oplus$ means bitwise XOR operation. d_t and σ are parameters determining the acceptable intra-centroid distance and the weighting magnitude, which are set to be 52 and 30, respectively.

To aggregate the effects of multiple layers, score fusion scheme is adopted as

$$S_h = \sum_l \sum_x s^l_h(x) / \sqrt{tf^l_{q(x)}}, \quad (8)$$

where $tf^l_{q(x)}$ denotes the Term Frequency (TF) stored in the inverted index of node $q(x)$ corresponding to layer l.

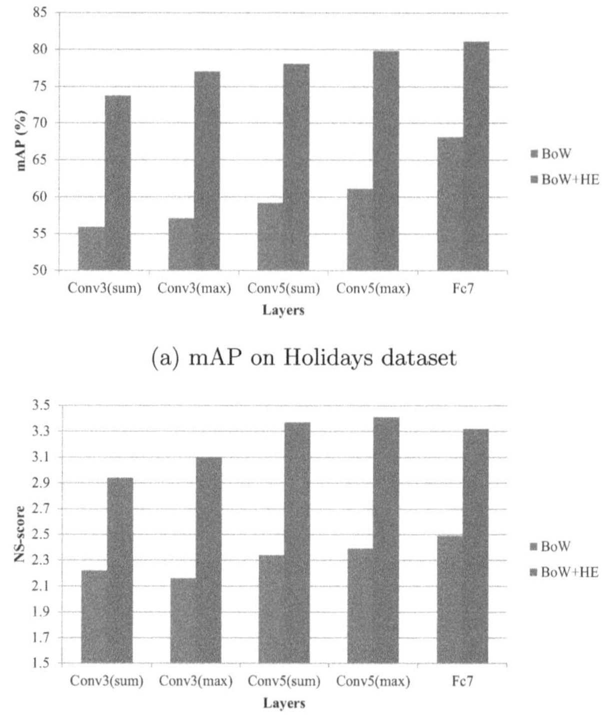

(a) mAP on Holidays dataset

(b) NS-score on UKBench dataset

Figure 2: Image retrieval performance with activations from different layers.

3. EXPERIMENTAL RESULTS

To evaluate the effectiveness of our approach, we perform retrieval experiments on two benchmark datasets, the Holidays dataset [10] and the UKBench dataset [16]. The Holidays datset contains 1,491 holiday images, of which 500 images are used as queries. Mean Average Precision (mAP) is used to evaluate the retrieval accuracy. On the UKBench dataset, there are 10,200 images from 2,550 object categories, with each containing 4 images. In this dataset, NS-score (average top 4 accuracy) is used to measure the retrieval accuracy.

In the following, we first compare the performance of activations from separate layers when applying the proposed local CNN based Bag-of-Words (BoW) framework with and without Hamming Embedding (HE). Then experiments on multiple layers are discussed to demonstrate the effectiveness of the Multi-layer Orderless Fusion (MOF) scheme. Finally, we compare our method with other CNN based works. In all experiments we use the pre-trained CNN-M-128 model [6].

3.1 Single Layer Evaluation

In our experiments, we choose activations from three layers in total, namely convolutional layers Conv3, Conv5, and fully-connected layer Fc7. For Conv3 and Conv5, we use sum-pooling and max-pooling to aggregate the convolutional layer feature maps, respectively. All activations undergo a square rooting for each dimension and L_2 normalization is performed to generate the final feature representation.

We summarize the image retrieval accuracies on Holidays and UKBench datasets in Figure 2 with respect to different

Table 1: MOF results of different layers

	Layers Comb.	Holidays sum	Holidays max	UKBench sum	UKBench max
BoW	Conv3+Conv5	67.23	69.80	2.67	2.68
BoW	Conv3+Fc7	72.60	75.14	2.85	2.75
BoW	Conv5+Fc7	74.05	75.36	2.74	2.93
BoW	Conv3+Conv5+Fc7	75.94	76.75	2.96	3.00
BoW+HE	Conv3+Conv5	79.74	82.34	3.22	3.39
BoW+HE	Conv3+Fc7	81.15	84.71	3.50	3.44
BoW+HE	Conv5+Fc7	83.58	83.85	3.26	3.51
BoW+HE	Conv3+Conv5+Fc7	83.78	**85.82**	3.38	**3.53**

layers, with or without applying Hamming Embedding (denoted as BoW+HE and BoW, respectively). From Figure 2 we observe that: 1) Except for BoW+HE on UKBench dataset, the activation from Fc7 layer generally achieves the best performance among all layers, demonstrating the effectiveness of the highly abstract feature representation in the CNN architecture; 2) For convolutional layer activations, max-pooling generally has a better performance compared to sum-pooling, which is probably because max-pooling is more robust to slight geometric transformations; 3) For activations from all layers, adding Hamming Embedding in our method dramatically improves the retrieval accuracy.

The best performance is achieved by Fc7 layer features on Holidays dataset, where the mAP value reaches up to 81.12%. While on UKBench dataset, max-pooled Conv5 layer features generate the highest NS-score as 3.41.

3.2 Multi-layer Orderless Fusion Results

While the proposed CNN feature representations of separate layers achieve satisfatory results on two benchmark datasets, we further perform Multi-layer Orderless Fusion (MOF) as described in Section 2.3 to boost the discriminative power of our method.

Since in the CNN architecture, low layers can extract some low-level visual patterns such as textures and shapes, while high layers usually extract high-level semantics, the fusion of different layers is expected to generate better results than the separate counterparts. The experimental results are in Table 1. We can see that the fusion of all three layers achieves the best performance for both BoW and BoW+HE, while the fusion of one convolutional layer and one fully-connected layer generally perform better than the fusion of two convolutional features. Applying Hamming Embedding greatly improves the BoW representation, and max-pooled features outperform the sum-pooled counterparts.

The best mAP result on Holidays dataset is 85.82% by using max-pooling and fusing three layers with Hamming Embedding. On UKBench dataset, NS-score 3.53 is achieved with the same experiment settings.

We compare the proposed Multi-layer Orderless Fusion (MOF) method with other state-of-the-art CNN-based algorithms, including Neural Codes [3], Multi-scale Orderless Pooling (MOP) [9] and Patch-CKN [17]. The comparison results are shown in Table 2. On the Holidays dataset, our method gains a remarkably improvement over the compared works for more than 5% in mAP, demonstrating that the Bag-of-Words quantization with Hamming Embedding works well with deep CNN features and outperforms the vector of locally aggregated descriptors (VLAD) [12] based pooling schemes used in previous works.

Table 2: The comparison with CNN-based methods

Methods	Holidays	UKBench
Neural Codes [3]	79.30	3.56
MOP [9]	80.18	-
Patch-CKN [17]	79.30	**3.76**
MOF	**85.82**	3.53

3.3 Comparisons

On the UKBench dataset, the result is still comparable. The possible reason affecting the results may be that the patches densely cropped include too much useless information. Specifically, different from natural scenes in the Holidays dataset, most of the images in UKBench have similar plain background with a single object in the center, so patches from background are of low discriminative power while they are great in amount. However, we may apply object detection or salience detection techniques to avoid such impact in the future work. In contrast, Patch-CKN [17] extracts local descriptors on detected interest areas, which can avoid background to a certain extent. Besides, several feature processing tools like Principal Component Analysis (PCA) and whitening adopted in MOP[9] and CKN-mix[17] boost the performance in 2%. These region proposal and postprocessing methods are to be studied in the future work.

4. CONCLUSIONS

This paper proposes a method called Multi-layer Orderless Fusion (MOF) for image retrieval. MOF aggregates hierarchical activations from different layers of the Convolutional Neural Network (CNN), with the activations from each layer incorporated into the Bag-of-Words (BoW) architecture separately. With the convenience that all activations from different layers can be extracted simultaneously by passing image patches through the deep network for only once, the proposed MOF approach is more efficient than previous multi-scale and multi-category feature fusion methods. Our experimental results on two benchmark datasets suggest that the CNN activations from different layers are complementary with each other. The fusion of them under the basic BoW framework can already achieve competitive performances against other state-of-the-art algorithms. It is worth mentioning that the proposed method can be easily extended by combining other improvements (*e.g.*, spatial information and postprocessing algorithms), which would be considered in the future.

5. ACKNOWLEDGMENTS

This work was supported by National Natural Science Foundation of China (NSFC) (Grant No. 61502073 and 61429201), the Foundation for Innovative Research Groups of the NSFC (Grant No. 71421001), the Open Projects Program of National Laboratory of Pattern Recognition (No. 201407349), and the China Scholarship Council. This work was supported in part to Dr. Qi Tian by ARO grants W911NF-15-1-0290 and Faculty Research Gift Awards by NEC Laboratories of America and Blippar. We thank Song Bai who provided insight and expertise that greatly assisted the research. We also thank Shaoyan Sun for assistance with the experiments, and Xiaopeng Zhang for comments that greatly improved the manuscript.

6. REFERENCES

[1] R. Arandjelović and A. Zisserman. Three things everyone should know to improve object retrieval. In *CVPR*, pages 2911–2918, 2012.

[2] A. Babenko and V. Lempitsky. Aggregating local deep features for image retrieval. In *ICCV*, pages 1269–1277, 2015.

[3] A. Babenko, A. Slesarev, A. Chigorin, and V. Lempitsky. Neural codes for image retrieval. In *ECCV*, pages 584–599, 2014.

[4] S. Bai and X. Bai. Sparse contextual activation for efficient visual re-ranking. *TIP*, 25(3):1056–1069, 2016.

[5] S. Bai, X. Bai, Z. Zhou, Z. Zhang, and L. J. Latecki. Gift: A real-time and scalable 3d shape search engine. In *CVPR*, 2016.

[6] K. Chatfield, K. Simonyan, A. Vedaldi, and A. Zisserman. Return of the devil in the details: Delving deep into convolutional nets. In *arXiv preprint arXiv:1405.3531*, 2014.

[7] O. Chum, J. Philbin, J. Sivic, M. Isard, and A. Zisserman. Total recall: Automatic query expansion with a generative feature model for object retrieval. In *ICCV*, pages 1–8, 2007.

[8] R. Girshick, J. Donahue, T. Darrell, and J. Malik. Rich feature hierarchies for accurate object detection and semantic segmentation. In *CVPR*, pages 580–587, 2014.

[9] Y. Gong, L. Wang, R. Guo, and S. Lazebnik. Multi-scale orderless pooling of deep convolutional activation features. In *ECCV*, pages 392–407, 2014.

[10] H. Jegou, M. Douze, and C. Schmid. Hamming embedding and weak geometric consistency for large scale image search. In *ECCV*, pages 304–317, 2008.

[11] H. Jégou, M. Douze, and C. Schmid. Improving bag-of-features for large scale image search. *IJCV*, 87(3):316–336, 2010.

[12] H. Jégou, M. Douze, C. Schmid, and P. Pérez. Aggregating local descriptors into a compact image representation. In *CVPR*, pages 3304–3311, 2010.

[13] H. Jégou, F. Perronnin, M. Douze, J. Sanchez, P. Perez, and C. Schmid. Aggregating local image descriptors into compact codes. *TPMAI*, 34(9):1704–1716, 2012.

[14] L. Liu, C. Shen, and A. van den Hengel. The treasure beneath convolutional layers: Cross-convolutional-layer pooling for image classification. In *CVPR*, pages 4749–4757, 2015.

[15] D. G. Lowe. Distinctive image features from scale-invariant keypoints. *IJCV*, 60(2):91–110, 2004.

[16] D. Nister and H. Stewenius. Scalable recognition with a vocabulary tree. In *CVPR*, pages 2161–2168, 2006.

[17] M. Paulin, M. Douze, Z. Harchaoui, J. Mairal, F. Perronin, and C. Schmid. Local convolutional features with unsupervised training for image retrieval. In *ICCV*, pages 91–99, 2015.

[18] J. Philbin, O. Chum, M. Isard, J. Sivic, and A. Zisserman. Object retrieval with large vocabularies and fast spatial matching. In *CVPR*, pages 1–8, 2007.

[19] J. Philbin, O. Chum, M. Isard, J. Sivic, and A. Zisserman. Lost in quantization: Improving particular object retrieval in large scale image databases. In *CVPR*, pages 1–8, 2008.

[20] J. Sánchez, F. Perronnin, T. Mensink, and J. Verbeek. Image classification with the fisher vector: Theory and practice. *IJCV*, 105(3):222–245, 2013.

[21] J. Yue-Hei Ng, F. Yang, and L. S. Davis. Exploiting local features from deep networks for image retrieval. In *CVPRW*, pages 53–61, 2015.

[22] S. Zhang, M. Yang, T. Cour, K. Yu, and D. N. Metaxas. Query specific rank fusion for image retrieval. *TPAMI*, 37(4):803–815, 2015.

[23] L. Zheng, S. Wang, Z. Liu, and Q. Tian. Packing and padding: Coupled multi-index for accurate image retrieval. In *CVPR*, pages 1939–1946, 2014.

[24] L. Zheng, S. Wang, L. Tian, F. He, Z. Liu, and Q. Tian. Query-adaptive late fusion for image search and person re-identification. In *CVPR*, pages 1741–1750, 2015.

[25] L. Zheng, S. Wang, and Q. Tian. Coupled binary embedding for large-scale image retrieval. *IEEE Transactions on Image Processing*, 23(8):3368–3380, 2014.

[26] L. Zheng, S. Wang, J. Wang, and Q. Tian. Accurate image search with multi-scale contextual evidences. *International Journal of Computer Vision*, pages 1–13, 2016.

A Deeply-Supervised Deconvolutional Network for Horizon Line Detection

Lorenzo Porzi
Fondazione Bruno Kessler
Trento, Italy
University of Perugia
Perugia, Italy
porzi@fbk.eu

Samuel Rota Bulò
Fondazione Bruno Kessler
Trento, Italy
rotabulo@fbk.eu

Elisa Ricci
Fondazione Bruno Kessler
Trento, Italy
University of Perugia
Perugia, Italy
eliricci@fbk.eu

ABSTRACT

Automatic skyline detection from mountain pictures is an important task in many applications, such as web image retrieval, augmented reality and autonomous robot navigation. Recent works addressing the problem of Horizon Line Detection (HLD) demonstrated that learning-based boundary detection techniques are more accurate than traditional filtering methods. In this paper we introduce a novel approach for skyline detection, which adheres to a learning-based paradigm and exploits the representation power of deep architectures to improve the horizon line detection accuracy. Differently from previous works, we explore a novel deconvolutional architecture, which introduces intermediate levels of supervision to support the learning process. Our experiments, conducted on a publicly available dataset, confirm that the proposed method outperforms previous learning-based HLD techniques by reducing the number of spurious edge pixels.

Keywords

Horizon detection; Convolutional Neural Network; Edge detection

1. INTRODUCTION

In the last decade several research efforts [10, 12] have been made to automatically analyze pictures of natural scenes. Mining images depicting natural landscapes is of interest in many applications, such as augmented reality, image retrieval and robot navigation. In this context, the analysis of pictures of mountainous landscapes represents an inherently challenging task. Indeed, the large variability of environmental and illumination conditions requires robust computer vision and image processing algorithms. Moreover, often traditional methods do not suffice and *ad hoc* solutions need to be developed (*e.g.* standard keypoints detectors and bag-of-words techniques are not appropriate for matching mountain profiles [3, 2]).

Recently, the overwhelming success of deep learning architectures [17] has opened new opportunities for research on natural scene analysis. In particular, Convolutional Neural Networks (CNNs) have been effectively applied to many tasks, such as scene recognition [21], prediction of visual attributes of places [10] and semantic segmentation [11]. Similarly, CNN architectures have been shown to be particularly effective in addressing low level tasks, such as contour detection [19, 8]. As demonstrated by previous works [1, 13], learning-based techniques for contour detection are significantly more accurate than traditional filtering methods and can be successfully used for the analysis of mountains images. In particular, the effectiveness of CNN-based solutions to detect mountains profiles have been shown in [1].

Inspired by these recent successes, in this paper we propose a novel approach for detecting the horizon line in mountainous pictures. Similarly to previous works [1], our approach is based on two-steps. First, a learning-based contour detection algorithm is applied to compute the boundary between sky and non-sky regions. Then, this initial estimate is refined via dynamic programming to find the most likely horizon line. Differently from previous methods, a novel neural network architecture is proposed to extract mountain profiles, which successfully combines ideas from recent deconvolutional [11] and deeply-supervised [9] nets. Our experimental evaluation, conducted on the publicly available CH1 dataset [14], demonstrates that our approach outperforms state-of-the-art, learning-based methods for HLD. Fig.1 shows a sample mountain image and the horizon line detected by our method.

Figure 1: (left) Picture depicting a mountainous landscape and (superimposed) the horizon line detected with the proposed approach. (right) Ground truth.

MM '16, October 15-19, 2016, Amsterdam, Netherlands

DOI: http://dx.doi.org/10.1145/2964284.2967198

The contribution of this paper is twofold. First, we demonstrate that deep deconvolutional networks can be effectively applied to the HLD task, outperforming previous learning-based solutions. Second, we show that by supporting deconvolutional networks with deep supervision, more accurate detections can be achieved compared to standard deconvolutional architectures with single supervision.

The paper is structured as follows. Section 2 discusses previous works on the analysis of mountains pictures and on learning-based approaches for contour detection. Section 3 introduces our deconvolutional architecture for horizon line detection, and in Section. 4 we report the results of our experimental evaluation. Finally, Section 5 outlines the main contributions of this paper and discusses future work.

2. RELATED WORKS

Most previous works on the automatic analysis of mountain pictures tackled the problem by designing robust methodologies for extracting peaks' profiles. Several works considered publicly available digital elevation maps (DEM), and proposed different solutions to the image-to-DEM matching problem. In fact, aligning images to synthetic profiles represents an essential step for mountain recognition and orientation identification. Baboud *et al.* [3] used edge maps computed with the Compass edge detector and a robust matching metric to calculate the rotation mapping an image to the terrain. As traditional edge detectors provides noisy estimates of mountain profiles, more recent works exploited learning-based solutions. Porzi *et al.* [13] proposed a two-steps method for detecting mountain profiles. First, the Sobel filter is applied to find putative pixels which belong to mountains edge. Then, a classifier based on Random Ferns is used to verify these hypothesis. Recently, Ahmad [1] exploited both CNN and SVM classifiers to detect pixels belonging to the horizon line. The initial estimates obtained with the learned classifier are then refined using a dynamic programming technique. A closely-related problem to HLD, *i.e.* sky segmentation for automatic picture geo-localization, was tackled in [14, 2]. Similarly, Tao *et al.* [16] focused on the identification of the sky seen in an image and proposed Skyfinder, a system to search for images with a specific sky appearance. Among previous works, the most related to ours is [1]. Similarly to [1], our approach is based on deep learning. However, our proposed network architecture is radically different from the one described in [1] and, as demonstrated in our experiments, significantly more accurate in detecting skyline pixels.

Learning-based edge detection has been explored in several previous works [5, 6, 18, 19, 8]. Dollar *et al.* [5] used a boosting-based approach to independently classify each pixel from its surrounding image patch. More recently in [6] improved results were obtained considering a Structured Random Forest classifier, such as to take into account correlations between adjacent output pixels. Ren *et al.* [18] proposed an approach based on sparse coding, which, however, suffers from high computational cost. Particularly relevant to our work are recent approaches using CNN architectures for detecting contours [19, 8].

Inspired by recent successful approaches for semantic segmentation [11], we propose a deconvolutional network, which however distinguishes from the other approaches by integrating a deeply-supervised training strategy [9, 19].

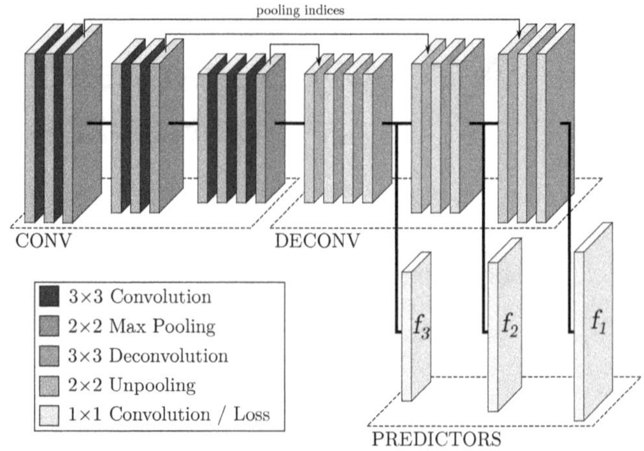

Figure 2: Schematic depiction of the proposed network architecture.

3. METHOD

A horizon line detector is a function $h : \mathcal{X} \to \mathcal{Y}$ that takes an image $X \in \mathcal{X}$ and returns a probability mask $Y \in \mathcal{Y}$ having the same size of the input image, each entry providing the probability of belonging to the horizon line. Accordingly, the input space $\mathcal{X}$ consists of $\mathrm{h} \times \mathrm{w}$ rgb images, *i.e.* $\mathcal{X} = \mathbb{R}^{\mathrm{h}\times\mathrm{w}\times 3}$, while the output space is given by $\mathrm{h}\times\mathrm{w}$ probability masks, *i.e.* $\mathcal{Y} = [0,1]^{\mathrm{h}\times\mathrm{w}}$.

3.1 Network architecture

In this paper we propose to model the detector h as a deep neural network that combines convolutional layers with deconvolutional layers[20] to produce the *entire* detection mask in output given the entire image in input. The actual topology that we consider is shown in Fig. 2 and described below.

CONV block. The first block of layers denoted by "CONV" is the well-known VGG network [15] truncated at the 3rd max pooling layer. This part of the network is composed by convolutional layers with RELU activation and max pooling layers arranged as depicted in Fig 2.

DECONV block. The second block of layers denoted by "DECONV" is composed by deconvolutional layers with RELU activation and unpooling layers (see Fig. 2 for the actual arrangement). Following the approach of [20], we use the locations of the maxima in the pooling layers to place the outputs of the corresponding unpooling layers. In the figure, this is denoted by arrows connecting each pooling layer in the "CONV" block to the corresponding unpooling layer in the "DECONV" block.

PREDICTORS block. Instead of considering a single output layer, we add also intermediate outputs in the deconvolutional block, denoted as "PREDICTORS" in Fig. 2, in order to provide a deeper supervision during the training phase. This positively impacts both the accuracy of the method, by introducing an implicit regularization, and the convergence of the network during the training phase [9]. Accordingly, the network incorporates three predictors that we denote by $f_j : \mathcal{X} \to \mathcal{Y}_j$, $j = 1, 2, 3$. The output dimensionality of each predictor is in general lower than the input dimensionality, excepting the last one. This motivates the use of the special notation $\mathcal{Y}_j$ to represent the output space of the jth predictor. Each output layer is composed by a

1×1 convolutional layer with a sigmoid activation function in order to produce probabilistic predictions for the output mask entries. The predictors are numbered in reversed order such that f_1 becomes the predictor that comprises the entire network (see Fig. 2).

3.2 Training

We train our network from labeled images $\{(X_i, Y_i)\}_{i=1}^{\mathrm{n}}$, where $X_i \in \mathcal{X}$ is the ith training image with the corresponding ground-truth mask given by $Y_i \in \mathcal{Y}$. Our training objective is the minimization of the empirical risk $R(\theta)$ given below with respect to the parameters of the network θ:

$$R(\theta) = \frac{1}{3\mathrm{n}} \sum_{i=1}^{\mathrm{n}} \sum_{j=1}^{3} L(f_j(X_i; \theta), Y_i \downarrow_{\mathcal{Y}_j}) . \qquad (1)$$

The empirical risk has separate loss terms for each predictor f_j. Due to the different dimensionality between the ground-truth mask $Y \in \mathcal{Y}$ and the mask predicted by f_j, we project Y into $\mathcal{Y}_j$ by downsampling Y to the proper size before evaluating the loss function. This operation is denoted by $Y_i \downarrow_{\mathcal{Y}_j}$ in (1). The loss function $L(\hat{Y}, Y)$ that measures the discrepancy between a predicted mask $\hat{Y} \in \mathcal{Y}$ and a ground-truth mask $Y \in \mathcal{Y}$ is given in terms of the following weighted cross-entropy:

$$L(\hat{Y}, Y) = -\sum_{u,v} [\beta_1 y_{uv} \log \hat{y}_{uv} + \beta_0 (1 - y_{uv}) \log(1 - \hat{y}_{uv})] . \qquad (2)$$

Here, the sum runs over all elements of Y, each denoted by y_{uv} (and similarly $\hat{y}_{uv}$ for $\hat{Y}$), β_0 is the fraction of edges in Y, while β_1 is the fraction of non-edges in Y. The same balancing scheme of the importance of edge/non-edge terms has been used in [19].

The minimization of the empirical risk is carried out via Stochastic Gradient Descent (SGD) with mini-batches and weight decay. More details about the parametrization of the optimizer are given in the experimental section.

3.3 Horizon detection

Once the network has been trained there are different ways to combine the three predictors f_1, f_2, f_3 to obtain the final horizon detector h. The one that is more consistent with the proposed empirical risk simply averages the outcome of the different predictors, by taking care of projecting the result to the right dimensionality first, *i.e.*

$$h_{\mathrm{avg}}(X) = \frac{1}{3} \sum_{j=1}^{3} f_j(X; \theta^*) \uparrow_{\mathcal{Y}} , \qquad (3)$$

where θ^* is the parametrization of the network obtained after the training procedure, and $\cdot \uparrow_{\mathcal{Y}}$ is the upsampling operator that projects the preceding argument into $\mathcal{Y}$. In addition to h^{avg} we evaluate also the performance of the single predictors. For each $j = 1, 2, 3$ we denote by h_j the horizon detector constructed from f_j, which is given by

$$h_j(X) = f_j(X; \theta^*) \uparrow_{\mathcal{Y}} . \qquad (4)$$

Post-processing. As a final step, we post-process the output of the horizon detector from the neural network, which is a probabilistic mask, to obtain a more accurate estimate of the horizon curve. Following [1], we construct a weighted graph on the elements of the horizon detector's output and find the final horizon curve by solving a shortest path problem. Differently from [1], we connect each node (u, v) to the nodes $\{(u', v + 1) \mid u' \in \{u - 3, \ldots, u + 3\}\}$, in order to account for steeper mountain profiles. Furthermore, we do not perform the "node reduction" step. The final output is a sequence of detected horizon points $P_v, v = 1, \ldots, \mathrm{w}$, one for each column of the input image.

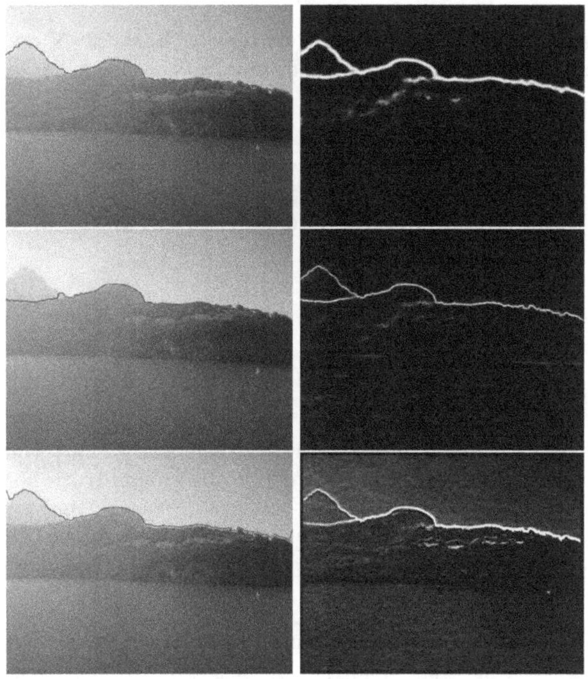

Figure 3: Detected horizon lines (left) and horizon probability maps (right) obtained with (from top to bottom): DCNN–DS1, Structured Forest [6] and the CNN in [1].

4. EXPERIMENTAL RESULTS

In this section we evaluate the HLD accuracy of the proposed method and variants thereof against other state-of-the-art approaches. The pixelswise detection mask obtained from each of the tested methods was fine-tuned with the dynamic programming approach described in Subsection 3.3 (post-processing). For each image, the HLD accuracy is evaluated using the error measure given in [1], *i.e.*

$$E = \sum_{v=1}^{\mathrm{w}} \|P_v - P_v^{\mathrm{gt}}\| , \qquad (5)$$

where P_v and P_v^{gt} are the predicted and ground-truth horizon points at the v-th column of the image, respectively. The results in the following are given in terms of the mean and standard deviation of the error in (5) on the test images.

4.1 Dataset

In our evaluation we consider the publicly-available CH1 dataset[1], first presented in the work of Saurer *et al.* [14]. This dataset comprises 203 photographs of mountainous landscapes taken from various locations in the Swiss Alps, depicting a wide variety of seasonal and weather conditions.

[1]https://cvg.ethz.ch/research/mountain-localization/

Table 1: **HLD error when using our best CNN configuration compared to previous methods.**

Method	Error (px) mean	std
DCNN–DS1	1.53	2.38
Structured Forest [6]	8.07	18.92
Random Ferns [13]	10.21	20.41
CNN in [1]	5.78	14.73
SVM in [1]	36.69	60.59

Each image is annotated with a ground truth sky/terrain segmentation, from which we derive the ground-truth horizon line. In our experiments we rescale each image to a resolution of 640×480 and randomly split the dataset into training and test subsets, comprising 60% and 40% of the images, respectively.

4.2 Implementation and training details

All the network architectures considered in the experimental evaluation are trained using the same setup and implemented using the Caffe library. Data augmentation is used to enrich the training set, which comprises only 121 images. In particular, from each image we select 16 patches of 256×256 pixels, each sampled after performing random scale, rotation, flip and translation transformations. At test time, thanks to the fully-convolutional nature of the architecture, we are able to evaluate the images in their original size (*i.e.* 640×480).

The training phase is performed using mini-batch SGD with the Adam [7] method. The "CONV" layers are initialized from a publicly available implementation of VGG16 [15] pre-trained on ImageNet. Each "DECONV" layer is initialized from a zero-mean Gaussian distribution with variance $\sqrt{2/fin}$, where *fin* is the layer's fan-in. Finally, the parameters of the output layers are initialized to zero. The training meta-parameters are as follows. The batch-size is set to 48. We perform 15 training epochs with a learning rate of 10^{-3} followed by 15 epochs with a learning rate of 10^{-4}. The weight decay is set to 0.0002.

4.3 Results and discussion

In a first set of experiments, we compare the proposed deeply-supervised deconvolutional network (DCNN-DS1) using the best-performing detector $h_1(\cdot)$ (see Sec. 3) with previous learning approaches used for detecting mountains profiles, *i.e.* structured forest [6], random ferns [13], and the CNN and SVM classifiers in [1]. The results in Table 1 indicate a clear advantage of our method, which outperforms the others by a considerable margin. Interestingly, the second best result is given by the CNN classifier in [1], which employs a very simple architecture with less than 1000 parameters. This result, together with the comparatively poorer performance obtained with traditional classifiers, suggests that the use of learned features is very important for the HLD task.

In our experiments, we also observe that the HLD pipeline is significantly less robust when traditional classifiers (not CNN-based) are employed. Figure 3 shows an example of this. Here, a peak in the background is covered by a light mist, which makes it look much fainter than the mountains in the foreground. In this case, the Structured Forest is not able to differentiate between the background peak-to-sky edge and the foreground mountain-to-background peak edge, producing an equally strong response for both. This forces the dynamic programming step to choose the second, straighter edge as the horizon. Conversely, our approach and CNN correctly give a stronger response for the first edge, producing the correct horizon line.

Table 2: **Horizon line detection error when using different CNN configurations.**

Method	Error (px) mean	std
DCNN–DSavg	2.03	2.32
DCNN–DS1	1.53	2.38
DCNN–DS2	2.25	2.47
DCNN–DS3	2.50	2.29
DCNN–No DS	3.94	8.76
CNN–DS	3.33	9.28

In a final set of experiments we compare several variants of our network architecture, specifically: i) the four detectors $h_1, h_2, h_3, h_{\text{avg}}$, denoted as DCNN–DSx, where x is one of 1, 2, 3 or avg; ii) a version of the net trained using only the f_1 predictor and its corresponding loss (*i.e.* with a single supervision), denoted as DCNN–No DS; iii) a deeply-supervised non-deconvolutional version of the net, denoted as CNN–DS. With reference to Fig. 2, CNN–DS is obtained by discarding the "DECONV" block and connecting each predictor to one of the convolutional layers immediately preceding a pooling layer in the "CONV" block. The final output is given by the average of the three predictions, as in DCNN-DSavg. This architecture is similar to the HED network in [19]. The results, summarized in Table 2, show a clear advantage of the deeply-supervised deconvolutional architecture compared to the other ones. Interestingly, DCNN–DS1 gives the best result among the DCNN–DSx nets, while DCNN–No DS gives the worst result overall. This fact, together with the relatively lower performance of DCNN–DSavg compared to DCNN–DS1, suggests that the beneficial effects of a deep supervision in our case are more related to its regularizing effects than to the availability of multiple outputs.

5. CONCLUSION

We presented a new method for horizon line detection. The main novelty of the proposed approach is a deeply-supervised deconvolutional network to detect horizon pixels. Our results demonstrate that the proposed approach outperforms previous learning-based HLD solutions. Future works include investigating alternative deeply-supervised architectures (*e.g.* to reduce the computational cost) and exploiting the proposed approach for image geo-localization [4].

6. ACKNOWLEDGMENTS

This research has received funding from the European Unions Horizon 2020 research and innovation programme under grant agreement No 687757.

7. REFERENCES

[1] T. Ahmad, G. Bebis, M. Nicolescu, A. Nefian, and T. Fong. An edge-less approach to horizon line detection. In *ICMLA*, 2015.

[2] G. Baatz, O. Saurer, K. Köser, and M. Pollefeys. Large scale visual geo-localization of images in mountainous terrain. In *ECCV*. 2012.

[3] L. Baboud, M. Čadík, E. Eisemann, and H.-P. Seidel. Automatic photo-to-terrain alignment for the annotation of mountain pictures. In *CVPR*, 2011.

[4] M. Bansal, H. S. Sawhney, H. Cheng, and K. Daniilidis. Geo-localization of street views with aerial image databases. In *ACM MM*, 2011.

[5] P. Dollár, Z. Tu, and S. Belongie. Supervised learning of edges and object boundaries. In *CVPR*, 2006.

[6] P. Dollár and C. L. Zitnick. Structured forests for fast edge detection. In *ICCV*, 2013.

[7] D. Kingma and J. Ba. Adam: A method for stochastic optimization. In *ICLR*, 2015.

[8] I. Kokkinos. Surpassing humans in boundary detection using deep learning. *ICLR*, 2016.

[9] C.-Y. Lee, S. Xie, P. Gallagher, Z. Zhang, and Z. Tu. Deeply-supervised nets. *AISTATS*, 2015.

[10] S. Lee, H. Zhang, and D. J. Crandall. Predicting geo-informative attributes in large-scale image collections using convolutional neural networks. In *WACV*, 2015.

[11] H. Noh, S. Hong, and B. Han. Learning deconvolution network for semantic segmentation. In *ICCV*, 2015.

[12] V. Ordonez and T. L. Berg. Learning high-level judgments of urban perception. In *ECCV*. 2014.

[13] L. Porzi, S. Rota Bulò, P. Valigi, O. Lanz, and E. Ricci. Learning contours for automatic annotations of mountains pictures on a smartphone. In *ICDSC*, 2014.

[14] O. Saurer, G. Baatz, K. Köser, M. Pollefeys, et al. Image based geo-localization in the alps. *IJCV*, pages 1–13, 2015.

[15] K. Simonyan and A. Zisserman. Very deep convolutional networks for large-scale image recognition. *CoRR*, abs/1409.1556, 2014.

[16] L. Tao, L. Yuan, and J. Sun. Skyfinder: attribute-based sky image search. In *ACM TOG*, volume 28, page 68, 2009.

[17] W. Wang, G. Chen, A. T. T. Dinh, J. Gao, B. C. Ooi, K.-L. Tan, and S. Wang. Singa: Putting deep learning in the hands of multimedia users. In *ACM MM*, 2015.

[18] R. Xiaofeng and L. Bo. Discriminatively trained sparse code gradients for contour detection. In *NIPS*, 2012.

[19] S. Xie and Z. Tu. Holistically-nested edge detection. In *ICCV*, 2015.

[20] M. D. Zeiler and R. Fergus. Visualizing and understanding convolutional networks. In *ECCV*. 2014.

[21] B. Zhou, A. Lapedriza, J. Xiao, A. Torralba, and A. Oliva. Learning deep features for scene recognition using places database. In *NIPS*, 2014.

Exploiting Objects with LSTMs for Video Categorization

Yongqing Sun[1], Zuxuan Wu[2], Xi Wang[2], Hiroyuki Arai[1], Tetsuya Kinebuchi[1], Yu-Gang Jiang[2]
[1]NTT Media Intelligence Laboratories, Japan
[2]School of Computer Science, Shanghai Key Laboratory of Intelligent Information Processing, Fudan University, China
{yongqing.sun, arai.hiroyuki, kinebuchi.t}@lab.ntt.co.jp, {zxwu, xwang10, ygj}@fudan.edu.cn

ABSTRACT

Temporal dynamics play an important role for video classification. In this paper, we propose to leverage high-level semantic features to open the "black box" of the state-of-the-art temporal model, Long Short Term Memory (LSTM), with an aim to understand what is learned. More specifically, we first extract object features from a state-of-the-art CNN model that is trained to recognize 20K objects. Then we leverage LSTM with the extracted features as inputs to capture the temporal dynamics in videos. In combination with spatial and motion information, we achieve improvements for supervised video categorization. Furthermore, by masking the inputs, we demonstrate what is learned by LSTM, namely (i) which objects are crucial for recognizing a class-of-interest; (ii) how the LSTM model could assist the temporal localization of these detected objects.

CCS Concepts

•**Information systems** → *Multimedia information systems;*

Keywords

Video Classification; Deep Learning; Objects; LSTM.

1. INTRODUCTION

Video classification based on semantic contents like human actions or complex events has been extensively studied in the multimedia community due to the rising needs from many practical applications, including video indexing, advertising and management. However, it remains a particularly challenging task since videos usually contain complicated interactions of human subjects and objects that evolve over time in the presence of cluttered backgrounds.

Traditional methods for video classification focus on learning robust classifiers with handcrafted features like STIP [13] and improved dense trajectory features [19]. Recently, deep neural networks, especially Convolutional Neural Networks (CNN), have achieved superior performance on a variety of tasks such as image classification [15, 18], object detection [5] and *etc.* Motivated by this great success, Karpathy *et al.* also applied CNNs to the video domain with stacked frames as inputs [11]. Simonyan *et al.* proposed a two-stream CNN operating on static frames and optical flow images to account for appearance and motion information respectively [14]. This framework is recently further extended using convolutional fusion [4]. Wang *et al.* proposed to learn transformations between actions [20] with CNN. However, CNN takes one frame/optical flow image as its input, and hence fails to consider the temporal coherence in videos. To better exploit the long-term temporal dynamics, a few recent studies adopted Long Short Term Memory (LSTM) [7] models with features extracted from fully-connected layers of CNNs (*e.g.*, fc_6) [3, 22, 17]. However, such features are usually not sufficient for categorization due to the semantic gap between low-level

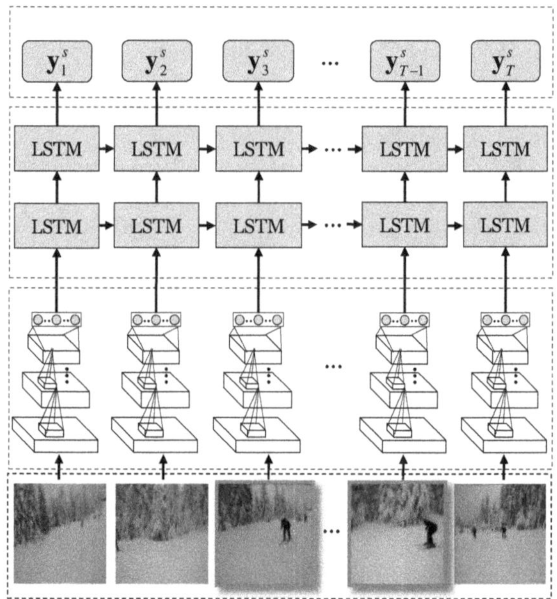

Figure 1: Illustration of the proposed framework. A two-layer LSTM is adopted for video categorization using high-level object features extracted from CNNs. The framework is able to discover highly related objects for a class-of-interest and to perform temporal localization (frames with red borders).

MM '16, October 15-19, 2016, Amsterdam, Netherlands
© 2016 ACM. ISBN 978-1-4503-3603-1/16/10...$15.00
DOI: http://dx.doi.org/10.1145/2964284.2967199

descriptors and high-level video semantics. In addition, the utilization of low-level features pose challenges to analyze what is learned by LSTM.

To address the above limitations, in this paper, we propose using high-level semantic features with LSTM to exploit how semantic concepts are evolving over time. More specifically, we first leverage a state-of-the-art CNN trained to recognize 20K objects to extract high-level object features, which are further utilized as inputs for LSTM to capture the temporal dynamics in videos. In combination with models capturing motion and spatial clues, we obtain improvements for supervised video categorization. Furthermore, by masking the inputs of LSTM models, we analyze what is learned in the classification process, namely (i) which objects are crucial for recognizing a class-of-interest; (ii) how the LSTM model could help for temporal localization of these detected objects.

2. OUR APPROACH

Object Detectors. We leverage the state-of-the-art VGG19 model [15] to compute the likelihood of objects presenting in a video frame. VGG19 consists of 16 convolutional layers with small convolutional filters capturing details, topped by three fully-connected layers that further boosts the discriminative capability, offering top-notch performance for image classification and object detection [15]. Motivated by the fact that humans can distinguish between more than 30K objects [1], we adopt the whole dataset of ImageNet [2] with more than 14M labeled images, on which a VGG19 model is fine-tuned to recognize 20,574 object categories. More concretely, we denote each video as a collection of frames $\mathbf{v} = \{v_1, v_2, \cdots, v_N\}$, where N is the number of frames for video $\mathbf{v}$. Then for the i-th frame v_i in the video clip, we simply run a feed-forward process through the network till the classification layer, and obtain a 20,574-d score vector $\mathbf{x}_i$, which indicates the probability of the corresponding objects. Finally, for the video clip $\mathbf{v}$, we attain a sequence of object scores $(\mathbf{x}_1, \mathbf{x}_2, \ldots, \mathbf{x}_N)$.

LSTM. Different from uniform pooling strategies that average features across frames into video-level representations, we resort to LSTM model to exploit the rich temporal structures in videos. LSTM is a type of RNN model that encompasses several control units, which enable the network to learn long sequences without suffering from the vanishing gradient effect. It is reasonable to adopt LSTM for sequential modeling task through mapping an input sequence $(\mathbf{x}_1, \mathbf{x}_2, \ldots, \mathbf{x}_T)$ to outputs $(\mathbf{y}_1, \mathbf{y}_2, \ldots, \mathbf{y}_T)$ by computing the following equations recursively from $t = 1$ to $t = N$:

$$
\begin{aligned}
\mathbf{i}_t &= \sigma(\mathbf{W}_{xi}\mathbf{x}_t + \mathbf{W}_{hi}\mathbf{h}_{t-1} + \mathbf{W}_{ci}\mathbf{c}_{t-1} + \mathbf{b}_i),\\
\mathbf{f}_t &= \sigma(\mathbf{W}_{xf}\mathbf{x}_t + \mathbf{W}_{hf}\mathbf{h}_{t-1} + \mathbf{W}_{cf}\mathbf{c}_{t-1} + \mathbf{b}_f),\\
\mathbf{c}_t &= \mathbf{f}_t\mathbf{c}_{t-1} + \mathbf{i}_t \tanh(\mathbf{W}_{xc}\mathbf{x}_t + \mathbf{W}_{hc}\mathbf{h}_{t-1} + \mathbf{b}_c),\\
\mathbf{o}_t &= \sigma(\mathbf{W}_{xo}\mathbf{x}_t + \mathbf{W}_{ho}\mathbf{h}_{t-1} + \mathbf{W}_{co}\mathbf{c}_t + \mathbf{b}_o),\\
\mathbf{h}_t &= \mathbf{o}_t \tanh(\mathbf{c}_t),
\end{aligned}
$$

where $\mathbf{x}_t, \mathbf{h}_t$ are the input and hidden vectors of the t-th time step, $\mathbf{i}_t, \mathbf{f}_t, \mathbf{c}_t, \mathbf{o}_t$ are the activation vectors of the input gate, forget gate, memory cell and output gate, $\mathbf{W}_{\alpha\beta}$ is the weight matrix between vector α and β (e.g., $\mathbf{W}_{xi}$ is weight matrix from the input $\mathbf{x}_t$ to the input gate $\mathbf{i}_t$), $\mathbf{b}_\alpha$ is the bias term of α and σ is the sigmoid function.

The major component that guarantees superior performance of LSTM unit is a memory cell that accumulates information over time, which is further regulated by different functional gates to determine whether to forget history clues or explore new information. Further, we can stack LSTM network, using the hidden units from one layer as inputs for the next layer, to further increase the discriminative ability of the network. A softmax layer is usually topped on the final LSTM network for predictions. To train the network, we adopt the Back-Propagation Through Time (BPTT) algorithm [6], which "unrolls" the model into a feed forward neural net and then back-propagates to learn network parameters.

Note that there exists a few works utilizing LSTM networks for video categorization [22, 3]. However, they all input low-level features extracted from fully-connected layers (*i.e.*, fc_6 or fc_7) to LSTMs sequentially. Hence, it remains hard to bridge the semantic gap and poses challenges understanding the working mechanism of LSTM models. Since videos depict appearance of objects and how they evolve over time, which could be modeled by LSTMs using object scores as high-level semantic features.

Relationship Mining. In order to investigate what is learned by LSTM models, we propose to mask the input object features by setting the probability of an object to be zero and then analyze the response of the output scores. If a certain object is crucial for recognizing the class-of-interest, we would expect a notable drop in the output score for that class. In particular, we adopt Alg 1 to understand the importance of the i-th object for the j-th video class at the t-th time step. We first reset the i-th dimension $\mathbf{x}_t(i)$ of the input feature to the average value $\mathbf{a}(i)$ over time N. Then we subtract the mean value $\mathbf{a}$ from the input to center the data around the origin for each dimension as in CNN training [12], which essentially sets the score of the i-th object to zero.

```
Data: K-dims high-level object features x_t
Data: K-dims mean value a of features over time N
Result: K × K-dims inputs M_t for the LSTM model
for i ← 1 to K do
    for j ← 1 to K do
        if i == j then
            M_t(i, j) = 0
        else
            M_t(i, j) = x_t(i) − a(i)
        end
    end
end
```

Algorithm 1: Masking the object features

Implementation Details. To fine-tune the VGG19 model on the whole ImageNet, we gradually decrease the learning rate from 10^{-2} to 10^{-3} after 20 epochs, then to 10^{-4} after 30 epochs. In addition, dropout is applied to the fully connected layers with a ratio of 0.5 to avoid over-fitting. The fine-tuning process took a month with 4 NVIDIA K40 cards using modified Caffe for multi-GPU parallelization.

For temporal modeling, we adopt a two-layers LSTM structure for the high-level sementic features. The LSTM structure has 256 hidden units in the bottom layer and 256 hidden units in the other layer. The network weights are learned using a parallel implementation of the BPTT algorithm with a mini-batch size of 10. In addition, the learning rate and momentum are set to 10^3 and 0.9 respectively. The training is stopped after 10 epochs for both datasets.

3. EXPERIMENTS

3.1 Experimental Setup

Datasets. We adopt two challenging video benchmarks on action recognition and event detection to evaluate the proposed approach.

UCF-101 [16] is a widely adopted action recognition benchmark, which consists of 13,320 video clips labeled into 101 action classes. Following [8], we conduct evaluations based on the popular 3 train/test splits. The results are measured by classification accuracy for each split and we report mean average accuracy across three splits.

Columbia Consumer Videos (CCV) [10] contains 9,317 videos collected from YouTube belonging to 20 classes. We divide the dataset evenly into a training set with 4,659 videos and a testing set with 4,658 videos as in [10]. And the results are measure by average precision (AP) for each class and mean average precision (mAP) across all classes.

Baselines. We compare with a number of approaches to evaluate the effectiveness of the proposed framework.

- Spatial CNN, utilizes RGB frames as inputs to capture static clues like shape and color for each video frame using a fine-tuned VGG_19 model and the final prediction for a video clip is obtained by averaging scores of 25 uniformly sampled frames.

- Motion CNN, models shot-term motion information in a short time window with a fine-tuned CNN_M model [15] using stacked optical flow images as inputs [14]. Similar to Spatial CNN, the final prediction score is produced by averaging 25 uniformly sampled stacked optical frames.

- Spatial LSTM, adopts the outputs from the first-fully connected layer (fc_6) of the spatial CNN as inputs for a two-layer LSTM to model the temporal dynamics in videos. We leverage the output from the last time step as the prediction score since it contains information from the entire sequence.

- Motion LSTM, is similar to Spatial LSTM but replaces the inputs with fc_6 features extracted from the motion CNN for a two-layer LSTM model. And the prediction score for a video is from the last time step of the LSTM as in Spatial LSTM.

- Object SVM, trains a linear SVM with the extract 20K high-level object features.

3.2 Results and Discussions

In this section, we first evaluate the performance of the proposed LSTM with object features and then conduct qualitative experiments to investigate what is learned by LSTM.

3.2.1 LSTM with Object Features

Table 1 summarizes the performance of our approach and comparisons with alternative baselines. On UCF-101, we can see that Object SVM and Object LSTM produce relatively lower results than other baselines. This might result from the fact that our Object LSTM directly utilizes 20K object features from a state-of-the-art deep model trained on images while both Motion and Spatial LSTM utilize the features from their corresponding CNN models that are fine-tuned on these two datasets. While on CCV, it is interesting to see that the Object LSTM outperforms Spatial and Motion LSTMs significantly and achieves similar performance with Motion CNN, which proves the robustness of the object features. In addition, the average duration of videos in CCV (80 seconds) is about 10 times longer than that of UCF-101 videos (8 seconds), and hence the contents in these long videos are usually diversified, which poses challenges for low-level features but could be captured by the high-level object features that contain sufficient objects. Comparing across both datasets, we observe that Object SVM attains better performance than Object LSTM, which we assume is due to the lack of sufficient video data to train LSTM models. The combination of Object SVM and Object LSTM offers 1% and 3.8% performance gain over Object SVM on UCF-101 and CCV respectively, since appearance and temporal clues are complementary as confirmed in [22].

	UCF-101	CCV
Spatial CNN	80.4	75.0
Motion CNN	78.3	59.1
Spatial LSTM	83.3	43.3
Motion LSTM	76.6	54.7
Object SVM	68.2	64.6
Object LSTM	56.0	59.8
Object (Object SVM & LSTM)	69.2	68.4
Spatial & Motion CNN	86.2	75.8
Spatial & Motion CNN + Object	88.4	79.8
Spatial & Motion LSTM	86.3	61.9
Spatial & Motion LSTM + Object	86.5	79.8
All Combined	90.9	85.9

Table 1: Performance of the proposed LSTM and comparisons with alternative methods.

To further investigate the complementarity of the object clues (Object SVM & LSTM) for other sources of information captured by baseline models, we simply average their classification scores linearly. The results are summarized in the last three groups of Table 1. On these two datasets, the integration of object features produces better results for both LSTMs and CNNs. The improvements on CCV are more prominent than UCF-101, especially for LSTMs where a 17% gain is obtained since CCV contains complicated events containing more objects than actions in UCF-101.

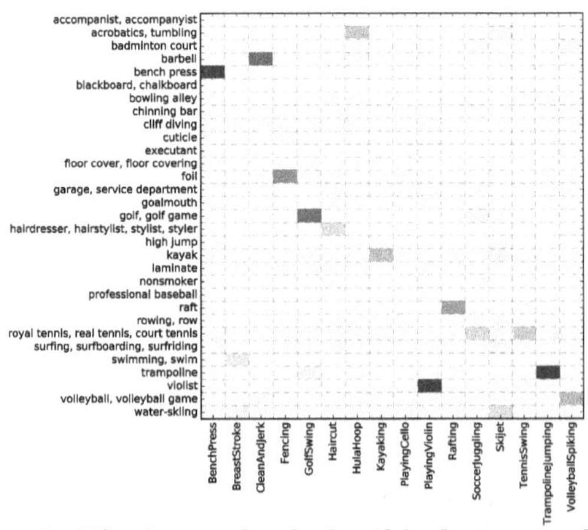

Figure 2: The learned relationship between objects and video categories on UCF-101, with each element indicating the response score.

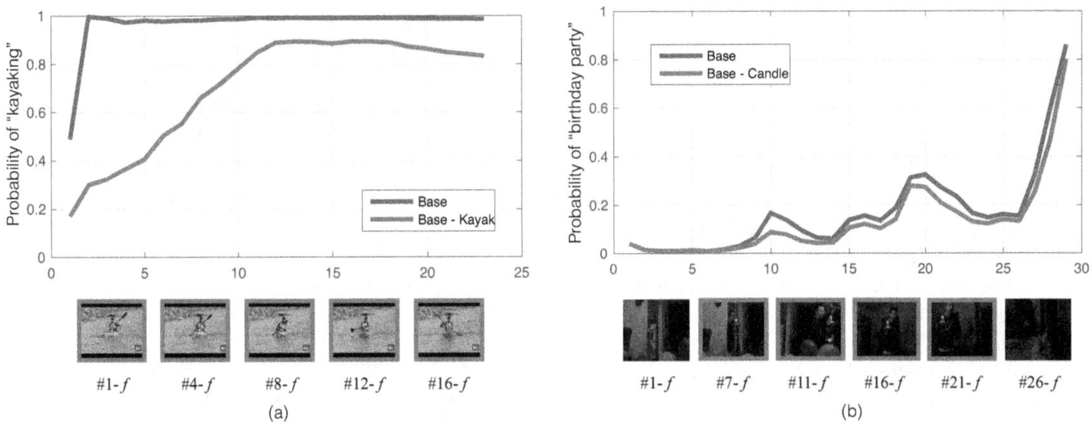

Figure 3: The probability of two video samples belonging to "kayaking" and "birthday party" respectively. Sampled frames are also presented with red border indicating the presence of a top related object and #i-*f* denotes the *i*-th frame. See text for discussion.

3.3 Relationship Mining

Relationship between Object and Video Classes. We first qualitatively investigate the relationship between video classes and objects. For each of the objects, we set its score to zero and if it is crucial for recognizing the class-of-interest, we would expect a notable drop in the output score for that class. Therefore, we visualize the objects that are most critical for recognizing action classes on UCF-101 in Fig. 2 with a heatmap as in [21, 9], where each element demonstrates the response score between each object and video class pair. Due to space limit, we show 16 action classes and the union of their most related object categories. For each video category, we observe that object categories with highest responses are semantically related to that class. For instance, "cleaning and jerk" has high scores from "barbell" while "playing violin" is closely related to "violist".

Object Temporal Localization. It is interesting to see that the LSTM could learn generic relationships between objects and video classes using the trained model itself without the need of additional knowledge. However, since LSTMs exploit long-term temporal dynamics by taking one feature representation at each time step, with the detected relationship, an obvious question arises: how do these crucial objects affect recognition over time and is it possible to perform object localization temporally? To answer these questions, we compute the probability of a target class with the trained LSTM model for a video clip, by setting the score of the most related object to zero. Figure 3 visualizes the prediction scores over time of two video samples .

Fig. 3 (a) presents the probability of the action class "kayaking" for a sample video from UCF-101. The object with highest response for this class is "kayak", which is expectedly highly related to the action. Its removal from the feature representation (Base - Kayak) leads to significant performance drop compared with the compact features representation (Base). It is also intriguing to see that for both features (Base and Base - Kayak), their probabilities gradually increase and then stabilize over time, which confirms the fact that LSTM model could store information along with time to exploit the temporal dynamics in sequences. Moreover, the gap between the masked feature with the compact feature tends to narrow down gradually, since LSTM could utilize other related objects like "paddle" to compensate the absence of "kayak".

Videos in UCF-101 are trimmed where all frames are related to an action class, to examine whether the scores could help the temporal localization of an object, we visualize the score of a video sample from CCV belonging to the category "birthday party" ("candle" is top related object) in Fig. 3 (b). At first, both features achieve similar performance since the beginning frames only contain backgrounds. Starting from the 7-th frame where a candle occurs, the Base representation begins to outperform the masked representation. We can observe the presence of a candle when their gap is relatively large. From the 25-th frame, the candle is blown out and hence the gap starts to close. Then with the help of "cake" detector and LSTM modeling temporal dynamics, the probability of "birthday party" progressively increases. Therefore, the LSTM model could assist the localization these detected objects temporally.

4. CONCLUSION

In this paper, we have demonstrated the effectiveness of LSTMs using high-level object features as inputs for video categorization. More specifically, we first extract object features from a state-of-the-art CNN that is pre-trained to recognize 20K objects on ImageNet. Then we leverage LSTM taking the extracted features as inputs to exploit the temporal information in videos. In combination with models capturing spatial and motion clues, we achieve competitive performance for supervised video categorization on two challenging video benchmarks. Furthermore, by masking the the score of an object in the feature representation, we demonstrate the trained LSTM model (i) contains valuable knowledge whether an object is crucial for recognizing a class-of-interest, and (ii) the model is able to perform temporal localization of the highly related objects without the need of additional information.

Acknowledgment

This work was supported in part by a China's National 863 Program (#2014AA015101).

5. REFERENCES

[1] I. Biederman. Recognition-by-components: a theory of human image understanding. *Psychological review*, 1987.

[2] J. Deng, W. Dong, R. Socher, L.-J. Li, K. Li, and L. Fei-Fei. ImageNet: A large-scale hierarchical image database. In *CVPR*, 2009.

[3] J. Donahue, L. A. Hendricks, S. Guadarrama, M. Rohrbach, S. Venugopalan, K. Saenko, and T. Darrell. Long-term recurrent convolutional networks for visual recognition and description. In *CVPR*, 2015.

[4] C. Feichtenhofer, A. Pinz, and A. Zisserman. Convolutional two-stream network fusion for video action recognition. In *CVPR*, 2016.

[5] R. Girshick, J. Donahue, T. Darrell, and J. Malik. Rich feature hierarchies for accurate object detection and semantic segmentation. In *CVPR*, 2014.

[6] A. Graves, A. Mohamed, and G. E. Hinton. Speech recognition with deep recurrent neural networks. In *ICASSP*, 2013.

[7] A. Graves and J. Schmidhuber. Framewise phoneme classification with bidirectional lstm and other neural network architectures. *Neural Networks*, 2005.

[8] H. Idrees, A. R. Zamir, Y.-G. Jiang, A. Gorban, I. Laptev, R. Sukthankar, and M. Shah. The thumos challenge on action recognition for videos" in the wild". *arXiv preprint arXiv:1604.06182*, 2016.

[9] M. Jain, J. C. van Gemert, and C. G. Snoek. What do 15,000 object categories tell us about classifying and localizing actions? In *CVPR*, 2015.

[10] Y.-G. Jiang, G. Ye, S.-F. Chang, D. Ellis, and A. C. Loui. Consumer video understanding: A benchmark database and an evaluation of human and machine performance. In *ACM ICMR*, 2011.

[11] A. Karpathy, G. Toderici, S. Shetty, T. Leung, R. Sukthankar, and L. Fei-Fei. Large-scale video classification with convolutional neural networks. In *CVPR*, 2014.

[12] A. Krizhevsky, I. Sutskever, and G. E. Hinton. Imagenet classification with deep convolutional neural networks. In *NIPS*, 2012.

[13] I. Laptev, M. Marszalek, C. Schmid, and B. Rozenfeld. Learning realistic human actions from movies. In *CVPR*, 2008.

[14] K. Simonyan and A. Zisserman. Two-stream convolutional networks for action recognition in videos. In *NIPS*, 2014.

[15] K. Simonyan and A. Zisserman. Very deep convolutional networks for large-scale image recognition. In *ICLR*, 2015.

[16] K. Soomro, A. R. Zamir, and M. Shah. UCF101: A dataset of 101 human actions classes from videos in the wild. *CoRR*, 2012.

[17] N. Srivastava, E. Mansimov, and R. Salakhutdinov. Unsupervised learning of video representations using LSTMs. In *ICML*, 2015.

[18] C. Szegedy, W. Liu, Y. Jia, P. Sermanet, S. Reed, D. Anguelov, D. Erhan, V. Vanhoucke, and A. Rabinovich. Going Deeper with Convolutions. In *CVPR*, 2015.

[19] H. Wang and C. Schmid. Action recognition with improved trajectories. In *ICCV*, 2013.

[20] X. Wang, A. Farhadi, and A. Gupta. Actions ~ transformations. In *CVPR*, 2016.

[21] Z. Wu, Y. Fu, Y.-G. Jiang, and L. Sigal. Harnessing object and scene semantics for large-scale video understanding. In *CVPR*, 2016.

[22] Z. Wu, X. Wang, Y.-G. Jiang, H. Ye, and X. Xue. Modeling spatial-temporal clues in a hybrid deep learning framework for video classification. In *ACM Multimedia*, 2015.

Assessing 3D Scan Quality Through Paired-comparisons Psychophysics

Jacob Thorn[1,2], Rodrigo Pizarro[1,3], Bernhard Spanlang[3], Pablo Bermell-Garcia[1], Mar Gonzalez-Franco [1*]

[1] Airbus Innovation Laboratories, Airbus Group, United Kingdom

[2] Department of Computer Science, University College London, United Kingdom

[3] Experimental Virtual Environments for Neuroscience and Technology Lab (EVENTLab), Universitat de Barcelona, Spain

*Corresponding author: margon@microsoft.com

ABSTRACT

Consumer 3D scanners and depth cameras are increasingly being used to generate content and avatars for Virtual Reality (VR) environments and avoid the inconveniences of hand modeling; however, it is sometimes difficult to evaluate quantitatively the mesh quality at which consumer available 3D scans should be exported, and whether the object perception might be affected by its shading. We propose using a paired-comparisons test based on psychophysics of perception to do that evaluation. As psychophysics is not subject to opinion, skill level, mental state, or economic situation it can be considered a quantitative way to measure how people perceive the mesh quality. In particular, we compare four different levels of mesh quality (1K, 5K, 10K and 20K triangles). We present two studies within subjects: in one we investigate the influences of seeing an object in a regular screen vs. in a Head Mounted Display (HMD); while in the second experiment we aim at detecting the effects of shading into quality perception. At each iteration of the pair-test comparisons participants pick the mesh that they think had higher quality; by the end of the experiment we compile a preference matrix. The results show a correlation between real and assessed quality, despite participants' reported uncertainty. We also find an interaction with quality and shading, which gains importance for quality perception when the mesh has high definition. Furthermore, we assess the subjective realism of the most/least preferred scans using an Immersive Augmented Reality (IAR) video-see-through setup to compare the real vs the 3D scanned object in the same HMD environment. Results show higher levels of realism were perceived through the HMD than when using a regular monitor, although the quality was similarly perceived in both systems.

Keywords

Virtual reality, mixed / augmented reality, scanners, metrics, mesh geometry models, perception, paired-test, psychophysics.

MM '16, October 15 - 19, 2016, Amsterdam, Netherlands

ACM 978-1-4503-3603-1/16/10...$15.00

DOI: http://dx.doi.org/10.1145/2964284.2967200

1. INTRODUCTION

Content creation and 3D modeling have long been a critical restriction to the VR expansion. In the game industry one approach to tackle this problem has been based on self-content creation, by providing tools for the users, they can generate and share their own content, scenes and avatars [1]. Thus, moving from the pre-modeled content to personalized environments with infinite content combinations. Similar ideas for content creation are appearing for VR setups, e.g. with digital sculpting [2], however some methods can get increasingly complex and require artistic skills from the users. With the appearance of depth sensors and 3D scans, we have seen a new boost in self-content creation. Using this technology users create new content out of real-life objects [3], own look-a-like avatars [4], [5] or complete scenes [6]. The quality of the scenes or objects created may vary across different scanning technologies and researchers have turned to the field of mesh quality evaluation in order to optimize the newly generated meshes so they can be used in scenarios such as Immersive Virtual Environments (IVE).

A classical evaluation approach in the domain of imaging that has been applied to computer rendering is the Visible Difference Predictor (VDP) [7], which assesses the dissimilarities with original inputs to estimate changes in perception [8]. Besides, research on mesh quality evaluation has also focused on geometric criteria or algebraic theories [9]. These approaches are able to quantify the results of meshing processes and influence the specifications of the mesh creation, optimization or smoothing algorithms. However, it is clear that the quality of the mesh is also bound to the fundamental limits of human perception, thus more subjective components have also been explored with questionnaires [9], or with ordered selections [10]. Some more complex approaches have created predictors of the subjective effect that a new rendering or lossy compression technique will have on the participants' perception [9]. Additionally, human perceptual evaluations can also be measured through behavioral responses [11], or even physiological measures [12], [13]; other research has looked at finding thresholds of perception through psychophysics [14], [15]. In fact, psychophysics is a good way to explore the fundamental limits of perception, since it involves the use of innate skills in estimation and sensory mechanisms [16]. For the case of mesh quality perception the psychophysics methodology can be borrowed from colorimetric matching [17]; where subjects determine equivalence classes of spectral content based on matching colors until they are perceptually indistinguishable, at Just-Noticeable-Differences [18] and bellow subjective thresholds. By analogy with the psychophysics of color matching, equivalence between different mesh qualities can be determined via a forced-choice pair-based comparison [19]. This method builds a full ranking of preference ordered mesh qualities instead of providing only absolute values.

In the current paper we present two experimental studies that explore the feasibility of the pair-based psychophysics approach to research mesh quality perception thresholds as well as to determine the importance of the two influencing factors (display and shading) [20].

2. Materials and Methods

2.1 Procedure

The primary investigation was to determine the extent to which participants were able to distinguish the different qualities of 3D scanned meshes using psychophysics (Figure 1). The secondary purpose of the study was to determine the influence of the use of HMD stereoscopic displays compared to traditional desktop screens (Experiment 1, n=20 participants aged 33.5 ± 8.9 years, 2 females), as well as the importance of shading (Experiment 2, n=21 participants aged 31.9 ± 8.9 years, 3 females). The two experiments were run within subjects, Experiment 2 also had a full factorial design with two factors: mesh quality (with 4 levels corresponding to the four exported models); and rendering mode (with 2 levels: unlit shader vs. Lambert diffuse shader) and was fully provided via HMD.

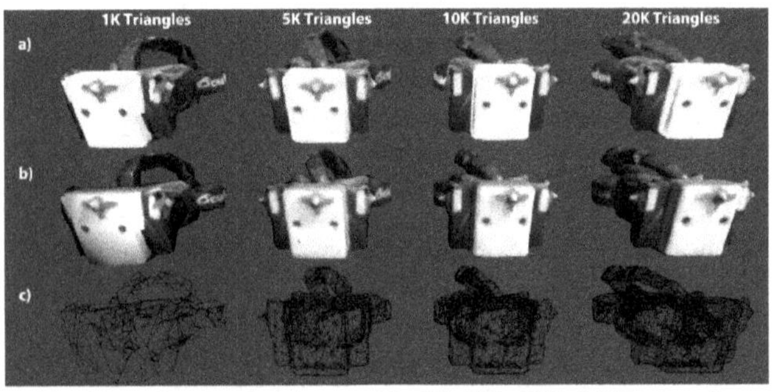

Figure 1. Scanned objects with 1K, 5K, 10K, 20K triangles (from left to right). (a) Unlit objects and (b) Lambert diffuse shaded objects are compared through paired-comparisons psychophysics. (c) Corresponding wireframe.

During the paired-comparisons, the 3D scanned objects were presented in random order appearing side by side and their position was also randomized. At each comparison participants were asked to select "which polygonal mesh had higher quality".

At the end of both experiments, participants were asked to measure the absolute realism of their most and least preferred meshes as described in the Measures section.

2.2 Apparatus

2.2.1 *Scan*

The models were scanned using an Asus Xtion PRO LIVE RGB and Depth Sensor camera and the software Skanect (see supplementary video). 3D models were trimmed and converted to watertight using the lowest smoothing option, they were also colour textured using the standard colourize settings within Skanect. Models were finally exported to the different resolutions of 1K, 5K, 10K and 20K to be used in the experiment. The scanned object was unknown to the participants.

2.2.2 *Display*

The mesh quality was tested in a monoscopic display HP LP2065 LCD running at a 1600x1200 pixel resolution, true life 32-bit at 60Hz. And in an Oculus Rift DK1 HMD. The scenario was built in Unity3D and rendered with a resolution of 1024x768, to match it of the HMD. The selections in the force-choice paired comparisons were done with a mouse click in the monoscopic display, and though a wand interaction on the HMD. Participants were allowed to explore the objects by moving the mouse in the monoscopic display and through real-time motion tracking in the HMD. The HMD head tracking was performed with a NaturalPoint Motive motion capture system (24 x Flex 13 cameras) running at 120Hz that streams the head's position and rotation providing a first person perspective to explore the object [21]. Since depth perception could also play a larger role in the selection, objects were equidistant at 20cm in both conditions (see supplementary video).

For the subjective comparisons with the real object in the stereoscopic condition we implement a video-see-through augmented reality rift [22], [23] (Figure 2), coupled to the HMD with a 3D printed body that holds two Logitech C310 cameras. The lenses were replaced by those of a Genius Widecam F100 to reduce the disparity in FOV between the HMD and the cameras. As a result, the setup features a 90° horizontal FOV and the aspect ratio is 1.33:1 for both the cameras and the Rift (the resulting FOV can be observed in Figure 2b). Although the frame rate of the cameras is less than the one featured by the HMD's (~45Hz and 60Hz respectively) the system is operative in real-time. The camera lenses optical distortion was corrected in real-time with a shader using pre-calculated camera calibrations [24].

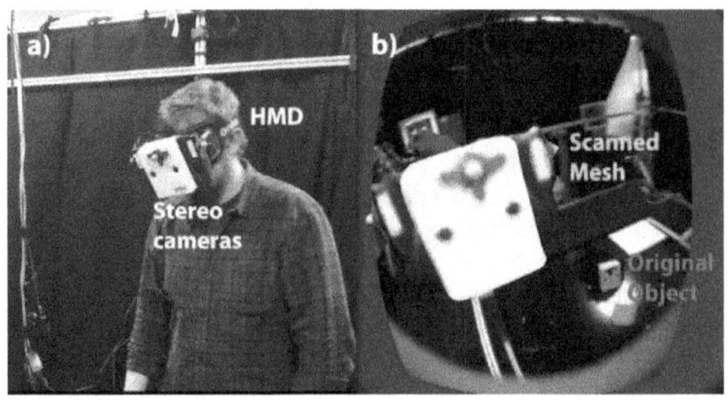

Figure 2. Augmented Reality Stereoscopic Setup: a) head tracked HMD and stereo cameras for video see through; b) the selected mesh can be seen together with the real object.

2.3 Measures

2.3.1 *Paired comparisons test*

Participants compared the different quality models exported from the scanning software in a forced-choice paired comparison psychometric task [19]. This comparative approach is based on context interpretation rather than abstract rankings and can be used to explore thresholds of perception while reaching statistical stability [19]; indeed paired comparisons can provide reliable rankings for an entire set of elements especially when participants are completely unable to subjectively determine a difference between the options at first glance [19]. The total number of comparisons presented is given by equation (1),

$$c = \frac{n\,(n-1)}{2} \qquad (1)$$

where n is the number of meshes in the set and c is the total number of comparisons between them.

During the experiments, the comparisons are performed twice for each pair, i.e. $2c$. If the participant's choice is not consistent in both comparisons, a third one is presented. This method results in a greater reliability of the final result. Therefore, the maximum number of comparisons c_{max} is given by equation (2).

$$c_{max} = \frac{3n\,(n-1)}{2} \qquad (2)$$

Therefore, in the first experiment with four meshes to be compared (n=4), participants had to do between 12 and 18 comparisons in each condition (stereoscopic and monoscopic). While in the second experiment with the full factorial design comparing four meshes and two shaders (n=8), participants had to perform between 56 and 84 comparisons in total.

While one way to determine confidence is to directly ask participants, this information can also be derived from the number of comparisons they underwent. Peterson and Brown's method accounts for the ambiguity of choices by creating a preference score that includes the number of comparisons that were needed at each step [19]. Therefore, the preference score *ps* between two meshes *A, B* corresponds to the difference in number of times the participant selected each mesh over the number of times the comparison was presented, represented by equation (3),

$$ps = \frac{(t_A - t_B)}{(t_A + t_B)} \qquad (3)$$

where t_A and t_B are the number of times the participant preferred meshes A and B correspondingly. I.e. if two meshes were compared and the same mesh was selected both times the preference score for that comparison would be (2-0)/(2+0)=1, if a third comparison was needed because no clear choice was found, the preference score would reduce and be (2-1)/(2+1)=0.333. The final preference score for a mesh would include the scores from all the comparisons within all the meshes: $\sum ps$. I.e, when comparing 4 meshes the maximum preference score for a mesh would be 3. Additionally Peterson and Brown also propose consistency checks on the decisions through the evaluation of circular triads in a person's choices [19].

2.3.2 *Subjective evaluation, realism and confidence*

In order to have a more absolute evaluation of the realism we select the most and least preferred mesh and asked for a comparison with the real object using the Immersive AR setup. In the monoscopic condition participants undergo a screen to real object comparison. "How much from 1 to 10 does this mesh look like the real object?" (From 1 not at all, 10 looks just like the real object).

Additionally, in the second experiment we also assessed participants' confidence level during the choices "How often were you certain of the answers or were you guessing?" (From 1 always certain to 10 always guessing).

3. Results

3.1 Experiment 1: Stereoscopy

3.1.1 *Paired-test comparison*

Participants compared the different quality models exported in a regular monitor condition and in the HMD condition, all under the same unlit shading conditions (Figure 1a). In both conditions we find a correlation between the mesh quality and the preference score in the force-choice paired test (Pearson correlation for monoscopic $r(78)=0.61$, $p<0.001$, and for stereoscopic $r(78)=0.55$, $p<0.001$), this correlation shows how the preference (number of times each mesh is selected) increases for higher mesh qualities (Figure 3). When looking into the data more in detail, we find that the thresholds of perception were not so clear for participants when comparing smaller quality changes such as 5K to 10K or 10K to 20K (Wilcoxon signed-rank test, Z <-1.3 p>0.1), but bigger mesh qualities where significantly differentiated such as 5K to 20K or 1K to the rest (Z <-2.7, p<0.01), both in the monoscopic and stereoscopic condition. Post-hoc comparisons between the two viewing conditions do not show significant differences (Z=0.37, p=0.7). Regarding confidence, the number of repeated comparisons needed both the monoscopic and the stereoscopic condition were similar (Z=-0.42, p=0.7).

3.1.2 *Subjective realism evaluation*

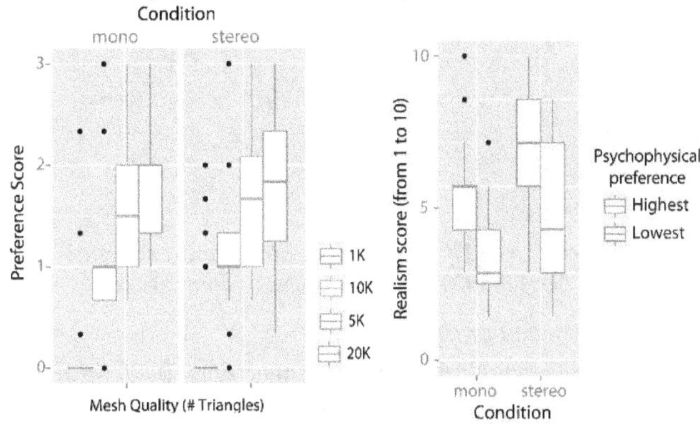

Figure 3. Left: boxplot representing distributions of the psychophysical preference score between the different meshes. Right: subjective realism of the most and least preferred meshes for both conditions. (Quartiles, median, standard deviation, and outliers marked).

Meshes seen in the stereoscopic condition were significantly perceived as more realistic than in the monoscopic condition (Wilcoxon paired signed rank test, Z=-2.5, p=0.01), independently of the quality mesh (Figure 3). Furthermore, as expected, the realism of the perceived highest quality mesh was ranked significantly higher than the one perceived as lowest quality mesh in both conditions (Z =-3.5, p<0.001). This result is a consistency check as when the quality mesh is increased so is the perceived realism of the object.

3.2 Experiment 2: Shading and Confidence

Participants compared the different quality meshes (5K, 10K and 20K) in two rendering conditions with an unlit shader vs. a Lambert diffuse shader, which computationally is not much more expensive than no shading. This experiment was run in the HMD and had a full factorial design, we analysed the results within and between class comparisons covariate by the subjective confidence level as a result to the question "How often were you certain of the answers or were you guessing?" (From 1 always certain to 10 always guessing). Participants were clustered as High Confidence (HC) if scored from 1 to 4, (n=8) and as Low Confidence (LC) if scored from 5 to 8 (n=13), nobody reported values higher than 8. Scores of 5 or higher can arguably be considered LC as it would represent guessing in 50% or more of the cases.

3.2.1 *Within comparisons*

We find that while the HC participants were able to suitably assess the mesh quality in the unlit meshes (significant Pearson correlation $r(24)=0.53$, p=0.007), the LC had a reduced ability to detect higher qualities (no correlation, Pearson p=0.85) (Figure 4).

Those differences were not found for the shaded models, where both HC and LC participants were not able to tell which mesh was better (no correlations, Pearson p>0.48). This can be interpreted as if the thresholds of perception where more diffused in the Lambert shaded condition, the original differences and correlations found in the Unlit condition disappear as if the different qualities of the mesh were harder to distinguish in the Lambert condition.

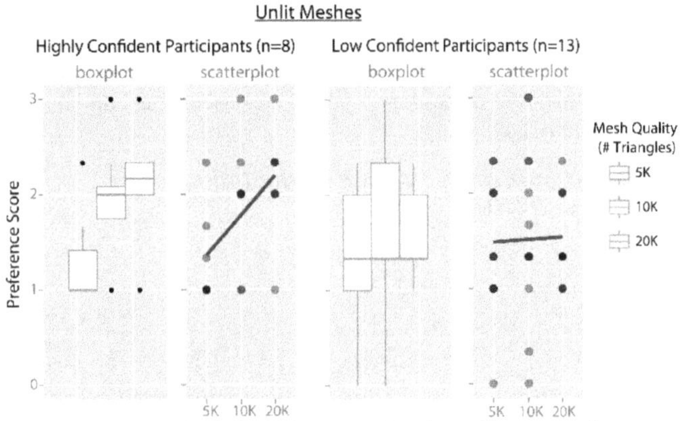

Figure 4. Left: HC preferences for the unlit comparisons. Right: LC results for the unlit comparisons.

3.2.2 Between comparisons

When considering all the between comparisons (unlit vs lit and different qualities) we did not find significant differences in preference between the two modes of shading per mesh quality, (Unlit and Lambert). No differences nor significant correlations were found when clustering the HC and LC participants' preferences (Figure 5). This can be interpreted as if participants were not taking shading into account to judge the mesh quality of 3D objects, although they might find higher realism in the Lambert shaded condition.

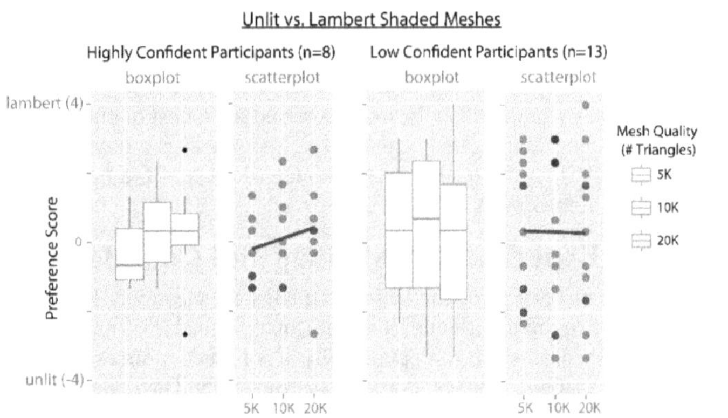

Figure 5. Left: HC participants' results for the Unlit vs. Lambert. Right: LC participants' results for the Unlit vs. Lambert. The boxplot represents the preference for the different mesh qualities. The Y axis goes from preferred Unlit to preferred Lambert, Zero means no preference.

4. Discussion

In the first experiment exploring mesh quality perception under two levels of immersion (monoscopic and stereoscopic viewing) we found a significant correlation between the quality of the mesh and the frequency of selection for both modalities. I.e. participants were equally good at estimating the quality of the meshes in both conditions. These results are consistent with previous studies comparing stereo to mono when performing different tasks (see recent review of over 70 papers [25]). Indeed, our study would be included into the "Finding/Identifying/Classifying Objects" group; over half of the papers in this group found that the stereoscopic view did not directly increase participant performance. Other tasks such as judging distances beneficiated more of stereoscopic viewing [25]. However, participants in our study consistently rated meshes in the stereoscopic view as more realistic than in the monoscopic view. This indicates that although they were not able to differentiate between the mesh qualities in both conditions, the stereoscopic view still made the meshes look more realistic overall. This is consistent with previous research that found clinicians assessing whether the optic disc of patients was presenting signs of glaucoma performed equally well on both viewing modes but had a slight preference towards the stereoscopic condition as being more realistic [26].

In a second experiment we analysed the effect of shading on the quality perception of a mesh with different levels of detail. We introduced an additional subjective assessment to compare high confident and low confident results. Results showed a decreased discernibility of mesh quality in the Lambert shaded condition that was not present in the Unlit comparisons. This perceptual glitch was particularly interesting for the case of the High Confident participants: their ability to discern the higher quality mesh significantly reduced only in the Lambert shading condition. Our results are in the same line as results obtained with VDPs [7] and visual equivalences [8]. Certain light directions can affect the quality perception and then higher and lower quality meshes cannot be distinguished well under shading [27]. In sum improved shading tends to mask lower definition and participants subjectively perceive objects as if they had the same quality as the high definition ones. However, participants did not show preference for the shaded models over the unlit ones. Other research has also shown that people are not actually so concerned when objects and scenes are Not Photorealistic (NPR) in Virtual Reality [28]. Suggesting that object rendering styles do not influence basic object identification, and mesh quality assessment could arguably qualify as basic object identification.

Our findings suggest that lower polygonal resolutions can achieve similar levels of quality perception when using shading. Indeed, the discernibility of the mesh quality dropped significantly when using shading; up to a point that even highly confident participants were unable of distinguishing the quality of meshes of 20K, 10K and 5K triangles.

5. Conclusions

Up to date several approaches have been presented to objectively and subjectively evaluate mesh quality [9], which are basic to the future of 3D scanning and self-content creation for VR. However, current objective techniques based on mathematical approaches do not always replicate the actual human perception of the meshes [9], while the subjective approaches have been mostly restricted to questionnaires that can be inadequate to measure differences at the level of perceptual thresholds [9]. The present approach based on psychophysics can help the community in that sense, and provide a more adequate methodology to discover the boundaries in human mesh quality perception [16].

Future research might include: more computationally expensive shading aimed at more realism; or the evaluation of the exported meshes with VDPs and mathematical methods to see how they compare to the psychophysiological results.

In general, we believe the findings and the methodology here presented are of great interest to the Multimedia and VR communities, as they can be used to help generate simpler meshes that are optimized for real-time rendering with fewer triangles and still be perceived as high quality.

6. REFERENCES

[1] J. Togelius, R. De Nardi, and S. M. Lucas, "Towards automatic personalised content creation for racing games," *Proc. 2007 IEEE Symp. Comput. Intell. Games, CIG 2007*, pp. 252–259, 2007.

[2] H. Chen and H. Sun, "Real-time Haptic Sculpting in Virtual Volume Space," in *Proceedings of the ACM Symposium on Virtual Reality Software and Technology*, 2002, pp. 81–88.

[3] F. Bruno, S. Bruno, G. De Sensi, M. L. Luchi, S. Mancuso, and M. Muzzupappa, "From 3D reconstruction to virtual reality: A complete methodology for digital archaeological exhibition," *J. Cult. Herit.*, vol. 11, no. 1, pp. 42–49, 2010.

[4] M. Dou, J. Taylor, H. Fuchs, A. Fitzgibbon, and S. Izadi, "3D Scanning Deformable Objects with a Single RGBD Sensor," *Proc. IEEE Conf. Comput. Vis. Pattern Recognit.*, pp. 493–501, 2015.

[5] H. Li, E. Vouga, A. Gudym, L. Luo, J. T. Barron, and G. Gusev, "3D self-portraits," *ACM Trans. Graph.*, vol. 32, pp. 1–9, 2013.

[6] M. Niessner, M. Zollhöfer, S. Izadi, and M. Stamminger, "Real-time 3D Reconstruction at Scale Using Voxel Hashing," *ACM Trans. Graph.*, vol. 32, no. 6, pp. 169:1–169:11, 2013.

[7] S. J. Daly, "Visible differences predictor: an algorithm for the assessment of image fidelity," in *SPIE/IS&T 1992 Symposium on Electronic Imaging: Science and Technology*, 1992, pp. 2–15.

[8] G. Ramanarayanan, J. Ferwerda, B. Walter, and K. Bala, "Visual equivalence: towards a new standard for image fidelity," *ACM Trans. Graph.*, vol. 26, no. 3, p. 76, 2007.

[9] D. Berjón, F. Morán, and S. Manjunatha, "Objective and subjective evaluation of static 3D mesh compression," *Signal Process. Image Commun.*, vol. 28, no. 2, pp. 181–195, 2013.

[10] S. Silva, C. Ferreira, J. Madeira, and B. S. Santos, "Perceived quality of simplified polygonal meshes: Evaluation using observer studies," *Proc. Ibero-American Symp. Comput. Graph. SIACG06*, no. August 2015, pp. 169–178, 2006.

[11] M. Gonzalez-Franco, D. Perez-Marcos, B. Spanlang, and M. Slater, "The contribution of real-time mirror reflections of motor actions on virtual body ownership in an immersive virtual environment," in *2010 IEEE Virtual Reality Conference (VR)*, 2010, pp. 111–114.

[12] M. González-Franco, T. C. Peck, A. Rodríguez-Fornells, and M. Slater, "A threat to a virtual hand elicits motor cortex activation.," *Exp. brain Res.*, vol. 232, no. 3, pp. 875–87, Mar. 2014.

[13] G. Padrao, M. Gonzalez-Franco, M. V Sanchez-Vives, M. Slater, and A. Rodriguez-Fornells, "Violating body movement semantics: Neural signatures of self-generated and external-generated errors," *Neuroimage*, vol. 124 PA, no. January, pp. 174–156, 2016.

[14] K. J. Blom, A. I. Bellido Rivas, X. Alvarez, O. Cetinaslan, B. Oliveira, V. Orvalho, M. Slater, and A. I. Bellido, "Achieving participant acceptance of their avatars," *Presence Teleoperators Virtual Environ.*, vol. 23, no. 3, 2014.

[15] M. Gonzalez-Franco and P. A. Chou, "Non-linear modeling of eye gaze perception as a function of gaze and head direction," in *Int'l Workshop on Quality of Multimedia Experience (QoMEX), IEEE*, 2014.

[16] S. S. Stevens, *Psychophysics*. Transaction Publishers, 1975.

[17] A. Blake and H. Bülthoff, "Does the brain know the physics of specular reflection?," *Nature*, vol. 343, no. 6254, pp. 165–168, 1990.

[18] I. Cheng and P. Boulanger, "A 3D Perceptual Metric using Just-Noticeable-Difference," pp. 97–100, 2005.

[19] G. L. Peterson and T. C. Brown, "Economic Valuation by the Method of Paired Comparison, with Emphasis on Evaluation of the Transitivity Axiom," *Land Econ.*, vol. 74(2), no. May, pp. 240–261, 1998.

[20] J. a Ferwerda, F. Pellacini, and D. P. Greenberg, "A psychophysically-based model of surface gloss perception," *Hum. Vis. Electron. Imaging*, vol. 4299, pp. 291–301, 2001.

[21] B. Spanlang, J.-M. Normand, D. Borland, K. Kilteni, E. Giannopoulos, A. Pomes, M. Gonzalez-Franco, D. Perez-Marcos, J. Arroyo-Palacios, X. N. Muncunill, and M. Slater, "How to Build an Embodiment Lab: Achieving Body Representation Illusions in Virtual Reality," *Front. Robot. AI*, vol. 1, no. November, pp. 1–22, Nov. 2014.

[22] W. Steptoe, S. Julier, and A. Steed, "Presence and discernability in conventional and non-photorealistic immersive augmented reality," in *ISMAR*, 2014, pp. 213–218.

[23] M. Gonzalez-Franco, J. Cermeron, K. Li, R. Pizarro, J. Thorn, P. Hannah, W. Hutabarat, A. Tiwari, and P. Bermell-Garcia, "Immersive Augmented Reality Training for Complex Manufacturing Scenarios," *arXiv.org*, p. 1602.01944, 2016.

[24] Z. Zhang, "A flexible new technique for camera calibration," *Pattern Anal. Mach. Intell. IEEE Trans.*, vol. 22, no. 11, pp. 1330–1334, 2000.

[25] J. P. McIntire, P. R. Havig, and E. E. Geiselman, "Stereoscopic 3D displays and human performance: A comprehensive review," *Displays*, vol. 35, no. 1, pp. 18–26, Jan. 2014.

[26] B. Parkin, G. Shuttleworth, M. Costen, and C. Davison, "A comparison of stereoscopic and monoscopic evaluation of optic disc topography using a digital optic disc stereo camera.," *Br. J. Ophthalmol.*, vol. 85, no. 11, pp. 1347–1351, 2001.

[27] B. E. Rogowitz and H. E. Rushmeier, "Are image quality metrics adequate to evaluate the quality of geometric objects?," *Photonics West 2001-Electronic Imaging*, pp. 340–348, 2001.

[28] P. Zimmons, A. Panter, and D. Ph, "The Influence of Rendering Quality on Presence And Task Performance in a Virtual Environment at Chapel Hill at Chapel Hill," vol. 2003, pp. 2–3, 2003.

Partial Multi-Modal Sparse Coding via Adaptive Similarity Structure Regularization

Zhou Zhao
College of Computer Science,
Zhejiang University, China
zhaozhou@zju.edu.cn

Hanqing Lu
College of Computer Science,
Zhejiang University, China
lhq110@zju.edu.cn

Deng Cai
State Key Lab of CAD&CG,
Zhejiang University, China
dengcai@gmail.com

Xiaofei He
State Key Lab of CAD&CG,
Zhejiang University, China
xiaofeihe@gmail.com

Yueting Zhuang
College of Computer Science,
Zhejiang University, China
yzhuang@zju.edu.cn

ABSTRACT

Multi-modal sparse coding has played an important role in many multimedia applications, where data are usually with multiple modalities. Recently, various multi-modal sparse coding approaches have been proposed to learn sparse codes of multi-modal data, which assume that data appear in all modalities, or at least there is one modality containing all data. However, in real applications, it is often the case that some modalities of the data may suffer from missing information and thus result in partial multi-modality data. In this paper, we propose to solve the partial multi-modal sparse coding problem via multi-modal similarity structure regularization. Specifically, we propose a partial multi-modal sparse coding framework termed *Adaptive Partial Multi-Modal Similarity Structure Regularization for Sparse Coding* (AdaPM^{2}SC), which preserves the similarity structure within the same modality and between different modalities. Experimental results conducted on two real-world datasets demonstrate that AdaPM^{2}SC significantly outperforms the state-of-the-art methods under partial multi-modality scenario.

1. INTRODUCTION

With the explosive growth of Internet, many real-world applications involve multi-modal data such as web images with related text descriptions and a news article with paired text and images. Multi-modal sparse coding is an essential problem for the representation of data with multiple modalities, which arises in many real applications such as cross-modal retrieval [16] and object recognition [4].

The problem of multi-modal sparse coding is to find succinct representation for multi-modal data using only a few coding coefficients, which has attracted considerable attention recently [10, 8, 16, 7, 4, 3, 2, 9, 12]. Most of the existing approaches (also known as multi-view or cross-view sparse coding) formulate the multi-modal sparse coding as the multi-modal data reconstruction via sparse regularization with l_1 penalty, and the multi-modal mapping function learning that preserves the modality correlation. Although existing multi-modal sparse coding methods have achieved promising performance, they assume that the data appear in all modalities, or at least there is one modality containing all data.

However, in real applications, it is often the case that some modalities of the data may suffer from missing information and thus result in partial multi-modality data [15, 9]. For example, not all web images are associated with text descriptions and some of the news articles may only contain textual contents. In order to apply the existing multi-modal spares coding methods to partial multi-modality data, we can either remove the data that suffer from missing information, or preprocess the partial multi-modal data by filling the missing information. The first strategy is not suitable since the goal of sparse coding is to learn the sparse representation for all data. On the other hand, our experimental results show that the existing multi-modal sparse coding methods with the second strategy does not achieve good performance.

Recently, the similarity structure regularization has shown excellent performance on both uni-modality data [14] and multi-modal sparse coding [11]. By exploiting the local similarity structure, the regularized sparse coding can have more discriminating power compared with traditional sparse coding algorithms, and thus the learning performance can be significantly enhanced [14]. However, to the best of our knowledge, the similarity structure regularization has not been fully exploited on partial multi-modal data. It is challenging to compute the explicit similarity structure of partial multi-modal data directly since the data information in some modalities are missing. One simple solution is to define some criterions to compute the similarity between the partial multi-modal data by using the existing multi-modal data as the bridge. However, the multi-modal data information are often noisy, which makes the computed similarity structure unreliable [6]. Therefore, it is important to develop the robust similarity structure regularization strategy for partial multi-modal sparse coding.

In this paper, we propose a novel partial multi-modal sparse coding framework termed *Partial Multi-Modal Similarity Structure Regularization for Sparse Coding* (AdaPM^{2}SC). AdaPM^{2}SC performs partial multi-modal similarity structure learning and unified sparse coding simultaneously. That is, AdaPM^{2}SC directly learns a similarity induced probability neighborhood [6], where the data similarity between different modalities is computed by joint probability strategy. We illustrate that the indirected similarity between partial data $\mathbf{x}_2$ and $\mathbf{x}_8$ can be computed through their directed similarity to multi-modal data $\mathbf{x}_4$ and $\mathbf{x}_5$ via joint probability strategy, as illustrated in Figure 1. The multi-modal similarity structure is adaptive learned from the unified sparse coding, and the sparse

MM '16, October 15-19, 2016, Amsterdam, Netherlands

DOI: http://dx.doi.org/10.1145/2964284.2967201

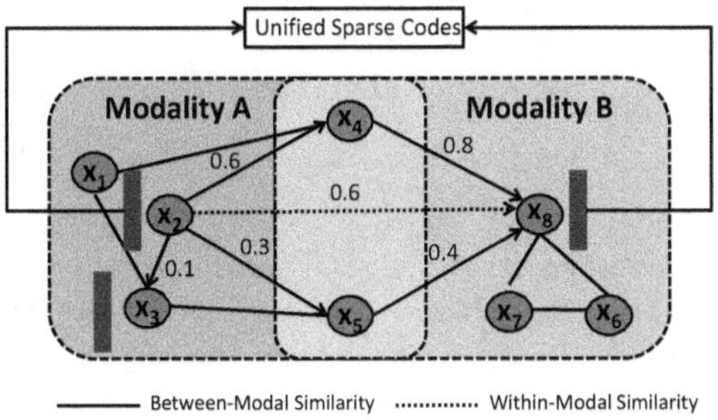

Figure 1: The Illustration of Partial Multi-Modal Similarity Learning.

coding is regularized by the adaptive structure. We summarize the contributions in this paper as follows: 1. We identify the partial multi-modality problem in sparse coding, and propose to tackle the problem via adaptive similarity structure regularization. To the best of our knowledge, this is the first study in the literature for this identified problem. 2. We propose a novel partial multi-modal sparse coding framework that performs partial multi-modal similarity structure learning and unified sparse coding simultaneously. We then develop a coordinate gradient descent algorithm for the optimization.

2. PARTIAL MULTI-MODAL SPARSE CODING

2.1 The Problem

Notations. For the ease of presentation, assume that we are dealing with the sparse coding with partial two-modality data. Given a set of N two-modal data samples $X = \{(\mathbf{x}_i^{(a)}, \mathbf{x}_i^{(b)}), i = 1, \ldots, N\}$, $\mathbf{x}_i^{(a)} \in R^{d_a}$ is the instance of the i-th sample in modality A and $\mathbf{x}_i^{(b)} \in R^{d_b}$ is the i-th sample in modality B (usually $d_a \neq d_b$). In partial modality setting, the data set is represented by $X = \{C, A, B\}$ where $C = \{(\mathbf{x}_1^{(a)}, \mathbf{x}_1^{(b)}), \ldots, (\mathbf{x}_c^{(a)}, \mathbf{x}_c^{(b)})\} \in R^{(d_a+d_b)}$ denotes the common samples presented in both modalities, $A = \{\mathbf{x}_{c+1}^{(a)}, \ldots, \mathbf{x}_{c+n_a}^{(a)}\} \in R^{d_a}$ denotes the samples only presented in modality A and $B = \{\mathbf{x}_{c+n_a+1}^{(b)}, \ldots, \mathbf{x}_{c+n_a+n_b}^{(b)}\} \in R^{d_b}$ denote the examples only presented in modality B. Note that the number of samples presented in both modalities, only in modality A, and modality B are c, n_a and n_b ($N = c + n_a + n_b$). We denote the representation of the common data examples in modality A and B by $\mathbf{X}_c^{(a)}$ and $\mathbf{X}_c^{(b)}$, respectively. We then denote the instances in each modality by $\hat{\mathbf{X}}^{(a)} = [\mathbf{X}_c^{(a)}, \mathbf{X}^{(a)}] \in R^{(c+n_a)\times d_a}$ and $\hat{\mathbf{X}}^{(b)} = [\mathbf{X}_c^{(b)}, \mathbf{X}^{(b)}] \in R^{(c+n_b)\times d_b}$.

Problem Definition. Given a set of N partial data samples with $\hat{\mathbf{X}}^{(a)}$ and $\hat{\mathbf{X}}^{(b)}$, the problem of partial multi-modal sparse coding is to learn the unified sparse codes $\boldsymbol{\alpha}$ together with the modality-specific dictionaries $\mathbf{D}^{(a)}$ and $\mathbf{D}^{(b)}$ by

$$
\begin{aligned}
\min_{\boldsymbol{\alpha},\mathbf{D}} \quad & \sum_{m\in\{a,b\}} \|\hat{\mathbf{X}}^{(m)} - \mathbf{D}^{(m)}\hat{\boldsymbol{\alpha}}^{(m)}\|_F^2 + \lambda\|\hat{\boldsymbol{\alpha}}^{(m)}\|_1 \\
s.t. \quad & \hat{\mathbf{X}}^{(a)} = \begin{pmatrix} \mathbf{X}_c^{(a)} \\ \mathbf{X}^{(a)} \end{pmatrix}, \hat{\mathbf{X}}^{(b)} = \begin{pmatrix} \mathbf{X}_c^{(b)} \\ \mathbf{X}^{(b)} \end{pmatrix} \\
& \hat{\boldsymbol{\alpha}}^{(a)} = \begin{pmatrix} \boldsymbol{\alpha}^{(c)} \\ \boldsymbol{\alpha}^{(a)} \end{pmatrix}, \hat{\boldsymbol{\alpha}}^{(b)} = \begin{pmatrix} \boldsymbol{\alpha}^{(c)} \\ \boldsymbol{\alpha}^{(b)} \end{pmatrix} \\
& \|\mathbf{d}_k^{(m)}\| \leq l, m \in \{a, b\}, \forall k, \qquad (1)
\end{aligned}
$$

which is in the unsupervised multi-modal sparse coding setting [10]. We denote that $\boldsymbol{\alpha}^{(c)}$ are the unified codes for common data examples, $\boldsymbol{\alpha}^{(a)}$ and $\boldsymbol{\alpha}^{(b)}$ are the codes for partial data examples. Thus, the sparse codes $\boldsymbol{\alpha} = \{\boldsymbol{\alpha}^{(c)}, \boldsymbol{\alpha}^{(a)}, \boldsymbol{\alpha}^{(b)}\}$ ensures the codes generated from different modalities are consistent. Furthermore, we want to preserve the data similarity within the same modality and between different modalities, and enforce that similar data examples are mapped to the similar codes. We note that our work can be easily extended to the supervised setting, and we consider it as the future work.

2.2 Unified Partial Multi-Modal Sparse Coding via Adaptive Similarity Structure Regularization

Unlike the existing graph regularized sparse coding approaches [13, 11], we introduce the probability neighborhood matrix [6] that learns the data similarity matrix and sparse coding simultaneously. The probability neighborhood matrix is learned by assigning the adaptive and optimal neighbors for each data sample $\mathbf{x}_i^{(a)}$ within the same modality A by $p_{ij}^{(a)}$ ($i, j \in A$ and $\mathbf{p}^a \in R^{n_a\times n_a}$), and between different modalities B by $p_{ij'}^{(a,b)}$ ($i \in A$ and $j' \in B$, $p_{ij'}^{(a,b)} \in R^{n_a\times n_b}$). Given a set of common data examples presented in both modalities C, the between-modal probability is define by $p_{ij}^{(a,b)} = \sum_{\mathbf{x}_k\in C} p_{ik}^{(a)} p_{kj}^{(b)}$, where the probabilities $p_{ik}^{(a)}$ and $p_{kj}^{(b)}$ are learned within the same modality A and B, respectively. Therefore, the adaptive similarity structure learning is given by

$$
\begin{aligned}
\min_{\mathbf{P}} \quad & \sum_{m\in\{a,b\},M\in\{A,B\}} \sum_{i,j\in M\bigcup C} \|\hat{\boldsymbol{\alpha}}_i{}^{(m)} - \hat{\boldsymbol{\alpha}}_j{}^{(m)}\|_2^2 p_{ij}^{(m)} \\
+ \quad & \gamma \sum_{i\in A,j\in B} \|\boldsymbol{\alpha}_i^{(a)} - \boldsymbol{\alpha}_j^{(b)}\|_2^2 p_{ij}^{(a,b)} \\
+ \quad & \nu(\|\mathbf{P}^{(a)}\|_2^2 + \|\mathbf{P}^{(b)}\|_2^2) \\
s.t. \quad & \mathbf{p}_i^{(m)}\mathbf{1}_{n_m} = 1, \mathbf{p}_i^{(m)} \geq \mathbf{0}, m \in \{a, b\}, \forall i \qquad (2)
\end{aligned}
$$

where $\mathbf{p}_i^{(m)} \in R^{n_m\times 1}$ is a vector with the j-th element as $p_{ij}^{(m)}$. We notice that a smaller distance $\|\hat{\boldsymbol{\alpha}}_i{}^{(m)} - \hat{\boldsymbol{\alpha}}_j{}^{(m)}\|_2^2$ should be assigned a larger probability $p_{ij}^{(m)}$, while a larger distance $\|\boldsymbol{\alpha}_i^{(a)} - \boldsymbol{\alpha}_j^{(b)}\|_2^2$ should be assigned a smaller probability $p_{ij}^{(a,b)}$.

Combining Equations (1) and (2), the objective function of unified partial multi-modal sparse coding via adaptive similarity structure regularization is given by

$$
\begin{aligned}
\min_{\boldsymbol{\alpha},\mathbf{D},\mathbf{P}} \quad & \sum_{m\in\{a,b\},M\in\{A,B\}} \{\|\hat{\mathbf{X}}^{(m)} - \mathbf{D}^{(m)}\hat{\boldsymbol{\alpha}}^{(m)}\|_F^2 \\
+ \quad & \beta \sum_{i,j\in M\bigcup C} \|\hat{\boldsymbol{\alpha}}_i{}^{(m)} - \hat{\boldsymbol{\alpha}}_j{}^{(m)}\|_2^2 p_{ij}^{(m)} \\
+ \quad & \lambda\|\hat{\boldsymbol{\alpha}}^{(m)}\|_1\} + \gamma \sum_{i\in A,j\in B} \|\boldsymbol{\alpha}_i^{(a)} - \boldsymbol{\alpha}_j^{(b)}\|_2^2 p_{ij}^{(a,b)} \\
+ \quad & \nu(\|\mathbf{P}^{(a)}\|_2^2 + \|\mathbf{P}^{(b)}\|_2^2) \\
s.t. \quad & \mathbf{p}_i^{(m)}\mathbf{1}_{n_m} = 1, \mathbf{p}_i^{(m)} \geq \mathbf{0}, m \in \{a, b\}, \forall i \\
& \|\mathbf{d}_k^{(m)}\| \leq l, m \in \{a, b\}, \forall k \qquad (3)
\end{aligned}
$$

where β, λ, γ and ν are the regularization parameters.

2.3 The Optimization

In this section, we derive an alternative algorithm to learn the unified sparse codes $\boldsymbol{\alpha}$, multi-modal dictionaries $\mathbf{D}$ and probabilistic neighborhood $\mathbf{P}$.

Algorithm 1 The Optimization of Problem (5)

Input: $\mathbf{q}_i \in R^n$

Sort $\mathbf{q}_i$ into $\mathbf{h}$ where $h_1 \geq h_2 \geq, \ldots, h_n$

Find $\rho = \max\{1 \leq j \leq n : h_j + \frac{1}{j}(1 - \sum_{k=1}^{j} h_k) > 0\}$

Define $\lambda = \frac{1}{\rho}(1 - \sum_{k=1}^{\rho} h_k)$

return $\mathbf{p}_i$, s.t., $p_{ij} = \max\{q_j + \lambda, 0\}, j = 1, \ldots, n$

Learning Probability Neighborhood P. First, when the unified sparse codes α and the multi-modal dictionaries $\mathbf{D}$ are fixed, the update for probabilistic neighborhood of data sample $\mathbf{x}_i$ in modality A (i.e., $\mathbf{p}_i^{(a)}$) is given by

$$\begin{aligned} \min_{\mathbf{p}_i^{(a)}} \quad & \sum_{j \in A} (\boldsymbol{\alpha}_i - \boldsymbol{\alpha}_j)^2 p_{ij}^{(a)} + \nu \|\mathbf{p}_i^{(a)}\|_2^2 \\ + \quad & \gamma \sum_{j' \in B, k \in C} (\boldsymbol{\alpha}_i - \boldsymbol{\alpha}_{j'})^2 p_{ik}^{(a)} p_{kj'}^{(b)} \\ s.t. \quad & \mathbf{p}_i^{(a)} \mathbf{1}_{n_a} = 1, \mathbf{p}_i \geq 0, \end{aligned} \tag{4}$$

where $\mathbf{1}_{n_a}$ is a $n_a \times 1$ vector of all elements equaling to 1. Let $D \in R^{n_a \times n_b}$ be a matrix with its entry

$$d_{ik}^{(a)} = \frac{(\boldsymbol{\alpha}_i - \boldsymbol{\alpha}_k)^2 + \gamma \sum_{j' \in B} (\boldsymbol{\alpha}_i - \boldsymbol{\alpha}_{j'})^2 p_{kj'}^{(b)} \times \mathbf{1}(k \in C)}{-2\nu}$$

, we then rewritten Problem (4) as follows:

$$\min_{\mathbf{p}_i^{(a)}} \frac{1}{2} \|\mathbf{p}_i^{(a)} - \mathbf{d}_i\|_2^2, s.t., \mathbf{p}_i^{(a)} \mathbf{1}_{n_a} = 1, \mathbf{p}_i \geq 0,, \tag{5}$$

which is an inequality constrained quadratic program (ICQP) problem [1] and can be efficiently solved by Algorithm 1 using Karush-Kuhn-Tucker (KKT) condition. The update for the probability neighborhood of data samples in modality B (i.e., $\mathbf{p}_i^{(b)}$) is similar.

Learning Unified Sparse Codes α. We then present the learning for unified sparse codes of the examples in both modalities $\alpha^{(c)}$, and the examples only in one modality $\alpha^{(a)}$ and $\alpha^{(b)}$, respectively. We note that the probability neighborhood matrix within the same modality can be seen as a similarity matrix of the graph with N data points. Therefore, it can be verified that

$$\sum_{i,j \in A, m \in \{a,b\}} \|\alpha_i^{(m)} - \alpha_j^{(m)}\|^2 p_{ij}^{(a)} = 2tr((\hat{\boldsymbol{\alpha}}^{(a)})^T \mathbf{L}^{(a)} \hat{\boldsymbol{\alpha}}^{(a)}),$$

where $\mathbf{L}^{(a)} = \mathbf{D}^{\mathbf{P}^{(a)}} - \frac{(\mathbf{P}^{(a)})^T + \mathbf{P}^{(a)}}{2}$ is called Laplacian matrix in graph theory, the degree matrix $\mathbf{D}^{\mathbf{P}^{(a)}} \in R^{n_a \times n_a}$ is defined as a diagonal matrix where the i-th diagonal element is $\sum_j \frac{p_{ij}^{(a)} + p_{ji}^{(a)}}{2}$. The adaptive regularizer $tr((\hat{\boldsymbol{\alpha}}^{(a)})^T \mathbf{L}^{(a)} \hat{\boldsymbol{\alpha}}^{(a)})$ can be rewritten as follows:

$$\begin{aligned} tr(\hat{\boldsymbol{\alpha}}^{(a)} \mathbf{L}^{(a)} (\hat{\boldsymbol{\alpha}}^{(a)})^T) &= tr(\sum_{i,j \in A} L_{ij}^{(a)} \hat{\boldsymbol{\alpha}}_i^{(a)} (\hat{\boldsymbol{\alpha}}_j^{(a)})^T) \\ &= \sum_{i,j \in A} L_{ij}^{(a)} \hat{\boldsymbol{\alpha}}_i^{(a)} (\hat{\boldsymbol{\alpha}}_j^{(a)})^T, \end{aligned} \tag{6}$$

and the reconstruction error of each modality $\|\hat{\mathbf{X}}^{(a)} - \mathbf{D}^{(a)} \hat{\boldsymbol{\alpha}}^{(a)}\|_F^2$ can be rewritten as:

$$\sum_{i \in A \bigcup C} \|\hat{\mathbf{x}}_i^{(a)} - \mathbf{D}^{(a)} \hat{\boldsymbol{\alpha}}_i^{(a)}\|_F^2. \tag{7}$$

By combining Equations (6) and (7), we obtain the objective function for the common example $\boldsymbol{\alpha}_i^{(c)}$ by fixing other codes $\{\boldsymbol{\alpha}_j\}_{j \neq i}$ by

$$\begin{aligned} \min_{\boldsymbol{\alpha}_i^{(c)}} \quad & \|[\mathbf{x}_i^{(a)}\ \mathbf{x}_i^{(b)}] - [\mathbf{D}^{(a)}\ \mathbf{D}^{(b)}] \boldsymbol{\alpha}_i^{(c)}\|_F^2 + 2\lambda \|\boldsymbol{\alpha}_i^{(c)}\|_1 \\ + \quad & \beta(L_{ii}^{(a)} + L_{ii}^{(b)}) \boldsymbol{\alpha}_i^{(c)} (\boldsymbol{\alpha}_i^{(c)})^T + 2(\boldsymbol{\alpha}_i^{(c)})^T \mathbf{h}_i^{(c)}, \end{aligned}$$

where $\mathbf{h}_i^{(c)} = \beta(\sum_{j \neq i} L_{ij}^{(a)} \boldsymbol{\alpha}_j^{(a)} + \sum_{j' \neq i} L_{ij'}^{(b)} \boldsymbol{\alpha}_{j'}^{(b)})$. By employing the feature-sign algorithm [5], we maintain an active set of potentially nonzero coefficients and corresponding signs for $\boldsymbol{\alpha}_i^{(c)}$, denoted by $\boldsymbol{\theta}_i^{(c)}$. Then, we can reduce the above objective function to the unconstrained quadratic programming. We then update $\boldsymbol{\alpha}_i^{(c)}$ at each step by

$$\begin{aligned} \boldsymbol{\alpha}_i^{(c)} \quad \leftarrow \quad & (\sum_{m \in \{a,b\}} (\mathbf{D}^{(m)})^T \mathbf{D}^{(m)} + \beta(L_{ii}^{(a)} + L_{ii}^{(b)}) \mathbf{I})^{-1} \\ \times \quad & (\sum_{m \in \{a,b\}} (\mathbf{D}^{(m)})^T \mathbf{x}_i^{(m)} - \lambda(\boldsymbol{\theta}_i^{(c)} + \mathbf{h}_i^{(c)})) \end{aligned} \tag{8}$$

Similarly, we can rewrite the objective function with respect to $\boldsymbol{\alpha}_i^{(a)}$ by

$$\begin{aligned} \min_{\boldsymbol{\alpha}_i^{(a)}} \quad & \|\mathbf{x}_i^{(a)} - \mathbf{D}^{(a)} \boldsymbol{\alpha}_i^{(a)}\|_F^2 + \lambda \|\boldsymbol{\alpha}_i^{(a)}\|_1 \\ + \quad & \beta L_{ii}^{(a)} \boldsymbol{\alpha}_i^{(a)} (\boldsymbol{\alpha}_i^{(a)})^T + (\boldsymbol{\alpha}_i^{(a)})^T \mathbf{g}_i^{(a)}, \end{aligned}$$

where $\mathbf{g}_i^{(a)} = 2(\beta \sum_{j \neq i} L_{ij}^{(a)} \boldsymbol{\alpha}_j^{(a)} - \gamma \sum_{j' \in B} p_{ij'}^{(a,b)} \boldsymbol{\alpha}_{j'}^{(b)})$. Following the feature-sign procedure, the update for $\boldsymbol{\alpha}_i^{(c)}$ is given by

$$\begin{aligned} \boldsymbol{\alpha}_i^{(a)} \quad \leftarrow \quad & ((\mathbf{D}^{(a)})^T \mathbf{D}^{(a)} + (\beta L_{ii}^{(a)} + \gamma) \mathbf{I})^{-1} \\ \times \quad & ((\mathbf{D}^{(a)})^T \mathbf{x}_i^{(a)} - \frac{\lambda \boldsymbol{\theta}_i^{(a)} + \mathbf{g}_i^{(a)}}{2}) \end{aligned} \tag{9}$$

where $\boldsymbol{\theta}_i^{(a)}$ is the corresponding sign of $\boldsymbol{\alpha}_i^{(a)}$.

Learning Multi-Modal Dictionaries D. Finally, we update dictionary $\mathbf{D}$ as follows:

$$\begin{aligned} \min_{\mathbf{D}} \quad & \sum_{m \in \{a,b\}} \|\hat{\mathbf{X}}^{(m)} - \mathbf{D}^{(m)} \hat{\boldsymbol{\alpha}}^{(m)}\|_F^2 \\ s.t. \quad & \|\mathbf{d}_k^{(m)}\| \leq l, m \in \{a,b\}, \forall k. \end{aligned} \tag{10}$$

This is a quadratically constrained quadratic program (QCQP) problem which can be solved using the method presented in [13].

3. EXPERIMENTS

3.1 Data Preparation

We evaluate our method on two popular public multi-modal datasets: Wiki Text-Image[1] and NUS-WIDE[2]. The Wiki Text-Image data contains 2,866 text-image pairs from ten different categories. The NUS-WIDE data consists of 12,072 text-image pairs from 31 different categories. We use the 500-dimension bag-of-visual-words (BoVW) based on SIFT features for the representation of each image and 1000-dimension bag-of-words (BoW) for the representation of each text.

Following the partial multi-modal settings in [9, 15], we randomly select a fraction of examples to be partial instances, i.e., they are described by only one modality, and the remaining ones appear in both modalities. We refer the fraction number of partial

[1]http://www.svcl.ucsd.edu/projects/cross-modal/

[2]http://lms.comp.nus.edu.sg/research/NUS-WIDE.htm

Table 1: Clustering Performance on Wiki Text-Image and NUS-WIDE datasets with PDR = 0.5. (The best scores are highlighted)

Algorithm	Criteria	SCDL	RMDL	VISP	MURL	SSMVE	AdaPM^{2}SC
WIKI	NMI	0.1736±0.0008	0.199±0.0002	0.2348±0.0003	0.2629±0.0002	0.2813±0.0002	**0.4385**±0.0002
	AC	0.3147±0.0005	0.3293±0.0009	0.3743±0.0005	0.3241±0.0006	0.499±0.0007	**0.5244**±0.0005
NUS-WIDE	NMI	0.0769±0.0005	0.0815±0.0003	0.0616±0.0006	0.0667±0.0004	0.0911±0.0007	**0.1007**±0.0003
	AC	0.1066±0.0009	0.1071±0.0001	0.1000±0.0002	0.1023±0.0003	0.1112±0.0003	**0.1164**±0.0004

examples as Partial Data Ratio (PDR) (e.g., $\frac{N-c}{N}$). Each time we randomly select 10% to 90% examples, with 10% as interval, as partial examples. Such process is repeated 10 times and the average results are recorded.

3.2 Performance Comparisons

We evaluate the performance of our proposed method by comparing with other five state-of-the-art unsupervised multi-modal (or multi-view) sparse representation methods as follows:

SCDL method [10] is an unsupervised semi-coupled sparse coding algorithm to learn a pair of dictionaries for multi-view data.

SSMVE method [3] is an unsupervised spectral sparse multi-view embedding algorithm that finds a low-dimensional consensus representation from multiple heterogeneous features.

RMDL method [2] is a probabilistic model-based robust multi-modal sparse coding method that generates the sparse codes via EM algorithm.

MURL method [9] is a multi-modal unified representation learning algorithm that preserves the data consistency among different modalities.

VISP method [12] is a view-invariant sparse representations that presents the data in each view using both the corresponding view-specific dictionary and the common dictionary.

In order to compare with the existing multi-modal sparse coding methods on the partial data, we have to recover the specific missing modalities of the data examples. Following the multi-modal data recovery approach [9], we complete the missing modality of the data examples using linear combination of its 5 nearest neighbors (weighted by their similarities) which have both modalities. Therefore, the compared multi-modal sparse coding algorithms can be directly applied on these extended data.

Table 1 shows the evaluation results with PDR = 0.5. The parameters which achieve the best performance are chosen to conduct the evaluation. We report the average value of all methods on both datasets using on NMI and AC criteria, respectively. The experiments reveal a number of interesting points: 1. The unified sparse representation methods SSMVE and MURL outperform the model-specific representation methods SCDL, RMDL and VISP, which suggests that the unified representation achieves better performance on the clustering task. 2. The SSMVE method achieves better performance than other baselines. This suggests that by exploiting the similarity structure of multi-modal data examples, the clustering performance can also be improved. 3. In all the cases, our AdaPM^{2}SC method achieves the best performance. This fact shows that by leveraging both unified sparse coding and adaptive similarity structure preserving within-modal and between-modal, we can further enhance the performance.

We then evaluate the effectiveness of our proposed AdaPM^{2}SC under different partial data ratios, we progressively increase the PDR from 0 to 90% with 10% as interval and compare with the other baselines. The clustering results on Wiki Text-Image dataset are shown in Figures 2(a) and 2(b). The clustering results on NUS-WIDE dataset are illustrated in Figures 3(a) and 3(b). As the PDR increases from 0 to 0.9, our proposed AdaPM^{2}SC always achieves the best performance. Although the missing modalities of some

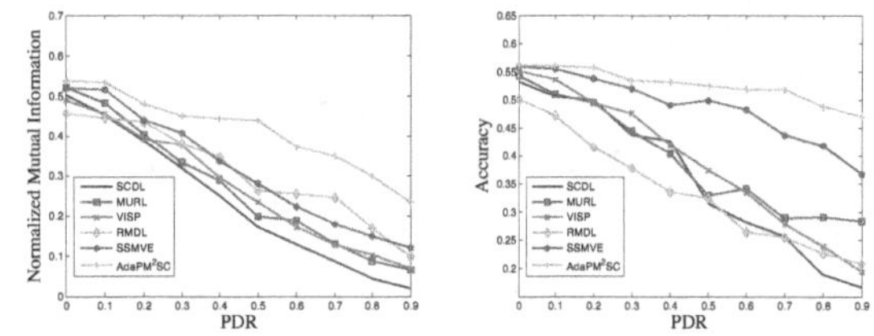

(a) NMI (b) Accuracy

Figure 2: Clustering Performance on Wiki Text-Image dataset with different PDRs

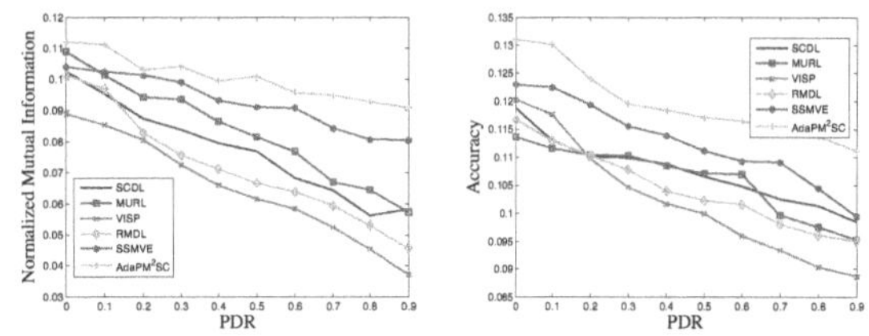

(a) NMI (b) Accuracy

Figure 3: Clustering Performance on NUS-WIDE dataset with different PDRs

data examples are recovered, the baseline methods still show to be less effective. Thus, we conclude that our method is better than other baseline methods on partial multi-modal data.

4. CONCLUSION

In this paper, we identify the problem of partial multi-modal sparse coding and propose a novel partial multi-modal sparse coding framework via adaptive similarity structure regularization, termed AdaPM^{2}SC. AdaPM^{2}SC performs partial multi-modal similarity structure learning and unified sparse coding simultaneously, which preserves the similarity structure within the same modality and between different modalities. We then develop a coordinate gradient descent algorithm for the optimization. We evaluate the performance of our method using two real-world datasets and the extensive experiments show that our method outperforms several state-to-the-art algorithm to this problem.

5. ACKNOWLEDGMENTS

This work was supported by National Basic Research Program of China (973 Program) under Grant 2013CB336500, National Program for Special Support of Top-Notch Young Professionals, National Natural Science Foundation of China under Grant 61233011 and Grant 61125203, Fundamental Research Funds for the Central Universities 2016QNA5015, and the China Knowledge Centre for Engineering Sciences and Technology.

6. REFERENCES

[1] S. Boyd and L. Vandenberghe. *Convex optimization*. Cambridge university press, 2004.

[2] T. Cao, V. Jojic, S. Modla, D. Powell, K. Czymmek, and M. Niethammer. Robust multimodal dictionary learning. In *Medical Image Computing and Computer-Assisted Intervention–MICCAI 2013*, pages 259–266. Springer, 2013.

[3] Y. Han, F. Wu, D. Tao, J. Shao, Y. Zhuang, and J. Jiang. Sparse unsupervised dimensionality reduction for multiple view data. *Circuits and Systems for Video Technology, IEEE Transactions on*, 22(10):1485–1496, 2012.

[4] X.-Y. Jing, R.-M. Hu, F. Wu, X.-L. Chen, Q. Liu, and Y.-F. Yao. Uncorrelated multi-view discrimination dictionary learning for recognition. In *AAAI*, 2014.

[5] H. Lee, A. Battle, R. Raina, and A. Y. Ng. Efficient sparse coding algorithms. In *Advances in neural information processing systems*, pages 801–808, 2006.

[6] F. Nie, X. Wang, and H. Huang. Clustering and projected clustering with adaptive neighbors. In *SIGKDD*, pages 977–986. ACM, 2014.

[7] S. Shekhar, V. M. Patel, N. M. Nasrabadi, and R. Chellappa. Joint sparse representation for robust multimodal biometrics recognition. *TPAMI*, 36(1):113–126, 2014.

[8] Y. Shi, Y. Gao, Y. Yang, Y. Zhang, and D. Wang. Multimodal sparse representation-based classification for lung needle biopsy images. *Biomedical Engineering, IEEE Transactions on*, 60(10):2675–2685, 2013.

[9] Q. Wang, L. Si, and B. Shen. Learning to hash on partial multi-modal data. In *IJCAI*, pages 3904–3910. AAAI Press, 2015.

[10] S. Wang, L. Zhang, Y. Liang, and Q. Pan. Semi-coupled dictionary learning with applications to image super-resolution and photo-sketch synthesis. In *CVPR*, pages 2216–2223. IEEE, 2012.

[11] J. Yu, Y. Rui, and D. Tao. Click prediction for web image reranking using multimodal sparse coding. *IEEE Transactions on Image Processing*, 23(5):2019–2032, 2014.

[12] J. Zheng and Z. Jiang. Learning view-invariant sparse representations for cross-view action recognition. In *Proceedings of the IEEE International Conference on Computer Vision*, pages 3176–3183, 2013.

[13] M. Zheng, J. Bu, C. Chen, C. Wang, L. Zhang, G. Qiu, and D. Cai. Graph regularized sparse coding for image representation. *TIP*, 20(5):1327–1336, 2011.

[14] S. Zheng, B. Xie, K. Huang, and D. Tao. Multi-view pedestrian recognition using shared dictionary learning with group sparsity. In *Neural Information Processing*, pages 629–638. Springer, 2011.

[15] S.-Y. L. Y. J. Zhi and H. Zhou. Partial multi-view clustering. In *AAAI*. AAAI Press, 2014.

[16] Y. T. Zhuang, Y. F. Wang, F. Wu, Y. Zhang, and W. M. Lu. Supervised coupled dictionary learning with group structures for multi-modal retrieval. In *AAAI*, 2013.

Improving Speaker Diarization of TV Series using Talking-Face Detection and Clustering

Hervé Bredin
LIMSI, CNRS
Université Paris-Saclay
F-91405 Orsay, France
bredin@limsi.fr

Grégory Gelly
LIMSI, CNRS, Univ. Paris-Sud
Université Paris-Saclay
F-91405 Orsay, France
gelly@limsi.fr

ABSTRACT

While successful on broadcast news, meetings or telephone conversation, state-of-the-art speaker diarization techniques tend to perform poorly on TV series or movies. In this paper, we propose to rely on state-of-the-art face clustering techniques to guide acoustic speaker diarization. Two approaches are tested and evaluated on the first season of *Game Of Thrones* TV series. The second (better) approach relies on a novel talking-face detection module based on bi-directional long short-term memory recurrent neural network. Both audio-visual approaches outperform the audio-only baseline. A detailed study of the behavior of these approaches is also provided and paves the way to future improvements.

Keywords

speaker diarization; face clustering; talking-face detection

1. INTRODUCTION

Speaker diarization is the task of partitioning an audio stream into homogeneous temporal segments according to the identity of the speaker. Followed by a supervised or unsupervised speaker identification step [15], it allows to answer the question "who speaks when?". Automatic speech transcription also benefits from speaker diarization to address the question "who speaks what?". Resulting augmented (or "rich") transcription can be very useful for multimedia documents structuring and indexing.

Speaker diarization has been successfully applied to various types of content: radio or TV broadcast news (mostly prepared speech and clean audio), telephone conversation (limited number of speakers) and meetings (spontaneous speech and lower audio quality). It is usually tackled using three cascading modules (speech activity detection, speaker change detection and unsupervised speech turns clustering) followed by an optional resegmentation step [2].

This paper investigates the application of speaker diarization on TV series content. As a matter of fact, it has been shown that current state-of-the-art approaches do not perform well when applied to TV series or movies [5, 9]. Several reasons might explain why this is the case. First, the number of speakers may vary a lot from one TV series to another (and even from one episode to another). For instance, *Game of Thrones* episodes range from 28 to 48 speakers, while *The Big Bang Theory* episodes only vary between 9 and 12 speakers. Then, the quality of the speech signal is often degraded because of background music or noise. Finally, though it is acted speech, one can classify speech interactions between TV series characters as spontaneous – as opposed to prepared or read speech in broadcast news, for instance. This leads to a lot of short speech turns for which the usual *2 seconds or more* assumption made by state-of-the-art speaker diarization system no longer holds. For instance, median speech turn duration is only 1.6 second for *Game Of Thrones* TV series.

In this paper, we aim at improving the clustering step by taking advantage of recent advances in deep learning for face recognition and clustering [20] combined with a novel talking-face detection module based on bi-directional long short-term memory (BLSTM) recurrent neural networks. Section 2 compares the approach we propose with existing work from the literature. Our novel approach to talking-face detection using recurrent neural networks is described in Section 3. The complete pipeline is described in details in Section 4, while Section 5 summarizes the first set of experiments applied to *Game Of Thrones* TV series. Finally, we conclude the paper in Section 6.

2. OVERVIEW AND RELATED WORKS

Figure 1 provides an overview of the approaches proposed in this paper. The main intuition is that, when a character is speaking, it is very likely that their face is visible and their voice is audible at the same time. Therefore, it should be possible to achieve (or at least guide) speaker diarization using *face clustering*. Obviously, the reciprocal is not true: the face of a character may be visible even if they do not speak. This is why we added the optional module dedicated to *talking-face detection* – which can be used to avoid tagging speech turns with non-speaking face labels. More details are available in Sections 3 and 4.

While a large number of papers addressed the problem of face recognition or clustering in TV series [12, 13, 23], only a handful of papers focused on speaker identification or diarization in TV series [7, 5]. [7] assumes that acoustic speaker models are available to perform supervised speaker identification. [5] is closer to our work as it aims at improv-

MM '16, October 15 - 19, 2016, Amsterdam, Netherlands

ACM 978-1-4503-3603-1/16/10...$15.00
DOI: http://dx.doi.org/10.1145/2964284.2967202

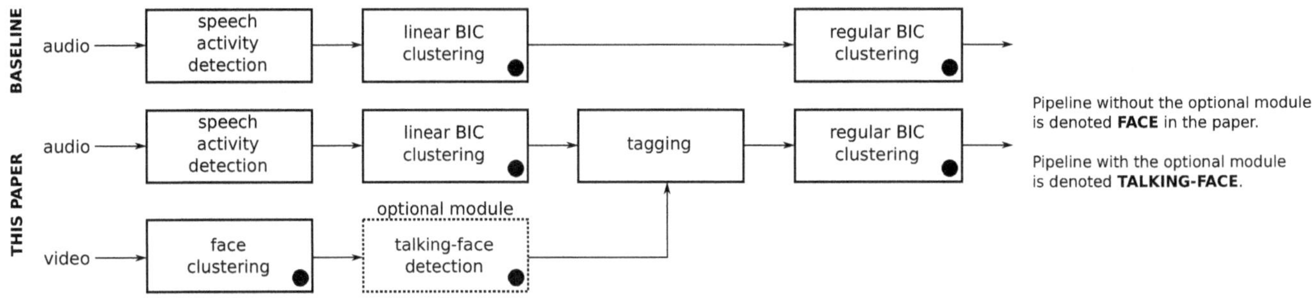

Figure 1: Overview of the proposed approaches. Every bullet ● corresponds to one hyper-parameter.

ing unsupervised acoustic speaker diarization using dialogue scenes detected automatically from repeating shot/reverse-shot patterns. Focusing on those dialogue scenes (which represents only half of the episode duration), they report a diarization error rate (DER) of 49.3% on one episode of *Game of Thrones*, even though they rely on manual speech turn segmentation. Other scenes are not processed nor part of the evaluation – DER of the full episode is therefore expected to be much higher.

Among face recognition papers referenced earlier, most of them rely on some kind of talking-face detection module to map subtitles and/or transcript to the current speaker. [12] computes the minimum pixelwise total difference between regions around the mouth determined via block matching, average it over the duration of the subtitle, and dual-threshold the resulting value into three classes: speaking, not sure, not speaking. They report a precision of around 94% and recall of 18% on this subtitle-to-face matching task. [13, 23] compute the spatial distance between lower and upper lips, apply band-pass filtering at the expected lip motion frequency (4-8Hz), accumulate it over the duration of the subtitles, and finally threshold it to perform the same task. Our talking-face detection module differs from these previous works in several ways: we do not assume that subtitles are available (and instead rely on detected acoustic speech regions) and we model this task as a sequence labeling task based on audio-visual features (instead of a binary classification task based on one single visual features).

3. TALKING-FACE DETECTION

Recurrent neural networks (RNN) and in particular those based on long short-term memory (LSTM-RNN) have been successfully applied to a wide range of classification tasks for which the discriminative information is embedded in a sequence. In particular, for (acoustic-only) voice activity detection (VAD), [14] showed that LSTM-RNN can outperform other VAD techniques. This section focuses on our first contribution: adapting the modified bidirectional long short-term memory recurrent neural networks (BLSTM-RNN) introduced in [14] to the talking-face detection problem.

3.1 Feature extraction

Each face track (defined in Section 4.2) is described by a sequence of audio-visual features, made of the concatenation of acoustic and visual features. Acoustic features are extracted every 20ms on a 32ms window. We concatenate 6 Mel-Frequency Cepstral Coefficients (MFCC), their first derivatives, their second derivatives, and the first and second derivative of the energy – leading to 20-dimensional acoustic features. Visual features are extracted every 40ms (videos are encoded at 25 frames per second) and interpolated linearly to reach a period of 20ms. We concatenate the normalized (x, y) coordinates of 18 facial landmarks [16] (those located around the lips), their first derivatives, their second derivatives, and the normalized mouth width with its first and second derivatives – leading to 111-dimensional visual features. The final 131-dimensional audio-visual features are used as input of the RNN described in the next paragraph.

3.2 Bidirectional long short-term memory recurrent neural networks

We use the modified version of the LSTM cell introduced in [14] and train the RNN using Quantum Particle Swarm Optimization (QPSO) [21] and Back-Propagation Through Time (BPTT) [24]. QPSO loss function is a weighted frame error rate defined as follows:

$$\text{loss} = (1-\alpha)\sum_{s\in S}(1-z_s) + \alpha\sum_{n\in N} z_n \tag{1}$$

where S is the set of talking-face frames, N is the set of non-talking-face frames, z is the binary output of the BLSTM-RNN classifier for each frame and α sets the relative importance between errors on the talking-face frames and errors on the non-talking-face frames. For BPTT, we used a similarly weighted version of the maximum likelihood loss function for a binary classifier. All details can be found in [14].

4. FACE-DRIVEN SPEAKER DIARIZATION

This section focuses on our second contribution: using face clustering (and optionally talking-face detection) to improve speaker diarization.

4.1 Speech detection and BIC clustering

Because we focused our work on clustering, we used reference speech activity detection as the first module of all approaches. It is obtained automatically by force-aligning manual speech transcripts with the audio stream. This first step results in a sequence of very short speech segments (one per spoken word): 230ms on average.

The same feature extraction step is used for both the *linear BIC clustering* and the *regular BIC clustering* modules: 12 MFCC coefficients and the energy are extracted every 16ms on a 32ms window. Both modules consist in the application of iterative agglomerative clustering using the Bayesian Information Criterion (BIC) as similarity measure [8]. Each iteration consists in three steps: merge the

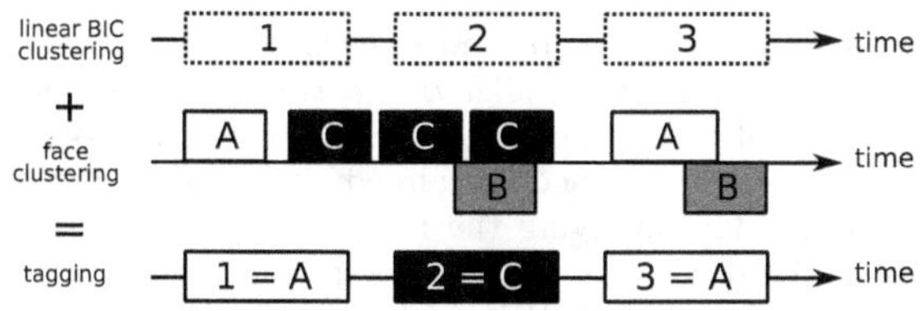

Figure 2: Each speech turn is tagged with the most co-occurring face cluster (e.g. C for turn #2).

two most similar clusters according to the Bayesian Information Criterion (BIC) [8], compute the resulting cluster model, and update the BIC criterion to all other clusters. This process is iterated until the BIC criterion is negative.

The main difference between *linear* and *regular BIC clustering* is that the former process the audio stream in chronological order and can only merge adjacent speech segments coming from the speech activity detection module. The second difference is that the BIC criterion is computed from Gaussian with diagonal covariance matrix for *linear BIC clustering*, while *regular BIC clustering* relies on full covariance matrix. Each module relies on its own penalty coefficient hyper-parameter (λ_{linear} and λ_{regular}) that controls how similar clusters must be to be mergeable.

4.2 Face tracking and clustering

The *face clustering* module in Figure 1 is actually built upon four submodules. First, shot boundaries are detected using optical flow and *displaced frame difference* [25]. Then, face tracking-by-detection is applied within each shot using a detector based on histogram of oriented gradients [10] and the correlation tracker proposed by *Danelljan et al.* [11]. Each face track is then described by its average *FaceNet* embedding and compared with all the others using Euclidean distance [20]. Finally, starting with one cluster per face track, we iteratively merge the two most similar clusters, compute the average *FaceNet* embedding of the resulting cluster and update the Euclidean distance to the other clusters. This process is repeated until the minimum distance between two clusters is higher than a threshold. Additionally, this hierarchical agglomerative clustering process is constrained not to merge co-occurring face track. Source code for this module is available in *pyannote-video* [6].

4.3 Tagging

Figure 2 illustrates what the tagging module does. In a nutshell, we propagate the labels resulting from the *face clustering* step onto co-occurring speech turns resulting from the *linear BIC clustering* step. As depicted by the dashed *talking-face detection* module in Figure 1, we tried two variants of this approach – with or without talking-face filtering. Without talking-face filtering, any face label can be propagated to the current speech turn. With talking-face filtering, only labels of talking faces are propagated.

5. EXPERIMENTS

5.1 Dataset

For this set of experiments, we relied on the reproducible corpus TVD [19] and focused on the first season of *Game Of Thrones* TV series. It contains ten episodes of approximately 55 minutes each. In particular, TVD provides the

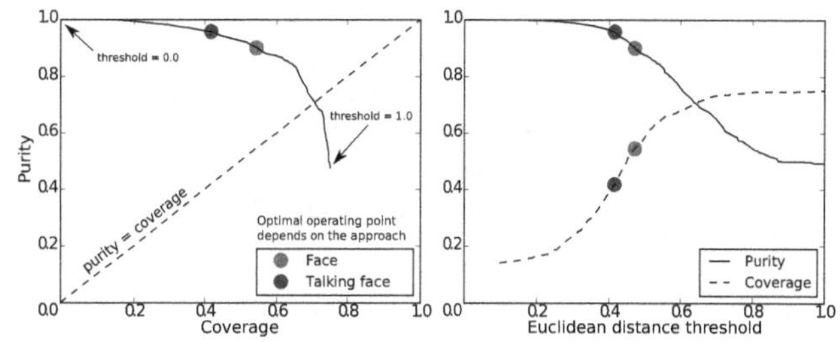

Figure 3: Performance of face track clustering.

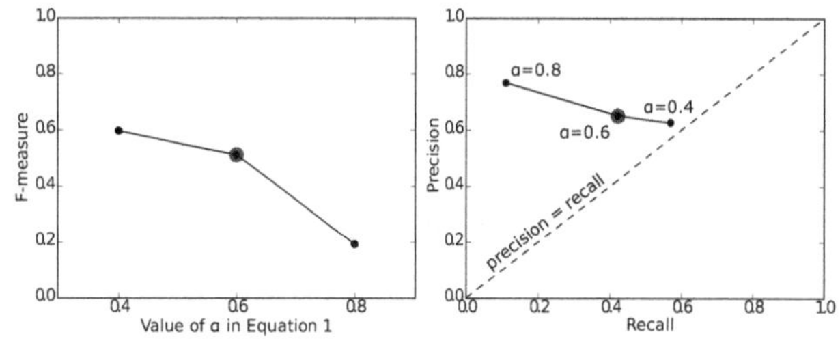

Figure 4: Performance of talking-face detection.

"who speaks when?" annotation obtained by forced alignement of the manual transcript with the audio track. Additionally, we relied on the manual face track annotation provided in [22] to train and evaluate the face clustering and talking-face detection modules.

For all experiments and unless otherwise stated, episodes 6 to 10 are used for training and reported evaluation metrics are averaged over episodes 1 to 5.

5.2 Face tracking and clustering

Figure 3 summarizes the performance obtained by the face clustering module. Pratically, we relied on *dlib* machine learning toolkit [17] for face detection [10] and tracking [11], and on *Openface* [1] for *FaceNet* embeddings [20]. Manual face track identities provided in [22] were used for evaluation.

The purity reported in Figure 3 is computed as the ratio of the accumulated total duration of the dominant class in each cluster over the accumulated total duration of each cluster. Complementarily, the coverage is the same as purity after (automatic) clusters and (manual) classes exchanged their role. A perfect clustering would lead to both purity and coverage equal to one. Setting the distance threshold to a value close to 0.0 would result in high purity and low coverage. The fact that coverage never reaches one (even with high distance threshold) is explained by the introduction of the constraint preventing co-occurring face tracks from being merged.

5.3 Talking-face detection

Figure 4 reports the performance obtained by the talking-face detection module. For each face track, the task is to decide when (if ever) the face is actually speaking. Groundtruth was generated by combining manual face track identities from [22] with *"who speaks when?"* annotations from [19]. We relied on *dlib* machine learning toolkit [17] for facial landmarks detection and *Yaafe* [18] for MFCC extraction.

Precision is computed as the ratio of the total duration

Table 1: Results (● is number of hyper-parameters).

	●	Purity	Coverage	DER
BASELINE	2	57.1 %	58.6 %	**54.5 %**
FACE	3	53.5 %	65.6 %	**53.1 %**
TALKING FACE	4	59.8 %	60.8 %	**51.8 %**

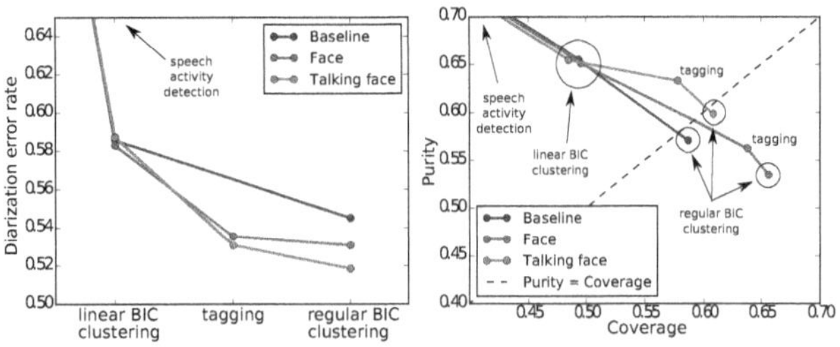

Figure 5: Behavior of tested approaches.

of face track correctly detected as speaking over the total duration of all face tracks. Recall is the ratio of the total duration of face track correctly detected as speaking over the total duration of speaking face tracks. Proper comparison of this approach with prior works on talking-face detection has yet to be done, as it was not the main focus of this paper. Note, however, that a simple baseline classifying all faces as talking would yield a precision of around 22% (i.e. the ratio of talking-faces in the corpus) and a F-measure of 36%.

5.4 Speaker diarization

Table 1 summarizes the performance obtained by the three tested speaker diarization approaches. BASELINE is the one from the upper part of Figure 1. FACE (respectively TALKING FACE) is the one from the lower part of Figure 1 without (resp. with) the *talking-face detection* module.

Diarization error rate (DER) is computed in two steps. First, the optimal one-to-one mapping between reference speaker labels and hypothesized speaker clusters is obtained using the Hungarian algorithm. Once hypothesized speaker clusters are mapped to reference speaker labels, the diarization error rate is the sum of three error rates: missed detection, false alarm and speaker confusion. Note that, in this paper, missed detection and false alarm are null because we rely on the reference speech/non-speech segmentation from [19]. Purity and coverage are defined in the same way as in Section 5.2, with the exception that speech regions replace face tracks.

For each approach, hyper-parameters were optimized jointly towards minimum diarization error rate on the training set, using tree-structured Parzen estimators [4]. Practically, we relied on the *hyperopt* hyper-parameters optimization toolkit [3]. The first observation is that the introduction of the face clustering module does improve the overall speaker diarization performance – whether non-talking faces are filtered (DER = 51.8%) or not (DER = 53.1%). Filtering out non-talking faces tends to improve both purity (+2.8%) and coverage (+2.2%); whereas keeping all faces seems to focus on improving coverage (+7.0%) at the expense of purity (−3.6%).

Figure 5 provides better insight at the internal behavior of each approach. The left (resp. right) part plots the value of the diarization error rate (resp. purity as a function of coverage) computed on the output of each module: *linear BIC clustering*, *tagging* and *regular BIC clustering*. It shows that the output of the face-driven *tagging* module in both *face* and *talking face* approaches is already better than the *baseline*, even before applying the final *regular BIC clustering* module. It also shows that *face* approach does not benefit from the final *regular BIC clustering* module as much as *talking face* does. This expected behavior can be explained by the fact that the *face tagging* module degrades purity a lot more than its *talking face tagging* counterpart – a state from which the subsequent *regular BIC clustering* step cannot recover.

Blue and green dots in Figure 3 correspond to the operating points selected through hyper-parameter optimization for the *face clustering* module of the TALKING FACE and FACE approaches respectively. The TALKING FACE approach "chooses" to stop face clustering earlier than the FACE approach does. Combined with a relatively precise *talking-face detection* module (blue dot in Figure 4), the resulting tagging module is able to increase coverage significantly (+9.1%) while leaving purity relatively stable (−3.1%).

The main limitation of the proposed approach is obviously the *linear BIC clustering* step. As a matter of fact, it appears that all three approaches converged towards the same hyper-parameter λ_{linear} that leads to a huge drop in purity (from 100% to 65%), from which subsequent clustering steps cannot (by design) recover. Future work will have to focus on this particular aspect.

6. CONCLUSIONS

In this paper, we aimed at improving audio speaker diarization applied to TV series using the visual stream. We used state-of-the-art face clustering based on neural network embeddings to initialize speaker diarization with co-occurring face labels, leading to improve diarization error rate (from 54.5% to 53.1%). Additionnaly, we designed a bi-directional long short-term memory recurrent neural network for talking-face detection and integrated it in the proposed framework to further improve the results (from 53.1% down to 51.8%).

Speaker diarization in TV series remains a scientific challenge, but achieving good results could lead to novel multimedia applications improving the audience experience. For instance, accessible subtitles as defined by BBC guidelines[1] could benefit greatly from such a multimodal speaker diarization output. For instance, one could use *"one color per speaker"*, *"horizontal positioning"* of subtitles closer to the current speaker's face thanks to the talking-face detection module, or even use mark *"single quotes for voice-over or out-of-vision speaker"* if no talking face is detected.

Future work will focus on improving the initial linear clustering (or speaker change detection) step, improving the talking-face detection module (and actually comparing it with existing approaches) and investigating joint audio-visual clustering techniques instead of the series of audio and visual clustering proposed in this paper.

Acknowledgements

This work benefited from the support of the CAMOMILE project (CHISTERA) and the MetaDaTV project (ANR).

[1] bbc.github.io/subtitle-guidelines

7. REFERENCES

[1] B. Amos, B. Ludwiczuk, and M. Satyanarayanan. Openface: A general-purpose face recognition library with mobile applications. Technical report, CMU-CS-16-118, CMU School of Computer Science, 2016.

[2] X. Anguera, S. Bozonnet, N. Evans, C. Fredouille, G. Friedland, and O. Vinyals. Speaker diarization: A review of recent research. *Audio, Speech, and Language Processing, IEEE Transactions on*, 20(2):356–370, 2012.

[3] J. Bergstra, D. Yamins, and D. D. Cox. Hyperopt: A Python Library for Optimizing the Hyperparameters of Machine Learning Algorithms. In *Proceedings of the 12th Python in Science Conference*, pages 13–20, 2013.

[4] J. Bergstra, D. Yamins, and D. D. Cox. Making a Science of Model Search: Hyperparameter Optimization in Hundreds of Dimensions for Vision Architectures. In *Proceedings of the 30th International Conference on Machine Learning, ICML 2013, Atlanta, GA, USA, 16-21 June 2013*, pages 115–123, 2013.

[5] X. Bost and G. Linares. Constrained Speaker Diarization of TV Series based on Visual Patterns. In *Spoken Language Technology Workshop (SLT), 2014 IEEE*, pages 390–395. IEEE, 2014.

[6] H. Bredin. pyannote-video: Face Detection, Tracking and Clustering in Videos. http://github.com/pyannote/pyannote-video. Accessed: 2016-07-04.

[7] H. Bredin, A. Roy, N. Pécheux, and A. Allauzen. "Sheldon speaking, bonjour!": Leveraging Multilingual Tracks for (Weakly) Supervised Speaker Identification. In *ACM MM 2014, 22nd ACM International Conference on Multimedia*, Orlando, USA, November 2014.

[8] S. Chen and P. Gopalakrishnan. Speaker, Environment and Channel Change Detection and Clustering via the Bayesian Information Criterion. In *Proc. DARPA Broadcast News Transcription and Understanding Workshop*, volume 8, pages 127–132. Virginia, USA, 1998.

[9] P. Clément, T. Bazillon, and C. Fredouille. Speaker Diarization of Heterogeneous Web Video Files: a Preliminary Study. In *Acoustics, Speech and Signal Processing (ICASSP), 2011 IEEE International Conference on*, pages 4432–4435. IEEE, 2011.

[10] N. Dalal and B. Triggs. Histograms of Oriented Gradients for Human Detection. In *Computer Vision and Pattern Recognition, 2005. CVPR 2005. IEEE Computer Society Conference on*, volume 1, pages 886–893 vol. 1, June 2005.

[11] M. Danelljan, G. Häger, F. Shahbaz Khan, and M. Felsberg. Accurate Scale Estimation for Robust Visual Tracking. In *Proceedings of the British Machine Vision Conference*. BMVA Press, 2014.

[12] M. Everingham, J. Sivic, and A. Zisserman. "Hello! My name is... Buffy" – Automatic Naming of Characters in TV Video. In *Proceedings of the British Machine Vision Conference*, 2006.

[13] M. Everingham, J. Sivic, and A. Zisserman. Taking the Bite out of Automatic Naming of Characters in TV Video. *Image and Vision Computing*, 27(5), 2009.

[14] G. Gelly and J.-L. Gauvain. Minimum Word Error Training of RNN-based Voice Activity Detection. *Interspeech*, 2015.

[15] V. Jousse, S. Petit-Renaud, S. Meignier, Y. Esteve, and C. Jacquin. Automatic named identification of speakers using diarization and asr systems. In *Acoustics, Speech and Signal Processing, 2009. ICASSP 2009. IEEE International Conference on*, pages 4557–4560. IEEE, 2009.

[16] V. Kazemi and J. Sullivan. One Millisecond Face Alignment with an Ensemble of Regression Trees. In *Proceedings of the IEEE Conference on Computer Vision and Pattern Recognition*, pages 1867–1874, 2014.

[17] D. E. King. Dlib-ml: A machine learning toolkit. *Journal of Machine Learning Research*, 10:1755–1758, 2009.

[18] B. Mathieu, S. Essid, T. Fillon, J. Prado, and G. Richard. YAAFE, an Easy to Use and Efficient Audio Feature Extraction Software. In *Proceedings of the 11th International Society for Music Information Retrieval Conference*, pages 441–446, Utrecht, The Netherlands, August 9-13 2010. http://ismir2010.ismir.net/proceedings/ismir2010-75.pdf.

[19] A. Roy, C. Guinaudeau, H. Bredin, and C. Barras. TVD: a Reproducible and Multiply Aligned TV Series Dataset. In *LREC 2014, 9th Language Resources and Evaluation Conference*, 2014.

[20] F. Schroff, D. Kalenichenko, and J. Philbin. FaceNet: a Unified Embedding for Face Recognition and Clustering. In *Proceedings of the IEEE Conference on Computer Vision and Pattern Recognition*, pages 815–823, 2015.

[21] J. Sun, X. Wu, V. Palade, W. Fang, C.-H. Lai, and W. Xu. Convergence Analysis and Improvements of Quantum-behaved Particle Swarm Optimization. *Information Sciences*, 193:81–103, 2012.

[22] M. Tapaswi, M. Bäuml, and R. Stiefelhagen. Book2Movie: Aligning Video scenes with Book chapters. In *IEEE Conference on Computer Vision and Pattern Recognition (CVPR)*, Jun. 2015.

[23] M. Tapaswi, M. Bäuml, and R. Stiefelhagen. Improved Weak Labels using Contextual Cues for Person Identification in Videos. In *IEEE International Conference on Automatic Face and Gesture Recognition (FG)*, May 2015.

[24] P. J. Werbos. Backpropagation Through Time: what it does and how to do it. *Proceedings of the IEEE*, 78(10):1550–1560, 1990.

[25] Y. Yusoff, W. Christmas, and J. Kittler. A Study on Automatic Shot Change Detection. In *Multimedia Applications, Services and Techniques*, pages 177–189. Springer, 1998.

Location-Independent WiFi Action Recognition via Vision-based Methods

Jen-Yin Chang*, Kuan-Ying Lee*, Yu-Lin Wei, Kate Ching-Ju Lin†, Winston Hsu

National Taiwan University, Taipei, Taiwan †National Chiao Tung University, Hsinchu, Taiwan
*Co-primary authors

ABSTRACT

Due to the characteristics of ubiquity, non-occlusion, privacy preservation of WiFi, many researchers have devoted to human action recognition using WiFi signals. As demonstrated in [1], Channel State Information (CSI), a fine-grained information capturing the properties of WiFi signal propagation, could be transformed into images for achieving a promising accuracy on action recognition via vision-based methods. However, from the experimental results shown in [1], the CSI is usually location dependent, which affects the recognition performance if signals are recorded in different places.

In this paper, we propose a location-dependency removal method based on Singular Value Decomposition (SVD) to eliminate the background CSI and effectively extract the channel information of signals reflected by human bodies. Experimental results show that our method considering the correlation of CSI streams could achieve promising accuracy above 90% in identifying six actions even testing in five different rooms.

1. INTRODUCTION

Action recognition aims to identify human actions automatically, which is essential to various applications. For example, in [2], Masaka et al. analyze the surveillance video for understanding what actions are performed, which is fundamental in video search and retrieval; in [3], Yan et al. work on egocentric video, which efficiently summarizes the long and redundant recorded video through activity recognition; in [4], a home video game console from Microsoft, Kinect, is proposed. It utilizes RGB-D camera to track human skeleton for users interacting with the fancy game world directly by moving body parts.

However, cameras are not feasible in every scenario. For example, cameras will breach privacy in bathroom or stop functioning in rooms without sufficient illumination. Nonetheless, action recognition is still vital in such places. For instance, prompt notice of emergency such as accidental falls could mitigate the damage. Thus, some works propose to analyze data from wearable or portable devices to detect

MM '16, October 15-19, 2016, Amsterdam, Netherlands

© 2016 ACM. ISBN 978-1-4503-3603-1/16/10...$15.00

DOI: http://dx.doi.org/10.1145/2964284.2967203

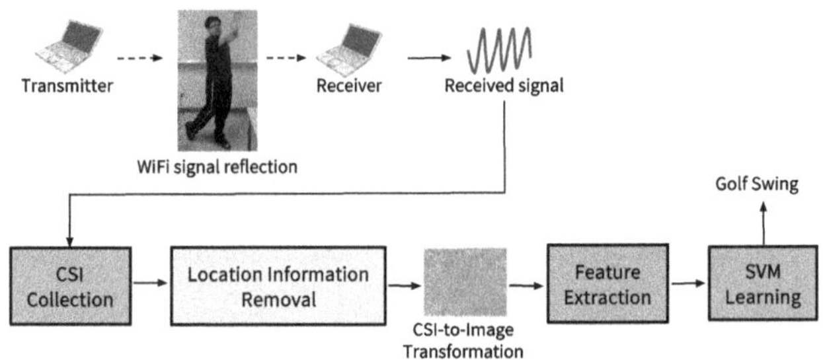

Figure 1: Framework Overview. Different from image/video-based action recognition, we utilize WiFi signals and propose location information removal method for location-independent WiFi action recognition.

user's movements [5, 6]. Still, the crucial limitation of wearable devices is the inconvenience in some scenarios like taking a shower. In comparison to previous approaches, WiFi is privacy-preserving, occlusion-free and non-contact. Also, WiFi is now almost available everywhere, making it the best choice of our media to achieve human action recognition.

In the pioneering stage, researchers analyze the frequency or amplitude changes of raw signals received by Universal Software Radio Peripheral (USRP) [7, 8]. Such raw signals, even though contain even more detailed channel information, can only be obtained by special hardware, nudging researchers toward CSI [9, 10, 11], which can, in practice, be accessed from today's commodity devices [12]. However, despite promising results, most prior works involve ad-hoc domain knowledge specifically related to the defined scenarios such as [9] primarily designed for fall detection, while [1] aims at investigating the general framework using the CSI-transformed image. However, their proposed framework cannot remove location information intrinsically embedded in CSI. That is, their performance drops if testing data are collected from different locations. Hence, we propose a location-independent method to remove static environment information that dominates the whole CSI, and thereby obtain the classifiers focusing more on human movements.

The rest of the paper is organized as follows. We give a background in Section 2 introducing how action recognition via CSI is realized, what is the relation between CSI and visual appearance, and why location information is embedded in CSI. The details of the proposed location-independent action recognition algorithm is described in Section 3. We show our experimental results in Section 4, and, finally, conclude this work in Section 5.

2. BACKGROUND

2.1 Channel State Information

As a transmitter (Tx) emits signals to the air, signals bump into objects and go through several reflections, absorptions, scatterings caused by human or objects before reaching a receiver (Rx). We can simply formulate the whole process as $Y = HX$, where X is the transmitted signals, Y is the received signals, and H is CSI, denoting the total influence of the environment to X. In the modern 802.11n protocol, the CSI contains both the amplitude and phase information of each OFDM (Orthogonal Frequency-Division Multiplexing) subcarrier. Due to the space limitation, we refer the readers to [13] for more details about OFDM.

2.2 CSI Amplitude and Visual Appearance

From [11], we know that the channel of a sub-carrier with frequency f at time t, denoted by $H(f,t)$, can be expressed as the sum of the channels of all static paths and dynamic paths as follows:

$$H(f,t) = e^{-j2\pi\Delta ft}\left(H_s(f) + H_d(f,t)\right), \quad (1)$$

where $H_s(f)$ is the sum channel of the static paths, $H_d(f,t)$ is the sum channel of the dynamic paths and Δf is the frequency offset between Tx and Rx. Specifically, the dynamic paths can be represented as $H_d(f,t) = \sum_{k\in P_d} a_k(f,t)e^{-j\frac{2\pi d_k(t)}{\lambda}}$, where P_d denotes the set of all the dynamic paths, $a_k(f,t)$ is the attenuation of the k_{th} path at frequency f and time t, and $d_k(t)$ is the distance of k_{th} path between Tx to Rx. Now we can see that the distance of k_{th} path is the main factor affecting the time-varying CSI. If an object moves at a certain speed which causes v_k of path k, $d_k(t)$ is equal to $d_k(0) + v_k t$, as a result altering $H(f,t)$ over time.

To provide more intuitive insight, we rewrite Eq. (1) as the following expression:

$$|H(f,t)|^2 = \quad (2)$$

$$\sum_{k\in P_d} 2|H_s(f)a_k(f,t)|\cos\left(\frac{2\pi v_k t}{\lambda} + \frac{2\pi d_k(0)}{\lambda} + \phi_{sk}\right) + C(f,t) +$$

$$\sum_{\substack{k,l\in P_d\\ k\neq l}} 2|a_k(f,t)a_l(f,t)|\cos\left(\frac{2\pi(v_k - v_l)t}{\lambda} + \frac{2\pi(d_k(0) - d_l(0))}{\lambda} + \phi_{kl}\right),$$

where $C(f,t)$ is a constant given a sub-carrier frequency and time, and ϕ_{sk} represents the initial phase offset between the aggregate static path s and a dynamic path k. (See [11] for the detailed derivation.) Then, we can observe that the frequency of sinusoidal waves in Eq. (2) is determined by v_k, which means that different speeds of actions cause different phase changes, and thus render various patterns on the transformed image, as shown in Figure 2.

2.3 Location-Dependent Information in CSI

Due to the property of CSI mentioned above, [1] transforms CSI into images for extracting visual features such as SIFT and Gabor. However, their results show performance degradation as involving data from different locations.

To elaborate on why CSI embeds location information, we transform a frequency-domain CSI profile collected from our testbed to the time domain by inverse fast Fourier transformation. As shown in Figure 3, the first tap usually represents the channel of the line-of-sight path (with the shortest delay), and, hence, has the strongest amplitude. The rest of weaker taps consist of other static paths, reflected by nearby objects, and dynamic paths, reflected by human bodies. We can observe that, even after removing the strongest line-of-sight path, the remaining signal patterns in the two rooms are still very different because the reflected static paths change with environments and, more importantly, still have a relatively strong power, as compared to those reflected by human. Hence, we argue that, to enable location-dependent recognition, we should remove those dominant environmental information and only transform the CSI of dynamic paths into images.

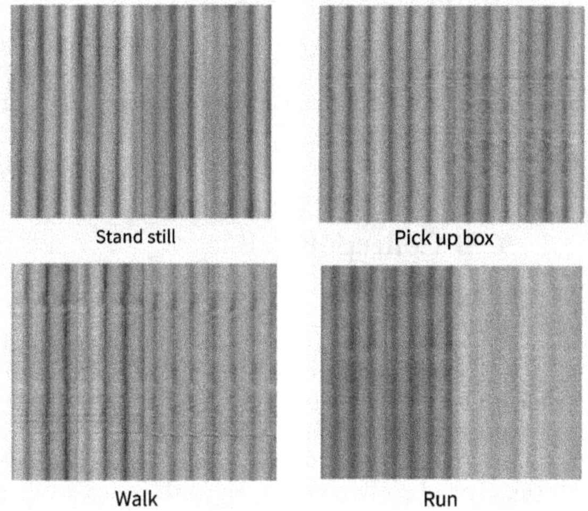

Figure 2: Examples of CSI-transformed images (X-axis: 30 sub-carriers × 4 antenna pairs, Y-axis: time stamps.)

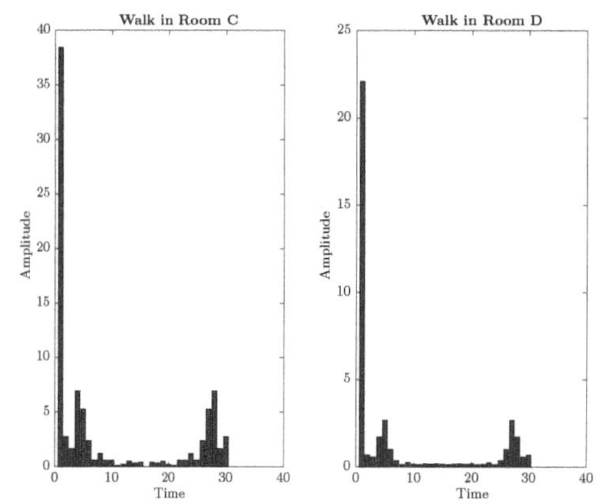

Figure 3: Each tap represents the aggregated time-domain channel of the paths with similar distances. A smaller time-domain index corresponds the signals from shorter paths, thereby causing a shorter delay.

3. PROPOSED METHOD

The main goal of our work is to develop a location-independent method that can allow the training model to learn human actions, exclusive of dominant environments. Our proposed method, considering transforming CSI to more representative space for background removal, is described in details in the following sections.

3.1 CSI Collection

We set up two laptops, ASUS U80v as Tx and Fujitsu SH560 as Rx, with two antennas for each of them. To operate in the injection mode, we install an Intel 5300 NIC in both laptops operating on channel 100, centered at frequency 5.5 GHz, which allows us to collect traces with a more stable data rate of around 2000 samples/sec. Each antenna pair produces CSI with dimension t (samples) by 30 (number of sub-carriers). Since there are two antennas at both Tx and Rx, we have four antenna pairs, generating four sets of CSI for each action recorded. We let d denote the total number of subcarriers $N_{\text{sub-carriers}} = 30 \times 4 = 120$.

3.2 Location Information Removal

In [11], Wei et al. consider the correlation between CSI streams and point out the fact that any effects to signals would be presented across CSI streams, inspiring us to apply SVD on CSI. In image processing techniques, SVD is an attractive algebraic transformation used to manipulate an image in two distinctive sub-spaces, i.e., data spaces and noise spaces. For example, we can apply SVD on an image and represent an image using low rank approximation to achieve image compression [14]. If we treat the CSI profile as a matrix H of dimension $t \times d$, after applying SVD, H is factorized into three matrices, U, S and V, where U is a $t \times t$ orthogonal matrix, V is a $d \times d$ orthogonal matrix, and S is a $t \times d$ matrix with the diagonal elements representing the singular values of H.

We can formulate low rank approximation of H as follows:

$$H' = \sum_{i=1}^{k} s_i u_i v_i^T = s_1 u_1 v_1^T + s_2 u_2 v_2^T + \cdots + s_k u_k v_k^T, \quad (3)$$

in which k is usually smaller than d for compression and s_i means the singular values (SV) in decreasing order corresponding to a pair of singular vectors u_i and v_i. Intuitively, this equation shows that H is a sum of different bases with its importance score for approximating the original H.

As shown in Figure 4, we can observe that if we set all SV in S to zero except for the largest one, denoted by $S = S_{SV_1 \neq 0}$, and reconstruct the channel information by $H_{SV_1 \neq 0} = U S_{SV_1 \neq 0} V^T$, then, the reconstructed channel $H_{SV_1 \neq 0}$ would be similar the CSI recorded in the quite environment, as shown in the first example of Figure 2. This example shows that the largest SV packs most of energy corresponding to the static paths. Therefore, we set the largest SV to zero so that the background can be mostly removed and the reconstructed channel $H_{SV_1=0}$ preserves only the human action part.

We illustrate how the SVD-based background removal method improves the performance by the examples shown in Figure 5. Before SVD is applied, even when the same action is performed, the power distribution of the whole CSI differs due to distinct static paths in different rooms, leading the models trained in one place not able to recognize actions recorded in other places. After removing the largest SV, as shown in the right ones in Figure 5, the remaining parts from two different rooms resemble each other. We will later investigate, via experiments, the two settings: (1) apply SVD on each set of CSI with dimension $t \times 30$ separately, and (2) apply SVD on all the CSI streams with dimension $t \times 120$, and explore which option performs better.

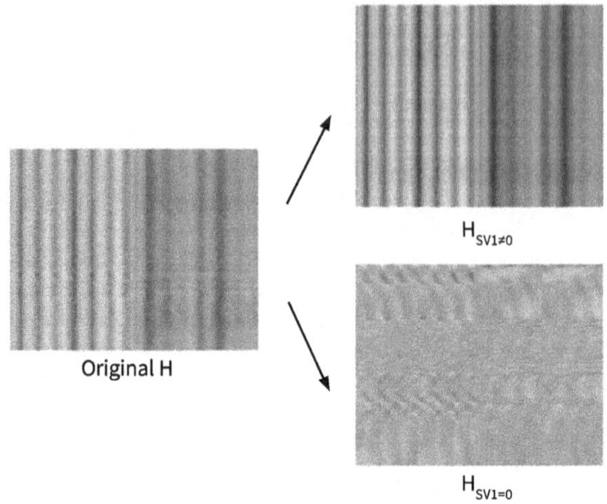

Figure 4: CSI-transformed images of picking up box from different reconstructed channels H.

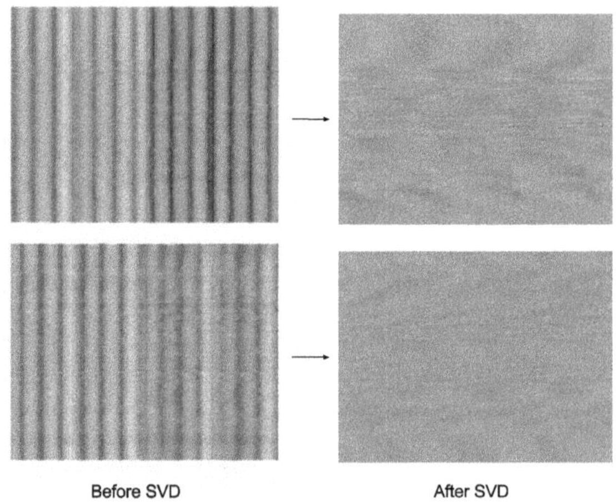

Figure 5: CSI-transformed images of the same action (pick up box) from two different rooms.

3.3 Feature Extraction for SVM Learning

After the reconstructed H is plotted, we obtain an image exclusive of noise and background. With the resemblance of textual appearances, the Gabor filters [15] are the first feature extractor we would like to experiment on. A Gabor filter is defined by a plane sine wave multiplied by a Gaussian function. To handle different textual appearances, a filter bank is needed by setting multiple scales and orientations. These filters are convoluted with a transformed image. When a local patch on the image resembles the filter, a high response will be obtained. Finally, a response map is produced, of which we then take two statistics, mean and standard deviation. In our implementation, we set $\#scale$,

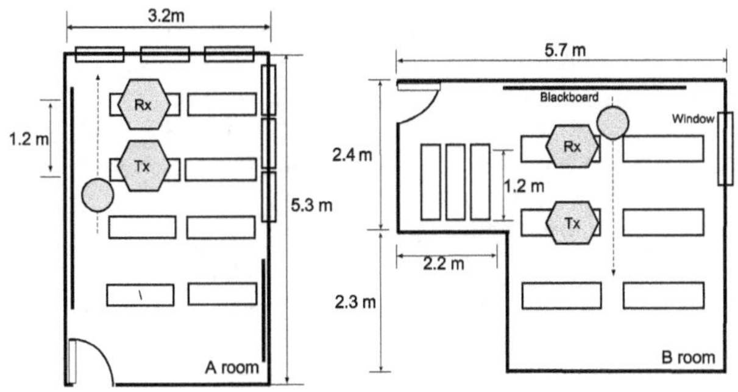

Figure 6: Examples of the seminar rooms. Subject performs actions along the trajectories and in circles.

Room	A	B	C	D	E
# of data	120	120	120	120	120
None-4SVM	30.00%	29.17%	26.67%	30.00%	30.83%
SVD30-1SVM	99.17%	97.50%	97.50%	96.67%	96.67%
SVD30-4SVM	98.33%	96.67%	99.17%	97.50%	95.83%
SVD120-1SVM	99.17%	98.33%	99.17%	99.17%	99.17%
SVD120-4SVM	99.17%	99.17%	98.33%	99.17%	100.00%

Table 1: Cross validation accuracy of each room. (Both training and testing data are at the same room.)

#orientation and size of the Gabor filters to 8, 6 and 15, respectively, which usually produce better accuracy. Hence, the dimension of our final Gabor feature is $8 \times 6 \times 2 = 96$.

For each antenna pair, we obtain a feature vector, so in total we have four feature vectors. In this early stage, we simply pick linear SVM as the classifier. In experiments, we investigate if data from different antenna pairs provide complementary information by two fusion schemes: (1) train one classifier using all four feature vectors, or (2) train four classifiers, each using one feature vector.

4. EXPERIMENTS

4.1 Dataset

We collect our dataset in five seminar rooms, such as the two shown in Figure 6, to verify if our method could recognize actions from different places. We define six actions: *Stand still*, *Walk*, *Run*, *Pick up box*, *Golf swing*, and *Jump*. A single subject performs each action 20 times so in total we have 120 traces for each room. All actions are performed in a 5-second period, each generating four sets of CSI with dimension $t \times 30$ and roughly more than 2000 samples/sec. We then transform them into four images of size 576×432.

4.2 Results

For each room, we evaluate the performance by 10-fold cross validation, as accuracy shown in Table 1. We experiment on four settings, in which SVDx-ySVM means applying SVD on x sub-carriers and training y SVM classifiers. Details about the settings are described in Section 3. If we do not apply SVD on CSI, performance debases significantly due to noises and background interference, showing that our method can also remove noises. With our setting and denoise strategy, the performance of 10-fold cross validation in one room is remarkably better than those in [1].

Testing room	A	B	C	D	E
None-4SVM	16.67%	16.67%	16.67%	16.67%	16.67%
SVD30-1SVM	80.83%	89.17%	89.17%	99.17%	98.33%
SVD30-4SVM	84.17%	53.33%	83.33%	90.83%	96.67%
SVD120-1SVM	76.67%	91.67%	97.50%	98.33%	95.83%
SVD120-4SVM	84.17%	75.83%	81.67%	84.17%	98.33%

Table 2: Accuracy of leave-one-out testing (all other rooms as training data).

Testing room	A	B	C	D	E
Train with 1 room	66.67%	40.00%	43.33%	31.67%	71.67%
Train with 2 rooms	66.67%	88.33%	95.83%	91.67%	96.67%
Train with 3 rooms	74.17%	95.00%	95.83%	95.83%	98.33%
Train with 4 rooms	76.67%	91.67%	97.50%	98.33%	96.67%

Table 3: Accuracy on SVD120-1SVM of increasing amount of training data (other rooms as training data).

Then, we also conduct cross room experiments with one room being testing data and others being training data, as shown in Table 2. The results of none pre-processing set are not even better than random guess, while those applying SVD achieve a promising accuracy. Moreover, we can observe that SVD120 outperforms SVD30 in average performance, inferring that 120 sub-carriers considered together capture more human action information. However, the results show that both fusion schemes produce similar performance.

Finally, we would like to explore whether the amount of training data affects the accuracy. Since the SVD120-1SVM obtains the better average performance in the previous experiment, we only list the results using SVD120-1SVM in Table 3. The results among all rooms show tendency that when more training data are involved, the higher accuracy may be achieved, implying the model is improved by investigating more data.

5. CONCLUSION

We observe the change of environments caused by human actions leads to specific fluctuation patterns on the CSI-transformed image. And, as presented in [1], applying vision-based methods on the image to achieve human action recognition is promising.

To remove the location dependency embedded in CSI, we propose a location-independent method to generalize the previous methods so that actions recorded in different locations could still be recognized by the trained classifiers.

In the future, we will investigate end-to-end training through deep neural network (DNN) models, such as convolutional neural networks which boost a prominent performance in image recognition tasks. Instead of hand-crafted features, we believe that we could achieve a better understanding of WiFi signals and identify more fine-grained human activities by DNN-based models.

Acknowledgement

This work is supported by grants MOST 104-2622-8-002-002, sponsored by MediaTek Inc, MOST 105-2633-E-002-001, NTU-105R104045, by NTU IoX Center, and MOST 104-2221-E-002-0490.

6. REFERENCES

[1] Jen-Yin Chang, Kuan-Yin Lee, Kate Ching-Ju Lin, and Winston Hsu. Wifi action recognition via vision-based methods. In *Acoustics, Speech and Signal Processing (ICASSP), 2016 IEEE International Conference on*. IEEE, 2016.

[2] Masaki Takahashi, Masahide Naemura, Mahito Fujii, and Shin'ichi Satoh. Human action recognition in crowded surveillance video sequences by using features taken from key-point trajectories. In *Computer Vision and Pattern Recognition Workshops (CVPRW), 2011 IEEE Computer Society Conference on*, pages 9–16. IEEE, 2011.

[3] Yan Yan, Elisa Ricci, Gaowen Liu, and Nicu Sebe. Egocentric daily activity recognition via multitask clustering. *Image Processing, IEEE Transactions on*, 24(10):2984–2995, 2015.

[4] Jamie Shotton, Toby Sharp, Alex Kipman, Andrew Fitzgibbon, Mark Finocchio, Andrew Blake, Mat Cook, and Richard Moore. Real-time human pose recognition in parts from single depth images. *Communications of the ACM*, 56(1):116–124, 2013.

[5] Pierluigi Casale, Oriol Pujol, and Petia Radeva. Human activity recognition from accelerometer data using a wearable device. In *Pattern Recognition and Image Analysis*, pages 289–296. Springer, 2011.

[6] Muhammad Shoaib, Stephan Bosch, Ozlem Durmaz Incel, Hans Scholten, and Paul JM Havinga. A survey of online activity recognition using mobile phones. *Sensors*, 15(1):2059–2085, 2015.

[7] Qifan Pu, Sidhant Gupta, Shyamnath Gollakota, and Shwetak Patel. Whole-home gesture recognition using wireless signals. In *Proceedings of the 19th annual international conference on Mobile computing & networking*, pages 27–38. ACM, 2013.

[8] Rajalakshmi Nandakumar, Bryce Kellogg, and Shyamnath Gollakota. Wi-fi gesture recognition on existing devices. *arXiv preprint arXiv:1411.5394*, 2014.

[9] Chunmei Han, Kaishun Wu, Yuxi Wang, and Lionel M Ni. Wifall: Device-free fall detection by wireless networks. In *INFOCOM, 2014 Proceedings IEEE*, pages 271–279. IEEE, 2014.

[10] Yan Wang, Jian Liu, Yingying Chen, Marco Gruteser, Jie Yang, and Hongbo Liu. E-eyes: device-free location-oriented activity identification using fine-grained wifi signatures. In *Proceedings of the 20th annual international conference on Mobile computing and networking*, pages 617–628. ACM, 2014.

[11] Wei Wang, Alex X Liu, Muhammad Shahzad, Kang Ling, and Sanglu Lu. Understanding and modeling of wifi signal based human activity recognition. In *Proceedings of the 21st Annual International Conference on Mobile Computing and Networking*, pages 65–76. ACM, 2015.

[12] Daniel Halperin, Wenjun Hu, Anmol Sheth, and David Wetherall. Tool release: gathering 802.11 n traces with channel state information. *ACM SIGCOMM Computer Communication Review*, 41(1):53–53, 2011.

[13] Taewon Hwang, Chenyang Yang, Gang Wu, Shaoqian Li, and Geoffrey Ye Li. Ofdm and its wireless applications: a survey. *Vehicular Technology, IEEE Transactions on*, 58(4):1673–1694, 2009.

[14] Rowayda A Sadek. Svd based image processing applications: state of the art, contributions and research challenges. *arXiv preprint arXiv:1211.7102*, 2012.

[15] Javier R Movellan. Tutorial on gabor filters. *Open Source Document*, 2002.

INRS Audiovisual Quality Dataset

Edip Demirbilek
Institut National de la Recherche Scientifique
800, de La Gauchetière
Montréal (Québec), Canada H5A 1K6
edip.demirbilek@emt.inrs.ca

Jean-Charles Grégoire
Institut National de la Recherche Scientifique
800, de La Gauchetière
Montréal (Québec), Canada H5A 1K6
gregoire@emt.inrs.ca

ABSTRACT

We present the INRS audiovisual quality dataset made of 160 unique configurations for audiovisual content including various media compression and network distortion parameters such as video frame rate, quantization and noise reduction parameters, and packet loss rate. The compression and network distortion parameter range values are selected to match real-time communications use cases. The H.264 video codec in 720p resolution and the AMR-WB audio codec are used for encoding video and audio streams. Thirty observers have rated the overall audiovisual quality on the Absolute Category Rating (ACR) 5-level quality scale in a controlled environment. The dataset includes MOS values, packet loss rates measured at bit stream level for both video and audio streams, compression parameters and various packet header information. We have used open source software for producing source audiovisual sequences, end-to-end streaming and a custom video player. These tools and the dataset are free to public access for research and development purposes.

CCS Concepts

•Information systems → Multimedia databases; Multimedia streaming; •Networks → Network measurement; *Network performance analysis;*

Keywords

Perceived Quality; Audiovisual Quality Dataset; MOS;

1. INTRODUCTION

The standard way of measuring perceived quality is to conduct subjective tests where several observer rates the system as a whole or rates individual system components on a continuous or discrete scale. However defining service quality by conducting subjective tests is resource intensive and not feasible in real-time communications. In order to develop models for accurate quality estimation, we need a reference point, in the form of datasets of audiovisual material at several quality levels. The existing audiovisual quality datasets have been created for streaming services in mind and do not span the range of configurations to train and validate the perceived quality estimation models in real-time communications. In this research, we present a dataset of audiovisual material with subjective scores for a wide range of audiovisual quality parameter values carefully selected to reflect real-time communication scenarios. Both the dataset [1] and the tools [2][3] used to create the dataset are free to public for research and development purposes.

The rest of this paper is organized as follows. In section 2, we list publicly available audiovisual quality datasets and compare them with the INRS audiovisual quality dataset created in this research. In section 3 we explain the INRS audiovisual quality dataset in details. In section 4 we analyze the dataset and discuss how certain parameters influence the perceived quality. We sum up the work in the conclusion section.

2. EXISTING AUDIOVISUAL DATASETS

Note first that the TVM [4] and P.NAMS training and validation [4] datasets have led to ITU-T standards P.1201 [9] and and G.1071 [7]. However they are not listed below since they are not open to public access at this time.

University of Plymouth Dataset (PLYM): Goudarzi et al. [5] have created an audiovisual quality database to discover methods for audiovisual quality predictions for video calls for wireless applications. They have conducted subjective tests for 60 audio, 60 video and 60 audiovisual test conditions. They have used 6 low-motion and different spatial complexity video sequences where each video had a 176×144 resolution and lasted between 7 and 14 seconds. They have used 2 video frame rates and 5 packet loss rates. The videos were encoded with the H.263 video codec and the G.711 μlaw audio codec. Absolute Category Rating (ACR) [8] with a discrete 9-level quality scale for low bit-rate evaluations was used during the experiments. They have conducted subjective tests to assess audio, video and audiovisual quality with 16 observers in each part.

TUM 1080p50 Dataset (TUM): Keimel et al. [10] have created subjective quality datasets for high definition videos in 1080p25 and 1080p50 formats. From these datasets, only the 1080p50 dataset consisted of both video and audio sequences. Five 10 seconds long source video sequences were encoded with the H.264/AVC video codec, each with one of the four chosen bitrates depending on the motion complexity of the source sequences in the range of 2 Mbit/s to 40 Mbit/s. The subjective test was carried with a projector and a 7.1 surround sound system following the single-

MM '16, October 15-19, 2016, Amsterdam, Netherlands
© 2016 ACM. ISBN 978-1-4503-3603-1/16/10. . . $15.00
DOI: http://dx.doi.org/10.1145/2964284.2967204

Table 1: Publicly Available Audiovisual Quality Datasets

	PLYM [5]	TUM [10]	VQEG [13][14]	Vienna [15]	VTT [11]	INRS
Sequences	6	5	5	19	12	1
Duration(s)	7 - 14	10	10	8 - 15	10	42
Motion	Low	Low - High	Low - High	Low - High	Low - High	Low
Bitrates	1x per Seq	4x per Seq	3x per Seq	1x per Seq	1x per seq	4x per Seq
Resolutions	144p	1080p	480p	480p	480p, 720p, 1080p	720p
Frame Rates	8, 15	50	30	25	25-30	4x (10 - 25)
PLR %	5x (0.01-0.20)	No	No	No	5x (0.3 - 4.8)	5x (0 - 5)
Mean Loss Burst	No	No	No	No	1.0, 2.0, 3.0	No
Noise Reduction	No	No	No	No	No	2x
Video Codec	H.263	H.264	H.264	H.264	H.264	H.264
Audio Codec	G.711	PCM	AAC	PCM	AAC	AMR-WB
Audio MOS	60	No	No	No	125	No
Video MOS	60	No	No	No	125	No
Audiovisual MOS	60	20	60 (per lab)	No	125	160
Observers per Test	16	21	9-35	18	24	30
Rating Scale	9	11	5	11	5	5

stimulus SSMM methodology. Twenty-one observers participated in the study and rated the perceived quality for 20 different data points using a discrete 11-level quality scale from 0 to 10. The encoding impairments introduced into the videos were blurring, visible blocking or ringing artifacts, and flicker and similar effects.

VQEG Dataset (VQEG): Pinson et al. [14] [13] have conducted subjective tests on the same audiovisual material at six different international laboratories to find out the most appropriate way to perform audiovisual quality testing. Overall ten different datasets were produced. Each dataset contained subjective scores for ten audiovisual source sequences lasting 10 seconds. Eight of audiovisual source sequences contained music or singing in English, and two contained speech with background noise. The video sequences had a 640x480 video resolution and a 30 fps frame rate. The H.264/AVC video codec with 6 bitrate levels was used for encoding. The Advanced Audio Coding (AAC) was used to encode audio streams at 8, 32, and 64 kbps. For each audio and video sequence, three coding qualities are selected: high, medium, and low coding quality. The experiment included five randomly picked impaired variant of each source and the original source sequences. Observers have rated the overall quality of 60 video clips on the ACR using a 5-point discrete quality rating scale. In each lab, a different number of observers, between 9 and 35, took part in the experiment. The authors inferred that the number of observers was the most substantial control variable for a reproducible subjective experiment. They have recommended to have 24 or more observers for ACR tests and to have 35 observers in the public environment to get the same Student's t-test sensitivity.

Made for Mobile Dataset (Vienna): Robitza et al. [15] have created a video dataset especially designed to evaluate content production rules and video quality between mobile and television. The Made for Mobile Database consisted of 19 pairs of extracted video sequences from 22 professionally produced clips. Researchers designed the experiment based on pair comparisons. 18 observers took part in the experiment. The experiment consisted of the pair of video clips: in each pair, one version made for mobile and another version made for television. The durations of the files were between 8-15 seconds. H.264 video codec's baseline profile used to encode the videos at an average bit rate of 500 Kbit/s and at the picture size of 854x480. The video sequence multiplexed with uncompressed PCM audio.

VTT Dataset (VTT): Maki et al. [11] have created an audiovisual quality dataset to predict the audiovisual quality in streaming services. They have conducted audiovisual quality assessment tests using H.264 video and AAC audio streams in streaming services. They have analyzed the influence of several quality factors. The video sequences were encoded with the H.264 baseline profile into different bitrates depending on their resolution. The audio was encoded with the AAC codec at two different bitrates. They have collected subjective audio, video and audiovisual scores in one assessment session from 24 observers for 125 streamed video sequences. Video samples varied by the impact of resolution, movement quantity (MQ), packet loss rate, and mean loss burst size. They have altered the Degradation Category Rating (DCR) method to collect audio, video and audiovisual ratings in one session. The content selected with the low, medium and high movement quantity.

Existing audiovisual datasets are invaluable for developing perceived quality estimation models for one-way streaming based services. However, they are not useful for real-time communication mainly because they have different scope. This research specifically targets one-to-one real-time communication and explores a number of parameters typically neglected in these datasets.

We often see the terms low, middle and high quality being used to address the various bitrates. This is vague for real-time communications where we need to be more specific about the encoder settings used and need to explicitly mention the quantization settings. It is tempting to address three motion complexity, three video resolutions levels and multiple content in the same subjective dataset. However, that approach significantly lessens the effective number of data points per motion complexity, resolution level and content type because of the practical limits. Audio and video codecs used influence the results obtained as well. The AAC audio codec or uncompressed audio are often used because they extend to music. However, in the telecommunication domain, a speech codec like Adaptive Multi-Rate Wide-Band (AMR-WB) is more often used. In this research, we concentrate on low motion complexity and a 720p reso-

Table 2: Media Compression parameters and Network impairments

	Video	Audio
FPS	10, 15, 20, 25	Mono, 16kHz, 24 kbps
QP	23, 27, 31, 35	Mono, 16kHz, 24 kbps
NR	0, 999	Mono, 16kHz, 24 kbps
PLR (%)	0, 0.1, 0.5, 1, 5	0, 0.1, 0.5, 1, 5

lution level only to produce the maximum number of data points in parameter space. We have kept frame rate and quantization range as large as possible alongside noise filter and network packet loss rate. We have also used AMR-WB to encode speech-only audio streams.

3. INRS AUDIOVISUAL DATASET (INRS)

The dataset has been designed to span the most important compression and network distortion influence factors. These factors are typically video frame rate, video quantization, filters and network packet loss rate. From the field study we have noted the range of these parameters for the H.264 video encoding as follows: (0, 0.1, 0.5, 1 and 5%) for network packet loss rate in both video and audio streams, (10, 15, 20 and 25 fps) for video frame rate, (23, 27, 31 and 35) for quantization, and (0 and 999) for the noise reduction filter.

3.1 Video Sequences and Test Setup

The original audiovisual sequence, ntia_HeadShoulders-Female15_original.avi file, has been downloaded from the Consumer Digital Video Library [12]. The video consists of low motion content with speech similar to a typical one-to-one audiovisual conversation.

The original 42 seconds long audiovisual source was encoded with the H.264/AVC video codec and the AMR-WB audio codec multiplexed into a 3gp video container with the GStreamer open source multimedia framework [16] to produce 32 reference audiovisual files. These reference files had various qualities in terms of selected video frame rate (FPS), quantization parameter (QP) and noise reduction (NR) values. These values are listed in Table 2. Video streams were encoded with the constrained-baseline profile using 720p progressive video resolution. Audio encoding settings were kept the same -mono channel, 16 kHz sample rate and 24kbps bit rate- for all audiovisual sequences.

One important setting that influences the overall perceived quality is the frequent use of I-frames. In the previously mentioned datasets, there is an I-frame every 1-2 seconds because of motion complexity as well as for uniformly spreading impairments under network packet loss. However, from a field study in one-to-one real-time communications we know that the duration between two following I-frames can be up-to the order of minutes. In this research, we have kept the default value for the I-frame periods, 10 s, for the low-motion videos set by the video encoder. This duration then obliged us to customize our test method.

The test sequences were prepared before the assessment by recording RTP-based video streams transmitted over an emulated network. The videos were streamed and recorded with the GStreamer based custom developed software which has enabled us to gather detailed RTCP statistics and report the exact network packet loss values for video and audio streams separately. This software is free to public access [2]. The Netem network emulator was deployed to produce net-

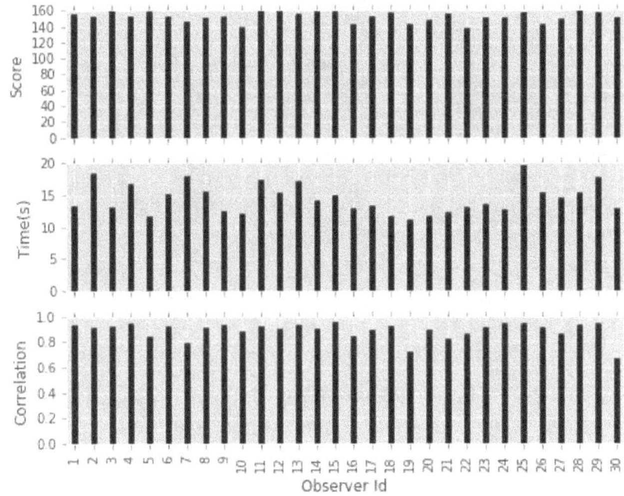

Figure 1: Accepted Subjective Scores, Average Time to Rate and Pearson Correlation Coefficient per Observer.

work packet loss conditions. Network packet loss was only activated after the first second of the audio and video transmission. This allowed us to get more realistic results. 160 unique combinations of compression and network impairments were captured in distinct A/V files. A custom video player was developed to collect the subjective scores [3].

3.2 Testing Methodology

Eleven female and nineteen male observers, ranging between 20 and 48 years old, took part in the study. Each observer was given written instructions in English and asked to rate the overall audiovisual quality on the 5-point ACR categorical quality scale. This scale tend to have a hedonic nature [17]. In order to reduce the potential biases introduced by the hedonic judgment, we took measures that are explained through the text below. Observers completed the tests in a sound isolated environment using headphones and a computer. Viewing and listening conditions mentioned in P.911 [8] were followed as close as possible. Observers were allowed to submit their subjective scores only after watching and listening to the first 10 seconds of video sequences. This period was selected because of the I-frame interval. The order of the presented sequences was drawn randomly before assessment but was the same for all observers. Observers at first performed a training session rating the quality of the various audiovisual files created from the same original sequence. Because of the high number of test conditions, observers completed the tests in two sessions. Each session took about 45 minutes and consisted of 4 parts to allow observers to have frequent pauses if needed. In each session, in the first two parts, 80 videos were rated by the observers. In the third and fourth parts, previously seen videos in the same session were rated again. Rating the same videos in the same session is done in order to reduce the bias due to mood [17]. This allowed us to collect two ACR scores for each file from each observer and measure the consistency of each observer independently. We have rejected both ACR scores for the same file from the same observers when the difference between both ACR scores was more than 1 by value. In Figure 1, the total number of accepted scores, the average time to rate as well as the Pearson correlation between the individual scores and the MOS values for each

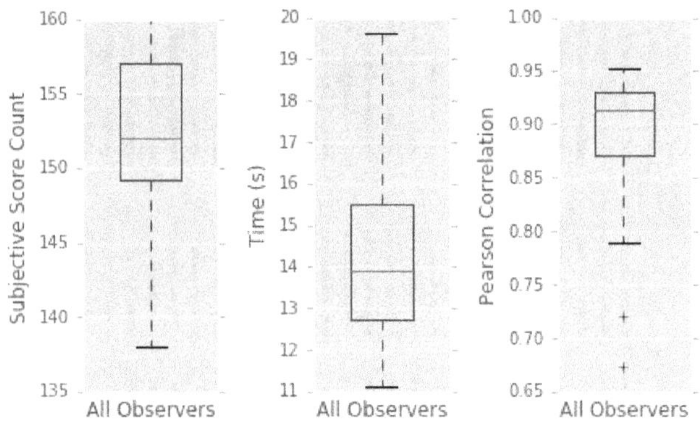

Figure 2: Variation for Accepted Subjective Scores Count, Average Time to Rate and Pearson Correlation Coefficient.

observer is given. When we look into the detailed scores submitted by each observer, specifically the observers that have 10 and more scores rejected, we observe short time periods where there are burst of rejected scores. This information shows that observers were not very attentive to the test during these short periods of time. Variation for accepted subjective scores count, the average time to rate and Pearson correlation coefficient for all observers is given in Figure 2. Here, the box extends from the lower to upper quartile values of the data with the line at the median and the whiskers extend from the box to show the range of the data. Flier points are those past the end of the whiskers (outliers) [6]. At the beginning of the first session, each observer was tested for normal visual acuity and color vision and it was noted that the observer with the id 20 had the red-green color deficiency.

3.3 Analysis

Figure 3 shows the variation in MOS value for various packet loss rate, video frame rate, quantization parameter and noise reduction values. Please note that each subfigure shows the variation in one factor in isolation from the other factors. The change in the network packet loss rate has dramatic effects on the perceived quality. Both the video frame rate and the quantization parameter, given the value range, have a moderate influence on the MOS value. Considering the best values for the lowest frame rate and quantization parameter that generate the smallest video bitrate, it seems that video frame rate has a minor advantage over the quantization parameter. However it is important to remember that this advantage is small and bound to specific parameter combinations. Detailed modeling attempts would reveal the complex relationship between those parameters. Changing the noise reduction parameter has the smallest effect on the outcome compared to the change in other parameters and should be used as the least favoured.

4. CONCLUSION

We have developed the INRS audiovisual quality dataset made of subjective scores for the combination of video frame rate, video quantization, noise reduction parameters and network packet loss rate. The value range of these parameters was set real-time communications in mind. Both the dataset [1] and the tools [2][3] used to create the dataset are publicly available for research and development purposes.

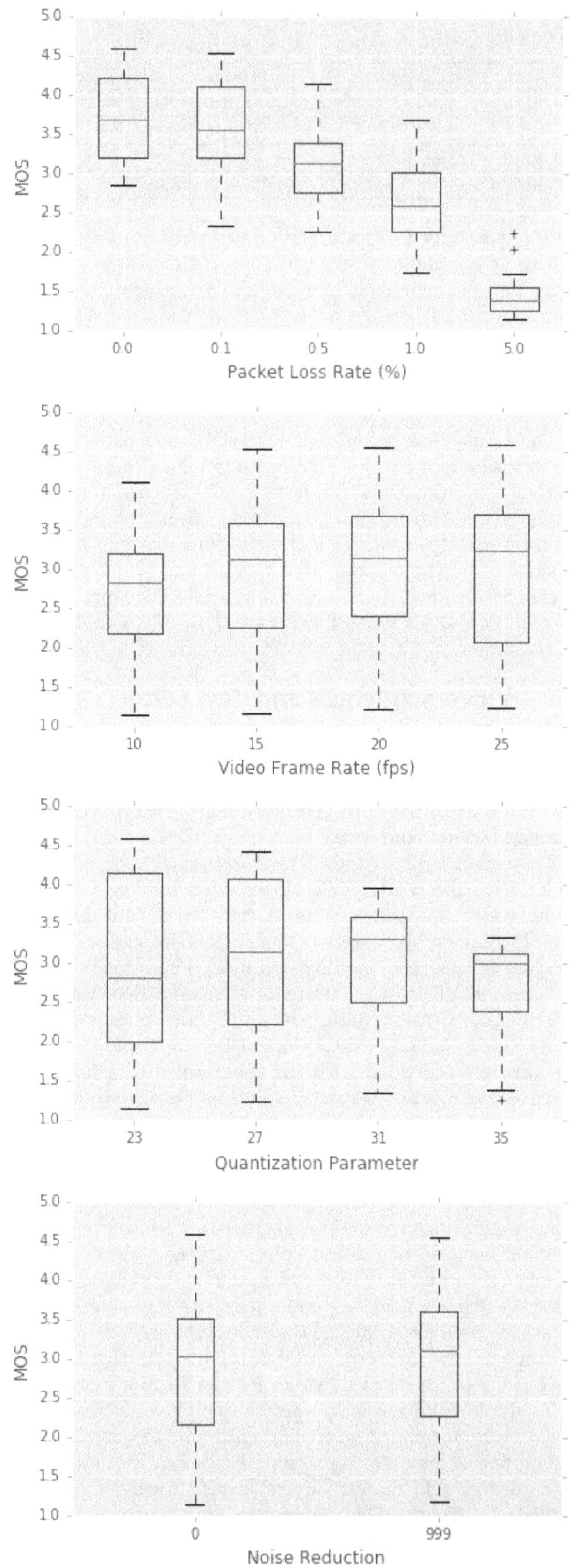

Figure 3: Variation in MOS value for Packet Loss Rate, Video Frame Rate, Quantization and Noise Reduction.

5. REFERENCES

[1] E. Demirbilek. The inrs audiovisual quality dataset. https://github.com/edipdemirbilek/TheINRSAudiovisualQualityDataset, 2016.

[2] E. Demirbilek. Gstreamer multimedia quality testbed. https://github.com/edipdemirbilek/GStreamerMultimediaQualityTestbed, 2016.

[3] E. Demirbilek. Subjective assesment video player. https://github.com/edipdemirbilek/SubjectiveAssesmentVideoPlayer, 2016.

[4] M.-N. Garcia. *Parametric Packet-based Audiovisual Quality Model for IPTV Services*. Springer, 2014.

[5] M. Goudarzi, L. Sun, and E. Ifeachor. Audiovisual quality estimation for video calls in wireless applications. In *Global Telecommunications Conference (GLOBECOM 2010), 2010 IEEE*, pages 1–5. IEEE, 2010.

[6] J. D. Hunter et al. Matplotlib: A 2d graphics environment. *Computing in science and engineering*, 9(3):90–95, 2007.

[7] G. ITU-T RECOMMENDATION. 1071: Opinion model for network planning of video and audio streaming applications. 2015.

[8] P. ITU-T RECOMMENDATION. 911: Subjective audiovisual quality assessment methods for multimedia applications. *International Telecommunications Union, Geneva*, 1998.

[9] P. ITU-T RECOMMENDATION. 1201: Parametric non-intrusive assessment of audiovisual media streaming quality. 2012.

[10] C. Keimel, A. Redl, and K. Diepold. The tum high definition video datasets. In *Quality of Multimedia Experience (QoMEX), 2012 Fourth International Workshop on*, pages 97–102. IEEE, 2012.

[11] T. Maki, D. Kukolj, D. Dordevic, and M. Varela. A reduced-reference parametric model for audiovisual quality of iptv services. In *Quality of Multimedia Experience (QoMEX), 2013 Fifth International Workshop on*, pages 6–11. IEEE, 2013.

[12] M. Pinson. The consumer digital video library [best of the web]. *Signal Processing Magazine, IEEE*, 30(4):172–174, 2013.

[13] M. Pinson, C. Schmidmer, L. Janowski, R. Pépion, Q. Huynh-Thu, P. Corriveau, A. Younkin, P. Le Callet, M. Barkowsky, and W. Ingram. Subjective and objective evaluation of an audiovisual subjective dataset for research and development. In *Quality of Multimedia Experience (QoMEX), 2013 Fifth International Workshop on*, 2013.

[14] M. H. Pinson, L. Janowski, R. Pépion, Q. Huynh-Thu, C. Schmidmer, P. Corriveau, A. Younkin, P. L. Callet, M. Barkowsky, and W. Ingram. The influence of subjects and environment on audiovisual subjective tests: An international study. *Selected Topics in Signal Processing, IEEE Journal of*, 6(6):640–651, 2012.

[15] W. Robitza, Y. Pitrey, M. Nezveda, S. Buchinger, and H. Hlavacs. Made for mobile: a video database designed for mobile television. In *Sixth International Workshop on Video Processing and Quality Metrics for Consumer Electronics (VPQM)*, 2012.

[16] G. Team. Gstreamer: open source multimedia framework.

[17] S. Zielinski. On some biases encountered in modern listening tests. *Proc. of Spatial Audio & Sensory Evaluation Techniques*, 2006.

Learning to Make Better Mistakes: Semantics-aware Visual Food Recognition

Hui Wu
IBM Research
wuhu@us.ibm.com

Michele Merler
IBM Research
mimerler@us.ibm.com

Rosario Uceda-Sosa
IBM Research
rosariou@us.ibm.com

John R Smith
IBM Research
jsmith@us.ibm.com

ABSTRACT

We propose a visual food recognition framework that integrates the inherent semantic relationships among fine-grained classes. Our method learns semantics-aware features by formulating a multi-task loss function on top of a convolutional neural network (CNN) architecture. It then refines the CNN predictions using a random walk based smoothing procedure, which further exploits the rich semantic information.

We evaluate our algorithm on a large "food-in-the-wild" benchmark [3], as well as a challenging dataset of restaurant food dishes with very few training images. The proposed method achieves higher classification accuracy than a baseline which directly fine-tunes a deep learning network on the target dataset. Furthermore, we analyze the consistency of the learned model with the inherent semantic relationships among food categories. Results show that the proposed approach provides more semantically meaningful results than the baseline method, even in cases of mispredictions.

Categories and Subject Descriptors H.3.3 [**Information Systems**]Information Storage and Retrieval-*Content Analysis and Indexing*; I.4 [**Computing Methodologies**]:Image Processing and Computer Vision
General Terms Hierarchical Deep Learning
Keywords Food Recognition, Multi-task Learning

1. INTRODUCTION

Food recognition has recently attracted a lot of attention in the multimedia and vision community, following the deluge of food pictures shared on the web and social media (either generic[1] or highly specific ones[2]). Meanwhile, with the growing popularity of fitness applications, the need for easy logging of calorie consumption on mobile devices has become increasingly relevant. While some preliminary work has been proposed to address the problem of nutrition assessment from images [10, 12], a full solution has yet to be achieved. We focus on developing a food recognition engine which can be used as a fundamental building block towards such applications for automatic nutrition intake tracking.

A range of different approaches have been proposed to address food recognition as an instance of a fine-grained classification problem [22], from random forests [3] to structured SVMs on top of extreme learning machines [13], from directly training or fine-tuning deep convolutional neural nets from food images [6, 9, 19] to using image captioning techniques [8]. When the geolocation information of a food picture is available, the scope of the problem is reduced from the recognition of food "in the wild" to matching items on a restaurant menu to enhance the recognition performance[1, 2, 17]. However, treating food recognition as a flat fine-grained classification problem disregards the rich semantic relationships among food classes. As shown in the examples in Figure 1, even when a food recognition engine fails to identify the exact class, it is preferable for a user if the system provides results consistent with the ground truth at a coarser category level. Based on this observation, we propose a deep CNN based food recognition framework that is aware of the semantic structured relationships among classes.

Multi-task learning has been extensively employed to op-

Figure 1: Examples of misclassified food items using CNN-FT and the proposed CNN-HL-LI. Ground truth labels are in green. While both methods misclassify the images, the predictions from CNN-HL-LI are semantically closer to the ground truth.

[1]www.instagram.com
[2]www.foodspotting.com, www.yummly.com

MM '16, October 15-19, 2016, Amsterdam, Netherlands

DOI: http://dx.doi.org/10.1145/2964284.2967205

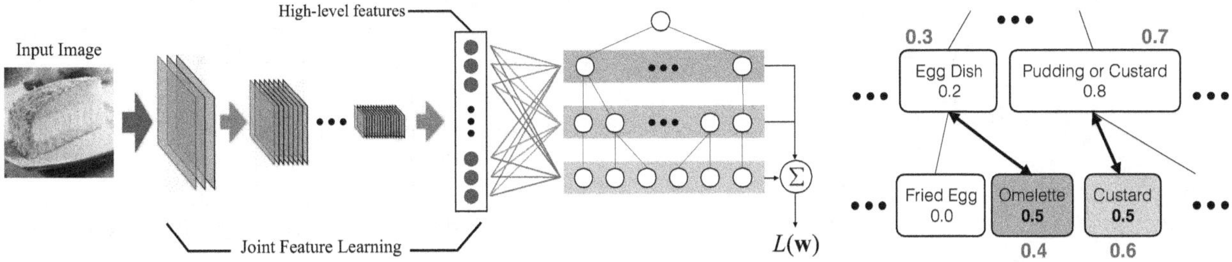

(a) Each semantic level has one separate fully connected layer. (b) The refined labels are in blue.

Figure 2: The proposed approach consists of (a) joint feature learning, where the semantic label hierarchy is embedded in the loss function, and (b) label refinement by explicitly utilizing relationships among classes.

timize for problems with a structured output, including as in our case a hierarchical one [5, 7]. However, such an approach is relatively new within the context of deep convolutional networks [20]. In terms of encoding label structures with CNNs, the proposed approach is similar to some existing techniques. Label structures within CNNs have been modeled as dedicated fully connected layers feeding each other (from coarse to fine) [18], and graphs linking fine-grained classes to auxiliary categories encompassing label or attribute relations [4, 16, 22]. Instead of class relationships, Zhang et al. [21] learn feature representations by jointly optimizing the fine-grained classification and hierarchical similarity constraints. However, most of those proposed approaches, while "deep" in network architecture, tend to be "shallow" in semantic hierarchy (they mostly handle a two-level hierarchy). Moreover, such approaches explicitly model semantic links between each pair of coarse and fine classes (for example, using triplet loss [21] or hierarchical weight regularization [16, 22]), which requires an extremely large amount of training examples and increases optimization complexity. Our proposed architecture, on the other hand, can easily generalize to an arbitrary number of levels in the hierarchical tree without demanding a substantial increase in the number of training examples. The main contributions of this work include:

- A flexible multi-task loss function that jointly learns CNN features across different semantic levels, which can be easily integrated with different CNN designs.
- A random walk based label refinement strategy that takes advantage of the semantic structure to improve consistent predictions at each semantic level.

2. PROPOSED METHOD

As shown in Figure 2, the proposed approach consists of two components, both utilizing the hierarchical semantic relationships among classes: a semantics-aware joint feature learning step based on multi-task learning, and a random walk based label refinement step.

2.1 Semantics-aware Joint Feature Learning

Given N training images, $\{\mathbf{x}_i, y_i\}_{i=1}^N$, where $\mathbf{x}_i$ is the vectorized pixel values of an image, and $y_i \in \mathcal{Y}$ is the corresponding image label, the classical softmax loss function used in CNN is formulated as:

$$L(\mathbf{w}) = \sum_{i=1}^{N} -\log\, p(y_i|\mathbf{x}_i, \mathbf{w}) \tag{1}$$

where $\mathbf{w}$ is a vector composed of the network parameters, and $p(y_i|\mathbf{x}_i, \mathbf{w})$ is the output at the y_i-th node in the output layer. While the above formulation applies to general fine-grained classification, it does not explicitly model structures such as semantic relationships among classes.

Suppose we are provided with a semantic structure, $\mathcal{T} = \{\mathcal{Y}^{(t)}\}_{t=0}^T$, where $\mathcal{Y}^{(t)} = \{0, 1, \cdots, c^{(t)}\}$ is the set of $c^{(t)}$ labels at the t-th level of the semantic hierarchy. $\mathcal{Y}^{(T)}$ is the root node, which represents a generic concept of "food". The leaf nodes, $\mathcal{Y}^{(0)} \equiv \mathcal{Y}$, correspond to the original input classes. By leveraging the semantic structure, $\mathcal{T}$, our goal is to learn high-level CNN features which can improve on fine-grained classification. Specifically, we propose the following multi-task learning based loss function:

$$\begin{aligned} L(\mathbf{w}) = & \sum_{i=1}^{N} -\log\, p(y_i^{(0)}|\mathbf{x}_i, \mathbf{w}_0, \mathbf{w}^{(0)}) \\ & + \lambda \cdot \sum_{t=1}^{T-1} \sum_{i=1}^{N} -\log\, p(y_i^{(t)}|\mathbf{x}_i, \mathbf{w}_0, \mathbf{w}^{(t)}) \end{aligned} \tag{2}$$

where $y_i^{(t)} \in \mathcal{Y}^{(t)}$ is the corresponding class label of image i at the t-th semantic level, $\mathbf{w} = [\mathbf{w}_0, \mathbf{w}^{(1)}, \cdots, \mathbf{w}^{(T)}]$, $\mathbf{w}_0$ represents the network parameters from the input layer to the high-level feature level, and $\mathbf{w}^{(t)}$ corresponds to the parameters of the fully-connected layer that maps from the high-level features to the output layer at the t-th level of the semantic tree. λ controls the trade-off between the contribution of the fine-grained classification from the leaf level, and the semantic relationships among super categories.

Given a semantic tree (Figure 3 shows the hierarchy used in this work), Equation 2 jointly optimizes the softmax output at each level of the hierarchy. As illustrated in Figure 2(a), the feature learning module is shared by different softmax output layers, each modeling a different level in the hierarchical tree. The joint feature learning design serves two purposes: (1) it ensures that high-level CNN features for fine-grained classification are also discriminant for super categories, and (2) it helps the model to produce more semantically coherent predictions. In fact, even in cases of misclassification, its predictions tend to fall within semantically related categories (see the examples in Figure 1).

During the learning process, the weights $\mathbf{w}_0$ of the shared feature layers were initialized using the values of a network pre-trained on ImageNet, while we initialize the fully connected layers using the uniform distribution. For each fully connected layer, the weight update is only related to its corresponding softmax term; for the previous layers, the gra-

Figure 3: The food semantic hierarchy.

dient can be computed as the weighted sum of the gradient related to each loss term in Equation 2. We optimize Equation 2 using standard stochastic gradient descent.

2.2 Label Inference in the Semantic Tree

Let $\mathbf{p} = [\mathbf{h}^{(0)\intercal}, \mathbf{h}^{(1)\intercal}, \cdots, \mathbf{h}^{(T-1)\intercal}]^\intercal$ be the probability outputs at each semantic level of the learned CNN, we propose to further incorporate the semantic relationships by inferencing the probability values on the semantic tree. We formulate the label inference problem as a random walk process: the initial probability scores are considered as initial values on each node. Each node takes random transitions to its parent or child in the semantic graph at each step until the node values converge. The goal is to incorporate the recognition results from super categories as well as from the leaf nodes, so that in difficult recognition cases, information at different semantic levels are considered simultaneously.

The process is exemplified in Figure 2 (b). The initial CNN predictions (values inside each box) might still present some errors/confusion (both *Omelette* and *Custard* have a 0.5 score). The random walk process enforces consistency by smoothing the prediction values over classes on the same semantic path. It thus drives the score of *Custard* (the correct prediction, in green) to a larger value of 0.6, thanks to the large initial prediction of its parent *Pudding or Custard.*

Let $\mathbf{A}_{n \times n}$ be the adjacency matrix defined over all the tree nodes, $\mathcal{V} = \{\mathcal{Y}^{(0)}, \mathcal{Y}^{(1)}, \cdots, \mathcal{Y}^{(T)}\}$, and $|\mathcal{V}| = \sum_{t=0}^{T} c^{(t)}$ is the total number of tree nodes. $A_{i,j} = 1$ when i-th node in $\mathcal{V}$ is the parent or a child of the j-th node; otherwise $A_{i,j} = 0$. Given the adjacency matrix, we construct a transitional probability matrix $\mathbf{T}$ by normalizing each column of $\mathbf{A}$ to have unit $L1$ norm. At the k-th step of the random walk process, the current node values are determined by both the initial input values, $\mathbf{p}_0$ (normalized to have unit $L1$ norm), and the previous values on each node:

$$\mathbf{p}^{(k)} = \alpha \cdot \mathbf{p}^{(0)} + (1 - \alpha) \cdot \mathbf{T}^\intercal \mathbf{p}^{(k-1)} \tag{3}$$

where α is a trade-off parameter between preserving input node values and semantic based label inference. Using the

Dataset		Classes	Images per class
Food-101		101	1000
5-Chain	Applebee's	50	8
	Dennys	56	6
	Olive Garden	55	8
	Panera Bread	79	28
	TGI Fridays	54	8

Table 1: Distribution of the experimental datasets.

constraint of unit $L1$ norm of $\mathbf{p}^{(k)}$, Equation 3 becomes

$$\begin{aligned}\mathbf{p}^{(k)} &= \alpha \cdot \mathbf{p}^{(0)} \mathbf{1}^\intercal \mathbf{p}^{(k-1)} + (1 - \alpha) \cdot \mathbf{T}^\intercal \mathbf{p}^{(k-1)} \\ &= \mathbf{T}'^\intercal \mathbf{p}^{(k-1)}\end{aligned} \tag{4}$$

where $\mathbf{T}'^\intercal = \alpha \cdot \mathbf{p}^{(0)} \mathbf{1}^\intercal + (1 - \alpha) \cdot \mathbf{T}^\intercal$. The final node values are taken as the stationary value of $\mathbf{p}^{(k)}$ as $k \to \infty$. It is readily seen that the stationary node values are proportional to the eigenvector (corresponding to the largest eigenvalue) of $\mathbf{T}'$. To calculate the stationary node values, $\mathbf{p}^*$, we used the Power Method [11] by continually multiplying $\mathbf{T}'$ to the node values until convergence. In each iteration, we apply $L1$ normalization to $\mathbf{p}^{(k)}$. The final prediction for an input image is obtained by taking the label with the largest value on the sub-vector in $\mathbf{p}^*$ corresponding to the leaf nodes.

3. EXPERIMENTS

3.1 Datasets and Experiment Setup

To thoroughly evaluate the proposed approach, we chose two types of datasets with different properties: (1) Food-101 [3]: a benchmark food dataset commonly used to evaluate food classification accuracy [12]; (2) 5-Chain: containing menu items from five popular restaurant chains among the top causal dining in the US. The images were collected from multiple web sources, such as search engines (Bing, Google) and social networks (Flickr, Foodspotting, Yelp), and manually labeled. As shown in Table 1, categories in the 5-Chain dataset contain very few images compared to Food-101, since they are very specific. On the other hand, Food-101 contains generic food classes with various composition styles, whereas 5-Chain food items have more standard food composition and less intra-class variance (Figure 4).

For Food-101, we trained a 101-way classifier; in 5-Chain, we trained a separate classifier for each restaurant independently. We constructed a generic food taxonomy (shown in Figure 3), and for each classification task, we only take into account the subset of the taxonomy that covers the corresponding food classes. For all the experiments, we randomly selected 75% of the images for training and the rest for testing. We adopted GoogLeNet [14] as the base network for the proposed hierarchical food recognition approach. Note that our framework is independent of the base deep architecture on top of which it is applied, and could be combined with any common CNN model.

We compared against a baseline model consisting of a pretrained GoogLeNet fine-tuned on each dataset (**CNN-FT**). This configuration has been proven to produce state of the art performance on the Food 101 dataset [12][3]. We denote

[3]Note that while we used the same network configuration as [12], the performance we present in Table 2 for Food 101 does not replicate what was reported in their paper. This might

Dataset		CNN-FT		CNN-HL		CNN-HL-LI	
		Accuracy	LCA	Accuracy	LCA	Accuracy	LCA
Food-101		69.64	0.80	72.09	**0.72**	**72.11**	**0.72**
5-Chain	Applebee's	72.55	0.93	**74.18**	**0.85**	73.91	0.86
	Dennys	57.74	1.31	59.68	1.27	**60.00**	**1.26**
	Olive Garden	78.10	0.77	79.52	0.72	**80.95**	**0.66**
	Panera Bread	91.03	0.27	90.98	0.26	**91.19**	**0.25**
	TGI Fridays	73.48	0.82	77.27	0.68	**77.78**	**0.66**

Table 2: Food recognition results from all methods across different food datasets.

(a) Hummus from Food-101

(b) TGI Fridays All American Stacked Burger

Figure 4: Example images of the datasets used.

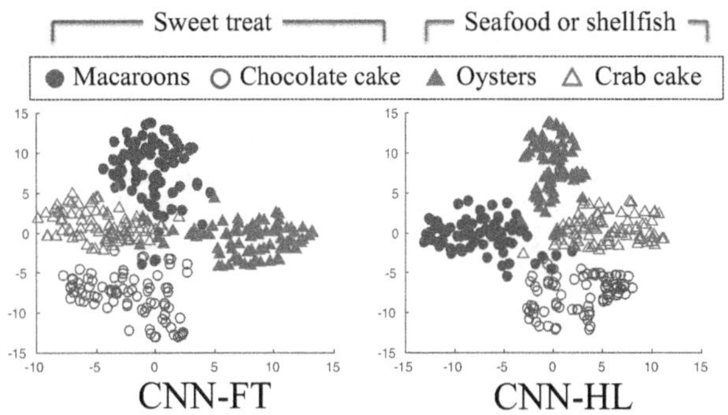

Figure 5: 2D embedding of the learned features in the proposed approach using T-SNE ([15]).

the CNN learned using the proposed multi-task *hierarchical loss* function as **CNN-HL**, and **CNN-HL-LI** with the addition of the *label inference* step.

We implemented the algorithm using the Lasagne library and the experiments were performed on a cluster with ~20 Nvidia K40 GPUs. In all experiments, we fixed $\lambda = 1$, $\alpha = 0.2$, which were obtained using the best cross validation performance on Food-101. The random walk process is considered to reach convergence when the $L1$ norm of the node values changes by less than .001. In our experiments convergence is typically achieved within 10 iterations.

3.2 Results and Discussion

Fine-grained Food Recognition Table 2 summarizes the top-1 classification accuracy of the three methods on Food-101 and 5-Chain datasets. Except on the Panera Bread experiment, **CNN-FT** produced lower classification performance than **CNN-HL**, which demonstrates that the proposed joint feature learning strategy improves upon learning with only softmax loss at the leaf semantic layer. Furthermore, the result from **CNN-HL-LI** ranks the highest except on Applebee's. This observation indicates the effectiveness of the explicit usage of the semantics in label refinement.

Hierarchical Learning Results In addition to directly evaluating the proposed approach on fine-grained food recognition, we are also interested in the consistency of the recognition result with the provided semantic structure. We visualize the learned features by taking the output of the high-level features layer of the learned CNN and projecting them to a 2D space using T-SNE [15]. Figure 5 shows that the two super categories (*Sweet Treat*, and *Seafood or Shellfish*) are better separated with the learned CNN using the proposed multi-task loss function. This demonstrates that the joint feature learning process enables learning features that can discriminate classes at different levels of the hierarchy. Such property is especially useful for a nutrition information estimation application, since in a misclassification scenario, a semantically close prediction provides more relevant nutrition estimation than an entirely unrelated prediction.

To quantitatively evaluate whether the learned model is consistent with the semantics, we measured the semantic distance between the ground truth label and the predicted label using the height of Lowest Common Ancestor (LCA), where 0 indicates a correct match, and 2 means the two nodes share a common grandparent. We calculate the mean LCA on each dataset (shown in Table 2). The results are in line with the fine-grained classification ones, where **CNN-FT** achieves the lowest performance and **CNN-HL-LI** outperforms **CNN-HL** on the majority of the tasks. Similar observations can be made from the qualitative results shown in Figure 1. Those results demonstrate that in misclassification cases, **CNN-HL-LI** can still provide recognition results that are semantically closer to the ground truth.

be due to differences in the implementations and parameter choices, which were not released by the authors.

4. CONCLUSIONS

We presented a framework that leverages hierarchical semantics for food recognition based on joint deep feature learning and semantic label inference. Experimental results show that the proposed framework not only improves upon the accuracy of basic flat fine-grained classification methods, but also produces more semantically coherent predictions. With the prevalence of fitness applications, such a food recognition algorithm is a first step towards visual food nutrition assessment. For future work, we plan to take advantage of the unified semantic hierarchy to transfer the knowledge learned from large datasets to small-scale ones that are challenging for fine-tuning CNNs.

5. REFERENCES

[1] O. Beijbom, N. Joshi, D. Morris, S. Saponas, and S. Khullar. Menu-match: Restaurant-specific food logging from images. In *IEEE Winter Conference on Applications of Computer Vision*, pages 844–851, 2015.

[2] V. Bettadapura, E. Thomaz, A. Parnami, G. Abowd, and I. Essa. Leveraging context to support automated food recognition in restaurants. In *IEEE Winter Conference on Applications of Computer Vision*, January 2015.

[3] L. Bossard, M. Guillaumin, and L. Van Gool. Food-101 – mining discriminative components with random forests. In *European Conference on Computer Vision*, 2014.

[4] J. Deng, N. Ding, Y. Jia, A. Frome, K. Murphy, S. Bengio, Y. Li, H. Neven, and H. Adam. Large-scale object classification using label relation graphs. In *European Conference on Computer Vision*, pages 48–64, 2014.

[5] T. Deselaers and V. Ferrari. Visual and semantic similarity in imagenet. In *IEEE Conference on Computer Vision and Pattern Recognition*, pages 1777–1784, 2011.

[6] Z. Ge, C. McCool, C. Sanderson, and P. I. Corke. Modelling local deep convolutional neural network features to improve fine-grained image classification. In *IEEE International Conference on Image Processing*, 2015.

[7] N. Goernitz, C. Widmer, G. Zeller, A. Kahles, G. Rätsch, and S. Sonnenburg. Hierarchical multitask structured output learning for large-scale sequence segmentation. In *NIPS*, pages 2690–2698, 2011.

[8] J. Hessel, N. Savva, and M. J. Wilber. Image representations and new domains in neural image captioning. *Conference on Empirical Methods in Natural Language Processing Vision + Learning workshop*, 2015.

[9] H. Kagaya, K. Aizawa, and M. Ogawa. Food detection and recognition using convolutional neural network. In *ACM Multimedia*, pages 1085–1088, 2014.

[10] Y. Kawano and K. Yanai. Foodcam: A real-time mobile food recognition system employing fisher vector. In *International Conference on MultiMedia Modeling*, pages 369–373, 2014.

[11] A. N. Langville and C. D. Meyer. A survey of eigenvector methods for web information retrieval. *SIAM review*, 47(1):135–161, 2005.

[12] A. Myers, N. Johnston, V. Rathod, A. Korattikara, A. Gorban, N. Silberman, S. Guadarrama, G. Papandreou, J. Huang, and K. Murphy. Im2calories: towards an automated mobile vision food diary. In *International Conference on Computer Vision*, 2015.

[13] C. M. Niki Martinel, Claudio Piciarelli and G. L. Foresti. A structured committee for food recognition. In *International Conference on Computer Vision*, 2015.

[14] C. Szegedy, W. Liu, Y. Jia, P. Sermanet, S. Reed, D. Anguelov, D. Erhan, V. Vanhoucke, and A. Rabinovich. Going deeper with convolutions. In *Proceedings of the IEEE Conference on Computer Vision and Pattern Recognition*, pages 1–9, 2015.

[15] L. Van Der Maaten. Accelerating t-sne using tree-based algorithms. *The Journal of Machine Learning Research*, 15(1):3221–3245, 2014.

[16] S. Xie, T. Yang, X. Wang, and Y. Lin. Hyper-class augmented and regularized deep learning for fine-grained image classification. In *IEEE Conference on Computer Vision and Pattern Recognition*, pages 2645–2654, 2015.

[17] R. Xu, L. Herranz, S. Jiang, S. Wang, X. Song, and R. Jain. Geolocalized modeling for dish recognition. *IEEE Transactions on Multimedia*, 17(8):1187–1199, Aug 2015.

[18] Z. Yan, H. Zhang, R. Piramuthu, V. Jagadeesh, D. DeCoste, W. Di, and Y. Yu. Hd-cnn: Hierarchical deep convolutional neural network for large scale visual recognition. In *International Conference on Computer Vision*, 2015.

[19] K. Yanai and Y. Kawano. Food image recognition using deep convolutional network with pre-training and fine-tuning. In *IEEE International Conference on Multimedia and Expo*, pages 1–6, 2015.

[20] T. Zeng and S. Ji. Deep convolutional neural networks for multi-instance multi-task learning. In *IEEE International Conference on Data Mining*, pages 579–588, 2015.

[21] X. Zhang, F. Zhou, Y. Lin, and S. Zhang. Embedding label structures for fine-grained feature representation. *IEEE Conference on Computer Vision and Pattern Recognition*, 2016.

[22] F. Zhou and Y. Lin. Fine-grained image classification by exploring bipartite-graph labels. In *IEEE Conference on Computer Vision and Pattern Recognition*, 2016.

Dictionary Learning Based Hashing for Cross-Modal Retrieval*

Xin-Shun Xu
School of Computer Science and Technology, Shandong University, Jinan 250101, China
xuxinshun@sdu.edu.cn

ABSTRACT

Recent years have witnessed the growing popularity of cross-modal hashing for fast multi-modal data retrieval. Most existing cross-modal hashing methods project heterogeneous data directly into a common space with linear projection matrices. However, such scheme will lead to large error as there will probably be some heterogeneous data with semantic similarity hard to be close in latent space when linear projection is used. In this paper, we propose a dictionary learning cross-modal hashing (DLCMH) to perform cross-modal similarity search. Instead of projecting data directly, DLCMH learns dictionaries and generates sparse representation for each instance, which is more suitable to be projected to latent space. Then, it assumes that all modalities of one instance have identical hash codes, and gets final binary codes by minimizing quantization error. Experimental results on two real-world datasets show that DLCMH outperforms or is comparable to several state-of-the-art hashing models.

Categories and Subject Descriptors

H.3.1 [**Information Storage and Retrieval**]: Content Analysis and Indexing—*indexing methods*; I.2.6 [**Artificial Intelligence**]: Learning

Keywords

Cross-Modal; Hashing; Dictionary Learning; Sparse Representation

1. INTRODUCTION

Nearest neighbor search lays the foundation for many important applications, such as computer vision, data mining, and information retrieval [15, 16]. Hashing is one of the most well-known methods that support approximate nearest neighbor (ANN) search. Such methods first map data points into hamming space; then make the comparison in hamming space. They have efficient constant query time and can also reduce storage by storing compact codes of data points. Thus, hashing based methods have garnered considerable interest in recent years [13, 14].

In addition, in many scenarios, people need to make similarity search across different modalities. For example, given an image as query, search engine can return some documents (text) to accurately describe the image. Recently, a few cross-modal hashing methods have been proposed for such task [17, 23, 19, 9, 7, 12]. These methods can be generally divided into two categories: modality-specific hashing methods and integrated hashing methods. Modality-specific hashing methods learn independent hash codes for each modality, e.g., [21, 18]. In [2], Bronstein et al. proposed a cross-modal similarity sensitive hashing method (CMSSH) which embeds incommensurable data into a common metric space; the hash functions for different modalities are learned by using eigen decomposition and standard AdaBoost. Kumar et al. [6] extended spectral hashing to the multi-view field and proposes a Cross-View Hashing model (CVH), which minimizes the inter-view and intra-view Hamming distance for similar points and maximizes that for dissimilar points. Inter-media Hashing (IMH) [11] introduces inter-media consistency and intra-media consistency to discover a common metric space, and uses linear regression with regularization model to learn hash functions for each modality. Integrated hashing methods learn unified hashing codes for different modalities. For instance, Zhang et al. [20] proposes the composite hashing with multiple information sources (CHMIS). Zhou et al. proposed LSSH [23] which uses sparse coding and matrix factorization to learn the latent spaces firstly and then projects the semantic spaces to a joint high level abstraction space. Kim et al. [5] proposed sequential spectral learning to hash with multiple representations. Ding et al. [4] proposed Collective Matrix Factorization Hashing which learns unified codes by collective matrix factorization with latent factor model from different modalities of each instance.

Although some attempts have been made towards effective cross-modal hashing, most of them linearly project different modalities data into a common space which will lead to large error as there will probably be some heterogeneous data with semantic similarity hard to be close in latent space. In this paper, we propose a novel cross-modal hashing method, which is referred to Dictionary Learning Cross-Modal Hashing (DLCMH). Instead of projecting data directly, DLCMH learns dictionaries for each modality and

*Jian Wang gave the original idea and code; Xin Luo conducted all experiments. Thus, they should be the first and second authors. Due to some reason, they are not included in the author list.

MM'16, October 15–19, 2016, Amsterdam, Netherlands.

DOI: http://dx.doi.org/10.1145/2964284.2967206

generates sparse representation for each data which will be more suitable to be projected to latent space. Moreover, DLCMH assumes that all modalities of one instance have identical hashing codes and minimizes quantization error in optimization stage. Thus, our proposed method in this paper is also an integrated one. Extensive experimental results on two benchmark datasets confirm the effectiveness of the proposed method in comparison with several state-of-the-art methods.

The remainder of this paper is organized as follows. In Section 2, the proposed method is introduced. In Section 3, we provide extensive experimental results on two real-world multimedia datasets. Conclusions are given in Section 4.

2. OUR METHODOLOGY

In this section, we describe the detail of the proposed method, i.e., Dictionary Learning Cross Modal Hashing (DLCMH). For simplicity of presentation, we give a description on bimodal case; but it is very easy to extend the proposed method to general cases with more than two modalities.

2.1 Notation and Problem Definition

Suppose that $\mathcal{O} = \{o_i\}_{i=1}^n$ is the given multi-modal training objects set. $X^1 \in \mathbb{R}^{d_1 \times n}$ and $X^2 \in \mathbb{R}^{d_2 \times n}$ are two different modal matrices of $\mathcal{O}$. Each feature point $x_i^1 (x_i^2)$ is located in the $d_1 (d_2)$ dimensional input feature space (usually, $d_1 \neq d_2$). We also have an inter-modality similarity matrix $S \in \{1, 0\}^{n \times n}$ where 1 and 0 denote similar and dissimilar relationship, respectively.

Given the binary code length r, DLCMH learns hash codes $Y \in \{+1, -1\}^{r \times n}$ whose column y_i corresponds to object o_i, $i = 1, 2, ..., n$, such that y_i, y_j preserve the similarity between o_i and o_j with high probability. Similar to integrated hashing methods, DLCMH forces different modalities of an object to have the same hash code.

2.2 Objective Function

[8] reveals the correlation between hash code inner product and Hamming distance:

$$code_r(x_i) \circ code_r(x_j) = r - 2\mathcal{D}_h(x_i, x_j), \tag{1}$$

where $code_r(x_i)$ is the r-bit hash code of x_i and $\mathcal{D}_h(x_i, x_j)$ is the Hamming distance between the hashing codes of x_i and x_j.

Based on the correlation mentioned above, similar to other methods, we can apply the similar scheme as that in KSH [8] to minimize the least-squares style objective function to learn the hash code matrix Y. Thus, the similarity preservation objective function is given as:

$$\tilde{\mathcal{O}}_{sp} = \min_{Y} \| Y^\top Y - r \cdot S \|_2^2, \tag{2}$$

To consider affine project functions which project feature points to Hamming space, we further give the following projection error objective function:

$$\tilde{\mathcal{O}}_{pe} = \min_{\tilde{R}^1, \tilde{R}^2} \| Y - sgn(\tilde{R}^1 X^1) \|_2^2 + \| Y - sgn(\tilde{R}^2 X^2) \|_2^2, \tag{3}$$

where $sgn(\cdot)$ denotes the element-wise sign function, $\tilde{R}^1 \in \mathbb{R}^{r \times d_1}$ and $\tilde{R}^2 \in \mathbb{R}^{r \times d_2}$ are projection matrices. However, $sgn(\cdot)$ will lead to intractable optimization problem and simply relaxing this objective function by replacing $sgn(x)$ with x will result in large error. Thus, to reduce such error, in this work, we adopt dictionary learning scheme to minimize the projection error:

$$\begin{aligned} \mathcal{O}_{pe} = & \min_{B^1, B^2, S^1, S^2, R^1, R^2} \| X^1 - B^1 S^1 \|_2^2 \\ & + \beta \cdot \| X^2 - B^2 S^2 \|_2^2 + \rho(\sum_{i=1}^n | S_i^1 | + \sum_{i=1}^n | S_i^2 |) \\ & + \lambda(\| Y - R^1 S^1 \|_2^2 + \| Y - R^2 S^2 \|_2^2) \end{aligned} \tag{4}$$

where $B^1 \in \mathbb{R}^{d_1 \times k}$ and $B^2 \in \mathbb{R}^{d_2 \times k}$ are dictionaries and k is the size of dictionary. $R^1 \in \mathbb{R}^{k \times d_1}$ and $R^2 \in \mathbb{R}^{k \times d_2}$ are projection matrices. S^1 and S^2 are sparse representations. In this paper, we set the size of dictionaries B^1, B^2 to the same, i.e., k; however, different size is acceptable.

We further relax $\tilde{\mathcal{O}}_{sp}$ by replacing binary code Y with sigmoid function $\varphi(H) = 2/(1 + exp(-H)) - 1$ with $H \in \mathbb{R}^{r \times n}$. $\varphi(x)$ is continuously differentiable and well approximates $+1$ and -1 when $|x| > 6$. Then, the overall objective function is as follows:

$$\begin{aligned} & \min_{B^1, B^2, S^1, S^2, R^1, R^2, Y} \| X^1 - B^1 S^1 \|_2^2 + \beta \| X^2 - B^2 S^2 \|_2^2 \\ & + \rho(\sum_{i=1}^n | S_i^1 | + \sum_{i=1}^n | S_i^2 |) + \lambda(\| H - R^1 S^1 \|_2^2 \\ & + \| H - R^2 S^2 \|_2^2) + \mu \| \varphi(H)^\top \varphi(H) - rS \|_2^2 \\ & s.t. \| B_{\cdot i}^1 \|_2 \leq 1, \| B_{\cdot i}^2 \|_2 \leq 1, \| R_{\cdot i}^1 \|_2 \leq 1, \| R_{\cdot i}^2 \|_2 \leq 1 \end{aligned} \tag{5}$$

where $\beta, \rho, \lambda, \mu$ are weight parameters, constraints are typically applied to avoid trivial solutions.

2.3 Optimization Algorithm

The optimization problem (5) is not convex with matrices variables $B^1, B^2, S^1, S^2, R^1, R^2, Y$. Fortunately, it is convex with respect to any one of $B^1, B^2, S^1, S^2, R^1, R^2$ while fixing the others, and Y can be solved by greedy optimization [8] while other variables are fixed. Therefore, the optimization problem can be solved by an iterative framework with the following listed steps until convergence.

Step 1: Learning sparse representation S^1 by fixing other variables, i.e., we solve the following problem:

$$\begin{aligned} & \min_{S^1} \| X^1 - B^1 S^1 \|_2^2 + \rho \sum_{i=1}^n | S_i^1 | + \lambda \| H - R^1 S^1 \|_2^2 \\ & \Rightarrow \min_{S^1} \| \begin{bmatrix} X^1 \\ \sqrt{\lambda} H \end{bmatrix} - \begin{bmatrix} B^1 \\ \sqrt{\lambda} R^1 \end{bmatrix} S^1 \|_2^2 + \rho \sum_{i=1}^n | S_i^1 | \end{aligned} \tag{6}$$

This problem can be efficiently solved by using standard toolboxes. Parameter S^2 could be solved in similar way.

Step 2: We learn the project matrix H in an incremental mode. Denoting the i-th row of H as H_i, then we have the following optimization problem for $i = 1, ..., r$.

$$\begin{aligned} & \min_{H_i} \lambda(\| H_i - (R^1 S^1)_i \|_2^2 + \| H_i - (R^2 S^2)_i \|_2^2) \\ & + \mu \| \varphi(H_i)^\top \varphi(H_i) - R_{i-1} \|_2^2 \end{aligned} \tag{7}$$

where $(R^1 S^1)_i$ and $(R^2 S^2)_i$ are the i-th rows of $(R^1 S^1)$ and $(R^2 S^2)_i$, respectively. $R_{i-1} = rS - \sum_{t=1}^{i-1} \varphi(H_t)^\top \varphi(H_t)$ and $R_0 = rS$. The gradient of formula (7) is as follows.

$$\begin{aligned} \frac{\partial}{\partial H_i} = & 2\lambda(H_i - (R^1 S^1)_i) + 2\lambda(H_i - (R^2 S^2)_i) \\ & - 2\mu R_{i-1} \varphi(H_i) \odot (\mathbf{1} - \varphi(H_i) \odot \varphi(H_i)) \end{aligned} \tag{8}$$

Table 1: mAP comparison on Wiki

Task	Method	Code Length 16 bits	24 bits	32 bits
Image Query v.s. Text Database	CVH	0.2016	0.1924	0.1740
	CMSSH	0.2147	0.2144	0.2091
	IMH	0.2156	0.2057	0.2126
	SCM-orth	0.2088	0.1899	0.1959
	SCM-seq	**0.2474**	0.2360	0.2363
	LSSH	0.2353	0.2306	0.2325
	DLCMH	0.2389	**0.2574**	**0.2473**
Text Query v.s. Image Database	CVH	0.3160	0.2471	0.2292
	CMSSH	0.2659	0.2710	0.2752
	IMH	0.2784	0.2761	0.2710
	SCM-orth	0.2702	0.2336	0.2543
	SCM-seq	0.3819	0.4280	0.4479
	LSSH	0.6210	0.6245	0.6375
	DLCMH	**0.6350**	**0.6418**	**0.6514**

Table 2: mAP comparison on NUS-WIDE

Task	Method	Code Length 16 bits	24 bits	32 bits
Image Query v.s. Text Database	CVH	0.4067	0.4061	0.4081
	CMSSH	0.4046	0.4114	0.4377
	IMH	0.5029	0.5150	0.5161
	SCM-orth	0.4875	0.4696	0.4553
	SCM-seq	0.5139	0.5130	0.5167
	LSSH	0.4837	0.4885	0.5066
	DLCMH	**0.5221**	**0.5301**	**0.5453**
Text Query v.s. Image Database	CVH	0.4049	0.4044	0.4040
	CMSSH	0.4775	0.4873	0.4299
	IMH	0.4622	0.4679	0.4686
	SCM-orth	0.4952	0.4678	0.4710
	SCM-seq	0.5568	0.5395	0.5412
	LSSH	0.5962	0.6263	**0.6373**
	DLCMH	**0.6090**	**0.6301**	0.6264

where **1** denotes a constant vector with n 1 entries and the symbol $\odot$ represents the Hadamard product (i.e., element-wise product). With the gradient, we apply L-BFGS (Limited memory BFGS) to look for a local minimum of H_i.

Step 3: In fact, the learning problem of B^1, B^2, R^1, R^2 is essentially similar; thus, we only show how to optimize B^1. With other variables fixed, the problem (5) becomes a least squares problem with quadratic constraints:

$$\min_{B^1} \| X^1 - B^1 S^1 \|_2^2 \quad s.t. \| B^1_{\cdot i} \|_2 \leq 1 \tag{9}$$

By introducing a diagonal matrix $\Theta \in \mathbb{R}^{k \times k}$ with diagonal elements being the Larangian multipliers, we have following Lagrangian dual function:

$$g(B^1, \Theta) = \| X^1 - B^1 S^1 \|_2^2 + Tr\{\Theta(B^\top B - I)\} \tag{10}$$

where $Tr\{\cdot\}$ denotes the trace of matrix and I is an identical matrix. Every element Θ_{ii} in the diagonal of Θ should be greater than or equal to zero. Deriving formula (10) with respect to B^1 and setting the derivation equal to zero, we have:

$$B^1 = X^1(S^1)^\top (S^1(S^1)^\top + \Theta)^{-1} \tag{11}$$

Replace B^1 in Eq. (10) with Eq. (11), we get the Lagrangian dual problem:

$$\min_{\Theta} Tr\{X^1(S^1)^\top (S^1(S^1)^\top + \Theta)^{-1} S^1 (X^1)^\top\} + Tr\{\Theta\}$$
$$s.t. \; \Theta_{ii} \geq 0, \; i = 1, ..., k \tag{12}$$

which can be solved by using Newton's method or conjugate gradient. After we get Θ, B^1 is easy to get through Eq. (11).

2.4 Out-of-Sample Extension

In query stage, a new query example q can be easily mapped to binary codes. In fact, the problem of encoding each modality is essentially the same; hence, we only show the case when modality 1 of q is given, denoted as x.

First, x can be represented by a sparse vector s by solving the following problem:

$$\min_{s} \| x - B^1 s \|_2^2 + \rho \mid s \mid \tag{13}$$

Then, we can project s with R^1 and the hash code of x is $y = sgn(R^1 s)$.

3. EXPERIMENTS

In this section, experiments on two real-world multimodal datasets, i.e., **Wiki** and **NUS-WIDE**, are conducted to test the performance of our DLCMH hashing method. Both datasets involve visual and textual modalities, and we retrieve relevant texts (images) by using images (texts) as queries.

3.1 Settings

We compare DLCMH with several state-of-the-art cross-modal hashing methods, including CVH [6], CMSSH [2], IMH [11], SCM-orth [19], SCM-seq [19] and LSSH [23]. Parameters in DLCMH are selected using cross-validation.

The dataset **Wiki** [10] consists of 2,866 Wikipedia documents, each of which is represented as an image-text pair and annotated with semantic labels of 10 categories. Each image is represented by 128-dimension SIFT feature vector and each text is represented by a 10-dimension topic vector generated by latent Dirichlet allocation (LDA) [1]. Documents are considered to be similar if they belong to the same category. Following [10], we use 2,173 documents as training pairs and the remaining 693 documents as the query set.

The **NUS-WIDE** [3] dataset contains 269,648 images crawled from Flickr, together with raw tags of these images. This dataset contains 81 concepts but some are scarce. We select 186,577 image-tag pairs from the 10 most common concepts. Each image is represented by a 500-dimensional SIFT codebook and each text is represented by a 1,000-dimensional tag occurrence feature vectors. The ground truth is defined based on whether two images share at least one common tag. Considering that CMSSH and IMH require too much resource to learn hash functions on NUS-WIDE with all samples, in this experiment, 3,000 instances are randomly selected as the training set from the database. All comparing methods adopt the same training data for fairness.

We use mean Average Precision (**mAP**) as one of performance measures. For a query q, the value of its average precision (AP) is defined as

$$AP = \frac{1}{L} \sum_{r=1}^{R} P(r)\delta(r) \tag{14}$$

where L is the number of ground-truth neighbors in retrieved set, $P(r)$ denotes the precision of top r retrieved instances, and $\delta(r)$ is an indicator function which equals to 1 if the

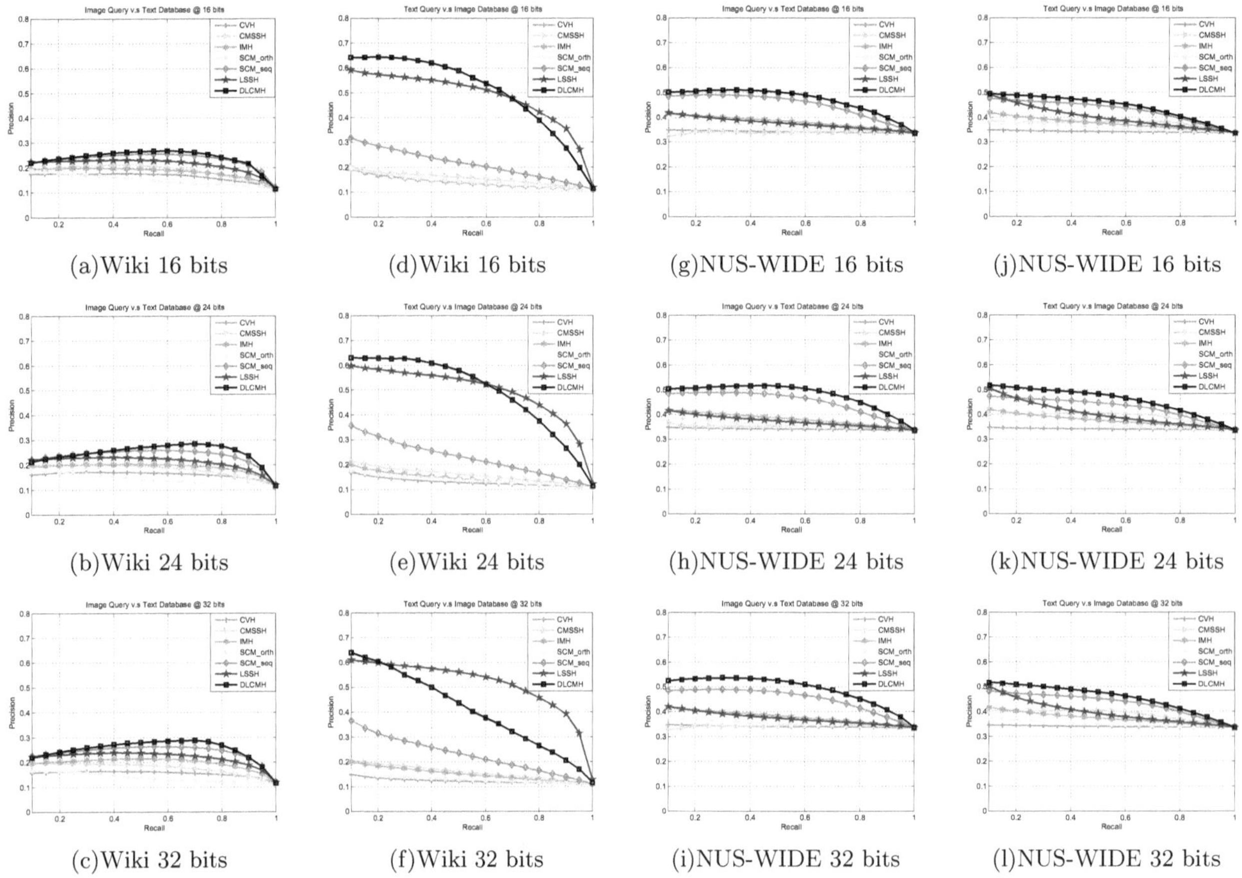

(a)Wiki 16 bits (d)Wiki 16 bits (g)NUS-WIDE 16 bits (j)NUS-WIDE 16 bits

(b)Wiki 24 bits (e)Wiki 24 bits (h)NUS-WIDE 24 bits (k)NUS-WIDE 24 bits

(c)Wiki 32 bits (f)Wiki 32 bits (i)NUS-WIDE 32 bits (l)NUS-WIDE 32 bits

Figure 1: Precision-recall curves on Wiki and NUS-WIDE

r-th instance is relevant to query, and 0 otherwise. Then, the AP of all queries is averaged to obtain the **mAP**. Furthermore, we also report *precision-recall* curve which shows the precision at different recall level. In the experiments, we set $R = 50$ and all of the results are averaged over 10 runs.

3.2 Results

The **mAP** results with various code lengths are summarized in Table 1 & 2. From these tables, we can find that

- On **Wiki**, there is only one case that DLCMH does not obtain the best result.
- On **NUS-WIDE**, DLCMH also obtains the best results on all other cases except the one of "Text Query v.s. Image Database" with 32 bits.
- The performance of many methods may degrade as the code length increases. A possible reason is that the learned methods will be farther from the optimal solutions when the code length gets longer which is also reported in [22].

To get more observations, we further plot *precision-recall* curves on both **Wiki** and **NUS-WIDE**. They are illustrated in Figure 1. From these figures, we have following observations:

- Except the cases of (d), (e) and (f), DLCMH obtains better results than all compared methods.
- DLCMH does not obtain the best results on the cases of (d), (e) and (f), however, it gets better precision when recall is small. This means that it can get more similar samples when the number of total retrieved samples is small.

From these results of Table 1 & 2 and Figure 1, we can find that DLCMH generally outperforms or is comparable to these state-of-the-arts.

4. CONCLUSIONS

In this paper, we have proposed a dictionary learning based hashing method for cross-modal retrieval. Experiments on two real-world datasets have demonstrated the effectiveness of the proposed method. For our future research, we will explore more efficient optimization algorithms to improve the scalability of DLCMH. In addition, we will also conduct more comparisons with more stat-of-the-art hashing methods.

5. ACKNOWLEDGEMENTS

This work was partially supported by National Natural Science Foundation of China (61173068, 61573212, 91546203), Program for New Century Excellent Talents in University of the Ministry of Education, the Key Science Technology Project of Shandong Province (2015GGE27033), the Independent Innovation Foundation of Shandong Province (2014CGZH1106).

6. REFERENCES

[1] D. M. Blei, A. Y. Ng, and M. I. Jordan. Latent dirichlet allocation. *Journal of Machine Learning Research*, 3:993–1022, 2003.

[2] M. M. Bronstein, A. M. Bronstein, F. Michel, and N. Paragios. Data fusion through cross-modality metric learning using similarity-sensitive hashing. In *Proceedings of IEEE International Conference on Computer Vision and Pattern Recognition*, pages 3594–3601, 2010.

[3] T.-S. Chua, J. Tang, R. Hong, H. Li, Z. Luo, and Y. Zheng. Nus-wide: a real-world web image database from national university of singapore. In *Proceedings of ACM International Conference on Image and Video Retrieval*, page 48, 2009.

[4] G. Ding, Y. Guo, and J. Zhou. Collective matrix factorization hashing for multimodal data. In *Proceedings of IEEE Conference on Computer Vision and Pattern Recognition*, pages 2075–2082, 2014.

[5] S. Kim, Y. Kang, and S. Choi. Sequential spectral learning to hash with multiple representations. In *Proceedings of European Conference on Computer Vision*, pages 538–551, 2012.

[6] S. Kumar and R. Udupa. Learning hash functions for cross-view similarity search. In *Proceedings of International Joint Conference on Artificial Intelligence*, pages 1360–1365, 2011.

[7] Z. Lin, G. Ding, M. Hu, and J. Wang. Semantics-preserving hashing for cross-view retrieval. In *Proceedings of the IEEE Conference on Computer Vision and Pattern Recognition*, pages 3864–3872, 2015.

[8] W. Liu, J. Wang, R. Ji, Y.-G. Jiang, and S.-F. Chang. Supervised hashing with kernels. In *Proceedings of IEEE Conference on Computer Vision and Pattern Recognition*, pages 2074–2081, 2012.

[9] M. Ou, P. Cui, F. Wang, J. Wang, W. Zhu, and S. Yang. Comparing apples to oranges: a scalable solution with heterogeneous hashing. In *Proceedings of ACM International Conference on Knowledge Discovery and Data Mining*, pages 230–238, 2013.

[10] N. Rasiwasia, J. Costa Pereira, E. Coviello, G. Doyle, G. R. Lanckriet, R. Levy, and N. Vasconcelos. A new approach to cross-modal multimedia retrieval. In *Proceedings of ACM International Conference on Multimedia*, pages 251–260, 2010.

[11] J. Song, Y. Yang, Y. Yang, Z. Huang, and H. T. Shen. Inter-media hashing for large-scale retrieval from heterogeneous data sources. In *Proceedings of ACM International Conference on Management of Data*, pages 785–796, 2013.

[12] D. Wang, X. Gao, X. Wang, and L. He. Semantic topic multimodal hashing for cross-media retrieval. In *Proceedings of International Joint Conference on Artificial Intelligence*, pages 3890–3896, 2015.

[13] J. Wang, X.-S. Xu, S. Guo, L. Cui, and X.-L. Wang. Linear unsupervised hashing for ann search in euclidean space. *Neurocomputing*, 171(C):283–292, 2016.

[14] S.-S. Wang, Z. Huang, and X.-S. Xu. A multi-label least-squares hashing for scalable image search. In *Proceedings of SIAM International Conference on Data Mining*, pages 954–962, 2015.

[15] Y. Yang, Z.-J. Zha, Y. Gao, X. Zhu, and T.-S. Chua. Exploiting web images for robust semantic video indexing via sample-specific loss. *IEEE Transactions on Multimedia*, 16(6):1677–1689, 2014.

[16] Y. Yang, H. Zhang, M. Zhang, F. Shen, and X. Li. Visual coding in a semantic hierarchy. In *Proceedings of ACM International Conference on Multimedia*, pages 59–68, 2015.

[17] Z. Yu, F. Wu, Y. Yang, Q. Tian, J. Luo, and Y. Zhuang. Discriminative coupled dictionary hashing for fast cross-media retrieval. In *Proceedings of ACM International Conference on Research and Development in Information Retrieval*, pages 395–404, 2014.

[18] D. Zhai, H. Chang, Y. Zhen, X. Liu, X. Chen, and W. Gao. Parametric local multimodal hashing for cross-view similarity search. In *Proceedings of International Joint Conference on Artificial Intelligence*, pages 2754–2760, 2013.

[19] D. Zhang and W.-J. Li. Large-scale supervised multimodal hashing with semantic correlation maximization. In *Proceedings of AAAI Conference on Artificial Intelligence*, pages 2177–2183, 2014.

[20] D. Zhang, F. Wang, and L. Si. Composite hashing with multiple information sources. In *Proceedings of ACM SIGIR International Conference on Research and Development in Information Retrieval*, pages 225–234, 2011.

[21] Y. Zhen and D.-Y. Yeung. Co-regularized hashing for multimodal data. In *Advances in Neural Information Processing Systems 25*, pages 1376–1384, 2012.

[22] Y. Zhen and D.-Y. Yeung. A probabilistic model for multimodal hash function learning. In *Proceedings of ACM International Conference on Knowledge Discovery and Data Mining*, pages 940–948, 2012.

[23] J. Zhou, G. Ding, and Y. Guo. Latent semantic sparse hashing for cross-modal similarity search. In *Proceedings of ACM International Conference on Research and Development in Information Retrieval*, pages 415–424, 2014.

SocialFX: Studying a Crowdsourced Folksonomy of Audio Effects Terms

Taylor Zheng
Northwestern University
EECS Department
tz0531@gmail.com

Prem Seetharaman
Northwestern University
EECS Department
prem@u.northwestern.edu

Bryan Pardo
Northwestern University
EECS Department
pardo@northwestern.edu

ABSTRACT

We present the analysis of crowdsourced studies into how a population of Amazon Mechanical Turk Workers describe three commonly used audio effects: equalization, reverberation, and dynamic range compression. We find three categories of words used to describe audio: ones that are generally used across effects, ones that tend towards a single effect, and ones that are exclusive to a single effect. We present select examples from these categories. We visualize and present an analysis of the shared descriptor space between audio effects. Data on the strength of association between words and effects is made available online for a set of 4297 words drawn from 1233 unique users for three effects (equalization, reverberation, compression). This dataset is an important step towards implementing of an end-to-end language-based audio production system, in which a user describes a creative goal, as they would to a professional audio engineer, and the system picks which audio effect to apply, as well as the setting of the audio effect.

Keywords

Interfaces; audio engineering; effects processing; signal processing; reverberation; equalization; compression; vocabulary; crowdsourcing

1. INTRODUCTION

Audio production is a critical part of the professional production of many forms of media. Audio production tools, such as reverberation, equalization, and compression, are used to process audio after it is recorded, transforming these raw recordings into polished final products. When communicating audio production goals in these settings, content creators often use language as the primary communication medium. Meaningful language is needed when communicating these goals, since the language used in this context has connotations that are particular to audio production tools.

People with little or no training on audio production tools often describe their creative audio goals with vocabulary that has no obvious path to realization using given audio production tools. Many such potential users of audio production tools (e.g. acoustic musicians, podcast creators) have sonic ideas that they cannot express in technical terms. They may not even be able to say which audio effect tool is used to achieve their goals. As a result, they have difficulty using such tools and interactions between audio production professionals and these content creators can be a frustrating experience, hampering the creative process.

The following quote from Jon Burton, of *Sound on Sound*, illustrates the communication problem audio engineers face: "...how can you best describe a sound when you have no technical vocabulary to do so? It's a situation all engineers have been in, where a musician is frustratedly trying to explain to you the sound he or she is after, but lacking your ability to describe it in terms that relate to technology, can only abstract. I have been asked to make things more 'pinky blue', 'Castrol GTX-y' and 'buttery'." [1]

In this work, we study a vocabulary that a population of non-experts in audio engineering produced to describe audio effects produced by three of the most widely used effects tools: equalization (EQ), reverberation, and dynamic range compression (compression). Equalization adjusts the gain of individual frequencies in a recording and can be used to make things sound brighter or warmer. Reverberation adjusts the spatial quality of an audio recording by adding echo effects to the audio and can be used to make things sound like they were recorded in a cave, or a church, or a stairwell, etc. Compression reduces the dynamic range of an audio recording by reducing the amplitude of parts of audio above a specified decibel value and can be used to increase the sustain of instruments, reduce sibilant and plosive frames of a vocal recording, and prevent clipping when multiple tracks are mixed together. The EQ and reverberation datasets were described and presented in [2] and [3]. This work adds another dataset consisting of a vocabulary for compression, describes a general framework for obtaining vocabularies for arbitrary audio effects, and makes a dataset available to the public for equalization, reverberation, and compression.

In this work, we consider the following questions:

1. How can we discover words used by laymen to describe arbitrary audio effects?
2. What words are associated with which audio effects?
3. What words are associated with audio effects in general, and can be achieved effectively using multiple audio effects?

MM '16, October 15-19, 2016, Amsterdam, Netherlands
© 2016 ACM. ISBN 978-1-4503-3603-1/16/10...$15.00
DOI: http://dx.doi.org/10.1145/2964284.2967207

We extend existing work ([2], [3]) into SocialFX, a crowdsourcing solution for discovering words used by a target population for describing an arbitrary audio effect. Importantly, this data collection doesn't merely collect words, it maps words onto concrete manipulations performed by EQ, reverberation and compression tools to make an actionable vocabulary that can be used to create effects tools to manipulate sounds in terms of these words. We look at the data collected using this approach to examine how words are used across multiple audio effects, offering the first insights into the shared descriptor space of audio effects.

2. RELATED WORK

There are several existing works for learning descriptors for audio. One common approach is to use text co-occurence, lexical similarity, and dictionary definitions (e.g. Wordnet [4]. These approaches are not sufficient, as we wish to examine the mappings between words and measurable sound features and controls for audio effect tools.

Psychologists have studied the mappings between descriptive terms and measurable signal characteristics for sound. Some terms, such as those for pitch (high, low) or loudness (loud, soft), have well defined mappings onto sounds [5], [6]. Others, such as "underwater", or "muffled", have no obvious connection onto audio tools. There have been numerous attempts since the 1950s that hope to find universal sound descriptors that relate to a set of canonical perceptual dimensions ([7], [6], [8], [9]). In recent years, researchers from many different backgrounds, such as recording engineering [10] [11], music composition [12], and computer science [13] have tried to find a universal set of descriptive terms for sound.

In [14], audio features are extracted from recordings from onomatopoeia and mapped into a perceptual space, where distance between terms is correlated with perceptual distance. This work focuses on onomatopoeia, rather than the broader range of all possible audio effects, and on a small population of four lab members, rather than the larger lay population.

In [15], [16], a reverberator is developed that can be controlled entirely through perceptual characteristics of the signal, rather than in terms of low-level audio signal processing. However, these works are limited to just a few words selected by the researcher, and is limited to reverberation. Our work finds many more words as elicited from a population of laymen, and works for arbitrary audio effects.

In [2] and [3], two distinct approaches to collecting effects vocabulary data were followed, with both approaches utilizing Amazon Mechanical Turk to crowdsource effect descriptor data. SocialEQ first asked users to provide a descriptor word, then to select one of three audio samples. The selected audio would have an effect applied to it (in this case, EQ), and users were asked to rate how well the resulting audio fit the descriptor they supplied. After 40 ratings, the system would have enough data to construct an effect with parameters that fit the supplied descriptor, resulting in a mapping of an effect's parameter space to a descriptor space over the course of many sessions.

In contrast, SocialReverb asked users to listen to an audio clip randomly chosen from a group of three clips, first with no effect applied and then with an effect applied, with parameters randomly chosen from a pool of 256 parameter configurations as specified in [2]. Users were then asked to describe the resulting effect, first with as many words as they freely desired, then with descriptors they agreed with, chosen from a pool of previously contributed words. Users then rated how strongly the applied effect affected the audio clip on a Likert scale. Much like SocialEQ, the resulting data maps the parameter space of an effect to a descriptor space over the course of many sessions. For our work, we chose to follow the approach used in SocialReverb, replacing reverberation with compression.

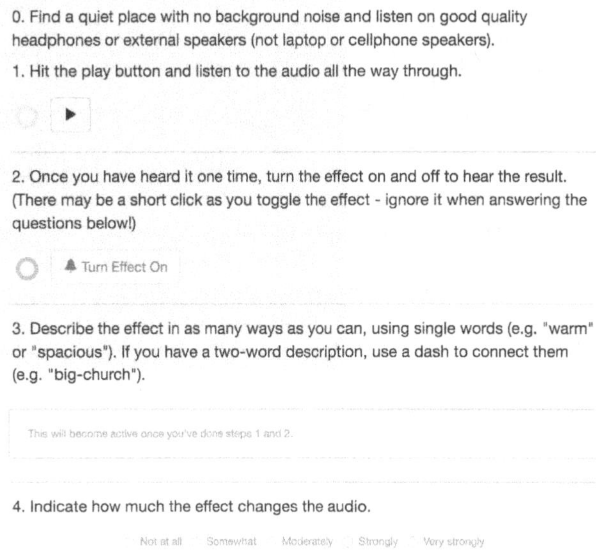

Figure 1: Part one of SocialFX: Participants are asked to listen to a dry recording, then a recording with an audio effect applied, and then describe it in their own words.

Taking into account exclusion criteria listed in [3], the data for Social-EQ was collected in 731 sessions from 481 individuals, resulting in a pool of 324 unique descriptors for equalization. Similarly, taking into account exclusion criteria listed in [2], the data for SocialReverb was collected from 513 individuals describing 256 unique instances of reverberation parameter configurations, resulting in 2861 unique descriptors for reverberation.

3. SOCIALFX

We build directly on the work in [2] and [3], extending it to SocialFX, a system for collecting descriptors for arbitrary audio effects from a population of laymen. In this work, we collect data on a new audio effect, compression. Then, we combine our compression vocabulary with the vocabularies previously collected for reverberation and EQ so as to analyze the relationships between descriptor spaces for these three different audio effects.

We used Amazon Mechanical Turk and the interface in Figures 1 and 2 to crowdsource data on how people describe compression. Taking into consideration exclusion criteria similar to that used in [2], our data was collected from 239 individuals describing 256 unique instances of compression parameter configurations, resulting in 1,112 unique descriptors.

When analyzing the shared descriptor space across EQ, reverberation, and compression, we were interested in learn-

Word category	EQ	Reverberation	Compression
General words	warm, loud, soft, happy, cool, clear, muffled, sharp, bright, calm, tinny		
Tending words	cold, happy, soothing, harsh, heavy, beautiful, mellow	distant, deep, hollow, large, good, grand, spacey	quiet, full, sharp, crisp, energetic, sutble, clean, fuzzy
Specific words	chunky, wistful, punchy, mischievous, aggravating	haunting, organ, big-hall, church-like, concert, cavernous, cathedral, gloomy	volume, sharpened, feel-good, rising, peppy, easy-going, earthy, clarified, snappy

Table 1: Descriptors and which audio effect they are related to. General words are used to describe audio effects produced by any of the three effects tools. Tending words are ones which were shown predominantly for a single audio effect, but appear in other audio effect vocabularies with low frequency. Specific words are ones that are used for a single audio effect and no others. The words shown above were found via inspection of the shared descriptor space between the three audio effects. The general words can be seen in Figure 3.

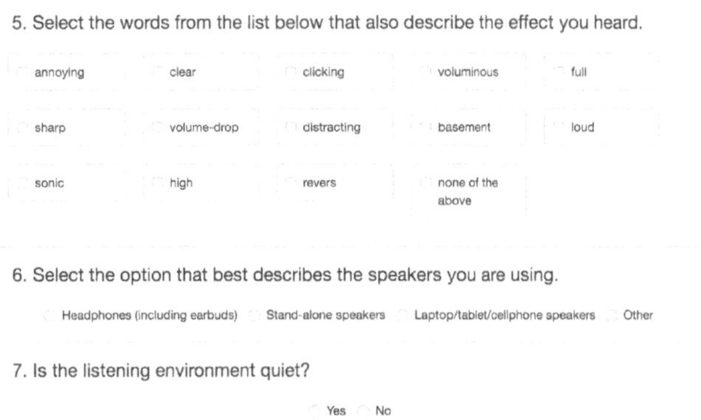

Figure 2: Part two of SocialFX: After completing part one of SocialFX, participants are asked to look at a set of words that other people used to describe the same audio effect, and check off which ones they agree describe the effect.

ing how strongly a descriptor is associated with each effect. Both audio effects experts (recording engineers) and non-experts (acoustic musicians, podcasters, videographers, etc) reach a shared understanding of what effect one is talking about when using a specific descriptor, reducing misunderstandings in the creative process.

To determine the particularity of a descriptor, we first calculate the frequency of appearance of a descriptor within an effect by dividing the number of occurrences of that descriptor within an effect by the total number of descriptor instances in the data set of that effect. Then we divide the descriptor space according to whether a descriptor is shared among all three effects or not. The descriptors in common with all three effects are further divided depending on how frequently they occurred for each effect; if a descriptor appeared with high frequency for reverberation but with low frequency for EQ and compression, we can conclude that the descriptor leans toward reverberation, while if a descriptor appeared with roughly equal frequency among all three effects, it is a more general descriptor.

We end up with three general categories of descriptors: ones that are specific to an effect, ones whose usage leans toward a particular effect, and ones that are general across all three effects. Examples of these are shown in Table 1.

4. DATASET ANALYSIS

Figure 3 visualizes the shared descriptor space across all three effects, with each axis representing the frequency of occurrence of each shared descriptor within the data set for each audio effect. In the shared descriptor space, we see certain words such as *warm* or *loud* are used broadly across compression, equalization, and reverberation, while other words, such as *soothing* or *full* tend towards one audio effect.

Within the shared data set, there are generic words such as *sound* and *normal* that have no strong connotations or associations with a particular effect. On the other hand, words such as *dark*, *bassy*, *tinny*, *bright*, and *warm* are all strongly associated with EQ. Their appearance as descriptors in both reverberation and compression can be explained by the fact that these two effects can alter the equalization of audio; in some cases, reverberation and compression can reduce the high frequency content of audio, leading to descriptors such as *warm* and *dark*.

Words that are usually associated with reverberation also appear in the list of common descriptors, such as *distant* and *spacey*. This can be explained in the case of EQ by the fact that reducing mid-range frequencies relative to treble and bass frequencies can create a greater perceived sense of distance from an audio source.

Smooth and *even* are words usually associated with compression that were used to describe EQ and reverberation as well. EQ and reverberation can potentially be used to reduce sibilants and transients in audio tracks, which can be perceived as *smooth* or *even*. Words like *quiet*, *soft*, and *loud* also all deal with volume levels, but can be achieved via reverberation by reducing the amount of direct sound or via equalization by damping prominent frequencies.

The list of shared descriptors also has bridge words, which are words that have different meanings in different contexts. For example, *hollow* in the context of EQ usually refers to a lack of mid-range frequencies, while in the context of reverberation, it can refer to the feeling of space generated by reverberation. *Crisp*, for EQ, refers to an abundance of upper treble frequencies, but for compression, it can refer to the preservation of transients under subtle compression settings. We find that the vocabularies of the three audio effects are often intertwined.

5. DATA SET

To facilitate the creation of word-based interfaces that use non-expert vocabulary to control audio production tools, we have created a data set which we will make available at http://bit.ly/1WmTP6v. The data set includes relative word frequency of 4297 words drawn from 1233 unique users across three effects (EQ, reverb, compression), as well as

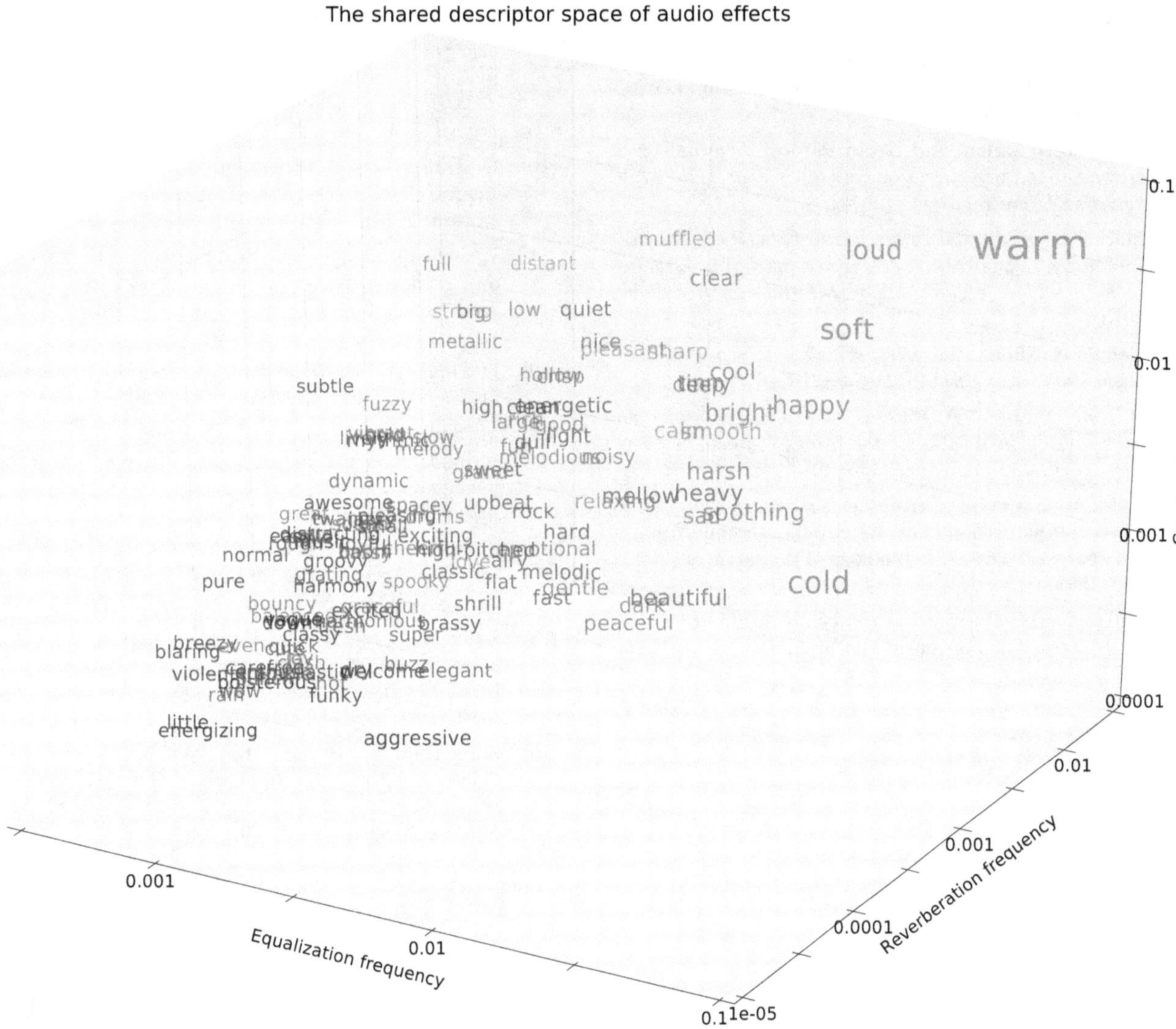

Figure 3: Shared descriptor space arranged in terms of frequency of occurrence in each effect data set. Towards the top right indicates high frequency across all audio effects (e.g. *warm*). The size of the word correlates with how often it was used across all three datasets. Words that tend towards an effect can be visualized along each axis. As words tend along the reverberation frequency axis, they become more transparent and become more red, to make the 3D effect easier to see.

the associated effects settings. We also plan to develop a Javascript library for the development of language-based audio production interfaces.

6. CONCLUSION

In this work, we have presented SocialFX, a crowdsourcing mechanism for discovering vocabulary related to audio effects. We have presented an analysis of three datasets, each collected for different audio effects - equalization, reverberation, and compression. We have found that there are three categories of words used to describe audio: ones that are generally used across effects, ones that tend towards a single effect, and ones that are exclusive to a single effect. We have shown examples of these three categories. Finally, we have visualized and presented an analysis of the shared descriptor space between audio effects. Our analysis of these descriptor spaces shows a way forward to alleviate communication difficulties in audio production environments that are caused by the use of language.

This analysis is a first step toward an end-to-end language-based audio production system, in which a user describes a creative goal, as they would to an audio engineer, and the system picks which audio effect to apply, in addition to adjusting that effect's parameters to achieve the user's goal.

7. ACKNOWLEDGMENTS

We would like to thank NSF Grants 1116384 and 1420971 for funding this work. Thanks to Alison Wahl for providing source audio for SocialFX.

References

[1] Jon Burton. *Ear Machine iQ: Intelligent Equaliser Plug-in.* June 2011. URL: http://www.soundonsound.com/sos/jun11/articles/em-iq.htm.

[2] Prem Seetharaman and Bryan Pardo. "Reverbalize: a crowdsourced reverberation controller". In: *ACM Multimedia, Technical Demo* (2014).

[3] Mark Cartwright and Bryan Pardo. "Social-eq: Crowdsourcing an equalization descriptor map". In: *14th International Society for Music Information Retrieval.* 2013.

[4] George A. Miller. *WordNet: a lexical database for English.* 1995. DOI: 10.1145/219717.219748.

[5] H. Helmholtz and A. Ellis. *On the sensations of tone as a physiological basis for the theory of music.* Dover, New York, 2nd english edition, 1954.

[6] S. McAdams et al. *Perceptual scaling of synthesized musical timbres: Common dimensions, specificities, and latent subject classes.* Psychological Research, 58(3):177-192, 1995.

[7] J. Grey. *Multidimensional perceptual scaling of musical timbres.* The Journal of the ASA, 61(5):1270-1277, 1977.

[8] L. Solomon. *Search for physical correlates to psychological dimensions of sounds.* The Journal of the ASA, 31(4):492-497, 1959.

[9] A Zacharakis, K Pastiadis, and G Papadelis. "An Investigation Of Musical Timbre: Uncovering Salient Semantic Descriptors And Perceptual Dimensions". In: *12th International Society for Music Information Retrieval Conference.* 2011.

[10] D. Huber and R. Runstein. *Modern recording techniques.* Focal Press/Elsevier, Amsterdam ; Boston, 7th edition, 2010.

[11] Ryan Stables et al. "SAFE: A system for the extraction and retrieval of semantic audio descriptors". In: *15th International Society on Music Information Retrieval* (2014).

[12] D. Smalley. *Spectromorphology: explaining sound-shapes.* Organised Sound, 2(02):107-126, 1997.

[13] M. Sarkar, B. Vercoe, and Y. Yang. "Words that describe timbre: a study of auditory perception through lan- guage". In: *Proc. of Language and Music as Cognitive Systems Conference.* 2007.

[14] S Sundaram and S Narayanan. "Analysis of audio clustering using word descriptions". In: *ICASSP: Acoustics, Speech and Signal Processing* (2007).

[15] Zafar Rafii and Bryan Pardo. "Learning to Control a Reverberator using Subjective Perceptual Descriptors". In: *10th International Society on Music Information Retrieval* (2009).

[16] Zafar Rafii and Bryan Pardo. "A Digital Reverberator Controlled through Measures of the Reverberation". In: *Northwestern Electrical Engineering and Computer Science Department* (2009).

SwiDeN : Convolutional Neural Networks For Depiction Invariant Object Recognition

Ravi Kiran Sarvadevabhatla, Shiv Surya*, Srinivas S S Kruthiventi, and Venkatesh Babu R.
Video Analytics Lab, Department of Computational and Data Sciences, Indian Institute of Science Bangalore, India
ravikiran@grads.cds.iisc.ac.in, shiv.surya314@gmail.com, kssaisrinivas@gmail.com, venky@cds.iisc.ac.in

ABSTRACT

Current state of the art object recognition architectures achieve impressive performance but are typically specialized for a single depictive style (e.g. photos only, sketches only). In this paper, we present SwiDeN: our Convolutional Neural Network (CNN) architecture which recognizes objects regardless of how they are visually depicted (line drawing, realistic shaded drawing, photograph etc.). In SwiDeN, we utilize a novel 'deep' depictive style-based switching mechanism which appropriately addresses the depiction-specific and depiction-invariant aspects of the problem. We compare SwiDeN with alternative architectures and prior work on a 50-category Photo-Art dataset containing objects depicted in multiple styles. Experimental results show that SwiDeN outperforms other approaches for the depiction-invariant object recognition problem.

Keywords

object category recognition, convolutional neural networks, deep learning, depiction-invariance

1. INTRODUCTION

Depiction-invariant object recognition is the ability to determine an object's category regardless of how the object is visually depicted (line drawing, realistic shaded drawing, photograph etc.). Given the varying level of abstraction and complexity in depiction (See Figure 1), this is a challenging task. Human beings easily accomplish depiction-invariant recognition but machine-based systems are nowhere close to a similar level of performance. Current state-of-the-art object recognition architectures do achieve good performance but they are specialized for a single depiction style (e.g. photos [8], sketches [19]). Therefore, designing architectures which recognize objects regardless of depiction style can facilitate progress towards matching human-level abilities. Moreover, the associated performance scores can also aid in quantitatively determining the semantic gap between human and machine capabilities [15].

Surprisingly, not much work exists for depiction-invariant object recognition. To address this gap, we propose a Convolutional Neural Network (CNN) architecture for depiction-invariant object category recognition which we call SwiDeN (Section 3). A novel aspect of our architecture is a 'deep' dynamic switching mechanism between two parallel CNN sub-architectures (Section 3.1.1). Our switch-based design not only reduces the overall burden of the generalized object recognition task but also enables the system to address depiction-specific and depiction-invariant aspects of the problem. We compare our approach with baselines, alternative architectures (Section 4.2) and previous work on a 50-category Photo-Art dataset containing multiple depictions of objects (Section 4). Experimental results show that our architecture outperforms other architectures, especially for non-photo object depictions (Section 5).

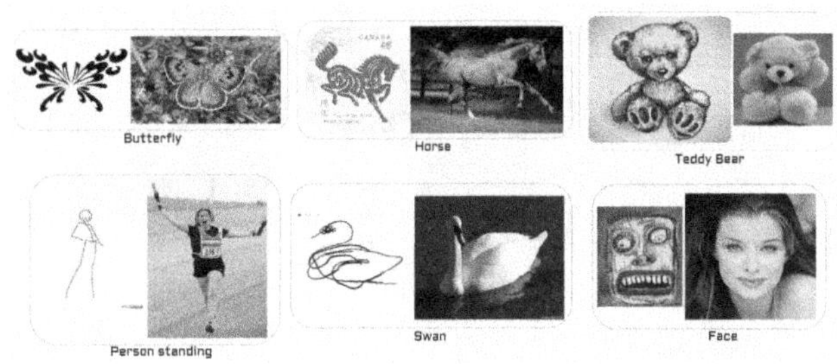

Figure 1: Sample images from the Photo-Art-50 dataset grouped by category. For each category, one image each from 'Art'(left in the pair) and 'Photo' depictive style are shown. Given the extreme changes in appearance, recognizing such images regardless of depiction is extremely challenging.

2. RELATED WORK

Object class (category) recognition, albeit restricted to photographic depictions, has been studied extensively by researchers [5, 6, 12]. However, little previous work exists for truly general multi- depiction object recognition. Wu et al. [16] construct multi-attribute part-graphs for object categories and use graph matching for classification on the same dataset we use. However, their evaluation procedure, also

*Equal contributor as the first author

MM '16, October 15-19, 2016, Amsterdam, Netherlands
© 2016 ACM. ISBN 978-1-4503-3603-1/16/10...$15.00
DOI: http://dx.doi.org/10.1145/2964284.2967208

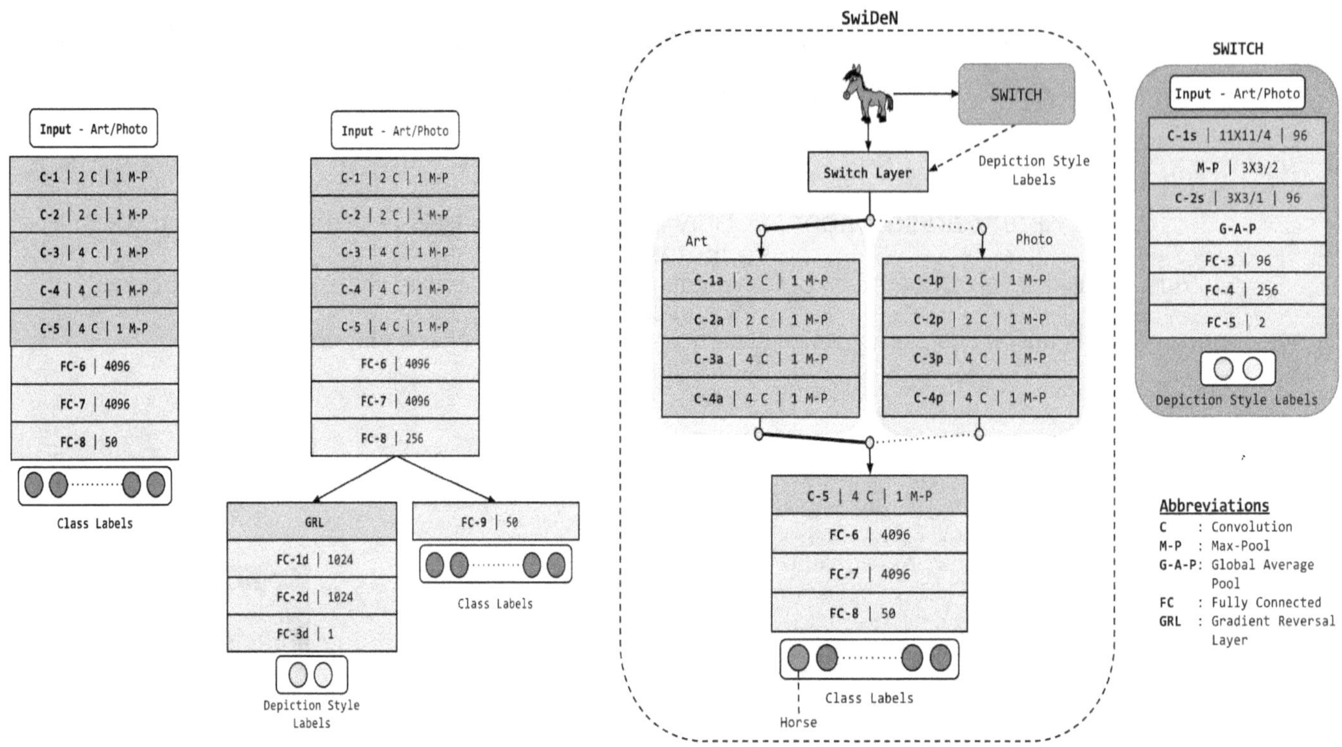

(a) Baseline (b) Gradient Reversal Network(GRN) (c) Switching Deep Networks(SwiDeN)

Figure 2: Our proposed architecture SwiDeN is shown in 2(c). The depictive style of the cartoon-ish horse image is determined as 'Art' by SWITCH (purple block). An associated switch layer relays it to the 'Art' sub-network (green block). The latter's output is passed via a series of shared layers and finally, a softmax classifier generates the label **Horse**. Figure 2(a) is the baseline architecture. Figure 2(b) (GRN) is a modification of architecture proposed by Ganin et al [ ]. VGG-19 [ ] is used as the base network for all architectures.

used by Cai et al. [,] , induces an unreasonable amount of category bias which makes comparison difficult. We present an alternative evaluation procedure which is more principled (See Section 4.1). Xiao et al. [ ] present a graph-based object modelling approach and evaluate it on 10 augmented classes of Caltech-256. Shrivastava et al [ ] utilize a depiction-invariant method for image matching. Domain adaption approaches have been also been tried [ ] . However, when the domain-specific identifiers (e.g. target domain labels) are available as in our case, a domain-adaptation procedure unnecessarily makes the overall problem harder since the objective in domain-adaptation is typically to "forget" the source domain.

All the approaches mentioned above utilize multiple hand-crafted modules in the recognition pipeline. To the best of our knowledge, ours is the first end-to-end deep learning approach for depiction-invariant recognition of object categories.

3. OUR FRAMEWORK

3.1 Motivation

Instead of learning from scratch, a common paradigm is to utilize pre-trained CNNs as a starting point while constructing deep networks of interest. We follow a similar paradigm in our approach.

In an effort to represent the sheer variety seen in image content, the convolutional layers in a CNN typically contain a large number of learnable filters. However, the filters are only sufficient to the extent that the depiction style remains unchanged (e.g. photographs). To accommodate the increase in variety when images from additional depiction styles need to be recognized, a naïve strategy would be to add additional learnable filters for each convolution layer of a pre-trained network[1] and perform fine-tuning. However, this strategy results in an unbalanced learning regime since convolutional layers now contain a mixture of learnt and non-learnt filters. In addition, the added filters necessitate an ad-hoc grouping of filter layers to ensure operational consistency which further complicates the overall framework.

An alternative design would be to learn the filters for each depictive style separately. In this design, a set of shallow layer sub-networks exist for each depictive style (see Figure 2(c)). Since our final objective is to achieve depiction-invariant recognition, we require our network to learn a depiction-invariant feature representation. This is achieved by having a final set of layers. To serve as a relay mechanism

[1]In this case, the network could be one pre-trained for a particular depiction style (e.g. photographs).

between the initial depiction-specific sub-network branches and the shared, deeper depiction-invariant fully-connected layers, we employ a custom-designed "switch" (Section 3.1.1). The switch is trained such that given an image, it determines its depictive style and selects the corresponding depiction-specific sub-network for processing the image. The output of this sub-network is then processed by the depiction-invariant layers of the network. The network culminates in a typical softmax-based classification layer which determines the image category, regardless of its depictive style (Figure 2(c)).

Next, we describe the depiction style-based switching mechanism. Subsequently, we delve into the architectural details of the main network pipeline which we dub SwiDeN (Switching Deep Network).

3.1.1 SWITCH

To realize the switching mechanism mentioned in Section 3.1, we design and train a switch network (see Figure 2 (c)), henceforth referred to as SWITCH, that determines the depiction style of the input image and passes the image to corresponding depiction sub-network (Photo or Art). The SWITCH has two convolution layers which capture depiction-discriminative features such as edges, textures, corners, colors and their conjunctions [20]. The first convolution layer is initialized from AlexNet [10]. The features from the first layer are max pooled while the features from the second convolution layer are average pooled globally [11]. The pooled features are processed by two fully connected layers and passed to a classifier layer which determines the depiction style of the input image as 'Art' or 'Photo'. For better generalization, we use dropout for fully connected layers with 0.5 as the dropout value. We trained SWITCH using stochastic gradient descent (SGD) [10] with a base learning rate $\alpha = 10^{-2}$ and momentum $\mu = 0.9$. Overall, SWITCH achieves an average accuracy of 83.7% (80.6% for 'Art' and 86.8% for 'Photo').

SWITCH's inability to achieve 100% accuracy can be attributed to the fact that some photo images have a predominantly artistic quality and vice-versa (see supplementary material). While this may seem like a liability, in practice, all we require is that SWITCH achieve a reasonably high accuracy which ensures an overall burden reduction for the filter learning process.

3.1.2 Switching Deep Network (SwiDeN)

The initial portion of SwiDeN consists of two separate sub-networks, one each for photo and art depiction style. During training, SWITCH (Section 3.1.1) selects the sub-network branch through which the input image is passed in the forward pass and ensures that the corresponding network loss is backpropagated through the branch selected during the forward pass. The layers after SWITCH are shared layers, designed to learn depiction-style invariant representations.

For our problem, we build SwiDeN using VGG-19 deep network [14] layers. We select a subset of initial convolutional layers of VGG-19 and utilize them as the sub-networks for each depictive style. The rest of the VGG-19 layers (except the final classification layer) are used as the shared layers of SwiDeN. Figure 2(c) illustrates a SwiDeN architecture where the first four convolutional layers of VGG-19 are used for the depictive style sub-networks (`C1a` - `C4a` for 'Art' and `C1p` - `C4p` for 'Photo') and the rest of VGG-19 layers (`C-5`,`FC-6`,`FC-7`) form the shared portion.

In our experiments, we systematically examined the effect on recognition performance when the first $k, 1 \leq k \leq 5$ convolutional layers of VGG-19 are used as depiction-style sub-networks (Section 5). For the rest of the paper, we refer to the corresponding architectures as **C1-S,C2-S,C3-S,C4-S** and **C5-S**. Thus, the architecture in Figure 2(c) is **C4-S**.

4. EXPERIMENTS

4.1 Dataset

We evaluate the classification performance on the Photo-Art-50 dataset [3]. This dataset contains 50 classes and 90 to 138 images in each class with approximately half photo and half art images. The authors also provide train-test splits for comparative evaluation. However, the splits are unbalanced and do not include a validation split, thus inducing significant class bias during evaluation. To avoid this issue, we create our own train, validation and test splits. We create five random splits, each containing 60 images from each category for training (30 art and 30 photo) and 20 images for testing (10 art and 10 photo). The remaining images from each category are used for validation. We augment the dataset by taking 5 crops of size 224×224 (four corner crops and the center crop) after rescaling the smallest side of the image to 256. For training images, the center crop alone is centered around the bounding box. Multiple objects of same class in a single image are ignored. We plan to release our balanced splits to the public.

4.2 Comparison architectures

4.2.1 Baseline

As a natural baseline, we fine-tune VGG-19 using the training data for the 50 classes described in Section 4.1. For training, we used a stochastic gradient descent (SGD) method with a base learning rate $\alpha = 10^{-5}$ and momentum $\mu = 0.9$ to learn the weights. The learning rate was stepped down by a factor of 10 when the validation accuracy plateaued.

4.2.2 Gradient Reversal Network

Ganin et al. [7] propose a deep network-based domain-adaptation framework. The authors aim to maximize the target domain accuracy by simultaneously minimizing the target-domain label loss function and maximizing the loss for domain type (target or source) classification. To achieve this, they introduce a gradient reversal layer which not only assists domain-adaptation but also helps learn a domain-invariant representation (FC-8 in Figure 2(b)). Intrigued by this domain-invariance feature, we wished to examine the architecture's suitability for our cross-depiction problem by viewing depictive styles as domains. However, in their original formulation, Ganin et al. maximize the accuracy for a single domain (depictive style). Therefore, we modify their formulation such that the overall network loss for *both* the domains ('Art' and 'Photo') is minimized. In addition, we replace Alexnet used by Ganin et al. with VGG-19. For the rest of the paper, we shall refer to this modified formulation as Gradient Reversal Network (GRN).

We initialize GRN with VGG-19 model weights and performed training using SGD with base learning rate of $\alpha = 10^{-5}$ and momentum $\mu = 0.9$. A uniform learning rate was maintained throughout training. For the gradient reversal

ARCH.	OVERALL ACC.	ART ACC.	PHOTO ACC.
Baseline	93.80%	89.80%	**97.80%**
GRN	92.64%	88.52%	96.76%
SwiDeN(Ours)	**94.42%**	**91.12%**	97.72%

Table 1: Classification accuracy for different architectures.

ARCH.	OVERALL ACC.	ART ACC.	PHOTO ACC.
Wu et al.[16]	89.67%	**89.06%**	90.29%
SwiDeN (Ours)	**93.02%**	88.47%	**97.56%**

Table 2: Classification accuracy on train-test splits by Cai et al. [3].

layer's scaling factor λ (see [ ] for details), we tried values of $1, 2, 3, 5, 10$ and found that $\lambda = 2$ gave the best result.

4.2.3 SwiDeN: training

The same training procedure and hyperparameters as in the baseline were used for training SwiDeN architectures **C1-S,C2-S...C5-S** (Section 3.1.2) with the exception of the the learning rates for the depictive style sub-networks. For the 'Art' sub-network, we used a learning rate scaled by a factor of 4 since the base network (VGG) is primarily trained for non-Art images. The learning rate was stepped down by a factor of 10 when the validation accuracy plateaued.

4.3 Evaluation

For evaluation, we determined the final label by pooling the results for five crops of the test image (four corner crops and one center crop) for all the architectures.

4.4 Implementation

We used Caffe [9] for all experiments on the baseline. For SwiDeN, we integrated the switch layer from a branch of Caffe [2] into the master branch [1] and customized it for our experiments involving SwiDeN. For experiments on GRN, we used the Caffe version provided by Ganin et al. [7].

5. RESULTS

For each architecture (baseline, GRN and SwiDeN (**C4-S**), we computed the average test set accuracy across all the classes and all the splits. We collate the results into three groups – accuracy regardless of depictive style ('Overall') and style-wise accuracies for 'Photo' (i.e. accuracy on photographic test images only) and 'Art'). The results can be seen in seen in Table 1. Our SwiDeN architecture outperforms the other two architectures overall and for 'Art' while remaining competitive for 'Photo'. In SwiDen, the depiction-style SWITCH guided sub-network learning reduces the overall burden for the deeper shared layers in learning a robust depiction-invariant representation, which in turn contributes to SwiDeN's performance.

GRN performs worse than the baseline and SwiDeN. Similar to SwiDeN, GRN also utilizes feedback from a depiction-style classifier. However, the feedback is provided coarsely and indirectly (in terms of loss). Moreover, the feedback is provided at a layer situated deep in the network. This hinders the fine-tuning of shallower (convolutional) filters to learn 'Art'-specific filters, thus affecting the performance on 'Art' in particular and overall performance in general.

We also observe that the baseline performs slightly better than other architectures for 'Photo' style. This is to be expected since the original filters are highly-tuned for photos. However, its performance for 'Art' is relatively lower compared to SwiDeN. This shows that the complexity involved in cross-depiction recognition cannot be addressed merely by employing typical transfer learning approaches such as fine-tuning.

In spite of the class-bias induced by the splits provided by Cai et al. [3], we compared the performance of our **C4-S** SwiDeN architecture against that of the multi-attribute part-graph model proposed by Wu et al. [16]. To aid training, we augment the training set by performing RGB jittering, horizontal flip on all images and morphological operations for 'Art' images. As Table 2 shows, SwiDeN achieves state-of-the-art results , outperforming the result of Wu et al. [16] overall and for 'Photo' images while remaining competitive for 'Art'.

Table 3 summarizes the performance of different SwiDeN architectures. As can be seen, **C4-S** outperforms other SwiDeN architectures. As an interesting observation, the trends in overall accuracy and 'Art' accuracy as the depth of depictive-style sub-networks increases resemble the patterns observed by Yosinski et al.[18] for deep networks but in the context of transfer learning.

SWIDEN ARCH.	OVERALL ACC.	ART ACC.	PHOTO ACC.
C1-S	94.22%	90.44%	**98.00%**
C2-S	94.36%	90.8%	97.92%
C3-S	93.96%	90.4%	97.52%
C4-S	**94.42%**	**91.12%**	97.72%
C5-S	92.64%	88.52%	96.76%

Table 3: Classification accuracy for different SwiDeN architectures **C1-S–C5-S**(see Section 3.1.2).

6. CONCLUSION

In this paper, we have described SwiDeN, our end-to-end deep learning framework for recognizing objects regardless of depiction. A key aspect of SwiDeN is the 'deep' depictive style-based switching mechanism which judiciously addresses depiction-specific and depiction-invariant aspects of the problem. Addressing these aspects enables us to achieve state-of-the-art results on a challenging dataset containing 'Photo' and 'Art' style object depictions. In future, we plan to explore unsupervised network learning approaches. Our code and pre-trained models can be accessed at https://github.com/val-iisc/swiden.

7. REFERENCES

[1] Caffe master branch. https://github.com/BVLC/caffe.

[2] Caffe switch layer branch. https://github.com/sguada/caffe-public/tree/switch_layer/src/caffe/layers.

[3] H. Cai, Q. Wu, T. Corradi, and P. Hall. The cross-depiction problem: Computer vision algorithms for recognising objects in artwork and in photographs. *arXiv preprint arXiv:1505.00110*, 2015.

[4] H. Cai, Q. Wu, and P. Hall. Beyond photo-domain object recognition: Benchmarks for the cross-depiction problem. In *Proceedings of the IEEE International Conference on Computer Vision Workshops*, pages 1–6, 2015.

[5] R. Fergus, P. Perona, and A. Zisserman. Object class recognition by unsupervised scale-invariant learning. In *Computer Vision and Pattern Recognition, 2003. Proceedings. 2003 IEEE Computer Society Conference on*, volume 2, pages II–264. IEEE, 2003.

[6] S. Fidler and A. Leonardis. Towards scalable representations of object categories: Learning a hierarchy of parts. In *Computer Vision and Pattern Recognition, 2007. CVPR'07. IEEE Conference on*, pages 1–8. IEEE, 2007.

[7] Y. Ganin and V. Lempitsky. Unsupervised domain adaptation by backpropagation. In *Proceedings of The 32nd International Conference on Machine Learning*, pages 1180–1189, 2015.

[8] K. He, X. Zhang, S. Ren, and J. Sun. Deep residual learning for image recognition. *arXiv preprint arXiv:1512.03385*, 2015.

[9] Y. Jia, E. Shelhamer, J. Donahue, S. Karayev, J. Long, R. Girshick, S. Guadarrama, and T. Darrell. Caffe: Convolutional architecture for fast feature embedding. *arXiv preprint arXiv:1408.5093*, 2014.

[10] A. Krizhevsky, I. Sutskever, and G. E. Hinton. Imagenet classification with deep convolutional neural networks. In *Advances in neural information processing systems*, pages 1097–1105, 2012.

[11] M. Lin, Q. Chen, and S. Yan. Network in network. *arXiv preprint arXiv:1312.4400*, 2013.

[12] J. Shotton, A. Blake, and R. Cipolla. Multiscale categorical object recognition using contour fragments. *Pattern Analysis and Machine Intelligence, IEEE Transactions on*, 30(7):1270–1281, 2008.

[13] A. Shrivastava, T. Malisiewicz, A. Gupta, and A. A. Efros. Data-driven visual similarity for cross-domain image matching. *ACM Transaction of Graphics (TOG) (Proceedings of ACM SIGGRAPH ASIA)*, 30(6), 2011.

[14] K. Simonyan and A. Zisserman. Very deep convolutional networks for large-scale image recognition. *CoRR*, abs/1409.1556, 2014.

[15] S. Ullman, L. Assif, E. Fetaya, and D. Harari. Atoms of recognition in human and computer vision. *Proceedings of the National Academy of Sciences*, 113(10):2744–2749, 2016.

[16] Q. Wu, H. Cai, and P. Hall. Learning graphs to model visual objects across different depictive styles. In *Computer Vision–ECCV 2014*, pages 313–328. Springer, 2014.

[17] B. Xiao, S. Yi-Zhe, and P. Hall. Learning invariant structure for object identification by using graph methods. *Computer Vision and Image Understanding*, 115(7):1023 – 1031, 2011. Special issue on Graph-Based Representations in Computer Vision.

[18] J. Yosinski, J. Clune, Y. Bengio, and H. Lipson. How transferable are features in deep neural networks? In *Advances in Neural Information Processing Systems*, pages 3320–3328, 2014.

[19] Q. Yu, Y. Yang, Y.-Z. Song, T. Xiang, and T. Hospedales. Sketch-a-net that beats humans. *BMVC*, 2015.

[20] M. D. Zeiler and R. Fergus. Visualizing and understanding convolutional networks. In *Computer vision–ECCV 2014*, pages 818–833. Springer, 2014.

Multi-Scale Triplet CNN for Person Re-Identification

Jiawei Liu[1], Zheng-Jun Zha[1], Qi Tian[2], Dong Liu[1], Ting Yao[3], Qiang Ling[1], Tao Mei[3]

[1]University of Science and Technology of China, China
[2]University of Texas at San Antonio, USA
[3]Microsoft Research Asia, China

{ljw368}@mail.ustc.edu.cn, {zhazj,dongeliu,qling}@ustc.edu.cn
{qi.tian}@cs.utsa.edu, {tiyao,tmei}@microsoft.com

ABSTRACT

Person re-identification aims at identifying a certain person across non-overlapping multi-camera networks. It is a fundamental and challenging task in automated video surveillance. Most existing researches mainly rely on hand-crafted features, resulting in unsatisfactory performance. In this paper, we propose a multi-scale triplet convolutional neural network which captures visual appearance of a person at various scales. We propose to optimize the network parameters by a comparative similarity loss on massive sample triplets, addressing the problem of small training set in person re-identification. In particular, we design a unified multi-scale network architecture consisting of both deep and shallow neural networks, towards learning robust and effective features for person re-identification under complex conditions. Extensive evaluation on the real-world Market-1501 dataset have demonstrated the effectiveness of the proposed approach.

Keywords: Person re-identification; Deep CNN

1. INTRODUCTION

Person re-identification is a pressing demand in automated video surveillance and attracts increasing attention from academia and industry. Given an image of a certain person taken from one camera, the task of re-identification is to identify the person images taken from different cameras [1, 2]. A person re-identification system could save a lot of human labour in exhaustively searching for a target person from a large number of video sequences.

Despite the encouraging progress in person re-identification, this task is still very challenging and remains unsolved due to camera setting variations, human pose changes, illumination changes as well as background clutter and occlusions [3]. In addition, persons may share similar visual appearance, making the re-identification more difficult. Figure 1 illustrates the matching of a probe image of a target person

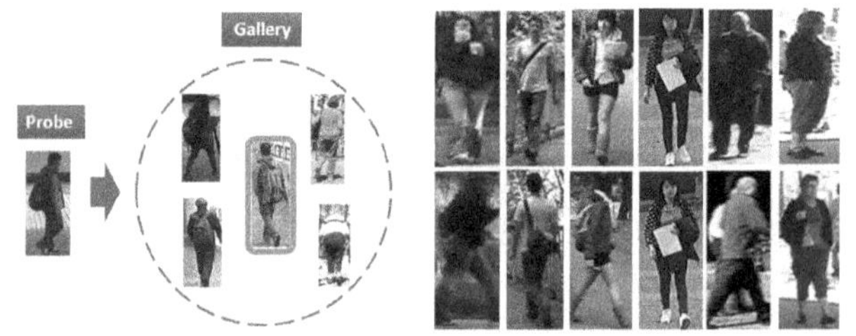

Figure 1. Illustration of (a)matching a probe image against gallery images. (b) image variations (left to right): low resolution, human pose changes, camera view changes, occlusions, illumination variation, and persons share similar appearance.

against a set of gallery images as well as several kinds of image variations.

To address these challenges, existing research focus on the development of effective features to describe visual appearance of persons and/or an appropriate metric to measure the similarity among person images. A number of hand-craft low-level features have been proposed to tackle the various image variations, including color histogram [4, 5, 6, 7], Local Binary Pattern (LBP) [8], Gabor feature [6], and SIFT [9], etc. Among these features, color representation is an important cue in person re-identification. Many sophisticated features have been developed in recent years to boost the re-identification performance. For example, Yang et al. [10] proposed a sophisticated color descriptor, termed salient color names. Farenzena et al. [11] proposed the Symmetry-Driven Accumulation of Local Features (SDALF) to exploit the symmetry property of human body to handle variations of camera views. Gary and Tao [12] proposed to select optimal descriptors from color and texture features by AdaBoost. Zhao et al. [13] exploited salience information and emphasized rare colors by giving them higher weights in matching. Ma et al. [14] and Zheng et al. [15] encoded local features to a final global representation. Song et al. [16] proposed to learn human attributes for person re-identification. Liao et al. [17] analyzed the horizontal occurrence of local features and maximized the occurrence to improve the robustness of features.

Recently, deep learning has obtained great successes in various computer vision tasks [18]. It has shown great ability for learning inconceivable and effective visual representation. However, there are few works that exploit deep

MM '16, October 15–19, 2016, Amsterdam, The Netherlands.
 ISBN 978-1-4503-3603-1/16/10...$15.00
DOI: http://dx.doi.org/10.1145/2964284.2967209

learning technique to facilitate person re-identification. Li et al. [19], Yi et al. [20], and Ahmed et al. [21] used a Convolutional Neural Network (e.g., "Siamese" network) to learn visual features from pedestrian image pairs. However, the number of generated negative pairs greatly outnumber the positive pairs. This may enforce the trained model biased towards negative pairs. And these networks were all designed with a relatively shallow architecture, which can not well exploit the effectiveness of deep learning.

Based on visual features, some existing works focus on learning an appropriate distance/similarity metric to compare the features across person images. The metric is expected to make the images of the same person close in feature space and separate the images from different persons far away from each other. For example, Dikmen et al. [22] proposed to learn a Mahalanobis distance metric through a maximum margin formulation. Sareesh et al. [23] learnt a distance metric by a Local Fisher Discriminant Analysis (LFDA) method. Martin et al. [24] introduced a simple, but effective strategy to learn a distance metric from equivalence constraints. Mignon et al. [5] developed a Pairwise Constrained Component Analysis (PCCA) method, which derives a projection from the original feature space into a low-dimensional space.

In this paper, we propose a multi-scale triplet convolutional neural network which captures visual appearance of a person at various scales. We design a unified multi-scale network architecture consisting of both deep and shallow neural networks, towards learning robust and effective features for person re-identification with various variations. We propose an integrated "end-to-end" learning procedure to learn deep features and similarity metric simultaneously. We optimize the network parameters based on a comparative similarity loss on massive sample triplets, addressing the problem of small training set in person re-identification. Extensive experiments on the real-world Market1501 data set have shown that the proposed approach achieves better performance than the state-of-the-art methods.

2. THE PROPOSED APPROACH

2.1 Comparative Similarity Loss

Person re-identification can be viewed as a person image matching problem. The objective is to learn an effective representation and an appropriate similarity metric to match images from the same person and distinguish images from different persons. Let $\mathcal{X} = \{x_i^p \mid i = 1, 2, ..., N\}$ denote a training set, where x_i^p represents the *p-th* image of *i-th* person and N is the number of pedestrians. For a probe image x of a person of interest, person re-identification system searches for the images from the same person by matching the probe image against a set of gallery images $\{\mathcal{G}\}$. The visual features and similarity metric are expected to give higher similarity score to the pair of images $\{x_i, x_i^+\}$ from the same person over the the pair $\{x_i, x_i^-\}$ from different persons. Hence, we design a comparative similarity loss on image triplets as follows:

$$L_{triplet} = \sum_{(x_i, x_i^+, x_i^-) \in \mathcal{X}} \max\left(1 - \frac{\|f_w(x_i) - f_w(x_i^-)\|_2^2}{\|f_w(x_i) - f_w(x_i^+)\|_2^2 + C}, 0\right) \quad (1)$$

where $f_w(x)$ is the feature representation from a CNN model, which projects the images from raw pixel space into a

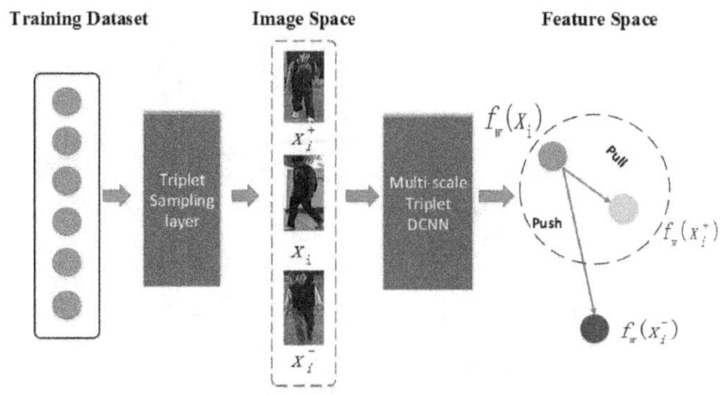

Figure 2. The minimization of comparative similarity loss on sample triplets leads to effective Deep CNN that generates similar features for the same person and dissimilar features for different ones.

feature space $\mathbb{R}^d$. The constant C is a predefined margin. The comparative triplet loss aims to enforce the distance among images from different persons larger than the images from the same person.

The above triplet loss dose not constrain the matching pair $(f_w(x_i), f_w(x_i^+))$ close to each other. As a result, the images belonging to the same person may form a cluster with large intra-class divergence in the learnt feature space. In other words, the learnt feature may be susceptible to the variations caused by illumination, human pose, camera view and occlusions, in visual matching. To address this problem, we design a loss term on image pairs to further constrain the distance among the intra-class image features as follows:

$$L_{pair} = \sum_{(x_i, x_i^+) \in \mathcal{X}} \|f_w(x_i) - f_w(x_i^+)\|_2^2 \quad (2)$$

By combining the above triplet and pair loss functions, the comparative similarity loss is obtained as follows:

$$\begin{aligned} L = \sum_{(x_i, x_i^+, x_i^-) \in \mathcal{X}} \max\left(1 - \frac{\|f_w(x_i) - f_w(x_i^-)\|_2^2}{\|f_w(x_i) - f_w(x_i^+)\|_2^2 + C}, 0\right) \\ + \mu \sum_{(x_i, x_i^+) \in \mathcal{X}} \|f_w(x_i) - f_w(x_i^+)\|_2^2 \end{aligned} \quad (3)$$

where μ is the weight parameter between the triplet and pair loss. This loss function together with the designed Deep CNN model as shown in Figure 2 is able to learn robust and effective visual features for person re-identification.

2.2 Multi-Scale Network

The proposed multi-scale triplet network is illustrated in Figure 3, consisting of three sub-networks: one deep convolutional neural network and two shallow networks. Due to the small scale of pedestrian image corpus, the traditional deep CNN model requiring a large amount of training samples can not be directly applied to person re-identification task. Therefore, we propose a triplet network architecture which shares same parameters with the proposed comparative loss on massive sample triplets instead of the traditional softmax loss. Given a training set $\{\mathcal{X}\}$, large number of sample triplets can be formed as the network input addressing the problem of limited training samples. Each sample triplet

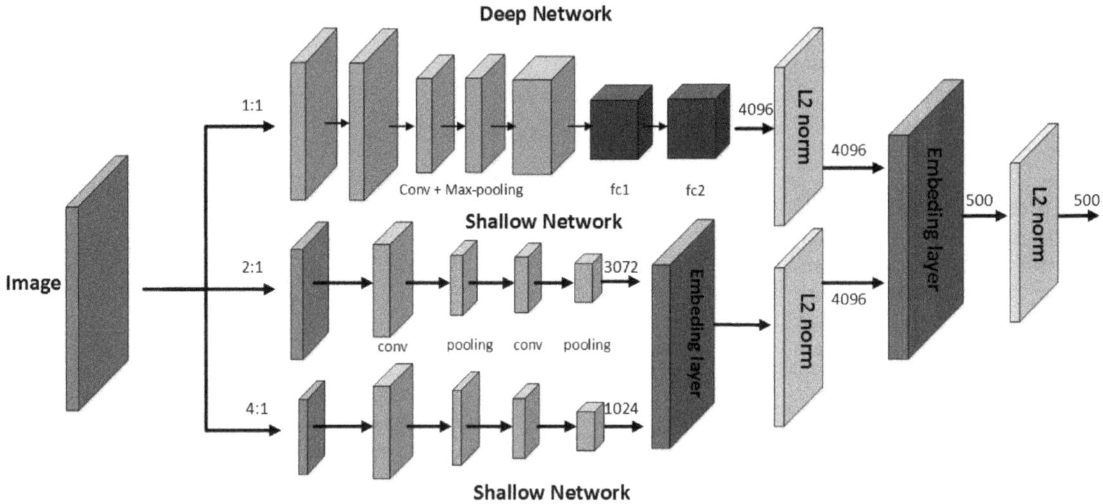

Figure 3. The multi-scale network architecture consist of one deep network and two shallow networks, which capture visual appearance of a person at various scales. The responses from the deep and shallow networks are embedded at an embedding layer to generate final feature representation.

includes a probe image x_i, an image of the same person x_i^+ , as well as an image from a different person x_i^-.

As the Alex network [18] has shown good performance in many compute vision tasks, we design the deep CNN according to Alex network. The two shallow networks take down-sample images with the rates of 2:1 and 4:1 as input respectively. The shallow networks can produce less invariance and low-level appearance features from images. After normalizing the outputs from the three networks with L_2 norm, the three feature vectors are fused into an embedding layer, leading to a final 500-dimensional feature vector from the entire network. The features from the deep and shallow networks capture image content at different scales and have complementary advantages. The fused feature is more robust and effective for representing pedestrian appearance under various conditions. In particular, the deep network contains five convolutional layers, five max-pooling layers, two local normalization layers, and three fully-connection layers. Each shallow network contains two convolutional layers followed by two pooling layers.

2.3 Training Strategy

We optimize the parameters of our CNN model by using the mini-batch stochastic gradient descent algorithm. The collection of training sample triplets is divided into a number of mini-batches of triplets. Given each mini-batch, the training errors are calculated based on the proposed loss function and the derivatives are obtained by back-propagation along the networks to update the parameters at each layer. The multi-scale triplet CNN model can be represented as follows:

$$f(x) = h_n(h_{n-1}(h_{n-2}(\cdots h_1(x)\cdots))) \tag{4}$$

where the h_i is the transfer function of the ith layer. The parameters of the transfer function are denoted as w_i. Given the objective function, we calculate the gradient of the loss with respect to the parameters at each layer by the chain rule as follows:

$$\frac{\partial T}{\partial w_l} = \frac{\partial T}{\partial f_w(x_i)} \times \frac{\partial f_w(x_i)}{\partial g_n} \times \frac{\partial g_n}{\partial g_{n-1}} \times \cdots \times \frac{\partial g_{l+1}}{\partial g_l} \times \frac{\partial g_l}{\partial w_l} \tag{5}$$

It should be note that the gradients ($\frac{\partial T}{\partial f_w(x_i)}$) of the loss for different samples in a triplet (x_i, x_i^+, x_i^-) are different.

3. EXPERIMENT

Our multi-scale triplet convolutional neural network was implemented based on the **Caffe** [1] framework. The overall network was trained using two NVIDIA K40 GPUs, Intel i7 CPU, and 32G memory.

Datasets - There are multiple pubic data sets established for person re-identification, including **Market1501, CUHK Campus, VIPeR,** and **PRID2011** etc. Among them, **Market1501** is the most challenging and realistic one. **Market1501** was collected from a total of six cameras, placed in front of campus supermarket. It contained 32,643 bounding boxes of 1,501 identities with Deformable Part Model (DPM) detector. Each identity was captured by six cameras at most and two cameras at least. Following to [14], the data set is divided into two parts. One part has 750 identities as training set and the other has 751 identities as testing set, in which there are 3,363 query images belong to the 750 identities, and each query has 14.8 ground-truth images in average in the gallery set.

Training Setting - The trained Caffe model was used to initialize the weights of our deep sub-network. The two shallow networks were trained from scratch. We started the stochastic gradient descent (SGD) method with learning rate of 0.001 and the weight decay of 0.0005. The parameters μ, C in Eq.(3) are set to 0.002 and 0.008 respectively in the experiments. Each mini-batch contains 160 sample triplets. The entire framework was trained for 150,000 iterations in total.

[1] http://caffe.berkeleyvision.org/

Performance on the Market1501 dataset - We compare our approach with several state-of-the-art methods, including Bag of words model[14], SDALF [10], eSDC[15], and XQDA[16]. Experimental results are shown in Table 1. It can be seen that our approach achieves the best performance among all the methods. Given a single query image, our approach achieves 45.1% rank-1 recognition rates and improves SDALF[10], eSDC[13], BOW(singleQ)[14], and XQDA[16] by 109.8%, 40.1%, 26.0%, and 3.0%, respectively. Given multiple query images, our approach outperforms existing BOW(MutiQ) method[14] with significant performance improvement in terms of rank-1 recognition rate. It can be also observed that the performance of our approach with multi-scale network performs better than that with a single Alex network. This demonstrates the effectiveness of the combination of deep and shallow networks on person re-identification task.

Table 1. Performance comparison with the state-of-the-art methods on the Market-1501 dataset

Method	Rank-1	Rank-5	Rank-10	Rank-30
BOW (singleQ)[14]	35.8	52.4	60.3	71.9
BOW (multiQ)[14]	44.4	60.2	66.5	76.2
SDALF[10]	21.5	34.5	42.3	50.7
eSDC[13]	32.2	47.1	55.2	64.1
XQDA[16]	43.8	-	-	-
Our Method (sin-network)	42.3	68.5	76.2	84.6
Our Method (singleQ)	45.1	70.1	78.4	88.7
Our Method (multiQ)	**55.4**	**78.9**	**85.6**	**93.7**

4. CONCLUSION

In this paper, we proposed a multi-scale convolutional neural network for person re-identification. A multi-scale triplet network architecture integrating deep and shadow networks was developed to capture visual appearance of a person at various scales and learn robust and effective features under complex conditions. A network learning method was proposed to optimize network parameters based on a comparative similarity loss over massive sample triplets. We have conducted extensive experiments on the real-world Market1501 data set and the experimental results have shown that the proposed approach outperforms the state-of-the-art methods.

5. ACKNOWLEDGMENTS

This work was supported in part by the National Natural Science Foundation of China (NSFC) under Contract 61472392 and 61429201. This work was also supported in part to Dr. Qi Tian by ARO grants W911NF-15-1-0290 and Faculty Research Gift Awards by NEC Laboratories of America and Blippar.

6. REFERENCES

[1] Roberto Vezzani, Davide Baltieri, and Rita Cucchiara. People reidentification in surveillance and forensics: A survey. *ACM Computing Surveys (CSUR)*, 46(2):29, 2013.

[2] Shaogang Gong, Marco Cristani, Shuicheng Yan, and Chen Change Loy. *Person re-identification*, volume 1. Springer, 2014.

[3] Sakrapee Paisitkriangkrai, Chunhua Shen, and Anton van den Hengel. Learning to rank in person re-identification with metric ensembles. In *Proceedings of the IEEE Conference on Computer Vision and Pattern Recognition*, pages 1846–1855, 2015.

[4] Alexis Mignon and Frédéric Jurie. Pcca: A new approach for distance learning from sparse pairwise constraints. In *Computer Vision and Pattern Recognition (CVPR), 2012 IEEE Conference on*, pages 2666–2672. IEEE, 2012.

[5] Fei Xiong, Mengran Gou, Octavia Camps, and Mario Sznaier. Person re-identification using kernel-based metric learning methods. In *Computer Vision–ECCV 2014*, pages 1–16. Springer, 2014.

[6] Wei-Shi Zheng, Shaogang Gong, and Tao Xiang. Reidentification by relative distance comparison. *Pattern Analysis and Machine Intelligence, IEEE Transactions on*, 35(3):653–668, 2013.

[7] Lianyang Ma, Xiaokang Yang, and Dacheng Tao. Person re-identification over camera networks using multi-task distance metric learning. *Image Processing, IEEE Transactions on*, 23(8):3656–3670, 2014.

[8] Wei Li and Xiaogang Wang. Locally aligned feature transforms across views. In *Proceedings of the IEEE Conference on Computer Vision and Pattern Recognition*, pages 3594–3601, 2013.

[9] Rui Zhao, Wanli Ouyang, and Xiaogang Wang. Unsupervised salience learning for person re-identification. In *Proceedings of the IEEE Conference on Computer Vision and Pattern Recognition*, pages 3586–3593, 2013.

[10] Yang Yang, Jimei Yang, Junjie Yan, Shengcai Liao, Dong Yi, and Stan Z Li. Salient color names for person re-identification. In *Computer Vision–ECCV 2014*, pages 536–551. Springer, 2014.

[11] Michela Farenzena, Loris Bazzani, Alessandro Perina, Vittorio Murino, and Marco Cristani. Person re-identification by symmetry-driven accumulation of local features. In *Computer Vision and Pattern Recognition (CVPR), 2010 IEEE Conference on*, pages 2360–2367. IEEE, 2010.

[12] Bryan Prosser, Wei-Shi Zheng, Shaogang Gong, Tao Xiang, and Q Mary. Person re-identification by support vector ranking. In *BMVC*, volume 2, page 6, 2010.

[13] Rui Zhao, Wanli Ouyang, and Xiaogang Wang. Person re-identification by salience matching. In *Proceedings of the IEEE International Conference on Computer Vision*, pages 2528–2535, 2013.

[14] Bingpeng Ma, Yu Su, and Frédéric Jurie. Local descriptors encoded by fisher vectors for person re-identification. In *Computer Vision–ECCV 2012. Workshops and Demonstrations*, pages 413–422. Springer, 2012.

[15] Liang Zheng, Liyue Shen, Lu Tian, Shengjin Wang, Jingdong Wang, and Qi Tian. Scalable person re-identification: A benchmark. In *Proceedings of the IEEE International Conference on Computer Vision*, pages 1116–1124, 2015.

[16] Xiao Liu, Mingli Song, Qi Zhao, Dacheng Tao, Chun Chen, and Jiajun Bu. Attribute-restricted latent topic model for person re-identification. *Pattern recognition*, 45(12):4204–4213, 2012.

[17] Shengcai Liao, Yang Hu, Xiangyu Zhu, and Stan Z Li. Person re-identification by local maximal occurrence representation and metric learning. In *Proceedings of the IEEE Conference on Computer Vision and Pattern Recognition*, pages 2197–2206, 2015.

[18] Alex Krizhevsky, Ilya Sutskever, and Geoffrey E Hinton. Imagenet classification with deep convolutional neural networks. In *Advances in neural information processing systems*, pages 1097–1105, 2012.

[19] Dong Yi, Zhen Lei, and Stan Z Li. Deep metric learning for practical person re-identification. *arXiv preprint arXiv:1407.4979*, 2014.

[20] Wei Li, Rui Zhao, Tong Xiao, and Xiaogang Wang. Deepreid: Deep filter pairing neural network for person re-identification. In *Proceedings of the IEEE Conference on Computer Vision and Pattern Recognition*, pages 152–159, 2014.

[21] Ejaz Ahmed, Michael Jones, and Tim K Marks. An improved deep learning architecture for person re-identification. In *Proceedings of the IEEE Conference on Computer Vision and Pattern Recognition*, pages 3908–3916, 2015.

[22] Mert Dikmen, Emre Akbas, Thomas S Huang, and Narendra Ahuja. Pedestrian recognition with a learned metric. In *Computer Vision–ACCV 2010*, pages 501–512. Springer, 2010.

[23] Sateesh Pedagadi, James Orwell, Sergio Velastin, and Boghos Boghossian. Local fisher discriminant analysis for pedestrian re-identification. In *Proceedings of the IEEE Conference on Computer Vision and Pattern Recognition*, pages 3318–3325, 2013.

[24] Martin Koestinger, Martin Hirzer, Paul Wohlhart, Peter M Roth, and Horst Bischof. Large scale metric learning from equivalence constraints. In *Computer Vision and Pattern Recognition (CVPR), 2012 IEEE Conference on*, pages 2288–2295. IEEE, 2012.

Multimodal Popularity Prediction of Brand-related Social Media Posts

Masoud Mazloom†, Robert Rietveld *, Stevan Rudinac †, Marcel Worring†*, Willemijn van Dolen*
†Informatics Institute, University of Amsterdam *Amsterdam Business School, University of Amsterdam

ABSTRACT

Brand-related user posts on social networks are growing at a staggering rate, where users express their opinions about brands by sharing multimodal posts. However, while some posts become popular, others are ignored. In this paper, we present an approach for identifying what aspects of posts determine their popularity. We hypothesize that brand-related posts may be popular due to several cues related to factual information, sentiment, vividness and entertainment parameters about the brand. We call the ensemble of cues *engagement parameters*. In our approach, we propose to use these parameters for predicting brand-related user post popularity. Experiments on a collection of fast food brand-related user posts crawled from Instagram show that: visual and textual features are complementary in predicting the popularity of a post; predicting popularity using our proposed *engagement parameters* is more accurate than predicting popularity directly from visual and textual features; and our proposed approach makes it possible to understand what drives post popularity in general as well as isolate the brand specific drivers.

1. INTRODUCTION

More than ever social media, where people are expressing their opinions through posts, is reshaping the business and marketing landscape. It has become an invaluable source for companies to understand the engagement of people with their brand or product. Instagram in particular, with its focus on self-expression and engagement, might provide an answer to the question of which aspects make some posts about brands more popular than other. Some of the information to answer this question is explicitly captured in parameters such as the number of likes. The bulk of information, however, is hidden in the text and visual content of the post. To benefit from the abundance of data in posts for understanding brand-related user post popularity, we need to be able to leverage both the explicit information in a post as well as the visual and textual content.

MM '16, October 15-19, 2016, Amsterdam, Netherlands

 ISBN 978-1-4503-3603-1/16/10...$15.00
DOI: http://dx.doi.org/10.1145/2964284.2967210

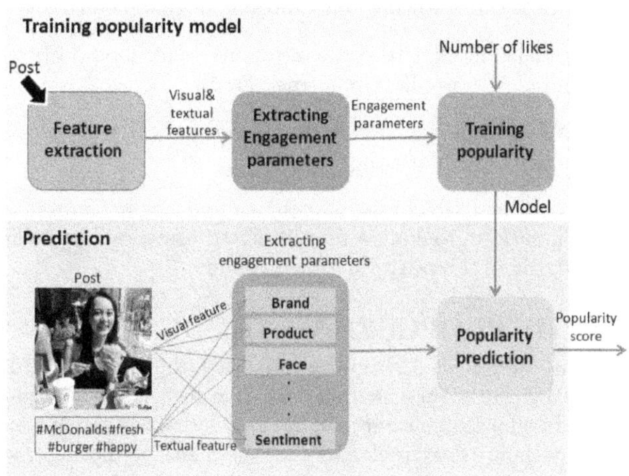

Figure 1: Our proposal for computing popularity of brand-related posts by considering a new layer consisting of *engagement parameters*.

Explicit parameters and textual content have been studied extensively to understand popularity of tweets on Twitter [1,8] and videos on YouTube [15]. In [8], Hong *et al.* show the importance of retweets for the prediction of message popularity on Twitter. The authors in [1] found a relation between the sentiment and popularity of tweets. Szabo et al. in [15] study the popularity of YouTube videos by analyzing the social cues, comments, and associated tags. All of these works successfully predict popularity using textual data. Visual content, which also holds a lot of information, is not addressed in these methods.

In recent years, various aspects of predicting the popularity of images have been studied by analyzing data from the photo-sharing site Flickr [3,6,9,12]. In [3], Cappallo *et al.* approach popularity prediction as a retrieval problem and learn a ranker that takes into account the distinctive visual cues in popular and unpopular images. Kholsa *et al.* [9] and McParalane *et al.* [12], model image popularity by learning regressors on both visual and textual context. Gelli *et al.* in [6] study the effect of visual sentiment features as well as contextual features. These methods demonstrate the potential of predicting the popularity for image content. Yet, in case of images from a photo-sharing site, the objective information as well as aesthetic quality are likely the determining factors for popularity. For Instagram, with its high portion of selfies and other forms of self-expression, different factors may determine the popularity and hence other or additional algorithms may be more appropriate.

We hypothesize that brand-related user posts may be popular due to several visual and textual cues such as the presence of the logo, products, faces, specific objective content descriptors, and sentiment evoked in the user posts. Therefore, we propose a new brand post popularity detection method by estimating the factual information, sentiment, vividness and entertainment parameters of the brand-related post. These aspects are based on frameworks from the context specific field, i.e. Marketing. The correlation between each of these parameters and the number of likes of each post (see Figure 1) provides a measure of predictive quality. By making the parameters contributing to brand post popularity explicit contributes to understanding the drivers of post popularity as well as increasing the prediction accuracy.

We make the following contributions in this paper:

- We are the first to study automatic multimodal brand popularity prediction on Instagram.
- We introduce a new layer of *engagement parameters* inspired by marketing research.
- We reveal which *engagement parameters* are most influential in making a brand-related user posts popular and how this varies between brands.

2. THE PROPOSED METHOD

In this section we describe our approach to popularity prediction by *engagement parameters*. We first define the parameters which play an important role in marketing. Then, we show how to extract and use them for predicting the popularity of brand-related posts.

2.1 Defining Engagement Parameters

We aim at developing an effective predictive model of post popularity in social media. We hypothesize that brand-related posts may be popular due to several reasons. For example, a marketeer analyzing the popularity of *McDonald's* posts in social media may wonder whether a post is popular because it comes from a famous person, the logo is visible, some brand specific products are present, or that it evokes a certain sentiment. We conjecture that the information needed to answer such questions may be implicitly or explicitly captured in the visual and textual channel of user posts. To study popularity, we first need to identify parameters that are context-specific to Marketing and are known from that field to influence popularity.

We are inspired by recent research in the marketing community for predicting the popularity of a post [4,14]. In [4], De Vries *et al.* consider information, entertainment and vividness as important sources for predicting brand post popularity. Smith *et al.* in [14] investigate the popularity by identifying four parameters in each post: promotional self-presentation, brand centrality, factually informative of the brand, and brand sentiment. We adapt and combine these parameters to define nine parameters, *engagement parameters*, which potentially impact the popularity of user generated brand related posts. Our *engagement parameters* are the following: *Brand* (brand centrality), *Product* (factual information about the brand), *Sentiment* (brand sentiment), *Image aesthetics* (vividness), *Concepts* (information and entertainment), *Face* (promotional self-presentation). We also combine *Product* and *Face* to produce *Person-Product* and *People-Product* which might reveal whether a brand may be perceived as more individual or social. At the end we consider number of *Followers* as a parameter which has direct effect on popularity. Different from [4,14], which rely on manual classification for extracting drivers of image popularity, we propose to automatically detect the parameters that drive post popularity and effectively incorporating them into a model for popularity prediction of brand-related posts.

2.2 Extracting Engagement Parameters

To detect the existence of *engagement parameters* in user posts, we analyse their visual and text content. For detecting the presence of a *Brand, Face(s)*, and *Product(s)* in the image of each post, we use the Google Vision API.

Brand: Binary indication of the *Brand* logo presence.

Face(s): The number of detected faces.

Product: In order to assess whether a *Product* is present in an image, we use the following procedure. We select the top 10 labels extracted by *Google Vision API* based on their confidence score. Each of the labels corresponds to an entry in Freebase. A label is considered to be a *Product* of the fast food restaurant if an entry was found in the food or dish category of Freebase. We consider a *Product* to be present in the image if at least one match was found.

Person-Product: Binary indication of the coincidence of exactly one *Face* and *Product.*

People-Product: The value of this parameter is 1 if there are 2 or more *Faces* and *Product* in image.

Sentiment: To detect the sentiment in user posts, we perform late fusion of *Visual-Sentiment* and *Textual-Sentiment.* We determine the *Visual-Sentiment*, similar to [6], using Sentibank detectors [2]. The ontology consists of a collection of 1,200 Adjective-Noun-Pairs (ANP). So we represent each image with a 1,200-dimensional vector in which each dimension shows the probability of the ANP being present in the image. *Textual-Sentiment* is determined by analyzing the text from hashtags, captions, and the comments associated with the images. Due to its effectiveness in extracting sentiment from short informal texts and for consistency with [2], we then deploy SentiStrength [17] to generate the positive (ranging from 1 to 5) and negative (ranging from -1 to -5) sentiment scores.

Image aesthetics: There are in total 42 filters in Instagram which the users can apply before sharing their images. We extract the information about the filters applied to the image from the contextual metadata of the post in to a 42-dimensional binary vector.

Concepts: we extract the convolutional neural network features, initially proposed in [16] and trained to identify those 15,293 ImageNet [5] concept categories, for which at least 200 positive examples are available. Similar to [10, 11], we represent the image of each post by the 15,293-dimensional output of the softmax layer of the network.

Followers: The number of contacts of the given user.

2.3 Post Popularity Measurement

Similar to [6,9], we treat the post popularity prediction as a ranking problem. As the measure of post popularity we use the number of likes it received. We find that the number of likes follows a power law distribution, where the majority of posts receive little or no likes and the minority of them receive a high number of likes. To deal with the large variation in the number of likes, we apply the log function to make it resemble a Gaussian distribution.

Table 1: **Experiment 1: Analysis of different visual and textual features on brand-related post popularity prediction.**

Datasets	Visual features: *CNN-Pool5*	*ConceptVec-15k*	*Visual-Sentiment*	Feature fusion: *Visual-Combi*	Multimodal fusion: *Visual-Textual-Combi*
Category-mix	0.201	0.187	0.224	0.233	*See*
Category-specific	0.220	0.196	0.264	0.270	*below*

Datasets	Textual features: *W2V*	*Textual-Sentiment*	*Term-based*	Feature fusion: *Textual-Combi*	Multimodal fusion: *Visual-Textual-Combi*
Category-mix	0.184	0.206	0.191	0.231	0.252
Category-specific	0.217	0.241	0.220	0.250	0,290

In order to predict post popularity, we use L2 regularized L2 loss Support Vector Regression (SVR) from the LIBLINEAR package. We train a popularity model on the training set and use it for predicting the popularity of a post at test time (see Figure 1). To find the optimal value of the regularization parameter C of SVM, we perform 5-fold cross-validation for $C \in \{0.001, 0.1, 1, 10, 100\}$.

3. EXPERIMENTAL SETUP

Dataset: We investigate the effectiveness of our proposed approach for post popularity prediction on an Instagram dataset. As mentioned in [7] the fast food category is one of the most popular categories on Instagram. As we are interested in analyzing brands, we select the six most popular fast food brands based on the annual revenue from 2014, namely: *McDonald's, Burger King, Culver's, Wendy's, Sonic Drive In*, and *Jack In The Box*. We created a dataset by crawling 75,000 user-posts related to these six categories.

In order to explore the effect of the *engagement parameters* on all user posts or in a specific brand category, we define two different settings:

Category-mix: In this setting the whole dataset is used to build a general model for popularity prediction.

Category-specific: For this setting, we perform the training and evaluation independently for each brand category.

In both settings we split the data randomly into two halves, one for training and the other for testing. We average the performance over 10 random splits to ensure consistency of the results.

Baseline features: *Visual features*, As low-level visual features we used the *CNN-Pool5*, the 1024-dimensional features from pooling the last fully connected layer of the Deep Net in [16]. We use also *Concepts*, and *Visual-Sentiment* explained in section 2.2 as high level features. We use three different representations based on the tags added to the posts as *Textual features*: *Term-based*, a sparse binary representation with a length of 22,110, where the length of the vector equals the number of unique tags in the dataset. Only the values of those elements corresponding to the tags of the post are set to one. The *W2V*, a state-of-the-art word embedding method which is a deep neural network trained on over a billion Google news documents [13]. Using this net, we compute a 300-dimensional vector by mapping each tag of a post to its word2vec representation. From there, average pooling is used to obtain the final 300-dimension representation of the post. At the end we use the *Textual-Sentiment* as explained in Section 2.2.

Evaluation metric: After predicting the popularity of each post at test time, we compute the Spearman's rank correlation between the prediction and ground truth which returns a value between [-1, 1]. A value close to 1 corresponds to perfect correlation.

3.1 Experiments

Experiment 1: ***Effect of multimodal features on post popularity*** In this experiment we evaluate the effect of different baseline features on predicting the popularity of a post in *Category-mix* and *Category-specific* datasets. In the *Category-specific* setting we report the average rank correlation score of all six brand categories. We also report the effect of combining *Visual features*, *Visual-Combi*, and *Textual features*, *Textual-Combi*, by average pooling in a late fusion scenario. We also report the result of combining *Visual-combi* and *Textual-combi*, denoted by *Visual-Textual-combi.*

Experiment 2: ***Effect of the engagement parameters on post popularity*** In this experiment we evaluate the post popularity prediction accuracy of our proposed *engagement parameters* on both settings of the dataset. Here, we attempt to quantify the extent to which the individual *engagement parameters* impact the popularity of a post. Finally by average pooling the rank of each post at test time we produce the *Late-fusion* results. To have a fair comparison with baseline features, we do not consider the follower parameter in the rank aggregation.

Experiment 3: ***Analysis of the engagement parameters on the popularity of each category*** In this experiment we analyze the effect of each *engagement parameter* on the popularity of brand-related posts in the *Category-specific* setting. We aim to understand which parameters make a brand become more popular. In particular, we try to understand the difference between the popularity of different brand categories. By analyzing the *engagement parameters* on brand-related posts we divide the brands into four categories: *Brand-based, Product-based, Social-based*, and *Individual-based.* The categorization is based on the parameter having the highest influence on the brand popularity, namely the presence of Brand identity (e.g., a logo), Product (e.g., fries or burger), People, and Person.

4. RESULTS

Experiment 1: ***Effect of multimodal features on post popularity*** We show the results of experiment 1 in Table 1. As we can see, the rank correlation performance using *Visual-Combi* reaches 0.233 and 0.270 in *Category-mix* and *Category-specific* respectively. In both settings, we find that the best visual feature is *Visual-Sentiment* which demonstrates the sentiment captured in the visual content of an image has a high impact on post popularity. We also observe that using *Textual-Combi* the results reach 0.231 and 0.250 on *Category-mix* and *Category-specific* respectively. To investigate whether the visual and textual features are

Table 2: **Experiment 2: The result of our proposal for post popularity detection.**

Datasets	*Brand*	*Product*	*Sentiment*	*Face*	*Concepts*	*Image ascetics*	*Person-Product*	*People-Product*	*Follower*	*Late-fusion without Follower*
Category-mix	0.322	0.263	0.305	0.321	0.187	0.192	0.382	0.401	0.542	0.441
Category-specific	0.361	0.293	0.335	0.375	0.196	0.203	0.414	0.425	0.555	0.462

complementary, we also combine *Visual-Combi* and *Textual-Combi* in a late fusion fashion. The result shows that they are indeed complementary, reaching 0.252 and 0.290 rank correlation accuracy on *Category-mix* and *Category-specific*.

The results of experiment 1, in general, confirm the importance of using both visual and textual features for predicting the popularity of a post in social media.

Experiment 2: ***Effect of the engagement parameters on post popularity*** We show the results of using different *engagement parameters* on the *Category-mix* and *Category-specific* in Table 2. The results demonstrate that our proposed approach has a positive effect on predicting popularity of posts where using the existence of a *Brand* results in 0.322 and 0.361 rank correlation accuracy on both *Category-mix* and *Category-specific* respectively. We also observe that by considering only the existence of a *Face* results in 0.321 and 0.375 in both settings. The results of post popularity prediction by *Person-Product* and *People-Product* in both settings show the effectiveness of these variables as compared to considering *Face* and *Product* separately. We observe that the fast food brand-related posts showing one person or people with products are more attractive and will likely get a higher number of likes. By fusing the rank correlation scores of our *engagement parameters* on each post by the average operator, the result reaches 0.441 and 0.462 popularity detection accuracy in *Category-mix* and *Category-specific* settings.

The results show a significant improvement in post popularity prediction against the baseline features. The results improve by a factor of two, 0.441 versus 0.252 on *Category-mix* and 0.462 versus 0.290 on *Category-specific*. Here we compare our proposal with *Visual-Textual-combi* which as shown in experiment 1 is the best performing baseline. It shows that for predicting the popularity of brand-related posts considering visual and textual features alone is not sufficient. The results confirm that post popularity prediction accuracy profits from using *engagement parameters*, which incorporate the correlation of different parameters with the popularity of posts.

Experiment 3: ***Analysis of the engagement parameters on the popularity of each category*** We plot the result of experiment 3 in Figure 2. The rank correlation of late fusion over all *engagement parameters* reaches to 0.520, 0.450, 0.424, 0.451, 0.421, and 0.511 for brand categories *Burger King, Culver's, Jack In The Box, Sonic Drive In, Wendy's,* and *McDonald's* respectively. By focusing on the correlation of the *Brand* parameter with the popularity of each category we find that for *McDonald's* and *Burger King*, the existence of the logo of the brand in user posts is more important in comparison with the other brands. This suggests that these two categories are more *Brand-based* in comparison with *Culver's* and *Jack In The Box* which are *Product-based.* We also observe that the existence of *Face* in all brand categories has a high impact on post popularity. It has a particularly high impact when combined with the *Product* parameter. The correlation score between the *People-Product* parameter and the popularity of *Burger King, Culver's, Jack In The Box, Wendy's,* and *McDon-*

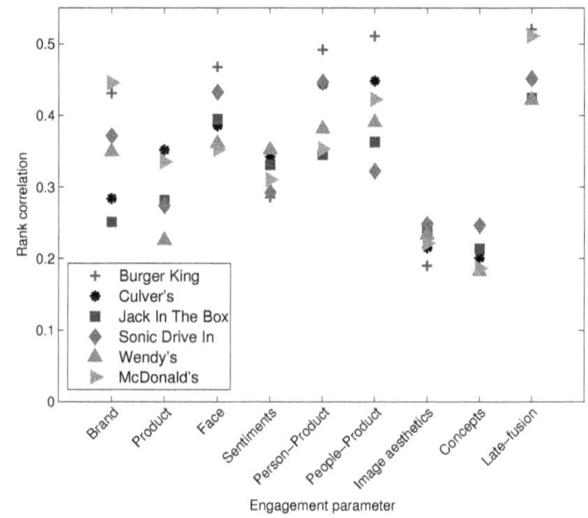

Figure 2: Experiment 3: The result of *engagement parameters* in prediction of brand post popularity for all six categories.

ald's shows the value of the social and cultural aspects of the brands. The posts for these brands show that users tend to enthusiastically socialize while consuming their product. On the other hand, the comparison of the rank correlation score of *Person-Product* and *People -Product* on *Sonic Drive In* shows the user's individual relationship with the product.

The results show that our approach is able to differentiate between the popularity of brands by analyzing the effect of *engagement parameters* on brand related user posts.

5. CONCLUSION

In this paper we study the drivers behind popularity of brand-related social media posts. Different from existing work, which simply models the popularity of a post directly from the visual and text features, in our approach we extract a set of parameters which are known to influence post popularity based on research frameworks in the filed of Marketing and directly embed them into the post popularity prediction model. Our proposed *engagement parameters* capture a number of factors of critical importance for studying the popularity of multimodal posts in a marketing setting. We evaluate the performance of our proposal by conducting a set of experiments on a collection of brand-related Instagram posts. The results of our experiments show that popularity prediction using the *engagement parameters* outperforms direct modelling of popularity using visual and text features only by up to a factor of two. Our *engagement parameters*, such as the existence of brand logo, sentiment and image aesthetics, all play important role in predicting post popularity. Moreover, the results show that utilizing the user *engagement parameters* gives us the ability not only to better predict the popularity of a post, but also to highlight the properties specific of each brand category.

Acknowledgments This research is supported by the Amsterdam Academic Alliance Data Science (AAA-DS) Program Award to the UvA and VU Universities.

6. REFERENCES

[1] Y. Bae and H. Lee. Sentiment analysis of twitter audiences: Measuring the positive or negative influence of popular twitterers. *J. Am. Soc. Inf. Sci. Technol.*, 63(12):2521–2535, 2012.

[2] D. Borth, R. Ji, T. Chen, T. Breuel, and S.-F. Chang. Large-scale visual sentiment ontology and detectors using adjective noun pairs. In *MM*, 2013.

[3] S. Cappallo, T. Mensink, and C. Snoek. Latent factors of visual popularity prediction. In *ICMR*, 2015.

[4] L. de Vries, S. Gensler, and P. S. H. Leeflang. Popularity of brand posts on brand fan pages: An investigation of the effects of social media marketing. *Journal of Interactive Marketing*, 26(2), 2012.

[5] J. Deng, W. Dong, R. Socher, L.-J. Li, K. Li, and L. Fei-Fei. ImageNet: A Large-Scale Hierarchical Image Database. In *CVPR*, 2009.

[6] F. Gelli, T. Uricchio, M. Bertini, A. Del Bimbo, and S.-F. Chang. Image popularity prediction in social media using sentiment and context features. In *MM*, 2015.

[7] K. Ginsberg. Instabranding: Shaping the personalities of the top food brands on instagram. *EJURC*, 6(1):78–91, 2015.

[8] L. Hong, O. Dan, and B. D. Davison. Predicting popular messages in twitter. In *WWW*, 2011.

[9] A. Khosla, A. Das Sarma, and R. Hamid. What makes an image popular? In *WWW*, 2014.

[10] M. Mazloom, A. Habibian, D. Liu, C. G. M. Snoek, and S.-F. Chang. Encoding concept prototypes for video event detection and summarization. In *ICMR*, 2015.

[11] M. Mazloom, X. Li, and C. G. M. Snoek. Tagbook: A semantic video representation without supervision for event detection. *TMM*, 18(7):1378–1388, 2016.

[12] P. J. McParlane, Y. Moshfeghi, and J. M. Jose. Nobody comes here anymore, it's too crowded; predicting image popularity on flickr. In *ICMR*, 2014.

[13] T. Mikolov, I. Sutskever, K. Chen, G. S. Corrado, and J. Dean. Distributed representations of words and phrases and their compositionality. In *NIPS*. 2013.

[14] A. Smith, E. Fischer, and C. Yongjian. How does brand-related user-generated content differ across youtube, facebook, and twitter? *Journal of Interactive Marketing*, 26(2), 2012.

[15] G. Szabo and B. A. Huberman. Predicting the popularity of online content. *Commun. ACM*, 53(8):80–88, 2010.

[16] C. Szegedy, W. Liu, Y. Jia, P. Sermanet, S. Reed, D. Anguelov, D. Erhan, V. Vanhoucke, and A. Rabinovich. Going deeper with convolutions. In *CVPR*, 2015.

[17] M. Thelwall, K. Buckley, G. Paltoglou, D. Cai, and A. Kappas. Sentiment in short strength detection informal text. *J. Am. Soc. Inf. Sci. Technol.*, 61(12), 2010.

Learning Multimodal Temporal Representation for Dubbing Detection in Broadcast Media

Nam Le[1,2], Jean-Marc Odobez[1,2]
[1] Idiap Research Institute, Martigny, Switzerland
[2] École Polytechnique Fédéral de Lausanne, Switzerland
{nle, odobez}@idiap.ch

ABSTRACT

Person discovery in the absence of prior identity knowledge requires accurate association of visual and auditory cues. In broadcast data, multimodal analysis faces additional challenges due to narrated voices over muted scenes or dubbing in different languages. To address these challenges, we define and analyze the problem of dubbing detection in broadcast data, which has not been explored before. We propose a method to represent the temporal relationship between the auditory and visual streams. This method consists of canonical correlation analysis to learn a joint multimodal space, and long short term memory (LSTM) networks to model cross-modality temporal dependencies. Our contributions also include the introduction of a newly acquired dataset of face-speech segments from TV data, which we have made publicly available. The proposed method achieves promising performance on this real world dataset as compared to several baselines.

Keywords

Multimodal, Person Diarization, Recurrent Neural Networks.

1. INTRODUCTION

Making large multimedia corpora easily accessible through search, retrieval and fast browsing tools is a crucial task given the daily production of broadcast TV and internet content. As the retrieval of information on people in videos is of high interest for users, research efforts have been devoted to unsupervised segmentation of videos into homogeneous segments according to person identity, like speaker diarization [21, 17, 29], face diarization [5, 35], and audio-visual (AV) person diarization [10, 25, 16, 8]. Combined with names extracted from overlaid text, AV person diarization makes it possible to identify people in videos [9].

Solving the AV person diarization and naming tasks requires associating visual person tracks or overlaid names with auditory voices, which has several difficulties. Firstly, the visible person may not be the current speaker. This issue occurs when anchors or invited speakers are commenting on video footage displaying famous people who might be talking or when several persons appear to be talking in the background. This cannot be solved with existing systems which visually detect talking faces [4, 1, 26, 8] to reinforce the AV association. Secondly, another recurrent issue in international TV is dubbing. The problem is common when an interviewed person, shown in the video, is speaking in a different language than that of the target audience, and is dubbed by a narrator. Such situations are problematic for person diarization, as they often lead to associating a face track (or a face cluster) or an overlaid person name with the wrong voice, potentially creating multiple ambiguities in person diarization and naming (e.g. if the same voice is dubbing several persons).

In this paper, we focus on dubbing detection in broadcast data, which involves modelling the synchrony of audio and lip motion. This task can be used to handle the two issues mentioned above, by detecting *which of the talking persons (if any) actually produces* the audio discourse. Although it is related to several research problems (AV speech recognition, voice over detection, spoofing in AV biometry), to the best or our knowledge, this dubbing problem has not been addressed previously. To initiate further research, we acquired the DW-dubbing corpus comprising 4722 segments of 2 seconds with the corresponding face track and audio. In addition, from a methodological perspective, we propose to exploit the recently revived LSTM networks to model the joint dynamics of synchronized AV segments in a multimodal space obtained via canonical correlation analysis (CCA). Experiments demonstrate the benefit of our method over several baselines. In summary, our contributions are:

- We address for the first time the problem of dubbing detection in broadcast data;
- We propose a method relying on LSTM and multimodal feature extraction, which achieves promising result on this problem;
- We make publicly available a dubbing dataset collected from TV news for future research.

MM '16, October 15 - 19, 2016, Amsterdam, Netherlands

ISBN 978-1-4503-3603-1/16/10...$15.00
DOI: http://dx.doi.org/10.1145/2964284.2967211

2. RELATED WORK

Dubbing detection shares some similarities to several problems discussed below along with the related works.

Talking faces. Person diarization and naming require matching audio segments with face tracks of talking people. To detect talking people, mean squared intensity differences [4] or motion entropy [1] within mouth regions were typically used, potentially combined with head motion [26]. Such

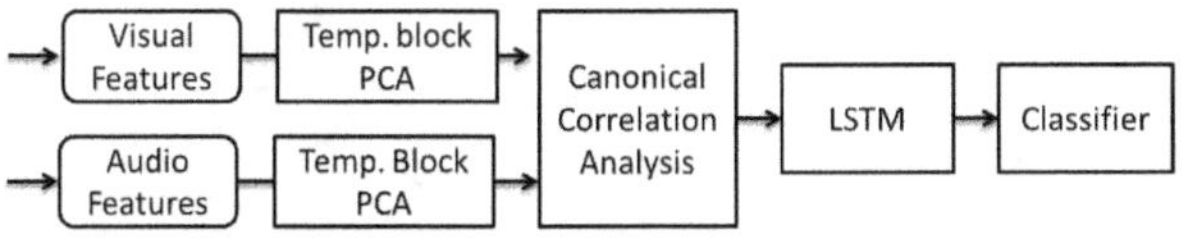

Figure 1: System overview: feature extraction, dimensionality reduction over concatenated feature from block of frames, mutual information extraction via Canonical-Correlation Analysis (CCA), and temporal modelling with LSTM.

visual-based approaches could be further enhanced using multimodal contextual information, like audio segment-face track overlap duration, or face size and position [8]. It is interesting to see that none of the existing systems relied on temporal models for this task. Also, when several persons are seen talking, or in dubbing situations, audio and video need to be jointly considered.

AV speech recognition. Modeling the relationship between audio and visual streams can be traced back to early researches in multimodal speech recognition [30]. Typical examples include coupled hidden Markov Model (CHMM) [22] or asynchronous HMM to model anticipation and retention phenomena. More recently, multimodal deep networks [23] showed good performance. However, the approach did not include temporal models: it relied on neural networks applied to groups of frames, whose outputs were averaged over time. Furthermore, the task is limited to the recognition of simple sounds [27] with little noise (head movements, illumination).

AV biometry and synchronization. The dubbing problem somehow resembles AV spoofing detection, where the task is to detect when visual attackers pretend to match with a playback audio. As an early work, cross-modal fusion with latent semantic analysis or canonical correlation analysis were applied, but only tested attacks composed of a single photograph, potentially animated with simple synthetic movements [3]. To deal with real face tracks with different voices, [32] investigated co-inertia or coupled HMM approaches to detected uncorrelated AV signals or unsynchronization. However, the method was applied to a constrained biometric environment, with specific test sentences used as input to the system. In addition, synchrony detection has also been addressed for speaker location & association [11, 7] in scenes with two people, and has focused more on mutual information modeling than temporal aspects. Mutual information was also shown to be important in monologue detection where a system needs to identify real speakers among sets of confusers [24, 15]. However, temporal modeling using HMM to evaluated likelihood of word utterance given joint AV distribution only yielded limited results [24]. Another related problem is to distinguish narrated vs genuine voices in TV news addressed in [19], where only primitive lip features were used without joint modality space or temporal modeling, and the dataset was very small (40 video clips). In contrast to the above works, our approach utilizes both cross-modal correlation analysis and temporal modeling with state-of-the-art LSTM. Furthermore, our dataset is collected from TV with unconstrained settings and unrestricted speech content.

AV modeling with Neural networks. In addition to the AV speech recognition [23], there has been more attention towards using deep neural networks (DNNs) for AV speaker naming with audio and visual streams. [14] used DNNs to jointly learn recognition models from 2 input streams. This work is further extended in the temporal domain with multimodal LSTM by [31]. Nevertheless, these works require identity information and are thus closer to biometric joint recognition than unsynchronization speech detection.

Figure 2: Example of mouth boxes. Mouth region is detected based on landmarks. Features are computed in 3×5 grid and grouped in a block of 5 frames.

3. MULTIMODAL FRAMEWORK

The overview of our system is illustrated in Fig. 1. First, features are extracted per frame for each modality. Subsequently, blocks of frames are concatenated and dimensionality reduction is applied. This is followed by cross-modality correlation modelling, whose outputs are modelled in the temporal domain using an LSTM to get the high level representation used for classification.

3.1 Feature extraction

Our goal is to build a full neural network to represent audio-visual speech. However, in this paper, we rely on standard features which should be sufficient for the task.

Visual stream. First, to obtain face tracks, we rely on the tracking-by-detection method described in [20]. Then, the mouth region is localized within each frame. This is done by detecting landmarks using the DLIB implementation of [18].

To characterise the mouth dynamics, dense optical flow is computed using the OpenCV implementation of [6]. The average flow is subtracted to remove head motion, and the residual flows are quantized into 8 bins based on their angular values, with 1 additional bin for close to static points. The mouth region is divided into 3×5 spatial regions in which flow histograms are computed, resulting in a vector of $3 \times 5 \times 9 = 135$ dimensions.

Audio stream. Every 10ms, we extract from 20ms windows Mel-frequency cepstral coefficient (MFCC) features with 13 coefficients and energy level together with first and second derivatives, resulting in a vector of 42 dimensions.

3.2 Multimodal processing

As often done in gesture recognition [28] and in NN-based AV speech recognition [23], we consider observations over a short interval (0.2s as in [28, 23]) to capture short-term temporal dynamics. Here, a block of 5 visual frames are grouped together (675-dim vector), which corresponds to 20 audio frames (840-dim vector). Principal component analysis (PCA) is applied separately to each modality to keep 95% of the variance, resulting in vectors of $N_{\rm V} = 100$ (visual) and $N_{\rm A} = 90$ (audio) dimensions.

Canonical-correlation analysis (CCA). The two modality streams contain different types of information. For example, audio may contain features about identity, semantics, or emotions which are irrelevant for our task and may have little correlation with the visual stream. To capture the synchrony between the two modalities, we use CCA, a powerful multivariate statistical technique. Its principle consists of learning matrices, one for each modality, which project the paired modality samples into a common space where

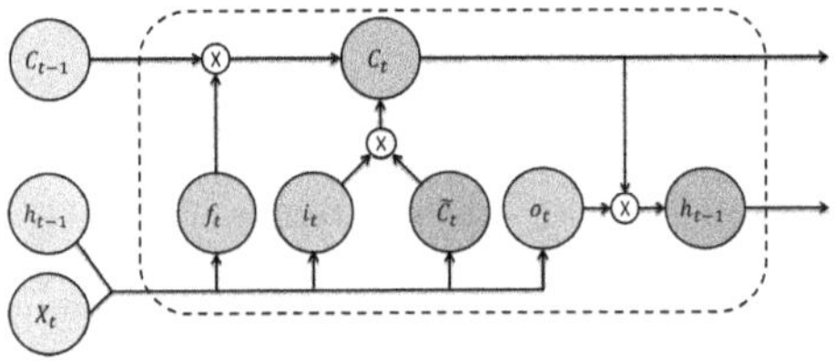

Figure 3: Temporal models. LSTM illustration. Red circles denote sigmoid activation of the gates while blue circles denote tanh activation of the states. × circles denote point-wise multiplication.

the cross-correlation between the projected samples is maximized. For instance, let $X_A \in \mathbb{R}^{N_A \times N}$ and $X_V \in \mathbb{R}^{N_V \times N}$ be N audio and visual samples, respectively. Looking at a one dimensional subspace, CCA looks for the projection weights $w_A \in \mathbb{R}^{N_A}$ and $w_V \in \mathbb{R}^{N_V}$ such that:

$$\max_{w_A, w_V} corr\left[w_A^T X_A, w_V^T X_V\right] \qquad s.t. \ ||w_A|| = 1, ||w_V|| = 1.$$

Such optimization is conducted by finding w_A and w_V using the eigenvalue decomposition method on the correlation matrix, and then generalized to find the common subspace in which the audio stream and visual stream are most correlated [13] Thus, features from this subspace can represent how two modalities harmonize with each other, which will be important to detect dubbing events.

3.3 Temporal modeling and classification

In this Section, we introduce the LSTM architecture and then describe how it is used in our dubbing detection task.

Long Short Term Memory. In sequence modelling, the typical challenge is to learn a model mapping an input sequence $\{x_0, x_1, ..., x_n\}$ to an output sequence $\{y_0, y_1, ..., y_n\}$ where predictions at step t should use the knowledge from x_0 to x_t. To tackle this challenge, RNNs were introduced and shown to learn both high level representation of input signals and temporal dependencies. However, due to gradients multiplications during back propagation through time, they suffered from *exploding* or *vanishing* gradients, making it hard to learn long range dependencies [2].

LSTMs were introduced to overcome these issues [12]. The key ideas were to add a memory cells C_t to store useful information to model long term dependencies, as well as explicit gating mechanisms to regulate the memory updates, as illustrated in Fig. 3 and indicated by the formulae below:

$$\begin{aligned}
Gates: \quad f_t &= sigm(W_{xf}x_t + W_{hf}h_{t-1} + b_f), && (1)\\
i_t &= sigm(W_{xi}x_t + W_{hi}h_{t-1} + b_i), && (2)\\
o_t &= sigm(W_{xo}x_t + W_{ho}h_{t-1} + b_o), && (3)\\
States: \quad \tilde{C}_t &= tanh(W_{xc}x_t + W_{hc}h_{t-1} + b_c), && (4)\\
C_t &= f_t \times C_{t-1} + i_t \times \tilde{C}_t, h_t = o_t \times c_t && (5)\\
Output: \quad y_t &= W_y h_t + b_y, && (6)
\end{aligned}$$

where $W_.$ and $b_.$ denote weight matrices and biases. The mechanism works as follows. First, new information are processed from current states x_t and h_{t-1} to yield $\tilde{C}_t$. Then, to update C_t, the LSTM can selectively decide how much information from the past needs to be "remembered" or forgotten by passing C_{t-1} through the forget gate f_t, and replaced (reset) by new information $\tilde{C}_t$ through the input gate i_t. Finally, through the output gate o_t, the LSTM selects which C_t components to use to generate the hidden states h_t, from which the LSTM output y_t is produced. Importantly, the strategy to open or close gates is data driven and automatically learned from the data through the trainable $W_.$ and $b_.$. Also, the weighted addition of $\tilde{C}_t$ and C_{t-1} is crucial for LSTMs to avoid the vanishing gradient issue and to propagate gradient through long intervals.

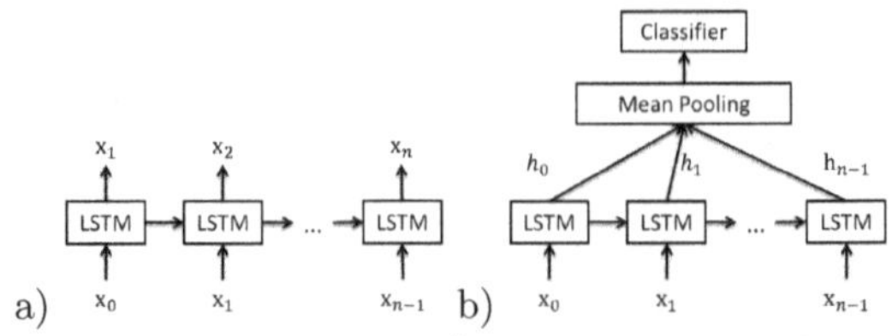

Figure 4: LSTM model. a) At each step i the LSTM learns to predict the feature vector x_{i+1} from the next time step. b) The LSTM is applied to the input sequence, and the sequence of hidden states h_i are averaged and used as input for classification.

Multimodal LSTM. Let $X = \{x_0, x_1, ..., x_n\}$ be a sequence of CCA projections for one segment. Because our task is binary, we have only one supervised signal denoting the class (Authentic or Dubbing). Straightforwardly, one could thus define the output sequence as a series of only 0s or of only 1s when appropriate and learn the LSTM classifier. However, such an approach does not constrain enough the network parameters, thus quickly leads to overfitting. Furthermore, in one dubbing segment, not all frames look asynchronous, thus forcing the label to 0 at every step can be misleading for the network to learn.

To overcome this challenge, similarly to [34, 33], we propose to train the LSTM in an unsupervised fashion with a bottleneck hidden layer h of size N_h: at each step t, the LSTM needs to predict the feature x_{t+1} of the next step, as shown in Fig. 4a. This architecture can learn good features for two related reasons. First, the hidden layer must be able to extract and compress the essential information from the input vector to make predictions. Since an input vector x_i is composed of two feature vectors of equal size coming from each modality, several hidden units will be able to capture the existing correlation between modalities, whereas others will perform intra-modality predictions (see Fig. 6). Second, to make better predictions and learn retention and anticipation temporal phenomena across modalities, the LSTM must also rely on features observed several steps in the past.

Finally, on a test sequence, the extracted hidden representations are mean pooled over the whole segment to form a single vector used for classification, as shown in Fig. 4b.

4. EXPERIMENTS

We describe below our experimental protocol and analysis of the talking face and dubbing detections results.

4.1 Experimental protocol

DW-Dubbing dataset[1]**.** We collect face tracks with their corresponding audio from Deutsche-Welle broadcast programs including debates and documentaries. Each track was divided into $2s$ segments. Segments with multiple arguing voices, inaudible speeches, or profile faces were discarded. The statistics of the dataset is shown in Tab. 1. Data from different videos were split into subsets used for unsupervised training, training and test data.The language of au-

[1] http://www.idiap.ch/scientific-research/resources

	Training set	Testing set	Unsupervised set
Authentic	617	444	1598
Dubbing	440	209	0
Silence	406	237	771

Table 1: Number of segments belonging to different splits and classes in the DW-dubbing dataset

	CV Acc.	Testing Acc.
MSD [4]	80.67	77.79
Mv [1]	78.92	82.16
HOF + SVM	78.39	79.06
HOF + LSTM	81.59	83.08

Table 2: Talking face detection results.

thentic speech/speaker segments was English, and dubbing segments taken from DW international documentaries had English voice dubbing a wide range of languages including Spanish, German, or other minority languages.

Protocol. For all models below, the authentic segments of the unsupervised set and of the training set were used to learn the PCA, CCA, and LSTM representations. Linear SVM classifiers were trained from the authentic and dubbing segments from the training set, using cross validation (CV) to determine hyperparameters. Evaluation was done on the test set, using accuracy as performance measures, along with recall and precision of authentic segments.

Models. To evaluate the contributions of the different elements, we tested several models. (i) **Audio.** This uses only MFCC features as the input for a SVM classifier. (ii) **PCA.** It consists of applying another PCA on the concatenation of the PCA representation of each modality. Keeping 95% of the representation, we obtained a 75 dimension vector for each block of frames, which were averaged and used as input to a SVM classifier. (iii) **CCA.** For each block, as shown in Fig. 1, the CCA projections (32 dimensions per modality) were computed, averaged and fed to a SVM. (iv) **PCA+LSTM.** It consists of a LSTM with $N_h = 16$ applied to the multimodal PCA representation of the PCA baseline. (v) **CCA+LSTM.** A LSTM with $N_h = 16$ is trained with the CCA projection vectors of the CCA baseline.

4.2 Experimental Results

Talking faces. In a preliminary experiment, we trained a LSTM model to detect talking faces from optical flow histograms computed at every frame. As in dubbing, the LSTM was trained to predict the next frame observations, and the average hidden state was used as input to a silent-vs-speaking classifier. Results in Tab. 2 demonstrate the benefit of the temporal information over other baselines (see Sec. 2 for details of [4] and [1]).

Dubbing. Tab. 3 displays the obtained results. Because one can possibly distinguish dubbing cases based on languages or quality of voices in the audio, Audio only can give some positive results. However, using both streams in

		Testing		
	CV Acc.	Acc.	Prec.	Recall
Audio	67.50	76.92	96.31	72.08
PCA	91.01	79.91	97.03	73.65
CCA	74.58	81.80	89.64	83.78
PCA + LSTM	85.44	83.76	94.69	81.53
CCA + LSTM	86.36	88.03	95.78	86.79

Table 3: Dubbing classification results on DW data.

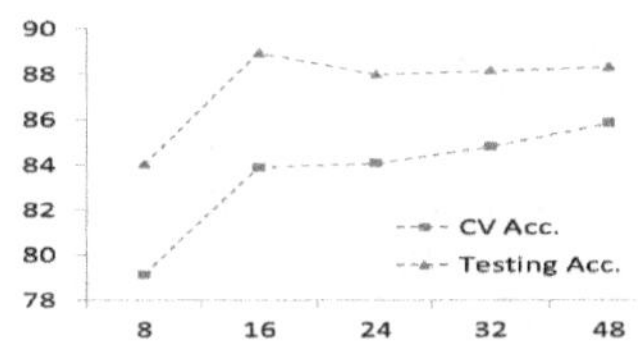

Figure 5: Training and testing accuracies for different values of N_h for the CCA+LSTM model.

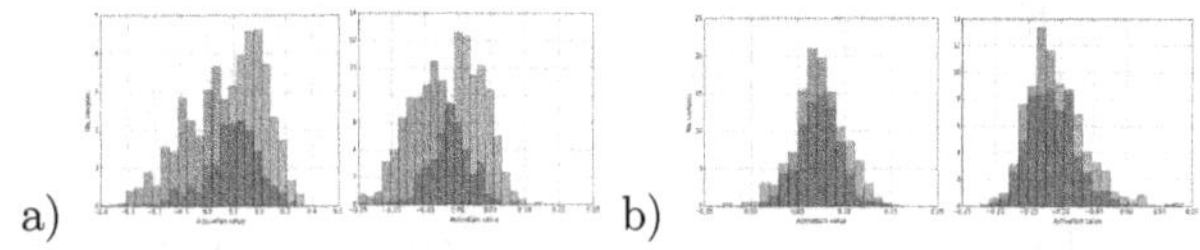

Figure 6: Hidden neurons activation distributions. Green distributions are from the authentic samples, red ones from dubbing samples. a) discriminative neurons. b) non-discriminative neurons.

PCA slightly improves the accuracy, this signifies the importance of multimodal analysis in this task. Nevertheless, the joint PCA subspace computed by maximizing variance is not expressive enough and results in confusing class observations, the classifier cannot be well generalized for the test set. CCA learns a better space where high or low correlation are expected depending on the class, leading to more stable results. By modeling the temporal dynamics within segments rather than averaging, the hidden state representation extracted from LSTM better discriminates the two classes and boosts the performance of both types of input. In this view, CCA offers a more suitable space for LSTM predictions of normal speech, and LSTM trained on CCA inputs outperforms LSTM trained from PCA.

This is confirmed by visualizing the activation distribution of the hidden neurons (i.e. each dimension of the hidden state). Typical examples are illustrated in Fig. 6 (CCA+LSTM with $N_h = 16$). The two left neurons fire stronger when the two streams are correlated (in green), and are inhibited otherwise (in red). Neurons on the right fire similarly regardless of the classes, suggesting that they are probably specialized to process single modality inputs, whereas left ones incorporate cross-modality information, thus contributing significantly to detecting asynchrony.

Finally, to explore the LSTM parameter space, we vary the hidden size N_h from 8 to 48. Results are shown in Fig. 5. As N_h increases, the cross validation training accuracy increases, but not the testing results. This shows that large hidden size can lead to overfitting on the training set.

5. CONCLUSION

We have addressed dubbing detection in broadcast data, which involves detecting asynchrony between a visible speaker and the actual audio. In this context we proposed a multimodal algorithm comprising a CCA step, to capture the correlation between the 2 modalities, and a LSTM to capture the joint evolution of audio and mouth features in the common CCA space. For further research, we have made our DW-dubbing dataset available. Future improvements may include features learned with deep networks and deep CCA, resulting in an end-to-end trainable network. In addition, to detect more challenging dubbing situations, semantic understanding of the asynchrony origin will be needed.

Acknowledgement This research was supported by the European Union project EUMSSI (FP7-611057).

6. REFERENCES

[1] M. Bendris, D. Charlet, and G. Chollet. Lip activity detection for talking faces classification in TV-Content. In *ICMV*, 2010.

[2] Y. Bengio, P. Simard, and P. Frasconi. Learning long-term dependencies with gradient descent is difficult. *IEEE Trans. on Neural Networks*, 1994.

[3] G. Chetty and M. Wagner. Audio-visual multimodal fusion for biometric person authentication and liveness verification. In *NICTA-HCSNet Multimodal User Interaction Workshop*, 2006.

[4] M. Everingham, J. Sivic, and A. Zisserman. Hello! my name is... Buffy–automatic naming of characters in TV video. In *BMVC*, 2006.

[5] M. Everingham, J. Sivic, and A. Zisserman. Taking the bite out of automated naming of characters in TV video. *Image and Vision Computing*, 2009.

[6] G. Farnebäck. Two-frame motion estimation based on polynomial expansion. In *Image analysis*. Springer, 2003.

[7] J. W. Fisher and T. Darrell. Speaker association with signal-level audiovisual fusion. *IEEE Trans. on Multimedia*, 6(3):406–413, 2004.

[8] P. Gay, E. Khoury, S. Meignier, J.-M. Odobez, and P. Deleglise. A Conditional Random Field approach for Audio-Visual people diarization. In *ICASSP*, 2014.

[9] P. Gay, S. Meignier, p. Deleglise, and J.-M. Odobez. Crf based context modeling for person identification in broadcast videos. *Frontiers in ICT*, 3, 2016.

[10] A. Giraudel, M. Carré, V. Mapelli, J. Kahn, O. Galibert, and L. Quintard. The {REPERE} Corpus: a multimodal corpus for person recognition. In *LREC*, 2012.

[11] J. Hershey and J. Movellan. Audio-vision: Using audio-visual synchrony to locate sounds. In *NIPS*, 2000.

[12] S. Hochreiter, S. Hochreiter, J. Schmidhuber, and J. Schmidhuber. Long short-term memory. *Neural computation*, 9(8):1735–80, 1997.

[13] H. Hotelling. Relations between two sets of variates. *Biometrika*, 28(3/4):321–377, 1936.

[14] Y. Hu, J. S. Ren, J. Dai, C. Yuan, L. Xu, and W. Wang. Deep multimodal speaker naming. In *ACM Multimedia*, 2015.

[15] G. Iyengar, H. J. Nock, and C. Neti. Audio-visual synchrony for detection of monologues in video archives. In *ICME*. IEEE, 2003.

[16] B. Jou, H. Li, J. G. Ellis, D. Morozoff-Abegauz, and S.-F. Chang. Structured exploration of who, what, when, and where in heterogeneous multimedia news sources. *ACM MM*, 2013.

[17] V. Jousse, S. Petit-Renaud, S. Meignier, Y. Esteve, and C. Jacquin. Automatic named identification of speakers using diarization and {ASR} systems. In *ICASSP*, 2009.

[18] V. Kazemi and J. Sullivan. One millisecond face alignment with an ensemble of regression trees. In *CVPR*, 2014.

[19] S. Kumagai, K. Doman, T. Takahashi, D. Deguchi, I. Ide, and H. Murase. Detection of inconsistency between subject and speaker based on the co-occurrence of lip motion and voice towards speech scene extraction from news videos. In *Multimedia (ISM), 2011 IEEE International Symposium on*, 2011.

[20] N. Le, D. Wu, S. Meignier, and J.-M. Odobez. Eumssi team at the mediaeval person discovery challenge. In *MediaEval 2015 Workshop*, 2015.

[21] C. Ma, P. Nguyen, and M. Mahajan. Finding speaker identities with a conditional maximum entropy model. In *ICASSP*, 2007.

[22] A. Morris, A. Hagen, H. Glotin, and H. Bourlard. Multi-stream adaptive evidence combination for noise robust asr. *Speech Communication*, 2001.

[23] J. Ngiam, A. Khosla, M. Kim, J. Nam, H. Lee, and A. Y. Ng. Multimodal deep learning. In *ICML*, 2011.

[24] H. J. Nock, G. Iyengar, and C. Neti. Assessing face and speech consistency for monologue detection in video. In *ACM Multimedia*, 2002.

[25] A. Noulas, G. Englebienne, and B. J. A. Krose. Multimodal speaker diarization. *TPAMI*, 2012.

[26] F. Patrona, A. Iosifidis, A. Tefas, N. Nikolaidis, and I. Pitas. Visual voice activity detection in the wild. *Transactions on Multimedia*, 2016.

[27] E. K. Patterson, S. Gurbuz, Z. Tufekci, and J. N. Gowdy. Cuave: A new audio-visual database for multimodal human-computer interface research. In *ICASSP*. IEEE, 2002.

[28] L. Pigou, A. Van Den Oord, S. Dieleman, M. V. Herreweghe, and J. Dambre. Beyond Temporal Pooling: Recurrence and Temporal Convolutions for Gesture Recognition in Video. *Arxiv*, pages 1–9, 2015.

[29] J. Poignant, L. Besacier, and G. Quénot. Unsupervised Speaker Identification in {TV} Broadcast Based on Written Names. *IEEE/ACM Trans. on Audio, Speech, and Language Processing*, 2014.

[30] G. Potamianos, C. Neti, G. Gravier, A. Garg, and A. W. Senior. Recent advances in the automatic recognition of audiovisual speech. In *Proceedings of the IEEE*, pages 1306–1325, 2003.

[31] J. S. Ren, Y. Hu, Y.-W. Tai, C. Wang, L. Xu, W. Sun, and Q. Yan. Look, Listen and Learn - A Multimodal LSTM for Speaker Identification. In *AAAI Conference on Artificial Intelligence*, 2016.

[32] E. A. Rúa, H. Bredin, C. G. Mateo, G. Chollet, and D. G. Jiménez. Audio-visual speech asynchrony detection using co-inertia analysis and coupled hidden markov models. *Pattern Analysis and Applications*, 2009.

[33] N. Srivastava, E. Mansimov, and R. Salakhutdinov. Unsupervised Learning of Video Representations using LSTMs. *Int. Conf. Machine Learning (ICML)*, 2015.

[34] I. Sutskever, O. Vinyals, and Q. V. Le. Sequence to sequence learning with neural networks. In *NIPS*, 2014.

[35] M. Tapaswi, O. M. Parkhi, E. Rahtu, E. Sommerlade, R. Stiefelhagen, and A. Zisserman. Total Cluster: A person agnostic clustering method for broadcast videos. In *ICVGIP*, 2014.

Joint Image-Text Representation by Gaussian Visual-Semantic Embedding

Zhou Ren[1]* Hailin Jin[2] Zhe Lin[2] Chen Fang[2] Alan Yuille[1,3]
[1]University of California, Los Angeles [2]Adobe Research, San Jose, CA
[3]Departments of Cognitive Science and Computer Science, Johns Hopkins University, Baltimore, MD
zhou.ren@cs.ucla.edu {hljin,zlin,cfang}@adobe.com alan.yuille@jhu.edu

ABSTRACT

How to jointly represent images and texts is important for tasks involving both modalities. Visual-semantic embedding models have been recently proposed and shown to be effective. The key idea is that by learning a mapping from images into a semantic text space, the algorithm is able to learn a compact and effective joint representation. However, existing approaches simply map each text concept to a single point in the semantic space. Mapping instead to a *density distribution* provides many interesting advantages, including better capturing uncertainty about each text concept, and enabling better geometric interpretation of concepts such as inclusion, intersection, *etc.* In this work, we present a novel Gaussian Visual-Semantic Embedding (GVSE) model, which leverages the visual information to model text concepts as Gaussian distributions in semantic space. Experiments in two tasks, image classification and text-based image retrieval on the large scale MIT Places205 dataset, have demonstrated the superiority of our method over existing approaches, with higher accuracy and better robustness.

Keywords

Visual-semantic embedding; gaussian embedding; image classification; text-based image retrieval

1. INTRODUCTION

Joint image-text representation is essential for tasks involving both images and texts, such as image captioning [8, 17], text-based image retrieval [7, 14], image classification [1, 3, 13], *etc.* In recent years, Visual-Semantic Embedding (VSE) models [2, 6, 10, 12] have shown impressive performance in those tasks. By leveraging the semantic information contained in unannotated text data, VSE models explicitly map images into a rich semantic space, with the goal that images of the same category are mapped to nearby locations around the corresponding text label, and text labels are embedded in such a smooth space with respect to some measure of similarity, that is, similar text concepts should be mapped into nearby locations.

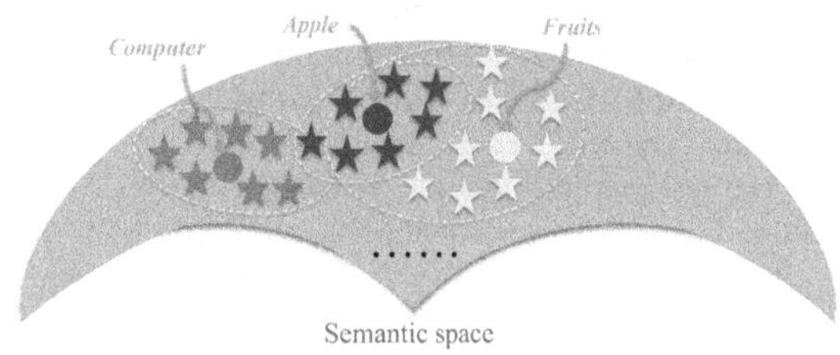

Figure 1: Existing Visual-Semantic Embedding models simply represent the text concepts as single points in the semantic space, as indicated by the circular symbols (we use different colors to indicate different categories). We propose the Gaussian Visual-Semantic Embedding (GVSE) model, which however leverages the visual information indicated as the pentagram symbols (pentagram symbols of the same color indicate various images of the same category) to model text concepts as Gaussian distributions. Modeling text concepts as densities innately represents uncertainties of text concepts, and has the benefit of geometric interpretation such as inclusion and intersection.

Although VSE models have shown remarkable results, representing text concepts as single points in semantic space carries some important limitations. Firstly, using an embedded vector to represent a text does not naturally express uncertainty about its concept with which the corresponding images may be associated. Even though various images may belong to the same text category, uncertainty is associated with them, which may reflect different aspects of a certain text concept. For instance, as shown in Fig.1, the *Computer* images may be from different brands, viewpoints, *etc.* Moreover, it is intrinsically problematic to map all images of a certain text label to a single point in semantic space, which would confuse the embedding function and thus harm the joint representation.

This paper advocates moving beyond modeling text concepts as single points to that as *densities* in semantic space. In particular, we explore Gaussian distributions (currently with diagonal covariance), in which the means are learned from unannotated text data online and variances are learned from the visual image data. Gaussians innately embody un-

*Part of this work was done when the author was an intern at Adobe Research.

MM '16, October 15–19, 2016, Amsterdam, The Netherlands.
© 2016 ACM. ISBN 978-1-4503-3603-1/16/10... $15.00
DOI: http://dx.doi.org/10.1145/2964284.2967212

certainty, and have a geometric interpretation, such as an inclusion or intersection relationships between text concepts, as shown in Fig.1. We name the proposed method Gaussian Visual-Semantic Embedding (GVSE) model.

To evaluate the proposed method, we have conducted experiments in two tasks on the large scale MIT Places205 dataset. In the image classification task, our model outperforms the VSE baseline [2] by 1-5%. In the task of text-based image retrieval, we illustrate the robustness of our method and the capability in generalizing to untrained texts.

1.1 Related Work

Multi-modal embedding models utilize information from multiple sources, such as images and texts. By leveraging the abundant textual data available on the Internet, several lexically distributed representations of texts have been proposed to capture the semantic meaning among texts, *e.g.*, the word2vec model [9] and GloVe model [11]. Image-sentence embedding models [5, 7] were proposed for image captioning. Recently, visual-semantic embedding models for image classification were proposed by leveraging the distributed representation of labels, *e.g.*, Frome *et al.* [2] and Norouzi *et al.* [10]. Ren *et al.* [12] proposed multiple instance visual-semantic embedding for multi-label image annotation. Vilnis *et al.* [16] presented Gaussian embedding model for word representation. The main difference between [16] and our model is that [16] is only for word representation learned from word data alone, while our model is for joint image-text representation.

2. OVERVIEW OF VISUAL-SEMANTIC EMBEDDING

We first review the background on visual-semantic embedding. Given an image dataset $\mathcal{D} \equiv \{(\mathbf{x}_i, y_i)\}_{i=1}^{N}$, each image is represented by a d-dimensional feature vector, $\mathbf{x}_i \in \mathcal{X} \stackrel{def}{=} \mathbb{R}^d$, and each image is associated with a text label, y_i. There are totally n distinct text labels in dataset $\mathcal{D}$, *i.e.*, $y_i \in \mathcal{Y} \equiv \{1, 2, ..., n\}$.

Previous methods [1, 3] associate images and texts as a classification problem, which predefine a fixed set of text labels $\mathcal{Y}$, and learn to predict the labels given image input, *i.e.*, $\mathcal{X} \rightarrow \mathcal{Y}$. However, these classification-based approaches do not provide a joint representation, thus they have limited applications. Moreover, they lack the ability of generalizing to unseen labels, and need to be retrained when a new label emerges. For example, given a training dataset $\mathcal{D}$ as above, and a test dataset $\mathcal{D}' \equiv \{(\mathbf{x}'_j, y'_j)\}_{j=1}^{N'}$ where $\mathbf{x}'_j \in \mathcal{X}$ and all test labels are distinct from the training labels in dataset $\mathcal{D}$, *i.e.*, $y'_j \in \mathcal{Y}' \equiv \{n+1, ..., n+n'\}$. The test labels are untrained as $\mathcal{Y} \cap \mathcal{Y}' = \emptyset$. Clearly, without side information about the relationships between labels in $\mathcal{Y}$ and $\mathcal{Y}'$, it is infeasible to generalize a classification-based method to unseen text labels without retraining it.

Fortunately, visual-semantic embedding models [2, 10, 12] have been proposed to address this issue. Instead of learning a mapping from images to labels ($\mathcal{X} \rightarrow \mathcal{Y}$), it aims to construct a continuous semantic space $\mathcal{S} \equiv \mathbb{R}^e$ which captures the semantic relationship among all text labels in $\mathcal{Y} \cup \mathcal{Y}'$, and explicitly learn the embedding function from images to such space, $f : \mathcal{X} \rightarrow \mathcal{S}$. The semantic space $\mathcal{S}$ is constructed such that two labels y and y' are semantically similar if and only if their semantic embeddings $s(y)$ and $s(y')$ are close in $\mathcal{S}$, where $s(y)$ is the semantic embedding vector of label y in $\mathcal{S}$. Thus the trained and unseen test labels become related via the semantic space $\mathcal{S}$. Once $f(\cdot)$ is learned, it can be applied to a test image $\mathbf{x}'$ to obtain $f(\mathbf{x}')$, and this image embedding vector of $\mathbf{x}'$ is then compared with the unseen label embedding vectors, $\{s(y'); y' \in \mathcal{Y}'\}$, to search for the most relevant test labels. This allows us to generalize the visual-semantic embedding models to unseen labels.

There are two key components of visual-semantic embedding models: One is how to learn the embedding function $f(\cdot)$. Various approaches [2, 10, 12] have validated the effectiveness of using ranking distance to learn $f(\cdot)$. The other key component is how to construct the continuous semantic space $\mathcal{S}$ of text labels.

3. GAUSSIAN VISUAL-SEMANTIC EMBEDDING

3.1 Constructing the semantic text space

We firstly introduce how we construct $\mathcal{S}$. Distributed representations [9, 11] has shown the capacity to provide semantically meaningful embedding features for text terms (including words and phrases), by learning from unannotated text data from the Internet. This method is able to learn similar embedding vectors for semantically related words because of the fact that those words are more likely to appear in similar semantic contexts.

Thus, we utilize the GloVe model [11] to construct a 300-dim text semantic space $\mathcal{S}$ which embodies the semantic relationship among labels.

3.2 Modeling text concepts as Gaussian distributions

Motivated by the success of ranking loss in state-of-the-art visual-semantic embedding [2, 10, 12], we employ ranking loss to learn the embedding function $f : \mathcal{X} \rightarrow \mathcal{S}$. The intuition is to encourage the embedding of an image to be closer to its ground truth text label than other negative labels:

$$L_{\mathrm{GVSE}}(\mathbf{x}_i, y_i) = \sum_{y_n \in \mathbf{y}_i^-} \max(0, m + D(f(\mathbf{x}_i), y_i) - D(f(\mathbf{x}_i), y_n)), \tag{1}$$

where m is the ranking loss margin that we cross-validate, $f(\mathbf{x})$ is the embedding vector of image $\mathbf{x}$ in $\mathcal{S}$, $\mathbf{y}_i^-$ denotes the negative labels excluding the ground truth label y_i, *i.e.*, $\mathbf{y}_i^- = \mathcal{Y}/y_i$, and $D(f(\mathbf{x}), y)$ is the distance measure between an image embedding point and a text concept. We will introduce how we compute $D(f(\mathbf{x}), y)$ later.

Existing visual-semantic embedding methods model texts as single points in the semantic space $\mathcal{S}$, thus $D(f(\mathbf{x}), y)$ in those methods is just the Euclidean distance between $f(\mathbf{x})$ and the text embedding vector $s(y)$. However, as claimed in the introduction, they are limited in representation capacity. Intrinsically, it is beneficial to model text concepts as densities, which can embody the uncertainty of concepts and also have better geometric interpretation.

In this paper, we model text concepts as Gaussian distributions with diagonal covariances, *i.e.*, $y_i \sim \mathcal{N}(\boldsymbol{\mu}_i, \Sigma_i)$. Thus, the distance between an image embedding vector $f(\mathbf{x}_i)$ and a text label y_i can be measured by Mahalanobis distance

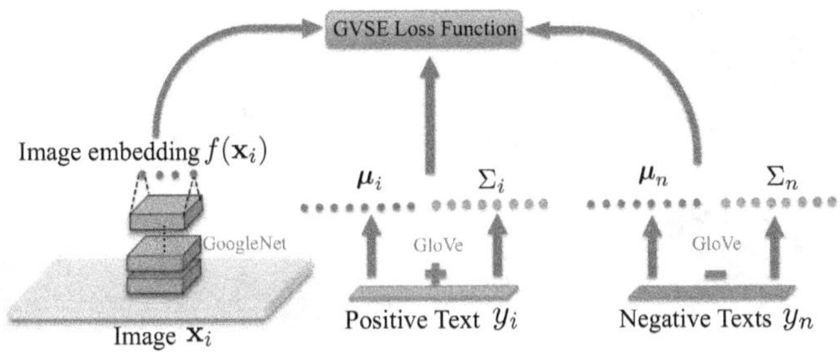

Figure 2: Training framework of the proposed Gaussian Visual-Semantic Embedding model.

as follows:

$$D(f(\mathbf{x}_i), y_i) = (f(\mathbf{x}_i) - \boldsymbol{\mu}_i)^T \Sigma_i^{-1} (f(\mathbf{x}_i) - \boldsymbol{\mu}_i). \quad (2)$$

Thus, our GVSE model could be effectively learned by the loss function in Eq.1.

3.3 Training and inference with GVSE

The learning framework is shown in Fig.2. We jointly learn the embedding function $f(\cdot)$ and the text density parameters $\{\boldsymbol{\mu}_i\}_{i=1}^n$, $\{\Sigma_i\}_{i=1}^n$ in two steps.

Firstly, the mean text embedding vectors $\{\boldsymbol{\mu}_i\}$ are learned using the unannotated text data online alone, as introduced in Section 3.1. Thanks to the similarity between text concepts captured in semantic space $\mathcal{S}$, our model is able to generalize to unseen text concepts, which will be illustrated in Section 4.3. Secondly, we learn $f(\cdot)$ and $\{\Sigma_i\}$ by end-to-end training. Note that we use GoogleNet [15] to extract image features $\mathbf{x}_i$. On top of the convolutional layers of GoogleNet, we add a fully connected layer to model the embedding function $f(\cdot)$. On the other hand, since Σ_i is a 300×300 diagonal matrix, we use a $300\times n$ fully connected layer to encode all parameters in $\{\Sigma_i\}_{i=1}^n$, where each column of the weight corresponds to a covariance matrix Σ_i.

Given a trained GVSE model, it is straightforward to do inference on either a query image or a query text, depending on the tasks. From either direction, we map the query and testing entries into the semantic space $\mathcal{S}$. And Mahalanobis distance between the query and each testing entry can be computed by Eq.2. Finally the result is computed based on such distances.

4. EXPERIMENTS

In this section, we report our experiments on image classification and text-based image retrieval, comparing the proposed GVSE model with visual-semantic embedding models.

4.1 Dataset and implementation

We test on a large-scale image dataset, MIT Places205 dataset [18], which has 2,448,873 images from 205 scene categories. We follow the train-test split provided in the dataset.

We use Caffe [4] to implement our model. The optimization of our network is achieved by Stochastic Gradient Descent with a momentum term of weight 0.9 and with mini-batch size of 100. The initial learning rate is set to 0.1, and we update it with the "steps" policy. A weight decay of 0.0005 is applied.

Figure 3: The top-9 image retrieval results of searching trained text "*airport terminal*". The incorrect image shares very similar visual appearance.

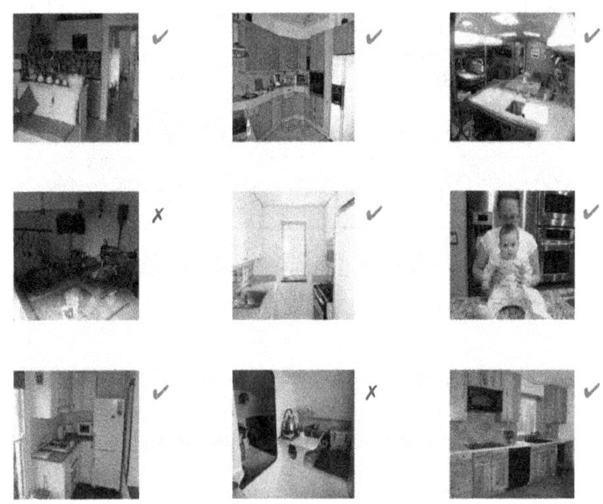

Figure 4: The top-9 image retrieval results of searching trained text "*kitchen*". The incorrect images belong to "*kitchenette*" which is a very close concept.

4.2 Image classification

To quantify the image classification performance, we use mAP@k as the evaluation metric, which measures the mean average precision of returning the ground truth label within top-k of the prediction list.

The results are shown in Table 1. We compare with two baseline models: one is visual-semantic embedding (VSE) model trained with L2 loss, the other is the DeViSE [2] model trained with ranking loss. These two models are state-of-the-art visual-semantic embedding models. As we see, with the basic nearest neighbor search in testing, the proposed GVSE model outperforms the best baseline for 0.93% on average, which validates the benefit of modeling text concepts as densities.

Moreover, we train a SVM classifier on top of the embedding representation that GVSE learned, and such classifying technique boosts the performance for 4.48% in mAP@1

Figure 5: The top-9 retrieval results of searching untrained text "*infant*". The returned images belong to "*nursery*" and "*hospital room*", which are conceptually related.

Figure 6: The top-9 retrieval results of searching untrained text "*sports*". The returned images belong to "*football stadium*", "*baseball stadium*" and "*stadium*", which are conceptually related.

Approach	mAP@1	mAP@5
1. nearest neighbor search		
VSE with L2 loss	41.33	68.02
DeViSE [2]	51.53	82.59
The proposed GVSE	52.38	83.60
2. SVM search		
The proposed GVSE	**56.86**	**84.46**

Table 1: Image classification results on the MIT Places205 dataset, shown in %.

and 0.86% in mAP@5. State-of-the-art classification-based method [18] (that uses deep learning and does not use explicitly modeling) reported mAP@1 performance 55.50%. Our performance is 1.36% higher. Note that classification-based methods [18] do not learn a joint representation and are not able to generalize to untrained classes, which is an advantage of our method, as shown in Fig.5, Fig.6 of Section 4.3.

4.3 Text-based image retrieval

Since GVSE model learns a joint embedding representation for both images and texts. We could either search labels given images (as in image classification of Section 4.2), or search images given text query. Thus we conduct a qualitative experiment on text-based image retrieval.

Thanks to the semantic space learned from unannotated text data, our model is able to search both trained or untrained texts, as discussed in Section 2 (searching by untrained texts is known as *zero-shot learning* [12], which is a challenging task.). Fig.3 and Fig.4 illustrate two examples of trained text searching, while Fig.5 and Fig.6 show two examples of untrained text searching.

As we see in Fig.3 and Fig.4, the retrieval results are very robust, except a few incorrect cases, which either share similar visual appearance with the query images or belong to very close text concept of the query. On the other hand, when we search untrained texts as shown in Fig.5 and Fig.6, the returned results are conceptually very related to the queries. For instance, "*sports*" is a text label that does not appear in the MIT Places205 training dataset. However, using the proposed GVSE model, the retrieved "*stadium*"s images are very related to "*sports*".

Both quantitative and qualitative experimental results validate the superiority of the proposed GVSE model in joint image-text representation.

4.4 Future work

From the experimental results above, we have validated the superiority of modeling text concepts as densities over single points. We explored our preliminary idea on Gaussian modeling. And for effective training, we constrained the densities to be diagonal Gaussians.

A straightforward improvement of our method is to model text concepts as more sophisticated density distributions, such as Gaussians with arbitrary covariances and Gaussian Mixture Models. Another future improvement over the proposed method is in the training process. We learned our model parameters by end-to-end training. However, with more complicated text modelings, such as GMM, iterative training can benefit the convergence.

5. CONCLUSION

In this paper, we have proposed a novel Gaussian Visual-Semantic Embedding model for joint image-text representation. Instead of modeling text concepts as single points in the semantic space, we move beyond to modeling that as densities. Effective end-to-end training framework and testing techniques have been introduced. Experiments on multimodal tasks in both directions of images and texts, including image classification and text-based image retrieval, have demonstrated that the proposed method outperforms existing visual-semantic embedding models with higher accuracy, better robustness, as well as the ability to generalize to untrained text concepts.

Acknowledgement

This work is partially supported by the Army Research Office ARO 62250-CS and a gift grant from Adobe Research. We also acknowledge the support of NVIDIA Corporation with the donation of GPUs used for this research.

6. REFERENCES

[1] J. Deng, W. Dong, R. Socher, L. Li, K. Li, and L. Fei-Fei. Imagenet: a large-scale hierachical image database. In *CVPR*, 2009.

[2] A. Frome, G. Corrado, J. Shlens, S. Bengio, J. Dean, M. Ranzato, and T. Mikolov. Devise: A deep visual-semantic embedding model. In *NIPS*, 2013.

[3] Y. Gong, Y. Jia, T. K. Leung, A. Toshev, and S. Ioffe. Deep convolutional ranking for multilabel image annotation. In *ICLR*, 2014.

[4] Y. Jia, E. Shelhamer, J. Donahue, S. Karayev, J. Long, R. Girshick, S. Guadarrama, and T. Darrell. Caffe: Convolutional architecture for fast feature embedding. *arXiv preprint arXiv:1408.5093*, 2014.

[5] A. Karpathy and L. Fei-Fei. Deep visual-semantic alignments for generating image descriptions. In *CVPR*, 2015.

[6] R. Kiros, R. Salakhutdinov, and R. Zemel. Unifying visual-semantic embeddings with multimodal neural language models. In *TACL*, 2015.

[7] R. Kiros, R. Salakhutdinov, and R. S. Zemel. Unifying visual-semantic embeddings with multimodal neural language models. In *TACL*, 2015.

[8] J. Mao, W. Xu, Y. Yang, J. Wang, Z. Huang, and A. L. Yuille. Deep captioning with multimodal recurrent neural networks (m-rnn). In *ICLR*, 2015.

[9] T. Mikolov, I. Sutskever, K. Chen, G. Corrado, and J. Dean. Distributed representations of words and phrases and their compositionality. In *NIPS*, 2013.

[10] M. Norouzi, T. Mikolov, S. Bengio, Y. Singer, J. Shlens, A. Frome, G. Corrado, and J. Dean. Zero-shot learning by convex combination of semantic embeddings. In *ICLR*, 2014.

[11] J. Pennington, R. Socher, and C. D. Manning. Glove: Global vectors for word representation. In *EMNLP*, 2014.

[12] Z. Ren, H. Jin, Z. Lin, C. Fang, and A. Yuille. Multi-instance visual-semantic embedding. In *arXiv preprint arXiv:1512.06963*, 2015.

[13] Z. Ren, C. Wang, and A. Yuille. Scene-domain active part models for object representation. In *ICCV*, 2015.

[14] Y. Rui, T. S. Huang, and S.-F. Chang. Image retrieval: Current techniques, promising directions, and open issues. *Journal of Visual Communication and Image Representation*, 1999.

[15] C. Szegedy, W. Liu, Y. Jia, P. Sermanet, S. Reed, D. Anguelov, D. Erhan, V. Vanhoucke, and A. Rabinovich. Going deeper with convolutions. In *CVPR*, 2015.

[16] L. Vilnis and A. McCallum. Word representations via gaussian embedding. In *ICLR*, 2015.

[17] O. Vinyals, A. Toshev, S. Bengio, and D. Erhan. Show and tell: A neural image caption generator. In *CVPR*, 2015.

[18] B. Zhou, A. Lapedriza, J. Xiao, A. Torralba, and A. Oliva. Learning deep features for scene recognition using places database. In *NIPS*, 2014.

A Domain Robust Approach for Image Dataset Construction

Yazhou Yao
Nanjing University of Science and Technology
University of Technology Sydney
yazhou.yao@outlook.com

Xian-sheng Hua
Alibaba Group
Hangzhou 310052, China
xiansheng.hxs@alibaba-inc.com

Fumin Shen
University of Electronic Science and Technology of China
Chengdu 610054, China
fumin.shen@gmail.com

Jian Zhang
University of Technology Sydney
NSW 2007, Australia
jian.zhang@uts.edu.au

Zhenmin Tang
Nanjing University of Science and Technology
Nanjing 210094, China
tzm.cs@njust.edu.cn

ABSTRACT

There have been increasing research interests in automatically constructing image dataset by collecting images from the Internet. However, existing methods tend to have a weak domain adaptation ability, known as the "dataset bias problem". To address this issue, in this work, we propose a novel image dataset construction framework which can generalize well to unseen target domains. In specific, the given queries are first expanded by searching in the Google Books Ngrams Corpora (GBNC) to obtain a richer semantic description, from which the noisy query expansions are then filtered out. By treating each expansion as a "bag" and the retrieved images therein as "instances", we formulate image filtering as a multi-instance learning (MIL) problem with constrained positive bags. By this approach, images from different data distributions will be kept while with noisy images filtered out. Comprehensive experiments on two challenging tasks demonstrate the effectiveness of our proposed approach.

Keywords

Domain robust, Multiple query expansions, Image dataset construction

1. INTRODUCTION

Labelled image datasets have played a critical role in high-level image understanding [4, 12, 29]. For example, ImageNet [7] has acted as one of the most important factors in the recent advance of developing and deploying visual representation learning models (e.g., deep CNN). However, the process of constructing ImageNet is both time consuming and labour intensive. Recently, there have been increasing research interests in automatically constructing image datasets by exploiting web images from the Internet. Existing methods [11, 13, 18, 25, 26, 28] usually take an iterative mechanism in the process of image selection. Due to the visual feature distributions of images collected by the iterative mechanism, these datasets tend to have statistical problems, which is known as the dataset bias problem [30]. Classifiers learned from these datasets usually have poor performance on domain adaptation [23]. To address this problem, a large number of domain adaptation approaches have been proposed [17, 19, 31], which explicitly coped with noisy labels of web images. Specifically, the images are partitioned into a set of clusters and each cluster is treated as a "bag" with the images in each bag as "instances". As a result, these tasks can be formulated as a multi-instance learning (MIL) problem and different MIL methods were proposed in [17, 19, 31]. The main difference of our work from previous domain robust works lies in the forming process of "bag". Existing works mainly take clustering based method to form the "bag" while our work use different query expansions. Our work is also related to the recent work for visual concept learning system [8] which achieves impressive performance on object detection. This method firstly find all related parts and then train a mixture DPM [10] detector.

In this work, we aim to construct a domain robust image dataset which can generalize well to unseen target domains. We propose to construct domain robust image dataset for given queries by three major steps: query expanding, noisy expansions filtering and noisy images filtering. Specifically, by searching in the GBNC [21], we firstly expand the given query to a set of semantically rich expansions, from which the visually non-salient and less relevant expansions are then filtered by exploiting both word-word and visual-visual similarity. After we obtain the candidate images by retrieving these unfiltered expansions with image search engine, we treat each expansion as a "bag" and the images in each bag as "instances". We then formulate this task as a MIL problem with constrained positive bags, in which noisy images will be filtered and domain robust image dataset will be constructed.

To verify the effectiveness of our proposed approach, we build an image dataset with 10 categories. We evaluate its

MM '16, October 15-19, 2016, Amsterdam, Netherlands

DOI: http://dx.doi.org/10.1145/2964284.2967213

object detection ability with several other baseline methods. To further demonstrate the domain robustness of our dataset, the cross-dataset generalization ability is compared between our dataset and two manually labelled image datasets.

2. IMAGE DATASET CONSTRUCTION

To build a large domain robust image dataset with Internet data, we must separate noisy images from useful images automatically and retain as much as possible images of different visual patterns. In this section, we propose our web supervised image dataset construction approach by three major steps: query expanding, noisy expansions filtering and noisy images filtering.

2.1 Query Expanding

Image datasets constructed by existing methods tend to have a higher accuracy, but usually have a weak domain adaptation ability [8]. In order to construct a domain robust image dataset, we expand query (e.g., "horse") to a set of query expansions (e.g., "jumping horse, walking horse, roaring horse", etc.) and then use these different query expansions (corresponding images) to reflect different "visual patterns" for the query. GBNC [21] cover almost all related queries at the text level. It's much more general and richer than WordNet [22]. We use GBNC to discover query expansions for the given query with Parts-Of-Speech (POS), specifically with NOUN, VERB, ADJECTIVE and ADVERB. Using GBNC help us to find all expansions for any possible query the human race has ever written down in books. In addition, POS tag helps us to partially purify these query expansions.

2.2 Noisy Expansions Filtering

Through query expanding, we get a richer semantic description for the given query. However, query expanding not only brings some useful query expansions, but also brings some noisy query expansions ("betting horse", "sea horse" and etc.). Using these noisy query expansions to retrieve images will result in a bad influence on dataset accuracy and robustness.

From the perspective of relevance, we want to identify both semantic and visual relevant expansions for the given query. The intuition is that relevant expansions should exhibit a small semantic and visual distance. We use combined word-word and visual-visual similarity based filtering method.

Words and phrases acquire meaning from the way they are used in society. For computers, the equivalent of "society" is "database", and the equivalent of "use" is "a way to search the database" [5]. Normalized Google Distance (NGD) constructs a method to extract semantic similarity distance from the World Wide Web (WWW) using Google page counts[5]. For a search term x and search term y, NGD is defined by:

$$NGD(x,y) = \frac{max\{logf(x), logf(y)\} - logf(x,y)}{logN - min\{logf(x), logf(y)\}} \quad (1)$$

where $f(x)$ denotes the number of pages containing x, $f(x,y)$ denotes the number of pages containing both x and y and N is the total number of web pages searched by Google.

We denote the semantic distance of all query expansions by a graph $G_g = \{N, D\}$ where each node represents a query expansion and its edge represents the NGD between the two nodes. We set the target query as center (x) and other query expansions have a score (D_{xy}) which corresponds to the distance to the target query. Similarly, we represent the visual distance of query and expansions by a graph $G_v = \{C, E\}$ where each node represents a query expansion and each edge represents the visual distance between query and expansions. Each node has a center C_y which corresponds to k = 1 Kmeans clustering center. The feature is 1000 dimensional Bag of visual words based on SIFT features. The edge weight E_{xy} correspond to the Euclidean distance.

The semantic distance and visual distance will be used to construct a new 2 dimensional feature $V = [D_{xy}; E_{xy}]$. Then the problem can be translated to calculate the importance weight w and bias penalty b in decision function $f(x) = w^T x + b$ to determine whether the expansion is relevant or not. There are lots of methods to obtain these coefficients w and b. Here we take linearSVM to solve this problem. Although linearSVM is not the prevailing state-of-the-art method for classification, we found our method to be effective in pruning irrelevant query expansions.

2.3 Noisy Images Filtering

Through query expanding and noisy expansions filtering, we get a richer semantic description for the given query. Then we use these unfiltered query expansions to retrieve images from Google Image search engine, constructing the raw image dataset for the given query.

Although Google Image search engine has ranked the returned images, some noisy images are still included. In addition, a few unfiltered noisy expansions will also bring some noisy images to the raw image dataset for the given query. MIL based methods are applied to filter these noisy images which caused by image search engine and unfiltered noisy expansions.

By treating each unfiltered expansion as a positive "bag" and the images corresponding to the expansion as "instances", we formulate a multi-instance learning problem by selecting a subset of images from each bag to construct the domain robust image dataset for the given query. Since the precision of images returned from Google Image search engine tend to have a relatively high accuracy, we define each positive bag at least has a portion of δ positive instances.

We denote each instance as x_i with its label $y_i \in \{\pm 1\}$, where i=1,...,n. We also denote the label of each bag B_I as $Y_I \in \{\pm 1\}$. The transpose of a vector or matrix is represented by superscript $'$ and the element-wise product between two matrices $\mathbf{P}$ and $\mathbf{Q}$ is represented by $\mathbf{P} \odot \mathbf{Q}$. Moreover, we define the identity matrix as $\mathbf{I}$ and $\mathbf{0}$, $\mathbf{1} \in \Re^n$ denote the column vectors of all zeros and ones, respectively. The inequality $\mathbf{u} = [u_1, u_2 ... u_n]' \geq \mathbf{0}$ means that $u_i \geq 0$ for i=1,...,n.

The decision function is assumed in the form of $f(x) = w'\varphi(x) + b$ and it is to be learned from the raw image dataset. Besides, the decision function will also be used to filter noisy images. We employ the formulation of Lagrangian SVM, in which the square bias penalty b^2 and the square hinge loss for each instance are used in the objective function. Then the decision function can be learned by minimizing the following structural risk functional:

$$\min_{\mathbf{y}, w, b, \rho, \varepsilon_i} \quad \frac{1}{2}\left(\|w\|^2 + b^2 + C\sum_{i=1}^{n} \varepsilon_i^2\right) - \rho \quad (2)$$

$$\text{s.t.} \quad y_i(w'\varphi(x_i) + b) \geq \rho - \varepsilon_i, i = 1, ...n. \quad (3)$$

$$\begin{aligned} \sum_{i:x_i \in B_I} \frac{y_i + 1}{2} \geq \delta |B_I| \quad & for \quad Y_I = 1, \\ y_i = -1 \quad & for \quad Y_I = -1 \end{aligned} \quad (4)$$

where φ is a mapping function that maps x from the original space into a high dimensional space $\varphi(x)$, $C > 0$ is a regularization parameter and ε_i values are slack variables. The margin separation is defined as $\rho / \|w\|$. $\mathbf{y} = [y_1 ... y_n]'$ means the vector of instance labels, $\lambda = \{\mathbf{y} | y_i \in \{\pm 1\}\}$ and $\mathbf{y}$ satisfies constraint (4). By introducing a dual variable α_i for inequality constraint (3) and kernel trick $k_{ij} = \varphi(x_i)'\varphi(x_j)$, we arrive at the below

Table 1: Object Detection Results (Average Precision) on PASCAL VOC 2007 (test)

Method	Supervised	bird	train	cat	cow	dog	horse	sheep	plane	bus	mbike	average
[26]	weak	3.1	**34.2**	7.1	9.3	1.5	29.4	0.4	13.4	31.2	**38.3**	16.79
[8]	web	**12.5**	23.5	8.4	17.5	12.9	30.6	**18.8**	14.0	35	27.5	16.62
our	**web**	12.3	25.5	**9.7**	**18.7**	**14.2**	**32.7**	15.3	**14.6**	**36.7**	28.5	**20.82**
[10]	full	10.3	45.2	22.5	24.3	12.6	56.5	20.9	33.2	52.0	48.5	32.6

optimization problem:

$$\min_{\mathbf{y}\in\lambda}\max_{\alpha} \quad -\frac{1}{2}\left(\sum_{i,j=1}^{n}\alpha_i\alpha_j y_i y_j k_{ij} + \sum_{i,j=1}^{n}\alpha_i\alpha_j y_i y_j + \frac{1}{C}\right) \quad (5)$$

where $\alpha_i \geq 0$, $\sum_{i=1}^{n}\alpha_i = 1$ and $\alpha = [\alpha_1, \alpha_2 ... \alpha_n]'$. By defining $\nu = \{\alpha|\alpha \geq \mathbf{0}, \alpha'\mathbf{1} = 1\}$, $\mathbf{K} = [k_{ij}]$ as an $n \times n$ kernel matrix and $\widetilde{\mathbf{K}} = \mathbf{K} + \mathbf{11}'$ as an $n \times n$ transformed kernel matrix for the augmented feature mapping $\widetilde{\varphi}(x) = [\varphi(x)'.\ \ 1]'$ of kernel $\widetilde{k_{ij}} = \widetilde{\varphi}(x_i)'\widetilde{\varphi}(x_j)$. (5) can be rewritten as follows:

$$\min_{\mathbf{y}\in\lambda}\max_{\alpha\in\nu} \quad -\frac{1}{2}\alpha'(\widetilde{\mathbf{K}} \odot \mathbf{yy}' + \frac{1}{C}\mathbf{I})\alpha \quad (6)$$

(6) is a mixed integer programming problem with respect to the instance labels $y_i \in \{\pm 1\}$. To solve this mixed integer programming problem, we take Label-Generating MMC (LG-MMC) algorithm which was proposed in [20].

We firstly consider interchanging the order of $max_{\alpha\in\upsilon}$ and $min_{\mathbf{y}\in\lambda}$ in (6) and get:

$$\max_{\alpha\in\nu}\min_{\mathbf{y}\in\lambda} \quad -\frac{1}{2}\alpha'(\widetilde{\mathbf{K}} \odot \mathbf{yy}' + \frac{1}{C}\mathbf{I})\alpha \quad (7)$$

According to the minmax theorem [15], the optimal objective of (6) is an upper bound of (7). We further rewrite (7) as:

$$\max_{\alpha\in\nu}\left\{\max_{\vartheta} - \theta|\theta \geq \frac{1}{2}\alpha'(\widetilde{\mathbf{K}} \odot \mathbf{y}^t\mathbf{y}^{t'} + \frac{1}{C}\mathbf{I})\alpha, \forall\mathbf{y}^t \in \lambda\right\} \quad (8)$$

$\mathbf{y}^t$ is any feasible solution in λ. For the inner optimization sub-problem, let $u_t \geq 0$ be the dual variable for inequality constraint. Its Lagrangian can be obtained as:

$$-\theta + \sum_{t:\mathbf{y}_t\in\lambda} u_t(\theta - \frac{1}{2}\alpha'(\widetilde{\mathbf{K}} \odot \mathbf{y}^t\mathbf{y}^{t'} + \frac{1}{C}\mathbf{I})\alpha) \quad (9)$$

Setting the derivative of (9) with respect to θ to zero, we have $\sum u_t = 1$. $\mathbf{M} = \{\mathbf{u}|\sum u_t = 1, u_t \geq 0\}$ is denoted as the domain of $\mathbf{u}$, where $\mathbf{u}$ is the vector of u_t. Then the inner optimization sub-problem is replaced with its dual and (8) be rewritten as:

$$\max_{\alpha\in\nu}\min_{\mathbf{u}\in\mathbf{M}} \quad -\frac{1}{2}\alpha'(\sum_{t:\mathbf{y}^t\in\lambda} u_t\widetilde{\mathbf{K}} \odot \mathbf{yy}' + \frac{1}{C}\mathbf{I})\alpha$$

or

$$\min_{\mathbf{u}\in\mathbf{M}}\max_{\alpha\in\nu} \quad -\frac{1}{2}\alpha'(\sum_{t:\mathbf{y}^t\in\lambda} u_t\widetilde{\mathbf{K}} \odot \mathbf{yy}' + \frac{1}{C}\mathbf{I})\alpha \quad (10)$$

Here, we can interchange the order of $max_{\alpha\in\nu}$ and $min_{\mathbf{u}\in\mathbf{M}}$ because the objective function is concave in α and convex in $\mathbf{u}$. Besides, (10) can be regarded as multiple kernel learning (MKL) problem [1], the target kernel matrix is a convex combination of base kernel matrices $\left\{\widetilde{\mathbf{K}} \odot \mathbf{y_t y_t}'\right\}$.

Although λ is finite and (10) is an MKL problem, we can't directly use existing MKL techniques like [24, 27] to solve this problem. The reason is that the exponential number of possible labelings $\mathbf{y}_t \in \lambda$ and the base kernels is also exponential in size makes direct MKL computes intractable.

Fortunately, not all the constraints in (8) are active at optimality, we can employ cutting-plane algorithm [14] to find a subset $\zeta \in \lambda$ of the constraints that can well approximate the original optimization problem. The detail solutions of cutting-plane algorithm for (10) are described in Algorithm 1.

Algorithm 1 Cutting-plane algorithm for (10)

1: Initialize $y_i = Y_I$ for $x_i \in B_I$ as $\mathbf{y}^1$, and set $\zeta = \{\mathbf{y}^1\}$;
2: Use MKL to solve α and $\mathbf{u}$ in (10) with ζ;
3: Select most violated $\mathbf{y}^t$ with α and set $\zeta = \mathbf{y}^t \cup \zeta$;
4: Repeat step 2 and step 3 until convergence.

Finding most violated constraint $\mathbf{y}^t$ is the most challenging part in the cutting-plane algorithm. According to (5), the most violated $\mathbf{y}^t$ is equivalent to the following optimization problem:

$$\max_{\mathbf{y}\in\lambda} \quad \sum_{i,j=1}^{n}\alpha_i\alpha_j y_i y_j k_{ij} \quad (11)$$

We take a similar process as in [19] to solve this integer optimization problem by enumerating all possible candidates of $\mathbf{y}^t$. Here we only enumerate the possible labeling candidates of the instances in positive bags as all instances in the negative bags are assumed to be negative in our paper.

Finally, we can derive the decision function from the raw image dataset for the given query as:

$$f(x) = \sum_{i:\alpha_i\neq 0}\alpha_i\widetilde{y}_i\widetilde{k}(x, x_i) \quad (12)$$

where $\widetilde{y}_i = \sum_{t:\mathbf{y}^t\in\lambda} u_t y_i^t$ and $\widetilde{k}(x, x_i) = k(x, x_i) + 1$. Then the decision function will be used to filter noisy images in each positive bag which corresponding to unfiltered query expansions.

One could expect that in our work there would be more visual patterns (responding to different query expansions) to represent the given query, and in return the constructed image dataset could achieve better domain adaptation ability than traditional image dataset which were constructed by iterative mechanism using one query.

3. EXPERIMENTS

In our experiments, for any given query (e.g.,"horse"), we first expand the given query to a set of query expansions with POS. We select n_+ positive training samples from these expansions which have small semantic distance or visual distance. The case of negative samples is more favorable: we calculate the semantic distance and visual distance between different query (e.g., "horse" and "cow") and get the n_- negative training samples. We don't choose to select the n_- negative training samples from these expansions which have a big semantic distance or visual distance because these expansions have a higher probability to be positive than other different query expansions. Here we set the $n = 1000$ and train a classifier based on linearSVM to filter noisy query expansions. The first 50 images are retrieved from Google Image search engine for each unfiltered query expansion to construct the raw image dataset. We treat the unfiltered query expansions as positive bags and images in bag as instances. We define each positive bag at least has a portion of $\delta = 0.8$ positive instances. While negative bags can be obtained by randomly sampling a few irrelevant images that are not associated with the given query. MIL based methods are applied to learn the decision function

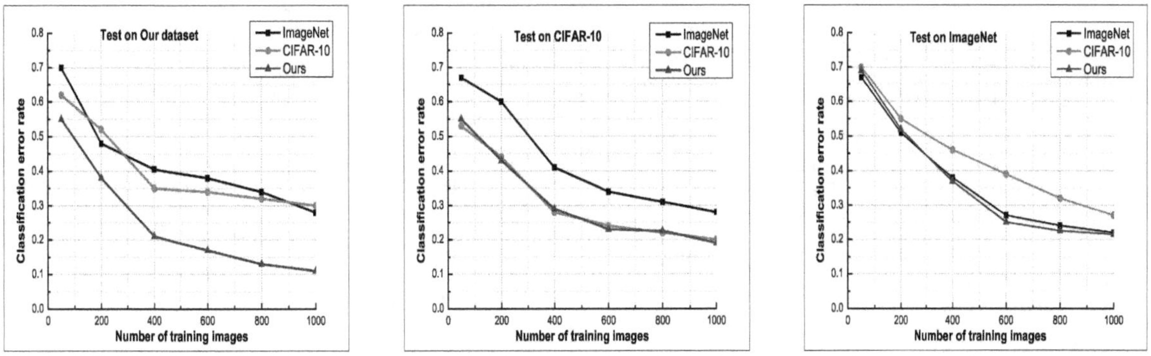

(a) (b) (c)

Figure 1: Cross-dataset generalization of HOG+SVM trained on our dataset, CIFAR-10 and ImageNet, then tested on: (a) Our dataset, (b) CIFAR-10 and (c) ImageNet.

(12), filtering noisy images in positive bags to construct the domain robust image dataset. In order to facilitate comparison with other algorithms, we choose 10 categories in PASCAL VOC 2007 to construct our dataset. Since existing automatically methods [11, 13, 18, 25, 26] didn't release their dataset, we can't directly compare our dataset with their extracted datasets. In our paper, we mainly take two below methods to evaluate the effectiveness and robustness of our dataset.

3.1 Performance Evaluation on Object Detection Ability

To compare the object detection ability of our dataset with three other baseline methods [8, 10, 26], we pick PASCAL VOC 2007 as the test data. The reason is recent state-of-the-art weakly and webly supervised methods have been evaluated on it. We resize images to a maximum of 500 pixels, discard all near-duplicates, and ignore images with extreme aspect ratios (aspect ratio > 2.5 or < 0.4). We initialize our bounding box to a sub-image within the image that ignores the image boundaries. Then the detector is trained using the default parameters of [10]. We evaluate the performance of our learned detection model on the PASCAL VOC 2007 test set [9] and Table 1 displays the results.

Compared to [26] which uses weak supervision and [10] which uses full supervision, the training set of our proposed method does not need to be labelled manually. Nonetheless, our results substantially surpass the previous best results in weakly supervised object detection method [26]. Compared to [8] which also uses web supervision, our method surpasses their results in most of the cases. By using the same feature and learning mechanism, our image dataset achieves a better performance than weakly and webly supervised method [26, 8]. The main reason for this is that our training data generated from unfiltered query expansions which contain much richer and accurate visual descriptions for these categories. In other words, our approach discovers query expansions that have much more useful linkages to the visual patterns for the given category.

3.2 Performance Evaluation on Cross-dataset Generalization Ability

Cross-dataset generalization ability measures the performance of classifiers learned from one dataset and tested on the other datasets. It indicates the efficiency and domain robustness of dataset [2, 30]. Here we compare the cross-dataset generalization ability of our dataset with two publicly available dataset CIFAR-10 [16] and ImageNet [7].

The CIFAR-10 dataset [16] consists of 10 categories. Each category has 5000 training images. ImageNet [7] is an image dataset organized according to the WordNet [22] hierarchy. It provides on average 1000 images to illustrate each category. To be fair, we only choose the five same categories (horse, bird, airplane, cat and dog) which are included in all three datasets to verify their cross-dataset generalization ability. Specifically, we randomly select 1000 training images from the CIFAR-10 dataset and our dataset (because the average number of training data in ImageNet is 1000). As the size of all images in the CIFAR-10 dataset are 32×32, we resize all images to $[32, 32]$ and convert all images to grayscale images. When training the image classification model, we set the same options for three datasets. Setting the type of SVM to be C-SVC, the type of kernel to be radial basis function and all other options to be the default LIBSVM [3] options. Then datasets are used to learn the image classification model based on same feature (HOG[6]) and learning method (SVM). We use the learned model to do image classification on these three image datasets. The results are shown in Fig. 1.

In all three cases, with the increase of training images, the best performance of classification is achieved by our dataset. When tested on our dataset, we achieves a much better performance than other two datasets. When tested on other two datasets, it shows that the generalization ability of our dataset is very close and our dataset performs slightly better than CIFAR-10 and ImageNet. From the perspective of cross-dataset generalization ability, it shows that our dataset has a much better domain adaptation ability than two other datasets. The reason is our dataset was constructed by multiple query expansions while other two dataset were constructed by only one query. Note, our dataset was constructed automatically while two other datasets were manually labelled.

4. CONCLUSION AND FUTURE WORK

In this work, we presented a new framework for domain robust image dataset construction. Three successive modules were employed in the framework including query expanding, noisy expansions filtering and noisy images filtering. To verify the effectiveness of our proposed method, we constructed an image dataset with 10 categories. The extensive experiments showed that our framework had a better object detection ability and can surpass [8, 26] in most of the cases. Finally, we evaluated the cross-dataset generation ability of our dataset with two manually labelled datasets CIFAR-10 and ImageNet. The results showed our image dataset outperformed the manually labelled datasets ImageNet and CIFAR-10 in terms of cross-dataset generalization ability.

Although good results were obtained, there is still room to improve the proposed dataset construction framework. For example, we can potentially use more sophisticated approaches to purify noisy query expansions, noisy images and that will be the focus of our future work.

Acknowledgments

This research was supported by the Natural Science Foundation of China (No. 61473154).

5. REFERENCES

[1] F. R. Bach, G. R. Lanckriet, and M. I. Jordan. Multiple kernel learning, conic duality, and the smo algorithm. In *Proceedings of the International conference on Machine learning*, pages 220–228. ACM, 2004.

[2] Y. Bai, K. Yang, W. Yu, C. Xu, W.-Y. Ma, and T. Zhao. Automatic image dataset construction from click-through logs using deep neural network. In *Proceedings of the ACM Conference on Multimedia*, pages 441–450. ACM, 2015.

[3] C.-C. Chang and C.-J. Lin. Libsvm: a library for support vector machines. *ACM Transactions on Intelligent Systems and Technology*, 2(3):27, 2011.

[4] F. Shen, W. Liu, S. Zhang, Y. Yang, and H. Shen, "Learning binary codes for maximum inner product search," In *Proceedings of IEEE International Conference on Computer Vision* , pages 4148–4156. IEEE, 2015.

[5] R. L. Cilibrasi and P. M. Vitanyi. The google similarity distance. *IEEE Transactions on Knowledge and Data Engineering*, 19(3):370–383, 2007.

[6] N. Dalal and B. Triggs. Histograms of oriented gradients for human detection. In *Proceedings of IEEE Conference on Computer Vision and Pattern Recognition*, pages 886–893. IEEE, 2005.

[7] J. Deng, W. Dong, R. Socher, L.-J. Li, K. Li, and L. Fei-Fei. Imagenet: A large-scale hierarchical image database. In *Proceedings of IEEE Conference on Computer Vision and Pattern Recognition*, pages 248–255. IEEE, 2009.

[8] S. K. Divvala, A. Farhadi, and C. Guestrin. Learning everything about anything: Webly-supervised visual concept learning. In *Proceedings of IEEE Conference on Computer Vision and Pattern Recognition*, pages 3270–3277. IEEE, 2014.

[9] M. Everingham, L. Van Gool, C. K. Williams, J. Winn, and A. Zisserman. The pascal visual object classes (voc) challenge. *International journal of computer vision*, 88(2):303–338, 2010.

[10] P. F. Felzenszwalb, R. B. Girshick, D. McAllester, and D. Ramanan. Object detection with discriminatively trained part-based models. *IEEE Transactions on Pattern Analysis and Machine Intelligence*, 32(9):1627–1645, 2010.

[11] R. Fergus, L. Fei-Fei, P. Perona, and A. Zisserman. Learning object categories from internet image searches. In *Proceedings of the IEEE*, 98(8):1453–1466, 2010.

[12] F. Shen, C. Shen, W. Liu, and H. Shen, "Supervised discrete hashing," In *Proceedings of the IEEE International Conference on Computer Vision and Pattern Recognition*, pages 37–45. IEEE, 2015.

[13] X.-S. Hua and J. Li. Prajna: Towards recognizing whatever you want from images without image labeling. In *Proceedings of AAAI Conference on Artificial Intelligence*, pages 137–144. AAAI, 2015.

[14] J. E. Kelley, Jr. The cutting-plane method for solving convex programs. *Journal of the Society for Industrial and Applied Mathematics*, 8(4):703–712, 1960.

[15] S.-J. Kim and S. Boyd. A minimax theorem with applications to machine learning, signal processing, and finance. *SIAM Journal on Optimization*, 19(3):1344–1367, 2008.

[16] A. Krizhevsky and G. Hinton. Learning multiple layers of features from tiny images, Citeseer, 2009.

[17] T. Leung, Y. Song, and J. Zhang. Handling label noise in video classification via multiple instance learning. In *Proceedings of IEEE International Conference on Computer Vision*, pages 2056–2063. IEEE, 2011.

[18] L.-J. Li and L. Fei-Fei. Optimol: automatic online picture collection via incremental model learning. *International journal of computer vision*, 88(2):147–168, 2010.

[19] W. Li, L. Duan, D. Xu, and I. W.-H. Tsang. Text-based image retrieval using progressive multi-instance learning. In *Proceedings of IEEE International Conference on Computer Vision*, pages 2049–2055. IEEE, 2011.

[20] Y.-F. Li, I. W. Tsang, J. T. Kwok, and Z.-H. Zhou. Tighter and convex maximum margin clustering. In *Proceedings of International Conference on Artificial Intelligence and Statistics*, pages 344–351, 2009.

[21] Y. Lin, J.-B. Michel, E. L. Aiden, J. Orwant, W. Brockman, and S. Petrov. Syntactic annotations for the google books ngram corpus. In *Proceedings of the ACL 2012 system demonstrations*, pages 169–174. Association for Computational Linguistics, 2012.

[22] G. A. Miller. Wordnet: a lexical database for english. *Communications of the ACM*, 38(11):39–41, 1995.

[23] L. Niu, W. Li, and D. Xu. Visual recognition by learning from web data: A weakly supervised domain generalization approach. In *Proceedings of IEEE Conference on Computer Vision and Pattern Recognition*, pages 2774–2783, IEEE, 2015.

[24] A. Rakotomamonjy, F. Bach, S. Canu, and Y. Grandvalet. Simplemkl. *Journal of Machine Learning Research*, 9:2491–2521, 2008.

[25] F. Schroff, A. Criminisi, and A. Zisserman. Harvesting image databases from the web. *IEEE Transactions On Pattern Analysis and Machine Intelligence*, 33(4):754–766, 2011.

[26] P. Siva and T. Xiang. Weakly supervised object detector learning with model drift detection. In *Proceedings of IEEE International Conference on Computer Vision*, pages 343–350. IEEE, 2011.

[27] S. Sonnenburg, G. Rätsch, C. Schäfer, and B. Schölkopf. Large scale multiple kernel learning. *The Journal of Machine Learning Research*, 7:1531–1565, 2006.

[28] Y. Yang, Z. Zha, Y. Gao, X. Zhu, and T. Chua, "Exploiting web images for semantic video indexing via robust sample-specific loss," *IEEE Transactions on Multimedia*, 16(6):1677–1689, 2014.

[29] Y. Yang, H. Zhang, M. Zhang, F. Shen, and X. Li, "Visual coding in a semantic hierarchy," in *Proceedings of the ACM International Conference on Multimedia*, pages 59–68. ACM, 2015.

[30] A. Torralba and A. A. Efros. Unbiased look at dataset bias. In *Proceedings of IEEE Conference on Computer Vision and Pattern Recognition*, pages 1521–1528. IEEE, 2011.

[31] V. Sudheendra and K. Grauman. Keywords to visual categories: Multiple-instance learning forweakly supervised object categorization. In *Proceedings of IEEE Conference on Computer Vision and Pattern Recognition*, pages 1–8. IEEE, 2008.

A Supervised Approach for Text Illustration

Harsh Jhamtani
Adobe Systems
jhamtani@adobe.com

Shubham Varma
IIT Varanasi
varmashubham2@gmail.com

Midhun Gundapuneni
IIT Kharagpur
g.midhun95@gmail.com

Siddhartha Kumar Dutta
IIT Bombay
siddhartha_dutta@live.com

ABSTRACT

In this paper we propose a novel method to illustrate text articles with pictures from a tagged repository. Certain types of documents, like news articles, are often accompanied by a few pictures only. Prior works leverage topics or key phrases from the text to suggest relevant pictures. We propose a supervised model based on features like readability, picturability, sentiment polarity, and presence of important phrases, to identify and rank key sentences. The proposed method then suggests some relevant pictures based on the top ranked sentences thus identified.

CCS Concepts

•**Information systems** → *Multimedia content creation;*

Keywords

Text Illustration; Supervised Approach;

1. INTRODUCTION

Since pictures often draw reader's attention, illustrating text articles with pictures is a positive way to engage readers of an article. Our work focuses on automatically illustrating a text article with limited number of relevant pictures from the available repository of pictures.

We propose a novel method which uses supervised learning approach to score sentences based on factors like presence of important phrases or keywords, 'picturability'[1] of sentence, sentiment polarity of sentence, and readability of sentence. These scores are then leveraged to retrieve relevant pictures. The major contribution of our work is as follows. We propose a novel method for text illustration which uses supervised learning to score and rank sentences. Our method identifies importance of above mentioned features in determining the pictures to accompany a text article.

[1] Picturability of a sentence or a phrase is the degree to which that semantics of a sentence or phrase can be represented through a picture

MM '16, October 15-19, 2016, Amsterdam, Netherlands

DOI: http://dx.doi.org/10.1145/2964284.2967214

2. RELATED WORK

Our problem involves various aspects spread over areas such as image retrieval, and natural language processing. There are some existing works focusing on translating short textual sentences to a structured series of pictures ([22, 6, 21]). However, our problem is different as we aim to illustrate articles, and not representing a single sentence through pictures.

Many existing works identify important keywords and phrases from text to retrieve relevant pictures ([3], [2]) . Zhu et al. ([22]), extract 'picturable' key phrases from a given text. Lu et al. ([14]) have proposed models for illustrating travelogues by extracting location specific topics from travelogues and finding relevant pictures from tagged picture repository. In contrast to this, we take a supervised approach to identify sentences to picturize based on a variety of textual features.

Some research efforts focus on retrieval and ranking of pictures for given text article. In the work by Aletras and Stevenson ([3]), a graph is created with pictures as nodes and similarity of visual features between pictures as edge weights. Then a graph-based algorithm is used to rank the pictures. Joshi et al. ([9]) use the keywords extracted from text for retrieving pictures from an annotated database. Similarity between the pictures is then calculated using integrated region matching and annotation based similarity. Finally, the pictures are ranked using the principle of mutual reinforcement.

Delgado et al. ([5]) propose a method where sentences are expressed as a word vector and pictures as a vector of tags, and the relevant pictures are found for each sentence using cosine similarity value between the two vectors. However, in our problem setting, only few pictures are to be added to an article - and not one picture for every sentence.

3. DATA SETS

To build our model and conduct our experiments, we used 120 news articles from Reuters (www.reuters.com) and CleanLeap (www.cleanleap.com) (60 from each). The news categories covered are politics, international news, and energy. There are a total of 5169 sentences in these articles. Apart from the pictures already present in these articles, we crawled pictures from other news domains like BBC (www.bbc.com) and CNN, from articles similar to the 120 articles in our data set. We also crawled pictures from about 1000 randomly chosen news articles from various news domains. We considered only those pictures which had accompanying descriptions.

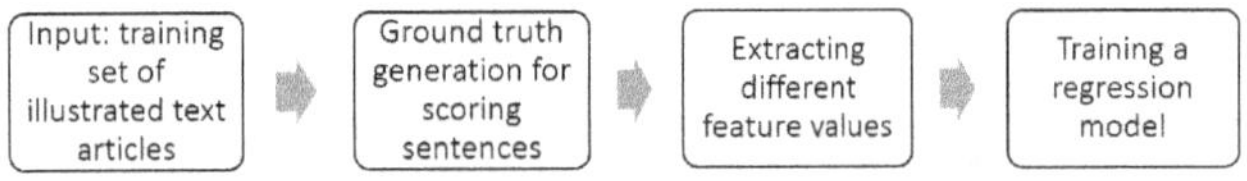

Figure 1: Steps in training a supervised model to score sentences

4. SOLUTION DESCRIPTION

In this section we describe our proposed approach. Figure 1 shows the major steps in building a supervised model to score sentences in a text article. Figure 2 shows the steps in ranking sentences of a text article, and finally obtaining the relevant pictures.

4.1 Picturizing Score

In our proposed approach, a score is assigned to every sentence in the article, which we shall refer to as ***picturizing score*** . A sentence with a higher *picturizing score* should be prioritized over a sentence with a lower *picturizing score* score, when identifying pictures to accompany text. To build a model to predict this score, we consider already illustrated news articles to obtain the ground truth data. The assumption here is that the content author or marketer is an expert, and has, through manual efforts, selected the relevant and significant pictures to accompany the text. To obtain the ground truth, we define 'picturizing score' (S_{ij}) of a sentence i to be the number of pictures (n_{ij}) found corresponding to the sentence in the original article j, divided by a normalizing factor. The formula used is as follows:

$$S_{ij} = \frac{n_{ij}}{\log_2(N_j + 1)} \tag{1}$$

Here, N_j refers to the total number of pictures corresponding to text in the jth article. Normalization is required since different articles have different number of accompanying pictures. Logarithm of the number of pictures in the document is used to prevent over penalization of heavily illustrated documents.

To obtain n_{ij} values, we designed an annotation task. We recruited 3 annotators for this purpose. The annotators were asked to identify the number of pictures in an article corresponding to each sentence in the same article. They were provided with task description and some examples. We considered only those annotations for which at least two annotators agreed, considering the agreed value as the final annotation. Since this was an easy task, there was high agreement among the annotators. Out of 5169 annotations, only 273 (5.28%) were discarded.

We build a regression model to predict the picturizing score of a sentence, which represents the degree to which the sentence should be associated with pictures in the article. The features, on which independent variables are based, will be described in Section 4.3.

4.2 Vector space representation of text

We use a term frequency-inverse document frequency based vector space based model ([18]) for representation of sentences as well as picture descriptions. Each sentence and each picture description is considered as a document. Inverse document frequency of a term (a 'word' in our case),

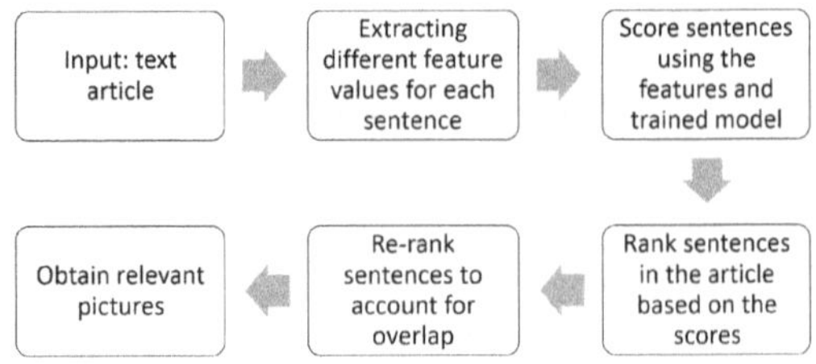

Figure 2: Steps in obtaining pictures after scoring sentences of a text article using the trained model

is calculated as follows:

$$IDF(t) = log_2(\frac{N_t}{|D|}) \tag{2}$$

Here, N_t is the number of documents containing the term t, and $|D|$ is the total number of documents. Then, TF-IDF of a term t for a document d is calculated as:

$$tfidf(t,d) = n_{t,d} * IDF(t) \tag{3}$$

Here, $n_{t,d}$ is the the count of term t in the document d normalized by the total number of terms in the document d. In order to find similarity between two sentences or a sentence and an image, one can compute certain measures like cosine similarity between corresponding vector representations.

4.3 Feature extraction from text

We consider following four types of features: (1) Readability of sentence (2) Picturability of sentence (3) Presence of keywords and important phrases (4) Sentiment polarity of sentence

4.3.1 Readability of sentence

Here we try to capture the readability of a sentence i.e. how easy will someone find reading and understanding the sentence. The intuition here is that sentences with low readability should be accompanied with pictures, to enhance the understanding. We consider following three features values corresponding to this:

Fog Index: Fog index computes a readability score of a sentence using the length of sentence and number of complex words with 3 or more syllables [1]. Higher fog index means lower readability. The formula used is as follows:

$$fogindex(sentence) = 0.4 \times number\_of\_words(sentence) + 40 \times \frac{no\_of\_complex\_words}{total\_no\_of\_words} \tag{4}$$

Sentence length: For a given sentence this feature value is equal to the number of words in the sentence. To break a sentence into words, we used white spaces as delimiters.

4.3.2 Picturability

Leong et al. ([12]) proposed a measure of 'picturability' of a sentence based on the tags of pictures in the picture repository . For our model, we measure the picturability of a sentence based on the maximum similarity it has across all the picture descriptions in repository, calculated using cosine similarity between corresponding vector space representations. The underlying intuition here is to identify sentences which can be easily picturized through pictures present in the repository. Note that *picturability* is not to be confused with *picturizing score*.

4.3.3 Importance phrases/keywords

Here we describe features capturing presence of various important phrases and keywords in a sentence. Such features have been used in many text mining tasks ([11],[7],[8]). The underlying intuition is that the sentences bearing more important words and phrases should be prioritized while ranking sentences to picturize.

Text Ranking: Text Rank [16] builds an undirected graph using sentences as vertices. Edges are a measure of similarity between the sentence vertices, for which we use cosine similarity between vector representations of corresponding two sentences. Once the graph is constructed, it is used to form a stochastic matrix, combined with a damping factor, and the scores of vertices are obtained using PageRank. Using this we are able to obtain score for each sentence, such that the score denotes the importance of the sentence.

LSA score: Latent semantic analysis (LSA) is a technique of analyzing relationships between a set of documents and the terms they contain by producing a set of concepts related to the documents and terms [20]. The method assigns significance scores to various concepts or topics, which is then used to determine sentence ratings. This is achieved by summing scores of various concepts present in a sentence.

TF-IDF based score: A score is obtained for each sentence by summing up the the TF-IDF values of unigrams, bigrams, and trigrams of words in the sentence. TF-IDF scores are obtained as described earlier in section 4.2.

4.3.4 Sentiment polarity

In many cases, we would not want to picturize a sentence comprising negative sentiment phrases and/or hate words. To capture this intuition, we generate a feature value for each sentence, which is the sentiment score of the sentence, as provided by Alchemy API [13]. The sentiment score is a real number between -1 and 1 (both inclusive). 1 represents the extreme positive sentiment polarity, while -1 represents the extreme negative polarity.

4.4 Training of model

Consider an **example** sentence: "A crewless cargo space ship burned up in the Earth's atmosphere after a communication failure, and a Proton-M carrier rocket carrying a Mexican satellite crashed in Siberia." Corresponding feature values are: lsa_score=5.71, fogindex=15.33, tfidf_score=0.63, sentence_length=36, picturability=0.43, and sentiment_score =0.0.

Normalization of feature values is done to bring the values to a scale of [0-1]. (Note that *picturizing score* is not to be confused with *picturability*). Regression models were trained using the normalized sentence features as independent variables and the sentence 'picturizing score' as dependent variable. The training involves learning various parameter values of the regression model using the annotated data.

4.5 Discounting for overlap among sentences

Since after ranking, the top sentences would be leveraged to obtain relevant pictures, overlap among top sentences should be minimized to avoid obtaining pictures depicting very similar ideas. We use Marginal Relevance (MMR) [4] to re-rank the sentences by combining picturizing scores and degree of overlap of the sentence with already selected sentences, using a linear combination function.

The following formula is used to obtain the best item from yet unselected items at any iteration:

$$\max_{D_i \epsilon R-S}[\lambda * Picturizing\_score_{D_i} - (1-\lambda)\max_{D_j \epsilon S} sim(D_i, D_j)] \quad (5)$$

Where R is the set of all sentences in the current text article. S is the subset of sentences in R already selected; $R-S$ is the set of as yet unselected sentences in R; $sim(D_i, D_j)$ is the cosine similarity score between vector space representations of D_i and D_j. Parameter λ takes a real value between 0 and 1. Higher the value of λ, more would be the importance given to *picturizing score* as compared to overlap between sentences. We used $\lambda = 0.5$ for our experiments.

4.6 Obtaining illustrated article

For a given sentence, the picture in the repository, corresponding to which the maximum similarity score is obtained, is selected. To compare similarity between a sentence and a picture, we calculate the cosine similarity between the vector representations of the sentence and the corresponding picture description. We inquire user about the number of pictures he wants to add, represented by K. We obtain a ranked list of sentences as explained above. Thereafter, we select one relevant picture for each of the top K sentences. The retrieved pictures are placed near the corresponding sentences to obtain the illustrated article.

5. EXPERIMENTS AND RESULTS

Here we describe various experiments we performed and report the obtained results. We have performed following two experiments: (1) Experiments to evaluate regression models to score sentences (2) Experiments to evaluate overall performance of the proposed text illustration system

5.1 Experiments to evaluate regression models

In Section 4.1, we had described how ground truth values of *picturizing score* are obtained. For evaluating the performance of the regression models, we randomly select 80% text articles, and the sentences in these articles are used to generate the training data. Sentences in the remaining articles constitute the test data. We experimented with Linear Regression, and Support Vector Regression (with linear and RBF kernels). Average MSE (Mean square error) values under five-fold cross validation for these models on the training set are **0.031**, 0.064, and 0.069 respectively, while average MSE values on test set are **0.033**, 0.046, and 0.035 respectively. We use Scikit [17] implementation of these regression models. Linear regression model performs the best. The mean square errors are low, and moreover, the testing errors are comparable to the training errors. Thus, it can be inferred that the regression model fits quite well on the data. The goodness of fit represented by R^2 is **0.87** for the Linear regression model, showing that 87% percentage of variance is explained by the chosen features.

The regression coefficient values of the features, corresponding to the Linear Regression model, are shown in Table 1. We also report significance of various features, which is calculated using hypothesis testing. The 'Null Hypothesis' is that the coefficient in question is 0. Note that a coefficient

Table 1: **Feature Coefficients and Significance levels for Linear Regression Model**

Feature name	Coefficient	Significance Level ($Pr > \|t\|$)
LSA Score	-0.03	0.510
Textrank Score	-0.03	0.670
Fog Index	0.09	0.037
TFIDF	0.23	3.46e-07
Picturability	0.08	0.002
Sentiment Value	0.05	0.049
Sentence Length	0.02	0.011

value of zero will mean that the corresponding feature is not a predictor of the *picturizing score*. We use Student's t-test ([15]) at 0.95 confidence level. Based on the test, those features will be significant for which $Pr > |t|$ is less than 0.05 TF-IDF, picturability score, fog index, sentiment score, and sentence length are found to be statistically significant. A surprising result is that LSA based score and Text Rank were found to be insignificant (All significant features are marked in bold in Table 1). One possible explanation for TextRank being insignificant is that those sentences score high for which there are other similar sentences in the the article, which may not be desirable.

For each article forming up the test data sentences, we rank the sentences as per the scores given by the regression model. We already have ground truth rank list for each article - obtained by sorting the sentences by the annotated score. We then compare two ranked lists for each article in the test set. Kendall Tau rank correlation coefficient τ [10] and Spearman's rank correlation coefficient ρ [19] for the Linear Regression model were found to be **0.856** and **0.699** respectively. This means that our method is able to provide a rank list very similar to the ground truth rank list.

5.2 Experiments to evaluate overall performance of the proposed system

For the baseline approach, we use Text Rank [16] to identify a ranked list of important terms. We build a graph with words (excluding stopwords) as vertices, such that an edge exists between two vertices if they occur within a window size of 8. Then PageRank is run on the graph to obtain top T significant vertices(words). Thereafter, contiguous significant words are coalesced, with score being the sum of scores of coalesced words. If the total number of pictures desired are K, then we consider the top K terms(words or coalesced set of words). For each term, we find a picture from repository containing the words in the term.

We created 24 sets of three articles each, of which one is illustrated using baseline method, one is illustrated using our method, and one is article without pictures. We recruited a total of 24 people, such that each one of them is assigned one set, and is then asked to rate each of the articles in the set on a scale of 1-7 on different aspects. The questions that were asked are shown in Table 2.

Analysis of responses: Table 3 shows the mean ratings for different questions for our approach, baseline approach, and non-illustrated articles (articles without pictures). Note that for non-illustrated articles, we only asked first two questions. It can be seen that our method received favorable scores in most cases, and outperforms the baseline approach. Moreover, we report the standard deviation for rating for different questions for our method as well as for baseline method in Table 3. On considering the standard deviation values, we observe that the mean value of ratings for our method differs from the baseline method by more than unit standard deviation for most cases.

[2]For questions 1,2,3,5,8 a higher score is more favorable (H) while a lower score is more favorable for questions 4,6,7 (L)

Table 2: Questionnaire for evaluation

Ques. no.	Question text (H/L) [2]
Q.1	The article was engaging (H)
Q.2.	The text of the article was easy to understand (H)
Q.3.	The pictures in the article were useful to understand the article (H)
Q.4.	The pictures were unhelpful in maintaining my interest in reading the article (L)
Q.5.	The pictures were relevant to the content of the article (
Q.6.	The pictures did not capture the main points of the article (L)
Q.7.	The two pictures in the article conveyed overlapping information (L)
Q.8.	Please take a look at the two pictures again. Then answ the following question: By themselves the two pictures told the story in the article (H)

Table 3: Mean rating values with corresponding standard deviations

Ques. no.	Our method: Mean (σ)[3]	Baseline: Mean (σ)	Without pictures: Mean (σ)
Q.1 (H) [2]	5.42 (0.71)	4.72 (0.41)	3.85 (0.75)
Q.2 (H)	5.05 (1.02)	4.20 (0.43)	3.35 (0.75)
Q.3 (H)	5.52 (0.79)	4.63 (0.63)	-
Q.4 (L)	2.62 (0.83)	3.95 (1.31)	-
Q.5 (H)	5.40 (0.98)	4.30 (0.58)	-
Q.6 (L)	2.78 (1.01)	3.88 (0.48)	-
Q.7 (L)	2.73 (0.60)	4.63 (0.39)	-
Q.8 (H)	4.85 (0.41)	3.85 (0.39)	-

6. CONCLUSION

We have proposed a novel approach based on supervised learning to identify key sentences, and then find relevant pictures. An advantage of our approach is that we consider a broad range of features beyond important phrases. Through experiments, we found that features like fog index (readability), picturability, sentence length, sentiment polarity of sentence, and TFIDF based presence of important terms, are significant predictors of key sentences for text illustration. In future, we would like to extend our work to consider features like position of sentence, font, etc.

[3]Standard Deviation

7. REFERENCES

[1] The gunning's fog index readability formula. Accessed: 2015-07-19.

[2] Agrawal, R., Gollapudi, S., Kannan, A., and Kenthapadi, K. Enriching textbooks with images. In *Proceedings of the 20th ACM international conference on Information and knowledge management* (2011), ACM, pp. 1847–1856.

[3] Aletras, N., and Stevenson, M. Representing topics using images. In *HLT-NAACL* (2013), pp. 158–167.

[4] Carbonell, J., and Goldstein, J. The use of mmr, diversity-based reranking for reordering documents and producing summaries. In *Proceedings of the 21st annual international ACM SIGIR conference on Research and development in information retrieval* (1998), ACM, pp. 335–336.

[5] Delgado, D., Magalhaes, J., and Correia, N. Automated illustration of news stories. In *Semantic Computing (ICSC), 2010 IEEE Fourth International Conference on* (2010), IEEE, pp. 73–78.

[6] Goldberg, A. B., Zhu, X., Dyer, C. R., Eldawy, M., and Heng, L. Easy as abc?: facilitating pictorial communication via semantically enhanced layout. In *Proceedings of the Twelfth Conference on Computational Natural Language Learning* (2008), Association for Computational Linguistics, pp. 119–126.

[7] Gupta, V., Varshney, D., Jhamtani, H., Kedia, D., and Karwa, S. Identifying purchase intent from social posts. In *ICWSM* (2014).

[8] Jhamtani, H., Chhaya, N., Karwa, S., Varshney, D., Kedia, D., and Gupta, V. Identifying suggestions for improvement of product features from online product reviews. In *International Conference on Social Informatics* (2015), Springer, pp. 112–119.

[9] Joshi, D., Wang, J. Z., and Li, J. The story picturing engine—a system for automatic text illustration. *ACM Transactions on Multimedia Computing, Communications, and Applications (TOMM) 2*, 1 (2006), 68–89.

[10] Kendall, M. G. A new measure of rank correlation. *Biometrika* (1938), 81–93.

[11] Kosala, R., and Blockeel, H. Web mining research: A survey. *ACM Sigkdd Explorations Newsletter 2*, 1 (2000), 1–15.

[12] Leong, C. W., Mihalcea, R., and Hassan, S. Text mining for automatic image tagging. In *Proceedings of the 23rd International Conference on Computational Linguistics: Posters* (Stroudsburg, PA, USA, 2010), COLING '10, Association for Computational Linguistics, pp. 647–655.

[13] LLC, O. Alchemyapi, 2009.

[14] Lu, X., Pang, Y., Hao, Q., and Zhang, L. Visualizing textual travelogue with location-relevant images. In *Proceedings of the 2009 International Workshop on Location Based Social Networks* (2009), ACM, pp. 65–68.

[15] Mankiewicz, R. *The story of mathematics.* Princeton University Press, 2000.

[16] Mihalcea, R., and Tarau, P. Textrank: Bringing order into texts. In *Proceedings of EMNLP 2004* (Barcelona, Spain, July 2004), D. Lin and D. Wu, Eds., Association for Computational Linguistics, pp. 404–411.

[17] Pedregosa, F., Varoquaux, G., Gramfort, A., Michel, V., Thirion, B., Grisel, O., Blondel, M., Prettenhofer, P., Weiss, R., Dubourg, V., et al. Scikit-learn: Machine learning in python. *The Journal of Machine Learning Research 12* (2011), 2825–2830.

[18] Salton, G., Wong, A., and Yang, C.-S. A vector space model for automatic indexing. *Communications of the ACM 18*, 11 (1975), 613–620.

[19] Spearman, C. The proof and measurement of association between two things. *The American journal of psychology 15*, 1 (1904), 72–101.

[20] Steinberger, J., and Jezek, K. Using latent semantic analysis in text summarization and summary evaluation. In *Proc. ISIM'04* (2004), pp. 93–100.

[21] UzZaman, N., Bigham, J. P., and Allen, J. F. Multimodal summarization of complex sentences. In *Proceedings of the 16th international conference on Intelligent user interfaces* (2011), ACM, pp. 43–52.

[22] Zhu, X., Goldberg, A. B., Eldawy, M., Dyer, C. R., and Strock, B. A text-to-picture synthesis system for augmenting communication. In *AAAI* (2007), vol. 7, pp. 1590–1595.

Learning Music Emotion Primitives via Supervised Dynamic Clustering

Yang Liu[1,2], Yan Liu[3], Xiang Zhang[3,4], Gong Chen[3], Kejun Zhang[4]
[1]Department of Computer Science, Hong Kong Baptist University, Kowloon Tong, Hong Kong SAR, P. R. China
[2]Institute of Research and Continuing Education, Hong Kong Baptist University, Shenzhen, P. R. China
[3]Department of Computing, The Hong Kong Polytechnic University, Hung Hom, Hong Kong SAR, P. R. China
[4]College of Computer Science and Technology, Zhejiang University, Hangzhou, 310027, P. R. China
csygliu@comp.hkbu.edu.hk, csyliu@comp.polyu.edu.hk, csxgzhang@comp.polyu.edu.hk
csgchen@comp.polyu.edu.hk, zhangkejun@zju.edu.cn

ABSTRACT

This paper explores a fundamental problem in music emotion analysis, i.e., how to segment the music sequence into a set of basic emotive units, which are named as emotion primitives. Current works on music emotion analysis are mainly based on the fixed-length music segments, which often leads to the difficulty of accurate emotion recognition. Short music segment, such as an individual music frame, may fail to evoke emotion response. Long music segment, such as an entire song, may convey various emotions over time. Moreover, the minimum length of music segment varies depending on the types of the emotions. To address these problems, we propose a novel method dubbed supervised dynamic clustering (SDC) to automatically decompose the music sequence into meaningful segments with various lengths. First, the music sequence is represented by a set of music frames. Then, the music frames are clustered according to the valence-arousal values in the emotion space. The clustering results are used to initialize the music segmentation. After that, a dynamic programming scheme is employed to jointly optimize the subsequent segmentation and grouping in the music feature space. Experimental results on standard dataset show both the effectiveness and the rationality of the proposed method.

Keywords

Music emotion analysis; emotion primitives; supervised dynamic clustering

1. INTRODUCTION

Music, laxly explained as the organized sound, can convey and evoke various emotions. Music emotion analysis, which attracts much attention of researchers from various disciplines such as musicology [4], psychology [11], and computer science [27], plays a crucial role in many real-world applications such as music recommendation [24] and music therapy [18].

With the huge amount of available musical data and the rapid development of computer resources, computational approaches to automate the process of music emotion analysis have taken on increasing interests and importance [15, 29, 22, 24, 25, 12]. Lu *et al.* [15] proposed a GMM-based model to detect the moods in music. Yang *et al.* [29] presented a regression approach for music emotion recognition. Trohidis *et al.* [22] formulated music emotion analysis as a multi-label classification problem. Wang *et al.* [24] built a probabilistic model for music recommendation. Wu *et al.* [25] proposed a multi-label multi-layer multi-instance multi-view learning scheme for music emotion recognition. Liu *et al.* [12] introduced a dimensionality reduction algorithm to model the relations between low-level music features and high-level emotions.

Although tremendous progress has been made in music emotion analysis, one of the fundamental problems, i.e., how to segment the music sequence into a set of plausible units according to the emotions, is seldom investigated. The inherent difficulty in the problem mainly stems from the variety and complexity of music emotion labels, a relatively large range of temporal scale for different music emotions, and the intra-emotion variation of the music sequences. In this paper, we work on this fundamental problem. We name these basic units as music emotion primitives and explore machine learning techniques to learn these primitives from the music data with human annotated emotions. To address aforementioned challenges, a novel computational model dubbed supervised dynamic clustering (SDC) is presented to jointly optimize the segmentation and clustering of music sequences under the supervision of the emotion information.

To the best of our knowledge, this is the first work to decompose the music sequences into plausible emotion primitives, although learning motion primitives for visual data has already achieved significant progress [6, 9, 13, 14, 30]. One latest related work is [7], which also modeled the dynamics of music emotions over time. However, the objective and methodology in [7] are totally different from those in our paper. The work in [7] aimed at performing emotion-based music retrieval via dynamic time warping [2], while the target of our work is to discover the emotion primitives of the music by the proposed SDC.

The rest of this paper is organized as follows. In Section 2, we propose SDC to learn the music emotion primitives. In Section 3, we schematically illustrate the learning outcomes and statistically evaluate the performance of proposed method on standard dataset. Finally, the paper is concluded with future work in Section 4.

2. SUPERVISED DYNAMIC CLUSTERING

Most of the computational models for music emotion analysis are based on two kinds of emotion representations: the categorical

MM '16, October 15-19, 2016, Amsterdam, Netherlands

DOI: http://dx.doi.org/10.1145/2964284.2967215

representation and the dimensional representation. The categorical representation describes the emotions of music sequences via a collection of labels, such as happy, sad, calming, and arousing [21, 23]. Although this kind of representation has clear semantic meaning, they are too general to represent the emotions of music since they ignore the variation of music emotions over time. Another kind of representation, called dimensional representation, describes the emotions in a Cartesian space with valence and arousal as two dimensions. Here valence means how positive or negative the affect appraisal is and arousal means how high or low the physiological reaction is [17, 28]. Although the valence-arousal (V-A) representation can provide dynamic information of music emotions, the individual V-A values at each frame are too trivial to represent the meaningful emotions since they fail to reflect the completeness of music emotions. In order to discover plausible units to represent music emotions, a novel method dubbed supervised dynamic clustering (SDC) is proposed to decompose the music sequence into music emotion primitives.

2.1 Problem Formulation

Given a music feature sequence $\mathbf{X} = [\mathbf{x}_1, ..., \mathbf{x}_n] \in \mathbb{R}^{d\times n}$ and its corresponding V-A label sequence $\mathbf{L} = [\mathbf{l}_1, ..., \mathbf{l}_n] \in \mathbb{R}^{2\times n}$, where d is the feature dimension of the music frame, n is the frame number of the sequence, and $\mathbf{l}_i = [v_i, a_i]^T$ denotes the valence value and arousal value at frame i of the given music, our target is to decompose $\mathbf{X}$ into m nonoverlapping segments, each of which represents one of the k music emotion primitives, i.e., belongs to one of the k primitive emotion clusters ($k \leq m$). The ith segment is denoted by $\mathbf{Y}_i = \mathbf{X}_{[s_i, s_{i+1})} = [\mathbf{x}_{s_i}, ..., \mathbf{x}_{s_{i+1}-1}]$. Let $\mathbf{s} = [s_1, ..., s_{m+1}]$ be the vector that contains the start and end of each segment, and $\mathbf{G} \in \{0,1\}^{k\times m}$ be the indicator matrix that assigns each music segment to one of the k clusters:

$$g_{ci} = \mathbb{1}(\mathbf{Y}_i \in \text{cluster } c), \tag{1}$$

where $c \in \{1, ..., k\}$, and $\mathbb{1}(\cdot)$ is an indicator function that equals one if the argument holds and zero otherwise. Then the objective of SDC can be formulated as follows:

$$\mathbf{G}, \mathbf{s} = \underset{\mathbf{G},\mathbf{s}}{\text{argmin}}\, J_{SDC}(\mathbf{G}, \mathbf{s}) = \underset{\mathbf{G},\mathbf{s}}{\text{argmin}}(1-\lambda)Q(\mathbf{G}, \mathbf{s}) + \lambda R(\mathbf{s}), \tag{2}$$

where $Q(\mathbf{G}, \mathbf{s})$ measures how "good" the clustering result is, $R(\mathbf{s})$ is the manifold regularization term to penalize the undesired segmentations between smoothly changed frames, and $\lambda \in [0, 1]$ is a trade-off parameter. Specifically, $Q(\mathbf{G}, \mathbf{s})$ is defined as:

$$Q(\mathbf{G}, \mathbf{s}) = \sum_{c=1}^{k}\sum_{i=1}^{m} g_{ci}\, dist^2(\mathbf{Y}_i, \mathbf{Z}_c), \tag{3}$$

where $dist(\mathbf{Y}_i, \mathbf{Z}_c)$ denotes the distance between the ith segment and the center of cluster c. In this paper, we use the dynamic time alignment kernel (DTAK) [19] as the distance metric because of its effectiveness in measuring the distance between segments of different lengths. Moreover, $R(\mathbf{s})$ is defined as follows:

$$R(\mathbf{s}) = \sum_{i=2}^{m} r(s_i), \tag{4}$$

where $r(s_i)$ denotes the penalization on the ith segmentation. To characterize both the feature smoothness and the label smoothness over time, we formulate $r(s_i)$ as follows:

$$r(s_i) = \sum_{j_1=s_i-n_{s_i}}^{s_i-1}\ \sum_{j_2=s_i}^{s_i+n_{s_i}-1} \Big(sim_f(\mathbf{x}_{j_1}, \mathbf{x}_{j_2}) + sim_l(\mathbf{l}_{j_1}, \mathbf{l}_{j_2}) \Big) \times e^{-\frac{(|j_1-j_2|-1)^2}{2\sigma^2}}, \tag{5}$$

where n_{s_i} denotes the size of the neighborhood of the ith segmentation, $sim_f(\mathbf{x}_{j_1}, \mathbf{x}_{j_2})$ denotes the similarity between two feature vectors $\mathbf{x}_{j_1}$ and $\mathbf{x}_{j_2}$, and $sim_l(\mathbf{l}_{j_1}, \mathbf{l}_{j_2})$ denotes the similarity between two label vectors $\mathbf{l}_{j_1}$ and $\mathbf{l}_{j_2}$. In this paper, we use the RBF kernel for sim_f and sim_l. Moreover, since the segment that represents music emotion primitives cannot be too long, we further add a constraint on the length of $\mathbf{Y}_i$, i.e., $n_i = s_{i+1} - s_i \in [1, n_{\text{max}}]$.

Obviously, the smaller the value of $Q(\mathbf{G}, \mathbf{s})$, the better the result of clustering; the smaller the value of $R(\mathbf{s})$, the smoother the obtained segments. By jointly optimizing both clustering and segmentation, a unified framework is established for learning the music emotion primitives.

2.2 V-A Supervised Clustering

In order to decompose a music sequence into music emotion primitives, two questions need to be answered: 1) How many emotion primitives exist in the given music sequence; and 2) How to determine which primitives a data point belongs to in the V-A space. The above issues can be naturally formulated as a clustering problem. Inspired by the work in [16], we introduce a clustering scheme, which is able to automatically determine the number of clusters and assign data points to the corresponding primitives in the V-A space.

Given the V-A label sequence $\mathbf{L} = [\mathbf{l}_1, ..., \mathbf{l}_n] \in \mathbb{R}^{2\times n}$, which can also be viewed as n data points in the V-A space, we first seek the candidates of cluster centers. Specifically, a cluster center should satisfy two conditions [16]: 1) Its density is relatively high; and 2) It is far from other data points whose density is higher than it. Accordingly, a density function and a distance function can be defined. For data point $\mathbf{l}_i$, we define the density function as:

$$\rho_i = \sum_{j=1, j\neq i}^{n} \left[e^{-\frac{d_l^2(\mathbf{l}_i, \mathbf{l}_j)}{2\epsilon^2}} \times \mathbb{1}(d_l(\mathbf{l}_i, \mathbf{l}_j) \leq \epsilon) \right], \tag{6}$$

where $d_l(\cdot,\cdot)$ is the Euclidean distance between two data points in the V-A label space, and $\epsilon > 0$ acts as a threshold. From Eq. (6), we can observe that the closer the data points, the more contributions they make to the density cumulation.

Moreover, the distance function for $\mathbf{l}_i$ is defined as:

$$\delta_i = \begin{cases} \max\limits_{j\in 1,...,n} d_l(\mathbf{l}_i, \mathbf{l}_j), & \text{if } \rho_i = \max\limits_{j\in 1,...,n} \rho_j; \\ \min\limits_{j:\rho_j > \rho_i} d_l(\mathbf{l}_i, \mathbf{l}_j), & \text{otherwise}, \end{cases} \tag{7}$$

which measures the distance from $\mathbf{l}_i$ to the closest data point of higher density. If a data point $\mathbf{l}_i$ has both large ρ_i and large δ_i, it has the reason to believe that $\mathbf{l}_i$ is a good candidate of cluster center. Hence, data points having large value of $v_i = \rho_i \delta_i$ are selected as the cluster centers of the V-A label sequence, and the number of clusters k is decided by:

$$k = \sum_{i=1}^{n} \mathbb{1}(v_i \geq \alpha v_{max}), \tag{8}$$

where $\alpha \in [0, 1]$ is a threshold parameter used to determine how large the v_i should be, and v_{max} denotes the maximum value among all v_i ($i = 1, ..., n$). Besides the above k cluster centers, each of the remaining $n-k$ data points is assigned to the same cluster as its nearest neighbor of higher density. Then a cluster indicator matrix $\mathbf{G}^L \in \{0,1\}^{k \times n}$ for $\mathbf{L}$ can be constructed accordingly:

$$g_{ci}^L = \mathbb{1}(\mathbf{l}_i \in \text{cluster } c). \tag{9}$$

2.3 Dynamic Segmentation

Based on the $\mathbf{G}^L$ learned from the previous step, we can easily initialize the cluster indicator matrix $\mathbf{G}$ and the segmentation vector $\mathbf{s}$ in Eq. (2). The idea of segmentation is simple: if the V-A labels of two music frames are different, it is likely that these two frames belong to different music emotion primitives. Consequently, we segment two consecutive frames $\mathbf{x}_{i-1}$ and $\mathbf{x}_i$ if and only if $\mathbf{l}_{i-1}$ and $\mathbf{l}_i$ belong to different clusters in the V-A space. After the initial segmentation, the frames in each segment belong to the same cluster in the V-A space. Then we assign the whole segment to the cluster which all the frames belong to, i.e.,

$$g_{ci}^{ini} = \mathbb{1}(\mathbf{l}_{s_i}, ..., \mathbf{l}_{s_{i+1}-1} \in \text{cluster } c). \tag{10}$$

Following the procedure in [30], we utilize a coordinate-descent algorithm to minimize the objective function in Eq. (2) iteratively:

$$\underset{\mathbf{G},\mathbf{s}}{\operatorname{argmin}}(1-\lambda)\sum_{c=1}^{k}\sum_{i=1}^{m} g_{ci}dist^2(\mathbf{Y}_i, \dot{\mathbf{Z}}_c) + \lambda R(\mathbf{s}), \tag{11}$$

where $\dot{\mathbf{Z}}_c$ is the center of cluster c computed using $(\dot{\mathbf{G}}, \dot{\mathbf{s}})$ obtained in the previous step. Since the exhaustive search of possible segmentations is time-consuming or even infeasible when n is large, we employ a dynamic programming (DP) scheme [3, 30] to solve the problem in polynomial time. Specifically, we introduce an auxiliary function $J : [1, n] \to \mathbb{R}$,

$$J(v) = \min_{\mathbf{G},\mathbf{s}} J_{SDC}(\mathbf{G},\mathbf{s})|_{\mathbf{X}_{[1,v]}}, \tag{12}$$

which satisfies the principle of optimality [3]:

$$J(v) = \min_{1<i\leqslant v}\Big(J(i-1) + \min_{\mathbf{G},\mathbf{s}} J_{SDC}(\mathbf{G},\mathbf{s})|_{\mathbf{X}_{[i,v]}}\Big). \tag{13}$$

This principle implies that the optimal decomposition of $\mathbf{X}_{[1,v]}$ is achieved only when the segmentations on both $\mathbf{X}_{[1,i-1]}$ and $\mathbf{X}_{[i,v]}$ are optimal and their sum is minimal. DP provides an efficient way to minimize $J(v)$ by using Bellman's equation:

$$\begin{aligned} J(v) = &\min_{v-n_{\max}<i\leqslant v}\Big(J(i-1) + \lambda r(i) \\ &+ (1-\lambda)\min_{\mathbf{g}}\sum_{c=1}^{k} g_c dist^2(\mathbf{X}_{[i,v]}, \dot{\mathbf{Z}}_c)\Big), \end{aligned} \tag{14}$$

where $r(i)$ penalizes the segmentation between the $(i-1)^{th}$ and the ith frames. Obviously, $J(n)$ denotes the minimum cost of the segmentation on the entire music sequence. We repeat the forward-backward steps [30] alternately until $J(n)$ converges.

The time costs of V-A supervised clustering and DP based segmentation are $O(n^2)$ and $O(n^2 n_{\max} t)$, respectively, where t is the number of iterations. Therefore, the total computational cost of SDC is $O(n^2 n_{\max} t)$.

3. EXPERIMENTS

We use the *Emotion in Music Database* [20] to train the proposed model since this database provides the audio files of the song, as well as the corresponding music features and V-A annotations of each frame along the timeline, all of which are of great importance in learning music emotion primitives.

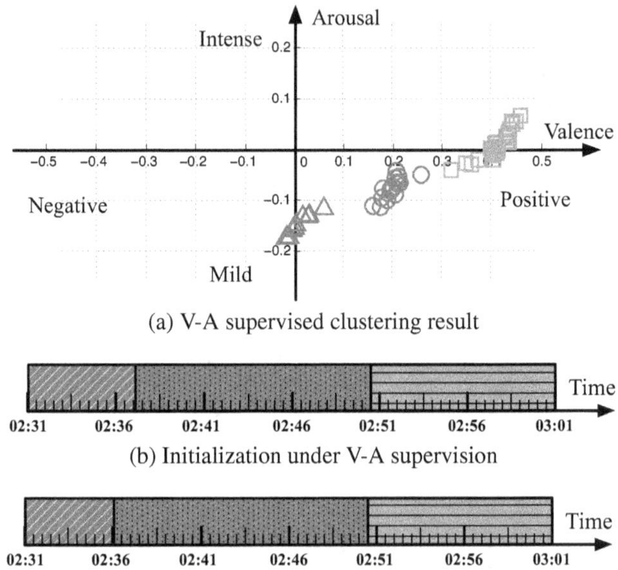

(a) V-A supervised clustering result

(b) Initialization under V-A supervision

(c) Final segmentation and clustering result of SDC

Figure 1: Schematic illustration of SDC on 30-second clip from the song "Butterfly".

The database contains 744 songs, all of which are royalty-free music selected from the Free Music Archive[1]. We use a subset of 431 songs with better inter-annotator agreement [1]. For each song, a 45-second clip is extracted from random (uniformly distributed) starting point and re-encoded to have the same sampling frequency, i.e, 44100Hz. For each clip, the openSMILE toolbox [8] is used to extract 260 features (e.g., MFCC and Mel-spectra) from nonoverlapping segments of 500ms, with frame size of 60ms with a 10ms step [1]. To annotate the emotions of the clips, the V-A representation is utilized. For each clip, the continuous V-A values are between -1 and $+1$, and the annotations are further resampled with 2Hz sampling rate. The annotations of the first 15 seconds are discarded due to instability of the annotations at the start of the clip. Therefore, for each of the 431 songs, we have a feature sequence composed of 61 feature vectors of 260 dimensions, and a V-A label sequence composed of 61 V-A annotation pairs. In our experiments, we set $\lambda = 0.1$, $\sigma = 1$, $\alpha = 0.05$, $n_{s_i} = 10$, and $n_{max} = \lceil n/2 \rceil = 31$. Moreover, we set ϵ to be the distance ranked at the 1% level (in the ascending order) among all the pair-wise distances $d_l(\mathbf{l}_i, \mathbf{l}_j)$.

3.1 Schematic Illustration

In order to intuitively illustrate the effect of the proposed method, we conduct the first experiment using the 30-second clip from the song "Butterfly". Fig. 1(a) shows the results of V-A supervised clustering on these 61 data points. According to the V-A values, these data points are automatically partitioned into three groups (noted as green triangles, red circles, and yellow squares, respectively). Fig. 1(b) visualizes the distribution of clusters on the time axis. It is so happened that data points belonging to the same cluster are also temporally coherent. This result is consistent with our intuition that the music emotion varies smoothly and gradually in a short period. Fortunately, most of the music clips in the database possess this continuity characteristic, which shows both the correctness of the proposed clustering scheme and the validity of using V-A clustering results as the supervision for further music seg-

[1]http://www.freemusicarchive.org

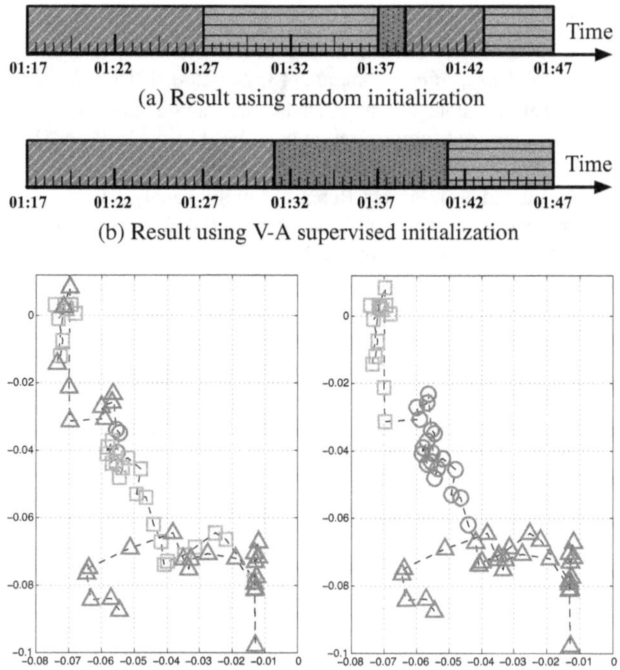

(a) Result using random initialization

(b) Result using V-A supervised initialization

(c) Result of (a) in V-A space (d) Result of (b) in V-A space

Figure 2: Comparison of music emotion segmentation results using random initialization and V-A supervised initialization on music sequence from the song "Borodin Butterfly".

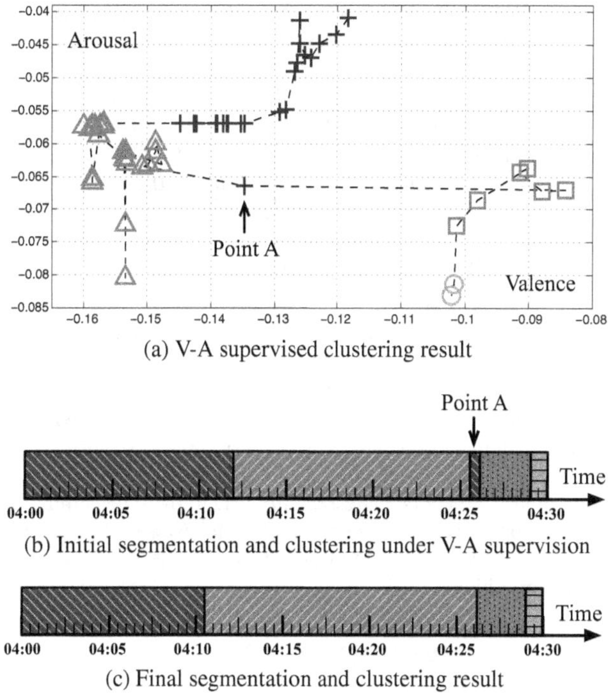

(a) V-A supervised clustering result

(b) Initial segmentation and clustering under V-A supervision

(c) Final segmentation and clustering result

Figure 3: Emotion clustering of isolate data point in V-A space.

mentation. Fig. 1(c) is the final segmentation result of SDC on the music feature space. Compared with the initial segmentation on the V-A emotion space, which is shown in Fig. 1(b), the segmentation boundary between the first segment and the second one has been moved backward. This interesting phenomenon is consistent with the daily-life observations that the feelings (i.e., emotion responses in our case) come with the corresponding experiences (i.e., the stimuli by music signal in our case), possibly within a short delay. In this example, the music clip is decomposed into three segments. According to the graphs of the valence-arousal model in [17], these three segments are roughly corresponding to the emotions of "sleepy" (green triangles), "relaxed" (red circles), and "satisfied" (yellow squares), respectively, which indicates that the proposed SDC is able to learn meaningful emotion primitives from music sequences.

In the second experiment, we show the role of V-A supervised clustering in learning the music emotion primitives. Specifically, we compare the segmentation and clustering results of the music clip from the song "Borodin Butterfly" with random initialization and V-A supervised initialization. Fig. 2(a) and Fig. 2(b) show the result with random initialization and the result guided by the V-A supervised initialization, respectively. To demonstrate the effect of V-A supervised initialization, in Fig. 2(c) and Fig. 2(d), we visualize the result of Fig. 2(a) and that of Fig. 2(b) in V-A space, respectively. For a fair comparison, we use the same number of clusters for both initializations. As can be seen in Fig. 2(c), the segments within the same cluster do not reflect the emotional similarity in V-A space while the segments from different clusters do not show emotional diversity well. Clearly, the clustering result in Fig. 2(d) is more reasonable than that in Fig. 2(c), which indicates that the V-A supervised clustering is able to generate favorable initialization for the subsequent dynamic segmentation.

The third experiment uses the music clip drawn from the song "Photosphere" to demonstrate the robustness of dynamic segmentation, even if the V-A supervised clustering results are not that reliable. Fig. 3(a) shows the V-A supervised clustering result. Data points are partitioned into four clusters (blue crosses, green triangles, red squares, and yellow circles). As shown in Fig. 3(a), data point A is grouped into the cluster of blue crosses in the V-A space. However, it might not be a reasonable assignment. As shown in Fig. 3(b), point A appears when the cluster of green triangles transfers to the cluster of red squares along the timeline. As the representation of an individual frame, point A is too trivial to generate a distinct emotional response. Instead, it is more reasonable to assign point A to either the cluster of green triangles or red squares intuitively. Fig. 3(c) shows the final segmentation and clustering result. Even though the V-A supervised clustering improperly assigns data point A, the dynamic segmentation adjusts it to the cluster of green triangles, which provides better emotion continuity.

3.2 Statistical Evaluation

In this subsection, we evaluate the performance of SDC by statistical comparison. In order to show that the segments generated by SDC are effective in representing the emotion primitives, we compare them with the individual frames (extreme segmentation) and 10-second segments (fixed-length segmentation) on the task of automatic music emotion prediction [1]. We use the long short-term memory (LSTM) [10] as our prediction tool since it has been widely used for dynamic music emotion prediction [5, 26]. We perform 10-fold cross validation and use the Root-Means-Squared Error (RMSE) as the evaluation criterion. Tables 1 shows the RMSE of three kinds of segments on both valence and arousal. By considering the emotion correlations among the consecutive music frames, both 10-second segments and SDC-generated segments show better performance than the individual frames. By decomposing the music sequence using a dynamic and emotion-based way, SDC-generated segments further demonstrate the superiority over 10-second segments.

Table 1: RMSE of individual frames, 10-second segments, and SDC-generated segments with LSTM.

	Valence	Arousal
Individual frames	0.182 ± 0.060	0.186 ± 0.071
10-second segments	0.155 ± 0.048	0.157 ± 0.059
SDC-generated segments	$\mathbf{0.131 \pm 0.053}$	$\mathbf{0.140 \pm 0.056}$

4. CONCLUSION

This paper proposes a novel supervised dynamic clustering algorithm to automatically decompose the music sequence into a set of emotion primitives with various lengths. Experiments on standard dataset demonstrate that emotion primitives provide meaningful base for further music emotion analysis. Moreover, dynamic segmentation in music feature space shows good noise immunity.

Future work will be explored from two aspects. First, we will explore musical factors that essentially lead to the same/similar or different/opposite emotion responses. Second, we will study the influence to the overall emotion from various structures with similar emotion primitives.

5. ACKNOWLEDGMENTS

This work was supported in part by the National Natural Science Foundation of China under Grants 61503317 and 61373122.

6. REFERENCES

[1] A. Aljanaki, Y.-H. Yang, and M. Soleymani. Emotion in music task at mediaeval 2015. In *Working Notes Proceedings of the MediaEval 2015 Workshop*, September 2015.

[2] D. J. Berndt and J. Clifford. Using dynamic time warping to find patterns in time series. In *Proc. Knowl. Discovery Data Mining Workshop*, pages 359–370. AAAI Press, 1994.

[3] D. P. Bertsekas. *Dynamic Programming and Optimal Control*. Athena Scientific, 1995.

[4] D. Cooke. *The Language of Music*. London: Oxford University Press, 1959.

[5] E. Coutinho, G. Trigeorgis, S. Zafeiriou, and B. Schuller. Automatically estimating emotion in music with deep long-short term memory recurrent neural networks. In *Working Notes Proceedings of the MediaEval 2015 Workshop*, September 2015.

[6] F. De la Torre, J. Campoy, Z. Ambadar, and J. Cohn. Temporal segmentation of facial behavior. In *IEEE 11th ICCV*, pages 1–8, 2007.

[7] J. J. Deng and C. H. C. Leung. Dynamic time warping for music retrieval using time series modeling of musical emotions. *IEEE Trans. Affect. Comput.*, 6(2):137–151, 2015.

[8] F. Eyben, F. Weninger, F. Gross, and B. Schuller. Recent developments in opensmile, the munich open-source multimedia feature extractor. In *Proc. 21st ACM Multimedia*, pages 835–838, 2013.

[9] A. Fod, M. J. Matarić, and O. C. Jenkins. Automated derivation of primitives for movement classification. *Autonomous Robots*, 12(1):39–54, 2002.

[10] S. Hochreiter and J. Schmidhuber. Long short-term memory. *Neural Comput.*, 9(8):1735–1780, 1997.

[11] P. N. Juslin and D. Vastfjall. Emotional responses to music: The need to consider underlying mechanisms. *Behavioral and Brain Sciences*, 31:559–575, 2008.

[12] Y. Liu, Y. Liu, Y. Zhao, and K. Hua. What strikes the strings of your heart? - feature mining for music emotion analysis. *IEEE Trans. Affect. Comput.*, 6(3):247–260, 2015.

[13] Y. Liu, F. Zhou, W. Liu, F. De la Torre, and Y. Liu. Unsupervised summarization of rushes videos. In *Proc. 18th ACM Multimedia*, pages 751–754, 2010.

[14] C. Lu and N. J. Ferrier. Repetitive motion analysis: segmentation and event classification. *IEEE Trans. Pattern Anal. Mach. Intell.*, 26(2):258–263, 2004.

[15] L. Lu, D. Liu, and H.-J. Zhang. Automatic mood detection and tracking of music audio signals. *IEEE Trans. Audio, Speech, Language Process.*, 14(1):5–18, 2006.

[16] A. Rodriguez and A. Laio. Clustering by fast search and find of density peaks. *Science*, 344(6191):1492–1496, 2014.

[17] J. A. Russell. A circumplex model of affect. *J. Pers. Soc. Psychol.*, 39:1161–1178, 1980.

[18] T. Särkämö, M. Tervaniemi, S. Laitinen, A. Forsblom, S. Soinila, M. Mikkonen, T. Autti, H. M. Silvennoinen, J. Erkkilä, M. Laine, I. Peretz, and M. Hietanen. Music listening enhances cognitive recovery and mood after middle cerebral artery stroke. *Brain*, 131(3):866–876, 2008.

[19] H. Shimodaira, K.-I. Noma, M. Nakai, and S. Sagayama. Dynamic time-alignment kernel in support vector machine. In *NIPS 14*, pages 921–928, 2001.

[20] M. Soleymani, M. N. Caro, E. M. Schmidt, C.-Y. Sha, and Y.-H. Yang. 1000 songs for emotional analysis of music. In *Proc. 2nd ACM CrowdMM*, pages 1–6, 2013.

[21] K. Trohidis, G. Tsoumakas, G. Kalliris, and I. Vlahavas. Multi-label classification of music into emotions. In *Proc. 9th ISMIR*, pages 325–330, 2008.

[22] K. Trohidis, G. Tsoumakas, G. Kalliris, and I. Vlahavas. Multi-label classification of music by emotion. *EURASIP J. Audio, Speech, and Music Process.*, 4:1–9, 2011.

[23] D. Turnbull, L. Barrington, D. Torres, and G. Lanckriet. Semantic annotation and retrieval of music and sound effects. *IEEE Trans. Audio, Speech, Language Process.*, 16(2):467–476, 2008.

[24] X. Wang, D. Rosenblum, and Y. Wang. Context-aware mobile music recommendation for daily activities. In *Proc. 20th ACM Multimedia*, pages 99–108, 2012.

[25] B. Wu, E. Zhong, A. Horner, and Q. Yang. Music emotion recognition by multi-label multi-layer multi-instance multi-view learning. In *Proc. 22nd ACM Multimedia*, pages 117–126, 2014.

[26] M. Xu, X. Li, H. Xianyu, J. Tian, F. Meng, and W. Chen. Multi-scale approaches to the mediaeval 2015 "emotion in music" task. In *Working Notes Proceedings of the MediaEval 2015 Workshop*, September 2015.

[27] Y.-H. Yang and H. H. Chen. Machine recognition of music emotion: A review. *ACM Trans. Intell. Syst. Technol.*, 3(3):40:1–40:30, 2012.

[28] Y. H. Yang, Y. C. Lin, H. T. Cheng, and H. H. Chen. Mr. emo: Music retrieval in the emotion plane. In *Proc. 16th ACM Multimedia*, pages 1003–1004, 2008.

[29] Y.-H. Yang, Y.-C. Lin, Y.-F. Su, and H. H. Chen. A regression approach to music emotion recognition. *IEEE Trans. Audio, Speech, Language Process.*, 16(2):448–457, 2008.

[30] F. Zhou, F. De la Torre, and J. K. Hodgins. Hierarchical aligned cluster analysis for temporal clustering of human motion. *IEEE Trans. Pattern Anal. Mach. Intell.*, 35(3):582–596, 2013.

Cross-modal Retrieval by Real Label Partial Least Squares

Jianfeng He[1,3], Bingpeng Ma[1,2,3]*, Shuhui Wang[2], Yugui Liu[1,3], Qingming Huang[1,2,3]
[1] School of Computer and Control Engineering, University of Chinese Academy of Sciences, China
[2] Key Laboratory of Intelligent Information Processing, Institute of Computing Technology, Chinese Academy of Sciences(CAS), China
[3] Key Laboratory of Big Data Mining and Knowledge Management, CAS, China
{jianfeng.he, shuhui.wang}@vipl.ict.ac.cn {bpma, liuyg, qmhuang}@ucas.ac.cn

ABSTRACT

This paper proposes a novel method named Real Label Partial Least Squares (RL-PLS) for the task of cross-modal retrieval. Pervious works just take the texts and images as two modalities in PLS. But in RL-PLS, considering that the class label is more related to the semantics directly, we take the class label as the assistant modality. Specially, we build two KPLS models and project both images and texts into the label space. Then, the similarity of images and texts can be measured more accurately in the label space. Furthermore, we do not restrict the label indicator values as the binary values as the traditional methods. By contraries, in RL-PLS, the label indicator values are set to the real values. Specially, the label indicator values are comprised by two parts: positive or negative represents the sample class while the absolute value represents the local structure in the class. By this way, the discriminate ability of RL-PLS is improved greatly. To show the effectiveness of RL-PLS, the experiments are conducted on two cross-modal retrieval tasks (Wiki and Pascal Voc2007), on which the competitive results are obtained.

Keywords

Cross-modal retrieval, multimedia, partial least squares, images and documents.

1. INTRODUCTION

With the development of Internet technology, the quantity of multimedia has increased dramatically. It is a great challenge to retrieve the information from the different modalities. Recently, more and more people pay their attention to the task of cross-modal retrieval [1] [9] [12] [20] [22] [24] [25]. The key problem of cross-modal retrieval is matching one modal feature to the other modal feature in the content-based area [13]. For example, in the image-text retrieval, given an image query, find the texts that best describe the image; or given a text document, return the most related images. However, the text features and the image features are in the different feature space so that they can't be matched directly with each other.

To solve the retrieval problem of the different feature spaces, recent works are devoted to the common subspace learning [8] [9] [13] [19]. These methods try to learn a common feature space so as to match the image and text features directly and preserve the correlations in the image-text pairs. As one of possible solutions, Canonical Correlation Analysis (CCA) projects two modal features to a shared latent space which maximizes the correlations between two modal features [7] [10] [13] [17]. Many extensions of CCA have been used in the similar area. For example, Semantic Correlation Match (SCM) was proposed to get the semantic subspace by using the logistic regressor based on CCA [13]. In [20], without no assumption on specific form of text, Correlated Semantic Representation (CSR) obtains a joint image-text representation and an unified formulation by learning a compatible function based on structural SVM.

Another classical method of subspace learning is Partial Least Squares (PLS) [2] [6] [14] [15] [16], aiming at learning two latent spaces by maximizing the correlations between them. Sharma *et al.* [17] and Kang *et al.* [9] applied PLS to build the relation between the latent variables of images and texts. Besides cross-modal retrieval, PLS and its extensions have been applied successfully on other problems. For an instance, in the task of cross-pose face recognition, the relation between the coupled faces are constructed by PLS [5] [11] [23]. In [18], bridge PLS was proposed by adding ridge-parameter to improve the efficiency in each iteration. Rosipal *et al.* [15] proposed the kernel PLS by mapping the input variables into high dimension space so as to solve the nonlinear problem in linear algorithm.

Moreover, most of the above algorithms don't use the label information. Generally speaking, cross-modal retrieval problem always exists semantic gap between the different modalities [4] [13] [21]. But by using the label information, the semantic gap can be decreased theoretically [4] [21]. Specially, using labels for extracting muliti-view features, GMLDA and GMMFA, constructed by framework based on Generalized Multiview Analysis (GMA), shown the competitive performance on the cross-modal retrieval problem [17]. In [9], which gains the state-of-art performance on cross-modal retrieval problem, the label information are used to close different modalities within the same class and far away between different modalities.

*Corresponding author.

MM '16, October 15-19, 2016, Amsterdam, Netherlands
 ISBN 978-1-4503-3603-1/16/10...$15.00
DOI: http://dx.doi.org/10.1145/2964284.2967216

In this paper, we propose a supervised algorithm named Real Label Partial Least Squares (RL-PLS), which projects two modal feature into a common space and reserves the label information and local structure while at the same time. Different with the above works [16] [17], we regard the label information as the assistant modality. Thus, we achieve a three modality shared feature space to obtain better performance than only using two modalities. Further, considering that the local structure of samples is ignored when all the samples existed in the different regions have the same label [9], RL-PLS constructs the class indicator matrix using real values to reserve the local structure. The label values in the matrix are comprised by two parts: character and value. Character represents the relationship between sample and class while the absolute value represents the local structure in the class. By using the probability belonging to the class, the different samples are given the different weights. Finally, the discriminative ability of RL-PLS is improved greatly.

2. KERNEL PARTIAL LEAST SQUARES

PLS can construct the relation between two different modalities by maximizing the correlation between the latent variables. Recently, it has gained great success in many areas [2] [6] [16]. Kernel partial least squares(KPLS), the extension of PLS, maps original feature into a new high dimension feature space to solve the nonlinear problem with linear algorithm. Because of reserving more information in nonlinear problem, KPLS often get better performance.

For the original feature of training set, its kernel feature as the input variables can be denoted by $\boldsymbol{X} \in \mathbb{R}^{n\times n}$, where n is the number of training samples. The latent variables of $\boldsymbol{X}$ are represented as $\boldsymbol{V} = [\boldsymbol{v}_1, \cdots, \boldsymbol{v}_n]^T \in \mathbb{R}^{n\times p}$, where p is the dimension of latent variables and far smaller than n. Similarly, $\boldsymbol{Z} = [\boldsymbol{z}_1, \cdots, \boldsymbol{z}_n]^T \in \mathbb{R}^{n\times d}$ denotes the output variables of training set, where d is the number of dimensions. It is represented by $\boldsymbol{U} = [\boldsymbol{u}_1, \cdots, \boldsymbol{u}_n]^T \in \mathbb{R}^{n\times p}$. Finally, KPLS can be built as:

$$\begin{cases} \boldsymbol{X} = \boldsymbol{V}\boldsymbol{P}^T + \boldsymbol{\varepsilon}_x \\ \boldsymbol{Z} = \boldsymbol{U}\boldsymbol{Q}^T + \boldsymbol{\varepsilon}_z \end{cases} \tag{1}$$

where the matrices $\boldsymbol{P}$ and $\boldsymbol{Q}$ represent the loading matrices, the matrices $\boldsymbol{\varepsilon_x}$ and $\boldsymbol{\varepsilon_z}$ are the residuals matrices. And according to [15], by means of the low dimension latent variables $\boldsymbol{V}, \boldsymbol{U}$, we can further get a regression coefficient matrix $\boldsymbol{B} \in \mathbb{R}^{n\times d}$ to get the relation between $\boldsymbol{X}$ and $\boldsymbol{Z}$:

$$\begin{cases} \boldsymbol{B} = \boldsymbol{X}^T\boldsymbol{U}(\boldsymbol{V}^T\boldsymbol{X}\boldsymbol{X}^T\boldsymbol{U})^{-1}\boldsymbol{V}^T\boldsymbol{Z} \\ \boldsymbol{Z} = \boldsymbol{X}\boldsymbol{B}^T + \boldsymbol{\varepsilon}_B \end{cases} \tag{2}$$

where $\boldsymbol{\varepsilon}_B$ is the matrix of residuals.

KPLS can be solved by Nonlinear Partial Least Squares (NIPALS) algorithm. More details about KPLS and NIPALS can be found in [15]. In Fig. 1 (a), we show the relation between different variables in KPLS model.

3. REAL LABEL PARTIAL LEAST SQUARES

In this section, we introduce the proposed method in details. In Fig. 1 (b), we show the structure diagram of the proposed method.

3.1 Labels in KPLS

From Eq. 2, we can know that in KPLS, the input modality $\boldsymbol{X}$ is projected into the space of the output modality $\boldsymbol{Z}$ and the similarity of the different modalities are measured in this space. Considering the semantic gap and the great discrepancy between texts and images in cross-model retrieval, the direct projection from the input modality to the output modality inevitably causes the information loss of the input modality and decreases the retrieval performance.

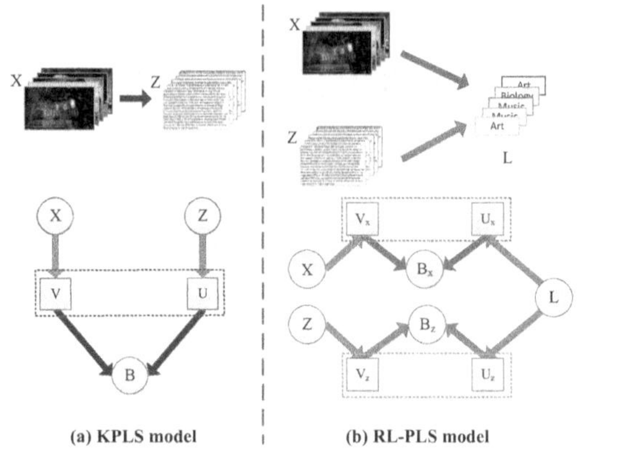

Figure 1: (a) The structure diagram of PLS. (b) The structure diagram of RL-PLS. The rectangles mean latent space.

Compared with texts and images, label information is more related to the semantic information. Many pairs of two modalities share the common labels in cross-modal problem. So, for the semantic gap between texts and images in cross-model retrieval, we argue that label information can help to build the relation between texts and images.

In this paper, we use $\boldsymbol{L}$ to denote the label indicator matrix. We take labels as the auxiliary modality and propose the RL-PLS method. In RL-PLS, we project images and texts into the semantic space simultaneously. By this way, the similarity of the different modalities can be measured more effectively in the semantic space. Specially, taking images as the input variables and labels as the output variables, $KPLS_{XL}$ constructs the relation between images and labels. Similarly, taking texts as the input variables and labels as the output variables, $KPLS_{ZL}$ constructs the relation between texts and labels:

$$KPLS_{XL}: \begin{cases} \boldsymbol{X} = \boldsymbol{V}_x\boldsymbol{P}_x^T + \boldsymbol{\varepsilon}_x \\ \boldsymbol{L} = \boldsymbol{U}_x\boldsymbol{Q}_x^T + \boldsymbol{\varepsilon}_{Lx} \end{cases} \tag{3}$$

$$KPLS_{ZL}: \begin{cases} \boldsymbol{Z} = \boldsymbol{V}_z\boldsymbol{P}_z^T + \boldsymbol{\varepsilon}_z \\ \boldsymbol{L} = \boldsymbol{U}_z\boldsymbol{Q}_z^T + \boldsymbol{\varepsilon}_{Lz} \end{cases} \tag{4}$$

where $\boldsymbol{V}_x$, $\boldsymbol{U}_x$, $\boldsymbol{V}_z$ and $\boldsymbol{U}_z$ are the latent variables; $\boldsymbol{P}_x$, $\boldsymbol{Q}_x$, $\boldsymbol{P}_z$ and $\boldsymbol{Q}_z$ represent the loading matrices; $\boldsymbol{\varepsilon}_x$, $\boldsymbol{\varepsilon}_{Lx}$, $\boldsymbol{\varepsilon}_z$ and $\boldsymbol{\varepsilon}_{Lz}$ are the residuals. Eq. 3 and Eq. 4 can be solved with NIPALS algorithm. According to Eq. 2, the regression coefficient matrix $\boldsymbol{B}_x$ in $KPLS_{XL}$ and $\boldsymbol{B}_z$ in $KPLS_{ZL}$ can be computed as follows:

$$KPLS_{XL}: \begin{cases} \boldsymbol{B}_x = \boldsymbol{X}^T\boldsymbol{U}_x(\boldsymbol{V}_x^T\boldsymbol{X}\boldsymbol{X}^T\boldsymbol{U}_x)^{-1}\boldsymbol{V}_x^T\boldsymbol{L} \\ \boldsymbol{L} = \boldsymbol{X}\boldsymbol{B}_x^T + \boldsymbol{\varepsilon}_{Bx} \end{cases} \tag{5}$$

$$KPLS_{ZL}: \begin{cases} \boldsymbol{B}_z = \boldsymbol{Z}^T\boldsymbol{U}_z(\boldsymbol{V}_z^T\boldsymbol{Z}\boldsymbol{Z}^T\boldsymbol{U}_z)^{-1}\boldsymbol{V}_z^T\boldsymbol{L} \\ \boldsymbol{L} = \boldsymbol{Z}\boldsymbol{B}_z^T + \boldsymbol{\varepsilon}_{Bz} \end{cases} \tag{6}$$

Finally, $\boldsymbol{B}_x$ and $\boldsymbol{B}_z$ map the input variables which are heterogenous features $\boldsymbol{X}$ and $\boldsymbol{Z}$ into the target feature space constructed by label information.

3.2 Real Labels

In $KPLS_{XL}$ and $KPLS_{ZL}$, the similarity of different modalities are computed in the label space. In the previous works, the class indicators often are the binary matrix. In other words, all the elements are zeros except for the corresponding classes [9]. Specially, if sample $\boldsymbol{a}$ is assigned to the kth class, its indicator vector $\boldsymbol{l}$ is constructed by $l_k = 1$, and $l_j = 0$ for $j \neq k$. For all the samples belonging to the same class, their class indicator vectors are the same. In fact, different samples exist in the different regions in the high dimensional space. The same labels mean that the local structure of samples is ignored.

In RL-PLS, we construct the class indicator matrix using real values to reserve the local structure. We assume that data points in each class can be modeled by several Gaussian distributions. The values in the class indicator matrix are set to the probabilities that samples belong to the clustering center. So, for the samples which near the class center, they have the bigger probability belonging to the class and their values are close to 1. For the samples which far away the class center, they have the bigger probability to be the outliers and their values are close to 0. In other words, by using the probability belonging to the class, we pay more attentions on the samples which near the clustering center and reduce the influence of the outliers.

Specially, there are five steps to compute class indicator matrix $\boldsymbol{L}$ in RL-PLS. Firstly, for each class in the modality $\boldsymbol{X}$, we use r Gaussian distributions to model it. So, for the total q classes in the training set, we can gain $s(= r \times q)$ Gaussian distributions $\{G_1, G_2, \cdots, G_s\}$. For the jth Gaussian distribution G_j, the class of its corresponding samples is c_j^g. The clustering center vector and covariance matrix of G_j is $\boldsymbol{\mu}_j$ and $\boldsymbol{\Sigma}_j$, respectively.

Secondly, we compute the Mahalanobis distance d_{ij} between $\boldsymbol{x}_i$ and $\boldsymbol{\mu}_j$ under the covariance matrix $\boldsymbol{\Sigma}_j$:

$$d_{ij} = (\boldsymbol{x}_i - \boldsymbol{\mu}_j)^T \boldsymbol{\Sigma}_j^{-1} (\boldsymbol{x}_i - \boldsymbol{\mu}_j) \tag{7}$$

Then, we compute the probability w_{ij} that $\boldsymbol{x}_i$ belongs to the j-th Gaussian distribution:

$$w_{ij} = \exp(-\frac{d_{ij}}{\sigma^2}) \tag{8}$$

where σ is the standard deviation of $\boldsymbol{D} = [\boldsymbol{d}_1, \boldsymbol{d}_2, \cdots, \boldsymbol{d}_s]^T$.

Fourthly, p_{ij} is designed to show the relation between the sample's class and the Gaussian distribution. Suppose c_i is the class label of sample x_i, the p_{ij} is set to 1 when c_i is equal to c_j^g. Otherwise, it is set to -1.

$$p_{ij} = \begin{cases} +1, & if \ \ c_i = c_j^g \\ -1, & otherwise. \end{cases} \tag{9}$$

Finally, l_{ij} is computed as:

$$l_{ij} = p_{ij} \times w_{ij} \tag{10}$$

Then, after the computation of the probabilistic class indicator vector of all the samples in the training set, the indicator matrix $\boldsymbol{L}$ can be gained by: $\boldsymbol{L} = [\boldsymbol{l}_1, \boldsymbol{l}_2, \cdots, \boldsymbol{l}_n]^T$ and $\boldsymbol{l}_i = (l_{i1}, l_{i2}, \cdots, l_{is})$.

From Eq. 10, we can know that the class indicator vector can be divided into two parts: character and value. For the samples whose class label is same to the label of the Gaussian distribution, the real values of class indicator can keep the local structure of the within-class. For the samples which has the different class label with the Gaussian distribution but it has the large probability w_{ij}, the negative value of the class indicator can increase the margin of the inter-classes. So, by the combination of the character and value, the discriminate ability of $\boldsymbol{L}$ is improved greatly.

It is must be noted that for images and texts, their class indicator matrices are different according to the computation process of $\boldsymbol{L}$. But considering that we try to find a common projection subspace for texts and images while the distributions of texts are not as complicated as images', we just construct $\boldsymbol{L}$ based on the texts modality.

3.3 Analysis of Computational Complexity

Lastly, we briefly analyze the computational complexity of RL-PLS, which involves h dimensions of latent variables, and each dimension is solved by NIPALS algorithm, in which the max iterations is set as g. Set n as the number of sample pairs in the training set, thus image feature and text feature are n dimensions as a result of RBF kernel. And set q as the number of total classes. The computational complexity of RL-PLS is $O(hgn^3 + n^2h^5q)$.

4. EXPERIMENTS

In this section, we test RL-PLS on two popular databases to show its performance on cross-modal retrieval.

4.1 Experimental Databases

Wiki [13] is constructed from Wikipedia including 2866 image-text pairs with 10 different classes. We randomly select 2173 image-text pairs for the training set and 693 image-text pairs for the testing set. The texts in Wiki are represented by the 10-dimensional Latent Dirichlet Allocation (LDA) features. For images, we use two different features to show the effectiveness of RL-PLS. On one hand, the images are represented by the traditional 128-dimensional vectors based on the SIFT descriptors; on the other hand, considering the success of deep learning, we also perform experiments using the Convolutional Neural Network (CNN). So the image features are also represented by the 4096-dimensional vectors output from the 'fc7' layer of convolutional neural network(CNN) based on central crop (no mirroring).

Pascal VOC2007 [3] consists of 5011/4952(training/testing) image-tag pairs with 20 classes. Taking account that some pairs of the database are multi-label, we choose single-label pairs in our experiment. As a result, training set includes 2808 image-tag pairs and testing set includes 2841 image-tag pairs. For feature representation, we use the 512-dimensional GIST features for images, and the 399-dimensional word frequency features for text.

4.2 Experimental Setting

We compare RL-PLS with PLS, KPLS, SCM, GMMFA, GMLDA and LGCFL in two retrieval tasks. PLS and KPLS are unsupervised learning methods while the other methods are supervised learning methods. In PLS and KPLS, we set the image features as input variables, and the text feature as output variables. As for SCM, it uses CCA to learn two maximally correlated subspaces, and then learns the logistic regressors in each subspaces. Both GMMFA and GMLDA use the framework of GMA[17]. LGCFL uses the valuable class information to jointly learn the consistent features and achieves the state-of-the-art performance.

Table 1: **MAP results on the Wiki database. Images are represented by SIFT features.**

Methods \ Tasks	im2txt	txt2im	Average
PLS [16]	0.207	0.192	0.199
KPLS [15]	0.260	0.201	0.231
SCM [13]	0.277	0.226	0.252
GMMFA [17]	0.264	0.231	0.248
GMLDA [17]	0.272	0.232	0.252
LGCFL [9]	0.277	0.229	0.253
RL-PLS	**0.316**	**0.238**	**0.277**

Table 2: **MAP results on the Wiki database. Images are represented by CNN features.**

Methods \ Tasks	im2txt	txt2im	Average
PLS [16]	0.302	0.272	0.287
KPLS [15]	0.374	0.322	0.348
SCM [13]	0.381	0.331	0.356
GMMFA [17]	0.373	0.340	0.357
GMLDA [17]	0.372	0.338	0.355
LGCFL [9]	0.399	0.351	0.375
RL-PLS	**0.425**	**0.363**	**0.394**

In our experiments, we use the Mean Average Precision (MAP) [9] [13] metric to evaluate the performance of the different methods. For Wiki, 5 Gaussian distributions are set for each class. But for Pascal VOC2007, since the number of samples are very limited for some classes, we set the number of Gaussian distributions to 3.

4.3 Results on the Wiki database

The MAPs of the different methods on the Wiki database where images are represented by SIFT features are shown in Tab. 1. From the table, we can find the following scenes:

Firstly, the performance of the supervised methods (SCM, GMMFA, GMLDA and LGCFL) outperforms those of the unsupervised methods (PLS and KPLS) by at least 7.4%. This indicates that the label information can provide the available information to improve the performance.

Secondly, the average MAP of KPLS outperforms 16.1% than PLS, which indicates that mapping original feature into a high dimensional feature space via kernel function can get better performance. The advantage of KPLS also motivates us to construct RL-PLS based on KPLS rather than PLS.

Thirdly, compared with KPLS, RL-PLS obtains 20.0% higher average MAP, which validates the effect of setting the label information as the output variables in RL-PLS. At the same time, the performance of RL-PLS outperforms the state-of-art method LGCFL by 9.5% higher average MAP. Because in RL-PLS, we break up the binary constraints in traditional class indicator matrix used in LGCFL and reserve the local structure and label information in RL-PLS. The results show the validity of RL-PLS.

Furthermore, we also repeat the experiments using CNN image features to verify our methods' high quality performance. The results are shown in Tab. 2. From the table, we can know that compared with using SIFT features, the performance of the different methods is improved when using CNN features. The experiments show the effectiveness of the CNN features. Besides, the results are consistent with the conclusion obtained form Tab. 1. It is mentionable that our methods achieve 5.1% higher average MAP than state-of-art method LGCFL, indicating that RL-PLS is also effective and competitive based on CNN features.

Table 3: **MAP results on the PASCAL VOC2007 database.**

Methods \ Tasks	im2txt	txt2im	Average
PLS [16]	0.320	0.251	0.286
KPLS [15]	0.347	0.266	0.307
SCM [13]	0.392	0.280	0.336
GMMFA [17]	0.343	0.280	0.311
GMLDA [17]	0.342	0.278	0.310
LGCFL [9]	0.401	0.320	0.360
RL-PLS	**0.429**	**0.358**	**0.393**

4.4 Results on the Pascal VOC2007 database

Tab. 3 shows the results on the Pascal database, from which, we can find as follow:

Firstly, it is remarkable that the average MAP of RL-PLS achieves 39.3%, which outperforms the state-of-art method, the LGCFL, for more than 9.2%. This verifies the effectiveness of RL-PLS again.

Secondly, the texts in the Pascal database have tags information, just using several words rather than paragraphs used by Wiki database. Under the condition, RL-PLS also gains the competitive results on the Pascal database, which indicates that RL-PLS is also viable on the texts constructed just by several words.

To sum up, we outperform above related methods and achieve competitive performance on two databases. Because of the advantages of RL-PLS, we draw the conclusion that RL-PLS can improve the performance on cross-modal retrieval via reducing the diversity in common space, through reserving the class information and local structure.

5. CONCLUSION

This paper proposes a novel method for the task of cross-modal retrieval. In our approach, we regard the label information as the assistant modality and construct two KPLSs. Furthermore, we design a novel class indicator matrix with real values which combines the class information and the local structure. Experiments carried out on two public databases show that our proposed method performs against the existing competitive methods.

There are several aspects to be further studied in the future. For example, we will look for more effective class indicator matrix to keep the local structure more well. We also can extend the proposed method to handle the multi-label and unpaired setting cross-modal retrieval task.

6. ACKNOWLEDGMENTS

This work was supported in part by National Basic Research Program of China (973 Program): 2012CB316400 and 2015CB351802, 863 Program of China: 2014AA015202, and Natural Science Foundation of China (NSFC): 61332016, 61572465 and 61303160. The authors also thank the suggestion and help from Liang Zhang and Chunfeng Wang.

7. REFERENCES

[1] J. Costa P, E. Coviello, G. Doyle, N. Rasiwasia, G. Lanckriet, R. Levy, and N. Vasconcelos. On the role of correlation and abstraction in cross-modal multimedia retrieval. *IEEE Transactions on Pattern Analysis and Machine Intelligence*, 36(3):521–535, 2014.

[2] B. Ding and R. Gentleman. Classification using generalized partial least squares. *Journal of Computational and Graphical Statistics*, pages 280–298, 2012.

[3] M. Everingham, L. Van Gool, C. Williams, J. Winn, and A. Zisserman. The pascal visual object classes challenge 2007 (voc 2007) results. 2008.

[4] Y. Gong and S. Lazebnik. Iterative quantization: A procrustean approach to learning binary codes. *Proc. IEEE Conference on Computer Vision and Pattern Recognition*, pages 817–824, 2011.

[5] G. Guo and X. Wang. A study on human age estimation under facial expression changes. *IEEE Conference on Computer Vision and Pattern Recognition*, pages 2547–2553, 2012.

[6] M. Haj, J. Gonzalez, and L. Davis. On partial least squares in head pose estimation: How to simultaneously deal with misalignment. *Proc. IEEE Conference on Computer Vision and Pattern Recognition*, pages 2602–2609, 2012.

[7] D. R. Hardoon, S. Szedmak, and J. Shawe-Taylor. Canonical correlation analysis: An overview with application to learning methods. *Neural computation*, 16(12):2639–2664, 2004.

[8] Y. Jia, M. Salzmann, and T. Darrell. Learning cross-modality similarity for multinomial data. *Proc. IEEE International Conference on Computer Vision*, pages 2407–2414, 2011.

[9] C. Kang, S. Xiang, S. Liao, C. Xu, and C. Pan. Learning consistent feature representation for cross-modal multimedia retrieval. *IEEE Transactions on Multimedia*, 17(3):370–381, 2015.

[10] A. Li, S. Shan, X. Chen, and W. Gao. Maximizing intra-individual correlations for face recognition across pose differences. *Proc. IEEE Conference on Computer Vision and Pattern Recognition*, pages 605–611, 2009.

[11] A. Li, S. Shan, X. Chen, and W. Gao. Cross-pose face recognition based on partial least squares. *Pattern Recognition Letters*, 32(15):1948–1955, 2011.

[12] X. Mao, B. Lin, D. Cai, X. He, and J. Pei. Parallel field alignment for cross media retrieval. *ACM Multimedia*, pages 897–906, 2013.

[13] N. Rasiwasia, J. C. Pereira, E. Coviello, G. Doyle, G. R. G. Lanckriet, R. Levy, and N. Vasconcelos. A new approach to cross-modal multimedia retrieval. *ACM Multimedia*, pages 251–260, 2010.

[14] R. Rosipal and N. Krämer. Overview and recent advances in partial least squares. *Subspace, latent structure and feature selection*, pages 34–51, 2006.

[15] R. Rosipal and L. J. Trejo. Kernel partial least squares regression in reproducing kernel hilbert space. *The Journal of Machine Learning Research*, 2:97–123, 2002.

[16] A. Sharma and D. W. Jacobs. Bypassing synthesis: Pls for face recognition with pose, low-resolution and sketch. *Proc. IEEE Conference on Computer Vision and Pattern Recognition*, pages 593–600, 2011.

[17] A. Sharma, A. Kumar, H. D. III, and D. W. Jacobs. Generalized multiview analysis: A discriminative latent space. *Proc. IEEE Conference on Computer Vision and Pattern Recognition*, pages 2160–2167, 2012.

[18] J. Tang, H. Wang, and Y. Yan. Learning hough regression models via bridge partial least squares for object detection. *Neurocomputing*, 152:236–249, 2015.

[19] J. B. Tenenbaum and W. T. Freeman. Separating style and content with bilinear models. *Neural computation*, 12(6):1247–1283, 2000.

[20] Y. Verma and C. Jawahar. Im2text and text2im: Associating images and texts for cross-modal retrieval. *Proc. British Machine Vision Conference*, 2014.

[21] J. Wang, S. Kumar, and S. Chang. Semi-supervised hashing for large-scale search. *IEEE Transactions on Pattern Analysis and Machine Intelligence*, 34(12):2393–2406, 2012.

[22] K. Wang, R. He, W. Wang, L. Wang, and T. Tan. Learning coupled feature spaces for cross-modal matching. *Proc. IEEE International Conference on Computer Vision*, pages 2088–2095.

[23] X. Wang, V. Ly, G. Guo, and C. Kambhamettu. A new approach for 2d-3d heterogeneous face recognition. *IEEE International Symposium on Multimedia*, pages 301–304, 2013.

[24] L. Xie, P. Pan, and Y. Lu. A semantic model for cross-modal and multi-modal retrieval. *ACM International Conference on Multimedia Retrieval*, pages 175–182, 2013.

[25] Y. Zhuang, Y. F. Wang, F. Wu, Y. Zhang, and W. Lu. Supervised coupled dictionary learning with group structures for multi-modal retrieval. *AAAI Conference on Artificial Intelligence*, 2013.

LSOD: Local Sparse Orthogonal Descriptor for Image Matching

Yiru Zhao, Yaoyi Li, Zhiwen Shao, Hongtao Lu*
Key Laboratory of Shanghai Education Commission for Intelligent Interaction and Cognitive Engineering
Department of Computer Science and Engineering, Shanghai Jiao Tong University, P.R.China
{yiru.zhao, dsamuel, shaozhiwen, htlu}@sjtu.edu.cn

ABSTRACT

We propose a novel method for feature description used for image matching in this paper. Our method is inspired by the autoencoder, an artificial neural network designed for learning efficient codings. Sparse and orthogonal constraints are imposed on the autoencoder and make it a highly discriminative descriptor. It is shown that the proposed descriptor is not only invariant to geometric and photometric transformations (such as viewpoint change, intensity change, noise, image blur and JPEG compression), but also highly efficient. We compare it with existing state-of-the-art descriptors on standard benchmark datasets, the experimental results show that our LSOD method yields better performance both in accuracy and efficiency.

Keywords

Image matching; autoencoder; local feature descriptor

1. INTRODUCTION

Local feature descriptor is basal research of many computer vision problems, such as image stitching [11], camera calibration [19], object detection [14], and so on. SIFT keypoint detector and descriptor [12], which was proposed a decade ago, has been proved effective in many image matching scenarios [18, 20], but it imposes a large computational cost, especially when used for real-time applications such as simultaneous localization and mapping (SLAM) systems. Many algorithms were proposed to improve SIFT in the following years, SURF [3] is one of them, which is faster but less accurate than SIFT. DSP-SIFT [5] raises a modification based on pooling gradient orientations. KAZE [1] introduces a feature detection and description algorithm in nonlinear scale spaces. It is accelerated in [2], by a descriptor called AKAZE.

On the other hand, machine learning and neural network are two of the rapidly growing fields in recent years and have achieved great success in many classical computer vision problems, such as image classification [9] and action recognition [8]. Inspired by sparse autoencoder, one of the well-known neural network models, we propose a new image local feature descriptor. With the orthogonal features learned from image dataset, autoencoder encodes an image patch as the descriptor. Our method is called Local Sparse Orthogonal Descriptor(LSOD), an example is shown in Figure 1. The main contributions of this paper include:

- Enhancing FAST detector with median filter scale pyramid and intensity centroid.
- Proposing a method of training a sparse orthogonal autoencoder used to describe the local image feature patch.

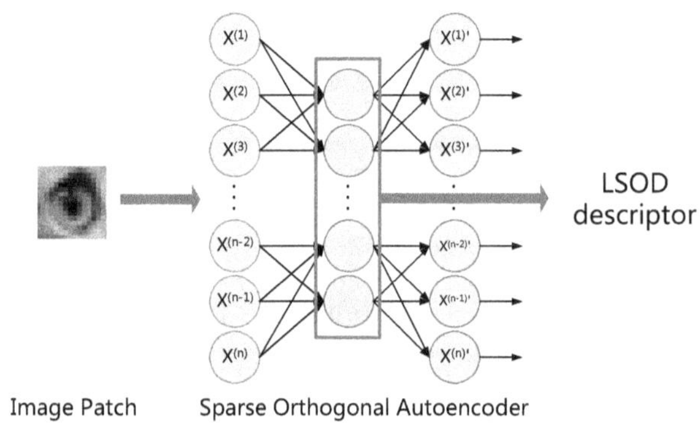

Figure 1: Illustration of calculating the LSOD descriptor for an image patch.

2. RELATED WORK

Detector: The first step in image matching is detecting interest points in the image and there have been many productive interest point detectors. Harris corner detector [7] gives a mathematical approach for determining whether an image patch is flat, edge or corner. SIFT calculates histograms of gray level gradient and chooses the peak orientation as the main direction. SURF uses approximation of block patterns, which is faster than computation of gradients. FAST and its extensions [16, 17] are good choices for keypoints detecting in real-time systems. They are stable and efficient to find corner keypoints, but sensitive to scale variance. Therefore the FAST detector is often applied with pyramid schemes for scale change.

*Corresponding author.

MM '16, October 15-19, 2016, Amsterdam, Netherlands
© 2016 ACM. ISBN 978-1-4503-3603-1/16/10...$15.00
DOI: http://dx.doi.org/10.1145/2964284.2967217

Descriptor: With one interest point and nearby patch pixels, we need a discriminative descriptor to calculate the local feature vector. SIFT generates feature descriptors by calculating histograms of oriented gradients (HOG), while SURF's descriptor is based on wavelet responses in horizontal and vertical direction. Some binary descriptors, such as BRIEF[4], use simple binary tests between pixels to represent features, which could use the Hamming distance instead of the Euclidean distance to search the matched pairs and reduce the time complexity.

3. THE PROPOSED METHOD

In our method, we use FAST detector in image pyramid to find interest points at different scale levels and train a sparse orthogonal autoencoder on a large image patch dataset to encode the local feature vector.

3.1 Enhanced FAST detector

FAST detector is famous for its light computational complexity. Its segment test criterion operates by comparing the intensity between the corner candidate p and a circle of sixteen pixels around it. If there exists a set of n contiguous pixels in the circle which are all brighter than $I_p + t$ or darker than $I_p - t$, p will be classified as a corner, where I_p is the intensity of the candidate pixel p and t is a manual threshold. However, FAST detector can not resist rotation and scale changes.

An usual approach for multiscale algorithm is generating an image pyramid by filtering the original image with an appropriate function over increasing scales. Gaussian kernel is frequently-used while with the drawback of loss of localization accuracy, because the natural boundaries of objects are smoothed to the same degree with details and noise. Alcantarilla *et al.* [1] performs feature detection in nonlinear scale pyramid, in which the noise in images is blurred but the object edges remain unaffected, the resulting algorithm is called KAZE. However the improvement brings out high computation complexity. To alleviate this drawback, we use median filter instead of Gaussian filter to build the image pyramid, which could obtain the similar result as KAZE without paying the high cost in computation. See the example in Figure 2. At high levels in pyramid, the details and noise in the original image (such as the texture on the brick wall) should be ignored and the prominent structure (like the edges of building or windows) should be maintained. This is well done in median filter pyramid and KAZE's nonlinear pyramid. However, the boundaries are blurred in Gaussian filter pyramid, resulting in a loss of localization and feature describing.

At each level of the image pyramid, we need to calculate main orientation of each detected point. The concept of intensity centroid was first proposed in [15]. It defines the moments as:

$$m_{pq} = \sum_{x,y} x^p y^q I(x,y) \tag{1}$$

where $I(x,y)$ denotes the intensity of pixel at the position (x,y), and the intensity centroid is located in:

$$C \triangleq (C_x, C_y) = \left(\frac{m_{10}}{m_{00}}, \frac{m_{01}}{m_{00}}\right) \tag{2}$$

Denoting the geometric center of a feature patch as $O \triangleq$

Figure 2: Comparison between the Gaussian filter, median filter and nonlinear diffusion scale pyramid. (a): original image. (b, c, d):Gaussian filter pyramid, KAZE's scale pyramid and median filter pyramid at the same scale level.

(O_x, O_y), direction of the vector $\overrightarrow{OC}$ is determined as the main orientation of the local interest point patch. We can calculate an angle θ by:

$$\theta = \begin{cases} \tan^{-1}\dfrac{O_y - C_y}{O_x - C_x}, & if \quad C_x \leq O_x \\ \tan^{-1}\dfrac{O_y - C_y}{O_x - C_x} + \pi, & if \quad C_x > O_x \end{cases} \tag{3}$$

Then the patch is rotated by θ degrees before calculating description, this can help resisting the influence of image rotation.

3.2 Sparse orthogonal autoencoder descriptor

The local information used to generate feature description varies from method to method. SIFT [12] counts the histogram of gradient orientation. While it is time consuming to calculate the gray level gradient. BRIEF and some other binary descriptors [4, 10] use simple binary tests between pixels to represent features, which is fast to generate but weak in expression ability.

In order to overcome these problems, here we propose a Local Sparse Orthogonal Descriptor (LSOD) for feature description. With a trained autoencoder we can encode the descriptor of a local image patch efficiently. Learning local features needs large amounts of image patches as the training data. Sampling patches in image database randomly is a common approach. But in our case, we only care about how the autoencoder will represent the interest point patches, such as the corners. So we construct a training set with 500k colored patches sampled from the PASCAL 2006 database [6], using the enhanced FAST detector introduced in section 3.1. We train an autoencoder on the image patch data, using the neural network shown in the Figure 3 (a).

Having one image patch $x = \left[x^{(1)}, x^{(2)}, \ldots, x^{(n)}\right]^T$ as the input layer 1, with the weight matrix $W^{(1)} \in R^{h \times n}$ and the activation function $f(x)$, often sigmoid function $f(x) = \dfrac{1}{1+e^{-x}}$ is used, we can get the output of the hidden layer

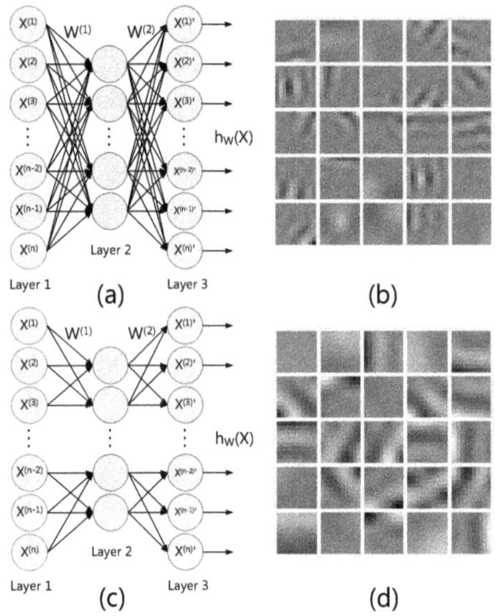

Figure 3: The neural network model and the visualization of features learned by the network. First Row: fully-connected autoencoder. Second Row: partially-connected autoencoder. Best viewed in color.

2 as: $a^{(2)} = f(W^{(1)}x)$, h is the number of hidden units. Similarly, we can calculate the output of layer 3 as: $a^{(3)} = f(W^{(2)}a^{(2)})$, $a^{(3)}$ is also denoted as $h_W(x)$.

A sparse autoencoder tries to learn a function $h_W(x) \approx x$ with some sparsity constraint. Given the training data set $X = [x_1, x_2, \ldots, x_N]$ of the interest point patches, we can calculate the average activation of the jth hidden unit as:

$$\hat{\rho}_j = \frac{1}{N}\sum_{i=1}^{N}\left[a_j^{(2)}(x_i)\right] \tag{4}$$

then enforce the constraint $\hat{\rho}_j = \rho$ to guarantee the sparsity of autoencoder, where ρ is a sparsity parameter, which is usually a small number close to zero. A relaxed penalty term is used here to replace the constraint $\hat{\rho}_j = \rho$:

$$\sum_j \rho \log\frac{\rho}{\hat{\rho}_j} + (1-\rho)\log\frac{1-\rho}{1-\hat{\rho}_j} \tag{5}$$

This term can also be written as the KL divergence:

$$\sum_j KL(\rho \| \hat{\rho}_j) \tag{6}$$

By means of gradient descent method, we can minimize the cost function and get the optimized encoding parameter $W^{(1)}$, which is visualized in the Figure 3 (b). It shows that the different hidden units have learned to detect edges in the image patch. However, in this fully-connected autoencoder, each hidden unit is only sensitive to a partial region of local image patch, and more than one units may detect the edges with same texture, color or orientation, just differing in position. This means that there exits high parameter redundancy in the fully-connected autoencoder. To cope with this problem, we propose a partially-connected autoencoder, as shown in Figure 3 (c). We split the whole network into m weight-sharing sub-networks, with the advantage that we only need to train the sub-autoencoder one time instead of training m different sub-autoencoders. Although the training data is m times bigger than the original data, we reduce the number of parameters by m^2 times. And the training time is reduced by about m times than the original autoencoder in our experiments. As shown in Figure 3 (d), the hidden units of partially-connected autoencoder detect more distinctive edge features, which can generate more discriminatory descriptions.

However, the partially-connected autoencoder still could not eliminate the similarity between the learned features totally. So we enforce another constraint that the weight matrix W must be an orthogonal matrix. In order to make the optimization tractable, we use a Frobenius norm as a relaxed penalty term added to the cost function. Finally the overall cost function of our problem is:

$$\begin{aligned} J(W) = & \frac{1}{N}\sum_{i=1}^{N}\|h_W(x_i) - x_i\|^2 + \beta\sum_j KL(\rho\|\hat{\rho}_j) \\ & + \gamma\|WW^T - I\|_F \end{aligned} \tag{7}$$

After training the sparse orthogonal autoencoder, a weight matrix $W^{(1)}$ is obtained and we can encode a local patch x with the descriptor $W_s^{(1)}R_\theta x$, where the rotation matrix R_θ makes the patch rotate to the main direction, and $W_s^{(1)}$ denotes the parameters $W^{(1)}$ resized to the corresponding scale level.

Thus, our LSOD descriptor becomes:

$$descriptor = \frac{W_s^{(1)}R_\theta x}{\|W_s^{(1)}R_\theta x\|} \tag{8}$$

The normalization ensures that patches in different scales return same descriptors, it also helps resisting the illumination variance.

4. EXPERIMENTS

In this section we present the evaluation results of our descriptor on standard datasets and its comparisons to state-of-the-art descriptors. For SIFT, SURF we use the implementations included in OpenCV. For KAZE, AKAZE and DSP-SIFT, the original codes provided by the authors were used. We set $\rho = 0.01, \beta = 5, \gamma = 1$ to train the autoencoder. All experiments results were obtained on a Core i5 Quad 3.0GHz laptop computer.

4.1 Interest point matching

In this section, we evaluate our descriptor on the standard Oxford dataset, which contains images with different geometric and photometric transformations, such as : viewpoint change, scale change, image rotation, image blur, illumination change and JPEG compression.

We use the evaluation criterion proposed by Mikolajczyk and Schmid [13] which is based on the number of correct and false matches between image pair. We use the nearest neighbor distance ratio (NNDR) as the matching strategy, which accepts a match if the distance ratio between the first and second nearest neighbors is below a threshold. The results are presented with recall versus 1-precision curves,

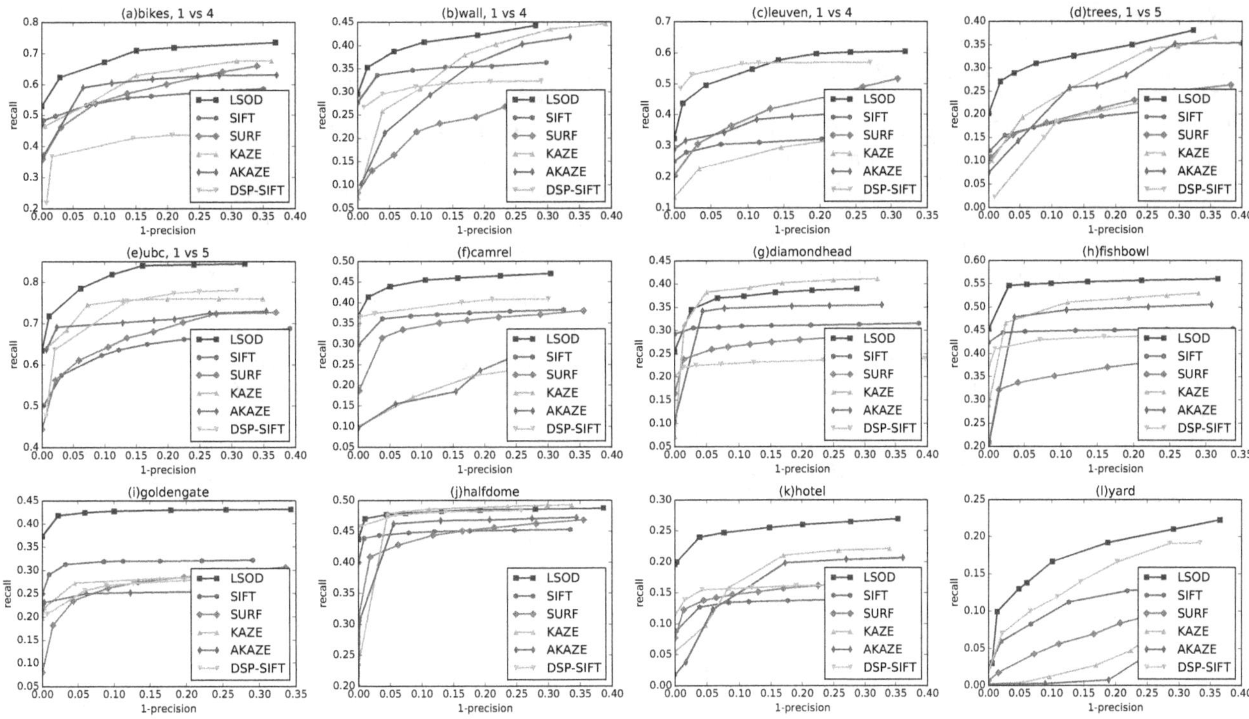

Figure 4: Interest points matching experiment results.(a)-(e): On Oxford dataset. (f)-(l): On Adobe Panorama dataset. Best viewed in color.

which is computed based on different matching thresholds:

$$recall = \frac{\#correct\,matches}{\#correspondences} \tag{9}$$

$$1 - precision = \frac{\#false\,matches}{\#allmatches} \tag{10}$$

The experiment results are plotted in Figure 4(a)-(e). Obviously, our LSOD gives the best results overall. Other methods, each with its strengths, rank 2nd to 6th on different image transformations. As can be observed, the proposed LSOD obtains a high discriminative power while staying robust to many image transformation.

4.2 Test on panorama dataset

One mainly application of image matching is panorama image stitching. Adobe Panoramas Dataset consists of several panorama image sets in different scenes, together with ground truth homographies for each overlapping image pair. We still use the same evaluation criterion as section 4.1. The results plotted in Figure 4(f)-(l) shows that our LSOD outperforms other descriptors on this panorama image dataset. It is appropriate for image stitching application and capable in variant scenes.

4.3 Timing Evaluation

In this section we perform a timing evaluation for a comparison between these feature descriptors. Considering that different methods detect different numbers of interest points, we record the total time of detecting and computing features divided by the number of detected points. The test uses the the first image of each scene in standard Oxford dataset.

Table 1 shows the average timing results in milliseconds

Table 1: Timing evaluation result.

Method	LSOD	SIFT	SURF	KAZE	AKAZE	DSP-SIFT
time(ms)	**0.038**	0.132	0.054	0.411	0.131	1.324

for detecting and computing each local feature patch. As can be observed, our LSOD feature is more computational efficient than other descriptors. It is about 4 times faster than SIFT and 1.5 times faster than SURF. KAZE is computational expensive due to the calculation of nonlinear scale pyramid. AKAZE is about 3 times faster than KAZE, but it is only comparable to SIFT. DSP-SIFT is the slowest may because its implementation is based on unoptimized MATLAB code.

5. CONCLUSIONS

In this paper we proposed a Local Sparse Orthogonal Descriptor (LSOD) for image matching. Compared with the previously proposed methods, experimental results show that LSOD is superior both in discriminative expression and efficient computational process.

6. ACKNOWLEDGMENTS

This paper is supported by NSFC (No. 61272247, 61533012, 61472075), the 863 National High Technology Research and Development Program of China (SS2015AA020501), the Basic Research Project of "Innovation Action Plan" (16JC1402800) and the Major Basic Research Program (15JC1400103) of Shanghai Science and Technology Committee.

7. REFERENCES

[1] P. F. Alcantarilla, A. Bartoli, and A. J. Davison. Kaze features. In *Computer Vision–ECCV 2012*, pages 214–227. Springer, 2012.

[2] P. F. Alcantarilla and T. Solutions. Fast explicit diffusion for accelerated features in nonlinear scale spaces. *IEEE Trans. Patt. Anal. Mach. Intell*, 34(7):1281–1298, 2011.

[3] H. Bay, T. Tuytelaars, and L. Van Gool. Surf: Speeded up robust features. In *Computer vision–ECCV 2006*, pages 404–417. Springer, 2006.

[4] M. Calonder, V. Lepetit, C. Strecha, and P. Fua. Brief: Binary robust independent elementary features. In *Computer Vision–ECCV 2010*, pages 778–792. Springer, 2010.

[5] J. Dong and S. Soatto. Domain-size pooling in local descriptors: Dsp-sift. In *Proceedings of the IEEE Conference on Computer Vision and Pattern Recognition*, pages 5097–5106, 2015.

[6] M. Everingham, A. Zisserman, C. Williams, and L. Van Gool. The pascal visual object classes challenge 2006 (voc 2006) results. 2006.

[7] C. Harris and M. Stephens. A combined corner and edge detector. In *Alvey vision conference*, volume 15, page 50. Citeseer, 1988.

[8] Q. V. Le, W. Y. Zou, S. Y. Yeung, and A. Y. Ng. Learning hierarchical invariant spatio-temporal features for action recognition with independent subspace analysis. In *Computer Vision and Pattern Recognition (CVPR), 2011 IEEE Conference on*, pages 3361–3368. IEEE, 2011.

[9] C.-Y. Lee, S. Xie, P. Gallagher, Z. Zhang, and Z. Tu. Deeply-supervised nets. *arXiv preprint arXiv:1409.5185*, 2014.

[10] S. Leutenegger, M. Chli, and R. Y. Siegwart. Brisk: Binary robust invariant scalable keypoints. In *Computer Vision (ICCV), 2011 IEEE International Conference on*, pages 2548–2555. IEEE, 2011.

[11] Y. Li, Y. Wang, W. Huang, and Z. Zhang. Automatic image stitching using sift, 2008.

[12] D. G. Lowe. Distinctive image features from scale-invariant keypoints. *International journal of computer vision*, 60(2):91–110, 2004.

[13] K. Mikolajczyk and C. Schmid. A performance evaluation of local descriptors. *Pattern Analysis and Machine Intelligence, IEEE Transactions on*, 27(10):1615–1630, 2005.

[14] P. Piccinini, A. Prati, and R. Cucchiara. Real-time object detection and localization with sift-based clustering. *Image and Vision Computing*, 30(8):573–587, 2012.

[15] P. L. Rosin. Measuring corner properties. *Computer Vision and Image Understanding*, 73(2):291–307, 1999.

[16] E. Rosten and T. Drummond. Machine learning for high-speed corner detection. In *Computer Vision–ECCV 2006*, pages 430–443. Springer, 2006.

[17] E. Rosten, R. Porter, and T. Drummond. Faster and better: A machine learning approach to corner detection. *Pattern Analysis and Machine Intelligence, IEEE Transactions on*, 32(1):105–119, 2010.

[18] N. Snavely, S. M. Seitz, and R. Szeliski. Skeletal graphs for efficient structure from motion. In *CVPR*, volume 1, page 2, 2008.

[19] B. Telle, M.-J. Aldon, and N. Ramdani. Camera calibration and 3d reconstruction using interval analysis. In *Image Analysis and Processing, 2003. Proceedings. 12th International Conference on*, pages 374–379. IEEE, 2003.

[20] X. Wang and W. Fu. Optimized sift image matching algorithm. In *Automation and Logistics, 2008. ICAL 2008. IEEE International Conference on*, pages 843–847. IEEE, 2008.

Frustratingly Easy Cross-Modal Hashing

Dekui Ma†, Jian Liang§,¶,*, Xiangwei Kong†, Ran He§,‡,¶
† School of Information and Communication Engineering, Dalian University of Technology
§ Center for Research on Intelligent Perception and Computing (CRIPAC),
National Laboratory of Pattern Recognition (NLPR), CASIA
‡ CAS Center for Excellence in Brain Science and Intelligence Technology (CEBSIT)
¶ University of Chinese Academy of Sciences (UCAS)
madk@mail.dlut.edu.cn, {jian.liang, rhe}@nlpr.ia.ac.cn, kongxw@dlut.edu.cn

ABSTRACT

Cross-modal hashing has attracted considerable attention due to its low storage cost and fast retrieval speed. Recently, more and more sophisticated researches related to this topic are proposed. However, they seem to be inefficient computationally for several reasons. On one hand, learning coupled hash projections makes the iterative optimization problem challenging. On the other hand, individual collective binary codes for each content are also learned with a high computation complexity. In this paper we describe a *simple yet effective* cross-modal hashing approach that can be implemented in just three lines of code. This approach first obtains the binary codes for one modality via unimodal hashing methods (e.g., iterative quantization (ITQ)), then applies simple linear regression to project the other modalities into the obtained binary subspace. Obviously, it is non-iterative and parameter-free, which makes it more attractive for many real-world applications. We further compare our approach with other state-of-the-art methods on four benchmark datasets (i.e., the Wiki, VOC, LabelMe and NUS-WIDE datasets). Despite its extraordinary simplicity, our approach performs remarkably and generally well for these datasets under different experimental settings (i.e., large-scale, high-dimensional and multi-label datasets).

CCS Concepts

•**Information systems** → **Top-k retrieval in databases;** *Novelty in information retrieval; Similarity measures;* Web indexing;

Keywords

cross-modal hashing; cross-media retrieval; image and text; double alignment

1. INTRODUCTION

With the fast development of the Internet, multi-modal data posted on the websites (e.g., Twitter and Facebook) are emerging, which makes retrieving heterogeneous content become more and more significant. Over the last decade, numerous cross-modal retrieval approaches [2, 31, 9] have been proposed, several unsupervised methods [10, 11] are also proposed. [15] first proposed a cross-modal retrieval method based on classification models. [14] further proposed a cross-modal learning method based pairwise classification, and obtained better retrieval performance. Recently owing to the benefits of lower storage costs and higher query speeds, hashing methods [25, 21, 27, 5] have gained even more popularity over traditional cross-modal retrieval methods. Since the text (i.e., articles, textual descriptions and tags) and image modality are even common in real-world web applications, we mainly focus on the text-image cross-modal retrieval in this work.

Cross-modal hashing (CMH) methods aim to map heterogeneous data into the common low-dimensional hamming space, where similarities among both intra- and inter- modalities are preserved. For semantic-preserving hashing methods, the heterogeneous data sharing the identical labels are required to be close to each other in the hamming space. The key issue for CMH is how to exploit the relationship of heterogeneous data efficiently for obtaining the hash projections.

Depending on whether the semantic labels for the observations are utilized or not, existing CMH methods can be roughly divided into two categories: supervised [32, 26, 13] and unsupervised [29, 3, 19] methods. Among the unsupervised ones, [8] extended [24] to the multimodal setting through minimizing the weighted distance, while [3] utilized collective matrix factorization from different modalities of one instance to obtain the hash functions with latent factor model. Besides, [29] captured the salient structures of images and learns latent concepts from texts through using sparse coding and matrix factorization respectively.

Supervised CMH methods make full use of provided semantic labels to learn discriminative hash functions via some other criterion like label-similarity preserving [6]. [28] tried to maximize the semantic correlation and learn the hash functions greedily. [13] made full use of the semantic similarity matrix to obtain the optimal binary codes for each observation. [1] was proposed to embed data from different feature space into a common metric space.

Furthermore, CMH methods can be optimized via two solutions, i.e., iterative and two-step optimization methods. When the former ones optimize the overall objective function iteratively, the two-step solutions first obtain an optimal binary code for each pair, then minimize the objective w.r.t. merely hash functions. Regarding of the time complexity, the iterative solution needs to optimize the binary codes and hash functions simultaneously, resulting in a higher time complexity. The two-step framework seems simple, however, it takes too much time in finding optimal binary codes for multiple modalities.

*The corresponding author; the first two authors contributed equally to this paper.

MM '16, October 15–19, 2016, Amsterdam, The Netherlands.

DOI: http://dx.doi.org/10.1145/2964284.2967218

Intuitively, unimodal hashing consists of two procedures, 1) finding the corresponding holes (binary codes) in hamming space, 2) solving the parameters of assumed hash functions which map origin features into known holes. The key issue for two-step CMH methods is how to obtain the code for each multimodal content efficiently. Here we propose a novel strategy double alignment based hashing (DASH) for the trivial two-step framework. The code generated by one single modality is reused for the other modality. In that way, we avoid the huge time-complexity and pass the semantic information from generated codes instead of explicit semantic labels, which proves effective for cross-modal learning. Extensive experimental results under large-scale, high-dimensional, multi-label settings are shown in the experiment section to validate the effectiveness and efficiency of our DASH method.

2. CORRELATION ALIGNMENT CROSS-MODAL HASHING

In this section, we first introduce some preliminary knowledge such as notations, terms and definition of hash function. Then we provide some motivations behind our proposed DASH and implementation details. Without loss of generality, we consider bimodal case (i.e., image-tag or image-text) for each instance, which is easy to present and understand.

2.1 Notations and Problem Definition

Supposing that we have n observations described in two modalities $X^{(m)} \in \mathbf{R}^{d_m \times n}$, $x_i^{(m)}$ denotes the i-th observation in the m-th modality, and d_m is the dimensionality of the m-th modality. Moreover, we also have *semantic labels* $y_i \in \{0,1\}^k$ for each observation $x_i = [x_i^{(1)}, x_i^{(2)}]$, $i \in [1, n]$, where k is the amount of semantic categories, and $y_{i,j} = 1$ denotes that the i-th observation belongs to the j-th category. Note that each observation is not limited to one semantic category (e.g., on multi-label datasets).

For each matrix $\mathbf{M} \in \mathbb{R}^{n \times m}$, its i-th row, j-th column are denoted by $\mathbf{m}^i$, $\mathbf{m}_j$ respectively, and $M_{i,j}$ lies in the i-th row and j-th column. The Frobenius norm of any matrix $\mathbf{M}$ is defined as $||\mathbf{M}||_F = \sqrt{\sum_{i=1}^n ||\mathbf{m}^i||_2^2}$, and the trace of the square matrix M is defined as $Tr(\mathbf{M}) = \sum_i \mathbf{M}_{i,i}$. Moreover, M^T denotes the transpose of a vector or matrix M.

The goal of CMH is to learn two hash functions $\{f_m(\cdot)\}_{m=1}^2$ for each modality. The functions $f_m(\cdot)$ are further defined as below: $f_m(x_i^{(m)}) = sgn(W_m^T x_i^{(m)})$, $sgn(\cdot)$ denotes the element-wise sign function, and $W_m \in \mathbf{R}^{d_m \times c}$ is the learned projection matrix, where c is the length of binary codes. Without loss of generality, we assume that the data points are all zero-centered, i.e., $\sum_{i=1}^n x_i^{(1)} = \mathbf{0}$, $\sum_{i=1}^n x_i^{(2)} = \mathbf{0}$.

2.2 Motivation and Framework

Recently, SePH [13] exploits Kullback-Leibler divergence with the semantic label similarities matrix to seek optimal binary codes for multiple observations, then applies logistic regression to obtain corresponding hash projections. This method resembles the framework of two-step unimodal hashing in [12], which also first learns the optimal binary code via semantic or locality preserving criterion, followed by learning hash functions via boosting tree or other various classifiers. However, both of them suffer from large computational complexity during the first stage, which are not flexible for large-scale data hashing.

ITQ [4] proposes a classic iterative quantization method to generate binary codes, which enjoys a linear time complexity $\mathcal{O}(n)$ in training data size n and achieves promising retrieval results at the same time. Inspired by the success achieved by the co-training strategy [30, 23], we attempt to directly utilize the binary codes generated by such fast unimodal hashing methods, and apply them to the other embedded modality to discover the optimal hash function. In this way, we can avoid the huge time complexity brought by seeking optimal binary codes and hash projections simultaneously. Besides, benefiting from the semantic embedding such as Canonical Correlation Analysis (CCA), we still preserve the semantic similarities in the hamming space. The overview of our proposed DASH is shown in Figure 1, and we summarize the algorithm in Algorithm 1.

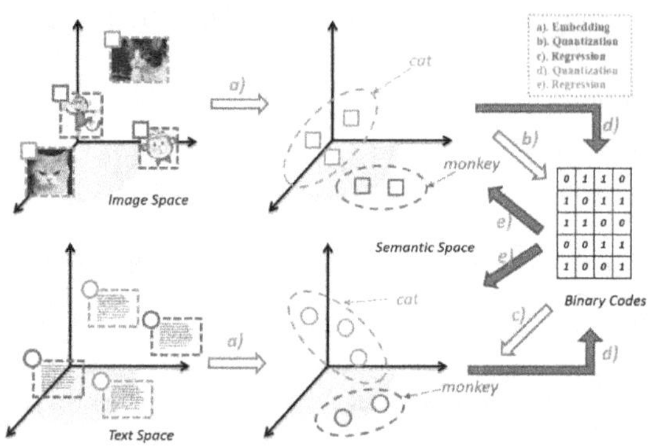

Figure 1: Overview of the proposed DASH, circles denote the text modality while squares denote the image modality. Red and green indicates two semantic categories, 'monkey' and 'cat', respectively. Our DASH follows unidirectional path *'a-b-c'* while traditional two-step methods go along with the path *'a-d-e'* and iterative methods follows the cycled path *'a-(d-e)$_n$'*. (Best viewed in colors).

2.3 Relationship to Iterative View-specific CMH Methods

Most previous view-specific works on CMH try to obtain the binary codes $B_m \in \{+1, -1\}^{c \times n}$ and hash function $W_m \in \mathbb{R}^{d_m \times c}$, $m = 1, 2$ in a unified framework as is shown below:

$$\min_{W_1, W_2, B_1, B_2} \mathcal{L} = ||B_1 - W_1^T X^{(1)}||_F^2 + ||B_2 - W_2^T X^{(2)}||_F^2 + \alpha\Omega(Y, B_1, B_2) + \beta\Phi(W_1, W_2), \tag{1}$$

where $\Omega(Y, B_1, B_2) = ||B_1 - B_2||_F^2$ is an ordinary alignment setting to keep codes close to each other. Note that $||B_1 - B_2||_F^2$ equals to $-2tr(B_1^T B_2) + const$ due to the hard discrete constraints.

Given B_1 and W_1 from last iteration, we minimize the following term versus B_2 and W_2 (here $\Phi(W_1, W_2) = \gamma \sum_i ||W_i||_F^2$),

$$\min_{B_2, W_2} ||B_2 - W_2^T X^{(2)}||_F^2 - 2\alpha tr(B_1^T B_2) + \gamma ||W_2||_F^2. \tag{2}$$

Then the optimal W_2 is explicitly given by following term,

$$\arg\min_{W_2} ||B_2 - W_2^T X^{(2)}||_F^2 = (X^{(2)} X^{(2)T} + \gamma I)^{-1} X^{(2)} B_2^T. \tag{3}$$

The term of miminizing B_2 is given below,

$$\min_{B_2} ||B_2 - W_2^T X^{(2)}||_F^2 - 2\alpha tr(B_1^T B_2) = -2tr((W_2^T X^{(2)} + \alpha B_1)^T B_2) + const. \tag{4}$$

When the trade-off parameter α becomes larger, the optimal code B_2 apparently equals to B_1. This result also corresponds with our

DASH, because the feedback from B_2 to B_1 is ignored due to the equivalence. Hence, we propose a rather simple approach to deal with cross-modal hashing problem. Note that γ is fixed to $1e^{-3}$, resulting in our DASH being a parameters-free method.

Algorithm 1 **D**ouble **A**lignment ba**S**ed **H**ashing (DASH)

Input: Data matrices $X^{(m)} \in \mathbf{R}^{d_m \times n}$, $m = 1, 2$, semantic label matrix $Y \in \mathbf{R}^{k \times n}$ and hash code length c.
Output: Hash projection matrices $W_m \in \mathbf{R}^{d_m \times c}$, $m = 1, 2$.
Procedure:
1. Obtain $\hat{X}^{(1)}$ and $\hat{X}^{(2)}$ via CCA with Y;
2. Solve B and W_1 with $\hat{X}^{(1)}$ via ITQ;
3. Compute W_2 with Eqn. 3.

2.4 Computation Complexity Analysis

During the training procedure, CCA semantic embedding of each modality occupy $\mathcal{O}(d_1^3 + d_2^3 + ncd_1 + ncd_2)$ due to the generalized eigenvalue decomposition problem, and ITQ occupies $\mathcal{O}(c^3 + ncd_1)$, where c is the code length. Besides, least-square linear regression occupies $\mathcal{O}(nd_2^2c)$. As a result, the overall time complexity is $\mathcal{O}(nd^2 + d^3)$, where d is the dimension of longer original features. It is linear with the training data size, guaranteeing that our DASH is suitable for large-scale datasets.

3. EXPERIMENTS

We compared our DASH with other start-of-the-art cross-modal hashing algorithms on four commonly used datasets: Wiki, LabelMe, VOC and NUS-WIDE. To compare the general retrieval performance on various settings, we extend these four basic datasets to seven different detailed datasets shown in Table 1.

3.1 Experimental Setting

3.1.1 Datasets

The **Wiki** dataset consists of 2,866 items which were collected from 'Wikipedia' and classified into 10 semantic categories. We adopt the same setting as [2]. The **Wiki++** extends the Wiki dataset with deep image features and high-dimensional text feature as [22].

The **LabelMe** dataset [17] consists of 2,686 fully annotated outdoor images from 8 scene categories. For the text modality, we generate the object account vector via the LabelMe toolbox the same as [11]. It is randomly split into training/testing set as 3:1.

The **VOC_full** dataset consists of 9,963 image-tag pairs classified as 20 different classes [7]. We choose images associated with only one object as [18] and obtain the **VOC** dataset. The CNN image features are extracted via Caffe[1] of the VOC_full dataset, denoted as **VOC_full+**.

The **NUS-WIDE** dataset [13, 3] is composed of 186,577 annotated web images associated with corresponding tags. Here we choose 1% of image-text pairs coming from the largest 10 classes randomly as our testing data, and the rest as training data.

3.1.2 Baseline Methods

Unsupervised methods: CVH [8], CMFH [3], PDH [16] and LSSH [29]; Supervised ones, SePH [13], IMH [20], CMSSH [1] and SCM [28]. For fair comparisons, all training instances are utilized for IMH and linear regression hash functions are adopted for SePH. All the source codes are kindly provided by the authors.

The methods of obtaining B with image and text are abbreviated as DASH_i and DASH_t, respectively. The definitions of

[1]http://caffe.berkeleyvision.org/.

Table 1: Statistics of several benchmark datasets (For label*, s denotes single-label, and m denotes multi-label).

Dataset	# training / testing	# image / text	# categories	labels*
Wiki	2,173 / 693	128 / 10	10	s
Wiki++	2,173 / 693	4,096 / 5,000	10	s
LabelMe	2,014 / 672	512 / 470	8	s
VOC	2,808 / 2,841	512 / 399	20	s
VOC_full	5,011 / 4,952	512 / 399	20	m
VOC_full+	5,011 / 4,952	4,096 / 399	20	m
NUS-WIDE	184,671 / 1,906	500 / 1,000	10	m

SCM_Orth and SCM_Seq are the same as [28]. We regard two items as true neighbors if they share one same class at least. In order to eliminate the effects of random initialization, all the results are averaged over 5 runs.

3.1.3 Evaluation Scheme

Performance of all the methods are measured with the mean average precision (MAP) that is widely used for retrieval methods and normalized discounted cumulative gain (NDCG), which is widely used for single-label and multi-label retrieval methods, respectively.

3.2 Experimental Results

3.2.1 Results for the Single-label Datasets

Table 2: MAP@100 result on three single-label datasets for different tasks. The best values are shown in boldface.

Image query	Wiki			LabelMe			VOC		
# of bits	16	24	32	16	24	32	16	24	32
CMSSH	23.1	18.9	17.3	53.1	55.4	57.9	22.5	20.3	24.1
CVH	21.3	20.3	19.6	33.2	32.8	31.5	19.8	19.0	18.9
IMH	20.4	19.2	18.5	41.5	38.4	31.5	27.4	24.6	22.9
PDH	21.6	20.5	22.6	50.6	51.3	54.7	20.0	20.3	20.0
CMFH	25.9	27.6	28.1	36.8	42.3	24.0	29.5	31.0	30.3
SCM_Orth	19.8	19.4	17.3	47.3	48.0	46.9	23.4	20.9	20.3
SCM_Seq	27.7	27.4	27.6	64.2	65.0	66.7	34.7	38.2	37.9
SePH	28.2	**30.9**	**31.1**	65.6	65.3	**70.1**	38.5	43.6	46.3
DASH_i	24.4	24.1	24.0	49.4	41.9	40.3	34.0	28.2	24.4
DASH_t	**28.9**	30.5	**31.1**	**67.7**	**68.6**	69.2	**45.0**	**49.2**	**52.1**
Text query	Wiki			LabelMe			VOC		
# of bits	16	24	32	16	24	32	16	24	32
CMSSH	22.3	22.5	19.2	53.7	57.6	57.7	26.9	27.2	27.6
CVH	19.7	19.4	18.3	34.7	34.2	33.3	20.3	19.5	19.3
IMH	21.2	19.5	18.4	43.1	39.5	36.6	27.9	24.9	23.0
PDH	19.4	18.2	19.4	50.7	51.7	53.0	19.1	18.9	19.2
CMFH	26.5	28.6	29.5	36.7	43.3	24.6	28.2	30.8	28.8
SCM_Orth	19.7	19.4	16.4	36.0	36.7	29.9	21.9	19.6	18.0
SCM_Seq	27.6	27.6	28.4	69.8	69.9	72.0	31.0	34.0	34.2
SePH	27.4	28.6	**31.1**	73.2	74.2	**77.8**	34.3	39.1	39.0
DASH_i	24.9	25.8	25.4	57.4	50.4	51.6	37.7	30.4	29.9
DASH_t	**27.8**	**29.6**	29.5	**74.7**	**74.3**	74.5	**38.1**	**39.2**	**39.8**

We compare DASH with other methods on three single-label datasets – Wiki, LabelMe and VOC. From Table 2, we can find that DASH_t and SePH achieve the best performances on all three datasets. Especially for the VOC dataset, our DASH outperforms the second best SePH at every bit.

3.2.2 Results for the High-dimensional Datasets

We evaluate DASH and other methods on two high dimensional datasets, Wiki++ and VOC_full+. From Table 3, we can summarize that DASH achieves the best MAP in all cases, especially on VOC_full+, its MAP value achieves nearly 90%. Compared with the second best method on Wiki++, the maximum gains of DASH_t reaches 14.2% for image query and 13.1% for text query. Note that DASH_i and DASH_t have similar performance. That is because the image is represented by 4,096 CNN features, which have rich semantic information.

Table 3: MAP@100 result on two high-dimensional datasets for different tasks. The best values are shown in boldface.

Image query	Wiki++			VOC_full+		
# of bits	16	24	32	16	24	32
CMSSH	31.1	29.3	29.7	70.4	73.7	73.8
CVH	14.3	14.3	14.3	74.2	72.4	66.7
IMH	28.6	28.4	27.7	68.5	65.2	63.7
CMFH	25.6	26.9	27.0	47.3	48.6	47.8
SCM_Orth	25.8	24.2	21.0	67.2	65.4	63.8
SCM_Seq	37.2	40.1	40.1	77.3	80.2	81.8
SePH	33.6	36.5	37.0	82.8	84.8	87.3
DASH_i	39.7	38.5	38.2	**84.9**	88.1	88.1
DASH_t	**42.5**	**41.7**	**41.6**	**84.9**	**88.9**	**89.2**
Text query	Wiki++			VOC_full+		
# of bits	16	24	32	16	24	32
CMSSH	37.0	31.2	32.4	70.4	77.1	79.2
CVH	15.0	14.7	14.3	80.5	75.9	65.6
IMH	28.9	29.0	28.0	71.1	66.2	61.3
CMFH	25.6	26.8	26.9	46.0	49.2	49.7
SCM_Orth	26.8	24.8	21.9	71.4	64.1	57.3
SCM_Seq	40.5	43.3	42.7	76.7	80.0	81.1
SePH	42.7	44.4	45.9	83.6	86.5	88.5
DASH_i	46.2	44.8	45.4	**91.8**	93.1	92.8
DASH_t	**48.3**	**47.8**	**47.5**	88.8	**93.6**	**94.2**

3.2.3 *Results for the Large-scale Datasets*

Table 4: Result on large-scale dataset (NUS-WIDE) for different tasks. The best values are shown in boldface.

Image query	MAP@100			NDCG@10		
# of bits	16	24	32	16	24	32
CMSSH	52.6	51.2	50.6	34.2	33.2	32.0
CVH	49.3	48.1	46.7	32.2	31.5	30.1
IMH	45.8	45.4	43.9	28.8	28.4	27.2
PDH	52.7	53.5	54.5	31.6	32.3	33.1
CMFH	41.2	40.7	42.7	23.9	23.8	25.6
SCM_Orth	49.8	47.7	47.9	32.6	31.1	31.4
SCM_Seq	**60.5**	**61.1**	**62.6**	40.3	40.1	**42.0**
SePH	55.0	56.7	56.0	35.1	35.7	36.1
DASH_i	55.7	55.3	55.9	34.4	33.7	34.5
DASH_t	60.3	57.9	59.1	**41.1**	**40.8**	41.6
Text query	MAP@100			NDCG@10		
# of bits	16	24	32	16	24	32
CMSSH	50.1	49.1	48.8	35.2	28.9	30.1
CVH	49.5	48.2	46.8	33.6	32.4	31.0
IMH	45.5	45.3	44.0	29.1	28.9	28.1
PDH	52.7	51.3	51.5	31.6	32.1	30.4
CMFH	41.2	41.8	42.7	24.3	26.2	27.1
SCM_Orth	49.1	45.4	47.3	30.9	28.8	27.9
SCM_Seq	58.2	60.6	61.4	36.8	38.7	40.8
SePH	57.5	58.6	57.2	38.5	36.8	37.5
DASH_i	**61.9**	**63.8**	**63.4**	**44.0**	**47.4**	**45.8**
DASH_t	58.4	57.3	56.6	38.9	37.6	37.2

From Table 4, we can easily find that our DASH performs best for text query. For image query, the MAP values of SCM are higher than that of DASH, while the NDCG values of SCM are smaller, which illustrates that DASH_t achieve better results with slight retrieval instances.

3.2.4 *Results for the Multi-label Datasets*

Cross-modal methods are evaluated on two multi-label datasets – NUS_WIDE and VOC_full. It is shown in Table 4 and Table 5 that DASH, SCM_Seq and SePH always perform better than other methods. In more than half of the cases, DASH achieves the best performance, especially in NUS_WIDE for text query.

Table 5: Result on multi-label dataset (VOC_full) for different tasks. The best values are shown in boldface.

Image query	MAP@100			NDCG@10		
# of bits	16	24	32	16	24	32
CMSSH	55.0	55.0	54.7	23.0	26.5	30.0
CVH	51.1	50.1	49.8	25.0	24.0	22.9
IMH	53.2	48.5	48.8	26.5	23.6	22.7
PDH	40.8	36.8	39.0	19.6	16.9	17.4
CMFH	50.5	52.6	52.6	25.1	25.9	26.0
SCM_Orth	51.2	49.3	49.4	24.5	23.4	23.4
SCM_Seq	56.1	60.1	61.3	27.8	**30.4**	**30.6**
SePH	**57.2**	58.9	**66.0**	25.8	26.7	27.3
DASH_i	55.8	54.1	54.4	**28.4**	27.4	26.7
DASH_t	**57.2**	**65.1**	65.3	28.3	30.1	29.7
Text query	MAP@100			NDCG@10		
# of bits	16	24	32	16	24	32
CMSSH	36.4	40.0	40.4	19.1	25.0	24.7
CVH	43.5	41.9	37.4	31.6	30.8	23.3
IMH	45.7	39.9	40.3	30.4	24.7	26.6
PDH	34.0	33.8	34.1	17.0	17.5	17.1
CMFH	41.6	44.3	43.3	26.7	31.2	28.5
SCM_Orth	42.5	38.6	35.1	29.9	25.1	21.8
SCM_Seq	47.7	50.5	52.2	32.5	32.9	36.5
SePH	50.2	52.8	**53.2**	35.7	38.0	37.6
DASH_i	**52.1**	48.1	46.3	**41.4**	35.8	33.0
DASH_t	51.4	**53.1**	51.8	40.4	**42.2**	**40.2**

3.2.5 *Training Time*

Table 6 shows the training time of the supervised hashing methods on three challenging datasets. Generally, CMSSH, SCM_Orth and DASH cost relatively less time, and DASH always performs better than the other two methods. Generally, the retrieval performance of SePH always follows SCM_seq and DASH in above tables. However, SePH is not applicable for the large-scale datasets. Even SePH randomly chooses 5,000 data as training set, the training time of SePH is still huge. By contrast, SCM has a strong ability to adapt to large-scale data, but it needs large training time cost in terms of processing high-dimensional data. For the VOC_full+ dataset, the training time of SePH and SCM is 100 times more than DASH. Moreover, the training time of SCM_seq is linear with the length of hash bits. Generally, our DASH is applicable for high-dimensional, large-scale datasets, and achieves the best or competitive cross-modal retrieval performance.

Table 6: Training time (in seconds) of supervised hashing methods on three datasets.

datasets	NUS-WIDE		VOC_full+		Wiki++	
# of bits	16	32	16	32	16	32
CMSSH	8	8	17	15	18	13
IMH	64	64	121	113	17	11
SCM_Orth	2	2	90	105	12	13
SCM_Seq	10	14	1,489	2,909	318	863
SePH	2,378	2,647	1,858	1,900	759	861
DASH_i	12	14	16	16	6	6
DASH_t	12	13	16	16	6	6

4. CONCLUSION

In this paper, we propose a *simple yet effective* approach named DASH for cross-modal hashing. This non-iterative and parameter-free DASH method is frustratingly easy to implement in three code lines. Extensive experimental results illustrate the advantages of our DASH over other existing state-of-the-art methods, which further confirms that DASH is flexible to various settings, including high-dimensional, large-scale and multi-label datasets.

5. ACKNOWLEDGMENTS

This work was supported by National Natural Science Foundation of China (Grant No. 61502073, 61473289), the Open Projects Program of National Laboratory of Pattern Recognition (No. 2014-07349) and the Strategic Priority Research Program of the Chinese Academy of Sciences (Grant No. XDB02070000).

6. REFERENCES

[1] M. M. Bronstein, A. M. Bronstein, F. Michel, and N. Paragios. Data fusion through cross-modality metric learning using similarity-sensitive hashing. In *Proc. CVPR*, pages 3594–3601, 2010.

[2] J. Costa Pereira, E. Coviello, G. Doyle, N. Rasiwasia, G. R. Lanckriet, R. Levy, and N. Vasconcelos. On the role of correlation and abstraction in cross-modal multimedia retrieval. *IEEE Transactions on Pattern Analysis and Machine Intelligence*, 36(3):521–535, 2014.

[3] G. Ding, Y. Guo, and J. Zhou. Collective matrix factorization hashing for multimodal data. In *Proc. CVPR*, pages 2083–2090, 2014.

[4] Y. Gong, S. Lazebnik, A. Gordo, and F. Perronnin. Iterative quantization: A procrustean approach to learning binary codes for large-scale image retrieval. *IEEE Transactions on Pattern Analysis and Machine Intelligence*, 35(12):2916–2929, 2013.

[5] R. He, Y. Cai, T. Tan, and L. S. Davis. Learning predictable binary codes for face indexing. *Pattern Recognition*, 48(10):3160–3168, 2015.

[6] X. He and P. Niyogi. Locality preserving projections. In *Proc. NIPS*, pages 153–160, 2003.

[7] S. J. Hwang and K. Grauman. Reading between the lines: Object localization using implicit cues from image tags. *IEEE Transactions on Pattern Analysis and Machine Intelligence*, 34(6):1145–1158, 2012.

[8] S. Kumar and R. Udupa. Learning hash functions for cross-view similarity search. In *Proc. IJCAI*, pages 1360–1365, 2011.

[9] J. Liang, D. Cao, R. He, Z. Sun, and T. Tan. Principal affinity based cross-modal retrieval. In *Proc. ACPR*, pages 126–130, 2015.

[10] J. Liang, R. He, Z. Sun, and T. Tan. Group-invariant cross-modal subspace learning. In *Proc. IJCAI*, pages 1739–1745, 2016.

[11] J. Liang, Z. Li, D. Cao, R. He, and J. Wang. Self-paced cross-modal subspace matching. In *Proc. SIGIR*, pages 569–578, 2016.

[12] G. Lin, C. Shen, and A. van den Hengel. Supervised hashing using graph cuts and boosted decision trees. *IEEE Transactions on Pattern Analysis and Machine Intelligence*, (11):2317–2331, 2015.

[13] Z. Lin, G. Ding, M. Hu, and J. Wang. Semantics-preserving hashing for cross-view retrieval. In *Proc. CVPR*, pages 3864–3872, 2015.

[14] A. K. Menon and D. Surian. Cross-modal retrieval : a pairwise classification approach. In *Proc. SDM*, pages 199–207, 2015.

[15] N. Rasiwasia, J. Costa Pereira, E. Coviello, G. Doyle, G. R. Lanckriet, R. Levy, and N. Vasconcelos. A new approach to cross-modal multimedia retrieval. In *Proc. MM*, pages 251–260, 2010.

[16] M. Rastegari, J. Choi, S. Fakhraei, D. Hal, and L. Davis. Predictable dual-view hashing. In *Proc. ICML*, pages 1328–1336, 2013.

[17] B. C. Russell, A. Torralba, K. P. Murphy, and W. T. Freeman. Labelme: a database and web-based tool for image annotation. *International Journal of Computer Vision*, 77(1-3):157–173, 2008.

[18] A. Sharma, A. Kumar, H. Daume III, and D. W. Jacobs. Generalized multiview analysis: A discriminative latent space. In *Proc. CVPR*, pages 2160–2167, 2012.

[19] X. Shen, F. Shen, Q.-S. Sun, and Y.-H. Yuan. Multi-view latent hashing for efficient multimedia search. In *Proc. MM*, pages 831–834, 2015.

[20] J. Song, Y. Yang, Y. Yang, Z. Huang, and H. T. Shen. Inter-media hashing for large-scale retrieval from heterogeneous data sources. In *Proc. SIGMOD*, pages 785–796, 2013.

[21] D. Wang, X. Gao, X. Wang, and L. He. Semantic topic multimodal hashing for cross-media retrieval. In *Proc. IJCAI*, pages 3890–3896, 2015.

[22] K. Wang, R. He, L. Wang, W. Wang, and T. Tan. Joint feature selection and subspace learning for cross-modal retrieval. *IEEE Transactions on Pattern Analysis and Machine Intelligence*, 2015. doi:10.1109/TPAMI.2015.2505311.

[23] W. Wang and Z.-H. Zhou. Analyzing co-training style algorithms. In *Proc. ECML*, pages 454–465, 2007.

[24] Y. Weiss, A. Torralba, and R. Fergus. Spectral hashing. In *Proc. NIPS*, pages 1753–1760, 2009.

[25] B. Wu, Q. Yang, W.-S. Zheng, Y. Wang, and J. Wang. Quantized correlation hashing for fast cross-modal search. In *Proc. IJCAI*, pages 3946–3952, 2015.

[26] Z. Yu, F. Wu, Y. Yang, Q. Tian, J. Luo, and Y. Zhuang. Discriminative coupled dictionary hashing for fast cross-media retrieval. In *Proc. SIGIR*, pages 395–404, 2014.

[27] D. Zhai, H. Chang, Y. Zhen, X. Liu, X. Chen, and W. Gao. Parametric local multimodal hashing for cross-view similarity search. In *Proc. IJCAI*, pages 2754–2760, 2013.

[28] D. Zhang and W.-J. Li. Large-scale supervised multimodal hashing with semantic correlation maximization. In *Proc. AAAI*, pages 2177–2183, 2014.

[29] J. Zhou, G. Ding, and Y. Guo. Latent semantic sparse hashing for cross-modal similarity search. In *Proc. SIGIR*, pages 415–424, 2014.

[30] Z.-H. Zhou and M. Li. Semi-supervised regression with co-training. In *Proc. IJCAI*, pages 908–913, 2005.

[31] F. Zhu, L. Shao, and M. Yu. Cross-modality submodular dictionary learning for information retrieval. In *Proc. CIKM*, pages 1479–1488, 2014.

[32] Y. Zhuang, Z. Yu, W. Wang, F. Wu, S. Tang, and J. Shao. Cross-media hashing with neural networks. In *Proc. MM*, pages 901–904, 2014.

Families in the Wild (FIW): Large-Scale Kinship Image Database and Benchmarks

Joseph P. Robinson, Ming Shao, Yue Wu, Yun Fu
Dept. of Electrical and Computer Engineering
Northeastern University
Boston, MA, USA
{jrobins1, mingshao, yuewu, yunfu}@ece.neu.edu

ABSTRACT

We present the largest kinship recognition dataset to date, Families in the Wild (FIW). Motivated by the lack of a single, unified dataset for kinship recognition, we aim to provide a dataset that captivates the interest of the research community. With only a small team, we were able to collect, organize, and label over 10,000 family photos of 1,000 families with our annotation tool designed to mark complex hierarchical relationships and local label information in a quick and efficient manner. We include several benchmarks for two image-based tasks, kinship verification and family recognition. For this, we incorporate several visual features and metric learning methods as baselines. Also, we demonstrate that a pre-trained Convolutional Neural Network (CNN) as an off-the-shelf feature extractor outperforms the other feature types. Then, results were further boosted by fine-tuning two deep CNNs on FIW data: (1) for kinship verification, a triplet loss function was learned on top of the network of pre-train weights; (2) for family recognition, a family-specific softmax classifier was added to the network.

1. INTRODUCTION

Automatic kinship recognition in visual media is essential for many real-world applications: *e.g.*, kinship verification [6, 8, 11, 26, 29, 30, 31, 32], automatic photo library management [21, 27], historic lineage and genealogical studies [2], social-media analysis [10], along with many of security applications addressing missing persons, human trafficking, crime scene investigations, and even our overall human sensing capabilities–ultimately, enhancing surveillance systems used in both real-time (*e.g.*, vBOLO [28] mission[1,2]) or offline (*e.g.*, searching for a subject in a large *gallery* [3, 23]). Thus, a gallery of imagery annotated with rich family information should lead to more powerful multimedia retrieval tools and complement many existing facial recognition systems (e.g., FBI's NGI[3]). However, even after several years (*i.e.*, since 2010 [8]) there are only a few vision systems capable of handling such tasks. Hence, kin-based technology in the visual domain has yet to truly evolve from research-to-reality.

[1]vBOLO: joint effort of two DHS Centers of Excellence, ALERT & VACCINE (http://www.northeastern.edu/alert)
[2]https://web-oup.s3-fips-us-gov-west-1.amazonaws.com/

MM '16, October 15-19, 2016, Amsterdam, Netherlands

DOI: http://dx.doi.org/10.1145/2964284.2967219

Figure 1: Sample faces chosen of 11 relationship types of FIW. *Parent-child*: (top row) Father-Daughter (F-D), Father-Son (F-S), Mother-Daughter (M-S) Mother-Son (M-S). *Grandparent-grandchild*: (middle row) same labeling convention as above. *Siblings*: (bottom row) Sister-Brother (SIBS), Brother-Brother (B-B), Sister-Sister (S-S).

We believe the reason that kinship recognition technology has not yet advanced to real-world applications is two-fold:

1. Current image datasets available for kinship tasks are not large enough to reflect the true data distributions of a family and their members.

2. Visual evidence for kin relationships are less discriminant than class types of other, more conventional machine vision problems (*e.g.*, facial recognition or object classification), as many hidden factors affect the similarities of facial appearances amongst family members.

To that end, we introduce a large-scale image dataset for kinship recognition called Families in the Wild (FIW). To the best of our knowledge, FIW is by far the **largest** and **most comprehensive** kinship dataset available in the vision and multimedia communities [see Table 1]. FIW includes 11,193 unconstrained family photos of 1,000 families, which is nearly 10x more than the next-to-largest, Family101 [7]. Also, it is from these 1,000 families that 418,060 image pairs for the 11 relationship types (see Figure 1 & Table 2).

Thus far, attempts at image-based kinship recognition have focused on facial features, as is the case for this work as well. Kinship recognition is typically conducted in one or more of the following modes: (1) kinship verification, which is a binary classification problem, *i.e.*, determine whether

[3]https://www.eff.org/2014/fbi-to-have-52M-face-photos

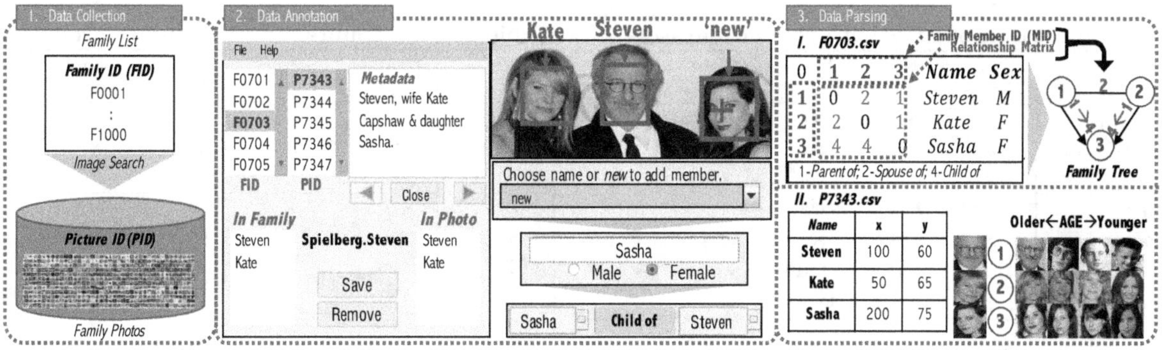

Figure 2: Method to construct FIW. ***Data Collection:*** **a list of candidate families (with an unique FID) and photos (with an unique PID) are collected.** ***Data Annotation:*** **a labeling tool optimized the process of marking the complex hierarchical nature of the 1,000 family trees of FIW.** ***Data Parsing:*** **post-processed the two sets of labels generated by the tool to partition data for kinship verification and family recognition.**

or not two or more persons are blood-related (kin or non kin); (2) family recognition, which is a multi-class classification problem where the aim is to determine the family of an individual in a photo; (3) kinship identification, which is a fine-grain categorization problem, as the aim is to determine the type of relationship shared between two or more people. We focus on the first and second modes in this paper, kinship verification and family recognition, which we briefly discuss next.

Kinship Verification. Previous efforts mainly focused on 4 *parent-child* pairs. As research in both psychology and computer vision revealed, different kin relations render different familiar features, and the 4 kin relations are usually modeled independently. Hence, it is important to have more kin relationship types accessible. Thus, FIW provides 11 pair-wise types (see Figure 1): 7 returning types (*i.e.*, *parent-child* and *siblings*), but in sample sizes scaling up 105x larger; and 4 types being offered to the research community for the first time (*i.e.*, *grandparent-grandchild*). Also, existing datasets contain, at most, only a couple of hundred pairs per category (*i.e.*, 1,000 in total). Such a insufficient amount leads to models overfitting the training data. Hence, existing models do not generalize well to new, unseen test data. However, FIW now makes 418,060 pairs available.

Family Recognition. A challenging task that grows more difficult with more families. This is because families contain large intra-class variations, often with overlaps between classes. Similar to conventional facial recognition, when the targets are unconstrained *faces in the wild* [12] (*i.e.*, pose, illumination, expression, and scene variant), the level of difficulty further increases, which is the same with kinship recognition. These are, unfortunately, challenges that need to be overcome. Thus, FIW poses realistic challenges needed to be surpassed before transitioning to real-world applications.

Contributions. We make three distinct contributions:

1. We introduce the largest visual kinship dataset to date, Families in the Wild (FIW).[4] FIW is complete with rich label information for 1,000 family trees, from which 11 kin relationship types were extracted in numbers that are orders of magnitude times larger than other datasets. This was made possible with an efficient annotation tool and procedure (Section 2).

2. We provide several benchmarks on FIW for both kinship verification and family recognition, including various low-level features, metric learning methods, and pre-trained Convolutional Neural Network (CNN) models. See Section 3 for experimental settings and results.

3. We fine-tune two CNNs: one with a triplet-loss layer on top, and the other with a softmax loss. Both yield a significant boost in performance over all other benchmarks for both tasks (Section 3.2).

[4]FIW will be available upon publication of this paper.

2. FAMILIES IN THE WILD

We now discuss the procedure followed to collect, organize, and label 11,193 family photos of 1,000 families with minimal manual labor. Then, we statistically compare FIW with other related datasets.

2.1 Building FIW

The goal for FIW was to collect approximately 10 photos for 1,000 families, each with at least 3 family members). We now summarize the method for achieving this in a three step process, which is visually depicted in Figure 2.

Step 1: Data Collection. A list of over 1,000 candidate families was made. To ensure diversity, we targeted groups of public figures worldwide by searching for <*ethnicity* OR *country*> AND <*occupation*> online (*e.g.*, *MLB* [Baseball] *Players*, *Brazilian Politicians*, *Chinese Actors*, *Denmark + Royal Family*). Family photos were then collected using various search engines (*e.g.*, Google, Bing, Yahoo) and social media outlets (*e.g.*, Pinterest) to widen the search space. Those with at least 3 family members and 8 family photos were added to FIW under an assigned Family ID (FID).

Step 2: Data Annotation. We developed a labeling tool to quickly annotate a large corpus of family photos. All photos for a given FID are labeled sequentially. Labeling is done by clicking a family member's face. Next, a face detector initializes a resizable box around the face. Faces unseen by the detector are discarded, as these are assumed to be poorly resolved. The tool then prompts for the name of the member via a drop-down menu. For starters, option new adds a member to a family under a unique member ID (MID), which prompts for the name, gender, and relationship types shared with others previously added to the current family (or FID). From there onward, labeling family members is just a matter of clicking.

Table 1: Comparison of FIW with related datasets.

Dataset	No. Family	No. People	No. Faces	Age Varies	Family Trees
CornellKin[8]	×	300	300	×	×
UBKinFace[20, 25]	×	400	600	✓	×
KFW-I[16]	×	1,066	1,066	×	×
KFW-II[16]	×	2,000	2,000	×	×
TSKinFace[18]	×	2,589	×	✓	✓
Family101[7]	101	607	14,816	✓	✓
FIW(Ours)	**1,000**	**10,676**	**30,725**	✓	✓

Step 3: Dataset Parsing. Two sets of labels are generated in Step 2: (1) *image-level*, containing names and corresponding facial locations; (2) *family-level*, containing a relationship matrix that represents the entire family tree. Relationship matrices are then referenced to generate lists of member pairs for the 11 relationship types. Next, face detections are normalized and cropped with [14], then are stored according the previously assigned *FID→ MID*. Lastly, lists of image pairs are generated for both kinship verification and family recognition.

2.2 Database Statistics

Our FIW dataset far outdoes its predecessors in terms of quantity, quality, and purpose. FIW contains 11,193 family photos of 1,000 different families. There are about 10 images per family that include at least 3 and as many as 24 family members. We compare FIW to related datasets in Table 1 and 2. Clearly, FIW provides more families, identities, facial images, relationship types, and labeled pairs– the pair count of FIW is orders of magnitude bigger than the next-to-largest (*i.e.*, KFW-II).

3. EXPERIMENTS ON FIW

In this section, we first discuss visual features and related methods used to benchmark the FIW dataset. We then report and review all benchmark results. Finally, we discuss the two methods used to fine-tune the pre-trained CNN model: (1) training a triplet-loss for kinship verification and (2) learning a softmax classifier for family recognition. Both obtain top scores in the respective task.

3.1 Features and Related Methods

All features and methods covered here were used to benchmark FIW. First, we review handcrafted features, Scale Invariant Feature Transformation (SIFT) and Local Binary Patterns (LBP), which are both widely used in kinship verification [16] and facial recognition [19]. Next, we introduce VGG-Face, the pre-trained CNN model used here as an off-the-shelf feature extractor. Lastly, we review other related metric learning methods.

SIFT [15] features have been widely applied in object and face recognition. As done in [16], we resized all facial images to 64×64, and set the block size to 16×16 with a stride of 8. Thus, there were a total of 49 blocks for each image, yielding a feature vector of length $128 \times 49 = 6,272$D.

LBP [1] has been frequently used for texture analysis and face recognition, as it describes the appearance of an image in a small, local neighborhood around a pixel. Once again, we followed the feature settings of [16] by first resizing each facial image to 64×64, and then extracting LBP features

Table 2: Pair counts for FIW and related datasets.

	KFW-II [16]	Sibling Face [10]	Group Face [10]	Family 101[7]	FIW (Ours)
B-B	×	232	40	×	**86,000**
S-S	×	211	32	×	**86,000**
SIB	×	277	53	×	**75,000**
F-D	250	×	69	147	**45,000**
F-S	250	×	69	213	**43,000**
M-D	250	×	62	148	**44,000**
M-S	250	×	70	184	**37,000**
GF-GD	×	×	×	×	**410**
GF-GS	×	×	×	×	**350**
GM-GD	×	×	×	×	**550**
GM-GS	×	×	×	×	**750**
Total	1,000	720	395	607	**418,060**

from 16×16 non-overlapping blocks with a radius of 2 pixels and number of neighbors (*i.e.*, samples) set to 8. We then generated a 256D histogram from each, yielding a final feature vector of length $256 \times 16 = 4,096$D.

VGG-Face CNN [17] uses a "Very Deep" architecture with very small convolutional kernels (*i.e.*, 3×3) and convolutional stride (*i.e.*, 1 pixel). This model was pre-trained on over 2.6 million images of 2,622 celebrity identities. For this, each face image was resized to 224×224 and then fed-forward to the second-to-last fully-connected layer (*i.e.*, fc7) of the CNN model, producing a 4,096D feature vector.

Metric Learning methods are commonly employed in the visual domain, some designed specifically for kinship recognition [5, 16, 18] and some as generic metric learning methods [4]. We chose two representative methods from these two categories to report benchmarks on, Neighborhood Repulsed Metric Learning (NRML) [16] and Information Theoretic Metric Learning (ITML) [4].

3.2 Fine-Tuned CNN Model

Weights of deep networks are trained on larger amounts of generic source data, then fine-tuned on target data, which utilize a wider, more readily available source domain that resembles the target in either modality, view, or both [9]. Following this notion, and motivated by recent success with deep learning on faces [17, 22, 24], we fine-tuned the VGG-Face model, improving results for both kinship verification and family recognition.

Kinship Verification. In kinship verification, for each fold we select the families which have more than 10 images in the rest four folds. 90% images of each family are used to fine-tune the model and the rest for validation. An average of 8,295 images are selected. The experimental results of this part can be found in Table 3 and Figure 3. This is so far the best results on FIW. Specifically, we remove the last fully-connected layer which is used to identify 2,622 people and employed a triplet-loss [19] as the loss function. The second-to-last fully-connected layer was the only non-frozen layer of the original CNN model, with an initial learning rate of 10^{-5} that decreased by a factor of 10 every 700 iterations (out of 1,400). Batch size was 128 images, and other network settings were the same as the original VGG-Face model. Training was done on a single GTX Titan X with about 10GB GPU memory. Fine-tuning was done using the renown Caffe [13] framework.

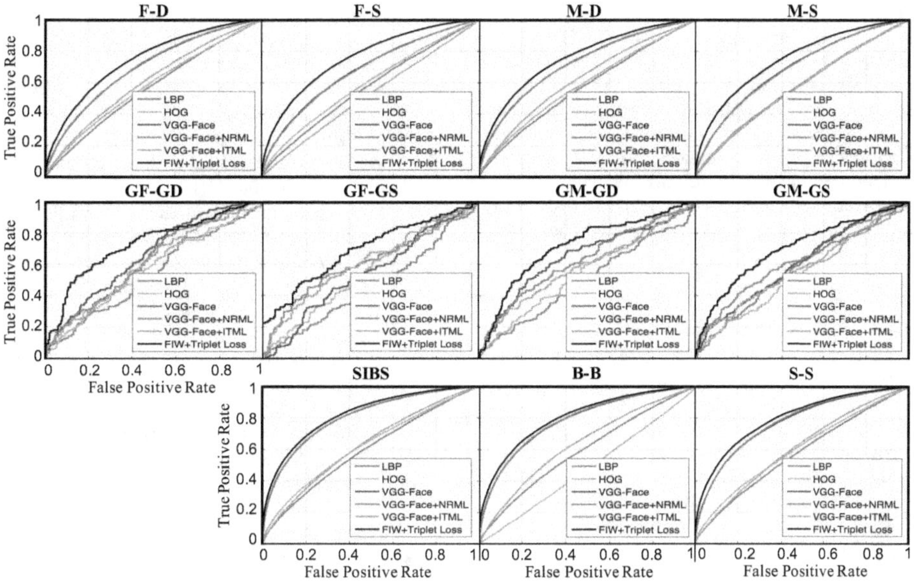

Figure 3: Relationship specific ROC curves depicting performance of each method.

Table 3: Verification accuracy scores (%) for 5-fold experiment on FIW. No family overlap between folds.

	F-D	F-S	M-D	M-S	SIBS	B-B	S-S	GF-GD	GF-GS	GM-GD	GM-GS	Avg.
SIFT	56.1	56.5	56.4	55.3	58.7	50.3	57.4	59.3	66.9	60.4	56.9	57.7±4.0
LBP	55.0	55.3	55.4	55.9	57.1	56.8	55.8	58.5	59.1	55.6	60.1	56.8±1.7
VGG-Face	64.4	63.4	66.2	64.0	73.2	71.5	70.8	64.4	68.6	66.2	63.5	66.9±3.5
Fine-Tuned CNN	**69.4**	**68.2**	**68.4**	**69.4**	**74.4**	**73.0**	**72.5**	**72.9**	**72.3**	**72.4**	**68.3**	**71.0±2.3**

Family Recognition. As visual kinship recognition is essentially related to facial features, we froze the weights in the lower levels of the VGG-Face network, and replaced with a new softmax layer to classify the 316 families. Other settings are the same as those used for kinship verification.

3.3 Experimental Settings

In this section, we provide benchmarks on FIW using all features and related methods mentioned in the previous section. Dimensionality of each feature is reduced to 100D using PCA. Experiments were done following a 5-fold cross-validation protocol. Each fold was of equal size and with no family overlap between folds.

Experiment 1: Kinship Verification. We randomly select an equal number of positive and negative pairs for each fold family. Cosine similarity is computed for each pair in the test fold. The average verification rate of all folds is reported in Table 3, showing that kinship verification is a challenging task. While some relation are relatively easy to recognize, *e.g.*, B-B, SIBS, S-S through SIFT, LBP, and VGG-Face features, results of other relations such as parent-child are still below 70.0%. Clearly, VGG-Face features are much better than hand-craft features. Notice grandparent-child pairs typically have higher accuracies than parent-child, which we believe is due to the differences in sample sizes. We also compare with the state-of-the-art metric learning methods, NRML and ITML [see Figure 3]. Showing improved scores for the low-level features, but still outperformed by the CNN model fine-tuned on FIW.

Table 4: Family Recognition accuracy scores (%) for 5-fold experiment on FIW (316 Families). No family overlap between folds.

	1	2	3	4	5	Avg.
VGG	9.6	14.5	11.6	12.7	13.1	12.3±1.8
Fine-tuned	**10.9**	**14.8**	**12.5**	**14.8**	**13.5**	**13.3±1.6**

Experiment 2: Family Recognition. We again follow the 5-fold cross-validation protocol with no family overlap. Families with 6 or more members, from which the 5 members with the most images were used. The results in Table 4 are from 316 families with 7,772 images. Folds were made up of one member for each family. Multi-class SVM was used to model VGG-Face features for each family (*i.e.*, one-vs-rest). We then improved the top-1 classification accuracy from 12.3±1.8 (%, VGG-Face) to 13.3±1.6 (%, our fine-tuned model).

4. DISCUSSION

We introduced a large-scale dataset of family photos captured in natural, unconstrained environments (*i.e.*, Families in the Wild). An annotation tool was designed to quickly generate rich label information for over 10,000 photos of 1,000 families. Emphasis was put on diversity (*i.e.*, families worldwide), data distribution (*i.e.*, at least 3 members and 8 photos per family), sample sizes (*i.e.*, multiple instances of each member, and at various ages), quality (*i.e.*, only faces seen by the detector), and quantity (*i.e.*, much more data and new relationship types).

There are many interesting directions for future work on our dataset. We currently only verify whether a pair of images is kin or non kin. However, also predicting the kin relationship type could lead to more value and practical usefulness. Thus, bringing us closer to doing fine-grain categorization on entire family trees. FIW will be an ongoing effort that will continually grow and evolve. See project page for downloads, updates, and to learn more about FIW.

Acknowledgements

This material is based upon work supported by the U.S. Department of Homeland Security, Science and Technology Directorate, Office of University Programs, under Grant Award 2013-ST-061-ED0001. The views and conclusions contained in this document are those of the authors and should not be interpreted as necessarily representing the official policies, either expressed or implied, of the U.S. Department of Homeland Security.

We would also like to thank all members of SMILE Lab who helped with the process of collecting and annotating the FIW dataset.

5. REFERENCES

[1] T. Ahonen, A. Hadid, and M. Pietikainen. Face description with local binary patterns: Application to face recognition. *IEEE Transactions on Pattern Analysis and Machine Intelligence (TPAMI)*, 28(12):2037–2041, 2006.

[2] M. Almuashi, S. Z. M. Hashim, D. Mohamad, M. H. Alkawaz, and A. Ali. Automated kinship verification and identification through human facial images: a survey. *Multimedia Tools and Applications*, pages 1–43, 2015.

[3] N. Crosswhite, J. Byrne, O. M. Parkhi, C. Stauffer, Q. Cao, and A. Zisserman. Template adaptation for face verification and identification. *arXiv preprint arXiv:1603.03958*, 2016.

[4] J. V. Davis, B. Kulis, P. Jain, S. Sra, and I. S. Dhillon. Information-theoretic metric learning. In *Proc. International Conference on Machine Learning (ICML)*, pages 209–216. ACM, 2007.

[5] A. Dehghan, E. Ortiz, R. Villegas, and M. Shah. Who do i look like? determining parent-offspring resemblance via gated autoencoders. In *Proc. IEEE Conference on Computer Vision and Pattern Recognition (CVPR)*, pages 1757–1764, 2014.

[6] H. Dibeklioglu, A. Salah, and T. Gevers. Like father, like son: Facial expression dynamics for kinship verification. In *Proc. IEEE International Conference on Computer Vision (ICCV)*, pages 1497–1504, 2013.

[7] R. Fang, A. Gallagher, T. Chen, and A. Loui. Kinship classification by modeling facial feature heredity. In *20th IEEE International Conference on Image Processing (ICIP)*, pages 2983–2987. IEEE, 2013.

[8] R. Fang, K. D. Tang, N. Snavely, and T. Chen. Towards computational models of kinship verification. In *IEEE International Conference on Image Processing (ICIP)*, pages 1577–1580. IEEE, 2010.

[9] R. B. Girshick, J. Donahue, T. Darrell, and J. Malik. Rich feature hierarchies for accurate object detection and semantic segmentation. *CoRR*, abs/1311.2524, 2013.

[10] Y. Guo, H. Dibeklioglu, and L. van der Maaten. Graph-based kinship recognition. In *International Conference on Pattern Recognition (ICPR)*, pages 4287–4292, 2014.

[11] J. Hu, J. Lu, J. Yuan, and Y.-P. Tan. *Large Margin Multi-metric Learning for Face and Kinship Verification in the Wild*, pages 252–267. Springer International Publishing, Cham, 2015.

[12] G. B. Huang, M. Ramesh, T. Berg, and E. Learned-Miller. Labeled faces in the wild: A database for studying face recognition in unconstrained environments. Technical Report 07-49, University of Massachusetts, Amherst, October 2007.

[13] Y. Jia, E. Shelhamer, J. Donahue, S. Karayev, J. Long, R. Girshick, S. Guadarrama, and T. Darrell. Caffe: Convolutional architecture for fast feature embedding. *arXiv preprint arXiv:1408.5093*, 2014.

[14] D. E. King. Dlib-ml: A machine learning toolkit. *Journal of Machine Learning Research*, 10:1755–1758, 2009.

[15] D. G. Lowe. Distinctive image features from scale-invariant keypoints. *International Journal of Computer Vision*, 60(2):91–110, 2004.

[16] J. Lu, X. Zhou, Y.-P. Tan, Y. Shang, and J. Zhou. Neighborhood repulsed metric learning for kinship verification. *IEEE Transactions on Pattern Analysis and Machine Intelligence (TPAMI)*, 36(2):331–345, 2014.

[17] O. M. Parkhi, A. Vedaldi, and A. Zisserman. Deep face recognition. In *Proc. British Machine Vision Conference (BMVC)*, 2015.

[18] X. Qin, X. Tan, and S. Chen. Tri-subject kinship verification: Understanding the core of A family. *CoRR*, abs/1501.02555, 2015.

[19] F. Schroff, D. Kalenichenko, and J. Philbin. Facenet: A unified embedding for face recognition and clustering. In *Proc. IEEE Conference on Computer Vision and Pattern Recognition (CVPR)*, pages 815–823, 2015.

[20] M. Shao, S. Xia, and Y. Fu. Genealogical face recognition based on ub kinface database. In *CVPR 2011 WORKSHOPS*, pages 60–65. IEEE, 2011.

[21] M. Shao, S. Xia, and Y. Fu. Identity and kinship relations in group pictures. In *Human-Centered Social Media Analytics*, pages 175–190. Springer, 2014.

[22] Y. Sun, X. Wang, and X. Tang. Deep learning face representation from predicting 10,000 classes. In *Proc. IEEE Conference on Computer Vision and Pattern Recognition (CVPR)*, pages 1891–1898, 2014.

[23] D. Wang, C. Otto, and A. K. Jain. Face search at scale: 80 million gallery. *CoRR*, abs/1507.07242, 2015.

[24] M. Wang, Z. Li, X. Shu, J. Tang, et al. Deep kinship verification. In *IEEE 17th International Workshop on Multimedia Signal Processing (MMSP)*, pages 1–6. IEEE, 2015.

[25] S. Xia, M. Shao, and Y. Fu. Kinship verification through transfer learning. In *Proc. International Joint Conferences on Artificial Intelligence (IJCAI)*, volume 22, pages 2539–2544, 2011.

[26] S. Xia, M. Shao, and Y. Fu. Toward kinship verification using visual attributes. In *Pattern Recognition (ICPR), 2012 21st International Conference on*, pages 549–552. IEEE, 2012.

[27] S. Xia, M. Shao, J. Luo, and Y. Fu. Understanding kin relationships in a photo. *IEEE Transactions on Multimedia*, 14(4):1046–1056, 2012.

[28] F. Xiong, M. Gou, O. Camps, and M. Sznaier. Person re-identification using kernel-based metric learning methods. In *European Conference on Computer Vision (ECCV)*, pages 1–16. Springer, 2014.

[29] H. Yan, J. Lu, W. Deng, and X. Zhou. Discriminative multimetric learning for kinship verification. *IEEE Transactions on Information Forensics and Security*, 9(7):1169–1178, 2014.

[30] H. Yan, J. Lu, and X. Zhou. Prototype-based discriminative feature learning for kinship verification. *IEEE Transactions on Cybernetics*, 45(11):2535–2545, 2015.

[31] X. Zhou, J. Hu, J. Lu, Y. Shang, and Y. Guan. Kinship verification from facial images under uncontrolled conditions. In *Proc. ACM International Conference on Multimedia*, pages 953–956. ACM, 2011.

[32] X. Zhou, J. Lu, J. Hu, and Y. Shang. Gabor-based gradient orientation pyramid for kinship verification under uncontrolled environments. In *Proc. ACM International Conference on Multimedia*, pages 725–728. ACM, 2012.

Enabling My Robot To Play Pictionary : Recurrent Neural Networks For Sketch Recognition

Ravi Kiran Sarvadevabhatla
ravikiran@grads.cds.iisc.ac.in

Jogendra Kundu*
jogendranathkundu@gmail.com

Venkatesh Babu R
venky@cds.iisc.ac.in

Video Analytics Lab
Department of Computational and Data Sciences
Indian Institute of Science
Bangalore, INDIA

ABSTRACT

Freehand sketching is an inherently sequential process. Yet, most approaches for hand-drawn sketch recognition either ignore this sequential aspect or exploit it in an ad-hoc manner. In our work, we propose a recurrent neural network architecture for sketch object recognition which exploits the long-term sequential and structural regularities in stroke data in a scalable manner. Specifically, we introduce a Gated Recurrent Unit based framework which leverages deep sketch features and weighted per-timestep loss to achieve state-of-the-art results on a large database of freehand object sketches across a large number of object categories. The inherently online nature of our framework is especially suited for on-the-fly recognition of objects as they are being drawn. Thus, our framework can enable interesting applications such as camera-equipped robots playing the popular party game Pictionary with human players and generating sparsified yet recognizable sketches of objects.

Keywords

object recognition, sketch, recurrent neural networks, deep features, sequence classification

1. INTRODUCTION

The process of freehand sketching has long been employed by humans to communicate ideas and intent in a minimalist yet almost universally understandable manner. In spite of the challenges posed in recognizing them [13], sketches have formed the basis of applications in areas of forensic analysis [11], electronic classroom systems [15], sketch-based retrieval [20, 13] etc.

Sketching is an inherently sequential process. The proliferation of pen and tablet based devices today enables us to capture and analyze the entire process of sketching, thus providing additional information compared to passive parsing of static sketched content. Yet, most sketch recognition approaches either ignore the sequential aspect or lack the ability to exploit it [20, 7, 18]. The few approaches which attempt to exploit the sequential sketch stroke data do so either in an unnatural manner [23] or impose restrictive constraints (e.g. Markov assumption) [1].

In our work, we propose a recurrent neural network architecture for sketch object recognition which exploits the long-term sequential and structural regularities in stroke data in a scalable manner. We make the following contributions:

- We propose the first deep recurrent neural network architecture which can recognize freehand sketches across a large number (160) of object categories. Specifically, we introduce a Gated Recurrent Unit (GRU)-based framework (Section 3.1) which leverages deep sketch features and weighted per-stroke loss to achieve state-of-the-art results.
- We show that the choice of deep sketch features and recurrent network architecture *both* play a crucial role in obtaining good recognition performance (Section 4.3).
- Via our experiments on sketches with partial temporal stroke content, we show that our framework recognizes the largest percentage of sketches (Section 4.3).

Given the on-line nature of our recognition framework, it is especially suited for on-the-fly interpretation of sketches as they are drawn. Thus, our framework can enable interesting applications such as camera-equipped robots playing the popular party game Pictionary [16] with human players, generating sparsified yet recognizable sketches of objects [17], interpreting hand-drawn digital content in electronic classrooms [15] etc.

2. RELATED WORK

To retain focus, we review approaches exclusively related to recognition of hand-drawn object sketches. Early datasets tended to contain either a small number of sketches and/or object categories [20, 14]. In 2012, Eitz et al. [7] released a dataset containing 20000 hand-drawn sketches across 250 categories of everyday objects. The dataset, currently the largest sketch object dataset available, provided the first opportunity to attempt the sketch object recognition problem at a relatively large-scale. Since its release, a number of approaches have been proposed to recognize freehand sketches of objects. The initial performance of hand-crafted feature-based approaches [13, 18] has been recently

---

*equal contribution as first author

MM '16, October 15-19, 2016, Amsterdam, Netherlands

DOI: http://dx.doi.org/10.1145/2964284.2967220

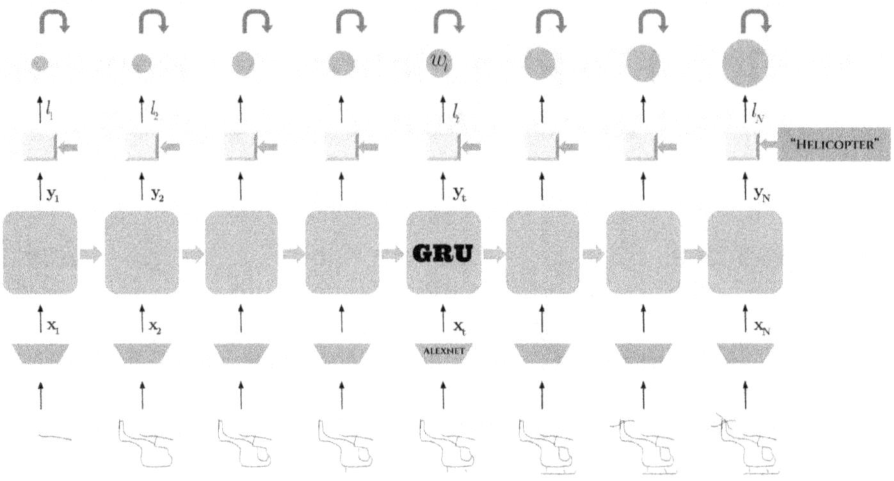

Figure 1: Overview of our sketch-recognition framework. Alexnet-based deep features $(\mathbf{x_1}, \mathbf{x_2}, \ldots, \mathbf{x_t}, \ldots)$ from each cumulative stroke image form the input to the GRU (blue), obtaining the corresponding prediction sequence $(\mathbf{y_1}, \mathbf{y_2}, \ldots, \mathbf{y_t}, \ldots)$. The per-timestep loss l_t is computed w.r.t ground-truth (green arrow) by the loss function (yellow box). This loss is weighted by a corresponding w_t (shown as proportionally sized gray circles) and backpropagated (purple curved arrow) for the corresponding time step t. Best viewed in color.

surpassed by deep feature-based approaches [17, 19], culminating in an custom-designed Convolutional Neural Network dubbed SketchCNN which achieved state-of-the-art results [23]. The approaches mentioned above are primarily designed for static, full-sketch object recognition. In contrast, another set of approaches attempt to exploit the sequential stroke-by-stroke nature of hand-drawn sketch creation [1, 22]. For example, Arandjelovic and Sezgin [1] propose a Hidden Markov Model (HMM)-based approach for recognizing military and crisis management symbol objects. Although mentioned above in the context of static object recognition, a variant of the SketchCNN [23] can also handle sequential stroke data. In fact, the authors demonstrate that exploiting the sequential nature of sketching process improves the overall recognition rate. However, given that CNNs are not inherently designed to preserve sequential "state", better results can be expected from a framework which handles sequential data in a more natural fashion. The approach we present in our paper aims to do precisely this. Our framework is based on Gated Recurrent Unit (GRU) networks recently proposed by Cho et al. [3]. GRU architectures share a number of similarities with the more popular Long Short Term Memory Networks [9] including the latter's ability to perform better [8] than traditional models (e.g. HMM) for problems involving long and complicated sequential structures. To the best of our knowledge, recurrent neural networks have not been utilized for online sketch recognition.

3. OUR RECOGNITION FRAMEWORK

3.1 Overview

Sketch creation involves accumulation of hand-drawn strokes over time. Thus, we require our recognition framework to optimally exploit object category evidence being accumulated on a per-stroke basis as well as temporally. Moreover, the variety in sketch-based depiction and intrinsic representational complexity of objects results in a large range for stroke-sequence lengths. Therefore, we require our recognition framework to address this variation in sequence lengths appropriately. To meet these requirements, we employ Gated Recurrent Unit (GRU) networks [3]. Our choice of GRU architecture is motivated by the observation that it involves learning a smaller number of parameters and performs better compared to LSTM in certain instances [4] including, as shall been seen (Section 4), our problem of sketch recognition as well.

A GRU network learns to map an input sequence $\mathbf{X} = (\mathbf{x_1}, \mathbf{x_2} \ldots \mathbf{x_N})$ to an output sequence $\mathbf{Y} = (\mathbf{y_1}, \mathbf{y_2} \ldots \mathbf{y_N})$. This mapping is performed by the following transformations which are applied at each time step:

$$r_t = \sigma(W_{xr}\mathbf{x_t} + W_{hr}h_{t-1} + b_r) \quad (1)$$

$$z_t = \sigma(W_{xz}\mathbf{x_t} + W_{hz}h_{t-1} + b_z) \quad (2)$$

$$\widetilde{h_t} = tanh(W_{xh}\mathbf{x_t} + U(r_t \odot h_{t-1}) + b_h) \quad (3)$$

$$h_t = (1 - z_t) \odot h_{t-1} + z_t \odot \widetilde{h_t} \quad (4)$$

$$\mathbf{y_t} = W_{hy}h_t \quad (5)$$

Here, $\mathbf{x_t}$ and $\mathbf{y_t}$ represent the t-th input and t-th output respectively, h represents the "hidden" sequence state of the GRU whose contents are regulated by parameterized gating units $r, z, \widetilde{h}$ and $\odot$ represents the elementwise dot-product. The subscripted Ws, bs and U represent the trainable parameters of the GRU. Please refer to Chung et al. [5] for details.

For each sketch, information is available at temporal stroke level. We use this to construct an image sequence $\mathcal{S} = (s_1, s_2 \ldots s_N)$ of sketch strokes cumulatively accumulated over time. Thus, s_N represents the full, final object sketch and N represents the number of sketch strokes or equivalently, time-steps (see Figure 1). To represent the stroke content for each $s_i \in \mathcal{S}$, we utilize deep features obtained when s_i is provided as input to Alexnet[1] [12]. The resulting

[1]Specifically, we remove classification layer and use outputs from final fully-connected layer of the resulting net as fea-

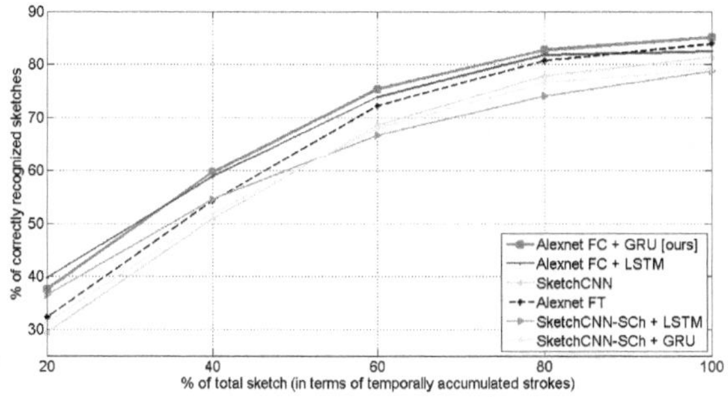

Figure 2: Comparison of online recognition performance for various classifiers. Our architecture recognizes the largest % of sketches at all levels of sketch completion. Best viewed in color.

deep feature sequence $\mathbf{X} = (\mathbf{x_1}, \mathbf{x_2} \ldots, \mathbf{x_N})$ forms the input sequence to GRU (see Figure 1). The GRU unit contains 3600 hidden units and its output is densely connected to a final softmax layer for classification. For better generalization, we include a dropout layer before the final classification layer which tends to benefit recurrent networks having a large number of hidden units. We used a dropout of 0.5 in our experiments.

3.2 Training

Our architecture produces an output prediction $\mathbf{y_t}$ for every time-step $t, 1 \leq t \leq N$ in the sequence. By comparing the predictions $\mathbf{y_t}$ with the ground-truth, we can determine the corresponding loss l_t for a fixed loss function (shown as a yellow box in Figure 1). This loss is weighted by a corresponding w_t and backpropagated) for the corresponding time step t. For the weighing function, we use

$$w_t = e^{-\alpha(1-\frac{t}{N})} \tag{6}$$

Thus, losses corresponding to final stages of sequence are weighted more to encourage correct prediction of the full sketch. Also, since w_t is non-zero, our design incorporates losses from all steps of the sequence. This has the net effect of encouraging correct predictions even in the early stages of the sequence. Overall, this feature enables our recognition framework to be accurate and responsive right from the beginning of the sketching process (Section 4) in contrast with frameworks which need to wait for the sketching to finish before analysis can begin. We additionally studied variations of the weighing function given in Equation (6) – using the final sequence member loss (i.e. $w_t = 0 \; \forall t \neq N$) and linearly weighted losses (i.e. $w_t = \frac{t}{N}$). We found that exponentially weighted loss[2] gave superior results.

To address the high variation of sequence length across sketches, we create batches of sketches having equal sequence length (i.e. N (Sec. 3.1)). These batches of varying size are randomly shuffled and delivered to the recurrent network during training. For each batch, categorical-cross-entropy loss is generated for each sequence by comparing the predictions with the ground-truth. The resulting losses are weighted (Equation (6)) on a per-timestep basis as described previously and back-propagated through the corresponding sequence during training. We used stochastic gradient descent with a learning rate of 0.001 for training.

tures.

[2]We used $\alpha = 10$ for our experiments.

CNN	RECURRENT NETWORK	#HIDDEN	AVG. ACC
Alexnet-FC	**GRU**	**3600**	**85.1%**
Alexnet-FC	LSTM	3600	82.5%
SketchCNN [23]	-	-	81.4%
Alexnet-FT	-	-	83.9%
SketchCNN-Sch-FC	LSTM	3600	78.8%
SketchCNN-Sch-FC	GRU	3600	79.1%

Table 1: Average recognition accuracy (rightmost column) for various architectures. #Hidden refers to the number of hidden units used in recurrent network. We obtain state-of-the-art results for sketch object recognition.

3.3 Category prediction

Suppose for a given input sequence $\mathbf{X} = (\mathbf{x_1}, \mathbf{x_2}, \ldots, \mathbf{x_N})$, the corresponding outputs at the softmax layer are $\mathbf{p_1}, \mathbf{p_2}, \ldots, \mathbf{p_N}$. Note that in our case, $\mathbf{x_t} \in \mathbb{R}^d$ where d is the dimension of deep feature $\mathbf{x_t}$ and $\mathbf{p_t} \in \mathbb{R}^K$ where K is the number of object categories (160). To determine the final category label $c_\mathbf{X}$, we perform a weighted sum-pooling of the softmax outputs as $c_\mathbf{X} = \arg\max_j \sum_{t=1}^{N} \mathbf{p_t}^j w_t$ where w_t is as given in Equation (6) and $1 \leq j \leq K$. We explored various other softmax output pooling schemes – last sequence member-based prediction ($c_\mathbf{X} = \arg\max_j \mathbf{p_N}^j$), max-pooling ($c_\mathbf{X} = \arg\max_j [\max_t \mathbf{p_t}^j]$), mean-pooling ($c_\mathbf{X} = \arg\max_j \sum_{t=1}^{N} \mathbf{p_t}^j / N$). From our validation experiments, we found weighted sum-pooling to be the best choice overall.

4. EXPERIMENTS

4.1 Data

In addition to obtaining the best results among approaches using handcrafted features, the work of Rosalia et al. [18] was especially instrumental in identifying a 160-category subset of the TU Berlin dataset which could be unambiguously recognized by humans. Consequently, our experiments are based on this curated 160-category subset of sketches. Following Rosalia et al. [18], we use 56 sketches from each of the 160 categories. To ensure principled evaluation, we split the 56 sketches of each category randomly into sets containing 57%, 18% and 25% of sketches to be used for training, validation and testing respectively[3]. Additionally, we utilized the validation set exclusively for making choices related to architecture and parameter settings and performed a one-shot comparative evaluation of ours and competing approaches on the test set.

4.2 Other architectures

We compared our performance with the following architectures:

Alexnet-FT: As a baseline experiment, we fine-tuned Alexnet using our 160-category training data. To ensure sufficient data, we augmented the training data on the lines of Sarvadevabhatla et al. [17]. We also used the final fully-connected 4096-dimensional layer features as input to our

[3]Thus, we have 32, 10 and 14 sketches from each category in the training, validation and test sets respectively.

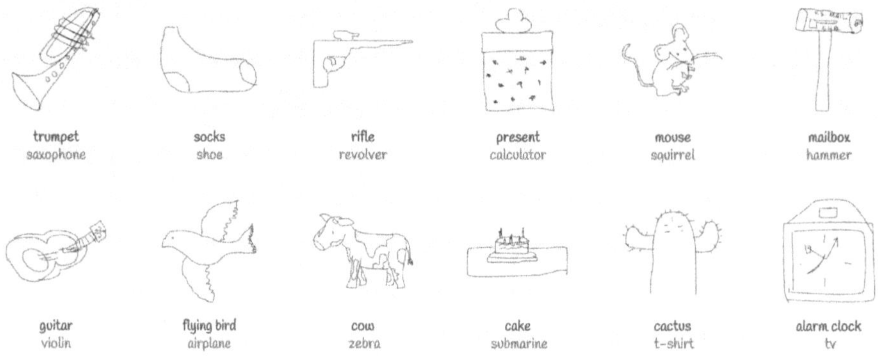

Figure 3: Examples of sketches misclassified by our framework. The ground-truth category is top label (blue) while the bottom label is our prediction (pink). Most of the misclassifications are reasonable errors.

recurrent architectures. We shall refer to such usage by ALEXNET-FC.

SketchCNN: This is essentially the deep architecture of Yu et al. [23] but retrained for the categories and splits mentioned in Section 4.1. Since CNNs do not inherently store "state", the authors construct six different sub-sequence stroke accumulation images which comprise the channels of the input representation to the CNNs. It comprises of five different CNNs, each trained for five different scaled versions of 256 × 256 sketches. The last fully-connected layer's 512-dimensional features from all the five CNNs are processed using a Bayesian fusion technique to obtain the final classification.

For our experiments, we also concatenated the 512 dimensional features from each scale of SKETCHCNN as the input feature to the recurrent neural network architectures that were evaluated. However, only the full 256 × 256 sketch was considered as the input to CNN (i.e. single-channel). For the rest of the paper, we refer to the resulting 2560-dimensional feature as SKETCHCNN-SCH-FC.

Recurrent architectures: We experimented with the number of hidden units, the number of recurrent layers, the type of recurrent layers (i.e. LSTM or GRU), the training loss function (Section 3.2) and various pooling methods for obtaining final prediction in terms of individual sequence member predictions (Section 3.3).

We built the software framework for our proposed architecture using Lasagne [6] and Theano [2] libraries. We also used MatConvNet [21] and Caffe [10] libraries for experiments related to other competing architectures.

4.3 Results

Overall performance: Table 1 summarizes the overall performance in terms of average recognition accuracy for various architectures. As can be seen, our GRU-based architecture (first row) outperforms SketchCNN by a significant margin even though it is trained on only 57% of the total data[4]. We believe our good performance stems from (a) being able to exploit the sequential information in a scalable and efficient manner via recurrent neural networks (b) the superiority of the deep sketch features provided by Alexnet [17] compared to the SketchCNN-FC features. The latter can be clearly seen when we compare the first two rows of Table 1 with the last two rows. In our case, the performance of GRU was better than that of LSTM when Alexnet features were used. Overall, it is clear that the choice of (sketch) features and the recurrent network *both* play a crucial role in obtaining state-of-the-art performance for the sketch recognition task.

On-line recognition: We also compared the various architectures for their ability to recognize sketches as they are being drawn (i.e. on-line recognition performance). For each classifier, we determined the fraction of test sketches t_x correctly recognized when only the first x% of the temporal sketch strokes are available. We varied x between 20 to 100 in steps of 20 and plotted t_x as a function of x. The results can be seen in Figure 2. Intuitively, the higher a curve on the plot, the better its online recognition ability. As can be seen, our framework consistently recognizes a larger fraction of sketches at all levels of sketch completion (except for very small x) relative to other architectures.

Semantic information: To determine the extent to which our architecture captures semantic information, we examined the performance of the classifier on misclassified sketches. As can be seen in Figure 3, most of the misclassifications are reasonable errors (e.g. `guitar` is mistaken for `violin`) and demonstrate that our framework learns the overall semantics of the object recognition problem.

5. CONCLUSION

In this paper, we have presented our deep recurrent neural network architecture for freehand sketch recognition. Our architecture has two prominent traits. *Firstly*, its design accounts for the inherently sequential and cumulative nature of human sketching process in a natural manner. *Secondly*, it exploits long-term sequential and structural regularities in stroke data represented as deep features. These two traits enable our system to achieve state-of-the-art recognition results on a large database of freehand object sketches. We have also shown that our recognition framework is highly suitable for on-the-fly interpretation of sketches as they are being drawn. Our framework source-code and associated data (pre-trained models) can be accessed at https://github.com/val-iisc/sketch-obj-rec.

6. ACKNOWLEDGEMENTS

We thank NVIDIA for their grant of Tesla K40 GPU.

[4]Typically, 75% of the data is used to report results in other approaches.

7. REFERENCES

[1] R. Arandjelović and T. M. Sezgin. Sketch recognition by fusion of temporal and image-based features. *Pattern Recognition*, 44(6):1225–1234, 2011. 1, 2

[2] F. Bastien, P. Lamblin, R. Pascanu, J. Bergstra, I. J. Goodfellow, A. Bergeron, N. Bouchard, and Y. Bengio. Theano: new features and speed improvements. Deep Learning and Unsupervised Feature Learning NIPS 2012 Workshop, 2012. 4.2

[3] K. Cho, B. van Merrienboer, Ç. Gülçehre, F. Bougares, H. Schwenk, and Y. Bengio. Learning phrase representations using RNN encoder-decoder for statistical machine translation. *CoRR*, abs/1406.1078, 2014. 2, 3.1

[4] J. Chung, C. Gulcehre, K. Cho, and Y. Bengio. Empirical evaluation of gated recurrent neural networks on sequence modeling. *arXiv preprint arXiv:1412.3555*, 2014. 3.1

[5] J. Chung, C. Gulcehre, K. Cho, and Y. Bengio. Gated feedback recurrent neural networks. *arXiv preprint arXiv:1502.02367*, 2015. 3.1

[6] S. Dieleman, M. Heilman, J. Kelly, M. Thoma, K. Rasul, E. Battenberg, H. Weideman, S. K. Sønderby, C. Raffel, J. Degrave, et al. Lasagne: First release. 2015. 4.2

[7] M. Eitz, J. Hays, and M. Alexa. How do humans sketch objects? *ACM Trans. Graph. (Proc. SIGGRAPH)*, 31(4):44:1–44:10, 2012. 1, 2

[8] A. Graves, M. Liwicki, S. Fernández, R. Bertolami, H. Bunke, and J. Schmidhuber. A novel connectionist system for unconstrained handwriting recognition. *Pattern Analysis and Machine Intelligence, IEEE Transactions on*, 31(5):855–868, 2009. 2

[9] S. Hochreiter and J. Schmidhuber. Long short-term memory. *Neural computation*, 9(8):1735–1780, 1997. 2

[10] Y. Jia, E. Shelhamer, J. Donahue, S. Karayev, J. Long, R. Girshick, S. Guadarrama, and T. Darrell. Caffe: Convolutional architecture for fast feature embedding. *arXiv preprint arXiv:1408.5093*, 2014. 4.2

[11] B. F. Klare, Z. Li, and A. K. Jain. Matching forensic sketches to mug shot photos. *Pattern Analysis and Machine Intelligence, IEEE Transactions on*, 33(3):639–646, 2011. 1

[12] A. Krizhevsky, I. Sutskever, and G. E. Hinton. Imagenet classification with deep convolutional neural networks. In *Advances in neural information processing systems*, pages 1097–1105, 2012. 3.1

[13] Y. Li, Y.-Z. Song, and S. Gong. Sketch recognition by ensemble matching of structured features. BMVC, 2013. 1, 2

[14] A. Lovett, M. Dehghani, and K. Forbus. Efficient learning of qualitative descriptions for sketch recognition. In *Proceedings of the 20th International Qualitative Reasoning Workshop*, 2006. 2

[15] B. Meyer, K. Marriott, A. Bickerstaffe, and L. Knipping. Intelligent diagramming in the electronic online classroom. In *Human System Interactions, 2009. HSI'09. 2nd Conference on*, pages 177–183. IEEE, 2009. 1

[16] Pictionary. https://en.wikipedia.org/wiki/Pictionary. 1

[17] R. K. Sarvadevabhatla and V. B. Radhakrishnan. Eye of the dragon: Exploring discriminatively minimalist sketch-based abstractions for object categories. In *Proceedings of the 23rd ACM International Conference on Multimedia*, MM '15, pages 271–280, New York, NY, USA, 2015. ACM. 1, 2, 4.2, 4.3

[18] R. G. Schneider and T. Tuytelaars. Sketch classification and classification-driven analysis using fisher vectors. *ACM Trans. Graph.*, 33(6):174:1–174:9, Nov. 2014. 1, 2, 4.1

[19] O. Seddati, S. Dupont, and S. Mahmoudi. Deepsketch: deep convolutional neural networks for sketch recognition and similarity search. In *Content-Based Multimedia Indexing (CBMI), 2015 13th International Workshop on*, pages 1–6. IEEE, 2015. 2

[20] Z. Sun, C. Wang, L. Zhang, and L. Zhang. Query-adaptive shape topic mining for hand-drawn sketch recognition. In *Proceedings of the 20th ACM international conference on Multimedia*, pages 519–528. ACM, 2012. 1, 2

[21] A. Vedaldi and K. Lenc. Matconvnet: Convolutional neural networks for matlab. In *Proceedings of the 23rd Annual ACM Conference on Multimedia Conference*, pages 689–692. ACM, 2015. 4.2

[22] X. Wang, H. Xu, and H. Wang. On-line sketch recognition for course of action diagrams. In *Mechatronics and Automation (ICMA), 2010 International Conference on*, pages 465–469. IEEE, 2010. 2

[23] Q. Yu, Y. Yang, Y.-Z. Song, T. Xiang, and T. Hospedales. Sketch-a-net that beats humans. *BMVC*, 2015. 1, 2, 3.3, 4.2

Experience Individualization on Online TV Platforms through Persona-based Account Decomposition

Payal Bajaj
Adobe Research Labs
Bengaluru, India
pabajaj@adobe.com

Sumit Shekhar
Adobe Research Labs
Bengaluru, India
sushekha@adobe.com

ABSTRACT

Online TV has seen rapid growth in recent years, with most of the large media companies broadcasting their linear content online. Access to the online TV accounts is protected by an authentication, and like the traditional cable TV subscription, users in the same household share the online TV credentials. However, as the standard data collection techniques have capability to collect only account level information, online TV measurements fail to capture individual level viewing characteristics in shared accounts. Thus, individual profile identification and experience individualization are challenging and difficult for online TV platforms. In this paper, we propose a novel approach to decompose online TV account into distinct personas sharing the account through analyzing viewing characteristics. A recommendation algorithm is then proposed to individualize the experience for each persona. Finally, we demonstrate the usefulness of the proposed approach through experiments on a large online TV database.

Keywords

Online TV measurement; Experience Individualization; Cluster Analysis; Recommendation; Personalization

1. INTRODUCTION

The online TV industry has seen a massive growth in the last few years. The users can now access TV program content over the Internet using a multitude of devices at any time unlike the traditional TV, where users watch as per channel schedules. Online TV is also different from the traditional television as it is built to provide a personalized TV experience to its users.

The access to the online TV platforms usually requires user authentication, and like the traditional TV, it is meant to be consumed by the members of the family. In this scenario, the multitude of analysis methods available on online platforms, lose the ability to track individual user behavior. This limits the ability of to create an individualized online TV experience for its viewers. For instance, consider a situation where the account is being shared between multiple members in the household with varied channel preferences. The father in the house might prefer *business* and *news* channels, the mother might prefer *travel* and *cooking* channels, the elder children may prefer *sports* channels whereas the younger kids might prefer *cartoon* and *anime* channels. Hence, decomposition of online TV accounts into individual viewing patterns is important to achieve the personalized TV experience.

This is a challenging problem due to ubiquitous access to online TV content available to users. Viewership was restricted to linear shows and followed a specific routine in traditional TV, but in online TV, users don't exhibit routine and periodic behavior as the content availability is not restricted like before. Therefore, it is difficult to disambiguate individual user viewing characteristics using routine or periodicity from online TV viewing logs. In this paper, we demonstrate that routine viewing patterns don't exist and propose an approach to individualize experience of users using shared accounts in online TV that does not rely on habitual and routine pattern of the programs.

To this end, we assume that users sharing an account have distinct video content and genre-driven preferences for program channels. We propose a novel method for persona identification to disambiguate between such users. Personas are defined as common viewing patterns observed in online TV, which we infer through mining user access logs. We further describe a recommendation algorithm to exploit the persona decomposition of online TV accounts and demonstrate its superiority over routine, like time of the day, decomposition on a large online TV dataset.

The remainder of the paper is organized as follows. Section 2 describes the prior literature related to user profile individualization in online TV domain. The problem statement and the proposed approach are discussed in Section 3. The dataset and experiments are then summarized, followed by results and evaluation in Section 4. The paper is concluded in Section 5.

MM '16, October 15–19, 2016, Amsterdam, The Netherlands.

DOI: http://dx.doi.org/10.1145/2964284.2967221

2. RELATED WORK

In this section, we discuss the prior literature for account decomposition and recommendation on online TV platforms.

2.1 Account Decomposition

Prior works in account disambiguation have focused on extracting routine behavior to decompose shared accounts. Iguchi *et al* [5] proposed a technique for account decomposition based on collective hourly viewing patterns. Wang et al [6] considered that user consuming behavior is periodic in IP-TV services and proposed a user identification algorithm based on captured preferences in continuous periods of non-overlapping sub-periods. User identification was also studied by Zhang et al. [4], where accounts were decomposed based on a subspace-based clustering method.

2.2 User Profiling using TV logs

User profiling plays a very important role for recommendation using online TV logs [8]. Online TV logs describe the content consumption behavior by the consumers, which can be used to infer their interests on watched TV programs.

Aroyo *et al* [1] presented a distributed personalization based method for TV personalization. A comprehensive context-sensitive user modeling method through monitoring user's actions was proposed by Pieter *et al* [2]. However, the context-sensitive user model created thus is independent of platform the content is being viewed on. For instance, the system assumes when a user sitting at his computer adds a program to his favorites, this will have a direct effect on his recommendation on the set top box application. But for online TV, users sharing the account would have different content preferences, hence this might not work well.

Zhiwen *et al* [3] proposed a method to construct a common profile for multiple viewers based on total distance minimization. They prove that merging can reflect the preferences of the majority of members within the group and recommendation strategy is effective for multiple viewers watching TV together. In contrast, we are trying to decompose the users within a shared account. Further, [3] requires multiple viewers to simultaneously log-in in order to identify who are watching the TV programs together.

Contributions: The contributions of this paper are -

- We propose a novel method to identify distinct personas sharing an account based on detecting the common viewing patterns across online TV users. We further demonstrate that habitual and routing watching patterns, assumed in prior literature, may not extend to online TV.
- We present a persona-based experience individualization method and demonstrate that it works better than context-based profiling method on a large online TV access logs dataset.

3. PERSONA-BASED INDIVIDUALIZATION

In this section, we describe the proposed approach for decomposing online TV accounts into personas followed by persona-based experience individualization. We also describe user profile and context-based profiling methods, against which we evaluate the proposed algorithm.

3.1 Notations

We denote the set of access logs by L, the set of program channels by Ch and the set of accounts in the dataset by A. Let the the total number of accounts be n, i.e., $n = |A|$. For each account $a \in A$, our problem is to identify distinct personas, a_p, sharing the account.

3.2 Persona Identification

We propose a method of account decomposition through persona identification. It distinguishes various users sharing an account by creating personas with distinct preferences. We define personas as the top common viewing patterns among the online TV accounts. Further, we assume that the viewing characteristics of individual users are governed by their genre preferences. For example, kids in the household might prefer to watch cartoons, teenagers might prefer movies and TV series whereas an elderly person might spend more time on news. We arrive at these characteristic viewing patterns through mining access logs of millions of online TV users. The steps for arriving at the personas are described below. Algorithm 1 summarizes the proposed method.

Algorithm 1 Proposed approach for persona identification from online TV access logs.

Input: L, A, Ch
Output: Distinct Personas $\{a_p\}\ \forall\ a \in A$
a. Create Frequency Matrix F
1: **for each** log $l \in L$ **do**
2: $a = Account(l)$
3: $ch = Channel(l)$
4: $F[a, ch] = F[a, ch] + 1$
5: **end for**
b. Create Correlation Matrix C
6: **for each** $ch_1 \in Ch$ **do**
7: $ch_1 = F[, ch_1]$
8: **for each** $ch_2 \in Ch$ **do**
9: $ch_2 = F[, ch_2]$
10: $corr(ch_1, ch_2) =$
11: $C[ch_1, ch_2] = CosineSimilarity(ch_1, ch_2)$
12: **end for**
13: **end for**
c. Channel Clustering
14: $Ch_{Clust} = HierarchicalClustering(C)$
15: $Clust_{Indx} = Indexes(Ch_{Clust})$
d. Splitting Accounts into Clusters
16: **for each** $a \in A$ **do**
17: Initialize set of cluster indexes, $a_c = \{\}$
18: **for each** $ch \in Ch$ **do**
19: **if** $F[a, ch] > 0$ **and** $Clust_{Indx} \notin a_c$ **then**
20: $a_c = a_c \cup Clust_{Indx}(ch)$
21: **end if**
22: **end for**
23: **end for**
e. Get Personas using Frequent Cluster Mining
24: $Clust_{Dataset} = \{\cup a_c \forall a \in A\}$
25: $Persona = Apriori(Clust_{Dataset}, support_{threshold})$
f. Decomposing Account into Personas
26: **for each** $a \in A$ **do**
27: $a_p = SetCover(a_c, Persona)$
28: **end for**

3.2.1 Similarity-based Channel Clustering

The algorithm begins with identifying the dominant viewing patterns over all accounts. We analyze all the channels and compute pairwise cosine similarity between them. A frequency matrix F is created which counts the videos viewed by each account for every channel (Lines $1-5$ in algorithm 1). A pairwise similarity matrix C is created (Lines $6-13$) using F (Line 10). Then we group them into clusters based on these similarity values. Clustering is performed on this matrix (Lines $14 - 15$) using hierarchical clustering

[12]. These clusters reflect the dominant channel viewing characteristics across all accounts.

3.2.2 Account Splitting

We split accounts into the clusters obtained in the previous step. Each account a is decomposed on the basis on which cluster's channels were viewed by the account (Lines $16-23$). If a channel ch is viewed by account a, the corresponding cluster that ch belongs to is added to patterns for accounts a, i.e., a_c.

3.2.3 Frequent Cluster Mining to obtain Personas

Next we identify top viewing patterns through running frequent cluster mining on the channel clusters, a_c identified for each account. We create a dataset, $Clust_{Dataset}$ of these clusters for all accounts (Line 24), and run Apriori algorithm [7] with a specified support threshold, $support_{threshold}$ to find top viewed cluster combinations (Line 25). These cluster combinations are then identified as unique personas, $Persona$. Note that these personas represent the common TV viewing patterns as envisioned in Section 1. Further, each persona may include multiple clusters, like news and sports, which may not have been fallen in the same cluster due to the presence of multiple popular sports as well as news channels online.

3.2.4 Decomposing Account into Personas

We replace the clusters a_c identified for each account a by the personas, $Persona$, using the greedy set cover approximation algorithm [10] (Lines $26-28$). For example, if an account is decomposed into three clusters {sports, cartoons, news, fashion}, and personas are identified as the clusters {sports, cartoons}, {fashion} and {cartoons, news}, then this account has three personas using the above mentioned greedy approach.

3.3 Experience Individualization

We assume that accounts are shared by multiple personas, but a TV session is usually driven by one persona. In other words, we assume that even when multiple users with varied interests may share the account, a session involves viewing channels catering to a particular persona. For this paper, we have defined session as a period of channel viewing activities until no activity is observed for an hour. For instance, the kids in the house would use the shared household account to watch cartoon channels in a session, whereas the sports enthusiasts would use the same account to view a match at a continuous stretch. Therefore, our hypothesis is that a session is usually driven by persona-based preferences. We validate this through a persona-based recommendation system.

To implement persona-based recommendation, we first recognize the persona to be leveraged for recommendation. We use the first channel viewed by the account in a session to identify the persona that owns the session. We have created persona in a way that every persona maps to a cluster of channels. These channels are referred to as the profile for that persona. We use this persona profile to recommend additional channels to the account through the session.

3.4 Comparisons

To evaluate persona-based recommendations, we create two account-based profiles. First, we create a profile to capture the overall account behavior. Second, we create contextual profiles of the accounts to study the impact of context, specifically, time of watching on recommendation. The account and contextual profiles are created by a normalized count of channel views from the training data. For a TV user account a, the account profile $AccProfile_a$ is computed in equation 1 below. F represents the frequency matrix as before.

$$AccProfile_a = \frac{\{F[a, ch_1], F[a, ch_2], \cdots, F[a, ch_n]\}}{\sum_{ch \in Ch} F[a, ch]} \quad (1)$$

To create contextual profiles, we divide the channel views from the accounts to create two time-dependent profiles of the account - day and night profiles. The two time-dependent profiles of the account are calculated using Equation 1, after separating the channels viewed at day and night. For recommendations using account-based profile, we use kNN algorithm [11] to identify the k most similar accounts based on that account's overall profile. For contextual profile, time of the session is used to identify the same separately for day and night profiles. We have used traditional cosine similarity for this purpose. The channels viewed by these top-k online TV accounts are then recommended.

4. EXPERIMENTS AND RESULTS

In this section, we present results on account decomposition based on persona identification and evaluate the performance of the persona based recommendation system.

4.1 Dataset

The experiments are performed on the access logs of during the period between December 1, 2014 till December 31, 2014. The logs provide information about the channels viewed, the time and day of viewing and devices used by online TV accounts. The dataset contains about 5 million accounts, with access to over 110 channels. The set of channels spans a variety of genres including sports, animation, fashion, movies, and news, etc.

4.2 Viewing Patterns on online TV

In this section, we analyze the online video viewing behavior of all the accounts. We demonstrate that the viewing behavior for online TV content doesn't follow routinely periodic patterns for majority of the accounts.

TV shows usually follow a weekly pattern, therefore for channels under consideration, we measure the weekly engagement of the accounts. We define the most engaging day for an online TV account to be the day of the week on which it was the most active, and then count the number of weeks the particular account was engaged the most on that day of the week. Previous works in this area [5] [6] have assumed weekly engagement as an important criteria for account disambiguation. However, as the Figure 1 shows, less than 13% of the accounts exhibit routine engagement for more than 2 weeks across different days of the week. Thus it is difficult to disambiguate accounts based on routine behavior. Note that this analysis is done for all the channels without hourly granularity. Adding these constraints will only increase the sparsity of the patterns. Therefore, we can not use weekly habitual viewing characteristics to decompose TV accounts because such patterns are not exhibited by the data.

Therefore, it is difficult to decompose online TV accounts based on habitual patterns as opposed to traditional TV.

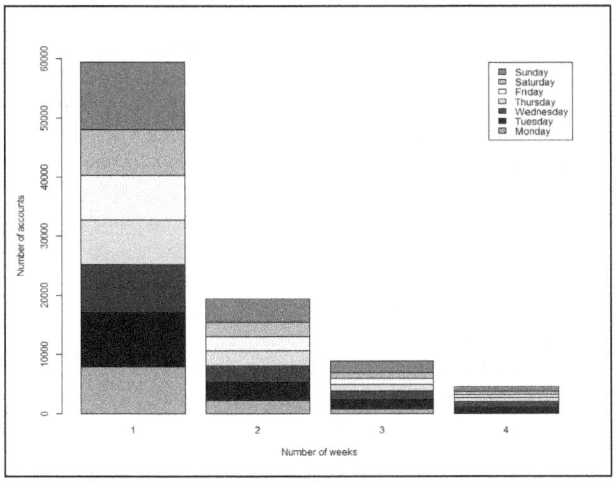

Figure 1: Plot of number of TV accounts with maximum engagement on a day of the week versus the number of active weeks for the account.

4.3 Experimental Set-up

In this section, we evaluate the proposed persona based recommendation algorithm. We took the logs for the first 20 days as training, and then evaluated the model for the remaining days of the month. For clustering, we have chosen the height of hierarchical clustering algorithm to be 1.4 empirically. Further, we keep the $support_{threshold}$ at 0.01 to discover representative personas for online TV accounts. Also, the value of k to create account and contextual profiles is chosen empirically to be 5.

We compare the channels recommended using account profiles, contextual profiles and persona profiles. For contextual profiles, we have used one of the day or night profiles depending on the time of the day in the test dataset. We report the recall and accuracy metrics [1] for comparing these algorithms.

4.4 Results

Figure 2 shows the output clusters of TV channels watched together (Line 14 in Algorithm 1). It can be observed that channels within many clusters have similar genre content. The final personas (Line 25) also reflect similar output (final persona outputs are not illustrated due to paucity of space). Thus, our assumption that distinct personas within an account are driven by content holds true.

The results of the recommendation algorithm are presented in Table 1. We took profiles with multiple discovered personas for testing the recommendations. The results are reported across accounts with 2, 3 and 4 discovered personas, along with the size of respective sets. It can be seen that the recall of persona-based recommendation outperforms the account and contextual profile-based methods, with only a slight decrease in accuracy. Contextual profiles do not improve the results at all. This validates our claim that online TV behavior is significantly different from traditional TV watching patterns.

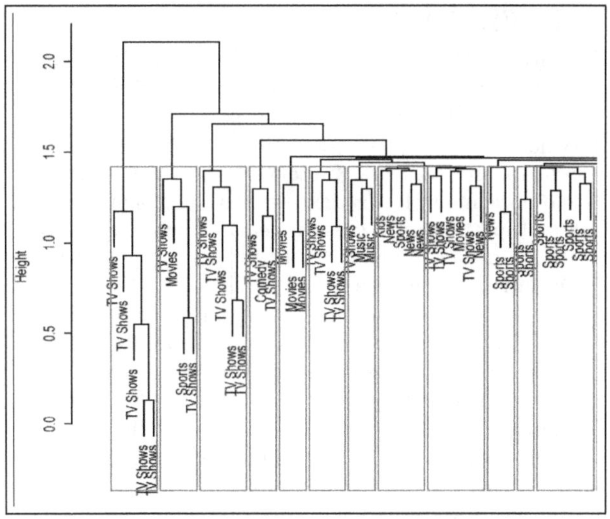

Figure 2: Clusters of different channels, showing their respective content genre, discovered through the proposed algorithm.

Algorithm	No. of Personas (Total count)	Recall	Accuracy
Account-based	2 (381,000)	0.4057	0.9872
Context-based	2 (381,000)	0.3945	0.9867
Persona-based	2 (381,000)	0.6973	0.9654
Account-based	3 (54,000)	0.3578	0.9852
Context-based	3 (54,000)	0.3422	0.9844
Persona-based	3 (54,000)	0.6226	0.9621
Account-based	4 (10,170)	0.2952	0.9826
Context-based	4 (10,170)	0.2948	0.9822
Persona-based	4 (10,170)	0.5878	0.9601

Table 1: Results for different channel recommendation algorithms.

5. CONCLUSION AND FUTURE WORK

In this paper, we present the problem of account disambiguation for online TV accounts. The patterns of online TV account usage make it difficult for time and routine based account decomposition. We present a novel approach which decomposes the TV accounts into distinct personas sharing the account through analyzing the channel viewing patterns. We further built a persona-based channel recommendation system, and demonstrate that it performs better than user-profile and contextual recommendation system on a large dataset of online TV logs.

Exploration of different methods to evaluate account decomposition into personas is a future work, as obtaining the ground truth is hard. Further, testing persona-based decomposition with advanced algorithms would highlight the significance of the proposed framework.

[1]

$$Recall = \frac{True\ Positive(TP)}{True\ Positive(TP)\ +\ False\ Negative(FN)}$$

$$Accuracy = \frac{True\ Positive(TP)\ +\ True\ Negative(TN)}{Totalnumber\ of\ channels}$$

6. REFERENCES

[1] Aroyo, L. M. "Distributed personalization: Bridging digital islands in museum and interactive TV." ERCIM News 72 (2008): 40.

[2] Bellekens, Pieter, Geert-Jan Houben, Lora Aroyo, Krijn Schaap, and Annelies Kaptein. "User model elicitation and enrichment for context-sensitive personalization in a multiplatform TV environment." Proceedings of the 7th European Conference on European interactive Television Conference. ACM, 2009.

[3] Yu, Zhiwen, Xingshe Zhou, Yanbin Hao, and Jianhua Gu. "TV program recommendation for multiple viewers based on user profile merging." User modeling and user-adapted interaction 16.1 (2006): 63-82.

[4] Zhang, Amy, Nadia Fawaz, Stratis Ioannidis, and Andrea Montanari. "Guess who rated this movie: Identifying users through subspace clustering." arXiv preprint arXiv:1208.1544 (2012).

[5] Iguchi, Koichi, Yoshinori Hijikata, and Shogo Nishida. "Individualizing user profile from viewing logs of several people for TV program recommendation." Proceedings of the 9th International Conference on Ubiquitous Information Management and Communication. ACM, 2015.

[6] Wang, Zhijin, Yan Yang, Liang He, and Junzhong Gu. "User Identification within a Shared Account: Improving IP-TV Recommender Performance." Advances in Databases and Information Systems. Springer International Publishing, 2014.

[7] Agrawal, Rakesh, and Ramakrishnan Srikant. "Fast algorithms for mining association rules." Proc. 20th International Conference on Very Large Databases, VLDB. Vol. 1215. 1994.

[8] Vèras, Douglas, et al. "A literature review of recommender systems in the television domain." Expert Systems with Applications 42.22 (2015): 9046-9076.

[9] Han, Jiawei, Wan Gong, and Yiwen Yin. "Mining Segment-Wise Periodic Patterns in Time-Related Databases." KDD. 1998.

[10] Chvatal, V. A. "Greedy Heuristic for the Set-Covering Problem." Mathematics of Operations Research Vol. 4, No. 3 (Aug., 1979), pp. 233-235

[11] Cover, Thomas M., and Peter E. Hart. "Nearest neighbor pattern classification." IEEE Transactions on Information Theory, 13.1 (1967): 21-27.

[12] Johnson, Stephen C. "Hierarchical clustering schemes." Psychometrika 32.3 (1967): 241-254.

Improved Dense Trajectory with Cross Streams

Katsunori Ohnishi
Graduate School of Information Science and Technology
The University of Tokyo
ohnishi@mi.t.u-tokyo.ac.jp

Masatoshi Hidaka
Graduate School of Information Science and Technology
The University of Tokyo
hidaka@mi.t.u-tokyo.ac.jp

Tatsuya Harada
Graduate School of Information Science and Technology
The University of Tokyo
harada@mi.t.u-tokyo.ac.jp

ABSTRACT

Improved dense trajectories (iDT) have shown great performance in action recognition, and their combination with the two-stream approach has achieved state-of-the-art performance. It is, however, difficult for iDT to completely remove background trajectories from video with camera shaking. Trajectories in less discriminative regions should be given modest weights in order to create more discriminative local descriptors for action recognition. In addition, the two-stream approach, which learns appearance and motion information separately, cannot focus on motion in important regions when extracting features from spatial convolutional layers of the appearance network, and vice versa. In order to address the above mentioned problems, we propose a new local descriptor that pools a new convolutional layer obtained from crossing two networks along iDT. This new descriptor is calculated by applying discriminative weights learned from one network to a convolutional layer of the other network. Our method has achieved state-of-the-art performance on ordinal action recognition datasets, 92.3% on UCF101, and 66.2% on HMDB51.

Keywords

Action recognition; Video representation; Local descriptor

1. INTRODUCTION AND RELATED WORK

Video representation is becoming increasingly important in today's online environment in which a massive amount of videos are uploaded on a daily basis. Various approaches have been proposed to efficiently and accurately represent the videos.

Dense trajectories [18] and improved dense trajectories (iDT) [19] have dominated action recognition. Extracting hand-crafted features [1, 10, 2] along these trajectories can provide effective local descriptors, and encoding these local descriptors with a Fisher vector (FV) [12] or a vector of locally aggregated descriptors (VLAD) [6] can provide an effective video representation [7].

Figure 1: Illustration of visualized iDT and feature map from convolutional layer in temporal net. We can see that there are some noisy trajectories in background due to camera shaking.

Fueled by the recent success of convolutional neural networks (CNN) in image classification, video representations based on CNN have also been developed in action classification. The two-stream approach [13] is one of the most successful methods that learns appearance information and motion information separately using one network whose input is RGB and the other network whose input is optical flow. The idea of this separate learning has been widely used in later works [5, 20, 22, 23, 25, 26].

Aiming at fully end-to-end learning, three-dimensional CNN learning methods that can capture spatial and temporal information simultaneously and automatically [16, 17] have been developed recently. However, three-dimensional CNN learning is still a very difficult task, and these methods have not yet achieved comparable performance to the state-of-the-art approach.

Trajectory-pooled deep-convolutional descriptors (TDD) [20] have shown state-of-the-art performance in action recognition by pooling convolutional two-stream layers along iDT. Because the convolutional layer retains position information, it is possible to combine it with iDT. However, TDD, which is based on iDT and the two-stream approach, has two main shortcomings: (1) as shown in Figure 1, iDT cannot completely remove the background image for videos captured by a shaking camera. This can be solved by giving modest weights to background trajectories. (2) Although each network in the two-stream approach captures important infor-

MM '16, October 15-19, 2016, Amsterdam, Netherlands
© 2016 ACM. ISBN 978-1-4503-3603-1/16/10...$15.00
DOI: http://dx.doi.org/10.1145/2964284.2967222

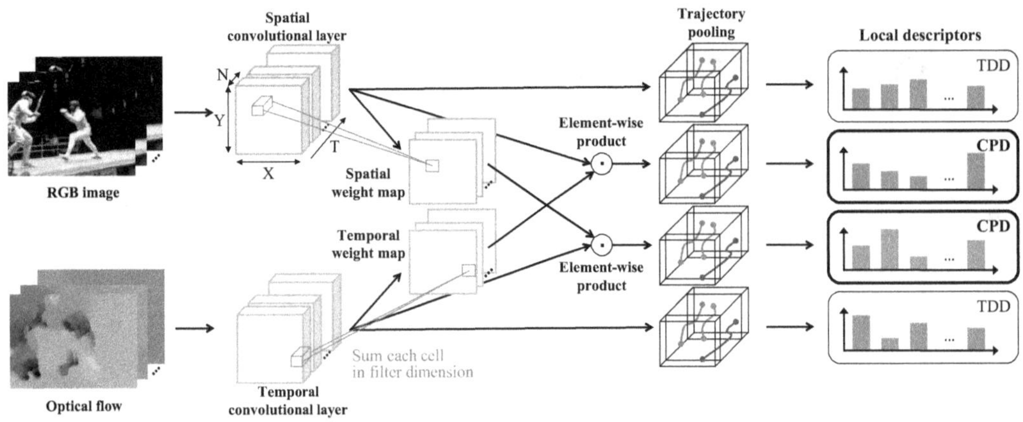

Figure 2: Illustration of the proposed local descriptors, named cross-stream pooled descriptors (CPD). After extraction, we encode these descriptors layer by layer and classify each of them. We then obtain final scores by simply summing all of their scores.

mation for action recognition, separate CNN learning sometimes lacks other important information that can be obtained only when spatial and temporal information are combined together.

For example, thinking about the action of pitching a ball, it is difficult for spatial CNN to focus on the region around the pitcher's hand from only a single RGB image. This shortcoming makes it difficult to discriminate between similar actions such as the difference between a soccer penalty kick and a field-hockey penalty shot, or between pitching a ball, a cricket shoot, a tennis serve, and a volleyball spike, especially when no background or context information is in the movie. Although iDT helps to solve this problem when recognizing action, iDT trajectories are hand-crafted so that they still contain both discriminative and non-discriminative trajectories. However, focusing on motion-important regions helps to extract more discriminative appearance features. When seeing a field hockey penalty, for example, the motion-important region is around the shooter's stick and the kipper. Extracting appearance features around these regions enables us to better recognize whether the player uses their own leg or the hockey stick or whether the kipper wears a protector or not. This can be also said in the case where spatial CNN and temporal CNN are reversed.

In order to address the above-mentioned problems, we utilize both networks in a two-stream approach by crossing two networks. Convolutional layers in spatial CNNs provide discriminative appearance features with position information while those in temporal CNNs provide discriminative motion features with position information. Thus, we propose a new descriptor that uses one network for the weights and gives these to the other network and pools along iDT, named cross-stream pooled descriptors (CPD). This is equivalent to pooling a convolutional layer of one network along iDT weighted by the convolutional layer of the other network, which leads to giving modest weights to iDTs in less discriminative regions. Our method has improved the performance of TDD on the ordinal action recognition datasets, UCF101 [15] and HMDB51 [8].

2. ACTION RECOGNITION REVISITED

In this section, we describe previous works on which our method is based.

2.1 Improved Dense Trajectories

Improved dense trajectories (iDT) [19] are the improved version of dense trajectories [18], which can remove dense trajectories in background images considering camera motion. A video whose size is (V_x, V_y, T) contains trajectories P^k $(k = 1 \dots K)$:

$$P^k = \{(x_1^k, y_1^k, t_1^k), (x_2^k, y_2^k, t_2^k), \cdots, (x_L^k, y_L^k, t_L^k)\}, \quad (1)$$

where K is the number of trajectories in a video, (x_l^k, y_l^k, t_l^k) is the position of the lth point in trajectory P^k, and L is the length of trajectory. Following other works [3, 9, 19, 20], we set $L = 15$ in this paper.

2.2 Two-Stream Approach

The two-stream approach [13] is a method that learns spatial information from RGB images and temporal information from optical flow images with each CNN separately. Since it is extremely difficult for a temporal net to learn motion only with a single flow image, a sequence of ten frames are used as input. In this paper, we call the network learned from RGB images a 'spatial network' and a network learned from optical flow images a 'temporal network.'

2.3 Trajectory-Pooled Deep-Convolutional Descriptors

Trajectory-pooled deep-convolutional descriptors (TDD) [20] combine iDT and the two-stream approach and achieves state-of-the-art performance on the UCF101 dataset. Given a ReLU applied convolutional layer $C \in \mathbb{R}^{X \times Y \times N \times T}$ from the two-stream approach, two normalization methods are applied to C, where X and Y are the width and height of the convolutional layer, N is the number of channels, T is the length of the video, and $C \geq 0$. Spatial normalization provides that $\widetilde{C}_{st}$ and channel normalization provides that $\widetilde{C}_{ch}$:

$$\widetilde{C}_{st}(x, y, n, t) = C(x, y, n, t)/\max_{x,y,t} C(x, y, n, t), \quad (2)$$

$$\widetilde{C}_{ch}(x, y, n, t) = C(x, y, n, t)/\max_{n} C(x, y, n, t), \quad (3)$$

where (x, y) is the position of the convolutional layer, n is the channel number of the convolutional layer, and t is the time in the video.

These $\widetilde{C}_{st}$ and $\widetilde{C}_{ch}$ are pooled along iDT instead of the originally pooled features (HOG [1], HOF [10], and MBH

[2]). Given a normalized convolutional layer $\widetilde{C}^a_b$, which is the convolutional layer after applying spatiotemporal normalization or channel normalization ($b \in \{st, ch\}$) from spatial or temporal nets ($a \in \{sp, tmp\}$), proposed descriptors $TDD(P^k, \widetilde{C}^a_b) \in \mathbb{R}^N$ are obtained as follows:

$$TDD(P^k, \widetilde{C}^a_b) = \sum_{l=1}^{L} \widetilde{C}^a_b(\overline{(r_x \times x^k_l)}, \overline{(r_y \times y^k_l)}, t^k_l), \quad (4)$$

where $\overline{(\cdot)}$ is the rounding operation and $(r_x, r_y) = (X/V_w, Y/V_h)$. These descriptors are encoded by FV. The final video representation is obtained by concatenating encoded vectors from both normalization methods.

3. IDT WITH THE CROSS STREAMS

As described to this point, separate CNN learning cannot always focus on truly important regions to capture an action's characteristics. Additionally, improved dense trajectories (iDT) cannot completely eliminate background trajectories from videos whose capturing camera experiences large motions. We address these problems to improve recognition performance using two equivalent methods. In this section, we describe both approaches in order to evaluate whether each problem can be improved by each calculation.

3.1 Cross-Stream Pooling Along iDT

In order to enhance motion-important regions in a spatial convolutional layer and appearance-important regions in a temporal convolutional layer, we propose a new convolutional layer for iDT pooling: the cross-stream layer. As shown in Figure 2, we produce spatial and temporal convolutional layers element-wise and pool the resulting four-dimensional matrix along iDT. We call this method cross-stream pooled descriptors (CPD). However, since each of the nth filters in C^{tmp} and C^{sp} do not have the same meaning, the simple element-wise product $C^{tmp}(x,y,n,t) \times C^{sp}(x,y,n,t)$ might not work well. A convolutional layer shows large activation for discriminative regions. Thus, we can obtain a discriminative weight map $W \in \mathbb{R}^{X \times Y \times T}$ by simply taking the sum in the n-direction:

$$W^{tmp}(x,y,t) = \sum_{n=1}^{N} \widetilde{C}^{tmp}(x,y,n,t), \quad (5)$$

where $\widetilde{C}^{tmp}$ is a normalized layer calculated from C^{tmp} as in equations (2) and (3). With this motion-based weight map, we can enhance the normalized spatial convolutional layer $\widetilde{C}^{sp}$, which contains appearance information:

$$D^{sp}(x,y,n,t) = \widetilde{C}^{sp}(x,y,n,t) \times W^{tmp}(x,y,t). \quad (6)$$

D^{sp} represents new appearance features enhanced by motion-important regions.

Similarly to motion-based weights, we can obtain appearance-based weights W^{sp} from C^{sp}, and D^{tmp} is calculated in the same way. The term ' cross stream ' originated from this cross utilization of two networks.

We then pool this D along iDT as in equation (4) to obtain $CPD(P^k, D^a_b) \in \mathbb{R}^N$ as follows:

$$CPD(P^k, D^a_b) = \sum_{l=1}^{L} D^a_b(\overline{(r_x \times x^k_l)}, \overline{(r_y \times y^k_l)}, t^k_l). \quad (7)$$

Table 1: Performance of each layer type on the UCF101 split1 dataset using parameters $(D, K) = (64, 128)$ for FV and $(D, K) = (128, 64)$ for VLAD.

Convolutional layer type	FV	VLAD
(a) Spatial	81.2%	81.8%
(b) Temporal	84.7%	85.5%
TDD: (a) + (b)	90.7%	91.5%
(c) Spatial weighted by temporal	81.3%	82.9%
(d) Temporal weighted by spatial	85.3%	85.9%
CPD (**ours**): (c) + (d)	90.4%	91.6%
TDD + CPD (**ours**)	90.8%	92.0%

Table 2: The combination of convolutional layers resulting in each network on the UCF101 split1 dataset when VLAD is applied using parameters $(D, K) = (128, 64)$. (a), (b), (c), and (d) represent spatial, temporal, spatial weighted by temporal, and temporal weighted by spatial cases.

	(a)	(b)	(c)	(d)
Conv3	71.9%	77.6%	74.1%	77.7%
Conv4	78.2%	82.2%	78.5%	82.0%
Conv5	76.3%	82.8%	75.7%	81.2%
Conv3 + Conv4	79.0%	82.5%	80.3%	83.2%
Conv4 + Conv5	81.3%	85.5%	81.5%	85.8%
Conv3 + Conv4 + Conv5	82.2%	85.8%	83.3%	86.5%

3.2 Two-Stream Pooling Along Weighted iDT

We next consider our method from a different point of view. Cross-stream pooled descriptors (CPD) can also be calculated as follows. In order to give modest weights to trajectories in the background region, we take advantage of the rest of the network. A convolutional layer C^{tmp} obtained from a temporal CNN in the two-stream approach, for example, has discriminative motion features without losing position information. Using this C^{tmp} as the weight and giving this weight to iDT, we can obtain new trajectories that are emphasized if they are in the region that contains motion-discriminative trajectories and are less emphasized if they are in regions that contain less motion-discriminative trajectories. As in equation (5), we obtain a discriminative weight map W^{tmp} by taking the sum in the n-direction. Each trajectory is weighted by this map W^{tmp}; then, we can obtain the weighted iDT. As for motion-based weights, an iDT weighted by an appearance-based map is calculated in the same way. We then pool the normalized convolutional layer $\widetilde{C}^a$ along the emphasized iDT whose weights are calculated from $W^{\overline{a}}$ and obtain the CPD as follows:

$$CPD(P^k, \widetilde{C}^a_b, W^{\overline{a}}_b) = \sum_{l=1}^{L} W^{\overline{a}}_b(x^k_l, y^k_l, t^k_l) \times \widetilde{C}^a_b(\overline{(r_x \times x^k_l)}, \overline{(r_y \times y^k_l)}, t^k_l). \quad (8)$$

This is equivalent to $CPD(P^k, D^a_b)$.

4. EXPERIMENTS

4.1 Datasets and Settings

We conducted experiments on widely used action recognition datasets, UCF101 [15] and HMDB51 [8]. We chose VGG16 [14] as our CNN and utilized publicly available models [21] that had been already trained on UCF101. Because UCF101 has more variety of actions and videos, we used a model learned on UCF101 split 1 as the initial model for HMDB51 training.The learning rate and other training set-

Table 3: Mean accuracy of CPD and other baseline methods on HMDB51 and UCF101. The score*[1] of two-stream (VGG16) on HMDB51 in our calculation.

Algorithm		HMDB51	UCF101
iDT & FV [19]		57.2%	85.9%
Two stream [13]		59.4%	88.0%
TDD & FV [20]		63.2%	90.3%
Two stream (VGG16)		61.9%*[1]	91.4% [21]
Spatial net	(VGG16 w/o flip&crop)	39.7%	75.5%
Temporal net	(VGG16 w/o flip&crop)	53.6%	81.0%
Two stream	(VGG16 w/o flip&crop)	59.3%	87.6%
TDD (VGG16) & FV		63.2%	91.3%
TDD (VGG16) & VLAD		65.0%	92.0%
CPD & VLAD (**ours**)		65.2%	91.8%
TDD (VGG16) & VLAD + CPD (**ours**) & VLAD		**66.2%**	**92.3%**

tings were the same as the training settings for UCF101[21]. We chose the models that showed the best validation scores during training.

As the convolutional layer for pooling, we chose conv3_3, conv4_3, and conv5_3 from VGG16. We call these conv3, conv4, and conv5 in this paper, respectively. A final video representation of each layer was obtained by concatenating st-normed and ch-normed Fisher vectors following TDD[20]. We fused SVM scores from each layer by taking the sum. Note that, in consideration of the calculation cost, we did not use multi-scale CNN, unlike TDD, and did not apply flipping or cropping to input images, unlike the original two-stream approach.

4.2 Analysis

Parameters and Coding Methods: We found the best coding method and parameters for TDD and CPD with UCF101 split1. Some previous works [7, 24] showed that VLAD encoding is also effective for action recognition. Thus, we tried both FV and VLAD for encoding. Through numerous experiments, we found that the best parameters for FV coding were $(D, K) = (64, 128)$, and those for VLAD coding were $(D, K) = (128, 64)$, where D is the dimension after compression by PCA and K is the number of clusters. Details are given in the supplemental material owing to limited space here.

Convolutional Type Combination: Table 1 shows that weighting the convolutional layer heightens accuracy for every layer and method, and combining our method with TDD improves the recognition accuracy of TDD. It is also shown that VLAD is more effective for all convolutional layer types than FV.

Layer Combination on Each Network: Table 2 presents the combination patterns of convolutional layers in each network. In all network types, we can see that using all layers showed the best performance. Thus, we simply employed all of them.

4.3 Evaluation of CPD

Table 3 represents the action accuracy of CPD and related methods on UCF101 [15] and HMDB51 [8], which are widely used action recognition datasets. Note that we did not flip and crop input images when predicting, unlike the original TDD. Although the two-stream approach of VGG16 without flipping and cropping shows worse performance than that of the original two-stream approach, as denoted in Table 3, the performance of TDD with FV is improved by replacing the CNN with VGG16. Encoding VLAD instead of FV also improves recognition accuracy. We then combine the scores of this TDD using VLAD with those of CPD, which increases the performance of TDD both on UCF101 and HMDB51.

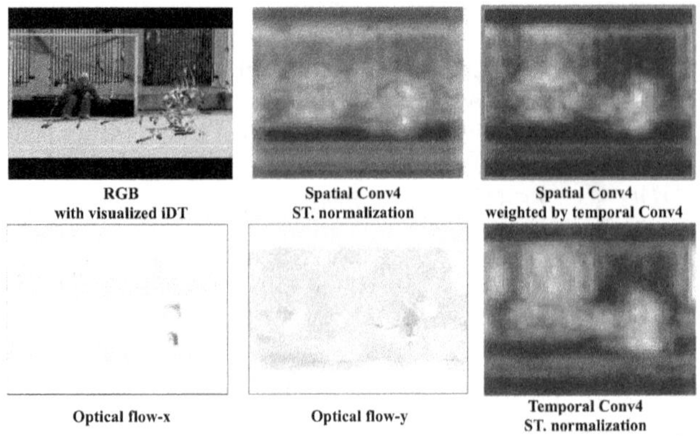

Figure 3: Sum of filter activations. We only show spatial layer weighted by temporal, because it will appear as the same image as temporal layer weighted by spatial with this visualization method.

Table 4: Comparison with the state-of-the-art methods. The scores written inside of () is the accuracy when combined with iDT & FV [19].

HMDB51		UCF101	
iDT & FV [19]	57.2%	iDT & FV [19]	85.9%
iDT & Stacked FV [11]	56.2%	C3D [17]	85.2%
+ iDT & FV	*(66.8%)*	+ iDT & FV	*(90.4%)*
$F_{ST}CN$ [16]	59.1%	$F_{ST}CN$ [16]	88.1%
LATE [3]	62.2%	MIFS [9]	89.1%
TDD & FV [20]	63.2%	TDD & FV [20]	90.3%
+ iDT & FV	*(65.9%)*	+ iDT & FV	*(91.5%)*
Video darwin [4]	63.7%	Hybrid LSTM [23]	91.3%
MIFS [9]	65.1%	Two stream (VGG16) [21]	91.4%
CPD (**ours**)	65.2%	CPD (**ours**)	91.8%
TDD + CPD (**ours**)	**66.2%**	TDD + CPD (**ours**)	**92.3%**

Fig. 3 shows an example of the visualized iDTs and convolutional layer activation. We can see that the spatial convolutional layer shows activation on many other objects whilst the convolutional layer weighted by the temporal convolutional layer shows activation mainly of the players. It can also be seen that some background iDTs still remain in the image due to camera shaking. However, the spatial layer weighted by the temporal layer activates mainly over the shooter and the kipper, ignoring their backgrounds. Thus, we can confirm that our method extracts appearance information mainly from motion-important regions and that these features capture different characteristics from those of TDD, which augments recognition performance.

4.4 Comparison with state-of-the-art

Table 4 shows the comparison of our method with other methods of action recognition on the UCF101 and HMDB51 datasets. On UCF101, the proposed method achieved state-of-the-art performance: 0.8% improvement over the combination of TDD [20] and iDT [19]. On HDMB51, our method achieved comparable performance to state-of-the-art methods. Considering the scores without adding iDT & FV [19], our method shows the best performance.

5. CONCLUSION

This study proposed a new type of local descriptors for action recognition, termed cross-stream pooled descriptors (CPD), that pools crossed convolutional layers along iDT. Our method achieved state-of-the-art performance on the widely used action recognition datasets UCF101 and HMDB51.

Acknowledgments

This work was supported by CREST, JST.

6. REFERENCES

[1] N. Dalal and B. Triggs. Histograms of oriented gradients for human detection. In *CVPR*, 2005.

[2] N. Dalal, B. Triggs, and C. Schmid. Human detection using oriented histograms of flow and appearance. In *ECCV*, 2006.

[3] C. Feichtenhofer, A. Pinz, and R. P. Wildes. Dynamically encoded actions based on spacetime saliency. In *CVPR*, 2015.

[4] B. Fernando, E. Gavves, J. M. Oramas, A. Ghodrati, and T. Tuytelaars. Modeling video evolution for action recognition. In *CVPR*, 2015.

[5] C. Gan, N. Wang, Y. Yang, D.-Y. Yeung, and A. G. Hauptmann. Devnet: A deep event network for multimedia event detection and evidence recounting. In *CVPR*, 2015.

[6] H. Jégou, M. Douze, C. Schmid, and P. Pérez. Aggregating local descriptors into a compact image representation. In *CVPR*, 2010.

[7] V. Kantorov and I. Laptev. Efficient feature extraction, encoding and classification for action recognition. In *CVPR*, 2014.

[8] H. Kuehne, H. Jhuang, E. Garrote, T. Poggio, and T. Serre. Hmdb: a large video database for human motion recognition. In *ICCV*, 2011.

[9] Z. Lan, M. Lin, X. Li, A. G. Hauptmann, and B. Raj. Beyond gaussian pyramid: Multi-skip feature stacking for action recognition. In *CVPR*, 2015.

[10] B. D. Lucas and T. Kanade. An iterative image registration technique with an application to stereo vision. *IJCAI*, 81:674–679, 1981.

[11] X. Peng, C. Zou, Y. Qiao, and Q. Peng. Action recognition with stacked fisher vectors. In *ECCV*, 2014.

[12] F. Perronnin and C. Dance. Fisher kernels on visual vocabularies for image categorization. In *CVPR*, 2007.

[13] K. Simonyan and A. Zisserman. Two-stream convolutional networks for action recognition in videos. In *NIPS*, 2014.

[14] K. Simonyan and A. Zisserman. Very deep convolutional networks for large-scale image recognition. In *ICLR*, 2015.

[15] K. Soomro, A. R. Zamir, and M. Shah. Ucf101: A dataset of 101 human actions classes from videos in the wild. *arXiv:1212.0402*, 2012.

[16] L. Sun, K. Jia, D.-Y. Yeung, and B. E. Shi. Human action recognition using factorized spatio-temporal convolutional networks. In *ICCV*, 2015.

[17] D. Tran, L. Bourdev, R. Fergus, L. Torresani, and M. Paluri. Learning spatiotemporal features with 3d convolutional networks. In *ICCV*, 2015.

[18] H. Wang, A. Kläser, C. Schmid, and C.-L. Liu. Action recognition by dense trajectories. In *CVPR*, 2011.

[19] H. Wang and C. Schmid. Action recognition with improved trajectories. In *ICCV*, 2013.

[20] L. Wang, Y. Qiao, and X. Tang. Action recognition with trajectory-pooled deep-convolutional descriptors. In *CVPR*, 2015.

[21] L. Wang, Y. Xiong, Z. Wang, and Y. Qiao. Towards good practices for very deep two-stream convnets. *arXiv:1507.02159*, 2015.

[22] X. Wang, A. Farhadi, and A. Gupta. Actions~ transformations. In *CVPR*, 2016.

[23] Z. Wu, X. Wang, Y.-G. Jiang, H. Ye, and X. Xue. Modeling spatial-temporal clues in a hybrid deep learning framework for video classification. In *ACMMM*, 2015.

[24] Z. Xu, Y. Yang, and A. G. Hauptmann. A discriminative CNN video representation for event detection. In *CVPR*, 2015.

[25] J. Yue-Hei Ng, M. Hausknecht, S. Vijayanarasimhan, O. Vinyals, R. Monga, and G. Toderici. Beyond short snippets: Deep networks for video classification. In *CVPR*, 2015.

[26] S. Zha, F. Luisier, W. Andrews, N. Srivastava, and R. Salakhutdinov. Exploiting image-trained cnn architectures for unconstrained video classification. In *BMVC*, 2015.

Joint Image and Text Representation for Aesthetics Analysis

Ye Zhou[1], Xin Lu[2], Junping Zhang[1*], James Z. Wang[3]
[1]Fudan University, China [2]Adobe Systems Inc., USA [3]The Pennsylvania State University, USA

ABSTRACT

Image aesthetics assessment is essential to multimedia applications such as image retrieval, and personalized image search and recommendation. Primarily relying on visual information and manually-supplied ratings, previous studies in this area have not adequately utilized higher-level semantic information. We incorporate additional textual phrases from user comments to jointly represent image aesthetics utilizing multimodal Deep Boltzmann Machine. Given an image, without requiring any associated user comments, the proposed algorithm automatically infers the joint representation and predicts the aesthetics category of the image. We construct the AVA-Comments dataset to systematically evaluate the performance of the proposed algorithm. Experimental results indicate that the proposed joint representation improves the performance of aesthetics assessment on the benchmarking AVA dataset, comparing with only visual features.

Keywords

Deep Boltzmann Machine, Image Aesthetics Assessment, Multimodal Analysis

1. INTRODUCTION

Image aesthetics assessment [2] aims at predicting the aesthetic value of images as consistent with a human population's perception as possible. It can be useful in recommendation systems by suggesting aesthetically appealing images to photographers. It can also serve as a ranking cue for both personal and cloud-based image collections.

In previous studies [3, 13], image aesthetics is commonly represented by an average rating or a distribution of ratings by human raters. Image aesthetics assessment is then formulated as a classification or regression problem. Under this framework, some effective aesthetics representations are proposed, such as manually-designed features [2, 4, 9, 1, 3, 13], generic visual features [10], and automatically learned features [8]. These approaches, including the more recent deep learning approaches [8, 17, 16], have generated good quality aesthetics ratings or categories (*e.g.*, high vs. low aesthetics).

Ratings alone, however, are limited as a representation of visual aesthetics. Many image sharing sites, *e.g.*, Flickr, Photo.net, and Instagram, support user comments on images, allowing explanations of ratings. User comments usually introduce rationale as to how and why users rate the aesthetics of an image. For example, many factors can result in high ratings on an image. Comments such as "interesting subject", "vivid colors", or "a fine pose" are much more informative than a rating. Similarly, comments such as "too small" and "blurry" explain why low ratings occur. Motivated by this observation, this work leverages comments in addition to images and their aesthetics ratings to study aesthetics assessment.

In this work, we first systematically examine effective visual and textual extraction approaches for image aesthetics assessment. We then propose a joint representation learning approach, building upon the most effective visual and textual feature extraction approaches found through this process. We jointly examine both the visual and textual information of images during training. In the testing stage, we only use the visual information of an image to derive the aesthetics prediction.

Forming a joint representation for image aesthetics assessment is nontrivial because aesthetics-related phrases are unstructured and can include a wide range of concepts. Our contribution is an approach for learning from both images and text for aesthetics assessment. We utilize multimodal Deep Boltzmann Machine (DBM) [15] to encode both images and text. We analyze and demonstrate the power of this joint representation, comparing with using only visual information.

As we were conducting our study, we generated a dataset that the research community can use. The AVA-Comments dataset contains all user comments extracted from the provided page links in the AVA dataset, and enables the extraction of aesthetics information from user comments. It complements the benchmark AVA dataset for aesthetics assessment.

*Correspondence should be addressed to Junping Zhang, School of Computer Science, Shanghai Key Laboratory of Intelligent Information Processing, Fudan University, Shanghai, China.
Emails: yezhou14@fudan.edu.cn, xinl@adobe.com, jpzhang@fudan.edu.cn, jwang@ist.psu.edu.

MM '16, October 15-19, 2016, Amsterdam, Netherlands

DOI: http://dx.doi.org/10.1145/2964284.2967223

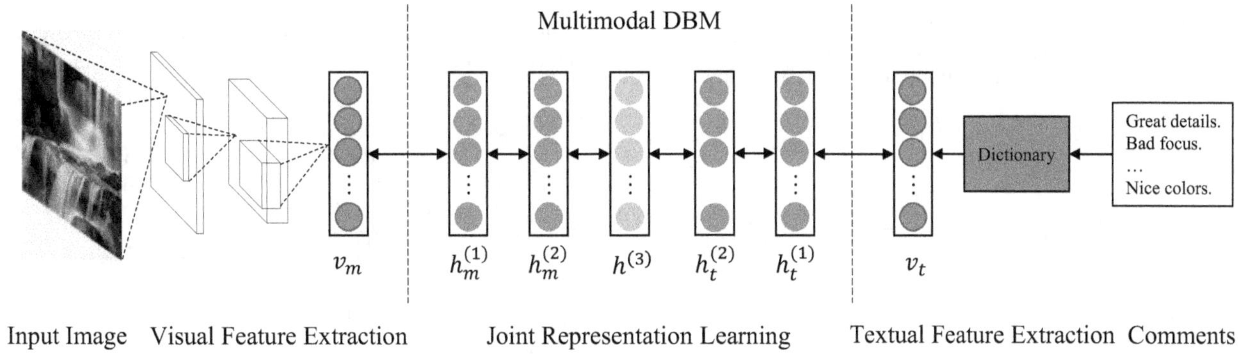

Figure 1: Approach Overview. Our approach consists of three modules: visual feature extraction, textual feature extraction, and joint representation learning.

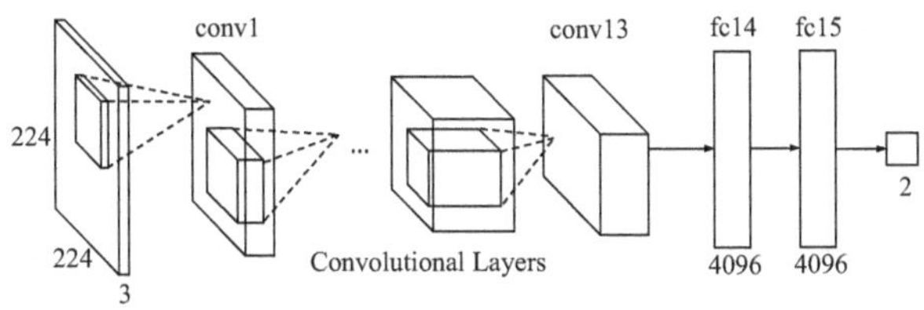

Figure 2: The architecture of the fine-tuned VGG-16 CNN model.

2. THE METHOD

We now provide technical details. As shown in Fig. 1, during training, we utilize a multimodal DBM to encode a joint representation with both visual and textual information, where visual information is extracted from deep neural network and textual information is collected from user comments. Importantly, test images are not associated with user comments. In testing, we leverage the learned representation to approximate the missing textual features and predict the aesthetic value of a given image.

2.1 Visual Feature Extraction

We demonstrate that pretrained VGG-16 model [14] on ImageNet can achieve reasonable performance for image aesthetics assessment, and a better performance is achieved by fine-tuning the VGG-16 model on an image aesthetics dataset. The detailed experimental results are discussed in Section 3.2.

We show the network structure during fine-tuning in Figure 2. It is noticeable that to deal with image aesthetics assessment as a binary classification problem, the last softmax layer with 1,000 classes on the ImageNet dataset is replaced by a 2-node softmax layer. The learning rate during fine-tuning process is lower than training from scratch, which avoids ruining the weights of the convolutional layer.

In testing, we adapt the multiview test performed in [6], and extracted 10 image patches from each testing image, which include the four corners and the central patch of the test input, and their horizontal flips.

We take the output of the fc15 layer (4,096-dimensional feature vector, illustrated in Fig. 2) of the fine-tuned network as the visual representation, and feature vectors from 10 patches are averaged to represent each image.

2.2 Textual Feature Extraction

Extracting aesthetics related information from user comments is not easy because user comments are unstructured and include discussions both about or beyond the content of the image. To examine the performance of different textual features on aesthetics classification, we build classifiers between the textual features and the aesthetics labels. Experimental results are shown in Section 3.3.

One of the most commonly used textual features is the word counts of a dictionary extracted from the original text. For the aesthetics assessment task, we extract a dictionary containing aesthetics-related words and phrases from user comments. In particular, we learn weights for all uni-grams, bi-grams and tri-grams occurred in user comments using a SVM variant with Naïve Bayes log-count ratios [18]. According to the experimental results discussed in [11], Naïve Bayes performs well on the snippets datasets and SVM is better at full-length reviews. A combination of Naïve Bayes like feature and SVM makes the model more robust.

Let $\mathbf{f}^{(i)} \in \{0,1\}^{|D|}$ indicate whether an item occurs, where D is the dictionary and $|D|$ is its cardinality. $\mathbf{f}_j^{(i)} = 1$ indicates that the dictionary item D_j occurs in the ith comment, otherwise $\mathbf{f}_j^{(i)} = 0$.

Denote $\mathbf{p} = \alpha + \sum_{i:y^{(i)}=1} \mathbf{f}^{(i)}$ and $\mathbf{q} = \alpha + \sum_{i:y^{(i)}=-1} \mathbf{f}^{(i)}$ as the positive and negative count vectors, repectively. α is a smooth parameter, which is usually set to $\alpha = 1$ for word counting vectors in the experiments. The log-count ratio is computed by $\mathbf{r} = \log((\mathbf{p}/||\mathbf{p}||_1)/(\mathbf{q}/||\mathbf{q}||_1))$, accordingly, the Naïve Bayes features $\mathbf{x}^{(i)}$ is derived by $\mathbf{x}^{(i)} = \mathbf{f}^{(i)} \circ \mathbf{r}$, where $\mathbf{a} \circ \mathbf{b}$ is the element-wise product of two vectors.

We train a L2-regularized L2-loss SVM to map the Naïve Bayes features to aesthetics labels. The Naïve Bayes features are sparse and high-dimensional because the dictionary size is large (over a million). We select a small dictionary by choosing several dimensions with maximum and minimum weight in $\hat{\mathbf{r}} = \mathbf{w} \circ \mathbf{r}$, where $\mathbf{w}$ is the weight vector in SVM. Then the word counts of the small dictionary can be calculated from user comments.

2.3 Multimodal Deep Boltzmann Machine

To perform a joint representation learning with visual and textual features, a multimodal DBM model [15] is built for aesthetics assessment and high-level semantics inference.

As shown in Fig. 1, the whole model contains three parts. For visual features, a DBM model is built between input units $\mathbf{v}_m$ and hidden units $\mathbf{h}_m^{(1)}, \mathbf{h}_m^{(2)}$. The layer between $\mathbf{v}_m$ and $\mathbf{h}_m^{(1)}$ is a Gaussian-Bernoulli RBM layer. For textual features, a DBM is built between input units $\mathbf{v}_t$ and hidden units $\mathbf{h}_t^{(1)}, \mathbf{h}_t^{(2)}$. The layer between $\mathbf{v}_t$ and $\mathbf{h}_t^{(1)}$ is a Replicated Softmax layer. The two models are combined with an additional hidden layer $\mathbf{h}^{(3)}$ between $\mathbf{h}_m^{(2)}$ and $\mathbf{h}_t^{(2)}$. The joint distribution over the multimodal input is as following.

$$P(\mathbf{v}_m, \mathbf{v}_t; \boldsymbol{\theta}) = \sum_{\mathbf{h}_m^{(2)}, \mathbf{h}_t^{(2)}, \mathbf{h}^{(3)}} \left(\left(\sum_{\mathbf{h}_m^{(1)}} P(\mathbf{v}_m, \mathbf{h}_m^{(1)}, \mathbf{h}_m^{(2)}) \right) \left(\sum_{\mathbf{h}_t^{(1)}} P(\mathbf{v}_t, \mathbf{h}_t^{(1)}, \mathbf{h}_t^{(2)}) \right) P(\mathbf{h}_m^{(2)}, \mathbf{h}_t^{(2)}, \mathbf{h}^{(3)}) \right) .$$

Both modality can be used in the training process. But during the testing process, user comments are not present. We therefore use variational inference [15] to approximate the posterior for the joint representation $P(\mathbf{h}^{(3)}|\mathbf{v}_m)$, or the missing textual representation $P(\mathbf{v}^t|\mathbf{v}^m)$.

3. EXPERIMENTS

3.1 The AVA and AVA-Comments Datasets

We adopted one of the largest image aesthetics dataset, the AVA [12], for evaluation. The AVA contains more than 255,000 user-rated images, each has an average of 200 ratings between 1 and 10. The dataset is divided into 235,000 images for training (including 167,000 high-quality images and 68,000 low-quality ones) and 20,000 images for testing without overlapping. The aesthetics assessment is formulated as a binary classification problem. Following the criteria in [12], images with a mean rating higher than 5 are labeled as high-quality images, the others as low-quality.

The user comments associated with each image are helpful for training aesthetics assessment model. For instance, images with smiling faces may not be visually appealing, but could still be rated with a high score; images with colorful content may still be rated low if they have boring content. Therefore, we crawled all the user comments for images in the AVA dataset to form the AVA-Comments dataset, where more than 1.5 million user comments were obtained from the original links. All user comments were tokenized, and all quotes and extra HTML tags such as links were removed. In our experiments, we found that user comments are particularly helpful in learning from these cases during network training. Moreover, the classification accuracy of aesthetics is improved without utilizing user comments during testing, as shown in Figs. 3 and 4. The AVA-Comments dataset is available to researchers.

3.2 Classification with Visual Features

We first evaluate the performance of the visual features used in this work. We compared the visual features discussed in Section 2.1 with pretrained VGG-16 [14] (denoted by Unmodified VGG-16), fine-tuned CaffeNet and VGG-16 presented in [17], and double-column CNN presented in [8]. For pretrained VGG-16 model, we built an L2-regularized L2-loss linear SVM to map features extracted from the layer fc15 of original VGG-16 model to aesthetics labels.

The classification results of these approaches are reported in Table 1. Our fine-tuned VGG-16 model performed the best, compared with other experimental settings. The fact that our fine-tuned model performed better than fine-tuned CaffeNet indicates that a larger capacity is required for the image aesthetics assessment task on the AVA dataset. Our fine-tuned VGG-16 is better than the result shown in [17] is because of one major setting difference: we fine-tuned VGG-16 with a larger batch size of 64 compared with 10. It means that a larger batch size may reduce the variance among mini-batches, resulting in better performance. Consequently, we use our fine-tuned VGG-16 as the visual feature extractor in the joint representation learning.

Table 1: Accuracy of Aesthetics Classification with Visual Features

Methods	Accuracy(%)
Double column CNN [8]	74.46
Unmodified VGG-16	74.12
Fine-tuned CaffeNet [17]	76.82
Fine-tuned VGG-16 [17]	77.09
Fine-tuned VGG-16 (Ours)	**78.19**

Table 2: Accuracy of Aesthetics Classification with Textual Features

Methods	Accuracy(%)
Recurrent Neural Networks [5]	79.36
Word2Vec [7]	79.62
Naïve Bayes SVM (whole dictionary)	80.90
Naïve Bayes SVM (3K small dictionary)	80.81

3.3 Classification with Textual Features

We now evaluate the performance of textual features on image aesthetics assessment. In both training and testing, user comments are available. For each image, we concatenate all user comments and generate textual input for feature extraction. We applied three commonly-adopted approaches for textual feature extraction, *i.e.*, Recurrent Neural Networks Language Model [5], Word2Vec [7], and Naïve Bayes features, on the AVA-Comments dataset.

To evaluate the performance of these feature extraction approaches, we built SVM classifier to map extracted features to aesthetics labels of images and examine the classification accuracy. Specifically, we trained a Recurrent Neural Networks Language Model [5] and a Word2Vec [7] model with the user comments. We then extracted textual features utilizing trained neural network models and built a L2-regularized L2-loss linear SVM classifier for aesthetics classification.

Meanwhile, we applied SVM on extracted Naïve Bayes features (denoted with "whole dictionary"). Since the dictionary size computed on the full training data is large (over a million), we further selected 2,000 items with the largest weights and 1,000 items with the smallest weights. These items indicate the most positive or negative phrases, forming a 3,000-item smaller dictionary. Note that we set number of positive and negative phrases according to the number of high and low quality images in the AVA dataset. A same classifier is built on word count vectors given the small dictionary and the results are shown in Table 2. The smaller dictionary is shown to keep aesthetics information to a large extent.

We present the classification results in Table 2, we found that Naïve Bayes SVM (whole dictionary) performed the best. We also found the Naïve Bayes SVM (3K small dictionary) achieved comparable performance. We thus adopted this scheme in the joint representation learning.

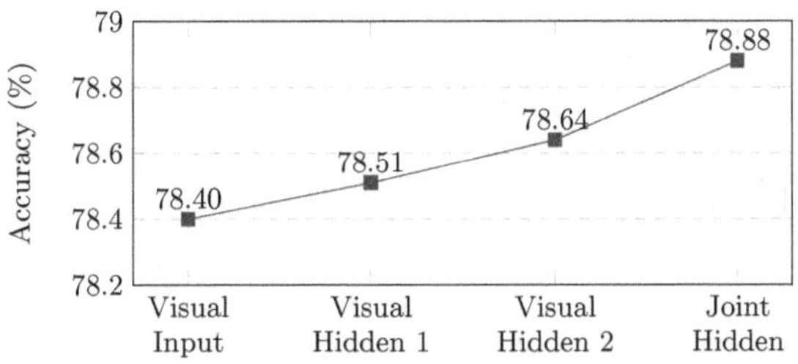

Figure 3: Classification accuracy of different layers in the multimodal DBM model with a single modality as input.

Figure 4: Test images correctly classified by the joint representation but misclassified by the visual feature. Images on the first row are high-aesthetics images and the second row are low-aesthetics images.

3.4 Classification with Joint Representation

We finally evaluate the performance of our proposed joint representation on image aesthetics assessment. The multimodal DBM model is trained as described in Section 2.3, where visual and textual features are extracted as discussed in Sections 3.2 and 3.3. The joint DBM model has three parts. The input dimension of a visual feature was 4,096, followed by a Gaussian RBM hidden layer with 3,072 nodes. The second hidden layer contained 2,048 nodes. Meanwhile, the word count vector of the 3,000-item dictionary was used as the textual input. The input dimension of a textual feature was 3,000, followed by a Replicated Softmax hidden layer of 1,536 nodes. The second hidden layer contained 1,024 nodes. To merge these two set of multimodal features, the joint hidden layer contains 3,072 nodes. The model was optimized using Contrastive Divergence (CD), and layer-wise pretraining described in [15] was performed. Finally, variational inference was used to generate the joint representation. Because we evaluate the aesthetic value of an image only based on its visual feature, the approach can be applied to situations where comments are not available.

To visualize the performance of neurons in each hidden layer in the multimodal DBM model, an L2-regularized L2-loss linear SVM that maps neurons in each layer to aesthetics labels is trained. As shown in Fig. 3, joint representation outperforms the visual feature representation, and the classification accuracy is gradually improved when utilizing representations from the input layer to the joint hidden layer.

To illustrate the difference between the visual feature representation and the joint representation of an image, we visualize several representative images that are correctly classified by the joint representation but misclassified by the visual feature in Fig. 4. The first row are high-aesthetics images and the second row are low-aesthetics ones.

Figure 5: Representative items in the dictionary with their top-related images.

To examine the power of the joint representation in inferring the textual representation of test images, we picked several representative words and show their most closely related images. As shown in Fig. 5, images accurately represent the semantic meaning of words/phrases in the dictionary (*e.g.*, blurry, dramatic sky, and pose). Notably, like any learning-based methods, ours is limited when a phrase has few training examples. For instance, images related to "technical success" are often just macro photos.

4. CONCLUSIONS

This paper presented a multimodal DBM model to encode both images and their users' comments into a joint representation to improve image aesthetics assessment. Features extracted from a single modality, either images or user comments, were systematically evaluated. A joint representation was then built upon most effective visual and textual features. A large dataset with images and user comments, the AVA-Comments dataset, was built. Experiments on the AVA-Comments dataset showed that the proposed joint representation could improve image aesthetics prediction results produced by merely visual feature. The relatively small improvement indicates that the problem is challenging and requires more fundamental technological advancements.

Acknowledgments

This material is based upon work partially supported by the National Natural Science Foundation of China under Grant No. 61273299 and the National Science Foundation under Grant No. 1110970.

5. REFERENCES

[1] S. Bhattacharya, R. Sukthankar, and M. Shah. A framework for photo-quality assessment and enhancement based on visual aesthetics. In *ACM International Conference on Multimedia (MM)*, pages 271–280, 2010.

[2] R. Datta, D. Joshi, J. Li, and J. Z. Wang. Studying aesthetics in photographic images using a computational approach. In *European Conference on Computer Vision (ECCV)*, pages III, 288–301, 2006.

[3] S. Dhar, V. Ordonez, and T. Berg. High level describable attributes for predicting aesthetics and interestingness. In *IEEE Conference on Computer Vision and Pattern Recognition (CVPR)*, pages 1657–1664, June 2011.

[4] Y. Ke, X. Tang, and F. Jing. The design of high-level features for photo quality assessment. In *IEEE Conference on Computer Vision and Pattern Recognition (CVPR)*, volume 1, pages 419–426, 2006.

[5] S. Kombrink, T. Mikolov, M. Karafiát, and L. Burget. Recurrent neural network based language modeling in meeting recognition. In *INTERSPEECH*, pages 2877–2880, 2011.

[6] A. Krizhevsky, I. Sutskever, and G. E. Hinton. ImageNet classification with deep convolutional neural networks. In *Advances in Neural Information Processing Systems (NIPS)*, pages 1097–1105, 2012.

[7] Q. Le and T. Mikolov. Distributed representations of sentences and documents. In *International Conference on Machine Learning (ICML)*, pages 1188–1196, 2014.

[8] X. Lu, Z. Lin, H. Jin, J. Yang, and J. Z. Wang. RAPID: Rating pictorial aesthetics using deep learning. In *ACM International Conference on Multimedia (MM)*, pages 457–466, 2014.

[9] Y. Luo and X. Tang. Photo and video quality evaluation: Focusing on the subject. In *European Conference on Computer Vision (ECCV)*, pages 386–399, 2008.

[10] L. Marchesotti, F. Perronnin, D. Larlus, and G. Csurka. Assessing the aesthetic quality of photographs using generic image descriptors. In *IEEE International Conference on Computer Vision (ICCV)*, pages 1784–1791, 2011.

[11] G. Mesnil, T. Mikolov, M. Ranzato, and Y. Bengio. Ensemble of generative and discriminative techniques for sentiment analysis of movie reviews. *arXiv:1412.5335*, 2014.

[12] N. Murray, L. Marchesotti, and F. Perronnin. AVA: A large-scale database for aesthetic visual analysis. In *IEEE Conference on Computer Vision and Pattern Recognition (CVPR)*, pages 2048–2415, 2012.

[13] M. Nishiyama, T. Okabe, I. Sato, and Y. Sato. Aesthetic quality classification of photographs based on color harmony. In *IEEE Conference on Computer Vision and Pattern Recognition (CVPR)*, pages 33–40, 2011.

[14] K. Simonyan and A. Zisserman. Very deep convolutional networks for large-scale image recognition. *CoRR*, abs/1409.1556, 2014.

[15] N. Srivastava and R. R. Salakhutdinov. Multimodal learning with deep boltzmann machines. In *Advances in Neural Information Processing Systems (NIPS)*, pages 2222–2230, 2012.

[16] X. Tian, Z. Dong, K. Yang, and T. Mei. Query-dependent aesthetic model with deep learning for photo quality assessment. *IEEE Transactions on Multimedia (TMM)*, 17(11):2035–2048, 2015.

[17] P. Veerina. Learning good taste: Classifying aesthetic images. Technical report, Stanford University, 2015.

[18] S. Wang and C. D. Manning. Baselines and bigrams: Simple, good sentiment and topic classification. In *Proceedings of the 50th Annual Meeting of the Association for Computational Linguistics*, pages 90–94, 2012.

Who is where? Matching People in Video to Wearable Acceleration During Crowded Mingling Events

Laura Cabrera-Quiros[1,2], Hayley Hung[1]
[1]Delft University of Technology, Netherlands
[2]Instituto Tecnológico de Costa Rica, Costa Rica
{l.c.cabreraquiros, h.hung}@tudelft.nl

ABSTRACT

We address the challenging problem of associating acceleration data from a wearable sensor with the corresponding spatio-temporal region of a person in video during crowded mingling scenarios. This is an important first step for multi-sensor behavior analysis using these two modalities. Clearly, as the numbers of people in a scene increases, there is also a need to robustly and automatically associate a region of the video with each person's device. We propose a hierarchical association approach which exploits the spatial context of the scene, outperforming the state-of-the-art approaches significantly. Moreover, we present experiments on matching from 3 to more than 130 acceleration and video streams which, to our knowledge, is significantly larger than prior works where only up to 5 device streams are associated.

Keywords

Mingling, wearable sensor, computer vision, association

1. INTRODUCTION

Mingling scenarios involve a dense concentration of people who come together to socialize. Examples of these events are parties, drinks receptions or networking events, and have the potential to hold rich information about how people could potentially influence each other. These kinds of events have received increasing interest from the multimedia, computer vision, and ubiquitous computing communities [6, 13, 5, 8, 1]. However, as the number of people participanting increases they become increasingly challenging to interpret with computer vision alone, due to the difficulties of analyzing the human form under appearance changes, shape deformations and body occlusions.

The use of other modalities, in addition to video, has proven to be a suitable alternative [2, 11]. Thus, each additional modalitiy acts as a complementary source of information in combination with video. For instance, Alameda-Pineda et al. [1] showed improvements in the detection and analysis of free-standing conversational groups by leveraging, along with video, speaking status and proximity using wearable audio and infrared (IR).

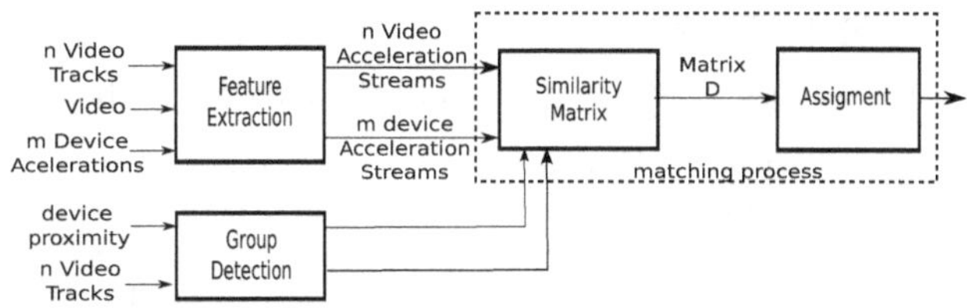

Figure 1: Overview of our approach

Although using wearable sensors as complementary source of information has many advantages, manually associating a specific device to a particular region of the video (where a person is wearing the device) quickly becomes unfeasible as the number of people to be associated increases. So, an automatic association is needed. However, with a higher number of samples to associate per modality the correct associations become harder to discriminate in a short time. Also, mingling events are challenging scenarios where people's social behavior, unlike simple actions like walking, does not tend to have a predictable and easily distinguishable pattern.

In this paper, we associate a time series signal from a wearable accelerometer to a video acceleration stream extracted from a region of video containing the person wearing the wearable device. We chose accelerometers as they are the simplest and most widespread sensors capturing movement.

The main contributions of this paper are: (i) we address large-scale data association in challenging crowded environments, (ii) we propose a novel method based on an extension of the Hungarian algorithm to automatically associate wearable devices via their acceleration reading to its wearer in video (spatio-temporal region) and (iii) we leverage the use of proximity information from the wearable devices and video as a spatial prior to the association process. Using the proximity, we can subdivide the association problem to areas in the real world sharing the same spatial-social context.

The closest works to our own are [15, 10, 9, 12]. Shigeta et al. [10] detected an object which contains an accelerometer out of many moving objects recorded by a single camera, using Normalized Cross-Correlations. Rofouei et al. [9] and Wilson and Benko [15] proposed similar methods to match the accelerometers and gyroscope of a smartphone to the pixels in a 3D video recorded with a Kinect. These approaches can only handle one device at a time and are conceived for scenarios where the person (or object) wearing the device is clearly moving in the video.

Finally, Teixeira et al.[12] identify and localize moving smartphones (by accelerometers and magnetometers) in a

MM '16, October 15 - 19, 2016, Amsterdam, Netherlands

ISBN 978-1-4503-3603-1/16/10...$15.00

DOI: http://dx.doi.org/10.1145/2964284.2967224

camera network using a Hidden Markov Models. Although they proposed a solution for more than one device, their experiments have one single person walking under the network of cameras, from which they later 'generate' more participants. They do not address the challenges from a crowded scene making their solution infeasible for mingling groups.

Compared to these works, our approach proposes a considerable increase in the number of accelerometers to be associated. To the best of our knowledge, we are the first to consider the association of video with multiple wearable devices in such crowded scenarios and with more than 5 device streams. In addition, we propose to solve the association problem in a much more challenging context where people's behavior can not be as easily characterized (e.g. walking).

2. OUR APPROACH

Our approach is summarized in Fig. 1 and detailed below.

2.1 Feature extraction

For a wearable device, a single acceleration stream is obtained using the magnitude of the 3 axes. Each axis is first normalized using its mean and variance over the entire time.

To associate each device stream with a region containing a person all the regions of interest (or bounding boxes), which include a person, are first extracted. Then, we concatenate the bounding boxes over time for each person, which results in the track (area over time) for that person. The Vatic tool [14] for video annotation was used to extract the bounding boxes. Using the SPOT tracker [16] gave us similar results but since this work only focuses on the already challenging problem of associating large numbers of streams and not in tracking we chose a manual labeling tool.

Next, for each track, an acceleration stream is calculated as follows. First, we extract dense optical flow for the video. Then, for each frame, we take the magnitude of all the flow vectors inside the box and compute the mean for those with a magnitude greater than zero. Thus, we obtain a vector of mean flow magnitudes for a given track over the entire video of length T samples, which represents the speed of movement for that person.This captures the influence of fine grained movements, originating from subtle social behavior such as gestures or laughter, as well as movement of the entire body. Fig. 2 illustrates the input and output of this step for 3 tracks (subjects). Finally, we compute the acceleration vector from the speed using finite difference approximation.

After we extract the acceleration streams from the video and wearable devices, we proceed to treat each stream as follows. First, we normalize the maximum value of all streams to one, so a comparison between video and wearable acceleration can be made. Next, we apply a sliding window calculating the variance over each stream. Using this instead of the raw acceleration gave us a better representation of changes in movement activity of each person.

2.2 Similarity measurements

Both video and acceleration streams are noisy because they capture only partially the behavior of a person. Therefore, we need measurements to assess how similar 2 streams are and not if they are equal. Different widely used [4] metrics are compared to quantify the affinity between the acceleration streams from video and the devices: covariance (COV), Dynamic Time Warping Distance (DTW) and Mutual Information (MI).

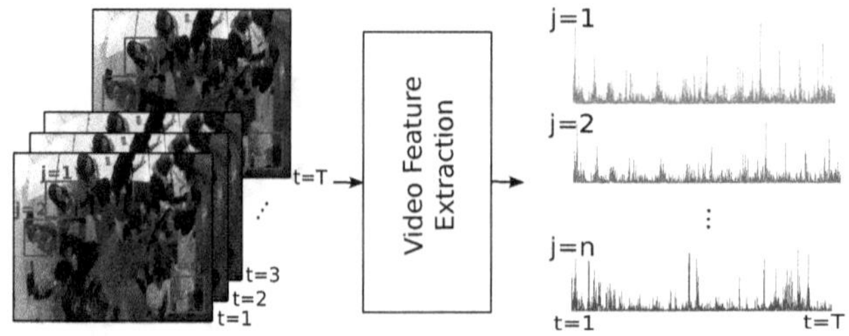

Figure 2: Feature extraction from video for 3 example tracks (subjects). Output: speed stream for each participant for interval of length T

2.3 Assignment methods

We consider the matching process to be an assignment problem where m elements of a set M (device streams) need to be associated with n elements of a set N (video streams), by fulfilling a given function or constraint. A distances matrix $\mathbf{D}$ (size $m \times n$) is formed by the pairwise distances between all possible combinations of m acceleration and n video streams, where

$$\mathbf{D}_{ij} = d(i,j), i \in \{1 \cdots m\} \text{ and } j \in \{1 \cdots n\} \quad (1)$$

and d is one of the similarity metrics from Section 2.2.

Winner-takes-all (greedy) association

State-of-the-art methods ([10, 9, 15]) use a greedy approach where the element in $\mathbf{D}$ that has the highest value determines the assignment. The corresponding column and row are removed from $\mathbf{D}$ and the assignment process is repeated, if applicable. This will be our baseline.

Hungarian method

Although the winner-takes-all method is a reasonable baseline, it does not consider that there is likely to be noise in both sensor streams. Hence, it may not be able to distinguish one possible assignment from the other. This is particularly problematic as the number of streams increases. Trying to optimize the assignments globally may help.

The Hungarian method [3] computes a solution for the assignment problem by optimally matching the elements m and n, based on a global optimization of $\mathbf{D}$. For this assignment problem, given the matrix of distances $\mathbf{D}$, the aim is to find the global cost c that minimizes

$$c = \min_{S^* \in S} \sum_{i=1}^{m} \sum_{j=1}^{n} d(i,j) w(i,j) \quad (2)$$

where $w(i,j)$ is the binary weight for matrix $\mathbf{W} \in \{0,1\}^{m \times n}$ for the element (i,j), and S is the set of all matrices $\mathbf{W}$ that fulfill 3 constraints: (i) no more than one weight equals to 1 per column so $\mathbf{W}\mathbf{1}_n \leq \mathbf{1}_m$, (ii) no more than one weight equals to 1 per row so $\mathbf{1}_m^T\mathbf{W} \leq \mathbf{1}_n^T$ and (iii) the total number of weights sums to one such that $\mathbf{1}_m^T\mathbf{W}\mathbf{1}_n = min(m,n)$. Thus, the elements of sets M and N can only be paired once and the method chooses the set of pairs with the lowest total pairing cost. Several solutions exist to solve this problem [3].

Hierarchical Hungarian method

As the number of people increases, there is a higher probability of finding similar streams. It is desirable for a potential real-time application to be able to rely on shorter time intervals to make the association. But if the streams are too short, we will not have enough observable behavior for the distance metric to be discriminative.

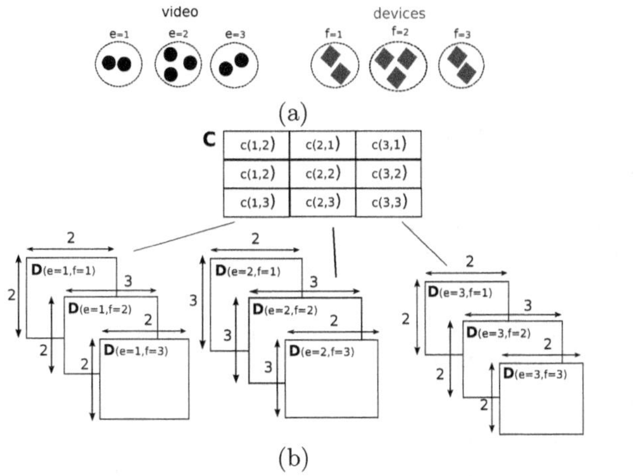

Figure 3: Example of assignment method. (a) Devices and Video streams representations. The dotted circles show the group detection. (b) Our proposed *Hierarchical Hungarian* method using the streams and clusters from (a).

As a solution, we hypothesize that subdividing the problem based on the local spatial neighborhood in each sensor modality can improve the numbers of correctly associated streams, which exploits the spatial and social context of the gathering. Thus, we propose an extension to the Hungarian method by performing the assignment in a hierarchical manner, using a divide-and-conquer strategy. All streams are subdivided into groups in each modality, reducing the initial assignment problem from a global to local optimization, defined by the number of groups in each modality.

So, the n video and m accelerometer streams are clustered into p groups for the acceleration and q groups for the video streams, as seen in Fig. 3(a). Then, $p \times q$ different distance matrices are generated; one for each group combination (e, f) where indices $e \in \{1 \cdots p\}$ and $f \in \{1 \cdots q\}$. For each of these matrices, the corresponding stream assignment is calculated. Within each group-to-group matching, the possible stream combinations are now reduced to $n'_e \times m'_f$, where n'_e and m'_f are the number of elements in the eth and f^{th} device and video groupings, respectively.

Each group-to-group assignment cost $c(e, f)$ is then obtained by Eq.2 and placed in a new matrix $\mathbf{C}$ (see Fig. 3(b)), which represents the costs of assigning the elements within each possible group combination e and f. Each cost $c(e, f)$ must be normalized by dividing by the number of assignments made so $\mathbf{C_{ef}} = c(e, f)/\min(m'_f, n'_e)$. For example, when comparing a group of 3 streams against a group of 2, only 2 costs from the 3×2 matrix are used for the final assignment. Finally, the Hungarian algorithm is applied to matrix $\mathbf{C}$ to find the optimal group-to-group assignment. The stream assignment for that specific group-to-group pairing is then chosen. Our Hierarchical Hungarian assignment procedure is illustrated in Fig. 3.

2.4 Clustering Devices and Video Streams

We propose to generate the groups by clustering based on their proximity over a particular time interval. The group detection must be performed independently per sensor type.

Each of the devices outputs a dynamic binary proximity graph (see Section 3), which is later refined to eliminate false neighbor detections using the method proposed by Martella et al. [7]. To do so, they apply a density-based clustering to group all the neighbor detections in time (see [7] for more details). Finally, maximal cliques are identified from the proximity graph to obtain p sets of fully connected nodes. We choose maximal cliques as this clustering method has proven to be an accurate approximation for conversational groups [6].

To cluster the video streams, we use the tracks extracted for each of the participants. For each frame of the video, an affinity matrix $\mathbf{A}$ is created, which defines a symmetric distance between person i and j $\mathbf{A}_{ij} = -e^{\frac{d_{ij}}{2\sigma^2}}$ where d_{ij} is the Euclidean distance in the image plane between the centroids of the bounding boxes for person i and j and σ is the width of the Gaussian kernel. In our experiments, σ was set to 150 pixels, as this was an approximate value for group distance given the image size and resolution of the camera. Then, we apply the group detection algorithm that extracts clusters as maximal cliques in edge-weighted graphs [6].

This is an iterative procedure that optimizes the group clustering based on the notion of a dominant set. If we have a graph G with each node representing the centroid of a person's bounding box and the affinity between people to be the edges, we can consider a representation of the closeness of a subset S of the graph as follows. We define a measure called the average weighted degree of a vertex $i \in S$ with respect to set S as $k_S(i) = \frac{1}{|S|}\sum_{j \in S} a_{ij}$. The relative affinity between node $j \notin S$ and i is defined as $\phi_S(i, j) = a_{ij} - k_S(i)$, and the weight of each i with respect to a set $S = R \cup \{i\}$ is defined recursively as

$$w_S(i) = \begin{cases} 1 & \text{if} |S| = 1 \\ \sum_{j \in R} \phi_R(j, i)\, w_R(j) & \text{otherwise} \end{cases} \quad (3)$$

$w_S(i)$ measures the overall relative affinity between i and the rest of the vertices in S, weighted by the overall affinity of the vertices in R. Therefore to find the cliques in the graph $w_S(i) > 0, \forall i \in S$. For every graph, only one maximal clique can be identified at a time and a peeling strategy is employed where the same conditions are repeatedly applied to the remaining sub-graph until no more cliques remain. Finally, the cliques identified per frame are combined into a single set of groupings using majority voting.

3. DATA

We collected video and wearable acceleration for 30 participants during a group gathering. This data was collected in a real mingling scenario after a speed dating event, where people were encouraged to mingle. Each person wore a wearable device hung around the neck which recorded triaxial acceleration at 20 Hz. These devices also have a binary proximity detector based on beacon communication with other devices. Thus, each device emits its own ID to all other devices around it allowing the devices to synchronize every second and detect each other from 2-3 meters away. The detection of a device is considered as a proximity detection (binary signal). Finally, overhead video was captured using 5 different GoPro Hero 3+ cameras that covered the whole mingling area with some overlap.

Due to hardware malfunction only 28 devices recorded data during the event. Also, people entering the field of view for just a small interval of time or those who's appearance was only captured partially for the camera (less than 50%) were excluded, as we do not intend to evaluate the impact of heavy visual occlusion in the matching process yet. After

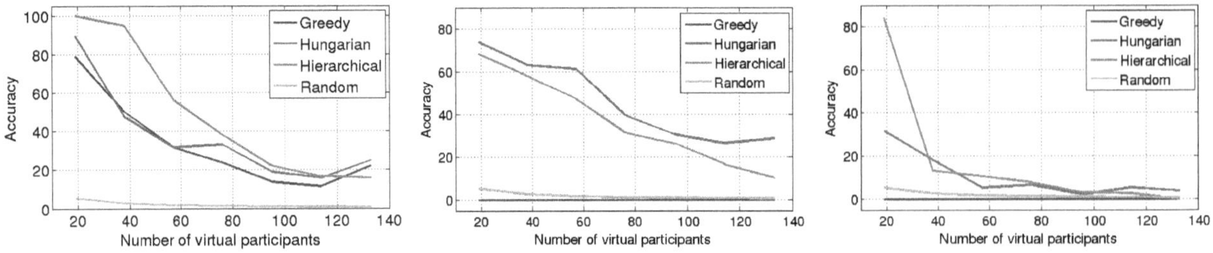

(a) (b) (c)

Figure 4: Accuracy of the stream association for our proposed method (Hierarchical), the state-of-the-art (Hungarian and Greedy) and a random baseline (Random) using (a) COV, (b) DTW and (c) MI.

Table 1: Association accuracy of the Hungarian and Hierarchical Hungarian method using 100s intervals using the COV

Nº Partic.	19	38	76
Hungarian	47.37	36.84	29.83
Hierarchical	**73.68**	**76.32**	**39.47**

these restrictions, we have video and acceleration streams for 19 subjects, for about 6 minutes.

4. EXPERIMENTS AND RESULTS

4.1 Generating virtual streams

Although significantly higher than those in previous works, our number of subjects is still rather low. To go further, we used *virtual streams*, similarly to Teixeira et al. [12], by splitting the total time interval of the streams into smaller intervals and treating each one as if they were occurring at the same time. Unlike [12], our data contains densely crowded mingling behavior so the dense crowding property holds across the virtual participants. From our 19 original streams, we created subsets with 38, 57, 76, 95, 114 and 133 virtual subjects, increasing significantly the number of streams we could associate. This leads inevitably to a reduction in the length of the streams, which is a trade-off that we also study in the following section.

4.2 Results

Fig. 4 shows the assignment accuracy against the number of participants for the 3 assignment methods in Section 2.3 and the metrics in Section 2.2. To stress test the number of streams to associate, we generate up to 133 virtual participants. Note that by repeatedly splitting the interval by a factor from 1 to 7 we have a time interval of 360s for 19 participants (original data), 180s for 38, and up to 51s for 133 participants for these figures.

Comparison between assignment methods

As seen in Fig.4, both Hungarian approaches performed significantly better than the random baseline when using the COV and the DTW metrics. Furthermore, our Hierarchical approach tends to have a higher accuracy than the other 2 methods when using the COV for less than 80 participants.

These results, although promising, are obtained using increasingly shorter intervals of the virtual streams. Due to this, Table 1 shows the accuracy for the two Hungarian-based methods using the same length of 100s for all streams and the COV as metric. For this test, given the data available, we can only split our data into 3 sets of virtual streams. Here, our Hierarchical Hungarian method still outperforms the Hungarian method, so the interval length is not necessarily the reason for the higher accuracies.

Table 2: Upper bound case: assignment accuracy using the Hierarchical Hungarian assignment where the correct group-to-group matching is known.*

	Nº Partic.	19	38	57	76	95	114	133
Acc(%)	COV	**100**	**94.7**	**89.5**	**82.9**	**81.1**	**86.0**	**79.7**
	DTW	**100**	89.5	80.7	82.9	75.8	82.5	75.2
	MI	84.2	76.3	56.1	64.5	67.4	66.7	66.9

*Group-to-group matching is manually annotated

Although outperforming the other methods, the accuracy for our Hierarchical Hungarian method decreases with a higher number of participants. We hypothesize that as the number of groups increases but the observation time remains low, the method will now have problems to discriminate between the groups instead of streams. Table 2 summarizes the assignment accuracy for all the metrics and different virtual streams using an ideal group-to-group matching, where the groups are matched manually based on the ground truth, instead of the matches chosen automatically by our method.

These results represent the upper bound for our Hierarchical method and suggests that the errors in Fig. 4(a) are introduced by the group-to-group matching, implying that a minimum time is needed to discriminate between groups.

Comparison between metrics

The performance for the Hierarchical Hungarian method is better overall than the Hungarian method when using for the COV but not so for the DTW distance. This implies that, unlike the COV, the costs chosen as globally optimal for assignments using the DTW are very similar between each other, making the matrix **C** noisy and difficult to discriminate for the Hierarchical Hungarian method. A particularly interesting result is the low accuracy achieved when using the MI as the similarity metric. However, previous works have shown that when 2 people interact, their MI tend to increase [4]. Thus, due to this and our rather short intervals, this metric it might not be adequate in our case.

5. CONCLUSION

We show a novel method for associating wearable devices to the region in the video of the person wearing the device, using its acceleration and radio-based proximity. We also have shown that using the spatial and social context as a preprocessing step for accelerometer and video stream matching increases the accuracy of our association method, particularly as the number of candidate streams increases. This leads to an increase in the matching accuracy of 47% when the spatial context was exploited for 38 participants. The number of devices used represents a considerable increase compared to previous efforts. In addition, we proposed an empirical validation for extending further the amount of devices to associate.

6. REFERENCES

[1] X. Alameda-Pineda, Y. Yan, E. Ricci, O. Lanz, and N. Sebe. Analizing free-standing convers. groups:a multimodal approach. *ACMMM*, 2015.

[2] G. Bahle, P. Lukowicz, K. Kunze, and K. Kise. I see you: How to improve wearable activity recognition by leveraging information from environmental cameras. *PerCom*, 2013.

[3] B. Burkard, M. D.'Amico, and S. Martello. *Assignment problems*. 2009.

[4] E. Delaherche, M. Chetouani, A. Mahdhaoui, C. Saint-Georges, S. Viaux, and D. Cohen. Interpersonal Synchrony: A Survey of Evaluation Methods across Disciplines. *Trans. on Affective Computing*, 2012.

[5] T. Gan, Y. Wong, D. Zhang, and M. Kankanhalli. Temporal encoded F-formation system for social interac. detection. In *ACMMM*, 2013.

[6] H. Hung and B. Krose. Detecting F-formations as dominant sets. *ICMI*, 2011.

[7] C. Martella, M. Dobson, A. van Halteren, and M. Van Steen. From proximity sensing to spatial-temporal social graphs. *PerCom*, 2014.

[8] C. Martella, E. Gedik, L. Cabrera-Quiros, G. Englebienne, and H. Hung. How Was It? Exploiting Smartphone Sensing to Measure Implicit Audience Responses to Live Performances. In *ACMMM*, 2015.

[9] M. Rofouei, A. Wilson, A. Brush, and S. Tansley. Your Phone or Mine? Fusing Body, Touch and Device Sensing for Multi-User Device-Display Interaction. In *CHI*, 2012.

[10] O. Shigeta, S. Kagami, and K. Hashimoto. Identifying a moving object with an accelerometer in a camera view. In *IROS*, 2008.

[11] S. Stein and S. Mckenna. Comb. embedded accelerometers with computer vision for recogn. food preparation activities. *UbiComp*, 2013.

[12] T. Teixeira, D. Jung, and A. Savvides. Tasking networked CCTV cameras and mobile phones to identify and localise multiple persons. *UbiComp*, 2010.

[13] S. Vascon, E. Mequanint, M. Cristani, H. Hung, M. Pelillo, and V. Murino. A Game-Theoretic Probabilistic Approach for Detecting Conversational Groups . In *ACCV*, 2014.

[14] C. Vondrick, D. Patterson, and D. Ramanan. Efficiently Scaling Up Crowdsourced Video Annotation. *IJCV*, 2012.

[15] A. Wilson and H. Benko. CrossMotion:fusing device and image motion for user identif., tracking and device association. In *ICMI*, 2014.

[16] L. Zhang and L. Van Der Maaten. Structure Preserving Object Tracking. *IEEE CVPR*, 2013.

Supervised Recurrent Hashing for Large Scale Video Retrieval

Yun Gu
School of Biomedical Engineering
Shanghai Jiao Tong University
Shanghai, China
geron762@sjtu.edu.cn

Chao Ma
Institute of Image Processing and Pattern Recognition
Shanghai Jiao Tong University
Shanghai, China
sjtu_machao@sjtu.edu.cn

Jie Yang*
Institute of Image Processing and Pattern Recognition
Shanghai Jiao Tong University
Shanghai, China
jieyang@sjtu.edu.cn

ABSTRACT

Hashing for large-scale multimedia is a popular research topic, attracting much attention in computer vision and visual information retrieval. Previous works mostly focus on hashing the images and texts while the approaches designed for videos are limited. In this paper, we propose a *Supervised Recurrent Hashing* (SRH) that explores the discriminative representation obtained by deep neural networks to design hashing approaches. The long-short term memory (LSTM) network is deployed to model the structure of video samples. The max-pooling mechanism is introduced to embedding the frames into fixed-length representations that are fed into supervised hashing loss. Experiments on UCF-101 dataset demonstrate that the proposed method can significantly outperforms several state-of-the-art methods.

Keywords

Video Retrieval; Recurrent Neural Networks; Supervised Hashing

1. INTRODUCTION

Finding the nearest neighbors of the query data is a fundamental problem in many applications of data mining, computer vision and information retrieval. Traditional search techniques are difficult to be directly used for large-scale database since the computational cost of similarity calculation with high-dimensional feature is very expensive. Recently, hashing techniques are increasingly popular for scalable similarity search. The basic task for hashing is to map the high-dimensional data into compact binary codes incorporating various machine learning approaches ranging from unsupervised [5, 6] to semi-supervised [14] to supervised methods [1, 10, 18]. Most of the existing approaches are designed for data (e.g. images or texts) with fixed length.

*Jie Yang is the corresponding author.

MM '16, October 15-19, 2016, Amsterdam, Netherlands

DOI: http://dx.doi.org/10.1145/2964284.2967225

However, with the increasing popularity of video-based services, fast retrieval for videos is in urgency. Unlike images and texts, videos are compromised with variable size of frames that are temporally related. Several attempts tend to address the video hashing approaches including multiple feature hashing [12] and submodular hashing [2]. Although the performance is promising, these method directly use the traditional LSH [3] and Spectral Hashing [15] to index each frame where the structure of video is not introduced; In order to generate fixed-length of binary codes, key frame selection are deployed in these approaches. However, how to determine the key frames in videos is a difficult task in computer vision community. Structure learning-based hashing [16] models the video structure with local and global temporal information. However, it is still a single frame-based approach that cannot generate fixed-length binary code based on variable-length videos. The similarity between two videos is measured by sum of the pairwise similarity between hash code of frames which leads to high storage and computation consumptions. Moreover, methods mentioned above are based on hand-crafted features (e.g. SIFT and HOG) designed for static images. These features cannot effectively represent the semantic content in frames.

The visual recognition for static images has been boosted by deep Convolutional Neural Networks (CNN) [9]. [11] shows that the output of layers in CNN can be used for visual features in many computer vision applications. Inspirited by recent advances in machine translation, the Recurrent Neural Network (RNN), which is proved to be a powerful sequence model, shows the state-of-the-art performance in video classification and captioning [4]. In their approaches, a fixed-length feature extracted by CNN is fed into the RNN as input. The combination of CNN and RNN can provide both discriminative frame-based features and long-term video structure information. Therefore, it arises a possibility to design a hashing system exploiting the deep structure of neural networks to effectively generate hash codes for videos.

In this paper, we propose a Supervised Recurrent Hashing (SRH) approach exploiting the deep neural networks for applications in video hashing. The main contributions of SRH are outlined as follows: (1) SRH is a supervised learning framework compromised with four key components. The first component is a deep convolutional neural network (CNN) to learn image representation from raw frames. The second component is a long-short term memory (LSTM) network which models the long-term video structure. The out-

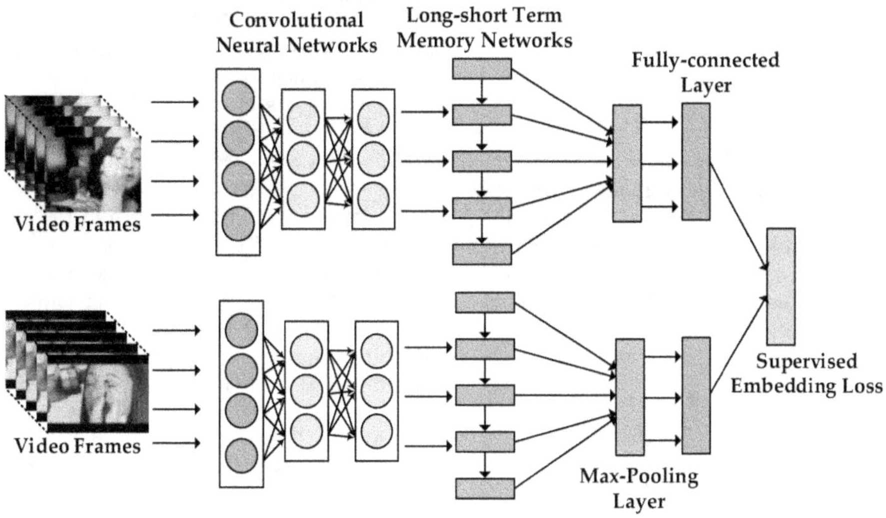

Figure 1: Workflow of the proposed framework.

put from LSTM is fed into the third component, a combination of max-pooling and fully-connected layer to obtain the fixed-length of hash code. And the fourth component is a loss function to measure the quality of hash codes guided by the pairwise labels. (2) Experiments on real datasets show that SRH method can outperform other methods to achieve the state-of-the-art performance in video retrieval tasks.

The reminder of this paper is organized as follows: The details of SRH is presented in Section 2. In Section 3, we conduct extensive experiments to evaluate the performance of SRH in comparisons with some state-of-the-art methods. The conclusion and the discussion on future work are presented in Section 4.

2. SUPERVISED RECURRENT HASHING

2.1 Notations

Suppose we have a training video collection $X = \{X_i; y_i\}$, $i = 1, \dots, N$ with N videos, where $X_i = \{x_i^{(j)}\}, j = 1, \dots, n_i$ is a video consisting of n_i successive frames, y_i is the label of video X_i which indicates the class assignment of samples. The task for our work is to obtain a hashing function $f(\cdot)$ to generate a K bits binary code $b_i \in \{0, 1\}^K$ for each video[1], i.e. $b_i = f(X_i)$. Unlike previous works [16] which generate frame-based binary codes, the proposed method can generate fixed-length binary codes from variable-length videos.

2.2 Model

Figure 1 depicts our framework using deep neural networks and pairwise embedding loss to generate binary hash codes from videos. Given a video, each frame is fed into the convolutional neural networks to generate discriminative representations. All frame-based features are sent to the long-short term memory network where a series of hidden states are obtained. The max-pooling layer integrates all hidden states into a fixed length of output and finally the binary codes are generated by the fully connected layer. To minimize the semantic reconstruction loss of hash codes, we introduce the pairwise embedding layer on top of the networks based on the labels of videos.

[1]It can also be in form of $b_i \in \{-1, +1\}^K$.

The first component of is a convolutional neural network to generate visual feature for each frame. In this paper, we follow the AlexNet architecture proposed in [9] which is originally designed for image classification. The first seven layers of AlexNet are deployed through which a 4096d feature can be obtained. For each video X_i, The CNN can be regarded as a non-linear function $f_{CNN}(\cdot)$ which generates a set of features $\{z_i^{(t)}\}, t = 1, \dots, n_i$ and:

$$z_i^{(t)} = f_{CNN}(x_i^{(t)}) \tag{1}$$

Given the frame-based features, previous works model the temporal structures in two ways: (1) manually design the weight or learn to select the key frames which are representative among all frames [2, 12] and (2) maximize the similarity between successive frames [16]. In this paper, we exploit the long short term memory networks (LSTM) [7], which is a successful variant of RNN, to keep both temporal and long-term information of the video. Relying on the LSTM unit in [17], the output $\{z_i^{(t)}\}, j = 1, \dots, N_i$ from the fc6 layer of CNN is fed into LSTM step-by-step to generate hidden states $\{h_i^{(t)}\}, j = 1, \dots, N_i$ as follows:

$$\begin{aligned}
i_t &= \sigma(W_{x^i} z_i^{(t)} + W_{h^i} h_i^{(t-1)} + b_i) \\
f_t &= \sigma(W_{x^f} z_i^{(t)} + W_{h^f} h_i^{(t-1)} + b_f) \\
o_t &= \sigma(W_{x^o} z_i^{(t)} + W_{h^o} h_i^{(t-1)} + b_o) \\
g_t &= \sigma(W_{x^g} z_i^{(t)} + W_{h^g} h_i^{(t-1)} + b_g) \\
c_t &= f_t \odot c_{t-1} + i_t \odot g_t \\
h_i^{(t)} &= o_t \odot \phi(c_t)
\end{aligned} \tag{2}$$

where c_t is a memory cell state, σ is the sigmoidal non-linearity, $\phi$is the hyperbolic tangent non-linearity, $\odot$ represents the element-wise product with the gate value, and the weight matrices denoted by W_{ij} and biases $b_j$are the trained parameters. As proved in [4], LSTM can well model the structure of videos for various applications. The output from LSTM is integrated into a fixed-length of hash codes by the max-pooling layer as follows:

$$\begin{aligned}\tilde{h}_i &= \mathcal{F}(\{h_i^{(t)}\}) \\ \tilde{h}_{i,j} &= \max\{|h_{i,j}^{(1)}|, \ldots, |h_{i,j}^{(t)}|, \ldots, |h_{i,j}^{(n_i)}|\}\end{aligned} \tag{3}$$

where $\mathcal{F}(\cdot)$ is the max-pooling function which is proved to outperform the average pooling in many literatures. Unlike the hand-crafted features based on static frames, the pooling operation is reasonable over hidden states from LSTM since it can indicate both long-term and short-term information of videos. The pooled feature is sent to a fully connected layer to generate K bit hash code as follows:

$$u_i = sgn(W_h \tilde{h}_i) \tag{4}$$

where $sgn(\cdot)$ is the sign function. However, the sign function leads to discontinuous and non-differentiable problems and thus is difficult to be optimized via gradient descent. To address this problem, we propose a *tanh*-like approximation $o(\nu)$ of the sign function:

$$o(\nu) = \frac{1 - e^{-\beta\nu}}{1 + e^{-\beta\nu}} \tag{5}$$

where β is a tuning parameter to control the smoothness. Therefore, we can obtain the final hash code u_i of video X_i.

Since the binary codes are used to fast video retrieval, the hashing functions should preserve the semantic similarity between videos. More specifically, we try to reconstruct the semantic similarity matrix by the learned hash codes. Hence, the final component of SRH is a supervised embedding loss which minimize the following squared error:

$$\min \mathcal{L} = \frac{1}{2} \sum_{i,j} (\frac{1}{K} u_i^T u_j - S_{i,j})^2 \tag{6}$$

where $S_{i,j}$ is the pairwise similarity based on labels of X_i and X_j:

$$S_{i,j} = \frac{y_i^T y_j}{\|y_i\|_2 \cdot \|y_j\|_2} \tag{7}$$

2.3 Learning

To learn the SRH model, we need to obtain the parameters of neural networks. Stochastic gradient descent (SGD) is used to learn the parameters. In particular, in each iteration we sample a minibatch of points from the whole training set, and then perform learning based on these sampled points. We use back-propagation (BP) to learn the parameters. For layers in CNN and LSTM, the derivatives of parameters have been derived by previous literatures. Here, we compute the derivatives of the loss function as follows:

$$\frac{\partial \mathcal{L}}{\partial u_i} = \frac{1}{K^2}(u_i^T u_j)u_j - S_{i,j}u_j \tag{8}$$

These derivatives can be fed into the former layers of the network to update the parameters through BP strategy.

2.4 Out-of-Sample Extension

For any video which is not in the training set, we can obtain its hash code by inputing all frames into the SRH network. Instead of using the *tanh*-like function in training, we directly replace it with the sign function to generate the final binary code.

3. EXPERIMENTS

In this section, we provide extensive experiments and comparison studies on UCF-101 dataset [13]. The UCF-101 dataset consists of over 12,000 videos categorized into 101 human action classes. We follow the settings in [4] where 9,537 videos are used for training and 3,783 videos for testing.

To demonstrate the strength of the proposed method, we compare SRH with several representative hashing methods on video retrieval task. The following three methods will be compared: Traditional Hashing techniques: Spectral Hashing (SH) [15] and Iteration Quantization (ITQ) [5]; Video Hashing approach: Structure Video Hashing (VHDT) [16][2]. Although [2] and [12] are also designed for video hashing, they are built on standard hashing techniques like LSH and require specific settings, like submodular and multiple-feature representations. Therefore, they are not considered as comparison in this paper which is also mentioned in [16].

3.1 Experimental Settings and Evaluation

In order to conduct fair comparison, we extract the 4096d deep convolutional feature from the fc-6 layer in our SRH neural networks for frame-based representation. We also extract the 256d output from LSTM of each frame as feature for SH and ITQ to demonstrate the power of LSTM in modeling the video structure. Therefore, SH and ITQ are denoted by SH-CNN/ITQ-CNN with CNN features and SH-LSTM/ITQ-LSTM with LSTM features. . For baseline methods, the similarity between videos is calculated as [16] does.

The performance of retrieval is evaluated with Mean Average Precision (MAP).For a query q,the average precision is defined as:

$$AP(q) = \frac{1}{L_q} \sum_{r=1}^{R} P_q(r)\delta_q(r) \tag{9}$$

where L_q is the number of ground truth neighbours in the retrieved list. $P_q(r)$ is the precision of the top r retrieved results and $\delta_q(r) = 1$ if the r-th result is the true neighbour and 0 otherwise. We also report the precision and recall with 128 bit hash codes according to different numbers of retrieved samples. The precision-recall curve is also provided.

All experiments are conducted on a workstation with Intel Xeon E5 CPU @3.70GHz, 16GB RAM and NVIDIA TitanX GPU. SRH is implemented with widely-used deep learning framework Caffe [8].

3.2 Results

We firstly report the MAP of all approaches in Table 1. The hash codes are generated with different length including 8, 16, 32, 64 and 128 bits. As can be seen, our method achieves the best performance over all the other methods in most cases. The performance improvements are consistent as the number of hash bits varies. Compared with SH-CNN and ITQ-CNN which are based on single frame features, the SRH significantly improves the MAP value. Although VHDT has considered the local and global structure of video samples, the performance is still not promising since it cannot capture long-term structure information. Another criti-

[2]The source code of this method is not public. We carefully implement it with MATLAB.

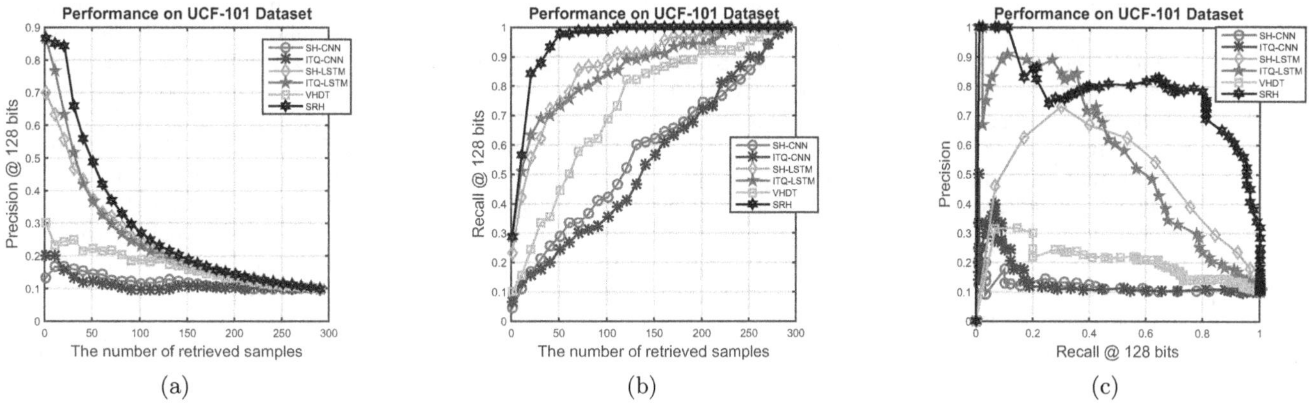

Figure 2: Performance comparison of different algorithms on the UCF-101 dataset. (a) Precision-Recall curve with 128 bits code (b) Recall with 128 bits code based on different numbers of retrieved samples. (c) Precision with 128 bits code based on different numbers of retrieved samples

cal observation is that the LSTM feature can largely improve the performance of original CNN feature. However, the proposed method introduce the supervised information which leads to better performance. Moreover, the hash codes for videos are generated in fixed length but not variable with the video length.

Table 1: MAP Result on UCF-101 Dataset. The best performance is shown in boldface.

Code Length (bit)	Methods		
	SH-CNN	ITQ-CNN	VHDT
$c = 8$	0.1141	0.1138	0.1890
$c = 16$	0.1281	0.1127	0.1665
$c = 32$	0.1312	0.1060	0.2711
$c = 64$	0.1352	0.1562	0.2137
$c = 128$	0.1235	0.1383	0.2060
Code Length (bit)	Methods		
	SH-LSTM	ITQ-LSTM	SRH
$c = 8$	0.2511	0.5383	**0.5578**
$c = 16$	0.5331	0.7140	**0.7161**
$c = 32$	0.5295	**0.7520**	0.6920
$c = 64$	0.5435	0.7186	**0.7537**
$c = 128$	0.4967	0.5674	**0.7808**

Figure 2 illustrates the performance on recall and precision of all approaches. It can be observed that SRH achieves better performance by comparing precision and recall with 128 bits hash codes. With the number of retrieved samples increases, the proposed SRH can achieve higher recall and precision than baseline methods.

4. CONCLUSION

In this paper, we propose a *Supervised Recurrent Hashing* (SRH) that explores the discriminative representation obtained by deep neural networks to design hashing approaches. The long-short term memory (LSTM) network is deployed to model the structure of video samples. The max-pooling mechanism is introduced to embedding the frames into fixed-length representations that are fed into supervised hashing loss to learn hash codes. As shown in experimental results, our framework can achieve better performance in video retrieval on UCF-101 dataset than the state-of-the-art approaches. Moreover, the exploiting of LSTM feature can also improve the traditional methods. Future work includes utilizing the motion cue from videos (e.g. Optical Flow) which can further improve the retrieval performance.

Acknowledgement

This work is partly supported by NSFC, China (No: 61572315) and 973 Plan, China (No. 2015CB856004).

5. REFERENCES

[1] M. M. Bronstein, A. M. Bronstein, F. Michel, and N. Paragios. Data fusion through cross-modality metric learning using similarity-sensitive hashing. In *Computer Vision and Pattern Recognition (CVPR), 2010 IEEE Conference on*, pages 3594–3601. IEEE, 2010.

[2] L. Cao, Z. Li, Y. Mu, and S.-F. Chang. Submodular video hashing: a unified framework towards video pooling and indexing. In *Proceedings of the 20th ACM international conference on Multimedia*, pages 299–308. ACM, 2012.

[3] M. Datar, N. Immorlica, P. Indyk, and V. S. Mirrokni. Locality-sensitive hashing scheme based on p-stable distributions. In *Proceedings of the twentieth annual symposium on Computational geometry*, pages 253–262. ACM, 2004.

[4] J. Donahue, L. Anne Hendricks, S. Guadarrama, M. Rohrbach, S. Venugopalan, K. Saenko, and T. Darrell. Long-term recurrent convolutional networks for visual recognition and description. In *Proceedings of the IEEE Conference on Computer Vision and Pattern Recognition*, pages 2625–2634, 2015.

[5] Y. Gong and S. Lazebnik. Iterative quantization: A procrustean approach to learning binary codes. In *Computer Vision and Pattern Recognition (CVPR), 2011 IEEE Conference on*, pages 817–824. IEEE, 2011.

[6] Y. Gu, H. Xue, J. Yang, and P. Shi. Cross-modality hashing with partial correspondence. In *Image*

Processing (ICIP), 2015 IEEE International Conference on, pages 1925–1929. IEEE, 2015.

[7] S. Hochreiter and J. Schmidhuber. Long short-term memory. *Neural computation*, 9(8):1735–1780, 1997.

[8] Y. Jia, E. Shelhamer, J. Donahue, S. Karayev, J. Long, R. Girshick, S. Guadarrama, and T. Darrell. Caffe: Convolutional architecture for fast feature embedding. In *Proceedings of the ACM International Conference on Multimedia*, pages 675–678. ACM, 2014.

[9] A. Krizhevsky, I. Sutskever, and G. E. Hinton. Imagenet classification with deep convolutional neural networks. In *Advances in neural information processing systems*, pages 1097–1105, 2012.

[10] S. Kumar and R. Udupa. Learning hash functions for cross-view similarity search. In *IJCAI Proceedings-International Joint Conference on Artificial Intelligence*, volume 22, page 1360, 2011.

[11] A. Razavian, H. Azizpour, J. Sullivan, and S. Carlsson. Cnn features off-the-shelf: an astounding baseline for recognition. In *Proceedings of the IEEE Conference on Computer Vision and Pattern Recognition Workshops*, pages 806–813, 2014.

[12] J. Song, Y. Yang, Z. Huang, H. T. Shen, and R. Hong. Multiple feature hashing for real-time large scale near-duplicate video retrieval. In *Proceedings of the 19th ACM international conference on Multimedia*, pages 423–432. ACM, 2011.

[13] K. Soomro, A. R. Zamir, and M. Shah. Ucf101: A dataset of 101 human actions classes from videos in the wild. *arXiv preprint arXiv:1212.0402*, 2012.

[14] J. Wang, S. Kumar, and S.-F. Chang. Semi-supervised hashing for large-scale search. *Pattern Analysis and Machine Intelligence, IEEE Transactions on*, 34(12):2393–2406, 2012.

[15] Y. Weiss, A. Torralba, and R. Fergus. Spectral hashing. In *Advances in neural information processing systems*, pages 1753–1760, 2009.

[16] G. Ye, D. Liu, J. Wang, and S.-F. Chang. Large-scale video hashing via structure learning. In *Proceedings of the IEEE International Conference on Computer Vision*, pages 2272–2279, 2013.

[17] W. Zaremba and I. Sutskever. Learning to execute. *arXiv preprint arXiv:1410.4615*, 2014.

[18] Y. Zhen and D.-Y. Yeung. Co-regularized hashing for multimodal data. In *Advances in Neural Information Processing Systems*, pages 1376–1384, 2012.

Adaptation of Word Vectors using Tree Structure for Visual Semantics

Nakamasa Inoue
Tokyo Institute of Technology, Tokyo, Japan
inoue@ks.cs.titech.ac.jp

Koichi Shinoda
Tokyo Institute of Technology, Tokyo, Japan
shinoda@cs.titech.ac.jp

ABSTRACT

We propose a framework of word-vector adaptation, which makes vectors of visually similar concepts close to each other. Here, word vectors are real-valued vector representation of words, e.g., *word2vec* representation. Our basic idea is to assume that each concept has some hypernyms that are important to determine its visual features. For example, for a concept *Swallow* with hypernyms *Bird*, *Animal* and *Entity*, we believe *Bird* is the most important since birds have common visual features with their feathers etc. Adapted word vectors are obtained for each word by taking a weighted sum of a given original word vector and its hypernym word vectors. Our weight optimization makes vectors of visually similar concepts close to each other, by giving a large weight for such important hypernyms. We apply the adapted word vectors to zero-shot learning on the TRECVID 2014 semantic indexing dataset. We achieved 0.083 of Mean Average Precision, which is the best performance without using TRECVID training data to the best of our knowledge.

1. INTRODUCTION

With advances in information and communication technologies, a large amount of image, video and text data have been made available on the Internet. Semantic analysis of such data has received a growing amount of attention since it has many multimedia applications such as search, surveillance, summarization, and robot vision. However, it has been a challenging topic due to the semantic gap [1], the lack of correspondence between low-level features and high-level semantic concepts such as objects, actions, and scenes.

For semantic analysis, knowing semantic relation between concepts is important. For example, relation between objects and/or scenes has shown to play important roles to bridge the semantic gap in recent works on zero-shot object recognition [2, 3, 4], concept localization [5], and event recounting [6].

A recent trend to extract semantic relation is to utilize word vectors [7, 8, 9], which represent a word by a real-valued vector. Since word vectors have interesting property that semantic regularities are captured by vector operations, e.g., the result of $v(\mathrm{King}) - v(\mathrm{Man}) + v(\mathrm{Woman})$ is close to $v(\mathrm{Queen})$ where $v(w) \in \mathbb{R}^d$ is a word vector of a word w, they can directly help to know the semantic relation between concepts. However, since word vectors are typically trained on a text corpus such as Wikipedia, similar words (concepts) found by them are not always visually similar to each other. This inspires us to propose a framework of word-vector adaptation for visual semantics.

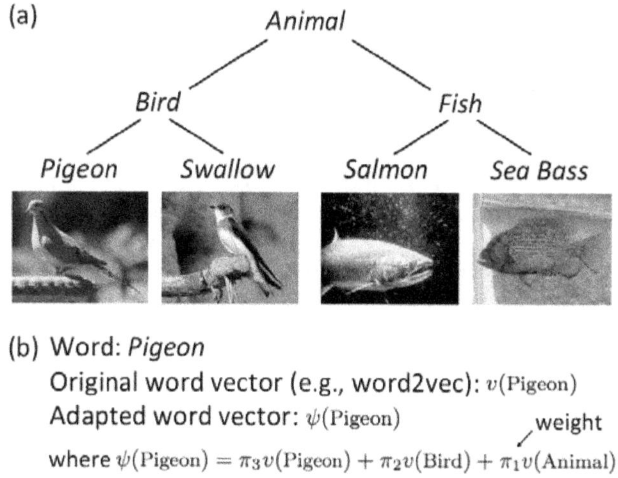

Figure 1: Adaptation of word vectors. (a) Example tree structure to obtain hypernyms of words. (b) An adapted word vector for *Pigeon*, which is obtained from weighted sum of original word vectors with its hypernyms. The weight coefficients are optimized on training data to make vectors of visually similar concepts close to each other.

To discuss visual similarity, let's have a question: *Why are Swallow and Pigeon visually similar?* If we answer to this question by *Because they are ____s*, which hypernym is appropriate for the blank: *Bird* or *Animal*? Because birds have common visual features with their feathers etc., we believe *Bird* is more appropriate. This implies that a hypernym *Bird* is an important word to explain the visual features of *Swallow* and *Pigeon*, and gives us an idea to use hyponyms for word-vector adaptation to image and video applications.

Our key contribution is a framework of word-vector adaptation based on hypernyms of words shown in Figure 1. From original word vectors given by a word embedding method such as Skip-gram model [7], our proposed framework ex-

MM '16, October 15 - 19, 2016, Amsterdam, Netherlands

ISBN 978-1-4503-3603-1/16/10...$15.00

DOI: http://dx.doi.org/10.1145/2964284.2967226

tracts adapted word vectors, which represent a word w by a weighted sum of its original word vector and its hypernym word vectors. Our weight optimization algorithm gives a large weight for important hyponyms, e.g., *Bird* for *Swallow*, to make vectors of visually similar concepts close to each other. In experiments, we apply adapted word vectors to zero-shot learning on the TRECVID Semantic Indexing dataset [10] to show the effectiveness of our framework. Here, zero-shot learning [2, 3, 4] is a type of learning which assumes that 1) target categories for training and testing are disjoint, and 2) traning images and/or videos are given only for training categories. We use 1,000 object categories from ImageNET [11] and 30 concept categories from TRECVID for training and testing, respectively.

The rest of this paper is organized as follows. Sec. 2 describes related works. Sec. 3 presents the proposed framework. Sec. 4 shows experimental evaluations, and Sec. 5 describes the conclusion with future work.

2. RELATED WORK

To extract word vectors, many word embedding methods have been proposed in the field of natural language processing with their applications such as machine translation [12] and web-document classification [13]. Latent semantic analysis [14] based on matrix factorization of a word frequency matrix is known to be a standard method. Some recent methods are focusing on the word analogy task, which aims to answer semantic questions about objects or places. The Skip-gram model proposed by Mikolov et al. [7] trains word vectors from a large-scale text corpus by using a neural network. The Global vector representation (GloVe) [9] introduces cooccurrence statistics to matrix factorization. With these methods, word analogies are represented by vector operations in the word-vector space. For example, the analogy of "Man is to Woman as King is to Queen" is represented by the fact that the result of $v(\text{King}) - v(\text{Man}) + v(\text{Woman})$ is close to $v(\text{Queen})$ where $v(w) \in \mathbb{R}$ is a word vector of a word w.

Since these word analogies include semantic relation between concepts such as objects and scenes, they can be directly introduced to visual applications. For example, zero-shot learning [15, 16] is known to be one of its major applications. Since zero-shot learning assumes sets of object categories for training and testing are disjoint, visual similarity between concepts often plays an important role. However, similar words (concepts) found by word vectors trained on a text corpus are not always visually similar to each other.

If we have labeled images and videos, a straightforward way to measure visual similarity is to use visual features. For feature extraction, a recent trend is to train visual features with a statistical model from large-scale datasets. For example, supervised learning of deep convolutional neural networks [17, 18] has been shown to be effective. The parameters of these networks are typically trained on ImageNET images [11], and are often fine-tuned on other data such as TRECVID videos [10]. For example, Snoek et al. have shown the effectiveness of deep neural networks in video semantic indexing and event detection [19].

Without using training images, it is also known that visual similarity between concepts can be obtained from specific metadata. For example, attribute metadata about colors and textures, which relates attributes with objects, has shown to be effective to detect objects such as animals [15, 16, 20]. Meta descriptions of events, which relate concepts to events, are often introduced to event detection [21, 22, 23]. The Skip-gram model [7] is also introduced in [24]. With these studies, visual similarity can be measured because detailed metadata often describes about visual information of objects, events, and scenes. However, manual attachment of such metadata is known to be costly.

In contrast, our framework of word-vector adaptation to visual applications aims to make word vectors of visually similar concepts close to each other without using metadata. Notably, our proposed framework is complementary to recent zero-shot learning techniques including domain adaptation [25, 26, 27, 28], distance modification [29], and joint learning [30, 31].

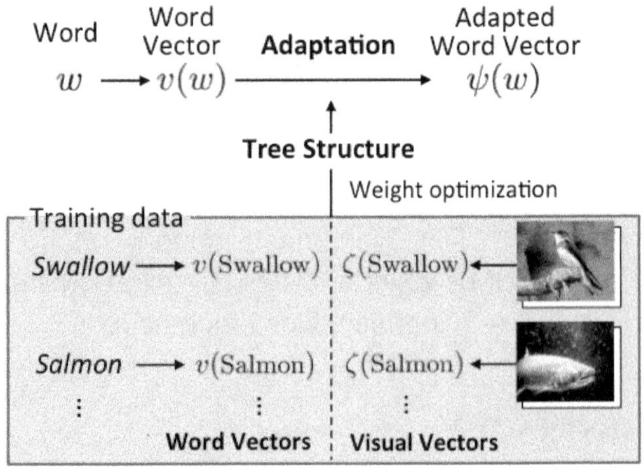

Figure 2: Overview of adaptation of word vectors. From training data, word vectors and visual vectors are extracted for each concept. They are used to optimize parameters for adaptation using tree structure.

3. PROPOSED FRAMEWORK

This section presents our proposed framework of word-vector adaptation shown in Figure 2. Let $v(w) \in \mathbb{R}^d$ be a word vector of a word w given by a word embedding method. The proposed framework represents a word w by an adapted word vector $\psi(w)$, which is defined by a weighted sum of an original word vector and its hypernym word vectors.

For example, two words *Swallow* and *Pigeon* with hypernyms *Bird* and *Animal* are represented by

$$\psi(\text{Swallow}) = \pi_3 v(\text{Swallow}) + \pi_2 v(\text{Bird}) + \pi_1 v(\text{Animal}), \quad (1)$$

$$\psi(\text{Pigeon}) = \pi_3 v(\text{Pigeon}) + \pi_2 v(\text{Bird}) + \pi_1 v(\text{Animal}), \quad (2)$$

where π is a weight coefficient. If *Bird* is an important hypernym to decide visual features of *Swallow* and *Pigeon* as discussed in Introduction, our algorithm will give $\pi_2 > \pi_1, \pi_3$ to make the two vectors, $\psi(\text{Swallow})$ and $\psi(\text{Pigeon})$, close to each other as a result.

In the following, word-vector adaptation using tree structure is presented in Sec. 3.1 and weight optimization algorithm is presented in Sec. 3.2. To the best of our knowledge, our framework to make word vectors of visually similar concepts close to each other based on hypernyms of words is novel.

3.1 Adaptation of Word Vectors

For each word w, we assume that a set of its hypernyms $A(w)$ is given by a lexical database such as WordNet [32], with hierarchical tree structure. The adapted word vector for w is defined by

$$\psi(w) = \sum_{a \in A(w) \cup \{w\}} \pi_{d(a)} v(a) \quad (3)$$

where $d(a)$ is the depth of a word a in the tree structure.

In Eq. (3), we introduced restriction for weight coefficients: all words with depth d have the same weight. This is for solving the data insufficiency problem in zero-shot learning. For example, if we have training samples for (hyponyms of) *Bird*, this helps to determine the weight for the other words at the same depth level, e.g., *Fish* in Figure 1, without training samples. This restriction is reasonable in practice with several ten thousand of training concepts available on recent image and video datasets such as ImageNET [11].

3.2 Weight Optimization

The goal here is to determine weight coefficients π_d in Eq. (3) from training data. Our idea is to minimize distance between the following two similarity matrixes.

1. $K_{ij} = k(\psi(y_i), \psi(y_j))$: word similarity matrix where $\psi(y)$ is an adapted word vector for a concept y with indexes $i, j = 1, 2, \cdots, |\mathcal{Y}|$ for the concepts for training.

2. $K'_{ij} = k'(\zeta(y_i), \zeta(y_j))$: visual similarity matrix where $\zeta(y)$ is a visual vector of a concept y discussed later.

Here, k and k' are kernel functions such as the RBF kernel. Weight coefficients are optimized by

$$\hat{\pi} = \underset{\pi}{\text{argmin}} \, \|K - K'\|. \quad (4)$$

The standard steepest descent method, in which the gradient is calculated by a finite difference approximation, is used to optimize π from an initial value of $\pi_d = 0$.

Finally, we discuss what the visual vector $\zeta(y_i)$ of a concept y_i is. With supervised learning methods, a concept is represented by a parametric classifier. This suggests that a concept can be represented by a vector of trained parameters. For example, for a softmax classifier, which is often used as the final layer of convolutional neural networks, is given by

$$\text{Softmax}(y_i|x) = \frac{\exp(f(y_i|x))}{\sum_j \exp(f(y_j|x))} \quad (5)$$

with a function

$$f(y_i|x) = a_i^T x + b_i. \quad (6)$$

Concatenation of the parameters a_i and b_i can be used as a visual vector, i.e., $\zeta(y_i) = (a_i^T, b_i)^T$.

4. EXPERIMENTS

We apply our word-vector adaptation to zero-shot learning experiments on two datasets, TRECVID and ImageNET. In the following, we first present a short summary of an application to zero-shot learning and then show our experimental settings and results.

Table 1: Evaluation on the TRECVID dataset. *Zero-shot baseline* uses the zero-shot learning framework in [28] with word vectors in [9] and Google Inception network [18]. *Ours* introduces the adapted word vectors to the baseline. The other three methods are from official submissions at TRECVID 2014. In the second column, *None* does not use training data, *Web Images* collects and uses training data from Google Search for each TRECVID concept, *TRECVID Videos* uses all training TRECVID videos. Mean Average Precision (Mean AP) for each method is reported.

Method	Training Data for TRECVID concepts	MeanAP(%)
Zero-shot baseline	None	6.37
Ours	None	**8.31**
Jiang et al.[33]	Web Images	1.21
McGuinness et al.[34]	Web Images	7.97
Snoek et al.[35]	TRECVID Videos	33.19

4.1 Application to Zero-shot Learning

Let $\mathcal{Y}$ and $\mathcal{Z}$ be disjoint sets of concepts for training and testing, respectively. In zero-shot learning [3, 5, 28], since training data is available only for concepts in $\mathcal{Y}$, a concept detector for $z \in \mathcal{Z}$ is build by a convex combination of trained detectors for $\mathcal{Y}$ as

$$f(z|x) = \frac{1}{C} \sum_{y \in \mathcal{Y}} \psi(y)^T \psi(z) f(y|x), \quad (7)$$

where $\psi(\cdot)$ is an adapted word vector, f is a detection function, $C = \|\psi(z)\| \|\sum_y \psi(y) f(y|x)\|$ is a normalization coefficient, and x is a testing image/video.

4.2 Experimental Settings

The TRECVID dataset consists of 800 hours of Internet videos with creative commons licenses used in the TRECVID 2014 semantic indexing task [10]. The goal is to detect 30 semantic concepts such as *Airplane*, *Dog*, and *Cityscape* from each video shot. Shot boundaries are provided with the dataset. The number of video shots is 547,634 for training and 107,806 for testing. For zero-shot experiments, we use the ImageNET images of 1,000 objects for training and TRECVID videos for testing. Note that TRECVID videos are not used for training. The evaluation measure is Mean Average Precision (Mean AP) over the 30 concepts, which is calculated by using the official toolkit and annotations.

The ImageNET dataset consists of 1,281,167 images for training, and 50,000 images for testing [1], with ground-truth labels of 1,000 object categories used at the ILSVRC 2012 competition [11]. We make a zero-shot learning task on this dataset under the following *leave-one-out* setting: repeat experiments 1,000 times so that 1) each category is selected once for testing, and 2) the rest 999 categories are used for training.

The word vectors in [9] trained on the Wikipedia dataset are used to extract adapted word vectors. The Google Inception Net [18] is used to train visual classifiers. RBF-kernels are used for the kernels in Sec. 3.2. We apply k-nearest

[1] We use the official "validation" set for testing, because the ground-truth labels for the official "test" set are not publicly available.

Table 2: Evaluation on the ImageNET dataset. *Zero-shot baseline* uses the zero-shot learning framework in [3] with word vectors in [9] and Google Inception network [18]. *Ours* introduces the adapted word vectors to the baseline. *Supervised* uses ImageNET training images. Mean Average Precision (Mean AP) and Top-5 Accuracy (Acc.) are reported.

Method	Mean AP (%)	Top-5 Acc. (%)
Zero-shot baseline	7.79	26.79
Ours	9.37	30.29
Supervised [18]	50.50	88.90

neighbor search to Eq.(7) by following the parameter settings in [3] and [28] for ImageNET and TRECVID, respectively.

4.3 Experimental Results

4.3.1 Performance Comparison

Table 1 and Table 2 show performance comparison on the TRECVID dataset and the ImageNET dataset, respectively. We see our method improves the performance on both datasets.

Compared with the other methods at the no-annotation semantic indexing task in TRECVID 2014 [10], which requires not to use TRECVID official training videos and allows to collect Web images by using search engines for supervised learning, we also see in Table 1 that our method outperforms its best performance of 7.97% in Mean AP. Note that our method did not use training images or videos for TRECVID concepts.

However, there is still a gap between supervised methods [18, 19] using official training data and our zero-shot method. To bridge the gap, improvement not only on word vectors, but also on visual classifiers is needed. For example, since we used detectors for 1,000 objects from ImageNET in our experiments, adding detectors for actions would be interesting as a next step. Audio analysis to detect concepts such as *Singing* and *MusicalInstruments* is also needed.

4.3.2 Analysis

Table 3 shows an example of tree structure for two object categories, *GoldFish* and *SnowBird*, with trained weight coefficients for each depth level. We see that the largest weight is given for the depth level of 12. From a biological point of view, this level mainly has *Classes* and *Orders* in the biological taxonomy, which are groups of animals whose physical features are similar to each other, e.g., *BonyFish* and *OscineBird*. Since physical features and visual features are often correlated, this supports our assumption that concepts have some hypernyms that decide their visual features.

Figure 3 shows the top 3 concepts from training data selected for *BoatShip* and *Baby*. We see that more visually similar concepts are selected with our method, such as *LifeBoat* and *OceanLiner* for *BoatShip*. For *Baby*, since its hypernyms or hyponyms are not included in the ImageNET dataset, the baseline method mainly selected animals, whose birth is often announced in news articles, e.g., *Panda*. On the other hand, our method improved the detection performance by selecting visually similar objects often seen with a baby, e.g. *Crib*.

Table 3: Tree structure for GoldFish and SnowBird. d: depth in the tree. π_d: obtained weights.

d	π_d	Tree structure	
1	0.03	*Entity*	
7	0.27	*Organism*	
8	0.30	*Animal*	
9	0.31	*Craniate*	
10	0.29	*AquaticVertebrate*	*Bird*
11	0.28	*Fish*	*PasseriformBird*
12	**0.43**	***BonyFish***	***OscineBird***
13	0.31	*Teleost*	*Finch*
14	0.35	*SoftFinnedFish*	*SnowBird*
15	0.27	*CypriniformFish*	
16	0.13	*CyprinidFish*	
17	0.06	*GoldFish*	

Figure 3: Top 3 ImageNET concepts selected by the baseline and our methods for two TRECVID concepts, (a) BoasShip and (b) Baby.

5. CONCLUSION

We proposed a framework of word-vector adaptation, which makes word vectors of visually similar concepts close to each other We applied our framework to zero-shot learning experiments on TRECVID and ImageNet datasets, and showed the performance improvement. Our future work will focus on audio and action analysis using word vectors.

Acknowledgments

This work was supported by JSPS KAKENHI 15K16019.

6. REFERENCES

[1] A.W.M. Smeulders, M. Worring, S. Santini, A. Gupta, and R. Jain. Content-Based Image Retrieval at the End of the Early Years. In IEEE Transactions on PAMI, vol.22, no.12, pp.1349–1380, 2000.

[2] T. Mensink, E. Gavves, and C.G.M. Snoek. Costa: Co-occurrence Statistics for Zero-shot Classification. *Proc. CVPR*, 2014.

[3] M. Norouzi, T. Mikolov, S. Bengio, Y. Singer, J. Shlens, A. Frome, G. Corrado, and J. Dean. Zero-shot Learning by Convex Combination of Semantic Embeddings. *Proc. ICLR*, 2014.

[4] A. Frome, G. S. Corrado, J. Shlens, S. Bengio, J. Dean, and T. Mikolov. Devise: A Deep Visual-semantic Embedding Model. *Proc. NIPS*, 2013.

[5] M. Jain, J.C. van Gemert, T.Mensink, and C.G.M. Snoek. Objects2action: Classifying and Localizing Actions without Any Video Example. *Proc. ICCV*, 2015.

[6] Q. Yu, J. Liu, H. Cheng, A. Divakaran, H. Sawhney. Multimedia event recounting with concept based representation. *ACM Multimedia*, 2012.

[7] T. Mikolov, K. Chen, G. Corrado, and J. Dean. Efficient Estimation of Word Representations in Vector Space. *Proc. ICLR*, 2013.

[8] T. Mikolov, I. lya Sutskever, Kai Chen, Greg Corrado, and Jeffrey Dean. Distributed Representations of Words and Phrases and their Compositionality. *Proc. NIPS*, 2013.

[9] J. Pennington, R. Socher, and C.D. Manning. GloVe: Global Vectors for Word Representation. *In Empirical Methods in Natural Language Processing*, pp.1532–1543, 2014.

[10] G. Awad, A. Smeaton, W. Kraaij, G. Quéenot, R. Ordelman, and R. Aly. TRECVID 2015 – An Overview of the Goals, Tasks, Data, Evaluation Mechanisms and Metrics. *Proc. TRECVID workshop*, 2015.

[11] O. Russakovsky, J. Deng, H. Su, J. Krause, S. Satheesh, S. Ma, Z. Huang, A. Karpathy, A. Khosla, M. Bernstein, A.C. Berg, and L. Fei-Fei. ImageNet Large Scale Visual Recognition Challenge. *In IJCV*, vol.115, no.3, pp.211–252, 2015.

[12] H. Schwenk. Continuous space language models. *In Computer Speech and Language*, vol. 21, 2007.

[13] C. Xing, D. Wang, X. Zhang, and C. Liu. Document classification with distributions of word vectors. *In Proc. APSIPA*, pp.1-5, 2014.

[14] S. Deerwester, S.T. Dumais, G.W. Furnas, T.K. Landauer, and R. Harshman, Indexing by Latent Semantic Analysis, *In Journal of the American Society for Information Science*, vol.41, 1990.

[15] C. Lampert, H. Nickisch, and S. Harmeling. Learning to Detect Unseen Object Classes by Between-Class Attribute Transfer. *Proc. CVPR*, 2009.

[16] Z. Akata, F. Perronnin, Z. Harchaoui, and C. Schmid. Label Embedding for Attribute-Based Classification. *Proc. CVPR*, 2013.

[17] A. Krizhevsky, I.Sutskever, and G.E. Hinton. ImageNet Classification with Deep Convolutional Neural Networks. *Proc. NIPS*, pp.1–9, 2012.

[18] C. Szegedy, W Liu, Y Jia, P. Sermanet, S. Reed, D. Anguelov, D. Erhan, V. Vanhoucke and A. Rabinovich. Going Deeper with Convolutions *Proc. CVPR*, 2015.

[19] C.G.M. Snoek, et al., Qualcomm Research and University of Amsterdam at TRECVID 2015: Recognizing Concepts, Objects, and Events in Video. *Proc. TRECVID workshop*, 2015.

[20] M. Rohrbach, M. Stark, and B. Schiele. Evaluating Knowledge Transfer and Zero-Shot Learning in a Large-scale Setting. *Proc. CVPR*, 2011.

[21] L. Jiang, D. Meng, T. Mitamura, and A.G. Hauptmann. Easy Samples First: Self-Paced Reranking for Zero-Example Multimedia Search. *Proc. ACM Multimedia*, 2014.

[22] A. Habibian, T. Mensink, and C.G.M. Snoek. Composite Concept Discovery for Zero-shot Video Event Detection. *Proc. ICMR*, 2014.

[23] S. Wu, S. Bondugula, F. Luisier, X. Zhuang, and P. Natarajan. Zero-shot Event Detection using Multi-modal Fusion of Weakly Supervised Concepts. *Proc. CVPR*, pp.2665–2672, 2014.

[24] L. Jiang, S.-I Yu, D. Meng, T. Mitamura, and A.G. Hauptmann. Bridging the Ultimate Semantic Gap: A Semantic Search Engine for Internet Videos. *Proc. ICMR*, 2015.

[25] E. Gavves, T. Mensink, T. Tommasi, C.G.M. Snoek, and T. Tuytelaars. Active Transfer Learning With Zero-Shot Priors: Reusing Past Datasets for Future Tasks. *Proc. ICCV*, 2015.

[26] E. Kodirov, T. Xiang, Z. Fu, and S. Gong. Unsupervised Domain Adaptation for Zero-Shot Learning. *Proc. ICCV*, 2015.

[27] Z. Zhang, and V. Saligrama. Zero-Shot Learning via Semantic Similarity Embedding. *Proc. ICCV*, 2015.

[28] N. Inoue, and K. Shinoda. Vocabulary Expansion using Word Vectors for Video Semantic Indexing. *Proc. ACM Multimedia*, 2015.

[29] Z. Fu, T. Xiang, E. Kodirov, and S. Gong. Zero-Shot Object Recognition by Semantic Manifold Distance. *Proc. CVPR*, 2015.

[30] J.L. Ba, K. Swersky, S. Fidler, and R. Salakhutdinov. Predicting Deep Zero-Shot Convolutional Neural Networks Using Textual Descriptions. *Proc. ICCV*, 2015.

[31] X. Li, Y. Guo, and D. Schuurmans. Semi-Supervised Zero-Shot Classification With Label Representation Learning. *Proc. ICCV*, 2015.

[32] G. A. Miller. WordNet: A Lexical Database for English. *In Communications of the ACM*, vol.38, no.11, pp.39–41, 1995.

[33] L. Jiang, et al., CMU-Informedia at TRECVID Semantic Indexing, *Proc. TRECVID workshop*, 2014.

[34] K. McGuinness, et al., Insight Centre for Data Analytics at TRECVid 2014: Instance Search and Semantic Indexing, *Proc. TRECVID workshop*, 2014.

[35] C.G.M. Snoek, et al., Video Concept Detection by Deep Nets with FLAIR (MediaMill at TRECVID 2014). *Proc. TRECVID workshop*, 2014.

Adaptive Bitrate Selection for Video Encoding with Reduced Block Artifacts

Min-Kook Choi, Hyun-Gyu Lee, Minseok Song, Sang-Chul Lee*
Department of Computer Engineering, Inha University, Incheon, Korea
{mkchoi,hg_lee}@inha.edu, {mssong,sclee}@inha.ac.kr

ABSTRACT

Blocking artifacts, commonly introduced during video encoding, are one of the major causes of reduced perceptual video quality. The trade-off between these artifacts and bitrate can be improved by adaptively selecting frames from a set of video copies encoded at different bitrates, prior to actual video encoding. We propose a new direction of constructing mixed bitrate video based on content-based image analysis on each video frame, which was posed as a problem of pre-analysis for the final video encoding step.

The proposed method consists of the following steps: First, we define a simple and fast impact metric in order to identify the blocking artifacts in each frame of multiple videos, encoded at different bitrates. Based on the impact metric, we generate a blocking artifact density functions for the available bitrates, on the whole video. Finally, we define and optimize our objective function from the blocking artifact density functions in order to select a bitrate with minimum perceptual blockiness and file size for each frame.

We validated our method throughout multiple types of videos, showing improved visual quality for the same file size based on commonly used quality assessment measures, such as MSU blocking, MSU blurring, SSIM, 3SSIM, and stSSIM. The reduction rates of average file size and average blocking artifact were about 4.9% and 8.3% over maximum bitrate encoding, respectively.

Keywords

Adaptive bitrate selection; video encoding; video quality measurement (VQM); blocking artifact

1. INTRODUCTION

Encoding is an essential process in the provision of video streaming services, and there has been a variety of approaches to improve efficiency and visual quality. Many new encoding tools and content-based metrics have been introduced

*Corresponding author (email: sclee@inha.ac.kr)

MM '16, October 15-19, 2016, Amsterdam, Netherlands
© 2016 ACM. ISBN 978-1-4503-3603-1/16/10... $15.00
DOI: http://dx.doi.org/10.1145/2964284.2967227

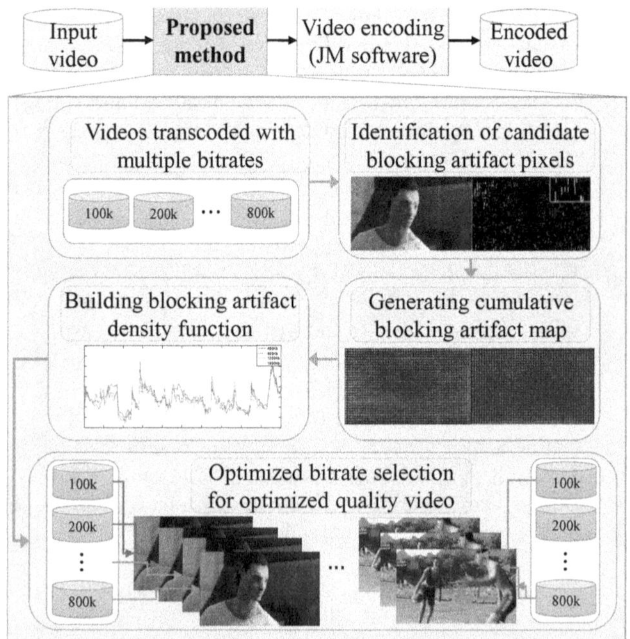

Figure 1: Overview of the proposed adaptive bitrate selection method.

to improve the compactness of video coding standards. Recently, the High Efficiency Video Coding (HEVC) [14] shows a significant improvement in compression over previous standards [12]. Another approach to improve the compactness of video coding is adaptive bitrate control, which also facilitates dynamic power control in embedded systems, network bandwidth adjustment, and video quality optimization. Initial work on adaptive bitrate control was mostly concerned with the support of network bandwidth renegotiation [13, 17]. For example, Javdtalab et al. [6] developed an algorithm that measures network bandwidth, frame size, PSNR and SSIM for rate-control under H.264 HEVC. Adaptive bitrate control has recently escaped from the network environment, and been used to improve the efficiency of video encoding and transcoding, and to reduce the power consumption of devices. Feghali et al. [4] proposed the variation of frame-rate and quantization parameters to achieve adaptive bitrate control in mobile video broadcasting, subject to a perceived-quality metric.

Closely related to our research, another lines of method to enhance encoding efficiency have been proposed to reduce blocking artifact. Li et al. presented blocking artifact measurement metric with no reference information using Tchebichef moments [9]. They used an observation of multiple orders of the Tchebichef kernels which have varying abilities to capture blockiness. On the other hands, Yoo et al. developed discrete cosine transform (DCT) based inter-block correlation for block artifact reduction algorithm[18].

We introduce a new approach of video quality optimization prior to actual video encoding. In specific, we propose a framework of constructing a multi-bitrate video based on content-based image analysis on each video frame, which is posed as a problem of pre-processing step before the actual video encoding step, as summarized in Figure 1. The proposed method has the following main differences from a multi-pass VBR: VBR is based on the motion changes, which does not necessarily reflect blocking artifacts, but the proposed method uses the pre-computed measures of blocking artifacts to select the video frames with optimal bitrates from the decoded videos that have been already encoded in different bitrates. Therefore, our method can measure/predict them before encoding the final video, whereas VBR cannot measure structural similarity before actually encoding the final video. It means that we can fine-tune the video to generate one with allowable levels of blocking artifacts associated with structural similarity, with budgeting file size. Since the proposed technique is an independent process of typical video quality enhancement techniques, that are typically applied after decoding process, our technique can still be applied as a standalone or along with other post processing techniques such as [7].

Although many different techniques can be applied for frame quality analysis problem, generally, blocking artifacts are known to be caused by quantization errors at the boundary location between adjacent macroblocks where there is a large difference in quantization levels, and to have a serious impact on the visual quality of videos [10]. First, we identify the blocking artifacts in each frame of the video, encoded at different bitrates, and quantify them using an impact metric. Then, we generate an artifact map for the whole video, consisting of blocking artifact density functions for the available bitrates. Finally, we construct an objective function from the blocking artifact density functions, and select a bitrate for each frame by L_1 and L_2 optimization of this objective function. Since we need to encode an input video into multiple bitrates before reconstructing a multi-bitrate video, note that the proposed method is intended for archived video contents, e.g., video-on-demand service, rather than real-time encoding, e.g., web casting. However, the proposed method is practical in real world application since once the videos in multiple bitrates are created, which is the most time consuming process, frame selection and reconstruction can be processed relatively in small amount of time. Furthermore, differently reconstructed videos can be generated in nominal amount of time.

The main contribution of the proposed method is twofold: First, we explored a new concept of optimizing visual video quality as a pre-processing step. The proposed method was validated throughout multiple types of videos in our experiments, showing improved visual quality for the same file size based on commonly used assessment measures, such as MSU blocking, MSU blurring, SSIM, 3SSIM, and stSSIM. Second, we introduced an optimization method with blocking artifact density function by incorporating a fast and effective blocking artifact detection method. By adjusting parameters, it is also possible to adjust detecting sensitivities according to different displaying environments. We tested multi-rate encoding on a well- known video dataset for testing MPEG-4 and mobile high-definition (HD) video. Our encoding method shows promising reduction rates in file size and decoding time, while improving visual quality when measured by standard video quality metrics (VQMs) .

2. BLOCKING ARTIFACTS

We search for blocking artifacts in multiple encodings of an input videos. After encoding at different bitrates, blocking artifacts are identified by examining the horizontal and vertical variations in one-dimensional derivative of pixel intensity in each frame. A cumulative map is then constructed from these candidate pixels, which is then used to locate the blocking artifacts in each frame. We will use $\mathbf{V} = (f^{(1)}, f^{(2)}, ..., f^{(k)})$ to denote an input video with k frames. By encoding $\mathbf{V}$ at h different bitrates, we obtain a set of h videos $\mathcal{V} = \{\mathbf{V}_1, \mathbf{V}_2, ..., \mathbf{V}_h\}$.

Artifacts Identification. Blocking artifacts typically occur where are large differences in quantization level between neighboring macroblocks, and the artifacts appear at the edges of each macroblock in the encoded frame. We calculate the one-dimensional derivatives of pixel intensity, in both horizontal and vertical directions $(f_x^{(i)}, f_y^{(i)})$, in the ith frame $f^{(i)} \in \mathbb{N}^{m \times n}$ of a video where m and n are the width and height of a frame. The frame $f^{(i)}$ belongs to the jth encoded video $\mathbf{V}_j$, and the derivatives $(f_x^{(i)}, f_y^{(i)})$ are defined as $f_x^{(i)}(u,v) = f^{(i)}(u,v) - f^{(i)}(u+1,v)$ and $f_y^{(i)}(u,v) = f^{(i)}(u,v) - f^{(i)}(u,v+1)$, where $f^{(i)}(u,v)$ is the intensity of the pixel at location (u,v) in the ith video frame.

A one-dimensional horizontal vector $\mathbf{v}_x(u,v) = [\Delta_x^1, \Delta_x^2, ..., \Delta_x^s]^T$ is constructed for the pixel at (u,v), and $\mathbf{v}_x(u,v)$ is the variation in intensity from $f_x^{(i)}(u,v)$ to $f_x^{(i)}(u,v+s)$, where s is the number of consecutive pixels with the same intensity which form the boundary of a visible block that has been detected. A second vector $\mathbf{v}_y$ is constructed in the vertical direction from $f_y^{(i)}(u,v)$ to $f_y^{(i)}(u+s,v)$. This process can be regarded as mapping $f_x^{(i)} \rightarrow \mathbf{W}_x^{(i)}$, where $\mathbf{W}_x^{(i)} \in \mathbb{N}^{m \times n \times s}$ is a 3D array. A matrix $\mathbf{D}^{(i)}$ can then be defined given as a constraint on $\mathbf{W}_x^{(i)}(u,v)$: $\mathbf{D}_x^{(i)}(u,v) = \begin{cases} 1, & \text{if } \Delta_x^1 = \Delta_x^2 = ... = \Delta_x^s \\ 0, & \text{otherwise} \end{cases}$, such that, $\mathbf{v}_x(u,v) \neq \mathbf{0}$. $\mathbf{D}^{(i)}(u,v) = \mathbf{D}_x^{(i)}(u,v) \vee \mathbf{D}_y^{(i)}(u,v)$ is a binary matrix of the same size as $f^{(i)}$, which indicates the likelihood of a pixel contributing to a blocking artifact.

Blocking Artifact Map. $\mathbf{C}_j$ is the blocking artifact map for the jth encoded video $\mathbf{V}_j$ in $\mathcal{V}$. The map $\mathbf{C}_j$ is constructed from $\mathcal{D}_j = \{\mathbf{D}_j^{(1)}, \mathbf{D}_j^{(2)}, ..., \mathbf{D}_j^{(k)}\}$ for all the pixel locations (u,v) on all the video frames, where $\mathcal{D}_j$ is a set of matrices of artifact pixels and k is the number of frames in $\mathbf{V}_j$: $\mathbf{C}_j(u,v) = \sum_{i=1}^{k} \mathbf{D}_j^{(i)}(u,v)$. We normalize this map to $\tilde{\mathbf{C}}_j = \mathbf{C}_j / \parallel \mathbf{C}_j \parallel$. By processing all the videos in $\mathcal{V}$, we obtain a set of blocking artifact maps $\mathcal{C} = \{\tilde{\mathbf{C}}_1, \tilde{\mathbf{C}}_2, ..., \tilde{\mathbf{C}}_h\}$, where the jth element in $\mathcal{C}$ corresponds to the encoded video $\mathbf{V}_j$. If the value at pixel location (u,v) in a normalized blocking artifact map $\tilde{\mathbf{C}}_j$ is greater than a threshold ρ then

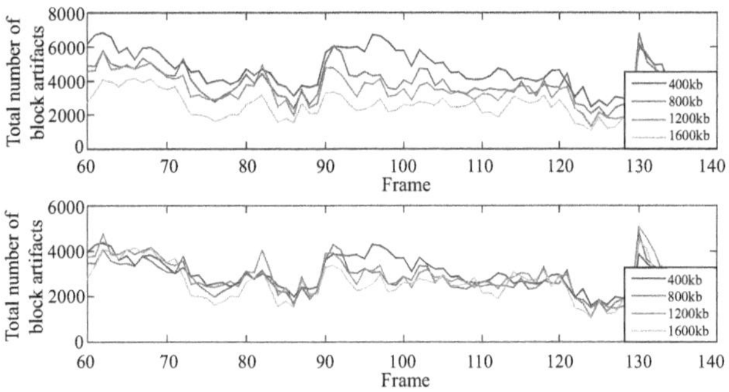

Figure 2: (a) An example blocking artifact density functions for 80 frames of a video encoded at four different bitrates ($s = 8$). (b) Scaled blocking artifact density functions $\mathcal{L}'$ ($h = 4$, $p = 2$). The block artifact functions with different bitrate are scaled by λ.

a visible blocking artifact can appear at (u, v). We consider $\tilde{\mathbf{C}}_j(u, v)$ to be the candidate location of a blocking artifact if it satisfies the constraint: $\mathbf{R}_j(u, v) = \{ \begin{array}{ll} 1, & \text{if } \tilde{\mathbf{C}}_j > \rho \\ 0, & \text{otherwise} \end{array}$. We call $\mathbf{R}_j \in \mathbb{N}^{m \times n}$ the region matrices corresponding to $\mathbf{V}_j$: we construct a set of region matrices $\mathcal{R} = \{\mathbf{R}_1, ..., \mathbf{R}_h\}$. We now obtain $\mathbf{A}^{(i)} \in \mathbb{N}^{m \times n}$ corresponding to the ith input video frame $f^{(i)}$ in $\mathbf{V}_j$ by intersecting $\mathbf{D}_j^{(i)}$ with the region matrix $\mathbf{R}_j$: $\mathbf{A}_j^{(i)}(u, v) = \mathbf{D}_j^{(i)}(u, v) \wedge \mathbf{R}_j(u, v)$. The set $\mathcal{A} = \{\mathbf{A}_1, ..., \mathbf{A}_h\}$ is later used to generate blocking artifact density functions, allowing us to select frames from $\mathcal{V}$ with the required visual quality.

3. BITRATE SELECTION

We now show how to generate blocking artifact density functions using the set of blocking artifact matrices $\mathcal{A}$, and how to choose the best bitrate for each frame optimizing an objective function.

Blocking Artifact Density Function. The outcome l_i is the visual impact of all the blocking artifacts occurring in the ith frame $f^{(i)}$, and can be expressed as $l_i = \sum_{u=1}^{m} \sum_{v=1}^{n} \mathbf{A}^{(i)}(u, v)$. After repeatedly applying this process, we assemble a density function $\mathbf{l}_j = [l_{1j}, l_{2j}, ..., l_{kj}]^T$, where k is the number of frames in $\mathbf{V}_j$. We also obtain a set of h vectors $\mathcal{L} = \{\mathbf{l}_1, \mathbf{l}_2, ..., \mathbf{l}_h\}$ from the set $\mathcal{V}$, and then generate h blocking artifact density functions. Figure 2 (a) shows an example of these functions when a video is encoded at four different bitrates ($h = 4$).

Objective Function Optimization. To select the best bitrate in each frame for an input video, we define an objective function that expresses the difference between the blocking artifact density functions at the lower bitrates and the same function at the highest bitrate:

$$\underset{\Lambda}{\operatorname{argmin}} \sum_{j=1}^{h-1} \parallel \mathbf{l}_h - \lambda_j \mathbf{l}_j \parallel_p . \quad (1)$$

where $\mathbf{l}_h$ is the blocking artifact density function for the highest bitrate in the set of density functions $\mathcal{L}$, and λ_j is a weight applied to the jth density function. We minimize this function using L_p distance to obtain a vector of weight coefficients $\Lambda = [\lambda_1, \lambda_2, ..., \lambda_{h-1}]^T$. The exponent of the p-norm is set to 1 or 2 in our experiments. Minimization produces a set $\mathcal{L}'$ of scaled density functions, as follows:

$$\mathcal{L}' = \{\mathbf{l}_1', \mathbf{l}_2', ..., \mathbf{l}_{h-1}'\}, \quad \mathbf{l}_j' = \lambda_j \mathbf{l}_j, \quad (2)$$

where the jth density function $\mathbf{l}_j'$ is the scaled density function from $\mathbf{l}_j$ by λ_j, and $1 \leq j \leq h - 1$. Figure 2 (b) shows an example of $\mathcal{L}'$ with $\mathbf{l}_h$ when h is 4 and p is 2. Since $\mathbf{l}_j'$ is a column vector with k elements, we obtain a $k \times h$ matrix $Q \in \mathbb{N}^{k \times h}$ from $\mathcal{L}'$ as follows:

$$\mathbf{Q} = \begin{bmatrix} l_{11}' & l_{12}' & \cdots & l_{1h-1}' & l_{1h}' \\ l_{21}' & l_{22}' & \cdots & l_{2h-1}' & l_{2h}' \\ \vdots & \vdots & \ddots & \vdots & \vdots \\ l_{k1}' & l_{k2}' & \cdots & l_{kh-1}' & l_{kh}' \end{bmatrix}. \quad (3)$$

Now, we select the best bitrates from the matrix $\mathbf{Q}$ as follows:

$$\hat{\mathbf{l}} = [\hat{l}_1, \hat{l}_2, ..., \hat{l}_k]^T, \quad \hat{l}_i = \min(l_{i1}', l_{i2}', \cdots, l_{ih}') \quad (4)$$

where the elements of $\hat{\mathbf{l}}$ are the selected bitrates for all the frames in a video. Finally, we apply a one-dimensional median filter to $\hat{\mathbf{l}}$ in order to prevent sudden changes of bitrate between two consecutive frames.

Video Generation with Variable Bitrates. Using the selected frame information vector $\hat{\mathbf{l}}$, we generate a new video $\hat{\mathbf{V}}$ from the h videos in $\mathcal{V}$. The new video $\hat{\mathbf{V}}$ has k frames, just like the original video $\mathbf{V}$: each frame $\hat{f}$ in $\hat{\mathbf{V}}$ is selected from the h available encoded frames based on the information vector $\hat{\mathbf{l}}$. The quality of the encoded video $\hat{\mathbf{V}}$ depends on the minimum and maximum bitrates of the encoded videos in $\mathcal{V}$ and the number of videos h with different bitrates in that range. The results of varying these two parameters are described in next section. Finally, the final video can be generated using a standard encoding technique either one-pass or two-pass VBR encoding approach.

4. EXPERIMENTAL RESULTS

To the best of our knowledge, there exists no other video pre-processing technique that can be directly compared with the proposed technique. The closest application may be MPEG-DASH (Dynamic Adaptive Streaming over HTTP), mainly used by Netflix, but it is still uncomparable since they change the bitrate depending on the network bandwidth, not to maintain the QoE. Our scheme aims at minimizing blocking artifact subject to the file size, which allows users in the DASH environment to receive higher-quality video segments, compared with simple VBR transcoding under the same network condition.

In our experiments, we compared our technique with the test videos encoded in multiple bitrates with H.264/AVC codec as baselines. We show the experimental results from our proposed technique applied to MPEG-4 [3] and mobile HD test datasets. The MPEG-4 dataset contains several types of video clip where each consists of frames at 352×288 standard definition (SD) resolution, with a frame-rate of 60fps. The mobile HD test dataset contains six videos with about 30 shots; their spatial resolution is 800×480, and there are $9,000$ frames at 30fps. This dataset is included to determine whether our method is applicable to rather

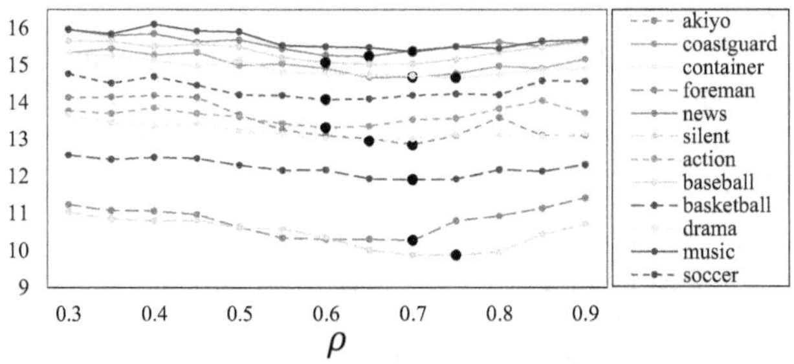

Figure 3: Parameter selection for the threshold ρ with all videos. Black dot indicates lowest MSU blocking values in each video.

long and high-resolution sequences. All the videos in both dataset are encoded using the standard H.264/AVC codec with the H.264/AVC JM reference software [15][2] after applying our preprocessing technique.

Parameter Selection. We set the number of bitrate levels h to 8, with the same interval between each bitrate. We created the h transcoded videos in $\mathcal{V}$ using the FFmpeg encoder [1]. The minimum bitrates for the videos in the MPEG-4 test dataset were selected between $40kb/s$ to $275kb/s$, and the maximum bitrates between $110kb/s$ to $625kb/s$, depending on the amount of data in the video. We encoded these mobile HD dataset videos at bitrates between $900kb/s$ and $1600kb/s$. The calculation of one-dimensional variation in intensity is controlled by the length s of the vectors $\mathbf{v}_x$ and $\mathbf{v}_y$ used to detect artifacts, and the distance metric p in the optimization. We tuned the parameters s and p to account for the average of blocky noise and file sizes, using the three videos in the mobile HD dataset with $h = 8$. As a result of this tuning exercise, we selected s to 8 and p to 2. Threshold ρ is a parameter to impose constraint to the normalized blocking artifact map in $\mathcal{C}$. We selected $\rho = 0.6791$ by considering average reduction amount of blocky noises in every video as shown in Figure 3.

Video Quality Measurement Results. We used five video quality metrics (VQMs) provided by the MSU quality measurement [5] for quantitative assessment of our technique: structural similarity (SSIM) [16], 3-component structural similarity (3SSIM) [8], spatio-temporal structural similarity (stSSIM) [11], MSU blurring, and MSU blocking [5]. The structural similarity metric compares the videos with a reference video (in this case an unencoded video) in terms of luminance, contrast and the structural properties of each frame. The 3SSIM augments the results from SSIM with edge, texture, and smoothness information; and stSSIM provides temporal information. All these similarity metrics have a value range of 0 to 1.0, with higher values corresponding to better perceptual quality. MSU blurring estimates sharpness, and again higher values are better. MSU blocking metric is particularly significant for our experiments, because our aim is to reduce the numbers of blocking artifacts. Higher values of this metric correspond to higher levels of blocking artifact noise.

Our result shows that the proposed method generated a video with comparable file size to the video encoded in the minimum bitrate, while achieving less or equal blocky noise than the video encoded the maximum bitrate. The structural similarity values are also comparable to the videos with maximum bitrate with meaningful reduction in file size. Table 1 shows the average file sizes and the VQMs for all the MPEG-4 test and mobile HD datasets, and Table 2 shows the average file size and blocking artifact reduction results depending on different categories and types of video clips. Proposed method achieves about 4.9% and 8.7% reduction in the average file size and the blocking artifacts in all video clips, respectively. It is also observable that the reduction rates are especially increased for videos with large movements in a video. The examples of visual results are available in the supplementary material.

Reduction rate(%)	MPEG-4	Mobile HD	Active	Inactive	Avg.
File size	5.103	4.752	4.711	5.144	4.927
MSU blocking	5.266	11.277	11.985	4.559	8.271

Table 1: The average file size and blocking artifact reduction rates in different categories of video clips. For example, the best reduction in blocking artifact was achieved in "active" video clips.

5. CONCLUSIONS

We proposed a novel video pre-processing framework for efficient video encoding with improved visual quality and reduced file size through the analysis of visible blocking artifacts. As well as reduced blocky noise, processed videos are compact and achieved good measures in multiple VQMs. Especially, the proposed method is practical for off-line video service, e.g., video-on-demand, since multiple versions of video reconstruction can be created relatively in small amount of time, once the videos in multiple bitrates are created. In order to apply the proposed method, multiple-encoded videos should be prepared by off-line processing. In spite of this prerequisite, our method can be used for many lines of real world applications on video encoding frameworks, such as video on demand and video achieving.

Since our technique does not directly modify any video encoding scheme, it is applicable to any recent encoding codecs such as H.265/MPEG-H HEVC. Other analysis metrics and optimization schemes might potentially improve our results, in terms of the estimation of visual quality and computational efficiency. It may also be possible to extract features reflecting different aspects of visual quality from the spatial and temporal domains of an encoded video in future work.

6. ACACKNOWLEDGMENT

This research was supported by Next-Generation Information Computing Development Program through the National Research Foundation of Korea(NRF) funded by the Ministry of Education, Science and Technology (No. 2012M3 C4A7032781) and Basic Science Research Program through the National Research Foundation of Korea(NRF) funded by the Ministry of Education(NRF-2015R1D1A1A01057968).

7. REFERENCES

[1] Ffmpeg. https://ffmpeg.org/.

[2] H.264/avc jm reference software. http://iphome.hhi.de/suehring/tml/download/.

[3] Xiph.org video test media. https://media.xiph.org/video/derf/.

Akiyo (kb/s)	File size (bytes)	MSU Blocking	MSU blurring	SSIM	3SSIM	stSSIM
40	43,361	14.078	9.2623	0.9776	0.9711	0.7697
50	45,340	14.025	9.3342	0.9833	0.9803	0.8280
60	46,648	13.936	9.4557	0.9868	0.9859	0.8645
70	47,801	14.112	9.4763	0.9888	0.9890	0.8882
80	48,430	14.181	9.5196	0.9907	0.9916	0.9078
90	48,826	13.996	9.5557	0.9919	0.9932	0.9218
100	48,898	13.880	9.5762	0.9928	0.9942	0.9324
110	49,131	13.656	9.6113	0.9937	0.9952	0.9409
Proposed	46,668	12.941	9.5110	0.9850	0.9870	0.8646

Coastguard (kb/s)	File size (bytes)	MSU Blocking	MSU blurring	SSIM	3SSIM	stSSIM
275	425,407	16.338	24.849	0.9319	0.9508	0.5248
325	435,965	15.382	25.152	0.9436	0.9601	0.5868
375	443,989	15.371	25.417	0.9525	0.9669	0.6376
425	450,475	15.129	25.614	0.9596	0.9724	0.6820
475	455,520	14.927	25.770	0.9658	0.9773	0.7213
525	457,271	14.986	25.871	0.9708	0.9807	0.7568
575	458,036	14.689	25.942	0.9747	0.9836	0.7861
625	459,262	14.643	26.020	0.9779	0.9858	0.8114
Proposed	426,723	14.671	25.293	0.9639	0.9771	0.7384

Container (kb/s)	File size (bytes)	MSU Blocking	MSU blurring	SSIM	3SSIM	stSSIM
50	72,731	16.468	20.042	0.9362	0.9408	0.4751
75	79,566	18.152	20.667	0.9567	0.9665	0.6138
100	86,080	16.052	21.144	0.9686	0.9790	0.7119
125	91,046	15.910	21.328	0.9765	0.9858	0.7792
150	93,809	15.827	21.456	0.9817	0.9898	0.8297
175	95,620	15.091	21.560	0.9852	0.9922	0.8654
200	96,704	15.520	21.673	0.9881	0.9941	0.8960
225	97,727	15.094	21.789	0.9901	0.9954	0.9156
Proposed	89,042	14.667	20.452	0.9627	0.9702	0.6699

Foreman (kb/s)	File size (bytes)	MSU Blocking	MSU blurring	SSIM	3SSIM	stSSIM
200	259,070	11.693	15.613	0.9605	0.9678	0.7130
225	263,581	11.508	15.787	0.9661	0.9728	0.7527
250	264,158	11.390	15.916	0.9706	0.9772	0.7858
275	266,008	11.354	16.005	0.9738	0.9803	0.8090
300	266,379	11.234	16.112	0.9770	0.9833	0.8332
325	266,445	11.156	16.193	0.9797	0.9859	0.8533
350	267,037	11.019	16.254	0.9816	0.9876	0.8680
375	267,453	10.992	16.317	0.9837	0.9894	0.8836
Proposed	261,235	10.274	16.242	0.9779	0.9852	0.8546

News (kb/s)	File size (bytes)	MSU Blocking	MSU blurring	SSIM	3SSIM	stSSIM
110	135,748	16.199	17.843	0.9792	0.9808	0.7651
125	139,613	15.639	17.938	0.9823	0.9844	0.7979
140	142,811	15.672	17.996	0.9852	0.9875	0.8323
155	144,531	16.168	18.037	0.9871	0.9894	0.8541
170	146,696	15.676	18.084	0.9890	0.9915	0.8792
185	147,696	15.859	18.126	0.9903	0.9929	0.8972
200	147,913	15.652	18.158	0.9916	0.9940	0.9114
215	148,046	15.539	18.194	0.9924	0.9948	0.9212
Proposed	144,312	15.244	17.772	0.9881	0.9916	0.8870

Silent (kb/s)	File size (bytes)	MSU Blocking	MSU blurring	SSIM	3SSIM	stSSIM
130	144,012	11.306	15.865	0.9666	0.9766	0.7385
145	147,470	11.563	16.009	0.9726	0.9817	0.7820
160	149,305	11.236	16.046	0.9763	0.9845	0.8113
175	151,144	11.056	16.105	0.9796	0.9872	0.8374
190	152,906	11.005	16.170	0.9820	0.9901	0.8565
205	153,158	10.792	16.254	0.9842	0.9905	0.8738
220	153,527	10.450	16.267	0.9816	0.9919	0.8887
235	154,385	10.591	16.321	0.9873	0.9926	0.9008
Proposed	152,487	9.873	16.250	0.9812	0.9890	0.8728

Table 2: Encoded file sizes and VQMs for the MPEG-4 dataset. Shaded entries are the closest values to the proposed method in each column. It can be interpreted that the file size and quality of the proposed method are comparable to the video encoded with the bitrate specified in the same row.

[4] R. Feghali, F. Speranza, D. Wang, and A. Vincent. Video quality metric for bit rate control via joint adjustment of quantization and frame rate. *IEEE Transactions on Broadcasting*, 53(1):441–446, 2007.

[5] C. M. Graphics and M. L. V. Group. Msu video quality measurement tool documentation. http://www.compression.ru/video/, 2011.

[6] A. Javdtalab, M. Omidyeganeh, S. Shirmohammandi, and M. Hosseini. A rate control algorithm for x264 high definition video conferencing. In *IEEE International Conference on Multimedia and Expo*, 2011.

[7] R. K. Lama, M. R. Choi, J. Y. Pyun, and G. R. Kwon. Post processing algorithm for reduction of blocking artifact in hdtv. In *IEEE International Conference on Consumer Electronics (ICCE)*, 2014.

[8] C. Li. Content-weighted video quality assessment using a three-component image model. *Journal of Electronic Imaging*, 19(1), 2004.

[9] L. Li, H. Zhu, G. Yang, and J. Qian. Referenceless measure of blocking artifacts by tchebichef kernal analysis. *IEEE Signal Processing Letter*, 21(1):122–125, 2014.

[10] Z. Li and E. J. Delp. Block artifact reduction using a transform-domain markov random field model. *IEEE Transactions on Circuits and Systems for Video Technology*, 15(12):1583–1593, 2005.

[11] A. K. Moorthy and A. C. Bovik. Efficient motion weighted spatio-temporal video ssim index. In *SPIE Proceedings Human Vision and Electronic Imaging*, 2010.

[12] A. Norkin, G. BjÃÿntegaard, A. Fuldseth, M. Narroschke, M. Ikeda, K. Andersson, M. Zhou, and G. V. Auwera. Hevc deblocking filter. *IEEE Transactions on Circuits and Systems for Video Technology*, 22(12):1746–1754, 2013.

[13] C. E. Rhee, J. S. Kim, and H. J. Lee. Bitrate control using a heuristic spatial resolution adjustment for a real-time h.264/avc encoder. *EURASIP Journal on Advances in Signal Processing*, 87, 2012.

[14] G. J. Sullivan, J. R. Ohm, J. W. Han, and T. Wiegand. Overview of the high efficiency video coding (hevc) standard. *IEEE Transactions on Circuits and Systems for Video Technology*, 22(12):1649–1668, 2012.

[15] A. M. Tourapis, K. Suhring, and G. Sullivan. H.264/14496-10 avc reference software manual, 2010.

[16] Z. Wang, A. C. Bovik, H. R. Sheikh, and E. P. Simoncelli. Image quality assessment: From error visibility to structural similarity. *IEEE Transactions on Image Processing*, 13(4):600–612, 2004.

[17] G. L. Wu, Y. J. Fu, S. C. Huang, and S. Y. Chien. Perceptual quality-regulable video coding system with region-based rate control scheme. In *In Proc. of International Conference of Image Processing*, 2009.

[18] S. B. Yoo, K. Choi, and J. B. Ra. Post-processing for blocking artifact reduction based on inter-block correlation. *IEEE Transactions on Multimedia*, 16(6):1536–1548, 2014.

What Makes Photo Cultures Different?

Miriam Redi
Yahoo
London, UK

Damon Crockett
University of California
San Diego, CA, USA

Lev Manovich
CUNY
New York, NY, USA

{miriam.redi, damoncrockett, manovich.lev} @ gmail.com

Simon Osindero
Flickr
San Francisco, CA, USA
osindero@cs.toronto.edu

ABSTRACT

Billions of photos shared online today are created by people with different socio-economic characteristics living in different locations. We introduce a number of methods for quantifying the differences between such "photo cultures" and apply them to a large collection of Instagram images shared in five mega-cities around the world. First, we extract image content and style features and use them to design a new visualization technique for qualitative analysis of photo cultures. We then use supervised learning to automatically recognize and compare visual activity at different locations and expose surprising connections between geographically distant photo cultures. Finally, we perform a low-level quantitative analysis to understand what makes photo cultures different from each other.

CCS Concepts

•**Human-centered computing → Social content sharing;**

1. INTRODUCTION

In sociology and media history, the term "culture" is used to characterize behaviors, beliefs or artifacts of a group of individuals in a particular time period and location(s). For example, rather than thinking of "photography" as a single phenomenon, it is more precise to consider it as a collection of many different "photo cultures", each with its set of distinct aesthetic rulesand defining mechanisms. Examples of photo cultures include the "New Vision" European photography in late 20s [10], the socially conscious photography practiced in New York in the 30s [4], or the snapshot-style fashion photography popular in the 90s.

How can this perspective that combines sociology of culture and media history inform studies of today's online communities? Just as photography did during its first 160 years, online photo sharing platforms such as Instagram could include many photo cultures: many individuals and groups might use Instagram to define their cultural identities. However, previous work analyzing Instagram images [6, 1] often approaches this medium as a single global photo culture. Existing works tend to use large samples drawn from Instagram as a whole, generic dataset, without considering possible differences in how Instagram is used by people with different backgrounds or geographic areas. Instagram users show very diverse socio-demographic characteristics (location, gender), and our hypothesis is that different users adopt this medium in different ways, making Instagram a collection of photo cultures sharing pictures with different subjects and stylistic attributes.

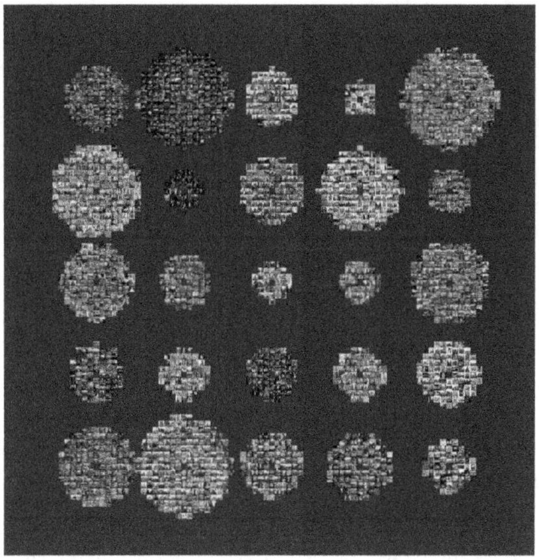

Figure 1: Stylistic clusters of Architecture images.

Our study explores this hypothesis by comparing for the first time Instagram images along one important variable: geographic location. Specifically, we use deep-learning based object detectors and computational aesthetics tools to analyze subjects and styles of 100K images from five well-known global megacities. Using such features, we design a visualization technique based on unsupervised clustering that allows us to qualitatively explore the visual activity of users in different locations, and to expose the existence of different photo cultures. We then design a supervised-learning framework and classify the collected data to understand differences and similarities between the visual preferences of photo cultures. Finally, we dive deep into the visual activity of photo cultures, drawing a map of stereotypical photographic subjects and styles, to understand what makes photo cultures different from each other.

Rather than confirming existing stereotypes, our analysis reveals new, unexpected patterns. For example, we find that Bangkok has the most distinctive photo culture in terms of photographic styles (very bright, unique pictures), while pictures in Berlin and Tokyo show the most unique subjects. While previous work showed [14] that city similarity and proximity are strongly related, we find that geographically distant photo cultures such as Bangkok and São Paulo show the most similar photographic subject patterns.

MM '16, October 15-19, 2016, Amsterdam, Netherlands
© 2016 ACM. ISBN 978-1-4503-3603-1/16/10. . . $15.00
DOI: http://dx.doi.org/10.1145/2964284.2967228

2. RELATED WORK

Our work closely relates to research that combines computational social science and computer vision to study the impact of social media images. Researchers have analyzed image diffusion [12], relations between image quality and popularity [11], the importance of faces for user engagement in Instagram[1], the content of Instagram posts [6]. These studies reveal many important patterns in Instagram usage, but, unlike our study, they do not consider possible differences due to the image geo-location thus possibly missing many local patterns. Also very related to ours, recent research works have explored the relation between visual features and image location. [9, 8, 3, 14]. The work in this paper differs from previous works on city identity recognition [14, 3] in that we do not focus on pure city elements: we use instead location information to analyze characteristics of photos shared on Instagram within the same geographic area, and to compare these characteristics between a number of photo cultures. We characterize users' pictures though *photographic* and *stylistic* attributes rather than *architectonical* or *urban* elements. As a matter of fact, as we shall see in Sec. 6, our findings differ from the ones in [14].

A set of online projects has used visualization tools to discover patterns in Instagram images from different cities[1] Although our study is inspired by these works, their main method for comparison between urban areas is based on visualizations arising from few basic visual features or face characteristics.

3. METHODOLOGY

To discover photo cultures and their activity, we first draw a sample of Instagram images at different locations, and then analyze their content and style through computer vision techniques.

3.1 Dataset

To explore the similarities and differences in photo cultures at different locations, we selected five cities located on 3 continents: Europe, Asia, and South America. We carefully selected cities that are very different in material and objective ways, as they are situated in different climates, they have different colors and architecture, different fashions, etc. These cities are Bangkok, Berlin, Moscow, Sao Paulo, and Tokyo. For each city, we identified the point coordinates corresponding to the official city center. We then used the Instagram API to collect images and their metadata in a 5km x 5km area around each point, thus capturing a significant part of a city[2]. In order to capture images and data from the same days of the week and hours from all cities, we used a single full week: Dec 4–Dec 12, 2013. The collection process resulted in 656K images, divided between the cities as follows. Bangkok: 162K, Berlin: 24K, Moscow: 140K, Sao Paulo: 123K, and Tokyo: 207K. We then randomly sample 20K images per city (100K in total).

3.2 Features

To understand photo cultures, we characterize various aspects of an image: we extract a group of *Subject* features that describe the image objects and scenes, and a group of *Stylistic* features that describe the image photo techniques and styles.

Subject Features. To describe picture subjects, we compute, for all images, the Flickr *machine tags*:[3] we run the Flickr deep learning-based object detectors, and obtain a set of object tags with their corresponding confidence scores (e.g. "flower, 0.6").

[1]phototrails.net/ , selfiecity.net/, on-broadway.nyc/.

[2]For example, in New York, it would cover parts of Brooklyn and all of Manhattan from downtown to Central Park

[3]http://www.fastcolabs.com/3037882/how-flickrs-deep-learning-algorithms-see-whats-in-your-photo

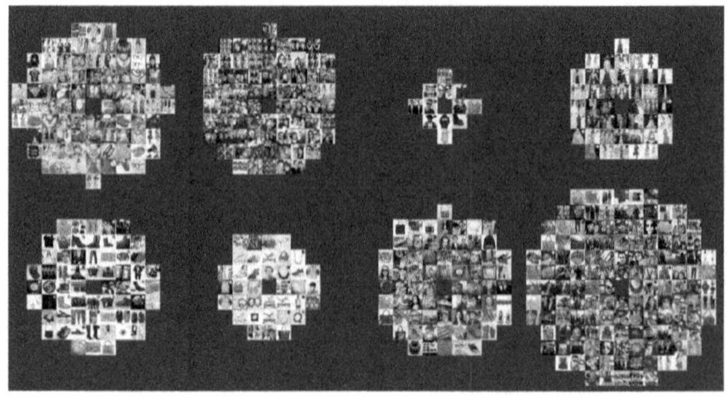

Figure 2: Details of clothing image clusters.

However, machine tag scores can be very sparse: an image contains only few of the possibly detectable objects. Moreover, object-level tag semantics are very fine-grained: for example, among the detectable objects, we can find a variety of different flower species. Such degree of specificity might not be useful to determine higher-level differences among photo cultures. We therefore manually organize object-level tag names into a smaller set of 14 groups, according to their semantics: *architecture, artifacts, fashion, furniture, tools, vehicles, animal, natural, plants, humans, food, activities, concepts, other.*. We associate each subject group with the maximum confidence score among the object-level tags falling inside a group: if an image had object tags "dog, 0.6" and "cat, 0.7", the subject group *animal* will get the score 0.7. The resulting subject feature vector is 14-dimensional.

Stylistic Features. We describe image style in two different ways. *Computational Aesthetics Features:* To help classifiers tell which images users will find more beautiful, computational aesthetic features are designed to describe how much an image follows standard rules for good photography.[2, 11]. In this work, we utilize them as a set of individual stylistic features. We first extract information regarding the *Color* distribution in the HSV colorspace (following Itten's Color wheel), together with three HSV-based indicators of emotional responses, namely *Pleasure, Arousal and Dominance*[7]. We then gather information regarding the homogeneity of the *Texture* using Haralick's features from the Gray-Level Co-occurrence Matrices [5]. We describe the overall image *Layout* by computing symmetry and object distribution features [11]. Finally, we collect features reflecting the image *Basic Photographic Quality*: the amount of balance in contrast and exposure, the amount of compression artifacts, and the sharpness of the foreground objects. *Stylistic Machine Tags:* To enrich the pool of features describing the stylistic patterns of photo cultures, we also include those machine tags that specifically refer to technical terms related to photography (e.g. black and white, monochrome, lens flare). The stylistic feature vector is 95-dimensional.

4. VISUALIZING PHOTO CULTURES

We present here a new visualization method specifically tailored for photo culture studies.We want to provide a visualization tool to explore subjects and style of large collections of images and spot visual patterns of photo cultures in different cities on a 2D canvas.

Pre-processing: Subject-Specific Photo Style Clustering After feature computation, each image is characterized over 110 (95 stylistic +14 subject + location) dimensions. To allow visualization on a 2D canvas, we must further compress the data characterizing each image, while preserving subject, style, and location information as much as possible. To preserve information regarding the **content**

of Instagram images, we partition the whole image collection according to the subject of the pictures. For each of the 14 subject groups, we create subject-based image subsets by selecting the images whose corresponding subject confidence score is above 0.8, thus ensuring that the image contains a certain subject. To preserve information about the image **style**, we cluster the stylistic features of the images in each subject group.This allows us to group images according to the dominant stylistic choices that photographers make when representing their subjects. We use hierarchical clustering and choose the number of clusters $k = 25$ by manually inspecting the quality of the visualizations resulting from varying k 5 to 50 in steps of 5. After these steps, each image is situated inside one of 14 subject groups, characterized by one of the 25 style clusters computed for each group, and labeled with its city location.

Data Visualization The visualization task is to present the computed clusters on a 2D canvas while incorporating geographic information. To do this, we generate a separate visualization for each of 14 subject groups. Each visualization shows all images in the group divided into 25 style clusters using the "growing entourage" plot, our own visualization technique designed to map high-dimensional image clusters onto a 2D canvas.

To "grow entourages", we first cluster centroids in the 95-d feature space, and then compute, for each image in a cluster, its Euclidean distance from the centroid. We then project the cluster centroids to 2D using t-distributed stochastic neighbor embedding (t-SNE), giving each cluster ("entourage") a location on a 2D map [13]. We plot 2D centroids on a 5x5 grid, and let the algorithm add members to each cluster, starting with those closest to its centroid. Each image added occupies the open grid square nearest its centroid. The images closest to the centroid on the 2D grid are therefore the images closest to the centroid in 95-dimensional space. Finally, we tag each image, in its upper-right corner, with a colored dot indicating its city of origin. Bangkok is green, Berlin is blue, Moscow red, Sao Paulo purple, and Tokyo yellow.

Visualization Properties The resulting plots (see Fig. 2) allow us to understand the dominant photographic styles (clusters) that different photo cultures (geolocation tag) tend to use when representing subjects (image subsets), as well as the extent to which different subjects are associated with each city by Instagram users. Geographic locations and subject groupings are fully preserved. Because images remain bound by their original cluster memberships, the plot preserves a significant amount of intra-cluster stylistic information between single images. Finally, because the clusters themselves are not arranged randomly on the canvas but instead are projected from the original feature space, some measure of inter-cluster similarity is likewise preserved. Our full set of 14 high-resolution visualizations showing all subject groups and style clusters can be found here: https://www.flickr.com/photos/137574408@N03/ .

Quantitative Cluster Analysis The data pre-processing allows not only for qualitative but also for quantitative analysis. By computing subject distributions across images, style clusters and locations, we can get an initial understanding of the trending patterns in photo cultures. We start observing that localized photo cultures actually exist. For example, around 50% of the photos containing food have been taken in Tokyo, 12% in Sao Paulo, 8% in Moscow, 12% in Berlin and 18% in Bangkok. This suggests that Tokyo's users tend to take pictures of food more than users in other cities. Similarly, we find that subjects such as architecture are more popular in Berlin. Bangkok's users tend to prefer fashion, and in Sao Paulo, we can find many pictures of people and activities.

We can also find some information about the style uniqueness of photo cultures. To do so, we look at city-specific clusters, namely stylistic clusters where at least 3/4 of the images come from the

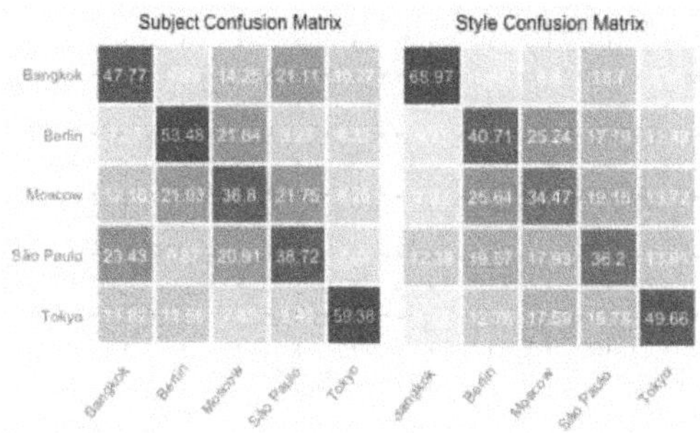

Figure 3: Prediction Task: classification rates for subject and stylistic features. The numbers inside the squares show percentages of photos from cities indicated on x-axis classified as belonging to cities indicated on y-axis.

same location. Photo cultures with high number of city-specific stylistic clusters will likely be more unique in terms of style. We find that around 5% of clusters are city-specific, out of which 42 % belongs to Tokyo, 42% to Bangkok, thus suggesting photo styles in Tokyo and Bangkok are more unique than in other cities.

5. ANALYZING PHOTO CULTURES

In the previous Section, we used clustering to visually compare photo cultures of different cities. In this Section, we use supervised learning to quantitatively compare the photo cultures in our dataset.

5.1 Detecting and Comparing Photo Cultures

To support our comparative analysis, we design a multi-class classification problem, similar to previous work [14]. Given groups of images randomly sampled from the same city, we want to train a classifier able to predict the location where such images originated. The intuition behind this is the following. A group of images sampled from a location should preserve the typical visual patterns of the photo culture from that location. If visual patterns of a city photo culture are clearly distinguishable from others, it will be easy for the classifier to identify the correct location of the image groups drawn from that city. On the other hand, the classifier will misclassify the image groups of cities with similar visual patterns.

Experimental Setup: We formulate the image group location detection problem as follows. We randomly split the images from each city into 50% train and 50% test sets. For both sets, we then randomly sample distinct groups of 10 images[4]. We then compute mean and standard deviation for both the stylistic and the subject features in each group, thus characterizing each group with a 28-d subject feature vector and a 190-d style vector. Next, we label each image group with a category corresponding to the city they have been sampled from, and train a multi-class 10-tree random forest classifier with the resulting data. We report in Fig. 3 the results in a confusion matrix: the number in each circle shows the percentage of image groups from the location indicated by the column label that were classified as belonging to the city indicated by the row label. The higher the percentage of correctly classified image groups for a given city, the more unique and distinctive are the visual patterns of that city's photo culture. Conversely, the higher the misclassification rate between two cities, the higher is the visual similarity of their photo cultures.

Experimental Results: Given that we use a balanced test set, the

[4]Although absolute accuracy numbers change when choosing a different group size, we found similar relational patterns between cities for all the group sizes considered

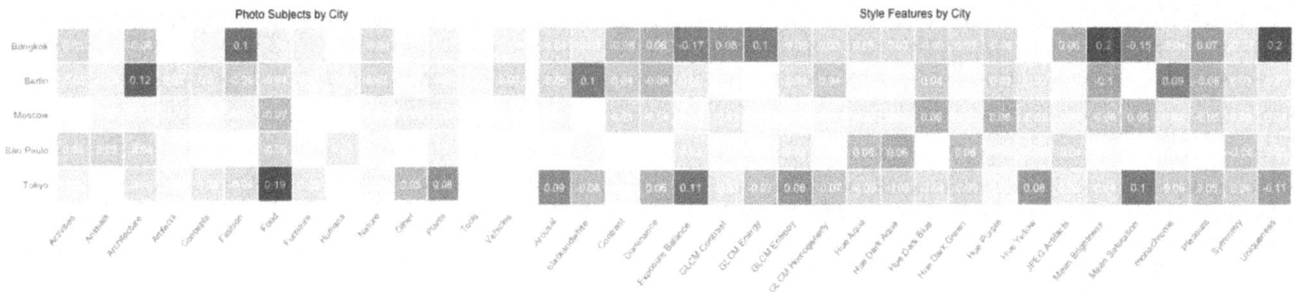

Figure 4: Stereotypical patterns of photo cultures. The squares show correlations between photo subjects and their locations. Correlation values range from -1 to +1. Red color indicates a negative value, white indicates 0, and blue indicates a positive value.

performances of the system (see Fig. 3) for this task are pretty high: while the accuracy of a random classifier would be around 20% for this task, the lowest performance that we get is 34% of correctly classified image groups. Overall, we can see that, in general, subjects are more discriminative than photographic styles for this task. The only exception is the style-based classification of Bangkok image groups, the most accurate among all, showing how unique Bangkok photo culture is.

Subject Features: As we can see from the confusion matrix, Tokyo has the most distinctive photo culture among the cities considered in terms of subjects represented. This is mainly due to the fact that, as we shall see in the next Section, food-related image abound in Tokyo's Instagram pictures, while architecture images common in other cities are missing. On the other hand, Moscow has the least distinguishable photo culture, often misclassified with Berlin or Sao Paulo. Moreover, we can see that, in the subjects depicted, Bangkok and Sao Paulo are the most similar photo cultures, unlike Bangkok and Berlin, whose photo cultures are rarely confused by the classifier. These findings are somewhat different from the ones in [14]: while that study found a high correlation between city identities and geographic proximities, we find here that photo cultures share similarities even though they belong to geographically distant cities, such as Bangkok and Sao Paulo.

Stylistic Features: As mentioned, Bangkok's photo culture has the most unique photo styles, followed by Tokyo: the classifier is able to correctly classify Bangkok's image groups (69%). Again, photo cultures from Moscow seem to be the least unique in terms of photographic styles used, and highly similar to Berlin's photo culture: around 25% of Berlin's image groups are classified as Moscow. We can also see that Bangkok and Berlin have the least similar stylistic patterns, similar to what we observed in the case of subjects.

5.2 What Makes Photo Cultures Different?

After looking at overall cross-photocultural patterns, we dive deep into each photo culture, looking at what makes localized photo cultures unique in terms of the subjects represented and styles used.

To discover the most *stereotypical* visual patterns for each photo culture, we look at how much visual features correlate with the location of the images in our collection. The higher this correlation between feature and city, the higher the unique presence of a given subject or style in the photo culture of the city. To do so, we correlate each feature with 5 binary city vectors, one for each location in our dataset. For a city c, for each image I in our data, the binary city vector will be 1 if the location of image I corresponds to c, and 0 otherwise. In Figures 4 we report the Pearson's ρ correlation coefficients (p-value < 0.05) of the subjects and styles that are statistically significantly related to each photo culture. In many cases, our findings confirm the intuitions suggested by our visualizations in Section 3. We observe the following.

Subject Features: As noticed in Section 4, Tokyo and Berlin have the most clearly distinctive characterizing subjects (see Fig. 4). People in Tokyo tend to take photos of food: by looking at the correlations of the individual object tags and the city vectors, we can see that objects such as *food, meal, meat, soup* are positively correlated ($\rho > 0.1$) with the Tokyo location. On the other hand, users in Berlin tend to depict the architectural aspect of the city (e.g. *building, house, palace*). Bangkok's images are characterized by the presence of clothes and fashion, for example *clothing, dress*, while Sao Paulo's photographers tend to focus on images of people and activities, showing high correlation with object tags such as *face, friends, people.* Among the 5 cities, Moscow shows the least prominent subject patterns, although at an individual object level, we found that the most related tags are *snow* and *night.*

Stylistic Features: By looking at Fig. 4, we can clearly see the distinctiveness of Bangkok's photo culture in terms of stylistic attributes. Images from Bangkok tend to be brighter, more unique, highly unbalanced in terms of exposure, more homogeneous (high GLCM Energy), and with more pleasant and dominant emotions. The second most unique photo culture in terms of style is Tokyo: less unique and highly balanced in terms of exposure, Tokyo's images show higher saturation compared to the others, and they tend to be more colorful (negative correlation *with black and white* and *monochrome* styles, high correlation with the *yellow* hue element). On the other hand, Berlin's images' distinctive pattern is monochromaticity (in particular, black and white). We find less prominent stylistic patterns for the remaining two cities, although, in terms of dominant colors, Sao Paulo's images tend to show more green/aqua subjects, while Moscow's tend to show dark blue and purple.

6. DISCUSSION AND CONCLUSIONS

How does a digital medium such as Instagram reflect cultural differences around the world? Our study, for the first time, presents a comprehensive comparison of Instagram photo cultures of different cities. Using a sample of 100K photos from 5 cities, we employ computer vision techniques to compare these photo cultures in terms of subjects and visual styles. We find significant and often unexpected differences between the cities. For example, despite being on different continents, Bangkok and Sao Paulo are most similar in terms of subjects shown. We also found that Bangkok and Tokyo have the most unique photo styles.

By equating the use of the Instagram medium and its reception with the "average" and the "most" (most frequently used, most popular), some of the previous research treated "Instagram" as a monoculture. The work presented in this paper is part of our effort to show that Instagram and other online media sharing platforms support many distinct photo cultures, and that we need to discover and describe more such different "Instagrams".

7. REFERENCES

[1] BAKHSHI, S., SHAMMA, D. A., AND GILBERT, E. Faces engage us: Photos with faces attract more likes and comments on instagram. In *Proceedings of the 32nd Annual ACM Conference on Human Factors in Computing Systems* (2014), CHI, ACM, pp. 965–974.

[2] DATTA, R., JOSHI, D., LI, J., AND WANG, J. Z. Studying aesthetics in photographic images using a computational approach. In *Proceedings of the 9th IEEE European Conference on Computer Vision* (2006), IEEE, pp. 288–301.

[3] DOERSCH, C., SINGH, S., GUPTA, A., SIVIC, J., AND EFROS, A. A. What makes paris look like paris? *ACM Transactions on Graphics (SIGGRAPH) 31*, 4 (2012), 101:1–101:9.

[4] DOHERTY, R. J. *Social-documentary Photography in the USA*. Amphoto, 1976.

[5] HARALICK, R. M. Statistical and structural approaches to texture. *Proceedings of the IEEE 67*, 5 (1979), 786–804.

[6] HU, Y., MANIKONDA, L., KAMBHAMPATI, S., ET AL. What we instagram: A first analysis of instagram photo content and user types. In *Proceedings of the 8th International AAAI Conference on Weblogs and Social Media* (2014), AAAI.

[7] MACHAJDIK, J., AND HANBURY, A. Affective image classification using features inspired by psychology and art theory. In *Proceedings of the 18th ACM International Conference on Multimedia* (2010), ACM, pp. 83–92.

[8] PORZI, L., ROTA BULÒ, S., LEPRI, B., AND RICCI, E. Predicting and understanding urban perception with convolutional neural networks. In *Proceedings of the 23rd Annual ACM Conference on Multimedia Conference* (2015), ACM, pp. 139–148.

[9] QUERCIA, D., O'HARE, N. K., AND CRAMER, H. Aesthetic capital: what makes london look beautiful, quiet, and happy? In *Proceedings of the 17th ACM Conference on Computer Supported Cooperative Work & Social Computing* (2014), ACM, pp. 945–955.

[10] SAHLI, J. *Filmische Sinneserweiterung: Lászlő Moholy-Nagys Filmwerk und Theorie*. Schüren Marburg, 2006.

[11] SCHIFANELLA, R., REDI, M., AND AIELLO, L. An image is worth more than a thousand favorites: Surfacing the hidden beauty of flickr pictures. In *Proceedings of the 9th International AAAI Conference on Web and Social Media* (2015), AAAI.

[12] TOTTI, L. C., COSTA, F. A., AVILA, S., VALLE, E., MEIRA, JR., W., AND ALMEIDA, V. The impact of visual attributes on online image diffusion. In *Proceedings of the 2014 ACM Conference on Web Science* (New York, NY, USA, 2014), WebSci '14, ACM, pp. 42–51.

[13] VAN DER MAATEN, L., AND HINTON, G. Visualizing data using t-sne. *Journal of Machine Learning Research 9*, 2579-2605 (2008), 85.

[14] ZHOU, B., LIU, L., OLIVA, A., AND TORRALBA, A. Recognizing city identity via attribute analysis of geo-tagged images. In *Proceedings of the 14th European Conference on Computer Vision*. Springer, 2014, pp. 519–534.

Synchronization among Groups of Spectators for Highlight Detection in Movies

Michal Muszynski
Computer Vision and Multimedia Laboratory
University of Geneva
Switzerland
michal.muszynski@unige.ch

Theodoros Kostoulas
Computer Vision and Multimedia Laboratory & Swiss Center for Affective Sciences
University of Geneva
Switzerland
theodoros.kostoulas@unige.ch

Patrizia Lombardo
Department of Modern French & Swiss Center for Affective Sciences
University of Geneva
Switzerland
patrizia.lombardo@unige.ch

Thierry Pun
Computer Vision and Multimedia Laboratory & Swiss Center for Affective Sciences
University of Geneva
Switzerland
thierry.pun@unige.ch

Guillaume Chanel
Swiss Center for Affective Sciences & Computer Vision and Multimedia Laboratory
University of Geneva
Switzerland
guillaume.chanel@unige.ch

ABSTRACT

Detection of emotional and aesthetic highlights is a challenge for the affective understanding of movies. Our assumption is that synchronized spectators' physiological and behavioral reactions occur during these highlights. We propose to employ the periodicity score to capture synchronization among groups of spectators' signals. To uncover the periodicity score's capabilities, we compare it with baseline synchronization measures, such as the nonlinear interdependence and the windowed mutual information. The results show that the periodicity score and the pairwise synchronization measures are able to capture different properties of spectators' synchronization, and they indicate the presence of some types of emotional and aesthetic highlights in a movie based on spectators' electro-dermal and acceleration signals.

Keywords

Synchronization; Grassmann manifolds; Persistent homology; Physiological and behavioral signals; Affective computing; Highlight detection

1. INTRODUCTION

Many studies have focused on matching spectators' physiological signals with affective states and the appearance of highlights in movies [5]. Since physiological reactions are considered to be an important component of emotions [15], [4], their measurements provide insight into spectators' aesthetic experience elicited by particular scenes [24]. In the field of affective computing, researchers have attempted to investigate emotion recognition in responses to multimedia content using electroencephalography (EEG) signals, peripheral physiological signals and facial expressions [14], [22]. The combination of spectators' physiological signals has been proposed in [5]. Because the spectators were watching separately a movie without any social context, they could not interact among themselves as it is the case in our studies.

Spectators can display similar behaviors or have similar physiological reactions when they are watching a movie together because: (*i*) the aesthetic choices of the filmmaker are made to elicit specific emotional reactions (e.g. special effects, empathy and compassion toward a character, etc.) and (*ii*) watching a movie together causes spectators' affective reactions to be synchronized through processes of emotional contagion [10]. For these reasons we gain insight on the impact of synchronization among group of spectators.

The first concept of synchronization came from the rhythm adjustment of oscillating objects [19]. In social sciences interpersonal synchrony consists of three components: rhythm, simultaneous movement and smooth meshing of interactions [2], [7]. One important step was made by [21] to introduce generalized synchronization of coupled chaotic systems. In [17], [18] the authors proposed that a level of the periodicity score can measure the amount of pattern repetitions in signals.

In this paper we propose to use periodicity score and baseline pairwise synchronization measures, such as the nonlinear interdependence [20] and the windowed mutual information [13] to uncover relations between occurrence of emotional and aesthetic highlights in films and spectators' physiological and behavioral reactions. Our goal is to verify if a level of synchronization that is computed over time windows of spectators' electro-dermal and acceleration signals

MM '16, October 15-19, 2016, Amsterdam, Netherlands

© 2016 ACM. ISBN 978-1-4503-3603-1/16/10...$15.00

DOI: http://dx.doi.org/10.1145/2964284.2967229

indicates the occurrence of different types of emotional and aesthetic highlights in movies. We then evaluate our results with respect to the annotations made by a movie critic.

In section 2 we detail the adaptation of synchronization measures to process spectators' physiological and behavioral signals. In section 3 we describe a movie watching in a ecological situation. In section 4 we present all the results. In section 5 we discuss and interpret the obtained results. In section 6 we provide the conclusions of our studies.

2. SYNCHRONIZATION MEASURES

In this section we propose to apply three synchronization measures: the periodicity score, the nonlinear interdependence and the windowed mutual information to spectators' physiological and behavioral signals in order to detect emotional and aesthetic highlights in movies. A high level of all synchronization measures reveals the synchronized reactions of spectators while watching a movie.

For spectators' electro-dermal and acceleration signals $\{x_i\}$ we consider time windows $\{x_i(l)\}$, $i = 1, ..., M$, $l = 1, ..., N$, where M is a number of spectators' signals and N is a number of time windows.

2.1 Contribution - Periodicity Score

In this subsection we detail the usage of the periodicity score to measure synchronization of signals [17], [18]. The overview is described in Figure 1. First, we map spectators' physiological or behavioral signals to the geometric framework of real Grassmann manifolds by applying the reduced singular value decomposition (RSVD) to their short time Fourier transform (STFT). We analyze time windows of spectators' signals as a sequence of points encoded on the Grassmann manifold preserving their intrinsic dependencies. Next, we associate a level of the periodicity score with the synchronized spectators' physiological and behavioral signals during emotional and aesthetic highlights in movies.

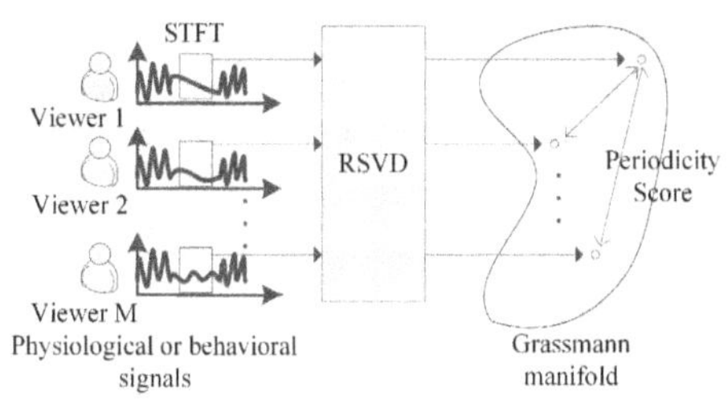

Figure 1: Physiological or behavioral signals are mapped to points on a Grassmann manifold applying RSVD to their STFT over time windows.

STFT. As shown in Figure 1 that we apply STFT to given time windows $x_i(l)$, $i = 1, ..., M$, and we yield $x_{t,f}^{i,l}$ in the time and frequency domain, where t is the time frame index and f is the frequency band index. Each time window $x_i(l)$ is split into segments with an overlap of 50% to apply STFT in this paper. Let $S_x^{i,l}(t, f)$ be the squared magnitude of the STFT, as follows

$$S_x^{i,l}(t, f) = ||x_{t,f}^{i,l}||^2. \tag{1}$$

RSVD. Then, we map time windows $\{x_i(l)\}$ of all signals on Grassmann manifolds to recover the intrinsic dependencies among them [6]. The real Grassmann manifold $G(k, n)$ parametrizes all $k-$dimensional subspaces of the vector space $\mathbb{R}^n$. A sequence of corresponding matrices $S_x^{i,l}(t, f)$, $i = 1, ..., M$ can be mapped to the points on the manifold $G(k, n)$ using RSVD as shown in the figure 1. If we compute RSVD of matrix $S_x^{i,l}(t, f)$, as follows:

$$S_x^{i,l}(t, f) = U^i \Sigma^i V^{iT}, \tag{2}$$

then the columns of the $n \times k$ orthogonal matrix U^i are a non-unique basis for the column space of $S_x^{i,l}(t, f)$. Thus, U^i can be used to represent the matrix $S_x^{i,l}(t, f)$, and can be identified with a point on the Grassmann manifold $G(k, n)$. Once the time windows are mapped to a sequence of points on $G(k, n)$, the pairwise distances between these points can be found using a function of the angles between subspaces. Let U^i and U^j be two $k-$ dimensional subspaces, we measure the similarity $d_{min}(U^i, U^j)$ of two points on the Grassmann manifold $G(k, n)$ using the minimum correlation distance [9]

$$d_{min}(U^i, U^j) = \sin\theta_k, \tag{3}$$

where $0 \leq \theta_1 \leq \theta_2 \leq ... \leq \theta_k \leq \frac{\pi}{2}$ are principle angles between two subspaces.

Periodicity Score. Finally, we introduce the basics of persistent homology: filtrations and persistence diagrams [17], [18], [8] plotted in Figure 2. Once the sequence of $S_x^{i,l}(t, f)$, $i = 1, ..., M$ matrices is mapped to $G(k, n)$ and defines a metric space $(U = \{U^1, ..., U^M\}, d_{min}(\cdot, \cdot))$, we recall the definition of the Vietoris-Rips complex $Rips_\alpha(U)$ as the set of the simplices $[U^1, ..., U^q]$ such that $d_{min}(U^i, U^j) \leq \alpha$ for $i, j = 1, ..., q$. There is an inclusion of $Rips_\alpha(U)$ in $Rips_\beta(U)$ for any $\alpha \leq \beta$. The sequences of inclusions are called filtrations $Filt_\alpha(U)$. An example is given in Figure 2(a). Persistence diagrams allow us to study the evolution of the topology of a filtration, and to capture properties of the metric which is used to generate the filtration. Existing connected components are merged for $0-$th homology, when α increases shown in Figure 2(b). Persistent homology tracks the birth (appearance) b and death (disappearance) d of all connected components shown in Figure 2(c).

The maximum persistence $mp(dgm(x_i(l)))$ of a persistence diagram $dgm(x_i(l))$ is defined as follows [18]

$$mp(dgm(x_i(l))) = \max_{(b,d)\in dgm(x_i(l))} pers(b, d), \tag{4}$$

where $pers(b, d) = d - b$ for $(b, d) \in dgm(x_i(l))$, and as ∞ otherwise. Finally, we can provide the periodicity score $S(x_i(l))$ [18]

$$S(x_i(l)) = \frac{mp(dgm(x_i(l)))}{\sqrt{3}}. \tag{5}$$

The normalized maximum persistence $mp(dgm(x_i(l)))$ of a persistence diagram $dgm(x_i(l))$ can help us to quantify synchronization among signals because it is capable of measuring their intrinsic geometric dependencies. The persistent score can measure synchronization among groups of signals based on the connectivity of signal clusters. Our approach to synchronization contains the multivariate measure which ascribes a single value to all signals in comparison with univariate measures, such as the nonlinear interdependence and the windowed mutual information which can only be computed over pairs of signals. When $S(x_i(l))$ equals 0, it means that we can not explore any structure in our data. If a value of $S(x_i(l))$ rises close to 1, we find some strong connectivity structure of data (synchronization).

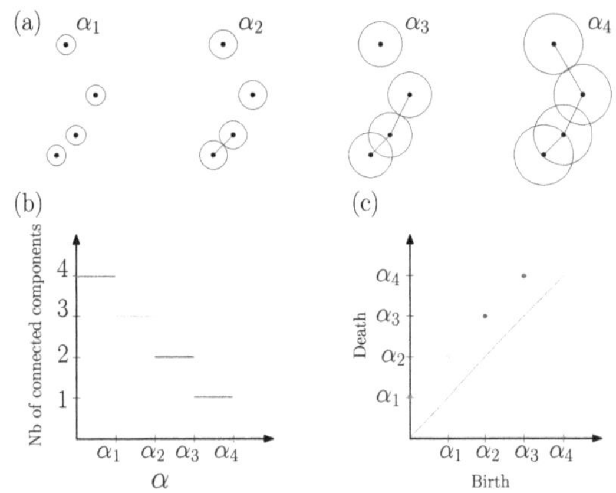

Figure 2: We show an example of : (a) the filtered Vietoris-Rips complex, (b) a number of connected components for different values of filtration parameter α, (c) the persistent diagram.

2.2 Nonlinear Interdependence

The nonlinear interdependence measures the geometrical similarity between the state space trajectories of two dynamical systems that are reconstructed from two time series $\{x_i\}$ and $\{x_j\}$ $i, j = 1, ..., M$ using time-delay embedding [23]. For each time window $x_i(l)$ the mean square Euclidean distance to its K nearest neighbours $x_i(n)$, $n = 1, ..., K$ is

$$R^K(x_i(l)) = \frac{1}{K}\sum_{n=1}^{K}(x_i(l) - x_i(n))^2, \qquad (6)$$

and the mean squared Euclidean distance conditioned by the equal time partners of the K nearest neighbours of $x_j(l)$ is

$$R^K(x_i(l)|x_j(l)) = \frac{1}{K}\sum_{n=1}^{K}(x_i(l) - x_j(n))^2. \qquad (7)$$

The nonlinear interdependence measure is defined as [20]

$$S^K(x_i(l)|x_j(l)) = \frac{R^K(x_i(l))}{R^K(x_i(l)|x_j(l))}. \qquad (8)$$

To make the nonlinear interdependence symmetric, we consider $S^K(x_j(l)|x_i(l))$ and we then average these parameters.

2.3 Windowed Mutual Information

From an information theory viewpoint, any signal can be treated as a collection of random variables which describes the evolution of a system over time. In this context, the windowed mutual information may capture nonlinear dependencies between signals that are not revealed in the covariance of signals [13]. The straightforward approach to estimation of the windowed mutual information consists of partitioning the supports of two time windows $x_i(l)$, $x_j(l)$ into finite size bins, and the approximation by the finite sum

$$I(x_i(l), x_j(l)) = \sum_{w,q} p(w,q)\log(\frac{p(w,q)}{p(w)p(q)}), \qquad (9)$$

where $p(w,q)$ is the joint probability density function of $x_i(l)$ and $x_j(l)$, $p(w)$ and $p(q)$ are the marginal probability density functions, respectively.

3. EXPERIMENT

The spectators' physiological and behavioral signals were recorded with a sampling frequency of 10 Hz during a movie projection (Taxi Driver, 1976) in a theater (Grütli cinema, Geneva) [12]. The duration of the movie is 113 min. In this paper we use 12 spectators' electro-dermal activity and acceleration (x,y, z axes, accelerometer attached to the hand of the spectator) signals ($M = 12$). All signals are filtered by third order lowpass Butterworth filter with cutoff frequency 0.3 Hz, and they are segmented into overlapping time windows with a time step and a window length equal 2 s and 5 s, respectively. The selection of these parameters was done to indicate highlights in meaningful time period for the whole duration of the movie.

Annotation of the movie was performed offline by a movie critic, who annotated the movie based on the following five types of emotional and aesthetic highlights [1], [3].
"Form-highlights" (the manner in which the subject is presented in the film):
- *H1*: Spectacular (technical choice, special effects);
- *H2*: Subtle (use of camera, lighting, music).
"Content-highlights" (the presented subject in the film):
- *H3*: Character development (characters' emotions and responses to dramatic events);
- *H4*: Dialogue (motivation of actions and tensions among characters);
- *H5*: Theme development (unusual close up, urban theme).
For each type of highlights, non-highlights are scenes without the particular type of the highlights (possibly, containing the other highlight type).
In these studies the periodicity score (PS) and pairwise synchronization measures: the nonlinear interdependence (NI) and the windowed mutual information (WMI) are applied to the spectators' physiological and behavioral signals to uncover different properties of their synchronization.

4. RESULTS

We employ the two side Welch's t-test at the significance level ($\alpha = 0.1$) to test the hypothesis. We verify if an increase/a drop of the synchronization of the spectators' physiological and behavioral reactions might appear during a particular type of highlights [16], [11].

Figure 3(a) shows the mean values of the PS which are computed over the spectators' physiological signals for all types of highlights. The values of the PS increase marginally significantly for the scenes in the movie containing spectacular highlights *H1* (t=1.77, p<0.1, r=0.12) and theme development highlights *H5* (t=1.90, p<0.1, r=0.14) in comparison to the scenes without those particular types of highlights. Figure 3(b) plots the results for the behavioral signals. The values of the PS rise significantly and marginally significantly for the scenes consist of spectacular highlights *H1* (t= 2.55, p=0.01, r=0.15) and subtle highlights *H2* (t=1.77, p<0.1, r=0.09), respectively. Moreover, the values of the PS drop marginally significantly for character development highlights *H3* (t=-1.71, p<0.1, r=0.11).

In Figure 3(c) the mean values of the NI for the electrodermal signals are plotted. The synchronization increases significantly and marginally significantly for spectacular highlights *H1* (t=4.99, p<0.01, r=0.52) and theme development highlights *H5* (t=1.91, p<0.1, r=0.14), respectively. Figure 3(d) gives information on the synchronization among the be-

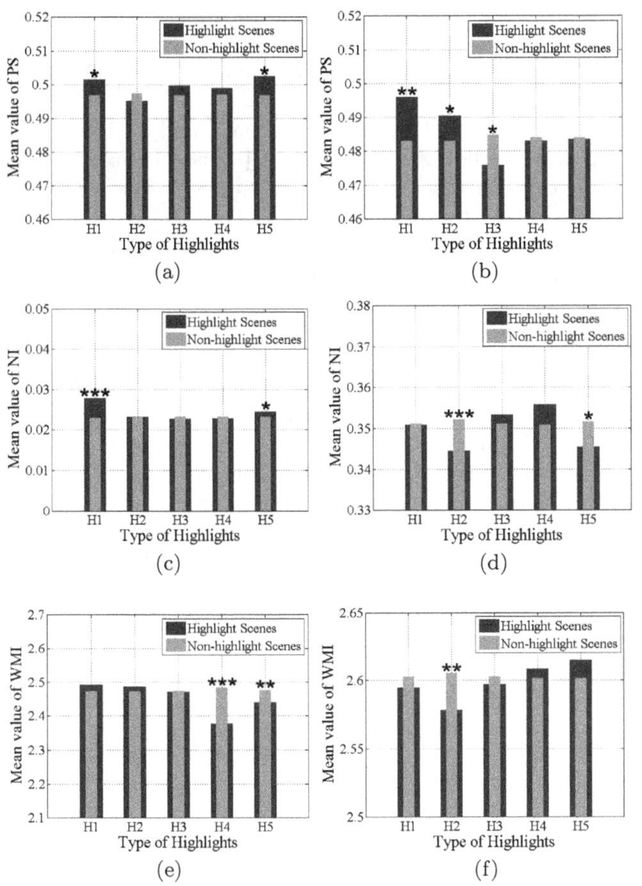

Figure 3: Mean values of synchronization measures: PS ((a), (b)), NI ((c), (d)), WMI ((e), (f)) for one particular type of highlight scenes (*H1*, *H2*, *H3*, *H4*, *H5*) versus scenes without the type of highlights in the movie. Left charts correspond to elctro-dermal activity signals and right charts correspond to acceleration signals. $\star$ stands for a p-value < 0.1, $\star\star$ for a p-value < 0.05 and $\star\star\star$ for a p-value < 0.01.

havioral signals. The values of the NI falls significantly and marginally significantly for subtle highlights *H2* (t=-3.55, p<0.01, r=0.16) and theme development highlights *H5* (t=-1.78, p<0.1, r=0.13), respectively.

Figure 3(e) for the WMI shows a significant decrease of dependencies among the physiological signals of the spectators for dialogue highlights *H4* (t=-10.9, p<0.01, r=0.55) and theme development highlights *H5* (t=-2.32, p<0.05, r=0.18). In Figure 3(f), we also observe a significant drop of dependencies among behavioral signals but only for subtle highlights *H2* (t=-2.58, p=0.01, r=0.14).

5. DISCUSSION

We can detect some types of highlights applying synchronization measures. The obtained results show that the values of the PS and NI increase marginally significantly and significantly, respectively, for spectacular highlights *H1*. These observations are in line with our previous works [16], [11], [12]. This can be justified by the nature of the scenes since *H1* corresponds to spectacular scenes where the director uses special effects, such as an increasing saturation of red color during final shooting scenes, playing with lights and a location of the camera. These may evoke strong emotional reactions and emotional contagion.

The slow movement of a camera and music during subtle highlights *H2* could decrease the spectators' behavioral reactions. Due to discrepancies among the spectators we observe a drop of the NI and the WMI while the PS might still capture some synchronization in their behaviors.

The PS falls marginally significantly for the spectators' behavioral reactions during character development highlights *H3* while the pairwise synchronization measures could not expose any marginally significant drop/increase of the synchronization. Some group of the spectators could only react similarly to the attitude of the main characters which could be caused by the ambiguity of their personality.

Also, we observe a significant drop of the WMI values for the spectators' physiological signals in the case of dialogue highlights *H4*. This can occur because of two reasons: long average duration of highlights *H4* may cause that the spectators' emotions fade in time, and the main character is also an ambiguous movie character who could elicit different reactions across the audience.

The results also report that the values of the PS and NI increase marginally significantly for the theme development highlights *H5*. The rise of spectators' synchronization might be caused partially by the overlapping of spectacular and theme development scenes in this particular movie. But the WMI also measures a significant drop in the statistical dependencies. It can be explained by a lack of any mutual dependence between signals.

6. CONCLUSIONS

In this paper we suppose that the occurrence of synchronized spectators' behaviors and physiological reactions are linked to the presence of emotional and aesthetic highlights in a movie. To detect these highlights, we propose to apply the periodicity score (PS) to measure synchronization among groups of spectators' signals that can not be identified by other measures. To explore the PS's properties, we compare it with the baseline pairwise synchronization measures: the nonlinear interdependence (NI) and the windowed mutual information (WMI). We show that the PS as well as the NI, can indicate the appearance of spectacular highlights *H1* and theme development highlights *H5* based on the spectators' physiological reactions. These results can be explained by special effects related to spectacular scenes in the urban landscape when strong physiological and behavioral reactions of spectators are supposed to be evoked. Also, the PS depicts the appearance of the spectacular highlights based on the spectators' behavioral signals. The PS as the NI and the WMI could identify the appearance of subtle highlights *H2* based on acceleration signals of the spectators. Moreover, the PS only decreases indicating character development highlights *H3* in comparison with the other methods.

In the future work, we will collect more multimodal signals to verify our preliminary studies. Also, we will attempt to reveal more topological features that could uncover different types of synchronization in spectators' physiological and behavioral data while watching different movies.

7. REFERENCES

[1] A. Bazin. *What is cinema?* University of California Press, 2004.

[2] F. J. Bernieri and R. Rosenthal. Interpersonal coordination: Behavior matching and interactional synchrony. 1991.

[3] D. Bordwell, K. Thompson, and J. Ashton. *Film art: an introduction.* McGraw-Hill New York, 1997.

[4] G. Chanel and C. Mühl. Connecting brains and bodies: applying physiological computing to support social interaction. *Interacting with Computers*, page iwv013, 2015.

[5] C. Chênes, G. Chanel, M. Soleymani, and T. Pun. Highlight detection in movie scenes through inter-users, physiological linkage. In *Social Media Retrieval*, pages 217–237, 2013.

[6] S. Chepushtanova, M. Kirby, C. Peterson, and L. Ziegelmeier. An application of persistent homology on grassmann manifolds for the detection of signals in hyperspectral imagery. In *Geoscience and Remote Sensing Symposium (IGARSS), 2015 IEEE International*, pages 449–452. IEEE, 2015.

[7] E. Delaherche, M. Chetouani, A. Mahdhaoui, C. Saint-Georges, S. Viaux, and D. Cohen. Interpersonal synchrony: A survey of evaluation methods across disciplines. *IEEE Transactions on Affective Computing*, 3(3):349–365, 2012.

[8] R. Ghrist. Barcodes: the persistent topology of data. *Bulletin of the American Mathematical Society*, 45(1):61–75, 2008.

[9] J. Hamm and D. D. Lee. Grassmann discriminant analysis: a unifying view on subspace-based learning. In *Proceedings of the 25th international conference on Machine learning*, pages 376–383. ACM, 2008.

[10] E. Hatfield, J. T. Cacioppo, and R. L. Rapson. *Emotional contagion.* Cambridge university press, 1994.

[11] T. Kostoulas, G. Chanel, M. Muszynski, P. Lombardo, and T. Pun. Dynamic time warping of multimodal signals for detecting highlights in movies. In *Proceedings of the 1st Workshop on Modeling INTERPERsonal SynchrONy And infLuence*, pages 35–40. ACM, 2015.

[12] T. Kostoulas, G. Chanel, M. Muszynski, P. Lombardo, and T. Pun. Identifying aesthetic highlights in movies from clustering of physiological and behavioral signals. In *Quality of Multimedia Experience (QoMEX), 2015 Seventh International Workshop on*, May 2015.

[13] A. Kraskov, H. Stögbauer, and P. Grassberger. Estimating mutual information. *Physical review E*, 69(6):066138, 2004.

[14] E. Kroupi, J.-M. Vesin, and T. Ebrahimi. Phase-amplitude coupling between eeg and eda while experiencing multimedia content. In *Affective Computing and Intelligent Interaction (ACII), 2013 Humaine Association Conference on*, pages 865–870. IEEE, 2013.

[15] T. Li, Y. Baveye, C. Chamaret, E. Dellandréa, and L. Chen. Continuous arousal self-assessments validation using real-time physiological responses. In *International Workshop on Affect and Sentiment in Multimedia (ASM)*, 2015.

[16] M. Muszynski, T. Kostoulas, G. Chanel, P. Lombardo, and T. Pun. Spectators' synchronization detection based on manifold representation of physiological signals: Application to movie highlights detection. In *Proceedings of the 2015 ACM on International Conference on Multimodal Interaction*, pages 235–238. ACM, 2015.

[17] J. A. Perea, A. Deckard, S. B. Haase, and J. Harer. Sw1pers: Sliding windows and 1-persistence scoring; discovering periodicity in gene expression time series data. *BMC bioinformatics*, 16(1):257, 2015.

[18] J. A. Perea and J. Harer. Sliding windows and persistence: An application of topological methods to signal analysis. *Foundations of Computational Mathematics*, 15(3):799–838, 2015.

[19] A. Pikovsky, M. Rosenblum, and J. Kurths. *Synchronization: a universal concept in nonlinear sciences*, volume 12. Cambridge university press, 2003.

[20] R. Q. Quiroga, J. Arnhold, and P. Grassberger. Learning driver-response relationships from synchronization patterns. *Physical Review E*, 61(5):5142, 2000.

[21] N. F. Rulkov, M. M. Sushchik, L. S. Tsimring, and H. D. Abarbanel. Generalized synchronization of chaos in directionally coupled chaotic systems. *Physical Review E*, 51(2):980, 1995.

[22] M. Soleymani, S. Asghari-Esfeden, M. Pantic, and Y. Fu. Continuous emotion detection using eeg signals and facial expressions. In *Multimedia and Expo (ICME), 2014 IEEE International Conference on*, pages 1–6. IEEE, 2014.

[23] F. Takens. Detecting strange attractors in turbulence. *Dynamical Systems and Turbulence, Lecture Notes in Mathematics*, 898:366–381, 1981.

[24] H. L. Wang and L.-F. Cheong. Affective understanding in film. *IEEE Transactions on Circuits and Systems for Video Technology*, 16(6):689–704, June 2006.

On Estimating Air Pollution from Photos Using Convolutional Neural Network

Chao Zhang
Beijing Normal University
IBM Research - China
zhangch@mail.bnu.edu.cn

Junchi Yan
East China Normal University
IBM Research - China
yanjc@cn.ibm.com

Changsheng Li*
IBM Research - China
lcsheng@cn.ibm.com

Xiaoguang Rui
IBM Research - China
ruixg@cn.ibm.com

Liang Liu
IBM Research - China
liuliang@cn.ibm.com

Rongfang Bie
Beijing Normal University
rfbie@bnu.edu.cn

ABSTRACT

Air pollution has raised people's intensive concerns especially in developing countries such as China and India. Different from using expensive or unreliable methods like sensor-based or social network based one, photo based air pollution estimation is a promising direction, while little work has been done up to now. Focusing on this immediate problem, this paper devises an effective convolutional neural network to estimate air's quality based on photos. Our method is comprised of two ingredients: first a negative log-log ordinal classifier is devised in the last layer of the network, which can improve the ordinal discriminative ability of the model. Second, as a variant of the Rectified Linear Units (ReLU), a modified activation function is developed for photo based air pollution estimation. This function has been shown it can alleviate the vanishing gradient issue effectively. We collect a set of outdoor photos and associate the pollution levels from official agency as the ground truth. Empirical experiments are conducted on this real-world dataset which shows the capability of our method.

1. INTRODUCTION

Air pollution is becoming more and more serious in many developing countries, which influences the human health and life significantly [22]. Thus, how to reduce the air pollution becomes an urgent problem in these countries. In order to achieve this goal, air quality estimation is an effective way to monitor the air pollution and can provide recommendations for decision makers. In the past, many methods have been proposed for predicting air quality. Chung [5] utilizes the satellites to detect the air pollution and its transport. Hodgeson et al. [10] use the spectroscopic technique to solve the complexity of the monitoring problems. Other works include filter-based gravimetric method [7], optical information of the atmospheric aerosol [23], social network based method [4], and mobile information based method [19]. However traditional air quality monitoring needs professional sensors or equipments deployed at representative sites, which is expensive in the cost. More importantly, their coverage is geographically limited, and thus the air pollution levels in those places far from air quality monitor sites can not be measured accurately. With the rapid development of smartphone, directly estimating air pollution from photos starts to gain the potential of being a convenient and less expensive approach because it can cover more areas in a crowd-sourcing manner. However, little work has been done for photo based air pollution estimation.

Feature learning based on convolutional neural networks (CNN) has been intensively studied in recent years, and many promising progresses have been made for solving typical computer vision problems [12]. In CNN based methods, designing a task-specific network structure is rather challenging. In this paper, we explore the way for how to design a CNN model for estimating air pollution by photos from mobile-phone. In particular, this paper focuses on two aspects in the CNN model design. First, one popular classifier in CNNs is Softmax [9] which is the generalization of the logistic regression. In addition, Softmax regression is a supervised learning algorithm, which can utilize the features derived from deep learning networks as input for prediction. Such combination has achieved prominent success in many tasks such as MNIST digit, CIFAR10 and CIFAR100 classification. However multinomial regression model like Softmax does not consider the ranking information at all during learning while ranking information is very important for ranking or regression problems [14, 15]. Therefore, designing a network structure to preserve the ranking information is necessary for air quality prediction.

Second, the activation function is another critical part for the success of CNN applications. The sigmoid suffers from the vanishing gradient problem [3]. The mean of ReLU [20] activation is larger than zero which may lead to bias for the next layer. PReLU [8] and LReLU [18] consider the nonzero slope for negative part but they do not consider change the slope of the positive part to improve model's flexibility.

In this paper, we propose a CNN based Photo Air Pollution Level Estimation algorithm, called PAPLE, for air pollution estimation. Specifically, a new function with two parameters $\theta = \{\alpha, \beta\}$ is first introduced as the activation operator followed by each convolutional layer. The positive parts α is

*Corresponding author.

MM '16, October 15 - 19, 2016, Amsterdam, Netherlands

ISBN 978-1-4503-3603-1/16/10...$15.00

DOI: http://dx.doi.org/10.1145/2964284.2967230

the slope and the negative part $\beta < 0$ is the constant term. The new activation layer enables our CNN model to be more flexible, less time-consuming and overcome the bias problem for the next layer. In the proposed convolutional neural network model, there are nine convolution layers, two pooling layers and two dropout layers. To capture the ranking information of the categories, we then involve in the ordinal classifier [6] in the last layer of network. Because most day's pollution levels are low and thus the cumulative probability for lower parts is high, we choose negative log-log as our link function [21].

In a nutshell, the main bullets of our method are:

- This paper is one of the first work for estimating the air pollution via image content. We collect a labeled dataset involving both photos taken in different air conditions and the pollution measurements from official agency. Empirical results show the feasibility of image based pollution estimation.

- A novel convolutional neural network is tailored to the air pollution estimation task with two ingredients. First, a modified activation function is introduced to effectively mitigate the problem of vanishing gradient and the bias for the next layer. Second, instead of the widely used Softmax classifier, a negative log-log ordinal classifier is adopted to better fit the pollution estimation problem.

2. POLLUTION ESTIMATION BY CNN

2.1 Convolutional Features Extractor

We first present the CNN features used in this work. The operator of the convolution layer can be summarized as

$$L_i = pool_P(\sigma(L_{i-1} * W_i + b_i)) \tag{1}$$

where L_{i-1} is the input feature layer, W_i are the weights and b_i are the biases. $\theta_i = \{W_i, b_i\}$ is the learned parameter set. The function *pool* is a sub-sampling operation. P is the size of the pooling region. $*$ represents the convolution operator, and σ is the activation function.

ReLU [20] has been proposed to replace saturated counterpart (e.g. sigmoid and tanh) activation function and achieves excellent performance. However, ReLU's mean activation is larger than zero which may lead to bias for the next layer. And ReLU's slope is 1 which is not flexible. Thus, we define a new activation as followed:

$$f(x) = \begin{cases} \beta, & if\ x < 0 \\ \alpha x, & otherwise \end{cases} \tag{2}$$

where $\theta = \{\alpha, \beta\}$ are the parameters. α is the slope and $\beta < 0$ is the constant term. The new activation only has two parameters and it is fast to train the model. Our proposed activation is similar to other ReLU family activation, like PReLU [8], LReLU [18]. But our function has one negative constant value. This simplifies our model and the slope parameter for positive part renders our function more flexible. Specifically when $\alpha = 1$ and $\beta = 0$, our activation function is reduced to standard ReLU. Fig.1 shows the shape of ReLU and our proposed activation function. The first derivative is derived as

$$f'(x) = \begin{cases} 0, & if\ x < 0 \\ \alpha, & otherwise \end{cases} \tag{3}$$

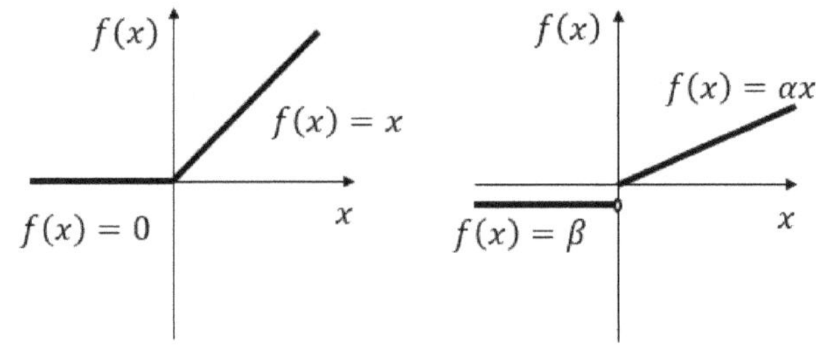

Figure 1: ReLU vs. the proposed activation function. The parameter $\theta = \{\alpha, \beta\}$, where α is the slope and β is the negative part.

The new activation function can be trained by backpropagation [13], the update rule for $\theta = \{\alpha, \beta\}$ is obtained from chain rule:

$$\frac{\partial O}{\partial \theta} = \sum_{x_i} \frac{\partial O}{\partial f(x_i)} \frac{\partial f(x_i)}{\partial \theta} \tag{4}$$

where O denotes the objective function, $\frac{\partial O}{\partial f(x_i)}$ is the gradient propagated from the higher layers. For the channel-shared variant, the gradient of θ is $\frac{\partial O}{\partial \theta} = \sum_i \sum_{x_i} \frac{\partial O}{\partial f(x_i)} \frac{\partial f(x_i)}{\partial \theta}$.

The gradients for the parameters α and β are

$$\frac{\partial f(x_i)}{\partial \alpha} = \begin{cases} 0, & if\ x < 0 \\ x_i, & otherwise \end{cases} \tag{5}$$

$$\frac{\partial f(x_i)}{\partial \beta} = \begin{cases} 1, & if\ x < 0 \\ 0, & otherwise \end{cases} \tag{6}$$

The momentum algorithm is used to update the $\theta = \{\alpha, \beta\}$

$$\Delta\theta := \mu\Delta\theta + \epsilon\frac{\partial O}{\partial \theta} \tag{7}$$

where μ is the momentum and ϵ is the learning rate.

To obtain features from CNN, we introduce a CNN based network structure: Estimation of Photo Air Pollution Level Network (EPAPLN). Its structure is summarized in Table 1. Our convolutional neural network includes 9 convolution layers, 2 pooling layers and 2 dropout layers. Our proposed activation function is used in each convolutional layer. In each convolution layer the first part shows the filter shape and the second part shows number of filters. The size of filters of pooling layers is set to 3×3. We utilize dropout [24] as the regularization method to prevent neural networks from overfitting. We set the probability of retaining a hidden unit to 0.5.

Stochastic gradient descent is applied to learn EPAPLN. The last two layers are used to represent the features because the high-level layers are more related to semantics [17].

2.2 Negative Log-log Ordinal Classifier

Softmax ignores data's order and treats all the categorical variables as nominal ones, which introduces bias for ordinal regression tasks. Hence we adopt the ordinal classifier to estimate the pollution level. Because pollution levels for most days are low and the cumulative probability for lower parts is high, we choose negative log-log as our link function. The negative log-log ordinal regression model is:

$$-\log(-\log(P(Y \leqslant j))) = \alpha_j + \sum \omega_i x_i \tag{8}$$

The log-likelihood function can be derived as below:

$$\ell = \sum_{j=1}^{J-1} \sum_{k=1}^{j} nk \log(\frac{\sum_l^j \pi_l}{\pi_{j+1}}) - \sum_{k=1}^{j+1} nk \log(\frac{\sum_l^{j+1} \pi_l}{\pi_{j+1}}) \tag{9}$$

Table 1: Network structure: each layer is a convolutional layer if not otherwise specified. Activation function is followed by each convolutional layer.

Input Size	EPAPLN (our model)
64×64	3×3, 32
64×64	3×3, 32
64×64	3×3, max pooling, /2
32×32	dropout, 0.5
16×32	3×3, 64
32×32	3×3, 64
32×32	3×3, 64
32×32	3×3, avg pooling, /2
16×8	dropout, 0.5
16×16	3×3, 96
16×16	3×3, 96
16×16	3×3, 96
16×16	3×3, 96

where n is the sum of all frequency weights. We denote the parameter vector as θ, which has $J-1+p$ parameters. $J=6$ is the level count and p is the feature number.

Newton-Raphson method can be used to estimate the parameters and let $theta_s$ be the parameter vector at step s and let A_s be a $(J-1+p)\times(J-1+p)$ matrix.

$$[A_s]_de = -\frac{\partial^2\ell}{\partial\theta_d\partial\theta_e} \tag{10}$$

For step $s+1$, the parameter vector θ_{s+1} can be obtained by:

$$A_s\theta_{s+1} = A_s\theta_s + \gamma\frac{\partial\ell}{\partial\theta_s} \tag{11}$$

where γ is the stepping scalar.

The first derivative of the log-likelihood regarding θ is:

$$\frac{\partial\ell}{\partial\theta_d} = \sum_{j=1}^{J-1}\left(\sum_{k=1}^{j} nk - \sum_{k=1}^{j+1} nk\frac{\sum_{l=1}^{j}\pi_l}{\sum_{l=1}^{j+1}\pi_l}\right)\frac{\sum_{l=1}^{j+1}\pi_l}{\sum_{l=1}^{j}\pi_l\pi_{j+1}} \left(\frac{\partial(\alpha_{j+1}+\sum\omega_i x_i)}{\partial\theta_d}\frac{\sum_{l=1}^{j}\pi_l}{\sum_{l=1}^{j+1}\pi_l}\sum_{l=1}^{j+1}\pi_l\log(\sum_{l=1}^{j+1}\pi_l) - \frac{\partial(\alpha_j+\sum\omega_i x_i)}{\partial\theta_d}\sum_{l=1}^{j}\pi_l\log(\sum_{l=1}^{j}\pi_l)\right) \tag{12}$$

where we set $\frac{\partial(\alpha_J+\sum\omega_i x_i)}{\partial\theta}=0$, $\sum_{l=1}^{J}\pi_l\log(\sum_{l=1}^{J}\pi_l)=0$ and $j=1,\cdots,J-1$, $d=1,\cdots,J-1+p$.

The second derivative of the log-likelihood w.r.t. θ is:

$$\frac{\partial^2\ell}{\partial\theta_d\partial\theta_e} = \sum_{j=1}^{J-1}(F_1 - F_2 + F_3F_4) \tag{13}$$

where F_1, F_2, F_3, F_4 can be computed as follows:

$$F_1 = Q_{je}\left(\sum_{k=1}^{j+1} nk\frac{\sum_{l=1}^{j}\pi_l}{\sum_{l=1}^{j+1}\pi_l} - \sum_{k=1}^{j} nk\right) \left(\frac{1}{(\sum_{l=1}^{j}\pi_l)^2}\frac{\sum_{l=1}^{j+1}\pi_l}{\sum_{l=1}^{j}\pi_l\pi_{j+1}}Q_{jd} + \frac{1}{\pi_{j+1}^2}\left(\frac{\sum_{l=1}^{j+2}\pi_l}{\sum_{l=1}^{j+1}\pi_l\pi_{j+2}}Q_{(j+1)d} - \frac{\sum_{l=1}^{j+1}\pi_l}{\sum_{l=1}^{j}\pi_l\pi_{j+1}}Q_{jd}\right)\right) \tag{14}$$

$$F_2 = \frac{\sum_{k=1}^{j+1} nk}{\sum_{l=1}^{j+1}\pi_l}\frac{\sum_{l=1}^{j+1}\pi_l}{\sum_{l=1}^{j}\pi_l\pi_{j+1}}Q_{jd}Q_{je} \tag{15}$$

$$F_3 = -\left(\sum_{k=1}^{j+1} nk\frac{\sum_{l=1}^{j}\pi_l}{\sum_{l=1}^{j+1}\pi_l} - \sum_{k=1}^{j} nk\right)\frac{\sum_{l=1}^{j+1}\pi_l}{\sum_{l=1}^{j}\pi_l\pi_{j+1}} \tag{16}$$

$$F4 = \frac{\partial(\alpha_j+\sum\omega_i x_i)}{\partial\theta_e}\left(1+\log\sum_{l=1}^{j}\pi_l\right) \sum_{l=1}^{j}\pi_l\log(\sum_{l=1}^{j}\pi_l)\frac{\partial(\alpha_j+\sum\omega_i x_i)}{\partial\theta_d} + \frac{\partial(\alpha_{j+1}+\sum\omega_i x_i)}{\partial\theta_e}\frac{Q_{jd}}{\sum_{l=1}^{j+1}\pi_l}\sum_{l=1}^{j+1}\pi_l\log(\sum_{l=1}^{j+1}\pi_l) + \frac{\partial(\alpha_{j+1}+\sum\omega_i x_i)}{\partial\theta_d}\frac{\sum_{l=1}^{j}\pi_l}{\sum_{l=1}^{j+1}\pi_l}\left(1+\log\sum_{l=1}^{j+1}\pi_l\right) \sum_{l=1}^{j+1}\pi_l\log(\sum_{l=1}^{j+1}\pi_l)\frac{\partial(\alpha_{j+1}+\sum\omega_i x_i)}{\partial\theta_d} \tag{17}$$

where $d,e=1,\cdots,(J-1)+p$ and Q_{jd} and Q_{je} are below:

$$Q_{jd} = \left(\frac{\partial(\alpha_{j+1}+\sum\omega_i x_i)}{\partial\theta_d}\frac{\sum_{l=1}^{j}\pi_l}{\sum_{l=1}^{j+1}\pi_l}\sum_{l=1}^{j+1}\pi_l\log(\sum_{l=1}^{j+1}\pi_l) - \frac{\partial(\alpha_j+\sum\omega_i x_i)}{\partial\theta_d}\sum_{l=1}^{j}\pi_l\log(\sum_{l=1}^{j}\pi_l)\right) \tag{18}$$

$$Q_{je} = \left(\frac{\partial(\alpha_{j+1}+\sum\omega_i x_i)}{\partial\theta_e}\frac{\sum_{l=1}^{j}\pi_l}{\sum_{l=1}^{j+1}\pi_l}\sum_{l=1}^{j+1}\pi_l\log(\sum_{l=1}^{j+1}\pi_l) - \frac{\partial(\alpha_j+\sum\omega_i x_i)}{\partial\theta_e}\sum_{l=1}^{j}\pi_l\log(\sum_{l=1}^{j}\pi_l)\right) \tag{19}$$

3. EXPERIMENTS

We evaluate our Photo Air Pollution Level Estimation (PAPLE) algorithm on the pollution images dataset which includes photos shots taken in Beijing by ourself. The dataset involves two major air pollutants in developing countries including Particulate Matter 2.5 (PM2.5) and Particulate Matter 10 (PM10) as the main targets for estimation, which have both 6 levels [1] as listed in Table 2. The associated ground truth, i.e. the air quality observation data, is collected from the website of Beijing environmental protection bureau [2].

Table 2: Air quality index for PM2.5 and PM10.

Level	1	2	3	4	5	6
PM2.5 Range	<35	35-75	75-115	115-150	150-250	>250
PM10 Range	<50	50-150	150-250	250-350	350-420	>420

We compare CNN-Softmax, PReLU-CNN-Softmax, LReLU-CNN-Softmax, ReLU-CNN-Softmax, PCA-Negative Log-log Ordinal Classifier (PCALL) and use their default parameters to train the model. Table 3 shows our proposed PAPLE performs competitively against the other methods on the

Table 4: Coincidence matrix for PM2.5 by different methods on the collected real-world dataset.

	1	2	3	4	5	6
1	326	13	3	1	3	2
2	63	48	11	1	0	4
3	33	23	23	8	4	1
4	11	10	4	5	8	3
5	15	4	2	10	43	9
6	3	2	2	4	12	44

(PAPLE)

	1	2	3	4	5	6
1	305	25	14	0	4	0
2	57	47	19	1	2	1
3	25	25	30	6	6	0
4	7	8	7	5	9	5
5	8	3	22	5	30	15
6	8	0	4	0	18	37

(CNN-Softmax)

	1	2	3	4	5	6
1	263	50	26	5	4	0
2	38	45	27	13	3	1
3	17	17	30	19	7	2
4	5	6	11	5	6	8
5	4	6	12	12	32	17
6	0	3	4	3	20	37

(PReLU-CNN-Softmax)

	1	2	3	4	5	6
1	296	44	0	0	8	0
2	53	68	0	0	5	1
3	28	56	0	0	7	1
4	4	22	0	0	13	2
5	6	24	0	0	46	7
6	5	5	0	0	28	29

(LReLU-CNN-Softmax)

	1	2	3	4	5	6
1	293	35	3	6	6	5
2	61	45	9	1	2	9
3	30	25	14	10	6	7
4	11	8	4	6	9	3
5	15	5	0	11	38	14
6	3	1	2	1	15	45

(ReLU-CNN-Softmax)

	1	2	3	4	5	6
1	293	46	4	0	5	0
2	62	59	2	0	3	1
3	37	43	6	0	5	1
4	7	21	0	0	11	2
5	6	30	2	0	37	8
6	2	3	5	0	27	30

(PCALL)

Table 3: Average error with different methods.

Methods	PM2.5	PM10
PAPLE	0.606	0.411
CNN-Softmax	0.644	0.47
PReLU-CNN-Softmax	0.691	0.492
LReLU-CNN-Softmax	0.694	0.511
ReLU-CNN-Softmax	0.699	0.526
PCALL	0.724	0.569

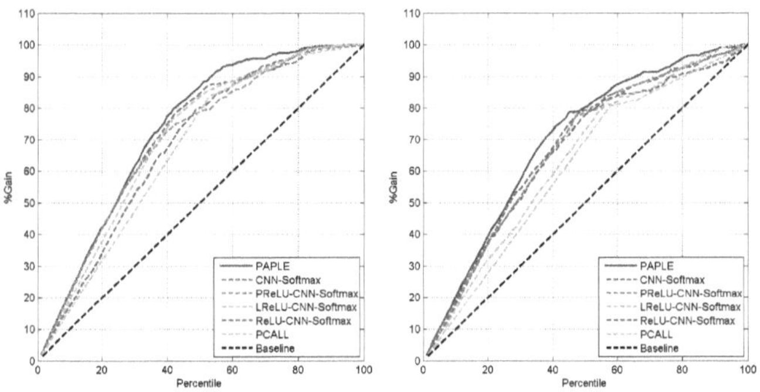

PM2.5 PM10

Figure 2: Cumulative gains for PM2.5, PM10.

average error which is defined by: $(\sum_{i=1}^{n} |predicted\ level - actual\ level|)/n$, where n is the number of testing samples. Table 4 shows the coincidence matrices which show the pattern of matches between each predicted level and its actual level with different methods for the PM2.5 as target. The rows refer to the actual PM2.5 levels, the columns show the predicted PM2.5 levels and the content of table shows the matching number of record. Larger diagonal numbers indicate better performance. Because of the space limitation, we do not list the PM10 results. In fact they are similar to the PM2.5 results.

Cumulative gain [11] is also adopted to measure the performance. It is calculated as the ratio between the results obtained with and without the model and it denotes the percentage of the overall number of cases in a given category "gained" by targeting a percentage of the total number of cases: $Gain = \frac{Expected\ Response\ Using\ Predictive\ Model}{Expected\ Response\ From\ Random\ Mailing}$. In Figure 2, y-axis shows the percentage of positive responses, and the result demonstrates PAPLE still outperforms all the other methods in terms of this metric.

4. CONCLUSION

In this paper, we have proposed an effective CNN based model for air pollution estimation from raw images. Our model involves a negative log-log ordinal classifier to fit the ordinal output well. We also empirically devise a new activation function for photo air pollution level estimation. The proposed approach is validated with qualitative and quantitative evaluations against several state-of-the-art methods. One important future work is to use crowd-sourced photos to trace contamination path. We will collect more photos from different places to study the influence of the diversity between the training and the testing dataset. We will also consider the image quality and noises in our model [16, 25].

5. ACKNOWLEDGMENT

This research is sponsored by National Natural Science Foundation of China (No.61171014, 61371185, 61401029, 11401028, 61571049) and the Fundamental Research Funds for the Central Universities (No.2014KJJCB32, 2013NT57, 2012LY-B46) and by SRF for ROCS, SEM and China Postdoctoral Science Foundation Funded Project (No.2016M590337).

6. REFERENCES

[1] http://210.72.1.216:8080/gzaqi/Document/gjzlbz.pdf. Accessed: 2016-07-19.

[2] http://zx.bjmemc.com.cn/. Accessed: 2016-07-19.

[3] Y. Bengio, P. Simard, and P. Frasconi. Learning long-term dependencies with gradient descent is difficult. *Neural Networks, IEEE Transactions on*, 5(2):157–166, 1994.

[4] J. Chen, H. Chen, G. Zheng, J. Z. Pan, H. Wu, and N. Zhang. Big smog meets web science: smog disaster analysis based on social media and device data on the web. In *Proceedings of the companion publication of the 23rd international conference on World wide web companion*, pages 505–510. International World Wide Web Conferences Steering Committee, 2014.

[5] Y. Chung. Air pollution detection by satellites: The transport and deposition of air pollutants over oceans. *Atmospheric Environment (1967)*, 20(4):617–630, 1986.

[6] S. Greenland. Alternative models for ordinal logistic regression. *Statistics in medicine*, 13(16):1665–1677, 1994.

[7] H. Hauck, A. Berner, B. Gomiscek, S. Stopper, H. Puxbaum, M. Kundi, and O. Preining. On the equivalence of gravimetric pm data with teom and beta-attenuation measurements. *Journal of Aerosol Science*, 35(9):1135–1149, 2004.

[8] K. He, X. Zhang, S. Ren, and J. Sun. Delving deep into rectifiers: Surpassing human-level performance on imagenet classification. In *Proceedings of the IEEE International Conference on Computer Vision*, pages 1026–1034, 2015.

[9] G. E. Hinton and R. R. Salakhutdinov. Replicated softmax: an undirected topic model. In *Advances in neural information processing systems*, pages 1607–1614, 2009.

[10] J. Hodgeson, W. McClenny, and P. Hanst. Air pollution monitoring by advanced spectroscopic techniques a variety of spectroscopic methods are being used to detect air pollutants in the gas phase. *Science*, 182(4109):248–258, 1973.

[11] K. J. and J. K. Cumulated gain-based evaluation of ir techniques. *ACM Transactions on Information Systems*, 20:2002, 2002.

[12] A. Krizhevsky, I. Sutskever, and G. E. Hinton. Imagenet classification with deep convolutional neural networks. In *Advances in neural information processing systems*, pages 1097–1105, 2012.

[13] Y. LeCun, B. Boser, J. S. Denker, D. Henderson, R. E. Howard, W. Hubbard, and L. D. Jackel. Backpropagation applied to handwritten zip code recognition. *Neural computation*, 1(4):541–551, 1989.

[14] C. Li, Q. Liu, J. Liu, and H. Lu. Learning ordinal discriminative features for age estimation. In *Computer Vision and Pattern Recognition (CVPR), 2012 IEEE Conference on*, pages 2570–2577, 2012.

[15] C. Li, Q. Liu, J. Liu, and H. Lu. Ordinal distance metric learning for image ranking. *IEEE transactions on neural networks and learning systems*, 26(7):1551–1559, 2015.

[16] Y. Li, Y. Zhou, J. Yan, J. Yang, and X. He. Tensor error correction for corrupted values in visual data. In *2010 IEEE International Conference on Image Processing*, pages 2321–2324. IEEE, 2010.

[17] C. Ma, J.-B. Huang, X. Yang, and M.-H. Yang. Hierarchical convolutional features for visual tracking. In *Proceedings of the IEEE International Conference on Computer Vision*, pages 3074–3082, 2015.

[18] A. L. Maas, A. Y. Hannun, and A. Y. Ng. Rectifier nonlinearities improve neural network acoustic models. In *Proc. ICML*, volume 30, page 1, 2013.

[19] S. Mei, H. Li, J. Fan, X. Zhu, and C. R. Dyer. Inferring air pollution by sniffing social media. In *Advances in Social Networks Analysis and Mining (ASONAM), 2014 IEEE/ACM International Conference on*, pages 534–539. IEEE, 2014.

[20] V. Nair and G. E. Hinton. Rectified linear units improve restricted boltzmann machines. In *Proceedings of the 27th International Conference on Machine Learning (ICML-10)*, pages 807–814, 2010.

[21] J. A. Nelder and R. J. Baker. Generalized linear models. *Encyclopedia of Statistical Sciences*, 1972.

[22] C. A. Pope III and D. W. Dockery. Health effects of fine particulate air pollution: lines that connect. *Journal of the air & waste management association*, 56(6):709–742, 2006.

[23] J. D. Smith and D. B. Atkinson. A portable pulsed cavity ring-down transmissometer for measurement of the optical extinction of the atmospheric aerosol. *Analyst*, 126(8):1216–1220, 2001.

[24] N. Srivastava, G. Hinton, A. Krizhevsky, I. Sutskever, and R. Salakhutdinov. Dropout: A simple way to prevent neural networks from overfitting. *The Journal of Machine Learning Research*, 15(1):1929–1958, 2014.

[25] J. Yan, M. Zhu, H. Liu, and Y. Liu. Visual saliency detection via sparsity pursuit. *IEEE Signal Processing Letters*, 17(8):739–742, 2010.

Cross-modal Retrieval with Label Completion

Xing Xu
University of Electronic Science and Technology of China
Chengdu, China
xing.xu@uestc.edu.cn

Fumin Shen
University of Electronic Science and Technology of China
Chengdu, China
fumin.shen@gmail.com

Yang Yang
University of Electronic Science and Technology of China
Chengdu, China
dlyyang@gmail.com

Heng Tao Shen
The University of Queensland
Brisbane, Australia
University of Electronic Science and Technology of China
Chengdu, China
shenhengtao@hotmail.com

Li He
Qualcomm R&D Center
San Diego, USA
lih@qti.qualcomm.com

Jingkuan Song
University of Trento
Trento, Italy
jingkuan.song@unitn.it

ABSTRACT

Cross-modal retrieval has been attracting increasing attention because of the explosion of multi-modal data, e.g., texts and images. Most supervised cross-modal retrieval methods learn discriminant common subspaces minimizing the heterogeneity of different modalities by exploiting the label information. However, these methods neglect the fact that, in practice, the given labels of training data might be incomplete (i.e., some of their labels are missing). The low-quality labels result in less effective subspace and consequent unsatisfactory retrieval performance. To tackle this, we propose a novel model that simultaneously performs label completion and cross-modal retrieval. Specifically, we assume the to-be-learned common subspace can be jointly derived through two aspects: 1) linear projection from modality-specific features and 2) enriching mapping from the incomplete labels. We thus formulate the subspace learning problem as a co-regularized learning framework based on multi-modal features and incomplete labels. Extensive experiments on two large-scale multi-modal datasets demonstrate the superiority of our model for both label completion and cross-modal retrieval over the state-of-the-arts.

Keywords

Cross-modal retrieval; label completion

1. INTRODUCTION

The past decade has witnessed the explosion of online imagery contents, especially on social photo-sharing websites such as Facebook, Flickr and Instagram. Usually, large-scale Internet photo collections consist of multi-modal data of images and texts. As the examples shown in Fig. 1, to describe the content of "Image", two types of textual data are usually associated: 1) "Text" that refers to descriptions from the surrounding web pages of the image or user-provided coarse tags; and 2) "Label" that represents the high-level semantic labels manually annotated by human annotators. Earlier research works, such as image search [30, 31, 21, 22] or document retrieval [5], try to explore the distinct characteristics in individual modality of "Image" or "Text". Recently, jointly modeling the statistics of images and associated textual data has continuously attracted much attention. Typical applications, such as automatic image annotation/caption [1, 17, 29, 27] and keyword-based image search [8, 23, 16], aim to build direct connection from "Image" to "Label" or the opposite. Due to the distinct statistical properties of "Image" and "Text", there have been increasing interests and efforts to model bidirectional connections across these two modalities. In this paper, we consider cross-modal retrieval problem on large-scale Image-Text datasets, where queries from one modality (e.g., "Image") are matched to database entries from another (e.g., "Text"). Since "Image" and "Text" reside in different feature spaces, the core issue of cross-modal retrieval is how to eliminate the diversity between the heterogeneous features.

To this end, many approaches have been proposed to learn a common latent subspace for cross-modal retrieval, where the projected features of different modalities are homogeneous and can be directly matched. In general, these methods can be classified into two categories: unsupervised and supervised. The unsupervised methods, including the classical ones such as Canonical Correlation Analysis (CCA) [12], Partial Least Square (PLS) [20] and their extensions [7, 9, 13, 19, 25], aim to directly build the correspondence and preserve the correlation of Image-Text pairs in the learned subspace. However, these approaches ignore the valuable label information ("Label") associated with the Image-Text pairs, resulting in less discriminative subspace.

On the other hand, the supervised methods [14, 24, 28] learn discriminant subspace from different modalities by fur-

MM '16, October 15-19, 2016, Amsterdam, Netherlands

DOI: http://dx.doi.org/10.1145/2964284.2967231

Figure 1: Two exemplars in Image-Text datasets: NUS-WIDE [3] (left) and Flickr30K [32] (right).

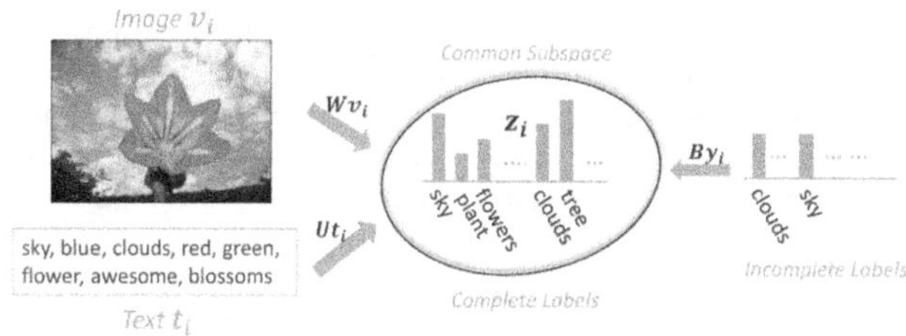

Figure 2: The joint learning framework of the proposed method.

ther exploiting the cues of "Label". However, most of these methods assume that each Image-Text pair contains a single label, which is not usually satisfied in practical Image-Text data with multi-label assumption as shown in Fig. 1. To overcome the shortcoming of these single-label approaches, several recent studies [4, 28] restrict the subspace to be decided by the label information and learn it under a linear classification framework with multi-label assumption. The latest work of [18] further extends the classic CCA to the multi-label situation under the supervision of multi-label information, achieving improved performance for cross-modal retrieval.

However, in practice the given labels are usually incomplete and insufficient as semantic description for corresponding images due to negligence or mistakes of the human annotators. For example, in Fig. 1 other proper labels such as $\langle flowers, tree, plant\rangle$, $\langle action, playing, room\rangle$, are missing for the two images respectively. Directly using these incomplete labels for subspace learning may not guarantee to achieve effective subspace for cross-modal retrieval. Therefore, it is necessary to first obtain complete labels via label completion before learning the discriminative subspace. Indeed, label completion is an attractive research topic in automatic image annotation problem. However, the existing studies [2, 15, 26] of label completion mainly focus on identifying the correct associations between the unimodal "Image" and "Label", not really suitable for multi-modal data containing both "Image" and "Text".

To tackle these challenges, we propose a novel method (as shown in Fig. 2) that performs label completion and cross-modal retrieval simultaneously. For cross-modal retrieval, linear regression is used to project data from different modalities into a common subspace; at the same time, for label completion, the common subspace is assumed to be defined exactly by the ideally complete label information, into which the incomplete labels can be transformed via enriching mapping. The two processes are integrated into a joint learning framework ensuring that the learned common subspace not only captures the intra- and inter-modality discrimination but also accounts for the ideally complete label information.

The main contributions of our work can be summarized as follows: 1) We propose a novel method to simultaneously tackle label completion and cross-modal retrieval problems. 2) Our method utilizes multi-modal data of image and text for label completion, which is an novel extension of traditional label completion approaches based on unimodal image data. 3) An iterative algorithm is presented to efficiently solve the complex minimization problem and can be applied to large-scale training data. 4) Experimental results on two large-scale multi-modal datasets have shown that our method obtains promising results on both label completion and cross-modal retrieval task.

2. THE PROPOSED METHOD

2.1 Problem Formulation

Assume that the multi-modal training data consists of n instances with image-text pairs, i.e. $\mathcal{X} = \{x_i\}_{i=1}^n$, $x_i = (\mathbf{v}_i, \mathbf{t}_i)$, where $\mathbf{v}_i \in \mathbb{R}^m$ is the i-th column of image feature matrix $\mathbf{V} \in \mathbb{R}^{m\times n}$, and $\mathbf{t}_i \in \mathbb{R}^d$ is the i-th column of the text feature matrix $\mathbf{T} \in \mathbb{R}^{d\times n}$. Here m and d are the dimensionality of image and text feature space, respectively. In addition, the incomplete labels $\mathbf{Y} = [\mathbf{y}_1, ..., \mathbf{y}_n] \in \mathbb{R}^{c\times n}$ of training instances $\mathcal{X}$ are also given, where c is the total number of labels and $\mathbf{y}_i = [y_{i,1}, ..., y_{i,c}] \in \mathbb{R}^c$ is the label vector for the i-th instance x_i. Note that, if x_i has the j-th label, then $y_{i,j} = 1$, otherwise $y_{i,j} = 0$. And x_i may have a single label or multiple labels. Unlike the previous subspace learning approaches [4, 18, 28] that define the common subspace by the given incomplete label information, here we consider to learn a common subspace that is defined by the ideally complete label information. The features of different modalities and the given incomplete labels can be simultaneously mapped to the subspace.

Specifically, our goal is to obtain a real-valued matrix $\mathbf{Z} \in \mathbb{R}^{c\times n}$ that satisfies the following three conditions simultaneously: 1) the i-th column vector $\mathbf{z}_i$ in $\mathbf{Z}$ is the common subspace feature representation of instance x_i, and it eliminates the heterogeneity between different features of $\mathbf{v}_i$ and $\mathbf{t}_i$; 2) $\mathbf{z}_i$ is sufficiently consistent with the provided incomplete labels $\mathbf{y}_i$, i.e. when performing label completion based on $\mathbf{z}_i$, $\mathbf{y}_i$ should be a subset of the ideally complete labels; 3) $\mathbf{z}_i$ preserves the discriminative properties of the ideally label information of different classes. We incorporate the three criteria simultaneously and integrate the label completion and cross-modal retrieval into a joint learning framework.

In particular, our learning framework (as shown in Fig. 2) contains two processes: 1) training modality-specific projections $\mathbf{W}\mathbf{v}_i \to \mathbf{z}_i$ and $\mathbf{U}\mathbf{t}_i \to \mathbf{z}_i$ to obtain the common subspace representation $\mathbf{z}_i$ from $\mathbf{v}_i$ and $\mathbf{t}_i$ of image and text modalities, respectively; 2) training an enriching mapping $\mathbf{B}\mathbf{y}_i \to \mathbf{z}_i$ to complete the provided incomplete labels $\mathbf{y}_i$ by recalling the missing labels that are likely to co-occur with those existing in $\mathbf{y}_i$. Therefore, for all the n instances, the loss function of the two sub-tasks can be written as

$$\frac{1}{n}\sum_{i=1}^{n}(\|\mathbf{z}_i - \mathbf{W}\mathbf{v}_i\|^2 + \|\mathbf{z}_i - \mathbf{U}\mathbf{t}_i\|^2 + \|\mathbf{z}_i - \mathbf{B}\mathbf{y}_i\|^2). \quad (1)$$

Here $\mathbf{W} \in \mathbb{R}^{c \times d}$ and $\mathbf{U} \in \mathbb{R}^{c \times m}$ are the projection matrices of image and text features, respectively, and $\mathbf{B} \in \mathbb{R}^{c \times c}$ is the enriching mapping matrix of given incomplete labels. To simplify Eq. 1, for each x_i, we force the output of the two sub-tasks to agree on $\mathbf{z}_i$, resulting in a *cross-modal co-regularized learning* problem by minimizing:

$$\min_{W,V,B} \frac{1}{n}\sum_{i=1}^{n}(\|\mathbf{B}\mathbf{y}_i - \mathbf{W}\mathbf{v}_i\|^2 + \|\mathbf{B}\mathbf{y}_i - \mathbf{U}\mathbf{t}_i\|^2). \quad (2)$$

In fact, the problem of Eq. 2 has a trivial solution at $\mathbf{B} = \mathbf{W} = \mathbf{U} = \mathbf{0}$. Therefore, it is necessary to add regularization terms for the model parameters $\mathbf{W}$, $\mathbf{U}$, and $\mathbf{B}$. In particular, for $\mathbf{W}$ and $\mathbf{U}$, we can simply add ℓ_2 regularizer for them due to their linear regression forms; for $\mathbf{B}$, because it is originally introduced to ensure the consistence between the given incomplete labels and the ideally complete labels during enriching mapping, it may be under constrained due to the absence of the ideally complete labels.

Inspired by [2], we constrain $\mathbf{B}$ by expanding the condition of enriching mapping, i.e. for the given incomplete labels $\mathbf{y}_i$ of instance x_i, $\mathbf{B}$ not only enriches $\mathbf{y}_i$ to its ideally complete labels, but also enriches a "corrupted" version of $\mathbf{y}_i$ (denoted as $\hat{\mathbf{y}}_i$) to $\mathbf{y}_i$. The idea is that if the consistence between $\mathbf{y}_i$ and its "corrupted" labels $\hat{\mathbf{y}}_i$ matches the consistence between $\mathbf{y}_i$ and its ideally complete labels, then applying $\mathbf{B}$ to $\mathbf{y}_i$ would recover the ideally complete labels.

Suppose that the "corrupted" labels $\hat{\mathbf{y}}_i$ are created by randomly removing each label in $\mathbf{y}_i$ with probability $p > 0$, the expected error of the enriching mapping between $\hat{\mathbf{y}}_i$ and $\mathbf{y}_i$ can be expressed as $\mathbb{E}[\|\mathbf{y}_i - \mathbf{B}\hat{\mathbf{y}}_i\|^2]_{p(\hat{\mathbf{y}}_i|\mathbf{y}_i)}$ under the corrupting distribution of $p(\hat{\mathbf{y}}_i|\mathbf{y}_i)$. Then the total expected error of all n instances can be computed as:

$$r(\mathbf{B}) = \frac{1}{n}\sum_{i=1}^{n}\mathbb{E}[\|\mathbf{y}_i - \mathbf{B}\hat{\mathbf{y}}_i\|^2]_{p(\hat{\mathbf{y}}_i|\mathbf{y}_i)}. \quad (3)$$

By defining $\mathbf{P} = \sum_{i=1}^{n}\mathbf{y}_i\mathbb{E}[\hat{\mathbf{y}}_i]^\top$ and $\mathbf{Q} = \sum_{i=1}^{n}\mathbb{E}[\mathbf{y}_i\mathbf{y}_i^\top]$, Eq. 3 can be expanded into

$$r(\mathbf{B}) = \frac{1}{n}trace(\mathbf{B}\mathbf{Q}\mathbf{B}^\top - 2\mathbf{P}\mathbf{B}^\top + \mathbf{Y}\mathbf{Y}^\top), \quad (4)$$

where $\mathbf{P} = (1-p)\mathbf{Y}\mathbf{Y}^\top$, $\mathbf{Q} = (1-p)^2\mathbf{Y}\mathbf{Y}^\top + p(1-p)\delta(\mathbf{Y}\mathbf{Y}^\top)$, and $\delta(\cdot)$ denotes the operation that sets all the entries except the diagonal of a matrix to zero. Then Eq. 4 can be considered as the regularization term for $\mathbf{B}$.

Finally, by integrating Eq. 2 and the regularization terms for $\mathbf{W}$, $\mathbf{U}$, and $\mathbf{B}$ discussed above, the proposed method can be formulated by minimizing:

$$\min_{\mathbf{W},\mathbf{U},\mathbf{B}} \frac{1}{n}\sum_{i=1}^{n}(\|\mathbf{B}\mathbf{y}_i - \mathbf{W}\mathbf{v}_i\|^2 + \|\mathbf{B}\mathbf{y}_i - \mathbf{U}\mathbf{t}_i\|^2) + \quad (5)$$
$$\lambda\|\mathbf{W}\|_2^2 + \mu\|\mathbf{U}\|_2^2 + \xi r(\mathbf{B}),$$

where λ, μ and ξ are the penalty coefficients of the regularization terms of each parameter.

2.2 Optimization

The minimization problem in Eq. 5 can be efficiently solved using block-coordinate descent algorithm by alternatively optimizing each variable by fixing the others. The detailed derivation for optimizing Eq. 5 is provided in supplementary. Here we depict the general optimization procedure of the parameters in each iteration as follows.

When fixing $\mathbf{U}$ and $\mathbf{B}$, optimizing $\mathbf{W}$ becomes a standard ridge regression problem that can be solved in closed-form:

$$\mathbf{W} = \mathbf{B}\mathbf{Y}\mathbf{V}^\top(\mathbf{V}\mathbf{V}^\top + n\lambda I)^{-1}. \quad (6)$$

Similarly, with fixed $\mathbf{W}$ and $\mathbf{B}$, $\mathbf{U}$ can also be optimized by solving the ridge regression problem, as:

$$\mathbf{U} = \mathbf{B}\mathbf{Y}\mathbf{T}^\top(\mathbf{T}\mathbf{T}^\top + n\mu I)^{-1}. \quad (7)$$

When fixing $\mathbf{W}$ and $\mathbf{U}$, $\mathbf{B}$ can be solved in closed-form as ordinary least squares:

$$\mathbf{B} = (\mathbf{W}\mathbf{V}\mathbf{Y}^\top + \mathbf{U}\mathbf{T}\mathbf{Y}^\top + \gamma\mathbf{P})[\mathbf{Y}\mathbf{Y}^\top + \gamma\mathbf{Q}]^{-1}, \quad (8)$$

where $\mathbf{P}$ and $\mathbf{Q}$ can be computed analytically with a predefined p. In practice, we can vary p in range $(0, 1)$ and choose appropriate value of p according to the resulting performance of label completion and cross-modal retrieval.

In summary, the objective function in Eq. 5 can be solved by updating variables $\mathbf{W}$, $\mathbf{U}$, and $\mathbf{B}$ iteratively until either convergence or a predefined number of iterations is reached. In each iteration, the time complexity is about $\mathcal{O}(kc^2n)$, where $k = \max\{m, d, c\}$ and usually we have $k \ll n$. Thus the training time complexity is linear to the size of training set, hence it is very efficient and scalable for large-scale training data.

2.3 Test Phase for Out-of-Instance

During the test phase, for a new test instance x' that contains features of one modality, i.e. $x' = (\mathbf{v}',)$ or $x' = (\mathbf{t}',)$, its subspace representation $\mathbf{z}'$ is computed as $\mathbf{z}' = \mathbf{W}\mathbf{v}'$ or $\mathbf{z}' = \mathbf{U}\mathbf{t}'$, respectively. For the the label completion task, we select the top-K labels that have top-ranked values in $\mathbf{z}'_i$ as the predicted label set of x', For the cross-modal retrieval task, we take $\mathbf{z}'$ as the query instance of one modality (e.g., image modality) to retrieve in the database of the other modality (text modality).

3. EXPERIMENTS

3.1 Experimental Setting

We apply the proposed method to both label completion and cross-modal retrieval tasks on two large-scale multi-modal datasets: NUS-WIDE [3] and Flickr30K [32]. The NUS-WIDE originally containing 269,648 instances, with each being an image with its associated textual tags. Each instance is manually annotated with at least one of 81 labels. For each instance, its image is represented as a 500-D bag-of-words (BOW) SIFT feature vector and its text as a binary tagging vector w.r.t. the top 1,000 most frequent tags. In our experiment, we take 267,613 instances as database and the remaining 2,035 instances as query. The Flickr30K consists of 31,783 instances, with each being an image with associated five textual sentences. In [10], the most frequent 350 keywords from the sentences in Flickr30K are selected as the labels, hence each instance is naturally assigned at least one of 350 labels. For each instance, its image is represented as a 4,096-D convolutional neural networks (CNN) feature extracted by Decaf model [6], and its text as a tf-idf-weighted tagging vector w.r.t the top 3,000 most frequent words that are crawled in [10]. In our experiment, we take 28,917 instances as database and the remaining 2,866 instances as query. It is worth mention that, for each instance in the two datasets, the average number of labels are 2.4 and 3.1, respectively, which is indeed incomplete.

To reduce the computational cost during training, we randomly select 10,000 instances from the database of each dataset and then apply the learned model to the other instances in database. Finally, the label completion task is performed on the query instances, and the cross-modal retrieval task is conducted between the query and database instances. In all experiments, the parameters λ, μ and ξ of the proposed model are empirically set to 10^{-5}, 10^{-5} and 10^{-2}, respectively. The experiments are conducted on a desktop which has 4-core 3.3GHz CPUs with 16GB RAM. It is worth noting that training the proposed method is highly efficient on the two large-scale datasets. For example, the training time of the proposed method on Flickr30K is about 10 minutes when using the high dimensional features of image and text modalities.

3.2 Results of Label Completion Task

We first compare the proposed method with several related methods on the label completion task. These methods are divided into three groups: 1) traditional image annotation methods using unimodal image for label prediction: JEC [17] and TagProp [11]; 2) label completion methods using unimodal image: Fasttag [2] and LSR [15]; 3) the cross-modal retrieval methods LCFS [24] and ml-CCA [18], which are capable to use multimodal data of image and text for label prediction. We implement the fast version of ml-CCA according to the instruction its original paper. We use the standard measures that are used in both traditional image annotation and label completion tasks, including average precision per label (P), average recall per label (R) and the number of labels that are recalled (N_+). For all the metrics, larger numerical value indicates better performance.

Table 1: Comparison of the proposed method with its counterparts on label completion task.

Dataset	NUS-WIDE			Flickr30K		
Method	P	R	N+	P	R	N+
JEC	0.031	0.102	54	0.263	0.312	249
TagProp	0.053	0.127	47	0.312	0.368	267
Fasttag	0.068	0.134	45	0.321	0.387	299
LSR	0.083	0.152	63	0.377	0.392	315
LCFS	0.398	0.478	69	0.417	0.491	319
ml-CCA	0.464	0.476	72	0.413	0.511	322
Proposed	**0.491**	**0.512**	**73**	**0.430**	**0.533**	**336**

Table 1 shows the overall results of different approaches on the two datasets. From Table 1, we have the following observations. Firstly, the multi-modal approaches (e.g., LCFS, ml-CCA) generally outperform the unimodal ones (e.g., JEC, TagProp, Fasttag, and LSR), since the additional text modality is helpful for label prediction. In addition, the visual feature of the NUS-WIDE dataset is less effective for the approaches that using unimodal images for label prediction. Secondly, these two datasets really suffer from missing labels, and the label completion approaches Fasttag and LSR improve the label prediction results of traditional image annotation methods JEC and TagProp. Moreover, the proposed method also outperforms the multi-modal approaches LCFS and ml-CCA that neglect missing labels. Thirdly, the proposed method achieves the best performance for label prediction on both datasets, showing the superiority of the proposed cross-modal co-regularized learning framework on capturing the hidden label correlation from multi-modal features of image and text.

3.3 Results of Cross-modal Retrieval Task

In this subsection, we evaluate the proposed method on cross-modal retrieval task. Specifically, we consider two standard scenarios (sub-tasks): Img2Txt and Txt2Img. We compare the proposed method with several subspace learning methods, including unsupervised ones: CCA [19], 3-view CCA [9] and supervised ones that can handle multi-label assumption: LCFS [24], CDL [28] ml-CCA [18]. We adopt the same evaluation metric of mean average precision (MAP) that is widely used in these methods for the two sub-tasks.

Table 2: Comparison of the proposed method with its counterparts on cross-modal retrieval task.

Dataset	NUS-WIDE		Flickr30K	
Method	Img2Txt	Txt2Img	Img2Txt	Img2Txt
CCA	0.265	0.278	0.228	0.245
3-view CCA	0.294	0.312	0.262	0.288
LCFS	0.349	0.363	0.271	0.296
CDL	0.358	0.366	0.293	0.301
ml-CCA	0.362	0.383	0.307	0.311
Proposed	**0.374**	**0.399**	**0.321**	**0.328**

Table 2 shows the MAP scores of all the methods on the two sub-tasks. We can observe that the results of unsupervised methods CCA and 3-view CCA are worse than the proposed method and other supervised ones LCFS, CDL, and ml-CCA. The main reason is that the unsupervised methods only use pairwise information of image and text modalities, ignoring the valuable label information. Furthermore, the proposed method outperforms the other supervised methods LCFS, CDL, and ml-CCA, indicating that it benefits from the label completion to learn more discriminant subspace for cross-modal matching.

4. CONCLUSION

In this paper, we studied the problem of cross-modal retrieval on multi-modal data with incomplete labels. We proposed a novel method that can simultaneously perform label completion and cross-modal retrieval. To achieve this, we introduced a common subspace as the ideally complete labels, which was jointly learned from two aspects: 1) linear projection from the modality-specific features; and 2) enriching mapping from the incomplete labels. This scheme ensures that the learned subspace was discriminant to account for the complete label information. We developed an efficient iterative algorithm for solving the optimization problem. Experiments on two large-scale datasets validated the advantages of the proposed method on both label completion and cross-modal retrieval tasks.

5. ACKNOWLEDGMENTS

This work was supported in part by the National Natural Science Foundation of China under Project 61572108 and Project 61502081, the National Thousand-Young-Talents Program of China, and the Fundamental Research Funds for the Central Universities under Project ZYGX2014Z007, Project ZYGX2015J055 and Project ZYGX2016KYQD114.

6. REFERENCES

[1] D. M. Blei and M. I. Jordan. Modeling annotated data. In *ACM SIGIR*, pages 127–134, 2003.

[2] M. Chen, A. Zheng, and K. Weinberger. Fast image tagging. In *ICML*, pages 1274–1282, 2013.

[3] T.-S. Chua, J. Tang, R. Hong, H. Li, Z. Luo, and Y.-T. Zheng. Nus-wide: A real-world web image database from national university of singapore. In *CIVR*, 2009.

[4] C. Deng, X. Tang, J. Yan, W. Liu, and X. Gao. Discriminative dictionary learning with common label alignment for cross-modal retrieval. *TMM*, 18(2):208–218, 2016.

[5] D. S. Doermann. The indexing and retrieval of document images: A survey. *Computer Vision and Image Understanding*, 70(3):287–298, 1998.

[6] J. Donahue, Y. Jia, O. Vinyals, J. Hoffman, N. Zhang, E. Tzeng, and T. Darrell. Decaf: A deep convolutional activation feature for generic visual recognition. In *ICML*, volume 32, pages 647–655, 2014.

[7] F. Feng, X. Wang, and R. Li. Cross-modal retrieval with correspondence autoencoder. In *ACM MM*, pages 7–16, 2014.

[8] R. Fergus, L. Fei-Fei, P. Perona, and A. Zisserman. Learning object categories from google's image search. In *ICCV*, volume 2, pages 1816–1823, 2005.

[9] Y. Gong, Q. Ke, M. Isard, and S. Lazebnik. A multi-view embedding space for modeling internet images, tags, and their semantics. *IJCV*, 106:210–233, 2014.

[10] Y. Gong, L. Wang, M. Hodosh, J. Hockenmaier, and S. Lazebnik. Improving image-sentence embeddings using large weakly annotated photo collections. In *ECCV*, volume 8692, pages 529–545, 2014.

[11] M. Guillaumin, T. Mensink, J. Verbeek, and C. Schmid. Tagprop: Discriminative metric learning in nearest neighbor models for image auto-annotation. In *CVPR*, pages 309 –316, 2009.

[12] D. R. Hardoon, S. R. Szedmak, and J. R. Shawe-taylor. Canonical correlation analysis: An overview with application to learning methods. *Neural Comput.*, 16(12):2639–2664, 2004.

[13] S. Hwang and K. Grauman. Learning the relative importance of objects from tagged images for retrieval and cross-modal search. *IJCV*, 100:134–153, 2012.

[14] C. Kang, S. Xiang, S. Liao, C. Xu, and C. Pan. Learning consistent feature representation for cross-modal multimedia retrieval. *TMM*, 17(3):370–381, 2015.

[15] Z. Lin, G. Ding, M. Hu, J. Wang, and X. Ye. Image tag completion via image-specific and tag-specific linear sparse reconstructions. In *CVPR*, pages 1618–1625, 2013.

[16] Y. Liu, D. Zhang, G. Lu, and W. Ma. A survey of content-based image retrieval with high-level semantics. *Pattern Recognition*, 40(1):262–282, 2007.

[17] A. Makadia, V. Pavlovic, and S. Kumar. A new baseline for image annotation. In *ECCV*, 2008.

[18] V. Ranjan, N. Rasiwasia, and C. V. Jawahar. Multi-label cross-modal retrieval. In *ICCV*, pages 4094–4102, 2015.

[19] N. Rasiwasia, J. Costa Pereira, E. Coviello, G. Doyle, G. Lanckriet, R. Levy, and N. Vasconcelos. A new approach to cross-modal multimedia retrieval. In *ACM MM*, 2010.

[20] R. Rosipal and N. Krämer. Overview and recent advances in partial least squares. In *Proc. SLSFS*, pages 34–51, 2006.

[21] F. Shen, W. Liu, S. Zhang, Y. Yang, and H. Tao Shen. Learning binary codes for maximum inner product search. In *ICCV*, pages 4148–4156, 2015.

[22] F. Shen, C. Shen, W. Liu, and H. T. Shen. Supervised discrete hashing. In *CVPR*, pages 37–45, 2015.

[23] H. Wang, S. Liu, and L.-T. Chia. Does ontology help in image retrieval?: a comparison between keyword, text ontology and multi-modality ontology approaches. In *ACM MM*, pages 109–112, 2006.

[24] K. Wang, R. He, W. Wang, L. Wang, and T. Tan. Learning coupled feature spaces for cross-modal matching. In *ICCV*, pages 2088–2095, 2013.

[25] W. Wang, R. Arora, K. Livescu, and J. Bilmes. On deep multi-view representation learning. In *ICML*, 2015.

[26] B. Wu, S. Lyu, and B. Ghanem. ML-MG: multi-label learning with missing labels using a mixed graph. In *ICCV*, pages 4157–4165, 2015.

[27] X. Xu, A. Shimada, H. Nagahara, and R. Taniguchi. Learning multi-task local metrics for image annotation. *Multimedia Tools Appl.*, 75(4):2203–2231, 2016.

[28] X. Xu, Y. Yang, A. Shimada, R.-i. Taniguchi, and L. He. Semi-supervised coupled dictionary learning for cross-modal retrieval in internet images and texts. In *ACM MM*, pages 847–850, 2015.

[29] Y. Yang, Y. Yang, and H. T. Shen. Effective transfer tagging from image to video. *ACM Trans. Multimedia Comput. Commun. Appl.*, 9(2):1–20, 2013.

[30] Y. Yang, Z. Zha, Y. Gao, X. Zhu, and T. Chua. Exploiting web images for semantic video indexing via robust sample-specific loss. *TMM*, 16(6):1677–1689, 2014.

[31] Y. Yang, H. Zhang, M. Zhang, F. Shen, and X. Li. Visual coding in a semantic hierarchy. In *ACM MM*, pages 59–68, 2015.

[32] P. Young, A. Lai, M. Hodosh, and J. Hockenmaier. From image descriptions to visual denotations: New similarity metrics for semantic inference over event descriptions. *TACL*, 2:67–78, 2014.

Objectness-aware Semantic Segmentation

Yuhang Wang[1,2], Jing Liu[1], Yong Li[1,2], Junjie Yan[3], Hanqing Lu[1]
[1]National Laboratory of Pattern Recognition, Institute of Automation, Chinese Academy of Sciences, Beijing, China
[2]University of Chinese Academy of Sciences, Beijing, China
[3]SenseTime Group Limited
{yuhang.wang, jliu, yong.li, luhq}@nlpr.ia.ac.cn, yanjunjie@sensetime.com

ABSTRACT

Recent advances in semantic segmentation are driven by the success of fully convolutional neural network (FCN). However, the coarse label map from the network and the object discrimination ability for semantic segmentation weaken the performance of those FCN-based models. To address these issues, we propose an objectness-aware semantic segmentation framework (OA-Seg) by jointly learning an object proposal network (OPN) and a lightweight deconvolutional neural network (Light-DCNN). First, OPN is learned based on a fully convolutional architecture to simultaneously predict object bounding boxes and their objectness scores. Second, we design a Light-DCNN to provide a finer upsampling way than FCN. The Light-DCNN is constructed with convolutional layers in VGG-net and their mirrored deconvolutional structure, where all fully-connected layers are removed. And hierarchical classification layers are added to multi-scale deconvolutional features to introduce more contextual information for pixel-wise label prediction. Compared with previous works, our approach performs an obvious decrease on model size and convergence time. Thorough evaluations are performed on the PASCAL VOC 2012 benchmark, and our model yields impressive results on its validation data (70.3% mean IoU) and test data (74.1% mean IoU).

Keywords

Semantic Segmentation; Deconvolutional Neural Network

1. INTRODUCTION

Semantic image segmentation is a core problem in computer vision, aiming at parsing images into several semantic regions and assigning them with correct semantic labels. In the past months, tremendous progresses in semantic segmentation have been made based on the framework of fully convolutional neural networks (FCN) [9]. The main advantage of FCN is that the network is an end-to-end network to solve semantic segmentation as a structured pixel-wise labeling problem, i.e., enabling pixel-wise category predictions from a whole image as input.

MM '16, October 15-19, 2016, Amsterdam, Netherlands
© 2016 ACM. ISBN 978-1-4503-3603-1/16/10...$15.00
DOI: http://dx.doi.org/10.1145/2964284.2967232

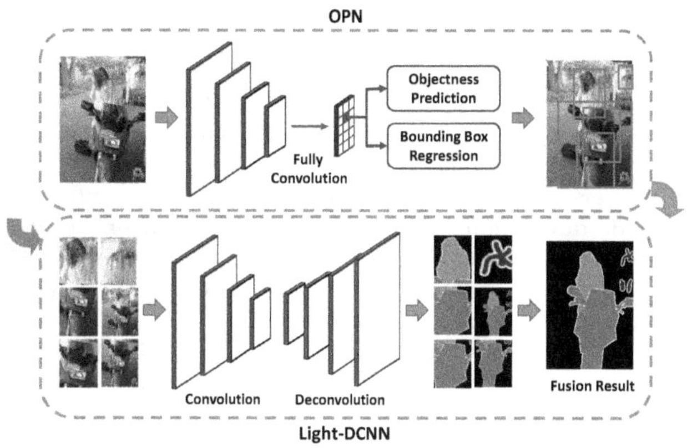

Figure 1: Overall architecture of OA-Seg framework.

However, the pixel-wise supervision in FCN is attached to the upsampled feature maps via large-span bilinear interpolation, thus the object boundaries are over smoothed in the results of segmentation. Besides, given a whole image as input, the fixed-size receptive fields possibly make foreground objects overwhelmed by a large area of diverse background parts. How to overcome the above limitations of FCN is the main motivation of our work. Simply, we aim to find a way to automatically discover region proposals with high objectness scores and segment them by mapping low resolution features to input resolution through a more refined method, where the boundary information is maintained as much as possible.

In view of such a motivation, we design an objectness-aware semantic segmentation framework (OA-Seg), which consists of two CNN-based networks. The first one is an object proposal network (OPN), which is a kind of fully convolutional network and trained end-to-end to generate candidate object regions. OPN takes an image as input and outputs a set of rectangular object proposals associated with their corresponding objectness scores. The second network is a lightweight deconvolutional neural network (Light-DCNN) which decodes convolutional feature maps into the same size of input image, to guarantee finer pixel-wise predictions. Light-DCNN is constructed on the top of convolutional layers in VGG-net with a mirrored deconvolutional and unpooling architecture, while the fully-connected layers are removed. Pooling indices in the convolutional part are employed during unpooling to ensure location consis-

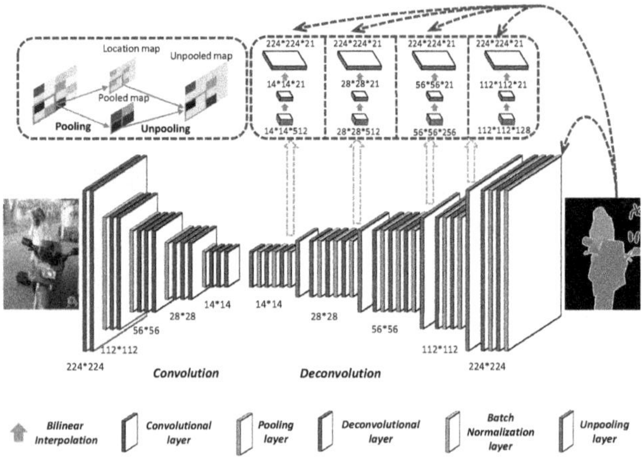

Figure 2: Network structure of Light-DCNN.

tency, which conducts a more refined unsampling operation than bilinear interpolation. Besides, hierarchical classification layers are presented by mapping multi-scale intermediate deconvolutional features to pixel-wise labeling maps, where unpooling and bilinear interpolation are cooperatively used. For the above two networks, we currently train them with object proposals as their connection, however alternative training schemes can also be further adopted to produce a unified network with sharable convolutional layers.

The network we propose above is a basic network for semantic segmentation, like FCN [9] and DeconvNet [11]. While compared with them, our model is much more lightweight with the model size decreased by 3 to 9 times and converges much faster, yet achieves better performance. Other improvements like CRF or MRF, which are always jointly used with FCN in state-of-the-art methods[1, 7, 19, 8], are actually orthogonal to our method. And they can also be combined with our method to further improve the performance. We simply use CRF as post-processing in this paper and evaluate our method on the PASCAL VOC 2012 benchmark [2], where our proposed OA-Seg produces impressive results on its validation data (70.3% mean IoU) and test data (74.1% mean IoU).

2. OUR APPROACH

Our model consists of two jointly learned neural networks as shown in Figure 1. One is an object proposal network (OPN) used to preliminarily locate objects in the image. And the other one is a lightweight deconvolutional neural network (Light-DCNN) for further semantic segmentation. With this framework, we enhance the performance of semantic segmentation with detection techniques, as massive background noises are eliminated during both training and testing.

2.1 Object Proposal Network

OPN is used here to help separating objects from overlapping ones and complex backgrounds, which makes the model more focused on single objects during training and testing. So we use "objectness" as our measurable indicator and make a rough judgment of whether the image region contains an object or not. The network is built on VGG 16-layer net [16] with a fully convolutional structure. All fully connected layers are removed, and the local features of the last convolutional layer are mapped to dense feature vectors through an extra convolutional layer. Thus each feature vector corresponds to a receptive field in the input image. We reuse it to represent multiscale image regions centering around the corresponding receptive field referring to [12], and simultaneously perform classification and bounding box regression to estimate objectness scores and region locations. The groundtruth used here are the circumscribed rectangles of segmentation groundtruth, and thus no extra information is used.

2.2 Light-DCNN

Unlike FCN [9] which obtains pixel-wise prediction through large-span bilinear interpolation, Light-DCNN provides a more refined reconstruction via progressively upsampling the feature maps to larger resolution. Illustration of our network structure is shown in Figure 2.

Light-DCNN is composed of two parts. The first part is a convolutional network that takes an image as input and encodes it into feature maps. And the second part is a deconvolutional network that takes the feature maps as input and propagates the responses back to each pixel. The two networks are spliced and optimized together. For the convolutional network, we directly inherit the network structure and parameters from VGG 16-layer net [16]. The deconvolutional network is built and the parameters are assigned following Zeiler *et al.* [17], which is a reverse process of the convolutional network with symmetrical structure. The main components of the deconvolutional network are deconvolutional and unpooling layers. Unlike convolutional layer that aggregates feature vectors in a local region into a single response, the deconvolutional layer attempts to disassemble the response back to each individual position. The unpooling layer carries out the inverse process of the pooling layer. As we use max pooling in the convolutional network, through the unpooling layer, we upsample the feature maps following max pooling indices and supplement 0 for the abandoned positions to ensure position correspondence.

Besides, our network is designed with several unusual features, which make it small-sized and easy to converge.

Parameter Inheritance: We use the parameters of the learned convolutional layers to initialize the deconvolutional layers in our network, rather than Gaussian random numbers. It supplies our network with applicable initial values during deconvolutional computation. And this treatment makes our network extremely easy to converge.

Discarding Fully Connected Layers: We discard the fully connected layers and reverse the net from the last convolutional layer, because the convolutional layers always show a much better ability for reserving spatial information compared with fully connected layer. And with this design, we decrease the model size by nearly 10 times, which makes our network more lightweight and easier to train because of the fewer parameters.

Asymmetrical Batch Normalization: We employ batch normalization [5] in our network to reduce the internal-covariate-shift during training, but we only add it in the deconvolutional part of Light-DCNN. In our framework, the convolutional network works as a feature extractor which encodes semantic information, and we don't want to break the correlations between the well-learned net layers. While the deconvolutional network is trained as a decoder, so we add a batch normalization layer after each deconvolutional layer for better optimization.

Table 1: Results of hierarchical predictions of Light-DCNN on PASCAL VOC 2012 val set.

Prediction	224×224	112×112	56×56	28×28	14×14
Mean IoU	60.0	62.3	62.8	62.2	60.0

Table 2: Results of OA-Seg with different object proposal settings on PASCAL VOC 2012 val set.

Object Proposal Addition	None	Train	Train&Inference
Mean IoU	63.1	66.7	69.6

Hierarchical Predictions: Although with strict positional correspondence, the unpooling layers tend to break some correlations within image regions for the reason of zero supplementary. To alleviate this, we connect a pixel-wise classification layer to each deconvolutional layer ahead of unpooling layers, and supervise it with pixel-wise groundtruth. In this way, we attempt to guarantee the discrimination and region correlations of our model before every unpooling. And the pixel-wise prediction is realized by feeding the deconvolutional feature maps into a fully convolutional classification layer and upsampling them with bilinear interpolation. It can be found that, with the hierarchical predictions, we are actually cooperatively using unpooling and bilinear interpolation to upsample feature maps to the resolution of input image. That is, the lower layer is attached greater scale change with bilinear interpolation, while the higher layer considers less scale change but more unpooling operations. It also inspires us with that, it is no need to reconstruct the deconvolutional feature maps to exact the same resolution with the input image, which is further discussed in section 3.1.

2.3 Implementation Details

For our current practice, the two networks of OPN and Light-DCNN are trained successively with the object proposals as connection. In our framework, the two networks can also be trained alternatively to share the convolutional layers and integrated into a unified model, as the training scheme of Faster R-CNN [12]. But in this paper, we make the two networks work in a sequential way, i.e., feed the object proposals generated from OPN into Light-DCNN. With this structure, we utilize more multiscale information and more notice is paid on tiny objects, which benefit the performance of our method.

In the training stage, the object proposals are selected to train Light-DCNN and those with little overlapping with groundtruth or oversized aspect ratios are discarded. While during testing, only the top n proposals with the highest objectness scores are input into Light-DCNN, as well as the entire image. Then we average the corresponding predictions for each pixel and achieve the final segmentation result. In this paper, we set n to 20.

Both of our two networks are implemented with Caffe [6]. For the training of OPN, the input image is rescaled to 600 pixels on its shorter side, in order to maintain the saliency of tiny objects. And nonmaximum suppression (NMS) is employed during inference to reduce highly overlapped proposals. While for Light-DCNN, we set a small batchsize of 1 in our experiment and average the gradients over all the pixels in a training batch for back propagation. The initial learning rate, momentum and weight decay used for standard stochastic gradient descent (SGD) are set to 2.5e-5, 0.99 and 0.0005 respectively.

3. EXPERIMENTS

Our experiments are conducted on the PASCAL VOC 2012 dataset [2] with extended annotations from [3], which contains 20 object categories and one background category. The extended dataset contains 10582 training images, 1449 validation images and 1456 testing images. We verify our approach on both the validation and test set with mean intersection-over-union (mean IoU) as our metrics.

3.1 Evaluation of Light-DCNN

We firstly evaluate the performance of Light-DCNN individually in this section. The network is trained and tested directly on entire images with no object proposals used.

• **Performance of Hierarchical Predictions**

Light-DCNN is connected to hierarchical classification layers by cooperatively using unpooling and bilinear interpolation, as discussed in section 2.2. If we reconstruct the network up to the resolution of input images, we will get 5 segmentation predictions from different deconvolutional layers with ×16, ×8, ×4, ×2, ×1 bilinear interpolation respectively, while the upsampling ratio through unpooling is just inverse. Thus, given an image of size 224×224, we indicate each of the 5 segmentation predictions with the sizes of their corresponding deconvolutional feature maps, which are 14×14, 28×28, 56×56, 112×112, and 224×224. The performance for each of them is listed in Table 1. It can be found that, the best result appears in the 56×56 layer. While the 224×224 layer, which is upsampled to the input image resolution all by unpooling, achieves poorer performance. So as to the 14×14 layer which is upsampled only with bilinear interpolation. The results proves the effectiveness of cooperatively using unpooling and bilinear interpolation. As two different upsampling methods, bilinear interpolation reserves local consistency but is easy to over smooth object edges, while unpooling restores more refined contexture features but tends to break up the correlations within local regions. The result of 56×56 layer benefits from appropriate proportions for each of them, which is achieved through two unpooling layers followed by ×4 bilinear interpolation.

Therefore, in the following experiments, we train our model with the deconvolutional network built only to the 56×56 layer and remove the upper larger-scale layers, yet the lower hierarchical supervision is still reserved. And only the result of the 56×56 layer is reported, which is the last output of the network.

• **Performance with Different Image Scales**

Considering the influence of image scales on training and inference, we reproduce our experiments with images rescaled to 224×224 and 512×512 respectively, with the network structure mentioned above. The results are shown in Table 5. The performance of our model is improved from 63.1% to 63.9% with larger images, yet with a cost of more training time and computing resource. On consideration of this, the following experiments are all conducted with the input scale of Light-DCNN set to 224×224.

3.2 Evaluation of OA-Seg

In this section, we accomplish the entire process of the proposed OA-Seg framework. During both training and infer-

Table 3: Comparison with state-of-the-art methods on PASCAL VOC 2012 val set.

Method	DeconvNet[11]	Zoom-out[10]	DeepLab[1]	Piecewise[7]	Deep-struct[13]	DPN[8]	OA-Seg	OA-Seg+CRF
Mean IOU	67.1	69.9	67.6	**70.3**	64.1	67.8	69.6	**70.3**

Table 4: Comparison with state-of-the-art methods on PASCAL VOC 2012 test set.

Method	areo	bike	bird	boat	bottle	bus	car	cat	chair	cow	table	dog	horse	mbk	person	plant	sheep	sofa	train	tv	mean
FCN-8s [9]	76.8	34.2	68.9	49.4	60.3	75.3	74.7	77.6	21.4	62.5	46.8	71.8	63.9	76.5	73.9	45.2	72.4	37.4	70.9	55.1	62.2
DeconvNet [11]	85.9	42.6	78.9	62.5	66.6	87.4	77.8	79.5	26.3	73.4	60.2	70.8	76.5	79.6	77.7	58.2	77.4	52.9	75.2	59.8	69.6
Zoom-out [10]	85.6	37.3	83.2	62.5	66.0	85.1	80.7	84.9	27.2	73.2	57.5	78.1	79.2	81.1	77.1	53.6	74.0	49.2	71.7	63.3	69.6
Piecewise [7]	87.5	37.7	75.8	57.4	72.3	88.4	82.6	80.0	**33.4**	71.5	55.0	79.3	78.4	81.3	**82.7**	56.1	79.8	48.6	77.1	66.3	70.7
DeepLab [1]	84.4	54.5	81.5	63.6	65.9	85.1	79.1	83.4	30.7	74.1	59.8	79.0	76.1	83.2	80.8	59.7	82.2	50.4	73.1	63.7	71.6
RNN [19]	87.5	39.0	79.7	64.2	68.3	87.6	80.8	84.4	30.4	78.2	60.4	80.5	77.8	83.1	80.6	59.5	82.8	47.8	78.3	**67.1**	72.0
DPN [8]	**87.7**	**59.4**	78.4	**64.9**	70.3	89.3	83.5	86.1	31.7	**79.9**	**62.6**	**81.9**	80.0	83.5	82.3	60.5	83.2	**53.4**	77.9	65.0	**74.1**
OA-Seg	83.3	44.3	85.3	58.6	**73.4**	91.1	83.6	85.4	31.6	78.5	61.0	78.4	80.9	84.3	80.4	61.8	85.3	52.8	82.3	66.7	73.5
OA-Seg+CRF	83.9	45.4	**86.9**	59.0	73.1	**91.6**	**83.8**	**86.5**	31.7	79.5	61.0	79.2	**81.4**	**85.3**	81.7	**63.3**	**86.3**	**53.4**	**82.8**	66.7	**74.1**

Table 5: Analysis on Model Size and Convergence on PASCAL VOC 2012 val set.

Method	Input Scale	Convergence Time	Model Size	Mean IOU
FCN-8s [9]	500	120 hours	513M	-
DeconvNet [11]	224	168 hours	961M	67.1
light-DCNN-224	224	11 hours	114M	63.1
light-DCNN-512	512	37 hours	114M	63.9
OA-Seg	224	77 hours	180M	**69.6**

ence, the performance of our model is improved with object proposals added. And state-of-the-art results are achieved on both the validation and test set.

• **Performance with Different Object Proposal Settings**

We verify the effectiveness of our proposed OA-Seg framework by progressively adding object proposals to training and inference processes. The results are shown in Table 2.

Firstly, we add object proposals only for training and evaluate on entire images, the performance of our model improves obviously by 3.6 percent. While with object proposals added to the testing process as well, our result achieves a further improvement by 2.9 percent, which verifies the effectiveness of OA-Seg. With object proposals provided, more focused samples are supplied during both training and inference and too large or tiny objects are rescaled to suitable sizes, which help improve the discrimination of our model.

• **Comparison with State-of-the-art Methods**

Performance of our proposed OA-Seg is compared with some of the best methods on validation and test sets, as shown in Table 3 and 4 [1]. We achieve state-of-the-art results with 70.3% mean IoU accuracy on validation set and 74.1% mean IoU accuracy on test set, with best results on 10 categories.

It should be noticed that, actually only FCN [9] and Deconvnet [11] can be directly compared with our model as basic segmentation networks. And our model obviously outperforms them by 11.3 percent and 3.9 percent respectively on test set, without the post-processing of CRF.

When combined with CRF/MRF, the FCN-based methods show improvements with CRF used just as post-processing [1]. And the results are further improved when jointly training CRF/MRF with FCN [7][19][8]. In this paper, we simply use CRF as post-processing and achieve state-of-the-art results on both the validation and test sets.

[1]The anonymous results links:
http://host.robots.ox.ac.uk:8080/anonymous/LGAA2D.html
http://host.robots.ox.ac.uk:8080/anonymous/ARIGY7.html

3.3 Analysis on Model Size and Convergence

We provide more indexes of our model in this section for comprehensive comparison with FCN [9] and DeconvNet [11], as all these three models work as basic networks in semantic segmentation. The detailed comparison is shown in Table 5. For our approach, we report the performance of Light-DCNN with image sizes of 224 and 512. Moreover, the performance of complete OA-Seg is reported with the input scale of Light-DCNN set to 224.

Under each of the settings, our approach always shows much faster convergence rate. With Light-DCNN trained with 224×224 images, we already achieve a result comparative with or better than FCN, referring to its test set result 62.2% [9]. But the convergence time is reduced more than 10 times. If we employ a similar image scale with FCN, our result further improves. When we accomplish the entire framework of OA-seg, the time cost increases to 77 hours which is still about half of the other two methods, yet the mean IoU result of our model obviously exceeds theirs.

Moreover, we decrease the model size by about 3 to 9 times compared with FCN and DeconvNet, which confirms that our models is more lightweight, flexible-to-use and effective in practice.

4. CONCLUSION

We propose an objectness-aware semantic segmentation framework in this paper, which consists of OPN and Light-DCNN. OPN is used to generate object proposals and make our model more focused on objects. While Light-DCNN provides more refined reconstruction to pixel-wise predictions and meanwhile lightens the network. The two networks are learned jointly to enhance the performance of semantic segmentation. We achieve impressive results on PASCAL VOC 2012 dataset with significant reduction on model size and convergence time, which confirms our approach as an effective and efficient framework for semantic segmentation.

5. ACKNOWLEDGMENTS

This work was supported by 863 Program (2014AA015104) and National Natural Science Foundation of China (61332016, 61272329, and 61472422).

6. REFERENCES

[1] L.-C. Chen, G. Papandreou, I. Kokkinos, K. Murphy, and A. L. Yuille. Semantic image segmentation with deep convolutional nets and fully connected crfs. In *ICLR*, 2015.

[2] M. Everingham, L. Van Gool, C. K. Williams, J. Winn, and A. Zisserman. The pascal visual object classes (voc) challenge. *IJCV*, 88(2):303–338, 2010.

[3] B. Hariharan, P. Arbeláez, L. Bourdev, S. Maji, and J. Malik. Semantic contours from inverse detectors. In *ICCV*, pages 991–998, 2011.

[4] S. Hong, H. Noh, and B. Han. Decoupled deep neural network for semi-supervised semantic segmentation. In *NIPS*, 2015.

[5] S. Ioffe and C. Szegedy. Batch normalization: Accelerating deep network training by reducing internal covariate shift. In *ICML*, pages 448–456, 2015.

[6] Y. Jia, E. Shelhamer, J. Donahue, S. Karayev, J. Long, R. Girshick, S. Guadarrama, and T. Darrell. Caffe: Convolutional architecture for fast feature embedding. *arXiv preprint arXiv:1408.5093*, 2014.

[7] G. Lin, C. Shen, I. Reid, and A. van den Hengel. Efficient piecewise training of deep structured models for semantic segmentation. *arXiv preprint arXiv:1504.01013*, 2015.

[8] Z. Liu, X. Li, P. Luo, C. C. Loy, and X. Tang. Semantic image segmentation via deep parsing network. In *ICCV*, 2015.

[9] J. Long, E. Shelhamer, and T. Darrell. Fully convolutional networks for semantic segmentation. In *CVPR*, 2015.

[10] M. Mostajabi, P. Yadollahpour, and G. Shakhnarovich. Feedforward semantic segmentation with zoom-out features. In *CVPR*, 2015.

[11] H. Noh, S. Hong, and B. Han. Learning deconvolution network for semantic segmentation. In *ICCV*, 2015.

[12] S. Ren, K. He, R. Girshick, and J. Sun. Faster r-cnn: Towards real-time object detection with region proposal networks. In *NIPS*, 2015.

[13] A. G. Schwing and R. Urtasun. Fully connected deep structured networks. *arXiv preprint arXiv:1503.02351*, 2015.

[14] J. Shotton, J. Winn, C. Rother, and A. Criminisi. Textonboost: Joint appearance, shape and context modeling for multi-class object recognition and segmentation. In *ECCV*, pages 1–15. 2006.

[15] K. Simonyan, A. Vedaldi, and A. Zisserman. Deep inside convolutional networks: Visualising image classification models and saliency maps. In *ICLR Workshop*, 2014.

[16] K. Simonyan and A. Zisserman. Very deep convolutional networks for large-scale image recognition. In *ICLR*, 2015.

[17] M. D. Zeiler and R. Fergus. Visualizing and understanding convolutional networks. In *ECCV*, pages 818–833. 2014.

[18] M. D. Zeiler, G. W. Taylor, and R. Fergus. Adaptive deconvolutional networks for mid and high level feature learning. In *ICCV*, pages 2018–2025, 2011.

[19] S. Zheng, S. Jayasumana, B. Romera-Paredes, V. Vineet, Z. Su, D. Du, C. Huang, and P. Torr. Conditional random fields as recurrent neural networks. In *ICCV*, 2015.

ReadMe: A Real-Time Recommendation System for Mobile Augmented Reality Ecosystems

Dimitris Chatzopoulos
Systems and Media Lab,
The Hong Kong University of Science and Technology, Hong Kong
dcab@cse.ust.hk

Pan Hui
Systems and Media Lab,
The Hong Kong University of Science and Technology, Hong Kong
panhui@cse.ust.hk

ABSTRACT

We introduce ReadMe, a real-time recommendation system (RS) and an online algorithm for Mobile Augmented Reality (MAR) ecosystems. A MAR ecosystem is the one that contains mobile users and virtual objects. The role of ReadMe is to detect and present the most suitable virtual objects on the mobile user's screen. The selection of the proper virtual objects depends on the mobile users' context. We consider the user's context as a set of variables that can be either drawn directly by user's device or can be inferred by it or can be collected in collaboration with other mobile devices.

1. INTRODUCTION

Mobile Augmented reality (MAR) is the research area that deals with the class of problems of supplement the reality of mobile users with virtual objects [9, 13, 17]. The amount of virtual objects can be huge and the selection of the most suitable ones [8, 23] is not trivial due to the limited screen sizes of the smartphones, or the wearable mobile devices like Google Glasses. Modern smartphones employ a variety of sensors and are able to sense: orientation, acceleration, location, temperature, can record audio and video and more importantly can connect to remote services. Therefore, they can share the collected data and exploit the resources offered by cloud services. Moreover, mobile devices can serendipitously work together and exchange context-aware data [4].

In this work we present *ReadMe*, a low complexity and scalable real-time Recommendation System (RS) that selects the most suitable virtual objects to visualise in the screen of the mobile device. Recommendation Systems have attracted research attention by both academia and industry [7, 1, 14, 19]. Julier *et al.* proposed information filtering to solve the problem of clutter and improve the effectiveness of display in MAR [11]. There are also many studies on object recommendation for location-based systems [15, 16, 6, 5, 22]. These studies focus on integrating spatial, temporal and social information into recommendation systems. By discovering correlations between users' check-ins and the factors above, they tried to improve the quality of recommended items with respect to a given user, time and location. There exist location-based recommendation systems, which apply augmented reality in order to enhance the experience of the users. Authors of [12] proposed a visualization method to recommend the most suitable restaurant in one area based on the preferences of the user and on online comments, while Zhang *et al.* presented an aggregated random walk algorithm incorporating personal preferences, location information, and temporal information in a layered graph to improve recommendation in MAR ecosystems [24].

ReadMe considers also enriched information, which are not taken into consideration in traditional recommendation systems, such as the user's *mood* or her *eye movement* can be used to improve the recommendation systems. Current research studies show that it is easily implementable by an eye tracking mechanism that follows the movement of the user's eyes [2, 10, 20]. We use the focus of user's eyes as an input to our recommendation system because it is meaningful to assume that if a user is looking at one object or to one area she is probably interested in specific type of objects[1]. The MAR ecosystems are by nature dynamic with virtual objects that are changing when the circumstances around the user are changing. The virtual objects can belong to different categories and should be treated differently. For example, any detected emergency (e.g. fire alarm) should be popped up immediately while shops would have high priority when *ReadMe* detects that the user is in a shop. On the contrary, restaurants would not be good candidates for recommendation if the user is already in a restaurant.

It is crutial for *ReadMe* to be able to process numerous candidate objects efficiently and for that reason we employ binary and general filters that decrease dramatically their number. Furthermore, our real-time hybrid algorithm keeps a sorted queue and has sublinear complexity in adding and removing virtual objects. Another technical constraint of MAR is the storage limitations of mobile devices. We can not assume that all the virtual objects can be stored in the smart device and for that reason we use a database as a service cloud service [3, 18]. *ReadMe* differs from the existing RS for MAR ecosystems in the following:

(1) it does not require any direct input from the user, **(2)** it separates past check-ins in short-term and long-term, **(3)** it categorises the virtual objects hierarchically and **(4)** it is not application specific.

MM '16, October 15-19, 2016, Amsterdam, Netherlands

DOI: http://dx.doi.org/10.1145/2964284.2967233

[1]In the case of not considering a smart glass device, the focus can be given as an input by the user via a tapping in the screen.

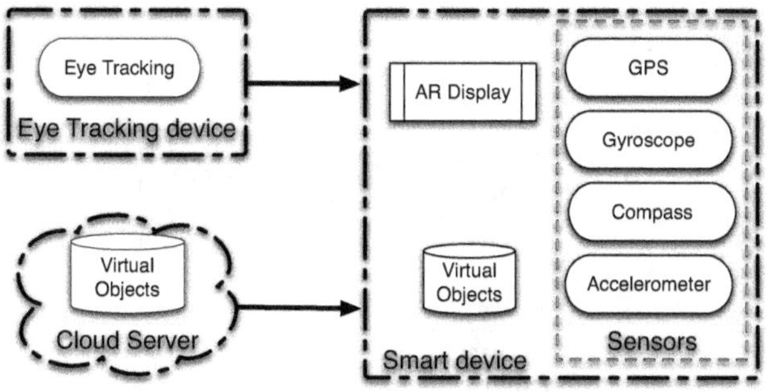

Figure 1: *ReadMe* architecture.

2. README ARCHITECTURE AND DESIGN

Architecture-wise, *ReadMe* is composed of three main components as depicted in Figure 1. The core component, which supports most of the functionalities, is the smart device and it is supported by two other components. A cloud DB component that deals with the huge amount of data that are related to the virtual objects and an eye tracking device that offers the user focus functionality. Before explaining how the real time algorithm works, we introduce the required notation and we explain how we categorise the virtual objects. Any user i at time t is described by the following tuple:

$$u_i(t) = \{u_i^H(t), u_i^h(t), u_i^s(t), u_i^O(t), u_i^o(t)\} \tag{1}$$

where $u_i^H(t), u_i^h(t)$ are the user's check-in long history between time $[t_0^i, t]$ and check-in short history between a time window $[t - t_s, t]$ respectively. $u_i^H(t)$ is the information the system has collected by users behaviour from the start of using the system (t_0) until now

$$u_i^H(t) = \{(t_0, l_{t_0}, o, R(t_0)), \ldots, (t, l_t, o, R(t))\} \tag{2}$$

l_t is the location of the check-in, o is the checked-in virtual object and $R_l(t)$ is the set of the recommended virtual objects at time t. $u_i^h(t)$ is user's behaviour at a short time window (e.g from the start of the day). So $u_i^h(t) \subseteq u_i^H(t)$. $u_i^s(t)$ denotes the user's social network information that is user's social connections, at time t, who also use the recommendation system. The user's social network is used to infer the user's preferences and interests. $u_i^O(t)$ contains all the virtual objects that are possible candidates for the user's recommendation list and finally $u_i^o(t)$ denotes the object that the user is focused on. We assume a set of virtual objects $\mathcal{O}(t) = \{(o_i, c_i)\}_{i=1}^{N_o}$ at time t, where o_i is the ith virtual object and c_i is its label. For instance, we have virtual object *Hilton* and its corresponding label *hotel*.

Figure 2 depicts our categorization. We first categorize virtual objects based on whether they are *user-independent* or *user-specific*. By *user-independent*, we mean the recommendations of these objects are irrelevant to who the user is. On the contrary, the system will recommend the *user-specific* objects based on user's profile as described in equation 1. For example, fire alarms are *user-independent* while restaurants are *user-specific*. Within the *user-independent* objects, we further classify them into *urgent* and *regular* ones, where for *urgent* objects the system recommends them whenever it detects them while *regular* objects are recommended on the condition that the user is looking for them.

Within *user-specific* class, we divide objects into *repeatable* and *unrepeatable*. The system should not recommend

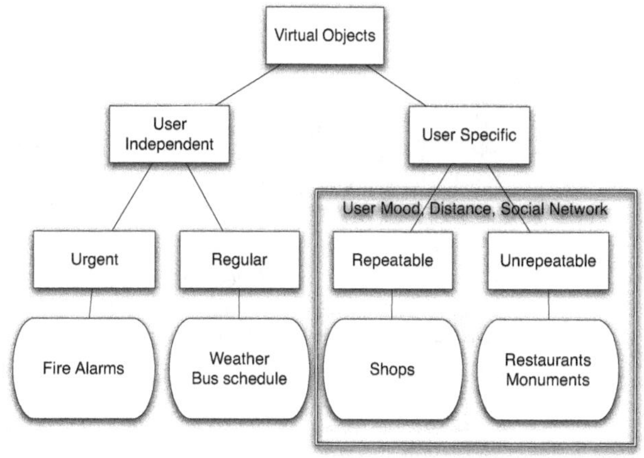

Figure 2: Object categorisation in *ReadMe*

objects belonging to *unrepeatable* if the user has already checked-in objects in this class within the time window $u_i^h(t)$. As for objects in class *repeatable*, the system encourages the user to the similar objects based on his short history check-ins $u_i^h(t)$. We define a set of filters $\mathcal{F} = \{f_1, f_2, \ldots, f_m\}$ to pick out the most relevant objects based on the user's mood, social network and the distance between the objects and users. For every virtual object $j \in u_i^O(t)$, our system assigns a weight w_{ij} which is a function of the following parameters: type of category combined with user's focus w_{ij}^c, user's short preferences w_{ij}^h, user's long preferences w_{ij}^H, social network preferences w_{ij}^s and physical distance w_{ij}^d.

$$w_{ij} = f\left(w_{ij}^c, w_{ij}^h, w_{ij}^H, w_{ij}^s, w_{ij}^d\right) \in [0, 1] \tag{3}$$

w_{ij} is changing when one of the input parameters is changing. It is worth mentioning that all the other weights apart from the distance are subjective to the user and their weights are not changing as fast as the distance. Depending on the user's focus w_{ij}^c equals to 0 or 1. If the user is focused in one object of the catecory c^*, $w_ij^{c^*} = 1$ for all objects in c^* category and 0 for all the objects in all the other categories. In case of no focus detected $w_{ij}^c = 1$ for all objects. The user's short preferences are used to check if w_{ij}^h is 0 if it belongs to a non-repeatable category and the user has already checked-in in an object of this category during a short time window or 1 otherwise. On the other hand, w_{ij}^H depends on the user's extracted statistics which came from the recommendation lists and the checked-in objects as described in equation 2. Furthermore, w_{ij}^s depends on the statistics coming from user's social network. Equation 3 can be rewritten as:

$$w_{ij} = (w_{ij}^c \&\& w_{ij}^h) \cdot f(w_{ij}^H, w_{ij}^s) \cdot w_{ij}^d \tag{4}$$

which means that the weight is proportional to the physical distance between the user and the object and it is zero if the user is focused on an other category or if she has checked-in recently to an object that belongs to the same category and the object belongs to a non-repeatable category. $f(w_{ij}^H, w_{ij}^s)$ depends on the historical data of the user and her social network and can become very sophisticated if we try to take into account all the possible parameters. However, our primal constraint is to keep the algorithm as simple as possible in terms of complexity. Our proposal for this function is a

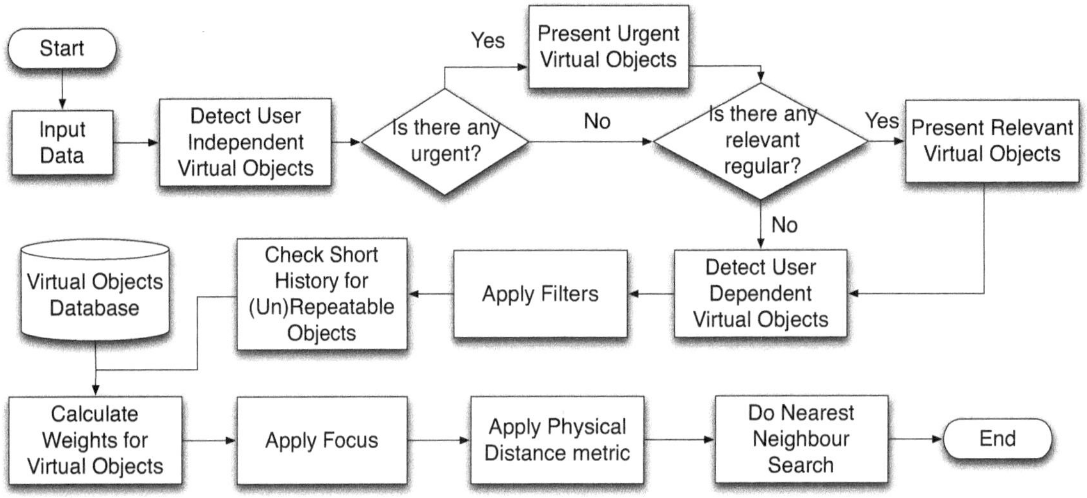

Figure 3: Flowchart of proposed algorithm. The main direction on the design of the algorithm is the abstraction between the factors that can affect the weight of virtual objects.

linear combination of the historical data and the social data with higher tuning parameter in the user's history. In both cases these weights are proportional to the number of times the object was selected by the user divided by the times it was in the recommendation list. Since the most frequently changing parameter is the physical distance we consider the two cases of a static user and a moving user separately.

Standing user: In this scenario we examine the case of a user who is standing in a specific location l and as a result the set of the possible virtual objects is fixed. The screen size of a smart device is limited and only a few objects should be selected. We split the time in periods of duration T (minutes) and we subdivide each period in slots of duration τ (seconds). In each slot a small fix number of objects, k, can be presented on the screen at the same time. So in each period at most $k\frac{T}{\tau}$ distinct virtual objects are presented in the screen. The first k objects that are presented are the objects with the biggest weight, after their presence, we decrease the weight of each one by the weight of the k-th object. The algorithm recalculates the weights either when all the weights become 0 or when the period expires.

Moving user: In this scenario, the user is browsing in one path and virtual objects are being enqueued and dequeued. We extend the aforementioned approach by dividing the path in zones where the set of virtual objects is static and the nearest objects to the user is the same to this path. This approach is similar to the continuous nearest neighbour search approach [21].

3. ALGORITHM

In this section, we formulate the problem we are studying. Given a user u_i, time t, location l and user dataset $\mathcal{U}(t)$, the goal of our system is to recommend a list of virtual objects $\subseteq u_i^O(t)$ which are most relevant to user u_i's current state. Our approach is the following: Given all the possible virtual objects, we calculate the weights of all the virtual objects in $u_i^O(t)$ and present all the objects with positive weight in a weighted round robin way. Figure 3 gives us a big picture of how our algorithm processes and recommends.

The system starts with the given data including the user's past information, time, location and all the other users' information (e.g. previous check-ins). Then, it retrieves all the *user-independent* virtual objects and presents the *urgent* ones if any. After that, it checks if there is any *regular* virtual objects related to the focus of the user u_i^o and shows them if so. Afterwards, the system searches and detects *user-specific* virtual objects. The system applies filters in $\mathcal{F}$ to remove any unqualified virtual objects. Then, the system removes any *unrepeatable* virtual object o_i if there exists another *unrepeatable* virtual object o_j such that $(t_k, l_{t_k}, o_j, R(t_k)) \in u_i^h(t_k) \wedge c_i = c_k$. *Repeatable* virtual objects are marked if the same labeled one has been checked-in in user's short history profile $u_i^h(t)$.

Weights of virtual objects, which are left after filtering and checking with short history, are calculated based on user's profile and his social network information. Note that in this stage, marked *repeatable* virtual objects in the previous stage tend to have higher weights. After weighing, the system applies focus to improve the weights of virtual objects that share the same label with $u_i^o(t)$, which the user is looking at. Then physical distance is taken into account since we assume user is not willing to walk a long way to the place. Intuitively, closer virtual objects get higher priority. The system combines the weights and the physical distance to a final virtual distance. At last, the system presents the remaining meaningful objects in a weighted round robin way. Figure 3 depicts our intention to design the system in an easily reconfigurable way and with abstract components that can be adapted to user's routine and personality.

4. EVALUATION AND RESULTS

In order to evaluate the performance of *ReadMe*, and see how good are its recommendations, we collected 100 objects via Google Street View, we categorised them in 9 categories and stored them in the following form: <ID, latitude, longitude, category>. We randomly pick a frame from each Google Street View snapshot we collected and retrieve the location of the user, the time and the user's profile at that frame. With these as an input and all the users' previous profiles, we generate our recommendation lists and checked whether our list hit the object the user saw in next frame. The used metrics are: **(1)** the mean reciprocal rank (MRR): $MRR = \frac{1}{m}\sum_{i=1}^{m}\frac{1}{rank_i}$,where $rank_i$ means the i-th recommended object is the correct answer, and **(2)** the number of hits (HIT_i): $HIT_i = \frac{\sum_{j=1}^{m} I_j}{m}$,where I_j is an indicator function, which is one if the correct object is in the top i recommended list and zero otherwise.

The time t is randomly generated from 9:00 am to 11:59 pm, the location l is randomly selected from the collected snapshots, and the focus y, which is one of the visible objects at location l in order to produce a test case (t, l, y). We want the recommended objects to be relevant and diversified regarding the test case. Also, high quality results should have higher rankings. For these reasons we let the users to evaluate the recommended objects and set 3 levels of scores. Score 0 means that the object is not related to the test case, score 1 refers to partially related to test case and score 2 represents strongly related to the test case object.

We test *ReadMe* in terms of: **(i)** Relevance: We calculate the average score of the recommendation list and **(ii)** Diversity: We calculate the Category-Cover@k (CC@k) [25] and we check how many different categories our recommendation list with k objects has cover as k varies.

We compare *ReadMe* with the following baselines: **(i)** k-Nearest Neighbors (KNN): KNN returns the k objects which are closest to the user, based on pure physical distance. **(ii)** Focus-Based Recommendation (Focus): This technique infers user's interests based on what the user is looking at and tries to find the most similar objects with current focus. In the next two subsections we present the performance of *ReadMe* compared with KNN and Focus in terms of Relevance and Diversity.

4.1 Evaluation of Relevance

We pick 10 representative and independent test cases. These cases consist of a timestamp, the user's location and her focus (t, l, f). We apply the 3 methods on them and get top N recommendation list, where N varies from 1 to 5. We let user decide whether the recommended objects are relevant to the test cases or not. The relevance score $r \in 0, 1, 2$, where 0 means irrelevant, 1 means partially irrelevant and 2 means relevant. We calculate the average score of top N for different recommendation list generated from different methods and we get Figure 4.

ReadMe outperforms the two baselines, especially when N equals to 1 or 2, which means the top ranked objects of our methods have high probability to be related to test cases. This is due to the fact that *ReadMe* considers time, location and focus. For example, one of the test case is (12:16, shopping center, XXX restaurant). *ReadMe* infers that there is a high probability that the user is looking for the focus related objects (restaurant) since 12:16 is lunch time. *ReadMe* searches for restaurants around the user and puts them in the front of the list. Besides, *ReadMe* also diversifies the result by recommending objects belonging to other categories. In this case, *ReadMe* recommends shops also. Focus may recommend good results in this case because it just looks for nearest restaurants. But it performs badly in other cases since the user is not always looking for focus related objects. KNN performs even worse since it just returns k nearest objects.

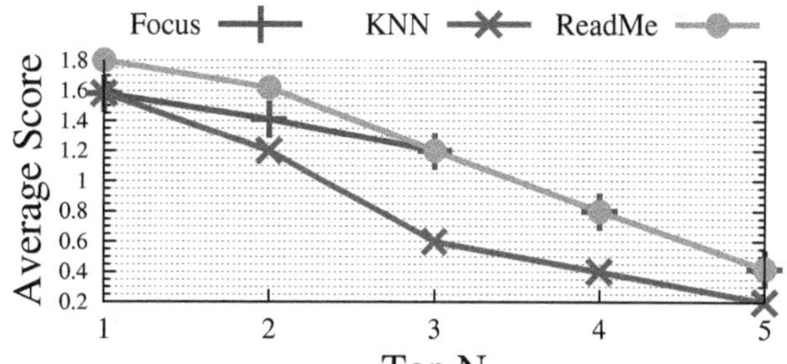

Figure 4: Relevance

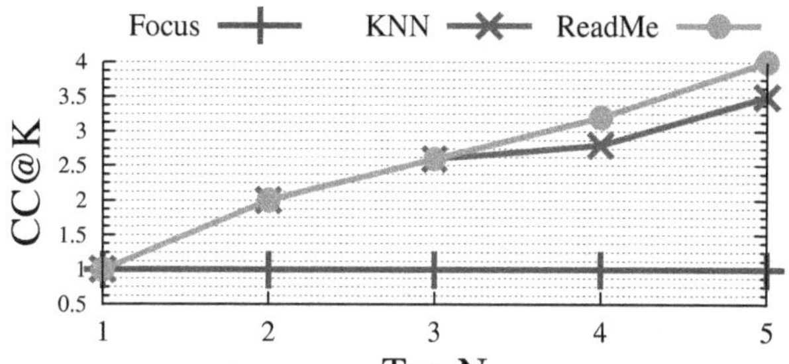

Figure 5: Diversity

4.2 Evaluation of Diversity

Figure 5 shows the results of the Category Cover (CC@k) when k varies from 1 to 5. For example, CC@2 equals 2, which means top 2 returned objects covered 2 categories. We can see CC@k of Focus is always 1 since Focus just returns objects belonging to the same category as focus. The diversity of recommended objects of KNN depends on the diversity of objects around the user, which is uncertain. On the other hand, *ReadMe* aims to return diversified results. From Figure 5, we can see *ReadMe* outperforms the other two methods.

5. CONCLUSION AND FUTURE WORK

In this paper, we propose a novel system architecture and a low complexity real-time algorithm for virtual object recommendation in MAR environments. We took into account user's characteristic as well as the dynamic features of the mobile environment in order to improve the quality of the recommendation list while at the same time we applied efficient filters in order to shrink the size of the huge number of the candidate virtual objects. Our current work is the implementation and the optimisation of this recommendation system in the android smartphones and on Google Glasses in order to produce more realistic and longer period results.

6. ACKNOWLEDGEMENTS

This research has been supported, in part, by General Research Fund 26211515 from the Research Grants Council of Hong Kong, the Innovation and Technology Fund ITS/369/14FP from the Hong Kong Innovation and Technology Commission, and the MRA15EG01 research grant from Microsoft Research Asia.

7. REFERENCES

[1] R. Burke. Knowledge-based recommender systems. *Encyclopedia of library and information systems*, 69(Supplement 32):175–186, 2000.

[2] M. R. Clark and L. Stark. Control of human eye movements: Iii. dynamic characteristics of the eye tracking mechanism. *Mathematical Biosciences*, 20(3):239–265, 1974.

[3] C. Curino, E. Jones, R. A. Popa, N. Malviya, E. Wu, S. Madden, H. Balakrishnan, and N. Zeldovich. Relational Cloud: A Database Service for the Cloud. In *5th Biennial Conference on Innovative Data Systems Research*, Asilomar, CA, January 2011.

[4] A. A. de Freitas and A. K. Dey. The group context framework: An extensible toolkit for opportunistic grouping and collaboration. In *Proceedings of the 18th ACM Conference on Computer Supported Cooperative Work & Social Computing*, CSCW '15, pages 1602–1611, New York, NY, USA, 2015. ACM.

[5] G. Ference, M. Ye, and W.-C. Lee. Location recommendation for out-of-town users in location-based social networks. In *Proceedings of the 22nd ACM international conference on Conference on information & knowledge management*, pages 721–726. ACM, 2013.

[6] H. Gao, J. Tang, X. Hu, and H. Liu. Exploring temporal effects for location recommendation on location-based social networks. In *Proceedings of the 7th ACM conference on Recommender systems*, pages 93–100. ACM, 2013.

[7] D. Goldberg, D. Nichols, B. M. Oki, and D. Terry. Using collaborative filtering to weave an information tapestry. *Communications of the ACM*, 35(12):61–70, 1992.

[8] G. Hu, J. Shao, L. Gao, and Y. Yang. Exploring viewable angle information in georeferenced video search. In *Proceedings of the 23rd ACM International Conference on Multimedia*, MM '15, pages 839–842, New York, NY, USA, 2015. ACM.

[9] Z. Huang, P. Hui, C. Peylo, and D. Chatzopoulos. Mobile augmented reality survey: a bottom-up approach. *CoRR*, abs/1309.4413, 2013.

[10] R. Jacob and K. S. Karn. Eye tracking in human-computer interaction and usability research: Ready to deliver the promises. *Mind*, 2(3):4, 2003.

[11] S. Julier, M. Lanzagorta, Y. Baillot, L. Rosenblum, S. Feiner, T. Hollerer, and S. Sestito. Information filtering for mobile augmented reality. In *Augmented Reality, 2000.(ISAR 2000). Proceedings. IEEE and ACM International Symposium on*, pages 3–11. IEEE, 2000.

[12] V. Kachitvichyanukul, H. Luong, and R. Pitakaso. Applying augmented reality to location-based restaurant recommendation for enhancing usability.

[13] H. Kimura, E. Tokunaga, and T. Nakajima. System support for mobile augmented reality services. In *Proceedings of the 2007 ACM Symposium on Applied Computing*, SAC '07, pages 1616–1623, New York, NY, USA, 2007. ACM.

[14] Y. Koren. Factorization meets the neighborhood: a multifaceted collaborative filtering model. In *Proceedings of the 14th ACM SIGKDD international conference on Knowledge discovery and data mining*, pages 426–434. ACM, 2008.

[15] K. W.-T. Leung, D. L. Lee, and W.-C. Lee. Clr: a collaborative location recommendation framework based on co-clustering. In *Proceedings of the 34th international ACM SIGIR conference on Research and development in Information Retrieval*, pages 305–314. ACM, 2011.

[16] B. Liu, H. Xiong, B. Liu, and H. Xiong. Point-of-interest recommendation in location based social networks with topic and location awareness. *Proc. of SDMâĂŽ13*, pages 396–404, 2013.

[17] J. Manweiler. Cloud-based mobile augmented reality, pitfalls and strategies in a realtime deployment. In *Proceedings of the 2014 Workshop on Mobile Augmented Reality and Robotic Technology-based Systems*, MARS '14, pages 21–21, New York, NY, USA, 2014. ACM.

[18] O. Mayor, Q. Llimona, M. Marchini, P. Papiotis, and E. Maestre. repovizz: A framework for remote storage, browsing, annotation, and exchange of multi-modal data. In *Proceedings of the 21st ACM International Conference on Multimedia*, MM '13, pages 415–416, New York, NY, USA, 2013. ACM.

[19] M. J. Pazzani and D. Billsus. Content-based recommendation systems. In *The adaptive web*, pages 325–341. Springer, 2007.

[20] M. Stengel, S. Grogorick, M. Eisemann, E. Eisemann, and M. A. Magnor. An affordable solution for binocular eye tracking and calibration in head-mounted displays. In *Proceedings of the 23rd ACM International Conference on Multimedia*, MM '15, pages 15–24, New York, NY, USA, 2015. ACM.

[21] Y. Tao, D. Papadias, and Q. Shen. Continuous nearest neighbor search. In *Proceedings of the 28th International Conference on Very Large Data Bases*, VLDB '02, pages 287–298. VLDB Endowment, 2002.

[22] M. Ye, P. Yin, and W.-C. Lee. Location recommendation for location-based social networks. In *Proceedings of the 18th SIGSPATIAL International Conference on Advances in Geographic Information Systems*, pages 458–461. ACM, 2010.

[23] H. Yin, B. Cui, Z. Huang, W. Wang, X. Wu, and X. Zhou. Joint modeling of users' interests and mobility patterns for point-of-interest recommendation. In *Proceedings of the 23rd ACM International Conference on Multimedia*, MM '15, pages 819–822, New York, NY, USA, 2015. ACM.

[24] Z. Zhang, S. Shang, S. R. Kulkarni, and P. Hui. Improving augmented reality using recommender systems. In *Proceedings of the 7th ACM conference on Recommender systems*, pages 173–176. ACM, 2013.

[25] X. Zhu, J. Guo, X. Cheng, P. Du, and H.-W. Shen. A unified framework for recommending diverse and relevant queries. In *Proceedings of the 20th International Conference on World Wide Web*, WWW '11, pages 37–46, New York, NY, USA, 2011. ACM.

Action Recognition Using Local Consistent Group Sparse Coding with Spatio-Temporal Structure

Yi Tian
Beijing Key Laboratory of Advanced Information Science and Network Technology
Institute of Information Science
Beijing Jiaotong University, China
11112062@bjtu.edu.cn

Qiuqi Ruan, Gaoyun An
Beijing Key Laboratory of Advanced Information Science and Network Technology
Institute of Information Science
Beijing Jiaotong University, China
{qqruan,gyan}@bjtu.edu.cn

Yun Fu
Department of Electrical and Computer Engineering
College of Engineering, and College of Computer and Information Science
Northeastern University, Boston, MA, 02115
yunfu@ece.neu.edu

ABSTRACT

This paper presents a novel and efficient framework for human action recognition through integrating the local consistent group sparse representation with spatio-temporal structure of each video sequence. We firstly propose a sparse encoding scheme named local consistent group sparse coding (LCGSC) to generate the sparse representation of each video sequence. The novel encoding scheme takes global structural information of features belonging to one group into consideration as well as the local correlations between similar features. In order to incorporate the spatio-temporal structures, an average location (AL) model is proposed to describe the distribution of each visual word along the spatio-temporal coordinates on the basis of the obtained sparse codes. Eventually, each video sequence is jointly represented by the sparse representation and the spatio-temporal layouts which fully model its motion, appearance and spatio-temporal information. Our framework is computationally efficient and achieves comparable performance on the challenging datasets with state-of-the-art methods.

Keywords

Action Recognition; Local Consistent Group Sparse Coding; Average Location Model

1. INTRODUCTION

Action recognition is one of the most popular and vivid research topic in the computer vision field, which has been widely applied in a number of applications [6][7][30]: human-computer interaction, video indexing and video surveillance systems, etc. Recently, the emergent of local spatio-temporal features [8][21][22][18] brings a great improvement to action recognition and the local feature based methods[15] have gained popularity and shown impressive results in this field.

MM '16, October 15-19, 2016, Amsterdam, Netherlands

© 2016 ACM. ISBN 978-1-4503-3603-1/16/10...$15.00

DOI: http://dx.doi.org/10.1145/2964284.2967234

The local feature is naturally effective as it carries abundant information: appearance, motion and spatio-temporal information. To integrate these information, a number of encoding variants have been proposed [16][29]. Especially, the concept of sparse representation has demonstrated promising performance. It's because that the sparse representation which describes each local feature as a linear combination of a small number of visual words is compact, such as standard sparse coding (SC)[5], locality-constrained linear coding [23], group sparse coding (GSC) [1], etc.

However, most of the sparse methods[15][3][23][1] ignore some useful information during their encoding operations, which directly degrades the discriminabilities of their representations. Firstly, the processing of each local feature in a video sequence is considered as separate encoding problem. Thus the correlations between features are ignored, which leads to the models being sensitive to feature variance and similar features being described with quite different words. These schemes always favor sparse representations of local features, yet do not ensure the sparsity of video sequence [1]. Secondly, given the sparse matrix of local features, pooling operations are used to obtain global representations of videos, which are always sensitive to the number of features and erase characters of some features[24][10]. Thirdly, most of the generated representations of videos are orderless and discard the spatio-temporal information of each local feature[15][25].

To make full use of the ignored information and better transform the low-level features into discriminative video-level representations, we propose a novel and effective framework for human action recognition by using local consistent group sparse coding scheme together with average location model, as shown in Fig.1. Motivated by group sparse coding (GSC) [1][2], the local consistent group sparse coding (LCGSC) scheme is firstly proposed, in which a group sparsity is applied to capture the underlying global structures of features within certain video and a local consistent term is added as a complement to preserve the local correlations between features. Once the sparse matrix is founded, a sparse representation of video is obtained by taking the p-norm of the code corresponding to each word. Meanwhile, an average location (AL) model is proposed to further collect the spatio-temporal information by calculating the distributions of visual words on the basis of obtained sparse

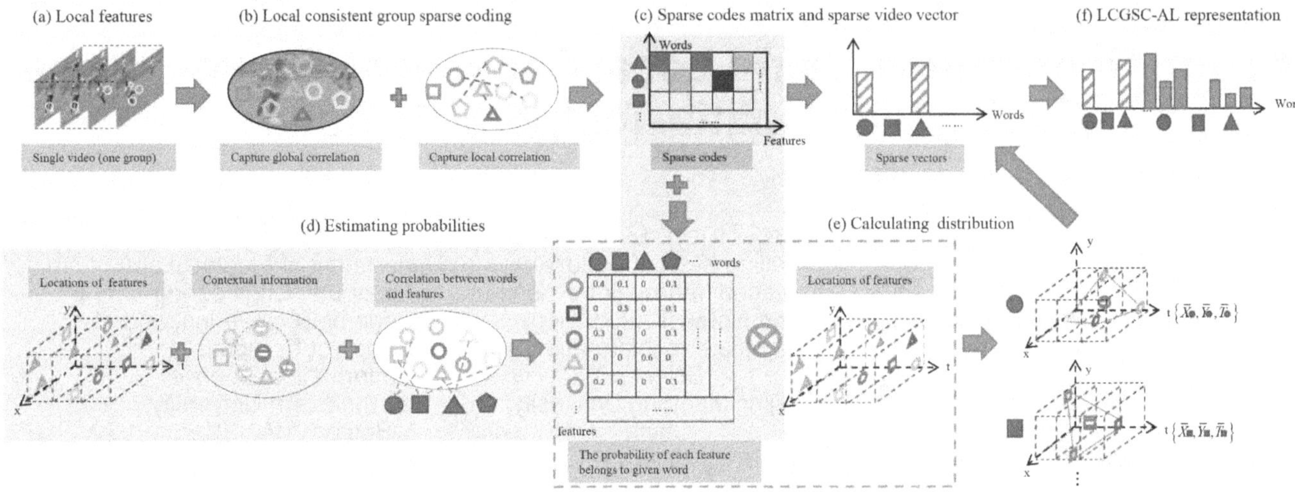

Figure 1: Flowchart of the proposed framework. (a) the detected local features in a video; (b) global structures and local correlations between features are captured during the LCGSC encoding operation; (c) features-level sparse codes are compressed into a video-level sparse vector; (d) the probabilities of local features belonging to each visual word are estimated on the basis of the four ingredients; (e) the estimated probabilities are multiplied with the locations to obtain the mean and variance of each word along the spatio-temporal axis; (f) LCGSC-AL representation is obtained by integrating the spatio-temporal descriptor with the local consistent group sparse represention.

codes, locations of features, contextual information of each single feature and correlations between features and words. Eventually, each video sequence is represented by integrating spatio-temporal representation with local consistent group sparse representation. The main contributions of the paper are made as follows:

1) All the features in specified group are treated as an integral object during the encoding operation. With the consideration of mixed-norm regular term and local consistent constraint, global structures and local correlations between features are captured by the proposed LCGSC scheme.

2) The pooling operations of sparse matrix are replaced by calculating the p-norm of the code corresponding to each word. It does not depend on the number of features and strengthens the characters of features.

3) A compact and effective AL model is proposed to characterize the global spatial-temporal layout of the whole video sequence as well as the local contextual information of each single feature.

2. METHODOLOGY

In this section, we introduce our framework in detail. The LCGSC-AL representation which jointly characterizes the motion, appearance and location information of each video is computed by employing the proposed encoding scheme together with average location model. The detailed procedures of them are described respectively in the followings.

2.1 Local Consistent Group Sparse Coding

Given C video sequences, each of which can be denoted as a collection of detected local features $X=[x_1, x_2, ..., x_N] \in R^{M\times N}$, M denotes the dimension of each feature and N is the number of them. In this paper, we gather all the features within the same video to form a video-based group. To encode the features in the same group integrally and capture global and local relationship between them, we propose a local consistent group sparse coding (LCGSC) scheme based on group sparse coding (GSC) [1]. The optimization problem is formulated as:

$$\min \sum_{i=1}^{N} \left\| x_i - \sum_{j=1}^{|D|} s_j^i b_j \right\|^2 + \lambda_1 \sum_{j=1}^{|D|} \|s_j\|_p + \lambda_2 \sum_{j=1}^{|D|} \|s_j - q_j\|_2^2$$
$$\text{s.t. } s_j^i \geq 0,\ q_j^i \in \{0,1\},\ x_i \in X \tag{1}$$

Where $B = [b_1, ..., b_{|D|}] \in R^{M\times|D|}$ is the visual dictionary with $|D|$ words. Sparse matrix $S \in R^{|D|\times N}$ consists of all the non-negative encodings of N local features in the video-based group. Each row $s_j = [s_j^1, ..., s_j^i, ..., s_j^N] \in R^{1\times N}$ of S specifies the contribution of the j_{th} word b_j to each feature. Compared to GSC which only contains the group sparsity (second term), LCGSC further takes a local consistent regularization term (third term) into consideration. λ_1, λ_2 control the sparsity of S and the contributions of the terms.

Group sparsity weighs the mixed l_1/l_p norm of S which preserves the global structural information of features in the same group. Once a visual word is chosen to describe one feature in group X, it will be selected to represent the others in the group as well. Hence, features within one group are prompted to select similar words to reconstruct themselves. However, GSC which only considers global structural information while neglecting local correlations between words and features will lead to several fatal confusions. 1) Features are likely to described by irrelevant words. 2) The different features belonging to the same group are enforced to select similar words.

As a complement for group sparsity constraint, the local consistent term which aims at preserving local correlations between features is added. To build this term, a local consistent matrix Q is defined in advance: $Q = [q_1, ..., q_j, ..., q_N] \in R^{|D|\times N}$ whose i_{th} column $q_i = [q_i^1, ..., q_i^{|D|}]^T \in R^{1\times|D|}$, $q_i^l \in \{0,1\}$ corresponds to a local consistent code of the i_{th} feature x_i. q_i indicates the relevances between x_i and all the words. To calculate it, the K ($K \ll |D|$) nearest visual words of x_i are chosen as its local neighbors in terms of Euclidean distances. The nonzero values of q_i occur at those indices where the corresponding words are the KNN neighbors of x_i. For example, assuming dictionary $B = [b_1, b_2, b_3, b_4, b_5, b_6]$ and features $X = [x_1, x_2, x_3]$, where b_1, b_2 are the neighbors of x_1; b_3, b_4 are corresponding to x_2; b_5, b_6 are adjacent to x_3, Q can be defined as $Q = \begin{bmatrix} 1 & 1 & 0 & 0 & 0 & 0 \\ 0 & 0 & 1 & 1 & 0 & 0 \\ 0 & 0 & 0 & 0 & 1 & 1 \end{bmatrix}^T$.

Therefore, the nearest K visual words of x_i contribute more to reconstruct it with the impact of local consistency. And the local correlations between similar features are preserved by sharing relevant and similar words. Furthermore, contributions of irrelevant words are reduced considerably which rectifies the confusions that caused by GSC. Compared to GSC, LCGSC generates much more informative and discriminative representations.

The proposed function (1) can be solved by coordinate descent method [1]. We firstly calculate the label consistent matrix Q and set norm factor p as 2. Doing some transformations and substitutions we can get that:

$$s_j = \begin{cases} 0 & \|\mu^+\| \leq \lambda_1 \\ \frac{1}{(\|b_j\|^2 + \lambda_2)}(1 - \frac{\lambda_1}{\|\mu^+\|})\mu^+ & \|\mu^+\| > \lambda_1 \end{cases} \tag{2}$$

$$\begin{aligned} &\mu_i^+ = \max\{0, \mu_i\} \\ &\mu_i = x_i \cdot b_j - \sum_{k \neq j} s_k^i (b_k b_j) + \lambda_2 q_j^i - \lambda_2 s_j^i \end{aligned} \tag{3}$$

Once we obtain the sparse matrix S of all the features in one group (video), the p-norm of each row of S is calculated to compress the video into a single $|D|$ dimensional vector as described in (4). Since the sparse codes of whole features within one group is zero or nonzero simultaneously, the yielded $|D|$ dimensional vector is as sparse as the codes. The sparse representation is much more robust and storage saving to action recognition framework.

$$\begin{aligned} &V = [v_1, v_2, ..., v_D] \in R^{1\times D} \\ &v_j = \text{Norm}_2(s_j) = \sqrt{\sum_{i=1}^{N} (s_j^i)^2} \end{aligned} \tag{4}$$

2.2 Average Location Model

It's concluded from Section 2.1 that similar features in one group prefer choosing similar visual words to reconstruct themselves. Therefore, distributions of the specified words would likely to be quite different in videos of diverse actions. To take advantage of the different distributions properly, an average location (AL) model which calculates the global mean and variance in spatio-temporal coordinates of each visual word is proposed based on the obtained sparse codes. The model also takes local contextual information of single feature into consideration while describing the global spatial-temporal layout of the whole features.

Superior to existent models (eg. spatio-temporal pyramid (STP) [9][21], super location vector (SLV) [25], LSTM [4], etc) which always ignore local contextual information of single feature or incorporate the spatio-temporal information at the cost of generating high dimensional representations. The proposed AL model gets discriminative spatio-temporal representations of videos in a compact way. The detailed operations of it are concluded into three steps.

Step 1. *Collecting contextual information.* Let Neib(x_i) $= \{x_i, n_{i1}, ..., n_{ik}, ..., n_{iK}\}$ denote set of feature x_i and its K nearest neighboring features. $s^{n_{ik}}$ denotes the sparse code of n_{ik}. The contextual information of x_i is collected by accumulating the neighboring sparse codes $\{s_{i1}, ..., s_{ik}, ..., s_{iK}\}$ with different weights, as formulated in Eq.(5). The feature which is closer to x_i has a greater effect on its context. The j_{th} index $c(x_i)_j$ of $c(x_i)$ indicates the contextual ingredient of x_i corresponding to the j_{th} word.

$$c(x_i) = \sum_{k=1}^{K} e^{-\beta_1 d_{ik}} \cdot s^{n_{ik}} \in R^{|D|} \tag{5}$$

Step 2. *Estimating probabilities.* Locations of local features are regarded as random variables. The probability of feature x_i belongs to given word b_j could be denoted as $\text{p}(x_i | b_j)$, which means the contribution of word b_j to the variable x_i. $L_i = (l_x, l_y, t)$ is the spatio-temporal location of feature x_i. Thus the likelihood of b_j falling on the location L_i is equivalent to $\text{p}(x_i | b_j)$. Analogous soft assignment (SA) method [15] is used to estimating the probability which is co-determined by the sparse codes, contextual information and correlations between features and visual words (Eq.6).

$$\text{p}(x_i | b_j) = \frac{(s_j^i + \beta_2 c(x_i)_j) \cdot \exp(-\alpha \|x_i - b_j\|_2^2)}{\sum_{n=1}^{N_n} (s_j^n + \beta_2 c(x_n)_j) \cdot \exp(-\alpha \|x_n - b_j\|_2^2)} \tag{6}$$

Step 3. *Calculating distribution.* The mean and variance of each word along spatio-temporal coordinates can be calculated by multiplying the estimated probabilities with features' locations (Eq.7), which describe the global spatio-temporal layout of video in a compact way.

$$\begin{aligned} &E_j = \sum_{i=1}^{N_i} \text{p}(x_i | b_j) L_i, \; R_j = \sum_{i=1}^{N_i} \text{p}(x_i | b_j)(L_i - E_j) \\ &s.t. \; \sum_{i=1}^{N_i} \text{p}(x_i | b_j) = 1 \end{aligned} \tag{7}$$

From the formulas we can find that, if a visual word has a small contribution to a feature, whose spatial-temporal locations are less affected by the feature. On the contrary, the feature which is mainly reconstructed by several few words conclusively influences the locations of these words. Meanwhile, the feature which is more relevant and closer to a word also determines the word's spatio-temporal distribution. The final spatio-temporal representation L of a video sequence with a dimensionality of $6|D|$ is described as Eq.8.

$$L = [E_1, ..., E_{[D]}, R_1, ..., R_{[D]}] \in R^{1\times 6|D|} \tag{8}$$

Eventually, the LCGSC-AL representation of each video which incorporates the local consistent group sparse representation with spatio-temporal structure is formulated as LCGSC-AL $= [\gamma V, L] \in R^{1\times 7|D|}$. γ is the factor that balances the two components.

Methods	UCF	Methods	Olympic	Methods	Youtube
BOW[15][8]	73.3%	BOW[15][8]	50.7%	BOW[15][8]	66.0%
Zhang *et al.*[27]	87.33%	Niebles1 *et al*[14]	72.1%	Zhao *et al*[28]	44.88%
Cho *et al.*[2]	90.3%	Li *et al.*[11]	78.2%	Yang *et al.*[25]	77.4%
Yuan *et al*[26]	86.67%	Sun *et al.*[20]	74.45%	Sun *et al.*[20]	72.09%
	87.33%			Liu *et al.*[13]	82.3%
Ours	**90.0%**	**Ours**	**80.0%**	**Ours**	**87.1%**

Table 2: Detailed comparison between proposed framework and some significant methods.

Table 1: Comparisons between LCGSC and other encoding schemes

Methods	UCF	Olympic	Youtube
VQ[19]	73.3%	50.7%	66.0%
SC[5]	81.0%	66.4%	77.3%
LLC[23]	82.0%	60.4%	71.0%
GSC[1]	84.0%	70.1%	81.2%
LCGSC	**88.7%**	**71.6%**	**82.5%**
LCGSC-AL	**90.0%**	**80.0%**	**87.1%**

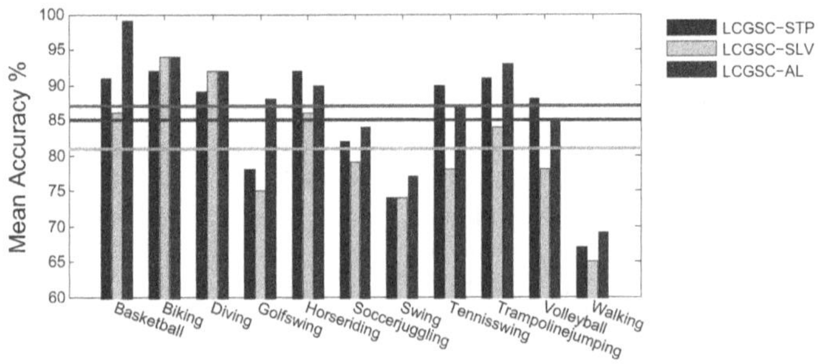

Figure 2: Comparisons between AL and other spatio-temporal methods on YouTube dataset.

3. EXPERIMENTS

In this section, we apply the novel action recognition framework on three challenging datasets, namely UCF sports dataset [17], Olympic sports dataset [14] and YouTube dataset [12]. The leave-one-out cross validation is conducted on UCF and Youtube datasets. The Olympic sport dataset is spitted as recommended by the authors [14]: 134 videos for testing and the rest for training. The initial codebooks are firstly generated by K-means method, the number of words are empirically set to 1000, 2000 and 2000 respectively. (λ_1, λ_2) are empirically set to (0.5, 0.1), (1.0, 0.1) and (1.0, 0.1) respectively. The spatial-temporal local features are firstly detected by Laptev [8], HOG and HOF are chosen as the local appearances of features. In the testing, SVM is implemented to assign query videos into corresponding categories.

Firstly, we evaluate the superior properties of LCGSC scheme. It's compared with several popular encoding schemes: VQ[19], stardand SC[5], LLC[23] and conventional GSC[1] with uniform setups. The detailed comparisons are shown in Table1. The LCGSC scheme achieves the highest accuracies on the three datasets which demonstrates firmly its effectiveness. The novel scheme which preserves the global structural information of features using group sparsity constraint and captures local correlations between features using local consistent constraint generates much more discriminative and informative representations. Compared to GSC, LCGSC gets 4.7%, 1.5% and 1.3% improvements on the three datasets respectively. It further proves the importance of local correlations between features and the superiority of local consistent constraint. In addition, we record the average computation time per feature of these two methods on Youtube dataset (the time is proportional to the numbers of visual words because of the using of coordinate descent method), which are 0.0227 seconds (GSC) and 0.0234 seconds (LCGSC) respectively. The approximately equal time demonstrates that LCGSC encodes features with more information, while it does not complicate the computation.

Secondly, we evaluate the performance of the proposed average location (AL) model. The cross-validation method is used to set the factor γ as 53, 50, 39 of the three datasets. The results of LCGSC-AL are listed in the last line of Table 1. From the table we can see that, the integrate representations consistently and significantly outperform LCGSC. It proves that the spatial-temporal vectors are effective to provide the complementary spatial-temporal information to the motion and appearance cues in LCGSC. To go to a further validation, we compare our method with the popular spatio-temporal pyramid (STP) [9] and super location vector (SLV) [25] representations on the YouTube dataset. In STP, we employ a $2*2$ grid for spatial domain and two segments for temporal domain. In SLV, the size of visual location dictionary is set to 5. Fig. 2 reports the average precisions (AP) per action class and average accuracies for all classes of the three methods. The average accuracies are 84.9%(LCGSC-STP), 81.0%(LCGSC-SLV) and 87.1%(LCGSC-AL) and the dims of their representations are $15|D|$, $16|D|$ and $7|D|$ respectively. Obviously LCGSC-AL achieves the highest average accuracy and excellent performances on the most of the action classes. Moreover, the advantages of our average location representation also manifests in low dimensionality as well as its contribution to fast training speed.

To further demonstrate the capabilities of our framework, we compare it with some significant methods as shown in Table2. The performance of the comparative methods are those published in their respective papers. In UCF sports datasets, our proposed method achieves comparable recognition accuracy 90.0%. In the wild Olympic sports dataset and YouTube dataset, our method achieves the highest recognition accuracy: 80.0% and 87.1%. It strongly demonstrates that the proposed framework using local consistent group sparse coding with spatio-temporal structures generates discriminative and informative representation of each video sequence. It makes full use of the global structural information of features, the local correlations between features and the spatio-temporal layouts of video sequence.

4. CONCLUSIONS

This paper proposed a novel action recognition framework which succeeded characteristics of sparse representation methods and overcame their weaknesses efficiently. Firstly, it preserved the global structural information and local correlations between features simultaneously during the encoding operation. Secondly, sparse representations of video sequences are obtained by calculating the p-norm of the code corresponding to each word, which made large-scale and online applications possible. Moreover, it integrated global spatio-temporal layout information and local contextual information with the sparse video representation. The compact and discriminative representation achieved promising results on the well-known datasets.

5. ACKNOWLEDGMENTS

This work was supported partly by the National Natural Science Foundation of China(61471032,61472030,61403024), National Key Basic Research Program of China(2012CB316304), Beijing Natural Science Foundation (4163075).

6. REFERENCES

[1] S. Bengio, F. Pereira, and Y. Singer. Group sparse coding. *NIPS*, 2009.

[2] J. Cho, M. Lee, H. J. Chang, and S. Oh. Robust action recognition using local motion and group sparsity. *Pattern Recognition*, 47(5):1813–1825, 2014.

[3] S. Gao, I. W. H. Tsang, L. T. Chia, and P. Zhao. Local features are not lonely laplacian sparse coding for image classification. *CVPR*, 2010.

[4] A. Grushin, D. D. Monner, J. A. Reggia, and A. Mishra. Robust human action recognition via long short-term memory. *IJCNN*, 2013.

[5] T. Guha and R. K. Ward. Learning sparse representations for human action recognition. *IEEE Transactions on Pattern Analysis and Machine Intelligence*, 34(8):1576–1588, 2012.

[6] Y. Kong and Y. Fu. Max-margin action prediction machine. *IEEE Transactions on Pattern Analysis and Machine Intelligence*, 2016.

[7] Y. Kong, Y. Jia, and Y. Fu. Interactive phrases: semantic descriptions for human interaction recognition. *IEEE Transactions on Pattern Analysis and Machine Intelligence*, 36(9):1775–1788, 2014.

[8] I. Laptev. On space-time interest points. *International journal of computer vision*, 64(2-3):107–123, 2005.

[9] I. Laptev, M. Marszalek, C. Schmid, and B. Rozenfeld. Learning realistic human actions from movies. *CVPR*, 2008.

[10] S. Lazebnik, C. Schmid, and J. Ponce. Beyond bags of features: Spatial pyramid matching for recognizing natural scene categories. *CVPR*, pages 2169–2178, 2006.

[11] W. Li, Q. Yu, H. Sawhney, and N. Vasconcelos. Recognizing activities via bag of words for attribute dynamics. *CVPR*, 2013.

[12] J. Liu, J. Luo, and M. Shah. Recognizing realistic actions from videos in the wild. *CVPR*, 2009.

[13] L. Liu, L. Shao, X. Li, and K. Lu. Learning spatio-temporal representations for action recognition: A genetic programming approach. *IEEE Transactions on Cybernetics*, 46(1), 2015.

[14] J. C. Niebles, C.-W. Chen, and L. F. Fei. Modeling temporal structure of decomposable motion segments for activity classification. *ECCV*, 2010.

[15] X. Peng, L. Wang, X. Wang, and Y. Qiao. Bag of visual words and fusion methods for action recognition: Comprehensive study and good practice. *Computer Vision and Image Understanding*, 2016.

[16] F. Perronnin, J. S'anchez, and T. Mensink. Improving the fisher kernel for large-scale image classification. *ECCV*, 2010.

[17] M. D. Rodriguez, J. Ahmed, and M. Shah. Action mach a spatio-temporal maximum average correlation height filter for action recognition. *CVPR*, 2008.

[18] P. Scovanner, S. Ali, and M. Shah. A 3-dimensional sift descriptor and its application to action recognition. *ACM MM*, pages 357–360, 2007.

[19] J. Sivic and A. Zisserman. Video google: A text retrieval approach to object matching in videos. *ICCV*, 2003.

[20] Q. Sun, H. Liu, L. Ma, and T. Zhang. A novel hierarchical bag-of-words model for compact action representation. *Neurocomputing*, 174:722–732, 2016.

[21] H. Wang, A. Klaser, C. Schmid, and C. L. Liu. Dense trajectories and motion boundary descriptors for action recognition. *International journal of computer vision*, 103(1):60–79, 2013.

[22] H. Wang and C. Schmid. Action recognition with improved trajectories. *ICCV*, 2013.

[23] J. Wang, J. Yang, K. Yu, F. Lv, T. Huang, and Y. Gong. Locality-constrained linear coding for image classification. *CVPR*, 2010.

[24] J. Yang, K. Yu, Y. Gong, and T. S. Huang. Linear spatial pyramid matching using sparse coding for image classification. *CVPR*, 2009.

[25] X. Yang and Y. Tian. Action recognition using super sparse coding vector with spatio-temporal awareness. *ECCV*, 2014.

[26] C. Yuan, X. Li, W. Hu, H. Ling, and S. J. Maybank. Modeling geometric-temporal context with directional pyramid co-occurrence for action recognition. *IEEE Transactions on Image Processing*, 23(2):658–672, 2014.

[27] Z. Zhang, C. Wang, B. Xiao, W. Zhou, and S. Liu. Action recognition using context-constrained linear coding. *Signal Processing Letters, IEEE*, 19(7):439–442, 2012.

[28] D. Zhao, L. Shao, X. Zhen, and Y. Liu. Combining appearance and structural features for human action recognition. *Neurocomputing*, 113:88–96, 2013.

[29] X. Zhou, K. Yu, T. Zhang, and T. S. Huang. Image classification using super-vector coding of local image descriptors. *ECCV*, 2010.

[30] G. Zhu, C. Xu, Q. Huang, W. Gao, and L. Xing. Player action recognition in broadcast tennis video with applications to semantic analysis of sports game. *ACM MM*, pages 431–440, 2006.

Super Resolution of the Partial Pixelated Images With Deep Convolutional Neural Network

Haiyi Mao[†], Yue Wu[‡], Jun Li[‡] , Yun Fu[‡†]
[†]College of Computer & Information Science, Northeastern University, Boston, USA
[‡]Department of Electrical & Computer Engineering, Northeastern University, Boston, USA
mao.hai@husky.neu.edu, junl.mldl@gmail.com {yuewu, yunfu}@ece.neu.edu

ABSTRACT

The problem of super resolution of partial pixelated images is considered in this paper. Partial pixelated images are more and more common in nowadays due to public safety etc. However, in some special cases, for instance criminal investigation, some images are pixelated intentionally by criminals and partial pixelate make it hard to reconstruct images even a higher resolution images. Hence, a method is proposed to handle this problem based on the deep convolutional neural network, termed depixelate super resolution CNN(DSRCNN). Given the mathematical expression pixelates, we propose a model to reconstruct the image from the pixelation and map to a higher resolution by combining the adversarial autoencoder with two depixelate layers. This model is evaluated on standard public datasets in which images are pixelated randomly and compared to the state of arts methods, shows very exciting performance.

Keywords

Super Resolution; Pixelate; Deep Learning; Adversarial Nets; Adversarial Autoencoder

1. INTRODUCTION

Super resolution, the process of from low resolution observations occupying high resolution images, has become a very tempting research topic in the past last two decades[12]. Neverthless, partial pixelates would damgage the process of super resolution. In this work, the problem is the super resolution for partial pixelated images. Figure 1 shows an example of our problem. Partial pixelated images appear more and more in people's daily life due to several reasons. The first one is public safety issues, which people want to hide personal identification information. Another reason is that image processing technologies introduce pixelates into images. Motivation of this paper is that on one hand it is necessary that in some cases we need to reconstruct the information hidden by the pixelates especially in criminal investigation. On the other hand for the super resolution issue, the performance of exsiting algorithms would be destroyed by even only small pixelates area and also makes it hard to recover information from pixlation. So regard of this, we propose a method to solve this specific problem.

MM '16, October 15-19, 2016, Amsterdam, Netherlands
© 2016 ACM. ISBN 978-1-4503-3603-1/16/10... $15.00
DOI: http://dx.doi.org/10.1145/2964284.2967235

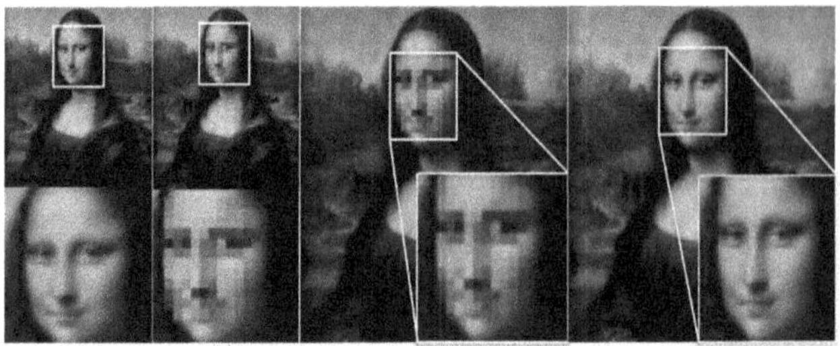

Figure 1: Illustration of the problem of partial pixelated images. (a) the image without pixelation. (b) the partial pixelated image. (c) the super reslution result of SCN [17] (scale = 2). (d) the result of DSRCNN(scale = 2). Notably our model DSRCNN can handle the partial pixelated images super resolution

Super resolution problem (SR) can be concluded as a process mapping from low resolution images observations to high resolution (HR) images observations [12]. Lately, a lot of proposed methods are aimed to solve Super Resolution. More recently, successful results have been achieved by data-driven approaches [21, 10]. However, the non-explicit form of the estimator leads to a more difficult bi-level optimization problem [10]. This difficulty can be mitigated by learning approximate inference mechanisms [9]. A generic neural network architecture is used as an inference step done by [3]. In [17], a learnt iterative shrinkage and thresholding algorithm (LISTA) network is used to approximate the sparse coding process. But none of previous model can solve partial pixelate images. In DSRCNN an autoencoder architecture is adopted, which try to learn a projection function from low resolution images to high resolutio images.

In the next section, pixelation can be formalized as a convolution operation. Naturally deconvolution can be used to solve pixelate problems. Deconvolution was studied in different fields due to its fundamentality in image restoration. For example Richardson-Lucy method [13, 18, 5, 8] is used to estimate the noise distribution for deconvolution. Another trend for image restoration is to leverage the deep neural network structure and big data to train the restoration function. For instance, [2, 19] show that a stacked denoise autoencoder (SDAE) structure [16] is a good choice

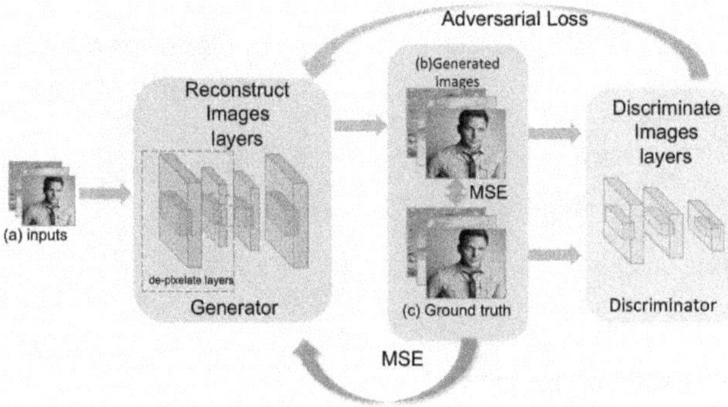

Figure 2: Architecture of DSRCNN. Input is a low resolution image with partial pixelation. Framework consists of generator and discriminator as [11]. The first two layers are depixelate layers from the idea[20].

for denoise and inpainting. Agostinelli et al. [1] generalizes it by combining multiple SDAE for handling different types of noise. In [7] and [4], the convolutional neural network (CNN) architecture [9] is used to handle strong noise such as raindrop and lens dirt. Schuler et al. [14] adds MLPs to a direct deconvolution to remove artifacts. Following [3], the deconvolution sub network are employed to do depixelate in our system. In this paper, we propose a Depixelatd Super Resolution convolutional Neural Network (DSRCNN). The DSRCNN is an end to end deep convolutional neural network framework mapping the low resolution images with partial pixelation to high resolution images. DSRCNN combines two functions depixelate with the super resolution in one adversarial autoencoder[11] architecture. The special two layers can borrow the pattern of non-pixelation area arround the pixelation to recover the original image. Figure 2 shows the general architecture of DSRCNN

2. THE ARCHITECTURE OF THE NETWORK AND ALGORITHM

The objective is to learn a mapping function from $\mathbf{Y}$ the low resolution image to an image $F(\mathbf{Y})$ and to try to make $F(\mathbf{Y})$ as similar as possible to $\mathbf{X}$, the ground truth high resolution image. The architecture is an autoencoder which is from [11] consisting of a generator and a discriminator. Generator is a network which maps from low resolution images to high resolution images. Discriminator is used to discern the ground truth and generated images. First the main loss function of whole model is proposed as following which is similar as [6]:

$$L = \min_{\Theta_1} \max_{\Theta_2} (L_G(\Theta_1) + \beta L_D(\Theta_2)), \tag{1}$$

where $L_G(\Theta_1)$ is the loss function of generator calculated by MSE. Θ_1 is the parameter sets of generator, for example, the kernel weights and biases. The same $L_D(\Theta_2)$ is the loss function of discriminator which calculated as cross-entropy named as adversarial loss. Θ_2 is the parameter sets of discriminator, for example, the kernel weights and biases. Finally, the loss function is a linear combination of L_G amd L_D, where β is setting to 0.01 empirically. In general, the model is trying to minimize MSE in generator and maximize the discriminator loss. The following is the details of every term in the loss function.

2.1 Generator(Super Resolution)

Super resolution is modeled as a process mapping from low resolution to high resolution [3]. The loss function of this part is modeled as follows:

$$L_G(\Theta_1) = \sum_{i=1}^{n} ||F(\mathbf{Y}_i;\Theta_1) - \mathbf{X}_i||^2, \tag{2}$$

Where Θ_1 is the set of parameters of the model, n is the number of samples.

2.2 Depixelate Network

Pixelate operation can be formalize as a linear convolution as shown in Eq.(3). In the light of this, we adopt previous work [20] which proposes a special convolutional network that approximates a deconvolution operator.

$$\mathbf{Y} = \mathbf{Y}' * \mathbf{K} \tag{3}$$

, where $\mathbf{Y}'$ is the image with pixelate, $\mathbf{Y}$ is the high resolution image without pixelates. $\mathbf{K}$ refers to the convolutional kernel function which is a average function. From previous work the kernel separability is achieved via singular value decomposition (SVD)[22]. Given the inverse kernel $\mathbf{K}^\dagger$, decomposition

$$\mathbf{K}^\dagger * \mathbf{Y}' = \mathbf{USV}^T, \tag{4}$$

Where $\mathbf{K}^\dagger$ is the deconvolutional kernel, and $\mathbf{Y}'$ is the image with pixelates. We denote by u_j and v_j the jth columns of $\mathbf{U}$ and $\mathbf{V}$, s_j the jth singular value. So we have

$$\mathbf{Y}_i = \sum_j s_j \cdot u_j * (v_j^T * \mathbf{Y}'_i), \tag{5}$$

where $\mathbf{Y}_i$ is the ith image, $\mathbf{Y}'_i$ is the ith image with pixelates.

In conclusion, depixelate problem can be written in following:

$$F(\mathbf{Y}_i;\Theta_1) = F(\sum_j s_j \cdot u_j * (v_j^T * \mathbf{Y}'_i), \Theta_1), \tag{6}$$

by combining Eq.(1) and Eq.(3), we have

$$\begin{aligned} L_G(\Theta_1) &= \sum_{i=1}^{n} ||F(\mathbf{Y}'_i, \Theta_1) - \mathbf{X}_i||^2 \\ &= \sum_{i=1}^{n} ||F(\sum_j s_j \cdot u_j * (v_j^T * \mathbf{Y}'_i), \Theta_1) - \mathbf{X}_i||^2 \end{aligned} \tag{7}$$

According to [20] we can use 1×121 and 121×1 special kernels to approximate the SVD decomposition.

2.3 Adversarial Loss

However if we only use the super resolution mapping network and the deconvolutional operators, the generated images have gaussian noise brought by the objective function and sometimes it is hard to get converged. In the light of generative advesarial nets [6] and [11] , we add one more discriminator in the architecture. Naturally the loss function is a combination of two loss as shown in the former equation

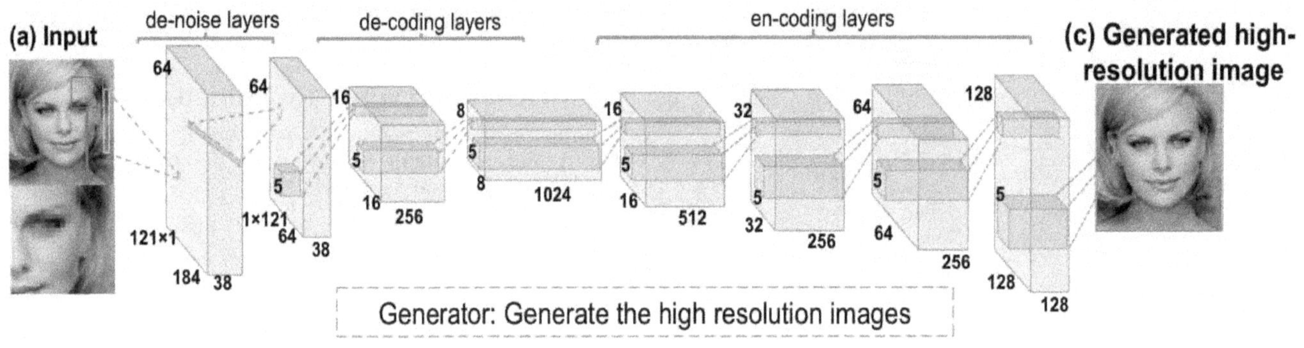

Figure 3: Details of the generator.Generator consists of de-noise layers, encoding layers, and decoding layers.

shown in Eq.(1). So we have two loss functions:

$$L_D(\Theta_2) = -\frac{1}{n}\sum_{i=1}^{m}[\mathbf{X}_i \ln D(F(\mathbf{Y}'_i;\Theta_1);\Theta_2) + (1-\mathbf{X}_i)\ln(1 - D(F(\mathbf{Y}'_i;\Theta_1);\Theta_2)] \quad (8)$$

where Θ_2 is the set of parameters in discriminator. L_D is the loss function of discriminator, which is cross-entropy.

Eq.(2) is the MSE calculated by generator, and Eq.(8) is the loss function of the discriminator. Eq.(1) from [6] is the main loss function of the image generator, which is a linear combination of Eq.(4) and Eq.(5).

The discriminator's architecture is the same as [11]. Kernels size are, $128\times5\times5$, $256\times5\times5$, $512\times5\times5$, $1024\times5\times5$, with padding 2 except first two layers. The loss of discriminator is cross-entropy which is given in Eq.[5] .

So the whole framework is one to minimize the MSE of generator loss then maximize the discriminator loss. During the training phases, the depixelate layers recovers the original information then the generator constructs the super resolution image. Then generated image and ground truth are both inputs of the discriminator. The discriminator will generate two scores for the ground truth with generated image and the ground truth with itself. The cross entropy of the two scores is used as the loss of the generator. However, during the testing phase, higher resolution images are only created by generator, no more discriminator gets involved.

Table 1: The result of Set5 measured by PSNR value. The comparison methods are Bicubic interpolation, SCN[17], SRCNN [3], K-SVD [23].

Set5 images (scale = 2)	Bicubic	SCN	SRCNN	K-SVD	DSRCNN
baby	33.91	34.79	35.03	34.59	**35.11**
bird	32.58	34.70	34.50	34.23	**35.06**
butterfly	24.04	27.31	27.30	26.65	**27.38**
head	32.88	33.55	33.41	33.23	**33.82**
woman	28.56	30.79	30.54	30.46	**30.79**
Set5 images (scale = 3)	Bicubic	SCN	SRCNN	K-SVD	DSRCNN
baby	32.49	32.95	33.85	32.89	**33.90**
bird	30.48	30.99	32.20	32.17	**32.51**
butterfly	23.80	24.01	24.08	24.89	**24.59**
head	32.24	32.39	32.40	32.33	**32.54**
woman	26.96	29.97	29.82	29.83	**30.41**
Set5 images (scale = 4)	Bicubic	SCN	SRCNN	K-SVD	DSRCNN
baby	31.78	33.09	33.13	32.25	**33.54**
bird	30.18	32.18	32.52	31.65	**32.37**
butterfly	22.10	25.06	25.46	24.76	**25.63**
head	31.59	32.55	32.44	31.62	**32.92**
woman	26.46	28.89	28.59	28.31	**28.91**

3. EXPERIMENTS

We evaluate our models on two public available standard data sets for super resolution. In this section, we first give a detailed decription of these data sets and how we add pixelation on the images. Then, the evaluation protocol used in the experiments is introduced. Next, the performance of several models is reported and some images as well.

We trained three scale sizes of network, they are 2, 3, 4. For the fair comparison the standard datasets Set5 and Set14 are used to evaluate the performance for our model and other methods.

3.1 Data Sets

The same training sets, test sets, and protocols are adopted as in [15] when compared with traditional example-based methods and CNN based methods. Be specific, the training set includes 1091 images which are from [3]. In addition for the 1091 images training set, we add pixelation square area randomly on all the training images with the size of the 0.2 times size of images. For every single image the pixelate operation would be done 4 times which means one image has 4 pixelated versions with different pixelation area location as inputs in training datasets. In order to evaluate the performance, upscaling factors 2, 3 are imposed on Set5 (5 images) and upscaling factor 2 and 3 are imposed on Set14 (14 images) to investigate the results. We compare DSRCNN with the Super Resolution methods related to convolutional neural network: SRCNN[3] and SCN[17]. Moreover K-SVD[22], and bicubic interpolation are also included in the comparison. The implementations are all from the publicly available codes provided by the authors.

3.2 Training Details

Specifically, in the training phase, the ground truth images are prepared as 184 pixel 6 subimages randomly cropped from the training images. Every image is pixelated with $0.2\times width, 0.2\times height$ rectangular area. And the location of the rectangular is randomly picked. Moreover, for ev-

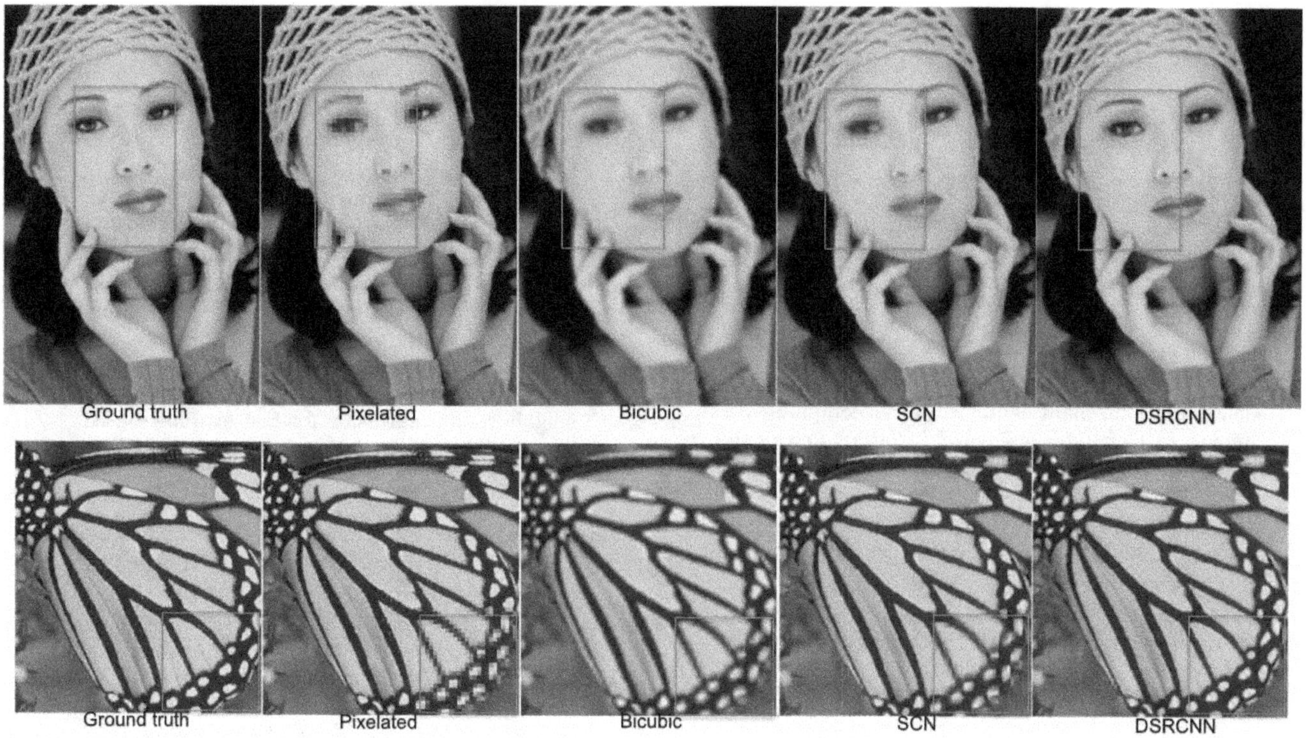

Figure 4: Results of woman. The comparison methods are Bicubic interpolation, SCN [17], ground truth and DSRCNN

Table 2: The result of Set14 measured by PSNR value. The comparison methods are Bicubic interpolation, SCN[17], SRCNN [3], K-SVD [23].

Set14 images (scale=2)	Bicubic	SRCNN	SCN	K-SVD	DSRCNN
banboo	24.13	24.86	24.64	24.26	**25.49**
babara	27.66	28.00	27.84	27.72	**28.29**
brindge	23.39	**26.58**	23.54	24.04	25.15
costguard	28.06	29.12	28.81	28.91	**30.58**
comic	24.62	**26.02**	25.63	25.62	28.65
face	34.06	34.83	34.42	34.33	**35.78**
flowers	28.82	30.37	29.67	28.91	**33.33**
foreman	32.05	34.14	33.26	33.12	**34.89**
lenna	32.65	34.70	33.25	33.13	**36.57**
man	28.13	29.25	29.00	28.51	**30.95**
monarc	29.97	32.94	30.47	29.76	**37.63**
peper	32.29	**34.97**	33.48	32.88	34.83
ppt3	25.85	26.87	27.45	26.13	**30.52**
zebra	27.77	30.63	28.15	27.74	**33.45**
Set14 images (scale=3)	Bicubic	SRCNN	SCN	K-SVD	DSRCNN
banboo	23.05	23.44	23.34	23.26	**23.58**
babara	26.20	26.46	25.96	25.18	**26.65**
brindge	23.82	24.47	24.63	24.04	**25.37**
costguard	25.84	26.36	26.22	25.91	**27.18**
comic	22.92	**24.18**	23.75	23.62	23.95
face	32.53	33.31	33.30	32.91	**33.47**
flowers	26.79	28.44	**28.48**	28.14	28.40
foreman	30.68	32.65	31.64	31.12	**33.32**
lenna	31.25	32.65	32.18	31.73	**33.12**
man	26.73	27.94	28.21	27.51	**28.33**
monarc	27.53	28.81	30.67	28.76	**28.94**
peper	32.00	**33.86**	32.43	31.88	33.83
ppt3	23.14	25.71	25.74	25.13	**25.69**
zebra	26.19	28.33	28.15	27.97	**28.54**

ery single image the pixelate operation will be done 4 times which means one image has 4 pixelated images as inputs in training datasets. In total, we have around 4k images to train the model. In order to get more solid model, we pre-trained the discriminator and generator with the code and data given by [11]

We extract subimages from original images by a stride of 14 the same as[3]. So the input images are 184×184 in RGB 3 channels. The kernel size in generator layers are 38 kernels with size of 121×1, 38 kernels with size of 1×121, other kernel size are shown in the figures 3.

3.3 Results

The PSNR values are evaluated in the testing data sets Set5 and Set14 shown in the table 1 and table 2. For the Set5 is tested under scale 2, 3 and 4, Set14 is tested under scale 2 and 3. Additionaly, the image results of woman and butterfly in Set5 are also shown in the next page. From the results, we can see the DSRCNN out-performs all images in Set5. For Set14 few images, for example comic, peper, flowers, fail to out perform SRCNN or SCN. The reason of failure is because images are relatively large to our kernel size, which leads that less information is gathered in deconvolutional phases. Generally, from the results, DSRCNN out-performs the previous algorithms. To extend, more work can be done which is based on different pixelation size, pixelation area sizes, or other kinds of blurriness.

Acknowledgement

This research is supported in part by the NSF CNS award 1314484, ONR award N00014-12-1-1028, ONR Young Investigator Award N00014-14-1-0484, and U.S. Army Research Office Young Investigator Award W911NF-14-1-0218.

4. REFERENCES

[1] F. Agostinelli, M. R. Anderson, and H. Lee. Adaptive multi-column deep neural networks with application to robust image denoising. In *Advances in Neural Information Processing Systems*, pages 1493–1501, 2013.

[2] H. C. Burger, C. J. Schuler, and S. Harmeling. Image denoising: Can plain neural networks compete with bm3d? In *Computer Vision and Pattern Recognition (CVPR), 2012 IEEE Conference on*, pages 2392–2399. IEEE, 2012.

[3] C. Dong, C. C. Loy, K. He, and X. Tang. Learning a deep convolutional network for image super-resolution. In *Computer Vision–ECCV 2014*, pages 184–199. Springer, 2014.

[4] D. Eigen, D. Krishnan, and R. Fergus. Restoring an image taken through a window covered with dirt or rain. In *Proceedings of the IEEE International Conference on Computer Vision*, pages 633–640, 2013.

[5] R. Fergus, B. Singh, A. Hertzmann, S. T. Roweis, and W. T. Freeman. Removing camera shake from a single photograph. *ACM Transactions on Graphics (TOG)*, 25(3):787–794, 2006.

[6] I. Goodfellow, J. Pouget-Abadie, M. Mirza, B. Xu, D. Warde-Farley, S. Ozair, A. Courville, and Y. Bengio. Generative adversarial nets. In *Advances in Neural Information Processing Systems*, pages 2672–2680, 2014.

[7] V. Jain and S. Seung. Natural image denoising with convolutional networks. In *Advances in Neural Information Processing Systems*, pages 769–776, 2009.

[8] D. Krishnan and R. Fergus. Fast image deconvolution using hyper-laplacian priors. In *Advances in Neural Information Processing Systems*, pages 1033–1041, 2009.

[9] Y. LeCun, L. Bottou, Y. Bengio, and P. Haffner. Gradient-based learning applied to document recognition. *Proceedings of the IEEE*, 86(11):2278–2324, 1998.

[10] J. Mairal, F. Bach, and J. Ponce. Task-driven dictionary learning. *Pattern Analysis and Machine Intelligence, IEEE Transactions on*, 34(4):791–804, 2012.

[11] A. Makhzani, J. Shlens, N. Jaitly, and I. Goodfellow. Adversarial autoencoders. *arXiv preprint arXiv:1511.05644*, 2015.

[12] K. Nasrollahi and T. B. Moeslund. Super-resolution: a comprehensive survey. *Machine vision and applications*, 25(6):1423–1468, 2014.

[13] W. H. Richardson. Bayesian-based iterative method of image restoration*. *JOSA*, 62(1):55–59, 1972.

[14] C. Schuler, H. Burger, S. Harmeling, and B. Scholkopf. A machine learning approach for non-blind image deconvolution. In *Proceedings of the IEEE Conference on Computer Vision and Pattern Recognition*, pages 1067–1074, 2013.

[15] R. Timofte, V. Smet, and L. Gool. Anchored neighborhood regression for fast example-based super-resolution. In *Proceedings of the IEEE International Conference on Computer Vision*, pages 1920–1927, 2013.

[16] P. Vincent, H. Larochelle, I. Lajoie, Y. Bengio, and P.-A. Manzagol. Stacked denoising autoencoders: Learning useful representations in a deep network with a local denoising criterion. *The Journal of Machine Learning Research*, 11:3371–3408, 2010.

[17] Z. Wang, D. Liu, J. Yang, W. Han, and T. Huang. Deep networks for image super-resolution with sparse prior. In *Proceedings of the IEEE International Conference on Computer Vision*, pages 370–378, 2015.

[18] N. Wiener. *Extrapolation, interpolation, and smoothing of stationary time series*, volume 2. MIT press Cambridge, MA, 1949.

[19] J. Xie, L. Xu, and E. Chen. Image denoising and inpainting with deep neural networks. In *Advances in Neural Information Processing Systems*, pages 341–349, 2012.

[20] L. Xu, J. S. Ren, C. Liu, and J. Jia. Deep convolutional neural network for image deconvolution. In *Advances in Neural Information Processing Systems*, pages 1790–1798, 2014.

[21] J. Yang, J. Wright, T. Huang, and Y. Ma. Image super-resolution as sparse representation of raw image patches. In *Computer Vision and Pattern Recognition, 2008. CVPR 2008. IEEE Conference on*, pages 1–8. IEEE, 2008.

[22] R. Zeyde, M. Elad, and M. Protter. On single image scale-up using sparse-representations. In *Curves and Surfaces*, pages 711–730. Springer, 2010.

[23] D. Zoran and Y. Weiss. From learning models of natural image patches to whole image restoration. In *Computer Vision (ICCV), 2011 IEEE International Conference on*, pages 479–486. IEEE, 2011.

Adaptive Visual Feedback Generation for Facial Expression Improvement with Multi-task Deep Neural Networks

Takuhiro Kaneko, Kaoru Hiramatsu, Kunio Kashino
NTT Communication Science Laboratories, NTT Corporation, Atsugi, Kanagawa, Japan
{kaneko.takuhiro, hiramatsu.kaoru, kashino.kunio}@lab.ntt.co.jp

ABSTRACT

While many studies in computer vision and pattern recognition have been actively conducted to recognize people's current states, few studies have tackled the problem of generating feedback on how people can improve their states, although there are many real-world applications such as in sports, education, and health care. In particular, it has been challenging to develop such a system that can adaptively generate feedback for real-world situations, namely various input and target states, since it requires formulating various rules of feedback to do so. We propose a learning-based method to solve this problem. If we can obtain a large amount of feedback annotations, it is possible to explicitly learn the rules, but it is difficult to do so due to the subjective nature of the task. To mitigate this problem, our method implicitly learns the rules from training data consisting of input images, key-point annotations, and state annotations that do not require professional knowledge in feedback. Given such training data, we first learn a multi-task deep neural network with state recognition and key-point localization. Then, we apply a novel propagation method for extracting feedback information from the network. We evaluated our method in a facial expression improvement task using real-world data and clarified its characteristics and effectiveness.

Keywords

Visual Feedback Generation; Facial Expression Improvement; Multi-task Learning; Deep Neural Networks

1. INTRODUCTION

Progress in computer vision and pattern recognition has recently been remarkable and enabled the development of reliable methods for *recognition*, e.g., facial expression recognition [28], *detection*, e.g., face detection [33], and *localization*, e.g., facial landmark localization [39] tasks. However, many studies have been focused on the problem of recognizing *what people do*, and few have been focused on the problem of generating feedback on *how people can improve* their states, although there are many real-world applications such as in sports, education, and health care. For example, facial expression feedback generation could be a useful application for individuals with challenges in emotional expression, e.g., with autism spectrum disorders. To explore research in this field, we are developing a *visual feedback generation* system that generates interpretable feedback on how people can improve their states, e.g., it displays an improvement guideline with arrows, as shown in Figure 1.

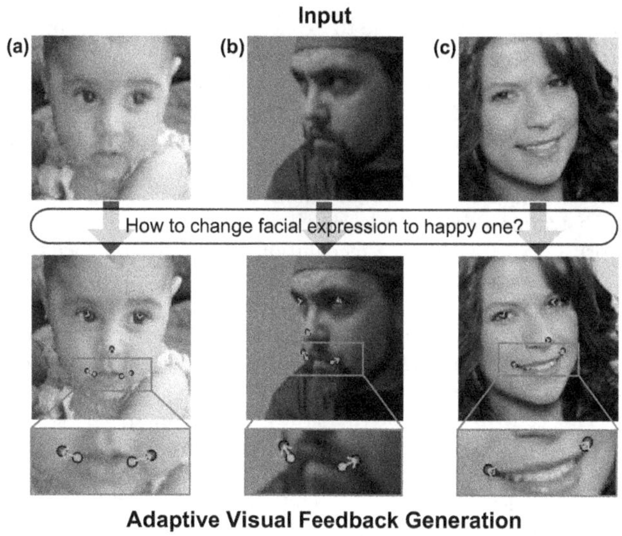

Figure 1: Practical examples of visual feedback generation with our developing system. Our goal is to develop a system for adaptively generating feedback for various input and target states. (a)(b) We change the arrow directions for feedback depending on pose and (c) decrease the amount of feedback when the present state is close to the target one.

To develop this system, we have to obtain the *rules* for generating feedback given an input image and target states. In human-computer interaction or sports science, many studies have defined the rules manually and implemented a state estimator for each rule, but using this approach under various situations requires defining various rules and implementing multiple state estimators. This problem is known as the *knowledge acquisition problem* in the field of expert systems.

We here propose a learning-based method to solve this problem. One main issue with this method is how to design training data considering the collection cost and ease of learning. If we can obtain a large amount of feedback

MM '16, October 15–19, 2016, Amsterdam, The Netherlands.
© 2016 ACM. ISBN 978-1-4503-3603-1/16/10...$15.00.
DOI: http://dx.doi.org/10.1145/2964284.2967236

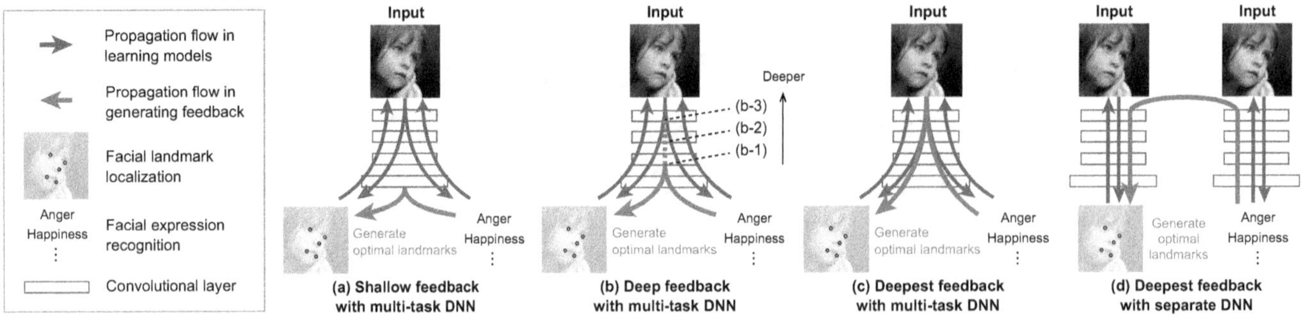

Figure 2: Models for comparison. They have different network architectures or propagation methods. We compared them to clarify characteristics of our method. (b) We prepared three models (b-1, b-2, b-3) where the optimized layers are different.

annotations, it is possible to explicitly learn the rules, but it is difficult to do so due to the subjective nature of the task. To mitigate this problem, our method implicitly learns the rules from training data consisting of input images, key-point annotations, e.g., facial landmark annotations, and state annotations, e.g., facial expression annotations, that do not require professional knowledge in feedback. Given such training data, we learn a multi-task deep neural network (DNN) with state recognition and key-point localization. In the resulting model, the feature space has relevance to input images, state classes and key-point locations that are key factors for generating feedback. Considering this, we apply a novel propagation method to extract the feedback information from the feature space.

The contributions of this study are summarized as follows. (i) To develop a system that adaptively provides interpretable feedback for various input and target states, we propose a learning-based method. (ii) Considering the data collection cost, we learn a multi-task DNN with state recognition and key-point localization and apply a novel propagation method for extracting feedback information from the network. (iii) We evaluated our method in a facial expression improvement task using real-world data and clarified its characteristics and effectiveness.

1.1 Related Work

Feedback System: In many feedback systems [3, 24, 32], the rules of feedback are manually fixed based on expert knowledge. They had the *knowledge acquisition problem*, as explained in Section 1. In several feedback systems [2, 4, 31], the difference between specific model data and input data is evaluated. They had a problem in defining the difference due to individual variations. We developed our learning-based method to solve this. In the field of computer vision, few studies have tackled this problem with learning-based methods. To the best of our knowledge, only Pirsiavash *et al.* [25] used a learning-based method similar to ours, but they required key-point locations to be obtained in advance, while we solve the problem simultaneously. As a result, they extracted the feedback information only from the locations, while we extract it from the more expressive feature space.

Multi-task DNNs: Several studies have used multi-task DNNs [1, 5, 20, 36, 37, 38] to accelerate the performance of each task. Their network architectures are similar to ours, but the motivation and propagation methods differ. Their goals were to accelerate the performance of each task by jointly learning multiple tasks, while our goal is to generate feedback by exploiting the relationship between multiple tasks. Moreover, they use typical backward and forward propagation methods for propagating between input and output, while we propose a different propagation method for extracting the relationship between multiple tasks.

Data Generation via DNNs: This is a hot topic in computer vision [6, 9, 10, 12, 14, 18, 26, 22, 35]. Most studies used DNNs with a single output, while we use a DNN with multiple outputs to exploit the relationship between multiple tasks and generate visual feedback.

2. ADAPTIVE VISUAL FEEDBACK GENERATION WITH MULTI-TASK DNN

2.1 Problem Setting

We define visual feedback as providing improvement guidelines as arrows, as shown in Figure 1. To generate such visual feedback, we first calculate the present key-point locations $\boldsymbol{y}^p$ given input image $\boldsymbol{x}^0$. We define the locations of K key points as $\boldsymbol{y}^p = (..., \boldsymbol{y}^{p_k T}, ...)^T$, $k \in \{1, ..., K\}$, where $\boldsymbol{y}^{p_k}$ contains the x and y coordinates of a k-th key point. We then calculate the optimal key-point locations $\boldsymbol{y}^{p*}$ given input image $\boldsymbol{x}^0$ and target state y^{s*}, where $y^{s*} \in \{1, ..., M\}$ indicates the class of states and M is the number of classes. Finally, we provide improvement guidelines as arrows by visualizing the difference between $\boldsymbol{y}^p$ and $\boldsymbol{y}^{p*}$.

In this problem, the main issue is how to calculate the optimal $\boldsymbol{y}^{p*}$ given $\boldsymbol{x}^0$ and y^{s*}. The problem is written as

$$\boldsymbol{y}^{p*} = f^f(\boldsymbol{x}^0, y^{s*}; \boldsymbol{w}^f) \quad (1)$$

with model parameter $\boldsymbol{w}^f$.

2.2 Model Formulation

Naive Method: To generate feedback, we have to obtain $\boldsymbol{w}^f$. If we can obtain the pair $(\boldsymbol{y}^{p*}, \boldsymbol{x}^0, y^{s*})$, i.e., feedback annotations, as training data, it is possible to learn the function explicitly. However, it is not easy to obtain the optimal $\boldsymbol{y}^{p*}$ for various input images since it requires professional knowledge in feedback.

Problem Mitigation: To mitigate this problem, we develop a method for representing f^f approximately. In particular, we exploit a multi-task DNN that shares the feature space between two tasks, key-point localization and state recognition, as shown in Figure 2 (b). In this model, the feature space has relevance to input images, state classes, and key-point locations that are key factors for generating feedback as described in Equation 1. We use this property to represent f^f approximately. Note that we must obtain the pair $(y^s, \boldsymbol{x}^0)$, i.e., state annotations, and the pair $(\boldsymbol{y}^p, \boldsymbol{x}^0)$, i.e., key-point annotations, as training data, but they are easier to collect than feedback annotations since they do not require professional knowledge in feedback. Such data can be collected via crowd sourcing [19, 30].

Model Formulation with Multi-task DNN: In a multi-task DNN, state recognition and key-point localization are written as

$$\boldsymbol{x}^0 \xrightarrow{f^{t_1}(\boldsymbol{x}^0;\boldsymbol{w}^{t_1})} \boldsymbol{x}^1 \xrightarrow{f^{t_2}(\boldsymbol{x}^1;\boldsymbol{w}^{t_2})} \dots \xrightarrow{f^{t_L}(\boldsymbol{x}^{L-1};\boldsymbol{w}^{t_L})} \boldsymbol{x}^L$$

$$\begin{aligned} y^s &= \arg\max_m f^s_m(\boldsymbol{x}^L;\boldsymbol{w}^s) \\ \boldsymbol{y}^p &= f^p(\boldsymbol{x}^L;\boldsymbol{w}^p), \end{aligned} \tag{2}$$

where f^{t_l}, $\boldsymbol{w}^{t_l}$, and $\boldsymbol{x}^l$ indicate the transformation function, model parameters, and intermediate features in the l-th layer. The last two equations are used for the last layer. We treat the problem of state recognition and that of key-point localization as classification and regression, respectively. In particular, we define $f^s_m(\boldsymbol{x}^L;\boldsymbol{w}^s)$ as a softmax function with $m \in \{1,...M\}$ and $f^p(\boldsymbol{x}^L;\boldsymbol{w}^p)$ as a linear function.

Learning: To obtain the optimal parameters in the network, cross entropy and least square can be used as the loss functions for logistic regression and linear regression, respectively. Suppose we have a set of feature vectors in the L-th layer $\{\boldsymbol{x}^L_i\}^N_{i=1}$ and their corresponding labels $\{y^s_i\}^N_{i=1}$, $\{\boldsymbol{y}^p_i\}^N_{i=1}$, where N is the number of training data. The loss functions can be written as

$$\begin{aligned} \mathcal{L}^s &= \sum_{i=1}^{N} \log f^s_{y^s_i}(\boldsymbol{x}^L_i;\boldsymbol{w}^s) \\ \mathcal{L}^p &= \frac{1}{2}\sum_{i=1}^{N} ||\boldsymbol{y}^p_i - f^p(\boldsymbol{x}^L_i;\boldsymbol{w}^p)||^2. \end{aligned} \tag{3}$$

The above parameters $\boldsymbol{w}^s$ and $\boldsymbol{w}^p$ as well as other network parameters $\boldsymbol{w}^{t_1},...,\boldsymbol{w}^{t_L}$ are optimized for the loss functions using a back-propagation algorithm.

2.3 Visual Feedback Generation

In a multi-task DNN, the feature space has relevance to input images, state classes and key-point locations that are key factors for generating feedback. Considering this, we apply a novel propagation method described in Algorithm 1 to extract the feedback information from the feature space. We first calculate the loss function for the target state. We then optimize the feature space in l^*-th layer for the loss function. Note that when conducting this procedure, the model parameters are fixed. Finally, we generate optimal $\boldsymbol{y}^{p*}$ using the optimal feature space.

In this algorithm, λ_{th} indicates the threshold for stopping optimization and is heuristically defined in the experiments. l^* indicates the layer index where the feature space is optimized. As l^* is smaller, propagation for feedback generation is deeper as shown in Figure 2 (a-c). We call the model with $l^* = L$ as *shallow feedback*, that with $l^* = 0$ as *deepest feedback*, and the others as *deep feedback*, respectively.

Algorithm 1 Feedback Generation with Multi-task DNN

```
X^0 ← input image
Y^{s*} ← target state
// Initialize feature space
for i = 1 to L do
    X^i ← f^{t_i}(X^{i-1}; W^{t_i})
end for
Y^p ← f^p(X^L; W^p) // present key-point locations
// Optimize feature space in l*-th layer
repeat
    L^s ← log f^s_{Y^{s*}}(X^L; W^s)
    X^{l*} +← −∇_{X_{l*}} L^s
    for i = l* + 1 to L do
        X^i ← f^{t_i}(X^{i-1}; W^{t_i})
    end for
until L^s < λ_th
// Calculate optimal key-point locations
Y^{p*} ← f^p(X^L; W^p)
// Generate visual feedback
Display arrows beginning at Y^p and ending at Y^{p*}
```

3. EXPERIMENTS

3.1 Experimental Setup

Dataset: We evaluated our method in a facial expression improvement task, assuming an application for individuals with challenges in emotional expression. To the best of our knowledge, there are no datasets for this task. Therefore, we combined the Multi-Task Facial Landmark (MTFL) dataset [37] and Facial Expression Recognition 2013 (FER-2013) dataset [11]. The MTFL dataset contains 10,000 images for training and 2,995 images for testing. The training images are from the CUHK Face Alignment dataset [29], and the testing images are from the AFLW dataset [16]. All images are annotated with five facial landmarks: centers of the eyes, nose, and corners of the mouth. The FER-2013 dataset contains 28,709, 3,589, and 3,589 images for training, public testing, and private testing, respectively. All the images are annotated with seven classes of facial expressions. We ignored the classes said to be nuanced and of which labeling is ambiguous [23] and selected three classes: anger, happiness, and neutral. During training, we first learned facial landmark localization using the training data in the MTFL dataset. We then learned facial expression recognition with the pre-trained features using the training and public testing data in the FER-2013 dataset. We evaluated our method using the testing data in the MTFL dataset.

Implementation Details: For the experiments, we used the convolutional architecture described in Table 1. The symbol ↓ represents down sampling. To downscale, we used convolutions with stride 2. The terms *BNorm* and *LReLU* indicate batch normalization [13] and leaky rectified activation [21, 34], respectively. During pre-processing, we converted the images to 48 × 48 gray-scale images. During training, we augmented the data by random translation, in-plane rotation, and zooming [7, 17] to improve generalization. During the evaluation, we augmented the data by flipping the images horizontally considering the balance of poses. We trained our model using the Adam optimizer [15] using an initial learning rate of 0.003 and batch of size 128.

Table 1: Network architecture

Input: 48 × 48 1 image
5 × 5 128 conv. ↓, LReLU
5 × 5 256 conv. ↓, BNorm, LReLU
5 × 5 512 conv. ↓, BNorm, LReLU
5 × 5 1024 conv. ↓, BNorm, LReLU
Output 1: 10 fully conn. for facial landmark localization
Output 2: 3 fully conn. for facial expression recognition

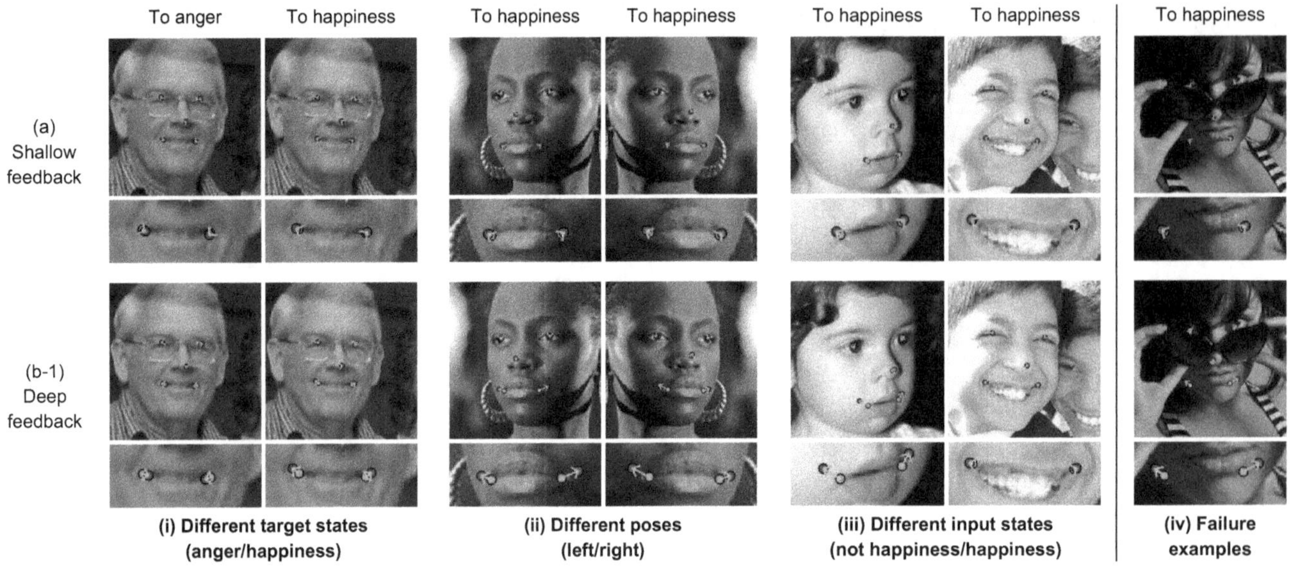

Figure 3: Generated visual feedback with shallow and deep feedback for various input data

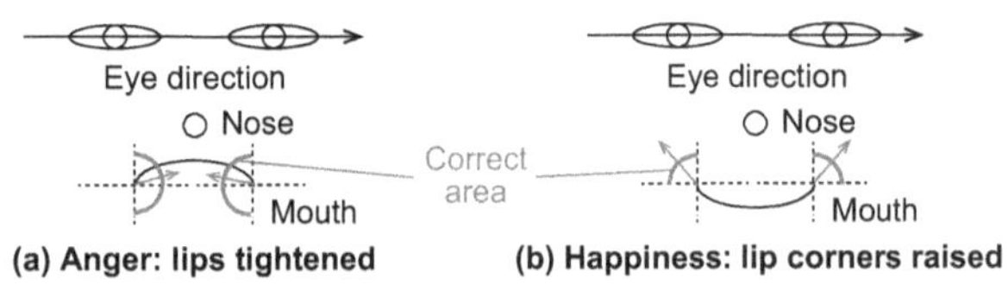

Figure 4: Evaluation metrics based on FACS.

Models for Comparison: To clarify the characteristics of our method, we compared models in which the network architectures or propagation methods are different, as shown in Figure 2.

3.2 Quantitative Analysis

We quantitatively evaluated the generated feedback based on the Facial Action Coding System (FACS) [8], which provides a common standard for systematically categorizing the physical expression of emotions. Using the standard, we selected those related to our detected key points, as shown in Figure 4. We then defined the direction of the axis on the basis of the eye direction and divided the orientations into four bins. When the generated feedback was contained in an area indicated with red, we regarded it as correct. Note that we evaluated coarsely as it is not easy to provide more detailed feedback annotations due to the subjective nature of this task. Table 2 lists the results. The comparison between using multi-task DNNs (a–c) and a separate DNN (d) indicates the importance of shared feature space for generating feedback. The comparison among multi-task DNNs (a–c) indicates that a propagation that is too deep lacks accuracy (b-3 and c), but others are competitive (a, b-1, b-2). This means that the relationship between facial landmark locations and facial expressions is maintained in these layers.

3.3 Qualitative Analysis

To analyze our method in more detail, we used the results in Figure 3. Due to limitations of space, we selected the results using the models shown in Figures 2 (a) and (b-1). The results indicate the following.

Shallow vs. Deep Feedback: As shown in (i), both (a) shallow and (b-1) deep feedback can generate feedback the directions of which satisfy the standards of FACS for different target states (anger/happiness). However, for various input data (ii–iii), shallow feedback generates similar feedback regardless of the states, while deep feedback adjusts the amount and direction of feedback depending on the states. The reason is considered to be that nonlinear transformation in deep feedback is useful for adopting feedback. Note that we did not explicitly provide pose information during training.

Table 2: Accuracy in direction of generated feedback. Bold indicates accuracy over 90%.

	Network	Propagation	Anger	Happiness
(a)	Multi-task	Shallow	**94.7**	**99.2**
(b-1)		↓	**93.9**	**97.6**
(b-2)		↓	**91.7**	**97.1**
(b-3)		↓	74.1	**90.8**
(c)		Deepest	71.5	**96.0**
(d)	Separate	Deepest	49.9	42.1

Limitation: As shown in (iv), our method cannot provide appropriate feedback when failing to localize key-points.

4. CONCLUSION AND FUTURE WORK

To develop a system that adaptively generates visual feedback, we proposed a learning-based method that learns the rules of feedback from data. Since it is difficult to collect a large amount of feedback annotations due to the subjective nature of the task, we learned a multi-task DNN with state and key-point annotations that do not require professional knowledge in feedback and applied a novel propagation method for extracting feedback information from the network. We evaluated our method in a facial expression improvement task using real-world data to clarify its characteristics and effectiveness.

We plan to extend our method on the basis of the findings of this experiment, i.e., (i) to increase the number of landmarks using a dense annotation dataset, e.g., the Helen [19] or 300-W [27] datasets, to provide more detailed feedback for more various expressions, (ii) conduct a user test for a qualitative evaluation, and (iii) make the method useful for other tasks in which the problem can be divided into key-point localization and state recognition, e.g., a pose improvement task.

5. REFERENCES

[1] A. Ahmed, K. Yu, W. Xu, Y. Gong, and E. Xing. Training hierarchical feed-forward visual recognition models using transfer learning from pseudo-tasks. In *ECCV*, 2008.

[2] D. S. Alexiadis, P. Kelly, P. Daras, N. E. O'Connor, T. Boubekeur, and M. B. Moussa. Evaluating a dancer's performance using kinect-based skeleton tracking. In *MM*, 2011.

[3] M. Bächlin, K. Förster, and G. Tröster. SwimMaster: A wearable assistant for swimmer. In *UbiComp*, 2009.

[4] J. C. P. Chan, H. Leung, J. K. T. Tang, and T. Komura. A virtual reality dance training system using motion capture technology. *Learning Technologies, IEEE*, 4(2):187–195, 2011.

[5] R. Collobert and J. Weston. A unified architecture for natural language processing: Deep neural networks with multitask learning. In *ICML*, 2008.

[6] A. Dosovistskiy, J. T. Springenberg, and T. Brox. Learning to generate chairs with convolutional neural networks. In *CVPR*, 2015.

[7] D. Eigen, C. Puhrsch, and R. Fergus. Depth map prediction from a single image using a multi-scale deep network. In *NIPS*. 2014.

[8] P. Ekman and W. Friesen. Facial action coding system: A technique for the measurement of facial movement. *Consulting Psychologists Press*, 1978.

[9] L. A. Gatys, A. S. Ecker, and M. Bethge. A neural algorithm of artistic style. *arXiv preprint arXiv:1508.06576*, 2015.

[10] I. Goodfellow, J. Pouget-Abadie, M. Mirza, B. Xu, D. Warde-Farley, S. Ozair, A. Courville, and Y. Bengio. Generative adversarial nets. In *NIPS*. 2014.

[11] I. J. Goodfellow, D. Erhan, P. L. Carrier, A. Courville, M. Mirza, B. Hamner, W. Cukierski, Y. Tang, D. Thaler, D.-H. Lee, et al. Challenges in representation learning: A report on three machine learning contests. *Neural Networks*, 64:59–63, 2015.

[12] G. E. Hinton, A. Krizhevsky, and S. D. Wang. Transforming auto-encoders. In *ICANN*, 2011.

[13] S. Ioffe and C. Szegedy. Batch normalization: Accelerating deep network training by reducing internal covariate shift. In *ICML*, 2015.

[14] D. P. Kingma, D. J. Rezende, S. Mohamed, and M. Welling. Semi-supervised learning with deep generative models. In *NIPS*, 2014.

[15] D. P. Kingma and M. Welling. Adam: A method for stochastic optimization. In *ICLR*, 2015.

[16] M. Kostinger, P. Wohlhart, P. M. Roth, and H. Bischof. Annotated facial landmarks in the wild: A large-scale, real-world database for facial landmark localization. In *ICCV Workshop*, 2011.

[17] A. Krizhevsky, I. Sutskever, and G. E. Hinton. Imagenet classification with deep convolutional neural networks. In *NIPS*. 2012.

[18] T. D. Kulkarni, W. Whitney, P. Kohli, and J. B. Tenenbaum. Deep convolutional inverse graphics network. In *NIPS*. 2015.

[19] V. Le, J. Brandt, Z. Lin, L. Bourdev, and T. S. Huang. Interactive facial feature localization. In *ECCV*. 2012.

[20] S. Li, Z.-Q. Liu, and A. B. Chan. Heterogeneous multi-task learning for human pose estimation with deep convolutional neural network. In *CVPR Workshop*, 2014.

[21] A. Maas, A. Y. Hannun, and A. Y. Ng. Rectifier nonlinearities improve neural network acoustic models. In *ICML*, 2013.

[22] A. Mahendran and A. Vedaldi. Understanding deep image representations by inverting them. In *CVPR*, 2015.

[23] H.-W. Ng, V. D. Nguyen, V. Vonikakis, and S. Winkler. Deep learning for emotion recognition on small datasets using transfer learning. In *ICMI*, 2015.

[24] N. Oliver and F. Flores-Mangas. MPTrain: A mobile, music and physiology-based personal trainer. In *MobileHCI*, 2006.

[25] H. Pirsiavash, C. Vondrick, and A. Torralba. Assessing the quality of actions. In *ECCV*, 2014.

[26] A. Radford, L. Metz, and S. Chintala. Unsupervised representation learning with deep convolutional generative adversarial networks. In *ICLR*, 2016.

[27] C. Sagonas, G. Tzimiropoulos, S. Zafeiriou, and M. Pantic. 300 faces in-the-wild challenge: The first facial landmark localization challenge. In *ICCV Workshop*, 2013.

[28] C. Shan, S. Gong, and P. W. McOwan. Facial expression recognition based on local binary patterns: A comprehensive study. *IVC*, 27(6):803–816, 2009.

[29] Y. Sun, X. Wang, and X. Tang. Deep convolutional network cascade for facial point detection. In *CVPR*, 2013.

[30] C. T. Tan, D. Rosser, and N. Harrold. Crowdsourcing facial expressions using popular gameplay. In *SIGGRAPH Asia 2013 Technical Briefs*, 2013.

[31] E. Velloso, A. Bulling, and H. Gellersen. MotionMA: Motion modelling and analysis by demonstration. In *CHI*, 2013.

[32] E. Velloso, A. Bulling, H. Gellersen, W. Ugulino, and H. Fuks. Qualitative activity recognition of weight lifting exercises. In *AH*, 2013.

[33] P. Viola and M. J. Jones. Robust real-time face detection. *IJCV*, 57(2):137–154, 2004.

[34] B. Xu, N. Wang, T. Chen, and M. Li. Empirical evaluation of rectified activations in convolutional network. *arXiv preprint arXiv:1505.00853*, 2015.

[35] J. Yim, H. Jung, B. Yoo, C. Choi, D. Park, and J. Kim. Rotating your face using multi-task deep neural network. In *CVPR*, 2015.

[36] C. Zhang and Z. Zhang. Improving multiview face detection with multi-task deep convolutional neural networks. In *WACV*, 2014.

[37] Z. Zhang, P. Luo, C. C. Loy, and X. Tang. Facial landmark detection by deep multi-task learning. In *ECCV*, 2014.

[38] Z. Zhang, P. Luo, C. C. Loy, and X. Tang. Learning deep representation for face alignment with auxiliary attributes. *IEEE Trans. PAMI*, 38:918–930, 2015.

[39] X. Zhu and D. Ramanan. Face detection, pose estimation, and landmark localization in the wild. In *CVPR*, 2012.

Fast Supervised LDA for Discovering Micro-Events in Large-Scale Video Datasets

Angelos Katharopoulos, Despoina Paschalidou, Christos Diou, Anastasios Delopoulos
Multimedia Understanding Group
ECE Department, Aristotle University of Thessaloniki, Greece
{katharas, pdespoin}@auth.gr; diou@mug.ee.auth.gr; adelo@eng.auth.gr

ABSTRACT

This paper introduces fsLDA, a fast variational inference method for supervised LDA, which overcomes the computational limitations of the original supervised LDA and enables its application in large-scale video datasets. In addition to its scalability, our method also overcomes the drawbacks of standard, unsupervised LDA for video, including its focus on dominant but often irrelevant video information (e.g. background, camera motion). As a result, experiments in the UCF11 and UCF101 datasets show that our method consistently outperforms unsupervised LDA in every metric. Furthermore, analysis shows that class-relevant topics of fsLDA lead to sparse video representations and encapsulate high-level information corresponding to parts of video events, which we denote "micro-events".

Keywords

video event detection; video micro-events; supervised topic modeling; variational inference

1. INTRODUCTION

Recently there have been significant advancements in video event detection with the two-stream models of [10, 15, 16] achieving high classification results. However, several related problems still exist (e.g. mapping motion to text descriptions, zero-shot detection) and seeking meaningful ways to analyse and represent video events remains a challenging and interesting problem. This paper aims to develop a method capable of decomposing actions or events from large-scale video data to a set of meaningful discriminative components, namely micro-events. To achieve that, we develop fsLDA, a variational inference algorithm that simultaneously preserves the computational efficiency of Latent Dirichlet Allocation (LDA) [2] and improves the discriminativeness of supervised LDA (sLDA) [1].

LDA was initially introduced as an unsupervised method, namely only the words in documents were considered to be the observed information. The goal was to infer topic distributions that maximized the likelihood of the data. Later on, Blei et al. [1] introduced a supervised variant of LDA in order to retain the discriminative information from the words with respect to the classes.

Supervised LDA has been successfully applied for classifying multimedia content mainly in the form of images [13, 8, 17]. Using a generative model is shown to be beneficial since it allows for different types of information to be encoded in a single latent space, resulting in improvements shared accross all predictions. For instance, modeling annotations in [13] marginally improves classification performance. However, it is shown in [3] that in sLDA the classes influence only lightly the latent topic assignments resulting in performance similar to LDA, which is an issue addressed in this paper. Furthermore, sLDA becomes computationally intractable for even moderately large video collections [9].

Regarding multimedia content, LDA has also been recently used, in a straightforward manner [9, 4], to combine information from different modalities and discover topics that span different vocabularies. To the best of our knowledge, there has been no attempt to train a discriminative LDA model on large-scale video data and this is probably due to computational issues in the traditional supervised LDA.

Unsupervised topic models encode the dominant structure in documents. In multimedia and especially in video data most content may refer to background movements and camera motion. This is less relevant to the depicted action than the foreground objects and their motion, thus our goal is to develop a method capable of encoding the most relevant information about the illustrated event rather than the most common.

The main contributions of this work are the following:

- We adopt topic modeling to infer both discriminative and semantic topics from large-scale video data, which encapsulate information about the micro-events that generate the events.
- We propose a supervised variation of LDA (fsLDA) that not only has lower asymptotic complexity than sLDA but is also able to adapt the influence of the supervised part on the final topic representation.

The rest of this paper is structured as follows. In section 2 the proposed method is presented. Experimental results are reported in section 3, followed by conclusions in section 4.

MM '16, October 15-19, 2016, Amsterdam, Netherlands
© 2016 ACM. ISBN 978-1-4503-3603-1/16/10... $15.00
DOI: http://dx.doi.org/10.1145/2964284.2967237

2. FAST SUPERVISED LDA

The key idea behind fsLDA is to reduce the computational complexity of sLDA so that it can infer topic distributions from large-scale video data, while at the same time increasing the influence the class information exerts on the topics to improve classification performance. Each video in the corpus corresponds to a mixture of visual and motion codewords, which are obtained by using a bag-of-words aggregation method on extracted local features. Every video belongs to one of C discrete classes, let it be y.

We suppose that the corpus consists of D documents and that there are V terms in the vocabulary. In addition, we denote two latent variables $\theta_{D\times K}$ and $z_{D\times N\times K}$, where K is the total number of topics and N is the number of codewords in a document d. The first hidden variable θ corresponds to the per-document topic distributions, while z corresponds to the per-codeword topic assignments. Moreover, α_K, $\beta_{K\times V}$ and $\eta_{K\times C}$ are the model parameters. sLDA assumes the following generative process for each document d in the corpus. For clarity, the subscript d is omitted when an equation refers to a single document (e.g. θ instead of θ_d and z_n instead of z_{dn}).

1. Draw topic proportions $\theta \sim \mathrm{Dir}(\alpha)$
2. For each codeword:
   (a) Draw topic assignment $z_n \mid \theta \sim \mathrm{Mult}(\theta)$
   (b) Draw word assignment $w_n \mid z_n, \beta_{1:K} \sim \mathrm{Mult}(\beta_{z_n})$
3. Draw class label $y \mid z_{1:N} \sim \mathrm{softmax}\left(\frac{1}{N}\sum_{n=1}^{N} z_n, \eta\right)$ where the softmax function provides the following distribution

$$p(y, \bar{z}, \eta) = \frac{\exp\left(\eta_y^T \frac{1}{N}\sum_{n=1}^{N} z_n\right)}{\sum_{\hat{y}=1}^{C} \exp\left(\eta_{\hat{y}}^T \frac{1}{N}\sum_{n=1}^{N} z_n\right)}$$

Given a document and the corresponding class label the posterior distribution of the latent variables is intractable, thus we use variational methods to approximate it. Following Blei et al. [1], our goal is to maximize the evidence lower bound (ELBO) $\mathcal{L}(\cdot)$, which is given in equation 1.

$$\begin{aligned}&\log p(w, y \mid \alpha, \beta, \eta) \geq \mathcal{L}(\gamma, \phi \mid \alpha, \beta, \eta) = \\ &\mathbb{E}_q[\log p(\theta \mid \alpha)] + \mathbb{E}_q[\log p(z \mid \theta)] + \mathbb{E}_q[\log p(w \mid \beta, z)] + \\ &H(q) + \mathbb{E}_q[\log p(y \mid z, \eta)]\end{aligned} \tag{1}$$

The expectation is taken with respect to a variational distribution $q(\theta, z_{1:N} \mid \gamma, \phi_{1:N}) = q(\theta \mid \gamma)\prod_{n=1}^{N} q(z_n \mid \phi_n)$, where ϕ_n is the variational multinomial parameter for the topic assignment z_n and γ is the variational Dirichlet parameter. Figure 1 depicts the probabilistic graphical model of sLDA.

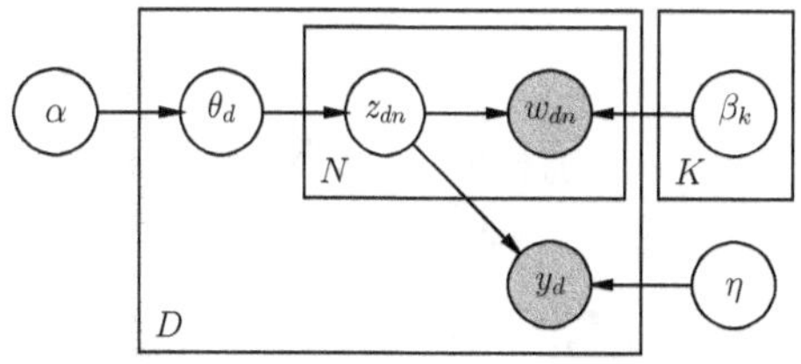

Figure 1: A graphical model representation of Supervised LDA

2.1 Inference approach of sLDA

In this section we present the inference approach of sLDA as it was introduced by Wang et al. in [13]. We point out the demerits of this approach, that motivated the development of our algorithm which is presented in section 2.2. In equation 1 the first three terms and the entropy $H(q)$ of the variational distribution are identical to the corresponding terms in the ELBO for unsupervised LDA [2]. The last term is the expected log probability of the class variable given the topic assignments, which can be computed from equation 2.

$$\mathbb{E}_q[\log p(y \mid z, \eta)] = \eta_y^T \sum_{n=1}^{N} \frac{\phi_n}{N} - \mathbb{E}_q\left[\log \sum_{\hat{y}=1}^{C} \exp(\eta_{\hat{y}}^T \bar{z})\right] \tag{2}$$

Following Wang et al. [13], the second term is approximated using Jensen's inequality, which results to the following update rules for ϕ and γ in the expectation step, where $\Psi(\cdot)$ is the first derivative of the $\log\Gamma(\cdot)$ and h is computed as in [13].

$$\begin{aligned}\gamma &= \alpha + \sum_{n=1}^{N} \phi_n \\ \phi_n &\propto \exp\left(\Psi(\gamma) + \frac{1}{N}\eta_y - (h^T \phi_n^{\text{old}})^{-1} h\right)\end{aligned} \tag{3}$$

Notice that in order to update ϕ_n once, one must compute the rule multiple times, since it is a fixed-point iteration method. The supervised part of this update rule is multiplied by $\frac{1}{N}$ and as a result, the influence of the supervised part is reduced for documents with more words, also noticed in [3]. Another drawback of the traditional inference approach of sLDA concerns the maximization step, where one must keep in memory all the variational parameters in order to compute the gradient of $\mathcal{L}$ with respect to η (e.g. for a moderately large video collection with 5000 videos, 4000 codewords and 50 topics, the variational parameter ϕ consists of 10^9 elements).

2.2 Inference approach of fsLDA

The main goal of our method is to improve the computation of the approximate variational distribution and reduce the memory requirements. $\mathcal{L}$ in terms of ϕ_n is:

$$\begin{aligned}\mathcal{L}_{\phi_n} = &\sum_{i=1}^{K} \phi_{n,i}\left(\Psi(\gamma_i) - \Psi(\sum_{j=1}^{K}\gamma_j)\right) + \\ &\sum_{i=1}^{K} \phi_{n,i} \log \beta_{i,n} - \sum_{i=1}^{K} \phi_{n,i} \log \phi_{n,i} + \\ &\eta_y^T \frac{\phi_n}{N} - \mathbb{E}_q\left[\log \sum_{\hat{y}=1}^{C} \exp(\eta_{\hat{y}}^T \bar{z})\right]\end{aligned} \tag{4}$$

The last term of equation 4 prevents a closed form solution for the update of ϕ_n. Using Jensen's inequality we can derive a lower bound for the expectation of the log normalizer and then approximate it with a second-order Taylor expansion, as shown in equation 5.

$$-\mathbb{E}_q\left[\log\sum_{\hat{y}=1}^{C}\exp(\eta_{\hat{y}}^T\bar{z})\right] \geq -\log\sum_{\hat{y}=1}^{C}\mathbb{E}_q\left[\exp(\eta_{\hat{y}}^T\bar{z})\right] \approx$$
$$-\log\sum_{\hat{y}=1}^{C}\exp(\eta_{\hat{y}}^T\mathbb{E}_q[\bar{z}])\left(1+\frac{1}{2}\eta_{\hat{y}}^T\mathbb{V}_q[\bar{z}]\eta_{\hat{y}}\right) \quad (5)$$

The expectation is $\mathbb{E}_q[\bar{z}] = \frac{1}{N}\sum_{n=1}^{N}\phi_n$, while the variance is $\mathbb{V}_q[\bar{z}] = \frac{1}{N^2}\left(\sum_{n=1}^{N}\sum_{m\neq n}\phi_n\phi_m^T + \sum_{n=1}^{N}\mathrm{diag}(\phi_n)\right)$. It can be observed that the variance term is multiplied with a very small number, especially in the case of multimedia. For instance, in case of video data, the corresponding number of codewords usually surpasses 20,000. Therefore, we decide to approximate the expectation of the log normalizer with the first-order expansion.

Finding a closed form solution to maximize $\mathcal{L}_{\phi_n}$ requires computing the derivative with respect to ϕ_n and adding Lagrange Multipliers, $\mathcal{L}'_{\phi_n} = \mathcal{L}_{\phi_n} + \lambda_n\left(\sum_{i=1}^{K}\phi_{n,i} - 1\right)$.

$$\frac{\mathrm{d}\mathcal{L}'_{\phi_n}}{\mathrm{d}\phi_n} = \left(\Psi(\gamma) - \Psi(\sum_{j=1}^{K}\gamma_j)\right) + \log\beta_n - \log\phi_n - 1 + \lambda_n +$$
$$\frac{1}{N}\left(\eta_y - \frac{\sum_{\hat{y}=1}^{C}\exp\left(\eta_{\hat{y}}^T\mathbb{E}_q[\bar{z}]\right)\eta_{\hat{y}}}{\sum_{\hat{y}=1}^{C}\exp\left(\eta_{\hat{y}}^T\mathbb{E}_q[\bar{z}]\right)}\right) \quad (6)$$

The last term of equation 6 can be written using $s = \mathrm{softmax}(\mathbb{E}_q[\bar{z}],\eta)$ as $\eta_y - \sum_{\hat{y}=1}^{C}s_{\hat{y}}\eta_{\hat{y}}$. Experiments show that s changes very slowly with respect to ϕ_n and therefore we derive the subsequent closed form update rule.

$$\phi_n \propto \beta_n\exp\left(\Psi(\gamma) + \frac{1}{N}\left(\eta_y - \sum_{\hat{y}=1}^{C}s_{\hat{y}}\eta_{\hat{y}}\right)\right) \quad (7)$$

Using the update rule from equation 7 we managed to alleviate the computational problems indicated in 2.1. We thus attain comparative computational complexity with the unsupervised LDA, while preserving the supervised part. However, the supervised part in this update rule is less dominant than the unsupervised one, due to the multiplication with the $\frac{1}{N}$ factor.

In order to address this problem we introduce the update rule shown in equation 8, where $\mathcal{C}$ is a free to change hyperparameter, which can influence the effect of the supervised part on the topics inference.

$$\phi_n \propto \beta_n\exp\left(\Psi(\gamma) + \frac{\mathcal{C}}{\max(\eta)}\left(\eta_y - \sum_{\hat{y}=1}^{C}s_{\hat{y}}\eta_{\hat{y}}\right)\right) \quad (8)$$

Intuitively, this update rule is justifiable if we consider that what actually matters is the relative proportions of the two terms and not the magnitude of their values, since ϕ_n is normalized. The update rule for γ remains the same as in the unsupervised LDA.

In the maximization step, we need to maximize $\mathcal{L}$ with respect to the model parameters β and η. The maximization with respect to the topics β remains the same as for the unsupervised LDA. To compute the classification parameters η we need to maximize $\mathcal{L}_\eta$.

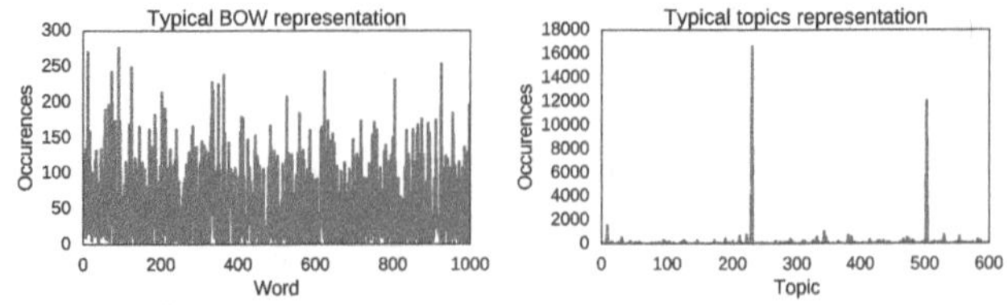

Figure 2: Typical Bag of Words and topics representations for a video

$$\mathcal{L}_\eta = \sum_{d=1}^{D}\eta_{y_d}^T\mathbb{E}_q[\bar{z_d}] -$$
$$\sum_{d=1}^{D}\log\sum_{\hat{y}=1}^{C}\exp(\eta_{\hat{y}}^T\mathbb{E}_q[\bar{z_d}])\left(1+\frac{1}{2}\eta_{\hat{y}}^T\mathbb{V}_q[\bar{z_d}]\eta_{\hat{y}}\right) \quad (9)$$

We have already mentioned that the influence of $\mathbb{V}_q[\bar{z}]$ is insignificant. In addition, in order to avoid computing and keeping the variance matrix in memory for every document, we adopt the first order approximation which amounts to multinomial logistic regression with respect to $\mathbb{E}_q[\bar{z}]$.

3. EXPERIMENTS

In this section, fsLDA is evaluated in two action recognition datasets of realistic videos. We assess its performance regarding two metrics, namely discriminativeness of the topic mixture representations and qualitative assessment of the semanticness of the inferred topics.

3.1 Experimental setup

Two datasets are used in our experiments, the UCF11-Youtube Action Dataset [5] and the UCF101-Action Recognition Dataset [12]. *UCF11* is composed of 11 action classes with 1600 videos, the majority of which contain heavy camera motion. *UCF101* is one of the state-of-the-art datasets for action recognition. It consists of 13320 videos, belonging to 101 categories.

We use both visual and motion features, in the conducted experiments, to establish that the proposed method is effective regardless of the nature of the local features. In order to represent motion information, Improved Dense Trajectories (IDT) [14] are extracted from each video for both datasets. In case of UCF11, Dense SIFT [6] are computed to encapsulate visual information. Regarding encoding visual information from UCF101, we decided to use the last two convolutional layers from [11] as local features in $\mathbb{R}^{512}$. The extracted local features are subsequently encoded using Bag of Words (BoW) representation with 1000 and 4000 codewords for UCF11 and UCF101 respectively.

In subsequent experiments, we measure the classification performance of a linear SVM by computing the mean accuracy score in three random splits. C for the SVM is chosen via cross-validation while the $\mathcal{C}$ hyperparameter of our method is selected by hand. We compare our method with both supervised and unsupervised LDA as well as with BoW.

3.2 Qualitative topic evaluation

It simply suffices to observe the topic versus word representation in Figure 2 to notice that topics are by far more sparse than words. Intuitively, this can be attributed to the topics encapsulating much more information than a sin-

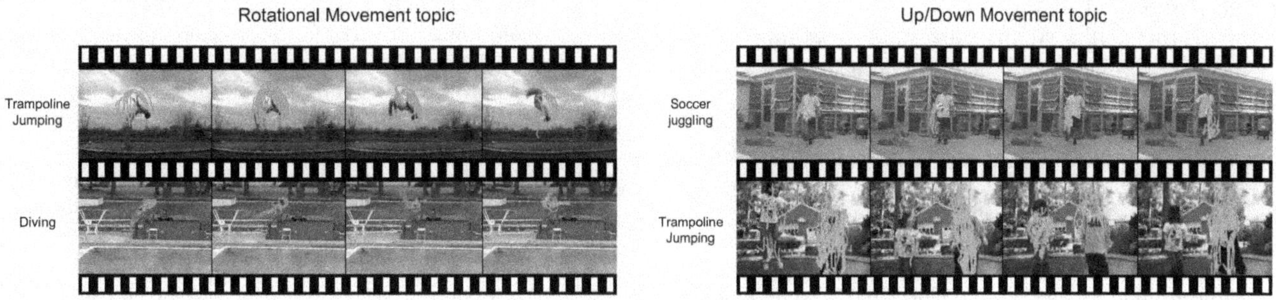

Figure 3: Visualization of rotational movement topic (orange) and vertical movement topic (light blue). The red bullet indicates the beginning of the trajectory.

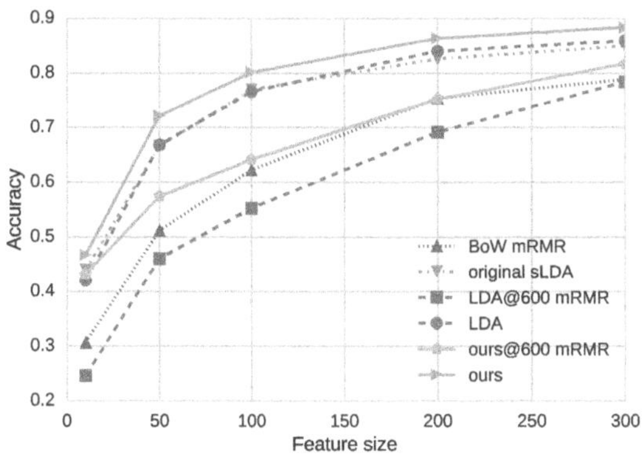

Figure 4: Classification accuracy using few dimensions to represent videos

gle word. In Figure 3, we draw the IDT trajectories that correspond to a codeword that belongs in the ten most common words of two different topics. It is noticeable that the inferred topics capture the specifics of different complex motions, such as rotational and vertical movements. These motions are discovered in videos from different classes, such as trampoline jumping and diving for rotational movement and soccer juggling and trampoline jumping for vertical movement. We have observed that many topics discovered with unsupervised LDA refer to background information, which is the dominant structure in the video. In contrast, the topics inferred using our method encapsulate high level information, which corresponds to micro-events.

In order to evaluate the class-relevant information encoded in each topic, we reduce feature dimensionality using either minimum Redundancy Maximum Relevance Feature Selection (mRMR) [7] or by simply training our method with a smaller number of topics. Figure 4 depicts the classification performance according to the aforementioned procedure on UCF11 using a single representative descriptor (idt-hog). Each of the topics discovered by fsLDA contains more class-relevant information compared to the ones inferred by both LDA and sLDA as well as to the codewords found by KMeans. This is established since the proposed method outperforms BoW using mRMR feature selection. The same results are observed when selecting features with other feature selection methods.

3.3 Evaluation of discriminativeness of topics

In this section, we evaluate the discriminativeness of the inferred topic distributions by measuring the classification performance on a variety of descriptors using the whole topic distribution or the concatenation of the topic distributions (denoted as combined) as a feature.

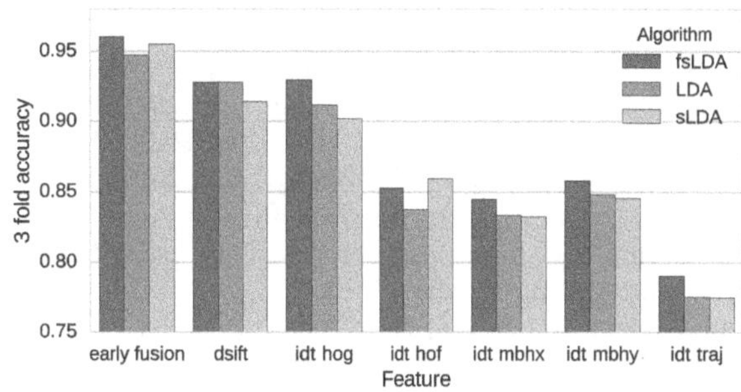

Figure 5: Comparison of fsLDA with unsupervised LDA and sLDA using 600 topics in UCF11

	LDA @ 1200	fsLDA @ 1200
conv5_2	56.03%	**62.37%**
idt-hof	52.72%	**56.07%**
combined	67.50%	**69.87%**

Table 1: Comparison of fsLDA with unsupervised LDA in UCF101 (the complexity of sLDA for UCF101 is prohibitive)

Figure 5 depicts the mean accuracy for every descriptor in UCF11. Our method outperforms LDA in every descriptor and sLDA in all but one while being 50 to 100 times faster. Table 1 presents the three-fold accuracy scores in the case of UCF101 for some indicative descriptors. Even in this more demanding large-scale dataset, fsLDA performs better in terms of classification accuracy especially for the conv5_2 features.

4. CONCLUSIONS

We have developed a new method to infer topics in a supervised manner which, in contrast to sLDA, is tractable on large-scale video datasets such as UCF101. Furthermore, we have shown that the proposed method outperforms unsupervised LDA and discovers topics which encapsulate high level information corresponding to micro-events, while containing more class-relevant information than words.

Future work includes the study of topics as rich descriptions of video attributes for video captioning and retrieval applications.

5. REFERENCES

[1] D. M. Blei and J. D. Mcauliffe. Supervised topic models. In *Advances in neural information processing systems*, pages 121–128, 2008.

[2] D. M. Blei, A. Y. Ng, and M. I. Jordan. Latent dirichlet allocation. *the Journal of machine Learning research*, 3:993–1022, 2003.

[3] M. Dixit, N. Rasiwasia, and N. Vasconcelos. Class-specific simplex-latent dirichlet allocation for image classification. In *Proceedings of the IEEE International Conference on Computer Vision*, pages 2672–2679, 2013.

[4] R. R. Iyer, S. Parekh, V. Mohandoss, A. Ramsurat, B. Raj, and R. Singh. Content-based video indexing and retrieval using corr-lda. *arXiv preprint arXiv:1602.08581*, 2016.

[5] J. Liu, J. Luo, and M. Shah. Recognizing realistic actions from videos in the wild. In *Computer Vision and Pattern Recognition, 2009. CVPR 2009. IEEE Conference on*, pages 1996–2003. IEEE, 2009.

[6] D. G. Lowe. Distinctive image features from scale-invariant keypoints. *International journal of computer vision*, 60(2):91–110, 2004.

[7] H. Peng, F. Long, and C. Ding. Feature selection based on mutual information criteria of max-dependency, max-relevance, and min-redundancy. *Pattern Analysis and Machine Intelligence, IEEE Transactions on*, 27(8):1226–1238, 2005.

[8] D. Putthividhya, H. T. Attias, and S. S. Nagarajan. Supervised topic model for automatic image annotation. In *Acoustics Speech and Signal Processing (ICASSP), 2010 IEEE International Conference on*, pages 1894–1897. IEEE, 2010.

[9] S. Qian, T. Zhang, C. Xu, and M. S. Hossain. Social event classification via boosted multimodal supervised latent dirichlet allocation. *ACM Transactions on Multimedia Computing, Communications, and Applications (TOMM)*, 11(2):27, 2015.

[10] K. Simonyan and A. Zisserman. Two-stream convolutional networks for action recognition in videos. In *Advances in Neural Information Processing Systems*, pages 568–576, 2014.

[11] K. Simonyan and A. Zisserman. Very deep convolutional networks for large-scale image recognition. *arXiv preprint arXiv:1409.1556*, 2014.

[12] K. Soomro, A. R. Zamir, and M. Shah. UCF101: A dataset of 101 human actions classes from videos in the wild. *arXiv preprint arXiv:1212.0402*, 2012.

[13] C. Wang, D. Blei, and F.-F. Li. Simultaneous image classification and annotation. In *Computer Vision and Pattern Recognition, 2009. CVPR 2009. IEEE Conference on*, pages 1903–1910. IEEE, 2009.

[14] H. Wang and C. Schmid. Action recognition with improved trajectories. In *Proceedings of the IEEE International Conference on Computer Vision*, pages 3551–3558, 2013.

[15] Z. Wu, X. Wang, Y.-G. Jiang, H. Ye, and X. Xue. Modeling spatial-temporal clues in a hybrid deep learning framework for video classification. In *Proceedings of the 23rd Annual ACM Conference on Multimedia Conference*, pages 461–470. ACM, 2015.

[16] J. Yue-Hei Ng, M. Hausknecht, S. Vijayanarasimhan, O. Vinyals, R. Monga, and G. Toderici. Beyond short snippets: Deep networks for video classification. In *Proceedings of the IEEE Conference on Computer Vision and Pattern Recognition*, pages 4694–4702, 2015.

[17] J. Zhu, A. Ahmed, and E. P. Xing. Medlda: maximum margin supervised topic models for regression and classification. In *Proceedings of the 26th annual international conference on machine learning*, pages 1257–1264. ACM, 2009.

Semantic Description of Timbral Transformations in Music Production

Ryan Stables
Digital Media Technology Lab
Birmingham City University
Birmingham, UK
ryan.stables@bcu.ac.uk

Brecht De Man
Centre for Digital Music
Queen Mary University of London
London, UK
b.deman@qmul.ac.uk

Sean Enderby
Digital Media Technology Lab
Birmingham City University
Birmingham, UK
sean.enderby@mail.bcu.ac.uk

Joshua D. Reiss
Centre for Digital Music
Queen Mary University of London
London, UK
joshua.reiss@qmul.ac.uk

György Fazekas
Centre for Digital Music
Queen Mary University of London
London, UK
g.fazekas@qmul.ac.uk

Thomas Wilmering
Centre for Digital Music
Queen Mary University of London
London, UK
t.wilmering@qmul.ac.uk

ABSTRACT

In music production, descriptive terminology is used to define perceived sound transformations. By understanding the underlying statistical features associated with these descriptions, we can aid the retrieval of contextually relevant processing parameters using natural language, and create intelligent systems capable of assisting in audio engineering. In this study, we present an analysis of a dataset containing descriptive terms gathered using a series of processing modules, embedded within a Digital Audio Workstation. By applying hierarchical clustering to the audio feature space, we show that similarity in term representations exists within and between transformation classes. Furthermore, the organisation of terms in low-dimensional timbre space can be explained using perceptual concepts such as size and dissonance. We conclude by performing Latent Semantic Indexing to show that similar groupings exist based on term frequency.

CCS Concepts

•**Information systems → Information systems applications; Multimedia information systems;** *Multimedia databases;*

Keywords

Semantic Audio, Timbre, Music Production, Hierarchical Clustering, Dimensionality Reduction

1. INTRODUCTION

Musical timbre refers to the properties of a sound, other than loudness and pitch, which allow it to be distinguished from other sounds [8]. Loudness and pitch can easily be measured in low-dimensional space, allowing sounds to be ordered from quiet to loud or low to high in frequency, whereas timbre is a more complex property of sound, requiring multiple dimensions [11]. To characterise perceptual attributes of musical timbre, listeners often attribute semantic descriptors such as *bright*, *rough* or *sharp* to describe latent dimensions [5]. A widely cited definition of timbre [1] shows it can be determined by a range of low level features of an audio signal, where the spectral content and temporal characteristics both affect the perceived timbre of a sound. Signal analysis techniques can be used to extract information about these elements of a signal. The contribution of these low level features to perceived timbre is often the focus of academic research, whereby dimensionality reduction techniques allow for the organisation of terms in an underlying subspace, with the intention of discovering some perceptually relevant representation of the data [2,4,6,17]. In music production, this is of particular interest as it can allow for the manipulation of audio processing modules, comprising multiple parameters using intuitive, low-dimensional controls [3,12,14,15].

In this paper we report our findings from the Semantic Audio Feature Extraction (SAFE) Project [13], and show that semantic descriptions of musical timbre can be grouped using both parameter and feature space representations, and can exhibit timbral similarities within and across audio processing types. We investigate the use of timbral descriptors to aid the retrieval of contextually relevant processing parameters given natural language descriptions of audio transformations. This allows for the development of intuitive and assistive music production interfaces, based on descriptive cues.

2. SAFE

The Semantic Audio Feature Extraction (SAFE) plug-ins[1] provide music producers with a platform to describe timbral transformations in a Digital Audio Workstation (DAW) using natural language [13]. The plugins (referred to herein as transform classes) consist of a five band parametric equaliser,

[1]Plugins and datasets available at semanticaudio.co.uk.

MM '16, October 15 - 19, 2016, Amsterdam, Netherlands

ISBN 978-1-4503-3603-1/16/10... $15.00

DOI: http://dx.doi.org/10.1145/2964284.2967238

	Num Instances		Confidence		Popularity		Generality	
N	term	n	term	c	term	p	term	g
0	warm	193	boxed	.250	warm	0.0019	sharp	.828
1	bright	153	splash	.250	bright	0.0014	deep	.819
2	punch	34	wholesome	.250	crunch	0.0006	boom	.809
3	air	31	pumping	.247	room	0.0005	thick	.806
4	crunch	29	rounded	.247	fuzz	0.0004	piano	.696
5	room	28	sparkle	.247	crisp	0.0004	strong	.596
6	smooth	22	atmosphere	.244	clear	0.0004	soft	.575
7	vocal	21	balanced	.244	cut	0.0004	bass	.555
8	clear	20	bass	.244	bass	0.0004	gentle	.525
9	fuzz	19	basic	.244	low	0.0004	tin	.483

Table 1: The highest ranking terms using confidence, popularity and generality measures.

a dynamic range compressor, amplitude distortion and a reverb effect. When a timbral transformation is recorded, the system extracts the descriptive terminology relating to the transform; a large set of temporal, spectral and abstracted audio features taken across a number of frames of the audio signal, both before and after processing (see [9] for a full list); the name and parameter settings of the audio effect; and a list of additional user data such as age, location, production experience, genre and instrument. This information is stored in an RDF triple store using an empirically designed ontology.

2.1 Dataset

The dataset used for the study comprised 2694 transforms, split into four groups according to their transform class. Overall, 454 were applied using a compressor, 303 using distortion, 1679 using an equaliser, and 258 using a reverb. The transforms were described using 618 unique terms taken from 263 unique users (averaging 2.35 terms per user), all of whom were music producers who participated by using the SAFE Plugins within their workflow.

We measure the *confidence* of a descriptor using the sum of its variance in feature space, where each of the features is mapped to a 6-dimensional space using Principal Component Analysis (PCA) in order to remove redundancy, whilst retaining $\geq 95\%$ of the variance:

$$c = \frac{1}{M} \sum_{n=0}^{N-1} \sum_{m=0}^{M-1} (PC_n(m) - \mu_n)^2 \tag{1}$$

To further identify the *popularity* of a descriptor, we weight the output of Eq. (1) with a coefficient representing the term as a proportion of the dataset:

$$p = c \cdot ln \frac{n(d)}{\sum_{d=0}^{D-1} n(d)} \tag{2}$$

where $n(d)$ is the number of entries for a descriptor d.

Finally, we evaluate the extent to which the descriptor is generalisable across a range of transform classes (*generality*) by finding the weighted mean of the term's sorted distribution. This is equivalent to finding the centroid of the density function across transform classes.

$$g = \frac{2}{K-1} \sum_{k=0}^{K-1} k \operatorname{sort}(x(d))_k \tag{3}$$

where the distribution of the term d is calculated as a proportion of the transform class (k) to which it belongs:

$$x(d)_k = \frac{n_d(k)}{N(k)} \frac{1}{\sum_{k=0}^{K-1} N(k)} \tag{4}$$

Here, $N(k)$ is the total number of entries in class k and $n_d(k)$ is the number of occurrences of descriptor d in class k. Using these metrics, the database is sorted and the top 10 descriptors are shown in Table 1. Similarly, Table 2 shows the most commonly used descriptors for each individual transform class. To group terms with shared meanings and variable suffixes, stemming conditions are applied using a Porter Stemmer [10]. This allows for the unification of terms such as *warm, warmer and warmth* into a parent category (*warm*).

Compressor	Distortion	EQ	Reverb
27 : punch	23 : crunch	440 : warm	30 : room
17 : smooth	20 : warm	424 : bright	13 : air
15 : sofa	6 : fuzz	16 : air	11 : big
14 : vocal	6 : destroyed	16 : clear	10 : subtle
12 : nice	5 : cream	12 : thin	9 : hall
9 : controlled	5 : death	11 : clean	9 : small
9 : together	5 : bass	11 : crisp	8 : dream
9 : crushed	5 : clip	10 : bass	7 : damp
8 : warm	5 : decimated	9 : boom	7 : drum
7 : comp	5 : distorted	9 : cut	6 : close

Table 2: The first ten descriptors per class, ranked by number of entries.

3. WITHIN-CLASS SIMILARITY

To find term-similarities within transform classes, hierarchical clustering is applied to differences (processed vs. unprocessed) in timbre space. To do this, the mean of the audio feature vectors from each unique descriptor is computed and PCA is applied, reducing the number of dimensions, whilst preserving $\geq 95\%$ of the variance. Terms with < 8 entries are omitted for readability and the distances between datapoints are calculated using Ward distance [16], the results of which are shown in Figure 1. In each transform class, clusters are intended to retain perceived latent groupings, based on underlying semantic representations.

From the term clusters, distances between groups of semantically similar timbral descriptions emerge. Among the Compressor terms, groups tend to exhibit correlation with the extent to which gain reduction is applied to the signal. *Loud*, *fat* and *squashed* generally refer to extreme compression, whereas *subtle*, *gentle* and *soft* tend to describe minor adjustments to the amplitude envelope. Distortion features tend to group based on the perceived dissonance of the

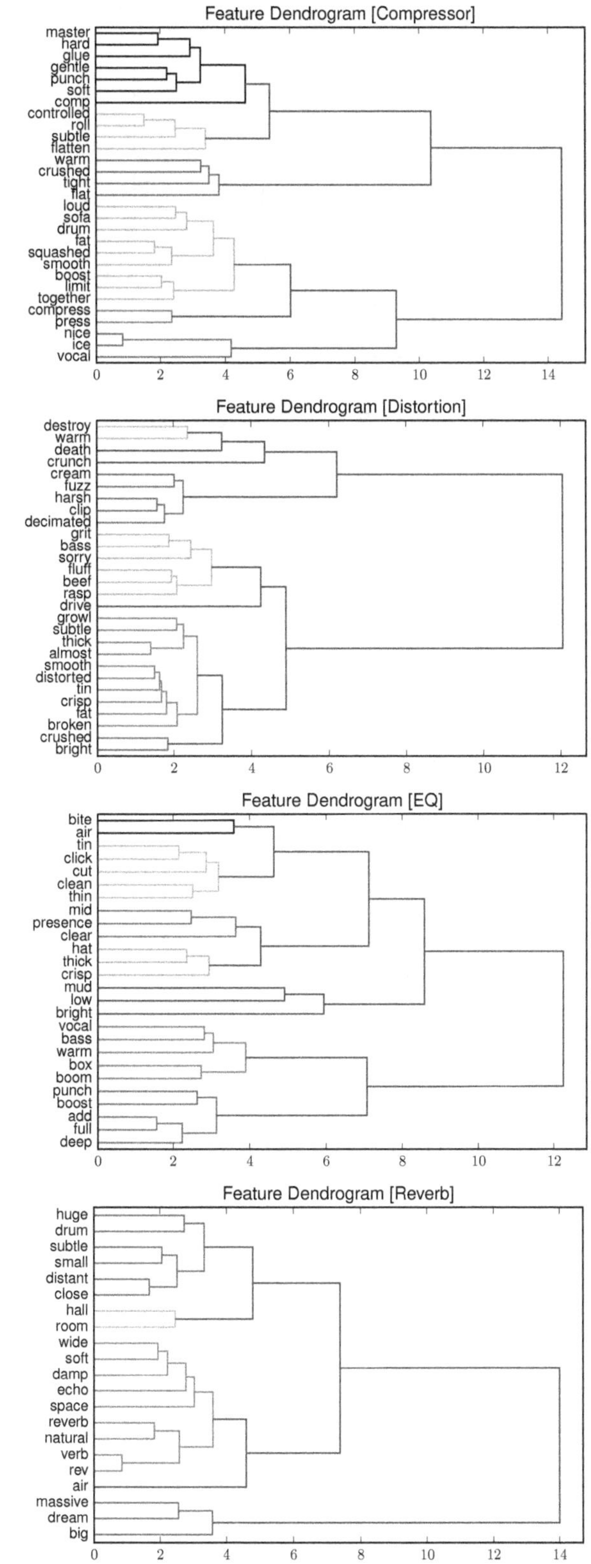

Figure 1: Dendrograms showing clustering based on feature space distances for each transform class.

transform, with terms such as *fuzz* and *harsh* clearly separated from *subtle*, *rasp* and *growl*. Equalisation comprises a wide selection of description-categories, although terms that generally refer to specific regions of spectral energy such as *bass*, *mid* and *full* tend to fall into separate partitions. Reverb terms tend to group based on size and descriptions of acoustic spaces. *Hall* and *room* for example exhibit similar feature spaces, while terms such as *soft*, *damp* and *natural* fall into the same group.

3.1 Parameter Space Representation

To illustrate the relevance of the within-class feature groups found using the hierarchical clustering algorithm, we can show that terms within clusters maintain similar characteristics in their parameter spaces. To demonstrate this, Figure 2 shows curves corresponding to two groups of descriptors taken from opposing clusters in the equaliser's feature-space: cluster 2 (*warm*, *bass*, *boom*, *box* and *vocal*) and cluster 8 (*thin*, *clean*, *cut*, *click* and *tin*). Curves in cluster 2 generally exhibit a boost around 500 Hz with a high-frequency roll-off, whereas terms in cluster 8 exhibit a boost in high-frequency energy centered around 5 kHz.

To further evaluate the organisation of terms based on their position in a parameter space, we use PCA to reduce the dimensionality of each space and overlay the parameter vectors. Figure 3 shows this for the distortion and reverb, where in 3(a) the bias is highly correlated with PC2, which tends to organise descriptors based on dissonance. Similarly in 3(b), the mix and gain parameters of the reverb class correlate with PC2 and tend to retain variance using size-based descriptors. These exhibit 0.68 and 0.81 cross-correlation values respectively.

4. INTER-TRANSFORM SIMILARITY

To investigate between-class similarities, we perform hierarchical clustering on the dataset, where transforms are grouped by unique terms and separated by transform class. Here, the organisation of terms into clusters is highly correlated with the organisation of terms into transform classes. Out of the 8 data partitions, the mean rank-order generality is 0.23, with a mean of 2.4 unique class labels per group.

To identify transform-agnostic descriptors, i.e. those with similar between-class transformations, we select the top 10 terms with the highest generality scores (defined in Table 1) and measure the variance across the transformations in reduced-dimensionality space. All terms had entries in all 4 transform classes, and had at least 10 entries overall. Ranked by between-class agreement: 1. *piano* (0.001), 2. *sharp* (0.012), 3. *soft* (0.013), 4. *thick* (0.018), 5. *tin* (0.021), 6. *deep* (0.022), 7. *bass* (0.033), 8. *gentle* (0.039), 9. *strong* (0.050), 10. *boom* (0.058).

4.1 Term Frequency Analysis

We measure term similarity independently of timbral or parameter space representations, using a term's association to a given transform class. Here, we use term frequency to define distributions across classes, resulting in four-dimensional vectors, e.g. $\mathbf{t} = [0.0, 0.5, 0.5, 0.0]$ has equal association with the distortion and equaliser, but no entries in the compressor or reverb classes. We then represent these using a Vector Space Model (VSM), and measure similarity between any two terms $(\mathbf{t_1}, \mathbf{t_2})$ using cosine distance:

$$\text{sim}(\mathbf{t_1}, \mathbf{t_2}) = \frac{\mathbf{t_1} \cdot \mathbf{t_2}}{\|\mathbf{t_1}\|\|\mathbf{t_2}\|} = \frac{\sum_{i=1}^{N} t_{1,i} t_{2,i}}{\sqrt{\sum_{i=1}^{N} t_{1,i}^2}\sqrt{\sum_{i=1}^{N} t_{2,i}^2}} \quad (5)$$

In order to better capture the true semantic relations of

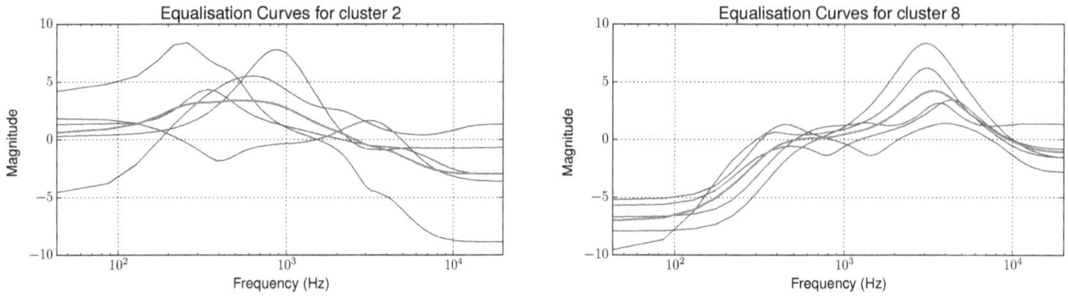

(a) *warm*, *bass*, *boom*, *box* and *vocal*   (b) *thin*, *clean*, *cut*, *click* and *tin*

Figure 2: Equalisation curves for two clusters of terms in the dataset.

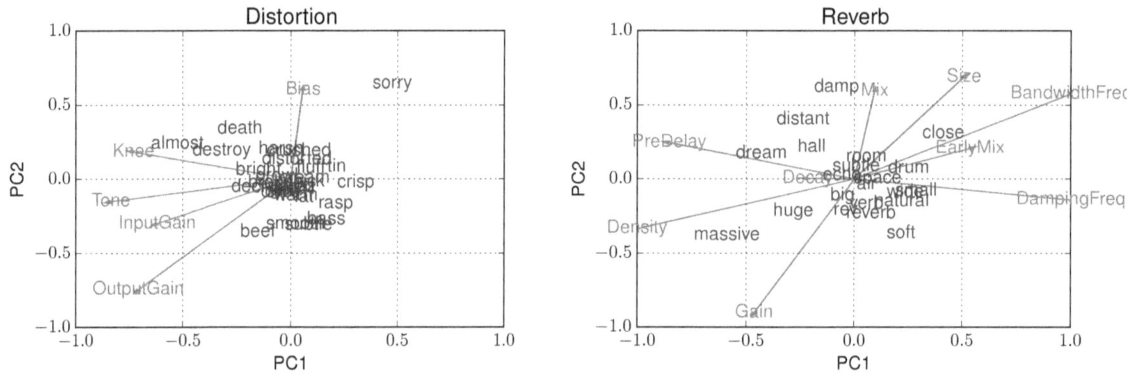

(a)   (b)

Figure 3: Biplots of the distortion and reverb classes, showing terms mapped onto 2 dimensions with overlaid parameter vectors.

the terms and the transforms they are associated with, we apply Latent Semantic Indexing (LSI) [7], a process that involves reducing the term-transform space from rank four to three by performing a singular value decomposition of the $N_{terms} \times 4$ occurrence matrix $\mathbf{M} = \mathbf{U\Sigma V}^*$, and setting the smallest singular values to zero before reconstructing it using $\mathbf{M}' = \mathbf{U\Sigma' V}^*$.

This process eliminates noise caused by differences in word usage, for instance due to synonymy and polysemy, whereas the 'latent' semantic relationships between terms and effects are preserved. Figure 4 shows the resulting pairwise similarities of the high-generality terms used in Section 4.

Here, the most similar terms are *bass* and *strong*, *deep* and *sharp* and *boom* and *thick* (all 0.99). Conversely, we can consider the similarity of transform types based on their descriptive attributes by transposing the occurrence matrix in the VSM. This is illustrated in Figure 4, in which terms used to describe equalisation transforms are similar to those associated with distortion (0.95), while equalisation and compression vocabulary is disjunct (0.641).

5. DISCUSSION/CONCLUSION

We have illustrated within- and between-class groupings of semantic descriptions of sound transformations taken from processing modules in a DAW. We showed that the groups represent meaningful subsets of entries by evaluating correlation in their parameter spaces, and that the parameters of each processing module can be used to organise terms in a similar fashion. To evaluate between-transform similarity, we demonstrated that transforms tend to form the basis of discrete clusters, and that terms such as *piano*, *sharp*, *soft*, *thick* and *tinny* have similar representations across a range of processing types. Finally, we measured the similarity of effects and terms based on their vector-space representations. This shows that equalisation and compression share a common vocabulary of terms, whilst reverb and distortion have a dissimilar description schema. The results are encouraging and show that timbre descriptors cluster in meaningful ways in the context of audio transformations. The findings thus provide useful insight into how to create semantic descriptor spaces for audio effects.

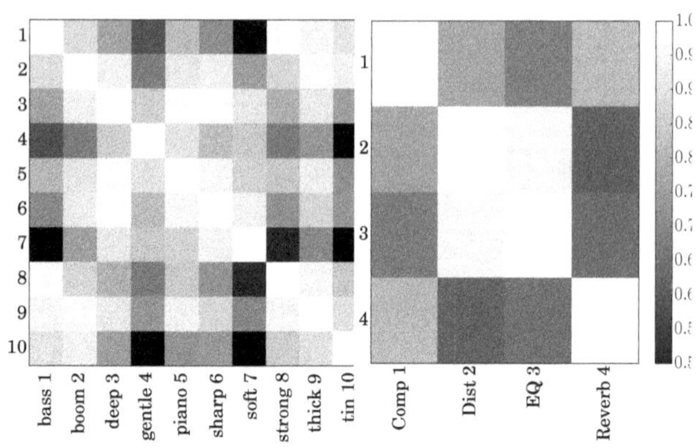

(a)   (b)

Figure 4: Vector-space similarity wrt. (a) high-generality terms and (b) transform-classes.

6. REFERENCES

[1] American Standards Association. American standard acoustical terminology (including mechanical shock and vibration). Technical report, 1960.

[2] A. Caclin, S. McAdams, B. Smith, and S. Winsberg. Acoustic correlates of timbre space dimensions: A confirmatory study using synthetic tones. *The Journal of the Acoustical Society of America*, 118(1):471–482, 2005.

[3] M. B. Cartwright and B. Pardo. Social-EQ: Crowdsourcing an equalization descriptor map. In *14th International Society for Music Information Retrieval Conference (ISMIR)*, 2013.

[4] J. Grey. Multidimensional perceptual scaling of musical timbres. *The Journal of the Acoustical Society of America*, 61(5):1270–1277, 1977.

[5] D. Howard and J. Angus. *Acoustics and Psychoacoustics*. Focal Press, 4th edition, 2009.

[6] R. Kendall and E. Carterette. Verbal attributes of simultaneous wind instrument timbres: I. von Bismarck's adjectives. *Music Perception: An Interdisciplinary Journal*, 10(4):445–467, 1993.

[7] T. A. Letsche and M. W. Berry. Large-scale information retrieval with latent semantic indexing. *Information sciences*, 100(1):105–137, 1997.

[8] M. Mathews. Introduction to timbre. In P. Cook, editor, *Music, Cognition, and Computerized Sound: An Introduction to Psychoacoustics*, chapter 7. MIT Press, 1999.

[9] G. Peeters. A large set of audio features for sound description (similarity and classification) in the CUIDADO project. Technical report, IRCAM, 2004.

[10] M. F. Porter. An algorithm for suffix stripping. *Program*, 14(3):130–137, 1980.

[11] T. Rossing, R. Moore, and P. Wheeler. *The Science of Sound*. Addison Wesley, 3 edition, 2002.

[12] P. Seetharaman and B. Pardo. Socialreverb: crowdsourcing a reverberation descriptor map. In *ACM International Conference on Multimedia*, November 2014.

[13] R. Stables, S. Enderby, B. De Man, G. Fazekas, and J. Reiss. SAFE: A system for the extraction and retrieval of semantic audio descriptors. In *15th International Society for Music Information Retrieval Conference (ISMIR)*, 2014.

[14] S. Stasis, R. Stables, and J. Hockman. A model for adaptive reduced-dimensionality equalisation. In *18th International International Conference on Digital Audio Effects (DAFx-15), Trondheim, Norway*, 2015.

[15] S. Stasis, R. Stables, and J. Hockman. Semantically controlled adaptive equalisation in reduced dimensionality parameter space. *Applied Sciences*, 6(4):116, 2016.

[16] J. H. Ward Jr. Hierarchical grouping to optimize an objective function. *Journal of the American statistical association*, 58(301):236–244, 1963.

[17] A. Zacharakis, K. Pastiadis, J. D. Reiss, and G. Papadelis. Analysis of musical timbre semantics through metric and non-metric data reduction techniques. In *12th International Conference on Music Perception and Cognition (ICMPC)*, pages 1177–1182, 2012.

Multimodal Learning via Exploring Deep Semantic Similarity

Di Hu
OPTIMAL in
Northwestern Polytechnical University
127 West Youyi Road
Xi'an Shaanxi, China
hdui831@mail.nwpu.edu.cn

Xiaoqiang Lu
OPTIMAL in
Chinese Academy of Sciences
Xi'an Institute of Optics and Precision Mechanics,
Xi'an Shaanxi, China
luxiaoqiang@opt.ac.cn

Xuelong Li
OPTIMAL in
Chinese Academy of Sciences
Xi'an Institute of Optics and Precision Mechanics
Xi'an Shaanxi, China
xuelong_li@opt.ac.cn

ABSTRACT

Deep learning is skilled at learning representation from raw data, which are embedded in the semantic space. Traditional multimodal networks take advantage of this, and maximize the joint distribution over the representations of different modalities. However, the similarity among the representations are not emphasized, which is an important property for multimodal data. In this paper, we will introduce a novel learning method for multimodal networks, named as *Semantic Similarity Learning* (SSL), which aims at training the model via enhancing the similarity between the high-level features of different modalities. Sets of experiments are conducted for evaluating the method on different multimodal networks and multiple tasks. The experimental results demonstrate the effectiveness of SSL in keeping the shared information and improving the discrimination. Particularly, SSL shows its ability in encouraging each modality to learn transferred knowledge from the other one when faced with missing data.

Keywords

Multimodal learning; Semantic similarity; Deep learning

1. INTRODUCTION

In the real world, information can be expressed in various kinds of modalities. Typically, images usually come with assigned accompanying tags for describing the same content [12, 19], regular speech contains audio signal and corresponding lip movements [6], and environment can be described in both image and 3D depth [17]. These modalities can jointly provide more valuable information than single modality, thus lots of tasks, including image-tag retrieval [15] and speech recognition [6], take consideration of multimodal input.

For each multimodal task, as data modalities generated from the same event are processed in different manners, they own distinct statistical properties which make it difficult to capture patterns across them. Recently, multimodal deep networks have been proposed to learn the shared representation across data modalities after learning each modality with single deep network, which takes advantages of the efficiency of deep network in producing useful representation for image, audio, and text [2]. In such multimodal networks, the generated features from different modalities are considered semantically relevant. Actually, as they share similar semantic information of the same entity, the association among data modalities can be enhanced and provide more valuable information for each one, especially in the case of missing modality. However, this property is not fully explored just by maximizing the joint distribution over modalities in the previous multimodal networks [11, 15, 7], so that the shared representation is easily affected by specific property of single modality and can not be held.

In this paper, we propose a novel learning algorithm for multimodal networks, which encourages the learned representation to keep the shared semantic information across modalities (e.g. audio, video, and text) and reduce the interference from specific modality. Specifically, as the generated high-level features of modalities are usually considered to have similar semantic, they should have similar contribution for the shared hidden layer. Based on this, we compare the hidden units activated by each modality, and enhance the semantic similarity by reducing the difference between them, which is named as *Semantic Similarity Learning* (SSL). To measure the similarity among modalities in different views, several functions are attempted, and the constituted algorithm is performed with multiple multimodal networks in several multimodal tasks. As expected, SSL keeps, even enhances the shared representation, which results in more discriminative representation. Besides, our algorithm shows its effectiveness in dealing with missing modality with the help of learned transferred knowledge.

In the following sections, we first survey the related work about multimodal deep networks in Section 2. In Section 3, we present our proposed learning algorithm for the networks. We then valid the algorithm on different tasks with audio, image, and text in Section 4. Section 5 concludes this paper.

2. RELATED WORK

In recent years, deep learning methods have performed its effectiveness in feature learning. And the features generated from multimodal networks are considered semantically

MM '16, October 15-19, 2016, Amsterdam, Netherlands
© 2016 ACM. ISBN 978-1-4503-3603-1/16/10...$15.00
DOI: http://dx.doi.org/10.1145/2964284.2967239

correlated [15]. In the early work of multimodal deep learning, Ngiam *et al.* [11] proposed a framework that learns the layers of modality-specific network firstly. Then the shared representation across the generated features of modalities are jointly learned using higher networks. Finally, the whole network is fine-tuned to minimize reconstruction errors of both modalities. This kinds of network is called *Multimodal Deep Auto-encoder* (MDAE). Different from the fusion strategy above, Andrew *et al.* [1] proposed *Deep Canonical Correlation Analysis* (DCCA) which measures the linear correlation between generated representations from each single network. They find that deep networks have the ability to transform complex nonlinear data into highly linear correlation and make them share more semantic information. Recently, Wang *et al.* [18] made a comparison between MDAE and DCCA, and attempted to combine them into a kind of *Deep Canonical Correlation Autoencoder* (DCCAE) that is expected to have advantages from both sides. But the simple combination has weakness in emphasizing the shared representation with the help of semantic similarity. Besides, Shu *et al.* [13] presented a multimodal framework to translate cross-domain knowledge based on the generated representations, but they used weakly parameter-shared setting instead of the general joint learning. This framework is more flexible but easier influenced by domain-specific features due to the relaxed constraint for parameters [13].

3. SEMANTIC SIMILARITY LEARNING

In this section, we first explore the property of the traditional *Maximum Joint Likelihood Learning* (MJLL) on the shared representation learning, then introduce our proposed learning method.

3.1 Multimodal Learning

The standard multimodal network is a modification of *Restricted Boltzmann Machine* (RBM), which is an undirected graphical model that defines a probability distribution of the generated features of different modalities using shared hidden layers [6], named as *Multimodal RBM* (MRBM[1]). The traditional MJLL for MRBM is to maximize the joint distribution over the high-level features of modalities, which contains not only the conditional likelihood across different modalities but also the likelihood of each modality [14]. Although the shared information exists in both modalities is more credible than the single modality, MJLL has weakness in keeping the shared information under the influence of specific modality.

To further explore the effect of single modality on the shared layer of MRBM with the MJLL training, we adopt the general multimodal task, *Audiovisual Speech Recognition* (AVSR), which makes use of the information from both audio and visual modalities for recognition. Inspired by denoising auto-encoders [16], we separately take audio and visual representation as the input to the MRBM and set the other one zero at testing time. Meanwhile, we also take the concatenation of them as the inputs as usual. Fig. 1 shows the activation state of the shared hidden units of MRBM. It's clear to find that both modalities have activated similar hidden units, which confirms the shared information between them, so that they have nearly common influence on

[1]Detailed presentation can be found in the supplementary material.

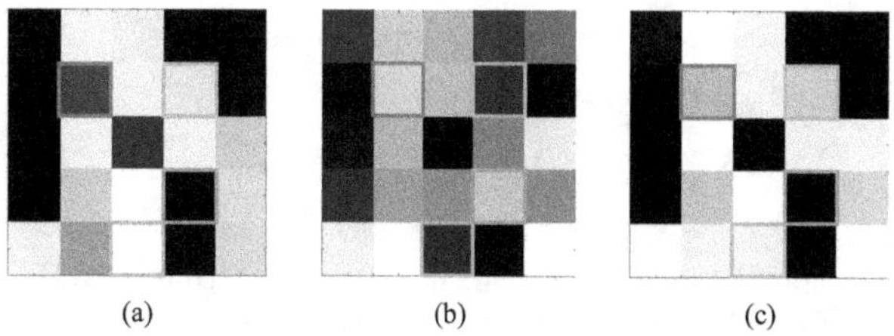

Figure 1: Visualization of activation state of the hidden units of MRBM with different inputs to the visible layer after MJLL learning. (a) Only audio modality. (b) Only visual modality. (c) Both audio and visual modality. The unit in complete white means fully activated state. Best viewed in color.

the shared representation, as shown in Fig. 1(c). However, there're also some units a bit different from them. To be specific, these units are separated into four groups with different colors. In these groups, different modalities have opposite influences on the shared representation. This is because some modality-specific properties are not relevant. For example, the shape size of mouth when a person is speaking or pronouncing a certain letter has little correlation with the corresponding voice. In fact, these cases may make the shared representation confused as described above, which should be penalized to keep the shared information across modalities. In this paper, we propose to learn the shared representation via reducing the differences between the high-level features based on the MJLL with the perspective of semantic similarity, which actually encourages the shared representation to keep the common information across modalities and reduce the influence from specific modality.

3.2 Objective Function

Suppose that $\mathbf{x}$ and $\mathbf{y}$ are the high-level representations obtained from two modality-specific networks. Let $\mathbf{H}^x \in R^{m\times n}$ and $\mathbf{H}^y \in R^{m\times n}$ denote the activation results of hidden layer $\mathbf{h}$ of the two modalities in MRBM framework, where m is the number of hidden units and n is the size of training set. They are used to evaluate the contribution of each modality to the shared representation, which should be similar. In this case, the goal is to enhance the similarity over $\mathbf{H}^x$ and $\mathbf{H}^y$, therefore, the objective function for MRBM becomes

$$\begin{aligned} &\text{minimize}_{\{\mathbf{W}^x,\mathbf{W}^y,\mathbf{b}^x,\mathbf{b}^y,\mathbf{b}^h\}} \\ &\qquad -\log p(\mathbf{x},\mathbf{y}) + \lambda\ \text{sim}(\mathbf{H}^{\text{x}},\mathbf{H}^{\text{y}}), \end{aligned} \tag{1}$$

where $p(\mathbf{x},\mathbf{y})$ is the joint likelihood over the two modalities based on the aforementioned MRBM, $\mathbf{W}^x$ is a matrix of pairwise weights between elements of $\mathbf{x}$ and $\mathbf{h}$, and similar for $\mathbf{W}^y$. $\mathbf{b}^x$, $\mathbf{b}^y$, $\mathbf{b}^h$ are bias vectors for $\mathbf{x}$, $\mathbf{y}$, and $\mathbf{h}$, respectively. And λ in Eq. 1 is a regularization constant. The regularization (i.e. $\text{sim}(\mathbf{H}^x, \text{H}^y)$, the similarity function) is a penalty to traditional objective function, which provides convenient fashion to control the similarity between the high-level representations of modalities. As the activation value of hidden units is between 0 and 1 when using the sigmoid activation function, it is intuitive to employ the cross-entropy to measure the similarity as follows,

$$\begin{aligned}\mathrm{sim}\left(\mathbf{H}^x, \mathbf{H}^y\right) &= \mathbb{H}(\mathbf{H}^x \parallel \mathbf{H}^y) \\ &= -\sum_{j,k}\left[\mathbf{H}^x_{jk}\log\mathbf{H}^y_{jk} + (1-\mathbf{H}^x_{jk})\log(1-\mathbf{H}^y_{jk})\right]. \end{aligned} \quad (2)$$

Note that the cross-entropy is not symmetry, that is $\mathbb{H}(\mathbf{H}^x \parallel \mathbf{H}^y) \neq \mathbb{H}(\mathbf{H}^y \parallel \mathbf{H}^x)$, so we also take the second form and make comparison between them.

As CCA is a standard statistical method to find a linear correlation of two kinds of data [5], we also employ it to measure the similarity via the following general solution to CCA [10],

$$\mathrm{sim}(\mathbf{H}^x, \mathbf{H}^y) = -\mathrm{corr}(\mathbf{H}^x, \mathbf{H}^y) = -\|\mathbf{T}\|_{tr}, \quad (3)$$

where $\mathbf{T} = \sum_{xx}^{-1/2}\sum_{xy}\sum_{yy}^{-1/2}$, and $\|\cdot\|_{tr}$ is the matrix trace norm. $\sum_{xx}$ and $\sum_{yy}$ denotes the auto-covariance of $\mathbf{H}^x$ and $\mathbf{H}^x$, respectively. And the cross-covariance $\sum_{xy}$ is over $\{\mathbf{H}^x, \mathbf{H}^y\}$. Finally, both the cross-entropy and CCA are treated as the similarity functions and considered in this paper.

For the optimization of Eq. 1, the gradient of the regularization term is performed based on batch-size following the *Contrastive Divergence* (CD) algorithm [4]. Due to space limit, we defer the details about the optimization to supplementary material. And we summarize the learning procedure in Algorithm 1.

Algorithm 1 SSL algorithm for MRBM

1: Initialize model parameters.
2: Update the parameters with respect to each modality $\{\mathbf{x}, \mathbf{y}\}$ using CD learning rule.
3: Update the parameters using the gradient of the regularization term[2].
4: Repeat above steps 2 and 3 until convergence or K steps.

4. EXPERIMENTS

In this section, we conduct sets of experiments for evaluating the SSL. Various kinds of modalities are experimented, including image, audio, and text. And for all the experiments, the parameter λ is fixed at 0.1 that is chosen from $\{10, 1, 0.1, 0.001, 0.0001\}$ and has been validated in the experiments.

4.1 Toy example

We first make a simple experiment on the MNIST handwritten digit recognition dataset [9], which consists of 60,000 train images and 10,000 test images. The 28×28 matrix of pixels in the original image is split into left and right part as two modalities, as these two parts constitute the whole image and share similar semantic information. In this experiment, the setting can be considered as a toy example of multimodal learning as in [1, 14]. Full image (left + right) is for both the training and testing, but we also test the algorithms with the single part. Table 1 shows the recognition errors obtained with different learning methods. Although the error of SSL is a little higher than MJLL in the case of full image input, it shows noticeable decreases for each single modality input, especially the SSL with cross-entropy function. Specifically, the improvements of error may come from the more exact gradient of MJLL with *Persistent CD* (PCD) compared with SSL that uses CD method. Nevertheless, we consider that the enhanced shared representations in SSL provide each modality more reliable discriminative information via the learned parameters and lead to the above decreases.

[2]The bias term has little influence on the activation of hidden units for MRBM in the experiments, so only the weight terms are considered in this case.

Table 1: The recognition error (%) obtained with different learning methods of MRBM on the MNIST dataset.

Method	Similarity function	Left+Right	Left	Right
MJLL [7]	-	**1.57**	14.98	18.88
SSL	$\mathbb{H}(\mathbf{H}^x \parallel \mathbf{H}^y)$	1.73	**11.93**	**15.87**
	$\mathbb{H}(\mathbf{H}^y \parallel \mathbf{H}^x)$	1.64	11.98	18.31
	$\mathrm{corr}(\mathbf{H}^x, \mathbf{H}^y)$	1.78	13.23	16.20

Table 2: The classification results (MAP) on the MIR-Flickr dataset. Both MJLL and SSL are implemented based on the MDBN.

Method	Similarity function	Text+Image	Image
MJLL [15]	-	59.77	45.78
SSL	$\mathbb{H}(\mathbf{H}^x \parallel \mathbf{H}^y)$	59.84	46.78
	$\mathbb{H}(\mathbf{H}^y \parallel \mathbf{H}^x)$	59.8	47.74
	$\mathrm{corr}(\mathbf{H}^x, \mathbf{H}^y)$	**60.29**	**53.29**

4.2 Image-text

In this experiment, we employ the MIR-Flickr Data set [8] to evaluate our method in the multimodal classification task. The dataset consists of 1 million images and corresponding user assigned tags from the photograpy website Flickr. Among the images, 25,000 are annotated for 24 potential topics and 14 strict category labels. We use the same visual and text features and follow the pre-processing in [15], where the image feature is processed into zero-mean and unit variance for each dimension and the text feature is represented using a word count of the 2000 most frequency tags. We use the random selected 15,000 for training and the rest 10,000 for testing. The performance metric adopts the *Mean Average Precision* (MAP). As for the model architecture, modality-specific deep network of [3857, 1024, 1024] and [2000, 1024, 1024] are built for image and text, respectively. And the shared hidden layer of MRBM consists of 2048 units. Thus, the network is truly a *Multimodal Deep Belief Network* (MDBN) [15].

Table 2 shows the MAP obtained by different learning methods in the cases of different inputs at testing time, i.e., multimodal input (image+text) and unimodal input (image). The proposed SSL outperforms the MJLL in all the settings. There are two points we should pay attention to. First, the improvement in the unimodal case is much higher than the multimodal case, that maybe come from the same reason as the toy example. The added regularization term reduces the uncertain parts and enhances the shared parts at the high-level representation of image modality, even makes

Table 3: Audiovisual speech classification performance (accuracy) implemented by different learning methods on two datasets.

Dataset	Method	Similarity function	AV	A
AVLetters2	MJLL[11]	-	59.89	70.88
	SSL	$\mathbb{H}(\mathbf{H}^x \parallel \mathbf{H}^y)$	68.68	74.18
		$\mathbb{H}(\mathbf{H}^y \parallel \mathbf{H}^x)$	64.28	73.62
		$\text{corr}(\mathbf{H}^x, \mathbf{H}^y)$	**70.88**	**75.82**
AVDigits	MJLL[11]	-	58.89	63.89
	SSL	$\mathbb{H}(\mathbf{H}^x \parallel \mathbf{H}^y)$	63.89	71.07
		$\mathbb{H}(\mathbf{H}^y \parallel \mathbf{H}^x)$	60.00	70.56
		$\text{corr}(\mathbf{H}^x, \mathbf{H}^y)$	**70.00**	**71.11**

the image network learn some transferred knowledge from text modality. Second, the CCA function performs much better than the other two, which may result from the efficient subspace learning of CCA, in which the image and text representations are embedded into highly linear correlation.

4.3 Audio-video

The last sets of experiments are conducted for AVSR, which is an interesting multimodal task. Two datasets are employed for testing, one is AVLetters2 [3] and the other is AVDigits [6]. AVLetters2 is about reading letters from A to Z, spoke by five people, seven times for each letter. Letters spoken by four people are for training and the rest one is for testing. Different from AVLetters2, AVDigits is about speaking digits from 0 to 9, spoke by six people, nine times for each digit. Letters spoken by four people are exploited to train and the rest two are exploited to test. Both datasets provide raw audio record and captured mouth movements.

The audio and visual data are preprocessed, respectively. We extract the spectrogram of the audio signal with 20ms hamming window and 10ms overlap. Then the obtained spectral coefficient is reduced to 50 dimensions using PCA whitening. As for the visual signal, the mouth shape is reshaped to 60×80 pixels and reduced to 100 principal components using PCA whitening as well. 4 audio frames and 1 video frame (almost the same duration) are used as the inputs to the networks. In this task, the MDAE framework [11] is chosen as the experimental network that is commonly used in AVSR.

In Table 3, we show the accuracy of different learning methods applied to the MDAE network, where the multimodal (audiovisual) and unimodal (audio) input setting are employed. There are three points we should pay attention to. First, similar to the above experimental results, the SSL outperforms the MJLL method on all the settings, which confirms the effectiveness of it in multimodal learning. Second, the SSL with cross-entropy of $\mathbb{H}(\mathbf{H}^x \parallel \mathbf{H}^y)$ performs better than $\mathbb{H}(\mathbf{H}^y \parallel \mathbf{H}^x)$, this is because the former is to force the visual modality to fit the expectation of the more reliable audio signal, which makes the shared representation more discriminative. Third, we also note that the audiovisual modality performs worse than single audio information. This is because the visual modality lowers the performance, which is a common situation [11]. But we can significantly reduce the gap between them via emphasizing the similar semantic, as shown in Table 3.

5. CONCLUSION

In this paper, we present a novel learning method for multimodal network in terms of the semantic similarity between the high-level representation of modalities. The conducted sets of experiments show that our method has remarkable improvements over traditional method on various multimodal deep networks. More importantly, the association among different modalities (i.e., image, audio, and text) are all enhanced, which demonstrates the efficient generalization of the method. But the learning is performed just in the M-RBM layers, a better solution may be found by searching the entire deep networks and inferring the modality-specific network with the SSL objective. Thus, a whole learning method of the multimodal deep networks should be derived in the future work.

6. ACKNOWLEDGEMENTS

This work is supported by the Fundamental Research Funds for the Central Universities (Grant no. 3102015BJ(II)JJZ01), the National Basic Research Program of China (973 Program) (Grant No. 2012CB719905), State Key Program of National Natural Science of China (Grant No. 61232010), the National Natural Science Foundation of China (Grant No. 61472413), and by the Open Research Fund of Key Laboratory of Spectral Imaging Technology, Chinese Academy of Sciences (Grant No. LSIT201408).

7. REFERENCES

[1] G. Andrew, R. Arora, J. Bilmes, and K. Livescu. Deep canonical correlation analysis. In *ICML*, pages 1247–1255, 2013.

[2] Y. Bengio, A. Courville, and P. Vincent. Representation learning: A review and new perspectives. *IEEE Transactions on PAMI*, 35(8):1798–1828, 2013.

[3] S. J. Cox, R. Harvey, Y. Lan, J. L. Newman, and B.-J. Theobald. The challenge of multispeaker lip-reading. In *AVSP*, pages 179–184, 2008.

[4] G. E. Hinton. Training products of experts by minimizing contrastive divergence. *Neural computation*, 14(8):1771–1800, 2002.

[5] H. Hotelling. Relations between two sets of variates. *Biometrika*, 28(3/4):321–377, 1936.

[6] D. Hu, X. Li, and X. Lu. Temporal multimodal learning in audiovisual speech recognition. In *CVPR*, 2016.

[7] J. Huang and B. Kingsbury. Audio-visual deep learning for noise robust speech recognition. In *ICASSP*, pages 7596–7599, 2013.

[8] M. J. Huiskes and M. S. Lew. The mir flickr retrieval evaluation. In *ACM MIR*, pages 39–43, 2008.

[9] Y. LeCun, L. Bottou, Y. Bengio, and P. Haffner. Gradient-based learning applied to document recognition. *Proceedings of the IEEE*, 86(11):2278–2324, 1998.

[10] K. V. Mardia, J. T. Kent, and J. M. Bibby. Multivariate analysis. 1980.

[11] J. Ngiam, A. Khosla, M. Kim, J. Nam, H. Lee, and A. Y. Ng. Multimodal deep learning. In *ICML*, pages 689–696, 2011.

[12] Y. Pang, Z. Ma, Y. Yuan, X. Li, and K. Wang. Multimodal learning for multi-label image classification. In *ICIP*, pages 1797–1800, 2011.

[13] X. Shu, G.-J. Qi, J. Tang, and J. Wang. Weakly-shared deep transfer networks for heterogeneous-domain knowledge propagation. In *ACM Multimedia*, pages 35–44, 2015.

[14] K. Sohn, W. Shang, and H. Lee. Improved multimodal deep learning with variation of information. In *NIPS*, pages 2141–2149, 2014.

[15] N. Srivastava and R. R. Salakhutdinov. Multimodal learning with deep boltzmann machines. In *NIPS*, pages 2222–2230, 2012.

[16] P. Vincent, H. Larochelle, Y. Bengio, and P.-A. Manzagol. Extracting and composing robust features with denoising autoencoders. In *ICML*, pages 1096–1103, 2008.

[17] A. Wang, J. Lu, G. Wang, J. Cai, and T.-J. Cham. Multi-modal unsupervised feature learning for rgb-d scene labeling. In *ECCV*, pages 453–467. 2014.

[18] W. Wang, R. Arora, K. Livescu, and J. Bilmes. On deep multi-view representation learning. In *ICML*, pages 1083–1092, 2015.

[19] Y. Zhen, Y. Gao, D.-Y. Yeung, H. Zha, and X. Li. Spectral multimodal hashing and its application to multimedia retrieval. *IEEE Transactions on cybernetics*, 46(1):27–38, 2016.

Multi-pose Facial Expression Recognition Using Transformed Dirichlet Process

Feifei Zhang†, Qirong Mao§, Ming Dong‡, Yongzhao Zhan†

† School of Computer Science and Communication Engineering
Jiangsu University
Zhenjiang, Jiangsu Province, 212013, China
susanzhang@ujs.edu.cn

§ Corresponding Author B
School of Computer Science and Communication Engineering
Jiangsu University
Zhenjiang, Jiangsu Province, 212013, China
mao_qr@ujs.edu.cn

‡ Corresponding Author A
Department of Computer Science
Wayne State University
Detroit, MI 48202, USA
mdong@cs.wayne.edu

ABSTRACT

Driven by recent advances in human-centered computing, Facial Expression Recognition (FER) has attracted significant attention in many applications. In this paper, we propose a novel graphical model, multi-level Transformed Dirichlet Process (ml-TDP), for multi-pose FER. In our approach, pose is explicitly introduced into ml-TDP so that separate training and parameter tuning for each pose is not required. In addition, ml-TDP can learn an intermediate facial expression representation subject to geometric constraints. By sharing the pool of spatially-coherent features over expressions and poses, we provide a scalable solution for multi-pose FER. Extensive experimental result on benchmark facial expression databases shows the superior performance of ml-TDP.

Keywords

Multi-pose facial expression recognition, Transformed Dirichlet process

1. INTRODUCTION

Facial expression is fundamental to human experience, influencing cognition, perception, and everyday tasks such as learning and communication. Driven by recent advances in human-centered computing, Facial Expression Recognition (FER) has attracted significant attention in applications such as human-computer interaction, face animation and analysis of social interaction.

Most of current models on FER are trained based on frontal or near-frontal face data. When a face turns sideways, the performance of these systems degenerates greatly. Although a handful of methods on multi-pose FER have been proposed recently [12], these models are typically learned and parameter-tuned separately for each pose. Thus, the system is not scalable, and its performance is heavily influenced by the model parameters.

MM '16, October 15-19, 2016, Amsterdam, Netherlands

DOI: http://dx.doi.org/10.1145/2964284.2967240

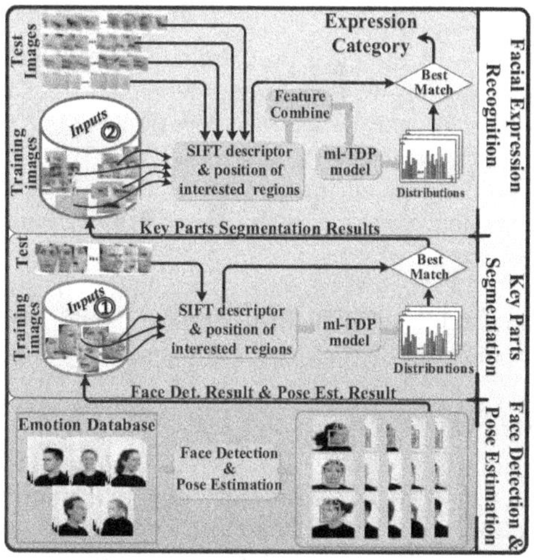

Figure 1: System Architecture

In FER, how to extract discriminative features from facial images is one of the central research issues. Features for FER can be roughly classified into three categories: 1) texture-based local features [2, 14, 3], 2) geometry-based global features [13, 3], and 3) hybrid features [20, 21]. In addition, texture features can be further classified into many subgroups, such as Gabor, Haar-like feature, Local Binary Patterns (LBP) and Scale Invariant Feature Transform (SIFT)-based descriptors. Bag of words models (e.g., probabilistic Latent Sematic Analysis) are frequently used to represent a face image as an orderless, independent collection of these features from local patches. This simplification completely ignores spatial information and thus does not work well with factors such as multi-poses [15].

FER usually employs a three-stage, sequential process consisting of feature extraction, feature selection and expression classification [20]. To achieve good recognition performance, extensive empirical studies are needed to search for an optimal combination of the three stages. The lack of a unified theoretical framework often leads to unsatisfactory results in multi-pose applications [11].

In this paper, we propose a novel graphical model, multi-level Transformed Dirichlet Process (ml-TDP), for unified multi-pose FER. In our approach, pose is explicitly introduced into a multi-level, spatially-coherent Transformed Dirichlet Process (TDP) model for robust key parts segmentation and expression recognition. The major contributions of this paper can be summarized as follows:

1. ml-TDP provides a unified model for multi-pose FER that mainly manifests in two aspects: 1) it integrates key parts segmentation and FER in a multi-level, unified graphical model and 2) pose is explicitly introduced in ml-TDP so that separate training and parameter tuning for each pose is not required. Thus, ml-TDP provides a scalable solution for multi-pose FER.
2. A facial image in our model is described by the segmented parts including the positions and corresponding appearance features. That is, the geometric constraints among different facial parts are implicitly encoded in our model and integrated with the appearance features to facilitate multi-pose FER. Thus, ml-TDP can obtain high recognition rate even with large pose variations.
3. TDP is a hierarchical probabilistic theme model with improvement on the feature independence assumption made in Latent Dirichlet Allocation (LDA) and Hierarchical Dirichlet Process (HDP) models. In FER, ml-TDP learns an intermediate facial expression representation, constrained by the spatial structure of a facial image.

The rest of the paper is organized as follows. In Section 2, we introduce ml-TDP for FER in details. The experimental results are given in Section 3. Finally, Section 4 concludes.

2. ML-TDP FOR MULTI-POSE FER

The architecture of our FER system is shown in Fig. 1, which cascades two levels of TDP to make coarse-to-fine prediction for key parts segmentation and expression recognition, one level per task. Before passing an image to our system, we first perform face detection and pose estimation using a tree-based part model [22]. After the preprocessing, in the first level of ml-TDP, we detect the key parts (e.g., eyes, nose, mouth) in the facial area using features extracted from Elliptical Interest Regions (EIRs) and the corresponding spatial locations. Then, in the second level, features from the key parts are used to build ml-TDP model for FER. Next, we first review Dirichlet Process (DP) [4] and then introduce our ml-TDP model for multi-pose FER in details.

2.1 Dirichlet Process and TDP

DP [4] is a Bayesian nonparametric probabilistic model where a Dirichlet random variable θ with k-dimensionality have the property: $\theta_i \geq 0, \sum_{i=1}^{k} \theta_i = 1$. DP describes the distribution of θ with the following probability density:

$$DP(\alpha,\theta) = \frac{\Gamma(\Sigma_{i=1}^{k}\alpha_i)}{\Pi_{i=1}^{k}\Gamma(\alpha_i)}\theta_1^{\alpha_1-1}...\theta_k^{\alpha_k-1}, \quad (1)$$

where the parameter α is a k-vector with components $\alpha_i > 1$ and Γ is the Gamma function. HDP [17] is an extension of the DP, mainly used to clustering grouped data. HDP uses a DP for each group of data, with the DPs for all groups sharing a base distribution which is itself drawn from a DP.

TDP [18] model generalizes HDP by applying a random set of transformations to each clustering center, and therefore the dependencies of the local patches are encoded. Our approach differs from the traditional TDP model in two aspects: 1) we introduce a variable c for pose in TDP to cope with the multi-pose FER, rather than using separated models for different poses; and 2) we build a multi-level structure to provide a unified solution of feature extraction and expression recognition.

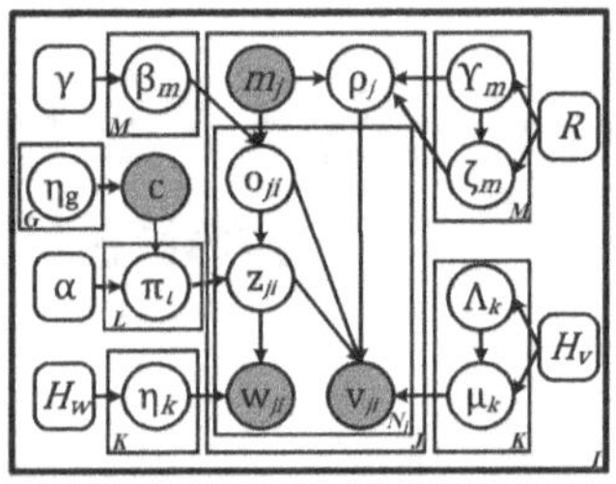

Figure 2: Graphical Model of ml-TDP

2.2 Structure of ml-TDP

Fig. 2 shows a graphical illustration of our ml-TDP model, in which variable I denotes the different levels, and variable c for poses. Pose is explicitly introduced as an observable variable because it is one of the factors that could influence the results of multi-pose FER. In addition, it can be estimated with high accuracy. Note that the graphical model of each level is the same, shown in the outermost rectangle. The only difference among the levels is the input. Next we use the expression recognition level as an example to present our model in details.

The input to the expression recognition level is the segmented key parts. After segmentation, suppose we have J facial parts (e.g., noses, mouths, eyes) in total, belonging to C poses and M expressions, our model can be described by the following generative process.

1. EIR is the basic unit of an image, and the ith EIR of image j is described by its detected location v_{ji} and discrete appearance feature w_{ji}, typically represented by the codewords in a codebook. That is $EIR_i = (v, w, t)$ with label $t = c \cdot m$, where $c = \{1, ..., C\}$ and $m = \{1, ..., M\}$ are the pose and facial expression labels, respectively.
2. The expression transformation ρ_j provides a reference to each of L latent objects o_{ji}, and is used to model their spatial relationship. Specifically, $\rho_j \sim N(\xi_m, \Upsilon_m)$ with normal-inverse-Wishart priors $(\xi, \Upsilon) \sim R$, where N is a Gaussian transformation distribution for each facial expression.
3. For a face image with pose c, draw a parameter π from the multinomial distribution $\pi \sim p(\pi|c, \alpha)$ to determine the distribution of the latent topics z, where α is a Dirichlet prior on the training sets.
4. An image is a collection of N EIRs, denoted by $j = (EIR_1, EIR_2, ..., EIR_N)$.
   4.1 Choose a latent topic $z \sim p(z|\pi)$, where $p(.)$ is a multinomial distribution. z is a K-dimensional unit vector and K is the number of latent topics.
   4.2 Choose a $EIR \sim p(EIR|z, \eta)$ with a latent topic z, where η is a $K \times T$ matrix, T is the total number of codewords in the codebook.

In our model, the Dirichlet parameter α is at the pose-levels, sampled once in the process of generating a pose. The multinomial variable π is at the theme-level, sampled once per face image. Through these parameters, the model can learn the relationships among different poses by sharing the pool of features.

Given the parameters ρ, π, c, o belonging to the ℓth latent object, the object features w, v and theme z are computed via a finite mixture model:

$$\begin{aligned} &p(w_{ji}, v_{ji}, z_{ji} | \rho_j, \pi_\ell, c, o_{ji} = \ell) \\ &= p(c|\eta) \sum_{k=1}^{K} \pi_{\ell k} \eta_k(w_{ji}) N(v_{ji}; \mu_k + \rho_{j\ell}, \Lambda_k) \\ &= p(c|\eta) \sum_{k=1}^{K} p(\pi_{\ell k} | c, \alpha) p(w_{ji} | z_{ji}, \eta_k) p(v_{ji} | \rho_j, \mu_k, \Lambda_k) \end{aligned} \quad (2)$$

2.3 Gibbs Sampling for ml-TDP

In this section, we describe a Markov Chain Monte Carlo (MCMC) [16] sampling scheme for ml-TDP. Our goal is to obtain a probability matrix and the theme distribution for every expression. Specifically, the sampling process can be described as follows. First, we remove feature (w_{ji}, v_{ji}) from the cached statistics for its current topic and expression category. Second, for each of the $L \cdot K$ pairs of latent object categories and themes, we determine the predictive likelihood as

$$f_{\ell k}^{t}(w_{ji} = w, v_{ji}) = (\frac{C_{kw} + \lambda/T}{\sum_{w'} C_{kw'} + \lambda}) \cdot N(v_{ji} - \rho_{jl}^{(t-1)}; \widehat{\mu}_k, \widehat{\Lambda}_k) \quad (3)$$

where $i \in \{\tau(1), ..., \tau(n_j)\}$, n_j is the number of features in image j, and $\tau(\cdot)$ denotes a random permutation. $v_{ji} - \rho_{jl}^{(t-1)}$ is the location parameter where the superscript t is the index of sampling iterations. $(\widehat{\mu}_k, \widehat{\Lambda}_k)$ is the scale parameter. C_{kw} is the number of times each appearance feature assigned to topic k, and T is the dictionary size through K-means clustering. Third, we sample new objects and topics from the following $L \cdot K$-dim multinomial distribution:

$$\begin{aligned} (o_{ji}, z_{ji}) \sim &\sum_{l=1}^{L} \sum_{K=1}^{k} (M_{m\ell} + \gamma/L) \\ &(\frac{N_{lk} + \alpha/K}{\sum_{k'} N_{lk'} + \alpha}) f_{lk}(w_{ji}, v_{ji}) \delta(o_{ji}, l) \delta(z_{ji}, k) \end{aligned} \quad (4)$$

where $M_{m\ell}$ is the number of the features associated with each latent object, and $N_{\ell k}$ represents the number of the features associated with each latent theme. Fourth, feature (w_{ji}, v_{ji}) is added to the cached statistics for its new object and topic. Finally, we fix (o_j, z_j) and sample a new reference transformation ρ_j^t, and update the features for theme $k = z_{ji}$ accordingly. The training process is stopped at the convergence of MCMC.

2.4 Bayesian Inference

In order to perform FER, we need to construct a probability matrix for each facial expressions m. Let θ_i^m denote the mixture components, which is decided by the multinomial distribution η_k for the appearance features and the Gaussian distribution for the location features $N(\mu_k + \rho_j, \Lambda_k)$. Specifically, the probability matrix can be represented by $p(w_j, v_j | \theta_i^m)$. Assuming that an unknown testing image j has N local EIRs, represented by features $(w_n, v_n), n = \{1, ..., N\}$, the probability $p(j|m)$ is calculated as,

$$\begin{aligned} p(j|m) &= \prod_{n=1:N} p(w_n, v_n | m) \\ &= \prod_{n=1:N} (\sum_i p(w_n, v_n | \theta_i^m) p(\theta_i^m | m)) \end{aligned} \quad (5)$$

Expression recognition is then achieved by maximizing the probability,

$$m = \arg\max_m p(j|m) \quad (6)$$

2.5 Expression Feature Extraction

Given an input image, we first detect a set of EIRs using Harris-affine region detectors. Then, SIFT features are extracted from these EIRs. Through k-means clustering, we identify a finite dictionary of the SIFT features, which later on are combined with the spatial location of EIRs to implicitly enforce facial geometric constraints. Finally, based on the collected training data, we build the ml-TDP model and obtain the distribution of codewords on latent themes and that of themes on each expression and pose.

These distributions are called intermediate features or latent expression themes. They provide a shared pool of spatially-coherent expression features in a unified framework, scalable to a large number of poses and expressions. For example, we can intuitively understand the intermediate features for disgust expression such as wrinkling nose and raised upper lip. The latent aspects of facial images, hidden behind the feature vector, once discovered, are well suited to reveal the distinctions between multi-pose facial expressions, and thus lead to higher accuracy of recognition.

3. EXPERIMENTS AND RESULTS

In this section, we evaluate ml-TDP on two well-known facial expression databases: BU-3DFE [19] and Radboud Faces Database (RAFD) [10]. In BU-3DFE, there are 100 3D subjects. We render 2D facial images at four levels of intensity and in five yaw views $(90°, 60°, 45°, 30°, 0°)$ with six facial expressions: anger, disgust, fear, happiness, sadness and surprise. Thus, we have $100 \times 6 \times 5 \times 4 = 12,000$ facial images in total for our experiment. RAFD contains a set of pictures of 67 actors displaying eight different emotions with five different poses $(180°, 135°, 90°, 45°$ and $0°)$, 8,040 face images in total. In our experiments, we consider all of the eight emotions with three yaw views $(135°, 90°, 45°)$. Consequently, we have $67 \times 8 \times 3 \times 3 = 4,824$ facial images. FER performance of ml-TDP is evaluated using ten-fold cross validation on both databases, and compared with several state-of-the-art FER methods in the literature.

3.1 Key Parts Segmentation

We first show some exemplar results of key parts segmentation on RAFD and BU-3DFE. First, a codebook is learned based on SIFT features from 2,400 images, 100 for each expression and pose, and the size of the codebook is fixed as 180. Then we iterate 500 rounds for each patch using MCMC, and α (Eq. 2) and γ (Eq. 4) are set at 0.1 and 1.5, respectively.

Fig. 3 gives several examples about the key parts segmentation. In Fig. 3, row A shows the input images; row B shows the EIRs detected and their initial latent topic assignments; row C gives the topic assignments after TDP learning; and row D gives the final results (key parts segmentation). From the images in row B, we can see that the EIRs are mainly distributed in the regions where the texture has significant changes. A closer look at row C clearly shows that most of the EIRs on the key facial subregions are colored in red, indicating that ml-TDP can successfully perform key parts segmentation on multi-pose images.

3.2 FER on BU-3DEF and RAFD

In this section, we report FER performance of ml-TDP on BU-3DFE and RAFD. In our experiments, a dictionary

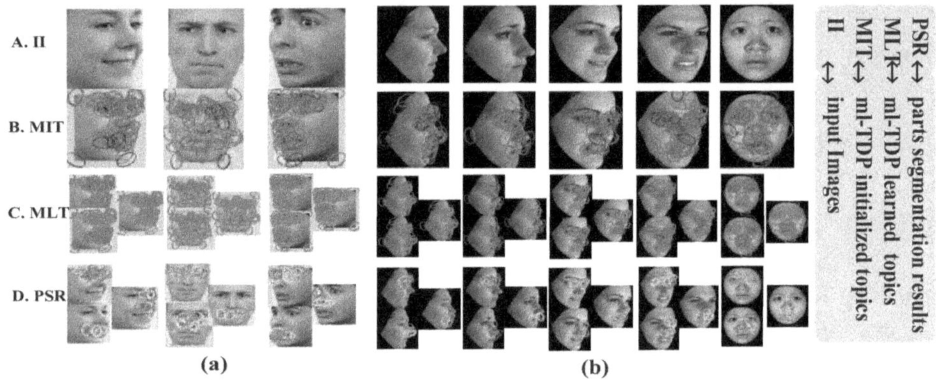

Figure 3: Key parts segmentation results on RAFD (a) and BU-3DFE (b)(this figure must be viewed in colors)

Method	Classifier	Features	Poses	Expressions		Recognition Rates(%)
				number	levels	
Hu et al.[6]	pose-wise svm	41 landmarks	5	6	1,2,3,4	66.7
Hu et al.[7]	single knn	SIFT+LPP	5	6	2,3,4	73.8
Zheng et al. [21]	knn	83 landmark points	5	6	1,2,3,4	78.3
Moore and Bowden [12]	pose-wise svm	LBP^{ms}(multi-scale LBP)	5	6	1,2,3,4	65.0
Moore and Bowden [12]	pose-wise svm	$LGBP$(Local Gabor BP)	5	6	1,2,3,4	68.0
Moore and Bowden [12]	pose-wise svm	LGBP/LBP^{ms}	5	6	1,2,3,4	71.1
Zheng et al. [20]	svm	Sparse SIFT	5	6	1,2,3,4	**78.9**
Jampour et al. [9]	svm	HOG+LBP	5	6	4	77.87
Jampour et al. [8]	svm	HOG+LBP	5	6	4	78.79
ml-TDP(ours)	TDP	SIFT with geometric constraints	5	6	1,2,3,4	**79.3**

Table 1: FER on BU-3DFE. The best and second best results are highlighted in bold.

of 150 codewords is built using 3,000 images and we iterate 800 epochs for each patch when sampling.

We first evaluate ml-TDP by comparing its performance with multi-pose FER results recently reported in the literature [6, 7, 21, 12, 20, 9, 8] on BU-3DEF. Details regarding each reported results, e.g., features, classifiers, the number of poses, and the number and level of expressions, are summarized in Table 1. ml-TDP is evaluated under the same experiment setting, and the FER accuracy is reported in the last column. The results clearly show that ml-TDP outperforms the existing methods with a 0.4% to 16.2% improvement on FER accuracy. Specifically, the average recognition accuracy on BU-3DFE of each pose are: 80.1% (0°), 80.9% (30°), 82.1% (45°), 77.6% (60°), and 75.8% (90°).

In order to evaluate the effect of pose estimation noises on FER accuracy, we performed additional experiments in which the face poses are set based on the ground truth provided in BU-3DEF, and obtained an average accuracy of 79.8%, slightly higher than our previous results at 79.3%. This shows that our system works well for both pose estimation and expression recognition.

Next, we conduct experiments on RAFD and compare ml-TDP with three well-known classification models: sLDA [1], TDP [16], and multi-SVM [5]. Specifically, sLDA and TDP are trained based on the facial images with expressions regardless of poses, while the multi-SVM model consists of 3 SVMs, each trained separately with expression images under the specific pose. The same set of features, SIFT with geometric constraints, are used in these experiments. Figures 4(a) and 4(b) provide recognition accuracy averaged over each pose and expression. Average recognition accuracy of the four methods is also reported in the right of figure 4(b) (75.00%, 63.32%, 63.74%, 66.15%, respectively). Overall, our method gets the highest recognition accuracy of

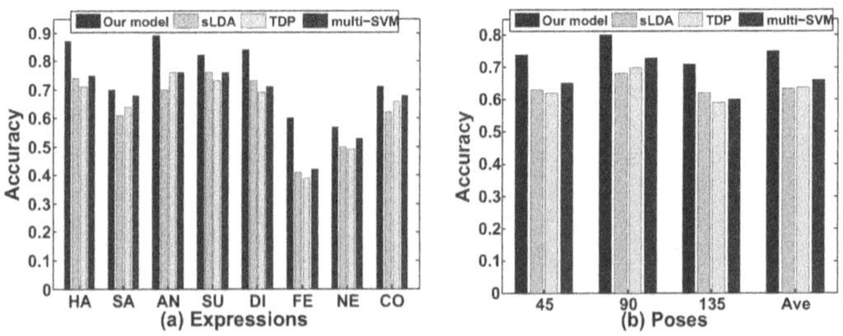

Figure 4: Performance comparison among our model, sLDA, TDP and multi-SVM on RAFD. (a): Recognition accuracy across eight expressions and (b): across three poses.

75.00%. The significant accuracy gain over sLDA and TDP shows the advantage of explicitly introducing poses in our model. In addition, our unified model avoids the separate training in multi-SVM model, and thus highly scalable to the large number of poses occurred in real-world environments.

4. CONCLUSIONS

In this paper, we proposed a novel graphical model, ml-TDP, for multi-pose FER. Pose is explicitly introduced into ml-TDP so that separate training and parameter tuning for each pose is not required. By sharing the pool of spatially-coherent features over expressions and poses, we provide a scalable solution for multi-pose FER. Experiments on benchmark facial expression databases show the superior performance of our model.

5. ACKNOWLEDGMENT

This work was partially supported by the National Nature Science Foundation of China (No. 61272211 and No. 61170126), by the Six Talent Peaks Foundation of Jiangsu Province under Grant DZXX-027 and by the General Financial Grant from the China Postdoctoral Science Foundation 2015M570413.

6. REFERENCES

[1] D. Blei and J. McAuliffe. Supervised topic models. *Proceedings of Advances in Neural Information Processing Systems*, pages 121–128, 2008.

[2] J. Chen and Y. Ariki. Robust facial expressions recognition using 3d average face and ameliorated adaboost. *Proceedings of the 21st ACM International Conference on Multimedia*, pages 661–664, 2013.

[3] S. Eleftheriadis, O. Rudovic, and M. Pantic. Discriminative shared Gaussian processes for multiview and view-invariant facial expression recognition. *IEEE Transactions on Image Processing*, 24(1):189–204, 2015.

[4] M. Escobar and M. West. Bayesian density estimation and inference using mixtures. *Journal of the American Statistical Association*, 90(430):577–588, 1995.

[5] N. Hesse, T. Gehrig, H. Gao, and H. Ekenel. Multi-view facial expression recognition using local appearance features. *Proceedings of the 21st International Conference on Pattern Recognition*, pages 3533–3536, 2012.

[6] Y. Hu, Z. Zeng, L. Yin, X. Wei, J. Tu, and T. Huang. A study of non-frontal-view facial expressions recognition. *Proceedings of the 19th International Conference on Pattern Recognition*, pages 1–4, 2008.

[7] Y. Hu, Z. Zeng, L. Yin, X. Wei, X. Zhou, and T. Huang. Multi-view facial expression recognition. *Proceedings of the 8th IEEE International Conference on Automatic Face and Gesture Recognition*, pages 1–6, 2008.

[8] M. Jampour, V. Lepetit, and T. Mauthner. Pose-specific non-linear mappings in feature space towards multiview facial expression recognition. *Image and Vision Computing*, 2016.

[9] M. Jampour, T. Mauthner, and H. Bischof. Pairwise linear regression: An efficient and fast multi-view facial expression recognition. *IEEE International Conference and Workshops on Automatic Face and Gesture Recognition*, 1:1–8, 2015.

[10] O. Langner, R. Dotsch, G. Bijlstra, D. Wigboldus, and S. Hawk. Ad van knippenberg: Presentation and validation of the radboud faces database. *Cognition Emotion*, 24(8):1377–1388, 2010.

[11] P. Liu, S. Han, Z. Meng, and Y. Tong. Facial expression recognition via a boosted deep belief network. *Proceedings of IEEE Conference on Computer Vision and Pattern Recognition*, pages 1805–1812, 2014.

[12] S. Moore and R. Bowden. Local Binary Patterns for multiview facial expression recognition. *Computer Vision and Image Understanding*, 115(4):541–558, 2011.

[13] O. Rudovic, M. Pantic, and I. Patras. Coupled Gaussian processes for pose-invariant facial expression recognition. *IEEE Transactions on Pattern Analysis and Machine Intelligence*, 35(6):1357–1369, 2013.

[14] E. Sangineto, G. Zen, and E. Ricci. We are not all equal: Personalizing models for facial expression analysis with transductive parameter transfer. *Proceedings of the 22nd ACM International Conference on Multimedia*, pages 357–366, 2014.

[15] X. Shen, Z. Lin, J. Brandt, and Y. Wu. Detecting and aligning faces by image retrieval. *Proceedings of IEEE Conference on Computer Vision and Pattern Recognition*, pages 3460–3467, 2013.

[16] E. Sudderth, A. Torralba, W. Freeman, and A. Willsky. Describing visual scenes using transformed objects and parts. *International Journal of Computer Vision*, 77(1-3):291–330, 2008.

[17] Y. Teh, M. Jordan, M. Beal, and D. Blei. Hierarchical Dirichlet processes. *Journal of the American Statistical Association*, 101:1566–1581, 2006.

[18] A. Torralba, A. Willsky, and E. Sudderth. Describing visual scenes using transformed Dirichlet processes. *Proceedings of Advances in Neural Information Processing Systems*, pages 1297–1304, 2005.

[19] L. Yin, X. Wei, Y. Sun, J. Wang, and M. Rosato. A 3d facial expression database for facial behavior research. *Proceedings of the 7th International Conference on Automatic Face and Gesture Recognition*, pages 211–216, 2006.

[20] W. Zheng. Multi-view facial expression recognition based on group sparse reduced-rank regression. *IEEE Transactions on Affective Computing*, 5(1):71–85, 2014.

[21] W. Zheng, H. Tang, Z. Lin, and T. Huang. A novel approach to expression recognition from non-frontal face images. *Proceedings of IEEE 12th International Conference on Computer Vision*, pages 1901–1908, 2009.

[22] X. Zhu and D. Ramanan. Face detection, pose estimation, and landmark localization in the wild. *Proceedings of IEEE Conference on Computer Vision and Pattern Recognition*, pages 2879–2886, 2012.

Neighborhood-Preserving Hashing for Large-Scale Cross-Modal Search

Botong Wu
Nat'l Engineering Laboratory for Video Technology
Cooperative Medianet Innovation Center
Key Laboratory of Machine Perception (MoE)
Sch'l of EECS, Peking University, Beijing, 100871, China
botongwu@pku.edu.cn

Yizhou Wang
Nat'l Engineering Laboratory for Video Technology
Cooperative Medianet Innovation Center
Key Laboratory of Machine Perception (MoE)
Sch'l of EECS, Peking University, Beijing, 100871, China
Yizhou.Wang@pku.edu.cn

ABSTRACT

In the literature of cross-modal search, most methods employ linear models to pursue hash codes that preserve data similarity, in terms of Euclidean distance, both within-modal and across-modal. However, data dimensionality can be quite different across modalities. It is known that the behavior of Euclidean distance/similarity between datapoints can be drastically different in linear spaces of different dimensionality. In this paper, we identify this "variation of dimensionality" problem in cross-modal search that may harm most of distance-based methods. We propose a semi-supervised nonlinear probabilistic cross-modal hashing method, namely Neighborhood-Preserving Hashing (NPH), to alleviate the negative effect due to the variation of dimensionality issue. Inspired by tSNE [19], rather than preserve pairwise data distances, we propose to learn hash codes that preserve neighborhood relationship of datapoints via matching their conditional distribution derived from distance to that of datapoints of multi-modalities. Experimental results on three real-world datasets demonstrate that the proposed method outperforms the state-of-the-art distance-based semi-supervised cross-modal hashing methods as well as many fully-supervised ones.

Keywords

Cross-Modal; Hashing; Neighborhood-Preserving

1. INTRODUCTION

Nowadays heterogeneous data are ubiquitous. For example, it is common to see an article on a webpage elucidating topics by embedding images, video clips and/or hyperlinks into text. Hence, there emerges a high demand on retrieving one type of data using data of another modality about similar topics, *e.g.*, using text to search for relevant images, or vice versa. Consequently, many cross-modal or cross-view retrieval methods have been proposed to solve the heterogeneous data retrieval problem *e.g.*, [30, 15, 32]. With the explosive growth of data, how to efficiently retrieve from large-scale datasets is a big challenge. Hashing based methods are proposed as an efficient means to tackle the challenge. However, most existing hashing methods (*e.g.*, [22, 12, 4, 24, 31, 9, 14]) are unimodal.

MM '16, October 15-19, 2016, Amsterdam, Netherlands

 ISBN 978-1-4503-3603-1/16/10...$15.00

DOI: http://dx.doi.org/10.1145/2964284.2967241

Recently, quite a number of cross-modal hashing methods have been proposed, *e.g.*, [2, 34, 27, 11, 33, 13, 35, 28, 29, 10, 5, 21, 23, 8]. Cross-modal hashing may be divided into supervised methods and semi-supervised ones by whether a method is using semantic information or not. In this paper, we propose a semi-supervised cross-modal hashing method for large-scale search. In the last years, several semi-supervised methods have been proposed. For example, Cross-View Hashing (CVH) [10] extends spectral hashing [24] to the cross-modal setting by preserving within-modal-similarity and cross-modal-similarity. Collective Matrix Factorization Hashing (CMFH) [5] and Semantic Topic Multimodal Hashing (STMH) [21] pursue a single set of hash codes to preserve data distance across modalities. CMFH method learns shared codes by collective matrix factorization with a latent factor model from different modalities. STMH method learns a set of hash codes of the text modality in accordance with the topics learned by a clustering based method. Similar to CVH and CMFH, Partial Multi-Modal Hashing ($\mathbf{PM^2H}$) [23] also learns shared hash codes by linear matrix decomposition to preserve data distance across different modalities. The within-modal-similarity is preserved using graph Laplacian as in CVH. Recently, many deep cross-modal hashing methods [36, 20] have been proposed. Most of them achieve outstanding performance, but they needed a large number of semantic labels. Whereas, in practice it is very hard or laborious to obtain complete and accurate semantic tags for all the objects in large-scale datasets. The only easy-getting cross-modal correlation is the datapoints belonging to the same object. The method, NPH, proposed in this paper falls into this category.

Most cross-modal hashing methods are linear models using techniques such as linear subspace learning and graph Laplacian to pursue hash codes that preserve data similarity both within-modal and across-modal. However, there is an important issue that requires further attention, *i.e.*, the variation of dimensionality across modalities may be drastic. We know that in spaces of different dimensionality the behavior (*e.g.*, distribution) of Euclidean distance between datapoints can be drastically different which prevents many projection-based/distance-based algorithms from being effective. This is a key reason inducing *the curse of dimensionality* [1]. However, this "variation of dimensionality" issue is largely ignored in the literature of cross-modal search.

In the literature of data visualization, dimensionality reduction and the like, people study methods to map high dimensional data to low dimensional space such that the local/global structure of data is preserved as well as possible. They also confront the above "variation of dimensionality" challenge. Rather than preserving the distance, "stochastic neighborhood embedding" [19] are proposed to place objects in a low dimensional space so as to optimally preserve neighborhood identity.

In this paper, motivated by [19], we propose a nonlinear probabilistic cross-modal hashing method, namely Neighborhood-Preserving Hashing (NPH) to alleviate the negative effect due to a large variation of dimensionality across modalities. Specifically, in order to preserve neighborhood relationship, we first convert the pairwise Euclidean distance between datapoints in each modality into conditional probabilities that represent their similarities, then learn a hashing function for each modality that projects datapoints to a common hash space. In the hash space, the shared hash codes preserve the data similarity, in terms of neighborhood relationship, in multi-modalities jointly. This is realized by minimizing the Kullback-Leibler divergence between the conditional distribution of hash codes and the collective conditional distributions of the datapoints from each modality. As in [19], we observe that taking different types of distributions (*e.g.*, heavy-tailed or light-tailed) can greatly compensate for the variation of dimensionality during matching the distributions across modalities. Hence we propose *distribution selection* when converting pairwise distance of datapoints/hash codes into conditional probabilities. Experiment results demonstrate that the proposed method outperforms the state-of-the-art cross-modal search methods by a notable margin. Especially on a large-scale dataset, CIFAR-580K, the proposed method achieves on average about 7% performance gain over the second best method.

2. NEIGHBORHOOD PRESERVING HASHING

Assuming that there are n objects, each is described by data of M modalities, $\mathbf{o}_i = (\mathbf{x}_i^{(1)}, \mathbf{x}_i^{(2)}, ..., \mathbf{x}_i^{(M)})$, where $i = 1, \cdots, n$, $m = 1, \cdots, M$. $\mathbf{x}_i^{(m)} \in \mathbf{R}^{d_m}$ denotes the datapoint of the m-th modality of the i-th object, and d_m is the dimensionality of the m-th modality. The data of each modality are zero-centered, i.e. $\sum_{i=1}^n \mathbf{x}_i^{(m)} = \mathbf{0}, \forall m$.

The goal of cross-modal hashing is to learn M hash functions that map the data of each modality to binary hash codes $\mathbf{B}^{(m)} \in \{-1,1\}^{c\times n}$, where c denotes the length of the hash codes. For example, the mapping/hash function can be defined as $f(\mathbf{x}_i^{(m)}) = \text{sgn}(\mathbf{W}^{(m)T}\mathbf{x}_i^{(m)})$, where $\mathbf{W}^{(m)} \in \mathbf{R}^{d_m \times c}$ denotes a projection matrix.

There are $M(M-1)$ tasks in a M-modal cross-search, *i.e.*, using data of one modality the model should be able to search for data of the other $M-1$ modalities.

The overall procedure of NPH is as follows: (i) In order to preserve neighborhood relationship, the pairwise Euclidean distances between datapoints in each modality are converted into conditional probabilities that represent their similarities in terms of probable neighbors. (ii) Optimal hash codes for training set are learned via minimizing M KL-divergences between the conditional distribution of the data from each modality (denoted as $\mathbf{P}^{(m)}$) and that of the hash codes (denoted as $\mathbf{Q}^{(m)}$). (iii) Learning hash functions to map datapoints to the hash codes for each modality via learning c binary classifiers of kernel logistic regression.

2.1 Formulation

Similar to SNE [6], we convert Euclidean distances between datapoints $\mathbf{x}_j^{(m)}$ and $\mathbf{x}_i^{(m)}$ into conditional probabilities $p_{j|i}^{(m)}$ as follows:

$$p_{j|i}^{(m)} = \frac{T(\mathbf{x}_i^{(m)}, \mathbf{x}_j^{(m)}; \theta)}{\sum_{k\neq i} T(\mathbf{x}_k^{(m)}, \mathbf{x}_i^{(m)}; \theta)}, \tag{1}$$

where $T(\mathbf{x}_i^{(m)}, \mathbf{x}_j^{(m)}; \theta)$ returns the probability from the distance between the two datapoints. θ denotes the parameter. The conditional distribution can be of different types:

(i) For Gaussian distribution,

$$T(\mathbf{x}_i^{(m)}, \mathbf{x}_j^{(m)}; \sigma_i) = \exp(-||\mathbf{x}_i^{(m)} - \mathbf{x}_j^{(m)}||^2/2\sigma_i^2) \tag{2}$$

where σ_i denotes the variance of the Gaussian that is centered on datapoint $\mathbf{x}_i^{(m)}$. The details of computing its value can be found in [6].

(ii) For Student t-distribution with one degree of freedom

$$T(\mathbf{x}_i^{(m)}, \mathbf{x}_j^{(m)}) = (1 + ||\mathbf{x}_i^{(m)} - \mathbf{x}_j^{(m)}||^2)^{-1} \tag{3}$$

We can adopt more type of distributions, *e.g.*, χ^2-distribution. In this paper, we only choose from Gaussian and Student t-distribution to demonstrate the idea. The conditional probability $p_{j|i}$ signifies the probable neighborhood relationship of the datapoints. We discuss distribution selection in Section 2.4. To simplify the problem, we make the relationship symmetric by $p_{ij} = (p_{j|i} + p_{i|j})/2$, also we set $p_{ii}^{(m)} = 0$.

Similarly, the distribution of hash codes $\mathbf{Q}$ can be computed as

$$q_{j|i}^{(m)} = \frac{T(\mathbf{b}_i, \mathbf{b}_j; \theta)}{\sum_{k\neq i} T(\mathbf{b}_k, \mathbf{b}_i; \theta)}, \tag{4}$$

where $\mathbf{b}_i \in \{-1,1\}^c$ and $\mathbf{b}_j$ denote the i-th and the j-th hash codes, T(.,.) returns the probability from their Hamming distance. We set $q_{ii}^{(m)} = 0$.

The objective of NPH is to learn a shared set of hash codes $\mathbf{B} = (\mathbf{b}_1, \cdots, \mathbf{b}_n)$ that can match its distribution $\mathbf{Q}^{(m)}$ to the datapoint distributions of each modality $\mathbf{P}^{(m)}$ jointly as well as possible. This matching optimizes the preservation of the neighborhood relationship between the hash codes and the datapoints in each modality.

We match the two distributions of the m-th modality, $\mathbf{P}^{(m)}$ and $\mathbf{Q}^{(m)}$, by minimizing their Kullback-Leibler(KL) divergence defined as follows

$$KL(\mathbf{P}^{(m)}||\mathbf{Q}^{(m)}(\mathbf{B})) = \sum_{i\neq j} p_{ij}^{(m)} \log \frac{p_{ij}^{(m)}}{q_{ij}^{(m)}} \tag{5}$$

To purse hash codes of m-th modality that preserves the neighborhood relationship in original space, we define the objective function as

$$O_m(\mathbf{B}) = \mathbf{KL}(\mathbf{P^{(m)}}||\mathbf{Q^{(m)}}(\mathbf{B})) \tag{6}$$

Hence, the final objective function which pursues the shared hash codes for all modalities is defined as

$$\min O(\mathbf{B}) = \sum_{m=1}^{M} \alpha_m O_m(\mathbf{B}) \quad s.t. \ \frac{1}{n}\mathbf{B}\mathbf{B}^T = \mathbf{I}_{c\times c} \tag{7}$$

where α_m are empirical parameters and $\sum_{m=1}^M \alpha_m = 1$, n is the number of training data. The constrain $\frac{1}{n}\mathbf{B}\mathbf{B}^T = \mathbf{I}_{c\times c}$ requires the hash codes to be uncorrelated. Since $\mathbf{B}$ is binary, optimizing the above objective is NP hard. Hence, we relax $\mathbf{B}$ to be real-value. To make the orthogonal constrain more concise, we denote the relaxed $\mathbf{B}$ as $\hat{\mathbf{B}} = \frac{1}{\sqrt{n}}\mathbf{B}$. The constrain turns to be $\hat{\mathbf{B}}\hat{\mathbf{B}}^T = \mathbf{I}_{c\times c}$.

2.2 Optimization

The gradient of the objective function O with respect to $\hat{\mathbf{b}}_i$ is distribution dependent. For Gaussian distribution, the gradient of

Task	Method	Wiki					NUS-WIDE					CIFAR-580K				
		c = 16	c = 32	c = 64	c = 96	c = 128	c = 16	c = 32	c = 64	c = 96	c = 128	c = 16	c = 32	c = 64	c = 96	c = 128
Task 1: Modality 1 to Modality 2	CMSSH*	0.2005	0.1938	0.1936	0.1861	0.1931	0.4544	0.5024	0.5024	0.4780	0.4942	0.1832	0.1694	0.1656	0.1652	0.1677
	SCM*	0.2359	0.2445	0.2520	0.2558	0.2553	0.5104	0.5114	0.5084	0.5065	0.5087	0.1723	0.1773	0.1780	0.1793	0.1791
	QCH*	0.2540	0.2566	0.2584	0.2455	0.2217	0.5571	0.5715	0.5713	0.5660	0.5620	0.1770	0.1934	0.1961	0.1950	0.1951
	CVH	0.2153	0.1743	0.1710	0.1767	0.1996	0.4712	0.4532	0.4510	0.4472	0.4461	0.1916	0.2380	0.2831	0.2481	0.2263
	CMFH	0.2458	0.2565	0.2623	0.2622	0.2636	0.5238	**0.5219**	**0.5244**	0.5165	**0.5169**	0.1587	0.1575	0.1565	0.1566	0.1557
	STMH	0.2006	0.2054	0.2343	0.2216	0.2255	**0.5272**	0.4776	0.4581	0.4374	0.4263	0.1819	0.1749	0.1664	0.1599	0.1596
	NPH	**0.2649**	**0.3358**	**0.3990**	**0.4172**	**0.4205**	0.5167	0.5059	0.5115	**0.5176**	0.5072	**0.2055**	**0.2434**	**0.3269**	**0.3850**	**0.4086**
Task 2: Modality 2 to Modality 1	CMSSH*	0.2397	0.2397	0.2486	0.2290	0.2254	0.4767	0.5175	0.5469	0.5278	0.5148	0.1650	0.1726	0.1650	0.1632	0.1697
	SCM*	0.3679	0.4026	0.4370	0.4432	0.4518	0.5624	0.5764	0.5909	0.5949	0.5968	0.1751	0.1766	0.1774	0.1765	0.1783
	QCH*	0.4176	0.4152	0.4034	0.3739	0.2895	0.5668	0.5900	0.5775	0.5708	0.5678	0.1709	0.1862	0.1917	0.1941	0.1940
	CVH	0.3127	0.2513	0.2194	0.2083	0.2341	0.4609	0.4472	0.4465	0.4496	0.4520	0.1911	0.2386	0.2837	0.2473	0.2246
	CMFH	0.6190	0.6461	0.6589	0.6526	0.6641	0.6565	0.7008	0.7218	0.7252	0.7277	0.1595	0.1578	0.1561	0.1566	0.1571
	STMH	0.6036	0.6157	0.6291	0.6496	0.6450	0.6536	0.6849	0.7071	0.7220	0.7252	0.1837	0.1746	0.1678	0.1662	0.1622
	NPH	**0.6715**	**0.6985**	**0.7132**	**0.7140**	**0.7172**	**0.6566**	**0.7421**	**0.7598**	**0.7688**	**0.7696**	**0.2033**	**0.2403**	**0.3193**	**0.3891**	**0.4144**

Table 1: Comparison of the Mean Average Precision (MAP) values of the state-of-the-art cross-modal hashing methods in different code-lengths on three datasets. The fully supervised cross-modal hashing methods are marked by $*$. The best MAP values of all the methods (semi-/full-supervised) are underlined, and the best semi-supervised results are highlighted in black-boldface.

O_m of the m-th modality is

$$\frac{\partial O_m}{\partial \hat{\mathbf{b}}_i} = 4\alpha_m \sum_j (p_{ij}^{(m)} - q_{ij}^{(m)})(\hat{\mathbf{b}}_i - \hat{\mathbf{b}}_j). \tag{8}$$

For Student t-distribution with one degree of freedom, the gradient

$$\frac{\partial O_m}{\partial \hat{\mathbf{b}}_i} = 4\alpha_m \sum_j (p_{ij}^{(m)} - q_{ij}^{(m)})(\hat{\mathbf{b}}_i - \hat{\mathbf{b}}_j)(1 + ||\hat{\mathbf{b}}_i - \hat{\mathbf{b}}_j||^2)^{-1}. \tag{9}$$

Hence, the gradient of the objective function O can be computed

$$\frac{\partial O}{\partial \hat{\mathbf{b}}_i} = \sum_{m=1}^{M} \alpha_m \sum_j \frac{\partial O_m}{\partial \hat{\mathbf{b}}_i} \tag{10}$$

The Lagrange of our objective function with orthogonal constrain is

$$L(\hat{\mathbf{B}}, \mathbf{\Lambda}) = O(\hat{\mathbf{B}}) - \frac{1}{2}\mathrm{tr}(\mathbf{\Lambda}(\hat{\mathbf{B}}\hat{\mathbf{B}}^{\mathrm{T}} - \mathbf{I})) \tag{11}$$

Then we set the gradient of Eqn.11 w.r.t. $\hat{\mathbf{B}}$ to be $\mathbf{0}$.

$$\frac{\partial L(\hat{\mathbf{B}}, \mathbf{\Lambda})}{\partial \hat{\mathbf{B}}} = \frac{\partial O(\hat{\mathbf{B}})}{\partial \hat{\mathbf{B}}} - \mathbf{\Lambda}\hat{\mathbf{B}} = \mathbf{0} \tag{12}$$

For convenience, denote $\mathbf{G} = \frac{\partial O(\hat{\mathbf{B}})}{\partial \hat{\mathbf{B}}}$. As $\mathbf{\Lambda}$ is symmetric, we can get $\mathbf{\Lambda} = \mathbf{G}\hat{\mathbf{B}}^T = \hat{\mathbf{B}}\mathbf{G}^T$ and $\frac{\partial L(\hat{\mathbf{B}},\mathbf{\Lambda})}{\partial \hat{\mathbf{B}}} = \mathbf{G} - \hat{\mathbf{B}}\mathbf{G}^T\hat{\mathbf{B}} = \hat{\mathbf{B}}\mathbf{A}$, where $\mathbf{A} = \hat{\mathbf{B}}^T\mathbf{G} - \mathbf{G}^T\hat{\mathbf{B}}$. Then $\hat{\mathbf{B}}$ can be updated by Crank-Nicolson-like method [17] as

$$\hat{\mathbf{B}} = \hat{\mathbf{B}} - \frac{\tau}{2}(\hat{\mathbf{B}} + \hat{\mathbf{B}}\mathbf{Q})\mathbf{A}, \tag{13}$$

where τ is the step size and $\mathbf{Q} = (\mathbf{I} + \frac{\tau}{2}\mathbf{A})^{-1}(\mathbf{I} - \frac{\tau}{2}\mathbf{A})$. We update $\hat{\mathbf{B}}$ with Barzilai-Borwein (BB) method as in [25]. After learning the relaxed hash codes $\hat{\mathbf{B}}$, the median vector of $\hat{\mathbf{B}}$ can be obtained

$$\mathbf{u} = \mathrm{median}(\hat{\mathbf{B}}) \in \mathbf{R}^c. \tag{14}$$

Then the shared binary hash code can be determined by the median vector, where $B_{ij} = 1$ when $B_{ij} \geq u_i$; $B_{ij} = -1$, otherwise. We binarizing $\hat{\mathbf{B}}$ with the median vector rather than directly using the sign function because balancing the labeled data can improve the classification performance when learning the hash function in Section 2.3.

2.3 Learning Hash Functions

After getting the hash codes $\mathbf{B}$ by optimizing Eqn. 7, here we introduce about how to learn a set of efficient hash functions to map data to the hash codes.

For each modality, we train c binary classifiers, each of which maps a datapoint $\mathbf{x}_i^{(m)}$ to the corresponding bit of its hash code. The classifiers are embodied by the Kernel Logistic Regression model [7], which is defined as

$$\mathbf{w}_k^{(m)*} = \arg\min \sum_{i=1}^{n} \log(1 + \exp(-B_{ki} \sum_{j=1}^{s} W_{jk}^{(m)} \cdot \kappa(\mathbf{m}_j^{(m)}, \mathbf{x}_i^{(m)}))) + \lambda||\mathbf{w}_k^{(m)}||_2^2 \tag{15}$$

where $B_{ki} \in \{-1, 1\}$ denotes the k-th row and the i-th column of $\mathbf{B}$, *i.e.*, the k-th bit of the i-th hash code, $k = 1, \cdots, c$. $\kappa(\mathbf{m}_j^{(m)}, \mathbf{x}_i^{(m)})$ is the kernel function that measures similarity between any pair of data $\mathbf{m}_j^{(m)}$ and $\mathbf{x}_i^{(m)}$, here, we utilize the RBF kernel. In order to reduce the computation in training and testing, $\mathbf{m}_j^{(m)}$ is the j-th cluster center of the training data obtained by k-means. We set $s = 500$ in each modality and set $\lambda = 0.01$. We learn $\mathbf{w}_k^{(m)}$ with the minFunc implemented by M. Schmidt *.

Given a datapoint in the m-th modality, say $\mathbf{x}^{(m)}$, using the learned Logistic function we obtain the probability of a hash bit $b_k^{(m)}$ being 1 and -1. Then the hash bit $b_k^{(m)}$ can be determined as

$$b_k^{(m)} = \mathrm{sign}\big(p(b_k^{(m)} = 1|\mathbf{x}^{(m)}) - p(b_k^{(m)} = -1|\mathbf{x}^{(m)})\big) \tag{16}$$

In this way, we can generate the hash code for any given datapoint.

2.4 Distribution Selection

As in [19], we also observe that different types of distributions (e.g., heavy-tailed or light-tailed) possess unique capabilities in depicting the neighborhood relationship of data in different dimensional spaces.

We employ two types of distributions — a heavy-tailed distribution (Student t-distribution) and a light-tailed distribution (Gaussian distribution) — and propose to choose distribution type for matching the neighborhood distributions between hash codes and datapoints of each modality. Notice that even for the same set of hash codes, when matching to different modalities, the type of $\mathbf{Q}^{(m)}$ may be different *w.r.t* its matched modality. During training, we adopt 5-fold cross-validation to choose the best combination of distributions for all modalities data and the hash codes.

Moreover, we find that the proposed NPH can achieve better performance on different tasks with different distribution selection. So for each task we learn a particular set of hash codes. Experiments show that this method greatly improves the performance.

*M. Schmidt. minFunc: unconstrained differentiable multivariate optimization in Matlab. http://www.cs.ubc.ca/ schmidtm/Software/minFunc.html, 2005.

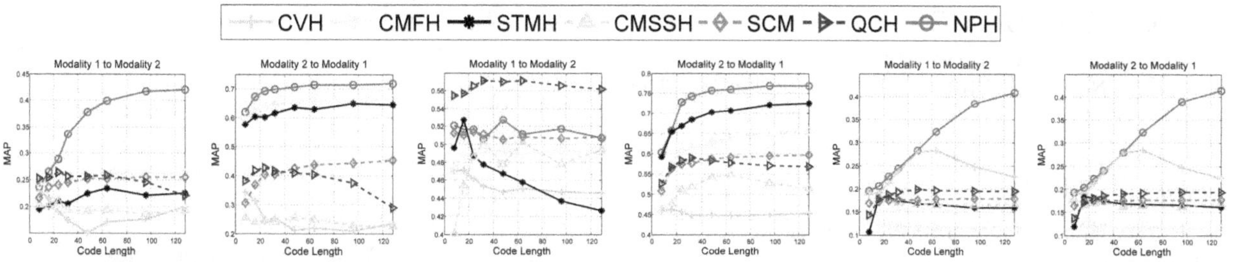

(a) On Wiki dataset (b) On NUS-WIDE dataset (c) On CIFAR-580K dataset

Figure 1: MAP results of different methods on three datasets with various hash code length.

3. EXPERIMENT

In this section, we will compare NPH with some state-of-the-art semi-supervised as well as fully-supervised cross-hashing methods on two widely used cross-modal datasets Wiki [16] and NUS-WIDE [3], and also on a large-scale cross-view dataset CIFAR-580K [26] sampled from 80M-Tiny image dataset [18].

In our experiment, ten runs of independent experiments are performed. In each run, training and testing sets are randomly sampled. The Mean Average Precision (MAP) is reported in this paper. All our experiments are conducted on a workstation with Intel(R) Xeon(R) E5-2620@2.0GHz CPUs, 128 GB RAM and 64-bit Ubuntu system.

3.1 Datasets and Evaluation

The Wiki dataset [16] contains 2,866 objects (which are described as image-text pairs) and ten semantic labels for each object. Each image is represented by a 128-dimensional Bag-of-Visual-Word (BoVW) feature and each text is denoted by a 10-dimensional vector. In our experiment, 80% of the data are randomly sampled for training and the rest are for testing.

The NUS-WIDE dataset [3] consists of 269,648 images and 5,018 raw tags in text. The semantic labels of 81 concepts are provided. We select 186,643 image-tag pairs belonging to 10 largest classes. Each image is denoted by a 500-dimensional Bag-of-Visual-Word (BoVW) vector, and each tag is 1000-dimensional most frequent tags from the raw tags. In our experiment, 1% of the data are randomly selected for testing. For training, the CMFH and STMH use 99% of the data and other algorithms use 5000 data.

The CIFAR-580K dataset consists of 580,804 images with ten class labels. As in [26], in order to construct multi-modal data, from each image a 384-dimensional GIST descriptor is extracted as one view and a 496-dimensional HOG descriptor is extracted as the other view. Similar to the NUS-WIDE dataset, we randomly select 1% data for testing. Due to large-scale, we randomly select 30% data as the training set for CMFH and STMH, and 5000 data as training set for other algorithms.

Since NPH is a semi-supervised method of cross-modal search, it is compared with the state-of-the-art semi-supervised cross-modal hashing methods including CVH [10], CMFH [5] and STMH [21]. Besides, we also compare it to some state-of-the-art fully supervised models including CMSSH [2], SCM [29] and QCH [26].

To evaluate the methods, we adopt widely used criterion, namely Mean Average Precision (MAP) with retrieval range R. In our experiment, we set $R = 50$, the same as [5, 21]. We set $\alpha_1 = \alpha_2 = 0.5$ in Eqn. 7 for all experiments of NPH. For distribution selection, we adopt 5-fold cross-validation to select from $2^{2\times2} = 16$ distribution combinations in total (see Section 2.4).

3.2 Results on the Three Datasets

From Table 1 and Figure 1(a), it can be seen that on the Wiki dataset NPH outperforms all other methods for all bits on all Tasks. NPH outperforms the second best method CMFH over 10% on Task 1 and over 5% on Task 2. From Figure 1(a), we can observe that on Task 1 the performance of NPH improves considerably with the increase of code length compared to the other methods.

From Table 1 and Figure 1(b), it can be seen that on NUS-WIDE the performance of NPH is comparable to CMFH and STMH on Task 1. However, when code length is over 32, NPH outperforms CMFH (the 2nd best semi-supervised method) by about 3% on Task 1. Meanwhile, NPH outperforms all other cross-modal hashing methods on Task 2 for all code lengths.

CIFAR-580K is a large-scale dataset, which is used to evaluate the scalability of the methods. Table 1 shows that NPH outperforms all the compared methods on both tasks by a large margin - over 7% gain on average of both tasks compared to CVH (the 2nd best). Particularly, the performance gain increases with the code length notably even compared to the supervised methods.

Task	Method	Wiki				
		c = 16	c = 32	c = 64	c = 96	c = 128
Modality 1 to Modality 2	NPH-SNE	0.2624	0.3324	0.3997	0.4199	0.4160
	NPH-tSNE	0.2502	0.2497	0.3016	0.3590	0.4005
	NPH	**0.2649**	**0.3358**	**0.3990**	**0.4172**	**0.4205**
Modality 2 to Modality 1	NPH-SNE	0.5294	0.5878	0.6415	0.6594	0.6696
	NPH-tSNE	0.6602	0.6890	0.6946	0.6955	0.6951
	NPH	**0.6715**	**0.6985**	**0.7140**	**0.7172**	**0.7725**

Table 2: MAP values of NPH with different distribution selection. The best values are highlighted in boldface.

3.3 Effect on Distribution Selection

The results of NPH in Table 1 and Figure 1 are the results of distribution selection for each modality and the hash codes. Here we compare distribution selection to two methods that adopt fixed distributions based on NPH, namely, NPH-SNE which adopts Gaussian distributions for both modality data and hash codes (as in SNE [6] for data visualization) and NPH-tSNE which adopts Gaussian distributions for modality data and Student t-distribution for hash codes (as in tSNE [19]). We report the results on Wiki dataset in Table 2. It can be seen that NPH achieves the best performance with the distribution selection and the strategy of training a particular set of hash codes for each task.

4. CONCLUSION

In this paper, we propose a semi-supervised cross-modal hashing, called Neighborhood Preserving Hashing (NPH). We propose to learn hash codes that preserve data neighborhood relationship via matching their distribution derived from distance to that of datapoints of multi-modalities. We further utilize cross-validation to select distributions to better match the modalities data and hash codes. Experiments show that the proposed model achieves superior performance over state-of-the-art cross-modal hashing methods.

5. ACKNOWLEDGMENTS

This work was supported in part by the following grants 973-2015CB351800, NSFC-61231010, NSFC-61527804, NSFC-61421062 and NSFC-61210005.

6. REFERENCES

[1] R. E. Bellman. *Dynamic Programming*. 1957.

[2] M. M. Bronstein, A. M. Bronstein, F. Michel, and N. Paragios. Data fusion through cross-modality metric learning using similarity-sensitive hashing. In *CVPR*, 2010.

[3] T.-S. Chua, J. Tang, R. Hong, H. Li, Z. Luo, and Y. Zheng. Nus-wide: a real-world web image database from national university of singapore. In *CIVR*, 2009.

[4] M. Datar, N. Immorlica, P. Indyk, and V. S. Mirrokni. Locality-sensitive hashing scheme based on p-stable distributions. In *SOCG*, 2004.

[5] G. Ding, Y. Guo, and J. Zhou. Collective matrix factorization hashing for multimodal data. In *CVPR*, 2014.

[6] G. E. Hinton and S. T. Roweis. Stochastic neighbor embedding. In *NIPS*, pages 833–840, 2002.

[7] S. S. Keerthi, K. Duan, S. K. Shevade, and A. N. Poo. A fast dual algorithm for kernel logistic regression. *JML*, 61(1-3):151–165, 2005.

[8] S. Kim and S. Choi. Multi-view anchor graph hashing. In *ICASSP*, 2013.

[9] B. Kulis and K. Grauman. Kernelized locality-sensitive hashing for scalable image search. In *ICCV*, 2009.

[10] S. Kumar and R. Udupa. Learning hash functions for cross-view similarity search. In *IJCAI*, 2011.

[11] Z. Lin, G. Ding, M. Hu, and J. Wang. Semantics-preserving hashing for cross-view retrieval. In *CVPR*, pages 3864–3872, 2015.

[12] W. Liu, J. Wang, R. Ji, Y.-G. Jiang, and S.-F. Chang. Supervised hashing with kernels. In *CVPR*, 2012.

[13] J. Masci, M. Bronstein, A. Bronstein, and J. Schmidhuber. Multimodal similarity-preserving hashing. *TPAMI*, 2013.

[14] M. Norouzi and D. M. Blei. Minimal loss hashing for compact binary codes. In *ICML*, 2011.

[15] N. Quadrianto and C. H. Lampert. Learning multi-view neighborhood preserving projections. In *ICML*, pages 425–432, 2011.

[16] N. Rasiwasia, J. Costa Pereira, E. Coviello, G. Doyle, G. R. Lanckriet, R. Levy, and N. Vasconcelos. A new approach to cross-modal multimedia retrieval. In *ACM MM*, 2010.

[17] G. D. Smith. Numerical solution of partial differential equations. 1965.

[18] A. Torralba, R. Fergus, and W. T. Freeman. 80 million tiny images: A large data set for nonparametric object and scene recognition. *TPAMI*, 30(11):1958–1970, 2008.

[19] L. Van der Maaten and G. Hinton. Visualizing data using t-sne. *JMLR*, 9(2579-2605):85, 2008.

[20] D. Wang, P. Cui, M. Ou, and W. Zhu. Deep multimodal hashing with orthogonal regularization. In *Proceedings of the 24th International Conference on Artificial Intelligence*, pages 2291–2297. AAAI Press, 2015.

[21] D. Wang, X. Gao, X. Wang, and L. He. Semantic topic multimodal hashing for cross-media retrieval. In *IJCAI*, pages 3890–3896, 2015.

[22] J. Wang, S. Kumar, and S.-F. Chang. Semi-supervised hashing for scalable image retrieval. In *CVPR*, 2010.

[23] Q. Wang, L. Si, and B. Shen. Learning to hash on partial multi-modal data. In *IJCAI*, pages 3904–3910. AAAI Press, 2015.

[24] Y. Weiss, A. Torralba, and R. Fergus. Spectral hashing. In *NIPS*, 2009.

[25] Z. Wen and W. Yin. A feasible method for optimization with orthogonality constraints. *Mathematical Programming*, 142(1-2):397–434, 2013.

[26] B. Wu, Q. Yang, W.-S. Zheng, Y. Wang, and J. Wang. Quantized correlation hashing for fast cross-modal search. In *IJCAI*, 2015.

[27] F. Wu, Z. Yu, Y. Yang, S. Tang, Y. Zhang, and Y. Zhuang. Sparse multi modal hashing. *T MultiMedia*, 2014.

[28] D. Zhai, H. Chang, Y. Zhen, X. Liu, X. Chen, and W. Gao. Parametric local multimodal hashing for cross-view similarity search. In *IJCAI*, 2013.

[29] D. Zhang and W.-J. Li. Large-scale supervised multimodal hashing with semantic correlation maximization. In *AAAI*, 2014.

[30] L. Zhang, Y. Zhang, R. Hong, and Q. Tian. Full-space local topology extraction for cross-modal retrieval. *TIP*, 24(7):2212–2224, 2015.

[31] K. Zhao, H. Lu, and J. Mei. Locality preserving hashing. In *AAAI*, 2014.

[32] Y. Zhen, P. Rai, H. Zha, and L. Carin. Cross-modal similarity learning via pairs, preferences, and active supervision. In *AAAI*, 2015.

[33] Y. Zhen and D.-Y. Yeung. Co-regularized hashing for multimodal data. In *NIPS*, 2012.

[34] Y. Zhen and D.-Y. Yeung. A probabilistic model for multimodal hash function learning. In *SIGKDD*, 2012.

[35] X. Zhu, Z. Huang, H. T. Shen, and X. Zhao. Linear cross-modal hashing for efficient multimedia search. In *Proceedings of the 21st ACM international conference on Multimedia*, pages 143–152. ACM, 2013.

[36] Y. Zhuang, Z. Yu, W. Wang, F. Wu, S. Tang, and J. Shao. Cross-media hashing with neural networks. In *ACM MM*, 2014.

Attention-based LSTM with Semantic Consistency for Videos Captioning

Zhao Guo
University of Electronic Science and Technology of China, Chengdu, China
guozhao@std.uestc.edu.cn

Lianli Gao
University of Electronic Science and Technology of China, Chengdu, China
lianli.gao@uestc.edu.cn

Jingkuan Song
Columbia University
New York, USA
jingkuan.song@columbia.edu

Xing Xu
University of Electronic Science and Technology of China, Chengdu, China
xing.xu@uestc.edu.cn

Jie Shao
University of Electronic Science and Technology of China, Chengdu, China
shaojie@uestc.edu.cn

Heng Tao Shen
The University of Queensland, Brisbane, Australia
University of Electronic Science and Technology of China, Chengdu, China
shenhengtao@hotmail.com

ABSTRACT

Recent progress in using Long Short-Term Memory (LSTM) for image description has motivated the exploration of their applications for automatically describing video content with natural language sentences. By taking a video as a sequence of features, LSTM model is trained on video-sentence pairs to learn association of a video to a sentence. However, most existing methods compress an entire video shot or frame into a static representation, without considering attention which allows for salient features. Furthermore, most existing approaches model the translating error, but ignore the correlations between sentence semantics and visual content. To tackle these issues, we propose a novel end-to-end framework named aLSTMs, an attention-based LSTM model with semantic consistency, to transfer videos to natural sentences. This framework integrates attention mechanism with LSTM to capture salient structures of video, and explores the correlation between multi-modal representations for generating sentences with rich semantic content. More specifically, we first propose an attention mechanism which uses the dynamic weighted sum of local 2D Convolutional Neural Network (CNN) and 3D CNN representations. Then, a LSTM decoder takes these visual features at time t and the word-embedding feature at time t-1 to generate important words. Finally, we uses multi-modal embedding to map the visual and sentence features into a joint space to guarantee the semantic consistence of the sentence description and the video visual content. Experiments on the benchmark datasets demonstrate the superiority of our method than the state-of-the-art baselines for video captioning in both BLEU and METEOR.

MM '16, October 15-19, 2016, Amsterdam, Netherlands

DOI: http://dx.doi.org/10.1145/2964284.2967242

Keywords

Video Description; Attention Mechanism; Multimodal Embedding; LSTM; Semantic Consistence

1. INTRODUCTION

Previously, visual content understanding [14, 7, 8] and natural language processing (NLP) are not correlative with each other. Integrating visual content with language learning to generate descriptions for images and videos has been regarded as a critical step towards machine intelligence and there are many applications such as video retrieval, video understanding, blind navigation and video subtitling.

Thanks to the rapid development of deep Convolutional Neural network (CNN), recent works have made significant progress for image description generation [22, 12, 24, 10, 6, 3, 9]. However, compared with image caption generation, video caption generation is more difficult for the diverse sets of objects, scenes, actions, attributes and salient content. Despite the difficulty of the video description generation, there have been a few attempts for video description generation [21, 20, 26, 11, 5, 23], which are mainly inspired by recent advances in translating with Long Short-Term Memory (LSTM). The LSTM is proposed to overcome the vanishing gradients problem by enabling the network to learn when to forget previous hidden states and when to update hidden states by integrating memory units. LSTM has been successfully adopted to several tasks, e.g., speech recognition, language translation and image caption [4, 21]. Thus, we follow this elegant recipe and choose to extend LSTM to generate the video sentence with rich semantic content.

Recently, many applications were proposed [21, 20, 26, 11] to directly connect a visual convolution model to deep LSTM networks. For example, Venugopalan *et al.* [21] translate videos to sentences by directly concentrating a deep neural network with a recurrent network. Ideally, video description not only requires modeling and integrating their sequence dynamic temporal attention information into a natural language but also needs to take into account the relationship between sentence semantics and visual content [15], which to our knowledge has not been simultaneously considered.

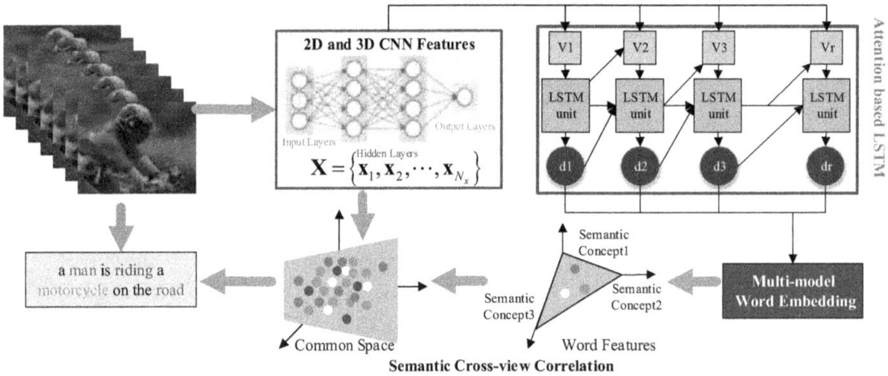

Figure 1: The framework of our proposed method aLSTMs.

Therefore, in this paper we propose a unified framework (Fig. 1), named aLSTMs, an attention-based Long Short-Term Memory model with semantic consistency. Firstly, we propose an attention mechanism which takes the dynamic weighted sum of local spatio-temporal 2D CNN feature vectors and 3D CNN feature vectors of the short spatial and temporal dynamics as the input for the LSTM decoder. Then, we integrate multi-word embedding and cross view methodology to project the generated words and the visual feature into a common space to bridge the semantic gap between videos and the corresponding sentences. It is worthwhile to highlight the following aspects for the proposed approach: 1) Our method incorporates the attention which allows for salient features by using the dynamic weighted sum of local 2D CNN and 3D CNN representations. 2) We use cross-modality model to enforce the consistency of generated sentence features with visual features. Therefore, aLSTMs can simultaneously explore the learning of LSTM and visual-semantic embedding. and 3) Experiments on the benchmark datasets demonstrate that our method outperforms the state-of-the-art methods in BLEU and METEOR.

2. THE PROPOSED APPROACH

In this section, we first introduce the Attention-based Long Short Term Memory, followed by the two components of the objective function which simultaneously considers video translation and semantic consistency. The final objective function and its solution are then illustrated.

Our goal is to generate language sentences for videos. Suppose we have a video $\mathbf{V}$ to be described by a textual sentence $D = \{d_1, \cdots, d_{N_d}\}$ consisting of N_d words. Let $\mathbf{X} = \{\mathbf{x}_1, \cdots, \mathbf{x}_{N_x}\} \in \mathbb{R}^{M \times N_x}$ and $\mathbf{D}^{'} = \left\{\mathbf{d}^{'}_1, \cdots, \mathbf{d}^{'}_{N_d}\right\} \in \mathbb{R}^{L \times N_d}$ denote the visual and the textual features, where $\mathbf{d}^{'}_i = \mathbf{E}d_i$ is the word representation of a single word d_i and N_x is the total number of feature vectors. Let M and L denote the dimension of visual feature and textual feature. $\mathbf{X}$ is extracted using deep neural networks, which will be described in the experimental part.

2.1 Attention-based LSTM Decoder

The main idea of Attention-based Long Short Term Memory is to integrate attention mechanism into the LSTM. A basic LSTM unit consists of a single memory cell, an input activation function, and three gates (input $\mathbf{i}_t$, forget $\mathbf{f}_t$ and output $\mathbf{o}_t$). $\mathbf{i}_t$ allows incoming signal to alter the state of the memory cell or block it. $\mathbf{f}_t$ controls what to be remembered and what to be forgotten by the cell and somehow can avoid the gradient from vanishing or exploding when back propagating through time. Finally, $\mathbf{o}_t$ allows the state of the memory cell to have an effect on other neurons or prevent it. Basically, the memory cell and gates in an LSTM block are defined as follows:

$$\begin{pmatrix} \mathbf{i}_t \\ \mathbf{f}_t \\ \mathbf{o}_t \\ \mathbf{g}_t \end{pmatrix} = \begin{pmatrix} \sigma \\ \sigma \\ \sigma \\ tanh \end{pmatrix} Z_{L+r,r} \begin{pmatrix} \mathbf{E}d_{t-1} \\ \mathbf{h}_{t-1} \end{pmatrix}$$
$$\mathbf{c}_t = \mathbf{f}_t \odot \mathbf{c}_{t-1} + \mathbf{i}_t \odot \mathbf{g}_t \qquad (1)$$
$$\mathbf{h}_t = \mathbf{o}_t \odot tanh(\mathbf{c}_t)$$

where $\mathbf{E}$ denotes an embedding matrix, $\sigma(x) = \frac{1}{1+e^{-x}}$ represents the logistic sigmoid non-linear activation function mapping real numbers to $(0, 1)$, $\odot$ is the element-wise product with the gate value, $Z_{m+r,r}$ denotes the parameters of the LSTM, Let L and r denote the embedding and LSTM dimensionality respectively.

Compared with images, videos contain more complex temporal attention information which should be aligned to language data. Thus we extend the attention mechanism introduced by [24] to support video captioning. LSTM becomes:

$$\begin{pmatrix} \mathbf{i}_t \\ \mathbf{f}_t \\ \mathbf{o}_t \\ \mathbf{g}_t \end{pmatrix} = \begin{pmatrix} \sigma \\ \sigma \\ \sigma \\ tanh \end{pmatrix} Z_{L+r+M,r} \begin{pmatrix} \mathbf{E}d_{t-1} \\ \mathbf{h}_{t-1} \\ \mathbf{v}_t \end{pmatrix}$$
$$\mathbf{v}_t = \sum_{i=1}^{N_x} \beta_i^t \mathbf{x}_i, \quad s_i^t = W_s \tanh\left(W_h \mathbf{h}_{t-1} + W_x \mathbf{x}_i + b_s\right) \qquad (2)$$
$$\beta_i^t = \frac{\exp\left(s_k^t\right)}{\sum_{k=1}^{N_x} \exp\left(s_k^t\right)}, \text{s.t,} \quad \sum_{i=1}^{N} \beta_i^t = 1$$

where $\mathbf{v}_t$ represents context vector which is a dynamic representation of the relevant representation of the video input at time t. M is the dimension of $\mathbf{v}_t$. In addition, β_i^t is the attention weights at time t describing the relevance of the i-th feature in the input video. Given the previous hidden state $\mathbf{h}_{t-1}$ of the LSTM decoder and the i-th video feature, it returns the unnormalized relevance score s_i^t. The W_s, W_h, W_x and b_s are the parameters that are estimated together with all the other parameters of the LSTM network. Once the relevance scores for all the features $\mathbf{X} = \{\mathbf{x}_1, \cdots, \mathbf{x}_{N_x}\}$ are computed, the LSTM is able to obtain β_i^t at time step t.

2.2 Loss 1: Translation of Videos to Words

In decoding phase, LSTM computes context vectors $\mathbf{v}_t$ given an input sequence $\mathbf{X} = \{\mathbf{x}_1, \cdots, \mathbf{x}_{N_x}\}$ and the hidden state $\mathbf{h}_{t-1}$. Inspired by the principle of translating images, we treat the activation value indexed by a training word d_t in the softmax layer of our sentence generator as the likelihood of generating that word:

$$P(d_t|\mathbf{v}_t; d_1, d_2, \cdots, d_{t-1}; \mathbf{E}) \tag{3}$$

The cost of generating that training word is then defined as the negative logarithm of the likelihood. We further define the cost of generating the words as:

$$Loss_1 = -\sum_{t=1}^{N_d} log(P(d_t|\mathbf{v}_t; d_1, d_2, \cdots, d_{t-1}; \mathbf{E})) \tag{4}$$

where N_d denotes the total number of words in sentence and d_i denotes the i-th word in sentence D. By minimizing the coherence $Loss_1$, the contextual relationship among the words in the sentence can be guaranteed, making the sentence coherent and smooth.

2.3 Loss 2: Bridging the Semantic Gap with Semantic Cross Correlation

Given a set of video visual features $\mathbf{X}$, we perform "mean pooling" process over all the feature vectors to generate a single M-dimensional visual feature $\mathbf{X}_{mean}$ for each video. Similarly, we perform "mean pooling" process over all the embedding vectors $\mathbf{D}'$ for constructing a single L-dimensional sentence feature $\mathbf{D}'_{mean}$ for each video (usually $M \neq L$). Then, the visual and sentence features are mapped into a common high level abstract space by a linear projection, which is the simplest isomorphic function:

$$R_I : R^M \to A^C \qquad R_D : R^L \to A^C \tag{5}$$

where $R_I \in \mathbb{R}^{M \times C}$ and $R_D \in \mathbb{R}^{L \times C}$. In order to construct a cross-correlation between two modalities, we require visual and sentence features of the same instance to be equal in A^C:

$$R_I(\mathbf{X}_{mean}) = R_D\left(\mathbf{D}'_{mean}\right) \tag{6}$$

Here, we let $M = C$, then the Eq.6 can be rewrite by left multiplication inverse R_D:

$$A_{.i} = {R_I}^{-1} R_D\left(\mathbf{D}'_{mean}\right) = R\mathbf{D}'_{mean}, \forall i \tag{7}$$

where $R = R_I^{-1} R_D$ is the linear projection. Therefore, we can approximate the above formulate by optimizing the cross-correlation:

$$Loss_2 = \left\| A - R\mathbf{D}'_{mean})\right\|_F^2 \tag{8}$$

where A is the mean pooling value of $\mathbf{X}$. By minimizing the semantic correlation score, the semantic consistence between the generated words and the video visual context can be guaranteed, making the sentence with rich semantic context.

2.4 Attention based LSTM with Semantic Cross Correlation

In our video description generation problem, on one hand, the generated descriptive words must be able to depict the main contents of a video precisely, and on the other hand, the generated words should be organized coherently in language. Therefore, we formulate the video description generation problem by minimizing the following energy function:

$$E(\mathbf{X}, D) = (1 - \lambda)\, Loss_2 + \lambda Loss_1 \tag{9}$$

Optimization: The above overall objective is optimized over the whole training video-sentence pairs using adadelta [27] which is an adaptive learning rate method. The training of aLSTMs is performed by simultaneously minimizing the coherent loss and semantic correlation loss. Through minimizing Eq.9, we can train our aLSTMs for translating videos to language.

Sentence generation: Sampling BeamSearch are two main approaches that used to generate a sentence given a video [24]. In this paper, we choose BeamSearch method which iteratively considers the set of the k best sentences up to time t as candidates to generate sentence of time $t+1$, and keeps only the resulting best k of them. Finally, we approximates $D = argmax_{D'} Pr(D'|X)$ as our best generated description. In our entire experiment, we set the beam size of BeamSearch as 10.

3. EXPERIMENTS

We evaluate our algorithm on the task of video captioning. We first study the influence of parameters on aLSTMs, and then compare our results with the state-of-the-art methods.

3.1 Experimental Settings

Youtube2Text. This video corpus consists of 1,970 short video clips, which is well suited for training and evaluating an automatic video description generation model. In total, this video corpus has approximately 80,000 description pairs and about 16,000 vocabulary words, which are provided by Microsoft Research [2]. Following [26, 20], we split the data set into a training, validation and testing set with 1,200, 100 and 670 videos respectively.

UCF101: We fine-tune C3D features on UCF101 dataset [16], following the work of [18]. The dataset consists of 13,320 videos of 101 human action categories. We use one of the three splits provided with this dataset for fine-tuning.

Features. Compared with images, videos fill with both static appearance and dynamic information. Thus, we extract spatial features from frame level and spatio-temporal features from shot level. For spatial features, as [26], we select equally-spaced 22 out of the first 240 from each video and fed them into CNN to obtain 1024-dimensional feature vectors which is extracted from the *pool5/7x7_s1* layer of GoogleNet [17]. For spatio-temporal features, we extract C3D features [18] every 16 frames as a shot from the videos. To extract 1024-dimensional features from $fc7\_1$ layer with rich representativeness, we use the C3D model which is pre-trained on the Sport1M dataset and fine-tuned on the UCF101 dataset. Then we select 6 equally-spaced shots of the whole video shots from each video. Finally, we put CNN and C3D features together as representation of the video.

Figure 2: Examples of video captioning results.

Baseline Methods and Evaluation Metrics. To evaluate the performance of our algorithm, we compare it with FGM [25], LSTM, SVC [11] and TA [26]. To evaluate the performance, we employ three different standard evaluation metrics: BLUE [13], METEOR [1] and CIDEr [19].

3.2 Experimental Results

The effect of λ. In our method, λ affects the performance of our algorithm. In this subsection, we study the performance variance with different λ values. Specifically, in order to make the performance curves falling into a comparable scale, we normalize BLEU and METEOR scores with the following function: $P' = \frac{P - min(P)}{min(P)}$ where P and P' represent the original and normalized performance values.

We tune λ from 0.1 to 1 and the results are shown in Fig.3. When λ is relatively small, e.g., 0.1, the worst performance is achieved. That is to say, if the impact of semantic cross correlation loss is dominant in constructing the final loss, the performance is unsatisfactory. With the increase of λ, the performance is improved until reaching the peak at $\lambda = 0.9$. Further raising λ will result in a slight drop.

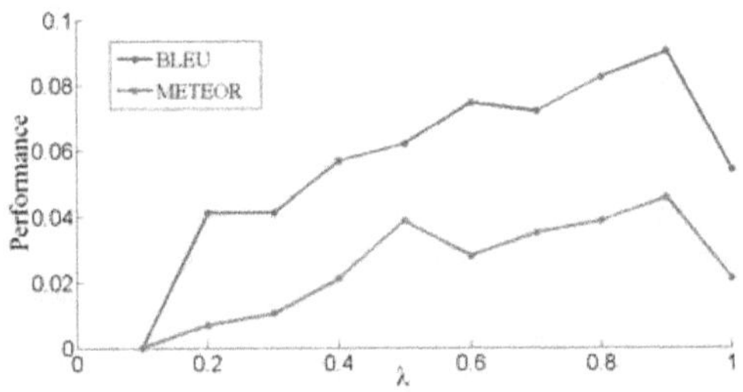

Figure 3: The effect of the λ.

Comparison Results. Tab.1 shows the comparison results and depicts the BLEU, METEOR, and CIDEr for the different methods. From Tab. 1, we have the following observations: 1) aLSTMs(2D+3D) that using 2D and 3D CNN features performs better than the one that only utilizing 2D CNN features, which proves that motion attention information is important for the video caption generation; 2) aLSTMs performs better than the method using temporal attention only (both 2D CNN and 2D+3D CNN features). This proves that our semantic consistency criterion can improve the performance of video translation; and 3) Our algorithm outperforms the other state-of-the-art methods, especially for the BLUE and CIDEr.

Table 1: Comparison of state-of-the-art algorithms with our proposed method on the Youtube2Text dataset.

Model	BLEU	METEOR	CIDEr
FGM[25]	13.68	23.90	-
LSTM[11]	31.19	26.87	-
SVC[11]	35.09	29.26	-
TA(2D)[26]	40.28	29.00	48.01
TA(2D+3D)[26]	41.92	29.60	51.67
aLSTMs (2D)	42.36	29.76	**61.20**
aLSTMs (2D+3D)	**44.87**	**30.38**	60.10

Example Results. In Fig.2 we show some examples of video caption results. Four videos are used for demonstration and four frames are extracted from each video. The top two examples demonstrate the influence of 3D CNN feature for caption generation. With 3D feature, it is possible to generate more precise verbs for video caption sentence. Moreover, in Fig.2, the relationship between words and the visual content is marked with different colors and the results show that our generated words has stronger correlation with the corresponding visual content. For instance, in the fourth video, 'women' is connected with the second frame and 'pot' is connected with the third frame. In addition, the bottom two examples prove that considering the semantic cross-view correlation will improve the generation of sentences with precise nouns. This nouns enable the description with rich context.

4. CONCLUSION

In this paper, we have proposed a framework aLSTMs, which simultaneously minimize the relevance loss and semantic cross-view loss. On two popular video description datasets, the results of our experiments demonstrate the success of our approach, outperforming the current state-of-the-art models on all three metrics.

5. ACKNOWLEDGMENTS

The work of Lianli Gao is partially supported by the Fundamental Research Funds for the Central Universities (Grant No.ZYGX2014J063) and the National Natural Science Foundation of China (Grant No. 61502080).

6. REFERENCES

[1] S. Banerjee and A. Lavie. Meteor: An automatic metric for mt evaluation with improved correlation with human judgments. In *Proceedings of the acl workshop on intrinsic and extrinsic evaluation measures for machine translation and/or summarization*, volume 29, pages 65–72, 2005.

[2] D. L. Chen and W. B. Dolan. Collecting highly parallel data for paraphrase evaluation. In *ACL*, pages 190–200. Association for Computational Linguistics, 2011.

[3] X. Chen and C. L. Zitnick. Learning a recurrent visual representation for image caption generation. *arXiv preprint arXiv:1411.5654*, 2014.

[4] K. Cho, A. Courville, and Y. Bengio. Describing multimedia content using attention-based encoder-decoder networks. *Multimedia, IEEE Transactions on*, 17(11):1875–1886, 2015.

[5] J. Donahue, L. A. Hendricks, S. Guadarrama, M. Rohrbach, S. Venugopalan, T. Darrell, and K. Saenko. Long-term recurrent convolutional networks for visual recognition and description. In *CVPR*, pages 2625–2634, 2015.

[6] H. Fang, S. Gupta, F. Iandola, R. K. Srivastava, L. Deng, P. Dollár, J. Gao, X. He, M. Mitchell, J. C. Platt, et al. From captions to visual concepts and back. In *CVPR*, pages 1473–1482, 2015.

[7] L. Gao, J. Song, F. Nie, Y. Yan, N. Sebe, and H. T. Shen. Optimal graph learning with partial tags and multiple features for image and video annotation. In *CVPR*, pages 4371–4379, 2015.

[8] L. Gao, J. Song, F. Nie, F. Zou, N. Sebe, and H. T. Shen. Graph-without-cut: An ideal graph learning for image segmentation. In *AAAI*, pages 1188–1194, 2016.

[9] X. Jia, E. Gavves, B. Fernando, and T. Tuytelaars. Guiding long-short term memory for image caption generation. *arXiv preprint arXiv:1509.04942*, 2015.

[10] A. Karpathy, A. Joulin, and F. F. F. Li. Deep fragment embeddings for bidirectional image sentence mapping. In *NIPS*, pages 1889–1897, 2014.

[11] G. Li, S. Ma, and Y. Han. Summarization-based video caption via deep neural networks. In *ACM Multimedia*, pages 1191–1194. ACM, 2015.

[12] J. Mao, W. Xu, Y. Yang, J. Wang, and A. L. Yuille. Explain images with multimodal recurrent neural networks. *arXiv preprint arXiv:1410.1090*, 2014.

[13] K. Papineni, S. Roukos, T. Ward, and W.-J. Zhu. Bleu: a method for automatic evaluation of machine translation. In *ACL*, pages 311–318. Association for Computational Linguistics, 2002.

[14] J. Song, Y. Yang, Z. Huang, H. T. Shen, and J. Luo. Effective multiple feature hashing for large-scale near-duplicate video retrieval. *IEEE Trans. Multimedia*, 15(8):1997–2008, 2013.

[15] J. Song, Y. Yang, Y. Yang, Z. Huang, and H. T. Shen. Inter-media hashing for large-scale retrieval from heterogeneous data sources. In *SIGMOD*, pages 785–796, 2013.

[16] K. Soomro, A. R. Zamir, and M. Shah. Ucf101: A dataset of 101 human actions classes from videos in the wild. *arXiv preprint arXiv:1212.0402*, 2012.

[17] C. Szegedy, W. Liu, Y. Jia, P. Sermanet, S. Reed, D. Anguelov, D. Erhan, V. Vanhoucke, and A. Rabinovich. Going deeper with convolutions. In *CVPR*, pages 1–9, 2015.

[18] D. Tran, L. Bourdev, R. Fergus, L. Torresani, and M. Paluri. Learning spatiotemporal features with 3d convolutional networks. *arXiv preprint arXiv:1412.0767*, 2014.

[19] R. Vedantam, C. Lawrence Zitnick, and D. Parikh. Cider: Consensus-based image description evaluation. In *CVPR*, pages 4566–4575, 2015.

[20] S. Venugopalan, M. Rohrbach, J. Donahue, R. Mooney, T. Darrell, and K. Saenko. Sequence to sequence-video to text. In *ICCV*, pages 4534–4542, 2015.

[21] S. Venugopalan, H. Xu, J. Donahue, M. Rohrbach, R. Mooney, and K. Saenko. Translating videos to natural language using deep recurrent neural networks. *arXiv preprint arXiv:1412.4729*, 2014.

[22] O. Vinyals, A. Toshev, S. Bengio, and D. Erhan. Show and tell: A neural image caption generator. In *CVPR*, pages 3156–3164, 2015.

[23] Q. Wu, C. Shen, A. v. d. Hengel, L. Liu, and A. Dick. Image captioning with an intermediate attributes layer. *arXiv preprint arXiv:1506.01144*, 2015.

[24] K. Xu, J. Ba, R. Kiros, A. Courville, R. Salakhutdinov, R. Zemel, and Y. Bengio. Show, attend and tell: Neural image caption generation with visual attention. *arXiv preprint arXiv:1502.03044*, 2015.

[25] R. Xu, C. Xiong, W. Chen, and J. J. Corso. Jointly modeling deep video and compositional text to bridge vision and language in a unified framework. In *AAAI*, pages 2346–2352. Citeseer, 2015.

[26] L. Yao, A. Torabi, K. Cho, N. Ballas, C. Pal, H. Larochelle, and A. Courville. Describing videos by exploiting temporal structure. In *ICCV*, pages 4507–4515, 2015.

[27] M. D. Zeiler. Adadelta: an adaptive learning rate method. *arXiv preprint arXiv:1212.5701*, 2012.

Efficient Mobile Implementation of A CNN-based Object Recognition System

Keiji Yanai Ryosuke Tanno Koichi Okamoto

Department of Informatics,
The University of Electro-Communications, Tokyo
1-5-1 Chofugaoka, Chofu, Tokyo 182-8585 JAPAN
{yanai,tanno-r,okamoto-k}@mm.inf.uec.ac.jp

ABSTRACT

Because of the recent progress on deep learning studies, Convolutional Neural Network (CNN) based method have outperformed conventional object recognition methods with a large margin. However, it requires much more memory and computational costs compared to the conventional methods. Therefore, it is not easy to implement a CNN-based object recognition system on a mobile device where memory and computational power are limited.

In this paper, we examine CNN architectures which are suitable for mobile implementation, and propose multi-scale network-in-networks (NIN) in which users can adjust the trade-off between recognition time and accuracy. We implemented multi-threaded mobile applications on both iOS and Android employing either NEON SIMD instructions or the BLAS library for fast computation of convolutional layers, and compared them in terms of recognition time on mobile devices. As results, it has been revealed that BLAS is better for iOS, while NEON is better for Android, and that reducing the size of an input image by resizing is very effective for speedup of CNN-based recognition.

Keywords

convolutional neural network, mobile implementation, network-in-network, iOS, Android

1. INTRODUCTION

Due to the recent progress of the studies on deep learning, convolutional neural network (CNN) based methods have outperformed conventional methods with a large margin. Therefore, CNN-based recognition should be introduced into mobile object recognition. However, since CNN computation is usually performed on GPU-equipped PCs, it is not easy for mobile devices where memory and computational power is limited.

In this paper, we explore the possibility of CNN-based object recognition on mobile devices, especially on iOS and Android devices including smartphones and tablets in terms of processing speed and required memory.

MM '16, October 15 - 19, 2016, Amsterdam, Netherlands

ISBN 978-1-4503-3603-1/16/10...$15.00

DOI: http://dx.doi.org/10.1145/2964284.2967243

First, we compare the CNN architectures for generic object recognition and select Network-in-Network (NIN) [1] as a basic architecture for our mobile CNN implementation. Next, we explore weight compression of NIN by Product Quantization (PQ) [2]. Regarding processing time, we describe fast mobile implementation and multi-scale recognition which allows users to adjust the trade-off between recognition time and accuracy. In addition, we modify the standard NIN architecture by introducing batch normalization (BN) [3] and adding layers to raise recognition performance. Finally we examine the above-mentioned points by the experiments.

To summarize our contributions in this paper, they are as follows:

- We compare basic CNN architectures and show the effectiveness of network-in-network for mobile implementation.
- We show multi-scale recognition of NIN is helpful to balance recognition time against accuracy.
- We have implemented NIN-based CNN recognition engines on both iOS and Android which can run in 32.6 ms in the fastest setting.

2. RELATED WORK

Recently the optional package of the OpenCV 3.1 library[1] distributed as "contrib" modules experimentally has supported a DNN module in which the network trained in Caffe [4] and Torch-7 [5] can be deployed. Since OpenCV supports both iOS and Android, anyone can implement a mobile deep learning system easily with the DNN module. However, no special optimization on the DNN module was carried out for mobile devices. To run AlexNet on iOS or Android it requires more than one second and much storage to store the trained weights. For example, 60 million weights are needed for AlexNet.

An open-source mobile deep learning software, DeepBeliefSDK[2] is optimized for Android and iOS where the BLAS library is employed on iOS and NEON SIMD instruction sets are used on Android. It took about 130 ms for one-time recognition on iPad Pro. In addition, to reduce memory to store the weights, one weight is represented in one byte by quantization [6]. Its drawback is that it is difficult to change CNN models from the built-in AlexNet to the others, since training function or importing function from other frameworks is not provided.

As academic studies, many researchers try to compress weights and reduce computational costs. Gong et al. [7] proposed to apply Product Quantization (PQ) [2] to convnets

[1]http://opencv.org/

[2]https://github.com/jetpacapp/DeepBeliefSDK

to compress their weights. However, they applied PQ-based compression to only fully connected (FC) layers in AlexNet and not to convolutional (conv) layers. Yang et al. [8] also proposed Fastfood transform and applied it for compression of FC layers in Alexnet, and Han et al. [9] proposed a method which combines pruning, quantization and Huffman Encoding, and applied it to both conv and FC layers in Alexnet and VGG-16. Courbariaux et al. [10] proposed a method to binarize network weights to reduce computational costs and required memory.

However, most of the authors did not implement their proposed method on actual mobile devices. Exceptionally, Wu et al. [11] implemented and tested Compressed AlexNet on an Android smartphone. However, it took 0.95 seconds for one-time recognition, which was much slower than our implementation.

In this paper, we aim to implement a practical CNN-based object recognition engine on both iOS and Android in terms of computational speed and required memory to store CNN weights.

Before the deep learning era got started, several local-feature-based mobile recognition systems were proposed. For example, Kawano *et al.* [12] proposed a mobile food recognition system which can classify 100 food classes in only 0.065 seconds employing Fisher Vector (FV) [13]. To realize fast recognition, they employed weight compression technique [14] and multi-threading implementation. This system was called "FoodCam" which was implemented as an interactive application taking advantage of their very quick recognition. One of our objectives in this paper is implementing such a fast mobile recognition system using a state-of-the-art CNN architecture. We propose "DeepFoodCam" which is a CNN-version of "FoodCam" as an example of CNN-based mobile recognition systems in the last part of this paper.

3. CNN ARCHITECTURE

As basic CNN architectures for object recognition, AlexNet [15], Network-in-Network (NIN) [1], GoogLeNet [16] and VGG-16 [17] are commonly used. For comparison, we show the basic characteristics of their CNN architecture regarding the number of layers, weights and computation on convolutional (conv) layers and fully-connected (FC) layers in Table 1 [3].

AlexNet is the first large-scale object recognition CNN which consists of 6 conv layers and 3 FC layers, while VGG-16 is a deeper version of AlexNet which has 13 conv layers and 3 FC layers. FC layers need a large number of weights, 59M for AlexNet and 129M for VGG-16. Although GoogLeNet also has a deep architecture consisting of 21 conv layers, it has only one FC layers with 1M parameters. While VGG-16 is a deep and high-performance but simple architecture which uses only 3×3 conv layers, GoogLeNet is quite complicated which consists of many "Inception modules" each of which consists of 5x5, 3x3, 1x1 conv layers and pooling layers.

For mobile implementation, these three architectures are not appropriate, because AlexNet and VGG-16 have too much parameters and GoogLeNet is a complicated architecture which is difficult for effective parallel implementation for mobile devices. Unlike these three architectures, Network-in-Network (NIN) has a simple architecture consisting of no FC layers and 12 conv layers. Instead of FC layers, NIN adopts Cascaded Cross Channel Parametric Pooling (CCCP Pooling) which is implemented by two consecutive 1 conv layers just after 3×3 or larger conv layers. The number of the total parameters of NIN are 7.6 million, and the number of the multiplication is 1.1 billion, which is relatively smaller than the other architectures.

[3]We referred to the open models at Caffe Model Zoo (https://github.com/BVLC/caffe/wiki/Model-Zoo).

Table 1: Comparison of CNN Architectures regarding the number of layers, weights and computation (multiplication). "ImageNet" means the top-5 error rate for the ImageNet Challenge data with a single model.

model		Alex	VGG-16	GoogLeNet	NIN
conv	layer	5	13	21	12
	weights	3.8M	15M	5.8M	7.6M
	comp.	1.1B	15.3B	1.5B	1.1B
FC	layer	3	3	1	0
	weights	59M	124M	1M	0
	comp.	59M	124M	1M	0
TOTAL	weights	62M	138M	6.8M	7.6M
	comp.	1.1B	15.5B	1.5B	1.1B
ImageNet	top-5 err.	17.0%	7.3%	7.9%	10.9%

Given these characteristics of NIN, we have decided to adopt NIN as a basic architecture of mobile implementation in this work. In addition, NIN can accept an image of any size as an input of the network by using global pooling instead of fixed-size pooling in the last pooling layer, because NIN is a CNN without FC layers. This is very helpful for mobile implementation, because users can adjust the balance between recognition speed and accuracy by their preference without changing the network weights. We will refer this point later.

4. COMPRESSION OF NIN WEIGHTS

In this paper, we adopt Network-in-Network (NIN) [1] as a basic CNN architecture, because both the amount of the parameters and computational costs are relatively smaller. However, 30 MByte at least is still needed to store 7.6 million weights in 32-bit single floating point representation. Then we introduce weight compression.

Inspired by Gong et al. [7], we apply product quantization (PQ) [2] for weight compression of conv layers of NIN, although Gong et al. applied PQ-based compression not to conv layers but only to FC layers in AlexNet. By the experiments, we confirm the effectiveness of PQ-based weight compression for conv layers of NIN.

5. FAST IMPLEMENTATION ON MOBILE DEVICES

In this work, we focus on iOS and Android devices including smartphones and tablets as target devices for mobile implementation.

For fast mobile implementation, it is essential to use (1) Multi-threading, (2) SIMD instruction sets and (3) iOS Accelerate Framework (only for iOS). In addition, it is possible to reduce computational costs by devising CNN architectures, computation algorithms, and introducing approximation into CNN computation. As the other easier way to reduce computational costs, we can reduce the size of an input image.

In this section, we describe (1), (2) and (3) which we consider are prerequisite for fast implementation of CNNs on mobile devices. Since so many works have been published regarding reducing computational costs of CNNs as mentioned in Sec.2, we like to keep introducing them for our future work. Instead, to verify the effectiveness of reducing

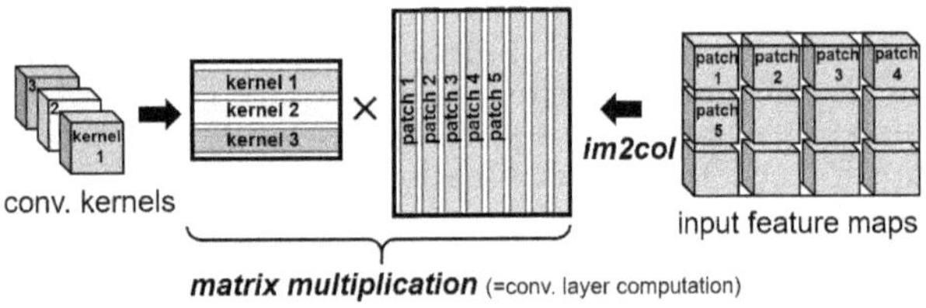

Figure 1: Computation of conv layers with "im2col" and "matrix multiplication".

of the size of an input image for speedup, we will examine the relations between input image sizes and recognition accuracy in the next section.

Because NIN has only conv layers as the layers having trained parameters, we need efficient mobile implementation of feed-forward computation of convolutional layers. In general, computation of conv layers is decomposed into "im2col" operation and matrix multiplications. In im2col operation, each patch to apply a conv kernel to is extracted from a given feature map, and place them in one column of a patch matrix, while each conv kernel is also placed in one row of a kernel matrix (See Figure 1). After that, we can obtain the output feature maps of the target conv layer by multiplying the kernel matrix by the im2col patch matrix. In general, this generic matrix multiplication (GEMM) is very time-consuming, since both matrices are large (sometime larger than 1000×1000). Although we can use GPU for fast GEMM calculation in case of PC or servers, for mobile devices we need to use CPU as effective as possible.

(1) Multi-threading: Most of the recent CPU on mobile devices have four CPU cores. By using four cores effectively, four times speedup can be expected. In our implementation, to use four CPU cores by multi-threading, we divide a kernel matrix into four sub-matrices along the row. As shown in Table 1, the number of conv kernels are usually multiples of four. Four GEMM operations are carried out in parallel. Note that most of the CPUs on iOS devices including the latest APPLE CPU, A9X, have only two cores. Therefore, only twice speedup is expected with multi-threading for iOS devices at most.

(2) SIMD instruction: Most of the recent mobile devices are equipped with ARM-based CPUs except for some devices having Intel Atom. Therefore, we focus only on NEON which is a SIMD instruction set of ARM processors. Among the NEON instruction set, we use "*vmla.f32*" which can execute four multiplications and accumulating calculations at once. This operations are frequently used for GEMM calculation. NEON instructions can be carried out in each CPU core independently. Therefore, by combining multi-threading and NEON, 16 times speedup for Android and 8 times for iOS are expected at most.

(3) iOS Accelerate Framework: In case of iOS, iOS Accelerate Framework which includes highly optimized BLAS (Basic Linear Algebra Subprograms) library is available. The GEMM function in the BLAS library ("*cblas_sgemm*") can be used for GEMM operations. BLAS in iOS probably uses NEON instructions inside the library. However, the detail is not disclosed. (2) and (3) are alternative to each other. We will compare them in the experiments.

Table 2: The original and variants of the NIN architectures.

layer no.	(1) original NIN	(2) 4layers + BN	(3) 5layers + BN
1	11x11x96 **conv1**	11x11x96 **conv1**	**11x11x96 conv1**
2	1x1x96 cccp1_1	1x1x96 cccp1_1	1x1x96 cccp1_1
3	1x1x96 cccp1_2	1x1x96 cccp1_2	1x1x96 cccp1_1
4	5x5x256 **conv2**	3x3x256 **conv2_1**	3x3x256 **conv2_1**
5	1x1x256 cccp2_1	3x3x256 **conv2_2**	3x3x256 **conv2_2**
6	1x1x256 cccp2_2	1x1x256 cccp2_1	1x1x256 cccp2_1
7	3x3x384 **conv3**	1x1x256 cccp2_2	1x1x256 cccp2_2
8	1x1x384 cccp3_1	3x3x384 **conv3**	3x3x384 **conv3**
9	1x1x384 cccp3_2	1x1x384 cccp3_1	1x1x384 cccp3_1
10	3x3x1024 **conv4**	1x1x384 cccp3_2	1x1x384 cccp3_2
11	1x1x1024 cccp4_1	3x3x768 **conv4**	3x3x768 **conv4**
12	1x1xN cccp4_2	1x1x768 cccp4_1	1x1x768 cccp4_1
13	avg. pool	1x1xN cccp4_2	1x1x768 cccp4_2
14	sofmax	avg. pool	3x3x1024 **conv5**
15		softmax	1x1x1024 cccp5_1
16			1x1x1024 cccp4_2
17			avg. poling
18			softmax
weights	7.6Million	5.5Million	15.8Million
computation	1.1Billion	1.2Billion	1.7Billion

6. MULTI-SCALE RECOGNITION FOR ADJUSTING TIME AND ACCURACY

The original NIN is designed so that the size of an input image of NIN is 227×227. However, by using global average pooling which accepts feature maps of any size in the final pooling layer, NIN can accept input images of any size, since NIN has no FC layers. This is a helpful characteristics for mobile implementation, since users can adjust processing speed by changing the size of an input image without changing CNN weights. The smaller the size of an input image becomes, the faster the NIN can recognize it. Instead, the accuracy will be degraded.

In the experiments, we examine the trade-off between recognition time and accuracy with input images of several sizes and two kinds of methods to generate smaller images. One is cropping smaller images from the original one without resizing, while the other is resizing original one to smaller images.

7. EXTENSION OF THE NIN ARCHITECTURE

The original NIN consists of four repetitive small structures each of which includes one conv layer and Cascaded Cross Channel Parametric Pooling (CCCP) layers which are equivalent to two consecutive 1×1 conv layers. When training, we added drop-out [18] to the two last 3×3 conv layers to make training easier.

Recently batch normalization (BN) [3] has been proposed, which can accelerate training without drop-out and make training of deeper networks possible. Then, we build two variant models of NIN by adding BN layers just after all the conv/cccp layers and one repetitive structures. One is "4-layers + BN" and the other is "5-layers + BN". In addition, we replaced 5x5 conv with two 3x3 conv layers, and reduced the number of kernels in conv_4 from 1024 to 768. The details of the original NIN and two variants are shown in Table 2. We will compare them regarding recognition performance in the experiments

Note that ReLUs (Rectified Linear Unit) exists just after all the conv/cccp layers, and in case of (2) and (3), BN (batch normalization) layers also exists just after all the conv/cccp layers and before ReLU, although they are not shown in the table.

Table 3: Recognition time [ms] on mobile devices.

	NIN(BLAS)	NIN(NEON)	NIN4	NIN5	D-Belief
iPad Pro	**66.0**	221.4	66.6	103.5	131.9
iPhone SE	**79.9**	251.8	77.6	116.6	137.7
Galaxy Note 3	1652	**251.1**	-	-	-

Table 4: Recognition accuracy (top-1/5) [%] of the trained models.

model	ImageNet2000		UEC-FOOD		
	top-1	top-5	top-1	top-5	weights
FV(HOG+color)[12]	-	-	65.3	86.7	5.6M
AlexNet	44.5	67.8	78.8	95.2	62M
NIN	41.9	65.9	75.0	93.7	7.6M
NIN(4layers+BN)	39.8	65.0	77.9	94.6	5.5M
NIN(5layers+BN)	45.8	70.5	80.8	95.4	15.8M

8. EXPERIMENTS

8.1 Implementation and Training

We have implemented a mobile deep learning framework which works on both iOS and Android. The framework supports only deployment of trained CNN models. We used Caffe [4] for training of CNN models on a PC with two Titan-X GPUs, and converted trained model files for our framework.

In the experiments, we mainly used the augmented UEC-FOOD100 dataset [19, 20] which is a 100-class food categories dataset containing at most 1000 food photos for each food class, because our objective is implementing practical CNN-based recognition engines. Following [20], before training with the food dataset, we pre-trained CNNs with ImageNet 2000 category images (totally 2.1 million images) which consisted of ILSVRC2012 1000 category images and 1000 food-related categories selected from all the 21,000 ImageNet categories.

For evaluation, we used 20% of ImageNet 2000 images and the images in the fold no.0 of the official split of UEC-FOOD100 as test images of ImageNet 2000 and augmented UEC-FOOD100, respectively. In the experiments, we measured processing time on mobile devices, while we evaluated recognition accuracy of the trained CNNs on a PC.

8.2 Recognition Time on Mobile Devices

We measured recognition times on iPad Pro 9.7inch (iOS 9.3), iPhone SE (iOS 9.3) and Galaxy Note3 (Android 5.0). We executed recognition more than twenty times and calculated the median of all the measured times for evaluation. Table 3 shows the processing time for one-time recognition with NIN with BLAS, NIN with NEON, NIN-4layers with BLAS, NIN-5layers with BLAS, and DeepBeliefSDK with BLAS (for comparison).

From these results, the BLAS library on iOS which was implemented as a part of iOS Accelerate Framework was very effective for speedup, while the OpenBLAS library which we used as BLAS implementation for Android was too slow. NEON implementation was moderate, although it was three times as slow as iOS BLAS implementation. For more speedup on Android, improvement of CNN models and computation such as reducing weights and approximation of CNN computation will be needed. This is one of our future works.

Although DeepBeliefSDK also employs BLAS, our NIN(BLAS) was twice as fast as it. One of the possible reason is that we used multi-threading, while they did not use.

For reference, we show the recognition accuracy for ImageNet2000 and UEC-FOOD with Fisher Vector (FV) based conventional method, AlexNet, NIN and two variants in Table 4. All the CNN based method outperformed the FV-based result [12] with a large margin. Both of two variants of NIN outperformed the original NIN except for NIN-4layers on ImageNet2000. Reducing the number of the kernels in the last conv layers for NIN-4layers is one of the possible reasons of this performance loss. NIN-5layers outperformed AlexNet, which showed that making a CNN deeper was effective for performance improvement.

Table 5: Time [ms] and top-1/5 accuracy [%] with images of various size.

(A) 4-layer + BN

Time	227x227		200x200		180x180		160x160	
iPad Pro	66.6		49.7		44.0		**32.6**	
iPhone SE	77.6		56.0		50.2		37.2	
Accuracy	top-1	top-5	top-1	top-5	top-1	top-5	top-1	top-5
resize	**78.8**	**95.2**	**77.3**	**95.1**	**76.0**	94.1	69.3	91.5
crop	**78.8**	95.2	75.8	93.9	72.0	92.1	63.0	87.7
multi-resize	74.7	93.9	74.0	94.6	74.4	**94.7**	**71.5**	**93.7**
multi-crop	74.7	93.9	70.8	92.2	69.8	92.2	61.4	87.2

(B) 5-layer + BN

Time	227x227		200x200		180x180		160x160	
iPad Pro	103.5		71.9		61.1		**46.6**	
iPhone SE	116.6		82.9		68.6		53.4	
Accuracy	top-1	top-5	top-1	top-5	top-1	top-5	top-1	top-5
resize	**81.5**	**96.2**	**80.2**	**95.7**	**78.4**	94.9	72.0	91.4
crop	**81.5**	**96.2**	78.3	95.1	75.1	93.6	65.3	87.3
multi-resize	78.2	95.3	78.2	95.1	78.2	**95.6**	**75.1**	**93.8**
multi-crop	78.2	95.3	75.8	93.2	73.1	92.2	66.3	88.3

Table 6: Accuracy (top-1/5) [%] with PQ-based weight compression.

	raw(32bit)	8bit	4bit	4bit(pair)	2bit(pair)
memory	30.4MB	7.6MB	3.8MB	3.8MB	1.9MB
top-1	75.0	74.5	66.8	72.9	50.3
top-5	93.7	93.5	89.7	92.9	78.1

8.3 Multi-scale Recognition

The advantage of NIN is that it can accept images of any size as input images. Table 5 shows relation between image size and time/accuracy. We used two methods to obtain smaller images, resizing and cropping. In addition, we trained NIN-4layers and NIN-5layers in multi-scale training where we resized training images with random magnification rate from 0.7 to 1.0 during training of the NIN models.

For the results, the processing time was proportional to the number of the pixels of an image. For example, in case of 160x160, the time was reduced by half. Although reducing the size from 227x227 to 180x180 brought only 2.8 point and 3.1 point accuracy loss for NIN-4layers and NIN-5layers, respectively, the processing time was reduced by two third.

As a method to reduce the size of an input image, resizing is much better than cropping in terms of accuracy.

The multi-scale trained models were not as effective as the normal models trained with 227x227 images except for 160x160 input images. The results by the multi-scale trained models are relatively uniform regardless the size of an input image, although the accuracy for the full-sized image was degraded compared to the normal models.

Until 180x180, reducing the size of an input image is effective and easy way to adjust the trade-off between accuracy and processing time.

8.4 Weight Compression

We applied Product Quantization (PQ) [2] to compress CNN weights for NIN to reduce required memory on mobile devices. Table 6 shows accuracy from no compres-

Figure 2: Screen-shots of food recognition app (left) and 2000-class recognition app (right).

sion to 1/16 compression. For "8bit" and "4bit", we applied quantization to each single element, while "4bit(pair)" and "2bit(pair)" means that we applied quantization to each pair of elements. Performance loss in case of "4bit(pair)" was only 2.1 point, although it brought 1/8 compression. From these results, PQ-based compression is helpful for NIN as well.

8.5 Mobile Applications

We have implemented two kinds of mobile CNN-based image recognition apps on iOS, a food recognition app, "DeepFoodCam", and a 2000-class object recognition app, which employ NIN trained with the augmented UEC-FOOD100 dataset including a additional non-food class, and NIN trained with 2000 ImageNet Food dataset, respectively. Both can recognize a 227x227 photo in 66ms and a 160x160 in 33ms.

We have released the iOS-version food recognition application on Apple App Store. Please search for "DeepFoodCam". The movies where two apps are working on iOS can be seen at our project page, http://foodcam.mobi/.

9. CONCLUSIONS

We proposed a mobile implementation of CNN which is based on Network-in-Network (NIN) [1]. For reducing the weights we examined PQ-based compression, while for fast recognition we adopted multi-threading and SIMD instruction or highly-optimized iOS Accelerate Framework for computation of convolutional layers. In addition, we examined NIN-based multi-scale recognition which enabled us to adjust the trade-off between time and speed. As results, it was turned out that reducing the size of input images was very effective. In addition, for a 160×160 input image, we achieved 32.6 ms recognition on iPad Pro, which is equivalent to the "real" real-time speed.

For future work, we plan to apply our mobile framework into real-time CNN-based mobile image processing such as super-resolution, semantic segmentation and neural style-transfer [21].

10. REFERENCES

[1] M. Lin, Q. Chen, and S. Yan, "Network in network," in *Proc. of International Conference on Learning Represenation Conference Track*, 2014.

[2] H. Jegou, M. Douze, and C. Schmid, "Product quantization for nearest neighbor search," *IEEE Transactions on Pattern Analysis and Machine Intelligence*, vol. 33, no. 1, pp. 117–128, 2011.

[3] S. Ioffe and C. Szegedy, "Batch normalization: Accelerating deep network training by reducing internal covariate shift," in *Proc. of International Conference on Machine Learning*, pp. 448–456, 2015.

[4] Y. Jia, E. Shelhamer, J. Donahue, S. Karayev, J. Long, R. Girshick, S. Guadarrama, and T. Darrell, "Caffe: Convolutional architecture for fast feature embedding," in *Proc. of ACM International Conference Multimedia*, pp. 675–678, 2014.

[5] R. Collobert, K. Kavukcuoglu, and C. Farabet, "Torch7: A matlab-like environment for machine learning," in *Proc. of NIPS Workshop on BIGLearn*, 2011.

[6] V. Vanhoucke, A. Senior, and M. Z. Mao, "Improving the speed of neural networks on CPUs," in *Proc. of NIPS Workshop on Deep Learning and Unsupervised Feature Learnings*, 2011.

[7] Y. Gong, L. Liu, M. Yang, and L. Bourdev, "Compressing deep convolutional networks using vector quantization," *arXiv preprint arXiv:1412.6115*, 2014.

[8] Z. Yang, M. Moczulski, M. Denil, N. de Freitas, A. Smola, L. Song, and Z. Wang, "Deep fried convnets," in *Proc. of IEEE International Conference on Computer Vision*, pp. 1476–1483, 2015.

[9] S. Han, H. Mao, and W. J. Dally, "Deep compression: Compressing deep neural networks with pruning, trained quantization and huffman coding," in *Proc. of International Conference on Learning Representation*, 2016.

[10] M. Courbariaux, Y. Bengio, and J. P. David, "BinaryConnect: Training deep neural networks with binary weights during propagations," in *Advances in Neural Information Processing Systems*, pp. 3123–3131, 2015.

[11] J. Wu, C. Leng, Y. Wang, Q. Hu, and J. Cheng, "Quantized convolutional neural networks for mobile devices," *arXiv preprint arXiv:1512.06473*, 2015.

[12] Y. Kawano and K. Yanai, "Foodcam: A real-time food recognition system on a smartphone," *Multimedia Tools and Applications*, vol. 74, no. 14, pp. 5263–5287, 2015.

[13] F. Perronnin, J. Sánchez, and T. Mensink, "Improving the fisher kernel for large-scale image classification," in *Proc. of European Conference on Computer Vision*, 2010.

[14] Y. Kawano and K. Yanai, "Ilsvrc on a smartphone," *IPSJ Transactions on Computer Vision and Applications*, vol. 6, pp. 83–87, 2014.

[15] A. Krizhevsky, I. Sutskever, and G. E. Hinton, "ImageNet classification with deep convolutional neural networks," in *Advances in Neural Information Processing Systems*, 2012.

[16] C. Szegedy, W. Liu, Y. Jia, P. Sermanet, S. Reed, D. Anguelov, D. Erhan, V. Vanhoucke, and A. Rabinovich, "Going deeper with convolutions," in *Proc. of IEEE Computer Vision and Pattern Recognition*, pp. 1–9, 2015.

[17] K. Simonyan, A. Vedaldi, and A. Zisserman, "Deep inside convolutional networks: Visualising image classification models and saliency maps," in *Proc. of International Conference on Learning Represenation Workshop Track*, 2014.

[18] N. Srivastava, G. Hinton, A. Krizhevsky, I. Sutskever, and R. Salakhutdinov, "Dropout: A simple way to prevent neural networks from overfitting," *Journal of Machine Learning Research*, vol. 15, no. 1, pp. 1929–1958, 2014.

[19] Y. Matsuda, H. Hoashi, and K. Yanai, "Recognition of multiple-food images by detecting candidate regions," in *Proc. of IEEE International Conference on Multimedia and Expo*, pp. 1554–1564, 2012.

[20] K. Yanai and Y. Kawano, "Food image recognition using deep convolutional network with pre-training and fine-tuining," in *Proc. of ICME Workshop on Multimedia for Cooking and eating Activities (CEA)*, 2015.

[21] J. Johnson, A. Alahi, and L. Fei-Fei, "Perceptual losses for real-time style transfer and super-resolution," *arXiv preprint arXiv:1603.08155*, 2016.

Context-aware Geometric Object Reconstruction for Mobile Education

Jinxin Zheng, Yongtao Wang*, Zhi Tang
Institute of Computer Science and Technology, Peking University
No.5 Yiheyuan Road, Haidian District
Beijing, China, 100871
zhengjinxin,wangyongtao,tangzhi@pku.edu.cn

ABSTRACT

The solid geometric objects in the educational geometric books are usually illustrated as 2D line drawings accompanied with description text. In this paper, we present a method to recover the geometric objects from 2D to 3D. Unlike the previous methods, we not only use the geometric information from the line drawing itself, but also the textual information extracted from its context. The essential of our method is a cost function to mix the two types of information, and we optimize the cost function to identify the geometric object and recover its 3D information. Our method can recover various types of solid geometric objects including straight-edge manifolds and curved objects such as cone, cylinder and sphere. We show that our method performs significantly better compared to the previous ones.

Keywords

3D reconstruction; geometric object; line drawing

1. INTRODUCTION

Many educational paper books, especially the textbooks for primary and secondary education, often contain a lot of illustrations of the three-dimensional (3D) geometric objects. Because these 3D geometric objects are illustrated as the two-dimensional (2D) line drawings with the loss of 3D information, sometimes it's too difficult to quickly understand the geometric objects by observing the 2D line drawings in the paper books.

This paper aims at helping the students understand the geometric objects in their books. Specifically, we recover the 3D geometric object from the 2D line drawing and its surrounding description text. Our algorithm is designed to be efficient enough to run on modern mobile devices (e.g. smart phones or tablets). By using just a mobile phone with a built-in camera, a student can view the recovered geometric object by photographing the line drawing on the book. The application of our method improves the student's experience in the mobile educational environment.

Some existing methods try to recover the 3D object from a line drawing by using its line configurations and lift the 2D line drawing into the 3D space by enforcing a variety of geometric regularities (parallelism, orthogonality, face planarity, minimal standard deviation of angles) [3, 9, 10, 11, 12, 1, 6, 7, 13]. These methods work quite well for the clear and accurate input line drawings. However, they only take into account the line drawing itself and try to recover the lost 3D information by merely guessing from the 2D positions of the vertices and the lines. Hence, the previous methods would perform very poorly when the input line drawing contains errors [18, 19].

Obviously, the inaccuracy of the line drawings is the main difficulty for the 3D reconstruction algorithms. Since it is so difficult to successfully recover an inaccurate line drawing, we seek for additional information that might help in identifying the correct object in the line drawing. Particularly, the geometric line drawings in the geometric books are usually accompanied with description text, which provides us with a hint of what the geometric object in the line drawing might be.

In this paper, we propose an algorithm to recover the 3D information of the solid geometric objects from single line drawing images taken from the geometric books. The core technical contribution of our work is the strategy to combine the geometrical information and the textual information. Moreover, we propose a solution to represent and recover some primitive curved objects (cones, cylinders and spheres). The rest of this paper is organized as follows. The related work is briefly reviewed in Section 2. An overview of the proposed method is given in Section 3, and details are introduced in Section 4. Experimental results are reported in Section 5 and conclusions are drawn in Section 6.

2. RELATED WORK

In the past two decades, a lot of researchers have made efforts to resolve the single line drawing-based 3D reconstruction problem. These methods include: (1) regularity-based methods which use some geometric rules as constraints to construct a cost function, and then minimize this function to obtain the 3D object [3, 9, 10, 11, 12, 1, 6, 7, 13]; (2) deduction-based methods which impose some assumptions over the input line drawing and deduce the reconstruction result based on these assumptions [4, 5, 19]; (3) divide-and-conquer-based methods which decomposes a complex line drawing into some simpler parts and conduct reconstruction

*Corresponding author.

MM '16, October 15–19, 2016, Amsterdam, The Netherlands.

DOI: http://dx.doi.org/10.1145/2964284.2967244

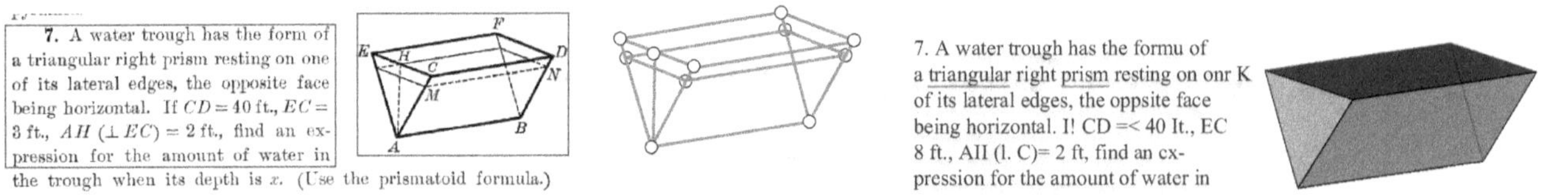

(a) Input (b) Extracted sketch (c) OCR text detection (d) Output

Figure 1: Overview of our method. (a) We take as input a line drawing image and an accompanied paragraph of description text. (b) We extract the sketch from the line drawing image and represent it as an undirected graph. The sketch might be under-complete or over-complete. The example shown is an over-complete one because of the extra lines. (c) We use OCR to detect the text from the input, and find some keywords from the text. The keywords "triangular" and "prism" are detected in this example. (d) The sketch and the keywords are combined in a formulation to estimate the pose of the object.

over each part and then combine all the partial results as the final result [2, 15, 16, 8, 17, 21, 20].

Among the methods listed above, our work is mostly related to Xue et al. [16]'s method (E3D) and our previous method (SGOR) [18]. Both of the methods have pre-defined a 3D model database from which to derive the most possible models for the input line drawing. The E3D method can handle complex objects based on divide-and-conquer approach. However, it requires the input to be a perfect line drawing. The SGOR method is more robust in that it can handle various inaccurate input line drawings. Both of them can not handle curved objects, such as cones, cylinders and spheres. In this paper, we propose a method which can handle both straight-edge manifolds and curved objects. Moreover, the context information is used to identify the correct geometric object the image contains.

3. OVERVIEW

Our algorithm takes a line drawing image and an optional image that contains a paragraph of text which describes the geometric object as input. Currently the user needs to manually select the area of the text which is related to the geometric object in the image.

Figure 1 shows the main steps of our method. For the input line drawing image, we extract the lines from it and convert them to an undirected graph, which is called the sketch. The details of the sketch extraction can be found in [18]. Note that due to the limitation of the sketch extraction algorithm, the extracted sketch is more likely to be inaccurate (i.e. under-complete or over-complete). In addition, we detect the ellipses (corresponding to curved objects) from the image and integrate them to the sketch. For the input text image, we perform OCR to extract the text information in it. We then find the keywords that has potential relationship with the geometric object in the extracted text. Finally, we mix the sketch and the keywords in an objective formulation to obtain the most possible geometric object and its pose, based on which we render the recovered object in 3D style.

4. 3D RECONSTRUCTION

The goal of our method is to convert the line drawing images that contain the primitive geometric objects to the vectorized line drawings and present them in 3D style. We follow our previous work [18] by extracting a 2D sketch of the image firstly, and then searching for the most possible 3D model in a pre-built 3D model database and compute the corresponding pose of the 3D model based on the extracted sketch.

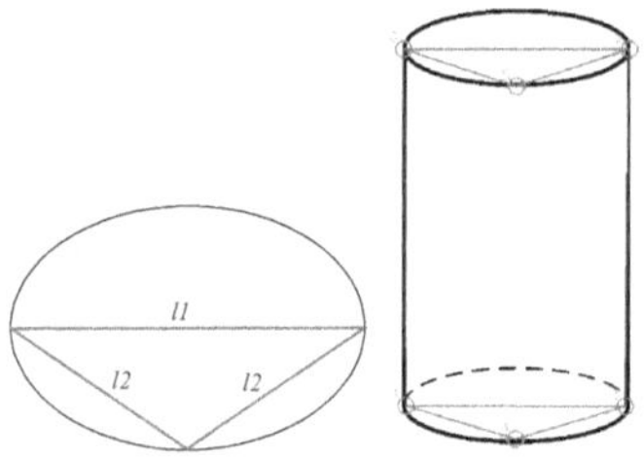

(a) (b)

Figure 2: (a) An ellipse is represented as an isosceles triangle. The base side of the triangle is the major axis of the ellipse and is labeled as $l1$. The other two equal sides connect the two endpoints of the major axis and one endpoint of the minor axis, and they are labeled as $l2$. (b) The sketch graph of the curved object contains unlabeled edges which are the normal straight lines and the labeled edges which come from the triangle of the ellipse.

4.1 Curved Object Models

If the line drawing contains curved objects, we use the algorithm in [14] to detect the ellipses in the image. Then each detected ellipse is represented as a triangle as shown in Figure 2(a). The triangle consists of three labeled sides: one side is the major axis of the ellipse, labeled as $l1$; each of the other two sides connects an endpoint of the major axis and an endpoint of the minor axis, labeled as $l2$. The labeled triangle is integrated into the sketch graph, as shown in Figure 2(b).

A curved object model is mostly the same as the 3D object model in [18], except that it has labeled triangles which represent the circles in the curved object model. For example, in Figure 3(a), the bottom circle is represented as the inscribed triangle whose base side is the axis of the circle and is isosceles. The three sides of the triangle are labeled as follows: the base side is labeled as $l1$, the two legs are labeled as $l2$. The labels in the curved object model are the same as the labels of the sketch graph shown in Figure 2(b). Besides the triangle, the cone model also has two unlabeled edges which represent the side face, corresponding to the 2D projection of the edges in the sketch graph. The

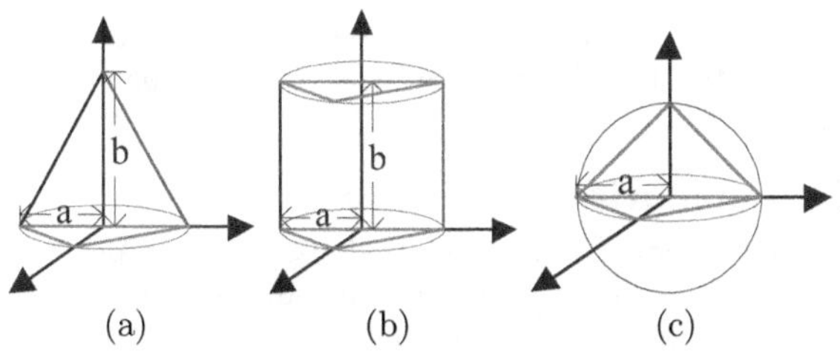

Figure 3: Examples of the curved object models. (a) Cone. (b) Cylinder. (c) Sphere.

cylinder object in Figure 3(b) is likewise. The sphere is just a bit different – as shown in Figure 3(c), it has two triangles sharing the same base side (the axis of the sphere), and the two triangles represent two perpendicular circles on the surface of the sphere, so they are perpendicular to each other in 3D space.

We impose strict labeling correspondence rule to the graph matching process: only unlabeled edges can be matched to unlabeled edges, and only the edges with the same labels can be matched(unlabeled matches unlabeled, $l1$ matches $l1$, $l2$ matches $l2$). This ensures that only curve object models can be selected if the image contains curve objects and the ellipses are detected from their 2D projections.

After the graph matching process [18], the candidate models are selected for the extracted sketch of the input image. With the triangular representation of the ellipses, the curved object models contain only straight edges (labeled and unlabeled). So the 3D reconstruction process in [18] can be easily applied to the curved objects in this paper. Figure 4 shows examples of the 3D reconstructions of curved objects.

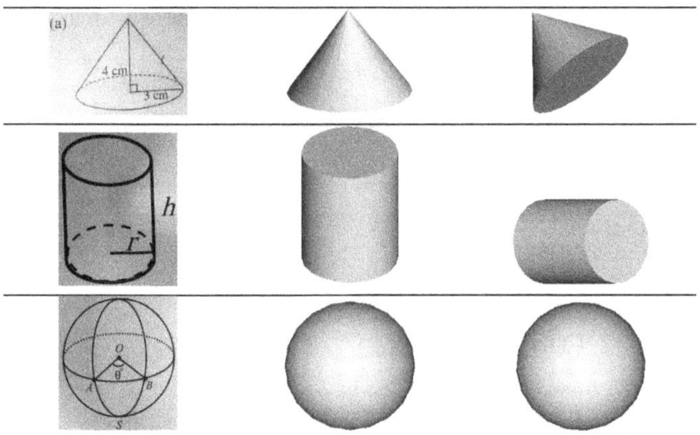

Figure 4: Examples of reconstruction results for the curved objects.

4.2 Keyword Identification

In this paper, we use the Ocropus[1] OCR algorithm to extract the text information from the images. We only identify the keywords that are related to the geometric objects, in English only. The interested keywords are listed as follows: `cuboid`, `cube`, `pyramid`, `tetrahedron`, `triangular`, `trihedral`, `quadrangular`, `parallelogram`, `parallelepiped`, `trapezoid`, `prism`, `oblique`, `frustum`, `pentagon`, `dodecahedron`, `cone`, `cylinder`, `sphere`. The extracted text information by OCR is not always correct due to the quality of the input image and the limitations of OCR algorithm. We calculate the edit distance d_{ij} between each of the interested keyword i and each word j in the space-delimited text. The keyword with the smallest edit distance and that satisfies $d_{ij} \leq 3$ is selected as the accepted keyword. We denote by k_i for each keyword identified from the input text and $\mathbf{k} = \{k_i\}$.

[1]https://github.com/tmbdev/ocropy

4.3 Formulation

Candidate models are first selected by using sub-graph isomorphism algorithm. Specifically, for a given sketch, sub-graph isomorphism are performed twice in order to handle both under-complete and over-complete sketches [18]. Moreover, if a keyword k_i is detected from the input text, we add the corresponding model to the candidate models list if it is not in the list.

The objective function for a candidate model m is defined as follows:

$$F_m = G(A, R, t) + \omega_1 P(A) + \omega_2 L(m, \mathbf{k}), \tag{1}$$

where $G(\cdot)$ evaluates the geometric coherence of the candidate model and the sketch, $P(\cdot)$ favors simpler model based on the number of model parameters, and $L(\cdot)$ is an add-on prior which incorporates the keyword detection. A denotes the set of model parameters, R and t are the rotation and transpose of the model in 3D space, k is the identified keywords, ω_1 and ω_2 balances these three terms.

Geometric term.

The geometric term is defined as the projection error as follows:

$$G(A, R, t) = \frac{1}{N} \sum_{k=1}^{N} \|K(RX_{i_k} + t) - x_{j_k}\|^2, \tag{2}$$

where N denotes the number of corresponding pairs of vertices in the mapping between the model and the sketch, K is the parallel projection matrix, X_{i_k} and x_{j_k} are the coordinates of the corresponding pairs of vertices in the model and the sketch respectively.

Parametric term.

We expect the selected model to be as simple as possible among the candidate models. Obviously, the fewer parameters a model has, the simpler it is. So we define the parametric term as the number of the model parameters as follows:

$$P(A) = |A|, \tag{3}$$

Keyword prior.

The keyword prior term should favor the model that matches the detected keyword.

$$L(m, \mathbf{k}) = \sum_{k_i \in \mathbf{k}} c(m, k_i), \tag{4}$$

where

$$c(m, k_i) = \begin{cases} \sigma_1 & m \text{ matches } k_i \\ \sigma_2 & \text{otherwise} \end{cases}, \tag{5}$$

where $\sigma_2 > \sigma_1 \geq 0$ and they are constant values that encourage the models matching the keywords. In this paper we set $\sigma_1 = 0$ and $\sigma_2 = 1$ for the whole experimental data set.

Let $\mathbf{M}$ denote the set of the candidate models. We minimize the objective function for each candidate model, and select the model with the smallest optimization value, as well as the optimal model parameters, rotation matrix and transpose vector as the final result, that is:

$$\tilde{A}, \tilde{R}, \tilde{t} = \arg \min_{m \in \mathbf{M}} \{F_m\}. \quad (6)$$

4.4 Optimization

Given the coordinates of the 2D sketch $\{\mathrm{x}_1 = (x_1, y_1)^{\mathrm{T}}, \mathrm{x}_2 = (x_2, y_2)^{\mathrm{T}}, \ldots, \mathrm{x}_n = (x_n, y_n)^{\mathrm{T}}\}$, and the correspondences between the vertices of the 2D sketch and the 3D model, we find the 3D coordinates $\{\mathrm{X}_1 = (x_1, y_1, z_1)^{\mathrm{T}}, \mathrm{X}_2 = (x_2, y_2, z_2)^{\mathrm{T}}, \ldots, \mathrm{X}_n = (x_n, y_n, z_n)^{\mathrm{T}}\}$ of the vertices of the model. Specifically, the objective function is a quadratic function with an orthogonal constraint of R. We use the algorithm in [16] to obtain the value of R, A and t. With R, A and t, we are able to generate the final result in 3D style. More details of the optimization algorithm can be found in [18].

5. EXPERIMENTS

Our experimental data set consists of the traditional printed geometric paper books and online documents that contain geometric objects including books, papers, teaching materials, slide shows and other types of documents. We use different brands of smart phones under different light environments to photograph the line drawings and text paragraphs. As a result, we capture 925 line drawing images as our testing data set, among which 679 contain normal geometric objects (containing only straight lines), and 246 contain the curved geometric objects.

5.1 Experiments Setup

The matching accuracy metric used in [18] is also used in this paper to evaluate the performances of our algorithm and previous ones. The matching accuracy is defined as

$$f_a = \frac{|\mathbf{F}_{correct}|}{|\mathbf{F}|}, \quad (7)$$

where $\mathbf{F}$ denotes the test image set, and $\mathbf{F}_{correct}$ denotes the set of correctly matched images.

We evaluate the parameters ω_1 and ω_2 with our testing data set. The ω_1 parameter controls the complexity of the selected model. A low value of ω_1 favors more complicated models (with more parameters) which produce lower values of the projection error, while a high value of ω_1 favors less complicated models (with fewer parameters) which produce higher values of the projection error. Lower value of the projection error means better fitting between the model and the sketch, but is more likely to be over fitting (e.g. by setting ω_1 to 0, for a cube, the cuboid model is always wrongly selected, because it can better fit the sketch no matter the object is in fact a cube or a cuboid). In practice we set $\omega_1 = 20.0$ for the whole data set.

The ω_2 parameter controls the impact of the matched keywords. If no keyword is found, the value of ω_2 has no difference between the models. By setting $\omega_2 = 0$, we completely discard the keyword detection results. A too high value of ω_2 may increase the negative impact of mis-detected keywords. In the experiments, we set $\omega_2 = 100.0$ for the whole data set.

5.2 Comparison

A strict comparison with previous works is not possible due to the different scenario of our method. Most of the existing methods take input as a perfect line drawing with only straight lines, while our method takes input as a roughly extracted line drawing which may contain some primitive curved objects and is possibly inaccurate, together with an image containing the context information. To provide a rough comparison (please note that this comparison is not strictly conducted due to the previous reasons. It can be seen as a reference to the performance of our method.), Table 1 shows the results of our method (with/without the keyword detections) and two previous methods (E3D [16] and SGOR [18]) on our testing data set. As we can see that the matching accuracy of our method is significantly higher than that of E3D and SGOR. The reason why E3D performs so poorly is that, as we have known, it can only handle complete sketches while our method can also handle incomplete or over-complete sketches. And in our experiment, we find that, for most of the testing line drawing images, the extracted sketch is inaccurate (i.e. incomplete or over-complete). Therefore, our method outperforms E3D significantly. The SGOR performs much better in terms of matching accuracy as it can handle inaccurate sketches. However, it can only handle the straight line drawing sketches (so does E3D) while our method can also handle the curved object sketches, plus that our method employs the contextual information, therefore it's still inferior to our method.

Table 1: Comparison between our method and previous ones

Method	Correct match	Incorrect match	Accuracy
E3D	126	799	13.6%
SGOR	537	398	57.4%
Ours w.o. keywords	675	250	72.9%
Ours	752	173	81.2%

6. CONCLUSION

We have presented a method to recover the 3D information of the solid geometric object from single line drawing image in the presence of contextual information. The core of our method is a formulation that incorporates the geometric information and the textual information. Extensive experimental results demonstrate that our method can achieve significantly better performance than the previous methods. In the future we plan to recover more complex line drawings, not just limited to the primitive geometric objects.

Acknowledgments

We'd like to thank the anonymous reviewers for providing encouraging and valuable comments to our work. This work is supported by National Natural Science Foundation of China under Grant 61300061 and Beijing Natural Science Foundation under Grant 4132033.

7. REFERENCES

[1] E. Brown and P. S. Wang. Three-dimensional object recovery from two-dimensional images: a new approach. In *Photonics East'96*, pages 138–147. International Society for Optics and Photonics, 1996.

[2] Y. Chen, J. Liu, and X. Tang. A divide-and-conquer approach to 3d object reconstruction from line drawings. In *Computer Vision, 2007. ICCV 2007. IEEE 11th International Conference on*, pages 1–8. IEEE, 2007.

[3] Y. G. Leclerc and M. A. Fischler. An optimization-based approach to the interpretation of single line drawings as 3d wire frames. *International Journal of Computer Vision*, 9(2):113–136, 1992.

[4] Y. T. Lee and F. Fang. 3d reconstruction of polyhedral objects from single parallel projections using cubic corner. *Computer-Aided Design*, 43(8):1025–1034, 2011.

[5] Y. T. Lee and F. Fang. A new hybrid method for 3d object recovery from 2d drawings and its validation against the cubic corner method and the optimisation-based method. *Computer-Aided Design*, 44(11):1090–1102, 2012.

[6] H. Lipson and M. Shpitalni. Optimization-based reconstruction of a 3d object from a single freehand line drawing. *Computer-Aided Design*, 28(8):651–663, 1996.

[7] J. Liu, L. Cao, Z. Li, and X. Tang. Plane-based optimization for 3d object reconstruction from single line drawings. *Pattern Analysis and Machine Intelligence, IEEE Transactions on*, 30(2):315–327, 2008.

[8] J. Liu, Y. Chen, and X. Tang. Decomposition of complex line drawings with hidden lines for 3d planar-faced manifold object reconstruction. *Pattern Analysis and Machine Intelligence, IEEE Transactions on*, 33(1):3–15, 2011.

[9] J. Liu and Y. T. Lee. Graph-based method for face identification from a single 2d line drawing. *Pattern Analysis and Machine Intelligence, IEEE Transactions on*, 23(10):1106–1119, 2001.

[10] J. Liu, Y. T. Lee, and W.-K. Cham. Identifying faces in a 2d line drawing representing a manifold object. *Pattern Analysis and Machine Intelligence, IEEE Transactions on*, 24(12):1579–1593, 2002.

[11] J. Liu and X. Tang. Evolutionary search for faces from line drawings. *Pattern Analysis and Machine Intelligence, IEEE Transactions on*, 27(6):861–872, 2005.

[12] T. Marill. Emulating the human interpretation of line-drawings as three-dimensional objects. *International Journal of Computer Vision*, 6(2):147–161, 1991.

[13] C. Tian, M. Masry, and H. Lipson. Physical sketching: Reconstruction and analysis of 3d objects from freehand sketches. *Computer-Aided Design*, 41(3):147–158, 2009.

[14] Y. Wang, Z. He, X. Liu, Z. Tang, and L. Li. A fast and robust ellipse detector based on top-down least-square fitting. *Computers & Electrical Engineering*, 40(4):1415–1428, 2014.

[15] T. Xue, J. Liu, and X. Tang. Object cut: Complex 3d object reconstruction through line drawing separation. In *Computer Vision and Pattern Recognition (CVPR), 2010 IEEE Conference on*, pages 1149–1156. IEEE, 2010.

[16] T. Xue, J. Liu, and X. Tang. Example-based 3d object reconstruction from line drawings. In *Computer Vision and Pattern Recognition (CVPR), 2012 IEEE Conference on*, pages 302–309. IEEE, 2012.

[17] L. Yang, J. Liu, and X. Tang. Complex 3d general object reconstruction from line drawings. In *Computer Vision (ICCV), 2013 IEEE International Conference on*, pages 1433–1440, Dec 2013.

[18] J. Zheng, Y. Wang, and Z. Tang. Recovering solid geometric object from single line drawing image. *Multimedia Tools and Applications*, pages 1–22, 2015.

[19] J. Zheng, Y. Wang, and Z. Tang. Solid geometric object reconstruction from single line drawing image. In *International Conference on Computer Graphics Theory and Applications (GRAPP 2015)*, 2015.

[20] C. Zou, S. Chen, H. Fu, and J. Liu. Progressive 3d reconstruction of planar-faced manifold objects with drf-based line drawing decomposition. *Visualization and Computer Graphics, IEEE Transactions on*, PP(99):1–1, 2014.

[21] C. Zou, H. Yang, and J. Liu. Separation of line drawings based on split faces for 3d object reconstruction. In *Computer Vision and Pattern Recognition (CVPR), 2014 IEEE Conference on*, pages 692–699, June 2014.

Automatic Music Video Generation Based on Emotion-Oriented Pseudo Song Prediction and Matching

Jen-Chun Lin
Academia Sinica
Taipei, Taiwan
jenchunlin@gmail.com

Wen-Li Wei
Academia Sinica
Taipei, Taiwan
lilijinjin@gmail.com

Hsin-Min Wang
Academia Sinica
Taipei, Taiwan
whm@iis.sinica.edu.tw

ABSTRACT

The main difficulty in automatic music video (MV) generation lies in how to match two different media (i.e., video and music). This paper proposes a novel content-based MV generation system based on emotion-oriented pseudo song prediction and matching. We use a multi-task deep neural network (MDNN) to jointly learn the relationship among music, video, and emotion from an emotion-annotated MV corpus. Given a queried video, the MDNN is applied to predict the acoustic (music) features from the visual (video) features, i.e., the pseudo song corresponding to the video. Then, the pseudo acoustic (music) features are matched with the acoustic (music) features of each music track in the music collection according to a pseudo-song-based deep similarity matching (PDSM) metric given by another deep neural network (DNN) trained on the acoustic and pseudo acoustic features of the positive (official), less-positive (artificial), and negative (artificial) MV examples. The results of objective and subjective experiments demonstrate that the proposed pseudo-song-based framework performs well and can generate appealing MVs with better viewing and listening experiences.

Keywords

Automatic music video generation, cross-modal media retrieval, deep neural networks.

1. INTRODUCTION

With the prevalence of mobile devices, video is widely used to record memorable moments of daily events such as wedding, graduation, and birthday parties. Websites such as YouTube or Vimeo have furthered the phenomenon as sharing becomes ever easy. In addition, people enjoy listening to music to release their emotions. In psychology, it is argued that a musical experience may evoke emotions when a listener conjures up images of things and events that have never occurred, in the absence of any episodic memory from a previous event in time [1]. Thus, music and video are often accompanied to complement each other to enhance emotional resonance in music videos (MVs), movies, and television programs. Accompanying a user-generated video (UGV) with music can enhance the entertaining quality and emotional resonance, and thus is desirable. For example, a wedding video accompanying with romantic music can enhance a sweet atmosphere. Nevertheless, to select good music for a video, music professionals are required. With the rapid growth of music collections, matching a video with suitable music becomes ever difficult. The advent of automatic MV generation systems is foreseeable.

MM'16, October 15–19, 2016, Amsterdam, Netherlands
© 2016 ACM. ISBN 978-1-4503-3603-1/16/10 ...$15.00
DOI: http://dx.doi.org/10.1145/2964284.2967245

In response to this trend, machine-aided MV composition has been studied in the past decade [2–8]. However, the performance of previous systems is usually limited, because most of them only consider the relationship between the low-level acoustic and visual features without considering any semantic constraints [2–4]. Since different semantics, e.g., emotion such as happy and sad, usually contain distinct MV properties, there is difficulty in establishing a direct relationship between the music and video modalities from the low-level features without considering such semantics. Moreover, there is a so-called semantic gap between the low-level acoustic (or visual) features and the high-level human perception. To narrow the gap, motivated by the recent development in affective computing of multimedia signals, some research has begun to map the low-level acoustic and visual features into an emotional space [5–8]. A music-accompanied video composed in this way is attractive, as the perception of emotion naturally occurs in video watching and music listening. However, most of the existing studies for automatic MV generation [5–8] model the relationship between the low-level acoustic (or visual features) and the emotion labels separately, whereas ignoring the correlation between music and video. Since the music and video contents in a professionally edited official music video (OMV) are always highly synchronized and carefully composed to match each other in terms of emotional storytelling, without considering the relationship between the music and video modalities in automatic MV generation may still result in bad viewing experiences.

Our idea to jointly handle the aforementioned problems is inspired by the recent computational models of the brain [9,10], in particular the memory-prediction framework [10], which emphasizes the notion of multisensory spatiotemporal predictions. For example, based on the input from one sense, e.g., vision, the brain can predict the current and future events in other senses, e.g., hearing. Similar findings have also been reported in psychology and cognitive science. For example, it has been suggested in [11] that visual information has a predictive role in processing audio information. Driven by these findings, we propose a novel automatic MV generation framework based on emotion-oriented pseudo song prediction and matching, as shown in Figure 1. Given a queried video, a shot change detection method is first used to segment the queried video into several video shots. For each video shot, a multi-task deep neural network (MDNN) [12,13], which is trained by jointly learning the relationship among acoustic (music) features, visual (video) features, and

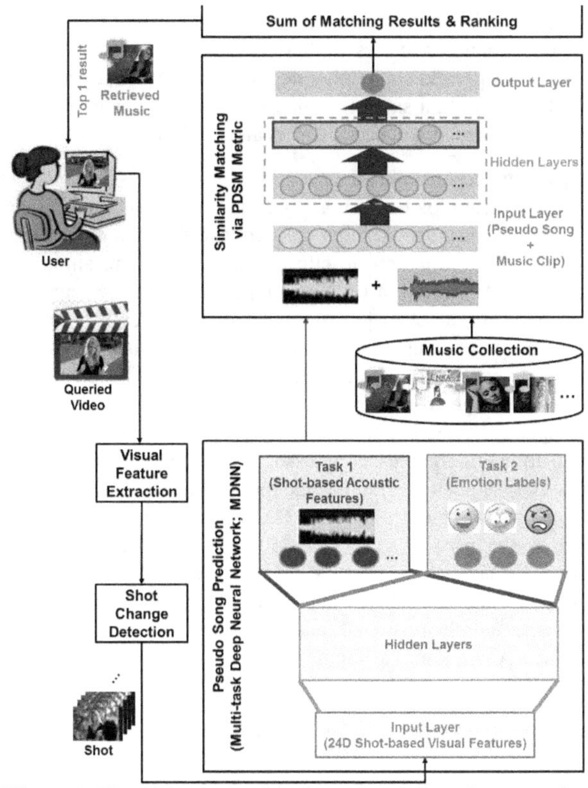

Figure 1. The MV generation framework based on emotion-oriented pseudo song prediction and matching.

emotion labels from an emotion-annotated OMV corpus, is adopted to predict the pseudo acoustic (music) features from the visual (video) features. For MV generation, a pseudo-song-based deep similarity matching (PDSM) metric is then applied to evaluate the similarity between the acoustic features of a music clip and the pseudo acoustic features of a shot of the queried video. The PDSM metric is realized by another deep neural network (DNN) trained on the positive (official), less-positive (artificial), and negative (artificial) MV examples. To the best of our knowledge, this is the first attempt to apply the multi-task deep neural network and pseudo song prediction and matching in automatic MV generation. The experimental results demonstrate that the proposed framework outperforms an existing system in both subjective and objective evaluations.

The remainder of this paper is organized as follows. Previous research on video soundtrack recommendation and MV generation is reviewed in Section 2. The methodology, including video shot change detection, pseudo song prediction, and pseudo-song-based deep similarity learning and matching, is described in Section 3. Finally, the experimental results are presented in Section 4, and conclusions are made in Section 5.

2. RELATED WORK

In this section, we briefly review the progress on video soundtrack recommendation and MV generation in the recent five years. Kuo et al. [4] employed multi-modal latent semantic analysis to learn the co-occurrence relationship between the low-level acoustic and visual features, such as Mel-frequency cepstral coefficients, loudness, spectral centroid, color, and motion, from the music and video contents for video soundtrack recommendation. To narrow the semantic gap between the low-level features and the high-level human perception, Wang et al. [5] proposed an acoustic-visual emotion Gaussians (AVEG) model to respectively map the acoustic features and the visual features into the same valence-arousal (VA) emotional space to measure the distance between a music clip and a video clip for MV generation. Shah et al. [6] employed a support vector machine (SVM) to model the categorical emotion, such as sweet, funny, and sad, from the acoustic, visual, and geographic features for video soundtrack recommendation. Lin et al. [7] adopted an emotional temporal course model (ETCM) to respectively model the temporal structure of emotional expression of music and video and a stream matching method to measure the similarity between the recognized emotional temporal phase sequences of music and video for MV generation. They further proposed an emotion-oriented deep similarity matching (EDSM) metric to measure the similarity between the recognized emotional temporal phase sequences [8].

3. METHODOLOGY

In the proposed MV generation system, as shown in Figure 1, shot change detection is first applied to segment a queried video into several video shots. For each video shot, a MDNN is used to predict the acoustic (music) features from the visual (video) features, called pseudo song prediction. Finally, a PDSM metric is used to match music and video based on the acoustic features.

3.1 Video Shot Change Detection

A queried video usually contains thousands of image frames. Consider that a video shot is usually captured by a single camera action, and that there are no significant content changes between successive frames in a shot [14], it would be more efficient to conduct pseudo song prediction and matching at the shot-level instead of the frame-level. In this study, we use 5-color themes [15] (a kind of dominant color representation) as features to segment the video into shots. The shot boundaries are determined according to the color theme difference CTD_i between two adjacent image frames I_{i-1} and I_i calculated as

$$CTD_i = \prod_{k=1}^{5}\prod_{j=1}^{5} CT_i(k) - CT_{i-1}(j), \tag{1}$$

where $CT_i(k)$ denotes the k-th color theme in the i-th frame and $CT_{i-1}(j)$ denotes the j-th color theme in the i-1-th frame. All the frames with $CTD_i \neq 0$ are considered shot boundaries. Figure 2 shows an example of the shot change detection results and the corresponding color themes. After shot change detection, the shot-based visual (or acoustic) features can be constructed by statistics of the component frame-based visual (or acoustic) features. If shot change detection fails to detect any boundaries, the whole video is used to predict a pseudo song.

3.2 Pseudo Song Prediction via Multi-Task Deep Neural Network

Multi-task learning [16] aims at improving the generalization performance of a learning task by jointly learning multiple related tasks together. It has been found that if the tasks are related and share some internal representation, then through joint learning, they can transfer knowledge to one another. The common internal representation learned in this way helps the models generalize better for the future unseen data. Consequently, for pseudo song prediction, we adopt the MDNN [12,13] to predict the acoustic (music) features from the visual (video) features by jointly

Figure 2. Shot change detection results of the OMV "love story" by Taylor Swift.

learning the relationship among the acoustic (music) features, visual (video) features, and emotion labels from an emotion-annotated OMV corpus.

Assume that there are K tasks $T \equiv \{T_1, T_2 ..., T_K\}$ to learn under the MDNN framework. The MDNN model parameters are represented by $\Lambda \equiv \{\lambda_0\} \cup \{\lambda_1, \lambda_2, ..., \lambda_K\}$, where λ_0 consists of model parameters shared by all tasks and λ_k consists of model parameters specific to task T_k. In this study, λ_0 represents the shared weights from all hidden layers, whereas λ_k represents the weights associated with the task-specific output layer of T_k. Without loss of generality, T_1 will always be taken as the primary task, and the rest are the secondary (or extra) tasks. The objective function ε for training is formulated as the weighted sum of the error functions of all the tasks as follows,

$$\varepsilon(D, \Lambda) = \sum_{x \in D} \left(\sum_{k=1}^{K} \beta_k \varepsilon_k (x; \lambda_0, \lambda_k) \right), \tag{2}$$

where ε_k and β_k are the error function and weight of task T_k subject to $\sum_{k=1}^{K} \beta_k = 1$, x is an input vector, and D is the whole set of training vectors for all tasks. After training, only the model parameters associated with the primary task T_1 (i.e., λ_0 and λ_1) are needed, and those of the secondary task(s) can be discarded.

In this study, we use emotion as the secondary task T_2 to learn the MDNN for predicting the acoustic features (the primary task T_1) from the input visual features x. The emotion can be regarded as the semantic constraint for MDNN learning, and is expected to be able to improve the prediction accuracy. β_k (k=1,2) is set to 0.5, and the error function ε_k of task T_k (k=1,2) is the sum of squared error as follows,

$$\varepsilon_k (x; \lambda_0, \lambda_k) = \sum_{i=1}^{N_k} \frac{1}{2} \times \left(d_i^{(k)} - s_i^{(k)} \right)^2, \tag{3}$$

where $d_i^{(k)}$ is the target value of the i-th output neuron for T_k, $s_i^{(k)}$ is the predicted value of the i-th output neuron for T_k, and N_k is the total number of output neurons for T_k. Specifically, x is the shot-based visual feature vector constructed from the component frame-based visual feature vectors, $d_i^{(1)}$ is the i-th element of the corresponding shot-based acoustic feature vector, $d_i^{(2)}$ is the emotion label, $s_i^{(1)}$ is the i-th element of the acoustic feature vector of the predicted pseudo song, while $s_i^{(2)}$ is the predicted emotion.

3.3 Pseudo-song-based Deep Similarity Learning and Matching for MV Generation

Recently, a similarity metric learning technique has been applied to the MV generation task [8]. The goal is to learn a flexible nonlinear similarity matching metric to alleviate the effect of emotion recognition errors in MV generation. Since inaccurate prediction of pseudo songs may degrade the performance of MV generation as well, a similarity metric capable of accommodating such pseudo song prediction errors is also desirable.

Again, we regard similarity learning as a regression learning problem. The goal is to learn a regression model (i.e., the PDSM metric) that can judge whether the acoustic features of a pseudo song and an arbitrary music clip of same length are similar. In PDSM metric learning, a DNN is adopted to learn the regression model based on a set of positive training examples v^{++}=(pseudo song, official music^{++}), less-positive training examples v^{+}=(pseudo song, official music^{+}), and negative training examples v^{-}=(pseudo song, official music^{-}) with labels y^{++}=3, y^{+}=2, and y^{-}=1, respectively. A positive training example is formed by the pseudo song and the music clip associated with a video shot of an OMV. A less-positive training example is constructed from the pseudo song of a video shot of an OMV and the music clip (same length as the pseudo song) of another OMV in the same VA emotional quadrant. A negative training example is constructed from the pseudo song of a video shot of an OMV and the music clip (same length as the pseudo song) of another OMV in a different VA emotional quadrant.

Denoting a training example v^{++}, v^{+} or v^{-} as v, we forward v layer-by-layer through a DNN to generate the representation of each layer, i.e., $v^{(1)}$,..., $v^{(L)}$. The l-th layer takes as input $v^{(l)}$ and uses a projection function to transform $v^{(l)}$ to $v^{(l+1)}$ as follows,

$$v^{(l+1)} = f^{(l)}(W^{(l)} v^{(l)} + b^{(l)}), \tag{4}$$

where $v^{(l)}$ and $v^{(l+1)}$ are the feature representation in the l-th and $l+1$-th layer, respectively; $W^{(l)}$ is a weight projection matrix; $b^{(l)}$ is a bias vector; and $f^{(l)}(.)$ is an activation function, which is a sigmoid function for l=1 to L-2, and a linear function for l=L-1. Given the label y, we use the sum of squared error as the loss function in the output layer:

$$\ell(v, y) = SSE(v^{(L)}, y). \tag{5}$$

The loss of the output layer will be back propagated to fine-tune the parameters W and b through the classical back-propagation method. Since the side-information (i.e., positive, less-positive or negative label) is considered for DNN to learn a nonlinear similarity matching metric, the resulting DNN regression model (i.e., the PDSM metric) is expected to alleviate the effect of errors in pseudo song prediction. The difference between the EDSM metric [8] and the proposed PDSM metric is that we regard similarity learning as a regression learning problem rather than a classification problem. By considering additionally the less-positive training examples, the learned PDSM metric should have a better generalization ability.

In the MV generation phase, given a queried video, the goal is to find a ranked list of music candidates for the query. Specifically, the queried video is paired with each music track from the target music database to form a testing pair. After video shot change detection, MDNN is applied to obtain the pseudo song for each video shot. Each paired music track is also divided into a sequence of music clips according to the time codes of the video shots. The PDSM metric is then applied to measure the similarity between the acoustic features of the pseudo song and the music clip, for each video shot. For each testing pair, the overall similarity score is summed from the similarity scores of all video shots. Finally, all the music tracks are ranked in

Table 1. Average ranking accuracy of the DEMV-matchmaker$_{com}$ and pseudo-song-based frameworks.

The Video Retrieving Music (V2M) Task	
DEMV-matchmaker$_{com}$ [8]	Pseudo-song-based MV Generation Framework
0.6519	0.7627

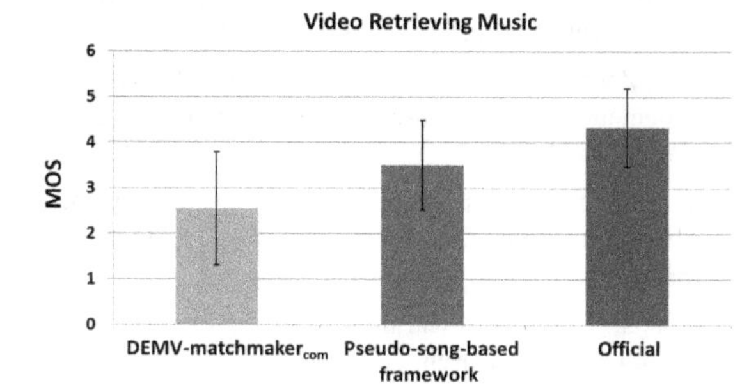

Figure 3. Results of the subjective MOS test.

descending order of scores, and the top one is regarded as the best recommendation for the queried video to generate the MV.

4. EXPERIMENTS

To evaluate the effectiveness of the proposed pseudo-song-based MV generation framework, we performed experiments on a set of OMVs downloaded from YouTube. 265 complete OMVs were collected, among which 65 OMVs downloaded according to the links provided in the DEAP database [17] were used to train the MDNN and the PDSM metric. Each OMV was assigned one (out of three) emotional quadrant based on the valence-arousal annotations provided in the DEAP database. The two emotional quadrants in the low arousal space were merged into one [7,8], since emotions mapped into the lower arousal space are difficult to differentiate [18]. The remaining 200 OMVs were used for testing.

For music, we used MIRToolbox to extract four types of frame-based acoustic features, namely dynamic, spectral, timbre, and tonal features [19,20]. In total, 46-dimensional acoustic features were extracted for each audio frame. Given a queried video, we extract the mean from the audio frames corresponding to a video shot as the 46-dimensional shot-based acoustic features. For video, the frame-based color themes and motion intensities were extracted as the 8-dimensional visual features [15,21]. The minimum, mean, and maximum values from the frame-based visual features in each video shot were extracted to generate 24-dimensional shot-based visual features. For the MDNN, there were 3 hidden layers, each with 230, 120, and 30 neurons, respectively. The size of mini-batch for the stochastic gradient descent algorithm was set to 20. For the PDSM metric, we used a DNN with 3 hidden layers, each with 230, 120, and 130 neurons, respectively. The size of mini-batch for the stochastic gradient descent algorithm was set to 1. For both DNNs, we applied random initialization for the weights, a constant learning rate of 0.05, and the L2 weight decay regularization to avoid over-fitting.

We compared the proposed pseudo-song-based MV generation framework with the state-of-the-art DEMV-matchmaker$_{com}$ framework [8]. In the experiments, the video of each testing OMV was used in turn to search for the best matched music from the music tracks of the 200 testing OMVs, and the one corresponding to the test video was regarded as the ground truth. The ranking accuracy [4] defined as

$$Ranking\ Accuracy = 1 - \frac{rank(g) - 1}{|C| + 1}, \qquad (6)$$

was adopted as the objective performance measure, where *rank(g)* is the rank of the ground truth *g*, and $|C|$ is the total number of candidates in the music set ($|C|$=200 in this study). We reported the average ranking accuracy over the testing set.

The results in Table 1 demonstrate that the proposed pseudo-song-based MV generation framework outperforms DEMV-matchmaker$_{com}$. We believe that it is because DEMV-matchmaker$_{com}$ did not consider the relationship between music and video modalities in the respective emotion recognition model construction. It may lose information useful for music (or video) emotion recognition, since the music and video contents in an OMV are always highly synchronized and carefully composed to match each other in terms of emotional storytelling. Even DEMV-matchmaker$_{com}$ has integrated a similarity learning metric to alleviate the effect of emotion recognition errors, the performance is still limited. The multi-task deep neural network (i.e., MDNN) used in the pseudo-song-based MV generation framework can indeed model the relationship among the acoustic (music) features, visual (video) features, and emotion labels. Overall, the pseudo-song-based MV generation framework pushed ahead the rank of ground truth music by approximately 22 (i.e., the average ranking accuracy was improved from 0.6519 to 0.7627), compared to DEMV-matchmaker$_{com}$.

Subjective evaluation[1] in terms of 5-point mean opinion score (MOS) was conducted on 6 MV sets. Each MV set contains the original official MV (ground truth) and the MVs generated by DEMV-matchmaker$_{com}$ and the proposed pseudo-song-based MV generation frameworks. Each MV was evaluated by thirteen subjects. The average MOS over all MVs and subjects is shown in Figure 3. It is clear that the pseudo-song-based MV generation framework outperforms DEMV-matchmaker$_{com}$. The results reveal that modeling the relationship among music, video, and emotion can indeed generate more attractive MVs to enhance subjects' viewing and listening experiences. The results also show that the MOS of the MVs generated by the pseudo-song-based MV generation framework is quite close to that of the ground truth MVs. We feel very excited for this result.

5. CONCLUSIONS AND FUTURE WORK

In this paper, a novel content-based MV generation system is proposed based on emotion-oriented pseudo song prediction and matching. The results of both subjective and objective evaluations have demonstrated that the proposed pseudo-song-based framework outperforms the state-of-the-art DEMV-matchmaker$_{com}$ framework, and can offer a satisfactory generated music video to enhance human viewing and listening experiences. Benefit from rich music video resources on the websites such as YouTube or Vimeo, developing an end-to-end deep neural network learning technique for automatic MV generation is desirable and will be studied in our future work.

6. ACKNOWLEDGMENTS

This work was supported in part by the Ministry of Science and Technology of Taiwan under Grant: NSC 102-2221-E-001-008-MY3.

[1] MOS results for individual MVs are available at https://sites.google.com/site/pseudosongpredictionmatching/

7. REFERENCES

[1] Juslin, P. N. and Västfjäll, D. Emotional responses to music: the need to consider underlying mechanisms. *Behavioral and Brain Sciences*, 31(5): 559–621, 2008.

[2] Hua, X.-S., Lu, L., and Zhang, H.-J. Automatic music video generation based on temporal pattern analysis. In *ACM MM*, 2004.

[3] Yoon, J.-C., Lee, I.-K., and Byun, S. Automated music video generation using multi-level feature-based segmentation. *Multimedia Tools and Application*, 41(2): 197–214, 2009.

[4] Kuo, F.-F., Shan, M.-K., and Lee, S.-Y. Background music recommendation for video based on multimodal latent semantic analysis. In *ICME*, 2013.

[5] Wang, J.-C., Yang, Y.-H., Jhuo, I.-H., Lin, Y.-Y., and Wang, H.-M. The acousticvisual emotion Gaussians model for automatic generation of music video. In *ACM MM*, 2012.

[6] Shah, R. R., Yu, Y., and Zimmermann, R. ADVISOR–personalized video soundtrack recommendation by late fusion with heuristic rankings. In *ACM MM*, 2014.

[7] Lin, J.-C., Wei, W.-L., and Wang, H.-M. EMV-matchmaker: emotional temporal course modeling and matching for automatic music video generation. In *ACM MM*, 2015.

[8] Lin, J.-C., Wei, W.-L., and Wang, H.-M. DEMV-matchmaker: emotional temporal course representation and deep similarity matching for automatic music video generation. In *ICASSP*, 2016.

[9] Friston, K. The free-energy principle: a unified brain theory?. *Nature Reviews Neuroscience*, 11(2): 127–138, 2010.

[10] Hawkins, J. and Blakeslee, S. *On intelligence*. Owl Books, 2005.

[11] Summerfield, Q. Some preliminaries to a comprehensive account of audio-visual speech perception. *Hearing by Eye: The Psychology of Lip Reading*, D. B. and C. R., Eds., 1987, 3–51.

[12] Chen, D. and Mak, Brian K.-W. Multitask learning of deep neural network for low-resource speech recognition. *IEEE/ACM Transactions on Audio, Speech, and Language Processing*, 23(7): 1172–1183, 2015.

[13] Xia, R. and Liu, Y. A multi-task learning framework for emotion recognition using 2D continuous space. *IEEE Transactions on Affective Computing*, 2015.

[14] Li, L., Zeng, X., Li, X., Hu, W., and Zhu, P. Video shot segmentation using graph-based dominant-set clustering. *ACM ICIMCS*, 2009.

[15] Wang, X., Jia, J., and Cai, L. Affective image adjustment with a single word. *The Visual Computer*, 29(11): 1121–1133, 2013.

[16] Caruana, R. Multitask learning. Ph.D. dissertation, Carnegie Mellon Univ., Pittsburgh, PA, USA, 1997.

[17] Koelstra, S., Mühl, C., Soleymani, M., Lee, J.-S., Yazdani, A., Ebrahimi, T., Pun, T., Nijholt, A., and Patras, I. DEAP: a database for emotion analysis using physiological signals. *IEEE Transactions on Affective Computing*, 3(1): 18–31, 2012.

[18] Soleymani, M., Kierkels, Joep J. M., Chanel, G., and Pun, T. A Bayesian framework for video affective representation. In *ACII*, 2009.

[19] Wang, J.-C., Yang, Y.-H., Wang, H.-M., and Jeng, S.-K. The acoustic emotion Gaussians model for emotion-based music annotation and retrieval. In *ACM MM*, 2012.

[20] Lartillot, O. and Toiviainen, P. A Matlab toolbox for musical feature extraction from audio. In *DAFx*, 2007.

[21] Chen, H.-W., Kuo, J.-H., Chu, W.-T., and Wu, J.-L. Action movies segmentation and summarization based on tempo analysis. In *MIR*, 2004.

Novel Word Embedding and Translation-based Language Modeling for Extractive Speech Summarization

Kuan-Yu Chen, Shih-Hung Liu, Berlin Chen[+], Hsin-Min Wang, Hsin-Hsi Chen[#]
Academia Sinica, Taiwan
[#]National Taiwan University, Taiwan
[+]National Taiwan Normal University, Taiwan
{kychen, journey, whm}@iis.sinica.edu.tw, [+]berlin@csie.ntnu.edu.tw, [#]hhchen@csie.ntu.edu.tw

ABSTRACT

Word embedding methods revolve around learning continuous distributed vector representations of words with neural networks, which can capture semantic and/or syntactic cues, and in turn be used to induce similarity measures among words, sentences and documents in context. Celebrated methods can be categorized as prediction-based and count-based methods according to the training objectives and model architectures. Their pros and cons have been extensively analyzed and evaluated in recent studies, but there is relatively less work continuing the line of research to develop an enhanced learning method that brings together the advantages of the two model families. In addition, the interpretation of the learned word representations still remains somewhat opaque. Motivated by the observations and considering the pressing need, this paper presents a novel method for learning the word representations, which not only inherits the advantages of classic word embedding methods but also offers a clearer and more rigorous interpretation of the learned word representations. Built upon the proposed word embedding method, we further formulate a translation-based language modeling framework for the extractive speech summarization task. A series of empirical evaluations demonstrate the effectiveness of the proposed word representation learning and language modeling techniques in extractive speech summarization.

Keywords

Word embedding, representation, interpretation, language model, speech summarization

1. INTRODUCTION

Owing to the popularity of various Internet applications, rapidly growing multimedia content, such as music video, broadcast news programs and lecture recordings, has been continuously filling our everyday life [1, 2]. Obviously, speech is one of the most important sources of information about multimedia. By virtue of speech summarization, one can efficiently browse multimedia content by digesting the summarized audio/video snippets and associated transcripts. Extractive speech summarization manages to select a set of salient sentences from a spoken document according to a target summarization ratio and subsequently concatenate them together to form a summary [3]. The wide spectrum of summarization methods developed so far may be roughly divided into three categories: 1) methods simply based on the sentence position or structure information [4], 2) methods based on unsupervised sentence ranking [5], and 3) methods based on supervised sentence classification [5]. Interested readers may refer to [5, 7, 8] for comprehensive reviews and new insights into the major methods that have been developed and applied with good success to a wide variety of text and speech summarization.

Orthogonal to the existing commonly-used methods, we explore in this paper the use of various word embedding methods [9-11] in extractive speech summarization, which have recently demonstrated excellent performance in many natural language processing (NLP) related tasks, such as machine translation [12], sentiment analysis [13] and sentence completion [14]. The central idea of these methods is to learn continuous, distributed vector representations of words using neural networks, which can probe latent semantic and/or syntactic cues, and in turn be employed to induce similarity measures among words, sentences and documents. According to the variety of the training objectives and model architectures, the classic methods can be roughly classified into the prediction-based and count-based methods [15]. Recent studies in the literature have evaluated these methods in several NLP-related tasks and analyzed their strengths and deficiencies [11, 16]. However, there are only a few studies in the literature that continue the line of research to crystalize an enhanced word embedding method that brings together the merits of these two major families. In addition, the interpretation of the learned value of each dimension in a learned word representation is a bit opaque. To satisfy the pressing need and complement the defect, we propose a novel modeling method, which not only inherits the advantages from the classic word embedding methods but also offers a clearer and more rigorous interpretation. Beyond the efforts to improve the representation of words, we also present a novel and efficient translation-based language modeling framework on top of the proposed word embedding method for extractive speech summarization. Unlike the common thread of leveraging word embedding methods in speech/text summarization tasks, which is to represent a document/sentence by averaging the corresponding word embeddings over all words in the document/sentence and estimate the cosine similarity measure of any given document-sentence pair, the proposed framework can authentically capture the finer-grained (i.e., word-to-word) semantic relationship to be effectively used in extractive speech summarization.

In a nutshell, the major contributions of the paper are twofold:

- **A novel word representation learning technique**, which not only inherits the advantages from the classic word embedding

MM '16, October 15-19, 2016, Amsterdam, Netherlands

DOI: http://dx.doi.org/10.1145/2964284.2967246

methods but also offers a clearer and more rigorous interpretation of word representations, is proposed.

- **A translation-based language modeling framework** on top of the proposed word embedding method, which can also be integrated with classic word embedding methods, is introduced to the extractive speech summarization task.

2. CLASSIC WORD EMBEDDING METHODS

Perhaps one of the most well-known seminal studies on developing word embedding methods was presented by Bengio et al. [9]. It estimated a statistical n-gram language model, formalized as a feed-forward neural network, for predicting future words in context while inducing word embeddings as a by-product. Such an attempt has already motivated many follow-up extensions to develop effective methods for probing latent semantic and syntactic regularities manifested in the representations of words. Representative methods can be categorized as prediction-based and count-based methods. The skip-gram model (SG) [10] and the global vector model (GloVe) [11] are well-studied examples of the two categories, respectively.

Rather than seeking to learn a statistical language model, the SG model is intended to obtain a dense vector representation of each word directly. The structure of SG is similar to a feed-forward neural network, with the exception that the non-linear hidden layer in the former is removed. The model thus can be trained on a large corpus efficiently, getting around the heavily computational burden incurred by the non-linear hidden layer, while still retaining good performance. Formally, given a word sequence, $w^1, w^2, \ldots, w^T$, the objective function of SG is to maximize the log-probability,

$$\sum_{t=1}^{T}\sum_{\substack{k=-c\\k\neq 0}}^{c}\log P(w^{t+k}\mid w^{t}), \tag{1}$$

where c is the window size of the contextual words for the central word w^t, and the conditional probability is computed by

$$P(w^{t+k}\mid w^{t})=\frac{\exp(\mathbf{v}_{w^{t+k}}\cdot\mathbf{v}_{w^{t}})}{\Sigma_{i=1}^{V}\exp(\mathbf{v}_{w_i}\cdot\mathbf{v}_{w^{t}})}, \tag{2}$$

where $\mathbf{v}_{w^{t+k}}$ and $\mathbf{v}_{w^t}$ denote the representations of the words at positions $t+k$ and t, respectively; w_i denotes the i-th word in the vocabulary; and V is the vocabulary size.

The GloVe model suggests that an appropriate starting point for word representation learning should be associated with the ratios of co-occurrence probabilities rather than the prediction probabilities. More precisely, GloVe makes use of a weighted least squares regression, with the aim of learning word representations that can characterize the co-occurrence statistics between each pair of words:

$$\sum_{i=1}^{V}\sum_{j=1}^{V}f(X_{w_iw_j})(\mathbf{v}_{w_i}\cdot\mathbf{v}_{w_j}+b_{w_i}+b_{w_j}-\log X_{w_iw_j})^2, \tag{3}$$

where w_i and w_j are any two distinct words in the vocabulary; $X_{w_iw_j}$ denotes the number of times words w_i and w_j co-occur in a pre-defined sliding context window; $f(\cdot)$ is a monotonic smoothing function used to modulate the impact of each pair of words involved in model training; and $\mathbf{v}_{w_i}$ and b_{w_i} denote the word representation and the bias term of word w_i, respectively. Interested readers may refer to [15, 16] for a more thorough and entertaining discussion.

3. METHODOLOGY

3.1 The Proposed Word Embedding Method

Although the prediction-based methods have shown their remarkable performance in several NLP-related tasks, they do not sufficiently utilize the statistics of the entire corpus since the models are usually trained on local context windows in a separate manner [11]. By contrast, the count-based methods leverage the holistic statistics of the corpus efficiently. However, a few studies have indicated their relatively poor performance in some tasks [16]. Among all the existing methods (both the prediction-based and count-based methods), the interpretation of the learned value of each dimension in the representation is not intuitively clear. Motivated by these observations, a novel modeling approach, which naturally brings together the advantages of the two major model families and results in interpretable word representations, is proposed.

We begin with the definition of terminologies and notations. As most classic embedding methods, we introduce two sets of word representations: one is the set of desired word representations, denoted by $\mathbf{M}$; the other is the set of separate context word representations, denoted by $\mathbf{W}$. $\mathbf{W}$ and $\mathbf{M}$ are $H\times V$ matrices, where the j-th columns of matrices $\mathbf{W}$ and $\mathbf{M}$, denoted by $\mathbf{W}_{w_j}\in\mathbb{R}^H$ and $\mathbf{M}_{w_j}\in\mathbb{R}^H$, correspond to the j-th word w_j in the vocabulary. H is a pre-defined dimension of the word embedding. To make the learned representation interpretable, we assume that each word embedding is a multinomial representation. Furthermore, to make the computation more efficient, we assume that each row vector of matrix $\mathbf{W}$ follows a multinomial distribution as well. To inherit the advantages from the prediction-based methods, the training objective is to obtain an appropriate word representation by considering the predictive ability of a given word occurring at an arbitrary position t of the training corpus (denoted w^t) to predict its surrounding context words:

$$\prod_{t}\prod_{\substack{k=-c\\k\neq 0}}^{c}P(w^{t+k}\mid w^{t})=\prod_{t}\prod_{\substack{k=-c\\k\neq 0}}^{c}\frac{\mathbf{W}_{w^{t+k}}\cdot\mathbf{M}_{w^{t}}}{\Sigma_{j=1}^{V}\mathbf{W}_{w_j}\cdot\mathbf{M}_{w^{t}}}. \tag{4}$$

The denominator can be omitted because it always equals to 1. In order to characterize the whole corpus statistics well, we train the model parameters in a batch mode instead of using a sequential learning strategy. Therefore, the objective function becomes

$$\sum_{i=1}^{V}\sum_{j=1}^{V}n(w_i,w_j)\log(\mathbf{W}_{w_i}\cdot\mathbf{M}_{w_j}), \tag{5}$$

where $n(w_i,w_j)$ denotes the number of times words w_i and w_j co-occur in a pre-defined sliding context window. Obviously, such a model not only bears a close resemblance to the prediction-based methods (e.g., SG) but also capitalizes on the statistics gathered from the entire corpus like the count-based methods (e.g., GloVe), in a probabilistic framework. The component distributions (i.e., $\mathbf{W}$ and $\mathbf{M}$) can be estimated using the expectation-maximization (EM) algorithm. Advanced algorithms, such as the triple jump EM algorithm [17], can be leveraged to accelerate the training process. Since the training objective of the proposed method is similar to that of the SG model, and it results a set of distributional word representations, we thus term the proposed model the distributional skip-gram model (DSG). The interpretive ability of DSG will be discussed in detail later in Section 4.3.

3.2 Translation-based Language Modeling for Summarization

Language modeling (LM) has proven its broad utility in many NLP-related tasks. In the context of using LM for extractive speech summarization, each sentence S of a spoken document D to be summarized can be formulated as a probabilistic generative model for generating the document, and sentences are selected based on the corresponding generative probability $P(D|S)$: the higher the probability, the more representative S is likely to be for D [18]. The major challenge facing the LM-based framework is how to accurately estimate the model parameters for each sentence. The simplest way is to estimate a unigram language model (ULM) on the basis of the frequency of each distinct word w occurring in the sentence S, with the maximum likelihood criterion:

$$P(w \mid S) = \frac{n(w,S)}{|S|}, \qquad (6)$$

where $n(w,S)$ is the number of times that word w occurs in sentence S, and $|S|$ is the length of the sentence.

There is a general consensus that merely matching terms in a candidate sentence and the document to be summarized may not always select summary sentences that can capture the important semantic intent of the document. Thus, in order to more precisely assess the representativeness of a sentence to the document, we suggest inferring the probability that the document would be generated as a translation of the sentence. That is, the generating probability is calculated based on a translation model of the form $P(w_j|w_i)$, which is the probability that a sentence word w_i is semantically translated to a document word w_j:

$$P(D \mid S) = \prod_{w_j \in D} \left[\sum_{w_i \in S} P(w_j \mid w_i) P(w_i \mid S) \right]^{n(w_j,D)}. \qquad (7)$$

Accordingly, the translation-based language modeling approach allows us to score a sentence by computing the degree of match between a sentence word and the semantically related words in the document. If $P(w_j|w_i)$ only allows a word to be translated into itself, Eq. (7) will be reduced to the ULM approach (cf. Eq. (6)). However, $P(w_j|w_i)$ would in general allow us to translate w_i into the semantically related words with non-zero probabilities, thereby achieving "semantic matching" between the document and its component sentences.

Based on the proposed DSG method, the translation probability $P(w_j|w_i)$ can be naturally computed by:

$$P(w_j \mid w_i) = \mathbf{W}_{w_j} \cdot \mathbf{M}_{w_i}. \qquad (8)$$

Consequently, the sentences offering the highest generated probability (cf. Eqs (7) and (8)) and dissimilar to those already selected sentences (for an already selected sentence S', computing $P(S|S')$ using Eq. (7)) will be selected and sequenced to form the final summary according to a desired summarization ratio. The proposed translation-based language modeling method is denoted by TBLM hereafter.

4. EXPERIMENTS

4.1 Dataset & Setup

We conduct a series of experiments on a Mandarin Benchmark broadcast new corpus [19]. The MATBN dataset is publicly available and has been widely used to evaluate several NLP-related tasks, including speech recognition [20], information retrieval [21] and summarization [18]. As such, we follow the experimental setting used by some previous studies for speech summarization. The average word error rate of the automatic transcripts of these broadcast news documents is about 38%. The reference summaries were generated by ranking the sentences in the manual transcript of a broadcast news document by importance without assigning a score to each sentence. Each document has three reference summaries annotated by three subjects. For the assessment of summarization performance, we adopted the widely-used ROUGE metrics (in F-scores) [22]. The summarization ratio was set to 10%. In addition, a corpus of 14,000 text news documents, compiled during the same period as the broadcast news documents, was used to estimate the parameters of the models compared in this paper.

Table 1. Summarization results achieved by various word-embedding methods in conjunction with the cosine similarity measure.

Cosine	MT		SRT	
	ROUGE-2	ROUGE-L	ROUGE-2	ROUGE-L
SG	0.239	0.311	0.215	0.311
GloVe	0.244	0.310	0.214	0.310
DSG	**0.281**	**0.351**	**0.234**	**0.330**
VSM	0.228	0.290	0.189	0.287
LSA	0.233	0.316	0.201	0.301
MMR	0.248	0.322	0.215	0.315

Table 2. Summarization results achieved by various word-embedding methods in conjunction with the translation-based language modeling method.

TBLM	MT		SRT	
	ROUGE-2	ROUGE-L	ROUGE-2	ROUGE-L
SG	0.320	0.385	0.225	0.322
GloVe	0.309	0.372	0.239	**0.332**
DSG	**0.333**	**0.389**	**0.244**	0.331
ULM	0.298	0.362	0.210	0.307

Table 3. Summarization results achieved by a few well-studied or/and state-of-the-art unsupervised methods.

	MT		SRT	
	ROUGE-2	ROUGE-L	ROUGE-2	ROUGE-L
MRW	0.282	0.332	0.191	0.291
LexRank	0.309	0.305	0.146	0.254
SM	0.286	0.332	0.204	0.303
ILP	**0.337**	0.348	0.209	0.306
DSG(TBLM)	0.333	**0.389**	**0.244**	**0.331**

4.2 Experimental Results

A common thread of leveraging word embedding methods in a summarization task is to represent a document/sentence by averaging the corresponding word embeddings over all words in the document/sentence. After that, the cosine similarity measure, as a straightforward choice, can be readily applied to determine the degree of relevance between any pair of representations [29, 30]. In the first place, we try to investigate the effectiveness of two state-of-the-art word embedding methods (i.e., SG and GloVe) and the proposed method (i.e., DSG), in conjunction with the cosine similarity measure for speech summarization. The experimental results are shown in Table 1, where MT denotes the results obtained based on the manual transcripts of spoken documents, and SRT denotes the results using the speech recognition transcripts of spoken documents that may contain speech recognition errors. Several observations can be made from these results. First, the two classic word embedding methods, though based on disparate model structures and learning strategies, achieve results competitive to each other in both the MT and SRT cases. Second, the proposed DSG method, which naturally brings together the advantages of the two major model families (i.e., prediction-based and count-based) in the literature, outperforms SG and GloVe (representatives of the two model families, respectively) by a significant margin in both the MT and SRT cases. Third, since the relevance degree between a document-sentence pair is computed by the cosine similarity measure, vector space-based methods, such as VSM [23], LSA [23] and MMR [24], can be treated as the principled baseline systems. Albeit that the classic word embedding methods (i.e., GloVe and SG) outperform the conventional VSM model, they achieve almost

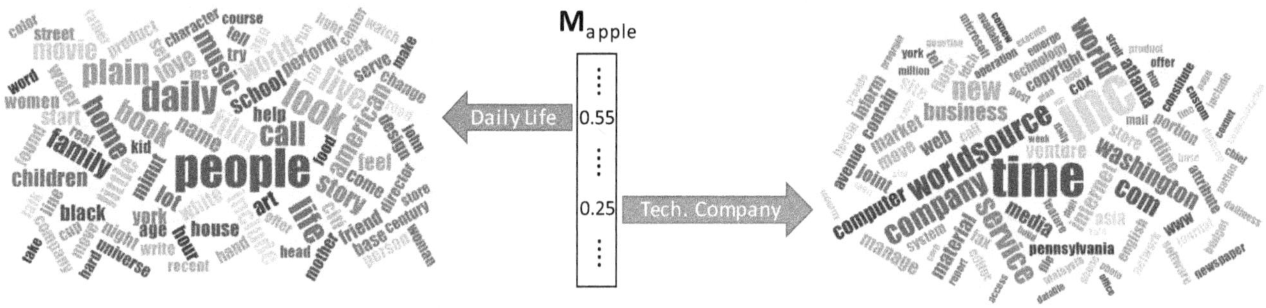

Figure 1. A running example for interpreting the word embeddings learned by DSG.

the same level of performance as LSA and MMR, which are considered two enhanced versions of VSM. It should be noted that the proposed DSG method not only outperforms VSM, but also is superior to LSA and MMR in both the MT and SRT cases.

Next, we evaluate the proposed TBLM method. It is worth mentioning that TBLM is well suitable for pairing with the DSG method since the translation probability can be easily obtained by lightweight calculation (cf. Eq. (8)). It can also be integrated with the classic word embedding methods (e.g. SG and GloVe), but with a heavier computational burden (cf. Eq. (2) for example). The experimental results are summarized in Table 2. Three observations can be made from the results. First, since the proposed DSG method inherits the advantages from prediction- and count-based methods, it outperforms both SG and GloVe, when all the three models are paired with the proposed TBLM method. Second, when integrated with TBLM, all the three word embedding methods outperform the baseline ULM method [18, 31] (cf. Section 3.2) by a remarkable margin in both the MT and SRT cases. Third, comparing the results in Tables 1 and 2, it is evident that TBLM is deemed a preferable vehicle to make use of powerful word embedding methods in speech summarization.

In the last set of experiments, we assess the performance levels of several well-practiced unsupervised summarization methods, including the graph-based methods (i.e., MRW [25] and LexRank [26]), the submodularity (SM) method [27], and the integer linear programming (ILP) method [28]. The corresponding results are illustrated in Table 3. The performance trends of these state-of-the-art methods in our study are quite in line with those observations made by other previous studies in different extractive summarization tasks. A noticeable observation is that speech recognition errors may lead to inaccurate similarity measures between a pair of sentences or document-sentence. Probably due to this reason, the two graph-based methods (i.e., MRW and LexRank) cannot perform on par with the vector-space methods (i.e., VSM, LSA, and MMR) (cf. Table 1) in the SRT case, but the situation is reversed in the MT case. Moreover, the SM and ILP achieve the best results in the MT case, but only offer mediocre performance among all methods in the SRT case. To sum up, the proposed DSG method, which inherits the advantages from both the prediction- and count-based methods, indeed outperforms classic word embedding methods when paired with different summarization strategies (i.e., the cosine similarity measure and TBLM). The proposed TBLM method further enhances the DSG method since it can authentically capture a finer-grained (i.e., word-to-word) semantic relationship to be effectively used in extractive speech summarization.

4.3 Further Analysis

SG, GloVe and the proposed DSG method can be analyzed from several critical perspectives. First, SG and DSG aim at maximizing the collection likelihood in training, while GloVe concentrates on discovering useful information from the co-occurrence statistics between each pair of words. It is worthy to note that GloVe has a close relation with the classic weighted matrix factorization approach, while the major difference is that the former concentrates on rendering the *word-by-word* co-occurrence matrix while the latter decomposes the *word-by-document* matrix [23, 32, 33]. Second, since the parameters (i.e., word representations) of SG are trained sequentially (i.e., the so-called *on-line* learning strategy), the sequential order of the training corpus may make the resulting models unstable. On the contrary, GloVe and DSG accumulate the statistics over the entire training corpus in the first place; the model parameters are then updated based on such censuses at once (i.e., the so-called *batch-mode* learning strategy). Finally, the word vectors learned by DSG are distributional representations, while SG and GloVe express each word by a distributed representation.

The classic embedding methods usually output two sets of word representations, but there is no particular use for the context word representations. Since DSG assumes that each row of the context word matrix $\mathbf{W}$ follows a multinomial distribution (i.e., a multinomial distribution over words), we can naturally interpret the semantic meaning of each dimension of a word embedding by referring to the words with higher probabilities in the corresponding row vector in $\mathbf{W}$. Since each word embedding in the desired word representations $\mathbf{M}$ is also a multinomial distribution, we can interpret a learned word embedding by first identifying the dimensions with higher probabilities and then identifying the context words with higher probabilities in the corresponding row vectors of $\mathbf{W}$. Figure 1 shows a running example for word "apple" learned by DSG on the LDC Gigaword corpus. The word cloud can be plotted with respect to the probabilities of individual context words for a selected dimension. It is obvious that "apple" is not only a kind of important matter in our daily life, but also is a famous technology company. The example shows that the word embeddings learned by DSG can be interpreted in a reasonable and systematical manner.

5. CONCLUSIONS

A novel distributional word embedding method and a translation-based language modeling method have been proposed and introduced for extractive speech summarization in this paper. Empirical results have demonstrated their respective and joint effectiveness and efficiency over several state-of-the-art summarization methods. In the future, we plan to further extend and apply the proposed framework to a wider range of summarization and NLP-related tasks. We will also concentrate on integrating a variety of prior knowledge for learning the word representations.

6. REFERENCES

[1] Mari Ostendorf. 2008. Speech technology and information access. *IEEE Signal Processing Magazine*, 25(3): 150–152.

[2] Sadaoki Furui, Li Deng, Mark Gales, Hermann Ney, and Keiichi Tokuda. 2012. Fundamental technologies in modern speech recognition. *IEEE Signal Processing Magazine*, 29(6): 16–17.

[3] Inderjeet Mani and Mark T. Maybury (Eds.). 1999. *Advances in automatic text summarization*. Cambridge, MA: MIT Press.

[4] P. B. Baxendale. 1958. Machine-made index for technical literature-an experiment. *IBM Journal*, 2(4): 354-361.

[5] Yang Liu and Dilek Hakkani-Tur. 2011. Speech summarization. *Chapter 13* in *Spoken Language Understanding: Systems for Extracting Semantic Information from Speech*, G. Tur and R. D. Mori (Eds), New York: Wiley.

[6] Ziqiang Cao, Furu Wei, Sujian Li, Wenjie Li, Ming Zhou, and Houfeng Wang. 2015. Learning Summary Prior Representation for Extractive Summarization. In *Proc. ACL*, pages 829–833.

[7] Ani Nenkova and Kathleen McKeown. 2011. Automatic summarization. *Foundations and Trends in Information Retrieval*, 5(2–3): 103–233.

[8] Gerald Penn and Xiaodan Zhu. 2008. A critical reassessment of evaluation baselines for speech summarization. In *Proc. ACL*, pages 470–478.

[9] Yoshua Bengio, Rejean Ducharme, Pascal Vincent, and Christian Jauvin. 2003. A neural probabilistic language model. *Journal of Machine Learning Research*, 3: 1137–1155.

[10] Tomas Mikolov, Kai Chen, Greg Corrado, and Jeffrey Dean. 2013. Efficient estimation of word representations in vector space. In *Proc. ICLR*, pages 1–12.

[11] Jeffrey Pennington, Richard Socher, and Christopher D. Manning. 2014. GloVe: Global vector for word representation. In *Proc. EMNLP*, pages 1532–1543.

[12] Will Y. Zou, Richard Socher, Daniel Cer, Christopher D. Manning. 2013. Bilingual word embeddings for phrase-based machine translation. In *Proc. ACL*, pages 1393–1398.

[13] Duyu Tang, Furu Wei, Nan Yang, Ming Zhou, Ting Liu, and Bing Qin. 2014. Learning sentiment-specific word embedding for twitter sentiment classification. In *Proc. ACL*, pages 1555–1565.

[14] Ronan Collobert and Jason Weston. 2008. A unified architecture for natural language processing: deep neural networks with multitask learning. In *Proc. ICLR*, pages 160–167.

[15] Marco Baroni, Georgiana Dinu, and German Kruszewski. 2014. Don't count, predict! A systematic comparison of context-counting vs. context-predicting semantic vectors. In *Proc. ACL*, pages 238–247.

[16] Omer Levy, Yoav Goldberg, and Ido Dagan. 2015. Improving distributional similarity with lessons learned from word embeddings. *Transactions of the Association for Computational Linguistics*, 3: 211–225.

[17] Han-Shen Huang, Bou-Ho Yang and Chun-Nan Hsu. 2005. Triple jump acceleration for the EM algorithm. In *Proc. ICDM*, pages 1–4.

[18] Shih-Hung Liu, Kuan-Yu Chen, Berlin Chen, Hsin-Min Wang, Hsu-Chun Yen, and Wen-Lian Hsu. 2015. Combining relevance language modeling and clarity measure for extractive speech summarization. *IEEE/ACM Transactions on Audio, Speech, and Language Processing*, 23(6): 957–969.

[19] Hsin-Min Wang, Berlin Chen, Jen-Wei Kuo, and Shih-Sian Cheng. 2005. MATBN: A Mandarin Chinese broadcast news corpus. *International Journal of Computational Linguistics and Chinese Language Processing*, 10(2): 219–236.

[20] Jen-Tzung Chien. 2015. Hierarchical Pitman-Yor-Dirichlet language model. *IEEE/ACM Transactions on Audio, Speech and Language Processing*, 23(8): 1259–1272.

[21] Chien-Lin Huang and Chung-Hsien Wu. 2007. Spoken Document Retrieval Using Multi-Level Knowledge and Semantic Verification. *IEEE Transactions on Audio, Speech, and Language Processing*, 15(8): 2551–2560.

[22] Chin-Yew Lin. 2003. ROUGE: Recall-oriented understudy for gisting evaluation. http://haydn.isi.edu/ROUGE/.

[23] Yihong Gong and Xin Liu. 2001. Generic text summarization using relevance measure and latent semantic analysis. In *Proc. SIGIR*, pages 19–25.

[24] Jaime Carbonell and Jade Goldstein. 1998. The use of MMR, diversity-based reranking for reordering documents and producing summaries. In *Proc. SIGIR*, pages 335–336.

[25] Xiaojun Wan and Jianwu Yang. 2008. Multi-document summarization using cluster-based link analysis. In *Proc. SIGIR*, pages 299–306.

[26] Gunes Erkan and Dragomir R. Radev. 2004. LexRank: Graph-based lexical centrality as salience in text summarization. *Journal of Artificial Intelligent Research*, 22(1): 457–479.

[27] Hui Lin and Jeff Bilmes. 2010. Multi-document summarization via budgeted maximization of submodular functions. In *Proc. NAACL HLT*, pages 912–920.

[28] Korbinian Riedhammer, Benoit Favre, and Dilek Hakkani-Tur. 2010. Long story short - Global unsupervised models for keyphrase based meeting summarization. *Speech Communication*, 52(10): 801–815.

[29] Mikael Kageback, Olof Mogren, Nina Tahmasebi, and Devdatt Dubhashi. 2014. Extractive summarization using continuous vector space models. In *Proc. CVSC*, pages 31–39.

[30] Kuan-Yu Chen, Shih-Hung Liu, Hsin-Min Wang, Berlin Chen, and Hsin-Hsi Chen. 2015. Leveraging word embeddings for spoken document summarization. In *Proc. INTERSPEECH*, pages 1383–1387.

[31] Kuan-Yu Chen, Shih-Hung Liu, Berlin Chen, Hsin-Min Wang, Ea-Ee Jan, Wen-Lian Hsu, and Hsin-Hsi Chen. 2015. Extractive broadcast news summarization leveraging recurrent neural network language modeling techniques. *IEEE/ACM Transactions on Audio, Speech, and Language Processing*, 23(8):1322–1334.

[32] Kuan-Yu Chen, Hsin-Min Wang, Berlin Chen, and Hsin-Hsi Chen. 2013. Weighted matrix factorization for spoken document retrieval. In *Proc. ICASSP*, pages 8530–8534.

[33] Omer Levy and Yoav Goldberg. 2014. Neural word embedding as implicit matrix factorization. In *Proc. NIPS*, pages 1–9.

Micro-Expression Recognition with Expression-State Constrained Spatio-Temporal Feature Representations

Dae Hoe Kim
Image and Video Systems Lab.
KAIST
Daejeon, Korea
dhkim10@kaist.ac.kr

Wissam J. Baddar
Image and Video Systems Lab.
KAIST
Daejeon, Korea
wisam.baddar@kaist.ac.kr

Yong Man Ro*
Image and Video Systems Lab.
KAIST
Daejeon, Korea
ymro@kaist.ac.kr

ABSTRACT

Recognizing spontaneous micro-expression in video sequences is a challenging problem. In this paper, we propose a new method of small scale spatio-temporal feature learning. The proposed learning method consists of two parts. First, the spatial features of micro-expressions at different expression-states (i.e., onset, onset to apex transition, apex, apex to offset transition and offset) are encoded using convolutional neural networks (CNN). The expression-states are taken into account in the objective functions, to improve the expression class separability of the learned feature representation. Next, the learned spatial features with expression-state constraints are transferred to learn temporal features of micro-expression. The temporal feature learning encodes the temporal characteristics of the different states of the micro-expression using long short-term memory (LSTM) recurrent neural networks. Extensive and comprehensive experiments have been conducted on the publically available CASME II micro-expression dataset. The experimental results showed that the proposed method outperformed state-of-the-art micro-expression recognition methods in terms of recognition accuracy.

Keywords

Micro-Expression Recognition; Recurrent Neural Networks; Long Short Term Memory

1. INTRODUCTION

Micro-expressions are spontaneous, brief and subtle facial movements that appear involuntarily reveling the genuine emotion of the subject [18]. Those brief micro-expressions are cumbersome to be recognized because they take a number of frames without significant motion [9]. Moreover, the subtlety of the micro-expressions can result in spatial features that are insufficient for recognizing the expressions, even at the apex frames.

Relatively few attempts on recognizing micro-expressions have been conducted [6; 7; 15; 16]. The methods tried to improve micro-expression recognition accuracy by extending hand-crafted spatial texture features (i.e., local binary pattern (LBP), local quantized pattern (LQP)) to spatio-temporal features, such as the LBP on three orthogonal planes (LBP-TOP), LBP mean orthogonal planes (LBP-MOP), LBP with six intersection points (LBP-SIP) and spatio-temporal completed LQP (STCLQP). However, the small scale of facial motion in micro-expressions results in feature vectors with low discriminative power. To improve the discriminative power of such descriptors, an integral projection technique [6] was proposed to preserve the property of micro-expressions and then enhance discrimination of micro-expressions. Authors in [13] reported adaptive motion magnification techniques to emphasize micro-expression motion. Although, motion magnification improves expression class separability, magnification parameters, such as frequency bands and magnification factors are sensitive to achieve a good performance. Moreover, the existing hand-crafted features have a limitation in the sense that they rely on a prior knowledge and heuristics [2].

In this paper, we propose a new micro-expression feature representation that is learned with expression-states. The proposed learning method consists of two-parts. First, the spatial features of micro-expression at different expression-states (i.e., onset, onset to apex transition, apex, apex to offset transition and offset) are encoded using convolutional neural networks (CNN). By adopting expression-states in the objective function at the spatial feature learning, the expression class separability of the learned micro-expression features is improved. After the micro-expression spatial feature representation is learned, the learned model is transferred to the second part to extract time scale dependent features from the micro-expression sequence. The temporal feature learning of micro-expression encodes the temporal characteristics of the different expression-states of the micro-expression using long short-term memory (LSTM) recurrent neural networks. Extensive and comprehensive experiments have been conducted on the CASME II micro-expression dataset [17]. The experimental results showed that the proposed method outperformed state-of-the-art micro-expression recognition methods in terms of recognition accuracy.

The remainder of this paper is organized as follows. Section 2 details the proposed micro-expression recognition with expression-state constrained spatio-temporal feature representations. Section 3 presents experimental setup and results. And the conclusions are drawn in section 4.

2. PROPOSED METHOD

Figure 1 shows an overview of the proposed expression-state constrained spatio-temporal feature representation learning for micro-expression recognition. As shown in the figure, the proposed method is composed of two parts. In the first part, spatial feature representation of the micro-expression is learned

* Corresponding author

MM '16, October 15-19, 2016, Amsterdam, Netherlands
© 2016 ACM. ISBN 978-1-4503-3603-1/16/10...$15.00
DOI: http://dx.doi.org/10.1145/2964284.2967247

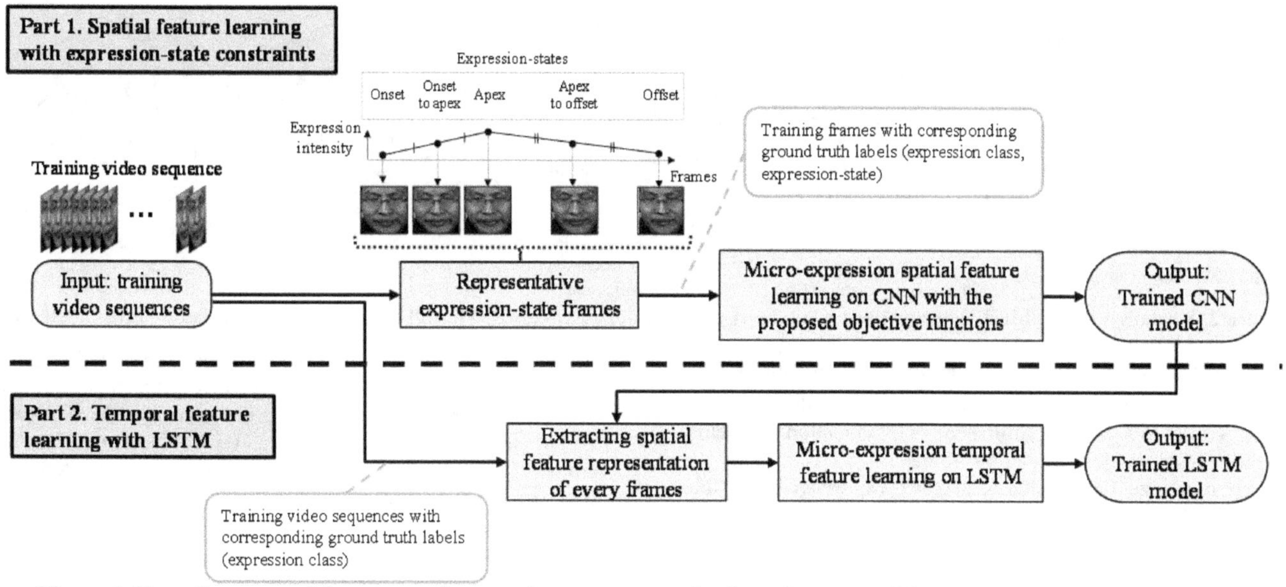

Figure 1. Overall process of the proposed expression-state constrained spatio-temporal feature representation learning for micro-expression recognition

using CNN. In this part, expression-states are taken into account in learning the CNN to differentiate expression classes, i.e., the expression-states dependent objective functions are devised in the learning. With the learned model in the first part, spatial features of all input frames are extracted and fed to the second learning part. In the second part, the temporal features of micro-expression are consequently encoded by using LSTM. The details of each part are described in the following subsections.

2.1 Learning Micro-Expression Spatial Features with Expression-State Constraints

In learning the spatial features, we consider expression-states including onset, apex and offset of expressions. We sample representative frames from video sequences that represent different expression-states of each expression. Specifically, 5 frames are selected in the learning; onset, the middle frame between onset and apex, apex, the middle frame between apex and offset, and offset are selected. To learn the spatial features of the micro-expression sequence frames, CNN is utilized. Recognition performance of spatial feature learned by CNN could vary depending on objective functions [14]. Thus, the design of the objective function based on a prior knowledge is important to determine the performance of CNN. In this paper, we propose a new objective function consisting of multiple objective terms to learn discriminative micro-expression spatial features that can encode subtle micro-expression regardless of subject variations and expression-state variations.

Figure 2 shows visualization of each objective term in the proposed objective function. The first term (E_1) of the objective function is responsible for recognizing the expression by minimizing the expression classification error. To that end, softmax loss function is utilized as:

$$E_1 = -\sum_i \sum_c t_i^c \log \hat{t}_i^c, \tag{1}$$

where c is the expression class index, t_i^c is the expression ground truth of the i-th sample (1 if c is the correct class and 0 otherwise), and $\hat{t}_i^c$ is the predicted probability that the sample belongs to the class c calculated at the last L-th layer.

To mitigate intra-class variations due to subject appearance variations, we devise the term E_2 as:

$$E_2 = \frac{1}{2}\sum_{c,p,i} g\left(\left\| \mathbf{y}_{c,p,i} - \overline{\mathbf{y}_c} \right\|_2^2 - (d_{\min}^c)^2 \right), \tag{2}$$

where $\mathbf{y}_{c,p,i}$ is the spatial feature vector of the i-th training sample ($\mathbf{x}_{c,p,i}$) of class c and the p-th expression-state extracted at the (L-1)-th layer (i.e., fully connected layer), $\overline{\mathbf{y}_c}$ is the mean of spatial feature vectors of training samples in class c calculated at the beginning of every epoch. $d_{\min}^c$ is half the minimum distance between $\overline{\mathbf{y}_c}$ and $\overline{\mathbf{y}_j}$ for $j \neq c$. The function $g(\omega)$ is a smoothed approximation of $[\omega]_+ = \max(0, \omega)$, defined as $g(\omega) = \log(1 + \exp(\beta\omega)) / \beta$ where β is a sharpness parameter [10]. By minimizing E_2, the spatial features included in each expression class are forced to be gathered in each multi-dimensional sphere, where the radius and the center of sphere are denoted by $d_{\min}^c$ and $\overline{\mathbf{y}_c}$, respectively. As a result, this term of the objective function reduces the within-class scatter of the learned spatial features and improves expression class classification.

Frames in a micro-expression sequence appear similar due to the subtlety of the expression motion. Such similarity between the frames can result in similar feature representations along the sequence frames. As a result, temporal changes become harder to model. To increase the distances between the learned features of different expression-states, we devise three objective terms (E_3, E_4 and E_5). E_3 is added to distinguish the expression-state by minimize the expression-state classification error as:

$$E_3 = -\sum_i \sum_p t_i^p \log \hat{t}_i^p, \tag{3}$$

where p is the expression-state index , t_i^p is the expression-state ground truth of the i-th sample (1 if p is the correct expression-

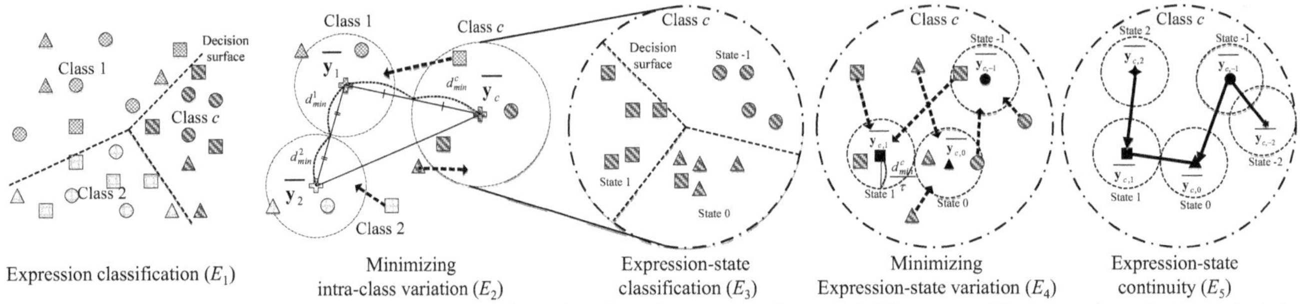

Figure 2. Visualizing the objective terms used when learning the micro-expression spatial features with expression-state constraints

state and 0 otherwise), and $\hat{t}_i^p$ is the predicted probability that the sample belongs to the expression-state p at the last L-th layer. Similar to E_1, E_3 is a softmax objective function that helps identify the expression-state of the frame.

To minimize the variations of each expression-state, the term E_4 is devised as:

$$E_4 = \frac{1}{2}\sum_{c,p,i} g\left(\left\|\mathbf{y}_{c,p,i} - \overline{\mathbf{y}_{c,p}}\right\|_2^2 - \left(\frac{d_{\min}^c}{\tau}\right)^2\right), \tag{4}$$

where $\overline{\mathbf{y}_{c,p}}$ is the mean of spatial feature vectors of training samples in the c-th class and the p-th expression-state calculated at the beginning of every epoch. τ is a parameter for determining the range of expression-state distribution. This term of the objective function helps cluster the features of the same expression according to the expression-states, which minimizes the effect of the expression-state variations on the micro-expression classification task.

The terms E_3 and E_4 improve the separability between expression-states. However, feature representations from adjacent frames could not be close to each other in feature space. This could degrade video classification performance in the next temporal learning (i.e., temporal feature learning with LSTM). Thus, the last term, E_5, is devised to regulate the expression-state continuity. As a result, features extracted from frames between two expression-states, which are used during the learning, could reside in the middle of two expression-states in the feature space. E_5 is calculated as:

$$E_5 = \frac{1}{2}\sum_{c}\sum_{p,p\neq 0} g\left(\left\|\overline{\mathbf{y}_{c,q}} - \overline{\mathbf{y}_{c,p}}\right\|_2^2 - \left(\frac{2d_{\min}^c}{\tau}\right)^2\right),\quad q = \begin{cases} p+1, & \text{if } p < 0 \\ p-1, & \text{if } p > 0, \end{cases} \tag{5}$$

where q represents the index of the adjacent expression-state in the learning stage. It should be noted that to enforce expression-state continuity, the expression-state indexes p and q were defined as (-2, -1, 0, 1 and 2) for onset, onset to apex transition, apex, apex to offset transition and offset expression-states, respectively.

2.2 Learning Micro-Expression Temporal Features with LSTM

In the first learning part, spatial feature representations are learned with the proposed objective function that improves expression class separability. In the second part, time scale dependent information that resides along the video sequences is consequently learned by using LSTM. LSTM is able to process long sequences of data efficiently [5]. Moreover, it can encode the temporal dependent characteristics of the variable length expression sequences without temporal normalization. The inputs for the LSTM are the spatial features extracted from all sequence frames using the model learned in the first part. The depth of LSTM structure in this paper is two layers, where each LSTM unit contains 512 hidden states. Note that spatio-temporal feature representation is learned with the CNN in the first part and consequent LSTM in the second part.

3. EXPERIMENTS

3.1 Experimental Setup

To verify the effectiveness of the proposed micro-expression recognition, experiments have been conducted on the CASME II dataset [17]. The dataset contains 246 spontaneous micro-expression sequences collected from 26 subjects with a temporal resolution of 200 fps. Each micro-expression sequence was categorized into one of five expression classes (i.e., happiness, disgust, repression, surprise, and others). The dataset also provides indexes of the onset, apex (peak), and offset frame in each sequence. In our experiments, micro-expression sequences from onset to offset were used, and the face region was cropped and aligned according the face region in the first frame [13].

The evaluations in our experiments were conducted with a leave-one-subject-out cross validation, such that the test subject was excluded from the training set. Due to the limited number of samples in the CASME II dataset, data augmentation was performed during the training to avoid overfitting [8]. In particular, each training video sequence was flipped horizontally, rotated between the angles [-10º, 10º] with an increment of 5º, translated along [(0, 0), (-2, -2), (-2, +2), (+2, -2), (+2, +2)] pixels in x and y axis, and scaled with scaling factors of 0.9, 1.0 and 1.1. As a result 150 augmented sequences from each training sequence were generated.

To implement the proposed micro-expression spatial feature learning with expression-state constrained CNN, ConvNet library [4] was utilized, while the LSTM was implemented using Keras [3]. The implemented CNN structure consisted of an input layer of size 64×64 pixels with RGB color channels, three convolutional layers with a 3×3 filters and the number of filters is 32, 64 and 64, respectively. Each convolutional layer was followed by a max pooling layer of kernel size 3x3, stride 2. Lastly, two fully-connected layers with 512 units were used. For the activation function, the rectified linear unit (ReLU) [11] was used. The CNN was trained for 40 epochs, then the learned model was transferred to the second part, such that the input features to the LSTM were extracted from the second fully connected layer.

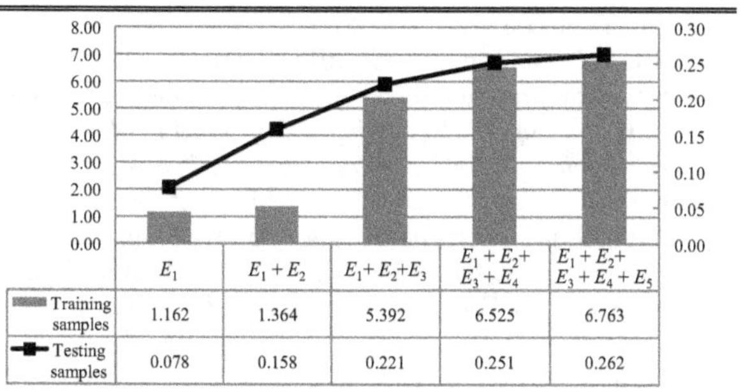

Figure 3. Fisher's discriminant ratio for class separability measure

Table 1. Micro-expression recognition accuracy (in the CNN) with different objective terms of spatial feature learning

Objective terms	Acc. (%)
E_1	40.65
E_1+E_2	48.37
$E_1+E_2+E_3$	54.07
$E_1+E_2+E_3+E_4$	54.88
All ($E_1+E_2+E_3+E_4+E_5$)	**58.54**

3.2 Performance of the Proposed Micro-Expression Spatial Feature Learning with Expression-State Constraints

In this experiment, a quantitative analysis was performed to evaluate the effect of each term of the objective function when learning the micro-expression spatial features with expression-state constraints. To that end, Fisher's discriminant ratio [1] was utilized for class separability measure. Fisher's discriminant ratio (J) measures the ratio of between-class scatter (S_b) and the within-class scatter (S_w) as follows:

$$J=\frac{trace(S_b)}{trace(S_w)},$$

$$S_b=\sum_{i=1}^{N_c}(\mathbf{m}_i-\mathbf{m})^{\mathrm{T}}(\mathbf{m}_i-\mathbf{m}),\quad S_w=\sum_{i=1}^{N_c}\sum_{j=1}^{N_i}(\mathbf{x}_{ij}-\mathbf{m}_i)^{\mathrm{T}}(\mathbf{x}_{ij}-\mathbf{m}_i), \qquad (6)$$

where N_c is the number of classes, N_i is the number of samples in class i, $\mathbf{m}_i$ is the mean of the samples in class i, $\mathbf{m}$ is the mean of all classes and $\mathbf{x}_{ij}$ is the feature vector of j-th sample in class i. Higher Fisher's discriminant ratio is achieved with larger S_b and smaller S_w which results in better expression class separability.

Figure 3 shows the Fisher's discriminant ratio according to various objective term combinations in the proposed micro-expression spatial features. As shown in the figure, with the term that minimizes expression classification error only (i.e., E_1), the Fisher's discriminant ratio is low. When employing E_2, which focuses on reducing the intra-class variations of each expression, the Fisher's discriminant ratio is increased. A more significant increase is observed when including terms related to the expression-state (i.e., E_3, E_4 and E_5) in the objective function.

To further evaluate the effectiveness of proposed objective terms, we perform expression recognition using the learned spatial features with expression-state constraints, by incrementally adding terms to the objective function. As a result, 5 models were learned as shown in table 1. Please note that the evaluation was performed using the CNN with apex frames from each sequence. From the recognition results, we can observe that E_2 improves recognition accuracy because it reduces the effect of intra-class variation of each expression, such as person identity variations. When employing expression-state related terms (E_3, E_4 and E_5) in the objective function, the micro-expression recognition accuracy improves due to the improvement of expression class separability by incorporating expression-state information.

Table 2. Micro-expression recognition accuracy comparison with existing state-of-the-art

Method	Acc. (%)
LBP-TOP [19]	44.12
LBP-TOP + adaptive motion magnification [13]	51.91
LBP-MOP [16]	45.75
Riesz wavelet [12]	46.15
Proposed method	**60.98**

3.3 Effectiveness of the Proposed Micro-Expression Spatio-Temporal Features

Table 2 shows the performance of the proposed micro-expression recognition with expression-state constrained spatio-temporal feature representations including the CNN and the LSTM (in Figure 1). Comparative results are shown with the state-of-the-art expression recognition methods as well. In this experiment, we evaluated the micro-expression recognition accuracies using the micro-expression video sequences. As shown in the table, the proposed method clearly outperformed existing state-of-the-art micro-expression recognition methods and the methods with CNN only (Table 1) on the same dataset. These results indicate that, the proposed method could improve the micro-expression recognition accuracy by incorporating spatial and temporal dependent information.

4. CONCLUSION

In this paper, we presented a method for recognizing micro-expressions by learning a spatio-temporal feature representation with expression-state constraints. First, CNN was utilized to encode the spatial characteristics of the facial expression at different expression-states. Then, the learned model with expression-state constraints was transferred to a micro-expression temporal feature learning stage which adopts LSTM. The experiments showed that employing the expression-states in the CNN objective function improves the expression class separability of the learned micro-expression features. Moreover, consequent temporal feature learning with LSTM was able to encode the temporal characteristics of the different states of the micro-expression, which generated sufficient representations of the underlying micro-expression. Finally, the experimental results showed that the proposed method was superior to existing state-of-the-art micro-expression recognition methods in terms of recognition accuracy. For future work, a more evaluation of the proposed method is to be conduct on additional datasets of spontaneous facial expression with various kinds of metrics (i.e., F1 score).

5. ACKNOWLEDGMENTS

This work was supported by the National Research Foundation of Korea (NRF) grant funded by the Korea government (MSIP) (No. 2015R1A2A2A01005724).

6. REFERENCES

[1] Bartlett, M.S., Movellan, J.R., and Sejnowski, T.J., 2002. Face recognition by independent component analysis. *Neural Networks, IEEE Transactions on 13*, 6, 1450-1464.

[2] Chherawala, Y., Roy, P.P., and Cheriet, M., 2013. Feature design for offline Arabic handwriting recognition: handcrafted vs automated? In *Document Analysis and Recognition (ICDAR), 2013 12th International Conference on* IEEE, 290-294.

[3] Chollet, F., 2015. Keras. Available: https://github.com/fchollet/keras

[4] Demyanov, S., ConvNet. Available: https://github.com/sdemyanov/ConvNet

[5] Gers, F.A., Schraudolph, N.N., and Schmidhuber, J., 2003. Learning precise timing with LSTM recurrent networks. *The Journal of Machine Learning Research 3*, 115-143.

[6] Huang, X., Wang, S.J., Zhao, G., Piteik, M., and Inen, 2015. Facial Micro-Expression Recognition Using Spatiotemporal Local Binary Pattern with Integral Projection. In *2015 IEEE International Conference on Computer Vision Workshop (ICCVW)*, 1-9.

[7] Huang, X., Zhao, G., Hong, X., Zheng, W., and Pietikäinen, M., 2016. Spontaneous facial micro-expression analysis using Spatiotemporal Completed Local Quantized Patterns. *Neurocomputing 175, Part A*(1/29/), 564-578.

[8] Khorrami, P., Paine, T., and Huang, T., 2015. Do Deep Neural Networks Learn Facial Action Units When Doing Expression Recognition? In *Proceedings of the IEEE International Conference on Computer Vision Workshops*, 19-27.

[9] Le Ngo, A.C., Liong, S.-T., See, J., and Phan, R.C.-W., 2015. Are subtle expressions too sparse to recognize? In *Digital Signal Processing (DSP), 2015 IEEE International Conference on* IEEE, 1246-1250.

[10] Mignon, A. and Jurie, F., 2012. Pcca: A new approach for distance learning from sparse pairwise constraints. In *Computer Vision and Pattern Recognition (CVPR), 2012 IEEE Conference on* IEEE, 2666-2672.

[11] Nair, V. and Hinton, G.E., 2010. Rectified linear units improve restricted boltzmann machines. In *Proceedings of the 27th International Conference on Machine Learning (ICML-10)*, 807-814.

[12] Oh, Y.-H., Le Ngo, A.C., See, J., Liong, S.-T., Phan, R.C.-W., and Ling, H.-C., 2015. Monogenic Riesz wavelet representation for micro-expression recognition. In *Digital Signal Processing (DSP), 2015 IEEE International Conference on* IEEE, 1237-1241.

[13] Park, S.Y., Lee, S.H., and Ro, Y.M., 2015. Subtle Facial Expression Recognition Using Adaptive Magnification of Discriminative Facial Motion. In *Proceedings of the 23rd Annual ACM Conference on Multimedia Conference* ACM, 911-914.

[14] Wan, L., Zeiler, M., Zhang, S., Cun, Y.L., and Fergus, R., 2013. Regularization of neural networks using dropconnect. In *Proceedings of the 30th International Conference on Machine Learning (ICML-13)*, 1058-1066.

[15] Wang, Y., See, J., Phan, R.C.-W., and Oh, Y.-H., 2014. LBP with Six Intersection Points: Reducing Redundant Information in LBP-TOP for Micro-expression Recognition. In *Computer Vision-ACCV 2014* Springer, 525-537.

[16] Wang, Y., See, J., Phan, R.C.-W., and Oh, Y.-H., 2015. Efficient Spatio-Temporal Local Binary Patterns for Spontaneous Facial Micro-Expression Recognition. *PloS One 10*, 5, e0124674.

[17] Yan, W.-J., Li, X., Wang, S.-J., Zhao, G., Liu, Y.-J., Chen, Y.-H., and Fu, X., 2014. CASME II: An improved spontaneous micro-expression database and the baseline evaluation. *PloS One 9*, 1, e86041.

[18] Yan, W.-J., Wu, Q., Liang, J., Chen, Y.-H., and Fu, X., 2013. How fast are the leaked facial expressions: The duration of micro-expressions. *Journal of Nonverbal Behavior 37*, 4, 217-230.

[19] Zhao, G. and Pietikainen, M., 2007. Dynamic texture recognition using local binary patterns with an application to facial expressions. *Pattern Analysis and Machine Intelligence, IEEE Transactions on 29*, 6, 915-928.

Multimodal Interest Level Estimation via Variational Bayesian Mixture of Robust CCA

Yuma Sasaka, Takhiro Ogawa and Miki Haseyama
Graduate school of information science and Technology, Hokkaido University
{sasaka, ogawa}@lmd.ist.hokudai.ac.jp, miki@ist.hokudai.ac.jp

ABSTRACT

This paper presents a method which estimates interest level while watching videos, based on collaborative use of facial expression and biological signals such as electroencephalogram (EEG) and electrocardiogram (ECG). To the best of our knowledge, no studies have been carried out on the collaborative use of facial expression and biological signals for estimating interest level. Since training data, which is used for estimating interest level, is generally small and imbalanced, Variational Bayesian Mixture of Robust Canonical Correlation Analysis (VBMRCCA) is newly applied to facial expression and biological signals, which are obtained from users while they are watching the videos. Unlike some related works, VBMRCCA is used to obtain the posterior distributions which represent the latent correlation between facial expression and biological signals in our method. Then, the users' interest level can be estimated by comparing the posterior distributions of the positive class data with those of the negative. Consequently, successful interest level estimation, via collaborative use of facial expression and biological signals, becomes feasible.

CCS Concepts

•**Human-centered computing** → **User studies**; *User centered design;*

Keywords

interest level; facial expression; biological signals; variational Bayesian mixture of robust canonical correlation analysis.

1. INTRODUCTION

In the field of video information retrieval, many recommendation methods have been studied in order to provide videos which match the desire of a user [3, 4, 8, 13, 23, 29, 33, 34]. Particularly, the recommendation methods that are based on individual video preference such as like/dislike and high/low interest, have been researched in recent years [4, 23, 34].

MM '16, October 15-19, 2016, Amsterdam, Netherlands
© 2016 ACM. ISBN 978-1-4503-3603-1/16/10...$15.00
DOI: http://dx.doi.org/10.1145/2964284.2967248

Specifically, these methods model individual video preference by extracting image and audio features from videos (hereafter video features), and effective video recommendation is realized by the video classification based on the model. However, these video features, which are generally not related to individual video preference, deteriorate the performance of the video classification. Furthermore, it is difficult to find a set of video features related to individual video preference since the element of a video that stimulates a user is dependent on each user. Therefore, it is necessary to introduce a new idea which solves the problem by estimating individual video preference based on alternative features.

Recently, with the development of various types of sensor technologies [6, 9, 25, 30, 32], some research has focused on psychopsysiological data, such as electroencephalogram (EEG), electrocardiogram (ECG) and facial expression, to estimate individual video preference [10, 22, 31]. For instance, Yeasin et al. reported in [31] that facial expression is a major cue in measuring interest level while users are watching videos. Meanwhile, biological signals, such as EEG and ECG, are also used to estimate interest level [5,10]. Furthermore, observation of biological signals has become easier, and the quality of observed signals has been improved due to the development and miniaturization of biological sensors [6, 9, 30]. From these studies, biological signals can also be considered effective cues to estimate interest level. Thus, both facial expression and biological signals are widely used, but separately, in measuring interest level.

However, a method which estimates interest level by using both facial expression and biological signals collaboratively, has not been researched as far as we know. Moreover, small and imbalanced training data is a significant problem, which is caused by the sparsity of the user-item interaction matrix [29] and a user's preference tendency in a standard mechanism of entrainment[1] [5].

Motivated by this discussion, taking small and imbalanced training data into account and maximizing the correlation between facial expression and biological signals are desirable to improve the performance of interest level estimation. In order to maximize the correlation, the most representative approach is the use of Canonical Correlation Analysis (CCA) [7]. Moreover, Local Discrimination CCA (LDCCA) [19] is a recently proposed CCA which uses class information. However, CCA and LDCCA cannot take noisy data, such as biological signals captured by sensors, into ac-

[1]Users tend to rate videos high without conscious realization.

count. As a result, the performance of estimating interest level is influenced for the worse.

In this paper, we propose a novel method of interest level estimation, which can be regarded as a psychological state evoked by multimedia [11], via the collaborative use of facial expression and biological signals for individual video recommendation. The proposed method utilizes Variational Bayesian Mixture of Robust CCA (VBMRCCA) [26] for the collaborative use since it can reveal the latent correlation and analyze complex data by using a Bayesian-based mixture model [24]. Moreover, with the Student's t-distribution which controls the variance of latent space, VBMRCCA can handle noisy data. CCA and LDCCA do not have these traits. With these traits, VBMRCCA is usually used for dimensionality reduction and data visualization. In the proposed method, we use VBMRCCA to obtain the posterior distributions which represent the latent correlation between facial expression and biological signals. Comparing the posterior distributions of positive class data with those of negative, we enable the estimation of the users' interest level as a binary fashion while they are watching videos even if the training data is small and imbalanced. In summary, the contributions of our work are twofold:

2. FEATURE EXTRACTION

In this section, we explain the extraction of the two different features: features of facial expression and those of biological signals used in our method.

2.1 Features of Facial Expression

In this subsection, we explain the feature extraction of facial expression. We obtain facial expression by using Kinect for Windows v2[2] which is playing a key role in the development of consumer depth sensors in various types of markets [25,32]. First of all, we detect the angular variation[3] and 17 landmark points on the face, with the landmark points being automatically selected by the Kinect. Since not all of the 17 features are correlated to interest level, we only use the angular variation of pitch and 6 landmark points on the face based on [14]. In particular, we use API which is called the Animation Unit[4] to capture the movement. In our method, we measure the degree of change from a continuous value that varies from 0 to 1. The details of these movements are shown in **Table 1**. We then capture the movements 15 times per second. In order to extract autonomic features, we calculate a mean and a standard deviation from 10 sec data windows, with a sliding window of 5 sec. In this way, we get the movements of each part of the face (12 dimensions) and the variation of pitch (2 dimensions) as facial expression features $\boldsymbol{x}_1 \in \mathbb{R}^{14}$.

2.2 Features of Biological Signals

In this subsection, we explain the feature extraction of biological signals. Biological signals are obtained by using a Silmee [21] and alphatec IV-s. In particular, Silmee is used for calculating heart rate. In order to extract autonomic features, we calculate a mean and a standard deviation from 10 sec data windows, with a sliding window of 5 sec. Furthermore, alphatec IV-s is used for obtaining EEG signals

[2]https://www.microsoft.com/en-us/kinectforwindows/
[3]pitch, yaw, roll
[4]https://msdn.microsoft.kinect.face.faceshapeanimations.aspx

Table 1: The landmark points used for calculating facial expression features in the proposed method.

AUs	DESCRIPTION	STATISTICS	DIMENSION
AU0	Jaw Open	Mean, Std	2
AU2	Jaw Slide Right	Mean, Std	2
AU3	Lip Stretcher Right	Mean, Std	2
AU4	Lip Stretcher Left	Mean, Std	2
AU13	Right eye brow Lowerer	Mean, Std	2
AU14	Left eye brow Lowerer	Mean, Std	2
	Pitch	Mean, Std	2

Table 2: Details of features calculated from signals obtained by biological sensors.

SENSOR	DISCRIPTION	DIMENSION
Silmee	Heart Rate	2
alphatec IV-s	θ wave (4-7Hz)	1
	slow-α wave (7-9Hz)	1
	mid-α wave (9-11Hz)	1
	slow-α wave (11-13Hz)	1
	β wave (13Hz-)	1

from Fp1, and EEG is closely related to the interest level of users [11]. Segmentation of EEG signal is performed at a fixed interval with an overlapped Hamming window. Note that the length of the window is also 10 seconds with a sliding window of 5 sec. We then apply short-time Fourier transform (SIFT) to each segment. Consequently, we obtain content percentage of θ wave (4-7Hz), slow-α wave (7-9Hz), mid-α wave (9-11Hz), slow-α wave (11-13Hz), β wave (13Hz-) from each segment. The measurements, which are obtained by using a Silmee and a alphatec IV-s, are shown in **Table 2**. In this way, we obtain biological signal features $\boldsymbol{x}_2 \in \mathbb{R}^7$.

3. INTEREST LEVEL ESTIMATION

In this section, we explain the method for estimating interest level via VBMRCCA. In **3.1**, we explain the training phase which integrates two features via VBMRCCA. We then describe the details of the estimation phase which estimates interest level in **3.2**. The overview of our proposed method is shown in **Fig.1**.

3.1 Training Phase

In this subsection, we explain the training phase which integrates two features via VBMRCCA [26]. The graphical model of the VBMRCCA used in our method is the same as that in [26]. Unlike some related works, we use VBMRCCA only for obtaining the posterior distributions which represent the latent correlation between facial expression and biological signals. Moreover, with the Student's t-distribution which controls the variance of latent space, VBMRCCA can handle noisy data. We denote the observed facial expression features and the biological signal features as $\boldsymbol{X} = \{\boldsymbol{x}_1 \in \mathbb{R}^{m_1}, \boldsymbol{x}_2 \in \mathbb{R}^{m_2}\}$, respectively. By setting $\boldsymbol{t}$ as the latent valuables representing the low-dimensional statistically dependent parts of $\boldsymbol{X}$, the prior distribution and the conditional probability distribution of $\boldsymbol{X}$ given $\boldsymbol{t}$ is denoted as follows:

$$u \sim \Gamma(v/2, v/2), \tag{1}$$

$$\boldsymbol{t}|u \sim N(0, u\boldsymbol{I}_d), \min\{m_1, m_2\} \geq d \geq 1, \tag{2}$$

$$\boldsymbol{x}_i|u, \boldsymbol{t} \sim N(\boldsymbol{W}_i\boldsymbol{t} + \boldsymbol{\mu}_i, u\boldsymbol{\Psi}_i),\ \boldsymbol{W}_i \in \mathbb{R}^{m_i \times d},\ \boldsymbol{\Psi}_i \geq 0, \tag{3}$$

where $i = 1, 2$. Note that u is a latent scale variable which implements robustness to outliers [15], and Γ is the gamma distribution with v degrees of freedom. In order to use the

Bayesian methodology based on [27], we set the prior distributions for the parameters described in Eq. (3) as follows:

$$p(\boldsymbol{\mu}_i) = N(0, {\beta_i}^{-1}\boldsymbol{I}_d), \tag{4}$$

$$p(\boldsymbol{W}_i|\boldsymbol{\alpha}_i) = \prod_{j=1}^{m_i} p(\boldsymbol{w}_{ij}|\boldsymbol{\alpha}_i), \tag{5}$$

$$p(\boldsymbol{w}_{ij}|\boldsymbol{\alpha}_i) = N(\boldsymbol{w}_{ij}|0, \mathrm{diag}(\boldsymbol{\alpha}_i)), \tag{6}$$

$$p(\boldsymbol{\alpha}_i) = \prod_{j=1}^{d} \Gamma(\alpha_{ij}|a, b), \tag{7}$$

$$p(\boldsymbol{\Psi}_i) = W(\gamma_i, \boldsymbol{K}_i^{-1}), \tag{8}$$

where β_i, a and b are hyper-parameters for α_{ij} which controls the number of the dependent parts of $\boldsymbol{X}$ [18]. Note that $\boldsymbol{w}_{ij}$ represents the jth column vector of $\boldsymbol{W}_i$. In addition, $\boldsymbol{K}_i = \beta_i \boldsymbol{I}$, $\gamma_i = \dim(\boldsymbol{x}_i) + 1$ and $W(\cdot)$ represents the Wishart distribution. We then apply mixture model to the above framework to handle complex data like sensor data. The probabilistic mixture is formulated by introducing a multinomial latent variable as follows:

$$\boldsymbol{z} \sim \mathrm{Multinomial}(\boldsymbol{z}|\pi), \tag{9}$$

where $\boldsymbol{z} = \{z_1, z_2, \cdots, z_K\}$ and $\sum_{k=1}^{K} z_k = 1$. Note that K denotes the number of clusters, and π is the probabilities of the clusters. By using Eqs. (1) $\sim$ (9), we obtain the optimal model parameters of the posterior distributions given by the training data as follows:

$$\boldsymbol{t} \sim N(0, \hat{u}\boldsymbol{I}_{\hat{d}}), \tag{10}$$

$$\boldsymbol{x}_i|\boldsymbol{t} \sim \sum_{k=1}^{\hat{K}} \hat{z}_k N(\hat{\boldsymbol{W}}_i^k \boldsymbol{t} + \hat{\boldsymbol{\mu}}_i^k, \hat{u}\hat{\boldsymbol{\Psi}}_i^k), \tag{11}$$

where $\hat{(\cdot)}^k$ represent a optimal parameter of k-th mixture component. Note that the detail of how to obtain the optimal posterior is shown in [26].

For all the above calculations, we can obtain the conditional probability distribution of $\boldsymbol{X}$ given $\boldsymbol{t}$. Based on the Bayes' theorem, the conditional probability distribution of $\boldsymbol{t}$ given $\boldsymbol{X}$ is denoted as follows:

$$\boldsymbol{t}|\boldsymbol{x}_i \sim \sum_{k=1}^{\hat{K}} \hat{z}_k N(\boldsymbol{W}_{x_i}^k(\boldsymbol{\mu}_{x_i} - \hat{\boldsymbol{\mu}}_i^k), \hat{\boldsymbol{M}}_i^k), \tag{12}$$

where $\hat{\boldsymbol{M}}_i^k = \{\boldsymbol{I}_{\hat{d}} + (\hat{\boldsymbol{W}}_i^k)^T(\hat{\boldsymbol{\Psi}}_i^k)^{-1}\hat{\boldsymbol{W}}_i^k\}^{-1}$ and $\boldsymbol{W}_{x_i}^k = \hat{\boldsymbol{M}}_i^k(\hat{\boldsymbol{W}}_i^k)^T(\hat{\boldsymbol{\Psi}}_i^k)^{-1}$. Note that $\boldsymbol{\mu}_{x_i}$ denotes the sample mean vectors of $\boldsymbol{X}$. In Eq. (12), $\boldsymbol{W}_{x_i}^k$ represents the projection matrix for $\boldsymbol{x}_i$ to the latent space at kth mixture component. As a result, we can obtain the two conditional distributions with taking the correlation between facial expression features and biological signal features into account.

3.2 Estimation Phase

In the proposed method, we estimate interest level by using the conditional distribution of $\boldsymbol{t}$ given $\boldsymbol{X}$ mentioned in the previous subsection. The overview of this phase is shown in **Fig.1**. First, we generate the conditional distributions, where the number of the distribution corresponds to the number of interest levels. For instance, we calculate l $(1, \cdots, L; L$ is the number of interest levels) conditional distributions if the number of interest levels is l. In this paper,

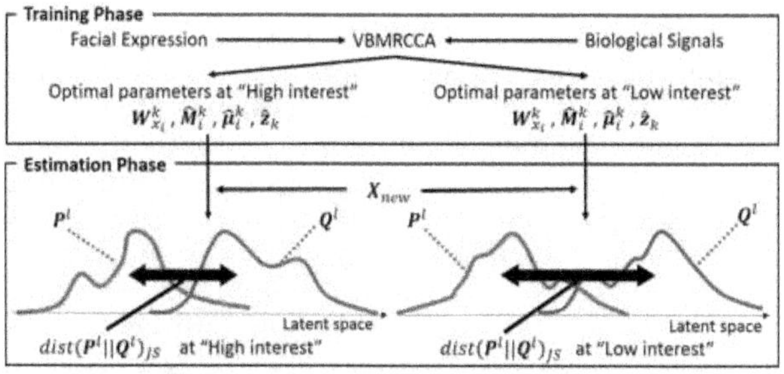

Figure 1: Overview of our proposed method.

l equals 2 since we estimate interest level as a binary fashion. We then estimate interest levels, which are represented by new facial expression and biological signal features $\boldsymbol{X}_{new} = \{\boldsymbol{x}_{new1}, \boldsymbol{x}_{new2}\}$, by comparing the similarity between two conditional probability distributions as follows:

$$\boldsymbol{t}^l|\boldsymbol{x}_{new_i} \sim \sum_{k=1}^{\hat{K}} \hat{z}_k N^l(\boldsymbol{W}_{x_i}^k(\boldsymbol{\mu}_{new_i} - \hat{\boldsymbol{\mu}}_i^k), \hat{\boldsymbol{M}}_i^k), \tag{13}$$

where $\boldsymbol{\mu}_{new1}$ and $\boldsymbol{\mu}_{new2}$ are sample means of $\boldsymbol{x}_{new1}$ and $\boldsymbol{x}_{new2}$. Note that $\boldsymbol{t}^l|\boldsymbol{x}_{new1}$ and $\boldsymbol{t}^l|\boldsymbol{x}_{new2}$ are the conditional probability distributions of $\boldsymbol{t}$ given $\boldsymbol{X}_{new} = \{\boldsymbol{x}_{new1}, \boldsymbol{x}_{new2}\}$ for interest level l. In the proposed method, we estimate $\boldsymbol{X}_{new}$ as representing interest level l based on the hypothesis which is reported in [17]. According to the hypothesis, if two different features are correlated, then their corresponding samples are closely distributed in the latent space. Hence, we estimate $\boldsymbol{X}_{new}$ as representing interest level l when the similarity between $\boldsymbol{t}^l|\boldsymbol{x}_{new_1}$ and $\boldsymbol{t}^l|\boldsymbol{x}_{new_2}$ is higher than those at any other interest levels.

In order to measure the similarity, we firstly calculate the Kullback-Leibler (KL) divergence [16, 28] between $\boldsymbol{t}^l|\boldsymbol{x}_{new_1}$ and $\boldsymbol{t}^l|\boldsymbol{x}_{new_2}$ as follows:

$$dist(\boldsymbol{P}^l||\boldsymbol{Q}^l) = D_{KL}(p(\boldsymbol{t}^l|\boldsymbol{x}_{new1})||p(\boldsymbol{t}^l|\boldsymbol{x}_{new2})), \tag{14}$$

$$dist(\boldsymbol{Q}^l||\boldsymbol{P}^l) = D_{KL}(p(\boldsymbol{t}^l|\boldsymbol{x}_{new2})||p(\boldsymbol{t}^l|\boldsymbol{x}_{new1})), \tag{15}$$

where $\boldsymbol{t} \in \mathbb{R}^{\hat{d}}$. Note that $\boldsymbol{P}^l$ and $\boldsymbol{Q}^l$ are the conditional distributions of $\boldsymbol{t}^l|\boldsymbol{x}_1$ and $\boldsymbol{t}^l|\boldsymbol{x}_2$ at interest level l. By using the KL divergence, we can consider both the mean and scatter information to calculate distribution differences [1]. Since the KL divergence is not a symmetric distance measure, we calculate the following Jensen-Shannon (JS) divergence [20, 28]:

$$dist(\boldsymbol{P}^l||\boldsymbol{Q}^l)_{JS} = \frac{1}{2}\{dist(\boldsymbol{P}^l||\boldsymbol{Q}^l) + dist(\boldsymbol{Q}^l||\boldsymbol{P}^l)\}. \tag{16}$$

When the value, which is calculated by Eq. (16), is higher than that of the other interest levels, we determine that $\boldsymbol{X}_{new} = \{\boldsymbol{x}_{new1}, \boldsymbol{x}_{new2}\}$ corresponds to interest level l.

4. EXPERIMENTS

In this section, we show the experimental results to verify the effectiveness of our method.

4.1 Experimental Conditions

In this subsection, we explain experimental conditions. In this experiment, a keyword "movie trailer" was given as a

Table 3: The details of the datasets used in the experiment per subject. Note that "INT" represents the number of interesting videos, and "NOINT" represents the number of not interesting videos.

Subject	A	B	C	D	E	F	G	H	I	J	K
INT	30	20	30	31	10	29	24	23	25	26	32
NOINT	20	30	20	19	40	21	26	27	25	24	18

Table 4: The details of the comparative methods.

Name	Training Phase	Estimation Phase
C1	VBCCA [27]	Based on our Estimation Phase
C2	VBMCCA [12]	
C3	CCA [7]	Support Vector Machine [2]
C4	LDCCA [19]	
C5	Without using any CCA[7]	
C6	Only facial expression[8]	
C7	Only biological signals[9]	

query to YouTube[5]. We then obtained 50 trailers of videos, and these 50 trailers consisted of five genres of film: science fiction, comedy, action, horror and romance. The subjects were 11 men between the ages of 22 and 24, and they watched all of the 50 trailers. Note that the length of each trailer is about 90 seconds, and each genre contained 10 trailers. They watched the trailers while sitting on a chair about 0.5-meters away from the display. The Kinect was set behind the display to obtain the subject's facial expression features. In addition, they wore a Silmee and alphatec IV-s on their chest and head respectively to obtain biological signals. The subjects then evaluated each of the trailers after watching in four grades[6]. The facial expression features and the biological signal features were calculated every second. As a result, the datasets including the four elements (trailer, rating, facial expression features, and biological signal features) could be obtained.

4.2 Experimental Results

We estimate interest level with respect to two classes, i.e., "Interesting" and "Not interesting". The class "Interesting" corresponds to the video evaluation rated 3 or 4 by subjects, and the class "Not interesting" corresponds to the video evaluation rated 1 or 2 by the subjects. The details about the prepared datasets are shown in **Table 3**. We compare the estimation results of our proposed method with seven comparative methods shown in **Table 4**. This is because C1 and C2 are used to verify the effectiveness of mixture framework and the robustness to outliers, respectively. Furthermore, C3 is a benchmark, and C4 which can consider k-nearest neighbors' class information of input data is a recently proposed CCA. The aim of using C5 - C7 is to show the effectiveness of the collaborative use. We evaluate the performance by using F-measure. As shown in **Table 5**, it is confirmed that our VBMRCCA-based method outperforms the other methods. In particular, the F-measures of C4 - C7 which use SVM in estimation phase are influenced by the imbalanced training data. We then estimate the interest level when the training data is small. First, we divide 50 groups (trailers) of facial expression and biological signals into 30 groups and 20 groups. In this estimation, we use the former 30 groups as test data and the later as training data, and the training data is not imbalanced. Thus, we evaluate the effectiveness of our method when the number of trailers used as training is changed from 10 to 20. Since the training data of subject E is too imbalanced to calculate F-measure, we do not use the data from subject E. As shown in **Fig.2**, our proposed method and C1 have robust performance despite changes in the amount of training data. Moreover, when the number of trailers used as training becomes 20, the performance of our proposed method is obviously high. In addition to the robustness, our proposed method gives a better performance as the number of trailers used as training increases (see **Table 5**). Therefore, our proposed method realizes effective interest level estimation even if the training data is small and imbalanced.

[5]http://www.youtube.com/

[6]1=Not at all interesting, 4=Extremely interesting

[7]Combining two features without any integration method

[8]Using only facial expression features in estimating interest level

[9]Using only biological signal features in estimating interest level

Table 5: F-measure of interest level estimation. Note that "SUB" represents subject and "AVE" represent average for all subjects.

SUB	Ours	C1	C2	C3	C4	C5	C6	C7
A	**0.645**	0.621	0.633	0.542	0.567	0.500	0.462	0.476
B	0.649	0.636	**0.683**	0.585	0.667	0.512	0.455	0.524
C	**0.643**	0.632	**0.643**	0.607	0.621	0.536	0.464	0.508
D	**0.679**	0.643	0.655	0.581	0.635	0.613	0.536	0.567
E	**0.522**	0.500	0.519	0.370	0.375	0.370	0.333	0.370
F	**0.678**	0.667	0.656	0.610	0.667	0.624	0.373	0.644
G	0.681	0.652	**0.696**	0.605	0.638	0.553	0.511	0.542
H	**0.692**	0.593	0.627	0.545	0.565	0.607	0.490	0.533
I	**0.679**	0.627	0.618	0.650	**0.679**	0.643	0.615	0.615
J	**0.717**	0.642	**0.717**	0.615	0.667	0.571	0.549	0.549
K	**0.508**	0.492	0.500	0.484	0.463	0.459	0.393	0.441
AVE	**0.645**	0.609	0.632	0.566	0.592	0.544	0.456	0.525

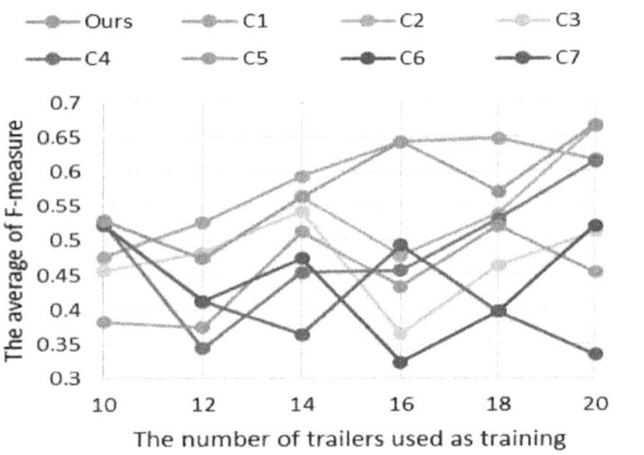

Figure 2: The average of F-measure for all subjects except E.

5. CONCLUSIONS

In this paper, we have proposed a method which estimates interest level while watching videos via collaborative use of facial expression and biological signals. In the proposed method, we use VBMRCCA to integrate the two features and obtain the posterior distributions. Experimental results indicate the validity of comparing the distributions. Consequently, we have realized successful interest level estimation via collaborative use of facial expression and biological signals even if the training data is small and imbalanced.

6. ACKNOWLEDGEMENT

This work was partly supported by Grant-in-Aid for Scientific Research(B) 25280036 from JSPS.

7. REFERENCES

[1] B. Chen, W. Lam, I. Tsang, and T.-L. Wong. Location and scatter matching for dataset shift in text mining. In *Proceedings of 2010 IEEE 10th International Conference on Data Mining (ICDM)*, pages 773–778, 2010.

[2] C. Cortes and V. Vapnik. Support-vector networks. *Machine learning*, 20(3):273–297, 1995.

[3] P. Cui, Z. Wang, and Z. Su. What videos are similar with you?: Learning a common attributed representation for video recommendation. In *Proceedings of the ACM International Conference on Multimedia*, pages 597–606, 2014.

[4] Z. Dai, G. Sheng, Z. Honggang, C. Guang, Z. Yongsheng, T. Jifeng, and G. Jun. A real-time video recommendation system for live programs. In *2014 4th IEEE International Conference on Network Infrastructure and Digital Content (IC-NIDC)*, pages 498–502. IEEE, 2014.

[5] S. H. Fairclough, A. J. Karran, and K. Gilleade. Classification accuracy from the perspective of the user: Real-time interaction with physiological computing. In *Proceedings of the 33rd Annual ACM Conference on Human Factors in Computing Systems*, pages 3029–3038, 2015.

[6] J. Hernandez, Y. Li, J. M. Rehg, and R. W. Picard. Bioglass: Physiological parameter estimation using a head-mounted wearable device. In *Proceedings of 2014 EAI 4th International Conference on the Wireless Mobile Communication and Healthcare (Mobihealth)*, pages 55–58, 2014.

[7] H. Hotelling. Relations between two sets of variates. *Biometrika*, pages 321–377, 1936.

[8] Q. Huang, B. Chen, J. Wang, and T. Mei. Personalized video recommendation through graph propagation. *ACM Transactions on Multimedia Computing, Communications, and Applications (TOMM)*, 10(4):32, 2014.

[9] S. Ishimaru, K. Kunze, K. Kise, J. Weppner, A. Dengel, P. Lukowicz, and A. Bulling. In the blink of an eye: combining head motion and eye blink frequency for activity recognition with google glass. In *Proceedings of the 5th Augmented Human International Conference*, 2014.

[10] E.-H. Jang, B.-J. Park, S.-H. Kim, M.-A. Chung, M.-S. Park, and J.-H. Sohn. Emotion classification based on bio-signals emotion recognition using machine learning algorithms. In *Proceedings of International Conference on Information Science, Electronics and Electrical Engineering (ISEEE)*, volume 3, pages 1373–1376, 2014.

[11] A. J. Karran and U. Kreplin. The drive to explore: physiological computing in a cultural heritage context. In *Advances in Physiological Computing*, pages 169–195. Springer, 2014.

[12] A. Klami and S. Kaski. Local dependent components. In *Proceedings of the 24th international conference on Machine learning*, pages 425–432, 2007.

[13] D. K. Krishnappa, M. Zink, C. Griwodz, and P. Halvorsen. Cache-centric video recommendation: an approach to improve the efficiency of youtube caches. *ACM Transactions on Multimedia Computing, Communications, and Applications (TOMM)*, 11(4):48, 2015.

[14] H. T. Le and L. A. Vea. A customer emotion recognition through facial expression using kinect sensors v1 and v2: A comparative analysis. In *Proceedings of the 10th International Conference on Ubiquitous Information Management and Communication*, page 80, 2016.

[15] C. Liu and D. B. Rubin. Ml estimation of the t distribution using em and its extensions, ecm and ecme. *Statistica Sinica*, pages 19–39, 1995.

[16] R. Miotto and N. Orio. A probabilistic model to combine tags and acoustic similarity for music retrieval. *ACM Transactions on Information Systems (TOIS)*, 30(2):8, 2012.

[17] H. Nakayama, T. Harada, and Y. Kuniyoshi. Canonical contextual distance for large-scale image annotation and retrieval. In *Proceedings of the First ACM workshop on Large-scale multimedia retrieval and mining*, pages 3–10, 2009.

[18] R. M. Neal. *Bayesian learning for neural networks*, volume 118. Springer Science & Business Media, 2012.

[19] Y. Peng, D. Zhang, and J. Zhang. A new canonical correlation analysis algorithm with local discrimination. *Neural processing letters*, 31(1):1–15, 2010.

[20] N. Rasiwasia, P. J. Moreno, and N. Vasconcelos. Bridging the gap: Query by semantic example. *IEEE Transactions on Multimedia,*, 9(5):923–938, 2007.

[21] T. Suzuki, H. Tanaka, S. Minami, H. Yamada, and T. Miyata. Wearable wireless vital monitoring technology for smart health care. In *Proceedings of International Symposium on Medical Information and Communication Technology (ISMICT)*, pages 1–4, 2013.

[22] M. Takahashi, S. Clippingdale, M. Naemura, and M. Shibata. Estimation of viewers' ratings of TV programs based on behaviors in home environments. *Multimedia Tools and Applications*, pages 1–16, 2014.

[23] R. M. A. Teixeira, T. Yamasaki, and K. Aizawa. Determination of emotional content of video clips by low-level audiovisual features. *Multimedia Tools and Applications*, 61(1):21–49, 2012.

[24] N. Ueda and Z. Ghahramani. Bayesian model search for mixture models based on optimizing variational bounds. *Neural Networks*, 15(10):1223–1241, 2002.

[25] R.-D. Vatavu. Audience silhouettes: peripheral awareness of synchronous audience kinesics for social television. In *Proceedings of the ACM International Conference on Interactive Experiences for TV and Online Video*, pages 13–22, 2015.

[26] J. Viinikanoja, A. Klami, and S. Kaski. Variational bayesian mixture of robust cca models. In *Machine Learning and Knowledge Discovery in Databases*, pages 370–385. Springer, 2010.

[27] C. Wang. Variational bayesian approach to canonical correlation analysis. *IEEE Transactions on Neural Networks*, 18(3):905–910, 2007.

[28] W. Wang, P. Barnaghi, and A. Bargiela. Probabilistic topic models for learning terminological ontologies. *IEEE Transactions on Knowledge and Data Engineering*, 22(7):1028–1040, 2010.

[29] M. Yan, J. Sang, and C. Xu. Unified youtube video recommendation via cross-network collaboration. In *Proceedings of the 5th ACM on International Conference on Multimedia Retrieval*, pages 19–26, 2015.

[30] H. Ye, M. Malu, U. Oh, and L. Findlater. Current and future mobile and wearable device use by people with visual impairments. In *Proceedings of the SIGCHI Conference on Human Factors in Computing Systems*, pages 3123–3132, 2014.

[31] M. Yeasin, B. Bullot, and R. Sharma. Recognition of facial expressions and measurement of levels of interest from video. *IEEE Transactions on Multimedia*, 8(3):500–508, 2006.

[32] S. Zennaro, M. Munaro, S. Milani, P. Zanuttigh, A. Bernardi, S. Ghidoni, and E. Menegatti. Performance evaluation of the 1st and 2nd generation kinect for multimedia applications. In *Proceedings of 2015 IEEE International Conference on Multimedia and Expo (ICME)*, pages 1–6, 2015.

[33] X. Zhao, H. Luan, J. Cai, J. Yuan, X. Chen, and Z. Li. Personalized video recommendation based on viewing history with the study on youtube. In *Proceedings of the 4th International Conference on Internet Multimedia Computing and Service*, pages 161–165, 2012.

[34] Q. Zhu, M.-L. Shyu, and H. Wang. Videotopic: Content-based video recommendation using a topic model. In *2013 IEEE International Symposium on Multimedia (ISM)*, pages 219–222. IEEE, 2013.

Transportation Mode Detection on Mobile Devices Using Recurrent Nets

Toan H. Vu
Department of Computer Science and Information Engineering
National Central University
Taoyuan, Taiwan
toanvuhong@gmail.com

Le Dung
School of Electronics and Telecommunications
Hanoi University of Science and Technology
Hanoi, Vietnam
dung.le@hust.edu.vn

Jia-Ching Wang
Department of Computer Science and Information Engineering
National Central University
Taoyuan, Taiwan
jcw@csie.ncu.edu.tw

ABSTRACT

We present an approach to the use of Recurrent Neural Networks (RNN) for transportation mode detection (TMD) on mobile devices. The proposed model, called Control Gate-based Recurrent Neural Network (CGRNN), is an end-to-end model that works directly with raw signals from an embedded accelerometer. As mobile devices have limited computational resources, we evaluate the model in terms of accuracy, computational cost, and memory usage. Experiments on the HTC transportation mode dataset demonstrate that our proposed model not only exhibits remarkable accuracy, but also is efficient with low resource consumption.

Keywords

Control gate-based recurrent neural network; CGRNN

1. INTRODUCTION

Transportation mode detection (TMD) has recently been incorporated into many mobile devices as it is a crucial component in a lot of applications that involve contextual understanding, especially in healthcare and fitness monitoring. For example, a healthcare assistant tells its user if he/she has been remaining in a particular state (such as sitting, running) for too long. A fitness program estimates the number of calories a person burns in a day by analyzing his/her travel diary built from predicted transportation modes [12]. TMD systems suggest a way to automatically collect travel routines from people. That information is very useful for transportation planning. This paper introduces a new method for detecting transportation modes using an accelerometer.

1.1 Related Work

Most TMD systems on mobile devices are based on various embedded sensors including accelerometers, gyroscopes, magnetometers, and GPS receivers [4, 9, 10, 12]. Existing works have attempted to extract good features from time-series signals of several sensors in many domains - time, frequency, and statistical- before finding out the best from a number of classifiers such as Support Vector Machines, Hidden Markov Models, and Decision Tree [4, 9, 10, 12]. Also, combining many sensors and sets of features frequently increases accuracy [9, 12]. However, these approaches cannot easily discover relevant features and the best classifiers for solving a given objective problem. Additionally, as more sensors and features are exploited, more computational resources are consumed.

Deep learning (DL) has been highly successful in a wide range of applications such as computer vision [6], speech recognition [3], and machine translation [1]. DL models are mostly end-to-end, so no gap exists between the feature extraction and classification stages. The DL models learn abstract features automatically from data to satisfy output conditions in the cases of either unsupervised or supervised learning. One important property of a DL system is the ability to handle big data by scaling up the model and making the model more non-linearly complex. Nonetheless, DL models that are applied on mobile devices may be computationally heavy if they are to be effective. The aim of this work is to build a DL model that is simple, accurate, and inexpensive.

1.2 Our Contribution

We propose a recurrent neural network model (RNN) for the TMD task that uses an accelerometer. The model manipulates directly sequential data that are collected from the accelerometer without any feature selection. We compare the model with implementations of several RNN structures such as Long Short-Term Memory (LSTM) [3, 5] and Gated Recurrent Unit (GRU) [1, 2]. The proposed model has a simpler structure and less burdensome computation than others, but with competitive performances, as can be seen in experiments on the HTC transportation mode dataset [12]. Moreover, the amount of power consumed by sensing components is very low since the system uses only an accelerometer.

The rest of paper is organized as follows. Section 2 presents general information about RNNs, and describes the proposed RNN design for the TMD task. In Section 3, experiments on the HTC transportation mode dataset with different RNN models are conducted and their results are analyzed in detail. Finally, Section 4 draws conclusions.

MM '16, October 15-19, 2016, Amsterdam, Netherlands

DOI: http://dx.doi.org/10.1145/2964284.2967249

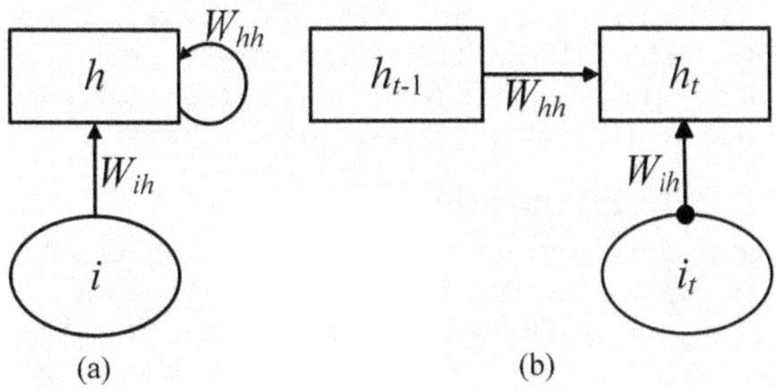

Figure 1: (a) A typical recurrent neural network; (b) the block diagram of a typical recurrent net at time *t*. Hidden state receives information from its previous state and current input.

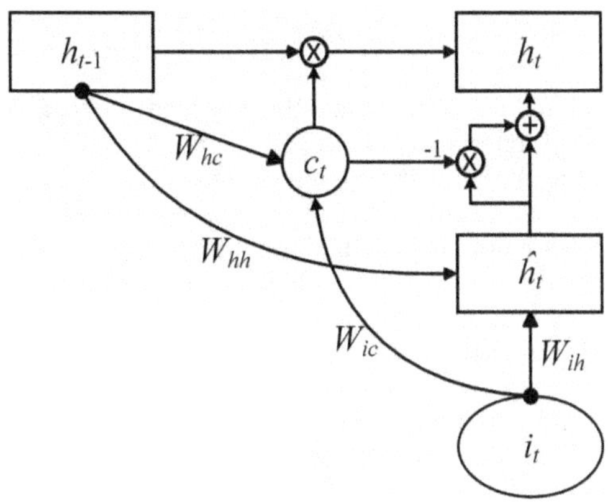

Figure 2: A control gate-based recurrent unit.

2. PROPOSED MODEL

In this section, general information about recurrent nets is presented, and then the proposed RNN model, called control gate-based recurrent neural network (CGRNN), is described in detail before an RNN architecture for detecting transportation modes is developed.

2.1 Recurrent Neural Networks

A recurrent neural network (RNN) is a neural network with self-connections whose delay is one. It is very efficient and powerful when used to time-series signals. In RNN models, a hidden layer with self-connections has the role of memory that accumulates information over time from an input sequence. Figure 1(a) shows a typical recurrent net structure in which the hidden layer is self-connected. The corresponding block diagram in Figure 1(b) illustrates how information is updated in the hidden layer at a specific time.

In standard RNNs, an input at time t is i_t, a typical hidden state is given by

$$h_t = f(W_{ih}i_t + W_{hh}h_{t-1}) \tag{1}$$

where f is an activation function that is used in the hidden layer, and is commonly a logistic sigmoid or hyperbolic tangent function; W_{ih} and W_{hh} represent weight matrices of connections between input and hidden and between hidden and hidden layers, respectively. For conciseness, biases are not included.

Simply, the back propagation through time (BPTT) method [11] is applied to compute gradients by unfolding the RNN structure. However, training RNNs is particularly difficult because of the exploding and vanishing gradient problem [8]. Thus, standard RNNs cannot easily learn long-range dependencies. To solve this problem, many works have attempted to discover better optimization techniques, such as gradient clipping method [8] and Hessian-Free optimization [7].

Another most interesting solution is to design new recurrent structures by using a gate mechanism, such as Long Short-Term Memory (LSTM) [3, 5] and Gated Recurrent Unit (GRU) [1, 2]. Gates are incorporated into a recurrent unit, which control information flows in the net. They are computed at each time step from the current input and previous recurrent states. Therefore, the network automatically learns and remembers relevant information into recurrent states over time. For instance, three gates in LSTM structure are the input gate, the forget gate, and the output gate, so information flows that are added to, are retained in, or being read from memory are strictly controlled. The gates inside RNN structures increase the capacity to learn long-range dependencies. More details of LSTM and GRU can be found elsewhere [1, 2, 3, 5].

Since gates are computed in a manner similar to the computation of a typical hidden state in standard RNNs, the computational cost of computing one gate is greater than or equal to that of computing a typical hidden state. Hence, more gates result in greater computational cost. This work will provide an effective gated RNN model that uses only a control gate and is cheap to implement on mobile devices. The model is introduced in the next subsection.

2.2 Control Gate-based Recurrent Neural Networks

Control gate-based recurrent neural networks (CGRNN) are constructed by integrating a control gate into the typical recurrent unit. Figure 2 displays a block diagram of the net, in which i_t represents the input at time t; h_{t-1} is the previous hidden state at time $t-1$; $\hat{h_t}$ can be seen as the typical hidden state at time t. The control gate c_t acts as a coordinator that calculates the proportions of information from the previous state and the typical state that contribute to the new state.

At a time step t, the typical state is computed as

$$\hat{h_t} = f(W_{ih}i_t + W_{hh}h_{t-1}) \tag{2}$$

and the equation of control gate is

$$c_t = \sigma(W_{ic}i_t + W_{hc}h_{t-1}) \tag{3}$$

The new hidden state is derived as

$$h_t = c_t \otimes h_{t-1} + (1 - c_t) \otimes \hat{h_t} \tag{4}$$

where f is an activation function; σ is a logistic sigmoid function, and W_{ih}, W_{hh}, W_{ic}, and W_{hc} are weight matrices. The symbol $\otimes$ denotes element-wise multiplication.

The value of control gate c_t varies in the range $[0, 1]$. If c_t is equal to zero, then the new hidden state forgets all its previous information and is charged by the current typical state. However, if c_t is close to one, then the new hidden state remains unchanged, and the current typical state has no effect.

Due to the integrated control gate, the computational cost of a CGRNN is approximately double that of a typical RNN

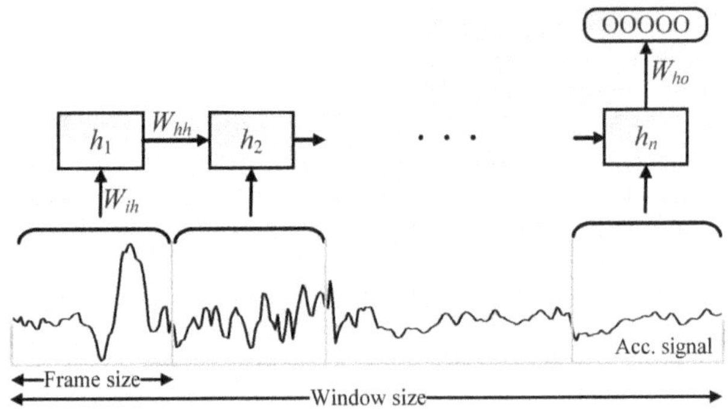

Figure 3: Recurrent neural network architecture for transportation mode detection using an accelerometer. Each input to the network corresponds to a frame that is divided from the window. (Acc. denotes accelerometer)

of the same size, but it is still lower than that of LSTM or GRU which employs more than one gate. In addition, we realize that a CGRNN can be regarded as a pruned version of GRU without a reset gate.

2.3 General Architecture for Detecting Transportation Modes

The TMD system that is presented herein relies on signals from an embedded accelerometer. The RNN models work directly with these time-series signals (Figure 3). Given a signal window, the hidden state reads temporal input at every step which corresponds to a frame that is divided from the window to obtain the final state before making a prediction from that state.

In the RNN-based TMD architecture, recurrent units can be of various types, such as typical RNN, LSTM, GRU, and CGRNN. The output layer is connected to the last state by a *softmax* connection that computes the probabilities of modes. The equation for the output layer is as follows.

$$P(l|h_n; W_{ho}) = \frac{exp(W_{ho}^{(l)} h_n)}{\sum_{i \in \{1,...,L\}} exp(W_{ho}^{(i)} h_n)} \quad (5)$$

where $P(l|h_n; W_{ho})$ is the probability of class l given the last hidden state h_n; W_{ho} is weight connection matrix between the output and hidden layers, and $W_{ho}^{(i)}$ is a connection matrix between the output unit of class i and the hidden layer. In addition, $\{1, ..., L\}$ is the set of labels.

Stacking up more layers on the hidden layer yields deeper recurrent neural nets. These architectures can learn more complex features from inputs, and so may perform better.

3. EXPERIMENTS

To evaluate the performance of the control gate-based recurrent network, experiments were carried out on the HTC transportation mode dataset [12] using various types of RNNs, including the typical recurrent net, GRU, LSTM, CGRNN, and their two-layer versions: RNN2L (RNN 2 layers), GRU2L (GRU 2 layers), and CGRNN2L (CGRNN 2 layers). LSTM 2 layers are not considered because they are computationally heavy even when implemented with a personal computer.

The dataset comprises signal logs from three sensors - an accelerometer, a magnetometer, and a gyroscope - with ten transportation modes - **Still**, **Walk**, **Run**, **Bike**, **Motorcycle**, **Car**, **Bus**, **Metro**, **Train**, and high speed rail (**HSR**). Similar to [12], the six latter modes are combined into the **Vehicle** mode, yielding five transportation modes.

3.1 Data Preparation

The training data are divided into the training set and the development set. The development set is constructed by taking at random 20 log files from all modes. The Vehicle mode has 120 files as it is made up of six original modes. The test data is provided independently.

In order to reduce the power consumed by sensors, we only employ data that are collected from an accelerometer. At each time-step, the magnitudes of the triaxial accelerometer signals are calculated since they are supposed to not be affected by the position of the device on the body.

$$A = \sqrt{A_x^2 + A_y^2 + A_z^2} \quad (6)$$

where A, A_x, A_y, and A_z are the magnitude, the x component, the y component, and the z component, respectively, of the accelerometer at the same time.

The global mean of magnitudes is computed from the training set before a global mean subtraction is applied for the entire database. The global mean is constant, so the subtraction can be performed immediately when signals are collected in real time.

Finally, we extract windows with size of 360 from both training and development set, equivalent to 12 seconds since the sampling rate of the sensors was 30 Hz. The window size has a large influence on accuracy of the system since small windows may not be sufficient and would be easily affected by noise, but very long windows lead to a longer response time. Approximately, 500 thousand windows are obtained from each mode in the training set.

3.2 Model and Training Details

Information about the RNN systems follows.

- Input: window size is 360; frame size is 5; global-mean subtraction is used.
- Hidden layers: number of hidden units in single-layer RNNs is 50. In two-layer RNNs, first layer has 30 units and second layer has 60 units.
- Output: size of output is 5; softmax connections.

The cross-entropy objective function is utilized for the classification task. Weights are initialized by sampling from $0.01N(0, 1)$, and biases are all initialized to zeros. To train the models, a combination of optimization methods including stochastic gradient descent (mini-batch size of 128, weight-decay of 0.0001), gradient clipping with a threshold value that varies in $\{1, 10, 100\}$, and ADADELTA (with hyper-parameters $\rho = 0.95$, $\varepsilon = 1e - 6$ as in[13]) is used. The optimal set of parameters is determined at the highest accuracy on the development set after 4 epochs.

3.3 Results

3.3.1 Evaluation of Accuracy

General approaches for the TMD task can only predict on each window. However, in this work, in RNN systems with

Table 1: Window-based test accuracy (B: Bike, R: Run, S: Still, W: Walk, V: Vehicle, *Avg*: Average)

Models	Accuracy (%)					
	B	R	S	W	V	*Avg*
RNN	86.73	97.99	91.14	95.12	72.43	88.68
GRU	91.90	98.19	92.70	98.12	83.24	**92.83**
LSTM	90.83	98.46	90.85	97.58	83.27	92.20
CGRNN	91.68	97.98	94.78	97.67	81.58	**92.74**
RNN2L	89.91	97.17	88.82	95.34	71.44	88.53
GRU2L	92.92	97.46	92.97	97.81	82.69	92.77
CGRNN2L	90.93	98.51	93.31	98.06	84.69	**93.10**

Table 2: Frame-based test accuracy (B: Bike, R: Run, S: Still, W: Walk, V: Vehicle, *Avg*: Average)

Models	Accuracy (%)					
	B	R	S	W	V	*Avg*
RNN	89.34	98.01	91.26	93.64	71.14	88.68
GRU	91.17	98.44	90.83	98.95	87.05	93.29
LSTM	50.86	47.33	80.70	81.39	62.62	**64.58**
CGRNN	91.98	98.11	95.03	98.91	82.89	**93.38**
RNN2L	90.70	97.31	88.89	96.04	71.87	88.96
GRU2L	94.21	97.77	92.49	98.75	88.61	94.37
CGRNN2L	93.13	98.56	90.47	99.06	92.40	**94.72**

the same set of parameters we also make predictions at every frame of an accelerometer signal by putting the *softmax* connections on top of the hidden state at every step (Figure 3). In a window-based test, the overlap between two consecutive windows is half of the window size. Tables 1 and 2 present our results herein on window-based and frame-based tests, respectively. The two tables reveal that the CGRNN and the CGRNN2L perform very well in both tests. Their results are competitive to the GRU and GRU2L. The best results yielded an average accuracy of 93.10 in the window-based test, and 94.72 in the frame-based test, and these were achieved using the CGRNN2L. The lowest accuracies were mostly obtained in the detection of Vehicle mode. The reason, we suppose, is that the accelerometer values are influenced by relative velocity so the Vehicle mode may be confused with other modes such as Still and Walk. Surprisingly, the accuracy of LSTM drops significantly from the window-based test to the frame-based test, suggesting that LSTM does not perform well on extended input sequences in this particular system. We believe LSTM could be made to work better in both testing cases by using another training strategy.

Another feature of the TMD systems on mobile devices is the latency between two predictions. For a window size of 360 (12 s), an overlap size of 180 (6 s), and a frame size of 5 (0.17 s) in our setting, the latency in the window-based test is 6 s while that in the frame-based test is only 0.17 s, suggesting that the frame-based approach can be used to make predictions in real time immediately after the system receives a new frame of signals.

3.3.2 Evaluation of Computational Cost and Memory Usage

For comprehensive evaluations, computational cost and memory usage of the models are considered. Computational cost is obtained as the time that is required by a model to make a prediction on a window. One computer and a fixed coding style are used to ensure fair evaluations of performance are obtained. Memory usage is estimated approximately to the model size. Table 3 compares models in terms of accuracy, memory usage, and computational cost. From Table 3, the single-layer and two-layer CGRNN are competitive in terms of accuracy with corresponding GRU models, but use less memory and have a lower computational burden. The computational cost of the CGRNN does not differ much from that of the GRU in the single-layer group, but CGRNN2L is clearly superior in the two-layer group. Besides, the standard RNN models, including the single-layer and two-layer versions, are low-cost but they are also the least accurate. LSTM requires much memory and has a high computational burden. These models are all therefore unsuited to the TMD task on mobile devices.

Table 3: Performance comparison between models

Models	Window -based accuracy	Memory usage (KB)	Computational cost (ms)
RNN	88.68	25	7.3
GRU	92.83	71	21.4
LSTM	92.20	153	24.7
CGRNN	**92.74**	**48**	**21.1**
RNN2L	88.53	56	11.8
GRU2L	92.77	162	36.8
CGRNN2L	**93.10**	**109**	**27.8**

4. CONCLUSIONS

This paper develops a control gate-based recurrent neural network for detecting transportation modes using an accelerometer. Signals from the sensor are processed directly by the system to make predictions. The proposed model works effectively not only at the window-based level, but also at the frame-based level, with a low computational consumption for each prediction. The model is simpler and cheaper than LSTM and GRU, but it is more accurate, as can be seen in the experiments using the HTC transportation mode dataset.

5. ACKNOWLEDGMENTS

The authors would like to thank HTC Research for providing the transportation mode dataset. We thank Meng-Chieh Yu for his support.

6. REFERENCES

[1] K. Cho, B. van Merrienboer, C. Gulcehre, D. Bahdanau, F. Bougares, H. Schwenk, and Y. Bengio. Learning phrase representations using RNN encoder-decoder for statistical machine translation. In *Proceedings of the 2014 Conference on Empirical Methods in Natural Language Processing (EMNLP)*, pages 1724–1734, 2014.

[2] J. Chung, Ç. Gülçehre, K. Cho, and Y. Bengio. Empirical evaluation of gated recurrent neural networks on sequence modeling. Technical Report Arxiv report 1412.3555, Université de Montréal, 2014.

Presented at the Deep Learning workshop at NIPS2014.

[3] A. Graves, A.-R. Mohamed, and G. Hinton. Speech recognition with deep recurrent neural networks. In *International Conference on Acoustics, Speech and Signal Processing (ICASSP)*, pages 6645–6649, 2013.

[4] S. Hemminki, P. Nurmi, and S. Tarkoma. Accelerometer-based transportation mode detection on smartphones. In *Proceedings of the 11th ACM Conference on Embedded Networked Sensor Systems - SenSys '13*, pages 1–14, 2013.

[5] S. Hochreiter, S. Hochreiter, J. Schmidhuber, and J. Schmidhuber. Long short-term memory. *Neural computation*, 9(8):1735–80, 1997.

[6] A. Krizhevsky, I. Sulskever, and G. E. Hinton. ImageNet classification with deep convolutional neural networks. In *Advances in Neural Information and Processing Systems (NIPS)*, pages 1–9, 2012.

[7] J. Martens and I. Sutskever. Learning recurrent neural networks with Hessian-free optimization. In *Proceedings of the 28th International Conference on Machine Learning, ICML 2011*, pages 1033–1040, 2011.

[8] R. Pacanu, T. Mikolov, and Y. Bengio. On the difficulties of training recurrent neural networks. In *Proceedings of the 30th International Conference on Machine Learning, ICML 2013*, pages 1310–1318, 2013.

[9] S. Reddy, M. Mun, J. Burke, D. Estrin, M. Hansen, and M. Srivastava. Using mobile phones to determine transportation modes. *ACM Transactions on Sensor Networks*, 6(2):1–27, 2010.

[10] M. A. Shafique and E. Hato. Use of acceleration data for transportation mode prediction. *Transportation*, 42(1):163–188, 2014.

[11] R. J. Williams and D. Zipser. Gradient-based learning algorithms for recurrent networks and their computational complexity. In Y. Chauvin and D. E. Rumelhart, editors, *Back-propagation: Theory, Architectures and Applications*, chapter 13, pages 433–486. Hillsdale, NJ: Erlbaum, 1995.

[12] M.-C. Yu, T. Yu, S.-C. Wang, C.-J. Lin, and E. Y. Chang. Big data small footprint: The design of a low-power classifier for detecting transportation modes. In *Proceedings of the VLDB Endowment (PVLDB)*, volume 7, pages 1429–1440, 2014.

[13] M. D. Zeiler. ADADELTA: An adaptive learning rate method. *CoRR*, abs/1212.5:6, 2012.

Deeply-Supervised Recurrent Convolutional Neural Network for Saliency Detection

Youbao Tang, Xiangqian Wu
School of Computer Science and Technology
Harbin Institute of Technology
Harbin, 150001 China
{tangyoubao, xqwu}@hit.edu.cn

Wei Bu
Department of New Media Technologies and Arts
Harbin Institute of Technology
Harbin, 150001 China
buwei@hit.edu.cn

ABSTRACT
This paper proposes a novel saliency detection method by developing a deeply-supervised recurrent convolutional neural network (DSRCNN), which performs a full image-to-image saliency prediction. For saliency detection, the local, global, and contextual information of salient objects is important to obtain a high quality salient map. To achieve this goal, the DSRCNN is designed based on VGGNet-16. Firstly, the recurrent connections are incorporated into each convolutional layer, which can make the model more powerful for learning the contextual information. Secondly, side-output layers are added to conduct the deeply-supervised operation, which can make the model learn more discriminative and robust features by effecting the intermediate layers. Finally, all of the side-outputs are fused to integrate the local and global information to get the final saliency detection results. Therefore, the DSRCNN combines the advantages of recurrent convolutional neural networks and deeply-supervised nets. The DSRCNN model is tested on five benchmark datasets, and experimental results demonstrate that the proposed method significantly outperforms the state-of-the-art saliency detection approaches on all test datasets.

Keywords
Saliency detection; deeply-supervised recurrent convolutional neural network; deeply-supervised learning; recurrent connection.

1. INTRODUCTION
Visual saliency detection, which aims to highlight the most important object regions in an image, is an important and challenging task in computer vision and has received extensive attentions in recent years. Numerous image processing applications incorporate the visual saliency to improve their performance, such as image segmentation [1] and cropping [2], object detection [3], and image retrieval [4], etc. A large number of visual saliency detection approaches [5-37] have been proposed by exploiting different salient cues recently. They can be roughly categorized as hand-designed features based approaches and CNN based approaches.

For the hand-designed features based approaches, the local and global features are extracted from pixels [5-7, 30] and regions [8-11, 18, 19, 23, 25, 27, 32-35, 37] for saliency detection. Generally,

MM '16, October 15-19, 2016, Amsterdam, Netherlands
© 2016 ACM. ISBN 978-1-4503-3603-1/16/10…$15.00
DOI: http://dx.doi.org/10.1145/2964284.2967250

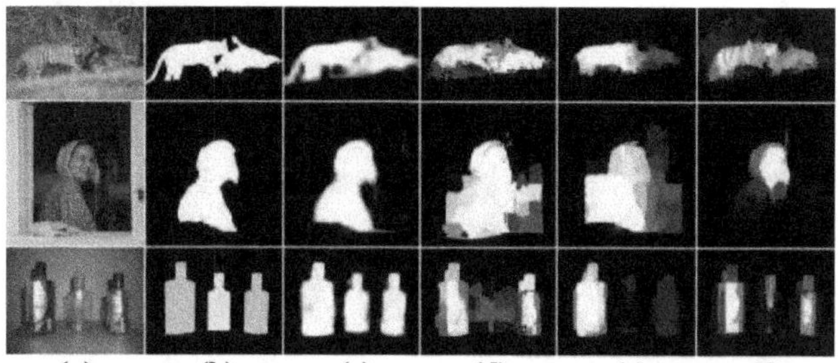

(a) (b) (c) (d) (e) (f)

Figure 1. Three examples of saliency detection results. (a) The input images. (b) The ground truths. (c) Our detection results. (d)-(f) The salient maps detected by the state-of-the-art CNN based approaches, i.e. MC [26], LEGS [28], and MDF [21], respectively.

the approaches extracted features from pixels highlight high-contrast edges instead of the salient objects, or get low contrast salient maps. That is because the extracted features are unable to reflect the complex relationship between pixels. The approaches extracted features from regions are much more effective than the ones from pixels to detect the saliency, since more sophisticated and discriminative features can be extracted from regions. Even so, the hand-designed features cannot capture the high-level and multi-scale information of salient objects.

Convolutional neural network (CNN) is powerful for high-level and multi-scale feature learning, which has been successfully used in many applications of computer vision, such as semantic segmentation [38, 39] and edge detection [40, 41]. In last year, several researchers [21, 26, 28] also propose CNN based approaches for saliency detection and get the state-of-the-art performance. That is because CNNs are able to extract more robust and discriminative features with considering the global contextual information of regions. All of these approaches [21, 26, 28] first segment images into a number of regions (such as sliding windows [28], multi-level decomposition regions [21], and superpixels [26]) and then use CNN to extract features from these regions, based on which the saliencies are estimated. Therefore, these approaches are complex and cannot generate the precise pixel-wise saliency prediction.

To overcome these problems, this work proposes a full image-to-image saliency prediction by developing a deeply-supervised recurrent convolutional neural network (DSRCNN), which is based on VGGNet-16 [42]. The DSRCNN combines the advantages of recurrent convolutional neural networks [43] and deeply-supervised nets [44] by incorporating the recurrent connections into each convolutional layer and adding side-output layers to supervise the feature learning of the intermediate layers. Therefore, an input image is fed into the DSRCNN model and a high quality salient map of the same size as the input image is directly produced after the feed-forward process. Figure 1 shows

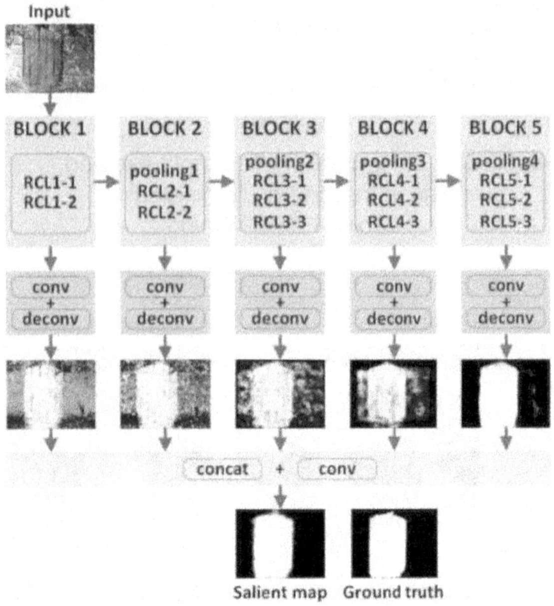

Figure 2. The architecture of the proposed deeply-supervised recurrent convolutional neural network for saliency detection.

some saliency detection results of the proposed method, which are very close to the ground truths.

2. DSRCNN FOR SALIENCY DETECTION

Recently, recurrent convolutional neural network (RCNN) has achieved state-of-the-art results of object recognition [43], and deeply-supervised nets (DSN) [44] have been successfully used in image classification [44] and edge detection [40]. RCNN has the ability to learn the contextual features, and DSN is able to learn more discriminative and robust features from local and global view. The contextual, local, and global features are important to extract a high quality salient map. Therefore, a deeply-supervised recurrent convolutional neural network (DSRCNN) is designed for saliency detection in this paper. In this section, we describe the DSRCNN in detail.

To obtain a precise saliency prediction, the CNN architecture should be deep and have multi-scale stages with different strides, so that we can learn discriminative and multi-scale features for pixels. Training such a deep network from scratch is difficult when there are few training samples. So this work chooses the VGGNet-16 [42] trained on the large-scale dataset as the pre-trained model for fine-tuning as done by [40]. The VGGNet-16 has six blocks. The first five blocks contain convolutional layers and pooling layers, and the last block contains a pooling layer and fully connected layers. The last block is removed in this work, since the pooling operation in this block makes the feature maps become too small (about $1/32$ of the input image size) to obtain fine full-size prediction and the fully connected layers are time and memory consuming. Based on the first five blocks of VGGNet-16, the deeply-supervised recurrent convolutional neural network (DSRCNN) is constructed as shown in Figure 2.

To make the model learn more contextual information, we use the recurrent convolutional layers (RCL) (as shown in Figure 3(b)) to replace the convolutional layers (as shown in Figure 3(a)) in the five blocks by incorporating the recurrent connections into each convolutional layer. Unfolding the recurrent convolutional layer for T time steps results in a feed-forward subnetworks of depth T+1, as shown in Figure 3(c) where T=2. In this work, we set T=2. While the recurrent input evolves over iterations, the feed-forward

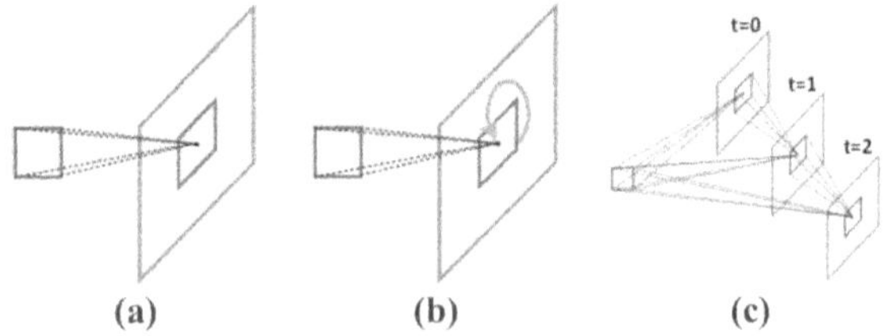

Figure 3. (a) Feed-forward convolutional layer. (b) Recurrent convolutional layer (RCL). (c) Subnetwork by unfolding the RCL.

input remains the same in all iterations. When t=0 only the feed-forward input is present. In the subnetwork, for a unit located at (i,j) on the kth feature map, its net input $z_{ijk}(t)$ at time step t is computed as [43] by:

$$z_{ijk}(t) = \left(\mathbf{v}_k^f\right)^T \mathbf{u}^{(i,j)}(t) + (\mathbf{v}_k^r)^T \mathbf{x}^{(i,j)}(t-1) + b_k \quad (1)$$

where $\mathbf{u}^{(i,j)}(t)$ and $\mathbf{x}^{(i,j)}(t-1)$ denote the feed-forward and recurrent input, $\mathbf{v}_k^f$ and $\mathbf{v}_k^r$ denote the feed-forward weights and recurrent weights, and b_k is the bias. More details about RCNN can be found in its reference [43]. As we can see, compared with the convolutional layer, the effective receptive field of an RCL unit in the feature maps of the previous layer expands when the iteration number increases. Therefore, the RCL is able to learn features which contain more contextual information.

To make the model learn more discriminative features from both local and global views, a side-output is generated to perform the deeply-supervised learning from the last RCL of each block by a convolutional layer and a deconvolutional layer, as shown in Figure 2. Another benefit of deeply-supervised learning is to alleviate the common problem of "vanishing" gradients during training such a deep network. The additional convolutional layer with one 1×1 convolutional kernel converts the feature maps to a salient map, and the additional deconvolutional layer is used to make the salient map have the same size with the input image. To make the final salient map consider the local and global information of salient objects and be robust to the size variation of salient objects, the side-outputs of the all five blocks are fused by concatenating them in the channel direction and using a convolutional kernel with size of 1×1 to convert the concatenation maps to the final salient map. Convolution with a 1×1 kernel is a weighted fusion process. So far, the whole architecture of DSRCNN has been constructed, as shown in Figure 2. All additional deconvolutional layer and the last convolutional layer are followed by a sigmoid activation function. And for each block, a dropout layer with the dropout ratio of 0.5 is followed to alleviate the overfitting.

For training of DSRCNN, the errors between all side-outputs and the ground truth should be computed and backward propagate. Therefore, we need to define a loss function to compute these errors. For most of images, the number of pixels in salient objects and background are heavily imbalanced. Here, given an image X and its ground truth Y, a cross-entropy loss function defined in [40] is used to balance the loss between salient and background classes as follows:

$$\begin{aligned} l_{side}^m(\mathbf{W}, \mathbf{w}^m) = -\alpha \sum_{i=1}^{|Y_+|} \log P(y_i = 1|X; \mathbf{W}, \mathbf{w}^m) \\ -(1-\alpha) \sum_{i=1}^{|Y_-|} \log P(y_i = 0|X; \mathbf{W}, \mathbf{w}^m) \end{aligned} \quad (2)$$

where $\alpha = |Y_-|/(|Y_+| + |Y_-|)$, $|Y_+|$ and $|Y_-|$mean the number of salient pixels and background pixels in ground truth, $\mathbf{W}$ denotes

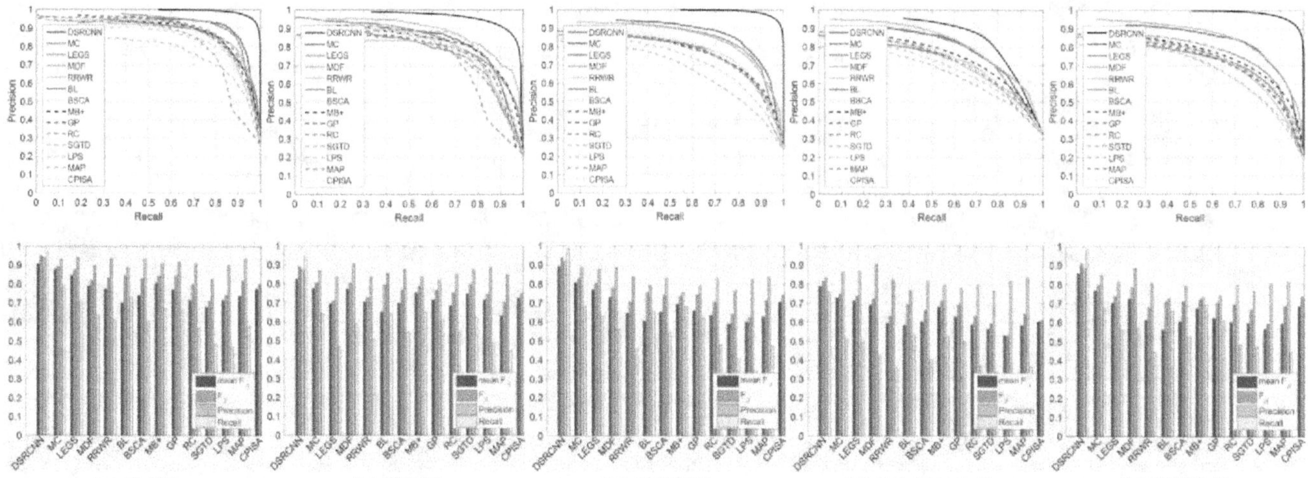

(a) SED1 (b) SED2 (c) ECSSD (d) PASCAL-S (e) HKU-IS

Figure 4: Results of all test approaches on five standard benchmark datasets, i.e. SED1, SED2, ECSSD, PASCAL-S, and HKU-IS. The first row presents the precision-recall curves. The second row presents the mean F-measures and the adaptive F-measures/precision/recall which are computed from the binary images obtained by binarizing the salient maps with adaptive thresholds computed by using Otsu algorithm.

Table 1. The weighted F-measure and MAE of different approaches on different test datasets (red, blue, and green texts respectively indicate rank 1, 2, and 3)

Approach	Year	SED1		SED2		ECSSD		PASCAL-S		HKU-IS	
		wF_β	MAE	wF_β	MAE	wF_β	MAE	wF_β	MAE	wF_β	MAE
DSRCNN	/	0.8935	0.0357	0.7924	0.0526	0.8718	0.0368	0.6974	0.1284	0.8330	0.0399
MC	CVPR2015	0.8242	0.0790	0.6959	0.1153	0.7293	0.1019	0.6064	0.1422	0.6899	0.0914
LEGS	CVPR2015	0.7671	0.1021	0.5911	0.1407	0.6722	0.1256	0.5791	0.1593	0.5911	0.1301
MDF	CVPR2015	0.6896	0.1284	0.6674	0.1152	0.6194	0.1377	0.5386	0.1633	0.6135	0.1152
RRWR	CVPR2015	0.6524	0.1412	0.5914	0.1615	0.5026	0.1850	0.4435	0.2262	0.4592	0.1719
BL	CVPR2015	0.5612	0.1850	0.4673	0.1905	0.4615	0.2178	0.4464	0.2478	0.4119	0.2136
BSCA	CVPR2015	0.6161	0.1546	0.5426	0.1591	0.5159	0.1832	0.4703	0.2220	0.4643	0.1760
MB+	ICCV2015	0.6956	0.1334	0.6354	0.1379	0.5632	0.1717	0.5307	0.1964	0.5438	0.1497
GP	ICCV2015	0.6449	0.1536	0.5688	0.1620	0.5180	0.1919	0.4823	0.2300	0.4680	0.1852
RC	TPAMI2015	0.6033	0.1642	0.5461	0.1562	0.5118	0.1868	0.4694	0.2253	0.4768	0.1714
SGTD	TIP2015	0.5743	0.1855	0.6453	0.1285	0.4689	0.2007	0.4385	0.2269	0.4785	0.1627
LPS	TIP2015	0.6029	0.1610	0.5950	0.1411	0.4585	0.1877	0.3882	0.2162	0.4252	0.1635
MAP	TIP2015	0.6339	0.1459	0.5181	0.1703	0.4953	0.1861	0.4361	0.2222	0.4533	0.1717
CPISA	TIP2015	0.6645	0.1458	0.5939	0.1482	0.5735	0.1596	0.4478	0.1983	0.5575	0.1374

the parameters of all network layers in the five blocks, $\mathbf{w}^m$ denotes the weights of the mth side-output layer including a convolutional layer and a deconvolutional layer, and $P(y_i = 1|X; \mathbf{W}, \mathbf{w}^m) \in [0,1]$ is computed using sigmoid function on the activation value at pixel j. So the whole loss of all side-outputs is defined as

$$L_{side}(\mathbf{W}, \mathbf{w}) = \sum_{m=1}^{5} l_{side}^{m}(\mathbf{W}, \mathbf{w}^m) \quad (3)$$

where $\mathbf{w} = (\mathbf{w}^1, \mathbf{w}^2, ..., \mathbf{w}^5)$. The loss between the fusion output and ground truth $L_{fuse}(\mathbf{W}, \mathbf{w}, \mathbf{h})$ is also computed by using the cross-entropy loss function, where $\mathbf{h}$ is the weights of the last fusion convolutional kernel. After computing all losses, the standard stochastic gradient descent algorithm is used to minimize the following objective function during training.

$$(\mathbf{W}, \mathbf{w}, \mathbf{h})^* = \operatorname{argmin}\left(L_{side}(\mathbf{W}, \mathbf{w}) + L_{fuse}(\mathbf{W}, \mathbf{w}, \mathbf{h})\right) \quad (4)$$

For testing of DSRCNN, given an image, we can use the trained model to predict a salient map, in which the salient object regions have larger values.

We use the popular Caffe deep leaning library [45] to implement the framework of DSRCNN. The THUS-10000 dataset [34] which contains 10,000 images and their corresponding ground truths is used for training. Since DSRCNN is a fully convolutional network, the images with arbitrary sizes can be the inputs without being resized during training and test. The training and test processes are conducted on a PC with an Intel i7-4790k CPU, a TESLA K40c GPU, and 32G RAM. The average runtime per image on the THUS-10000 dataset is about 0.23 second.

3. EXPERIMENTAL RESULTS

3.1 Datasets and Evaluation Criteria

We evaluate the proposed method, denoted as DSRCNN, on five standard benchmark datasets: SED1 [46], SED2 [46], ECSSD [8], PASCAL-S [20], and HKU-IS [21].

SED1 [46] and **SED2** [46] contain 100 images with one and two salient object, respectively, in which objects have largely different sizes and locations.

ECSSD [8] contains 1,000 images with complex backgrounds, which makes the detection tasks much more challenging.

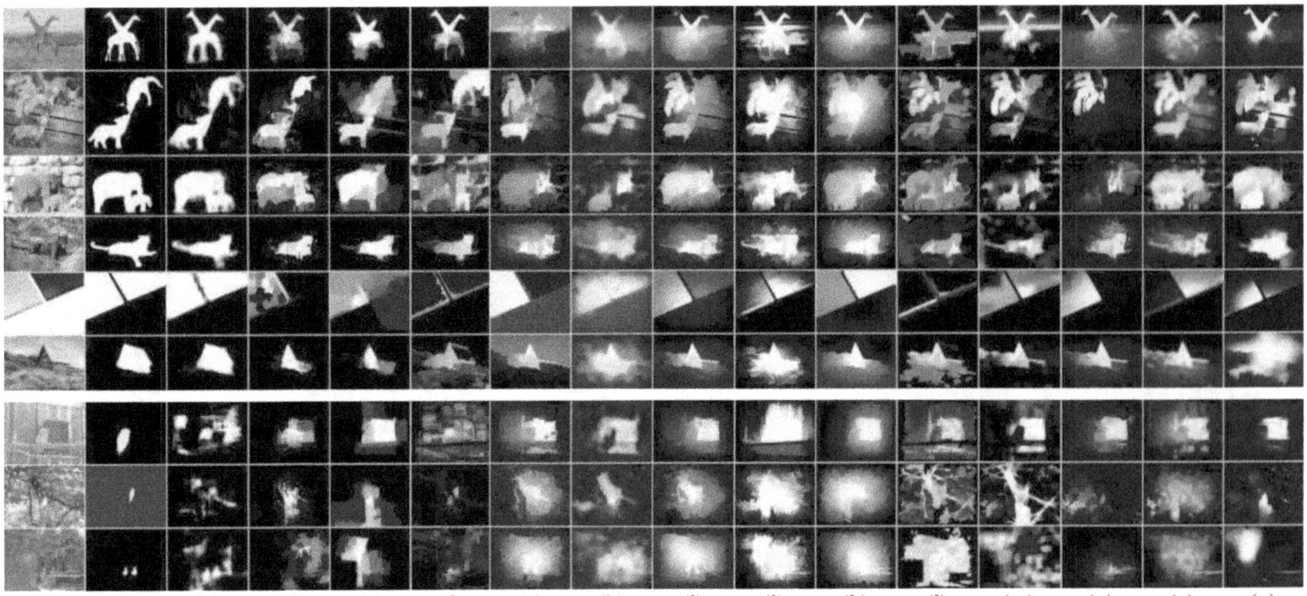

Figure 5: Visual Comparisons of different saliency detection approaches in various challenging scenarios. Our method is successful and failed in the first six rows and the last three rows, respectively. (a) Original images, (b) Ground truth, (c) DSRCNN, (d) MC, (e) LEGS, (f)MDF, (g) RRWR, (h) BL, (i) BSCA, (j) MB+, (k) GP, (l) RC, (m) SGTD, (n) LPS, (o) MAP, (p) CPISA.

PASCAL-S [20] is constructed on the validation set of the PASCAL VOC 2012 segmentation challenge. This dataset contains 850 natural images with multiple complex objects and cluttered backgrounds. The PASCAL-S data set is arguably one of the most challenging saliency data sets without various design biases (e.g., center bias and color contrast bias).

HKU-IS [21] contains 4447 challenging images, which is newly developed by considering at least one of the following criteria: 1) there are multiple disconnected salient objects, 2) at least one of the salient objects touches the image boundary, 3) the color contrast (the minimum Chi-square distance between the color histograms of any salient object and its surrounding regions) is less than 0.7.

All datasets provide the corresponding ground truth in the form of accurate pixel-wise human-marked labels for salient regions.

For evaluation, the popular criteria, i.e. the standard precision-recall (PR) curves, F-measure (denoted as F_β), the mean absolute error (MAE), and the weighted F-measure (denoted as wF_β) [47], are used to test the performance of the proposed method.

3.2 Performance Comparison

We compare the proposed method (denoted as DSRCNN) with thirteen state-of-the-art saliency detection approaches on five datasets, including MC [26], LEGS [28], MDF [21], RRWR [27], BL [23], BSCA [25], MB+ [30], GP [36], RC [34], SGTD [35], LPS [32], MAP [33], CPISA [31]. For fair comparison, the source codes of these approaches released by the authors are used for test with recommended parameter settings in this work.

Figure 4 shows the PR curve and F_β of different approaches on all test datasets, and Table 1 lists the MAE and wF_β of different approaches on all test datasets. From Figure 4 and Table 1, we can see that the proposed method significantly outperforms all of the state-of-the-art approaches on all test datasets in terms of all evaluation criteria, which convincingly demonstrates the effectiveness of the proposed method. All methods get the worst performance on the PASCAL-S dataset. That is because PASCAL-S is the most complex one in these five test datasets, and different salient objects get different saliencies in the ground truths. Therefore, we believe that if a large-scale dataset containing complex images and different saliencies for different salient objects is used to train the DSRCNN model, the performance will be further improved. Also, we qualitatively compare our detected salient maps with those detected by other approaches in the first six rows of Figure 5. As we can see, the proposed method is able to highlight saliencies of salient objects and suppress the saliencies of background better, and the results of our salient maps are much close to the ground truth in various challenging scenarios.

The last three rows of Figure 5 show some cases in which the proposed method fails to correctly detect the salient regions. For example, the colors of salient objects and backgrounds are very similar, the backgrounds are too complex, and the salient objects are too small. In these cases, the other approaches also cannot correctly detect the salient objects.

4. CONCLUSIONS

In this paper, we have developed a deeply-supervised recurrent convolutional neural network (DSRCNN) for saliency detection, which integrates the ideas of recurrent convolutional neural networks and deeply-supervised networks. DSRCNN not only learns the explicit contextual and high-level information, but also combines multi-scale discriminative information. All of these information is important for saliency detection, so the proposed DSRCNN based saliency detection method is able to generate high quality salient maps for various challenging scenarios. Extensive experiments on five standard benchmark datasets demonstrate that the proposed method get the best performance compared with the state-of-the-art approaches, convincingly demonstrating the effectiveness of the proposed method.

5. ACKNOWLEDGEMENTS

This work was supported by the Natural Science Foundation of China under Grant 61472102. The authors would like to thank the founders of the publicly available datasets and the support of NVIDIA Corporation with the donation of the Tesla K40 GPU used for this research.

6. REFERENCES

[1] Jung, C. and Kim, C. A unified spectral-domain approach for saliency detection and its application to automatic object segmentation. *TIP*, 21(3):1272-1283, 2012.

[2] Rother, C., Bordeaux, L., Hamadi, Y., and Blake, A. Autocollage. *TOG*, 25(3):847-852, 2006.

[3] Luo, P., Tian, Y., Wang, X., and Tang, X. Switchable deep network for pedestrian detection. *CVPR*, 2014.

[4] Gao, Y., Wang, M., Zha, Z., Shen, J., Li, X., and Wu, X. Visual-textual joint relevance learning for tag-based social image search. *TIP*, 22(1):363-376, 2013.

[5] Rosin, P. A simple method for detecting salient regions. *PR*, 42(11):2363-2371, 2009.

[6] Achanta, R., Hemami, S., Estrada, F., and Susstrunk, S. Frequency-tuned salient region detection. *CVPR*, 2009.

[7] Liu, T., Yuan, Z., Sun, J., Wang, J., Zheng, N., Tang, X., and Shum, H. Learning to detect a salient object. *TPAMI*, 33(2):353-367, 2011.

[8] Yan, Q., Xu, L., Shi, J., and Jia, J. Hierarchical saliency detection. *CVPR*, 2013.

[9] Yang, C., Zhang, L., Lu, H., Ruan, X., and Yang, M. Saliency detection via graph-based manifold ranking. *CVPR*, 2013.

[10] Li, X., Lu, H., Zhang, L., Ruan, X., and Yang, M. Saliency detection via dense and sparse reconstruction. *ICCV*, 2013.

[11] Jiang, H., Wang, J., Yuan, Z., Wu, Y., Zheng, N., and Li, S. Salient object detection: A discriminative regional feature integration approach. *CVPR*, 2013.

[12] Cheng, M., Warrell, J., Lin, W., Zheng, S., Vineet, V., and Crook, N. Efficient salient region detection with soft image abstraction. *ICCV*, 2013.

[13] Zhang, J. and Sclaroff, S. Saliency detection: A boolean map approach. *ICCV*, 2013.

[14] Jiang, B., Zhang, L., Lu, H., Yang, C., and Yang, M. Saliency detection via absorbing markov chain. *ICCV*, 2013.

[15] Li, X., Li, Y., Shen, C., Dick, A., and Van Den Hengel, A. Contextual hypergraph modeling for salient object detection. *ICCV*, 2013.

[16] Liu, R., Cao, J., Lin, Z., and Shan, S. Adaptive partial differential equation learning for visual saliency detection. *CVPR*, 2014.

[17] Lu, S., Mahadevan, V., and Vasconcelos, N. Learning optimal seeds for diffusion-based salient object detection. *CVPR*, 2014.

[18] Zhu, W., Liang, S., Wei, Y., and Sun, J. Saliency optimization from robust background detection. *CVPR*, 2014.

[19] Kim, J., Han, D., Tai, Y., and Kim, J. Salient region detection via high-dimensional color transform. *CVPR*, 2014.

[20] Li, Y., Hou, X., Koch, C., Rehg, J., and Yuille, A. The secrets of salient object segmentation. *CVPR*, 2014.

[21] Li, G. and Yu, Y. Visual saliency based on multiscale deep features. *CVPR*, 2015.

[22] Frintrop, S., Werner, T., and García, G. Traditional saliency reloaded: A good old model in new shape. *CVPR*, 2015.

[23] Tong, N., Lu, H., Ruan, X., and Yang, M. Salient object detection via bootstrap learning. *CVPR*, 2015.

[24] Gong, C., Tao, D., Liu, W., Maybank, S., Fang, M., Fu, K., and Yang, J. Saliency propagation from simple to difficult. *CVPR*, 2015.

[25] Qin, Y., Lu, H., Xu, Y., and Wang, H. Saliency detection via cellular automata. *CVPR*, 2015.

[26] Zhao, R., Ouyang, W., Li, H., and Wang, X. Saliency detection by multi-context deep learning. *CVPR*, 2015.

[27] Li, C., Yuan, Y., Cai, W., Xia, Y., and Feng, D. Robust saliency detection via regularized random walks ranking. *CVPR*, 2015.

[28] Wang, L., Lu, H., Ruan, X., and Yang, M. Deep networks for saliency detection via local estimation and global search. *CVPR*, 2015.

[29] Li, N., Sun, B., and Yu, J. A weighted sparse coding framework for saliency detection. *CVPR*, 2015.

[30] Zhang, J., Sclaroff, S., Lin, Z., Shen, X., Price, B., and Mech, R. Minimum barrier salient object detection at 80 fps. *ICCV*, 2015.

[31] Wang, K., Lin, L., Lu, J., Li, C., and Shi, K. Pisa: Pixelwise image saliency by aggregating complementary appearance contrast measures with edge-preserving coherence. *TIP*, 24(10):3019-3033, 2015.

[32] Li, H., Lu, H., Lin, Z., Shen, X., and Price, B. Inner and inter label propagation: Salient object detection in the wild. *TIP*, 24(10):3176-3186, 2015.

[33] Sun, J., Lu, H., and Liu, X. Saliency region detection based on markov absorption probabilities. *TIP*, 24(5):1639-1649, 2015.

[34] Cheng, M., Mitra, N.J.M., Huang, X., Torr, P.H.S., and Hu, S. Global contrast based salient region detection. *TPAMI*, 37(3):569-582, 2015.

[35] Scharfenberger, C., Wong, A., and Clausi, D. Structure-guided statistical textural distinctiveness for salient region detection in natural images. *TIP*, 24(1):457-470, 2015.

[36] Jiang, P., Vasconcelos, N., and Peng, J. Generic promotion of diffusion-based salient object detection. *CVPR*, 2015.

[37] Tang, Y., Wu, X., and Bu, W. Saliency detection based on graph-structural agglomerative clustering. *ACMMM*, 2015.

[38] Zheng, S., Jayasumana, S., Romera-Paredes, B., Vineet, V., Su, Z., Du, D., Huang, C., and Torr, P. Conditional random fields as recurrent neural networks. *ICCV*, 2015.

[39] Long, J., Shelhamer, E., and Darrell, T. Fully convolutional networks for semantic segmentation. *CVPR*, 2015.

[40] Xie, S. and Tu, Z. Holistically-nested edge detection. *CVPR*, 2015.

[41] Bertasius, G., Shi, J., and Torresani, L. Deepedge: A multi-scale bifurcated deep network for top-down contour detection. *CVPR*, 2015.

[42] Simonyan, K. and Zisserman, A. Very deep convolutional networks for large-scale image recognition. *arXiv preprint arXiv:1409.1556*, 2014.

[43] Liang, M. and Hu, X. Recurrent convolutional neural network for object recognition. *CVPR*, 2015.

[44] Lee, C.-Y., Xie, S., Gallagher, P., Zhang, Z., and Tu, Z. Deeply-supervised nets. *AISTATS*, 2015.

[45] Jia, Y., Shelhamer, E., Donahue, J., Karayev, S., Long, J., Girshick, R., Guadarrama, S., and Darrell, T. Caffe: Convolutional architecture for fast feature embedding. *ACMMM*, 2014.

[46] Alpert, S., Galun, M., Basri, R., and Brandt, A. Image segmentation by probabilistic bottom-up aggregation and cue integration. *CVPR*, 2007.

[47] Margolin, R., Zelnik-Manor, L., and Tal, A. How to evaluate foreground maps. *CVPR*, 2014.

Deep Correlation Features for Image Style Classification

Wei-Ta Chu
National Chung Cheng University, Chiayi, Taiwan
wtchu@ccu.edu.tw

Yi-Ling Wu
National Chung Cheng University, Chiayi, Taiwan
amtommy6@gmail.com

ABSTRACT

This paper presents a comprehensive study of deep correlation features on image style classification. Inspired by that correlation between feature maps can effectively describe image texture, we design and transform various such correlations into style vectors, and investigate classification performance brought by different variants. In addition to intra-layer correlation, we also propose inter-layer correlation and verify its benefit. Through extensive experiments on image style classification and artist classification, we demonstrate that the proposed style vectors significantly outperforms CNN features coming from fully-connected layers, as well as outperforms the state-of-the-art deep representation.

Keywords

Deep correlation features; image style; paintings; Gram matrix

1. INTRODUCTION

Despite various studies on visual features and semantic concept detection, some image properties are difficult to extract, for the purposes of image/video classification or retrieval. Some bio-inspired properties, like sentiment [2] and emotion, are apparently perceived by human, but are hard to be modeled in a computational way. In this work, we focus on *image style* property that emerges recently and is believed to be a promising extension of current classification/retrieval works. We take oil painting images as the main target, and attempt to propose features based on a deep learning framework to classify images according to styles, such as Academicism, Baroque, and Cubism.

Foreseeing the potential of image style analysis, several inspiring works have been proposed. Karayev et al. [6] proposed two image datasets respectively consisting of photos from Flickr and artist images from Wikiart.org, and investigated various visual features on image style classification. They found that Convolutional Neural Network (CNN) features, though trained based on object class categories (ImageNet), outperforms hand-crafted features like color histogram and GIST. Specific to painting images, Khan et al. [7] constructed a large-scale painting image dataset consisting of paintings from 91 different artists. They studied how local and global features perform in three applications, i.e., artist categorization, style classification, and saliency detection. Most recently, Tseng et al. [10] proposed a ranking model for style identification based on random forests. Based on visual features like Lab color histogram and GIST, they more concentrate on mitigating the overfitting problem and the ambiguity problem by using random forests.

To describe image styles, how to represent images is obviously the key. In [6], Karayev et al. reported that deep features, which have been demonstrated to achieve promising performance in various fields, also yield performance much better than hand-crafted features like color histogram, GIST, and visual saliency. However, the complex interplay between visual appearance and perceived image style is still not clear. Recently, Gatys [5] proposed a feature space that was originally designed for texture synthesis [4] on top of the filter responses in each layer of a convolutional neural network. Particularly, the correlations between different filter responses over the spatial extend to feature maps are calculated, as the important clues for them to transfer a photograph into a painting of some artist's style. This work excitingly inspires us to extract image style descriptors based on correlations between feature maps.

In this paper we focus on painting style classification and investigate performance variations obtained based on different deep correlation features. Figure 1 shows sample images of styles from Academicism to Rococo. Given a painting image, we extract its style descriptor and classify it into one of the style classes. Contributions of this work come from the following experimental studies:

- We transform the exciting findings of [5] (correlations between feature maps) into image style descriptors. Descriptors derived from different layers with different settings are comprehensively experimented.
- In addition to correlations between feature maps at the same layer (intra correlations), we further propose descriptors from correlations across multiple layers (inter correlations). Benefits of jointly considering various correlations are extensively verified.

MM '16, October 15-19, 2016, Amsterdam, Netherlands
© 2016 ACM. ISBN 978-1-4503-3603-1/16/10...$15.00
DOI: http://dx.doi.org/10.1145/2964284.2967251

2. BASIC DEEP CORRELATION FEATURE

Deep Framework. In this work we utilize the very deep convolutional neural network [9] that consists of sixteen con-

Figure 1: Sample painting images of different styles. Left to right: Academicism, Baroque, Expressionism, High Renaissance, Low Renaissance, Impressionism, Neoclassicism, Realism, and Rococo.

Table 1: Style classes and the numbers of images in each class in the OilPainting dataset.

Style	Academicism	Art Nouveau	Baroque	Cubism	Expressionism	High Renaissance
#img	342	263	1892	349	1127	408
Style	Impressionism	Mannerism	Naive Art	Neoclassicism	Northern Renaissance	Post-Impressionism
#img	4557	607	373	442	549	2183
Style	Realism	Rococo	Romanticism	Surrealism	Symbolism	
#img	2766	1097	1532	794	506	

Table 2: Performance variations of style vectors from different layers, based on the OilPainting dataset (average poolings were applied in the framework).

Layer	Ori. dim.	Rdu. dim.	Avg. Accuracy
fc	4096	4096	52.86%
conv1_1	4096	4096	32.71%
conv2_1	16384	4096	34.24%
conv3_1	65536	4096	40.77%
conv4_1	262144	4096	47.87%
conv5_1	262144	4096	**57.19%**

Table 3: Performance variations of style vectors from different layers, based on the OilPainting dataset (max poolings were applied in the framework).

Layer	Ori. dim.	Rdu. dim.	Avg. Accuracy
fc7	4096	4096	56.83%
conv1_1	4096	4096	30.08%
conv2_1	16384	4096	35.05%
conv3_1	65536	4096	44.70%
conv4_1	262144	4096	50.60%
conv5_1	262144	4096	**58.13%**

volutional layers and three fully-connected layers. At each convolutional layer, the receptive field is fixed to 3×3 with convolution stride 1 pixel. Spatial pooling is carried out by five max-pooling layers, which respectively follow the 2nd, the 4th, the 8th, the 12th, and the 16th convolutional layers (note that not every convolutional layer is followed by a pooling layer). Max-pooling is performed over 2×2 pixel window, with stride 2. Because of the pooling layers, convolutional layers in this framework can be divided into five groups. The work in [5] utilized the 19-layer very deep network, and named convolutional layers as 'conv1_1', 'conv1_2', 'conv2_1', 'conv2_2', and so on. The 'conv2_1' layer, for example, are the 3rd convolutional layer that just follows the first pooling layer. In this work, we use the imagenet-vgg-verydeep-19 model trained for the MatConvNet toolbox [11] to conduct the following studies.

Deep Correlation Features. With the findings in [4], Gatys et al. built a style representation based on the correlations between filter responses (feature maps), in order to transfer a photo into a painting image with a targeted style. In [5], the correlations are measured by the Gram matrix $G^l \in R^{N_l \times N_l}$, where G^l_{ij} is the inner product between the vectorized feature map i and j in layer l, i.e.,

$$G^l_{ij} = \sum_k F^l_{ik} F^l_{jk}, \tag{1}$$

where F^l_{ik} is the activation of the ith filter at position k in layer l.

In order to achieve image style classification, we traverse the Gram matrix G^l by raster scan and transform the matrix into a *style vector*, which is then classified by an SVM classifier (support vector machine) pre-trained for image styles. In the next section, we will comprehensively study how variants of deep correlation features work on image style classification.

3. EXPERIMENTAL STUDY

3.1 Datasets

From WikiArt.org, we collected totally 19,787 oil painting images belonging to 17 image styles for the following evaluation. Table 1 shows detailed information of the collected OilPainting dataset, where each style class contains at least 200 images. To fairly do performance comparison, we also evaluate performance on the Wikipaintings dataset [6] and the Painting-91 dataset [7]. The former consists of 82,442 images belonging to 25 styles, and the latter consists of 2,338 oil painting images belonging to 13 styles.

3.2 Performance of Style Vectors from Different Layers

We first investigate performance variations yielded by deep correlation features computed from different layers. According to [5], we especially focus on the Gram matrices derived from 'conv1_1', 'conv2_1', 'conv3_1', 'conv4_1', and 'conv5_1', which are all the first convolutional layer after the pool layer (except for 'conv1_1'). The five Gram matrices are of different dimensions, and so do the transformed style vectors. To fairly compare performance of style vectors from different layers, we adopt principal component analysis (PCA) to reduce all style vectors into 4096-dimensional.

Table 2 and Table 3 show performance variations obtained by style vectors from different layers, when average pooling and max pooling are adopted in the deep framework, respectively. The experiments were conducted based on the Oil-

Table 4: Performance variations of different deep correlation features, based on the OilPainting dataset.

Correlation	fc7	**Gram matrix**				
Avg. Acc.	56.83%	**58.13%**				
Correlation	Spearman	Pearson	Covariance	Chebychev dist.	Euclidean dist.	**Cosine Sim.**
Avg. Acc.	44.92%	44.96%	45.51%	46.05%	51.33%	**53.34%**
Correlation	Pear.-Spear.	Pear.-Cos.	Gram-Pear.	Gram-Cos.	Gram.-Eud.	**Gram-Cov.**
Avg. Acc.	47.36%	55.68%	60.22%	60.36%	60.42%	**60.56%**
Correlation	Eud. dot Cos.	**Gram dot Cos.**				
Avg. Acc.	51.17%	**61.28%**				

Table 5: Performance variations of style vectors derived from intra-layer correlation only and intra-inter correlation.

Correlation	Average accuracy
fc7	56.83%
Gram matrix (from 'conv5_1')	58.13%
Gram matrix + Gram of Gram	**59.91%**

Painting dataset with the five-fold cross validation scheme, and the average classification accuracies are reported. As can be seen from both tables, we see that style vectors derived from the 16th convolutional layer, i.e., 'conv5_1', perform the best. The 'conv5_1' layer is thus widely used in the following experiments. The 'fc7' row shows the performance obtained by vectors coming the second fully-connected layer (other than convolutional layers, before this layer there are five max pooling layers and one fully-connected layer, and this is why it is called fc7), which was commonly used in many classification tasks. Comparing fc7 with others, fc7 outperforms most except for 'conv5_1'. This shows that output of the fully-connected is quite effective. However, more performance gain can be obtained if we extract style vectors from an appropriate layer, e.g., 'conv5_1'. By comparing Table 2 and Table 3, we found that the network with max pooling performs better.

3.3 Performance of Various Correlations

After verifying the effectiveness of Gram-matrix-based features, we would like to further investigate the possibility of other correlation features. In [5], only the inner products between feature maps (Gram matrix) are used. Here we further evaluate style vectors calculated based on (1) Spearman correlation, (2) Pearson correlation, (3) covariance, (4) Chebychev distance, (5) Euclidean distance, and (6) Cosine similarity between feature maps, respectively. Combinations of some of them are also extensively evaluated.

Table 4 shows performance variations of different deep correlation features. This table can be divided into four parts. The first part is just the subset of Table 3, showing the best performance obtained by Gram matrices. The second part shows average accuracies obtained by six different style vectors derived from six correlations, respectively. Note that each individual style vector is reduced to 4096-dimensional by PCA. By comparing the first two parts, we see no other correlation works better than Gram matrices. This verifies the choice in [5] is really good. Among the correlations other than Gram matrix, Euclidean distances and Cosine similarity are relatively better.

The third part of Table 4 verifies the conjecture: will better performance be obtained if we jointly consider multiple style vectors derived from different correlations? For example, the cell 'Gram-Cos.' means that we concatenate the style vector derived from Gram matrices with that derived from Cosine similarity. Note that in order to make fair comparison, we reduce dimensionality of each kind of style vector into 2048-dimensional, so that concatenation of two different style vectors form a 4096-dimensional vector. The third part of Table 4 shows that by concatenating style vectors derived from Gram matrices and covariance outperforms other combinations (accuracy=60.56%), and it also verifies that combining two different style vectors outperforms the best individual one (Gram matrix, accuracy=58.13%).

Since considering multiple correlations yields performance gain, how about calculating *correlation between multiple correlations* and viewing it as a style vector? The fourth part of Table 4 shows performances obtained by style vectors derived from correlation (measured by inner product) between Euclidean distances and Cosine similarity (denoted by 'Eud. dot Cos.'), and correlation between Gram matrices and Cosine similarity (denoted by 'Gram dot Cos.'). Surprisingly, we obtain further performance gain (61.28% vs. 60.56%), by comparing the 'Gram dot Cos.' with 'Gram-Cov.' shown in the third part. Other 'correlation between correlations' were also experimented, but performance gains are not significant and are not shown here. We can thus push the idea proposed in [5] one step further: *correlation between deep correlation features even works better.*

3.4 Intra-Layer and Inter-Layer Correlations

The Gram matrices mentioned above are calculated based on feature maps of the 'conv5_1' convolutional layer. They are 'intra-layer' correlations because only information within the 'conv5_1' layer is considered. We are wondering if *correlations between feature maps across layers* also benefit style classification. To verify this, we calculate Gram matrices of feature maps at each convolutional layer, and then calculate inner products between intra-layer Gram matrices (after dimension reduction) to measure the inter-layer correlation, i.e., the Gram matrix of Gram matrices.

Table 5 shows performances obtained by style vectors derived from 'conv5_1' only, and by the concatenation of style vectors from 'conv5_1' and the Gram matrix of Gram matrices. As can be seen, by further considering inter-layer correlation, performance gain can be obtained (59.91% vs. 58.13%). There may be many ways to jointly consider intra-layer and inter-layer correlations. We, however, show simple experimental results in Table 5 due to space limitation, and will provide deeper investigation in the future.

Table 6: Average accuracies obtained by different style vectors, based on the Painting-91 dataset.

	[7]	[8]	fc7	Gram	Gram-Cov.	**Gram dot Cos**
Avg. accuracy	62.20%	69.21%	68.35%	71.86%	72.41%	**73.59%**

Table 7: Average accuracies obtained by different style vectors, based on the Wikipaintings dataset.

	Fusion × Content [6]	DeCAF6 [6]	[1]	fc7	Gram	**Gram dot Cos.**
Avg. accuracy	47.30%	35.60%	57.00%	52.67%	56.58%	**58.19%**

Table 8: Average artist classification accuracies obtained by different style vectors.

OilPainting Artist dataset						
	fc7	Gram	Gram-Cov.	**Gram dot Cos**		
Avg. Accuracy	52.59%	60.61%	60.72%	**63.33%**		
Painting-91 Artist dataset						
	[7]	[8]	fc7	Gram	Gram-Cov.	**Gram dot Cos**
Avg. Accuracy	53.10%	56.40%	55.59%	60.90%	61.06%	**63.17%**

3.5 Performance Comparison

To verify superiority of the proposed style vectors, we compare our features with the state-of-the-art based on the Painting-91 dataset. Table 6 shows average accuracies obtained by different style vectors. Khan et al. [7] integrated hand-crafted local and global features as image representation, which is surpassed by [8] that considered features extracted from multiple layers of CNN. Comparing 'fc7' (result of one convolutional layer) and [8] (68.35% vs. 69.21%), we confirm that considering multiple layers yields better performance. However, if we construct the style vector based on the Gram matrix between feature maps, clear improvement can be obtained (71.86% vs. 69.21%). If we combine multiple correlations (Gram-Cov. and Gram dot Cos), significant improvement can be made over [8].

Table 7 shows performance comparison between our methods and [6] [1], based on the Wikipaintings dataset. In [6], deep features from a fully-connected layer are used as image representation (DeCAF6). They also utilized class confidences of high-level attribute classifiers [3] as image presentation, by further considering the inter-correlation of four aggregated classifier confidence (Fusion × Content). A very recent work [1], which was developed independently of our work and was just accepted to ICMR 2016, is very similar to ours in that they also used Gram matrix of feature maps (in the VGG-16 framework, while we use the VGG-19 framework) as image representation. Their work, however, did not thoroughly study the influence of different types of intra-layer correlations and the inter-layer correlation. As can be seen from Table 7, correlation between Gram matrices and Cosine similarity again yields the best performance, which surpasses the most recent results reported in [1].

3.6 Artist Classification

Different artists have their unique styles in producing artworks. Several previous works thus also study classifying images according to artists. In this paper, we also study this issue based on two datasets. We select the artists who produced more than 50 images from the OilPainting dataset, and construct the OilPainting Artist dataset that includes totally 15,357 images produced by 104 artists. Another dataset is from [7], called the Painting-91 Artist dataset, and contains 4,266 images produced by 91 artists.

The top part of Table 8 shows average classification accuracies for the OilPainting Artist dataset. It again shows the superiority of the correlation between Gram matrices and Cosine similarity, yielding 63.33% accuracy that significantly outperforms the fully-connected layer (52.59%). The bottom part of Table 8 shows performance comparison between ours and [7] [8] based on the Painting-91 Artist dataset. By considering the correlation between Gram matrices and Cosine similarity, the best performance with average accuracy 63.17% can be obtained for this challenging dataset, significantly outperforming previous works [7] and [8].

4. CONCLUSION

Inspired by the interesting work [5] that showed the effectiveness of correlation between feature maps, we transform such correlations into style vectors, and utilize them to achieve image style classification. We comprehensively study performance variations brought by correlations in different layers, performance variations of different correlations, and the idea of inter-layer correlation. We demonstrated effectiveness of the proposed style vectors through image style classification and artist classification, as well as performance comparison with the state of the art. In the future, deeper studies about the essential characteristics of such descriptors and how to devise better deep features will be conducted.

5. ACKNOWLEDGMENTS

The work was partially supported by the Ministry of Science and Technology of Taiwan under the grants MOST 103-2221-E-194-027-MY3, MOST 104-2221-E-194 -014, and MOST 105-2628-E-194-001-MY2.

6. REFERENCES

[1] CNN-based style vector for style image retrieval. In *Proceedings of ACM International Conference on Multimedia Retrieval*, 2016.

[2] D. Borth, R. Ji, T. Chen, T. Breuel, and S.-F. Chang. Large-scale visual sentiment ontology and detectors

using adjective noun pairs. In *Proceedings of ACM Multimedia Conference*, 2013.

[3] S. Dhar, V. Ordonez, and T. L. Berg. High level describable attributes for predicting aesthetics and interestingness. In *Proceedings of IEEE International Conference on Computer Vision and Pattern Recognition*, 2011.

[4] L. Gatys, A. S. Ecker, and M. Bethge. Texture synthesis using convolutional neural networks. In *Proceedings of Neural Information Processing Systems*, 2015.

[5] L. A. Gatys, A. S. Ecker, and M. Bethge. A neural algorithm of artistic style. Aug 2015.

[6] S. Karayev, M. Trentacoste, H. Han, A. Agarwala, T. Darrell, A. Hertzmann, and H. Winnemoeller. Recognizing image style. In *Proceedings of British Machine Vision Conference*, 2014.

[7] F. Khan, S. Beigpour, J. van de Weijer, and M. Felsberg. Painting-91: A large scale database for computational painting categorization. *Machine Vision and Application*, 25(6):1385–1397, 2014.

[8] K.-C. Peng and T. Chen. Cross-layer features in convolutional neural networks for generic classification tasks. In *Proceedings of IEEE International Conference on Image Processing*, 2015.

[9] K. Simonyan and A. Zisserman. Very deep convolutional networks for large-scale image recognition. In *Proceedings of International Conference on Learning Representation*, 2015.

[10] T.-E. Tseng, W.-Y. Chang, C.-S. Chen, and Y.-C. F. Wang. Style retrieval from natural images. In *Proceedings of IEEE International Conference on Acoustics, Speech and Signal Processing*, 2016.

[11] A. Vedaldi and K. Lenc. Matconvnet: Convolutional neural networks for matlab. In *Proceedings of ACM International Conference on Multimedia*, pages 689–692, 2015.

CNN vs. SIFT for Image Retrieval: Alternative or Complementary?

Ke Yan[1,2], Yaowei Wang[*,3], Dawei Liang[1,2], Tiejun Huang[1,2], Yonghong Tian[*,1,2]
[1]National Engineering Laboratory for Video Technology, School of EE&CS, Peking University, Beijing, China
[2]Cooperative Medianet Innovation Center, China
[3]Department of Electronic Engineering, Beijing Institute of Technology, China
{keyan, dwliang, tjhuang, yhtian}@pku.edu.cn;yaoweiwang@bit.edu.cn

ABSTRACT

In the past decade, SIFT is widely used in most vision tasks such as image retrieval. While in recent several years, deep convolutional neural networks (CNN) features achieve the state-of-the-art performance in several tasks such as image classification and object detection. Thus a natural question arises: for the image retrieval task, can CNN features substitute for SIFT? In this paper, we experimentally demonstrate that the two kinds of features are highly complementary. Following this fact, we propose an image representation model, complementary CNN and SIFT (CCS), to fuse CNN and SIFT in a multi-level and complementary way. In particular, it can be used to simultaneously describe scene-level, object-level and point-level contents in images. Extensive experiments are conducted on four image retrieval benchmarks, and the experimental results show that our CCS achieves state-of-the-art retrieval results.

Keywords

Multi-level image representation; CNN; SIFT; Complementary CNN and SIFT (CCS)

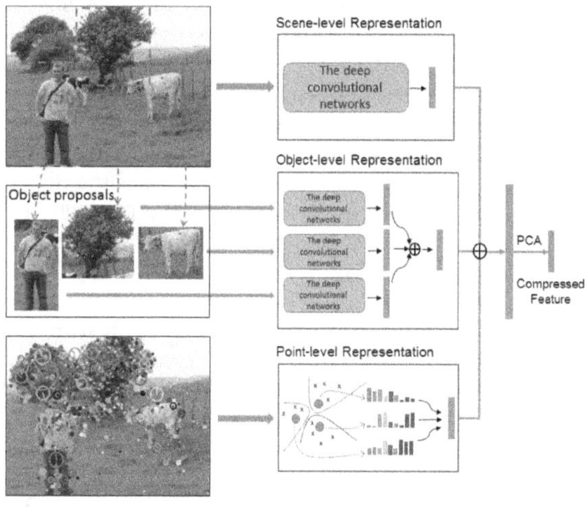

Figure 1: The demonstration of our proposed complementary CNN and SIFT (CCS). The CCS aggregates three level contents, i.e., scene-level, object-level and point-level representations.

1. INTRODUCTION

Scale-invariant feature transform (SIFT) [1] has been the most widely-used hand-crafted feature for content-based image retrieval (CBIR) in the past decade. Technologically, SIFT is intrinsically robust to geometric transformations and shows good performance for near-duplicate image retrieval [2] [3]. Meanwhile, there are also many works (e.g., Fisher vector [4], VLAD [5] and their variants [6] [7] [8]), that attempt to construct semantically-richer mid-level image representations so as to improve the retrieval performance. However, in spite of significant efforts, it is still difficult to fully bridge the semantic gap between such feature representations and human's understanding of an image only with SIFT-based features.

Recently, deep convolutional neural networks (CNN) have achieved the state-of-the-art performance in several tasks, such as image classification [9] [10], object detection [11] [12] and saliency detection [13]. Compared with hand-crafted features, CNN features learned from numerous annotated data (e.g., ImageNet [14]) in a deep learning architecture, carry richer high-level semantic information. Several attempts in CBIR [15] [16] [17] showed that CNN features work well for image retrieval as a scene-level representation. Gong *et al.* [18] proposed an approach called Multi-scale Orderless Pooling (MOP) to represent local information by aggregating CNN features at three scales respectively. Konda *et al.* [19] and Xie *et.al.* [20] detected object proposals and extracted CNN features for each region at the object-level. Besides, there are also some researchers who paid attention to deep convolutional layers to derive representations [21] [22] [23] [24] for image retrieval. Although CNN features achieve good performance, we can not say that C-NN will always outperform SIFT yet. Vijay *et al.* [25] had showed that no one was better than the other consistently and the retrieval gains can be obtained by combining the two features.

*Corresponding author: Yaowei Wang and Yonghong Tian.

MM '16, October 15-19, 2016, Amsterdam, Netherlands
© 2016 ACM. ISBN 978-1-4503-3603-1/16/10...$15.00
DOI: http://dx.doi.org/10.1145/2964284.2967252

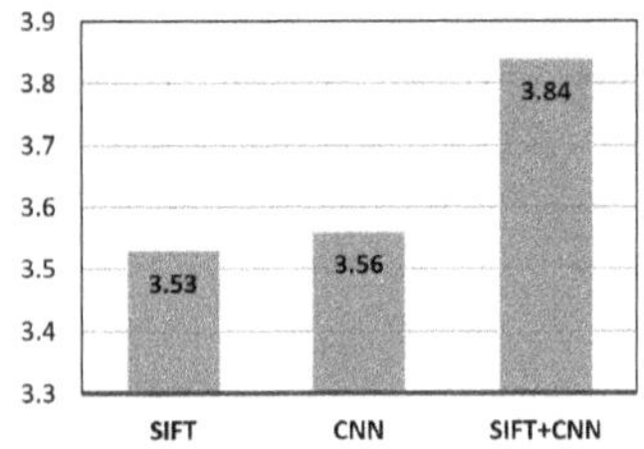

Figure 2: The overall performance comparison of SIFT, CNN, and their naive combination.

Inspired by these pioneering works and our preliminary experiments described in section 2, we demonstrate that C-NN and SIFT features are highly complementary for image retrieval tasks. Following this fact, a complementary CNN and SIFT (CCS) image representation is proposed in this paper. A similar work is Zheng *et al.* [26], which also fused CNN and SIFT from multiple levels. But [26] utilized CNN features derived from regional and global patches as auxiliary cues to BoW model to improve the matching accuracy of local feature, while our method focuses on getting a unified and powerful representation integrating CNN and SIFT coequally. As shown in Fig. 1, CNN features from scene and object levels and SIFT features from point-level are fused to form a compact image representation: First, features from the top layer of CNN are utilized as the scene-level representation. Secondly, we obtain the deep CNN features of each region generated by the object proposal method, and pool them to a fixed-length object-level representation with VLAD. Note that the pooling method really influences the power of object-level representation. It is demonstrated that VLAD pooling outperforms other pooling in our experimental results. Thirdly, a VLAD representation of SIFT features serve as the point-level representation. Finally, we concatenate all the three level representations and then leverage PCA to reduce redundancies so as to obtain the final compact representation.

Experiments are conducted on four image retrieval benchmarks, i.e., INRIA Holidays [27], Oxford5K [28], Paris6K [29] and UKBench [30]. Experimental results show that the proposed CCS outperforms the state-of-the-art methods on three datasets, and achieves comparable performance on the INRIA Holidays dataset (the smallest one).

2. PRELIMINARY EXPERIMENTS

In this section, we qualitatively discuss the complementarity between CNN and SIFT through a preliminary experiment. We conduct the experiment on the UKBench dataset [30]. As a widely-used image retrieval benchmark, this dataset consists of 10,200 images of 2,550 objects, each containing 4 images. By using every image as the query, the performance is reported as the average recall at top four results.

We obtain CNN and SIFT features by using standard settings. Specifically, we extract global activation values provided by the pool5 layer in GoogLeNet [10] as CNN features. VLAD is adopted to aggregate SIFT features. The two features hold the same dimension after adopting PCA to compress the corresponding representations.

The overall result is shown in Fig. 2. From the results, we can see that CNN and SIFT achieve nearly comparable performance. To investigate the complementarity, we conduct an experiment by simply concatenating CNN and SIFT features, and the performance is significantly boosted.

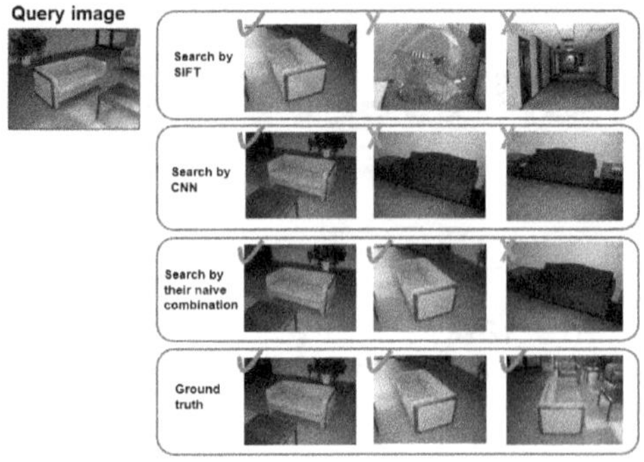

Figure 3: An image retrieval example from UK-Bench. Each image has three most similar images.

An example of results is shown in Fig. 3. CNN and SIFT return one similar image respectively. However, the returned similar images are not the same one. Their naive combination returns two similar images, demonstrating that they are indeed highly complementary. From another perspective, this example also shows that the naive combination of CNN and SIFT may not work perfectly since one similar image is also missed in this result.

3. CCS: A MULTI-LEVEL REPRESENTATION OF COMPLEMENTARY CNN AND SIFT

In this section, we describe the proposed CCS image representation. As shown in Fig. 1, it mainly consists of three level representations and a fusion method. In what follows, we introduce each component in detail respectively.

3.1 Scene-level representation

Scene-level features are used to mainly capture global and high level information for an image. It is well known that the deep learning features, especially those from the high layers, are suitable to represent semantic information [9]. In this study, we obtain CNN features from the pool5 layer in GoogLeNet [10], which is a recent deep convolutional network that ranked as the top one at the image classification task in ILSVRC 2014. Here, we denote the scene-level semantic features as $f_s \in R^{1024}$.

3.2 Object-level representation

We obtain the object-level representation using the following three steps: First, we take advantage of an object proposal approach to produce numbers of candidate object regions. Secondly, we extract deep features for each selected region. Finally, these features are pooled to a fixed-length feature vector using an appropriate pooling method.

Object proposals. Considering the trade-off between efficiency and effectiveness, we adopt edgebox [31] to produce a set of object proposals. Unlike [19] which achieved good performance by choosing the best number of proposal regions from 100 to 2,000, we choose only top 100 regions ranked by their scores considering the computational efficiency.

Features for regions. After obtaining the regions of object proposals, we also extract CNN features from the pool5 layer in GoogLeNet for them:

$$F_o = \{f_{o1}, f_{o2}, f_{o3}, \cdots, f_{oN}\}, \quad (1)$$

where F_o is the set of object features for an image, f_{o_i} is the CNN features of the i-th proposal region, N is the number of proposals (100 in our experiments).

Pooling methods. We introduce three pooling methods *i.e.*, max pooling, sum or average pooling and VLAD pooling.

(1) Max pooling: Girshick *et al.* [11] have illuminated that at the intermediate layers of the CNN, a high activation of a node indicates a specific type of visual input. Therefore, this pooling method mainly stores the high activation for each visual content. It can be represented as

$$f_o = [max\{f_{o_n}^{(1)}\}_{n=1}^N, \cdots, max\{f_{o_n}^{(D)}\}_{n=1}^N], \quad (2)$$

where f_o is the final representation after pooling the features of all regions, $max\{f_{o_n}^{(i)}\}_{n=1}^N$ represent the max value at the i-th dimension of all features, and D is the dimension of each feature, which is also the final dimension in the component (1024 in our experiments).

(2) Sum or average pooling: This pooling method retains the sum/average activation for each visual content. It pools CNN features by

$$f_o = [\sum_{n=1}^{N} f_{o_n}^{(1)}, \cdots, \sum_{n=1}^{N} f_{o_n}^{(D)}], \quad (3)$$

where $\sum_{n=1}^{N} f_{o_n}^{(i)}$ represents the sum value at the i-th dimension of all region features. The formulation for average pooling only needs to replace $\sum_{n=1}^{N} f_{o_n}^{(i)}$ by $\frac{1}{N}\sum_{n=1}^{N} f_{o_n}^{(i)}$.

(3) VLAD pooling: As for VLAD pooling, we first utilize k-means to obtain $c_1, c_2, \cdots, c_k$ of k visual word centers. For each image, a region feature f_{o_i} is assigned to its nearest center $c_m = NC(f_{o_i})$. After subtracting the corresponding cluster center, the residuals of each region feature are retained. An VLAD description for an image can be represented as follows:

$$F_v = [\sum_{NC(f_{o_i})=c_1} (f_{o_i} - c_1), \cdots, \sum_{NC(f_{o_i})=c_k} (f_{o_i} - c_k)], \quad (4)$$

where F_v is an aggregated feature after pooling all object-level features for an image. And we represent the VLAD features by accumulating the residuals on each visual word center. Therefore, the dimensionality of such a representation is $k * d$, which is too high to describe an image efficiently for retrieval. We subsequently apply $L2$ normalization and PCA to obtain a fixed dimension, and then derive the object-level representation f_o.

3.3 Point-level representation

Preserving geometric invariance in image representation is important for image retrieval, since some images are obtained through scaling, rotating and other geometric transformations. Additionally, considering that the hand-crafted features can keep stable performance without the need of supervised training on a large dataset, we introduce the SIFT descriptor to represent point-level information.

RootSIFT [32] is adopted to generate the descriptors surrounding interest points for an image, and then VLAD is used to obtain the point-level representation. We also apply post-processing methods on this VLAD representation, *i.e.*, $L2$ normalization and PCA, to derive a fixed dimensionality. Finally, the point-level representation is denoted by f_p.

3.4 Fusing three-level representations

To fuse the three level features, we directly concatenate them to generate the integrated representation f with

$$f = [f_s, f_o, f_p]. \quad (5)$$

Note that this integrated representation has relatively high dimensionality (i.e., three times as much as each component). Aiming to represent an image more compactly, we conduct a series of post-processing operations on the integrated representation. First, PCA and whitening are performed on f after the $L2$ normalization, which can be represented as below:

$$f_{whiten} = diag(1./sqrt(v_1, v_2, \cdots, v_h)) * U * \frac{f}{||f||_2}, \quad (6)$$

where U is the PCA transformation matrix, h is the number of the retained dimensions after PCA, and v_i is the ith corresponding singular value. At last, $L2$ re-normalization is performed to obtain the final compact representation $f_{final} = \frac{f_{whiten}}{||f_{whiten}||_2}$ for an image.

4. EXPERIMENTS AND RESULTS

We perform extensive experiments on commonly used benchmarks to show the effectiveness of CCS. Two sets of experiments are conducted, including the evaluation of different pooling methods for object-level and the holistic performance compared with state-of-the-art methods.

4.1 Datasets and evaluation

Four image retrieval benchmarks are used in experiments, including INRIA Holidays [27], Oxford5K [28], Paris6K [29] and UKBench [30]. Following the corresponding standard evaluation protocols, we report the performance using mean average precision (mAP) on INRIA Holidays, Oxford5K and Paris6K, and report recall at top four results on UKBench.

4.2 Experiments of object-level pooling

In Sec. 3.2, we have introduced three pooling methods. Obviously, the pooling method will remarkably influence the retrieval performance. Compared with the other two methods, the VLAD pooling method needs more parameters. We utilize k-means to generate 500 centers, and then adopt PCA to reduce the dimensionality to 1024 ultimately. In our experiments, we follow [7] which uses the soft assignment to get a more powerful representation.

We experimentally compared these pooling methods on Holidays and UKBench datasets. The results are shown in Table 1. We can see that the VLAD pooling method is the best method to aggregate object-level semantic features. A reasonable interpretation of the results is that VLAD can capture the 0th and 1st order statistics as advocated in [5]. Whereas, max pooling and sum/average pooling lack 1st order statistics. According to the experimental results and the analysis, we adopt VLAD for aggregating object-level CNN features.

Table 1: Comparison of different pooling methods aggregating object-level contents

Method	Dimension	Holidays	UKBench
Max	1024	66.89	3.70
Sum/average	1024	62.89	3.62
VLAD	1024	**71.66**	**3.77**

Table 2: The retrieval results (mAP) on INRIA Holidays dataset.

Method	Dimension						
	32	64	128	256	512	1024	2048
VLAD [5]	48.4	52.3	55.7	-	59.8	-	62.1
TE [6]	-	-	61.7	-	-	72.0	-
NC [15]	68.3	72.9	78.9	74.9	74.9	-	-
SPoC [21]	-	-	-	81.8	-	-	-
MOP [18]	-	-	-	-	78.38	-	80.18
LC [22]	-	-	83.6	-	-	-	-
SP [17]	-	-	-	74.2	-	-	-
OC [19]	73.96	**80.67**	**85.09**	**87.77**	**88.46**	**86.58**	85.94
$f_s + f_o$:	68.87	75.09	78.57	80.39	80.56	79.34	79.46
$f_s + f_p$:	71.36	78.46	81.74	83.96	84.84	83.79	83.83
$f_o + f_p$:	67.94	75.57	81.08	83.21	84.86	82.25	82.56
f_{final}	**74.65**	79.16	84.13	86.32	87.43	85.79	**86.09**

4.3 Comparison with state-of-the-arts

To make fair comparison, we evaluate the overall retrieval performance at different dimensions from 32 to 2048. Since the original dimension of our CCS image representation is 3072, we perform PCA on the CCS representation so as to derive its low-dimension variants. The experimental results are presented in Tables 2, 3, 4, 5. The best performance at each dimension is shown in bold.

Several observations can be drawn from these results. First, after performing PCA, features at relatively low dimensions may achieve better performance since PCA eliminates the influences of redundancies. Secondly, the combination of two level features can approach or outperform the pervious state-of-the-art methods, demonstrating that multi-level representation is very powerful. However, their performance is slightly unstable. For example, $f_s + f_p$ achieves better performance on Holidays, but the other two combinations achieve better performance on Oxford5K. Finally, compared with two level features, our method almost outperforms all the possible combinations of two level features on the four datasets (apart from the Paris6K dataset at 512 and 2048 dimensionalities). Moreover, ours outperforms all these state-of-the-art methods on the Oxford5K, Paris6K and UKBench datasets. In particular, our CCS reaches 3.91 on the UKBench dataset in term of recall. We also achieve comparable performance on the Holidays dataset, which is the smallest dataset containing only 1491 images.

Table 3: The retrieval results (mAP) on Oxford5K dataset

Method	Dimension						
	32	64	128	256	512	1024	2048
VLAD [5]	-	-	28.7	-	-	-	-
TE [6]	-	-	43.3	-	-	56.0	57.1
gVLAD [8]	-	-	60	-	-	-	-
NC [15]	39.0	42.1	43.3	43.5	43.5	-	-
SPoC [21]	-	-	-	59.3	-	-	-
LC [22]	-	-	59.3	-	-	-	-
SP [17]	-	-	-	53.3	-	-	-
OC [19]	40.1	48.02	56.24	59.78	60.71	59.42	58.92
$f_s + f_o$:	45.99	53.59	58.97	62.43	62.69	62.06	61.98
$f_s + f_p$:	43.98	50.19	55.02	58.14	59.59	60.46	60.04
$f_o + f_p$:	46.87	54.67	63.78	65.13	63.47	62.17	61.04
f_{final}	**48.71**	**56.78**	**64.84**	**67.62**	**67.26**	**66.41**	**65.43**

Table 4: The retrieval results (mAP) on Paris6K dataset

Method	Dimension						
	32	64	128	256	512	1024	2048
gVLAD [8]	-	-	59.2	-	-	-	-
LC [22]	-	-	59.0	-	-	-	-
SP [17]	-	-	-	67.0	-	-	-
OC [19]	65.38	71.47	70.39	68.43	66.23	64.11	62.84
$f_s + f_o$:	74.84	76.67	75.14	72.71	70.44	69.44	69.46
$f_s + f_p$:	70.52	75.35	75.22	73.94	**72.42**	71.02	**70.99**
$f_o + f_p$:	66.17	68.54	65.76	61.76	58.55	56.49	55.91
f_{final}	**76.34**	**78.27**	**76.76**	**74.35**	72.22	**71.07**	70.72

Table 5: The retrieval results on UKBench dataset.(* *indicates the recall result transformed from precision at top 4.*)

Method	Dimension						
	32	64	128	256	512	1024	2048
VLAD [5]	-	-	3.35	-	-	-	-
TE [6]	-	-	3.4	3.45	3.49	3.51	-
SP [17]	-	-	-	3.54*	-	-	-
SPoC [21]	-	-	-	3.65	-	-	-
NC [15]	3.3	3.53	3.55	3.56	3.56	-	-
OC [19]	3.4	3.61	3.71	3.77	3.81	3.84	3.84
$f_s + f_o$	3.51	3.66	3.73	3.78	3.80	3.82	3.83
$f_s + f_p$	3.48	3.65	3.74	3.79	3.82	3.83	3.84
$f_o + f_p$	3.50	3.69	3.78	3.83	3.87	3.89	3.89
f_{final}	**3.61**	**3.75**	**3.81**	**3.86**	**3.89**	**3.91**	**3.91**

5. CONCLUSION AND FUTURE WORK

In this paper, we verify the complementarity between C-NN and SIFT features for image retrieval tasks. To benefit from the complementarity, we propose the CCS model to represent scene-level, object-level and point-level visual content simultaneously. By compressing the CCS representation with simple PCA, it outperforms or achieves comparable performance over several state-of-the-art methods on four benchmarks. This paper also provides an insightful observation that the conventional hand-crafted features can be integrated with deep learning features so as to obtain better representation of an image. In the future, we will consider a different strategy of feature combination instead of simple PCA so as to further improve the performance for image retrieval, e.g., bayesian fusion.

6. ACKNOWLEDGEMENTS

This work is partially supported by grants from the National Basic Research Program of China under grant 2015CB-351806, the National Natural Science Foundation of China under contract No. 61390515, No. 61425025 and No. 61471042, Beijing Municipal Commission of Science and Technology under contract No. Z151100000915070 and the National Key Technology Research and Development Program of China under contract No. 2014BAK10B02. This work is also supported by Microsoft Research Asia Collaborative Research Program 2016, project ID FY16-RES-THEME-034.

7. REFERENCES

[1] D.G. Lowe. Distinctive image features from scale-invariant keypoints. *IJCV*, 60(2):91–110, 2004.

[2] J.J. Foo and R. Sinha. Pruning sift for scalable near-duplicate image matching. In *ADC*, pages 63–71. Australian Computer Society, Inc., 2007.

[3] Y. Ke and R. Sukthankar. Pca-sift: A more distinctive representation for local image descriptors. In *CVPR*, volume 2, pages II–506. IEEE, 2004.

[4] F. Perronnin and C. Dance. Fisher kernels on visual vocabularies for image categorization. In *CVPR*, pages 1–8. IEEE, 2007.

[5] H. Jégou, F. Perronnin, M. Douze, J. Sanchez, P. Perez, and C. Schmid. Aggregating local image descriptors into compact codes. *TPAMI*, 34(9):1704–1716, 2012.

[6] H. Jégou and A. Zisserman. Triangulation embedding and democratic aggregation for image search. In *CVPR*, pages 3310–3317. IEEE, 2014.

[7] A. Bergamo, S. N. Sinha, and L. Torresani. Leveraging structure from motion to learn discriminative codebooks for scalable landmark classification. In *CVPR*, pages 763–770. IEEE, 2013.

[8] Z. Wang, W. Di, A. Bhardwaj, V. Jagadeesh, and R. Piramuthu. Geometric vlad for large scale image search. *arXiv preprint arXiv:1403.3829*, 2014.

[9] A. Krizhevsky, I. Sutskever, and G. E. Hinton. Imagenet classification with deep convolutional neural networks. In *NIPS*, pages 1097–1105, 2012.

[10] C. Szegedy, W. Liu, Y. Jia, P. Sermanet, S. Reed, D. Anguelov, D. Erhan, V. Vanhoucke, and A. Rabinovich. Going deeper with convolutions. *arXiv preprint arXiv:1409.4842*, 2014.

[11] R. Girshick, J. Donahue, T. Darrell, and J. Malik. Rich feature hierarchies for accurate object detection and semantic segmentation. In *CVPR*, pages 580–587. IEEE, 2014.

[12] S. Ren, K. He, R. Girshick, and J. Sun. Faster r-cnn: Towards real-time object detection with region proposal networks. In *NIPS*, pages 91–99, 2015.

[13] X. Huang, C. Shen, X. Boix, and Q. Zhao. Salicon: Reducing the semantic gap in saliency prediction by adapting deep neural networks. In *ICCV*, pages 262–270, 2015.

[14] J. Deng, W. Dong, R. Socher, L. Li, K. Li, and L. Fei-Fei. Imagenet: A large-scale hierarchical image database. In *CVPR*, pages 248–255. IEEE, 2009.

[15] A. Babenko, A. Slesarev, A. Chigorin, and V. Lempitsky. Neural codes for image retrieval. In *ECCV*, pages 584–599. Springer, 2014.

[16] J. Wan, D. Wang, S. C. H. Hoi, P. Wu, J. Zhu, Y. Zhang, and J. Li. Deep learning for content-based image retrieval: A comprehensive study. In *Multimedia*, pages 157–166. ACM, 2014.

[17] A. S. Razavian, J. Sullivan, A. Maki, and S. Carlsson. Visual instance retrieval with deep convolutional networks. *arXiv preprint arXiv:1412.6574*, 2014.

[18] Y. Gong, L. Wang, R. Guo, and S. Lazebnik. Multi-scale orderless pooling of deep convolutional activation features. In *ECCV*, pages 392–407. Springer, 2014.

[19] Reddy M. K. and Venkatesh B. R. Object level deep feature pooling for compact image representation. In *CVPRW*, pages 62–70, 2015.

[20] L. Xie, R. Hong, B. Zhang, and Q. Tian. Image classification and retrieval are one. In *ICMR*, pages 3–10. ACM, 2015.

[21] A. Babenko and V. Lempitsky. Aggregating local deep features for image retrieval. In *ICCV*, pages 1269–1277. IEEE, 2015.

[22] J. Y. Ng, F. Yang, and L. S. Davis. Exploiting local features from deep networks for image retrieval. *arXiv preprint arXiv:1504.05133*, 2015.

[23] L. Zheng, Y Zhao, S. Wang, J. Wang, and Q. Tian. Good practice in cnn feature transfer. *arXiv preprint arXiv:1604.00133*, 2016.

[24] G. Tolias, R. Sicre, and H. Jégou. Particular object retrieval with integral max-pooling of cnn activations. *arXiv preprint arXiv:1511.05879*, 2015.

[25] V. Chandrasekhar, J. Lin, O. Morère, H. Goh, and A. Veillard. A practical guide to cnns and fisher vectors for image instance retrieval. *arXiv preprint arXiv:1508.02496*, 2015.

[26] L. Zheng, S. Wang, J. Wang, and Q. Tian. Accurate image search with multi-scale contextual evidences. *IJCV*, pages 1–13, 2016.

[27] H. Jegou, M. Douze, and C. Schmid. Hamming embedding and weak geometric consistency for large scale image search. In *ECCV*, pages 304–317. Springer, 2008.

[28] J. Philbin, O. Chum, M. Isard, J. Sivic, and A. Zisserman. Object retrieval with large vocabularies and fast spatial matching. In *CVPR*, pages 1–8. IEEE, 2007.

[29] J. Philbin, O. Chum, M. Isard, J. Sivic, and A. Zisserman. Lost in quantization: Improving particular object retrieval in large scale image databases. In *CVPR*, pages 1–8. IEEE, 2008.

[30] D. Nister and H. Stewenius. Scalable recognition with a vocabulary tree. In *CVPR*, volume 2, pages 2161–2168. IEEE, 2006.

[31] C. L. Zitnick and P. Dollár. Edge boxes: Locating object proposals from edges. In *ECCV 2014*, pages 391–405. Springer, 2014.

[32] R. Arandjelović and A. Zisserman. Three things everyone should know to improve object retrieval. In *CVPR*, pages 2911–2918. IEEE, 2012.

Looking Good With Flickr Faves: Gaussian Processes for Finding Difference Makers in Personality Impressions

Xiaoyu Xiong
School of Computing Science
University of Glasgow
Sir A.Williams Bldg.
G12 8QQ Glasgow, UK
x.xiong.1@research.gla.ac.uk

Maurizio Filippone
Department of Data Science
EURECOM
Campus SophiaTech
06410 Biot, FRANCE
maurizio.filippone@eurecom.fr

Alessandro Vinciarelli
School of Computing Science
University of Glasgow
Sir A.Williams Bldg.
G12 8QQ Glasgow, UK
vincia@dcs.gla.ac.uk

ABSTRACT

Flickr allows its users to generate galleries of "faves", i.e., pictures that they have tagged as favourite. According to recent studies, the faves are predictive of the personality traits that people attribute to Flickr users. This article investigates the phenomenon and shows that faves allow one to predict whether a Flickr user is perceived to be above median or not with respect to each of the Big-Five Traits (accuracy up to 79% depending on the trait). The classifier - based on Gaussian Processes with a new kernel designed for this work - allows one to identify the visual characteristics of faves that better account for the prediction outcome.

Keywords

Personality; Social Media; Computational Aesthetics

1. INTRODUCTION

Every trace left on social media - pictures, posts, videos, comments, etc. - reaches a large number of unacquainted observers: "*[...] the audience layer sits beyond the weak ties layer. It is made up of strangers [that] can play constructive roles when they are activated*" [7]. Employers gathering information about job candidates are a typical case. According to the Harvard Business Review, the outcome of the interviews depends, to a significant extent, on the impression that the employers develop by watching the online material posted by the candidates [2]. Such an example shows that it is important to investigate the interplay between, on the one hand, the observable traces people leave online and, on the other hand, the impressions that these traces convey. For this reason, this article investigates the relationship between "*faves*" - the pictures that Flickr users tag as favourite - and personality impressions.

The experiments of this work show that faves can be used to predict whether a Flickr user is perceived to be above median or not with respect to each of the Big-Five personality traits [10]. The accuracies range between 58% and 79% depending on the particular trait. The task has been performed with a classifier based on Gaussian Processes [9]. The main novelty of the approach is the *Group Automatic Relevance Determination* (G-ARD) kernel. Its accuracies are comparable, if not superior, to those achieved with Support Vector Machines, a widely applied state-of-the-art classifier. However, the most important advantage of the G-ARD kernel is that its parameter set includes weights - set automatically during the training process - capable of identifying the feature groups that better account for the classification outcome. In this respect, the G-ARD kernel is inspired by the *Automatic Relevance Determination* (ARD) one [6]. The main difference is that this latter has a weight for each individual feature and, therefore, the number of its parameters tends to be larger. For this reason, the G-ARD kernel appears to be more suitable when the amount of training material is limited like in the case of this work.

In the experiments, the analysis of the G-ARD weights shows that the classification outcome depends, to a significant extent, on the following characteristics of the faves: presence of human faces, composition, textural properties and, finally, number and size of visually homogeneous regions. Furthermore, weight differences across personality assessors of different national origins provide indications about cultural effects. The prediction of personality traits has been addressed extensively in the literature (see [12] for an extensive survey). However, this is the first work, to the best of our knowledge, that tries to go beyond simple classification to provide insights about the actual interplay between data and attributed traits. This applies, in particular, to previous results obtained over the publicly available data used in this work [3, 11].

The rest of this article is organised as follows: Section 2 describes the data and the personality model adopted in this work, Section 3 presents the features and the G-ARD approach, Section 4 reports on experiments and results and the final Section 5 draws some conclusions.

2. DATA AND PERSONALITY

The experiments of this work have been performed over *PsychoFlickr*, a publicly available corpus of 60,000 pictures tagged as favourite by 300 Flickr users (200 faves per user), the subjects hereafter [3, 11]. For every subject, the Corpus includes two personality assessments (see below): the

MM '16, October 15–19, 2016, Amsterdam, The Netherlands.

DOI: http://dx.doi.org/10.1145/2964284.2967253

first is the average of the traits attributed by 11 British assessors, the second is the average of the traits attributed by 11 Asian assessors. This makes it possible to investigate cultural effects. The personality assessments are presented in terms of the *Big Five Traits* (BF). These are five behavioural dimensions that are known to capture most individual differences and are recognised as the most effective personality model proposed so far [10]. The BFs are as follows: *Openness* (tendency to have wide interests and to be intellectually curious), *Conscientiousness* (tendency to be responsible, thorough and planful), *Extraversion* (tendency to be active and establish social relationships), *Agreeableness* (tendency to act according to the benefit of others) and *Neuroticism* (tendency to experience only the negative side of life).

From a computing point of view, the main advantage of the BF is that it represents personalities as five-dimensional vectors, a format particularly suitable for computer processing. Each component of the vector is a score that accounts for how well the behaviour of an individual fits the tendencies associated to a particular trait. The scores can be obtained with questionnaires designed for personality assessment. In the experiments of this work, the questionnaire is the *Big Five Inventory 10* (BFI-10) [8]. Once the BF scores are available for all persons in a corpus, it is possible to estimate the median for every trait. In this way, the subjects can be split into two classes, namely those who are above the median versus the others. Hereafter, the two classes are referred to as *high* and *low*, respectively.

3. THE APPROACH

The approach proposed in this work includes two main steps, namely feature extraction and classification into *high* or *low* (see Section 2). The rest of this section presents both steps in detail.

3.1 Feature Extraction

Every picture of the corpus is represented with a set of 82 features inspired by Computational Aesthetics, the domain aimed at predicting whether people consider an image visually appealing or not [5]. The main reason behind this choice is that these features capture the visual appearance of the faves, the only information that the assessors have at disposition to attribute personality traits to the 300 subjects of the Corpus. Furthermore, the features have been shown to be effective in tasks similar to the one addressed in this work [3, 11]. In view of the G-ARD approach (see Section 3.2), the features have been split into 9 groups corresponding to the main visual properties of a picture (see [11] for a full description of the features):

- *G1: Faces.* Number of human faces (1 feature);
- *G2: Colour Properties.* Statistics on the distribution of Hue, Saturation and Value (5 features), valence, arousal and dominance of the emotions elicited by the colours (3 features), variety of colours (1 feature);
- *G3: Colour Distribution.* Fraction of pixels that can be mapped into each of the 11 basic colour categories (red, yellow, pink, etc.) (11 features);
- *G4: Homogeneous Regions.* Amount of edge pixels, number and size of homogeneous regions, image size (4 features);
- *G5: Composition.* Depth of field and use of the rule of thirds (2 features);
- *G6: Texture Wavelets.* Wavelets coefficients (12 features);
- *G7: GIST filters.* Coefficients of GIST filters (24 features);
- *G8: Gray Level Co-occurrence Matrix.* Statistics of pixel values co-occurrences in 3×3 patches (12 features);
- *G9: Texture Statistics.* Tamura features and gray level distribution entropy (4 features).

The feature set is designed to account for content independent visual characteristics and, hence, cope with the wide semantic variability of the pictures posted online. The only content dependent feature is the number of human faces (Group G1) because these are ubiquitous in pictures. A subject of the PsychoFlickr Corpus is represented with the average of the 200 feature vectors extracted individually from every fave. In this way, the whole PsychoFlickr Corpus is represented by 300 vectors, one per subject (see Section 2).

3.2 Trait Classification

The classification approach proposed in this work is based on Gaussian Processes (GPs) [9]. These share with Support Vector Machines - the classifier that achieves state-of-the-art results in most tasks addressed in the literature - the important property of being nonparametric. However, GPs have at least two major advantages. The first is that an appropriate definition of their kernel allows one to explain the role played by the different feature groups in the classification (without explicit knowledge of the mapping between features and labels). The second is that GPs are formulated in probabilistic terms and, hence, a Bayesian treatment allows one to incorporate confidence levels when making predictions.

Consider the vector $\mathbf{y}$ where the ith component y_i is the actual class of training vector $\mathbf{x}_i$ ($y_i = 1$ when the class is *high* and $y_i = -1$ when the class is *low*). The assumption underlying GP classifiers is that the y_i's are independently Bernoulli distributed conditioned on a set of N latent variables f_i evaluated in correspondence of the training vectors $\mathbf{x}_i$, where N is the size of the training set. As a result, the expression of the likelihood is as follows: $p(\mathbf{y} \mid \mathbf{f}) = \prod_{i=1}^{N} p(y_i \mid f_i(\mathbf{x}_i))$, where $p(y_i \mid f_i(\mathbf{x}_i))$ is equal to the normal cumulative distribution $\Phi(y_i f_i(\mathbf{x}_i))$.

Under the GP assumption, the latent values $\mathbf{f}$ are jointly Gaussian distributed with $p(\mathbf{f} \mid \boldsymbol{\theta}) \sim \mathcal{N}(\mathbf{0}, \mathbf{K})$, where $\mathbf{K}$ is the kernel matrix and $\boldsymbol{\theta}$ is the parameter vector of the kernel function. The main novelty of this work is the *Group-Automatic Relevance Determination* (G-ARD) kernel function, a new kernel parametrisation designed to quantify the role played by the feature groups identified in Section 3.1 or any other meaningful partitions of the features:

$$k(\mathbf{x}_i, \mathbf{x}_j) = \sigma \exp\left\{ -\sum_{r=1}^{N_g} \frac{1}{N_r \tau_r{}^2} \left[\sum_{s \in \mathcal{G}_r} (\mathbf{x}_{i(s)} - \mathbf{x}_{j(s)})^2 \right] \right\}, \quad (1)$$

where σ is the marginal variance of the latent values, τ_r is the length-scale parameter for group r (it ensures, on the one hand, that the weights do not depend on the number of features in the groups and, on the other hand, that different weights are comparable even if the respective groups include different numbers of features), N_r is the number of features in group r, N_g is the number of groups, $\mathbf{x}_{i(s)}$ is the sth component of vector $\mathbf{x}_i$, and $\mathcal{G}_r$ is the set of the indexes of the features that belong to group r. Compared to the ARD kernel, the G-ARD allows one to reduce the number of weights from 82 (the number of features) to 9 (the number of groups).

3.3 Fully Bayesian Inference and Predictions

Let $\boldsymbol{\theta}$ denote the parameters of the G-ARD kernel. For a new input vector $\mathbf{x}_\star$ with latent function $f_\star$, a fully Bayesian treatment of the $y_\star$ prediction requires solving:

$$p(y_\star \mid \mathbf{y}) = \int p(y_\star \mid f_\star)p(f_\star \mid \mathbf{f}, \boldsymbol{\theta})p(\mathbf{f}, \boldsymbol{\theta} \mid \mathbf{y})df_\star d\mathbf{f}d\boldsymbol{\theta} \quad (2)$$

where $p(\mathbf{f}, \boldsymbol{\theta} \mid \mathbf{y})$ is the posterior over $(\mathbf{f}, \boldsymbol{\theta})$. The integral with respect to $f_\star$ is univariate and is not problematic, whereas integration over $\mathbf{f}$ and $\boldsymbol{\theta}$ is intractable. Common practice is to approximately integrate out $\mathbf{f}$ and replace the integral over $\boldsymbol{\theta}$ with a fixed point estimate $\boldsymbol{\theta}$, usually obtained by optimising an approximation to the marginal likelihood $p(\mathbf{y} \mid \boldsymbol{\theta})$. While this yields a tractable formulation of the model, it can potentially underestimate uncertainty or cause inaccurate evaluation of the relative influence of different features [4]. We propose to account for the posterior $p(\mathbf{f}, \boldsymbol{\theta} \mid \mathbf{y})$, which encodes the uncertainty in model parameters, enabling us to gain an understanding of the importance of different features with an associated level of confidence.

Sampling from $p(\mathbf{f}, \boldsymbol{\theta} \mid \mathbf{y})$ requires the design of highly nontrivial Markov Chain Monte Carlo (MCMC) algorithms. In this work, predictions are carried out using an adaptive importance sampling-based approach, and in particular the Pseudo-Marginal Adaptive Multiple Importance Sampling (PM-AMIS) proposed in [14], which has been shown to be faster than state-of-the-art MCMC approaches at computing predictions for GP models. The intuition is that the algorithm adaptively constructs an approximate posterior over $\boldsymbol{\theta}$ that is used to build an increasingly more accurate importance sampling estimator of the predictive distribution (2). The importance weights have the following form:

$$w_i^t = p(\boldsymbol{\theta}_i^t) / \frac{1}{\sum_{t=0}^{T-1} N_t} \sum_{t=0}^{T-1} N_t q_t(\boldsymbol{\theta}_i^t; \widehat{\gamma_t}), \quad (3)$$

where T is the total number of iterations, $p(.)$ denotes the posterior of $\boldsymbol{\theta}$ up to a constant, $q_t(.)$ denotes the importance density at iteration t with sequentially updated parameters $\widehat{\gamma_t}$, and $\boldsymbol{\theta}_i^t$ are samples drawn from $q_t(.)$ with $0 \leq t \leq T-1$, $1 \leq i \leq N_t$. At each iteration of PM-AMIS, all the importance weights get updated, including those computed at previous iterations. Because in GP classification the marginal likelihood $p(\mathbf{y} \mid \boldsymbol{\theta})$ cannot be computed analytically, PM-AMIS resorts to an unbiased estimate of the marginal likelihood using a "nested" importance sampling estimation procedure. Even though the computation of the weights is now approximate, because of the fact that $p(\mathbf{y} \mid \boldsymbol{\theta})$ is estimated unbiasedly, it can be shown that PM-AMIS does not introduce any bias in predictions [14].

4. EXPERIMENTS AND RESULTS

The experiments address the task of predicting whether a subject belongs to class *high* or *low* for the Big-Five (see Section 2). The main reason behind this choice is that it corresponds to the natural tendency to compare others in terms of who is higher or lower along a given dimension: "*a compelling argument can be made for emphasising comparisons among individuals, which we do in everyday life (Who is more assertive? Who is more responsible?) and which is useful for such practical purposes as deciding whom to hire for a particular job*" [1].

Table 1: Prediction accuracy.

	Ope	Con	Ext	Agr	Neu
GPs (UK)	65%	58%	71%	73%	79%
SVM (UK)	59%	62%	71%	74%	77%
GPs (Asia)	68%	52%	74%	68%	69%
SVM (Asia)	68%	47%	68%	69%	70%

The experiments have been performed using a k-fold validation approach ($k = 10$) and the same subject never appears in training and test set. The classification has been performed with both the G-ARD approach (see section 3.2) and an SVM with radial basis functions kernel (one parameter). The SVM classifier optimises the kernel parameters by minimising the cross-validation error across a set of candidate values, which is generally not feasible for large parameter sets and / or small amounts of data like the one adopted in this work (300 subjects in total). In contrast, the proposed G-ARD GPs can integrate the uncertainty in the kernel parameters by means of a Bayesian approach when they make predictions. As a result, Table 1 shows that the G-ARD is competitive with the SVM even if the number of its kernel parameters is larger. The accuracy differences across the traits are in line with results typically observed in Personality Computing [12], where different traits can be predicted with different degrees of accuracy depending on the particular data. This parallels the psychological concept of *relevance* according to which the traits emerge with different evidence in different contexts (e.g., Extraversion is easier to observe at a party than at a funeral) [13].

Besides achieving high accuracies, the G-ARD provides information about the feature groups that better account for the classification outcomes. Figure 1 shows the G-ARD weights for both Asian and British assessors. Overall, the presence of human faces (group G1) plays the most important role for all traits and both cultures. The only exception is Extraversion, where the role of G1 is significant, but comparable to those of other groups. The probable reason is that in the case of this trait, strongly associated to social interactions, it is important not only that there are other faces, but also in what type of image they appear (e.g., the face is the main element in a portrait, but it is just a detail in the picture of a crowded public space). Overall, faces appear to be more important for British assessors than for Asian ones for all traits except Neuroticism (the difference between the G1 weights is always statistically significant). The other feature groups for which the weights are large are those that correspond to high level aspects of a picture, namely amount and size of visually homogeneous regions (G4), composition (G5) and textural properties (G9). The other groups have a non-negligible role, but appear to be less important. One possible reason of these results is that visual features accessible at first glance, like those included

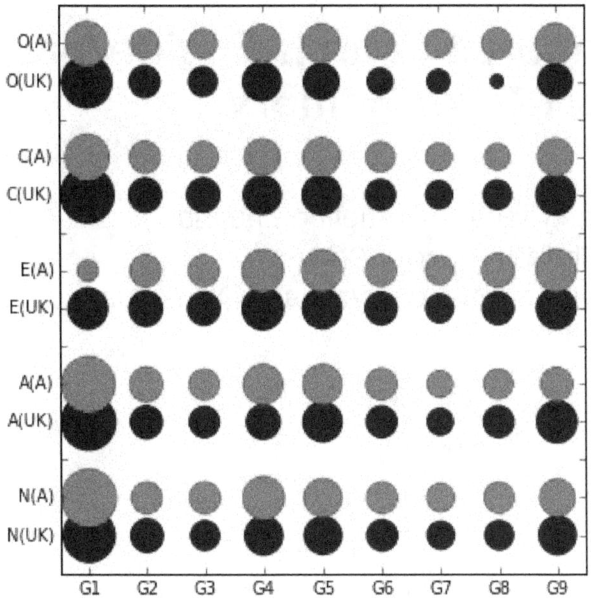

Figure 1: The plot shows the coefficients of the G-ARD for the five traits (O,C,E,A,N) and the two cultures, namely Asia (A) and UK.

in the groups above, are probably more likely than others to drive the personality impressions of the assessors.

The difference between the weights resulting from British and Asian assessors is always statistically significant except in the case of G5 for Neuroticism ($p < 0.01$ after Bonferroni Correction according to a weighted two-sample t-test). These results suggest that there is a cultural effect on personality perception. The largest differences can be observed for G1 (see above). Furthermore, British assessors are less sensitive to number and size of visually homogeneous regions for Agreeableness and Neuroticism while they are more sensitive to the texture properties for Conscientiousness and Agreeableness (conversely for Openness). Overall, Figure 1 suggests that UK and Asian assessors are sensitive to the same visual characteristics, but with different relative importance. One probable explanation is that there is no cultural difference for the physiological aspects - hence all assessors are sensitive to the same visual features - but there are cultural differences when it comes to the association between visual features and personality traits.

5. CONCLUSIONS

This article has shown that Flickr faves can be used to predict whether a Flickr user is perceived to be above median with respect to the Big-Five traits. The results show that the new G-ARD kernel designed for the experiments of this work allows a GP based classifier to achieve comparable accuracies as state-of-the-art SVMs. Furthermore, the parameters of of the G-ARD kernel allow one to identify the groups of features that better account for the classification outcome while detecting cultural differences between UK and Asian personality assessors.

The classification accuracies, well above chance for all traits, show that the weights of the G-ARD kernel provide reliable information about the interplay between low-level, visual characteristics of faves and attribution of personality traits. According to recent sociological investigations [7], this is important because the impression people convey online can change the outcome of important issues like, e.g., getting or not getting a job [2]. For this reason, future work will concentrate on how to use the information provided by the G-ARD weights to ensure that items posted online do not convey a wrong impression, whether it comes to faves or other types of online material.

6. REFERENCES

[1] S. Cloninger. Conceptual issues in personality theory. In P.J. Corr and G. Matthews, editors, *The Cambridge handbook of personality psychology*, pages 3–26. Cambridge University Press, 2009.

[2] D. Coutu. We googled you. *Harvard Business Review*, 85(6):1–8, 2007.

[3] M. Cristani, A. Vinciarelli, C. Segalin, and A. Perina. Unveiling the multimedia unconscious: Implicit cognitive processes and multimedia content analysis. In *Proceedings of the ACM International Conference on Multimedia*, pages 213–222, 2013.

[4] M. Filippone and M. Girolami. Pseudo-marginal Bayesian inference for Gaussian processes. *IEEE Transactions on Pattern Analysis and Machine Intelligence*, 36(11):2214–2226, 2014.

[5] F. Hoenig. Defining computational aesthetics. In *Proceedings of the Eurographics Conference on Computational Aesthetics in Graphics, Visualization and Imaging*, pages 13–18, 2005.

[6] David J.C. MacKay. Bayesian non-linear modelling for the prediction competition. In *In ASHRAE Transactions, V.100, Pt.2*, pages 1053–1062. ASHRAE, 1994.

[7] L. Rainie and B. Wellman. *Networked.* MIT Press, 2012.

[8] B. Rammstedt and O.P.P John. Measuring personality in one minute or less: A 10-item short version of the Big Five Inventory in English and German. *Journal of Research in Personality*, 41(1):203–212, 2007.

[9] C.E. Rasmussen and C. Williams. *Gaussian Processes for Machine Learning.* MIT Press, 2006.

[10] G. Saucier and L.R. Goldberg. The language of personality: Lexical perspectives on the five-factor model. In J.S. Wiggins, editor, *The Five-Factor Model of Personality*, pages 21–50. Guilford Press, 1996.

[11] C. Segalin, A. Perina, M. Cristani, and A. Vinciarelli. The pictures we like are our image: continuous mapping of favorite pictures into self-assessed and attributed personality traits. *IEEE Transactions on Affective Computing (to appear)*, 2016.

[12] A. Vinciarelli and G. Mohammadi. A survey of personality computing. *IEEE Transactions on Affective Computing*, 5(3):273–291, 2014.

[13] A. Wright. Current directions in personality science and the potential for advances through computing. *IEEE Transactions on Affective Computing*, 5(3):292–296, 2014.

[14] X. Xiong, V. Šmídl, and M. Filippone. Adaptive Multiple Importance Sampling for Gaussian Processes. *eprint arXiv:1508.01050v2*, 2016.

Ad Recommendation for Sponsored Search Engine via Composite Long-Short Term Memory

Dejiang Kong Fei Wu Siliang Tang Yueting Zhuang
College of Computer Science, Zhejiang University, China
{kdjysss, siliang.tang}@gmail.com wufei@cs.zju.edu.cn yzhuang@zju.edu.cn

ABSTRACT

Search engine logs contain a large amount of users' click-through data that can be leveraged as implicit indicators of relevance. In this paper we address ad recommendation problem that finding and ranking the most relevant ads with respect to users' search queries. Due to the click sparsity, the conventional methods can hardly model the both inter- and intra-relations among users, queries and ads. We utilize the long-short term memory(LSTM) network to effectively encode two kinds of sequences: the (user, query) sequence and the query word sequence to represent users' query intention in a continuous vector space and decode them as distributions over ads respectively. Further more, we combine these two LSTM networks in an appropriate way to build up a more robust model referred as composite LSTM model(cLSTM) for ad recommendation. We evaluate the proposed cLSTM on real world click-through data set comparing with two baseline methods, the results demonstrate that our proposed model outperforms two baselines and mitigate the click sparsity problem to a certain degree.

Keywords

Ad recommendation; Long-short term memory; Click-through data; Web logs

1. INTRODUCTION

Search advertising has been one of the major revenue sources of the Internet industry for years. A key technology behind search advertising is to predict the click-through rate (pCTR) of ads, since the economic model behind search advertising utilizes pCTR values to rank ads and to price clicks.

Recently, click prediction(ad recommendation) has received much attention from both industry and academia[9] and many works[1, 16, 14, 18] have been done to improve the prediction accuracy. For example, [1] uses their fine-designed query-ad click graph to better discover similarities between queries and leverage the Collaborative Filtering(CF) approach to make a better ad recommendation. [14] concentrates on modeling user psychological desire using special textual patterns and condenses them into powerful features to improve the prediction performance. Unlike [14] and [1], [16] opens another way to the problem, they pay attention to the relations between ads which are proved an important factor in predicting click probability.

MM '16, October 15-19, 2016, Amsterdam, Netherlands
© 2016 ACM. ISBN 978-1-4503-3603-1/16/10...$15.00
DOI: http://dx.doi.org/10.1145/2964284.2967254

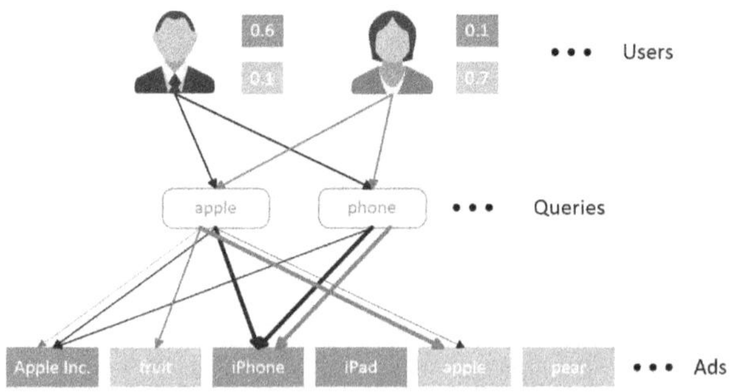

Figure 1: One example of interactions among users, queries and ads. The colored rectangles represent the categories of ads(e.g. blue for tech ad and green for food ad), and colored arrows stand for different users' query intentions(e.g., one user clicks his/her favorite ads after submitting a query).

All of aforementioned works merely modeled one or two kinds of relations among users, queries and ads, while we find that the inter- and intra-relations among them are complicated as Figure 1 illustrated. (1) Different users with the same query may have their favorite desires, i.e. the man in Figure 1 prefers tech more than food, when he issues a query "apple", it is more likely that he will click the "iPhone" ad rather than fruit apple ad, while the woman with another preference is more likely to click the latter one. (2) Different users with different queries may have the same intention. Two different queries "apple" and "phone" are individually issued but both of them result in strong intention to click the "iPhone" ad. (3) Same user with different queries may have the same intention, i.e., the man issues different queries "apple" and "phone" but both have a high probability to click the "iPhone" ad as he desires to buy a phone at that time.

The click tuple (user, query, ad) can be regarded as a three-dimensional data, which is then natural to use Tensor Factorization(TF) based methods[13, 10] to model them for prediction, but these methods are intrinsically prone to perform badly when data is sparse. Long-Short Term Memory(LSTM) network[8] has shown its ability in modeling sequential data in many fields recently[5, 6, 12]. To our problem, we have two kinds of sequences: the global sequences (user, query, ad) and the local query word sequences(e.g. "apple latest released products"). In this paper, we leverage LSTM networks to model these two sequences in order to reveal the inter- and intra-relations among users, queries and ads. All of our contributions in this paper can be concluded as follows:

1.We implement two kinds of LSTM models, one emphasizes on local query contents and another focuses on global relations among users, queries and ads. By this way we can encode users' query intentions and decode them as distributions over ads respectively. To the best of our knowledge, we are the first one to employ LSTM networks in ad recommendation problem for sponsored search engine.

2.We combine aforementioned two LSTM models to build up a more powerful composite LSTM network(cLSTM) to solve the ad recommendation problem.

3.Finally, we show empirically that our proposed model outperforms two baselines on a real world click data set.

2. AD RECOMMENDATION VIA CLSTM

2.1 Problem Introduction

Sponsored search engine can be seen as interaction between three involved factors: user, query and ad. In general a user issues a query to a search engine to seek information, search engine returns highly ranked items and the corresponding ads according to user's query intention. One user may click the returned ad if it is highly relevant to the user's preference. Therefore, lots of these click-through (user, query, ad) tuples are accumulated in search engine. The underlying mission of this paper can be stated as follows: *Given a user and his/her search query, we want to model user's query intention and then recommend the most likely ads to the user.* In this problem, we have two kinds of sequences – query word sequences and (user, query) sequences, it is effective to use Recurrent Neural Networks[15] to encode them. LSTM[8] is an optimized RNN model that avoids the vanishing and exploding gradients problem[2, 7] by introducing *input gate*, *forget gate*, *output gate* and *memory cell.* These multiple gates allow the memory cell in LSTM to keep, update or forget information over time. LSTM model has shown a great ability in modeling sequential data[5, 6, 12] recently and we will discuss how to utilize LSTM model to effectively encode aforementioned two kinds of sequences in following subsections.

2.2 Local LSTM Model

Our local LSTM(Figure 2) model emphasizes on local query contents and encodes the relations between queries and ads. Given the ith query $\boldsymbol{q}^i = \{v_1^i, v_2^i, ..., v_k^i\}$ by a user with k words, $k = |\boldsymbol{q}^i|$ and $v \in V$ where V is a vocabulary consisting of all of individual query words. We first transform each query word v in terms of one-hot representation into a latent vector $\boldsymbol{v}$ via the transformation word embedding matrix $\boldsymbol{W}_v$, then our local LSTM sequentially takes these query word vectors as input and learns the hidden output vectors as follows:

$$\begin{aligned} \boldsymbol{h}_{l,j}^i &= LSTM(\boldsymbol{h}_{l,j-1}^i, \boldsymbol{v}_j^i) \\ \boldsymbol{h}_{l,0}^i &= \boldsymbol{0}; j = 1, ..., k \end{aligned} \tag{1}$$

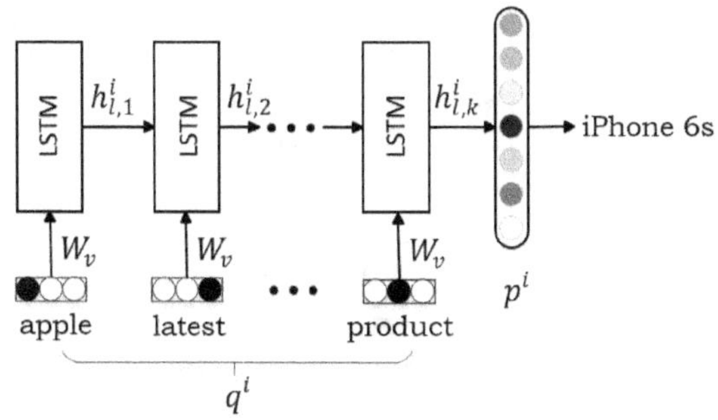

Figure 2: The encoding of query sequence via local LSTM. For simplicity, we only give out one query sequence with k words $\boldsymbol{q}^i = \{apple, latest, released, products\}$ as well as its clicked ads "iPhone 6s". Here $\boldsymbol{h}_{l,j}^i (j = 1, ..., k)$ is the output after encoding first j query words, $\boldsymbol{W}_v$ is the learned word embedding matrix which used to transform one-hot representation words into latent vectors and $\boldsymbol{p}^i$ is the probability distribution of ads. We can see the last hidden layer $h_{l,k}^i$ of $\boldsymbol{q}^i$ is employed to classify the query sequence as "iPhone 6s".

$$\boldsymbol{h}_l^i \equiv \boldsymbol{h}_{l,k}^i \tag{2}$$

where $LSTM(\cdot)$ denotes one step forward pass of the encoding and $\boldsymbol{v}_j^i$ is the jth word of $\boldsymbol{q}^i$. We assume that the output $\boldsymbol{h}_l^i$ of the local LSTM describes the intention of query $\boldsymbol{q}^i$ and can be decoded as a distribution over the clicked ads:

$$\boldsymbol{p}^i = softmax(\boldsymbol{W}_l \cdot \boldsymbol{h}_l^i + \boldsymbol{b}_l) \tag{3}$$

where $\boldsymbol{p}^i$ is the probability distribution with respect to query $\boldsymbol{q}^i$, $\boldsymbol{W}_l$ is the transformation matrix and $\boldsymbol{b}_l$ is the corresponding bias. The probability of the most likely clicked ad for $\boldsymbol{q}^i$ is predicted as follows:

$$p^i = max(\boldsymbol{p}^i) \tag{4}$$

2.3 Global LSTM Model

Our global LSTM model(Figure 3) is proposed to learn the interactions among users, queries and users. After given user u^i and his/her corresponding query q^i, we first transform u^i and q^i into latent vectors $\boldsymbol{u}^i$ and $\boldsymbol{q}^i$ via user embedding matrix $\boldsymbol{W}_u$ and query embedding matrix $\boldsymbol{W}_q$ respectively. Then the global LSTM encodes (user, query) sequence as follows:

$$\begin{aligned} \boldsymbol{h}_{g,u}^i &= LSTM(\boldsymbol{h}_{g,0}^i, \boldsymbol{u}^i) \\ \boldsymbol{h}_{g,0}^i &= \boldsymbol{0} \end{aligned} \tag{5}$$

$$\boldsymbol{h}_{g,q}^i = LSTM(\boldsymbol{h}_{g,u}^i, \boldsymbol{q}^i) \tag{6}$$

$$\boldsymbol{h}_g^i \equiv \boldsymbol{h}_{g,q}^i \tag{7}$$

where $LSTM(\cdot)$ denotes one step forward pass of the encoding. $\boldsymbol{h}_g^i$ is the encoding output of (u^i, q^i) via global LSTM and can been decoded into a distribution over ads as follows:

$$\boldsymbol{p}^i = softmax(\boldsymbol{W}_g \cdot \boldsymbol{h}_g^i + \boldsymbol{b}_g) \tag{8}$$

where $\boldsymbol{W}_g$ and $\boldsymbol{b}_g$ are the transformation matrix and the corresponding bias. The probability of the most likely clicking ad for u^i q^i is calculated as local LSTM does.

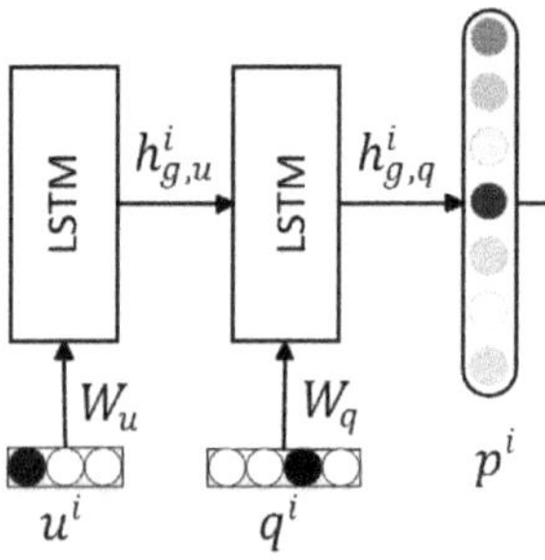

Figure 3: The encoding of *user-query* sequence via global LSTM. For simplicity, we only give out one user-query sequence $\{u^i, q^i\}$ as well as the clicked ad a^i here. $\boldsymbol{W}_u$ is the user embedding matrix, $\boldsymbol{W}_q$ is the query embedding matrix.

2.4 The Composite LSTM Model

The local LSTM encodes query word sequences and decodes them as distributions over ads. By this way, local LSTM can learn the intra-relations among queries (i.e., how is searching mission is formulated) and the inter-relations between queries and ads (i.e., users' searching intention). The global LSTM encodes (user, query) sequences and decodes them as local LSTM does. In this way, global LSTM can disentangle the inter-relations among users, queries and ads.

In order to fully utilize the interactions between users, queries and ads, we propose composite LSTM here. Generally speaking, we send the last hidden layer output h_l of the local LSTM (i.e., the encoding of query sentences) to the global LSTM via a linear transformation(Figure 4):

$$\boldsymbol{q}' = \boldsymbol{W}_{lg} \cdot \boldsymbol{h}_l + \boldsymbol{b}_{lg} \tag{9}$$

where $\boldsymbol{W}_{lg}$ is the transformation matrix and the new generated $\boldsymbol{q}'$ can be taken as a stronger representation of each query than original $\boldsymbol{q}$. In composite LSTM, the local LSTM keeps predicting ads and at the same time is used as one auxiliary network encoding queries for the master one – global LSTM. During the back-propagation of training process, $\boldsymbol{h}_l$ receives two gradients from both the gobal and local LSTM networks, we define the composite gradient as follows:

$$\triangle \boldsymbol{h}_l = c \cdot \triangle \boldsymbol{h}_m + (1-c) \cdot \triangle \boldsymbol{h}_a \tag{10}$$

where $\triangle \boldsymbol{h}_m$ and $\triangle \boldsymbol{h}_a$ are the gradients from the master and auxiliary network respectively, c is a weight parameter to balance these two gradients.

2.5 Learning

Given all of training examples $T = \cup_{(u,q,a)}$, the objective function of composite LSTM can be defined as follows:

$$J(\theta) = \sum \log p(y|x, \theta) \tag{11}$$

where x represents input sequence(query word sequence for local LSTM and (user, query) sequence for global LSTM) and y is the ground truth clicked ads. θ represents all of the model parameters which are learned by maximizing the log-likelihood of $J(\theta)$ and the gradients of the objective function are computed using the back-propagation through time (BPTT) algorithm[11].

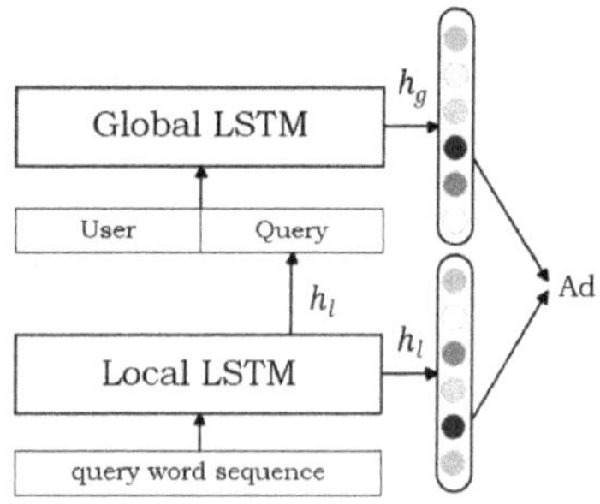

Figure 4: The composite LSTM model for ad recommendation. $\boldsymbol{h}_l$ and $\boldsymbol{h}_g$ are the outputs of local LSTM and global LSTM respectively. The local LSTM receives query word sequence as input, while the global one takes two kinds of inputs, one is the user and another is the encoding of query sequence $\boldsymbol{h}_l$ (learned via local LSTM).

3. EXPERIMENTS

3.1 Experiments Settings

Dataset. The data set 2012 KDD Cup[1] is used in this paper. The original data set is derived from session logs of the Tencent proprietary search engine - soso.com, which contains 149,639,105 records with 23,669,283 distinct users, 26,243,606 distinct queries and 22,238,277 ads. We remove some trivial users, queries and ads. Finally, we obtain our experimental data set with total 57,540 click-through tuples consist of 9,791 distinct users, 7,228 distinct queries and 8,435 distinct ads. The obtained data set is still sparse that over fifty percent of users, queries and ads appear only one click-through tuple. The experiment data are divided into three parts: 42,540 for training, 7,500 for validation and 7,500 for testing. The 7,228 distinct query word sequences have a vocabulary with size of 8,122.

Parameter Settings. For all original input u, q and v we take the one-hot representation and then translate them to the same input dimension d_i using transformation embedding matrix $\boldsymbol{W}_u, \boldsymbol{W}_q, \boldsymbol{W}_v$ respectively. All of embedding matrices are learned with a random initialization. The LSTM cell dimension is denoted as d_c. Parameter optimization is done using mini-batch RMSPROP[4] and the training is terminated when the likelihood of the validation set does not improve for 5 consecutive iterations. The best results of our model reported in section 3.2 has following parameter settings: $d_i = 300$, $d_c = 600$ and the balance weight c is set to 0.7.

Baseline Methods. We implement two baseline methods: (1) Collaborative filtering(CF). We divide our click-through tuple (u, q, a) into two 2-dimension pairs (u, a) and (q, a) and apply collaborative filtering method to discover user-ad and query-ad interrelation respectively. (2) Tensor factorization(TF). As our click-through tuple (u, q, a) is a 3-dimensional data, it is natural to represent the tuple by a 3-order tensor and then factorize and reconstruct the tensor to discover the missing part for prediction. Our TF experiments use HOSVD proposed in [3].

Evaluation Criteria. We evaluate the performance of the model and the baselines in terms of two kinds of criteria.

[1]http://www.kddcup2012.org/c/kddcup2012-track2/data

Table 1: The overall performance for ad recommendation with $d_i = 300$, $d_c = 600$ and $c = 0.7$

Methods	Accuarcy@1	Accuarcy@3	Accuarcy@5	Accuarcy@10	Accuarcy@15	Accuarcy@20	MRR
CF - (q, a)	0.002	0.006	0.009	0.014	0.018	0.022	0.006
CF - (u, a)	0.003	0.010	0.021	0.049	0.074	0.097	0.021
HOSVD	0.198	0.355	0.403	0.474	0.519	0.541	0.296
local LSTM	0.164	0.379	0.514	0.663	0.742	0.788	0.320
global LSTM	0.369	0.607	0.700	0.801	0.842	0.867	0.516
cLSTM	**0.451**	**0.684**	**0.765**	**0.849**	**0.888**	**0.909**	**0.591**

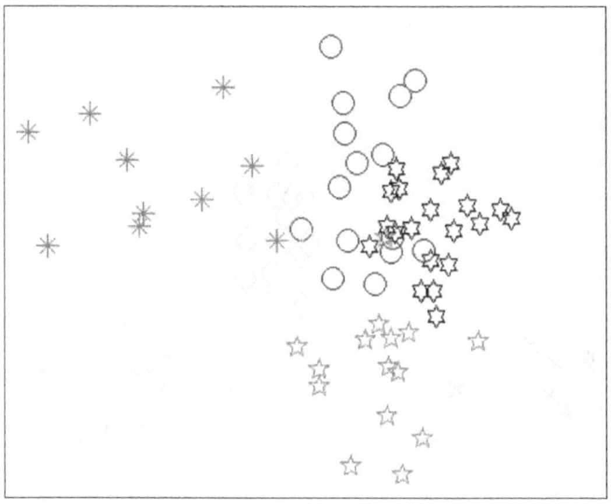

Figure 5: The projection of encoding of query sentences via cLSTM in the 2-dimensional space. The data points with the same colors and shapes indicate that they come from a same category (i.e., different query sentences click a same ads). Here we can see that the encoding exhibits a discriminative embedding representation. Blue circle queries have some overlapping regions in the vicinity with dark hexagon queries since we find in data set that two kinds of clicked ads share many of describing words.

The first one is Accuracy@k proposed in [17] which can be defined as:

$$Accuracy@k = \frac{\#hit@k}{\#tests}$$

where $\#hit@k$ means the number of predicted ads ranking at top k and $\#test$ stands for the number of total testing tuples. Another evaluation criteria is mean reciprocal rank(MRR), which is common for tasks with one ground truth instance.

3.2 Experiments Results

We give out the overall results in Table 1 and analyze them from the following two aspects.

LSTMs *vs.* **CF & TF.** The LSTM models outperform the CF & TF methods much more. For both user-based and query-based CF methods, there are over 8 thousands ads to be predicted while only around 40 thousands training instances used (i.e., data sparisty). The CF-based models even can not accomplish the task due to the data sparsity. TF-based method HOSVD solves the sparsity problem better than CF-based models as it simultaneously utilizes 3-dimensional information. HOSVD gets about **0.275** MRR gain over best performed CF-bases methods. LSTM models show a great superiority to handle data sparsity, the MRR value of the cLSTM comes up to **0.591** and the *Accuracy*@20 of it is around **91%**. The LSTM models learn the interactions between users, queries and clicked ads, and therefore are attractive to perform ads prediction. The worst performed LSTM model – local LSTM that only models the interactions between queries and clicked ads, is still better than conventional CF and TF-based models as the results demonstrated.

cLSTM *vs.* **local & global LSTMs.** The experiment results indicate that the cLSTM model perform better than both the local LSTM and global LSTM in terms of all evaluation criteria. More specifically, the composite model achieves **14.5%** and **84.7%** gains over global and local models in MRR respectively, and in *Accuracy*@20 the performance improvement are **4.8%** and **15.4%**. Comparing the local and global models we find that the latter solves the recommendation problem better, which proves that users are an essential role in recommendation (e.g., different users have similar query intentions). In cLSTM, the local LSTM works like a regularization network by sending the appropriate query encoding to the global LSTM and overcomes the over fitting problem. The cLSTM can learn the encodings of query sentences.

In Figure 5, we embed the encoding learned into a 2D space. In total 107 query sentences belonging to 7 clicked ads are chosen. From Figure 5, we observe that the encodings of query sentences has implicit margins according to their belonging clicked ads(i.e.,categories), which means that the query sentences from the same category are grouped together.

4. CONCLUSIONS

This paper proposes a composite LSTM(cLSTM) model to learn the inter and intra-relations among users, queries and ads. The composite model consists of two sub LSTM networks: global LSTM and local LSTM. The global LSTM works as a master network to encode user and query information while the local LSTM works as an auxiliary network to give a richer representation of query sentences for the global LSTM. The experiment results show the effectiveness of our proposed model and outperform much of the conventional CF and TF-based methods.

5. ACKNOWLEDGMENTS

This work was supported in part by the National Basic Research Program of China under Grant 2015CB352300, NSFC(61402401, U1509206), and the Zhejiang Provincial NSFC(LQ14F010004), in part by the China Knowledge Centre for Engineering Sciences and Technology, and in part by the Fundamental Research Funds for the Central Universities, Qianjiang Talents Program of Zhejiang Province.

6. REFERENCES

[1] T. Anastasakos, D. Hillard, S. Kshetramade, and H. Raghavan. A collaborative filtering approach to ad recommendation using the query-ad click graph. In *Proceedings of the 18th ACM conference on Information and knowledge management*, pages 1927–1930. ACM, 2009.

[2] Y. Bengio, P. Simard, and P. Frasconi. Learning long-term dependencies with gradient descent is difficult. *Neural Networks, IEEE Transactions on*, 5(2):157–166, 1994.

[3] L. De Lathauwer, B. De Moor, and J. Vandewalle. A multilinear singular value decomposition. *SIAM journal on Matrix Analysis and Applications*, 21(4):1253–1278, 2000.

[4] A. Graves. Generating sequences with recurrent neural networks. *arXiv preprint arXiv:1308.0850*, 2013.

[5] A. Graves, A.-r. Mohamed, and G. Hinton. Speech recognition with deep recurrent neural networks. In *Acoustics, Speech and Signal Processing (ICASSP), 2013 IEEE International Conference on*, pages 6645–6649. IEEE, 2013.

[6] A. Graves and J. Schmidhuber. Offline handwriting recognition with multidimensional recurrent neural networks. In *Advances in neural information processing systems*, pages 545–552, 2009.

[7] S. Hochreiter, Y. Bengio, P. Frasconi, and J. Schmidhuber. Gradient flow in recurrent nets: the difficulty of learning long-term dependencies, 2001.

[8] S. Hochreiter and J. Schmidhuber. Long short-term memory. *Neural computation*, 9(8):1735–1780, 1997.

[9] B. J. Jansen and T. Mullen. Sponsored search: an overview of the concept, history, and technology. *International Journal of Electronic Business*, 6(2):114–131, 2008.

[10] S. Rendle, L. Balby Marinho, A. Nanopoulos, and L. Schmidt-Thieme. Learning optimal ranking with tensor factorization for tag recommendation. In *Proceedings of the 15th ACM SIGKDD international conference on Knowledge discovery and data mining*, pages 727–736. ACM, 2009.

[11] D. E. Rumelhart, G. E. Hinton, and R. J. Williams. Learning representations by back-propagating errors. *Cognitive modeling*, 5(3):1, 1988.

[12] M. Sundermeyer, R. Schlüter, and H. Ney. Lstm neural networks for language modeling. In *INTERSPEECH*, pages 194–197, 2012.

[13] P. Symeonidis, A. Nanopoulos, and Y. Manolopoulos. Tag recommendations based on tensor dimensionality reduction. In *Proceedings of the 2008 ACM conference on Recommender systems*, pages 43–50. ACM, 2008.

[14] T. Wang, J. Bian, S. Liu, Y. Zhang, and T.-Y. Liu. Psychological advertising: exploring user psychology for click prediction in sponsored search. In *Proceedings of the 19th ACM SIGKDD international conference on Knowledge discovery and data mining*, pages 563–571. ACM, 2013.

[15] R. J. Williams and D. Zipser. A learning algorithm for continually running fully recurrent neural networks. *Neural computation*, 1(2):270–280, 1989.

[16] C. Xiong, T. Wang, W. Ding, Y. Shen, and T.-Y. Liu. Relational click prediction for sponsored search. In *Proceedings of the fifth ACM international conference on Web search and data mining*, pages 493–502. ACM, 2012.

[17] H. Yin, B. Cui, Y. Sun, Z. Hu, and L. Chen. Lcars: A spatial item recommender system. *ACM Transactions on Information Systems (TOIS)*, 32(3):11, 2014.

[18] Y. Zhang, H. Dai, C. Xu, J. Feng, T. Wang, J. Bian, B. Wang, and T.-Y. Liu. Sequential click prediction for sponsored search with recurrent neural networks. In *Twenty-Eighth AAAI Conference on Artificial Intelligence*, 2014.

Learning a Multi-class Discriminative Dictionary with Nonredundancy Constraints for Visual Classification

Zhao Liu[1,3], Yuwei Wu[1,2], Junsong Yuan[2], Yap-peng Tan[2]
[1]Beijing Laboratory of Intelligent Information Technology, Beijing Institute of Technology, Beijing, China
[2]School of Electrical and Electronics Engineering, Nanyang Technological University, Singapore
[3]Collaborative Innovation Center of Security and Law for Cyberspace, PPSUC, Beijing, China
liuzhao@ppsuc.edu.cn; wuyuwei@bit.edu.cn; jsyuan@ntu.edu.sg; eyptan@ntu.edu.sg

ABSTRACT

Recent studies have demonstrated advantages of sparse representation in providing an appealing paradigm for visual classification tasks. However, how to effectively learn a compact dictionary of superior reconstruction and discrimination power is still a challenging problem. In this paper, we concurrently exploit both the intra-class and the inter-class visual correlations to learn a multi-class discriminative dictionary. The intra-nonredundancy constraint prevents zero entities from appearing in the class-specific bases, thereby making the learned dictionary more stable. The inter-nonredundancy constraint effectively separates the common visual patterns from all the class-specific bases, yielding a more compact dictionary. Combining nonredundancy constraints with the reconstruction error and the classification error to form a unified objective function, our method can learn a superior dictionary and an optimal linear classifier simultaneously. Extensive experimental results demonstrate that the proposed algorithm achieves notable improvement over the state-of-the-art methods in image classification and visual tracking tasks.

Keywords

Discriminative dictionary learning; Nonredundancy constraints; Visual tracking;Image classification

1. INTRODUCTION

Dictionary learning (DL) has received considerable attention in signal processing and computer vision community with a wide range of applications including visual tracking [17, 27], face recognition [34, 30], and image classification [9, 5, 37, 18, 16, 14]. The goal of traditional DL is to find an *overcomplete* dictionary, such that each input signal can be linearly reconstructed by a relatively small subset of bases, while keeping the reconstruction error as small as possible. However, the conventional DL methods often lack of discriminative ability as they are only optimal for reconstruction but not classification. Over the past years, tremendous efforts have been made to overcome this issue. Nevertheless, how to effectively learn a compact dictionary of superior reconstruction and discrimination power is still a challenging problem. In this paper, we focus on learning a multi-class discriminative dictionary with nonredundancy constraints for visual analysis.

To enhance the discrimination power of the dictionary, a great number of methods have been proposed to learn the class-specific dictionary for different classes [19, 30, 37], where the representation residual associated with each class is used for classification. However, most algorithms still have difficulties in discriminating the similar visual attributes, especially for objects sharing similar shape and/or visual appearances. Many DL models often fail to distinguish the differences successfully. The reason can be explained as follows. Since the visually similar classes could share some common patterns, the eventually learned dictionary (*i.e.,* an overcomplete dictionary) is likely to be governed by these common patterns. Samples from different classes may be encoded by same bases. As a result, the representations will share many similar codes and the proportion of discriminative codes may be very small [5]. Such a property causes the loss of subtle image information that is critical to differentiate the highly similar object classes.

In addition, although an overcomplete dictionary allows the existence of more sparse codes to effectively encode the input data, accurately estimating these codes becomes computationally demanding and needs a larger storage cost. This limits the scenarios where the algorithm can be applied. In visual tracking, for example, the appearance of an object could be continuously changing and thus it is impossible to be independent and identically distributed (*i.i.d*). A good tracker often needs a large number of labeled samples to adequately fit the real data distribution. However, precisely labeled samples only come from the first frame during tracking, *i.e.*, the number of labeled samples is very small. If the dimensionality of the sparse representation is larger compared to the number of the samples, then sparsity-based tracking methods predict overfitting due to the "curse of dimensionality".

It is thus desirable that a reconstructive, compressive, and discriminative dictionary should be established for visual analysis. To achieve this goal, we propose a new dictionary learning method based on the following observations: **(1)** The class-specific bases usually share some coherent or even the same bases (*i.e.,* common patterns) because of inter-class visual correlations. The redundant information does not contribute to boosting the discrimination power of the dictionary, but may even degrade the classification accuracy. Directly cleaning up the shared bases is inadvisable, as the discarded bases could be essential for the reconstruction-based representation of the object. We are thus motivated to use the inter-nonredundancy constraint which effectively separates the common visual patterns from all the class-specific bases, yielding a more compact dictionary. **(2)** To facilitate the optimization, a vast majority of DL methods update the dictionary bases without considering the norm 1 constraint. Therefore the class-specific dic-

MM '16, October 15-19, 2016, Amsterdam, Netherlands
© 2016 ACM. ISBN 978-1-4503-3603-1/16/10...$15.00
DOI: http://dx.doi.org/10.1145/2964284.2967255

tionary may contain many zero entities, *i.e.,* the bases are sparse, which produces unstable spare coefficients with a high absolute value corresponding to other non-zero ones, and thus degrades the classification accuracy. To alleviate this effect, we incorporate the intra-nonredundancy constraint to stabilize the learned dictionary for each class, *i.e.,* the bases are dense. In this way, the similarity among the sparse codes is guaranteed during sparse coding.

Motivated by these observations, we propose a multi-class discriminative dictionary learning method that exploits both the intra-class and inter-class visual correlations. To enhance the discrimination power of the dictionary, the classification error and nonredundancy constraints are incorporated into a unified objective function. Our model can jointly learn class-specific bases, while effectively discovering the commonly shared visual bases from the class-specific ones. The class-specific bases are able to capture the most discriminative feature among different classes, and the shared ones can reconstruct the common patterns among all samples. The nonredundancy constraints ensure that the learned dictionary bases are diverse, such that the dictionary is full rank to preserve the consistence of sparse codes for the similar input signals. Therefore, our dictionary is more compact and discriminative, which can achieve better classification performance. Note that our method can work with any feature, including convolutional neural network (CNN) features [10]. In addition, our method does not use external dataset for pre-training, and it also obtains promising results in family of dictionary learning, as evidenced in Section 4.

2. OUR METHOD

In this paper, we use $\boldsymbol{x}$ and $\mathbf{X}$ to denote a vector and a matrix, respectively. Given C classes of individual samples, let $\mathbf{X} = [\mathbf{X}_1, \cdots, \mathbf{X}_c, \cdots, \mathbf{X}_C] \in \mathbb{R}^{d\times N}$ be a training set with N samples. Here $\mathbf{X}_c \in \mathbb{R}^{d\times N_c}$ contains samples of each class and N_c is the number of samples from the c-th class. The class-specific dictionary is denoted by $\mathbf{B}_c \in \mathbb{R}^{d\times K_c}$ with $c = 1, 2, \cdots, C$, and the shared dictionary is denoted by $\mathbf{B}_0 \in \mathbb{R}^{d\times K_0}$, respectively. K_0 and K_c are the number of bases in the shared dictionary and c-th class-specific dictionary, respectively. $\mathbf{B}_c$ is responsible for describing the class-specific visual properties of each class. $\mathbf{B}_0$ is used to describe the commonly shared visual patterns for all classes. Thus the complete learned dictionary is $\mathbf{B} = [\mathbf{B}_0, \mathbf{B}_1, \cdots, \mathbf{B}_c, \cdots, \mathbf{B}_C] \in \mathbb{R}^{d\times K}$, where K is the number of the bases with $K = \sum_{c=0}^{C} K_c$. Denote by $\mathbf{A}$ the sparse coefficient matrix of $\mathbf{X}$ over $\mathbf{B}$, *i.e.,* $\mathbf{X} \approx \mathbf{BA}$. Here, $\mathbf{A}$ can be expressed as $\mathbf{A} = [\mathbf{A}_1, \cdots, \mathbf{A}_c, \cdots, \mathbf{A}_C] \in \mathbb{R}^{K\times N}$, where $\mathbf{A}_c \in \mathbb{R}^{K\times N_c}$ is the coefficients matrix of $\mathbf{X}_c$ over $\mathbf{B}$.

The first consideration is that the learned dictionary $\mathbf{B}$ should well represent $\mathbf{X}_c$, *i.e.,* $\mathbf{X}_c \approx \mathbf{BA}_c$. For each class samples, the representation $\mathbf{A}_c$ can be rewritten as $\mathbf{A}_c = \left[\mathbf{A}_c^0; \mathbf{A}_c^1; \cdots; \mathbf{A}_c^c; \cdots; \mathbf{A}_c^C\right] \in \mathbb{R}^{K\times N_c}$, where $\mathbf{A}_c^0 \in \mathbb{R}^{K_0\times N_c}$ is the coding coefficients of $\mathbf{X}_c$ over the shared dictionary $\mathbf{B}_0$, and $\mathbf{A}_c^c \in \mathbb{R}^{K_c\times N_c}$ is the coding coefficient of $\mathbf{X}_c$ over the sub-dictionary $\mathbf{B}_c$. So there exists $\mathbf{X}_c \approx \mathbf{BA}_c = \sum_{i=0}^{C} \mathbf{B}_i\mathbf{A}_c^i$. In addition, ideally each class sample $\mathbf{X}_c$ should be well represented by $\mathbf{B}_0$ and $\mathbf{B}_c$. That is, only the coefficients associated with $\mathbf{B}_0$ and $\mathbf{B}_c$ can be non-zero, such that $\mathbf{X}_c \approx \mathbf{B}_0\mathbf{A}_c^0 + \mathbf{B}_c\mathbf{A}_c^c$. Mathematically, the data fidelity term is formulated as

$$
\begin{aligned}
\mathcal{C}(\mathbf{X}, \mathbf{A}, \mathbf{B}) &= \sum_{c=1}^{C} \mathcal{C}(\mathbf{X}_c, \mathbf{A}_c, \mathbf{B}, \mathbf{B}_0, \mathbf{B}_c) \\
&= \sum_{c=1}^{C} \left(\|\mathbf{X}_c - \mathbf{BA}_c\|_F^2 + \|\mathbf{X}_c - [\mathbf{B}_0, \mathbf{B}_c][\mathbf{A}_c^0; \mathbf{A}_c^c]\|_F^2 \right).
\end{aligned} \tag{1}
$$

The first term is able to guarantee the good representation power of the overall dictionary, and the second term ensures that samples of each class can be favorably reconstructed by $\mathbf{B}_0$ and $\mathbf{B}_c$. Obviously, only using the first term is impractical to learn the discriminative class-specific bases. While only adopting the second term is impossible to obtain an optimal shared dictionary $\mathbf{B}_0$, as there exist some commonly shared visual bases between $\mathbf{B}_0$ and $\mathbf{B}_c$. In what follows, we will introduce three constraints imposed on the dictionary to enhance its discrimination power.

(1) To make the dictionary more discriminative, it is desired that each class-specific dictionary has poor representation ability for other classes, *i.e.,* $\mathbf{A}_c^j$ should have nearly zero coefficients such that $\sum_{j\neq c, j=1}^{C} \left\|\mathbf{B}_j\mathbf{A}_c^j\right\|_F^2$ is as small as possible. In this case, we consider a strong constraint $\sum_{j\neq c, j=1}^{C} \|\mathbf{A}_c^j\|_F^2 \approx 0$. That is, for samples of the c-th class, it amounts to forcing the coefficients to be zero except the ones corresponding to both the c-th class-specific bases and the shared ones.

(2) However, the constraint mentioned above does not mean that the learnt individual dictionary bases only contain the visual properties of its corresponding class. The commonly shared visual bases may appear in the different individual dictionaries, which makes the individual dictionary bases redundant and thereby resulting in poor performance [2]. The mutual coherence among all class-specific bases and the shared bases should be as small as possible. Inspired by the incoherence penalty term in [19], the inter-nonredundancy constraint is $\min \sum_{j\neq c, j=0}^{C} \left\|\mathbf{B}_c^\top\mathbf{B}_j\right\|_F^2$. Note that j starts with $j = 0$, which means we also consider the nonredundancy of shared bases with all class-specific ones. Clearly, the sub-dictionary among the class-specific bases and the shared ones are nonredundant, and in this case we regard the learnt dictionary $\mathbf{B}$ as most incoherent. Furthermore, an intra-nonredundancy constraint is introduced to encourage low mutual coherence of the same class dictionary, which is defined as $\min \left\|\mathbf{B}_c^\top\mathbf{B}_c - \mathbf{I}_{K_c}\right\|_F^2$. This constraint makes the learnt class-specific dictionary more stable, which benifits to improve reconstruction accuracy, as validated in experiments. Without this constraint, many bases in the class-specific dictionary will be zeros.

Therefore, the complete $\mathcal{C}(\mathbf{X}, \mathbf{A}, \mathbf{B})$ is given by

$$
\begin{aligned}
\sum_{c=1}^{C} \mathcal{C}(\mathbf{X}_c, \mathbf{A}_c, \mathbf{B}, \mathbf{B}_0, \mathbf{B}_c) &= \sum_{c=1}^{C} \Big(\|\mathbf{X}_c - \mathbf{BA}_c\|_F^2 \\
&+ \|\mathbf{X}_c - [\mathbf{B}_0, \mathbf{B}_c][\mathbf{A}_c^0; \mathbf{A}_c^c]\|_F^2 + \|\mathbf{A}_c^{/0,c}\|_F^2 \\
&+ \lambda_1\|\mathbf{B}_c^\top\mathbf{B}_{/c}\|_F^2 + \lambda_2\|\mathbf{B}_c^\top\mathbf{B}_c - \mathbf{I}_{K_c}\|_F^2 \Big).
\end{aligned} \tag{2}
$$

Here λ_1 and λ_2 are the trade-off parameters between constraints. $\mathbf{A}_c^{/0,c}$ indicates the submatrix by removing $\mathbf{A}_c^0$ and $\mathbf{A}_c^c$ from $\mathbf{A}_c$, *i.e.,* $\mathbf{A}_c^{/0,c} = \left[\mathbf{A}_c^1; \cdots; \mathbf{A}_c^{c-1}; \mathbf{A}_c^{c+1} \cdots; \mathbf{A}_c^C\right] \in \mathbb{R}^{(K-K_0-K_c)\times N_c}$. $\mathbf{B}_{/c}$ is the submatrix by removing $\mathbf{B}_c$ from $\mathbf{B}$, *i.e.,* $\mathbf{B}_{/c} = [\mathbf{B}_0, \mathbf{B}_1, \cdots, \mathbf{B}_{c-1}, \mathbf{B}_{c+1}, \cdots, \mathbf{B}_C] \in \mathbb{R}^{d\times(K-K_c)}$.

Eq.(2) seems to be incremental, but it is not a trivial combination. The first two terms guarantee the good representation power of the learnt dictionary, and they can discover the hidden patterns shared by the visually correlated classes. The third term ensures that each class-specific dictionary has poor representation ability for other classes. More importantly, the inter-nonredundancy and the intra-nonredundancy constraints are considered in the last two terms. These two constraints are meaningful, and make the learnt dictionary non-redundant and more stable. We evaluate the effectiveness of each term in our experiments.

The final objective function for the multi-class discriminative DL model with nonredundancy constraints is given by

$$\langle \mathbf{A}_c^*, \mathbf{B}_0^*, \mathbf{B}_c^*, \mathbf{W}^* \rangle = \arg \min_{\mathbf{A}_c, \mathbf{B}_0, \mathbf{B}_c, \mathbf{W}} \left\{ \sum_{c=1}^{C} \mathcal{C}(\mathbf{X}_c, \mathbf{A}_c, \mathbf{B}, \mathbf{B}_0, \mathbf{B}_c) + \|\mathbf{H} - \mathbf{W}\mathbf{A}\|_F^2 + \beta \|\mathbf{W}\|_F^2 + \eta \sum_{c=1}^{C} \|\mathbf{A}_c\|_1 \right\}. \tag{3}$$

Here, β is a trade-off parameter controlling the relative contribution of the corresponding terms, and η is a scalar parameter which involves the sparsity of the coefficients. $\|\mathbf{H} - \mathbf{W}\mathbf{A}\|_F^2$ represents the classification error. $\mathbf{W} \in \mathbb{R}^{C \times K}$ denotes the classifier parameters. $\mathbf{H} = \{\boldsymbol{h}_1, \boldsymbol{h}_2, \cdots, \boldsymbol{h}_N\} \in \mathbb{R}^{C \times N}$ is the class labels of $\mathbf{X}$, where class label vector $\boldsymbol{h}_i = [0, 0, \cdots, 1, \cdots, 0, 0]^\top \in \mathbb{R}^C$. For each sample $\boldsymbol{x}_i \in \mathbb{R}^d$, if $\boldsymbol{x}_i$ belongs to the c-th class ($1 \leq c \leq C$), the c-th entry in $\boldsymbol{h}_i$ is 1 and all the other entries are 0's.

The objective function in Eq. (3) is not jointly convex concerning all variables $\mathbf{A}_c, \mathbf{B}_0, \mathbf{B}_c, \mathbf{W}$, however, it is convex with respect to each variable when others are fixed. Therefore, the optimization procedure of our DDL model can be divided into four sub-procedures by solving $\mathbf{A}_c, \mathbf{B}_0, \mathbf{B}_c$, and $\mathbf{W}$ alternatively. The alternative procedure is iteratively implemented to find the local optimum of each variable. Following [19], we use a stochastic gradient descent algorithm to optimize $\mathbf{B}_0$ and $\mathbf{B}_c$, and adopt the method of orthogonal matching pursuit (OMP) to update $\mathbf{A}_c$. Meanwhile, given updated $\mathbf{A}$ and $\mathbf{B}$, we can readily obtain the closed-form solution of $\mathbf{W}$.

3. CLASSIFICATION APPROACH

After getting $\mathbf{B} = [\boldsymbol{b}_1, \boldsymbol{b}_2, \cdots, \boldsymbol{b}_K] \in \mathbb{R}^{d \times K}$, and $\mathbf{W} = [\boldsymbol{w}_1, \boldsymbol{w}_2, \cdots, \boldsymbol{w}_K] \in \mathbb{R}^{C \times K}$, as discussed in [34], we cannot directly use $\mathbf{B}$ and $\mathbf{W}$ for testing since they are normalized jointly in the optimization. The desired normalized dictionary and the corresponding classifier can be obtained with the method provided in [34]. Given an input sample $\boldsymbol{x} \in \mathbb{R}^{d \times 1}$, we encode it over the normalized dictionary $\mathbf{B}$ by solving $\arg\min_{\boldsymbol{\nu}} \|\boldsymbol{x} - \mathbf{B}\boldsymbol{\nu}\|_2^2 + \eta \|\boldsymbol{\nu}\|_1$, where the sparse coefficient $\boldsymbol{\nu} \in \mathbb{R}^{K \times 1}$. The final classification of a test sample is based on its sparse coefficient $\boldsymbol{\nu}$. We simply apply the linear classifier to estimate the label vetor $\boldsymbol{h} = \mathbf{W}\boldsymbol{\nu} \in \mathbb{R}^{C \times 1}$. The label of test sample $\boldsymbol{x}$ is decided by the index corrresponding the largest element of $\boldsymbol{h}$, *i.e.*, $c = \arg\max_{j \in \{1, 2, \cdots, C\}} \boldsymbol{h}_j$.

4. EXPERIMENTS

In this section, we experimentally evaluate our method on two visual classification applications, *i.e.*, visual tracking and image classification. *Note that we fix the parameters of our model for all following experiments to demonstrate its robustness and stability.* The nonredundancy constraint parameters are set as $\lambda_1 = 0.15$ and $\lambda_2 = 0.1$. The parameter of the linear regression model is set as $\beta = 1e - 10$. And the regularization parameter of sparse coding $\eta = 0.15$. Our approach is implemented in Matlab. The experiments are performed on an Intel Core2 3.2 GHz processor with 32GB RAM.

4.1 Application 1: Visual Tracking

Considering visual tracking as a binary classification problem, our goal is to distinguish the object from the background. In this case, $C = 2$. With the learned dictionary introduced in Section 2, we propose a new tracker based on Bayesian inference where the classification score $\mathbf{W}\boldsymbol{\nu}$ is used to construct the observation model. In our tracker, a candidate with the highest score is considered as the tracking result.

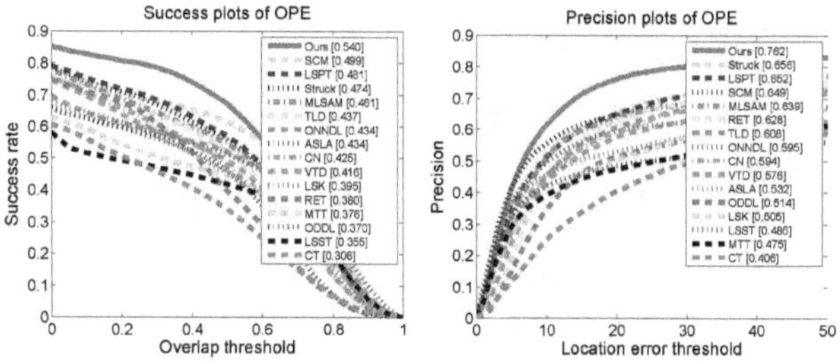

Figure 1: Overall performance comparisons of precision plot and success rate (best viewed on high-resolution display).

Experimental setup: We run our tracker on the benchmark dataset [26] including 51 challenging image sequences. The total number of frames on the benchmark is more than 25000. We evaluate the proposed tracker against 15 state-of-the-art tracking algorithms including ONNDL [24], RET [1], CT [33], MLSAM [27], ODDL [28], CN [3], VTD [12], SCM [36], Struck [7], TLD [11], ASLA [8], LSST [22], MTT [35], LSK [15], and LSPT [31]. For fair comparisons, we use the source codes provided by the benchmark with the same parameters except ONNDL, RET, LSST, MLSAM, ODDL, CN and LSPT which are provided by the authors with the same initialization and whose parameters of the particle filter are the same as our tracker.

The number of particles is 600 and the state transition matrix is $[8, 8, 0.015, 0, 0.005, 0]$ in the particle filter. We resize the object image to 16×16 pixels. 256 dimensional gray scale feature and 128 dimensional HOG feature are extracted from each candidate, and they are concatenated into a single feature vector of 384 dimensions. In the first frame, $N_p = 50$ positive samples and $N_n = 200$ negative samples are used to initialize the dictionary. Once the tracked object is located, 10 positive samples and 80 negative samples are used for dictionary updating.

Comparison results: Followed by [26], one pass evaluation (OPE) is employed to evaluate the overall performance for 16 trackers on 51 sequence. The OPE curve of both the precision plot and success rate are shown in Figure 1. For precision plots, we use the results at error threshold of 20 pixels for ranking these 16 trackers. The AUC score for each tracker is shown in the legend. Our tracker is 4.1% above the SCM in success rate, and outperforms the Struck by 10.6% in precision plot.

Apart from summarizing the performance on the whole sequences, we also construct 11 subsets corresponding to different attributes to test the tracking performance under specific challenging conditions. Our approach performs favorably on 8 out of 11 attributes: background clutter (BC), illumination variation (IV), motion blur (MB), deformation (DEF), out-of-view (OV), in-plane rotation (IPR), out-of-plane rotation (OPR) and occlusions (OCC). Figure 2 illustrates the SP of two attributes which occur more frequently in the benchmark.

4.2 Application 2: Image Classification

We evaluate our method on the Caltech101 dataset [1] and Oxford flower dataset [2]. The spatial pyramid feature [13] is computed as the representation of an image. On the Caltech101 dataset, we compare our approach with SPM [13], D-KSVD [34], SRC [25], GLP [4], ScSPM [29], LLC [23], LC-KSVD2 [9], and other competing methods [21], [20]. We randomly select 30 images per category as

[1] http://www.vision.caltech.edu/Image_Datasets/Caltech101/
[2] www.robots.ox.ac.uk/ vgg/data/flowers/17/index.html

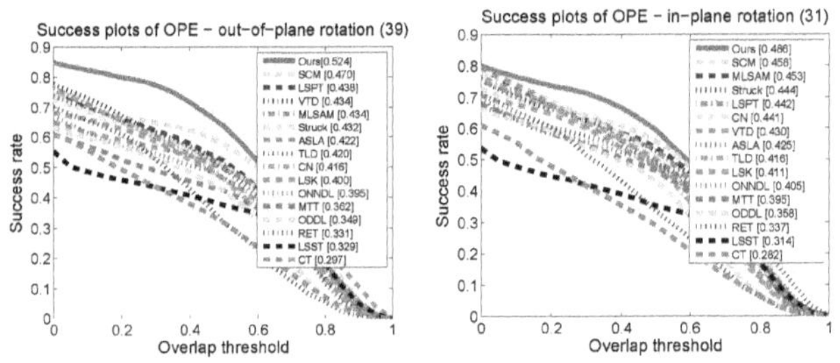

Figure 2: Attribute-based performance analysis in success rate (best viewed on high-resolution display).

Table 1: Comparison of the classification accuracies (%) on the Caltech101 dataset.

Method	♯ Training samples per class					
	5	10	15	20	25	30
D-KSVD	49.60	59.50	65.10	68.60	71.10	73.00
SPM	-	-	56.44	-	-	64.60
GLP	59.35	-	70.34	-	-	82.60
SRC	48.80	60.10	64.90	67.70	69.20	70.70
ScSPM	-	-	67.00	-	-	73.20
Wang	-	-	75.10	-	-	83.26
LLC	51.15	59.77	65.43	67.74	70.16	73.44
Shabou	-	-	-	-	-	73.23
LC-KSVD2	54.0	63.1	67.7	70.5	72.3	73.6
Ours	52.7	59.6	68.4	**76.2**	**81.5**	**83.7**

training data. As a trade-off between computational efficiency and effectiveness, the size of each class-specific dictionary is 20 while fixing the shared dictionary size to be 128. The comparative results are shown in Table 1. Compared with LC-KSVD2, we can observe that the performance improvement brought by our model is nearly 10.1% when using 30 training samples. Different from the works of [4, 21], in which sophisticated SVM classifiers are trained to obtain good performance. In comparison, our results are obtained by using only a simple linear classifier, but the performance of our approach is slightly better than methods in [4, 21].

On the Oxford flower dataset, we randomly select 40 images per category as training data and use the rest as test data. The size for each category-specific dictionary is fixed to 60 and shared dictionary is set to be 128. We compare our method with ScSPM [29], JDL [37], D-KSVD [34], FDDL [30], CSDL [5], MCLP [6], and MTJSRC [32]. We show the experimental results in Table 2. It is clearly seen that our algorithm outperforms other dictionary learning algorithms. Since this dataset has strong visual correlation among different classes, the proposed algorithm is able to learn a more discriminative dictionary concurrently using the intra-class visual information and inter-class visual correlations.

Effectiveness of $\mathbf{B}_0$: The shared dictionary $\mathbf{B}_0$ is designed in our dictionary learning method to discover the hidden visual patterns shared by the visually correlated categories. Since the common patterns may make the learnt class-specific bases redundant, they do not benefit classification performance, but may even degrade the classification accuracy. Separating them from the class-specific bases enables our model to learn more discriminative and more compact dictionaries. To evaluate the effectiveness of the shared dictionary $\mathbf{B}_0$, we train class-specific bases without considering the shared ones explicitly in three datasets mentioned above.

Table 2: Average classification rate (%) on the Oxford flower dataset.

Methods	Accuracy	Methods	Accuracy
JDL	68.69	ScSPM	52.35
FDDL	66.47	MCLP	66.74
CSDL	72.65	D-KSVD	61.47
MTJSRC	69.95	**Ours**	**74.2**

Table 3: Average classification rate (%) comparisons of our method with and without separating the shared bases from the class-specific bases.

	Caltech101	Oxford flower
Ours without $\mathbf{B}_0$	81.1	72.8
Ours	83.7	74.2

Table 4: Average classification rate (%) comparisons of our method with and without nonredundancy constraints.

	Caltech101	Oxford flower
Baseline1	72.8	62.9
Baseline2	82.5	73.9
Baseline3	74.9	64.4
Ours	83.7	74.2

The simple linear classifier is used for classification once the learned dictionary is available. Table 3 shows that separating the hidden visual patterns from the class-specific ones is effective to ameliorate the discrimination of the dictionaries.

The importance of nonredundancy constraints: In the BaseLine1, we do not consider the inter-nonredundancy constraint in Eq. (2), *i.e.*, $\lambda_1 = 0$. In the BaseLine2, we do not consider the intra-nonredundancy constraint is not be considered in Eq. (2), *i.e.*, $\lambda_2 = 0$. In the BaseLine3, the two nonredundancy constraints are both not exploited in Eq. (2), *i.e.*, $\lambda_1 = 0$, $\lambda_2 = 0$. The comparison results are presented in Table 4. Clearly, Baseline1 and Baseline3 are marginally worse than our method, as the redundancy of the dictionary does not benefit classification performance, but may even degrade the classification accuracy. Encouraging low mutual coherence among dictionary bases can necessarily improve the discrinimative power of sparse codes. Although Baseline2 is comparable to our method, the intra-nonredundancy constraint can avoid many entities of the class-specific dictionary being zeros, and make the learnt dictionary more stable.

5. CONCLUSION

In this paper, we have presented a multi-class discriminative dictionary method with nonredundancy constraints for visual tracking and image classification. The proposed method can jointly learn the shared bases and the class-specific ones, while effectively separating the commonly shared visual patterns from the class-specific ones. Incorporating the classification error and nonredundancy constraints into the objective function, our model is able to obtain a prominent dictionary, discriminative sparse coefficients, and classifier parameters simultaneously. We have conducted extensive comparative studies on the challenging benchmarks and shown that our method can boost the classification performance with only one simple linear classifer to outperform or be comparable with the state-of-the-art methods. As suggested in [10], we will take our model as a direct supervision information and embed it into the late hidden layers of the deep convolutional neural network in our future work.

6. ACKNOWLEDGMENTS

This work was supported in part by Singapore Ministry of Education Academic Research Fund Tier 2 MOE2015-T2-2-114 and the Natural Science Foundation of China (NSFC) under Grant No. 61375044. Part of this work was carried out at the Rapid-Rich Object Search (ROSE) Lab at the Nanyang Technological University, Singapore. The ROSE Lab is supported by the National Research Foundation, Prime Ministers Office, Singapore, under its IDM Futures Funding Initiative and administered by the Interactive and Digital Media Programme Office.

7. REFERENCES

[1] Q. Bai, Z. Wu, S. Sclaroff, M. Betke, and C. Monnier. Randomized ensemble tracking. In *ICCV*, pages 2040–2047, 2013.

[2] D. Barchiesi and M. D. Plumbley. Learning incoherent dictionaries for sparse approximation using iterative projections and rotations. *TSP*, 61(8):2055–2065, 2013.

[3] M. Danelljan, F. Shahbaz Khan, M. Felsberg, and J. Van de Weijer. Adaptive color attributes for real-time visual tracking. In *CVPR*. IEEE, 2014.

[4] J. Feng, B. Ni, Q. Tian, and S. Yan. Geometric ℓ_p-norm feature pooling for image classification. In *CVPR*, pages 2609–2704. IEEE, 2011.

[5] S. Gao, I.-H. Tsang, and Y. Ma. Learning category-specific dictionary and shared dictionary for fine-grained image categorization. *TIP*, 23(2):623–634, Feb 2014.

[6] P. Gehler and S. Nowozin. On feature combination for multiclass object classification. In *ICCV*, pages 221–228. IEEE, 2009.

[7] S. Hare, A. Saffari, and P. H. Torr. Struck: Structured output tracking with kernels. In *ICCV*, pages 263–270, 2011.

[8] X. Jia, H. Lu, and M. Yang. Visual tracking via adaptive structural local sparse appearance model. In *CVPR*, pages 1822–1829, 2012.

[9] Z. Jiang, Z. Lin, and L. S. Davis. Label consistent k-svd: learning a discriminative dictionary for recognition. *TPAMI*, 35(11):2651–2664, 2013.

[10] Z. Jiang, Y. Wang, L. Davis, W. Andrews, and V. Rozgic. Learning discriminative features via label consistent neural network. *arXiv preprint arXiv:1602.01168*, 2016.

[11] Z. Kalal, K. Mikolajczyk, and J. Matas. Tracking-learning-detection. *TPAMI*, 34(7):1409–1422, 2012.

[12] J. Kwon and K. Lee. Visual tracking decomposition. In *CVPR*, pages 1269–1276, 2010.

[13] S. Lazebnik, C. Schmid, and J. Ponce. Beyond bags of features: Spatial pyramid matching for recognizing natural scene categories. In *CVPR*, volume 2, pages 2169–2178. IEEE, 2006.

[14] S. Li, M. Shao, and Y. Fu. Cross-view projective dictionary learning for person re-identification. In *IJCAI*, pages 2155–2161, 2015.

[15] B. Liu, J. Huang, L. Yang, and C. Kulikowsk. Robust tracking using local sparse appearance model and k-selection. In *CVPR*, pages 1313 – 1320, 2011.

[16] G. Liu, Y. Yan, E. Ricci, Y. Yang, Y. Han, S. Winkler, and N. Sebe. Inferring painting style with multi-task dictionary learning. In *IJCAI*, 2015.

[17] X. Mei, Z. Hong, D. Prokhorov, and D. Tao. Robust multitask multiview tracking in videos. *TNNLS*, page in press, 2015.

[18] Q. Qiu, V. Patel, and R. Chellappa. Information-theoretic dictionary learning for image classification. *TPAMI*, 36(11):2173–2184, 2014.

[19] I. Ramirez, P. Sprechmann, and G. Sapiro. Classification and clustering via dictionary learning with structured incoherence and shared features. In *CVPR*, pages 3501–3508. IEEE, 2010.

[20] A. Shabou and H. LeBorgne. Locality-constrained and spatially regularized coding for scene categorization. In *CVPR*, pages 3618–3625. IEEE, 2012.

[21] D. Wang and S. Kong. A classification-oriented dictionary learning model: Explicitly learning the particularity and commonality across categories. *PR*, 47(2):885–898, 2014.

[22] D. Wang, H. Lu, and M.-H. Yang. Least soft-thresold squares tracking. In *CVPR*, pages 2371–2378, 2013.

[23] J. Wang, J. Yang, K. Yu, F. Lv, T. Huang, and Y. Gong. Locality-constrained linear coding for image classification. In *CVPR*, pages 3360–3367. IEEE, 2010.

[24] N. Wang, J. Wang, and D.-Y. Yeung. Online robust non-negative dictionary learning for visual tracking. In *ICCV*, pages 657–664. IEEE, 2013.

[25] J. Wright, A. Y. Yang, A. Ganesh, S. S. Sastry, and Y. Ma. Robust face recognition via sparse representation. *TPAMI*, 31(2):210–227, 2009.

[26] Y. Wu, J. Lim, and M.-H. Yang. Online object tracking: A benchmark. In *CVPR*, pages 2411–2418. IEEE, 2013.

[27] Y. Wu, B. Ma, M. Yang, Y. Jia, and J. Zhang. Metric learning based structural appearance model for robust visual tracking. *TCSVT*, 24(5):865–877, 2014.

[28] F. Yang, Z. Jiang, and L. S. Davis. Online discriminative dictionary learning for visual tracking. In *WACV*, 2014.

[29] J. Yang, K. Yu, Y. Gong, and T. Huang. Linear spatial pyramid matching using sparse coding for image classification. In *CVPR*, pages 1794–1801. IEEE, 2009.

[30] M. Yang, L. Zhang, X. Feng, and D. Zhang. Sparse representation based fisher discrimination dictionary learning for image classification. *IJCV*, pages 1–24, 2014.

[31] R. Yao, Q. Shi, C. Shen, Y. Zhang, and A. van den Hengel. Part-based visual tracking with online latent structural learning. In *CVPR*, pages 2363–2370, 2013.

[32] X.-T. Yuan, X. Liu, and S. Yan. Visual classification with multitask joint sparse representation. *TIP*, 21(10):4349–4360, 2012.

[33] K. Zhang, L. Zhang, and M.-H. Yang. Real-time compressive tracking. In *ECCV*, pages 864–877. Springer, 2012.

[34] Q. Zhang and B. Li. Discriminative k-svd for dictionary learning in face recognition. In *CVPR*, pages 2691–2698. IEEE, 2010.

[35] T. Zhang, B. Ghanem, S. Liu, and N. Ahuja. Robust visual tracking via multi-task sparse learning. In *CVPR*, pages 2042–2049, 2012.

[36] W. Zhong, H. Lu, and M. Yang. Robust object tracking via sparsity-based collaborative model. *TIP*, 23(5):2356–2368, 2014.

[37] N. Zhou and J. Fan. Jointly learning visually correlated dictionaries for large-scale visual recognition applications. *TPAMI*, 36(4):715–730, April 2014.

A Compact Binary Aggregated Descriptor via Dual Selection for Visual Search

Yuwei Wu[1], Zhe Wang[1], Junsong Yuan[1], Lingyu Duan[2]
[1]School of Electrical and Electronics Engineering, Nanyang Technological University, Singapore
[2]School of Electronics Engineering and Computer Science, Institute of Digital Media, Peking University, Beijing, China
wuyuwei@bit.edu.cn; wangzhe@ntu.edu.sg;jsyuan@ntu.edu.sg;lingyu@pku.edu.cn

ABSTRACT

To achieve high retrieval accuracy over a large scale image/video dataset, recent research efforts have demonstrated that employing extremely high-dimensional descriptors such as the Fisher Vector (FV) and the Vector of Locally Aggregated Descriptors (VLAD) can yield good performance. To enable fast search, the FV (or VLAD) is usually compressed by product quantization (PQ) or hashing. However, compressing high-dimensional descriptors via PQ or hashing may become intractable and infeasible due to both the storage and computation requirements for the linear/nonlinear projection of PQ or hashing methods. We develop a novel compact aggregated descriptor via dual selection for visual search. We utilize both sample-specific Gaussian component redundancy and bit dependency within a binary aggregated descriptor to produce its compact binary codes. The proposed method can effectively reduce the codesize of the raw aggregated descriptors, without degrading the search accuracy or introducing additional memory footprint. We demonstrate the significant advantages of the proposed binary codes in solving the approximate nearest neighbor (ANN) visual search problem. Experimental results on extensive datasets show that our method outperforms the state-of-the-art methods.

Keywords

Aggregated descriptors;Visual search; Dual selection; Compact binary code

1. INTRODUCTION

With the advent of the era of Big Data, huge body of resources can be easily found on the multimedia sharing platforms such as *YouTube*, *Facebook* and *Flickr*. Visual search is attracting considerable attention in the multimedia and computer vision literature. It refers to the discovery of images contained within a large dataset that describes the same objects as those depicted by query terms. There exists a wide variety of emerging applications, *e.g.*, searching buildings for location recognition and 3D reconstruction [13], searching logos for the estimation of brand exposure [22], and rapidly locating and tracking of criminal suspects from masses of surveillance videos [15]. The basic idea of visual search is to extract visual descriptors from images/videos, then perform descriptor matching between the query and dataset to find relevant items. Towards an effective and efficient visual search system, the visual descriptors need to be discriminative and resource-efficient (*e.g.*, low memory footprint). The discriminability determines the search accuracy, while the resource involves the scalability of a visual search system. In this paper, our goal is to design a new compact binary coding method which can achieve satisfactory search accuracy, search efficiency, and memory cost simultaneously.

More recently, various visual tasks are being performed on the larger and larger dataset, and visual search is no exception. To achieve high retrieval accuracy on such datasets, it is necessary to employ extremely high-dimensional descriptors such as the Fisher Vector (FV) [21] and the Vector of Locally Aggregated Descriptors (VLAD) [12]. In retrieval tasks, the FV (or VLAD) is usually compressed to binary aggregated descriptors because the binarized FV (or VLAD) allows for fast Hamming distance computation as well as light storage of visual descriptors [20, 2, 19, 16, 30].

Product quantization (PQ) [10, 18, 5, 29, 1, 23] and hashing [15, 6, 7, 17, 27, 26, 24] are popularly used techniques to obtain binary aggregated descriptors. In PQ and Hashing methods, the linear (or nonlinear) projection is usually employed to convert high dimensional features (*e.g.,* feature $\mathbf{f} \in \mathbb{R}^N$) into binary embeddings or product codes. However, both the space and computational complexity of the projection is $\mathcal{O}(N^2)$ [14, 6, 27]. For instance, assume that a 426-dimensional dense trajectory feature is extracted from a video and then PCA is employed to project it to the dimensionality 213, we will obtain a $54,528$-dimensional FV when the number of Gaussion components $K = 128$. In the case of $N = 54,528$, projection matrix alone will take more than 10 GB memory footprint and projecting one vector would spend 800 ms on a single core. As the number of Gaussion components K increases, binarizing high-dimensional descriptors directly using PQ or hashing may become intractable and infeasible due to the computational cost and memory requirements.

It is thus desirable that a discriminative and compact aggregated descriptor should be established for visual search over a large scale dataset when only limited hardware resources are available. To achieve this goal, we consider the following observations: (1) As discussed in [21], since each residual vector of the FV (or VLAD) is aggregated from local features being assigned to the corresponding Gaussian component, not all the components are of equal importance to distinguish a sample. (2) Although the redundancy from the component-level is removed, the bit-wise dependency within each selected component may be further reduced.

Motivated by these observations, we propose a novel compact binary coding method for visual search. A sample-specific component selection scheme is introduced to remove the redundant Gaus-

MM '16, October 15-19, 2016, Amsterdam, Netherlands

DOI: http://dx.doi.org/10.1145/2964284.2967256

sian components, and a global structure preserving sparse subspace learning method is presented to suppress the bit-wise dependency within a selected component. Specifically, given a raw Fisher vector with K Gaussian components, to fulfill the constraint of compression complexity, we first binarize the FV by a sign function, leading to a binarized Fisher vector (BFV). Both sample-specific Gaussian component redundancy and bit dependency within a component are then introduced to produce compact binary codes. The obtained binary codes, as required, are discriminative, and yet compact, capable of efficiently handling the large scale dataset, as validated in Section 5.

2. BINARY AGGREGATED DESCRIPTOR

In the FV method, a Gaussian Mixture model (GMM) $p_\lambda(x) = \sum_{i=1}^{K} \omega_i p_i(x)$ with K Gaussians is to estimate the distribution of local features over a training set. We denote the set of Gaussian parameters as $\lambda_i = \{\omega_i, \mu_i, \sigma_i^2, i = 1, ..., K\}$, where ω_i, μ_i and σ_i^2 are the weight, mean vector and variance vector of the i-th Gaussian p_i, respectively. Let $\mathbf{F} = \{\mathbf{f}_1, ..., \mathbf{f}_T\}$ denote a collection of T SIFT local features extracted from an image. Employing PCA to project the dimensionality of SIFT or trajectory to dimension D is beneficial to the overall performance [11, 12]. By concatenating of the sub-vector $\mathbf{g}(i)$ of all the K components, we form the FV $\mathbf{g} = [\mathbf{g}(1), ..., \mathbf{g}(K)] \in \mathbb{R}^{KD}$, where $\mathbf{g}(i) \in \mathbb{R}^{D}$. Similarly, the VLAD can be derived from FV by replacing the GMM soft clustering with k-means clustering [12].

Following the compressed fisher vectors[20], we choose a one-bit quantizer to binarize the high dimensional $\mathbf{g} \in \mathbb{R}^{KD}$, such that superior retrieval performance with nearly zero memory footprint can be achieved. We generate binary aggregated descriptors by quantizing each dimension of FV or VLAD into a single bit $0/1$ based on a sign function. Formally speaking, $sgn(\mathbf{g})$ is used to map each element g_j of the descriptor $\mathbf{g}$ to 1 if $g_j > 0$, $j = 1, 2, \cdots, KD$; otherwise, 0, yielding a Binary Aggregated Descriptor (BAD) $\mathbf{b} = \{\mathbf{b}(1), ..., \mathbf{b}(K)\}$ with $N = KD$ bits, where $\mathbf{b}(i) \in \mathbb{R}^{D}$.

3. COMPACT BINARY AGGREGATED DESCRIPTOR VIA DUAL SELECTION

In this paper, our goal is to compress aggregated descriptors into binary codes, without sacrificing considerable loss of search accuracy. In addition, the encoding process should satisfy small memory footprint and low computational complexity. We formulate the compact binary coding as a resource-constrained (*e.g.*, bit rate, memory footprints and computational complexity) feature compression problem. Although the BAD method supports ultra-fast Hamming distance computation (XOR operation and bit count), it has a fixed codesize and thus cannot meet the given constraints. Moreover, the coarse binary quantization would probably drop the search accuracy of uncompressed aggregated descriptors. To address these issues, we propose a dual selection model which utilizes both sample-specific component selection and component-specific bit selection to explore the informative bits. Since the VLAD is a simplified non-probabilistic version of FV, in what follows, we take the FV as an example to elaborate how to obtain the compact Fisher codes via dual selection.

3.1 Sample-specific Component Selection

We note that FV exhibits the natural 2-D structure due to the Gaussian component based feature aggregation, as shown in Figure 1. The aggregated FV is formed by concatenating residual vectors computed for all Gaussian components, while each residual

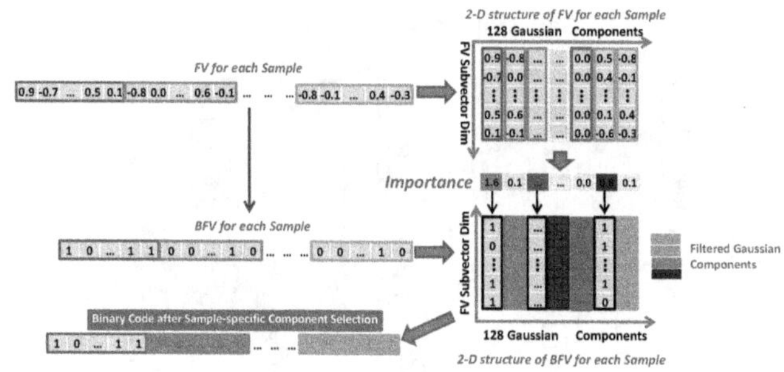

Figure 1: Sample-specific component selection. The aggregated FV is partitioned into disjoint components by Gaussian components. We select all the bits of Gaussian components with high *importance* and the rest of components are discarded. In this work, the *importance* is defined as the sum of posterior probabilities of local features being assigned to the i-th Gaussion component.

vector is aggregated from local features being assigned to the corresponding Gaussian component. In other words, not all Gaussian components equally contribute to describing a sample. Assume that the occurrence of a Gaussian component is the number of local features quantized to that component. The occurrence of different Gaussian components may vary for each sample. Gaussian components with low occurrence are supposed to be less discriminative for describing the sample. In an extreme case, if none of local features is assigned to a Gaussian component i, then all the elements of the corresponding subvector $\mathbf{g}(i)$ are zero. Our method thus considers the sample-specific component selection within an individual sample, which uses local statistics to discard the redundant Gaussian components.

Specifically, we can partition the FV into disjoint components by Gaussian components and select all the bits of those with high importance. Here, the importance means that which Gaussian components are activated and how large the amplitudes of their responses are. In particular, we adopt the soft assignment $\gamma(\mathbf{f}_t, i)$ of local features as the importance of Gaussian i to adaptively select part of discriminative components for each sample. The importance, *i.e.*, $I(\lambda_i)$, is defined as the sum of posterior probabilities of local features $\{\mathbf{f}_1, ..., \mathbf{f}_T\}$ being assigned to the i-th Gaussian component, given by

$$I(\lambda_i) = \sum_{t=1}^{T} \gamma(\mathbf{f}_t, i). \tag{1}$$

Sample-specific component selection can be implemented efficiently by applying a sorting algorithm to the set $\{I(\lambda_i), i = 1, 2, \cdots, K\}$, *i.e.*, the subvector of the binary Fisher vector (BFV) $\mathbf{b}(i)$ with the largest $I(\lambda_i)$ is first selected to generate Fisher codes, followed by the $\mathbf{b}(j)$ with the second largest one. In this way, we can compute the importance of components for each sample using Eq. (1) and select a subset of components with high importance. The rest of components are discarded, as shown in Figure 1. The number of the selected components will be discussed in Section ??. Since noisy components are removed from the original aggregated FV, the required number of shortlisted candidates can be largely reduced. Meanwhile, it is not necessary to maintain a Gaussian selection mask for all samples. Accordingly, the sample-specific component selection is memory free, and the computational cost of Gaussian selection is $\mathcal{O}(N)$.

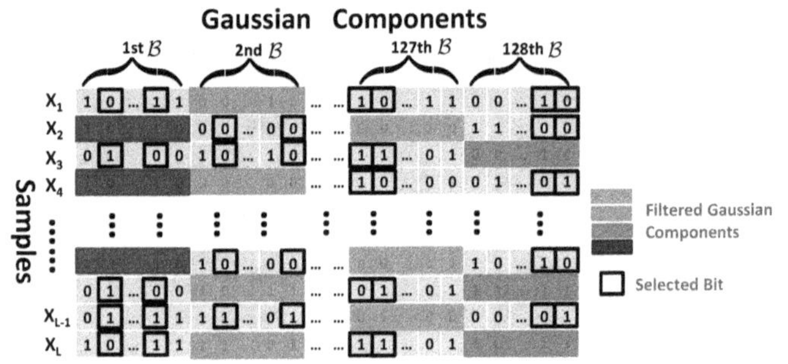

Figure 2: Componet-specific bit selection. The bits that carry as much information as possible are selected by the global structure preserving sparse subspace learning. For each sample, the bits in black bounding boxes are the final compact Fisher codes. L denotes the number of training samples.

3.2 Component-specific Bit Selection

After sample-specific component selection, although the redundancy from a component-level is removed, there probably exists bit-level redundancy within each selected component. Therefore, we need to further reduce the dimensionality of each component, while maintaining search performance. Inspired by [25], in this paper, we introduce a component-specific bit selection scheme by global structure preserving sparse subspace learning to select bits that carry as much information as possible.

Without loss of generality, let $\mathcal{B} \in \{0,1\}^{\Theta \times D}$ denote a subset of the BAD from the i-th Gaussian component corresponding to the whole dataset. Here Θ represents how many samples treating the i-th component as an *important* one, as shown in Figure 2. $\Theta \leq L$, where L is the number of training samples. The goal of bits selection is to find a small set of bits that can capture most useful information of $\mathcal{B}$. One natural way is to measure how close the original data samples are to the learned subspace spanned by the selected bits. Mathematically, the component-specific bit selection is formulated as

$$\begin{aligned} &\min_{\mathbf{W},\mathbf{H}} ||\mathcal{B} - \mathcal{B}\mathbf{W}\mathbf{H}||_F^2. \\ &s.t. \mathbf{W} \in \{0,1\}^{D \times D'} \\ &\quad \mathbf{W}^\top \mathbf{1}_{D\times 1} = \mathbf{1}_{D' \times 1} \\ &\quad ||\mathbf{W}\mathbf{1}_{D'\times 1}||_0 = D' \end{aligned} \tag{2}$$

Here, $\mathbf{W}$ is a selection matrix with entries of 0 or 1. $\mathbf{W}^\top \mathbf{1}_{D\times 1} = \mathbf{1}_{D'\times 1}$ enforces that each column of $\mathbf{W}$ has only one 1, *i.e.*, at most the D' bits are selected for each Gaussian component. $||\mathbf{W}\mathbf{1}_{D'\times 1}||_0 = D'$ guarantees that $\mathbf{W}$ has the D' nonzero rows, and thus exact D' bits will be selected. $\mathbf{H}$ is the optimal subspace. Hence, Eq.(2) denotes the distance of $\mathcal{B}$ to the learned subspace $\mathbf{H}$.

A major difficulty of solving Eq. (2) lies in handling the discrete constraints imposed on $\mathbf{W}$, which typically makes bits selection problem very challenging. In this work, we relax the 0-1 constraint of $\mathbf{W}$ to nonnegativity constraint and the hard constraints both $\mathbf{W}^\top \mathbf{1}_{D\times 1} = \mathbf{1}_{D'\times 1}$ and $||\mathbf{W}\mathbf{1}_{D'\times 1}||_0 = D'$ to a $L_{2,1}$ norm constraint. Therefore, optimizing Eq. (2) is equivalent to solving

$$\begin{aligned} &\min_{\mathbf{W},\mathbf{H}} ||\mathcal{B} - \mathcal{B}\mathbf{W}\mathbf{H}||_F^2 + \beta||\mathbf{W}||_{2,1}, \\ &s.t. \mathbf{W} \in \mathbb{R}_+^{D\times D'} \end{aligned} \tag{3}$$

where $\mathbb{R}_+^{D\times D'}$ denotes a set of $D \times D'$ nonnegative matrices and β is a parameter. After obtaining a solution $\mathbf{W}$, we choose the bits corresponding to the D' rows of $\mathbf{W}$ that have the largest norms.

In this work, we employ the accelerated block coordinate update (ABCU) method [28] to alternatingly update $\mathbf{W}$ and $\mathbf{H}$ with

$$\begin{cases} f(\mathbf{W},\mathbf{H}) = ||\mathcal{B} - \mathcal{B}\mathbf{W}\mathbf{H}||_F^2 \\ g(\mathbf{W}) = \beta||\mathbf{W}||_{2,1}. \end{cases} \tag{4}$$

Due to the space limit, interested readers refer to [28] for details.

Normalizing each column of $\mathbf{W}$, we sort $||\mathbf{W}_{i,\cdot}||_2, i = 1, 2, \cdots, D$ and select bits corresponding to the D' largest ones . Since the Gaussian components are independent of each other, the component-specific bit selection can be implemented in a parallel fashion. In addition, the number of selected bits D' is fixed and applied to all samples, so both the memory footprint the computational cost of bits selection are $\mathcal{O}(N)$.

4. HAMMING DISTANCE MATCHING

In online search, we apply the dual selection scheme to query samples as well and perform search using the selected bits. As the selected components may vary in different samples, we have to address a challenging issue of matching descriptor across different Gaussian components. That is, given a query $\mathbf{x}_q$ and a dataset sample $\mathbf{x}_r$, if the selected Gaussian components are different, the similarity cannot be compared directly using standard Hamming distance. We adopt a normalized cosine similarity score Sc to calculate the distance matching, given by

$$Sc = \frac{\sum_{i=1}^{K} s_i^q s_i^r \left(D' - 2 * h\big(sgn(\mathbf{g}_i^{\mathbf{x}_q}), sgn(\mathbf{g}_i^{\mathbf{x}_r})\big)\right)}{D'\sqrt{||s^q||_0||s^r||_0}}, \tag{5}$$

where s_i^q and s_i^r denote whether the i-th Gaussian component is chosen for $\mathbf{x}_q$ and $\mathbf{x}_r$, respectively, and $h(\cdot,\cdot)$ is the Hamming distance between binarized Fisher subvectors. In practice, Sc is computed based on the overlapping Gaussians $s^q \bigcap s^r$ between $\mathbf{x}_q$ and $\mathbf{x}_r$.

5. EXPERIMENTS

In this section, extensive experiments are conducted to evaluate the proposed method in both computational efficiency and search performance. Our approach is implemented in C++. The experiments are performed on an Dell Precision workstation 7400-E5440 with 2.83GHz Intel XEON processor and 32GB RAM in a mode of single core and single thread.

5.1 Comparison with the state-of-the-art

We carry out retrieval experiments on MPEG-7 CDVS datasets and the publicly available INRIA Holidays dataset [9]. The MPEG-7 CDVS benchmark data set consists of 5 classes: graphics, paintings, video frames, landmarks, and common objects [4].

To fairly evaluate the performance over a large-scale dataset, we use *FLICKR1M* [8] as the distractor dataset, containing 1 million distractor images collected from Flickr. In the training phase, the codebook of GMM and component-specific bit selection matrix $\mathbf{W}$ are typically learned on the *FLICKR1M*. The retrieval performance is measured by mean Average Precision (mAP). We evaluate the proposed method against LSH [3], BPBC [6], PQ [10], RR+PQ [5, 18], ITQ [7] and BFV [1]. The SIFT from each image is extracted and then the dimensionality of SIFT is reduced to 64 by PCA. We employ FV encoding to aggregate the dim-reduced SIFT features

[1]In the BFV method, the raw FV is directly sign binarized to produce binary codes whose dimensionality is the same as the original FV, as described in Section 2.

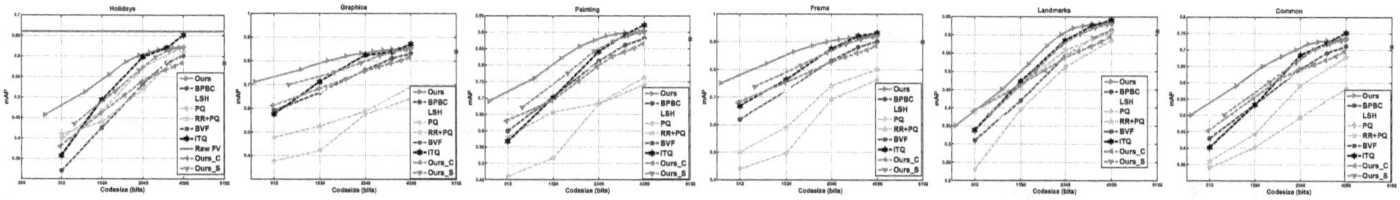

Figure 3: Retrieval performance in terms of mAP vs. descriptor codesize over various benchmark datasets. Note that we evaluate the uncompressed FV on the INRIA Holidays dataset. For MPEG CDVS datasets, we perform large scale retrieval by combining them with the 1 million FLICKR distractor dataset. In the BFV method, the raw FV is directly binarized by a sign function and thus the length of BFV is only 8192 (best viewed on high-resolution display).

Table 1: Comparison of descriptor compression ratio, additional compression time and memory footprint for FV compression between the proposed method and the baseline schemes, with comparable retrieval mAP, *e.g.*, about 51% on the INRIA Holidays dataset. Note that N, P, Q denote the dimensionality of FV, the target codesize and the size of vector quantization codebooks for the PQ method, respectively.

Method	Compression Ratio	Memory Cost		Compression Time	
		Theoretical	Practice (MB)	Theoretical	Practice (ms)
LSH	93.6	$\mathcal{O}(NP)$	91.8	$\mathcal{O}(NP)$	151
BPBC	154.2	$\mathcal{O}(\sqrt{N}\sqrt{P})$	0.031	$\mathcal{O}(N\sqrt{P}+P\sqrt{N})$	17
PQ	65.5	$\mathcal{O}(NQ)$	8.4	$\mathcal{O}(NQ)$	25
RR+PQ	65.5	$\mathcal{O}(NQ+N^2)$	277	$\mathcal{O}(NQ+N^2)$	278
ITQ	256	$\mathcal{O}(N^2)$	254	$\mathcal{O}(N^2)$	257
Ours	374.5	$\mathcal{O}(N)$	0.015	$\mathcal{O}(N)$	< 1

with 128 Gaussian components. Therefore, the total dimensionality of FV is $128 \times 64 = 8192$. Note that for compared methods, we apply power law ($\alpha = 0.5$) followed by $L2$ normalization to the raw FV feature.

Figure. 3 presents an extensive comparison between the proposed method and both the product quantization approaches and hashing algorithms, in terms of mAP vs. different codesize over different datasets. As it is computational expensive for $L2$ distance between uncompressed FV, we only present the retrieval accuracy of uncompressed FV on the INRIA Holidays dataset. We can see that RR+PQ obtains better mAP than PQ, but both of them perform significantly worse than the hashing algorithms (*e.g.,* LSH, ITQ and BPBC). The proposed method achieves superior accuracy than the other schemes, especially for small codesizes. Compared with the BFV, the codesize of our method can save about 3 times, while obtaining better retrieval performance. It should be emphasized that ITQ obtain best mAP for all datasets with large codesize such as 4096 bits. This is reasonable since ITQ is fine tuned for learning a projection to minimize the mean square error. However, ITQ suffers from the huge memory and computational footprints because of the projection matrix computation explained in Section 1.

5.2 Effectiveness of Dual Selection

In this section, we analyze two aspects of our method that are important for good retrieval results, *i.e.*, sample-specific component selection and component-specific bit selection. Note that the proposed method can be degraded to two simple models: Ours_S denotes an algorithm in which only the sample-specific component selection scheme is employed described in Section 3.1. Ours_C only uses the component-specific bit selection presented in Section 3.2.

From Figure 3, we observe that the Ours_S performs consistently better than Ours_C at the same codesize over all datasets (except the Landmarks at small codesize). In contrast, the proposed method significantly outperforms both Ours_S and Ours_C. For example, At codesize of 1920 bits, Ours_S and Ours_C yield mAP 79.2% and 75.6% on Graphics dataset, while our method achieves 83.2%. This gain may be attributed to the fact that the dual selection scheme is complementary to each other, which can select more informative bits. With more bits, Ours_S, Ours_C and the proposed schemes progressively improve the retrieval accuracy. In particular, Ours_S and our methods approach to the retrieval mAP of uncompressed FV at large codesize. They obtain mAP 62.1% at codesize of 3840 bits on the Holidays dataset, which is comparable with the mAP 66% of uncompressed FV.

5.3 Computational Complexity

We evaluate the compression complexity on the "Holidays + 1M Flickr" dataset [9]. Table 1 compares the compression ratio, memory and time complexities of the proposed method and other baselines, with comparable retrieval accuracy. With comparable retrieval mAP, we observe that the compression ratio of the proposed method is 2 to 6 times larger than the baseline schemes, resulting in much smaller compact codes. The memory footprint introduced by the our method is extremely low, *i.e.*, 0.015 MB (16 KB) for the globally bit selection mask. By contrast, RR+PQ and LSH cost over hundreds of megabytes to store the projection matrix. In addition, compression time of the proposed method is ultra fast, as there are only binarization and selection operations, while hashing methods and PQ involve a large amount of floating point multiplications.

6. CONCLUSION

In this paper, we have proposed an efficient and effective solution for learning compact binary codes to address the ANN problem with the long binary aggregated descriptor. We utilize both the sample-specific Gaussian component selection and the component-specific bit selection to produce a compact binary code. The proposed method exhibits extremely low compression memory and time complexity, and supports fast Hamming distance matching. Extensive experimental results demonstrate that our method has superior retrieval accuracy against the state-of-the-art methods such as hashing and PQ algorithms, while with fewer bits.

7. ACKNOWLEDGMENTS

This work was supported in part by Singapore Ministry of Education Academic Research Fund Tier 2 MOE2015-T2-2-114 and the National Basic Research Program of China (973 Program): No. 2015CB351806.

This research was carried out at the Rapid-Rich Object Search (ROSE) Lab at the Nanyang Technological University, Singapore. The ROSE Lab is supported by the National Research Foundation, Prime Ministers Office, Singapore, under its IDM Futures Funding Initiative and administered by the Interactive and Digital Media Programme Office.

8. REFERENCES

[1] A. Babenko and V. Lempitsky. Tree quantization for large-scale similarity search and classification. In *CVPR*, pages 4240–4248, 2015.

[2] D. Chen, S. Tsai, V. Chandrasekhar, G. Takacs, R. Vedantham, R. Grzeszczuk, and B. Girod. Residual enhanced visual vector as a compact signature for mobile visual search. *SP*, 93(8):2316–2327, 2013.

[3] M. Datar, N. Immorlica, P. Indyk, and V. S. Mirrokni. Locality-sensitive hashing scheme based on p-stable distributions. In *Proceedings of the twentieth annual symposium on Computational geometry*, pages 253–262. ACM, 2004.

[4] L.-Y. Duan, V. Chandrasekhar, J. Chen, J. Lin, Z. Wang, T. Huang, B. Girod, and W. Gao. Overview of the mpeg-cdvs standard. *TIP*, 25(1):179–194, Jan 2016.

[5] T. Ge, K. He, Q. Ke, and J. Sun. Optimized product quantization for approximate nearest neighbor search. In *CVPR*, pages 2946–2953. IEEE, 2013.

[6] Y. Gong, S. Kumar, H. Rowley, S. Lazebnik, et al. Learning binary codes for high-dimensional data using bilinear projections. In *CVPR*, pages 484–491. IEEE, 2013.

[7] Y. Gong, S. Lazebnik, A. Gordo, and F. Perronnin. Iterative quantization: A procrustean approach to learning binary codes for large-scale image retrieval. *TPAMI*, 35(12):2916–2929, 2013.

[8] M. J. Huiskes, B. Thomee, and M. S. Lew. New trends and ideas in visual concept detection: The mir flickr retrieval evaluation initiative. In *ACM MIR*, pages 527–536, 2010.

[9] H. Jegou, M. Douze, and C. Schmid. Hamming embedding and weak geometric consistency for large scale image search. In *ECCV*, pages 304–317. Springer, 2008.

[10] H. Jegou, M. Douze, and C. Schmid. Product quantization for nearest neighbor search. *TPAMI*, 33(1):117–128, 2011.

[11] H. Jégou, M. Douze, C. Schmid, and P. Pérez. Aggregating local descriptors into a compact image representation. In *CVPR*, pages 3304–3311. IEEE, 2010.

[12] H. Jégou, F. Perronnin, M. Douze, J. Sanchez, P. Perez, and C. Schmid. Aggregating local image descriptors into compact codes. *TPAMI*, 34(9):1704–1716, 2012.

[13] R. Ji, Y. Gao, W. Liu, X. Xie, Q. Tian, and X. Li. When location meets social multimedia: A survey on vision-based recognition and mining for geo-social multimedia analytics. *ACM TIST*, 6(1):1, 2015.

[14] P. Li, A. Shrivastava, J. L. Moore, and A. C. König. Hashing algorithms for large-scale learning. In *NIPS*, pages 2672–2680, 2011.

[15] Y. Li, R. Wang, Z. Huang, S. Shan, and X. Chen. Face video retrieval with image query via hashing across euclidean space and riemannian manifold. In *CVPR*, pages 4758–4767, 2015.

[16] J. Lin, L.-Y. Duan, Y. Huang, S. Luo, T. Huang, and W. Gao. Rate-adaptive compact fisher codes for mobile visual search. *SPL*, 21(2):195–198, 2014.

[17] W. Liu, C. Mu, S. Kumar, and S.-F. Chang. Discrete graph hashing. In *NIPS*, pages 3419–3427, 2014.

[18] M. Norouzi and D. J. Fleet. Cartesian k-means. In *CVPR*, pages 3017–3024. IEEE, 2013.

[19] O. M. Parkhi, K. Simonyan, A. Vedaldi, and A. Zisserman. A compact and discriminative face track descriptor. In *CVPR*, pages 1693–1700. IEEE, 2014.

[20] F. Perronnin, Y. Liu, J. Sánchez, and H. Poirier. Large-scale image retrieval with compressed fisher vectors. In *CVPR*, pages 3384–3391. IEEE, 2010.

[21] J. Sánchez, F. Perronnin, T. Mensink, and J. Verbeek. Image classification with the fisher vector: Theory and practice. *IJCV*, 105(3):222–245, 2013.

[22] R. Tao, A. W. Smeulders, and S.-F. Chang. Attributes and categories for generic instance search from one example. In *CVPR*, pages 177–186, 2015.

[23] J. Wang, J. Wang, J. Song, X.-S. Xu, H. T. Shen, and S. Li. Optimized cartesian k-means. *TKDE*, 27(1):180–192, 2015.

[24] Q. Wang, L. Si, and B. Shen. Learning to hash on structured data. In *AAAI*, 2015.

[25] S. Wang, W. Pedrycz, Q. Zhu, and W. Zhu. Subspace learning for unsupervised feature selection via matrix factorization. *PR*, 48(1):10–19, 2015.

[26] Z. Wang, L.-Y. Duan, J. Lin, X. Wang, T. Huang, and W. Gao. Hamming compatible quantization for hashing. In *AAAI*, pages 2298–2304, 2015.

[27] Y. Xia, K. He, P. Kohli, and J. Sun. Sparse projections for high-dimensional binary codes. In *CVPR*, pages 3332–3339, 2015.

[28] Y. Xu and W. Yin. A block coordinate descent method for regularized multiconvex optimization with applications to nonnegative tensor factorization and completion. *SIAM Journal on imaging sciences*, 6(3):1758–1789, 2013.

[29] T. Zhang, G.-J. Qi, J. Tang, and J. Wang. Sparse composite quantization. In *CVPR*, pages 4548–4556, 2015.

[30] Y. Zhang, J. Wu, and J. Cai. Compact representation for image classification: To choose or to compress? In *CVPR*, pages 907–914. IEEE, 2014.

Capped ℓ_p-Norm Graph Embedding for Photo Clustering

Mengfan Tang
mengfant@uci.edu
University of California, Irvine

Feiping Nie
feipingnie@gmail.com
Northwestern Polytechnical University, China

Ramesh Jain
jain@ics.uci.edu
University of California, Irvine

ABSTRACT

Photos are a predominant source of information on a global scale. Cluster analysis of photos can be applied to situation recognition and understanding cultural dynamics. Graph-based learning provides a current approach for modeling data in clustering problems. However, the performance of this framework depends heavily on initial graph construction by input data. Data outliers degrade graph quality, leading to poor clustering results. We designed a new capped ℓ_p-norm graph-based model to reduce the impact of outliers. This is accomplished by allowing the data graph to self adjust as part of the graph embedding. Furthermore, we derive an iterative algorithm to solve the objective function optimization problem. Experiments on four real-world benchmark data sets and Yahoo Flickr Creative Commons data set show the effectiveness of this new graph-based capped ℓ_p-norm clustering method.

Keywords

Photo clustering, unsupervised learning, capped ℓ_p-norm, Yahoo Flickr Creative Commons data

1. INTRODUCTION

As the web continually becomes more visual [6], photos serve dual roles. They are important for capturing, saving, sharing, and reminiscing memories of events and people. Moreover, photos have become a crucial objective resource of events [15]. They have been used for emerging applications such as event recognition [19], trend analysis [7], and cultural dynamics [5]. Social events and trends are usually detected by the concurrences of photo visual concepts. For example, "Olympics Games" is always associated with concepts of people, sport, bar and stadium, etc, evolving in a certain pattern. The event model of "Olympics Games" can be defined as bag of these photo visual concepts. Detection of events is then transformed to a photo clustering problem, in which each cluster represents an event [15].

MM '16, October 15-19, 2016, Amsterdam, Netherlands

DOI: http://dx.doi.org/10.1145/2964284.2967257

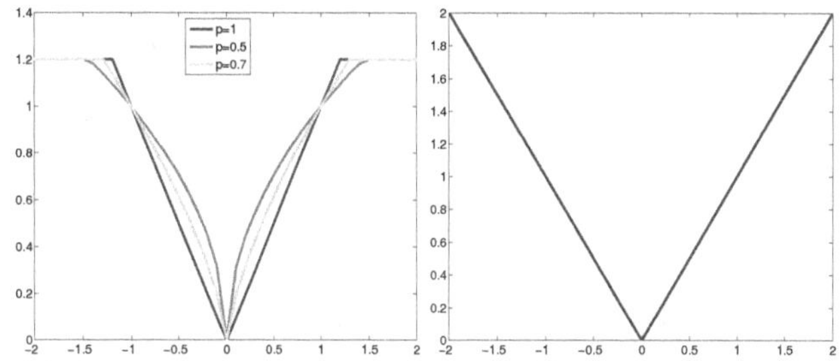

(a) Capped ℓ_p-norm loss with $\theta = 1$ (b) ℓ_1-norm loss

Figure 1: Comparison of Capped ℓ_p-norm and ℓ_1-norm

In the context of event and trend detection, photo clustering assigns photos to groups which share the same semantic concepts of the contents of photo. As an important topic in multimedia and vision, clustering analysis has been well studied. Many approaches from various angles have been proposed for efficient clustering analysis, such as K-means, support vector clustering, and spectral clustering. Among these approaches, spectral clustering, which has shown the state-of-the-art performance, models data into an efficient manifold. For instance, ratio cut clustering can be approximated by Laplacian embedding [2], and normalized cut clustering can be approximated by a generalized eigenvectors of Laplacian matrix [16]. Thus, graph-based learning provides an efficient way for modeling data in clustering problems. An important advantage of working with a graph is its capacity to incorporate diverse types of information, such as the relationship between data points [17]. Some of the existing graph-based models use a quadratic form of graph embedding. However, a major drawback is the sensitivity of results to outliers. A robust graph-based unsupervised learning method can alleviate this drawback through manipulation of metrics in noisy data. Among these methods, an important improvement is ℓ_0-norm. The ℓ_0-norm of vector F is defined as $\|F\|_0 = |\{i : f_i \neq 0\}| = n$, where n represents the number of important variables in the measurement. Models using this norm have demonstrated effective performance [21]. Unfortunately, computational expense increases when subset selection problems find the number of subset of cardinality n. To reduce the computational burden, the ℓ_0-norm has been replaced by some relaxations which approximate it. For example, ℓ_1-norm is a standard convex relaxation for ℓ_0-norm, in which ℓ_1-norm based objective functions lead to sparse and direct clustering results [22].

Other studies also use $\ell_{2,1}$-norm based objective function to reduce the impact of outliers [11]. Still these methods suffer from extreme data outliers. Thus, the performance of event and trend detection from these methods is also easily influenced by noisy outliers.

In this paper, we propose a novel noise resistant model. This model learns an efficient graph embedding by utilizing capped ℓ_p-norm to remove data outliers. As shown in Figure 1, the capped ℓ_p-norm loss function is $\min(|x|^p, \theta)$, where $0 < p \leq 2$. This function gives the value of $|x|^p$, when $|x|^p < \theta$, and θ, otherwise. The capped ℓ_p-norm effectively removes outliers and noise beyond the parameter θ. We use this property in projecting data into a manifold where the similarity of data points is adjusted without input from outliers. If the distance of a label vector is large, the corresponding similarity value is not updated. Additionally, an efficient iterative algorithm is adopted to solve the optimization problem. To verify the effectiveness and efficiency of the proposed model, we apply it to a few benchmark data sets and Yahoo Flickr Creative Commons data. This proposed method outperforms state-of-the-art approaches.

2. THE PROPOSED APPROACH

In this section, we present the noise resistant capped ℓ_p-norm unsupervised learning model. First, we introduce graph Laplacian unsupervised learning. Second, we give the formulation of the proposed model, followed by the optimized solutions.

2.1 Problem Formulation and Motivation

Suppose we have n data points $\{x_1, x_2, \cdots, x_n\} \in \mathcal{R}^{d\times 1}$. The main task of clustering is to group these n data points into c different clusters. Denote the cluster assignment matrix by $F = [f_1, \cdots, f_n]^T \in \{0,1\}^{n\times c}$, where f_i is the cluster assignment vector for the data point x_i. The j-th element of f_i is 1 if x_i belongs to cluster j, and is 0, otherwise. Given the data, a similarity matrix $W \in \mathcal{R}^{n\times n}$ can be defined. The element w_{ij} reflects affinity of x_i and x_j, which is the ij-th entry of matrix W. The Laplacian matrix L is defined as $L = D - W$, where D is a diagonal matrix with diagonal elements as $D_{ii} = \sum_j w_{ij}, \forall i$. Denote $Tr(L)$ as the trace operator of matrix L. The multi-way graph ratio-cut clustering is formulated to minimize $Tr(F^T LF)$. It's not a trival problem because the cluster assignment matrix is constrained to be an integer solution. With the relaxed continuous clustering assignment matrix $F \in \mathcal{R}^{n\times c}$, the relaxation form of the multi-way graph ratio-cut clustering is written in the following form,

$$\min_{F^T F=I} \sum_{i,j=1}^{n} w_{ij} \left\| f^i - f^j \right\|_2^2. \tag{1}$$

Another similar spectral clustering is Normalized Cut, and it can be written as,

$$\min_{F^T DF=I} \sum_{i,j=1}^{n} w_{ij} \left\| f^i - f^j \right\|_2^2. \tag{2}$$

The ideal solution of F is that $f^i = f^j$ if x_i and x_j are in the same cluster. In this case, rows of F are equal and thus F represents clustering structure. These two graph-based models use quadratic form of graph embedding, thus the results are sensitive to outliers. In order to overcome this problem, more robust graph-based unsupervised learning methods are proposed to handle such noisy data. Because ℓ_1-norm is more robust to outliers, some studies build models on top this norm. In [12], the authors propose ℓ_1-norm of spectral embedding in the following form.

$$\min_{F^T DF=I} \sum_{i,j=1}^{n} w_{ij} \left\| f^i - f^j \right\|_2. \tag{3}$$

However, this model still suffers from the effect of extreme outliers. Besides that, ℓ_1-based model is not stable comparing to ℓ_2-based model [20].

2.2 Graph-based Capped ℓ_p-Norm Method

Capped norm based loss function has been used for various purposes. For example, capped ℓ_1-norm is used for sparsity regularization [23]. Capped $\ell_{1,1}$-norm is proposed for multi-task learning [4]. Here, we use ℓ_p-norm as a robust and stable loss function to resist outliers and propose a new graph embedding model using this norm.

Capped norm based loss function of a c-dimensional vector $u \in \mathcal{R}^{1\times c}$ is $\min(\|u\|_2^p, \theta)$, where θ is a parameter. The value of this loss function is $\|u\|_2^p$, if $\|u\|_2^p$ is smaller than θ, and is θ, otherwise. This loss function is more robust to outliers than ℓ_1-norm because it has threshold θ for outliers.

The Proposed Capped ℓ_p-Norm Method is expressed as,

$$\min_{F^T F=I} \sum_{i,j} w_{ij} \min(\|f_i - f_j\|_2^p, \theta), \tag{4}$$

where w_{ij} is the similarity measurement in graph between x_i and x_j, $0 < p \leq 2$ and θ is a parameter.

The above formulation benefits from the input control of input data. The clustering results are dependent on the quality of input data graph. Most of time, they are sensitive to the particular graph construction methods. We overcome this problem from two perspectives, graph initialization and graph similarity adaptation. Because the objective function is not convex, when $p < 1$. It may not converge to the global minimum. The minimum value depends on the initialization. One of the ways to overcome the problem is to select some "good" graph initialization. We will introduce a method to give a "good" initialization. For the graph similarity adaptation, if distance of label vector is large, then the corresponding similarity value is not updated because of the capped norm.

2.3 Optimization Algorithm

In this subsection, we introduce the optimization algorithm to solve problem (4). Because the proposed model is a weighted sum of a concave function, it can be solved in a general re-weighted optimization framework [14].

The general re-weighted optimization problem is,

$$\min_{x\in\mathcal{C}} f(x) + \sum_i h_i(g_i(x)), \tag{5}$$

where $h_i(x)$ is an arbitrary concave function with the domain of $g_i(x)$. This general problem can be solved by Algorithm 1.

For problem (4), denote $h(x) = \min(x^{\frac{p}{2}}, \theta)$ and $x = \|f_i - f_j\|_2^2$. Because $h(x)$ is a concave function with respect to x, the supergradient of $h(x)$ can be obtained.

Algorithm 1: Solve Problem (5)

Initialize $X \in \mathcal{C}$;
repeat
  Calculate $D_i = h_i'(g_i(x))$
  Solve the following problem
  $\min_{x \in \mathcal{C}} f(x) + \sum_i Tr(D_i^T g_i(x))$
until *converge*;

$$h'(x) = \begin{cases} \frac{p}{2} x^{\frac{p-2}{2}} & x^{\frac{p}{2}} \leq \theta \\ 0 & \text{otherwise} \end{cases} \tag{6}$$

Problem (4) can be solved using Algorithm 1, because $h(x)$ is concave. The proposed model can be written in the following form,

$$\begin{aligned} \min_{F^T F = I} \sum_{i,j} w_{ij} h'(x) x &= \min_{F^T F = I} \sum_{i,j} w_{ij} s_{ij} \|f_i - f_j\|_2^2 \\ &= \min_{F^T F = I} \sum_{i,j} \tilde{s}_{ij} \|f_i - f_j\|_2^2 \\ &= \min_{F^T F = I} Tr(F^T L_{\tilde{s}} F), \end{aligned} \tag{7}$$

where $\tilde{s_{ij}} = w_{ij} s_{ij}$.

In the objective function, because an initial graph similarity matrix $W \in \mathcal{R}^{n \times n}$ is required, and the construction of graph plays key role in performance of graph-based clustering. We use the following Constrained Laplacian Rank method [13] to generate initial graph for the proposed model.

$$\min_{w_i^T 1 = 1, w_i \geq 0, w_{ii} = 0} \sum_{j=1}^{n} \|x_i - x_j\|_2^2 w_{ij} + \lambda \sum_{j=1}^{n} w_{ij}^2.$$

where w_i is the i-th row of similarity matrix W. Denote $e_{ij} = \|x_i - x_j\|_2^2$, and use Lagrangian method, the optimal similarities can be obtained,

$$\hat{w_{ij}} = \begin{cases} \frac{e_{i,m+1} - e_{ij}}{k e_{i,k+1} - \sum_{m=1}^{k} e_{ik}} & j \leq k \\ 0 & j > k \end{cases} \tag{8}$$

where k is the number of neighbors. Computing the similarity matrix always involves parameters, such as Gaussian functions. This above method has only one integer parameter: the number of neighbors, which is easier to tune. Besides that, because of the simplicity of computation of $\hat{w_{ij}}$, comparing to Gaussian functions, it can also be applied to construct large-scale graphs.

According to Algorithm 1, we have the following Algorithm 2 to solve Problem (4).

Algorithm 2: Solve Problem (4)

Initialize s_{ij} and set $s_{ij} = 1$;
Construct graph for $w_{ij} \in W$ using Equation (8).
repeat
  Calculate $\tilde{s}$ by $\tilde{s} = w_{ij} s_{ij}$
  Update F by $\min_{F^T F = I} Tr(F^T L_{\tilde{s}} F)$;
  Calculate $s_{ij} = \begin{cases} \frac{p}{2} \|f_i - f_j\|_2^{p-2} & \|f_i - f_j\|_2^p \leq \theta \\ 0 & \text{otherwise} \end{cases}$
until *converge*;

Table 1: Data Descriptions

Data set	# sample	# feature	# class
USPS	1000	784	10
BinAlpha	1014	320	36
COIL20	1440	1024	20
MNIST	2000	784	10
YFCC	3000	4096	10

We apply an iterative algorithm to solve the optimization problem (4). One of the most important aspects of iterative algorithm is convergence. Because the objective function is fit into the general optimization problem. Naturally, it is theoretically proved to converge [14].

3. EXPERIMENTS

In this section, we perform experiments on photo data sets to demonstrate the effectiveness of the proposed approach. For simplicity, we denote the proposed Capped ℓ_p-norm graph embedding method as CGE. The proposed model is compared with K-means, Ratio Cut [2], Normalized Cut [16] and ℓ_1-norm graph [12].

3.1 Data Description

Four benchmark data sets COIL20 [10], BinAlpha [3], USPS [8] and MNIST [9], one recent released multimedia data set YFCC100M [18] are used.

BinAlpha data contains 26 binary hand-written alphabets and 39 photos for each alphabet.

USPS is a handwritten digit database. We randomly select 100 photos for each digit, and totally 1000 photos for our experiments.

COIL20 contains different objects imaged at different angles in a 360 rotation.

MNIST is handwritten digits database. We randomly sample 200 photos for each group, and 2000 photos in total for the experiments.

YFCC contains around 99.2 million photos and nearly 800,000 videos from Flickr. For the purpose of experiments, we sample 3000 photos from ten concepts, "architecture", "plant","sport", "car", "food", "animal", "bike", "field game", "landscape" and "cloud". In addition, we use CaffeNet Hybrid-CNN as features for the experiments which is in 4096 dimension [1].

A summary of data information is shown in Table 1.

3.2 Experimental Settings

In this section, we present experimental study on various unsupervised methods such as K-means, ratio cut and normalized ratio cut, graph-based ℓ_1-norm model and the proposed model for clustering.

There are two parameters θ and p in CGE. We do cross validation to select the best parameter combination from the range $\theta = (0.1, 1, 10, 100, 1000)$ and $p = (0.5, 0.7, 1, 1.5, 1.7, 2)$.

Clustering algorithm K-means is used to get the final clustering results. Because the results of K-means depend on the initializations, we repeat K-means with 100 random initializations and report the results with the best objective values. We set K as the number of classes in the data sets. Clustering accuracy and normalized mutual information (NMI) are used to evaluate the performances.

Figure 2: Examples of outliers in YFCC data

Table 2: Clustering accuracy using K-means, Rcut [2], Ncut [16], L1G [12] and the proposed model CGE on five data sets.

Data	Accuracy				
	K-means	Rcut	Ncut	L1G	CGE
COIL20	0.6299	0.7896	0.8174	0.8229	**0.8451**
USPS	0.5910	0.6330	0.6220	0.6320	**0.6420**
BinAlpha	0.4131	0.5164	0.4986	0.4466	**0.5321**
MNIST	0.6015	0.6660	0.6605	0.6380	**0.6825**
YFCC	0.6534	0.7259	0.6099	0.5789	**0.7827**

Table 3: Clustering NMI K-means, Rcut [2], Ncut [16], L1G [12] and the proposed model CGE on the five data sets.

Data	Normalized Mutual Information				
	K-means	Rcut	Ncut	L1G	CGE
COIL20	0.7704	0.8950	0.8960	0.9052	**0.9136**
USPS	0.5827	0.7351	0.7136	0.7407	**0.7470**
BinAlpha	0.5758	0.6457	0.6107	0.6054	**0.6537**
MNIST	0.5042	0.6530	0.6508	0.6160	**0.6608**
YFCC	0.5940	0.6821	0.5486	0.5478	**0.6910**

3.3 Results

Next we evaluate the performance of the proposed model on four benchmark data sets by comparing it with other established models. Accuracy and normalized mutual information as listed in Tables 2 and 3 are utilized to measure the differences between the labels predicted by each model, and the benchmark labels actually observed. With respect to the accuracy, the proposed model CGE outperforms all other compared methods. For example, compared with the baseline Normalized Ratio Cut, CGE reduces testing error by 3.39%, 3.22%, 6.72% and 3.33%, respectively, on the four data sets. These results demonstrate the effectiveness of CGE in learning the intrinsic manifold projection. Similar to the performance on the accuracy, CGE holds the promise of enhancing NMI accuracy as well. Compared with its baseline Normalized Ratio Cut, the proposed model reduces error by 1.96%, 4.68%, 7.04% and 1.54%, respectively, as presented in Table 3, which further proves the effectiveness of our method in learning the intrinsic manifold projection.

We also experiment with data with extreme outliers, in particular, YFCC data. Each photo in YFCC is given a concept label, however, some photos are mislabeled. We call these photos outliers. Figure 2 shows example of outlier photos in dash red box from each concept. It is very clearly shown that outlier photos are irrelevant to the concept cluster they belong to. Regarding the established methods, L1G method obtains lower accuracy than K-means, and is not robust on YFCC. The main reason is that L1G is defined on ℓ_1-norm. Theories and experiments in [20] show that ℓ_1-based model cannot be stable. The proposed method leverages both stability and robustness to outliers to improve clustering of photos by using capped ℓ_p-norm. For example, compared with the baseline Ratio Cut, CGE reduces clustering error by 7.82%.

4. CONCLUSION

We present a new graph-based capped ℓ_p-norm model for photo clustering. It utilizes the properties of capped norm to remove the effect of outliers, and explore the underlying data structure in manifold to improve the performance of clustering. We develop an efficient iterative algorithm to solve the optimization problem for the proposed objective function. This algorithm updates similarity matrix in an adaptive way by ignoring the outliers and noise and performs effective data mapping in the nonlinear manifold. The experiments on photo data demonstrate effectiveness of the proposed method. A stream of photos from different people and different places creates a mosaic of world wide events as they happen. Accurate photo clustering will facilitate situation recognition in emerging applications in Web. The ℓ_p-norm model can also be used in semi-supervised learning setting. The semi-supervised learning framework can be applied to photo annotation, photo semantic index and search.

5. REFERENCES

[1] J. Bernd, D. Borth, C. Carrano, J. Choi, B. Elizalde, G. Friedland, L. Gottlieb, K. Ni, R. Pearce, D. Poland, et al. Kickstarting the commons: The yfcc100m and the yli corpora. In *Proceedings of the 2015 Workshop on Community-Organized Multimodal Mining: Opportunities for Novel Solutions*, pages 1–6. ACM, 2015.

[2] P. K. Chan, M. D. Schlag, and J. Y. Zien. Spectral k-way ratio-cut partitioning and clustering. *Computer-Aided Design of Integrated Circuits and Systems, IEEE Transactions on*, 13(9):1088–1096, 1994.

[3] O. Chapelle, B. Schölkopf, and A. Zien, editors. *Semi-Supervised Learning*. MIT Press, Cambridge, MA, 2006.

[4] P. Gong, J. Ye, and C.-s. Zhang. Multi-stage multi-task feature learning. In *Advances in Neural Information Processing Systems*, pages 1988–1996, 2012.

[5] N. Hochman and L. Manovich. Zooming into an instagram city: Reading the local through social media. *First Monday*, 18(7), 2013.

[6] R. Jain. Let's weave the visual web. *MultiMedia, IEEE*, 22(3):66–72, 2015.

[7] X. Jin, A. Gallagher, L. Cao, J. Luo, and J. Han. The wisdom of social multimedia: using flickr for prediction and forecast. In *Proceedings of the international conference on Multimedia*, pages 1235–1244. ACM, 2010.

[8] Y. LeCun, J. S. Denker, S. A. Solla, R. E. Howard, and L. D. Jackel. Optimal brain damage. In *NIPs*, volume 89, 1989.

[9] T. M. Mitchell. Machine learning. *Computer Science Series (McGraw-Hill, Burr Ridge, 1997) MATH*, 1997.

[10] S. A. Nene, S. K. Nayar, H. Murase, et al. Columbia object image library (coil-20). Technical report, technical report CUCS-005-96, 1996.

[11] F. Nie, H. Huang, X. Cai, and C. H. Ding. Efficient and robust feature selection via joint l2,1-norms minimization. In *Advances in neural information processing systems*, pages 1813–1821, 2010.

[12] F. Nie, H. Wang, H. Huang, and C. Ding. Unsupervised and semi-supervised learning via l1-norm graph. In *ICCV*, pages 2268–2273. IEEE, 2011.

[13] F. Nie, X. Wang, M. I. Jordan, and H. Huang. The constrained laplacian rank algorithm for graph-based clustering. In *AAAI*, 2016.

[14] F. Nie, J. Yuan, and H. Huang. Optimal mean robust principal component analysis. In *ICML*, pages 1062–1070, 2014.

[15] S. Pongpaichet, M. Tang, L. Jalali, and R. Jain. Using photos as micro-reports of events. In *Proceedings of the 2016 ACM on International Conference on Multimedia Retrieval*, pages 87–94. ACM, 2016.

[16] J. Shi and J. Malik. Normalized cuts and image segmentation. *Pattern Analysis and Machine Intelligence, IEEE Transactions on*, 22(8):888–905, 2000.

[17] M. Tang, P. Agrawal, F. Nie, S. Pongpaichet, and R. Jain. A graph based multimodal geospatial interpolation framework. In *2016 IEEE International Conference on Multimedia and Expo (ICME)*, pages 1–6. IEEE, 2016.

[18] B. Thomee, B. Elizalde, D. A. Shamma, K. Ni, G. Friedland, D. Poland, D. Borth, and L.-J. Li. Yfcc100m: The new data in multimedia research. *Communications of the ACM*, 59(2):64–73, 2016.

[19] Y. Wang and M. S. Kankanhalli. Tweeting cameras for event detection. In *Proceedings of the 24th International Conference on World Wide Web*, pages 1231–1241. International World Wide Web Conferences Steering Committee, 2015.

[20] H. Xu, C. Caramanis, and S. Mannor. Sparse algorithms are not stable: A no-free-lunch theorem. *Pattern Analysis and Machine Intelligence, IEEE Transactions on*, 34(1):187–193, 2012.

[21] M. Yang, L. Zhang, J. Yang, and D. Zhang. Robust sparse coding for face recognition. In *Computer Vision and Pattern Recognition (CVPR), 2011 IEEE Conference on*, pages 625–632. IEEE, 2011.

[22] G. Ye, M. Tang, J.-F. Cai, Q. Nie, and X. Xie. Low-rank regularization for learning gene expression programs. *PloS one*, 8(12):e82146, 2013.

[23] T. Zhang. Analysis of multi-stage convex relaxation for sparse regularization. *The Journal of Machine Learning Research*, 11:1081–1107, 2010.

Bidirectional Long-Short Term Memory for Video Description

Yi Bin[†], Yang Yang[†], Fumin Shen[†], Xing Xu[†], Heng Tao Shen[§,†]
[†]University of Electronic Science and Technology of China, Chengdu, China
[§]The University of Queensland, Brisbane, Australia
yi.bin@hotmail.com, {dlyyang, fumin.shen}@gmail.com
xing.xu@uestc.edu.cn, shenht@itee.uq.edu.au

ABSTRACT

Video captioning has been attracting broad research attention in multimedia community. However, most existing approaches either ignore temporal information among video frames or just employ local contextual temporal knowledge. In this work, we propose a novel video captioning framework, termed as *Bidirectional Long-Short Term Memory* (BiLSTM), which deeply captures bidirectional global temporal structure in video. Specifically, we first devise a joint visual modelling approach to encode video data by combining a forward LSTM pass, a backward LSTM pass, together with visual features from Convolutional Neural Networks (CNNs). Then, we inject the derived video representation into the subsequent language model for initialization. The benefits are in two folds: 1) comprehensively preserving sequential and visual information; and 2) adaptively learning dense visual features and sparse semantic representations for videos and sentences, respectively. We verify the effectiveness of our proposed video captioning framework on a commonly-used benchmark, i.e., Microsoft Video Description (MSVD) corpus, and the experimental results demonstrate that the superiority of the proposed approach as compared to several state-of-the-art methods.

CCS Concepts

•Computing methodologies → Visual content-based indexing and retrieval; Neural networks;

Keywords

Video captioning; bidirectional long-short term memory

1. INTRODUCTION

With the development of digital media technology and popularity of Mobile Internet, online visual content has increased rapidly in recent couple of years. Subsequently, visual content analysis for retrieving and understanding becomes a fundamental problem in the area of multimedia research, which has motivated world-wide researchers to develop advanced techniques. Most previous works, however, have focused on classification task [19, 20], such as annotating an image [9, 31, 32] or video [5, 17, 22, 29, 30] with given fixed label sets. With some pioneering methods [4, 14] tackling the challenge of describing images with natural language proposed, visual content understanding has attracted more and more attention. State-of-the-art techniques for image captioning have been surpassed by new advanced approaches in succession [2, 3, 8, 26, 28]. Recent researches [11, 15, 18, 24, 25, 34, 35] have been focusing on describing videos with more comprehensive sentences instead of simple keywords. Different from image, video is sequential data with temporal structure, which may pose significant challenge to video caption. Most of the existing works in video description employed max or mean pooling across video frames to obtain video-level representation, which failed to capture temporal knowledge. To address this problem, Yao et al. proposed to use 3-D Convolutional Neural Networks to explore local temporal information in video clips, where the most relevant temporal fragments were automatically chosen for generating natural language description with attention mechanism [34]. In [24], Venugopanlan et al. implemented a Long-Short Term Memory (LSTM) network, a variant of Recurrent Neural Networks (RNNs), to model the global temporal structure in whole video snippet. However, these methods failed to exploit bidirectional global temporal structure, which could benefit from not only previous video frames, but also information in future frames. Also, existing video captioning schemes cannot adaptively learn dense video representation and generate sparse semantic sentences.

In this work, we propose to construct a novel bidirectional LSTM (BiLSTM) network for video captioning. More specifically, we design a joint visual modelling to comprehensively explore bidirectional global temporal information in video data by integrating a forward LSTM pass, a backward LSTM pass, together with CNNs features. In order to enhance the subsequent sentence generation, the obtained visual representations are then fed into LSTM-based language model as initialization. We summarize the main contributions of this work as follows: (1) To our best knowledge, our approach is one of the first to utilize bidirectional recurrent neural networks for exploring bidirectional global temporal structure in video captioning; (2) We construct two sequential processing models for adaptive video representation learning and language description generation, respectively, rather than using the same LSTM for both video frames encoding and text decoding in [24]; and (3) Exten-

MM '16, October 15-19, 2016, Amsterdam, Netherlands
© 2016 ACM. ISBN 978-1-4503-3603-1/16/10...$15.00
DOI: http://dx.doi.org/10.1145/2964284.2967258

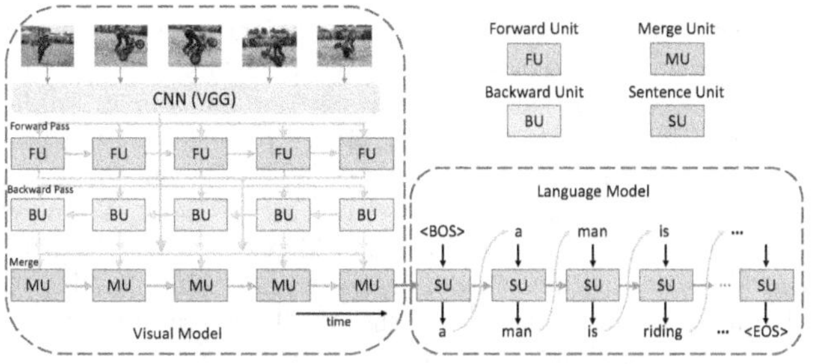

Figure 1: The overall flowchart of the proposed video captioning framework. We first extract CNNs features of video frames and feed them into forward pass networks (FU, green box) and backward pass networks (BU, yellow box). We then combine the outputs of hidden states together with the original CNNs features, and pass the integrated sequence to another LSTM (MU, blue box) to generate final video representation. We initialize language model (SU, pink box) with video representation and start to generate words sequentially with <BOS> token, and terminate the process until the <EOS> token is emitted.

sive experiments on a real-world video corpus illustrate the superiority of our proposal as compared to state-of-the-arts.

2. THE PROPOSED APPROACH

In this section, we elaborate the proposed video captioning framework, including an introduction of the overall flowchart (as illustrated in Figure 1), a brief review of LSTM-based Sequential Model, the joint visual modelling with bidirectional LSTM and CNNs, as well as the sentence generation process.

2.1 LSTM-based Sequential Model

With the success in speech recognition and machine translation tasks, recurrent neural structure, especially LSTM and its variants, have dominated sequence processing field. LSTM has been demonstrated to be able to effectively address the gradients vanishing or explosion problem [6] during back-propagation through time (BPTT) [27] and to exploit temporal dependencies in very long temporal structure. LSTM incorporates several control gates and a constant memory cell, the details of which are following:

$$i_t = \sigma\left(W_{ix}x_t + W_{ih}h_{t-1}\right), \quad (1)$$

$$f_t = \sigma\left(W_{fx}x_t + W_{ih}h_{t-1}\right), \quad (2)$$

$$o_t = \sigma\left(W_{ox}x_t + W_{oh}h_{t-1}\right), \quad (3)$$

$$c_t = f_t \odot c_{t-1} + i_t \odot \phi\left(W_{cx}x_t + W_{ch}h_{t-1}\right), \quad (4)$$

$$h_t = o_t \odot \phi\left(c_t\right), \quad (5)$$

where W_{mn}-like matrices are LSTM weight parameters, σ and ϕ are denote the sigmoid and hyperbolic non-linear functions, respectively, and $\odot$ indicates element-wise multiplication operation. Inspired by the success of LSTM, we devise an LSTM-based network to investigate the video temporal structure for video representation. Then initializing language model with video representation to generate video description.

2.2 Bidirectional Video Modelling

Different from other video description approaches that represent video by implementing pooling across frames [25] or 3-D CNNs with local temporal structure [15], we apply BiLSTM networks to exploit the bidirectional temporal structure of video clips. Convolutional Neural Networks (CNNs) has demonstrated overwhelming performance on image recognition, classification [9, 33] and video content analysis [3, 24]. Therefore, we extract caffe [7] $fc7$ layer of each frame through VGG-16 layers [21] caffemodel. Following [24, 25], we sample one frame from every ten frames in the video and extract the $fc7$ layer, the second fully-connected layer, to express selected frames. Then a T-by-4096 feature matrix generated to denote given video clip, where T is the number of frames we sampled in the video. As in Figure 1, we then implement two LSTMs, forward pass and backward pass, to encode CNNs features of video frames, and then merge the output sequences at each time point with a learnt weight matrix. What is interesting is that at each time point in bidirectional structure, we not only "see" the past frames, but also "peek" at the future frames. In other words, our bidirectional LSTM structure encodes video by scanning the entire video sequence several times (same as the number of time steps at encoding stage), and each scan is relevant to its adjacent scans. To investigate the effect of reinforcement of original CNNs feature, we combine the merged hidden states of BiLSTM structure and $fc7$ representation time step-wise. We further employ another forward pass LSTM network with incorporated sequence to generate our video representation. We represent the entire video clip using the state of memory cell and output of the last time point, and feed them into description generator as initialization of memory cell and hidden unit respectively.

2.3 Generating Video Description

Existing video captioning approaches usually share common part of visual model and language model as representation [15, 24], which may lead to severe information loss. Besides, they also input the same pooled visual vector of the whole video into every sentence processing unit, thereby ignoring temporal structure. Such methods may easily result in undesirable outputs due to the duplicate inputs in every time point of the new sequence [25]. To address these issues, we generate descriptions for video clips using a sequential model initialized with visual representation. Inspired by the superior performance of probabilistic sequence generation machine, we generate each word recurrently at each time point. Then the log probability of sentence S can be expressed as below:

$$\log p\left(S|V\right) = \sum_{t=1}^{t=N} \log p\left(w_t|V, w_1, ...w_{t-1}; \theta\right), \quad (6)$$

where θ denotes all parameters in sentence generation model and V is the representation of given video, and N indicates the number of words in sentence. We identify the most likely sentence by maximizing the log likelihood in Equation (6), then our object function can be described as:

$$\theta^* = \underset{\theta}{\operatorname{argmax}} \sum_{t=1}^{t=N} \log p\left(S|V; \theta\right). \quad (7)$$

The optimizer updates θ with θ^* across the entire training process applying Stochastic Gradient Descent (SGD). During training phrase, the loss is back propagated through time and each LSTM unit learns to derive an appropriate hidden representation h_t from input sequence. We then implement the Softmax function to get the probability distribution over the words in the entire vocabulary.

At the beginning of the sentence generation, as depicted in Figure 1, an explicit starting token (<BOS>) is needed and we terminate each sentence when the end-of-sentence token (<EOS>) is feeding in. During test phrase, similar to [24], our language model takes the word w_{t-1} with maximum likelihood as input at time t repeatedly until the <EOS> token is emitted.

3. EXPERIMENTS

3.1 Dataset

Video Dataset: We evaluate our approach by conducting experiments on the Microsoft Research Video Description (MSVD) [1] corpus, which is description for a collection of 1,970 video clips. Each video clip depicts a single action or a simple event, such as "shooting", "cutting", "playing the piano" and "cooking", which with the duration between 8 seconds to 25 seconds. There are roughly 43 available sentences per video and 7 words in each sentence at average. Following the majority of prior works [15, 24, 25, 34], we split entire dataset into training, validation and test set with 1200, 100 and 670 snippets, respectively.

Image Dataset: Comparing to other LSTM structure and deep networks, the size of video dataset for caption task is small, thereby we apply transferring learning from image description. COCO 2014 image description dataset [13] has been used to perform experiments frequently [2, 3, 8, 28], which consists of more than 120,000 images, about 82,000 and 40,000 images for training and test respectively. We pre-train our language model on COCO 2014 training set first, then transfer learning on MSVD with integral video description model.

3.2 Experimental Setup

3.2.1 Preprocessing

Description Processing: Some minimal preprocessing has been implemented to the descriptions in both MSVD and COCO 2014 datasets. We first employ *word_tokenize* operation in NLTK toolbox[1] to obtain individual words, and then convert all words to lower-case. All punctuation are removed, and then we start each sentence with <BOS> and end with <EOS>. Finally, we combine the sets of words in MSVD with COCO 2014, and generate a vocabulary with 12,984 unique words. Each word input to our system is represented by one-hot vector.

Video Preprocessing: As previous video description works [15, 24, 25] , we sample video frames once in every ten frames, then these frames could represent given video and 28.5 frames for each video averagely. We extract frame-wise caffe $fc7$ layer features using VGG-16 layers model, then feed the sequential feature into our video caption system.

3.2.2 Models

We employ a bidirectional S2VT [24] and a joint bidirectional LSTM structure to investigate the performance of our bidirectional approach. For convenient comparison, we set the size of hidden unit of all LSTMs in our system to 512 as [15, 24], except for the first video encoder in unidirectional joint LSTM. During training phrase, we set 80 as maximum number of time steps of LSTM in all our models and a mini-batch with 16 video-sentence pairs. We note that over 99% of the descriptions in MSVD and COCO 2014 contain no more than 40 words, and in [24], Venugopalan et al. pointed out that 94% of the YouTube training videos satisfy our maximum length limit. To ensure sufficient visual content, we adopt two ways to truncate the videos and sentences adaptively when the sum of the number of frames and words exceed the limit. If the number of words is within 40, we arbitrarily truncate the frames to satisfy the maximum length. When the length of sentence is more than 40, we discard the words that beyond the length and take video frames with a maximum number of 40.

Bidirectional S2VT: Similar to [24], we implement several S2VT-based models: S2VT, bidirectional S2VT and reinforced S2VT with bidirectional LSTM video encoder. We conduct experiment on S2VT using our video features and LSTM structure instead of the end-to-end model in [24], which need original RGB frames as input. For bidirectional S2VT model, we first pre-train description generator for image caption. We next implement forward and backward pass for video encoding and merge the hidden states step-wise with a learnt weight while the language layer receives merged hidden representation with null padded as words. We also pad the inputs of forward LSTM and backward LSTM with zeros at decoding stage, and concatenate the merged hidden states to embedded words. In the last model, we regard merged bidirectional hidden states as complementary enhancement and concatenate to original $fc7$ features to obtain a reinforced representation of video, then derive sentence from new feature using the last LSTM. The loss is computed only at decoding stage in all S2VT-based models.

Joint-BiLSTM: Different from S2VT-based models, we employ a joint bidirectional LSTM networks to encode video sequence and decode description applying another LSTM respectively rather than sharing the common one. We stack two layers of LSTM networks to encode video and pre-train language model as in S2VT-based models. Similarly, unidirectional LSTM, bidirectional LSTM and reinforced BiLSTM are executed to investigate the performance of each structure. We set 1024 hidden units of the first LSTM in unidirectional encoder so that the output could pass to the second encoder directly, and the memory cell and hidden state of the last time point are applied to initialize description decoder. Bidirectional structure and reinforced BiLSTM in encoder are implemented similarly to the corresponding type structure in S2VT-based models, respectively, and then feed the video representation into description generator as the unidirectional model aforementioned.

3.3 Results and Analysis

BLEU [16], METEOR [10], ROUGE-L [12] and CIDEr [23] are common evaluation metrics in image and video description, the first three were originally proposed to evaluate machine translation at the earliest and CIDEr was proposed to evaluate image description with sufficient reference sentences. To quantitatively evaluate the performance of our bidirectional recurrent based approach, we adopt METEOR metric because of its robust performance. Contrasting to

[1]http://www.nltk.org

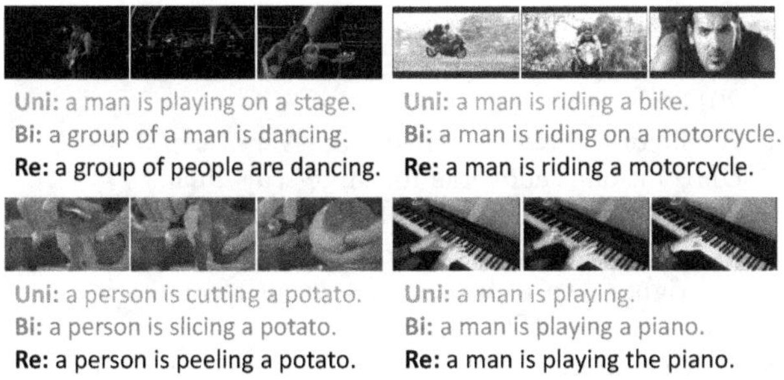

Figure 2: Video captioning examples of our proposed method. "Uni" in color blue, "Bi" in color brown and "Re" in color black are unidirectional Joint-LSTM, bidirectional Joint-LSTM and reinforced Joint-BiLSTM model, respectively.

Table 1: Comparison results of unidirectional, bidirectional structures and reinforced BiLSTM in both S2VT-based and joint LSTMs structure with METEOR (reported in percentage, higher is better).

Model	METEOR
S2VT-unidirectional	28.7
S2VT-bidirectional	28.6
S2VT-BiLSTM reinfored	**29.5**
Joint-LSTM unidirectional	29.5
Joint-LSTM bidirectional	29.9
Joint-BiLSTM reinforced	**30.3**

the other three metrics, METEOR could capture semantic aspect since it identifies all possible matches by extracting exact matcher, stem matcher, paraphrase matcher and synonym matcher using WordNet database, and compute sentence level similarity scores according to matcher weights. The authors of CIDEr also argued for that METEOR outperforms CIDEr when the reference set is small [23].

We first compare our unidirectional, bidirectional structures and reinforced BiLSTM. As shown in Table 1, in S2VT-based model, bidirectional structure performs very little lower score than unidirectional structure while it shows the opposite results in joint LSTM case. It may be caused by the pad at description generating stage in S2VT-based structure. We note that BiLSTM reinforced structure gains more than 3% improvement than unidirectional-only model in both S2VT-based and joint LSTMs structures, which means that combining bidirectional encoding of video representation is beneficial to exploit some additional temporal structure in video encoder (Figure 2). On structure level, Table 1 illustrates that our Joint-LSTMs based models outperform all S2VT based models correspondingly. It demonstrates our Joint-LSTMs structure benefits from encoding video and decoding natural language separately.

We also evaluate our Joint-BiLSTM structure by comparing with several other state-of-the-art baseline approaches, which exploit either local or global temporal structure. As shown in Table 2, our Joint-BiLSTM reinforced model outperforms all of the baseline methods. The result of "LSTM" in first row refer from [15] and the last row but one denotes the best model combining local temporal structure using C3D with global temporal structure utilizing temporal attention in [34]. From the first two rows, our unidirectional joint LSTM shows rapid improvement, and comparing with S2VT-VGG model in line 3, it also demonstrates some superiority. Even LSTM-E jointly models video and descriptions representation by minimizing the distance between video and corresponding sentence, our Joint-BiLSTM reinforced obtains better performance from bidirectional encoding and separated visual and language models.

Table 2: Comparing with several state-of-the-art models (reported in percentage, higher is better).

Model	METEOR
LSTM	26.9
Joint-LSTM unidirectinal (ours)	29.5
S2VT [24]	
-RGB (VGG)	29.2
-RGB (VGG)+Flow (AlexNet)	29.8
LSTM-E (VGG) [15]	29.5
LSTM-E (C3D) [15]	29.9
Yao et al. [34]	29.6
Joint-BiLSTM reinforced (ours)	**30.3**

We observed that while our unidirectional S2VT has the same deployment as [24], our model gives a little poorer performance(line 1, Table 1 and line 3, Table 2). As mentioned in Section 3.2.2, they employed an end-to-end model reading original RGB frames and fine-tuning on the VGG caffemodel. The features of frames from VGG $fc7$ layer are more compatible to MSVD dataset and the description task. However, our joint LSTM demonstrates better performance with general features rather than specific ones for data, even superior to their model with multiple feature aspects (RGB + Flow, line 4, Table 2), which means that our Joint-BiLSTM could show more powerful descriptive ability in end-to-end case. Certainly, We would investigate effect of end-to-end type of our Joint-BiLSTM in future works.

4. CONCLUSION AND FUTURE WORKS

In this paper, we introduced a sequence to sequence approach to describe video clips with natural language. The core of our method was, we applied two LSTM networks for the visual encoder and natural language generator component of our model. In particular, we encoded video sequences with a bidirectional Long-Short Term Memory (BiLSTM) network, which could effectively capture the bidirectional global temporal structure in video. Experimental results on MSVD dataset demonstrated the superior performance over many other state-of-the-art methods.

We also note some limitations in our model, such as end-to-end framework employed in [24] and distance measured in [15]. In the future we will make more effort to fix these limitations and exploit the linguistic domain knowledge in visual content understanding.

5. ACKNOWLEDGMENTS

This work was supported in part by the National Natural Science Foundation of China under Project 61572108 and Project 61502081, the National Thousand-Young-Talents Program of China, and the Fundamental Research Funds for the Central Universities under Project ZYGX2014Z007 and Project ZYGX2015J055.

6. REFERENCES

[1] D. L. Chen and W. B. Dolan. Collecting highly parallel data for paraphrase evaluation. In *ACL*, pages 190–200, 2011.

[2] X. Chen and C. Lawrence Zitnick. Mind's eye: A recurrent visual representation for image caption generation. In *CVPR*, pages 2422–2431, 2015.

[3] J. Donahue, L. Anne Hendricks, S. Guadarrama, M. Rohrbach, S. Venugopalan, K. Saenko, and T. Darrell. Long-term recurrent convolutional networks for visual recognition and description. In *CVPR*, pages 2625–2634, 2015.

[4] A. Farhadi, M. Hejrati, M. A. Sadeghi, P. Young, C. Rashtchian, J. Hockenmaier, and D. Forsyth. Every picture tells a story: Generating sentences from images. In *ECCV*, pages 15–29. 2010.

[5] C. Gan, N. Wang, Y. Yang, D.-Y. Yeung, and A. G. Hauptmann. Devnet: A deep event network for multimedia event detection and evidence recounting. In *CVPR*, pages 2568–2577, 2015.

[6] S. Hochreiter and J. Schmidhuber. Long short-term memory. *Neural computation*, 9(8):1735–1780, 1997.

[7] Y. Jia, E. Shelhamer, J. Donahue, S. Karayev, J. Long, R. Girshick, S. Guadarrama, and T. Darrell. Caffe: Convolutional architecture for fast feature embedding. In *ACM Multimedia*, pages 675–678, 2014.

[8] A. Karpathy and L. Fei-Fei. Deep visual-semantic alignments for generating image descriptions. In *CVPR*, pages 3128–3137, 2015.

[9] A. Krizhevsky, I. Sutskever, and G. E. Hinton. Imagenet classification with deep convolutional neural networks. In *NIPS*, pages 1097–1105, 2012.

[10] M. D. A. Lavie. Meteor universal: language specific translation evaluation for any target language. 2014.

[11] G. Li, S. Ma, and Y. Han. Summarization-based video caption via deep neural networks. In *ACM Multimedia*, pages 1191–1194, 2015.

[12] C.-Y. Lin. Rouge: A package for automatic evaluation of summaries. In *ACL*, 2004.

[13] T.-Y. Lin, M. Maire, S. Belongie, J. Hays, P. Perona, D. Ramanan, P. Dollár, and C. L. Zitnick. Microsoft coco: Common objects in context. In *ECCV*, pages 740–755. 2014.

[14] V. Ordonez, G. Kulkarni, and T. L. Berg. Im2text: Describing images using 1 million captioned photographs. In *NIPS*, pages 1143–1151, 2011.

[15] Y. Pan, T. Mei, T. Yao, H. Li, and Y. Rui. Jointly modeling embedding and translation to bridge video and language. In *CVPR*, pages 4594–4602, 2016.

[16] K. Papineni, S. Roukos, T. Ward, and W.-J. Zhu. Bleu: a method for automatic evaluation of machine translation. In *ACL*, pages 311–318, 2002.

[17] V. Ramanathan, P. Liang, and L. Fei-Fei. Video event understanding using natural language descriptions. In *ICCV*, pages 905–912, 2013.

[18] A. Rohrbach, M. Rohrbach, N. Tandon, and B. Schiele. A dataset for movie description. In *CVPR*, pages 3202–3212, 2015.

[19] F. Shen, W. Liu, S. Zhang, Y. Yang, and H. T. Shen. Learning binary codes for maximum inner product search. In *ICCV*, pages 4148–4156, 2015.

[20] F. Shen, C. Shen, W. Liu, and H. Tao Shen. Supervised discrete hashing. In *CVPR*, pages 37–45, 2015.

[21] K. Simonyan and A. Zisserman. Very deep convolutional networks for large-scale image recognition. *CoRR*, abs/1409.1556, 2014.

[22] K. Tang, B. Yao, L. Fei-Fei, and D. Koller. Combining the right features for complex event recognition. In *ICCV*, pages 2696–2703, 2013.

[23] R. Vedantam, C. Lawrence Zitnick, and D. Parikh. Cider: Consensus-based image description evaluation. In *CVPR*, pages 4566–4575, 2015.

[24] S. Venugopalan, M. Rohrbach, J. Donahue, R. Mooney, T. Darrell, and K. Saenko. Sequence to sequence-video to text. In *ICCV*, pages 4534–4542, 2015.

[25] S. Venugopalan, H. Xu, J. Donahue, M. Rohrbach, R. Mooney, and K. Saenko. Translating videos to natural language using deep recurrent neural networks. In *NAACL HLT*, 2015.

[26] O. Vinyals, A. Toshev, S. Bengio, and D. Erhan. Show and tell: A neural image caption generator. In *CVPR*, pages 3156–3164, 2015.

[27] P. J. Werbos. Backpropagation through time: what it does and how to do it. *Proceedings of the IEEE*, 78(10):1550–1560, 1990.

[28] K. Xu, J. Ba, R. Kiros, K. Cho, A. Courville, R. Salakhudinov, R. Zemel, and Y. Bengio. Show, attend and tell: Neural image caption generation with visual attention. In *ICML*, pages 2048–2057, 2015.

[29] X.-S. Xu, Y. Jiang, X. Xue, and Z.-H. Zhou. Semi-supervised multi-instance multi-label learning for video annotation task. In *ACM Multimedia*, pages 737–740, 2012.

[30] X.-S. Xu, X. Xue, and Z.-H. Zhou. Ensemble multi-instance multi-label learning approach for video annotation task. In *ACM Multimedia*, pages 1153–1156, 2011.

[31] Y. Yang, Y. Gao, H. Zhang, J. Shao, and T.-S. Chua. Image tagging with social assistance. In *ICMR*, page 81, 2014.

[32] Y. Yang, Z.-J. Zha, Y. Gao, X. Zhu, and T.-S. Chua. Exploiting web images for semantic video indexing via robust sample-specific loss. *IEEE Transactions on Multimedia*, 16(6):1677–1689, 2014.

[33] Y. Yang, H. Zhang, M. Zhang, F. Shen, and X. Li. Visual coding in a semantic hierarchy. In *ACM Multimedia*, pages 59–68, 2015.

[34] L. Yao, A. Torabi, K. Cho, N. Ballas, C. Pal, H. Larochelle, and A. Courville. Describing videos by exploiting temporal structure. In *ICCV*, pages 4507–4515, 2015.

[35] H. Yu, J. Wang, Z. Huang, Y. Yang, and W. Xu. Video paragraph captioning using hierarchical recurrent neural networks. In *CVPR*, pages 4584–4593, 2016.

A Robust Distance with Correlated Metric Learning for Multi-Instance Multi-Label Data

Yashaswi Verma
CVIT, IIIT Hyderabad, India
yashaswi.verma@research.iiit.ac.in

C. V. Jawahar
CVIT, IIIT Hyderabad, India
jawahar@iiit.ac.in

ABSTRACT

In multi-instance data, every object is a bag that contains multiple elements or instances. Each bag may be assigned to one or more classes, such that it has at least one instance corresponding to every assigned class. However, since the annotations are at bag-level, there is no direct association between the instances within a bag and the assigned class labels, hence making the problem significantly challenging.

While existing methods have mostly focused on Bag-to-Bag or Class-to-Bag distances, in this paper, we address the multiple instance learning problem using a novel Bag-to-Class distance measure. This is based on two observations: (a) existence of outliers is natural in multi-instance data, and (b) there may exist multiple instances within a bag that belong to a particular class. In order to address these, in the proposed distance measure (a) we employ L_1-distance that brings robustness against outliers, and (b) rather than considering only the most similar instance-pair during distance computation as done by existing methods, we consider a subset of instances within a bag while determining its relevance to a given class. We parameterize the proposed distance measure using class-specific distance metrics, and propose a novel metric learning framework that explicitly captures inter-class correlations within the learned metrics. Experiments on two popular datasets demonstrate the effectiveness of the proposed distance measure and metric learning.

CCS Concepts

•**Computing methodologies** → *Computer vision tasks; Machine learning;*

Keywords

Multiple instance learning; Distance metric learning

1. INTRODUCTION

In the conventional image categorization task, each image is considered as a single instance, and is assigned to one (single-instance single-label problem) or more (single-instance multi-label problem) classes. However, this ignores the fact that usually only some region(s) in an image correspond(s) to a particular semantic concept. E.g., as shown in Figure 1, though the images are tagged with several classes, each of these concepts represent only few specific region(s).

Figure 1: Samples from IAPR TC-12 dataset [6], which show that a whole image is not representative of all the assigned classes. Moreover, there could be multiple instances within an image that denote a particular semantic concept. E.g., there are multiple segments in the left and right pairs that belong to the classes "people" and "car" respectively.

Multiple Instance Learning (MIL) [2] is a machine learning paradigm that has lately achieved significant attention [17, 8, 10, 11, 1, 19, 14, 16, 15]. In MIL, each object/sample is assumed to be a bag consisting of a collection of instances, and is assigned to one or more classes such that there is at least one instance corresponding to every assigned class. MIL framework has been shown to be particularly useful for capturing inherent structure in data, such as indirect associations between an image's regions and its assigned classes [8, 14, 15], or reducing the labeling cost of videos [16]. However, along with these advantages, it also presents several challenges [8, 10, 14, 16, 15]. First, computing distance between two object-bags is not straightforward since they are *bags* of multiple instances rather than a single instance, and traditional distance measures such as Manhattan distance or Euclidean distance cannot be applied directly. Second, there exists a weak association between the instances of a bag and the classes assigned to it. Due to this, learning class-specific models remains non-trivial. And third, by the definition of MIL, an object bag is assigned to a class if at least one of its instances belongs to that class. In such a scenario, most of the other instances which do not represent that class act as outliers for the class under consideration.

MM '16, October 15-19, 2016, Amsterdam, Netherlands
© 2016 ACM. ISBN 978-1-4503-3603-1/16/10...$15.00
DOI: http://dx.doi.org/10.1145/2964284.2967259

Most of the existing MIL methods [17, 8, 10, 19, 14, 16, 15] have focused on developing sophisticated distance measures, and/or learning dataset-specific or class-specific distance metrics (also called metric learning) for MIL. While metric learning for single-instance data (single-label [5, 4, 18] or multi-label [7, 13]) is a well-studied topic, there have been few attempts that perform metric learning for multi-instance data. The first metric learning formulation for multi-instance data was proposed in [10]. Since it is based on computing bag-to-bag (or B2B) distance, there exists no direct association between instances within a bag and their class labels. Hence, to overcome this, it learns a single distance metric by simultaneously learning associations between instances and class labels, which results into a complex optimization problem. After this, few other methods have focused on learning distance metric for multi-instance data by using either B2B distance [8] or class-to-bag (or C2B) distance [14, 16, 15]. Since [14, 16, 15] are based on C2B distance, they were able to learn class-specific distance metrics unlike [10]. They represent every class by a *super-bag*, which consists of all the instances from the object-bags that belong to that class. Given a new object bag and a particular class, its distance from every instance of the corresponding super-bag is computed using the class-specific distance metric. Finally, the classes are assigned based on decreasing order of their distance from that object bag.

In this paper, we present a novel bag-to-class (or B2C) distance measure for computing distance of an object-bag from a super-bag. The major differences between the proposed distance measure and those in the earlier works are:
(1) Instead of using L_2-distance [17, 8, 10, 14, 16, 15], we propose to use L_1-distance while computing distance between two instances. This is because L_1-distance is known to be more robust against outliers than L_2-distance, which are frequent in multi-instance data.
(2) Rather than using C2B distance [14, 15, 16] or B2B distance [10, 8], our distance measure is based on computing B2C distance. This is because while C2B distance may be affected by the presence of large number of outliers within a super-bag, B2B distance complicates learning distance metrics since it requires computing distance between bags belonging to different classes which involves distance metrics from different classes (as also mentioned in [15]).
(3) While existing methods such as [8, 10, 14, 16, 15] consider only the single most similar pair of instances for computing C2B or B2B distance, we compute the distance of an object-bag from a given super-bag based on a subset of top few instances from both the sets that are most similar to each other, with similarity being computed from object-bag towards super-bag. This is based on the observation that there could be multiple instances within a bag that denote a particular semantic concept (Figure 1). Each of these in turn may match with a potentially different subset of instances within the super-bag under consideration. We believe that this further adds robustness to our distance measure since instead of relying only on the most similar instance which may be an outlier, we consider a set of top few most similar instances while computing the B2C distance.

Due to these considerations specifically adopted to introduce robustness while computing distance in MIL setting, we call our proposed distance as Robust B2C (or RB2C) distance. Other important contributions of this work are: (1) Similar to [14, 16, 15], we integrate class-specific distance metrics into RB2C-distance. (2) We formulate a novel metric learning framework that explicitly captures inter-class correlations, which are particularly observed in multi-label datasets. To our knowledge, this is the first metric learning formulation of its kind in this domain.

To validate our approach, we extensively experiment on two popular multi-label datasets: Corel-5K [3] and IAPR TC-12 [6]. Experiments demonstrate that the baseline RB2C-distance itself outperforms most of the existing techniques, and achieves further improvements after incorporating learned distance metrics.

2. PROPOSED DISTANCE MEASURE

In this section, first we briefly discuss the multi-instance setting [14, 15, 16]. Then, we describe the proposed RB2C-distance for multi-instance data.

2.1 Preliminaries

Let $\mathcal{D} = \{(X_1, \mathbf{y}_1), \dots, (X_{|\mathcal{D}|}, \mathbf{y}_{|\mathcal{D}|})\}$ be a dataset consisting of $|\mathcal{D}|$ input-output pairs and L classes. Each $X_i = [\mathbf{x}_{i1}, \dots, \mathbf{x}_{in_i}]$ is a bag of n_i instances, where $\mathbf{x}_{ij}$ is the jth instance of X_i and is represented by an N-dimensional feature vector ($\mathbf{x}_{ij} \in \mathbb{R}^N \ \forall j = \{1, \dots, n_i\}$). Each output vector $\mathbf{y}_i \in \{0, 1\}^L$ is a binary vector. Under the MIL setting, for a given bag X_i, if $\exists j \in \{1, \dots, n_i\}$ such that the instance $\mathbf{x}_{ij}$ belongs to the lth class ($1 \leq l \leq L$), then the whole bag X_i belongs to the lth class and $\mathbf{y}_i(l) = 1$; otherwise $\mathbf{y}_i(l) = 0$. Also, if $\sum_{l=1}^{L} \mathbf{y}_i(l) = 1, \forall i \in \{1, \dots, |\mathcal{D}|\}$, then each bag X_i belongs to exactly one class and the dataset $\mathcal{D}$ is a single-label dataset. While, if $\sum_{l=1}^{L} \mathbf{y}_i(l) \geq 1 \ \forall i \in \{1, \dots, |\mathcal{D}|\}$, then each bag X_i may belong to one or more classes, and the dataset $\mathcal{D}$ is a multi-label dataset. Thus, single-label data is a special case of multi-label data.

2.2 Robust B2C Distance for MIL

Let each class l be represented by a super-bag U_l that consists of all instances from all the training bags that belong to that class [14, 15, 16]. Precisely,

$$U_l = \{\mathbf{x}_{ij} \mid \mathbf{y}_i(l) = 1\} \tag{1}$$

Let $m_l = |U_l| = \sum_{i \mid \mathbf{y}_i(l)=1} n_i$ be the size of the super-bag U_l. In case of single-label data where each bag belongs to exactly one class, all the super-bags are non-overlapping; i.e., (i) $\sum_{j=1}^{|\mathcal{D}|} n_j = \sum_{l=1}^{L} m_l$, and (ii) $|U_g \cap U_h| = 0, \forall\, g \neq h$. Whereas, in case of multi-label data where each bag may be labeled with one or more classes, there may be an overlap among different super-bags; i.e., (i) $\sum_{j=1}^{|\mathcal{D}|} n_j \leq \sum_{l=1}^{L} m_l$, and (ii) $|U_g \cap U_h| \geq 0, \forall\, g \neq h$.

Based on this, now we present the RB2C-distance for MIL. Given an object bag $A = [\mathbf{a}_1, \dots, \mathbf{a}_{n_A}]$ and a class l, let $\mathbf{d}_{ilj}^{A} \in \mathbb{R}^N$ denote element-wise L_1-distance between an instance $\mathbf{a}_i$ of A and an instance $\mathbf{x}_{lj} \in U_l$. Precisely,

$$\mathbf{d}_{ilj}^{A}(k) = |\mathbf{a}_i(k) - \mathbf{x}_{lj}(k)|, \ \forall\, k \in \{1, \dots, N\} \tag{2}$$

Using this, distance between the instances $\mathbf{a}_i$ and $\mathbf{x}_{lj}$ (instance-to-instance distance or D_{i2i}) is defined as

$$D_{i2i}(\mathbf{a}_i, \mathbf{x}_{lj}) = \sum_{k=1}^{N} |\mathbf{a}_i(k) - \mathbf{x}_{lj}(k)| = \mathbf{e}^T \mathbf{d}_{ilj}^{A}\ , \tag{3}$$

where $\mathbf{e} = [1, \dots, 1]^T$ is a vector with all entries equal to 1. Let $\mathcal{N}_{il}^{K_1} \subseteq U_l$ be the set of the top K_1 nearest-neighbours of

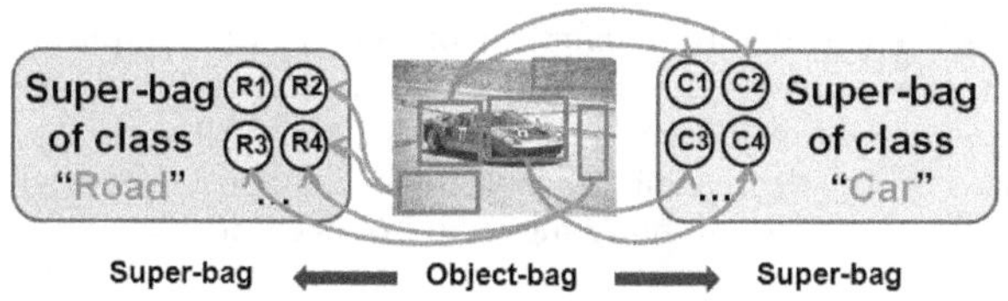

Figure 2: The proposed RB2C-distance is based on the assumption that a bag may have multiple instances (illustrated by red boxes) that represent some particular class. Additionally, each of these instances may match with a potentially different (may or may not be disjoint) subset of instances within the super-bag of the concerned class. E.g., in this figure, there are two instances in the object-bag that match with the super-bag of "car". Moreover, each of these matched instances match with two distinct sets of instances $\{C_1, C_2\}$ and $\{C_3, C_4\}$. Note that in both the datasets used in our experiments, an instance is a segment of an image. Here we use box just for illustrative purpose.

$\mathbf{a}_i$ from the super-bag U_l determined using Eq. 3. Then, the distance of instance $\mathbf{a}_i$ from super-bag U_l (instance-to-class distance or D_{i2c}) is defined as:

$$D_{i2c}(\mathbf{a}_i, U_l) = \frac{1}{K_1} \sum_{\mathbf{x}_{lj} \in \mathcal{N}_{il}^{K_1}} D_{i2i}(\mathbf{a}_i, \mathbf{x}_{lj}) \,. \tag{4}$$

Now, let $\mathcal{N}_l^{K_2}$ be the set that contains the top K_2 instances of A with least distance from super-bag U_l computed using Eq. 4. Then, distance of A from U_l (bag-to-class distance or D_{b2c}) is defined as:

$$D_{b2c}(A, U_l) = \frac{1}{K_2} \sum_{\mathbf{a}_i \in \mathcal{N}_l^{K_2}} D_{i2c}(\mathbf{a}_i, U_l) \,. \tag{5}$$

Substituting Eq. 3 and Eq. 4 into the above equation gives

$$D_{b2c}(A, U_l) = \frac{1}{K_1 K_2} \; \mathbf{e}^T \left(\sum_{\mathbf{a}_i \in \mathcal{N}_l^{K_2}} \sum_{\mathbf{x}_{lj} \in \mathcal{N}_{il}^{K_1}} \mathbf{d}_{ilj}^A \right) . \tag{6}$$

The distance function defined by the above equation is our proposed RB2C-distance. Intuitively, it computes distance of a given object from a class based on distance between the few instances from both the bags that are most similar to each other, with similarity being computed from object bag towards super-bag. Figure 2 illustrates the gist of RB2C-distance for multi-instance data.

3. METRIC LEARNING FOR RB2C

The distance function defined in Eq. 6 is based on simple L_1-distance that considers every dimension of a feature vector as equally important. However, it is well-known that computing distance in a learned projected space better captures data properties as compared to unprojected space, and hence also improves quantitative performance. Here we discuss how to learn linear distance metrics for the proposed RB2C-distance. Also, since there exists large diversity among samples from different classes, we learn L different class-specific metrics $\mathbf{w}_l \in \mathbb{R}^N$, $\forall\, l \in \{1, \ldots, L\}$. For this, we re-define the distance in Eq. 6 as:

$$\overset{\mathbf{w}}{D}_{b2c}(A, U_l) = \frac{1}{K_1 K_2} \; \mathbf{w}_l^T \left(\sum_{\mathbf{a}_i \in \mathcal{N}_l^{K_2}} \sum_{\mathbf{x}_{lj} \in \mathcal{N}_{il}^{K_1}} \mathbf{d}_{ilj}^A \right) . \tag{7}$$

We shall refer this as metric based RB2C-distance (or M-RB2C). To learn the metrics $\mathbf{w}_l$ $\forall l \in \{1, \ldots, L\}$, we follow the approach of metric learning using pair-wise comparisons [18, 4, 5, 13]. For a given bag A, let $L_A^+ \subseteq \{1, \ldots, L\}$ be the set of classes to which it belongs; and $L_A^- = \{1, \ldots, L\} \setminus L_A^+$ be the set of classes to which it does not belong. We are interested in learning $\mathbf{w}_l$'s such that the distance of A from U_l $\forall\, l \in L_A^+$ is less than its distance from U_k $\forall\, k \in L_A^-$ by a margin. This results in the following constraints:

$$\forall l \in L_A^+, \forall\, k \in L_A^- : \;\; \overset{\mathbf{w}}{D}_{b2c}(A, U_k) - \overset{\mathbf{w}}{D}_{b2c}(A, U_l) \geq 1 - \xi_{kl}^A \tag{8}$$

Let $\mathbf{W} = [\mathbf{w}_1, \ldots, \mathbf{w}_L] \in \mathbb{R}^{N \times L}$ be the concatenation of all class-specific metrics. Based on the above constraints, we solve the following convex optimization problem:

$$OP1: \min_{\mathbf{W}, \xi_{kl}^A \geq 0} \; \frac{1}{2} Trace(\mathbf{W}^T \mathbf{W}) + C \sum_{A, l \in L_A^+, k \in L_A^-} \xi_{kl}^A$$

$$s.t. \;\; \forall A, l \in L_A^+, k \in L_A^- : \overset{\mathbf{w}}{D}_{b2c}(A, U_k) - \overset{\mathbf{w}}{D}_{b2c}(A, U_l) \geq 1 - \xi_{kl}^A$$
$$\forall\, 1 \leq l \leq L, \; 1 \leq i \leq N : \;\; \mathbf{w}_l(i) \geq 0$$

where ξ_{kl}^A are slack variables, and $C > 0$ is a constant that controls the trade-off between the two terms. The second set of constraints impose non-negativity on the elements of $\mathbf{w}_l$. This is necessary since it is used to define a distance metric, which should be a positive semi-definite operator. We optimize $OP1$ in the primal form itself using a batch gradient-descent and projection method similar to [18]. In the beginning, we initialize $\mathbf{w}_l = \mathbf{e}$, $\forall\, l \in \{1, \ldots, L\}$.

4. CORRELATED METRIC LEARNING (CML)

In multi-label datasets where each bag may belong multiple classes, presence of one class gives hint about the presence of its correlated classes. E.g., presence of "car" may imply presence of "road". In $OP1$, a linear metric $\mathbf{w}_l$ is learned corresponding to every class l. However, it ignores to capture inter-class correlations into the learned metrics. In this section, we extend $OP1$ by explicitly incorporating inter-class correlations within the metric learning framework.

Consider the distance computation of a bag A from super-bag U_l as given in Eq. 7. There, let $\tilde{\mathbf{d}}_l^A \in \mathbb{R}^N$ denote the normalized sum of all distance vectors; i.e.,

$$\tilde{\mathbf{d}}_l^A = \frac{1}{K_1 K_2} \sum_{\mathbf{a}_i \in \mathcal{N}_l^{K_2}} \sum_{\mathbf{x}_{lj} \in \mathcal{N}_{il}^{K_1}} \mathbf{d}_{ilj}^A \tag{9}$$

Now, let $\tilde{\mathbf{D}}^A = [\tilde{\mathbf{d}}_1^A, \ldots, \tilde{\mathbf{d}}_L^A] \in \mathbb{R}^{N \times L}$. Also, $\forall l \in \{1, \ldots, L\}$, let $\mathbf{e}_l \in \mathbb{R}^L$ be a binary vector with $\mathbf{e}_l(l) = 1$ and rest all entries being 0. Then, it is easy to verify that the constraints given by Eq. 8 are equivalent to

$$\forall l \in L_A^+, \forall\, k \in L_A^- : (\mathbf{W}\mathbf{I}\mathbf{e}_k)^T \tilde{\mathbf{D}}^A \mathbf{e}_k - (\mathbf{W}\mathbf{I}\mathbf{e}_l)^T \tilde{\mathbf{D}}^A \mathbf{e}_l \geq 1 - \xi_{kl}^A$$

where $\mathbf{I}$ denotes the identity matrix. Let $\mathbf{P} \in \mathbb{R}^{L \times L}$ be a matrix such that $\mathbf{P}(k, l)$ denotes the correlation between the kth and l^{th} classes. Using $\mathbf{P}$, we introduce inter-class correlations into the above constraints as follows:

$$\forall l \in L_A^+, \forall\, k \in L_A^- : (\mathbf{WPe}_k)^T \tilde{\mathbf{D}}^A \mathbf{e}_k - (\mathbf{WPe}_l)^T \tilde{\mathbf{D}}^A \mathbf{e}_l \geq 1 - \xi_{kl}^A$$

Now, let $\mathbf{V} = \mathbf{WP} \in \mathbb{R}^{N \times L}$, and $\mathbf{R} = \mathbf{P}^T\mathbf{P} \succ 0$. Then, the above constraints and the identity $Trace(\mathbf{G}_1\mathbf{G}_2\mathbf{G}_3) = Trace(\mathbf{G}_3\mathbf{G}_1\mathbf{G}_2)$ result into the following optimization:

$$OP2: \min_{\mathbf{V}, \xi_{kl}^A \geq 0} \quad \frac{1}{2} Trace(\mathbf{V}\mathbf{R}^{-1}\mathbf{V}^T) + C \sum_{A, l \in L_A^+, k \in L_A^-} \xi_{kl}^A$$

$$s.t.\ \forall A, l \in L_A^+, k \in L_A^- : (\mathbf{Ve}_k)^T \tilde{\mathbf{D}}^A \mathbf{e}_k - (\mathbf{Ve}_l)^T \tilde{\mathbf{D}}^A \mathbf{e}_l \geq 1 - \xi_{kl}^A$$
$$\forall\, 1 \leq l \leq L,\ 1 \leq i \leq N: \quad \mathbf{v}_l(i) \geq 0$$

where $\mathbf{v}_l$ denotes the lth column of $\mathbf{V}$. Similar to $OP1$, we use a batch gradient-descent and projection method to solve $OP2$. Thus, $\mathbf{v}_l$ is the new learned distance metric that explicitly encodes correlations of the lth class with all other classes. Moreover, since each of these metrics are learned jointly in a max-margin discriminative manner, it also ensures optimal predictive performance. One can observe that if the prior matrix $\mathbf{P}$ is taken to be $\mathbf{I}$ (i.e., there are no prior correlations among the classes), then $OP2$ becomes the same as $OP1$, which makes $OP1$ a special case of $OP2$. Also, since there is no particular restriction on the matrix $\mathbf{R}$ except that it must be a positive-definite matrix, it can be either sparse or dense depending on the given application.

Using these new class-correlated metrics, we update the distance function of Eq. 7 by replacing $\mathbf{w}_l$ with $\mathbf{v}_l$ as below:

$$D_{b2c}^{\mathbf{v}}(A, U_l) = \mathbf{v}_l^T \left(\sum_{\mathbf{a}_i \in \mathcal{N}_l^{K_2}} \sum_{\mathbf{x}_{lj} \in \mathcal{N}_{il}^{K_1}} \mathbf{d}_{ilj}^A \right). \quad (10)$$

We shall refer the above distance as correlated metric based RB2C (or CM-RB2C). We believe ours is the first work that incorporates inter-class correlations into metric learning framework for multi-instance multi-label data.

The proposed CML formulation is motivated by [9] that incorporates inter-class correlations into SVM classifiers. Our framework differs from theirs in two important ways: (1) Their approach is meant to learn binary one-vs.-rest SVM classifiers, while our aim is to learn class-specific distance-metrics in a nearest-neighbour scenario. (2) Since they learn one-vs.-rest SVM classifiers, their optimization problem boils-down into disjoint optimization problems for individual classes, which can be optimized easily. However, in our case, the pair-wise constraints defined over pairs of positive and negative classes for each bag (Eq. 10) result in a more complex optimization problem, where we need to learn metrics for all the classes simultaneously in a joint manner.

Defining P: Since $\mathbf{R}$ is a positive-definite matrix, the capacity of the prior correlation matrix $\mathbf{P}$ is quite large (it can also have negative entries to model negative correlations). We define the correlation between k^{th} and l^{th} class as [12]:

$$\mathbf{P}(k, l) = \frac{f_{kl}}{f_k + f_l - f_{kl}}, \quad (11)$$

where f_k and f_l denote the frequencies of the kth and l^{th} classes respectively, and f_{kl} denotes their co-occurrence frequency. Higher the value of $P(k, l)$, more is the correlation between these two classes, and vice-versa.

Label Prediction: Given an object A, we compute its distance from every class using Eq. 6, 7, and 10 for different forms of parameterization. Then we rank all the classes based on the decreasing order of their distance from A, with smaller distance implying higher relevance and vice-versa.

5. EXPERIMENTS

Now we evaluate and compare different variants of the proposed distance measures (Eq. 6, Eq. 7 and Eq. 10).

5.1 Datasets and Experimental Details

We use two popular multi-instance multi-label datasets Corel-5K [3] and IAPR TC-12 [6]. In both these datasets, each image (bag) consists of multiple segments (instances), and each segment is represented by a feature vector. We use the same train/test partitions for both the datasets as in [7, 13]. Corel-5K dataset consists of 4500 training images, 500 testing images, and a vocabulary of 260 classes. IAPR TC-12 dataset consists of 17665 training images, 1962 testing images, and a vocabulary of 291 classes. In all our experiments, we consider the top 20 most frequent classes from each dataset since others have very few occurrences.

We compare with following benchmark methods: (a) Citation kNN [17], (b) MIMLSVM [19], (c) MildML [8], (d) S-C2B and its variants (C2B and M-C2B) [15], (e) TagProp [7], and (f) 2PKNN [13]. For MIMLSVM [19], MildML [8], TagProp [7] and 2PKNN [13], we use publicly available codes. For Citation-kNN [17] and S-C2B (and its variants) [15], we have implemented these methods by following the details from the respective papers. For RB2C and its variants, we keep $K_1 = 5$ and $K_2 = 8$ for Corel-5K dataset, and $K_1 = 10$ and $K_2 = 4$ for IAPR TC-12 dataset.

Note that both TagProp and 2PKNN consider whole image as a single instance and used a set of 15 features [7]. This gives a 37152-dimensional feature vector per image, which is more than 100 times the number of features used by all other methods listed above. Since this would result in an unfair comparison, we project each of these 15 features using Principle Component Analysis (PCA) and keep only the top 5% dimensions from every feature. This gives a 1858-dimensional feature vector per image.

For quantitative evaluations, we use five popular metrics: Hamming loss (HL), One-error (OE), Coverage (Co), Ranking loss (RL) and Average precision (AP). More details on these measures can be found in [15, 16, 10]. Among these, while HL and OE measure multi-label classification performance, Co, RL and AP measure multi-label ranking performance, Also, for HL, OE, Co and RL, smaller score means better performance; and for AP, higher score means better performance. Since Hamming loss is based on binary assignment of classes, we assign the top μ classes to each test-bag while computing it. Here, μ is set to be the (rounded) average number of classes per bag in training data ($\mu = 2$ for Corel-5K dataset, and $\mu = 3$ for IAPR TC-12 dataset).

5.2 Results and Discussion

Table 1 compares the performance of different methods. We can observe that: (1) Citation-kNN, which although is quite old, achieves very competitive results and performs either better than or comparable to several recent methods. This demonstrates the effectiveness of this classical MIL method, and also reflects the need of revisiting such methods for developing better methods. (2) The simple RB2C-

Table 1: Performance using different methods (↓: lower is better; ↑: higher is better).

Method	Corel-5K HL ↓	Corel-5K OE ↓	Corel-5K Co ↓	Corel-5K RL ↓	Corel-5K AP ↑	IAPR TC-12 HL ↓	IAPR TC-12 OE ↓	IAPR TC-12 Co ↓	IAPR TC-12 RL ↓	IAPR TC-12 AP ↑
Citation-kNN [17]	0.088	0.514	5.288	0.193	0.558	0.121	0.502	7.682	0.249	0.521
MIMLSVM [19]	0.100	0.590	5.849	0.195	0.530	0.133	0.593	8.929	0.281	0.456
MildML [8]	0.090	0.511	5.851	0.210	0.548	**0.120**	0.520	7.968	0.262	0.504
S-C2B [16]	0.519	0.669	7.094	0.240	0.438	0.487	0.608	9.706	0.304	0.420
C2B [16]	0.479	0.671	7.016	0.237	0.438	0.452	0.605	9.611	0.300	0.422
M-C2B [16]	0.465	0.664	6.988	0.229	0.445	0.439	0.597	9.497	0.293	0.431
TagProp [7]	0.122	0.603	5.217	0.174	0.520	0.168	0.546	7.406	0.223	0.516
2PKNN [13]	0.120	0.628	5.524	0.188	0.516	0.172	0.591	7.748	0.240	0.498
RB2C (this work)	0.107	0.468	4.207	0.131	0.607	0.148	0.480	6.912	0.199	0.554
M-RB2C (this work)	0.095	0.462	4.124	0.126	0.613	0.142	0.469	6.727	0.190	0.562
CM-RB2C (this work)	**0.087**	**0.457**	**4.086**	**0.119**	**0.620**	0.139	**0.460**	**6.659**	**0.184**	**0.568**

distance itself outperforms (sometimes significantly) most of the other methods, and the performance of M-RB2C is consistently better than RB2C. It further improves by using distance metrics learned with inter-class correlations (CM-RB2C), thus validating the utility of the proposed CML formulation. (3) CM-RB2C provides the best performance for both the tasks, except on IAPR TC-12 where its HL is slightly inferior to competing methods.

6. CONCLUSION

We have introduced a novel RB2C-distance for multi-instance multi-label data, and integrated class-specific distance metrics into it. Additionally, we have presented a novel metric learning framework that explicitly takes into account inter-class correlations in multi-label datasets, and also provide its principled interpretation. Our method demonstrates marginal improvements in performance on multi-label ranking and classification tasks compared to several benchmark techniques, thus confirming its effectiveness. Though in this work we have focused only on multi-instance multi-label data, the proposed CML framework can be adopted for single-instance multi-label data as well.

Acknowledgement: Yashaswi Verma is partially supported by Microsoft Research India PhD fellowship 2013.

7. REFERENCES

[1] Y. Chen and J. Z. Wang. Image categorization by learning and reasoning with regions. *The Journal of Machine Learning Research*, 5:913–939, 2004.

[2] T. Dietterich, R. Lathrop, and T. Lozano-Pérez. Solving the multiple-instance problem with axis-parallel rectangles. *Artificial Intelligence*, 89(1–2):31–71, 1997.

[3] P. Duygulu, K. Barnard, J. D. Freitas, and D. Forsyth. Object recognition as machine translation: Learning a lexicon for a fixed image vocabulary. In *ECCV*, 2002.

[4] A. Frome, Y. Singer, and J. Malik. Image retrieval and classification using local distance functions. In *NIPS*, 2007.

[5] A. Frome, Y. Singer, F. Sha, and J. Malik. Learning globally-consistent local distance functions for shape-based image retrieval and classification. In *ICCV*, 2007.

[6] M. Grubinger. *Analysis and Evaluation of Visual Information Systems Performance.* PhD thesis, Victoria University, Melbourne, Australia, 2007.

[7] M. Guillaumin, T. Mensink, J. Verbeek, and C. Schmid. Tagprop: Discriminative metric learning in nearest neighbor models for image auto-annotation. In *ICCV*, 2009.

[8] M. Guillaumin, J. Verbeek, and C. Schmid. Multiple instance metric learning from automatically labeled bags of faces. In *ECCV*, 2010.

[9] B. Hariharan, L. Z.-Manor, S. V. N. Vishwanathan, and M. Varma. Large scale max-margin multi-label classification with priors. In *ICML*, 2010.

[10] R. Jin, S. Wang, and Z. H. Zhou. Learning a distance metric from multi-instance multi-label data. In *CVPR*, 2009.

[11] O. Maron and A. L. Ratan. Multiple-instance learning for natural scene classification. In *ICML*, 1998.

[12] B. Sigurbjörnsson and R. van Zwol. Flickr tag recommendation based on collective knowledge. In *WWW*, 2008.

[13] Y. Verma and C. V. Jawahar. Image annotation using metric learning in semantic neighbourhoods. In *ECCV*, 2012.

[14] H. Wang, H. Huang, F. Kamangar, F. Nie, and C. Ding. Maximum margin multi-instance learning. In *NIPS*, 2011.

[15] H. Wang, F. Nie, and H. Huang. Learning instance specific distance for multi-instance classification. In *AAAI*, 2011.

[16] H. Wang, F. Nie, and H. Huang. Robust and discriminative distance for multi-instance learning. In *CVPR*, 2012.

[17] J. Wang and J. D. Zucker. Solving the multiple-instance problem: A lazy learning approach. In *ICML*, 2000.

[18] K. Q. Weinberger and L. K. Saul. Distance metric learning for large margin nearest neighbor classification. *The Journal of Machine Learning Research*, 10:207–244, 2009.

[19] Z. H. Zhou and M. L. Zhang. Multi-instance multi-label learning with application to scene classification. In *NIPS*, 2007.

Multiview Video Super-Resolution via Information Extraction and Merging

Yawei Li, Xiaofeng Li, Zhizhong Fu, Wenli Zhong
School of Communication and Information Engineering
University of Electronic Science and Technology of China, Chengdu, China
lywuestc@163.com, {xfli, fuzz}@uestc.edu.cn, zwluestc@163.com

ABSTRACT

Multiview video super-resolution provides a promising solution to the contradiction between the huge data size of multiview video and the degraded video quality due to mixed-resolution compression. This algorithm consists of two different functional layers. An information extraction layer draws relevant high-frequency information from the high-resolution views via depth-image-based rendering and interpolation. A merging layer fuses multiview high-frequency information to refine the low-resolution view. In this paper, we introduce kernel regression and non-local means to improve the two layers, respectively. Kernel regression adapts to the local image structure and thus outperforms basic interpolation methods. Non-local means exploits the similarity between different views of multiview videos to restore the high-frequency component of a low-resolution image. We constrain non-local means by limiting the pixels used to restore a pixel. The experimental results show the effectiveness of the proposed algorithm.

Keywords

Super-resolution; kernel regression; non-local means; multiview video processing

1. INTRODUCTION

Super-resolution (SR) algorithms aim at recovering the high-frequency component of a low-resolution (LR) image and creating its high-resolution (HR) counterpart. Since the rediscovery by Huang *et al.* [9], SR algorithms have shown a promising prospect in medical image processing, video compression, three-dimensional television (3DTV), and free-viewpoint television (FTV). Compared with expensive hardware capture system, SR algorithms provide an economic alternative to generate HR images and videos.

SR algorithms are divided into reconstruction-based methods and example-based methods [13]. Reconstruction-based methods use subpixel displacement among successive LR images. Goldlueche *et al.* first proposed a 3D multiview SR approach that led to a total variation energy for the texture map [7]. By solving the Euler-Lagrange equation on the surface, the texture map could be recovered. Example-based methods establish a library from a set of training samples, which guides the learning phase of the SR algorithm [4].

When applied to a video sequence, SR algorithms exploit the temporal or spatial redundancy of the video instead of establishing libraries from irrelevant training samples. Brandi *et al.* proposed an algorithm that super-resolved non-key frames of a video sequence with the assisted information from key frames [2]. Ancuti *et al.* used HR still photographs of the same scene to refine a LR video [1]. In addition, mixed-resolution (MR) multiview video allows one to exploit the spatial redundancy of videos to increase the sharpness of a LR view [6]. MR video coding is proposed to save the cost and bandwidth used to capture, transmit, and store multiview videos. However, this video format fails to offer satisfactory viewing experience in different perspectives due to the inherent LR views. Fortunately, multiview video SR algorithms solve the problem [6, 12].

Multiview video SR methods mainly contain an information extraction layer and an information merging layer. The extraction layer is based on depth-image-based rendering (DIBR) that projects high-frequency content from a HR view to a LR view [3, 6]. On the other hand, the merging layer is a mechanism that fuses all of the available high-frequency information to recover a LR view. Since the algorithm proposed by Garcia *et al.* resulted in projection errors in case of noisy depth map [6], Richter *et al.* proposed an algorithm that was based on displacement-compensated high frequency synthesis and aimed at correcting the errors [12]. Besides the algorithms extracting information in spatial domain, Fu *et al.* extracted high-frequency content in discrete cosine transform (DCT) domain and devised an optimal weight distribution to merge multiview information [5]. Jin *et al.* proposed a decision mechanism to determine whether to fill the missing pixels in the super-resolved frame by HR-view pixels or by interpolated LR-view pixels [10].

In this paper, we propose to use kernel regression and non-local means (NLM) to improve the two functional layers of multiview SR algorithms, respectively. Kernel regression is based on the assumption of the local continuity of natural images and changes the shape of the kernel according to the local image structure [8]. Thus, it can avoid introducing irrelevant pixels into predicting an unknown pixel and improves the performance of the extraction layer. Due to the occlusion of objects and the displacement of cameras, the derived images by the extraction layer usually contain holes

MM '16, October 15-19, 2016, Amsterdam, Netherlands

DOI: http://dx.doi.org/10.1145/2964284.2967260

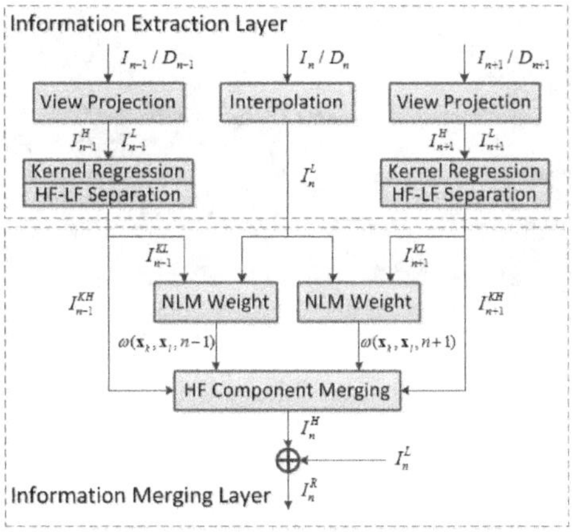

Figure 1: Flowchart of the proposed algorithm.

and cracks that cannot be filled by a single view. Thus, the information merging layer is needed to fuse the multiview images. Contrary to the assumption of local continuity of kernel regression, NLM assumes that a similar patch can repeat within a non-local area of an image [11]. We impose constraints on the number of available pixels to reject the dissimilar ones which may be misused to recover a pixel.

The rest of the paper is organized as follows. Section 2 describes the proposed algorithm in detail. Section 3 shows the experimental results. Section 4 concludes the paper.

2. THE PROPOSED ALGORITHM

Multiview video plus depth (MVD) format is used for the SR algorithm. Let I_n be the LR image, I_{n-1} and I_{n+1} be the HR images in the adjacent view. In addition, each view is provided with a depth map D (See Fig. 1). The video format is not limited to just two HR views and can be extended to any possible HR configurations. Since the operations of I_{n-1} and I_{n+1} are symmetric, we mainly talk about I_{n-1}.

The proposed algorithm contains two layers: an information extraction layer and a merging layer. In the information extraction layer, the LR image is enlarged by bicubic interpolation, resulting in its full-resolution counterpart I_n^L. However, I_n^L lacks high-frequency information and needs to be enhanced with the aid of I_{n-1} and I_{n+1}. Thus, the HR images undergo view projection, kernel regression. View projection establishes coordinate correspondences between I_n^L and I_{n-1} and projects high-frequency information from I_{n-1} to the image plane of I_n^L. As is shown in Fig. 2, the derived coordinates are irregular samples (blue stars) instead of the regular samples (red points). Thus, kernel regression is used to restore the regular samples. Meanwhile, component separation is implemented along with kernel regression, resulting in a high-frequency component I_{n-1}^{KH} and a low-frequency component I_{n-1}^{KL}.

The primitively refined images by kernel regression have some unavoidable holes and cracks. Therefore, the merging layer is used to combine the multiview images and to alleviate the cracks and holes. The high-frequency component I_{n-1}^{KH} and the low-frequency component I_{n-1}^{KL} are used differently in NLM, which is detailed in Subsection 2.2. After NLM, the derived detail information and structure information are added to complete the whole algorithm.

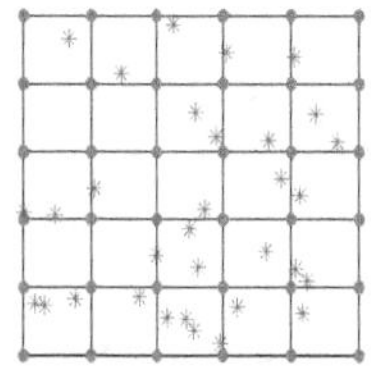

Figure 2: Regular samples (red points) and irregular samples (blue stars).

2.1 The Information Extraction Layer

2.1.1 *View Projection*

View projection is a fundamental technology in MR-MVD processing. It establishes coordinate correspondences between a LR view and its adjacent HR view.

We assume a basic pinhole model where points in space and points in an image plane are linked via central projection. To start with, a point (x_1', x_2') in the HR image plane of I_{n-1} is projected to its space position

$$(u_1, u_2, u_3)^T = R_{n-1}^{-1} A_{n-1}^{-1} D(x_1', x_2')(x_1', x_2', 1)^T + t_{n-1} \tag{1}$$

where A_{n-1}, R_{n-1}, and t_{n-1} are the intrinsic matrix, rotation matrix, and translation vector of the camera, respectively. $D(x_1', x_2')$ is the physical depth which can be derived from the depth map, i.e.

$$\frac{1}{D(x_1', x_2')} = \frac{d(x_1', x_2')}{255}\left(\frac{1}{D_{min}} - \frac{1}{D_{max}}\right) + \frac{1}{D_{max}} \tag{2}$$

where $d(x_1', x_2')$ is the 8-bit entry in the depth map, D_{max} and D_{min} define the physical depth range. Then the space point is projected onto the image plane of I_n^L, i.e.

$$w(x_1, x_2, 1)^T = A_n R_n \left[(u_1, u_2, u_3)^T - t_n\right] \tag{3}$$

Therefore, a point (x_1', x_2') in I_{n-1} is uniquely associated with a point (x_1, x_2) in the image plane of I_n^L. Ideally, the pixel information of (x_1', x_2') can be directly used to recover that of (x_1, x_2). However, the derived points are irregular samples(Fig. 2). In order to obtain the regular samples, different methods are used. Fu *et al.* directly rounded irregular samples to their regular positions, thus incurring at most half-pixel error along each axis [5]. Garcia *et al.* obtained regular samples via bilinear interpolation [6]. In the following subsection, we will introduce kernel regression to obtain regular samples.

2.1.2 *Kernel Regression*

Kernel regression assumes the local continuity of natural images and exploits this local regularity to restore images and videos. It's suitable not only for interpolation of regularly sampled images but also for restoration of irregularly sampled images. We discuss recovering regular samples from irregular samples here (Fig. 2). For the simplicity of notation, we use a coordinate vector $\mathbf{x}$ to denote a pixel position. Kernel regression is generalized as a least-square optimization problem, i.e.

$$\hat{z}(\mathbf{x}_i) = \arg\min_z \sum_{\mathbf{x}_j \in \mathcal{N}(\mathbf{x}_i)} (I_{n-1}(\mathbf{x}_j) - z)^2 K_{\mathbf{x}_i}(\mathbf{x}_j - \mathbf{x}_i) \tag{4}$$

where $K_{\mathbf{x}_i}(\mathbf{x}-\mathbf{x}_i)$ is the steering kernel, $\mathcal{N}(\mathbf{x}_i)$ is the neighborhood of $\mathbf{x}_i$, $\mathbf{x}_i$ and $\mathbf{x}_j$ denote the regular and irregular samples. Solving the optimization problem gives

$$\widehat{z}(\mathbf{x}_i) = \frac{\sum_{\mathbf{x}_j \in \mathcal{N}(\mathbf{x}_i)} I_{n-1}(\mathbf{x}_j) K_{\mathbf{x}_i}(\mathbf{x}_j - \mathbf{x}_i)}{\sum_{\mathbf{x}_j \in \mathcal{N}(\mathbf{x}_i)} K_{\mathbf{x}_i}(\mathbf{x}_j - \mathbf{x}_i)} \quad (5)$$

Thus, the irregular neighbors $\mathbf{x}_j$ constitute the regression basis of $\mathbf{x}_i$. The essence of kernel regression is to develop a steering kernel adapted to the local structure of an image. An adaptive Gaussian kernel can be constructed, i.e.

$$K_{\mathbf{x}_i}(\mathbf{x}-\mathbf{x}_i) = \frac{\{\det(C_i)\}^{1/2}}{2\pi\sigma_k^2} \exp\left\{\frac{(\mathbf{x}-\mathbf{x}_i)^T C_i^{-1}(\mathbf{x}-\mathbf{x}_i)}{-2\sigma_k^2}\right\} \quad (6)$$

where C_i is the diffusion tensor at $\mathbf{x}_i$ controlling the shape of the kernel, σ_k controls the bandwidth of the kernel [15].

2.1.3 *Component Separation*

The bicubic interpolation I_n^L of the LR image offers convincing low-frequency (structure) information although it lacks high-frequency (detail) information. Instead of restore the overall pixel value, one only need to recover the detail information of the LR image I_n. Therefore, a proper separation of the detail and structure information becomes an important task for the information extraction layer.

The component separation of regular samples is implemented simultaneously with kernel regression, i.e.

$$\widehat{z}(\mathbf{x}_i) = I_{n-1}^{KL}(\mathbf{x}_i) + I_{n-1}^{KH}(\mathbf{x}_i) \quad (7)$$

where $I_{n-1}^{KL}(\mathbf{x}_i)$ and $I_{n-1}^{KH}(\mathbf{x}_i)$ are the detail and structure components of $\mathbf{x}_i$. These two components are computed as

$$I_{n-1}^{KL}(\mathbf{x}_i) = \frac{\sum_{\mathbf{x}_j \in \mathcal{N}(\mathbf{x}_i)} I_{n-1}^{L}(\mathbf{x}_j) K_{\mathbf{x}_i}(\mathbf{x}_j - \mathbf{x}_i)}{\sum_{\mathbf{x}_j \in \mathcal{N}(\mathbf{x}_i)} K_{\mathbf{x}_i}(\mathbf{x}_j - \mathbf{x}_i)} \quad (8a)$$

$$I_{n-1}^{KH}(\mathbf{x}_i) = \frac{\sum_{\mathbf{x}_j \in \mathcal{N}(\mathbf{x}_i)} I_{n-1}^{H}(\mathbf{x}_j) K_{\mathbf{x}_i}(\mathbf{x}_j - \mathbf{x}_i)}{\sum_{\mathbf{x}_j \in \mathcal{N}(\mathbf{x}_i)} K_{\mathbf{x}_i}(\mathbf{x}_j - \mathbf{x}_i)} \quad (8b)$$

where I_{n-1}^L and I_{n-1}^H are the low-frequency and high-frequency parts of the HR image I_{n-1}. I_{n-1}^L is derived from I_{n-1} by blurring, decimation, and interpolation. I_{n-1}^H is the difference between I_{n-1} and I_{n-1}^L [2]. In the information extraction layer, the low-frequency component guides the fusion of multiview high-frequency components.

2.2 The Information Merging Layer

2.2.1 *Image Merging*

The images derived from kernel regression have annoying artifacts of holes and cracks. For example, Fig. 3 shows this phenomenon in two complementary views. Each of the views has artifacts that cannot be filled with information from a single HR view. However, if the two images in Fig. 3 are merged, the resultant image will overcome this problem. Since I_n^L has convincing low-frequency information, we only need to merge multiview high-frequency information via NLM.

In MR multivew setup, NLM exploits the similarity between a LR image and its adjacent HR views to recover the missing high-frequency information of I_n^L. For a pixel in I_n^L, its high-frequency component is computed as a weighted sum of those of its neighbors in the HR images, i.e.

(a) (b)

Figure 3: (a) and (b) are two complementary views.

$$I_n^H(\mathbf{x}_k) = \frac{\sum_v \sum_{\mathbf{x}_l \in \mathcal{S}(\mathbf{x}_k, v)} I_v^{KH}(\mathbf{x}_l)\omega(\mathbf{x}_k, \mathbf{x}_l, v)}{\sum_v \sum_{\mathbf{x}_l \in \mathcal{S}(\mathbf{x}_k, v)} \omega(\mathbf{x}_k, \mathbf{x}_l, v)} \quad (9)$$

where $\mathcal{S}(\mathbf{x}_k, v)$ is the similarity patch that contains the neighbors of pixel $\mathbf{x}_k$ in the HR view v, $\mathbf{x}_l$ is a pixel in the patch, and $\omega(\mathbf{x}_k, \mathbf{x}_l, v)$ is a weight that reflects the similarity of $\mathbf{x}_k$ and $\mathbf{x}_l$. The weight is computed by comparing the two low-frequency parts, i.e.

$$\omega(\mathbf{x}_k, \mathbf{x}_l, v) = \exp\left(\frac{-\left\|(R_{\mathbf{x}_k} I_v^{KH} - R_{\mathbf{x}_l} I_n^L)G_\sigma\right\|_2^2}{2\sigma_l^2}\right) \quad (10)$$

where the operator $R_{\mathbf{x}}$ extracts a patch around $\mathbf{x}$, σ_l is a smoothing factor, G_σ is a Gaussian kernel with standard deviation σ.

2.2.2 *Constrained NLM*

One major problem of the described algorithm is that it involves too many pixels in the recovery of a pixel in the LR image. Although a dissimilar pixel can be assigned with a small weight, it still participates in the weighted-averaging process. In the extreme case, considerable dissimilar pixels that are used to recover a pixel will accumulate restoration errors. Thus, we choose no more than ρ pixels in the weighting process to reject the dissimilar pixels. The selected ρ pixels are those with the largest possible weights.

2.3 Discussion

From (5) and (9), kernel regression and NLM have similar computing structures. However, they act differently in the method. First, the basic assumption of the two methods are different. Kernel regression uses local continuity and smoothness to interpolate regular samples while NLM exploits the similarity of multiview video. Second, as mentioned above, they play different roles in the proposed method.

Some other work is also related to combining the advantages of kernel regression and NLM [15, 16]. However, the multiview setup makes the discussed algorithm distinct. The MR format allows the algorithm to learn detail information

Table 1: Parameter Setup

Parameter	σ_k	σ_l	σ	ρ	$\mathcal{N}(\mathbf{x})$ size	$\mathcal{S}(\mathbf{x})$ size
Value	2.6	1.6	1	12	3	7

Table 2: Comparison of Intermediate Results and the Final Result

Method	PSNR(dB)	SSIM
Bilinear Interpolation	36.6643	0.9882
No separtion, no constraint	36.6854	0.9709
Only Constraint	37.1654	0.9806
Final Result	**38.7299**	**0.9925**

Table 3: PSNR (dB) and SSIM of Frame 20

Method	Ballet PSNR/SSIM	Breakdancers PSNR/SSIM
Bicubic	37.0085/ 0.9890	36.8104/0.9883
SRTD	37.3724/ 0.9893	37.1304/0.9884
SRDM	38.5339/ 0.9927	38.0414/0.9894
Proposed	**39.0107/ 0.9933**	**38.8205/0.9925**

from the HR view although no learning library is trained. View projection establishes relative accurate coordinate correspondences, which makes it possible for kernel regression to compute regular samples. Component separation guarantees accurate high-frequency information is extracted.

3. EXPERIMENTAL RESULTS

In this section, we validate the proposed approach by experimental results. We use the sequences *Ballet* and *Breakdancers* for our tests [17]. The parameter setups are given in Table 1. For all of the SR algorithms, View 3 is the LR view to be refined with the aid of HR View 0, View 2, View 4, and View 6. In order to simulate the LR view, the original full-resolution images in View 3 are down-sampled with a sampling rate of 2.

We conduct two experiments with different purposes. The first experiment compares the intermediate results and the final result of the proposed algorithm to show how each technique improves the method's performance. The results in comparison are bicubic interpolation, result without component separation and constrained NLM (No separtion, no constraint), result only with constrained NLM (Only Constraint), and the final result. The Peak Sigal-to-Noise Rate (PSNR) and Structure SIMilarity (SSIM) [14] of *Breakdancers* are shown in Table 2.

In the second experiment, we compare the proposed algorithm with bicubic interpolation, SR in transform domain (SRTD) [5], and SR for multiview images using depth map (SRDM) [6]. Table 3 shows the PSNR and SSIM results of Frame 20 of the two sequences. SRTD can only provide limited improvement over bicubic interpolation. The PSNR gains are only 0.3639dB and 0.33dB for *Ballet* and *Breakdancers*, respectively. Compared with SRTD, SRDM has relative better result. Among the SR algorithms, the propsed has the best performance. The PSNR gain of the proposed algorithm over the other methods are 2.0022dB, 1.6381 dB and 0.4768 dB for *Ballet*. Fig. 4 shows the PSNR result of 30 frames of *Ballet*. The proposed algorithm has the best performance under all the circumstances.

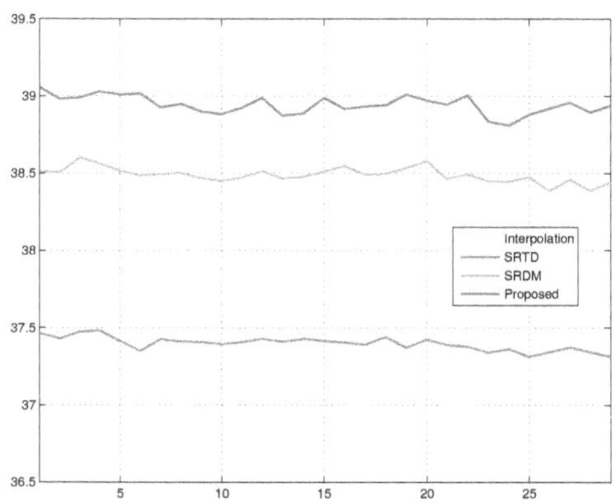

Figure 4: PSNR (dB) of 30 frames for *Ballet*

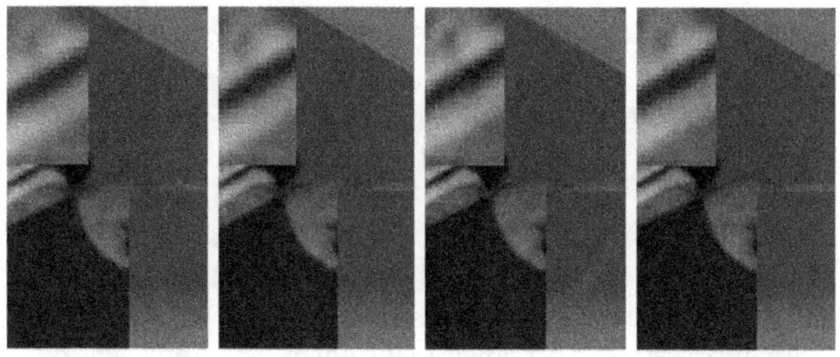

(a) (b) (c) (d)

Figure 5: (a) - (d) are the details of bicubic interpolation, SRTD, SRDM, and the proposed method for *Breakdancers*.

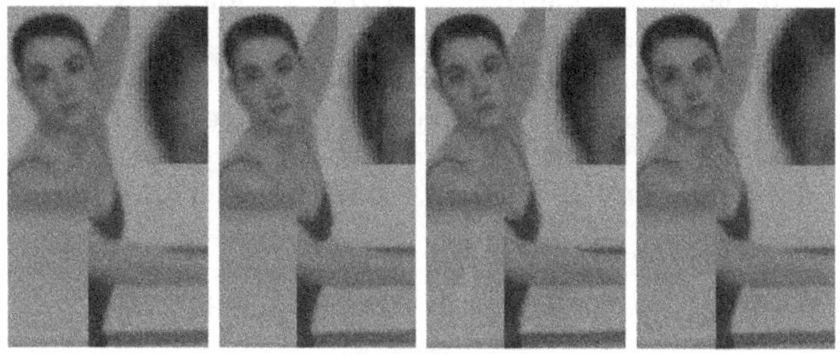

(a) (b) (c) (d)

Figure 6: (a) - (d) are the details of bicubic interpolation, SRTD, SRDM, and the proposed method for *Ballet*.

Fig. 5 and Fig. 6 shows the details of the SR images. Both SRDM and the proposed algorithm can recover satisfactory high-frequency information for the LR image. However, SRDM has some artifacts around the edges of the images.

4. CONCLUSION

In this paper, we proposed a multiview SR algorithm that improves the performance of the information extraction layer and the merging layer. Kernel regression adapted to the local structure extracts more accurate high-frequency information, compared with basic interpolation. NLM is used to merge the extracted high-frequency information from HR views. The constraints imposed on the number of available pixels avoid incorporating mismatched pixels into the restoration of a pixel. The experimental results show the effectiveness of the main techniques used in the proposed algorithm. The comparison with other multiview SR algorithms shows the improvement of the proposed algorithm.

5. REFERENCES

[1] C. Ancuti, C. O. Ancuti, and P. Bekaert. Video super-resolution using high quality photographs. In *Proc. ICASSP*, pages 862 – 865, 2010.

[2] F. Brandi, R. d. Queiroz, and D. Mukherjee. Super-resolution of video using key frames and motion estimation. In *Proc. ICIP*, pages 321 – 324, 2010.

[3] C. Fehn. Depth-image-based rendering (DIBR), compression and transmission for a new approach on 3D-TV. *Proc. SPIE*, 5291:93 – 104, 2004.

[4] W. T. Freeman, T. R. Jones, and E. C. Pasztor. Example-based super-resolution. *IEEE Comput. Graph. Appl.*, 22(2):56 – 65, 2001.

[5] Z. Fu, Y. Li, J. Xu, H. Wu, and Y. Lai. Super resolution for multiview mixed resolution images in transform-domain with optimal weight. *Multimed. Tools Appl.*, pages 1–15, 2016.

[6] D. C. Garcia, C. Dorea, and R. L. de Queiroz. Super resolution for multiview images using depth information. *IEEE Trans. Circuits Syst. Video Technol.*, 22(9):1249 – 1256, 2012.

[7] B. Goldluecke and D. Cremers. Superresolution texture maps for multiview reconstruction. In *Proc. CVPR*, pages 1677 – 1684, 2009.

[8] T. Hiroyuki, F. Sina, and M. Peyman. Kernel regression for image processing and reconstruction. *IEEE Trans. Image Process.*, 16(2):349 – 366, 2007.

[9] T. S. Huang and R. Y. Tsai. Multi-frame image restoration and registration. *Adv. Comput. Vis. Image Process.*, 1:317 – 339, 1984.

[10] Z. Jin, T. Tillo, C. Yao, and J. Xiao. Virtual view assisted video super-resolution and enhancement. *IEEE Trans. Circuits Syst. Video Technol.*, PP(99):1, 2015.

[11] P. Matan, E. Michael, T. Hiroyuki, and M. Peyman. Generalizing the nonlocal-means to super-resolution reconstruction. *IEEE Trans. Image Process.*, 18(1):36 – 51, 2009.

[12] T. Richter, J. Seiler, W. Schnurrer, and A. Kaup. Robust super-resolution for mixed-resolution multiview image plus depth data. *IEEE Trans. Circuits Syst. Video Technol.*, PP(99):1, 2015.

[13] H. Su, L. Tang, Y. Wu, D. Tretter, and J. Zhou. Spatially adaptive block-based super-resolution. *IEEE Trans. Image Process.*, 21(3):1031 – 1045, 2012.

[14] Z. Wang, A. C. Bovik, H. R. Sheikh, and E. P. Simoncelli. Image quality assessment: from error visibility to structural similarity. *IEEE Trans. Image Process.*, 13(4):600 – 612, 2004.

[15] H. Zhang, J. Yang, Y. Zhang, and T. S. Huang. Image and video restorations via nonlocal kernel regression. *IEEE Trans. Cybern.*, 43(3):1035 – 1046, 2013.

[16] K. Zhang, X. Gao, D. Tao, and X. Li. Single image super-resolution with non-local means and steering kernel regression. *IEEE Trans. Image Process.*, 21(11):4544 – 4556, 2012.

[17] C. L. Zitnick, S. B. Kang, M. Uyttendaele, S. Winder, and R. Szeliski. High-quality video view interpolation using a layered representation. *SIGGRAPH*, 23(3):600 – 608, 2004.

InnerView: Learning Place Ambiance from Social Media Images

Darshan Santani
Idiap Research Institute
EPFL, Lausanne, Switzerland
dsantani@idiap.ch

Rui Hu
Idiap Research Institute
rhu@idiap.ch

Daniel Gatica-Perez
Idiap Research Institute
EPFL, Lausanne, Switzerland
gatica@idiap.ch

ABSTRACT

In the recent past, there has been interest in characterizing the physical and social ambiance of urban spaces to understand how people perceive and form impressions of these environments based on physical and psychological constructs. Building on our earlier work on characterizing ambiance of indoor places, we present a methodology to automatically infer impressions of place ambiance, using generic deep learning features extracted from images publicly shared on Foursquare. We base our methodology on a corpus of 45,000 images from 300 popular places in six cities on Foursquare. Our results indicate the feasibility to automatically infer place ambiance with a maximum R^2 of 0.53 using features extracted from a pre-trained convolutional neural network. We found that features extracted from deep learning with convolutional nets consistently outperformed individual and combinations of several low-level image features (including Color, GIST, HOG and LBP) to infer all the studied 13 ambiance dimensions. Our work constitutes a first study to automatically infer ambiance impressions of indoor places from deep features learned from images shared on social media.

1. INTRODUCTION

There is increasing interest in characterizing the physical and social ambiance of urban spaces (both indoor and outdoor), to understand how people perceive these environments based on physical and psychological constructs [7, 21, 22, 23]. Ambiance, formally defined as the "character and atmosphere of a place" [4], is the human way of relating to places. Consequently, understanding ambiance of places in cities has been proposed as a new topic in multimedia research [22]. Characterizing place ambiance has many applications ranging from hyper-local, ambiance-driven place search and discovery (e.g., a *trendy* place for a night-out or a *romantic* place for the wedding anniversary) to data-driven recommendations for place owners to improve the presentation (e.g., architecture design and style) of their venues.

In hospitality research, there is a significant body of work that investigates the effect of ambiance on patrons' dining experience, perception, and customer retention [1, 25, 8], but most of these studies are small-scale and based on in-situ interviews and questionnaires, which may have limitations with respect to generalization or recall biases. To overcome these limitations, researchers have used geo-tagged images from Google Street View or taken by volunteers to measure the perceptions of outdoor spaces for several urban dimensions including safety, quietness, etc. [21, 16, 19, 23].

Until recently, most of the studies examining urban perceptions using online images were focused on outdoor spaces. From the perspective of urban design, studying elicited impressions for indoor places should involve examination of different variables when compared to outdoor spaces; for instance, "formal" is a meaningful ambiance construct in an indoor venue, but not necessarily so in an outdoor space. As a brave new topic in [22], we presented a crowdsourcing methodology to examine the suitability of social media images for the characterization of indoor ambiance impressions across 13 dimensions (including artsy, romantic, formal, loud and trendy, among others) in 300 popular Foursquare places. We found that reliable estimates of ambiance were obtained for several of the dimensions, suggesting the presence of visual cues that allow to create such impressions. In this paper, we extend our earlier work to automatically characterize place ambiance using visual cues from images.

To infer human perception of outdoor spaces, recent works have used a variety of low-level image features including Color, GIST, HOG, LBP, SIFT and generic deep convolutional activation features. Using these features on geo-tagged images from Google Street View, high-level attributes (e.g., wealthy, uniqueness, and safety) for outdoor scenes are inferred in two US cities [11, 14]. Using the same dataset, in [15], a CNN architecture is proposed to predict and discover mid-level visual patterns which correlate with the perceived safety of an outdoor scene. Building upon these works, in this paper we focus on studying places across 13 dimensions appropriate for the indoor environment. Specifically, we address two research questions:

RQ1: Can judgments of ambiance of an indoor place be automatically inferred using low-level image and generic deep features extracted from social media images?

RQ2: What visual categories represent popular places on Foursquare in connection to indoor ambiance?

To address these questions, we build upon our earlier work and dataset [22]. For automatic characterization and inference, we build upon prior work in object classification and scene understanding using deep learning techniques [20, 17, 26]. Our contributions are two-fold. First, we devised a methodology to automatically infer ambiance impressions of popular Foursquare places, using generic deep features extracted from images. We base our methodology using a corpus of over 45,000 images from 300 popular places on

MM '16, October 15 - 19, 2016, Amsterdam, Netherlands

ISBN 978-1-4503-3603-1/16/10... $15.00

DOI: http://dx.doi.org/10.1145/2964284.2967261

(a) Restaurant, Eating Place

(b) Stage

(c) Library

(d) Grocery Store

Figure 1: Sample of random images from the *50K image* corpus which were classified as (a) Restaurants/Eating Place, (b) Stage, (c) Library, and (d) Grocery Store. For each class, from top to bottom, images are sorted in decreasing order of ImageNet dominant class probability (Section 4.1).

Foursquare spread across six cities. The results indicate the feasibility to automatically infer the ambiance of these places with a maximum R^2 of 0.53 using features extracted from a pre-trained convolutional neural network, precisely GoogLeNet model trained on ImageNet data. Furthermore, we found that CNN features consistently outperform individual and combinations of several low-level image features for all the 13 studied dimensions. Second, to better understand the image corpus, we studied the distribution of the most likely ImageNet class assigned to each image. We find that most of the top-10 dominant classes are associated with either food or drinks, but also contains images which represent the physical environment with clear and unoccluded views of the indoor space. These findings point towards the nature of images shared on Foursquare, which to our knowledge have not been analyzed before at such a scale from the perspective of ambiance [7].

2. DATASET

We use the image corpora and place ambiance annotations collected as part of our prior work [22], which contains data from 300 popular places on Foursquare in six cities – Barcelona, Mexico City, New York City, Paris, Seattle, and Singapore. For each city, we chose 50 popular places among restaurants, cafes, bars, or nightclubs. Below we describe the data:

Image Corpora: For each selected place, there are two image corpora: a) *Physical Environment Image Corpus*: this corpus was manually curated to contain images with clear views of the physical environment of a place. It contains three images per place, which show the indoor space from different angles, resulting in a total of 900 images for all 300 places; b) *50K Image Corpus*: the second image corpus contains all publicly available images shared on Foursquare for each place, resulting in a total of 45,848 images for 280 places (an average of 164 images per place). Note that the 50K image corpus contains images for 280 places, as opposed to 300 places, due to changes in the Foursquare API [6]. Figure 1 shows a sample of images selected randomly across four ImageNet categories from this corpus.

Ambiance Annotations: In addition to images, the data contains the results of an online crowdsourcing study to collect ambiance impressions for each place, based on *physical environment image* corpus. Ambiance ratings were elicited across 13 physical and psychological dimensions (shown in Table 1), where images served as stimuli to form place impressions. Ambiance ratings were obtained using the three manually selected images for each place. For this study, we used the mean annotation ratings for each place and dimension as described in [22].

3. METHODOLOGY

3.1 Feature Extraction

Building upon recent work in the literature, we have extracted the following set of low-level and deep visual features:

1. Color: We computed global color histogram in RGB space. Each channel was quantized into 8-bins, resulting in 8^3 possible color combinations and a 512-dimensional color feature vector.

2. GIST: This descriptor captures the dominant spatial structure of a scene from a set of perceptual dimensions (e.g., naturalness, openness, roughness, etc.) [13]. We use the standard setting of this descriptor, resulting in a 512-dimensional vector.

3. Texture (LBP): Texture captures the spatial arrangement of color and intensities in an image. We apply the local binary pattern (LBP) descriptor [12], which encodes local texture information (such as spots, edges, and corners) by comparing each pixel with its neighborhood pixels, resulting in a 256-dimensional vector.

4. Gradient (HOG): Histogram of oriented gradients (HOG) computes occurrences of gradient orientations in localized region of an image [10]. We apply the pyramid HOG implementation, where images are first represented in pyramid hierarchies, then the HOG descriptor is computed on each level, and finally the final descriptor is the concatenation of vectors across all levels [2]. We compute the pyramid HOG descriptor for levels $l = 0$ to $l = 3$. Images are divided into 2^{2*l} regions, and a 8-bin histogram is computed within each region, which results in a 680-dimensional feature vector.

5. CNN: The availability of large-scale image datasets [20] and the performance of deep neural networks for object classification and scene understanding [17, 26], have opened opportunities to explore these features for our problem. We have used the features extracted using a pre-trained convolutional neural networks model (CNNs) using the Caffe framework [9]. Specifically, we used the GoogLeNet CNN [24] trained on ImageNet data. ImageNet data contains over 14 million images across 1,000 categories. To extract the CNN descriptors, for each image, we obtained the final layer class probabilities across all 1,000 ImageNet classes, resulting in a 1000-dimensional feature vector.

We chose to use a pre-trained model trained on a large and diverse data (ImageNet in our case), as opposed to training a CNN model on our data for two reasons. First, it has been shown that features extracted using pre-trained CNN models can potentially provide discriminative features for multiple visual recognition tasks [5, 17]. ImageNet categories are well suited for our problem as they are descriptive of visual cues typically present in restaurants, bars, etc. (refer to Figures 1 and 2). Second, using a pre-trained model avoids the need to train, adapt or fine-tune a CNN on our dataset, which can be computationally expensive and resource intensive.

Feature Aggregation: As stated in Section 2, ambiance ratings were given for each place and each place had an average of 164 images. We extracted all the previously described visual features for each image. Then, in order to obtain a representative feature vector for each place, we apply an early feature fusion approach by computing the mean feature vectors of all images describing the same place, for each feature set.

3.2 Inference Method and Evaluation

We are interested in examining the predictive power of both the low-level image features and deep CNN features to automatically infer the perceptions of social ambiance for the studied dimensions. We approach this problem as a regression task, where the objective is to infer the mean annotation scores of each place. For regression, we use Random Forest, a tree-based supervised learning method that guards against overfitting to the training data [3]. In all our experiments we used a 10-fold cross-validation approach. To evaluate the performance of different feature sets, we used two standard measures: the root-mean-square error ($RMSE$) and coefficient of determination (R^2) between the perceived ground-truth and inferred ambiance scores for each label and feature set. Furthermore, we have used variable importance measures from random forests to understand the relative importance of visual cues for each dimension (see Section 4). To understand and compare the predictive performance of each feature set, we choose the baseline model to be the mean annotated score as the predicted value for each label.

4. RESULTS AND DISCUSSION

4.1 Visual Categories

We begin our analysis by examining the distribution of the most likely ImageNet class assigned to each image. As stated before, the last layer of the GoogLeNet CNN model outputs the probability distribution of the image across all 1,000 ImageNet classes. Given this probability distribution, we chose the ImageNet class with the highest probability as the dominant class for each image. In Figure 2, we show the distribution of the top-10 dominant classes for both image corpora. For the *50K image* corpus, most of the top ten dominant categories are associated with either food (e.g., plate, meatloaf, ice-cream, chocolate) or drinks (e.g., beer glass, espresso, eggnog), as shown in Figure 2a. These results are consistent with previous findings [22] and expected given that all places are restaurants, bars, cafes, or nightclubs (Section 2).

While analyzing the top-10 class distribution for the *physical environment image* corpus, we observe that most of the dominant classes relate to the physical attributes of the indoor environment (e.g., stage, library, dining table, bakery, etc.) and do not contain food or drinks categories, which is in contrast with the class distribution for the *50K image* corpus (Figure 2b). These findings are not surprising given that all images in this corpus were manually selected to show clear views of the indoor scene (Section 2) [22]. Some of the recognized categories in *physical environment image* corpus may seem intriguing at first glance (e.g., library, grocery store, or barbershop), but after manually browsing the images belonging to these categories, we found that these classes describe various attributes of the indoor environment and are misclassified yet makes sense visually. For instance, most of the images belonging to "library" class contain images showing wall shelves typically found in cafes and bars (Figure 1c); while some of the "grocery store" images contain transparent window shelves displaying food or drink items (Figure 1d).

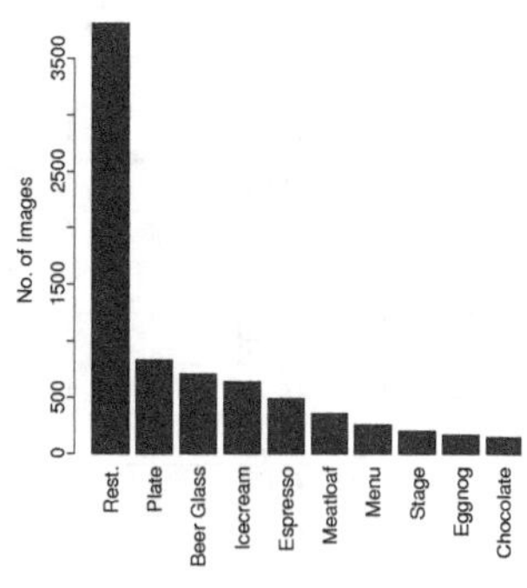

(a) 50K Image Corpus

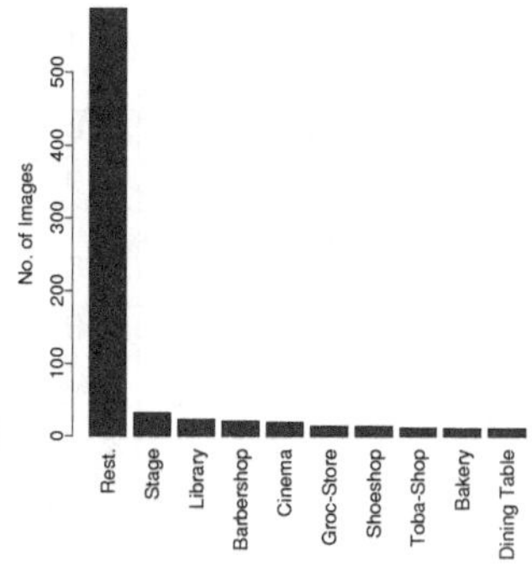

(b) Phy. Env. Image Corpus

Figure 2: Histogram of Top 10 recognized ImageNet classes for a) *50K Image* Corpus, and b) *Physical Environment Image* Corpus

Further, we observe that the top class in both image corpora is "restaurant/eating place". For the *50K* and *physical environment* image corpora, this class respectively contains 8% and 65% of total images. At first, it looks like a generic class but after manually browsing these images (Figure 1a), we found that most of the images represent the physical environment well, providing clear and unoccluded views of the indoor space. These findings point towards the feasibility to automate the selection of images for indoor ambiance characterization. As we previously reported, human observers preferred views of the physical environment of places to make impressions of ambiance [22]. However, as we show in the following subsection, other image categories are also exploited by the learning algorithm.

While the plots shown in Figure 2 are focused on illustrating the dominant visual class, many other classes are also informative of ambiance for a given image (e.g., a photo of someone eating an ice cream in a restaurant or drinking an espresso in a coffee shop are not likely to be generated in a club). This is the reason why we use the 1000-dimensional probability vector to infer the ambiance dimensions, as described in the next subsection. Overall, these findings point towards the nature of images shared on Foursquare, which to our knowledge has not been analyzed before at such a scale from the perspective of ambiance.

4.2 Regression

In this section, we evaluate the performance of both low-level image features and deep CNN features to automatically infer impressions of place ambiance. In Table 1, we report the R^2 values between ground-truth and inferred ambiance scores for each label and feature set. For the baseline model and the model learned using CNN features, we also report the $RMSE$ values. All the low-level visual features (Color, GIST, HOG, and LBP) are computed on the *50K image* corpus, while the CNN features are computed for both image corpora.

Overall, the results indicate that a maximum R^2 of 0.53 can be obtained by the CNN-based regressor (for the *loud* dimension), while low R^2 values are obtained for other dimensions (*creepy*, *dingy*, *off the beaten path*). For six out of 13 dimensions, the obtained R^2 exceeds 0.30. On the *50K image* corpus, we find that CNN features consistently outperform individual and combinations of several low-level image features (including Color, GIST, HOG, and LBP) for all labels, consistent with results reported in the vision and multimedia literature [17]. Note that in Table 1, we have not shown the results for the combination of low-level image features due to space constraints. The results highlight the suitability of pre-trained CNN models to infer perceptual judgments in indoor

	Baseline-50K		Color-50K	GIST-50K	HOG-50K	LBP-50K	CNN-Phy-Env		CNN-50K	
	R^2	$RMSE$	R^2	R^2	R^2	R^2	R^2	$RMSE$	R^2	$RMSE$
Artsy	0.0	0.69	0.01	0.02	0.04	0.05	0.12	0.66	**0.22**	0.63
Bohemian	0.0	0.55	0.08	0.05	0.11	0.09	0.08	0.54	**0.24**	0.50
Conservative	0.0	0.67	0.21	0.20	0.19	0.11	0.24	0.60	**0.30**	0.57
Creepy	0.0	0.29	0.05	0.04	0.01	0.00	0.06	0.29	**0.14**	0.28
Dingy	0.0	0.50	0.04	0.02	0.01	0.05	0.05	0.50	**0.17**	0.47
Formal	0.0	0.82	0.10	0.07	0.03	0.10	0.28	0.72	**0.37**	0.70
Loud	0.0	0.73	0.33	0.29	0.26	0.31	**0.53**	0.51	0.52	0.51
Off the beaten path	0.0	0.61	0.05	0.01	0.01	0.00	0.15	0.47	**0.17**	0.47
Old-fashioned	0.0	0.50	0.16	0.11	0.10	0.08	**0.24**	0.54	0.22	0.55
Romantic	0.0	0.67	0.10	0.15	0.03	0.08	0.36	0.57	**0.39**	0.56
Sophisticated	0.0	0.79	0.11	0.10	0.04	0.10	0.26	0.72	**0.38**	0.67
Trendy	0.0	0.64	0.19	0.1	0.12	0.15	0.17	0.61	**0.32**	0.54
Up-scale	0.0	0.78	0.14	0.11	0.03	0.13	0.29	0.69	**0.40**	0.65

Table 1: Inference results for 13 ambiance dimensions for all feature sets, using R^2 and $RMSE$ as evaluation measures. Cells marked in **bold** correspond to the best R^2 result obtained for each dimension across all feature sets.

places; our finding complements what has been shown in recent literature regarding deep learning of high-level perception of outdoor scenes [14, 15].

While evaluating the performance of deep features between the *50K* and *physical environment* image corpora, we observe that the CNN-50K model outperforms the CNN-Phy-Env model in terms of higher R^2 and lower $RMSE$ values for most of the dimensions except the *loud* and *old-fashioned* dimensions. When examining the differences in more detail, we find that for some labels (e.g., *loud, romantic, old-fashioned, off the beaten path*), R^2 values are comparable, while for some dimensions (e.g., *artsy, bohemian, trendy*), the difference between R^2 values across image corpora is relatively high. Note that the ambiance ratings were obtained using just three manually selected images. These findings suggest that it is difficult to automatically represent some dimensions with just three images (compared to the human ability to infer and generalize from very few examples), and that the availability of more images provide additional informative visual cues to characterize some of these labels at high level. Future work will investigate the effect of the amount of data used for learning ambiance.

The performance of low-level features indicates that all feature sets perform the best for the *loud* feature (Table 1). Amongst the low-level feature sets, color features achieve the highest R^2 for most of the ambiance dimensions, including *trendy* and *up-scale* places, which corroborates results reported in [18], that attempted to infer ambiance for a 50-place dataset from profile pictures of Foursquare users rather than using photos of the venues. HOG and GIST also perform moderately for the *conservative* label.

While examining individual labels, the *loud* label achieves the highest performance with $R^2 \geq 0.26$ for all feature sets, suggesting visual patterns such as texture cues associated with the perception of loudness e.g., presence of crowd, an elevate stage, etc. (see Figure 1b). On the other hand, *creepy* achieves the lowest predictive performance ($R^2 \leq 0.14$). The low R^2 values for *creepy* can be attributed to a combination of lower inter-rater agreement and lowest mean annotation scores across all labels [22]. Overall, positively phrased (*romantic, up-scale, sophisticated*) and negatively phrased labels (*creepy, dingy*), which likely correspond to different ambiances, achieve in each case similar R^2 values.

Moreover, the *romantic* label achieves promising prediction performance ($R^2 = 0.39$) with CNN features, and relatively poor performance with low-level image features. We further analyze the relative importance of visual categories for different labels using the variable importance measures taken from random forests [3]. Using these measures, we find that "dining table" and "table lamp" are the top two discriminative visual categories for *romantic* places (see Figure 3a and 3b); "suit of clothes" and "red wine" for places perceived as *upscale* and *formal* (see Figure 3c); and "altar" for *artsy* places (see Figure 3d). In summary, the regression results suggest the feasibility to automatically infer place ambiance with promising prediction performance for some of the dimensions.

(a) Dining Table (b) Table Lamp (c) Suits (d) Altar

Figure 3: Sample of images from the *50K image* corpus which are recognized to belong to the visual category of a) Dining Table, b) Table Lamp, c) Suits of clothes, and d) Altar. For privacy reasons, images showing faces have been pixelated.

5. CONCLUSIONS

In this paper, we presented a methodology to automatically infer human impressions of place ambiance from social media images. Our results demonstrated the feasibility to automatically infer place ambiance using visual cues extracted from a pre-trained CNN model. We found that CNN features consistently outperformed low-level image features. Our work constitutes a first study to automatically characterize ambiance impressions of popular indoor places from deep features learned from social media images. Future work includes understanding the specific combination of different image types (food, people, environment) to ambiance inference, as well as the effect of the amount of available data.

6. ACKNOWLEDGMENTS

This work was supported by the Swiss National Science Foundation through the Youth@Night project. We thank Laurent Nguyen (Idiap) for discussions.

7. REFERENCES

[1] Julie Baker, Dhruv Grewal, and Ananthanarayanan Parasuraman. 1994. The Influence of Store Environment on Quality Inferences and Store Image. *Journal of the Academy of Marketing Science* 22, 4 (1994), 328–339.

[2] Anna Bosch, Andrew Zisserman, and Xavier Munoz. 2007. Representing Shape with a Spatial Pyramid Kernel. In *Proceedings of the 6th ACM International Conference on Image and Video Retrieval (CIVR '07)*. ACM, New York, NY, USA, 401–408.

[3] Leo Breiman. 2001. Random Forests. *Machine learning* 45, 1 (2001), 5–32.

[4] Oxford Dictionary. 2015. Definition of Ambiance in English. http://bit.ly/1dAy80r. (2015). Retrieved July 24, 2016.

[5] Jeff Donahue, Yangqing Jia, Oriol Vinyals, Judy Hoffman, Ning Zhang, Eric Tzeng, and Trevor Darrell. 2014. DeCAF: A Deep Convolutional Activation Feature for Generic Visual Recognition. In *ICML*. 647–655.

[6] Foursquare. 2015. Foursquare API August 2014 Update. https://developer.foursquare.com/docs/2014update. (2015). Retrieved July 24, 2016.

[7] L Graham and S Gosling. 2011. Can the Ambiance of a Place be Determined by the User Profiles of the People Who Visit It?. In *Proceedings of AAAI International Conference on Weblogs and Social Media (ICWSM)*.

[8] Vincent Heung and Tianming Gu. 2012. Influence of Restaurant Atmospherics on Patron Satisfaction and Behavioral Intentions. *International Journal of Hospitality Management* 31, 4 (2012), 1167–1177.

[9] Yangqing Jia, Evan Shelhamer, Jeff Donahue, Sergey Karayev, Jonathan Long, Ross Girshick, Sergio Guadarrama, and Trevor Darrell. 2014. Caffe: Convolutional Architecture for Fast Feature Embedding. In *Proceedings of the ACM International Conference on Multimedia*. ACM, 675–678.

[10] Frederic Jurie and Bill Triggs. 2005. Creating Efficient Codebooks for Visual Recognition. In *Proceedings of the Tenth IEEE International Conference on Computer Vision (ICCV '05)*. IEEE Computer Society, Washington, DC, USA, 604–610.

[11] Nikhil Naik, Jade Philipoom, Ramesh Raskar, and Cesar Hidalgo. 2014. Streetscore – Predicting the Perceived Safety of One Million Streetscapes. In *Proceedings of the 2014 IEEE Conference on Computer Vision and Pattern Recognition Workshops (CVPRW '14)*. IEEE Computer Society, Washington, DC, USA, 793–799.

[12] Timo Ojala, Matti Pietikainen, and Topi Maenpaa. 2002. Multiresolution Gray-Scale and Rotation Invariant Texture Classification with Local Binary Patterns. *IEEE Trans. Pattern Anal. Mach. Intell.* 24, 7 (July 2002), 971–987.

[13] Aude Oliva and Antonio Torralba. 2001. Modeling the Shape of the Scene: A Holistic Representation of the Spatial Envelope. *International Journal of Computer Vision* 42, 3 (2001), 145–175.

[14] Vicente Ordonez and Tamara L Berg. 2014. Learning High-Level Judgments of Urban Perception. In *European Conference on Computer Vision*. Springer, 494–510.

[15] Lorenzo Porzi, Samuel Rota Bulò, Bruno Lepri, and Elisa Ricci. 2015. Predicting and Understanding Urban Perception with Convolutional Neural Networks. In *Proceedings of the 23rd Annual ACM Conference on Multimedia Conference*. ACM, 139–148.

[16] Daniele Quercia, Neil Keith O'Hare, and Henriette Cramer. 2014. Aesthetic Capital: What makes London Look Beautiful, Quiet, and Happy?. In *Proceedings of the 17th ACM Conference on Computer Supported Cooperative Work & Social Computing*. ACM.

[17] Ali Razavian, Hossein Azizpour, Josephine Sullivan, and Stefan Carlsson. 2014. CNN Features off-the-shelf: an Astounding Baseline for Recognition. In *Proceedings of the IEEE Conference on Computer Vision and Pattern Recognition Workshops*. 806–813.

[18] Miriam Redi, Daniele Quercia, Lindsay Graham, and Samuel Gosling. 2015. Like Partying? Your Face Says It All. Predicting the Ambiance of Places with Profile Pictures. In *Ninth International AAAI Conference on Web and Social Media*.

[19] Salvador Ruiz-Correa, Darshan Santani, and Daniel Gatica-Perez. 2014. The Young and the City: Crowdsourcing Urban Awareness in a Developing Country. In *Proceedings of the First International Conference on IoT in Urban Space (URB-IOT '14)*. ICST (Institute for Computer Sciences, Social-Informatics and Telecommunications Engineering), ICST, Brussels, Belgium, Belgium, 74–79.

[20] Olga Russakovsky, Jia Deng, Hao Su, Jonathan Krause, Sanjeev Satheesh, Sean Ma, Zhiheng Huang, Andrej Karpathy, Aditya Khosla, Michael Bernstein, and others. 2015. Imagenet Large Scale Visual Recognition Challenge. *International Journal of Computer Vision* 115, 3 (2015), 211–252.

[21] Philip Salesses, Katja Schechtner, and Cesar A. Hidalgo. 2013. The Collaborative Image of The City: Mapping the Inequality of Urban Perception. *PLoS ONE* 8, 7 (07 2013).

[22] Darshan Santani and Daniel Gatica-Perez. 2015. Loud and Trendy: Crowdsourcing Impressions of Social Ambiance in Popular Indoor Urban Places. In *Proceedings of the 23rd Annual ACM Conference on Multimedia Conference*. ACM, 211–220.

[23] Darshan Santani, Salvador Ruiz-Correa, and Daniel Gatica-Perez. 2015. Looking at Cities in Mexico with Crowds. In *Proceedings of the 2015 Annual Symposium on Computing for Development*. ACM, 127–135.

[24] Christian Szegedy, Wei Liu, Yangqing Jia, Pierre Sermanet, Scott Reed, Dragomir Anguelov, Dumitru Erhan, Vincent Vanhoucke, and Andrew Rabinovich. 2015. Going Deeper with Convolutions. In *Proceedings of the IEEE Conference on Computer Vision and Pattern Recognition*. 1–9.

[25] Lou W Turley and Ronald E Milliman. 2000. Atmospheric Effects on Shopping Behavior: A Review of the Experimental Evidence. *Journal of Business Research* 49, 2 (2000), 193–211.

[26] Bolei Zhou, Agata Lapedriza, Jianxiong Xiao, Antonio Torralba, and Aude Oliva. 2014. Learning Deep Features for Scene Recognition Using Places Database. In *Advances in Neural Information Processing Systems*. 487–495.

Quartet-net Learning for Visual Instance Retrieval

Jiewei Cao, Zi Huang, Peng Wang, Chao Li, Xiaoshuai Sun, and Heng Tao Shen
The University of Queensland, Australia
{j.cao3, p.wang6, c.li1, x.sun1}@uq.edu.au, {huang, shenht}@itee.uq.edu.au

ABSTRACT

Recently, neuron activations extracted from a pre-trained convolutional neural network (CNN) show promising performance in various visual tasks. However, due to the domain and task bias, using the features generated from the model pre-trained for image classification as image representations for instance retrieval is problematic. In this paper, we propose quartet-net learning to improve the discriminative power of CNN features for instance retrieval. The general idea is to map the features into a space where the image similarity can be better evaluated. Our network differs from the traditional Siamese-net in two ways. First, we adopt a double-margin contrastive loss with a dynamic margin tuning strategy to train the network which leads to more robust performance. Second, we introduce in the mimic learning regularization to improve the generalization ability of the network by preventing it from overfitting to the training data. Catering for the network learning, we collect a large-scale dataset, namely GeoPair[1], which consists of 68*k* matching image pairs and 63*k* non-matching pairs. Experiments on several standard instance retrieval datasets demonstrate the effectiveness of our method.

Keywords

Convolutional Neural Networks; Feature Learning

1. INTRODUCTION

The neuron activations of a convolutional neural network (CNN), serving as image features, are used in various visual tasks [5, 18]. For visual instance retrieval, i.e., finding images containing the same object or scene as in a query image, mounting evidences [3, 19] demonstrate that the CNN features show superior performance compared to the traditional handcrafted features (e.g., SIFT), especially in the case of low dimensionality. However, due to the domain and task bias (e.g., most CNNs are trained on ImageNet [20] for classification), directly using the features generated from the pre-trained model as image representations for instance retrieval is not an ideal option. One treatment to this problem is to fine-tune the deep model in a target domain.

In this paper, we propose a novel feature learning strategy called *quartet-net* learning. The general idea is to map the image features into an embedding space where the similarity can be better evaluated. Siamese-net [4] can be regarded as a special case of our method and our framework differs from it in two ways: 1) Instead of using single-margin loss as in the standard Siamese-net, we adopt double-margin loss [14, 21] with the margins being dynamically tuned during training. Comparing to single-margin loss, double-margin loss pushes the feature distances between images of the same object under a threshold rather than to be zero. This idea is similar to the triplet loss [25, 22] which allows the learned features of the same object to live on a manifold instead of being projected onto a single point in the embedding space. The rationality behind is that we empirically find it difficult to map the features of positive pairs onto the same point especially in complex scenes and the double-margin relaxation turns out to be crucial in the feature learning. Different from [14, 21], we propose to tune the margins progressively which enhances the discriminative power of network during training; 2) Another advantage of our network is that we introduce in the mimic learning regularization [2, 7]. Specifically, we use two CNNs (i.e., teacher CNN) with fixed parameters to regularize the networks (i.e., student CNN) in order to prevent them from overfitting to the training data and consequently improve the generalization ability of the learned features.

Catering for the network training, we collect a large-scale geo-related dataset, namely *GeoPair*, which consists of 68*k* visually matching image pairs and 63*k* non-matching pairs. Extensive experiments conducted on several standard instance retrieval benchmarks demonstrate the effectiveness of our feature learning method.

[1]https://goo.gl/reg8M9

MM '16, October 15–19, 2016, Amsterdam, The Netherlands.

DOI: http://dx.doi.org/10.1145/2964284.2967262

2. QUARTET-NET LEARNING

The instance retrieval framework is illustrated in Fig. 1. During training, both matching and non-matching image pairs are fed into the network. After training, the activations of a specific layer are used as image representations to perform instance retrieval.

2.1 Network Structure

Given a pre-trained CNN, we duplicate its network structure four times within a quartet-net (see Fig. 1). The middle

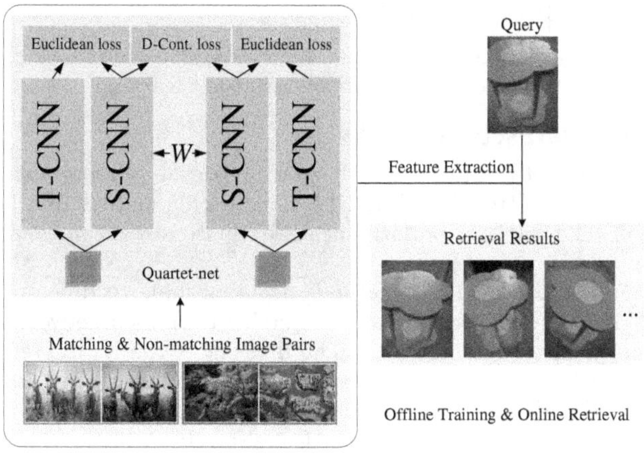

Figure 1: The framework of the proposed retrieval system.

two CNNs, similar to Siamese-net, share the same learned parameters W. We name these two CNNs "student CNNs" (S-CNNs) because during training they gradually learn the image similarities from the input image pairs. Different from [4] where single-margin contrastive loss is employed, we adopt double-margin contrastive loss [14] on the S-CNNs' top layers (e.g., the first fully connected layer). Inspired by the mimic learning in [2], the other two outside CNNs with fixed parameters act as "teacher CNNs" (T-CNNs) where their outputs are used as synthetic labels for "guiding" the S-CNNs. The advantages of these settings will be explained later. The inputs of a quartet-net are image pairs. The parameters are updated using standard back propagation algorithm and stochastic gradient descent.

2.2 Double-margin Contrastive Loss

Given a pair of images $(\mathbf{x}_\alpha^0, \mathbf{x}_\beta^0)$, the single-margin contrastive loss S_l for layer l is defined as:

$$S_l(\mathbf{x}_\alpha^0, \mathbf{x}_\beta^0) = y||\mathbf{x}_\alpha^l - \mathbf{x}_\beta^l||_2^2 + (1-y)\max(m - ||\mathbf{x}_\alpha^l - \mathbf{x}_\beta^l||_2^2, 0), \quad (1)$$

where $y = 1$ if $(\mathbf{x}_\alpha^0, \mathbf{x}_\beta^0)$ is a matching pair or $y = 0$ otherwise, $\mathbf{x}_\alpha^l$ and $\mathbf{x}_\beta^l$ are image $\mathbf{x}_\alpha^0$'s and $\mathbf{x}_\beta^0$'s feature representations in layer l respectively, and $m > 0$ is a margin parameter affecting non-matching pairs. This loss function can be interpreted as applying a contractive force between elements of any matching image pairs and a repulsive force between elements of non-matching pairs whose feature distances are smaller than margin $\sqrt{m}$. In contrast, the double-margin contrastive loss D_l adds another margin parameter to affect matching pairs:

$$D_l(\mathbf{x}_\alpha^0, \mathbf{x}_\beta^0) = y\max(||\mathbf{x}_\alpha^l - \mathbf{x}_\beta^l||_2^2 - m_1, 0) + (1-y)\max(m_2 - ||\mathbf{x}_\alpha^l - \mathbf{x}_\beta^l||_2^2, 0), \quad (2)$$

where $m_1 > 0$ and $m_2 > 0$ are margins affecting matching and non-matching pairs respectively. Therefore, double-margin contrastive loss only applies a contractive force between elements of matching pairs whose feature distances are larger than $\sqrt{m_1}$. The reason why double-margin contrastive loss is preferred rather than the single-margin one in instance retrieval is as follow: Given two matching images, they are probably far apart in the high-dimensional feature space [14]. Hence, we modify the loss to only penalize matching pairs whose distances are larger than a certain threshold. Similar mechanisms are involved in large margin nearest neighbor classification [26] and triplet loss [25, 22], but here we use two different margins to control how image pairs should be separated.

Instead of fixed margins, we use a dynamic margin tuning strategy, namely multistage margins control (MMC), during training. The process is to decrease the margin m_1 for matching pairs and increase m_2 for non-matching pairs in Eq.2 after certain learning epochs. This adjustment can be performed multiple times during training. Each time we change the margins in this manner, it will impose a contractive force between elements of any matching pairs whose feature distances are larger than the new $\sqrt{m_1}$, and a repulsive force between elements of non-matching pairs whose feature distances are smaller than the new $\sqrt{m_2}$. Double-margin loss with MMC can better separate the distribution of matching and non-matching image pairs in the feature space by progressively adjusting the margins, and as a result the retrieval accuracy is improved (see Sec. 4.3).

2.3 Mimic Learning Regularization

In [2], the authors show that it is possible to train a shallow net with high accuracy via mimic learning by training the shallow net (student net) to mimic a deep net (teacher net) with high fidelity. The process is first to train a state-of-the-art deep net using the original training data, and then pass the unlabeled data through this net to collect the produced outputs as labels. These synthetically labeled data is then used to train the shallow net. Experiments in [2] show that the student net can achieve comparable accuracy while it requires fewer parameters and shorter training time. A more general version of this kind of learning, called "knowledge distillation", is proposed in [7].

In this paper, we show that mimic learning can also be used as an effective regularization for quartet-net learning to avoid overfitting. Specifically, given an image $\mathbf{x}$, we denote its probability predictions produced by a CNN as $\mathbf{p} \in \mathbb{R}^K$, where K is the number of output units in the last layer. Normally, $\mathbf{p}$ are the outputs of the last softmax layer, i.e. $p_k = e^{z_k} / \sum_j^K e^{z_j}$. Here the log probability values $\mathbf{z}$, also called logits, are the probability values before the softmax layer. The teacher CNNs consume the same input image pairs as student CNNs do and conduct high-level "guidance" via regressing logits with the Euclidean loss. For example, given the same input image $\mathbf{x}$, the mimic learning loss between a teacher and student CNNs pair is:

$$E(\mathbf{x}) = \frac{1}{2}||\mathbf{z}_S - \mathbf{z}_T||_2^2, \quad (3)$$

where $\mathbf{z}_S$ and $\mathbf{z}_T$ are the logits generated by S-CNN and T-CNN respectively. In [2], regressing logits are preferred, rather than the output probability predictions, in order to avoid the information loss that occurs after passing through the logits to probability space.

Finally, given a pair of images $(\mathbf{x}_\alpha^0, \mathbf{x}_\beta^0)$, the loss function $\mathcal{L}$ for quartet-net learning is defined as:

$$\mathcal{L}(\mathbf{x}_\alpha^0, \mathbf{x}_\beta^0) = \sum_{l \in L} D_l(\mathbf{x}_\alpha^0, \mathbf{x}_\beta^0) + E(\mathbf{x}_\alpha^0) + E(\mathbf{x}_\beta^0), \quad (4)$$

where L is the set of layers that double-margin contrastive loss is applied on. With this loss function, we impose constrains that both S-CNNs would mimic the behaviors of their

Figure 2: GeoPair dataset samples. Images in each row are taken at the same spot within 100 meters by different users and share high visual similarities.

T-CNNs while learning discriminative features for matching and non-matching image pairs. This behavior is similar to the idea of "learning without forgetting" recently proposed in [13]. Experiments in section 4.3 verify that the extended mimic learning regularization can help prevent overfitting.

3. GEOPAIR DATASET

Images of the same object/scene with various visual variations are desired for our network training. Driven by the proliferation of GPS-enabled devices and media-sharing platforms, people have been creating large collections of images with geo-coordinates [24]. We use the images crawled from Flickr to construct our image pair dataset, namely GeoPair. Note that the geo-locations and user information allow us to apply an automatic method (described below) to construct a large collection of image dataset where images of the same object/scene are captured at different viewpoints and share high visual similarities.

We first use k-means to cluster all the images into 500 clusters according to their geo-coordinates. For every image in a cluster, we find a set of visually similar images from the same cluster [2], which is considered as a finer spot in this coarse cluster. To refine the result, only the images uploaded by different users and geographically within 100 meters are selected. In this way, we filter out most redundant images uploaded by the same user and collect diverse viewpoints of the same object/scene from different users. We obtain 28,418 spots with 109,725 images in total. Each spot has two similar images at minimum, and five images on average. Fig. 2 gives some examples of the collected dataset.

We create the matching image pairs by selecting images from the same spot and non-matching pairs by randomly pickup images from different spots. As a result, we generate 68,248 matching pairs and 63,432 non-matching pairs from the whole corpus. We randomly shuffle all image pairs and select 80% (105,344 pairs) for training and the rest 20% (26,336 pairs) for validation. In the following experiments, GeoPair dataset is used for quartet-net learning.

[2]SIFT and RANSAC verification [16] are used in our work.

4. EXPERIMENTS

In this section, we evaluate the retrieval performance of CNN features before and after quartet-net learning.

4.1 Datasets & CNNs

We report results on four instance retrieval datasets: Oxford5k [16], Paris6k [17], INRIA Holidays [8], and UKBench [15]. The retrieval performance is evaluated by mean average precision (mAP).

To demonstrate our methods are applicable to different CNNs, we used two publicly available pre-trained networks implemented by Caffe [11]. The first one is the BVLC reference CaffeNet which is similar the one proposed in [12]. The second one is the OxfordNet [23] which has 16 layers in total and is much deeper than CaffeNet. Both of them are pre-trained on the ILSVRC2012 dataset [20].

4.2 Quartet-net Learning Settings

In quartet-net learning, we apply the double-margin contrastive loss on the first and second fully connected layers of the two S-CNNs, namely $FC6$ and $FC7$ layers. We set the two margin parameters m_1 and m_2 in Eq.2 equal and their values are the average median distance of matching and non-matching pairs calculated from the GeoPair validation set. For example, the margin for CaffeNet's $FC6$ layer is the average of matching pairs' median distance and non-matching pairs' median distance in the $FC6$ layer's feature space (i.e., $m_1 = m_2 = 72105.6$ in this case). Note that we do not apply dropout [12] on $FC6$ and $FC7$ layers since we need to calculate the squared ℓ_2 norm of their outputs (i.e., $||\mathbf{x}_\alpha^l - \mathbf{x}_\beta^l||_2^2$ in Eq.2). For mimic learning regularization, the Euclidean loss is applied on each teacher and student CNNs pair's last fully connected layers, namely $FC8$ layers, via regressing logits before the softmax activation.

During training, one can decide to tune all the layers within a S-CNN or only a partial of them, such as $FC6$, $FC7$ and $FC8$ on which the loss functions are applied and keep other layers' parameters fixed. In the following experiments, we compare the performance of different combinations of network settings. Specifically, we denote the baseline Siamese-net learning for all layers in CaffeNet as CaffeNet$_{\times 2}$. Similarly, we denote CaffeNet$_{\times 4}$ as quartet-net learning for all the layers in CaffeNet. Due to the size and time consumption of OxfordNet, we only perform fine-tuning for its fully connected layers (i.e., $FC6$, $FC7$, $FC8$ layers), which is denoted as OxfordNet$_{\times 4}$.

We set the initial learning rate to $1e^{-8}$. This value is chosen through trial and error by keep reducing the learning rate by a factor of 10 from its initial value 0.01 until we observe a steady decrease in the validation error rate at the beginning of learning steps. Follow the parameters settings as in [12, 6] for training, we set momentum to 0.9, weight decay to $5e^{-4}$, and train on the GeoPair dataset for a maximum 200 epochs[3]. After every 20 epochs, we decrease the learning rate by a factor of 10. And after every 50 epochs, we decrease m_1 (margin for matching pairs) and increase m_2 (margin for non-matching pairs) in Eq.2 by a factor of 10. Finally, we use the activations of $FC6$ (or $FC7$) layer in the S-CNN as global image descriptors. Given a query image, we extract the query feature for the whole image and

[3] The training time depends on the network size and computing hardware. For CaffeNet, it takes about 14 hours for 50 learning epochs on the GTX Titan Black.

Table 1: The retrieval performance of CaffeNet's features with different learning settings. "Org." are the mAPs before fine-tuning. "CaffeNet$^{(S)}_{\times 2}$(CaffeNet$^{(D)}_{\times 2}$)" are the mAPs after Siamese-net learning with single(double)-margin loss, and CaffeNet$_{\times 4}$ are the mAPs after quartet-net learning using the GeoPair dataset.

		Org.	CaffeNet$^{(S)}_{\times 2}$	CaffeNet$^{(D)}_{\times 2}$	CaffeNet$_{\times 4}$
FC6	Ox5k	0.407	0.233	0.415	**0.426**
	Pa6k	0.584	0.372	0.586	**0.619**
	Hol.	0.681	0.393	**0.687**	0.679
	UKB.	0.849	0.549	0.837	**0.866**
FC7	Ox5k	0.387	0.220	0.407	**0.412**
	Pa6k	0.587	0.343	0.593	**0.604**
	Hol.	0.681	0.338	0.685	**0.701**
	UKB.	0.856	0.493	0.830	**0.867**

return a list of images ranked by the dot product of the ℓ_2-normalized feature in descending order.

4.3 The Performance of Quartet-net Learning

We evaluate the effects of different components of quartet-net learning and compare it with Siamese-net learning as shown in Tab. 1. 1) *Effects of double-margin contrastive loss*: The results of CaffeNet$^{(S)}_{\times 2}$ show that Siamese-net learning with single-margin contrastive loss significantly decreases retrieval accuracies, which means that the distribution of matching and non-matching image pairs is not distinguishable after fine-tuning. This result is consistent with the previous findings in [14]. In contrast, the mAPs are slightly improved when Siamese-net is equipped with double-margin contrastive loss (CaffeNet$^{(D)}_{\times 2}$), which confirms the effectiveness of this loss function. 2) *Effects of mimic learning regularization*: CaffeNet$_{\times 4}$ outperforms CaffeNet$^{(D)}_{\times 2}$ on all the datasets except for the case of *FC*6 on Holiday dataset. With the help of mimic learning regularization between student and teacher CNNs, quartet-net learning can maximize the learning capacity and representational power of the tuned CNN. These results demonstrate the effectiveness of our proposed network structure.

Next, we evaluate the effect of dynamic margin turning. We decrease m_1 (margin for matching pairs) and increase m_2 (margin for non-matching pairs) in Eq. 2 by a factor of 10 after 50 epochs before continuing training. Fig. 3 shows the retrieval accuracy of CaffeNet's *FC*6 features on Oxford5k after quartet-net learning with MMC. We observe that MMC provides consistent improvements for both Siamese-net and quartet-net learning. But it downgrades the discriminative power of the CNN features after certain epoch (e.g., the 200-th epoch). Therefore, our total training epochs is set to 200. "CaffeNet$_{\times 4}$(*nommc*)" uses fixed margins and trains the same amount of learning epochs but there is no significant improvement, which means the performance gains of S-CNN are not due to the longer training time. In addition, if we use the best margin values for fixed margins training, as demonstrated by "CaffeNet$_{\times 4}$(#200)", the mAP steadily increases. Therefore, MMC can also be used to determine the best margins for training.

4.4 Comparisons with Existing Work

According to the previous experiments, we use the *FC*6 layer's features as image descriptors. We report the results of CaffeNet$_{\times 4}$ and OxfordNet$_{\times 4}$. Tab. 2 shows the comparisons between our method with existing work. Note that for a fair comparison, we only report results on features with the same dimension. We also use PCA to reduce the original feature dimensionality to much lower ones to further compare the performance in different dimensional feature spaces. Note that KTH [18] also uses the *FC*6 features as image descriptors, but their results are not directly comparable since their CNN is different from us. When comparing with other optimized handcraft features [9, 10, 1], our method outperforms them under different dimensionalities on all datasets.

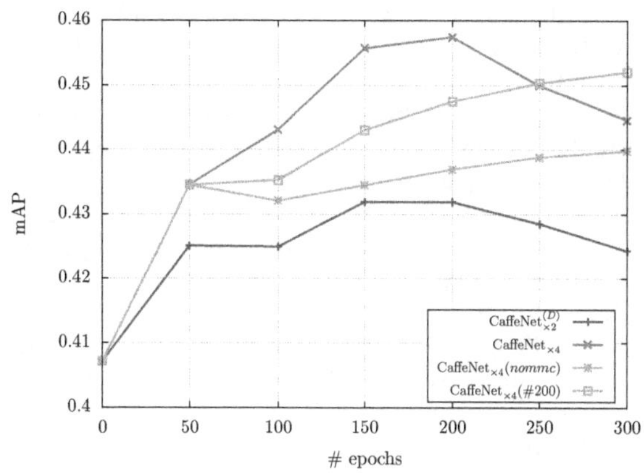

Figure 3: The performance of CaffeNet's *FC*6 features on Oxford5k dataset during different learning stages. CaffeNet$_{\times 4}$(*nommc*) stands for quartet-net learning without MMC, and CaffeNet$_{\times 4}$(#200) uses the fixed margin values of m_1 and m_2 at the 200-th epoch.

Table 2: Comparisons with existing work.

	Dim.	Oxford5k	Paris6k	Holidays	UKBench
KTH [18]	4096	32.2	49.5	64.2	76.0
VLAD [9]	4096	37.8	-	55.6	-
FV [9]	4096	41.8	-	59.9	-
CaffeNet$_{\times 4}$	4096	45.7	69.2	70.2	86.6
OxfordNet$_{\times 4}$	4096	**48.3**	**71.5**	**71.5**	**88.2**
Inria [10]	256	47.2	-	65.7	86.3
CaffeNet$_{\times 4}$	256	47.3	47.4	71.6	86.3
OxfordNet$_{\times 4}$	256	**49.7**	**48.8**	**72.5**	**88.3**
VLAD-intra [1]	128	44.8	-	62.5	-
CaffeNet$_{\times 4}$	128	46.9	47.7	**71.6**	85.6
OxfordNet$_{\times 4}$	128	**48.5**	**48.8**	71.2	**87.5**

5. CONCLUSION

In this paper, we present quartet-net learning to improve the discriminative power of CNN features for visual instance retrieval. By incorporating the double-margin contrastive loss and mimic learning regularization, quartet-net learning can help avoid overfitting when training on large image pairs dataset. Our proposed method can be applied to different CNNs and outperforms existing methods on various datasets. Besides, we release the GeoPair dataset, a large-scale dataset consisting of matching/non-matching image pairs, to facilitate future studies.

6. REFERENCES

[1] R. Arandjelovic and A. Zisserman. All about VLAD. In *CVPR*, 2013.

[2] J. Ba and R. Caruana. Do deep nets really need to be deep? In *NIPS*, 2014.

[3] A. Babenko, A. Slesarev, A. Chigorin, and V. Lempitsky. Neural codes for image retrieval. In *ECCV*. 2014.

[4] S. Chopra, R. Hadsell, and Y. LeCun. Learning a similarity metric discriminatively, with application to face verification. In *CVPR*, 2005.

[5] J. Donahue, Y. Jia, O. Vinyals, J. Hoffman, N. Zhang, E. Tzeng, and T. Darrell. Decaf: A deep convolutional activation feature for generic visual recognition. In *ICML*, 2014.

[6] R. B. Girshick, J. Donahue, T. Darrell, and J. Malik. Rich feature hierarchies for accurate object detection and semantic segmentation. In *CVPR*, 2014.

[7] G. E. Hinton, O. Vinyals, and J. Dean. Distilling the knowledge in a neural network. *CoRR*, abs/1503.02531, 2015.

[8] H. Jégou, M. Douze, and C. Schmid. Hamming embedding and weak geometric consistency for large scale image search. In *ECCV*, 2008.

[9] H. Jégou, F. Perronnin, M. Douze, J. Sánchez, P. Pérez, and C. Schmid. Aggregating local image descriptors into compact codes. *TPAMI*, 2012.

[10] H. Jégou and A. Zisserman. Triangulation embedding and democratic aggregation for image search. In *CVPR*, 2014.

[11] Y. Jia, E. Shelhamer, J. Donahue, S. Karayev, J. Long, R. B. Girshick, S. Guadarrama, and T. Darrell. Caffe: Convolutional architecture for fast feature embedding. In *MM*, 2014.

[12] A. Krizhevsky, I. Sutskever, and G. E. Hinton. Imagenet classification with deep convolutional neural networks. In *NIPS*, 2012.

[13] Z. Li and D. Hoiem. Learning without forgetting. *CoRR*, abs/1606.09282, 2016.

[14] J. Lin, O. Morere, V. Chandrasekhar, A. Veillard, and H. Goh. Deephash: Getting regularization, depth and fine-tuning right. *CoRR*, abs/1501.04711, 2015.

[15] D. Nister and H. Stewenius. Scalable recognition with a vocabulary tree. In *CVPR*, 2006.

[16] J. Philbin, O. Chum, M. Isard, J. Sivic, and A. Zisserman. Object retrieval with large vocabularies and fast spatial matching. In *CVPR*, 2007.

[17] J. Philbin, O. Chum, M. Isard, J. Sivic, and A. Zisserman. Lost in quantization: Improving particular object retrieval in large scale image databases. In *CVPR*, 2008.

[18] A. S. Razavian, H. Azizpour, J. Sullivan, and S. Carlsson. CNN features off-the-shelf: an astounding baseline for recognition. In *CVPRW*, 2014.

[19] A. S. Razavian, J. Sullivan, A. Maki, and S. Carlsson. A baseline for visual instance retrieval with deep convolutional networks. In *ICLRW*, 2015.

[20] O. Russakovsky, J. Deng, H. Su, J. Krause, S. Satheesh, S. Ma, Z. Huang, A. Karpathy, A. Khosla, M. Bernstein, A. C. Berg, and L. Fei-Fei. ImageNet Large Scale Visual Recognition Challenge. *IJCV*, 2015.

[21] F. Sadeghi, C. L. Zitnick, and A. Farhadi. Visalogy: Answering visual analogy questions. In *NIPS*, 2015.

[22] F. Schroff, D. Kalenichenko, and J. Philbin. Facenet: A unified embedding for face recognition and clustering. In *CVPR*, 2015.

[23] K. Simonyan and A. Zisserman. Very deep convolutional networks for large-scale image recognition. *CoRR*, abs/1409.1556, 2014.

[24] B. Thomee, D. A. Shamma, G. Friedland, B. Elizalde, K. Ni, D. Poland, D. Borth, and L. Li. YFCC100M: the new data in multimedia research. *Commun. ACM*, 2016.

[25] J. Wang, Y. Song, T. Leung, C. Rosenberg, J. Wang, J. Philbin, B. Chen, and Y. Wu. Learning fine-grained image similarity with deep ranking. In *CVPR*, 2014.

[26] K. Q. Weinberger, J. Blitzer, and L. K. Saul. Distance metric learning for large margin nearest neighbor classification. In *NIPS*, 2005.

AKSDA-MSVM: A GPU-accelerated Multiclass Learning Framework for Multimedia

Stavros Arestis-Chartampilas
CERTH-ITI
Thermi 57001, Greece
stav_ares@iti.gr

Nikolaos Gkalelis
CERTH-ITI
Thermi 57001, Greece
gkalelis@iti.gr

Vasileios Mezaris
CERTH-ITI
Thermi 57001, Greece
bmezaris@iti.gr

ABSTRACT

In this paper, a combined nonlinear dimensionality reduction and multiclass classification framework is proposed. Specifically, a novel discriminant analysis (DA) technique, called accelerated kernel subclass discriminant analysis (AKSDA), derives a discriminant subspace, and a linear multiclass support vector machine (MSVM) computes a set of separating hyperplanes in the derived subspace. Moreover, within this framework an approach for accelerating the computation of multiple Gram matrices and an associated late fusion scheme are presented. Experimental evaluation in five multimedia datasets, on tasks such as video event detection and news document classification, shows that the proposed framework achieves excellent results in terms of both training time and generalization performance.

Keywords

Discriminant analysis; GPU; multiclass classification; SVM

1. INTRODUCTION

In high-dimensional machine learning problems such as multimedia classification, the curse-of-dimensionality becomes a major challenge: the complexity of the pattern recognition model grows exponentially with the dimensionality of the space [8, 25]. A key observation for solving the curse-of-dimensionality problem is that most physical processes observed in some high-dimensional ambient space adhere to another, low-dimensional manifold. Hence, the curse-of-dimensionality can be alleviated by first identifying and then operating in this "intrinsic" low-dimensional space. Based on this fact, a major research direction is the investigation of frameworks that combine manifold learning with classification approaches [3, 29, 12, 15, 22, 19].

Kernel discriminant analysis (KDA) is a powerful class of manifold learning techniques (e.g. KFD [20], GDA [2]) that combined with linear (or piece-wise linear) classifiers have provided very good results in very challenging tasks. Moreover, further performance improvements have been achieved by subclass extensions of conventional KDA approaches, which by imposing a less strict requirement for the feature mapping are able to identify a more discriminant subspace (e.g. KSDA [28], KMSDA [13]). In the resulting subspace, it is then possible to use lower-capacity classifiers, such as linear SVMs (LSVMs), improving the generalization performance of the overall system [25].

Despite the above advances, the application of subclass-based KDA approaches to large-scale problems remains computationally challenging. The core of this limitation lies in the computation of the Gram matrix and the solution of the generalized eigenvalue problem. Recently, accelerated generalised subclass discriminant analysis (AGSDA) and its GPU implementation have been proposed, alleviating the above drawbacks and achieving state-of-the-art results in a variety of problems [1]. For example, its combination with LSVM (AGSDA-LSVM) has resulted in increased precision and orders of magnitude faster training times over LSVM and KSVM [1] in the problems of concept and event detection in video. Furthermore, earlier approaches such as SRKDA [4] and GSDA [10] (upon which AGSDA was based) were previously already shown to provide improved performance over many other KDA approaches.

The AGSDA-LSVM described above resolves many problems of subclass-based KDA approaches, but still suffers from the following limitations: i) it has been developed only for two-class problems and zero-mean datasets, ii) the GPU acceleration of AGSDA-LSVM has been proposed only in conjunction with the Gaussian RBF kernel. To this end, in this paper we propose AKSDA-MSVM that extends AGSDA-LSVM for multiclass classification, and datasets that are not necessarily normalized to have zero mean. Moreover, by carefully reformulating the Gram matrices of three popular kernels, we show how they can be simultaneously computed, exploiting both GPU and multi-core CPU acceleration. The experimental evaluation of AKSDA-MSVM on several large-scale datasets for both multimedia classification and retrieval tasks shows that the proposed approach achieves excellent performance in terms of both training time and generalization accuracy. Summarizing, the main contributions of this paper are:

- To the best of our knowledge, this is the first work that combines nonlinear discriminant analysis with multiclass support vector machines for multimedia classification.
- A method for the parallel computation of multiple Gram matrices is proposed, exploiting GPU and multicore CPU acceleration.

MM '16, October 15-19, 2016, Amsterdam, Netherlands

DOI: http://dx.doi.org/10.1145/2964284.2967263

- The proposed approach achieves very good performance in terms of training time and generalization performance. Moreover, its software implementation is made freely available to the scientific community[1].

The rest of the paper is structured as follows: In Section 2, the proposed AKSDA-MSVM approach is described. Experimental results are presented in Section 3, while Section 4 concludes the paper.

2. AKSDA-MSVM

2.1 AKSDA

Let $\mathcal{X} = \{(\mathbf{x}_n, (\omega_n, \upsilon_n)), n = 1, \ldots, N\}$ be a subclass partition of an annotated training set, where $\mathbf{x}_n \in \mathbb{R}^L$ is the n-th training observation in the L-dimensional input space, $\omega_n \in \{1, \ldots, \Omega\}$, $\upsilon_n \in \{1, \ldots, \Upsilon_{\omega_n}\}$ are its class and subclass labels, Υ_{ω_n} is the number of subclasses of class ω_n, and Ω, N are the total number of classes and observations respectively. The partitioning of classes to subclasses can be performed fully automatically (in our experiments this is done using k-means). Moreover, the training set is ordered in ascending order according to the class and subclass labels (i.e., $\omega_n \leq \omega_{n+1}$, and within a given class it is $\upsilon_n \leq \upsilon_{n+1}$). Given $\mathcal{X}$, AKSDA solves the generalized eigenvalue problem:

$$\mathbf{K}_c\mathbf{A}\mathbf{K}_c\boldsymbol{\Psi}_c = \mathbf{K}_c\mathbf{B}\mathbf{K}_c\boldsymbol{\Psi}_c\boldsymbol{\Lambda}_c, \tag{1}$$

where, $\mathbf{K}_c$, $[\mathbf{K}_c]_{r,q} = k_c(\mathbf{x}_r, \mathbf{x}_q)$ is the Gram matrix of the training set associated with a Mercer kernel function $k_c(\cdot,\cdot) : \mathbb{R}^L \times \mathbb{R}^L \to \mathbb{R}$, $\mathbf{A}$ is the between-subclass factor matrix, whose element $[\mathbf{A}]_{r,q}$ corresponding to samples $\mathbf{x}_r$, $\mathbf{x}_q$ is defined as

$$[\mathbf{A}]_{r,q} = \begin{cases} \frac{\hat{P}(\omega_r,\upsilon_r)(1-\hat{P}(\omega_r))}{N^2_{\omega_r,\upsilon_r}}, & \text{if } (\omega_r, \upsilon_r) = (\omega_q, \upsilon_q), \\ 0 & \text{if } \omega_q = \omega_r, \upsilon_q \neq \upsilon_r, \\ -\frac{\hat{P}(\omega_r,\upsilon_r)\hat{P}(\omega_q,\upsilon_q)}{N_{\omega_r,\upsilon_r}N_{\omega_q,\upsilon_q}}, & \text{otherwise,} \end{cases}$$

N_{ω_r}, $\hat{P}(\omega_r)$, N_{ω_r,υ_r}, $\hat{P}(\omega_r, \upsilon_r)$ are the number of observations and estimated prior probabilities of class ω_r and subclass (ω_r, υ_r) respectively, $\mathbf{B} = \mathbf{I} - \frac{1}{N}\mathbf{J}$ is the total factor matrix, $\mathbf{I}$ and $\mathbf{J}$ are $N \times N$ identity and all-ones matrices, $\boldsymbol{\Psi}_c \in \mathbb{R}^{N\times D}$ is the column-orthogonal eigenvector matrix, $\boldsymbol{\Lambda}_c \in \mathbb{R}^{D\times D}$ is the diagonal matrix with sorted eigenvalues in its diagonal, $D = \Upsilon - 1$ is the dimensionality of the projection subspace[2], and Υ is the total number of subclasses. Following [11], the above problem can be solved in two steps: a) identifying the eigenpairs $(\mathbf{V}, \boldsymbol{\Delta})$, $\mathbf{V} \in \mathbb{R}^{N\times D}$, $\boldsymbol{\Delta} \in \mathbb{R}^{D\times D}$ of $\mathbf{A}$, b) obtaining $\boldsymbol{\Psi}_c$ by solving the following linear matrix system

$$\mathbf{K}_c\boldsymbol{\Psi}_c = \mathbf{V}. \tag{2}$$

The eigenvector matrix $\mathbf{V}$ in the first step of AKSDA can be efficiently computed following [11]. The projection $\mathbf{z}$ of an observation $\mathbf{x}$ in the discriminant subspace can then be computed as $\mathbf{z} = \boldsymbol{\Psi}_c^T[k_c(\mathbf{x}_1, \mathbf{x}), \ldots, k_c(\mathbf{x}_N, \mathbf{x})]^T$.

2.2 GPU-accelerated computation of multiple Gram matrices

One of the most computationally expensive parts of AKSDA (and of most kernel-based approaches) in terms of both memory consumption and learning time is the calculation of the Gram matrix $\mathbf{K}_c$. In [1], a tiled general matrix multiplication (GEMM) approach was proposed for the efficient computation of the Gram matrix with Gaussian RBF kernel. Inspired from [1], we propose a method for accelerating the computation of multiple Gram matrices. For illustration purposes, we examine the application of the proposed method in accelerating the computation of the Gram matrices associated with the Gaussian RBF, t-student and Cauchy kernels

$$\begin{aligned} k_1(\mathbf{x}_r, \mathbf{x}_q) &= \exp(-\gamma\|\mathbf{x}_r - \mathbf{x}_q\|^2), \\ k_2(\mathbf{x}_r, \mathbf{x}_q) &= (1 + \|\mathbf{x}_r - \mathbf{x}_q\|^d)^{-1}, \\ k_3(\mathbf{x}_r, \mathbf{x}_q) &= (1 + \|\mathbf{x}_r - \mathbf{x}_q\|^2/\sigma)^{-1}, \end{aligned} \tag{3}$$

where exp() is the exponential function, and γ, d, σ are the respective kernel parameters. Rearranging the above we get

$$k_1(\mathbf{x}_r, \mathbf{x}_q) = \exp(-\gamma u_{rq}), \qquad k_2(\mathbf{x}_r, \mathbf{x}_q) = \mathrm{sgm}_{d/2}(u_{rq}),$$
$$k_3(\mathbf{x}_r, \mathbf{x}_q) = \mathrm{sgm}_1(u_{rq}/\sigma),$$

where $\mathrm{sgm}_\iota(\upsilon) = (1+\upsilon^\iota)^{-1}$ is a sigmoid scalar function, and $u_{rq} = \|\mathbf{x}_r - \mathbf{x}_q\|^2$. Considering exp(), $\mathrm{sgm}_\iota()$ as element-wise matrix operators, the respective Gram matrices can be expressed as

$$\mathbf{K}_1 = \exp(-\gamma\mathbf{D}),\ \mathbf{K}_2 = \mathrm{sgm}_{d/2}(\mathbf{D}),\ \mathbf{K}_3 = \mathrm{sgm}_1(\mathbf{D}/\sigma). \tag{4}$$

The most computationally expensive part above is the computation of matrix $\mathbf{D}$, defined as $\mathbf{D} = \mathbf{X}^T\mathbf{X} + \mathbf{E}$, where $\mathbf{X}$ is the training data matrix, $\mathbf{E} = \mathbf{F} + \mathbf{C}$, $\mathbf{C} = \mathbf{F}^T$, and the elements of $\mathbf{F}$ are defined as $[\mathbf{F}]_{rq} = \mathbf{x}_r^T\mathbf{x}_r$, $\forall\, r, q$. As shown in [1], $\mathbf{D}$ can be easily partitioned to an arbitrary number of tiles, which can be computed in parallel by exploiting the GEMM function of CUDA's cuBLAS library. Furthermore, the element-wise matrix operations in (4) can also be parallelized by exploiting a multi-core CPU. Note that by appropriately formulating other kernel functions (e.g. the Inverse Multi-quadric kernel[3]) an arbitrary number of different Gram matrices can be parallelized.

2.3 Classification

Let $\mathcal{Z} = \{\mathcal{Z}_c, c = 1, \ldots, C\}$ be a training dataset of C subsets, where each subset $\mathcal{Z}_c = \{(\mathbf{z}_{n,c}, \omega_n), n = 1, \ldots, N\}$, $\mathbf{z}_{n,c} = \boldsymbol{\Psi}_c^T[k_c(\mathbf{x}_1, \mathbf{x}_n), \ldots, k_c(\mathbf{x}_N, \mathbf{x}_n)]^T \in \mathbb{R}^D$ is derived from $\mathcal{X}$ using AKSDA and a specified kernel function $k_c(\cdot,\cdot)$. Given the above dataset, we define a linear model for each class and kernel function

$$f_{i,c}(\mathbf{z}_{n,c}) = \mathbf{w}_{i,c}^T\mathbf{z}_{n,c}, \tag{5}$$

where $\mathbf{w}_{i,c} \in \mathbb{R}^D$ is the weight vector referring to i-th class and c-th kernel function[4]. For the identification of the weight vectors we utilize the linear MSVM approach [16, 6]. That is, the following optimization problem is solved

[1]Software: http://mklab.iti.gr/project/aksda

[2]$\mathbf{K}_c$ may be semidefinite positive matrix and in this case $D \leq \Upsilon - 1$. However, we assume that $\mathbf{K}_c$ is positive definite, which can be easily accomplished through regularization [11].

[3]More details in http://crsouza.blogspot.com/2010/03/kernel-functions-for-machine-learning.html

[4]Note that a bias term is not included in (5). However, this can be easily solved by using augmented weight vectors or appropriate kernel functions as explained in [6].

using the respective training subset $\mathcal{Z}_c$

$$\min_{\mathbf{w}_{i,c},\boldsymbol{\xi}_{n,c}} \frac{1}{2}\sum_{i=1}^{\Omega} \mathbf{w}_{i,c}^T\mathbf{w}_{i,c} + R\sum_{n=1}^{N} \xi_{n,c},$$

subject to the constraints

$$(\mathbf{w}_{\omega_n,c} - \mathbf{w}_{i,c})^T\mathbf{z}_{n,c} \geq e_{i,n} - \xi_{n,c},\ \forall i,n$$

where, $\xi_{n,c} \geq 0$ is the slack variable corresponding to $\mathbf{z}_{n,c}$, $R > 0$ is the penalty term, $e_{i,n} = 1-\delta_{i,n}$, and $\delta_{i,n}$ is the class indicator function, i.e., $\delta_{i,n} = 1$ if $\omega_n = i$, $\delta_{i,n} = 0$ otherwise. Given the learned models in (5) a test observation $\mathbf{x}_t$ can be then classified according to the following rule

$$\omega_t = \arg\max_{i=1,\ldots,\Omega}(f_{i,c}(\mathbf{z}_{t,c})),$$

where $\mathbf{z}_{t,c} = \mathbf{\Psi}_c^T[k_c(\mathbf{x}_1,\mathbf{x}_t),\ldots,k_c(\mathbf{x}_N,\mathbf{x}_t)]^T$. However, the above rule does not combine the different kernel modalities. To this end, following [18] the parameters α, β of the sigmoid function below are estimated in order to be able to map class similarities to posterior class probabilities

$$\hat{P}_c(i|\mathbf{x}_n) = \frac{1}{1+\exp(\alpha f_{i,c}(\mathbf{z}_{n,c})+\beta)}.$$

Then, assuming equiprobable priors for each class, the sum rule [17] can be applied to yield the overall posterior probability for the i-th class

$$\dot{P}(i|\mathbf{x}_t) = \sum_{c=1}^{C}\hat{P}_c(i|\mathbf{x}_t),$$

and the following rule is used for classifying test observations

$$\omega_t = \arg\max_{i=1,\ldots,\Omega}(\dot{P}(i|\mathbf{x}_t)). \quad (6)$$

3. EXPERIMENTAL RESULTS

3.1 Compared methods

We experimentally compare the following methods:

i) MSVM-1: Multiclass LSVM implementation of libsvm [5]. We use the Matlab version (compiled again in our evaluation workstation, so that all cores of the machine are exploited[5]). Matlab makes use of Intel's state-of-the-art numerical libraries, which speed up this method significantly.

ii) MSVM-2: Same as MSVM-1, with multiclass KSVM instead of multiclass LSVM.

iii) MSVM-3: Multiclass LSVM implementation of liblinear (out-of-the-box Matlab multi-core version) [7], which is among the fastest MSVM implementations.

iv) AKSDA-MSVM-1: The proposed method, using only the Gaussian RBF kernel. The liblinear MSVM [7] is employed for learning the separating hyperplanes.

v) AKSDA-MSVM-2: Same as AKSDA-MSVM-1, but with four kernels. Specifically, the Gaussian RBF, T-Student, Cauchy and Inverse Multi-quadric.

3.2 Datasets

One TRECVID, two UCI[6] (Amazon, YouTube) and two libsvm[7] (News20, Sector) datasets are used for the evaluation of the proposed method, described in the following:

i) MED12: This is an annotated subset of the TRECVID MED 2012 video corpus, where each video is represented in $\mathbb{R}^{101376}$ using improved dense trajectories [1, 14, 21, 26]. It consists of 25 target events and 13249 videos. The overall set is divided to 8824 training and 4425 evaluation videos.

ii) Amazon: It consists of 1500 reviews posted by 50 Amazon customers. Each review is represented by a 10000-dimensional vector. A random partition to 1200 training and 300 test observations is used.

iii) YouTube: It consists of 30 video game classes and up to 13 feature types per observation. We only use the audio MFCC features (2000-dimensional), and a subset of 20000 observations from the overall training set. For evaluation, the entire test set of 17177 instances is employed.

iv) News20: A collection of approximately 20000 news documents from 20 different newsgroups, used for text classification. A partition of 15935 training and 3993 test observations in $\mathbb{R}^{62061}$ is provided, already scaled. It is a very sparse dataset with approximately 0.13% non-zero elements.

v) Sector: A collection of 9619 corporate web pages organized into 105 categories based on each company's commercial activity. The scaled version of the dataset, partitioned to 6412 training and 3207 test observations in $\mathbb{R}^{55197}$, is used. It is very sparse, with only 0.3% non-zero elements.

3.3 Experimental setup

For all tested methods, model selection is done using 3-fold cross-validation, where at each fold the training set is split to 30% learning set and 70% validation set. For both AKSDA-MSVM (-1 & -2) and the KSVM of libsvm (MSVM-2), the kernel and SVM penalty parameters are searched in {0.5, 1, 1.5, ..., 10} and {0.1, 1, 10, 100}, respectively. For the penalty term of the LSVMs a broader set of candidate values is used according to relevant literature, i.e., {0.01, 0.03, 0.1, 0.3, 1, 3, 10} for the News20 and Sector, and {0.1, 1, 10, 100} for the YouTube and Amazon datasets. Moreover, class balancing is applied to each SVM classifier using a weight $(N-N_i)/N_i$, where N_i, N are the number of observations in i-th class and the total number of observations, respectively. The PC used for the evaluation is an Intel i7 3770K@3.5Ghz with 32 GB RAM, Windows 7, and a low-end Nvidia GPU (GTX 650). The experiments with AKSDA-MSVM were also repeated on a high-end GPU (GTX TITAN).

Figure 1: Training time along different parts of AKSDA-MSVM-1 on GTX TITAN

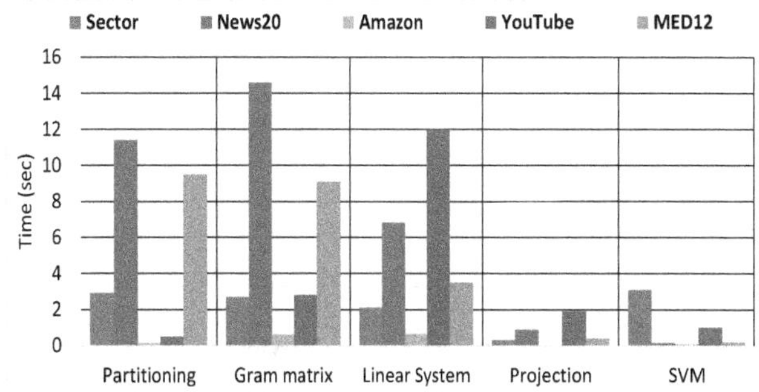

3.4 Results

The retrieval evaluation results in terms of mean average precision (MAP) and the respective times on GTX 650 are

[5]As advised in http://www.csie.ntu.edu.tw/~cjlin/libsvm/faq.html#f8032

[6]http://archive.ics.uci.edu/ml

[7]https://www.csie.ntu.edu.tw/~cjlin/libsvmtools/datasets/

Table 1: Performance evaluation on YouTube

Method	MAP	Train/Test(minutes)
MSVM-1 [5]	38.94%	81.14/7.3
MSVM-2 [5]	49.14%	118.7/7.58
MSVM-3 [7]	28.14%	0.78/**0.018**
AKSDA-MSVM-1	49.28%	**0.57**/0.087
AKSDA-MSVM-2	**51.6%**	2.45/0.337

Table 2: Performance evaluation on MED12

Method	MAP	Train/Test(minutes)
AGSDA-LSVM [1]	41.20%	23.4/18.6
LSVM (from [1])	38.73%	75.5/2
AKSDA-MSVM-1	41.20%	**0.85/0.66**
AKSDA-MSVM-2	**41.87%**	1.01/0.80

Table 3: Performance evaluation on three datasets (CCR %, Train/Test time in minutes)

Method	Amazon	News20	Sector
MSVM-1 [5]	66%	84.52%	91.89%
	0.65/0.020	3.1/0.16	2.12/0.18
MSVM-2 [5]	66.33%	84.62%	91.64%
	0.657/0.020	4.8/0.18	2.14/0.19
MSVM-3 [7]	72.3%	84.59%	93.73%
	0.08/**0.001**	**0.71/0.04**	4.75/**0.03**
AKSDA-	77.33%	86.3%	94.17%
MSVM-1	**0.008**/0.002	1.51/0.49	**0.31**/0.15
AKSDA-	**79.3%**	**86.6%**	**94.44%**
MSVM-2	0.023/0.003	2.48/0.58	0.65/0.16

Table 4: Performance evaluation on GTX TITAN (Train/Test time in minutes)

Dataset	AKSDA-MSVM-1	AKSDA-MSVM-2
Amazon	0.008/ 0.001	0.011/0.0016
News20	0.36/0.073	0.79/0.1
Sector	0.12/0.03	0.45/0.045
YouTube	0.27/0.05	0.93/0.2
MED12	0.18/0.09	0.3/0.11

Figure 2: Scalability analysis of AKSDA-MSVM-1 along different datasets and GPU cards. Training times on GTX 650 (top value) and GTX TITAN (bottom value) are reported, in minutes.

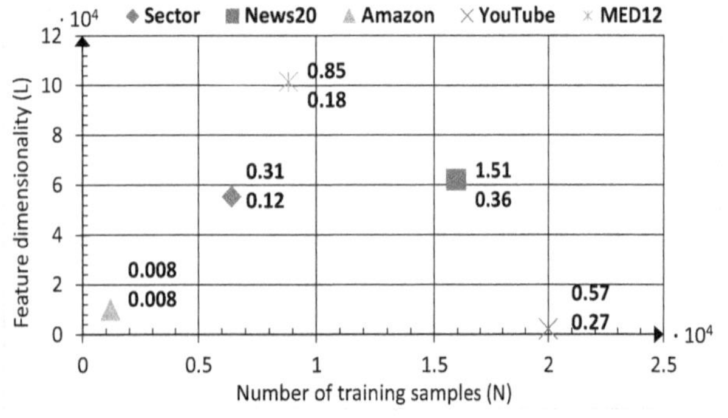

shown for the YouTube and MED12 video datasets, in Tables 1 and 2. It should be noted that due to higher RAM size requirements, MSVM-1 to -3 could not run for the MED12 dataset. The classification results in terms of correct classification rate (CCR) and the respective times (on GTX 650) for the Amazon, News20 and Sector datasets, are presented in Table 3. The training and test times of AKSDA-MSVM-1 & -2 on GTX TITAN, for all datasets, are shown in Table 4. Finally, the distribution of the training time of AKSDA-MSVM-1 along its individual components for each dataset, and the overall training time on GTX 650 and GTX TITAN, are shown in Figures 1 and 2, respectively. From the obtained results we observe the following:

i) AKSDA-MSVM-2, followed by AKSDA-MSVM-1, achieve the best generalization performance in all datasets.

ii) In terms of training time (even on GTX 650), AKSDA-MSVM-1 outperforms the state-of-the-art liblinear SVM implementation (MSVM-3) in three out of four datasets, while AKSDA-MSVM-2 (despite the computation of four Gram matrices) is still much faster than the MSVMs of libsvm (MSVM-1 & -2) in all datasets (Tables 1 & 3). Moreover, an impressive training time speedup (more than one order of magnitude) of the proposed method over the GPU accelerated AGSDA-LSVM [1] is observed in the MED12 dataset (Table 2). This is mainly due to the fact that AKSDA-MSVM solves one large eigenproblem (which is done efficiently using the proposed GPU-accelerated framework) to obtain a transformation matrix $\mathbf{\Psi}_c$ common for all (Ω) classes (see Sections 2.1, 2.2), while AGSDA-LSVM computes the GPU-accelerated solution of Ω eigenproblems to obtain one transformation matrix for each class. Finally, as expected, further improvement in training/test times is observed with the high-end GTX TITAN GPU (Table 4).

iii) From the analysis in Figure 1 we observe that the subclass partitioning, Gram matrix computation and linear system solver are the most intensive parts of the proposed method. Moreover, we can see that the linear system solver and the Gram matrix computation are mostly affected by the number of training observations and the feature vector dimensionality, respectively.

iv) In Figure 2, it is shown that in terms of training time the proposed method scales very well both with the number of training observations N and with feature dimensionality L. Specifically, considering the training times required for Sector and News20 when using GTX TITAN (thus overlooking any hardware limitations of the GTX 650), we see that for a similar feature vector size, doubling the number of training samples results in a $\times 3$ increase in training time, instead of the expected $\times 8$ increase of conventional KDA (due to its $O(N^3)$ complexity). Additionally, comparing the results for Sector and MED12, we see that despite a +100% increase in feature vector size and +50% increase in number of samples, the training time increases only by +50%.

4. CONCLUSIONS

A GPU-accelerated multiclass learning framework was presented providing very good performance in several multimedia-centered machine learning tasks. Future work directions include the extension of the proposed framework for multiple kernel learning [27, 9, 23] and the combination of AKSDA and MSVM in a single optimization problem [24].

5. ACKNOWLEDGEMENTS

This work was supported by the EU's FP7 and Horizon 2020 research and innovation programmes under grant agreements FP7-600826 ForgetIT and H2020-687786 InVID.

6. REFERENCES

[1] S. Arestis-Chartampilas, N. Gkalelis, and V. Mezaris. GPU accelerated generalised subclass discriminant analysis for event and concept detection in video. In *Proc. ACM Multimedia*, pages 1219–1222, Brisbane, Australia, 2015.

[2] G. Baudat and F. Anouar. Generalized discriminant analysis using a kernel approach. *Neural Comput.*, 12(10):2385–2404, Oct. 2000.

[3] P. N. Belhumeur, J. P. Hespanha, and D. J. Kriegman. Eigenfaces vs. Fisherfaces: Recognition using class specific linear projection. *IEEE Trans. Pattern Anal. Mach. Intell.*, 19(7):711–720, Jul. 1997.

[4] D. Cai, X. He, and J. Han. Speed up kernel discriminant analysis. *VLDB J.*, 20(1):21–33, Mar. 2011.

[5] C.-C. Chang and C.-J. Lin. LIBSVM: A library for support vector machines. *ACM Trans. on Intelligent Systems and Technology*, 2:27:1–27:27, 2011.

[6] K. Crammer and Y. Singer. On the algorithmic implementation of multiclass kernel-based vector machines. *J. Mach. Learn. Res.*, 2:265–292, Mar. 2002.

[7] R.-E. Fan, K.-W. Chang, C.-J. Hsieh et al. LIBLINEAR: A library for large linear classification. *J. Mach. Learn. Res.*, 9:1871–1874, 2008.

[8] K. Fukunaga. *Introduction to statistical pattern recognition (2nd ed.).* Academic Press Professional, Inc., San Diego, CA, USA, 1990.

[9] M. G. Genton. Classes of kernels for machine learning: A statistics perspective. *J. Mach. Learn. Res.*, 2:299–312, Mar. 2002.

[10] N. Gkalelis and V. Mezaris. Video event detection using generalized subclass discriminant analysis and linear support vector machines. In *Proc. ACM ICMR*, pages 25:25–25:32, Glasgow, UK, 2014.

[11] N. Gkalelis and V. Mezaris. Accelerated nonlinear discriminant analysis. *arXiv preprint arXiv:1504.07000*, 2015.

[12] N. Gkalelis, V. Mezaris, and I. Kompatsiaris. Mixture subclass discriminant analysis. *IEEE Signal Process. Lett.*, 15(5):319–332, May 2011.

[13] N. Gkalelis, V. Mezaris, I. Kompatsiaris, and T. Stathaki. Mixture subclass discriminant analysis link to restricted gaussian model and other generalizations. *IEEE Trans. Neural Netw. Learn. Syst.*, 24(1):8–21, Jan 2013.

[14] A. Habibian et al. Recommendations for video event recognition using concept vocabularies. In *Proc. ACM ICMR*, pages 89–96, Dallas, Texas, USA, 2013.

[15] T. Hofmann, B. Schölkopf, and A. J. Smola. Kernel methods in machine learning. *Ann. Statist.*, 36(3):1171–1220, 2008.

[16] S. S. Keerthi, S. Sundararajan et al. A sequential dual method for large scale multi-class linear SVMs. In *Proc. 14th ACM SIGKDD*, pages 408–416, Las Vegas, USA, Aug. 2008.

[17] J. Kittler, M. Hatef, R. P. W. Duin, and J. Matas. On combining classifiers. *IEEE Trans. Pattern Anal. Mach. Intell.*, 20(3):226–239, Mar. 1998.

[18] H.-T. Lin, C.-J. Lin, and R. C. Weng. A note on platt's probabilistic outputs for support vector machines. *Mach. Learn.*, 68(3):267–276, oct 2007.

[19] Y. Liu, Y. Liu, S. Zhong, and K. C. Chan. Semi-supervised manifold ordinal regression for image ranking. In *Proc. ACM Multimedia*, pages 1393–1396, 2011.

[20] S. Mika, G. Ratsch, J. Weston, B. Scholkopf, and K. R. Mullers. Fisher discriminant analysis with kernels. In *Neural Networks for Signal Processing IX, 1999. Proc. of the 1999 IEEE Signal Processing Society Workshop*, pages 41–48, 1999.

[21] P. Over, G. Awad et al. TRECVID 2012 - an introduction to the goals, tasks, data, evaluation mechanisms and metrics. In *Proc. TRECVID 2012 Workshop*, Gaithersburg, MD, USA, Nov. 2013.

[22] F. Radenović, H. Jégou, and O. Chum. Multiple measurements and joint dimensionality reduction for large scale image search with short vectors. In *Proc. ACM ICMR*, pages 587–590, Shanghai, China, 2015.

[23] S. Sonnenburg, G. Rätsch, C. Schäfer, and B. Schölkopf. Large scale multiple kernel learning. *J. Mach. Learn. Res.*, 7:1531–1565, Dec. 2006.

[24] A. Tefas, C. Kotropoulos, and I. Pitas. Using support vector machines to enhance the performance of elastic graph matching for frontal face authentication. *IEEE Trans. Pattern Anal. Mach. Intell.*, 23(7):735–746, Jul. 2001.

[25] V. Vapnik. *Statistical learning theory.* New York: Willey, 1998.

[26] H. Wang and C. Schmid. Action recognition with improved trajectories. In *Proc. IEEE Int. Conf. on Computer Vision (ICCV)*, pages 3551–3558, Sydney, Australia, Dec. 2013.

[27] J. Ye, S. Ji, and J. Chen. Multi-class discriminant kernel learning via convex programming. *J. Mach. Learn. Res.*, 9:719–758, Jun. 2008.

[28] D. You, O. C. Hamsici, and A. M. Martinez. Kernel optimization in discriminant analysis. *IEEE Trans. Pattern Anal. Mach. Intell.*, 33(3):631–638, Mar. 2008.

[29] M. Zhu and A. M. Martinez. Subclass discriminant analysis. *IEEE Trans. Pattern Anal. Mach. Intell.*, 28(8):1274–1286, Aug. 2006.

Automatic Reflection Removal using Gradient Intensity and Motion Cues

Chao Sun
University of Electronic Science and Technology of China
chaorensx@126.com

Shuaicheng Liu*
University of Electronic Science and Technology of China
liushuaicheng@uestc.edu.cn

Taotao Yang
University of Electronic Science and Technology of China
taotaoyangt@gmail.com

Bing Zeng
University of Electronic Science and Technology of China
eezeng@uestc.edu.cn

Zhengning Wang
University of Electronic Science and Technology of China
zhengning.wang@uestc.edu.cn

Guanghui Liu
University of Electronic Science and Technology of China
guanghuiliu@uestc.edu.cn

ABSTRACT

We present a method to separate the background image and reflection from two photos that are taken in front of a transparent glass under slightly different viewpoints. In our method, the SIFT-flow between two images is first calculated and a motion hierarchy is constructed from the SIFT-flow at multiple levels of spatial smoothness. To distinguish background edges and reflection edges, we calculate a motion score for each edge pixel by its variance along the motion hierarchy. Alternatively, we make use of the so-called superpixels to group edge pixels into edge segments and calculate the motion scores by averaging over each segment. In the meantime, we also calculate an intensity score for each edge pixel by its gradient magnitude. We combine both motion and intensity scores to get a combination score. A binary labelling (for separation) can be obtained by thresholding the combination scores. The background image is finally reconstructed from the separated gradients. Compared to the existing approaches that require a sequence of images or a video clip for the separation, we only need two images, which largely improves its feasibility. Various challenging examples are tested to validate the effectiveness of our method.

1. INTRODUCTION

We study in this paper how to separate reflections when images are taken in front of a transparent glass. In this circumstance, we end up with a mixture of two scenes: the scene beyond the glass and the scene reflected by the glass. Intuitively, one solution is to separate the blended image into the background layer and the reflectance layer, so that they can be observed separately [17].

Some previous methods require a polarizer to capture multiple images with a static camera under different polarized angles [5, 6, 13, 16]. These methods employ different models and priors, and can achieve good results if the underlying models/priors are well-fitted. However, a polarizer is often not common in practice. Several methods have attempted to apply a flash [1] and varying focuses [15]. Moreover, Levin *et al.* [7, 9] proposed to add user interactions to manually label pixels into two layers, in which image gradients are marked to either the background or the foreground and the result is reconstructed by an optimization in the gradient domain. However, manual labelling is tedious. Meanwhile, Levin *et al.* [9] also proposed an automatic approach by minimizing the total number of edges and corners in the recovered layers according to image's intrinsic statistics.

Another class of methods tries to utilize motions, i.e., misalignments of image contents between two layers be used as effective cues for the layer separation. For instance, Szeliski *et al.* [17] and Irani *et al.* [14] employed misalignments in the intensity domain, while Gai *et al.* [3, 4] utilized misalignments in the gradient domain. More recently, Li *et al.* [10] used SIFT-flow [12] to align several images which automatically labels the registered gradient edges, and Xue *et al.* [18] proposed a computational approach for obstruction separation using video clips. In summary, these methods have made use of motion differences in different layers for optimization. However, they either require several images or a video clip, which may not be practical.

In our work, we propose an approach that only requires a minimum number of images, namely, two images, for providing motion cues. Instead of aligning images using a standard SIFT-flow [10], we propose to compute a motion hierarchy from the SIFT-flow with a number of varying spatial smoothness levels. Our observation is that the background edges tend to have uniform motions across the hierarchy while the reflected edges possess larger motion variations. Thus, motion scores are derived for the edge pixels to distinguish background edges from reflection ones. Edge pixels can further be grouped into edge segments according to the so-called image superpixels [2], and motion scores are averaged over each segment for a better smoothness.

In the meantime, background edges usually have larger intensities compared to reflection edges, which would yield the edge intensity scores. Then, we leverage the gradient intensities and motion cues for the separation. After labelling edges as either background or reflection, the background can be recovered by an optimization under sparsity priors [7, 9].

*The corresponding author

MM '16, October 15-19, 2016, Amsterdam, Netherlands

DOI: http://dx.doi.org/10.1145/2964284.2967264

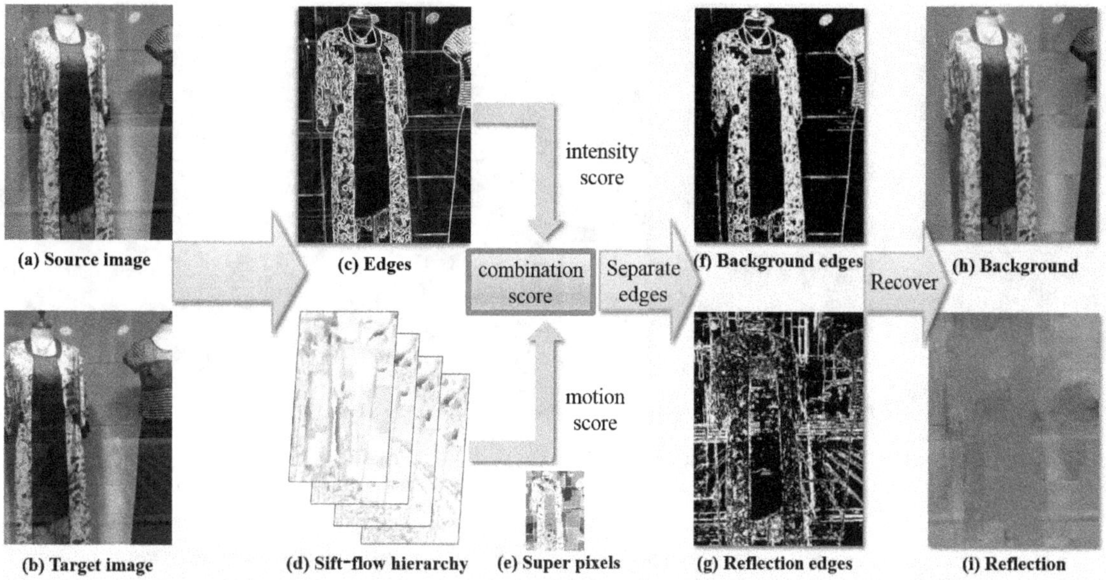

Figure 1: Pipeline of our system. (a) and (b) are the source and target input images. (c) An intensity score is derived from gradient edges. (d) SIFT-flow hierarchy is computed with different levels of smoothness, which produces motion scores for edge segments that are grouped by image superpixels (shown in (e)). We combine two scores to separate the edges into (f) reflectance edges and (g) background edges. (h) The final background image is recovered through the background edges. Optionally, a reflectance image (i) can also be reconstructed. Note that the light spot located at the upper right corner of the image is the background, which is labeled correctly due to the use of the motion score

2. OUR METHOD

Figure 1 shows our pipeline. The inputs to our system are two images that are taken in front of a glass with two slightly varying viewpoints. One image is selected as the source image and the other is specified as the target image. Without loss of generality, we only describe the method of removing reflectance of the source image. Notably, the source and target images can be exchanged so that the same method can also be applied to remove relection in the target image.

We first generate the edge image (the image gradients) by *Sobel* operator, as shown in Fig. 1(c). We also generate the motion hierarchy (from the SIFT-flow) as shown in Fig. 1(d). Intensity scores and motion scores are then calculated for the separation. The former is motivated from our observation that the reflected edges are relatively weaker as compared to the background edges. The later is obtained from the SIFT-flow through superpixel-based edge segments (Fig. 1(e)). The final background (Fig. 1(h)) is reconstructed from the separated background edges (Fig. 1(f)).

Let's denote the source image as I, and its reflectance and background layers as I_R and I_B such that

$$I = I_R + I_B. \tag{1}$$

The gradient magnitude of I is denoted as G. Similarly, G is composed of the reflectance component G_R and background component G_B:

$$G = G_R + G_B. \tag{2}$$

Here, our goal is to find a binary labelling (0 for reflectence edge or 1 for background edge) for each pixel in G, i.e., to label it as either G_R or G_B. To achieve this goal, each pixel in G is assigned with two scores, namely, the intensity score and the motion score, as described in the following.

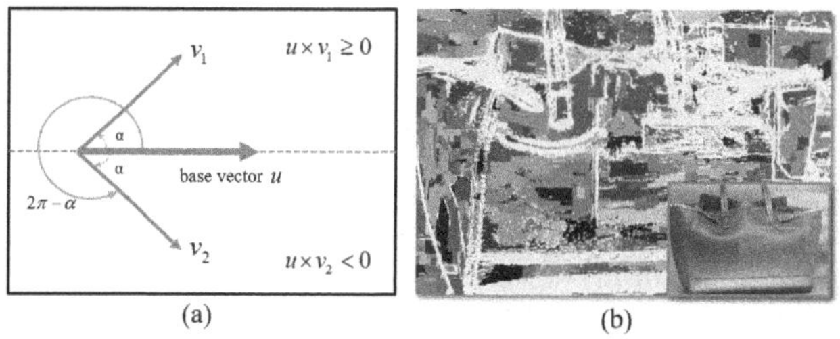

Figure 2: (a) Vector angles are calculated in $[0, 360^o]$ to avoid ambiguities. (b) Edge segments in superpixels.

2.1 Intensity score

By observations, we notice that most of reflection edges have lower intensities as compared to background edges. While being a simple prior, it provides an effective discrimination. Therefore, we utilize pixel intensities of edges as the intensity score and denote it as $S_{intensity} \in [0, 255]$.

We also notice that there exist some violating cases. That is, reflection edges sometimes have larger intensities at some regions than background edges when, for example, light sources are reflected or reflected objects are exposed under strong illumination. Therefore, we need another image so that we can exploit the motions between them for improvements.

2.2 Motion score

SIFT-flow [12] has been utilized in [10] to warp multiple input images to a reference image. Here, we adopt the SIFT-flow for the motion calculation between two images. As the background layer is more prominent than the reflectance layer, motions are dominated by the back-

Figure 3: Comparison with the methods in [10] [11]. In each example, the first, second, third and fourth columns show the input, the results of [11], the results of [10], and our results, respectively.

ground [10]. In other words, if the source image is warped to the target image by the SIFT-flow, ideally, the backgrounds will be well aligned. However, due to interferences of the reflected edges, the quality of alignment is limited, especially at regions where the reflected edges intersect with the background edges. Thus, rather than warping images by SIFT-flows [10], motions are recorded at the edge positions.

The smooth constraint in the SIFT-flow can enforce the neighborhood smoothness such that the noisy motions due to image noises can be well regularized, creating a smoothed flow field [12]. Different levels of noises demand different strengths of smoothness. In our problem, the interferences from reflected edges can be considered as a strong "noise". To produce a smoothed flow field, regions with only backgrounds require a weak regularization while regions with reflections desire a strong regularization. To capture the variations, we propose to calculate SIFT-flows with 10 different levels of smoothness, yielding a SIFT-flow hierarchy. Our observation is that a background pixel tends to have similar motion vectors across the SIFT-flow hierarchy while a reflected pixel will have different motion vectors.

Let's define a motion vector of pixel i at the k-th hierarchy level as v_i^k. We choose $u = (0, 1)$ as a base vector. We calculate the angle between the motion vector v_i^k and the base vector u:

$$\alpha_i^k = \arccos\left(\frac{u \cdot v_i^k}{\|u\|\|v_i^k\|}\right). \quad (3)$$

Note that there are 10 such angles calculated for each pixel. Next, we compute the standard deviation of angles of each pixel. Notably, as the range of α_i^k is $[0, 180^o]$, two vectors equally located at different sides of the base vector would produce 0 variance, see Fig. 2(a) for an example. To fix it, we extend the angle range to $[0, 360^o]$ by adjusting the relative position of motion vectors to the base vector through the vector outer product:

$$\hat{\alpha}_i^k = \begin{cases} \alpha_i^k & u \times v_i^k \geq 0 \\ 360^o - \alpha_i^k & u \times v_i^k < 0 \end{cases} \quad (4)$$

where $\hat{\alpha}_i^k$ is the angle with range of $[0, 360^o]$. Next, the standard deviation σ_i of $\hat{\alpha}_i^k$ $(k = 1, \cdots, 10)$ is calculated for each edge pixel. We use σ_i as our *motion score* $S_{motion}(i)$.

2.3 Average of motion scores

The calculation of σ_i is independent at each edge pixel. To enforce the spatial smoothness, we propose to group edge pixels into edge segments. To this end, we compute image superpixels [2], and then edge pixels are grouped into an edge segment if they belong to the same superpixel. Fig. 2(b) shows an example of edge segments that are generated according to superpixels. Then, we would like to encourage the pixels in the same segment to have the same motion score, which can be obtained by taking an average, because the spatial smoothness can be improved in this way.

2.4 Combination score

The two scores described above are complementary to each other. For example, reflections with strong intensities will be considered as the backgrounds if only the intensity score is involved. However, large motion variations of reflections can help us to make the right decision. Therefore, a more suitable score is a combination of these two scores. A combination score $S_{combine}(i)$ at pixel i is obtained as:

$$S_{combine}(i) = S_{intensity}(i) - \varepsilon S_{motion}(i), \quad (5)$$

where ε balances two scores and it is set to 0.5 in our implementation. The minus is used here because edges with large intensity scores are more likely to belong to background but edges with small motion scores are more likely to belong to reflectence.

The edge separation is performed by thresholding the combination scores, which gives the binary labelling $E(i)$ as:

$$E(i) = \begin{cases} 1 & c_{i,j} \geq \tau \\ 0 & c_{i,j} < \tau \end{cases} \quad (6)$$

where τ is set to be 80 in our implementation.

2.5 Image reconstruction

After the separation of gradient edges, we follow the approach in [7, 8, 10] to reconstruct the background image from the gradients.

Levin *et al.* showed that the long-tailed gradient distribution of natural images is an effective prior for reconstruction in the gradient domain [7, 8]. The Laplacian distribution is thus adopted to approximate the long tailed distribution. For reconstruction, the probability $P(I_B, I_R)$ is maximized, which is equal to minimizing $-\log P(I_B, I_R)$. Similar to [7, 8, 10], the energy function is defined as:

(a) (b) (c) (d) (e)

Figure 4: More results of our method. Please find some more in the supplementary file.

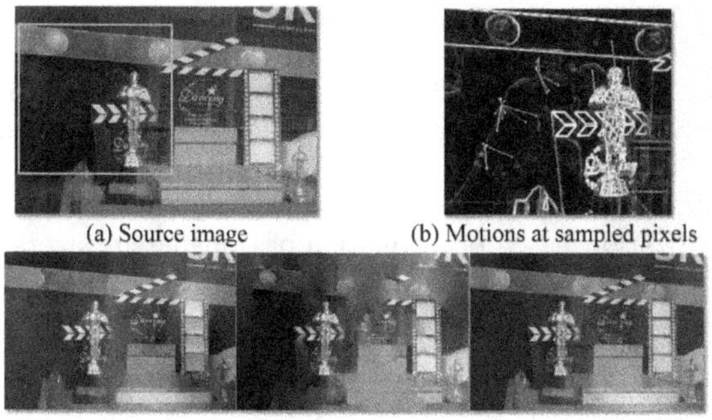

(a) Source image (b) Motions at sampled pixels

(c) Intensity score only (d) Motion score only (e) Our result by two scores

Figure 5: The effect of different scores.

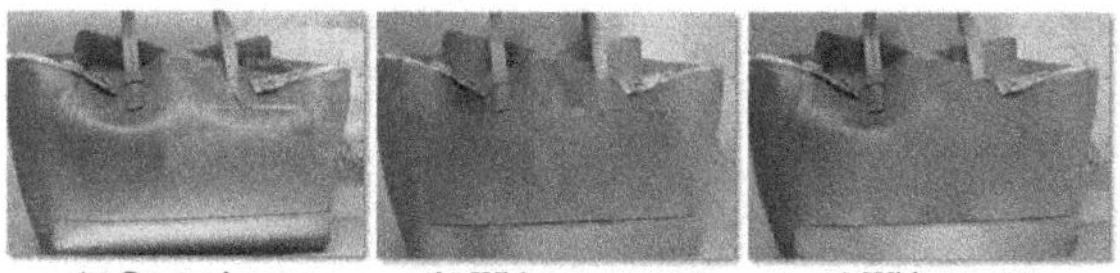

(a) Source image (b) Without average (c) With average

Figure 6: The effect of grouping edge pixels.

$$\begin{aligned} J(I_B) = & \sum_{x,n} |(f_n * I_B)(x) + ((I_L - I_B) * f_n(x))| \\ & + \lambda \sum_{x \in E_B, n} |((I_L - I_B) * f_n)(x)| \\ & + \lambda \sum_{x \in E_R, n} |(I_B * f_n)(x)|, \end{aligned} \tag{7}$$

where f_n denotes the derivative filter and $*$ is the convolution operator. E_B and E_R denote edges that are labeled to background and reflectance, respectively. Here, we use two orientations and two degrees of derivative filters. The first term enforces the sparsity while the last two terms require the recovered image gradients to follow our separation. This energy can be minimized efficiently using iterative reweighted least squares.

3. EXPERIMENTS

Figure 3 shows the comparison between our method and the methods in [10] and [11]. Note that 5 images and one image are used in [10] and [11], respectively, to produce the results, whereas our method selects two from 5 images used in [10]. It can be seen that our method has produced better results - notice the strong reflectance residuals in the results of [10]. Figure 4 presents some more results of our method. Especially, Fig. 4(a),(b) and (c) show three traditional examples where the glass is placed between the background and the reflected objects. In Fig. 4(d), we capture a reflective screen of a laptop. Finally, a synthetic example is shown in Fig. 4(e).

Next, we evaluate our method by turning off each component one by one.

3.1 Effect of motion and intensity scores

Figure 5 shows the effect of different scores. Fig 5(b) shows the gradient edges of a green window in Fig 5(a). Here, we sample several points and draw the motions by color lines. As can be seen in Fig 5(b), pixels at the reflected edges (edges of the camera man) have different motions while pixels at the background (the trophy) have uniform motions. Fig 5(c) shows the result by using only the intensity score. It can be seen that the detail of bulbs are lost due to their low intensities. Fig 5(d) shows the result by using only the motion score. It can be seen that some parts of the image are contaminated due to the inaccuracy of the motion estimation. The result obtained by using both scores is shown in Fig 5(e). It is clear that the shadow of the camera man is wiped off, the contaminated region in Fig 5(d) is restored, and the detail of bulbs is preserved.

3.2 Effect of grouping edge pixels

For the source image shown in Fig. 6(a), we show in Fig. 6(b) and (c) the results without and with motion score averaging in edge segments, respectively. Clearly, the average strategy has removed the reflectance residuals quite successfully.

4. CONCLUSIONS

We have presented an effective method for reflection removal by using two input images that are taken in front of a transparent glass under two slightly different view angles. Our method first computes two priors for each edge pixel, namely, the intensity score (gradient magnitude) and the aggregated motion score (from a SIFT-flow hierarchy built upon a number of smoothness levels). Two scores are composed into a combination score, which is then used to distinguish background and reflection. We have presented several examples to demonstrate the necessity of each of these two scores and the combination score. We have also presented some results to show that our method can achieve a better performance compared to some existing works.

5. ACKNOWLEDGMENTS

This work has been supported by National Natural Science Foundation of China (61502079 and 61370148).

6. REFERENCES

[1] A. Agrawal, R. Raskar, S. K. Nayar, and Y. Li. Removing photography artifacts using gradient projection and flash-exposure sampling. In *ACM Trans. Graph.*, volume 24, pages 828–835, 2005.

[2] P. F. Felzenszwalb and D. P. Huttenlocher. Efficient graph-based image segmentation. *Int. J. Comput. Vis.*, 59(2):167–181, 2004.

[3] K. Gai, Z. Shi, and C. Zhang. Blindly separating mixtures of multiple layers with spatial shifts. In *Proc. CVPR*, pages 1–8, 2008.

[4] K. Gai, Z. Shi, and C. Zhang. Blind separation of superimposed moving images using image statistics. *IEEE Trans. Pattern Anal. Mach. Intell.*, 34(1):19–32, 2012.

[5] N. Kong, Y.-W. Tai, and S. Y. Shin. High-quality reflection separation using polarized images. *IEEE Trans. on Image Processing*, 20(12):3393–3405, 2011.

[6] N. Kong, Y.-W. Tai, and S. Y. Shin. A physically-based approach to reflection separation. In *Proc. CVPR*, pages 9–16, 2012.

[7] A. Levin and Y. Weiss. User assisted separation of reflections from a single image using a sparsity prior. *IEEE Trans. Pattern Anal. Mach. Intell.*, (9):1647–1654, 2007.

[8] A. Levin and Y. Weiss. User assisted separation of reflections from a single image using a sparsity prior. *IEEE Trans. Pattern Anal. Mach. Intell.*, (9):1647–1654, 2007.

[9] A. Levin, A. Zomet, and Y. Weiss. Separating reflections from a single image using local features. In *Proc. CVPR*, 2004.

[10] Y. Li and M. Brown. Exploiting reflection change for automatic reflection removal. In *Proc. CVPR*, pages 2432–2439, 2013.

[11] Y. Li and M. Brown. Single image layer separation using relative smoothness. In *Proc. CVPR*, pages 2752–2759, 2014.

[12] C. Liu, J. Yuen, and A. Torralba. Sift flow: Dense correspondence across scenes and its applications. *IEEE Trans. Pattern Anal. Mach. Intell.*, 33(5):978–994, 2011.

[13] N. Ohnishi, K. Kumaki, T. Yamamura, and T. Tanaka. Separating real and virtual objects from their overlapping images. In *Proc. ECCV*, pages 636–646. 1996.

[14] B. Sarel and M. Irani. Separating transparent layers of repetitive dynamic behaviors. In *Proc. ICCV*, pages 26–32, 2005.

[15] Y. Y. Schechner, N. Kiryati, and R. Basri. Separation of transparent layers using focus. *Int. J. Comput. Vis.*, 39(1):25–39, 2000.

[16] Y. Y. Schechner, J. Shamir, and N. Kiryati. Polarization-based decorrelation of transparent layers: The inclination angle of an invisible surface. In *Proc. ICCV*, volume 2, pages 814–819, 1999.

[17] R. Szeliski, S. Avidan, and P. Anandan. Layer extraction from multiple images containing reflections and transparency. In *Proc. CVPR*, pages 246–253, 2000.

[18] T. Xue, M. Rubinstein, C. Liu, and W. T. Freeman. A computational approach for obstruction-free photography. *ACM Trans. Graph.*, 34(4):79, 2015.

Personal Multi-view Viewpoint Recommendation based on Trajectory Distribution of the Viewing Target

Xueting Wang, Kensho Hara, Yu Enokibori, Takatsugu Hirayama, Kenji Mase
Graduate School of Information Science, Nagoya University
Furo-cho, Chikusa-ku, Nagoya, Aichi, Japan
{wang, kensho}@cmc.ss.is.nagoya-u.ac.jp, {enokibori, hirayama, mase}@is.nagoya-u.ac.jp

ABSTRACT

Multi-camera videos with abundant information and high flexibility are expected to be useful in a wide range of applications, such as surveillance systems, web lecture broadcasting, concerts and sports viewing, etc. Viewers can enjoy a high-presence viewing experience of their own choosing by means of virtual camera switching and controlling viewing interfaces. However, some viewers may feel annoyed by continual manual viewpoint selection, especially when the number of selectable viewpoints is relatively large. In order to solve this issue, we propose an automatic viewpoint-recommending method designed especially for soccer games. This method focuses on a viewer's personal preference for viewpoint-selection, instead of common and professional editing rules. We assume that the different trajectory distributions cause a difference in the viewpoint selection according to personal preference. We therefore analyze the relationship between the viewer's personal viewpoint selecting tendency and the spatio-temporal game context. We compare methods based on a Gaussian mixture model, a general histogram+SVM and bag-of-words+SVM to seek the best representation for this relationship. The performance of the proposed methods are verified by assessing the degree of similarity between the recommended viewpoints and the viewers' edited records.

Keywords

multi-view video recommendation; user preference; Gaussian mixture model

1. INTRODUCTION

Multi-view videos taken by multiple cameras from different angles are playing an important role in video services with the development of video capturing, processing and delivering technologies [1, 2]. Furthermore, free-view videos can be generated to provide more viewpoint options by interpolating scenes or modeling 3D scenes [8, 10, 13]. Because of the diverse information and viewing options, viewers can enjoy more interesting contents in their own way than that provided by the professional TV broadcasters with a single forced viewpoint. Thus, multi-view videos are suitable to represent events as diverse as web lectures, concerts and sports viewing.

However, the continual selection of appropriate viewpoints by a completely manual process on the existing multi-view video interface [11, 12] could be annoying, especially when the selection options are relatively numerous. A high level of viewer stress could occur when viewing a dynamic event in a wide-scale field. Thus, an automatic viewpoint recommendation based on a viewer's personal preference is important for multi-view video watching in such situations. In this work, we focus on the viewpoint recommendation for the sports game, in particular, the soccer game.

There are several related studies on automatic viewpoint selecting. In works [4, 15, 18], camera selecting are based mainly on audio feature, face trajectory and speaker position for web lectures and meeting broadcasts. The audio context are not suitable for sports games due to the noise of the crowd and far distance of wide-angle cameras. Saini et.al. [16] proposed a framework for the automatic mashup of dance performance videos taken by mobile phones. They chose the best angle based on view quality context depending on such as illumination and shakiness, and professional editing rules. We assume that game context consisting of individual object information, such as positions of the ball and players, is more reliable than the audio-visual information used in the above methods for sports games.

Other researchers have also focused on the game context. In work [5, 6] Daniyal et al. presented an algorithm for viewpoint-quality ranking based on object scoring for *frame-level* features including size and location of the players in a basketball game. The extended approach in work [17] optimized the viewpoint transition by viewpoint-quality evaluation with dynamic measurements corresponding to game context represented by the object position calculated in each frame. Muramatsu et al. [14] selected viewpoint by learning the average of object features, such as position, distance to the camera and size in the view among a short time from user's viewpoint-selection records. However, these approaches are processed either without or with poorly represented past and future object dynamics such as trajectory and temporal behavior. We assume that the game context is described better by information about the object's trajectory than by frame-level information, and that the recent machine-learning representation is more effective than simple average processing.

MM '16, October 15-19, 2016, Amsterdam, Netherlands

DOI: http://dx.doi.org/10.1145/2964284.2967265

Most of the related studies discussed above focus mainly on common preferences [4, 5, 6, 15, 18] such as assigning the viewpoint evaluation score in proportion to the size and number of players visible in the view, and professional editing rules [16] such as learning the shot length from the directors' viewpoint transition. However, viewers might prefer viewing that is based on their own preferences and styles. There are only a few existing studies on user-dependent viewpoint recommendation [14, 17]. They learn the object's features and optimize the weight parameters for feature combination from each user's viewpoint-selection record. The performance of these approaches is limited due to the lack of representation of the object's temporal information.

We therefore aim to achieve a personal viewpoint recommendation considering the spatio-temporal game context represented by the trajectory of the main viewing target, i.e., the ball. We assume that different viewers show different viewpoint-selection tendency for different trajectory distributions. Thus, we apply a machine leaning to learn the relationship between the trajectory distribution of the viewing target and each viewer's viewpoint-selection tendency to achieve an effective personal viewpoint recommendation. We first divide short video sequences into cuts. We then use the ball-trajectory distribution in each cut as a feature vector to learn each viewer's viewpoint selection preference for the spatio-temporal game context. We compare and seek the best one from three methods each based on a Gaussian mixture model(GMM), a two-dimensional histogram with SVM, and a bag-of-words(BoW) with SVM to achieve the best performance for personal recommendation based on the viewer's viewpoint-selection records.

Contributions. We now summarize our contribution in this paper as follows.

- We realize personal viewpoint recommendation using the trajectory distribution of the main viewing target in order to featuring spatio-temporal context for personal preference learning.
- We achieve the better performance over other representations by using GMM-based method.

2. PERSONAL VIEWPOINT RECOMMENDATION

The proposed method describes trajectory distribution of the viewing target as feature vectors in order to learn each viewer's preference from viewpoint-selection records of the viewer's in cuts dividing the video sequences. Most viewers of a soccer game have a trend to view the game by following the ball [9]. Thus, we use the ball as the main viewing target, and we use its trajectory to represent the game context that is required for a personal viewpoint recommendation.

In this section, we first detail the analysis of the relationship between the ball trajectory distribution and each viewer's viewpoint-selection tendency. Then, we discuss three methods for describing the relationship. We also discuss two definitions of cut unit includes several frames segmented from the video sequence. In the following discussion, we represent the ball trajectory by $B = \{T_i\}$, where i is the trajectory index of each cut. The trajectory of each cut is $T = \{\mathbf{x}_f\}_{f=1}^{F}$ is the trajectory of each cut, where $\mathbf{x}_f \in \mathbb{R}^2$ is the point on the field coordinate system at frame $f(1 \leq f \leq F)$.

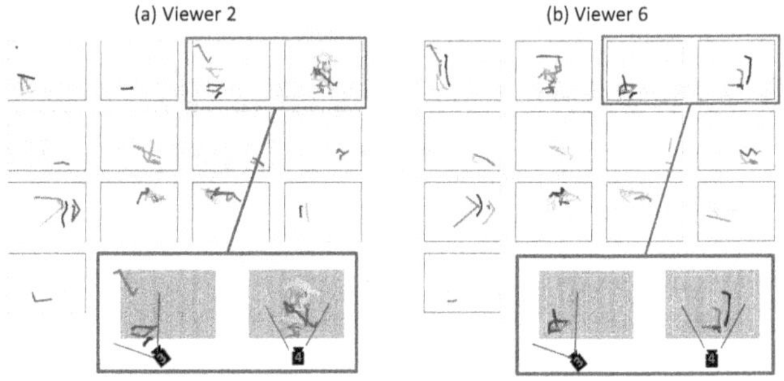

Figure 1: Ball-trajectory distribution for each selected viewpoint of two viewers in Game 2. Lines of different colors show the trajectories during cuts unit in overall soccer field.

2.1 Qualitative Analysis of Trajectory Distribution and Viewpoint-selection Tendency

We assume that viewers select the appropriate viewpoints based on the game context, which can be represented by the spatio-temporal movement of the main object, i.e., the ball in the case of a soccer game. We analyze the relationship between the ball trajectory and each viewpoint-selection records acquired in our video-editing experiment. Figure 1 shows that the ball trajectories centered around a location in the soccer field when each viewer selected each viewpoint. In other words, the ball trajectories have different trends for the different viewpoints that are selected. Thus, we consider that using the ball-trajectory distribution is effective to learn different viewpoint-selection tendency.

2.2 Learning Personal Preference

Personal preference can be represented by the relationship between personal viewpoint-selection tendency and distribution of ball trajectories. We compare three methods each based on GMM, a two-dimensional histogram with SVM and BoW with SVM to seek the best representation for the relationship.

2.2.1 Gaussian Mixture Model based Method

GMM is the linear combination of several Gaussian components, and it is widely used to express an object-position distribution. In this work, we use it to represent the different ball-trajectory distributions of the different viewpoints for each viewer. For each viewpoint c, we gather the ball trajectories B_c while it is selected. We express the points in the gathered trajectories using GMM with EM algorithm to estimate the parameters (mean and covariance).

We generate the model of each viewpoint for each viewer from the training data. For each video sequence in the test data, we first divide the video sequence into cuts and extract the ball trajectory T from each cut. We calculate the grand total of the log-likelihood of each trajectory T under the generated GMM of each viewpoint for the viewer. We recommend the viewpoint with the largest likelihood for each trajectory. The number of components is based on the experimentally varied results, as discussed later.

2.2.2 Histogram with SVM based Method

We also employ a method based on two-dimensional histogram with SVM called Hist-SVM for short. We spatially divide the soccer field equally into $M * N$ bins. We calculate the histogram of the ball trajectory T in each cut. A histogram normalization is conducted in consideration of the differences in the length of a cut.

In the training steps, we use the normalized histogram as s feature vector and perform the learning by SVM with a RBF kernel. The supervised signals are the viewpoint-selection records of each viewer. Thus, we build the multi-class classifiers corresponding to each viewpoint in order to recommend viewpoints. For the test data, the SVM assigns a viewpoint to the trajectory T in each cut in the same way as in the training step. In this study, M and N are set to their optimum values based on the experimentally varied results.

2.2.3 BoW with SVM based Method

Finally, we employ a bag-of-words technique with SVM [3] called BoW-SVM for short. We first cluster all the points in the ball trajectory B of the training data to cordwords using the Gaussian Mixture Model. A codeword in this work is defined as each Gaussian distribution in the Gaussian Mixture Model. We then apply a soft assignment to generate the histogram of codewords in the cut. The scores of bins of the codewords histogram are calculated by the sum of the normalized likelihood under each Gaussian distribution for points of the trajectory T in the cut. We generate the codewords histogram as a feature vector. We then learn the relationship between the feature vectors and the selected viewpoints by each viewer with RBF kernel based SVM using the viewpoint-selection records as the supervised signals. Thus, we build the multi-class classifiers as with Hist-SVM. In the test step, the SVM assigns a viewpoint to the feature vector. The number of codewords is set to the optimum value based on the experimentally varied results.

2.3 Video Cut Segmentation

In this study, we take care to reflect the fact that viewers select viewpoints according to the game context in past and future periods, and not only solely on the current frame. We use the cut consisting of multiple frames to represent the spatio-temporal game context. Therefore, it is necessary to determine how the video sequence should be segmented. In this study, we consider the following two kinds of segmentation.

2.3.1 Ideal Segmentation

Here, ideal segmentation is a result that the game context is appropriately classified according to personal preference, which causes viewer's viewpoint selecting. We call this segmentation SegU for short. It is unavailable for viewpoint recommendation in practice. In this study, we record the viewer's viewpoint switching timing to segment the video sequences to verify the upper bound of recommendation accuracy.

2.3.2 Equal Segmentation

Equal segmentation is a result that the video sequence is segmented into cuts of a fixed length, which can be easily realized in practice. We call this segmentation SegS for short. We adopt the sliding-window method to compensate for the overlap in each cut. Concretely, we generate the cut with a window size around each frame. The recommended viewpoint based on the trajectory distribution in the cut unit is assigned to the center frame of the cut. The window size, which is the length of the cut, is set to the optimum value based on the experimentally varied results.

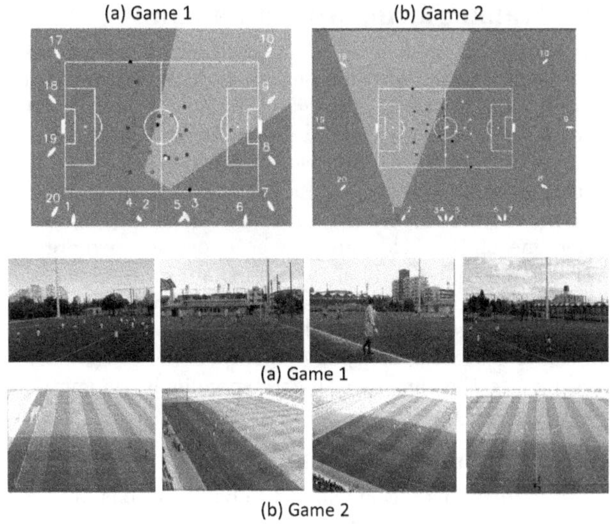

Figure 2: Camera position and sample viewpoint images.

3. EXPERIMENT

In this study, we collect the viewers' viewpoint-selection records through video-editing experiment using soccer game multi-view videos dataset. Construction of the proposed methods and effectiveness evaluation are carried out using the same dataset.

3.1 Multi-view Video Dataset

We use multi-view video datasets of two soccer games in different venues with different camera settings to evaluate the proposed method. The games were filmed using 13 digital cameras (CASIO EX-F1, at 30 fps 1920 × 1080 pixels) with no pan, tilt, or zoom) around the soccer field. The camera settings and sample viewpoint images are shown in Figure 2. The video sequences were synchronized after filming. We obtained the position of the ball through manual labeling and an interpolation procedure since our main focus is the viewpoint selection but not automatic ball tracking. Some vision-based and sensor-based tracking techniques are being researched separately for this purpose [7].

3.2 Collection of Viewers' Selection Records

We conducted a multi-view video editing experiment to collect viewers' records. The participants in this experiment comprised six males and four females of ages between 20-39. They were all occasional viewers of soccer games, with no particular expertise. In view of the difficulty of participants performing video editing work for long periods of time, we randomly presented 11 and 10 short video sequences (of about 30 seconds each) containing typical play scenes to the participants for each game in the experiment. The participants could repeatedly replay each scene, select viewpoints, and confirm the selected viewpoints with a simple action on a graphical user interface. The editing record of each participant would reflect their personal preference so that could be used for personal preference learning.

3.3 Training Using Mirror Samples

In a practical application of the method, we assume that training data acquired from viewers are limited because we can only use a few parts of the game for this purpose without annoying the viewer. Thus, we introduce a useful method to increase the training data as follows.

Since soccer field is symmetrical in the left-right direction, the mirror-reversed positions of the ball with respect to the center line of the field can also be expected to represent virtual game context. Thus, we add the mirror trajectories to the training data. Besides, since the cameras surrounding the field are also symmetrical in most games, we transfer the viewer's selected viewpoint corresponding to the mirror trajectory to the camera in a correspondingly symmetrical position as the new records.

3.4 Comparative Methods

AveragePos uses centroid of the ball positions during a cut as the feature, which is used in [14] as mentioned in the first section.

WeightOptm uses context-dependent optimized weights to combine the features in each frame, which is used in [17] as mentioned in the first section.

3.5 Evaluation Framework

We conducted a leave-one-sequence-out cross-validation as the evaluation by using one sequence of each participant's viewing records as testing data until all the sequences are used as test data. We then compared the viewpoints recommended by each method and each participant's viewing records and calculated the average concordance rate of all the test data on each frame.

4. RESULTS

We use the evaluation framework mentioned above to verify the performance of each method.

4.1 Parameters

The proposed methods achieved the highest average concordance rate using the following parameters. The number of component in GMM were 4 and 1, the number of notecodes in BoW-SVM were 31 and 36 for the two games separately. With regard to Hist-SVM, $7 * 3 = 21$ bins was the best for both games.

4.2 Concordance Rate

The average concordance rates of 10 participants with different methods for the two games are shown in Figure 3(a) and (b). From these figures, we find that the method based on GMM with ideal segmentation (GMM+SegU) achieved the best concordance rates 66.46% and 56.65% for the two games, separately. With regard to the game-context representation, GMM was more effective than those based on Hist-SVM and BoW-SVM. The lower result of the comparative methods (i.e., AveragePos and WeightOptm) show that using the spatio-temporal game context was effective. All the proposed methods achieved higher concordance rates than those of AveragePos for the two games. This result shows that the centroid of the ball position during a cut could not represent the game context.

In addition, Figure 4(c) and (d) show the concordance rates of GMM for each participant obtained in the experiment of the two games. In the figure, we show the result

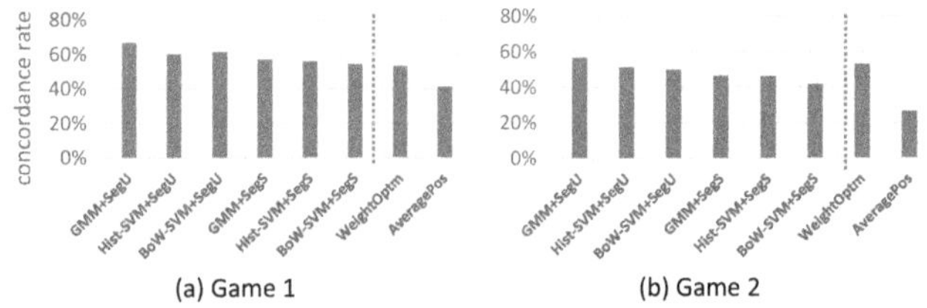

Figure 3: Concordance rates of different methods with different segmentation for the two games

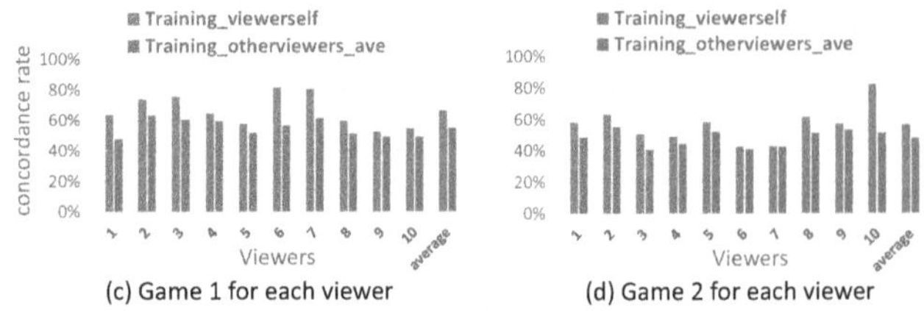

Figure 4: Comparision with results of training using other viewers' records for each viewer.

of leave-one-participant-out cross validation as the average performance. The performance of learning from each participant through the leave-one-sequence-out cross-validation was better than that of the average one. This result shows that each participant had a different viewing tendency and our recommendation reflected their personal preference.

The performance when using the mirror trajectories in the training step was evaluated in the same way. The concordance rates for GMM based method increased from 66.46% and 56.65% to 67.70% and 61.96% of the two games respectively, showing the effectiveness of increasing the training data.

5. CONCLUSIONS

In this study, we proposed an automatic viewpoint recommendation method based on personal preference. We predicted the personal recommendation by learning the relationship between personal viewpoint-selection tendency and the spatio-temporal game context in the form of the trajectory distribution of the main viewing target. The experimental results showed the GMM based method outperformed other methods. In the future, we intend to include the spatio-temporal features of other objects related to the main target and to discuss on better methods for segmentation.

6. ACKNOWLEDGMENTS

This work was supported by JSPS KAKENHI Grant Number 26280074.

7. REFERENCES

[1] I. Ahmad. Multi-view video: get ready for next-generation television. *IEEE Distributed Systems Online*, 8(3):6–6, 2007.

[2] R. T. Collins, O. Amidi, and T. Kanade. An active camera system for acquiring multi-view video. In *in Proc. International Conference on Image Processing*, 2002.

[3] G. Csurka, C. Dance, L. Fan, J. Willamowski, and C. Bray. Visual categorization with bags of keypoints. In *Workshop on statistical learning in computer vision, ECCV*, volume 1, pages 1–2. Prague, 2004.

[4] R. Cutler, Y. Rui, A. Gupta, J. J. Cadiz, I. Tashev, L.-w. He, A. Colburn, Z. Zhang, Z. Liu, and S. Silverberg. Distributed meetings: A meeting capture and broadcasting system. In *Proceedings of the tenth ACM international conference on Multimedia*, pages 503–512. ACM, 2002.

[5] F. Daniyal and A. Cavallaro. Multi-camera scheduling for video production. In *European Conference on Visual Media Production (CVMP)*, pages 11–20, 2011.

[6] F. Daniyal, M. Taj, and A. Cavallaro. Content and task-based view selection from multiple video streams. *Multimedia tools and applications*, pages 235–258, 2010.

[7] T. D'Orazio and M. Leo. A review of vision-based systems for soccer video analysis. *Pattern Recognition*, 43(8):2911–2926, 2010.

[8] M. Goesele, N. Snavely, B. Curless, H. Hoppe, and S. M. Seitz. Multi-view stereo for community photo collections. In *IEEE 11th International Conference on Computer Vision(ICCV)*, pages 1–8, 2007.

[9] A. Iwatsuki, T. Hirayama, and K. Mase. Analysis of soccer coach's eye gaze behavior. In *Pattern Recognition (ACPR), 2013 2nd IAPR Asian Conference on*, pages 793–797, Nov 2013.

[10] J. Kilner, J. Starck, and A. Hilton. A comparative study of free viewpoint video techniques for sports events. In *European Conference on Visual Media Production (CVMP)*, pages 87–96, 2006.

[11] J.-G. Lou, H. Cai, and J. Li. A real-time interactive multi-view video system. In *Proceedings of the 13th annual ACM international conference on Multimedia*, pages 161–170. ACM, 2005.

[12] K. Mase, K. Niwa, and T. Marutani. Socially assisted multi-view video viewer. In *Proceedings of the 13th international conference on multimodal interfaces*, pages 319–322. ACM, 2011.

[13] T. Matsuyama, S. Nobuhara, T. Takai, and T. Tung. *3D video and its applications*. Springer, 2012.

[14] Y. Muramatsu, T. Hirayama, and K. Mase. Video generation method based on user's tendency of viewpoint selection for multi-view video contents. In *5th Augmented Human International Conference, AH '14*, pages 1:1–1:4, 2014.

[15] A. Ranjan, R. Henrikson, J. Birnholtz, R. Balakrishnan, and D. Lee. Automatic camera control using unobtrusive vision and audio tracking. In *Proceedings of Graphics Interface*, pages 47–54. Canadian Information Processing Society, 2010.

[16] M. K. Saini, R. Gadde, S. Yan, and W. T. Ooi. Movimash: online mobile video mashup. In *Proceedings of the 20th ACM international conference on Multimedia*, pages 139–148. ACM, 2012.

[17] X. Wang, T. Hirayama, and K. Mase. Viewpoint sequence recommendation based on contextual information for multiview video. *IEEE MultiMedia*, (4):40–50, 2015.

[18] C. Zhang, Y. Rui, J. Crawford, and L.-W. He. An automated end-to-end lecture capture and broadcasting system. *ACM Transactions on Multimedia Computing, Communications, and Applications (TOMM)*, 4(1):6, 2008.

Motion Segmentation using Visual and Bio-mechanical Features

Stefano Alletto, Giuseppe Serra, Rita Cucchiara
Dept. of Engineering, University of Modena and Reggio Emilia
Modena, Italy
name.surname@unimore.it

ABSTRACT

Nowadays, egocentric wearable devices are continuously increasing their widespread among both the academic community and the general public. For this reason, methods capable of automatically segment the video based on the recorder motion patterns are gaining attention. These devices present the unique opportunity of both high quality video recordings and multimodal sensors readings. Significant efforts have been made in either analyzing the video stream recorded by these devices or the bio-mechanical sensor information. So far, the integration between these two realities has not been fully addressed, and the real capabilities of these devices are not yet exploited. In this paper, we present a solution to segment a video sequence into motion activities by introducing a novel data fusion technique based on the covariance of visual and bio-mechanical features. The experimental results are promising and show that the proposed integration strategy outperforms the results achieved focusing solely on a single source.

Keywords

Egocentric vision, wearable devices, multimodal sensor analysis

1. INTRODUCTION

Due to the wide spreading of head-mounted cameras, systems dealing with an egocentric perspective are arousing a growing interest in industries and in the research community. Egocentric videos captured with wearable cameras are long and unstructured, and their continuous nature yields no evident shot boundaries. Information such as events and personal experiences cannot be comfortably reviewed but require a manual search through the video sequences, which can be several hours long. For this reason, the need for automated tools that assist users in accessing to the information in such videos is clear.

Several works tackle with problems such as activity and gesture recognition, social interactions or object recognition exploiting the unique perspective of wearable cameras [6, 1, 2]. Although these approaches are robust enough in specialized contexts and short activities they are not designed to analyze long and unconstrained videos in order to identify interesting segments of video that contain relevant information.

Recently, Lu and Grauman [10] handled egocentric video summarization partitioning videos into relevant sub-shots on the basis of motion features analysis. They segment the video in three classes: *static*, *moving the head*, *in tansit* and smooth the classification results with a Markov Random Field. Kitani *et al.* [8] present an unsupervised learning approach that uses motion-based histograms in order to classify ego-action categories. Poleg *et al.* [12] propose to temporally segment an egocentric video into twelve long time activities (such as *walking*, *running* and *wheels*) using classifiers trained on feature vectors derived from the cumulative displacement curves.

While these methods address a key problem of egocentric video, they are doing so disregarding a major feature of many modern wearable devices. From smartphones to Google Glass, many of these devices equip bio-mechanical sensors such as accelerometers and gyroscopes. In fact, the low costs, low power requirements and small dimensions of these sensors make them perfect for embedded and wearable applications. A new range of applications and techniques arise from their use: Li *et al.* [9] employ gyroscope and accelerometer to detect the posture of a subject, focusing on harmful situations like falls. Recently, the high precision of these sensors has been exploited by Hernandez *et al.* [7] to predict in real-time physiological parameters of their user such as heart and respiration rates. Differently, Brunetto *et al.* [3] exploit sensor information in a SLAM framework where accelerometer and gyroscope are combined with a RGB-D camera and are employed to enforce the orientation estimation, effectively improving the keyframe extraction process.

In this paper, we propose a novel approach to integrate a robust visual motion descriptor, namely Optical Flow (the key descriptor exploited in the aforementioned ego-vision video segmentation approaches [10, 8, 12]), with heterogeneous sensor data. In particular, our proposal is to build a descriptor based on the covariance of visual and inertial information. In contrast with common early fusion approaches which directly combine (e.g concatenating the resulting feature vectors) heterogeneous data, our strategy allows to capture the correlation between visual and inertial features. The results obtained are encouraging and demon-

MM '16, October 15-19, 2016, Amsterdam, Netherlands

DOI: http://dx.doi.org/10.1145/2964284.2967266

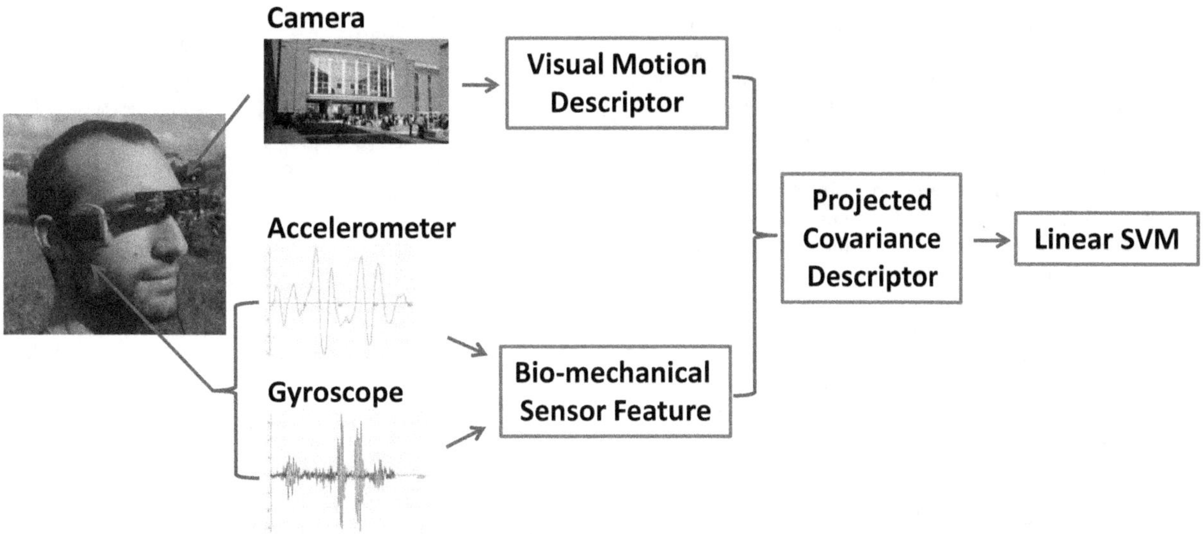

Figure 1: A schematization of the proposed solution.

strate clear benefits in the integration between visual and bio-mechanical features.

Furthermore, due to the novelty of the proposed study, we contribute to further research efforts on the matter releasing both the dataset and the source code. The dataset, referred as EGO-SENSORS in the following, features several hours of egocentric video coupled with tri-axial accelerometer and gyroscope data, fully annotated at a frame level with the current motion label.

2. MOTION SEGMENTATION

To segment egocentric videos into motion classes, we analyze the visual and bio-mechanical data stream coming from a glass-mounted wearable device, which features a camera, a tri-axial accelerometer and a tri-axial gyroscope. The Figure 1 depicts a schematization of our solution.

In particular, we analyze the multimodal stream using a sliding window approach. Two different sets of windows are considered: a smaller window $\mathbf{W} = \{\mathbf{f}_1, \ldots, \mathbf{f}_N\}$ that aggregates motion features for each frame, and a larger one $\mathbf{S} = \{\mathbf{W}_1, \ldots, \mathbf{W}_M\}$ that aggregates windows (N and M are the size of the two windows respectively). The frame-level window W allows to compute metrics over small temporal intervals: this choice balances the trade-off between fine information grain and noise, and the 50% overlap between windows has demonstrated to improve sampling robustness [14]. For each window W, motion features are extracted from the visual content and from the tri-axial accelerometer and gyroscope respectively (see subsection 2.1 and subsection 2.2). The windows **S** aggregates small windows into larger and more temporally relevant sequences spanning a few seconds of video.

To deal with these heterogeneous data we propose an approach that efficiently integrates and captures the correlation between them. In particular, let **S** be a set of descriptors extracted on a large window, where $\mathbf{W}_i = [\mathbf{mv}_i \mathbf{mb}_i]$ is the concatenation of heterogeneous features of the sub-window $\mathbf{W}_i$, we represent them by a covariance matrix **C**. It encodes information about the variance of the features and their correlations and is computed as follows:

$$\mathbf{C} = \frac{1}{N-1} \sum_{i=1}^{N} (\mathbf{W}_i - \mathbf{m})(\mathbf{W}_i - \mathbf{m})^T, \quad (1)$$

where $\mathbf{m}$ is the mean vector of the set $\mathbf{W}_i$. Although the space of covariance matrices can be formulated as a differentiable manifold, it does not lie in a vector space (e.g the covariance space is not closed under multiplication with a negative scalar) and Euclidean distance between image descriptors can not be computed. Therefore to use this descriptive feature vector, we need to define a suitable transformation. We exploit a projection from the Riemannian manifold to an Euclidean tangent space, called Log-Euclidean metric as suggested by [13]. The basic idea of the Log-Euclidean metric is to construct an equivalent relationship between the Riemannian manifold and the vector space of the symmetric matrix.

The first step is the projection of the covariance matrix on an Euclidean space tangent to the Riemannian manifold, on a specific tangency matrix **T**. The second one is the extraction of the orthonormal coordinates of the projected vector. In the following, matrices (points in the Riemannian manifold) will be denoted by bold uppercase letters, while vectors (points in the Euclidean space) by bold lowercase ones. The projection of **C** on the hyperplane tangent to **T** becomes:

$$\mathbf{c} = \mathrm{vec}_{\mathbf{I}}\left(\log\left(\mathbf{T}^{-\frac{1}{2}}\mathbf{C}\mathbf{T}^{-\frac{1}{2}}\right)\right), \quad (2)$$

where log is the matrix logarithm operator and **I** is the identity matrix, while the vector operator on the tanget space at identity of a symmetric matrix **Y** is defined as:

$$\mathrm{vec}_{\mathbf{I}}(\mathbf{Y}) = \left[y_{1,1}\ \sqrt{2}y_{1,2}\ \sqrt{2}y_{1,3} \ldots y_{2,2}\ \sqrt{2}y_{2,3} \ldots y_{d,d}\right]. \quad (3)$$

As observed in [11], by computing the sectional curvature of the Riemmanian manifold, the natural generalization of the classical Gaussian curvature for surfaces, it is possible to show that this space is almost flat. This means that the neighborhood relation between the points on the manifold remains unchanged, wherever the projection point **T** is located. Therefore, from a computational point of view, the best choice for **T** is the identity matrix, which simply translates the mapping into applying the $\text{vec}_\mathbf{I}$ operator to the standard matrix logarithm. This also frees us from the problem of optimizing the projection point for the specific data under consideration, leading to a generally applicable descriptor. Since the projected covariance is a symmetric matrix of $d \times d$ values, the image descriptor is a $(d^2 + d)/2$-dimensional feature vector.

The feature vectors resulting from this analysis are extremely descriptive and can be used to train a linear SVM classifier. This is particularly favorable due to the considered setting of embedded wearable devices that often features limited hardware capabilities and real-time processing needs.

2.1 Visual Motion Descriptor

To represent the visual components of apparent motion in each sub-window **W**, we extract features based on optical flow and blurriness following [10]. The optical flow descriptor can both measure forward travel and effectively capture the fast head movements that so often occur in ego-vision. We compute dense optical flow for each couple of consecutive frames, using Farneback algorithm [5], obtaining the relative apparent velocity of each pixel (V_x, V_y). These values can be expressed in polar coordinates (magnitudes and orientations) as in the following:

$$M = \sqrt{V_x^2 + V_y^2} \quad \theta = \arctan(V_y/V_x) \tag{4}$$

We quantize both the orientations and magnitudes into eight bins. The final visual feature vector is then obtained concatenating the magnitude and the orientation histograms, where the latter is weighed by its magnitude.

To compute the blurriness descriptor we adopt the solution proposed by Roffet *et al.* [4], which evaluating the line and row difference between the original image and the image obtained applying to it a horizontal and a vertical strong low-pass filter.

The visual motion feature vector, i.e. the concatenation of the two visual descriptors, is used to compute the frame window W descriptor applying an *average pooling* strategy followed by a l^2 normalization.

2.2 Bio-mechanical Sensor Feature

The bio-mechanical descriptor is composed by data obtained from the accelerometer and the gyroscope. The raw data consists of three values corresponding to the head acceleration along x-axis, y-axis and z-axis expressed in $\frac{m}{s^2}$ and other three values that represent the orientations (azimuth, pitch and roll) expressed in $\frac{degree}{sec}$. However, classifiers are demonstrated to perform poorly on raw sensor data and require a representation that captures the predominant characteristics that are intrinsic to this kind of data [9]. In fact, Figure 2 shows a plot of the raw data obtained from the x-axis of the accelerometer. It can be seen how, aside from two peaks, no clear and discriminative information can be directly inferred from such data. Therefore, for each window W we compute different features for both data sensors: minimum and maximum values inside the window; mean and standard deviation of acceleration and orientation values along the three axes; amount of zero-crossings inside the window, that is the amount of changes in sign of the considered metric. The dimensionality of this descriptor can vary depending on which of these features are considered and is $30 - \textit{dimensional}$ when all of them are employed together.

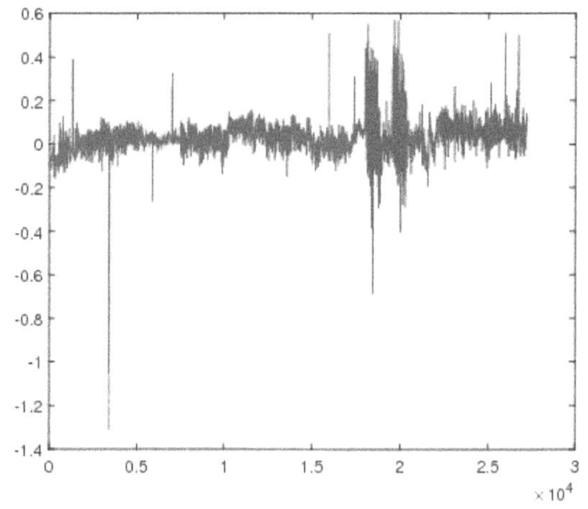

Figure 2: An example of raw data acquired from the x-axis of an accelerometer over 25.000 frames.

3. EXPERIMENTAL RESULTS

To thoroughly evaluate the proposed approach, we record the novel dataset EGO-SENSORS. It was collected by using glass-mounted device that consists of a tri-axial accelerometer and a tri-axial gyroscope embedded in the EXLs1 sensor node, a camera and an Odroid-XU developer board used as data-processing and storage unit.

The developer board we use embeds the ARM Exynos 5 SoC, that hosts a Quad big.LITTLE ARM processor (Cortex A15 and A7). Since the wearable camera acquires data at 30 frames per second and the EXLs1 sensor streams at 100 Hz, we synchronize the two by sub-sampling the sensor readings at 30 Hz as to have one reading per frame. This dataset features 300,000 high quality egocentric frames, each with a timestamp and its relative sensor reading. The dataset is fully annotated with six different motion classes: *biking*, *jogging*, *running*, *standing*, *walking* and *wandering*. The dataset is composed of videos captured in unconstrained real environments such as outdoor and indoor locations, captured by different people spanning various ages and in significantly different timespan featuring both night and day illumination conditions. Currently, there is no record of a publicly available egocentric video collection provided with accelerometer and gyroscope readings. Hence, being EGO-SENSORS the first significant dataset tackling with this problem, we publicly release it along with both the code[1].

The experiments are conducted in an incremental way: first, we evaluate the contribution of different sets of features individually and then, the performance resulting from their combination is evaluated. To highlight the contribution of our data fusion strategy, results are reported with and without the use of our covariance descriptor, where the latter concatenates the different feature vectors (commonly referred to as early fusion). The features considered

[1] http://imagelab.unimore.it/sensors

	Linear SVM			
	Early Fusion		Our Approach	
Features	Acc.	Std	Acc.	Std
Blur + Optical Flow	0.724	0.017	0.741	0.015
A + G	0.762	0.054	0.921	0.009
Blur + A + G	0.792	0.059	0.909	0.009
Optical Flow + A + G	0.837	0.045	0.937	0.009
Blur + Opt. Flow + A + G	0.864	0.039	0.939	0.008

Table 1: Comparison of fusion strategies for different combinations of visual and bio-mechanical features. The first column describes the type of feature used, where A: Accelerometer, G: Gyroscope.

are: blur, optical flow, gyroscope and accelerometer information. Table 1 reports the results of the described evaluation in terms of classification accuracy and standard deviation. These metrics are obtained from a cross validation with a $80-20$ ratio between training and testing data where each test is repeated 100 times. All the experiments have been performed fixing the window sizes to $N=4$ and $M=40$, values identified with preliminary tests.

The table reports the contributions of different combination of visual and bio-mechanical descriptors. It can be noticed how the combination of different sensors can outperform their stand-alone usage in both fusion strategies. As expected, due to the unconstrained experimental setting solely adopting visual features results in poor performance. In fact, the table shows that the final feature vector that combines both visual and sensor data achieves the best results. It also shows that our solution, based on a covariance mapping, largely outperforms the standard early fusion strategy in all types of feature combinations. For example comparing the result of the final descriptor, we can observe that the propose solution improves over the early fusion approach by more than 8%.

For a more detailed analysis of the motion segmentation problem, we refer to the confusion matrices reported in Figure 3. In particular, Figure 3a reports the classification results using visual features in an early fusion fashion similar to what proposed for ego-motion segmentation by Lu *et al.* [10]. It can be seen how in this situation the class *walking* has a low accuracy rating due to the low discrimative capability of visual information to predict this particular class. On the other hand, Figure 3b reports results obtained using solely bio-mechanical features and shows a reduced risk of misclassifiying *walking* thanks to motion classification capabilities inherent of inertial sensors. Furthermore, the opposite situation occurs when classifying *biking* sequences, where visual information has better performance due to the fact that part of the bicycle is often visible in the scene. This shows the complementarity of the two information sources.

Considering the combination of features obtained from both visual and bio-mechanical sources, Figures 3c and 3d report the results obtained by using an early fusion approach (3c) and our covariance descriptor (3d). The Figures show how, given our descriptors' ability to capture the correlation between heterogeneous features, it can significantly reduce the error in the most ambiguous classes. For example, while the *jogging* class is recognized with a 66% accuracy using an early fusion strategy, our covariance descriptor can achieve a relative improvement of 32%.

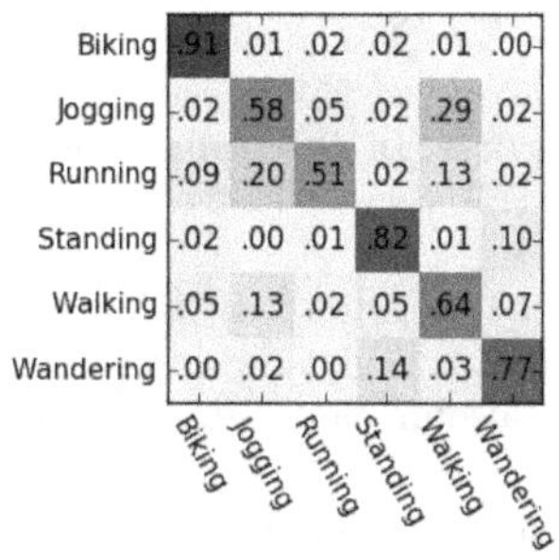

(a) Confusion matrix of the results obtained using visual features in an early fusion fashion

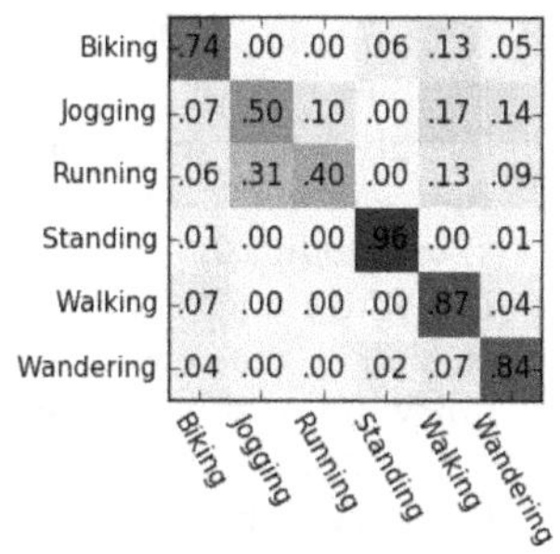

(b) Confusion matrix of the results using bio-mechanical data with an early fusion strategy

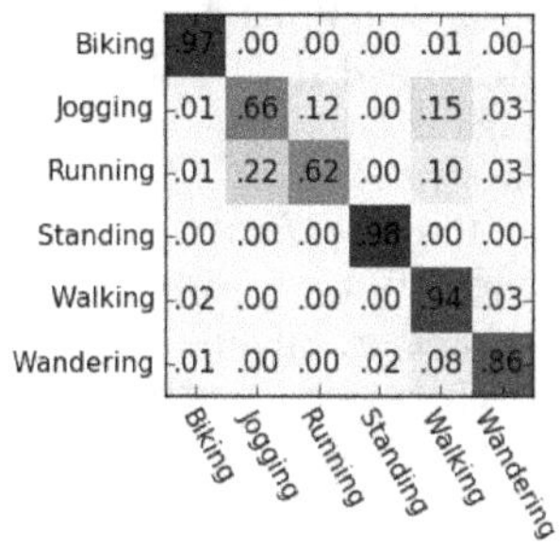

(c) Confusion matrix obtained by merging visual and bio-mechanical features through early fusion

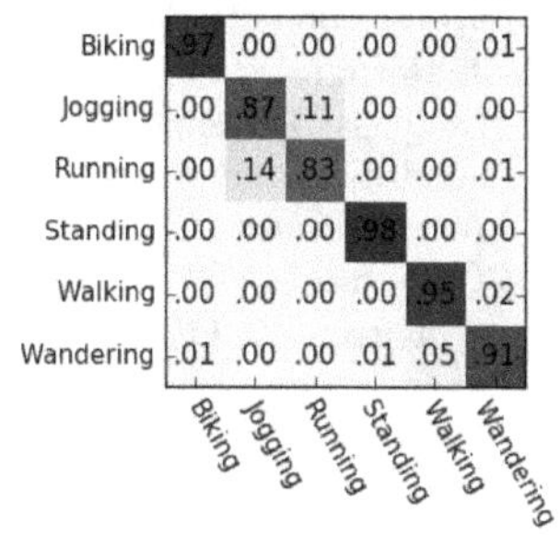

(d) Confusion matrix obtained by merging visual and bio-mechanical features through our covariance descriptor

Figure 3: Confusion matrices of different features

4. CONCLUSION

In this paper we presented a thorough analysis of the multimodal acquisition capabilities of new egocentric wearable devices. We demonstrated that the main feature traditional computer vision focuses on, while providing a useful insight on the motion patterns present in the scene, can greatly benefit from the additional information resulting from bio-mechanical sensors. In particular, we design a novel data fusion strategy based on the projected covariance descriptor, which can better capture relations between visual and inertial information. Experimental results on a new and unconstrained egocentric dataset show that, when compared to the traditional early fusion strategy, our solution can improve the overall performance and significantly lower the error in the most ambiguous motion classes. Furthermore, due to the novelty of the task at hand, this work contributes to further research by releasing a real world unconstrained dataset annotated with motion activities and featuring both high quality video and bio-mechanical sensor readings.

5. REFERENCES

[1] S. Alletto, G. Serra, S. Calderara, F. Solera, and R. Cucchiara. From ego to nos-vision: Detecting social relationships in first-person views. In *Proc. of Egocentric (First-Person) Vision Workshop, CVPRW*, 2014.

[2] A. Betancourt, P. Morerio, C. Regazzoni, and M. Rauterberg. The evolution of first person vision methods: A survey. *IEEE Transactions on Circuits and Systems for Video Technology*, PP(99):1–1, 2015.

[3] N. Brunetto, S. Salti, N. Fioraio, T. Cavallari, and L. Stefano. Fusion of inertial and visual measurements for rgb-d slam on mobile devices. In *Proc. of the IEEE International Conference on Computer Vision Workshops*, 2015.

[4] F. Crété-Roffet, T. Dolmiere, P. Ladret, M. Nicolas, et al. The blur effect: Perception and estimation with a new no-reference perceptual blur metric. In *Proc. of SPIE*, 2007.

[5] G. Farnebäck. Two-frame motion estimation based on polynomial expansion. In *Image Analysis*, pages 363–370. Springer, 2003.

[6] A. Fathi, A. Farhadi, and J. Rehg. Understanding egocentric activities. In *Proc. of ICCV*, 2011.

[7] J. Hernandez, Y. Li, J. M. Rehg, and R. W. Picard. Bioglass: Physiological parameter estimation using a head-mounted wearable device. In *Proc. of International Conference on Wireless Mobile Communication and Healthcare*, 2014.

[8] K. Kitani, T. Okabe, Y. Sato, and A. Sugimoto. Fast unsupervised ego-action learning for first-person sports videos. In *Proc. of CVPR*, 2011.

[9] Q. Li, J. A. Stankovic, M. A. Hanson, A. T. Barth, J. Lach, and G. Zhou. Accurate, fast fall detection using gyroscopes and accelerometer-derived posture information. In *Proc. of International Workshop on Wearable and Implantable Body Sensor Networks*, 2009.

[10] Z. Lu and K. Grauman. Story-driven summarization for egocentric video. In *Proc. of CVPR*, 2013.

[11] S. Martelli, D. Tosato, M. Farenzena, M. Cristani, and V. Murino. An FPGA-based Classification Architecture on Riemannian Manifolds. In *Proc. of DEXA Workshops*, 2010.

[12] Y. Poleg, C. Arora, and S. Peleg. Temporal segmentation of egocentric videos. In *Proc. of CVPR*, 2014.

[13] O. Tuzel, F. Porikli, and P. Meer. Pedestrian Detection via Classification on Riemannian Manifolds. *IEEE Transactions Pattern Analysis and Machine Intelligence*, 30(10):1713–1727, 2008.

[14] S. D. Richard W. DeVaul. Real-time motion classification for wearable computing applications. In *Technical report, MIT Media Laboratory*, 2001.

Locality-preserving K-SVD Based Joint Dictionary and Classifier Learning for Object Recognition

Yuan-Shan Lee
kg934283@gmail.com

Chien-Yao Wang
102582011@cc.ncu.edu.tw

Seksan Mathulaprangsan
mr.sekk@gmail.com

Jia-Hao Zhao
ross800127@gmail.com

Jia-Ching Wang
jcw@csie.ncu.edu.tw

Department of Computer Science and Information Engineering
National Central University, Taoyuan, Taiwan

ABSTRACT

This paper concerns the development of locality-preserving methods for object recognition. The major purpose is consideration of both descriptor-level locality and image-level locality throughout the recognition process. Two dual-layer locality-preserving methods are developed, in which locality-constrained linear coding (LLC) is used to represent an image. In the learning phase, the discriminative locality-preserving K-SVD (DLP-KSVD) in which the label information is incorporated into the locality-preserving term is proposed. In addition to using class labels to learn a linear classifier, the label-consistent LP-KSVD (LCLP-KSVD) is proposed to enhance the discriminability of the learned dictionary. In LCLP-KSVD, the objective function includes a label-consistent term that penalizes sparse codes from different classes. For testing, additional information about the locality of query samples is obtained by treating the locality-preserving matrix as a feature. The recognition results that were obtained in experiments with the Caltech101 database indicate that the proposed method outperforms existing sparse coding based approaches.

Keywords

K-SVD; D-KSVD; locality-preserving; joint dictionary learning; object recognition

1. INTRODUCTION

Object recognition is that aspect of computer vision that involves recognizing objects from photographs or videos. Although humans can recognize objects with ease, machines face numerous difficulties in so doing: for example the variable orientation of objects relative to a camera may have a huge effect on recognition performance, and the variation of the size of a target object with the distance from the object to the camera can greatly affect the accuracy of recognition. These difficulties make object recognition a highly challenging task.

Generally, the process of object recognition can be divided into two main steps, which are feature extraction and classification. Diverse methods exist for extracting the features from image files. Scale-invariant feature transformation (SIFT) [12] is a method that solves the problem of the rotated image. Another famous approach to resolving scale- and rotation-invariance is based on speeded-up robust features (SURF) [1]; the method creates a SURF descriptor using a precomputed integral image. Spatial pyramid matching (SPM) [8] is a technique that solves the problem of scale variation. SPM splits an image into blocks and computes histograms of low-level descriptors, such as SIFT, for each block. The histograms of each block are then concatenated into a feature vector to represent the image. Originally, a codebook that is generated by vector quantization (VQ) was utilized to compute the histograms of descriptors. To avoid the quantization loss that is associated with VQ, Yang *et al.* [17] proposed a linear SPM that is based on sparse coding (ScSPM). The ScSPM has been proven to be effective with simple linear SVMs. Yu *et al.* [19] indicated that locality is more important than sparsity in nonlinear learning. Based on the work of Yu *et al.* [19], locality-constrained linear coding (LLC) was developed [14]. Zhang *et al.* [22] presented low-rank sparse coding (LRSC), which jointly codes the local region of descriptors for image classification. More recently, locality-constrained low-rank coding (LCLR) [5] which benefits from joint coding and locality, has also been developed. The aforementioned locality-based representations [5, 14, 19, 22] provide favorable classification accuracy, even with linear classifiers.

In the classification step, the extracted image representations are fed into classifiers such as the support vector machine (SVM) [2], the sparse representation-based classification (SRC) [16] and others. Recently, the advent of supervised dictionary-based methods [3, 7, 10, 18, 20, 21] has massively improved object recognition; of these methods, discriminative K-SVD (D-KSVD) [21] is regarded as one of the most representative. D-KSVD jointly learns the dictionary and the linear classifier. The classification error term is incorporated into the reconstruction error term in the objective function. This scheme improves the discriminative power of the dictionary in face recognition task. Label-consistent K-SVD (LC-KSVD) [6] was developed by adding a label-consistent term to D-KSVD to improve the distinguishability of the learned sparse codes. To preserve

MM '16, October 15-19, 2016, Amsterdam, Netherlands

 ISBN 978-1-4503-3603-1/16/10...$15.00

DOI: http://dx.doi.org/10.1145/2964284.2967267

the local structure of data in dictionary learning, Wei *et al.* [15] proposed a locality-sensitive SRC (L-SRC), which has a close-form solution throughout the learning process. Liu *et al.* [11] developed a locality-preserving K-SVD (LP-KSVD), which integrates the locality penalty term into the D-KSVD framework. However, to the best of our knowledge, although various locality-based methods have been proposed, most consider either locality on SIFT descriptors [5, 14, 19, 22], or locality on image representations [11, 15].

To exploit fully the potential of the locality-preserving technique for object recognition task, this paper develops two dual-layer locality-preserving methods. First, the discriminative LP-KSVD (DLP-KSVD), which incorporates the label information into locality-preserving term, is proposed. Second, the label-consistent LP-KSVD (LCLP-KSVD) is developed to improve the discriminability of the learned dictionary. By employing the LLC for image representation, the proposed methods take both descriptor-level locality and image-level locality into consideration.

The rest of this paper is organized as follows. Section 2 describes works relevant to the developed model. Section 3 elucidates details of the proposed model. Section 4 presents experimental results. Finally, section 5 draws conclusions and summarizes possibilities for future work.

2. RELATED WORKS

2.1 Locality-preserving Projections

LPP [4] is a linear dimensionality reduction algorithm. It finds a linear transformation that exposes the locality of the input signals. The objective function of the LPP can be presented as,

$$\min \sum_{ij}(x_i - x_j)\mathbf{L}_{ij} \tag{1}$$

where x_i is the low-dimensional representation of input signal y_i. $\mathbf{L}$ is a similarity matrix which is defined as:

$$\mathbf{L}_{ij} = \begin{cases} exp(\frac{-\|y_i - y_j\|^2}{\rho}) & ; e(y_i, y_j) = 1 \\ 0 & ; e(y_i, y_j) = 0 \end{cases} \tag{2}$$

where $e(y_i, y_j) = 1$ for k-nearest y_j according to y_i. ρ denotes a tunable parameter.

2.2 Sparse Representation Classifier

Sparse representation classifier (SRC) [16] is a classifier that exploits sparse representation. The dictionary comprises training data. Following sparse coding, the reconstruction error of each class can be calculated. The recognition results are obtained by minimizing the reconstruction error.

Let $\mathbf{Y}$ be a training dataset that has N signals, each of which has d dimensions, so $\mathbf{Y} = [\mathbf{y}_1, ..., \mathbf{y}_N] \in R^{d \times N}$. For the reconstruction of $\mathbf{Y}$, the optimization formula of dictionary learning can be conducted by solving the following equation.

$$< \mathbf{D}, \mathbf{X} >= \arg \min_{\mathbf{D},\mathbf{X}} \|\mathbf{Y} - \mathbf{DX}\|_F^2 \quad s.t. \forall i, \|\mathbf{x}_i\|_0 \leq T \tag{3}$$

where $\mathbf{X} = [\mathbf{x}_1, ..., \mathbf{x}_N] \in R^{m \times N}$ represents the sparse codes of $\mathbf{Y}$, $\mathbf{D} = [\mathbf{d}_1, ..., \mathbf{d}_m] \in R^{d \times m}$ is the trained overcomplete dictionary. m denotes the total number of dictionary atoms. The sparse constraint T is applied to control the sparseness of nonzero items in each sparse code.

2.3 Joint Dictionary Learning

Pham and Venkatesh [13] developed joint dictionary learning (JDL) as a method that combines dictionary learning and classifier learning. The objective function is defined as,

$$< \mathbf{W}, \mathbf{b} >= \arg \min_{\mathbf{W},\mathbf{b}} \|\mathbf{H} - \mathbf{WX} - \mathbf{b}\|_2^2 + \gamma \|\mathbf{W}\|_2^2 \tag{4}$$

where $\mathbf{W}$ and $\mathbf{b}$ are parameters of the linear classifier $\mathbf{H} = \mathbf{WX} + \mathbf{b}$. $\mathbf{H}$ is the target matrix of the linear classifier. Each column in $\mathbf{H}$ is a vector for which $\mathbf{h}_i = [0, ...1, ..., 0, 0]$ is class number that is associated with each input sample. $\|\mathbf{H} - \mathbf{WX} - \mathbf{b}\|_2^2$ is the recognition error. $\|\mathbf{W}\|_2^2$ is the regularization penalty term. To simplify the objective function, $\mathbf{b}$ is set to zero.

The dictionary learning objective function is based on the combination of l_0-norm and the linear classifier objective function in (4):

$$< \mathbf{D}, \mathbf{X}, \mathbf{W} >= \arg \min_{\mathbf{D},\mathbf{X},\mathbf{W}} \|\mathbf{Y} - \mathbf{DX}\|_2^2 + \beta \|\mathbf{H} - \mathbf{WX}\|_2^2 + \gamma \|\mathbf{W}\|_2^2 \quad s.t. \forall i, \|\mathbf{x}_i\|_0 \leq T \tag{5}$$

where the parameters β and γ are used to balance the influence of each term.

2.4 Discriminative K-SVD

Zhang and Li [21] developed a method of simultaneously training the dictionary and the classifier, called discriminative K-SVD. The objective function of D-KSVD is defined as,

$$< \mathbf{D}, \mathbf{X}, \mathbf{W} >= \arg \min_{\mathbf{D},\mathbf{X},\mathbf{W}} \|\mathbf{Y} - \mathbf{DX}\|_2^2 + \beta \|\mathbf{H} - \mathbf{WX}\|_2^2 \quad s.t. \forall i, \|\mathbf{x}_i\|_0 \leq T \tag{6}$$

where $\mathbf{H} \in R^{c \times N}$ is the object matrix of c-classes linear classifier. Each column in $\mathbf{H}$ is a vector such that $\mathbf{h}_i = [0, ...1, ..., 0, 0]$ is the class number for each input data. $\mathbf{W}$ is a linear classifier. β is a parameter that modifies the influence between reconstruction error and recognition error. Notably, the regularization penalty term $\|\mathbf{W}\|_2^2$ in joint dictionary learning is discarded to simplify the objective function.

To obtain the dictionary, sparse codes, and linear classifier simultaneously, the objective function in (6) is modified as,

$$< \mathbf{D}, \mathbf{X}, \mathbf{W} >= \arg \min_{\mathbf{D},\mathbf{X},\mathbf{W}} \left\| \begin{pmatrix} \mathbf{Y} \\ \sqrt{\beta}\mathbf{H} \end{pmatrix} - \begin{pmatrix} \mathbf{D} \\ \sqrt{\beta}\mathbf{W} \end{pmatrix} \mathbf{X} \right\|_2^2 \quad s.t. \forall i, \|\mathbf{x}_i\|_0 \leq T \tag{7}$$

K-SVD can be used to obtain dictionary $\mathbf{D}$ and linear classifier $\mathbf{W}$ at the same time. After training, the sparse code $\mathbf{x}'$ of the query $\mathbf{y}'$ can be identified. The recognition result is computed by multiplying the linear classifier $\mathbf{W}$ by the sparse code $\mathbf{x}'$:

$$\mathbf{l} = \mathbf{Wx}' \tag{8}$$

where $\mathbf{l}$ is the recognition result.

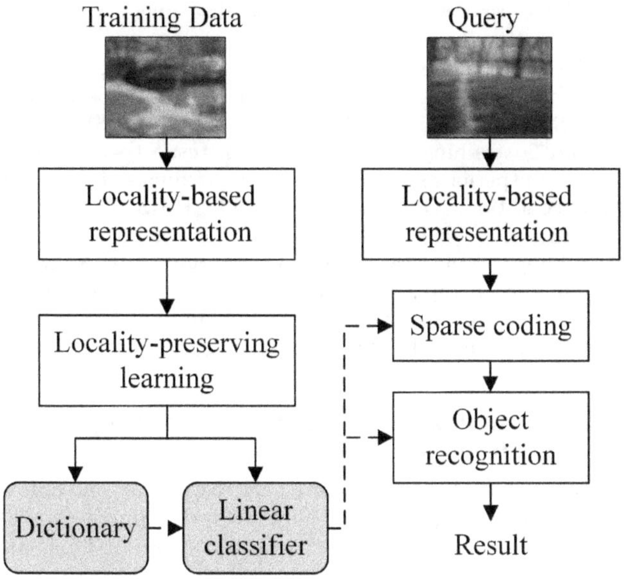

Figure 1: An overview of the proposed method.

3. DUAL-LAYER LOCALITY-PRESERVING K-SVD FOR OBJECT RECOGNITION

This work developed two dual-layer locality-preserving methods for object recognition. Sections 3.1 and 3.2 address the difference between them. Both of the proposed methods comprise two main stages, which are feature extraction and classifier learning. In the first stage, LLC [14] features are extracted from the images. In the second stage, the sparse codes are learned from LLC features based on the proposed methods, DLP-KSVD and LCLP-KSVD. Thereafter, the linear classifier is used with the learned sparse codes to recognize objects. In so doing, both descriptor-level locality and image-level locality are considered. Figure 1 displays an overview of the proposed dual-layer locality-preserving methods.

3.1 Discriminative LP-KSVD (DLP-KSVD)

The proposed DLP-KSVD is derived by combining the preservation of locality with dictionary learning. Unlike the work of Liu *et al.* [11], a discriminative target matrix is proposed to preserve locality. Label information is incorporated into the proposed locality target matrix to further enhance the discrimination of learned sparse codes. Adding the locality-preserving term into the original D-KSVD yields the objective function as,

$$< \mathbf{D},\mathbf{P},\mathbf{W},\mathbf{X} >= \arg\min_{\mathbf{D},\mathbf{P},\mathbf{W},\mathbf{X}} \|\mathbf{Y}-\mathbf{D}\mathbf{X}\|_2^2 + \alpha \left\|\check{\mathbf{L}}-\mathbf{P}\mathbf{X}\right\|_2^2 + \beta\|\mathbf{H}-\mathbf{W}\mathbf{X}\|_2^2 \quad s.t. \forall i, \|\mathbf{x}_i\|_0 \le T \tag{9}$$

where α and β are parameters that fine-tune the effects of reconstruction term, locality term, and recognition term on each other. $\mathbf{P}$ denotes a linear transformation matrix that maps $\mathbf{X}$ into locality-preserving code space. $\mathbf{W}$ denotes the linear classifier. $\check{\mathbf{L}}$ indicates the discriminative locality-preserving matrix, defined as,

$$\check{\mathbf{L}}_{ij} = \begin{cases} exp(\frac{-\|y_i-y_j\|^2}{\rho}) & ;\breve{e}(y_i,y_j)=1 \\ -(1-exp(\frac{-\|y_i-y_j\|^2}{\rho})) & ;\breve{e}(y_i,y_j)=0 \end{cases} \tag{10}$$

where $\breve{e}(y_i,y_j)=1$ for k-nearest y_j, which belongs to the same class as y_i, and $\breve{e}(y_i,y_j)=0$ for k-nearest y_j, which belongs to a different class from y_i.

Equation (9) can be rewritten by using K-SVD to minimize the objective function as,

$$< \mathbf{D},\mathbf{P},\mathbf{W},\mathbf{X} >= \arg\min_{\mathbf{D},\mathbf{P},\mathbf{W},\mathbf{X}} \left\| \begin{pmatrix} \mathbf{Y} \\ \sqrt{\alpha}\check{\mathbf{L}} \\ \sqrt{\beta}\mathbf{H} \end{pmatrix} - \begin{pmatrix} \mathbf{D} \\ \sqrt{\alpha}\mathbf{P} \\ \sqrt{\beta}\mathbf{W} \end{pmatrix} \mathbf{X} \right\|_2^2 \quad s.t. \forall i, \|\mathbf{x}_i\|_0 \le T \tag{11}$$

3.2 Label-consistent LP-KSVD (LCLP-KSVD)

Except for using class labels to learn a linear classifier, the label consistent term is utilized to improve the discriminability of the learned dictionary. Following the work of Zhang and Li [21], the label information is associated with each dictionary atom in the learning process. Adding the label consistent term into the original LP-KSVD yields the objective function as,

$$< \mathbf{D},\mathbf{P},\mathbf{W},\mathbf{A},\mathbf{X} >= \arg\min_{\mathbf{D},\mathbf{P},\mathbf{W},\mathbf{A},\mathbf{X}} \|\mathbf{Y}-\mathbf{D}\mathbf{X}\|_2^2 + \alpha\|\mathbf{L}-\mathbf{P}\mathbf{X}\|_2^2 + \beta\|\mathbf{H}-\mathbf{W}\mathbf{X}\|_2^2 + \gamma\|\mathbf{Q}-\mathbf{A}\mathbf{X}\|_2^2 \quad s.t. \forall i, \|\mathbf{x}_i\|_0 \le T \tag{12}$$

where α, β and γ are parameters that fine-tune the effects of reconstruction term, locality term, recognition term, and label consistent term on each other. $\mathbf{Q}$ denotes the discriminative sparse codes of input signals [21].

Similarly, Eq. (12) can be rewritten by using K-SVD to minimize the objective function as,

$$< \mathbf{D},\mathbf{P},\mathbf{W},\mathbf{A},\mathbf{X} >= \arg\min_{\mathbf{D},\mathbf{P},\mathbf{W},\mathbf{A},\mathbf{X}} \left\| \begin{pmatrix} \mathbf{Y} \\ \sqrt{\alpha}\mathbf{L} \\ \sqrt{\beta}\mathbf{H} \\ \sqrt{\gamma}\mathbf{Q} \end{pmatrix} - \begin{pmatrix} \mathbf{D} \\ \sqrt{\alpha}\mathbf{P} \\ \sqrt{\beta}\mathbf{W} \\ \sqrt{\gamma}\mathbf{A} \end{pmatrix} \mathbf{X} \right\|_2^2 \quad s.t. \forall i, \|\mathbf{x}_i\|_0 \le T \tag{13}$$

3.3 Locality-incorporated Dictionary Learning

For a query sample $\mathbf{z}$, the corresponding sparse code can be obtained as,

$$\mathbf{x}' = \arg\min_{\mathbf{x}'} \|\mathbf{z}-\mathbf{D}\mathbf{x}'\|_2^2 \quad s.t. \forall i, \|\mathbf{x}'_i\|_0 \le T \tag{14}$$

Finally, after the training step, the recognition result can be computed using Eq. (8). To incorporate the locality information into the query, the locality-preserving matrix is regarded as a new feature. The objective function is rewritten as,

$$< \mathbf{D}',\mathbf{P},\mathbf{W},\mathbf{X}, >= \arg\min_{\mathbf{D},\mathbf{P},\mathbf{W},\mathbf{X}} \|\mathbf{Y}'-\mathbf{D}'\mathbf{X}\|_2^2 + \beta\|\mathbf{H}-\mathbf{W}\mathbf{X}\|_2^2 \quad s.t. \forall i, \|\mathbf{x}_i\|_0 \le T \tag{15}$$

Table 1: Accuracy rates of different training data sizes on Caltech101 dataset

# of Tr. Images	5	10	15	20	25	30
SRC	49.00	58.81	63.90	66.96	69.47	71.83
D-KSVD	52.59	62.08	66.94	69.66	72.00	74.21
LC-KSVD	52.49	62.14	66.80	69.35	71.49	73.67
LP-KSVD	52.51	62.09	66.90	69.65	71.99	74.23
LCLP-KSVD	55.69	64.59	**69.95**	71.90	74.50	75.72
LCLP-KSVD+	55.66	**64.78**	69.59	71.86	74.63	75.62
DLP-KSVD	**55.73**	64.75	69.57	72.02	74.80	76.67
DLP-KSVD+	55.67	64.67	69.48	**72.26**	**74.95**	**76.79**

where $\mathbf{Y}' = \begin{pmatrix} \mathbf{Y} \\ \sqrt{\alpha}\hat{\mathbf{L}} \end{pmatrix}$, $\mathbf{D}' = \begin{pmatrix} \mathbf{D} \\ \sqrt{\alpha}\mathbf{P} \end{pmatrix}$. K-SVD was used to solve the objective function as in (11). The locality-preserving feature $\hat{\mathbf{L}}$ is set to $\check{\mathbf{L}}$ in DLP-KSVD, whereas it is set to set to $\mathbf{L}$ in LCLP-KSVD.

When a query sample $\mathbf{z}$ is addressed, the training data $\mathbf{Y}$ were utilized to calculate locality-preserving feature which is defined as,

$$\bar{\mathbf{L}}_j = \begin{cases} exp(\frac{-\|z-y_j\|^2}{\rho}) & ; e(z, y_j) = 1 \\ 0 & ; e(z, y_j) = 0 \end{cases} \quad (16)$$

where $e(z, y_j) = 1$ for k-nearest y_j according to z.

We combine the query $\mathbf{z}$ and $\bar{\mathbf{L}}$. Extracting sparse code $\bar{\mathbf{x}}$ and then utilize (8) to obtain the recognition result. The objective function is defined as,

$$\bar{\mathbf{x}} = \arg\min_{\bar{\mathbf{x}}} \left\| \begin{pmatrix} \mathbf{z} \\ \sqrt{\alpha}\bar{\mathbf{L}} \end{pmatrix} - \mathbf{D}'\bar{\mathbf{x}} \right\|_2^2 \quad s.t. \forall i, \|\bar{\mathbf{x}}_i\|_0 \leq T \quad (17)$$

where $\mathbf{D}'$ denotes the locality-incorporated dictionary for coding the query.

4. EXPERIMENTS

Experiments were performed on Caltech101 [9] database. Caltech101 contains 102 classes (101 main classes and a background class) and a total of 9144 images. Each class is associated with 31 to 800 images of various sizes and the sizes vary hugely among classes. SRC [16], D-KSVD [21], LC-KSVD [6], and LP-KSVD [11] were selected as baseline algorithms for comparison. SPM [8] was used to extract the features in the SRC, D-KSVD, LC-KSVD, and LP-KSVD methods. For simplicity, the proposed methods with locality-incorporated dictionary learning are abbreviated as DLP-KSVD+ and LCLP-KSVD+, respectively. LP-KSVD, DLP-KSVD and LCLP-KSVD used 60 nearest neighbors ($k = 60$) in the calculation of the locality-preserving matrix. The parameters α, β, and γ are set to 0.001. To obtain a reliable result, all of the experiments were carried out ten times and the mean value of the results was obtained.

4.1 Comparison of Effects of Variously Sized Training Data

To determine the effect on the size of the training dataset, 5, 10, 15, 20, and 25 images per class were selected at random for training with dictionary size 510, 1020, 1530, 2040, 2550, and 3060 respectively, and the remaining images were used as the testing data.

The experimental results, presented in Table 1, confirm that the proposed DLP-KSVD performed best. Specifically, LCLP-KSVD is 1.5% to 2.5% better than LP-KSVD with 25 and 30 training samples per class, respectively. DLP-KSVD outperforms LP-KSVD by approximate 1% in the same condition. DLP-KSVD+ and LCLP-KSVD+ underperformed DLP-KSVD and LCLP-KSVD when the number of training samples was small but outperformed them when the number of training samples was large. This observation indicates that the incorporated locality information becomes more important as the number of training samples increases.

4.2 Comparison of Effects of Variously Sized Dictionaries

To elucidate the effect of dictionary size on the Caltech101 dataset, 30 images were randomly selected to provide training data. The dictionary size was set to 510, 1020, 1530, 2040, 2550, or 3060. As shown in Table 2, the proposed methods achieve the most accuracy for all dictionary sizes. The proposed DLP-KSVD (76.79%) is much better than the other sparse coding based methods in Table 3, which are SRC (71.83%), D-KSVD (74.21%), LC-KSVD (73.67%), and is approximately 1.5% better than the LPKSVD.

Table 2: Accuracy rates of different dictionary sizes on Caltech101 dataset

Dictionary Size	510	1020	1530	2040	2550	3060
SRC	71.57	72.00	71.75	71.50	71.60	71.83
D-KSVD	72.03	72.42	71.97	70.81	72.00	74.21
LC-KSVD	72.16	72.22	71.19	71.32	71.19	73.67
LP-KSVD	71.89	72.35	71.96	72.01	71.95	74.23
LCLP-KSVD	73.10	74.19	74.17	73.79	74.33	75.72
LCLP-KSVD+	73.02	74.21	74.43	73.76	74.42	75.62
DLP-KSVD	73.11	74.34	**74.48**	74.62	74.91	76.67
DLP-KSVD+	**73.40**	**74.75**	74.47	**74.68**	**75.30**	**76.79**

5. CONCLUSIONS AND FUTURE WORKS

This work developed the dual-layer locality-preserving model, which improves conventional dictionary learning approaches by jointly considering descriptor-level locality and image-level locality. The addition of a locality-preserving term improves the distinguishability of the classifier for object recognition problems. Specifically, label information is incorporated into the locality-preserving matrix. A label-consistent term is utilized to enhance the discrimination of learned sparse codes. Experimental results demonstrate the superiority of the proposed DLP-KSVD and LCLP-KSVD with Caltech101 database. The locality-incorporated dictionary learning has been shown to play an important role when the training dataset is sufficiently large. Possible future work includes extending the presented approach to the online dictionary learning, which is highly applicable to large-scale data processing. Also, treating the locality-preserving matrix as the target of another nonlinear classifier to perform discriminative feature extractions, will be of interest.

6. REFERENCES

[1] H. Bay and A. Ess. Speeded-up robust features (SURF). *Comput. Vision and Image Understanding*, 110:346–359, 2008.

[2] C. Cortes and V. Vapnik. Support-vector networks. *Mach. Learning*, 20:273–297, 1995.

[3] M. J. Gangeh, A. Ghodsi, and M. S. Kamel. Kernelized Supervised Dictionary Learning. *IEEE Trans. on Signal Process.*, 61(19):4753–4767, 2013.

[4] X. He and P. Niyogi. Locality preserving projections. In *Proc. Conf. Advances in Neural Inform. Process. Syst.*, pages 153–160, 2003.

[5] Z. Jiang, P. Guo, and L. Peng. Locality-constrained low-rank coding for image classification. In *Proc. the Twenty-Eighth AAAI Conf. Artificial Intell.*, pages 2780–2786, 2013.

[6] Z. Jiang, Z. Lin, and L. S. Davis. Learning a discriminative dictionary for sparse coding via label consistent. In *Proc. IEEE Conf. Comput. Vision and Pattern Recognition (CVPR)*, pages 1697–1704, 2011.

[7] S. Lazebnik and M. Raginsky. Supervised learning of quantizer codebooks by information loss minimization. *IEEE Trans. on Pattern Anal. and Mach. Intell.*, 31(7):1294–1309, 2009.

[8] S. Lazebnik and C. Schmid. Beyond bags of features: spatial pyramid matching for recognizing natural scene categories. In *Proc. IEEE Conf. Comput. Vision and Pattern Recognition (CVPR)*, pages 2169–2178, 2006.

[9] F. F. Li, R. Fergus, and P. Perona. Learning generative visual models from few training examples: an incremental Bayesian approach tested on 101 object categories. *Comput. Vision and Image Understanding*, 106(1):59–70, 2007.

[10] X. C. Lian, Z. Li, C. Wang, B. L. Lu, and L. Zhang. Probabilistic models for supervised dictionary learning. In *Proc. IEEE Conf. Comput. Vision and Pattern Recognition (CVPR)*, pages 2305–2312, 2010.

[11] W. Liu, Z. Yu, M. Yang, L. Lu, and Y. Zou. Joint kernel dictionary and classifier learning for sparse coding via locality preserving k-svd. In *Proc. IEEE Int. Conf. Multimedia Expo (ICME)*, pages 1–6, 2015.

[12] D. G. Lowe. Distinctive image features from scale-invariant keypoints. *Int. J. of Comput. Vision*, 60(2):91–110, 2004.

[13] D. S. Pham and S. Venkatesh. Joint learning and dictionary construction for pattern recognition. In *Proc. IEEE Conf. Comput. Vision and Pattern Recognition (CVPR)*, 2008.

[14] J. Wang, J. Yang, K. Yu, F. Lv, T. Huang, and Y. Gong. Locality-constrained linear coding for image classification. In *Proc. IEEE Conf. Comput. Vision and Pattern Recognition (CVPR)*, pages 3360–3367, 2010.

[15] C.-P. Wei, Y.-W. Chao, Y.-R. Yeh, and Y.-C. F. Wang. Locality-sensitive dictionary learning for sparse representation based classification. *Pattern Recognition*, 46(5):1277–1287, 2013.

[16] J. Wright, A. Y. Yang, A. Ganesh, S. S. Sastry, and Y. Ma. Robust face recognition via sparse representation. *IEEE Trans. on Pattern Anal. and Mach. Intell.*, 31(2):210–227, 2009.

[17] J. Yang, K. Yu, Y. Gong, and T. Huang. Linear spatial pyramid matching using sparse coding for image classification. In *Proc. IEEE Conf. Comput. Vision and Pattern Recognition (CVPR)*, pages 1794–1801, 2009.

[18] M. Yang, L. Zhang, X. Feng, D. Zhang, and H. Kong. Fisher discrimination dictionary learning for sparse representation. In *Proc. IEEE Conf. Comput. Vision*, pages 543–550, 2011.

[19] K. Yu, T. Zhang, and Y. Gong. Nonlinear learning using local coordinate coding. In *Advances Neural Inf. Proc. Syst. 22*, pages 2223–2231, 2009.

[20] H. Zhang, Y. Zhang, and T. S. Huang. Simultaneous discriminative projection and dictionary learning for sparse representation based classification. *Pattern Recognition*, 46(1):346–354, 2013.

[21] Q. Zhang and B. Li. Discriminative K-SVD for dictionary learning in face recognition. In *Proc. IEEE Conf. Comput. Vision and Pattern Recognition (CVPR)*, pages 2691–2698, 2010.

[22] T. Zhang, B. Ghanem, S. Liu, C. Xu, and N. Ahuja. Low-rank sparse coding for image classification. In *Proc. IEEE Int. Conf. Comput. Vision (ICCV)*, pages 281–288, 2013.

Label Tree Embeddings for Acoustic Scene Classification

Huy Phan
Institute for Signal Processing
University of Lübeck
phan@isip.uni-luebeck.de

Lars Hertel
Institute for Signal Processing
University of Lübeck
hertel@isip.uni-luebeck.de

Marco Maass
Institute for Signal Processing
University of Lübeck
maass@isip.uni-luebeck.de

Philipp Koch
Institute for Signal Processing
University of Lübeck
koch@isip.uni-luebeck.de

Alfred Mertins
Institute for Signal Processing
University of Lübeck
mertins@isip.uni-luebeck.de

ABSTRACT

We present in this paper an efficient approach for acoustic scene classification by exploring the structure of class labels. Given a set of class labels, a category taxonomy is automatically learned by collectively optimizing a clustering of the labels into multiple meta-classes in a tree structure. An acoustic scene instance is then embedded into a low-dimensional feature representation which consists of the likelihoods that it belongs to the meta-classes. We demonstrate state-of-the-art results on two different datasets for the acoustic scene classification task, including the DCASE 2013 and LITIS Rouen datasets.

Keywords

acoustic scene classification; label tree embedding; spectral clustering

1. INTRODUCTION

Acoustic scene classification (ASC) is an important problem of computational auditory scene analysis [26, 16]. Solving this problem will allow a device to recognize a surrounding environment via the sound it captures, and hence, enables a wide range of applications, such as surveillance [22], robotic navigation [8], and context-aware services [27, 11]. A recognized scene can also be used as a prior information to improve the performance of sound event detection [13].

Excluding the background noise, an acoustic scene usually involves various kinds of foreground sounds. Due to its complex sound composition, it is challenging to obtain a good representation for classification. Different features adapted from the related problems, such as speech recognition and audio event classification, have been used to characterize an acoustic scene, for instance MFCC [19, 24] and Gammatone filters [25]. Some hand-crafted features tailored for the task have also been proposed and demonstrated good performance, like Histogram of Oriented Gradients (HOG) [23, 4, 28] and Gabor dictionaries [17]. At a higher semantic level, foreground sound events [2, 14, 7], background noise [9], and their combination [28] can be used as a footprint to represent a scene [2, 14, 7].

MM '16, October 15 - 19, 2016, Amsterdam, Netherlands

ISBN 978-1-4503-3603-1/16/10...$15.00

DOI: http://dx.doi.org/10.1145/2964284.2967268

However, most (if not all) previous methods considered the "flat" classification scheme. Thus far, to the best of the authors' knowledge, no studies have explored the structured nature of the scene categories for classification. In this work, we incorporate a class taxonomy by learning to group similar categories into meta-classes on a tree structure. Going beyond that, we construct explicit embeddings to map each acoustic scene instance into the semantic space that underlies the class hierarchy. It turns out that two similar scene instances are expected to be close to each other in the semantic space. We study the class hierarchy learned from the acoustic scene data themselves as well as the one learned from external speech data [20, 21]. Both of them show good empirical performance even with simple linear classifiers. In addition, combining them with a simple fusion scheme leads to state-of-the-art performance on both target datasets: DCASE 2013 [24] and LITIS Rouen datasets [23].

2. THE PROPOSED APPROACH

In this section, we firstly present the framework to learn the label trees and the label tree embeddings for feature mapping. Afterwards, we elaborate different label tree embeddings derived from the framework and the final classification step.

2.1 Learning a Label Tree

Consider a database (e.g. scene database) with the label set $\mathcal{L} = \{1, \dots, C\}$ where C indicates the number of target categories. In order to explore the structure of class labels, we learn a label tree similar to [3]. The learning algorithm collectively partitions the label set into disjoint subsets in such a way that they are easy to distinguish from one another. Given the set of samples $\mathcal{S} = \{(\mathbf{x}_n, c_n)\}_{n=1}^{|\mathcal{S}|}$ extracted from the training data, where $\mathbf{x} \in \mathbb{R}^M$ denotes the vector of some M low-level features, $c \in \mathcal{L}$ indicates the class label, and $|\cdot|$ represents the set cardinality.

The label tree is constructed recursively so that each node

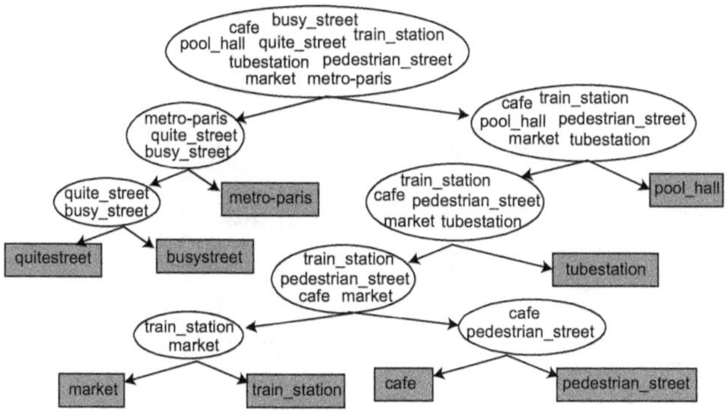

Figure 1: A subtree extracted from the label tree learned from the LITIS Rouen dataset [23].

is associated with a set of class labels. Consider a node with a label set ℓ (and therefore, the root node is assigned with the label set $\mathcal{L}$), our goal is to split ℓ into two subsets ℓ^L and ℓ^R that hold the following requirements: $\ell^L \neq \emptyset$, $\ell^R \neq \emptyset$, $\ell^L \cup \ell^R = \ell$, and $\ell^L \cap \ell^R = \emptyset$. There are totally $2^{|\ell|-1}-1$ such possible partitions $\{\ell^L, \ell^R\}$. The optimal partition is then adopted such that a binary classifier designed to separate ℓ^L and ℓ^R makes as few errors as possible.

In order to find the optimal partitioning, we rely on the multi-class confusion matrix which indicates how good a class is separated from the others. Let $\mathcal{S}^\ell \subset \mathcal{S}$ denote the set of samples corresponding to the label set ℓ. Furthermore, suppose that we have changed and sorted the label set ℓ so that $\ell = \{1, \ldots, |\ell|\}$. In addition, we divide $\mathcal{S}^\ell$ into two equal halves: $\mathcal{S}^\ell_{\text{train}}$ for training a classifier and $\mathcal{S}^\ell_{\text{eval}}$ for evaluation. We train the multi-class classifier $\mathcal{M}^\ell$ using random forest classification [6] with 200 trees using $\mathcal{S}^\ell_{\text{train}}$ and then evaluate it on the evaluation set $\mathcal{S}^\ell_{\text{eval}}$ to obtain the confusion matrix $\mathbf{A} \in \mathbb{R}^{|\ell|\times|\ell|}$. Each element $\mathbf{A}_{ij}$ of the matrix $\mathbf{A}$ is computed by:

$$\mathbf{A}_{ij} = \frac{1}{|\mathcal{S}^\ell_{\text{eval},i}|} \sum_{\mathbf{x}\in\mathcal{S}^\ell_{\text{eval},i}} P(j|\mathbf{x}, \mathcal{M}^\ell). \quad (1)$$

Here, $\mathcal{S}^\ell_{\text{eval},i} \subset \mathcal{S}^\ell_{\text{eval}}$ is the set of samples with the label i. $P(j|\mathbf{x}, \mathcal{M}^\ell)$ denotes the probability that the classifier $\mathcal{M}^\ell$ predicts the sample $\mathbf{x}$ as class j. $\mathbf{A}_{ij}$ implies how likely a sample of the class i is wrongly predicted to belong to the class j by the classifier. Since $\mathbf{A}$ is not symmetric, we symmetrize it as

$$\bar{\mathbf{A}} = (\mathbf{A} + \mathbf{A}^\mathsf{T})/2. \quad (2)$$

Eventually, the optimal partitioning $\{\ell^L, \ell^R\}$ is selected to maximize:

$$E(\ell) = \sum_{i,j\in\ell^L} \bar{\mathbf{A}}_{ij} + \sum_{m,n\in\ell^R} \bar{\mathbf{A}}_{mn}. \quad (3)$$

By this, we tend to group the ambiguous classes into the same subset, as a result, produce two meta-classes $\{\ell^L, \ell^R\}$ that are easy to separate from each other. We apply spectral clustering [18] on the matrix $\bar{\mathbf{A}}$ to solve a relaxed version of the optimization problem in (3). The subsets ℓ^L and ℓ^R are then directed to the left and right child nodes, respectively. The splitting process is recursively repeated to grow the tree until a leaf node with a single class label is reached.

We demonstrate in Figure 1 a subtree extracted from the label tree learned from the LITIS Rouen dataset [23] (more details in Section 2.3).

2.2 Label Tree Embedding (LTE)

Via the learned label tree, we have formed $(C-1)\times 2$ meta-classes in total from the original label set $\mathcal{L}$. Two of them are associated with the left and right child nodes of one out of $(C-1)$ split nodes. For clarity, suppose that we have indexed the split nodes of the label tree as $\{\ell_i\}_{i=1}^{C-1}$. Our objective is then to learn a representation for a test sample by embedding them into the space of the meta-class labels. Formally, we then want to obtain an explicit mapping $\Psi : \mathbb{R}^M \to \mathbb{R}^{(C-1)\times 2}$ to map the test sample $\mathbf{x} \in \mathbb{R}^M$ to a feature vector $\Psi(\mathbf{x}) = \left(\psi_1^L(\mathbf{x}), \psi_1^R(\mathbf{x}), \ldots, \psi_{C-1}^L(\mathbf{x}), \psi_{C-1}^R(\mathbf{x})\right)$. The entries of $\psi_i^L(\mathbf{x})$ and $\psi_i^R(\mathbf{x})$ denote the likelihoods that $\mathbf{x}$ belongs to two meta-classes on the left and right child nodes of the split node ℓ_i.

To obtain the likelihoods, at a split node ℓ_i with the optimal partition $\{\ell_i^L, \ell_i^R\}$, we train the binary random-forest classifier $\mathcal{M}_i^\ell$ with 200 trees using the whole set S^{ℓ_i} as training data. The samples with their labels in ℓ_i^L are considered as negative examples and others with their labels in ℓ_i^R are considered as positive ones. The likelihoods are then given by:

$$\psi_i^L(\mathbf{x}) = P(\text{negative}|\mathbf{x}, \mathcal{M}^{\ell_i}), \quad (4)$$

$$\psi_i^R(\mathbf{x}) = P(\text{positive}|\mathbf{x}, \mathcal{M}^{\ell_i}). \quad (5)$$

Here, $P(\text{negative}|\mathbf{x}, \mathcal{M}^{\ell_i})$ and $P(\text{positive}|\mathbf{x}, \mathcal{M}^{\ell_i})$ are the classification probabilities outputted by $\mathcal{M}^{\ell_i}$ when evaluating on $\mathbf{x}$, thanks to the probability support of the random forest classification [6].

2.3 Scene and Speech LTEs

Using the above-described framework, we study following LTEs to cope with the acoustic scene classification task: (1) the LTE derived from a target scene database itself (Scene-LTE), (2) the LTE learned from an external speech data (Speech-LTE), and (3) their combination (Fusion-LTE).

Scene-LTE. Given a target scene database (e.g. LITIS Rouen), the Scene-LTE is formed following the framework. However, we do not consider the whole 30-second snippet of an acoustic scene instance as a sample. Instead, in order to capture meaningful events happening in a scene whose lengths are in order of hundreds of milliseconds, we use segments of length 500 ms with an overlap of 250 ms as the samples for further processing. Each segment is decomposed into 50 ms frames with 50% overlap, each of which is described by $M = 128$ Gammatone cepstral coefficients [25, 10] in the frequency range of 1-11025 Hz. A segment is then represented by a 128-dimensional feature vector computed by averaging the feature vectors of its constituent frames. Furthermore, each audio segment is labeled by the label of the scene where it is taken from.

The learned Scene-LTE is then applied on a test audio segment, resulting in a Scene-LTE feature vector. To compute the global Scene-LTE features for the 30-second scene snippet, we employ average pooling on the Scene-LTE features of its constituent segments.

Speech-LTE. Speech signals have been shown to bear potential to serve as a generic representation for nonspeech audio events [20, 21]. We show here that they can also

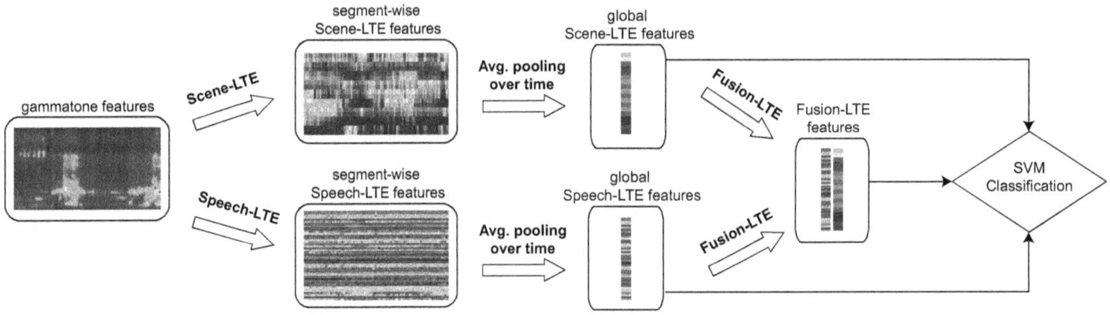

Figure 2: Overview of the proposed acoustic scene classification schemes.

Table 1: *Scene-LTE:* Performance in terms of accuracy (%) (DCASE) and F1-score (%) (LITIS).

	linear	χ^2	hist.	RBF
DCASE	84.0±5.5	85.0±5.5	84.0±2.2	86.0 ± 4.2
LITIS	94.3±0.9	94.9±1.0	94.5±1.0	94.8 ± 0.8

been used to represent acoustic scenes. The Speech-LTE is learned from a set of *phone triplets* [21] selected from TIMIT speech data [12]. We rely on the closeness measure between a phone triplet category and a scene category for the selection. From the training 500 ms segments obtained from the target scene database, we train a 200-tree multi-class random-forest classifier $\mathcal{M}_{\text{scene}}$. The closeness $\kappa(c, y)$ of a scene category c and a phone triplet category y and is then computed as

$$\kappa(c, y) = \frac{1}{|\mathcal{S}^y|} \sum_{\mathbf{x}^y \in \mathcal{S}^y} P(c|\mathbf{x}^y, \mathcal{M}_{\text{scene}}). \tag{6}$$

Here, $\mathcal{S}^y = \{\mathbf{x}_i^y\}_{i=1}^{|\mathcal{S}^y|}$ denotes the sample set of the phone triplet category y. We then rank closeness measures and select top $N = \{5, 10, 15, 20, 25\}$ phone triplet categories for each scene class. The Speech-LTE is finally applied on the audio segments of a scene snippet, followed by the average pooling to produce the global Speech-LTE feature vector for the scene instance. Note that, instead of the Gammatone cepstral coefficients used in the Scene-LTE, we utilized the same low-level feature set in [21] for the Speech-LTE.

Fusion-LTE. In order to take advantage of representations from different perspectives, i.e. Scene-LTE and Speech-LTE, we combine them using the extended Gaussian-χ^2 kernel [15] given by

$$K(\mathbf{x}_i, \mathbf{x}_j) = \exp\Big(- \sum_k \frac{1}{\bar{D}^k} D\big(\Psi^k(\mathbf{x}_i), \Psi^k(\mathbf{x}_j)\big)\Big), \tag{7}$$

where $D\big(\Psi^k(\mathbf{x}_i), \Psi^k(\mathbf{x}_j)\big)$ is the χ^2 distance between the embedded scene instances $\Psi^k(\mathbf{x}_i)$ and $\Psi^k(\mathbf{x}_j)$ with respect to the k-th channel where $k \in \{\text{Scene-LTE}, \text{Speech-LTE}\}$. $\bar{D}^k$ is the mean χ^2 distance of the embedded scene instances in training data for the k-th channel.

2.4 Final Acoustic Scene Classification

An overview of the final classification schemes is illustrated in Figure 2. For a test acoustic scene instance, we obtain its representations using the Scene-LTE and Speech-LTE as above. To extract representations for the training instances, we conducted 10-fold cross-validation on training

Table 2: *Speech-LTE:* Performance in terms of accuracy (%) (DCASE) and F1-score (%) (LITIS).

	N	linear	χ^2	hist.	RBF
DCASE	5	78.0±4.5	80.0±3.5	84.0 ± 2.2	82.0± 2.7
	10	84.0±2.2	83.0±2.7	86.0 ± 6.5	86.0± 5.5
	15	85.0±5.0	85.0±3.5	79.0±10.8	79.0 ±4.2
	20	83.0±7.6	85.0±6.1	86.0 ± 6.5	83.0 ±7.6
	25	87.0±2.7	85.0±6.1	86.0 ± 4.2	85.0 ±5.0
LITIS	5	85.4±1.0	85.9±1.3	86.4 ± 0.9	87.9± 1.4
	10	87.1±1.2	88.2±1.0	87.8 ± 0.9	89.3± 1.2
	15	87.8±1.0	88.5±1.1	89.1 ± 1.2	89.9± 1.0
	20	88.2±1.3	89.2±1.1	89.1 ± 0.8	89.7± 1.1
	25	88.6±1.2	89.7±1.1	89.5 ± 0.7	90.1± 1.2

Table 3: *Fusion-LTE:* Performance in terms of accuracy (%) (DCASE) and F1-score (%) (LITIS).

N	DCASE	LITIS
5	84.0 ± 6.5	96.1 ± 1.0
10	86.0 ± 6.5	96.2 ± 0.9
15	86.0 ± 5.5	96.2 ± 0.9
20	86.0 ± 5.5	96.1 ± 1.0
25	87.0 ± 6.7	96.2 ± 0.9

data. Lastly, we trained the final scene classification systems using one-vs-one support vector machines (SVM) with different kernels, including linear, χ^2, histogram intersection (*hist* for short), and radial basis function (RBF) kernels. For Fusion-LTE, we used nonlinear SVMs with the extended Gaussian kernel given in (7). The hyperparameters of the SVMs were tuned via 10-fold cross-validation.

3. EXPERIMENTS

3.1 Datasets

We employed the following datasets in our experiments:

DCASE 2013 dataset [2, 24]. This dataset was used in the DCASE 2013 challenge [24]. It consists of ten scene categories recorded in different locations in London at different time points. The dataset has two subsets: public and private subsets, each contains 100 30-second-long scene instances with ten examples for each class. The former was released during the challenge for participants to tune their classification systems. The latter was used to evaluate the submissions and also made public after the challenge. The submitted systems were evaluated with five-fold stratified cross validation on the private subset [24]. We follow the cross validation setting, however, at each time, we combined the public set and the training folds of the private set to make the training data.

LITIS Rouen dataset [23]. This dataset contains 3026 30-second-long examples of 19 scene categories recorded with the total duration of 1500 minutes. Each class is specific to a location such as a train station, an airplane, or a market. To our knowledge, this is so far the largest publicly available dataset for the task. We follow the standard training/testing splits in [23] (for more details, please refer to [23]) and report average performances over 20 splits of the data.

3.2 Experimental Results

The classification performance obtained by Scene-LTE, Speech-LTE, and Fusion-LTE are shown in Tables 1, 2, and 3. For the DCASE dataset, the performance is reported in terms of classification accuracy as in the DCASE 2013 challenge [24] whereas we used average class-wise F1-score for the LITIS dataset since it exhibits significant imbalance in the numbers of samples per class.

Using Scene-LTE, our systems achieve an accuracy of 86% and a F1-score of 94.9% on the DCASE and LITIS datasets, respectively. These results surpass the best reported performance on the DCASE dataset (85% in terms of accuracy [1]) while being just marginally below the best performance on the LITIS dataset (95.6% in terms of F1-score [5]). Regarding Speech-LTE, we obtain the best accuracy, 87%, with $N = 25$ and linear kernel which is even better than that of Scene-LTE on the DCASE 2013 dataset. For the LITIS dataset, although Speech-LTE maintains good F1-score near 90% in most of the cases, these results are not as good as with those of Scene-LTE. It is also noticeable that adding more selected phone triplet categories per scene class seems to bring up the performance, however, the gains are insignificant in most of the cases. Lastly, for both DCASE and LITIS datasets, the performance of the linear systems are comparable with the nonlinear ones with χ^2, hist., and RBF kernels. This is good since the linear systems are computationally much cheaper to train and evaluate compared to the nonlinear ones.

For the fusion of Scene-LTE and Speech-LTE into Fusion-LTE with the extended Gaussian-χ^2 kernel, we obtain average accuracy gains of 0.8% and 2.2% compared to individual Scene-LTE and Speech-LTE with the χ^2 kernel on the DCASE dataset. Similarly, the average F1-score gains on the LITIS dataset are 1.3% and 7.9%. These results indicate that speech signals are not only able to represent well the scene audio signals but also provide a valuable external source to enhance the performance of a classification system built on the scene data itself.

Finally, we present a comprehensive performance comparison of our systems and other reported results on the DCASE and LITIS datasets in Tables 4 and 5, respectively. We mark in bold where the performance of our systems outperforms all the opponents. Since the results on the LITIS dataset were reported with different metrics, i.e. average class-wise precision [23, 19], average class-wise F1-score [4, 5], and overall accuracy [4, 28], we provide our performance on all of these metrics to make a proper comparison. We also would like to notice that although there exists other works on the DCASE dataset after the challenge, we only mention here those with performance equivalent or higher than that of the best submission in the challenge. For the details of the competitive systems, please refer to the respective references. As can be seen for the DCASE dataset, our systems consistently outperform the best submission to the challenge (RNH [24]) with a large margin of about 10% and also outrun the best reported performance in [1] from 1% to 2%. For the LITIS dataset, our systems with Scene-LTE alone show better performance than most of the compared systems. Moreover, our Fusion-LTE systems set state-of-the-art performance on all evaluation metrics and outperform the best reported results by 3.7%, 0.6%, and 0.4% in terms of precision, F1-score, and accuracy, respectively.

Table 4: Performance comparison on the DCASE 2013 dataset.

Systems	Accuracy
Scene-LTE	**86.0**
Speech-LTE	**87.0**
Fusion-LTE	**87.0**
RNH [24]	76.0
MV [24]	77.0
Human [2]	75.0
HOG [23]	76.0
AMS+LDA [1]	85.0

Table 5: Performance comparison on the LITIS Rouen dataset.

Systems	Prec.	F1-score	Acc.
Scene-LTE	**94.6**	94.9	94.9
Speech-LTE	89.7	90.1	90.3
Fusion-LTE	**95.9**	**96.2**	**96.4**
HOG [23]	91.7	–	–
HOG+SPD [4]	93.3	92.8	93.4
DNN+MFCC [19]	92.2	–	–
Sparse NMF [5]	–	94.1	–
Convolutive NMF [5]	–	94.5	–
Kernel PCA [5]	–	95.6	–
HOG+ProbSVM [28]	–	–	96.0

4. CONCLUSIONS

In this paper, we present efficient schemes for acoustic scene classification. We explore the structure of the class labels by automatically learning class-label hierarchies and then the label-tree embeddings to map scene instances into the semantic space underlying the class hierarchy. We study both the label tree embedding intrinsically learned from the scene data as well as the one learned from the external TIMIT speech data. Both of them demonstrate good empirical performance on the experimental datasets, including the DCASE 2013 and LITIS Rouen datasets. Furthermore, fusing them with a simple scheme leads to state-of-the-art performance.

5. ACKNOWLEDGMENTS

This work was supported by the Graduate School for Computing in Medicine and Life Sciences funded by Germany's Excellence Initiative [DFG GSC 235/1].

6. REFERENCES

[1] S. Ağcaer, A. Schlesinger, F.-M. Hoffmann, and R. Martin. Optimization of amplitude modulation features for low-resource acoustic scene classification. In *Proc. European Signal Processing Conference (EUSIPCO)*, pages 2556–2560, 2015.

[2] D. Barchiesi, D. Giannoulis, D. Stowell, and M. Plumbley. Acoustic scene classification: Classifying environments from the sounds they produce. *IEEE Signal Processing Magazine*, 32(3):16–34, 2015.

[3] S. Bengio, J. Weston, and D. Grangier. Label embedding trees for large multi-class tasks. In *Proc. Advances in Neural Information Processing Systems (NIPS)*, pages 163–171, 2010.

[4] V. Bisot, S. Essid, and G. Richard. HOG and subband power distribution image features for acoustic scene classification. In *Proc. European Signal Processing Conference (EUSIPCO)*, pages 719–723, 2015.

[5] V. Bisot, R. Serizel, S. Essid, and G. Richard. Acoustic scene classification with matrix factorization for unsupervised feature learning. In *Proc. IEEE International Conference on Acoustics, Speech and Signal Processing (ICASSP)*, pages 6445–6449, 2016.

[6] L. Breiman. Random forest. *Machine Learning*, 45:5–32, 2001.

[7] R. Cai, L. Lu, and A. Hanjalic. Co-clustering for auditory scene categorization. *IEEE Trans. Multimedia*, 10(4):596–606, 2008.

[8] S. Chu, S. Narayanan, C.-C. J. Kuo, and M. J. Mataric. Where am I? Scene recognition for mobile robots using audio features. In *Proc. IEEE International Conference on Multimedia and Expo (ICME)*, pages 885–888, 2006.

[9] S. Deng, J. Han, C. Zhang, T. Zheng, and G. Zheng. Robust minimum statistics project coefficients feature for acoustic environment recognition. In *Proc. IEEE International Conference on Acoustics, Speech and Signal Processing (ICASSP)*, pages 8232–8236, 2014.

[10] D. P. W. Ellis. Gammatone-like spectrograms, 2009.

[11] A. J. Eronen, V. T. Peltonen, J. T. Tuomi, A. P. Klapuri, S. Fagerlund, T. Sorsa, G. Lorho, and J. Huopaniemi. Audio-based context recognition. *IEEE Trans. Audio, Speech, and Language Processing*, 14(1):321–329, 2006.

[12] W. Fisher, G. Doddington, and K. Goudie-Marshall. The DARPA speech recognition research database: Specifications and status. In *Proc. DARPA Workshop on Speech Recognition*, pages 93–99, 1986.

[13] T. Heittola, A. Mesaros, A. Eronen, and T. Virtanen. Context-dependent sound event detection. *EURASIP Journal on Audio, Speech, and Music Processing*, 2013.

[14] T. Heittola, A. Mesaros, A. J. Eronen, and T. Virtanen. Audio context recognition using audio event histogram. In *Proc. European Signal Processing Conference (EUSIPCO)*, pages 1272–1276, 2010.

[15] I. Laptev, M. Marszałek, C. Schmid, and B. Rozenfeld. Learning realistic human actions from movies. In *Proc CVPR*, pages 1–8, 2008.

[16] R. F. Lyon. Machine hearing: An emerging field. *IEEE Signal Processing Magazine*, 27(5):131–139, 2010.

[17] R. Mogi and H. Kasaii. Noise-robust environmental sound classification method based on combination of ICA and MP features. *Artificial Intelligence Research*, 2(1):107–121, 2013.

[18] A. Y. Ng, M. I. Jordan, and Y. Weiss. On spectral clustering: Analysis and an algorithm. In *Proc. NIPS*, pages 849–856, 2001.

[19] Y. Petetin, C. Laroche, and A. Mayoue. Deep neural networks for audio scene recognition. In *Proc. European Signal Processing Conference (EUSIPCO)*, pages 125–129, 2015.

[20] H. Phan, L. Hertel, M. Maass, R. Mazur, and A. Mertins. Representing nonspeech audio signals through speech classification models. In *Proc. Interspeech*, pages 3441–3445, 2015.

[21] H. Phan, L. Hertel, M. Maass, R. Mazur, and A. Mertins. Learning representations for nonspeech audio events through their similarities to speech patterns. *IEEE/ACM Trans. Audio, Speech, and Language Processing*, 24(4):807–822, April 2016.

[22] R. Radhakrishnan, A. Divakaran, and P. Smaragdis. Audio analysis for surveillance applications. In *Proc. IEEE Workshop on Applications of Signal Processing to Audio and Acoustics (WASPAA)*, pages 158–161, 2005.

[23] A. Rakotomamonjy and G. Gasso. Histogram of gradients of time-frequency representations for audio scene classification. *IEEE/ACM Trans. Audio, Speech, and Language Processing*, 23(1):142–153, 2015.

[24] D. Stowell, D. Giannoulis, E. Benetos, M. Lagrange, and M. D. Plumbley. Detection and classification of acoustic scenes and events. *IEEE Trans. Multimedia*, 17(10):1733–1746, 2015.

[25] X. Valero and F. Alías. Gammatone cepstral coefficients: biologically inspired features fro non-speech audio classification. *IEEE Trans. Multimedia*, 17(6):1684–1689, 2012.

[26] D. Wang and G. J. Brown. *Computational Auditory Scene Analysis: Principles, Algorithms, and Applications*. Wiley-IEEE Press, 2006.

[27] Y. Xu, W. J. Li, and K. K. Lee. *Intelligent Wearable Interfaces*. Hoboken, NJ: Wiley, 2008.

[28] J. Ye, T. Kobayashi, M. Murakawa, and T. Higuchi. Acoustic scene classification based on sound textures and events. In *Proc. ACM Multimedia*, pages 1291–1294, 2015.

Deep Learning for Image Memorability Prediction: the Emotional Bias

Yoann Baveye, Romain Cohendet, Matthieu Perreira Da Silva, Patrick Le Callet
IRCCyN UMR CNRS 6597
Université de Nantes, France
{yoann.baveye, romain.cohendet, matthieu.perreiradasilva, patrick.lecallet}@univ-nantes.fr

ABSTRACT

Image memorability prediction is a recent topic in computer science. First attempts have shown that it is possible to computationally infer from the intrinsic properties of an image the extent to which it is memorable. In this paper, we introduce a fine-tuned deep learning-based computational model for image memorability prediction. The performance of this model significantly outperforms previous work and obtains a 32.78% relative increase compared to the best-performing model from the state of the art on the same dataset. We also investigate how our model generalizes on a new dataset of 150 images, for which memorability and affective scores were collected from 50 participants. The prediction performance is weaker on this new dataset, which highlights the issue of representativity of the datasets. In particular, the model obtains a higher predictive performance for arousing negative pictures than for neutral or arousing positive ones, recalling how important it is for a memorability dataset to consist of images that are appropriately distributed within the emotional space.

CCS Concepts

•Computing methodologies → Computer vision; *Scene understanding;* **•Human-centered computing →** *Human computer interaction (HCI);*

Keywords

Image memorability; Affect; Deep learning

1. INTRODUCTION

The study of image memorability has recently attracted the interest of computer vision researchers [4, 13, 22]. Previous work has found that individuals share a tendency to remember and forget the same images [12], which paves the way for the design of frameworks predicting the image memorability from intrinsic information. The first attempts at such a prediction used a handcrafted set of low-level features extracted from images to predict their memorability scores (*i.e.*, the degree to which the image is remembered or forgotten) [13]. Results show that image memorability prediction is possible using intrinsic features only. However, this approach performs moderately and could be improved by using higher-level – *e.g.* semantic – information. In particular, the introduction of deep learning for memorability prediction may disrupt this field of study by substantially increasing the prediction performance of memorability prediction systems.

The second issue addressed in this work is the memorability prediction performance for new images labeled with emotional scores. The emotion a stimulus conveys can be considered as a key element to predict how well it will be memorized. The psychological literature provides evidence that emotional images are generally associated with better memory performance than neutral ones [5, 7, 15]. However, datasets composed of images associated with memorability scores are not designed according to their distribution in the emotional space.

Our contributions mainly focus on these two aspects and can be summarized as follows. In this work, we introduce "MemoNet": a deep learning-based computational model for image memorability prediction significantly outperforming the performance of the models proposed in previous work. The performance of MemoNet is also evaluated on a new dataset of 150 images, for which we collected through a laboratory experiment emotional ratings and memorability scores. Results show that the performance of the model is tied to the emotional scores of images: the deep learning framework obtains a higher predictive performance for pictures inducing arousing and negative emotions than for pictures inducing neutral or positive ones.

The paper is organized as follows. Section 2 provides background material on image memorability prediction work, as well as Convolutional Neural Networks (CNNs). In Section 3, a deep learning-based framework to predict image memorability is introduced and its performance is compared with previous work. The influence of emotions on the performance of image memorability prediction is studied and discussed in Section 4, while the paper ends in Section 5 with conclusions.

MM '16, October 15-19, 2016, Amsterdam, Netherlands

DOI: http://dx.doi.org/10.1145/2964284.2967269

2. BACKGROUND

Isola *et al.* pioneered the prediction of image memorability by mapping a combination of global image features using a support vector regression (SVR) [12, 13]. These global features are standard features that have been previously found to be effective at scene and objects recognition tasks. Indeed, Isola *et al.* shown that object and scene semantics tends to be a primary substrate of memorability [12]. Thus, the global features are GIST, spatial pyramid histograms of SIFT, HOG2x2, SSIM, and pixel color histograms.

More recently, Mancas and Le Meur showed that attention-related features can advantageously replace low-level features in image memorability prediction by considerably reducing the size of the input features while performing slightly better [22]. Attention-based features perform 2% better by using 17 dimensions instead of the 512 dimensions of the GIST feature, in addition to the other features introduced in [13], namely SIFT, HOG2x2, SSIM, and pixel color histograms.

Previous work thus relies on a predefined set of handcrafted features extracted from images. However, building complex handcrafted features requires strong domain knowledge and is highly problem-dependent. Obtaining a satisfying feature set is thus not a trivial issue. In contrast with previous work using handcrafted features, in this work we focus on CNNs to predict image memorability scores. Beginning with LeNet-5 [20], CNNs followed a classic structure: they are composed of stacked convolutional layers followed by one or more fully-connected layers. So far, best results on the ImageNet classification challenge have been achieved using CNN-based models [17, 24]. However, large labeled datasets are crucial to train such large CNN frameworks and there is currently no large image datasets with memorability labels. Nevertheless, fine-tuning is an effective paradigm for learning high-capacity CNNs when data is scarce [9]. The fine-tuning strategy consists in pre-training a deep CNN on a large-scale external dataset (*e.g.*, ImageNet) and fine-tuning the pre-trained network by continuing the back-propagation on the small-scale target data to fit the specific classification task.

3. MEMORABILITY PREDICTION

Fine-tuning pre-trained models originally predicting object and scene semantics is particularly suitable for image memorability prediction since both concepts are inherently related to each other [12, 16]. Neural networks have also successfully modeled the biologically inspired memory processes [1, 3, 23]. Consequently, we fine-tune the GoogleNet model introduced by Szegedy *et al.*, that became in 2014 the new state of the art performance on the ImageNet dataset [24].

3.1 Fine-tuned Convolutional Neural Network

The GoogleNet architecture is a concatenation of nine similar "Inception" networks. An Inception network consists in 1×1, 3×3, and 5×5 convolutions stacked upon each other, with max-pooling layers to reduce the resolution. Given the depth of the network, two auxiliary losses are connected to intermediate layers to increase the back-propagated gradient and to prevent the vanishing gradient problem. During training, the auxiliary losses are added to the total loss of the network with a discount weight. Training is stopped after a specific number of training iterations is reached. At test time, the auxiliary losses are no longer needed and are thus removed from the network. In our fine-tuning approach, the two auxiliary and the final softmax activations are replaced by a fully-connected layer composed of a unique neuron. The loss functions associated to the model are the Euclidean loss.

All the layers of the pre-trained model are fine-tuned, but the learning rate associated to the original layers is ten times smaller than the one associated with the new last neuron. Indeed, we want the pre-trained layers to change very slowly, but let learn faster the new layer. The weights of the new layer are initialized using the xavier algorithm that automatically determines the scale of initialization based on the number of input and output neurons [10]. The biases are all initialized as constant, with the default filling value 0.

Table 1: Global performance for image memorability prediction models in terms of Spearman's Rank Correlation Coefficient (ρ) and Mean Square Error (MSE)

	ρ	MSE
Isola *et al.* [12]	0.462	0.017
Mancas and Le Meur [22]	0.479	X
MemoNet 1k	0.522	0.017
MemoNet 10k	0.620	0.012
MemoNet 30k	0.636	0.012

The proposed fine-tuned model for image memorability prediction is denoted MemoNet in the remaining of this paper.

3.2 Experimental Results

In order to obtain results that are fully comparable with previous work, we use in this paper the same data and the same train/test protocol used by Isola *et al.* [12] and Mancas and Le Meur [22]. The dataset is composed of 2,222 images with memorability labels collected by Isola *et al.* using crowdsourcing [13]. The images were randomly selected from the SUN dataset [26] and represent various scene categories. Object and scene categories are thus available for each image (see [8] for details). A memorability score, used as "ground truth" to train and test MemoNet, is defined as the percentage of correct detections of an image when it is repeated once in a stream of images by a set of participants. MemoNet is trained 25 times using the training sets defined by Isola *et al.* composed of one half of the images, and tested on the other half of the images.

Similarly to Isola *et al.*, global performance is defined as the mean of the Spearman's Rank Correlation Coefficient (ρ) between the ground truths and the predictions obtained for each of the 25 trained models [13]. In addition, global Mean Square Error (MSE) is assessed. The performance of MemoNet for several training iterations numbers (*i.e.*, 1k, 10k, 30k), as well as the performance of previous work, are indicated in Table 1.

Results show that the performance of MemoNet significantly outperforms the performance obtained by both Isola *et al.* [12] and Mancas and Le Meur [22]. More particularly, MemoNet 30k obtains a 32.78% relative increase in term of Spearman's Rank Correlation Coefficient compared to the approach of Mancas and Le Meur. Table 2 shows the best performing object and scene categories for categories composed of over 100 pictures. Interestingly, best performing object categories are similar to the best performing ones obtained by Isola *et al.* [12]. No significant linear correlation was found between the size of the object categories and their performance ($r = -0.018, t(25) = -0.092, p = 0.46$).

4. THE ROLE OF AFFECT

Affect is a key factor in determining the memorability of images [2, 5]. This section thus investigates if the performance of trained models is the same no matter the emotion elicited by the image given as input.

Table 2: Influence of the object and scene semantics composed of over 100 pictures on the prediction performance of MemoNet 30k. The size and the mean of the memorability scores (GT) for each category are also indicated.

Rank	Category	Size	GT	ρ
1	person sitting	165	0.753	0.655
2	person	554	0.725	0.628
3	pole	108	0.667	0.613
4	mountain	272	0.593	0.606
5	painting	101	0.696	0.593
6	wall	989	0.718	0.581
7	window	589	0.662	0.580
8	table	212	0.703	0.580
9	sign	147	0.664	0.572
10	door	361	0.668	0.570
11	chair	268	0.712	0.564
12	fence	181	0.656	0.554
13	sky	1080	0.628	0.550
14	tree	814	0.630	0.548
15	plant	417	0.640	0.543
16	floor	766	0.727	0.537
17	ground	269	0.637	0.521
18	ceiling	571	0.713	0.514
19	water	151	0.631	0.511
20	road	297	0.647	0.497
21	sidewalk	163	0.643	0.493
22	building	699	0.630	0.492
23	ceiling lamp	289	0.713	0.491
24	box	121	0.719	0.489
25	steps	115	0.659	0.477
26	grass	341	0.630	0.464
27	car	192	0.649	0.464

4.1 Memorability for IAPS Images

A subset of 150 images randomly selected from the International Affective Picture System (IAPS) dataset [19] is used in this work to analyze the performance of MemoNet for emotional images. Affective scores are available for these images in terms of valence, arousal, and dominance [14, 19]. Valence ranges from negative (*e.g.*, sad, disappointed) to positive (*e.g.*, joyous, elated), whereas arousal can range from inactive (*e.g.*, tired, pensive) to active (*e.g.*, alarmed, angry), and dominance ranges from dominated (*e.g.*, bored, sad) to in control (*e.g.*, excited, delighted).

The experimental protocol presented by Isola *et al.* [13] is reproduced in a laboratory environment to collect memorability scores for each of the 150 selected images. Participants had to perform a memory task and an emotional rating task.

4.1.1 Memory task

The memory task consists of a memory encoding phase interlaced with a recognition memory test. The task instruction is to press the space bar whenever an image reappears in a sequence of images. A black frame is displayed between each image for 1 second. During the task, 50 targets (*i.e.*, images repeated once selected from the subset of 150 images) and 200 fillers are displayed, each of them being displayed for 2 seconds. The fillers, composed of other images randomly selected from IAPS, provide spacing between the first display of a target image and its repetition. Images are displayed pseudo-randomly: the spacing between a target image and its repetition has to be separated by at least 70 images (*i.e.*, 3.30 min) in order to measure memorability corresponding to a long-term memory performance. Whenever the space bar is pushed, the image is framed by a green rectangle to show the participants that their answer is taken into account. Responses that may occur during the 1 second-long inter-stimuli black frame following the target image are also considered. The task is preceded by a training phase to familiarize the participants with the task.

4.1.2 Emotional rating task

An emotional rating task was set up to collect arousal and valence scores for 100 images displayed for 6 seconds. Before the display of each image, the participant is invited to get prepared for the rating process of the next image. The ratings are collected on the 9-point Self-Assessment Manikin (SAM) scales for arousal and valence [6], which is a powerful and easy to use pictorial system regardless of age, educational or cultural background due to its non-verbal design. The images are randomly displayed, for a total task duration of about 30 minutes. Similarly to the memorability task, the emotional rating task starts with instructions, followed by a training phase composed of training images spanning the entire arousal-valence emotional space to familiarize the participants with the task but also with the rating scales.

4.1.3 Procedure

The images were displayed on a 40 inch monitor (TV-LOGIC LVM401) with a display resolution of 1,920 × 1,080. The participants were seated at a distance of 150 centimeters from the screen (three times the screen height). The 1,024 × 768 images were centered on a black background; at a viewing distance of 150 cm, the stimuli subtended 18.85 degrees of vertical visual angle. Fifty participants (18-41 years of age; $mean = 22.54$; $SD = 5.01$; 60% of them female) compensated for their participation were recruited in Nantes, France. All participants have either normal or corrected-to-normal visual acuity. Correct visual acuity was assured prior to this experiment through near and far vision tests using Parinaud and Monoyer charts respectively. The first experimental phase was then launched, corresponding to the memory task. The next day, participants performed the emotional rating task. For each task, displayed images were selected to ensure that each memorability score is generated from at least 16 annotations and that each affective score is generated from at least 32 annotations.

4.2 Results

From Section 4.1, a set of 150 images selected from IAPS with memorability and emotional scores is created. The 150 images are pre-processed in order to be given as input to MemoNet 30k. Indeed, MemoNet 30k is fed with the resized 224 × 224 center crop of each image. Black bands added to several pictures by Lang *et al.* [19] to obtain the same ratio for each image are removed before cropping the image. As expected, the global performance of MemoNet 30k for this new dataset is lower than the performance of the model measured on the dataset created by Isola *et al.* [13] ($\rho = 0.251$; $MSE = 0.033$).

A local performance of MemoNet 30k is defined as the difference between the ground truth memorability score and the mean of the predictions from the 25 trained models for an image. Table 3 shows the rank correlation between the local performances of MemoNet 30k and the affective scores

Table 3: Spearman's Rank Correlation Coefficient (ρ) between the local performances of MemoNet 30k for the subset of IAPS images and their affective labels ($^{*}p < .05$; $^{**}p < .01$; $^{***}p < .001$)

Dimension	Data origin	ρ
Valence	Lang *et al.* [19]	-0.285***
	Ito *et al.* [14]	-0.248**
	Ours	-0.284***
Arousal	Lang *et al.* [19]	0.096
	Ito *et al.* [14]	0.222*
	Ours	0.198**
Dominance	Lang *et al.* [19]	-0.221**

collected either in the experiment detailed in Section 4.1, or in previous work [14, 19]. These correlations measure the relation between the considered emotional dimension and the fact that the model predicts a memorability score higher or lower than the ground truth. Please note that the local performances using Ito *et al.*'s data are computed on the subset of images from IAPS selected both in this work and Ito *et al.*'s work, corresponding to 104 images. The local performances of MemoNet 30k and the emotional scores collected in this work are shown in Figure 1. The rank correlations exhibit a moderate, but coherent, relationship between the performance of MemoNet 30k and the valence, arousal and dominance scores for the emotional ratings collected in both previous work [14, 19] and our work. Valence is negatively correlated with the local performances of MemoNet 30k, while arousal is positively correlated. Similarly to valence, dominance exhibits a negative correlation with the local performances of MemoNet 30k. Valence and arousal account for most of the independent variance [11, 18]. Consequently, dominance is not taken into account in the following analysis.

To provide a deeper analysis of the relationship between the accuracy of the predicted memorability scores and the affective properties of the pictures collected in this work, the k-means clustering algorithm is used to separate the 150 images into three clusters in the valence-arousal space (see Figure 1(c)). The three clusters separate the images inducing arousing and negative emotions (cluster 1) from the images inducing neutral emotions (cluster 2) and from those inducing moderately arousing and positive emotions (cluster 3). It is important to note that arousal and valences scores of the 150 images are significantly correlated ($r = -0.522, t(148) = -7.445, p < .0001$). A one-way ANOVA revealed that the local performances of MemoNet 30k is significantly different for the three clusters ($F(2, 147) = 5.82; p < .005$). The Tukey's multiple comparison test confirmed that the local performances for the pictures in the first cluster is in average closer to zero – *i.e.* the optimal performance – ($mean = 0.0298$) than for images in the second ($mean = -0.0536$) or third ($mean = -0.0847$) clusters. In other words, this result shows that MemoNet 30k has the highest predictive performance for arousing negative pictures. For the other groups (*i.e.*, neutral and positive) the model is less reliable to predict the memorability.

The results suggest that affect should be taken into account in datasets of images labeled with memorability scores to ensure they induce a large variety of emotions. Indeed, emotion and memorability being related, the performance of

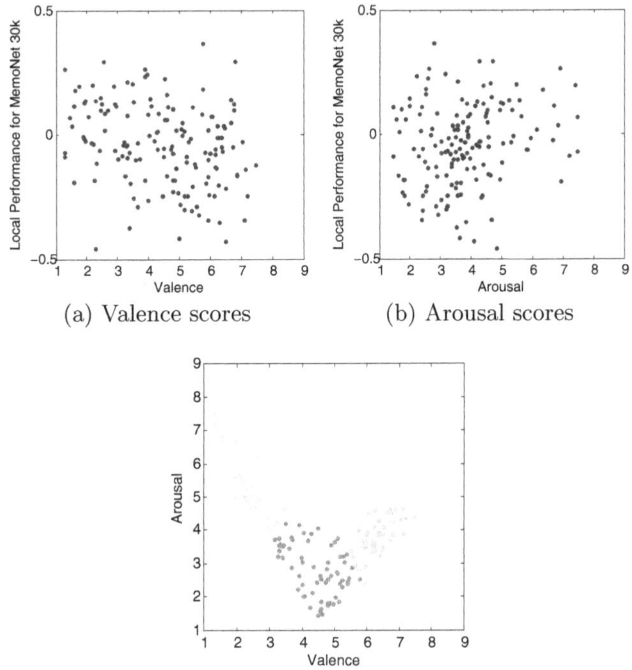

(a) Valence scores

(b) Arousal scores

(c) k-means clustering result

Figure 1: Local performance of MemoNet 30k with (a) valence and (b) arousal scores collected in our experiment for each of the 150 images selected from IAPS, as well as (c) the result of the k-means clustering ($k = 3$).

a memorability model depends on the emotions induced by the images used to train the model. The results also suggest that emotional information could be a valuable feature to increase the performance of the model for neutral and positive pictures, especially as it is possible to computationally infer emotional information from pictures [21, 25].

5. CONCLUSIONS

The study reported in this paper focuses on the image memorability prediction using deep learning. The proposed model significantly outperforms previous work and obtains a 32.78% relative increase in performance compared to the best-performing model from the state of the art. An experimental protocol has also been set up to collect memorability and emotional scores in a laboratory environment. However, the generalization of the performance of the deep learning model to this new dataset is a mitigated success. In particular, an emotional bias appears to influence the performance of the proposed model: the deep learning framework obtains a higher predictive performance for arousing negative pictures than for neutral or positive ones. This underlines the importance for an image dataset used for memorability prediction to consist in images appropriately distributed within the emotional space.

Because memorability is also subjective, the memorability prediction is doomed to inaccuracy if one is only interested in the intrinsic information of the images. Our current work focuses on the integration of context-dependent and observer-dependent information for the purpose to personalize the memorability prediction.

6. REFERENCES

[1] W. C. Abraham and A. Robins. Memory retention–the synaptic stability versus plasticity dilemma. *Trends in neurosciences*, 28(2):73–78, 2005.

[2] J. Abrisqueta-Gomez, O. F. A. Bueno, M. G. M. Oliveira, and P. H. F. Bertolucci. Recognition memory for emotional pictures in alzheimerŠs patients. *Acta Neurologica Scandinavica*, 105(1):51–54, 2002.

[3] B. Ans and S. Rousset. Neural networks with a self-refreshing memory: knowledge transfer in sequential learning tasks without catastrophic forgetting. *Connection science*, 12(1):1–19, 2000.

[4] W. A. Bainbridge, P. Isola, and A. Oliva. The intrinsic memorability of face photographs. *Journal of Experimental Psychology: General*, 142(4):1323–1334, 2013.

[5] M. M. Bradley, M. K. Greenwald, M. C. Petry, and P. J. Lang. Remembering pictures: pleasure and arousal in memory. *Journal of experimental psychology: Learning, Memory, and Cognition*, 18(2):379–390, 1992.

[6] M. M. Bradley and P. J. Lang. Measuring emotion: the self-assessment manikin and the semantic differential. *Journal of behavior therapy and experimental psychiatry*, 25(1):49–59, 1994.

[7] L. Cahill and J. L. McGaugh. A novel demonstration of enhanced memory associated with emotional arousal. *Consciousness and Cognition*, 4(4):410–421, 1995.

[8] M. J. Choi, J. J. Lim, A. Torralba, and A. S. Willsky. Exploiting hierarchical context on a large database of object categories. In *2010 IEEE Conference on Computer Vision and Pattern Recognition (CVPR)*, pages 129–136, June 2010.

[9] R. Girshick, J. Donahue, T. Darrell, and J. Malik. Rich feature hierarchies for accurate object detection and semantic segmentation. In *The IEEE Conference on Computer Vision and Pattern Recognition (CVPR)*, pages 580–587, June 2014.

[10] X. Glorot and Y. Bengio. Understanding the difficulty of training deep feedforward neural networks. In *International conference on artificial intelligence and statistics*, pages 249–256, 2010.

[11] M. K. Greenwald, E. W. Cook, and P. J. Lang. Affective judgment and psychophysiological response: Dimensional covariation in the evaluation of pictorial stimuli. *Journal of psychophysiology*, 3(1):51–64, 1989.

[12] P. Isola, J. Xiao, D. Parikh, A. Torralba, and A. Oliva. What makes a photograph memorable? *IEEE Transactions on Pattern Analysis and Machine Intelligence*, 36(7):1469–1482, 2014.

[13] P. Isola, J. Xiao, A. Torralba, and A. Oliva. What makes an image memorable? In *IEEE Conference on Computer Vision and Pattern Recognition (CVPR)*, pages 145–152, 2011.

[14] T. A. Ito, J. T. Cacioppo, and P. J. Lang. Eliciting affect using the international affective picture system: Trajectories through evaluative space. *Personality and Social Psychology Bulletin*, 24(8):855–879, 1998.

[15] E. A. Kensinger, B. Brierley, N. Medford, J. H. Growdon, and S. Corkin. Effects of normal aging and alzheimer's disease on emotional memory. *Emotion*, 2(2):118–134, 2002.

[16] T. Konkle, T. F. Brady, G. A. Alvarez, and A. Oliva. Scene memory is more detailed than you think the role of categories in visual long-term memory. *Psychological Science*, 21(11):1551–1556, 2010.

[17] A. Krizhevsky, I. Sutskever, and G. E. Hinton. Imagenet classification with deep convolutional neural networks. In F. Pereira, C. J. C. Burges, L. Bottou, and K. Q. Weinberger, editors, *Advances in Neural Information Processing Systems 25*, pages 1097–1105. Curran Associates, Inc., 2012.

[18] P. J. Lang, M. M. Bradley, and B. N. Cuthbert. International affective picture system (iaps): Technical manual and affective ratings. *NIMH Center for the Study of Emotion and Attention*, pages 39–58, 1997.

[19] P. J. Lang, M. M. Bradley, and B. N. Cuthbert. International affective picture system (iaps): Affective ratings of pictures and instruction manual. *Technical report A-8*, 2008.

[20] Y. LeCun, B. Boser, J. S. Denker, D. Henderson, R. E. Howard, W. Hubbard, and L. D. Jackel. Backpropagation applied to handwritten zip code recognition. *Neural computation*, 1(4):541–551, 1989.

[21] N. Liu, E. Dellandréa, B. Tellez, and L. Chen. Associating textual features with visual ones to improve affective image classification. In *4th International Conference on Affective Computing and Intelligent Interaction*, pages 195–204, Oct 2011.

[22] M. Mancas and O. L. Meur. Memorability of natural scenes: The role of attention. In *2013 20th IEEE International Conference on Image Processing (ICIP)*, pages 196–200, Sept 2013.

[23] J. L. McClelland, B. L. McNaughton, and R. C. O'Reilly. Why there are complementary learning systems in the hippocampus and neocortex: insights from the successes and failures of connectionist models of learning and memory. *Psychological review*, 102(3):419–457, 1995.

[24] C. Szegedy, W. Liu, Y. Jia, P. Sermanet, S. Reed, D. Anguelov, D. Erhan, V. Vanhoucke, and A. Rabinovich. Going deeper with convolutions. In *IEEE Conference on Computer Vision and Pattern Recognition (CVPR)*, pages 1–9, June 2015.

[25] W. Wang and Q. He. A survey on emotional semantic image retrieval. In *2008 15th IEEE International Conference on Image Processing*, pages 117–120, Oct 2008.

[26] J. Xiao, J. Hays, K. A. Ehinger, A. Oliva, and A. Torralba. Sun database: Large-scale scene recognition from abbey to zoo. In *2010 IEEE Conference on Computer Vision and Pattern Recognition (CVPR)*, pages 3485–3492, June 2010.

Demand-adaptive Clothing Image Retrieval Using Hybrid Topic Model

Zhengzhong Zhou, Jingjin Zhou and Liqing Zhang
MOE-Microsoft Key Laboratory for Intelligent Computing and Intelligent Systems
Department of Computer Science and Engineering
Shanghai Jiao Tong University
Shanghai, China
{tczhouzz, zhoujingjin}@sjtu.edu.cn, zhang-lq@cs.sjtu.edu.cn

ABSTRACT

This paper proposes a novel approach to meet users' multi-dimensional requirements in clothing image retrieval. It enables users to add search conditions by modifying the color, texture, shape and attribute descriptors of the query images to further refine their requirements. We propose the Hybrid Topic (HT) model to learn the intricate semantic representation of the descriptors above. The model provides an effective multi-dimensional representation of clothes and is able to perform automatic image annotation by probabilistic reasoning from image search. Furthermore, we develop a demand-adaptive retrieval strategy which refines users' specific requirements and removes users' unwanted features. Our experiments show that the HT method significantly outperforms the deep neural network methods. The accuracy could be further improved in cooperation with image annotation and demand-adaptive retrieval strategy.

Keywords

Content-based Image Retrieval; Clothing Image Retrieval; Topic Model

1. INTRODUCTION

Content-based image retrieval (CBIR) [11, 6, 15] has been employed to apparel e-commerce in recent years. It enables us to search similar clothes from daily photos or images on fashion websites, providing great convenience for online shopping. However, sometimes customers are not satisfied with the retrieved products based on low level features. They tend to refine their specifications on the color, texture, shape or attribute of the selected clothing images. For example, "I would buy this T-shirt if its collar type was round and its material was cotton". Therefore, such a system should allow users to modify the visual and attribute descriptors of the query images (see Fig. 1). Utilizing color or attribute constraints to filter out unnecessary images is inappropriate, because the attribute descriptors in the image data are not directly related to the visual features. In particular, a user who lacks prior knowledge may ask for a business suit with *colored dots*. Such unreasonable demands will cause the inconsistency among different channel descriptors, leading to unsatisfactory results eventually.

MM '16, October 15 - 19, 2016, Amsterdam, Netherlands

ISBN 978-1-4503-3603-1/16/10...$15.00
DOI: http://dx.doi.org/10.1145/2964284.2967270

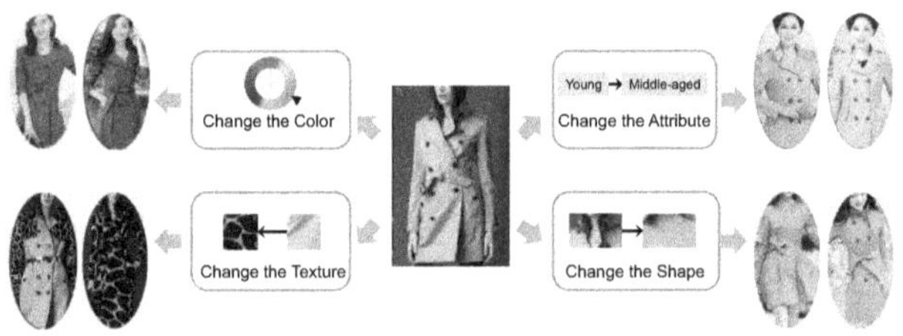

Figure 1: User Requirements for Searching Clothes.

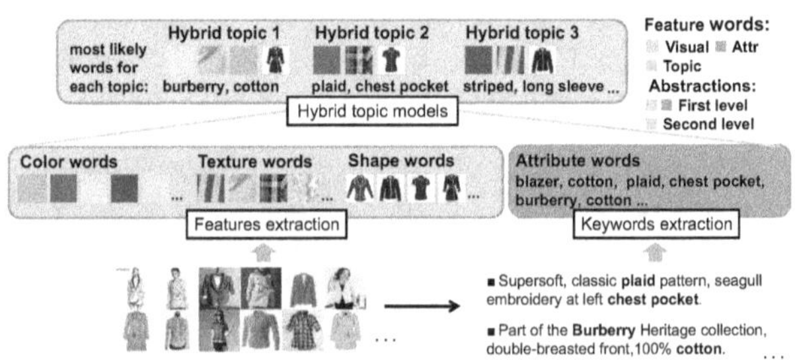

Figure 2: The Concept of Our Two-level Abstraction.

There exist a number of works for clothing image retrieval. Liu *et al.* and Kalantidis *et al.* [8, 5] eliminated the cluttered background by object detection [2, 14] and concatenated visual descriptors to search products. However, the semantic information of images is not taken into account.

Junshi *et al.* and Lin *et al.* [3, 4, 7] trained convolutional neural networks (CNN) to extract high level features. Though these methods bridge the *semantic gap*, they do not support interaction with users. Mizuochi *et al.* [9] evaluated the global similarity of clothes by the local similarities with multiple regions. Users could modify the detail of query images for further retrieval, yet it disregards the inconsistency caused by unreasonable modification.

In this paper, we propose a novel approach to meet the multi-dimensional users' search specifications utilizing topic model [1, 12, 13]. As is shown in Fig. 2, the feature extraction procedure is described as a two-level abstraction. For the first level abstraction, we extract clothing descriptors including color, texture, shape and text around images. We convert them into the bag of words (BOW) formats.

For the second level abstraction, we present a probabilistic network to combine the multi-channel descriptors into a unified framework, *i.e.* Hybrid Topic (HT) model. In this model, each image is depicted as a linear combination of hybrid topics. While each topic is described as the distributions over various codewords. The HT model learns the intricate semantic representation among different descriptors, which benefits us in the following ways: Firstly, it derives an effective representation of clothing images. Secondly, it can be used to infer the missing values of attribute descriptors, *i.e.* to automatically annotate the images. Last but not least, we utilize it to design a demand-adaptive retrieval strategy which refines users' specific requirements and removes users' unwanted features. Our experiments show that the HT model method achieves better performance than deep neural network methods, while the accuracy could be further improved in conjunction with image annotation and demand-adaptive retrieval strategy.

2. THE FIRST-LEVEL ABSTRACTION

Image preprocessing. Before extracting descriptors, we localize the region of clothes in image and split it into several local regions. This procedure aims to improve the robustness against cluttered backgrounds and increase the recall rate in image search. First, we train two independent Faster R-CNN [10] detectors to identify the torso and sleeve regions respectively. Then, we resize the sleeve regions to 64×64 and the torso region to 192×128. Two slide windows (128×64 and 64×128) are further used to sample the torso region with the stride 16. Hence, totally 17 local regions can be obtained from each image, including 14 overlapping regions cropped from the torso region, two sleeve regions and the torso region itself.

Feature extraction and quantization. For each local region we extract 3 types of visual descriptors: HOG, LBP, and color histogram, which represent the shape, texture and color information respectively. We denote these descriptors as $\vec{d}^j$s, $j \in \{h(hog), l(lbp), c(color)\}$. By k-means clustering, we generate the vocabulary list of $\vec{d}^j$ with size D^j: $V^j = \{w_i^j\}_{i=1}^{D^j}$, here w_i^j is the ith visual codewords of V^j. Utilizing non-negative sparse coding, we project each $\vec{d}^j$ to the space spanned by V^j: $\vec{d}^j \approx \sum_i u_i^j w_i^j$ and get its BOW representation $\vec{u}^j = (u_1^j, ..., u_{Dj}^j)^T$.

Meanwhile, we analyze the clothing product description $\vec{d}^t$s and collect the frequently used tag w_i^ts to compose the vocabulary list $V^t = \{w_i^t\}_{i=1}^{D^t}$. In our experiments, V^t contains 118 common tags including 9 kinds of clothing attributes (color, shape, pattern, material, collar, sleeve, placket, style and category). Utilizing the vocabulary list, we quantize $\vec{d}^t$ into BOW representation: $\vec{u}^t = (u_1^t, ..., u_{D^t}^t)^T$, where u_i^t equals to 1 iff $\vec{d}^t$ contains tag w_i^t, otherwise 0.

3. HYBRID TOPIC MODEL

In this section, we present a Hybrid Topic (HT) model for the second level abstraction. We elaborate the model generation process and its parameter estimation method. We will also introduce how to extract image search features with our model.

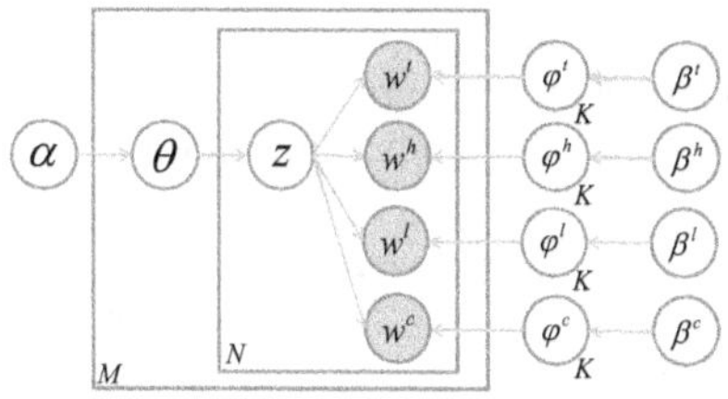

Figure 3: The Graphical Model of HT.

Generation process. The HT model integrates both visual and attribute information of clothing images into a model in order to extract semantic features together. It constructs the statistical relationship of the fore-mentioned codewords and achieves an effective representation of clothes as the image search feature. Fig. 3 shows the graphical model of HT. Assume that M is the total number of images in our database $\{I_m\}_{m=1}^M$ and K is the number of topics in our HT model. We extract various descriptors $F = \{t(text), h, l, c\}$ from these images as mentioned in Section 2. For each topic k and each descriptor channel j, we draw the mixture component $\vec{\varphi}_k^j$ which follows the Dirichlet distribution with prior $\vec{\beta}^j$. Meanwhile, we represent each image I_m as a list of N phrases, and each phrase is defined as a set of terms $\{w_r^j | j \in F\}$. Here $r = (m, n)$ denotes the index of the phrase. For each image I_m, we draw a topic mixture proportion $\vec{\theta}_m$ which follows the Dirichlet distribution with prior $\vec{\alpha}$. For each phrase p_r, we assign a topic $z_r \in [1, K]$ which follows the Multinomial distribution $\vec{\theta}_m$. Finally, the term w_r^j is generated by Multinomial distribution $\vec{\varphi}_{z_r}^j$. The generation process of our model is given as follows:

For each descriptor channel $j \in F$
    For each topic $k \in [1, K]$
        sample mixture component $\vec{\varphi}_k^j \sim Dir(\vec{\beta}^j)$
For each image $I_m, m \in [1, M]$
    sample mixture proportion $\vec{\theta}_m \sim Dir(\vec{\alpha})$
    For each phrase p_r, $r = (m, n)$
        sample topic index $z_r \sim Mult(\vec{\theta}_m)$
        For each descriptor channel $j \in F$
            sample term $w_r^j \sim Mult(\vec{\varphi}_{z_r}^j)$

Our model describes the clothing concepts with various visual and attribute descriptors. It depicts the intricate semantic representation of different codewords with a small number of topics. In this way, we reduce the dimension of feature space and achieve the highly abstracted representation for clothing images.

Parameter estimation. The parameters of HT model are estimated by Gibbs sampling. Let us denote $n_k^{(j,i)}$ as the count of codeword w_i^j in topic k, $n_m^{(k)}$ as the count of topic k in image I_m, and $\vec{w}^j$ as the word assignment in descriptor channel j. Given the parameters $\vec{\alpha}$ and $\underline{\vec{\beta}} = \{\vec{\beta}^j | j \in F\}$, we obtain the joint distribution of $\underline{\vec{w}} = \{\vec{w}^j | j \in F\}$ and $\vec{z}$:

$$P(\underline{\vec{w}}, \vec{z}|\vec{\alpha}, \underline{\vec{\beta}}) = P(\vec{z}|\vec{\alpha}) \prod_{j\in F} P(\vec{w}^j|\vec{z}, \vec{\beta}^j) = \left(\prod_{m=1}^{M} \frac{\Delta(\vec{n}_m+\vec{\alpha})}{\Delta(\vec{\alpha})}\right) \prod_{j\in F} \prod_{k=1}^{K} \frac{\Delta(\vec{n}_k^j+\vec{\beta}^j)}{\Delta(\vec{\beta}^j)}, \quad (1)$$

where $\vec{n}_k^j = (n_k^{j,1}, ..., n_k^{j,D^j})^T$, and $\vec{n}_m = (n_m^1, ..., n_m^K)^T$. $\Delta(\cdot)$ denotes the Dirichlet delta function.

With Eq. 1, the Gibbs updating rule for HT model can be derived as:

$$P(z_r = k|\vec{z}_{\neg r}, \underline{\vec{w}}/\{\vec{w}^j|j \in H\}, \vec{\alpha}, \underline{\vec{\beta}}) \propto \frac{n_{m,\neg r}^{(k)} + \alpha_k}{\sum_{z=1}^{K} (n_{m,\neg r}^{(z)} + \alpha_z)} \prod_{j \in F, j \notin H} \frac{n_{k,\neg r}^{(j,w_r^j)} + \beta_{w_r^j}^j}{\sum_{g=1}^{D^j} (n_{k,\neg r}^{(j,g)} + \beta_g^j)}. \tag{2}$$

Here, the counts $n_{\cdot,\neg r}^{(\cdot)}$ indicates that the phrase r is excluded from the corresponding image or topic and the hyperparameters are omitted. H is the set of unavailable descriptors when we extract features, *e.g.* a user may submit a gray query image without text description.

Utilizing Eq. 2, we iteratively evaluate the $\vec{z}$ until it converges. The parameter $\vec{\theta}_m$ and $\vec{\varphi}_k^j$ are estimated according to $\vec{z}$ and $\vec{w}^j$:

$$P(\vec{\varphi}_k^j|\vec{z}, \vec{w}^j, \vec{\beta}^j) \propto Dir(\vec{\varphi}_k^j|\vec{n}_k^j + \vec{\beta}^j). \tag{3}$$

$$P(\vec{\theta}_m|\vec{z}, \vec{\alpha}) \propto Dir(\vec{\theta}_m|\vec{n}_m + \vec{\alpha}). \tag{4}$$

Finally, we substitute the expectation of the Dirichlet distribution $\langle Dir(\vec{x})\rangle = x_i/\sum_i x_i$ into Eq. 3 and Eq. 4, and get:

$$\varphi_{k,i}^j = \frac{n_k^{(j,i)} + \beta_i^j}{\sum_{g=1}^{D^j} n_k^{(j,g)} + \beta_g^j}. \tag{5}$$

$$\theta_{m,k} = \frac{n_m^{(k)} + \alpha_k}{\sum_{z=1}^{K} n_m^{(z)} + \alpha_z}. \tag{6}$$

Retrieval feature extraction. We now describe the method to extract retrieval features using the above model. As noted, the clothing image is divided into multiple local regions. For each region, we train a HT model to learn its representation. Given an image I_q, we first extract descriptors as mentioned in Section 2. Then, we feed these descriptors into the pre-trained models to infer the topic proportion $\vec{\theta}_q$ for each region. We denote the achieved $\vec{\theta}_q$s as the local representations of I_q and concatenate all of them as our retrieval features. The similarity measure of two images is the L1-norm distance of their features. We return the images with top similarity as the retrieval result.

The difference between our method and CNN methods [3, 4, 7] is that we estimate retrieval features by probabilistic reasoning. Each element in the feature vector is represented as the weights of corresponding topics. Meanwhile, the features of CNNs are represented as the outputs of the network models, which are not likely to provide the semantic interpretation. Hence, CNN methods usually project images to higher dimensional spaces and it is not flexible to modify the local descriptors of images in the space of the deep network.

4. APPLICATIONS

In this section, we verify that our model can be leveraged for two applications: image annotation and demand-adaptive retrieval.

Image annotation. The automatic image annotation is to evaluate the missing attributes of query images and remove the irrelevant tags in database. Assume that the image I_q needs to be tagged. For each local region model,

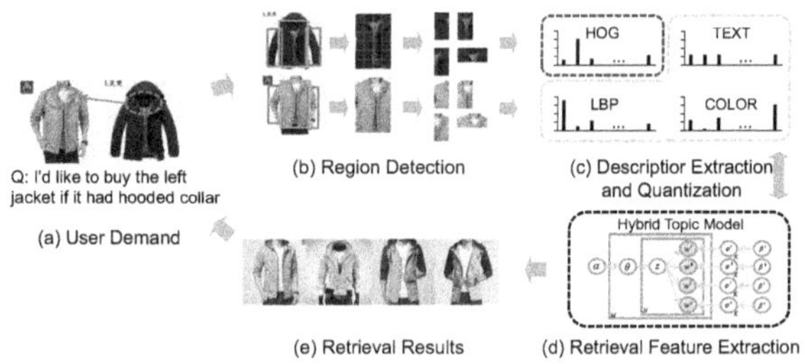

Figure 4: A toy example of the demand-adaptive retrieval.

we sample the parameter $\vec{z}_q$s using Eq. 2 and estimate the probability that I_q is tagged with w_i^t:

$$P(w_i^t|\vec{z}_q, \vec{\alpha}, \vec{\beta}^t) = \sum_{k=1}^{K} \left(\frac{n_k^{(t,i)} + \beta_i^t}{\sum_{g=1}^{D^t} n_k^{(t,g)} + \beta_g^t} \frac{n_q^{(k)} + \alpha_k}{\sum_{z=1}^{K} n_q^{(z)} + \alpha_z} \right). \tag{7}$$

We adopt adaboost strategy to combine the predictions from each model. The recommended tags can be used to improve our retrieval.

Demand-adaptive retrieval. The demand-adaptive retrieval improves the retrieval results by further refining the reasonable requirements. However, it is difficult to distinguish whether a requirement is reasonable or not. Our strategy can be divided into following steps: First, we integrate the demand of modification into the query image representation. Since our feature is defined as the concatenation of local representation $\vec{\theta}$s, we recalculate $\vec{\theta}$s in the designated regions via mixing the modified and unmodified descriptors. Fig. 4 illustrates a toy example of our strategy, where we modify the shape descriptors of the original query.

Algorithm 1 Demand-adaptive Representation Optimization

Input: the bag-of-words representations $\vec{u}^j$s, $j \in F$.
for each descriptor channel $j \in F$ **do**
  • Set $\vec{\gamma}^j = \vec{u}^j / \|\vec{u}^j\|_1$.
end for
repeat
  • Sample all the terms: $w_r^j \sim Mult(\vec{\gamma}^j)$.
  • Sample $\vec{z}$ using Eq. 2.
  • Evaluate $\vec{\theta}$ using Eq. 6.
  for each descriptor channel $j \in F$ **do**
    for each codeword $w_i^j \in V^j$ **do**
      • Evaluate the frequency of w_i^j:
      $P(w_i^j|\vec{z}) = \sum_{k=1}^{K} \left(\frac{n_k^{(j,i)} + \beta_i^j}{\sum_{g=1}^{D^j} n_k^{(j,g)} + \beta_g^j} \frac{n_q^{(k)} + \alpha_k}{\sum_{z=1}^{K} n_q^{(z)} + \alpha_z} \right)$.
    end for
    • Set $\vec{\gamma}^j = (P(w_1^j|\vec{z}), ..., P(w_{D^j}^j|\vec{z}))^T$.
  end for
until $\vec{\theta}$ converges
Output: the demand-adaptive representation $\vec{\theta}$.

Second, we mitigate the inconsistency caused by unreasonable modification. As noted, all the clothing descriptors are converted into BOW format. The inconsistency among descriptors will result in irrelevant weights of the codewords. To this end, we offer a concise algorithm which iteratively

Table 1: The Retrieval Accuracy of Each Method.

$NDCG@k$	HT	HT-nt	HT-an	CNN-hs	CNN-ds
$k = 20$	0.784	0.565	0.678	0.532	0.551

evaluates $\vec{\theta}$ until convergence (see Algorithm 1). The irrelevant weight values will be adaptively smoothed by probability reasoning, while the other values will remain basically unchanged. Thus, we reduce the negative impact of the unreasonable demands and optimize the image representations with reasonable ones.

5. EXPERIMENTS

Dataset. We collect over 200,000 upper-body clothing images and corresponding text descriptions from e-commerce platforms (*e.g.* Taobao.com and JD.com) as our dataset. These images contain different human poses and various backgrounds. We manually label the bounding boxes of 10,000 images among them to train the Faster R-CNN detectors mentioned in Section 2.

Clothing Retrieval Evaluation. We randomly divide our dataset into two equal-size parts: one for training and the other for testing. In training process, we discard about 2,000 images whose text information is seriously missing. For each HT model, we set the parameter $N = 100$ and $K = 50$, hence the dimension of our feature is $50 \times 17 = 850$. In testing process, we use CNN-hs [7] and CNN-ds [4] as the baselines. We compare our results with them under different configurations: (1) HT: We extract the features of query images as show in Section 3. (2) HT-nt: We assume the image tags of queries are unavailable and sample the parameters of models by Eq. 2. (3) HT-an: We infer the unavailable tags with our annotation strategy and combine them with other descriptors. We adopt Normalized Discounted Cumulative Cain to measure the performance: $NDCG@k = \sum_{j=1}^{k} \frac{2^{r(j)}-1}{\log(j+1)}$, $r(j)$ is the number of matched tags between query and the jth image divided by the total number of query tags.

Table 1 shows the result of our experiments. As we see, The precision of HT-nt is close to CNN based methods. Though we ignore the image tags while extracting features, the pre-trained models have learned the semantic information from the training set. Meanwhile, HT-an improves 11.3% compared with HT-nt, which verifies the effectiveness of our annotation strategy. HT uses the real tags of images to extract features. It performs best among all the methods, which is consistent with our expectations.

Demand-adaptive Retrieval Evaluation. In this experiment, we compare four kinds of strategies: (1) HT-in: We retrieve the query image using HT feature which integrates the user demand regardless of its rationality. (2) HT-op: On the basis of the second strategy, we optimize the HT feature with the algorithm mentioned in Section 4. (3) CNN-hs and (4) CNN-ds: We retrieve the query image using CNN features and filter the results by search constraints.

We invite 10 subjects to perform 100 constrained retrieval tasks. For each task, subjects submit a clothing image and corresponding tags as the query. Then, they can refine their requirements by modifying the visual content or clothing attributes of the query images. Finally, we obtain the top-20 retrieval results based on the above strategies. The accuracy is denoted as the average proportion of the images which meets the subjects' demand in the top-20 results of all tasks.

Table 2: The Demand-adaptive Retrieval Accuracy.

$AP@k$	HT-in	HT-op	CNN-hs	CNN-ds
$k = 20$	0.648	0.779	0.365	0.374

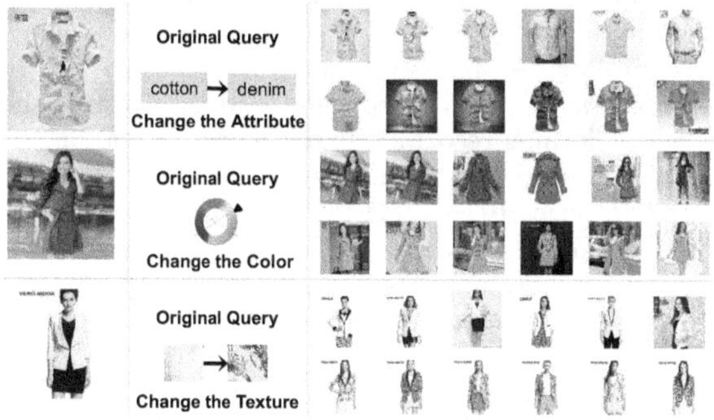

Figure 5: Several Groups of User Requirements and Corresponding Results.

Table 2 shows the accuracy of demand-adaptive retrieval strategies. We discover that the accuracies of CNN-hs and CNN-ds are much lower than that of HT-in. The original features extracted from query could not describe the modification made by users. Even if we use simple filters to filter the images, the result is still unsatisfactory. Meanwhile, HT-in recalculates the feature of query, which reduces the distance between query and user desired images in the feature space. This strategy is more in line with human vision mechanism. Furthermore, HT-op uses Algorithm 1 to mitigate the inconsistency among descriptors and achieves another 13.1% increment. Fig. 5 shows some examples of our retrieved results.

6. CONCLUSIONS

In this paper, we propose a novel clothing image retrieval framework to meet users' multi-dimensional requirements. It offers a two-level abstraction for clothing images and constructs hybrid topic models to link the relationship among visual and attribute descriptors. We apply the proposed model to two applications including image annotation and demand-adaptive retrieval strategy. Experiment results show that our method achieves much better performance than the state-of-the-art methods.

7. ACKNOWLEDGMENTS

The work was supported by the National Basic Research Program of China (Grant No. 2015CB856004), the Key Basic Research Program of Shanghai Municipality(15JC1400103) and the National Natural Science Foundation of China (Grant No. 91420302, 61272251).

8. REFERENCES

[1] D. M. Blei, A. Y. Ng, and M. I. Jordan. Latent dirichlet allocation. *JMLR*, 3:993–1022, 2003.

[2] R. B. Girshick, P. F. Felzenszwalb, and D. Mcallester. Object detection with grammar models. *NIPS*, 33:442–450, 2010.

[3] J. Huang, R. S. Feris, Q. Chen, and S. Yan. Cross-domain image retrieval with a dual attribute-aware ranking network. In *ICCV*, pages 1062–1070, 2015.

[4] J. Huang, W. Xia, and S. Yan. Deep search with attribute-aware deep network. In *ACM MM*, pages 731–732, 2014.

[5] Y. Kalantidis, L. Kennedy, and L. J. Li. Getting the look: Clothing recognition and segmentation for automatic product suggestions in everyday photos. In *ICMR*, pages 105–112, 2013.

[6] M. Kokare, B. N. Chatterji, and P. K. Biswas. A survey on current content based image retrieval methods. *Iete Journal of Research*, 48(3-4):261–271, 2015.

[7] K. Lin, H. F. Yang, K. H. Liu, J. H. Hsiao, and C. S. Chen. Rapid clothing retrieval via deep learning of binary codes and hierarchical search. In *ICMR*, pages 499–502, 2015.

[8] S. Liu, Z. Song, G. Liu, C. Xu, H. Lu, and S. Yan. Street-to-shop: Cross-scenario clothing retrieval via parts alignment and auxiliary set. In *CVPR*, pages 3330–3337, 2012.

[9] M. Mizuochi, A. Kanezaki, and T. Harada. Clothing retrieval based on local similarity with multiple images. In *ACM MM*, pages 1165–1168, 2014.

[10] S. Ren, K. He, R. Girshick, and J. Sun. Faster r-cnn: Towards real-time object detection with region proposal networks. In *NIPS*, pages 1440–1448, 2015.

[11] A. W. M. Smeulders, M. Worring, S. Santini, A. Gupta, and R. Jain. Content-based image retrieval at the end of the early years. *IEEE Transactions on Pattern Analysis Machine Intelligence*, 22(12):1349–1380, 2000.

[12] Z. Sun, C. Wang, L. Zhang, and L. Zhang. Query-adaptive shape topic mining for hand-drawn sketch recognition. In *ACM MM*, pages 519–528, 2012.

[13] C. Wang, D. M. Blei, and F. Li. Simultaneous image classification and annotation. In *CVPR*, 2009.

[14] Y. Yang and D. Ramanan. Articulated pose estimation with flexible mixtures-of-parts. In *CVPR*, pages 1385–1392, 2011.

[15] R. Zhou, L. Chen, and L. Zhang. Sketch-based image retrieval on a large scale database. In *ACM MM*, pages 973–976, 2012.

Deep Multi-task Learning with Label Correlation Constraint for Video Concept Detection

Foteini Markatopoulou[1,2]
markatopoulou@iti.gr

Vasileios Mezaris[1]
bmezaris@iti.gr

Ioannis Patras[2]
i.patras@qmul.ac.uk

[1] Information Technologies Institute (ITI), CERTH, Thermi 57001, Greece
[2]Queen Mary University of London, Mile end Campus, UK, E14NS

ABSTRACT

In this work we propose a method that integrates multi-task learning (MTL) and deep learning. Our method appends a MTL-like loss to a deep convolutional neural network, in order to learn the relations between tasks together at the same time, and also incorporates the label correlations between pairs of tasks. We apply the proposed method on a transfer learning scenario, where our objective is to fine-tune the parameters of a network that has been originally trained on a large-scale image dataset for concept detection, so that it be applied on a target video dataset and a corresponding new set of target concepts. We evaluate the proposed method for the video concept detection problem on the TRECVID 2013 Semantic Indexing dataset. Our results show that the proposed algorithm leads to better concept-based video annotation than existing state-of-the-art methods.

Keywords

Concept detection; deep learning; video analysis

1. INTRODUCTION

Semantic concept detection in video refers to the task of assigning one or more semantic concepts to video fragments (e.g., video keyframes) based on a predefined concept list (e.g., "car", "running") [24]. In a typical process, the video is initially segmented into meaningful fragments, called shots; each shot may be represented by one or more characteristic keyframes; and, these keyframes are passed through a pre-trained deep convolutional neural network (DCNN) that performs the final class label prediction directly, using typically a softmax or a hinge loss layer [22, 10].

The small number of labeled training examples is a common problem in video datasets, making it difficult to train a deep network from scratch without over-fitting its parameters on the training set [23]. For this reason, it is common to use transfer learning. I.e., to take a network that has been trained on a large-scale source dataset (e.g., ImageNet [21]) and fine-tune its parameters for the target dataset. Furthermore, the tasks in the target dataset may be related, and so their relations can be exploited to further improve the video concept detection accuracy. Concept correlations obtained by the ground-truth annotation can provide a source of information regarding the relations between tasks. Additionally, concepts, besides label relations, can be related in terms of their feature representation or the task parameters, i.e., the parameters of the binary classifier learned from the training data. Multi-task learning (MTL) refers to those methods that learn many tasks together at the same time.

In this work we append a MTL-like loss to a neural network and we minimize the entire network end-to-end. In addition, we incorporate a label-based constraint related to the concept correlations. We refer to the proposed method as deep multi-task learning with label constraint (DMTL_LC) and we apply it on a transfer learning scenario. Specifically, we extend the two-sided neural network, proposed in [27] for MTL, in the following ways: i) We use the network jointly with a pre-trained network in order to perform transfer learning, instead of using it as a standalone network that takes as input hand-crafted or DCNN-based features. ii) We introduce a new label-based constraint that considers concept correlations. We evaluate DMTL_LC on the TRECVID 2013 semantic indexing (SIN) task's dataset of 38 different semantic concepts [20]. Our results show that the proposed algorithm leads to better concept-based annotation than existing state-of-the-art methods.

2. RELATED WORK

MTL and transfer learning are two strategies to improve learning by sharing knowledge across different but related tasks or domains. Let us define two domains with their learning tasks: the source domain D_{so} with a set of learning tasks T_{so} (the set of concepts that need to be detected), and the target domain D_{ta} with a set of learning tasks T_{ta}. On the one hand, transfer learning aims to improve the learning in D_{ta} by using the knowledge in D_{so}, without considering potential improvements to the tasks of D_{so}. The latter is the focus of multi-domain learning (MDL). On the other hand, MTL methods learn the relations across the learning tasks T_{so} or T_{ta} together at the same time. It should be noted that the terms MTL and MDL are sometimes used interchangeably. However, it is useful to distinguish them clearly: MDL refers to shared knowledge about the same tasks across different domains, while MTL refers to shared knowledge about different tasks in the same domain. The

MM '16, October 15-19, 2016, Amsterdam, Netherlands

DOI: http://dx.doi.org/10.1145/2964284.2967271

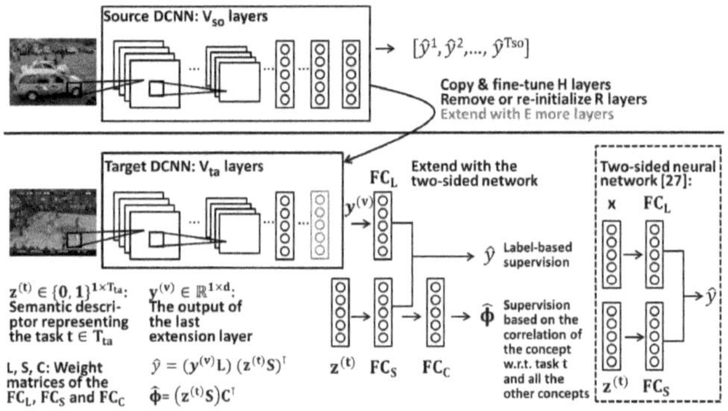

Figure 1: Transfer learning using the proposed DMTL_LC method.

latter is the focus of this work, so we do not further discuss methods that focus on MDL, such as [12].

Noisy and incomplete annotations are common in video datasets (e.g., TRECVID SIN [20]), which makes it difficult to train a deep neural network from scratch [23]. Many works investigate which features within a pre-trained network are sufficiently generic, and develop approaches that effectively transfer this knowledge to new target datasets. The typical approach for transfer learning is to start with a DCNN trained in D_{so}, replace its classification layer with a new T_{ta}-dimensional classification layer and train it towards the D_{ta} domain [4, 29, 8]. The way that the parameters of the source DCNN will be used has been examined in many works. For example, in [18, 29], the first H layers of the pre-trained DCNN are copied and remain frozen, and the rest of the layers are randomly initialized. In addition, [29] fine-tunes the H layers, instead of freezing them, which leads to improved accuracy. Fine-tuning begins with the parameter weights of the source-domain DCNN and modifies them in order to adjust the network to the target domain. A different approach was proposed in [23, 15, 18] that extends a pre-trained DCNN by one or more fully-connected layers placed on the bottom of the classification layer.

MTL methods learn the relations across many tasks together at the same time. The main difference between MTL methods is the way they define task relatedness. Some methods identify shared features between different task and use regularization to model task relatedness [1, 17, 16]. Others identify a shared subspace over the task parameters [6, 5, 2]. The methods above make the strong assumption that all tasks are related; some newer methods consider the fact that some tasks may be unrelated. For example, the clustered MTL algorithm (CMTL) [31] uses a clustering approach to assign to the same cluster parameters of tasks that lie nearby in terms of their L2 distance. Adaptive MTL (AMTL) [25] decomposes the task parameters into a low-rank structure that captures task relations, and a group-sparse structure that detects outlier tasks. The GO-MTL algorithm [11] (i.e, for Grouping and Overlap in Multi-Task Learning) and the online version of it [14] use a dictionary-based method that allows two tasks from different groups to overlap by having one or more basis in common.

Deep learning is well suited for MTL; in [27] a two-sided neural network that addresses the MTL problem is proposed. Specifically, this method unifies several MTL methods that use a predictor matrix factorization approach, e.g., $\boldsymbol{w}^{(t)} = \boldsymbol{L}\boldsymbol{s}^{(t)^{\top}}$ [11], in order to learn their parameters using a two-sided neural network. $\boldsymbol{L}$ correspond to the parameter vectors of k latent tasks, while $\boldsymbol{s}^{(t)} \in \mathbb{R}^{1\times k}$ is a task-specific weight vector that contains the coefficients of the linear combination. MTL in deep learning architectures has also been proposed for facial landmark detection [30] and human pose estimation [19]. In [30] the task of facial landmark detection is optimized with the assistance of an arbitrary number of related/auxiliary tasks. This is a special case of the conventional MTL that typically maximizes the performance of all tasks. In this work the two sided neural-network proposed by [27] is modified and extended, for devising a deep learning method suitable for transferring a network that has been originally trained on a large-scale image dataset for concept detection, to a target video dataset and a corresponding new set of target concepts.

3. PROPOSED APPROACH

3.1 Problem Formulation

A video concept detection system needs to learn a number of supervised learning tasks T_{ta}, one for each target concept. Each task t is associated with the training set available for this concept $X^{(t)} = (\boldsymbol{x}_i^{(t)}, y_i^{(t)})_{i=1}^{N_t}$, where $\boldsymbol{x}_i^{(t)} \in \mathbb{R}^d, y_i^{(t)} \in \{\pm 1\}$. When the training set is small, it is common to take a DCNN that has been trained on a large-scale source dataset for T_{so} tasks, and transfer its parameters on a target DCNN to be trained on the target dataset $X = \{X^{(t)}\}_{t=1}^{T_{ta}}$ for a different set of T_{ta} tasks. With respect to the target dataset, the task parameters of related tasks may share similar knowledge, but also concept correlations obtained by the ground-truth annotation provide another source of information regarding the relations between tasks. In this section, considering all the above, we append a GO-MTL-like loss to a neural network and we incorporate a label-based constraint that considers concept correlations. We minimize the entire network end-to-end using stochastic gradient descent (SGD). We refer to the proposed method as deep multi-task learning with label constraint (DMTL_LC) and we apply it on a transfer learning scenario.

3.2 Deep Multi-task Learning with Label Constraint: DMTL_LC

Figure 1 presents the proposed approach for transferring a pre-trained DCNN network that consists of V_{so} layers (upper part) on a target DCNN to be trained to a target dataset (lower part). Starting with the DCNN trained on the source domain, the first H layers are copied to the target DCNN and fine-tuned on the target dataset. The remaining R layers are completely removed or randomly initialized; consequently, $H + R \leq V_{so}$. Subsequently, the target network can be extended with $E \geq 0$ fully-connected layers. Finally, the target network is trained using the DMTL_LC method.

The DMTL_LC algorithm unifies the GO-MTL algorithm [11] in the target DCNN by using and extending the two-sided neural network proposed in [27] as follows: i) The two-sided neural network is placed on the top of the V_{ta}-th fully-connected layer (where $V_{ta} = H + R + E$ is the number of layers before the two-sided network), instead of using it as a standalone network that takes as input hand-crafted or DCNN-based features. ii) The two-sided network is extended with a new label-based constraint in order to incorporate statistical information of pairwise correlations between concepts that we can acquire from the ground-truth annotation.

Specifically, the upper side of the target DCNN in Fig. 1, contains a fully-connected layer $FC_{\boldsymbol{L}}$ that takes as input the output of the V_{ta}-th layer. $FC_{\boldsymbol{L}}$ consists of k neurons, each representing one latent task. The parameter matrix $\boldsymbol{L} \in \mathbb{R}^{d \times k}$ of this layer constitutes a shared knowledge basis for all task models T_{ta}. The concept related to each task t is represented by a semantic descriptor $\boldsymbol{z}^{(t)} \in \{0,1\}^{1 \times T_{ta}}$, which is a binary vector of length T_{ta} that has zeros in every position except for position t. The lower side of the target DCNN contains a fully-connected layer $FC_{\boldsymbol{S}}$ that consists of k neurons and takes as input the semantic descriptor $\boldsymbol{z}^{(t)}$. Each row of the parameter matrix $\boldsymbol{S} \in \mathbb{R}^{T_{ta} \times k}$ of this layer contains a task-specific weight vector of the coefficients of the linear combination with the shared basis $\boldsymbol{L}$. This linear combination indicates for each concept which latent tasks describe it. The label-based constraint is placed on the top of the task-specific layer $FC_{\boldsymbol{S}}$. The network predicts a single output, which is equal to $y^{(t)} = (\boldsymbol{y}^{(V_{ta})}\mathbf{L})(\boldsymbol{z}^{(t)}\mathbf{S})^{\mathsf{T}}$, where $\boldsymbol{y}^{(V_{ta})}$ is the output of the V_{ta} layer. The higher the output, the more likely that the concept learned w.r.t. task t is depicted in the input keyframe.

The above problem can be formulated by two separate objective functions:

$$\min_{(\mathbf{L},\mathbf{S},f \in F)} \frac{1}{T_{ta}} \sum_{t=1}^{T_{ta}} \left\{ \frac{1}{N_t} \sum_{i=1}^{N_t} \mathcal{L}\left(y_i^{(t)}, \hat{y}_i^{(t)} \right) \right\} \quad (1)$$

where $y_i^{(t)} = (\boldsymbol{y}_i^{(v)}\mathbf{L})(\boldsymbol{z}^{(t)}\mathbf{S})^{\mathsf{T}}$ is the prediction w.r.t task t, and $\boldsymbol{y}_i^{(v)} = \alpha(\boldsymbol{W}^{(v)}\boldsymbol{y}_i^{(v-1)} + \boldsymbol{b}^{(v)})$ is the output of the v-th layer, with α referring to the layer's activation functions. E.g., $\alpha(x) = max(0,x)$ for the ReLU function.

In the above equation $\mathcal{L}$ refers to the loss function calculated between the prediction $y_i^{(t)}$ and ground-truth annotation $\hat{y}_i^{(t)}$. $f^{(v)} = \{\boldsymbol{W}^{(v)}, \boldsymbol{b}^{(v)}\}$ is the pair of the network parameters for the v-th layer and $F = \{f^{(v)}\}_{v=1}^{V_{ta}}$ is the set of network parameters for the first V_{ta} layers.

The second objective function that is placed on the top of the task-specific layer $FC_{\boldsymbol{S}}$ can be formulated as follows:

$$\min_{\mathbf{S}} \beta \left(\frac{1}{T_{ta}} \sum_{t=1}^{T_{ta}} \left\{ \frac{1}{N_t} \sum_{i=1}^{N_t} \mathcal{L}\left(\boldsymbol{\phi}^{(t)}, \hat{\boldsymbol{\phi}}^{(t)} \right) \right\} \right) \quad (2)$$

The role of this objective function is to approximate the correlation matrix $\boldsymbol{\Phi} \in [-1,1]^{T_{ta} \times T_{ta}}$. Each position of this matrix corresponds to the ϕ-correlation coefficient between two concepts regarding two different tasks t and t', calculated from the ground-truth annotation of the training set. Consequently, $\hat{\boldsymbol{\phi}}^{(t)} \in [-1,1]^{1 \times T_{ta}}$ refers to the t'th row of $\boldsymbol{\Phi}$ that contains the correlations of task t with all the other tasks. $\boldsymbol{\phi}^{(t)} \in \mathbb{R}^{1 \times T_{ta}}$, where $\boldsymbol{\phi}^{(t)} = (\boldsymbol{z}^{(t)}\mathbf{S})\mathbf{C}^{\mathsf{T}}$, is the network's prediction for this row. Finally, $\boldsymbol{C} \in \mathbb{R}^{T_{ta} \times k}$ is the weight matrix to train for approximating the correlation matrix. To train $\boldsymbol{C}$, back propagation can be performed by the loss $\mathcal{L}$ between $\boldsymbol{\phi}^{(t)}$ and $\hat{\boldsymbol{\phi}}^{(t)}$.

We use the sigmoid cross entropy loss given by the following equation: $\mathcal{L} = \hat{\phi} log(\sigma(\phi)) + (1 - \hat{\phi}) log(1 - \sigma(\phi))$, where $\sigma(.)$ refers to the sigmoid function $\sigma(x) = 1/(1 + exp(-x))$. We scale the target vector $\hat{\boldsymbol{\phi}}$ in [0,1] in order to deal with the negative values.

This second objective function takes the form of a constraint over the task-specific parameters $\mathbf{S}$ of the network. Specifically, the rows of the correlation matrix $\boldsymbol{\Phi}$ of two correlated concepts will be similar and we want the corresponding rows of $\boldsymbol{S}$ to be similar, too. During training, this second loss (Eq. 2) gets added to the total loss of the network (Eq. 1) with a discount weight β. At inference time, this auxiliary constraint is discarded.

4. EXPERIMENTS

4.1 Dataset and Experimental Setup

Our experiments were performed on the TRECVID 2013 SIN dataset [20], which consists of approximately 800 and 200 hours of internet archive videos for training and testing, respectively. The training set is partially annotated and highly imbalanced; approximately 100K positive keyframes are available for the 60 TRECVID SIN concepts, which is insufficient for training a DCNN from scratch. In our experiments, we used the 8-layer AlexNet [10] that was trained on 1000 ImageNet categories [21] as the source DCNN, and fine-tuned it on the 60 TRECVID SIN concepts. We evaluated all the methods on the test set using the subset of 38 concepts that were also evaluated as part of the TRECVID 2013 SIN task [20]. The video indexing problem was examined; that is, given a concept, we measure how well the top retrieved video shots for this concept truly relate to it. We analyze our results in terms of mean extended inferred average precision (MXinfAP) [28], which is an approximation of the mean average precision suitable for the partial ground-truth that accompanies the TRECVID dataset [20].

A first set of experiments was ran, where we examined different approaches of using the pre-trained AlexNet [10] to fine-tune a target-DCNN towards the 60 TRECVID SIN concepts [20]: i) The baseline approach (Fig. 1: H=7, R = E=0), that copies the first 7 layers [4, 29, 8]. ii) The extension approach (Fig. 1: H=7, R=0, E=1), that copies the first 7 layers and extends the network by one more layer [23, 15, 18]. iii) The re-initialization approach (Fig. 1: H=6, R=1, E=0), that copies the first 6 layers and randomly initializes the 7th layer [29]. For each approach we evaluated a) the typical transfer learning method (Default-TL) that replaces the classification layer of AlexNet [10] with a new 60-dimensional layer; b) the proposed DMTL_LC method that uses a two-sided network and considers concept correlations. The H layers, in all cases, were copied and fine-tuned towards the target dataset. To train the proposed method, for each concept, a training set was assembled that included all positive annotated training examples for the given concept, and negatives to a maximum of 15:1 ratio. For the Default-TL method we used the positive examples for each concept following an one-vs-all strategy. Subsequently, we applied each of the fine-tuned networks on the TRECVID keyframes and we evaluated the direct output of each network that corresponds to the class label prediction for 60 categories (Table 1).

We also compared (Table 2) the proposed method with the following ones: i) Single-task learning (STL) using a) Logistic regression (LR), b) LSVM and c) kernel SVM with radial kernel (KSVM). ii) MTL using: a) AMTL [25], b) CMTL [31] and c) the two-sided neural network instantiated with the GO-MTL algorithm [27]. We refer to the latter method as 2S-NN. STL refers to the typical approach of training one classifier e.g., SVMs, per concept, with features extracted from one or more layers of DCNNs [13, 4],

Table 1: MXinfAP (%) for 38 concepts, for different fine-tuning processes of the pre-trained 8-layer AlexNet [10] towards the 60 TRECVID SIN concepts [20]: i) The baseline [4, 29, 8]. ii) The extension [23, 15, 18]. iii) The re-initialization [29]. For each approach we evaluate a) the typical transfer learning method (Default-TL) that replaces the classification layer of AlexNet [10] with a new 60-dimensional layer; b) the proposed DMTL, DMTL_LC methods that use a two-sided network. The H AlexNet layers, in all cases, are copied and fine-tuned towards the target dataset.

fine-tuning process	(i) Baseline [4, 29, 8]	(ii) Extension [23, 15, 18]			(iii) Re-initialization [29]	
	(a)	(b)	(c)	(d)	(e)	(f)
fine-tuning parameters		#Neurons for the extension layer:			#Neurons for the re-initialization layer	
		1096	2048	4096	1096	2048
DefaultTL-Softmax	**16.76**	16.22	15.53	14.79	16.24	16.68
DefaultTL-Hinge	13.26	19.91	19.89	18.76	19.20	15.30
Proposed-DMTL	12.71	15.82	14.89	19.93	18.39	19.47
Proposed-DMTL_LC	15.78	**20.13**	**22.60**	**20.84**	**22.54**	**21.47**

instead of performing the final class label prediction directly, using a softmax/hinge loss layer [22, 10]. To train the compared methods, we applied the pre-trained AlexNet on the TRECVID keyframes and we used as a feature the network's last fully-connected layer (fc8). Subsequently, we used the same training set of positive/negative examples as described above.

Regarding the proposed method, the value of k was set to 157 and the regularization parameter β in Eq. (2) was set to 0.3. These parameters are expected to depend on the dimensionality of the feature space and the number of examples, and according to preliminary experiments seem to work well for the employed dataset. The hinge loss was used in Eq. (1) and a ReLU function was placed on the top of $\boldsymbol{S}$ to encourage sparse models. We used stochastic gradient descent (SGD) with 0.9 momentum and cross-validated the learning rate between 10^{-5} and 10^{-2} by a multiplicative step-size $10^{0.5}$. The Caffe software [9] was used for training the DCNN networks on a Tesla K40 GPU. The LibLINEAR library [7] was used as the source of learning LSVM and LR models and the LibSVM [3] for learning KSVMs. The MALSAR library [32] was used for learning the CMTL [31] and AMTL [25].

4.2 Experimental Results

Tables 1 and 2 present the results of our experiments in terms of MXinfAP. DMTL is an intermediate version of the proposed DMTL_LC that solves the objective function of DMTL (eq. 1) without using the label constraint of DMTL_LC (eq. 2). In Table 1 we examine the best way of using the layers of the pre-trained AlexNet by comparing three different fine-tuning processes. For completeness, we also report how these processes affect the typical way of transferring learning that replaces the classification layer of AlexNet with a new 60-dimensional classification layer (Default-TL). Based on these results, which

Table 2: MXinfAP (%) for 38 concepts for different STL and MTL methods using two pre-trained DCNNs.

	Methods	AlexNet	AlexNet Default-TL (best from Table 1)
	Direct output	-	19.91
STL e.g., [13, 4]	LR	18.57	22.34
	LSVM	20.59	22.21
	KSVM	18.81	21.79
MTL	AMTL [25]	20.44	22.21
	CMTL [31]	18.18	22.38
	2S-NN [27]	20.19	23.12
	Proposed DMTL_LC	**22.60**	**25.04**

refer to the direct output of the fine-tuned networks, we can see that the proposed DMTL_LC performs better than the Default-TL alternative independently of the utilized fine-tuning process, with only one exception in the case of the baseline fine-tuning. Furthermore, adding the label constraint (DMTL_LC) further improves the DMTL method for all of the fine-tuning processes. The proposed DMTL_LC is overall the best performing method, reaching a MXinfAP of 22.60% (Table 1: col(c)). This result is important, considering that the pre-trained AlexNet was used as the source DCNN; by incorporating in our DMTL_LC framework better performing DCNN architectures such as GoogLeNet [26] instead of AlexNet, further performance gains are expected.

In Table 2 we compare the proposed DMTL_LC method with different STL and MTL methods. The pre-trained AlexNet and the best Default-TL fine-tuned network of Table 1, i.e., Table 1: col. (b), are used as the source DCNNs. The proposed DMTL_LC fine-tunes each of these networks towards the 60 TRECVID SIN concepts. To train the other methods, the output of the last fully-connected layer of each source DCNN was used as a feature. Regarding the AlexNet source DCNN, the proposed DMTL_LC is the best performing method, reaching a MXinfAP of 22.60%. We also observe that fine-tuning is a procedure that significantly improves the precision of all the compared methods, by increasing the MXinfAP, when the best Default-TL is used as the source DCNN. As the Default-TL approach does not consider the correlations of the concepts and the relations across tasks, in contrast to the proposed DMTL_LC, the latter reaches the highest performance by fine-tuning once again the former network (MXinfAP equal to 25.04%).

5. CONCLUSIONS

In this work we presented deep multi-task learning method for video concept detection. Extensive experiments reveal the usefulness of fine-tuning a deep network by directly learning the relations between many task models (one per concept) in combination with the concept correlations that can be captured from the ground-truth annotation.

6. ACKNOWLEDGEMENTS

This work was supported by the EU's Horizon 2020 research and innovation programme under grant agreements H2020-687786 InVID and H2020-693092 MOVING, and by Nvidia corporation with the donation of a Tesla K40 GPU.

7. REFERENCES

[1] A. Argyriou, T. Evgeniou, and M. Pontil. Multi-task feature learning. *Advances in Neural Information Processing Systems (NIPS 2007)*, 2007.

[2] A. Argyriou, T. Evgeniou, and M. Pontil. Convex multi-task feature learning. *Machine Learning*, 73(3):243–272, 2008.

[3] C.-C. Chang and C.-J. Lin. LIBSVM: A library for support vector machines. *ACM Trans. on Intelligent Systems and Technology*, 2:27:1–27:27, 2011.

[4] K. Chatfield, K. Simonyan, A. Vedaldi, and A. Zisserman. Return of the devil in the details: Delving deep into convolutional nets. In *British Machine Vision Conference*, 2014.

[5] H. Daumé, III. Bayesian multitask learning with latent hierarchies. In *the 25th Conf. on Uncertainty in Artificial Intelligence (UAI 2009)*, pages 135–142, Quebec, Canada, 2009. AUAI Press.

[6] T. Evgeniou and M. Pontil. Regularized multi–task learning. In *the 10th ACM SIGKDD Int. Conf. on Knowledge Discovery and Data Mining (KDD 2004)*, pages 109–117, Seattle, WA, 2004.

[7] R.-E. Fan, K.-W. Chang, C.-J. Hsieh, X.-R. Wang, and C.-J. Lin. LIBLINEAR: A library for large linear classification. *Journal of Machine Learning Research*, 9:1871–1874, 2008.

[8] R. Girshick, J. Donahue, T. Darrell, and J. Malik. Rich feature hierarchies for accurate object detection and semantic segmentation. In *the IEEE Conf. on Computer Vision and Pattern Recognition (CVPR 2014)*, 2014.

[9] Y. Jia, E. Shelhamer, J. Donahue, S. Karayev, J. Long, R. Girshick, S. Guadarrama, and T. Darrell. Caffe: Convolutional architecture for fast feature embedding. *arXiv preprint arXiv:1408.5093*, 2014.

[10] A. Krizhevsky, S. Ilya, and G. Hinton. ImageNet classification with deep convolutional neural networks. *Advances in Neural Information Processing Systems (NIPS 2012)*, pages 1097–1105, 2012.

[11] A. Kumar and H. Daume. Learning task grouping and overlap in multi-task learning. In *the 29th ACM Int. Conf. on Machine Learning (ICML 2012)*, pages 1383–1390, Edinburgh, Scotland, 2012.

[12] M. Long and J. Wang. Learning multiple tasks with deep relationship networks. *CoRR*, abs/1506.02117, 2015.

[13] F. Markatopoulou, V. Mezaris, and I. Patras. Cascade of classifiers based on binary, non-binary and deep convolutional network descriptors for video concept detection. In *the IEEE Int. Conf. on Image Processing (ICIP 2015)*, pages 1786–1790, Quebec, Canada, 2015.

[14] F. Markatopoulou, V. Mezaris, and I. Patras. Online Multi-Task Learning for Semantic Concept Detection in Video. In *the IEEE Int. Conf. on Image Processing (ICIP 2016)*, Phoenix, AZ, USA, 2016.

[15] F. Markatopoulou et al. ITI-CERTH in TRECVID 2015. In *TRECVID 2015*. NIST, USA, 2015.

[16] H. Mousavi, U. Srinivas, V. Monga, Y. Suo, M. Dao, and T. Tran. Multi-task image classification via collaborative, hierarchical spike-and-slab priors. In *the IEEE Int. Conf. on Image Processing (ICIP 2014)*, pages 4236–4240, Paris, France, 2014.

[17] G. Obozinski and B. Taskar. Multi-task feature selection. In *the 23rd Int. Conf. on Machine Learning (ICML 2006). Workshop of Structural Knowledge Transfer for Machine Learning*, Pittsburgh, PA, 2006.

[18] M. Oquab, L. Bottou, I. Laptev, and J. Sivic. Learning and transferring mid-level image representations using convolutional neural networks. In *the IEEE Conf. on Computer Vision and Pattern Recognition (CVPR 2014)*, Columbus, OH, 2014.

[19] W. Ouyang, X. Chu, and X. Wang. Multi-source deep learning for human pose estimation. In *the IEEE Conf. on Computer Vision and Pattern Recognition (CVPR 2014)*, pages 2337–2344, Columbus, OH, 2014.

[20] P. Over et al. TRECVID 2013-An overview of the goals, tasks, data, evaluation mechanisms and metrics. In *TRECVID 2013*. NIST, USA, 2013.

[21] O. Russakovsky, J. Deng, and H. S. et al. ImageNet Large Scale Visual Recognition Challenge. *Int. Journal of Computer Vision (IJCV 2015)*, 115(3):211–252, 2015.

[22] K. Simonyan and A. Zisserman. Very deep convolutional networks for large-scale image recognition. *arXiv technical report*, 2014.

[23] C. Snoek, D. Fontijne, K. E. van de Sande, and H. e. a. Stokman. Qualcomm research and University of Amsterdam at TRECVID 2015: Recognizing concepts, objects, and events in video. In *TRECVID 2015*. NIST, USA, 2015.

[24] C. G. M. Snoek and M. Worring. Concept-Based Video Retrieval. *Foundations and Trends in Information Retrieval*, 2(4):215–322, 2009.

[25] G. Sun, Y. Chen, X. Liu, and E. Wu. Adaptive multi-task learning for fine-grained categorization. In *the IEEE Int. Conf. on Image Processing (ICIP 2015)*, pages 996–1000, Quebec, Canada, 2015.

[26] C. Szegedy et al. Going deeper with convolutions. In *the IEEE Conf. on Computer Vision and Pattern Recognition (CVPR 2015)*, Boston, MA, 2015.

[27] Y. Yang and T. M. Hospedales. A unified perspective on multi-domain and multi-task learning. In *the Int. Conf. on Learning Representations (ICLR 2015)*, San Diego, California, 2015.

[28] E. Yilmaz, E. Kanoulas, and J. A. Aslam. A simple and efficient sampling method for estimating AP and NDCG. In *the 31st ACM Int. Conf. on Research and Development in Information Retrieval (SIGIR 2008)*, pages 603–610, Singapore, 2008.

[29] J. Yosinski, J. Clune, Y. Bengio, and H. Lipson. How transferable are features in deep neural networks? *Advances in Neural Information Processing Systems (NIPS 2014)*, pages 3320–3328, 2014.

[30] Z. Zhang, P. Luo, C. C. Loy, and X. Tang. Facial landmark detection by deep multi-task learning. In *the 13th Europ. Conf. on Computer Vision (ECCV 2014)*, pages 94–108, Zurich, Switzerland, 2014. Springer.

[31] J. Zhou, J. Chen, and J. Ye. Clustered multi-task learning via alternating structure optimization. *Advances in Neural Information Processing Systems (NIPS 2011)*, 2011.

[32] J. Zhou, J. Chen, and J. Ye. MALSAR: Multi-task learning via structural regularization. *Technical report*, 2011.

Application-Layer Rate-Adaptive Multicast Video Streaming over 802.11 for Mobile Devices

Raheeb Muzaffar[*†], Evşen Yanmaz[▽], Christian Bettstetter[*], Andrea Cavallaro[†]
[*]Institute of Networked and Embedded Systems, Alpen-Adria-Universität Klagenfurt, Austria
[▽]Lakeside Labs GmbH, Klagenfurt, Austria
[†]Centre for Intelligent Sensing, Queen Mary University of London, United Kingdom

ABSTRACT

Multicast video streaming over IEEE 802.11 is unreliable due to the lack of feedback from receivers. High data rates and variable link conditions require feedback from the receivers for link estimation to improve reliability and rate adaptation accordingly. In this paper, we validate on a test platform an application-layer rate-adaptive video multicast streaming framework using an 802.11 ad-hoc network applicable for mobile senders and receivers. Experimental results serve as a proof of concept and show the performance in terms of goodput, delay, packet loss, and received video quality.

Keywords

Rate-adaptive multicast, wireless video streaming, 802.11

1. INTRODUCTION AND MOTIVATION

This paper addresses the problem of reliably multicasting a video stream over an IEEE 802.11 ad-hoc network with mobile nodes to satisfy the receivers' quality of experience (QoE). Our work has been motivated by the use of micro aerial vehicles (MAV) for civil applications, such as search and rescue, surveillance, and disaster management [3, 9, 19]. Such applications benefit from multicast wireless video streaming to transmit identical data to multiple users (see Fig. 1). However, achieving reliability, fairness among nodes, communication performance, and adhering to delay bounds is challenging [4, 5, 11, 15, 22, 23]. In particular, aerial mobility leads to dynamic network topologies with frequent link outages [2, 6, 10].

While existing license-based wireless communication technologies can in principle be used for MAVs, they bear infrastructure requirements that may not be available in disaster areas. In contrast, IEEE 802.11 does not require an infrastructure, is easy to setup, operates in the unlicensed spectrum [7], and is supported by many MAV platforms [10]. However, IEEE 802.11 was not designed for our scenario.

This work was partly supported by the EACEA Agency of the European Commission under EMJD ICE FPA n° 2010-0012; the ERDF, KWF, and BABEG under grant KWF-20214/24272/36084 (SINUS); and the Artemis JU and the UK Technology Strategy Board (Innovation UK) through the COPCAMS Project, under Grant 332913.

MM '16, October 15-19, 2016, Amsterdam, Netherlands
© 2016 ACM. ISBN 978-1-4503-3603-1/16/10...$15.00
DOI: http://dx.doi.org/10.1145/2964284.2967272

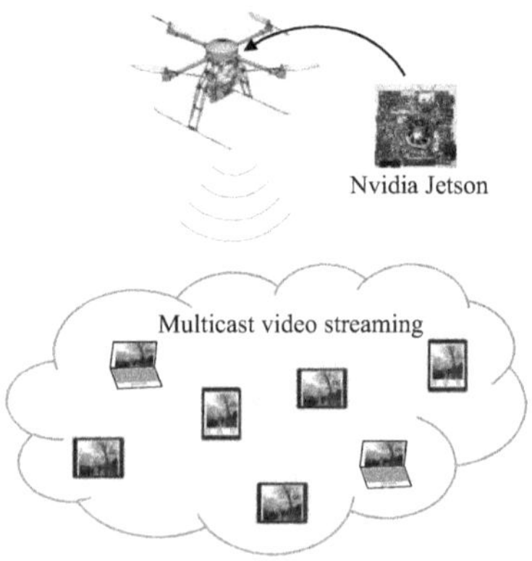

Figure 1: Multicast video streaming from a micro aerial vehicle (MAV).

Because the multicast frames in 802.11 are group addressed and are not acknowledged by the receivers, the ability to gain feedback from receivers about packet reception is a major issue [22]. In fact, without feedback, the source is not aware of packet losses and cannot retransmit lost packets or adapt the transmission rate. Approaches to provide feedback include promiscuous reception of unicast packet [8, 21], polling-based schemes [16, 18], and leader-based approaches [4, 12, 17]. However, these approaches require modifications in the medium access control (MAC) layer. Given the constraints of multicasting over 802.11 with mobility, the node providing feedback may at times lose connectivity with the source. This may make all other multicast recipients suffer from a possible smooth video reception. A feedback mechanism for retransmission and rate adaptation is required to achieve reliability and to satisfy receivers' QoE without any MAC layer modifications.

We discuss and validate an application-layer solution to gain feedback from the receiver nodes that works for any 802.11 wireless ad-hoc setup. The feedback received is not only used to retransmit lost packets but also to adapt the *video encoding* rate, the *link transmission* rate, and the *video frame* rate to obtain a smooth video reception. We refer to the combination and adaptation of these three parameters as

Table 1: Comparison of schemes for multicasting over 802.11 (extended from [14])

Ref.	Scheme	Changes to MAC?	Reliability	Scalability	Rate adaptation	Evaluation
[16]	Polling based	Yes	None	Low	Joint reception correlation	Testbed
[18]	Polling based	Yes	None	Low	User experience in time	Simulation ns-2
[4]	Leader based	Yes	High	Low	Auto rate fallback	Simulation ns-2
[17]	Leader based	Yes	None	High	Beacon Signal	Simulation ns-2
[13, 20]	Directed multicast	Yes	High	Low	None	Testbed
[13, 20]	Unsolicited retries	Yes	Implementation dependent	High	None	Testbed
[13, 20]	Block ACK	Yes	Implementation dependent	Implementation dependent	None	Testbed
Ours	Dynamic leader	**No**	Medium	High	RTP packet feedback	Testbed

ELF rate adaptation. Our framework was initially presented and validated with simulations in [14] and it is extended and validated in this paper through testbed experiments that quantify performance in terms of achieved goodput, delay, and received video quality.

The paper is organized as follows. Section 2 covers existing approaches for multicasting and rate adaptation in wireless networks. Section 3 presents the proposed rate adaptation scheme for video multicasting. Section 4 discusses the experimental evaluation and Section 5 concludes the paper.

2. RELATED WORK

Approaches that can be used to multicast over 802.11 include the legacy 802.11 multicast, 802.11aa amendments, and schemes to gain feedback on packet reception from members of a multicast group.

The 802.11aa GATS specifies the directed multicast service (DMS), the groupcast with retries (GCR) unsolicited retries, and GCR Block ACK besides the legacy multicast service [20]. The legacy multicast mechanism is No-Ack/No-Retry service that uses the basic fixed transmission rate. The DMS converts multicast traffic to unicast frames intended for individual recipients. Reliability is ensured through retransmissions until frames are received correctly by all the recipients. While this scheme is the most reliable, it has a higher overhead and is not scalable.

The GCR unsolicited retries does not use an acknowledgment mechanism and retransmits the same frame several times. This method offers smaller overhead, higher scalability but lower reliability [13].

The GCR Block ACK scheme sends a burst of multicast frames and requests a block acknowledgment (ACK) of the transmitted frames from one or more recipients. The choice and number of recipients from which to gain a feedback is left to the specific implementation. Frames that are not received correctly by one or more recipients can be retransmitted until the retry limit is reached. This scheme offers a trade-off between reliability, overhead, and scalability [13].

In a multicast group, feedback on packet reception can be obtained via promiscuous reception of unicast transmission, polling schemes, and leader-based protocols [22]. With *promiscuous reception*, a member receives data from the source as unicast traffic, while other members listen in promiscuous mode [8, 21]. Each member needs to know the MAC and IP address of the node receiving the unicast traffic and, when this node leaves the group, the other members experience a total packet loss.

The *polling scheme* asks each receiver to acknowledge the reception of the packet that is re-multicast when an ACK is missing [16, 18]. This solution is not efficient for our problem as considerable network resources are needed.

Leader-based schemes select a member that is tasked to send the ACKs. The other members can send negative acknowledgments (NACKs) when packets are not received [4, 12, 17]. While these approaches address reliability by sending feedback through the ACK/NACK mechanism, they do not address the challenges of mobility and video streaming requirements of resilience to jitter and packet losses [14].

Table 1 compares existing schemes and our proposed approach, which is described in the next section.

3. ELF RATE ADAPTIVE MULTICAST

We use an application-layer ELF rate adaptation applicable to 802.11 ad-hoc networks. We advance our work in [14] by (*i*) adapting the video frame rate in addition to the encoding and transmission rates, (*ii*) performing an experimental evaluation on a real testbed, and (*iii*) identifying parameters that are applicable for outdoor real-time multicast video streaming. The notation we use in this section is listed in Table 2.

Members of the multicast group are assigned as *designated nodes* based on their signal quality from the source. Upon receiving a packet, the designated nodes provide feedback through an application-layer acknowledgment, `AL-ACK`, or else provide a negative acknowledgment, `AL-NACK`. The member with the highest signal quality becomes the *primary* designated node, P. Other members with good signal quality become part of the set of *secondary* designated nodes, S, which serve as backup of P. Non-designated nodes are part of the set of *best effort* nodes, B, which do not provide feedback and receive videos on a best effort basis [14].

Feedback received by the source is used for rate adaptation to reduce video distortion and for retransmission upon packet loss (see Fig. 2). Similarly to the leader-based schemes, the source assigns the roles to the receivers based on the signal quality [14]. However, we allow feedback from multiple receivers (designated nodes) and not from a single leader only. Unlike our work [14], which used the signal-to-interference-noise-ratio (SINR), we use here as indicator for signal quality to the connected devices the received signal strength (RSS).

To minimize feedback delays and channel contention time, the roles are assigned in a hierarchy. The source can adjust the ELF rate when the reception conditions of the receivers change, thus facilitating a smooth video playback.

The source assesses the signal quality of the member nodes to assign the feedback responsibility dynamically to a member node, accounting for the change in reception conditions due to mobility of both the source and receivers. The role assignment procedure is defined in Algorithm 1.

The first node joining the multicast group becomes P. Fewer than half of the nodes in the multicast group M can

Table 2: Notation

Symbol	Definition
M	Multicast group
V	A new mobile receiver node
R_X	RSS of node X
P	Primary designated node
$S = \{S_1, \cdots, S_{n_1}\}$	Secondary designated nodes S_i
$B = \{B_1, \cdots, B_{n_2}\}$	Best effort nodes B_i
card(.)	Cardinality of a set

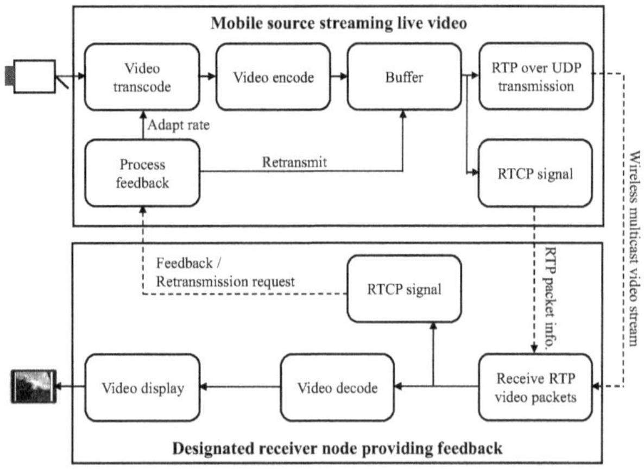

Figure 2: Source multicasts live video stream over the wireless medium as RTP packets. RTCP signaling provides RTP packet information to the receiver nodes. Designated nodes provide feedback about packet reception or packet loss. The source retransmits lost packets and adapts ELF rates.

be designated nodes. A node is assigned to S if [14]

$$\frac{\text{card}(S)+1}{\text{card}(M)+1} < 0.5. \tag{1}$$

A node joining can change between P and S_i, if $R_V > R_P$ or $R_V > R_{S_i}$, respectively. However, the role for P is assigned to another group member (the one with the highest signal quality) in case two consecutive AL-NACKs are received from P while an S_i responds with an AL-ACK. Otherwise, it is added as a member to M as B.

While P is responsible for sending AL-ACKs upon packet reception, either P or an S_i node can send an AL-NACK to request retransmission of lost packets.

To make the approach scalable, the number of designated nodes can be adjusted based on the network density.

The encoder has to choose the video encoding and frame rates for the next Group of Picture (GoP). We use the real-time transport protocol (RTP) for video streaming and its control protocol RTCP for signaling feedback about reception of RTP packets.

These following values are chosen experimentally: The *link transmission rate* is increased upon ten consecutive AL-ACKs from the designated nodes. It is decreased upon signal loss, i.e., when no feedback is received from any of the designated nodes. We use rates as 6, 9, 12, 18, 24, 36, 48, and 54 Mbit/s. The *video encoding rate* is initially set to 512 kbit/s and it is increased by 5 % upon receiving an AL-ACK (up to a maximum of 8192 kbit/s). It is decreased by 5 %

Algorithm 1: Role assignment

```
Notation: See Table 2.
Input: V, R_V, R_P, R_{S_i}, R_{B_i}, card(S), card(M).
Output: Role is assigned to V joining muticast group M.
if card(M) > 0 then
    if card(S) > 0 then
        if (card(S)+1)/(card(M)+1) > 0.5 then
            if R_V > R_P then
                M ← V, B ← S_n, S ← P, P = V
            else if R_V > R_{S_i} then
                M ← V, B ← S_n, S ← V
            else
                M ← V, B ← V
            end
        else if R_V > R_{S_i} then
            M ← V, B ← S_n, S ← V
        else
            M ← V, B_i = V
        end
    else if card(M) ≥ 2 then
        if R_V > R_{B_1} then
            M ← V, S_1 = V
        else
            M ← V, S_1 = B_1, B_1 = V
        end
    else
        M ← V, B_1 = V
    end
else
    M ← V, P = V
end
```

upon receiving three consecutive AL-NACKs (down to a minimum of 128 kbit/s). The source retransmits the packet in the latter case. The *frame rate* is initially set to 25 frames/s and it is decreases by one frame/s (down to a minimum of 10 frames/s) upon three consecutive AL-NACKs if the video encoding rate is already at its minimum. It is increased again upon one AL-ACK.

4. TESTBED EVALUATION

We built an 802.11a ad-hoc network using Atheros AR9462 wireless cards, which support 802.11abgn and independent basic service set (IBSS). To capture videos, Logitech C920 cameras that support full HD 1080p video quality at 30 frames/s with H.264 video compression are used. NVIDIA Jetson TK1 boards [1] are used for processing and video streaming; they have a quad-core 2.3 GHz ARM Cortex-A15 CPU and energy consumption of 1–5 W.

We evaluate our framework with a mobile source and three static receivers (N_1, N_2, and N_3). All nodes are on approximately one meter above the ground. We analyze the effect of the motion of the source on the received video stream quality at distances from 5 to 80 m. The three receivers are placed 5 m apart. We manually select the closest receiver node to the source as P, the second closest as S_1, and the farthest as B_1.

Our rate adaptive approach is compared with a fixed transmission rate of 6 Mbit/s and constant encoding rates of 128 kbit/s and 256 kbit/s. We evaluate performance in terms of received video quality, packet loss, and delay.

Figure 3 shows the mean values from five experimental runs. The cumulative goodput is calculated by adding the received bytes as the RSS decreases in order to observe the

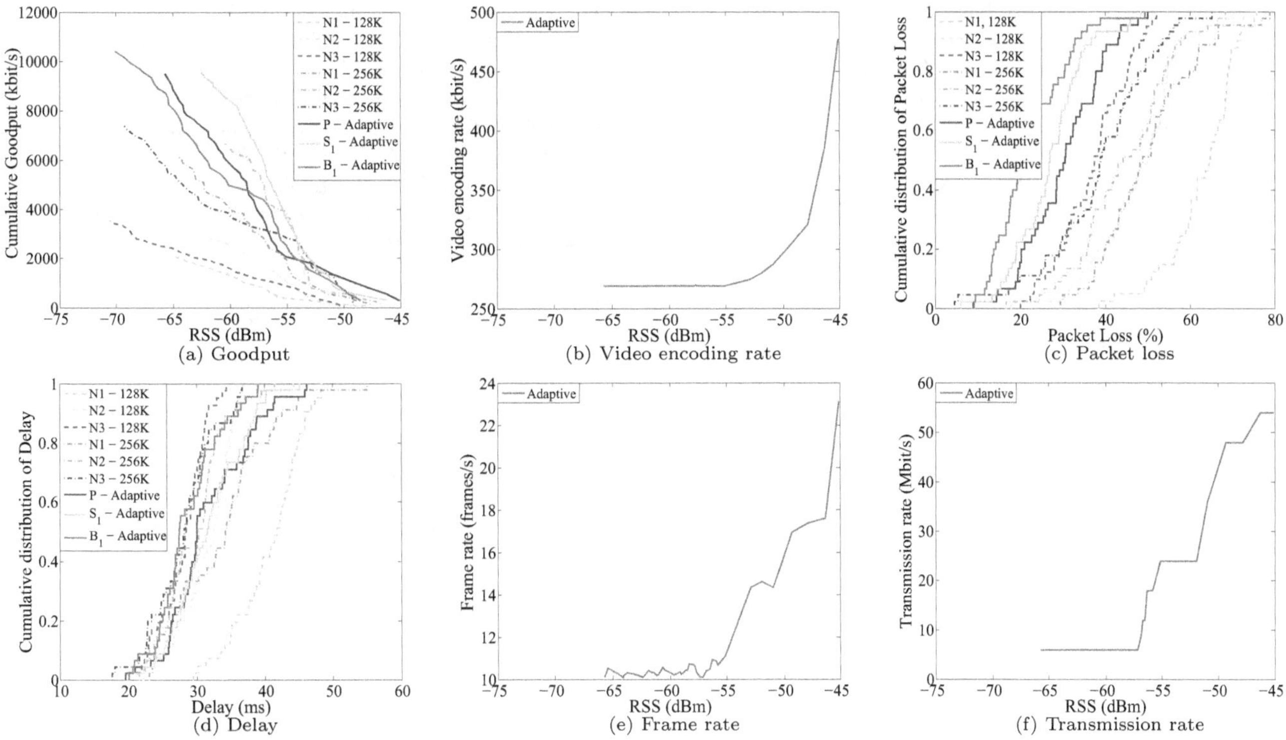

Figure 3: Performance of multicast video streaming with the source moving away from the receivers.

Figure 4: Sample frames representing received video quality with CBR 6 Mbit/s encoded at 128 kbit/s (top row) and our rate adaptive scheme (bottom row) for a multicast video stream.

trend of the received packets with and without the feedback mechanism. The RSS is measured in decibel-milliwatts (dBm). The cumulative goodputs (Fig. 3(a)) of the receiver nodes P compared to N_1, S_1 compared to N_2, and B_1 compared to N_3 remain higher due to higher and adaptive encoding rate. As it moves away from the receivers, the source adapts the video encoding rate (Fig. 3(b)), frame rate (Fig. 3(e)), and transmission rate (Fig. 3(f)). The packet loss (Fig. 3(c)) of the receiver nodes remains lower with our approach compared to the fixed 6 Mbit/s transmission due to the feedback and retransmission mechanism. Due to a reduced packet loss, a smoother video is observed compared to the video of the legacy multicast. Balanced delays under bounds are observed in all cases (Fig. 3(d)).

To compare the received video quality of legacy multicast and our approach, sample frames captured at 5 s intervals are shown in Fig. 4. A high distortion is noticeable with the fixed rate transmission, while an acceptable video stream is received with the proposed rate adaptive approach.

5. CONCLUSIONS

We validated the feasibility of an application-layer rate-adaptive multicast video stream on an experimental testbed that does not require any modifications of the MAC layer and is suitable for mobile platforms equipped with cameras. Transmission, video encoding, and frame rates are adapted based on the received feedbacks from designated nodes. Reliability is achieved by retransmissions of lost packets, resulting in fewer packet losses. The proposed framework enables a smooth video reception and outperforms legacy multicast in terms of packet loss and video quality.

6. REFERENCES

[1] Nvidia Jetson TK1 developer kit. http://www.nvidia.com/object/jetson-tk1-embedded-dev-kit.html. Last accessed 25 April 2016.

[2] T. Andre, K. A. Hummel, A. P. Schoellig, E. Yanmaz, M. Asadpour, C. Bettstetter, P. Grippa, H. Hellwagner, S. Sand, and S. Zhang. Application-driven design of aerial communication networks. *IEEE Communications Magazine*, 52(5):129–137, 2014.

[3] G. Chmaj and H. Selvaraj. Distributed processing applications for UAV/drones: a survey. In *Springer Progress in Systems Engineering*, 2015.

[4] S. Choi, N. Choi, Y. Seok, T. Kwon, and Y. Choi. Leader-based rate adaptive multicasting for wireless LANs. In *IEEE GLOBECOM*, 2007.

[5] C. de Morais Cordeiro, H. Gossain, and D. P. Agrawal. Multicast over wireless mobile ad hoc networks: present and future directions. *Network*, 17(1):52–59, 2003.

[6] E. W. Frew and T. X. Brown. Airborne communication networks for small unmanned aircraft systems. *Proceedings of the IEEE*, 96(12), 2008.

[7] X. Fu, W. Ma, and Q. Zhang. The IEEE 802.16 and 802.11 a coexistence in the license-exempt band. In *IEEE WCNC*, 2007.

[8] P. Ge and P. K. McKinley. Comparisons of error control techniques for wireless video multicasting. In *IEEE IPCCC*, 2002.

[9] S. Gupte, P. I. T. Mohandas, and J. M. Conrad. A survey of quadrotor unmanned aerial vehicles. In *IEEE SoutheastCon*, 2012.

[10] S. Hayat, E. Yanmaz, and R. Muzaffar. Survey on unmanned aerial vehicle networks for civil applications: A communications viewpoint. *IEEE Communications Surveys & Tutorials*, in press, 2016.

[11] P. Jacquet and G. Rodolakis. Multicast scaling properties in massively dense ad hoc networks. In *IEEE ICPADS*, 2005.

[12] J. Kuri and S. K. Kasera. Reliable multicast in multi-access wireless LANs. *Wireless Networks*, 7(4):359–369, 2001.

[13] K. Maraslis, P. Chatzimisios, and A. Boucouvalas. IEEE 802.11 aa: Improvements on video transmission over wireless LANs. In *IEEE ICC*, 2012.

[14] R. Muzaffar, V. Vukadinovic, and A. Cavallaro. Rate-adaptive multicast video streaming from teams of micro aerial vehicles. In *IEEE ICRA*, 2016.

[15] A. Nafaa. Provisioning of multimedia services in 802.11-based networks: facts and challenges. *Wireless Communications*, 14(5):106–112, 2007.

[16] S. Paris, N. Facchi, F. Gringoli, and A. Capone. An innovative rate adaptation algorithm for multicast transmissions in wireless LANs. In *IEEE VTC*, 2013.

[17] Y. Park, Y. Seok, N. Choi, Y. Choi, and J. Bonnin. Rate-adaptive multimedia multicasting over IEEE 802.11 wireless LANs. In *IEEE CCNC*, 2006.

[18] K. Piamrat, A. Ksentini, J. Bonnin, and C. Viho. Q-DRAM: QoE-based dynamic rate adaptation mechanism for multicast in wireless networks. In *IEEE GLOBECOM*, 2009.

[19] M. Quaritsch, E. Stojanovski, C. Bettstetter, G. Friedrich, H. Hellwagner, B. Rinner, M. Hofbaur, and M. Shah. Collaborative microdrones: applications and research challenges. In *ACM Autonomics*, 2008.

[20] P. Salvador, L. Cominardi, F. Gringoli, and P. Serrano. A first implementation and evaluation of the IEEE 802.11 aa group addressed transmission service. *ACM SIGCOMM Computer Communication Review*, 44(1):35–41, 2013.

[21] J. Tourrilhes. Robust broadcast: improving the reliability of broadcast transmissions on CSMA/CA. In *IEEE, PIMRC*, 1998.

[22] J. Vella and S. Zammit. A survey of multicasting over wireless access networks. *IEEE Communications Surveys & Tutorials*, 15(2):718–753, 2013.

[23] H. Zhu, M. Li, I. Chlamtac, and B. Prabhakaran. A survey of quality of service in IEEE 802.11 networks. *Wireless Communications*, 11(4):6–14, 2004.

Scalable Compression of Deep Neural Networks

Xing Wang
Simon Fraser University, BC, Canada
AltumView Systems Inc., BC, Canada
xingw@sfu.ca

Jie Liang
Simon Fraser University, BC, Canada
AltumView Systems Inc., BC, Canada
jiel@sfu.ca

ABSTRACT

Deep neural networks generally involve some layers with millions of parameters, making them difficult to be deployed and updated on devices with limited resources such as mobile phones and other smart embedded systems. In this paper, we propose a scalable representation of the network parameters, so that different applications can select the most suitable bit rate of the network based on their own storage constraints. Moreover, when a device needs to upgrade to a high-rate network, the existing low-rate network can be reused, and only some incremental data are needed to be downloaded. We first hierarchically quantize the weights of a pre-trained deep neural network to enforce weight sharing. Next, we adaptively select the bits assigned to each layer given the total bit budget. After that, we retrain the network to fine-tune the quantized centroids. Experimental results show that our method can achieve scalable compression with graceful degradation in the performance.

CCS Concepts

•**Computing methodologies** → **Neural networks;** *Discrete space search;* •**Information systems** → Clustering and classification;

Keywords

Deep neural network, scalable compression

1. INTRODUCTION

Deep neural networks (DNN) or deep learning have evolved into the state-of-the-art technique for many artificial intelligence tasks including computer vision [9], [14]. In this paper, we focus on the convolutional neural network (CNN), which was originally developed in 1998 by LeCun et al. with less than 1M parameters (weights) to classify handwritten digits [10]. In 2012, CNN was used as a key component in [9] to achieve the breakthrough in ImageNet Large Scale Visual Recognition Challenge 2012 (ILSVRC2012), and the proposed AlexNet has 60M parameters and needs 240MB of storage space. In 2014, Simonyan et al. further improved the accuracy by 10% [14], and the VGG-16 model they developed has 138M parameters.

Although the performance of DNN is very promising, its application in low-end devices such as mobile phones faces some challenges. For example, many devices have limited storage spaces. Therefore storing millions of DNN parameters on these devices could be a problem. If the DNN network needs to be updated, usually via wireless channels, downloading the large amount of network parameters will cause excessive delay. Moreover, running large-scale DNNs with floating-point parameters could consume too much energy and slow down the algorithm. Therefore, efficient compression of the DNN parameters without sacrificing too much the performance becomes an important topic.

There have been some recent works on the compression of neural networks. Vanhoucke et al. [11] proposed a fixed-point implementation with 8-bit integer (vs 32-bit floating-point) activations. Denton et al. [3] exploited the linear structure of the neural network by finding an appropriate low-rank approximation of the parameters and keeping the accuracy within 1% of the original model. Kim et al. [7] applied tensor decomposition to the network parameters and proposed an one-shot whole network compression scheme that can achieve significant reductions in model size, runtime and energy consumption.

Many works focus on binning the network parameters into buckets, and only the values in the bucket need to be stored. HashedNets [2] is a recent technique to reduce model size by using a hash function to randomly group connection weights, so that all connections within the same hash bucket share a single parameter value. Gong et al. [4] compressed deep convnets using vector quantization, which resulted in 1% accuracy loss. Both methods studied the fully-connected (FC) layer in the CNN, but ignored the convolutional (CONV) layers. Recently, Han et al. [5] introduced a deep neural network compression pipeline by combining pruning, quantization and Huffman encoding, which can reduce the storage requirement of neural network by 35 × or 49 × without affecting their accuracy.

In this paper, motivated by the successful applications of scalable coding in various image and video coding standards such as JPEG 2000, H.264, and H.265/HEVC [16, 13, 15], we propose a scalable compression framework for DNNs, which has not been addressed before. Our goal is to represent the DNN parameters in a scalable fashion such that we can easily truncate the representation of the network according

MM '16, October 15-19, 2016, Amsterdam, Netherlands
© 2016 ACM. ISBN 978-1-4503-3603-1/16/10...$15.00
DOI: http://dx.doi.org/10.1145/2964284.2967273

to the storage constraint and still get near-optimal performance at each rate. Moreover, if the network needs to be upgraded with higher rate and better performance, the existing low-rate network can be reused, and only some incremental data are needed. This is better than recompressing and re-transmitting the network as in [5, 7].

To achieve this goal, we propose a three-stage pipeline. First, a hierarchical representation of weights in DNNs is developed. Second, we propose a backward greedy search algorithm to adaptively select the bits assigned to each layer given the total bit budget. Finally, we fine-tune the compressed model.

The rest of the paper is organized as follows. Sec. 2 is devoted to hierarchical quantization of the DNN parameters. In Sec. 3 we formulate the bit allocation as an optimization problem and propose a backward search solution. A fine-tuning method is presented in Sec. 4. Experimental results on MNIST, CIFAR-10 and ImageNet datasets are reported in Sec. 5, followed by conclusions in Sec. 6.

2. HIERARCHICAL QUANTIZATION

The K-means clustering-based quantization is a popular technique in the compression of DNN [4], [5]. Therefore, in this paper, we also choose K-means clustering with linear initialization [5] to compress the weights in DNN. However, the framework developed in this paper is quite general and can also be applied to other quantization techniques, e.g., the fixed-point quantization in [11] and other similar tasks besides classification, e.g., regression problems.

In [5], the authors quantize the weights to enforce weight sharing with K-means clustering, e.g., they assign 8 bits (256 shared weights) to each CONV layer and 5-bits (32 shared weights) to each FC layer. However, every time a CONV layer is assigned a different bit, the K-means clustering has to be performed again, rendering scalable compression infeasible. On the other hand, some DNN layers have a large number of weights, e.g., the number of weights in the fc6 layer of AlexNet is 38M. Therefore the K-means clustering can be quite slow, even with the help of GPU.

To address this problem, we adopt the scalable coding concept in image/video coding [16, 13, 15], and represent the weights hierarchically, i.e., each weight is represented by a base-layer component and several enhancement-layer components; hence, we only need to perform the quantization step once during the entire scalable compression process, which also benefits the adaptive bit allocation in Sec. 3. Note that there are two different kinds of layers in this paper: the network layers in DNN, and the hierarchical quantization layers in the scalable representation of the weights.

Suppose we want to allocate n bits to each weight in a pre-trained DNN layer. We first perform K-means clustering of all weights with $K = 2$ (1-bit quantization), and record the corresponding cluster indices and centroids. We also record the corresponding quantization error. This yields the 1-bit base-layer approximations of all weights. Next, we perform another K-means clustering with $K = 2$ on all quantization errors, and record the corresponding cluster indices, centroids, and quantization errors. The gives us the 1-bit first-enhancement-layer representations of all weights. By repeating this procedure, we can obtain a n-layer hierarchical representation of a weight, i.e.,

$$w \approx b_1 + e_1 + ... + e_{n-1}, \tag{1}$$

where w is a uncompressed weight, b_1 and e_i are the centroid of the base layer and the i-th enhancement layer respectively.

This hierarchical quantization only needs to be performed once, which facilitates future network updating, as we only need to add or delete certain quantization layers to meet the new bit rate constraint. For the tradition K-means clustering used in [4] and [5], we have to perform K-means clustering every time a new bit budget is required.

After the hierarchical quantization, we can build a codebook that stores the centroid and cluster index information of all quantization layers. For a network layer of DNN with N weights, there are $2n$ centroids, and the number of cluster indices is Nn. If each uncompressed weight or centroid is represented by b bits (b=32 for single-precision floating-point number), the compression rate of the n-bit hierarchical quantization scheme is

$$r = \frac{Nb}{Nn + 2nb}. \tag{2}$$

In contrast, in the conventional K-means method [5], given the same n-bit quantization, the compression rate is $r = Nb/(Nn + 2^n b)$.

Note that the storage cost is dominated by Nn, compared to $2nb$ or $2^n b$, because the number of connections N in a DNN is usually very large.

3. ADAPTIVE BIT ALLOCATION

In DNN, the redundancies in different network layers are different [5, 11]. Therefore it is necessary to design an optimal bit allocation algorithm, i.e., given a bit budget, how to allocate the bits to different network layers in order to get the best performance. In this paper, we formulate the following optimization problem.

$$\begin{aligned} &\arg \min_{\{\mathbf{n},\mathbf{C},\mathbf{G}\}} f(\mathbf{n},\mathbf{C},\mathbf{G}) \\ &\text{s.t.} \sum_{i=1}^{L} N_i n_i + 2n_i b \le \mu. \end{aligned} \tag{3}$$

where $\mathbf{n} = \left[\, n_1 \;\; ... \;\; n_L \,\right]$ is a vector containing the bits allocated to L network layers, $\mathbf{C}$ is the centroid vector, $\mathbf{G}$ is the cluster-by-index matrix for the network layers, N_i is the number of weights in the i-th network layer, and μ is the bit budget. We use the cross entropy between the pdf of the predicted labels and true labels as the cost function $f(\cdot)$, which is frequently used in classification tasks.

It is hard to solve the combinatorial optimization in Eq. (3), since the number of bits assigned to each network layer n_i has to be integer and the number of entries in the cluster-by-index matrix $\mathbf{G}$ is $\sum_{i=1}^{L} N_i n_i$, even larger than the number of weights $\sum_{i=1}^{L} N_i$ in the pre-trained DNN. Therefore, we use a similar method to [5] to first approximate the original uncompressed weights with high-rate quantized weights. More specifically, we first use the hierarchical method in Sec. 2 to assign M bits to each CONV layer weight and P bits to each FC layer weight. This is used as the initialization step. The centroid vector $\mathbf{C}$ and the cluster-by-index matrix $\mathbf{G}$ are then determined and fixed. We use E to denote the number of bits to store this initial network.

Next, we adaptively allocate bits to network layers such

that $u < \text{E}$. The problem in Eq. (3) is simplified to

$$\begin{aligned} &\arg\min_{\{\mathbf{n}\}} f(\mathbf{n}) \\ &\text{s.t. } B = \sum_{i=1}^{L} (N_i + 2b) n_i \leq \mu. \end{aligned} \tag{4}$$

For small-scale problems, the optimization above can be solved by exhaustive grid search, where configurations that violate the bit constraint are skipped, and the others are evaluated to find the best solution. The process can be accelerated by parallel computing, since different configurations are independent. However, for large-scale problems, exhaustive search becomes infeasible, as the number of configurations grows exponentially with the number of bits. For example, in AlexNet, there are 5 CONV layers and 3 FC layers. If 10 bits are assigned to each CONV layer and 5 bits are assigned to each FC layer, the total number of configurations would be $10^5 \times 5^3 = 12.5\text{M}$.

One way to speed up the process is to use random search [1], since the number of bits assigned to each network layer can be treated as a hyper-parameter for the DNN. Theoretical analysis in [1] shows that randomly selecting 60 configurations can ensure that the top 5% result can be achieved with a probability of 0.95. For the bit allocation problem here, we should randomly select a number of configurations that satisfy the bit constraint. In Sec. 5, random search is used as a baseline algorithm for comparison.

In this paper, we propose a backward greedy search algorithm to address the bit constraint explicitly and solve the problem in Eq. (4). We start from the initial high-rate quantized network as discussed above. Denote the bit allocation in the t-th iteration as $\mathbf{n}^t = [n_1^t, \ldots, n_L^t]$, whose corresponding total bit cost is B^t. To find $\mathbf{n}^{t+1}$ at iteration $t+1$, we follow the spirit of the gradient descent method by assigning one less bit to each network layer respectively, calculating the corresponding gradient of the total bit cost, and choosing the configuration that has the maximum gradient. In other words, let $\mathbf{n}^{t,j} = [n_1^t, \ldots, n_{j-1}^t, n_j^t - 1, n_{j+1}^t, \ldots, n_L^t]$, the bit allocation in the $(t+1)$-th iteration is obtained by

$$\begin{aligned} &\arg\max_{\mathbf{n}^{t,j}} \tfrac{f(\mathbf{n}^{t,j}) - f(\mathbf{n}^t)}{B^{t,j} - B^t} \\ &\text{s.t. } \mathbf{n}^{t,j} \subset \{\mathbf{n}^{t,1}, \mathbf{n}^{t,2}, \ldots, \mathbf{n}^{t,L}\}, \\ &\quad B^{t,j} = \sum_{i=1}^{L} (N_i + 2b) n_i^{t,j}. \end{aligned} \tag{5}$$

The iteration terminates until the bit constraint is satisfied. The entire backward greedy search algorithm is summarized in Alg. 1. The intuition behind the gradient defined above is twofold. First, if two bit allocations have the same cost function value, the one with smaller total bit cost should be chosen. Second, if two bit allocations have the same total bit cost, we should choose the one with lower cost function value and use the maximum function in Eq. (5) due to $B^{t,j} < B^t$.

Algorithm 1 Backward Greedy Search Algorithm

Initialization: Quantize the network with M bits for each CONV layer and P bits for each FC layer. Let $t = 0$.
while $B^t > \mu$ **do**
  for each network layer $j \leq L$ **do**
    $n_j^{t,j} \leftarrow n_j^t - 1, n_p^{t,j} \leftarrow n_p^t$ for $p \neq j$.
    Update the weights of DNN based on the hierarchical framework in Sec. 2
    Test with the validation data and record $B^{t,j}$ and $f(\mathbf{n}^{t,j})$
  end for
  Select $\mathbf{n}^{t+1}$ based on Eq. (5)
  $t \leftarrow t + 1$
end while

4. FINE TUNING (FT)

It is shown in [5, 11] that fine-tuning (FT) of the centroids after the quantization of DNN can significantly improve the classification performance. In this paper, we also perform fine-tuning after the adaptive bit allocation to update the centroids based on Eq. (3) in [5].

The advantage of the proposed scalable compression of the DNN is that for each target bit rate, we can find a near-optimal bit allocation. If later on the DNN bit rate on a device needs to be updated, instead of re-transmitting a new set of the DNN parameters, we only need to transmit some incremental data, including the centroid vector $\mathbf{C}$ and cluster-by-index matrix $\mathbf{G}$. The required bit rate is thus much lower than replacing the entire network.

During the update, some additional bits caused by the fine-tuning are needed to update the centroids of the previous compressed model. However, according to the analysis in Sec. 2, the centroid update will cost $2b \sum_{i=1}^{L} n_i$ at most, while the minimal bits needed to update the cluster-by-index matrix are $\min\{N_1, N_2, \ldots, N_L\}$. The storage cost is dominated by the cluster indices instead of centroids; hence the overhead introduced by the fine-tuning is negligible. Take AlexNet as an example, if we use 10 bits to quantize CONV layers and 5 bits for FC layers, at most 0.52KB are needed to update these centroids, while we may use at least 5KB to update the cluster-by-index matrix every time a different bit budget is given.

5. EXPERIMENTAL RESULTS

We test the proposed scalable compression on 3 networks designed for the MNIST [10], CIFAR-10 [8] and ImageNet [12] datasets respectively. We implement the network training based on the CNN toolbox MatConvNet [17] with our own modifications. The training is done on a desktop with a NVIDIA TIAN X GPU with 12GB memory.

5.1 LeNet-5 for MNIST

We use the *cnn_mnist_experiment.m* function in MatConvNet to train LeNet-5 for MNIST dataset. There are 2 CONV layers and 2 FC layers. The pre-trained model can achieve 0.88% Top-1 error and needs a storage of 1720KB. We use 8 bits to hierarchically quantize each CONV layer and 5 bits for each FC layer. The initial quantized model can achieve 0.97% Top-1 error, and the corresponding storage cost is 279KB. In Fig. 1(a), we compare the proposed backward greedy search method (BS) with the exhaustive grid search method (GS). We also present the number of configurations tested on the validation set in Table 1 to compare the computational complexity. We can see that our proposed backward search algorithm can achieve comparable compression performance to the grid search with much smaller computational complexity. The only exception happens when the compression rate is extremely large,

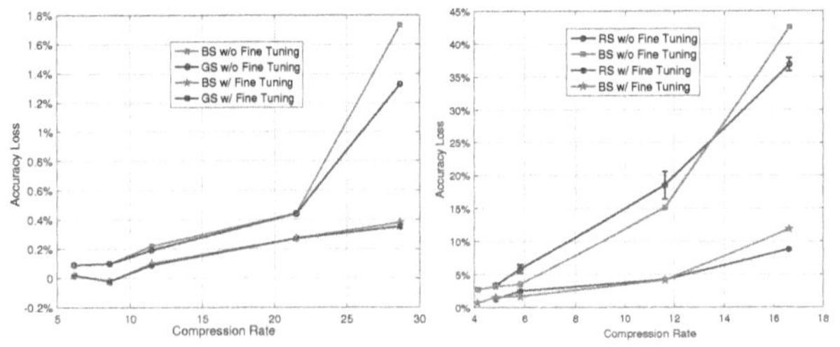

(a) (b)

Figure 1: Top-1 accuracy loss of compressed DNNs under different bit allocation methods. (a) LeNet-5 and (b) CIFAR-10-quick.

LeNet-5 for MNIST				
Bit Budget (KB)	200	150	80	60
Compression Rate	8.60	11.47	21.50	28.67
BS Number	26	51	101	115
GS Number	960	640	320	79
CIFAR-10-quick for CIFAR-10				
Bit Budget (KB)	120	100	50	30
Compression Rate	4.85	5.82	11.64	19.40
BS Number	26	51	101	115
RS Number	120			

Table 1: Number of configurations tested on MNIST and CIFAR-10 validation set v.s. compression rate.

e.g., 28.67 in Fig. 1(a). However, after fine tuning, the performance is still very close to the original one.

5.2 CIFAR-10-quick for CIFAR-10

We use the provided *cnn_cifar.m* in MatConvNet to train CIFAR-10-quick for CIFAR-10 dataset. There are 3 CONV layers and 2 FC layers in the network. The reference model can achieve 19.97% Top-1 error and needs a storage space of 582KB. We use 10 bits to quantize each CONV layer and 5 bits for each FC layer. The initial quantized model can achieve 22.70% Top-1 error and needs 141KB storage space. Since there are at most 25K configurations which takes too much time to evaluate, instead of using grid search as a comparison, we use the random search method (RS) [1]. In each trial, we randomly choose 120 configurations that satisfy the bit constraint from the configuration pool.

The compression performance is shown in Fig. 1(b) and the computational complexity is presented in Table 1. It can be seen that the proposed backward search algorithm can achieve similar or even better performance than random search with much smaller computational complexity, especially when the bit rate is close to that of the initial quantized network. The only exception happens when the compression rate is extremely large, e.g., 20 in Fig. 1(b). For the fine-tuning in the random search method, we fine-tune the result that achieves the median classification accuracy in the 10 trials.

5.3 AlexNet for ILSVRC12

We use the provided *cnn_imagenet.m* to train AlexNet for ILSVRC12. The reference model is slightly different from that of the original AlexNet in [9], where the order of pooling layer and norm layer are swapped. It contains 5 CONV layers and 3 FC layers. This reference model can achieve 41.39% Top-1 error, 18.85% Top-5 error, and needs 240 MB

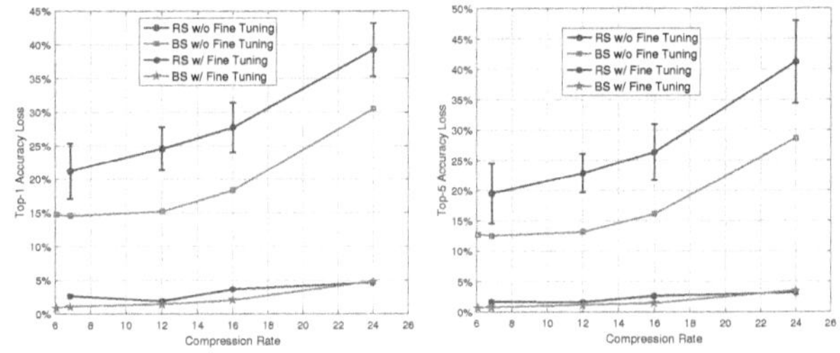

(a) (b)

Figure 2: Accuracy loss of compressed AlexNet v.s. compression rate.

Bit Budget (MB)	35	20	15	10
Compression Rate	6.86	12	16	24
BS Number	25	81	89	126
RS Number	150			

Table 2: Number of configurations tested on ILSVRC12 validation set v.s. compression rate.

to store. We use 10 bits to quantize each CONV layer and 5 bits for each FC layer. This initial quantized model can achieve 56.09% Top-1 error, 31.63% Top-5 error, and needs 39.5 MB to store. The number of configurations in each trial of RS is 150. The number of trials is 5 in order to get 0.95 confidence interval. The result that achieves the median classification accuracy in the 5 trials is fine-tuned.

The compression performance is shown in Fig. 2, and the computational complexity is shown in Table 2. We can see that with much smaller computational complexity, the proposed backward search can achieve better compression performance than random search. Moreover, the classification performance of proposed scalable compression framework drops little when the compression rate is within 10. The compression performance is comparable to state-of-the-art algorithms at fixed rate, e.g., AlexNet is compressed to 47.6 MB with more than 1% Top-1 accuracy loss in [3].

6. CONCLUSIONS AND FUTURE WORK

In this paper, we discuss the scalable compression of deep neural networks, and propose a three-stage pipeline: hierarchical quantization of weights, backward search for bit allocation, and fine-tuning. Its efficacy is tested on three different DNNs. In [5], the authors can compress AlexNet to 6.9 MB without loss of accuracy, much smaller than what is achieved in this paper, due to network pruning is used [6], which removes many small-weight connections from the network. This not only compresses the network, but also reduces the complexity of the implementation. In addition, entropy coding is used in [5]. However, the quantization in [5] is fixed and not scalable. This paper focuses on the scalable quantization and adaptive bit allocation. It is also shown from Fig. 7 in [5] that pruning does not hurt quantization. Therefore the pruning and entropy coding can also be used in our scheme to further improve the performance.

Acknowledgement

This work was supported by by NSERC of Canada under grant RGPIN312262, STPGP447223, and RGPAS478109, and NVIDIA University Partnership Program.

7. REFERENCES

[1] J. Bergstra and Y. Bengio. Random search for hyper-parameter optimization. *J. Mach. Learn. Res.*, 13:281–305, Feb. 2012.

[2] W. Chen, J. Wilson, S. Tyree, K. Q. Weinberger, and Y. Chen. Compressing neural networks with the hashing trick. In *Proceedings of the 32nd International Conference on Machine Learning (ICML-15)*, pages 2285–2294. JMLR Workshop and Conference Proceedings, 2015.

[3] E. L. Denton, W. Zaremba, J. Bruna, Y. Lecun, and R. Fergus. Exploiting linear structure within convolutional networks for efficient evaluation. In *Advances in Neural Information Processing Systems 27*, pages 1269–1277. Curran Associates, Inc., 2014.

[4] Y. Gong, L. Liu, M. Yang, and L. Bourdev. Compressing deep convolutional networks using vector quantization. In *arXiv*, page arXiv:1412.6115, 2014.

[5] S. Han, H. Mao, and W. J. Dally. Deep compression: Compressing deep neural networks with pruning, trained quantization and huffman coding. In *International Conference on Learning Representations (ICLR)*, 2016.

[6] S. Han, J. Pool, J. Tran, and W. Dally. Learning both weights and connections for efficient neural network. In *Advances in Neural Information Processing Systems 28*, pages 1135–1143. 2015.

[7] Y.-D. Kim, E. Park, S. Yoo, T. Choi, L. Yang, and D. Shin. Compression of deep convolutional neural networks for fast and low power mobile applications. In *International Conference on Learning Representations (ICLR)*, 2016.

[8] A. Krizhevsky and G. Hinton. Learning multiple layers of features from tiny images. *Master's thesis, Department of Computer Science, University of Toronto*, 2009.

[9] A. Krizhevsky, I. Sutskever, and G. E. Hinton. Imagenet classification with deep convolutional neural networks. In *NIPS*, pages 1097–1105, 2012.

[10] Y. LeCun, L. Bottou, Y. Bengio, and P. Haffner. Gradient-based learning applied to document recognition. *Proceedings of the IEEE*, 86(11):2278–2324, 1998.

[11] D. D. Lin, S. S. Talathi, and V. S. Annapureddy. Fixed point quantization of deep convolutional networks. In *arXiv*, page arXiv:1511.06393, 2015.

[12] O. Russakovsky, J. Deng, H. Su, J. Krause, S. Satheesh, S. Ma, Z. Huang, A. Karpathy, A. Khosla, M. Bernstein, A. C. Berg, and L. Fei-Fei. ImageNet Large Scale Visual Recognition Challenge. *International Journal of Computer Vision (IJCV)*, 115(3):211–252, 2015.

[13] H. Schwarz, D. Marpe, and T. Wiegand. Overview of the scalable video coding extension of the h.264/avc standard. *IEEE Trans. Circ. Syst. Video Tech.*, 17(9):1103–1120, 2007.

[14] K. Simonyan and A. Zisserman. Very deep convolutional networks for large-scale image recognition. In *arXiv*, page arXiv:1409.1556, 2014.

[15] G. J. Sullivan, J. M. Boyce, Y. Chen, J.-R. Ohm, C. A. Segall, and A. Vetro. Standardized extensions of high efficiency video coding. *IEEE Journal on Selected Topics in Signal Processing*, 7(6):1001–1016, Dec. 2013.

[16] D. Taubman and M. Marcellin. *JPEG 2000: image compression fundamentals, standards, and practice.* Kluwer Academic Publishers, Boston, MA, 2002.

[17] A. Vedaldi and K. Lenc. Matconvnet – convolutional neural networks for matlab. In *Proceeding of the ACM Int. Conf. on Multimedia*, 2015.

UnitBox: An Advanced Object Detection Network

Jiahui Yu[1,2] Yuning Jiang[2] Zhangyang Wang[1] Zhimin Cao[2] Thomas Huang[1]
[1]University of Illinois at Urbana–Champaign
[2]Megvii Inc
{jyu79, zwang119, t-huang1}@illinois.edu, {jyn, czm}@megvii.com

ABSTRACT

In present object detection systems, the deep convolutional neural networks (CNNs) are utilized to predict bounding boxes of object candidates, and have gained performance advantages over the traditional region proposal methods. However, existing deep CNN methods assume the object bounds to be four independent variables, which could be regressed by the ℓ_2 loss separately. Such an oversimplified assumption is contrary to the well-received observation, that those variables are correlated, resulting to less accurate localization. To address the issue, we firstly introduce a novel Intersection over Union (*IoU*) loss function for bounding box prediction, which regresses the four bounds of a predicted box as a whole unit. By taking the advantages of *IoU* loss and deep fully convolutional networks, the UnitBox is introduced, which performs accurate and efficient localization, shows robust to objects of varied shapes and scales, and converges fast. We apply UnitBox on face detection task and achieve the best performance among all published methods on the FDDB benchmark.

Keywords

Object Detection; Bounding Box Prediction; *IoU* Loss

1. INTRODUCTION

Visual object detection could be viewed as the combination of two tasks: object localization (where the object is) and visual recognition (what the object looks like). While the deep convolutional neural networks (CNNs) has witnessed major breakthroughs in visual object recognition [3] [11] [13], the CNN-based object detectors have also achieved the state-of-the-arts results on a wide range of applications, such as face detection [8] [5], pedestrian detection [9] [4] and etc [2] [1] [10].

Currently, most of the CNN-based object detection methods [2] [4] [8] could be summarized as a three-step pipeline: firstly, region proposals are extracted as object candidates from a given image. The popular region proposal methods include Selective Search [12], EdgeBoxes [15], or the early stages of cascade detectors [8]; secondly, the extracted proposals are fed into a deep CNN for recognition and categorization; finally, the bounding box regression technique is employed to refine the coarse proposals into more accurate object bounds. In this pipeline, the region proposal algorithm constitutes a major bottleneck in terms of localization effectiveness, as well as efficiency. On one hand, with only low-level features, the traditional region proposal algorithms are sensitive to the local appearance changes, e.g., partial occlusion, where those algorithms are very likely to fail. On the other hand, a majority of those methods are typically based on image over-segmentation [12] or dense sliding windows [15], which are computationally expensive and have hamper their deployments in the real-time detection systems.

MM '16, October 15-19, 2016, Amsterdam, Netherlands

DOI: http://dx.doi.org/10.1145/2964284.2967274

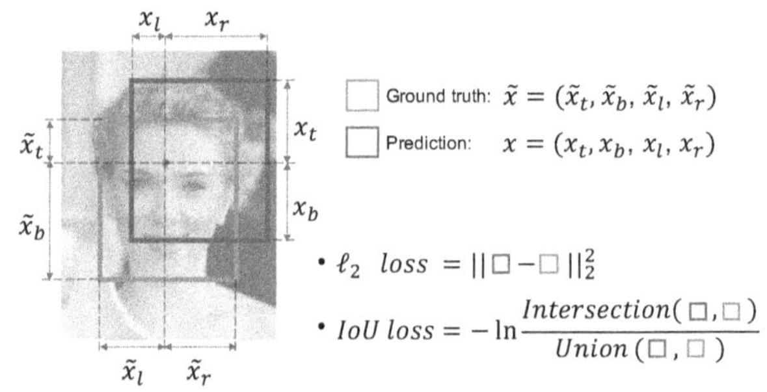

Figure 1: Illustration of *IoU* loss and ℓ_2 loss for pixel-wise bounding box prediction.

To overcome these disadvantages, more recently the deep CNNs are also applied to generate object proposals. In the well-known Faster R-CNN scheme [10], a region proposal network (RPN) is trained to predict the bounding boxes of object candidates from the *anchor* boxes. However, since the scales and aspect ratios of *anchor* boxes are pre-designed and fixed, the RPN shows difficult to handle the object candidates with large shape variations, especially for small objects.

Another successful detection framework, DenseBox [5], utilizes every pixel of the feature map to regress a 4-D distance vector (the distances between the current pixel and the four bounds of object candidate containing it). However, DenseBox optimizes the four-side distances as four independent variables, under the simplistic ℓ_2 loss, as shown in Figure 1. It goes against the intuition that those variables are correlated and should be regressed jointly.

Besides, to balance the bounding boxes with varied scales,

DenseBox requires the training image patches to be resized to a fixed scale. As a consequence, DenseBox has to perform detection on image pyramids, which unavoidably affects the efficiency of the framework.

The paper proposes a highly effective and efficient CNN-based object detection network, called UnitBox. It adopts a fully convolutional network architecture, to predict the object bounds as well as the pixel-wise classification scores on the feature maps directly. Particularly, UnitBox takes advantage of a novel Intersection over Union (*IoU*) loss function for bounding box prediction. The *IoU* loss directly enforces the maximal overlap between the predicted bounding box and the ground truth, and jointly regress all the bound variables as a whole unit (see Figure 1). The UnitBox demonstrates not only more accurate box prediction, but also faster training convergence. It is also notable that thanks to the *IoU* loss, UnitBox is enabled with variable-scale training. It implies the capability to localize objects in arbitrary shapes and scales, and to perform more efficient testing by just one pass on singe scale. We apply UnitBox on face detection task, and achieve the best performance on FDDB [6] among all published methods.

2. IOU LOSS LAYER

Before introducing UnitBox, we firstly present the proposed *IoU* loss layer and compare it with the widely-used ℓ_2 loss in this section. Some important denotations are claimed here: for each pixel (i, j) in an image, the bounding box of ground truth could be defined as a 4-dimensional vector:

$$\widetilde{\boldsymbol{x}}_{i,j} = (\widetilde{x}_{t_{i,j}}, \widetilde{x}_{b_{i,j}}, \widetilde{x}_{l_{i,j}}, \widetilde{x}_{r_{i,j}}), \tag{1}$$

where $\widetilde{x}_t$, $\widetilde{x}_b$, $\widetilde{x}_l$, $\widetilde{x}_r$ represent the distances between current pixel location (i, j) and the top, bottom, left and right bounds of ground truth, respectively. For simplicity, we omit footnote i, j in the rest of this paper. Accordingly, a predicted bounding box is defined as $\boldsymbol{x} = (x_t, x_b, x_l, x_r)$, as shown in Figure 1.

2.1 L2 Loss Layer

ℓ_2 loss is widely used in optimization. In [5] [7], ℓ_2 loss is also employed to regress the object bounding box via CNNs, which could be defined as:

$$\mathcal{L}(x, \widetilde{x}) = \sum_{i \in \{t,b,l,r\}} (x_i - \widetilde{x}_i)^2, \tag{2}$$

where $\mathcal{L}$ is the localization error.

However, there are two major drawbacks of ℓ_2 loss for bounding box prediction. The first is that in the ℓ_2 loss, the coordinates of a bounding box (in the form of x_t, x_b, x_l, x_r) are optimized as four independent variables. This assumption violates the fact that the bounds of an object are highly correlated. It results in a number of failure cases in which one or two bounds of a predicted box are very close to the ground truth but the entire bounding box is unacceptable; furthermore, from Eqn. 2 we can see that, given two pixels, one falls in a larger bounding box while the other falls in a smaller one, the former will have a larger effect on the penalty than the latter, since the ℓ_2 loss is unnormalized. This unbalance results in that the CNNs focus more on larger objects while ignore smaller ones. To handle this, in previous work [5] the CNNs are fed with the fixed-scale image patches in training phase, while applied on image pyramids in testing phase. In this way, the ℓ_2 loss is normalized but the detection efficiency is also affected negatively.

2.2 IoU Loss Layer: Forward

In the following, we present a new loss function, named the *IoU* loss, which perfectly addresses above drawbacks. Given a predicted bounding box $\boldsymbol{x}$ (after ReLU layer, we have $x_t, x_b, x_l, x_r \geq 0$) and the corresponding ground truth $\widetilde{\boldsymbol{x}}$, we calculate the *IoU* loss as follows:

Algorithm 1: *IoU* loss Forward

```
Input: x̃ as bounding box ground truth
Input: x as bounding box prediction
Output: L as localization error
for each pixel (i, j) do
    if x̃ ≠ 0 then
        X = (x_t + x_b) * (x_l + x_r)
        X̃ = (x̃_t + x̃_b) * (x̃_l + x̃_r)
        I_h = min(x_t, x̃_t) + min(x_b, x̃_b)
        I_w = min(x_l, x̃_l) + min(x_r, x̃_r)
        I = I_h * I_w
        U = X + X̃ − I
        IoU = I / U
        L = −ln(IoU)
    else
        L = 0
    end
end
```

In Algorithm 1, $\widetilde{\boldsymbol{x}} \neq \boldsymbol{0}$ represents that the pixel (i, j) falls inside a valid object bounding box; X is area of the predicted box; $\widetilde{X}$ is area of the ground truth box; I_h, I_w are the height and width of the intersection area I, respectively, and U is the union area.

Note that with $0 \leq IoU \leq 1$, $\mathcal{L} = -ln(IoU)$ is essentially a cross-entropy loss with input of *IoU*: we can view *IoU* as a kind of random variable sampled from Bernoulli distribution, with $p(IoU = 1) = 1$, and the cross-entropy loss of the variable *IoU* is $\mathcal{L} = -pln(IoU) - (1-p)ln(1 - IoU) = -ln(IoU)$. Compared to the ℓ_2 loss, we can see that instead of optimizing four coordinates independently, the *IoU* loss considers the bounding box as a unit. Thus the *IoU* loss could provide more accurate bounding box prediction than the ℓ_2 loss. Moreover, the definition naturally norms the *IoU* to $[0, 1]$ regardless of the scales of bounding boxes. The advantage enables UnitBox to be trained with multi-scale objects and tested only on single-scale image.

2.3 IoU Loss Layer: Backward

To deduce the backward algorithm of *IoU* loss, firstly we need to compute the partial derivative of X w.r.t. x, marked as $\nabla_x X$ (for simplicity, we notate x for any of x_t, x_b, x_l, x_r if missing):

$$\frac{\partial X}{\partial x_t (\textbf{or } \partial x_b)} = x_l + x_r, \tag{3}$$

$$\frac{\partial X}{\partial x_l (\textbf{or } \partial x_r)} = x_t + x_b. \tag{4}$$

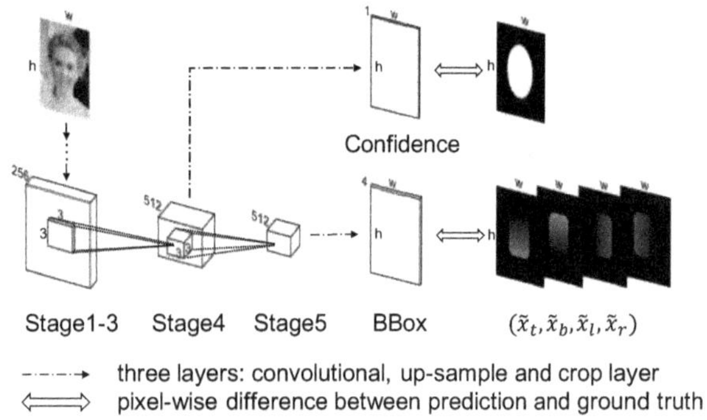

Figure 2: The Architecture of UnitBox Network.

To compute the partial derivative of I w.r.t x, marked as $\nabla_x I$:

$$\frac{\partial I}{\partial x_t(\textbf{or } \partial x_b)} = \begin{cases} I_w, & \text{if } x_t < \widetilde{x}_t(\textbf{or } x_b < \widetilde{x}_b) \\ 0, & \text{otherwise,} \end{cases} \tag{5}$$

$$\frac{\partial I}{\partial x_l(\textbf{or } \partial x_r)} = \begin{cases} I_h, & \text{if } x_l < \widetilde{x}_l(\textbf{or } x_r < \widetilde{x}_r) \\ 0, & \text{otherwise.} \end{cases} \tag{6}$$

Finally we can compute the gradient of localization loss $\mathcal{L}$ w.r.t. x:

$$\begin{aligned} \frac{\partial \mathcal{L}}{\partial x} &= \frac{I(\nabla_x X - \nabla_x I) - U \nabla_x I}{U^2 IoU} \\ &= \frac{1}{U}\nabla_x X - \frac{U+I}{UI}\nabla_x I. \end{aligned} \tag{7}$$

From Eqn. 7, we can have a better understanding of the IoU loss layer: the $\nabla_x X$ is the penalty for the predict bounding box, which is in a positive proportion to the gradient of loss; and the $\nabla_x I$ is the penalty for the intersection area, which is in a negative proportion to the gradient of loss. So overall to minimize the IoU loss, the Eqn. 7 favors the intersection area as large as possible while the predicted box as small as possible. The limiting case is the intersection area equals to the predicted box, meaning a perfect match.

3. UNITBOX NETWORK

Based on the IoU loss layer, we propose a pixel-wise object detection network, named UnitBox. As illustrated in Figure 2, the architecture of UnitBox is derived from VGG-16 model [11], in which we remove the fully connected layers and add two branches of fully convolutional layers to predict the pixel-wise bounding boxes and classification scores, respectively. In training, UnitBox is fed with three inputs in the same size: the original image, the confidence heatmap inferring a pixel falls in a target object (positive) or not (negative), and the bounding box heatmaps inferring the ground truth boxes at all positive pixels.

To predict the confidence, three layers are added layer-by-layer at the end of VGG stage-4: *a convolutional layer* with stride 1, kernel size $512 \times 3 \times 3 \times 1$; *an up-sample layer* which directly performs linear interpolation to resize the feature map to original image size; *a crop layer* to align the feature map with the input image. After that, we obtain a 1-channel feature map with the same size of input image, on which we use the sigmoid cross-entropy loss to regress the generated confidence heatmap; in the other branch, to predict the bounding box heatmaps we use the similar three stacked layers at the end of VGG stage-5 with convolutional kernel size 512 x 3 x 3 x 4. Additionally, we insert a ReLU layer to make bounding box prediction non-negative. The predicted bounds are jointly optimized with IoU loss proposed in Section 2. The final loss is calculated as the weighted average over the losses of the two branches.

Some explanations about the architecture design of UnitBox are listed as follows: 1) in UnitBox, we concatenate the confidence branch at the end of VGG stage-4 while the bounding box branch is inserted at the end of stage-5. The reason is that to regress the bounding box as a unit, the bounding box branch needs a larger receptive field than the confidence branch. And intuitively, the bounding boxes of objects could be predicted from the confidence heatmap. In this way, the bounding box branch could be regarded as a bottom-up strategy, abstracting the bounding boxes from the confidence heatmap; 2) to keep UnitBox efficient, we add as few extra layers as possible. Compared to DenseBox [5] in which three convolutional layers are inserted for bounding box prediction, the UnitBox only uses one convolutional layer. As a result, the UnitBox could process more than 10 images per second, while DenseBox needs several seconds to process one image; 3) though in Figure 2 the bounding box branch and the confidence branch share some earlier layers, they could be trained separately with unshared weights to further improve the effectiveness.

With the heatmaps of confidence and bounding box, we can now accurately localize the objects. Taking the face detection for example, to generate bounding boxes of faces, firstly we fit the faces by ellipses on the thresholded confidence heatmaps. Since the face ellipses are too coarse to localize objects, we further select the center pixels of these coarse face ellipses and extract the corresponding bounding boxes from these selected pixels. Despite its simplicity, the localization strategy shows the ability to provide bounding boxes of faces with high accuracy, as shown in Figure 3.

4. EXPERIMENTS

In this section, we apply the proposed IoU loss as well as the UnitBox on face detection task, and report our experimental results on the FDDB benchmark [6]. The weights of UnitBox are initialized from a VGG-16 model pre-trained on ImageNet, and then fine-tuned on the public face dataset WiderFace [14]. We use mini-batch SGD in fine-tuning and set the batch size to 10. Following the settings in [5], the momentum and the weight decay factor are set to 0.9 and 0.0002, respectively. The learning rate is set to 10^{-8} which is the maximum trainable value. No data augmentation is used during fine-tuning.

4.1 Effectiveness of IoU Loss

First of all we study the effectiveness of the proposed IoU loss. To train a UnitBox with ℓ_2 loss, we simply replace the IoU loss layer with the ℓ_2 loss layer in Figure 2, and reduce the learning rate to 10^{-13} (since ℓ_2 loss is generally much larger, 10^{-13} is the maximum trainable value), keeping the other parameters and network architecture unchanged. Figure 4(a) compares the convergences of the two losses, in which the X-axis represents the number of iterations and the Y-axis represents the detection miss rate. As we can see, the model with IoU loss converges more quickly and steadily than the one with ℓ_2 loss. Besides, the UnitBox has

Figure 3: Examples of detection results of UnitBox on FDDB.

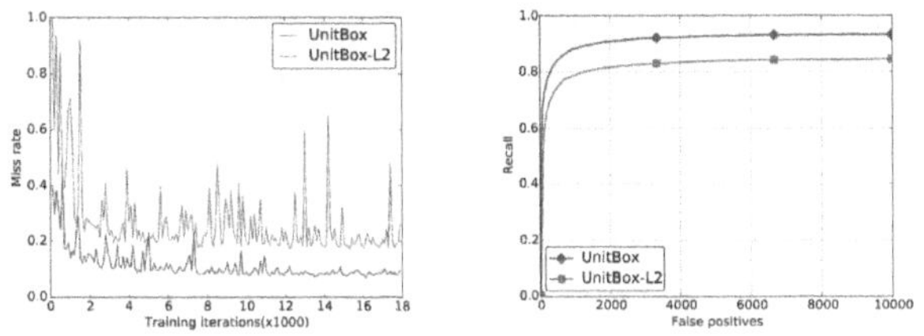

(a) Convergence (b) ROC Curves

Figure 4: Comparison: IoU vs. ℓ_2.

a much lower miss rate than the UnitBox-ℓ_2 throughout the fine-tuning process.

In Figure 4(b), we pick the best models of UnitBox ($\sim$ 16k iterations) and UnitBox-ℓ_2 ($\sim$ 29k iterations), and compare their ROC curves. Though with fewer iterations, the UnitBox with IoU loss still significantly outperforms the one with ℓ_2 loss.

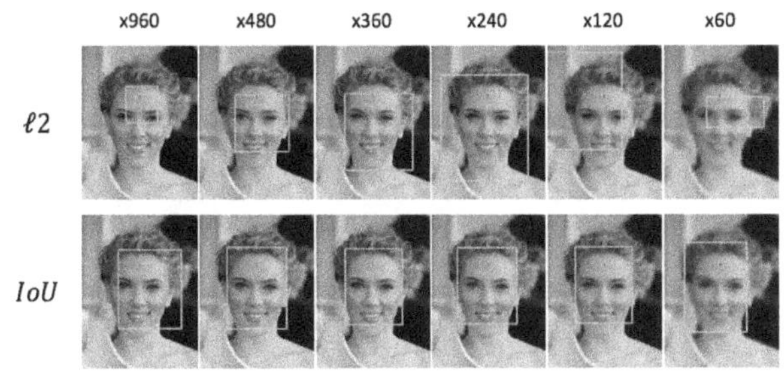

Figure 5: Compared to ℓ_2 loss, the IoU loss is much more robust to scale variations for bounding box prediction.

Moreover, we study the robustness of IoU loss and ℓ_2 loss to the scale variation. As shown in Figure 5, we resize the testing images from 60 to 960 pixels, and apply UnitBox and UnitBox-ℓ_2 on the image pyramids. Given a pixel at the same position (denoted as the red dot), the bounding boxes predicted at this pixel are drawn. From the result we can see that 1) as discussed in Section 2.1, the ℓ_2 loss could hardly handle the objects in varied scales while the IoU loss works well; 2) without joint optimization, the ℓ_2 loss may regress one or two bounds accurately, e.g., the up bound in this case, but could not provide satisfied entire bounding box prediction; 3) in the x960 testing image, the face size is even larger than the receptive fields of the neurons in UnitBox (around 200 pixels). Surprisingly, the UnitBox can still give a reasonable bounding box in the extreme cases while the UnitBox-ℓ_2 totally fails.

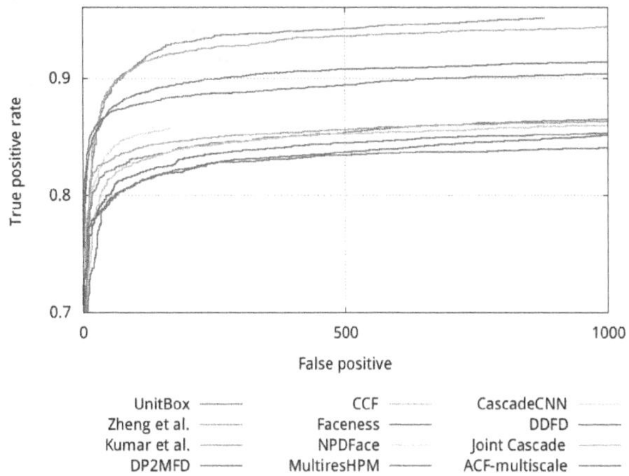

Figure 6: The Performance of UnitBox comparing with state-of-the-arts Methods on FDDB.

4.2 Performance of UnitBox

To demonstrate the effectiveness of the proposed method, we compare the UnitBox with the state-of-the-arts methods on FDDB. As illustrated in Section 3, here we train an unshared UnitBox detector to further improve the detection performance. The ROC curves are shown in Figure 6. As a result, the proposed UnitBox has achieved the best detection result on FDDB among all published methods.

Except that, the efficiency of UnitBox is also remarkable. Compared to the DenseBox [5] which needs seconds to process one image, the UnitBox could run at about 12 fps on images in VGA size. The advantage in efficiency makes UnitBox potential to be deployed in real-time detection systems.

5. CONCLUSIONS

The paper presents a novel loss, i.e., the IoU loss, for bounding box prediction. Compared to the ℓ_2 loss used in previous work, the IoU loss layer regresses the bounding box of an object candidate as a whole unit, rather than four independent variables, leading to not only faster convergence but also more accurate object localization. Based on the IoU loss, we further propose an advanced object detection network, i.e., the UnitBox, which is applied on the face detection task and achieves the state-of-the-art performance. We believe that the IoU loss layer as well as the UnitBox will be of great value to other object localization and detection tasks.

6. REFERENCES

[1] V. Belagiannis, X. Wang, H. Beny Ben Shitrit, K. Hashimoto, R. Stauder, Y. Aoki, M. Kranzfelder, A. Schneider, P. Fua, S. Ilic, H. Feussner, and N. Navab. Parsing human skeletons in an operating room. *Machine Vision and Applications*, 2016.

[2] R. Girshick, J. Donahue, T. Darrell, and J. Malik. Rich feature hierarchies for accurate object detection and semantic segmentation. In *Computer Vision and Pattern Recognition*, 2014.

[3] K. He, X. Zhang, S. Ren, and J. Sun. Deep Residual Learning for Image Recognition. *ArXiv e-prints*, Dec. 2015.

[4] J. Hosang, M. Omran, R. Benenson, and B. Schiele. Taking a deeper look at pedestrians. In *Proceedings of the IEEE Conference on Computer Vision and Pattern Recognition*, pages 4073–4082, 2015.

[5] L. Huang, Y. Yang, Y. Deng, and Y. Yu. DenseBox: Unifying Landmark Localization with End to End Object Detection. *ArXiv e-prints*, Sept. 2015.

[6] V. Jain and E. Learned-Miller. Fddb: A benchmark for face detection in unconstrained settings. Technical Report UM-CS-2010-009, University of Massachusetts, Amherst, 2010.

[7] Z. Jie, X. Liang, J. Feng, W. F. Lu, E. H. F. Tay, and S. Yan. Scale-aware Pixel-wise Object Proposal Networks. *ArXiv e-prints*, Jan. 2016.

[8] H. Li, Z. Lin, X. Shen, J. Brandt, and G. Hua. A convolutional neural network cascade for face detection. In *Proceedings of the IEEE Conference on Computer Vision and Pattern Recognition*, pages 5325–5334, 2015.

[9] J. Li, X. Liang, S. Shen, T. Xu, and S. Yan. Scale-aware Fast R-CNN for Pedestrian Detection. *ArXiv e-prints*, Oct. 2015.

[10] S. Ren, K. He, R. Girshick, and J. Sun. Faster R-CNN: Towards real-time object detection with region proposal networks. In *Advances in Neural Information Processing Systems (NIPS)*, 2015.

[11] K. Simonyan and A. Zisserman. Very Deep Convolutional Networks for Large-Scale Image Recognition. *ArXiv e-prints*, Sept. 2014.

[12] J. R. R. Uijlings, K. E. A. van de Sande, T. Gevers, and A. W. M. Smeulders. Selective search for object recognition. *International Journal of Computer Vision*, 104(2):154–171, 2013.

[13] Z. Wang, S. Chang, Y. Yang, D. Liu, and T. S. Huang. Studying very low resolution recognition using deep networks. *CoRR*, abs/1601.04153, 2016.

[14] S. Yang, P. Luo, C. C. Loy, and X. Tang. Wider face: A face detection benchmark. In *IEEE Conference on Computer Vision and Pattern Recognition (CVPR)*, 2016.

[15] C. L. Zitnick and P. Dollár. Edge boxes: Locating object proposals from edges. In *ECCV*. European Conference on Computer Vision, September 2014.

Alone versus In-a-group: A Comparative Analysis of Facial Affect Recognition

Wenxuan Mou
Queen Mary
University of London, UK
w.mou@qmul.ac.uk

Hatice Gunes
University of Cambridge
Cambridge, UK
hatice.gunes@cl.cam.ac.uk

Ioannis Patras
Queen Mary
University of London, UK
i.patras@qmul.ac.uk

ABSTRACT

Automatic affect analysis and understanding has become a well established research area in the last two decades. Recent works have started moving from individual to group scenarios. However, little attention has been paid to comparing the affect expressed in individual and group settings. This paper presents a framework to investigate the differences in affect recognition models along arousal and valence dimensions in individual and group settings. We analyse how a model trained on data collected from an individual setting performs on test data collected from a group setting, and *vice versa*. A third model combining data from both individual and group settings is also investigated. A set of experiments is conducted to predict the affective states along both arousal and valence dimensions on two newly collected databases that contain sixteen participants watching affective movie stimuli in individual and group settings, respectively. The experimental results show that (1) the affect model trained with group data performs better on individual test data than the model trained with individual data tested on group data, indicating that facial behaviours expressed in a group setting capture more variation than in an individual setting; and (2) the combined model does not show better performance than the affect model trained with a specific type of data (i.e., individual or group), but proves a good compromise. These results indicate that in settings where multiple affect models trained with different types of data are not available, using the affect model trained with group data is a viable solution.

Keywords

Affect recognition; arousal and valence recognition; individual affect recognition; group settings

1. INTRODUCTION

Automatic affect analysis has attracted increasing attention and has seen much progress in recent years [5, 6, 11, 17, 13]. Recent works in affective content analysis and affect recognition fields have started focusing on the analysis of naturalistic affect displayed and collected in more diverse and complex scenarios, such as dyadic interactions [1] and a group of people in a scene or involved in an interaction [8, 4]. Human behaviours are largely dependent on social context [7, 16]. Specifically, the way humans behave alone is different from the way humans behave in a group setting. Consequently, we hypothesize that being alone versus being in-a-group setting will affect the performance and the effectiveness of the automatic analysers that heavily depend on the type of data utilised for training.

Pioneering works in this direction have recently emerged in disengagement analysis. In [7], the individual disengagement was studied in different types of settings (i.e., individual vs. group human-robot interactions). However, little attention has been paid to these diverse settings in the affective computing community.

In this paper, we introduce a framework to analyse individual affect using both individual and group videos. We analyse the affective states along both arousal and valence dimensions by training and testing three different models. To achieve this, we trained different affect models using two different datasets, i.e., individual and group. Individual dataset refers to data collected from one participant watching affective movie stimuli, while group dataset refers to data collected from a group of participants watching affective movie stimuli together. Using these datasets we trained three affect recognition models: one model is trained with individual data only, i.e., *Individual Model*; one model is trained with group data only, i.e., *Group Model*; and another model is trained using both individual and group data, i.e., *Combined Model*. Our analysis shows that (1) although the model trained with a specific type of data shows the best testing performance within the corresponding data, *Group Model* can perform better with individual data than the other way around; and (2) *Combined Model* provides a good compromise between the *Individual Model* and *Group Model*.

The rest of the paper is organized as follows: the proposed framework is illustrated in Section 2; the experiments and results are presented and discussed in Section 3; and conclusions and future work are described in Section 4.

2. THE PROPOSED FRAMEWORK

We propose a framework for the prediction of individual valence and arousal in both individual and group videos by using spatio-temporal facial features. The proposed framework is illustrated in Fig. 1. Our goal is to investigate

MM'16 October 15–19, 2016, Amsterdam, The Netherlands

DOI: http://dx.doi.org/10.1145/2964284.2967276

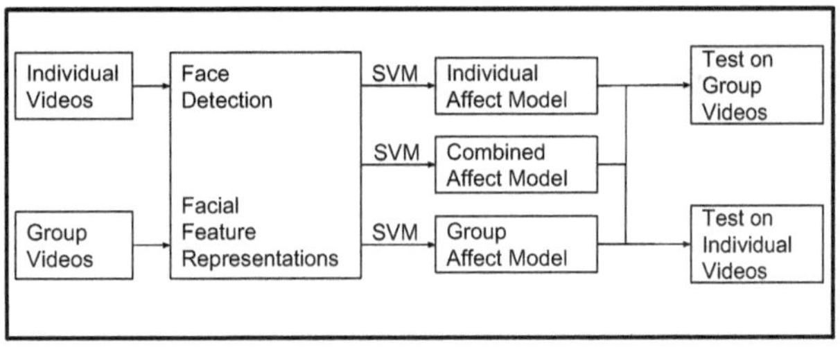

Figure 1: Illustration of the proposed framework.

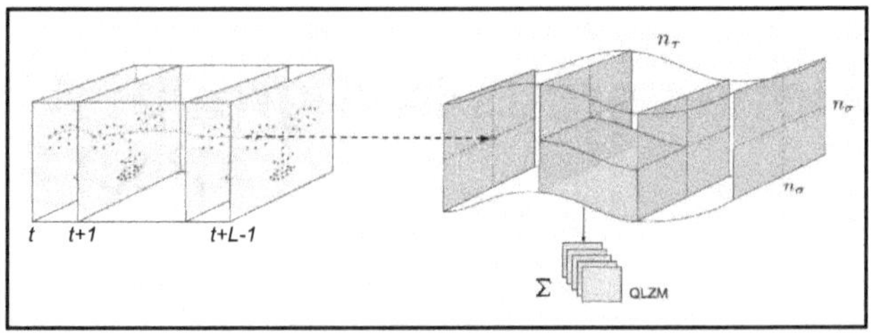

Figure 2: Illustration of the vQLZM feature extraction process. Left: Facial landmark points are detected. Facial landmark point tracking is in the spatial scale over L frames. Right: Appearance and motion information over a local neighbourhood of $N \times N$ pixels along each facial landmark point are extracted, where $N = 24$. In order to embed the structure information, the local volume is subdivided into a spatio-temporal grid of size $n_\tau \times n_\sigma$. Based on [14], parameters are set to $n_\tau = 3$, $n_\sigma = 2$ and $L = 15$.

whether and how affect recognition differs when training a model using the expressive data of individuals when they are alone versus when they are in a group setting. More specifically, how do the data for the same individual acquired in different settings influence affect recognition? Is it possible to obtain a similar performance on group data using a model trained with individual data and *vice versa*? To this end, we train three different classification models, including one model trained with data from the individual dataset (i.e., *Individual Model*), one model trained with data from the group dataset (i.e., *Group Model*) and a third model trained with data from both the individual and the group datasets (i.e., *Combined Model*). When training the different models, we use the same feature representation, i.e., facial spatio-temporal representations. We carry out multiple experiments to investigate the performance of different models on different types of data.

2.1 Facial Feature Extraction

Intraface [15] is used to detect all faces in the videos and 49 facial points are obtained for each face. Due to illumination and head pose variations in such a naturalistic scenario, it is difficult to detect all faces. As a result, manual inpsection showed that 99% faces were detected in the individual database, while 96% of faces were detected in the group database.

In our previous work [9] showed that Volume Quantised Local Zernike Moments (*vQLZM*) facial representation outperformed other facial and body representations. Therefore, in this work, we use *vQLZM* for facial representation. After faces are detected, Quantised Local Zernike Moments (QLZM) [12] are obtained from the local patch around each facial landmark point as the appearance representation. QLZM is used as a low-level representation that is extracted by first calculating local Zernike Moments (ZMs) in the neighbourhood of each pixel of the input image. Then the accumulated local features are converted into position dependent histograms. Each ZM coefficient describes the texture variation at a unique scale and orientation. Once the ZMs are computed for all pixels, the QLZM descriptors are obtained by quantising all ZM coefficients around a pixel into a single integer. The QLZM [12], by design, takes into account only static spatial information, that is, it is designed for static images/frames [12]. In this paper, we used the extended volume representation to embed both appearance and temporal information as illustrated in Fig. 2. More details about *vQLZM* representation can be found in [9].

2.2 Fisher Vector Encoding

Fisher Vector (FV) encoding [10] has been widely used in computer vision problems such as action recognition [14] and depression analysis [3]. It encodes both the first and the second order statistics between the low-level (local) video/image descriptors and a Gaussian Mixture Model (GMM). To reduce the dimensionality, Principal Component Analysis (PC-A) is first applied to the descriptors. A GMM is then fitted to the extracted descriptors, *vQLZM*. The number of Gaussians is set to $K = 256$ and a subset of 256000 descriptors is randomly sampled to fit a GMM. Subsequently, each clip is represented by a $(2D + 1)K$ dimensional Fisher Vector, where D is the dimensionality of the descriptor after performing PCA. In this way, we obtained Fisher Vectors from *vQLZM* (*vQLZM-FV*).

3. DATASETS AND EXPERIMENTS

3.1 Data Collection and Annotation

Two datasets were collected and annotated, namely the individual dataset and the group dataset. Sixteen participants (8 females and 8 males), aged between 25 and 38 were recorded while watching affective movies. Each participant was recorded in both individual and group settings. In order to avoid familiarity with the stimuli, they watched different movies in these two settings. For the individual dataset, each participant watched sixteen short movies separately. For the group dataset, the participants were arranged into four groups with four participants in each group, watching four long videos together. The setup for these two settings is shown in Fig. 3.

Independent observer annotations were obtained from external human labellers who are all researchers working on affect analysis. An in-house emotion annotation tool, that requires the labellers to scroll a bar between a range of values (0 and 1), was used. Individual (short) videos were divided into 10-second clips. All clips were annotated except the first and last 10s of each video. For the group (long) videos, 10-second clips were annotated for every 2 minutes starting from the first minute, e.g., the interval for 00:50~1:00

(a) Individual

(b) Group

Figure 3: The setup for individual and group data acquisition. In individual settings, each participant watched the movie stimuli alone, while in group settings, a group of four participants watched the movie stimuli together.

Table 1: The distribution of samples for individual and group videos along both arousal and valence dimensions after quantisation.

Dimensions	Arousal		Valence	
Labels	High	Low	Positive	Negative
Group Data	197	379	171	405
Individual Data	326	937	438	825

min, 2:50∼3:00 min etc. Each labeller was presented with that 10-second clip of each participant separately and was asked to observe the non-verbal behaviors without hearing any audio. A single annotation was given by each labeller after watching one 10-second clip. In order to avoid confusion, arousal and valence annotations were obtained separately. The average of annotations from all labellers was calculated and used as thresholds (i.e., 0.5 for both arousal and valence in individual dataset, and 0.4 for arousal and 0.5 for valence in group dataset) to quantize the arousal and valence annotations into two classes – *high* and *low* arousal and *positive* and *negative* valence. The distribution of samples for individual and group videos along both arousal and valence dimensions after quantisation is shown in Table 1. Annotations from three labellers were obtained for group videos, but annotations from only one labeller were available for the individual videos. Details of the annotation and the inter-labeller agreement can be found in [9].

3.2 Experiments

Experimental setup. For the individual setup, data from 16 participants with 14 recordings were used providing us a total number of 1263 clips. For the group setup, data from the same 16 participants (4 groups) were used as follows: 3 groups (12 participants) with 4 recordings and 1 group (4 participants) with 2 recordings. As a result, there were data from 16 participants and 14 sessions in total. During each session, each group watched one movie. From each session, we used 10-second clips extracted every 2 minutes in line with the annotations obtained. The total number of samples from all subjects used in the experiments was 576.

Classifier. As we aim to investigate the effects of different settings (i.e., individual and group) in automatic recognition of affect rather than focus on improving recognition accuracy by testing with different feature representations and different machine learning techniques, we conducted experiments using the same classification technique and the same facial representation. We used Support Vector Machines (SVMs) and the LibSVM library [2], widely used in affect analysis [18, 5].

Evaluation. To evaluate the models, we used *leave-one-subject-out* cross-validation and *subject-specific* validation. Each time the parameters of the classifier were optimized over the training-validation samples. *Leave-one-subject-out* refers to, in each fold, using 15 participants for training-validation and the remaining one participant for testing. *Subject-specific* model was built by applying *leave-one-sample-out* cross-validation for each participant separately. Affect classification was evaluated in terms of average of $F1$ score across all samples (average of $F1$ score for both classes).

Experiments. Linear-SVM was used for classification with respect to the dimensions of arousal (i.e., high and low) and valence (i.e., positive and negative). Prior to feeding the facial features to the classifier, PCA was first applied to reduce the dimensionality. In each case, we trained two binary linear-SVM classifiers, one using the individual dataset and the other one using the group dataset, which we refer to as *Individual Model* and *Group Model* respectively. We also tested the *Individual Model* on the group data and the *Group Model* on the individual data. Specifically, for *leave-one-subject-out* cross validation, we trained the model with group data from 15 participants, and tested with individual data from the remaining one participant, and *vice versa.* For *subject-specific* validation, we trained the model with group data from each participant, and then tested it with individual data from the same participant, and *vice versa.* In addition, we also trained a third model with data from both group and individual settings using *leave-one-subject-out* cross-validation. As the goal is to recognize the affect of each individual separately, the group model does not include any features/information of the other group members. In this way, we can have a fairer comparison between individual and group models, and can avoid some cases in which information of the other participants in the same group is lost due to occlusions or other challenging conditions.

3.3 Results and Analysis

The classification results of the *Individual Model* (M_I) and *Group Model* (M_G) are shown in Table 2. We can see that overall, *vQLZM-FV* proves to be a good representation for classifying affect along arousal and valence dimensions in both individual and group settings.

On one hand, for both *leave-one-subject-out* and *subject-specific* setups, we can see that the M_I shows slightly better performance than the M_G when classifying the data collected from the same type of settings. For instance, the recognition results are 0.78 for arousal and 0.80 for valence in terms of $F1$ score obtained with the M_I in *subject-specific* setup, while those obtained with the M_G are 0.74 for arousal and 0.78 for valence. On the other hand, M_G shows an advantage in dealing with data collected from different types of settings (i.e., individual data). For example, arousal recognition results obtained on group test data with the M_I with *leave-one-subject-out* cross-validation is $F1$=0.51, while on individual test data with M_G the result obtained is $F1$=0.58.

In light of these findings we further hypothesise that the *Group Model* tested with individual data (M_{GI}) performs better than the *Individual Model* tested with group data (M_{IG}), and perform t-test to see the statistical significance

Table 2: **Classification results obtained with *Individual Model* and *Group Model* on both individual and group datasets in terms of $F1$ score in *leave-one-subject-out cross-validation* and *subject-specific* setups**

Models	Individual Model			
Test Data	**Individual Data**		**Group Data**	
Dimensions	Arousal	Valence	Arousal	Valence
Sub-specific	0.78	0.80	0.50	0.58
One-sub-out	0.63	0.68	0.51	0.53
Models	**Group Model**			
Test Data	**Individual Data**		**Group Data**	
Dimensions	Arousal	Valence	Arousal	Valence
Sub-specific	0.54	0.58	0.74	0.78
One-sub-out	0.58	0.57	0.61	0.70

Table 3: Classification results obtained with M_{GI} and M_{IG} in terms of $F1$ score for 10 sets of randomly sampled balanced data in *leave-one-subject-out cross-validation* and *subject-specific* setups. (3rd column) p-value obtained for comparisons between M_{GI} / M_{IG} and chance level (0.5); (last column) p-value obtained for each pair of M_{GI} / M_{IG} comparisons.

Arousal	**One-subject-out**										**mean**	**p-value**
M_{GI}	0.57	0.53	0.61	0.55	0.54	0.54	0.51	0.53	0.55	0.57	0.55(p<0.05)	<0.05
M_{IG}	0.46	0.56	0.49	0.48	0.49	0.44	0.44	0.54	0.55	0.35	0.49(p=0.3)	
Valence												
M_{GI}	0.63	0.56	0.58	0.59	0.57	0.58	0.52	0.60	0.59	0.59	0.58(p<0.05)	<0.05
M_{IG}	0.51	0.37	0.56	0.50	0.45	0.38	0.53	0.38	0.60	0.61	0.49(p=0.7)	
Arousal	**Subject-specific**											
M_{GI}	0.54	0.55	0.58	0.57	0.54	0.53	0.53	0.54	0.52	0.57	0.55(p<0.05)	<0.05
M_{IG}	0.49	0.54	0.51	0.46	0.50	0.48	0.53	0.47	0.46	0.56	0.50(p=1)	
Valence												
M_{GI}	0.59	0.57	0.53	0.54	0.59	0.54	0.52	0.52	0.60	0.54	0.55(p<0.05)	<0.05
M_{IG}	0.51	0.37	0.56	0.50	0.45	0.38	0.53	0.38	0.60	0.61	0.49(p=0.7)	

of these results. We randomly sample the data to make it balanced between individual and group data as well as between the two classes along each dimension. Based on the data we have, each time we randomly select 171 samples for high and low arousal and 197 samples for positive and negative valence for both individual and group data. Then we train the M_{GI} model with randomly selected group data and test it with individual data, and vice versa for M_{IG}, for ten times. We perform (1) two-sample right-tail t-test for each pair of M_{GI} set and M_{IG} set to see whether M_{GI} is significantly better than M_{IG} and (2) one-sample t-test for each M_{GI} set and M_{IG} set to see whether they are significantly different from chance level, i.e., 0.5. The results presented in Table 3 confirm that our hypothesis is indeed correct. M_{GI} is significantly better than M_{IG} and M_{GI} performs significantly different from chance level, while M_{IG} does not. A possible explanation is that although group settings are relatively more complex and challenging, the group model ends up modelling a larger variety of affective behaviors. In group settings, each participant behaves in a multitude of ways, they might behave similarly to when they are recorded alone, or they might end up talking to others expressing their opinions.

The *Combined Model* (M_C) is trained with both individual and group datasets. The classification results obtained with the M_C are shown in Table 4. We can see that the M_C shows better performance than the M_I (M_G) tested with group data (individual data), but not as good as theM_G (M_I) tested with group data (individual data). Note that,

Table 4: Classification results of the combined model on both individual and group datasets in terms of $F1$ score using *leave-one-subject-out* cross-validation

Models	Combined Model			
Test Data	**Individual Data**		**Group Data**	
Dimensions	Arousal	Valence	Arousal	Valence
One-sub-out	0.59	0.68	0.59	0.61

the M_C is trained with all data from both individual and group datasets, only excluding the participant used as the test data at each round. Therefore, it is trained with more data than both the M_I and the M_G. However, more training data does not always provide a better model. A possible explanation is that the M_C has to make a compromise when modelling different types of data simultaneously, which results in decreased performance when compared to the M_I and the M_G tested on the same type of data.

4. CONCLUSION AND FUTURE WORK

In this paper, we proposed a framework to investigate the effects of affect expressed in different settings (alone vs. in-a-group) on the automatic recognition performance. We conducted a set of experiments on two newly collected datasets. We trained three different SVM-based recognition models using different types of affect data, namely one model trained with data from one participant watching movie stimuli alone (i.e., *Individual Model*), one model trained with data from a group of four participants watching movie stimuli together (i.e., *Group Model*) and another model with the combined dataset (i.e., *Combined Model*).

The experimental results show that the best performance can be achieved by using data from the same type of setting (i.e., individual or group) than using data from different settings for training and testing. The best solution would be to provide multiple affect models trained with different types of data and settings. However, our experimental results also show that a model trained with group data is more generic than a model trained with individual data. Specifically, a model trained with group data has a better performance on individual data than vice versa. Similar results are also reported for the analysis of disengagement in human-robot interaction settings [7]. Our results indicate that in settings where multiple affect models trained with different types of data are not available, using the affect model trained with group data is a viable solution.

Although the experiments reported in this paper have been conducted in an audience context (i.e., participants watching movie stimuli), the proposed feature representation and classification methods can be applied to other types of settings, including human-robot interactions. Despite the promising results obtained, the impact of unbalanced data and feature representation needs to be investigated further by utilising a larger balanced dataset and other feature representations including audio and physiological signals.

Acknowledgements

The work of Wenxuan Mou is supported by CSC/Queen Mary joint PhD scholarship. The work of Hatice Gunes and Wenxuan Mou is partially funded by the EPSRC under its IDEAS Factory Sandpits call on Digital Personhood (grant ref: EP/L00416X/1).

5. REFERENCES

[1] C. Busso, M. Bulut, C.-C. Lee, A. Kazemzadeh, E. Mower, S. Kim, J. N. Chang, S. Lee, and S. S. Narayanan. Iemocap: Interactive emotional dyadic motion capture database. *Language Resources and Evaluation*, 2008.

[2] C.-C. Chang and C.-J. Lin. LIBSVM: A library for support vector machines. *ACM Trans. on Intelligent Systems and Technology*, 2011.

[3] A. Dhall and R. Goecke. A temporally piece-wise fisher vector approach for depression analysis. In *Proc. of Int. Conf. on Affective Computing and Intelligent Interaction (ACII)*, 2015.

[4] A. Dhall, R. Goecke, and T. Gedeon. Automatic group happiness intensity analysis. *IEEE Trans. on Affective Computing*, 2015.

[5] H. Gunes and B. Schuller. Categorical and dimensional affect analysis in continuous input: Current trends and future directions. *Image and Vision Computing*, 2013.

[6] S. Koelstra and I. Patras. Fusion of facial expressions and eeg for implicit affective tagging. *Image and Vision Computing*, 2013.

[7] I. Leite, M. McCoy, D. Ullman, N. Salomons, and B. Scassellati. Comparing models of disengagement in individual and group interactions. In *Proc. of ACM/IEEE Int. Conf. on Human-Robot Interaction*, 2015.

[8] W. Mou, O. Celiktutan, and H. Gunes. Group-level arousal and valence recognition in static images: Face, body and context. In *Proc. of IEEE Int. Conf. on Automatic Face and Gesture Recognition and Workshops (FG)*, 2015.

[9] W. Mou, H. Gunes, and I. Patras. Automatic recognition of emotions and membership in group videos. In *Proc. of IEEE Conf. on Computer Vision and Pattern Recognition and Workshops (CVPRW)*, 2016.

[10] J. Sánchez, F. Perronnin, T. Mensink, and J. Verbeek. Image classification with the fisher vector: Theory and practice. *International Journal of Computer Vision*, 2013.

[11] E. Sariyanidi, H. Gunes, and A. Cavallaro. Automatic analysis of facial affect: A survey of registration, representation, and recognition. *IEEE Trans. on Pattern Analysis and Machine Intelligence*, 2015.

[12] E. Sariyanidi, H. Gunes, M. Gökmen, and A. Cavallaro. Local Zernike Moment representation for facial affect recognition. In *Proc. of Brithish Machine and Vision Conference (BMVC)*, 2013.

[13] M. Soleymani, S. Koelstra, I. Patras, and T. Pun. Continuous emotion detection in response to music videos. In *Proc. of IEEE Conf. on Automatic Face and Gesture Recognition and Workshops (FG)*, 2011.

[14] H. Wang, A. Kläser, C. Schmid, and C.-L. Liu. Dense trajectories and motion boundary descriptors for action recognition. *International Journal of Computer Vision*, 2013.

[15] X. Xiong and F. De la Torre. Supervised descent method and its applications to face alignment. In *Proc. of IEEE Conf. on Computer Vision and Pattern Recognition (CVPR)*, 2013.

[16] R. B. Zajonc et al. *Social facilitation*. Research Center for Group Dynamics, Institute for Social Research, University of Michigan, 1965.

[17] Z. Zeng, M. Pantic, G. I. Roisman, and T. S. Huang. A survey of affect recognition methods: Audio, visual, and spontaneous expressions. *IEEE Trans. on Pattern Analysis and Machine Intelligence*, 2009.

[18] G. Zhao and M. Pietikainen. Dynamic texture recognition using local binary patterns with an application to facial expressions. *IEEE Trans. on Pattern Analysis and Machine Intelligence*, 2007.

Local Diffusion Map Signature for Symmetry-aware Non-rigid Shape Correspondence

Meng Wang
NYU Multimedia and Visual Computing Lab
Dept. of ECE, NYU Abu Dhabi, UAE
Dept. of CSE, NYU Tandon School of Engineering, USA

Yi Fang*
NYU Multimedia and Visual Computing Lab
Dept. of ECE, NYU Abu Dhabi, UAE
Dept. of ECE, NYU Tandon School of Engineering, USA

ABSTRACT

Identifying accurate correspondences information among different shapes is of great importance in shape analysis such as shape registration, segmentation and retrieval. This paper aims to develop a paradigm to address the challenging issues posed by shape structural variation and symmetry ambiguity. Specifically, the proposed research developed a novel shape signature based on local diffusion map on 3D surface, which is used to identify the shape correspondence through graph matching process. The developed shape signature, named local diffusion map signature (LDMS), is obtained by projecting heat diffusion distribution on 3D surface into 2D images along the surface normal direction with orientation determined by gradients of heat diffusion field. The local diffusion map signature is able to capture the concise geometric essence that is deformation-insensitive and symmetry-aware. Experimental results on 3D shape correspondence demonstrate the superior performance of our proposed method over other state-of-the-art techniques in identifying correspondences for non-rigid shapes with symmetry ambiguity.

Keywords

3D shape correspondence; non-rigid shape matching; 3D shape signature

1. INTRODUCTION

1.1 Background

Shape correspondence provides important information for many shape analysis such as shape alignment and registration, texture mapping, information transformation among shapes, shape morphing, statistical shape modelling and so on. It is therefore of great interest to develop the efficient

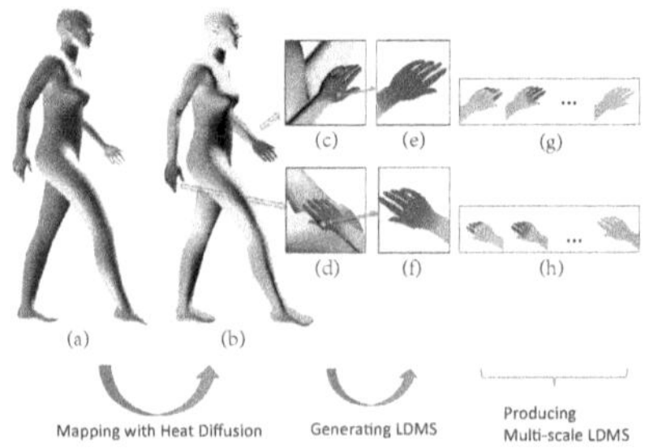

Figure 1: Pipeline of our method.

shape correspondence algorithm that, given a pair of shapes, return the corresponding regions on surface. The accuracy of shape correspondence algorithm is ultimately determined by the quality and characteristics of the shape signature that captures the geometric essence of points on 3D surface. While many advancements have been made for shape correspondence over the years, there remain challenges in the development of effective and discriminative shape signature. Two such challenges are shape structural variations and symmetry ambiguity and both can significantly degrade the performance of a shape correspondence technique[13, 12, 7, 18]. Therefore, a robust shape signature should be able to address the following issues.

- Structural variation in 3D models.
- Symmetry ambiguity in 3D shapes.
- Noise and incompleteness present in 3D shape description.

1.2 Related Work

3D non-rigid shape correspondence has been received considerable attention from computer vision and graphics areas. Many 3D objects contain dynamical units with their 3D shape flexibility and variations play an essential role in certain types of functional processes. The non-rigid shape correspondence methods often attempt to find correspondence information through a feature matching process. The process starts with computing a certain type of shape signature that capture geometric characteristics for representative

*Corresponding author. Email: yfang@nyu.edu

MM '16, October 15-19, 2016, Amsterdam, Netherlands

DOI: http://dx.doi.org/10.1145/2964284.2967277

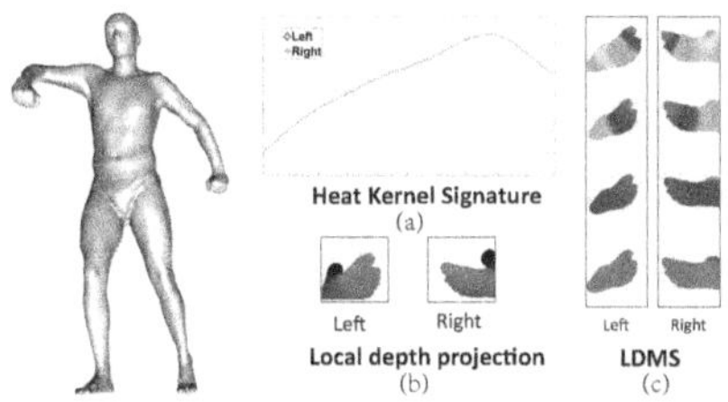

Figure 2: Local descriptor comparison between HKS(middle up), local depth descriptor(middle bottom) and multi-scale HKS projection descriptor(right). HKS cannot separate left and right foot, local depth projection is not discriminative, multi-scale HKS projection is discriminative between left and right foot.

points sampled on shape surface, then identifies a sparse correspondence by solving an assignment problem which maximize the similarity between the set of shape signatures with a certain type of spatial constrains such as preservation of geometric distance among corresponding pairs[17, 16]. Since a complete survey of non-rigid shape correspondence techniques is beyond the scope of this research paper, we refer the interested readers to review papers [17] for a comprehensive summary of the detailed techniques. As we can see from the feature matching process, the non-rigid shape correspondence can essentially boils down to two key components: the shape signature and assignment algorithm. Given an assignment algorithm, the accuracy of shape correspondence algorithm is ultimately determined by the quality and characteristics of the shape signature.

There have been a significant works on shape signatures in computer graphics community. [15, 3] Although those shape signatures are able to robustly capture the deformation invariant feature, all of them face with the symmetry ambiguity challenge. Early attempt to address the symmetry ambiguity takes advantage of the distortion measures based on conformal mapping[8, 10] or symmetry information[12]. However, these methods are restricted to meshes with same genus and require the mesh to be quite close to each other. Most recently, Yoshiyasu presented an orientation-aware local shape descriptors that be used for finding correspondence for shapes present incompleteness and symmetry [18].

1.3 Our shape signature: Local Diffusion Map Signature

Based on the diffusion geometry, we proposed a local diffusion map signature (LDMS) based on a novel strategy of projecting heat diffusion distribution on 3D surface into 2D image along the direction determined by gradients of heat diffusion field. Figure 1 illustrates the pipeline of generating LDMS, which mainly includes three steps. The first step is mapping a 3D surface with heat diffusion distribution. A variety of heat diffusion distribution, such as HKS, SIHKS, and Heat Kernel Matrix, can be chosen for this purpose. HKS is chosen in our development. The Figure 1(b) is a mapping of HKS on 3D surface shown on Figure 1(a). And Figure 1(c) and Figure 1(d) are closeup view of left and right hand region for human model. The second step is generating LDMS for repressive points sampled from 3D shape. The Figure 1(e) and Figure 1(f) illustrate the LDMS for points sampled from left and right hand respectively. The third step is producing a multi-scale LDMS for repressive points sampled from 3D shape. The multi-scale LDMS is produced by concatenating 2D images by projecting HKS based heat diffusion distribution at different scales. As we can see from Figure 2, the HKS (Figure 2(a))for sampled points from left and right hand are almost identical, whereas the local depth projection (Figure 2(b)) and LDMS (Figure 2(c)) can differentiate those points. In addition, multi-scale LDMS shown in Figure 2(c) provides much more discriminative power compared to local depth projection (shown in Figure 2(b)).

2. METHOD

2.1 Heat diffusion and heat kernel signature

Heat kernel signature[15], which is developed based heat diffusion, has been widely used for 3D shape processing [15]. Heat kernel signature is defined by:

$$HKS(x) = (h_{t_1}(x,x), h_{t_2}(x,x), \ldots, h_{t_n}(x,x)) \qquad (1)$$

where x denotes a point on the surface, $HKS(x)$ denotes the heat kernel signature at point x, $h_t(x,x)$ denotes the heat kernel value at point x, t_n denotes the nth sample point in time. A number of attractive attributes, including invariance to isometric transformation, robustness to noise, and multi-scale representation, make HKS a popular signature in community[15]. Our LDMS is developed based on HKS as described below.

2.2 Local diffusion map signature (LDMS)

LDMS is proposed primarily to address two challenging shape correspondence issues: structural variations and symmetry ambiguity. As shown in Figure 1, there are three main steps in producing a LDMS and multi-scale LDMS for a sampled point on 3D surface. Subsections below, which include representative points sampling, local diffusion map, stable orientation direction, and generation of LDMS, provide with detailed descriptions for LDMS computation.

Representative points sampling: A triangulated 3D mesh normally contains a large number of vertex on its surface. It is therefore very time-consuming and computationally inefficient for a shape correspondence algorithm considering all of the vertex to establish a dense correspondence between a pair of shapes. In our work, DoG detector [4] is used to identify the representative samples on surface and a density-invariant smoothing strategy [4] is employed to reduce the influence due to the sampling density. With result of correspondence of sampled points, a dense shape correspondence can be established by various approaches like [14].

Local diffusion map: In this paper, we define local diffusion map as a regional heat diffusion distribution of HKS values for a specific point at a time scale. For each point on the surface (for example, a sampled point on right hand as shown in Figure 1(d)), a local diffusion map reflects two important information 1)the HKS values for its neighbour points, 2) the spatial orientation of its neighbour points. As described in [15], HKS capture intrinsic geometric feature for points on surface. However, it loses the spatial orientation information. This explains why HKS values for points sampled from left and right hands are almost identical as shown in Figure 2(a). Therefore, to capture symmetry-aware information, we need to further exploit the spatial orientation

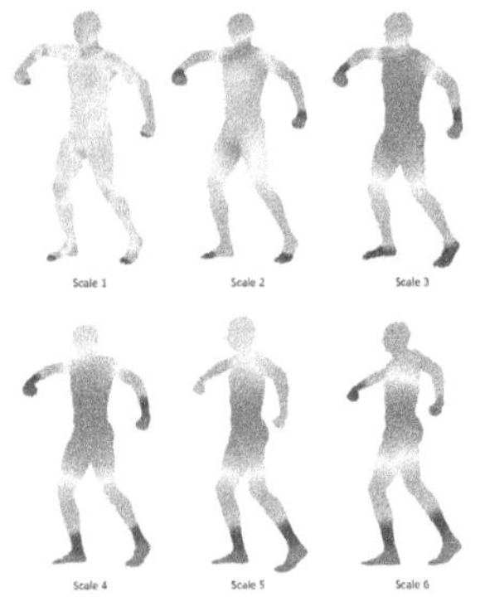

Figure 3: Diffusion map on a 3D surface at different scales.

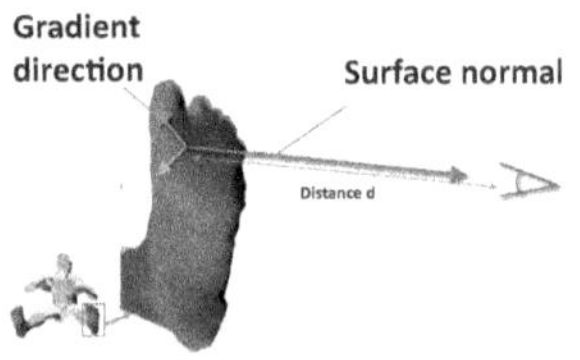

Figure 4: Demonstration of projecting a local diffusion map to 2D image.

information contained in local diffusion map. In this paper, we developed a method of determining a stable orientation from gradients of heat diffusion field, which is explained in the following subsection. Note that local diffusion map also has multi-scale property due to the multi-scale nature of HKS. Figure 3 illustrate the diffusion map for the entire 3D surface at six different scales.

Stable orientation direction: Previous work [4] suggests the principle component vector based PCA analysis is able to provide a reasonable orientation direction for a surface point. However, this direction is not stable especially for points on the surface of non-rigid shapes with the local deformations. In [18], the authors suggest that the gradients of average diffusion distance field will give a more stable orientation direction compared to the principle component vector. In this paper, we develop a way to determine the orientation from gradients of heat diffusion field which is computed by averaging diffusion maps at all scales. Although the determination of orientation direction is similar to the approaches in [4, 18], our experimental experience indicates that our orientation direction is more stable probably due to multi-scale nature of diffusion map.

Generation of LDMS: The newly proposed LDMS is generated by projecting local diffusion map into 2D image. To perform a projection from a local diffusion map on 3D surface to a 2D image, we require to have three critical parameters to set up a camera: camera position, viewing direction and camera rotation (up direction). As shown in Figure 4, the viewing direction is the opposite direction of surface normal, the camera is placed at some position on the normal direction line with a distance of d to the surface point, and the camera rotation is set as the stable orientation direction determined in subsection above. The LDMS for a surface point is generated by projecting a local diffusion map to a 2D image based on the camera setting. In addition, the multi-scale property of the local diffusion map can naturally give rise to a multi-scale nature for LDMS by projecting multi-scale local diffusion map as shown in Figure 1(g). The multi-scale LDMS is able to boost the discriminative power of the shape signature.

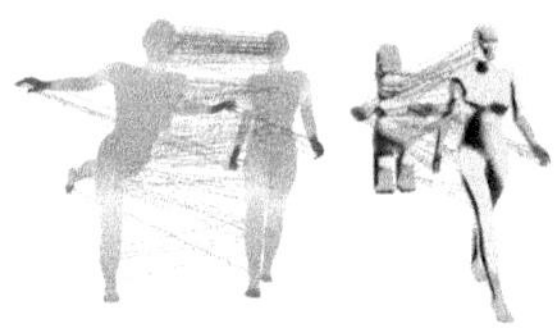

Figure 5: Shape correspondence over nonrigid models

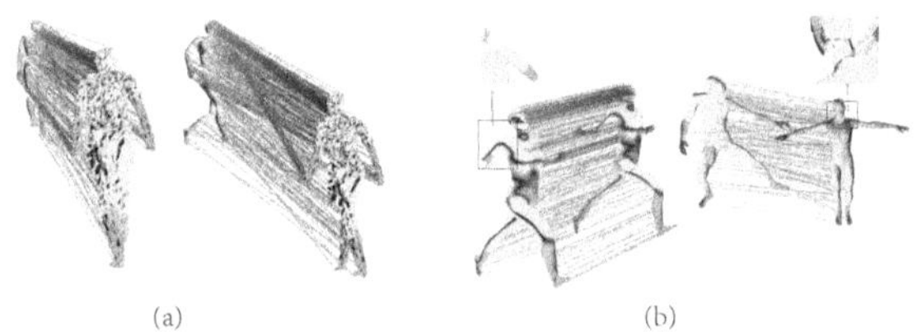

Figure 6: Shape correspondence over noise models and partial models

3. EXPERIMENT

We carry out a set of experiments for finding shape correspondence and assessed the performance of our LDMS. The 3D models were chosen from the following databases: SCAPE [5], TOSCA [2], and Watertight [6] database. The SCAPE library has 71 human meshes in total, which is 3D human surface library with realistic muscle deformation in different poses. The 3D models from datasets have undergone different types of geometric transformations which lead to various levels of structural variations. Models in Figure 5, 6 are from TOSCA [2] and Watertight [6] database.

In the experiments, all the shapes are resampled to have approximately the same amount of faces. The represented sample points are selected by the DoG detector or by consistent selection from ground truth correspondence. For the heat diffusions we sampled 101 scales in time interval of 0.0065. For each sample point, we generate six LDMS by choosing local diffusion map at six different time scales (1,21,41,61,81,101). We normalized the shape coordinates to $1/max(max(\mathbf{X}-average(X)), max(\mathbf{Y}-aver(Y)), max(\mathbf{Z}-aver(Z)))$ of original magnitude, where $\mathbf{X}, \mathbf{Y}, \mathbf{Z}$ are physical coordinates of all the input points. Each LDMS has a resolution of 50 pixel $\times$ 50 pixel.

3.1 Shape correspondence for non-rigid models

In this experiment, we test the performance of LDMS for finding correspondence on nonrigid shape models. We carry out two sets of tests using 3D models present in different types of nonrigid deformation. In the first test, we aim to establish the shape correspondence between 3D models with articulated deformation. We selected a pair of 3D human models at different poses as shown on the left side of Figure 5. In the second test, we aim to identify the shape correspondence between 3D models with non-isometric deformation, which is generally considered as much more challenging deformation for a shape correspondence method. We chosen a 3D human model and a 3D homer model as shown on the right side of Figure 5. All of the 3D models selected in this experiment are present in symmetry. The shape correspondence results can be found in Figure 5, where the red lines link the corresponding points between two models. The accurate correspondence shown in Figure 5 indicates that our LDMS captures deformation-insensitive and symmetry-aware geometric essence.

3.2 Shape correspondence for noise models

In this experiment, we will demonstrate that LDMS is robust to numerical noise. To prepare the noisy model, we simulate noise on the 3D model by randomly perturbing the vertices of original models. As we can see from the Figure 6(a), there are a original model is a 3D human model without noise and a noisy models generated from the original model at a moderate noise level. We can see that the geometric features of the noisy human model have significantly altered and deteriorated. As indicated by the results in Figure 6(a), our method performs very well in identifying correspondence between models with moderate level of noise suggested by the accurate corresponding pair of points linked by red lines in the Figure.

3.3 Shape correspondence for incomplete models

In this experiment, we will design the test that validate the performance of LDMS under the context of incomplete models. To prepare the incomplete 3D models, we select clean models from TOSCA dataset and manually remove some parts from the clean models as shown in Figure 6(b). The figure on left in Figure 6(b) illustrates a pair of 3D human models with one model missing the right arm part. The figure on right in Figure 6(b) displays a pair of 3D human models with one model having a hole on the neck. The close-up figures provide a better view of the incompleteness in original models. As indicated by the results in Figure 6(b), our method works very well for finding the shape correspondence as demonstrated by the accurate corresponding pair of points linked by red lines in the figure.

Methods	Average Geodesic Error
LDMS	**0.039**
Blended	0.081
Mobius Voting	0.162
Best Conformal	0.113
GMDS	0.276
HKM 1 corr	0.272
HKM 2 corr	0.256

Table 1: Result average geodesic error on SCAPE library. 100 uniform vertices are sampled.

3.4 Comparisons with state-of-the-art signatures

In this section, we will conduct an experiment to compare the performance of LDMS to those of other state-of-the-art shape signature. We compared the proposed method with other methods including Blended Intrinsic Maps [8], Mobius Voting [10], GMDS [1] and heat kernel map matching [11] in the benchmark and the most recent SAM method published in CVPR 2014 [18]. The geodesic distortion is defined as the a distance shift from the identified corresponding point to the true one. We provide two quantitative evaluation based on geodesic distortion: 1) Average geodesic error, 2) Geodesic error vs Percentage of corresponding points Curve (GP-curve). The average error measures the overall performance of a shape correspondence based on the mean geodesic errors produced by all corresponding points. As we can see in Table 1, LDMS gives the best correspondence performance as indicated the smallest average geodesic error. The GP-curve evaluates the performance of a shape correspondence at a given level of geodesic error. For each level of geodesic error, GP-curve provides with a percentage of corresponding points that have a lower geodesic error than the given one. In Figure 7, we plot all GP-curves for five different methods. As we can see from the figure, LDMS consistently gives the best performance at all levels of geodesic errors as indicated by the fact that red GP-curve consistently stays on the top of all other GP-curves. The results quantitatively validate the superior performance of our proposed method over other state-of-the-art techniques in identifying correspondences for non-rigid shapes with symmetry ambiguity.

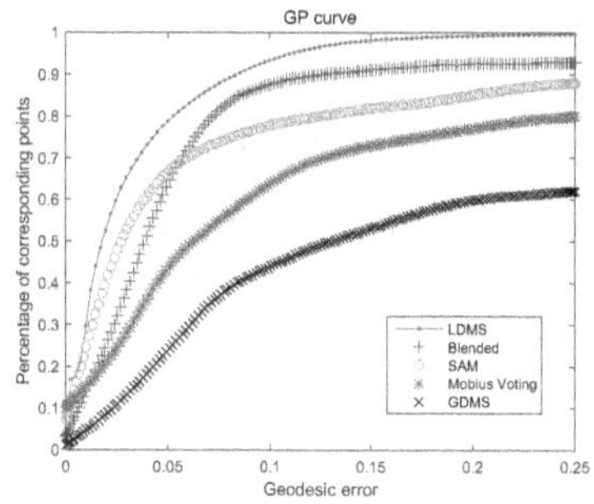

Figure 7: Geodesic error for shape correspondence on SCAPE. 100 uniform vertices are sampled.

4. CONCLUSION

Identifying accurate correspondence information among shapes is of great importance in shape analysis such as shape registration, segmentation and retrieval. In this paper, we proposed a shape signature, named local diffusion map signature (LDMS), that capture the deformation-insensitive and symmetry-aware geometric essence. Driven by LDMS, a shape correspondence paradigm is developed to address the challenging issues posed by shape structural variations and symmetry ambiguity. Experimental results on 3D shape correspondence demonstrate the superior performance of our proposed method over other state-of-the-art techniques in identifying correspondences for non-rigid shapes with symmetry ambiguity.

5. ACKNOWLEDGMENTS

This material is partly based upon work supported by New York University Abu Dhabi institute (AD131 and REF131).

6. REFERENCES

[1] A. M. Bronstein, M. M. Bronstein, and R. Kimmel. Generalized multidimensional scaling: a framework for isometry-invariant partial surface matching. *Proceedings of the National Academy of Sciences of the United States of America*, 103(5):1168–1172, 2006.

[2] A. M. Bronstein, M. M. Bronstein, and R. Kimmel. *Numerical geometry of non-rigid shapes*. Springer Science & Business Media, 2008.

[3] A. M. Bronstein, M. M. Bronstein, R. Kimmel, M. Mahmoudi, and G. Sapiro. A gromov-hausdorff framework with diffusion geometry for topologically-robust non-rigid shape matching. *Int. J. Comput. Vision*, 89:266–286, 2010.

[4] T. Darom and Y. Keller. Scale-invariant features for 3-d mesh models. *Image Processing, IEEE Transactions on*, 21(5):2758–2769, 2012.

[5] P. S. Dragomir Anguelov, H.-C. Pang, D. Koller, and J. D. Sebastian Thrun. The correlated correspondence algorithm for unsupervised registration of nonrigid surfaces. In *Advances in Neural Information Processing Systems 17: Proceedings of the 2004 Conference*, volume 17, page 33. MIT Press, 2005.

[6] D. Giorgi, S. Biasotti, and L. Paraboschi. Shrec: shape retrieval contest: Watertight models track. *Online]: http://watertight. ge. imati. cnr. it*, 2007.

[7] Q.-X. Huang, B. Adams, M. Wicke, and L. J. Guibas. Non-rigid registration under isometric deformations. In *Computer Graphics Forum*, volume 27, pages 1449–1457. Wiley Online Library, 2008.

[8] V. G. Kim, Y. Lipman, and T. Funkhouser. Blended intrinsic maps. In *ACM Transactions on Graphics (TOG)*, volume 30, page 79. ACM, 2011.

[9] C. Li and A. B. Hamza. Spatially aggregating spectral descriptors for nonrigid 3d shape retrieval: a comparative survey. *Multimedia Systems*, 20(3):253–281, 2014.

[10] Y. Lipman and T. Funkhouser. Möbius voting for surface correspondence. In *ACM Transactions on Graphics (TOG)*, volume 28, page 72. ACM, 2009.

[11] M. Ovsjanikov, Q. Mérigot, F. Mémoli, and L. Guibas. One point isometric matching with the heat kernel. In *Computer Graphics Forum*, volume 29, pages 1555–1564. Wiley Online Library, 2010.

[12] M. Ovsjanikov, Q. Mérigot, V. Pătrăucean, and L. Guibas. Shape matching via quotient spaces. In *Computer Graphics Forum*, volume 32, pages 1–11. Wiley Online Library, 2013.

[13] Y. Sahillioğlu and Y. Yemez. Coarse-to-fine isometric shape correspondence by tracking symmetric flips. In *Computer Graphics Forum*, volume 32, pages 177–189. Wiley Online Library, 2013.

[14] A. Sharma, R. Horaud, J. Cech, and E. Boyer. Topologically-robust 3d shape matching based on diffusion geometry and seed growing. In *Computer Vision and Pattern Recognition (CVPR), 2011 IEEE Conference on*, pages 2481–2488. IEEE, 2011.

[15] J. Sun, M. Ovsjanikov, and L. Guibas. A concise and provably informative multi-scale signature based on heat diffusion. *SGP '09: Proceedings of the Symposium on Geometry Processing*, pages 1383–1392, 2009.

[16] A. Tevs, M. Bokeloh, M. Wand, A. Schilling, and H.-P. Seidel. Isometric registration of ambiguous and partial data. In *Computer Vision and Pattern Recognition, 2009. CVPR 2009. IEEE Conference on*, pages 1185–1192. IEEE, 2009.

[17] O. van Kaick, H. Zhang, G. Hamarneh, and D. Cohen-Or. A survey on shape correspondence. *Computer Graphics Forum*, 30(6):1681–1707, 2011.

[18] Y. Yoshiyasu, E. Yoshida, K. Yokoi, and R. Sagawa. Symmetry-aware nonrigid matching of incomplete 3d surfaces. In *Computer Vision and Pattern Recognition (CVPR), 2014 IEEE Conference on*, pages 4193–4200. IEEE, 2014.

How Cosmopolitan Are Emojis?

Exploring Emojis Usage and Meaning over Different Languages with Distributional Semantics

Francesco Barbieri
Universitat Pompeu Fabra
Barcelona, Spain
francesco.barbieri@upf.edu

German Kruszewski
University of Trento
Trento, Italy
germank@gmail.com

Francesco Ronzano
Universitat Pompeu Fabra
Barcelona, Spain
francesco.ronzano@upf.edu

Horacio Saggion
Universitat Pompeu Fabra
Barcelona, Spain
horacio.saggion@upf.edu

ABSTRACT

Choosing the right emoji to visually complement or condense the meaning of a message has become part of our daily life. Emojis are pictures, which are naturally combined with plain text, thus creating a new form of language. These pictures are the same independently of where we live, but they can be interpreted and used in different ways. In this paper we compare the meaning and the usage of emojis across different languages. Our results suggest that the overall semantics of the subset of the emojis we studied is preserved across all the languages we analysed. However, some emojis are interpreted in a different way from language to language, and this could be related to socio-geographical differences.

Keywords

Emojis, Natural Language Processing, Distributional Semantics

1. INTRODUCTION

The information society has considerably changed the way in which we communicate with each other mainly due to the advent of Social Media. Social networking platforms such as Twitter allow users to post short text messages to update followers on current affairs, sentiments, emotions and express opinions on any topic. During the last few years, Twitter users have started to extensively use emojis in their posts[1]. Emojis are pictures that can be naturally combined with plain text to create a new form of language[2]; a practice also adopted in other networking platforms such as Facebook, Whatsapp and Instagram. Emojis pose important challenges for researchers in multimedia information systems, since their meaning remains for the time being unexplored. In spite of their assumed universality, the sense of an emoji may change from language to language and culture to culture. Understanding the meaning of emojis with respect to their context of use is important for multimedia information indexing, retrieval, or content extraction systems.

In this paper we investigate the use of emojis across languages from a natural language processing viewpoint. We adopt an empirical research methodology relying on current vector space representation modelling [22, 15] to understand the "semantics" of these important elements of multimedia communication. More specifically, we collected a corpus of more than 30 million tweets in four languages, American English (USA), British English (UK), Peninsular Spanish (ESP), and Italian (ITA), and carried out various experiments to compare emojis. Despite the languages have different vocabularies and syntactic structures, we were able to find a way to compare the use of emojis across languages. Our results demonstrate that the semantics of the 150 most popular emojis is somehow preserved across different languages. Nevertheless, for some emojis we observed interesting language specific usage patterns. For instance, the emojis 🔥, 👏, and 🙌 seem to be used in different contexts across distinct languages, while there is a relative agreement on the cross-language use and meaning of 🎶 and 🌳.

In the next section we overview previous studies on emojis. In Section 3, we describe the dataset we have collected and the text processing tools we use to model the meaning of emojis across languages. By relying on this dataset, we run two experiments: in the first one (Section 4.1) for each emojis we compare the most similar ones in different languages. In our second experiment (Section 4.2) we focus on the comparison of the similarity of pairs of emojis across languages: in particular we analyse the language-dependent similarity matrices of the 150 most popular emojis. We find that the matrices that describe the four language variations considered are strongly correlated[3]. We conclude the pa-

[1]Realtime Emoji use on Twitter can be tracked at http://emojitracker.com/

[2]A complete list can be found at http://emojipedia.org/

[3]Detailed and complete results can be found at http://sempub.taln.upf.edu/tw/cosmopolitan/

MM '16, October 15 - 19, 2016, Amsterdam, Netherlands

ISBN 978-1-4503-3603-1/16/10...$15.00

DOI: http://dx.doi.org/10.1145/2964284.2967278

Rank	USA		UK		ESP		ITA	
1	😂	350	😂	32	😍	46	❤	55
2	❤	301	❤	27	❤	38	😂	35
3	😍	213	😍	22	😂	34	😍	34
4	🔥	166	🎄	20	💕	24	🇮🇹	16
5	💯	104	😊	13	👌	23	😊	12
6	😊	101	🎅	11	😘	22	🔝	12
7	🙌	89	🎉	10	🎉	22	😘	11
8	😘	86	👍	10	💪	21	😁	10
9	🎄	85	👌	10	😊	19	☀	10
10	💕	84	🇬🇧	9	👏	16	😎	10
11	🎉	80	😘	9	🔝	14	🎉	9
12	😭	79	✨	8	💃	12	💙	8
13	💙	77	❄	8	💙	12	😜	8
14	✨	75	😁	8	👫	12	🌹	7
15	❄	72	💕	8	💞	11	✌	7

Table 1: The 15 most frequent emojis across the four languages studied. For each language, next to each emoji, we show the thousand of occurrences in the our dataset.

per with a summary of our findings and avenues for further research.

2. RELATED WORK

Currently, emojis represent a widespread and pervasive global communication device largely adopted by almost any Social Media service and instant messaging platform [12, 19, 18]. Emojis, like the older emoticons, support the possibility to express diverse types of contents in a visual, concise and appealing way that is perfectly suited to the informal style of Social Media communication. The meaning expressed by emoticons has been exploited to enable or improve several tasks related to the automated analysis of Social Media contents, like sentiment analysis [10, 9]. In this context, emoticons have also been often exploited to label and thus characterize the textual excerpts where they occur. As a consequence, by analyzing all the textual contents where a specific emoticon appears several sentiment and emotional lexicons have been build [23, 21, 21, 4]. Go et al. [8] and Castellucci et al. [7] use distant supervision over emotion-labeled textual contents in order to respectively train a sentiment classifier and build a polarity lexicon. Aoki et al.[1] describe a methodology to represent each emoticon as a vector of emotions and Jiang [11] proposed a sentiment and emotion classifier based on semantic spaces of emojis in the Chinese Website Sina Weibo.

Novak et al. [17] built a lexicons and drew a sentiment map of the 751 most frequently used emojis. Cappallo et al. [5] proposed Image2Emoji, a multimodal approach for generating emoji labels for images (they also presented a demo [6]). Miller et al. [16] explored whether emoji renderings or differences across platforms (e.g. Apple's iPhone vs. Google's Nexus phone) give rise to diverse interpretations of emojis. Pavalanathan and Eisenstein [20] used a matching approach from causal inference to test whether the adoption of emojis causes individual users to employ fewer emoticons in their text on Twitter.

Finally, we explored meaning of Twitter emojis in American English with Distributional Semantics [3]. We tested our models with semantic similarity experiments, comparing our models with human assessment. We also carried out a qualitative evaluation, exploring cluster of emojis and the most related words to each emoji (the models can be found online[4]). We also explored the usage of the emojis in Madrid and Barcelona [2].

3. DATASET AND TEXT ANALYSIS

To support the creation of the semantic vectorial models presented in this paper we gathered a dataset composed of more than 30 million tweets retrieved with the Twitter APIs. We retrieved geo-located tweets that were posted from United States of America, United Kingdom, Spain, and Italy. We collected tweets from October 2015 to April 2016. We used geo-located tweets in order to retrieve tweets from real user, filtering out spam and bot generated tweets. The total number of tweets is 28,8 millions for USA, 2.1 for United Kingdom, 1.56 for Spain and 1.63 for Italy. Table 1 shows, for each language, the 15 most frequent emojis together with the number of times each emoji occurs. We can see that 😂, ❤ and 😍 are the most common emojis in each one of the four languages considered.

In order to preprocess the text of each tweet we follow the same procedure of Barbieri et al. [3]. We modelled in the same vectorial space both the words and the emojis of tweets by means of embeddings, by relying on the skip-gram embedding model introduced by Mikolov et al. [14] with 300 dimensions and a window size of 6 tokens (we previously found out that this is the best configuration to model emojis [3]). We built 4 models, one per language.

4. EXPERIMENTS AND EVALUATION

We run several experiments to compare the way the semantics of emojis varies across languages. In a first experiment (Section 4.1) we investigate if the meaning of single emojis is preserved across language variations. In a second experiment (Section 4.2), we compare the overall semantic models of the 150 most frequent emojis across languages.

4.1 Experiment 1

In our first experiment, we quantify how the meaning of an emoji A is preserved across different languages by measuring to what extent the emojis that are most similar to A overlap across languages. We exploit the vectorial representation of each emojis in a specific language to select the ones with similar vectors and thus presumably closest in meaning. We define the Nearest Neighbours $NN_l(e)$ of the emoji e in the language l, as the set of the 10 nearest emojis[5] to the emoji e in the semantic space of language l. We retrieve the nearest neighbours of each emojis with respect to its cosine similarity with other emojis. Note that the semantic vectors are derived from co-occurrence statistics extracted from both emojis and words. However, since an emoji is defined by other similar emojis, we are able to compare these representations across different languages. In order to see if an emoji is similarly defined in two languages,

[4]http://sempub.taln.upf.edu/tw/emojis/

[5]In average the cosine similarity drops after the 10th closest emoji and for each emoji the cosine similarity of the ten most similar emojis is always greater than 0.4.

	Rank	USA UK	USA ESP	USA ITA	UK ESP	UK ITA	ESP ITA	s_{all}
	23	9	9	9	9	9	9	9
	91	9	9	9	9	9	9	9
	118	9	9	9	9	9	9	9
	126	9	9	9	9	9	9	9
	146	9	8	9	8	9	8	8
	150	8	9	9	9	8	8	8
	128	8	8	8	8	8	8	8
	74	8	9	8	8	7	9	7
	77	7	7	8	9	9	8	7
	80	7	7	7	9	9	9	7
	72	7	7	7	9	9	8	7
	79	8	8	7	8	7	7	7
	84	8	7	9	7	9	8	6
	144	8	7	8	8	7	6	6
	60	6	9	8	6	6	8	6
	39	3	5	4	2	2	3	0
	55	4	1	5	1	4	3	0
	14	5	3	0	4	0	1	0
	57	2	2	2	3	1	2	0
	85	3	3	2	2	1	1	0
	87	1	5	2	2	0	2	0
	30	0	0	1	3	3	3	0
	95	0	4	2	0	1	2	0
	149	3	4	0	1	0	1	0
	148	3	0	0	1	1	3	0
	100	3	1	2	2	0	0	0
	69	3	0	0	0	0	3	0
	97	1	0	0	0	4	0	0
	78	1	1	0	0	1	0	0
	110	1	0	1	0	0	0	0

Table 2: Experiment 1, emojis with high sim_{all} (indicated as s_{all} in the table) on the top, and emojis with low sim_{all} in the bottom.

we look at the common elements in the *NN* representation of that emoji in the two languages. If the representations of the emoji in different languages share many elements it would mean that the emoji is defined and thus used in a similar way. If there are not common elements among the two representations, the emoji is more likely to mean something different in the two languages. More precisely, to determine if emoji e is similar in language l_1 and l_2 we measure the size of the intersection of the NN sets:

$$sim_{l_1 l_2}(e) = |NN_{l_1}(e) \bigcap NN_{l_2}(e)|$$

We assume that if $sim_{l_1 l_2}$ is equal to 10, the emoji e has the same meaning in the languages l_1 and l_2. On the other hand, if $sim_{l_1 l_2}$ is equal to 0 the emoji means something different in the two languages.

Moreover, we also measure whether an emoji means the same across all the languages by looking at the overlap of all the sets of emojis that are most similar to the emoji e in each language:

$$sim_{all}(e) = |NN_{l_1}(e) \bigcap NN_{l_2}(e) \bigcap ... \bigcap NN_{l_n}(e)|$$

where n is the number of languages.

In the top half of Table 2 we report the results of Experiment 1 for the emojis with highest sim_{all}. For each emoji are indicated the rank (where 1 is the most common emoji over the four languages and 150 is the least used emoji), the six combinations of $sim_{l_1 l_2}$, and the sim_{all}. The emojis that seem to keep the same meaning independently from the language are the music, nature and food related ones. In the bottom half of Table 2 are reported the emojis with the lowest sim_{all} (all emojis have a sim_{all} score equal to 0): these emojis meanings are probably language dependent. Looking at the bottom of the table we can see that the emojis and are used in a very different way across all the languages, and each language seems to have its own way to define them. Also the emojis , , and do not seem to keep their meaning across different languages (the number 100 for example might be just a number or a excellent grade). For the waving-hand emoji , we also plot the NN for USA and UK, (Figure 1) and we can observe that these two emojis are interpreted in different ways. In the case of American English the waving-hand seems to mean *bye/see you later* (smiles and people waving), while for British English the waving-hand emojis is related to travelling (countries flags, train and airplane are included in the NN). On the other hand, , , , and are concrete objects but they are exploited to convey different meanings across different languages.

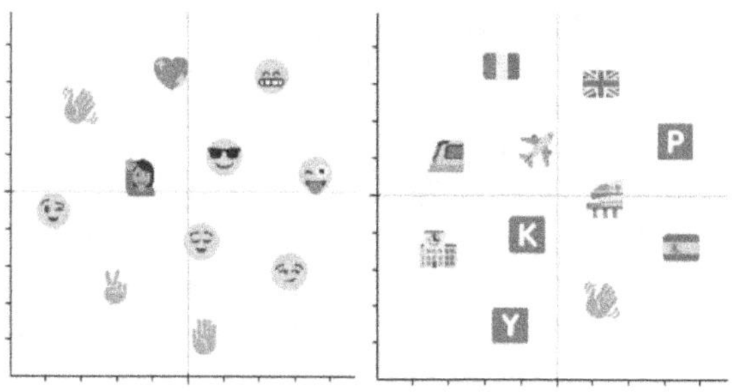

Figure 1: tSNE of nearest neighbours of the waving-hand emoji for USA (left) and UK (right)

	USA	UK	ESP	ITA	AVG
USA	1	**0.76**	0.743	0.698	0.734
UK	0.76	1	0.719	0.702	0.727
ESP	0.743	0.719	1	0.739	0.734
ITA	0.698	0.702	0.739	1	0.713

Table 3: Experiment 2, Pairwise Pearson's Correlation between similarity matrices.

4.2 Experiment 2

In order to understand the use and the similarity of pairs of emojis across different languages we compute for each language the similarity matrix of the 150 emojis that we are studying. The value of each cell of this matrix is equal to the cosine similarity of the corresponding pair of emojis. We

		USA	UK			USA	ESP			USA	ITA			UK	ESP			UK	ITA			ESP	ITA
😩	👵	0.54	0.06	🔥	💥	0.39	0.73	🍴	🍕	0.35	0.67	👫	🍀	0.2	0.68	😣	😬	0.29	0.62	🎉	💟	0.22	0.57
⭐	😣	-0.01	0.4	😩	👵	0.54	-0.01	✌	🔝	0.37	0.6	🍀	👫	0.24	0.66	🎉	💟	0.25	0.57	😏	💎	0.57	0.14
🎁	🎄	0.26	0.62	🍀	👫	0.35	0.66	🍀	🌸	0.35	0.59	😈	🐂	0.35	0.75	😡	😬	0.27	0.58	✨	👏	0.57	0.16
😈	😮	0.72	0.25	😈	🐂	0.47	0.75	😣	😬	0.4	0.62	🌊	🌅	0.43	0.81	🌊	🌅	0.43	0.68	😈	😚	0.48	0.11
✨	🎄	0.25	0.61	💯	🔝	0.46	0.72	👍	🔝	0.38	0.59	💫	🍀	0.22	0.61	🌞	🌊	0.43	0.68	😈	💎	0.5	0.13
❤	😃	0.21	0.57	👫	🍀	0.41	0.68	🎉	💣	0.23	0.48	💯	💎	0.18	0.58	👍	🔝	0.32	0.59	🐾	☁	0.48	0.11
🎅	🎁	0.58	0.9	💎	🍀	0.26	0.56	🍀	🌿	0.42	0.61	🌊	🌴	0.47	0.82	❤	😃	0.57	0.11	💕	🍺	0.47	0.11
✨	⛄	0.16	0.51	💫	🍀	0.33	0.61	😍	🔝	0.21	0.46	😏	💎	0.18	0.57	🍺	🍔	0.39	0.64	‼	🔴	0.17	0.47
☕	🎂	0.39	0.71	✨	👏	0.29	0.57	🍷	🍴	0.6	0.73	💘	🍀	0.25	0.59	💯	💝	0	0.33	😈	🐂	0.75	0.36
❄	🎁	0.23	0.57	💥	🐂	0.28	0.56	🔝	🍔	0.12	0.39	💎	🍀	0.22	0.56	❤	💝	0.37	0.61	💕	❤	0.5	0.15
😮	🐾	0.44	0.03	🍕	🍔	0.47	0.71	🍺	🍕	0.36	0.56	💯	🔝	0.41	0.72	🌊	🌴	0.47	0.68	💎	😇	0.43	0.09
✨	❄	0.17	0.51	🍺	🔝	0.2	0.5	💦	😚	0.35	-0.06	🌴	🌅	0.42	0.72	🎄	🌳	0.69	0.85	👫	🍀	0.68	0.31
🐾	💝	0.26	0.59	😅	‼	0.49	0.04	💯	💄	0.21	0.45	👫	💝	0.34	0.65	😉	⚡	0.11	0.4	🍺	🎊	0.68	0.32
🎁	⛄	0.37	0.69	😱	😜	0.53	0.08	✌	👍	0.43	0.6	💕	🍀	0.27	0.59	😈	😬	0.25	0.51	💕	😳	0.39	0.06

Table 4: Experiment 2, pair of emojis with highest similarity difference between two languages.

normalise the cosine similarity values by the average cosine similarity of all the pairs of emojis.

4.2.1 Correlation Between Languages

We take advantage of the similarity matrices to analyse whether two languages represent emojis in similar ways. The Pearson's correlation of the similarity matrices of the four languages are reported in Table 3. We can see that most of the languages are strongly correlated to each other. This is an interest finding, as vocabularies of the languages are different, and the context words modelled by the semantic spaces too, but the semantic of the emojis we studied is in some way preserved. American English and Spanish are the languages that interpret emojis in the most universal way, with high correlation to all the other languages (both with an average of 0.734). British English has a lower similarity matrix correlation with other languages (average of 0.727) and Italian scores an even lower average correlation, 0.713. This suggests that these two latter languages interpret emojis in a slightly different way than the other languages, especially Italian.

Looking at the single emoji-pairs similarities, the strongest correlation is between USA and UK (0.760), probably supported by similar vocabularies, and the weakest is between USA and ITA (0.698). On the other hand, Italian has high correlation with Spanish (0.739), while Spanish correlates better with Italian and American English than British English.

4.2.2 Emoji Differences

Even if we observed that in most of the cases the semantics of emojis is somehow preserved across languages, we can also spot some interesting difference in the language-specific use of these pictograms. In particular, in this section we explore the disagreement in the similarity matrices of the four languages (using a method similar to [13]). We analyse the pairs of emojis that have different similarities across two languages. Table 4 shows the similarity matrix scores of pairs of emojis for all the possible language combinations. We report pairs of emojis which are semantically related in one language (e.g. USA) but unrelated in the other (e.g. UK).

The emojis with higher differences in American and British English are 😩 👵 and 😮 🐾 that are similar in USA but not in UK. On the other hand the emoji 🎁 seems to be used in a different ways in UK, as it scores higher than USA with the emojis 🎅, ❄, and 🎄. It seems that the gift emoji is used mostly as Christmas gift in UK. Other interesting combinations are 😱 and 😜 that apparently are very similar in USA but not in Spain, and the pizza emoji 🍕 which highly correlates with 🍴 in Italian but not in USA, probably for the different way to eat pizza in these two countries.

An interesting pattern in the UK results are the emojis related to the beach and the good weather: emojis like 🌊, 🌅, 🌴, and 🌞 are similar to each other in Italian and Spanish, but not in British English, and this is probably related to the countries geographical location.

Two emojis that are used in a different way in Spain are 🍀 and 👫. They both appear in various combinations in the disagreement table (Table 4) of the Spanish language. The sly smile 😏 and 💎 are similar in Spain but not in UK and Italy, suggesting that the combination is frequently used only in Spain. One of the differences between Spanish and Italian is the emoji 🍺 that in Spanish is similar to 💕, and 🎊, but not in Italian. One last interesting pattern is the emoji 🔝 that in Italian means approvement as it is similar to emojis like 👍 and ✌, but it is not the case in USA and UK (where probably the emoji 💯 is used instead).

5. CONCLUSIONS

In this paper we explore the meaning and usage of emojis across four languages: American English, British English, Peninsular Spanish and Italian. We use distributional semantic models to represent the semantics of the emojis in the four languages, and we compare the language-specific models of each emoji. Our results suggest that in spite of differences in use of emojis across the languages we studied, the overall semantics of the most frequent emojis is similar. These are only preliminary results, and we are planning to run further, more extensive analyses of the cross-language meaning of emojis in the near future.

Acknowledgements

We thank the three anonymous reviewers for their useful comments, especially for the future work. We received partial support from the TUNER project (TIN2015-65308-C5-5-R, MINECO/FEDER, UE) and the Maria de Maeztu Units of Excellence Programme (MDM-2015-0502). First author also acknowledges the COST Action IC1307 iV&L Net (European Network on Integrating Vision and Language), supported by COST (European Cooperation in Science and Technology).

6. REFERENCES

[1] S. Aoki and O. Uchida. A method for automatically generating the emotional vectors of emoticons using weblog articles. In *Proc. 10th WSEAS Int. Conf. on Applied Computer and Applied Computational Science, Stevens Point, Wisconsin, USA*, pages 132–136, 2011.

[2] F. Barbieri, L. Espinosa-Anke, and H. Saggion. Revealing Patterns of Twitter Emoji Usage in Barcelona and Madrid. In *International Conference of the Catalan Association for Artificial Intelligence, CCIA*, Barcelona, Spain, October 2016.

[3] F. Barbieri, F. Ronzano, and H. Saggion. What does this Emoji Mean? A Vector Space Skip-Gram Model for Twitter Emojis. In *Language Resources and Evaluation conference, LREC*, Portoroz, Slovenia, May 2016.

[4] M. Boia, B. Faltings, C.-C. Musat, and P. Pu. A:) is worth a thousand words: How people attach sentiment to emoticons and words in tweets. In *Social Computing (SocialCom), 2013 International Conference on*, pages 345–350. IEEE, 2013.

[5] S. Cappallo, T. Mensink, and C. G. Snoek. Image2emoji: Zero-shot emoji prediction for visual media. In *Proceedings of the 23rd Annual ACM Conference on Multimedia Conference*, pages 1311–1314. ACM, 2015.

[6] S. Cappallo, T. Mensink, and C. G. Snoek. Query-by-emoji video search. In *Proceedings of the 23rd Annual ACM Conference on Multimedia Conference*, pages 735–736. ACM, 2015.

[7] G. Castellucci, D. Croce, and R. Basili. Acquiring a large scale polarity lexicon through unsupervised distributional methods. In *Natural Language Processing and Information Systems*, pages 73–86. Springer, 2015.

[8] A. Go, R. Bhayani, and L. Huang. Twitter sentiment classification using distant supervision. *CS224N Project Report, Stanford*, 1:12, 2009.

[9] A. Hogenboom, D. Bal, F. Frasincar, M. Bal, F. de Jong, and U. Kaymak. Exploiting emoticons in sentiment analysis. In *Proceedings of the 28th Annual ACM Symposium on Applied Computing*, pages 703–710. ACM, 2013.

[10] A. Hogenboom, D. Bal, F. Frasincar, M. Bal, F. De Jong, and U. Kaymak. Exploiting emoticons in polarity classification of text. *J. Web Eng.*, 14(1&2):22–40, 2015.

[11] F. Jiang, Y.-Q. Liu, H.-B. Luan, J.-S. Sun, X. Zhu, M. Zhang, and S.-P. Ma. Microblog sentiment analysis with emoticon space model. *Journal of Computer Science and Technology*, 30(5):1120–1129, 2015.

[12] T. A. Jibril and M. H. Abdullah. Relevance of emoticons in computer-mediated communication contexts: An overview. *Asian Social Science*, 9(4):201, 2013.

[13] N. Kriegeskorte, M. Mur, and P. A. Bandettini. Representational similarity analysis-connecting the branches of systems neuroscience. *Frontiers in systems neuroscience*, 2:4, 2008.

[14] T. Mikolov, K. Chen, G. Corrado, and J. Dean. Efficient estimation of word representations in vector space. *arXiv preprint arXiv:1301.3781*, 2013.

[15] T. Mikolov, Q. V. Le, and I. Sutskever. Exploiting similarities among languages for machine translation. *arXiv preprint arXiv:1309.4168*, 2013.

[16] H. Miller, J. Thebault-Spieker, S. Chang, I. Johnson, L. Terveen, and B. Hecht. "Blissfully happy" or "ready to fight": Varying Interpretations of Emoji. *ICWSM'16*, 2016.

[17] P. K. Novak, J. Smailović, B. Sluban, and I. Mozetič. Sentiment of Emojis. *PloS one*, 10(12):e0144296, 2015.

[18] J. Park, Y. M. Baek, and M. Cha. Cross-cultural comparison of nonverbal cues in emoticons on twitter: Evidence from big data analysis. *Journal of Communication*, 64(2):333–354, 2014.

[19] J. Park, V. Barash, C. Fink, and M. Cha. Emoticon style: Interpreting differences in emoticons across cultures. In *ICWSM*, 2013.

[20] U. Pavalanathan and J. Eisenstein. Emoticons vs. emojis on twitter: A causal inference approach. *arXiv preprint arXiv:1510.08480*, 2015.

[21] D. Tang, F. Wei, B. Qin, M. Zhou, and T. Liu. Building large-scale twitter-specific sentiment lexicon: A representation learning approach. In *COLING*, pages 172–182, 2014.

[22] P. D. Turney, P. Pantel, et al. From frequency to meaning: Vector space models of semantics. *Journal of artificial intelligence research*, 37(1):141–188, 2010.

[23] C. Yang, K. H.-Y. Lin, and H.-H. Chen. Building emotion lexicon from weblog corpora. In *Proceedings of the 45th Annual Meeting of the ACL on Interactive Poster and Demonstration Sessions*, pages 133–136. Association for Computational Linguistics, 2007.

Online Weighted Clustering for Real-time Abnormal Event Detection in Video Surveillance

Hanhe Lin Jeremiah D. Deng Brendon J. Woodford Ahmad Shahi
Department of Information Science, University of Otago
PO Box 56, Dunedin 9054, New Zealand
{hanhe.lin,jeremiah.deng,brendon.woodford}@otago.ac.nz
ahmad.shahi@postgrad.otago.ac.nz

ABSTRACT

Detecting abnormal events in video surveillance is a challenging problem due to the large scale, stream fashion video data as well as the real-time constraint. In this paper, we present an online, adaptive, and real-time framework to address this problem. The spatial locations in a frame is partitioned into grids, in each grid the proposed Adaptive Multi-scale Histogram Optical Flow (AMHOF) features are extracted and modelled by an Online Weighted Clustering (OWC) algorithm. The AMHOFs which cannot be fit to a cluster with large weight are regarded as abnormal events. The OWC algorithm is simple to implement and computational efficient. In addition, we improve the detection performance by a Multiple Target Tracking (MTT) algorithm. Experimental results demonstrate our approach outperforms the state-of-the-art approaches in pixel-level rate of detection at a processing speed of 30 FPS.

CCS Concepts

•Computing methodologies → Scene anomaly detection; •Information systems → *Data stream mining;* **•Theory of computation →** *Online learning algorithms;*

Keywords

online adaptive learning, abnormal event detection, video surveillance, multiple target tracking, real-time

1. INTRODUCTION

Abnormal Event Detection (AED) in video surveillance is attracting increasing attention along with the growing importance of public security and safety. However, it is subject to a number of challenges, including the large volumes and streaming nature of the data, and the real-time data processing requirements. As a result, most existing anomaly detection algorithms [3, 12] cannot be applied directly as they operate by nature in batch mode, which requires the entire dataset to be made available in advance so that these algorithms can proceed. Essentially, an ideal video anomaly detector is required to track slow changes of normal patterns in an online adaptive manner, and detect abrupt changes of abnormal patterns in real time.

A broad spectrum of approaches have been proposed for AED. In [11, 9], Mixture of Dynamic Textures (MDT) is adopted to detect both spatial and temporal anomalies. By performing a Conditional Random Field (CRF) filter on multi-scale anomaly maps, [9] improves the detection performance significantly compared with [11]. Sparse Reconstruction Cost (SRC) [4] has been introduced for anomaly detection in crowd scenes as well, based on the idea that normal events are more likely to be reconstructed from a learnt dictionary, whereas anomalous events are not. A similar idea is found in [10], where the processing cost was reduced significantly by introducing the Sparse Combination Learning (SCL) as well as resizing the frame resolution to a really small scale (i.e., 120×160). A "video parsing" approach is proposed in [1], which first finds a set of hypotheses using foreground detection with a linear SVMs. A probabilistic graphical model is built using the hypotheses obtained from training videos. Abnormalities are then detected from testing videos using hypothesis tests based on the graph model. Although the above approaches have achieved comparable detection results, they still cannot meet all the aforementioned three challenges.

Inspired by the ideas of Gaussian Mixture Model (GMM) used in background subtraction [13, 15], we propose an online, adaptive, and real-time framework for AED. With the assumption that most of events in video surveillance are normal while only a small portion is abnormal, we propose a novel OWC algorithm to model the recent history of events, where the clusters with large weights represent normal events and events that cannot match well to these clusters are detected as anomalies. Meanwhile, the detection performance has improved by a MTT algorithm. The approach is simple to implement, achieves better or comparable results in comparison with the-state-of-the-art approaches, and operates in a real-time speed.

MM '16, October 15-19, 2016, Amsterdam, Netherlands

DOI: http://dx.doi.org/10.1145/2964284.2967279

2. THE COMPUTATIONAL FRAMEWORK

2.1 Pre-processing

After modeling the background via the GMM [15], a sliding window is used to scan through the detected foreground of current frame and detect Region Of Interest (ROI) which

(a) (b) (c)

Figure 1: ROI extraction using background subtraction. (a) Incoming frame. (b) Foreground. (c) ROIs.

may be related to AED. Specifically, for all pixels inside the sliding window, if the proportion of foreground pixels is greater than a threshold (empirically set as 0.2 in experiments), then the window is highlighted as a ROI. Figure 1 displays the process of ROI extraction. As can been seen, this process filters most of the background out, reducing the computational cost as well as enhancing the robustness of the anomaly detector.

Due to the fact that an anomaly does not occur only in one frame, we employ a sliding window centred at time t: $\{t-n, \cdots, t-1, t, t+1, \cdots, t+n\}$, to extract the AMHOF descriptor. Specifically, in each ROI the optical flow of each pixel is calculated using Horn and Schunck's method [6]. The flow vector containing two directional components is denoted as $\{f_x, f_y\}$, where its orientation a and magnitude f are calculated through $\phi = \arctan(f_y/f_x)$ and $f = \sqrt{f_x^2 + f_y^2}$. Then, all flow vectors are quantized into $M \times N$ bins, where M is number of directions, and N is the discretization level of motion intensities. The discretization centres of motion intensities are determined by performing k-means clustering ($k = N$) of a random subset of magnitude f of flow vectors from the training set.

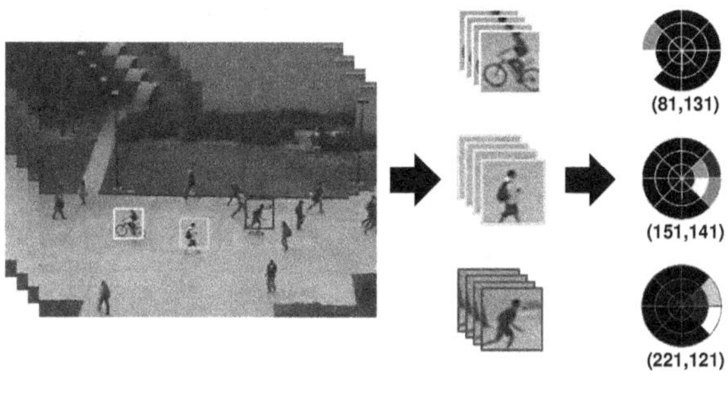

Figure 2: Feature extraction from three different ROIs ($M = 8$, $N = 3$), where the colours Yellow, Green and Blue correspond to biker, pedestrian, and skateboarder, respectively.

Besides motion information, we also keep the spatial location (i.e., x and y coordinates) of each ROI. A ROI is denoted as $\mathbf{r}_i = \{\mathbf{d}_i, \mathbf{l}_i\}$ from now on, where $\mathbf{d}_i$ and $\mathbf{l}_i$ correspond to AMHOF and spatial location respectively. Figure 2 shows features extracted from three ROIs, where the AMHOF discriminates motion patterns by capturing both direction and motion intensity information.

2.2 Online Weighted Clustering (OWC)

The spatial position in a frame is divided into $2^{L-1} \times 2^{L-1}$ grids, where L is the granularity level, the ROIs that are located in the same grid are clustered by online learning.

Algorithm 1 OWC

Input: $\mathbf{d}_i$, $\{\omega_k\}_{k=1}^K$, $\{\mathbf{C}_k\}_{k=1}^K$, α, T, δ, θ

```
Initialize matched(d_i) ← False    label_{d_i} ← abnormal
totalWeight ← 0
for k in 1...K do
    ω_k ← (1 − α)ω_k
    if matched(d_i)==False then
        D ← ||d_i − C_k||
        if D < θ then
            matched(d_i) ← True
            ω_k ← ω_k + α    C_k ← C_k + (α/ω_k)(d_i − C_k)
            if totalWeight < δ then
                label_{d_i} ← normal
            end if
        end if
    end if
    totalWeight ← totalWeight + ω_k
end for
if matched(d_i)==False then
    ω_{min(K+1,T)} ← α    C_{min(K+1,T)} ← d_i
end if
Sort ω_k, C_k in descending order of ω_k and renormalize ω_k
```

Output: $\text{label}_{\mathbf{d}_i}$, $\{\omega_k\}_{k=1}^K$, $\{\mathbf{C}_k\}_{k=1}^K$

This step helps to overcome perspective distortion which may result in scale variation of the extracted features.

In each grid, we model the recent history of motion features through the OWC algorithm. Specifically, let $\omega_1, \ldots, \omega_K$ be the weights and $\mathbf{C}_1, \ldots, \mathbf{C}_K$ be the centroids of K ($K \leq T$) clusters in a grid, where $\sum_{k=1}^K \omega_k = 1$, K and T are the number of existing clusters and a specified maximum number of clusters respectively. For a new $\mathbf{r}_i$, we first assign its $\mathbf{d}_i$ to a grid using $\mathbf{l}_i$ and the clusters in the grid are updated as [15]:

$$\omega_k \leftarrow \omega_k + \alpha(o_k - \omega_k), \tag{1}$$

$$\mathbf{C}_k \leftarrow \mathbf{C}_k + o_k(\alpha/\omega_k)(\mathbf{d}_i - \mathbf{C}_k), \tag{2}$$

where α is the learning rate ($0 < \alpha < 1$), and o_k is set to 1 if the Euclidean distance from $\mathbf{d}_i$ to $\mathbf{C}_k$ is less than a threshold θ, otherwise is 0.

If no existing cluster is fit for $\mathbf{d}_i$, a new cluster with $\omega_{K+1} = \alpha$ and $\mathbf{C}_{K+1} = \mathbf{d}_i$ is generated. If $K < T$, the new cluster is added to the existing clusters straightforwardly. If $K = T$, the cluster with smallest ω_k is replaced by the new cluster. The weights are renormalized after this step.

In general, clusters that belong to normal AMHOFs are supposed to have large weights whereas additional clusters that represent abnormal AMHOFs have small weights. Therefore, if the clusters are sorted by descending order of ω_k, we define the first B clusters as *normality*:

$$\text{Normality} = \arg\min_B \left(\sum_{k=1}^{B} \omega_k > \delta \right), \tag{3}$$

where δ is the threshold to determine the minimum portion of the clusters that can represent normal AMHOFs. In other words, if $\mathbf{d}_i$ is able to match one of the first B clusters, it is detected as normal, otherwise is abnormal. Algorithm 1 details the online clustering process.

One significant advantage of this algorithm is that it is adaptive. From Eq. (1) we have a conclusion that a cluster that represents normal AMHOFs will be regarded as an abnormal cluster if it cannot be fit for a new $\mathbf{d}_i$ in approximate $\log\delta/\log(1-\alpha)$ updates [15]. Likewise, if we detect some similar abnormal AMHOFs all the time, the weights of clusters that represent these AMHOFs will increase gradually and eventually become normal clusters.

2.3 Multiple Target Tracking (MTT)

Although we have detected abnormal ROIs in each frame, there are still some false and missing detections due to the serious occlusion of moving objects. With the hypothesis that an abnormal event is supposed to appear in a continuous spatial-temporal locations, we adopt a simplified MTT algorithm [2] to improve the final detection performance.

At time t, we have an available set of existing tracks $\mathcal{T} = \{\mathbf{t}_1, \dots, \mathbf{t}_m\}$, where the state of each track is modelled by a Kalman filter [7], denoted as $\mathbf{t}_i = \{\mathbf{x}_{i,t-1}, P_{i,t-1}, A, H, Q, R\}$, using the notation in Table 1. Meanwhile, we also have a new set of blobs, which are extracted from the foreground pixels of the detected abnormal ROIs through a connected-component labeling algorithm [14]. The centroids of the blobs are denoted as $\mathcal{Z} = \{\mathbf{z}_{1,t}, \dots, \mathbf{z}_{n,t}\}$. For an existing track $\mathbf{t}_i$, we first predict its new state $\hat{\mathbf{x}}_{i,t}$ and state covariance $\hat{P}_{i,t}$ using the estimated state $\mathbf{x}_{i,t-1}$ and estimated state covariance $P_{i,t-1}$ at time $t-1$:

$$\begin{aligned} \hat{\mathbf{x}}_{i,t} &= A\mathbf{x}_{i,t-1}, \\ \hat{P}_{i,t} &= AP_{i,t-1}A^T + Q. \end{aligned} \tag{4}$$

Next, we associate an existing track $\mathbf{t}_i$ with a blob $\mathbf{z}_{j,t}$ by gating computation. Specifically, a distance matrix D is constructed, where D_{ij} measures the squared Mahalanobis distance between $\hat{\mathbf{x}}_{i,t}$ and $\mathbf{z}_{j,t}$:

$$D_{ij} = (\mathbf{z}_{j,t} - H\hat{\mathbf{x}}_{i,t})^T (H\hat{P}_{i,t}H^T + R)^{-1} (\mathbf{z}_{j,t} - H\hat{\mathbf{x}}_{i,t}). \tag{5}$$

A blob $\mathbf{z}_{j,t}$ is the candidate to be associated with a track $\mathbf{t}_i$ only if $D_{ij} \le G$, where G is the gate size. When there are multiple blobs within the gate, we adopt the Global Nearest Neighbor (GNN) scheme to assign the nearest blob to the track. It works well in our approach due to the sparse distributed blobs and the proposed robust anomaly detector. However, multiple hypothesis tracking [5, 8] may be considered under some more complicated environments.

A blob can either be assigned to an existing track or initiate a new track. If a blob $\mathbf{z}_{j,t}$ is assigned to an existing track $\mathbf{t}_i$, the track is updated as:

$$\begin{aligned} K &= \hat{P}_{i,t}H^T(H\hat{P}_{i,t}H^T + R)^{-1}, \\ \mathbf{x}_{i,t} &= \hat{\mathbf{x}}_{i,t} + K(\mathbf{z}_{j,t} - H\hat{\mathbf{x}}_{i,t}), \\ P_{i,t} &= (I - KH)\hat{P}_{i,t}, \end{aligned} \tag{6}$$

otherwise it initiates a new track.

If no blob is assigned to an existing track $\mathbf{t}_i$, the track is updated as:

$$\begin{aligned} \mathbf{x}_{i,t} &= \hat{\mathbf{x}}_{i,t}, \\ P_{i,t} &= \hat{P}_{i,t}, \end{aligned} \tag{7}$$

which provides a level of support for temporary occlusion.

We delete an existing track if no blob is assigned to it in a certain number of frames, this track can either disappear or be noise, depending on the track length. To improve the detection results, we only keep the tracks whose length is greater than 20 and the proportion of visible frames in a track is greater than 0.6 empirically.

Table 1: Notation of the Kalman filter

Symbol	Description
$\mathbf{x}_{i,t}$	Estimated state of track i at time t
$\hat{\mathbf{x}}_{i,t}$	Predicted state of track i at time t
$\mathbf{z}_{j,t}$	The centroid of blob j at time t
$P_{i,t}$	Estimated state covariance of track i at time t
$\hat{P}_{i,t}$	Predicted state covariance of track i at time t
K	Kalman gain
A	State transition matrix, constant
H	Measurement matrix, constant
Q	Process noise covariance, constant
R	Measurement noise covariance, constant
I	Identity matrix

3. EXPERIMENTAL RESULT

3.1 Setup

We have carried out experiments on the UCSD anomaly detection dataset[1], which contains two subsets from two different pedestrian walkways. The first set, denoted as "Ped1", has 34 training clips and 36 testing clips, each with 158×238 resolution (i.e., height $\times$ width) and a fixed length of 200 frames, while the second, denoted as "Ped2", has 16 training clips and 12 testing clips, each with a resolution of 240×360, and the length varying from 120 to 180 frames.

The same as in [11, 9], two performance metrics are employed for evaluation: area under the ROC curve (AUC) and Rate of Detection (RD). The latter is defined as RD = 1 − EER, where EER stands for the Equal Error Rate (EER)[2]. We use the same evaluation methodology in [11, 9] to compare the performance: frame level and pixel level. For the former an anomaly detection is counted correct if a frame is related to an abnormal event regardless of the anomaly location within the frame, while for the latter the anomaly detection is counted correct only if at least 40% of the true anomaly-related pixels are detected.

The orientation bin number M in AMHOF is set as 8 empirically. To reduce computational cost, we first resize the frame resolution of both sets to 160×240. Then a 20×10 sliding window with 1/2 overlap is applied to extract ROIs, whose temporal length in both sets is set as 6.

In the following experiments, the threshold θ to match a cluster is set as 0.15. Meanwhile, to obtain the optimal performance, four parameters, i.e., quantization level N, granularity level L, maximum number of cluster T, and learning rate α, have to be evaluated. We use a grid search scheme to find the optimal parameters. Specifically, N is chosen from $\{2, 4, 6, 8, 10\}$, L from $\{1, 2, 3, 4, 5\}$, T from $\{3, 5, 10, 15, 20\}$, and α from $\{0.1, 0.01, 0.001, 0.0001\}$, we try all the possible settings and report the best results of both subsets obtained using $N = 8$, $L = 4$, $T = 15$, and $\alpha = 0.001$.

3.2 Results on UCSD

Figure 4 illustrates some detection results on the Ped1 dataset. By comparison with the results of OWC, OWC-MTT improves the detection results on several aspects. First, with the help of background subtraction and blob extraction, OWC-MTT displays more accurate anomaly localiza-

[1]http://www.svcl.ucsd.edu/projects/anomaly/dataset.html

[2]The error rate at the point on the ROC curve where true positive rate equals to true negative rate (i.e., 1 - false positive rate).

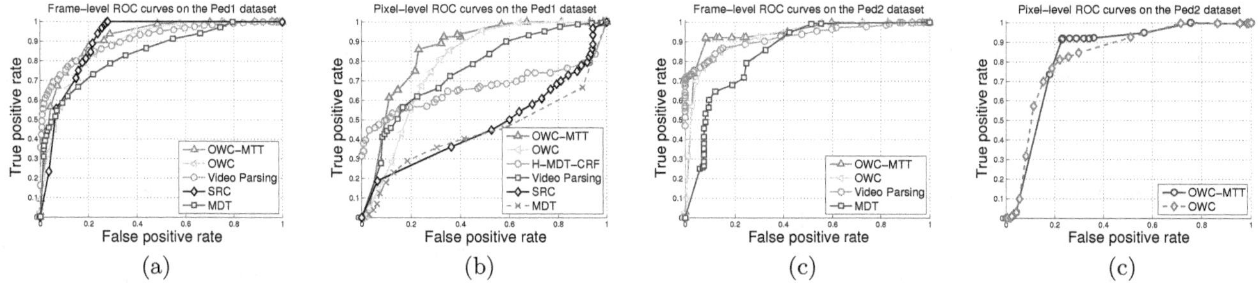

Figure 3: Comparison of ROC curves on the UCSD dataset. (a) Frame-level on Ped1. (b) Pixel-level on Ped1. (c) Frame-level on Ped2. (d) Pixel-level on Ped2.

Figure 4: Detection results on some sample frames from the Ped1 dataset. First row: OWC. Second row: OWC-MTT, where the annotation number corresponds to the track id.

Table 2: Performance comparison on Ped1.

Method	Frame-level (%) AUC	Frame-level (%) RD	Pixel-level(%) AUC	Pixel-level(%) RD
MDT [11]	83.8	75.6	44.0	49.4
H-MDT-CRF [9]	-	82.2	66.2	64.9
Video Parsing [1]	90.5	81.9	75.6	67.6
SRC [4]	90.2	80.8	47.1	46.0
SCL [10]	91.8	85.0	63.8	59.1
OWC	88.2	80.2	79.0	71.6
OWC-MTT	**91.2**	**82.9**	**85.4**	**76.7**

tion than OWC. Besides, the MTT algorithm not only filters out noise (Figure 4(a)(c)) by removing short tracks, it also has the capability to endure temporary occlusion; for instance, in Figure 4(b), where the abnormal target disappears in a few frames due to occlusion.

We compare our approach with the-state-of-art approaches on Ped1 data, including MDT [11], H-MDT-CRF [9], Video Parsing [1], SRC [4], and SCL [10] on both the ROC curves in Figure 3(a-b) and the RD metric in Table 2. In short, OWC-MTT achieves the comparable RD on frame-level, and best RD on pixel-level annotation, attaining **76.7**%.

On the other hand, the ROC curve comparison on Ped2 data is illustrated in Figure 3(c-d), and the RD metric comparison is shown in Table 3. As can be seen, OWC-MTT achieves the best AUC and RD metrics in both frame-level and pixel-level, where the pixel-level RD has been improved by around **9**% over H-MDT-CRF [9]. Figure 5 displays some detection results on Ped2 data.

3.3 Running time analysis

Our approach is implemented using MATLAB R2014a

Figure 5: Detection results on Ped2. First row: OWC. Second row: OWC-MTT.

Table 3: Performance comparison on Ped2.

Method	Frame-level (%) AUC	Frame-level (%) RD	Pixel-level (%) AUC	Pixel-level (%) RD
MDT [11]	84.8	74.0	-	45.0
H-MDT-CRF [9]	-	81.5	-	70.1
Video Parsing [1]	91.0	85.8	-	-
OWC	92.5	85.2	83.1	77.9
OWC-MTT	**94.0**	**86.1**	**83.6**	**78.9**

and runs on a 2.7GHZ Intel Core i5 with 8GB RAM. The average computation time is 27.2 FPS on Ped1, and 31.2 FPS on Ped2. Compared with the state-of-the-art approaches in Table 4, our approach is much faster than H-MDT-CRF, Video parsing, and SRC, with an exception of SCL. However, note that SCL resizes the frame resolution from 158×238 to 120×160, which reduces computational cost significantly.

Table 4: Computational time comparison on UCSD dataset (seconds/frame).

	H-MDT-CRF	Video parsing	SRC	SCL	OWC-MTT
Ped1	1.11	$5 \sim 10$	3.8	0.007	0.037
Ped2	1.38	$5 \sim 10$	-	-	0.032

4. CONCLUSION

In this paper, we introduce a novel framework for AED. The OWC algorithm is not only computationally efficient, but also adaptive to possible concept drifts in video surveillance. Meanwhile, we adopt the MTT algorithm to filter noise. We employ our framework on a benchmark dataset and achieve better or comparable results as well as a 30 FPS processing speed.

5. REFERENCES

[1] B. Antić and B. Ommer. Video parsing for abnormality detection. In *Computer Vision (ICCV), 2011 IEEE International Conference on*, pages 2415–2422. IEEE, 2011.

[2] S. S. Blackman. Multiple hypothesis tracking for multiple target tracking. *Aerospace and Electronic Systems Magazine, IEEE*, 19(1):5–18, 2004.

[3] M. M. Breunig, H.-P. Kriegel, R. T. Ng, and J. Sander. Lof: identifying density-based local outliers. In *ACM sigmod record*, volume 29, pages 93–104. ACM, 2000.

[4] Y. Cong, J. Yuan, and J. Liu. Abnormal event detection in crowded scenes using sparse representation. *Pattern Recognition*, 46(7):1851–1864, 2013.

[5] L. J. Cox and S. L. Hingorani. An efficient implementation of reid's multiple hypothesis tracking algorithm and its evaluation for the purpose of visual tracking. *Pattern Analysis and Machine Intelligence, IEEE Transactions on*, 18(2):138–150, 1996.

[6] B. K. Horn and B. G. Schunck. Determining optical flow. In *1981 Technical Symposium East*, pages 319–331. International Society for Optics and Photonics, 1981.

[7] R. E. Kalman. A new approach to linear filtering and prediction problems. *Journal of basic Engineering*, 82(1):35–45, 1960.

[8] C. Kim, F. Li, A. Ciptadi, and J. M. Rehg. Multiple hypothesis tracking revisited. In *Proceedings of the IEEE International Conference on Computer Vision*, pages 4696–4704, 2015.

[9] W. Li, V. Mahadevan, and N. Vasconcelos. Anomaly detection and localization in crowded scenes. *Pattern Analysis and Machine Intelligence, IEEE Transactions on*, 36(1):18–32, Jan 2014.

[10] C. Lu, J. Shi, and J. Jia. Abnormal event detection at 150 fps in matlab. In *Computer Vision (ICCV), 2013 IEEE International Conference on*, pages 2720–2727. IEEE, 2013.

[11] V. Mahadevan, W. Li, V. Bhalodia, and N. Vasconcelos. Anomaly detection in crowded scenes. In *Computer Vision and Pattern Recognition (CVPR), 2010 IEEE Conference on*, pages 1975–1981. IEEE, 2010.

[12] B. Schölkopf, J. C. Platt, J. Shawe-Taylor, A. J. Smola, and R. C. Williamson. Estimating the support of a high-dimensional distribution. *Neural Computation*, 13(7):1443–1471, 2001.

[13] C. Stauffer and W. E. L. Grimson. Adaptive background mixture models for real-time tracking. In *Computer Vision and Pattern Recognition, 1999. IEEE Computer Society Conference on.*, volume 2, pages 246–252. IEEE, 1999.

[14] K. Suzuki, I. Horiba, and N. Sugie. Linear-time connected-component labeling based on sequential local operations. *Computer Vision and Image Understanding*, 89(1):1–23, 2003.

[15] Z. Zivkovic. Improved adaptive gaussian mixture model for background subtraction. In *Pattern Recognition, 2004. ICPR 2004. Proceedings of the 17th International Conference on*, volume 2, pages 28–31. IEEE, 2004.

Accelerating Convolutional Neural Networks for Mobile Applications

Peisong Wang
National Laboratory of Pattern Recognition, CASIA, Beijing, China
University of Chinese Academy of Sciences, Beijing, China
peisong.wang@nlpr.ia.ac.cn

Jian Cheng
National Laboratory of Pattern Recognition, CASIA, Beijing, China
University of Chinese Academy of Sciences, Beijing, China
CAS Center for Excellence in Brain Science and Intelligence Technology
jcheng@nlpr.ia.ac.cn

ABSTRACT

Convolutional neural networks (CNNs) have achieved remarkable performance in a wide range of computer vision tasks, typically at the cost of massive computational complexity. The low speed of these networks may hinder real-time applications especially when computational resources are limited. In this paper, an efficient and effective approach is proposed to accelerate the test-phase computation of CNNs based on low-rank and group sparse tensor decomposition. Specifically, for each convolutional layer, the kernel tensor is decomposed into the sum of a small number of low multilinear rank tensors. Then we replace the original kernel tensors in all layers with the approximate tensors and fine-tune the whole net with respect to the final classification task using standard backpropagation.

Comprehensive experiments on ILSVRC-12 demonstrate significant reduction in computational complexity, at the cost of negligible loss in accuracy. For the widely used VGG-16 model, our approach obtains a 6.6× speed-up on PC and 5.91× speed-up on mobile device of the whole network with less than 1% increase on top-5 error.

Keywords

Convolutional Neural Networks; Acceleration; Image Classification; Tensor Decomposition

1. INTRODUCTION

In recent years, convolutional neural networks (CNNs) is continuously setting new state-of-the-art performance in computer vision tasks such as image classification and object detection. However, to a certain extent these breakthroughs have become possible through adding layers and increasing the size of feature maps. One drawback of the resulting networks is that the computation time increases significantly at both training and testing phase. Thanks to specialized hardwares like NVIDIA GPUs and CPU clusters, these CNN models can be trained offline within a relatively affordable time. But the real-world systems may still suffer from long testing time, especially for real-time but computation-limited systems, such as smart phones and automated vehicles. Therefore, it is of central importance to speed up test-phase computation of CNN models.

There have been a banch of studies for CNN model acceleration. One of the most widely used techniques is low-rank approximation. Many low-rank based approaches [3, 6] have been investigated since Denil et al.'s work [2] on reducing redundancy of CNN models. Among these studies, Zhang et al.'s work [18] achieved 3.8× speed-up on VGG-16 model. Low-rank tensor decomposition based methods have also been developed. Lebedev et al. [11] utilized CP-decomposition to approximate the 4D convolutional kernel tensor. But they only handled a single layer for AlexNet. Kim et al. [8] proposed to use Tucker decomposition to reduce the computational complexity of CNN models. Network pruning [4, 12] is another widely used technique for CNN compression and acceleration. The main idea of these methods is to remove low-saliency parameters or small-weight connections [4]. These methods achieve significant theoretical speed-up ratio, but the resulting unstructured sparse connections do not fit well in parallel computation. Beyond the methods mentioned above, many other approaches are proposed. Wu et al. [17] proposed to use product quantization for CNN compression and acceleration at the same time. FFT-based method was also investigated in [13].

In this paper, we propose an acceleration method for CNN models based on tensor low-rank and group sparse decomposition. The resulting architecture gains efficiency from both low-rank and sparsity. We evaluate our proposed method on one of the largest image classification benchmark of ILSVRC-12 [14]. Our approach achieves 6.6× speed-up with less than 1% drop in top-5 classification accuracy. Our contributions can be summarized as follows:

- We propose a tensor Block Term Decomposition (BTD) based acceleration method for convolutional neural networks, which benefits from both low-rank and group sparsity.
- A new alternative least square method, i.e., Principle Component Iteration (PCI), is proposed for efficient tensor block term decomposition.

MM '16, October 15-19, 2016, Amsterdam, Netherlands

DOI: http://dx.doi.org/10.1145/2964284.2967280

- Our method achieves significant speed-up for CNN models. For the widely used VGG-16 [15] model, we obtain 6.6× actual speed-up on PC and 5.91× speed-up on smart phone with less than 1% drop on top-5 classification accuracy.

2. PROPOSED METHOD

Throughout this paper vectors are denoted boldface lowercase letters, e.g., $\mathbf{x}$. Boldface capital letters, e.g., $\mathbf{X}$, are utilized to represent matrices. Euler script letters are used to denote higher-order tensors, e.g., $\mathcal{X}$. The symbol $\times_n$ represent n-mode product of a tensor with a matrix [9].

2.1 Low-rank and Group Sparse Tensor Approximation

In CNN models, the convolutional kernel is a 4-way tensor of size W×H×S×T, where W/H is the width/height of the kernel and S/T is the number of input/output channels. For simplicity, we combine width/height together and denote the spatial dimension as P(=WH). Thus the kernel tensor becomes a 3D tensor. The proposed method exploits low-rank and group sparse decomposition on the 3D convolutional kernel tensor.

Our assumption is twofold. First, we assume that the learned kernel tensors are low rank along the input and output channels. The resulting architecture is called *bottleneck* [5]. Bottleneck architecture consists of three layers where the first 1×1 convolution is used to reduce input channel dimension, the last 1×1 convolution layer is responsible for restoring output channel dimension, and the middle layer is a regular W×H convolution but with smaller input/output dimensions.

We also assume that connections of the second layer of the bottleneck architecture is sparse in group. The resulting architecture is a layer with multiple convolutions which is (channel-wise) locally connected. We refer to this architecture as *group* like in the implementation of Caffe [7].

The approach presented here benefits from both low-rank and group sparsity. The method proposed has the form of tensor block term decomposition [1]. Thus we denote our acceleration method as BTD.

2.2 Block Term Decomposition on Convolutional Kernels

Throughout this paper we represent convolutional kernels as a 3D tensor $\mathcal{T} \in \mathbb{R}^{S\times T\times P}$, where S and T are the numbers of input and output channels and P is the spatial dimension, e.g., for a 3×3 kernel, P equals to 9.

The basic idea of tensor block term decomposition is to approximate a tensor as a sum of several low-rank tensors. Each low-rank tensor is in the form of a core tensor multiplied by a factor matrix along each dimension. For the convolutional kernel tensor $\mathcal{T}$, the block term decomposition is

$$\mathcal{T} \approx \sum_{r=1}^{R} \mathcal{G}_r \times_1 \mathbf{A}_r \times_2 \mathbf{B}_r \times_3 \mathbf{C}_r \tag{1}$$

where $\mathcal{G}_r \in \mathbb{R}^{s\times t\times p}$ is the core tensor of r-th subtensor and $\mathbf{A}_r \in \mathbb{R}^{S\times s}$, $\mathbf{B}_r \in \mathbb{R}^{T\times t}$ and $\mathbf{C}_r \in \mathbb{R}^{P\times p}$ are factor matrices along each dimension. Here the lower-case letter s, t and p represent the rank in each dimension respectively.

In our method, we don't exploit the low rank of spatial

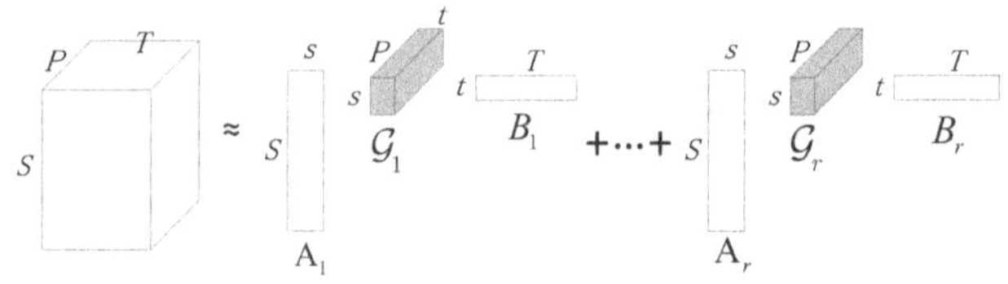

Figure 1: Visualization of tensor block term decomposition.

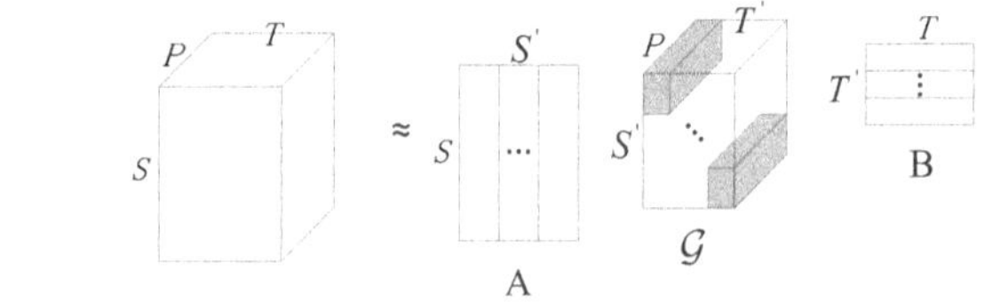

Figure 2: Visualization of tensor block term decomposition with a group sparse core tensor.

dimension, thus we utilize the decomposition of the following form:

$$\mathcal{T} \approx \sum_{r=1}^{R} \mathcal{G}_r \times_1 \mathbf{A}_r \times_2 \mathbf{B}_r \tag{2}$$

where $\mathcal{G}_r \in \mathbb{R}^{s\times t\times P}$ is the core tensor of r-th subtensor and $\mathbf{A}_r \in \mathbb{R}^{S\times s}$ and $\mathbf{B}_r \in \mathbb{R}^{T\times t}$ are factor matrices along input and output channel dimensions respectively. We can think that the factor matrix along spatial dimension in (2) is an identity matrix. The decomposition is visualized in Figure 1.

The next section will discuss how to solve this decomposition problem efficiently. If the decomposition is known, each component of the subtensors can be concatenated, i.e., concatenating $\mathbf{A}_1, \cdots, \mathbf{A}_r$ into a big matrix $\mathbf{A}$, and $\mathbf{B}_1, \cdots, \mathbf{B}_r$ into a big matrix $\mathbf{B}$, and $\mathcal{G}_1, \cdots, \mathcal{G}_r$ into a big core tensor $\mathcal{G}$. Here the resulting big core tensor $\mathcal{G}$ is group sparse, i.e., non-zero values are along the diagonal blocks, as shown in Figure 2. The matrices $\mathbf{A}$ and $\mathbf{B}$ correspond to the first and last 1×1 convolutional layers of the bottleneck architecture, and the core tensor $\mathcal{G}$ is the second convolution kernel of size $W \times H$ which can be constructed using multiple groups. Figure 3 shows how convolution layers can be replaced by new layers for speed-up.

2.3 Principle Component Iteration

Tensor decomposition can be seen as a generalization of matrix decomposition to multidimensional case and has been actively studied in recent years. Many approaches are proposed for tensor decomposition, however, few of them consider the block term decomposition. An intuitive method for solving the decomposition problem of (1) is in the greedy way, e.g., greedily finding a best Tucker approximation of

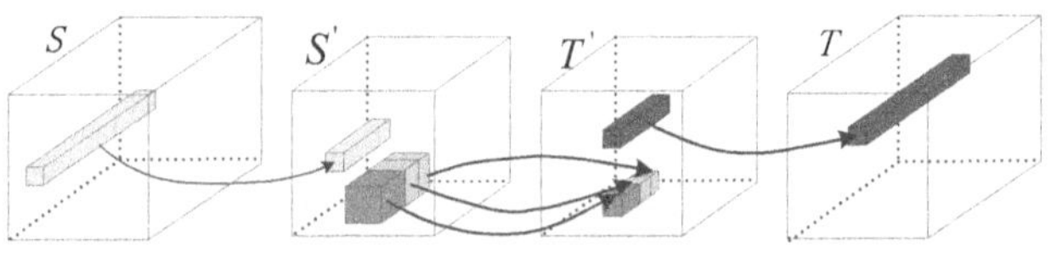

Figure 3: Block term decomposition used for speeding-up convolution.

the residual tensor. But this greedy method may suffer from high approximation error. In our experiment we find that a minor increase of the approximation error may result in a huge drop on the final accuracy.

The authors of [1] gives an alternating least squares (ALS) algorithms. But in our experiments, we find that this method has a large memory consumption and runs quite slow, which is prohibitive for practical use. Nonlinear least squares (NLS) algorithms are also quite slow.

In this section, a much more efficient algorithm called Principle Component Iteration (PCI) is proposed, which is a generalization of higher order orthogonal iteration (HOOI) [9] used in the Tucker decomposition. The basic idea of PCI is to find the principle component (a subtensor) of residual tensor approximated using other components at every iteration. PCI is much more efficient than existing methods. For example, the decomposition time of a single layer for VGG-16 model is more than ten hours using NLS algorithm, while PCI can achieve comparable approximation error within half an hour. The details of our proposed PCI method is presented in Algorithm 1.

Algorithm 1 Principle Component Iteration

```
procedure PCI(𝒯)
    initialize 𝒯_r ← 0 for r = 1, ··· , R
    repeat
        for r = 1 to R do
            𝒯_res ← 𝒯 − sum(𝒯_1, ··· , 𝒯_{r−1}, 𝒯_{r+1}, ··· , 𝒯_R)
            𝒯_r ← HOOI(𝒯_res)
        end for
        𝒯_res ← 𝒯 − sum(𝒯_1, ··· , 𝒯_R)
    until 𝒯_res ceases to decrease or maximum iterations reached
    return 𝒯_1, ··· , 𝒯_R
end procedure
```

2.4 Complexity Analysis

For every spatial position and every convolutional layer of the original networks, the normal convolution requires $S \times T \times W \times H$ multiplication-addition operations. While in our method, the required operations of the corresponding three layers (note that we replace the original convolutional layer with three convolutional layers) are $S \times S'$, $S' \times T' \times W \times H/R$, and $T \times T'$ respectively, where R represents the number of groups. Thus the theoretical speed-up ratio is given by:

$$ratio = \frac{STWH}{SS' + S'T'WH/R + TT'} \tag{3}$$

3. EXPERIMENTS

In this section, we evaluate our approach on ILSVRC-12 [14] image classification benchmark. Experiments are conducted on two of the mostly used CNN models, i.e., AlexNet [10] and VGG-16 [15]. Single-layer performance for AlexNet is firstly evaluated using our approach. Based on the experimental results, we further show the power of our method on whole-model acceleration of very deep VGG model [15]. Through out this section, we use Berkeley's *Caffe* [7] routines for our experiments. We utilize Intel MKL and Eigen3 library for PC and smart phone respectively.

3.1 Speed-Up Results for AlexNet

In this subsection, we evaluate the acceleration performance on AlexNet. We process the second convolutional layer of AlexNet, as in [3, 6, 11, 17], because the second convolution is the most time-consuming layer during test-phase. Table 1 shows the comparison with existing methods. All results in Table 1 are the best results reported by the authors in their papers except for [6], which is reproduced by [11]. For our method, we set the selected rank $S' = 40, T' = 120$ and the group number R is set to be 20.

Table 1: Comparison with other methods for the second convolutional layer of AlexNet.

Method	Speed-up	Top-5 Err. ↑
Biclustering + SVD [3]	2.7×	0.95%
CP Decomposition [11]	4.5×	1.22%
Q-CNN [17]	6.1×	0.31%
Low rank [6]	6.6×	≈1%
BTD	8.1×	0.98%

From Table 1 we can conclude that with about 1% drop in accuracy, our method achieves more than 8× speed-up, which is much higher than other methods.

3.2 Whole-Model Acceleration for VGG-16

In this subsection, we evaluate our approach on VGG-16 model for ImageNet classification. We mainly focus on the convolutional layers in our experiments. But our approach can be directly combined with other approaches e.g., the product quantization method [17] or SVD used in [3, 18]. We report actual running time and speed-up ratio for each layer as well as for the whole VGG-16 model in Table 2. All results in this subsection are conducted on personal computer with i7 CPU (3.4GHz). We don't process the first convolutional layer because of the small complexity.

As can been seen from Table 2, our method can achieves about $6 \sim 13\times$ CPU speed-up. Our method obtains 6.6× whole-model speed-up (column denoted by "Whole") even without accelerating the fully connected layers at the cost of 1% drop in accuracy. Note that the first fully connected layer can be treated as convolution with large filters. Thus we can further improve speed-up ratio to 7.4× (last column denoted by "Whole*"), which is almost twice as much of the best existing method as shown in Table 3. Note that the theoretical speed-up ratios shown in Table 3 are calculated using the multiplication-addition operations of all convolutional layers before and after accelerating. Non-convolutional layers, such as pooling layers, are also time-consuming. Thus the actual speed-up ratios are much lower than the theoretical ones, especially at higher speed-up ratios.

Comparison with current state-of-the-art methods are illustrated in Table 3. All results are the best results reported by the authors except for the method used in [6], which is the result reproduced by the authors of [18]. The different theoretical speed-up ratio are got by setting different hyperparameters, for example the rank used by these methods.

From Table 3, we find that our method outperforms all the rest methods significantly. Even without accelerating fully connected layers, our method can still achieves 6.6× actual speed-up, which is much higher compared to the 3.8× acceleration of [18].

Table 2: Performance of accelerating VGG-16 model. Runing time is in milliseconds for a single view on CPU using Intel MKL (single thread, with SSE).

Layers	$C1_1$	$C1_2$	$C2_1$	$C2_2$	$C3_1$	$C3_2$	$C3_3$	$C4_1$	$C4_2$	$C4_3$	$C5_1$	$C5_3$	$C5_3$	Whole	Whole*
VGG-16	10.9	200.4	86.4	171.2	79.0	159.7	159.9	76.9	154.1	153.6	42.8	42.8	42.7	1442.0	1442.0
BTD	10.95	33.25	9.46	18.87	7.58	12.41	14.01	6.20	10.40	13.00	6.64	6.63	6.62	218.33	194.88
Speed-up	1×	6.0×	9.1×	9.0×	10.4×	12.9×	11.4×	12.4×	14.8×	11.8×	6.4×	6.5×	6.5×	6.6×	7.4×

Table 3: Comparison with other methods for whole-model acceleration of VGG-16. BTD*/BTD is obtained with/without processing the fully connected layer. Different theoretical speed-up ratios result from different hyper-parameters

Method	Theoretical	Actual	Top-5 Err. ↑
Zhang [18]	4×	3.8×	0.3%
	5×	-	1.0%
Jaderberg [6]	3×	-	2.3%
	4×	3.8×	9.7%
	5×	-	29.7%
Tai [16]	3×	2.1×	0.3%
Q-CNN [17]	4×	-	0.5%
BTD	12.1×	6.6×	1.0%
BTD*	12.2×	7.4×	1.3%

3.3 Results on Mobile Device

In this subsection, we evaluate the performance of our method on smart phone. Results are conducted on Huawei Mate 7 which is equipped with a 1.8GHz Kirin 925 CPU. We adapt the code of Caffe onto Android and use Eigen3 library for matrix operations. We use the same accelerated model as in previous subsection. Thus the accuracy drop for mobile devices is the same as reported in previous subsection. The results are shown in Table 4. Speed-up ratio are based on runing time of VGG-16 on smart phone using single thread.

Table 4: Comparison on time consumption of the original and the accelerated VGG-16 model on smart phone.

Model	#threads	Time (s)	speed-up
VGG-16	1	10.52	1×
	4	4.29	2.45×
BTD	1	1.78	5.91×
	4	0.96	10.95×

From Table 4 we can see that our model runs much faster than the original VGG-16 model. The actual speed-up is 5.91× using single thread.

4. CONCLUSIONS

In this paper, we propose an acceleration method for CNN models based on tensor low-rank and group sparse decomposition. The resulting architecture gains efficiency from both low-rank and sparsity that cannot be matched by either method. We also propose a new alternative least square method, i.e., priciple componant iteration, for tensor block term decomposition, which is much more efficient. Comprehensive experiments conducted on ILSVRC-12 benchmark [14] demonstrate significant reduction in computational complexity, at the cost of negligible loss in accuracy.

Acknowledgements

This work was supported in part by National Natural Science Foundation of China (No.61332016) and Beijing Brain Science Research Project (No.Z161100000216146).

5. REFERENCES

[1] L. De Lathauwer and D. Nion. Decompositions of a higher-order tensor in block terms-part iii: Alternating least squares algorithms. *SIAM journal on Matrix Analysis and Applications*, 30(3):1067–1083, 2008.

[2] M. Denil, B. Shakibi, L. Dinh, N. de Freitas, et al. Predicting parameters in deep learning. In *Advances in Neural Information Processing Systems*, pages 2148–2156, 2013.

[3] E. L. Denton, W. Zaremba, J. Bruna, Y. LeCun, and R. Fergus. Exploiting linear structure within convolutional networks for efficient evaluation. In *Advances in Neural Information Processing Systems*, pages 1269–1277, 2014.

[4] S. Han, J. Pool, J. Tran, and W. Dally. Learning both weights and connections for efficient neural network. In *Advances in Neural Information Processing Systems*, pages 1135–1143, 2015.

[5] K. He, X. Zhang, S. Ren, and J. Sun. Deep residual learning for image recognition. *IEEE Conference on Computer Vision and Pattern Recognition (CVPR)*, 2016.

[6] M. Jaderberg, A. Vedaldi, and A. Zisserman. Speeding up convolutional neural networks with low rank expansions. *arXiv preprint arXiv:1405.3866*, 2014.

[7] Y. Jia, E. Shelhamer, J. Donahue, S. Karayev, J. Long, R. Girshick, S. Guadarrama, and T. Darrell. Caffe: Convolutional architecture for fast feature embedding. In *Proceedings of the ACM International Conference on Multimedia*, pages 675–678. ACM, 2014.

[8] Y.-D. Kim, E. Park, S. Yoo, T. Choi, L. Yang, and D. Shin. Compression of deep convolutional neural networks for fast and low power mobile applications. *arXiv preprint arXiv:1511.06530*, 2015.

[9] T. G. Kolda and B. W. Bader. Tensor decompositions and applications. *SIAM review*, 51(3):455–500, 2009.

[10] A. Krizhevsky, I. Sutskever, and G. E. Hinton. Imagenet classification with deep convolutional neural networks. In *Advances in neural information processing systems*, pages 1097–1105, 2012.

[11] V. Lebedev, Y. Ganin, M. Rakhuba, I. Oseledets, and V. Lempitsky. Speeding-up convolutional neural networks using fine-tuned cp-decomposition. *arXiv preprint arXiv:1412.6553*, 2014.

[12] B. Liu, M. Wang, H. Foroosh, M. Tappen, and M. Pensky. Sparse convolutional neural networks. In

IEEE Conference on Computer Vision and Pattern Recognition (CVPR), pages 806–814, 2015.

[13] M. Mathieu, M. Henaff, and Y. LeCun. Fast training of convolutional networks through ffts. *arXiv preprint arXiv:1312.5851*, 2013.

[14] O. Russakovsky, J. Deng, H. Su, J. Krause, S. Satheesh, S. Ma, Z. Huang, A. Karpathy, A. Khosla, M. Bernstein, et al. Imagenet large scale visual recognition challenge. *International Journal of Computer Vision*, 115(3):211–252, 2015.

[15] K. Simonyan and A. Zisserman. Very deep convolutional networks for large-scale image recognition. *arXiv preprint arXiv:1409.1556*, 2014.

[16] C. Tai, T. Xiao, X. Wang, et al. Convolutional neural networks with low-rank regularization. *arXiv preprint arXiv:1511.06067*, 2015.

[17] J. Wu, C. Leng, Y. Wang, Q. Hu, and J. Cheng. Quantized convolutional neural networks for mobile devices. *IEEE Conference on Computer Vision and Pattern Recognition (CVPR)*, 2016.

[18] X. Zhang, J. Zou, K. He, and J. Sun. Accelerating very deep convolutional networks for classification and detection. *IEEE Transactions on Pattern Analysis and Machine Intelligence (TPAMI)*, 2015.

News Program Detection in TV Broadcast Videos

Raghvendra Kannao Durgaprasad Dandi Swamy Yellapu
Prithwijit Guha

Department of Electronics and Electrical Engineering
Indian Institute of Technology Guwahati
Guwahati - 781039, Assam, India
{raghvendra, durga.dandi, swamy.yellapu, pguha}@iitg.ernet.in

ABSTRACT

Television news channels broadcast different kinds of content like debates, interviews, commercials along with news presentations. Real time detection of these news programs or their retrieval from large volumes of stored broadcast videos is a challenging problem and is a necessary first step for broadcast analytics. News program detection is even harder in Indian context where closed caption text or program markers are not provided by TV news channels (not mandated by law). We propose a two stage approach to classify news video segments. First, broadcast video shots are classified with multiple labels based on a set of audio-visual features. Second, sequences of these shot features are modeled to detect news programs. Another contribution of this work is the construction of a dataset of 120 hours of shot categories and news programs from Indian English news channels. We have experimented with SVM, HMM and CRF based classifiers and achieved a $F1$ score of 99% in detecting news programs while experimenting on our dataset.

Keywords

News Program Detection; Semantic Shot Classification; CRF; HMM; SVM

1. INTRODUCTION

Rapid rise in number of 24 × 7 TV news channels have mandated the use of automatic video analysis systems for news monitoring. Segmentation of videos into suitable logical units is a prerequisite for such video analysis [16]. News channels broadcast news bulletins and a wide variety of programs of different genres including debates, interviews and documentaries along with ads. However, only a small set of programs (e.g. news bulletins) may be of interest to the monitoring agencies. Thus, real time broadcast monitoring applications have to keep track of large number of program schedules of multiple channels for selective processing of broadcast videos.

MM '16, October 15-19, 2016, Amsterdam, Netherlands

 ISBN 978-1-4503-3603-1/16/10...$15.00

DOI: http://dx.doi.org/10.1145/2964284.2967281

Schedule of programs aired on a broadcast day is determined by certain demographic segments and engagement of targeted audience in different activities. This is achieved by roughly dividing a broadcast day into seven parts. These parts are late fringe (23 : 00 - 02 : 00 hrs), graveyard (02 : 00 - 06 : 00 hrs), early morning (06 : 00 - 10 : 00 hrs), daytime (10 : 00 - 17 : 00 hrs), early fringe (17 : 00 - 20 : 00 hrs) and prime time slot (20 : 00 - 23 : 00 hrs) [15]. Prime time and early morning slots have highest viewer-ship. followed by early and late fringe slots. Broadcast schedule for these slots is decided well ahead of time and remains unchanged. The daytime, graveyard and post late fringe slots have least viewer-ship throughout the day. Thus, these slots are usually filled with live telecast of some events, rebroadcast of programs, local news bulletins, syndicated news programs etc. These three slots, spanning over almost twelve hours, have very flexible schedule and often deviate from predefined electronic programming guides due to last moment changes [15]. This makes schedule based acquisition of programs uncertain. However, programs can still be identified by using program markers present in closed caption text. In USA, Canada and some countries of European Union, broadcast of closed caption (CC) text is mandated by law. However, this is not the case for most other nations (e.g. South Asian countries). Uncertain scheduling and absence of synchronized CC text mandates broadcast analysis systems to have an automatic program segmentation and genre detection module for processing on-line as well as archival data.

Various shows broadcast on news channels are characterized by unique spatio-temporal presentation formats and are governed by the channel's edit policies. Spatial format corresponds to the studio setup, placement of on screen overlay text, info-graphics, channel logo etc. Whereas, temporal presentation format represents the order in which different types of shots are presented over time. We observe that, spatio-temporal format of different shows are repetitive irrespective of the content. Thus, the spatio-temporal format of these shows can be exploited to identify the genre and type of programs.

Previous Work – Genre classification in context of movies is a well studied problem in multi-media community and several works exist on the same [5, 19]. However, program genre detection in news videos is still comparatively unexplored. Li et al. [10] proposed a program segmentation system in news broadcast and have used the electronic program guides and the markers present in CC text. However, this

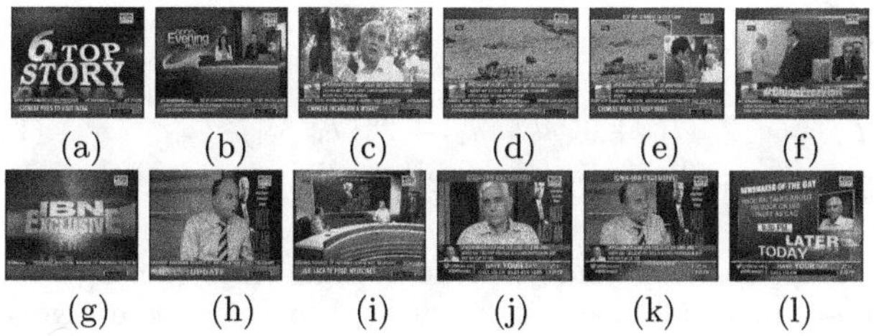

Figure 1: (a)–(f) and (g)–(l) are the key-frames extracted from a news program and debate (non-news) respectively. (e-f) – Multi-view (multiple videos boxes in single frame), (a,g,l) – Graphics (synthetic frame), (l) – Informative Graphics (contains headlines or useful information), (a,g) – Non-Informative Graphics (program or channel logo animation)a,g), (b, h-k) – Studio (program recorded in studio settings), (c,d) – Field (footage acquired by field reporters in indoor/outdoor settings), (b, h-l) – Indoor, (c,d) – Outdoor, (c,h,j,k) – Face Shots (scenes having human faces taken from close or medium distance).

approach fails in many countries like India where CC text is absent. Moreover, news channels often broadcast the live content while reporting various events. Such live broadcast and programs aired during graveyard and daytime slots are not included in the electronic program guides. Thus, this approach may not be applicable to general program segmentation. Zlitni et al. [20] have recently proposed to use a video grammar based on prior knowledge of news channels to achieve news block detection and story segmentation. They have used manually identified shot templates to detect program boundaries. Thus, this approach for segmentation of videos is news channel specific. In this work we have introduced a pure learning based approach while modeling the spatio-temporal presentation format of the news programs.

In our proposal, broadcast videos are shot segmented first and commercial are removed [7] to obtain non-commercial segments as shot sequences. We propose a two stage process for modeling the spatio-temporal presentation format of these shot sequences. **First**, we classify the video shots into following six semantic categories (Figure 1) – **(a)** Multi-view vs. Uni-view **(b)** Graphics vs. Natural **(c)** Non-informative graphics vs. Info-graphics **(d)** Studio vs. Field **(e)** Indoor vs. Outdoor and **(f)** Face Shots vs. Non-face Shots. These semantic categories capture the spatial presentation format. We have experimented with different low level features and feature fusion techniques to train the classifiers. It may be noted that we generate six labels for each video shot. In the **second** stage, the sequence of semantic labels are modeled using Conditional Random Fields (CRFs) to learn the temporal format. We have also experimented with SVMs and HMMs to benchmark the performance of CRF based modeling. Another contribution of this work is the construction of a shot semantic category and news program dataset from roughly 120 hours of TV broadcast from Indian English news channel CNN-IBN.

The rest of the paper is organized in the following manner. Section 2 briefly describes the features and classifiers used for shot categorization. News block detection through sequence classification is explained in Section 3. The experimentations and results are presented in Section 4. Finally, we conclude in Section 5 and sketch the scope of future extensions.

2. VIDEO SHOT CATEGORIZATION

Continuous stream of video data available from TV broadcast is first subjected to video shot segmentation based on color distribution consistency between consecutive video frames. These shot sequences are then preprocessed for removing commercials (using [7]) to obtain non-commercial blocks as temporally ordered shot sequences. The aim of video shot categorization is to provide information on spatial presentation formats. To achieve this, we extract a set of audio-visual features [7, 8, 17] from each shot and classify it into following six categories. These categories are **(a)** Multi-view vs. Uni-view **(b)** Graphics vs. Natural **(c)** Non-informative graphics vs. Info-graphics **(d)** Studio vs. Field **(e)** Indoor vs. Outdoor and **(f)** Face Shots vs. Non-face Shots. All visual features are extracted from video frames and are aggregated over the entire shot. These features are briefly described next.

Color Features – We have used **Distinct Color Score** [3] (single dimensional), **Ranked Histogram** [3] having 512 bins, **Farthest Neighbor Histogram** [3] having 766 bins, **HSV Histogram** with 256 bins per channel [8], **Grid Color Moments** [17], **Ohta Histogram** having 32 bins for each of the three channels [13], **Saturation Metric Score** (single dimensional) [3] and **Color Oriented Histogram (COH)** having 256 bins [8]. These features are mainly useful in discriminating graphics, indoor and studio shots from others [6].

Gradient Features – Natural videos usually have smoother gradients as compared to synthetic video shots [6]. Moreover, Info-graphics and Multi-view shots have peculiar pattern of edges due to presence of text and multiple windows. To capture this information, we have computed **Grid-wise Edge Oriented Histogram** (GEOH) as distribution of edge orientations by dividing video frame into cells. From each cell of 5×5 grid, we have computed a 4 bin histogram edge orientation histogram (EOH). All these EOHs are then concatenated to form GEOH. Additionally, we have also combined 256 bin COH and EOH (by placing bins alternately) from each cell of 5×5 grid to form Grid-wise ECOH (GECOH) [8].

Motion Distribution – Outdoor, field and non-informative graphic shots have significant motion content compared to others [6]. Thus, motion features can be used to discriminate these shots from others. We compute dense optical flow (Horn-Schunk) between consecutive frames to construct a distribution of flow magnitudes over the entire shot with 40 uniformly divided bins in range of $[0, 40]$. Along with optical flow, **Frame Difference Distribution** is also computed. We obtain the frame difference by averaging absolute frame difference in each of 3 color channels and the distribution is constructed with 32 bins in the range of $[0, 255]$.

Overlay Text Distribution – Text distribution is an important cue for identifying Info-graphics, face and multi-view shots as broadcasters use a specific layout for these shots [7, 6]. Following existing works [7], we have divided the frame into a 5×3 grid and have constructed a 30 dimensional feature vector (TD) storing mean and variance of the fractions of text area in each grid block of every frame over the entire shot.

Face Area Statistics – We have derived several features from the scene distribution of faces. This is a strong feature in identifying face shots and works moderately in identify natural shots. We have used number of detected faces (single dimensional), **Face Detection Features** represented with centroid (two dimensional) and area (single dimensional) of detected face for top 10 faces arranged in decreasing order of area, grid-wise distribution of face area extracted from 5×5 grid and **Histogram of Normalized Face Area** having 10 exponentially divided bins averaged over the entire shot as features [17].

Audio Features – Audio features can be used to discriminate non-informative graphics and field shots from others as former will have non-pure speech. We have used 6 low level audio features to discriminate between speech, music and non-pure speech. These are **Short Time Energy**, **Zero Crossing Rate**, **Fundamental Frequency**, **Spectral Centroid**, **Flux** and **Roll-Off Frequency** [18]. For all above mentioned audio features, we have used non-overlapping frames of 20 msec duration and sampling frequency of 8 kHz. The mean and standard deviation of each low level audio feature over the shot resulted in a $2D$ vector for each feature.

We have trained six independent classifiers using these audio-visual features. We fuse these features using three different schemes viz. SVM based early fusion [1], late fusion ($F1$-score weighted ensemble of SVM classifiers) [1] and intermediate fusion (Success weighted multiple kernel combination) [7]. The performances of various feature fusion experiments are reported in Table 1[1]. We observe that the multiple kernel combination based intermediate feature fusion has outperformed the other two feature fusion schemes.

Semantic category labels predicted by these six classifiers are used for modeling the temporal format in either of following two ways. First, we concatenate the likelihoods predicted by category classifiers to get a real valued six dimensional feature vector ($\mathbf{D}_j$ for shot $\mathbf{s}_j$). This feature vector is then used to train models for each of two categories viz. news bulletins and others (non-news). In second case, six shot categories are binary encoded to get a single symbol for each shot. These encoded labels are then used as feature to model the temporal format. Binary encoding of shot categories generates unique labels for each possible combination of shot categories. To illustrate, consider a shot $\mathbf{s}_j$ extracted from video $\mathbf{V}$. Let, the classifiers $\mathbf{C}_1, \mathbf{C}_2, \dots \mathbf{C}_6$ predict labels $l_{1j}, l_{2j}, \dots l_{6j}$ ($l_{ij} \in \{0, 1\}$) for shot $\mathbf{s}_j$. Then encoded semantic category label L_j is given as $L_j = 2^5 \cdot l_{1j} + 2^4 \cdot l_{2j} + 2^3 \cdot l_{3j} + 2^2 \cdot l_{4j} + 2^1 \cdot l_{5j} + 2^0 \cdot l_{6j}$ Shot s_j is evaluated by all of six classifiers. However, very few combinations are possible and valid due to inherent hierarchy present in shot types. Thus, we modify the binary encoding scheme according to assumptions in following order to avoid invalid conditions.

- Shots are first evaluated by Multi-view (1) vs. Uni-view (0) classifier ($\mathbf{C}_1$). Multi-view shots are evaluated by Face (1) vs. Non-face (0) classifiers ($\mathbf{C}_6$). Whereas Uni-view shots are processed further.
- Only Uni-view shots are evaluated by Graphics (1) vs. Natural (0) classifier ($\mathbf{C}_2$).
- Only Graphics shots are evaluated by Non-informative graphics (1) vs. Info-graphics (0) classifier ($\mathbf{C}_3$).
- Only Natural shots are evaluated by Studio (1) vs. Field (0) ($\mathbf{C}_4$), Indoor (1) vs. Outdoor (0) ($\mathbf{C}_5$) and Face (1) vs. Non-face (0) classifiers ($\mathbf{C}_6$).

[1]We have also reported feature-wise performance in supplementary material

Accordingly, $\hat{L}_j$ can be modified as

$$\begin{aligned} \hat{L}_j \;=\; & 2^5 \cdot l_{1j} + 2^4 \cdot \bar{l}_{1j} \cdot l_{2j} + 2^3 \cdot l_{3j} \cdot \bar{l}_{1j} \cdot l_{2j} \\ & + 2^2 \cdot l_{4j} \cdot \bar{l}_{1j} \cdot \bar{l}_{2j} + 2^1 \cdot l_{5j} \cdot \bar{l}_{1j} \cdot \bar{l}_{2j} + 2^0 \cdot l_{6j} \cdot \bar{l}_{2j} \end{aligned} \quad (1)$$

where, $\bar{l}_{ij}$ is negation of label l_{ij}. Each video shot s_j from non-commercial blocks is represented by semantic category encoded label $\hat{L}_j$. Now, non-commercial blocks can be visualized as strings of symbols and can be processed using existing sequence modeling methods. In next section, we briefly describe different shot sequence classification techniques to discriminate news programs from others.

3. SHOT SEQUENCE CLASSIFICATION

Programs of different genres have their own temporal presentation format governed by edit policies of news channels. This temporal presentation format can be exploited for genre classification of non-commercial shot sequences. Consider a sequence of N non-commercial shots $\mathbf{S} = \{s_1, s_2, \dots s_N\}$ extracted from a video $\mathbf{V}$ after commercial detection [7]. Each shot s_j is represented either by low level audio-visual features ($\mathbf{a}_j$) or shot semantic category labels ($\mathbf{D}_j$ or $\hat{L}_j$ (Section 2). Shot sequence $\mathbf{S}$ along with its features is then used to model the temporal presentation formats of various programs. In this work, we restrict ourselves to discriminating news bulletins from other shows. Several sequence classification algorithms are proposed in literature [4]. In this work we have experimented with three machine learning algorithms for modeling the non-commercial blocks. These are Hidden Markov Models (HMM), Support Vector Machines (SVM) and Conditional Random Fields (CRF).

Hidden Markov Models (HMMs, henceforth) [11] are generative probabilistic models and are widely used for applications involving sequence modeling and classification [20, 16]. In our experimentation we have tried two different sets of features for describing the video shots (Section 2). In first approach (RF-HMM), each shot is represented by concatenated low level raw audio-visual features $\mathbf{a}_j$ (Section 2). This approach does not require the semantic categorization of shots. In second case (LH-HMM), we have used vectors $\mathbf{D}_j$ obtained after concatenating likelihoods predicted by six semantic shot classifiers. We have trained two different models – one for news (λ_{news}), and second, for other genres (λ_{other}). In both cases, feature vector is real valued. Given a new non-commercial shot sequence $\mathbf{S}$, it is first segmented in overlapping and fixed length subsequence $\mathbf{S}_k$. Genre G_k of this subsequence is given by $G_k = \mathbf{argmax}_\lambda \Big(p(\mathbf{S}_k|\lambda_{news}), p(\mathbf{S}_k|\lambda_{other}) \Big)$. Sub-sequence labels G_k are then combined to get genre of shot sequence $\mathbf{S}_k$.

Support Vector Machines with String Kernel (SK-SVM) have been used successfully in previous works for sequence classification [14]. String kernel measures the structural similarity between two given sequences. Whereas, SVM learns the discriminative boundary between two classes. We have used the binary encoded semantic shot label $\hat{L}_j$ using Equation 2 to describe each video shot s_j (Section 2). In case of SVM also, we segment the shot sequence $\mathbf{S}$ into overlapping and fixed length subsequences $\mathbf{S}_k$. The genre(s) for sequence $\mathbf{S}$ is obtained by aggregating the genres predicted for individual subsequences.

Conditional Random Fields (SC-CRF) [9] use a log-linear model representing the conditional distribution of the observation labels. It has lately received significant attention in machine learning as it outperforms HMMs in a variety of sequential data labeling tasks [2]. The CRF model overcomes the label bias problem and generalizes well for unseen data while considering the contextual features [9]. We have used binary encoded semantic labels $\hat{L}_j$ (Equation 2) to describe the shots. Let, shots in sequence $\mathbf{S}$ be respectively described by encoded semantic label sequence $\mathbf{L} = \{\hat{L}_j, j = 1, 2, \ldots N\}$ for shot class sequence $\mathbf{G} = \{g_j, j = 1, 2, \ldots N\}$. Here, g_j may take unique values equal to the number of shot classes (two in our case). CRFs model the conditional distribution $p(\mathbf{G}|\mathbf{L})$ [9]. In CRF, the relationship between adjacent pairs of shot genres g_{j-1} and g_j is modeled as a Markov random field conditioned on the feature $\mathbf{L}$ [4]. Thus, the way in which the adjacent shot genres influence each other is determined by the input features $\mathbf{L}$. The probability assigned to sequence of labels $\mathbf{G}$ for an input shot sequence $\mathbf{S}$ by a linear-chain CRFs is given by

$$p(\mathbf{G}|\mathbf{L}) = \frac{1}{Z(\mathbf{L})} exp\left(\sum_{j=1}^{N}\sum_{m=1}^{M} \lambda_m \cdot f_m\left(g_{j-1}, g_j, L_j\right)\right)$$

$$\text{where, } Z(\mathbf{L}) = \sum_{g_j \in \mathbf{G}} exp\left(\sum_{j=1}^{N}\sum_{m=1}^{M} \lambda_m \cdot f_m\left(g_{j-1}, g_j, L_j\right)\right)$$

and $f_m(\cdot)$ are the boolean functions jointly encoding information about (g_{j-1}, g_j) and (L_j, g_j). These feature functions are determined empirically while, λ_m are estimated during training using gradient descent. Theoretically, current label g_j may depend on the feature vector of all shots. However, to restrict the calculations we use feature vectors from immediate neighbors only. M denotes the number of neighbors whose feature vectors are used to predict the label of current shot. We call the set of neighbors around current shot as template. Given a sequence $\mathbf{S}$, genre of each shot g_j is determined such that sequence $\mathbf{G}$ maximizes $p(\mathbf{G}|\mathbf{L})$. In our experimentation template size is determined experimentally to maximize the performance. It may be noted that, ideally the template size is not restricted to only neighboring shots. However, to optimize the training time we follow the approach proposed in [16] and restrict the template size.

4. EXPERIMENTATION AND RESULTS

We have created a **TV News Programs Dataset**[2] consisting of 120 hours of broadcast videos recorded from Indian English news channel **CNN-IBN**. These videos are recorded in chunks of 1 hour. Each one hour video is first segmented into shots based on color histogram consistency between consecutive frames. This resulted in a total of 89,036 shots. This follows detection and removal of TV commercial shots. Non-commercial shots are then marked to get news and non-news blocks[3]. Our dataset consists of 336 news and 130 non-news blocks spanning over 57.32 hours (3439.2 minutes) and 15.01 hours (901 minutes) respectively. Moreover, we have also marked shots for six semantic categories. We have divided this dataset into training and training sets consisting of 60% and 40% of non-commercial blocks with stratification. This training set is used for training shot category-wise classifiers and sequence models.

[2]Dataset available on request

[3]we call consecutive set of shots having same genre as block

For semantic shot categorization, we have experimented with early (EF) [1, 12], late (LF) [1, 12] and intermediate (IF) [7] feature fusion schemes. In early fusion we have used SVM with RBF kernel as classifier on concatenated audio-visual features. In late fusion scheme we have used SVM with RBF and linear kernels trained on each feature as base classifiers. The decision of these base classifiers are then combined using their $F1$-scores to get semantic category labels. For intermediate fusion [7] of features we have used base kernels defined on individual features using linear and radial basis similarity functions. Performances of semantic category-wise classifiers on these three feature fusion schemes are presented in Table 1. We have reported $F1$-scores for positive and negative classes for each semantic category. Hyper-parameters for these SVMs are determined by grid search. We observe that intermediate feature fusion scheme has better performance compared to the other two methods. Thus, for sequence modeling we have used shot classifiers trained using intermediate fusion.

Table 1: Performance of different feature fusion techniques in terms of $F1$-scores of positive (F+) and negative (F-) classes for category-wise classifiers. It may be noted that intermediate feature fusion (IF) technique outperforms all other methods.

Classifiers → / Methods ↓		C_1	C_2	C_3	C_4	C_5	C_6
EF	F+	0.89	0.94	0.96	0.94	0.91	0.96
	F-	0.92	0.96	0.96	0.92	0.91	0.95
LF	F+	0.87	0.93	**0.97**	0.91	0.81	0.97
	F-	0.91	0.95	0.94	0.88	0.89	0.96
IF	F+	**0.91**	**0.94**	0.95	**0.98**	**0.94**	**0.97**
	F-	**0.96**	**0.96**	**0.97**	**0.97**	**0.97**	**0.96**

C_1 - Multi-view (+) vs. Uni-view, C_2 - Graphics (+) vs. Natural, C_3 - Non-informative graphics (+) vs. Info-graphics, C_4 - Studio (+) vs. Field, C_5 - Indoor (+) vs. Outdoor and C_6 - Face (+) vs. Non-face

For modeling the temporal presentation format we have experimented with HMM (HTK Toolkit), SVM (Lib SVM) with string kernel and CRF (CRF++ Toolkit) as described in Section 3. SVMs are sensitive to class imbalances and thus, we have re-sampled the training data to have equal number of instances from news and non-news blocks. For HMM and SVM we have used sub-sequences of length 30 shots with a overlap of 20 shots. We set number of states and mixtures for HMM to 12 and 5 respectively. For CRFs we have used template size of 10 shots on either sides. Experimental results supporting selection of these parameters are reported in supplementary material. We call a predicted block (either news or non-news) correctly classified, if Jaccard similarity coefficient (intersection over union) between duration of predicted and ground truth blocks, is greater than 0.8 (overlap of more than 80%). We report the performance of news program detection using block-wise precision, recall and $F1$-scores for news and non-news blocks. These results are tabulated in Table 2. We observe that, CRF outperformed the remaining two methods by a large margin.

Discussions – We observe that HMM and SVM based models are biased towards detecting news blocks (positive class). In case of HMM, inferior performance may be attributed to large variability present in non-news class and inability of GMMs in modeling the complex feature space. Moreover, performance of HMM decreased further when used with raw features (1000+ dimensions) due to insufficient

Table 2: Performance of different shot sequence modeling schemes described in Section 3. We observe that conditional random fields based modeling outperforms other approaches in detecting the news blocks

	News Blocks			Non-news Blocks		
	P	R	F	P	R	F
RF-HMM	0.67	0.57	0.61	0.37	0.55	0.43
LH-HMM	0.72	0.74	0.71	0.61	0.48	0.49
SK-SVM	0.53	0.84	0.65	0.60	0.23	0.33
SC-CRF	**1.00**	**0.98**	**0.99**	**0.95**	**1**	**0.97**

data available for estimating large number of parameters. In case of SVMs, imbalance in number of training instances from two classes and variability in non-news class resulted in performance degradation. Furthermore, string kernel does not have provision of matching two sequences with edits. This results in string mismatch even due to change in symbol for a single shot. All these in combination with large variability in negative class resulted in poor recall (of SK-SVM) for non-news blocks. CRFs on the other hand are known to overcome the label bias problem [16]. Moreover, it has the ability of automatic selection of template size around a shot thereby giving flexibility in matching symbol sequences. Additionally, CRFs can also learn to detect start and end of sequences [16]. Thus, entire test sequence can be evaluated at once to obtain labels for each shot in the sequence.

5. CONCLUSION AND FUTURE WORK

Existing works in program genre detection in TV broadcasts have relied on channel specific prior knowledge based assumptions, indicators in close caption text or electronic program guides. In our proposal, broadcast videos are preprocessed to remove commercials for obtaining non-commercial blocks as temporally ordered shot sequences. The spatial format of these shots are modeled first by classifying (MKL-SVM with audio-visual features) them with six semantic labels. The temporal format is leaned (using CRF) from the sequence of these shot semantic labels. The CRF based modeling is found to outperform (in terms of $F1$ scores) HMM and SVM (with string kernel) based sequence classification. We have constructed a shot and news program labeled broadcast video dataset of 120 hours. Experimentations on this dataset have provided us with a $F1$ measure of 0.99 in detecting news programs.

We have only demonstrated the success of the proposed approach in detecting news programs. However, we believe that this approach can be applied to recognition of other program genres (interviews, debates, weather reports etc.) in TV news channel broadcasts. Also, We are presently removing commercials using a shot-wise classification technique [7]. This methodology can be further extended to detect and filter commercials in the same framework.

6. REFERENCES

[1] P. K. Atrey, M. A. Hossain, S. A. El, and M. S. Kankanhalli. Multimodal fusion for multimedia analysis: a survey. *Multimedia systems*, 16(6):345–379, 2010.

[2] S. P. Chatzis and Y. Demiris. The infinite-order conditional random field model for sequential data modeling. *Pattern Analysis and Machine Intelligence*, 35(6):1523–1534, 2013.

[3] Y. Chen, Z. Li, M. Li, and W.-Y. Ma. Automatic classification of photographs and graphics. In *ICME*, pages 973–976. IEEE, 2006.

[4] T. G. Dietterich. Machine learning for sequential data: A review. In *Structural, syntactic, and statistical pattern recognition*, pages 15–30. Springer, 2002.

[5] N. Dimitrova, L. Agnihotri, and G. Wei. Video classification based on hmm using text and faces. In *European Signal Processing Conference*, 2000.

[6] L. Elin and A. Lapides. *Designing and Producing the Television Commercial.* Pearson/A and B, 2004.

[7] R. Kannao and P. Guha. Tv commercial detection using success based locally weighted kernel combination. In *MultiMedia Modeling*, pages 793–805. Springer, 2016.

[8] W. Kim, J. Park, and C. Kim. A novel method for efficient indoor–outdoor image classification. *Journal of Signal Processing Systems*, 61(3):251–258, 2010.

[9] J. Lafferty, A. McCallum, and F. C. Pereira. Conditional random fields: Probabilistic models for segmenting and labeling sequence data. 2001.

[10] H. Li, B. Jou, J. G. Ellis, D. Morozoff, and S.-F. Chang. News rover: Exploring topical structures and serendipity in heterogeneous multimedia news. In *ACM MM*, pages 449–450. ACM, 2013.

[11] L. R. Rabiner and B.-H. Juang. An introduction to hidden markov models. *ASSP Magazine, IEEE*, 3(1):4–16, 1986.

[12] L. Rokach. Ensemble-based classifiers. *Artif. Intell. Rev.*, 33(1-2):1–39, 2010.

[13] M. Szummer and R. W. Picard. Indoor-outdoor image classification. In *Workshop on Content-Based Access of Image and Video Database*, pages 42–51. IEEE.

[14] S. Vishwanathan, A. J. Smola, et al. Fast kernels for string and tree matching. *Kernel methods in computational biology*, pages 113–130, 2004.

[15] Wikipedia. Dayparting — Wikipedia, the free encyclopedia. https://en.wikipedia.org/wiki/Dayparting, 2016. [Online; accessed 22-July-2016].

[16] S. Xu, B. Feng, Z. Chen, and B. Xu. A general framework of video segmentation to logical unit based on conditional random fields. In *ICMR*, pages 247–254, 2013.

[17] A. Yanagawa, W. Hsu, and S.-F. Chang. Anchor shot detection in trecvid-2005 broadcast news videos. Technical report, Columbia ADVENT Technical Report, 2005.

[18] L. Zhang, Z. Zhu, and Y. Zhao. Robust commercial detection system. In *ICME*, pages 587–590, 2007.

[19] H. Zhou, T. Hermans, A. V. Karandikar, and J. M. Rehg. Movie genre classification via scene categorization. In *ACM MM*, pages 747–750. ACM, 2010.

[20] T. Zlitni, B. Bouaziz, and W. Mahdi. Automatic topics segmentation for tv news video using prior knowledge. *Multimedia Tools and Applications*, pages 1–28, 2015.

Detecting Arbitrary Oriented Text in the Wild with a Visual Attention Model

Wenyi Huang[†]
harrywy@gmail.com

Dafang He[†]
duh188@psu.edu

Xiao Yang[‡]
xuy111@psu.edu

Zihan Zhou[†]
zzhou@ist.psu.edu

Daniel Kifer[‡]
dkifer@cse.psu.edu

C. Lee Giles[†‡]
giles@ist.psu.edu

[†]Information Sciences and Technology, [‡]Computer Science and Engineering
The Pennsylvania State University
University Park, PA 16802

ABSTRACT

Text embedded in images provides important semantic information about a scene and its content. Detecting text in an unconstrained environment is a challenging task because of the many fonts, sizes, backgrounds, and alignments of the characters. We present a novel attention model for detecting arbitrary oriented and curved scene text. Inspired by the attention mechanisms in the human visual system, our model utilizes a spatial glimpse network to processes the attended area and deploys a recurrent neural network that aggregates the information over time to determine the attention movement. Combining this with an off-the-shelf region proposal method, the model achieves the state-of-the-art performance on the highly cited ICDAR2013 dataset, and the MSRA-TD500 dataset which contains arbitrary oriented text.

Keywords

Scene Text Detection; Visual Attention; Deep Learning

1. INTRODUCTION

Text in natural scenes usually provides important semantic information about the scene and its content. A system that reads text in the wild will enable numerous multimedia applications such as improving automatic object recognition and image categorization [34], multimedia document indexing and retrieval, and assisting the visually impaired.

Although there have been numerous work on reading text in the wild [26, 27, 18, 11], the problem remains unsolved because of the insufficient accuracy in real-world applications. Especially, localizing text in natural scenes is extremely difficult because of the unconstrained fonts, sizes, backgrounds, inconsistent illumination, and occlusions. In addition, text in the wild is mostly captured with different orientations, perspective distortion and curved shapes. Most existing works on text detection have focused on horizontal or near-horizontal text. While a few works target localizing text with arbitrary orientations, perspectives, and skews [30, 6], these approaches still rely on hand-crafted features or rules for grouping oriented or skewed text.

Inspired by the presence of attention mechanisms in the visual system [20, 8] where humans recognize objects by moving attention to the next relevant parts of the object, we designed our text detection model to imitate this attention mechanism. Our attention-based model processes the scene text character by character in a sequential manner. Fig. 1 shows an example of how our model processes scene text. Specifically, our model is build up on a recurrent neural network (RNN) in combination with a convolutional neural network (CNN) [14]. At each step of the RNN, a CNN is deployed on a small area (the attended area) to perform local feature extraction. The extracted feature is input to the RNN, which aggregates the information over time, to determine the attended area for the next character. The model will stop when the last character of the word is encountered. Thus, the model follows the character sequence and localizes the word. Because of the attention mechanism, our model is able to localize arbitrarily oriented and skewed text.

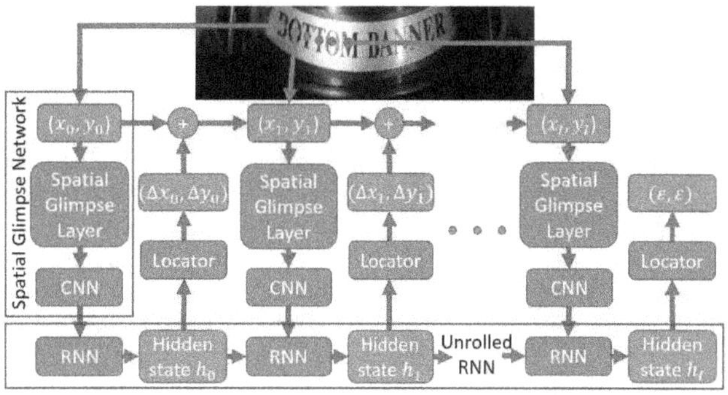

Figure 1: The architecture of the proposed attention model for text localization with an example of scene text detection.

For evaluation, our model was trained on a synthetically generated text in the wild dataset with ground truth locations of each character. We then conducted the experiments on two most cited datasets: the ICDAR2013 and the MSRA-TD500. We show that our model is capable of localizing arbitrarily oriented and skewed text without heuris-

MM '16, October 15 - 19, 2016, Amsterdam, Netherlands

ISBN 978-1-4503-3603-1/16/10...$15.00

DOI: http://dx.doi.org/10.1145/2964284.2967282

tically designed features and rules for grouping characters. Comparing with other baseline methods, our model achieves the state-of-the-art results. For oriented and skewed text, our method generates more accurate polygons as bounding boxes, some of them are even better than human labels.

2. RELATED WORK

2.1 Scene Text Detection

There are at least two major approaches in text localization. The first is sliding window based methods [7, 26, 27, 11] which slide a classifier over the entire image. The second is connected components methods, which group pixels into character regions using local properties such as color, gradient, intensity, stroke-width, etc. Pixels are group by algorithms such as Stroke Width Transform [9, 30], Extremal Regions [17, 18, 15], and Gradient Vector Flow [19]. The latter approaches have recently become more popular because they are usually more efficient and relatively insensitive to scale and orientation. However, most existing work has been focused on detecting horizontal or near-horizontal text. A few papers have considered detecting text with arbitrary orientations, perspectives, and skews [30, 6] based on hand-crafted features or rules for grouping oriented text.

2.2 Visual Attention

Attention mechanisms in human visual system has been proposed and studied in neuroscience [25, 20, 8]. Inspired by the mechanisms, various visual attention-based computer vision models have been proposed on tasks such as object recognition [1, 16, 2], object tracking [4], and image captioning [29]. In particular, our work extends the work of [16] and [2]. Mnih et al. [16] proposed a recurrent attention model for single object recognition which successfully learns the attention sequences on the MNIST dateset. Ba et al. [2] extends the recurrent attention model to recognize multi-digit on the SVHN dataset. The model is designed to recognize one big object (house number) with multiple components (multiple digits). The attention strategies are learnt based on a Cartesian coordinate that is centered at the middle of the input image. A hyper-parameter ratio that is used to convert unit width in the coordinate system to the number of pixels, however, limits the scalability of these models.

Different from these models, our model is relatively insensitive to the scale of text and the size of the image. In addition, instead of using reinforcement learning, our model is trained on synthetic text in the wild images, where ground truth locations are used for learning attention movement.

3. ATTENTION MODEL FOR TEXT LOCALIZATION

We approach the text localization task as a sequential process of attention pursuit. As in Fig. 1, at each step, a spatial glimpse network observes a limited area. It extracts the local information of the attended character area with different sizes and resolutions. Since the scene environment is partially observed by the spatial glimpse network, a recurrent neural network is deployed on top to aggregate the information over time. The integrated feature of the RNN is used by a locator network to determine where the model should attend to at the next step.

3.1 Model Components

Spatial Glimpse Network.

When a human recognize objects, the focus of our attention is within a small area. Meanwhile, we also maintain a blurry sense of the surrounding environment [25]. The spatial glimpse network is designed to imitate this visual attention mechanism. It is composed of two parts: a spatial glimpse layer [16] and a multi-column CNN.

Given an input image and a focusing coordinate (x, y), the spatial glimpse layer crops d image patches centered at (x, y) with multiple size and resolutions. The first image patch is $w \times w$ with the original resolution. This patch is considered as the focusing area where the model "sees" the most clearly. Each successive image patch is cropped twice the size of its previous image patch size then re-scaled to $w \times w$. Thus the model catches the surrounding environments of the focusing area. Fig. 2 shows an example of the input and the output of a glimpse layer with $d = 3$ and $w = 32$.

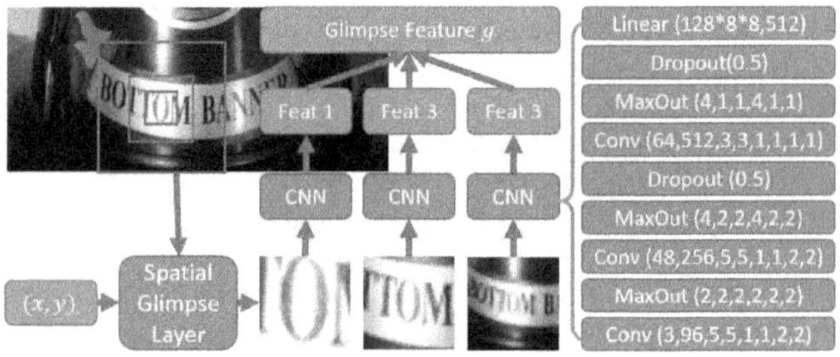

Figure 2: Input and output of a spatial glimpse layer with $d = 3$ and $w = 32$ and the details of the glimpse network.

The d glimpse patches are then input to a d-column convolutional neural network for feature extraction. Each column is a deep CNN and these CNNs do not share parameters. The output feature vectors from these d columns are concatenated as one feature vector which we refer to as the glimpse feature g. Details of the glimpse network and the structures of the CNNs are shown in Fig. 2.

Recurrent Neural Network.

In a cognitive visual attention mechanism, our brain aggregates aggravates the previously captured information over time to comprehend the whole picture of the environment [20, 8]. The integrated information helps us to determine the next location to move our attention to. Our attention model for text localization is designed to process words character by character, i.e. in a sequential manner. The location of the next character is determined by the sequence of characters that appears before. We use an RNN to aggregate the information extracted by the spatial glimpse network. At each step, the glimpse feature is input to the RNN. Meanwhile, the previous hidden state of the RNN is also the input to the current step. In our model, we use a simple RNN:

$$h_t = \mathrm{ReLU}(W_{ih} \cdot g_t + W_{hh} \cdot h_{t-1} + b_r) \tag{1}$$

where h_t and h_{t-1} is the hidden state of the RNN at step t and $t-1$ respectively, g_t is the glimpse feature extracted by the spatial glimpse network at step t, W_{ih} is the weighting matrix from input to hidden, W_{hh} is the weighting matrix from hidden to hidden. We use the rectified linear unit (ReLU) as the activation function for the RNN.

Locator Network.

The hidden state of the RNN h_t is used to predict where to deploy the spatial glimpse network for the $t+1$ step. A locator network takes h_t as input and predicts where to attend to by outputing the movement offset (Δx_t,Δy_t). It consists of a fully connected layer that projects the hidden state h_t to a 2-dimensional vector, a tanh activation layer that rescales the numbers to [-1, 1] and a scaling layer that multiplies the vector by the maximal step length s_l.

$$(\Delta x_t, \Delta y_t) = s_l \tanh(W_l \cdot h_t + b_l) \tag{2}$$

and the next location is computed by:

$$(x_{t+1}, y_{t+1}) = (x_t, y_y) + (\Delta x_t, \Delta y_t) \tag{3}$$

Ideally, a well-trained model will move the attention to the location of the successive characters in the text.

3.2 Training

The training criterion is to minimize the Euclidian distance between the predicted location and ground truth location of each character in the word. The parameters of the glimpse network, the recurrent network, and the locator network are tuned by the loss function:

$$Loss_t = \frac{1}{2}\left[(x_t - \hat{x}_t)^2 + (y_t - \hat{y}_t)^2\right] \qquad \forall t \in [1, l] \tag{4}$$

where (x_t, y_t) is the predicted location at step t and $(\hat{x}_t, \hat{y}_t)$ is the ground truth center of the tth character. For a word of length l, there will be $l-1$ backpropagation through time.

Curriculum Learning.

Since the predicted location at step t depends on all the previous moving strategies, the error will accumulate over steps. It will be meaningless if a prediction is made based on a wrong glimpse of a no-text area (i.e. the previous predicted attention area is far from the ground truth location). To solve this problem, we adapted the curriculum learning strategy [5] that we start with easy examples: The model starts training with data samples of sequence length 2. The sequence length increases as the average loss drops to a acceptable range (averaged Euclidian loss less than 9.00, i.e. 3 pixels away from ground truth). During the attention moving process, we will stop moving forward and start backpropagation when the current predicted center is far from the ground truth (i.e. larger than 3 pixels).

Two models.

Our attention model requires an initial location of a character in the text. However, there is no guarantee that the region proposal methods can always capture the first character of a word. To make our model robust, we enrich the training sequences to not only start from the very first character of a word, but also start from each character in the word. In addition, we trained two models that learn to localize text from left to right and right to left respectively. Given a proposed region, we apply the two models to localize the left part and the right part simultaneously.

3.3 Synthetic Data Generation

In order to train the attention model, we need a text in the wild dataset with ground truth locations of each character. However, existing datasets that meet the requirement contain too few images; also the variation of text orientation is limited. Considering the inaccuracy and the cost of human labeling, it's impractical to manually create a large training dataset that meet the requirement. Thus, we create our own synthetically generated text in the wild images with ground truth locations. The data generation process is similar to [10]. First, a font is randomly chosen from over 1,400 Google Fonts to generate the foreground text. Then several rendering effects, such as border/shadow rendering, rotation, perspective transformation, and Gaussian noise, are added to the generated images with random parameters. Based on the glyph metrics of each individual character as well as the kerning information of the font, we are able to calculate the exact bounding box and the center location of each letter. In the last step, we remove the text areas in ICDAR2013 and MSRA-TD500 training images, and blend the generated text into these natural scenes images.

All words are randomly selected from a pre-defined dictionary which contains over 90,000 common English words. Each generated image has a range of 1 to 3 lines of text with each line contains 1 to 3 words. Fig. 3 shows some examples of the synthetic text in the wild images.

Figure 3: Examples of synthetic text in the wild images with bounding boxes and character centers.

4. TEXT LOCALIZATION PIPELINE

A full text localization pipeline involves three steps:

Region Proposal. We utilize an off-the-shelf region proposal method, Extremal Regions (ER) [18], to generate candidate character regions. The output regions of ER are then filtered by a CNN text/no-text classifier that we trained using the same architecture as in [11]. After filtering, we will have a set of proposed regions.

Localization with Attention Model. For each proposed region, we rescale the image so that the size of the region fits in $w \times w$. Then the left-to-right and the right-to-left models are applied to predicted the attended area of each character in the word. If the center of a predicted attended area by the model is within 3 pixels of a proposed region's center, we will remove the proposed region so that we do not have multiple detections of a same word. After this step, we will have several text line candidates.

Text line filtering. To remove the false positive text line candidates, we again use the text/no-text classifier to slide through the text lines. We will filter out a text line candidate if less than half of the text line regions are classified as text.

5. EXPERIMENTS

We set the number of cropped image patches d=3, the focusing area size w=32, and the maximal step length s_l=64. 30,000 synthetic images are generated with 90,000 most frequently used English words for training. For optimization, all model components are tuned with rmsprop [24] with batches of size 50. The initial learning rate is set to 0.005 and we halved the learning rate every 20 epoches. Our model is trained and tested on a single NVIDIA Tesla K40 GPU.

5.1 Dataset

We measure the performance of the proposed model on the ICDAR2013 [13] and the MSRA Text Detection 500 (MSRA-TD500) [30] datasets. ICDAR2013 mainly consists of horizontal text. The testing set contains 233 images. We evaluate our result on the ICDAR online evaluation system[1]. MSRA-TD500 is a multi-orientation text dataset containing text in both Chinese and English. The testing set consists of 200 images. We follow the evaluation protocols as in [30] and apply DetEval [28] to calculate the Precision, Recall and F-measure of our detection result.

5.2 Results

We first test our model on the ICDAR2013 dataset, which is the most cited horizontal text detection dataset. As in Table 1, the proposed method achieves 88%, 72%, 79% in Precision, Recall, and F-measure. Compared with the most recent methods that are only designed for horizontal text, our model achieve the best precision as the state-of-the-art method. The recall is a bit lower because we used an off-the-shelf region proposal method without fine-tuning.

	Precision	Recall	F-measure
Neumann and Matas [18]	73	65	69
Shi et al. [22]	83	63	72
Bai et al. [3]	79	68	73
Zamberletti et al. [32]	86	70	77
Tian et al. [23]	85	**76**	**80**
Zhang et al. [33]	**88**	74	**80**
Our model	**88**	72	79

Table 1: Localization performances on ICDAR2013(%).

We then experiment on the MSRA-TD500 dataset to validate our model's capability in localizing arbitrary oriented and skewed text in the wild. For each detection, our model outputs a sequence of centers. The final bounding box of a text line is created to be a polygon which is the union of all focusing areas in the sequence. Table 2 compares the results of our model with other baseline methods. The results show that the proposed method outperforms most of the other baselines in precision and F-measure. Compared to [31], our method does not sacrifice the recall to get a higher precision. With the same highest recall as in [21], our method achieves a much better precision result.

	Precision	Recall	F-measure
Chen et al. [7]	5	5	5
Epshtein et al. [9]	25	25	25
Yao et al. [30]	63	63	63
Risnumawan et al. [21]	70	**68**	69
Yin et al. [31]	**81**	63	**71**
Kang et al. [12]	71	62	66
Our model	74	**68**	**71**

Table 2: Localization performances on MSRA-TD500(%).

Besides the quantitative results, we also show the detection examples of some challenging cases from the MSRA-TD500 in Fig. 4. The yellow boxes indicate the ground truth. The red ones and the green ones are generated from our model, where a green polygon means a hit and a red polygon indicates a false positive detection. It is important to note that although our models are trained on synthetic dataset that only contains English words, the model shows the ability to localize Chinese characters as well.

[1]http://rrc.cvc.uab.es/

(a) Succeed cases of the proposed method

(b) Failed cases of the proposed method.

(c) Cases we failed following the evaluation protocol. However, our proposed model generates better bounding boxes.

Figure 4: Loalization results on MSRA-TD500 test set.

In Fig. 4a, we show that our proposed model is able to localize text of arbitrary orientation, perspective distortion, different scales, and inconsistent illumination. We also show that our generated polygons are tighter and more accurate than the ground truth boxes. Fig. 4b shows several failed cases of the proposed model, most of the failures are due to the fact that region proposal method, ER, sometimes cannot capture an entire Chinese character. Thus we would expect higher precision and recall if better region proposal methods are used. Fig. 4c shows some cases that our model failed the test following the evaluation protocol. However, we argue that in these cases, our method generates more accurate polygon bounding boxes than the human labeled ground truth. For example, in the first figure, "WELCOME" is broken into pieces, whereas "COME" and "TO EC" is merged as one box in the ground truth. Our model successfully detected "WELCOME" as one text region. In the second figure, our detection for the skewed text "AZONA" is much more accurate than the human labeled box. Our model's detections on the Chinese words in the last figure are more accurate than the loose boxes provided by the ground truth. In sum, by showing these detection results, we demonstrate that our proposed model generates more accurate polygons as bounding boxes for oriented and skewed text. Some of them are even better than human labels.

6. CONCLUSIONS

We propose a novel attention model for text detection in the natural scenes. The visual attention mechanism, implemented with CNNs and RNNs, provides a natural solution for localizing arbitrary oriented and skewed text. Evaluation results on two benchmark datasets show that our model generates more accurate bounding boxes for both horizontal and oriented text. For future work, we are going to explore our model's ability in the word recognition task.

Acknowledgments

This work was funded by NSF grant CCF-1317560 and a GPU donation by NVIDIA.

7. REFERENCES

[1] B. Alexe, N. Heess, Y. W. Teh, and V. Ferrari. Searching for objects driven by context. In *Proc. of NIPS'12*, pages 881–889, 2012.

[2] J. Ba, V. Mnih, and K. Kavukcuoglu. Multiple object recognition with visual attention. In *Proc. of ICLR'15*, 2015.

[3] B. Bai, F. Yin, and C. L. Liu. Scene text localization using gradient local correlation. In *Proc. of ICDAR'13*, pages 1380–1384. IEEE, 2013.

[4] L. Bazzani, N. de Freitas, H. Larochelle, V. Murino, and J.-A. Ting. Learning attentional policies for object tracking and recognition in video with deep networks. In *Proc. of ICML'11*, pages 937–944. ACM, 2011.

[5] Y. Bengio, J. Louradour, R. Collobert, and J. Weston. Curriculum learning. In *Proc. of ICML'09*, pages 41–48. ACM, 2009.

[6] M. Bušta, T. Drtina, D. Helekal, L. Neumann, and J. Matas. Efficient character skew rectification in scene text images. In *Proc of ACCV'14 Workshops*, pages 134–146. Springer, 2014.

[7] X. Chen and A. L. Yuille. Detecting and reading text in natural scenes. In *Proc. of CVPR'04*, pages 366–373. IEEE Computer Society, 2004.

[8] M. Corbetta and G. L. Shulman. Control of goal-directed and stimulus-driven attention in the brain. *Nature reviews neuroscience*, 3(3):201–215, 2002.

[9] B. Epshtein, E. Ofek, and Y. Wexler. Detecting text in natural scenes with stroke width transform. In *Proc. of CVPR'10*, pages 2963–2970. IEEE, 2010.

[10] M. Jaderberg, K. Simonyan, A. Vedaldi, and A. Zisserman. Synthetic data and artificial neural networks for natural scene text recognition. In *Workshop on Deep Learning, NIPS*, 2014.

[11] M. Jaderberg, A. Vedaldi, and A. Zisserman. Deep features for text spotting. In *Proc. of ECCV 2014*, pages 512–528. Springer, 2014.

[12] L. Kang, Y. Li, and D. Doermann. Orientation robust text line detection in natural images. In *Proc. of CVPR'14*, pages 4034–4041. IEEE, 2014.

[13] D. Karatzas, L. Gomez-Bigorda, A. Nicolaou, S. Ghosh, A. Bagdanov, M. Iwamura, J. Matas, L. Neumann, V. R. Chandrasekhar, S. Lu, et al. Icdar 2015 competition on robust reading. In *Proc. of ICDAR'15*, pages 1156–1160. IEEE, 2015.

[14] Y. LeCun, L. Bottou, Y. Bengio, and P. Haffner. Gradient-based learning applied to document recognition. In *Intelligent Signal Processing*, pages 306–351. IEEE Press, 2001.

[15] J. Mao, H. Li, W. Zhou, S. Yan, and Q. Tian. Scale based region growing for scene text detection. In *Proc, of ACM MM'13*, pages 1007–1016. ACM, 2013.

[16] V. Mnih, N. Heess, A. Graves, et al. Recurrent models of visual attention. In *Proc. of NIPS'14*, pages 2204–2212, 2014.

[17] L. Neumann and J. Matas. A method for text localization and recognition in real-world images. In *Proc. of ACCV'10*, pages 770–783. Springer, 2010.

[18] L. Neumann and J. Matas. Real-time scene text localization and recognition. In *Proc. of CVPR'12*, pages 3538–3545. IEEE, 2012.

[19] T. Q. Phan, P. Shivakumara, and C. L. Tan. Detecting text in the real world. In *Proc. of ACM MM'12*, pages 765–768. ACM, 2012.

[20] R. A. Rensink. The dynamic representation of scenes. *Visual cognition*, 7(1-3):17–42, 2000.

[21] A. Risnumawan, P. Shivakumara, C. S. Chan, and C. L. Tan. A robust arbitrary text detection system for natural scene images. *Expert Systems with Applications*, 41(18):8027–8048, 2014.

[22] C. Shi, C. Wang, B. Xiao, Y. Zhang, and S. Gao. Scene text detection using graph model built upon maximally stable extremal regions. *Pattern recognition letters*, 34(2):107–116, 2013.

[23] S. Tian, Y. Pan, C. Huang, S. Lu, K. Yu, and C. Lim Tan. Text flow: A unified text detection system in natural scene images. In *Proc. of ICCV'15*, pages 4651–4659, 2015.

[24] T. Tieleman and G. Hinton. Lecture 6.5-rmsprop: Divide the gradient by a running average of its recent magnitude. *COURSERA: Neural Networks for Machine Learning*, 4:2, 2012.

[25] H. von Helmholtz and J. P. C. Southall. *Treatise on Physiological Optics: Translated from the 3rd German Ed.* Optical Society of America, 1925.

[26] K. Wang, B. Babenko, and S. Belongie. End-to-end scene text recognition. In *Proc. of ICCV'11*, pages 1457–1464. IEEE, 2011.

[27] T. Wang, D. J. Wu, A. Coates, and A. Y. Ng. End-to-end text recognition with convolutional neural networks. In *Proc. of ICPR'12*, pages 3304–3308. IEEE, 2012.

[28] C. Wolf and J.-M. Jolion. Object count/area graphs for the evaluation of object detection and segmentation algorithms. *IJDAR*, 8(4):280–296, 2006.

[29] K. Xu, J. Ba, R. Kiros, K. Cho, A. Courville, R. Salakhutdinov, R. Zemel, and Y. Bengio. Show, attend and tell: Neural image caption generation with visual attention. In *Proc. of ICML'15*, 2015.

[30] C. Yao, X. Bai, W. Liu, Y. Ma, and Z. Tu. Detecting texts of arbitrary orientations in natural images. In *Proc. of CVPR'12*, pages 1083–1090. IEEE, 2012.

[31] X.-C. Yin, W.-Y. Pei, J. Zhang, and H.-W. Hao. Multi-orientation scene text detection with adaptive clustering. *IEEE Transactions on PAMI*, 37(9):1930–1937, 2015.

[32] A. Zamberletti, L. Noce, and I. Gallo. Text localization based on fast feature pyramids and multi-resolution maximally stable extremal regions. In *Proc. of ACCV'14*, pages 91–105. Springer, 2014.

[33] Z. Zhang, W. Shen, C. Yao, and X. Bai. Symmetry-based text line detection in natural scenes. In *Proc. of CVPR'15*, June 2015.

[34] Q. Zhu, M.-C. Yeh, and K.-T. Cheng. Multimodal fusion using learned text concepts for image categorization. In *Proc. of ACM MM'06*, pages 211–220. ACM, 2006.

Global Consistent Shape Correspondence for Efficient and Effective Active Shape Models

Meng Wang
NYU Multimedia and Visual Computing Lab
Dept. of ECE, NYU Abu Dhabi, UAE
Dept. of CSE, NYU Tandon School of Engineering, USA

Yi Fang*
NYU Multimedia and Visual Computing Lab
Dept. of ECE, NYU Abu Dhabi, UAE
Dept. of ECE, NYU Tandon School of Engineering, USA

ABSTRACT

Finding the accurate corresponded landmarks from a collection of shape instances plays critical role in constructing active shape models (ASMs). We have developed a global consistent shape correspondence paradigm for efficient and effective active shape models to address challenging issues in statistical shape modelling. Specifically, in this paper, we developed techniques to perform a fast multiple shape matching to identify global consistent shape correspondence from a set of training shape instances via efficient low-rank recovery optimization. High quality ASMs can then be constructed based on the identified corresponded points. The entire process is unsupervised without manual annotation as well as free of selection of anatomically significant point. Experimental results on mobile hand image data demonstrate the superior performance of our proposed method over other state-of-the-art techniques like MDL in constructing active shape models.

Keywords

Active shape model; Shape correspondence; Joint shape matching

1. INTRODUCTION

1.1 Background

Active shape models (ASMs) are statistical models that are widely used to quantitatively represent various shape structures and their possible variations [6]. With the active shape models, a new shape can be generally reconstructed via a iterative fitting a process. The ASMs have been widely used in many computer vision applications such as object tracking and classification [7, 16].

However, it is well known that the automatic identification of an accurate set of corresponded landmark points among training shape instances often poses challenges for existing techniques towards constructing active shape models. A small correspondence error in identified landmark points might significantly deteriorate the quality of constructed ASMs [8]. To address the correspondence challenges, most previous research firstly obtain the corresponded landmarks by manual annotation. Although the manually labelled landmarks can provide a decent set of correspondence points among shapes, it is a laborious process of manually annotating the shapes. In addition, due to the variety of individual backgrounds, the labelled landmarks are not always consistent each time and not be coincident with any anatomically significant point of a shape structure, resulting in an inefficient and ineffective construction of ASMs. Shape correspondence is therefore a well known challenging problem, especially for shape instances with large non-rigid shape variation and corrupted with great noise.

1.2 Related Works

There have been several prior works that were developed to address the shape correspondence challenge as discussed above [1, 2, 9, 10, 5, 18, 13]., We will briefly review two representative works, the minimum description length (MDL) method [10, 11] and the spherical harmonics descriptors method (SPHARM) [5]. One of widely used technique was developed based on MDL [10, 11] to establish shape correspondence through minimizing the errors measured by the required bit-length to transmit the constructed new shape model and all of the training shape models. Despite the effectiveness of MDL, it suffers the high complexity due to the nature of shape correspondence error measure and the local optimal solution if the training shape instances present a large structural variations and noise, leading to inconsistent and local shape correspondence among training instances. In [5], authors identify the shape correspondence using spherical parametrization of shape instances. In spite of the good performance in 3D shape correspondence, SPHARM requires expensive computation because of the conformal mapping transformation.

Recent work has indicated that optimizing the consistency of a collection of pairwise shape correspondences is able to give rise to a global consistent shape correspondence [15] among the population of shape instances. The hidden constraint used for joint multiple shape registration is the cycle consistency, that is, correct correspondences along different

*Corresponding author. Email: yfang@nyu.edu

MM '16, October 15-19, 2016, Amsterdam, Netherlands
© 2016 ACM. ISBN 978-1-4503-3603-1/16/10...$15.00
DOI: http://dx.doi.org/10.1145/2964284.2967283

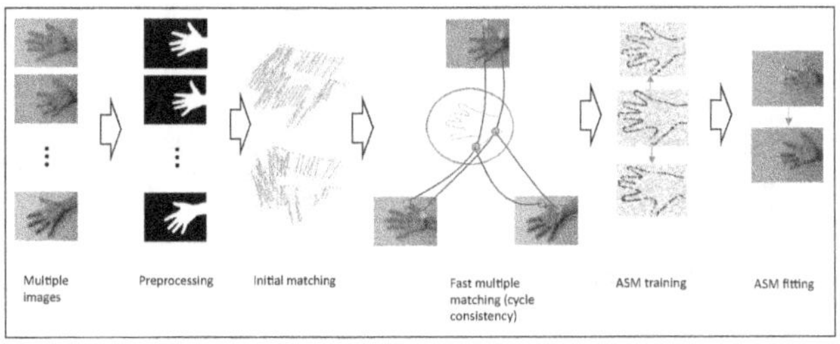

Figure 1: Pipeline of global consistent shape correspondence for active shape model.

walking paths of a collection of shapes should always be identical. By enforcing this constraint on multiple shape correspondence, most of the incorrect correspondences will be detected and replaced by correct maps along other paths, and missing maps will be filled up by the help of intermediate shapes. In addition, dissimilar shapes can be corresponded through the set of similar shapes between them. However, this constraint can not be modelled easily as the number of possible paths are often very large and the number of consistent cycles could be very small [20]. [15, 14] propose that the cycle consistency can be modelled as a positive semi-definite and low-rank optimization process for the global binary correspondence matrix. However, unfortunately the semi-definite programming (SDP) employed is not computational efficient when the matrix is large, which limits the application to a small scale collection of shapes instances.

1.3 Our method

In this paper, to efficiently find global consistent shape correspondence for better constructing active shape models with higher quality without manually annotating the landmark points, we introduce a fast low-rank matrix recovery optimization using the nuclear-norm relaxation for rank minimization via a fast alternating optimization to address the computational limitation of SDP in registering a large number of shapes of many sampling points from each shape [20]. There are three major attractive features in our proposed method:

- Global consistent shape correspondence: our method is able to find the corresponding landmarks that are globally consistent among all of training shape instances,
- Unsupervised learning: our method is able to automatically find anatomically significant corresponding landmarks without manual annotation,
- Efficient modelling: our method is able to quickly find consistent correspondence from a reasonable size of shape instances.

The pipeline of our method can be seen in Figure 1. In the first step the images are preprocessed to extract sample points on the contour. Second, an initial matching is performed based on the extracted descriptors of the sample points. Then the fast multiple matching are performed on the initial matching result to generate more consistent correspondences. Fourth, ASM is constructed using the well-corresponded training set. At last, the trained model is used for analysis or fitting. The pipeline is applicable to different ASMs, for simplicity we take hand image processing as an example.

2. METHOD

2.1 Fast Multiple Shape Matching via Low-rank Recovery Optimization

2.1.1 Preprocessing

The purpose of this step is to extract the contour of the shape. Skin detection is an efficient way to extract the foreground when it comes to human skin such as hands. The specific skin color is defined so that the satisfying pixels can be picked up. The range of human skin can be adjusted according to the lighting conditions. The pixels just picked can be discontinuous and noisy, a morphological operation such as image close operation (dilate then erode) can be used to smooth and denoise the extracted foreground (remove isolated pixels, fill small holes). At last, the contour can be obtained from the extracted foreground with the isocontour geometry extraction method.

2.1.2 Initial Matching

Shape correspondences are normally calculated using shape descriptors as a similarity measure. A shape descriptor is a representation of structure information of the shape. For the hand image we are considering, shape context [3] descriptor is an efficient method. Shape context is calculated based on the context of sampling points, which is a robust and simple algorithm for finding correspondences between shapes. The extracted shape context descriptor can be used to calculate the similarity between points and perform matching task between contour images. Typical matching methods include greedy matching, Hungarian assignment, graph matching. As the number of initially sampled points is often not consistent, greedy matching performs better as we do not require a one-to-one matching.

2.1.3 Multiple Matching

Similar to fast optimization strategy used in [20, 19] for multi-view and multi-image matching, we introduce fast alternating minimization to solve the low-ranking matrix recovery optimization in order to handle practical problems with a large scale of shapes. As reported in [20], the fast alternating minimization used in [20] is about 20 times faster than the one used in [15] for joint registering 20 shapes with each shape of 500 samples. The computational time for the method in [15] exponentially increase as the size of shape descriptors increase. As we discussed before, the cycle consistency is an important constraint used in matching a set of shapes. It can be defined as:

$$\mathbf{X}_{ac} = \mathbf{X}_{ab}\mathbf{X}_{bc} \tag{1}$$

where a, b, c are any three shapes from the shape set, $\mathbf{X}_{ij} \in \{0,1\}^{(m \times n)}$ is a binary matrix indicating whether a pair of vertices from two shapes i, j is a match, m, n are the number of sampled vertices in shape i, j.

The cycle consistency can be more concisely described by introducing a virtual set of unique vertices in the set of shapes. The virtual set of vertices can be utilized as intermediate vertices by many vertices in the same time. The cycle consistency can be refined as:

$$\mathbf{X}_{ij} = \mathbf{A}_i \mathbf{A}_j^T, \mathbf{A}_i \in \{0,1\}^{m \times k}, k \geq m \tag{2}$$

where $\mathbf{A}_i$ denotes the mapping from shape i to the virtual set, m is the number of vertices in shape i.

All the $\mathbf{X}_{ij}$ matrices can be tiled together into one giant matrix $\mathbf{X}$.

$$\mathbf{X} = \begin{pmatrix} \mathbf{X}_{11} & \mathbf{X}_{12} & \cdots & \mathbf{X}_{1n} \\ \mathbf{X}_{21} & \mathbf{X}_{22} & \cdots & \mathbf{X}_{2n} \\ \vdots & \vdots & \ddots & \vdots \\ \mathbf{X}_{n1} & \mathbf{X}_{n2} & \cdots & \mathbf{X}_{nn} \end{pmatrix} \tag{3}$$

where n is the number of 3D shapes. Now $\mathbf{X}$ can be denoted as $\mathbf{X} = \mathbf{A}\mathbf{A}^T$. From this equation, we can see that $\mathbf{X}$ should be both positive semi-definite ($\mathbf{X} \geq 0$) and in low-rank ($rank(\mathbf{X}) \leq k$). Imposing a constraint on $\mathbf{X}$ can avoid checking cycle-consistency over all the possible paths.

The cycle consistency has been formulated as an optimization problem to do matrix recovery. The overall cost function can be formulated as:

$$f(\mathbf{X}) = -\Sigma_{i=1}^{n}\Sigma_{j=1}^{n}\mathbf{S}_{ij} \cdot \mathbf{X}_{ij} + \lambda||\mathbf{X}||_* = -\mathbf{S} \cdot \mathbf{X} + \lambda||\mathbf{X}||_* \tag{4}$$

where $\mathbf{S}$ is a global affinity matrix, $\lambda||\mathbf{X}||_*$ is the nuclear norm of $\mathbf{X}$. The nuclear term is the sum of singular values in $\mathbf{X}$, which is a relaxation for the rank of $\mathbf{X}$. Here we set $\mathbf{S} = \mathbf{M}$, where $\mathbf{M}$ is the matching result from pair-wise correspondence, and $\mathbf{M}$ is constructed from many pair-wise correspondences like Equation 3. It is proven that the positive semi-definite constraint can be fulfilled in the same time if λ is large enough [21]. The nuclear norm minimization problem is convex and the proximal method [17] and ADMM [4] can be used to solve the problem. A fast alternating [21] is proposed to solve this problem much more faster.

2.2 Active Shape Model

To build the ASM models, well-corresponded examples we obtained from multiple matching are used as a representative training set.

2.2.1 Alignment

In most cases among different shapes the position, scale, and rotation are different, so an alignment is a necessity to the training set. We make transformations (translation, scaling, and rotation) to each shape compared to the first shape such that they become as similar as possible. Then all the shapes are aligned to the mean shape. The Procrustes method is used to find the transformation that best aligned the shapes.

2.2.2 Applying Principal Component Analysis

A set of aligned vectors in the form of Eq 5 is obtained after shape alignment.

$$\mathbf{x} = [x_1, x_2, ..., x_n, y_1, y_2, ...y_n] \tag{5}$$

where n is the number of sampled points in the matching, x_i, y_i are coordinates of point i. Now a shape can be represented by a vector in a $2n$-dimensional space. As a result, the training set can be fully characterized by a distribution of m vectors, where m is the size of the training set. Principal Components Analysis (PCA) is then used to extract the directions of independent variation in the cloud of points. The most significant directions with largest eigenvalues are

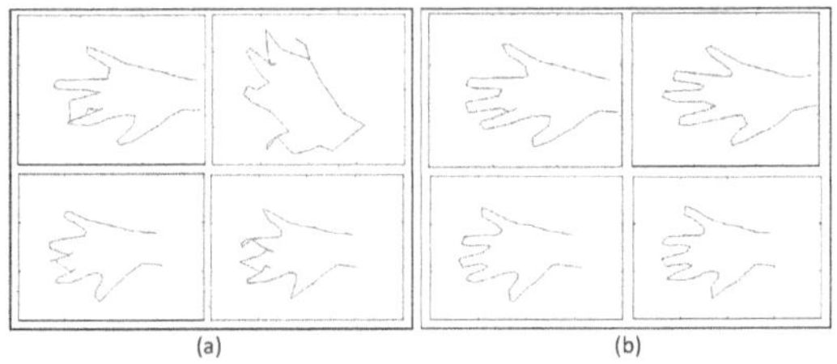

Figure 2: Results of multiple shape matching. First the corresponding points from the points in the first shape are plotted, then the points are connected according to the connection of corresponding points of the first shape. (a)Shapes generated from the initial matching. (b)Shapes generated from the refined multiple matching.

retained and the shape can be approximated without losing a lot of information by:

$$\mathbf{x} \approx \bar{\mathbf{x}} + \mathbf{P}\mathbf{b} \tag{6}$$

where $\mathbf{P} = \mathbf{p}_1\mathbf{p}_2...\mathbf{p}_t$ is the eigenvectors, $\mathbf{b} = [b_1 b_2 ... b_t]$ is the coefficient. t is chosen so that 98% of the variance is represented (98% of the total eigenvalues are used). $\mathbf{b}$ is a set of parameters to deform a shape and generate new plausible shapes.

2.2.3 Generate shapes

Suppose for model that the different parameters b_i are independent, gaussian distributed with zero mean, then 95% of the distribution of one parameter is covered in the range [-2SD, 2SD], where SD is the standard deviation of the training vectors. By constricting b to $[-2\sqrt{\lambda_i}, 2\sqrt{\lambda_i}]$, where λ_i is the variance of the i_th parameter, the shape generated is similar to the shapes in the training set. t is the number of modes needed to describe the shape properly.

2.2.4 Adjust ASM to fit a shape in the image

An ASM of the hand consists a mean shape $\bar{\mathbf{x}}$, a parameter vector $\mathbf{b}$, and eigenvectors. Through certain variations on the $\mathbf{b}$ and transformation, we can generate a plausible shape that best fit a new input shape.

Plausible points selection. It is important to select plausible points that both keep the basic shape of the trained model and keep close to the new shape. For each point in the mean shape, the candidate points are selected along the boundary normal within a certain range to keep the basic shape. After inputting the new shape, candidates points that are the most similar in gradient textures to the point in the new shape are selected. The selected plausible points will form a new target shape.

Adjust the model parameters to best fit selected points. Given a new set of points $\mathbf{x}$, we can translate, rotate, scale and deform our model in order that it best fits $\mathbf{x}$. This can be done by applying a transformation to find the best alignment, and compute some new shape parameters $\mathbf{b}$ to find the best deformation. Given the mean shape $\mathbf{x}$ and the set of new points $\mathbf{s}$, the shape parameters can be obtained.

These two processes will be executed alternatively until there are no big updates on transformation and $\mathbf{b}$.

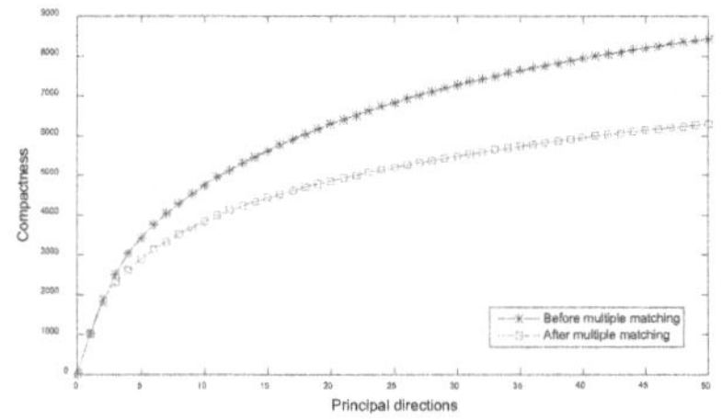

Figure 3: Quantitative evaluation of ASMs using compactness.

Table 1: Quantitative evaluation of ASMs using AIC

Method	AIC value
MDL	12.54
Shape Context	12.32
Our method	**11.10**

3. EXPERIMENT

3.1 Dataset and Settings

A set of experiments are performed to evaluate our method. The hand image data is selected from mobile hand images database (MOHI) [12]. MOHI is a database of hands created using mobile phones, which has modest qualities. 110 images are used to perform the multiple matching and active shape model training. The running time for 110 shapes with 200 samples per shape is about one hour, which is significantly (about 20 times) faster than other SDP-based matrix recovery method. For experiment purpose, equal number of points (200 points per shape) are sampled from the edge. In multiple matching, λ is set to 50.

3.2 Results

First a shape matching experiment is conducted before and after multiple matching to test the performance of multiple matching. As in Figure 2, the shapes are generated using the corresponding points to the first shape. The shapes in Figure 2(a) are generated using the correspondence of initial matching, which are problematic due to incorrect correspondences. We show matching result after multiple matching in Figure 2 (b), the shapes generated have much improved quality as the correspondence errors are largely decreased. As can be seen from the matching result, the multiple matching is effective in improving the correspondences.

We use two measures as evaluation criteria to evaluate our method quantitatively: compactness and Akaike's Information Criterion (AIC). Compactness suggests the cumulative variance of the input vector. A good model is normally trained from data with as little variance as possible. Compactness is defined as:

$$compact(M) = \Sigma_{m=1}^{M} \lambda_m \tag{7}$$

where λ_m is the m_{th} largest eigenvalue. AIC is an evaluation criterion for evaluating and selecting models, which can also be used to evaluate the ASMs. We are using the form of Eq 8.

$$AIC = -log(\frac{n}{R}) + 2\frac{k}{n} \tag{8}$$

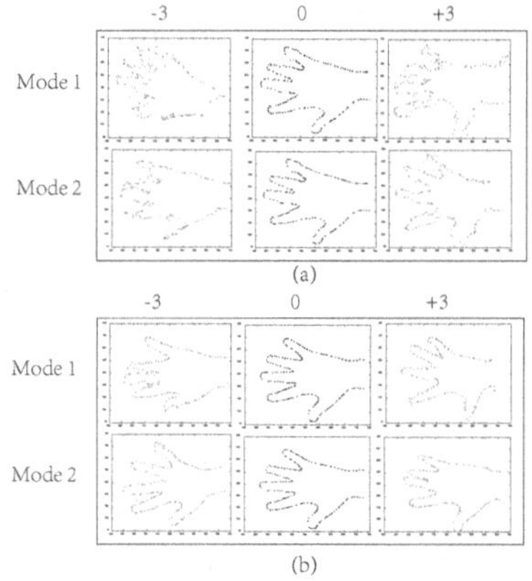

Figure 4: Comparisons of generated plausible shapes. (a)Shape context. (b)Our method of refined multiple matching. Shapes generated of first two modes varying from -3SD to 3SD are displayed.

where n is the size of the training set, R is the construction residual reconstructing using the first k principal directions. We set k to be 3 for all the methods. Smaller value of AIC indicates higher quality of the model. Quantitative results are shown in Table 1 and Figure 3. As we can see in Table 1, our method gives the best ASM among the three methods as indicated by the smallest AIC value. As we can see in Figure 3, our method gives a better performance as indicated by lower curve. The results quantitatively validate the superior performance of our proposed method over other techniques in constructing ASM.

To test the performance of the trained ASM, we also conduct an experiment on the plausible shapes generated from ASM. In Figure 4, plausible shapes generated are compared for ASMs based on correspondences before and after multiple matching. As indicated by Figure 4 (a) and (b), our method show great improvement in terms of the quality of generated plausible shapes. Shapes in (a) are inconsistent and many points of them does not lie on edge of hands. Shapes in (b) are more similar to hands contour edges in plausible variations from the mean shape. The global multiple shape matching has greatly improved the quality of ASM.

4. CONCLUSION

In this paper, we developed techniques to perform a fast multiple shape matching to identify global consistent shape correspondence from a set of training shape instances via efficient low-rank recovery optimization. High quality ASMs can then be constructed based on the identified corresponded points. The entire process is unsupervised without manual annotation as well as free of selection of anatomically significant point. Both quantitative and qualitative evaluation results on mobile hand image data demonstrate the superior performance of our proposed method in constructing active shape models.

5. ACKNOWLEDGMENTS

This material is partly based upon work supported by New York University Abu Dhabi institute (AD131 and REF131).

6. REFERENCES

[1] X. Bai, S. Bai, Z. Zhu, and L. J. Latecki. 3d shape matching via two layer coding. *Pattern Analysis and Machine Intelligence, IEEE Transactions on*, 37(12):2361–2373, 2015.

[2] X. Bai, C. Rao, and X. Wang. Shape vocabulary: A robust and efficient shape representation for shape matching. *Image Processing, IEEE Transactions on*, 23(9):3935–3949, 2014.

[3] S. Belongie, J. Malik, and J. Puzicha. Shape context: A new descriptor for shape matching and object recognition. In *NIPS*, volume 2, page 3, 2000.

[4] S. Boyd, N. Parikh, E. Chu, B. Peleato, and J. Eckstein. Distributed optimization and statistical learning via the alternating direction method of multipliers. *Foundations and Trends® in Machine Learning*, 3(1):1–122, 2011.

[5] C. Brechbühler, G. Gerig, and O. Kübler. Parametrization of closed surfaces for 3-d shape description. *Computer vision and image understanding*, 61(2):154–170, 1995.

[6] T. F. Cootes, G. J. Edwards, and C. J. Taylor. Active appearance models. *IEEE Transactions on Pattern Analysis & Machine Intelligence*, (6):681–685, 2001.

[7] T. F. Cootes, C. J. Taylor, D. H. Cooper, and J. Graham. Active shape models-their training and application. *Computer vision and image understanding*, 61(1):38–59, 1995.

[8] P. Dalal, B. C. Munsell, S. Wang, J. Tang, K. Oliver, H. Ninomiya, X. Zhou, and H. Fujita. A fast 3d correspondence method for statistical shape modeling. In *2007 IEEE Conference on Computer Vision and Pattern Recognition*, pages 1–8. IEEE, 2007.

[9] R. H. Davies, T. F. Cootes, C. J. Twining, and C. J. Taylor. An information theoretic approach to statistical shape modelling. In *BMVC*, pages 1–10, 2001.

[10] R. H. Davies, C. J. Twining, T. F. Cootes, J. C. Waterton, and C. J. Taylor. A minimum description length approach to statistical shape modeling. *Medical Imaging, IEEE Transactions on*, 21(5):525–537, 2002.

[11] G. Gerig, M. Styner, D. Jones, D. Weinberger, and J. Lieberman. Shape analysis of brain ventricles using spharm. In *Mathematical Methods in Biomedical Image Analysis, 2001. MMBIA 2001. IEEE Workshop on*, pages 171–178. IEEE, 2001.

[12] A. Hassanat, M. Al-Awadi, E. Btoush, A. Al-Btoush, G. Altarawneh, et al. New mobile phone and webcam hand images databases for personal authentication and identification. *Procedia Manufacturing*, 3:4060–4067, 2015.

[13] A. Hill and C. J. Taylor. A method of non-rigid correspondence for automaticlandmark identification. In *BMVC*, pages 1–10, 1996.

[14] Q.-X. Huang, S. Flöry, N. Gelfand, M. Hofer, and H. Pottmann. Reassembling fractured objects by geometric matching. *ACM Transactions on Graphics (TOG)*, 25(3):569–578, 2006.

[15] Q.-X. Huang and L. Guibas. Consistent shape maps via semidefinite programming. In *Computer Graphics Forum*, volume 32, pages 177–186. Wiley Online Library, 2013.

[16] M. E. Leventon, W. E. L. Grimson, and O. Faugeras. Statistical shape influence in geodesic active contours. In *Computer Vision and Pattern Recognition, 2000. Proceedings. IEEE Conference on*, volume 1, pages 316–323. IEEE, 2000.

[17] N. Parikh and S. Boyd. Proximal algorithms. *Foundations and Trends in optimization*, 1(3):123–231, 2013.

[18] H. H. Thodberg and H. Olafsdottir. Adding curvature to minimum description length shape models. In *British Machine Vision Conference, BMVC*, 2003.

[19] J. Yan, J. Wang, H. Zha, X. Yang, and S. M. Chu. Multi-view point registration via alternating optimization. In *Proceedings of the Twenty-Ninth AAAI Conference on Artificial Intelligence*, AAAI'15, pages 3834–3840. AAAI Press, 2015.

[20] X. Zhou, M. Zhu, and K. Daniilidis. Multi-image matching via fast alternating minimization. *CoRR*, abs/1505.04845, 2015.

[21] X. Zhou, M. Zhu, and K. Daniilidis. Multi-image matching via fast alternating minimization. *arXiv preprint arXiv:1505.04845*, 2015.

Towards Ultra-Low-Bitrate Video Conferencing Using Facial Landmarks

Pin-Chun Wang[1], Ching-Ling Fan[1], Chun-Ying Huang[2], Kuan-Ta Chen[3], and Cheng-Hsin Hsu[1]

[1]Department of Computer Science, National Tsing Hua University
[2]Department of Computer Science, National Chiao Tung University
[3]Institute of Information Science, Academia Sinica

ABSTRACT

Providing high-quality video conferencing experience over the best-effort Internet and wireless networks is challenging, because 2D videos are bulky. In this paper, we exploit the common structure of conferencing videos for an ultra-low-bitrate video conferencing system. In particular, we design, implement, optimize, and evaluate a video conferencing system, which: (i) extracts facial landmarks, (ii) transmits the selected facial landmarks and 2D images, and (iii) warps the untransmitted 2D images at the receiver. Several optimization techniques are adopted for minimizing the running time and maximizing the video quality, e.g., the image and warping frames are optimally determined based on network conditions and video content. The experiment results from real conferencing videos reveal that our proposed system: (i) outperforms the state-of-the-art x265 by up to 11.05 dB in PSNR (Peak Signal-to-Noise Ratio), (ii) adapts to different video content and network conditions, and (iii) runs in real-time at about 12 frame-per-second.

Keywords: Data compression; facial landmarks; facial models; video conferencing; video codecs; optimization

1. INTRODUCTION

Recent market research [19] depicts that the market share of video conferencing systems is expected to grow from 3.31 billion USD in 2013 to 6.40 billion in 2020, at a compound annual growth rate of 9.3%. Providing high-quality video conferencing experience, however, is challenging, because video conferencing, like many other real-time interactive applications, is resource demanding. For example, Skype recommends bitrates between 700 Kbps and 2.5 Mbps for 1280x720 video calls using H.264 codecs [13]. Guaranteeing such a high end-to-end bandwidth requirement is no easy task in the best-effort Internet; and doing so in shared wireless networks, such as WiFi and cellular networks, is even more difficult due to congestion, channel fading, shadowing, and interference.

In this paper, we design an *ultra-low-bitrate high-quality video conferencing system* for commodity computers by analyzing the structures of typical conference video frames and *aggressively* skipping redundant information. By *typical* conference videos, we consider a talking head in a conference room, while our system can be generalized for multiple participants in the same conference room. We make a crucial observation: in these videos, the major movements come from talking heads. To leverage this observation for bitrate reduction, we may: (i) transmit a snapshot image of talking heads at the beginning of each video conferencing session as a reference image, which is referred to as a *base image*, and (ii) describe the talking heads using facial landmarks [17], in order to synthesize facial expressions without sending (bulky) 2D images in all video frames. In particular, we propose such a system (one-way for brevity) in Fig. 1. We divide all video frames from the Webcam into two groups: (i) image frames that are transmitted as regular video frames encoded with video codecs and (ii) warped frames that are synthesized using image frames and facial landmarks, such as key feature points on edges of eyes, nose, and mouth. Selected landmarks and image frames are sent to the receiver. The receiver reconstructs the warped frames and sequentially plays all video frames. Fig. 1 also presents sample reconstructed frames from our proposed system and those from a conventional (image-based) video codec at 25 Kbps. The blocking features of the sample frames from the image-based video codec are clear, leading to degraded video conferencing quality.

We emphasize that our goal is very aggressive, as we aim to provide *acceptable* video conferencing quality at 30 Kbps, which is even lower than some audio codecs, such as G.711. To cope with this challenge, we carefully design and implement the individual components in the proposed system. The crux of the whole system is the *frame type selector*, which analyzes the expected video quality of sending the current video frame as: (i) an image frame or (ii) a warped frame under the bandwidth constraints. The frame type selector then makes the decision based on the analysis results, so as to maximize the overall video quality and thus the conferencing experience. We implement the proposed system and conduct experiments with real conferencing videos from several subjects. The experiment results show the merits of our system, for example, it: (i) outperforms the state-of-the-art x265 by up to 11.05 dB in PSNR (Peak Signal-to-Noise Ratio), (ii) adapts to different video content and network conditions, and (iii) runs in real-time at about 12 fps (frame-per-second).

2. RELATED WORK

Qi et al. [16] propose to skip transmitting some video frames at the sender, and employ 2D interpolation to synthesize the skipped video frames at the receiver. Different from our system, their solution ignores the fact that facial expressions of the talking head are the most crucial content in video conferences, and may lose the opportunity to exploit the redundancy among faces in adjacent frames. Facial models may be used to convey more facial details, e.g., Allen et al. [2] extract facial model parameters for higher compression

MM '16, October 15-19, 2016, Amsterdam, Netherlands

DOI: http://dx.doi.org/10.1145/2964284.2967284

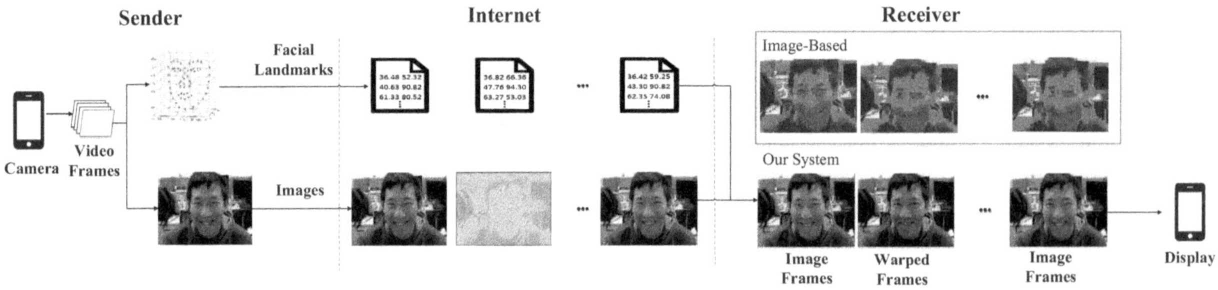

Figure 1: Illustrations of our low-bitrate video conferencing system. Only one-way video streaming is shown for brevity. Sample reconstructed video frames from our and image-based (x265) systems are given.

ratios, and Zeng et al. [23] propose a solution to emphasize the appearance of mouths and eyes during video conferences. These studies [2,23] transmit potentially duplicated texture parameters across adjacent video frames. In contrast, we aggressively avoid sending repeated information by using image frames and landmark coordinates. An early study [10] transmits images from three different angles of a face, and uses manually-selected landmark coordinates for frame interpolation. The authors find the facial expressions are not clear, and apply Principle Component Analysis (PCA) to transmit the regions of eyes and mouth. Our work also leverages base images similar to Koufakis and Buxton [10]; however, their system requires human interventions, and thus is not suitable to interactive video conferences. MPEG-4 [14] provides coding tools for face animation. In particular, the high-level expressions, like, joy, anger, and sadness, can be encoded with a given facial model. However, extracting these high-level expressions is time-consuming (3.72 fps at 352x288 on smartphones [18]), rendering it not suitable for real-time video conferences. MPEG-4 also supports low-level expressions, which are encoded using six parameters, such as the distance between upper and lower eyelids. Six parameters are too few, and lead to degraded facial expressions, as reported in Zeng et al. [23]. Compared to the high- and low-level MPEG-4 coding tools, our system runs faster and encodes more facial details, respectively.

3. FACIAL LANDMARK-BASED VIDEO CONFERENCING SYSTEM

3.1 Overview

Fig. 2 presents the architecture of our ultra-low-bitrate video conferencing system. Different from conventional video conferencing systems, the proposed system consists of five unique components: (i) *Landmark Detector*, (ii) *Video Codec*, (iii) *Landmark Codec*, (iv) *Image Warper*, and (v) *Frame Type Selector*. The interactions among those components are as follows. The original video frames are captured by a Webcam, and sent to the landmark detector, which outputs the coordinates of detected landmarks. Afterwards, the landmark codec quantizes and compresses the landmarks and transmits them to the image warper. The image warper synthesizes the latest image frame based on the quantized landmark and passes the image to the frame type selector. We assume the very first base image is sent to the receiver right before each video conference, which is used to bootstrap frame warping. The frame type selector compares the video quality between the warped frame and the image frame to decide the frame type. Following the decision, the image frames and facial landmarks are transmitted as needed. At the receiver side, the image frames are decoded by the video codec and the warped frames are reconstructed by the uncompressed landmarks and the last received image frame. Among the five components, the frame type selector hosts the intelligence of maximizing video quality. We present the designs of the other four components in Sec. 3.2, and the details on frame type selector in Sec. 3.3.

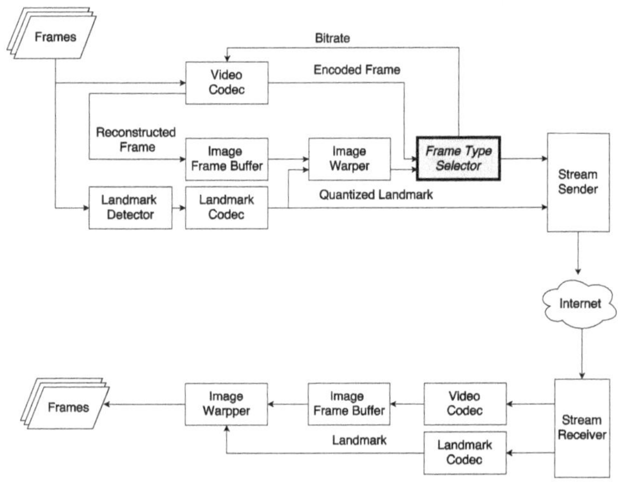

Figure 2: The architecture of our proposed system.

3.2 Component Designs (Except Frame Type Selector)

Landmark Detector. We use facial models to derive the landmarks on each frame. Facial models can be roughly classified into 3D [3,5] and 2D [7,8] ones. We adopt 2D facial models since the illumination and talking head features are rather static in video conferencing. In particular, we consider two most popular 2D facial models: Active Appearance Model [7] (AAM) and Constrained Local Model [8] (CLM). The goal of AAM is to fit a static shape and appearance model to a new image. Through iterations, AAM fits the models and computes the coordinates of the landmarks. In contrast, CLM builds shape models by labeled training data. Generally, AAM preforms better on face alignment and rotated faces, and CLM provides more delicate changes on different expressions. Considering the properties of conferencing videos (more facial expressions, fewer changes on face orientations), we choose CLM with 68 landmarks [4] for better video quality.

Image Warper. Image Warper synthesizes frames based on landmarks and prior image frames. We first use Delaunay Triangulation algorithm [11] to divide faces (excluding the background region) into triangles based on the landmarks. Then, an affine transformation is applied to those triangles. This process can be viewed as if those triangles are projected onto new surfaces pixel by pixel. Moreover, the affine function is ideal for image mapping when the transformed regions are small due to its geometric properties. In our application, the affine transformation not only solves the deformation problem on facial regions, but also incurs lower computational complexity because of its linear property.

Video Codec. We adopt the state-of-the-art H.265 codec, which achieves higher coding efficiency than earlier codecs, such as H.264 and MPEG-4. For example, Ohm et al. [12] report that H.265 achieves 50% bitrate reduction compared to H.264 in objective tests. Their subjective tests show even larger gaps. If codec availability is a concern, any other low-complexity 2D video codec can also be used in our system.

Landmark Codec. Since coordinates of the same landmark impose temporal redundancy across neighboring frames, we encode the landmark coordinates in *deltas* instead of raw numbers, as detailed below. First, we send the number of landmarks in each video frame, which is an 8-bit unsigned integer. This is followed by a series of video frames. Each frame starts with a timestamp as a 16-bit unsigned integer, followed by a series of landmarks. The landmarks are first normalized to the width/height of the video resolution (i.e., between 0 and 100%), and then quantized into the unit of ten thousand. For the first frame, we store each landmark as a 14-bit integer. The landmarks in the following frames are stored in deltas, which can be either a *short* or *long* delta, as indicated by a flag bit. Using real conferencing videos (detailed in Sec. 4), we analyze the distributions of landmark deltas. We find that 4-bit short deltas cover 76.2% of all landmark deltas, and 7-bit long deltas cover additional 24.5% of them. Since there are only 0.3% remaining landmark deltas, we decide to encode them in 7-bit, and carry over the residues to the next frame in the worst case. With the proposed representation format, we reduce the size of landmark coordinates by about 30%. The resulting landmark representations are compressed by the 7z [1] algorithm before being transmitted.

3.3 Maximizing Video Quality Using Frame Type Selector

We design the frame type selector to be content dependent and network adaptive. It dynamically instructs: (i) the sender to transmit an image frame or (ii) the receiver to synthesize a warped frame, so as to maximize the video quality of every single frame. In particular, the sender keeps track of the available bitrate, or *bit budget*, of each video frame. The sender encodes the current video frame using the bit budget and also simulates the warping procedure at the receiver side. The frame type selector then chooses the type (image or warped frame) that leads to higher video quality. Notice that we only transmit the landmarks whenever needed. This is because warping each frame only requires the landmarks of the latest image frame and the current frame. By deferring the transmission of the landmarks of image frames, we never transmit the landmarks that will not be used. We note that our frame type selector implicitly determines the frequency of sending an image frame based on the video content characteristics and network resource availability, which is the core research problem to optimize the proposed ultra-low-bitrate video conferencing system.

4. EXPERIMENTS

4.1 Setup

We have implemented our proposed video conferencing system using CLM [4] and OpenCV [6] libraries, and in C++. Our system has five components: (i) *landmark detector*, which analyzes video frames and generates the landmarks for each video frame, (ii) *frame type selector*, for selecting whether it is an image frame or a warped frame under different total bitrate constraints, (iii) *encoder*, which compacts and compresses landmarks, and invokes x265 [22] to encode images frames according to frame type and the per-frame bitrate constraints, (iv) *decoder*, which decodes the images and landmarks, and (v) *warper*, which generates intermediate synthesized images with OpenCV [6]. The base images are compressed into JPEG, and the x265 configurations are ultrafast preset, zero latency tuning, and IPPP $\cdots$ structure, if not otherwise specified.

We recruit nine subjects in our university, and record nine videos at 1280x720 using commodity Webcams and computers for our experiments[1]. When recording the videos, we ask the subjects to talk as if they are in video conferences. Each video has 300 frames and lasts for 10 seconds. We adopt the following performance metrics:

- **Video quality:** the video quality in PSNR and SSIM (Structured Similarity Index [21]), computed by comparing the original video at the sender against the reconstructed one at the receiver.
- **Warping ratio:** the ratio between the number of the warped frames and the total frames.
- **Running time:** the execution time of each software component, derived by instrumenting our prototype system.

We conduct the experiments with the abovementioned conferencing videos in our ultra-low-bitrate system (denoted as Our System in figures). Our system adaptively sends encoded images and landmarks according to the expected video quality. To our best knowledge, our system is the first complete system of its own kind, e.g., although Zeng et al. [23] also use facial models, they do not propose rate control mechanism, and thus their work cannot serve as the baseline system. For comparisons, we also run the same experiments with the x265 [22] codec, which is the state-of-the-art image-based codec (denoted as Image-Based in figures). For each conferencing video, we vary the bitrate at $\{25, 30, 40, 50, 60, 100\}$ Kbps, and the base image size at $\{20, 40, 80\}$ KB. We let the bitrate be 40 Kbps and the image size be 80 KB if not otherwise specified. We run the experiments on a Linux workstation with an Intel i7 CPU at 3.6 GHz and 8 GB RAM. Our system works with different video quality metrics. Results from optimizing video quality in PSNR are shown by default; only some SSIM results are presented due to the space limitations.

4.2 Results

Our system outperforms the image-based system. Fig. 3 plots the PSNR values of a sample video under different bitrates. In both systems, higher bitrates lead to better conferencing video quality. However, our system constantly outperforms the image-based system. For example, our system achieves 30 dB in PSNR at merely 25 Kbps[2], while the image-based system requires 60 Kbps (2.4 times). Next, we calculate the quality improvements in PSNR and SSIM of all conferencing videos and plot the mean improvements with 95% confidence intervals in Fig. 4. This figure shows that our system always outperforms the image-based system at all bitrates. The mean PSNR improvement of all conferencing videos is up to 7.5 dB, while the mean SSIM improvement is up to 0.08. For individual conferencing videos, the maximal PSNR improvement is 11.05 dB, and the maximal SSIM improvement is 0.15.

Our system adapts to network conditions and video content. We plot the average warping ratios at different bitrates in Fig. 5(a).

[1]To be realistic, we consider users who feel comfortable talking in diverse ways, e.g., some of them constantly move their heads, and others are rather static.

[2]30 dB is considered as good quality [20].

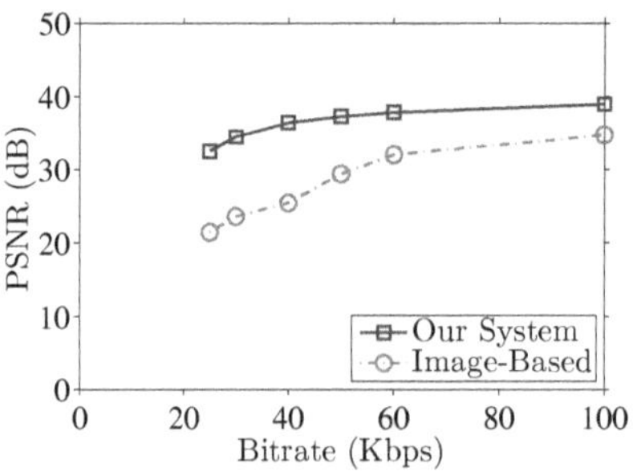

Figure 3: The video quality of a sample video under different bitrates.

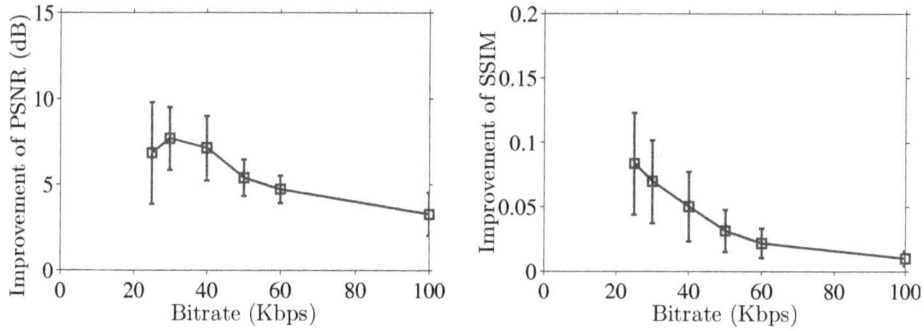

(a) (b)

Figure 4: Our system outperforms the image-based system in terms of conferencing video quality, in: (a) PSNR and (b) SSIM.

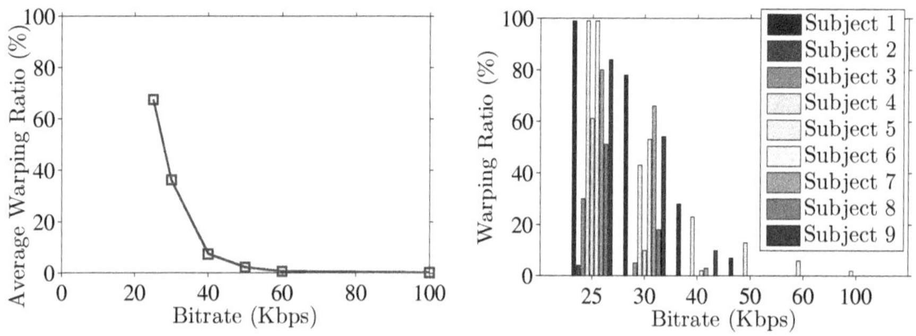

(a) (b)

Figure 5: Our system automatically adapts to diverse: (a) network conditions and (b) video content.

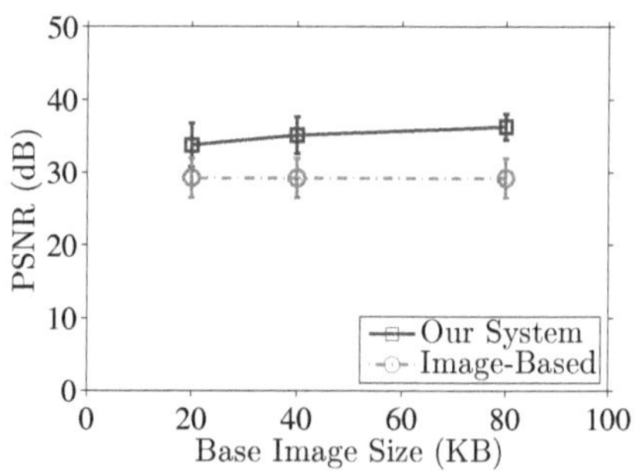

Figure 6: Better base image quality leads to higher conferencing video quality. Sample results in PSNR are shown.

In this figure, the average warping ratio increases as the total bitrate decreases. This shows the effectiveness of our system under different network conditions, because warped frames consume smaller bit budgets. Fig. 5(b) plots the ratio of the warped frames of all conferencing videos under different bitrates. This figure shows that our system results in diverse warping ratios with different video content. A closer look indicates that our system selects more warped frames when sending more active conferencing videos; and it selects fewer warped frames when sending more static ones. Hence, our system is effective under different video content.

Implications of base image quality. We plot the average PSNR values across all conferencing videos with 95% confidence intervals in Fig. 6. We observe that, compared to the image-based system, our system achieves higher average video quality with all considered base image sizes, and the gap becomes slightly smaller if we reduce the base image size from 80 to 20 KB. More precisely, among all conferencing videos, our system outperforms the image-based system in 100%, 91%, and 83% of the conferencing videos, with the base image size of 80, 40, and 20 KB.

Running time. We measure and report the per-component running time. On average, the running times of the landmark detection, landmark encoding/decoding, image warping, image encoding/decoding, and the video quality assessment are 38, 1, 28, 13, and 5 ms, respectively. We note that some components are not invoked for every single video frame and some components may be pipelined. Our analysis reveals that the current (unoptimized) prototype system achieves up to 12 fps. Several optimization techniques can be applied to further increase the frame rate, e.g., H.265 codec chips may become commodity soon, which run much faster than the x265 software used in our experiments.

5. CONCLUSION AND FUTURE WORK

In this paper, we designed, implemented, optimized, and evaluated an ultra-low-bitrate video conferencing system that extracts facial landmarks, compresses and transmits facial landmarks and images, and warps the untransmitted images. Various optimization techniques were proposed to maximize the video quality. Using real conferencing videos, we conducted experiments to quantify the performance and limitations of our proposed system. The results show that our system: (i) outperforms the state-of-the-art x265 by up to 11.05 dB in PSNR, (ii) adapts to different video content and network conditions, and (iii) runs in real-time at 12 fps. We believe the lessons learned when developing the proposed system will stimulate future research in this direction.

The presented work can be extended in several directions. First, multiple base images, e.g., with different facial expressions, may be sent and cached, so that the frame type selector may choose the base image that produces the highest warped frame quality. Second, a compression algorithm specifically designed for landmarks can be developed. Currently, landmarks are encoded using generic compression algorithm, leading to 21 Kbps bitrate on average. A customized compression algorithm that takes the landmark structure into considerations or even drops some less-critical landmarks may achieve lower landmark bitrate. Last, we plan to further speed up the individual components, especially the warper, using multithreading, GPU, and techniques proposed in the literature [9, 15].

6. ACKNOWLEDGEMENTS

This work was partially supported by the Ministry of Science and Technology of Taiwan under the grants: 103-2221-E-001-023-MY2, 103-2221-E-009-230-MY2, 102-2221-E-007-062-MY3.

7. REFERENCES

[1] 7-zip official site, 2015. http://www.7-zip.org.

[2] N. Allen, B. Naidoo, and S. McDonald. Model-based compression for low-bitrate comms: A statistical approach to facial video encoding. In *Proceedings of Southern Africa Telecommunication Networks and Applications Conference (SATNAC)*, Sep. 2006.

[3] A. Ansari and A. Mohamed. 3D face modeling using two views and a generic face model with application to 3D face recognition. In *Proceedings of IEEE Advanced Video and Signal Based Surveillance (AVSS)*, Jul. 2003.

[4] T. Baltruvsaitis, P. Robinson, and L. Morency. 3D constrained local model for rigid and non-rigid facial tracking. In *Proceedings of IEEE Conference on Computer Vision and Pattern Recognition (CVPR)*, Jun. 2012.

[5] V. Blanz and T. Vetter. A morphable model for the synthesis of 3D faces. In *Proceedings of the Annual Conference on Computer Graphics and Interactive Techniques (SIGGRAPH)*, Aug. 1999.

[6] G. Bradski. The OpenCV Library. *Dr. Dobb's Journal of Software Tools*, 2000.

[7] T. Cootes, G. Edwards, and C. Taylor. Active appearance models. *IEEE Transactions on Pattern Analysis and Machine Intelligence*, (6):681–685, Jun. 2001.

[8] D. Cristinacce and T. Cootes. Feature detection and tracking with constrained local models. In *Proceedings of the British Machine Vision Conference (BMVC)*, Sep. 2006.

[9] V. Fuetterling, C. Lojewski, and F. Pfreundt. High-performance delaunay triangulation for many-core computers. In *Proceedings of the ACM SIGGRAPH Symposium on High Performance Graphics (HPG)*, Aug. 2014.

[10] I. Koufakis and B. Buxton. Very low bit rate face video compression using linear combination of 2D face views and principal components analysis. *Image and Vision Computing*, 17(14):1031–1051, Jan. 1999.

[11] D. Lee and B. Schachter. Two algorithms for constructing a delaunay triangulation. *International Journal of Computer and Information Sciences*, 9(3):219–242, Feb. 1980.

[12] J. Ohm, G. Sullivan, H. Schwarz, T. Tan, and T. Wiegand. Comparison of the coding efficiency of video coding standards including high efficiency video coding HEVC. *IEEE Transactions on Circuits and Systems for Video Technology*, 22(12):1669–1684, Dec. 2012.

[13] Plan network requirements for Skype for business 2015, Sep 2015. https://technet.microsoft.com/en-us/library/gg425841.aspx.

[14] A. Puri and A. Eleftheriadis. MPEG-4: An object-based multimedia coding standard supporting mobile applications. *Mobile Networks and Applications*, 3(1):5–32, Jun. 1998.

[15] M. Qi, T. Cao, and T. Tan. Computing 2D constrained delaunay triangulation using the GPU. *IEEE Transactions on Visualization and Computer Graphics*, 19(5):736–748, May. 2013.

[16] X. Qi, Q. Yang, D. Nguyen, G. Zhou, and G. Peng. LBVC: towards low-bandwidth video chat on smartphones. In *Proceedings of ACM Multimedia System Conference (MMSys)*, Mar. 2015.

[17] D. Rathod, A. Vinay, S. Shylaja, and S. Natarajan. Facial landmark localization - a literature survey. *International Journal of Current Engineering and Technology*, 4(3):1901–1907, Jun. 2014.

[18] M. Suk and B. Prabhakaran. Real-time facial expression recognition on smartphones. In *Proceedings of the IEEE Applications of Computer Vision (WACV)*, Jan. 2015.

[19] Video conferencing market to expand at 9.3% CAGR to 2020 thanks to increasing usage in healthcare and defense, Jul. 2015. http://www.transparencymarketresearch.com/pressrelease/video-conferencing-market.htm.

[20] Y. Wang, J. Ostermann, and Y. Zhang. *Video Processing and Communications*. Prentice Hall, 2001.

[21] Z. Wang, L. Lu, and A. Bovik. Video quality assessment based on structural distortion measurement. *Signal Processing: Image Communication*, 19(2):121–132, Feb. 2004.

[22] x265 HEVC Encoder official site. http://x265.org.

[23] W. Zeng, M. Yang, and Z. Cui. Ultra-low bit rate facial coding hybrid model based on saliency detection. *Journal of Image and Graphics*, 3(1):25–29, Jun. 2015.

Generating Diverse Image Datasets with Limited Labeling

Niluthpol Chowdhury Mithun, Rameswar Panda, Amit K. Roy-Chowdhury
University of California, Riverside, CA 92521, USA
nmithun@ece.ucr.edu, rpand002@ucr.edu, amitrc@ece.ucr.edu

ABSTRACT

Image datasets play a pivotal role in advancing multimedia and image analysis research. However, most of these datasets are created by extensive human effort and extremely expensive to scale up. There is high chance that we may have no instances for some required concepts in these data-sets or the available instances do not cover the diversity of real-world scenarios. In this regard, several approaches for learning from web images and refining them have been proposed, but these approaches either include significant redundant instances in the dataset or fail to guarantee a diverse enough set to train a robust classifier. In this work, we propose a semi-supervised sparse coding framework to collect a diverse set of images with minimal human effort, which can be used to both create a dataset from scratch or enrich an existing dataset with diverse examples. To evaluate our method, we constructed an image dataset with our framework, which is named as DivNet. Experiments on this dataset demonstrate that our method not only reduces manual effort, but also the created dataset has excellent accuracy, diversity and cross-dataset generalization ability.

Keywords

Image dataset construction, Sparse coding, Active learning.

1. INTRODUCTION

The efficiency of several visual recognition tasks depends upon the ability to identify suitable training examples to learn initial models. The majority of the success in this regard has been achieved by models trained on large-scale hand-labeled image datasets (e.g., SUN [34], ImageNet[24]). Although, these datasets cover large numbers of categories, expanding them to new categories or providing new examples to an existing category, is extremely costly and labor-intensive [20]. Moreover, there exist various types of bias in the popular image datasets and hence, they do not demonstrate satisfactory cross-dataset generalization (training on a dataset, testing on a different dataset) capability [19, 30].

MM '16, October 15-19, 2016, Amsterdam, Netherlands

DOI: http://dx.doi.org/10.1145/2964284.2967285

Future multimedia and image analysis research requires examining even a greater number of visual categories and adapt to higher intra-class variation present within a category[7]. Complexity of the models will increase over time to cope with this. Hence, creating high-quality image dataset and continuously updating existing datasets with new diverse examples is becoming more important over time. Complete human labeling based solution is unlikely to keep pace with this growing need.

To address the issues stated above and inspired by streams of images available on the web, there has been lot of recent interest in learning directly from noisy web data [20, 28, 18, 4, 14, 15, 5] or automatically curating web images for creating a dataset [33, 23, 31, 6, 1]. These methods reduce labeling cost and show promising results in recognition tasks by having a noise-aware model. However, these methods usually assume that most of the returned images from the web will be relevant to the query. It may work well for simple categories, (e.g. bike, car) but it is unlikely to be true for the complex categories, (e.g. birthday party, concert), especially when looking beyond the top few matches. Furthermore, most of these approaches consider images from a single search engine (e.g. Google [20, 14], Flickr [4]), or generate synthetic data from a clean set [28]. This may bring up issues of bias, low accuracy and lack of diversity.

A few semi-supervised approaches have been developed that minimize human effort for dataset creation using an active learning framework [35, 9, 7]. However, there is no guarantee that the images collected represent a diverse enough set to train a robust classifier. Similar to automatic approaches, most of the semi-automatic approaches primarily aim at collecting as many relevant images as possible. Hence, in spite of causing serious wastage of space, the dataset loses quality and training with these images may not provide expected performance gain. Moreover, these approaches [7, 35] may select many samples for human labeling that have significant information overlap [12].

Motivated by the above, the main goal of this work is to develop a method for construction of high-quality image datasets with limited budget (e.g. labeling, storage etc). The images in each category of the dataset should be relevant and diverse. The second goal, is to provide an online framework, that is capable of collecting more discriminative images continuously as new data becomes available, which is suitable for enriching existing image datasets. In order to achieve these goals, *we propose a novel sparse coding framework with human in the loop*. Our method builds upon several machine learning tools, e.g., active learning [25, 17, 2], sparse coding [11, 32, 36] and deep learning [22, 21].

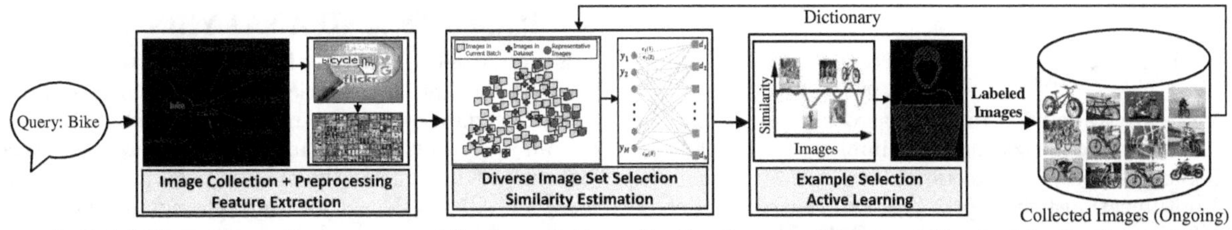

Figure 1: Brief illustration of our proposed framework for collecting images. Please see the text in Section 2 for details.

Contributions. The main contributions of this work are following. **First,** our proposed diversity aware sparse representative selection based active learning approach considers both images in current unlabeled batch and images in existing dataset to select the best subset for further processing. Hence, our approach efficiently minimizes the chance of including redundant instances in dataset and utilizes human effort in labeling most informative and discriminative instances. **Second,** the proposed framework is a generalized one which makes high-precision image dataset creation feasible with no initial cost (e.g. providing positive and/or negative seeds for categories) and limited labeling budget. Moreover, our approach can efficiently update an already created dataset, when new data becomes available. **Third,** experiments demonstrate that the dataset created by our method shows excellent cross-dataset performance, diversity and scalability. Additionally, it is worth mentioning that, even with no human labeling, our method shows high-precision in collecting images automatically.

2. PROPOSED METHODOLOGY

Overview. In our framework, collecting images of one category is independent of other categories. Hence, images for different categories can be collected in parallel. Fig. 1 summarizes our incremental image collection framework for a category 'bike'. Initially, we collect images related to the category from different web-sources. If no image of the category is available beforehand, a set of top ranked images from a reliable search engine is considered as initial dataset. During each run of incremental update, we process a small batch from the collected images. First, we employ a diversity aware sparse representative selection approach to choose a smaller set of representative images that not only best represents this batch, but also is discriminative to the images in current dataset. Then, we calculate similarity of each representative images with the images in dataset. Based on the similarity score, we employ active learning to decide whether to label an image manually or not. As collecting images for one category is independent of others, we ask only binary questions to annotator. We continuously update the dataset with new images labeled by the system.

2.1 Image Collection and Feature Extraction

Since the number of returned images from a web search based on a query is limited, we use a query expansion scheme. The expansion is done using Google Search and ConceptNet [27]. We select only synonyms and derived phrases as expanded queries, as these are highly relevant. For example, given a query 'Bike', we expand to queries such as 'Bicycle', 'Ride Bike', 'Mountain Bike' etc. The expanded queries are used to collect images from different web sources. We filter out the images having sufficiently low quality, e.g., out-of-focus or blurred, too white or black, empty or too small. A mini batch of images from the remaining collection is processed during each run of incremental update until required number of images for the category is selected. Batch-size is chosen experimentally and depends on available resources.

We apply deep CNN to extract features, as they are now the state-of-the-art image features [22, 21]. The best performance among CNN models has been achieved by very deep networks with large number of layers [26, 29], but the processing time per image in such networks can be very high. Hence, to keep dataset construction scalable, we use the architecture proposed in [21], which requires significantly less processing time. It is worth mentioning that our method does not depend on this particular choice of CNN, except for the scalablity issue mentioned above. We remove the last classification layer of the CNN [21] and treat rest of the network as a fixed feature extractor. For an image f at the input layer, we extract feature vector x_f ($x_f \in R^d$, $d = 4096$) from fc7 layer of the CNN.

2.2 Diverse Representative Set Selection

The goal of this step is to find an optimal subset of the current batch of images. In particular, we are trying to represent the current batch of images by selecting only a few representative images, which are also dissimilar to the images in current dataset. Therefore, our natural goal is to establish a image level sparsity which can be induced by performing l_1 regularization on rows of the sparse coefficient matrix. By introducing the row sparsity regularizer, the problem can now be succinctly formulated as

$$\begin{aligned} \min \; & ||X - XZ||_F^2 \\ \text{s.t.} \; & ||Z||_{2,1} \leq \tau, \; ||D^T XZ||_F^2 \leq \kappa \end{aligned} \tag{1}$$

Here, $X \in \mathbb{R}^{B\times N}$ is the feature matrix for all images in current batch, where $X = \{x_i \in \mathbb{R}^B, i = 1, \cdots, N\}$. Each x_i represents the feature descriptor of an image in current batch in B-dimensional feature space. N denotes the number of images in the batch. $Z \in \mathbb{R}^{N\times N}$ is the sparse coefficient matrix and $\|Z\|_{2,1} \triangleq \sum_{i=1}^{N} \|z_i\|_2$ is the row sparsity regularizer, i.e., sum of l_2 norms of the rows of Z. τ and κ are trade-off parameters. $D \in \mathbb{R}^{B\times M}$ is the feature matrix of current dataset, where $D = \{d_j \in \mathbb{R}^B, j = 1, \cdots, M\}$. M denotes the number of images of the category in current dataset.

The objective function in Eq. 1 is intuitive: the first constraint i.e., $l_{2,1}$ regularizer is to induce row level sparsity in representative selection [8, 11], whereas the second constraint tries to select images that are less correlated with images in current dataset. Minimization of Eq. 1 leads to a sparse solution for Z in terms of rows, *i.e.*, the sparse coefficient matrix Z contains few nonzero rows which constitute the representative set. Optimization of Eq. 1 attempts to obtain a sparse set of images non-redundant with previously selected images.

Optimization. Here, we briefly describe the strategy to solve the convex optimization problem in Eq. 1. Using Lagrange multipliers, optimization problem in Eq. 1 can be written as

$$\min \frac{1}{2}||X - XZ||_F^2 + \lambda||Z||_{2,1} + \frac{\alpha}{2}||D^T XZ||_F^2 \quad (2)$$

where λ and α are trade-off parameters associated with sparsity and diversity regularization. We implement the algorithm using an Alternating Direction Method of Multipliers (ADMM) optimization framework [3]. We refer the reader to check [3] for more details on the ADMM. We choose columns of X corresponding to the nonzero rows of final Z and denote the feature matrix of the representative set as Y. Here, $Y \in \mathbb{R}^{B \times K}$ is the feature matrix for all images in representative set, where $Y = \{y_i \in \mathbb{R}^B, i = 1, \cdots, K\}$. y_i represents the feature descriptor of ith representative sample in B-dimensional feature space. K denotes the total number of images in selected representative set.

2.3 Active Learning for Image Labeling

After we have a diverse representative set Y, the next goal is to estimate the similarity of each image in Y to the images in the dataset D. Based on the similarity score, active learning module will determine images to be labeled.

Our goal here is to find how likely a sample image belongs to a particular class, given only some examples of the same class. Specifically, given a sample y_i, we compute its sparse representation c_i based on dictionary D.

Then, we select a sample y_i as relevant based on how well the nonzero entries in the estimate c_i are associated with the columns of D. Given the above stated goals, the optimization problem can be written as,

$$\min \; ||Y - DC||_F^2 \;\; \text{s.t.} ||c_i||_1 \leq s \quad (3)$$

Here, $C \in \mathbb{R}^{M \times K}$ is the sparse coefficient matrix, where $C = \{c_i \in \mathbb{R}^M, i = 1, \cdots, K\}$. s is a tradeoff parameter.

In Eq. 3, the constraint, i.e., l_1 regularizer is to induce element wise sparsity in a column. The objective is logical as any new sample of a category will approximately lie in the linear span of some samples in dataset associated with the same category. We require the coefficient matrix C to be sparse by solving the optimization program in Eq. 3. We use similar ADMM procedure stated in Sec. 2.2, to solve this optimization problem.

After calculating C, the similarity score for each image in representative set is calculated as follows,

$$\zeta_i = 1 - \frac{||y_i - Dc_i||_2}{||y_i||_2} \quad (4)$$

Here, ζ_i is similarity score of ith sample. $||y_i - Dc_i||_2$ indicates the residual between y_i and Dc_i, which is reconstruction of y_i using samples of same category from dataset.

For an instance $y_i \in Y$, if the corresponding similarity score ζ_i is greater than a threshold δ, we assume that our system is highly confident about this instance. Hence, we label the instance y_i using the label of the query and add to the dataset. Number of instances obtained without any human supervision is not fixed and depends on the value of δ, which we set sufficiently large so that irrelevant instances are less likely to be added to the dataset. We remove instances, which have a similarity score ζ_i smaller than a threshold γ (say $\gamma = 0.3$), as we believe there is high chance of these examples to be irrelevant. Among the remaining samples, we choose the instances with lowest similarity score first for human labeling, as these examples have greater chance to increase diversity in our dataset. We sequentially choose maximum b instances like this and request for human annotation. Here, b is our labeling budget per iteration.

3. RESULTS AND ANALYSIS

Experimental Setup. For feature extraction, in all of the experiments, we use Alexnet-CNN, which is trained on ImageNet dataset, under the network architecture of [21]. For all the results shown in this paper, we have used the features extracted from the pre-trained CNN[21] and trained SVM classifiers. We set all the Lagrangian multipliers $\lambda = \lambda_0/\mu$, where $\mu > 1$ and λ_0 is computed from the input data [11]. For fair comparison, in all the experiments, except dataset enrichment, we considered no image related to the concept word is available beforehand. We take advantage of the high-precision of few top returned images for the query from Google search by utilizing them as initial dataset.

3.1 Constructed Dataset by our Framework

We constructed a dataset using the proposed framework to verify our approach, which we name as DivNet. We are continuously adding more categories in this dataset. Now, it contains images for 550 categories, averaging 1K images per category. The dataset is publicly available to download in http://www.ee.ucr.edu/~amitrc/datasets.php. We crawled images from Bing, Google and Flickr. The categories are mainly chosen from ILSVRC2016 object detection and scene classification challenge [24].

The ratio of human labeling used, compared to the total number of images in the dataset is 11.7%. The average accuracy of the labels in DivNet is estimated by manually inspecting 5.5K images (10 random images per concept) from the entire dataset. The average accuracy has been found to be 97.2%, which is slightly lower than 99.7%, reported in ImageNet. However, for collecting same number of images for any category, the manual labeling is about 9 times lower in our case on average. Fig.2 shows human labeling statistics of 35 categories from our dataset.

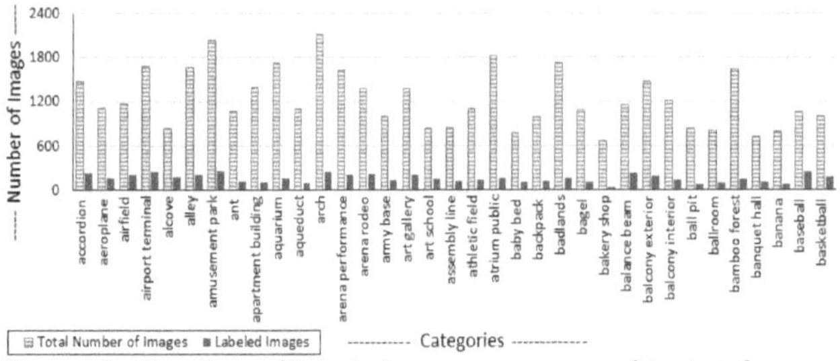

Figure 2: Number of labeled images compared to total number of selected images for 35 categories in DivNet.

3.2 Cross-Dataset Generalization

To evaluate the generalization ability of our constructed dataset, we compare the dataset with two popular hand-labeled image datasets, e.g., VOC2012 [13] and ImageNet[24]. We select all twenty categories from VOC2012 dataset [13] for this experiment. We collect images from all three datasets for these categories and train classifiers. The result for different training and testing data combinations is shown in Fig. 3. Training and testing on the same dataset provides the best performance most of the times for a fixed number of samples. However, training with DivNet shows the best generalization among datasets, as the average cross dataset performance drop (e.g. training and testing on VOC, compared to training on ours and testing on VOC) is minimum. Initially with few training samples, the performance of DivNet is lower as it has very few manually labeled samples. However, as we continuously select more diverse images to be labeled by our system, the performance improves at a higher

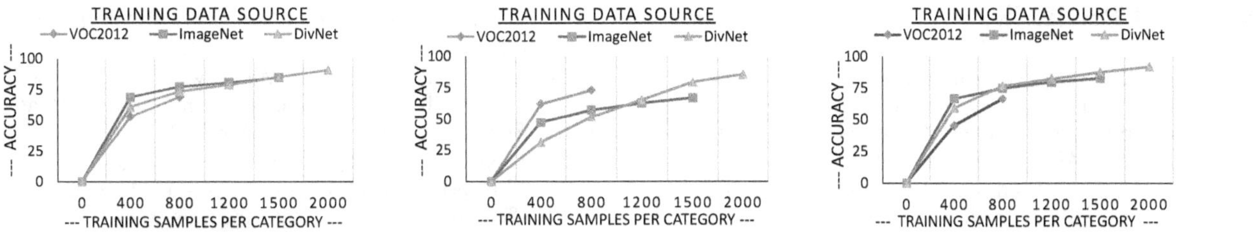

(a) Test on ImageNet (b) Test on VOC2012 (c) Test on DivNet

Figure 3: Cross dataset performance of classifier trained on different datasets with different number of samples per category.

rate. We can compare the performance of the datasets at the point of 1500 training samples (since state of the art ImageNet has on average 1500 images per category) and see the generalization ability of DivNet is better. The comparison at the same number of training samples shows the cross-dataset generalization ability of DivNet. Moreover, DivNet can achieve even better generalization performance because of its ability to scale up with limited labeling effort.

3.3 Diversity

In order to illustrate the diversity of images in our collected dataset, we follow [10, 7], which computes the average image of each category and measure lossless JPG file size which reflects the amount of information in an image. A diverse image set should result in a blurrier average image, and the JPG file size of average image should be smaller. We resize all images to 256X256, and create average images for each category from all images of the category. Fig. 4 shows the average images and the corresponding JPG image size comparison of four categories: person, dog, monitor and airoplane. The average image of DivNet is blurrier and hard to recognize out the object, while the average image of Caltech-256 [16] is more structured and sharper. DivNet has slightly smaller JPG file size than ImageNet, but significantly smaller than Caltech-256. This phenomenon is common for almost all of the categories. For randomly selected 10 categories, the average lossless JPG size has been found to be 2.3 KB in DivNet, 2.5 KB in ImageNet and 3.9 KB in Caltech-256.

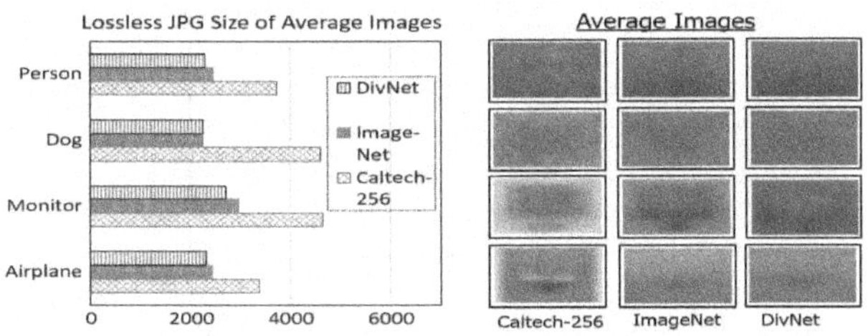

Figure 4: Average images of DivNet, ImageNet and Caltech-256 for four categories. Left chart shows the lossless JPG file sizes of average images in Bytes.

3.4 Dataset Enrichment

To evaluate the performance of our approach in dataset enrichment, we enrich ImageNet, VOC2012 and Caltech-256 by our method. For this experiment, we pick eight categories that are common in these datasets: airplane, bike, bird, car, dog, horse, monitor and person. For each category, we start our dataset construction method with images from a particular dataset as initial dataset and collect 1000 more images using our framework automatically with no labeling (Enrich Dataset-Auto) and also with a labeling budget of 50 (Enrich Dataset-50). We train image classifier on these categories with initial dataset images and also with enriched dataset images. The result in Fig. 5 shows that the performance of classifier improves after enriching dataset with our framework. Hence, our method is suitable for extending existing image collections with discriminative examples.

Figure 5: Change in image classifier performance after enriching datasets with our framework.

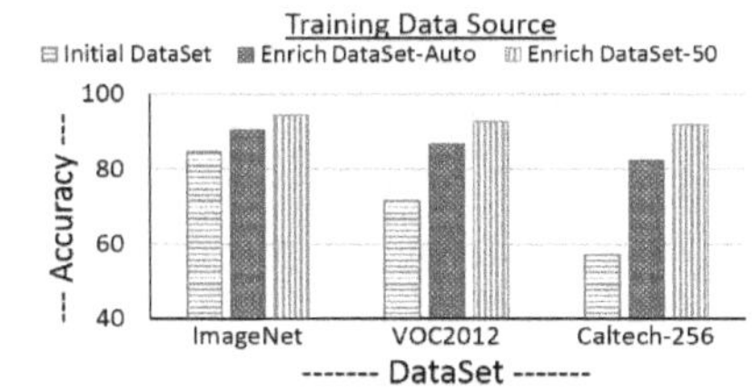

3.5 Scalability

Different from static dataset construction, our method can be used to dynamically update datasets. One can collect images based on desired dataset size and labeling budget. Such property makes sense as one user may be interested in collecting more image for a category, compared to others. It is also likely that a user may want to spend more time labeling images from some particular category than other categories. We investigate the scalability in labeling by collecting fixed number of images with different labeling budget. The accuracy of the classifier per category increases by 3.2% on average initially, as we increase labeling budget by 25. However, the performance improvement usually saturates after labeling around 100-200 examples(the actual number varies by category).

4. CONCLUSIONS

In this paper, we propose a semi-supervised framework for collecting images from web, which is suitable for dataset construction, or enriching existing datasets with discriminative examples. Our system provides flexibility that permits us to filter out irrelevant images and obtain a reliable set of diverse images based on resource and labeling budget available, so that a high-precision large-scale image classifier can be trained. The experimental results demonstrate that our approach is not only useful in reducing the manual annotation efforts, but also successful in collecting images with high precision and diversity, and robust image classifiers can be trained from these images. Future works will investigate domain-adaptation techniques and other image metadata available on the web to further improve the dataset construction framework in terms of budget and quality.

Acknowledgments: This work was partially supported by US NSF grants IIS-1316934 and CPS-1544969. We would like to thank Andrew Kwon, Cody Simons and Nishanth Babu, three current UCR undergraduate students, for helping in the construction of the DivNet dataset.We also thank NVIDIA for donating a Tesla K40 GPU.

5. REFERENCES

[1] Y. Bai, K. Yang, W. Yu, C. Xu, W.-Y. Ma, and T. Zhao. Automatic image dataset construction from click-through logs using deep neural network. In *Proc. ACM Conf. Multimedia*, pages 441–450. ACM, 2015.

[2] J. H. Bappy, S. Paul, and A. K. Roy-Chowdhury. Online adaptation for joint scene and object classification. In *ECCV*. Springer, 2016.

[3] S. Boyd, N. Parikh, E. Chu, B. Peleato, and J. Eckstein. Distributed optimization and statistical learning via the alternating direction method of multipliers. *Foundations and Trends® in Machine Learning*, 3(1):1–122, 2011.

[4] X. Chen and A. Gupta. Webly supervised learning of convolutional networks. In *ICCV*, pages 1431–1439, 2015.

[5] X. Chen, A. Shrivastava, and A. Gupta. Neil: Extracting visual knowledge from web data. In *ICCV*, pages 1409–1416, 2013.

[6] D. S. Cheng, F. Setti, N. Zeni, R. Ferrario, and M. Cristani. Semantically-driven automatic creation of training sets for object recognition. *Computer Vision and Image Understanding*, 131:56–71, 2015.

[7] B. Collins, J. Deng, K. Li, and L. Fei-Fei. Towards scalable dataset construction: An active learning approach. In *ECCV*, pages 86–98. Springer, 2008.

[8] Y. Cong, J. Yuan, and J. Luo. Towards scalable summarization of consumer videos via sparse dictionary selection. *IEEE Trans. Multimedia*, 14(1):66–75, 2012.

[9] Y. Cui, F. Zhou, Y. Lin, and S. Belongie. Fine-grained categorization and dataset bootstrapping using deep metric learning with humans in the loop. *arXiv preprint arXiv:1512.05227*, 2015.

[10] J. Deng, W. Dong, R. Socher, L.-J. Li, K. Li, and L. Fei-Fei. Imagenet: A large-scale hierarchical image database. In *CVPR*, pages 248–255. IEEE, 2009.

[11] E. Elhamifar, G. Sapiro, and R. Vidal. See all by looking at a few: Sparse modeling for finding representative objects. In *CVPR*, pages 1600–1607. IEEE, 2012.

[12] E. Elhamifar, G. Sapiro, A. Yang, and S. Sasrty. A convex optimization framework for active learning. In *ICCV*, pages 209–216, 2013.

[13] M. Everingham, L. Van Gool, C. K. Williams, J. Winn, and A. Zisserman. The pascal visual object classes (voc) challenge. *IJCV*, 88(2):303–338, 2010.

[14] R. Fergus, L. Fei-Fei, P. Perona, and A. Zisserman. Learning object categories from google's image search. In *ICCV*, volume 2, pages 1816–1823. IEEE, 2005.

[15] R. Fergus, Y. Weiss, and A. Torralba. Semi-supervised learning in gigantic image collections. In *NIPS*, pages 522–530, 2009.

[16] G. Griffin, A. Holub, and P. Perona. Caltech-256 object category dataset. California Institute of Technology, 2007.

[17] M. Hasan and A. K. Roy-Chowdhury. Context aware active learning of activity recognition models. In *ICCV*, pages 4543–4551, 2015.

[18] H. Izadinia, B. C. Russell, A. Farhadi, M. D. Hoffman, and A. Hertzmann. Deep classifiers from image tags in the wild. In *Proc. of the Workshop on Community Organized Multimodal Mining: Opportunities for Novel Solutions*, pages 13–18. ACM, 2015.

[19] A. Khosla, T. Zhou, T. Malisiewicz, A. A. Efros, and A. Torralba. Undoing the damage of dataset bias. In *ECCV*, pages 158–171. Springer, 2012.

[20] J. Krause, B. Sapp, A. Howard, H. Zhou, A. Toshev, T. Duerig, J. Philbin, and L. Fei-Fei. The unreasonable effectiveness of noisy data for fine-grained recognition. *arXiv preprint arXiv:1511.06789*, 2015.

[21] A. Krizhevsky, I. Sutskever, and G. E. Hinton. Imagenet classification with deep convolutional neural networks. In *NIPS*, pages 1097–1105, 2012.

[22] Y. LeCun and Y. Bengio. Convolutional networks for images, speech, and time series. *The handbook of brain theory and neural networks*, 3361(10):1–14, 1995.

[23] L.-J. Li and L. Fei-Fei. Optimol: automatic online picture collection via incremental model learning. *IJCV*, 88(2):147–168, 2010.

[24] O. Russakovsky, J. Deng, H. Su, J. Krause, S. Satheesh, S. Ma, Z. Huang, A. Karpathy, A. Khosla, M. Bernstein, et al. Imagenet large scale visual recognition challenge. *IJCV*, 115(3):211–252, 2015.

[25] B. Settles. Active learning literature survey. *Univ. of Wisconsin, Madison*, 52(55-66):11, 2010.

[26] K. Simonyan and A. Zisserman. Very deep convolutional networks for large-scale image recognition. *arXiv preprint arXiv:1409.1556*, 2014.

[27] R. Speer and C. Havasi. Conceptnet 5: A large semantic network for relational knowledge. In *The Peoples Web Meets NLP*, pages 161–176. Springer, 2013.

[28] S. Sukhbaatar, J. Bruna, M. Paluri, L. Bourdev, and R. Fergus. Training convolutional networks with noisy labels. *arXiv preprint arXiv:1406.2080*, 2014.

[29] C. Szegedy, W. Liu, Y. Jia, P. Sermanet, S. Reed, D. Anguelov, D. Erhan, V. Vanhoucke, and A. Rabinovich. Going deeper with convolutions. In *CVPR*. IEEE, 2015.

[30] A. Torralba, A. Efros, et al. Unbiased look at dataset bias. In *CVPR*, pages 1521–1528. IEEE, 2011.

[31] S.-Y. Wang, W.-S. Liao, L.-C. Hsieh, Y.-Y. Chen, and W. H. Hsu. Learning by expansion: Exploiting social media for image classification with few training examples. *Neurocomputing*, 95:117–125, 2012.

[32] J. Wright, A. Y. Yang, A. Ganesh, S. S. Sastry, and Y. Ma. Robust face recognition via sparse representation. *IEEE Trans. Pattern Analysis and Machine Intelligence*, 31(2):210–227, 2009.

[33] Y. Xia, X. Cao, F. Wen, and J. Sun. Well begun is half done: Generating high-quality seeds for automatic image dataset construction from web. In *ECCV*, pages 387–400. Springer, 2014.

[34] J. Xiao, J. Hays, K. Ehinger, A. Oliva, A. Torralba, et al. Sun database: Large-scale scene recognition from abbey to zoo. In *CVPR*, pages 3485–3492. IEEE, 2010.

[35] F. Yu, Y. Zhang, S. Song, A. Seff, and J. Xiao. Construction of a large-scale image dataset using deep learning with humans in the loop. *arXiv preprint arXiv:1506.03365*, 2015.

[36] M. Zheng, J. Bu, C. Chen, C. Wang, L. Zhang, G. Qiu, and D. Cai. Graph regularized sparse coding for image representation. *IEEE Trans. Image Processing*, 20(5):1327–1336, 2011.

Multi-modal Conditional Attention Fusion for Dimensional Emotion Prediction

Shizhe Chen, Qin Jin*
School of Information, Renmin University of China
{cszhe1, qjin}@ruc.edu.cn

ABSTRACT

Continuous dimensional emotion prediction is a challenging task where the fusion of various modalities usually achieves state-of-the-art performance such as early fusion or late fusion. In this paper, we propose a novel multi-modal fusion strategy named conditional attention fusion, which can dynamically pay attention to different modalities at each time step. Long-short term memory recurrent neural networks (LSTM-RNN) is applied as the basic uni-modality model to capture long time dependencies. The weights assigned to different modalities are automatically decided by the current input features and recent history information rather than being fixed at any kinds of situation. Our experimental results on a benchmark dataset AVEC2015 show the effectiveness of our method which outperforms several common fusion strategies for valence prediction.

Keywords

Continuous dimensional emotion prediction; Multi-modal Fusion; LSTM-RNN

1. INTRODUCTION

Understanding human emotions is a key component to improve human-computer interactions [1]. A wide range of applications can benefit from emotion recognition such as customer call center, computer tutoring systems and mental health diagnoses.

Dimensional emotion is one of the most popular computing models for emotion recognition [2]. It maps an emotion state into a point in a continuous space. Typically the space consists of three dimensions: arousal (a measure of affective activation), valence (a measure of pleasure) and dominance (a measure of power or control). This representation can express natural, subtle and complicated emotions. There have been many research works on dimensional emotion analysis for better understanding human emotions in recent years [3, 4, 5].

Since emotions are conveyed through various human behaviours, past works have utilized a broad range of modalities for emotion recognition including speech [6], text [7], facial expression [8], gesture [9], physiological signals [10], etc. Among them, facial expression and speech are the most common channels to transmit human emotions. It is beneficial to use multiple modalities for emotion recognition.

Fusion strategies for different modalities in previous works can be divided into 3 categories, namely feature-level (early) fusion, decision-level (late) fusion and model-level fusion [11]. Early fusion uses the concatenated features from different modalities as input features for classifiers. It has been widely used in the literature to successfully improve performance [12]. However, it suffers from the curse of dimensionality. Also it's not very useful when features are not synchronized in time. Late fusion eliminates some disadvantages of early fusion. It combines the predictions of different modalities and trains a second level model such as RVM [13], BLSTM [14]. But it ignores interactions and correlations between different modality features. Model-level fusion is a compromise between the two extremes. The implementation of model-level fusion depends on the specific classifiers. For example, for neural networks, model-level fusion could be concatenation of different hidden layers from different modalities [15]. For kernel classifiers, model-level fusion could be kernel fusion [16]. As for Hidden Markov Model (HMM) classifiers, novel forms of feature interactions have been proposed [17].

In this paper, we propose a novel architecture for the fusion of different modalities called conditional attention fusion. We use Long-short term memory recurrent neural networks (LSTMs) as the basic model for each uni-modality since LSTMs are able to capture long time dependencies. For each time step, the fusion model learns how much of attentions it should put on each modality conditioning on its current input multi-modal features and recent history information. This approach is similar to human perceptions since humans can dynamically focus on more obvious and trustful modalities to understand emotions. Unlike early fusion, we dynamically combine predictions of different modalities, which avoids the curse of dimensionality and synchronization between different features. And unlike late fusion, the input features are interacted in a higher level to learn the current attention instead of being isolated without any interactions among different modalities. The main architecture is shown in Figure 2. We use the AVEC2015 dimensional

*Qin Jin is the corresponding author

MM '16, October 15-19, 2016, Amsterdam, Netherlands

DOI: http://dx.doi.org/10.1145/2964284.2967286

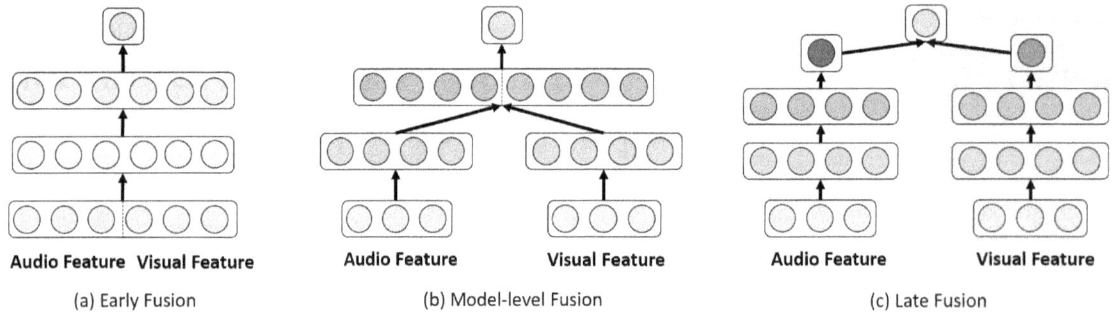

Figure 1: Three typical multi-modality fusion strategies. (a) Early fusion: concatenation of features from different modalities. (b) Model-level fusion: concatenation of high level feature representations from different modalities. (c) Late fusion: fusion of predictions from different modalities.

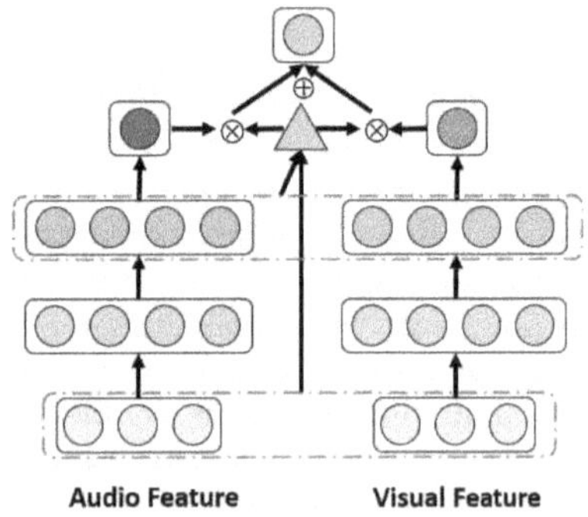

Figure 2: Conditional attention fusion model. The units in the dashed red line is concatenated together as the input of the triangle to learn the attention weights. ⊗ and ⊕ denote the element multiplication and addition respectively.

emotion dataset [5] to evaluate our methods. The results shows the effectiveness of our new fusion architecture.

2. MULTI-MODAL FEATURES

2.1 Audio Features

We utilize the OpenSMILE toolkit [18] to extract low-level features including MFCCs, loudness, F0, jitter and shimmer. All the features are extracted using 40ms frame window size without overlap to match with the groundtruth labels since it is demonstrated in [19] that short-time features can reveal more details and thus boost performance for affective prediction using LSTMs. The low-level acoustic features are in 76 dimensions.

2.2 Visual Features

Two sets of visual features are extracted from facial expression: appearance-based features and geometric-based features [5]. The appearance-based features are computed by using Local Gabor Binary Patterns from Three Orthogonal Planes (LGBP-TOP) and are compressed to 84 dimensions via PCA. The geometric-based features in 316 dimensions are computed from 49 facial landmarks. Frames where no face is detected are filled with zeros. We concatenate appearance-based features and geometric-based features as our visual feature representations.

3. EMOTION PREDICTION MODEL

3.1 Uni-Modality Prediction Model

Long short term memory (LSTM) architecture [20] is the state-of-the-art model for sequence analysis and can exploit long range dependencies in the data. In this paper, we use the peephole LSTM version proposed by Graves [21]. The function of hidden cells and gates are defined as follows.

$$\begin{aligned} i_t &= \sigma(W_{xi}x_t + W_{hi}h_{t-1} + W_{ci}c_{t-1} + b_i) \\ f_t &= \sigma(W_{xf}x_t + W_{hf}h_{t-1} + W_{cf}c_{t-1} + b_f) \\ c_t &= f_t \cdot c_{t-1} + i_t \cdot tanh(W_{xc}x_t + W_{hc}h_{t-1} + b_c) \\ o_t &= \sigma(W_{xo}x_t + W_{ho}h_{t-1} + W_{co}c_{t-1} + b_o) \\ h_t &= o_t \cdot tanh(c_t) \end{aligned} \tag{1}$$

where i, f, o and c refers to the input gate, forget gate, output gate, and cell state respectively. $\sigma(\cdot)$ is the sigmoid function and $tanh(\cdot)$ is the tangent function.

3.2 Conditional Attention Fusion Model

Let x_t^a and x_t^v refer to the audio features and visual features respectively at the tth frame. h_t^a and h_t^v refer to the outputs of the last hidden layer from uni-modality model with audio or visual features respectively. f_{θ_a} and f_{θ_v} refer to the uni-modality model which maps the audio or visual features into predictions. We define the conditional attention fusion of the predictions from the two modalities at timestep t as:

$$\widehat{y_t} = \lambda_t \cdot f_{\theta_a}(x_t^a, h_{t-1}^a) + (1 - \lambda_t) \cdot f_{\theta_v}(x_t^v, h_{t-1}^v) \tag{2}$$

$$\lambda_t = \sigma(W_g[h_t^a|h_t^v|x_t^a|x_t^v]) \tag{3}$$

where $[h_t^a|h_t^v|x_t^a|x_t^v]$ is the concatenation of the representations inside the bracket.

The λ_t is calculated based on the current audio and visual features and their high-level history information for two reasons. Firstly, the current input features are the most direct indicators to show whether the modality is reliable. For example, for facial features, inputs filled with 0s suggest that the current face detection fails and thus should be assigned with less confidence. Secondly, the weights assigned to each modality would be smoothed by considering high-level history features h_t^v and h_t^a in addition to current input features. In this way, the model can dynamically pay attention to different modalities, which could improve the stability in different situations.

3.3 Model Learning

Intuitively, the acoustic features are more reliable when the acoustic energy is higher, because the headset microphone can record speech from both the subject speaker and other speakers in conversations. Higher energy may refers to higher confidence that the speech is from the target subject. Similarly the facial features are reliable only when faces are correctly detected. So adding such side information might be beneficial to learn the attention weights.

We transform the acoustic energy into scale [0, 1], and we use g_t^a to denote its value at the tth timestep. For visual features, we use $g_t^v \in \{0, 1\}$ to indicate whether the subject's face is detected since the face detection provided in the dataset has no detection confidence. We therefore define the final loss function for one sequence as follows:

$$L_t^g = \frac{1}{2}(\alpha(g_t^a - \lambda_t)^2 + \beta(g_t^v - (1 - \lambda_t))^2) \quad (4)$$

$$L = \sum_t \frac{1}{2}(\widehat{y_t} - y_t)^2 + L_t^g \quad (5)$$

where α and β are hyper-parameters and are optimized on the development set. In practice, α and β are usually set to small values around 10^{-2} to avoid L_t^g over-affecting on λ_t.

The derivative of L_t^g with respect to λ_t is as follows:

$$\frac{\partial L_t^g}{\partial \lambda_t} = \beta g_t^v - \alpha g_t^a - \beta + (\alpha + \beta)\lambda_t \quad (6)$$

When g_t^a is high and g_t^v is low, (6) is close to $(\alpha+\beta)(\lambda_t - 1)$ (the extreme case when $g_t^a = 1$ and $g_t^v = 0$). The derivative is less than 0, which will push λ_t to increase to give acoustic features more confidence. But when $g_t^a \to 0$ and $g_t^v \to 1$, (6) is close to $(\alpha + \beta)\lambda_t$, which is larger than 0 and will push λ_t to decrease to focus on visual features. When $g_t^a \approx g_t^v$, the absolute value of the derivative would be small and thus L_t^g has less influence on λ_t.

4. EXPERIMENTS

4.1 Dataset

The AVEC2015 dimensional emotion dataset is a subset of the RECOLA dataset [22], a multimodal corpus of remote and collaborative affective interactions. There are 27 subjects in the dataset and are equally divided into training, development and testing sets. Audio, video and physiological data are collected for each participant for the first 5 minutes of interactions. Arousal and valence are annotated in scale [-1, 1] for every 40ms [5]. Since the submission times on testing set are limited, we carry out cross validation on the development set. We randomly select 5 subjects as the development set to optimize hyper parameters and the remained 4 speakers are used as the test set. We do the experiments 8 times. The concordance correlation coefficient (CCC) [5] works as the evaluation metric.

4.2 Experimental Setup

Annotation delay compensation [13] is applied because there exists a delay between signal content and groundtruth labels due to annotators' perceptual processing. We drop first N groundtruth labels and last N input feature frames.

Table 1: CCC performance of uni-modal features

	audio feature	visual feature
arousal	0.787	0.432
valence	0.595	0.620

Table 2: CCC performance of different loss functions on valence prediction

	mean	std
without L_t^g, $\alpha = \beta = 0$	0.672	0.046
with L_t^g, $\alpha = 0.04, \beta = 0.02$	0.684	0.041

N is optimized by non-temporal regression model SVR on training set. In this paper, N is optimized to be 20 frames for both audio and visual features. When predicting the result, the outputs of the model are shifted back by N frames. The missing predictions in the first N frames are filled with zeros. Finally, a binomial filter is applied to smooth the predictions. Annotation delay compensation and smoothing is applied in all the following experiments.

The input features are normalized into the range [-1,1]. For acoustic features, the LSTM has 2 layers and 100 cells for each layer. For visual features, the LSTM has 2 layers and 120 cells for each layer. The size of mini-batch is 256 and truncated backpropagation through time (BPTT) [23] is applied. The initial learning rate is set to be 0.01 with learning rate decay. Dropout is used as regularization. The training epochs are 100 and the model that achieves the best performance in development set is used as the final model.

We compare the conditional attention fusion model with early fusion, late fusion and model-level fusion. For early fusion, the LSTM has 150 units each layer, which has the similar size of parameters to other fusion methods. For late, model-level and conditional attention fusion, the parameters in LSTM are initialized with the trained uni-modal LSTMs. In order to avoid overfitting, we only fine-tune the network for 10 epochs with smaller initial learning rate 0.001. The hyper-parameters α and β are set to zeros for arousal prediction and 0.04, 0.02 respectively for valence prediction.

4.3 Experimental Results

Table 1 shows the prediction performance using uni-modality features. Acoustic features achieve the best performance on

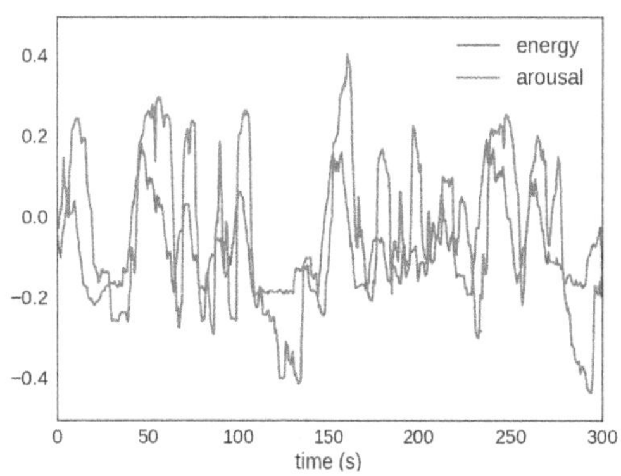

Figure 3: The relationship between arousal labels and acoustic energy on an example from dev set

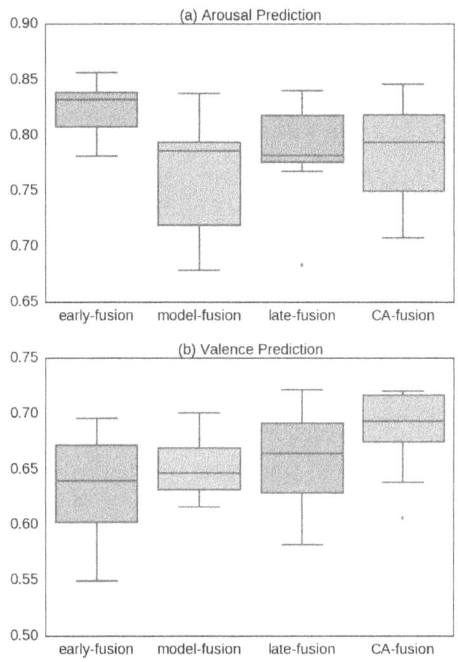

Figure 4: Performance of different fusion strategies

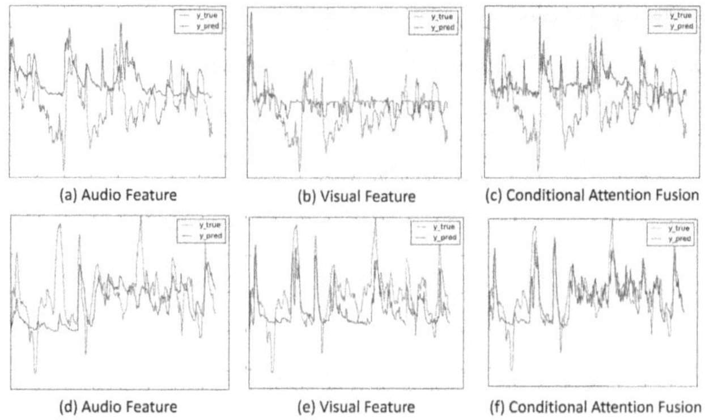

Figure 5: Examples of valence prediction on dev set. The red line is the groundtruth label and the blue line is the prediction.

Table 3: Valence prediction performance on test set

	rmse	pcc	ccc
Chen et al. [19]	0.111	0.59	0.567
Chao et al. [24]	0.103	0.627	0.618
CA-fusion	0.090	0.716	0.664

the arousal prediction and visual features are slightly better than acoustic features on valence prediction.

The performance of different fusion methods on arousal prediction is shown in Figure 4(a). Early fusion achieves the average best performance and our proposed fusion method performs the second best among all the fusion strategies. However, there is no significant difference between early fusion prediction and acoustic uni-modality prediction comparing Figure 4(a) with Table 1 (Student t-test with p-value = 0.07). We find that there exists a strong correlation between arousal and the acoustic energy, as shown in Figure 3 where we smooth the acoustic energy with window 100 and shift and scale it according to the mean and standard deviation between energy and arousal labels. And their Pearson Correlation Coefficient on development set is high to 0.558 and CCC is 0.4. This suggests that humans' perception of arousal may mainly base on acoustic features so fusing other modalities may bring less benefit.

But for valence prediction, all the fusion strategies outperform the original uni-modality models (as shown in Table 1). An interesting finding is that the higher level the fusion strategy applies, the better performance is achieved as shown in Figure 4(b). Among them, our proposed conditional attention fusion model achieves the best performance and significantly surpasses other fusion strategies by t-test ($p<0.02$ compared with the second best fusion strategy late fusion, and $p<0.007$ compared with others). This indicates that dynamically adapting fusion weights for different modalities is beneficial.

Table 2 shows the CCC performance with and without L_t^g in loss function. We can see that considering L_t^g in loss function can further improve performance since it helps to guide the importance of different modalities. It is might because of the insufficiency of data that the model is unable to learn the attention weights effectively without any supervised information. We also observe in our experiments that when α and β are around 10^{-2}, there is no significant change in prediction performance.

Figure 5 shows some examples of the emotion predictions from the conditional attention fusion method. The upper row shows the case where most of the visual features are missing and the bottom row is another case where the visual features can be extracted in most frames. We can see that the fusion method can make use of the complementary information automatically from audio and visual features in these two situations.

The valence prediction performance of the conditional attention fusion method on testing set is shown in Table 3. Chen et al. [19] use the same feature set as ours and Chao et al. [24] use more features including CNNs for valence prediction. The comparison further demonstrates the effectiveness of the conditional attention fusion method.

5. CONCLUSIONS

In this paper we propose a multi-modal fusion strategy named conditional attention fusion for continuous dimensional emotion prediction based on LSTM-RNN. It can dynamically pay attention to different modalities according to the current modality features and history information, which increases the model's stability. Experiments on benchmark dataset AVEC 2015 show that our proposed fusion approach significantly outperform the other common fusion approaches including early fusion, model-level fusion and late fusion for valence prediction. In the future, we will use more features from different modalities and apply strategies to express the correlation and independence of different modality features better.

6. ACKNOWLEDGEMENTS

This work is supported by National Key Research and Development Plan under Grant No. 2016YFB1001202.

7. REFERENCES

[1] Rosalind W. Picard. Affective computing: challenges. *International Journal of Human-Computer Studies*, 59(1-2):55–64, 2003.

[2] Stacy Marsella and Jonathan Gratch. Computationally modeling human emotion. *Communications of the ACM*, 57(12):56–67, 2014.

[3] Martin Wöllmer, Moritz Kaiser, Florian Eyben, Björn Schuller, and Gerhard Rigoll. Lstm-modeling of continuous emotions in an audiovisual affect recognition framework. *Image and Vision Computing*, 31(2):153–163, 2013.

[4] Michel Valstar, Björn Schuller, Kirsty Smith, Timur Almaev, Florian Eyben, Jarek Krajewski, Roddy Cowie, and Maja Pantic. Avec 2014: 3d dimensional affect and depression recognition challenge. In *Proceedings of the 4th International Workshop on Audio/Visual Emotion Challenge*, pages 3–10. ACM, 2014.

[5] Fabien Ringeval, Björn Schuller, Michel Valstar, Shashank Jaiswal, Erik Marchi, Denis Lalanne, Roddy Cowie, and Maja Pantic. Av+ec 2015: The first affect recognition challenge bridging across audio, video, and physiological data. In *International Workshop on Audio/visual Emotion Challenge*, pages 3–8, 2015.

[6] Moataz El Ayadi, Mohamed S Kamel, and Fakhri Karray. Survey on speech emotion recognition: Features, classification schemes, and databases. *Pattern Recognition*, 44(3):572–587, 2011.

[7] Richard Socher, Alex Perelygin, Jean Y Wu, Jason Chuang, Christopher D Manning, Andrew Y Ng, and Christopher Potts. Recursive deep models for semantic compositionality over a sentiment treebank. In *Proceedings of the conference on empirical methods in natural language processing (EMNLP)*, volume 1631, page 1642. Citeseer, 2013.

[8] Beat Fasel and Juergen Luettin. Automatic facial expression analysis: a survey. *Pattern recognition*, 36(1):259–275, 2003.

[9] Stefano Piana, Alessandra Stagliano, Francesca Odone, Alessandro Verri, and Antonio Camurri. Real-time automatic emotion recognition from body gestures. *arXiv preprint arXiv:1402.5047*, 2014.

[10] Xiao-Wei Wang, Dan Nie, and Bao-Liang Lu. Emotional state classification from EEG data using machine learning approach. *Neurocomputing*, 129:94–106, 2014.

[11] Chung-Hsien Wu, Jen-Chun Lin, and Wen-Li Wei. Survey on audiovisual emotion recognition: databases, features, and data fusion strategies. *APSIPA Transactions on Signal and Information Processing*, 3:e12, 2014.

[12] Viktor Rozgic, Sankaranarayanan Ananthakrishnan, Shirin Saleem, Rohit Kumar, Aravind Namandi Vembu, and Rohit Prasad. Emotion recognition using acoustic and lexical features. In *INTERSPEECH 2012, 13th Annual Conference of the International Speech Communication Association, Portland, Oregon, USA, September 9-13, 2012*, pages 366–369, 2012.

[13] Zhaocheng Huang, Ting Dang, Nicholas Cummins, Brian Stasak, Phu Le, Vidhyasaharan Sethu, and Julien Epps. An investigation of annotation delay compensation and output-associative fusion for multimodal continuous emotion prediction. In *The International Workshop on Audio/visual Emotion Challenge*, 2015.

[14] Lang He, Dongmei Jiang, Le Yang, Ercheng Pei, Peng Wu, and Hichem Sahli. Multimodal affective dimension prediction using deep bidirectional long short-term memory recurrent neural networks. In *Proceedings of the 5th International Workshop on Audio/Visual Emotion Challenge, AVEC 2015, Brisbane, Australia, October 26, 2015*, pages 73–80, 2015.

[15] Zuxuan Wu, Yu-Gang Jiang, Jun Wang, Jian Pu, and Xiangyang Xue. Exploring inter-feature and inter-class relationships with deep neural networks for video classification. In *Proceedings of the ACM International Conference on Multimedia, MM '14, Orlando, FL, USA, November 03 - 07, 2014*, pages 167–176, 2014.

[16] JunKai Chen, Zenghai Chen, Zheru Chi, and Hong Fu. Emotion recognition in the wild with feature fusion and multiple kernel learning. In *Proceedings of the 16th International Conference on Multimodal Interaction, ICMI 2014, Istanbul, Turkey, November 12-16, 2014*, pages 508–513, 2014.

[17] Kun Lu and Yunde Jia. Audio-visual emotion recognition with boosted coupled HMM. In *Proceedings of the 21st International Conference on Pattern Recognition, ICPR 2012, Tsukuba, Japan, November 11-15, 2012*, pages 1148–1151, 2012.

[18] Florian Eyben, Martin llmer, and Björn Schuller. Opensmile: the munich versatile and fast open-source audio feature extractor. *Acm Mm*, pages 1459–1462, 2010.

[19] Shizhe Chen and Qin Jin. Multi-modal dimensional emotion recognition using recurrent neural networks. In *Proceedings of the 5th International Workshop on Audio/Visual Emotion Challenge, AVEC 2015, Brisbane, Australia, October 26, 2015*, pages 49–56, 2015.

[20] Sepp Hochreiter and Jürgen Schmidhuber. Long short-term memory. *Neural Computation*, 9(8):1735–1780, 1997.

[21] Alex Graves. Generating sequences with recurrent neural networks. *Eprint Arxiv*, 2013.

[22] Fabien Ringeval, Andreas Sonderegger, Jürgen S. Sauer, and Denis Lalanne. Introducing the RECOLA multimodal corpus of remote collaborative and affective interactions. In *10th IEEE International Conference and Workshops on Automatic Face and Gesture Recognition, FG 2013, Shanghai, China, 22-26 April, 2013*, pages 1–8, 2013.

[23] P. J. Werbos. Backpropagation through time: what it does and how to do it. *Proceedings of the IEEE*, 78(10):1550–1560, 1990.

[24] Linlin Chao, Jianhua Tao, Minghao Yang, Ya Li, and Zhengqi Wen. Long short term memory recurrent neural network based multimodal dimensional emotion recognition. In *Proceedings of the 5th International Workshop on Audio/Visual Emotion Challenge, AVEC 2015, Brisbane, Australia, October 26, 2015*, pages 65–72, 2015.

Video Generation Using 3D Convolutional Neural Network

Shohei Yamamoto
Grad. School of Information
Science and Technology
The University of Tokyo
yamamoto@mi.t.u-tokyo.ac.jp

Tatsuya Harada
Grad. School of Information
Science and Technology
The University of Tokyo
harada@mi.t.u-tokyo.ac.jp

ABSTRACT

Recently, content generation using neural network has been widely studied. Motivated by this recent progress, we studied the generation of videos using only a label as input. In our method, we iteratively minimize two objective functions at the same time : an objective function to evaluate how close the video is to the target class and another to evaluate how natural-appearing the video is. Our proposed method uses the cross-entropy error between the target label and the output of 3D convolutional neural network (C3D) as the objective function for evaluating how close the video is to the target class and uses the Euclidean distance between the input video and the video decoded from our temporal convolutional auto-encoder ("tempCAE") as the objective function for evaluating how natural-appearing the video is. We conducted an experiment evaluating the generated videos using a crowdsourcing service and confirmed the utility of our method.

Keywords

Video Generation; 3D Convolutional Neural Network; Temporal Convolutional Auto-encoder

1. INTRODUCTION

Content generation from neural networks (NNs) has been widely studied. It can be considered that we can recognize the characteristics of an NN by generating an image from it. Simonyan et al. [1] studied the generation of images from convolutional neural networks (CNNs) and Gregor et al. [2] proposed the Deep Recurrent Attentive Writer (DRAW) neural network architecture for image generation. As another approach, image reconstruction from NNs has also been studied [3, 4].

However, studies of content generation have been limited primarily to the case of image generation; video generation has been little studied yet. Addressing this lack, this paper proposes a novel method for generating videos using only a label as input. In this method, we iteratively minimize the cross-entropy error between the target label and the output score of a 3D convolutional neural network (C3D) [5], as an objective measure of how close the video is to the target class, and simultaneously minimize the Euclidean distance between the input video and the video decoded from our proposed temporal convolutional auto-encoder "tempCAE", as a measure of how natural-appearing the video is. The idea of tempCAE is an extension of the idea of convolutional auto-encoder (CAE) [6] to video. We created a very simple dataset of moving objects and conducted generating experiments on it; some generated results are shown in Figure 1.

MM '16, October 15-19, 2016, Amsterdam, Netherlands
© 2016 ACM. ISBN 978-1-4503-3603-1/16/10...$15.00
DOI: http://dx.doi.org/10.1145/2964284.2967287

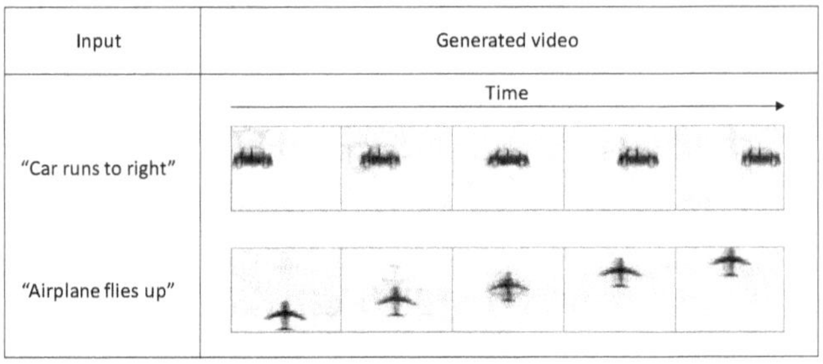

Figure 1: Some examples of video generated by our method. Input is the target label of the video and output is a video of the target label.

Our contributions are the following:

1. We propose a novel method for generating videos from a label alone; the method works by minimizing the cross-entropy error between the target label and the output score of a C3D and minimizing the Euclidean distance between the input video and the video decoded using our proposed temporal convolutional auto-encoder.
2. We propose "temporal convolutional auto-encoder" for extracting temporally local features of videos.
3. We propose a novel method for improving the naturalness of the appearance of generated videos using our temporal convolutional auto-encoder.
4. We demonstrate video generation on a dataset we created and conduct an evaluation experiment using a crowdsourcing service.

2. RELATED WORK

In this section, we introduce the relevant concepts of image reconstruction, image generation, and video reconstruction.

Simonyan et al. [1] studied image generation using CNNs trained on the ImageNet dataset [7]; they computed the target score of the output of the CNN and took the image whose score was highest as the generated result. Gregor et al. [2] proposed the Deep Recurrent Attentive Writer (DRAW) neural network architecture for image generation; their method incorporates attention mechanisms into recurrent neural network (RNN) architectures. Mansimov et al. [8]

extended Gregor et al.'s architecture for generating images from captions with attention.

Image reconstruction using CNNs has also been studied. Reconstruction is different from generation in that the network is given an image as input. Mahendran and Vedaldi [3] reconstructed input images from an intermediate layer of the CNN by minimizing the Euclidean distance of a feature at that layer. In addition, Dosovitskiy and Brox [4] reconstructed input images from an intermediate layer of AlexNet [9] by using an up-convolutional neural network.

As for research in video reconstruction, although Srivastava et al. [10] investigated video reconstruction and future prediction using long short-term memory (LSTM), they focused only on video reconstruction with a video given as an input to LSTM and did not focus on generating video from a label alone.

In this way, as the topic of the content generation, image reconstruction, image generation, video reconstruction have been studied. However, the video generation has not been studied yet. Then, this paper proposes a novel method for generating videos from a label alone, and we conduct an experiment evaluating the generated videos using a crowdsourcing service and confirmed the utility of our method.

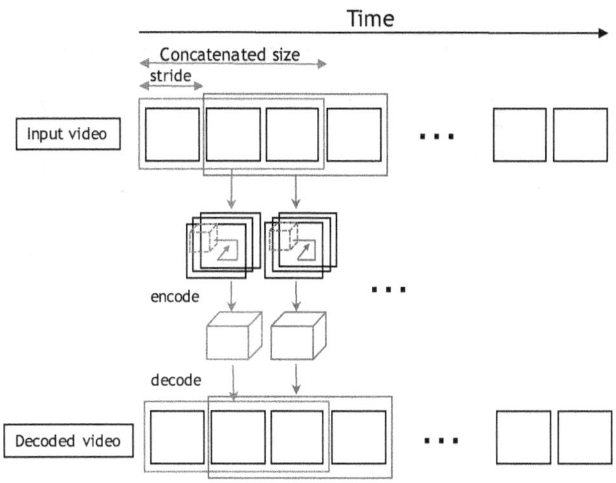

Figure 2: Our proposed temporal convolutional auto-encoder. In this module, we concatenate several frames (concatenated size) of the video to an input 'multi-channels image' and encode and decode input video.

3. METHOD

In this section,after describing an existing image-generation method, C3Ds, convolutional auto-encoder (CAE), and our temporal convolutional auto-encoder ("tempCAE"), we introduce our video-generation method. A C3D and tempCAE are modules of our system for video generation.

3.1 Image Generation

As an existing method for image generation, we introduce Simonyan et al.'s method [1]. Simonyan et al. studied image generation using a CNN trained on the ImageNet dataset [7]. They regarded an image X in the following expression as a generated image:

$$\underset{X}{\operatorname{argmax}}\, S_\theta(X) - \lambda\|X\|^2, \tag{1}$$

where θ is the target label, S_θ is the score of the target label in the classification layer of the CNN, and λ is a regularization parameter. In other words, they sought an L2-regularized image such that the score S_θ is high. By this method, we can find an image that the CNN strongly favors as a target image. In our evaluation experiment, we demonstrate the video-generation by an extension of Simonyan et al.'s method to video generation as a comparison method.

3.2 3D Convolutional Neural Network

A 3D convolutional neural network (C3D) is a classifier for video classification using CNN. In the conventional method for image classification, we convolve only for the horizontal and vertical directions (= 2D convolution). We can extract the spatial information of the input image by 2D convolution. In the C3D method, by contrast, we convolve not only for the horizontal and vertical directions but also for the temporal directions. From experiments conducted by Tran et al. (the C3D developers), it is known that 3D convolution can preserve the temporal information of the input signals in the resulting output features.

3.3 Convolutional Auto Encoder

Convolutional auto encoder (CAE) [6] is an application of AE. In the method of CAE, we convolve the input image in the same way as CNN and reconstruct the input image from feature map. So, the formula of CAE is as follows.

$$encode : \boldsymbol{h}^k = \sigma(\boldsymbol{x} * W^k + b^k) \tag{2}$$

$$decode : \boldsymbol{y} = \sigma(\sum_{k \in H} \boldsymbol{h}^k * W'^k + b'^k) \tag{3}$$

Therein, $\boldsymbol{x}, \boldsymbol{y}$, and $\boldsymbol{h}^k$ respectively denote the input image, the output image, and the k-th feature map. Also, H identifies the group of feature map, and $*$ denotes the 2D convolution. So, when we train the CAE, we train the parameters W^k, W'^k, b^k, and b'^k in the above formula.

3.4 Temporal Convolutional Auto Encoder

As an auto-encoder for video, we propose the temporal auto-encoder "tempCAE". The idea of tempCAE is an extension of the idea of CAE [6] to the case of video. We show an overview of the method in Figure 2. In this method, we concatenate some frames (concatenated size) of the video to an input "multi-channels image" and encode the input to the feature map in the same way as 3D convolution. After encoding, we decode in the same way as normal auto encoder (AE). So, the formula of tempCAE is as follows.

$$encode : \boldsymbol{h}[i, CS] = \sigma(\boldsymbol{x}[i, CS] * W + b) \tag{4}$$

$$decode : \boldsymbol{y}[i, CS] = \sigma(\boldsymbol{h}[i, CS] \cdot \tilde{W} + b') \tag{5}$$

Therein, CS denotes the size of concatenation (= concatenated size). Also, $\boldsymbol{x}[i, CS]$, $\boldsymbol{h}[i, CS]$, and $\boldsymbol{y}[i, CS]$ respectively denote an input "multi-channels image" to which we concatenated the some frames (from the i-th frame to the $i+CS$-th frame of the video), the feature map, and the output image. Also, $*$ and $\cdot$ respectively denote the 3D convolution and the linear multiplication. In the training step of tempCAE, we train the parameters W, W', b, and b' in the above formula. We can extract temporally local features of videos using tempCAE.

3.5 Video Generation

We establish two objective functions as follows.

$$L_{\mathrm{C3D}}(X) = -\sum_{\theta}^{N} \mathrm{C3D}(X, \theta) \log Y(\theta) \tag{6}$$

$$L_{\mathrm{tempCAE}}(X[i, CS]) = \|\mathrm{tempCAE}(X[i, CS]) - X[i, CS]\|^2 \tag{7}$$

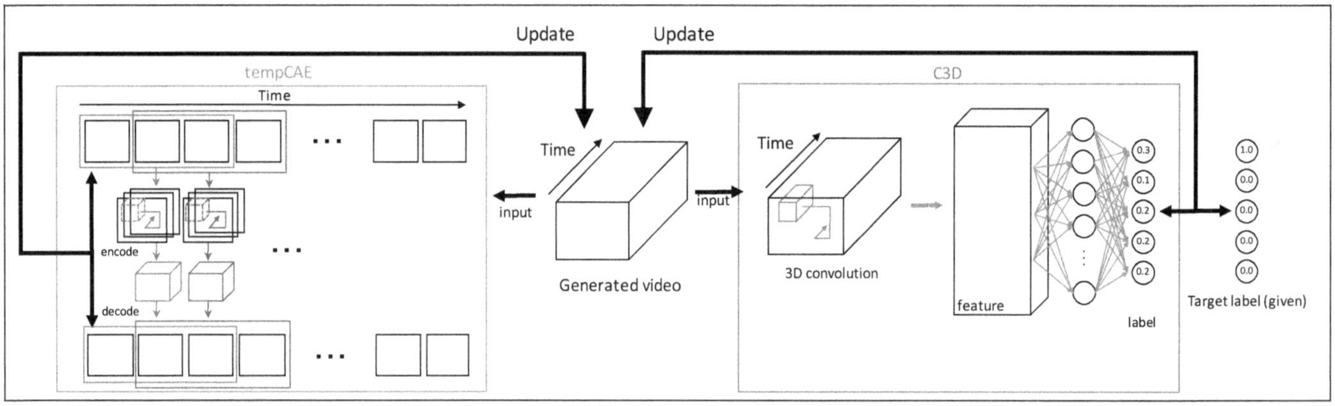

Figure 3: System for generation of videos from a label alone. In this system, we generate video by iteratively minimizing two objective functions (the cross-entropy error between the target label and C3D output, as an objective measure of how close the video is to the target class, and the Euclidean distance between the input video and the video decoded from tempCAE, as a measure of how natural-appearing the video is) at the same time.

Therein, $\mathrm{C3D}(X, \theta)$ denotes the output score of category θ when the video X is input to C3D, and $\mathrm{tempCAE}(X[i, CS])$ denotes the decoded video when the some frames (= from the i-th frame to the $i + CS$-th frame) of video is input to tempCAE, and $Y(\theta)$ denotes the target score of θ (so, $Y(\theta)$ will be 1.0 or 0.0). In short, Function (6) represents the cross-entropy error between the target label and output score of C3D (we call this the "target error"), and Function (7) represents the square of the Euclidean distance between the generated video and video decoded from tempCAE (we call this the "decoded error"). N denotes the number of classes.

The reason we establish the above objective functions is as follows. If the target error is minimized, it means that the video has features similar to the target video. However, just the fact that the target error is minimized doesn't necessarily mean that the generated video appears natural to people who view it. Therefore, we use the decoded error of the video. If the decoded error is minimized, it means that the generated video has features similar to the entire training datasets and that the video looks natural to people. For these reasons, we regard a video X that minimizes above objective functions as a generated result.

After we trained C3D and tempCAE on a video dataset, we use these trained networks to generate videos. For the video generation process, we started with a random video and updated it so that it approached the target class depending on the values of the above objective functions. As the updating method, we used a gradient descent (GD) method as follows.

$$X_{t+1} = X_t - \eta_{C3D}\frac{\partial L_{C3D}}{\partial X_t} - \eta_{tempCAE}\frac{\partial L_{tempCAE}}{\partial X_t} \qquad (8)$$

Therein, η_{C3D}, $\eta_{tempCAE}$ respectively denote updating weight of C3D and tempCAE. We show an overview of our system in Figure 3.

4. EXPERIMENTS

We experimented on a simple video dataset that we created for the purpose.

4.1 Datasets

Although large video datasets such as HMDB51 [11] and UCF101 [12] already exist, these datasets are too complicated to use for generating videos, and it is unreasonable to do video-generation experiments on them. As a dataset to use in our video-generation experiments to confirm the utility of our method, it is desirable that the objects of each class are simple and the moving of each class is easy-to-understand. Thus, we created a simple dataset to use in our video-generation experiments. The details of the dataset are as follows.

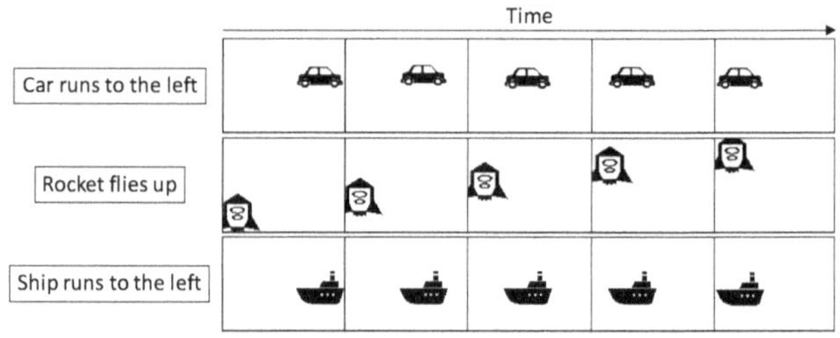

Figure 4: Some examples from the dataset we created.

- the number of classes : 11 classes (a car runs to the right/left, a rocket flies up/down, an airplane flies up/down, a ship runs to the right/left, a bicycle runs to the right/left, a balloon flies up)
- size of dataset : 200 data for each class
- size of videos : 128 * 96 px, 16 frames

We show some examples from our dataset in Figure 4 and other examples in supplemental material.

4.2 Comparison Method

As the comparison method in our video-generation experiments, we set the following two objective functions:

$$L_{\mathrm{C3D}}(X) = -\sum_{\theta}^{N} \mathrm{C3D}(X, \theta) \log Y(\theta) \qquad (9)$$

$$L_{\mathrm{norm}}(X) = ||X||^2 \qquad (10)$$

The function (9) represents the cross-entropy error between the target label and the output score of C3D, and the function (10) represents the L2 norm of the generated video. So, in this method, we would like to find an L2-regularised video such that the cross-entropy error between the target label and the output score of C3D is minimized. In short, it can be considered that this method is extension of Simonyan et al.'s image-generation method (mentioned in Section 1) to video-generation. As the updating method, we used a gradient descent (GD) method as follows.

$$X_{t+1} = X_t - \eta_{C3D}\frac{\partial L_{C3D}}{\partial X_t} - \eta_{norm}\frac{\partial L_{norm}}{\partial X_t} \quad (11)$$

Therein, η_{norm} is a regularization parameter.

4.3 Results

We experimented on our simple video dataset. It took 30 minutes for generating a video using suitable GPU. Although the dataset may look like too simple, in terms of computational cost, it can be considered that such a simple dataset is appropriate for experiments on new method.

We show some of the generated videos in Figure 5 and others in supplemental material. As shown in the figure, the videos generated by our method with tempCAE are more natural-appearing than those generated by the comparison method, and we can easily recognize the video categories. Furthermore, we can see difference in the backgrounds of the generated videos : whereas the backgrounds in the videos generated by the comparison method are very noisy, videos generated by our method have backgrounds that are close to white. However, we can also see faint images of objects of other classes (*e.g.*, an airplane appears in the background of the video of a car). It is reasonable to assume that the features of the other classes appear because the dataset features were generated by using tempCAE trained on the entire dataset.

4.4 Evaluation

To evaluate our method quantitatively, it is desirable to have a human check the generated results. Thus, we used CrowdFlower [13] which is a crowdsourcing service where we can ask a member (called a "contributor") to do a variety of tasks using CrowdFlower. We showed contributors some videos generated by the two methods and a list of categories and asked them to choose the appropriate category for each video. The list of categories consisted of 11classes of the dataset, "Other", and "Unclear" (13 classes in total). The number of contributors who participated in our experiment was 300. We show the results and parameters on Table 1. We can clearly see the notable difference in the accuracy: the accuracy of our method was more than twice that of the comparison method.

Table 1: Parameters and accuracy of CrowdFlower.

Method	Iteration	η_{C3D}	$\eta_{tempCAE}$	η_{norm}	Accuracy
Ours	50000	10.0	10.0	none	88.2 %
Comparison	50000	10.0	none	5.0	42.7 %

5. APPLICATION

As an application of our method, we generated new videos as shown in Figure 6. In this application, we generated videos from multiple labels at the same time (*e.g.*, "Car runs to the right" and "Rocket flies up"). In this way, our method can be applied to a system for the generation of new videos.

6. CONCLUSION

We have proposed a novel method for generating videos by iteratively minimizing two objective functions at the same time: the objective function for evaluating how close the video is to the target class and another function for evaluating how natural-appearing the video is. As the objective function for evaluating how close the video is to the target class, our proposal uses the cross-entropy error between the target label and the output of C3D, and for evaluating how natural-appearing the video is, the Euclidean distance between the input video and the video decoded from tempCAE is used. We conducted a video-generation experiment on our video dataset and quantitatively evaluated the results using a crowdsourcing service, and thereby confirmed the utility of our method. In our future research, we plan to generate a larger video dataset and develop an architecture for generating videos not only from words but also from short captions.

7. ACKNOWLEDGEMENT

This work was funded by ImPACT Program of Council for Science, Technology and Innovation (Cabinet Office, Government of Japan).

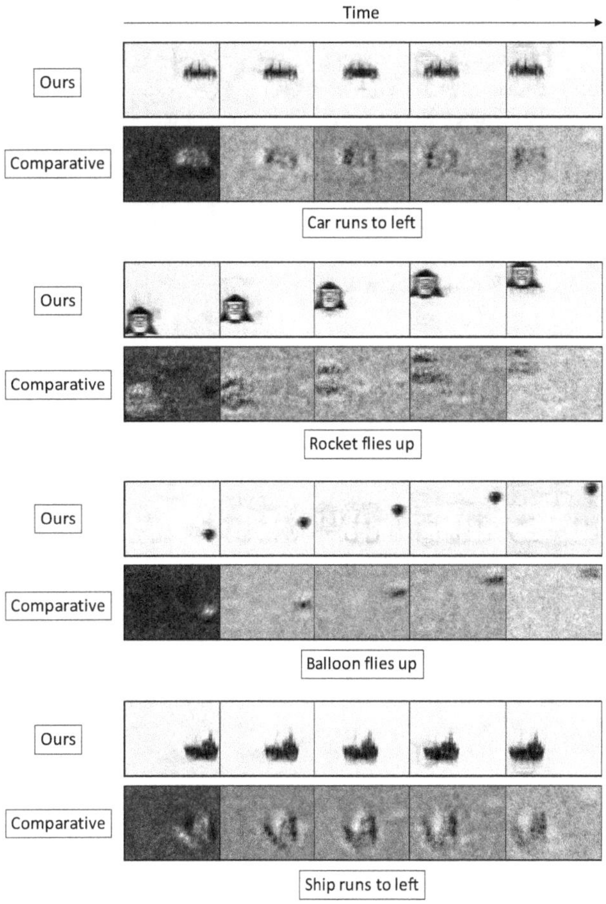

Figure 5: Some videos generated by our method and comparative method.

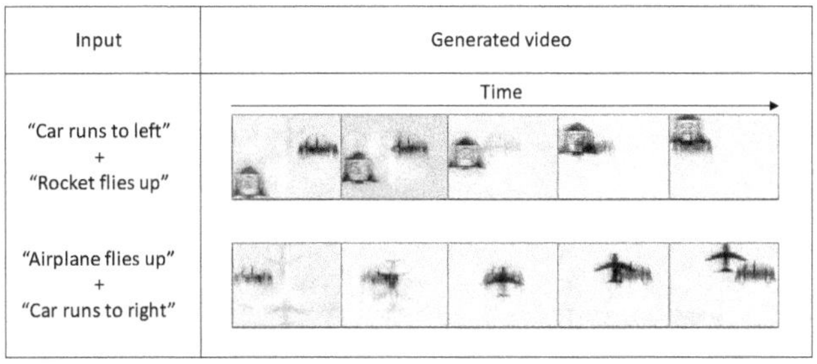

Figure 6: Some examples of videos generated from multiple labels.

8. REFERENCES

[1] Karen Simonyan, Andrea Vedaldi, and Andrew Zisserman. Deep inside convolutional networks: Visualising image classification models and saliency maps. *arXiv preprint arXiv:1312.6034*, 2013.

[2] Karol Gregor, Ivo Danihelka, Alex Graves, Danilo Jimenez Rezende, and Daan Wierstra. Draw: A recurrent neural network for image generation. In *ICML*, 2015.

[3] Aravindh Mahendran and Andrea Vedaldi. Understanding deep image representations by inverting them. In *CVPR*, 2015.

[4] Alexey Dosovitskiy and Thomas Brox. Inverting visual representations with convolutional networks. In *CVPR*, 2016.

[5] Du Tran, Lubomir Bourdev, Rob Fergus, Lorenzo Torresani, and Manohar Paluri. Learning spatiotemporal features with 3d convolutional networks. In *ICCV*, 2015.

[6] Jonathan Masci, Ueli Meier, Dan Cireşan, and Jürgen Schmidhuber. Stacked convolutional auto-encoders for hierarchical feature extraction. In *Artificial Neural Networks and Machine Learning–ICANN 2011*, pp. 52–59. Springer, 2011.

[7] Jia Deng, Wei Dong, Richard Socher, Li-Jia Li, Kai Li, and Li Fei-Fei. Imagenet: A large-scale hierarchical image database. In *CVPR*, 2009.

[8] Elman Mansimov, Emilio Parisotto, Jimmy Lei Ba, and Ruslan Salakhutdinov. Generating images from captions with attention. In *ICLR*, 2016.

[9] Alex Krizhevsky, Ilya Sutskever, and Geoffrey E Hinton. Imagenet classification with deep convolutional neural networks. In *NIPS*, 2012.

[10] Nitish Srivastava, Elman Mansimov, and Ruslan Salakhutdinov. Unsupervised learning of video representations using lstms. In *ICML*, 2015.

[11] Hildegard Kuehne, Hueihan Jhuang, Estíbaliz Garrote, Tomaso Poggio, and Thomas Serre. Hmdb: a large video database for human motion recognition. In *ICCV*, 2011.

[12] Khurram Soomro, Amir Roshan Zamir, and Mubarak Shah. Ucf101: A dataset of 101 human actions classes from videos in the wild. *arXiv preprint arXiv:1212.0402*, 2012.

[13] CrowdFlower. http://www.crowdflower.com/.

Processing-Aware Privacy-Preserving Photo Sharing over Online Social Networks

Weiwei Sun
Department of CIS
University of Macau
yb57457@umac.mo

Jiantao Zhou
Department of CIS
University of Macau
jtzhou@umac.mo

Ran Lyu
Department of CIS
University of Macau
mb45442@umac. mo

Shuyuan Zhu
School of EE
UESTC
eezsy@uestc.edu.cn

ABSTRACT

With the ever-increasing popularity of mobile devices and online social networks (OSNs), sharing photos online has become extremely easy and popular. The privacy issues of shared photos and the associated protection schemes have received significant attention in recent years. In this work, we address the problem of designing privacy-preserving, high-fidelity, storage-efficient photo sharing solution over Facebook. We first conduct an in-depth study on the manipulations that Facebook performs to the uploaded images. With the awareness of such information, we suggest a DCT-domain image encryption scheme that is robust against these lossy operations. As validated by our experimental results, superior performance in terms of security, quality of the reconstructed images, and storage cost can be achieved.

Keywords

Social networks; Facebook; privacy-preserving; photo sharing; JPEG

1. INTRODUCTION

With the wide-adoption of mobile devices equipped with high-resolution on-board cameras, online photo sharing has become an extremely easy and popular activity. Nowadays, users can conveniently share photos through OSNs such as Facebook and Google+, or dedicated photo sharing platforms such as Instagram. As these images contain significant amount of personal information, they are privacy-sensitive in nature. This has triggered the research on the problem of privacy protection arisen from online photo sharing.

Some works focused on designing access control protocols such that the shared photos can only be accessed by a selected group of users [2, 1, 3]. However, as pointed out by [7], the existing privacy controls are far from adequate, leading to severe information leakage when users fail to understand the complex privacy settings, or when the OSN cannot implement the access control polices correctly.

Another category of privacy protection schemes aims at encrypting the image data, before uploading them to the OSN for sharing. Essentially, stronger protection could be offered, as in this case even the OSN itself cannot get the information of the original images. A challenging issue under this framework, however, is the design of an end-to-end image encryption/decryption mechanism that is robust against the lossy operations conducted by the OSN. For instance, Facebook converts all uploaded images to JPEG, choosing quality factor (QF) adaptively without user input.

Along this line, Ra *et al.* proposed the P3 [5], a privacy-preserving photo sharing system, which splits an image into a public part and a private part. The public part is shared over the OSN in the plaintext, and the secret part is encrypted and stored in a cloud storage server. The introduction of an additional cloud server dramatically complicates the file management system. More importantly, the public part of P3 leaks significant visual information of the original image. Alternatively, Tierney *et al.* designed a system called Cryptagram, enabling users to encrypt photos with traditional block ciphers and then embed the encrypted bit stream into a JPEG file. However, the desirable properties of Cryptagram are realized at the cost of a significantly increased storage burden in the OSN, as the use of cover image results in significant file expansion. Furthermore, selective image encryption was employed to provide privacy protection for online photo sharing [9, 10]. Unfortunately, they are not robust against the lossy operations in Facebook.

In this work, we focus on the privacy protection issues of the online photo sharing over Facebook. For simplicity and without loosing generality, we here only consider the grayscale images. The proposed technique could be readily extended to the other OSNs and color images as well. We first conduct an in-depth study on the manipulations that Facebook performs to the uploaded images. With the awareness of such information, we suggest a DCT-domain image encryption scheme that is robust against these lossy operations. As validated by our experimental results, superior performance in terms of security, quality of the reconstructed images, and storage cost can be achieved.

MM '16 October 15–19, 2016, Amsterdam, The Netherlands.

DOI: http://dx.doi.org/10.1145/2964284.2967288

2. PROBE INTO FACEBOOK

It has been observed that almost all the existing OSNs apply various lossy operations to the uploaded images [5, 4]. To design a robust privacy-preserving photo sharing scheme, it is very important to know how the OSN manipulates the uploaded images. In this work, we focus on a representative OSN: Facebook, because 1) Facebook is one of the most popular OSNs that integrates image sharing. In the first quarter 2015 earnings announcement, Facebook revealed that it now has more than 1.44 billion monthly active users, and this number is still growing. 2) According to [4], the operations conducted by Facebook are much more complex than the other OSNs such as Google+ and Twitter. The results obtained over Facebook could be easily extended to other platforms. Though [4] investigated this problem, some of their results are not accurate and many are no longer valid, probably due to the system update of Facebook.

Facebook converts the uploaded images into pixel domain, regardless of their original formats, and then applies the following types of operations when necessary: 1) resizing, and 2) JPEG compression, and 3) enhancement.

Resizing It is found that Facebook performs resizing when the resolution of the upload image is too large. As resizing could cause significant information losses, it is crucial to limit the resolution of the uploaded image such that no resizing is performed. To know the maximum tolerable resolution, we upload a series of images of different resolutions to Facebook, and compare with the downloaded versions. We observe that when both the length and width dimensions are less than 2048 pixels, the image resolution will remain intact. Otherwise, resizing is conducted.

JPEG Compression All the uploaded images are applied to an additional round of JPEG compression, in which the users *cannot* choose the value of QF. As the distortion caused by JPEG compression is directly related to the employed QF, it is of great importance to know the mechanism of assigning QF for different images. Some prior works [4] only roughly studied this issue, and claimed that the employed QF values are in the range of [76, 86].

To gain more accurate and up-to-date information, we upload all the 1338 images from UCID-v2 [6] to Facebook, and then extract the quantization tables from the downloaded images. It is observed that the quantization tables match exactly with the ones included in the International JPEG Group standard [8]. The employed QF values are image dependent and range from 71 to 92, as can be seen from Fig. 1. Generally, for images with rich amount of activities, the QF values tend to be low, while for those with large portion of homogenous regions, the QF values seem to be high. This is reasonable to better limit the sizes of the compressed files. We also have another very important observation: for encrypted images, no matter which type of encryption algorithm is applied, the QFs adopted are *consistently* 71. Essentially, Facebook treats encrypted images as high-activity ones, and apply the lowest QF.

Enhancement Filtering Besides JPEG compression, Facebook also applies additional enhancement filtering to improve the appearance of the images. Unfortunately, we find that it is very challenging to know such enhancement filtering exactly, as they are applied locally and are highly adaptive. The designed privacy-preserving photo sharing scheme should be robust to these unknown lossy operations as well.

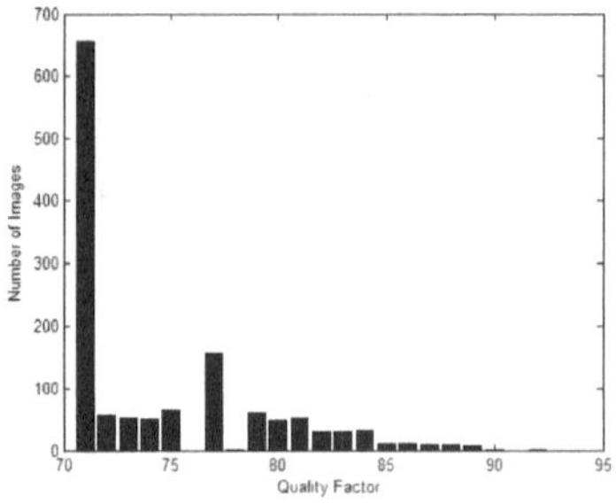

Figure 1: Distribution of the employed QFs.

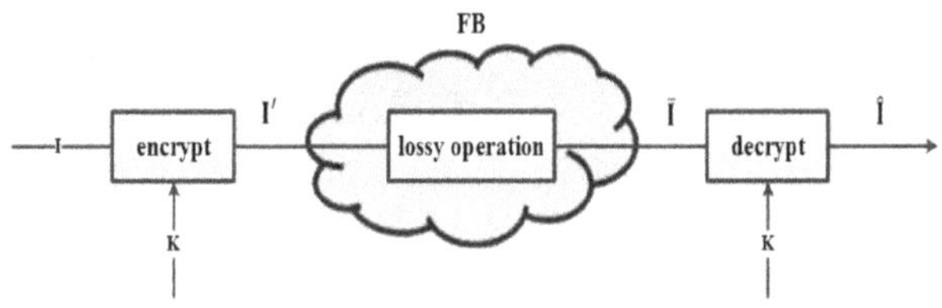

Figure 2: Schematic diagram of the proposed privacy-preserving image sharing scheme.

3. SYSTEM MODEL AND DESIGN GOALS

The schematic diagram of the whole system is depicted in Fig. 2. A user Alice first encrypts the original image $\mathbf{I}$ into $\mathbf{I}'$ by using an encryption function $\texttt{Encry}$

$$\mathbf{I}' = \texttt{Encry}(\mathbf{I}, K) \tag{1}$$

where K is the secret key shared between Alice the recipient Bob. Alice then uploads the encrypted $\mathbf{I}'$ to Facebook for sharing purpose. Facebook converts the received $\mathbf{I}'$ to the pixel domain, and then applies JPEG compression. As discussed in Section 2, the employed QF for JPEG compression is 71. The processed image $\bar{\mathbf{I}}$ of JPEG format is stored in the Facebook server, and shared over the Internet. At the client side, Bob downloads $\bar{\mathbf{I}}$ from Facebook and applies the following decryption function to produce an estimated $\mathbf{I}$.

$$\mathbf{I} = \texttt{Decry}(\bar{\mathbf{I}}, K) \tag{2}$$

The key components of the privacy-preserving photo sharing scheme are the encryption and decryption functions $\texttt{Encry}$ and $\texttt{Decry}$. The design goals are summarized as follows.

i) *Reasonably high level of security*: Those parties that do not access the secret key K cannot get meaningful information about the original image. This is the fundamental requirement for any privacy-preserving photo sharing scheme.

ii) *High quality of the reconstructed image*: The reconstructed image $\mathbf{I}$ should be of high quality.

iii) *High efficiency of storage on Facebook*: We also would like to minimize the storage cost in Facebook, as the number of photos shared becomes astonishingly large. This is also related to the bandwidth consumption in the client's side.

4. PROPOSED IMAGE ENCRYPTION AND DECRYPTION

After knowing the processing conducted over Facebook, we now present the key components of the proposed privacy-

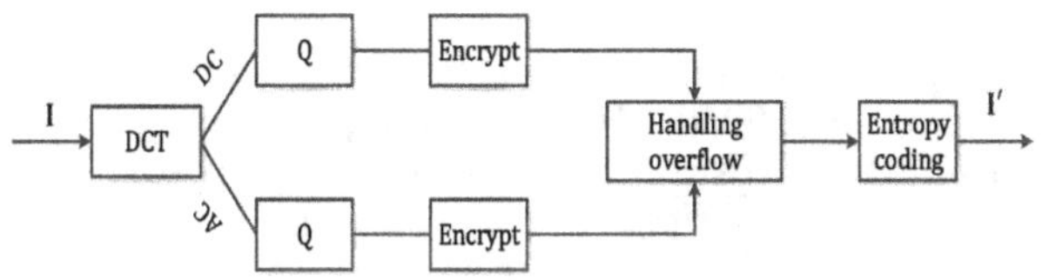

Figure 3: Processing-aware Image Encryption

preserving photo sharing scheme: image encryption and decryption modules. We should bear in mind that these two modules should be designed in a way to be robust against the lossy operations performed in Facebook. As the dominating degradation source in Facebook is the JPEG compression carried out over the DCT domain, it is natural to choose the DCT domain for performing encryption, so as to better limit the distortion incurred. Note that the encrypted file will be converted into pixel domain before JPEG is applied by Facebook. Such DCT-pixel domain conversion could cause severe pixel overflow problem that has to be tackled to ensure the high-quality of the reconstructed images.

Fig. 3 depicts the design of our proposed image encryption scheme. We first divide image $\mathbf{I}$ into a series of non-overlapping blocks of size 8×8. Let $\mathbf{B} = \{B_{r,s}\}$ be a generic 8×8 pixel block, where $0 \leq r, s \leq 7$. For each $\mathbf{B}$, we apply the DCT transform and obtain the DCT coefficient block $\mathbf{D} = \{D_{i,j}\}$, where $0 \leq i, j \leq 7$. Clearly, $D_{0,0}$ corresponds to the DC component, while the remaining ones are AC components. We then quantize $D_{i,j}$ with the JPEG quantization table associated with QF=71. As will be proved in our forthcoming work, this strategy of choosing the quantization table minimizes the end-to-end distortion $d = \|\mathbf{I} - \mathbf{I}\|_2^2$. Due to the different characteristics of DC and AC components, we encrypt them separately, as detailed below.

4.1 Encryption of DC coefficients

We can easily get the quantized DC coefficients of all the blocks of the input image $\mathbf{I}$, and form a DC vector

$$\mathbf{DC} = (DC_0, DC_1, \cdots, DC_{n-1})' \tag{3}$$

where n is the number of blocks in $\mathbf{I}$. We reshape the vector $\mathbf{DC}$ into a 2-D block having four columns and $\lceil n/4 \rceil$ rows. We then perform two key-driven cyclical shift operations to the resulting 2-D block of DC components, and read out the data in raster-scan order to obtain the permuted DC vector $\tilde{\mathbf{DC}} = (\tilde{DC}_0, \tilde{DC}_1, \cdots, \tilde{DC}_{n-1})$. The key vectors controlling the column and the row shift offsets for $\mathbf{DC}$ are obtained from a stream cipher, which implies that the employed key vectors could be different, even for the same image encrypted at different sessions. Note that such permutation operations can be realized via circular shifts, which can be easily implemented in either hardware or software.

4.2 Encryption of AC coefficients

In JPEG compression, AC coefficients are encoded by run-length coding, implying that the coding efficiency is determined by the locations of none-zero coefficients and their code lengthes. To minimize the storage overhead of the encrypted images, our strategy of encrypting the AC coefficients is to randomize the non-zero coefficients using a stream cipher, while maintaining the location and the binary length of each non-zero AC coefficient. The steps of performing the AC coefficients encryption are as follows.

Step 1: Generate a binary key stream $\mathbf{KA}$ using the secret key K through a stream cipher, and partition it into $\mathbf{KA} = \mathbf{KA}(0), \mathbf{KA}(1), \cdots$, where each $\mathbf{KA}(i)$ is of length 12 bits.

Step 2: Convert each non-zero AC coefficient AC_i into a bit sequence $\mathbf{W}_i$ of length l_i.

Here, the way of converting the bit sequence is the same as that done by JPEG.

Step 3: Encrypt AC_i by bit-wise XORing $\mathbf{W}_i$ with the first l_i bits of $\mathbf{KA}(i)$, i.e.,

$$\mathbf{W}'_i = \mathbf{W}_i \oplus \mathbf{KA}_{1 \to l_i}(i) \tag{4}$$

where $\mathbf{W}'_i$ is the encrypted version of $\mathbf{W}_i$ and $\mathbf{KA}_{1 \to l_i}(i)$ represents the first l_i bits of $\mathbf{KA}(i)$. The reason why we assign 12 bits for each $\mathbf{KA}(i)$ is to achieve better robustness. The lossy operations in Facebook could make some of the zero AC coefficients be non-zero, or may even change the lengthes of some non-zero AC coefficients. To address the challenging issue of achieving synchronization between the encoder and the decoder, we associate each AC coefficient, regardless zero or non-zero, with a key stream $\mathbf{KA}(i)$ of length 12, which is longer than the maximum length of any AC coefficient [8]. It can be easily seen that the local de-synchronization only affects the decryption/decoding of the local AC coefficient; but such error will not propagate to influence the subsequent AC coefficients.

Step 4: Convert each binary sequence $\mathbf{W}'_i$ into signed decimal number, denoted as AC'_i.

A desirable property of the proposed AC encryption scheme is that the positions and the lengths of the non-zero AC coefficients are kept intact. This property makes the encrypted file readily compressible by Facebook without the need of accessing the secret key K.

4.3 Handling pixel overflow

As mentioned earlier, Facebook converts the uploaded images to the pixel domain, before applying JPEG compression. Due to the DCT-domain randomization, it is very likely that some of the pixel values are outside the range [0,255] after converting, causing the pixel overflow problem. This could severely affect the quality of the reconstructed images in the user end. To solve this challenging issue, we here propose a solution through DCT coefficient shrinkage.

Specifically, after applying the above DCT-domain encryption, we mimic the operations of Facebook by converting the encrypted blocks to the pixel domain. We then record the blocks that contain the overflow pixels in a location map $\mathbf{M} = \{M_{i,j}\}$. In general, the location map is sparse and hence compressible. Let $\mathbf{D} = \{D_{i,j}\}$ be a generic DCT block having the overflow problem. Our strategy of solving the overflow is to multiply each $D_{i,j}$ with a shrinkage factor $\alpha_{i,j} \in [0, 1]$, reducing the energy of the whole block. Smaller $\alpha_{i,j}$ can more effectively eliminate the overflow problem; but at the same time kills more small AC elements to zeros, leading to another type of distortion. The determination of $\alpha_{i,j}$ can be formulated as an optimization problem to balance the distortion caused by the overflow and the one caused by killing small AC elements. We leave the detailed discussion on the optimal determination of $\alpha_{i,j}$ to our future work. In this work, we set $\alpha_{0,0}$=0.20, and $\alpha_{i,j}$=0.40. The processed

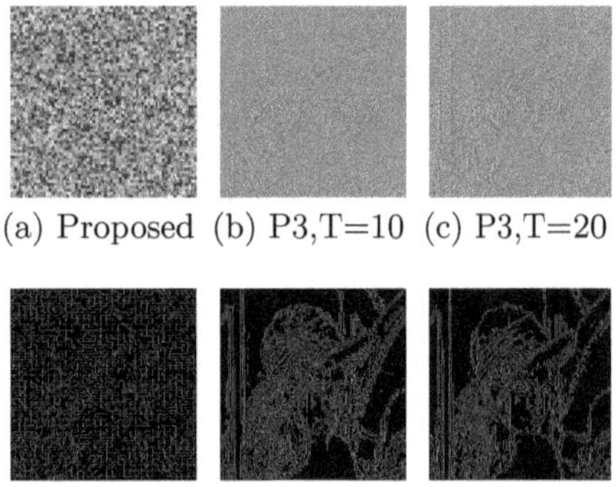

(a) Proposed (b) P3,T=10 (c) P3,T=20

(d) Proposed (e) P3,T=10 (f) P3,T=20

Figure 4: Visual security comparison with P3 for the test image `Lena`. The first row gives the images that are exposed to Facebook. The second row represents the versions obtained by edge detection.

DCT blocks are subject to entropy coding to produce the final encrypted and compressed file $\mathbf{I}'$

4.4 Decryption function `Decry`

After downloading the encrypted JPEG file from Facebook, Bob aims to decrypt and decode it to the pixel domain with the assistance of the secret key K. The encrypted file can be parsed into blocks of DCT coefficients. We first check the location map $\mathbf{M}$, in which we record the overflow blocks. If the current block does not contain any overflow pixels, we can decrypt the DC and AC components by applying the reverse operations as those performed in the encryption stage. While if the current block is recorded in $\mathbf{M}$, we first need to divide the shrinkage factors applied to DC and AC coefficients, and then apply the decryption as a normal block. After decrypting all the DC and AC components, the pixel values can be recovered by applying the inverse DCT.

5. EXPERIMENTAL RESULTS

In this section, we experimentally evaluate the performance of our proposed privacy-preserving photo sharing scheme. The test set is composed of 100 images randomly selected from UCID-v2 [6].

We first compare the visual security of our proposed scheme with P3, while leaving the theoretical security analysis for our future work. In Fig. 4, we show the images that are accessible to Facebook for the test image `Lena`. As can be seen, Facebook can hardly get any meaningful information from the encrypted version of our proposed scheme, even after edge detection. In contrast, for P3, the public part stored in Facebook reveals significant visual information of the original image. The edge detected version could be treated as a sketch of great fidelity, and the quality is improved by increasing the parameter T. Similar observations can be obtained for the other test images as well.

We then investigate the quality of the reconstructed images. In Table 1, we show the PSNR results of offline JPEG with QF=71, our proposed method, P3, and the one based on secure JPEG [10]. Compared with the offline JPEG, the PSNR drop of our method is around 1.5 dB on average, due to the lossy operations performed by Facebook. In contrast, the method in [10] leads to severe PSNR degradation, with average PSNR drop being 7.94 dB. P3, on the other hand,

Table 1: The Comparison of Reconstruction Quality in terms of PSNR. Here, Average is obtained by averaging the results of the 100 images from UCID.

	JPEG	Proposed	[10]	P3
`Lena`	37.40	36.32	28.85	36.84
`Baboon`	30.64	30.63	24.51	30.63
`Goldhill`	35.27	34.67	29.24	35.24
`Truck`	32.96	32.75	28.31	32.95
`Elaine`	33.94	33.61	28.49	33.81
`Airplane`	38.58	37.18	29.10	38.23
`Couple`	35.34	34.15	27.20	34.96
Average	34.56	33.02	26.62	34.12

Table 2: The Comparison of Storage Overhead

	Proposed	P3(T=10)	[10]
`Lena`	3.2%	20.2%	5.7%
`Baboon`	1.4%	13.8%	2.2%
`Goldhill`	3.7%	15.2%	8.8%
`Truck`	2.3%	12.6%	3.3%
`Elaine`	3.1%	15.9%	5.2%
`Airplane`	6.0%	25.5%	17.5%
`Couple`	1.9%	18.0%	3.3%
Average	2.0%	16.0%	5.6%

has its inherent advantages in terms of the quality of the reconstituted images because most of the parts are stored in an error-free cloud server. The PSNR gap between our method and P3 is not big; less than 1 dB on average. It should be noted that the higher reconstruction quality of P3 is achieved through the introduction of a third-party cloud server, which may not be realistic in many situations.

We finally study the storage overhead in the Facebook, which becomes an important evaluation criterion due to the huge number of shared images. In Table 2, we show the overhead incurred by the privacy protection for different methods, where the overhead is calculated with respect to the offline JPEG with QF=71. On average, the overhead of our proposed method is 2%, which is only 1/8 and 1/2.8 of the counterparts given by the competing P3 and secure JPEG.

6. CONCLUSION

In this work, we have addressed the problem of designing privacy-preserving, high-fidelity, and storage-efficient photo sharing scheme over Facebook. Based on a DCT-domain image encryption method robust to various lossy operations conducted by Facebook, we have achieved superior performance in terms of security, quality of the reconstructed images, and storage cost, compared with the state-of-the-art competing solutions.

7. ACKNOWLEDGMENTS

This work was supported in part by the Macau Science and Technology Development Fund under grants FDCT/009 /2013/A1, FDCT/046/2014/A1, in part by the Research Committee at University of Macau under grants MYRG2014-00031-FST, MYRG2015-00056-FST,and in part by the National Science Foundation of China under grant 61402547.

8. REFERENCES

[1] L. A. Cutillo, R. Molva, and M. Önen. Privacy preserving picture sharing: Enforcing usage control in distributed on-line social networks. In *Proc. SNS'12*, page 6. ACM, 2012.

[2] P. Klemperer, Y. Liang, M. Mazurek, M. Sleeper, B. Ur, L. Bauer, L. F. Cranor, N. Gupta, and M. Reiter. Tag, you can see it!: using tags for access control in photo sharing. In *Proc. CHI'12*, pages 377–386. ACM, 2012.

[3] M. L. Mazurek, Y. Liang, W. Melicher, M. Sleeper, L. Bauer, G. R. Ganger, N. Gupta, and M. K. Reiter. Toward strong, usable access control for shared distributed data. In *Proc. FAST'14*, pages 89–103. USENIX Association, 2014.

[4] J. Ning, I. Singh, H. V. Madhyastha, S. V. Krishnamurthy, G. Cao, and P. Mohapatra. Secret message sharing using online social media. In *Proc. CNS'14*, pages 319–327. IEEE, 2014.

[5] M.-R. Ra, R. Govindan, and A. Ortega. P3: Toward privacy-preserving photo sharing. In *Proc. NSDI'13*, pages 515–528. USENIX Association, 2013.

[6] G. Schaefer and M. Stich. UCID - An uncompressed colour image database. In *Proc. SPIE: Storage and Retrieval Methods and Applications for Multimedia*, volume 5307, pages 472–480, 2004.

[7] M. Tierney, I. Spiro, C. Bregler, and L. Subramanian. Cryptagram: Photo privacy for online social media. In *Proc. COSN'13*, pages 75–88. ACM, 2013.

[8] G. K. Wallace. The jpeg still picture compression standard. *IEEE Transactions on Consumer Electronics*, 38(1):xviii–xxxiv, 1992.

[9] L. Yuan, P. Korshunov, and T. Ebrahimi. Privacy-preserving photo sharing based on a secure jpeg. In *Proc. INFOCOM WKSHPS'15*, pages 185–190. IEEE, 2015.

[10] L. Yuan, P. Korshunov, and T. Ebrahimi. Secure jpeg scrambling enabling privacy in photo sharing. In *Proc. FG'15*, volume 4, pages 1–6. IEEE, 2015.

Detecting Violence in Video using Subclasses

Xirong Li[1,2,3] Yujia Huo[2] Qin Jin[1,2*] Jieping Xu[1,2]
[1]Key Lab of Data Engineering and Knowledge Engineering, Renmin University of China
[2]Multimedia Computing Lab, School of Information, Renmin University of China
[3]Shanghai Key Laboratory of Intelligent Information Processing
{xirong,qjin,xjieping}@ruc.edu.cn

ABSTRACT

This paper attacks the challenging problem of violence detection in videos. Different from existing works focusing on combining multi-modal features, we go one step further by adding and exploiting subclasses visually related to violence. We enrich the MediaEval 2015 violence dataset by *manually* labeling violence videos with respect to the subclasses. Such fine-grained annotations not only help understand what have impeded previous efforts on learning to fuse the multi-modal features, but also enhance the generalization ability of the learned fusion to novel test data. The new subclass based solution, with AP of 0.303 and P100 of 0.55 on the MediaEval 2015 test set, outperforms the state-of-the-art. Notice that our solution does not require fine-grained annotations on the test set, so it can be directly applied on novel and fully unlabeled videos. Interestingly, our study shows that motion related features (MBH, HOG and HOF), though being essential part in previous systems, are seemingly dispensable. Data is available at http://lixirong.net/datasets/mm2016vsd.

CCS Concepts

•**Computing methodologies** → **Scene understanding;**

Keywords

Video violence detection, subclass annotation, fusion

1. INTRODUCTION

Detecting violence in videos is important for protecting children against offensive content. Viewing violence as a specific concept, one might treat violence detection as a showcase of video concept detection, an extensively studied topic in the literature [12, 22]. The MediaEval affective task defines violence as *one would not let an 8 years old child see because of their physical violence* [15]. Scenes of violence lack consistent visual patterns, see Fig. 1. Moreover,

Figure 1: Visual examples of ten violence subclasses. We enrich the MediaEval 2015 violence data [15] by providing video-level annotations with respect to these subclasses.

the perception of violence varies over subjects. Another evidence showing the different landscape of violence detection is that state-of-the-art video concept detection uses deep image features alone [16]. By contrast, a violence detection system often involves a number of multi-modal features related to image, audio and motion [2, 8, 23]. We also use multi-modal features, but go one step further by adding and exploiting subclasses visually related to violence, for better performance and deeper insight.

Progress on video violence detection. Thanks to the MediaEval benchmark effort [3, 4, 15], data for violence detection research has been substantially expanded in terms of types of violence and the amount of videos, compared to earlier work on a specific type of violence, e.g., fight in hockey games [1]. Consequently, different from previous works that mainly utilize motion related features such as motion SIFT and histogram of optical flow [1, 20], current solutions embrace multi-modal features to describe video content in terms of visual appearance, audio channel and motion over the temporal dimension. A common package, as reported in [2,6,8,23], consists of image features extracted by pre-trained deep convolutional neural networks [14, 17], MFCC based audio features [5], and local descriptors derived from improved dense trajectories [19].

As for combining the many features, although late fusion is consistently found to improve over models derived from single features [6, 7, 23], the success so far has been limited to average weighting, i.e., all the underlying models are treated equally. As the effectiveness of the features varies [8], average fusion is unlikely to be the optimal so-

*Corresponding author

MM '16, October 15 - 19, 2016, Amsterdam, Netherlands

ISBN 978-1-4503-3603-1/16/10...$15.00

DOI: http://dx.doi.org/10.1145/2964284.2967289

lution. Nonetheless, efforts on learn-to-fuse are found to be inferior to the average-fusion baseline [6]. While current works simply attribute this to divergence between training and test data [6,7], we believe a more in-depth analysis is required to understand what impedes the use of learn-to-fuse for video violence detection.

Contributions of this work. In order to better understand the difficulty in generalizing models learned on a given dataset to a novel test set, we first enrich the MediaEval 2015 violence set, an up-to-date benchmark for video violence detection, by providing video-level manual annotations with respect to ten subclasses of violence. We are inspired by the work from Tan and Ngo [18], which makes an interesting attempt to express violence by a number of middle-level concepts. Nonetheless, as they target at learning these concepts from YouTube videos to derive a semantic feature, the two works are driven by completely different motivations. As we will show in Section 2, the newly added subclass annotations help interpret cross-dataset divergence and consequently the difficulty of generalizing the learned fusion to previously unseen test data. Moreover, we show in Section 3 how this difficulty can be resolved to some extent using subclass based violence detection, and learned fusion of multiple features and multiple subclasses outperforms several state-of-the-art alternatives.

2. SUBCLASS ANNOTATION

Video sets. We use the official release of the MediaEval 2015 affective task [15]. Containing 10,900 short video clips extracted from 199 professional and amateur movies, this benchmark dataset is much larger and more diverse than those narrow-domain videos used in previous works [1, 20]. The MediaEval dataset consists of two disjoint subsets: a development set of 6,144 clips and a test set of 4,756 clips. Notice that the videos were not originally selected for violence, so they have low occurrence of violence, with 4.4% in the development set and 4.8% in the test set.

Manual labeling procedure. We aim to provide fine-grained annotations of violence videos by manually assigning visual concepts that are highly relevant to violence. Such a concept is supposed to have relatively consistent visual appearance and thus more easy to be detected. We take the 52 middle-level concepts from [18] as our initial concept vocabulary. Given the subjective definition of video violence, the vocabulary may expand with novel concepts as the manual labeling process goes on. We watched all violence videos in the development set, eventually yielding a vocabulary of 95 concepts. For a specific concept, there shall be a reasonable amount of positive instances, otherwise modeling this concept is very likely to be futile. We empirically set the threshold to be 20, i.e., a concept needs to have over 20 occurrences in the development set. This results in ten subclasses of violence, as exemplified in Fig. 1. Four of them, namely 'bind', 'aim', 'weapon' and 'death', are not covered by the initial 52 concepts. A video can be labeled with multiple subclasses. Some subclasses tend to co-occur with some others in the same video clips, e.g., 'rope' to 'bind' and 'blood' to 'death'. However, 'death' and 'fight' seldom co-occur, as a fight hardly ends with death in this dataset.

In order to reveal potential divergence between the development set and the test set, we repeat the above procedure to annotate all violence videos in the test set. Fig. 2 shows the occurrence rate of each subclass, which clearly varies across the two datasets. Such divergence suggests the challenge of applying a fusion model trained on the development set to the (unseen) test set.

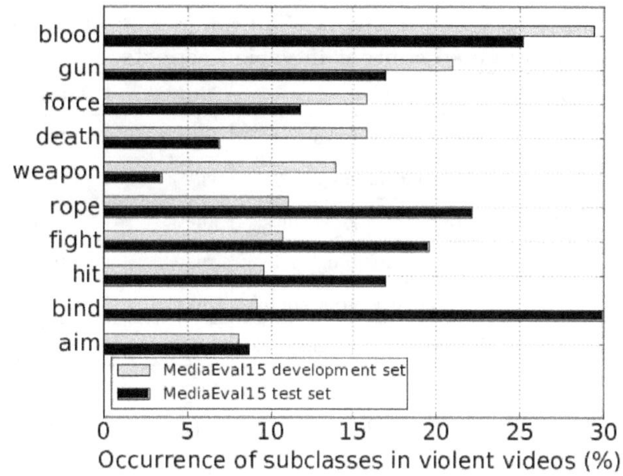

Figure 2: Occurrence of each subclass in violence videos, varying across datasets. Such divergence adds difficulty of generalizing models trained on the development set to the previously unseen test set.

Note that the fine-grained annotations of the test set are meant for cross-dataset analytics only. They are not used for violence detection. So, similar to existing works [2, 4, 23], our subclass based violence detection solution is directly applicable to novel video data that are completely unlabeled.

3. USING SUBCLASSES FOR VIOLENCE DETECTION

To verify the viability of subclass based violence detection, we build two systems, with and without subclasses, respectively.

3.1 Setup

Following the current practice [2,7,23], we employ multimodal video representations including image features extracted by deep convolutional neural networks [14,17], audio features [5], and motion features [19]. They are described as follows, and summarized in Table 1.

Image CNN features. Given a video, we uniformly extract its frames with an interval of 0.5 second, resulting in 131,441 and 101,587 frames in the development and test sets, respectively. For each frame we extract deep features using three pretrained CNN models, i.e., VGGNet [14], GoogleNet [17], and GoogletNet4k [11], a very recent variant of GoogleNet trained on a bottom-up reorganization of the ImageNet hierarchy. By taking the last fully connected layer of VGGNet and the pool5 layer of the two GoogleNets, we obtain three frame-level features

A video-level representation substantially reduces the amount of training/test examples and is commonly used in event detection [21, 22]. We obtain three video-level features by average pooling on the corresponding frame-level features.

Audio features. We use the Mel-frequency Cepstral Coefficients (MFCCs) [5], computed over a sliding short-time window of 25ms with a 10ms shift. An audio segment is then

Table 1: Fourteen features used in our experiments, describing video content in varied aspects.

Modality	Feature	Notation	Dim.
Image	frame-level vggnet	$vnet_f$	4,096
	video-level vggnet	$vnet_v$	4,096
	frame-level googlenet	$gnet_f$	1,024
	video-level googlenet	$gnet_v$	1,024
	frame-level googlenet4k	$g4k_f$	1,024
	video-level googlenet4k	$g4k_v$	1,024
Audio	mfcc + bow	$mfcc_b$	4,096
	mfcc + fisher vector	$mfcc_{fv}$	19,968
Motion	mbh + bow	mbh_b	4,000
	mbh + fisher vector	mbh_{fv}	98,304
	hog + bow	hog_b	4,000
	hog + fisher vector	hog_{fv}	49,152
	hof + bow	hof_b	4,000
	hof + fisher vector	hof_{fv}	55,296

Table 2: Performance of the indiviudal features, sorted in descending order by AP scores of the *learn* run on the test set. For each feature, top performers on a given dataset are shown in bold font.

	MediaEval15 validation set			MediaEval15 test set		
Feature	*w/o subclass*	*avg*	*learn*	*w/o subclass*	*avg*	*learn*
$g4k_f$	0.321	0.260	**0.365**	0.190	0.179	**0.216**
$g4k_v$	0.284	0.237	**0.292**	**0.213**	0.195	0.199
$vnet_v$	0.295	0.263	**0.316**	0.120	0.137	**0.156**
$gnet_f$	0.245	0.210	**0.316**	0.097	**0.164**	0.156
hog_b	0.164	0.132	**0.174**	0.160	**0.175**	0.153
$vnet_f$	**0.347**	0.226	0.339	0.118	**0.147**	0.145
$mfcc_{fv}$	0.313	0.270	**0.316**	0.100	**0.138**	0.136
$gnet_v$	0.296	0.258	**0.312**	**0.152**	0.142	0.130
mbh_b	0.119	0.109	**0.197**	0.122	**0.129**	0.092
hof_b	0.127	0.130	**0.170**	**0.113**	0.109	0.092
$mfcc_b$	**0.320**	0.234	0.295	**0.090**	0.075	0.077
mbh_{fv}	**0.199**	0.075	0.159	**0.099**	0.064	0.067
hof_{fv}	**0.134**	0.083	0.096	**0.102**	0.050	0.054
hog_{fv}	**0.225**	0.070	0.101	**0.078**	0.047	0.049

represented by a set of MFCC features. In order to transform these features into a fixed-dimension vector, we adopt two encoding schemes, i.e., bag-of-audio-words by hard assignment and Fisher Vector encoding [13].

Motion features. The Improved Dense Trajectory (IDT) [19] is used to capture actions in a video. We use three trajectory based descriptors, namely Motion Boundary Histogram (MBH), Histogram of Oriented Gradient (HOG), and Histogram of Optical Flow (HOF). In a similar manner to the audio features, bag-of-words and Fisher Vector encodings are used to quantize each of the descriptors, resulting in six motion related features.

Classification Models. For each of the ten subclasses as well as the holistic violence class, we train binary linear SVMs classifiers. To effectively learn from the large amounts of imbalanced examples, we leverage the Negative Bootstrap algorithm [9], which iteratively and adaptively finds negative training examples that better improve classification than negatives selected at random. For each frame-level classifier, we obtain its prediction on a given video by first scoring every frame, smoothing the scores along the temporal dimension, and then taking the maximal response.

The developement set is randomly divided into two disjoint subsets, 70% for training the SVM models and 30% as a validation set to optimize hyper-parameters.

Strategies for multi-feature multi-subclass fusion. We investigate late fusion with two weighting strategies. One is average weighting, i.e., assigning equal weights to the base classifiers. Despite its simplicity, the average strategy is found to be effective for multi-feature fusion for violence detection [8]. The second strategy is learning to fuse. In particular, we optimize the weights on the validation set using coordinate ascent, which optimizes a chosen weight per iteration. A recent study in the context of image classification [10] shows that compared to more complicated fusion algorithms such as multiple kernel learning, coordinate ascent is more effective by directly optimizing (non-differential) performance metrics.

Putting all the features and subclasses together, we need to learn weights for up to 140 classifiers. By contrast, for the system without subclasses, we only need to optimize weights for 14 classifiers at maximum. Hence, comparing the two systems shall allow us to conclude whether the introduction of subclasses makes sense.

Evaluation criteria. Following the protocol [15], we report Average Precision (AP), Precision at the top 10 ranked videos (P10), and P100.

3.2 Experiments

Experiment 1. The impact of subclasses in a single-feature setting. Table 2 shows the performance of the individual features, where *w/o class* indicates runs without considering subclasses, *avg* means average fusion of the ten subclasses, and *learn* is fusion with weights tuned on the validation set. In the *w/o class* setting, the best motion feature hog_b, with AP of 0.160, outperforms the best standard CNN feature, i.e., $gnet_v$. This is consistent with a recent result reported in [8]. Nonetheless, $g4k_v$ with AP of 0.213 is the top performer.

Half of the features improve by combining subclass classifiers, with the best performance obtained by $gnet_f$ + *learn*. Interestingly, the majority of the features for which fusion does not work are motion related. By looking in combinations of one subclass and one feature for violence detection, we find that the motion features are in general less effective for modeling subclasses when compared with image CNN features.

Experiment 2. The impact of subclasses in a multi-feature setting. We now move to the setting where multiple features are combined together with subclasses. Given that there are over 16k combinations, we take a more practical approach by starting with using all the features. Specific

Table 3: **Performance of feature-subclass fusion, sorted in descending order according to AP scores of the *learn* run on the test set. For each feature-fusion setting, top performers on a given dataset are shown in bold font.**

Varied settings of feature fusion														MediaEval15 val set				MediaEval15 test set			
Image CNN						Audio MFCC		Motion IDT						w/o subclass		with subclass		w/o subclass		with subclass	
$vnet_f$	$vnet_v$	$gnet_f$	$gnet_v$	$g4k_f$	$g4k_v$	$mfcc_b$	$mfcc_{fv}$	mbh_b	mbh_{fv}	hog_b	hog_{fv}	hof_b	hof_{fv}	*avg*	*learn*	*avg*	*learn*	*avg*	*learn*	*avg*	*learn*
✔	✔	✔	✔	✔	✔	✔	✔	✘	✘	✘	✘	✘	✘	0.484	**0.511**	0.386	0.510	0.274	0.251	0.288	**0.303**
✘	✘	✘	✘	✔	✔	✔	✔	✔	✘	✔	✘	✔	✘	0.376	0.492	0.293	**0.493**	0.269	0.275	0.277	**0.296**
✘	✘	✘	✘	✔	✔	✔	✔	✘	✘	✘	✘	✘	✘	0.455	0.473	0.397	**0.491**	0.248	0.236	0.283	**0.290**
✔	✔	✔	✔	✔	✔	✔	✔	✔	✔	✔	✔	✔	✔	0.442	**0.531**	0.279	0.522	0.248	0.270	0.226	**0.279**
✔	✔	✔	✔	✔	✔	✔	✘	✔	✘	✔	✘	✔	✘	0.440	**0.527**	0.282	0.511	**0.300**	0.260	0.259	0.275
✔	✔	✔	✔	✔	✔	✘	✘	✔	✘	✔	✘	✔	✘	0.394	**0.482**	0.254	0.435	**0.280**	0.225	0.249	0.263
✔	✔	✔	✔	✔	✔	✔	✘	✘	✘	✘	✘	✘	✘	0.468	0.495	0.353	**0.512**	**0.266**	0.228	0.250	0.263
✔	✔	✔	✔	✔	✔	✘	✘	✘	✘	✘	✘	✘	✘	0.427	**0.449**	0.291	0.419	0.244	0.233	0.239	**0.255**
✔	✔	✔	✔	✔	✔	✘	✘	✔	✔	✔	✔	✔	✔	0.373	**0.479**	0.226	0.447	0.229	0.249	0.202	**0.253**
✔	✔	✔	✔	✔	✔	✘	✘	✘	✔	✘	✔	✘	✔	0.434	**0.468**	0.250	0.444	0.238	**0.253**	0.171	0.231
✘	✘	✘	✘	✘	✘	✔	✔	✔	✔	✔	✔	✔	✔	0.308	0.424	0.194	**0.446**	**0.164**	0.141	0.141	0.141
✘	✘	✘	✘	✘	✘	✔	✔	✘	✘	✘	✘	✘	✘	0.347	0.348	0.273	**0.353**	0.107	0.106	0.111	**0.117**
✘	✘	✘	✘	✘	✘	✘	✘	✔	✔	✔	✔	✔	✔	0.206	0.279	0.146	**0.296**	**0.143**	0.111	0.116	0.114

features are progressively removed with preference given to slower and longer features. E.g., fisher vectors are removed in advance to their bag-of-words counterparts. Moreover, in order to study complementariness of distinct modalities, features of an unchosen modality are left out. Eventually we obtain 13 feature combinations with their performance reported in Table 3.

Comparing with the single feature setting, multi-feature fusion improves the performance. In the *w/o subclass* setting, however, fusion weights learned on the validation set often yields lower AP than average weighting. As shown in Table 3, for only 4 out of 13 times *learn* is better than *avg*. By contrast, the use of subclasses makes *learn* beats *avg* 11 out of 13 times. This result shows the importance of subclasses for learning to fuse.

We observe that some subclasses are more easier to detect, e.g., 'blood', 'gun' and 'death', than some others, e.g., 'aim', 'rope', and 'bind'. Due to page limit, more detailed analysis concerning the subclass detection will be presented in the future extension of this work.

Concerning the complementariness of distinct modalities, all the modalities are required for deriving a holistic violence detector, as in the *w/o subclass* scenario. However, once subclasses are taken into account, the joint use of image and audio modalities (with motion excluded) performs the best.

Finally, we make a system level comparison between the proposed subclass based system and three state-of-art systems as demonstrated in the MediaEval 2015 evaluation. The result shown in Table 4 further confirms the effectiveness of subclass based violence detection.

Table 4: **Comparing with front-runners in the MediaEval 2015 violence detection task.**

System	**AP**	**P10**	**P100**
Fudan-Huawei [2]	0.296	1.0	0.46
MIC-TJU [23]	0.285	0.8	0.49
NII-UIT [7]	0.268	0.6	0.44
this work, w/o subclass	0.275	0.9	0.42
this work, with subclass	**0.303**	**1.0**	**0.55**

4. SUMMARY AND CONCLUSIONS

We contribute to video violence detection as follows. First, we enrich the MediaEval 2015 violence dataset by providing video-level annotations with respect to ten subclasses of violence. The clear divergence between subclass distributions of the MediaEval dev and test sets explains why existing learn-to-fuse attempts did not work. Second, by a systematic comparison between violence detection with and without subclasses, we re-justify the effectiveness of learn-to-fuse for violence detection. The new solution beats the state-of-the-art on the MediaEval 2015 test set. Moreover, decomposing violence into subclasses results in novel findings concerning complementariness of distinct modalities. The conclusion of [8] that visual and motion features are better than audio features holds when modeling violence in a holistic manner. For fusion of multiple subclasses and multi-modal features, motion related features appear to be ignorable.

Acknowledgments. The authors are grateful to the MediaEval 2015 Affective Impact of Movies Task organizers [15] for making video data available for this research. The work was supported by the Fundamental Research Funds for the Central Universities and the Research Funds of Renmin University of China (No. 14XNLQ01), NSFC (No. 61303184, No. 71531012), SRFDP (No. 20130004120006), BJNSF (No. 4142029), and Shanghai Key Laboratory of Intelligent Information Processing, China (Grant No. IIPL-2013-002).

5. REFERENCES

[1] E. Bermejo, O. Deniz, G. Bueno, and R. Sukthankar. Violence detection in video using computer vision techniques. In *CAIP*, 2011.

[2] Q. Dai, R. Zhao, Z. Wu, X. Wang, Z. Gu, W. Wu, and Y. Jiang. Fudan-Huawei at MediaEval 2015: Detecting Violent Scenes and Affective Impact in Movies with Deep Learning. In *MediaEval Workshop*, 2015.

[3] C. Demarty, C. Penet, M. Schedl, B. Ionescu, V. L. Quang, and Y. Jiang. The MediaEval 2013 Affect Task: Violent Scenes Detection. In *MediaEval Workshop*, 2013.

[4] C. Demarty, C. Penet, M. Soleymani, and G. Gravier. VSD, a public dataset for the detection of violent scenes in movies: design, annotation, analysis and evaluation. *Multimedia Tools Appl.*, 74(17):7379–7404, 2015.

[5] T. Ganchev, N. Fakotakis, and G. Kokkinakis. Comparative evaluation of various MFCC implementations on the speaker verification task. In *SPECOM*, 2005.

[6] Q. Jin, X. Li, H. Cao, Y. Huo, S. Liao, G. Yang, and J. Xu. RUCMM at MediaEval 2015 affective impact of movies task: Fusion of audio and visual cues. In *MediaEval Workshop*, 2015.

[7] V. Lam, S. P. Le, D. Le, S. Satoh, and D. A. Duong. NII-UIT at MediaEval 2015: Affective Impact of Movies Task. In *MediaEval Workshop*, 2015.

[8] V. Lam, S. Phan, D.-D. Le, D. A. Duong, and S. Satoh. Evaluation of multiple features for violent scenes detection. *Multimedia Tools Appl.*, 2016. in press.

[9] X. Li, C. G. Snoek, M. Worring, D. Koelma, and A. W. Smeulders. Bootstrapping visual categorization with relevant negatives. *IEEE Trans. Multimedia*, 15(4):933–945, 2013.

[10] S. Liao, X. Li, H. T. Shen, Y. Yang, and X. Du. Tag features for geo-aware image classification. *IEEE Trans. Multimedia*, 17(7):1058–1067, 2015.

[11] P. Mettes, D. C. Koelma, and C. G. M. Snoek. The ImageNet Shuffle: Reorganized Pre-training for Video Event Detection. In *ICMR*, 2016.

[12] M. Naphade, J. R. Smith, J. Tesic, S.-F. Chang, W. Hsu, L. Kennedy, A. Hauptmann, and J. Curtis. Large-scale concept ontology for multimedia. *IEEE MultiMedia*, 13(3):86–91, 2006.

[13] J. Sánchez, F. Perronnin, T. Mensink, and J. J. Verbeek. Image classification with the fisher vector: Theory and practice. *International Journal of Computer Vision*, 105(3):222–245, 2013.

[14] K. Simonyan and A. Zisserman. Very Deep Convolutional Networks for Large-Scale Image Recognition. In *ICLR*, 2015.

[15] M. Sjöberg, Y. Baveye, H. Wang, V. L. Quang, B. Ionescu, E. Dellandrea, M. Schedl, C.-H. Demarty, and L. Chen. The MediaEval 2015 affective impact of movies task. In *MediaEval Workshop*, 2015.

[16] C. Snoek, S. Cappallo, D. Fontijne, D. Julian, D. Koelma, P. Mettes, K. van de Sande, A. Sarah, H. Stokman, and R. Towal. Qualcomm Research and University of Amsterdam at TRECVID 2015: Recognizing Concepts, Objects, and Events in Video. In *NIST TRECVID Workshop*, 2015.

[17] C. Szegedy, W. Liu, Y. Jia, P. Sermanet, S. E. Reed, D. Anguelov, D. Erhan, V. Vanhoucke, and A. Rabinovich. Going deeper with convolutions. In *CVPR*, 2015.

[18] C. C. Tan and C.-W. Ngo. The Vireo team at MediaEval 2013: Violent scenes detection by mid-level concepts learnt from Youtube. In *MediaEval Workshop*, 2013.

[19] H. Wang and C. Schmid. Action Recognition with Improved Trajectories. In *ICCV*, 2013.

[20] L. Xu, C. Gong, J. Yang, Q. Wu, and L. Yao. Violent video detection based on MoSIFT feature and sparse coding. In *ICASSP*, 2014.

[21] Z. Xu, Y. Yang, and A. Hauptmann. A discriminative CNN video representation for event detection. In *CVPR*, 2015.

[22] G. Ye, Y. Li, H. Xu, D. Liu, and S.-F. Chang. EventNet: A large scale structured concept library for complex event detection in video. In *ACMMM*, 2015.

[23] Y. Yi, H. Wang, B. Zhang, and J. Yu. MIC-TJU in MediaEval 2015 Affective Impact of Movies Task. In *MediaEval Workshop*, 2015.

Deep Representation for Abnormal Event Detection in Crowded Scenes

Yachuang Feng[1,2]
fengyachuang@opt.cn

Yuan Yuan[1]
yuany@opt.ac.cn

Xiaoqiang Lu[1]
luxq666666@gmail.com

[1]Center for OPTical IMagery Analysis and Learning (OPTIMAL),
State Key Laboratory of Transient Optics and Photonics, Xi'an Institute of Optics and Precision Mechanics,
Chinese Academy of Sciences, Xi'an 710119, Shaanxi, P. R. China
[2]University of Chinese Academy of Sciences, Beijing 100049, P. R. China

ABSTRACT

Abnormal event detection is extremely important, especially for video surveillance. Nowadays, many detectors have been proposed based on hand-crafted features. However, it remains challenging to effectively distinguish abnormal events from normal ones. This paper proposes a deep representation based algorithm which extracts features in an unsupervised fashion. Specially, appearance, texture, and short-term motion features are automatically learned and fused with stacked denoising autoencoders. Subsequently, long-term temporal clues are modeled with a *long short-term memory* (LSTM) recurrent network, in order to discover meaningful regularities of video events. The abnormal events are identified as samples which disobey these regularities. Moreover, this paper proposes a spatial anomaly detection strategy via manifold ranking, aiming at excluding false alarms. Experiments and comparisons on real world datasets show that the proposed algorithm outperforms state of the arts for the abnormal event detection problem in crowded scenes.

Keywords

Video surveillance; crowded scene; abnormal event detection; deep representation

1. INTRODUCTION

Abnormal event detection aims to identify abnormal events in surveillance videos automatically. In recent years, anomaly detection has attracted a surge of interest from both academia and industry. However, it is still quite challenging to design a general framework for abnormal event detection. This is because the definition of an anomaly varies in different applications. An abnormal event in one scene probably is normal in another. To deal with this problem, one common solution is to extract normal event patterns from training (normal) videos, and detect abnormal ones by finding events which diverge from these patterns.

In the past decade, significant improvements have been achieved by designing various valid video event features. For example, tracking [6] is usually carried out to analyse individual moving objects. Trajectory-based features are born with simplicity and high-level semantics. But they are limited by factors such as shadows and occlusion in crowded scenes. As alternatives, recent works extract event patterns at pixel-level, 2D patches or 3D blocks. For example, Reddy et al. [9] split video frames into non-overlapping cells, from which features of motion, size and texture are extracted. In [13], spatio-temporal interest points are described by the *histogram of gradient* (HoG) and *histogram of optical flow* (HoF). There are also many other video event features widely used for anomaly detection. One commonality of these features is that they are hand-crafted. Generally, designing an effective descriptor is time-consuming and difficult. Moreover, it is hard to decide which kind of feature is suitable for a specific situation.

Nowadays, deep learning [12] has become a hot topic, which learns features automatically from raw data. In many computer vision tasks, deep learning has demonstrated strong performance, such as object detection, image segmentation, and activity recognition. The reason why deep learning achieves inspiring performance is that meaningful and discriminative features can be adaptively extracted through multi-layer non-linear transformations. In consequence, abnormal event detection is expected to benefit from deep learning algorithms.

Recently, Xu et al. [11] propose a novel deep learning framework for abnormal event detection. In [11], appearance, motion, and their joint representations are learned via three *stacked denoising autoencoders* (SDAEs). Then anomaly scores are calculated by three one-class support vector machine classifiers with these learned features. Although they have learned effective video event features, there are still some shortcomings. 1) Only short-term motion information is considered, i.e. optical flow maps. As is well known, video events are highly complex. Static frames and short-term motion clues are insufficient to represent video events. Therefore, long-term temporal clues are crucial for learning meaningful regularities of video events. 2) Context information is ignored. In crowded scenes, moving objects are highly related to each other. In this case, discovering relationships among adjacent video events ought to be helpful for anomaly detection in crowded scenes.

MM '16, October 15-19, 2016, Amsterdam, Netherlands
© 2016 ACM. ISBN 978-1-4503-3603-1/16/10...$15.00
DOI: http://dx.doi.org/10.1145/2964284.2967290

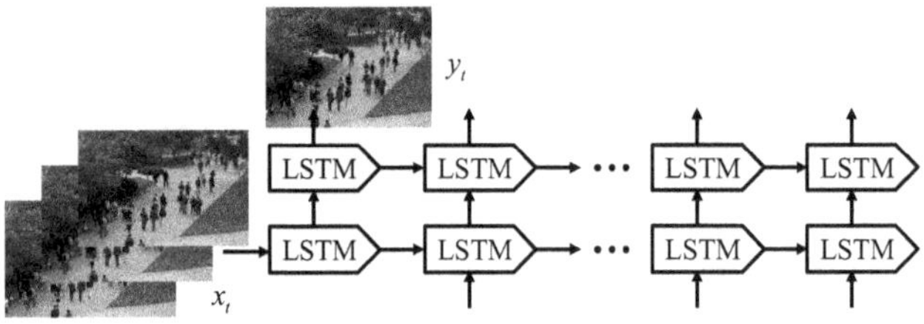

Figure 1: The illustration for learning long-term dependencies in video events.

In order to cope with these issues, this paper proposes a different deep learning framework for abnormal event detection. Similarly with [11], an SDAE model is trained to learn and fuse features from appearance, texture, and short-term motion clues. As for long-term temporal clues, Li et al. [4] model dynamics and appearances of crowds with the dynamic texture, which is a linear dynamical system. Due to the complexity of video events, one linear model might be insufficient. To improve the representation ability, multiple dynamic textures are mixed to model video events in [4]. However, this introduces more parameters and increases the complexity. In contrast, this paper models event regularities with a recurrent neural network, which adopts non-linear transformation and considers both the current input and the previous hidden state. Specifically, LSTM [10] is utilized in this paper because it is capable of learning long-term dependencies in video events. These dependencies are learned by an LSTM based prediction framework, as is shown in Fig. 1. The last three video frames are taken as the input to the LSTM, and the current frame is the predicted output.

The LSTM neural network learns meaningful regularities of video events, and dissimilarities in testing videos are treated as temporal anomalies. In order to incorporate the spatial context of individual moving objects, Li et al. [4] compute feature responses for surrounding annular windows, and detect anomalies as center-surround salient objects. In this paper, a much simpler and more effective strategy is proposed to make use of spatial contextual information. Based on the input video frame, a graph is constructed. In this graph, only adjacent samples in the spatial context are connected, and the weights are estimated as similarities in the feature space. After that, a graph-based manifold ranking algorithm is designed to identify anomalies. Since normal video frames contain no anomalies, we select some totally normal samples as queries and rank the rest according to their relevances to these queries. Samples with small ranking scores are treated as spatial anomalies. Furthermore, an adaptive weight is assigned to each sample in order to improve the distinctiveness between abnormal and normal events. As a result, false alarms are excluded and the identification of anomalies gets easier.

2. THE PROPOSED METHOD

2.1 Video Event Modeling

Inspired by [11], we use SDAEs to adaptively extract video event features. Specifically, we extract features from appearance, texture, and short-term motion clues, which are respected by image sequences, gradients and optical flows on

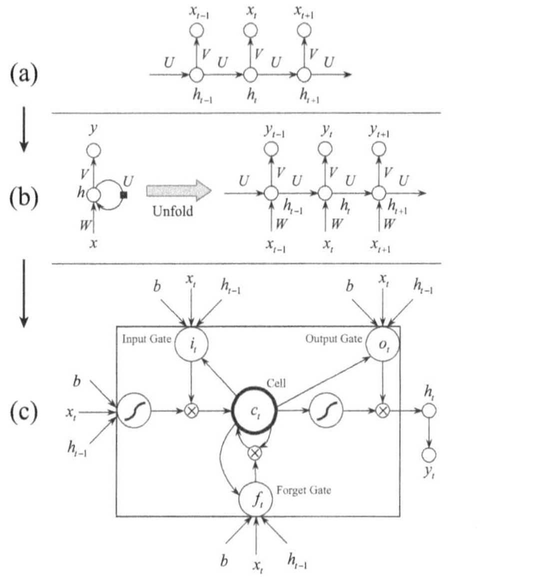

Figure 2: Frameworks for video event modeling. U, V, W are weight matrices. (a) Linear dynamic texture; (b) RNN; (c) LSTM.

horizontal and vertical directions, respectively. After that, another SDAE is learned to fuse these features.

In order to learn long-term dependencies in video events, an LSTM based prediction model is developed. Fig. 2 illustrates our motivation. Compared with linear dynamic textures, RNN is much more preferable because of its non-linear character, as well as taking both observations and hidden states as inputs to predict time dependencies. Equations related to the LSTM based prediction model are listed as follows.

$$
\begin{aligned}
g_t &= \varphi(\mathbf{W}_{xg}\mathbf{x}_t + \mathbf{W}_{hg}\mathbf{h}_{t-1} + \mathbf{b}_g), && (1)\\
i_t &= \sigma(\mathbf{W}_{xi}\mathbf{x}_t + \mathbf{W}_{hi}\mathbf{h}_{t-1} + \mathbf{b}_i), && (2)\\
f_t &= \sigma(\mathbf{W}_{xf}\mathbf{x}_t + \mathbf{W}_{hf}\mathbf{h}_{t-1} + \mathbf{b}_f), && (3)\\
o_t &= \sigma(\mathbf{W}_{xo}\mathbf{x}_t + \mathbf{W}_{ho}\mathbf{h}_{t-1} + \mathbf{b}_o), && (4)\\
C_t &= f_t \odot C_{t-1} + i_t \odot g_t, && (5)\\
\mathbf{h}_t &= o_t \odot \varphi(C_t), && (6)\\
\mathbf{y}_t &= \mathbf{W}_y\mathbf{h}_t + \mathbf{b}_y. && (7)
\end{aligned}
$$

φ denotes the *tanh* function, and σ represents the *sigmoid* function. $\odot$ stands for the element-wise multiplication. These gates (i_t, f_t, and o_t) ensure the capture of temporal dependencies. The objective function is minimizing

$$L(\mathbf{y},\mathbf{y}) = \frac{1}{2}\sum_t \|\mathbf{y}_t - \mathbf{y}_t\|_2^2, \qquad (8)$$

where $\mathbf{y}_t$ and $\mathbf{y}_t$ are the predicted and true outputs at time t, respectively.

2.2 Abnormal Event Detection

With these normal event regularities, video events which disobey these rules are treated as temporal anomalies. The temporal anomaly score for sample $\mathbf{y}$ is computed as

$$\mathcal{T}(\mathbf{y}) = \frac{1}{2}\|\mathbf{y} - \mathbf{y}\|_2. \qquad (9)$$

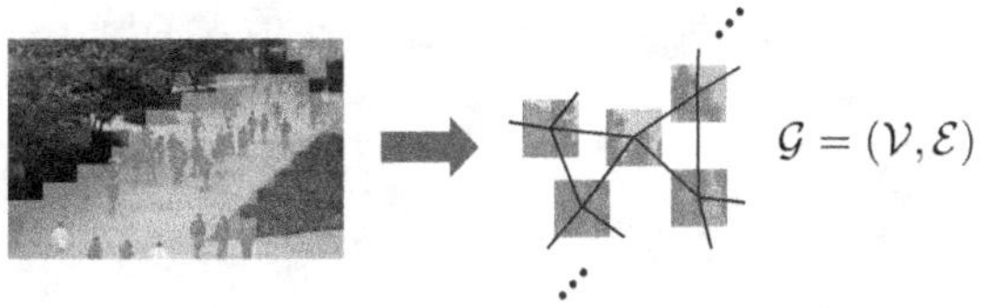

Figure 3: The graph model for manifold ranking.

In order to improve the detection accuracy using the spatial contextual information, a manifold ranking algorithm is designed. Firstly, a graph $\mathcal{G} = (\mathcal{V}, \mathcal{E})$ is constructed from the motion region of an input frame. Vertices $\mathcal{V}$ are samples in the motion region, and edges $\mathcal{E}$ only connect adjacent samples in the spatial context, as is shown in Fig. 3. These edges are weighted by

$$\mathbf{W}_{ij} = \begin{cases} e^{-\frac{\|\mathbf{y}_i - \mathbf{y}_j\|^2}{2\sigma_y^2}}, & \mathbf{y}_j \in \mathcal{N}(\mathbf{y}_i) \\ 0, & otherwise, \end{cases} \tag{10}$$

where $\mathcal{N}(\mathbf{y}_i)$ stands for neighbors of $\mathbf{y}_i$, and σ_y is a scale parameter. Subsequently, a ranking method is developed. Since normal video frames contain no anomalies, we select several normal ones as queries by

$$\widetilde{\mathcal{T}} = \begin{cases} 1, & \mathcal{T} < \tau \\ 0, & otherwise, \end{cases} \tag{11}$$

where τ is a threshold which can be estimated from training samples. The rankings for testing samples are evaluated by solving

$$\arg\min_{\mathcal{S}} \frac{1}{2} \sum_{i,j} \mathbf{W}_{ij} \|\mathcal{S}_i - \mathcal{S}_j\|^2 + \frac{\mu}{2} \sum_i \gamma_i \|\mathcal{S}_i - \widetilde{\mathcal{T}}_i\|^2. \tag{12}$$

The parameter μ controls the balance of the smoothness and fitting constraints. γ_i is an adaptive weight, which aims to improve the discrimination between abnormal and normal events. To this end, γ_i is set as

$$\gamma_i = \begin{cases} 1, & \mathcal{T} < \tau \\ \mathcal{T}_i / Z, & otherwise, \end{cases} \tag{13}$$

where Z is the maximum value of $\mathcal{T}$. Mathematically, Eq. (13) assigns large weights to normal ($\mathcal{T}_i < \tau$) and suspicious events (large $\mathcal{T}$), while small weights to others. In this case, temporal anomaly scores are preserved with large γ_i, and false alarms are smoothed. The spatial anomaly scores can be computed by

$$\mathcal{S} = \frac{\mu}{2} (\mathbf{D} - \mathbf{W} + \frac{\mu}{2} \mathbf{\Gamma})^{-1} \mathbf{\Gamma} \widetilde{\mathcal{T}}, \tag{14}$$

where $\mathbf{\Gamma}$ and $\mathbf{D}$ are both diagonal matrices, with $\mathbf{\Gamma}_{ii} = \gamma_i$ and $\mathbf{D}_{ii} = \sum_j \mathbf{W}_{ij}$.

The final detection results are computed as

$$\mathcal{AE} = \mathcal{T} \odot (1 - \overline{\mathcal{S}}), \tag{15}$$

where $\overline{\mathcal{S}}$ is the normalized value of $\mathcal{S}$.

3. EXPERIMENTS

In order to verify the effectiveness of the proposed algorithm, qualitative and quantitative comparisons are provided on two real world datasets.

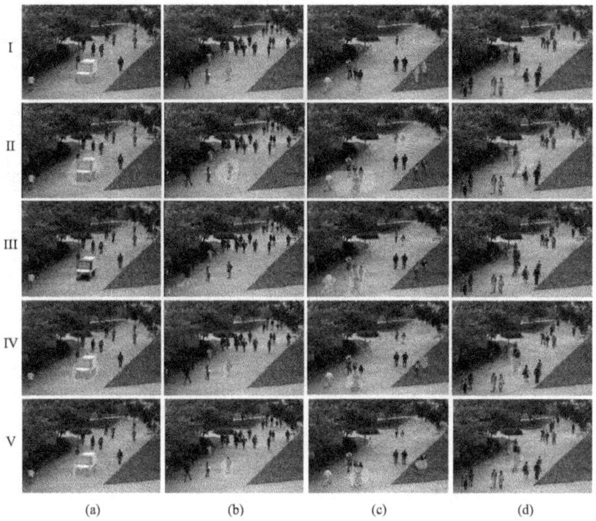

Figure 4: Examples of detected abnormal events on the UCSD ped1 dataset. (I) the ground-truth; (II) the MDT algorithm [7]; (III) the SF-MPPCA algorithm [7]; (IV) the SRC algorithm [2]; and (V) the proposed algorithm.

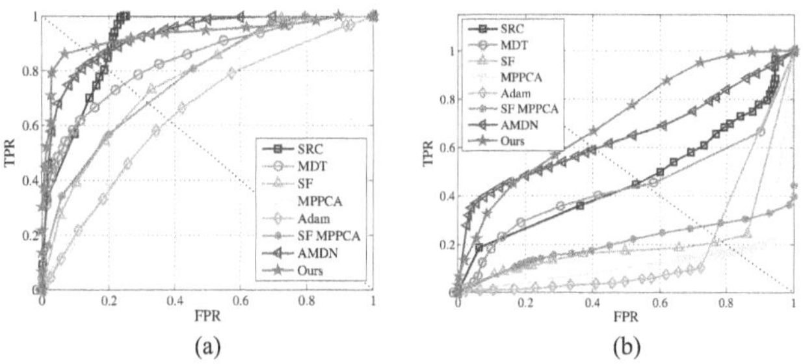

Figure 5: ROC curves for the UCSD Ped1 dataset. (a) Frame-level ROC; (b) Pixel-level ROC.

3.1 UCSD Ped1 Dataset

The UCSD Ped1 dataset[1] is taken from a surveillance camera overlooking a pedestrian walkway. The crowd density in the scene varies from sparse to extremely crowded. There are 34 and 36 video clips in the training and testing sets, respectively. In the testing dataset, all clips have frame-level labels, and 10 clips are provided with pixel-level ground-truth. Each short video clip is composed of 200 frames, with spatial resolution of 158×238.

We compare the proposed algorithm with some state of the art algorithms. Some visualized comparison results are shown in Fig. 4, in which detected abnormal events are labeled with red masks. The abnormal events include car, skater, biker, and so on. The proposed algorithm achieves competitive performance compared with others. The quantitative evaluations are measured on frame and pixel levels.

ROC Curve Comparison According to [4], as long as one pixel is detected as an anomaly in a testing frame, it is labeled as an abnormal frame. If the ground-truth is also abnormal, it is a true positive. Otherwise, it is a false pos-

[1]http://www.svcl.ucsd.edu/projects/abnormality/dataset.html.

Table 1: **Comparisons on the UCSD Ped1 dataset.**

	Frame-level		Pixel-level	
	EER	AUC	EDR	AUC
MDT [7]	25.0%	81.8%	45.0%	44.1%
MPPCA [3]	40.0%	67.0%	18.0%	13.3%
SF-MPPCA [7]	32.0%	76.9%	28.0%	20.5%
SF [8]	31.0%	76.8%	21.0%	21.3%
Adam [1]	38.0%	64.9%	24.0%	19.7%
SRC [2]	19.0%	86.0%	46.0%	46.1%
Lu [5]	15.0%	91.8%	59.1%	63.8%
H-MDT [4]	17.8%	–	64.8%	66.2%
AMDN [11]	16.0%	92.1%	59.9%	67.2%
SDAE+LSTM	13.5%	92.7%	61.9%	70.3%
Ours	11.1%	93.2%	63.5%	71.7%

itive. By altering the detection threshold, we produce a frame-level ROC curve as shown in Fig. 5(a). The proposed algorithm has obvious high *true positive rate* (TPR) when the *false positive rate* (FPR) is low. This is vital for real applications.

As for the pixel-level measurement, a detected abnormal frame is true positive if and only if more than 40% abnormal pixels are detected. A normal frame is false positive as long as one pixel is detected as abnormal. In Fig. 5(b), we compare the pixel-level ROC curves. The proposed algorithm achieves the best performance.

AUC, EER, and EDR Based on these ROC curves, three evaluation criteria are taken as quantitative indexes. *Area under curve* (AUC) is the area under the ROC curve; *Equal error rate* (EER) is the ratio of misclassified frames when the false positive rate equals the miss rate, i.e. the FPR at which FPR $= 1 - $ TPR; *Equal detected rate* (EDR) is the detection rate at EER, i.e. EDR $= 1 -$ EER. In Table 1, we report EER and AUC at frame-level, meanwhile EDR and AUC at pixel-level. These results indicate that the proposed algorithm outperforms AMDN by 1.1% and 4.5% at AUC values of frame-level and pixel-level, respectively. Moreover, we also verify the impact of the manifold ranking algorithm by comparing with the results without ranking, which is denoted as "SDAE+LSTM" in Table 1.

3.2 Avenue Dataset

The Avenue dataset[2] contains 14 kinds of abnormal events, including running, loitering, and throwing objects, etc. There are 16 video clips for training and 21 clips for testing. All testing clips have object-level ground-truth, i.e. labeling anomalies with rectangle regions. This dataset has 30,652 frames totally, with spatial resolution of 360×640.

Some visualized comparison results are shown in Fig. 6. "3D Gradient" is the result of the proposed algorithm replacing the SDAE features with 3D gradient features. We can find that both "3D Gradient" and the proposed algorithm exclude false detections. In Table 2, we compare accuracies under different detection thresholds. According to [5], it is a correct detection if the ratio $\frac{\text{Detected Anomaly} \bigcap \text{True Anomaly}}{\text{Detected Anomaly} \bigcup \text{True Anomaly}}$ exceeds θ. As is shown in Table 2, deep representation (SDAE) is better than hand-crafted features (3D gradient).

[2]http://appsrv.cse.cuhk.edu.hk/~cwlu/Anormality_1000_FPS/dataset.html.

Figure 6: Examples of detected anomalies on the Avenue dataset. Abnormal regions are labeled with red masks. (I) the ground-truth; (II) Lu's algorithm [5]; (III) 3D Gradient; and (IV) the proposed algorithm.

Table 2: Comparisons on the Avenue dataset.

θ	Lu [5]	3D Gradient	SDAE+LSTM	Ours
0.2	70.0%	72.8%	73.7%	75.2%
0.3	67.3%	70.7%	71.9%	73.5%
0.4	63.3%	67.8%	68.4%	71.0%
0.5	59.3%	65.0%	67.6%	68.9%
0.6	57.5%	62.9%	65.7%	66.9%
0.7	55.7%	62.4%	63.8%	64.6%
0.8	54.4%	62.3%	63.2%	63.7%

Meanwhile, the manifold ranking algorithm improves the detection accuracies.

4. CONCLUSIONS

This paper presents a novel video abnormal event detection method based on unsupervised deep learning. Video event features are adaptively extracted and fused from appearance, texture, and short-term motion clues. In order to model long-term dependencies in video events, an LSTM based prediction model is proposed. Furthermore, a graph-based manifold ranking algorithm is designed to make use of the spatial contextual information. As a result, the discrimination between abnormal and normal events is increased, and false alarms are excluded. Experimental results on two surveillance video datasets demonstrate the effectiveness of the proposed algorithm, and show competitive performance compared with existing methods.

Acknowledgments

This work is supported by the National Basic Research Program of China (Youth 973 Program) (Grant No. 2013CB336500), the State Key Program of National Natural Science of China (Grant No. 61232010), the National Natural Science Foundation of China (Grant Nos. 61172143 and 61472413), the National Basic Research Program of China (973 Program) (Grant No. 2012CB719905), the Key Research Program of the Chinese Academy of Sciences (Grant No. KGZD-EW-T03), and the Open Research Fund of the Key Laboratory of Spectral Imaging Technology, Chinese Academy of Sciences (Grant No. LSIT201408).

5. REFERENCES

[1] A. Adam, E. Rivlin, I. Shimshoni, and D. Reinitz. Robust real-time unusual event detection using multiple fixed-location monitors. *IEEE TPAMI*, 30(3):555–560, 2008.

[2] Y. Cong, J. Yuan, and J. Liu. Sparse reconstruction cost for abnormal event detection. In *IEEE CVPR*, pages 3449–3456, 2011.

[3] J. Kim and K. Grauman. Observe locally, infer globally: A space-time MRF for detecting abnormal activities with incremental updates. In *IEEE CVPR*, pages 2921–2928, 2009.

[4] W. Li, V. Mahadevan, and N. Vasconcelos. Anomaly detection and localization in crowded scenes. *IEEE TPAMI*, 36(1):18–32, 2014.

[5] C. Lu, J. Shi, and J. Jia. Abnormal event detection at 150 FPS in MATLAB. In *IEEE ICCV*, pages 2720–2727, 2013.

[6] X. Lu, Y. Yuan, and P. Yan. Robust visual tracking with discriminative sparse learning. *Pattern Recognition*, 46(7):1762–1771, 2013.

[7] V. Mahadevan, W. Li, V. Bhalodia, and N. Vasconcelos. Anomaly detection in crowded scenes. In *IEEE CVPR*, pages 1975–1981, 2010.

[8] R. Mehran, A. Oyama, and M. Shah. Abnormal crowd behavior detection using social force model. In *IEEE CVPR*, pages 935–942, 2009.

[9] V. Reddy, C. Sanderson, and B. C. Lovell. Improved anomaly dtection in crowded scenes via cell-based analysis of foreground speed, size and texture. In *IEEE CVPR*, pages 55–61, 2011.

[10] Z. Wu, X. Wang, Y.-G. Jiang, H. Ye, and X. Xue. Modeling spatial-temporal clues in a hybrid deep learning framework for video classification. In *ACM Multimedia*, pages 461–470, 2015.

[11] D. Xu, E. Ricci, Y. Yan, J. Song, and N. Sebe. Learning deep representations of appearance and motion for anomalous event detection. In *BMVC*, pages 1–12, 2015.

[12] Y. Yuan, L. Mou, and X. Lu. Scene recognition by manifold regularized deep learning architecture. *IEEE TNNLS*, 26(10):2222–2233, 2015.

[13] B. Zhao, L. Fei-Fei, and E. P. Xing. Online detection of unusual events in videos via dynamic sparse coding. In *IEEE CVPR*, pages 3313–3320, 2011.

Exploration of Large Image Corpuses in Virtual Reality

Sanket Khanwalkar
University of California, Irvine
skhanwal@uci.edu

Shonali Balakrishna
University of California, Irvine
shonalib@uci.edu

Ramesh Jain
University of California, Irvine
jain@ics.uci.edu

ABSTRACT

With the increasing capture of photos and their proliferation on social media, there is a pressing need for a more intuitive and versatile image search and exploration system. Image search systems have long been confined to the binds of the 2D legacy screens and the keyword text-box. With the recent advances in Virtual Reality (VR) technology, a move towards an immersive VR environment will redefine the image navigation experience. To this end, we propose a VR platform that gathers images from various sources, and addresses the 5 Ws of image search - what, where, when, who and why. We achieve this by providing the user with two modes of interactive exploration - (i) A mode that allows for a graph based navigation of an image dataset, using a steering wheel[1] visualization, along multiple dimensions of time, location, visual concept, people, etc. and (ii) Another mode that provides an intuitive exploration of the image dataset using a logical hierarchy of visual concepts. Our contributions include creating a VR image exploration experience that is intuitive and allows image navigation along multiple dimensions.

Keywords

Multimedia, Image Exploration, Big Data, Virtual Reality

1. INTRODUCTION

More data has been created in the 21st century than in all of human history. Estimates say that 2.5 quintillion bytes of data is generated each day [1]; So much so that 90% of the data in the world today has been created in the last two years alone. With the wide proliferation of photos and videos from phone cameras, the Web has also become increasingly visual. To put numbers in perspective for photos, in 2015 alone, for every minute on an average, Instagram users liked more than 1.7 million photos, Pinterest users pinned nearly 10,000 images and Facebook users uploaded nearly 136,000 photos [2, 4].

Information was initially represented in text documents. With the advent of the World Wide Web, it became possible to make the document corpus available to everyone, and most importantly, traverse from one document to the other using hyperlinks. The current information age needs to capitalize on the exponentially expanding image corpus by creating an interlinked visual web [18]. At present, the images cannot be interlinked with each other based on their contents or contextual metadata, making it extremely tedious and unintuitive to explore massive image datasets, whether personal or global, available on photo sharing applications like Google, Facebook, Instagram, Flickr or Pinterest. For example, Google Image Search only allows a spading-fork traversal in one direction, compelling users to query repeatedly to traverse in a different direction.

The image content and context (time, location) are becoming major sources of information for situation recognition [18, 24], with advanced techniques like deep learning being developed in computer vision for recognizing key concepts from the image content and easy availability of contextual information through the use of sensors like GPS, accelerometers etc. Therefore, these visual concepts and contextual features can now be leveraged in image search and exploration in order to implement an associative means of navigating through image datasets.

Until now, data visualization was limited to the representation of textual data, mainly on 2D interfaces. But as data evolves from text to multimedia (Eg. images), representing this data in 2D interfaces in an easily comprehensible manner becomes a challenge. Traditional visualization approaches when applied to large image datasets provide limited usability due to the constrained space on the visualization plane and the lack of interactivity for the user.

The platform on which data can be visualized is undergoing a transformation, from browsers on PCs to mobile devices to the upcoming Virtual Reality (VR) devices. VR could prove to be a powerful and engaging platform for image search and exploration, as it provides infinite environment space, multimodal user inputs (gaze, voice, head/hand motion) and distributed connectivity. VR, finally, offers an exciting possibility for applications in image exploration, because (i) with the advent of Google Cardboard and other such affordable and accessible VR devices compatible with smartphones, VR applications are now feasible for the typical user in terms of cost and size, (ii) there has been ex-

[1]In this paper, making a selection on a curved plane containing multiple options is equivalent to moving a 'steering wheel' in a particular direction.

MM '16, October 15-19, 2016, Amsterdam, Netherlands

DOI: http://dx.doi.org/10.1145/2964284.2967291

tensive research in academia and industry towards the facilitation of VR as an effective environment. In this paper, we propose a VR image exploration system that provides the user with two modes of exploration - Steering Wheel browsing and Hierarchical browsing. Steering wheel browsing allows the user to explore image datasets using a graph structure, along multiple dimensions like time, location, concepts, people, etc. Hierarchical browsing allows the user to explore image datasets using hierarchies that are based on visual concepts.

This paper is organized as follows: Section 2 describes related work in this domain. Section 3 discusses our proposed method, with the two modes of visualization, our image graph, system architecture, system implementation and evaluation. Section 4 discusses the conclusions of this paper, followed by a discussion of future work in Section 5.

2. RELATED WORK

While a lot of work has been done on content based image retrieval techniques, the existing semantic gap [27] is still a challenge and approaches like query-by-example [13] have limited application in practice. The most primitive image browsing visualizes a limited number of thumbnails on a 2D screen, requiring the user to continually go back and forth to view more images. More intuitive interfaces have been proposed for navigating image collections [25, 16], which can be broadly classified into mapping based, clustering based and graph based visualizations [22]; These visualizations are created using dimensionality reduction [27, 19], grouping based on image characteristics [11, 15] and interlinked image graphs [12, 28] respectively with similar images placed closer to each other. Visualizations represent clusters using a representative image, upon whose selection all images in the clusters are displayed to the user [8, 9, 10, 14, 23].

Traditional browsing techniques include horizontal browsing (within a particular level of the hierarchy), vertical browsing (navigation to a different level of the hierarchy) and time based browsing [21]. A spherical visualization approach to image exploration is proposed in [26], where image databases are handled in a hierarchical approach, with visually similar images placed together; Zooming operations reveal images on a deeper level of the tree structure, with the user being allowed to modify the browsing interactively.

In the past, image exploration systems like 3D MARS have been implemented in VR to leverage the infinite virtual space for displaying image query results using low-level image properties like color, texture and structure. However, such features for query-by-example render image exploration unintuitive limiting the accuracy in retrieving the semantic relationships between the images [20].

3. PROPOSED METHODS

As a first step in the direction of implementing an immersive image exploration system, we present a proof-of-concept in this section, with an overview of the image graph, the two modes, system architecture, implementation and evaluation. In our prototype, we provide the user with two exploratory modes - Steering Wheel browsing and Hierarchical browsing.

3.1 Image Graph

In recent years, with considerable research in deep learning techniques for concept extraction in images, and availability of more sensor information offering detailed context, the creation of an interlinked image graph is now a possibility. Such a visual web [18] can then provide traversal along multiple dimensions providing insights on what, where, when and who, thereby making intuitive image exploration a reality.

In our approach, we create the link structure using content and context based relationships between images, thus allowing navigation along multiple dimensions. We have used a university research dataset for image exploration in our system, which contains time and location information as part of the image EXIF metadata. Furthermore, this dataset is augmented with concepts that are mined from the images using a deep learning API (Clarifai [3]), location information that is retrieved via a location web service (Foursquare [5]) and people were extracted using pre-existing name tags, available for several images. Links are created by tagging image metadata based on time, location, concepts and people and navigation between images is based on similarity between these tags.

3.2 Steering Wheel Browsing Mode

In this approach, we arrange the image corpus as a graph with each image acting as a node, interconnected with other image nodes through edges. The edges between the graph nodes may represent connections based on time, location, concepts and people.

To implement this approach in VR, we begin with randomly generated images from the dataset. The currently viewed image is larger in size and placed exactly in front of the user, while other images are placed around it in the environment in a panoramic fashion. In this mode, the tiles on the steering wheel at the bottom represent the important entities present in the currently displayed image. These entities include time information, location information, concepts derived from the image and people present in the image. The location information is displayed via a static map and a place banner (if applicable) while people and concepts are displayed in a vertical menu.

In the example shown in Figure 1, the image identified 2 different persons viz. *Steve Jobs* and *Bill Gates* as people, *WWDC '08* as the place in *San Francisco*, which is the geographical location and dinner as a concept. If the user is interested in exploring photos involving one of the people or the city in the photo, he can simply make a selection using gaze-and-select mechanism in the direction of his choice on the steering wheel. A new set of photos are then rendered and the corresponding options on the steering wheel are updated, based on the current image. This style of exploration provides the user with valuable details present in the image and also the ability to traverse along the given dimensions (location, concept or people) in the image graph.

3.3 Hierarchical Browsing Mode

In this approach, we arrange the image corpus in logical hierarchies based on concepts present in the images. Each level in the hierarchy contains images belonging to the same concept category. Iteratively, each category at any given level, may further contain subcategories of images.

To implement this approach in VR, we begin our navigation with a predefined set of high-level categories. At each level in the hierarchy, images that belong to the same category are displayed in the environment and subcategories

Figure 1: VR application showing graph-based image exploration

Figure 2: VR application showing hierarchy-based image exploration

are depicted by representative images on the bottom panel. With every selection on the panel, the system updates the environment with corresponding images belonging to that category and updates the panel with its subcategories. Once the user reaches the bottom of the hierarchy, the user is offered two options: (i) Traverse one level up in the hierarchy using the voice command 'back' or (ii) Jump into a conceptually related category using suggested options displayed on the right pane.

For example, we begin with popular search categories like Music, Hollywood, Sports, Politics, etc. placed as individual tiles on the bottom panel. As shown in Figure 2, selecting a representative tile at a given layer of the hierarchy, like Sports in this example, loads the subsequent options of the hierarchy like Tennis, Soccer, Baseball, etc. The user can refine his exploratory search by selecting any of these sports categories, say Soccer, by a gaze-and-select mechanism, thereby loading the next set of subcategories like players, teams, tournaments etc. on the bottom panel. Iteratively, after following a path like Sports –> Soccer –> Players –> *Lionel Messi* and reaching the end of this hierarchy, the user can either move back using a 'back' voice command or simply jump to related options like *Diego Maradona*, *Barcelona FC*, Golden Boot, etc. displayed on the right pane, and in this manner, continue his exploration infinitely.

3.4 System Architecture

Our system relies on the intricate integration between 4 components - data (image datasets, link structures), user input (voice, gaze-and-select), network (low latency, reliability) and VR display (aesthetic, intuitive, seamless rendering). Our system has a hybrid design that takes advantages of both client-side and server-side capabilities [17].

As shown in Figure 3, depending on the mode selected, the user is presented with the corresponding visualizations containing options to start his image exploration. The user provides his navigation input to the controller using voice or gaze-and-select. The controller communicates the user input to the backend and fetches the images and the corresponding link structures, for rendering in the virtual environment.

Our backend consists of servers and a data store; The data store contains the image corpus that will be explored. The servers are used to extract the link structure between images, from the image content and metadata, by querying external web services. We have utilized external web services for extracting visual concepts from image content, and possible locations from the spatial metadata.

3.5 System Implementation

3.5.1 Frontend Implementation

For developing and rendering a platform-independent application that can be deployed in the web, mobile or VR devices like Google Cardboard, we used MozVR [7]. This WebVR framework uses HTML elements to run the applica-

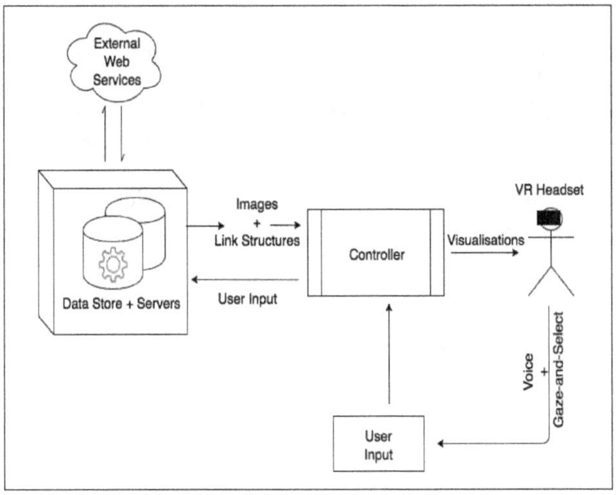

Figure 3: System Architecture

tion in a WebGL-enabled browser. This framework provides the gaze-and-select feature enabling users to choose options available in the VR space. Additionally, Google Voice API was integrated with this framework, thereby providing secondary assistance for user input.

3.5.2 Backend Implementation

We created a REST API to retrieve images from an existing university research dataset, and have further processed these images to create the link structures using external web services. The backend is designed to query external web services like ClarifAI [3] for extracting visual concepts from image content and Foursquare [5] for extracting possible locations from the spatial metadata. Our backend technology stack is Python based, and we use a Python web framework called Flask to create the REST API. For rendering static maps in our browser, we send location details in a HTTP request to Google Maps and receive static images as the response. All the other visualizations are processed in the backend and only their output is rendered in the browser as images.

3.6 Evaluation

For a general evaluation of our system, we conducted a pilot study with 11 participants (age group of 21-30). We deployed the application on a web browser in an iPhone, with a Google Cardboard as the VR device.

The following steps were performed in carrying out this study: (i) The user was initially asked to explore images from Flickr, Instagram and Pinterest feeds on a computer or smartphone. (ii) The user was then asked to explore images in our VR application rendered on Google Cardboard. (iii) During his exploration, we provide guidance to the user to help him understand his VR environment better. (iv) Post our study, with each participant taking around 10 minutes exploring our system, they were requested to answer a few questions, on a number scale of 1-5 (5 being most satisfied), related to their experience, concerns, usefulness, etc. Results of our study can be found in Table 1.

Our evaluation results suggest that there is definitely a need for a better image exploration system. The rather average score of 3.3 for the gaze-and-select mechanism can be attributed to the lack of sophistication in the UI/UX of our preliminary prototype as well as the novelty of the VR environment in general. However, the evaluation study for the remaining 4 questions clearly suggests that there is considerable potential in such a system and a willingness among participants to use this image exploration system, especially for social media and personal photos.

Questions	Score
How satisfied are you with legacy image search using keywords in textboxes?	2.7
How positive was your experience with gaze-and-select for image exploration?	3.3
How intuitive was image exploration using the steering wheel browsing?	4.4
How positive was your experience exploring images in infinite virtual space?	4.3
Would you use such a VR application in the future for image exploration?	Yes (91%)

Table 1: Evaluation Results

4. CONCLUSION

We propose an approach that provides two modes to the user - first, a mode for browsing through an interlinked image graph structure along dimensions like time, location, concepts, people; second, a mode that allows an intuitive navigation through conceptual hierarchies of images for a simpler exploratory search and browsing experience in VR. The advantage of using our proposed approach is two fold - (i) it provides interlinking between images along many dimensions by incorporating contextual and conceptual information into the navigation. (ii) it provides the user with an interactive and immersive exploration experience in VR space, where he gets to engage and set the tone of the navigation.

5. FUTURE WORK

Based on our literature survey and current work, supported by the pilot study, we strongly believe that further work on the following areas will lead to the successful convergence of image exploration and virtual reality. Firstly, a knowledge graph can be applied to the objects or concepts present in an image for more insightful exploration of large image datasets. In order to infer deeper meaning from plain text queries, Google's Knowledge Graph considers the semantic meaning behind the query and fetches improved search results. This graph is built by finding entities and relationships associated with each word with the help of sources like Wikipedia [6]. Thus, creation of a knowledge graph for images will enable efficient exploration of large image datasets by offering semantically meaningful directions of exploration. Second, the nature of VR technology creates opportunities in collaborative image viewing/exploration experience, which was not possible before. With multimodal user input, infinite environment space, remote and distributed connectivity and sophisticated sensors, collaborating and sharing your image exploration can certainly become a reality. Third, this system can be extended as a platform to incorporate social media feeds like Instagram, Pinterest, Flickr, etc. along with personal image collections to create a unified image exploration experience.

6. REFERENCES

[1] Big Data Statistics. http://www.vcloudnews.com/every-day-big-data-statistics-2-5-quintillion-bytes-of-data-created-daily/.

[2] Big Data Usage Per Minute. http://www.inc.com/larry-kim/15-mind-blowing-statistics-reveal-what-happens-on-the-internet-in-a-minute.html.

[3] ClarifAI. https://developer.clarifai.com/.

[4] Facebook Data Statistics. https://zephoria.com/top-15-valuable-facebook-statistics/.

[5] FourSquare. https://developer.foursquare.com/.

[6] Google Knowledge Graph. https://en.wikipedia.org/wiki/Knowledge_Graph.

[7] MozVR Framework. http://mozvr.com/#developers.

[8] I. Bartolini, P. Ciaccia, and M. Patella. Adaptively browsing image databases with pibe. *Multimedia Tools and Applications*, 31(3):269–286, 2006.

[9] J.-Y. Chen, C. A. Bouman, and J. C. Dalton. Hierarchical browsing and search of large image databases. *Image Processing, IEEE Transactions on*, 9(3):442–455, 2000.

[10] Y.-X. Chen and A. Butz. Photosim: Tightly integrating image analysis into a photo browsing ui. In *Smart Graphics*, pages 224–231. Springer, 2008.

[11] M. Cooper, J. Foote, A. Girgensohn, and L. Wilcox. Temporal event clustering for digital photo collections. *ACM Transactions on Multimedia Computing, Communications, and Applications (TOMM)*, 1(3):269–288, 2005.

[12] M. Dontcheva, M. Agrawala, and M. Cohen. Metadata visualization for image browsing. In *18th annual ACM symposium on user interface software and technology*, 2005.

[13] C. Faloutsos, R. Barber, M. Flickner, J. Hafner, W. Niblack, D. Petkovic, and W. Equitz. Efficient and effective querying by image content. *Journal of intelligent information systems*, 3(3-4):231–262, 1994.

[14] A. Gomi, R. Miyazaki, T. Itoh, and J. Li. Cat: A hierarchical image browser using a rectangle packing technique. In *Information Visualisation, 2008. IV'08. 12th International Conference*, pages 82–87. IEEE, 2008.

[15] B. Gong, U. Westermann, S. Agaram, and R. Jain. Event discovery in multimedia reconnaissance data using spatio-temporal clustering. In *Proc. of the AAAI Workshop on Event Extraction and Synthesis (EES'06)*, 2006.

[16] D. Heesch. A survey of browsing models for content based image retrieval. *Multimedia Tools and Applications*, 40(2):261–284, 2008.

[17] B. Huang, B. Jiang, and H. Li. An integration of gis, virtual reality and the internet for visualization, analysis and exploration of spatial data. *International Journal of Geographical Information Science*, 15(5):439–456, 2001.

[18] R. Jain. Let's weave the visual web. *MultiMedia, IEEE*, 22(3):66–72, 2015.

[19] B. Moghaddam, Q. Tian, N. Lesh, C. Shen, and T. S. Huang. Visualization and user-modeling for browsing personal photo libraries. *International Journal of Computer Vision*, 56(1-2):109–130, 2004.

[20] M. Nakazato and T. S. Huang. 3d mars: Immersive virtual reality for content-based image retrieval. In *ICME*, 2001.

[21] W. Plant and G. Schaefer. Navigation and browsing of image databases. In *Soft Computing and Pattern Recognition, 2009. SOCPAR'09. International Conference of*, pages 750–755. IEEE, 2009.

[22] W. Plant and G. Schaefer. Visualising image databases. In *Multimedia Signal Processing, 2009. MMSP'09. IEEE International Workshop on*, pages 1–6. IEEE, 2009.

[23] J. C. Platt, M. Czerwinski, and B. A. Field. Phototoc: Automatic clustering for browsing personal photographs. In *Information, Communications and Signal Processing, 2003 and Fourth Pacific Rim Conference on Multimedia. Proceedings of the 2003 Joint Conference of the Fourth International Conference on*, volume 1, pages 6–10. IEEE, 2003.

[24] S. Pongpaichet, M. Tang, L. Jalali, and R. Jain. Using photos as micro-reports of events. In *Proceedings of the 2016 ACM on International Conference on Multimedia Retrieval*, pages 87–94. ACM, 2016.

[25] S. D. Ruszala and G. Schaefer. Visualisation models for image databases: A comparison of six approaches. In *Irish machine vision and image processing conference*, pages 186–191. Citeseer, 2004.

[26] G. Schaefer. A next generation browsing environment for large image repositories. *Multimedia Tools and Applications*, 47(1):105–120, 2010.

[27] A. W. Smeulders, M. Worring, S. Santini, A. Gupta, and R. Jain. Content-based image retrieval at the end of the early years. *Pattern Analysis and Machine Intelligence, IEEE Transactions on*, 22(12):1349–1380, 2000.

[28] M. Worring, O. de Rooij, and T. van Rijn. Browsing visual collections using graphs. In *Proceedings of the international workshop on Workshop on multimedia information retrieval*, pages 307–312. ACM, 2007.

HEVC-compliant Tile-based Streaming of Panoramic Video for Virtual Reality Applications

Alireza Zare[1], Alireza Aminlou[1,2], Miska M. Hannuksela[2], Moncef Gabbouj[1]
[1]Department of Signal Processing, Tampere University of Technology, [2]Nokia Technologies
[1]{ali.zare, moncef.gabbouj}@tut.fi, [2]{alireza.aminlou, miska.hannuksela}@nokia.com

ABSTRACT

Delivering wide-angle and high-resolution spherical panoramic video content entails a high streaming bitrate. This imposes challenges when panorama clips are consumed in virtual reality (VR) head-mounted displays (HMD). The reason is that the HMDs typically require high spatial and temporal fidelity contents and strict low-latency in order to guarantee the user's sense of presence while using them. In order to alleviate the problem, we propose to store two versions of the same video content at different resolutions, each divided into multiple tiles using the High Efficiency Video Coding (HEVC) standard. According to the user's present viewport, a set of tiles is transmitted in the highest captured resolution, while the remaining parts are transmitted from the low-resolution version of the same content. In order to enable selectively choosing different combinations, the tile sets are encoded to be independently decodable. We further study the trade-off in the choice of tiling scheme and its impact on compression and streaming bitrate performances. The results indicate streaming bitrate saving from 30% to 40%, depending on the selected tiling scheme, when compared to streaming the entire video content.

CCS Concepts

• **Multimedia and Vision→Video coding and streaming in support of vision applications**.

Keywords

Video Coding; HEVC; Tiles; Panoramic Video Streaming; Virtual Reality; Head-mounted Display (HMD).

1. INTRODUCTION

This work is motivated by the fact that in many displaying situations only part of the whole video frame is displayed while the remaining parts are decoded but not displayed. For example, this occurs in applications where the same wide-angle high-resolution video content serves a number of devices with different specifications (e.g. display size). One approach would be to deliver a spatially down-sampled representation of the entire video to suit the end-user device's capability. However, this approach results in a decreased sense of immersion at the client terminal, which contradicts with the gist of virtual reality (VR) applications where an immersive viewing experience is the main goal. This paper studies such condition in panoramic video streaming for VR applications using head-mounted displays (HMD). The field of view (FOV) in the current commercially available HMDs is in the range of 96° to 110° [4]. Considering the limited HMD's FOV, only part of the video frame is needed to be displayed at a time, while the input video for HMDs consumption often covers the entire 360°.

MM '16, October 15-19, 2016, Amsterdam, Netherlands
© 2016 ACM. ISBN 978-1-4503-3603-1/16/10...$15.00
DOI: http://dx.doi.org/10.1145/2964284.2967292

When using HMDs, as the user turns his/her head, an appropriate view, corresponding to the user's viewport, has to be presented. Latency to presenting a new perspective of the scene severely affects the usability of such devices. In fact, one of the most important attributes of the HMDs is to provide fast dynamic response to the user's interaction. This results in well synchronization of user's movements with the displayed scene. The conventionally streaming of the full 360° video content entails a high streaming bitrate, and may also cause a risk of network and/or access link congestion and re-buffering, which is an impediment to providing low enough latency operation. Furthermore, in the end-user device the coded pictures have to be fully decoded, since they have strong dependencies including: spatial dependencies (e.g., intra prediction), entropy coding dependencies, in-loop filtering dependencies, and spatio-temporal dependencies (i.e., motion vectors pointing to different parts of the reference pictures).

Tile-based panoramic video streaming is a particular way of panoramic video streaming, in which only part of the whole picture is transmitted, instead of the full picture. In the server side, an encoder is configured to divide video pictures into a desired number of tiles with various possible arrangements in order to meet the requirements of the application under consideration. In the client side, each user receives a set of tiles on the basis of, for example, the present viewing orientation or a region of interest (ROI). This approach relies on motion-constrained tile sets (MCTS) concept which enables the support for decoding a freely-selected set of tiles. MCTSs have been utilized for different applications in the literature. Both [2] and [7] propose compressed-domain approaches for merging different video contents using a combination of tiles and slices. These approaches were proposed to serve several purposes including: transport complexity reduction and enabling support for devices with a single hardware decoder. In [8] a tile-based panoramic streaming solution is presented, with the aim of reducing the transmission bitrate at ROI switching points.

This paper takes advantage of MCTSs for streaming panorama video to a HMD. In our work, similar encoder restrictions as proposed in [2] and [7] are used. Contrary to them, we allow motion vectors to point outside tile boundaries within a specific set of tiles which are always streamed together. In order to guarantee low latency operation, we propose to transmit the tile sets corresponding to the user's current viewport in the highest captured resolution and the remaining parts from a low-resolution representation of the captured scene.

The proposed method in this paper uses the standard HEVC decoding, unlike [2], which requires modifications to the candidate list derivation for HEVC motion vector prediction. Furthermore, we present methods to construct an HEVC full-picture-compliant bitstream out of a MCTS such that standard HEVC decoders can cope with that, as opposed to requiring a specialized decoder to process only the MCTS from the original panorama bitstream. We also study different tile partitioning arrangements for 360° panorama video and discuss the related practical limitations and respective solutions.

The rest of paper is organized as follows. Section 2 presents background. In Section 3, an overview of the proposed VR streaming system is provided and the proposed tiling schemes along with their practical limitations and respective solutions are described. The simulation results are evaluated in Section 4 and finally the paper is concluded in Section 5.

2. BACKGROUND

In the HEVC standard [6], a video picture is partitioned into square-shaped regions called coding tree unit (CTU) which represents the basis of the coding process. Similar to the slices, as already known from the Advanced Video Coding (AVC) standard, an integer number of CTUs are aggregated into a tile [5] to form CTU-aligned picture partitioning. When tiling is enabled, a video picture is horizontally and vertically divided into columns and rows. Compared to slices, tiles are always rectangular. Furthermore, tiles provide more flexibility to partitioning and appear to incur less compression penalty since tiles do not contain any header.

Intra-picture prediction does not cross tile boundaries and entropy coding state is re-initialized at the beginning of every tile [9]. Hence, each constructed tile is independently decodable from other tiles within the same picture. In terms of inter-picture prediction, however, motion vectors can freely point to any predictor beyond the co-located tile boundaries in the reference pictures. Nevertheless, following the spirit of isolated regions suggested in [3], motion vectors are restricted in encoding to only point to the co-located tiles in the reference pictures. This results in constructing motion-constrained tiles (MCT). Extending the restriction further onto a set of tiles leads to the concept of motion-constrained tile set (MCTS) in which motion vectors are allowed to cross tile boundaries within the tile set but not across the tile set.

3. APPROACH

3.1 Overview of the System

An overview of the proposed VR streaming system is depicted in Figure 1, where the proposed tile-based streaming approach is employed. In the server side, we propose to store two versions of the same panoramic video content at different resolutions. An HEVC encoder, in which tile sets are motion constrained, is configured to divide video pictures into a desired number of tiles based on the tiling schemes described in the next subsection. The encoding may be performed offline or in real-time for live content. The encoding results in two separate HEVC-conforming bitstreams.

According to the present viewing orientation, a tile set request is signaled to the server by the end-user device. The server dynamically identifies the requested tile sets from the client based on a sensory feedback. An intermediate extractor, which may for example be a script running in an origin or edge server, extracts the tile set corresponding to present viewing orientation from the high-resolution bitstream. The remaining parts are collected from the low-resolution bitstream, in order to cover the entire captured FOV. The extractor then constructs two independent full-picture bitstreams including the requested MCTS from the high- and low-resolution bitstreams. The outgoing bitstreams are HEVC-compliant. This allows to realize the proposed approach in real-world applications using HEVC Main Profile hardware decoders, available today in the market.

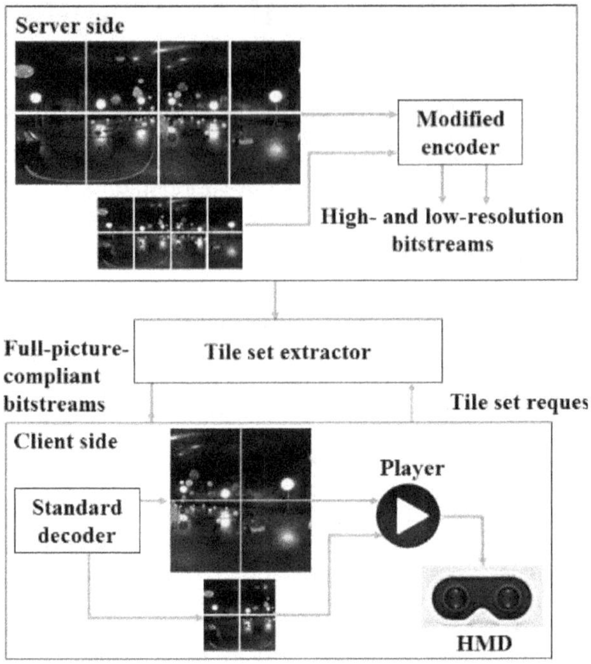

Figure 1. System overview (with 8-grid tiling)

3.2 Proposed Tiling Schemes

Assuming panoramic video playback in HMDs, three tiling arrangements are considered as follows: 1) the horizontal FOV is split into 6 tile columns with each having 60° FOV and the vertical FOV is divided into three tile rows with 45°-90°-45° FOVs, resulting into an 18-grid partitioning, 2) while in vertical direction the same tiling scheme as in 1 is considered, the horizontal FOV is split into 4 tile columns with each having 90° FOV, resulting into a 12-grid partitioning, and 3) in both directions a 90° FOV partitioning is performed, resulting into 4 tile columns and 2 tile rows, in total 8 tiles. The abovementioned tiling arrangements are depicted in Figure 2a, Figure 2b, and Figure 1, respectively.

The idea behind the first two selected tiling schemes is that looking significantly upwards and downwards is rare while using HMDs. Therefore, the most top and bottom parts form separate tile rows from the middle tile row which comprises tiles with higher heights. This arrangement allows to either stream the top and bottom parts at a lower bitrate or avoid streaming them. The idea is further supported by typical trait of panoramic videos in which pixels at the top and bottom appear stretched. The third partitioning scheme is suggested to study the trade-off between simplifying the proposed approach and the cost introduced by the simplification. There are some cases where tiles are not CTU-aligned in the tiled high- and low-resolution video sequences. This may occur, for example, because of the considered restriction on the minimum tile width in the HEVC standard. Consequently, this results in different

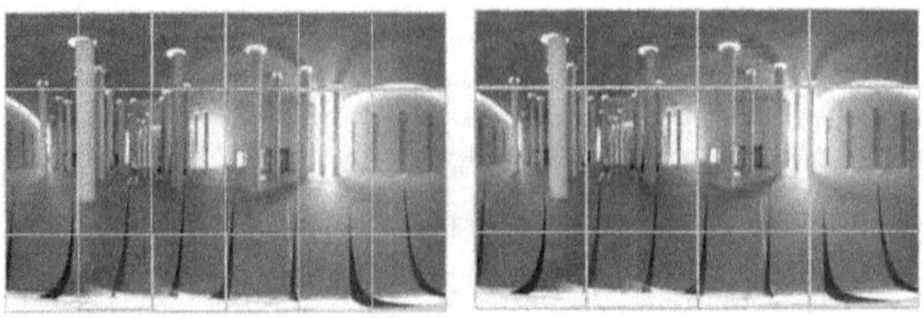

Figure 2. a) 18-grid tiling b) 12-grid tiling

tiling scheme in the low-resolution video sequence than in the high-resolution one. This introduces some overlap area between the selected tile sets from high- and low-resolution bitstreams. The third scheme allows avoiding such situation. In addition, it is adequate for applications in which wide FOV in both vertical and horizontal directions is required (e.g., because video sequences do not have the abovementioned trait). Furthermore, we assume that it is relatively rare that the user would peek straight at the middle of tiles, in which case a single tile would often be sufficient to cover central part of FOV while periphery area are taken from a low-resolution bitstream. Consequently, in most cases, a 2x2 set of high-resolution tiles need to be transmitted (see Figure 1).

In the first two selected tiling scheme, the proposed MCTS is realized in such way that top and bottom tile rows are allowed to be predicted from the middle tile row within the same tile column. However, motion vectors from the middle tile row are restricted to point to the top and bottom tile rows. This is suggested based on the fact that tiles from the middle tile row within a tile set are always subject to be transmitted. In the third scheme, motion vectors are restricted within tile boundaries and are not allowed to break tile set boundaries.

3.3 Practical Limitations and Solutions

There are some limitations which have to be addressed in order to deploy the proposed approach in real-world applications. These limitations and respective solutions are discussed in the following:

1) At view switching points, the switching between tile sets can only take place at an intra-coded picture. As a solution, the entire low-resolution video sequence, which contains all view orientations, can be transmitted in order to provide no latency at view switching points. In this case, the entire low-resolution bitstream is streamed along with the selected tile set from high-resolution bitstream at all times.

2) There are some cases in which the extracted tile set from the low-resolution bitstream cannot be arranged within a single picture (e.g., because of having tiles with different widths/heights). Here the extractor uses an artificially generated tile with the minimal bitstream size in order to provide a conforming extracted bitstream.

3) In the HEVC standard, the end of a slice is indicated using entropy-coded *end_of_slice_flag* which is set to one if the current CTU is the last CTU in the slice. This causes the extractor to construct a non-confirming bitstream in cases where the right-most tile, in which the flag is set, in the high-resolution bitstream is not included in the extracted tile set. The reason is that the decoder does not meet the end of slice condition while decoding the last CTU within the picture in the extracted bitstream. We propose two alternatives to deal with this problem. The first solution is to attach a dummy tile of minimal size at the end of each picture in the compressed domain, such that the end of slice condition is met. The second solution is to use a combination of tiles and slices in a way that each tile contains one slice (i.e., their boundaries match). Both solutions come along with a cost of increase in bitrate because of dummy tile or slice header overhead, respectively. However, in our experiments, the dummy tile solution is shown to incur lower compression penalty at the cost of increasing complexity because of the required processes for attaching and decoding dummy tile.

4. EXPERIMENTS

4.1 Experimental Conditions

The performance of the proposed tile-based streaming approach was evaluated in terms of storage and streaming bitrate measurements. The approach was also analyzed based on its benefit on decoding complexity reduction in an end-user device. The proposed approach was compared against two legacy solutions: 1) an end-user device receives a panoramic video sequence with the entire captured FOV and 2) all possible tile sets are cropped from high- and low-resolution sequences, in pixel domain, and encoded as separate bitstreams in server side, in which no tiling is required.

The encoder was configured to divide the video sequences in a regular manner, in which each tile occupies the same spatial region over all pictures. MCTSs were implemented into the HEVC reference software (HM) version 16.7 [10]. The standard HM decoder was used to examine HEVC conformance. The reported experiments were conducted on eight equirectangular video sequences with divergent contents in different spatial resolutions, namely, MyShelter-sta, MyShelter-mov, Daisy, Lisboa, Sheriff, VRC-concert, Kremlin, and Moscow. The first five sequences contain large and slow-motion objects. VRC-concert sequence captured a detailed scene with slow-motion objects. The two last sequences show detailed scenes containing fast-motion objects, which in the case of Kremlin are caused due to the sequence being a time-lapse video clip. MyShelter-mov, Lisboa, and VRC-concert sequences were acquired by moving cameras. All sequences were captured in real world except the Sheriff sequence which is a computer animated sequence. The high-resolution sequences were down-sampled by a factor of two in both horizontal and vertical directions in order to obtain the low-resolution versions. The simulations were performed using Main profile random access configuration with 49 frames per sequence and quantization parameters (QP) values 22, 26, 30, and 34. The compression performance and streaming bitrate saving measurements are expressed in terms of Bjøntegaard Delta-rate (BD-rate) criterion [1] for luma pictures, where positive/negative values indicate how much the bitrate is increased/reduced for the same peak signal-to-noise (PSNR) value.

4.2 Result Analysis

The usage of tiles and constraining motion within the tile set boundaries incur compression efficiency penalty since the imposed restrictions reduce the correlation among pixel samples. Table 1 shows that on average the incurred penalties for the 18-grid, 12-grid, and 8-grid partitioning schemes are 5.82%, 3.70%, and 3.18%, respectively. The finer the partitioning is, the higher compression loss occurs. As can be seen from Table 1, the compression loss is higher for sequences containing large object motion. In addition, the highest costs occur for sequences which were captured by moving cameras. This is explained due to crossing objects among tile sets that increases percentage of intra-coded blocks.

The basic alternative to the MCTS is pixel-domain cropping of all possible tile sets and encoding each tile set as separate sequence. The compression performance of this technique is shown in Table 2, only average result is presented due to the lack of space. The result indicates that its compression penalty is very close to that of the proposed tile-based approach. However, if full panorama versions were to be also provided with this alternative, e.g. to serve legacy clients, the server-side storage requirement would be roughly doubled, compared to the proposed approach.

Table 3 shows the streaming bitrate saving achieved by using the proposed approach, when compared with transmitting the entire captured FOV in high resolution. It shows significant reduction in streaming bitrate by 40.64%, 33.44%, and 29.58% on average for the 18-grid, 12-grid, and 8-grid partitioning schemes, respectively. It is expected to have less streaming bitrate saving as coarser partitioning scheme is used since the extracted high-resolution tile sets cover a higher FOV. For example, each extracted tile set in 18-grid tiling scheme covers 120° horizontal FOV, while in case of 12-grid tiling it covers 180° horizontal FOV. However, coarser partitioning allows higher switching view latency because of the provided extraneous peripheral vision.

As can also be observed from Table 3, in 18-grid scheme, the streaming bitrate saving is less for MyShelter-sta and MyShelter-mov sequences compared to the other sequences. This is because of the overlapping problem between the selected tile sets from high- and low-resolution bitstreams, as discussed in Section 3.2. Furthermore, in order to address the problem of strict low-latency requirement at view switching points, one proposed solution (see Section 3.3) is to transmit the entire low-resolution bitstream, which contains all view orientations. In this experiment, this causes on average 12% streaming bitrate overhead compared with the case where the low-resolution is transmitted partially.

By comparing the results presented in Table 3 and Table 4, we can see that both tile-base streaming approaches (i.e., the proposed tile-based streaming and its alternative, pixel-domain cropping of all possible tile sets) provide very close streaming bitrate saving. This is expected by noticing that both techniques provide similar compression performance, as discussed above.

In Figure 3, rate-distortion curve for the Daisy sequence is illustrated. It can be observed that higher streaming bitrate saving is achieved at higher bitrates. This is appreciated in HMDs which typically consume high-quality content. Although only the RD curve related to the Daisy sequence is presented, the similar behavior is observed for the other video sequences.

Although a comparison of decoder complexity between the proposed tile-base streaming approach and the case where the decoder receives entire captured FOV is not presented, it is obvious that the proposed solution provides a much lower decoding complexity by lowering the computational burden of decoding. The number of pixels to be decoded is reduced by approximately 69%, 47%, and 37% for 18-, 12-, and 8-grid partitioning schemes, respectively, when compared to decoding of high-resolution panorama video clips.

5. CONCLUSION AND FUTURE WORK

In this paper, we proposed an HEVC-compliant approach for efficient streaming of panoramic video clips for virtual reality applications using motion-constrained tile sets. The encoder restrictions necessary to enable the proposed tile-based streaming technique were discussed. We studied the performance of the proposed approach based on three tiling variants that are adequate to be utilized in head-mounted displays. While smaller tile size enables higher streaming bitrate saving, it introduces more compression loss. The incurred compression penalty in order to enable the proposed solution ranged from 3% to 6%, depending on the selected tiling scheme. However, a significant streaming bitrate saving from 30% to 40% was achieved. This enables greater flexibility of streaming VR content in high fidelity over various access networks. In addition, the proposed approach considerably reduces the computational burden of decoding. This leads to battery power saving in end-user devices. The simulation results demonstrated the approach practical to be deployed in the real-world applications in the future. As the next step in our future work, we plan to enable the proposed approach for stereoscopic panoramic video contents. Additionally, we plan to assess and validate the perceived user experience of the proposed approach.

Table 1. Compression performance of MCTS (BD-Rate (%))

Sequences	Resolution (WxH)	18-grid tiling	12-grid tiling	8-grid tiling
MyShelter-sta.	2048x1024	5.42	4.16	3.16
MyShelter-mov.	2048x1024	12.08	7.14	6.02
Daisy	3072x1536	4.20	2.78	3.35
VRC-concert	3072x1536	10.42	5.95	3.97
Kremlin	4096x2048	1.27	0.87	0.59
Lisboa	4096x2048	8.02	5.11	4.91
Moscow	4096x2048	1.59	1.14	1.16
Sheriff	4096x2048	3.53	2.42	2.29
Average loss		5.82	3.70	3.18

Table 2. Compression performance of pixel-domain cropping tile sets technique (BD-Rate (%))

	18-grid tiling	12-grid tiling	8-grid tiling
Average loss	5.73	3.73	3.18

Table 3. Streaming bitrate performance of tile-based streaming technique using MCTS (BD-Rate (%)), compared with transmitting the entire captured FOV

Sequences	18-grid tiling	12-grid tiling	8-grid tiling
MyShelter-sta.	-34.60	-31.99	-27.57
MyShelter-mov.	-32.10	-30.44	-26.47
Daisy	-41.90	-34.64	-27.74
VRC-concert	-41.85	-34.23	-29.56
Kremlin	-42.66	-33.87	-30.28
Lisboa	-44.96	-34.66	-32.43
Moscow	-44.14	-34.43	-31.69
Sheriff	-42.90	-33.29	-30.91
Average gain	-40.64	-33.44	-29.58

Table 4. Streaming bitrate performance of pixel-domain cropping tile sets technique (BD-Rate (%)), compared with transmitting the entire captured FOV

	18-grid tiling	12-grid tiling	8-grid tiling
Average gain	-40.49	-33.88	-31.89

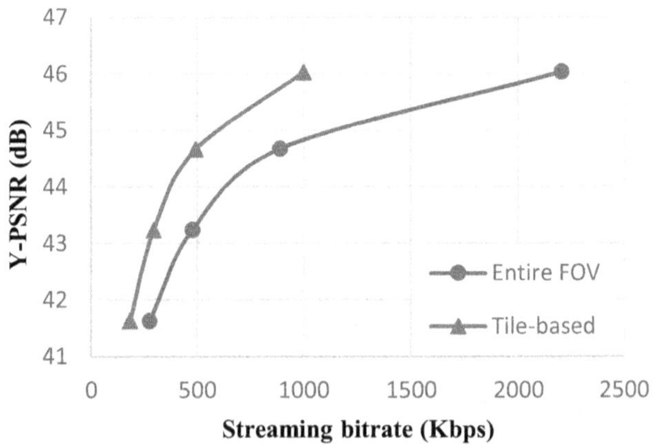

Figure 3. RD-curve, tile-based vs. entire FOV streaming, for Daisy sequence

6. REFERENCES

[1] Bjøntegard, G. 2001. Calculation of average psnr differences between rd-curves, document VCEG-M33. Austin.

[2] Feldmann, C., Bulla, C., and Cellarius, B. 2013. Efficient stream-reassembling for video conferencing applications using tiles in HEVC. In *MMEDIA 2013, The Fifth International Conferences on Advances in Multimedia*, Venice, Italy.

[3] Hannuksela, M. M., Wang, Y.-K., and Gabbouj, M. 2004. Isolated regions in video coding. *IEEE Trans. on Multimedia,* vol. 6, p. 259–267.

[4] Mason, W. 2016. VR HMD Roundup: Technical Specs. Accessed April 20 from http://uploadvr.com/vr-hmd-specs/.

[5] Misra, K. M., Segall, C. A., Horowitz, M., Xu, S., Fuldseth, A., and Zhou, M. 2013. An overview of tiles. *IEEE Journal of Selected Topics in Sig-nal Processing,* (Dec. 2013), vol. 7 , no. 6, pp. 969-977.

[6] Rosewarne , C., Bross, B., Naccari, M., Sharman, K., and Sullivan, G. 2015. High Efficiency Video Coding (HEVC) test model 16 (HM 16), Document JCTVC-U1002. Warsaw, (Jun. 2015).

[7] Sanchez, Y., Globisch, R., Schierl, T., and Wiegand, T. 2014. Low complexity cloud-video-mixing using HEVC. In *IEEE CCNC - Multimedia Networking, Services and Applications*. Las Vegas, NV, USA.

[8] Sánchez, Y., Skupin, R., and Schierl, T. 2015. Compressed domain video processing for tile based panoramic streaming using HEVC. In *IEEE International Conference onImage Processing (ICIP)*, Quebec City, QC.

[9] Schwarz, H., Schierl, T., and Marpe, D. 2014. Block structures and parallelism features in HEVC. In *High Efficiency Video Coding (HEVC): Algorithms and Architectures*, Springer, pp. 49-90.

[10] High Efficiency Video Coding (HEVC) reference software HM. 2016. Fraunhofer Institute for Telecommunications, Heinrich Hertz Institute. DOI= https://hevc.hhi.fraunhofer.de/.

MatchDR: Image Correspondence by Leveraging Distance Ratio Constraint

Rui Wang, Dong Liang, Wei Zhang*, Xiaochun Cao
State Key Laboratory of Information Security, Institute of Information Engineering, Chinese Academy of Sciences, Beijing 100093, China
wangrui@iie.ac.cn, dongliang.ucas@gmail.com, wzhang.cu@gmail.com, caoxiaochun@iie.ac.cn

ABSTRACT

Image correspondence is to establish the connections between coherent images, which can be quite challenging due to the visual and geometric deformations. This paper proposes a robust image correspondence technique from the perspective of spatial regularity. Specifically, the visual deformation is addressed by introducing the spatial information by enforcing the distance ratio constrain. At the same time, the geometric deformation is tolerated by adopting a smoothness term. Subsequently, image correspondence is formulated as permutation problem, for which, we propose a Gradient Guided Simulated Annealing method for robust optimization. Furthermore, our method is much more memory efficient, where the storage complexity is reduced from $O(n^4)$ to $O(n^2)$. The experiments on several datasets indicate that our proposed formulation and optimization significantly improve the baselines for both visually-similar and semantically-similar images, where both visual and geometric deformations are present.

Keywords

Image Correspondence; Spatial Regularity; Distance Ratios; Discrete Optimization

1. INTRODUCTION

Image correspondence is to establish the connections between similar points across different images. Due to its wide applications in many other high-level visual problems, image correspondence has been extensively studied in the past decade as rigid scene matching, image registration / alignment, optical / SIFT flow, and dense correspondences. Traditional correspondence problems mainly focus on images that are spatially overlap or temporally adjacent, where images are closely related by similar visual appearances, e.g., the stereo correspondence problem.

Image correspondence is challenging as pictures taken by different persons for different purposes may look differently, the image pairs can be semantically similar images, images with blur / quality changes, images with occlusions, images taken from different views of the same 3D object, to name a few. For example, two cars with different models can be visually dissimilar, and thus difficult to relate. However, matching images with diverse appearances is a critical technique for various applications.

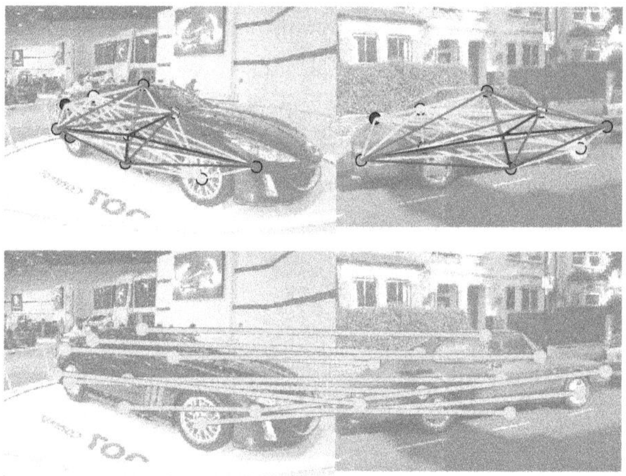

Figure 1: The distance ratio gives clues for the spatial regularity in image correspondence. The top image pair plots the distances between all landmark points. The lines with the same color indicate corresponding edges. Note that distances are more stable than angles for complex cases such as semantically similar cars. The bottom pair shows the result by our method MatchDR by enforcing the distance ratio constraint.

The challenges of this problem can be summarized into two types of deformations. The first one is the visual deformation. The image pairs could exhibit diverse visual appearances in different background, colors or models, as shown in Fig 1. Matching based on visual similarities can be very difficult. The second one comes from the geometric deformation. The same object could show different sizes, shapes and poses, where the Planar Homography does not hold anymore. For example, cars viewed from different viewpoints will also deform in shape.

The problem is traditionally formulated as a quadratic assignment problem (QAP), which is known to be NP-hard, and it incorporate both *node-to-node* and *edge-to-edge* similarity as structural information in a bulky way. The memory cost is huge for coping with large images. This paper proposes a new formulation which requires much less memory, and a geometric based method addressing the aforementioned challenges. We define the problem using the Distance Ratio (DR) matrix. And the proposed method is named "Match via Distance Ratio" (MatchDR). Based on the

*Corresponding author

MM '16, October 15-19, 2016, Amsterdam, Netherlands
© 2016 ACM. ISBN 978-1-4503-3603-1/16/10...$15.00
DOI: http://dx.doi.org/10.1145/2964284.2967293

observation that the locations of the corresponding points on pairwise images should be structurally similar, we use the constant that the distance ratios between correspondences should be a constant. Specifically, the objective is to find the permutation matrix to minimize the variance of the distance ratios. Note that we discard the absolute locations and only use the relative distances between points, This kind of information is actually strong enough to recover the original locations of points as stated in [25].

On one hand, we introduce the spatial regularity to the correspondence problem by enforcing the DR matrix, which improves the quality of visual correspondence where elements are with small variance. On the other hand, by introducing a smoothness term, the geometric deformation is modeled by tolerating local spatial jitters. Compared to other methods using spatial information, our method is much more memory efficient, due to the DR matrix encoding all the weight information is of $n \times n$, rather than $n^2 \times n^2$, where n is the number of landmarks on each image.

Our contributions can be summarized as follows: First, we propose an effective geometric method by enforcing consistent distance rations. The problem can be modeled as a permutation problem. Second, we achieve the state-of-the-art performance on both visually similar and semantically similar datasets.Third, we proposed a Gradient Guided Simulation Annealing method for robust optimization of the proposed method. The discovery of new solutions is directed by the gradient, making the optimization more accurate and effective.

2. RELATED WORKS

Image correspondence is one of the fundamental problems in computer vision and multimedia, which has been widely studied through the past decades [8]. According to the information exacted from the images, previous literatures can be divided into visual based and geometric based methods.

2.1 Visual-based methods

Visual-based correspondence is a reliable method for image correspondence and has already been used in many applications. A tremendous number of research efforts have been conducted in various forms. In computer vision, early correspondence method is often called the stereo correspondences [20, 23]. There are two different ways dealing with the problem in the literature. Many algorithms on image correspondence are based on comparing the differences of the appearance of the landmark points, leading to area-based matching (ABM) [2, 16] or feature-based matching (FBM) [7, 9, 12], which are classical and well-developed.

Many works have been done since then and there are quite a lot new techniques for detecting landmarks and generating local features [17]. For example, the invention of SIFT for detecting and describing the local features of the landmarks in the images. Visual-based methods of both pairwise matching [19,24] and multimatching [14, 26] are based on the feature detection. Recently, the Convolutional Neural Network is used to detect and describe features and gets a better result. Furthermore, [3] trains the LDA classifier for every pixel to exclude the false matches. [27] trains a convolutional neural network to predict how well two image patches match. [30] introduces the universe to simplify the calculation.

2.2 Geometric-based methods

Though visual based methods make up a large proportion in the literature, the geometric-based methods are widely found in various computer vision problems, e.g., image retrieval [10, 28, 29]. In the literature, the spatial information is used as a kind of feature the same as visual feature ponderously [1]. Spatial rigidity is usually preferred, i.e., selecting the correct corresponding pair of edges by QAP, which is well known as a graph matching problem. While QAP is NP-hard, many efficient algorithms have been proposed to solve it approximately. The earliest approach for QAP is the spectral methods [11]. [6] introduces a random walk view on the problem, and the result is relatively noise-robust. Another weakness for QAP is that the dimension of the affinity matrix equals the number of the possible point pairs. Usually, the landmark of an image is several hundreds, making the affinity matrix very large.

3. METHODOLOGY

3.1 Problem formulation

The image correspondence problem is defined on two related images. For each image $k \in \{1, 2\}$, we define an undirected graph as $\mathcal{G}^k = (\mathcal{V}^k, \mathcal{E}^k, \mathcal{W}^k)$, where $\mathcal{V}^k, \mathcal{E}^k, \mathcal{W}^k$ denote the nodes, edge, and attributes of edge respectively.

The pairwise match problem between a graph pair $\mathcal{G}^1$ and $\mathcal{G}^2$ is to find a one-to-one correspondence τ between $\mathcal{V}^1$ and $\mathcal{V}^2$ which minimizes some costs between them. p_k is the number of nodes in the graph $\mathcal{G}^k$. We represent the correspondence τ by a partial permutation matrix $\mathbf{X} \in \{0, 1\}^{p_1 \times p_2}$. "One-to-one" constraint is assumed, that is, one node in graph $\mathcal{G}^1$ can match at most one node in graph $\mathcal{G}^2$ and vice versa. The assumption can be formulated as the doubly stochastic constraints:

$$0 \le \mathbf{X1} \le 1, \;\; 0 \le \mathbf{X}^\top \mathbf{1} \le 1. \tag{1}$$

3.2 Approach overview and algorithm details

The geometric information of images can be encoded as a graph. For each image k, we extract p_k features, and let $\mathcal{V}^k$ denote the set of feature points. The coordinate of the centre point of the ith$(i \le p_k)$ feature in image k is (x_i^k, y_i^k). $\mathcal{E}^k$ denotes each pair of nodes. As we want to extract the distance information in every images, $\mathcal{W}^k(v_i^k, v_j^k)$ is regarded as the Euclidian distance on image k between two nodes i and j, i.e. $\mathcal{W}^k(v_i^k, v_j^k) = \sqrt{(x_i^k - x_j^k)^2 + (y_i^k - y_j^k)^2}$.

The adjacency matrix $D_k \in \mathbb{R}^{p_k \times p_k}$ encodes the geometric information of graph $\mathcal{G}^k$,

$$\mathbf{D}_k = [d_{i,j}^k] = \begin{cases} d_{i,j}^k = \mathcal{W}^k(\mathcal{V}_i^k, \mathcal{V}_j^k) & i \ne j; \\ d_{i,j}^k = \frac{1}{p_k} \sum\limits_{l=1, l \ne i}^{p_k} \mathcal{W}^k(\mathcal{V}_i^k, \mathcal{V}_l^k) & i = j. \end{cases} \tag{2}$$

To avoid zeros in $\mathbf{D}_k$, we replace the zeros in the original affinity matrix with the mean distance.

For image correspondence, the main problem is to find the correct correspondence between two graphs $\mathcal{G}^k$. As shown in Fig. 1, for the graphs with the same spatial structures, the ratio of distances should be roughly consistent, i.e.

$$\frac{d_{1,2}^1}{d_{1,2}^2} \approx \frac{d_{1,3}^1}{d_{1,3}^2} \approx \cdots \approx \frac{d_{i,j}^1}{d_{i,j}^2} \approx \cdots \approx \frac{d_{p_1,p_1}^1}{d_{p_2,p_2}^2} \approx \mathrm{C}. \tag{3}$$

To represent the ratios efficiently, we fill the ratios in a matrix:

$$\mathbf{Q} = \mathbf{X}^\top \mathbf{D}_1 \mathbf{X} \circ \mathbf{D}_2^{\circ -1}, \tag{4}$$

where $\circ$ denotes the Hadamard product. The matrix $\mathbf{Q}$ is called the distance ratio matrix.

Ideally, the elements in $\mathbf{Q}$ should be the same for a pair of graphs. So it is clear that the variance of all elements in $\mathbf{Q}$ should be minimized:

$$J_1(\mathbf{X}) = \mathrm{tr}((\mathbf{Q} - E(\mathbf{Q}))^\top (\mathbf{Q} - E(\mathbf{Q}))) \tag{5}$$

To compute the variance, $E(\mathbf{Q})$ is a matrix with the mean of all elements in $\mathbf{Q}$. Particularly, all the elements in $E(\mathbf{Q})$ equal to $\frac{\langle \mathbf{1},\mathbf{Q}\rangle}{\langle \mathbf{1},\mathbf{X}\rangle^2}$, where $\langle \cdot, \cdot \rangle$ denotes inner product of matrices.

Moreover, the estimated $\mathbf{X}$ should be sparse since at most one value in each row of $\mathbf{X}$ can be nonzero. To introduce sparsity, we minimize the summation of values in $\mathbf{X}$. The problem can be formulated as:

$$\begin{aligned} \min_{\mathbf{X}} J(\mathbf{X}) &= J_1(\mathbf{X}) + J_2(\mathbf{X}) \\ s.t. \mathbf{X} &\in \mathcal{C} \end{aligned} \tag{6}$$

where $J_2(\mathbf{X}) = \alpha\langle \mathbf{1}, \mathbf{X}\rangle$, α is the trade-off weight for sparsity, $\mathcal{C}$ denotes the set of matrices satisfying the constraints in Eqn. (1).

The affinity matrix defined here is much smaller comparing with the the formulation of QAP. The storage complexity of the affinity matrix of the proposed formula is reduced from $O(n^4)$ to $O(n^2)$.

3.3 Optimization

3.3.1 Gradient Guided Simulated Annealing (GGSA)

The solution space of the problem is discrete (see Eqn. (1)) and the problem is NP-hard. Usually, such problem is relaxed to real space by treating $\mathbf{X}$ as a real matrix. But the methods in real space e.g. Gradient Descent is slow to converge, and always stucks to inferior local minimum solution in our case. In this paper, we propose a Gradient Guided Simulated Annealing algorithm to find solutions in large discrete space. Basically, we follow the framework of the Simulated Annealing algorithm [4] and improve neighbor generation using the gradient information.

To optimize Eqn. (6), we first compute the gradient as follow:

$$\begin{aligned} \frac{dJ}{d\mathbf{X}} &= \frac{4}{\langle \mathbf{1},\mathbf{X}\rangle^2}(\mathbf{D}_1\mathbf{X})(\mathbf{X}^\top\mathbf{D}_1\mathbf{X}) \circ \mathbf{D}_2^{\circ -2} \\ &+ 4\frac{\langle \mathbf{1},\mathbf{Q}\rangle}{\langle \mathbf{1},\mathbf{X}\rangle^6}(p^2 - 2\langle \mathbf{1},\mathbf{X}\rangle^2)\mathbf{D}_1\mathbf{X} \circ \mathbf{D}_2^{\circ -1} \\ &+ 2\frac{\langle \mathbf{1},\mathbf{Q}\rangle^2}{\langle \mathbf{1},\mathbf{X}\rangle^7}(4\langle \mathbf{1},\mathbf{X}\rangle^2 - 3p^2)\mathbf{X} - 2\frac{\langle \mathbf{1},\mathbf{Q}^{\circ 2}\rangle}{\langle \mathbf{1},\mathbf{X}\rangle^3}\mathbf{X} + \alpha\mathbf{X} \end{aligned} \tag{7}$$

Although the problem can not be trivially optimized with gradient descent, $\frac{dJ}{d\mathbf{X}}$ gives clues on generating neighbors:

- According to the gradient, the minimum element of the gradient matrix infers that the corresponding element of $\mathbf{X}$ is most likely to be 1. To keep $\mathbf{X}$ a valid permutation matrix, a 0 changes to 1 at the same time. This new permutation is included in the neighborhood set $\mathcal{X}$.

- Meanwhile, the maximum element of the gradient matrix infers $1 \rightarrow 0$ in the expected solution $\mathbf{X}$. While the corresponding element change $0 \rightarrow 1$ has $\max(p_1, p_2)$ possible choices. We collect them in the neighborhood set $\mathcal{X}$.

The $\mathbf{X} \in \mathcal{X}$ minimizing the Eqn. (6) is an approach to get the neighbor of the simulated annealing algorithm.

Another approach for the neighbor is random permutation. As the non-convexity of the problem, the gradient does not always point to the right direction. To avoid being caught in a local minimum, we randomly generate a permutation matrix as the neighbor with a probability ρ. Upon our experimental observation, we set $\rho = 0.2$ in the experiment. Because, in most conditions, the gradient guided neighbor is trustable. In our paper, the Gradient Guided neighbor finding method is denoted $GGN(\mathbf{D}_1, \mathbf{D}_2, \mathbf{X})$.

3.3.2 Initialization

Many algorithms have been proposed based on visual matching or spatial matching. It is hard to match two images with a random initialization due to several reasons. First, the optimization of Eqn. (6) is discrete and NP-hard. The solution-space is essentially $O(n!)$ where n is the number of nodes in the graph. Second, even the relaxed version (discrete to continuous space) of Eqn.(6) is non-convex, such that the initialization impacts the result prominently. To solve the problem, it is necessary to make full use of both visual and spatial information jointly. Therefore in practice, we mostly initialize our algorithm with the result of another algorithm to ease the optimization difficulty. In the experiments, we observe significant improvements over a range of state-of-the-arts based on this strategy.

3.3.3 Smoothness term

As the existence of very short edges, the error can be magnified even with very small geometric deformation, which makes the optimization difficult. In such case, the gradient becomes unstable due to the division by a small (e.g., close to zero) value in Eqn. (4). The cost of $J(\mathbf{X})$ will change a lot when the denominator slightly changes. To avoid these errors, we add a smoothness term λ for both sides of the fraction in the distance ratio matrix $\mathbf{Q}$. That equals to adding λ to each element of the affinity matrices $\mathbf{D}_1$ and $\mathbf{D}_2$. Moreover, the smoothness term also tolerates some geometric jitters for the correspondences.

Above all, the proposed algorithm can be written as Algorithm. 1, where $P(E(\mathbf{X}), E(\mathbf{X}^{new}), t) = \exp((J(\mathbf{X}) - J(\mathbf{X}^{new}))/t)$.

Algorithm 1 GGSA: Gradient Guided Simulated Annealing

```
Input: D1, D2, X^0: initialization, T : maximum iterations.
Output: Solution X
X ← X^0;
for t = T···0 do
    //generate a neighbor based on the gradient in Eqn. (7).
    X^new ← GGN(D1, D2, X);
    if P(E(X), E(X^new), t) ≥ rand(0, 1) then
        X ← X^new; //update solution
        if converge then
            break;
        end if
    end if
end for
```

4. EXPERIMENTAL EVALUATION

4.1 Datasets and Evaluation Metric

In the real-data experiment we apply our method on image correspondence problems using local feature detectors. The dataset used is listed as bellow.

The Building dataset [18] contains images taken from the the frame of a sequence, where the view of a building gradually changes. The image pairs are visually similar for temporally adjacent frames. The landmark are points marked by [15][1].

Willow Object class dataset [5] It includes images of five object classes. The appearance of images varies significantly, since the instances are only loosely related to the same semantic object, e.g., different models of car. We use SIFT [13] to extract interesting points and represent the node and edge attributes.

[1]http://pages.cs.wisc.edu/~pachauri/perm-sync/

Table 1: Performance Comparison with Other Methods in Error-Rates(%)

		K-M [15]	MatchALS [30]	SM [11]	RRWM [6]	SMCM [22]	SMCP [21]
The Building	w/o, MatchDR	81.44	79.72	85.47	78.83	86.02	76.36
	MatchDR	**30.49**	74.95	47.52	39.30	47.33	35.78
Willow Object	w/o, MatchDR	88.75	91.63	80.17	68.02	81.08	67.55
	MatchDR	47.70	41.21	39.48	35.01	45.26	**32.37**

(a) Kuhn-Munkres(0.89) (b) Kuhn-Munkres(0.95)
(c) MatchALS(0.89) (d) MatchALS(0.89)
(e) SM(0.89) (f) SM(0.95)
(g) RRWM(0.75) (h) RRWM(0.89)
(i) SMCM(0.67) (j) SMCM(0.95)
(k) SMCP(0.75) (l) SMCP(0.89)
(m) rnd-init MatchDR(0.0) (n) rnd-init MatchDR(0.0)

Figure 2: Example results motocycle and car in the Willow. Our approach is randomly initialized. The numbers in parentheses are the corresponding Error-Rates(%).

We adopt the evaluation metric used in [30]. Given a solution $\mathbf{X}^{alg}$ and the ground-truth $\mathbf{X}^{gt}$: We measure the error rate by intersection over union:

$$\text{Error-Rate} = 1 - \frac{|\tau(\mathbf{X}^{alg}) \cap \tau(\mathbf{X}^{gt})|}{|\tau(\mathbf{X}^{alg}) \cup \tau(\mathbf{X}^{gt})|}, \quad (8)$$

where τ denotes the correspondence defined by the permutation matrix $\mathbf{X}^{alg}$ or $\mathbf{X}^{gt}$, and $|\cdot|$ is the cardinality of the set.

4.2 Performance Comparison

The methods compared are released, and the codes used in the comparison are from the corresponding websites. Table. 1 shows the error-rates of the image correspondence in both datasets, with both visual based methods (MatchALS [30][2], Kuhn-Munkres algorithm [15][1]) and geometric based methods (SM [11][3], RRWM [6][4], SMCM [22][5], SMCP [21])[6] in the first row, while the error-rates of our method (MatchDR) based on the corresponding initialization are shown in the second row.

The Building dataset is designed for homographic image correspondence. The local feature of images provides a good initialization, and Kuhn-Munkres with MatchDR achieves the best performance. Though their error rate seems high, their results implicit more visual correspondence information. The geometric-based methods cannot leverage the visual information and fail in most run.

The Willow Object class dataset is mainly for semantic correspondence, where visual-based correspondence is almost invalid. In table. 1, the geometric based methods offer better initialization, and our method contributes an obvious improvement for them. As shown in the example correspondence in Fig. 2, random initialization is qualified for the proposed method.

5. CONCLUSIONS

In this paper, we have introduced a novel technique addressing the visual and geometric deformation problems in image correspondence, by leveraging the consistent distance ratio constraint. For the visual deformation, we add the spatial regularity into the correspondence and achieved significant improvement. For the geometric deformation, a smooth term is introduced to adapt the spatial perturbation. Our experiments on several datasets, show the effectiveness of the proposed method. However, the permutation problem is essentially difficult to optimize, and sensitive to initialization. Our future direction is to find a more robust optimization technique and more reliable initialization.

6. ACKNOWLEDGMENTS

This work was supported by National Key Research and Development Plan(No. 2016YFB0800603), National Natural Science Foundation of China (No. 61422213), "Strategic Priority Research Program" of the Chinese Academy of Sciences (XDA06010701), and National Program for Support of Top-notch Young Professionals.

7. REFERENCES

[1] A. C. Berg, T. L. Berg, and J. Malik. Shape matching and object recognition using low distortion correspondences. In

[2] https://fling.seas.upenn.edu/~xiaowz/dynamic/wordpress/my-uploads/codes/MatchALS.zip

[3] The code of this work can be found in the project of RRWM[4]

[4] http://cv.snu.ac.kr/research/~RRWM/

[5] http://cv.snu.ac.kr/research/~SMCM/

[6] http://cv.snu.ac.kr/research/~SMCP/

2005 IEEE Computer Society Conference on Computer Vision and Pattern Recognition (CVPR 2005), 20-26 June 2005, San Diego, CA, USA, pages 26–33, 2005.

[2] R. Berthilsson. Affine correlation. In *Pattern Recognition, 1998. Proceedings. Fourteenth International Conference on*, volume 2, pages 1458–1460 vol.2, Aug 1998.

[3] H. Bristow, J. Valmadre, and S. Lucey. Dense semantic correspondence where every pixel is a classifier. In *2015 IEEE International Conference on Computer Vision, ICCV 2015, Santiago, Chile, December 7-13, 2015*, pages 4024–4031, 2015.

[4] V. Černý. Thermodynamical approach to the traveling salesman problem: An efficient simulation algorithm. *Journal of Optimization Theory and Applications*, 45(1):41–51.

[5] M. Cho, K. Alahari, and J. Ponce. Learning graphs to match. In *Proceedings of the IEEE Interational Conference on Computer Vision*, 2013.

[6] M. Cho, J. Lee, and K. M. Lee. Reweighted random walks for graph matching. In *Computer Vision - ECCV 2010 - 11th European Conference on Computer Vision, Heraklion, Crete, Greece, September 5-11, 2010, Proceedings, Part V*, pages 492–505, 2010.

[7] W. Eric and L. Grimson. Computational experiments with a feature based stereo algorithm. *IEEE Trans. Pattern Anal. Mach. Intell.*, 7(1):17–34, 1985.

[8] P. Foggia, G. Percannella, and M. Vento. Graph matching and learning in pattern recognition in the last 10 years. *IJPRAI*, 28(1), 2014.

[9] W. Förstner. A feature based correspondence algorithm for image matching. *International Archives of Photogrammetry and Remote Sensing*, 26(3):150–166, 1986.

[10] H. Jegou, M. Douze, and C. Schmid. Hamming embedding and weak geometric consistency for large scale image search. In *Computer Vision - ECCV 2008, 10th European Conference on Computer Vision, Marseille, France, October 12-18, 2008, Proceedings, Part I*, pages 304–317, 2008.

[11] M. Leordeanu and M. Hebert. A spectral technique for correspondence problems using pairwise constraints. In *10th IEEE International Conference on Computer Vision (ICCV 2005), 17-20 October 2005, Beijing, China*, pages 1482–1489, 2005.

[12] C. Liu and H. Wechsler. Gabor feature based classification using the enhanced fisher linear discriminant model for face recognition. *IEEE Trans. Image Processing*, 11(4):467–476, 2002.

[13] D. G. Lowe. Object recognition from local scale-invariant features. In *ICCV*, pages 1150–1157, 1999.

[14] A. Nguyen, M. Ben-Chen, K. Welnicka, Y. Ye, and L. J. Guibas. An optimization approach to improving collections of shape maps. *Comput. Graph. Forum*, 30(5):1481–1491, 2011.

[15] D. Pachauri, R. Kondor, and V. Singh. Solving the multi-way matching problem by permutation synchronization. In C. J. C. Burges, L. Bottou, M. Welling, Z. Ghahramani, and K. Q. Weinberger, editors, *Advances in Neural Information Processing Systems 26*, pages 1860–1868. Curran Associates, Inc., 2013.

[16] W. K. Pratt. *Digital Image Processing (2Nd Ed.)*. John Wiley & Sons, Inc., New York, NY, USA, 1991.

[17] A. S. Razavian, H. Azizpour, J. Sullivan, and S. Carlsson. CNN features off-the-shelf: An astounding baseline for recognition. In *IEEE Conference on Computer Vision and Pattern Recognition, CVPR Workshops 2014, Columbus, OH, USA, June 23-28, 2014*, pages 512–519, 2014.

[18] R. Roberts, S. N. Sinha, R. Szeliski, and D. Steedly. Structure from motion for scenes with large duplicate structures. In *The 24th IEEE Conference on Computer Vision and Pattern Recognition, CVPR 2011, Colorado Springs, CO, USA, 20-25 June 2011*, pages 3137–3144, 2011.

[19] H. Sarnel and Y. Senol. Accurate and robust image registration based on radial basis neural networks. *Neural Computing and Applications*, 20(8):1255–1262, 2011.

[20] N. Snavely, S. M. Seitz, and R. Szeliski. Modeling the world from internet photo collections. *Int. J. Comput. Vision*, 80(2):189–210, Nov. 2008.

[21] Y. Suh, K. Adamczewski, and K. M. Lee. Subgraph matching using compactness prior for robust feature correspondence. In *Conference on Computer Vision and Pattern Recognition*, 2015.

[22] Y. Suh, M. Cho, and K. M. Lee. Graph matching via sequential monte carlo. In *Computer Vision - ECCV 2012 - 12th European Conference on Computer Vision, Florence, Italy, October 7-13, 2012, Proceedings, Part III*, pages 624–637, 2012.

[23] R. Szeliski. Computer vision: Algorithms and applications, 2010.

[24] A. Taimori and A. Behrad. A new deformable mesh model for face tracking using edge based features and novel sets of energy functions. *Multimedia Tools Appl.*, 74(23):10735–10759, Dec. 2015.

[25] Y. Terada and U. V. Luxburg. Local ordinal embedding. In *Proceedings of the 31st International Conference on Machine Learning (ICML-14)*, pages 847–855, 2014.

[26] C. Zach, M. Klopschitz, and M. Pollefeys. Disambiguating visual relations using loop constraints. In *The Twenty-Third IEEE Conference on Computer Vision and Pattern Recognition, CVPR 2010, San Francisco, CA, USA, 13-18 June 2010*, pages 1426–1433, 2010.

[27] J. Zbontar and Y. LeCun. Computing the stereo matching cost with a convolutional neural network. In *IEEE Conference on Computer Vision and Pattern Recognition, CVPR 2015, Boston, MA, USA, June 7-12, 2015*, pages 1592–1599, 2015.

[28] W. Zhang and C. Ngo. Topological spatial verification for instance search. *IEEE Trans. Multimedia*, 17(8):1236–1247, 2015.

[29] W. Zhang, L. Pang, and C. Ngo. Snap-and-ask: answering multimodal question by naming visual instance. In *Proceedings of the 20th ACM Multimedia Conference, MM '12, Nara, Japan, October 29 - November 02, 2012*, pages 609–618, 2012.

[30] X. Zhou, M. Zhu, and K. Daniilidis. Multi-image matching via fast alternating minimization. In *2015 IEEE International Conference on Computer Vision, ICCV 2015, Santiago, Chile, December 7-13, 2015*, pages 4032–4040, 2015.

A Novel Shadow-Free Feature Extractor for Real-Time Road Detection*

Zhenqiang Ying, Ge Li†, Xianghao Zang, Ronggang Wang, and Wenmin Wang
School of Electronic and Computer Engineering
Shenzhen Graduate School, Peking University, China
zqying@pku.edu.cn,gli@pkusz.edu.cn,zangxh@pku.edu.cn,{rgwang,wangwm}@pkusz.edu.cn

ABSTRACT

Road detection is one of the most important research areas in driver assistance and automated driving field. However, the performance of existing methods is still unsatisfactory, especially in severe shadow conditions. To overcome those difficulties, first we propose a novel shadow-free feature extractor based on the color distribution of road surface pixels. Then we present a road detection framework based on the extractor, whose performance is more accurate and robust than that of existing extractors. Also, the proposed framework has much low-complexity, which is suitable for usage in practical systems.

Keywords

road detection; shadow removal; feature extraction; driver assistance system

1. INTRODUCTION

Road detection constitutes a basis for many intelligent vehicle applications such as lane departure warning and lane keeping assistance. The main task of road detection is to detect the road area from an image captured by a camera mounted behind a car windshield. Although many efforts have been devoted using feature-based methods in this area, most detection methods suffer from the interference of shadow [3]. To overcome those difficulties, some researchers proposed illumination-robust feature extractors [17, 27] while others introduced shadow-free feature extractors [2, 16]. Although the shadow-free feature extractors can help improve the performance of illumination-sensitive road detection, they still cannot perform well in severe shadow conditions. Meanwhile, shadow removal methods, which may perform better, are too time-consuming for the real-time road detection task. In this paper, we propose a low-complexity shadow-free feature extractor with better performance, especially in severe shadow conditions (cf. Fig.1). Besides, we set up a general framework for road detection based on the proposed extractor. Experiments show that road surfaces can be detected accurately and efficiently through our extractor.

Figure 1: Comparison of various feature extractors. illumination-sensitive: Y. Illumination-robust: H, S and S'. Shadow-free: $\mathcal{I}'_\theta$, $\mathcal{I}'_\alpha$ and $\mathcal{I}'_b(ours)$.

2. RELATED WORK

2.1 Existing Road Detection Methods

Existing road detection techniques can be divided into two broad categories: feature-based [4, 11, 14, 18, 19, 20, 21, 23, 24, 25] and model-based methods [12, 13, 15, 28]. Feature-based methods utilize local visual features of interest, such as gradient, color [11, 18, 20, 22], brightness [21, 24], texture [14], orientation [4] and their combinations [19, 23, 25], which are relatively insensitive to road shapes but are sensitive to illumination effects. Especially, those methods are vulnerable to the interference of severe shadows, which may lead to false alarms in edge detection, texture extraction, color segmentation [3], etc. On the contrary, model-based methods apply global road models to match low-level features, which are more robust against illumination effects but sensitive to road shapes. The reason lies in that the number of predefined models is limited compared to practical scenarios. For example, the geometrical model proposed in [28] contains only thirteen curvatures, which may not match all kinds of road shapes such as *S-curve*. Besides, those methods may totally fail under severe shadow scenarios because of model mismatch. As a conclusion, both existing feature-based and model-based road detection methods suffer from severe shadows, thus a more robust method is critical to real applications.

*This project was supported by Science and Technology Planning Project of Guangdong Province, China (No. 2014B090910001), Shenzhen Peacock Plan (20130408-183003656), China 863 project of 2015AA015905 and Shenzhen Research Project (JCYJ20150331100658943).

†Corresponding author.

MM '16, October 15-19, 2016, Amsterdam, Netherlands

 ISBN 978-1-4503-3603-1/16/10. . . $15.00
DOI: http://dx.doi.org/10.1145/2964284.2967294

2.2 Feature Extractors in Severe Shadow Cases

To fight for the severe shadow interferences, feature extractors are employed in the pre-processing stage to obtain a grayscale feature image, in which illumination effects are reduced. Two kinds of feature extractors are studied: illumination-robust and shadow-free extractors.

Illumination-robust feature extractors. In RGB space, the brightness and color information are mixed together for three components, thus they are vulnerable to the impact of shadow. To solve this problem, color space conversion is often employed [11, 18, 20] to extract the brightness information into a separate component, such as I of HSI, L of Lab and Y of YUV. The remaining two components are suitable for road detection since they only contain color information which is relatively illumination-insensitive. Take HSI as an example, H component can be employed to extract road features [20], and S component is suitable to extract roadside vegetation [26]. However, color components are unstable in severe shadow cases (cf. Fig.1). An illumination-robust feature called S' is presented in [27] to accommodate both the severe shadow cases and weak shadow cases.

Shadow-free feature extractors. Since shadows still exist in the extracted component via illumination-robust extractors, the road boundary may not be recovered well in some cases [27]. To completely remove the shadow interferences, some researchers try to find underlying features which are invariant to illumination effects. *Log-chromaticity space (LCS)* [7] is often employed to recover a shadow-free image. Under the condition that an image is captured by a narrow-band camera with approximately *Planckian illumination* and *Lambertian surfaces*, Finlayson *et al.*[7] show that the set of color surfaces of different chromaticities forms parallel straight lines in the LCS. The band-ratio chromaticity is defined as

$$\chi_j = \frac{\rho_q}{\rho_p}, \quad q \epsilon \{1,2,3\}, q \neq p, \quad j = 1, 2, \tag{1}$$

where ρ_1, ρ_2 and ρ_3 are matrices respectively representing the red(R), green(G) and blue(B) components of the raw image, p is the index of the normalizing components and index q points to the remaining two components. The shadow-free image $\mathcal{I}$ proposed in [7] is derived from the aforementioned linear relationship as

$$\mathcal{I} = exp(cos\theta \cdot log(\chi_1) + sin\theta \cdot log(\chi_2)), \tag{2}$$

where θ is a camera-dependent parameter.

Álvarez and Ĺopez [2] applied that method to their shadow-free extractor $\mathcal{I}'_\theta$ for road detection. As shown in Eq.3, G is used for normalization ($p = 2; q = 1,3$) and the outermost exponential operation is removed to improve the speed.

$$\mathcal{I}'_\theta = cos\theta \cdot log(R/G) + sin\theta \cdot log(B/G) \tag{3}$$

Maddern *et al.*[16] proposed another form of illumination invariant imaging and applied it to vision-based localization, mapping and classification for autonomous vehicles. Their extractor $\mathcal{I}'_\alpha$ is defined as

$$\mathcal{I}'_\alpha = (1-\alpha) \cdot log(R) + \alpha \cdot log(B) - log(G) + 0.5, \tag{4}$$

where α is a camera dependent parameter ($\alpha = \frac{sin\theta}{cos\theta + sin\theta}$) and 0.5 is an offset term.

As shown in Fig.1, shadow-free feature extractors perform better than illumination-robust extractors in weak shadow cases since the shadows are completely removed. However,

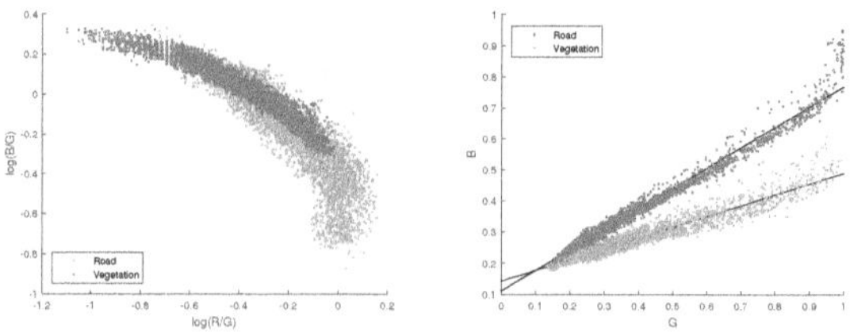

Figure 2: Road and vegetation pixels on $log\frac{R}{G}$-$log\frac{B}{G}$ (left) and G-B (right) plane.

their performance in severe shadow cases still needs to be improved. To find why existing shadow-free extractors [2, 16] fail in severe shadow cases, we choose a shadowy road image from ROMA dataset [21] and then map pixels of road and vegetation regions into LCS. According to their basic assumption, the set of color surfaces of different chromaticities will form parallel straight lines in LCS. However, the distribution is more like a quadratic function in severe shadow conditions, and the two classes are mixed together indistinguishably (cf. Fig.2 (left)).

3. OUR APPROACH

To obtain a new shadow-free feature extractor which is robust against severe shadows, a more proper relationship is required. Healey *et al.*[10] proved that the measured colors of homogeneous dielectric surfaces lie on a line passing through the origin of RGB space. To verify that, we map the road and vegetation pixels from aforementioned shadowy road image into RGB space. Since road and vegetation can be treated as homogeneous dielectric surfaces, their corresponding pixels should be arranged in line shapes. Our experimental results are in agreement with [10] except for an offset between the intersection and origin (cf. Fig.3).

To see the offset more clearly, we project the pixels onto the GB plane (cf. Fig.2 (right)), where the G and B components of the same material are distributed along a straight line with an offset shown as the intercept of B axis. That offset is ignored in [10]. We can use a linear function to accurately describe the relationships among road surface pixels as

$$G_{r,c} \approx k * B_{r,c} + b, \quad (r,c) \in road, \tag{5}$$

where r and c are the indexes of row and column indicating the location of a road pixel, k is the slope of the straight line and b is the intercept.

Define a matrix K as

$$K \triangleq \frac{G-b}{B}, \tag{6}$$

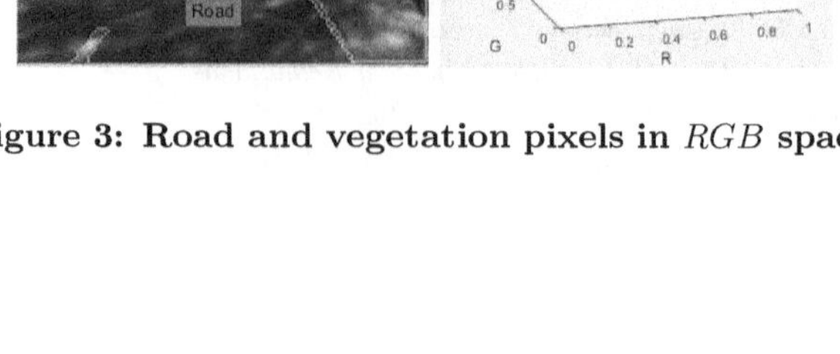

Figure 3: Road and vegetation pixels in RGB space.

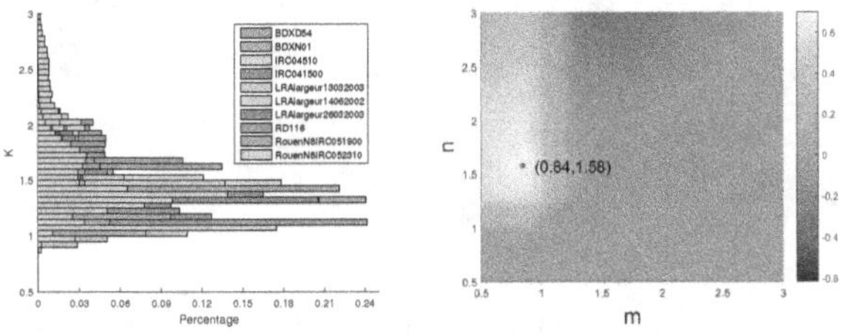

Figure 4: Histogram of K (left) and the optimal range (m^*, n^*) for ROMA dataset (right).

whose elements in the road area are approximately a constant (cf. Eq.7). The intercept b can be obtained by polynomial fitting among the road pixels on GB plane. Besides, experiments show that all images captured by the same camera can share one b, so b can be explained as an intrinsic parameter of each color camera like θ of $\mathcal{I}'_\theta$ (Eq.3) and α of $\mathcal{I}'_\alpha$ (Eq.4). Therefore, we only need to do an off-line calibration once for one camera.

$$\forall (r, c) \in road \rightarrow K_{r,c} = \frac{G_{r,c} - b}{B_{r,c}} \approx k \tag{7}$$

To design an efficient extractor, we need to analyze the distribution of K. For each sub-dataset of ROMA, we plot the histogram of K to each pixel in all images as shown in Fig.4 (left). Let K_{min} and K_{max} be the minimum and maximum of K. Unevenly distributed of K makes it inefficient to use the whole range $[K_{min}, K_{max}]$ to form the shadow-free component. Thus, we need to choose a dominant subrange (m, n) to make it more compact.

Let $\mathcal{H}$ be the overall histogram of ROMA dataset. We compute the optimal range $[m^*, n^*] \subset [K_{min}, K_{max}]$ for ROMA dataset via

$$(m^*, n^*) = \underset{(m,n)}{\operatorname{argmax}}\{g(m, n) - c(m, n)\}, \tag{8}$$

where $g(m, n)$ is defined as

$$g(m, n) \triangleq \sum_{i=m}^{n} \mathcal{H}(i) / \sum_{i=K_{min}}^{K_{max}} \mathcal{H}(i), \tag{9}$$

and $c(m, n)$ is defined as

$$c(m, n) \triangleq (m - n)/(K_{max} - K_{min}). \tag{10}$$

Figure 5: Shadowy images and the results of extractors. Complete results can be found on our website.

We find that the optimal range for ROMA dataset is $[m^*, n^*] = [0.84, 1.58]$, as shown in Fig.4 (right). To facilitate normalization (cf. Eq.11) and make our extractor more concise, $[m, n] = [1, 2]$ are used to approximate the $[m^*, n^*]$ and our extractor $\mathcal{I}'_b$ is derived (cf. Eq.12).

$$1 \leqslant K \leqslant 2 \Rightarrow 0 \leqslant 2 - K \leqslant 1 \tag{11}$$

$$\mathcal{I}'_b \triangleq 2 - K \tag{12}$$

To apply our extractor to road detection task, we present a general road detection framework based on feature extractors. The framework takes an RGB image as input and outputs a binary image where 1 denotes road pixel and 0 denotes non-road pixel. Our road detection framework is summarized as follows:

1. Region of interest (ROI) determination. Limit the following processing in ROI to avoid meaningless opera tions on irrelevant regions.
2. Feature Extraction. Apply an extractor to the image in ROI and output a grayscale image.
3. Filtering. Remove the noise introduced when performing feature extraction.
4. Segmentation. Segment the grayscale image into several regions (set of pixels) and output a labeled image.
5. Connected Component Analysis. Find the region with the largest area (cardinality of set) and output a binary image indicating that region.
6. Morphological Filtering. Applying morphology image operation using a structuring element to separate the road from other areas.
7. Holes filling. Road markings will produce holes in the obtained area. Filling the holes to obtain a complete road area.

4. EXPERIMENTAL RESULTS

4.1 Shadow-Free Extractor

Effectiveness. We test our extractor on a public dataset [9]. Different from all other extractors, our results look like a natural image except that the shadows are disappeared. As sample images shown in Fig. 6, our extractor is robust against images of a wide range of materials and surface textures. It also retains the texture (e.g. road, brick and wood) and details (e.g. handwriting) well compared to other extractors, as shown in Fig.5.

Time Efficiency. We measure the average time and variance ($\mu \pm \sigma$) for extractors implemented with MATLAB to process an image having 1280 × 1024 dots with a PC equipped with an i7-3770 3.40 GHz CPU and 16GB RAM (GPU acceleration is not used). Due to the low-complexity of our extractor, it achieves the fastest speed compared with others (cf. Table 1).

Table 1: Processing speed of feature extractors.

Extractors	S' [27]	$\mathcal{I}'_\theta$ [2]	$\mathcal{I}'_\alpha$ [16]	$\mathcal{I}'_b$ (Ours)
Time/ms	21.3±0.2	52.2±0.4	54.9±3.6	**12.9±0.1**

Table 2: Pixel-wise measures (right) defined using entries of a contingency table (left).

		Ground-truth	
		Others	Road
Result	Others	TN	FN
	Road	FP	TP

Measure	Definition
Quality	$\hat{g} = \frac{TP}{TP+FP+FN}$
Precision	$DR = \frac{TP}{TP+FP}$
Recall	$DA = \frac{TP}{TP+FN}$
Effectiveness	$F = \frac{2DR \times DA}{DR+DA}$
Valid	$VRI = \frac{TP+TN}{TP+TN+FP+FN} \geq 0.8$

4.2 Road Detection

To evaluate the performance of road detection, we adopt pixel-wise measurements shown in Table 2. Quantitative evaluations are provided using four error measurements: quality $\hat{g}$, precision DR (also known as detection rate), recall DA (also known as detection accuracy) and effectiveness F. We also use a qualitative measurement called valid road result index VRI [1]: a detection result is valid ($VRI = 1$) if and only if at least 80% of pixels are correctly classified. As [1] suggested, road boundary pixels should be discarded when computing those measurements to reduce the inherent error of manual segmentation.

ROMA dataset. There are 10 sub-datasets of various scenes, road types and illumination conditions in ROMA.We manually labeled road area ground truth of all sub-datasets. To make a fair comparison, different extractors are employed in the same road detection framework under the same parameter settings. In our implementation, the lower half of image is selected as ROI in step 1. A graph-based image segmentation algorithm introduced in [6] with the parameters $\sigma = 1.2$, $k = 300$ and $min = 1000$ is employed in step 4. Since the algorithm already has a parameter σ to smooth the image, a 5×5 median filter is employed in step 3 to filter the extracted feature image. Finally, morphology opening using a structuring element of 8×8 disk is applied in step 6 to separate the road from other areas. As shown in Table 3, detection results based on the proposed extractor outperform the others in both quantitative and qualitative measurements, especially in adverse lighting conditions.

KITTI-ROAD dataset [8]. To test the performance on challenging KITTI-ROAD dataset, we compare our result with that of the state-of-art top 3 methods accessible on the KITTI benchmark website[1]. As shown in Fig.6, our detection result shows more accuracy than that of the state-of-art methods. Besides, we test three edge detectors (Sobel, Canny and Structured Edge [5]) in severe shadow cases. As shown in Fig.7, using the shadow-free image obtained by our extractor can achieve a better result. Also, the false color segmentation caused by severe shadow can be avoided by employing our extractor as a preprocessing step, as shown in Fig.8.

To encourage future works, we make the source code open, as well as our labeled ground-truth for ROMA. More testing results can be found on our project website[2].

Table 3: Performance on ROMA Dataset.

	Complete dataset				
	$\hat{g}$	DR	DA	F	VRI
Y	$.79 \pm .17$	$.91 \pm .12$	$.86 \pm .17$	$.87 \pm .12$	63%
S' [26]	$.85 \pm .18$	$.94 \pm .11$	$.90 \pm .17$	$.91 \pm .12$	75%
$\mathcal{I}'_\theta$ [2]	$.82 \pm .23$	$.94 \pm .12$	$.87 \pm .23$	$.88 \pm .18$	72%
$\mathcal{I}'_\alpha$ [16]	$.79 \pm .14$	$.83 \pm .13$	$.95 \pm .11$	$.87 \pm .09$	59%
$\mathcal{I}'_b$ (Ours)	**$.92 \pm .11$**	**$.96 \pm .07$**	**$.96 \pm .09$**	**$.96 \pm .07$**	**93%**
	Adverse lighting conditions				
	$\hat{g}$	DR	DA	F	VRI
Y	$.76 \pm .16$	$.88 \pm .14$	$.85 \pm .18$	$.85 \pm .12$	48%
S' [26]	$.81 \pm .20$	$.91 \pm .14$	$.88 \pm .19$	$.88 \pm .14$	67%
$\mathcal{I}'_\theta$ [2]	$.81 \pm .20$	$.93 \pm .11$	$.87 \pm .21$	$.88 \pm .14$	65%
$\mathcal{I}'_\alpha$ [16]	$.77 \pm .14$	$.81 \pm .14$	$.95 \pm .10$	$.86 \pm .09$	48%
$\mathcal{I}'_b$ (Ours)	**$.92 \pm .09$**	**$.96 \pm .07$**	**$.96 \pm .07$**	**$.96 \pm .05$**	**96%**

Figure 6: Comparison with state-of-art methods. Red areas denote false negatives, blue areas correspond to false positives and green areas represent true positives.

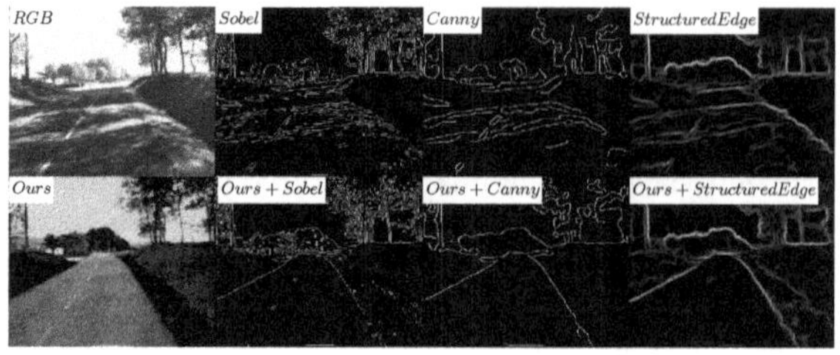

Figure 7: Improve edge detection via our extractor.

Figure 8: Improve segmentation via our extractor.

5. CONCLUSIONS

In this paper, we propose a novel shadow-free feature extractor to improve the performance of road detection under severe shadow conditions. The proposed extractor shows robustness against different materials and illumination conditions. A road detection framework based on the proposed extractor is built. Experimental results on public datasets demonstrate the superior performance compared to other existing extractors. As a result, the novel extractor is well suitable to other computer vision tasks as well as autonomous driving applications by its good performance and computational efficiency.

[1] http://www.cvlibs.net/datasets/kitti/eval_road.php
[2] https://github.com/baidut/OpenVehicleVision/

6. REFERENCES

[1] J. M. Álvarez, T. Gevers, and A. M. Lopez. 3d scene priors for road detection. In *Computer Vision and Pattern Recognition (CVPR), 2010 IEEE Conference on*, pages 57–64. IEEE, 2010.

[2] J. M. Álvarez and A. M. Ĺopez. Road detection based on illuminant invariance. *Intelligent Transportation Systems, IEEE Transactions on*, 12(1):184–193, 2011.

[3] A. Bar Hillel, R. Lerner, D. Levi, and G. Raz. Recent progress in road and lane detection: a survey. *Machine Vision and Applications*, 25(3):727–745, 2014.

[4] B. Benligiray, C. Topal, and C. Akinlar. Video-based lane detection using a fast vanishing point estimation method. In *Multimedia (ISM), 2012 IEEE International Symposium on*, pages 348–351, Dec 2012.

[5] P. Dollár and C. Zitnick. Structured forests for fast edge detection. In *Proceedings of the IEEE International Conference on Computer Vision*, pages 1841–1848, 2013.

[6] P. F. Felzenszwalb and D. P. Huttenlocher. Efficient graph-based image segmentation. *International Journal of Computer Vision*, 59(2):167–181, 2004.

[7] G. D. Finlayson, S. D. Hordley, C. Lu, and M. S. Drew. On the removal of shadows from images. *Pattern Analysis and Machine Intelligence, IEEE Transactions on*, 28(1):59–68, 2006.

[8] J. Fritsch, T. Kuhnl, and A. Geiger. A new performance measure and evaluation benchmark for road detection algorithms. In *Intelligent Transportation Systems-(ITSC), 2013 16th International IEEE Conference on*, pages 1693–1700. IEEE, 2013.

[9] H. Gong and D. Cosker. Interactive shadow removal and ground truth for variable scene categories. In *BMVC 2014-Proceedings of the British Machine Vision Conference 2014*. University of Bath, 2014.

[10] G. Healey. Segmenting images using normalized color. *Systems, Man and Cybernetics, IEEE Transactions on*, 22(1):64–73, 1992.

[11] J. Huang, B. Kong, B. Li, and F. Zheng. A new method of unstructured road detection based on hsv color space and road features. In *Information Acquisition, 2007. ICIA '07. International Conference on*, pages 596–601, July 2007.

[12] S.-N. Kang, S. Lee, J. Hur, and S.-W. Seo. Multi-lane detection based on accurate geometric lane estimation in highway scenarios. In *Intelligent Vehicles Symposium Proceedings, 2014 IEEE*, pages 221–226, June 2014.

[13] Z. Kim. Robust lane detection and tracking in challenging scenarios. *Intelligent Transportation Systems, IEEE Transactions on*, 9(1):16–26, March 2008.

[14] H. Kong, J.-Y. Audibert, and J. Ponce. General road detection from a single image. *Image Processing, IEEE Transactions on*, 19(8):2211–2220, 2010.

[15] Z. Li, Z. xing Cai, J. Xie, and X. ping Ren. Road markings extraction based on threshold segmentation. In *Fuzzy Systems and Knowledge Discovery (FSKD), 2012 9th International Conference on*, pages 1924–1928, May 2012.

[16] W. Maddern, A. Stewart, C. McManus, B. Upcroft, W. Churchill, and P. Newman. Illumination invariant imaging: Applications in robust vision-based localisation, mapping and classification for autonomous vehicles. In *Proceedings of the Visual Place Recognition in Changing Environments Workshop, IEEE International Conference on Robotics and Automation (ICRA), Hong Kong, China*, 2014.

[17] C. Oh, J. Son, and K. Sohn. Illumination robust road detection using geometric information. In *Intelligent Transportation Systems (ITSC), 2012 15th International IEEE Conference on*, pages 1566–1571. IEEE, 2012.

[18] C. Rotaru, T. Graf, and J. Zhang. Color image segmentation in hsi space for automotive applications. *Journal of Real-Time Image Processing*, 3(4):311–322, 2008.

[19] T. Scharwachter and U. Franke. Low-level fusion of color, texture and depth for robust road scene understanding. In *Intelligent Vehicles Symposium (IV), 2015 IEEE*, pages 599–604. IEEE, 2015.

[20] T.-Y. Sun, S.-J. Tsai, and V. Chan. Hsi color model based lane-marking detection. In *Intelligent Transportation Systems Conference, 2006. ITSC '06. IEEE*, pages 1168–1172, Sept 2006.

[21] T. Veit, J.-P. Tarel, P. Nicolle, and P. Charbonnier. Evaluation of road marking feature extraction. In *Intelligent Transportation Systems, 2008. ITSC 2008. 11th International IEEE Conference on*, pages 174–181, Oct 2008.

[22] B. Wang, V. Frémont, and S. A. Rodríguez. Color-based road detection and its evaluation on the kitti road benchmark. In *Intelligent Vehicles Symposium Proceedings, 2014 IEEE*, pages 31–36. IEEE, 2014.

[23] J. Wang, Z. Ji, and Y.-T. Su. Unstructured road detection using hybrid features. In *Machine Learning and Cybernetics, 2009 International Conference on*, volume 1, pages 482–486. IEEE, 2009.

[24] J. Wang, T. Mei, B. Kong, and H. Wei. An approach of lane detection based on inverse perspective mapping. In *Intelligent Transportation Systems (ITSC), 2014 IEEE 17th International Conference on*, pages 35–38, Oct 2014.

[25] Y. U. Yim and S. young Oh. Three-feature based automatic lane detection algorithm (tfalda) for autonomous driving. *Intelligent Transportation Systems, IEEE Transactions on*, 4(4):219–225, Dec 2003.

[26] Z. Ying and G. Li. Robust lane marking detection using boundary-based inverse perspective mapping. In *2016 IEEE International Conference on Acoustics, Speech and Signal Processing (ICASSP)*, pages 1921–1925, March 2016.

[27] Z. Ying, G. Li, and G. Tan. An illumination-robust approach for feature-based road detection. In *2015 IEEE International Symposium on Multimedia (ISM)*, pages 278–281, Dec 2015.

[28] S. Zhou, Y. Jiang, J. Xi, J. Gong, G. Xiong, and H. Chen. A novel lane detection based on geometrical model and gabor filter. In *Intelligent Vehicles Symposium (IV), 2010 IEEE*, pages 59–64, June 2010.

Facial Expression Recognition with Deep two-view Support Vector Machine

Chongliang Wu, Shangfei Wang*, Bowen Pan, Huaping Chen
University of Science and Technology of China, Hefei, Anhui, China
clwzkd@mail.ustc.edu.cn, sfwang@ustc.edu.cn,
o0helloworld0o@outlook.com, hpchen@ustc.edu.cn

ABSTRACT

This paper proposes a novel deep two-view approach to learn features from both visible and thermal images and leverage the commonality among visible and thermal images for facial expression recognition from visible images. The thermal images are used as privileged information, which is required only during training to help visible images learn better features and classifier. Specifically, we first learn a deep model for visible images and thermal images respectively, and use the learned feature representations to train SVM classifiers for expression classification. We then jointly refine the deep models as well as the SVM classifiers for both thermal images and visible images by imposing the constraint that the outputs of the SVM classifiers from two views are similar. Therefore, the resulting representations and classifiers capture the inherent connections among visible facial image, infrared facial image and target expression labels, and hence improve the recognition performance for facial expression recognition from visible images during testing. Experimental results on the benchmark expression database demonstrate the effectiveness of our proposed method.

CCS Concepts

•Human-centered computing → HCI design and evaluation methods;

Keywords

deep two-view learning; visible images; thermal images; facial expression recognition

1. INTRODUCTION

Recently, facial expression recognition has attracted increasing attention due to its wide application in many areas of human-computer interaction, and achieved considerable progress [1, 2, 3]. Most current facial expression recognition works detect expressions from visible images, or videos, and are not robust to illumination changes, since illumination changes can significantly influence the appearance of visible images. While, thermal infrared images, which record temperature distribution, are not sensitive to illumination conditions. Hence, several researchers have turned to expression recognition from thermal images[4, 5, 6, 7, 8, 9, 10, 11, 12, 13, 14].

Although thermal images possess robustness to illumination changes, they are sensitive to the surrounding temperature and opaque to glass [4], while visible images are not. Therefore, it is intuitive thinking to combine visible and thermal images for facial expression recognition. Yet, only very recently, a little attention has been paid to facial expression recognition by fusing visible and thermal images with feature-level fusion or decision-level fusion. For example, Sharma et al. [9] proposed to detect stress by feature-level fusion of visible and thermal videos. Support vector machine (SVM) is adopted to integrate visible and thermal features for stress detection. Yoshitomi et al. [15] proposed to classify five expressions (i.e. anger, happiness, neutral, sadness and surprise) through decision-level fusion of voices, visual and infrared facial images. Two neural network classifiers are trained for visual and thermal features respectively, and hidden Markov models are adopted for emotion detection from voices. The recognition results of the three classifiers were integrated by a simple weighted voting. All these researches demonstrate that the fusion of thermal and visual image data for expression classification outperforms either of the individual modality.

In fact, visible cameras are widely used in our daily life, while thermal cameras are available in laboratory environment. Thus, the use of thermal imaging for facial expression recognition in real world situations is questionable. It is promising to integrate thermal and visible images for expression recognition by using thermal images as privileged information [16], which is only required during training to help visible images construct a better expression classifier, and not required during testing. Furthermore, current feature-level and decision-level fusion either concatenate visible features and thermal features into one feature vector, or combine the recognition results from two classifiers directly. They can not fully exploit the inherent dependencies between thermal and visible images for expression recognition. To address it, two-view learning [17] [18]should be considered, since it introduces one function to model a particular view, such as visible images, and jointly optimizes all the functions, i.e. classifiers from thermal and visible features.

*This author is the corresponding author.

MM '16, October 15–19, 2016, Amsterdam, The Netherlands.

DOI: http://dx.doi.org/10.1145/2964284.2967295

Only very recently, Shi et al. [19] proposed a method of expression recognition from visible images with the help of thermal images. First, active appearance model features and temperature features are extracted from visible and thermal images respectively. Then, canonical correlation analysis (CCA) is used for feature representation and SVM is adopted as the classifier on the constructed visible feature space. Their proposed method integrated thermal images and visible images to learn a new representation of visible images during training. The new representation is expected to be more discriminative for expression recognition. Thermal images are only required during training to construct better visible image representation. Their proposed method uses thermal images as privileged information, and adopts CCA, a two-view learning method, to model the inherent dependencies among visible and thermal images for performance improvement.

Although their constructed representation reflects thermal infrared images' supplementary role for visible images, it has no direct relationship to target expression labels. Furthermore, the hand-craft visible and thermal features may not thoroughly reflect the expression patterns embedded in images. Therefore, in this paper, we propose a new deep two-view approach to learn features from both visible and thermal images and leverage the commonality among visible and thermal images for expression recognition. Specifically, we first separately learn a deep model from visible images and thermal images. After that, we jointly refine the deep models as well as the SVM classifiers for both visible images and thermal images by imposing the constraint that the outputs of the SVM classifiers from visible images and thermal images are similar. Thus, the resulting representations and classifiers capture the inherent connections among visible images, thermal images and expression labels, and hence improve the performance of expression recognition from visible images. Experimental results on the MAHNOB laughter database demonstrate the effectiveness of our proposed method.

2. PROPOSED METHOD

2.1 Problem Statement

We develop a method for expression recognition by using two views of data, i.e. visible images and thermal images, to represent the same category of expressions. Denote $v \in R^{|V|}$ and $t \in R^{|T|}$ as visible and thermal image data, respectively, where $|V|$ and $|T|$ are dimension of visible and thermal image data. Assuming we have two different categories of expressions, labeled as $y \in \{-1, 1\}$. The training data consists of visible image, thermal image and the corresponding facial expression labels, denoted as $D = \{v_l, r_l, y_l\}, l = 1, ..., L$, where L is the number of samples in training set.

The goal of expression recognition is to find a classifier that projects input data into its expression label. In the situation of two-view, there are two different kinds of input data for one sample, each view can train a classifier to recognize expression category of the sample. The proposed method is based on SVM classifier, which first projects input into a real value, i.e. $f_x : R^{|X|} \to R$, and then use a decision function, $d_x : R \to \{-1, 1\}$. Denote f_v and f_r as the trained SVM projection of visible image data and thermal image data. Since f_v and f_r are projections to the same expression category, we assume that informativeness of them for classification are similar. Motivated by Farquhar *et.al*'s[20] work, we introduce a constraint of similarity of f_v and f_r to refine the performance of the related classifiers. The similarity constraint of f_v and f_r can be expressed as 1.

$$|f_v(v_l) - f_r(r_l)| \leq \eta_l + \epsilon \tag{1}$$

where, η_l is the slack variable to measure the amount that l^{th} sample fails to meet ϵ similarity between projection f_v and f_r.

2.2 Background: SVM2K and Deep Network

Assuming ϕ_v and ϕ_r are feature projections of two views, visible image and thermal image, with corresponding kernels. By considering SVM as a 1-dimensional projection of input data followed by a threshold, constraints of similarity between projections of SVMs for two views are introduced to combine KCCA and SVM into a single optimization. With training data D, the similarity constraint of SVM2K [20] is defined as

$$|f_v(v_l) - f_r(r_l)| \leq \eta_l + \epsilon \tag{2}$$

where

$$f_v(v_l) = \langle w_v, \phi_v(v_l)\rangle + b_v \quad f_r(r_l) = \langle w_r, \phi_r(r_l)\rangle + b_r \tag{3}$$

for all $l = 1, ..., L$, where η_l is slack variable that measures the amount of point l fails to meet ϵ similarity, (w_v, b_v) and (w_r, b_r) are parameters of SVM for visible image data and thermal image data. The optimization of SVM2K combines similarity constraints with usual 1-normal SVM:

$$\begin{aligned} \min_{w_v, w_r, b_v, b_r} \quad & \frac{1}{2}\|w_v\|^2 + \frac{1}{2}\|w_r\|^2 + C^v \sum_{l=1}^{L} \xi_l^v + C^r \sum_{l=1}^{L} \xi_l^r + D \sum_{l=1}^{L} \eta_l \\ s.t. \quad & |\langle w_v, \phi_v(v_l)\rangle + b_v - \langle w_r, \phi_r(r_l)\rangle - b_t| \leq \eta_l + \epsilon \\ & y_l(\langle w_v, \phi_A(v_l)\rangle + b_v) \geq 1 - \xi_l^v \\ & y_l(\langle w_r, \phi_A(r_l)\rangle + b_r) \geq 1 - \xi_l^r \\ & \xi_l^v \geq 0,\ \xi_l^r \geq 0,\ \eta_l \geq 0 \ all\ for\ 1 \leq l \leq L \end{aligned} \tag{4}$$

Lagrange multiplier is applied to solve this optimization problem. During testing, the final decision function is a linear combination of projections from SVMs for visible and thermal image data.

Comparing with SVM2K, in the proposed method, in stead of applying kernel method for feature representation, deep networks are used. Deep network consists of multiple layers of restricted Boltzmann machine (RBM). We adopt two different deep networks for nonlinearly transform two views of data, i.e. visible and thermal image data. As shown in Figure 1(a) and 1(b), the output of deep networks can be computed layer by layer through a series of nonlinear functions. Assuming in deep network for visible image data, $t \in \{1, 2, ..., T\}$ represents the index of layers of the network, n_t^v represents the number of nodes at t^{th} layer. For an input sample $v_l \in R^{|V|}$ $(l = 1, ..., L)$, n^v represents the number of input nodes. Output of the first layer of the network can be computed as $h_1^{v,l} = s(\langle w_1^v, v_l\rangle + b_1^v) \in R^{n_1^v}$, where $\{w_1^v, b_1^v\}$ are parameters of the first layer of deep network for the first view of data, $s : R^{|V|} \to R^{n_1^A}$ is the nonlinear function of the transformation.

Then h_1^v is used as input of second layer of the network, the output of second layer can be computed similarly, and so on. At the final layer, $h_T^{v,l}$ is obtained as: $h_T^{v,l} = s(< w_T^v, h_{T-1}^{v,l} > +b_T^v) \in n_T^v$, where $h_T^{v,l}$ is the learned representation of visible

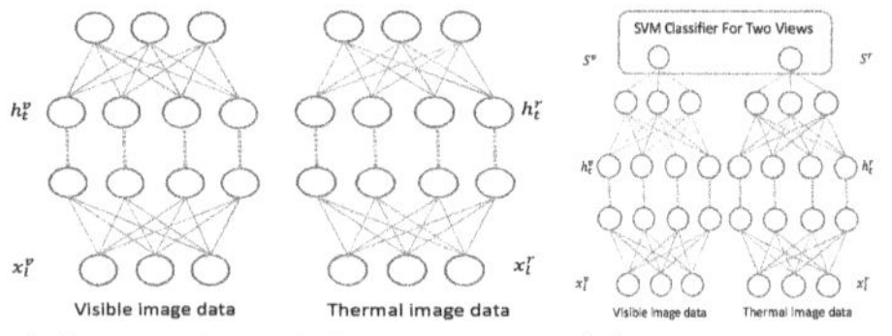

(a) Visible (b) Thermal (c) Our Model

Figure 1: The scheme of deep network for visible image data, thermal image data and the scheme of the proposed model.

image data and can be computed as the final projection. Deep network for thermal image data is similar.

2.3 Deep Two-view Support Vector Machine

In deep two-view SVM, deep network is applied to learn feature representations for each view of data. By introducing similarity constraints, we construct optimization that aims to find maximally correlated feature represents and to optimize common SVM classifiers for both views of data simultaneously. We add a layer at the top of each deep network which contains only one node, denoted as S^v and S^r, as show in Figure 1(c). The value of S^v and S^r is linear combination of the output of deep networks

$$S^v = \langle w_S^v, h_T^v \rangle + b_S^v; \quad S^r = \langle w_S^r, h_T^r \rangle + b_S^r \tag{5}$$

where w_S^v, b_S^v (w_S^r, b_S^r) is weights and bias of the added layer of deep networks which are also parameters of SVM classifier for both views of data, here. We define constraint of similarity between S^v and S^r as

$$|S^v - S^r| \leq \eta_l \tag{6}$$

where η_l is slack variable that measures the amount of dissimilarity of sample l from two views.

Combining similarity constraint defined above and common SVM constraints the optimization of our model expressed as:

$$\begin{aligned} \min_{\Theta_v,\Theta_r} L = & \frac{1}{2} \parallel w_S^v \parallel_2^2 + \frac{1}{2} \parallel w_S^r \parallel_2^2 \\ & + C^v \sum_{l=1}^{L} (\xi_l^v)^2 + C^r \sum_{l=1}^{L} (\xi_l^r)^2 + D \sum_{l=1}^{L} (\eta_l)^2 \\ s.t.\ & |S^v - S^r| \leq \eta_l, \quad y_l \cdot S^v \geq 1 - \xi_l^v, \\ & y_l \cdot S^r \geq 1 - \xi_l^r, \quad \xi_l^v \geq 0,\ \xi_l^r \geq 0,\ \eta_l \geq 0, \\ & all\ for\ 1 \leq l \leq L. \end{aligned} \tag{7}$$

where $\Theta_v = \{\theta^v, w_S^v, b_S^v\}$ and $\Theta_r = \{\theta^r, w_S^r, b_S^r\}$ are parameters of the extended deep networks, ξ_l^v, ξ_l^r are slack variable of common SVMs, η_l is the slack for similarity constraint. According to [21], using squared slacks is slightly better, thus in Eq.7 use $(\xi_l^v)^2$, $(\xi_l^r)^2$ and $(\eta_l)^2$ instead. By substituting the slack variables from the constraints into the objective function, Eq.7 can be rewritten as the minimization of Eq.8.

$$\begin{aligned} F(\Theta_v, \Theta_r) = & \frac{1}{2} \parallel w_S^v \parallel_2^2 + \frac{1}{2} \parallel w_S^r \parallel_2^2 + C^v \sum_{l=1}^{L} [1 - y_l \cdot S^v]_+^2 \\ & + C^r \sum_{l=1}^{L} [1 - y_l \cdot S^r]_+^2 + D \sum_{l=1}^{L} (S^v - S^r)^2 \end{aligned} \tag{8}$$

where, $[\cdot]_+$ is the hinge function.

Back propagation is used for optimization. The key is to compute gradient of objective function, Eq.8, with respect to all weight and bias parameters at each layer of deep networks, including the added layer. For parameters corresponding to view A, gradient of objective function Eq.8 to the weight and bias at the top layer (SVM parameters) can be computed as

$$\begin{aligned} \frac{\partial F}{\partial w_S^v} &= \frac{\partial F}{\partial S^v} \cdot \frac{\partial S^v}{\partial w_S^v} = w_S^v + \delta_S^v \cdot h_T^v; \\ \frac{\partial F}{\partial b_S^v} &= \frac{\partial F}{\partial S^v} \cdot \frac{\partial S^v}{\partial b_S^v} = \delta_S^v \cdot \mathbf{1} \end{aligned} \tag{9}$$

where δ_S^v is backward error at the top layers that will be passed to previous layer, $\mathbf{1}$ is a vector with all ones.

$$\delta_S^v = \frac{\partial F}{\partial S^v} = -2C^v \cdot Y \times [1 - Y \times S^v]_+ + 2D \cdot (S^v - S^r) \tag{10}$$

For other layers, the gradients can be computed as normal back propagation algorithm.

$$\frac{\partial F}{\partial w_t^v} = \sum_{l=1}^{L} \frac{\partial F}{\partial h_t^{v,l}} \cdot \frac{\partial h_t^{v,l}}{\partial w_t^v} \tag{11}$$

all for $t = 1, ..., T$. For parameters corresponding to thermal image data, all derivative is similar.

All deep network parameters are initialized through "pretraining" process using contrastive divergence algorithm, according to [22]. Weights of SVM are randomly initialized. During testing, the decision function of our model is $d(x) = sign(f(x))$, where $f(x)$ can estimate using both views or any one of them.

DCCA and the proposed method both applied deep networks for feature representation. DCCA learns complex nonlinear transformations of two views of data such that the resulting representations are highly linearly correlated. However, unlike DCCA, the learned representations of our method captures not only the relations among multiple view of data, but also the relations between data and expression labels by training deep networks and SVMs simultaneously through Eq.7. Comparing our method with SVM2K, instead of learning two related classifiers directly from views of data, our proposed method trained classifiers from a hidden layer of the deep network, as shown in Figure 1(c), which are the complex nonlinear transformations of two views subjecting to the inherit relations among multiple view of data and expression labels. The learned classifier may be better due to the good representation of deep networks.

3. EXPERIMENTS

3.1 Experimental condition

As mentioned in section 1, there exists one work, which uses thermal image data as privileged information to help facial expression recognition from visible images [19]. Shi *et al* proposed to use CCA to construct visible features with the help of thermal images, and adopt SVM as a classifier to recognize expressions from visible images. Their experiments were conducted on the NVIE database and the Equinox database. Since the number of image samples adopted in their experiments is not large enough for deep model training, instead of using the same data as theirs, we conduct experiments of laughter-vs-speech discrimination from

Table 1: Results on the MAHNOB database

Experiment	Accuracy(%)	F1-score
NN (Stavros [23] visual-only)	83.9	0.772
DCCA+SVM	86.42	0.8117
SVM2K	91.40	0.8852
Single view using DNN with SVM	93.98	0.9208
Ours (multi-view)	**94.14**	**0.9230**

images on the MAHNOB laughter database [23] to validate the effectiveness of the proposed method.

The MAHNOB laughter database consists of audio, visible videos and thermal videos of spontaneous laughter from 22 subjects during their watching funny video clips. The database also includes subjects' speech visible videos and thermal videos during their speaking in English and their mother languages. Since three subjects don't have thermal videos during their speech, we selected visible and thermal videos from 19 subjects for our experiments of laughter-vs-speech discrimination. First, we locate facial area for every frame in visible and thermal videos using face detection algorithm implemented in OpenCV [24]. Then, facial images are converted to gray scale and resized into 28×28. Finally, 8252 laughter images and 12914 speech images are obtained. A leave-one-subject-out cross-validation is adopted.

Four experiments are conducted, i.e., laughter-vs-speech discrimination from visible images only, laughter-vs-speech discrimination from visible images with the help of thermal images using DCCA with SVM, SVM2K and our method. For the laughter-vs-speech discrimination experiment from visible images only (i.e. single view using DNN with SVM), the same deep neural network as shown in the left part of Figure 1(c) is adopted to learn features and the SVM classifier simultaneously from visible images during training. For the laughter-vs-speech discrimination from visible images with the help of thermal images, during training, both visible and thermal images are used. During testing, only visible image data are required. For SVM2K and DCCA with SVM experiments, the codes provided by Farquhar *et al*[20] and Wang*et al*[25] are adopted. DCCA with SVM is a classification method using DCCA for feature representation and SVM for classification.

3.2 Experimental results and analyses

Experimental results on the MAHNOB laughter database are shown in Table 1. From Table 1, we can find the following observations:

First, the proposed method outperforms other methods with the highest recognition accuracy and the F1-score. It demonstrates that the proposed method captures inherent relations among visible, thermal facial images and their corresponding labels successfully, and hence improves visible expression recognition with the help of thermal images. Compared with DCCA, the proposed method captures relations among visible images, thermal images and expression labels, and leverages them for expression recognition directly. Although DCCA captures relations between visible and thermal image, feature representations learned by DCCA are not specific for expression recognition. Compared with SVM2K, the proposed model uses deep network for feature representation instead of kernel function. Deep network has been proved more advance than kernel method in feature representation [26]. Although SVM2K trains classifiers for recognition directly, it is unable to capture complex structure in visible and thermal image as deep network does. Compared with laughter-vs-speech discrimination from visible images only, the better performance of the proposed method demonstrate that the proposed method can exploit thermal images during training effectively to construct better visible features and expression classifier.

Second, laughter-vs-speech discrimination from visible images only using deep neural network with SVM outperforms laughter-vs-speech discrimination from visible images with the help of thermal images using DCCA with SVM and SVM2K. Comparing with SVM2K, the single-view model using DNN with SVM can take advantage of the ability of feature learning with DNN. While compared with DCCA with SVM, the single-view model using DNN with SVM learns features in a supervised way and those features are more suitable for classification. This may further demonstrate the power of feature learning using deep models and the importance of learning features and classifier together.

Most experiments conducted on the MAHNOB database are for laughter-vs-speech discrimination. In order to demonstrate the effectiveness of the proposed method, we use their results as a baseline for reference. Stavros *et al* [23] conducted laughter-vs-speech discrimination experiments from visual information, audio information and their combination. They used neural network (NN) as the classifier. Since only visual information is used in our experiments, we compare our results with their visual-only results. As shown in Table 1, both recognition accuracy and F1-score of our method are better than theirs, further demonstrating the effectiveness of our proposed method.

4. CONCLUSION

This paper proposes a deep two-view learning approach for expression recognition. Visible and thermal facial image are viewed as two view of expression. First, for feature representation, two deep networks are trained for visible and thermal image data. Two support vector machines are trained for classification. During deep network pre-training, layer-wise RBM training method is applied. Deep network refine and SVM parameter learning are integrated into a single optimization problem through similarity constraint between outputs of two SVMs. Thermal image data is used as privileged information to help expression recognition on visible image data. During testing, only visible image data used for classification. Experimental result on the MAHNOB laughter database demonstrate that the proposed method can capture relationships among two view data and their labels and can recognize expression on visible image effectively.

5. ACKNOWLEDGMENTS

This work has been supported by the National Science Foundation of China (grant nos. 61175037, 61228304, and 61473270) and Natural Science Foundation of Anhui Province (1508085SMF223).

6. REFERENCES

[1] Vinay Bettadapura. Face expression recognition and analysis: the state of the art. *arXiv preprint arXiv:1203.6722*, 2012.

[2] Zhihong Zeng, Maja Pantic, Glenn I Roisman, and Thomas S Huang. A survey of affect recognition methods: Audio, visual, and spontaneous expressions. *Pattern Analysis and Machine Intelligence, IEEE Transactions on*, 31(1):39–58, 2009.

[3] Evangelos Sariyanidi, Hatice Gunes, and Andrea Cavallaro. Automatic analysis of facial affect: A survey of registration, representation, and recognition. *Pattern Analysis and Machine Intelligence, IEEE Transactions on*, 37(6):1113–1133, 2015.

[4] Avinash Wesley, Pradeep Buddharaju, Robert Pienta, and Ioannis Pavlidis. A comparative analysis of thermal and visual modalities for automated facial expression recognition. In *Advances in Visual Computing*, pages 51–60. Springer, 2012.

[5] Shangfei Wang, Shan He, Yue Wu, Menghua He, and Qiang Ji. Fusion of visible and thermal images for facial expression recognition. *Frontiers of Computer Science*, 8(2):232–242, 2014.

[6] Lijun Yin Peng Liu. Spontaneous facial expression analysis based on temperature changes and head motions. In *FG2015*, 2015.

[7] Hung Nguyen, Kazunori Kotani, Fan Chen, and Bac Le. Estimation of human emotions using thermal facial information. In *Fifth International Conference on Graphic and Image Processing*, pages 90690O–90690O. International Society for Optics and Photonics, 2014.

[8] Sophie Jarlier, Didier Grandjean, Sylvain Delplanque, Karim N'diaye, Isabelle Cayeux, Maria Inés Velazco, David Sander, Patrik Vuilleumier, and Klaus R Scherer. Thermal analysis of facial muscles contractions. *Affective Computing, IEEE Transactions on*, 2(1):2–9, 2011.

[9] Nandita Sharma, Abhinav Dhall, Tom Gedeon, and Roland Goecke. Modeling stress using thermal facial patterns: A spatio-temporal approach. In *Affective Computing and Intelligent Interaction (ACII), 2013 Humaine Association Conference on*, pages 387–392. IEEE, 2013.

[10] Yasunari Yoshitomi, Taro Asada, Ryota Kato, and Masayoshi Tabuse. Facial expression recognition using facial expression intensity characteristics of thermal image. *Journal of Robotics, Networking and Artificial Life*, 2(1):5–8, 2015.

[11] Marina Gavrilova Ahmad Poursaberi, Svetlana N. Yanushkevich. An efficient facial expression recognition system in infrared images. In *2013 Fourth International Conference on Emerging Security Technologies*, pages 25 – 28, 2013.

[12] Benjamin Hernandez, Gustavo Olague, Riad Hammoud, Leonardo Trujillo, and Eva Romero. Visual learning of texture descriptors for facial expression recognition in thermal imagery. *Computer Vision and Image Understanding*, 106(2):258–269, 2007. Special issue on Advances in Vision Algorithms and Systems beyond the Visible Spectrum.

[13] Shan He, Shangfei Wang, Wuwei Lan, Huan Fu, and Qiang Ji. Facial expression recognition using deep boltzmann machine from thermal infrared images. In *Affective Computing and Intelligent Interaction (ACII), 2013 Humaine Association Conference on*, pages 239–244. IEEE, 2013.

[14] Verónica Pérez-Rosas, Alexis Narvaez, Mihai Burzo, and Rada Mihalcea. Thermal imaging for affect detection. In *Proceedings of the 6th International Conference on PErvasive Technologies Related to Assistive Environments*, PETRA '13, pages 36:1–36:4, New York, NY, USA, 2013. ACM.

[15] Yasunari Yoshitomi, Sung-Ill Kim, Takako Kawano, and T Kilazoe. Effect of sensor fusion for recognition of emotional states using voice, face image and thermal image of face. In *Robot and Human Interactive Communication, 2000. RO-MAN 2000. Proceedings. 9th IEEE International Workshop on*, pages 178–183. IEEE, 2000.

[16] Vladimir Vapnik and Akshay Vashist. A new learning paradigm: Learning using privileged information. *Neural Networks*, 22(5):544–557, 2009.

[17] Chang Xu, Dacheng Tao, and Chao Xu. A survey on multi-view learning. *CoRR*, abs/1304.5634, 2013.

[18] Shiliang Sun. A survey of multi-view machine learning. *Neural Computing and Applications*, 23(7-8):2031–2038, 2013.

[19] Xiaoxiao Shi, Shangfei Wang, and Yachen Zhu. Expression recognition from visible images with the help of thermal images. In *Proceedings of the 5th ACM on International Conference on Multimedia Retrieval, Shanghai, China, June 23-26, 2015*, pages 563–566, 2015.

[20] Jason Farquhar, David Hardoon, Hongying Meng, John S Shawe-taylor, and Sandor Szedmak. Two view learning: Svm-2k, theory and practice. In *Advances in neural information processing systems*, pages 355–362, 2005.

[21] Shi-Xiong Zhang, Chaojun Liu, Kaisheng Yao, and Yifan Gong. Deep neural support vector machines for speech recognition. In *Acoustics, Speech and Signal Processing (ICASSP), 2015 IEEE International Conference on*, pages 4275–4279. IEEE, 2015.

[22] Geoffrey E Hinton, Simon Osindero, and Yee-Whye Teh. A fast learning algorithm for deep belief nets. *Neural computation*, 18(7):1527–1554, 2006.

[23] Stavros Petridis, Brais Martinez, and Maja Pantic. The mahnob laughter database. *Image and Vision Computing*, 31(2):186–202, 2013.

[24] Paul Viola and Michael Jones. Rapid object detection using a boosted cascade of simple features. In *Computer Vision and Pattern Recognition, 2001. CVPR 2001. Proceedings of the 2001 IEEE Computer Society Conference on*, volume 1, pages I–511. IEEE, 2001.

[25] Weiran Wang, Raman Arora, Karen Livescu, and Jeff Bilmes. On deep multi-view representation learning. In *Proceedings of the 32nd International Conference on Machine Learning (ICML-15)*, pages 1083–1092, 2015.

[26] Galen Andrew, Raman Arora, Jeff Bilmes, and Karen Livescu. Deep canonical correlation analysis. In *Proceedings of the 30th International Conference on Machine Learning*, pages 1247–1255, 2013.

Mental Visual Indexing: Towards Fast Video Browsing

Richang Hong[†], Jun He[†], Hanwang Zhang[‡] and Tat-Seng Chua[‡]
[†]School of Computer and Information, Hefei University of Technology
[‡]School of Computing, National University of Singapore
{hongrc.hfut, hyj.hfut.mail, hanwangzhang}@gmail.com, dcscts@nus.edu.sg

ABSTRACT

Video browsing describes an interactive process where users want to find a target shot in a long video. Therefore, it is crucial for a video browsing system to be fast and accurate with minimum user effort. In sharp contrast to traditional Relevance Feedback (RF), we propose a novel paradigm for fast video browsing dubbed Mental Visual Indexing (MVI). At each interactive round, the user only needs to select one of the displayed shots that is most visually similar to her mental target and then the user's choice will further tailor the search to the target. The search model update given a user feedback only requires vector inner products, which makes MVI highly responsive. MVI is underpinned by a sequence model in terms of Recurrent Neural Network (RNN), which is trained by automatically generated shot sequences from a rigorous Bayesian framework, which simulates user feedback process. Experimental results on three 3-hour movies conducted by real users demonstrate the effectiveness of the proposed approach.

Keywords

Mental Search, Video Browsing, RNN, Temporal Model, Query intent

1. INTRODUCTION

A common scenario is that we have seen a movie long time ago and one day we are eager to seek an interesting shot that just suddenly comes to our mind. Then, we might have to scroll the progress bar in a video player that forward/rewind to find our target shot, which is a video browsing issue in the temporal space. When the movie is long, *e.g.* over 2 hours, the procedure is sometimes frustrating since it is very time-consuming and tricky, especially on small-screen mobile devices. We argue that the conventional interactive search by scrolling in most commercial players is less intelligent since it neglects the inherent visual information of videos.

In fact, many video shots are close to each other in the feature space or visually similar although they are far apart in the temporal space. To exploit visual features may accelerate the video browsing process. Be aware that exploiting visual features of videos has been extensively studied in multimedia community [7, 8, 18, 19, 20, 22], *e.g.* TRECVID Instance Search task (INS) has been run for five years since 2010 to address the need of finding more video segments of a certain person, object, or place in a video collection, given one or more visual examples of the specific item [11]. Video Browsing Showdown (VBS) is another event which focuses on video analysis and retrieval. To be concrete, VBS is a live video browsing competition where researchers evaluate and demonstrate the efficiency of their video browsing tools. The VBS participants use their own systems to perform an interactive search in the specified video files taken from a common data set and try to find the desired segment as fast as possible [14].

Relevance Feedback (RF) is a feature of some information retrieval systems [13] and is widely used in different kinds of works [1, 2, 5, 9, 10]. The intuitive idea behind RF is to involve users in the retrieval process so as to improve the final result [23]. Typically, users are asked to label the top candidates returned by the search model as "relevant" or "irrelevant". The feedbacks are then used to refine the search model. Through iterative feedback and model refinement, relevance feedback attempts to capture the information needs of users and improve search results gradually [21]. The main drawback is that RF suffers from a lot of user efforts which prevent a system from being easy-to-use. In a retrieval system, for instance, a user is usually asked to refine her query by telling the system whether a human face detector is needed or not, or by pinpointing and submitting several toy examples. Moreover severely, computation cost of RF is high. So, it would not support many users doing RF simultaneously. Since RF involves transmitting more data,

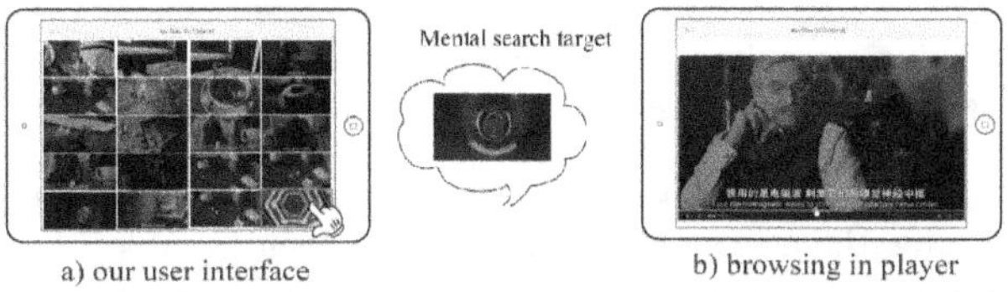

Figure 1: Two different modes of interaction: a) user selects one shot according to the visual similarity, see the one marked in the red box; b) user scrolls the progress bar to find the target shot.

MM '16, October 15–19, 2016, Amsterdam, The Netherlands.
 ISBN 978-1-4503-3603-1/16/10...$15.00
DOI: http://dx.doi.org/10.1145/2964284.2967296

it leads to a more expensive Internet traffic than traditional retrieval methods.

To this end, we propose an spectacularly fast and effective method for video browsing. In the interactive process, the only user effort required is to click one shot which most visually relates to the target, out of 20 displayed shots. Every time when asked to make a selection, the user is involved in a new search session. It is obvious that a shot which is closely related to traffic will never be chosen if the user wants the one that is about a banquet. Since the user selection reflects her query intent, we can assist the user to find the target as quickly as possible if we succeed in capturing the query intent conveyed in the user selections. In other words, it's possible to learn about the target from user feedbacks. Thus, we propose a fast and traffic-economic video browsing paradigm called Mental Visual Indexing (MVI). The core of MVI is a temporal model, specifically a RNN model referenced as char-RNN [6]. The model receives the user feedback and takes the corresponding shot ID as input, indexing the user's query intent in its hidden variables. The output of the model is a prediction which indicates the probability of one shot being the user's search target. The model can quickly response since it requires no heavy real-time similarity comparison. To train the model, we first select every shot in the shot repository as the mental target and generate 40 pseudo user feedback sequences using the statistical model detailed in Section 2.3. A pseudo user feedback sequence is a sentence which is composed of at least two shot IDs, starting and ending with the target shot ID. Then we feed all the sequences to our char-RNN model. Experiments show that our char-RNN based framework is accurate, fast, and user-friendly.

Our contributions are summarized as follows:

- We propose a very fast and traffic-economic video browsing paradigm called Mental Visual Indexing (MVI). It only requires user click from mental.

- MVI is built on a deep temporal model: char-RNN, to index the long-term visual relationships among click-through user feedbacks. It is automatically trained by sampling machine-generated visual feedback steps. Once trained, it can quickly calculate the next candidate video shots.

- We develop a video browsing interface. Experiments on real-world movies show that user can find a target in 3-5 steps.

2. THE PROPOSED METHOD

2.1 System Overview

Given a long video and a mental target shot, our goal is to assist the user to find the target via minimum interactions. To achieve this goal, we proposed a framework which consists of two main components: a statistical framework and a Character-Level Language Model, *i.e.* the char-RNN model. The statistical framework is employed to generate pseudo user feedbacks or click histories based on visual similarity. These feedbacks accumulate into a large training data set for char-RNN network training. The char-RNN model is employed to analyze the interrelationships between video shots. Once well trained, the model is able to successfully infer user's query intent during the procedure of video browsing. See Figure 2 for a general understanding about our framework.

Our system is divided into two parts: off-line part and online part. In the off-line part, we cut a video into shots which are represented by their VGG19 [15] features. Then, we feed all the Shots-Target pairs to the statistical framework which results in a bunch of pseudo user feedback sequences. Each Shots-Target pair here is composed of all the shots and a randomly selected target. A sequence indicates that all the video shots contained in the sequence have some sort of inner connection in the visual feature space. We trained the char-RNN model on the sequences. In the on-line part, we initially show the user some shots, then the user selects the one that is most similar to her mental target. The system receives the user's choice and feeds the corresponding shot ID to the well trained RNN model. The model, then, predicts the next candidate shots for display. The process lasts until the user meets her target.

2.2 Mental Visual Indexing

Suppose there are N shots segmented from a long video, denoted as $\mathcal{V} = \{1...i...N\}$ for simplicity. Let $\mathcal{M} \subset \mathcal{V}$ denotes the possible subset of the long video shots, *i.e.*, it can be considered as candidates of users' target mental shots. Generally, $\mathcal{M}$ is unknown or even imaginary to the system. We assume that if a member of $\mathcal{M}$ is displayed, the user can easily find the target by using this shot as a starting point for precise localization in the long video.

We denote the user feedback history as $\mathcal{H}_t = \mathcal{H}_{t-1} \cup \{c_t = k, k \in \mathcal{D}_t\}$, of which $\mathcal{D}_t$ is the shots displayed during search session t and $\mathcal{H}_{t-1}$ stands for the previous history. The essence of MVI lies in its ability to learn about the user's query intent from $\mathcal{H}_t$ gradually in the process of user interaction with the system. Eq (1) is the update formula for query intent modeling, where s_{t-1} is the intent guessed after the previous interaction, c_t donates the user's feedback in the current round and s_t stands for the updated intention.

$$s_t = f(c_t, s_{t-1}). \tag{1}$$

Inspired by [16], we employed the char-RNN [6] model to automatically learn about the inherent query information as the search session lasts. Originally, the model is designed to take character sequence as input and predict the next character. In this work, we extend the model to take a shot ID as input and output the IDs of the candidate shots for next display. The model is trained with a dictionary file which is a text file with unique shot ID per line and a text file containing all the pseudo user feedback sequences. Each sequence is a machine-generated sentence with shot IDs as the words. All the sequences are generated by randomly selecting one shot as the target and feeding all the shots and the pseudo target as a Shots-Target pair to our statistical framework. The statistical framework then builds the sequence by continuously comparing visual similarity until the target is found (see Figure 2).

When trained on the sequences, the RNN model is reliable to grasp the inner connections among video shots because only relevant shots appear in the same sequence. Therefore, the model guarantees the output shots are always very related with the input one and captures user intent by updating its hidden variables, *i.e.* s_t. The model is very fast in that the heavy computation is done in the off-line part

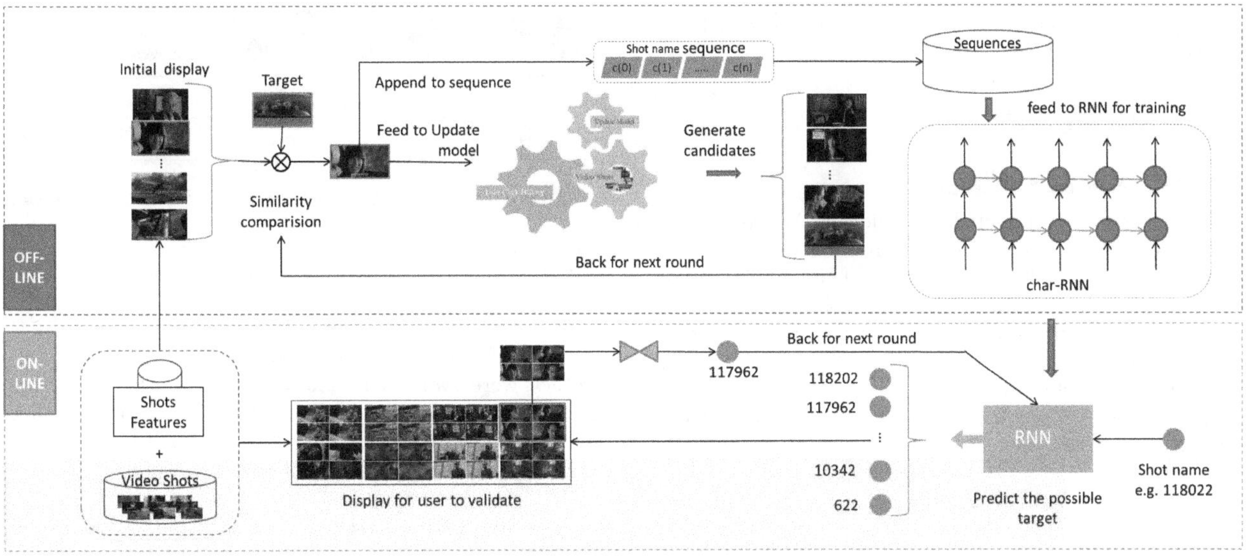

Figure 2: The framework is divided into off-line part and on-line part: 1) In off-line part, we generate training by simulating user feedback and train the char-RNN model; 2) In on-line part, the model takes the user feedback as input and predicts the candidates for next display.

and in the on-line part, the only required computation is one step of vector inner product.

2.3 Statistical Framework for Training

The statistical framework is a variant of the one proposed in [2] which is inspired by [1, 17]. Given the Shots-Target pair, the framework is employed to generate the pseudo user feedback sequences in the off-line part which form the training data for our char-RNN model. To be concrete, imaging this is a real user feedback procedure, we maintain N-independent Bayesian system $p_t(i)$ for each video shot i. In particular, $p_t(i)$ is the estimated probability of shot i belonging to the target set $\mathcal{M}$:

$$p_t(i) = P(i \in \mathcal{M}|\mathcal{H}_t). \tag{2}$$

Since we have no prior knowledge about $\mathcal{M}$, we take $p_0(i) = 0.5$ as the starting state.

By applying Bayes rule, we can rewrite the definition in Eq (2) as:

$$p_t(i) = \frac{P\left(c_t = k|\mathcal{H}_{t-1}, i \in \mathcal{M}, k \in \mathcal{D}_t\right) P\left(i \in \mathcal{M}|\mathcal{H}_{t-1}, k \in \mathcal{D}_t\right)}{P\left(c_t = k|\mathcal{H}_{t-1}, k \in \mathcal{D}_t\right)}. \tag{3}$$

In order to further simplify the above model for computability, we should note several statistical sufficiency and assumptions. First, $c_t = k$ is a sufficient statistic for $k \in \mathcal{D}_t$ since it is obvious that once the user clicks on k, k must be in $\mathcal{D}_t$. Second, the fact $i \in \mathcal{M}$ is unrelated to the display set $\mathcal{D}_t$. Third, once given the display $\mathcal{D}_t$, the history $\mathcal{H}_{t-1}$ is no longer informative to the user click $c_t = k$. Based on these statistical properties, we have the update model for $p_t(i)$ as:

$$\begin{aligned} p_t(i) &= \frac{P\left(c_t = k|i \in \mathcal{M}, k \in \mathcal{D}_t\right) p_{t-1}(i)}{P\left(c_t = k|k \in \mathcal{D}_t\right)} \\ &= \frac{P_+(k|i, D) p_{t-1}(i)}{P_+(k|i, D) p_{t-1}(i) + P_-(k|i, D)\left(1 - p_{t-1}(k)\right)}. \end{aligned} \tag{4}$$

where

$$\begin{cases} P\left(c_t = k|i \in \mathcal{M}, k \in \mathcal{D}_t\right) = P_+(k|i, D), \\ P\left(c_t = k|i \notin \mathcal{M}, k \in \mathcal{D}_t\right) = P_-(k|i, D). \end{cases} \tag{5}$$

Therefore, all we need to update $p_t(i)$ is to model the user feedback $P_+(k|i, D)$ and $P_-(k|i, D)$. We assume that the user always selects the shot that most matches her mental target from the shots displayed, the click probability can be modeled as:

$$\begin{cases} P_+(k|i, D) = \dfrac{s(i, k)}{\sum_{j \in \mathcal{D}_t} s(j, k)}, \\ P_-(k|i, D) = \dfrac{d(i, k)}{\sum_{j \in \mathcal{D}_t} d(j, k)}. \end{cases} \tag{6}$$

where $d(\cdot, \cdot)$ and $s(\cdot, \cdot)$ denote the distance and similarity in the feature space, respectively. The intuition behind the above definitions is that if i is the target shot, the probability is enhanced by the similarity between i and k; if i is not the target, the probability is depressed by the distance between i and k.

Now the problem is how to choose D_{t+1} given the user feedback and D_t. The simplest approach may be to select several shots that are most likely to belong to M. Unfortunately, it's not efficient in the real user interactive procedure. For example, usually two very similar shots are probably either both in M or both not in M, which may lead to the unexpected situations where both of the shots are displayed in the next round or none of them are displayed. Both of the situations will prevent the user from getting more information about the shot repository. To avoid this case, we select the most informative subset $\mathcal{D}_{t+1} \subset \mathcal{V}$ by minimizing $\min_{\mathcal{D} \subset \mathcal{V}} \text{Entropy}(z_{t+1}|\mathcal{H}_t)$. Intuitively, the selection attempts to make an optimal Voronoi partition for the video shots. The detailed calculation of the probability z_{t+1} is given in [1].

The situation is a little different when it comes to our user feedback simulation. A simple machine does not have an imaginary target and, of course, does not have the ability to tell visual similarity intelligently as we humans do. The workaround is to select the one that is closest to the target in the feature space as the feedback. We keep recording the feedback until the predetermined target is found and treat each record as a sequence.

3. EXPERIMENTS

3.1 Experiment Settings

Experiments were conducted on 3 videos: Ant-Man, Life of PI and a product launch video from Microsoft. We first produced three sets with about 8200, 7780 and 12500 frames respectively by extracting one frame every 20 frames. Then, Caffe toolbox [4] and the model discussed in [15] were employed to generate a high level representation (VGG19) for each frame. The 4096-dimension VGG19 feature we used in our experiments is the output of full-connection layer "fc7" before RELU and dropout layer.

Video was cut into shots by comparing frame-level features. For each frame, we compared its feature with the previous one to see how similar they are. After that consecutive frames with high similarity were restructured into one shot by averaging frame-level features. In order to give users a clearer picture of the shot, an informative thumbnail was generated. For computability, the frame-level features as well as the shot features were normalized. Unlike our baseline, feature dimension reduction is not required in that no copious real-time feature comparisons are needed. Even in the baseline, only when high precision was not strictly demanded did we apply PCA-whitening [3, 12] to reduce the dimension into 512 [2].

We chose to set $rnn\_size = 128$, $num\_layers = 1$, $seq\_len = 20$, $learning\_rate = 0.01$ and the other training parameters to their default values after comparing the performance under different model settings. The most important parameter is seq_len which specifies the length of each stream and, as well, limits the back-propagation of the gradients. For instance, if $seq\_len = 10$, then the gradients will never back-propagate more than 10 time steps, and the model might not find dependencies longer than this length in number of characters. Because the mean sequence length over all training sequences is about 10, we set $seq\_len = 20$. Although it is recommended to use num_layers of either 2/3, we found a better performance could be achieved when we set $num\_layers = 1$ [6].

3.2 Experiment Results

In this section we first evaluated the efficiency of our approach, then we compared our approach with the one proposed in [2], finally we conducted a user study to identify the effectiveness of our approach. All the experiments were based on the 10 randomly selected targets (see Figure 3).

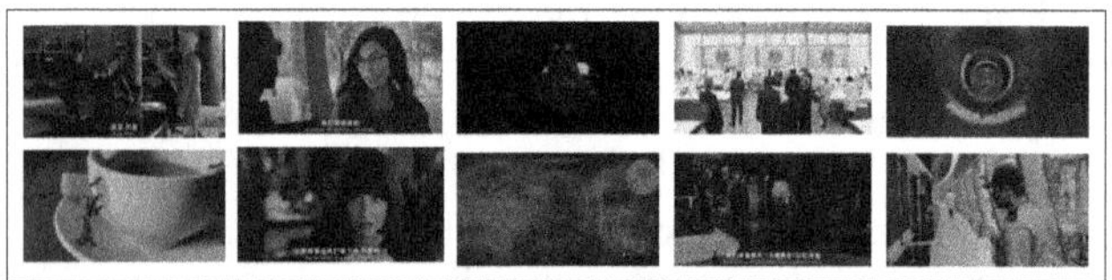

Figure 3: The 10 randomly selected target shots

To have a basic understanding about the efficiency of our framework, we selected 4 target shots from Figure 3 and conducted a general validation. Table 1 lists the result. It

4	3	7	4	iterations
yes	yes	yes	yes	found

Table 1: Efficiency validation of our framework

shows that our approach is effective and, in average, we can find a target in 4 iterations.

The next set of experiment was performed on each of the shots in Figure 3. Both the baseline method and our approach were evaluated. The result shows that ,by average, our approach can locate the target in 30 seconds with 96% accuracy within 4 iterations which is much better than the baseline (70s, 8 iterations and 88% accuracy).

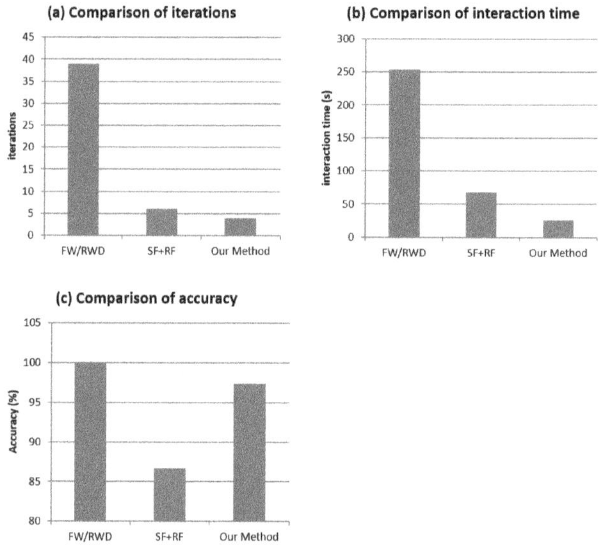

Figure 4: User study results: a) mean iterations comparison; b) mean interaction time comparison; c) mean retrieval accuracy comparison.

Eight students were involved in our user study, with five of them are enrolled in computer vision studies and the others are enrolled in natural language processing (NLP) studies, which means about half of the student are novices. Three tasks have been conducted: 1) find all the targets in any common video player; 2) find all the target shots in the system proposed in [2]; 3) find all the target shots in our system. The general comparison of three tasks is shown in Figure 4. The result shows that our approach can measurably improve system performance.

4. CONCLUSIONS

In the paper, we extended the char-RNN temporal model to video browsing task by a new interactive search paradigm named Mental Visual Indexing (MVI). The intuition behind MVI is to learn the inherent connections between video shots automatically and capture user query intent gradually by analyzing the user feedbacks. When trained on a large set of simulated user feedbacks, the proposed model responses quickly and accurately to the user query. Our results show that the char-RNN based model improves system performance by shortening system response time, decreasing interactive iterations and increasing prediction accuracy.

5. ACKNOWLEDGMENTS

This work was supported in part by the Anhui Fund for Distinguished Young Scholars under Grant 1508085J04, in part by the National High-Tech Development Program of China under Grant 2014AA015104, in part by the National Natural Science Foundation of China under Grant 61472116.

We are grateful to all study participants for their contributions and to NExT for the supply of lab facilities. NExT research is supported by Nation Research Foundation, Prime Minister's Office, Singapore under its IRC@SG Funding Initiative.

6. REFERENCES

[1] M. Ferecatu and D. Geman. A statistical framework for image category search from a mental picture. *Pattern Analysis and Machine Intelligence, IEEE Transactions on*, 31(6):1087–1101, 2009.

[2] J. He, X. Shang, H. Zhang, and T.-S. Chua. Mental visual browsing. In *MultiMedia Modeling*, pages 424–428. Springer, 2016.

[3] H. Jégou and O. Chum. Negative evidences and co-occurences in image retrieval: The benefit of pca and whitening. In *Computer Vision–ECCV 2012*, pages 774–787. Springer, 2012.

[4] Y. Jia, E. Shelhamer, J. Donahue, S. Karayev, J. Long, R. Girshick, S. Guadarrama, and T. Darrell. Caffe: Convolutional architecture for fast feature embedding. *arXiv preprint arXiv:1408.5093*, 2014.

[5] L. Jiang, T. Mitamura, S.-I. Yu, and A. G. Hauptmann. Zero-example event search using multimodal pseudo relevance feedback. In *Proceedings of International Conference on Multimedia Retrieval*, page 297. ACM, 2014.

[6] Karpathy. Multi-layer recurrent neural networks (lstm, gru, rnn) for character-level language models in torch. https://github.com/karpathy/char-rnn. Accessed April 4, 2016.

[7] Z. Ma, Y. Yang, Z. Xu, S. Yan, N. Sebe, and A. Hauptmann. Complex event detection via multi-source video attributes. In *Proceedings of the IEEE Conference on Computer Vision and Pattern Recognition*, pages 2627–2633, 2013.

[8] V. Mezaris, A. Dimou, and I. Kompatsiaris. Local invariant feature tracks for high-level video feature extraction. In *11th International Workshop on Image Analysis for Multimedia Interactive Services, WIAMIS 2010, Desenzano del Garda, Italy, April 12-14, 2010*, pages 1–4, 2010.

[9] I. Mironica, B. Ionescu, J. Uijlings, and N. Sebe. Fisher kernel based relevance feedback for multimodal video retrieval. In *Proceedings of the 3rd ACM conference on International conference on multimedia retrieval*, pages 65–72. ACM, 2013.

[10] A. Nordin. Improving an information retrieval system by using machine learning to improve user relevance feedback. 2016.

[11] P. Over, J. Fiscus, G. Sanders, D. Joy, M. Michel, G. Awad, A. Smeaton, W. Kraaij, and G. Quénot. Trecvid 2014–an overview of the goals, tasks, data, evaluation mechanisms and metrics. In *Proceedings of TRECVID*, page 52, 2014.

[12] A. Razavian, H. Azizpour, J. Sullivan, and S. Carlsson. Cnn features off-the-shelf: an astounding baseline for recognition. In *Proceedings of the IEEE Conference on Computer Vision and Pattern Recognition Workshops*, pages 806–813, 2014.

[13] J. J. Rocchio. Relevance feedback in information retrieval. 1971.

[14] K. Schoeffmann, D. Ahlström, W. Bailer, C. Cobârzan, F. Hopfgartner, K. McGuinness, C. Gurrin, C. Frisson, D.-D. Le, M. Del Fabro, et al. The video browser showdown: a live evaluation of interactive video search tools. *International Journal of Multimedia Information Retrieval*, 3(2):113–127, 2014.

[15] K. Simonyan and A. Zisserman. Very deep convolutional networks for large-scale image recognition. *CoRR*, abs/1409.1556, 2014.

[16] I. Sutskever, J. Martens, and G. E. Hinton. Generating text with recurrent neural networks. In *Proceedings of the 28th International Conference on Machine Learning (ICML-11)*, pages 1017–1024, 2011.

[17] M. Wang, Y. Gao, K. Lu, and Y. Rui. View-based discriminative probabilistic modeling for 3d object retrieval and recognition. *IEEE Transactions on Image Processing*, 22(4):1395–1407, 2013.

[18] Z. Zha, M. Wang, Y. Zheng, Y. Yang, R. Hong, and T. Chua. Interactive video indexing with statistical active learning. *IEEE Trans. Multimedia*, 14(1):17–27, 2012.

[19] H. Zhang, X. Shang, W. Yang, H. Xu, H. Luan, and T.-S. Chua. Online collaborative learning for open-vocabulary visual classifiers. *IEEE International Conference on Computer Vision and Pattern Recognition*, 2016.

[20] H. Zhang, F. Shen, W. Liu, X. He, H. Luan, and T.-S. Chua. Discrete collaborative filtering. In *Proc. of SIGIR*, volume 16, 2016.

[21] H. Zhang, Z.-J. Zha, S. Yan, J. Bian, and T.-S. Chua. Attribute feedback. In *Proceedings of the 20th ACM international conference on Multimedia*, pages 79–88. ACM, 2012.

[22] X. Zhang, Y. Yang, Y. Zhang, H. Luan, J. Li, H. Zhang, and T. Chua. Enhancing video event recognition using automatically constructed semantic-visual knowledge base. *IEEE Trans. Multimedia*, 17(9):1562–1575, 2015.

[23] X. S. Zhou and T. S. Huang. Relevance feedback in image retrieval: A comprehensive review. *Multimedia systems*, 8(6):536–544, 2003.

One Sensor is not Enough: Adapting and Fusing Sensors for the Quality Assessment of User Generated Video

Stefan Wilk
TU Darmstadt, Germany
stefan.wilk@cs.tu-darmstadt.de

Manisha Luthra
TU Darmstadt, Germany
manisha.luthra@kom.tu-darmstadt.de

Wolfgang Effelsberg
TU Darmstadt, Germany
wolfgang.effelsberg@cs.tu-darmstadt.de

ABSTRACT

In comparison to professional productions, User Generated Video (UGV) often suffers from quality degradations such as camera shakes or harmful occlusions. Quick and reliable algorithms are needed to detect and assess the impact of these quality degradations. Recently, researchers leverage data from auxiliary sensors such as gyroscope readings or accelerometer values for quality assessment. In comparison to video-based approaches, auxiliary sensor-based ones achieve results more quickly but often lack precision.

This work proposes a framework for the combined analysis of UGV which leverages the strength of video-based and auxiliary sensor-based algorithms. In addition, we propose a hybrid algorithm for camera shake detection, which dynamically adapts which *sensor* readings to use for the assessment. A hybrid algorithm achieves an improved precision and a reduced runtime in comparison to the usage of a single sensor.

1. INTRODUCTION

Despite the popularity of User Generated Video (UGV), its quality assessment has not been adequately addressed. Recently, researchers proposed solutions to identify specific degradations such as noisy audio recordings [6], over- or underexposed video frames [9]. The algorithms rely on either an analysis of the video frames using image processing or on leveraging data from auxiliary sensors, which is sampled during the recording, e.g., from the accelerometer or the gyroscope. Whereas video-based approaches are usually highly accurate, they consume significant computational time. Thus, only a limited number of these algorithms can be executed in real-time. Auxiliary sensor-based approaches offer quick results, but their performance significantly suffers from imprecisions of the sensors, e.g., white noise and requires calibration for reliable quality assessment. Our vision is to design an hybrid approach, which leverages multiple sensors for quality analysis in UGV. We propose a framework for fusing multiple sensors for quality assessment, which generates accurate estimations at a low runtime.

MM '16, October 15-19, 2016, Amsterdam, Netherlands

DOI: http://dx.doi.org/10.1145/2964284.2967297

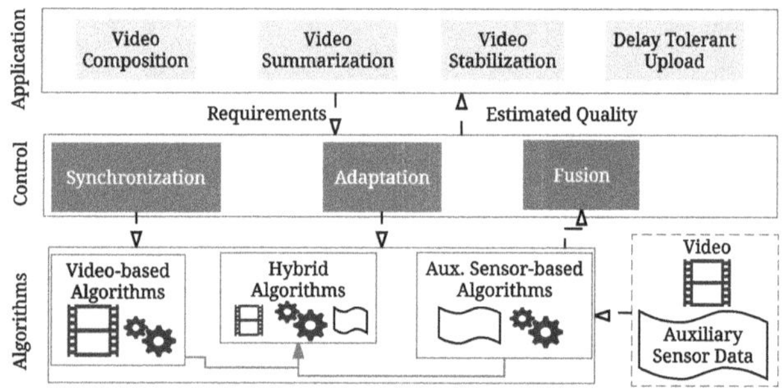

Figure 1: Layers of the Multi-Sensor Quality Assessment.

To this end we make the following contributions: (1) We propose a multi-sensor fusion based framework for UGV (see Fig. 1), by adaptation between auxiliary sensors and video signals for video quality assessment, (2) we overcome shortcomings of existing camera shake detection algorithm by proposing improvements, and (3) we show the benefits of the proposed hybrid approach by evaluating the two public datasets: Jiku [10] and CMDG [1].

Quality assessment of UGV is addressed in this work as these videos often suffer from different degradations such as camera shaking, encoding artifacts or bad lighting conditions. Quality assessment steps of multimedia applications usually rely on long-running image processing algorithms analyzing specific degradations such as camera shakes [9, 11] or compression effects such as proposed by Mittal et al. [7] or VideoBLINDS [8]. Recently proposed algorithms focus on real-time analysis relying on auxiliary sensors as proposed by Cricri et al. [3] using a accelerometer sensor or the gyroscope-based algorithm of Bano et al. [1].

All these algorithms are designed using a specific sensor as input and decide for a suitable trade-off between precision and runtime of the algorithm. Yet, no algorithm proposes a combination of different sensors for the reliable and quick analysis of quality impairments, even though it is promising, as, e.g., demonstrated for video genre classification [4].

2. MULTI-SENSOR QUALITY ASSESSMENT

The central idea of this work is to propose a scheme for designing hybrid quality assessment algorithms. Hybrid implies that at least two sensors are used by an algorithm for the video quality assessment. We assume that a runtime environment for quality assessment is available, which is structured into the application, the control and the algorithm layer. Multimedia applications which need a quality assessment include video composition [13, 14], summarization or stabilization systems. These applications are part of our decoupled application layer. Applications are unaware of the used algorithms, but leverage the control layer to request a quality assessment (see Fig. 1). The control layer coordinates algorithms which leverage different sensors as input and hides the associated complexity from the application. This includes the synchronization of media with auxiliary sensors, the adaptation between different sensor inputs and the fusion of sensor samples. Adaptation is used if over the time of a video recording session, one sensor input degrades in terms of reliability, as the noise in the sensing increases. A hybrid algorithm should detect this situation and adapt the input to another sensor, as the camera. Fusion combines the results of different sensors in order to improve the precision of a quality assessment. The algorithm layer is invoked by the control layer and offers the runtime for the quality assessment algorithms. The description on the algorithm layer as well as the concepts of adaptation and fusion are given in the next subsections.

2.1 Design of a Multi-Sensor Algorithm

The idea of using multiple sensors as input for quality assessment is illustrated using a novel camera shake detection algorithm combining a video-based and an auxiliary sensor-based algorithm.

2.1.1 Video-based Algorithm

We propose a video-based algorithm for camera shake detection, which performs an intensity-based projection of consecutive video frames and the calculation of a global motion between the video frames. Based on this analysis, repetitive changes in motion are classified as camera shakes. Figure 2 gives an overview of the algorithm, which extracts in a window of N frames, two consecutive video frames per iteration. A fast intensity-based approach is applied which is derived from the Fast Sub-Block Gray Projection Algorithm (FSGPA) [5]. For detecting the motion, 64×64 pixel subblocks of the intensity representations of the video frames are extracted from each video frame. Therefore, the subblock detection or sifting step filters subblocks whose average intensity per pixel is below $T_{lowerGray} = 98$. All subblocks which have such a low intensity are not considered for motion calculation. The rationale behind this step is that motion cannot be reliably determined in a low intensity range.

The global motion between two filtered frames is estimated by analyzing the horizontal and vertical projections of a video frame independent of each other. Vertical and horizontal motion vectors are determined by finding the minimal, common movement of all subblocks—indicated by a minimal error when mapping the two intensity frames. Therefore, in a search breadth of $m = 1$ for each subblock it is determined whether it has moved not at all or up to $2*m+1$ blocks. The minimum of the sum of absolute differences indicates the steps a subblock has moved, i.e., in the horizontal $d_x = m + 1 - w_{min,h}$ and vertical translation by $d_y = m + 1 - w_{min,v}$. Here, $w_{min,h}$ indicates the alignment to compensate motion in the horizontal direction—similarly $w_{min,v}$ exists for the vertical projection. Based on this motion estimation, which is repeatedly calculated for all frames i in a window of video frames, the number of direction changes can be determined. As soon as at least two direction changes are detected, a camera shake is identified.

2.1.2 Auxiliary Sensor-based Algorithm

On the auxiliary sensor side, we leverage linear accelerometer values. The idea of the algorithm is to identify camera shakes by at least two direction changes in a sensor sample window, and is an advancement of the algorithm proposed in our previous work [13]. To reduce the computational burden, a subset of 15 samples (f = 15Hz) in a window of 1s are gathered by linear accelerometers. Therefore, a low pass filter is applied to both reduce the window size and avoid noise generated by the highly sensitive sensors.[1] The filtered values are then used to determine camera shakes as depicted in Algorithm 1.

Algorithm 1 Algorithm for the Detection of Camera Shakes [13].

function sgn(p,q): 3D-Signum-Function - calculates the sign of the difference of p to q for each dimension of a 3D vector and returns a 3D vector.
function MAX($p[]$): Calculates highest absolute acceleration in the array $p[]$ of three-dimensional vectors
Require: $s[]$: Three-dimensional sample array (x,y,z) of size m filled with linear accelerometer sensor samples
Require: t: Latest sample index
Require: T_S: Threshold for identifying significant camera shaking

```
c_d ← 0
if s_{t,x} ≠ s_{t-1,x} or s_{t,y} ≠ s_{t-1,y} or s_{t,z} ≠ s_{t-1,z} then
    for i ← 0..t − 3 do
        if sgn(s_i, s_{i+1}) ≠ sgn(s_{i+1}, s_{i+2}) then
            c_d ← c_d + 1
        end if
    end for
    if c_d ≥ 2 and MAX(s[]) ≥ T_S then
        return true
    end if
end if
return false
```

The algorithm applies a signum function to determine the direction of linear accelerometer values. The number of direction changes are counted, where two or more direction changes indicates a camera shake. To compensate small and imperceivable changes a threshold $T_S = 0.2\frac{m}{s^2}$ determines the minimum acceleration, which indicates a harmful shake.

The described video-based and the auxiliary sensor-based algorithms indicate if a camera shake is present or not. The quantification of its impact on the perceived quality can be achieved by determining its amplitude, speed and duration. Our previous works offers the respective quality model indicating a subjectively validated Mean Opinion Score (MOS) [12].

2.2 Adaptation

An adaptation between sensors is beneficial, if the single sensor algorithms perform differently well for different

[1]The low pass filter uses a threshold of $\alpha = 0.3$ and iterates linear accelerometer samples a with index i by applying $a_i = a_{i-1} + \alpha * (a_i - a_{i-1})$.

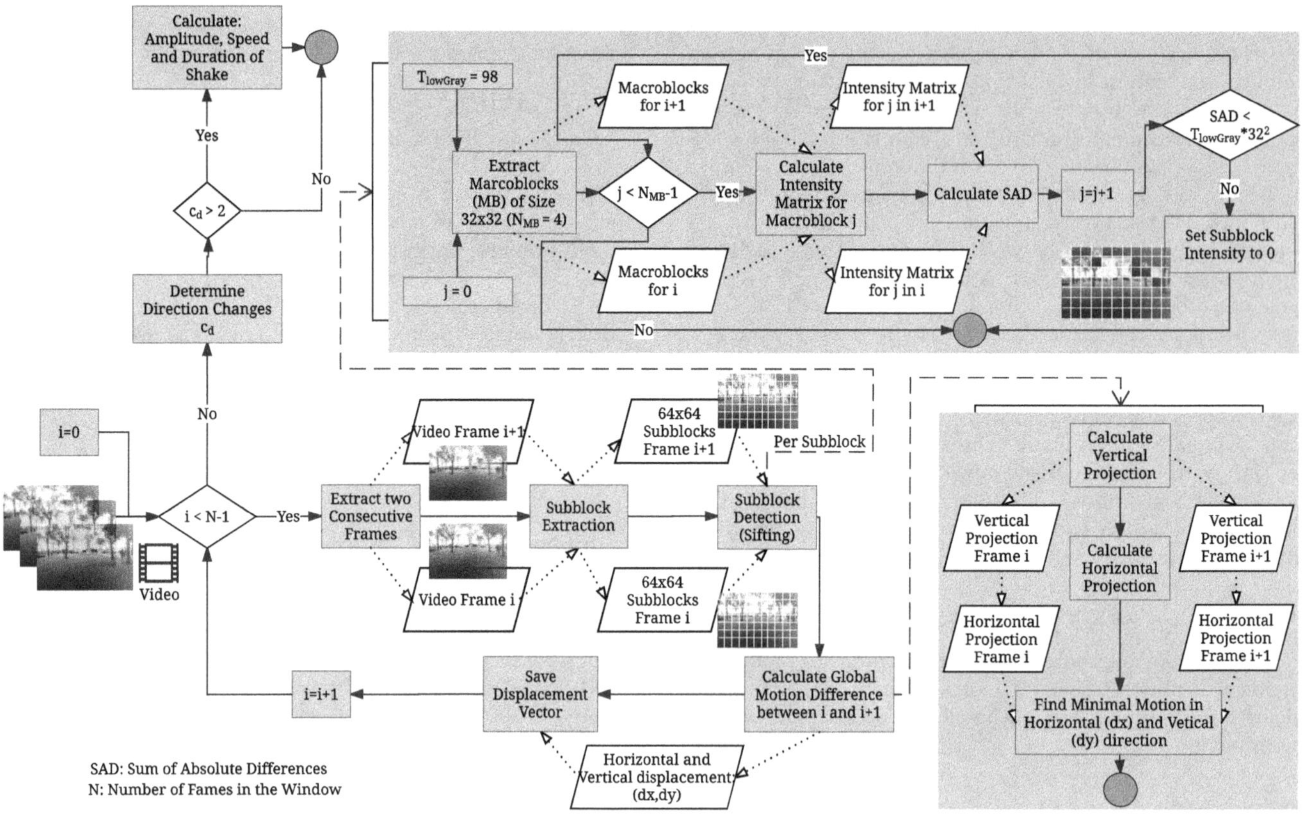

Figure 2: Overview on the camera shake detection algorithm relying on the analysis of the video.

environmental conditions. For example, feature extraction methods are known for their weaknesses, if lighting changes rapidly. Bano et al. [1] have recently identified that for camera movement analysis using image processing algorithms, the luminance value significantly affects the precision. To compensate for this, we propose to dynamically determine whether a video-based algorithm is suitable, e.g., for camera shake detection, by analyzing the luma intensity of a video. Video-based algorithms are able to determine the luma in a video reliably, but are time-consuming. Therefore, we propose to use the built-in light sensors in today's smartphones for determining approximate luma of a video. The light sensor samples are averaged in order to retrieve one luma value per video frame.

$$V_{j,w_i} = \begin{cases} 1, & \text{if } \mathcal{L}j, w_i \geq T_{L,D} \\ 0, & \text{otherwise} \end{cases} \tag{1}$$

Here, V_{w_i} represents a binary indicator whether the video-based algorithm shall be considered for a specific video frame j in the sample window w_i. Note that the set of all w_i represents the complete video stream. $\mathcal{L}j, w_i$ depicts the average light intensity for j in window w_i, determined by samples from the light sensor in a smartphone. A decision, whether a video-based algorithms can be applied is based on whether the majority of frames in w_i fulfill $V_{j,w_i} = 1$ or not. $T_{L,D}$ is a device-specific threshold, as the sensed samples vary significantly between manufacturers of the light sensors embedded in smartphones [1], as, e.g., the LG Nexus 5 shows good ambient light conditions at around 2.0, whereas a Samsung Galaxy S2 senses under same conditions around 100.0. The values were gathered based on the video and sensor dataset of Bano et al. [1].

2.3 Fusion

The second concept used by hybrid algorithms is fusion, which helps to reliably determine camera shakes, if the adaptation decision is unclear. In contrast to adaptation, fusion leverages for a given time in a video both: auxiliary sensor and video frames. To detect situations in which fusion should be applied, the auxiliary sensor sample window $w_{i,AS}$ and the video frame window $w_{i,V}$ are used. It is triggered when, within a given sample window, the sensor does not uniformly detect a degradation.

The entries of both windows need to be synchronized based on the timestamps associated with the sensor samples and the video frames. The resulting scores $S_{A_V,w_{i,V}}$ and $S_{A_{AS},w_{i,AS}}$ of simultaneously executed algorithms are then considered for fusion. Here, A_V represents the video-based algorithm and A_{AS} the auxiliary sensor-based algorithm. The scores can be either binary values as indicated in Algorithm 1, which solely indicate if a camera shake is present or not, or calculate a camera shakiness score, which quantifies the degradation as described in our previous work [12].

$S_{V,AS}$ represents the fused score which is calculated by:

$$S_{V,AS} = o_V * S_{A_V,w_{i,V}} + o_{AS} * S_{A_{AS},w_{i,AS}} \tag{2}$$

Here, o_{IP} represents the weight for the shake score calculated by the video-based algorithm and o_{AS} the score based on auxiliary sensors. The scores $S_{A_{AS},w_{i,AS}}$ and $S_{A_V,w_{i,V}}$ as well as the weights o_V and o_{AS} are normalized between

Table 1: Algorithm performance for different datasets. 'H' represents the proposed, hybrid algorithm and shows its performance in comparison to state-of-the-art algorithms. Metrics used include P: precision; R: recall; F1: F1 score; T: runtime for analyzing 10 video seconds; ◦: no valid results.

	CMDG			JIKU			
Algo.	P	R	*F*1	P	R	*F*1	T
H	0.53	0.73	**0.65**	0.92	0.99	**0.97**	4.02s
[9]	0.10	0.70	0.18	0.92	0.81	0.86	13.0s
[2]	0.11	0.82	0.19	0.92	0.97	0.94	13.39s
[1]	0.41	0.57	0.48	◦	◦	◦	0.008s

$[0, 1]$ and the condition $o_{IP} + o_{AS} = 1$ must hold. Thus, fusion introduces the opportunity for algorithm developers to adjust the influence of sensors on the final results.

3. EVALUATION

We evaluate the proposed, hybrid quality assessment of UGV using other state-of-the-art algorithms and run them under the same conditions for public video datasets. We assess its performance in terms of precision, recall, F1 score and the runtime.

3.1 Evaluation Setup

The public JIKU dataset [10] and CMDG dataset [1] are used for assessing the characteristics of our proposed algorithm, as both dataset contain UGV annotated by auxiliary sensor samples. In the JIKU dataset, we analyze the 'NAF160312' event which consists of 66 concert video clips with a duration between 0:49 minutes and 40:18 minutes and a resolution of either 480p or 720p at a frame rate of 25 to 29 frames per second. We manually added a ground truth on whether a human perceivable camera shakes occur. The CMDG dataset was specifically designed to evaluate camera motion using the gyroscope sensor in a smartphone, with an available ground-truth. The authors annotated the dataset consisting of 24 videos with a total duration of 70 minutes by a ground truth on whether camera shakes occur. The resolution of the videos is 480p and a frame rate of 29 to 30 frames per second. We compare our algorithm with different state-of-the-art camera shake detection algorithms by Saini et al. [9] (Video-based), Campanella et al. [2] (Video-based) and Bano et al. [1] (Gyroscope Sensor).

3.2 Parameter Study

In a parameter study we determined the best settings for the video-based part by iterating different parameter settings with the goal of a maximized F1 score.

T_S is used to compensate for very small movements detected by the linear accelerometer. Any value above $0.2\frac{m}{s^2}$ is perceived as significant motion, which can lead to camera shake. A shake is then detected by the linear accelerometer of within a window of 1 second at $f = 15$Hz, if two or more direction changes are detected. For fusion the values $o_{IP} = 0.5$ and $o_{AS} = 0.5$, equal weights are used. The other algorithms [9, 2, 1] were configured accordingly.

3.3 Evaluation Results

In comparison to any prior work, we evaluate the proposed and competitive approaches on multiple, public video datasets, which incorporate recordings from different devices and videos created under varying conditions, as, e.g., concerts, art festivals, out- and indoor recordings.

As depicted in Table 1, for the CMDG dataset the proposed algorithm performs better than any prior work in terms of precision and F1 score. Only in terms of the recall rate the approach of Campanella et al. [2], which solely relies on video-based processing, is better as tested on CMDG dataset. Yet, the video-based algorithm of Campanella et al. [2] possess only low precision and F1 score in comparison to our proposed approach. As identified by Bano et al. [1], the video-based methods are susceptible towards moving objects in the video. We tend to minimize this effect by leveraging auxiliary sensor algorithm results. In comparison to video-based algorithms, the algorithm achieves comparably high gains in terms of precision by 0.43 in comparison to [9] and 0.42 in comparison to [2].

The robustness of our algorithm is measured in terms of varying image and auxiliary sensor conditions. Whereas in the CMDG dataset a low resolution of 480p, but a high sampling rate of the auxiliary sensors, the JIKU dataset contains 480p and 720p recordings but only a limited number of samples per second ($f = 5.1Hz$). The results in Table 1 depict that in terms of the F1 score, in both datasets, the proposed, hybrid algorithm outperforms single sensor-based algorithms. In presence of high quality video content at a resolution of 720p and low sensor sample rates, the approach of Saini achieves a slightly higher precision, but a reduced recall rate at a significantly increased runtime.

The algorithms differ not only in terms of precision and recall, but also in terms of run-time. Therefore, the algorithms were run over both datasets on a Intel Xeon CPU E5-1650 and 8GB of dedicated memory. We averaged the runtime per one second of video and depict the results in Table 1. The quickest approach is proposed by Bano et al. [1], which can be executed in less than a second (0.08s), followed by the proposed, hybrid algorithm with a run-time of 4.02s. The investigated video-based algorithms achieve a runtime, which is significantly larger than real-time.

In summary, the proposed algorithm outperforms related approaches in terms of the F1 score and precision and achieves real-time computation on retail hardware.

4. CONCLUSION

This work describes a multi-sensor approach towards quality assessment in UGV. In contrast to existing approaches we propose to adapt and fuse the sensors in order to achieve reliable results in short time. We show that such a hybrid camera shake detection algorithm has significant advantages in comparison to state-of-the-art algorithms. In future, additional algorithms shall be designed using different sensors in order to analyze the potential of hybrid quality assessment algorithms.

Acknowledgements

This work has been co-funded by the German Research Foundation (DFG) as part of the projects C03 within the Collaborative Research Center (CRC) 1053 – MAKI as well as by the project LiViU funded by the German Federal Ministry of Education and Research with grant no. 01IS12054.

5. REFERENCES

[1] S. Bano, A. Cavallaro, and X. Parra. Gyro-based Camera-motion Detection in User-generated Videos. In *ACM Conference on Multimedia Conference*, pages 1303–1306, 2015.

[2] M. Campanella, H. Weda, and M. Barbieri. Edit while Watching: Home Video Editing Made Easy. *SPIE Electronic Imaging*, 2007.

[3] F. Cricri, I. D. Curcio, S. Mate, K. Dabov, and M. Gabbouj. Sensor-Based Analysis of User Generated Video for Multi-camera Video Remixing. In K. Schoeffmann, B. Merialdo, A. Hauptmann, C.-W. Ngo, Y. Andreopoulos, and C. Breiteneder, editors, *Advances in Multimedia Modeling*, pages 255–265. Springer lecture notes edition, 2012.

[4] F. Cricri, M. Roininen, J. Leppanen, and S. Mate. Sport Type Classification of Mobile Videos. *IEEE Transactions on Multimedia*, 16(4):917–932, 2014.

[5] W. Hao, D. Hong-bin, and Z. Xuan. Study on a Fast Motion Estimation Algorithm of Video Stabilization System. *Journal of Convergence Information Technology*, 2013.

[6] Z. Li, J.-C. Wang, J. Cai, Z. Duan, H.-M. Wang, and Y. Wang. Non-reference Audio Quality Assessment for Online Live Music Recordings. In *ACM International Conference on Multimedia*, pages 63–72, 2013.

[7] A. Mittal, A. Moorthy, and A. Bovik. Blind/Referenceless Image Spatial Quality Evaluator. In *IEEE Conference on Signals, Systems and Computers*, 2011.

[8] M. Saad, A. Bovik, and C. Charrier. Blind Prediction of Natural Video Quality. *IEEE Transactions on Image Processing*, 23(3):1352–1365, 2014.

[9] M. Saini, R. Gadde, S. Yan, and W. Ooi. MoViMash: Online Mobile Video Mashup. In *ACM International Conference on Multimedia*, 2012.

[10] M. Saini, S. Venkatagiri, W. Ooi, and M. Chan. The Jiku Mobile Video Dataset. In *ACM Multimedia Systems Conference*, 2013.

[11] P. Shrestha, P. de With, H. Weda, M. Barbieri, and E. Aarts. Automatic Mashup Generation from Multiple-camera Concert Recordings. In *International Conference on Multimedia*, 2010.

[12] S. Wilk and W. Effelsberg. The Influence of Camera Shakes, Harmful Occlusions and Camera Misalignment on the Perceived Quality in User-generated Video. In *IEEE International Conference on Multimedia and Expo*, pages 1–6, 2014.

[13] S. Wilk, S. Kopf, and W. Effelsberg. Video Composition by the Crowd: A System to Compose User-generated Videos in Near Real-time. *ACM International Multimedia Systems Conference*, 2015.

[14] S. Wilk, R. Zimmermann, and W. Effelsberg. Leveraging Transitions for the Upload of User-generated Mobile Video. In *ACM International Workshop on Mobile Video*, 2016.

Boosting Video Description Generation by Explicitly Translating from Frame-Level Captions

Yuan Liu, Zhongchao Shi
Ricoh Software Research Center (Beijing) Co., Ltd., Beijing, China
yuanliu.ustc@gmail.com; Zhongchao.Shi@srcb.ricoh.com

ABSTRACT

Automatically describing video content with natural language is a fundamental challenge of computer vision. The recent advanced technique that approaches this problem is Recurrent Neural Networks (RNN). The need to train RNN on large-scale complex and diverse videos and their associated language, however, makes the task human-labeling intensive and computationally expensive. Moreover, the results can suffer from robustness problem, especially when there are rich of temporal dynamics in the sequence of video frames.

We demonstrate in this paper that the above two limitations can be mitigated by jointly exploring the largely available data from image domain and representing each frame by high-level attributes rather than visual features. The former leverages the learnt models on image captioning benchmark to generate caption for each video frame, while the latter explicitly incorporates the obtained captions which are regarded as the attributes of each frame. Specifically, we propose a novel sequence to sequence architecture to generate descriptions for videos, in a sense that the inputs are the captions of sequential frames and it outputs words sequentially. On a widely used YouTube2Text dataset, our proposal is shown to be powerful with superior performance over several state-of-the-art methods including both architectures that are purely developed on video data and RNN-based models which translate directly from visual features to language.

Keywords

Video Captioning; Image Captioning; Recurrent Neural Networks; Deep Convolutional Neural Networks.

1. INTRODUCTION

Due to the easy availability of digital equipments and various ways for propagating media resources, there are large amount of video data (e.g., news videos, sports videos, speeches and tutorials) proliferating over Internet, TV channels and mobile devices. This has encouraged the development of advanced techniques for a broad range of video understanding applications. A fundamental issue that underlies the success of these technological advances is the recognition. Previous research has predominantly focused on recognizing videos with a predefined set of individual words (tags). Recently, researchers have strived to automatically describe video content with a complete and natural sentence, which can be regarded as the ultimate goal of video understanding. Nevertheless, the problem itself has been taken as an open challenge, as the description generation model should be powerful enough not only to recognize scenes and objects in the video, but also be capable of modeling their spatio-temporal relationships and the dynamics expressed in a natural sentence.

Despite the difficulty of this problem, there have been several attempts being proposed for attacking the video sentence generation [11][15] and its closely related task of image captioning [13]. The main inspiration of those works comes from the advances by using Recurrent Neural Networks (RNN) [1], which has achieved great success on sequence to sequence tasks such as speech recognition and machine translation [9]. A widely used type of RNN model among these successful attempts is Long Short-Term Memory (LSTM) [4], and thus we follow this recipe for generating descriptions of videos in this work.

While encouraging performances are reported, the fact that current video captioning benchmarks only focus on specific domains with very limited scale of training videos and simple descriptions has made the learnt LSTM based models still unpractical. This is because collecting and annotating large-scale complex video dataset requires immense human labor and training on a large amount of videos also demands huge computational resources. Instead, the intensive research on image captioning has also made several benchmarks publically available (e.g. Microsoft COCO (MSCOCO) [5]), where tens of thousands of images are annotated with natural sentences. A valid question is whether we can leverage largely available image captioning benchmarks to generalize and boost video description generation. Furthermore, different from the common inputs of visual features to existing LSTM based models, another alternative inputs are in the form of explicit representations of high-level attributes which are more understandable to humans. We investigate particularly the impact of passing from these high-level attributes of each video frame to video description in LSTM based architecture.

By consolidating the idea of leveraging image captioning data and representing each video frame by semantic

MM '16, October 15-19, 2016, Amsterdam, Netherlands

DOI: http://dx.doi.org/10.1145/2964284.2967298

attributes, we propose a novel sequence to sequence architecture for video description generation, as shown in Figure 1. Given a video, a pre-learnt model on image captioning benchmark is utilized to generate the caption for each selected video frame. The generated caption is regarded as explicit representations of attributes of each frame. Then, a LSTM first encodes the attributes (caption) of each frame one by one. Once all captions are read, the LSTM generates a sentence word by word. The encoding of the attributes of each frame and decoding of each word in video description are jointly learnt in the architecture.

The major contributions of this paper are several folds: We show that boosting and generalizing video description generation becomes much easier and cheaper if we leverage largely available and accessible image captioning data. Instead of representing each video frame by visual features, we investigate the translation from high-level attributes of each frame to video description. A novel sequence to sequence architecture is proposed for video description generation.

2. VIDEO DESCRIPTION GENERATION

Our goal is to generate natural sentences for videos. Unlike the general techniques for video captioning [6][11][12][14] which take visual representations as the input to translation systems, we explicitly utilize the frame-level captions generated by image captioning system as the input sequence and then decode the target description from these sequential captions. The architecture overview is illustrated in Figure 1.

2.1 Notation

Suppose we have a video $\mathcal{V}$ with N_v sample frames (uniform sampling) to be described by a natural sentence $\mathcal{S}$, where $\mathcal{V} = \{f_1, f_2, ..., f_{N_v}\}$ consisting of N_v sample frames and $\mathcal{S} = \{w_1, w_2, ..., w_{N_s}\}$ consisting of N_s words. Let $\mathbf{f}_m \in \mathbb{R}^{D_v}$ and $\mathbf{w}_t \in \mathbb{R}^{D_w}$ denote the D_v-dimensional visual features of the m-th sample frame of video $\mathcal{V}$ and the D_w-dimensional textual features of the t-th word in sentence $\mathcal{S}$ represented by one-hot vector, respectively.

2.2 Frame-level caption generation

To generate frame-level caption for each sample frame, the state-of-the-art image captioning model NIC [13], is exploited here. Specifically, NIC encodes image into visual representations through a pre-trained CNN and then generates corresponding sentence based on the input visual representations by LSTM. Hence, given the input video $\mathcal{V} = \{f_1, f_2, ..., f_{N_v}\}$, we can generate its corresponding frame-level captions $\mathcal{C} = \{s_1, s_2, ..., s_{N_v}\}$ using NIC, where s_m is the generated corresponding caption for m-th sample frame f_m. It is worth noticing that due to limited training data for video captioning, we leverage much larger image captioning benchmark, MSCOCO [5], to pre-train the NIC model, which exploits the knowledge learnt from image domain to enhance video understanding for description generation. Let $\mathbf{s}_m \in \mathbb{R}^{D_w}$ denote the integrated word representations of entire sentence s_m with the same dimension of $\mathbf{w}_t$.

2.3 Sequence to sequence: frame-level caption to video description

Given the frame-level caption sequence, a sequence to sequence model is proposed for video description generation, where the input is the sequence of frame-level captions $\mathcal{C} = \{s_1, s_2, ..., s_{N_v}\}$ and the output is the sequence

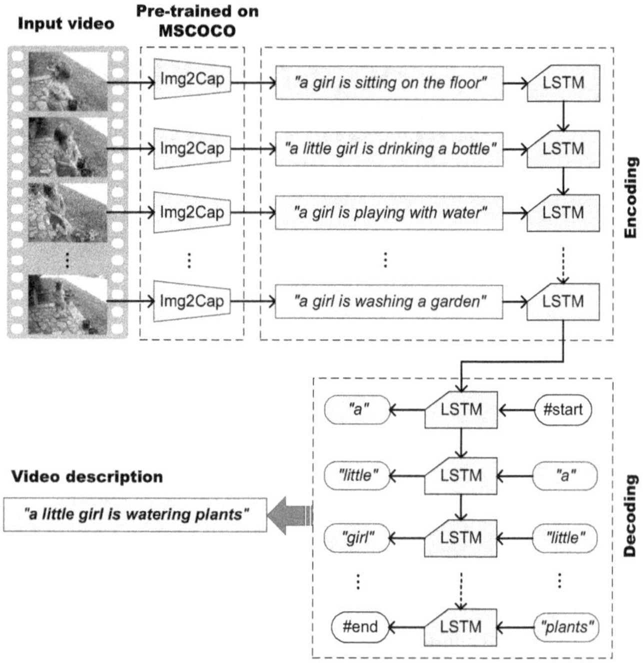

Figure 1: An overview of our architecture for video description generation.

of target words $\mathcal{S} = \{w_1, w_2, ..., w_{N_s}\}$. Hence, given the input frame-level caption sequence $\{s_1, s_2, ..., s_{N_v}\}$, we aim to estimate the conditional probability of the output word sequence $\{w_1, w_2, ..., w_{N_s}\}$, i.e.,

$$\Pr(w_1, w_2, ..., w_{N_s} | s_1, s_2, ..., s_{N_v}). \quad (1)$$

Inspired by the recent successes of sequence to sequence model leveraged in machine translation [9] and video captioning [11], we follow this elegant recipe and extend the LSTM-based sequence to sequence model to solve the problem in Eq.(1). The main idea is to first encode the input sequence of frame-level captions, one caption at a time, representing the input video using multiple frame-level semantics (high-level attributes) captured by image captioning and then decode from these frame-level captions to the target video description, one word at each time step.

Next, we will briefly introduce the standard LSTM, which addresses the vanishing gradients problem in traditional RNN training. It consists of a single memory cell, an input activation function, an output activation function, and three gates (input, forget and output). The vector formulas for a LSTM layer forward pass are given below. For timestep t, $\mathbf{x}^t$ and $\mathbf{h}^t$ are the input and output vector respectively, $\mathbf{T}$ are input weights matrices, $\mathbf{R}$ are recurrent weight matrices and $\mathbf{b}$ are bias vectors. Sigmoid σ and hyperbolic tangent ϕ are element-wise non-linear activation functions. The dot product and sum of two vectors are denoted with $\odot$ and $+$, respectively. Given inputs $\mathbf{x}^t$, $\mathbf{h}^{t-1}$ and $\mathbf{c}^{t-1}$, the LSTM unit updates for timestep t are:

$$\begin{array}{ll}
\mathbf{g}^t = \phi(\mathbf{T}_g\mathbf{x}^t + \mathbf{R}_g\mathbf{h}^{t-1} + \mathbf{b}_g) & \textit{cell input} \\
\mathbf{i}^t = \sigma(\mathbf{T}_i\mathbf{x}^t + \mathbf{R}_i\mathbf{h}^{t-1} + \mathbf{b}_i) & \textit{input gate} \\
\mathbf{f}^t = \sigma(\mathbf{T}_f\mathbf{x}^t + \mathbf{R}_f\mathbf{h}^{t-1} + \mathbf{b}_f) & \textit{forget gate} \\
\mathbf{c}^t = \mathbf{g}^t \odot \mathbf{i}^t + \mathbf{c}^{t-1} \odot \mathbf{f}^t & \textit{cell state} \\
\mathbf{o}^t = \sigma(\mathbf{T}_o\mathbf{x}^t + \mathbf{R}_o\mathbf{h}^{t-1} + \mathbf{b}_o) & \textit{output gate} \\
\mathbf{h}^t = \phi(\mathbf{c}^t) \odot \mathbf{o}^t & \textit{cell output}
\end{array} . \quad (2)$$

Thus, in the encoding stage, given the input sequential captions $\mathcal{C} = \{s_1, s_2, ..., s_{N_v}\}$, LSTM computes a sequence of hidden states $\{h_1, h_2, ..., h_{N_v}\}$. During decoding stage, the log probability of the sentence $\mathcal{S} = \{w_1, w_2, ..., w_{N_s}\}$ is given by the sum of the log probabilities over the word and can be expressed as

$$\log \Pr(\mathcal{S}|\mathcal{C}) = \sum_{t=1}^{N_s} \log \Pr(w_t | h_{N_v+t-1}, w_{t-1}), \quad (3)$$

where the distribution of $\Pr(w_t | h_{N_v+t-1}, w_{t-1})$ is measured by Softmax function over all the words in the vocabulary.

Training and Inference. During the first N_v time steps in encoding stage, LSTM receives the sequence of frame-level captions and encodes them. There is no loss calculated in this stage. After all the frame-level captions in $\mathcal{C}$ have been injected into LSTM, we feed the start sign word $\#start$ into LSTM, which indicates the starting of decoding process. When training in decoding stage, we aim to maximize the log probability of the output video description $\mathcal{S}$ given the hidden representations of the frame-level caption sequence, the pervious words it has seen and the model parameters θ, which can be formulated as

$$\theta^* = \underset{\theta}{argmax} \sum_{t=1}^{N_s} \log \Pr(w_t | h_{N_v+t-1}, w_{t-1}; \theta). \quad (4)$$

This log probability is only calculated in decoding stage and optimized over the whole training dataset using stochastic gradient descent. Note that the end sign word $\#end$ is required to terminate the description generation in decoding stage. Hence, after encoding the inputs of frame-level caption sequence, we choose the next word with maximum probability at each decoding step and set it as LSTM input in next time step until the end sign word is emitted.

3. EXPERIMENTS

We evaluate and compare with state-of-the-art approaches for video description generation task on the most widely used dataset, YouTube2Text [2].

3.1 Dataset and Settings

Dataset. We conduct our experiments on Microsoft Research Video Description Corpus (YouTube2Text), which contains 1,970 YouTube snippets. There are roughly 40 available English descriptions per video. In our experiments, following the settings used in previous works [11][15], we take 1,200 videos for training, 100 for validation and 670 for testing.

Settings. In the experiment, we uniformly sample $N_v = 20$ frames for each video. We take the output of 4096-way fc7 from 16-layer VGG [8] network pre-trained on ImageNet ILSVRC12 dataset [7] as the frame visual representations. The size of hidden layer in LSTM is set as 1,024.

3.2 Compared Approaches

We compare the following approaches for performance evaluation:

- Mean Pooling (MP) [12]: MP attempts to directly translate from video pixels to natural language with a single deep neural network. The video representations are by performing mean pooling over the frame-level representations extracted by VGG. This run is named as MP. Moreover, the model can be pre-trained on MSCOCO image captioning dataset and then fine-tuned on YouTube2Text. This variant of mean pooling model is named as MP-COCO.
- Soft-Attention (SA) [15]: SA combines the frame representations from GoogleNet [10] and video clip representations based on a 3-D CNN trained on handcrafted descriptors. Furthermore, a weighted attention mechanism is used to dynamically select the most relevant temporal segments of the video while generating sentence. It is worth noting that for fair comparison with these models which focus on frame-level representations, we only use frame representations extracted by GoogleNet with attention mechanism in this baseline.
- Sequence to Sequence - Video to Text (S2VT) [11]: S2VT incorporates both RGB and optical flow as inputs. The encoding of the inputs and decoding of each word in the description are learnt jointly in a parallel manner. To ensure the performance comparable, we only employ the frame-level RGB input in this run.
- Sequence to Sequence - Frame-level Captions to text (S2FT): We design this run for our proposed approach.

Table 1: METEOR scores (%) on YouTube2Text.

Model	METEOR
MP [12]	27.7
MP-COCO [12]	29.3
SA [15]	29.0
S2VT [11]	29.2
S2FT (Ours)	**29.9**

3.3 Performance Comparison

Table 1 shows the METEOR [3] performance of five runs on YouTube2Text dataset. Overall, our proposed S2FT outperforms the other runs. In particular, the METEOR can achieve 0.299, which is so far the highest performance reported on YouTube2Text dataset when solely relying on frame-level information.

MP-COCO, which is pre-trained on MSCOCO image captioning dataset, leads to a performance boost against MP. Similar in spirit, S2FT by additionally leveraging image captioning is superior to S2VT. The results basically indicate the advantage of utilizing image captioning for boosting video description generation. There is a performance gap among three runs MP, SA and S2VT. Though three runs are all purely based on YouTube2Text dataset, they are fundamentally different in the way of modeling temporal structure in the video. The performance of MP and SA is as a result of linearly fusing visual representations of video frames by mean pooling and soft attention respectively, while S2VT is by encoding the video frames in a sequential manner. As indicated by our results, the strategy of sequence to sequence learning performs better. Compared to MP-COCO in which video frame is represented by visual features, S2FT is benefited from generating explicit representations of high-level attributes (frame-level caption in our case) for video frame and exhibits better performance.

Figure 2 shows a few sentence examples generated by our method and two sampled human-annotated ground truth

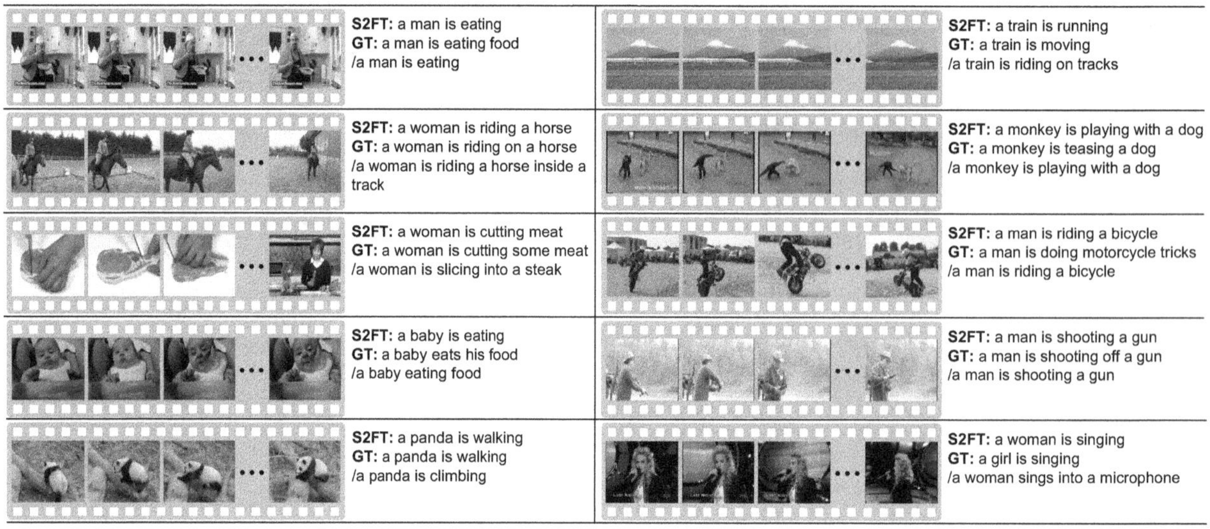

Figure 2: Sentence generation results on YouTube2Text. The videos are represented by sampled frames. The output sentences are generated by our S2FT and two sampled ground truth (GT) sentences.

Table 2: The effect of hidden layer size of LSTM for our S2FT framework on YouTube2Text.

Hidden layer size	METEOR	Parameter number
128	28.5	3.6M
256	29.3	7.5M
512	29.7	16.0M
1024	29.9	36.2M

(GT) sentences. From these exemplar results, it is easy to see that our method can generate accurate sentences, which encapsulate the video content clearly.

3.4 The Size of Hidden Layer of LSTM

In order to show the relationship between the performance and hidden layer size of LSTM, we compare the results of the hidden layer size in the range of 128, 256, 512 and 1024. The results shown in Table 2 indicate increasing the hidden layer size can generally lead to performance improvements. Considering that the number of parameters increases exponentially at the meantime, the hidden layer size is empirically set to 1,024 and no further increased in our experiments.

4. CONCLUSION

In this paper, we have investigated video description generation by leveraging largely image captioning data and proposed a novel sequence to sequence architecture. Particularly, a pre-learnt image captioning model is utilized to generate caption for video frame. As an explicit representation of high-level attributes of video frame, our architecture first encodes the generated caption of frame sequentially and then outputs the video description sentence word by word in decoding stage. Experiments conducted on a widely used video to language dataset validate our proposal and analysis. Performance improvements are observed when comparing to other architectures such as model learning purely on video data and representing video frame by visual features.

5. REFERENCES

[1] D. Bahdanau, K. Cho, and Y. Bengio. Neural machine translation by jointly learning to align and translate. In *ICLR*, 2015.

[2] D. L. Chen and W. B. Dolan. Collecting highly parallel data for paraphrase evaluation. In *ACL*, 2011.

[3] M. Denkowski and A. Lavie. Meteor universal: Language specific translation evaluation for any target language. In *EACL*, 2014.

[4] S. Hochreiter and J. Schmidhuber. Long short-term memory. *Neural Computation*, 9(8):1735–1780, 1997.

[5] T.-Y. Lin, M. Maire, S. Belongie, J. Hays, P. Perona, D. Ramanan, P. Dollár, and C. L. Zitnick. Microsoft coco: Common objects in context. In *ECCV*. 2014.

[6] Y. Pan, T. Mei, T. Yao, H. Li, and Y. Rui. Jointly modeling embedding and translation to bridge video and language. In *CVPR*, 2016.

[7] O. Russakovsky, J. Deng, H. Su, J. Krause, S. Satheesh, S. Ma, Z. Huang, A. Karpathy, A. Khosla, M. Bernstein, A. C. Berg, and L. Fei-Fei. ImageNet Large Scale Visual Recognition Challenge. *IJCV*, 2015.

[8] K. Simonyan and A. Zisserman. Very deep convolutional networks for large-scale image recognition. In *ICLR*, 2015.

[9] I. Sutskever, O. Vinyals, and Q. V. Le. Sequence to sequence learning with neural networks. In *NIPS*, 2014.

[10] C. Szegedy, W. Liu, Y. Jia, P. Sermanet, S. Reed, D. Anguelov, D. Erhan, V. Vanhoucke, and A. Rabinovich. Going deeper with convolutions. In *CVPR*, 2015.

[11] S. Venugopalan, M. Rohrbach, J. Donahue, R. Mooney, T. Darrell, and K. Saenko. Sequence to sequence - video to text. In *ICCV*, 2015.

[12] S. Venugopalan, H. Xu, J. Donahue, M. Rohrbach, R. Mooney, and K. Saenko. Translating videos to natural language using deep recurrent neural networks. In *HLT-NAACL*, 2015.

[13] O. Vinyals, A. Toshev, S. Bengio, and D. Erhan. Show and tell: A neural image caption generator. In *CVPR*, 2015.

[14] J. Xu, T. Mei, T. Yao, and Y. Rui. MSR-VTT: A large video description dataset for bridging video and language. In *CVPR*, 2016.

[15] L. Yao, A. Torabi, K. Cho, N. Ballas, C. Pal, H. Larochelle, and A. Courville. Describing videos by exploiting temporal structure. In *ICCV*, 2015.

Artist-based Classification via Deep Learning with Multi-scale Weighted Pooling

Kevin Alfianto Jangtjik*
Dept. of CSIE
Taiwan Tech.
Taipei, Taiwan
m10315813@mail.ntust.edu.tw

Mei-Chen Yeh*
Dept. of CSIE
Nat'l Taiwan Normal Univ.
Taipei, Taiwan
myeh@csie.ntnu.edu.tw

Kai-Lung Hua
Dept. of CSIE
Taiwan Tech.
Taipei, Taiwan
hua@mail.ntust.edu.tw

ABSTRACT

For analyzing digital images of paintings we propose a new approach to categorize them based on artist. Determining the authorship of a painting is challenging because common subjects are illustrated in paintings, and paintings of an artist may not have a unique style. The proposed approach is built upon convolutional neural networks (CNN)—a class of biologically inspired vision model that recently demonstrates near-human performance on several visual recognition tasks. However, training a CNN model requires large scale training data of a fixed input image size (e.g. 224×224). In this paper, we propose to construct a multi-layer pyramid from an image, providing 21X more features than using a single layer (i.e., the original image) alone. We train a CNN model for each layer, and propose a new weighted fusion scheme to adaptively combine the decision results. To evaluate the proposed methods, we collect a new painting image dataset, categorized into 13 artists. As demonstrated in the experimental results, the proposed method achieves a promising result—88.08% recall rate in top-2 retrieval on the challenging classification task.

CCS Concepts

•**Computing methodologies** → **Neural networks;** *Image representations;*

Keywords

Digital painting image classification; deep learning; spatial pyramid representation; convolutional neural network

1. INTRODUCTION

The increasing volume of digitized art images on the Internet provides an opportunity to immerse in the artwork at arbitrary place and time. However, online paintings often lack detailed information (e.g., artist's name, year), unlike those archived in museum collections. It therefore demonstrates a need to analyze, classify and understand the paintings in an automatic manner. One of the crucial information is the authorship. Artist-based classification can be utilized to create index for organizing and retrieving painting collections, identify unknown paintings, and gain insights into the artistic style of an artist from his/her artwork.

Determining the authorship of unattributed paintings is a challenging task because of the following factors. First, the content of paintings, even illustrated by different artists, can be similar. For example, we often find faces in portrait paintings and flowers in still life paintings. Second, similar techniques can be applied to create paintings of similar style. Figure 1 shows a few examples of a painting image dataset (detailed in section 4). Portrait paintings in class 5 and class 9 have similar pose, style, and color. Third, paintings of an artist can have more than one style (e.g., sample paintings in class 7). The large intra- and inter-variations inherited in paintings create challenges for artist-based painting classification. An initial observation reveals that the low-level or middle-level features may not be sufficient to differentiate the classes shown in Figure 1.

Convolutional neural networks (CNN) [7] have shown breakthrough performance on various visual recognition tasks in recent studies, including scene recognition [13], image style analysis [4], semantic segmentation [8] and visual description generation [1]. The trend of using CNN starts when Krizhevsky et al. showed CNN outperformed previous methods by a large margin in the ImageNet classification task [5]. Krizhevsky's CNN can also be used as a generic feature extractor (e.g., using the output of the fc-7 layer). For example, Kummerer et al. recently present a new saliency model based on Krizhevsky's CNN that significantly outperforms state-of-the-art models on the MIT saliency benchmark [6].

Although extraordinary performance by using CNN has been reported in recent studies, the prevalent CNN requires a fixed input image size (e.g. 224 x 224). When the CNN is applied to images of arbitrary sizes, there are several manners of fitting the input image to the fixed size, but the best one remains unclear. In this paper, we use artist-based painting classification as a study case, and present a spatial-pyramid approach for CNN-based painting classification. Specifically, an image is represented by using a pyramid of increasingly fine sub-regions, as shown in Figure 2. For each layer we train a CNN model, and adaptively aggregate the class probabilities of each model in testing.

*The first two authors contributed equally to this work.

MM'16, October 15–19, Amsterdam, Netherlands.

DOI: http://dx.doi.org/10.1145/2964284.2967299

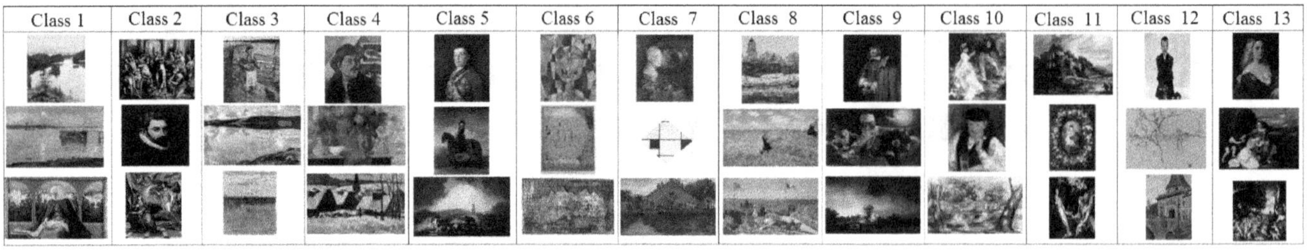

Figure 1: Samples of our artist-based painting image dataset.

We present a digital painting image dataset containing 1300 images of 13 artists, and validate the effectiveness of the proposed method using the dataset. A CNN method coupled with a multi-scale pyramid representation and an adaptive fusion scheme significantly outperforms Krizhevsky's CNN on the challenging artist-based painting classification task.

In the reminder of the paper, we first describe related work on painting classification. Section 3 presents the main approach, including the spatial pyramid representation for fitting an input image to CNN and a weighting scheme for aggregating the classification results from several models. We then demonstrate its performance on a new painting image dataset and conclude the paper with a discussion.

2. RELATED WORK

Recently, researchers have started to develop computational methods to study painting authorship. For example, Hanchao and Shannon suggested paintings' background is an important feature to classify paintings based on artist [2]. The study found that a painter is likely to bear unconscious signature at background rather than the main object. Several methods including wavelet transform, linear regression and hidden Markov model were used to distinguish the painter. The support vector machine (SVM) was used as the classifier, and outliers were detected by a thresholding scheme. Their experiment involved a binary classification task (van gogh or non van gogh), while we deal with a more challenging task of 13 artist classes.

Another work on digital painting classification is presented in [11]. In particular, Chinese painting images categorized into six classes were used in the experiment. Several features such as edge-based brush strokes and CNN features were designed. The classifier was implemented using sparse group lasso. As revealed in the title, the study was limited to Chinese paintings.

In [12] Zhao et al. studied the affective image classification problem with paintings. The painting images were classified into eight emotional categories: anger, disgust, fear, sadness, amusement, awe, contentment, and excitement. The authors used several features in their work such as GIST, color, texture, line and principle features (balance, contrast, harmony, variety, gradation, and movement). A number of classifiers were examined in the study, including global weight, KNN weighting, softmax regression and shared sparse learning.

A CNN-based method was proposed in [10] to classify digital painting images. Authors released the constraint that features were solely extracted from the topmost layer. Instead, they proposed to leverage the features extracted from different layers. Experiments showed that the cross-layer features outperformed Krizhevsky's CNN on three different

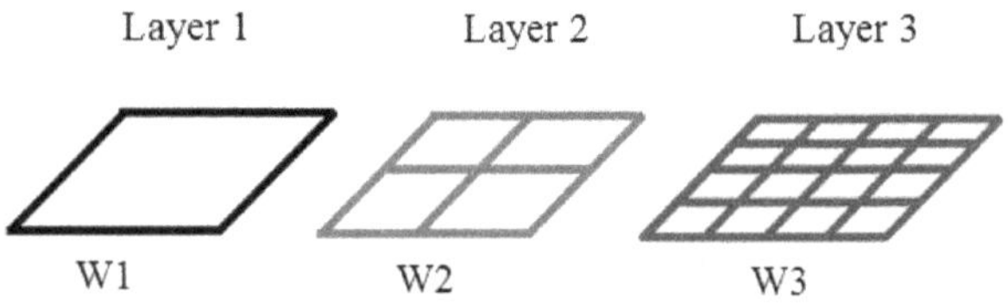

Figure 2: Spatial pyramid representation.

image classification tasks. Similar to this work, we propose to create more features from a CNN. Unlike [10] that uses cross layers, we use topmost layer alone but create features by decomposing an image into a multi-scale pyramid.

3. APPROACH

Training a recognition model using CNN usually requires large scale training data because the model is complex in terms of the number of parameters in the deep architecture [5]. It also requires a fixed input image size (e.g. 224×224) because the network architecture is not flexible to cope with images with varied sizes. In this section we propose to use spatial pyramid representation to address both issues. Technical details are described in the next subsections.

3.1 Training of Multi-scale Networks

For the training stage, a multi-scale pyramid is constructed. We let the 1st layer has a fixed size of a CNN and 2nd layer and 3rd layer scaled images have four and sixteen times larger resolution than the 1st layer scale image, as illustrated in Figure 2. For the 1st layer, all the training images are fed into the ImageNet-trained CNN model [5] to fine-tune the weights of the pre-trained network by continuing the backpropagation. Similarly, the higher layer models are also fine-tuned with the same technique. Note that for higher layers, instead of one patch for each training image where 1st layer applies, we now have 4 and 16 patches for each training data for 2nd layer and 3rd layer, respectively.

3.2 Adaptive Fusion for Artist-based Classification

After the multi-scale networks are computed, for any input testing image, individual single-scale classification results for each patch could be obtained, as illustrated in Figure 3. To obtain the final resultant classification decision, multi-scale CNN results need to be aggregated together. Our strategy for aggregating multi-scale results is to rely more on the decisions of a set of scales relatively performing well. However, the selection of good scales is in general challenging and data-dependent. In this paper, we propose to

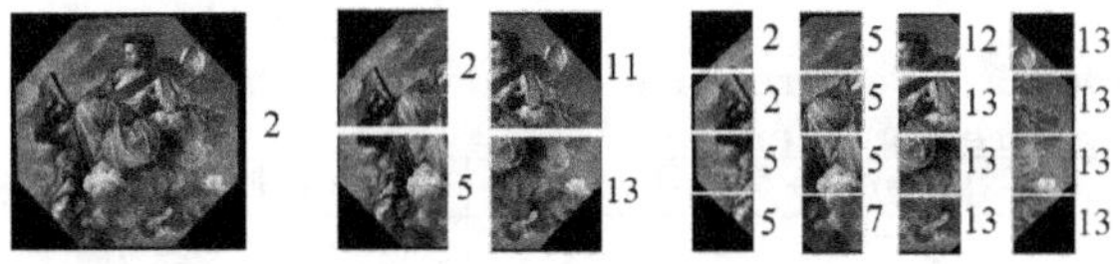

Figure 3: Classification results (shown at the right-hand side of each sub-region image) for layer 1 (left), layer 2 (middle), and layer 3 (right).

utilize entropy information to determine the decision quality for multi-scale layers. To be more specific, we first compute the class probability values for each layer. Let p_i^j denote the probability of being identified as class i at layer j, the corresponding entropy of multiple probabilities H^j of layer j is then computed as follows:

$$H^j = -\sum p_i^j \log(p_i^j). \tag{1}$$

(a) Sample image

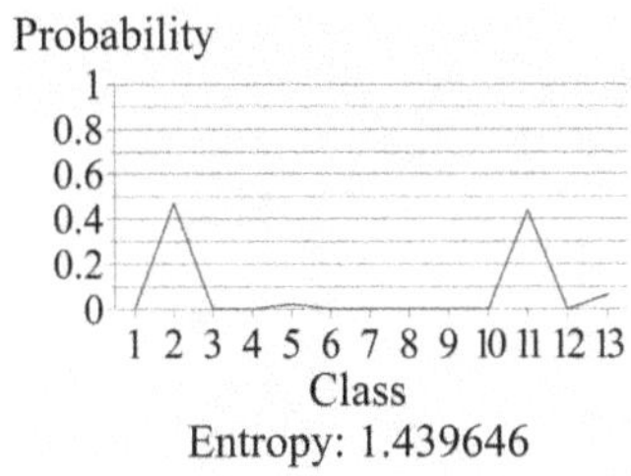

(b) Histogram layer 1

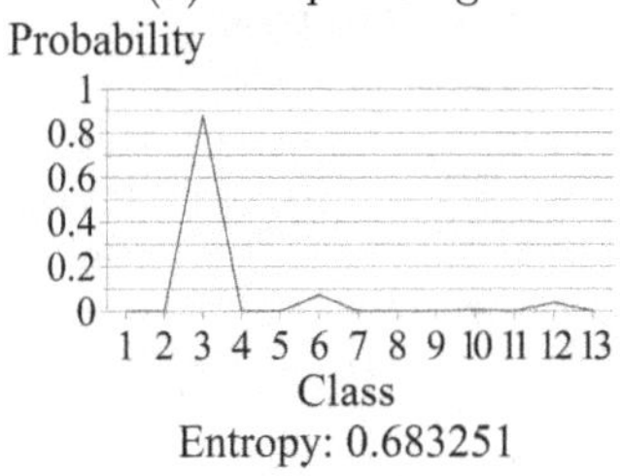

(c) Histogram layer 2

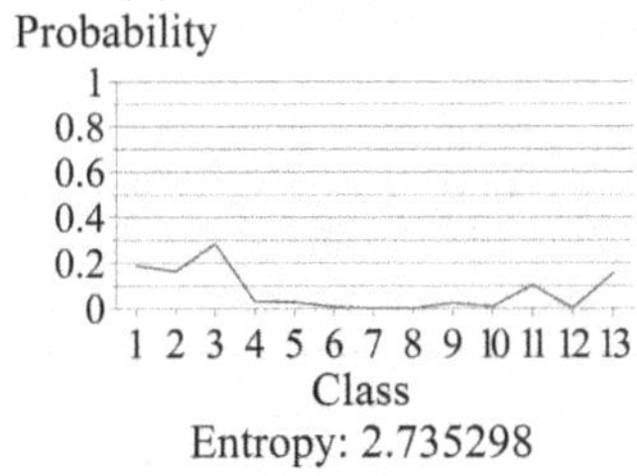

(d) Histogram Layer 3

Figure 4: Class probability values from layer 1, layer 2 and layer 3.

In Figure 4, we show the class probability and entropy values for each layer for one test image. Note that the 3rd model (lower-right one) shows a relatively diverse distribution and hence its importance should be considered less as compared to the other two models. Since the entropy value is proportional to the level of distribution diversity, we define the weight of layer j as the inverse value of entropy, that is,

$$W^j = 1/H^j. \tag{2}$$

Hence the final aggregated multi-scale class probability value of class i, p_i, is computed as follows:

$$p_i = \frac{\sum_j W^j \times p_i^j}{\sum_i \sum_j W^j \times p_i^j}. \tag{3}$$

The final decision is then obtained via

$$i^* = \operatorname*{argmax}_i = \{p_i\}. \tag{4}$$

Table 1: Performance Evaluation

Top-1			
Experiment	Precision	Recall	F Score
Pre trained model (baseline)	65.26%	66.15%	65.7%
Multi-scale pyramid (hard)	70.48%	71.92%	71.2%
Multi-scale pyramid (soft)	70.83%	71.92%	71.4%
Multi-scale pyramid (adaptive)	71.22%	72.30%	71.7%

(a)

Top-2			
Experiment	Precision	Recall	F Score
Pre trained model (baseline)	83.72%	83.46%	83.59%
Multi-scale pyramid (hard)	84.58%	85%	84.79%
Multi-scale pyramid (soft)	87.61%	87.69%	87.65%
Multi-scale pyramid (adaptive)	88.10%	88.08%	88.09%

(b)

4. EXPERIMENTS

In this section, we evaluate the performance of the proposed classification method. We collected a digital painting image dataset from [9] and categorized the images based on artist. This dataset contains 1300 digital painting images of artists, i.e., each artist has 100 images. A few samples of the dataset are displayed in Figure 1. We randomly sample 80 images per category for training and 20 images per category for testing. The performance is evaluated by precision, recall and F-scores, where precision is the ability of the classifier not to label as positive a sample that is negative, recall is the ability of the classifier to find all the positive samples, F-score is the weighted average of the precision and recall.

4.1 Baseline

We start our experiment from a baseline setting that simply employs ImageNet-trained CNN model [5] and fine-tune the weights of the pre-trained network by continuing the backpropagation via Caffe framework [3]. The employed pre-trained model has rich variety auxiliary data, so it is ideal to initialize the CNN parameters. The first row of Table 1(a) summarizes the baseline results.

4.2 Multi-scale Pyramid with Hard Decision

We employ a multi-scale pyramid of three layers. For the 1st layer, it is identical to the baseline. As described in Section 3, each image in the pyramid has twice resolution than the previous scale starting from the standard size defined at layer 1. Therefore, for layer 2 and layer 3, we would have $80\times13\times4$ and $80\times13\times16$ total training images, respectively, for each category. Max pooling operation is performed on each input patch of each layer to obtain the classification result, as illustrated in Figure 3. Finally, we fuse the classification results from each layer via weighted average. Since there are 1, 4, and 16 votes for layer 1, 2, and 3, respectively, three layer weights are selected as $(16, 4, 1)$ for layer 1, 2, and 3 to normalize the influence. The second row of Table 1(a) summarizes the results of multi-scale pyramid with hard decision.

4.3 Multi-scale Pyramid with Soft Decision

Identical to the previous setting, we construct a multi-scale pyramid of three layers in this experiment. However, instead of max pooling operation, soft decision is considered to fuse the overall classification result. To be more specific,

Actual Class	Predicted Class												
	1	2	3	4	5	6	7	8	9	10	11	12	13
1	40	0	10	0	15	0	0	5	10	10	5	0	5
2	0	95	0	0	0	0	0	0	0	0	5	0	0
3	15	0	20	5	0	15	15	15	0	0	5	5	5
4	10	0	5	75	0	0	0	0	0	0	0	5	5
5	0	0	0	0	55	0	0	0	35	5	5	0	0
6	0	0	0	5	0	90	5	0	0	0	0	0	0
7	5	0	0	5	0	0	85	0	0	0	0	5	0
8	0	0	5	0	0	0	0	85	0	10	0	0	0
9	0	0	0	0	5	5	0	0	80	0	0	0	10
10	10	0	0	0	0	0	0	0	0	85	5	0	0
11	5	0	5	0	0	0	0	0	0	10	80	0	0
12	0	0	0	0	0	0	5	0	0	0	0	95	0
13	0	0	5	0	5	0	0	0	10	0	25	0	55

Figure 5: Percentage confusion matrix of the multi-scale pyramid (adaptive) approach.

based on the previous hard decision experiment, we also computed the class probability value for each test of each layer. We first aggregate the class probability values for each layer by simply summing its corresponding class probability values for each class from the corresponding sub-region images. When fusing the soft results from three layers, similar to hard decision experiment, we employ $(16, 4, 1)$ as the weight for layer 1, 2, and 3, respectively, to normalize the influence. The third row of Table 1(a) summarizes the results of multi-scale pyramid with soft decision.

4.4 Multi-scale Pyramid with Soft Decision and Adaptive Pooling

Based on the experiments of Subsection 4.3, we obtained the soft decision results of each test image from three layers. When fusing the soft results from three layers, unlike previous setting that employes constant weights for three layers, we now adaptively apply the weights based on the decision quality for multi-scale layers according to the corresponding entropy information as explained in Section 3.2. The final classification result is determined by selecting the class that has the maximum weighted average probability value. The fourth row of Table 1(a) summarizes the results of multi-scale pyramid with soft decision and adaptive pooling operation.

4.5 Results and Discussion

We perform comprehensive experiments to compare various methods on the target classification task. The comparison results for the collected dataset are summarized in Table 1(a). As expected, the baseline approach [5] (1st row) performs the worst. The multi-scale approach with hard decision improves the performance by 5.22%, 5.77%, and 5.5% in terms of precision, recall, and F-score, respectively. This improvement verifies that exploiting multi-scale activations is beneficial for the artist-based classification performance.

When we replace the hard-decision with constant weight soft-decision for multi-scale approach, the performance (2nd row) could be further improved marginally for 0.35%, 0%, and 0.2% in terms of precision, recall, and F-score, respectively. Furthermore, if we employ the proposed entropy-based adaptive weight scheme for the multi-scale soft decision approach, the performance (3rd row) could be improved for 0.74%, 0.38%, and 0.5% in terms of precision, recall, and F-score, as compared to the hard decision approach and for significant 5.96%, 6.15%, and 6% in terms of precision, recall, and F-score, as compared to the baseline. Based on this significant improvement, the effectiveness of the proposed method is verified.

In addition to top-1 experiments, we show top-2 experiments in Table 1(b). It could be observed that when top-2 results are considered, the F-score would achieve satisfactory 88.09%. To explore the contribution from multi-scale pyramid, Table 2 shows the performance when different scales are considered. It could be observed that with more layers, better performance could be achieved by considering the scale characteristic of neural activations.

Table 2: Performance evaluation when different scales are considered.

Experiment	Precision	Recall	F Score
Layer 1	65.26%	66.15%	65.7%
Layer 1 + 2	68.53%	69.61%	69.1%
Layer 1 + 2 + 3	71.22%	72.30%	71.7%

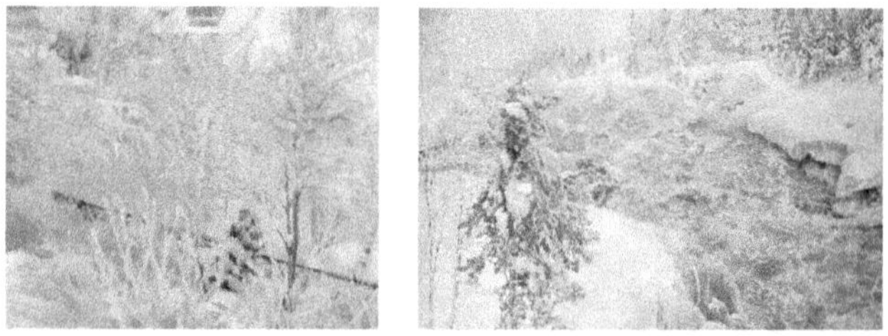

Figure 6: One example image pair of class 1 (left side) and class 3 (right side) that look similar.

Finally, we show the confusion matrix of the multi-scale pyramid (adaptive) approach in Figure 5. Note that the blue blocks show the correct classification result. From this confusion matrix, it could be observed that the performance of class 3 is not good. Testing images from class 3 are likely to be misclassified as class 1. Interestingly, with our investigation, we found that the author of class 3 (Akseli Gallen-Kallela) has strong relation to the author of class 1 (Albert Edelfelt). These two artists were not only friends, but they both attended drawing classes at the Finnish Art Society and studied under Mr. Adolf von Becker once, therefore their paintings show certain similar drawing skills and are difficult to be differentiated. To show the similarity between these two artist, Figure 6 demonstrates one example pair of the paintings, from class 1 and class 3, that are misclassified.

5. CONCLUSION

In this paper, we present a new method for artist-based digital painting image classification. We collect a new digital painting image dataset categorized into 13 artists, which should be broadly useful to the community studying related problems. We decompose an image into a spatial pyramid of increasingly fine sub-regions, and train a CNN model for each layer. We further propose a weighted fusion scheme, which adaptively combines the models based on their estimated posteriori probability. The experiments using a challenging dataset demonstrate that the proposed method achieves a promising result (88.08% recall rate in top-2 image retrieval) and significantly improves the baseline method (Krizhevsky's CNN).

6. REFERENCES

[1] J. Donahue. Long-term recurrent convolutional networks for visual recognition and description. *Computer Vision and Pattern Recognition*, pages 2625–2634, 2015.

[2] Q. Hanchao and H. Shannon. A new method for visual stylometry on impresionist paintings. *IEEE International Conference on Acoustics, Speech and Signal Processing*, pages 2036–2039, 2011.

[3] Y. Jia, E. Shelhamer, J. Donahue, S. Karayev, J. Long, R. Girshick, S. Guadarrama, and T. Darrel. Caffe: convolutional architecture for fast feature embedding. *ACM International Conference in Multimedia*, pages 675–678, 2014.

[4] S. Karayev. Recognizing image style. *British Machine Vision Conference*, 2014.

[5] A. Krizhevsky, I. Sutskever, and G. Hinton. Imagenet classification with deep convolutional neural networks. *Advances in Neural Information Processing Systems 25*, pages 1097–1105, 2012.

[6] M. Kummerer, L. Theis, and M. Bethge. Deep gaze i: Boosting saliency prediction with feature maps trained on imagenet. *ICLR Workshop*, 2015.

[7] Y. LeCun, B. Boser, J. Denker, D. Henderson, R. Howard, W. Hubbard, and L. Jackel. Backpropagation applied to hand-written zip code recognition. *Neural Computing*, 1(4):541–551, 1989.

[8] J. Long, E. Shelhamer, and T. Darrel. Fully convolutional networks for semantic segmentation. *Computer Vision and Pattern Recognition*, pages 3431–3440, 2015.

[9] PaintingDb. PaintingDb fastest growing art gallery in the web, 2015.

[10] K. Peng and T. Chen. Cross-layer features in convolutional neural networks for generic classification tasks. *International Conference in Image Processing*, pages 3057–3061, 2015.

[11] M. Sun, D. Zhang, J. Ren, Z. Wang, and J. S.Ji. Brushstroke based sparse hybrid convolutional neural networks for author classification of chinese ink-wash paintings. *IEEE International Conference on Image Processing*, pages 626–630, 2015.

[12] S. Zhao, H. Yao, X. Jiang, and X. Sun. Predicting discrete probability distribution of image emotion. *IEEE International Conference on Image Processing*, pages 2459–2463, 2015.

[13] B. Zhou, A. Lapedriza, J. Xiao, A. Torralba, and A. Oliva. Learning deep features for scene recognition using places database. *Advances in Neural Information Processing System*, 2014.

CrowdNet: A Deep Convolutional Network for Dense Crowd Counting

Lokesh Boominathan
Video Analytics Lab
Indian Institute of Science
Bangalore, INDIA - 560012
boominathanlokesh@gmail.com

Srinivas S S Kruthiventi
Video Analytics Lab
Indian Institute of Science
Bangalore, INDIA - 560012
kssaisrinivas@gmail.com

R. Venkatesh Babu
Video Analytics Lab
Indian Institute of Science
Bangalore, INDIA - 560012
venky@cds.iisc.ac.in

ABSTRACT

Our work proposes a novel deep learning framework for estimating crowd density from static images of highly dense crowds. We use a combination of deep and shallow, fully convolutional networks to predict the density map for a given crowd image. Such a combination is used for effectively capturing both the high-level semantic information (face/body detectors) and the low-level features (blob detectors), that are necessary for crowd counting under large scale variations. As most crowd datasets have limited training samples (<100 images) and deep learning based approaches require large amounts of training data, we perform multi-scale data augmentation. Augmenting the training samples in such a manner helps in guiding the CNN to learn scale invariant representations. Our method is tested on the challenging UCF_CC_50 dataset, and shown to outperform the state of the art methods.

Keywords

Crowd Density; Convolutional Neural Networks

1. INTRODUCTION

In the light of problems caused due to poor crowd management, such as crowd crushes and blockages, there is an increasing need for computational models which can analyse highly dense crowds using video feeds from surveillance cameras. Crowd counting is a crucial component of such an automated crowd analysis system. This involves estimating the number of people in the crowd, as well as the distribution of the crowd density over the entire area of the gathering. Identifying regions with crowd density above the safety limit can help in issuing prior warnings and can prevent potential crowd crushes. Estimating the crowd count also helps in quantifying the significance of the event and better handling of logistics and infrastructure for the gathering.

In this work, we propose a deep learning based approach for estimating the crowd density as well as the crowd count from still images. Counting crowds in highly dense scenarios (>2000 people) poses a variety of challenges. Highly dense crowd images suffer from severe occlusion, making the traditional face/person detectors ineffective. Crowd images can be captured from a variety of angles introducing the problem of perspective. This results in non-uniform scaling of the crowd necessitating the estimation model to be scale-invariant to large scale changes. Furthermore, unlike other vision problems, annotating highly dense crowd images is a laborious task. This makes the creation of large-scale crowd counting datasets infeasible and limits the amount of training data available for learning-based approaches.

Hand-crafted image features (SIFT [13], HOG etc. [6]) often fail to provide robustness to challenges of occlusion and large scale variations. Our approach for crowd counting relies instead on deep learnt features using the framework of fully convolutional neural networks(CNN). We tackle the issue of scale variation in the crowd images using a combination of a shallow and deep convolutional architectures. Further, we perform extensive data augmentation by sampling patches from the multi-scale image representation to make the system robust to scale variations. Our approach is evaluated on the challenging UCF_CC_50 dataset [8] and has achieved state of the art results.

Actual Count: 1115 Estimated: 1143

Actual Count:440 Estimated:433

Figure 1: Crowd images with head annotations marked using red dots and their corresponding estimated crowd density maps

MM '16, October 15-19, 2016, Amsterdam, Netherlands

DOI: http://dx.doi.org/10.1145/2964284.2967300

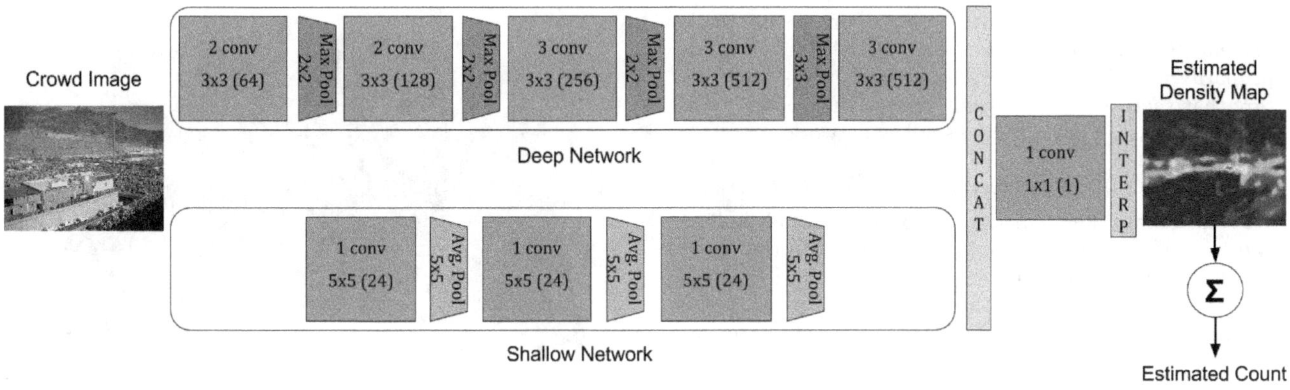

Figure 2: Overview of the proposed architecture for crowd counting

2. RELATED WORK

Some works in the crowd counting literature experiment on datasets having sparse crowd scenes [2, 10], such as UCSD dataset [2], Mall dataset [3] and PETS dataset [7]. In contrast, our method has been evaluated on highly dense crowd images which pose the challenges discussed in the previous section. Methods introduced in [1] and [15] exploit patterns of motion to estimate the count of moving objects. However, these methods rely on motion information which can be obtained only in the case of continuous video streams with a good frame rate, and do not extend to still image crowd counting.

The algorithm proposed by Idrees *et al.* [8] is based on the understanding that it is difficult to obtain an accurate crowd count using a single feature. To overcome this, they use a combination of handcrafted features: HOG based head detections, Fourier analysis, and interest points based counting. The post processing is done using multi-scale Markov Random Field. However, handcrafted features often suffer a drop in accuracy when subjected to variances in illumination, perspective distortion, severe occlusion etc.

Though Zhang *et al.* [19] utilize a deep network to estimate crowd count, their model is trained using perspective maps of images. Generating these perspective maps is a laborious process and is infeasible. We use a simpler approach for training our model, yet obtain a better performance. Wang *et al.* [18] also train a deep model for crowd count estimation. Their model however is trained to determine only the crowd count and not the crowd density map, which is crucial for crowd analysis. Our network estimates both the crowd count as well as the crowd density distribution.

3. PROPOSED METHOD

3.1 Network Architecture

Crowd images are often captured from varying view points, resulting in a wide variety of perspectives and scale variations. People near the camera are often captured in a great level of detail i.e., their faces and at times their entire body is captured. However, in the case of people away from camera or when images are captured from an aerial viewpoint, each person is represented only as a head blob. Efficient detection of people in both these scenarios requires the model to simultaneously operate at a highly semantic level (faces/body detectors) while also recognizing the low-level head blob patterns. Our model achieves this using a combination of deep and shallow convolutional neural networks. An overview of the proposed architecture is shown in Fig. 2. In the following subsections, we describe these networks in detail.

3.1.1 Deep Network

Our deep network captures the desired high-level semantics required for crowd counting using an architectural design similar to the well-known VGG-16 [17] network. Although the VGG-16 architecture was originally trained for the purpose of object classification, the learned filters are very good generic visual descriptors and have found applications in a wide variety of vision tasks such as saliency prediction [11], object segmentation [5] etc. Our model efficiently builds up on the representative power of the VGG network by fine-tuning its filters for the problem of crowd counting. However, crowd density estimation requires per-pixel predictions unlike the problem of image classification, where a single discrete label is assigned for an entire image. We obtain these pixel-level predictions by removing the fully connected layers present in the VGG architecture, thereby making our network fully convolutional in nature.

The VGG network has 5 max-pool layers each with a stride of 2 and hence the resultant output features have a spatial resolution of only 1/32 times the input image. In our adaptation of the VGG model, we set the stride of the fourth max-pool layer to 1 and remove the fifth pooling layer altogether. This enables the network to make predictions at 1/8 times the input resolution. We handle the receptive-field mismatch caused by the removal of stride in the fourth max-pool layer using the technique of holes introduced in [4]. Convolutional filters with holes can have arbitrarily large receptive fields irrespective of their kernel size. Using holes, we double the receptive field of convolutional layers after the fourth max-pool layer, thereby enabling them to operate with their originally trained receptive field.

3.1.2 Shallow Network

In our model, we aim to recognize the low-level head blob patterns, arising from people away from the camera, using a shallow convolutional network. Since blob detection does not require the capture of high-level semantics, we design this network to be shallow with a depth of only 3 convolutional layers. Each of these layers has 24 filters with a kernel size of 5×5. To make the spatial resolution of this network's prediction equal to that of its deep counterpart, we use pooling layers after each convolution layer. Our shallow network is primarily used for the detection of small head-blobs. To ensure that there is no loss of count due to max-pooling, we use average pooling layers in the shallow network.

3.1.3 Combination of Deep and Shallow Networks

We concatenate the predictions from the deep and shallow networks, each having a spatial resolution of 1/8 times the input image, and process it using a 1x1 convolution layer. The output from this layer is upsampled to the size of the input image using bilinear interpolation to obtain the final crowd density prediction. The total count of the people in the image can be obtained by a summation over the predicted density map. The network is trained by back-propagating the $l2$ loss computed with respect to ground-truth.

3.2 Ground Truth

Training a fully convolutional network using the ground-truth of head annotations, marked as a binary dot corresponding to each person, would be difficult. The exact position of the head annotations is often ambiguous, and varies from annotator to annotator (forehead, centre of the face etc.), making CNN training difficult.

In [18], the authors have trained a deep network to predict the total crowd count in an image patch. But using such a ground truth would be suboptimal, as it wouldn't help in determining which regions of the image actually contribute to the count and by what amount. Zhang *et al.* [19] have generated ground truth by blurring the binary head annotations, using a kernel that varies with respect to the perspective map of the image. However, generating such perspective maps is a laborious task and involves manually labelling several pedestrians by marking their height.

We generate our ground truth by simply blurring each head annotation using a Gaussian kernel normalized to sum to one. This kind of blurring causes the sum of the density map to be the same as the total number of people in the crowd. Preparing the ground truth in such a fashion makes the ground truth easier for the CNN to learn, as the CNN no longer needs to get the exact point of head annotation right. It also provides information on which regions contribute to the count, and by how much. This helps in training the CNN to predict both the crowd density as well as the crowd count correctly.

3.3 Data Augmentation

As CNNs require a large amount of training data, we perform an extensive augmentation of our training dataset. We primarily perform two types of augmentation. The first type of augmentation helps in tackling the problem of scale variations in crowd images, while the second type improves the CNN's performance in regions where it is highly susceptible to making mistakes i.e., highly dense crowd regions.

In order to make the CNN robust to scale variations, we crop patches from the multi-scale pyramidal representation of each training image. We consider scales of 0.5 to 1.2, incremented in steps of .1, times the original image resolution (as shown in Fig.3) for constructing the image pyramid. We crop 225×225 patches with 50% overlap from this pyramidal representation. With this augmentation, the CNN is trained to recognize people irrespective of their scales.

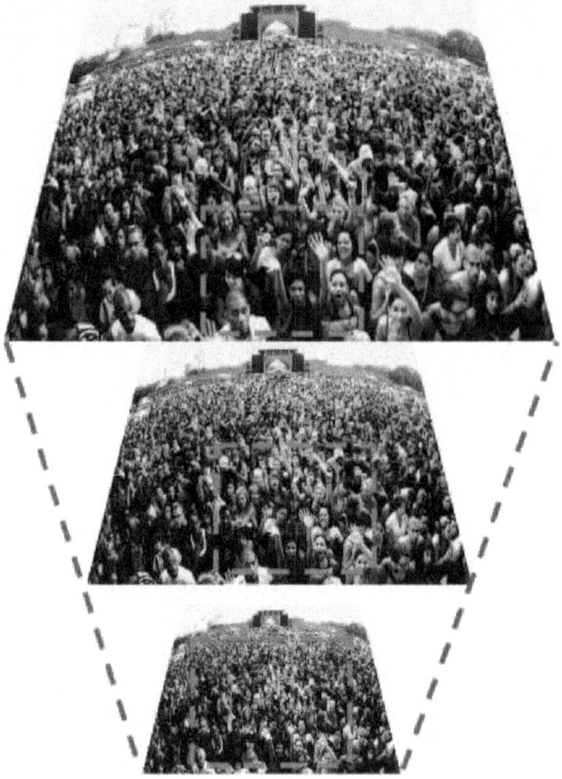

Figure 3: Our network is designed to be robust to scale variations by training it with patches cropped from multi-scale image pyramid.

We observed that CNNs find highly dense crowds inherently difficult to handle. To overcome this, we augment the training data by sampling high density patches more often.

4. EXPERIMENTS

We evaluate our approach for crowd counting on the challenging UCF_CC_50 [8] dataset. This dataset contains 50 gray scale images, each provided with head annotations. The number of people per image varies between 94 and 4543, with an average of 1280 individuals per image. The dataset comprises of images from a wide range of scenarios such as concerts, political rallies, religious gatherings, stadiums etc.

In a manner similar to recent works [19, 8], we evaluate the performance of our approach using 5-fold cross validation. We randomly divide the dataset into five splits with each split containing 10 images. In each fold of the cross validation, we consider four splits (40 images) for training the network and the remaining split (10 images) for validating its performance. We sample 225×225 patches from each of the 40 training images following the previously described data augmentation method. This procedure yields an average of 50,292 training patches per fold. We train our deep convolutional network using the Deeplab [5, 14] version of Caffe [9] deep learning framework, using Titan X GPUs. Our network was trained using Stochastic Gradient Descent (SGD) optimization with a learning rate of $1e-7$ and momentum of 0.9. The average training time per fold is about 5 hours.

4.1 Results

We use Mean Absolute Error (MAE) to quantify the performance of our method. MAE computes the mean of absolute difference between the actual count and the predicted count for all the images in the dataset. The results of the proposed approach along with other recent methods are shown in Table. 4.1. The results shown do not include any post-processing methods. The results illustrate that our approach achieves state-of-the-art performance in crowd counting.

Method	Mean Absolute Error
Learning to Count [12]	493.4
Density-aware Detection [16]	655.7
FHSc [8]	468.0
Cross-Scene Counting [19]	467.0
Proposed	**452.5**

Table 1: Quantitative results of our approach along with other state-of-the-art methods on UCF_CC_50 Dataset.

We also show the predicted count for each image in the dataset along with its actual count in Fig. 4. For most of the images, the predicted count lies close to the actual count. However, we observe that the proposed approach tends to underestimate the count in cases of images with more than 2500 people. This estimation error could possibly be a consequence of the insufficient number of training images with such large crowds in the dataset.

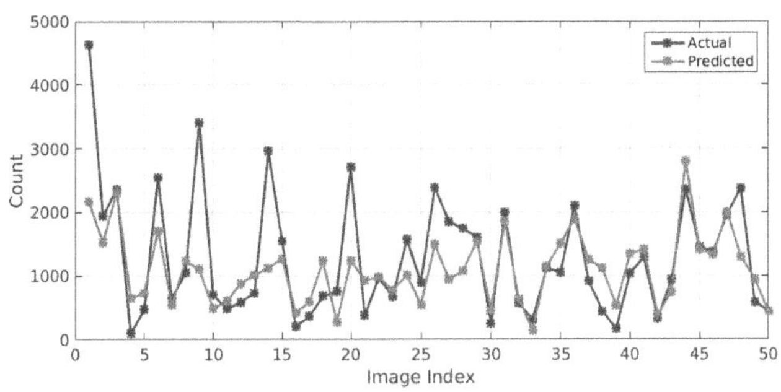

Figure 4: Actual count vs. Predicted Count for each of the 50 images in the UCF_CC_50 dataset.

4.2 Analysis

In this section, we analyse the following aspects of our approach using the hardest of the 5-folds.

Deep and Shallow Networks: Here, we experimentally show that combining both the deep and shallow networks, effectively captures individuals at multiple scales, thereby reducing the MAE. The experiment was performed on the hardest of 5 folds, and it was observed that using a combination of shallow and deep network gives a quantitative improvement over using just either one of them, as shown in Table 2.

Count based Augmentation: Augmenting the training samples in favour of highly dense patches is observed to be effective at mitigating the lack of sufficient training samples with large crowds. Augmenting in such a fashion for the hardest fold, almost doubles the number of patches from 26,385 to 50,891. The quantitative advantage obtained by this augmentation is shown in the Table 3.

Method	Mean Absolute Error
Shallow Network	1107
Deep Network	681
Proposed (Deep + Shallow)	645

Table 2: Quantitative results on the performance of the individual deep and shallow networks for crowd counting as opposed to the combined network, evaluated on the hardest of 5 folds.

Method	Mean Absolute Error
Without augmentation	725
Proposed (with augmentation)	645

Table 3: Quantitative results showing the advantage of augmenting data in favour of highly dense crowd patches, evaluated on the hardest of 5 folds.

5. CONCLUSION

In this paper, we proposed a deep learning based approach to estimate the crowd density and total crowd count from highly dense crowd images. We showed that using a combination of a deep network as well as a shallow network is essential for detecting people under large scale variations and severe occlusion. We also show that the challenge of varying scales, and inherent difficulties in highly dense crowds, can be effectively tackled by augmenting the training images. Our method outperforms the state-of-the-art methods on the challenging UCF_CC_50 dataset.

6. ACKNOWLEDGMENTS

This work was supported by Science and Engineering Research Board (SERB), Department of Science and Technology (DST), Govt. of India (Proj No. SB/S3/EECE/0127/2015).

7. REFERENCES

[1] G. J. Brostow and R. Cipolla. Unsupervised bayesian detection of independent motion in crowds. In *IEEE Conference on Computer Vision and Pattern Recognition*, 2006. 2

[2] A. B. Chan, Z.-S. J. Liang, and N. Vasconcelos. Privacy preserving crowd monitoring: Counting people without people models or tracking. In *IEEE Conference on Computer Vision and Pattern Recognition*, 2008. 2

[3] K. Chen, C. C. Loy, S. Gong, and T. Xiang. Feature mining for localised crowd counting. In *BMVC*, 2012. 2

[4] L.-C. Chen, G. Papandreou, I. Kokkinos, K. Murphy, and A. L. Yuille. Semantic image segmentation with deep convolutional nets and fully connected crfs. *arXiv preprint arXiv:1412.7062*, 2014. 3.1.1

[5] L.-C. Chen, G. Papandreou, I. Kokkinos, K. Murphy, and A. L. Yuille. Semantic image segmentation with deep convolutional nets and fully connected crfs. In *ICLR*, 2015. 3.1.1, 4

[6] N. Dalal and B. Triggs. Histograms of oriented gradients for human detection. In *IEEE Computer Society Conference on Computer Vision and Pattern Recognition, 2005.*, volume 1, pages 886–893. IEEE, 2005. 1

[7] J. Ferryman and A. Ellis. Pets2010: Dataset and challenge. In *IEEE International Conference on Advanced Video and Signal Based Surveillance (AVSS)*, 2010. 2

[8] H. Idrees, I. Saleemi, C. Seibert, and M. Shah. Multi-source multi-scale counting in extremely dense crowd images. In *IEEE Conference on Computer Vision and Pattern Recognition*, 2013. 1, 2, 4, 4.1

[9] Y. Jia, E. Shelhamer, J. Donahue, S. Karayev, J. Long, R. Girshick, S. Guadarrama, and T. Darrell. Caffe: Convolutional architecture for fast feature embedding. *arXiv preprint arXiv:1408.5093*, 2014. 4

[10] D. Kong, D. Gray, and H. Tao. A viewpoint invariant approach for crowd counting. In *International Conference on Pattern Recognition, 2006.* 2

[11] S. S. Kruthiventi, K. Ayush, and R. V. Babu. Deepfix: A fully convolutional neural network for predicting human eye fixations. *arXiv preprint arXiv:1510.02927*, 2015. 3.1.1

[12] V. Lempitsky and A. Zisserman. Learning to count objects in images. In *Advances in Neural Information Processing Systems*, 2010. 4.1

[13] D. G. Lowe. Distinctive image features from scale-invariant keypoints. *International journal of computer vision*, 60(2):91–110, 2004. 1

[14] G. Papandreou, L.-C. Chen, K. Murphy, and A. L. Yuille. Weakly- and semi-supervised learning of a dcnn for semantic image segmentation. *arxiv:1502.02734*, 2015. 4

[15] V. Rabaud and S. Belongie. Counting crowded moving objects. In *IEEE Computer Society Conference on Computer Vision and Pattern Recognition*, 2006. 2

[16] M. Rodriguez, I. Laptev, J. Sivic, and J.-Y. Audibert. Density-aware person detection and tracking in crowds. In *IEEE International Conference on Computer Vision*, 2011. 4.1

[17] K. Simonyan and A. Zisserman. Very deep convolutional networks for large-scale image recognition. *arXiv preprint arXiv:1409.1556*, 2014. 3.1.1

[18] C. Wang, H. Zhang, L. Yang, S. Liu, and X. Cao. Deep people counting in extremely dense crowds. In *Proceedings of the 23rd Annual ACM Conference on Multimedia Conference*, 2015. 2, 3.2

[19] C. Zhang, H. Li, X. Wang, and X. Yang. Cross-scene crowd counting via deep convolutional neural networks. In *IEEE Conference on Computer Vision and Pattern Recognition*, 2015. 2, 3.2, 4, 4.1

Do Textual Descriptions Help Action Recognition?

Matteo Bruni, Tiberio Uricchio, Lorenzo Seidenari, and Alberto Del Bimbo
Media Integration and Communication Center, Università degli Studi di Firenze
{name.surname}@unifi.it

ABSTRACT

We present a novel method to improve action recognition by leveraging a set of captioned videos. By learning linear projections to map videos and text onto a common space, our approach shows that improved results on unseen videos can be obtained. We also propose a novel structure preserving loss that further ameliorates the quality of the projections. We tested our method on the challenging, realistic, Hollywood2 action recognition dataset where a considerable gain in performance is obtained. We show that the gain is proportional to the number of training samples used to learn the projections.

CCS Concepts

•Information systems → Video search; •Computing methodologies → Activity recognition and understanding;

Keywords

Action recognition, Multi-modal learning

1. INTRODUCTION

Imagine listening to someone describing a movie clip. When watching the actual footage afterwards, there will be many divergences from what one may have pictured. Many of the missing visual details from the description will likely appear different in pictures, having been filled in by one's brain. That is because text and videos are very much different domains.

A sentence describing a video clip will inevitably not illustrate every detail of a scene, usually focusing on the relevant semantic entities. A video, instead, carries plenty of information. In particular, the semantic of a video is still hardly represented through visual features due to the well known *semantic gap* [20]. Features are designed to capture appearance and motion, with invariance to lighting, camera movements and viewpoint. They are not usually geared to represent meaning in the form of objects and actions, unless some learning is involved. Consequently, both representations have natural limitation on the information they may deliver. Yet two video sequences with similar descriptions should share semantic properties.

MM '16, October 15-19, 2016, Amsterdam, Netherlands
© 2016 ACM. ISBN 978-1-4503-3603-1/16/10...$15.00
DOI: http://dx.doi.org/10.1145/2964284.2967301

We believe that the semantics of a text associated with a video can be exploited to improve the visual features. This approach has been successfully applied to image annotation [1]. Textual descriptions of videos have some interesting properties. First they contain a high level representation that is hard to obtain from the bare visual data. Second they have a strong sequential structure that in some cases, visual feature representation struggle to maintain.

In this paper we try to give an answer to the question: "Do textual descriptions help action recognition?" To satisfy this curiosity we devise a learning scheme to incorporate the textual information into the video representation. We require this process to be done once in advance, so that textual descriptions are not needed when attempting to predict actions in a new video.

Our learning scheme has a first step, creating a connection between visual and textual features, in the form of a feature transformation. Finally this transformation is applied to visual feature vectors on which we want to learn human action classifiers. When testing new videos only the transformation and the classifier are needed.

The main contributions of this paper are:

- A method exploiting paired visual and textual data to learn a common space, in which text semantic improves visual features, leading to better action recognition performance.
- A novel structure preserving loss, that is able to avoid excessive distortion of the relationships in the initial feature spaces.

To the best of our knowledge, this is the first work that incorporates textual information into the video representation for the task of action recognition. Experiments on the challenging Hollywood2 dataset show several benefits of our approach, obtaining state of the art performance. Even more, we show that performance increases with the amount of training data and that such benefit is observable even with relatively few samples.

2. PREVIOUS WORK

There are few contributions on cross-modal representation for video and there is no previous work on action recognition exploiting joint multi-modal representations. For this reason we briefly review works pertaining cross-modal space learning and action recognition and highlight the few intersections in these two lines of research.

2.1 Multimodal Joint Spaces

There is little prior art on video-text embedding. Das *et al.* use latent topics modeling and a tripartite template graph to map visual features to words and finally to generate a textual description [2]. Xu *et al.* jointly model language and visual space to improve retrieval [29]. Zhu *et al.* [31] proposed to use a context-aware CNN to combine video and text for the task of aligning books and movies.

Additionally, embedding visual and textual features into a common space has been done for other tasks.

For the task of image annotation, Ballan *et al.* [1] proposed to use Kernel Canonical Correlation Analysis to fuse labels with image features into a semantic space. Considering that the top k ranked list of annotations are usually transferred when annotating a novel image, in [28] a novel embedding built with a rank loss is proposed. They show that optimizing the precision at k in a joint word-image embedding is useful. A deep visual semantic embedding model is proposed in [4] to train visual models exploiting both labeled image data and semantic information gathered from unannotated text. Socher *et al.* [21] proposed to employ a neural network to map the training images to their respective word vectors, in order to perform zero-shot learning on novel image categories.

For the task of captioning, in [22] the authors proposed to use Recurrent Neural Networks (RNN) on dependency trees, together with a learned multimodal representation for describing images with sentences. In [8], another approach based on RNN for describing images is proposed. They perform alignment of textual descriptions with an embedding that is learned on training pairs of images and descriptions.

Differently from all these works, we address the task of action recognition in video. We propose a novel loss to learn a structure preserving common space in which action classification is easier, thanks to the incorporation of knowledge from the textual space.

2.2 Action Recognition

Action recognition has received significant attention in the past. The majority of the works follow a standard pipeline where features are first extracted from the video and then used as inputs to a classifier.

Since videos provide a huge amount of information through motion, many works focused on the development of features such as the improved Dense Trajectories (iDT) [26] and the recent Convolutional Neural Networks (CNN) [12, 23].

Improved Dense Trajectories exploit optical flow to perform feature tracking and extract consistent local descriptors. Optical flow is estimated compensating camera movements, registering subsequent frames with a transformation [26]. They are considered state-of-the-art of video handcrafted features.

After local feature extraction, generic action recognition methods typically apply a pooling strategy to obtain a global feature of a video. As in the image domain, Fisher Vectors [17] obtain the best performance [26].

In addition to handcrafted features, CNNs have been recently found to be very good at learning meaningful features [3, 23]. In [23], 3D convolutions are used to extend an AlexNet CNN [12] to videos, with the aim of obtaining learned features from its activations. They show performance comparable to iDT features on datasets obtained from YouTube.

Classification is usually performed using SVM. Only recently few works began to employ CNN to train end-to-end classifiers [9, 19].

3. FUSING TEXT AND VIDEO

In this section we introduce our embedding model which learns, via linear projections, a novel representation for videos.

3.1 Common Space

Given a pair made of a video $x \in \mathbb{R}^D$ and a sentence $y \in \mathbb{R}^V$, we define $W_v \in \mathbb{R}^{K\times D}$ and $W_t \in \mathbb{R}^{K\times V}$ respectively as the video and sentence projection matrices, where K is the dimensionality of the common space. The pair embedded representation is:

$$u = W_v \cdot x \qquad v = W_t \cdot y \tag{1}$$

Similarly as [8, 31], the idea is that paired elements should be located very near in the projected space while unpaired ones should be more distant. In particular, we require that the cosine similarity $\cos(x, y) = x\cdot y/(||x||\cdot||y||)$ between two paired elements (u_i, v_i) versus any other unpaired elements should be greater than $\alpha \in (0, 1)$. To this end, we learn matrices W_v and W_t solving an unconstrained problem, by minimizing the following contrastive ranking loss:

$$\begin{aligned}\mathcal{L}_{rank} = & \sum_i\sum_k \max\{0, \alpha - \cos(u_i, v_i) + \cos(u_i, v_k)\} + \\ & \sum_i\sum_k \max\{0, \alpha - \cos(v_i, u_i) + \cos(v_i, u_k)\}\end{aligned} \tag{2}$$

where v_k and u_k are contrastive terms, respectively incorrect videos and sentences that should not be associated to u_i and v_i.

3.2 Structure Preserving Space

One shortcoming of the pairwise ranking-loss defined in Equation 2 is that no information of the original manifolds of visual and textual features is preserved in the common space. For instance, similar videos with close visual features can be mapped far apart in the common space or, conversely, dissimilar videos may end up close together.

We address this shortcoming by defining additional constraints that, in contrast to Equation 2, preserve the original similarities in the common space. Thus, they act as a regularizer that induces some structure of the original manifolds into the common space.

We consider the constraint:

$$|\cos(x_i, x_k) - \cos(u_i, u_k)| < \beta_v \tag{3}$$

which enforces solutions that keep the similarity between two videos, before and after the projection, within a margin β_v. Similarly, we formulate the following constraint for sentences:

$$|\cos(y_i, y_k) - \cos(v_i, v_k)| < \beta_s \tag{4}$$

We add these constraints to the problem defined by the minimization of loss in Equation 2. In order to maintain an unconstrained problem, we relax the constraints defined in

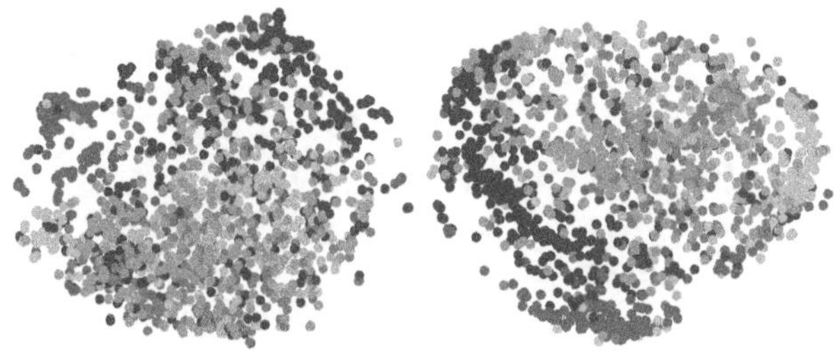

(a) Video Space (b) Embedding Space

Figure 1: Effect of our projection, using t-SNE visualization on Hollywood2 dataset. Each color corresponds to a different label.

Equation 3 and Equation 4 into a structure preserving loss. For videos, we define:

$$\Omega = \sum_i \sum_k \max\{0, -\beta_v + \cos(x_i, x_k) - \cos(u_i, u_k)\} + \sum_i \sum_k \max\{0, -\beta_v - \cos(x_i, x_k) + \cos(u_i, u_k)\} \quad (5)$$

and for sentences, we define:

$$\Theta = \sum_i \sum_k \max\{0, -\beta_s + \cos(y_i, y_k) - \cos(v_i, v_k)\} + \sum_i \sum_k \max\{0, -\beta_s - \cos(y_i, y_k) + \cos(v_i, v_k)\} \quad (6)$$

We add both terms to the ranking loss in Equation 2 and define our novel structure preserving loss:

$$\mathcal{L}_{struct} = \mathcal{L}_{rank} + \Omega + \Theta \quad (7)$$

We show in Figure 1 a t-SNE [25] visualization of the original video features and their projection in the common space. It can be seen that a structure emerges in the embedding space. Compared to the original features, video sharing the same labels (i.e. the same colors) are put closer. This suggests that a classification algorithm may be able to find a better hypothesis.

Our embedding procedure uses a vector representation for videos and descriptions. In the following we detail the visual and textual features we have used in our experiments.

3.3 Video Representations

We explore two different video representations: learned spatio-temporal features and handcrafted features. The former is based on recent developments in deep learning, specifically we used the temporal extension of convolutional neural network obtained by performing 3D convolutions on video volumes namely C3D, proposed by Tran [23]. The latter is the well known improved dense trajectory (iDT) features proposed by Wang *et al.* [27].

For each video we compute C3D features on subsequences of 16 frames using the network pre-trained on Sports-1M [9]. Specifically, we obtain the activations of the sixth network layer which is Fully Connected (FC6). To obtain a global video representation, we use average-pooling of the FC6 over the whole sequence, ending with a 4096-dimensional vector.

We use all iDT descriptors, namely HOG, HOF, MBH_x, MBH_y, MBH_{xy} and trajectories coordinates, encoding them with Fisher Vectors [17]. First we learn a PCA projection on 200k randomly selected descriptors for each local feature. We retain the first 80 components of each feature (except for trajectories which is compressed to 20). Then we concatenate the space-time coordinates of the central trajectory point, normalized in $[-1, 1]$, to the PCA compressed features. This adds spatial context to each local feature.

We estimate the GMM using the same subset on which we have learned PCA. We consider 256 Gaussians as previous work [26]. This results in a high dimensional representation that can be prone to overfitting. Thus, we further compress this representation to 4,096 dimensions with PCA, the same of C3D representation.

3.4 Textual Representation

We employ the Skip-Thought representation [11] which learns a distributed sentence representation using a neural model similar in the spirit to Word2Vec [15]. Skip-Thought are learned through an encoder-decoder architecture. A sentence s_i is fed to the encoder one word w_i^t at a time to produce a hidden state h_i representing the entire sentence. Then, the decoder has to output the previous s_{i-1} and the next s_{i+1} sentence of the corresponding text, exploiting the encoder output h_i. Thus, the model is learned optimizing the sum of the log-probabilities for the forward and backward sentences conditioned on the encoder representation.

Given sentences s_i, s_{i-1} and s_{i+1}, the log loss to be optimized is:

$$\sum_t \log p(w_{i+1}^t | w_{i+1}^{<t}, h_i) + \sum_t \log p(w_{i-1}^t | w_{i-1}^{<t}, h_i) \quad (8)$$

where notation $w^{<t}$ indicates all words before w_t, in the same sentence. We use the combine-skip model that has a hidden state h_i dimensionality of 4,800.

3.5 Learning Details

We initialize matrices weights, with random uniform distribution, $w_{ij} \propto \mathcal{U}\left(-\sqrt{(2/n_{in})}, \sqrt{(2/n_{in})}\right)$, where n_{in} is the input dimensionality of each domain. We set the projection space dimensionality K to 1000. Parameters α and β were both set to 0.2.

We optimize all losses using ADAM [10]. Considering all the contrastive pairs is unfeasible on large datasets, thus we only select a set of random pairs at each iteration.

We set the batch size to 100 and randomly sample 50 contrastive elements for each batch element. We run no more than 20 epochs and keep the model yielding the highest action classification mAP. We measure the mAP using 5-fold cross-validation on Hollywood2 training set.

After computing textual and visual features, we learn an embedding space for each type of feature. Afterwards, we apply the relative projections defined in Equation 1 to obtain new visual features. We learn a one-vs-rest linear SVM for each action class. For iDT we use late fusion, i.e. we sum SVM scores of each single-feature classifier.

4. EXPERIMENTS

4.1 Datasets

Since no public dataset with textual descriptions and action classes is publicly available, we consider one dataset to learn the embedding and one to perform the actual action recognition.

(a) iDT

Approach	mAP
Wang [26] *et al.*	65.7
Jain [6] *et al.*	62.5
Zhu [30] *et al.*	61.4
Mathe [14] *et al.*	61.0
Jiang [7] *et al.*	59.5
Gaidon [5] *et al.*	54.0
iDT+Fisher	56.4
iDT+Fisher+PCA	58.4
ours	66.2
ours + structure	**67.4**

(b) CNN

Approach	mAP
Max pooled LSTM [18]	43.2
Soft attention model [18]	43.9
C3D	44.7
ours	48.1
ours + structure	**48.7**

Table 1: Comparison with state-of-the art on Hollywood2.

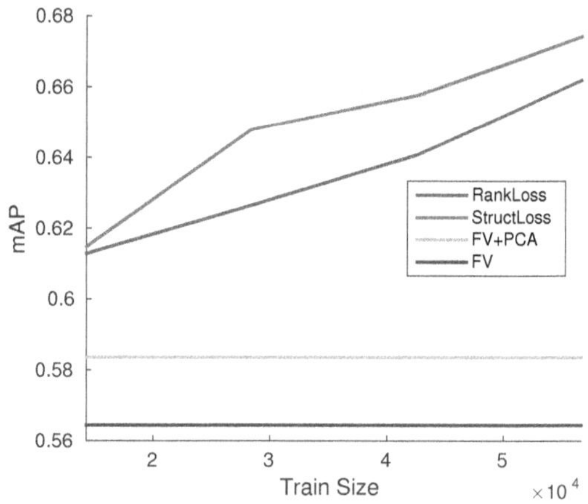

Figure 2: MAP on Hollywod2 varying the training set size compared to baseline.

The MPII Video Description Dataset [16] contains 68,337 short video sequences with associated textual descriptions, gathered from 94 HD movies. The particularity of this dataset is the availability of aligned Audio Descriptions. They are textual descriptions of video sequences that, read by a professional narrator, make movies accessible to visually impaired people. We use this dataset to learn the embedding.

The Hollywood2 [13] dataset contains 1,707 video snippets gathered from 69 HD movies labeled with 12 different actions. It is a difficult dataset since actions have high variation in appearance, context and motion. We used the clean training dataset with the provided train and test split. We use this dataset to measure the actual action recognition performance.

Both datasets are built from movies. We keep the datasets independent by removing from MPII all clips extracted from movies that are used in both datasets. We are left with 57,613 clips.

4.2 Results

We compare classification performance on Hollywood2 of baseline features and their projected counterparts.

First, we report in Table 1 (a) the performance of our approach using iDT features, compared to the state-of-the-art. Our baseline is similar to the approach of Wang *et al.* in [26]. However, for the sake of simplicity we do not use Spatio-Temporal Pyramids in conjunction with Spatial Fisher Vector. We just rely on the concatenation of local feature coordinates to each descriptor to inject contextual information. Thus, our implementation reaches 56.4 vs 65.7 of [26].

Applying PCA to the baseline does not compromise performance in classification, actually slightly improving the mAP. This behavior has been reported previously in image retrieval tasks [24]. Our projection, learned with the structure preserving loss, obtains an improvement of more than 9 mAP points with respect to the FV+PCA baseline.

In Table 1 (b) we report classification results using the C3D descriptor, compared with other CNN based approaches. Unfortunately convolutional representations do not perform very well on this challenging dataset. Our baseline is slightly superior to the Soft attention model by Sharma *et al.* [18]. Nonetheless, using our re-projected features improves mAP by 4 points. The structure preserving loss adds a slight improvement.

For both visual features we obtain a substantial improvement by learning a novel representation from video-text pairs. Moreover our structure preserving loss helps in not corrupting the video similarity in the starting space consistently improving the performance on both features.

We also analyze how the size of embedding training set affects the action classification performance. Increasing the set of captioned videos should increment the quality of the common space. We are also interested to understand if the learning method saturates. We perform this analysis using the late fusion of iDT descriptors, that performed better than C3D.

Interestingly, using 25% of the training set, we already get a sensible improvement in classification performance. Even more intriguing is the fact that the quality of the features steadily increases until the whole training set is used, with no observable saturation, as can be seen in Figure 2. We believe that further increasing the amount of captioned videos may lead to even better projections.

5. CONCLUSIONS

Our intuition that textual description can improve visual features for action recognition in video proved correct. The proposed method can easily leverage large sets of videos paired with a description to improve action recognition. Projections in structure preserving common space, can be profitably learned even with a smaller data set and performance improvement, in our experiments, does not show saturation.

Acknowledgments. This work is partially supported by the "Social Museum and Smart Tourism" project (CTN01_00034_231545).

6. REFERENCES

[1] L. Ballan, T. Uricchio, L. Seidenari, and A. Del Bimbo. A cross-media model for automatic image annotation. In *Proc. of ICMR*. ACM, 2014.

[2] P. Das, C. Xu, R. Doell, and J. Corso. A thousand frames in just a few words: Lingual description of videos through latent topics and sparse object stitching. In *Proc. of the CVPR*, pages 2634–2641, 2013.

[3] J. Donahue, Y. Jia, O. Vinyals, J. Hoffman, N. Zhang, E. Tzeng, and T. Darrell. Decaf: A deep convolutional activation feature for generic visual recognition. *arXiv preprint arXiv:1310.1531*, 2013.

[4] A. Frome, G. S. Corrado, J. Shlens, S. Bengio, J. Dean, T. Mikolov, et al. Devise: A deep visual-semantic embedding model. In *Proc. of NIPS*.

[5] A. Gaidon, Z. Harchaoui, and C. Schmid. Activity representation with motion hierarchies. *International Journal of Computer Vision*, pages 1–20, 2013.

[6] M. Jain, H. Jégou, and P. Bouthemy. Better exploiting motion for better action recognition. In *Proc. of CVPR*, 2013.

[7] Y.-G. Jiang, Q. Dai, X. Xue, W. Liu, and C.-W. Ngo. Trajectory-based modeling of human actions with motion reference points. In *Proc. of ECCV*. 2012.

[8] A. Karpathy and L. Fei-Fei. Deep visual-semantic alignments for generating image descriptions. In *Proc. of CVPR*, 2015.

[9] A. Karpathy, G. Toderici, S. Shetty, T. Leung, R. Sukthankar, and L. Fei-Fei. Large-scale video classification with convolutional neural networks. In *Proc. of CVPR*, 2014.

[10] D. P. Kingma and J. Ba. Adam: A method for stochastic optimization. *CoRR*, abs/1412.6980, 2014.

[11] R. Kiros, Y. Zhu, R. R. Salakhutdinov, R. Zemel, R. Urtasun, A. Torralba, and S. Fidler. Skip-thought vectors. In *Proc. of NIPS*, 2015.

[12] A. Krizhevsky, I. Sutskever, and G. E. Hinton. Imagenet classification with deep convolutional neural networks. In *NIPS*, 2012.

[13] M. Marszalek, I. Laptev, and C. Schmid. Actions in context. In *Proc. of CVPR*, 2009.

[14] S. Mathe and C. Sminchisescu. Dynamic eye movement datasets and learnt saliency models for visual action recognition. In *Proc. of ECCV*. 2012.

[15] T. Mikolov, I. Sutskever, K. Chen, G. Corrado, and J. Dean. Distributed representations of words and phrases and their compositionality. *CoRR*, abs/1310.4546, 2013.

[16] A. Rohrbach, M. Rohrbach, N. Tandon, and B. Schiele. A dataset for movie description. In *Proc. of CVPR*, 2015.

[17] J. Sánchez, F. Perronnin, T. Mensink, and J. Verbeek. Image classification with the fisher vector: Theory and practice. *International journal of computer vision*, 105(3):222–245, 2013.

[18] S. Sharma, R. Kiros, and R. Salakhutdinov. Action recognition using visual attention. *NIPS Workshop on Time Series*, 2015.

[19] K. Simonyan and A. Zisserman. Two-stream convolutional networks for action recognition in videos. *CoRR*, abs/1406.2199, 2014.

[20] A. W. Smeulders, M. Worring, S. Santini, A. Gupta, and R. Jain. Content-based image retrieval at the end of the early years. *Pattern Analysis and Machine Intelligence, IEEE Transactions on*, 22(12):1349–1380, 2000.

[21] R. Socher, M. Ganjoo, C. D. Manning, and A. Ng. Zero-shot learning through cross-modal transfer. In *Proc. of NIPS*, 2013.

[22] R. Socher, A. Karpathy, Q. V. Le, C. D. Manning, and A. Y. Ng. Grounded compositional semantics for finding and describing images with sentences. *Transactions of the Association for Computational Linguistics*, 2:207–218, 2014.

[23] D. Tran, L. Bourdev, R. Fergus, L. Torresani, and M. Paluri. Learning spatiotemporal features with 3d convolutional networks. *CoRR*, abs/1412.0767, 2014.

[24] T. Uricchio, M. Bertini, L. Seidenari, and A. Del Bimbo. Fisher encoded convolutional bag-of-windows for efficient image retrieval and social image tagging. In *Proc. of ICCV Workshops*, 2015.

[25] L. van Der Maaten. Accelerating t-SNE using tree-based algorithms. *Journal of Machine Learning Research*, 15(1):3221–3245, 2014.

[26] H. Wang, D. Oneata, J. Verbeek, and C. Schmid. A robust and efficient video representation for action recognition. *International Journal of Computer Vision*, pages 1–20, 2015.

[27] L. Wang, Y. Qiao, and X. Tang. Action recognition with trajectory-pooled deep-convolutional descriptors. *CoRR*, abs/1505.04868, 2015.

[28] J. Weston, S. Bengio, and N. Usunier. Large scale image annotation: learning to rank with joint word-image embeddings. *Machine learning*, 81(1):21–35, 2010.

[29] R. Xu, C. Xiong, W. Chen, and J. J. Corso. Jointly modeling deep video and compositional text to bridge vision and language in a unified framework. In *In Proc. of AAAI*. Citeseer, 2015.

[30] J. Zhu, B. Wang, X. Yang, W. Zhang, and Z. Tu. Action recognition with actons. In *Proc. of ICCV*, 2013.

[31] Y. Zhu, R. Kiros, R. S. Zemel, R. Salakhutdinov, R. Urtasun, A. Torralba, and S. Fidler. Aligning books and movies: Towards story-like visual explanations by watching movies and reading books. *CoRR*, abs/1506.06724, 2015.

Frame Untangling for Unobtrusive Display-Camera Visible Light Communication

Xiao Shu
McMaster University
shux@mcmaster.ca

Xiaolin Wu
Shanghai Jiao Tong University
xwu510@sjtu.edu.cn

ABSTRACT

Pairing displays and cameras can open up convenient and "free" visible light communication channels. But in realistic settings, the synchronization between displays (transmitters) and cameras (receivers) can be far more involved than assumed in the literature. This study aims to analyze and model the temporal behaviors of displays and cameras to make the visible light communication channel between the two more robust, while maintaining perceptual transparency of the transmitted data.

Keywords

Visible light communication, information display

1. INTRODUCTION

A new, intriguing modality of visible light communication (VLC) is the use of optoelectronic displays as transmitters and digital cameras as receivers [7, 8, 4, 5, 6, 9]. This display-camera VLC modality has the advantage of data specificity: communicating information pertaining to displayed contents on screen; in addition, the modality is convenient to use, thanks to the ubiquity of displays and cameras in modern life. An example of display-camera VLC is QR code, which has rapidly gained popularity in recent years. QR code is suitable for consumer applications when only a very small amount of information needs to be communicated, such as sending web addresses or contact information among smart devices. QR code encodes the information as a still binary image, which is a two-dimensional extension of barcode. The main design criteria of QR code are simplicity and easy decoding. But the QR code design has two obvious drawbacks. First, QR code completely ignores the great potential of temporal dimension in code capacity, despite in practice most displays and cameras operate in video mode; as such, QR code offers very low bandwidth for the large screen real estate taken. Second, QR code is visually intrusive because it compromises the integrity of the original image on screen.

Recently, research efforts have been reported on exploring the temporal dimension to greatly increase the communication bandwidth in display-camera VLC. Some temporal modulation techniques were proposed to embed data stream in displayed video for VLC [2, 12, 11, 1]. Moreover, some researchers strive to make the embedded data invisible on screen to human viewers, by exploiting the limited temporal resolution of the human visual system (HVS) [7, 4, 9]. These authors demonstrated the possibility of opening up a hidden display-camera communication channel without interference with normal functionalities of optoelectronic displays.

All techniques to visually hide embedded data in display-camera VLC are based on the following simple idea. A 2D data pattern is added to one frame and then subtracted from the next frame. This quick flip-and-flop between the positive (addition) and negative (subtraction) states makes the screen flicker and transmits the data. The screen flickering due to the sequence of data-modulated frames becomes invisible to human viewers if the display runs at a sufficiently high refresh rate; the HVS cannot discern the high frequency flickering, instead it only perceives the fusion of adjacent frames. This fusion cancels out the positive and negative modulation patterns and renders the embedded data transparent to human eyes. On the other hand, if a high frame rate camera matching the refresh rate of the display can capture all the modulated frames, embedded data can be detected and recovered from the high-frequency optical signal by comparing the difference of every two adjacent frames.

Although the above approach of visually transparent display-camera VLC can support high bandwidth transmission in theory, none of the published works of this category is able to sustain a low enough bit error rate outside ideal lab environments. The bit error rates of some techniques can often go beyond 15% even if the camera is placed right in front of the screen on a tripod [7, 4], greatly limiting the effective bandwidth. The high bit error rate is caused by poor quality of the display-camera communication channel that has not been studied in depth. The most serious challenge is that both display and camera are row-by-row scanning devices, making it very difficult to synchronize data frames in display-camera VLC, which is an issue completely overlooked by previous works. Other non-ideal device characteristics, such as, slow response time of liquid crystal displays (LCDs), which are by far the main stream displays in use,

This research is supported by National Natural Science Foundation of China (NSFC 61331014).

MM '16, October 15-19, 2016, Amsterdam, Netherlands

DOI: http://dx.doi.org/10.1145/2964284.2967302

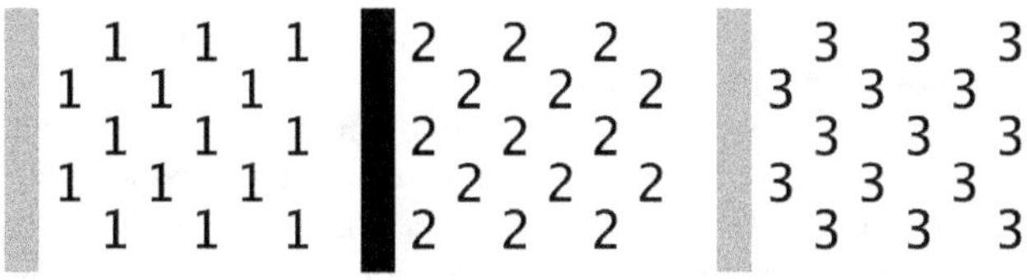

(a) 3 consecutive frames displayed on screen

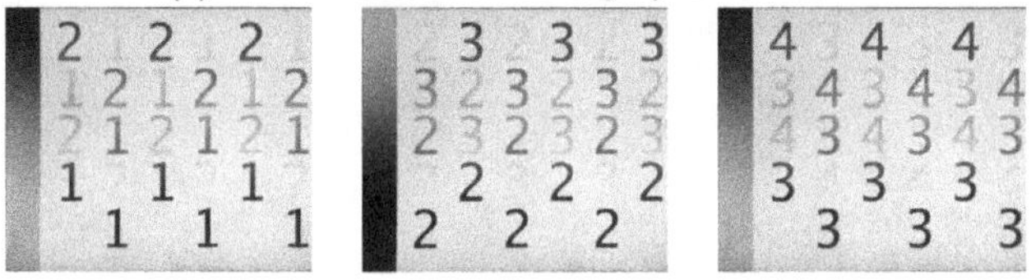

(b) 3 consecutive images captured by camera

Figure 1: Each captured image of the screen is a blend of two frames rather than a clean shot of a single, complete frame.

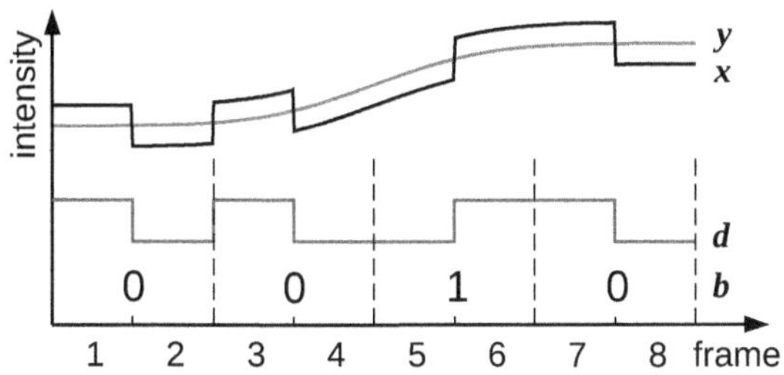

Figure 2: Display-camera VLC methods hide data $\boldsymbol{b}$ in video $\boldsymbol{x}$ by adding a fast flipping signal $\boldsymbol{d}$ in original video $\boldsymbol{y}$.

and long camera exposure time further complicate the matter. As demonstrated in Fig. 1, getting a clean image of any frame displayed on screen can be surprisingly difficult due to the frame tangling effects. Without properly compensating for these device imperfections, directly comparing the difference of two adjacent camera frames can only yield correct results for parts of the screen, resulting unacceptably high error rate.

The goal of this work is to analyze and model how displayed frames are mingled in camera-captured frames so that we can reverse the process and restore the true data frames. Previous attempts on synchronizing captured images with displayed frames all rely on visible markers that block some parts of the screen, defeating the visual transparency property of the display-camera VLC communication. In developing the mathematical model for the formation of a frame of the camera capturing the display, we find that the seam of two displayed frames exhibits some unique statistical fingerprint. This fingerprint can be used to localize the seam position reliably, and consequently untangle mingled data frames.

2. PRACTICAL CHALLENGES

As shown in Fig. 2, most unobtrusive display-camera VLC methods realize hidden data transmission by adding a fast flipping signal modulated by the data to the original frames

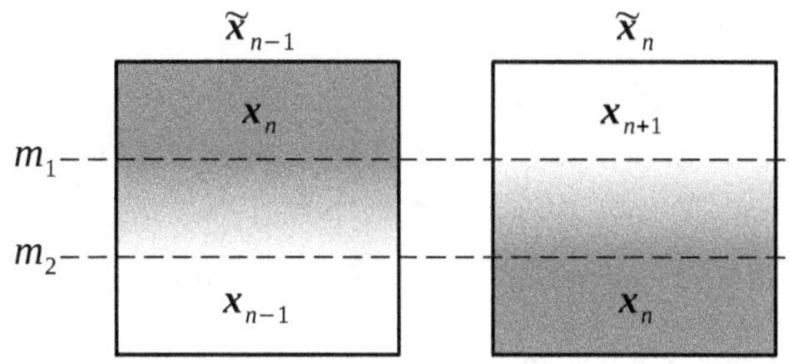

Figure 3: Two consecutive captured images of the display with two data frames mingled together in each image.

as follows,

$$\begin{aligned} \boldsymbol{x}_{2n-1} &= \boldsymbol{y}_{2n-1} + \boldsymbol{d}_n \\ \boldsymbol{x}_{2n} &= \boldsymbol{y}_{2n} - \boldsymbol{d}_n, \end{aligned} \tag{1}$$

where $\boldsymbol{y}_n$ and $\boldsymbol{x}_n$ are the n-th original and modified frames, respectively, and $\boldsymbol{d}_n$ is the added signal. There are multiple ways to encode a data sequence $\boldsymbol{b}$ into signal $\boldsymbol{d}$, for instance, using Manchester code,

$$\boldsymbol{d}_n(i) = \delta \cdot (-1)^{\boldsymbol{b}(n*M+i)}, \tag{2}$$

where M is the number of pixels in each frame, $0 \leq i < M$ is a pixel and δ is the strength of the signal. If the modified frames $\boldsymbol{x}$ are displayed on a screen refreshing at least twice as fast as the flicker fusion frequency [10, 13], the added flipping signal becomes completely transparent to most people. But a camera capable of capturing an image $\tilde{\boldsymbol{x}}_n$ for each frame $\boldsymbol{x}_n$ on screen can still see the added signal,

$$\tilde{\boldsymbol{d}}_n = \frac{1}{2}(\tilde{\boldsymbol{x}}_{2n-1} - \tilde{\boldsymbol{x}}_{2n}) \approx \frac{1}{2}(\boldsymbol{x}_{2n-1} - \boldsymbol{x}_{2n}) = \boldsymbol{d}_n, \tag{3}$$

and decode it to recover the embedded data $\boldsymbol{b}$.

Unfortunately, this simple scheme is flawed in real world setting: a captured image of the display is most likely a blend of two or more frames rather than a clean image of a single frame as assumed in Eq (3), even if the frame rate of the camera matches the refresh rate of the display. This problem is a result of the physical and practical limitations of modern camera and display systems. For example, instead of showing every pixel of a new frame on the screen all at once, most display devices update a frame row by row from top to bottom in sequence. In the middle of this refreshing process, the top part of the screen might have updated to a new frame $\boldsymbol{x}_n$ while the bottom rest is still showing the old frame $\boldsymbol{x}_{n-1}$. A picture $\tilde{\boldsymbol{x}}_{n-1}$ taken at this moment would then be a patchwork with the top part of $\boldsymbol{x}_n$ and the bottom part of $\boldsymbol{x}_{n-1}$, as illustrated in Fig. 3. On a typical liquid crystal display (LCD), the above scenario can easily occur, as the time required to update all pixels (the refresh time) often takes a significant portion of each frame duration [3].

Another factor that hinders display-camera synchronization is the screen response time, which is the time for a pixel to transit from one intensity to another. If a fast changing content, like a video with added flipping signal $\boldsymbol{d}$, is displayed on a LCD, a picture of the screen would capture many pixels in the middle of transitions, like the pixels in the region between m_1 and m_2 in Fig. 3. Since display-camera VLC encodes the data in the small differences $\boldsymbol{d}_n$ between every two adjacent frames while keeps their average true to the original as in Eq. (1), a pixel captured in the middle of intensity transition,

$$\begin{aligned}\tilde{\boldsymbol{x}}_{2n-1}(i) &= [\boldsymbol{x}_{2n-1}(i) + \boldsymbol{x}_{2n}(i)]/2 \\ &= [\boldsymbol{y}_{2n-1}(i) + \boldsymbol{d}_n(i) + \boldsymbol{y}_{2n} - \boldsymbol{d}_n(i)]/2 \\ &= [\boldsymbol{y}_{2n-1}(i) + \boldsymbol{y}_{2n}]/2, \end{aligned} \tag{4}$$

would be the average of original frames, erasing the embedded signal $\boldsymbol{d}_n$.

Cameras are not ideal receivers either for display-camera VLC. For instance, a camera must have a sufficiently long exposure time in order to capture enough photons to overcome sensor noise. As a result, a captured screen image is not the true content at a particular moment but an integral of the displayed frames over the period of camera exposure time. In display-camera VLC, if the camera captures the transition from one frame to the next during the exposure time, the added opposite data pulses in the two adjacent frames cancel out in the captured image, making the embedded data unrecoverable. This problem has the similar effects as the long response time in LCDs.

Last but not least, most digital video cameras use rolling shutter technique to scan a scene in a row-by-row fashion. This technique is similar to the refreshing mechanism of a display, which leads to the same problem of capturing multiple frames within the same image [2]. Due to this scanning nature of both display and camera, it can be very difficult or even impossible to untangle individual frames from captured images in display-camera VLC. The worst case scenario happens when a camera scans a display from top to bottom at the same pace as the refreshing speed of the display. In this case, if one displayed row is scanned by the camera during its transition, then every row in the captured image is in this undecodable state due to synchronized scanning of the display and camera.

Given all these intricacies in display-camera synchronization, modeling and detecting how frames are mingled in a captured screen image is crucial to the performance of display-camera VLC. If the seam of every two adjacent frames can be located accurately, restoring a complete frame is simply cutting out all the pieces of the frame scattered across captured images and then pasting them together. With a complete frame, the decoding process in display-camera VLC becomes simple and less error-prone. Moreover, since the seam of two frames indicates the pixel intensity transition from one frame to the other, captured pixels around the seam are likely in the middle of transition with poor signal strength. This knowledge of data reliability is useful to design robust coding strategies.

3. DETECTING SEAM OF FRAMES

Our design objective is a generic method for detecting and repairing data frame fragments from a captured video in flickering-based display-camera VLC as presented in Eq. (1). This method pre-processes captured video for the next decoding process and should be compatible with most existing display-camera VLC coding schemes. But a few assumptions about the video and coding scheme must be made: first, the captured video is taken using roughly the same frame rate as the refresh rate of the display; second, the original video intended for human viewers is relatively smooth, i.e., $\boldsymbol{y}_n \approx \boldsymbol{y}_{n+1}$; last, the added signal $\boldsymbol{d}_n(i)$ is either $-\delta$ or δ and independent with $\boldsymbol{d}_{n+1}(i)$. All these conditions are either already required by all the existing display-camera VLC techniques or easy to achieve.

Now, suppose that each captured image $\tilde{\boldsymbol{x}}_n$ is a fusion of two consecutive frames with part of the new frame $\boldsymbol{x}_{n+1}$ on the top and part of the old frame $\boldsymbol{x}_n$ on the bottom, as shown in Fig. 3; and each pixel $m_1 \leq i < m_2$ in the middle part of the screen is in transition state with its intensity $\tilde{\boldsymbol{x}}_n(i)$ being a weighted average of $\boldsymbol{x}_n(i)$ and $\boldsymbol{x}_{n+1}(i)$. Thus, the intensity of each pixel i in image $\tilde{\boldsymbol{x}}_n$ can be written as,

$$\tilde{\boldsymbol{x}}_n(i) = (1 - \lambda(i))\boldsymbol{x}_{n+1}(i) + \lambda(i)\boldsymbol{x}_n(i) \tag{5}$$

where for $m_1 \leq i < m_2$, $0 \leq \lambda(i) \leq 1$ is a monotonically increasing function, and for $i < m_1$ and $i \geq m_2$, $\lambda(i)$ equals to 0 and 1, respectively. Since the frame rate of the camera is the same as the refresh rate of the display, the frames are mingled in the same way in each captured image, thus, the same function $\lambda(i)$ in Eq. (5) applies to every image. If we define the seam of two consecutive frames as the place where the intensity transition is right in the half way, then pixel i on the seam must have $\lambda(i) = 1/2$ by this definition.

Pixels with $\lambda(i) = 1/2$ have some strong statistical pattern in the difference image of two captured consecutive frames. By the imaging model in Eq. (5), this difference image, which contains the added data signal, is,

$$\begin{aligned} f_{2n-1}(i) &= \tilde{\boldsymbol{x}}_{2n-1}(i) - \tilde{\boldsymbol{x}}_{2n}(i) \\ &= (1 - \lambda(i))[\boldsymbol{x}_{2n}(i) - \boldsymbol{x}_{2n+1}(i)] \\ &\quad + \lambda(i)[\boldsymbol{x}_{2n-1}(i) - \boldsymbol{x}_{2n}(i)]. \end{aligned} \tag{6}$$

By substituting $\boldsymbol{x}_n$ using the encoding equation in Eq. (1) and assuming that $\boldsymbol{y}_n \approx \boldsymbol{y}_{n+1}$, the difference image $f_{2n-1}(i)$ can be approximated as,

$$\tilde{f}_{2n-1}(i) = (1-\lambda(i))[-\boldsymbol{d}_n(i) - \boldsymbol{d}_{n+1}(i)] + 2\lambda(i)\boldsymbol{d}_n(i), \tag{7}$$

and if $|\boldsymbol{d}_n(i)| = |\boldsymbol{d}_{n+1}(i)| = \delta$ as assumed, then,

$$|\tilde{f}_{2n-1}(i)| = \begin{cases} 2\delta \cdot \lambda(i) & \boldsymbol{d}_n(i) \neq \boldsymbol{d}_{n+1}(i) \\ 2\delta \cdot |2\lambda(i) - 1| & \boldsymbol{d}_n(i) = \boldsymbol{d}_{n+1}(i). \end{cases} \tag{8}$$

Since $\boldsymbol{d}_n(i), \boldsymbol{d}_{n+1}(i)$ are independent, $\boldsymbol{d}_n(i) \neq \boldsymbol{d}_{n+1}(i)$ and $\boldsymbol{d}_n(i) = \boldsymbol{d}_{n+1}(i)$ are equally probable. Therefore, the expected value and standard deviation of $|\tilde{f}_{2n-1}(i)|$ are,

$$\begin{aligned} \mu_{2n-1}(i) &= \mathrm{E}[|\tilde{f}_{2n-1}(i)|] \\ &= \delta(\lambda(i) + |2\lambda(i) - 1|), \end{aligned} \tag{9}$$

$$\begin{aligned} \sigma_{2n-1}(i) &= \sqrt{\mathrm{E}[(|\tilde{f}_{2n-1}(i)| - \mu_{2n-1}(i))^2]} \\ &= \delta\,|\lambda(i) - |2\lambda(i) - 1||\,. \end{aligned} \tag{10}$$

Similarly, the approximation of $\tilde{\boldsymbol{x}}_{2n}(i) - \tilde{\boldsymbol{x}}_{2n+1}(i)$ has absolute value,

$$|\tilde{f}_{2n}(i)| = \begin{cases} 2\delta \cdot (1 - \lambda(i)) & \boldsymbol{d}_n(i) \neq \boldsymbol{d}_{n+1}(i) \\ 2\delta \cdot |2\lambda(i) - 1| & \boldsymbol{d}_n(i) = \boldsymbol{d}_{n+1}(i), \end{cases} \tag{11}$$

and the expected value and standard deviation of $|\tilde{f}_{2n-1}(i)|$ are,

$$\mu_{2n}(i) = \delta(1 - \lambda(i) + |2\lambda(i) - 1|), \tag{12}$$

$$\sigma_{2n}(i) = \delta|1 - \lambda(i) - |2\lambda(i) - 1||. \tag{13}$$

As shown in a plot of $\mu_{2n-1}(i), \sigma_{2n-1}(i), \mu_{2n}(i)$ and $\sigma_{2n}(i)$ as functions of $\lambda(i)$ in Fig. 4, all the four functions have the same value if and only if $\lambda(i) = 1/2$. Thus, if the values

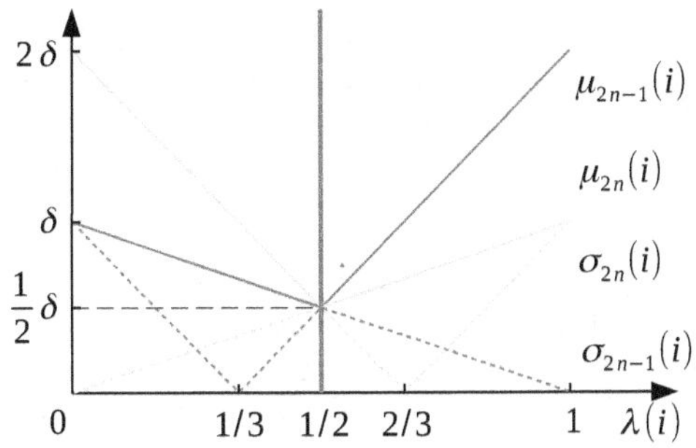

Figure 4: The values of $\mu_{2n-1}(i), \sigma_{2n-1}(i), \mu_{2n}(i), \sigma_{2n}(i)$ are all equal if and only if $\lambda(i) = 1/2$ (the red vertical line).

of the four functions at some pixel i are sufficiently close to each other, $\lambda(i)$ should be near 1/2, which indicates pixel i being on the seam of two frames. This observation gives raise to our seam detection method as in Algorithm 1.

Algorithm 1 Detect seam of frames

Input: 3 consecutively captured image $\tilde{\boldsymbol{x}}_1, \tilde{\boldsymbol{x}}_2, \tilde{\boldsymbol{x}}_3$

```
α = 0.15                                          ▷ Threshold
f1 = |x̃1 − x̃2|; f2 = |x̃2 − x̃3|                    ▷ Eq. (6)
for n = 1 to 2 do
    for each the i-th row r_i in f_n do
        μ_n(i) = mean(r_i)                        ▷ Eq. (9)
        σ_n(i) = std(r_i)                         ▷ Eq. (10)
    end for
end for
for i = 1 to number_of_elements(μ1) do
    h(i) = std([μ1(i), μ2(i), σ1(i), σ2(i)])
end for
h = h/[mean(μ1) + mean(μ2)]                       ▷ Normalize h
Find k such that h(k) = min(h)
```

Output: k if $h(k) < \alpha$, otherwise, "Not Found"

Since the camera scans the display row by row in this case, $\lambda(i)$ is approximately the same for every pixel in the same row. Therefore, the expect values and standard deviations, for example $\mu_{2n-1}(i)$ and $\sigma_{2n}(i)$, can be estimated using mean and sample standard deviation of all the samples $|\tilde{f}_{2n}(i)|$ in the same row.

4. EXPERIMENTAL RESULTS

To evaluate the performance of our proposed method, we captured several data-embedded video segments displayed on a 120Hz LCD (ASUS VG278HE) with a camera (Apple iPhone 6) shooting at 120fps. The transmitted data is a random binary sequence, which is encoded using the technique in [9]. A sample image sequence from one of the captured video segments is shown in Fig. 5a with the seams of frames detected and marked in red lines by using the proposed method. In this example, it is easy to spot the frame transition regions: pixels in these regions look blurred due to the added signals cancelling out each other. Clearly, the proposed method accurately marked all these regions. The statistical information collected from this sample by the proposed method is plotted in Fig. 5b. The mean and standard deviation of the absolute difference between two captured images well coincide with the theoretical analysis presented in Fig. 3.

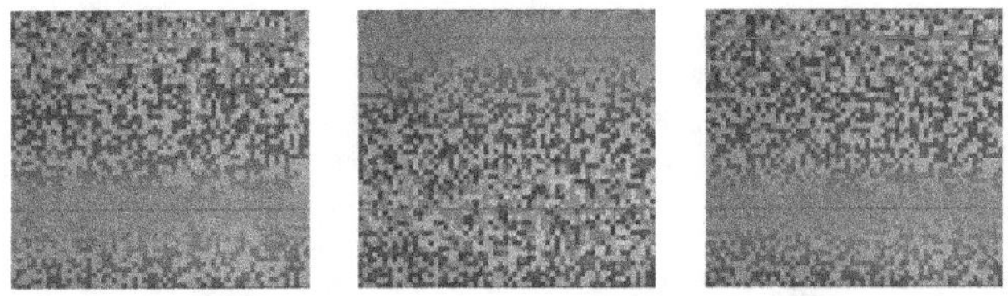

(a) 3 consecutively captured image, $\tilde{\boldsymbol{x}}_1, \tilde{\boldsymbol{x}}_2, \tilde{\boldsymbol{x}}_3$

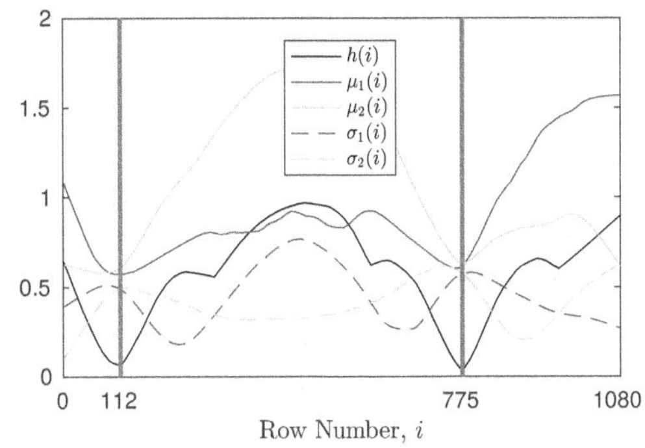

(b) Vectors $h, \mu_1, \mu_2, \sigma_1, \sigma_2$ in Algorithm 1.

Figure 5: A sample input and the corresponding result of seam detection by the proposed method. Red vertical lines mark the seams of frames.

Fig. 6 shows the decoding performance of the proposed method for 66 video segments collected from movie trailers embedded with random signals of four different strength levels. We group video segments by the average energy level of the difference image between two adjacent frames, measured by root mean square error (RMSE). In general, the faster the scene, the larger the RMSE. A large difference between frames in the original video breaks the assumption that $\boldsymbol{y}_n \approx \boldsymbol{y}_{n+1}$ in our analysis. However, in such a case, the proposed method still works well. To quantify the performance of our method, we first find the optimal way, by brutal force, to untangle the frames so that the resulting images achieves highest correct ratio of decoded data. Then this ratio is used as a benchmark to compare against our method. On average, the correct ratio of our method is about 95% of the optimal regardless of the strength of the added signal.

5. CONCLUSION

This paper reveals some unique statistical fingerprint indicating how two frames are mingled in a captured screen image. As demonstrated by experiments, this fingerprint can be used to localize the seam position reliably, and consequently untangle the data frames.

6. REFERENCES

[1] R. Carvalho, C.-H. Chu, and L.-J. Chen. Ivc: Imperceptible video communication. *Proc. of HotMobile (poster)*, 2014.

[2] W. Hu, H. Gu, and Q. Pu. LightSync: Unsynchronized visual communication over screen-camera links. In *Proceedings of the 19th annual*

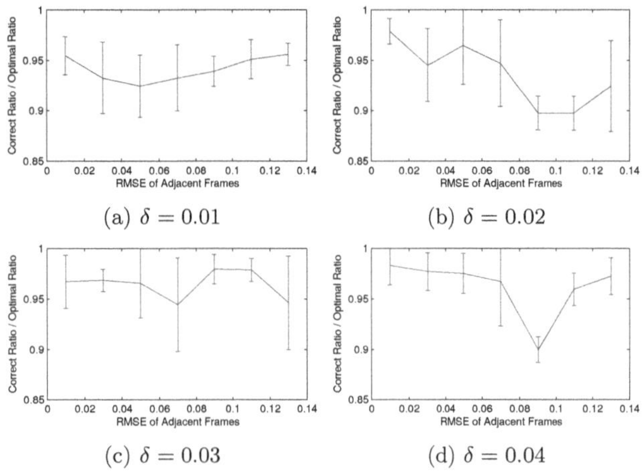

(a) $\delta = 0.01$ (b) $\delta = 0.02$ (c) $\delta = 0.03$ (d) $\delta = 0.04$

Figure 6: The performance of the proposed method is insensitive to signal strength δ and the speed of the original video measured by the RMSE of adjacent frames.

international conference on Mobile computing & networking, pages 15–26. ACM, 2013.

[3] L. Jiao, X. Shu, Y. Cheng, X. Wu, and N. Burini. Optimal backlight modulation with crosstalk control in stereoscopic display. *Display Technology, Journal of*, 11(2):157–164, Feb 2015.

[4] T. Li, C. An, X. Xiao, A. T. Campbell, and X. Zhou. Real-time screen-camera communication behind any scene. In *Proceedings of the 13th Annual International Conference on Mobile Systems, Applications, and Services*, pages 197–211. ACM, 2015.

[5] V. Nguyen, Y. Tang, A. Ashok, M. Gruteser, K. Dana, W. Hu, E. Wengrowski, and N. Mandayam. High–rate flicker–free screen–camera communication with spatially adaptive embedding. In *IEEE INFOCOM*, volume 2, 2016.

[6] S. Shi, L. Chen, W. Hu, and M. Gruteser. Reading between lines: high-rate, non-intrusive visual codes within regular videos via ImplicitCode. In *Proceedings of the 2015 ACM International Joint Conference on Pervasive and Ubiquitous Computing*, pages 157–168. ACM, 2015.

[7] A. Wang, Z. Li, C. Peng, G. Shen, G. Fang, and B. Zeng. InFrame++: Achieve simultaneous screen-human viewing and hidden screen-camera communication. In *Proceedings of the 13th Annual International Conference on Mobile Systems, Applications, and Services*, pages 181–195. ACM, 2015.

[8] A. Wang, C. Peng, O. Zhang, G. Shen, and B. Zeng. InFrame: Multiflexing full-frame visible communication channel for humans and devices. In *Proceedings of the 13th ACM Workshop on Hot Topics in Networks*, page 23. ACM, 2014.

[9] X. Wu and X. Shu. Combining information display and visible light wireless communication. In *40th IEEE International Conference on Acoustics, Speech, and Signal Processing (ICASSP)*, Apr 2015.

[10] X. Wu and G. Zhai. Temporal psychovisual modulation: A new paradigm of information display. *Signal Processing Magazine, IEEE*, 30(1):136–141, 2013.

[11] W. Yuan, K. Dana, A. Ashok, M. Gruteser, and N. Mandayam. Dynamic and invisible messaging for visual MIMO. In *Applications of Computer Vision (WACV), 2012 IEEE Workshop on*, pages 345–352. IEEE, 2012.

[12] W. Yuan, K. Dana, M. Varga, A. Ashok, M. Gruteser, and N. Mandayam. Computer vision methods for visual MIMO optical system. In *Computer Vision and Pattern Recognition Workshops (CVPRW), 2011 IEEE Computer Society Conference on*, pages 37–43. IEEE, 2011.

[13] G. Zhai and X. Wu. Multiuser collaborative viewport via temporal psychovisual modulation. *Signal Processing Magazine, IEEE*, 31(5):144–149, 2014.

Performance Measurements of Virtual Reality Systems: Quantifying the Timing and Positioning Accuracy

Chun-Ming Chang[1], Cheng-Hsin Hsu[2], Chih-Fan Hsu[1], and Kuan-Ta Chen[1]

[1]Institute of Information Science, Academia Sinica
[2]Department of Computer Science, National Tsing Hua University

ABSTRACT

We propose the very first non-intrusive measurement methodology for quantifying the performance of commodity Virtual Reality (VR) systems. Our methodology considers the VR system under test as a black-box and works with any VR applications. Multiple performance metrics on timing and positioning accuracy are considered, and detailed testbed setup and measurement steps are presented. We also apply our methodology to several VR systems in the market, and carefully analyze the experiment results. We make several observations: (i) 3D scene complexity affects the timing accuracy the most, (ii) most VR systems implement the dead reckoning algorithm, which incurs a non-trivial correction latency after incorrect predictions, and (iii) there exists an inherent trade-off between two positioning accuracy metrics: precision and sensitivity.

Keywords: Measurement; Head Mounted Display; Virtual Reality; Quality of Experience; latency; accuracy; sensitivity

1. INTRODUCTION

Virtual Reality (VR) renders computer-generated objects to create virtual environments for users [7], which enables many applications, such as military, healthcare, and video games, and thus becomes more and more popular. In fact, market research [3] indicates that the VR's annual market could grow to $80 billion in 10 years, compared to the current laptop computer market at $111 billion and game console market at $14 billion. The main driving force behind such a high growth rate is the *commodity* Head-Mounted Displays (HMDs) recently built for *desktop* and *mobile* VR systems, including Sony Morpheus, Microsoft HoloLens, Oculus Rift, and HTC Vive [1].

VR systems with HMDs were first built in research labs decades ago [14], using miniature Cathode Ray Tubes (CRTs) for displaying and mechanical/ultrasonic sensors for head tracking, in order to change the rendered images when the user moves. Over years, various hardware components have been enhanced for better VR experience at lower costs. Among these components, the compact and inexpensive Micro-Electro-Mechanical System (MEMS) sensors and high-resolution displays, which are also adopted by smartphones, allow VR developers, such as Oculus [8], to build commodity HMDs for VR systems. In these HMDs, the cumbersome mechanical/ultrasonic head-tracking sensors are replaced by MEMS inertial sensors with accelerometers and gyroscopes. However, these commodity VR systems suffer from *drifting* due to integration over potentially biased inertial sensor readings [15], which may be nontrivial as the sensors are likely to be inexpensive. This kind of drifting leads to *inaccurate* head-tracking results, which in turn cause cybersickness, like nausea, disorientation, headaches, sweating, and eye strain [4]. Hence, quantifying the performance of the commodity VR systems is crucial for faster and wider adoption.

Measuring the performance of the commodity VR systems is no easy task, because these HMDs are consumer-grade products with limited, if any, hardware and software accessibility. Moreover, these VR systems consist of multiple entities, including HMDs, rendering desktops or smartphones, VR applications, and dead reckoning algorithms. Since these entities all directly affect the system performance, we propose a system-wide black-box measurement methodology in this paper. Our methodology is general, because it does not: (i) instrument the VR systems (e.g., VR applications and HMDs) nor (ii) assume the existence of a specific (easy to recognize) virtual object. In other words, our methodology works with off-the-shelf VR systems, which to our best knowledge, is not possible in prior studies [5, 6, 10, 13]. Furthermore, our measurement methodology quantifies several variations of the *timing* and *positioning accuracy* metrics, which were not discussed in the literature. Timing accuracy, like delay, quantifies the temporal gaps between physical and virtual worlds. On the other side, positioning accuracy quantifies the spatial gaps like precision. We apply the methodology to several commodity VR systems, and analyze the measurement results. Several observations are made from our experiment results: (i) 3D scene complexity affects the timing accuracy the most, showing the importance of rendering desktops or smartphones, (ii) most VR systems (3 out of 4) implement the dead reckoning algorithm, which shortens the time of reacting to head movements, but incurs a non-trivial correction latency after incorrect predictions, and (iii) there exists an inherent trade-off between two positioning accuracy metrics: some VR systems opt for higher precision, while others opt for higher sensitivity.

2. RELATED WORK

The implications of low-level VR system performance, such as latency, on high-level user experience have been studied using carefully-designed subjective tests. For example, Papadakis et al. [9] investigate the relation between spatial memory performance and latency. Young et al. [16] compare the performance of two VR systems by asking subjects to perform diverse tasks, such as sorting and searching, and provide opinion scores. Samaraweera et al. [12]

MM '16, October 15-19, 2016, Amsterdam, Netherlands

DOI: http://dx.doi.org/10.1145/2964284.2967303

study whether mobility impaired patients are less vulnerable to cybersickness due to the latency. These subjective experiments are complementary to our work that focuses on objective experiments on commodity VR systems.

There are few existing work proposing methodologies to measure the latency of VR systems. Papadakis et al. [10] present a system with photodiodes, an oscilloscope, and a servo-motor to measure the latency of a head-tracking (inertial) sensor. They manually read the measurement results from the oscilloscope, which may be error-prone. Steed [13] proposes to create a virtual pendulum, and configures it to follow a head-tracking sensor that moves in a sinusoidal pattern. The measured results of the pendulum and the head-tracking sensor are fit to sinusoidal functions, which are then used to calculate the latency. Di Luca [5] proposes to use two photodiodes to capture the position of the head-tracking sensor based on gradient images. The signals from photodiodes need to be processed, which may result in additional and unknown latency, and over-estimated latency. Friston and Steed [6] propose an automated frame counting approach to measure latency using an easily-recognized virtual object that follows the movement of a head-tracking sensor. They assume that this virtual object is never occluded by other objects. Compared to prior arts [5,6,10,13], our work: (i) considers a wider spectrum of performance metrics, and (ii) works with off-the-shelf VR applications in arbitrary scenes.

3. METHODOLOGY

Our proposed methodology controls the movements of an HMD, and measure the differences between the physical and virtual world states using off-the-shelf VR applications. We describe the design of testbed, performance metrics, measurement procedures, and post-processing steps in the rest of this section.

3.1 Testbed Setup

The measurement testbed comprises a number of components: (i) a rotating platform [2] to emulate head (HMD) movements, (ii) an external display that mirrors the view in the HMD, and (iii) a high-speed camera that captures both the HMD device and the HMD view. We aim to support both desktop and mobile VR systems. Desktop VR systems (such as Oculus Rift) have dedicated HMD devices, while mobile VR systems (such as Samsung Gear VR) directly use smartphones within cases that work as HMD devices. For brevity, we use HMD devices to refer to the devices that provide VR view in both desktop and mobile VR systems.

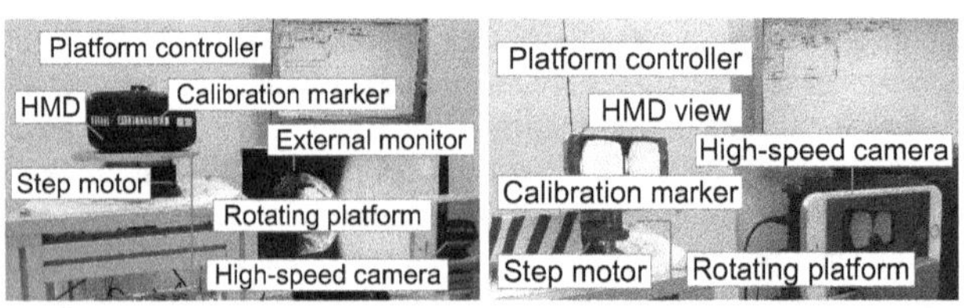

(a) With Oculus Rift (b) With Google Cardboard

Figure 1: Testbed setup.

Figure 1 shows the testbed for Oculus Rift and Google Cardboard HMDs. As shown in this figure, the HMD device is mounted on the rotating platform. For desktop VR systems, we redirect the HMD view to an external display via an HDMI cable. For mobile VR systems, no external display is used, because the smartphone (Samsung S6) used in our testbed does not support any HDMI output. In either cases, the high-speed camera needs to shoot both the HMD device and the HMD view (either on the external monitor or the smartphone display). We use Apple iPhone 6 as the high-speed camera, which supports continuous 240 fps (frame-per-second) video recording. To emulate the movement of HMDs in action, a rotating platform is used to mimic various human head motions. The platform comes with a high-quality step motor, and is fast and accurate even when it is loaded with up to 10 KG objects. More specifically, the platform can rotate at angular speed from 0.001 rpm (revolutions per minute) to 200 rpm with a stepping resolution of 0.007°.

3.2 Performance Metrics

The basic requirement of a VR system is to track the physical motions and provide corresponding visual/multimodal feedbacks as realistic as possible. Hence, we quantify the performance of the VR systems in two aspects: timing and positioning accuracy.

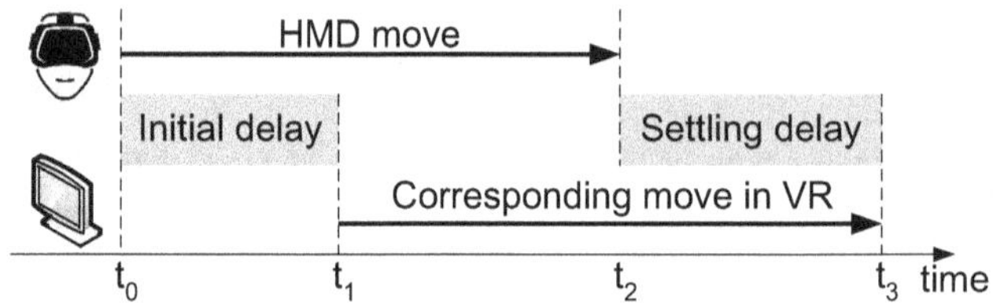

Figure 2: Illustrations of initial and settling delays in VR systems.

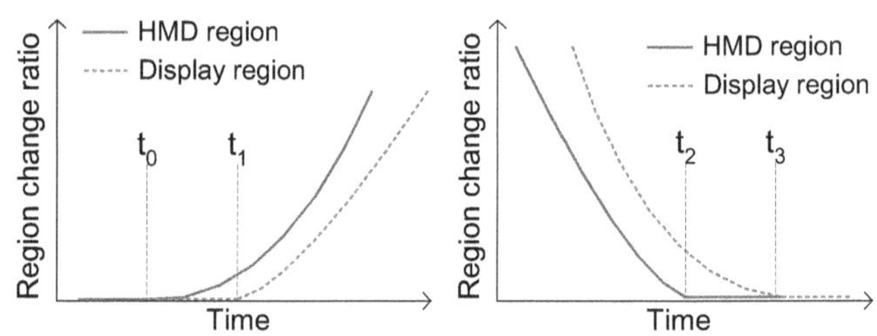

(a) Based on the initial reference frame (b) The settled reference frame

Figure 3: Detection of change points on the region change ratio time series.

Timing accuracy. Timing accuracy is critical as it is highly related to a variety of cybersickness, such as nausea, disorientation, and headaches. We define the following two metrics to quantify timing accuracy, which are also illustrated in Figure 2.

1. *Initial delay*: The time difference between the start of head motion (t_0) and that of the corresponding feedback in the virtual world (t_1).
2. *Settling delay*: The time difference between the stop of head motion (t_2) and that of the corresponding feedback in the virtual world (t_3).

Positioning accuracy: The spatial inconsistency between physical moves and visual feedback is another major cause of cybersickness. We accordingly define two metrics as follows.

3. *Precision*: The angular positioning consistency between physical moves and visual feedbacks in the virtual world in terms of degrees.
4. *Sensitivity*: The capability of HMD inertial sensors to perceive subtle motions and subsequently provide feedbacks to users.

3.3 Measurement Procedures

The measurement procedures for the four performance metrics are all similar, and are presented in the following. First, we select a VR application as the experiment scenario. Second, we configure the desired motion parameters that will be performed by the rotating platform, such as (angular) velocity and rotation angle. Last, we start both the rotating platform and high-speed camera to record the motion of the HMD and the HMD view. We recommend repeating each experiment at least 20 rounds for statistically meaningful results.

Table 1: The Considered Commodity VR Systems

Type	Desktop VR Systems		Mobile VR Systems	
Name	3Glasses D2	Oculus Rift DK2	Google Cardboard	Samsung Gear VR
Dim. (mm)	192.5×88×88	181×120.5×91	154.5×88.5×81	201.9×166.4×92.6
Weight (g)	246	440	213	446
FoV (°)	110	100	96	96
Display	2560×1440, 60 Hz	2560×1440, 75 Hz	2560×1440, 60 Hz	
CPU	Intel i7-4790 CPU 3.60 GHz		4-core Cortex-A57 2.1 GHz and 4-core Cortex-A53 1.5 GHz	
GPU	GeForce GTX 645		Mali-T760 MP8	
RAM	32 GB		3 GB	

Since we rely on video recordings to monitor the HMD motions and the corresponding visual feedbacks on HMD view, it is important for the HMD view needs to be fully observable by the high-speed camera when the rotation starts and ends. This becomes an issue if the HMD does not support the mirroring of its view to an external display. For example, as Samsung S6 does not support external displays, its view would leave the capture range of the high-speed camera when the rotation starts, and thus the corresponding visual feedback on the HMD view cannot be captured. A possible workaround is to fixate the high-speed camera on the rotating platform, but the vibrations of the platform lead to blur videos, in our experience. Hence, currently the initial delay is not measured for mobile VR systems that do not support external monitors.

3.4 Post-processing Steps

Several post-processing steps need to be performed to extract the performance results. The input to the post-processing steps is the recorded video from the high-speed camera. Since each experiment consists of multiple repeated rounds (say N), we leverage the sound made by the rotating platform (i.e., the step motor) to cut the video recording in N clips. Furthermore, the video clips are converted to gray scale before the content analysis, which is detailed below.

First, we need to derive two reference frames from each video clip. The *initial reference frame* is derived as the average of the first K frames[1], where the *settled reference frame* is derived as the average of the last K frames in each video clip. For each reference frame, we define two regions: (i) *the HMD region*, which comprises the calibration marks on the HMD or on the upper tray of the rotating platform (see Figure 1) across video frames. The purpose of the calibration marks is to add some salient points on the rotating platform and HMD so that the angular changes of HMDs can be easily identified; (ii) *the display region*, which comprises the HMD view on the video frame.

Next, for a reference-frame-and-region pair (F, R), we compute the *region change ratio* in percentage of the changed pixels in the region R compared with the reference frame F, where a pixel is considered changed if the pixel's gray level is significantly different from that of the same pixel on the reference frame F[2].

Timing accuracy. We first obtain four time series based on the combinations of two regions and two reference frames. We then apply the change point detection algorithm [11] to automatically identify t_0 and t_2 from the region change ratios based on the initial reference frame, and t_1 and t_3 from those based on the settled reference frame. The derivations are summarized in Figure 3.

Positioning accuracy. The precision is computed as the region change ratio of the display region by comparing the initial and settled reference frames. The sensitivity is computed as the ratio of *sensible rounds* in all the rounds; a round is considered as sensible, if we can find any difference in the display region between the initial and settled reference frames.

4. EXPERIMENTS

4.1 Considered VR Systems

We compare the performance of four commodity VR systems, as illustrated in Table 1, which are available at the time of writing. 3Glasses D2 (3GD2) and Oculus Rift DK2 (ORDK2) are desktop VR systems connected to an Intel i7 PC via HDMI and USB cables for rendering 3D scenes. Google Cardboard (GC) and Samsung Gear VR (SGVR) are mobile VR systems that work with smartphones. GC is a chassis that holds a smartphone and lenses for low-cost VR experience. In contrast, SGVR dictates a Samsung smartphone connected via micro USB. We use Samsung S6 in GC and SGVR for rendering 3D scenes, because it is supported by both VR systems. Besides, the off-the-shelf VR application used in our experiment is Titans of Space, because it is available for the four VR systems under test and also provides a common ground for further comparisons.

4.2 Experiment Results

We repeat each experiment 20 times with individual VR systems. The two major parameters are rotation angle (in rad) and velocity (in rad/s) If not otherwise specified, we set the angle as $\pi/2$ and the velocity as π.

Initial delay. We compare the initial delay of desktop VR systems under different rotation angles from 2π to 20π rad. We find the initial delay remains very similar: about 44 ms and 48 ms for 3GD2 and ORDK2[3]. We also compare the initial delay under different velocities from $\pi/8$ to π rad/s, and observe no clear difference. Figure 4 shows the initial delay under different scene complexities, which are quantified by compressing each screenshot image into jpeg at quality level of 85%. We observe that: (i) higher complexity results in longer initial delay, and (ii) ORDK2 tends to have a slightly longer initial delay.

Settling delay. We next compare the settling delay of all four VR systems. Figure 5 reports the settling delay under different rotation angles. This figure shows that most VR systems (except ORDK2) suffer from longer settling delay under larger rotation angles. The unique behavior of ORDK2 may be attributed to the unique *kinematic constraints* [8] implemented in it. The implication of velocity on the settling delay is not clear in our experiments. The VR systems sorted in the descending order of settling delay are GC (90 ms), SGVR (80 ms), ORDK2 (75 ms), and 3GD2 (60 ms). Figure 6 gives the settling delay under different scene complexities. We observe that, similar to initial delay, higher complexity leads to longer settling delay. Moreover, desktop VR systems generally result in shorter settling delay than mobile VR systems, which can be attributed to: (i) less expensive inertial sensors and (ii) lower computational power of smartphones.

Correction latency. We observe that when the motion of an HMD stops, the wrong estimation of the dead reckoning algorithm

[1]We empirically choose $K = 100$ and find that the results are not sensitive to the K values.

[2]The threshold for the gray level difference is empirically set to 30 (in the range of 0–255).

[3]Figures that carry less information are not shown throughout this paper, due to the space limitations.

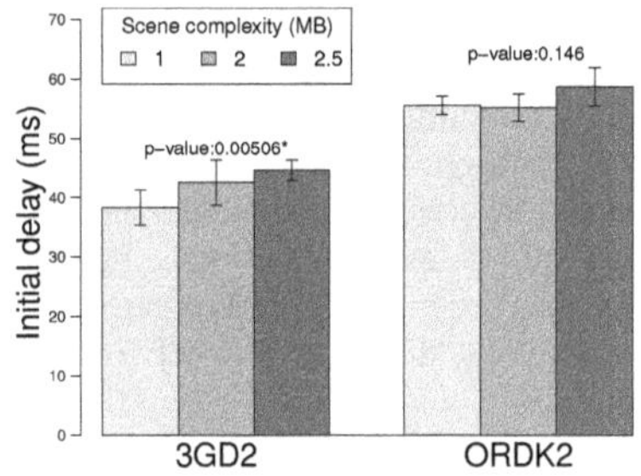

Figure 4: Initial delay under different scene complexities.

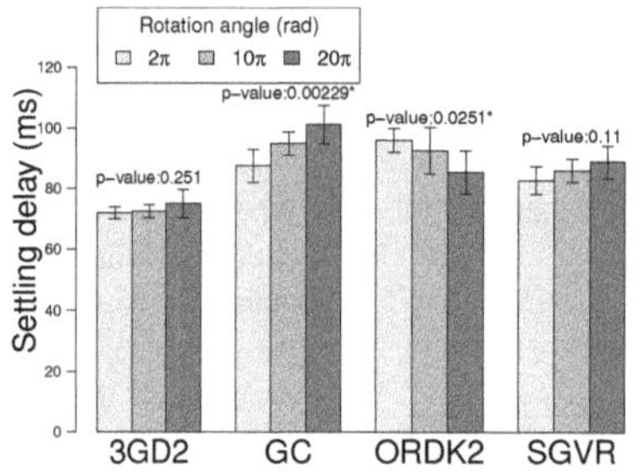

Figure 5: Settling delay under different rotation angles.

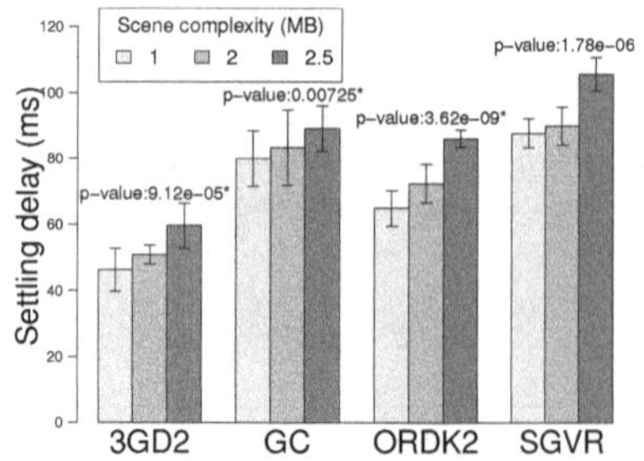

Figure 6: Settling delay under different scene complexities.

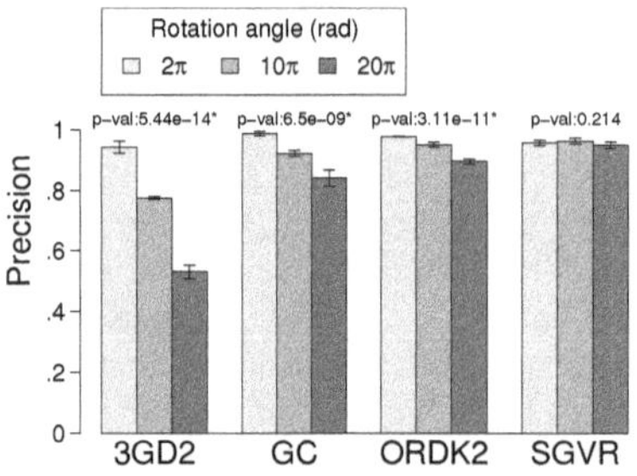

Figure 7: Precision under different rotation angles.

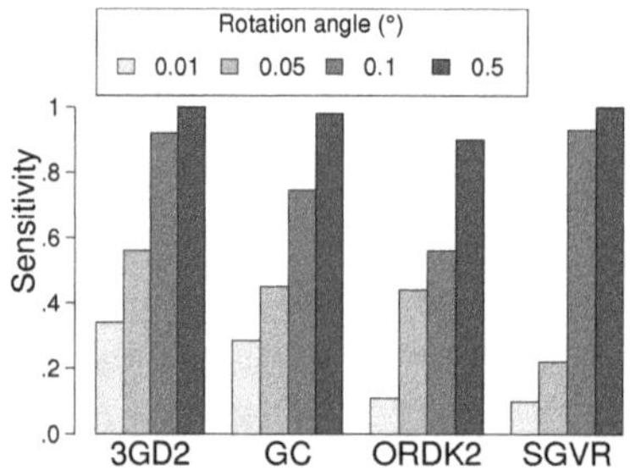

Figure 8: Sensitivity under different degrees per move.

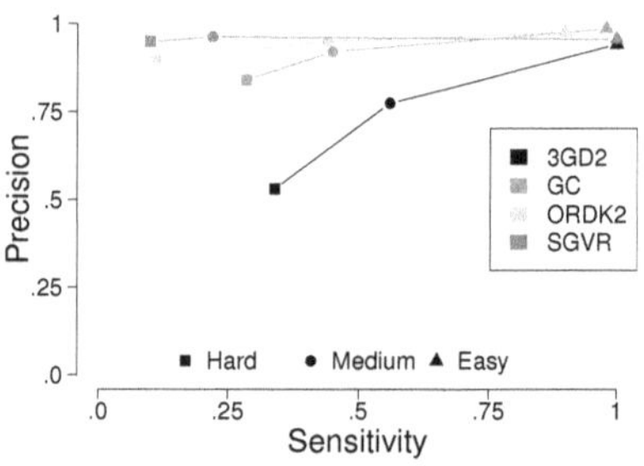

Figure 9: Trade-off between precision and sensitivity under 3 sample settings.

at that time would make the HMD view overstep the right position and take additional time to correct. During settling down, the time spent on correcting is defined as *correction latency*. Figure 10 gives the fraction of the correction latency in the settling delay, and 3GD2 always has *zero* correction latency, showing that *no* dead reckoning algorithm is implemented in 3GD2. This figure also reveals that in most VR systems (except 3GD2), especially mobile VR systems, correction latency represents a nontrivial portion of settling delay. Moreover, we find the correction latency is quite diverse on different VR systems: from about 40 ms in ORDK2 to about 80 ms and 90 ms in SGVR and GC. The correction latency is one of the side effect of the dead reckoning algorithm. We also conduct rigorous experiments to quantify the benefit of the dead reckoning algorithm. Due to the space limitation, we only give a high-level sample observation: thanks to the dead reckoning algorithm, ORDK2 reacts to head movements sooner and displays the same 3D scenes about 10 ms earlier than 3GD2 on average.

Precision and sensitivity. We vary the rotation angles from 2π to 20π rad, and plot the precision of the four VR systems in Figure 7. This figure depicts that the VR systems sorted by the precision in the descending order are SGVR, ORDK2, GC, and 3GD2. Such diversity of precision may be attributed to the design choices, e.g., some developers may prefer very high precision and filter out small noises (or movements). To verify this, we next vary the degree per move from 0.01 to 0.5, and plot the sensitivity of the four VR systems in Figure 8. This figure confirms our conjecture: VR systems that achieve higher precision, also suffer from lower sensitivity in general. To better visualize such trade-off, we select three sample settings on precision and sensitivity as follows. *Hard* is 20π rad and 0.01 degree per move; *medium* is 5π and 0.05; and *easy* is π and 0.5. The results are given in Figure 9. We make two observations from this figure. First, all VR systems perform well under the easy setting. Second, curves closer to the lower-right corner represent more sensitive, but less precise VR systems. In other words, 3GD2 is the most sensitive VR system, while SGVR is the most precise one.

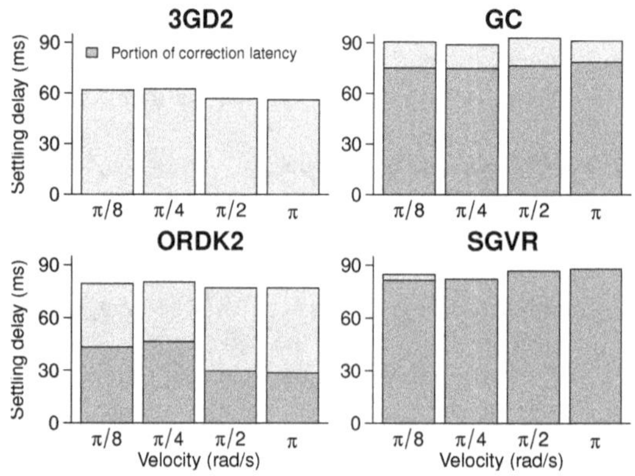

Figure 10: Portion of correction latency in settling delay.

5. CONCLUSION

We presented a measurement methodology to quantify the timing and positioning accuracy of commodity VR systems. Our methodology considers the VR system under test as a black-box and works with any VR applications without code instruments and system modifications. We applied the methodology to four commodity VR systems to demonstrate its effectiveness. Several interesting observations were made from our experiments. For example, some VR systems opt for higher precision at the expense of lower sensitivity, while others prefer higher sensitivity and lower precision. Our proposed methodology may be leveraged by VR researchers and developers to better quantify the system-wide performance in both objective and subjective experiments.

6. ACKNOWLEDGEMENTS

This work was partially supported by the Ministry of Science and Technology of Taiwan under the grants: 103-2221-E-001-023-MY2 and 102-2221-E-007-062-MY3.

7. REFERENCES

[1] HTC Vive vs Oculus Rift vs PlayStation VR. http://www.itpro.co.uk/desktop-hardware/25186/htc-vive-vs-oculus-rift-vs-playstation-vr-big-three-set-to-drive-just-13-per.

[2] Rotating platform specification. http://www.extion.com.tw/c/pdf/1/usc.pdf.

[3] Virtual reality could become an $80b industry: Goldman. http://www.cnbc.com/2016/01/14/virtual-reality-could-become-an-80b-industry-goldman.html.

[4] S. Davis, K. Nesbitt, and E. Nalivaiko. A systematic review of cybersickness. In *Proc. of Australasian Conference on Interactive Entertainment (IE'14)*, pages 1–9, Newcastle, Australia, December 2014.

[5] M. Di Luca. New method to measure end-to-end delay of virtual reality. *Presence*, 19(6):569–584, December 2010.

[6] S. Friston and A. Steed. Measuring latency in virtual environments. *IEEE Transactions on Visualization and Computer Graphics*, 20(4):616–625, April 2014.

[7] D. Krevelen and R. Poelman. A survey of augmented reality technologies, applications and limitations. *The International Journal of Virtual Reality*, 9(2):1–20, January 2010.

[8] S. LaValle, A. Yershova, M. Katsev, and M. Antonov. Head tracking for the Oculus Rift. In *Proc. of IEEE International Conference on Robotics and Automation (ICRA'14)*, pages 187–194, Hong Kong, China, May 2014.

[9] G. Papadakis, K. Mania, M. Coxon, and E. Koutroulis. The effect of tracking delay on awareness states in immersive virtual environments: An initial exploration. In *Proc. of ACM International Conference on Virtual Reality Continuum and Its Applications in Industry (VRCAI'11)*, pages 475–482, Hong Kong, China, December 2011.

[10] G. Papadakis, K. Mania, and E. Koutroulis. A system to measure, control and minimize end-to-end head tracking latency in immersive simulations. In *Proc. of ACM International Conference on Virtual Reality Continuum and Its Applications in Industry (VRCAI'11)*, pages 581–584, Hong Kong, China, December 2011.

[11] K. Rebecca and E. Idris. changepoint: An R package for changepoint analysis. *Journal of Statistical Software*, 58(3):1–19, 2014.

[12] G. Samaraweera, R. Guo, and J. Quarles. Head tracking latency in virtual environments revisited: Do users with multiple sclerosis notice latency less? *IEEE Transactions on Visualization and Computer Graphics*, 22(5):1630–1636, May 2016.

[13] A. Steed. A simple method for estimating the latency of interactive, real-time graphics simulations. In *Proc. of ACM Symposium on Virtual Reality Software and Technology (VRST'08)*, pages 123–129, Bordeaux, France, October 2008.

[14] I. Sutherland. A head-mounted three dimensional display. In *Proc. of Fall Joint Computer Conference (AFIPS'68)*, pages 757–764, San Francisco, CA, December 1968.

[15] G. Welch and E. Foxlin. Motion tracking: No silver bullet, but a respectable arsenal. *IEEE Computer Graphics and Applications*, 22(6):24–38, November/December 2002.

[16] M. Young, G. Gaylor, S. Andrus, and B. Bodenheimer. A comparison of two cost-differentiated virtual reality systems for perception and action tasks. In *Proc. of ACM Symposium on Applied Perception (SAP'14)*, pages 83–90, Vancouver, Canada, August 2014.

Synthesizing Emerging Images from Photographs

Cheng-Han Yang
Dept. of Computer Science
National Tsing Hua University
Hsinchu 300, Taiwan
b9932028@gmail.com

Ying-Miao Kuo
Dept. of Computer Science
National Tsing Hua University
Hsinchu 300, Taiwan
jollytreeskuo@gmail.com

Hung-Kuo Chu
Dept. of Computer Science
National Tsing Hua University
Hsinchu 300, Taiwan
hkchu@cs.nthu.edu.tw

ABSTRACT

Emergence is the visual phenomenon by which humans recognize the objects in a seemingly noisy image through aggregating information from meaningless pieces and perceiving a whole that is meaningful. Such an unique mental skill renders emergence an effective scheme to tell humans and machines apart. A recent state-of-the-art work proposes to synthesize images of 3D objects that are detectable by human but difficult for an automatic algorithm to recognize. However, using 3D objects as inputs brings drawbacks. For instance, the quality of results is sensitive to the viewing and lighting conditions in the 3D domain. The available resources of 3D models are usually limited, and thus restricts the scalability. This paper presents a novel synthesis technique to automatically generate emerging images from regular photographs, which are commonly taken with decent setting and widely accessible online. We adapt the previous system to the 2D setting of input photographs and develop a set of image-based operations. Our algorithm is also designed to support the difficulty level control of resultant images through a limited set of parameters. We conducted several experiments to validate the efficacy and efficiency of our system.

Keywords

Emergence, Gestalt psychology, image segmentation, image synthesis

1. INTRODUCTION

Emergence refers to the unique mental skill of humans to perceive objects in a seemingly noisy image not by recognizing the object parts, but as a whole. A classic example of emerging image can be found in Figure 1. Typically, the local windows in such an image reveal only meaningless, complex and random patterns. Only when observed in its entirety, the main subject (e.g., The Dalmatian dog) suddenly *emerges* and is perceived as a whole. Although this special phenomenon has been studied extensively in Gestalt psychology with simple synthetic patterns, the process of how exactly the humans perceive complex objects is still unknown. It means that modeling an automatic recognition will be extremely challenging, or not even possible. This makes emergence an effective scheme for Turing test (e.g., Captcha [14]) to distinguish between humans and automated machines. Moreover, a system that can synthesize an infinite number of emerging images can be valuable for exploring and understanding the factors involving in both cognitive psychology and computer vision techniques.

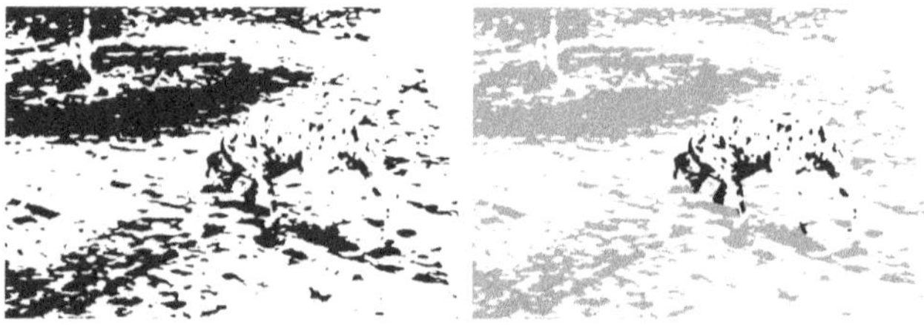

Figure 1: *A classic example of an emerging image by R. C. James. Although the left image reveals meaningless patterns in small local neighborhoods, we can still perceive a Dalmatian dog sniffing around as shown on the right.*

Inspired by the Dalmatian dog image (see Figure 1), Mitra *et al.* [12] presented a pioneer work to investigate the problem of synthesizing images containing subjects that can be recognized by humans, but are extremely difficult for automatic machines. Their system takes 3D objects with well-defined viewpoint and lighting as inputs, and renders the 3D scene according to two guiding principles. To generate images that are easy for human, the system renders complex splats that capture the silhouette and shading of subjects. Those long coherent splats are further broken and utilized to introduce clutter in the remainder of the image to make segmentation harder for machines. Results are validated by conducting experiments to test against humans and state-of-the-art computer vision methods. However, using 3D objects as inputs imposes several limitations: (i) the image quality may degrade quickly as the viewing and lighting conditions changing in the 3D domain; (ii) available resources of 3D model repository are limited, and (iii) operations on the 3D domain are computationally expensive. Thus, the existing system is still far behind a practical and scalable solution for a massive production of emerging images.

In this work, we present an automatic method that synthesizes emerging images from regular photographs. The idea is mainly motivated by two observations. First, it is much more easier to acquire photographs than 3D models. For example,

MM '16, October 15-19, 2016, Amsterdam, Netherlands

DOI: http://dx.doi.org/10.1145/2964284.2967304

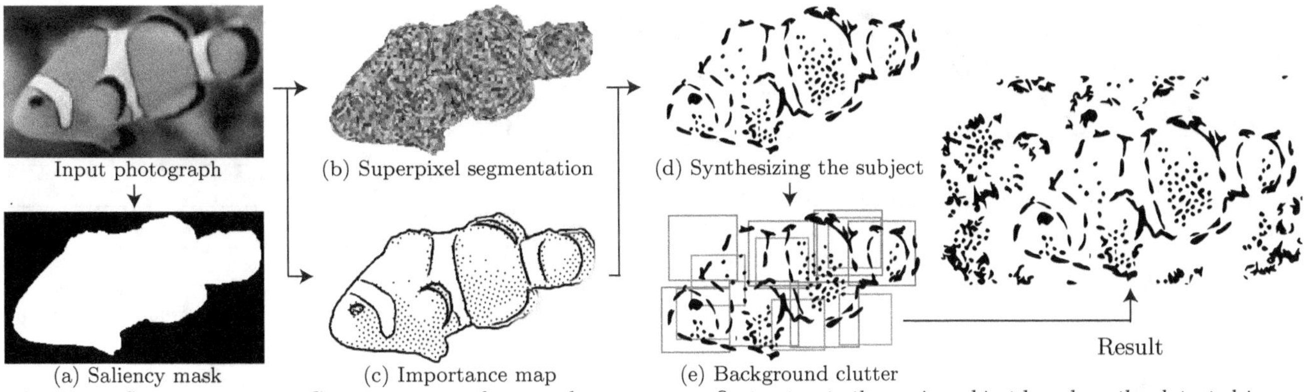

Figure 2: *System overview. Given an input photograph, our system first extracts the main subject based on the detected image saliency. Then the foreground subject is over-segmented into superpixels, which correspond to unit splat used for rendering. An importance map that captures edge features and luminance distribution of subject is computed. To synthesize the subject, we use the importance map to determine which superpixels should be colored in black, followed by breaking long coherent splats and performing spatial perturbation. Lastly, we adopt a simple copy-perturb-paste algorithm to copy splats within random windows on the subject to fill the remainder parts of image, and obtain the final result.*

we can effortlessly take the photographs via smart phone or download from public photo sharing spaces such as flickr. Second, most of photographs, especially those taken by professionals, are composed of clear subjects with decent viewpoint and lighting. To generate effective emerging images, our system follows the model of previous system, and lies the technical novelty in developing a set of operations tailored for 2D image setting. The algorithm is carefully designed to guarantee the synthesized subjects can be recognized using the principle of emergence, at controllable difficulty levels.

We tested our system on a wide variety of input photographs, ranging from human portrait, animals, cartoon, etc, and generated over 900 emerging images so far. Please refer to the supplementary file for a subset of 100 examples. For validation, we performed a user study to evaluate the effectiveness of our results. We also conducted experiments to evaluate how the performance of current state-of-the-art object recognition methods is impaired by our results.

2. RELATED WORK

How the humans perceive subjects in the emerging images is closely related to Gestalt theory, which consists of several principles to describe the relationships between the parts and the whole [10]. Among all the principles, our system is based on two principles, *closure* and *continuity*, to design algorithm for synthesizing emerging images. Other principles such as symmetry, proximity, which have been extensively studied, are worthy exploring to provide additional cues for recognition.

There are other kinds of drawings that illustrate interesting emergence in different contexts. Gal *et al.* [7] present a 3D collage system for creating compound shapes by juxtaposing different fruit models to mimic Arcimboldo's painting. The idea is further extended by Huang *et al.* [8] who utilize the internet images to compose a 2D figure that resembles the input image. Yoon *et al.* [8] present a hidden-picture puzzle generator that aims at finding suitable places to hide small objects in a clutter background image. Chu *et al.* [4] propose to camouflage a target subject by synthesizing its appearance using the textures sampled from the surrounding. Rather working in the spatial domain, Tong *et al.* [13] show that comparable camouflage images can be created through the composition in the frequency domain. Note that while above works all aim to conceal the subjects in the images to a certain degree, they are not designed to model the special phenomenon of emergence where the local neighborhoods reveal little.

Captcha, a kind of Turning test to distinguish between humans and automated machines, was originated from the work of Ahn *et al.* [14]. Not surprisingly, the intriguing nature of emergence leads to a potential new Captcha scheme that might outperform existing text-based systems. With the supports of publicity available photo database, our system can benefit the Captcha applications in terms of puzzles numbers and instant feedbacks. However, there are other system-level considerations for building a mature Captcha scheme, which is beyond the scope of this work.

3. ALGORITHM

Preprocessing. Given an input photograph, our system first extracts the foreground subject using automatic saliency cut [3] (see Figure 2(a)). The user can optionally provide scribbles to refine the saliency mask. Then it performs an image over-segmentation [1] to obtain superpixels on the foreground subject (see Figure 2(b)). We refer to each superpixel as a *splat*, which is used as a basic rendering unit. The problem of synthesizing an emerging foreground is formulated as assigning binary color (black or white) to these splats. Note that the size (d_s) and compactness (d_c) of superpixels might vary as changing the image resolution. For the sake of simplicity, we resize the input image to fit the resolution of 640×480 and use the setting of $d_s = 30$ pixels and $d_c = 4$ across the experiments.

Importance map. The importance map captures the necessary visual cues of subject for humans to recognize, and is constructed using two feature maps (see Figure 2(c)). The first one represents the salient edge features computed by applying the flow-based image filter [11]. The other one models the luminance distribution (e.g., shading) with a set of sampling points. This is done by applying the Poisson Disk Sampling [2] on the luminance map of subject. The density of sampling points is controlled by α and β, indicating respectively the minimum and maximum valid distance among sampling points.

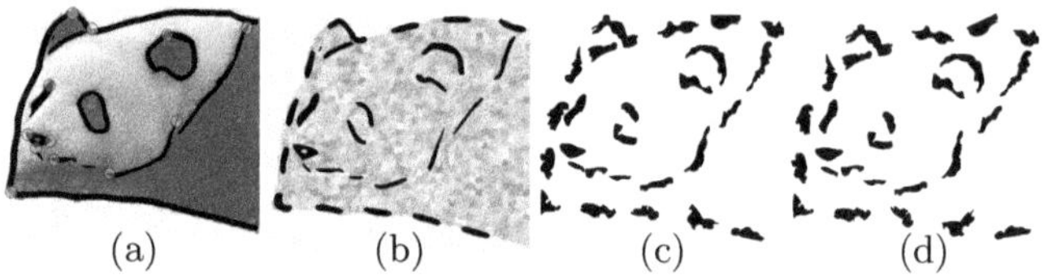

Figure 3: *Edge perturbation. (a) Original image and edge map. The yellow circles indicate the detected corners. (b) The edges are broken into line segments and (c) the corresponding complex splats. (d) Applying 2D space perturbation to complex splats.*

	easy	medium	difficult
edge perturbation $[a{:}b]$*D (preserve:break length(pixels))	[0.06:0.04]	[0.04:0.06]	[0.02:0.08]
sampling density distance $[\alpha{:}\beta]$*D (minimum:maximum (pixels))	[0.01:0.10]	[0.02:0.08]	[0.03:0.06]
rand. perturb. angle θ (degree)	[-10,10]	[-15,15]	[-20,20]
rand. perturb. displacement δ*D (along x, y direction (pixels))	0.01	0.02	0.03
rand. repel field distance d*D (pixels)	[0.03:0.02]	[0.02:0.01]	[0.01:0.00]

Table 1: *Parameters used to generate emerging images at easy, medium and difficult levels. D is the diagonal length of subject's bounding box.*

Synthesizing the subject. Once we have the superpixels and importance map, an initial rendering of subjects is obtained by superimposing two maps and assigning black to those superpixels hit by the black pixels in the importance map. We refer to the grouping of superpixels as *complex splats*. However, such a naive approach reveals important information about subject's silhouette, which can possibly be identified by machines using boundary extraction (see Figure 3(a)). Hence, we break long coherent complex splats along silhouettes into smaller parts in a manner such that the machines can not restore the original shape via interpolating and extrapolating between parts. To this end, we first compute central line segments of the complex splats using image thinning and detect corners on the line segments. Then, starting from each corner point, we move along the line segments and iteratively break the complex splat by removing the atomic splats in a controlled manner. More specifically, we use two parameters a and b to control the length of retained complex splats and the gap between consecutive complex splats, respectively. An example of edge breaking can be found in Figure 3(b,c). To null the chance of using interpolation and extrapolation algorithm, we further apply a 2D space perturbation with random rotation and positional jitters to the complex splats (see Figure 3(d)).

Background clutter. In this step, we employ the *copy-perturb-paste* procedure by Mitra *et al.* [12] to fill the remainder parts of image. In brief, we add controlled clutter to make it harder for machines to identify where the subject may lie by making the rest of the image look similar when observed from a local window. We simply copy small regions of the subjects, randomly perturb the interior splats, and paste the them to other regions of image. During the procedure, we further apply a repel field to cancel the paste of background splats if they are close to the subject contour. A parameter d', representing the minimum proximity distance, is used to control the difficulty level.

Difficulty level control. As we can see our algorithm involves several stages, some of which can be used to control the difficulty level of synthesized emerging images. They are: (i) sampling density of importance map ($[\alpha, \beta]$); (ii) degree of edge perturbation ($[a, b], \theta, \delta$); and (iii) background clutter (d). Table 1 lists the default values used for generating emerging images at easy, medium, and difficult settings.

4. EXPERIMENT AND RESULTS

We have tested our system with a wide variety of input photographs, ranging from human portrait to man-made objects. Our algorithm is efficient, which takes less than 0.3 second to generate an emerging image from a photograph with resolution 640×480 using a moderate PC. This enable us to interactively craw photographs from internet and generate corresponding emerging images. As a result, we have generated over 900 emerging images at three difficulty levels. Figure 5 shows six examples generated by our system. Please refer to the supplementary file for a collection of 100 examples. In the following, we conducted experiments to validate the effectiveness of our system.

Exp I: user study. A good emerging image synthesis algorithm should generate images reliably perceived by humans, at an easily controllable difficulty level. To evaluate our algorithm, we conducted a user study involving 20 participants. Users were shown a sequence of 20 images with different subjects (only one subject per image) and are synthesized at different difficulty levels. During the trial, the users were asked to type what they saw. Elapsed time starting from showing the image until the user type her answer is recoded as response time. Each image was shown for a maximum of one minute.

As shown in Figure 4 (Left), the user response indicates that we can generate perceivable emerging images at controllable difficulty levels. We use one-way analysis of variance (ANOVA) [15] to evaluate the statistical significance of the results. The analysis shows that the recognition accuracy is significant at the $p < 0.05$ level, $F(2,398) = 3.51$. The response time is significant at the $p < 0.01$ level, $F(2,398) = 494$. As far as the recognition accuracy and the response time are concerned, the correlation is significant with controllable difficulty levels.

Exp II: validation with machines. We test our results against two popular learning based systems, Caffe [9] and Bag-of-features [5], to evaluate how difficult the current state-of-the-art to crack the emergence.

Caffe [9] is a deep learning framework made with expression, speed, and modularity. We prepared 50 examples, which are used as queries to Caffe for recognizing the sub-

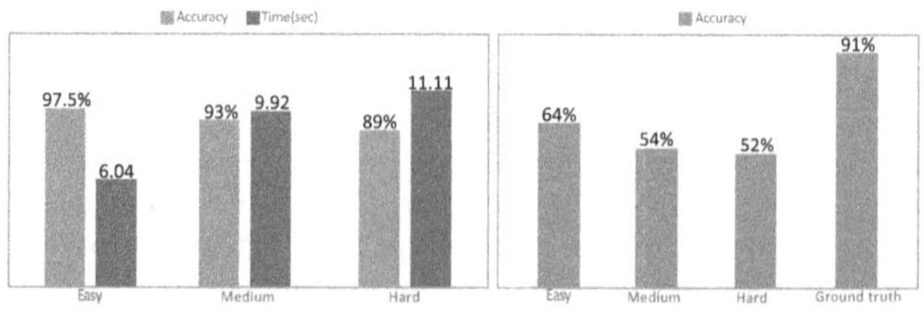

Figure 4: *(Left) Recognition accuracy and response time on three difficulty levels of generated emerging images as observed in course of our user study. (Right) Performance of a learning based image recognition systems operating on regular and emerging images.*

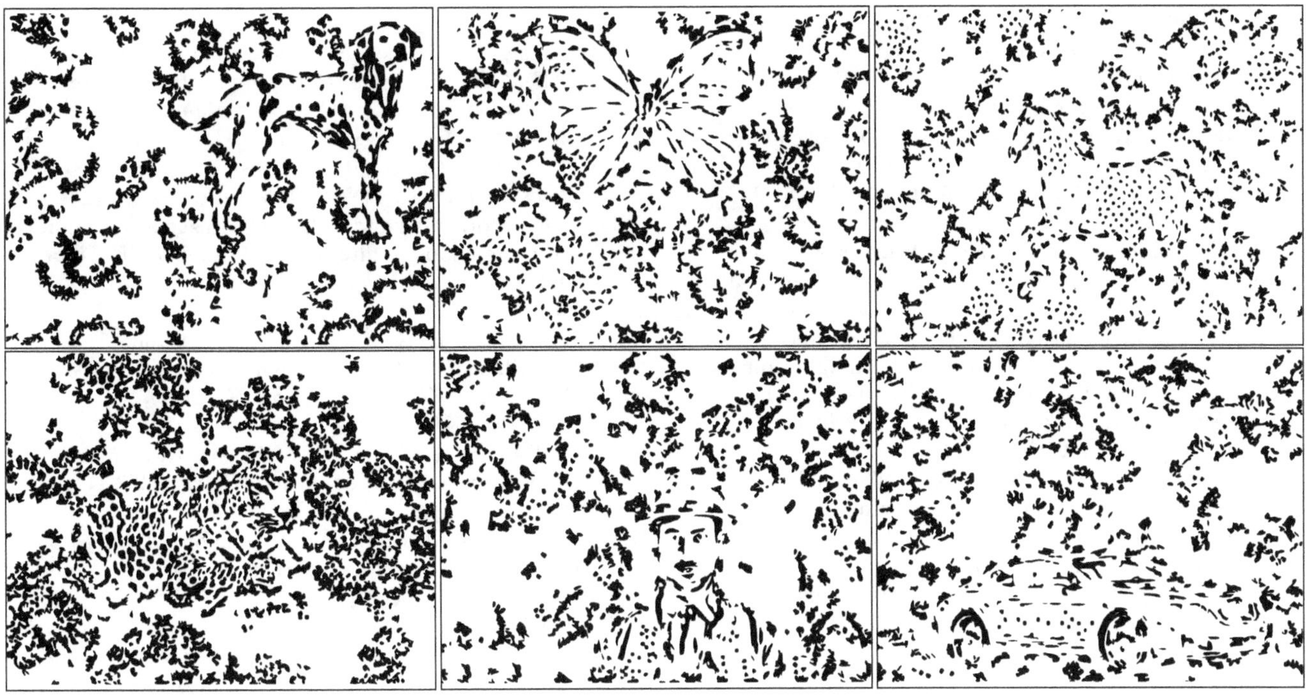

Figure 5: *Six emerging images generated by our system at, from left column to right column, easy, medium, and hard difficulty levels.*

jects therein based on the pre-defined models. The result indicates that while a 100 percent accuracy was returned by Caffe when using the original image as queries, Caffe failed to identify any of subjects in the emerging image even at easy difficulty level.

Bag-of-features is a kind of visual image categorization that assigns a category label to a query image. To learn bag of features used for image category classification, we used the most widely used Caltech 101 [6] as target image data set. We selected the three categories (cat, hawksbill and leopards), each of which contains 100 images using [training: verification] with [4:6] ratio, randomly picked for extraction and classification features. For each image, we generated corresponding emerging images at three three difficulty levels. The verification results are shown in Figure 4 (Right), indicating that the performance of system drops significantly (30% $\sim$ 40%) when dealing with our results.

Limitation. Our system still has several limitations. (i) The quality of synthesized image depends on the quality of extracted saliency mask (see Figure 6(a)). (ii) If the foreground subject occupies a large portion of image regions, the difficult control is less effective due to the central-fixation (see Figure 6(b)). (iii) Our system can not generate effective results for the subjects with textureless appearance (see Figure 6(c)).

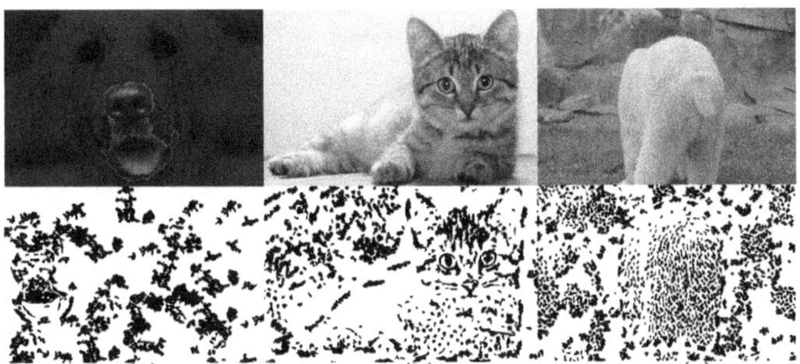

(a) (b) (c)

Figure 6: *Limitations. (a) Saliency cut fails to extract correct foreground mask. (b) Central-fixation problem. (c) Textureless subject.*

5. CONCLUSIONS

We present an automatic method to synthesize emerging images from photographs at controllable difficulty level. We conducted several experiments to evaluate the efficiency and efficacy of our system. The experimental results shows that our system is efficient and is capable of generating a massive production of emerging images, which may benefit to future development of new Captcha system.

Acknowledgements

We thank the anonymous reviewers for their invaluable comments and suggestions. The project was supported in part by the Ministry of Science and Technology of Taiwan (102-2221-E-007-055-MY3, 103-2221-E-007-065-MY3 and 105-2221-E-007-104-MY2).

6. REFERENCES

[1] R. Achanta, A. Shaji, K. Smith, A. Lucchi, P. Fua, and S. SÃijsstrunk. Slic superpixels compared to state-of-the-art superpixel methods. *IEEE Trans. Pattern Anal. Mach. Intell.*, 34(11):2274–2282, 2012.

[2] R. Bridson. Fast poisson disk sampling in arbitrary dimensions. In *ACM Trans. Graph. (Proc. SIGGRAPH)*. ACM, 2007.

[3] M. M. Cheng, N. J. Mitra, X. Huang, P. H. S. Torr, and S. M. Hu. Global contrast based salient region detection. *IEEE Trans. Pattern Anal. Mach. Intell.*, 37(3):569–582, March 2015.

[4] H.-K. Chu, W.-H. Hsu, N. J. Mitra, D. Cohen-Or, T.-T. Wong, and T.-Y. Lee. Camouflage images. *ACM Trans. Graph. (Proc. SIGGRAPH)*, 29:51:1–51:8, 2010.

[5] G. Csurka, C. Dance, L. Fan, J. Willamowski, and C. Bray. Visual categorization with bags of keypoints. In *ECCV*, volume 1, pages 1–2. Prague, 2004.

[6] L. Fei-Fei, R. Fergus, and P. Perona. Learning generative visual models from few training examples: An incremental bayesian approach tested on 101 object categories. *Computer Vision and Image Understanding*, 106(1):59–70, 2007.

[7] R. Gal, O. Sorkine, T. Popa, A. Sheffer, and D. Cohen-Or. 3D collage: Expressive non-realistic modeling. In *Proc. of NPAR*, page 14. ACM, 2007.

[8] H. Huang, L. Zhang, and H.-C. Zhang. Arcimboldo-like collage using internet images. *ACM Trans. Graph. (Proc. SIGGRAPH Asia)*, 30(6):155:1–155:8, Dec. 2011.

[9] Y. Jia, E. Shelhamer, J. Donahue, S. Karayev, J. Long, R. Girshick, S. Guadarrama, and T. Darrell. Caffe: Convolutional architecture for fast feature embedding. In *Proc. ACM International Conference on Multimedia*, pages 675–678. ACM, 2014.

[10] G. Kanizsa. *Organization in Vision: Essays on Gestalt Perception.* Praeger New York, 1979.

[11] J. E. Kyprianidis and J. Döllner. Image abstraction by structure adaptive filtering. In *Proc. EG UK Theory and Practice of Computer Graphics*, pages 51ÂřV–58, 2008.

[12] N. J. Mitra, H.-K. Chu, T.-Y. Lee, L. Wolf, H. Yeshurun, and D. Cohen-Or. Emerging images. *ACM Trans. Graph. (Proc. SIGGRAPH)*, 28(5):163:1–163:8, 2009.

[13] Q. Tong, S.-H. Zhang, S.-M. Hu, and R. R. Martin. Hidden images. In *Proc. of NPAR*, pages 27–34. ACM, 2011.

[14] L. von Ahn, M. Blum, and J. Langford. Telling humans and computers apart automatically. *Commun. ACM*, 47(2):56–60, 2004.

[15] B. Watson, A. Friedman, and A. McGaffey. Measuring and predicting visual fidelity. In *ACM Trans. Graph. (Proc. SIGGRAPH)*, pages 213–220. ACM, 2001.

Predicting and Optimizing Image Compression

Oleksandr Murashko
School of Computer Science
University of St Andrews, UK
om21@st-andrews.ac.uk

John Thomson
School of Computer Science
University of St Andrews, UK
j.thomson@st-andrews.ac.uk

Hugh Leather
School of Informatics
University of Edinburgh, UK
hleather@inf.ed.ac.uk

ABSTRACT

Image compression is a core task for mobile devices, social media and cloud storage backend services. Key evaluation criteria for compression are: the quality of the output, the compression ratio achieved and the computational time (and energy) expended. Predicting the effectiveness of standard compression implementations like libjpeg and WebP on a novel image is challenging, and often leads to non-optimal compression.

This paper presents a machine learning-based technique to accurately model the outcome of image compression for arbitrary new images in terms of quality and compression ratio, without requiring significant additional computational time and energy. Using this model, we can actively adapt the aggressiveness of compression on a per image basis to accurately fit user requirements, leading to a more optimal compression.

Keywords

Image compression; machine learning; JPEG; WebP

1. INTRODUCTION

Photography is one of the key use scenarios for mobile devices. The demands of the modern consumer are ever increasing – a single photo might now be expected to be automatically uploaded to multiple cloud services, re-compressed, edited, and shared with others via social media apps. This combined with the trend for high resolution sensors in mobile cameras means significantly increased pressure on cellular networks and storage requirements. Similarly, social media and cloud storage services frequently serve images at different resolutions, requiring multiple server-side compressions of the uploaded source, often on-the-fly. There is a clear incentive to minimize file size of images, while maintaining a required level of quality, and not increasing energy consumption, which is so critical to both mobile and cloud services.

MM '16, October 15–19, 2016, Amsterdam, The Netherlands.

ISBN 978-1-4503-3603-1/16/10...$15.00

DOI: http://dx.doi.org/10.1145/2964284.2967305

This paper presents a machine learning-based technique to accurately predict the outcome of image compression from an uncompressed source like a camera sensor, or a resized image, in terms of image quality and compression ratio. Using our models, we can actively adapt the aggressiveness of compression on a per image basis to accurately fit user requirements in terms of required image quality (as measured by PSNR or MSSIM [21]) or compression ratio, while maximizing the free objective.

User requirements are essentially arbitrary, but our technique can adapt to any desired quality level or target file size. Taking a common usage scenario where a mobile device compresses 16 MP image into JPEG at *quality factor* (QF) 90, we observe the 5th percentile of quality over a large dataset. Assuming this as a minimum acceptable quality, we can maintain the same minimum quality while reducing the average file size by 38%, resulting in consequent savings in bandwidth, storage and energy of transmission.

We employ a classic machine learning approach to build a statistical model – extracting features from uncompressed images using a fast analysis pass, and mapping these features and compression parameters to compression ratio. By building the model based on a dataset of 50 000 different images, from 0.24 MP to 24 MP, we are able to adequately characterise the space of images, such that new, unseen images can be predicted accurately. We implement our technique for both *libjpeg* [2] and Google's *WebP* [1] compressors, with each requiring its own models.

2. RELATED WORK

The most well known open source JPEG codecs, *libjpeg* at the time of writing, [2] has no explicit means to control target file size or quality. Instead, the user is asked to select a *quality factor* between 0 and 100, which scales the quantization table. Importantly, the user is effectively asked to parametrize an intricacy of an algorithm, rather than specifying their actual needs in a meaningful or measurable way. It is well known that both compression ratio and quality of output are highly dependant on the content of the input image when using JPEG [4]. Some image processing suites attempt to solve this problem by performing an exhaustive or binary search with different compression options, but this is unsatisfactory – such a search increases the compression time linearly with the number of iterations, and while this may have limited effect when compressing a single image, the effect is considerable when batch processing. Additionally, *energy consumption* is a key metric in multimedia from embedded systems to data centers, and in the general case, execution time and energy consumption are known to be highly correlated [9].

Google's WebP compressor does provide options to more accurately target a particular image quality (specified in PSNR) or target file size, but at the expense of significantly longer compression time. The WebP manual [1] explains this additional time by making 'several passes of partial encoding' to fit the given constraints. By contrast, our work requires no additional recompressions.

Several papers have looked at the problem of predicting the effects of recompressing already compressed images.

Chandra et al. consider JPEG image transcoding [4]. Their method involves generating a statistical table to determine if recompressing a particular image is worthwhile in terms of predefined tradeoff between reduced size and lower quality. To navigate this table, they use parameters of the compressed JPEG image obtained from manipulating DCT coefficients. The idea of using coefficients of image spectral transformations has inspired our feature design.

Coulombe and Pigeon present their own predictor of file size and image complexity for JPEG over a number of papers describing similar techniques [14, 5, 15, 16, 17, 11, 18]. The key idea underpinning these works is to use the compression ratio of an already encoded image as input to nearest neighbor and table-based predictors, under the assumption that file size and quality grow monotonically with increasing quality factor, and neighbor values of quality factor correspond to similar compression ratio and quality level. Our approach differs as it does not require the input image to be compressed and instead works on uncompressed images. Nevertheless, we compare experimentally with their work and show a significantly lower error in our model, despite having less information as input.

There are a number of papers that discuss image feature extraction for a range of purposes. Many of these features are complex and related mostly to computer vision problems like in [12]. However, others consider low-level features – in particular, discrete wavelet transform coefficients are used by Hanghang et al. [19] to indicate the amount of blur in the images and by Viola et al. [20] to detect faces. We do not believe that features designed for vision are likely to be transferable to our problem.

3. METHODOLOGY

In order to predict the image quality and file size of our compressed images, we employ a classical machine learning approach. We gathered a dataset of 500 000 uncompressed images – a set of 100 different image resolutions logarithmically distributed by size in the range [0.24; 24] megapixels. These images were resampled down from larger photographs to the desired size using the Fant method [6], which is a geometrically accurate anti-aliasing technique. The original images of different sizes from 24 MP to approximately 36 MP were collected from a wide selection of image-hosting websites and personal archives. None of the images were duplicates, which we engineered by design, and verified using an external tool – "Awesome Duplicate Photo Finder" [8]. The dataset was equally split into standard training (50 000 images), validation (50 000) and testing (400 000) sets. The experiments were conducted on an Intel Core i7 5820K @ 4.0 GHz, 16 GB RAM running Ubuntu 14.04 64-bit with GCC 4.8 compiler. The software used was libjpeg-turbo-1.4.2 and libwebp-0.4.3.

3.1 Feature description

Descriptive features are the key to any successful machine learning approach. We designed a feature set to capture the complexity and compression characteristics of the image from its pixel data.

The features were devised manually, based on the assumption that highly detailed and noisy images are less compressible – *e.g.* the average magnitude of the image gradient, the amplitude of high-frequency components of different spectral transformations like discrete cosine transform, discrete Haar wavelet transform and the Walsh-Hadamard transform [13, fig. 3]. The assumption behind the selection was that some high-frequency image characteristics correlate with the amount of noise in the image.

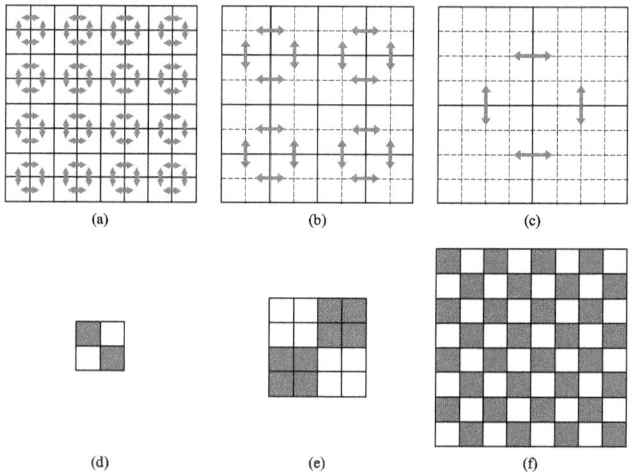

Figure 1: Differences between pixels and blocks for calculating features: (a) f_1 and f_4, (b) f_2 and f_5, (c) f_3 and f_6; and convolutions for features (d) f_7, (e) f_8, (f) f_9

The first step in calculating a set of content features for an image is to divide it onto fragments 8×8 pixels. This facilitates usage of Intel AVX instructions in program implementation. Subsequently, the raw pixel values in RGB format are converted to YC_bC_r color space following ITU-R BT.601 standard [7], but using full range for luminance and chrominance components.

We define feature f_1 as a mean absolute neighbor pixel difference. Figure 1a shows selected differences in 8×8 fragment with arrows. More simply, if a and b are brightness levels of adjacent pixels, then this feature is an arithmetical average of $|a - b|$. In our implementation we consider only some of possible differences in the fragment to optimize for specific AVX instructions like horizontal subtraction.

Feature f_2 is a mean absolute difference between neighbor blocks of 2×2 pixels. It can be considered as a "lower frequency" modification of the f_1. Conceptually f_2 is the same as f_1, but instead of pixels a and b we use mean values for adjacent blocks 2×2 (figure 1b). Again, not all possible differences are considered due to usage of AVX instructions.

Feature f_3 is a mean absolute difference between neighbor blocks of 4×4 pixels. f_3 is an analogue of f_1 and f_2 (figure 1c).

Features f_4, f_5 and f_6 are very similar to the described f_1, f_2, f_3. They only use squared differences instead of absolute, for example, $\boldsymbol{f_4}$ is a mean squared neighbor pixel difference.

Features $\boldsymbol{f_7}$ and $\boldsymbol{f_9}$ are mean absolute values of "checkboard" convolutions in all non-overlapping blocks of 2×2 and 8×8 pixels respectively (fig. 1d and 1f). By "checkboard" convolution we mean the last high-frequency basis function in 2-dimensional Walsh-Hadamard transform (WHT) of the respective size [13, fig. 3]. Feature $\boldsymbol{f_8}$ is another WHT coefficient of lower frequency calculated in blocks of 4×4 pixels (fig. 1e).

$\boldsymbol{f_{10}}$ is the only feature calculated for chrominance components of the image. $\boldsymbol{f_{10}}$ is exactly the same as $\boldsymbol{f_2}$, but it is calculated and averaged for both color components C_b and C_r instead of luminance Y.

The dynamic range of these features is quite large, and the majority of values are close to zero (but always > 0). Consequently the coverage of the feature space is very irregular. Therefore, we logarithmize all 10 features to make them suitable for regression: $\boldsymbol{f_i} \leftarrow ln(\boldsymbol{f_i} + 1)$. Increment is required to avoid $ln(0)$. Logarithmizing makes feature values distribution close to normal.

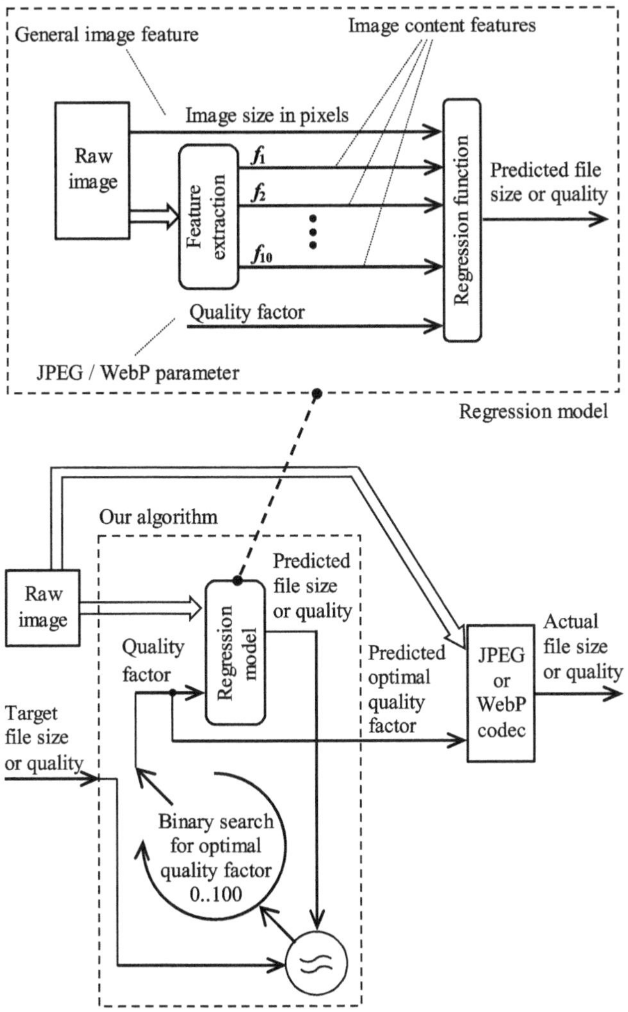

Figure 2: Sketch of our method.

3.2 Modelling

We construct our models empirically from the training data set, modelling the mapping from uncompressed input image and quality factor to either quality or file size. We do this for both *libjpeg* and WebP, meaning we use four models in total. As described in figure 2, the inputs to the model consist of: the image size in pixels, the quality factor used for compression and ten features extracted from the raw image as described above. In addition, all inputs to the regression models should be statistically standardized as we do not know which are the most important, so we assume that they have approximately the same influence on the result during training process. For this purpose we use z-score standardization [10, p. 524]:

$$standardized\_input\_value = \frac{input\_value - mean}{standard\_deviation}.$$

We employ a classic feedforward, back propogation multilayer perceptron with one hidden layer, using gradient descent, as described by Bishop [3]. Initially, we trained a simple linear regression model [3], but the results were poor, justifying the more complex non-linear approach. We also trained both linear regressors and MLPs with just the image size and quality factor as inputs, ignoring the features altogether. This approach was also unsuccessful, illustrating the importance of features in the regression. The best parametrization of the model was selected using the validation set, and the results reported on the testing set as is standard practice.

Once the models are trained, they can be used as a proxy to quickly search the optimization space for specified user requirement, as show in figure 2.

4. RESULTS

We present results in terms of the accuracy of predictions, and in real-world use case scenarios where we use the models to actually find optimal compression parameters. We demonstrate the technique and its universality using both JPEG and WebP formats.

A summary of the prediction error of the core regression models is presented in table 1. These models map input image and quality factor to the objective. The real-world compression results which follow all use these models.

Table 1: Mean errors of core regression functions

Objective	Average test set error
JPEG file size	3.06% (percentage error)
JPEG MSSIM	0.008 (absolute error)
WebP file size	4.75% (percentage error)
WebP PSNR	0.22 dB (absolute error)

4.1 JPEG

We evaluate the accuracy of our system for predicting an optimal JPEG quality factor in two real-world scenarios: targeting a file size and *mean SSIM* (MSSIM) value. We calculate the difference in file size and quality metric of the compressed image with the predicted quality factor from a sensible range of target values across our dataset, and compare average errors in our method with the respective values for the JPEG transcoding predictor.

We compare against a reimplementation of the Coulombe and Pigeon's JPEG transcoding method [5]. This method works only for recompressing already compressed images, so we initially compress the input image with random QF 60–95 as input for their model, requiring an additional compression. Nevertheless, we outperform Coulombe and Pigeon substantially in both prediction of file size, and quality as shown in figure 3.

Using our method, the file size mean absolute percentage error for the entire test set is 3.2%, which is expectedly similar to the error of the respective regression model in table 1. JPEG transcoding performed considerably worse, producing 10.3% error (fig. 3). The mean absolute error of fitting the MSSIM requirement in our method was much smaller than in JPEG transcoding: 0.008 versus 0.023.

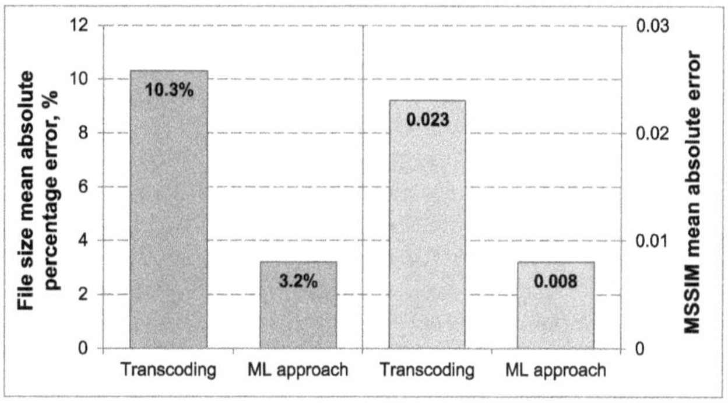

Figure 3: Error in objectives between target and actual JPEG images

The accuracy of the model allows users to confidently ask more from the compressor while maintaining important constraints. A potential use case might be a requirement for the minimum quality of compression not to drop below 0.94 MSSIM in more than 5% of cases. This is roughly the effect of selecting a QF of 90 for *libjpeg* – a commonly used setting. Using our accurate predictor, we can compress more aggressively in general, moving the error distribution, while maintaining the minimum quality constraint.

Figure 4 illustrates this on a dataset of 1000 unseen images of 16 MP – a common camera phone resolution. More aggressive compression gives a mean file size of 1.94 MB per image, compared to 3.12 MB for QF 90.

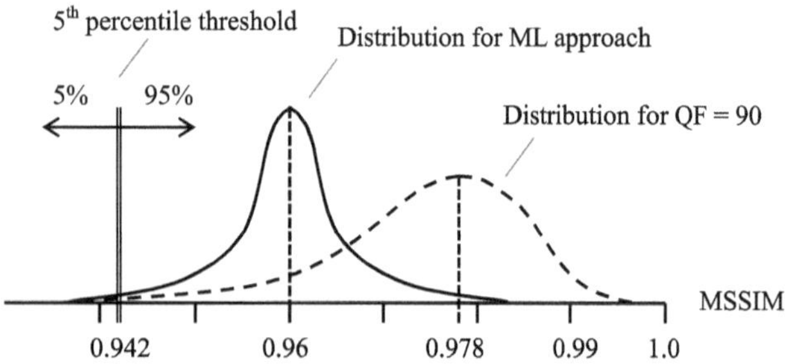

Figure 4: Distributions of quality for 16 MP images

4.2 WebP

Unlike *libjpeg*, WebP encoder already supports targeting quality and file size, allowing us to compare directly with the existing implementation. Here we use PSNR as the image quality metric as that is the metric used by WebP for quality targeting. In order to increase the accuracy of prediction, WebP supports a multiple pass option, which performs partial recompressions to facilitate a search to fit the objective, at the cost of increased compression time.

Figures 5 and 6 show a comparison of our approach with WebP's pass options for compressing 4000 images of 24 MP. Our approach greatly outperforms WebP in terms of accuracy for both quality and file size prediction, with a mean absolute error in PSNR of 0.63 dB compared to 5.36 dB, and a mean absolute percentage error of 5% compared to 109%. It is slightly slower however, due to the feature extraction stage. Allowing WebP four passes closes the gap significantly at the cost of longer compression time, but it is still outperformed by our technique. In an energy sensitive environment, such an increase is likely to be unacceptable.

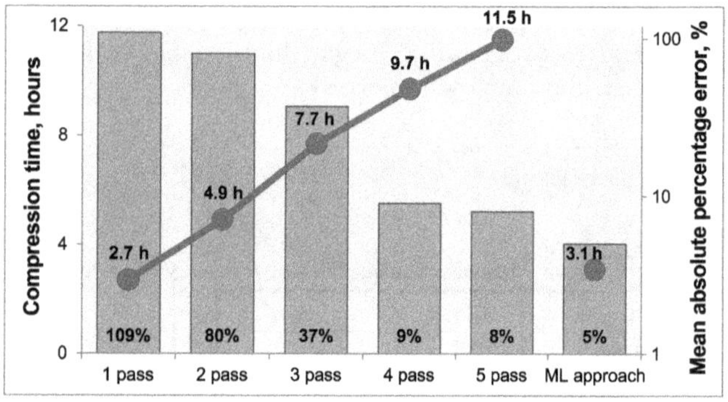

Figure 5: Error in file size between target and actual WebP images against time

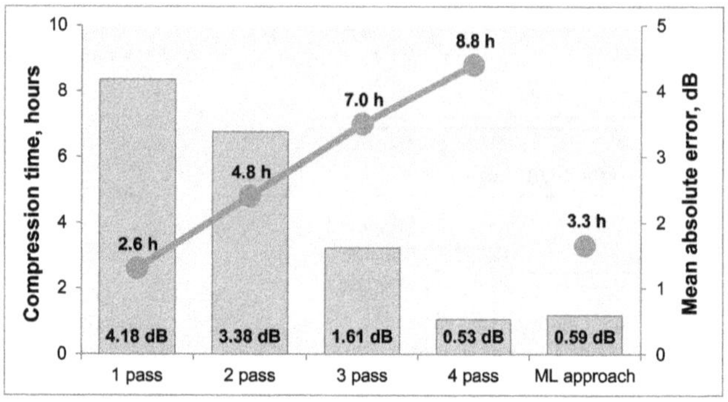

Figure 6: Error in image quality between target and actual WebP images against time

5. CONCLUSION

This paper presents a methodology to predict the results of image compression, based only on an uncompressed source. Building models for two standard compressors, *libjpeg* and WebP, we can automatically control image compression aggression to accurately fulfil user requirements for file size and quality. We significantly improve upon previous approaches for JPEG, even from an uncompressed source, and we are able to obtain higher accuracy of prediction than WebP's implementation while taking significantly less time.

6. REFERENCES

[1] WebP manual, Google Developers. https://developers.google.com/speed/webp/docs/cwebp, December 2015.

[2] Independent JPEG group. http://www.ijg.org/, January 2016.

[3] C. M. Bishop. *Neural Networks for Pattern Recognition.* Oxford University Press, Inc., New York, NY, USA, 1995.

[4] S. Chandra and C. S. Ellis. JPEG compression metric as a quality aware image transcoding. In *2nd USENIX Symposium on Internet Technologies & Systems (USITS'99)*, 1999.

[5] S. Coulombe and S. Pigeon. Low-complexity transcoding of JPEG images with near-optimal quality using a predictive quality factor and scaling parameters. *Image Processing, IEEE Transactions on*, 19(3):712–721, 2010.

[6] K. Fant. A nonaliasing, real-time spatial transform technique. *Computer Graphics and Applications, IEEE*, 6(1):71–80, January 1986.

[7] ITU. Recommendation ITU-R BT.601-7. https://www.itu.int/dms_pubrec/itu-r/rec/bt/R-REC-BT.601-7-201103-I!!PDF-E.pdf, March 2011.

[8] U. Javaid. Find & remove similar photos instantly. http://www.addictivetips.com/windows-tips/find-remove-similar-photos-instantly, June 2010.

[9] A. Lewis, S. Ghosh, and N.-F. Tzeng. Run-time energy consumption estimation based on workload in server systems. In *Proceedings of the 2008 Conference on Power Aware Computing and Systems*, HotPower'08, pages 4–4, Berkeley, CA, USA, 2008. USENIX Association.

[10] T. Little. *The Oxford Handbook of Quantitative Methods, Vol. 2: Statistical Analysis.* Oxford Library of Psychology. Oxford University Press, 2013.

[11] H. Louafi, S. Coulombe, and U. Chandra. Efficient near-optimal dynamic content adaptation applied to JPEG slides presentations in mobile web conferencing. In *Advanced Information Networking and Applications (AINA), 2013 IEEE 27th International Conference on*, pages 724–731, March 2013.

[12] L. Marchesotti, F. Perronnin, D. Larlus, and G. Csurka. Assessing the aesthetic quality of photographs using generic image descriptors. In *Computer Vision (ICCV), 2011 IEEE International Conference on*, pages 1784–1791, Nov 2011.

[13] M. Montgomery. Next generation video: Introducing daala part 3. https://people.xiph.org/~xiphmont/demo/daala/demo3.shtml, August 2013.

[14] S. Pigeon and S. Coulombe. Computationally efficient algorithms for predicting the file size of JPEG images subject to changes of quality factor and scaling. In *Communications, 2008 24th Biennial Symposium on*, pages 378–382, June 2008.

[15] S. Pigeon and S. Coulombe. Efficient clustering-based algorithm for predicting file size and structural similarity of transcoded JPEG images. In *Multimedia (ISM), 2011 IEEE International Symposium on*, pages 137–142, Dec 2011.

[16] S. Pigeon and S. Coulombe. Optimal quality-aware predictor-based adaptation of multimedia messages. In *Intelligent Data Acquisition and Advanced Computing Systems (IDAACS), 2011 IEEE 6th International Conference on*, volume 1, pages 496–499, Sept 2011.

[17] S. Pigeon and S. Coulombe. K-means based prediction of transcoded JPEG file size and structural similarity. *International Journal of Multimedia Data Engineering and Management (IJMDEM)*, 3(2):41–57, 2012.

[18] S. Pigeon and S. Coulombe. Quality-aware predictor-based adaptation of still images for the multimedia messaging service. *Multimedia tools and applications*, 72(2):1841–1865, 2014.

[19] H. Tong, M. Li, H. Zhang, and C. Zhang. Blur detection for digital images using wavelet transform. In *Multimedia and Expo, 2004. ICME '04. 2004 IEEE International Conference on*, volume 1, pages 17–20 Vol.1, June 2004.

[20] P. Viola and M. Jones. Rapid object detection using a boosted cascade of simple features. In *Computer Vision and Pattern Recognition, 2001. CVPR 2001. Proceedings of the 2001 IEEE Computer Society Conference on*, volume 1, pages I–511–I–518 vol.1, 2001.

[21] Z. Wang, A. Bovik, H. Sheikh, and E. Simoncelli. Image quality assessment: from error visibility to structural similarity. *Image Processing, IEEE Transactions on*, 13(4):600–612, April 2004.

Spectral and Cepstral Audio Noise Reduction Techniques in Speech Emotion Recognition

Jouni Pohjalainen[1], Fabien Ringeval[1,2], Zixing Zhang[1], Björn Schuller[1,3]
[1]Chair of Complex and Intelligent Systems, University of Passau, Germany
[2]Laboratoire d'Informatique de Grenoble, Université Grenoble Alpes, France
[3]Department of Computing, Imperial College London, UK
{firstname.lastname}@uni-passau.de

ABSTRACT

Signal noise reduction can improve the performance of machine learning systems dealing with time signals such as audio. Real-life applicability of these recognition technologies requires the system to uphold its performance level in variable, challenging conditions such as noisy environments. In this contribution, we investigate audio signal denoising methods in cepstral and log-spectral domains and compare them with common implementations of standard techniques. The different approaches are first compared generally using averaged acoustic distance metrics. They are then applied to automatic recognition of spontaneous and natural emotions under simulated smartphone-recorded noisy conditions. Emotion recognition is implemented as support vector regression for continuous-valued prediction of arousal and valence on a realistic multimodal database. In the experiments, the proposed methods are found to generally outperform standard noise reduction algorithms.

Keywords

noise reduction; denoising; speech emotion recognition

1. INTRODUCTION

Audio signals are commonly affected by factors other than the signal of interest. Additive noise arises due to other sound sources competing with the target signal and due to the combined effects of the recording equipment and the transmission channel. Convolutive variation appears due to the channel and acoustic reverberation. The performance of machine learning systems is generally negatively affected by these effects, because they may mask target signals, such as speech, and cause mismatch in feature statistics between the training and recognition conditions.

Additive noise is a ubiquitous problem that affects the performance of machine-learning speech systems in many common environments. In the field of automatic speech recognition (ASR), this is addressed on different stages of the system, including feature extraction, feature enhancement, machine learning models and their training [13, 29] and also by using better hardware or multiple microphones.

Noise reduction for speech audio is often evaluated from the viewpoint of listeners in terms of enhancing either the subjective quality or speech intelligibility [16]. Of these, intelligibility, whose improvement is the more difficult problem [16], is potentially relevant for ASR. Computational paralinguistic analysis of speech, whose general aim is to uncover various external attributes of speech not related to its linguistic message (the concern of ASR), has emerged as an active field of research within the past decade [28]. Two of its most central topics are speaker recognition (identification and verification) and, more recently, automatic recognition of emotion in speech. These applications, which are important for multimedia content analysis, retrieval and processing, do not have an obvious connection with the traditional objectives of speech enhancement. Nevertheless, in speaker recognition, traditional single-channel noise reduction systems are frequently found helpful as preprocessing in improving system performance under noisy or mismatched conditions [9, 19, 25, 26]. General-purpose signal-based denoising methods, such as power spectral subtraction and minimum-mean-square-error estimation of log-spectral amplitude, have been found to improve speaker recognition performance quite reliably across different back-end machine learning systems, test conditions (type and level of degradation) and training conditions (noise-matched or mismatched), even more so than auditory-based methods designed to improve subjective quality [9]. In general, the relative performance of different denoising methods is quite strongly affected by the aforementioned factors [9, 25].

In this paper, following on the results of the studies focusing on signal denoising in text-independent speaker recognition [9, 25], a machine learning task that is commonly based on identifying the distribution of the short-time magnitude spectrum, we compare denoising techniques from the viewpoint of audio and multimedia content analysis in speech emotion recognition. It is another central paralinguistic problem with other applications ranging from ASR systems and call centers to intelligent user interfaces [28]. Work on noise robustness in speech emotion recognition has also been started [27, 32], but to our knowledge, signal denoising has not been explicitly studied for this purpose. As emotional or stressed speech often coincides with acoustically noisy environments, it is worthwhile to investigate the performance of general-purpose noise reduction solutions in improving short-time spectral representation of the two pri-

MM '16, October 15-19, 2016, Amsterdam, Netherlands
© 2016 ACM. ISBN 978-1-4503-3603-1/16/10...$15.00
DOI: http://dx.doi.org/10.1145/2964284.2967306

mary emotion dimensions – activation (arousal), i. e., the intensity of emotional expression, and valence, i. e., the positive/negative affective dimension [10].

We propose a family of general-purpose, adaptive signal denoising techniques that can be simply configured with respect to spectral smoothing, temporal smoothing and adaptation rate of the noise model in order to tackle different nonstationary noise conditions and application requirements. They operate in a log-spectral or cepstral domain, which differ in terms of spectral smoothing facilitated by the cepstral representation. These methods are compared against published implementations of baseline methods suggested by the previous studies, firstly by using general, objective signal enhancement quality measures. The most promising variants are then compared as preprocessing for an emotion recognition system performing continuous-valued prediction of arousal and valence. In this study, we focus on relatively similar noise conditions in the training and testing phase, so that denoising is used to recover important information in both training and testing.

2. NOISE REDUCTION

2.1 Previous Work

Classical single-channel noise reduction methods include variants of spectral subtraction [2, 3], where an averaged noise (magnitude or power) spectrum is subtracted from the noisy signal spectrum while keeping the resultant spectral magnitudes positive, and Wiener filtering [16], often implemented in practice using an iterative approach [12].

The performance of the minimum mean square error (MMSE) [7] and log-spectral amplitude MMSE (Log-MMSE) estimators [8] still remains among the best of the published methods [20]. In part, this can be attributed to their decision-directed estimation approach, which bases the spectral estimate of each frame partially on the estimates from previous frames via the *a priori* SNR estimate updated by using a memory coefficient [5]. Spectral subtraction [21] and the decision-directed MMSE [20] methods have also been applied in the spectral modulation domain in order to better handle nonstationary noise.

In recent comprehensive evaluations looking at noise reduction preprocessing techniques to combat mismatch in speaker recognition, MMSE, Log-MMSE and spectral subtraction have performed well [9, 25]. Power spectral subtraction also resulted in large performance gains in [26]. Therefore, as the baseline noise reduction methods in this study, we choose two published implementations of spectral subtraction, one working in the power spectral domain (SS-P [16]) and one in the magnitude spectral domain (SS-M [4]), and two published implementations of Log-MMSE (MMSE-1 [16]; MMSE-2 [4]).

2.2 Methods Under Study

The methods proposed in this study are based on obtaining the noise model by averaging over low-energy frames in the representation domain – log-spectral or cepstral – and, optionally, by adapting the noise model constantly based on the (Gaussian) similarity of the short-term moving average of the representation to the initial noise model. A general overview is presented in Fig. 1.

The audio signal is processed in Hann-windowed frames of 30 ms extracted every 10 ms. The discrete Fourier transform

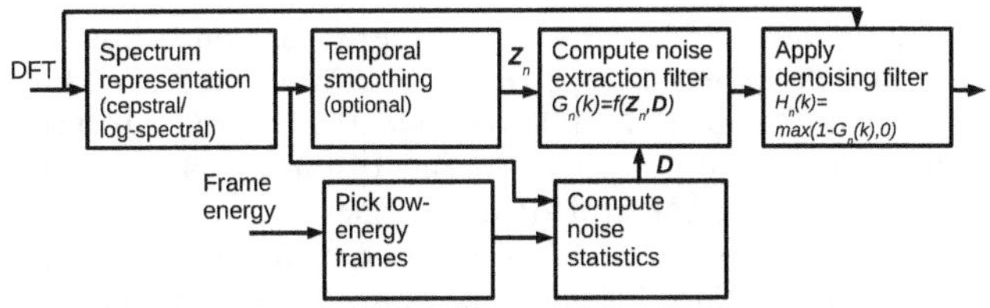

Figure 1: *The noise reduction framework.*

(DFT) of each audio frame is first transformed into either a logarithmic magnitude spectrum or a truncated cepstrum [6, 22]. The real cepstrum is a frequency transform (specifically, the inverse Fourier transform) of the logarithmic spectrum. A truncated cepstrum, where only the lower-order coefficients are retained, thus represents a smoothed version of the original logarithmic spectrum [22]. With the sampling rate of 44100 Hz used in this study, we choose to retain the first $J = 50$ cepstral coefficients in accordance to a rule of thumb of choosing the length of the truncated cepstrum to be less than an expected pitch period [22].

In the lower branch of Fig. 1, low-energy frames within the analysis block of six seconds are automatically found by clustering the frame logarithmic energies into two clusters by using k-means and selecting the frames assigned to the cluster with the lower mean value. The *initial noise model* $D = \{\mu_j, \sigma_j^2\}$, consisting of a mean and variance for each (spectral or cepstral) coefficient, is then obtained by averaging over these frames. In the upper branch, temporal smoothing is applied to the complete sequence of the noisy vectors $\{\boldsymbol{Y}_n\}$ by using the equation

$$\boldsymbol{Z}_n = \beta \boldsymbol{Z}_{n-1} + (1-\beta)\boldsymbol{Y}_n, \qquad (1)$$

where n is the frame index, $\beta = (w-1)/w$ and w is an "equivalent rectangular window length" of the moving average integrator in the sense that the contribution of each new observation is weighted by $1/w$. Setting $w = 1$ causes no temporal integration to be performed. In the next stage, the similarity of the noisy representation $\boldsymbol{Z}_n = (Z_{n,1}, \ldots, Z_{n,J})$ with the initial noise model is evaluated as

$$\gamma_{n,j} = \exp(-(Z_{n,j} - \mu_j)^2/\sigma_j^2), \qquad 1 \le j \le J, \qquad (2)$$

yielding scores in the range $(0, 1)$. The components of the *current* noise model at the nth frame $\mu_{n,j}$ (initially, $\mu_{0,j} = \mu_j$) are then *adapted* towards the direction of the current smoothed noisy representation $\boldsymbol{Z}_n$, in proportion α to the similarity $\gamma_{n,j}$ of the latter to the *initial* noise model:

$$\mu_{n,j} = \mu_{n-1,j} + \alpha\gamma_{n,j}(Z_{n,j} - \mu_{n-1,j}). \qquad (3)$$

In both log-spectral and cepstral domains, spectral-domain division corresponds to subtraction. Therefore, the DFT-domain *noise extraction filter* $G_n(k)$ is represented by $\mu_{n,j} - Z_{n,j}$ in the analysis domain, and can be obtained by transforming this quantity back to the DFT domain. It is then used to create the noise suppression filter, with the lower limit of suppression at zero: $H_n(k) = \max(1 - G_n(k), 0)$. The modified frames are combined using an overlap-add method to produce the enhanced signal.

One motivation for processing the signal in one of these domains is to be able to apply cepstral smoothing in generating the noise and noisy signal models by temporal averaging and integration. The log-spectral representation is both an intermediate stage in cepstrum computation and a special case in the sense that it is equivalent to a non-truncated cepstral representation. Considering distance metrics in the cepstral and log-spectral domains, the cepstral Euclidean distance can be shown to be a lower bound for the root-mean-square (RMS) log-spectral distance; with the inclusion of more cepstral coefficients in the truncated cepstrum, more spectral fine structure information is preserved and the cepstral Euclidean distance approaches the RMS log-spectral distance from below [11]. The logarithmic spectrum representation is frequently used in audio signal analysis due to the large dynamic range of hearing in the amplitude dimension [33], and is also used in denoising by the Log-MMSE method [8]. In this paper, methods using the two representations are distinguished by referring to them as cepstral noise reduction (CNR) and log-spectral noise reduction (LNR). The variants of these main types are further distinguished from each other based on the temporal smoothing parameter w and the adaptation rate α (Eqs. 1-3), which control the focus of the noise suppression filter on different modulation frequencies of the nonstationary noise and the target signal.

3. EXPERIMENTS

3.1 Overview and Material

We evaluate the denoising methods on the RECOLA multimodal affective interaction corpus [24]. It includes 46 multimodal (audio, video and physiological data) recordings of French-speaking participants involved in a dyadic collaborative task. Affective dimensions expressed by the participants were evaluated by six annotators for the first five minutes of each recording. This was done for arousal and valence separately. Obtained labels were then resampled to a constant 40 ms frame rate and averaged over all raters by considering inter-evaluator agreement, to provide a 'gold standard' [23]. In order to ensure speaker-independence in the experiments, the corpus was split into three partitions, by balancing the gender and the age of the subjects: training (16 subjects), validation (15 subjects) and testing (15 subjects).

In adding noise to the audio material, the recordings were convolved with the impulse response of a smartphone [18]. This step was performed to simulate talking over a smartphone in different places. Different types of additive noise were then added, using the CHiME-2013 database [1] for simulating a living room environment (*CHiME*), and data collected from the freesound platform[1] to simulate public transport (*trains*) environments. We collected, in total, 230 minutes of noise, to match the duration of the RECOLA database. In order to provide realistic conditions, we concatenated all the recordings of noise into three independent partitions and added them to the smartphone-simulated recordings of the RECOLA database, with two different signal-to-noise ratios (SNRs): 0 and 6 dB.

In the first part dealing with acoustic distance measures (Section 3.2), we use the first six recordings of the RECOLA training set (30 minutes in total) and study the quality of noise reduction using these distance measures. The original audio is used as reference signal.

An emotion recognition system is then equipped with different types of noise reduction preprocessing, in both the training and evaluation phase, using the most promising variants of the proposed methods and the relevant baseline methods. The different systems are trained on the training set of RECOLA to predict continuous-valued arousal and valence using support vector regression (SVR) on the mean and variance of 13 mel-frequency cepstral coefficients (MFCCs). In the training phase, we adjust the windowing for mean and variance computation to be optimal according to the validation set, as in [31]. For SVR, we use a linear kernel and also tune the complexity on the validation partition [32]. Post-processing of the predictions is applied using the same methodology as described in [30]. Performance in emotion recognition is evaluated with the concordance correlation coefficient (CCC) [15, 31].

3.2 Acoustic Quality Measures

Several quality measures exist for automatically evaluating denoising and enhancement results for speech signals. These include simple energy-based measures such as SNR and segmental SNR, perceptual measures such as PESQ and distance measures in different representation domains of the magnitude spectrum [16].

The short-time magnitude spectrum is the basis of most audio feature extraction techniques. Audio pattern recognition and machine learning systems generally aim to distinguish sound classes based on the distributions of the *shape* of the short-time magnitude spectrum, and typically are not concerned with the true sound level or its psychoacoustical counterpart, loudness [33]. Therefore, in this study, we choose not to use measures that depend on the signal level in any manner, and whose results would depend on proper gain adjustment applied to the enhanced signal. These include the SNR measures as well as the RMS log-spectral distance [11]. We also do not use perceptual measures that explicitly aim to predict subjective quality or intelligibility. Instead, we focus on the preservation of the information about the shape of the short-time magnitude spectrum. These considerations resulted in the choice of two measures. Firstly, we apply the Itakura distance [6, 14], given by $d_{\text{ITA}} = \log(\boldsymbol{a}\boldsymbol{R}_0\boldsymbol{a}'/\boldsymbol{a}_0\boldsymbol{R}_0\boldsymbol{a}_0')$, where $\boldsymbol{a}=(1, a_1, \ldots, a_p)$ is the all-pole model under test for its similarity to the reference model $\boldsymbol{a}_0 = (1, a_{0,1}, \ldots, a_{0,p})$, estimated using the Toeplitz autocorrelation matrix $\boldsymbol{R}_0$ [17]. The numerator represents the total squared prediction error of the reference signal using the test model and the denominator represents the error using the reference model. In this study, $\boldsymbol{R}_0$ and the reference model $\boldsymbol{a}_0$ are obtained from the original, i. e., not noisified signal. This is a purely signal-based, non-perceptual distance measure that focuses on accuracy in all-pole modeling, which in turn is known to focus on spectral peaks and formants [17, 22]. As another measure, we apply the Euclidean distance between two mel-frequency cepstral vectors, the noisy test vector and the reference vector obtained from the original signal, consisting of 12 MFCCs while excluding the zeroth coefficient [13]; we denote this measure by d_{MFCC}. This measure has the perceptual aspect of an auditory-based warped frequency scale and it is also connected to the feature extraction procedure of many machine learning systems, including the one used in the present study.

Fig. 2 shows the Itakura and MFCC distances, averaged over a large number of speech frames, computed such that denoised frames are compared against corresponding reference frames in the original signal. Three conditions are con-

[1]https://www.freesound.org/

sidered: smartphone speech, and smartphone with *CHiME* and *trains* noise, each added at 6 dB SNR.

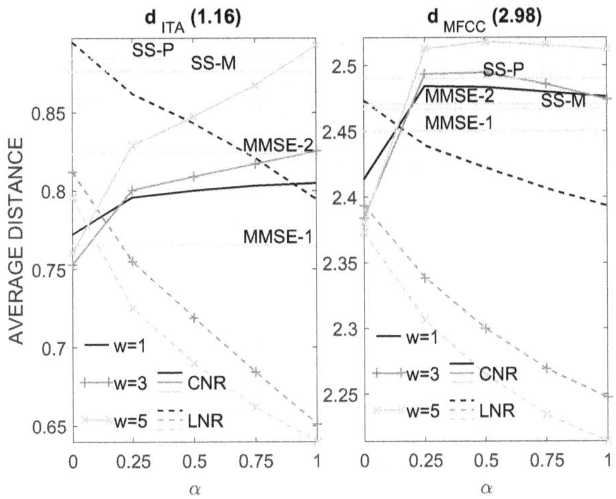

Figure 2: Signal degradation (left: Itakura distance, right: MFCC distance) evaluated for denoised signals against original, frame by frame, averaged over three noise conditions and the 25 % frames with most target signal energy. The performance of the proposed methods is shown with respect to the temporal smoothing parameter w and the noise model adaptation rate α. Corresponding averages for unprocessed noisy signals are shown in parentheses.

3.3 Emotion Recognition

Table 1 shows the emotion recognition results in various noise conditions with approximately matched training. When training is performed with the original audio material, the system is evaluated with the original and smartphone-processed material. For *CHiME* and *trains* noise, the training is performed with 6 dB SNR and the system is evaluated with 0 dB and 6 dB SNR of the same type of noise corruption. This setup requires the noise reduction preprocessing methods to preserve emotion-related information to a sufficient precision in both the training and recognition phases.

The two leftmost results columns indicate that denoising clean speech generally degrades recognition performance. A similar observation has been made in a recent study on feature enhancement with the same data [32]. An exception here, however, is the cepstral approach with moderate adaptation and no temporal smoothing (CNR/1,0.5), which actually improves prediction of the arousal dimension. None of the evaluated methods improve the prediction of arousal under the nonstationary *CHiME* noise; this might be explained by highly variable residual noise corrupting spectral energy trajectories. Otherwise, the proposed methods (CNR, LNR) outperform both the not denoised approach and the standard baseline noise reduction methods.

4. CONCLUSIONS

Noise reduction methods were evaluated with a focus on paralinguistic machine learning applications (two emotion recognition tasks). Baseline methods were chosen based on earlier, related studies and compared with a proposed new approach, which can be configured according to the specific learning task and the noise conditions using a small number of parameters. The experiments involved objective signal degradation measures and recognition of emotions on a multimodal interaction corpus. In the former evaluation, the proposed approach is shown to perform competitively to the standard noise reduction methods (spectral subtraction and MMSE, recommended as robust baseline methods in the field of speaker recognition [9]) over most of the range of the parameter values. By increasing the temporal smoothing and adaptation rate in noise modeling, the log-spectral approach clearly outperforms the standard techniques.

In emotion recognition evaluations, arousal and valence are noticed to place somewhat different requirements on the denoising scheme. Denoising improves the results in a majority of the evaluated training/test setups and in these cases, the proposed methods outperform the standard baselines. The cepstral approach without temporal smoothing of the noise leads to noticeable improvement in the high-SNR conditions. In noisy training and test conditions, temporal smoothing combined with adaptation outperforms all other evaluated approaches. Therefore, it is noted that the proposed methods show promise in audio noise reduction and audio content analysis. In future work, the relationships of different learning tasks, noise conditions and noise reduction approaches can be further investigated.

Table 1: Correlation (CCC) between predicted and ground-truth arousal and valence over the test set for closely matched training while using a given denoising method in both training and testing. The cases in which denoising improves upon the not denoised case are indicated in bold.

Training	Original		*CHiME* 6 dB		*trains* 6 dB	
Noise reduction method (w,α)	Test: Orig.	phone	*CHiME* 6 dB	0 dB	*trains* 6 dB	0 dB
	–	–				
	AROUSAL					
none	0.735	0.728	0.670	0.557	0.483	0.379
SS-P	0.704	0.697	0.634	0.553	**0.538**	**0.441**
SS-M	0.708	0.701	0.637	0.535	**0.564**	**0.488**
MMSE-1	0.672	0.680	0.601	0.490	**0.566**	**0.488**
MMSE-2	0.679	0.698	0.620	0.510	**0.514**	**0.430**
CNR (1,0.5)	**0.753**	**0.755**	0.599	0.502	**0.535**	**0.438**
CNR (20,1.0)	0.676	0.650	0.642	0.539	**0.547**	**0.440**
LNR (1,0.5)	0.706	0.664	0.635	0.538	**0.532**	**0.435**
LNR (20,1.0)	0.676	0.650	0.641	0.535	**0.701**	**0.637**
	VALENCE					
none	0.400	0.342	0.173	0.120	0.154	0.108
SS-P	0.328	0.262	0.112	0.107	**0.195**	**0.228**
SS-M	0.386	0.303	0.128	0.114	**0.190**	**0.177**
MMSE-1	0.318	0.294	0.098	0.066	**0.218**	**0.190**
MMSE-2	0.340	0.292	0.087	0.071	**0.219**	**0.160**
CNR (1,0.5)	0.308	0.308	**0.180**	**0.127**	**0.243**	**0.156**
CNR (20,1.0)	0.207	0.179	**0.261**	**0.227**	**0.252**	**0.198**
LNR (1,0.5)	0.359	0.288	**0.174**	**0.124**	0.147	0.107
LNR (20,1.0)	0.278	0.250	0.137	0.109	**0.241**	**0.218**

5. ACKNOWLEDGMENTS

This work has been supported by the European Community's Seventh Framework Programme through the ERC Starting Grant No. 338164 (iHEARu).

6. REFERENCES

[1] J. Barker, E. Vincent, N. Ma, C. Christensen, and P. Green. The PASCAL CHiME speech separation and recognition challenge. *Computer Speech and Language*, 27(3):621–633, Nov. 2013.

[2] M. Berouti, R. Schwartz, and J. Makhoul. Enhancement of speech corrupted by acoustic noise. In *Proc. ICASSP*, Washington, D.C., USA, Apr. 1979.

[3] S. F. Boll. Suppression of acoustic noise in speech using spectral subtraction. *IEEE Trans. Acoustics, Speech, and Signal Processing*, 27(2):113–120, Apr. 1979.

[4] M. Brookes. VOICEBOX: Speech processing toolbox for MATLAB, speech enhancement functions. http://www.ee.ic.ac.uk/hp/staff/dmb/voicebox/voicebox.html#enhance. Accessed: 2016-04-26.

[5] O. Cappé. Elimination of the musical noise phenomenon with the Ephraim and Malah noise suppressor. *IEEE Trans. Speech and Audio Processing*, 2(2):345–349, Apr. 1994.

[6] J. R. Deller, J. G. Proakis, and J. H. L. Hansen. *Discrete-Time Processing of Speech Signals.* Macmillan Publishing Company, 1993.

[7] Y. Ephraim and D. Malah. Speech enhancement using a minimum mean-square error short-time spectral amplitude estimator. *IEEE Trans. Acoustics, Speech, and Signal Processing*, 32(6):1109–1121, Dec. 1984.

[8] Y. Ephraim and D. Malah. Speech enhancement using a minimum mean-square error log-spectral amplitude estimator. *IEEE Trans. Acoustics, Speech, and Signal Processing*, 23(2):443–445, Apr. 1985.

[9] K. W. Godin, S. O. Sadjadi, and J. H. L. Hansen. Impact of noise reduction and spectrum estimation on noise robust speaker identification. In *Proc. Interspeech*, Lyon, France, Aug. 2013.

[10] M. Goudbeek and K. Scherer. Beyond arousal: Valence and potency/control cues in the vocal expression of emotion. *Journal of the Acoustical Society of America*, 128(3):1322–1336, Sept. 2010.

[11] A. H. Gray and J. D. Markel. Distance measures for speech processing. *IEEE Trans. Acoustics, Speech, and Signal Processing*, 24(5):380–391, Oct. 1976.

[12] J. H. L. Hansen and M. A. Clements. Constrained iterative speech enhancement with application to speech recognition. *IEEE Trans. Signal Processing*, 39(4):795–805, Apr. 1991.

[13] X. Huang, A. Acero, and H.-W. Hon. *Spoken Language Processing.* Prentice Hall PTR, 2001.

[14] F. Itakura. Minimum prediction residual principle applied to speech recognition. *IEEE Trans. Acoustics, Speech, and Signal Processing*, 23(1):67–72, Feb. 1975.

[15] L. Lin. A concordance correlation coefficient to evaluate reproducibility. *Biometrics*, 45(1):255–268, Mar. 1989.

[16] P. C. Loizou. *Speech Enhancement: Theory and Practice.* CRC Press, 2007.

[17] J. Makhoul. Linear prediction: A tutorial review. *Proceedings of the IEEE*, 63(4):561–580, Apr. 1975.

[18] M. Mauch and S. Ewert. The audio degradation toolbox and its application to robustness evaluation. In *Proc. ISMIR*, Curitiba, Brazil, Nov. 2013.

[19] J. Ortega-Garcia and J. Gonzalez-Rodriguez. Overview of speech enhancement techniques for automatic speaker recognition. In *Proc. ICSLP*, Philadelphia, PA, Oct. 1996.

[20] K. Paliwal, B. Schwerin, and K. Wójcicki. Speech enhancement using a minimum mean-square error short-time spectral modulation magnitude estimator. *Speech Communication*, 54(2):282–305, Feb. 2012.

[21] K. Paliwal, K. Wójcicki, and B. Schwerin. Single-channel speech enhancement using spectral subtraction in the short-time modulation domain. *Speech Communication*, 52(5):450–475, May 2010.

[22] L. R. Rabiner and R. W. Schafer. *Digital Processing of Speech Signals.* Prentice-Hall, 1978.

[23] F. Ringeval, F. Eyben, E. Kroupi, A. Yuce, J.-P. Thiran, T. Ebrahimi, D. Lalanne, and B. Schuller. Prediction of asynchronous dimensional emotion ratings from audiovisual and physiological data. *Pattern Recognition Letters*, 66:22–30, Nov. 2015.

[24] F. Ringeval, A. Sonderegger, J. Sauer, and D. Lalanne. Introducing the RECOLA multimodal corpus of remote collaborative and affective interactions. In *Proc. FG*, Shanghai, China, Apr. 2013.

[25] S. O. Sadjadi and J. H. L. Hansen. Assessment of single-channel speech enhancement techniques for speaker identification under mismatched conditions. In *Proc. Interspeech*, Makuhari, Japan, Sept. 2010.

[26] R. Saeidi, J. Pohjalainen, T. Kinnunen, and P. Alku. Temporally weighted linear prediction features for tackling additive noise in speaker verification. *IEEE Signal Processing Letters*, 17(6):599–602, June 2010.

[27] B. Schuller, D. Arsic, F. Wallhoff, and G. Rigoll. Emotion recognition in the noise applying large acoustic feature sets. In *Proc. Speech Prosody*, Dresden, Germany, May 2006.

[28] B. Schuller, S. Steidl, A. Batliner, F. Burkhardt, L. Devillers, C. Müller, and S. Narayanan. Paralinguistics in speech and language - state-of-the-art and the challenge. *Computer Speech and Language*, 27:4–39, 2013.

[29] B. Schuller, M. Wöllmer, T. Moosmayr, and G. Rigoll. Recognition of noisy speech: A comparative survey of robust model architecture and feature enhancement. *EURASIP J. on Audio, Speech, and Music Processing*, 2009:17 pages, 2009.

[30] G. Trigeorgis, F. Ringeval, R. Bruckner, E. Marchi, M. Nicolaou, B. Schuller, and S. Zafeiriou. Adieu features? End-to-end speech emotion recognition using a Deep Convolutional Recurrent Network. In *Proc. ICASSP*, Shanghai, China, Mar. 2016.

[31] M. Valstar, J. Gratch, B. Schuller, F. Ringeval, D. Lalanne, M. T. Torres, S. Scherer, G. Stratou, R. Cowie, and M. Pantic. AVEC 2016 – depression, mood, and emotion recognition workshop and challenge. In *Proc. AVEC*, Amsterdam, Oct. 2016.

[32] Z. Zhang, F. Ringeval, J. Han, J. Deng, E. Marchi, and B. Schuller. Facing realism in spontaneous emotion recognition from speech: Feature enhancement by LSTM neural autoencoders. In *Proc. Interspeech*, San Francisco, CA, Sept. 2016.

[33] E. Zwicker and H. Fastl. *Psychoacoustics, Facts and Models.* Springer-Verlag, Berlin, 1990.

AntiLoiter: A Loitering Discovery System for Longtime Videos across Multiple Surveillance Cameras

Jianquan Liu, Shoji Nishimura, and Takuya Araki
System Platform Research Laboratories, NEC Corporation
1753 Shimonumabe, Nakahara-ku, Kawasaki, Kanagawa 211-8666, Japan
{j-liu@ct, s-nishimura@bk, t-araki@dc}.jp.nec.com

ABSTRACT

Since loitering is a suspicious behavior that often leads to abnormal situations, such as pickpocketing and terrorist attacks, its analysis attracts increasing research attention. In this paper, we present AntiLoiter, a practical loitering discovery system for surveillance. AntiLoiter can efficiently discover loitering candidates from longtime videos across multiple cameras. Most of existing systems mainly focus on how to detect or identify loiterers by behavior tracking techniques. However, the difficulties of tracking-based methods are known as that their analysis results are heavily influenced by occlusions, overlaps, and shadows. Moreover, tracking-based methods need to track the human appearance continuously. Therefore, they are not readily applied to longtime videos across multiple cameras due to the appearance discontinuity of criminal loitering. For instance, a suspect would probably come to the same place several times on different dates for preliminary inspections before a terrorist attack happens, where the loitering behavior is discontinuous. To solve this problem, we abandon the tracking method, instead, design a novel approach to efficiently discover loiterers based on their frequent appearance patterns for longtime videos across multiple cameras. Our approach simply yet effectively adopts existing face recognition techniques for loitering discovery. We conducted extensive experiments on both synthetic and real surveillance videos to evaluate the efficiency and efficacy of our approach. The experimental results show that our system can find out loitering candidates correctly and outperforms existing method by 100 times in terms of runtime.

CCS Concepts

•Information systems → Multimedia databases; Video search; *Search engine indexing;* **•Social and professional topics → Surveillance;**

Keywords

Loitering discovery; Video surveillance; Multimedia database

1. INTRODUCTION

Nowadays surveillance cameras are installed everywhere, such as in shopping malls, buildings, stations, and other public places, for security monitoring. As a result, surveillance has become a ubiquitous aspect of the modern urban landscape [1]. The majority of researches in the computer vision, multimedia, and artificial intelligence communities usually focus on typical tasks of video analysis for general purposes, including object detection, recognition, tracking and behavior analysis [2]. However, we are aware of the changing international situation for public safety such as terrorism. We cannot forget the Paris Attacks that happened in November, 2015 [3]. Researchers in both industry and academia are required to pay attention on the researches for public safety including the monitoring of suspicious and criminal activities.

MM '16, October 15-19, 2016, Amsterdam, Netherlands
© 2016 ACM. ISBN 978-1-4503-3603-1/16/10... $15.00
DOI: http://dx.doi.org/10.1145/2964284.2970927

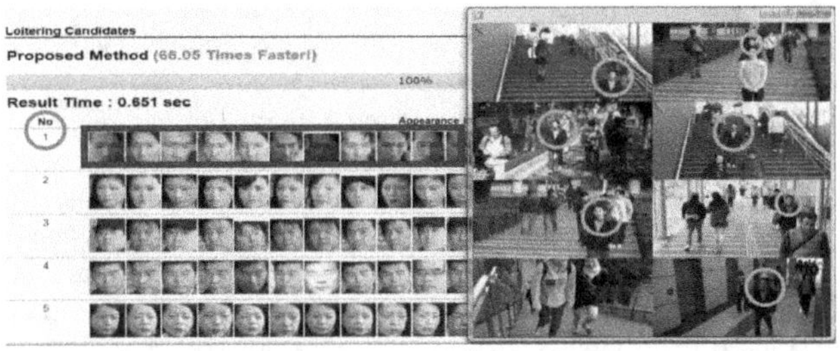

Figure 1: Visualization result [4] of loiterer candidates discovered by AntiLoiter from the videos captured by eight surveillance cameras; The person simulating as a pickpocket (marked in green circles) keeps loitering in multiple surveillance cameras; He is discovered and ranked as a candidate at No.1 (marked in a red circle and blue rectangle).

Recently, loitering detection (or analysis) has attracted increasing attention for crime prevention and investigation [5, 6, 7, 8], because loitering is a suspicious behavior that often leads to abnormal situations, such as pickpocketing. Most of researchers mainly focus on how to detect or identify loitering individuals by *micro-approaches.* It means that the loitering analysis is dealt with in a micro manner, such as manually monitoring frame by frame, tracking human behavior by a set of repeated actions [7], pedestrian tracking based on spatiotemporal changes [8], etc. Since such kinds of analysis are carried out deeply in vertical direction for a short time, or a single view in videos, we categorize them as micro-approaches.

However, the difficulties of micro-approaches are known as that the results of tracking analysis are heavily influenced by occlusions, overlaps, and shadows [1]. One worse limit is that tracking-based methods need to track the human appearance continuously. While in real-world environments, multiple cameras are installed for longtime surveillance, such a kind of continuous tracking is not readily applied. For example, a suspect would probably come to the same place several times on different dates separately for preliminary inspections before a terrorist attack happens. In this case, the loitering behavior of a suspect is discontinuous and extended to some days, thus continuous tracking is time-consuming and not applicable. Developing an automated system for analyzing loitering in longtime videos across multiple cameras remains a challenge. Since tracking-based methods are

Table 1: **Characteristics comparison between our macro-approach and existing micro-approaches [5, 6, 7, 8]**

	macro-approach	micro-approaches
duration	long	short
camera	multiple	single
analysis	horizontal (wide-range)	vertical (deep-level)
efficiency	super fast	time-consuming
efficacy	high	low

not applicable, *can we find out loitering candidates without any human behavior tracking?*

Motivated by the above-mentioned challenge, we propose AntiLoiter, a loitering discovery system for surveillance, which takes into account longtime videos and multiple cameras. In AntiLoiter, we abandon the tracking-based micro-approaches. Instead, we design a novel *macro-approach* that enables a horizontal loitering discovery[1] only utilizing face features extracted from videos without any behavior tracking or vertical analysis. AntiLoiter is realized according to a common knowledge that the loitering behavior is usually considered as a pattern of repeated frequent appearance. Thus we just retrieve the top k frequently appeared persons across multiple cameras as loitering candidates in this work. The challenging question can be answered by this simple yet reasonable idea.

For example, as shown in Figure 1, the person simulating as a pickpocket keeps loitering around a certain place. AntiLoiter discovers the person as a loiterer candidate and ranks him at No.1 because he most frequently appeared across multiple surveillance cameras. Our macro-approach is simple and straightforward, but the discovery result is really surprising.

To realize this simple yet effective idea, we still face another one challenge: *how to complete such a loitering discovery task efficiently across longtime multiple videos.* For this challenge, we propose a novel index, Luigi[2], to perform efficient similarity search that is applied for loitering discovery. The detail will be introduced in Section 2.

The main contributions of this paper are summarized as follows. In addition, the characteristics comparison is summarized in Table 1 to clarify the difference between our macro-approach and existing micro-approaches [5, 6, 7, 8].

- We design and implement a real system, named AntiLoiter, to perform loitering discovery without vertical video analysis such as human activity tracking.
- In AntiLoiter, we propose a novel index, Luigi, for similarity search and algorithms to enable efficient loitering discovery across longtime multiple videos.
- We conduct extensive experiments on synthetic and real datasets to evaluate the efficacy and the efficiency of AntiLoiter. The results indicate that our system can find out loitering candidates correctly and outperforms existing method by 100 times in terms of runtime.

2. SYSTEM DESIGN & ALGORITHMS

In this section, we introduce the design and algorithms of our system in detail. As shown in Figure 2, AntiLoiter consists of five modules depicted in rectangular boxes, including frame splitter, feature extractor, metadata store, loitering discovery and web-based retrieval GUI.

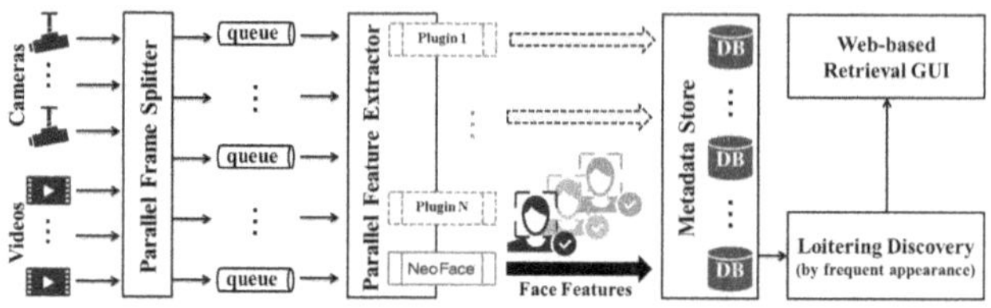

Figure 2: System overview of AntiLoiter

In AntiLoiter, the historical or real-time videos captured by multiple surveillance cameras are input into the frame splitter module. The frame splitter receives multiple videos and splits them into separate frames in a parallel way. Subsequently, all splitted frames are delivered to parallel queues awaiting pickup by feature extractor in next phase. The feature extractor is also designed in a parallel manner and has pluggable interfaces connecting to any existing feature extraction techniques, such as the popular descriptors SIFT [9], HoG [10], etc. These extracted features are stored in the metadata store and utilized for loitering discovery. The results of loitering discovery can be retrieved by the web-based retrieval GUI. As we know, the processing bottleneck in most image/video processing systems is the computation for feature extraction and matching. To reduce such a bottleneck, in the design of AntiLoiter, we adopt parallel mechanism to maximize the utilization of multithread architecture in modern computer systems.

2.1 Luigi index

As shown in Figure 2, the databases inside metadata store receive different kinds of features for loitering discovery. This motivates us to propose a novel and generic method for indexing arbitrary features. Therefore, in this section, we introduce the key idea of designing the Luigi index, and algorithms of building the index structure in detail.

Key ideas. Our approach is inspired by the *similarity transitivity* inside similar data. Before discussing the similarity transitivity, we first introduce two important definitions as follows. They will be used to clarify the similarity transitivity.

Definition 1 (SIMILAR). *Given a similarity threshold* δ*, two features* f_a *and* f_b*, and a blackbox similarity function* $sim(\cdot,\cdot)$*, if* $sim(f_a, f_b) \geq \delta$ *is satisfied, the relation between* f_a *and* f_b *is called similar. It is notated as* $f_a \overset{\delta}{\sim} f_b$.

Definition 2 (REPRESENTATIVE). *Given a similarity threshold* δ*, a feature* f_r*, and a feature set* $f \in F$*, if* $\forall f \in F$*,* $f_r \overset{\delta}{\sim} f$ *is satisfied,* f_r *is called as a representative of* F*. It is notated as* $f_r \overset{\delta}{\rightsquigarrow} F$.

Property 1 (SIMILARITY TRANSITIVITY). *Given three features* f_a*,* f_b*, and* f_c*, if having* $f_a \overset{\delta}{\sim} f_b$ *and* $f_b \overset{\delta}{\sim} f_c$*, then* f_a *and* f_c *can be approximately considered as* $f_a \overset{\delta}{\sim} f_c$.

The Property 1 is not always true, but the possibility of being true is high, which is well observed in [11]. Such a property probably being true is based on the observation results from the examined small-world theorem [12], i.e., well-known as "six degrees of separation". For example in a social network, a friend of a friend is also likely to be a friend. In this paper, we employ this simple principle to help design

[1]We use the word, *discovery*, instead of analysis or detection, to differ our approach from existing micro-approaches.

[2]Luigi is a fictional character appeared in the worldwide famous video game, *Super Mario Bros*. He is the younger brother of Mario. As its pronunciation is the same as the word "similar" in Japanese, we take it as naming.

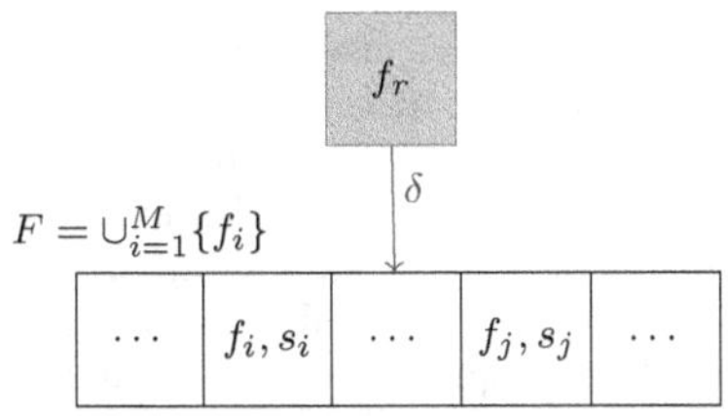

Figure 3: Basic unit of data structure used in Luigi

the Luigi index and heuristic pruning strategy for similarity search.

Subsequently, we design an important data structure as shown in Figure 3 to realize the representative relation in Definition 2. It is a basic unit and recursively constructed inside the Luigi index. As shown in Figure 3, the representative feature f_r is pointing its child node, where the link is associated with the similarity threshold δ. The child node storing the feature set F, contains M entries, in each of which the feature f_i and the similarity value $s_i = sim(f_r, f_i)$ are stored. The representative feature f_r is stored as an entry in parent node. This basic unit of data structure can be also confirmed in the example shown in Figure 4. Its basic structure must be maintained in any node of the tree. By adopting approximate similarity transitivity, we design two strategies for tree traversal as follows.

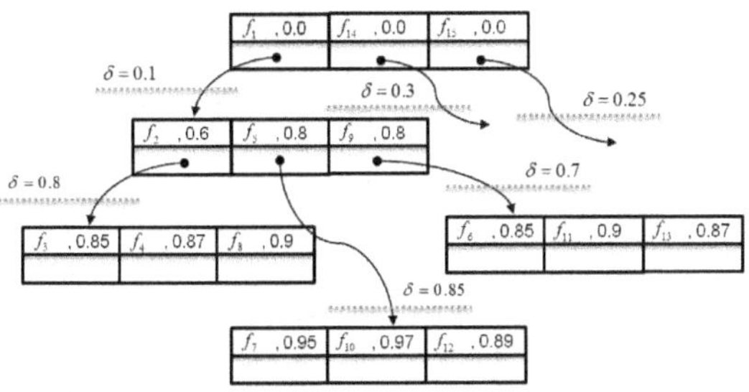

Figure 4: A hierarchical example of Luigi index.

Strategy 1 (PRUNING). *Given a feature f, a current visiting entry e, if $sim(f, e.f_r) < e.\delta$ is satisfied, the forward path from entry e can be pruned without further traversal.*

Strategy 2 (REFINING). *Given a feature f, a current visiting entry e, if $sim(f, e.f_r) \geq e.\delta$ is satisfied, the forward path from entry e must continue to visit for further refinement.*

Construction algorithms. Having the aforementioned key ideas, we can propose algorithms to construct the Luigi index in the manner of recursively embedding the basic unit (Figure 3) into a hierarchical tree (Figure 4). In Algorithm 1, we demonstrate the procedure of building Luigi index. The algorithm iteratively picks up each feature f from the data set *db* (line 2), and sequentially insert f into an appropriate node (line 3, 4). After an insertion is completed, the algorithm examines whether the number of entries in current node exceeds the node capacity M (line 5). If so, the algorithm calls Algorithm 3 to split the current node (line 6).

The Algorithm 2 is designed to position an appropriate node for performing an insertion of feature f. It is called by Algorithm 1 in line 3. In Algorithm 2, the current Luigi T is traversed in the manner of depth-first-search (DFS) by utilizing a stack L to keep the current visiting node (line 2 – 4). Inside each visiting node, the algorithm loops to compute the similarity between feature f and each entry e, and selects the right entry holding maximum similarity to feature f (line 6). Here, the refining Strategy 2 is applied to determine whether go to visit forward path or not. Until it cannot find a better candidate, the algorithm will terminate immediately to return the selected best node for insertion operations (line 7 – 9).

Algorithm 1: BuildIndex(Data set *db*, **Luigi** T)

Input: Data set *db* containing features ($db = \cup_i^N\{f_i\}$).
Output: **Luigi** T constructed by this algorithm.

```
1  begin
2      foreach f ∈ db do
3          Node ← findNodeToInseart( T, f ) ;
4          T.insert( Node, f ) ;
5          if Node.size > M then
6              T.splitNode( Node ) ;
7      return T ;
```

Algorithm 2: findNodeToInsert(**Luigi** T, feature f)

Input: Current **Luigi** T, feature f to be inserted.
Output: Appropriate node.

```
1  begin
2      Initialize stack L ← ∅ ;
3      L.push( root node of T ) ;
4      while L is not empty do
5          Node ← L.pop() ;
6          e ← arg max_{e∈Node} {s|s ← sim(e, f) ∧ s ≥ e.δ} ;
7          if e ≠ NIL then
8              L.push( child node of e ) ;
9      return Node ;
```

When overflow happens after an insertion, the Algorithm 3 will be called to adjust the overflowed node and to maintain the basic unit recursively. As shown in line 2, a new representative entry f_r in the current node n is selected randomly. To our empirical analysis, a random selection would generally perform better than other strategies, at the view point of tree balancing. After the new representative f_r is determined, pairwise similarities between f_r and all entries $\forall e_i \in n$ have to be recomputed (line 3). All results are stored into an array $s[\cdot]$. In order to split all entries half by half, a strategy of selecting the median values in $s[\cdot]$ is used to dynamically determine the new threshold δ (line 4). By having f_r and δ, we now can put half of all entries into a new child node n_c, and leave the other half into the current node n. In such a simple way, we can maintain the basic unit structure shown in Figure 3 by one-pass processing, thus it is quite efficient.

Algorithm 3: splitNode(Node n)

Input: Current node n.

```
1   begin
2       f_r ← Randomly pickup entry ∃e ∈ n ;
3       s[·] ← Recompute sim(f_r, e_i), ∀e_i ∈ n \ f_r ;
4       δ ← Median value of s[·] ;
5       n_c ← Create a new empty node ;
6       if s[i] ≥ δ then
7           Insert (e_i, s[i]) into n_c ;
8       else
9           Keep (e_i, s[i]) into n ;
10      Maintain the basic unit structure f_r ~δ~> n_c ;
```

Searching algorithm. In this section, we design an algorithm to perform efficient similarity search using Luigi index. In Algorithm 4, the Luigi index is depth-first traversed to retrieve the answer set of an issued similarity search. It is worth noting that the Strategy 1 and Strategy 2 are applied in line 8 – 9 to filter out negative results but refine positive results.

Similar to the complexity analysis of Algorithm 2, the Algorithm 4 also runs in the manner of depth-first-search (DFS). The different point is that the Algorithm 4 traverses the tree structure of Luigi in multiple paths. Therefore, its computational complexity of a similarity search is near to $O(c \log_M(N))$ with a linear factor c. In this sense of theoretical analysis, the ideal efficiency of the proposed searching Algorithm 4 is very high comparing to the traditional sequential scan that needs $O(N)$ complexity.

Algorithm 4: SimilaritySearch (q, r, T)

```
   Input: Query feature q, Range threshold r, Luigi T.
   Output: Answer set S of similarity search.
1  begin
2      Initialize answer set S ← ∅ ;
3      Initialize stack L ← ∅ ;
4      L.push( root node of T ) ;
5      while L is not empty do
6          Node ← L.pop() ;
7          foreach Entry e in Node do
8              if sim(q, e) ≥ e.δ then
9                  L.push( child node of e ) ;
10             if sim(q, e) ≥ r then
11                 S ← {e} ∪ S ;
12     return S ;
```

In our system, we initially employ face recognition technique to identify individuals. As we know, there are a number of existing features that can be used for face recognition, such as SIFT descriptor. However, in our system, we have to guarantee high credibility and accuracy for face recognition. We thus adopt a commercial product NeoFace®[3] for facial feature extraction and matching.

2.2 Loitering discovery

In this section, by taking the advantage of the Luigi index, we propose a novel algorithm to realize the efficient loitering discovery across longtime multiple videos.

First, we generally discuss how to handle the loitering discovery without tracking but only having facial features. A naive approach coming to mind is shown in Figure 5. Since we have all facial features extracted frame by frame in the previous phase, we can probe pairwise matching of facial features to group similar faces. For example, we can identify two individuals as the same person when the similarity of their face features is over than a given threshold δ (e.g., δ=0.8). It means the two individuals are similar over 80%.

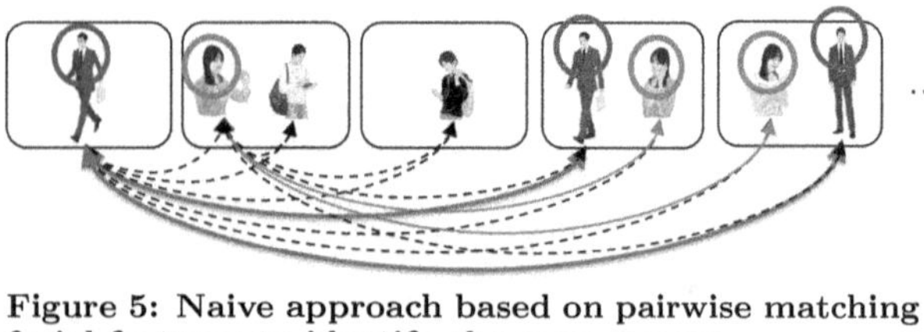

Figure 5: Naive approach based on pairwise matching of facial features to identify the same person.

[3]NeoFace® is the world's best face recognition technology [13], which can provide No.1 precision and No.1 speed for facial feature extraction and feature matching, respectively.

Subsequently, all face features can be grouped into different persons based on all pairwise similarities. We can count the appearance frequency of the same person, and rank all persons according to their frequencies in descending order. According to the common knowledge mentioned in Section 1, the loitering behavior is usually considered as a pattern of repeated frequent appearance. Thus we retrieve the top k ranked persons as loitering candidates. The naive approach sounds simply accomplishing our goal. However, as we know, the naive approach is not practical due to its high complexity of $O(N^2)$ for pairwise matching, where N is the number of facial features.

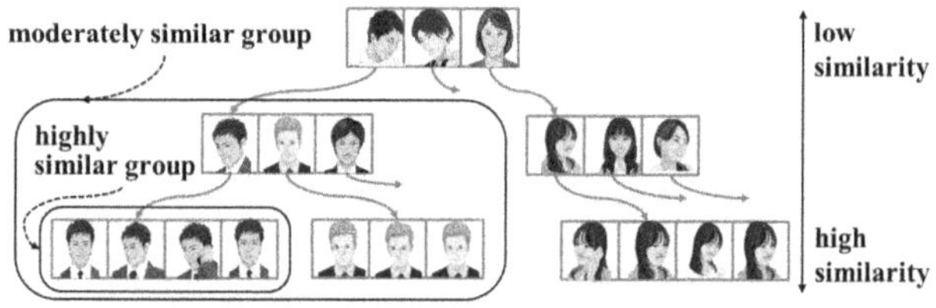

Figure 6: Face grouping by Luigi index.

To reduce the computational complexity of the naive approach, we propose an efficient algorithm to perform approximate face grouping by adopting the Luigi index for similarity search. The algorithmic processing is shown in Algorithm 5. As shown in Figure 6, the Luigi can dynamically index similar data in a hierarchical tree, where moderately similar group and highly similar group can be differentiated by the hierarchical similarities inside the tree structure. We introduce two similarity thresholds δ_1, δ_2 in Algorithm 5 to utilize this novel characteristic for face grouping. From line 2 to 5, the algorithm picks up those moderately similar facial features ($\geq \delta_1$) from the tree T. Whereafter, the algorithm creates an empty tree $T2$ to iteratively insert all facial features from the queue Q, and incrementally divides them into different groups ($\geq \delta_2$) (line 6-14).

According to the pseudo codes in Algorithm 5, it can be easily analyzed that its computational complexity is $O(|Q| \log |Q|)$, where $|Q|$ is the length of the queue Q and $\log |Q|$ is the cost of probing a similarity search at line 10. In the worst case of relaxing δ_1=0, the size of $|Q|$ is equal to N, and the total complexity becomes $O(N \log N)$. Comparing to the complexity of naive approach, the efficiency of Algorithm 5 is improved from $O(N^2)$ to $O(N \log N)$.

3. EXPERIMENTS

In this section, we report the evaluation results of experiments conducted on synthetic and real datasets to show the efficiency and the efficacy of AntiLoiter.

Our experiments are conducted in the Ubuntu 12.10 OS with 11GB memory and Intel® Xeon® E5504 @ 2.00GHz CPU. The synthetic data is 15-minute videos recorded from the simulation of a pickpocketing usecase. A person appeared frequently, kept loitering around a certain place, and was captured by multiple cameras. The real world dataset is provided by one of our oversea customers, which contains 24-hour videos recorded by multiple real surveillance cameras that are installed around a public area. We extracted 10 thousand and 1 million facial features from synthetic and real datasets, respectively. We feed the two dataset into AntiLoiter system to evaluate the results of loitering discovery and its runtime speed. The parameters are set to δ_1=0.65, δ_2=0.80, and k=20 as default values.

Algorithm 5: GroupBy(Threshold δ_1, δ_2, **Luigi** T)

Input: δ_1, used to cut moderately similar faces; δ_2, used to exactly group similar faces; **Luigi** T.
Output: G, a list of groups of different persons.

```
begin
    Queue Q ← ∅ ;
    foreach Node e ∈ T do
        if e.δ ≥ δ1 then
            Q.inqueue(e) ;
    Luigi T2 ← ∅ ;
    while Q is not empty do
        Node e ← Q.dequeue() ;
        foreach Data d ∈ e do
            if SimilaritySearch(d, δ2, T2) ≠ ∅ then
                G.insertToExistingGroup(d) ;
            else
                G.insertToNewGroup(d) ;
            T2.insertData(d) ;
    return G ;
```

Results on synthetic dataset. As we know, there is one simulated suspect acting as a pickpocket and keeping loitering across multiple cameras. The experiment result is demonstrated in Figure 7. The simulated suspect is correctly suggested as a loitering candidate and ranked at No.1. Therefore, our system achieved 100% recall and 100% precision at top-1 result for loitering discovery. Besides, Figure 7 indicates that our proposed method (right) outperforms the naive approach (left) by 100 times in terms of runtime.

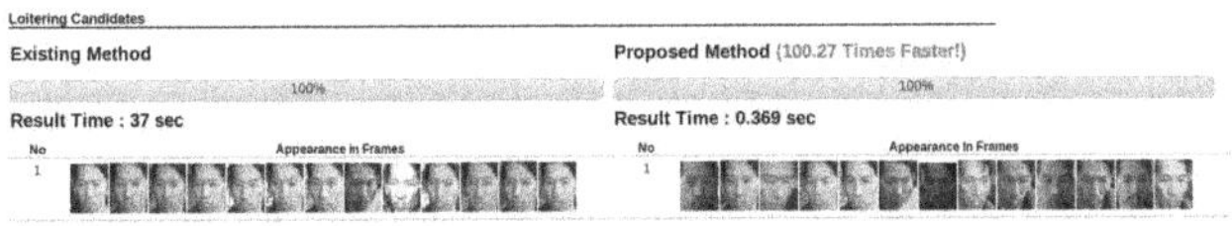

Figure 7: Efficiency evaluation on synthetic data.

Results on real dataset. After submitting the top 20 loitering candidates discovered by AntiLoiter to the customer, we received their feedback. The feedback told that the whole 7 loiterers were correctly listed up in our results, thus the customer felt very surprising. It means that our system achieved 100% recall for loitering discovery on the real dataset. Due to privacy and security issue, we are only informed the number of loiterers as ground truth by the customer, but without knowing their details. Therefore, we cannot compute the precision at top-7 of the results of loitering discovery.

Table 2: The scalability of our method for loitering discovery compared with the naive method.

N (# of facial features)	Our method	Naive method
10K	0.369 (sec)	37 (sec)
135K	5 (sec)	$\approx$ 60,750 (sec)
1M	10 (sec)	$\approx$ 46 (days)

Regarding the scalability of runtime speed for loitering discovery, we randomly selected two smaller subset from the real dataset to conduct the evaluation. The results are shown in Table 2. It is worth noting that the speeds of naive method running on the 135K and 1M datasets are estimated values. It is too time-consuming to perform real testing.

Discussion. Although our experimental results indicate that AntiLoiter system is efficient and effective for loitering discovery, it still faces some issues to be solved. The most critical one is how to differ loiterers from normal people who just happen to appear frequently. For example, it is helpful to define a time window to filter out normal cases.

4. CONCLUSION

We designed and implemented a real system, AntiLoiter, to perform loitering discovery without tracking based analysis. Our experiments examined its efficiency and efficacy for loitering discovery on both synthetic and real datasets. In future, we aim to follow the above discussed issues to improve the system performance.

5. REFERENCES

[1] Tomi Räty. Survey on contemporary remote surveillance systems for public safety. *IEEE Trans. Systems, Man, and Cybernetics, Part C*, 40(5):493–515, 2010.

[2] Mubarak Shah, Omar Javed, and Khurram Shafique. Automated visual surveillance in realistic scenarios. *IEEE MultiMedia*, 14(1):30–39, 2007.

[3] Paris attacks: What happened on the night, 9 Dec. 2015. www.bbc.com/news/world-europe-34818994.

[4] Jianquan Liu, Shoji Nishimura, and Takuya Araki. Visloiter: A system to visualize loiterers discovered from surveillance videos. In *The 43rd International Conference and Exhibition on Computer Graphics & Interactive Techniques (SIGGRAPH)*, 2016.

[5] N. D. Bird, O. Masoud, P. Papanikolopoulos, and A. Isaacs. Detection of loitering individuals in public transportation areas. *IEEE Tran. on Intelligent Transportation Systems*, 6(2):167–177, 2005.

[6] Shian-Ru Ke, Le Uyen Thuc Hoang, Yong-Jin Lee, Jenq-Neng Hwang, Jang-Hee Yoo, and Kyoung-Ho Choi. A review on video-based human activity recognition. *Computers*, 2(2):88–131, 2013.

[7] Héctor F. Gómez A., Rafael Martínez-Tomás, Susana Arias Tapia, Antonio Fernández-Caballero, Sylvie Ratté, Alexandra González Eras, and Patricia Ludeña González. Identification of loitering human behaviour in video surveillance environments. In *International Work-Conference on the Interplay Between Natural and Artificial Computation (IWINAC)*, pages 516–525, 2015.

[8] Yunyoung Nam. Loitering detection using an associating pedestrian tracker in crowded scenes. *Multimedia Tools Application*, 74(9):2939–2961, 2015.

[9] David G. Lowe. Distinctive image features from scale-invariant keypoints. *International Journal of Computer Vision*, 60(2):91–110, 2004.

[10] Navneet Dalal and Bill Triggs. Histograms of oriented gradients for human detection. In *IEEE Conference on Computer Vision and Pattern Recognition (CVPR)*, pages 886–893, 2005.

[11] Wei Dong, Moses Charikar, and Kai Li. Efficient k-nearest neighbor graph construction for generic similarity measures. In *Proceedings of the 20th International Conference on World Wide Web (WWW)*, pages 577–586, 2011.

[12] Stanley Milgram. The Small World Problem. *Psychology Today*, 2:60–67, 1967.

[13] NIST. Multiple Biometrics Evaluation, 2010. www.nist.gov/itl/iad/ig/mbe.cfm.

Magic Mirror: A Virtual Fashion Consultant

Yejun Liu[12], Jia Jia[1]*, Jingtian Fu[12], Yihui Ma[1], Jie Huang[1], Zijian Tong[3]
[1]Department of Computer Science and Technology, Tsinghua National Laboratory for Information Science and Technology (TNList), Tsinghua University, Beijing, China
[2]Academy of Arts & Design, Tsinghua University, Beijing, China
[3]Sogou Corporation, Beijing, China
jjia@mail.tsinghua.edu.cn

ABSTRACT

What should I wear? We present Magic Mirror, a virtual fashion consultant, which can parse, appreciate and recommend the wearing. Magic Mirror is designed with a large display and Kinect to simulate the real mirror and interact with users in augmented reality. Internally, Magic Mirror is a practical appreciation system for automatic aesthetics-oriented clothing analysis. Specifically, we focus on the clothing collocation rather than the single one, the style (aesthetic words) rather than the visual features. We bridge the gap between the visual features and aesthetic words of clothing collocation to enable the computer to learn appreciating the clothing collocation. Finally, both object and subject evaluations verify the effectiveness of the proposed algorithm and Magic Mirror system.

Keywords

Clothing Collocation, Aesthetics Learning

1. INTRODUCTION

You are what you wear. People reinforce their mood and express their feelings through their clothing. What to wear is inevitable, however, most people have no great aesthetics and appreciation for fashion and can not follow the fashion trend. So they usually struggle with what to wear.

To solve the problems, we need to figure out what makes dressing different. Instead of a single piece of clothing, the collocation of clothing plays a more important role in dressing. As well, in Nina Garcia's books, style [1] [2] is determinant of what to wear, which is the aesthetic feeling of wearing. Thus, the style of clothing collocation is the focus to appreciate the wearing.

Meanwhile, it is not appropriate to make a decision of what to wear for people, but it is helpful to provide the professional appreciation and consultation of wearing, then let people make their own decision.

*Corresponding author: J.Jia(jjia@mail.tsinghua.edu.cn)

MM '16, October 15–19, 2016, Amsterdam, The Netherlands.
© 2016 ACM. ISBN 978-1-4503-3603-1/16/10. . . $15.00
DOI: http://dx.doi.org/10.1145/2964284.2970928

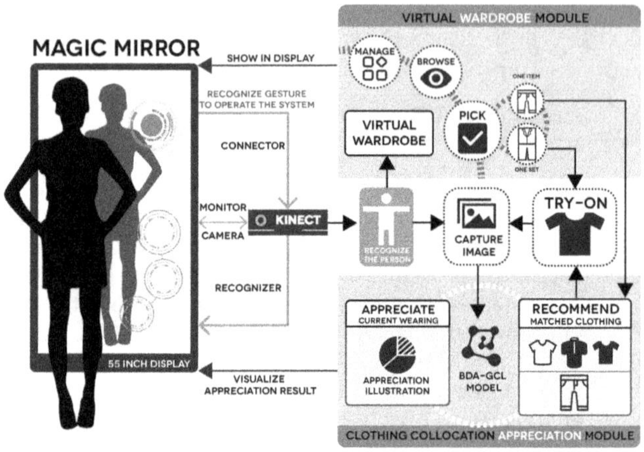

Figure 1: Overview of Magic Mirror.

So, in this paper, we designed a practical appreciation system, Magic Mirror, to be a virtual fashion consultant to parse, appreciate and recommend the clothing collocation. Magic Mirror is designed with the large display and Kinect, which simulates the real mirror and interacts with users in AR (augmented reality). Magic Mirror automatically appreciates the collocation of clothing and suggests the wearing. Through Magic Mirror, users can build their own virtual wardrobe and manage the clothing in it. As well, users can get the recommendation of matched collocation after picking one piece of clothing.

To appreciate clothing collocation, we built the association between the visual features of single-clothing and aesthetic words of collocation by proposing a three-level framework (VF-ISS-AWS). Then, the system is based on the model of Bimodal Deep Autoencoder Guided by Correlative Label (BDA-GCL), which can deeply combine visual features of tops and bottoms in the collocation and describe the mapping between combined visual features and image-scale space.

Finally, we conducted the experiments to verify the validity of algorithm and performed the user study to observe the satisfaction of appreciation and the effectiveness of recommendation.

2. MAGIC MIRROR

In normal life, people always use mirror to appreciate their own wearing directly in an other sight. To improve immersion and authenticity, Magic Mirror is not only designed to simulate the real mirror, but also empowered to appreciate and recommend the fashion collocation in AR.

2.1 System Architecture

2.1.1 Hardware

Magic Mirror consists of a 55-inch large display, a Kinect and a computing device. The 55-inch display is placed on end like a true mirror and connected to the Kinect. Especially, Kinect is a monitor, a camera, a recognizer and a connector. It shows what is in front of the display like a real mirror, especially capturing some key image in which there is a person wearing clothing. Meanwhile, Kinect can recognize the skeleton and the gestures to optimize the interaction between users and Magic Mirror.(Figure 1)

2.1.2 Interactive experience with Kinect

In order to give users the natural experience, we designed the interaction by body languages and gestures. Users operate the Magic Mirror with the natural responding gestures. Additional, Magic Mirror can trigger the functions naturally by recognizing the appearance or disappearance of users(skeleton). Moreover, the appreciating results and suggestions are shown as tips in Magic Mirror, which are attaching to and going with the skeleton of users. Specifically, we will introduce the interactive details in chapter 2.2.1.

2.2 System Modules

To be a virtual fashion consultant, Magic Mirror, the appreciation system, has two modules: the *virtual wardrobe* module and the *appreciation* module. (Figure 1)

2.2.1 Virtual Wardrobe Module

In the wardrobe module, users can get into a virtual wardrobe and have a simple try-on looking in Magic Mirror.

First, Users can open the virtual closet by the gesture of pushing open, then browse the tops and bottoms in the wardrobe by opening or closing the hands. If users want to see the details of one piece of tops, they need to close the bottom drawer through holding and dragging down the handle of the bottom drawer. As well, the clothes in the wardrobe can be managed such as adding or deleting. Users add the clothing by hanging on one piece in display, and Magic Mirror will take a photo automatically as soon as users leaving from the mirror. Well, users delete the picked clothing by crossing gesture to confirm and tearing it apart.

In addition, the virtual wardrobe allows users to pick and match the clothes themselves and shows the simple try-on looking in the display. Hence, the virtual wardrobe module is the basic library for users to copy their real clothes to the virtual, supporting the appreciation module.

2.2.2 Appreciation Module

In the appreciation module, there are two main functions: appreciation function and recommendation function.

In appreciation, user can get the appreciating analysis of current wearing in mirror with vivid visualization. As soon as Kinect recognizes the person (skeleton) in the display, the system will capture the image and analyze the clothing collocation on it. There are several conclusions:(Figure 2)

1.Basic attributes, including color combination, suited seasons and appropriate occasions of the collocation.

2.Style distribution. It shows the distribution of relevant styles of the wearing.

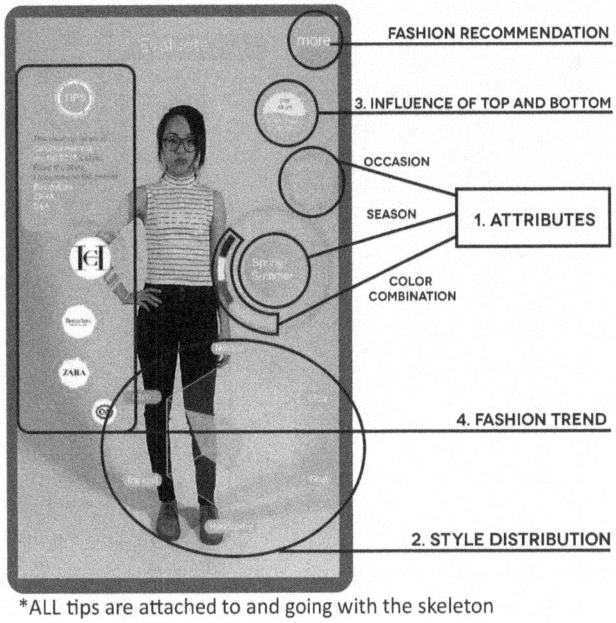

Figure 2: Introduction of Appreciation Illustration.

3.The influence of the top and bottom on style. The top and bottom of wearing will have different contribution to the style analysis.

4.Fashion trend. Based on the styles of the wearing, we can analyze which season of which brand is similar.

In recommendation, user can get several matched top/ bottom after picking certain piece of clothes in wardrobe, dividing into different relevant styles. First, user can pick one piece in virtual wardrobe and request the recommendation of matched one. Hence, Magic Mirror will give several relevant styles to choose and show the recommended collocation in different styles. Then, user will pick the willing recommended one. In the end, it will show a simple try-on looking of the combination and give the appreciation.

3. CLOTHING COLLOCATION APPRECIATION VIA BDA-GCL MODEL

How to appreciate and recommend the clothing collocation? Internally, we aimed at a clothing appreciation system, which uses the clothing photos as the input, then automatically parses the collocation of clothing.

3.1 Aesthetic Theory and Framework

In order to analyze the aesthetic style of collocation of tops and bottoms, we formulate the task to a three level framework: visual features (VF) - image-scale space (ISS) - aesthetic words space (AWS). We employ the ISS as an intermediate layer and map both visual features and aesthetic words space into it. In this way, we can label clothing images with aesthetic words automatically.

The visual features of clothing in this paper are defined from two aspects : the pattern features and color features. The pattern features of tops include collar shape, sleeve length and cut shape, of bottoms include waist height and both include sexy, length, patterns and materials. We extract pattern features by a deep neural network. The color

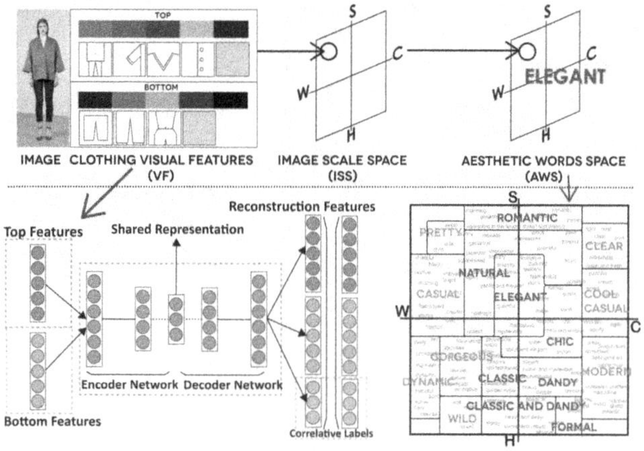

Figure 3: Framework and BDA-GCL Model.

features include five-color combination, brightness and its contrast, saturation and its contrast. ISS based on Kobayashi's aesthetic theory is a two-dimensional space (warm-cool and hard-soft), which has been used in appreciating menswear before and is proven to work effectively[3]. AWS consists of the words used to describe clothing in Amazon. Kobayashi proposed 180 keywords in 16 aesthetic categories and defined their coordinate values in ISS, considered as seed words. For a new word, we pick three of the most similar seed words depending on the semantic distances and calculate their mean value as the new coordinate value.(Figure 3)

3.2 Map visual feature to image scale space

In order to map visual features to the image-scale space (ISS), we divide the task into two steps. First, we propose a novel Bimodal Deep Autoencoder Guided by Correlative Labels (BDA-GCL) for feature learning. Second, we use several regression methods to make the new constructed features cast into two-dimensional coordinates in ISS.

A critical challenge of our task is how to calculate the specific influence of the aesthetic style by the relationship between tops and bottoms. We get several inspirations of multimodal learning[4]. More specifically, we consider the visual features of tops and bottoms as two different modals and put them into the autoencoder. We triple the training data and discard the top and bottom features separately as the other two parts data. In this way, our autoencoder can recover the whole clothing by only top or bottom features. The loss of the autoencoder can be counted as the indicator of the collocation. A smaller loss means that the tops and bottoms clothing match better.

Compared to classical autoencoder, we introduce correlative labels of clothing into the original symmetrical structure as another improvement. We choose the categories of clothing (e.g., sweater, shirt) as correlative labels. Then we use the network to regain the visual features and correlative labels at the same time. This method can be considered as a semi-supervised learning process.

As shown in the figure 3, the orange and green nodes present the top and bottom features of clothing, while the yellow nodes present the correlative labels. Through an encoder network and a decoder network indicated by the blue nodes, we regain the reconstruction features and correlative labels. And we consider the middle layer of the network as the results of feature learning.

Formally, we use the vector $x = [x_t, x_b]$ to indicate the visual features of a clothing image and c to indicate the correlative labels. The relationship between two adjacent hidden layers $h^{(l+1)}$ and h^l can be presented as:

$$h^{(l+1)} = s(W^{(l)}h^{(l)} + b^{(l)}) \tag{1}$$

where $W^{(l)}$ and $b^{(l)}$ are the parameters between lth layer and $(l+1)$th layer and s is the sigmoid function ($s(x) = \frac{1}{1+e^{-x}}$). Specially, $h^{(0)} = [x_t, x_b]$ and $[\hat{x_t}, \hat{x_b}, \hat{c}] = h^{(N_h+1)}$.

The loss function to evaluate the difference between $[x_t, x_b, c]$ and $[\hat{x_t}, \hat{x_b}, \hat{c}]$ is defined as:

$$J(W,b) = \frac{\lambda_1}{2m}\sum_{i=1}^{m}||x_t - \hat{x_t}||^2 + \frac{\lambda_2}{2m}\sum_{i=1}^{m}||x_b - \hat{x_b}||^2$$
$$+\frac{\lambda_3}{2m}\sum_{i=1}^{m}||c - \hat{c}||^2 + \frac{\lambda_4}{2}\sum_{l}(||W^{(l)}||_F^2 + ||b^{(l)}||_2^2) \tag{2}$$

where m is the number of samples, $\lambda_1, \lambda_2, \lambda_3, \lambda_4$ is a regularization hyperparameter and $||\cdot||_F$ denotes the Frobenius norm.

We define $\theta = (W, b)$ as our parameters. The training of BDA-GCL is optimized to minimize the cost function:

$$\theta^* = arg\min_{\theta} J(W,b) \tag{3}$$

To map visual features to the image-scale space, we further make the new constructed features produced by our model cast into two-dimensional coordinate. This step can be considered as a regression problem. We try using several regression models (e.g. K-Nearest Neighbor, Support Vector Machine, Linear Regression, Decision Tree).

3.3 Experiment

We conducted several objective experiments to validate the model by evaluating the mapping results between visual features(VF) of clothing images and coordinate values in image-scale space(ISS). In the experiment, we firstly compared the performances of different feature learning methods including denosing autoencoder(DA), bimodal strategy(B), guiding strategy(-GCL). Then we compare several regression algorithms with the output of BDA-GCL.

We employed clothing images from online clothing shop [1] and fashion website[2] as our experimental data. The dataset contains 100000 clothing images. Cooperating with Sougou company, we employ a group to manually label the dataset with the coordinate values in the ISS. In the evaluation of the mapping effects, we calculated the error between predicted coordinate values and labeled coordinate values. The error is formulated by mean squared error (MSE[3]). All the experiments are performed on five-folder cross-validation.

The experiment results are shown in Table 1 and Table 2. It is clear that our model BDA-GCL (MSE:0.1854) performs better than the baselines. And the results support the effectiveness of our guiding strategy and bimodal strategy. Comparing among several regression algorithms, we find that SVM and LR have the best results.

[1]http://www.Amazon.com
[2]http://www.style.com
[3]https://en.wikipedia.org/wiki/MSE

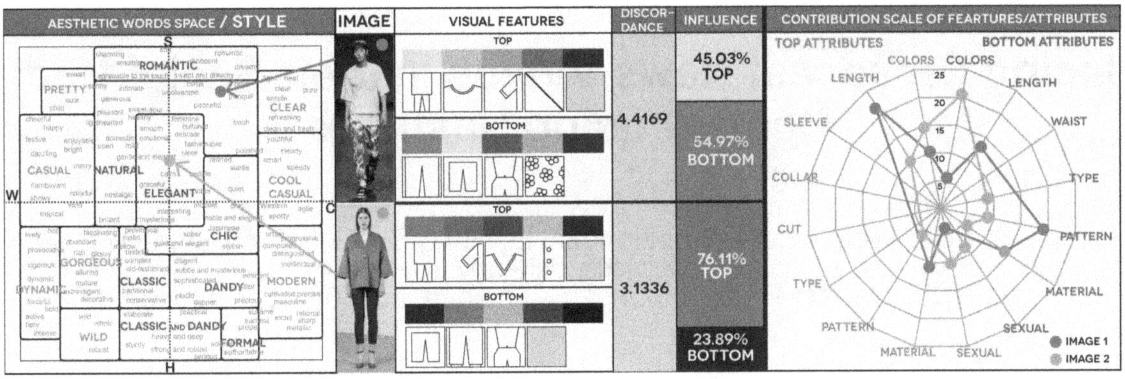

Figure 4: The Statement of Analysis Results.

Table 1: Comparison among different feature learning methods

Autoencoder	Regression	MSE
None		0.1927
DA		0.1928
DA-GCL	SVM	0.1860
BDA		0.1881
BDA-GCL		0.1854

Table 2: Comparison among different regression models

Autoencoder	Regression	MSE
BDA-GCL	D-Tree	0.3378
	KNN	0.3324
	LR	0.1854
	SVM	0.1854

3.4 Analysis Results

Using our framework, we can not only analyze the style of certain clothing image, but also conclude several interesting aesthetic rules to support our recommendation:(Figure 4)

1. The distribution of relevant styles of the wearing. The collocation of the top and bottom locates at a coordinate in the aesthetic words space. We can calculate the correlation between the coordinate and rounded styles.

2. The different roles of tops and bottoms clothing playing in the aesthetics effect. We compare the errors between using whole features and using single tops or bottoms features to analyze the different contributions of them.

3. The discordance of tops and bottoms. We use the value from zero to infinite to measure the discordance that if the value close to the infinite, the collocation is more discordant.

4. The different contributions of various visual features. For example, as shown in the Figure 4, the length of tops have larger influence in the Image 1 than that in Image 2, while the color features play a more important in role in the Image 2 than Image 1.

5. The indicator of the collocation. Our autoencoder can measure the harmony of tops and bottoms. So even with the loss of piece, we can get the matched one.

6. The aesthetic style of brands. We analyze the aesthetic style distribution of brands and take them into consideration when we recommend clothing.

4. USER STUDY

We employed 11 people, 5 males and 6 females, to participant the user study. First, participants try to use Magic Mirror to appreciate the current wearing. Then we investigated their satisfaction of appreciation that 10/11 participants thought Magic Mirror gave them great appreciation about wearing. Next, we provided them some pieces of top that let them choose the matched bottom in several limited styles from the wardrobe. We compared their choices with the first five recommended ones by Magic Mirror. 89 percent choices are in the first five. Hence, the recommendation of Magic Mirror is appropriate and rational. According to the study, we can conclude that the Magic Mirror truly gave the similar wearing suggestions of the participants and make them feel appreciated.

5. FUTURE WORK

In this work, Magic Mirror mainly focused on mining general rules based on the popular aesthetics and fashion trend to guide users wearing. In fact, personal factors have no small impact on wearing in daily life, such as user's taste and figure. In the future, we will investigate such personalization thoroughly.

6. ACKNOWLEDGMENTS

This work is supported by National Key Research and Development Plan(2016YFB1001200), the National Basic Research Program (973 Program) of China (2012CB316401) and National Natural, and Science Foundation of China (61370023).

7. REFERENCES

[1] N. Garcia. *The little black book of style.* Harper Collins, 2010.

[2] N. Garcia. *Nina GarciaâĂŹs Look Book: What to Wear for Every Occasion.* Harper Collins, 2010.

[3] J. Jia, J. Huang, G. Shen, T. He, Z. Liu, H. Luan, and C. Yan. Learning to appreciate the aesthetic effects of clothing. In *Thirtieth AAAI Conference on Artificial Intelligence*, 2016.

[4] J. Ngiam, A. Khosla, M. Kim, J. Nam, H. Lee, and A. Y. Ng. Multimodal deep learning. In *Proceedings of the 28th international conference on machine learning (ICML-11)*, pages 689–696, 2011.

Placing Broadcast News Videos in their Social Media Context using Hashtags

Joseph G. Ellis, Svebor Karaman, Hongzhi Li, Hong Bin Shim and Shih-Fu Chang
Columbia University
{jge2105, svebor.karaman, hongzhi.li, h.shim, sc250}@columbia.edu

ABSTRACT

With the growth of social media platforms in recent years, social media is now a major source of information and news for many people around the world. In particular the rise of hashtags have helped to build communities of discussion around particular news, topics, opinions, and ideologies. However, television news programs still provide value and are used by a vast majority of the population to obtain their news, but these videos are not easily linked to broader discussion on social media. We have built a novel pipeline that allows television news to be placed in its relevant social media context, by leveraging hashtags. In this paper, we present a method for automatically collecting television news and social media content (Twitter) and discovering the hashtags that are relevant for a TV news video. Our algorithms incorporate both the visual and text information within social media and television content, and we show that by leveraging both modalities we can improve performance over single modality approaches.

Keywords

video analysis; video news; hash tagging; social media

1. INTRODUCTION

Social media platforms are a primary source of news information for many users. Twitter, in particular, is one of the most popular social media platform for news consumption and dissemination. Indeed, information about an event is often first posted on Twitter, oftentimes through first hand accounts of a news event. After this an engaging discussion is then added to and commented on by news agencies or other media outlets. Twitter users are often very active and post their opinions about news event by posting new tweets or reposting the existing popular tweets, enabling quick and wide spread dissemination of any information deemed valuable. To help build a conversation around a particular event, topic, or idea, Twitter users link their tweets to a subject by using hashtags. A hashtag, is a short word or acronym preceded by the "#" sign. Hashtags can then be searched easily within social media sites, making it simple to quickly obtain cogent information about a possibly very narrow topic or opinion in an efficient manner. This is the simplest way

MM '16, October 15 - 19, 2016, Amsterdam, Netherlands

ISBN 978-1-4503-3603-1/16/10. . . $15.00

DOI: http://dx.doi.org/10.1145/2964284.2970929

Table 1: Examples of found hashtags for a set of news programs using our multimodal algorithm. Hashtags in red were found predominantly using our text pipeline, and those in blue were found using predominantly visual pipelines.

Frame from video	Found hashtags
	#politics, #trump2016, #realdonaldtrump, #goptownhall, #votetrumpsc
	#politics, #dumptrump, #realdonaldtrump, #gopdebate
	#iphone, #apple, #cybersecurity

to link related content into threads on social media platforms. As the discussion grows and evolve, different hashtags can be used in relation to a subject and the meaning of some hashtags may not be obvious given only the hashtag. Twitter users often like to use short hashtags due to the restriction on the number of characters in a tweet. Thus, to engage efficiently in the discussion requires some understanding of the hashtags related to a subject.

Although social media platforms have become major sources of news, especially for young people, traditional TV news still provides a unique value to customers. The news videos usually provide rich video footage and professional commentators' opinion which many not be covered by social media. Twitter attracts attentions from major news agencies and TV channels as it can provide an increased reach for their content. However, the content from TV broadcasts has to be properly integrated in the social media context in order to maximize this reach. By linking the broadcast news videos to hashtags, we let Twitter users have easy access to high quality content and can help TV news channels with a unique opportunity to reach a much wider audience.
The contributions of this paper are as follows:

- We present a pipeline and algorithms for automatically collecting social media and television news video and linking hashtags used on Twitter to the videos.
- We show improved performance for linking hashtags to television news when leveraging a multimodal approach over single visual or text modalities, demonstrating the importance of taking into account multiple modalities for this task.

2. RELATED WORKS

Twitter is one of the largest and fastest paced information channels on the Internet. For example, during the 2011 Tohoku earthquake information traveled throughout Twitter incredibly fast [19, 7]. Thanks to its rich amount and quick spreading of information, Twitter data attracts researchers from many different areas. Twitter data can be used to predict and respond to customers' complaints [10, 16], to predict election results, gather and spread breaking news, and even crime prediction [24].

An interesting and challenging problem using Twitter data is event detection and tracking. Topic Detection and Tracking (TDT) is a traditional research topic, which focus on finding events and linking documents to the related event in broadcast news streams [26, 25, 1]. However, TDT on twitter data faces new challenges due to the limited number of characters used in twitter messages and also the large number of noise and meaningless messages on twitter [9]. Several advanced methods have been developed recently to address the event detection and tracking problem on twitter data, to detect unspecified types of events [20, 18, 17], or discover predefined types of events from twitter messages [19, 4, 15].

Hashtags are used by social media users to convey an idea, event or feeling that is associated with a post. Recently, researchers have worked on automatically tagging a user's images with hashtags based on their user specific information [6, 2, 3]. In this application, we use hashtags [22, 5, 21, 23, 8] to organize tweets as topics and link them to broadcasting TV news events.

3. DATA COLLECTION

In this section we will describe the collection of data used for this work. We have collected a large scale multimodal dataset from twitter and broadcast news videos. The data that we have collected consists of content from the dates of 02/15/2016 - 02/24/2016.

3.1 Video news

To collect our set of video news programs we have built a recording infrastructure that automatically processes 100 hours of broadcast television news per day [13]. We begin by segmenting each of the full television programs into smaller semantically coherent segments that tend to be between 1-8 minutes long, and consist of one distinct topic. This segmentation is done using multimodal inputs, such as audio silence, anchor scenes, and text cues [11]. We have collected 3823 videos from this time window that should be used for matching to social media hashtags. Each of the videos include the closed caption transcripts that are associated with the video, and these are used for text matching.

3.2 Tweets

We collect tweets from the same 02/15/2016-02/24/2016 timeframe. To perform our tweet collection we have set up an infrastructure for downloading and crawling the freely available twitter public stream [1]. The Twitter public stream is a random sampling of the full twitter dataset, and therefore should be a reasonable representation of all of the information that flows through Twitter. The information from the public stream is returned in json formatted strings, and each tweet representation can consist of but is not limited to the following categories: images, videos, text, hashtags, usernames, geotags, timepoints, retweet status. Any tweets that did not contain hashtags were not used in our dataset. The collection statistics of our full dataset can be seen in Table 2. We can see that our dataset has over 2 million tweets, and more than 1 million images.

[1]https://dev.twitter.com/streaming/public

Table 2: Twitter Dataset Statistics

Hashtags	355,403
Tweets	2,778,052
Word Vocabulary Size	327,442
Images	1,000,941
Users	422,947

4. VIDEO HASHTAGGING

In this section we will detail the algorithms and pipeline that we have used for processing the videos. Our goal is to link hashtags collected from Twitter to our video dataset. When attempting to process information on Twitter and in other microblogging formats, the information contained in one piece of information (tweet, post, etc.) tends to be very sparse, due to the small nature of each particular instance compared to the entire search space of the whole dataset. To solve this issue we have developed a framework that helps to densify the representation of social media data. Hashtags represent the idea, content, and feeling of a particular post and are therefore important for posting and searching social media. We thus organize all our Twitter content into hashtag representations.

We develop the following framework and representation for a hashtag. The ith hashtag in our dataset is represented by a vector of the words (H_i^w) that are contained in tweets that have been marked with this hashtag. The images that are from tweets with this hashtag are represented as the set, (H_i^v). We read over each of the tweets in our dataset, and augment the representation for each (H_i^w) using the words from the tweet if a hashtag appears in that particular tweet. Through this approach, we are able to build a dense representation for each hashtag based on all of the tweets that contain the hashtag. This allows for a more complete and robust representation of a topic than standard tweet-only approaches. We discard any hashtags that do not contain *at least* 300 tweets or *at least* 50 images as we are looking for popular hashtags. We represent the video news segments with a set of subsampled frames appearing in the segment (V_j^v), and the full closed caption transcript (V_j^w).

4.1 Text modalities

In this section we will describe how we link hashtags to broadcast news using text content. In our text matching frameworks we use unigram text features. In this work we have implemented two separate but related pipelines for performing text mapping. First, we have implemented a classic bag of words mapping pipeline that leverages the words that appear in each hashtag and the transcript for each video. This method, which we refer to as "bag-of-words", tends to work well for hashtags that have densely sampled our word vocabulary. However, for hashtags that have fewer tweets the bag of words representation can be quite sparse, and this can cause spurious matches to video transcripts.

Therefore, to overcome this issue we have developed a novel pipeline for matching hashtag text to video transcript. Our second method, which we will call "hashtag-probing" relies on first finding the most important words for each particular hashtag, and then using these words as a "probe" to find which videos contain information associated with this hashtag.

4.1.1 Bag-of-Words

For the "bag-of-words" representation of hashtags, we first filter all stopwords and words from our vocabulary that do not have at least 30 occurrences within our dataset. This filtering aims at removing words that appear only sparsely in social media. After this filtering our vocabulary size is $30,845$.

Let our word count vector for the i'th hashtag be defined as:

$$H_i^c = \{c_{i1}, c_{i2}, ..., c_{in}\},$$

where n is the number or words in our vocabulary, and c_{ik} represents the frequency of the k'th term of the vocabulary w_{ik} in the i'th hashtag. We build similarly the representation for the j'th video transcript, represented by V_j^c, using the same vocabulary as generated from our hashtags. We compute the *idf* weight of each word over all of the hashtags, and then apply a *tf-idf* weighting scheme on both the transcript representations and hashtags representations. Finally, we define the bag of words scoring function as the cosine similarity between the two *tf-idf* transformed vectors.

$$S_{BoW}(H_i^c, V_j^c) = \cos(\mathit{tfidf}(H_i^c), \mathit{tfidf}(V_j^c)), \tag{1}$$

4.1.2 *Hashtag-Probing*

We begin by finding the most relevant k unigram terms from all words associated with a hashtag, H_i^w. To accomplish this, we use *tf-idf* with logarithmic weighting over each term in the vector to represent each hashtag, which can be seen below,

$$\mathit{log\text{-}tfidf}(w_{ik}) = \frac{\log(c_{ik})}{(1 + log(df_{ht}(w_{ik})))}, \tag{2}$$

where $df_{ht}(w_{ik})$ is the number of hashtags this word appears in. We then take the top-k magnitude terms to represent each hashtag. In our experiments we set k to 40, and we represent the 40 probe-terms in used for this hashtag as H_i^{pr}.

Finally, we have developed the following hashtag scoring function representing how closely a hashtag relates to a given transcript:

$$S_{pr}(H_i^{pr}, V_j^w) = \sum_{t_x \in V_j^w} \mathcal{I}_{H_i^{pr}}(t_x) \frac{1}{1 + log(df_{ht}(t_x))}, \tag{3}$$

where V_j^w is the set of words that appear in the j'th video transcript, t_x is a word in the transcript, and $\mathcal{I}_{H_i^{pr}}$ is an indicator function that denotes if t_x appears in H_i^{pr}. We will compare this methodology to the "bag-of-words" approach in Sec. 5.

4.2 Visual modalities

In addition to the use of text analysis detailed above, we are looking into finding similarities between the broadcast news videos and the visual content posted on social media. We rely on three different types of representation: full images, faces and mid-level patterns. We detail in this section how each representation is computed and used to obtain a similarity score between videos and hashtags.

4.2.1 *Full image matching*

We first are looking for video frames and images posted on social media that may be depicting the same scene. We extract a global descriptor from each image in our dataset, either video frames or social media images. We decided to use the pre-trained *hybrid-CNN* model [30], which follows Caffe reference network architecture and has been trained on both the ImageNet and Places datasets, as it is a generic global feature able to cope with the variations of scene that can be depicted in news video and in images posted on social media. The *hybridCNN* feature of an image is extracted from the *fc7* layer and lies in $\mathbb{R}^{4096}$. The *hybridCNN* features are $l2$-normalized and compared with Euclidean distances.

Figure 1: Example of face matching. Left column: frames of news videos, right column: images from Twitter. Detected matching faces are overlaid as green rectangles.

The *full* similarity $S_F(H_i^F, V_j^F)$ between a hashtag i and a video j is defined as:

$$S_F(H_i^F, V_j^F) = \sum_{v_j^k \in V_j^F} \sum_{h_i^l \in H_i^F} \mathbf{I}(d(v_j^k, h_i^l) < t_F) \frac{1}{d(v_j^k, h_i^l)}, \tag{4}$$

where t_F is a threshold on the distance set to 0.6 in our experiments, v_j^k is the feature of keyframe i in video j, h_i^l is the feature from image l of a hashtag i, V_j^F is the set of features for the keyframes of video j and H_i^F is the set of features from images in a hashtag H_i.

4.2.2 *Face matching*

A topic or event is often heavily related to a small set of key persons. When analyzing the visual content, the most reliable information to identify people are their faces. Face bounding boxes are obtained through the face detector NPD [14] run on all the keyframes of the videos and on all images of hashtags selected for visual matching. Each bounding box is then described by a binary code of 512 bits, enabling fast face matching computation using the hamming distance. We trained a deep network for face classification on the CASIA Webface dataset [27]. We use the architecture defined in [27], with one additional fully connected layer of 512 nodes with sigmoid activation, namely the "hash layer" between the *pool5* and *fc6* layers. Given a cropped face image using the NPD bounding box, we extract the activations of the hash layer and binarize it by thresholding the output at 0.5. An example of face match obtained is given in Figure 1. The *face* similarity $S_{fa}(H_i^{fa}, V_j^{fa})$ between a hashtag i and a video j is defined similarly as Eq. (4) but restricted to the single best match using the hamming distance and setting the *face* acceptance threshold (t_f) to 0.2.

4.2.3 *Image Pattern Matching*

Visual patterns are discriminative and representative image patches in a given image set. Visual patterns are often used as mid level image feature representation in image retrieval and classification tasks [28, 29]. We follow the pipeline proposed in [12] to discover visual

Figure 2: Example of matched image pairs using the pattern bank. Left column: frames of news videos, right column: images from Twitter. Some faces in the second row were blurred.

patterns in the images associated with each hashtag. Visual patterns are aggregated to form a *pattern bank*. We then detect visual patterns from all images in twitter and all frames in news videos. Each image or frame is represented by the set of visual patterns which are detected in it. The similarity of a twitter hashtag and video is defined as the Jaccard similarity between their detected pattern sets, where V_j^{pa} is the patterns extracted from the jth video, and H_k^{pa} are the patterns extracted from the kth hashtag, see below. Only hashtags with similarity values higher than 0.25 are considered.

$$S_{pa}(V_i^{pa}, H_k^{pa}) = \frac{P_{V_i^{pa}} \cap P_{H_k^{pa}}}{P_{V_i^{pa}} \cup P_{H_k^{pa}}}. \quad (5)$$

4.3 Multimodal Fusion

Each of our particular matching methods have strength and weaknesses to link hashtags to the video content. Some hashtags may have iconic images but few tweets, hence having sparse text representations that are hard to match, but may match well using the visual modalities. Leveraging a combination of each methods should provide a performance gain over one single approach. We include a normalizing constant for each component so that the each of the scoring functions produce results of similar magnitudes for their best matches. Therefore, we propose the following linear combination of our 5 scoring functions, to obtain the final multi-modal score $S_{mm}(H_k, V_i)$:

$$\begin{aligned} S_{mm}(H_k, V_i) = &\alpha_{BoW} S_{BoW}(H_k^w, V_i^w) + \alpha_{pr} S_{pr}(H_k^{pr}, V_i^w) \\ &+ \alpha_F S_F(H_k^F, V_i^F) + \alpha_{fa} S_{fa}(H_k^{fa}, V_i^{fa}) \\ &+ \alpha_{pa} S_{pa}(H_k^{pa}, V_i^{pa}), \end{aligned} \quad (6)$$

where the α_* are normalization weights estimated from all hashtags as $\alpha_{pr} = \frac{1}{\max(S_{pr}(\cdot, V_i^w))}$, $\alpha_{BoW} = \frac{1}{\max(S_{BoW}(\cdot, V_i^w))}$, $\alpha_{pa} = \frac{1}{\max(S_{pa}(\cdot, V_i^{pa}))}$, $\alpha_{fa} = \frac{1}{\max(S_{fa}(\cdot, V_i^{fa}))}$, and $\alpha_F = \frac{0.5}{\max(S_F(\cdot, V_i^F))}$ as the full image matching is the noisiest modality. Note that these weights are video specific.

Table 3: Evaluation results.

Methods	MAP@1	MAP@2	MAP@3	MAP@5
BoW (text)	0.64	0.66	0.63	0.56
Probing (text)	0.80	0.67	0.62	0.50
Full (image)	0.24	0.20	0.16	0.13
Face (image)	0.51	0.39	0.31	0.25
Patterns (image)	0.49	0.39	0.37	0.32
Multimodal	**0.89**	**0.82**	**0.72**	**0.64**

5. EXPERIMENTS

5.1 Experimental setting

To evaluate the performance of our hashtagging algorithms we have annotated part of our dataset with relevant hashtags for each video. To obtain a very high recall of relevant hashtags for each video, we return all hashtags that are possible candidates according to any of our modalities. For example, we return all hashtags for which a word in the transcript can be found in the set of words of our hashtag probing algorithm. We obtain a large set of possible hashtags for each video to be pruned through manual annotation.

A hashtag is considered "relevant" to a video if the tweets and concepts behind the hashtag are closely related to the video content. We have developed a website for annotation in which the annotators can search tweets and photos from a hashtag, and then can decide if the hashtag is relevant for the given video. We annotated 47 news segments across a variety of different topics, and over 30 different news programs. We use mAP@K as our evaluation metric for the performance of our hashtagging algorithms. We present results for K equal to 1, 2, 3, and 5 as we are only looking for a small set of relevant hashtags.

5.2 Results

We can see the results from our methods in Table. 3. The text based methods have the highest performance for this task, which makes sense as a large portion of news is text-based. Our probing method performs better than the standard BoW approach for the top results in our retrieved hashtags. Whereas, the BoW method begins performing better when comparing hashtags we are not as confident about i.e. that are lower in the retrieved hashtag results. The visual content can also do a reasonable job of finding and predicting hashtags for videos, especially the face matching approach that gives the best visual mAP@1 performance and the pattern based approach which can find important local image patches within hashtags and then find these patches in the news frames.

However, our multimodal method performs the best across each of the different levels of mAP evaluation. The visual and text information are indeed complementary in nature for this task, which leads to improved performance, examples are shown in Table 1. With the high precision of our method we could enable a TV news channel to link their video content to social media discussions.

6. CONCLUSIONS

We have presented a new research challenge of linking television video content to its proper context within social media using hashtags. Our approach demonstrates the value of leveraging the visual and text modalities within both television and social media as they bring disparate but complimentary information for this task. We believe that automatically leveraging hashtags to place traditional media in its social media context is a useful and important challenge. We plan to extend the annotation and release our dataset in the future to foster research on this problem.

7. ACKNOWLEDGMENTS

This material is based upon work supported by the National Science Foundation Graduate Research Fellowship under Grant No. DGE-11-44155 and the Office of the Director of National Intelligence (ODNI), Intelligence Advanced Research Projects Activity (IARPA), via IARPA R&D Contract No. 2014-14071600012. Any opinion, views, findings, and conclusions expressed in this material are those of the authors and should not be interpreted as necessarily representing the views, official policies or endorsements, either expressed or implied, of the National Science Foundation, the ODNI, IARPA, or the U.S. Government. The U.S. Government is authorized to reproduce and distribute reprints for Governmental purposes notwithstanding any copyright annotation thereon.

8. REFERENCES

[1] J. Allan, J. G. Carbonell, G. Doddington, J. Yamron, and Y. Yang. Topic detection and tracking pilot study final report. 1998.

[2] S. Amer-Yahia, S. Anjum, A. Ghenai, A. Siddique, S. Abbar, S. Madden, A. Marcus, and M. El-Haddad. Maqsa: a system for social analytics on news.

[3] L. Ballan, M. Bertini, T. Uricchio, and A. Del Bimbo. Data-driven approaches for social image and video tagging. *Multimedia Tools and Applications*, 74(4):1443–1468, 2015.

[4] H. Becker, M. Naaman, and L. Gravano. Beyond trending topics: Real-world event identification on twitter. 2011.

[5] H.-C. Chang. A new perspective on twitter hashtag use: Diffusion of innovation theory. *Proc. of the American Society for Information Science and Technology*, 47(1):1–4, 2010.

[6] E. Denton, J. Weston, M. Paluri, L. Bourdev, and R. Fergus. User conditional hashtag prediction for images.

[7] S. Doan, B.-K. H. Vo, and N. Collier. An analysis of twitter messages in the 2011 tohoku earthquake. In *Electronic Healthcare*, pages 58–66. Springer, 2011.

[8] F. Godin, V. Slavkovikj, W. De Neve, B. Schrauwen, and R. Van de Walle. Using topic models for twitter hashtag recommendation. In *Proc. of the International Conference on World Wide Web*, pages 593–596, 2013.

[9] J. Hurlock and M. L. Wilson. Searching twitter: Separating the tweet from the chaff. In *ICWSM*, pages 161–168, 2011.

[10] L. Jiang, M. Yu, M. Zhou, X. Liu, and T. Zhao. Target-dependent twitter sentiment classification.

[11] B. Jou, H. Li, J. G. Ellis, D. Morozoff-Abegauz, and S.-F. Chang. Structured exploration of who, what, when, and where in heterogeneous multimedia news sources. In *Proc. of the 21st ACM international conference on Multimedia*, pages 357–360. ACM, 2013.

[12] H. Li, J. G. Ellis, H. Ji, and S.-F. Chang. Event specific multimodal pattern mining for knowledge base construction. In *Proceedings of the 24th ACM international conference on Multimedia*. ACM, 2016.

[13] H. Li, B. Jou, J. G. Ellis, D. Morozoff, and S.-F. Chang. News rover: Exploring topical structures and serendipity in heterogeneous multimedia news. In *Proc. of the 21st ACM international conference on Multimedia*, pages 449–450. ACM, 2013.

[14] S. Liao, A. Jain, and S. Li. A fast and accurate unconstrained face detector. *Transactions on Pattern Analysis and Machine Intelligence*, 2014.

[15] K. Massoudi, M. Tsagkias, M. De Rijke, and W. Weerkamp. Incorporating query expansion and quality indicators in searching microblog posts. In *Advances in information retrieval*, pages 362–367. Springer, 2011.

[16] A. Pak and P. Paroubek. Twitter as a corpus for sentiment analysis and opinion mining. In *LREc*, volume 10, pages 1320–1326, 2010.

[17] S. Petrović, M. Osborne, and V. Lavrenko. Streaming first story detection with application to twitter. In *Human Language Technologies: The 2010 Annual Conference of the North American Chapter of the Association for Computational Linguistics*, pages 181–189, 2010.

[18] S. Phuvipadawat and T. Murata. Breaking news detection and tracking in twitter. In *Web Intelligence and Intelligent Agent Technology (WI-IAT), 2010 IEEE/WIC/ACM International Conference on*, volume 3, pages 120–123. IEEE, 2010.

[19] T. Sakaki, M. Okazaki, and Y. Matsuo. Earthquake shakes twitter users: real-time event detection by social sensors. In *Proc. of the 19th international conference on World wide web*, pages 851–860. ACM, 2010.

[20] J. Sankaranarayanan, H. Samet, B. E. Teitler, M. D. Lieberman, and J. Sperling. Twitterstand: news in tweets. In *Proc. of the 17th acm sigspatial international conference on advances in geographic information systems*, pages 42–51. ACM, 2009.

[21] T. A. Small. What the hashtag? a content analysis of canadian politics on twitter. *Information, Communication & Society*, 14(6):872–895, 2011.

[22] O. Tsur and A. Rappoport. What's in a hashtag?: content based prediction of the spread of ideas in microblogging communities. In *Proc. of the fifth ACM international conference on Web search and data mining*, pages 643–652. ACM, 2012.

[23] A. Tumasjan, T. O. Sprenger, P. G. Sandner, and I. M. Welpe. Predicting elections with twitter: What 140 characters reveal about political sentiment. *ICWSM*, 10:178–185, 2010.

[24] X. Wang, M. S. Gerber, and D. E. Brown. Automatic crime prediction using events extracted from twitter posts. In *Social Computing, Behavioral-Cultural Modeling and Prediction*, pages 231–238. Springer, 2012.

[25] Y. Yang, J. G. Carbonell, R. D. Brown, T. Pierce, B. T. Archibald, and X. Liu. Learning approaches for detecting and tracking news events. *IEEE Intelligent Systems*, (4):32–43, 1999.

[26] Y. Yang, T. Pierce, and J. Carbonell. A study of retrospective and on-line event detection. In *Proc. of the 21st annual international ACM SIGIR conference on Research and development in information retrieval*, pages 28–36. ACM, 1998.

[27] D. Yi, Z. Lei, S. Liao, and S. Z. Li. Learning face representation from scratch. *arXiv preprint arXiv:1411.7923*, 2014.

[28] J. Yuan, Y. Wu, and M. Yang. Discovery of collocation patterns: from visual words to visual phrases. In *Computer Vision and Pattern Recognition, 2007. CVPR'07. IEEE Conference on*, pages 1–8. IEEE, 2007.

[29] J. Yuan, M. Yang, and Y. Wu. Mining discriminative co-occurrence patterns for visual recognition. In *Computer Vision and Pattern Recognition (CVPR), 2011 IEEE Conference on*, pages 2777–2784. IEEE, 2011.

[30] B. Zhou, A. Lapedriza, J. Xiao, A. Torralba, and A. Oliva. Learning deep features for scene recognition using places database. In *Advances in neural information processing systems*, pages 487–495, 2014.

MARIM: Mobile Augmented Reality for Interactive Manuals

Tam V. Nguyen
Department of Computer Science
University of Dayton
vantam@gmail.com

Dorothy Tan, Bilal Mirza, Jose Sepulveda
ARTIC Research Center, Singapore Polytechnic
bilal2@e.ntu.edu.sg, {dorothy_tan, sepulveda_jose}@sp.edu.sg

ABSTRACT

In this work, we present a practical system which uses mobile devices for interactive manuals. In particular, there are two modes provided in the system, namely, expert/trainer and trainee modes. Given the expert/trainer editor, experts design the step-by-step interactive manuals. For each step, the experts capture the images by using phones/tablets and provide visual instructions such as interest regions, text, and action animations. In the trainee mode, the system utilizes the existing object detection and tracking algorithms to identify the step scene and retrieve the respective instruction to be displayed on the mobile device. The trainee then follows the displayed instruction. Once each step is performed, the trainee commands the devices to proceed to the next step.

Keywords

Augmented Reality, Authoring Tool, Interactive Manuals

1. INTRODUCTION

Today, thanks to the massive coverage of the Internet, people are able to access to useful do-it-yourself materials to help them in their work and daily lives. Situations where individuals need to get quick instructions can range from fixing consumer devices to cooking or baking. Some of these do-it-yourself materials can be found from popular video websites, *i.e.*, YouTube [1]. Others can be found from the websites such as Instructables [2] and wikiHow [3]. However, people are usually impatient to follow the full instruction videos and the instructions are not well organized which causes the users to get lost at some point. Also, there is a lack of interactive method to deliver the instructions to trainees in the conventional methods.

In recent years, the rapid proliferation of smartphones and tablets is profoundly changing the way that we behave, consume content and conduct commerce. Almost all of inexpensive smartphones are equipped with cameras, wireless network, gyroscope, and accelerometer. The improvements in imaging capabilities and computational power have given a rise to many exciting mobile applications. Augmented Reality (AR) is a technology applied for training purpose. Although there are many AR systems for learning, researchers do not usually use the most important feature of AR - showing an explicit relationship between the virtual learning content and real objects found in the natural environment.

MM '16 October 15-19, 2016, Amsterdam, Netherlands

ACM ISBN 978-1-4503-3603-1/16/10.

DOI: http://dx.doi.org/10.1145/2964284.2973807

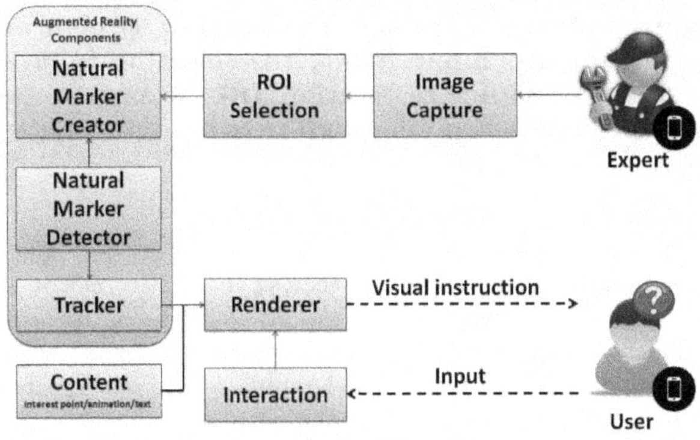

Figure 1: The flowchart of MARIM system.

Witnessing the demand of users and the growth of mobile devices, we would like to create a mobile AR-based system that serves as a platform where experts can create and upload manual instructions that can be used by the user to train themselves for the tasks. This new type of training will be based on mobile platforms tapping on all the capabilities. As a solution we propose a system named MARIM, known as Mobile Augmented Reality for Interactive Manuals, which guides the trainees to do things and at the same time ensures that they are doing it right. A short video about our system is available at https://www.youtube.com/watch?v=3LkwO41eXrM.

2. TECHNICAL DETAILS

Figure 1 depicts the major components of our system. Our proposed system supports two modes, namely, trainer editor mode where the experts can design the manuals, and the trainee mode where the users can use the created manuals to solve their problems.

2.1 Expert/Trainer Editor

The actual flowchart of the editor mode is illustrated in Fig. 2. First, the image is retrieved from mobile camera. The expert chooses the interactive points on the image and

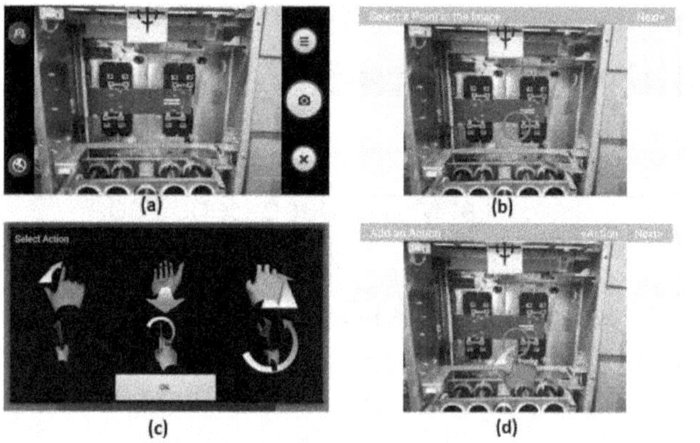

Figure 2: The screenshots of our expert/trainer editor mode. (a) input frame, (b) selecting interest point, (c) providing instruction, (d) the superimposition of instruction and interest point.

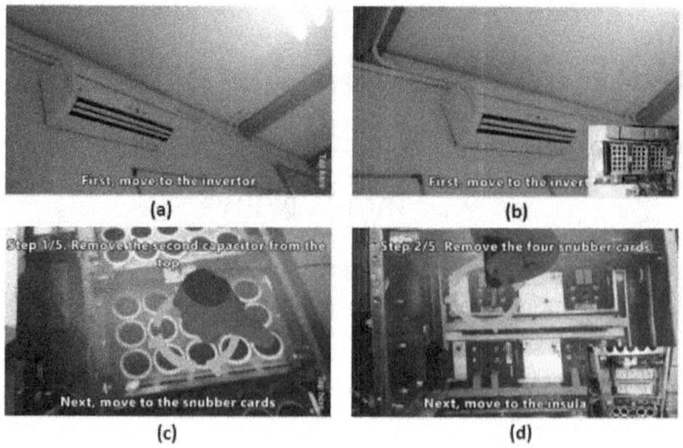

Figure 3: The screenshots of our user/trainee usage mode. (a) the instruction in the text form, (b) the reference photo to guide the trainee, (c) the superimposition of the action animation and text in the video frame, (d) the following step is displayed.

selects the corresponding instructions, *i.e.*, text and action animation. When the system receives these information, it finds the region of interests of the input image by incorporating its saliency map from the real-time AH method [6] and the interactive points (with applied Gaussian kernel) input by the experts. The regions with high salient values will be kept while a Guassian blur [7] is applied to the other regions. This is to ensure that the image matching and tracking functions focus more on the main object and the interactive points. Next, the feature extraction is applied to extract the keypoint descriptors, *i.e.*, SIFT [5], of the feature points. Note that the chosen descriptors are invariant to noise, scale, and rotation. Lastly, all the fine-tuned images, instruction information and keypoint descriptors are stored on the manual database.

2.2 User/Trainee Guidance

The trainees log into the system and select the appropriate manuals for their repairing tasks. As shown in Fig. 3, the trainee mode shows the instruction in the text form. In addition, the trainee mode shows the reference photo to guide the trainee point to the correct scene. Meanwhile, the video frame from the live streaming of mobile camera undergoes the feature extraction, namely, keypoint descriptors. Next, the keypoints of the current video frame are matched with the ones of the stored images in the scenario. Once the frame is matched, the system performs image tracking and compute the camera pose to the scene. Then, then instruction information associated with the current step is delivered back to the user's device, and the information is superimposed on top of the video image. Once each step is done, the trainee commands the devices to proceed to the next step via touch screen interface.

It is worth noting that the interactive manuals implicitly support reparation step verification. In other words, it means that the users will be reminded if they forget to perform any step. Our system is also supported on head mounted display [4], a mobile augmented reality device that provides an immersive augmented reality experience, and frees user's hands to do the task. The actual usage of the trainee mode is illustrated in Fig. 3.

3. DEMONSTRATION PLAN

For the demonstration, we will show our system with two modes, expert/editor and trainee modes. Demo presenters provide all necessary items for the demo, such as laptops, smart phones and tablets. Given the demo application, the participants are encouraged to generate interesting manuals in the editor mode and actually exploit the created scenarios to amend things. During the demonstration, we will also provide users guidance through steps by steps as shown in Fig. 2 and Fig. 3.

4. CONCLUSIONS

We have developed a user-friendly application creating interactive manuals from mobile devices. Given a reparation scenario, the MARIM system allows the expert to create the interactive manuals. In the meantime, the trainee can download the manuals to repair his/her own stuffs. Limited by the current performance of image matching and object tracking, some sudden camera movements may make the object mistracked. This issue can be further alleviated along with the development of state-of-the-art tracking methods. We believe this work can inspire more research in the future.

5. ACKNOWLEDGEMENTS

This work was supported by Singapore Ministry of Education under research Grant MOE2014-TIF-1-G-007.

6. REFERENCES

[1] YouTube. http://www.youtube.com/.
[2] Instructables. http://www.instructables.com/.
[3] WikiHow. http://www.wikihow.com/.
[4] Epson Moverio glasses. https://www.epson.com/cgi-bin/Store/jsp/Landing/moverio-bt-2000-smart-headset.do.
[5] D. Lowe. Distinctive image features from scale-invariant keypoints. *International Journal of Computer Vision*, 60(2):91–110, 2004.
[6] T. V. Nguyen and J. Sepulveda. Salient object detection via augmented hypotheses. In *International Joint Conference on Artificial Intelligence*, pages 2176–2182, 2015.
[7] G. Stockman and L. G. Shapiro. *Computer Vision.* Prentice Hall PTR, Upper Saddle River, NJ, USA, 1st edition, 2001.

A Live Face Swapper

Shengtao Xiao [1,2] *
xiao_shengtao@u.nus.edu

Luoqi Liu [2]
liuluoqi@360.cn

Xuecheng Nie [1,2]
niexuecheng@gmail.com

Jiashi Feng [1]
elefjia@nus.edu.sg

Ashraf A. Kassim [1]
ashraf@nus.edu.sg

Shuicheng Yan [2,1]
eleyans@nus.edu.sg

[1] Department of Electrical and Computer Engineering, National University of Singapore
[2] Artificial Intelligence Institute, 360

ABSTRACT

In this technical demonstration, we propose a face swapping framework, which is able to interactively change the appearance of a face in the wild to a different person/creature's face in real time on a mobile device. To realize this objective, we develop a deep learning-based face detector which is able to accurately detect faces in the wild. Our face feature points tracking system based on progressive initialization ensures accurate and robust localization of facial landmarks under extreme poses and expressions in real time. Relying on the advances of our face detector and face feature points tracker, we construct the Face Swapper which can smoothly replace the face appearance of a user in real time.

Categories and Subject Descriptors

J.5 [**Arts and Humanities**]: Arts, fine and performing

Keywords

Face replacement; Facial animation

1. INTRODUCTION

Facial animation is one of the key components in the entertainment industries. To transform an actor/actress's facial appearance to that of a different person/creature, in most computer aided imagery movies, e.g. Planet of the Apes and Avatar, an actor/actress is required to wear a facial expression capturing device which usually consists of markers on the face and a wearable camera. The markers aim to provide accurate tracking of facial landmarks. With recent progress of face detection and facial points tracking, we believe that these devices are indeed unnecessary. In this demonstration, we show that without these expensive devices, face replacement can be achieved practically on a mobile device.

*This work was performed when Mr. Shengtao Xiao was an intern at Artificial Intelligence Institute, 360

MM '16 October 15-19, 2016, Amsterdam, Netherlands

ACM ISBN 978-1-4503-3603-1/16/10.

DOI: http://dx.doi.org/10.1145/2964284.2973808

Our demonstration consists of three key tasks: face detection, facial landmarks tracking and face swapping. For a given image from a video stream, our application first detects the locations of possible face images. Based on the detected face bounding box, we first localize the 95 predefined face feature points. Our feature points tracker then smoothly track all feature points in a few milliseconds. Face swapper is then applied to the input face with a selected target face mask. All tasks can be performed in real time on a recent mainstream mobile device.

2. SYSTEM

2.1 System Overview

Fig. 1 shows the flowchart of the entire system. The face detection module is triggered periodically to save computational resources and ensure detection of new faces. Detection process is also turned on immediately when the landmark tracking fails. When a new face is detected, landmarks will be first localized. For coming frames, landmark tracking process will utilize the location information of landmarks detected/tracked in the previous frame. This tracking performance is automatically evaluated to ensure the accuracy of landmark locations. The detected/tracked landmarks are passed to the face swapper, by which the correspondence between the source face and the target face can be established. Image manipulation is then performed between the input face and the target face.

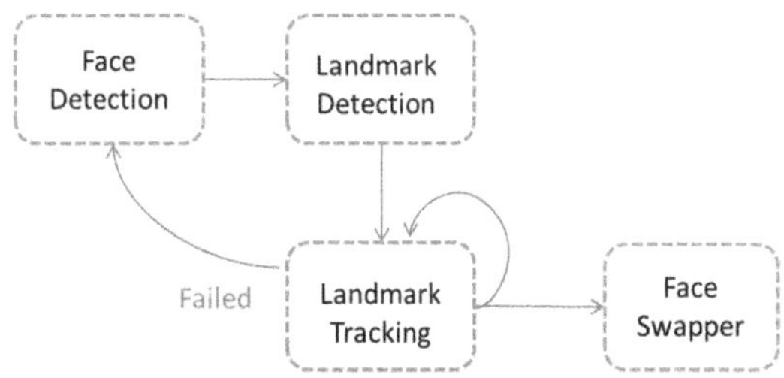

Figure 1: System flowchart.

2.2 Face Detection

We train our face detection model on the AFLW and Wider Face datasets with a framework similar to Faster R-CNN [2]. However, images from both data sets are from the

Internet, mostly with good lighting conditions. The training set is expanded by adding extra face images collected by ourselves based on application requirements. We train our detection model on the Caffe [1] platform. A deeply optimized version of key convolutional neural networks components, e.g. convolutional layer, pooling layer, fully connected layer, is realized for testing on the mobile devices. Our face detection model achieves 80% recall rate with 50 false positives on the FDDB dataset. It runs at around 20 FPS on an iPhone 6s Plus.

2.3 Facial Landmark Tracker

Accurate landmark locations and smooth tracking of the detected landmarks are essential for a good face swapper application. We follow the general framework proposed by [3] for facial landmark detection and tracking. The shape regressors are trained on a much larger training set. Each face image is annotated with 95 key points including face contour, eyebrows, eyes, nose and mouth lips. Xiao et al [3] used the variance of multiple regressed shapes as a measure of accuracy for the landmarks localized in the tracking process. We find that it is not very robust as it may easily reject face images with large poses. It also requires manually tuning the variance threshold which is not user friendly. We revised this process by introducing an adaption mechanism. This makes the landmark tracking process more robust to face images with large poses. Our optimized and revised version of [3] runs at the speed of 125 FPS on an iPhone 6s Plus, which shows dramatic enhancement on robustness, accuracy and speed. Fig. 2 shows that our framework can accurately and robustly track the facial points even under challenging conditions. Please refer to [3] for details of facial landmarks tracking.

Figure 2: Facial landmark tracking under challenging simulations, e.g. large poses, backlit, motion and half face. The green box indicates the face bounding box tracked with our framework and white dots are the localized landmarks.

2.4 Face Swapper

Based on the facial landmarks, a triangular mesh can be easily constructed with the Delaunay triangulation algorithm. In our framework, additional five points are used to create a face bounding box and a forehead reference point for morphing. Fig. 3 shows how the five additional points (in red) and the triangular mesh are generated. Now we can directly apply the triangular mesh based face morphing method. However, directly transforming the target face to a source face may distort the shape of the target face especially when the two faces have different face sizes. To maintain the target face's appearance, i.e. dimension, an additional step of warping the source face to a similar size of the target face is performed before we transform the source face to the target face. Face Swapper runs at a speed of 160 FPS on the iPhone 6s Plus.

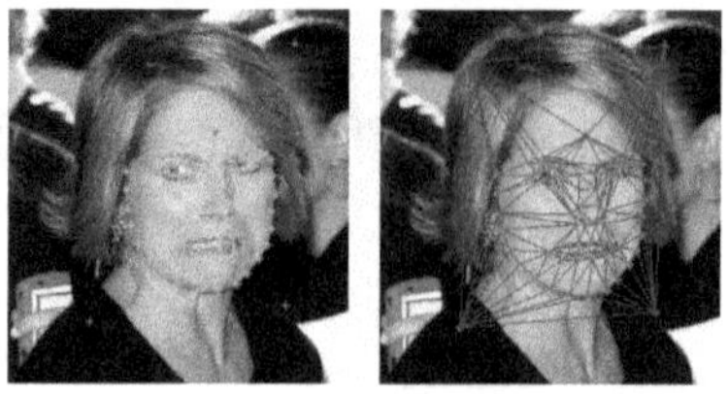

Figure 3: Key points (red and cyan dots) and triangular mesh (blue lines) used for face morphing.

3. INTERFACE

Fig. 4 shows the user interface and some selected results of the swapped face image. The user is able to select a face mask to change his/her facial appearance. This application can also show the facial landmarks tracked. Fig. 4 demonstrates that our application can seamlessly swap the face of the input image to a target face even under large poses and expressions. More results can be found in the supplementary material.

Figure 4: Interface of demonstration. A few masks that have been used in this demonstration. The visual effects after face swapping for corresponding face masks are shown here.

4. CONCLUSION

In this demonstration, we showcase an interactive face swapper framework which runs on a mobile device in real time. Based on our robust, accurate and computationally efficient face detection and landmark tracking modules, our face swapper system shows stable and nearly real facial appearance. In the future, we will introduce more features to the face swapper, e.g. hair style.

5. REFERENCES

[1] Y. Jia, E. Shelhamer, J. Donahue, S. Karayev, J. Long, R. Girshick, S. Guadarrama, and T. Darrell. Caffe: Convolutional architecture for fast feature embedding. *arXiv preprint arXiv:1408.5093*, 2014.

[2] S. Ren, K. He, R. Girshick, and J. Sun. Faster r-cnn: Towards real-time object detection with region proposal networks. In *Advances in Neural Information Processing Systems*, pages 91–99, 2015.

[3] S. Xiao, S. Yan, and A. Kassim. Facial landmark detection via progressive initialization. In *Proceedings of the IEEE International Conference on Computer Vision Workshops*, pages 33–40, 2015.

WorkCache: Salvaging siloed knowledge

Scott Carter, Laurent Denoue, Matthew Cooper
FX Palo Alto Laboratory, Inc.
3174 Porter Drive
Palo Alto, California 94304 USA
carter,denoue,cooper@fxpal.com

ABSTRACT

The proliferation of workplace multimedia collaboration applications has meant on one hand more opportunities for group work but on the other more data locked away in proprietary interfaces. We are developing new tools to capture and access multimedia content from any source. In this demo, we focus primarily on new methods that allow users to rapidly reconstitute, enhance, and share document-based information.

CCS Concepts

Information systems → Information systems applications → Multimedia information systems → Multimedia content creation

Keywords

Multimedia capture and access; image processing; video processing; interactive documents

1. INTRODUCTION

New multimedia messaging tools (such as Slack) and an explosion of real-time video services have changed the landscape of everyday knowledge work, which is now increasingly collaborative and distributed. At the same time, this proliferation of group support applications has increased the amount of multimedia data tied to specific protocols and representations, counter-intuitively siloing data within work cliques that use a particular subset of tools. Overall, these trends can make it more difficult to share knowledge between disparate work groups, potentially limiting productivity as well as mitigating the type of spontaneous connections that can drive innovation [1].

Similarly, previous work we conducted investigating the uptake of real-time collaboration tools in the enterprise showed that workers use an array of different synchronous and asynchronous multimedia communication tools [2]. Typically, users have a set of applications that they prefer for personal use, but have to use a different set of applications for different work contexts because of various institutional or third-party demands. Furthermore, study participants reported that they often struggled to extract meaningful information from these siloed, and often unstructured data sources.

As a first step toward remedying this issue, we present WorkCache, a tool to capture, analyze, and index any screen-based content. With WorkCache, users can capture either multimedia or document-based content using a browser extension (Figure 1). Multimedia content is uploaded or streamed directly to

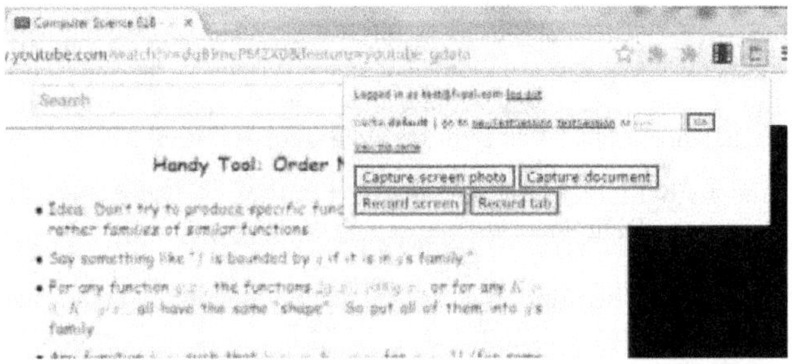

Figure 1. WorkCache includes an extension that allows users to capture multimedia screen content or documents. Screen content is uploaded to a back end server, indexed automatically, and added to a search-based user interface. Documents are sent to a separate service (see Figure 3).

a backend server, which then runs image- and video-based analysis to automatically index multimedia content (see [3] for details). Document-based content is handled using a new tool we developed to capture documents via screen recordings. Using image stitching techniques, the system analyses the screen recording and produces a copy of the original document that is immediately available online as a Web page, viewable on any device with a basic web browser. This web-based viewer shows each page as an image, including any interaction and voice comments that the author added while recording.

2. CREATING WORKCACHE DOCUMENTS

To record a document, users launch the document capture tool from the WorkCache extension and pick one window on their desktop that displays the document to capture, e.g. a window showing a Word file, and click a "Start" recording button.

They then interact freely with the document inside the application window, scrolling up and down through pages they wish to capture and share. During the recording, they have full access to the functions provided by the application, such as selecting text passages and moving their pointer over areas of the document. The system is able to recognize the two major kinds of document viewing metaphors: scrolling and pagination. All word processors or PDF viewers typically implement scrolling, while pagination is used for showing slide decks, e.g. PowerPoint. Using the same system, users can also pick a browser window showing a video of a lecture, in which the speaker is showing slides. At the end of the session, the user will have a reconstituted copy of the slides that were shown during the video lecture.

During users' interactions, the system analyses in real-time every captured frame of the window and turns them into an enhanced copy of the original document[1].

[1] See video at https://youtu.be/MTMpHwXj4dY

MM '16, October 15-19, 2016, Amsterdam, Netherlands
ACM 978-1-4503-3603-1/16/10.
http://dx.doi.org/10.1145/2964284.2973809

In order to generate this copy, the system applies four important steps: 1) Region of Interest (ROI) detection, 2) Image stitching, 3) Interaction lifting, and 4) Document generation.

ROI detection: Once the user is done recording, the system processes the first frame, binarizes it, and looks for long vertical and horizontal segments. It combines them to determine the largest rectangle as the ROI for that window.

If the system has correctly detected this ROI, the user simply clicks over the identified region and the system proceeds to the next step. Alternately, users simply drag a rectangle to manually specify what ROI to use. Some document types such as web pages do not have clear paginated layout, making it hard or impossible for an automatic ROI detector to find the correct rectangle.

Image stitching: Image stitching is a critical analytical step for the system. Brute force comparisons between frames to determine their vertical shift would be very CPU intensive. Instead, we borrow techniques from the image stitching literature [4] that use key point detection and matching as the basis for finding generic transformations between pairs of images and adapt it to our domain (Figure 2). These methods are fast and robust to some noise, making them appealing for a real-time implementation.

Figure 2. Vectors are matched in a vertical shift up: left previous frame, right next frame; blue lines join matching key-points (3 outliers); red dots show detected key-points.

Interaction lifting: Because the system records the screen as a video, users can also talk at the same time, e.g. to describe a figure that needs to be modified or express a feeling about a particular passage in the document. Authors can also interact with the document. These two features allow authors to add annotations to the document, a key component of active reading [5]. For example, an author can highlight specific words for revision with a co-author, or a teacher can explain a chart or figure by moving her cursor, or a lawyer can circle a whole section with her mouse cursor and ask a question verbally.

To detect these actions, it is enough to recognize when people only move their cursor and stop scrolling or paginating through the document.

Document generation: Given the set of frames and estimated shifts between them, the system generates a single composite image. Each frame is then copied at its corresponding Y position based on the accumulated delta offsets until that index. Special attention needs to be paid for cases when the user started recording her window at a later page and scrolls up.

Once the composite image is created, the system identifies likely page breaks: long horizontal lines that cross the whole ROI's width. Special attention is paid to small interrupted fragments; while recording, the mouse cursor has sometimes been found to overlap page boundaries, thus creating little discontinuities in the horizontal segments. To speed up implementation, our fast binarization step only computes the vertical gradient of the composite image so that it only detects horizontal edges.

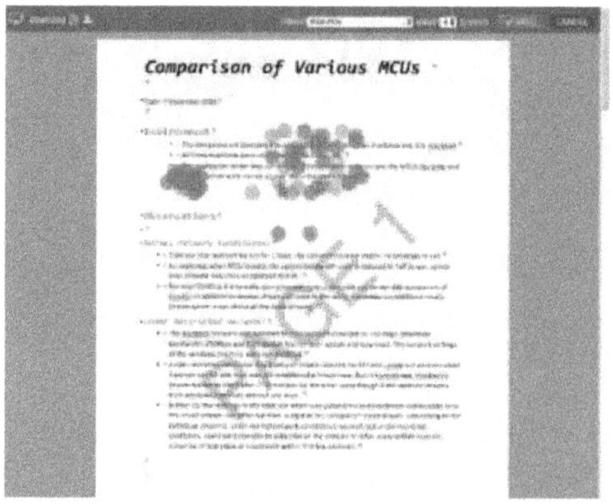

Figure 3. A sample reconstituted document; mouse actions and pages are preserved.

Once page breaks have been found, the system cuts the tall image into as many smaller page images as necessary, padding the last one with white space in case the user had not completely captured it, thus giving the inferred document pages a more uniform look.

Finally, detected actions are overlaid on the corresponding page images as a DIV element that depicts a mouse pointer (Figure 3). When clicked, the original motion path is used to play an animation of the fake mouse cursor. The corresponding voice segment is played at the same time by seeking the audio track to the start time and playing it until the end of the segment.

All image-processing algorithms run in real-time inside the user's web browser in JavaScript. The video frames are captured using the MediaDevices API available to modern web apps, allowing us to capture either the full desktop or individual windows.

3. CONCLUSION

We built WorkCache to ameliorate the increasingly siloed nature of multimedia content. In this demonstration, we will present our capture and analysis methods, focusing in particular on features to reconstitute and annotate digital documents.

4. REFERENCES

[1] I. Nonaka and H. Takeuci. The Knowledge-Creating Company: How Japanese Companies Create the Dynamics of Innovation. Oxford Press, Oxford. 1945.

[2] J. Marlow, S. Carter, N. Good, and J-W. Chen. Beyond Talking Heads: Multimedia Artifact Creation, Use, and Sharing in Distributed Meetings. In Proceedings of ACM CSCW, 1703-1715. 2016.

[3] S. Carter, L. Denoue, and M. Cooper. Searching and Browsing Live, Web-based Meetings. In Proceedings of ACM MM, 791-792. 2015.

[4] L. Zhu, Y. Wang, B. Zhao and X. Zhang. A Fast Image Stitching Algorithm Based on Improved SURF. In proceedings of CIS, 171-175. 2014.

[5] A. Adler, A. Gujar, B. L. Harrison, K. O'Hara, and A. Sellen. A diary study of work-related reading: design implications for digital reading devices. In Proceedings of ACM CHI, 241–248. 1998.

Hypervideo Production Using Crowdsourced Youtube Videos

Stefan John[1], Christian Handschigl[2], Britta Meixner[3], Michael Granitzer[2]
[1]Philipps-Universität Marburg, Hans-Meerwein-Straße 6, 35032 Marburg, Germany
[2]University of Passau, Innstraße 43, 94032 Passau, Germany
[3]FX Palo Alto Laboratory, 3174 Porter Drive, Palo Alto, CA 94304, USA
[1]stefan.john@uni-marburg.de, [2]firstname.lastname@uni-passau.de,
[2]meixner@fxpal.com

ABSTRACT

Hypervideos, consisting of media enriched and linked video scenes, have proven useful in many scenarios. Software solutions exist that help authors make hypervideos from media files. However, recording and editing video scenes for hypervideos is a tedious and time consuming job. Huge video databases like YouTube exist that can provide rich sources of video material. Yet it is often illegal to download and re-purpose videos from these sites, requiring a solution that links whole videos or parts of videos and plays them in an embedded player. This work presents the SIVA Web Producer, a Chrome extension for the creation of hypervideos consisting of scenes from YouTube videos. After creating a project, the SIVA Web Producer embeds YouTube videos or parts thereof as video clips. These can then be linked in a scene graph and extended with annotations. The plug-in provides a preview space for testing the hypervideo. Finalized videos can be published on the SIVA Web Portal or embedded in a Web page.

CCS Concepts

•Human-centered computing → Hypertext / hypermedia; Graphical user interfaces;

Keywords

Hypervideo; Crowdsourcing; Authoring; Chrome Extension

1. INTRODUCTION

Hypervideos consist of linked video scenes. A scene graph provides an underlying structure which connects video scenes in a meaningful way. The viewer can choose a path through the scenes by selecting one of the next available scenes. Another way to navigate is with a table of contents, which allows the user to jump to a specific scenes in the scene graph and play the hypervideo from there without having to navigate through the scene graph again.

MM '16 October 15-19, 2016, Amsterdam, Netherlands

ACM ISBN 978-1-4503-3603-1/16/10.

DOI: http://dx.doi.org/10.1145/2964284.2973810

While hypervideos have proven to be useful in many different scenarios, it is a tedious job to film all needed scenes, cut and edit them, and maintain a high quality for further usage. However, "as of July 2015, more than 400 hours of video were uploaded to YouTube every minute" [10]. Reusing these videos can reduce hypervideo production time significantly. Our previous hypervideo authoring tool, the SIVA Producer [3, 4, 5, 6], provided all functions to create hypervideos. But it also required storing the video on a local hard disk. A more practical solution is to web-link the video clips and play them directly from their source.

2. RELATED WORK

While hypervideo systems have been implemented since 1996 [9], very few authoring tools are currently available. The SIVA Producer [3, 4, 5, 6] allowed the creation of annotated interactive non-linear videos, a special form of hypervideos. However, all videos had to be available on ones hard-disk making it difficult to legally use large video pools like YouTube with current copyright restrictions. Klynt [2], a tool for interactive storytelling, also provides many features for hypervideo creation and allows the integration of YouTube videos. However, only the whole video can be embedded, not shorter sequences from within the clip. YouTube video annotations, which appear in different shapes in the video (like speech bubbles or notes), can allow videos to be linked with each other [15]. However, no view is provided that shows links between videos (like a scene graph). This makes it hard to create and maintain larger projects. When a user clicks one of the hotspots, a new web-page with the linked video is loaded. This destroys the impression of a coherently presented the hypervideo. Our research has not discovered other platforms that allow easy linking of user generated video from platforms like YouTube.

3. SIVA WEB PRODUCER

The SIVA Web Producer is implemented as a Chrome Plug-in [8] which can be activated on YouTube video pages and opens in the lower part of the browser. The application is organized in a tab concept with six tabs.

The **Select Project** tab provides an overview of one's projects. New projects can be created or already existing ones can be selected and loaded for editing. This area also provides functions to export the hypervideo structure and publish the hypervideo on our online platform [11]. Apart from a direct link to the exported video, an embed code is also provided allowing users to embed their hypervideo into

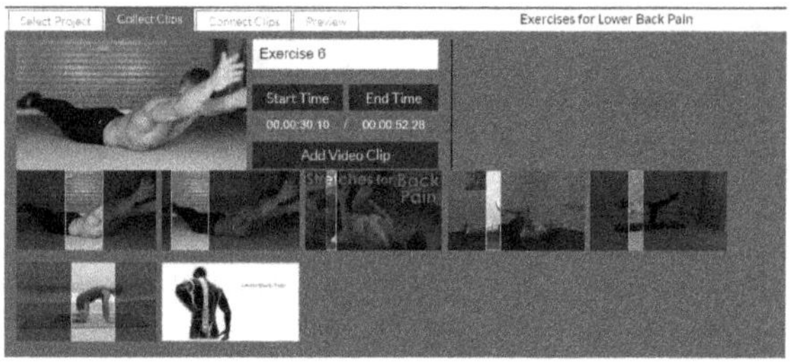

Figure 1: Collect clips tab (media repository)

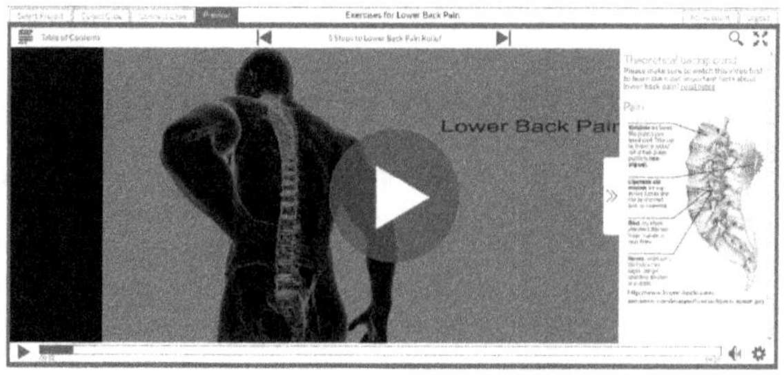

Figure 3: Preview tab (player)

other web-pages. During playback, the SIVA Web Player loads the videos directly from the YouTube web-page using the YouTube API [14].

The **Collect Clips** tab has two areas (see Figure 1). In the upper left area, the currently displayed YouTube video can be named and added to the scene repository below. If only a part of the video is needed, start and end time of the desired clip can either be defined manually or selected with corresponding buttons while watching the video. The lower part of the screen contains a repository where the already created clips are shown. An orange box on the preview thumbnail indicates which part of the video is selected from the respective clip. The unselected parts are grayed-out.

The **Connect Clips** tab also consists of two sub-areas (see Figure 2). The right side shows a list of all previously created clips. Each clip is represented by a preview thumbnail, the name, an assigned number, and a colored rectangular frame. Each frame has a unique color which helps to better identify the clip in the scene graph on the left side of the tab. The clip is dragged from the list on the right onto the graph area on the left. Doing this changes its appearance, eliminating the thumbnail image making the box smaller. Two connectors are added. A scene graph is created by clicking the outgoing connector area of one scene and then clicking the incoming connector area of another scene. A valid scene graph has at least one connection from the start node to one scene, and each scene is reachable from the start node. The elements in the graph area can be re-sized, providing a better overview of larger graphs. A right-click on a scene in the scene graph opens an annotation editor that allows adding text or image annotations to the scene. Annotations can be arranged in a desired order and are shown over the whole duration of a scene.

The **Preview** tab uses the same player as our hypervideo platform and allows the author to test the video without having to export it first (which was a major shortcoming

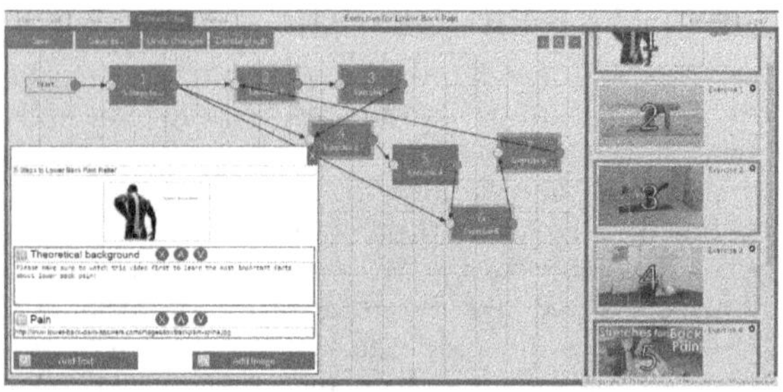

Figure 2: Connect clips tab (scene graph)

of our desktop version of the SIVA Producer [3, 4, 5, 6]). The video is shown centered. It may be overlayed by a selection panel on the left side at the end of a scene where the viewer has to decide on how to proceed in the hypervideo. Additionally, an annotation area on the right side of the screen can be opened and closed by using its handle. The player furthermore provides all elements of the SIVA HTML5 Player [3]. Along with the title of the current scene, buttons for the table of contents, search, and full screen mode are shown in the top pane of the player. The play/pause or repeat button (depending on the state of the video), the video time line, the volume control and the settings button are shown in the bottom pane of the player.

The My Account tab allows users to administer their personal data. Users log out of the system by clicking on the log-out tab.

4. DEMONSTRATION

The demonstration of our SIVA Web Producer Chrome extension describes its use in a physical exercise scenario. Personal trainers or physiotherapists can create fitness videos with existing materials from YouTube. A search on May 4, 2016 showed about 2,220,000 results for the term "fitness exercises" and about 75,300 results for the term "physio exercises". Linking selected videos or parts of videos results in a training program that can be fitted to the needs and daily condition of the user (for an example see [7]). Existing training programs can be extended or new ones may be created. We can imagine using the system in other scenarios like e-learning courses or tutorials. A demo video is available [1], as well as a tutorial [12].

5. CONCLUSION

The SIVA Web producer, a Chrome extension, is an authoring tool for the creation of hypervideos that links externally stored videos and annotations (from sources like YouTube) to scene graphs that are read and played by a web player. This eliminates the need for hypervideo authors to download, reconstruct, and store media locally. These completed hypervideos are then be published on our hypervideo platform or embedded in web pages. While our current version only accesses YouTube, future work will include integrating videos from other platforms like Vimeo [13].

6. ACKNOWLEDGMENTS

This work was funded by the Bundesministerium für Bildung und Forschung (German Federal Ministry of Education and Research) (BMBF) under project number 03V0633. We thank John Doherty for producing the demo video.

7. REFERENCES

[1] FX Palo Alto Laboratory. Demo video. Website, https://vimeo.com/167556235/df8bba958e. (accessed July 20, 2016).

[2] Honkytonk Films. Klynt. Website, http://www.klynt.net/, 2015. (accessed April 27, 2015).

[3] B. Meixner, S. John, and C. Handschigl. Siva suite: Framework for hypervideo creation, playback and management. In *Proceedings of the 23rd ACM International Conference on Multimedia*, MM '15, pages 713–716, New York, NY, USA, 2015. ACM.

[4] B. Meixner, S. John, and C. Handschigl. Annotated interactive non-linear video - software suite, download and cache management. *SIGMultimedia Rec.*, 8(1):14–15, Mar. 2016.

[5] B. Meixner, K. Matusik, C. Grill, and H. Kosch. Towards an easy to use authoring tool for interactive non-linear video. *Multimedia Tools and Applications*, 70(2):1251–1276, 2012.

[6] B. Meixner, B. Siegel, G. Hölbling, F. Lehner, and H. Kosch. Siva suite: Authoring system and player for interactive non-linear videos. In *Proceedings of the 18th ACM International Conference on Multimedia*, MM '10, pages 1563–1566, New York, NY, USA, 2010. ACM.

[7] B. Meixner, K. Tonndorf, S. John, C. Handschigl, K. Hofmann, and M. Granitzer. A multimedia help system for a medical scenario in a rehabilitation clinic. In *Proceedings of the 14th International Conference on Knowledge Technologies and Data-driven Business*, i-KNOW '14, pages 25:1–25:8, New York, NY, USA, 2014. ACM.

[8] mirkul. Siva web producer. Website, https://chrome.google.com/webstore/detail/siva-web-producer/iekikdlghfmiomfaboebdmlahnhcjfkc. (accessed May 3, 2016).

[9] N. Sawhney, D. Balcom, and I. Smith. Hypercafe: Narrative and aesthetic properties of hypervideo. In *Proceedings of the the Seventh ACM Conference on Hypertext*, HYPERTEXT '96, pages 1–10, New York, NY, USA, 1996. ACM.

[10] statista. Hours of video uploaded to youtube every minute as of july 2015. Website, http://www.statista.com/statistics/259477/hours-of-video-uploaded-to-youtube-every-minute/. (accessed May 3, 2016).

[11] University of Passau. Siva web portal. Website, https://hypertube.fim.uni-passau.de/. (accessed May 3, 2016).

[12] University of Passau. Tutorial. Website, https://www.youtube.com/watch?v=i8dUHbjkLCs. (accessed July 20, 2016).

[13] Vimeo, Inc. Vimeo - make life worth watching. Website, https://vimeo.com/, 2016. (accessed May 19, 2016).

[14] YouTube. Api resources - apis and tools that let you bring the youtube experience to your webpage, application, or device. Website, https://www.youtube.com/yt/dev/api-resources.html. (accessed May 3, 2016).

[15] YouTube. Youtube help - create and edit annotations. Website, https://support.google.com/youtube/answer/92710?hl=en. (accessed May 6, 2016).

SceneTextReg: A Real-Time Video OCR System

Haojin Yang, Cheng Wang, Christian Bartz, Christoph Meinel
Hasso Plattner Institute (HPI), University of Potsdam, Germany
P.O. Box 900460,
D-14440 Potsdam
{haojin.yang, cheng.wang, meinel}@hpi.de
{christian.bartz}@student.hpi.uni-potsdam.de

ABSTRACT

We showcase a system for real-time video text recognition. The system is based on the standard workflow of text spotting system, which includes text detection and word recognition procedures. We apply deep neural networks in both procedures. In text localization stage, textual candidates are roughly captured by using a Maximally Stable Extremal Regions (*MSERs*) detector with high recall rate, false alarms are then eliminated by using Convolutional Neural Network (*CNN*) verifier. For word recognition, we developed a skeleton based method for segmenting text region from its background, then a CNN based word recognizer is utilized for recognizing texts. Our current implementation demonstrates a real time performance for recognizing scene text by using a standard laptop with webcam. The word recognizer achieves competitive result to state-of-the-art methods by only using synthetical training data.

CCS Concepts

•Computing methodologies → Computer vision; Visual content-based indexing and retrieval; •Computer systems organization → *Real-time systems;*

Keywords

Video OCR; Multimedia Indexing; Deep Neural Networks

1. INTRODUCTION

The amount of video data available on the World Wide Web (*WWW*) is growing rapidly. According to the official statistic-report of YouTube, 100 hours of video are uploaded every minute. Therefore, how to efficiently retrieve video data on the WWW or within large video archives has become a very important and challenging task.

On the other hand, due to the rapid popularization of smart mobile and wearable devices, large amounts of self-recorded "lifelogging" videos are created. Generally, it lacks metadata for indexing such video data, since the only searchable textual content is often the title given by the uploader, which is typically brief and subjective. A more general solution is highly desired for gathering video metadata automatically.

Text in video is one of the most important high-level semantic feature, which directly depicts the video content. In general text displayed in a video can be categorized into scene text and overlay text (or artificial text). In contrast to overlay text, to detect and recognize scene text is often more challenging. There are numerous problems affecting the recognition results, as e.g., texts appeared in a nature scene image can be in a very small size with high variety of contrast; motion changes of the camera may affect the size, shape and brightness of text content, and may lead to geometrical distortion. All of those factors have to be considered in order to obtain a correct recognition result.

Most of proposed scene-text recognition methods can be briefly divided into two categories, either based on connected components (*CCs*) or sliding windows. The CCs based approaches include Stroke Width Transform (*SWT*) [4], MSERs [11], Oriented Stroke [12] etc. One of the significant benefits of CCs based method is its computational efficiency since the detection is often a one pass process across image pixels. The sliding window based methods as e.g., [14, 3, 13, 7] usually apply representative visual features to train a machine learning classifier for text detection. Here hand-crafted features [13, 9, 1] as well as deep features [14, 7] can be applied, and text regions will be detected by scanning the whole image with a sub-window in multiple scales with a potential overlapping. In [14, 3, 7], sliding window based methods with deep features achieved promising accuracy for end-to-end text recognition. [15] propose to consider scene text detection as a semantic segmentation problem, by which their Fully Convolutional Network (*FCN*) performs per-pixel prediction for classifying text and background. However, their proposed approaches may hard to achieve sufficient performance for real-time application due to the expensive computation time.

In our approach, we intended to take advantages from both categories, i.e. the computation benefit of CCs based algorithm and the powerful text-classification ability of deep features. The demonstrated system achieves real-time performance[1] on a standard laptop (3.2 GHz CPU×4, 8G RAM, NVIDIA GeForce 860M) with webcam.

[1]Similar to [11], we consider the real-time ability of a video text recognition system if its response time is comparable to a human.

MM '16 October 15-19, 2016, Amsterdam, Netherlands

ACM ISBN 978-1-4503-3603-1/16/10.
DOI: http://dx.doi.org/10.1145/2964284.2973811

2. SYSTEM DESIGN

In this section, we will briefly describe the main work flows of the system, and report evaluation results on ICDAR 2015 Robust Reading Competition Challenge 2 - Task 3 "Focused Scene Word Recognition".

2.1 Text Detection

In [14, 8, 7], the authors were intended to achieve the best end-to-end text recognition accuracy. Therefore in text detection step, their systems have been tuned to produce text candidates with high recall, and the subsequent recognition engines will further eliminate the false alarms. Since recognition procedures are often time consuming, we thus keep the text detection result as accurate as possible, and only pass the text candidates with high confidence to the recognition stage. We apply MESRs [10] based detector to roughly detect character candidates from the input video frame with high recall rate. All candidate regions are further verified by using a grouping method and CNN classifier. The applied binary CNN classifier has been trained by using deep network similar to [5].

2.2 Text Segmentation

We developed a novel skeleton-based approach for text segmentation, which will simplify the further OCR process. In short, we determine the text gradient direction for each text candidate by analyzing the content distribution of their skeleton maps. We then calculate the threshold value for seed-selection by using the skeleton map which has been created with the correct gradient direction. Subsequently, a seed-region growing procedure starts from each seed pixel and extends the seed-region in its north, south, east, and west directions. The region grows iteratively until it reaches the character boundary. This method achieved the first place in ICDAR 2011 text segmentation challenge for born digital images.

2.3 Word Recognition

In this step verified text candidates are first separated into words. Word recognition is accomplished by performing joint-training of CNN and LSTM [6] based Recurrent Neural Network, followed by a standard spell checker. In order to train the deep network we developed a data engine, which created several millions of synthetical training data by considering different scene factors such as font style, background, lighting effect, contrast ratio etc.

2.4 Evaluation Result

We evaluated our word recognizer by using ICDAR 2015 Robust Reading Competition Challenge 2 - Task 3 "Focused Scene Word Recognition" dataset (refer to IC15) in the unconstrained manner[2]. Since the output of our word recognizer is case-insensitive, we thus only consider the evaluation results of the category "Word Recognition Rate (Uppercase)" (WRR-U) from the ICDAR 2015 online evaluation system. We also created evaluation result ignored capitalization and punctuation differences using this dataset (refer to I.C.P), and compared with the best known methods [2, 7].

Table 1 shows the comparison results to previous methods on IC15 dataset. In *I.C.P* evaluation, our current result outperforms JOINT-model from [7], but comes behind Google's photoOCR by 1.9%. We didn't considered the DICT-model from [7], since its result is constrained to lexicons. According to the *IC15 ranking* results, our approach is currently not able to outperform the results created by commercial organizations such as SRC-B, Baidu-IDL, Megvii and Google, but improves on the next best one (NESP) by almost 18% of WRR-U. Our result is still competitive to commercial organizations, regarding that we have only used synthetical training data, and applied more succinct network architecture by taking into account of the execution speed. In contrast, [2] applied several millions of manually labelled samples, and the processing time of their system is around 1.4 secs per image. To process a 640 × 480 image, the system from [15] needs about 20 secs on CPU or 1 sec on GPU only for text localization. Therefore, our system is obviously superior regarding running time. This can be proved by our demo video captured by using a laptop and a video camera[3]. The OCR analysis has been performed on every input frame from the camera.

[2]The OCR results are not constrained to a given lexicon.

	Description	WRR-U
I.C.P	PhotoOCR [2]	0.876
	Our result	**0.857**
	Jaderberg's JOINT-model [7]	0.818
IC15	SRC-B-TextProcessingLab*	0.8895
	Baidu-IDL*	0.872
	Megvii-Image++ [15]	0.8603
	PhotoOCR [2]	0.853
	Our result	**0.826**
	NESP	0.6484
	PicRead	0.6192
	PLT	0.6311
	MAPS	0.6329
	Feild's Method	0.5233
	PIONEER	0.5571
	Baseline	0.4658
	TextSpotter	0.2813

Table 1: Evaluation result on IC15. The baseline method is from a commercially available OCR system. We are intended to include results that are not constrained to a pre-defined lexicon. However the methods marked with * are not published, therefore they are not distinguishable. (Last check: 20/05/2016)

3. DEMO SETUP

We will show case the proposed video ocr system in an interactive manner. The input video stream will be captured by using a live camera, and the ocr result will be directly displayed on the computer screen. The hardware needed to be prepared by the authors are a laptop and a video camera.

4. REFERENCES

[1] H. Bay, A. Ess, T. Tuytelaars, and L. Van Gool. Speeded-up robust features (surf). *Comput. Vis. Image Underst.*, 110(3):346–359, June 2008.

[2] A. Bissacco, M. Cummins, Y. Netzer, and H. Neven. Photoocr: Reading text in uncontrolled conditions. In

[3]https://vimeo.com/140059065
http://www.tudou.com/programs/view/hMkGCsWEe2Y/

The IEEE International Conference on Computer Vision (ICCV), December 2013.

[3] A. Coates, B. Carpenter, C. Case, S. Satheesh, B. Suresh, T. Wang, D. J. Wu, and A. Y. Ng. Text detection and character recognition in scene images with unsupervised feature learning. In *Proc. of International Conference on Document Analysis and Recognition*, ICDAR '11, pages 440–445, Washington, DC, USA, 2011. IEEE Computer Society.

[4] B. Epshtein, E. Ofek, and Y. Wexler. Detecting text in natural scenes with stroke width transform. In *Proc. of International Conference on Computer Vision and Pattern Recognition*, pages 2963–2970, 2010.

[5] I. J. Goodfellow, Y. Bulatov, J. Ibarz, S. Arnoud, and V. Shet. Multi-digit number recognition from street view imagery using deep convolutional neural networks. *arXiv preprint arXiv:1312.6082v4*, 2014.

[6] S. Hochreiter and J. Schmidhuber. Long short-term memory. *Neural Comput.*, 9(8):1735–1780, Nov. 1997.

[7] M. Jaderberg, K. Simonyan, A. Vedaldi, and A. Zisserman. Deep structured output learning for unconstrained text recognition. In *International Conference on Learning Representations*, 2015.

[8] M. Jaderberg, A. Vedaldi, and A. Zisserman. Deep features for text spotting. In *Proc. of European Conference on Computer Vision (ECCV)*. Springer, 2014.

[9] D. G. Lowe. Distinctive image features from scale-invariant keypoints. *Int. J. Comput. Vision*, 60(2):91–110, Nov. 2004.

[10] J. Matas, O. Chum, M. Urban, and T. Pajdla. Robust wide-baseline stereo from maximally stable extremal regions. *Image and Vision Computing*, 22(10):761 – 767, 2004. British Machine Vision Computing 2002.

[11] L. Neumann and J. Matas. Real-time scene text localization and recognition. In *Computer Vision and Pattern Recognition (CVPR), 2012 IEEE Conference on*, pages 3538–3545, June 2012.

[12] L. Neumann and J. Matas. Scene text localization and recognition with oriented stroke detection. In *Computer Vision (ICCV), 2013 IEEE International Conference on*, pages 97–104, Dec 2013.

[13] K. Wang, B. Babenko, and S. Belongie. End-to-end scene text recognition. In *Computer Vision (ICCV), 2011 IEEE International Conference on*, pages 1457–1464, Nov 2011.

[14] T. Wang, D. Wu, A. Coates, and A. Ng. End-to-end text recognition with convolutional neural networks. In *Pattern Recognition (ICPR), 2012 21st International Conference on*, pages 3304–3308, Nov 2012.

[15] C. Yao, J. Wu, X. Zhou, C. Zhang, S. Zhou, Z. Cao, and Q. Yin. Incidental scene text understanding: Recent progresses on icdar 2015 robust reading competition challenge. *arXiv preprint arXiv:1511.09207v2*, 2016.

Beauty eMakeup: a Deep Makeup Transfer System

Xinyu Ou[1,2,3], Si Liu[1]*, Xiaochun Cao[1], Hefei Ling[2]
[1]SKLOIS, Institute of Information Engineering, Chinese Academy of Sciences
[2]School of Computer Science and Technology, Huazhong University of Science and Technology
[3]YNGBZX, Yunnan Open University
ouxinyu@hust.edu.cn, {liusi,caoxiaochun}@iie.ac.cn, lhefei@hust.edu.cn

ABSTRACT

In this demo, we present a Beauty eMakeup System to automatically recommend the most suitable makeup for a female and synthesis the makeup on her face. Given a before-makeup face, her most suitable makeup is determined automatically. Then, both the before-makeup and the reference faces are fed into the proposed Deep Transfer Network to generate the after-makeup face. Our end-to-end makeup transfer network have several nice properties including: **(1)** with complete functions: including foundation, lip gloss, and eye shadow transfer; **(2)** cosmetic specific: different cosmetics are transferred in different manners; **(3)** localized: different cosmetics are applied on different facial regions; **(4)** producing naturally looking results without obvious artifacts; **(5)** controllable makeup lightness: various results from light makeup to heavy makeup can be generated. Extensive experimental evaluations and analysis on testing images well demonstrate the effectiveness of the proposed system.

Keywords

Beauty eMakeup System; Face Parsing; Makeup Recommendation; Makeup Transfer

1. INTRODUCTION

Makeup is a key factor that influence people's judgment about one's look, especially for female. By choosing proper makeup, one may look more attractive. This demo presents a novel Beauty eMakeup system, which helps users to automatically recommend the most suitable makeup for a female and synthesis the makeup on her face.

As shown in Fig.1, we simulate an applicable makeup process with two functions. **I:** The first function is *makeup recommendation*, where personalization is taken special cares. More specifically, females with similar face, eye or mouth shapes are suitable for similar makeups. The similarity is measured by the Euclidean distance between deep features produced by an off-the-shelf deep face recognition network.

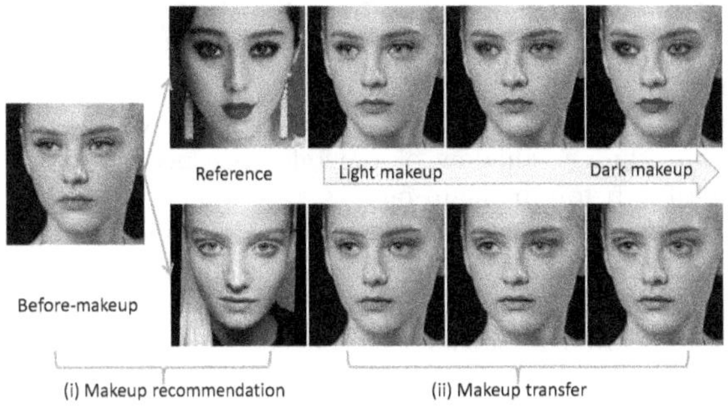

Figure 1: System flowchart.

To sum up, the recommendation is personalized, data-driven and easy to implement. **II:** The second function is *makeup transfer* from the reference face to the before-makeup face. We propose a Deep Localized Makeup Transfer Network(DLMTnet) to achieve face parsing, makeup learning and makeup transfer. Firstly, both before-makeup and reference faces are fed into a face parsing network to generate two corresponding labelmaps. The DLMTnet is based on the Fully Convolutional Networks by (i) emphasizing the makeup relevant facial parts, such as eye shadow and (ii) considering the symmetry structure of the frontal faces. Based on the parsing results, the local region of the before-makeup face (e.g., mouth) corresponds to its counterpart (e.g., lip) in the reference face. Secondly, three most common cosmetics, i.e, eye shadow, lip gloss and foundation are transferred in their own manners. The after-makeup face is initialized as the before-makeup face, then gradually updated via Stochastic Gradient Descent to produce naturally looking results. By tuning up the weight of each cosmetic, a series of after-makeup faces with increasingly heavier makeup can be generated. In this way, our system can produce various results with controllable makeup lightness.

2. TECHNOLOGY

In this Section, we sequentially introduce our makeup recommendation and makeup transfer methods in detail.

Makeup Recommendation Given a before-makeup face, we find several similar faces from the reference dataset. The similarities are defined as the Euclidean distances between the deep features extracted by feeding the face into an off-the-shelf face recognition model named VGG-Face. The experiment shows that the recommended reference faces have similar facial shapes with the before-makeup faces, and therefore the recommendation is personalized.

Facial Parts vs. Cosmetics Correspondence In or-

*Si Liu is the corresponding author.

MM '16 October 15-19, 2016, Amsterdam, Netherlands

ACM ISBN 978-1-4503-3603-1/16/10...$15.00
DOI: http://dx.doi.org/10.1145/2964284.2973812

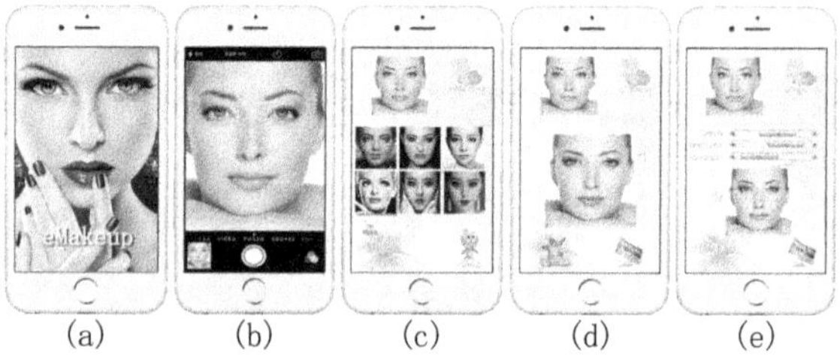

Figure 2: The user interface of Beauty eMakeup system on a mobile devices. (a) welcome,(b) photo taking, (c) makeup recommendation and choice, (d) synthesis, (e) Lightness Control.

der to transfer the makeup, we need build the correspondence between facial parts of the before-makeup face and the cosmetic regions of the reference face. As a result, the cosmetic can be between the matched pairs. Most of the correspondences can be obtained by the face parsing results. But, the eye shadow of the reference need to warp to match the before-makeup face.

(1) **Face parsing** model is based on the Fully Convolution Network, but we pay more attention to the makeup relevant labels. we propose a *weighted cross-entropy loss* which is a weighted sum over the spatial dimensions of the final layer:

$$\ell\left(x;\theta\right)=\sum\nolimits_{ij}\ell'\left(y_{ij},p\left(x_{ij};\theta\right)\right)\cdot w\left(y_{ij}\right), \tag{1}$$

where ℓ' is the cross entropy loss defined on each pixel. y_{ij} and $p\left(x_{ij};\theta\right)$ are the ground truth and predicted label of the pixel x_{ij}, and $w\left(y_{ij}\right)$ is the label weight. The weight is set empirically by maximizing the F1 score in the validation set.

(2) **Eye shadow warping** are used to handle the problem of the shapes of eyes and eye brows are different in before-makeup photo and reference photo.

Makeup Transfer Makeup transfer is conducted based on the correspondences among image pairs. In this work, the **Overall Makeup Transfer** considers eye shadow, lip gloss and foundation, and also preserves the face structure.

$$\begin{aligned}A^{*}=\ &\underset{A\in R^{H\times W\times C}}{\arg\min}\ \lambda_e\left(R_l(A)+R_r(A)\right)+\lambda_f R_f(A)\\&+\lambda_l\left(R_{up}(A)+R_{low}(A)\right)+\lambda_s R_s(A)+R_{V^{\beta}}(A)\end{aligned} \tag{2}$$

To make the results more natural, the total variance term $R_{V^{\beta}}=\sum_{i,j}\left(\left(A_{i,j+1}-A_{ij}\right)^2+\left(A_{i+1,j}-A_{ij}\right)^2\right)^{\frac{\beta}{2}}$ is added. $R_l(A)$, $R_r(A)$, $R_f(A)$, $R_{up}(A)$, $R_{low}(A)$ and $R_s(A)$ are the left, right eye shadow, foundation, upper, lower lip gloss and face structure loss. And λ_e, λ_f, λ_l and λ_e are the weights to balance different cosmetics. By tuning these weights, the lightness of makeup can be adjusted. For example, by increasing the λ_e, the eye shadow will be darker. The overall energy function (2) is optimized via Stochastic Gradient Descent (SGD) by using momentum.

3. USER INTERFACE

The Beauty eMakeup system is a mobile APP, it has multiple screens. After entering the welcome screen in Fig.2(a), the user can choose to take or upload a non-makeup photo, shown in Fig.2(b). After that, system will automatically enter the makeup recommendation screen, and a set of the most suitable makeup girls are displayed to user, as shown in Fig.2(c). In this screen, user can choose a favourite model and press the "Makeup" button to synthesize the makeup photo or press the "More" button to automatic replace another group of the makeup girls. Fig.2(d) shows the makeup photo, which is synthesized by non-makeup photo and reference photo. A "Save" button allows user to save the makeup photo, while the "Lightness" button permit user to adjust the lightness of each makeup part, such as lip gloss, eye shadow, and foundation in Fig.2(e). Another "save" button is designed on this screen to allow user to save her/his photo.

Besides, we will develop a eMakeup system for PC user.

4. DEMONSTRATION

We compare with DFace [3], NerualStyle [1], the results is conducted both qualitatively and quantitatively. Furthermore, in order to show our method can generate after-makeup face with various makeup lightness, ranging from light makeup to dark makeup, we gradually increase certain makeup weights λ_e, λ_f and λ_l, one result is shown in Fig.1 For each before-makeup face, we select serval most similar looking reference girls, and transfer their makeup to the before-makeup face, Fig.3 shown the effect picture. This function is quite useful in real application, because the users can virtually try different makeup and choose the favorite one. More experiment details, please refer to [4].

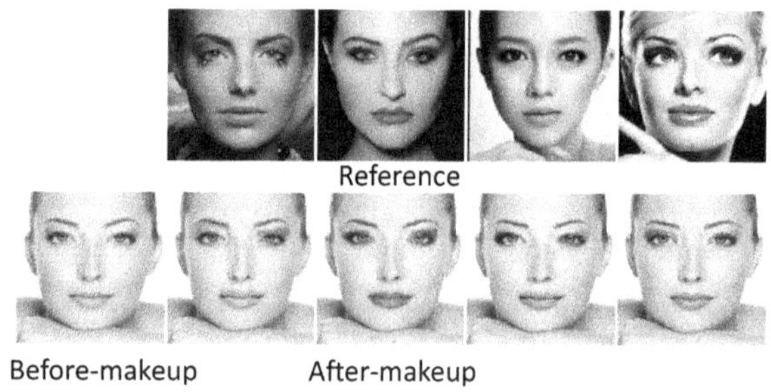

Figure 3: The same girl wears different makeups.

5. CONCLUSIONS

In this demo, we showcase a novel Deep Localized Makeup Transfer Network to automatically transfer the makeup from a reference face to a before-makeup face. In the future, we plan to explore the extensibility of the network. For example, one before-makeup face can be combined with two reference faces. The after-makeup face has the eye shadow of one reference face and lip gloss of another reference face. Moreover, we also want to integrate the makeup system into human parsing [2].

6. ACKNOWLEDGMENTS

This work was supported in part by the Natural Science Foundation of China under Grant U1536203 and 61272409, in part by the Major Scientific and Technological Innovation Project of Hubei Province under Grant 2015AAA013.

7. REFERENCES

[1] L. A. Gatys, A. S. Ecker, and M. Bethge., A neural algorithm of artistic style. *CoRR*, abs/1508.06576, 2015.

[2] S. Liu, X. Liang, L. Liu, X. Shen, J. Yang, C. Xu, L. Lin, X. Cao, and S. Yan. Matching-cnn meets knn: Quasi-parametric human parsing. *In Computer Vision and Pattern Recognition*, pages 1419-1427, 2015.

[3] D. Guo and T. Sim. Digital face makeup by example. *In Computer Vision and Pattern Recognition*, pages 73-79, 2009.

[4] S. Liu, X. Ou, R. Qian, W. Wang, and X. Cao. Makeup like a superstar: Deep localized makeup transfer network. 2016.

Real-time Wearable Computer Vision System for Improved Museum Experience

Giovanni Taverriti*, Stefano Lombini*, Lorenzo Seidenari,
Marco Bertini and Alberto Del Bimbo
Media Integration and Communication Center, Università degli Studi di Firenze
Viale Morgagni 65 - 50134 Firenze, Italy
{*name.surname*}@unifi.it

ABSTRACT

The goal of this demo is to perform real-time object classification and artwork recognition using a wearable device, to improve user experience during a museum visit by providing contextual information and performing user profiling. We propose the use of a compact CNN network that performs object classification and artwork localization and, using the same CNN features, we perform a robust artwork recognition. Shape based filtering, artwork tracking and temporal filtering further improve recognition accuracy.

Keywords

Object recognition; Context recognition; cultural heritage

1. INTRODUCTION

The goal of this work is to implement a real-time computer vision system that can run on wearable devices to perform object classification and artwork recognition, to improve the experience of a museum visit through understanding the interests of users. Object classification helps to understand the context of the visit, e.g. differentiating when a visitor is talking with people, or just wandering through the museum, or if he is looking at an exhibit that interests him. Artwork recognition allows to provide automatically information of the observed item or to create a user profile based on what and how long a user has observed artworks.

2. THE SYSTEM

We base our wearable computer vision system on the YOLO [1] algorithm. To adhere to the real-time requirement on a NVIDIA Jetson TK1 board, we use an architecture derived from the *Tiny Net* proposed by authors of [1].

YOLO has an interesting structure since it combines recent advancements in deep convolutional neural network design with the novel idea of dealing with object detection as a regression problem.

*Equal contribution, {*name.surname*}@stud.unifi.it

MM '16 October 15-19, 2016, Amsterdam, Netherlands

ACM ISBN 978-1-4503-3603-1/16/10...$15.00

DOI: http://dx.doi.org/10.1145/2964284.2973813

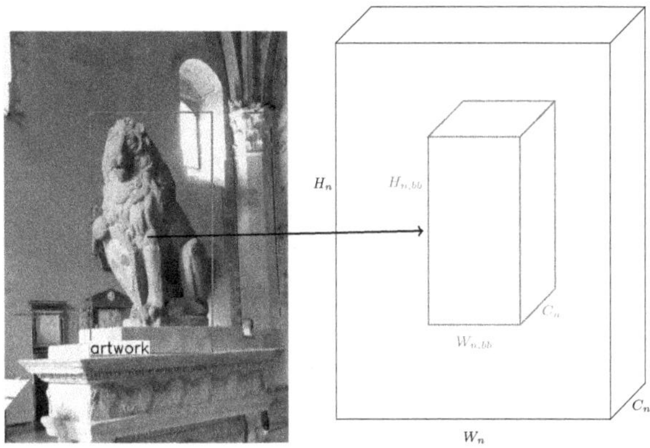

Figure 1: Feature extraction procedure for an artwork detection on a single convolutional feature map.

The network is designed taking inspiration from GoogleNet inception modules, which exploits 1×1 convolution to reduce the dimensionality and the amount of computation.

Given a convolutional feature map, computed after a set of non-linear transformations, the final Fully Connected (FC) layer for each of the evaluated windows generate a bounding box and a vector of class probabilities. After remapping this $|C| \times |B| \times 5$ tensor to a set of windows, non-maximal suppression is applied to get rid of redundant detections.

We fine-tuned the network to recognize artworks and people using our publicly available dataset[1]. The CNN features computed for classification are then used to recognize specific artworks, e.g. to provide informations through an automatic audio guide, and to understand users behaviours and interests, based on how long an artwork is observed.

2.1 Artwork recognition

To obtain a lightweight but descriptive visual feature to perform artwork recognition we re-map artwork detections onto convolutional feature maps and apply a global max-pooling (Fig. 1). Consider our network architecture in Fig. 2. Layers on the left are high-resolution and very correlated with low-level image features, while layers on the right end are low-resolution, highly semantic representation of the image content. We use feature maps 3 and 4, for a descriptor of size 768, obtained concatenating the max-pooled tensors extracted from the rescaled regions.

[1]https://www.micc.unifi.it/resources/

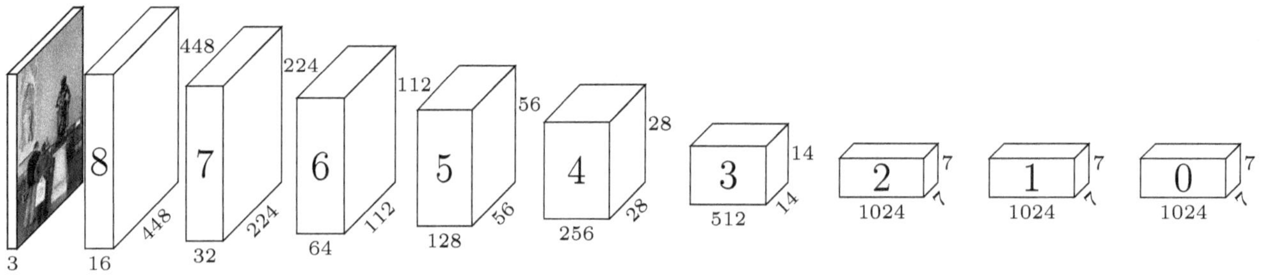

Figure 2: Our network architecture, with tensor size and layer numbering.

Considering a dataset of artwork patches $p_i \in \mathcal{D}$ and their artwork labels y, we annotated each artwork detection d finding the nearest neighbor patch

$$\hat{p} = \arg\max_i \langle p_i, d \rangle \tag{1}$$

and associating the respective label $\hat{y}$. According to our experimental evaluation layer 3 was the best performing alone. The coupling with layer 4 gave the best result.

We aim at high recognition accuracy, since mistaking an artwork for another may result in a bad user experience, e.g. due to the audio guide that presents an artwork different from the one that is actually observed.

We avoid recognizing detected artwork which are evaluated to be too distant to be of interest. Not having any camera calibration we rely on a simple heuristic comparing the artwork bounding box area with the frame area:

$$\frac{w_{bb}h_{bb}}{WH} > \alpha \tag{2}$$

where WH is the frame area and w_{bb} and h_{bb} are bounding box width and height respectively, and α is a threshold (Fig. 3). In our experiments we obtained the best results for $\alpha = 0.05$, that allows to reduce false recognitions by 50% w.r.t. not using the heuristic, at the cost of introducing a small number of missed recognitions.

Figure 3: Shape based filtering: artwork in yellow (left) is not considered for recognition, not satisfying Eq. 2, while the other is recognized as "marzocco".

2.2 Temporal Smoothing

We apply two different strategies to improve the stability of our recognition.

We continuously predict artwork labels according to Eq. 1, but we consider a prediction only after it persist for M frames. We implement this by tracking all artwork detection boxes with a greedy data association tracking-by-detection algorithm.

To further improve recognition result we apply the following strategy. We increment a counter p every time the recognition label for a box is unchanged, keeping track of the most frequent label $\overline{y}$. Every time a label $y*$ different from $\overline{y}$ we decrement p. We predict the artwork identity as $y*$ only if $p > P > M$. This technique greatly reduces the number of false recognitions. In our experiments best results were obtained for $M = 15$ and $P = 20$.

2.3 Dataset

We collected people images from PASCAL VOC2007 and an in house dataset comprising images from museums. Artwork images have been collected shooting videos inside the Bargello Museum. 8 masterpieces of Donatello have been selected as artworks to be recognized. A tool to easily add artwork descriptors from videos has also been developed, to ease development in other museums.

3. CONCLUSIONS

We have presented a system running on the NVIDIA Jetson TK1 SoC. Our approach jointly solves two problems: contextual analysis and object recognition. We apply our efficient pipeline to improve museum experience. Our method allows to profile in real-time visitor interest and to provide instantaneous feedback on the artworks of interest.

Acknowledgments.

This work is partially supported by the "Social Museum and Smart Tourism" project (CTN01_00034_231545).

4. REFERENCES

[1] J. Redmon, S. Divvala, R. Girshick, and A. Farhadi. You only look once: Unified, real-time object detection. *arXiv preprint arXiv:1506.02640*, 2015.

An Intention-Aware Interactive System for Mobile Video Browsing

Jun He[†], Hanwang Zhang[‡], Ling Shen[†], Richang Hong[†] and Tat-Seng Chua[‡]
[†]School of Computer and Information, Hefei University of Technology
[‡]School of Computing, National University of Singapore
{hyj.hfut.mail, hanwangzhang, sammiling315, hongrc.hfut}@gmail.com,
dcscts@nus.edu.sg

ABSTRACT

Video browsing describes an interactive process where the user wants to find a target shot in a long video. Therefore, it is crucial for a video browsing system to be fast and accurate with minimum user effort. Previously, video browsing systems suffered from either lots of user efforts or heavy computation cost, which makes them less effective. We propose an RNN-based *intention-aware* system to overcome these limitations. At each interactive round, the user only needs to select one of the displayed shots that is most visually similar to her mental target and then the user's choice will further tailor the search to the target. The search model update merely requires vector inner products which means the system is highly responsive.

Keywords

Video Browsing, RNN, Temporal Model, Intention-Aware, Mental Search

1. INTRODUCTION

A common scenario is that we have seen a movie a long time ago and one day, we are eager to seek an interesting shot that suddenly appears in our mind. Then, we might have to scroll the progress bar in a video player which supports fast forward or rewind (FW/RWD) to find the target shot. When the movie is long, *e.g.*, over 2 hours, the procedure is sometimes frustrating since it is very time-consuming and tricky, especially on the small screen of mobile devices. We argue that the conventional interactive search by scrolling in most commercial players is less intelligent since it neglects the inherent visual information of videos.

Content-based video browsing describes the methodologies about applying computer vision techniques to improve the performance of modern video browsing tools or systems. In fact, it has drawn a lot of attention since the early 1990s [1]. Some examples for video browsing tailored for mobile devices are given in [2, 6, 7, 9]. An informal observation is that most of the video browsing systems rely on user feedbacks to refine the search model, *e.g.* [1, 2, 6]. The drawback is Relevance Feedback (RF) may suffer from lots of user efforts and usually requires expert abilities, which prevents a system from being easy-to-use. Moreover, most systems cause heavy computation when responding to user query or updating the search model.

MM '16 October 15-19, 2016, Amsterdam, Netherlands

ACM ISBN 978-1-4503-3603-1/16/10.
DOI: http://dx.doi.org/10.1145/2964284.2973814

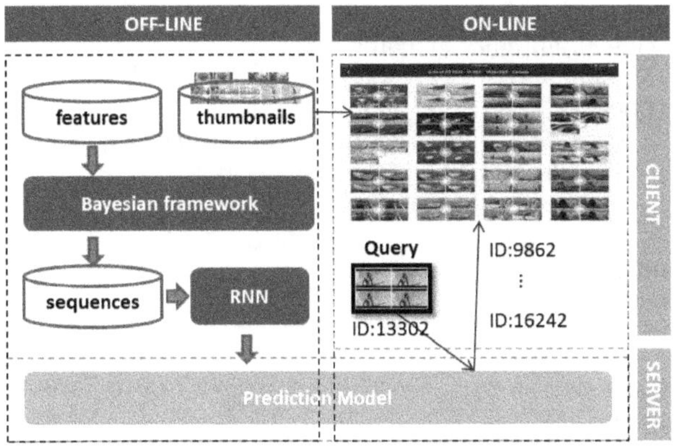

Figure 1: The basic system architecture

In this demonstration we present an interactive content-based video browsing system. In contrast to traditional RF, throughout the interaction process, the only user effort required is to click one shot which most visually relates to the one in mind, out of 20 displayed shots. The core of the system is a temporal model, specifically, a char-RNN [8] model which is trained to capture user query intention from user feedbacks. As far as we know, it is the first attempt to apply RNN in video browsing task even though it is widely used in action detection, event recognition and natural language processing, *etc.* [3, 10, 12].

2. SYSTEM ARCHITECTURE

The direct precursor of our system is the one proposed in [5], which adapts [4] to video browsing task. What makes our system more competitive is that an RNN temporal model is embedded to infer the query intention intelligently while the user is interacting with the system. In other words, given a feedback sequence, the system can figure out what kind of target the user tries searching for, and output the relevant shots as potential targets. The intuitive idea behind this implementation is that the query intention can be learned from user feedbacks since they essentially reflect the information needs of the user. Additionally, it is obvious that a feedback sequence consists of chronological user feedbacks which are correlated both in visual feature space and semantic space. Thus, we train our RNN model with a large set of machine-generated user feedback sequences to capture the interrelationships between video shots and gain an insight into the video structure. The trained model can be deployed to deduce user query intention during the procedure of video browsing.

Algorithm 1: Feedback sequences generation algorithm

```
Input: s: target video shot; S: video shot set
Output: seq: sequence of shots
P = [p1, p2...pN], pi = 0.5, for i = 1...N, N is the
   number of shots in S.
seq = [], initialize an empty sequence
D0, randomly select 8 shots from S
repeat
   similarity comparison between s and D_t^i, append D_t^i
     which yields the highest similarity to seq
   update P
   update Dt
until s in Dt;
return seq
```

Our video browsing system is composed of two parts, as illustrated in Figure 1. In the off-line part, we first create an abstraction of the original video by extracting one frame from every 20 continuous frames, then cut the video into shots according to visual feature similarity. Each shot is represented with the 4096-dimensional VGG19 [11] feature and an informative thumbnail generated by uniting 4 randomly selected frames. After that, we feed all the Shots-Target pairs to the Bayesian framework specified in [5] for generating pseudo user feedback sequences which are further used to train the RNN model. Each Shots-Target pair here is composed of all the shots and a randomly selected target. Algorithm 1 details the method for pseudo user feedback sequence generation. The methods for updating P and D_t in the algorithm are functions inspired by the update model and display model discussed in [5] respectively. Eventually, the off-line part ends up with video-specific prediction models.

When it comes to the on-line part, we simply maintain a client/server (C/S) subsystem in which the client is responsible for handling user interaction, making queries and presenting information in a user-friendly way, while the server handling user queries and updating session status. In order to achieve better user experience, the client is designed to be an iOS-based native application for use with iPad. Meanwhile, for simplicity, the server is implemented to supply web services using lua programming language. The client and server communicate with each other via HTTP protocol. Initially, the server loads the corresponding prediction model trained in the off-line part and sends 20 randomly selected shots to the client. After receiving user feedback, the server feeds it to the prediction model, sends back the predicted results and marks them as presented to avoid repeat in the future. During the entire interaction process, the system only concerns with shot IDs without involving high-dimensional features and the only required computation is one step of vector inner product.

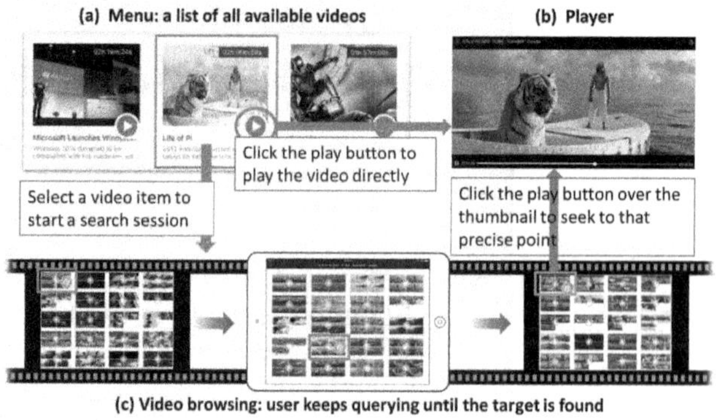

Figure 2: User interaction schematic illustration

3. USER INTERFACE

The UI could be simple and generous in that we only take into account the high-level visual characteristic instead of miscellaneous low-level characteristics, such as color, texture, shapes, *etc.* Figure 2 offers a glimpse of the thumbnail-based grid layout used in our system for information presentation. A list of available videos are presented to users as the application starts. Users can click the play button to watch or skim the video in the conventional manner or click the remaining area to start the intelligent video browsing procedure in which the user always chooses the one that is most visually similar to her mental target, out of 20 displayed shots, and then the client updates user interface according to the newly predicted candidates. During the browsing procedure, users are free to choose whether to combine the current search with the previous one or not. Because it is not always good to inherit the result model of previous search, it is recommended to break off the connection when an acceptable candidate shows up. The procedure lasts until the user meets her target, at which point the user can click the play button over the thumbnail for directly jumping to the corresponding video point.

4. CONCLUSIONS

In the work, we extended the RNN temporal model to video browsing task and introduced our intention-aware video browsing system. The system, employing a char-RNN model to learn the inherent connections between video shots automatically and infer user query intention gradually by analyzing user feedbacks, can help to find a target in 3-5 steps. Theoretically, the system is suitable for browsing among several videos as well.

5. ACKNOWLEDGMENTS

This work was supported in part by the Anhui Fund for Distinguished Young Scholars under Grant 1508085J04, in part by the National High-Tech Development Program of China under Grant 2014AA015104, in part by the National Natural Science Foundation of China under Grant 61472116. We are grateful to NExT for the supply of lab facilities. NExT research is supported by Nation Research Foundation, Prime Minister's Office, Singapore under its IRC@SG Funding Initiative.

6. REFERENCES

[1] F. Arman, R. Depommier, A. Hsu, and M.-Y. Chiu. Content-based browsing of video sequences. In *Proceedings of the second ACM international conference on Multimedia*, pages 97–103, 1994.

[2] C. Cobârzan, M. A. Hudelist, and M. Del Fabro. Content-based video browsing with collaborating mobile clients. In *MultiMedia Modeling*, pages 402–406. Springer, 2014.

[3] D. Eck and J. Schmidhuber. Finding temporal structure in music: Blues improvisation with lstm recurrent networks. In *Neural Networks for Signal Processing, 2002. Proceedings of the 2002 12th IEEE Workshop on*, pages 747–756. IEEE, 2002.

[4] M. Ferecatu and D. Geman. A statistical framework for image category search from a mental picture. *Pattern Analysis and Machine Intelligence, IEEE Transactions on*, 31(6):1087–1101, 2009.

[5] J. He, X. Shang, H. Zhang, and T.-S. Chua. Mental visual browsing. In *MultiMedia Modeling*, pages 424–428. Springer, 2016.

[6] W. Hürst and D. Darzentas. History: a hierarchical storyboard interface design for video browsing on mobile devices. In *Proceedings of the 11th International Conference on Mobile and Ubiquitous Multimedia*, page 17. ACM, 2012.

[7] W. Hürst and K. Meier. Interfaces for timeline-based mobile video browsing. In *Proceedings of the 16th ACM international conference on Multimedia*, pages 469–478. ACM, 2008.

[8] Karpathy. Multi-layer recurrent neural networks (lstm, gru, rnn) for character-level language models in torch. https://github.com/karpathy/char-rnn. Accessed July 15, 2016.

[9] S. Pongnumkul, J. Wang, G. Ramos, and M. Cohen. Content-aware dynamic timeline for video browsing. In *Proceedings of the 23nd annual ACM symposium on User interface software and technology*, pages 139–142. ACM, 2010.

[10] S. Reiter, B. Schuller, and G. Rigoll. A combined lstm-rnn-hmm-approach for meeting event segmentation and recognition. In *Acoustics, Speech and Signal Processing, 2006. ICASSP 2006 Proceedings. 2006 IEEE International Conference on*, volume 2, pages II–II. IEEE, 2006.

[11] K. Simonyan and A. Zisserman. Very deep convolutional networks for large-scale image recognition. *CoRR*, abs/1409.1556, 2014.

[12] I. Sutskever, J. Martens, and G. E. Hinton. Generating text with recurrent neural networks. In *Proceedings of the 28th International Conference on Machine Learning (ICML-11)*, pages 1017–1024, 2011.

A Multimodal Gamified Platform for Real-Time User Feedback in Sports Performance *

David Monaghan[a], Freddie Honohan[a], Amin Ahmadi[a],
Troy McDaniel[b], Ramin Tadayon[b], Ajay Karpur[b],
Kieran Moran[a], Noel E. O'Connor[a] and Sethuraman Panchanathan[b]
[a]Insight Centre for Data Analytics, Dublin City University, Ireland
[b]Center for Cognitive Ubiquitous Computing, Arizona State University, Tempe, Arizona 85281 USA
monodavids@gmail.com

ABSTRACT

In this paper we introduce a novel platform that utilises multi-modal low-cost motion capture technology for the delivery of real-time visual feedback for sports performance. This platform supports the expansion to multi-modal interfaces that utilise haptic and audio feedback, which scales effectively with motor task complexity. We demonstrate an implementation of our platform within the field of sports performance. The platform includes low-cost motion capture through a fusion technique, combining a Microsoft Kinect V2 with two wrist inertial sensors, which make use of the accelerometer and gyroscope sensors, alongside a game-based Graphical User Interface (GUI) for instruction, visual feedback and gamified score tracking.

Categories and Subject Descriptors

I.4.5 [**Computing Methodologies**]: Image Processing and Computer Vision—*Reconstruction*

Keywords

Motion capture, Human-Computer Interaction, Multimodal Interfaces, Sports Performance

1. INTRODUCTION

As sensing and feedback technology have become increasingly prevalent worldwide, motor learning has become a critical topic of study and research in the field of Human-Computer Interaction. Of particular interest is unsupervised motor learning, wherein motor function is improved in the absence of a trainer. To date, there remains a critical need in the rehabilitation applications for an effective automated method for motor learning in the home environment [12], or any such environment without the direct supervision of a qualified trainer. There are heavy limits on trainer availability in general, and consequently, unsupervised training is required outside of sports training sessions. Moreover, it is also apparent that guidance and frequent, informative feedback are necessary in real-time to catalyze motor learning [1]. Furthermore, motor tasks are often repetitive and monotonous, resulting in reduced compliance without some form of engagement or interaction [10].

Providing feedback on human motion presents a number of research challenges including: capturing bio-mechanically accurate motion outside a laboratory environment, automatic classification and extraction of different actions within a movement sequence, analysis and interpretation of motion data of each action, communication of the analysis results and suggestions for modification/improvement back to the end user. The feedback that is delivered to the end user also depends upon a number of factors including the nature of the movement being measured (e.g. day-long activity vs a specific exercise), complexity of the action (e.g. simple single limb movement vs whole body action), user context (e.g. location and time) and user experience (e.g. novice vs expert). A further over-arching research challenge of course is that all of this should be accomplished in real-time (i.e. during a movement) or near real-time (i.e. immediately after a movement has been performed).

In this paper, we present the design of an interactive platform for motion sensing and feedback delivery in a home based setting, which is capable of delivering real-time visual feedback, with an emphasis on performance.

2. MOTION CAPTURE

Motion Capture (MoCap) is a field of science that primarily deals with the recording, reconstructing and analysis of motion, and is a well-studied and broad area of research [13]. Marker based Vicon MoCap[1] generally represents the gold-standard and offers excellent results but carries a high price tag and requires complex post-processing, leaving it out of reach for most. For this reason, significant research is being performed into the area of low-cost alternatives [8, 6], using either marker-less based methods such computer vision [14] based analysis or by using depth cameras like the Microsoft Kinect [7, 15]. However, many of these systems suffer from tracking errors due to marker occlusions.

*This work was funded by the ASU-DCU Catalyst Fund. Part of this work was supported by Science Foundation Ireland under grant number SFI/12/RC/2289.

MM '16 October 15-19, 2016, Amsterdam, Netherlands

ACM ISBN 978-1-4503-3603-1/16/10.
DOI: http://dx.doi.org/10.1145/2964284.2973815

[1]See: http://www.vicon.com/

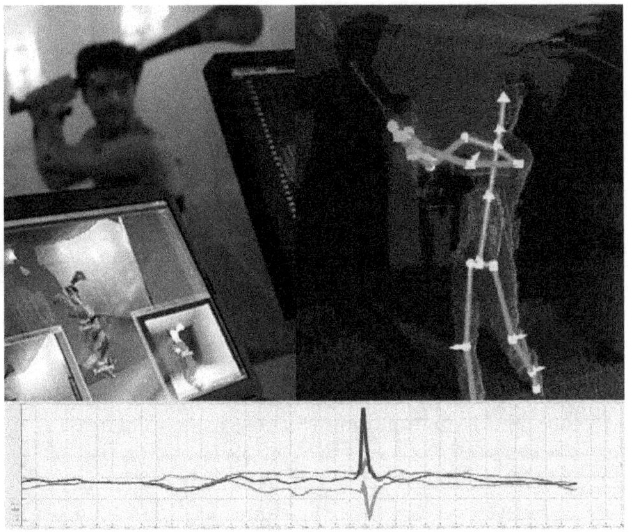

Figure 1: ***The authors demonstrating the comparison between a Gold-Standard Vicon system, on the left, with their low cost Kinect-IMU fusion approach.***

Inertial Measurement Units (IMUs) offer an accurate MoCap alternative [9, 3] and have been developed into commercially successful systems, such as XSens [11], however they are still prone to drift in accuracy over time, a common limitation of inertial sensing. IMUs are low power, light weight, offer high sample rates and do not suffer from occlusions, but they are susceptible to orientation and position errors if not corrected over time. Furthermore, commercially available IMU MoCap solutions are still relatively high in price, approx. 50K Euro. During the last few years, a number of low-cost alternatives have been proposed, the majority of which are based upon fusing data received from different cheap sensor modalities (e.g. fusion of Kinect & wearables) [5, 4] to provide inexpensive yet accurate systems.

Previous research [2] carried out by the authors has investigated a low-cost platform that utilises 3 IMU sensors together with advanced analysis algorithms, multiple IMU calibration and inverse kinematics for detecting the stance phase of the gait cycle. This allows for the reduction of integration drift error of the IMU system and creates an accurate 3-D gait analysis platform for the lower limbs.

In this paper the described platform utilises low-cost sensor fusion to produce a skeletal reconstruction that combines the global joint positioning of the Microsoft Kinect together with the joint-rotational accuracy of inertial sensors.

3. THE PLATFORM

The platform consists of two IMUs, a Microsoft Kinect V2 and software written in C# through the open-source Unity3D game engine. The IMUs are connected via Bluetooth to a computer and are set with a sample frequency of 256Hz. Only the accelerometer and gyroscope channels are used. After a brief T-pose to calibrate the IMUs to the local coordinate system of the Kinect, a skeleton fusion technique is employed, based on [2, 5, 4], that uses the skeleton extraction/tracking from the Microsoft Kinect for all joints except the wrists where the joint position and orientations are calculated from the IMUs (note that the Hand, Hand-Tip and Thumb joints from the Kinect SDK were not used here). The platform can be seen in Figure 2.

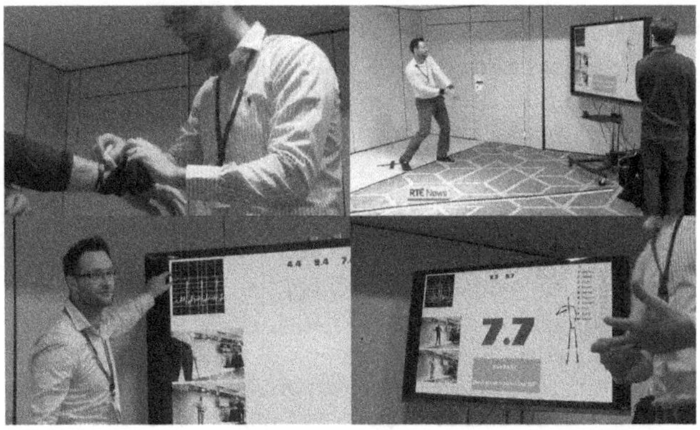

Figure 2: ***Clockwise from the top left: An IMU is strapped to each wrist of the user's wrists for use with the platform; the user is being recorded using the platform whilst attempting to copy the selected motion; Accelerometer data graphed against the target acceleration of the correct technique is displayed for the user; A gamified score feedback is given to the user after each of their three attempts and a leader-board of the top scores records the total.***

A sample movement of a trainer or athlete performing a desired motion is demonstrated for the user through a video, skeleton visualisation and an IMU acceleration graph. The user is then prompted to perform the movement. A comparison module compares the user's accelerations from each wrist to the sample movement and visual feedback is given. A score based on the a ratio of the user data to the sample data is recorded for this attempt and feedback is given instructing the user to speed up or slow their movement. The user performs two subsequent attempts and then the overall score is recorded on a system score board for comparison. This platform demonstrates an example of providing feedback soon after a movement, where the goal is not to change the technique as it is being produced but rather to indicate to an end user that he/she has attained a specific performance level associated with a fast complex movement.

4. CONCLUSION

We wish to understand the most optimum way of delivering multimodal feedback to a user both during slow moving rehabilitation sessions and also throughout fast moving sporting sessions. If a user can be informed through out a session about their performance, this can allow them to make the necessary adjustments to their technique in order to perform better, both in sports performance and in muscular-skeletal rehabilitation.

5. DEMONSTRATION

The demonstration will consist of a laptop, a Kinect, two wrist worn IMUs, a bluetooth receiver and a large screen. The platform will be showcased using a pre-recorded sporting movement from an Irish national Hurling champion and users will be shown how to engage with the system in order to replicate the precise sporting motion. Then they can proceed to play the game, having three attempts and finally being given a score based on their performance. A poster detailing the motivations behind and current state of our research on low-cost motion capture and gaming technologies will also be shown.

6. REFERENCES

[1] Patient Motivation and Adherence to Postsurgery Rehabilitation Exercise Recommendations: The Influence of Physiotherapists' Autonomy-Supportive Behaviors. 90.

[2] A. Ahmadi, F. Destelle, D. Monaghan, K. Moran, N. E. O'Connor, L. Unzueta, and M. Linaza. Human gait monitoring using body-worn inertial sensors and kinematic modelling. pages 1–4, 2015.

[3] A. Ahmadi, E. Mitchell, C. Richter, F. Destelle, M. Gowing, N. E. O'Connor, and K. Moran. Toward automatic activity classification and movement assessment during a sports training session. *Internet of Things Journal, IEEE*, 2(1):23–32, 2015.

[4] F. Destelle, A. Ahmadi, K. Moran, N. E. O'Connor, N. Zioulis, A. Chatzitofis, D. Zarpalas, P. Daras, L. Unzueta, and J. Goenetxea. A multi-modal 3d capturing platform for learning and preservation of traditional sports and games. *ACM*, pages 747–748, 2015.

[5] F. Destelle, A. Ahmadi, N. E. O'Connor, K. Moran, A. Chatzitofis, D. Zarpalas, and P. Daras. Low-cost accurate skeleton tracking based on fusion of kinect and wearable inertial sensors. pages 371–375, 2014.

[6] J. E. Deutsch, M. Borbely, J. Filler, K. Huhn, and P. Guarrera-Bowlby. Use of a low-cost, commercially available gaming console (wii) for rehabilitation of an adolescent with cerebral palsy. *Physical Therapy*, 88:1196–1207, 2008.

[7] S. Essid, D. Alexiadis, R. Tournemenne, M. Gowing, P. Kelly, D. Monaghan, P. Daras, A. Drémeau, and N. E. O'Connor. An advanced virtual dance performance evaluator. *IEEE*, 2012.

[8] E. Farella, L. Benini, B. Ricco, and A. Acquaviva. A low-power, low-cost motion capture system based on integrated accelerometers. *Advances in Multimedia*, 1, 2007.

[9] H. Liu, X. Wei, J. Chai, I. Ha, and T. Rhee. Realtime human motion control with a small number of inertial sensors. *Symposium on Interactive 3D Graphics and Games. ACM*, pages 133–140, 2011.

[10] D. Reinkensmeyer and S. Housman. "If I can't do it once, why do it a hundred times?": Connecting volition to movement success in a virtual environment motivates people to exercise the arm after stroke. In *Virtual Rehabilitation, 2007*, pages 44–48, Sept. 2007.

[11] D. Roetenberg, H. Luinge, and P. Slycke. Xsens mvn: Full 6dof human motion tracking using miniature inertial sensors. *Xsens Motion Technologies BV, Tech.Rep.*, 2009.

[12] N. SkjÃęret, A. Nawaz, T. Morat, D. Schoene, J. L. Helbostad, and B. Vereijken. Exercise and rehabilitation delivered through exergames in older adults: An integrative review of technologies, safety and efficacy. *International Journal of Medical Informatics*, 85(1):1–16, Jan. 2016.

[13] G. Welch and E. Foxlin. Motion tracking: No silver bullet, but a respectable arsenal. *Computer Graphics and Applications, IEEE*, 22:24–38, 2002.

[14] M. Windolf, N. GÃűtzen, and M. Morlock. Systematic accuracy and precision analysis of video motion capturing systemsâĂŤexemplified on the vicon-460 system. *Journal of Biomechanics*, 41:2776–2780, 2008.

[15] Z. Zhang. Microsoft kinect sensor and its effect. *MultiMedia, IEEE*, 19:4–10, 2012.

PlaylistCreator: An Assisted Approach for Playlist Creation

Ricardo Dias, Daniel Gonçalves
INESC-ID, Instituto Superior Técnico,
Universidade de Lisboa, Portugal
{ricardo.dias,daniel.j.goncalves}@ist.utl.pt

Manuel J. Fonseca
LaSIGE, Faculdade de Ciências,
Universidade de Lisboa, Portugal
mjfonseca@ciencias.ulisboa.pt

ABSTRACT

In this demo paper we describe PlaylistCreator, an assisted approach for supporting the creation of music playlists. Our solution allows creators to express song selection and browsing through a visual representation of their intents in a unified view, which relies on a set-based model for representing sources of songs. Creators can convey their purposes by seamlessly combining criteria for song selection from either manual or automatic sources, such as artists and albums, or similarity measures between artists or songs.

CCS Concepts

•**Human-centered computing** → **Graphical user interfaces;** •**Information systems** → *Search interfaces;*

Keywords

Assisted Playlist Creation; Song Selection; Set Theory; Visual Representation

1. INTRODUCTION

During the last years, music playlists have received increasingly attention from researchers because of their use in streaming services as a mechanism to promote song discovery, and as a strategy for browsing music libraries, and for social affirmation. Most recent efforts in the research of playlist creation have been directed at the creation of algorithms to automatically generate playlists without human control and intervention [1]. However, assisted techniques that rely on visualization techniques for supporting a hybrid playlist creation have gained attention, mostly driven by recent findings from a few studies reporting that people enjoy creating playlists manually [3], and that listeners trust and prefer handmade playlists over those automatically generated [5]. Assisted techniques promise to bridge the gap between manual and automatic approaches and address the lack of control existent in automatic techniques.

MM '16 October 15-19, 2016, Amsterdam, Netherlands

ACM ISBN 978-1-4503-3603-1/16/10.

DOI: http://dx.doi.org/10.1145/2964284.2973816

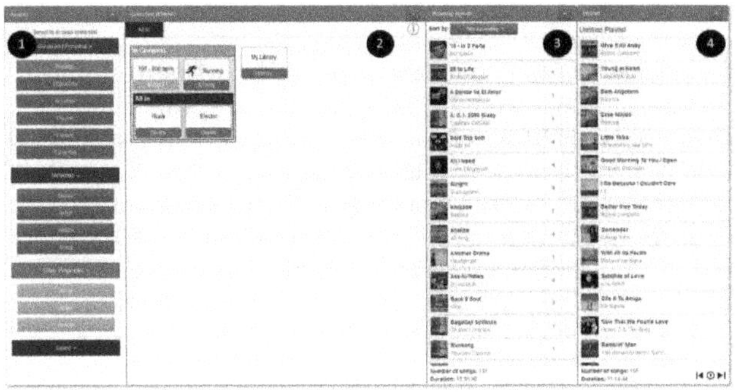

Figure 1: PlaylistCreator User Interface.

In this paper we present PlaylistCreator[1], an assisted approach for supporting the interactive creation of playlists. This solution allows creators to perform song selection by seamlessly combining heterogeneous criteria, either from manual and automatic sources (Figure 1), in a composite box-like visual representation, similar to faceted techniques. It combines strategies for manual song selection, like for example, looking for songs using metadata (song title, artist name, and album name), with algorithms that automatically suggest songs, based on content-based features, for instance. This application implements a set-based model that provides the background for the design of complex queries through the combination of heterogeneous sources of songs with the recourse to binary operations from set theory [4].

2. SONG SELECTION

Assisted approaches typically rely on visualization techniques to support playlist creation. In PlaylistCreator, we propose a set-based model and a composite box-like visualization to support song selection for creating playlists.

2.1 Set-based Model

In our model, every *source of songs (or entry point)* is considered a *set*. Songs can belong to one or more sets, and a set can have zero or more songs. The sets of songs can either come from a manual source, like the songs from an artist or an album, or from an automatic approach, such as the tempo, mood or similarity. Some sets can be a subset of others, and the result of combining them depends on the criteria used to create (filter) them.

To support the creation of more complex queries, sets can

[1]http://web.ist.utl.pt/ricardo.dias/playlistcreator

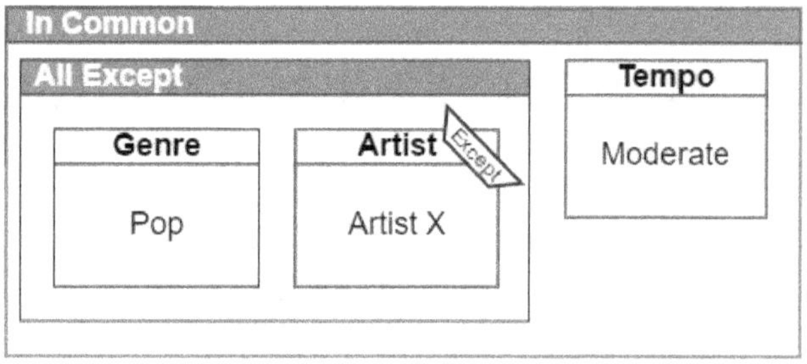

Figure 2: Visual representation of a query, with three sources of songs and the application of the set binary operations.

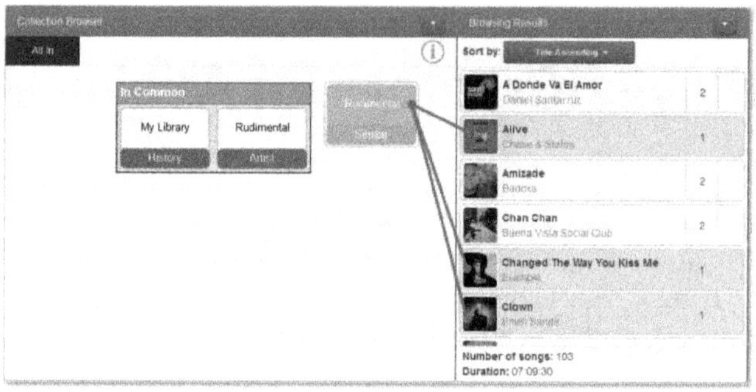

Figure 3: Brushing and Highlighting mechanisms.

be combined using the binary operations from set theory [4]. To improve readability, speak the users language and facilitate recognition of the different operations, we defined a nomenclature closely related to song selection for each of the set operators: i) Union - **All In**, ii) Intersection - **In Common**, iii) Symmetric Difference - **Not In Common**, and iv) Set Difference - **All Except**. Despite their provenance, either manual selection or automatic algorithms, all sources are treated and represented equally.

2.2 Visual Representation

To represent the proposed set-based model we adopted a composite box-like diagram, in a similar fashion to what is presented in *UML diagrams* or in some faceted techniques [2]. We chose this representation because it provides an easy to read visualization, and supports the combination of different criteria in more complex queries by applying box composition (for manual and automatic sources).

Each *source* or set is drawn as a *box*, in a similar fashion to *Classes* in *UML diagrams*. This representation provides a visual mapping of the *source*, by showing the type that it represents and a description or parametrization of the source (Figure 2 - Genre, Artist and Tempo). Set operations are also drawn using a box representation that encodes the *type of the operation and its parameters* (Figure 2 - In Common and All Except). We applied box composition in a similar fashion to *object composition* in *UML diagrams*, to capture the essence of the operations and improve query readability.

3. PLAYLISTCREATOR PROTOTYPE

PlaylistCreator is the prototype developed for supporting an assisted playlist creation (Figure 1), using the proposed set-based model to allow the combination of both manual and automatic criteria for browsing and song selection. It was implemented using the Play Framework for the backend, and HTML, CSS, Javascript, and GO.JS[2] for the front-end. Communication is handled using JSON requests.

3.1 User Interface

The user interface of PlaylistCreator is divided into four main parts as depicted in Figure 1: 1) consists of a toolbar representation that allows creators to select songs from a list of predefined filters or criteria grouped into different categories, and that encode the sources of songs described in the set-based model; 2) the *Collection Browser*, depicted in area 2, is where creators combine the sources of songs to browse the music collection and select songs, using the visual representation proposed; 3) consists of a sortable list of songs that contains the result of the visual query created, and highlights the relationship between the sources of songs used in the *Collection Browser* and the results (bidirectional brushing and highlighting mechanism); 4) represents the playlist being created, offering the possibility to add, remove, reorder and position songs, as well as exporting the playlist.

[2]https://gojs.net/

3.2 Song Selection and Playlist Creation

In PlaylistCreator, each playlist is created and managed manually, with creators having the final decision about which songs appear in it. To select songs from the music collection, creators drag the sources of songs from the *toolbar* to the *collection browser*, and compose them using the available operations. This creates visual queries like the ones depicted in Figure 2 and 3 and filters out songs that respect all the criteria (Figure 1-3). The combination of results follows a bottom-up approach, by first selecting the songs for the sources (Figure 1- Genre, Artist, Tempo) and then performing the binary combination operations (Figure 1 - All Except, In Common). Each song is related to a list of the sets that originally selected it, which supports the brushing and highlighting mechanisms (Figure 3), that promote transparency of the combination process and trust in the final results. In this approach, the higher the number of sources that suggest a song, the more probable that song fits the intents of the creator entirely. Finally, creators pick the songs they want for the playlist, either by randomly or individually selecting them.

4. CONCLUSIONS

PlaylistCreator is an assisted approach for playlist creation that proposes the use of a flexible and scalable set-based model and its visual representation to seamlessly support the heterogeneous combination of music sources for the task of song selection.

5. ACKNOWLEDGMENTS

This work was supported by national funds through Fundação para a Ciência e Tecnologia, under INESC-ID multi-annual funding - PEst-OE/EEI/LA0021/2013 and LaSIGE Strategic Project - UID/CEC/00408/2013. Ricardo Dias was supported by FCT, grant reference SFRH/BD/70939/-2010.

6. REFERENCES

[1] G. Bonnin and D. Jannach. Automated generation of music playlists: Survey and experiments. *ACM Computing Surveys (CSUR)*, 47(2):26, 2015.

[2] R. Dachselt, M. Frisch, and M. Weiland. Facetzoom: a continuous multi-scale widget for navigating hierarchical metadata. In *Proceedings of the SIGCHI Conference on Human Factors in Computing Systems*, pages 1353–1356. ACM, 2008.

[3] M. Kamalzadeh, D. Baur, and T. Möller. A survey on music listening and management behaviours. In *Proceedings of the International Conference on Music Information Retrieval*, pages 373–378, 2012.

[4] V. J. Katz. *A History of Mathematics.* Pearson/Addison-Wesley, 2004.

[5] A. Laplante and J. S. Downie. Everyday life music information-seeking behaviour of young adults. In *Proceedings of the International Conference on Music Information Retrieval*, pages 381–382, 2006.

WIMBY: What's in My Backyard?

Michael Dorkhom
Queensland University of Technology
Brisbane, Australia
michael.dorkhom@connect.qut.edu.au

Alan Woodley
Queensland University of Technology
Brisbane, Australia
a.woodley@qut.edu.au

Shlomo Geva
Queensland University of Technology
Brisbane, Australia
s.geva@qut.edu.au

Richi Nayak
Queensland University of Technology
Brisbane, Australia
r.nayak@qut.edu.au

ABSTRACT
Location-aware social media is increasingly being used to inform decisions in a spatiotemporal context. However, collecting, fusing, processing and merging information from different social media platforms is a challenge because of diversity of information between different platforms. Here, we present the WIMBY, which is able to access multiple social media platforms to help users answer the question "What's in my Backyard?". In doing so, the WIMBY helps to address the challenge of dealing with diverse social media information. It is believed that the WIMBY can be extended to include more information sources (including other social media platforms) to help inform decision makers in a wider array of applications.

CCS Concepts
Information systems → Information retrieval → Specialized information retrieval → Environment-specific retrieval → Web and social media search.

Keywords
Georeference; social media; data fusion.

1. INTRODUCTION
Decision makers, ranging from the general population to governments and companies, are increasingly relying on spatially tagged information to inform their decisions. The volume and diversity of spatially tagged information is increasing. For example, spatially tagged information can be: textual or non-textual, static or streaming, structured or unstructured and occur across multiple spatiotemporal scales. This creates increased complexity to collect, fuse, process and analyze this information, particularly from a user friendly perspective.

Here, we describe the WIMBY, a prototype web application that allows users to rapidly intuitively answer the question "What's in my backyard". To use the WIMBY, users identify an area of interest (for example, their current location). The WIMBY mines social media platforms to identify, collect and fuse together information about points of interest (for example, pubs, restaurants, nightclubs) within the specified area. The WIMBY is able process a diverse range of datasets, including: textual, multimedia, streaming, structured and unstructured information. Finally, the WIMBY presents this information to the user in an intuitive manner.

Here, we describe the WIMBY in detail. The WIMBY accesses three diverse social media platforms. For our initial research, we have specifically chosen a general purpose use case. Given the need to understand complex spatiotemporal data sets it is easy to see how the use case could be extended for more sophisticated use cases involving individuals, companies or governments that need to make personal, commercial or policy decisions.

2. BACKGROUND
Understanding spatiotemporal context is often vital for a wide variety of decision makers. For example, policy makers will need to know where are the best places to invest in schools, hospitals or infrastructure [2], industries will need to understand the environmental and social impacts caused by their actions [4] and individuals will use spatiotemporal information when making life-changing decisions such as where to live, work or receive an education.

Social media is more frequently being used as a resource for general research purposes, that is, those outside of the traditional text or multimedia retrieval domains, such as understanding natural disaster response and recovery [3; 7; 9], estimating aesthetic and ecological values [6] and capturing a community's response to industrial growth [1].

For spatiotemporal research social media seems particularly useful, since social media posts are often georeferenced, either through implicit geolocation tagging through the device used to upload the post (for example by using GPS co-ordinates on a mobile device or reverse IP geolocation on a desktop) or explicit geolocation tagging (via user generated hashtags). There is also a benefit in accessing and combining multiple social media sources as this increase the size of data that can be analyzed. However, fusing different social media is difficult as information across platforms is inherently diverse. Some of the diversity contained in social media includes:

- **Media**: Information can consist of text, images, audio or video;
- **Format**: Information can either be unstructured (such as free text) or structured (consisting of field names, values and types);
- **Velocity**: Information can be generated at different rates ranging from streaming information (information that is continuously being generated), static information

MM '16, October 15-19, 2016, Amsterdam, Netherlands
ACM 978-1-4503-3603-1/16/10.
DOI: http://dx.doi.org/10.1145/2964284.2973818

(information that does not change) or information that is updated at various rates.

Here, we present the WIMBY – a location-aware social monitoring and fusion application. The WIMBY identifies and collects information about points of interest for a user. The WIMBY is similar to other location-aware applications such as Geofeedia [5] and WeLink [8] but advances on these applications because it is able to fuse together multiple social media posts about a single point of interest.

3. WIMBY DESIGN

3.1 Social Media Sources

The WIMBY is able to collect, fuse, process and merge information from social media posts. A key motivation for the WIMBY is to address the challenge of fusing together posts from a diverse range of social media, therefore, the chosen social media platforms contain a diverse range of media, format and velocity. These platforms are presented in Table 1. Since the WIMBY is currently a prototype, only three platforms were chosen. However, additional platforms and other types of sources could be used by the WIMBY in the future.

Table 1. Social media sources

Platform	Foursquare	Twitter	Tumblr
Media	Text	Text	Text and Images
Format	Structured	Unstructured	Unstructured
Velocity	Non-streaming	Streaming	Streaming

3.2 System Design

The WIMBY operates via the following eight steps:

1. **Identifying an area of interest:** Users select a specific area on the map or enter a specific address and the respective georeferenced location is identified.
2. **Identifying points of interests:** The area is submitted to Foursquare, which returns points of interest within that area. Each point of interest is represented as a marker on the map.
3. **Points of interest selection:** The user selects a particular point of interest from the map.
4. **Information extraction.** For the selected point of interest information including its name, city and country are extracted from Foursquare.
5. **Searching for information:** Twitter and Tumblr are searched for the names of the points of interests. The queries search for names both as free text (that is, appearing 'as is' in the Tweet or Tumblr text) and as a hashtag. These platforms return a set of posts which are returned to the WIMBY.
6. **Sorting information**: The social media posts are sorted according to the number of times each post has been shared, commented or retweeted.
7. **Information analysis:** For optimization purposes, the posts are filtered and re-ranked. Georeferenced posts that have a geolocation greater than fifty kilometers from the point of interest are removed, since they are likely to be irrelevant. Posts that mention the same city or country as the point of interest are given a higher rank, since they are more likely to be relevant.
8. **Presentation of information**: The final information is presented to the user as a ranked list of posts. Separate tabs are used for each platform.

Figure 1 presents a screenshot of the WIMBY for the user selecting an area of interest (Step 1), while Figure 2 presents the screenshot of the WIMBY after a point of interest has been selected and information about the point of interest has been retrieved (Steps 2 to 8).

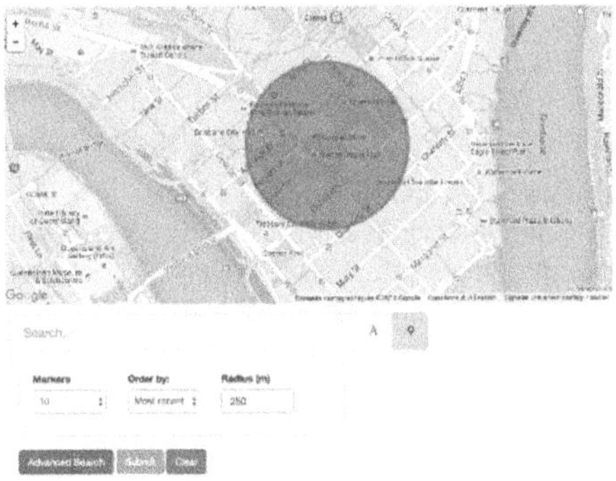

Figure 1. Selecting an area of interest

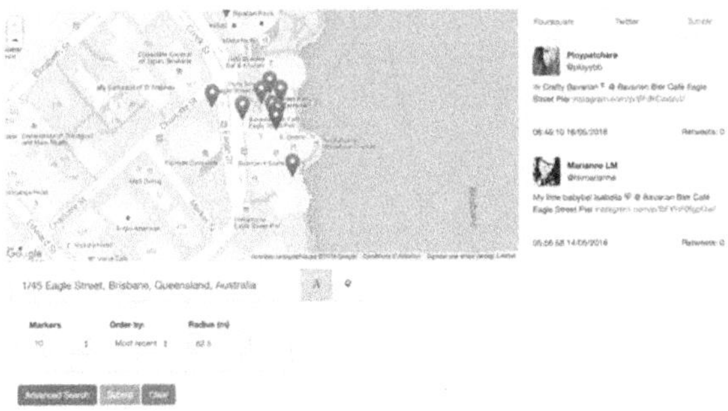

Figure 2. Points of interests and results

4. CONCLUSION

Here we have presented the WIMBY. The WIMBY is able to respond to a user's location with information about local points of interest – informing the user about "What's in my Backyard?" The WIMBY is able to collect, fuse, process and merge a diverse range of social media posts, thereby, addressing a significant challenge. The WIMBY presents this information in a user friendly and intuitive interface.

The WIMBY is currently in its prototype stage of development. However, the WIMBY could be extended to include further spatiotemporal datasets, including information beyond social media platforms. These additional datasets would allow governments, companies and individuals to make better informed personal, commercial or policy decisions.

5. SOURCE CODE

The source code for the WIMBY is available at: https://github.com/MichaelDorkhom/WIMBY. A video on how to use the WIMBY is available at: https://www.youtube.com/watch?v=83aRPvqJ9OO.

6. REFERENCES

[1] Bice, S., Bortz, M., Sullivan, H., and Haines, F., 2015. Fear and licensing in Australia: Exploring a social licence to

operate for an emerging coal seam gas industry. In *Proceedings of the International Conference on Public Policy* (Milian, Italy, 4 July 2015 2015).

[2] Cramb, S.M., Mengersen, K.L., and Baade, P.D., 2011. *Atlas of Cancer in Queensland: Geographical variation in incidence and survival, 1998 to 2007.* Viertel Centre for Research in Cancer Control, Cancer Council Queensland.

[3] Dashti, S., Leysia Palen, L., Heris, M.P., Anderson, K.M., Anderson, T.J., and Anderson, S., 2014. Supporting disaster reconnaissance with social media data: A design-oriented case study of the 2013 colorado floods. In *Proceedings of the Proceedings of the 11th International ISCRAM Conference* (Pennsylvania, United States of America2014).

[4] Franks, D.M., Brereton, D., and Moran, C.J., 2010. Managing the cumulative impacts of coal mining on regional communities and environments in Australia. *Impact Assessment and Project Appraisal 28*, 4, 299-312.

[5] Geofeedia, 2016. Geofeedia: Location-based intelligence platform.

[6] Keeler, B.L., Wood, S.A., Polasky, S., Kling, C., Filstrup, C.T., and Downing, J.A., 2015. Recreational demand for clean water: evidence from geotagged photographs by visitors to lakes. *Frontiers in Ecology and the Environment 13*, 76–81. DOI= http://dx.doi.org/10.1890/140124.

[7] Turpin, E. and Holderness, T., 2015. From social media to geosocial intelligence: experiments with crowdsourcing civic co-management for flood response Jakarta, Indonesia. In *Social Media for Government Services*, S. Nepal, C. Paris and G. D. Eds. Springer, United States, 115-134.

[8] Welink, 2016. WeLink - Location based social media monitoring and engagement platform.

[9] Xiao, Y., Huang, Q., and Wu, K., 2015. Understanding social media data for disaster management. *Natural Hazards 79*, 1663-1679.

SuperSelect – An Interactive Superpixel-Based Segmentation Method for Touch Displays

Christoph Korinke
OFFIS - Institute for Information Technology
Oldenburg, Germany
korinke@offis.de

Tim Claudius Stratmann, Tim Laue, Susanne Boll
University of Oldenburg
Oldenburg, Germany
firstname.lastname@uol.de

ABSTRACT

We present the concept of an interactive image segmentation method, which allows a fast and precise extraction of foreground objects from natural images. The method is especially suited for mobile, touch-based devices. The approach combines automatic image segmentation with interactive refinement. In a first step, the user extracts an object using the first stage of the GrabCut algorithm [6]. Any errors in the resulting segmentation can then be corrected via a novel correction step in which the underlying image is over-segmented into superpixels using the SLIC algorithm [1]. The user can select individual superpixels in order to adjust the image segmentation. This image segmentation method is implemented as a full working demo on a Microsoft Surface Pro 3.

Keywords

segmentation; user interface; human computer interaction

1. INTRODUCTION

The usage of mobile devices is increasing and getting more and more popular. As the majority of today's mobile devices also have a camera the number of photos taken with mobile devices has superseded the number of photos taken with regular cameras. Photos are then shared via social media platforms such as Instagram. Often, they are edited first, e.g. by blurring or graying out the background to focus on the important parts. There are many algorithms today supporting the user to modify photos by adjusting simple parameters. However, the accurate segmentation of areas in a photo still demands a lot of effort from a user, as an automatic segmentation is often imprecise and the segmentation often requires a tedious interactive process. Especially on mobile devices, accurate image segmentation can be a challenge as most segmentation algorithms are optimized for the usage on a desktop computer. But today photos are often used and shared directly after the shot. Consequently, there is a need for intuitive and easy to use segmentation applications on mobile devices.

We present a novel approach for image segmentation on mobile devices. The first step of our approach is based on the first step of the Grabcut algorithm [6]. The user performs a simple rectangular selection as input for the first stage of Grabcut. In a second step, we utilize superpixels in a second segmentation step by showing a superpixel mask to the user. A superpixel forms a cluster of pixels within a limited space and homogeneous color. Superpixels can hence be understood as a perceptual grouping of pixels in an image. The superpixels are generated with the SLIC algorithm [1]. The segmentation can be refined by selecting or deselecting superpixels. The user can zoom and pan to perform a more precise segmentation. The superpixel mask is recalculated based on the zoom level and viewport of the image maintaining a fixed superpixel size. The iterative selection process is continued until the results satisfy the users demands.

MM '16 October 15-19, 2016, Amsterdam, Netherlands

ACM ISBN 978-1-4503-3603-1/16/10.
DOI: http://dx.doi.org/10.1145/2964284.2973819

2. RELATED WORK

Reese et al. characterize in [5] interactive segmentation methods as an adjustment of seed points, boundaries or tuning parameters to incrementally refine a selection. Li et al. classify the methods in two main approaches for interactive image segmentation, region based and boundary based [3].

In *boundary based methods*, the user encircles an object with an adjustable curve. One approach has been presented by Mortensen and Berrett in intelligent scissors [4]. In this approach, the user sets points around the object and the algorithms tries to adjust a line between these points to the object boundary. In texture rich regions many alternative paths exist which can lead to wrong selections. For a better result, the user has to set more points in this region. As the user has to enclose the entire boundary this can lead to an increased amount of user interaction for good results.

Region based methods use loose hints of foreground objects and background parts for an optimization algorithm which tries to extract the object boundary by these hints. The hints can be given e.g. by clicking or drawing lines. In several iterations the user can give more hints to improve the result. An prominent example of a region based method is GrabCut [6]. In this approach, the user gives a first estimation by a bounding box by which everything outside the box is labelled as background everything inside the box as unknown. The algorithm then classifies the unknown pixels into foreground and background based on the knowledge of background pixels. In further steps, the user can draw lines for foreground and background on wrongly classified pixels to improve the results.

There exists a number of approaches for image segmentation, but most of these focus primarily on algorithms rather than input and refinement methods. In our previous work we explored different input methods for interactive image segmentation on mobile devices in [2]. We found that drawing an outline or a bounding box are intuitively used by users on touch displays to segment an object. Appropriate input methods for the result refinement, especially on mobile touch-based devices, are not evaluated. Following we present an approach for an input method to easily improve the result based on oversegmentation with SLIC [1].

3. DESIGN

Our proposed method is based on two steps – a region-based approach combined with an interactive segmentation method based on superpixels. Previous and related work shows [2] that a bounding box is an intuitive input method for segmentation. We use the GrabCut algorithm by [6]. Therefore, we decided that a user draws a bounding box around the desired object that should be segmented by GrabCut in the first step. The result can then be iteratively refined in the second step. The refinement process is illustrated in Figure 1.

First, the image is oversegmented with the SLIC algorithm [1]. SLIC uses homogeneous cluster centres to cluster pixels with a spatial limit for k-means clustering to create homogeneous superpixels. These homogeneous superpixels fit good to the edges of the object. These superpixels can be easily added to or removed from the foreground by simply clicking on them. The colors of the superpixel edges display how many foreground or background pixels belong to each superpixel.

We designed two interaction variants to fit the selected foreground pixels to the object edges using the superpixel mask.

Static zoom, dynamic superpixels In this variant of the refinement step the user marks a wrongly segmented region using a drawing tool. The view port automatically zooms into the selected region, filling the screen. The zoomed region then is oversegmented in superpixels. The user can dynamically change the size of the superpixels using a slider. After the selection, the viewport changes back to the full view of the segmented object. It is important to define lower and upper boundaries for the superpixel size in this approach.

Dynamic zoom, static superpixels The image is then divided up into a number of superpixels. The size of the superpixels is calculated depending on the size and pixel density of the display as well as the current size of the visible image region. Thereby, we maintain a minimal but still comfortably touchable superpixel size to ensure a high precision and a good usability. The interaction with the superpixel mask is implemented analogue to the first variant. The user can zoom and move the view port freely by using pinch and spread gestures. The superpixel mask is then recalculated and adjusted to the current viewport when the viewport is changed by the user. We implemented a small delay before the recalculation to avoid unnecessary calculations during the zooming and moving process.

As a steady superpixel size resulted in an easier and intuitive handling, we implemented the second variant. We

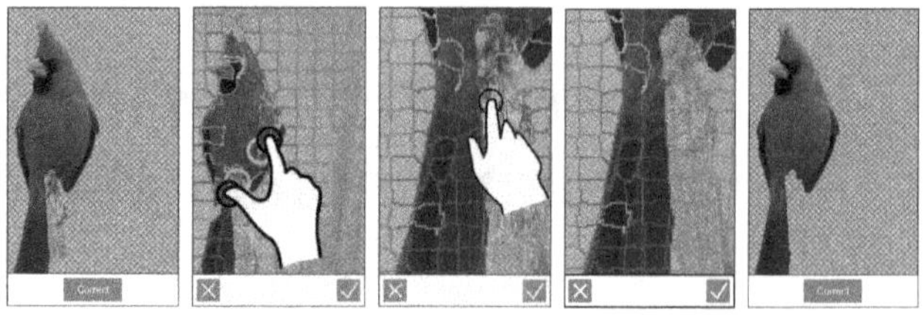

Figure 1: Illustration of refinement step (variant 2)

chose the SLIC algorithm to create our superpixel mask, as it provides a good precision and homogeneity and the possibility to weight both properties. Figure 2 shows a screenshot of the prototype implementation of our approach.

Figure 2: Screenshot of the User Interface for interactive adjustment of the segmentation

4. USAGE

After an image is loaded, the user can drag a bounding box around the object that shall be cut out. Two circles, top left and bottom right, show the touch points for adapting the dimension of the bounding box. When the object fits into the bounding box, the extraction button shall be pressed. A first result is shown with hidden background. If needed, the bounding box can be adapted again. The result can be refined by entering the correction view. In this view, the background is transparent and a superpixel mask is shown. With a zoom gesture, the object size changes and the superpixels remain in their average size. Thus, the superpixels can be adapted to the object border. In a menu the user can change if touching a superpixel will add or remove it from the foreground or toggle between fore- and background. After pressing the confirm button, the result without the background is shown.

5. CONCLUSIONS

We present a semi-automated segmentation approach for touch displays that supports user refinement of the segmentation by utilizing a static superpixel mask that can be dynamically zoomed to select and deselect parts of the fore- or background. Our prototype demonstrates, superpixel masks are a good visualization tool for humans to interactively correct and refine the segmentation of images.

6. REFERENCES

[1] R. Achanta, A. Shaji, K. Smith, A. Lucchi, P. Fua, and S. Süsstrunk. Slic superpixels. Technical report, 2010.

[2] C. Korinke, N. S. Worzyk, and S. Boll. Exploring touch interaction methods for image segmentation on mobile devices. In *Proceedings of the 14th International Conference on Mobile and Ubiquitous Multimedia*, MUM '15, pages 84–93, New York, NY, USA, 2015. ACM.

[3] Y. Li, J. Sun, C.-K. Tang, and H.-Y. Shum. Lazy snapping. In *ACM SIGGRAPH 2004 Papers*, SIGGRAPH '04, pages 303–308, New York, NY, USA, 2004. ACM.

[4] E. N. Mortensen and W. A. Barrett. Intelligent scissors for image composition. In *Proceedings of the 22nd annual conference on Computer graphics and interactive techniques*, SIGGRAPH '95, pages 191–198, New York, NY, USA, 1995. ACM.

[5] L. Reese and W. Barrett. Image editing with intelligent paint. In *Proceedings of Eurographics*, volume 21, pages 714–724, 2002.

[6] C. Rother, V. Kolmogorov, and A. Blake. Grabcut: interactive foreground extraction using iterated graph cuts. In *ACM SIGGRAPH 2004 Papers*, SIGGRAPH '04, pages 309–314, New York, NY, USA, 2004. ACM.

ThePlantGame: Actively Training Human Annotators for Domain-specific Crowdsourcing

Maximilien Servajean
INRIA Zenith team
LIRMM
servajean@lirmm.fr

Alexis Joly
INRIA Zenith team
LIRMM
alexis.joly@inria.fr

Dennis Shasha
NYU
shasha@courant.nyu.edu

Julien Champ
INRIA Zenith team
LIRMM
champ@lirmm.fr

Esther Pacitti
INRIA Zenith team
LIRMM
pacitti@lirmm.fr

ABSTRACT

In a typical citizen science/crowdsourcing environment, the contributors label items. When there are few labels, it is straightforward to train contributors and judge the quality of their labels by giving a few examples with known answers. Neither is true when there are thousands of domain-specific labels and annotators with heterogeneous skills. This demo paper presents an *Active User Training* framework implemented as a serious game called ThePlantGame. It is based on a set of data-driven algorithms allowing to (i) actively train annotators, and (ii) evaluate the quality of contributors' answers on new test items to optimize predictions.

1. ACTIVE USER TRAINING

Classical crowdsourcing algorithms for multi-label classification tasks [1, 3, 5, 6] are typically based on the Bayesian inference of the most probable labels according to the confusion matrix of each worker. Applying such approaches in the context of classification tasks with very large number of classes and expert knowledge is however challenging in two principle ways. First, the very high number of classes, *e.g.* thousands of plant species, makes it impossible to train a complete confusion matrix for each participant as it would require them to answer a huge number of queries (typically quadratic in the number of classes). Furthermore, the brute-force approach consisting of a quiz across the full list of classes is not tractable for non-specialist contributors. To address these issues, we propose an *Active User Training* framework where the training hypothesis space is adaptively and dynamically chosen for each user and observation, through machine learning techniques. Figure 1 describes the framework architecture. It is composed of five modules:

1. Automatic annotation: when a new data item i is added to the system, a machine learning model (*i.e.* a convolutional neural network in our experiment) predicts the probability of its true label t_i. Once the probability $p(t_i = j)$ of one class overcomes a system defined threshold (*i.e.* 99%), the item is automatically tagged as validated. Otherwise, it is processed by steps 2, 3 and 4 to reduce its uncertainty.

2. Active Training: to actively train the annotators, the system automatically creates quizzes of size $k << n$ classes in which the probability of appearance of a class j is proportional to its likelihood $p(t_i = j)$ given an item i. Thus, the annotators actually learn how to disambiguate the classes that are the most confused in the unvalidated data. Using such Monte-Carlo sampling rather than a hard selection of the top-k classes allows to train more complementary the annotators and avoids sticking on the current bias of the system (*e.g.* the true class might not be in the top-k).

3. Skills-aware Assignment: to classify as many data as possible based on the current known confusion of each annotators, the system assigns unvalidated items to users – up to a system defined threshold – that are very likely – given a threshold – to be able to disambiguate them. This is done by solving the following optimization problem (using *e.g.* Cplex solver):

$$\begin{aligned} \underset{x_{ik}}{\text{maximize}} \quad & \sum_{i=0}^{N}\sum_{k=0}^{K} x_{ik}p_{ik} \\ \text{subject to} \quad & \sum_{i=0}^{N} x_{ik} < n_k \;\forall k, \sum_{k=0}^{K} x_{ik} < m_i \;\forall i \\ & x_{ik} \in \{0,1\} \;\forall i,k. \end{aligned}$$

where $x_{ik} \in \{0, 1\}$ indicates if item i has been assigned to user k or not, p_{ik} is the likelihood of user k to give a correct classification proposition for item i (according to her/his confusion matrix as discussed in step 4). x_{ik} is constrained by n_k and m_i to limit the number of assignments per user and per object. Solving this optimization problem will result in maximizing the number of assignment that will receive a correct classification proposition.

4. Classification inference: Once classification propositions have been given by the annotators to a set of items, an inference model will update their probability distributions. This model initializes the confusion of each user based on their performance during the training and the probabilities of each class based on the validated data. The model then infer the actual confusion of each worker using a Bayesian network. It has the following joint probability distribution:

$$p(\kappa, \Pi, t, c, \theta | A, B, \nu) = \prod_{i=1}^{N}\{\kappa_{t_i} \prod_{k=1}^{K} \pi^{(k)}_{t_i, c_i^{(k)}}\} p(\kappa|\nu) \\ p(\Pi|\theta)p(\theta|A, B) \tag{1}$$

MM '16 October 15-19, 2016, Amsterdam, Netherlands

ACM ISBN 978-1-4503-3603-1/16/10.

DOI: http://dx.doi.org/10.1145/2964284.2973820

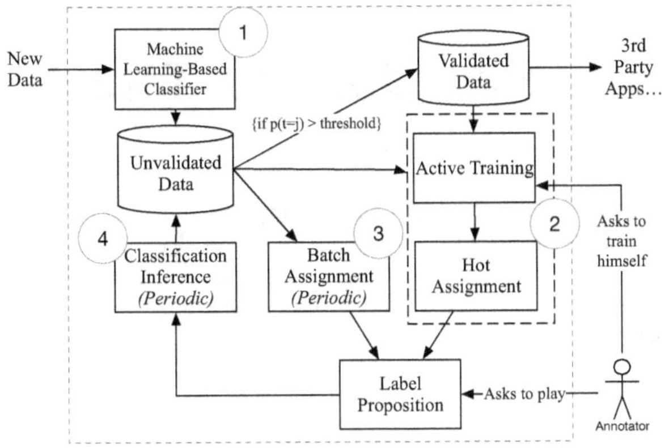

Figure 1: Framework Architecture.

Where κ is the global distribution of each class that follows a Dirichlet distribution of parameters ν, Π represents all confusion matrices where $\pi_{jl}^{(k)}$ is the probability that the user k would answer class l if the true class was j. Each row of a confusion matrix has a Dirichlet distribution of parameters $\theta_j^{(k)}$. t is the set of true labels of all items following a multinomial distribution of parameters κ. Finally, all θ_{jl} follow independent gamma distributions of parameter α_{jl} and β_{jl}. More details about the model are available in the following paper [4].

2. THE PLANT GAME

The proposed framework was implemented within a real playful platform (*The Plant Game*[1]) focused on the specific and complex problem of plants classification. We used the dataset released for the plant task of the LifeCLEF 2015 challenge [2]. Training images were used for the automatic creation of the quizzes (*i.e.* for the active training of the annotators) whereas test images were used as the unannotated data to be classified. To play, each user has to create an account and to self-evaluate his current expertise (*i.e.* beginner, intermediate, expert or expert+). The Plant Game then offers three game modes: (i) **Training mode**, *i.e.* the active training approach, (ii) **The Plant Game mode** where the player can annotate the unvalidated observations assigned to him, and (iii) the **Duel mode** in which two players can challenge each others based on randomly assigned items. After an item has become validated (thanks to one or several inference rounds), the player can see can see if she/he was wrong or not in The Plant Game mode view. Additionally, all users can check their ranking to see how well they perform.

3. EXPERIMENTS

Figure 2 shows a global overview of the benefits of our contributions. First, it is clear that complex classification tasks are impossible without training. Second, training only is not sufficient. The annotators can actually not learn all classes. Combining training and a correct assignment strategy is necessary to obtain the best results. Also, a correct aggregation method based on a Bayesian network enables even better Results.

Figure 3 shows that our contributions enable a clear gain in terms of data quality compared to a fully automated solution. For instance, we obtain a precision of 0.98 while the *CNN* only obtains 0.85.

[1]http://theplantgame.com

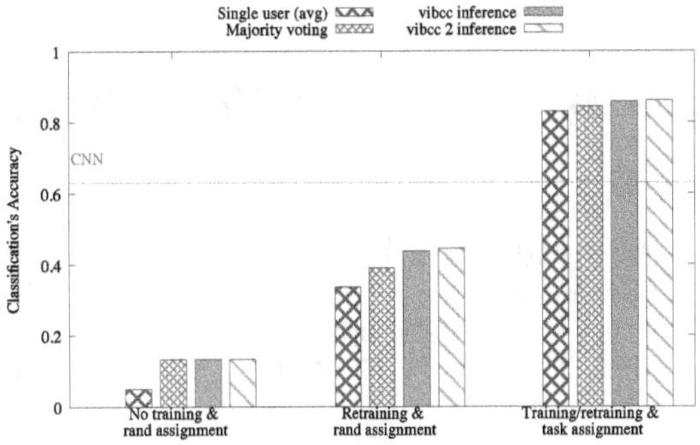

Figure 2: Classification quality with several assignment and training approaches combination.

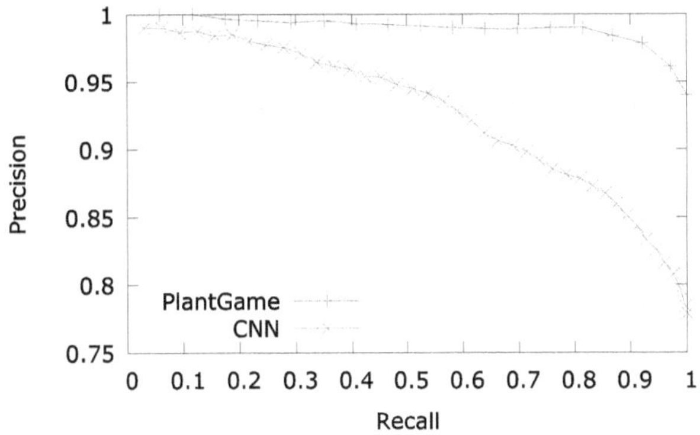

Figure 3: Recall precision curves (CNN alone vs. ThePlantGame)

4. REFERENCES

[1] A. P. Dawid and A. M. Skene. Maximum likelihood estimation of observer error-rates using the em algorithm. *Applied statistics*, pages 20–28, 1979.

[2] H. Goëau, A. Joly, and P. Bonnet. Lifeclef plant identification task 2015. In *CLEF 2015*, 2015.

[3] H.-C. Kim and Z. Ghahramani. Bayesian classifier combination. In *International conference on artificial intelligence and statistics*, pages 619–627, 2012.

[4] M. Servajean, A. Joly, D. Shasha, J. Champ, and E. Pacitti. Thousands-of-labels crowdsourcing: an active bayesian approach. *IEEE Trans. on Multimedia (submitted)*, 2016.

[5] E. Simpson, S. Roberts, I. Psorakis, and A. Smith. Dynamic bayesian combination of multiple imperfect classifiers. In *Decision Making and Imperfection*, pages 1–35. Springer, 2013.

[6] M. Venanzi, J. Guiver, G. Kazai, P. Kohli, and M. Shokouhi. Community-based bayesian aggregation models for crowdsourcing. In *Proc. of WWW conference*, pages 155–164. ACM, 2014.

A Multi-Video Browser for Endoscopic Videos on Tablets

Marco A. Hudelist
Institute for Information Technology
Klagenfurt University
Klagenfurt, Austria
marco@itec.aau.at

Sabrina Kletz
Institute for Information Technology
Klagenfurt University
Klagenfurt, Austria
sabrina@itec.aau.at

Klaus Schoeffmann
Institute for Information Technology
Klagenfurt University
Klagenfurt, Austria
ks@itec.aau.at

ABSTRACT

We present a browser for endoscopic videos that is designed to easily navigate and compare scenes on a tablet. It utilizes frame stripes of different levels of detail to quickly switch between fast and detailed navigation. Moreover, it uses saliency methods to determine which areas of a given keyframe contain the most information to further improve the visualization of the frame stripes. As scenes with much movement can be non-relevant *out-of-patient* scenes, the tool supports filtering for scenes of low, medium and high motion. The tool can be especially useful for patient debriefings as well as for educational purposes.

Keywords

Video Browsing; Mobile; Endoscopic Videos; User Interface

1. INTRODUCTION & RELATED WORK

Powerful mobile devices like tablets and smartphones have had a large impact on the medical sector over the last years. For example, they enable doctors to get updates about their patients on-the-go when they are moving from patient to patient and surgery to surgery. Nevertheless, there is still room for improvement. Intuitive and effective inspection of endoscopic videos is challenging, as traditional video players are not optimized for this specific task. They can not support users in navigating such videos in a fast and effortless way. Moreover, if surgeons try to compare two recordings of endoscopic procedures the user experience is very cumbersome, as they have to operate two different players at the same time. On smaller screens it may be even necessary to constantly switch between two player windows or applications all the time.

Therefore, we propose a video browsing tool for tablets that improves the experience on two fronts: First, it utilizes the concept of *frame stripes* [15, 12] at different levels of detail to speed up navigation and enable iterative browsing approaches. Users are able to start at a coarse but fast navigation level and gradually refine their search by switching to slower but detailed browsing. Moreover, they can switch between uniform sampled segments and content-based segmentation. Filtering segments is also possible by choosing between four options of detected motion in the content, i.e., to exclude out-of-patient segments.

Second, the tool enables users to open two videos at the same time and compare them side-by-side. This feature can be especially useful for comparing the same procedure of different patients or comparing earlier vs. later conditions during a surgery. Navigation and playback can also be synchronized between both videos, so that users do not need to control playback for each individually.

While video browsing for mobile devices tailored for endoscopic recordings is still a rather new field, there is a lot of related work for general video content. ProPane presented by Ganhör [2] is a smartphone video navigation tool that enables fast and very precise browsing at the same time by using various touch gestures. Huber et al. [3] present with *Wipe'n'Watch* an interface for smartphones that focuses on browsing interrelated eLearning video collections. A hierarchical storyboard is utilized by *HiStory*, a tablet interface shown by Hürst and Darzentas [8] that uses a hierarchical storyboard for exploring video content. Hürst et al. also show various other approaches for mobile video browsing like timeline-based interface optimization or even one-handed video navigation for smartphones [9, 10]. Karrer et al. [11] show a system that is using direct manipulation of objects for navigation in a video. Other examples for tablet video browsing interfaces are an interactive 3D filmstrip, a thumb-optimized interface, an interface that uses sub-shot visualization and an advanced tablet video filtering tool utilizing frame stripes shown by Hudelist et al. [4, 5, 6, 7], a smartphone interface that utilizes a *scrubbing wheel* and a tablet interface where users control playback speed using wipe gestures presented by Schoeffmann et al. [13, 14].

2. INTERFACE

At the top of the interface two playback windows are placed. The two windows can show the same video file at varied positions or two different videos, e.g., to compare the same type of surgery of two different surgeons. A blue border around a window indicates which one will respond to navigational input.

At the bottom of the interface two stripes of frames are visible. This visualization is inspired by frame stripes shown by Schoeffmann et al. [15], which are inspired by MO-images, shown by Mueller-Seelich and Tan [12]. Each frame represents a video segment and the stripes can be used to

MM '16 October 15-19, 2016, Amsterdam, Netherlands

ACM ISBN 978-1-4503-3603-1/16/10.

DOI: http://dx.doi.org/10.1145/2964284.2973821

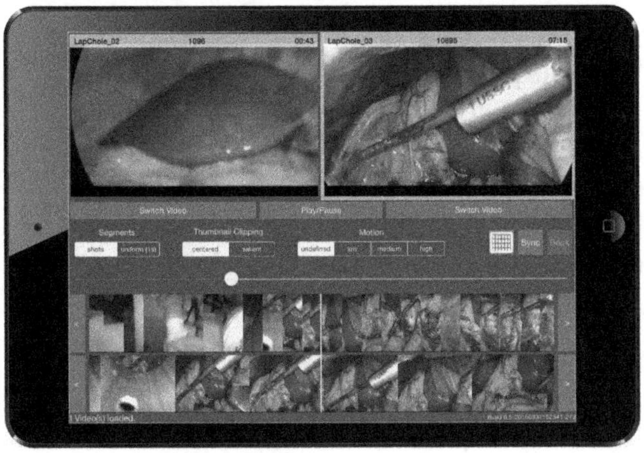

Figure 1: Screenshot of the interface with player windows at top, settings controls in the middle and browsing stripes at the lower half.

navigate inside a video. For this, users just have to drag the stripes with touch gestures or use the arrow buttons on either sides of the stripes. The stripes are always in sync with each other, so that when users navigate with one of them the other one instantly reorients. As a result the the same content is always below a virtual play head indicated by a yellow line in the middle on the stripes (see Fig. 2).

To offer different navigation approaches the two stripes show the same keyframes but with varying slice sizes. This enables users to traverse between fast but coarse browsing with the top stripe to slower but more detailed browsing with the lower stripe. Moreover, users can always tap on any of the frames to directly navigate to the appropriate position in the video. They can also page through the keyframes by using arrow buttons at each side of the stripes.

In the middle interface section, additional settings of the browsing experience can be changed. On one hand, the type of segmentation can be alternated between shot-based browsing and uniformly sampled segments of one second of length.

To provide users a simple but effective filtering option it is possible to restrict the shown segments according to their contents motion. As *out-of-patient* scenes are often not relevant but contain a high degree of motion due to handling the instrument the setting can be used to focus on more important sections of the video.

Furthermore, three additional buttons let users: (i) switch to an overview browsing mode, (ii) synchronize playback of both video windows, and (iii) undo any earlier performed navigational action like navigating by tapping on a frame. In overview mode the top stripe visualizes the segments by small thumbnails. This enables users to browse a video event faster, as more segments can segments can be inspected at a single glance.

Users can navigate a video also by utilizing a traditional seeker bar in the middle of the screen. This UI control was added in order to give users an additional interaction element that they know from traditional video players. Moreover, it enables even faster seeking through videos if required without the advantages of instant content insight provided by the navigation stripes. As users interact with it, the stripes re-position themselves accordingly.

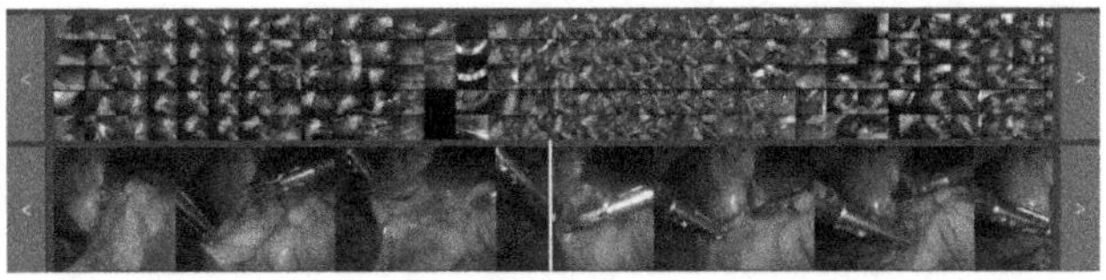

Figure 2: Overview-Mode: Segments are visualized by small thumbnails in the upper stripe for even faster browsing.

2.1 Keyframe Clipping

The way the frames are clipped to the slices can be changed. As it can be important to which area of a given keyframe this clipping is applied users can switch between always clipping to the center of a frame or clipping to the salient region. To detect salient regions in the frame we use the frequency-based method proposed by Achanta et al. [1]. Therefore, we compute the saliency map S for each frame F of size $(W \times H)$ based on the following formula:

$$S(x, y) = |F_\mu - F_G(x, y)| \tag{1}$$

where F_μ is the arithmetic mean pixel value of the image and F_G is a Gaussian blurred version (see [1] for details). In that saliency map we find the horizontal area P_w with a predefined width $W_P \leq W$ that has the maximum average saliency for the complete vertical area:

$$P_w(W_P, H) = \underset{x \in W_P, y \in H}{\arg\max} \frac{\sum S(x, y)}{W_P \times H} \tag{2}$$

3. CONCLUSIONS

We have presented a video browser for tablets that focuses on easy navigation and comparison of different phases of a recorded endoscopic surgery. Two video player windows can be used to navigate freely in two different recordings or to compare different phases of one surgery. For improving navigation it uses two frame stripes with different levels of granularity. One can be used for fast but coarse navigation while the other supports detailed inspection. An additional stripe visualization uses a grid organization of small thumbnails to speed up navigation even more. Moreover, it supports filtering video content for different levels of movement to remove i.e., non-relevant out-of-patient sequences. At our demo booth conference participants will be able to go hands-on with our prototype and test its functionality.

4. ACKNOWLEDGMENTS

This work was supported by Universität Klagenfurt and Lakeside Labs GmbH, Klagenfurt, Austria and funding from the European Regional Development Fund and the Carinthian Economic Promotion Fund (KWF) under grant KWF 20214 u. 3520/ 26336/38165.

5. REFERENCES

[1] R. Achanta, S. Hemami, F. Estrada, and S. Susstrunk. Frequency-tuned salient region detection. In *Computer vision and pattern recognition, 2009. cvpr 2009. ieee conference on*, pages 1597–1604. IEEE, 2009.

[2] R. Ganhör. Propane: Fast and precise video browsing on mobile phones. In *Proc. of the 11th International Conference on Mobile and Ubiquitous Multimedia*, MUM '12, pages 20:1–20:8, New York, NY, USA, 2012. ACM.

[3] J. Huber, J. Steimle, R. Lissermann, S. Olberding, and M. Mühlhäuser. Wipe'n'watch: Spatial interaction techniques for interrelated video collections on mobile devices. In *Proc. of the 24th BCS Interaction Specialist Group Conference*, BCS '10, pages 423–427, Swinton, UK, UK, 2010. British Computer Society.

[4] M. A. Hudelist, K. Schoeffmann, and L. Boeszoermenyi. Mobile video browsing with a 3d filmstrip. In *Proc. of the 3rd ACM Conference on Int. Conf. on Multimedia Retrieval*, ICMR '13, pages 299–300, New York, NY, USA, 2013. ACM.

[5] M. A. Hudelist, K. Schoeffmann, and L. Boeszoermenyi. Mobile video browsing with the thumbbrowser. In *Proc. of the 21st ACM International Conference on Multimedia*, MM '13, pages 405–406, New York, NY, USA, 2013. ACM.

[6] M. A. Hudelist, K. Schoeffmann, and Q. Xu. *Proc. of the 21st Int. Conf. on MultiMedia Modeling*, chapter Improving Interactive Known-Item Search in Video with the Keyframe Navigation Tree, pages 306–317. Springer, Cham, 2015.

[7] M. A. Hudelist and Q. Xu. *The Multi-stripe Video Browser for Tablets*, pages 272–277. Springer International Publishing, Cham, 2015.

[8] W. Hürst and D. Darzentas. History: A hierarchical storyboard interface design for video browsing on mobile devices. In *Proc. of the 11th Int. Conf. on Mobile and Ubiquitous Multimedia*, MUM '12, pages 17:1–17:4, New York, NY, USA, 2012. ACM.

[9] W. Hürst, G. Götz, and M. Welte. A new interface for video browsing on pdas. In *Proc. of the 9th Int. Conf. on Human Computer Interaction with Mobile Devices and Services*, MobileHCI '07, pages 367–369, New York, NY, USA, 2007. ACM.

[10] W. Hürst and P. Merkle. One-handed mobile video browsing. In *Proc. of the 1st Int. Conf. on Designing Interactive User Experiences for TV and Video*, UXTV '08, pages 169–178, New York, NY, USA, 2008. ACM.

[11] T. Karrer, M. Wittenhagen, and J. Borchers. Pocketdragon: A direct manipulation video navigation interface for mobile devices. In *Proc. of the 11th Int. Conf. on Human-Computer Interaction with Mobile Devices and Services*, MobileHCI '09, pages 47:1–47:3, New York, NY, USA, 2009. ACM.

[12] H. Mueller-Seelich and E. Tan. Visualizing the semantic structure of film and video, 2000.

[13] K. Schoeffmann and L. Burgstaller. Scrubbing wheel: An interaction concept to improve video content navigation on devices with touchscreens. In *IEEE Int. Symposium on Multimedia (ISM)*, pages 351–356, Dec 2015.

[14] K. Schoeffmann, K. Chromik, and L. Boeszoermenyi. Video navigation on tablets with multi-touch gestures. In *IEEE Int. Conf. on Multimedia and Expo Workshops (ICMEW)*, pages 1–6, July 2014.

[15] K. Schoeffmann, M. Taschwer, and L. Boeszoermenyi. The video explorer: A tool for navigation and searching within a single video based on fast content analysis. In *Proc. of the First Annual ACM SIGMM Conference on Multimedia Systems*, MMSys '10, pages 247–258, New York, NY, USA, 2010. ACM.

A Tablet Annotation Tool for Endoscopic Videos

Marco A. Hudelist
Institute for Information Technology
Klagenfurt University
Klagenfurt, Austria
marco@itec.aau.at

Sabrina Kletz
Institute for Information Technology
Klagenfurt University
Klagenfurt, Austria
sabrina@itec.aau.at

Klaus Schoeffmann
Institute for Information Technology
Klagenfurt University
Klagenfurt, Austria
ks@itec.aau.at

ABSTRACT

We present a tool for mobile browsing and annotation tailored for endoscopic videos. Professional users can utilize this tablet app for patients debriefings or educational purposes. It supports text input, free-hand and shape drawing as well as angle measurements, e.g. for comparing instrument orientation. It is possible to annotate single frames as well as user-defined video sections. Moreover, it provides easy and efficient navigation via a zoom-able navigation bar that is based on frame stripes. Frame stripes are created by extracting a single, one pixel wide vertical stripe from every keyframe. The stripes are then arranged next to each other to form a uniform bar. This gives users great overview of the content of a given video. Furthermore, the app supports creation of custom reports based on the entered annotations that can be directly mailed or printed for further usage.

Keywords

Video Browsing; Mobile; Endoscopic Videos; User Interface

1. INTRODUCTION & RELATED WORK

Mobile devices like tablets are an integral part of the day to day work routine in the health care system. Doctors and other medical staff are using them to easily plan, review and communicate medical data between each other, the management as well as with the patients. For example, in case of endoscopic videos doctors are in need of an easy-to-use, mobile application that can be used in surgery debriefings and for educational purposes.

Intuitive and effective inspection of endoscopic videos is challenging, as traditional mobile video players are not optimized for this specific task. They can not support users in navigating such videos fast and effortless. Moreover, if surgeons would like to quickly annotate certain areas in a video, e.g. to highlight specific elements for patients or when training other surgeons, they may even have to copy the frame and switch to a different application.

MM '16 October 15-19, 2016, Amsterdam, Netherlands

ACM ISBN 978-1-4503-3603-1/16/10.

DOI: http://dx.doi.org/10.1145/2964284.2973822

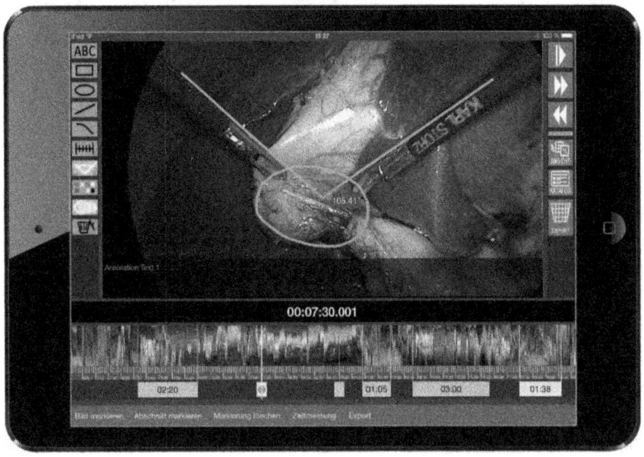

Figure 1: Screenshot of the interface.

In this paper we present an interface tailored for the special needs of surgeons and endoscopists. Users are able to annotate single frames as well as user-defined segments in a given endoscopic recording. They have options to add textual descriptions, shapes, free-hand drawings and angle measurements. Moreover, it provides capabilities to generate reports based on all or only selected annotations that can be shared via e-mail or directly printed. To make navigation easier the tablet app provides an enhanced navigation bar that utilizes *frame stripe visualization* [15, 12] to let users directly identify interesting sections of the video. The navigation bar is also zoom-able to give users better control on the level of detail that is displayed.

Although mobile video browsing tailored for endoscopic purposes is in its early stages there are of course other comparable approaches for mobile video browsing in case of other, more general content. With ProPane Ganhör [3] shows a mobile video navigation tool for fast and very precise browsing. Huber et al. [4] show Wipe'n'Watch, an interface for browsing interrelated video collections. It is similar to the approach of De Rooij et al. [2] for desktop computers. With *HiStory*, Hürst and Darzentas [8] show a tablet video browser that uses a hierarchical storyboard. Moreover, Hürst et al. also show various approaches for timeline-based or one-handed interaction on mobile devices [9, 10]. Hudelist et al. [5] present a browser that uses a metaphor of a 3D filmstrip for browsing videos on a tablet device. Also, they show a thumb-optimized interface [6] and a combination of multiple navigation bars of keyframes with different granularity levels based on sub-shot segmentation [7]. In addition, Schoeffmann et al. present browsing via a *scrubbing wheel* [13] and by using wipe gestures for controlling playback speed [14]. Furthermore, Karrer et al. [11] propose using direct manipulation of objects in a scene for navigation instead of traditional seeker bars.

2. INTERFACE

For navigation in a video users can either use the traditional play/pause, fast forward and fast rewind buttons on the right hand side or interact with the frame stripe navigation bar at the lower part of the interface by simple tap gestures. The navigation bar shows on one hand a visualization of the current videos' content as well as annotation markings below the frame stripes. The content is visualized by uniformly sampling frames from the video and extracting a single, one pixel wide stripe from the center of the image. This *frame stripe* visualization is inspired by the works of Schoeffmann et al. [15] - also known as MO-images as shown by Mueller-Seelich and Tan [12]. Of all keyframes an one pixel wide vertical strip is extracted. The extracted stripes are arranged consecutively in a vertical manner. This visualization enables users to quickly identify content changes in the video, e.g., the beginning of a new phase of a surgery. It is also very easy to identify scenes with a unique color pattern, e.g., out-of-patient scenes where the camera records shots from the operation room. In contrast to typical scenes with a color palette ranging from orange to red, such scenes typically generate green or gray patterns, as can be seen Fig. 2.

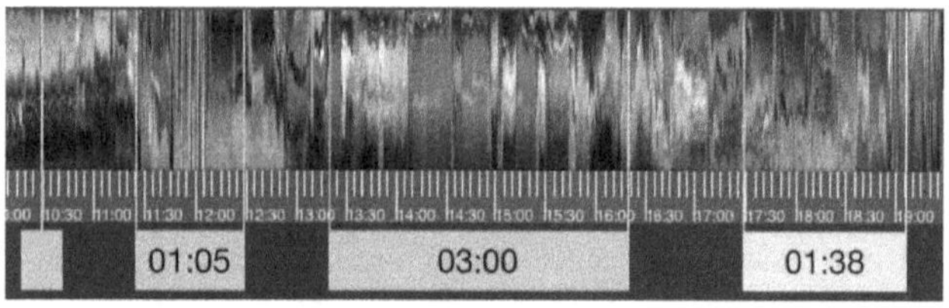

Figure 2: Zoomed screenshot of a portion of the navigation bar.

As the stripe can become quite dense when used with longer videos it is also possible to use pinch gestures to zoom in and out. In such a case the stripe becomes Below the stripe, ruler-like markings give an indication about time. Furthermore, below the time marks an area is reserved for visualizing single as well as range annotations. When selected via a single tap the player re-positions accordingly and loads drawings, measurements and text annotations.

New annotations can be added by first navigating to the appropriate position and then either using dedicated buttons to annotate the frame or a range at the lower part of the interface. A frame or a range can be annotated textually as well as with drawings and measurements. For instance, users can add shapes like circles and rectangles, freehand drawings but also measurements of angles. Such drawings are displayed directly in the player window as an overlay, while textual annotations are displayed at the bottom of the player window in a semi-transparent box (see Fig. 1).

It is also possible to measure time between two events in the video. For this, users have to activate the appropriate button and adjust a displayed range marking on the navigation stripe accordingly.

Moreover, the app supports exporting frame and range annotations for generating a report with screenshots. The report can be directly printed by using an AirPrint-ready[1] printer. To add an annotation to the report users need to select the appropriate annotation in the navigation bar and select the export button at the bottom of the interface. It is also possible to add any current frame of the player window by using the same method. A preview of the report and options for printing are accessible via a dedicated export button on the right hand side of the interface.

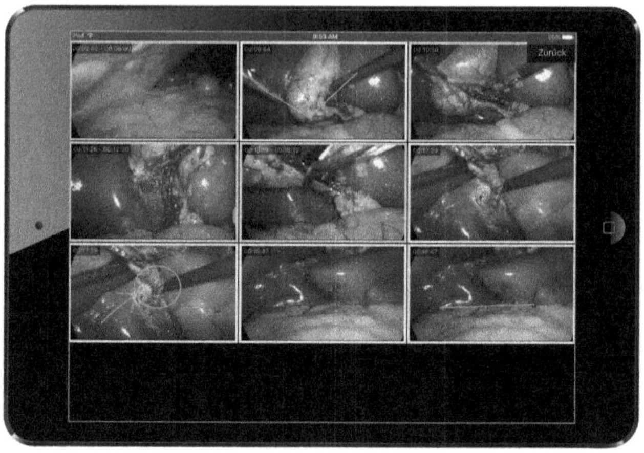

Figure 3: Grid visualization of all added annotations by their respective keyframes.

To quickly access annotations it is further possible to change the interface to a grid visualization of all already added annotations (see Fig. 3). For this, another dedicated button is available on the right side of the screen.

3. CONCLUSIONS

In this paper a tablet tool for browsing and annotation of endoscopic videos has been presented. It supports surgeons and other medical staff to easily debrief patients after procedures as well as it can be used for educational purposes. Textual annotations are supported as well as free-hand and shape drawings. Moreover, users are able to quickly navigate in the video by using a zoom-able navigation bar that utilizes frame stripe visualization. It is able to provide visual access to a videos' content in a very compact way.

4. ACKNOWLEDGMENTS

This work was supported by Universität Klagenfurt and Lakeside Labs GmbH, Klagenfurt, Austria and funding from the European Regional Development Fund and the Carinthian Economic Promotion Fund (KWF) under grant KWF 20214 u. 3520/ 26336/38165.

[1]Apple AirPrint [1] is a technology that enables iOS devices to directly send data to supported printers via WiFi connections.

5. REFERENCES

[1] About airprint - apple support. https://support.apple.com/en-jo/HT201311. Accessed: 2016-05-22.

[2] O. de Rooij, C. G. M. Snoek, and M. Worring. Mediamill: Semantic video search using the rotorbrowser. In *Proc. of the 6th ACM Int. Conf. on Image and Video Retrieval*, CIVR '07, pages 649–649, New York, NY, USA, 2007. ACM.

[3] R. Ganhör. Propane: Fast and precise video browsing on mobile phones. In *Proc. of the 11th International Conference on Mobile and Ubiquitous Multimedia*, MUM '12, pages 20:1–20:8, New York, NY, USA, 2012. ACM.

[4] J. Huber, J. Steimle, R. Lissermann, S. Olberding, and M. Mühlhäuser. Wipe'n'watch: Spatial interaction techniques for interrelated video collections on mobile devices. In *Proc. of the 24th BCS Interaction Specialist Group Conference*, BCS '10, pages 423–427, Swinton, UK, UK, 2010. British Computer Society.

[5] M. A. Hudelist, K. Schoeffmann, and L. Boeszoermenyi. Mobile video browsing with a 3d filmstrip. In *Proc. of the 3rd ACM Conference on Int. Conf. on Multimedia Retrieval*, ICMR '13, pages 299–300, New York, NY, USA, 2013. ACM.

[6] M. A. Hudelist, K. Schoeffmann, and L. Boeszoermenyi. Mobile video browsing with the thumbbrowser. In *Proceedings of the 21st ACM International Conference on Multimedia*, MM '13, pages 405–406, New York, NY, USA, 2013. ACM.

[7] M. A. Hudelist, K. Schoeffmann, and Q. Xu. *Proc. of the 21st Int. Conf. on MultiMedia Modeling*, chapter Improving Interactive Known-Item Search in Video with the Keyframe Navigation Tree, pages 306–317. Springer, Cham, 2015.

[8] W. Hürst and D. Darzentas. History: A hierarchical storyboard interface design for video browsing on mobile devices. In *Proc. of the 11th Int. Conf. on Mobile and Ubiquitous Multimedia*, MUM '12, pages 17:1–17:4, New York, NY, USA, 2012. ACM.

[9] W. Hürst, G. Götz, and M. Welte. A new interface for video browsing on pdas. In *Proc. of the 9th Int. Conf. on Human Computer Interaction with Mobile Devices and Services*, MobileHCI '07, pages 367–369, New York, NY, USA, 2007. ACM.

[10] W. Hürst and P. Merkle. One-handed mobile video browsing. In *Proc. of the 1st Int. Conf. on Designing Interactive User Experiences for TV and Video*, UXTV '08, pages 169–178, New York, NY, USA, 2008. ACM.

[11] T. Karrer, M. Wittenhagen, and J. Borchers. Pocketdragon: A direct manipulation video navigation interface for mobile devices. In *Proc. of the 11th Int. Conf. on Human-Computer Interaction with Mobile Devices and Services*, MobileHCI '09, pages 47:1–47:3, New York, NY, USA, 2009. ACM.

[12] H. Mueller-Seelich and E. Tan. Visualizing the semantic structure of film and video, 2000.

[13] K. Schoeffmann and L. Burgstaller. Scrubbing wheel: An interaction concept to improve video content navigation on devices with touchscreens. In *IEEE Int. Symposium on Multimedia (ISM)*, pages 351–356, Dec 2015.

[14] K. Schoeffmann, K. Chromik, and L. Boeszoermenyi. Video navigation on tablets with multi-touch gestures. In *IEEE Int. Conf. on Multimedia and Expo Workshops (ICMEW)*, pages 1–6, July 2014.

[15] K. Schoeffmann, M. Taschwer, and L. Boeszoermenyi. The video explorer: A tool for navigation and searching within a single video based on fast content analysis. In *Proceedings of the First Annual ACM SIGMM Conference on Multimedia Systems*, MMSys '10, pages 247–258, New York, NY, USA, 2010. ACM.

News Archive Exploration Combining Face Detection and Tracking with Network Visual Analytics

Benjamin Renoust
National Institute of Informatics
& JFLI CNRS UMI 3527
renoust@nii.ac.jp

Thanh Duc Ngo
University of Information Technology
VNU-HCM
thanhnd@uit.edu.vn

Duy-Dinh Le and Shin'Ichi Satoh
National Institute of Informatics
{ledduy, satoh} @nii.ac.jp

ABSTRACT

Visual analytics helps analytical reasoning and exploration of complex systems, for which it combines the means of interactive visualization, with the power of data analytics. The recent progress in computer vision techniques opens wide applications in real world video archives. Particularly, recent advances in face detection and recognition have been put under the spotlight. The applications of such techniques are often concern intelligence, or peer recognition in photo posted in social networks. We propose to combine those two domains by demonstrating a visual exploration of over a decade of the news program from the Japanese broadcaster NHK News 7. We derive social networks from face detection and tracking of this large dataset. With the help of a little domain knowledge, we monitor the activity of political public figures and explore the archive. This allows understanding and comparison of the politico-media scene presented by NHK under different Prime Minister's governance. The social networks are interactive, and to explore the multimedia database and its video content.

Keywords

Face detection and tracking; visual analytics; media analytics; social networks analysis; politics; NHK; Japan

1. INTRODUCTION

Media monitoring is a discipline which holds a strategic importance for media professionals, politicians and other public figures. This monitoring can help people manage their public image, broaden the scope of a news story, survey the impact of decision, or even predict market behavior. It requires then to mine the ever producing sources of information that constitutes the media. A traditional way is to look at the semantics behind the stories and Visual analytics often tackled news media analysis by combining topic analysis, named entity recognition, and time series analysis to show trends, reveal important individuals, summarize stories, or do predictions. However, news media are often conveyed through video and the use of the images became as strategic as the language that tells a story.

Because computer vision tools are becoming mature enough, we propose to go beyond these traditional approaches and to work solely on the visual content conveyed by the news. Through face detection and tracking, we want to monitor the activity of political figures. Since 2001, we have archived thousands of hours of news from NHK, and we propose a visual exploration of these news. We explore the news from a social networks perspective which gives an understanding the politico-media scene presented by the NHK over the different cabinets led by different Prime Ministers. Users can then explore the social networks over different time frames, compare the activity of the different political actors and finally access the video segments in which politicians have been detected.

2. DESCRIPTION OF THE SYSTEM

Our system first combines news segments with a large scale face detection and tracking framework as illustrated

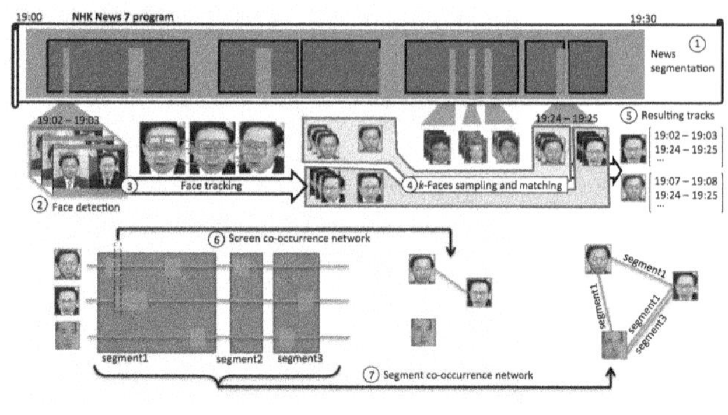

Figure 1: Network construction from face-tracking. 1- The video data is segmented given topical distribution, a topic roughly corresponding to a news segment. 2- Faces are detected in the video with Viola-Jones. 3- Faces are tracked using the KLT point tracker. 4- We use GreedyRSC to cluster the faces which are later manually annotated, resulting in face-tracks (5). This allows us to generate two forms of links between annotated people: we can connect people when they simultaneously co-appear on screen (6) and when they appear during the same news segment (7).

MM '16 October 15-19, 2016, Amsterdam, Netherlands

ACM ISBN 978-1-4503-3603-1/16/10.
DOI: http://dx.doi.org/10.1145/2964284.2973823

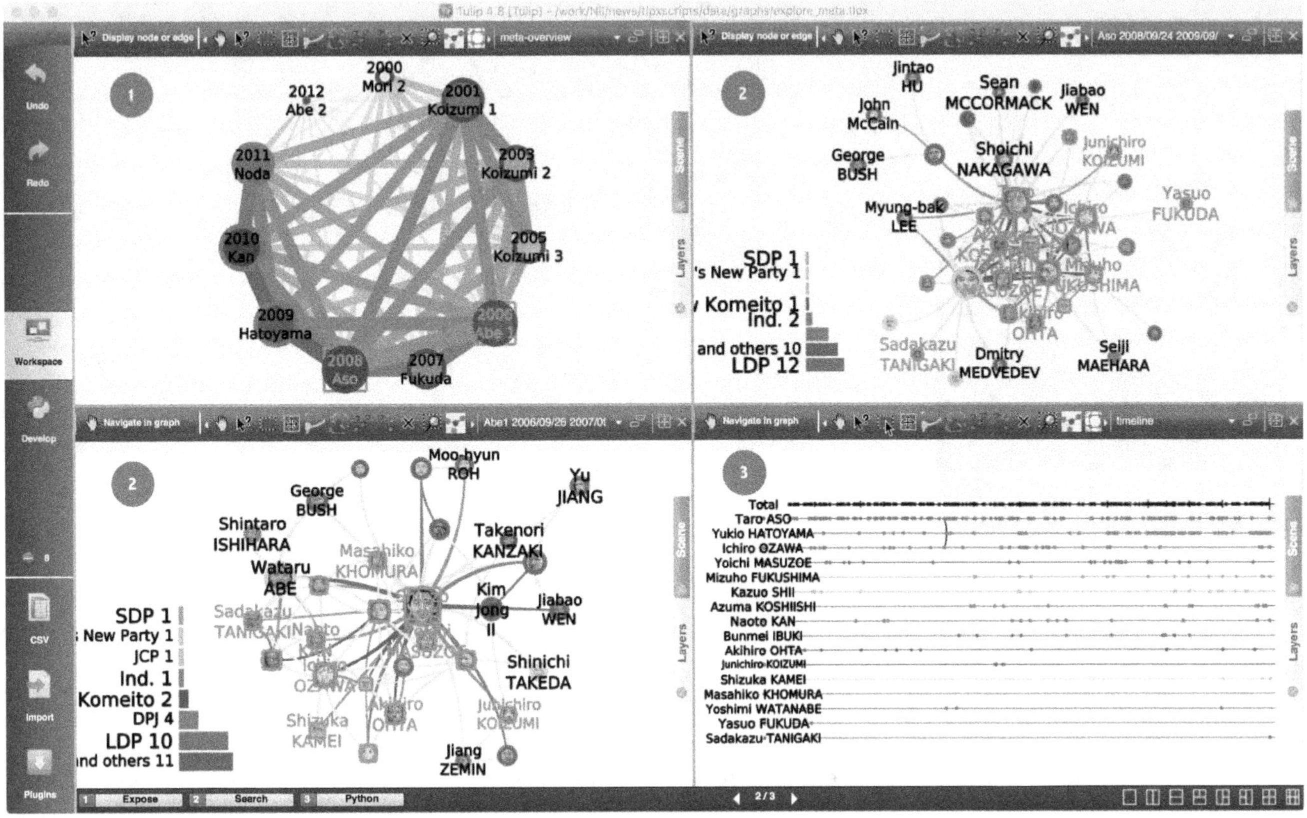

Figure 2: Network visualization. 1- The visualization offers first an overview of the cabinets ordered in time, with links showing similarity among politico-media scenes. 2- Selecting two cabinets in the previous view opens two network views corresponding to each selected cabinet. The common political figures are highlighted in pink. 3- The timelines of appearance of the selected political figure during Aso's cabinet. Political leaning colors the line, and crossing connections (in black) correspond to screen co-occurrence.

in Fig. 1, so we can identify in which stories are the different political actors participating in, in order to construct relevant social networks.

A news program traditionally presents different topics in a succession of news stories that we call news segments. We first enrich our videos with meta-data and automatically extract news segment boundaries (Fig. 1-1), kindly provided by the authors of [2].

We then proceed with a large scale face detection and tracking. We first detect faces in each frame using Viola-Jones[6] (Fig. 1-2). We create face-tracks by regrouping faces instances matching through the KLT point tracker [5] (Fig. 1-3). Each face-track is temporally sampled using k-faces [4], and we extract their average point in the OpenFace 128-dimensional feature space [1]. Face-tracks are finally clustered using GreedyRSC [3] (Fig. 1-4), and manually annotated. We finally obtained about 150 different public figures (Fig. 1-5) over 15k facetracks in 3370 clusters.

From this process we can extract two types of relationships. Relationships appear when two individuals co-appear on screen (Fig. 1-6). Although strong, the meaning of this relationship is ambivalent: it often means that people appeared on the same place at the same time, however, news often place multiple people on screen to express an opposition of ideas. This links are sparse, and because our videos often focus on one individual rather than on a group.

The second type of relationship is derived from the news segment boundaries (Fig. 1-7). Indeed, different politicians appear during a same news segment when they took part in a same news event. We thus create a link between two people each time they appeared during a same news segment.

From the 150 public figures annotated, we recognized 75 people involved in politics, including the different Prime Ministers leading Japan at the moment of capture. We can segment time, creating a time frame for each of these Prime Ministers' cabinets, each corresponding to a sub-network. We additionally gathered party affiliation for each of the cabinets to enrich the visualization.

3. A MULTI-LEVEL VISUALIZATION

We first[1] offer a meta-view where each node corresponds to a cabinet's time-frame (Fig. 2-1). Links between nodes correspond to the (Jaccard) proximity between cabinets in terms of political actors we have detected, mapped to size and color. Similarly, the size and color of nodes correspond to the number of politicians detected during the cabinet.

With interaction, the user can explore these cabinets, for which the social network is displayed (Fig. 2-2), a node corresponding to a politician. The user can select political parties and politicians, and linked highlighting (Fig. 2-2

[1]Work implemented using the Tulip framework *tulip.labri.fr*

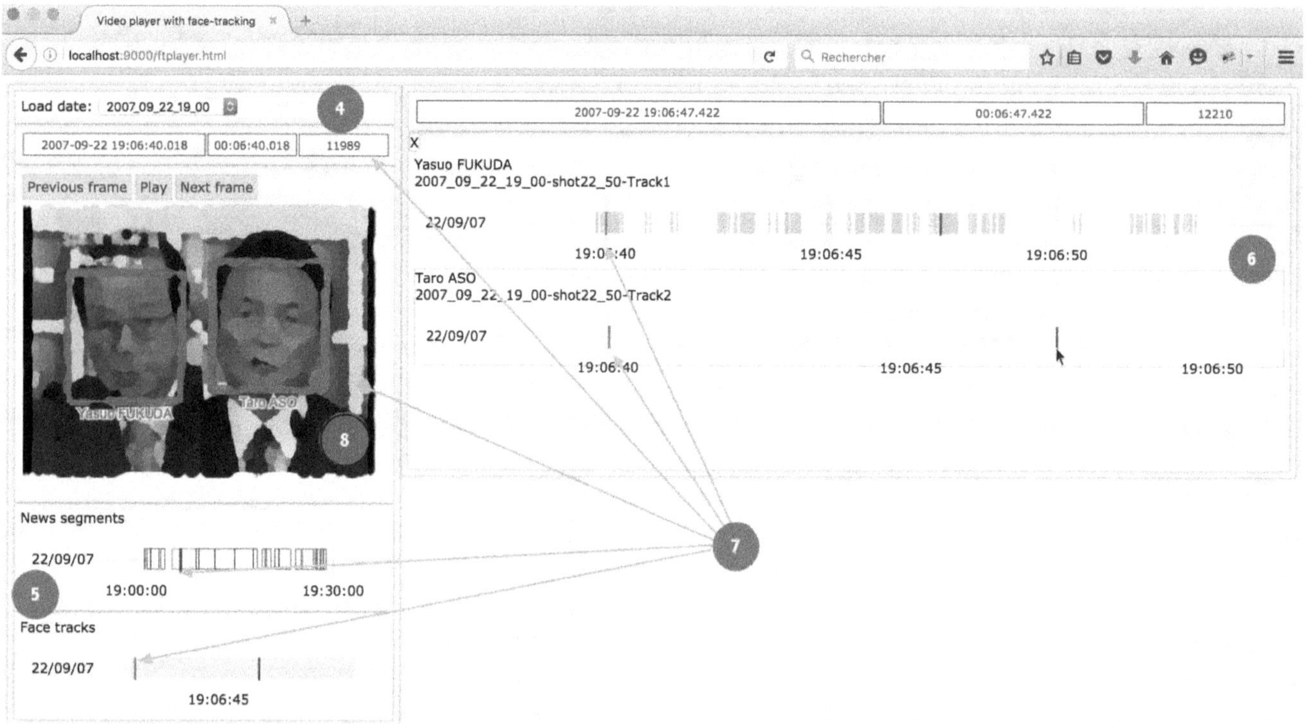

Figure 3: The face-track video player. Selecting sections in the timeline (Fig. 2-3) loads a playlist corresponding to the dates of detection (4). For a given date, we display timelines corresponding to topic segmentations (5) and individual face-tracks (6), all interactively linked highlighted independently to scales (7). Upon interaction, the video is played and face bounding boxes are displayed accordingly (8).

in pink) displays the selection in other views, to compare cabinets between one another.

Interaction also allows the user to compare the activity of the different politicians using timelines (Fig. 2-3). Each bin of the timeline corresponds to a day of detection of a politician, its height being mapped to the number of news segments appearances. Eventually, we also displays co-appearance links when available.

Finally, another interaction in the timeline allows for exploration of individual news programs. It opens a player[2] and loads a playlist corresponding to the selection (Fig. 3-4). The player displays multiple timelines corresponding to news segments (Fig. 3-5) and face-tracks (Fig. 3-6). The different timelines are all linked highlighted over hovering and video playing (Fig. 3-7) for a precise face-track exploration. Face-track boundaries are then displayed over the video (Fig. 3-8), allowing users to identify holes and duplicates in the face detection.

4. CONCLUSION

This system allows for a didactic discovery of the politico-media scene presented by NHK during our period of capture. Through exploration, we can overview different phenomena, such as: the changes of network topology between when Japan's leading party changes; the rise of (future Prime Minister) Shinzo Abe during Jun'Ichiro Koizumi's cabinets; and the identification the very peculiar Ichiro Ozawa.

[2]Implemented over Canvas and D3 *d3js.org*

Acknowledgements

This material is based on work supported by the Japanese Society for the Promotion of Science (JSPS) under grant P14773. Any opinions, findings, and conclusions or recommendations expressed in this material are those of the authors and do not necessarily reflect those of the JSPS.

5. REFERENCES

[1] B. Amos *et al.* OpenFace: Face Recognition with Deep Neural Networks. http://github.com/cmusatyalab/openface. Accessed: 2016-01-11.

[2] I. Ide *et al.* Topic threading for structuring a large-scale news video archive. *Image and Video Retrieval*, 1(1):123–131, 2004.

[3] D. D. Le and S. Satoh. Indexing faces in broadcast news video archives. In *2011 IEEE 11th ICDM Workshops*, pages 519–526, Dec 2011.

[4] T. D. Ngo *et al.* Face retrieval in large-scale news video datasets. *IEICE TRANSACTIONS on Information and Systems*, 96(8):1811–1825, 2013.

[5] J. Shi and C. Tomasi. Good features to track. In *Proceedings CVPR'94.*, pages 593–600. IEEE, 1994.

[6] P. Viola and M. J. Jones. Robust real-time face detection. *International journal of computer vision*, 57(2):137–154, 2004.

A New Tool for Collaborative Video Search via Content-based Retrieval and Visual Inspection

Wolfgang Hürst,
Algernon Ip Vai Ching
Utrecht University
Utrecht, The Netherlands
huerst@uu.nl

Marco A. Hudelist,
Manfred J. Primus,
Klaus Schoeffmann
Klagenfurt University
Klagenfurt, Austria
{marco, mprimus,ks}@itec.aau.at

Christian Beecks
RWTH Aachen University
Aachen, Germany
beecks@cs.rwth-aachen.de

ABSTRACT
We present a new approach for collaborative video search and video browsing relying on a combination of traditional, index-based video retrieval complemented with large-scale human-based visual inspection. In particular, a traditional PC interface is used for query-based search using advanced indexing and querying methods (e.g., concept search), whereas a visualization of the database on a tablet is used for pure human-based browsing. Both parts are coupled to compensate for mutual disadvantages; human visual inspection allows for a better, more detailed analysis of the data – also bridging the semantic gap – but comes at the price of an unfiltered database – a disadvantage that is resolved by using the results from the query engine to change visualization order.

Keywords
Video retrieval; feature signatures; collaborative search; human-computer interaction

1. INTRODUCTION
State-of-the-art content-based retrieval tools allow for high quality search in video databases. When entering information about color distribution, concepts, or other features, users are generally presented with a filtered and ranked subset of the data that should contain the information one is looking for. While this works well in many situations, there are still limitations and issues such as the semantic gap [7]. Problems with ambiguous queries or a lack of knowledge about the search goals make it likely that not all of these will ever be resolved completely. Thus, the interface and interaction design plays a crucial role for effective video search. Common standard representations of search results work well if and only if the search engine's ranked results are reliable. Yet, providing more content information to a user can be helpful in situations when this is not the case (e.g., when the target segment is in the same file but at a different position than the one returned by the retrieval tool). We therefore present a combined approach for collaborative video search that takes advantage of both worlds. A high-performing content-based search engine is used for video search by querying. It is coupled with a second tool, operated by a collaborating user. Here, the search results are represented in more detail using a visualization technique optimized for quick, large-scale visual data skimming under consideration of established knowledge about human visual perception.

MM '16, October 15-19, 2016, Amsterdam, Netherlands
ACM 978-1-4503-3603-1/16/10.
http://dx.doi.org/10.1145/2964284.2973824

The basic concept was used in the Video Browser Showdown (VBS) competition [6] in 2016 where it achieved the 2nd place. In this demo, we present its latest incarnation with an extended content-based search, a further optimized visualization tool, and an improved communication between the two collaborating systems. In the following, we will shorty describe the content-based video retrieval part of the system (2.1), illustrate the visualization concept and related interaction of the tablet-based search tool (2.2), and describe how they are integrated in a beneficial way for optimal collaborative video search (2.3).

2. SYSTEM DESCRIPTION
2.1 Content-based Video Retrieval

Figure 1. PC-based CBVR tool.

The content-based video retrieval (CBVB) tool features various query processing functionality, including temporal feature signatures entered via sketching (Fig. 1, top right), concept filtering tools (Fig. 1, top) and chronological segment browsing. Content analysis is done by, for example, using CNNs for concept detection and temporal feature signatures which in turn utilize a variant of the Signature Matching Distance for video shot comparisons [1,5]. The high performance of these search algorithms was demonstrated at the VBS 2016 competition [2] and newer tests done with an enhanced version of the system. Results returned by the search engine are represented in a standard way by ranked segments (Fig. 1, left). Users can further inspect individual results in a small playback area (Fig. 1, bottom right).

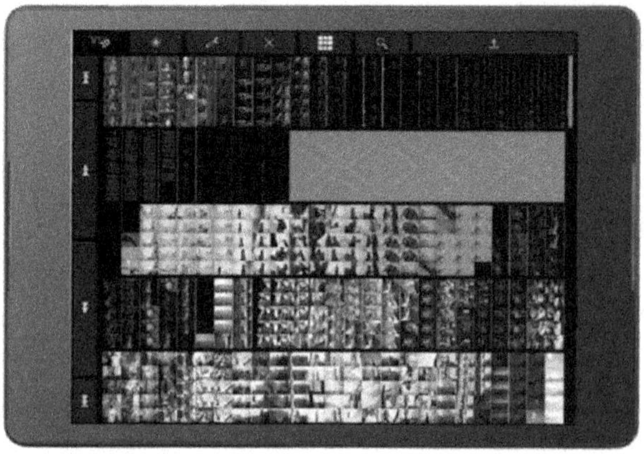

Figure 2. Tablet-based visual inspection tool.

2.2 Large-scale Visual Inspection

The traditional way of representing potentially relevant parts of a video as search results is efficient if and only if the target location is part of these visualized segments. Other situations though might require more details. Navigating individual clips using the small playback window to explore a particular video is possible, but often cumbersome and not flexible enough due to the enforced sequential navigation structure. Fig. 2 shows a screenshot of our tablet-based tool for visual inspection that is optimized for quick, efficient visual skimming of large amounts of video at detailed levels. The whole database is visualized as a storyboard representing all videos. The blue bar in Fig. 2 illustrates the end of a single video file. For each video, a key frame is extracted every second and shown as a small thumbnail. Thumbnail sizes are kept extremely small to make maximum usage of the limited screen estate, yet being large enough to ensure a good human classification performance with respect to visual perception [3]. In order to better identify scenes in such a miniaturized visualization, thumbnails are not arranged in the common line-by-line representation, but instead they are shown from left to right in columns of five thumbnails. Fig. 2 illustrates that this results in "clusters" of scenes that are easier and faster to spot. This visualization approach has proven to perform extremely well for known item search tasks (KIS). In the VBS 2015 competition, a similar interface was used with a storyboard containing all 100 hours of the database in a fixed but random order. Although it did not feature any content-based indexing or querying at all but enforced the user to visually skim the entire database, it achieved a remarkable 3rd place in the end [4].

2.3 Combined Collaborative Approach

The results from [4] have proven that an optimized visualization method performs extremely well even at database sizes of up to 100 hours. Yet, it does not scale indefinitely and there are obvious limits to how much data can be visually inspected in a given amount of time (e.g., at VBS 2015, the time limit per task was 5 minutes). Thus, we present an integrated system that combines both approaches in a way that copes with the respective disadvantages and maximizes the benefits of each individual search concept (Fig. 3). In particular, results from the CBVR tool are sent to the tablet and used to update the order of videos in the storyboard. Likewise, files that have been inspected on the tablet and classified as irrelevant are excluded from future retrieval request thus reducing the database and increasing the likelihood of finding relevant results quickly. In our research [8], we investigated different ways to resort the visualizations in the storyboard on the tablet based on the CBVR tool results as well as how the information sent via the back channel from the tablet to the PC tool can be used in optimal ways.

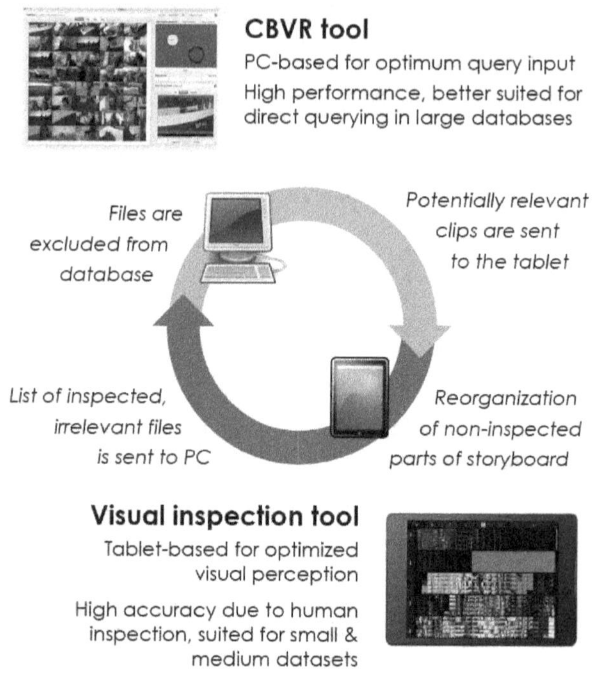

Figure 3. Collaboration between CBVR & tablet tool.

3. REFERENCES

[1] Christian Beeks, Steffen Kirchhoff, Thomas Seidl. 2013. Signature matching distance for content-based image retrieval. In *Proceedings of the 3rd ACM International conference on multimedia retrieval* (ICMR'13), 41-48.

[2] Marco A. Hudelist, Claudiu Cobârzan, Christian Beecks, Rob van de Werken, Sabrina Kletz, Wolfgang Hürst, Klaus Schoeffmann. 2016. Collaborative Video Search Combining Video Retrieval with Human-based Visual Inspection. *MultiMedia Modeling*, Vol 9517 of Lecture Notes in Computer Science, 400-405.

[3] Wolfgang Hürst, and Rob van de Werken. 2015. Human-based Video Browsing – Investigating interface design for fast video browsing. In *Proceedings of IEEE International Symposium on Multimedia* (ISM 2015), 363-368.

[4] Wolfgang Hürst, Cees G.M. Snoek, Willem-Jan Spoel, and Mate Tomin. 2010. Keep moving!: revisiting thumbnails for mobile video retrieval. In *Proceedings of the 18th ACM international conference on Multimedia* (MM '10). ACM, New York, NY, USA, 963-966.

[5] Jakub Lokoč, Adam Blažek, and Tomáš Skopal. 2014. Signature-Based Video Browser. *MultiMedia Modeling*, Vol 8326 of Lecture Notes in Computer Science, 415-418.

[6] Klaus Schoeffmann. 2014. A User-Centric Media Retrieval Competition: The Video Browser Showdown 2012-2014. *IEEE Multimedia*, Vol. 21, No. 4, Oct.-Dec., 2014, 8-13.

[7] Arnold W. M. Smeulders, Marcel Worring, Simone Santini, Amarnath Gupta, and Ramesh Jain. 2000. Content-Based Image Retrieval at the End of the Early Years. *IEEE Trans. Pattern Anal. Mach. Intell.* 22, 12 (December 2000), 1349-1380.

A Browsing and Retrieval System for Broadcast Videos using Scene Detection and Automatic Annotation

Lorenzo Baraldi[1], Costantino Grana[1], Alberto Messina[2] and Rita Cucchiara[1]

[1]Università degli Studi di Modena e Reggio Emilia
name.surname@unimore.it

[2]RAI - Radiotelevisione Italiana - Centre for Research and Technological Innovation
alberto.messina@rai.it

ABSTRACT

This paper presents a novel video access and retrieval system for edited videos[1]. The key element of the proposal is that videos are automatically decomposed into semantically coherent parts (called *scenes*) to provide a more manageable unit for browsing, tagging and searching. The system features an automatic annotation pipeline, with which videos are tagged by exploiting both the transcript and the video itself. Scenes can also be retrieved with textual queries; the best thumbnail for a query is selected according to both semantics and aesthetics criteria.

Keywords

Video Browsing; Temporal Video Segmentation; Retrieval

1. INTRODUCTION

Video sharing and browsing platforms like Youtube allow to upload, search and access user-generated videos. Retrieval is usually performed using tags and descriptions given by the content provider, and thumbnails are static, meaning that the same thumbnail is shown when a video is searched with different queries. This paradigm fits well for short user-generated videos, in which the content is quite uniform and it is easy to get a glimpse of it. The same does not apply to broadcast videos, which are usually longer and more complex. Beside the length, those have indeed more complex story lines and may contain different topics.

The system we present in this paper addresses these limitations with three novelties: first, it lets the user browse and retrieve videos with a finer granularity level, by decomposing them into sets of *scenes*, which are parts of video with uniform semantic content. Secondly, it does not require manually generated tags or descriptions, as it extract annotations using visual content and transcripts. Lastly, given a textual query it retrieves the most significant scenes by presenting them with the most appropriate thumbnail, according to both semantics and aesthetics.

[1]Demo is available at http://imagelab.ing.unimore.it/neuralstory

MM '16 October 15-19, 2016, Amsterdam, Netherlands

ACM ISBN 978-1-4503-3603-1/16/10.

DOI: http://dx.doi.org/10.1145/2964284.2973825

2. THE SYSTEM

Our system comprises three main components: a scene detection module, a concept detection algorithm, which visually detects the presence of concepts expressed in the transcript, and a retrieval algorithm with which users can search for scenes inside a video collection.

Scene detection To segment a video into a set of scenes, we apply the algorithm described in [1]. Given a ground-truth temporal segmentation of a set of videos, it runs a shot detector and trains a Siamese Neural network to predict whether two shots should belong to the same scene. Each branch of the Siamese network is composed by a Convolutional Neural Network (CNN), whose penultimate layer is concatenated with features extracted from the transcript of the video. Training is done using a contrastive loss function, which computes the distance between two input shots. At test time, distances between shots given by the Siamese network are arranged into a similarity matrix, which is then used with Spectral Clustering to obtain the final scene limits.

Automatic concept detection Sentences in the transcript of a video are parsed with the Stanford CoreNLP tagger [3]. Each unigram tagged as noun, proper noun or foreign word is converted to its lemmatized form, and then matched with the most semantically similar class in the Imagenet database [4], which contains more than 40.000 categories. This is achieved with a Word2Vec model [5], which assigns each word to a vector in a semantic space.

Having mapped each unigram to an Imagenet class, we build a classifier to detect the presence of a visual concept in a shot. Images from Imagenet are represented using feature activations from pre-trained CNNs; a linear probabilistic SVM is then trained for each concept, using randomly sampled negative images from other classes. The probability output of each classifier is used as an indicator of the presence of a concept in a shot. Given the temporal coherency of a video, it is unlikely for a visual concept to appear in a shot which is far from the point in which the concept found in the transcript. For this reason, we run a classifier only on shots which are temporally near to its corresponding term, and apply a Gaussian weight to the probability of each term, based on the temporal distance.

Retrieval Given a textual query, we build a retrieval

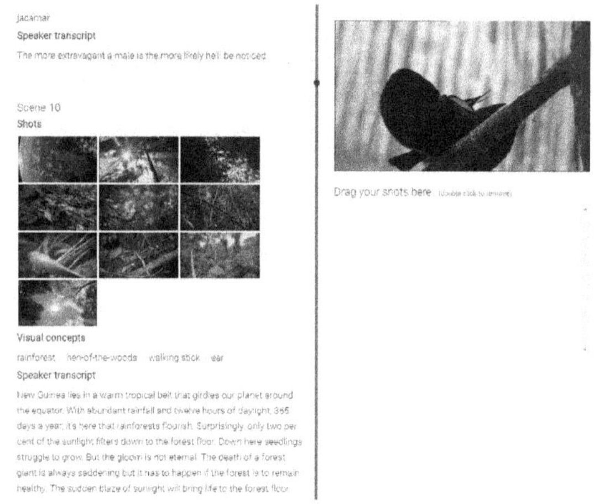

Figure 1: Browsing interface.

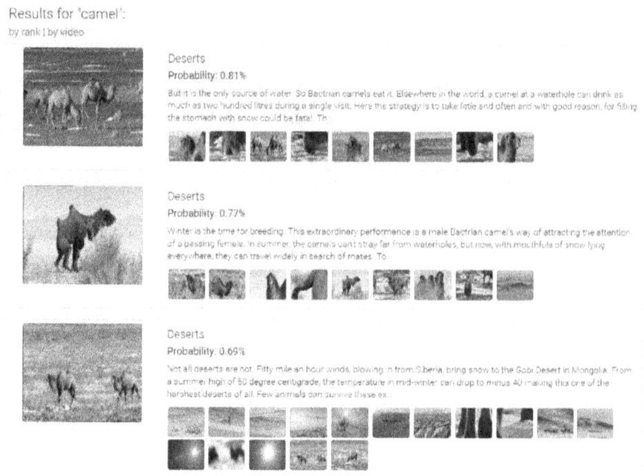

Figure 2: Retrieval interface (for query *camel*).

strategy which exploits automatically detected concepts. Details can be found in [2].

We first match the query with the most similar detected concept, using the Word2Vec embedding. If the query is composed by more than one word, the mean of the embedded vectors is used. Given a query q, each scene inside the video collection is then assigned a score according to the following function:

$$R_{scene}(q) = \max_{s \in scene} \left(\alpha P(s,u) + (1-\alpha) \max_{d \in s} E(d) \right) \quad (1)$$

where s is a shot inside the given scene, u is the most similar concept found in transcripts to query q, according to the Word2Vec embedding, and d represent all keyframes extracted from a given shot. $P(s,u)$ is the probability that shot s contains concept u, computed as described above. $E(d)$ is the aesthetic ranking of key-frame d, computed according to [2]. Parameter α tunes the relative importance of semantic representativeness and aesthetic beauty. The final retrieval results is a collection of scenes, ranked according to $R_{scene}(q)$, each one represented with the keyframe that maximizes the second term of the score.

It is worth to notice that most of the proposed pipeline is executed off-line. Scenes boundaries are detected only once when a video is uploaded, while probabilities $P(s,u)$ are computed offline for each unigram found in the transcript of a video and stored in an inverted index. $E(d)$, as well, are computed in advance for each key-frame, thus greatly reducing the computational needs in the on-line stage. The off-line stage requires on average the duration of the video.

3. INTERFACE

Given automatically extracted scenes, a video is presented in a time-line fashion (see Fig. 1), where users can get an insight of the content of the video by scrolling the timeline. For each scene, a carousel of shots is also presented, along with the speaker transcript and automatically detected concepts. On the right-hand side of the timeline, a video player is put, and users can navigate from one point to another of the video by clicking on shot thumbnails. A drag-and-drop zone is finally placed under the video player, in which users can drop shots or entire scenes, to build new videos from watched ones.

Figure 2 depicts the retrieval interface. Given the query, a ranked list of scenes is reported: for each scene, the title of the corresponding video and the transcript of the scene is reported, along with a confidence score. The full set of shots in the scene is also shown, as well as the thumbnail which maximized the conceptual and aesthetic criterion.

The system is presented with a collection of videos from the BBC educational series *Planet Earth* as well as a portion of the first season of the TV-Series *Ally McBeal*.

4. CONCLUSIONS

We described a video browsing and retrieval system specifically designed for collections of edited videos. Videos are presented as sequences of scenes to enhance browsing, and a retrieval strategy based on automatically detected concepts is used to let the user search inside the collection.

Acknowledgments This work has been partially founded by the project "Città educante" (CTN01_00034_393801) of the National Technological Cluster on Smart Communities (cofunded by the Italian Ministry of Education, University and Research - MIUR).

5. REFERENCES

[1] L. Baraldi, C. Grana, and R. Cucchiara. A deep siamese network for scene detection in broadcast videos. In *ACM MM*, pages 1199–1202. ACM, 2015.

[2] L. Baraldi, C. Grana, and R. Cucchiara. Scene-driven retrieval in edited videos using aesthetic and semantic deep features. In *ACM ICMR*, 2016.

[3] M.-C. De Marneffe, B. MacCartney, C. D. Manning, et al. Generating typed dependency parses from phrase structure parses. In *Proceedings of LREC*, volume 6, pages 449–454, 2006.

[4] J. Deng, W. Dong, R. Socher, L.-J. Li, K. Li, and L. Fei-Fei. Imagenet: A large-scale hierarchical image database. In *CVPR*, pages 248–255. IEEE, 2009.

[5] T. Mikolov, I. Sutskever, K. Chen, G. S. Corrado, and J. Dean. Distributed representations of words and phrases and their compositionality. In *ANIPS*, pages 3111–3119, 2013.

First-Person Shooter Game for Virtual Reality Headset with Advanced Multi-Agent Intelligent System

Ilya Makarov[*]
iamakarov@hse.ru,
revan1986@mail.ru

Mikhail Tokmakov[†]
matokmakov@gmail.com

Pavel Polyakov[‡]
polyakovpavel96@gmail.com

National Research University Higher School of Economics,
School of Data Analysis and Artificial Intelligence,
125319, 3 Kochnovskiy Proezd, Moscow, Russia Federation

ABSTRACT

We present a multiplayer first-person shooter (FPS) game with advanced intelligent non-playable characters (NPC) under computer control. The game is specially adapted for playing in VR headset so the simulator sickness symptoms are significantly reduced. The demo allows users to play with the other human and NPC players in a shooter game made in Unreal Engine 4. User can verify his/her game skills versus evolving human-like NPCs with a level adjusting model. The humanness of NPC was verified with Alan Turing game test beating 52% record from BotPrize'12 competition.

Keywords

Game artificial intelligence; reinforcement learning; virtual reality; first-person shooter; Unreal Engine

1. INTRODUCTION

Multimedia sources often declare that playing video-games leads to such negative effects as aggression, obesity and addiction. However, recent research proved positive influence of such activity on player's cognitive skills [2]. In [1] authors have shown that playing strategic video-games increases the impact. The only way to improve the importance of strategic planning component in command FPS is to make enemies more challenging. In a current state-of-art NPC usually acts as scripted/predetermined and uses full information from the computer engine, unavailable to a human player. Multiple synthetic algorithms were presented to compensate BOT (enemy NPC) supremacy over human drawing balancing entertainment and game challenge in virtual world.

[*]Corresponding author; project head.

[†]Team leader; core programmer.

[‡]BOT motion and tactical map.

MM '16 October 15-19, 2016, Amsterdam, Netherlands

ACM ISBN 978-1-4503-3603-1/16/10.

DOI: http://dx.doi.org/10.1145/2964284.2973826

Figure 1: Computer controlled player

We developed a comprehensive intelligent agent for FPS game learning its skills from in-game experience and making decision through the same cognitive patterns as humans. Frequently playing improves people's skills like training improve sportsman's indicators. So, instead of giving redundant information on environment state, we improved BOT playing skills by teaching it to make optimal decisions during game. We also created human-computer intelligent teams, in which each player could make its own decisions under supervision of a team goal expert system.

2. MODEL DESCRIPTION

2.1 Interaction in a Team

The environment state reflects all the information about the game state. BOT could obtain game states in the way human plays. Game states contain teammates health levels, amount of weapons, presence of an enemy in line of sight, etc. BOT can perform such actions as moving to strategic point, entering teammates group, looking around, targeting at enemy in line of sight (shooting or not), reloading.

We focused on a single mode behavior influenced by restrictions from cooperative strategy. At each tic BOT decides whether to continue current action or start another one according to environment state and fuzzy logic rules. We also improved results of [5] using reinforcement learning for cooperative planning of wining policies.

2.2 Motion and Tactical Waypoints

When developing a BOT with a human-like behavior, path planning, movement and its' smoothing appear to be almost the most essential parts of the AI. A human player can overlook some tactical mistakes made by AI but even minor unnatural movement can become a decisive factor to assess its' quality or distinguish it from a human player. Constraint path planning is also computationally very hard problem.

In [3] authors apply navigation via human traces such that BOT walks exactly like humans with some randomness. It does not solve the problem of BOT having its own decision pattern without direct imitation of human players' motions.

We use Voronoi-based navigation mesh combined with composite Bezier curves to smooth produced randomized paths. It leads to a better representation of map topology and provides an opportunity of tactical path finding. We use visibility and cover positions, curvature of path trajectory and general penalties for traveling in particular areas to implement tactical map properties. In addition, a path computed as a sequence of Voronoi cells tends to have a natural look even without further post processing stages.

2.3 Weapon Selection

During game session BOT should be able to select weapons for current in-game situation, depending on distance between the BOT and its opponent, players' motions, ammo, accuracy, etc. We train BOT using neural network that performs reinforcement learning [6]. There is a variety of benefits in such approach: BOT's behavior will be non-deterministic and similar to human players adapting combat tactics to different situations in ever-changing game environment. Combined with Kohonen self-organising maps for local goal selection and enemy position prediction, neural networks make FPS gameplay satisfy human player expectations of NPC skills.

2.4 Object Recognition and Targeting

The process of targeting and shooting is decomposed into the enemy recognition, targeting with respect to motor reflexes, and shooting after player's crosshair aim at recognized enemy. For the first part we use a toolkit for enemy recognition that outputs probability of an object to be an enemy player and its cover area [4]. The targeting was reconstructed via series of experiments with analysing mouse-tracking in game tests. Finally, we discovered correlation between in-game events and aiming techniques, and use the following three: target lock (locking the player's crosshairs on the closest target by manipulating his pitch and yaw), target gravity (choosing an area of targeting and then the closest target, if several enemies are recognized), or sticky targets (aiming at the moving targets following its motion).

3. PLAYER EXPERIENCE

We give a user HTC Vive headset and controllers, emulating real weapons. User participates in a deathmatch competition with limited time. We allow user to play with both, humans via Internet and BOTs with human-like behavior. The BOTs' skills set is adapted to human-player game level during the game. We implement technical demo providing AAA graphics quality with the use of Unreal Engine 4 under custom license agreement.[1] We evaluate the BOT model through game Turing test obtaining 80% humanness judged by humans playing the demo FPS game.

[1]`https://www.unrealengine.com/custom-licensing`

Figure 2: VR FPS Game Demo

The demo exhibits a first-person shooter video-game with reduced simulator sickness and advanced intelligent enemies. We present a challenging gameplay that may be of great interest to game developers and users of any game experience.

4. ACKNOWLEDGMENTS

The authors would like to thank Maxim Vergazov from `virtuality.club` for granting access to VR equipment.

5. ADDITIONAL AUTHORS

National Research University Higher School of Economics, School of Data Analysis and Artificial Intelligence :
P. Zyuzin (Weapon selection) `peter95zyuzin@gmail.com`,
M. Martynov (VR, UE4) `martynov.maxim@gmail.com`,
O. Konoplya (VR adaptation) `olegkonoplya@gmail.com`,
G. Kuznetsov (Balancing) `goniakuznetsov@gmail.com`,
I. Guschenko-Cheverda, M. Uriev (Moving-target seek),
I. Mokeev (Local goal), O. Gerasimova (Reasoning),
L. Tokmakova, A. Kosmachev (Targeting recognized enemy).

6. REFERENCES

[1] P. J. C. Adachi and T. Willoughby. More than just fun and games: The longitudinal relationships between strategic video games, self-reported problem solving skills, and academic grades. *Journal of Youth and Adolescence*, 42(7):1041–1052, 2013.

[2] I. Granic, A. Lobel, and R. C. Engels. The benefits of playing video games. *American Psychologist*, 69(1):66–78, 2014.

[3] I. V. Karpov, J. Schrum, and R. Miikkulainen. *Believable Bots: Can Computers Play Like People?*, chapter Believable Bot Navigation via Playback of Human Traces, pages 151–170. Springer Berlin Heidelberg, Berlin, Heidelberg, 2012.

[4] I. Makarov, M. Tokmakov, and L. Tokmakova. Imitation of human behavior in 3D-shooter game. In *4th International Conference on Analysis of Images, Social Networks and Texts*, pages 64–77, 2015.

[5] M. Smith, S. Lee-Urban, and H. M. noz Avila. Retaliate: Learning winning policies in first-person shooter games. In *Proceedings of the 19th National Conference on Innovative Applications of Artificial Intelligence - Volume 2*, IAAI'07, pages 1801–1806. AAAI Press, 2007.

[6] D. Wang and A. H. Tan. Creating autonomous adaptive agents in a real-time first-person shooter computer game. *IEEE Transactions on Computational Intelligence and AI in Games*, 7(2):123–138, June 2015.

SuperStreamer: Enabling Progressive Content Streaming in a Game Engine

Yong Xue Eu, Jermyn Tanu, Justin Jieting Law, Muhammad Hanif B Ghazali
Shuan Siang Tay, Wei Tsang Ooi, Anand Bhojan
School of Computing, National University of Singapore
bhojan@comp.nus.edu.sg

ABSTRACT

This technical demonstration presents the SuperStreamer project, which enables progressive game assets streaming to players while games are played, reducing the startup time required to download and start playing a cloud-based game. SuperStreamer modifies a popular game engine, Unreal Engine 4, to support developing and playing games with progressive game asset streaming. With SuperStreamer, developers can mark the minimal set of files, containing only the game content essential to start playing the game. When a player plays the game, these minimal set of files will be downloaded to the player's device. SuperStreamer also generates low resolution textures automatically when a developer publishes a game, and these low resolution textures are transmitted first into the game client. As players move through a game level, high quality textures required for the game will be downloaded. In our demo game, we are able to decrease the time taken to startup and load the first game level by around 30%.

1. INTRODUCTION

Cloud gaming is a form of on-demand service that allows players to run a game of their choice as quickly as possible, with the game content being streamed to the player from a remote server rather than the player having the entire game already in their local drive.

Most game streaming services are now offering game streaming through video streaming (or pixel streaming). The player uses a client provided by the service to access the game. The game runs on on a remote server and a video stream depicting the rendered content of the game is streamed to the player. The client runs on the player's device, takes in his or her input, and sends it back to the server where it is relayed into the game, effectively behaving as if the player is in control of the game. This form of game streaming allows the player to run high- end games on low-end devices, and removes the need to download the game content onto the player's device before being able to play.

Real-time interactive games, however, requires low interaction latency for the game to be playable. Various research recommends a round trip latency of 50 ms for optimal player experience in first person shooter games, a game genre that requires quick reflexes and fast responses. This is a challenge faced by game streaming services as they have to satisfy their customers by providing low latency video streaming of games. To achieve low latency, companies set up servers in various locations globally to cater to geographically distributed customers. The lack of an Internet infrastructure that is good enough to entice gamers to try out cloud gaming is speculated to be one of the reasons behind cloud gaming pioneer OnLive's recent demise.

MM '16 October 15-19, 2016, Amsterdam, Netherlands

ACM ISBN 978-1-4503-3603-1/16/10.

DOI: http://dx.doi.org/10.1145/2964284.2973827

1.1 Cloud Gaming through File Streaming

An alternative form of cloud game streaming has emerged since, focusing on streaming the game content rather than the rendered content [2, 3]. This form of streaming allows players to begin playing the game as soon as a small subset of the game content has been downloaded. Since the game runs locally on the player's device, this approach reduces the need for a low latency Internet connection, at the cost of requiring capable devices to run the game, since the game's processing is no longer offloaded to a remote server.

File streaming game services such as Spawnapps usually determine the minimal set of files required for the game to function to create a small initial download package for the player, before proceeding to stream the remaining files on demand. The methods to achieve file streaming in games are, however, proprietary, and thus the benefits of this form of streaming cannot be shared with the general public.

1.2 Our Solution: SuperStreamer

We set out to modify an existing open source game engine so that developers can build games that can stream its files progressively, giving players a relatively seamless gameplay experience without a long download time. Choosing an open source game engine allows others to learn from, and build on, what we have done. Integrating file streaming into a game engine opens the possibility of making it compatible for more games in the future.

Our solution, SuperStreamer, is a set of tools that will aid game developers using Unreal Engine 4 to package and deploy their games so that progressive file streaming will work off the bat for players of the games. We are targeting single player games.

SuperStreamer is intended to be the first part of a two step approach to future cloud gaming technology, Gamelets [1]. At the point of its conception, the client portion of SuperStreamer enabled games were to be stored and run on modified wireless access points or micro-servers in the network (known as Gamelet nodes), which in turn streams video (pixel streaming) to the resource limited clients few hops away. Gamelets system is a micro-cloud based hybrid system that combines the benefits of both file streaming and pixel streaming.

2. SYSTEM OVERVIEW

SuperStreamer consists of (i) a SuperStreamer server, (ii) a SuperStreamer client (not to be confused with game client), and (iii) a game builder. The SuperStreamer server is essentially a web server responsible for serving game files (referred to as assets from here onwards) to the player. The SuperStreamer client is a modified, lightweight, Unreal Engine client that is able to stream game assets from the SuperStreamer Server. The game builder contains modifications and additions to the Unreal Editor that aid in making the published game ready for distribution to the SuperStreamer Server and the player.

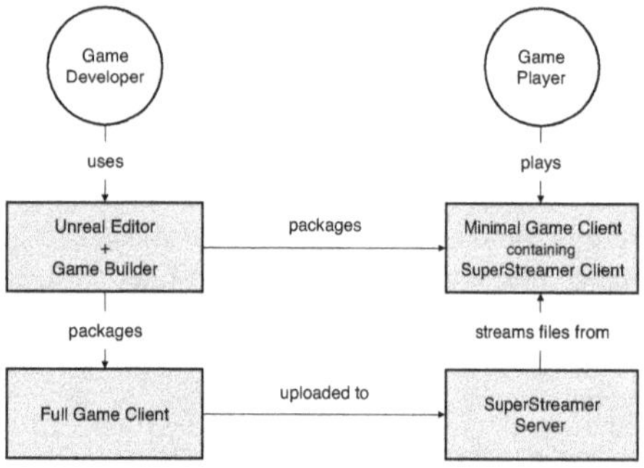

Figure 1: Users' High Level Interactions with SuperStreamer

To build a game, a game developer uses the Unreal Engine editor as per normal, except that they need to mark certain game assets as essential. These are the asset that must be present before a player can play the game. The developer then package the game for publishing using the game builder. The game builder generates lower quality textures for non-essential game assets used in the game, and include these in the game to be downloaded (initially) by the player. The high quality version of the textures are uploaded to the SuperStreamer server. It also generates asset mappings that will be used by the Server to locate the correct assets to send to the player.

To play a game, the SuperStreamer client first downloads the essential game files. Once all the files are loaded, the game is launched, and as the game is played, the SuperStreamer client predicts the high-quality textures that will be needed and prefetches them. Low quality version of the textures are rendered if the high quality version is not downloaded in time.

To prefetch the game assets, we use a combination of distance-based and frequency-based approach to prioritize which assets (i.e., high-quality textures) to download first. For distance-based approach, SuperStreamer periodically determine the distance of objects from the player current position, and assets that are closer are given higher priority than those that are further away. Assets that are referenced more times throughout the entire game are also given higher priority than those that are less frequently referenced, since the gain of downloading these assets are higher.

3. RESULTS

To evaluate the performance of the SuperStreamer Client, we measure (i) the initial download size, which is the total file size of the minimal set of files needed to run the game; (ii) the level load time, which is the time taken before a level is loaded and playable by the user.

We built a demo game using our modified version of Unreal Engine. Most assets (meshes and textures) were taken from the built-in *Starter Content* as well as the free-to-use *Infinity Blade Collection* released by Epic Games. The demo game contained 873 textures, materials, and meshes. The first level to be loaded in this game consists of 75 objects, with different textures on each object. The objects were spread out across the level.

The SuperStreamer-enabled game's initial download size is 139 MB compressed (434 MB uncompressed). At 1.5 MBps, it takes 92 secs to download the initial set of files. The level load time for the first map is 234 seconds. Giving a total of 326 seconds before the game can be played.

In constrast, the same game without using SuperStreamer has an initial download size of 688 MB compressed (1340 MB uncompressed), about 5 times larger. The level load time of the first map is only 10 secs, but it takes 459 seconds to download all the game content, giving a total of 469 seconds before the game can be played. Thus, in the case of our demo game, we achieve a 30% reduction in game loading time.

Note that, players playing the SuperStreamer-enabled game may see low-quality textures when the game starts playing and thus experience lower QoE compared to those playing the non-SuperStreamer version. SuperStreamer, however, caches high quality game assets that are downloaded. Thus, on the next launch of the game, players using the SuperStreamer-enabled game will likely have higher QoE.

4. CONCLUSION

We present SuperStreamer, a system that enabled progressive game asset streaming, with the goal of reducing game play startup time for games that are served from the cloud. Our system uses and modifies Unreal Engine 4, a popular commercial game engine, thus making the SuperStreamer approach potentially available to a large number of game developers.

Beyond this initial proof of concepts, we plan to improve upon the asset prioritization algorithms, taking into consideration multiple players, the server load, the network condition, and the QoE of players. We also plan to integrate SuperStreamer into Gamelets micro-cloud environment to support low-latency video-based cloud gaming.

5. ACKNOWLEDGMENT

This work is supported by Singapore Ministry of Education Academic Research Fund Tier 1 T1 251RES1506 "Cloud-based Multi-user Interactive Virtual Environments".

6. REFERENCES

[1] B. Anand and A. J. H. Edwin. Gamelets – multiplayer mobile games with distributed micro-clouds. In *The 7th International Conference on Mobile Computing and Ubiquitous Networking (ICMU), 2014*, pages 14–20. IEEE, 2014.

[2] A. Jurgelionis, P. Fechteler, P. Eisert, F. Bellotti, H. David, J.-P. Laulajainen, R. Carmichael, V. Poulopoulos, A. Laikari, P. Perälä, et al. Platform for distributed 3D gaming. *International Journal of Computer Games Technology*, 2009:1, 2009.

[3] L. Lin, X. Liao, G. Tan, H. Jin, X. Yang, W. Zhang, and B. Li. LiveRender: A cloud gaming system based on compressed graphics streaming. In *Proceedings of the 22nd ACM International Conference on Multimedia*, pages 347–356. ACM, 2014.

DeepSketch2Image: Deep Convolutional Neural Networks for Partial Sketch Recognition and Image Retrieval

Omar Seddati
UMONS
Computer science – TCTS LAB
Mons, Belgium
+32 (0) 65 37 47 32
omar.seddati@umons.ac.be

Stéphane Dupont
UMONS
TCTS LAB
Mons, Belgium
+32 (0) 65 37 47 39
stephane.dupont@umons.ac.be

Saïd Mahmoudi
UMONS
Computer science
Mons, Belgium
+32 (0) 65 37 40 56
said.mahmoudi@umons.ac.be

ABSTRACT
Freehand sketches are an interesting universal form of visual representation. Sketching has become easily accessible with many of the devices that we use on a daily basis. In this paper, we propose a system for real-time sketch recognition and similarity search. Our system is able to recognize partial sketches from 250 object categories. It is then able to retrieve similar sketches but also images/photographs. In this work, we propose to use deep convolutional neural networks (ConvNets) for partial sketch recognition and feature extraction. Features are extracted from sketches and image contours in order to be used as a basis for similarity search using k-Nearest Neighbors (kNN). Our system demonstrates promising results in identifying similar images, and could be integrated in larger content-based search engines.

General Terms
Algorithms, Performance, Experimentation.

Keywords
ConvNets, sketches, recognition, retrieval.

1. INTRODUCTION
Freehand sketches are a simple and powerful tool commonly used by humans to record ideas, or to communicate. The universality of this kind of representation attracts more and more interest in the research community. Research works in the field of sketch recognition goes back to the development of SketchPad [5]. Ever since, different computer vision approaches were used in order to achieve better results in multiple application domains (mathematical sketches [7], chemical structure drawings [8]). Cao et al. [1] proposed a low dimensional symmetry aware flip invariant descriptor for sketches. Li et al. [3] exploited local feature representations and global structures to address local and global variations.

In the last few years, ConvNets significantly improved performance in the field of image recognition [13, 14]. They have also been used recently for sketch recognition [15, 16, 18, 20] and achieved beyond state-of-the-art results [20, 21]. ConvNet-based sketch recognition research is challenging in part due to the lack of large scale data sets, both for model training but also more generally for benchmarking. To address this issue, Eitz et al. [2] defined a taxonomy of 250 common object categories and gathered 20000 unique sketches, forming the first large scale dataset of human sketches (TU-Berlin benchmark). Sarvadevabhatla et al. [15] used two popular ConvNets architectures (ImageNet ConvNet and a modified LeNet ConvNet) and fine-tuned their parameters on a subset of the TU-Berlin sketch database. In contrast, Yang et al. [16] trained a ConvNet from scratch instead of fine tuning existing ones. In [20], we also proposed a system for sketch recognition and similarity search (using ConvNets + kNN) fully trained on the TU-Berlin data set. We then further improved the system to support partial sketch recognition [21]. In [18], the authors used a multi-scale multi-channel ConvNet for sketch recognition.

In the last two decades, many sketch based image retrieval (SBIR) methods have been proposed. One of the main challenges in this area is to find a common feature representation that enables to match sketches and images. Eitz et al. [4] introduced a benchmark for SBIR performance evaluation and proposed new descriptors based on bag-of-features. Szanto et al. [6] used edge histogram descriptors (EHD) and the histogram of oriented gradients (HOG). Wang et al. [9] used edge map descriptors and wavelet transform features to match sketches and images. Zhou et al. [10] used a saliency-based approach to select the main object in the image and extract features only for the salient region. Jin et al. [11] presented an approach based on a visual region descriptor where sketch-like representations are generated from images by using edge map generation and edge pixel screening. Then, the sketch-like representation was used for sketch-image matching.

The system presented here is based on the use of ConvNets from our previous work [20,21], but goes beyond sketched object recognition, as it enables real-time sketch and image search. More precisely, it can achieve real-time recognition of partial sketches, estimation of sketch completeness and sketch-based image search. In contrast to other approaches that rely on the use of edges for SBIR, our method uses ConvNet features as a common feature representation for sketch-image matching. The system will be demonstrated live on a tablet device at the conference.

2. METHODOLOGY
As mentioned before, we use a ConvNet for sketch recognition and feature extraction. The TU-Berlin dataset sketches are available in SVG (Scalable Vector Graphics) format, with the

MM '16, October 15-19, 2016, Amsterdam, Netherlands
ACM 978-1-4503-3603-1/16/10.
http://dx.doi.org/10.1145/2964284.2973828

stroke order also provided. This enables to generate partial sketch images as if we had taken picture snapshots of the sketches as they were being drawn. We generate five instances of increasing completeness per sketch: the first instance contains 20% of the original sketch strokes, the second 40%, the third 60%, the fourth 80%, and the last one 100%. The generated partial sketches are then used to train our ConvNet [21]. This ConvNet is trained in a multi-task learning scheme (Figure 1) to address partial sketch recognition and completeness prediction (Table 1). We can notice that the first 20% of the strokes are enough to get the correct category in the top-5 recognition results 62% of the time.

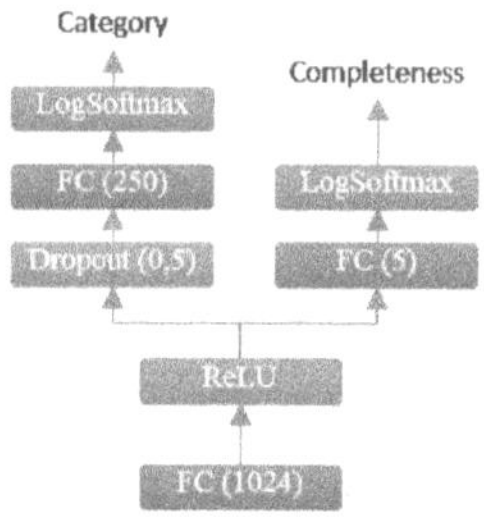

Figure 1. Our multi-task classifier.

Table 1. Our multi-task ConvNet top-1 and top-5 mean results on TU-Berlin benchmark.

	mAP (%)				
completeness	20	40	60	80	100
Top-1	32.12	52.58	64.48	71.29	74.12
Top-5	61.85	80.04	87.29	91.16	92.18

The obtained ConvNet forms the core of our retrieval system. When the user is querying the system (i.e. drawing a sketch), the ConvNet is used to predict the top-5 object categories on one side, and to extract a feature vector representing the sketch on the other side. The outputs of the last convolutional layer are actually used as features. kNN is used to find the most similar sketches in a sketch collection, where the search for neighbors is bounded to the sketches in the collection belonging to the top-5 predicted categories. All this is run periodically with retrieved results refreshed in real-time.

For SBIR now, kNN is also used to retrieve images, which requires finding a feature representation where the distance between a sketch and an image can be computed. For this, we processed the images to extract their contour, making them look closer to sketches, hence enabling to use the same ConvNet for image feature extraction, and finally kNN search. The exact preparation process is described here. We extract contours from the images in the collection using the canny edge detection algorithm [22]. For each image we generate six propositions for the contours by using different values for the canny algorithm upper and lower thresholds. We use an upper-lower ratio equal to 3 and a Gaussian kernel of size equal to 3. The six sketch-like propositions are then presented as input to our ConvNet. The proposition for which the ConvNet produces the highest probability for the object category actually present in the image is kept for similarity search. Again, retrieval is hybrid semantic and metric-based, as the search for neighbors is bounded to the images belonging to the top-5 predicted categories from the sketch query, while the similarity search enable to retrieve pictures which have a similar compositions (and contours) than the drawn sketch.

3. DEMO SYSTEM

Our system is based on the use of the publicly available Torch toolbox [17]. We also used OpenCV [19] for both contour extraction and kNN search. In this section, we introduce the GUI of our application. On the top right of the GUI (Figure 2), we have five boxes that show the closest sketch for each of the top-5 predicted categories. Down left, it shows the probabilities predicted by the ConvNet for the top-5 categories for the current sketch query. Also, a bar chart indicates the predicted completeness probabilities for this query.

Figure 2. Sample of query with additional details related to environment and adjacent objects.

Finally, the application displays the three closest images for each of the top-5 categories, based on the approach we described. The application updates suggestions two times per second until the user stops drawing. At any moment, the user can select one of the output categories and keep adding details to the sketch, in order to find images that fit better what the user has in mind. This option is meant to be used in case the user wants to add additional information related to the environment around the object for example. However, as the sketch database used to train our ConvNet contains only one object per image, adding more details to the current drawing could hurt performance and finally end up reducing the quality of the top-5 retrieved categories. To prevent this, the user can at any point select one of the suggested categories from the top-5 by clicking on it. After that, the progressing sketch query will be used only for refining sketch-image matching, not for updating the top-5 list of categories used for the "semantic" part of the retrieval. Adding such details can provide quite impressive search results. Such a system can be especially useful in the context of known-item search tasks.

4. CONCLUSION

In this paper, we have presented a novel approach for partial sketch recognition and similarity search, for searching both sketches but also images, from sketch-only queries. The system runs in real-time and is based on the use of a ConvNet that achieves state-of-the-art results for partial and complete sketch recognition. Similarity content-based sketch search is achieved using features extracted with this ConvNet together with kNN. We have also shown that these features can be used to match sketches with images, with automatic contour extraction being applied on these images before computing their features. Our approach yields promising results. Sketch classification has been benchmarked on the current largest available research dataset, but SBIR still need to be benchmarked fully. In the future, we plan to propose such an evaluation. Also, it would be interesting to address some of the limitations of the system, in particular the fact that it currently works on so-called iconic pictures only (with one main object occupying most of the picture space).

5. REFERENCES

[1] CAO, Xiaochun, ZHANG, Hua, LIU, Si, et al. Sym-fish: A symmetry-aware flip invariant sketch histogram shape descriptor. In: Computer Vision (ICCV), 2013 IEEE International Conference on. IEEE, 2013. p. 313-320.

[2] EITZ, Mathias, HAYS, James, et ALEXA, Marc. How do humans sketch objects?. ACM Trans. Graph., 2012, vol. 31, no 4, p. 44.

[3] LI, Yi, SONG, Yi-Zhe, et GONG, Shaogang. Sketch recognition by ensemble matching of structured features. In: In British Machine Vision Conference (BMVC). 2013.

[4] EITZ, Mathias, HILDEBRAND, Kristian, BOUBEKEUR, Tamy, et al. Sketch-based image retrieval: Benchmark and bag-of-features descriptors.Visualization and Computer Graphics, IEEE Transactions on, 2011, vol. 17, no 11, p. 1624-1636.

[5] SUTHERLAND, Ivan E. Sketch pad a man-machine graphical communication system. In: Proceedings of the SHARE design automation workshop. ACM, 1964. p. 6.329-6.346.

[6] SZÁNTÓ, B., POZSEGOVICS, P., VÁMOSSY, Z., et al. Sketch4match—Content-based image retrieval system using sketches. In : Applied Machine Intelligence and Informatics (SAMI), 2011 IEEE 9th International Symposium on. IEEE, 2011. p. 183-188.

[7] LAVIOLA JR, Joseph J. et ZELEZNIK, Robert C. MathPad 2: a system for the creation and exploration of mathematical sketches. In: ACM SIGGRAPH 2007 courses. ACM, 2007. p. 46.

[8] OUYANG, Tom Y. et DAVIS, Randall. ChemInk: a natural real-time recognition system for chemical drawings. In: Proceedings of the 16th international conference on intelligent user interfaces. ACM, 2011. p. 267-276.

[9] WANG, Yuxin, YU, Miao, JIA, Qi, et al. Query by sketch: An asymmetric sketch-vs-image retrieval system. In : Image and Signal Processing (CISP), 2011 4th International Congress on. IEEE, 2011. p. 1368-1372.

[10] Zhou R, Chen L, Zhang L (2012) Sketch-based image retrieval on a large scale database. In: ACM international conference on Multimedia.

[11] JIN, Cheng, WANG, Zheming, ZHANG, Tianhao, et al. A Novel Visual-Region-Descriptor-based AJIN, Cheng, WANG, Zheming, ZHANG, Tianhao, et al. A Novel Visual-Region-Descriptor-based Approach to Sketch-based Image Retrieval. In : Proceedings of the 5th ACM on International Conference on Multimedia Retrieval. ACM, 2015. p. 267-274.pproach to Sketch-based Image Retrieval. In: Proceedings of the 5th ACM on International Conference on Multimedia Retrieval. ACM, 2015. p. 267-274.

[12] J. Deng, A. Berg, S. Satheesh, H. Su, A. Khosla, and L. Fei-Fei. ILSVRC-2012, 2012. URL http://www.image-net.org/challenges/LSVRC/2012/.

[13] KRIZHEVSKY, Alex, SUTSKEVER, Ilya, et HINTON, Geoffrey E. Imagenet classification with deep convolutional neural networks. In : Advances in neural information processing systems. 2012. p. 1097-1105.

[14] SZEGEDY, Christian, LIU, Wei, JIA, Yangqing, et al. Going deeper with convolutions. arXiv preprint arXiv:1409.4842, 2014.

[15] SARVADEVABHATLA, Ravi Kiran et BABU, R. Venkatesh. Freehand Sketch Recognition Using Deep Features. arXiv preprint arXiv:1502.00254, 2015.

[16] YANG, Yongxin et HOSPEDALES, Timothy M. Deep Neural Networks for Sketch Recognition. arXiv preprint arXiv:1501.07873, 2015.

[17] Collobert, R., Kavukcuoglu, K., & Farabet, C. (2011). Torch7: A matlab-like environment for machine learning. In BigLearn, NIPS Workshop (No.EPFL-CONF-192376).

[18] YU, Qian, YANG, Yongxin, SONG, Yi-Zhe, et al. Sketch-a-net that beats humans. In : Proceedings of the British Machine Vision Conference (BMVC). 2015. p. 7.1-7.12.

[19] OPENCV, Learning. Computer vision with the OpenCV library. GaryBradski & Adrian Kaebler-O'Reilly, 2008.

[20] SEDDATI, Omar, DUPONT, Stephane, et MAHMOUDI, Said. Deepsketch: deep convolutional neural networks for sketch recognition and similarity search. In : Content-Based Multimedia Indexing (CBMI), 2015 13th International Workshop on. IEEE, 2015. p. 1-6.

[21] SEDDATI, Omar, DUPONT, Stephane, et MAHMOUDI, Said. DeepSketch 2: Deep Convolutional Neural Networks for Partial Sketch Recognition. In : Content-Based Multimedia Indexing (CBMI), 2016 14th International Workshop on. IEEE, 2016. p. 1-6.

[22] J. Canny. A Computational Approach to Edge Detection, IEEE Trans. on Pattern Analysis and Machine Intelligence, 8(6), pp. 679-698 (1986).

A Fast Cattle Recognition System using Smart devices

Santosh Kumar, Sanjay Kumar Singh, Tanima Datta, and Hari Prabhat Gupta
{santosh.rs.cse12, sks.cse, tanima.cse, hariprabhat.cse}@iitbhu.ac.in
Department of Computer Science and Engineering
Indian Institute of Technology (B.H.U.) Varanasi, India -221005

ABSTRACT

A recognition system is very useful to recognize human, object, and animals. An animal recognition system plays an important role in livestock biometrics, that helps in recognition and verification of livestock in case of missed or swapped animals, false insurance claims, and reallocation of animals at slaughter houses. In this research, we propose a fast and cost-effective animal biometrics based cattle recognition system to quickly recognize and verify the false insurance claims of cattle using their primary muzzle point image pattern characteristics. To solve this major problem, users (owner, parentage, or other) have captured the images of cattle using their smart devices. The captured images are transferred to the server of the cattle recognition system using a wireless network or internet technology. The system performs preprocessing on the muzzle point image of cattle to remove and filter the noise, increases the quality, and enhance the contrast. The muzzle point features are extracted and supervised machine learning based multi-classifier pattern recognition techniques are applied for recognizing the cattle. The server has a database of cattle images which are provided by the owners. Finally, One-Shot-Similarity (OSS) matching and distance metric learning based techniques with ensemble of classifiers technique are used for matching the query muzzle image with the stored database. A prototype is also developed for evaluating the efficacy of the proposed system in term of recognition accuracy and end-to-end delay.

Keywords

Cattle Recognition; Muzzle Point Pattern; Object Recognition; Machine Learning; Feature Extraction; Classification

1. INTRODUCTION

The cattle recognition is an emerging field of the animal biometrics, computer vision, and pattern recognition [1, 2]. It prevents the manipulations, swapping of cattle and helps to recognize the parentage or ownership of each cattle. The cattle recognition system identifies and controlling the widespread of critical animal diseases. It also provides a way to ensure animal food safety, to validate various sources, pro-

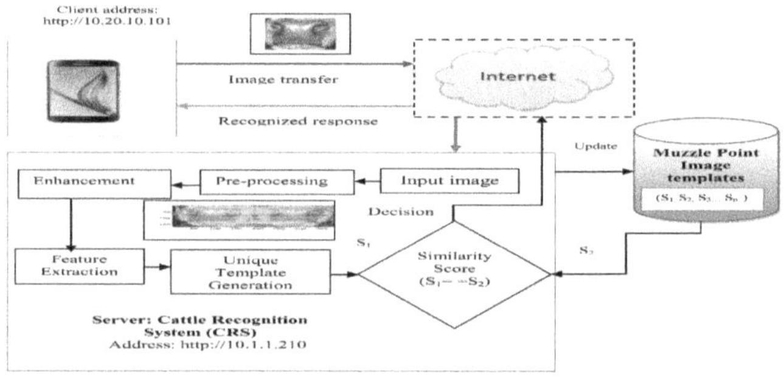

Figure 1: Block diagram of the cattle recognition using smart devices.

used to recognize the cattle, cattle recognition techniques can be classified into the following categories: permanent, semi-permanent, and temporary identification based techniques [2]. An example of permanent identification technique is ear-tagging of cattle, where recognition techniques apply a unique label on the cattle ear with identification numbers. Other examples of semi-permanent recognition techniques are ear tips-notches, embedding microchips, tattoos, and freeze-branding. The temporary recognition techniques are collar tags, paint/dye and RFID based identification system, respectively [2, 3]. With the recent advancement of hardware and cameras in smart devices, capturing and transmitting images have become easy and widespread. The authors in [1] proposed a system for wirelessly tracking cows using RFID tags and devices. The RFID reader is connected to the ZigBee wireless networking node. However, RFID tags, embedding microchips and devices are required which increases the cost of the system. In [3], a matching refinement technique was proposed based on the keypoint's orientation and the Scale Invariant Feature Transform (SIFT) technique eliminates the miss-matched key point for the recognition of cattle.

In this paper, we address the problem of cattle recognition and monitoring. To solve this problem, we use a smartphone for capturing the muzzle point images of cattle. We apply the WiFi (IEEE 802.11) protocol for transferring the captured images to the server. The system performs preprocessing on the muzzle point images to mitigate the artifacts (noises). The preprocessing technique increases the image quality, and enhance the contrast of muzzle images. The muzzle point image consists of beads and ridges features as shown in Fig. 2. The features are extracted from the muzzle point images. After that, supervised machine learning techniques based multi-classifiers are applied for recognizing the

MM '16 October 15-19, 2016, Amsterdam,Netherlands

ACM ISBN 978-1-4503-3603-1/16/10.
DOI: http://dx.doi.org/10.1145/2964284.2973829

cattle. Finally, One-Shot Similarity (OSS) matching and distance metric based learning techniques are applied for matching the query muzzle image with the stored database. The advantages proposed system are fast, cost-effective, and remotely accessible. The rest of the paper is organized as follows: Section 2 proposes a cattle recognition system. Section 4 illustrates the experimental results. Finally, paper is concluded in section 5.

2. CATTLE RECOGNITION SYSTEM

In this section, the proposed cattle recognition system is illustrated in detail. The system uses SIFT and muzzle point image pattern technique for extracting and matching the features as shown in Fig. 1.

2.1 Data Acquisition and Communication

The proposed cattle recognition system consists of two phases: (1) training phase, and (2) testing phase. During the training phase, the system creates a database to store the valuable information of cattle and their owner in the server of the proposed system. The stored owner information includes owner's name, date-of-birth(DOB), and address. The system assigns a unique identification number to each cattle. In the testing phase, captured muzzle point as the query image matches with stored muzzle point image database for the recognition of cattle. The proposed system wirelessly transfers the cattle muzzle images and owner information to the server. The benefits of the proposed system are fast, cost-effective, and remotely accessible, *i.e.*, a user in testing phase requires only to capture and transfer the cattle image to the server for the recognition of cattle.

2.2 Preprocessing and Enhancement

The muzzle point images of cattle are captured in the unconstrained environment. These images can be defective, poor quality, contrast, and blurred. In addition, wireless transmission of the images also added noises in the muzzle images. The proposed system performs the preprocessing to mitigate and filter the noise and increases the quality. The contrast Limited Adaptive Histogram Equalization (CLAHE) technique is applied to enhance the contrast of the muzzle images.

3. FEATURE EXTRACTION AND CLASSIFICATION

After preprocessing and enhancement, the proposed system first extracts the salient features from the images. We extract the ridges, SIFT, and SURF feature points of muzzle images as salient features as shown in Fig. 2. After feature

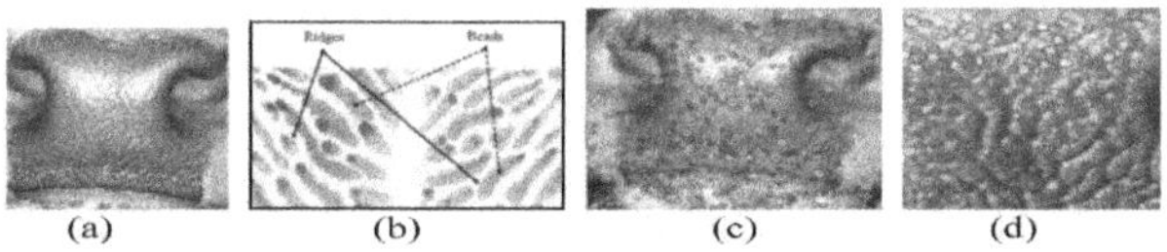

(a) (b) (c) (d)

Figure 2: Feature extraction: (a) input muzzle image, (b) ridges, (c) SIFT feature, and (d) SURF features.

extraction, the proposed cattle recognition system adopted an ensemble of classifiers approach, such as Bagging, Random Subspace, and AdaBoost classification methods along with conventional supervised classification methods, namely, Binary Tree, Linear Discriminant Analysis (LDA) classifier, Naive Bayes classifier, k-Nearest Neighbor (k-NN) classifier, and Adaptive Neuro Fuzzy Inference System (ANFIS) classifier. Such ensemble classifiers are updated periodically to adapt the variations of the extracted features. Therefore, the system successively eliminates a number of histories of samples and restore several new samples. Finally, OSS matching and distance metric learning based techniques with ensemble of classifiers technique are applied for matching the query image with the stored database.

4. EXPERIMENTAL RESULTS

We used four breeds of cattle, *i.e.*, Balinese cow, Hybrid Ongole cow, Holstein Friesian cow, and Cross breed evaluate the accuracy of the proposed system. The prepared muzzle image database of the cattle was segmented training and test part, where 6 muzzle point images of each subject (cattle) out of 5000 muzzle image from 500 subjects (e.g., 500 subjects $\times$ 10 image of each subject) were randomly chosen for the training phase and the remaining were used as a test image. A cumulative match score [2] curve is applied to the evaluation of accuracy of the proposed system. Fig. 3(a) illustrates the impact of the change in the resolution of the image with the end-to-end delay of the system. The required time of the system is the information transfer time and processing time to recognize the cattle using muzzle images. Fig. 3(b) illustrates the impact of the change in the resolution of the image with the accuracy of the recognition system. High-resolution muzzle images cater more features (information) and therefore increases the accuracy of the system.

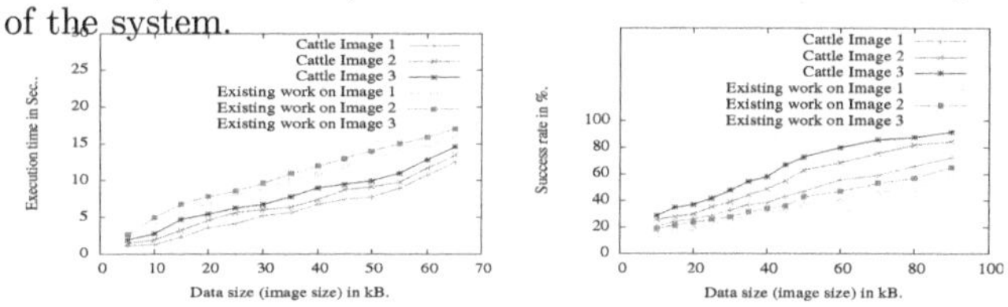

(a) (b)

Figure 3: Impact of the size of images on (a) end-to-end delay and (b) accuracy of the system.

5. CONCLUSIONS

In this paper, we propose a fast and cost-effective system for cattle recognition using smart devices. The muzzle point images of cattle are captured and transferred to the server using wireless (internet). The system performed image preprocessing on muzzle point to remove noise, increase the image quality, and enhance the contrast of muzzle images. Feature extraction and supervised machine learning techniques based multi-classifier pattern recognition technique is used for recognition. We developed a prototype for evaluating the end-to-end delay of the system. The prototype shows that the system provides the desired accuracy within the given processing time. This work can be used in the planning and design of large scale livestock recognition.

6. REFERENCES

[1] G. Byrd. Tracking cows wirelessly. *Computer*, 48(6):60–63, 2015.

[2] S. Kumar, S. Tiwari, and S. K. Singh. Face recognition of cattle: Can it be done? *Proceedings of the National Academy of Sciences, India Section A: Physical Sciences*, 86(2):137–148, 2016.

[3] A. Noviyanto and A. M. Arymurthy. Beef cattle identification based on muzzle pattern using a matching refinement technique in the sift method. *Comput. Electron. Agric.*, 99:77–84, Nov. 2013.

Vibrotactile Experiences for Augmented Reality

Wolfgang Hürst
Utrecht University
Utrecht, The Netherlands
huerst@uu.nl

Nina Rosa
Utrecht University
Utrecht, The Netherlands
N.E.Rosa@uu.nl

Jean-Paul van Bommel
Utrecht University
Utrecht, The Netherlands
j.g.vanbommel@students.uu.nl

ABSTRACT

This demo illustrates several use cases for utilizing vibrotactile feedback, i.e., tactile sensations created by small, body-worn vibration motors, in an augmented reality setting with head-mounted displays. In particular, we address how such feedback can be used to create different experiences and also how it can be applied to provide additional information to a user that might be beneficial when performing certain tasks, such as interactions requiring a high accuracy that is hard to achieve with pure visual feedback (e.g., correct placement of virtual objects at a specific location in the real world).

Keywords

Augmented reality, mixed-reality, multimodal interaction, haptics, vibrotactile feedback, human-computer interaction.

1. INTRODUCTION

Current augmented reality (AR) systems using head-mounted displays (HMDs) allow for the integration of graphical 3D objects into the real world (cf. Fig. 1) thus offering tremendous opportunities for various application fields. While this technology has reached a high level of realism, the experience is commonly still restricted to our visual senses and, to a much lesser degree, audio feedback, but lacks the full richness of how humans experience the real world. For example, tactile perception is an important aspect, especially when interacting with our environment. This naturally includes the experience of touching something or being touched. Yet, tactile feedback can also be used in general, more "abstract" ways. Think about the vibration of a smartphone to notify its user or a vibrating game controller providing additional information to players, for example, about hitting an object in the game or loosing health points. In our research, we are investigating different ways in which tactile feedback can be integrated in AR to provide better experiences or other benefits such as improved performance for certain tasks.

Tactile senses are very rich and related experiences are difficult to simulate. Yet, even simple tactile feedback, such as the one provided by the small vibration motors commonly integrated in mobile phones allows us to create interesting and useful tactile sensations. For example, in [4] we demonstrated how such devices can be used to simulate different experiences in a virtual reality setting when combined with a certain visual feedback. Erp et al. [1] showed how they can be used as navigation aid. In this demo, we present scenarios where vibrotactile feedback, i.e., the tactile sensation created with body-attached vibration motors provides a potential benefit for interaction in AR; either by creating a richer experience (e.g., similar to [4]) or by, for example, presenting additional information (e.g., similar to [1]). In the following, we describe the basic setup using a simple example (Section 2.1), discuss a performance-related, "abstract" usage of vibrotactile AR (Section 2.2), and shortly address a few other potential usage scenarios (Section 2.3).

MM '16, October 15-19, 2016, Amsterdam, Netherlands
ACM 978-1-4503-3603-1/16/10.
http://dx.doi.org/10.1145/2964284.2973830

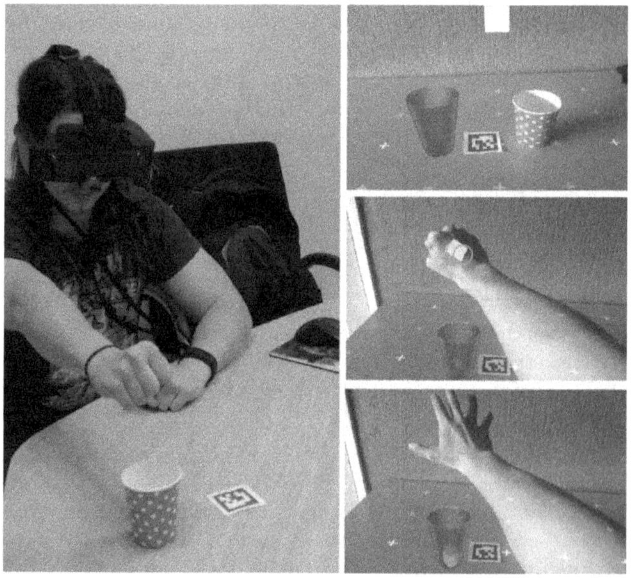

Figure 1. AR scene with a real cup and a virtual one that is only visible to the person wearing the HMD.

2. VIBROTACTILE FEEDBACK IN AR

2.1 Basic Usages and Setup

As discussed in the introduction, tactile feedback in AR can serve the purpose to make the experience more realistic, to improve and enrich it in other ways (e.g., by increasing subjective experience even in non-natural usages), or to provide additional information, which, for example, might lead to performance improvements in certain situations. Creating a natural haptic experience with vibrotactile feedback in AR seems unrealistic due to the limited tactile experience provided by these units and the lack of a similar counterpart in real-life situations. Yet, even if not resembling, for example, the experience of touching a real object, it might be beneficial to provide vibrotactile feedback at the point of contact when interacting with it (Fig. 2a). Such experiences resemble the vibrotactile feedback we have when hitting buttons on the touch screen on some smartphones (cf., e.g., [2]), although it is still unexplored if such sensations provide a benefit in AR and what are useful implementations (e.g., with respect to intensity or frequency of the tactile signal). Because most current AR HMDs render virtual objects at a fixed focal point, touching or grabbing them can be difficult. Thus, it could be beneficial to not just provide tactile feedback when directly touching an object but already when approaching it, similarly to a visual feedback when hovering over a location (Fig. 2b). Again, it is a question of ongoing research if such a setting provides a real benefit and what kind of implementation is most suitable. For example, is it better to provide discrete tactile feedback or should it increase when approaching the object? And if so, how (e.g., modification of intensity, frequency, or both)? Taking this to an extreme, we can also provide tactile feedback at other locations than the place of contact (Fig. 2c). While this does not resemble a realistic tactile experience, such feedback might still be helpful when used in the right context and for the right tasks (cf. Richter et al. [3] who studied such a situation in relation to interaction with horizontally mounted interactive surfaces). Notice that these three usages of vibrotactile feedback resemble the scenarios discussed at the beginning; feedback upon touch compares, at least to some degree, to a more natural situation, feedback when approaching extends this by providing additional information, whereas remote tactile feedback does not have a direct relation to a realistic scenario at all, but just provides additional, "abstract" information.

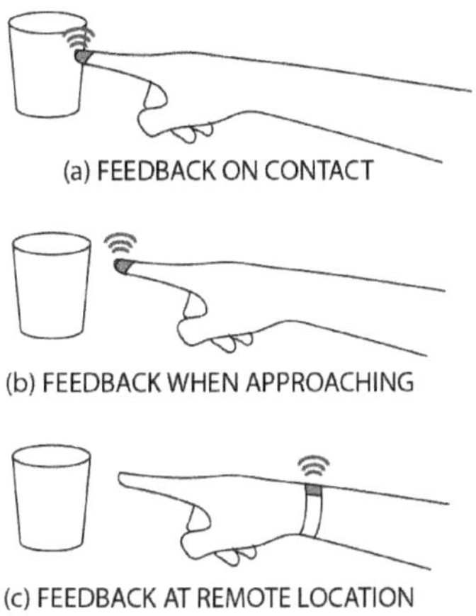

Figure 2. Simple use cases for vibrotactile feedback in AR. Parameters for implementation include vibration intensity, frequency, and duration, as well as location of tactile feedback (cf. (b) vs. (c)) and time of activation (cf. (a) vs. (b)).

2.2 Vibrotactile Depth Perception

In our latest research, we investigated if and how vibrotactile feedback can be used to improve depth perception when interacting with virtual objects in an AR scenario with HMDs. In particular, using a setup with six vibration motors distributed over one's forearm and thumb (Fig. 3, right), we used different tactile feedbacks to illustrate distance from a virtual object; "intensity gradient", where intensity of vibration increased at locations 1 and 2, and "positional gradient", where vibration was activated at locations 1 to 6 depending on the distance from the target. In a comparative study with conditions "visual", "pure tactile", and "tactile and visual" we evaluated depth perception with a reaching task, where subjects had to accurately place their thumb at the location of a virtual object (Fig. 3, left). Our results prove that such abstract, additional tactile feedback can indeed be used to determine a virtual object's depth. Under certain conditions, pure tactile feedback even outperformed the pure visual condition.

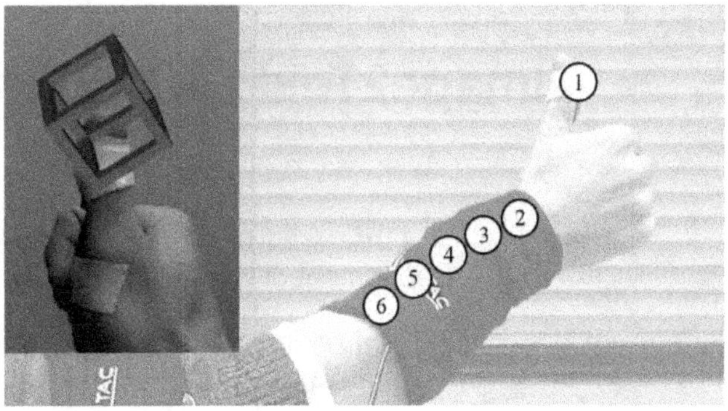

Figure 3. Setup for tactile depth perception experiment.

2.3 Other Use Cases

The two preceding subsections introduced different types of vibrotactile usage in AR and gave a concrete example where such feedback can be used in an abstract way as some sort of additional information channel to improve performance (here: depth perception in reaching tasks). Our demonstration framework illustrates different other use cases, including more playful experiences (e.g., variations of tactile feedback when touching different types of visuals) as well as further cases where tactile feedback is used to provide further information. An example for the latter includes indication of virtual objects that are out of the current field of view. In such a setup directional tactile feedback can not only be used to draw people's attention, but also to steer them into the right direction. Interesting variations to study and experience include the aforementioned modifications of tactile feedback (duration, frequency, intensity) and the influence of its location or when it is activated (e.g., touching or approaching; cf. Fig. 2). An important aspect of ongoing research is also how tactile feedback can accommodate for differences that appear when interacting with both real and virtual objects (cf. the real and virtual cup in Fig. 1 and the task of grabbing and dropping an object into either of them or using them to catch a falling object).

3. REFERENCES

[1] Erp, J.B.F. van, & Werkhoven, P. 2006. Validation of Principles for Tactile Navigation Displays. In *Proceedings of the 50th annual Human Factors and Ergonomics Society Conference,* (HFES 2006), October 2006, San Francisco, USA, 1687-1691.

[2] Dan Odell. 2015. On-screen keyboards: does the presence of feedback or tactile landmarks improve typing performance? In *Proceedings of the 17th International Conference on Human-Computer Interaction with Mobile Devices and Services* (MobileHCI '15). ACM, New York, NY, USA, 131-136.

[3] Richter, H., Loehmann, S., Weinhart, F., & Butz, A. 2012. Comparing direct and remote tactile feedback on interactive surfaces. In *Haptics: Perception, Devices, Mobility, and Communication*, Springer Berlin Heidelberg, 301-313.

[4] Nina Rosa, Wolfgang Hürst, Wouter Vos, and Peter Werkhoven. 2015. The Influence of Visual Cues on Passive Tactile Sensations in a Multimodal Immersive Virtual Environment. In *Proceedings of the 2015 ACM on International Conference on Multimodal Interaction* (ICMI '15). ACM, New York, NY, USA, 327-334.

Image2Text: A Multimodal Caption Generator

Chang Liu[1]*, Changhu Wang[2], Fuchun Sun[1], Yong Rui[2]
[1]Department of Computer Science, Tsinghua University, Beijing, P.R. China
[2]Microsoft Research, Beijing, P.R. China
cliu13@mails.tsinghua.edu.cn, chw@microsoft.com
fcsun@mail.tsinghua.edu.cn, yongrui@microsoft.com

ABSTRACT

In this work, we showcase the Image2Text system, which is a real-time captioning system that can generate human-level natural language description for any input image. We formulate the problem of image captioning as a multimodal translation task. Analogous to machine translation, we present a sequence-to-sequence recurrent neural networks (RNN) model for image caption generation. Different from most existing work where the whole image is represented by a convolutional neural networks (CNN) feature, we propose to represent the input image as a sequence of detected objects to serve as the source sequence of the RNN model. Based on the captioning framework, we develop a user-friendly system to automatically generated human-level captions for users. The system also enables users to detect salient objects in an image, and retrieve similar images and corresponding descriptions from a database.

CCS Concepts

•Information systems → Language models; •Computing methodologies → Neural networks; 5

Keywords

Image Captioning; Object Detection; Deep Neural Networks

1. INTRODUCTION

Image captioning is a challenging research topic due to the requirements of the knowledge of both vision modality and natural language modality. The ultimate goal of image captioning is to generate natural language description for any given image in a real-time manner, just like what we humans do. Moreover, the generated language should be capable of describing the objects and their relations in the image in a grammar error-free and fluent way.

*This work was performed at Microsoft Research Asia.

MM '16 October 15-19, 2016, Amsterdam, Netherlands

ACM ISBN 978-1-4503-3603-1/16/10.

DOI: http://dx.doi.org/10.1145/2964284.2973831

Figure 1: Example results of the system. Given any image, the system is able to generate human-level caption sentences, show detected objects with bounding boxes and labels, and return similar images with corresponding sentences in real time.

Despite the difficulty of this task, there have been emerging efforts recently due to the success of introducing the deep neural networks to this field. Most existing work leverages the deep convolutional neural networks (CNN) and the recurrent neural networks (RNN) in an encoding-decoding scheme [6, 4, 1, 5, 3]. In these work, the input image is usually encoded by a fixed length of CNN feature vector, functioning as the first time-step input to the RNN; the description is generated by conditioning the output word at each time step on the input visual vector as well as the previous generated words.

However, since the power of RNN lies in its capability in modeling the contextual information between each time step [2], the encoded visual vector extracted from the whole image may weaken the RNN's memory of the visual information as it contains no temporal concept. To encode more visual information to balance the source and the target sequence of the recurrent neural networks, a natural idea is to leverage the object information in the image. We propose in this work to leverage the high-level features of the detected objects in the image, in order to enrich the visual part of the source sequence. The objects are arranged in a sequence manner according to their saliency, and thus expand the encoding phase of the recurrent neural networks for the image from one time step to multiple time steps. The object features are then mapped into a common hidden

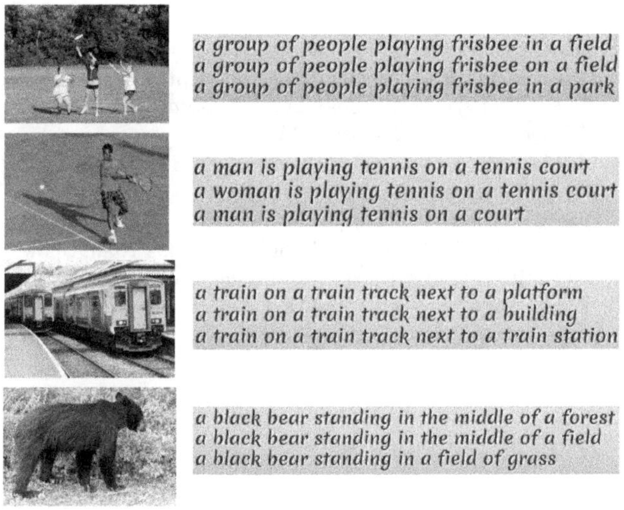

Figure 2: Examples of image caption generation. Given any image, the model can generate the natural language description of the image in real time.

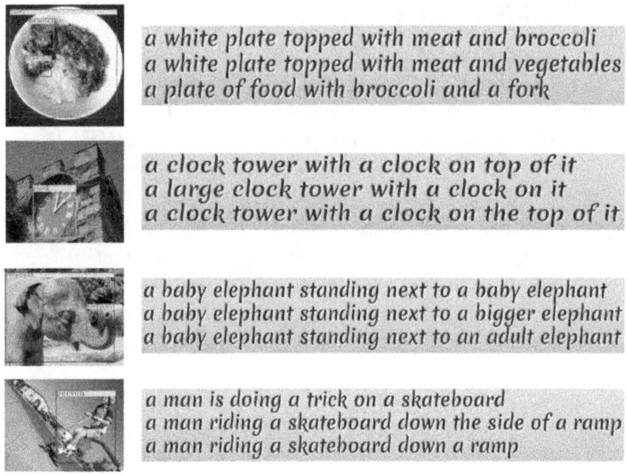

Figure 3: Alongside the image caption generation, the system is also capable of detecting objects in the image, whose bounding boxes and labels are shown at the same time.

space to serve as the 'visual words' in the source sequence. Thus the problem is formulated as a multimodal translation problem, in which we use the detected objects in the image to serve as the source input 'language', and the corresponding words as the target language.

We develop an image captioning system, which allows the users to 1) generate human-level natural language description of any input image, 2) detect objects in the given image alongside caption generation, and 3) retrieve similar images and descriptions from a database, which holds over 120,000 image-description pairs, all in real time. The core of the system is a combination of pre-trained deep convolutional neural networks for object detection, and recurrent neural networks for caption generation.

2. SYSTEM OVERVIEW

Func.1 Examples The first function of the system is a simple example section, which demonstrates the basic image captioning task by presenting several example images for users to choose. Once the user selects some image among example images, a caption for the image will be generated in the background process of the system, and the response time is generally less than 0.2s. The main purpose of this function is to provide users with ease to use the system at a glance.

Func.2 Capioning The system provides an interface for the users to upload an image or copy the image URL for futher captioning. Once uploaded, a human-level description result of the image will be shown, also in a real-time manner. The results contain three best candidates given by the model, ordered by the log probability of the generation result, as shown in Fig. 2.

Func.3 Detection and Captioning The third part of the system provides a further functionality for the input image. Beyond generating the caption of the image, the model will also detect the objects in the image, and presents the detection result by drawing bounding boxes around the detected objects. The object names are also shown on top of the bounding boxes. Similar to the captioning function, three candidate captions will be shown on the bottom of the image, with the same ordering strategy, as shown in Fig. 3.

Func.4 Retrieval The system enables users to retrieve similar images and corresponding descriptions from a database given any input image. The user can have a glimpse of the retrieved image by clicking one of them, and a pop-up box will present a sharper version of the image, with the caption below it, as shown in Fig. 4

Figure 4: Examples of image retrieval. Similar images to the query image and corresponding sentences are returned.

3. REFERENCES

[1] J. Donahue, L. Anne Hendricks, S. Guadarrama, M. Rohrbach, S. Venugopalan, K. Saenko, and T. Darrell. Long-term recurrent convolutional networks for visual recognition and description. In *The IEEE Conference on Computer Vision and Pattern Recognition (CVPR)*, June 2015.

[2] S. Hochreiter and J. Schmidhuber. Long short-term memory. *Neural computation*, 9(8):1735–1780, 1997.

[3] X. Jia, E. Gavves, B. Fernando, and T. Tuytelaars. Guiding long-short term memory for image caption generation. *arXiv preprint arXiv:1509.04942*, 2015.

[4] A. Karpathy and L. Fei-Fei. Deep visual-semantic alignments for generating image descriptions. In *The IEEE Conference on Computer Vision and Pattern Recognition (CVPR)*, June 2015.

[5] J. Mao, W. Xu, Y. Yang, J. Wang, Z. Huang, and A. Yuille. Deep captioning with multimodal recurrent neural networks (m-rnn). *ICLR*, 2015.

[6] O. Vinyals, A. Toshev, S. Bengio, and D. Erhan. Show and tell: A neural image caption generator. In *The IEEE Conference on Computer Vision and Pattern Recognition (CVPR)*, June 2015.

History Rhyme: Searching Historic Events by Multimedia Knowledge

Yifan Xiong[1], Jia Chen[2], Qin Jin[1]*, Chao Zhang[1]
[1]School of Information, Renmin University of China
{xiongyf, qjin, 2010202526}@ruc.edu.cn
[2]School of Computer Science, Carneige Mellon University
jiac@cs.cmu.edu

ABSTRACT

This demo shows a novel system "History Rhyme" which searches historic events by multimedia knowledge. Different from existing historic events related works, we focus on the retrieval of historic events by semantic related multimedia knowledge. Our system can not only search historic events based on keyword queries, but also retrieve similar historic events to a given event based on chosen facets. In both cases, the system returns top retrieval results and shows the image profiles of each historic event. To build such functions, we automatically mine knowledge from multimedia data and index each historic event. Our online demo is available at http://222.29.193.164/HistoryRhyme.

Keywords

Historic Event Search; Multimedia Knowledge

1. INTRODUCTION

A famous quote says "History does not repeat itself, but it does rhyme". It not only shows that history knowledge is valuable but also indicates that searching similar historic events is an important tool in exploring and studying history. Work [2] focuses on preserving multimedia history knowledge through image profiling. Work [1] links images to phases of historic events by semantic image profiling. In this demo, we propose a system to mine finer multimedia knowledge and use such knowledge to index historic events for retrieval. We name our system "History Rhyme". Different from work [3] which focuses on searching for historic events based on the location inferred from the query photo, our work focuses on retrieval of historic events by semantic related multimedia knowledge.

The multimedia knowledge includes three types: text knowledge, visual knowledge and cross-media knowledge. The text knowledge consists of exact detailed information related to the event, including person, location and time. Such knowledge could be used to measure similarity in event facets such as whether a certain person is involved in both events, or whether both events happened in the same year. The visual knowledge consists of rich concepts, including objects and scenes. Such knowledge could be used to measure the similarity in event facets such as whether planes are involved in both events, or whether both events happened in railway stations. The cross-media knowledge is represented by a set of image-phrase pairs with each pair describing which image in the historic event image profile corresponds to which phrase in the event text description. It is very useful when users are exploring a specific historic event. It links the knowledge in the image media to that in the text media.

We integrate the above three types of knowledge in one system for users to:

1. use keywords to search historic events. We provide a keyword query input interface since it is the standard input interface of the state-of-the-art search engines and users are already familiar with it. Furthermore, we provide keyword suggestion functions to ease the requirement of history background knowledge for users. Both text and visual knowledge is used in this function.

2. search similar historic events to a given event in the chosen facets/aspects. This function is particularly useful for browsing the historic event dataset. Users can use this function to discover the rhyme of history by fixed facets, or to compare events under certain facets. Both text and visual knowledge is used in this function.

3. explore the image profiles of a historic event Our system organizes images related a historic event based on the cross-media knowledge. To be specific, we group images according to image-phrase pairs which are mined from the historic events multimedia data. All images linked to the same phrase are grouped together, which is a concise interface for users to browse the image-phrase pairs under a historic event.

2. SYSTEM OVERVIEW

There are three key functions in our system: (1) keyword search function, (2) similar events search function and (3) image profile explore function. As shown in figure 1, all functions are based on events indexing and ranking using historic knowledge mined from multimedia data. The keyword search function and similar events search function use text and visual knowledge while image profile explore function uses cross-media knowledge.

Use keyword to search historic events: As shown in Figure 2, users can input a keyword query to search his-

*Qin Jin is the corresponding author

MM '16 October 15-19, 2016, Amsterdam, Netherlands

ACM ISBN 978-1-4503-3603-1/16/10.
DOI: http://dx.doi.org/10.1145/2964284.2973832

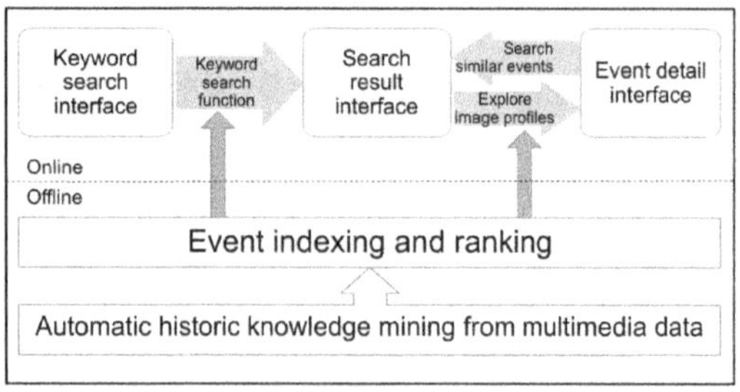

Figure 1: Framework of History Rhyme System

toric events in the keyword-search interface. There are three input fields in this interface, users can choose to input an object/scene class (area 1), or input a historical person's name (area 2), or select a history period (area 3). Inputs in one or more fields are allowed. Real-time suggestions are provided for a better experience if users choose to type the keywords. Additionally, to show the typical events in our dataset, we provide some query examples (area 4). Once the search-button is clicked, our system will return search results using both text and visual knowledge and users will be brought to the search-results interface as shown in Figure 3. The search-results interface shows the ranked results according to the user's query. The top input field shows keyword query (area 1), while the rest area shows the ranked results. Each result record corresponds to one historic event in our historic events corpus. Each event is shown by its text description (area 3) and key phrases (area 4), detailed image profile under this event will be shown after clicking on the header link (area 2).

Search similar historic events to a given event in the chosen facets: Once users click on a historic event's header link, our system will show the event-details interface whose top part is shown in Figure 4. Users can read the detailed event description (area 1), choose certain facets in this event (area 2) and click on the search button (area 3) to retrieve similar events to discover the rhyme of history with respect to this event. Results will be shown in the search-results interface which is similar to Figure 3.

Explore the image profile of a historic event: To explore every facet of a certain event, users can look through the image profile part in the event-details interface as shown in Figure 5. In this interface, grouped images will be shown using cross-media knowledge. Some famous images are shown in a cascade layout (area 1) to represent this event. Image-phrase pairs are browsed by phrases (area 2) and images related to certain phrase are grouped together (area 3).

3. TECHNICAL DETAILS

The "History Rhyme" system is built based on our previous work [1], technical implementation and algorithms can be found at that work.

Automatic knowledge mining from multimedia data:

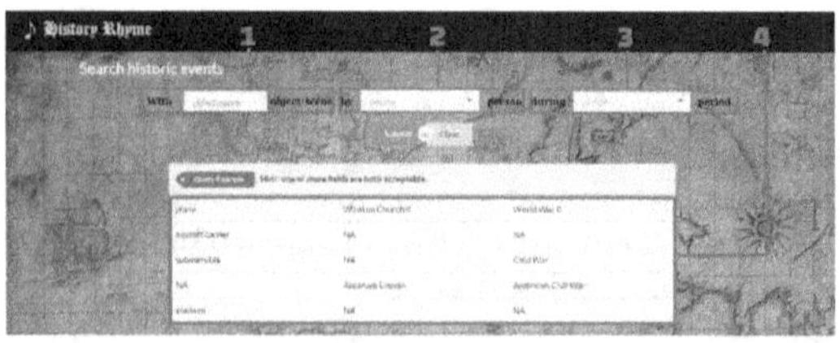

Figure 2: Keyword-search interface

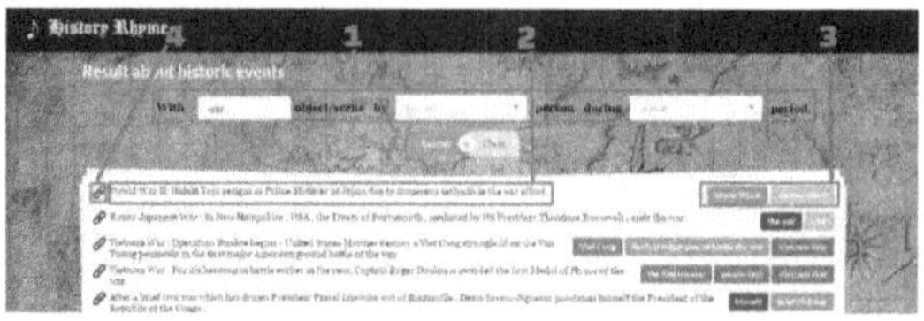

Figure 3: Search-results interface

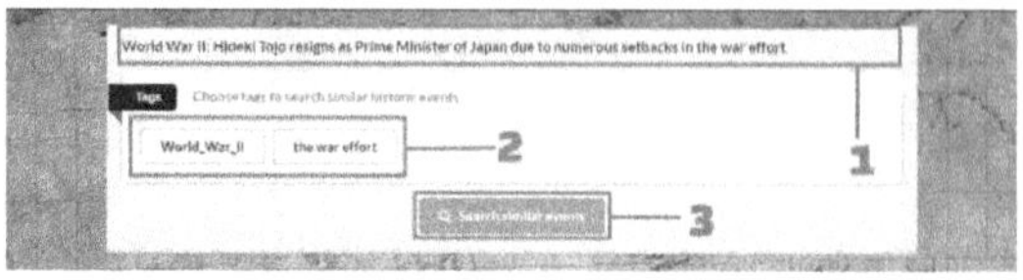

Figure 4: Text part in the event-details interface

Having crawled multimedia data of historic events from Internet, we extract person and period knowledge from text media using natural language processing method [4], object and scene knowledge from image media using pre-trained DCNN [6]. We design a score to automatically evaluate the similarity between a phrase and an image under certain event so that to link a phrase to an image for automatic knowledge mining. The evaluation details are available at our previous work [1].

Event indexing and ranking: Altogether 1,080 historic events and about 23,352 image-phrase pairs are indexed in our system using cross-media knowledge. We use word2vec [5] to calculate the similarity between the user query and key phrases and rank the top retrieved events.

4. CONCLUSION

The main contributions of the proposed system are summarized as follows:

1. It's the first application to retrieve historic events by semantic related multimedia knowledge.
2. Our system has automatically mined multimedia knowledge from 23,352 image-phrase pairs in 1,080 historic events.
3. Our system provides convenient interfaces for users to search historic events by keywords, explore image profiles of historic events and discover the rhyme of history by fixed facets.

5. ACKNOWLEDGEMENTS

This work was partially supported by the Beijing Natural Science Foundation (No. 4142029) and the Fundamental Research Funds for the Central Universities and the Research Funds of Renmin University of China (No. 14XNLQ01).

Figure 5: Image profile part in the event-details interface

6. REFERENCES

[1] J. Chen, Q. Jin, and Y. Xiong. Semantic image profiling for historic events: Linking images to phrases. In *Proceedings of the 24th Annual ACM Conference on Multimedia Conference, MM '16, Amsterdam, The Netherlands, October 15 - 19, 2016.*

[2] J. Chen, Q. Jin, Y. Yu, and A. G. Hauptmann. Image profiling for history events on the fly. In *Proceedings of the 23rd Annual ACM Conference on Multimedia Conference, MM '15, Brisbane, Australia, October 26 - 30, 2015*, pages 291–300, 2015.

[3] J. Chen, Q. Jin, W. Zhang, S. Bao, Z. Su, and Y. Yu. Tell me what happened here in history. In *ACM Multimedia Conference, MM '13, Barcelona, Spain, October 21-25, 2013*, pages 467–468, 2013.

[4] C. D. Manning, M. Surdeanu, J. Bauer, J. Finkel, S. J. Bethard, and D. McClosky. The Stanford CoreNLP natural language processing toolkit. In *Association for Computational Linguistics (ACL) System Demonstrations*, pages 55–60, 2014.

[5] T. Mikolov, I. Sutskever, K. Chen, G. S. Corrado, and J. Dean. Distributed representations of words and phrases and their compositionality. In *Advances in Neural Information Processing Systems 26*, pages 3111–3119. 2013.

[6] K. Simonyan and A. Zisserman. Very deep convolutional networks for large-scale image recognition. *CoRR*, abs/1409.1556, 2014.

Intelli-Wrench: Smart Navigation Tool for Mechanical Assembly and Maintenance

Toru Takahashi, Yuta Kudo and Rui Ishiyama
Data Science Research Laboratories, NEC Corporation
Shimonumabe 1753, Nakahara-ku, Kawasaki, Kanagawa, 211-8666 Japan
{t-takahashi@hg, y-kudo@bc, r-ishiyama@bl}.jp.nec.com

ABSTRACT
We present Intelli-Wrench, a smart tool for providing just-in-time information for mechanical assembly and maintenance workers, which releases the workers from miss-operation and annoying manual documents. The Intelli-Wrench captures the image of a bolt head as its "fingerprint" by using FIBAR (Fingerprint Imaging by Binary Angular Reflection) imaging method. The fingerprint image is then uploaded to a cloud server and matched with parts databases in order to provide the specific information associated with the bolt. Receiving the information, the Intelli-Wrench informs the workers about the designated location and torque requirements of the bolt. This direct integration of information retrieval into a tangible tool provides immediate access to relevant information otherwise found in manual documents. Furthermore, the Intelli-Wrench automatically logs the interaction and eliminates the annoying pointing-and-calling procedure which is the traditional way of secure servicing. We demonstrate a working prototype and interaction scenario.

CCS Concepts

· *Computing methodologies~Object identification* • Human-centered computing~Ubiquitous and mobile devices

Keywords
IoT, Traceability, Image recognition, Individual identification, Fingerprint of things, FIBAR

1. INTRODUCTION
Precise torque-settings are critical in the context of mechanical tasks such as tightening wheel lug nuts of a car wheel. If they are too loose, they bear the risk of shipping off. On the other hand, if they are too tight, the material gets damaged. As in most mechanical contexts, aircraft maintenance also requires each of numerous bolts to be securely checked to keep the right torque. Traditionally the correct values are indicated in the accompanying manual document. In order to assist the process of setting the right torque of bolts, this paper proposes Intelli-Wrench, a smart tool which is able to (i) uniquely identify each individual bolt by means of image recognition, (ii) inform the designated place and torque requirement of each bolt, and (iii) log all the interaction for checking human error as shown in Fig. 1.

There are some studies which propose smart tools. The basic idea of these studies is enhancing functions of traditional hand-held tools by using computational power. For example, a positioning tool for 2D digital fabrication which reduces human errors by means of computer vision techniques is proposed [1]. And also, for 3D fabrication, the smart hand-held digital milling device is proposed [2]. On the side of image recognition, an innovative imaging technique named FIBAR makes it possible to robustly identify individual bolts of mass-production [3]. The Intelli-Wrench is a smart industrial tool enhanced by image recognition with FIBAR imaging method. The Intelli-Wrench combines different operations such as identification, information retrieval, and bolt tightening which previously required separate devices, into one process.

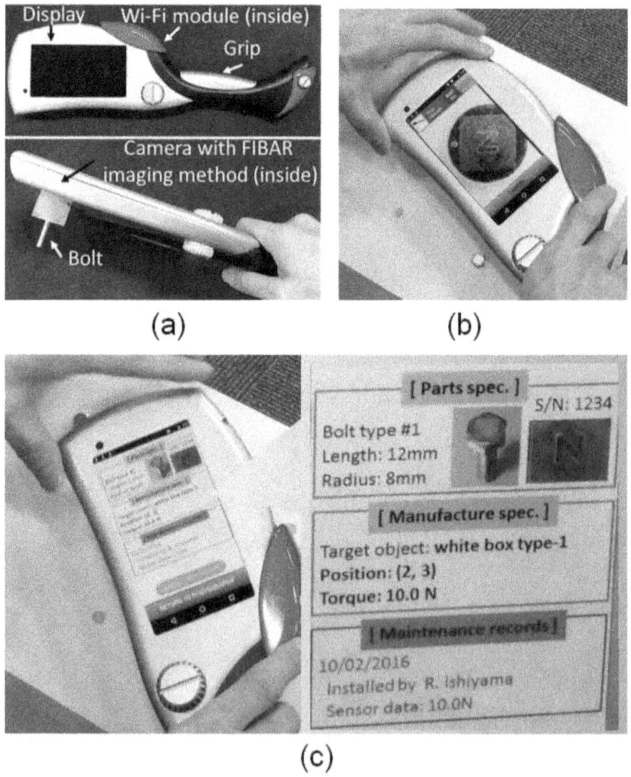

Figure 1: "Intelli-Wrench" Hand-Tool and its interaction scenario. (a) A prototype of "Intelli-Wrench" hand-held tool. The tool captures "fingerprints" of metal bolts by using an integrated camera with FIBAR imaging method and transfers the image to a "fingerprints" cloud data server. (b) An usage example of "Intelli-Wrench": maintenance of the installed bolt. (c) Provided information of a specific bolt from the cloud data server.

MM '16, October 15-19, 2016, Amsterdam, Netherlands
ACM 978-1-4503-3603-1/16/10.
DOI: http://dx.doi.org/10.1145/2964284.2973833

2. INTELLI-WRENCH SYSTEM

Figure 2 (a) shows overview of the *Intelli-Wrench System.* The *Intelli-Wrench System* consists of the following three subsystems.

2.1 Bolt Fingerprint Database

We developed an automated process to enroll numerous bolts' fingerprints into a database with parts information. In this process, the individual bolts get scanned automatically by a custom machine (see Fig. 2 (b)). Once a mass of bolts is poured into the bucket, the machine automatically picks up each bolt to slide in front of the camera. Thus, the fingerprint images of the individual bolts are captured and uploaded to the cloud server database. The machine also enrolls each bolt's specification data and their designated position on the target object, i.e. work-piece or aircraft.

2.2 Intelli-Wrench

The Intelli-Wrench hand-held tool is a traditional wrench-like device that has a built-in camera module that captures a top-view of a bolt head in compliance with the FIBAR requirements. This enables the precise identification of individual bolts by matching the "fingerprint" images (see Fig. 2 (c)). The Intelli-Wrench is also equipped with a bolt socket, Wi-Fi module connecting to the cloud server and a touch-panel display, which are built in a chassis made by 3D printing as shown in Fig. 1 (a). This tool enables integration of the identification of the bolt at hand, the assistive feedback to the worker, the torque setting and logging the interaction in one seamless process.

From the user perspective, operation is the same as the traditional wrench; first the user puts the bolt into the socket. Here, the Intelli-Wrench automatically displays the designated location and the proper torque of the bolt without the need to individually remember or look up the required specifications. By automatically indicating the required action, the process is simplified and quality-controlled. It prevents miss-operation, thus both quality and efficiency are improved. Additionally all actions are logged automatically in order to check for compliance with the safety requirements. This relieves users from the annoying pointing-and-calling procedure for checking human errors.

2.3 Cloud-based Fingerprint Matching

A server-based application provides the means for matching the enrolled fingerprints with the fingerprint captured with the Intelli-Wrench on site. FIBAR technology can capture the micro bumps on the metal bolt as useful image features to identify the individual bolts. We employ the method to match the local features of the fingerprints of bolts, described in [3] as shown in Fig. 2 (d). The server matches the received fingerprint image with each of the previously enrolled images in the database. The server sends back the identifier of the best matched bolt and its corresponding information such as the designated location and required torque setting as well as information from previous maintenance history of the particular bolt.

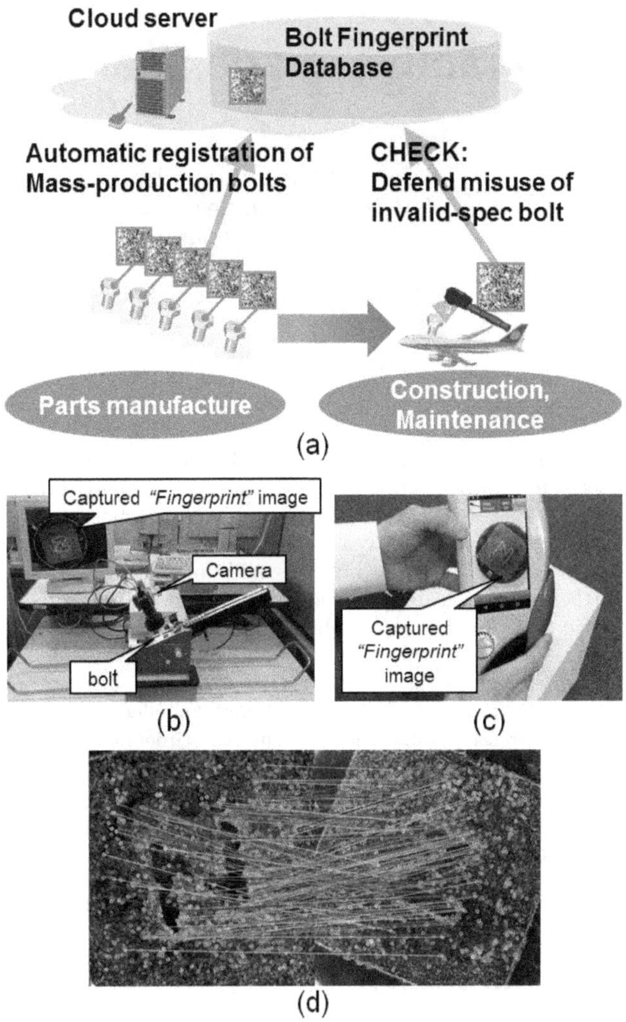

Figure 2: Overview of Intelli-Wrench system: (a) A Concept of Intelli-Wrench system. (b) Prototype of automatic bolt-scanning machine for registration of mass-production bolts. (c) Checking process by using Intelli-Wrench hand-held tool. (d) Example of image matching result (the same individual pair).

3. CONCLUSION AND FUTURE WORK

Augmenting traditional tools for direct assistance during the work process have a lot of future potential. The *Intelli-Wrench system* combines traditional tool usage and informative assistance to the user into the simple mechanical work process. The user can fully focus on the task, due to being relieved from pulling the required information from manual documents, logging their activities and checking for errors. For future work, field studies are planned to verify the effectiveness and gain more insights on how meaningful information and feedback can be provided without overloading the user.

4. REFERENCES

[1] A. Rivers, I. E. Moyer and F. Durand, Position-correcting tools for 2d digital fabrication, *ACM Trans. Graph.* 31, 4, 88:1 – 88:7, July 2012.

[2] A. Zoran, R. Shilkrot, S. Nanyakkara, and J. Paradiso, The hybrid artisans: A case study in smart tools, *ACM Trans. Comput.-Hum, Interact.* 21, 3, 15:1 – 15:29, June 2014.

[3] T. Takahashi and R. Ishiyama, FIBAR: Fingerprint Imaging by Binary Angular Reflection for Individual Identification of Metal Parts, *Proceedings of the 5th International Conference on Emerging Security Technologies (EST-2014),* pp.48–51, 2014.

Interactive Image Search for Clothing Recommendation

Zhengzhong Zhou, Yifei Xu, Jingjin Zhou and Liqing Zhang
MOE-Microsoft Key Laboratory for Intelligent Computing and Intelligent Systems
Department of Computer Science and Engineering
Shanghai Jiao Tong University, Shanghai, China
{tczhouzz, fei960922, zhoujingjin}@sjtu.edu.cn, zhang-lq@cs.sjtu.edu.cn

ABSTRACT

This demo delivers a novel retrieval system which meets users' multi-dimensional requirements in clothing image search. In this system, users are able to use both image and keywords as query inputs. We employ the color, texture, shape and attributes as additional descriptors to further refine the requirements. We propose the Hybrid Topic (HT) model, a probabilistic network integrating the multi-channel descriptors into a unified framework, to learn the intricate semantic representation of the descriptors above. The proposed model provides an effective multi-modal representation of clothes. Our experiments show that the HT method significantly outperforms the CNN-based deep search methods.

Keywords

Content-based Image Retrieval; Clothing Image Retrieval; Topic Model

1. INTRODUCTION

Using image retrieval technology to search for clothing products provides great convenience in apparel e-commerce [7, 5, 6]. When a user gravitates to someone's attire in a photo, he can simply submit the photo to the retrieval system to get a group of garments similar to the photo for selection.

However, there still exist two major problems. The first one is "semantic gap". Due to the intra-class variation and inter-class ambiguity in image space, low-level visual features could not describe the semantic concept like category or style explicitly. The second one is "multi-dimensional requirements". Since the appropriate query images are not always available, users tend to further refine their demands by modifying the color, texture, shape and attribute descriptors of the original queries.

In this demo, we present a novel interactive retrieval system (see Fig. 1) to tackle both problems utilizing topic model [1, 2, 9]. Our feature extraction procedure

Figure 1: Illustration of System Interface.

is described as a two-level abstraction. For the first level abstraction, we extract multiple clothing descriptors from images and convert them into the bag of words (BOW) formats. The BOW format enables us to use topic model for semantic analysis. Meanwhile, it benefits us to modify the local details of image descriptions.

For the second level abstraction, we present a probabilistic network to combine the multi-channel descriptors into a unified framework, *i.e.* Hybrid Topic (HT) model. In this model, each image is depicted as a linear combination of hybrid topics, while each topic is described as distributions over various codewords. The HT model learns the intricate relationship among different descriptors, which can derive an effective representation of clothing images.

We develop an interactive retrieval system on the server with 2 Intel Xeon 2.6GHz processors and 128GB memory. It contains about 120,000 upper-body clothing images crawled from online shopping platform JD.com. Experiments show that our system not only achieves better performance than the CNN-based deep search method [6], but also provides a more personalized interaction for online customers. The average retrieval time for a query is within 1 second.

2. SYSTEM FRAMEWORK

Fig. 2 shows the flowchart of our system. Given a query image and corresponding search conditions, the region of clothes is cropped using object detection algorithm [10, 4, 8] as a preprocessing stage. We extract multiple visual descriptors from the detected region and quantize them into BOW representation. Furthermore, we adjust the codeword weights of the modified feature to meet users' requirement. Using the pre-trained hybrid topic model, we integrate

MM '16 October 15-19, 2016, Amsterdam, Netherlands

ACM ISBN 978-1-4503-3603-1/16/10.
DOI: http://dx.doi.org/10.1145/2964284.2973834

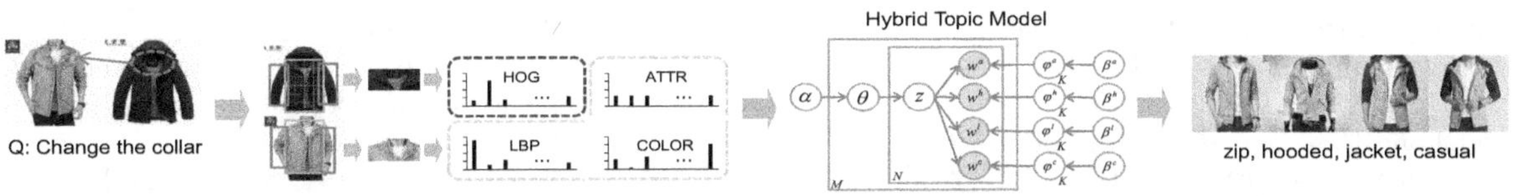

(a) User Demand (b) The First-level Abstraction (c) The Second-level Abstraction (d) Result and Predicted Tags

Figure 2: The Framework of Our Two-level Abstraction.

the above descriptors into effective retrieval features and infer the attributes of query image to improve the user interaction. Finally, we calculate the similarity between the query image and images in database. Those top-ranked images are returned as the retrieval result.

The First-level Abstraction. In the pre-processing stage, we adopt Faster R-CNN [8] to localize the torso and sleeve regions in clothing images. We resize the torso region to 192×128 and use two slide windows (128×64 and 64×128) to sample it (stride 16). In this way, we split the image into 17 local regions (2 sleeve regions, 1 torso region and 14 overlapping regions cropped from the torso region). For each local region, we extract 3 types of visual descriptors: The histogram of oriented gradients (HOG) [3], Local binary patterns (LBP), and color histogram (COL). We also extract the keywords from the text description as attribute descriptor (ATTR). Using sparse coding, we convert all these descriptors into BOW formats, so that we can simply modify the codeword weights of descriptors instead of image contents.

HT Model for the Second-level Abstraction. As noted, we present a novel topic model, *i.e.* Hybrid Topic (HT) to integrate both visual and attribute information of clothing images. Fig. 2(c) shows the graphical model of HT. Images are represented as a list of "phrases". A phrase is a set of codewords w^j in different descriptor channels ($j \in \{a(ATTR), h(HOG), l(LBP), c(COL)\}$). For each image, we draw a topic mixture proportion θ to describe its high-level concept. For each phrase, we assign a topic z to determine its meaning. We assume that w^js and z follow the Multinomial distribution with prior φ^js and θ. While φ^j and θ follow the Dirichlet distribution with prior β^js and α. The above parameters of HT model are estimated by Gibbs sampling. To achieve an effective image representation, we train 17 HT models (one for each local region) on the dataset, and denote the topic proportion θs as local descriptions of images. Thus, we concatenate the θs extracted from 17 local regions of a clothing image as its retrieval feature.

Image annotation. To further facilitate the users, we automatically add tags to the query image in our retrieval system. The HT model is able to evaluate the missing values of attribute descriptors by the Bayesian reasoning. Meanwhile, users could modify these recommended tags to confirm their requirements.

3. EXPERIMENTS

To evaluate the performance of our approach, we realize a CNN based method called Deep Search [6] as the baseline. We invite 10 subjects to perform 100 retrieval tasks in our retrieval system. For each task, we upload a clothing image and modify its color, shape, texture or attributes to refine the requirement. We measure the performance by Normalized Discounted Cumulative Cain: $NDCG@k = \sum_{j=1}^{k} \frac{2^{r(j)}-1}{\log(j+1)}$, where $r(j) = 1$ iff the jth returned image satisfies the subject's demand, otherwise 0.

Table 1: The Retrieval Accuracy of HT.

	$NDCG@20$
Deep Search	0.42
Hybrid Topic	0.66

Figure 3: Several Groups of User Requirements and Corresponding Results.

Our experiment result is shown in Table 1. As we see, the hybrid topic method improves the precision by 24% compared with the Deep Search. It integrates the demand of modification into image representation, which reduces the distances between a query image and user desired images in feature space. Fig. 3 shows some examples of our retrieved results.

4. CONCLUSIONS

In this demo, we present a novel interactive clothing image retrieval system to meet users' multi-dimensional requirements which can be refined through editing both visual features and attributes. It offers a two-level abstraction for clothes and constructs hybrid topic models to link the relationship among multiple descriptors. Based on our framework, more diversified retrieval applications can be designed in further research.

5. ACKNOWLEDGMENTS

The work was supported by the Key Basic Research Program of Shanghai Municipality (15JC1400103), the National Basic Research Program of China (2015CB856004), and the National Natural Science Foundation of China (91420302).

6. REFERENCES

[1] D. M. Blei, A. Y. Ng, and M. I. Jordan. Latent dirichlet allocation. In *NIPS*, pages 601–608, 2001.

[2] W. Chong, D. Blei, and F.-F. Li. Simultaneous image classification and annotation. In *CVPR*, pages 1903–1910, 2009.

[3] N. Dalal and B. Triggs. Histograms of oriented gradients for human detection. In *CVPR*, volume 1, pages 886–893, 2005.

[4] R. Girshick. Fast r-cnn. In *ICCV*, pages 1440–1448, 2015.

[5] J. Huang, R. S. Feris, Q. Chen, and S. Yan. Cross-domain image retrieval with a dual attribute-aware ranking network. In *ICCV*, pages 1062–1070, 2015.

[6] J. Huang, W. Xia, and S. Yan. Deep search with attribute-aware deep network. In *ACM MM*, pages 731–732, 2014.

[7] S. Liu, Z. Song, G. Liu, C. Xu, H. Lu, and S. Yan. Street-to-shop: Cross-scenario clothing retrieval via parts alignment and auxiliary set. In *CVPR*, pages 3330–3337, 2012.

[8] S. Ren, K. He, R. Girshick, and J. Sun. Faster r-cnn: Towards real-time object detection with region proposal networks. In *NIPS*, pages 91–99, 2015.

[9] Z. Sun, C. Wang, L. Zhang, and L. Zhang. Query-adaptive shape topic mining for hand-drawn sketch recognition. In *ACM MM*, pages 519–528, 2012.

[10] C. Wang, L. Zhao, S. Liang, L. Zhang, J. Jia, and Y. Wei. Object proposal by multi-branch hierarchical segmentation. In *CVPR*, pages 3873–3881, 2015.

Video ChatBot: Triggering Live Social Interactions by Automatic Video Commenting*

Yehao Li [†], Ting Yao [‡], Rui Hu [‡], Tao Mei [‡], Yong Rui [‡]
[†] Sun Yat-Sen University, Guangzhou, China
[‡] Microsoft Research, Beijing, China
yehaoli.sysu@gmail.com; {tiyao, ruhu, tmei, yongrui}@microsoft.com

ABSTRACT

We demonstrate a video chatbot, which can generate human-level emotional comments referring to the videos shared by users and trigger a conversation with users. Our video chatbot performs a large-scale similar video search to find visually similar videos w.r.t. a given video using approximate nearest-neighbor search. Then, the comments associated with the searched similar videos are ranked by learning a deep multi-view embedding space for modeling video content, visual sentiment and textual comments. The top ranked comments are selected as responses to the given video and trigger the succeeding text-based chat between users and the chatbot. The demonstration is conducted on a newly collected dataset with over 102K videos and 10.6M comments. Moreover, our video chatbot has great potential to increase live social interactions.

Keywords

Video Commenting; Multi-View Embedding; Deep Convolutional Neural Networks.

1. INTRODUCTION

The advent of video sharing sites and rapid development of video technologies have led to the unprecedented delivery of online video content. Nowadays, millions of daily users are broadcasting, consuming and communicating via videos. Video has become a predominant media for the booming live social interactions, e.g., Vine, Instagram, and Periscope. Automatic generation of emotional comments to a video has great potential to significantly increase user engagement in many socio-video applications (e.g., chatbot).

A comment is usually a natural sentence that expresses the emotional reaction and feelings after viewing a video. We demonstrate a video chatbot, which is capable of generating comments for videos. Figure 1 shows two use cases of our video chatbot. Specifically, users first share their videos in any social platform. Our video chatbot will then generate comments to the videos for the purpose of social engagement. Take the first video as an example, a comment is presented, e.g., "What a cute and beautiful baby. How old is he?" The generated comment can further trigger the succeeding text-based chat between users and our chatbot, e.g., "He was 2 years old in this video." and "Oh my! He's growing up fast!" Therefore, it is of great potential to increase social interactions and thus enhance user engagement.

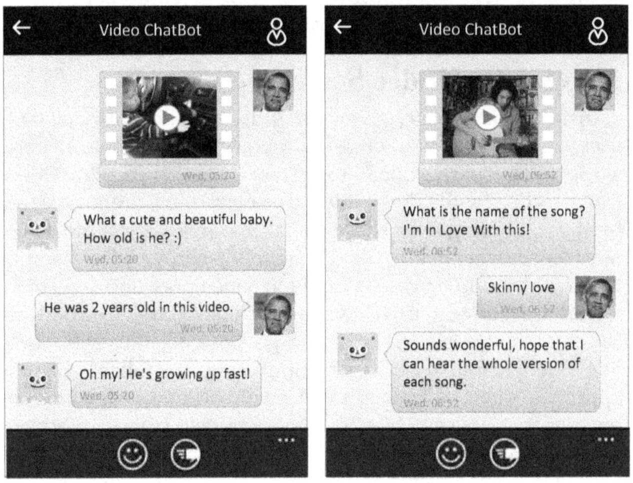

Figure 1: The use cases of our video chatbot.

Our video chatbot is novel by enabling automatic commenting on videos. To the best of our knowledge, the work represents the first effort towards this target in the multimedia research community. Furthermore, a text-based chatbot is integrated into our video chatbot, which is capable of supporting the succeeding text-based chat with users triggered by video commenting.

2. VIDEO COMMENTING SYSTEM

The key technology of our video chatbot is automatic video commenting. The system overview is given in Figure 2, which is composed of two components: similar video search (VS) and comment dynamic ranking (DR). The former efficiently finds the visually similar videos, while the latter effectively ranks the comments associated with the searched similar videos in a learnt deep multi-view embedding space.

* This work was performed when Yehao Li was visiting Microsoft Research Asia as a research intern.

MM '16 October 15-19, 2016, Amsterdam, Netherlands

ACM ISBN 978-1-4503-3603-1/16/10.
DOI: http://dx.doi.org/10.1145/2964284.2973835

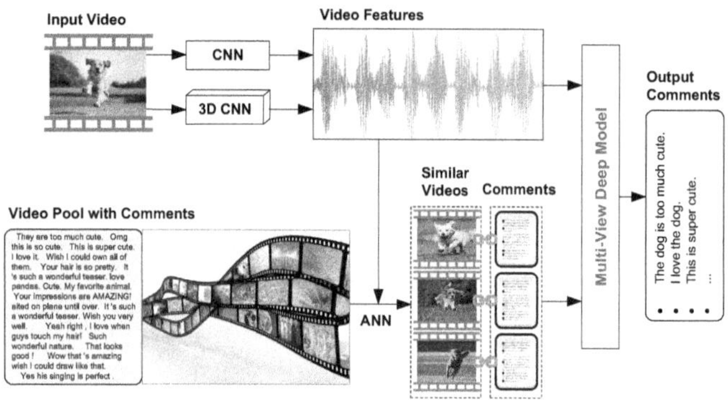

Figure 2: An architecture overview of video commenting system in our video chatbot.

2.1 Similar Video Search

In this component, given the video uploaded by an end user, the 2-D [2] and/or 3-D [3] convolutional neural networks (CNNs) are utilized to extract visual features of video frames/clips, while deep video representations are produced by mean pooling over these visual features. Next, approximate nearest neighbor (ANN) search is employed to search the visually similar videos from our video pool and the comments associated with these similar videos are regarded as candidates. Specifically, for the purpose of efficiently similar video search with fast computation, we follow [4] and apply the query-driven iterated neighborhood graph search model for ANN search, which contains two stages. A video neighborhood graph on video visual representations is first built and then a query-driven iterated neighborhood graph search approach is exploited to locate the ANNs. Note that our video pool here consists of 96,752 videos with their corresponding human-generated comments collected from Vine[1]. It covers a wide variety of video categories (12 general categories, e.g., animal, entertainment and sports). Hence, with this large-scale video pool, we can leverage the "crowdsourcing" human intelligence to easily collect the comment candidates consisting of real user comments associated with these similar videos.

2.2 Comment Dynamic Ranking

After we obtain the comment candidates in VS stage, how to select the most relevant one in DR stage? As textual comment and video content are of different views, they cannot be directly compared. Inspired by the success of multi-view embedding [5], we utilize our deep multi-view embedding model to learn a latent space where the direct comparison of text comments and videos are allowed. Specifically, our deep multi-view embedding model is learnt based on three views: (1) video content view which depicts objects and temporal dynamics in video, (2) visual sentiment view which represents the visual emotions evoked on video, and (3) textual comment view which expressed the reaction and feelings from users. With the learnt three mappings for the above three views, we can directly calculate the distance between each pair of comment and video, which reflects how relevant the candidate comment could be presented to the given video. Thus, given the uploaded video, a rank list of candidate comments is produced by sorting the relevance scores of video-comment pairs.

[1]https://vine.co/

The comment with the highest relevance score will be taken as the final comment in our video commenting system, which can further trigger the succeeding text-based interactions/chat between the user and our chatbot.

3. SYSTEM AND USER INTERFACE

Our video chatbot can be accessed through a software operated on a PC client. As shown in Figure 1, an end user first uploads a video to our system and then the video chatbot will generate the comment w.r.t the uploaded video automatically. Based on the comment presented by video chatbot, the user could further chat with our chatbot, which is supported by integrating a real text-based chatbot.

The whole system is currently run on a regular PC (Intel dual-core 3.39GHz CPU and 16GB RAM). Given a five seconds' video, the time of feature extraction of the video is about 4.3 sec, the similar video search basically completes a search within 0.02 sec, and the dynamic ranking takes about 0.50 sec. Overall, it takes around 4.82 sec to complete the comment generation by our video chatbot, which is less than the duration of the video.

4. EVALUATIONS

To evaluate the performance of our video chatbot, we collected 4,000 and 1,000 videos from Vine as validation and testing samples, respectively. Eight evaluators from different education backgrounds are invited to annotate the comments for testing samples generated by our video chatbot. Each comment was annotated on a five point ordinal scale: 5-Very Good; 4-Good; 3-Normal; 2-Bad; 1-Very Bad. Note that only the comments with their scores more than 3 points are regarded as relevant and satisfying ones for evaluation. The rate of satisfying result for our video chatbot is 54.9%.

Furthermore, to verify the merit of video commenting by search, we further conducted the experiments on this task when it is treated as a problem of sentence generation. Following [1], a LSTM-based model is learnt over all the video-comment pairs in training set. When we apply the model to our testing set, most of the predicted comments to the videos are very general-purpose phrases, e.g., "cute" and "it is amazing." This is expected, as these phrases often appear in the comments of different videos, making the predicted probabilities of these phrases very high for any input videos. This comparison further validates our proposal of video commenting by search.

5. REFERENCES

[1] Y. Pan, T. Mei, T. Yao, H. Li, and Y. Rui. Jointly modeling embedding and translation to bridge video and language. In *CVPR*, 2016.

[2] K. Simonyan and A. Zisserman. Very deep convolutional networks for large-scale image recognition. In *ICLR*, 2015.

[3] D. Tran, L. D. Bourdev, R. Fergus, L. Torresani, and M. Paluri. C3d: generic features for video analysis. In *ICCV*, 2015.

[4] J. Wang and S. Li. Query-driven iterated neighborhood graph search for large scale indexing. In *ACM MM*, 2012.

[5] T. Yao, T. Mei, and C.-W. Ngo. Learning query and image similarities with ranking canonical correlation analysis. In *ICCV*, 2015.

bBridge:
A Big Data Platform for Social Multimedia Analytics

Aleksandr Farseev*, Ivan Samborskii**, and Tat-Seng Chua*
farseev@u.nus.edu; samborskiy.ivan@gmail.com; chuats@nus.edu.sg
*School of Computing, National University of Singapore; **Computer Technologies Department, ITMO University

ABSTRACT

In this technical demonstration, we propose a cloud-based Big Data Platform for Social Multimedia Analytics called bBridge [9] that automatically detects and profiles meaningful user communities in a specified geographical region, followed by rich analytics on communities' multimedia streams. The system executes a community detection approach that considers the ability of social networks to complement each other during the process of latent representation learning, while the community profiling is implemented based on the state-of-the-art multi-modal latent topic modeling and personal user profiling techniques. The stream analytics is performed via cloud-based stream analytics engine, while the multi-source data crawler deployed as a distributed cloud jobs. Overall, the bBridge platform integrates all the above techniques to serve both business and personal objectives.

Keywords

Multiple Sources Integration; Community Detection; User Profiling; Stream Analytics; Cloud computing

1. INTRODUCTION

The past decade has recorded a rapid development and change in the Internet. We are currently witnessing an explosive growth in social networking services, where users are publishing and consuming online contents. In such a context, millions of users publish their posts regularly on different online social platforms, such as Twitter, Facebook, Foursquare, and Instagram. The increasing amounts of published user-generated content (UGC) provides opportunities as well as challenges for its consumers — users and data analysts. At the *users level*, the biggest problem is *information filtering*, due to the growing amount of irrelevant content, such as advertisement and spam. At the data analytics level, *data-preprocessing, fusion, and modeling* pose the greatest challenges to address. A comprehensive solution of these problems provide users with meaningful social-multimedia insights at both the individual and group levels [6]. For example, the group-level analytics can be utilized in Facilities Planning, Brand Monitoring, Marketing, and Geo-Enabled Advertisement domains, while the personal analytics, can be used for Personal Content Filtering and Interest-Based Recommendation.

In our previous works, we proposed the frameworks for venue category recommendation via user community detection [11], and multi-source user profile learning [6, 8]. However, the adopted user community detection techniques [11] cannot be directly applied to our current problem of multi-source community detection due to the data representation and multi-source integration issues. Thus, for this demonstration, we enriched the previously utilized techniques by implementing the so-called multi-source regularized spectral clustering [5]. Furthermore, to perform user community profiling, we exploited the multi-modal topic modeling [16] and our earlier developed multi-source user profiling [8] techniques. Eventually, all the above approaches were integrated into the Big Social Multimedia Analytics Platform bBridge, which delivers the live stream analytics to its users.

The overall data processing pipeline in bBridge is as follows: (a) the distributed cloud crawlers harvest recently posted UGC from multiple social networks [6]; (b) the community detection framework extracts user communities in a latent cross-social network space [5, 11]; (c) multi-source user profile learning [8] and multi-modal topic modeling [16] techniques construct comprehensive profiles of each detected user community and prepare it for further visualization; and (d) the stream analytics engine aggregates communities' multimedia UGC streams [1], which enables various T-SQL queries to be performed into live multimedia data [3, 13]. To the best of our knowledge, the bBridge is one of the first online solutions that offers Big Social Multimedia Analytics at both personal and group levels.

2. BBRIDGE

2.1 Platform Description

We now briefly describe the bBridge platform. The details of the adopted community detection approach were elaborated in previous works [5, 11]; the utilized user profile learning techniques were also described in our previous studies [8, 6]; while the multi-modal topic learning framework was outlined by Vorontsov et al. [16]. The block diagram of the bBridge platform is shown in Figure 1.

In the bBridge cloud platform, the user communities and its' corresponding profiles are re-computed every 12 hours, while the stream analytics and multi-source crawling are executed continuously. At any given time frame, the following

MM '16, October 15–19, 2016, Amsterdam, The Netherlands.

ACM ISBN 978-1-4503-3603-1/16/10..

DOI: http://dx.doi.org/10.1145/2964284.2973836

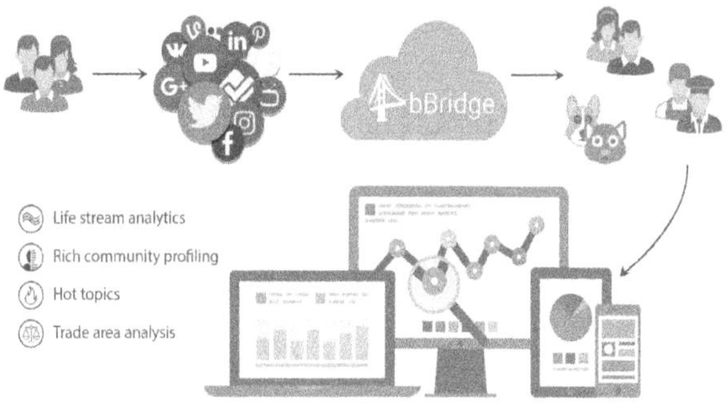

Figure 1: Block diagram of the bBridge platform

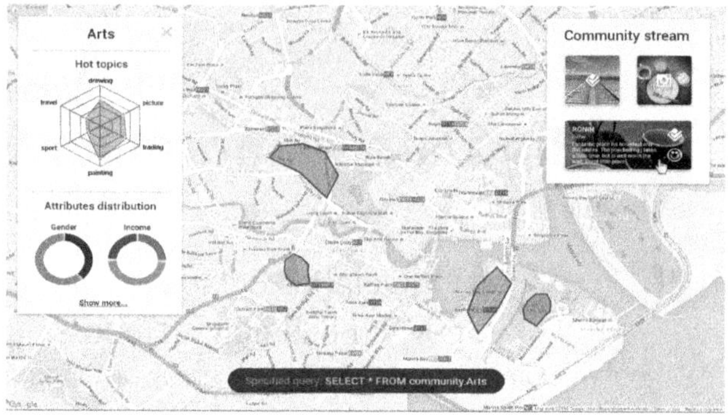

Figure 2: The bBridge online GUI snapshot

steps are taken (the continuously executing operations are marked with the "*"):

I. Multi-Source Distributed Crawling*: The crawling process consists of two steps: (a) a set of active users who have recently posted tweets through the cross-linking functionality [8] of multimedia social networks is collected; and (b) Twitter Stream APIs [15] are used to perform tweets streaming with respect to specified geographical regions, so that cross-social network account mapping can be performed when users publish tweets that contain posts from other social networks (i.e. publish Instagram images on Twitter). By following the described user identification approach, we continuously harvest the data from Twitter, Instagram, Foursquare, and Facebook. In the current technical demonstration setup, we continuously monitor about 170 thousand Twitter users from Singapore, which were active (post cross-linking tweets) near Singapore region during the recent one month time frame.

II. Multi-Modal Feature Extraction: We represented data as follows: visual data (Instagram and Twitter images) is represented in a form of image concept distribution [4]; location data (Foursquare check-ins) is represented in a form of distribution among venue categories and mobility patterns [6, 8]; textual data (Twitter tweets, Instagram image captions, and Foursquare check-in comments) is represented in a form of latent topics [16], LIWC distribution [14] and writing style features [8]. The detailed description of the adopted feature extraction processes is given in Farseev et al. [8].

III. Multi-Source Community Detection: The user communities are detected via regularized spectral clustering [5] on a multi-layer graph. Each layer in the graph is constructed based on UGC similarity between users, which is estimated as a cosine distance between data representations in each social network [6].

IV. User Communities Profiling: User Community Profiling is performed in three steps: (a) individual user profile learning [6] is applied to each community member, which results in a set of personal users' attributes, such as Age, Gender, Occupation Industry, Education Level, Income Level, Relationship Status, etc.; (b) the extracted attributes are summarized among all community members for further visualization in a form of "Pie" diagrams; and (c) top K (where $K = 6$) hot multi-modal latent topics [16] are detected for each user community for further visualization in a form of "Radar" diagrams.

V. Live Stream Analytics*: Except for sentiment analysis for every post [8], the live stream analytics is performed in a form of T-SQL queries [3] into a real-time social multimedia stream. bBridge adopts the Windows Azure Stream Analytics cloud service [1], which allows for using various query constructions such as "Like/Not Like patterns", "CASE statements", "Embedded procedures", etc. A typical query into bBridge Platform could be expressed as below:

```
SELECT Topics, Content FROM MultimediaStream
TIMESTAMP BY CreatedAt GROUP BY SLIDINGWINDOW(s, 30)
WHERE Sentiment='Positive' AND Community='Arts'
AND Region='Downtown'
```

The above query will output distribution among extracted latent topics, and content of all the multimedia posts published from "Downtown" district during the last 30 seconds by the "Arts" community with the "Positive" sentiment score. From the example, it can be seen that the aforementioned querying approach can be used to query multimedia data at both global and local levels.

2.2 Architecture

To take advantage of parallel processing, we have implemented bBridge platform as a multi-role cloud service [2]. Each crawler runs as a separate Windows Azure worker role, which enables us to harvest multiple social multimedia venues simultaneously. The community detection and profiling modules are implemented as multi-instance Windows Azure worker roles, so that it can be performed for different time frames at the same time. The stream analytics module utilizes Azure Stream Analytics engine [1] that can perform complex real-time queries [3] into the live social multimedia stream. All worker roles and stream engine are synchronized via the Windows Azure Service Bus.

3. THE DEMONSTRATION

Using our web GUI [10], bBridge users can select one of the recently detected communities in a specified geographical region. Based on the selected user community, the following features are provided: (a) observe geo-activity of the community members; (b) discover hot multi-modal topics that were discussed by the community members; (c) view the distribution of the community members among automatically inferred user attributes (such as age, gender, occupation industry, education level, relationship status, and income level); and (d) perform queries of different complexity into the live social multimedia stream, which is generated by the community members.

A snapshot of the GUI is shown in Figure 2. The UI shows the map of a Singapore region and the opened visualization console for the "Arts" community. The map shows

Table 1: User Profiling Results in Terms of Macro Accuracy

Attribute	Age Gr.	Gender	Rel.	Edu.	Occ.
Macro Acc.	0.509	0.878	0.659	0.689	0.107

the polygons that describe recent community members' geo-activity; the left pane displays the hot topics, discussed by the community members and the distribution of the community members among the detected personal user attributes; while the right pane lists the recent cross-network posts of the community members, which are filtered according to the specified query. bBridge users can select different user communities, view visualization, specify real-time queries into the community stream via the query UI control.

4. EVALUATION

To quantify the efficiency of the core technologies behind the bBridge platform, we utilize a subset of Multi-Source Cross-Region Social Dataset NUS-MSS [8] (Singapore region) for testing user community detection and personal user profiling performance.

As in Farseev et al. [7], the user community detection is implicitly evaluated via performing venue category recommendation, where the user-based collaborative filtering is only applied to users from the same pre-detected user community [11]. Multi-source user communities were detected on a multi-layer users' relatedness graph (constructed based on user-generated data similarities for each data source) via the Grassmann subspace analysis clustering [5]. The venue category recommendation was completed via our previously proposed community constrained collaborative filtering approach [11]. The user community detection results are presented in Figure 2. It can be seen that the user-based collaborative filtering, which is performed over pre-detected user communities, can achieve higher recommendation performance as compared to other multi-source recommendation approaches. This suggests that the bBridge user community detection approach can detect relevant and meaningful user communities from multiple social media sources.

The personal user profiling performance is explicitly evaluated by predicting the following individual user attributes: Age Group (< 20, $20-30$, $30-40$, > 40), Gender (Male/Female), Education Level (School/University), Occupation Industry (14 classes from NUS-MSS [8] test set), and Relationship Status (In a Relationship/Single). To do so, we utilized our previously proposed multi-source ensemble learning approach [8], which can handle imbalanced multi-source data for the inference purposes. The personal user profiling performance results are presented in Table 1. It can be seen, that the Age Group, Gender, Relationship Status, and Education Level attributes can be inferred with the sufficiently high Macro Recall (Macro Accuracy) [8], while the Occupation Industry inference [12] requires further elaboration. The above suggests that the automatically inferred personal user attributes can be used for visualization of the detected user communities in an aggregated form.

5. ACKNOWLEDGMENTS

This research is supported by the Singapore National Research Foundation under its International Research Center @ Singapore Funding Initiative and administered by the IDM Programme Office. This research is partially supported by the Government of Russian Federation, Grant 074-U01.

We thank Prof. Konstantin Vorontsov (MIPT, Russia), Ms. Nadezhda Chirkova, Mr. Arseniy Pendryak, Mr. Maksym Sihida, and Mr. Alexei Vasilyev for assistance with demo evaluation and implementation.

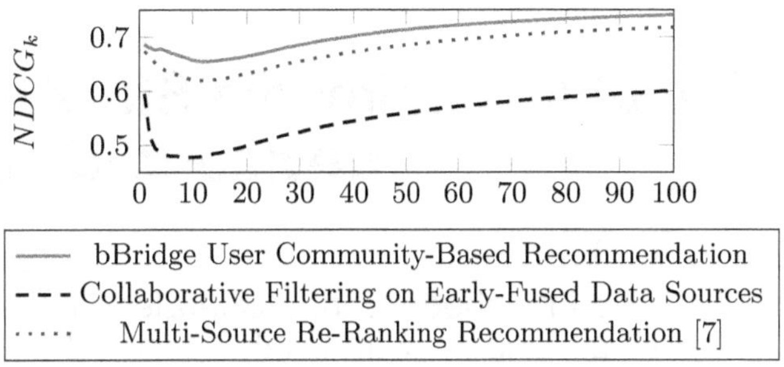

Figure 3: User Community Detection Results (via Venue Category Recommendation) in Terms of $NDCG_k$

6. REFERENCES

[1] M. Azure. Microsoft azure stream analytics service. https://azure.microsoft.com/en-us/services/stream-analytics/. Online; accessed 3 Aug 2016.

[2] M. Azure. Microsoft cloud services overview. https://azure.microsoft.com/en-us/documentation/articles/cloud-services-choose-me/. Online; accessed 3 Aug 2016.

[3] M. Azure. Stream analytics query language reference. https://msdn.microsoft.com/en-us/library/azure/dn834998.aspx. Online; accessed 3 Aug 2016.

[4] J. Deng, W. Dong, R. Socher, L.-J. Li, K. Li, and L. Fei-Fei. Imagenet: A large-scale hierarchical image database. In *Proceedings of the IEEE Conference on Computer Vision and Pattern Recognition, 2009*. IEEE, 2009.

[5] X. Dong, P. Frossard, P. Vandergheynst, and N. Nefedov. Clustering on multi-layer graphs via subspace analysis on grassmann manifolds. *IEEE Transactions on Signal Processing*, 2014.

[6] A. Farseev, M. Akbari, I. Samborskii, and T.-S. Chua. 360° user profiling: past, future, and applications. *ACM SIGWEB Newsletter*, (Summer), 2016.

[7] A. Farseev, D. Kotkov, A. Semenov, J. Veijalainen, and T.-S. Chua. Cross-social network collaborative recommendation. *Proceedings of the 7th ACM International Conference on Web Science*, 2015.

[8] A. Farseev, L. Nie, M. Akbari, and T.-S. Chua. Harvesting multiple sources for user profile learning: a big data study. In *Proceedings of the 5th ACM International Conference on Multimedia Retrieval*, 2015.

[9] A. Farseev, I. Samborskii, and T.-S. Chua. bbridge: A big social multimedia analytics platform. https://bbridge.net. Online; accessed 3 Aug 2016.

[10] A. Farseev, I. Samborskii, and T.-S. Chua. bbridge: A big social multimedia analytics platform demo. https://demo.bbridge.net. Online; accessed 3 Aug 2016.

[11] A. Farseev, N. Zhukov, I. Gossoudarev, and U. Zarichnyak. Cross-platform online venue and user community recommendation based upon social networks data mining. *Computer Tools in Education*, 6, 2014.

[12] L. Nie, L. Zhang, M. Wang, R. Hong, A. Farseev, and T.-S. Chua. Learning user attributes via mobile social multimedia analytics. *ACM Transactions on Intelligent Systems and Technology*, 8, 2016.

[13] I. Nikolaidis, K. Iniewski, B. Malhotra, H. Jeung, T. Kister, S. Bressan, and K.-L. Tan. Maritime data management and analytics. In *Building Sensor Networks: From Design to Applications*. CRC Press, 2013.

[14] J. W. Pennebaker, M. E. Francis, and R. J. Booth. Linguistic inquiry and word count: Liwc 2001. *Mahway: Lawrence Erlbaum Associates*, 2001.

[15] Twitter. The streaming apis. https://dev.twitter.com/streaming/overview. Online; accessed 3 Aug 2016.

[16] K. Vorontsov, O. Frei, M. Apishev, P. Romov, M. Suvorova, and A. Yanina. Non-bayesian additive regularization for multimodal topic modeling of large collections. In *Proceedings of the Workshop on Topic Models: Post-Processing and Applications*. ACM, 2015.

Scalable Multimedia Streaming in Wireless Networks with Device-to-Device Cooperation

Karim Jahed[1], Sanaa Sharafeddine[1], Abdallah Moussawi[2], Abbas Abou Daya[2], Hassan Dbouk[2], Saadallah Kassir[2], Zaher Dawy[2], Preethi Valsalan[3], Wael Cherif[3] and Fethi Filali[3]

[1] Lebanese American University (LAU), Beirut, Lebanon
[2] American University of Beirut (AUB), Beirut, Lebanon
[3] Qatar Mobility Innovation Center (QMIC), Doha, Qatar

{karim.jahed, sanaa.sharafeddine}@lau.edu.lb, {aam68, aia29, had27, sak54}@mail.aub.edu, zd03@aub.edu.lb, {preethiv, waelc, filali}@qmic.com

ABSTRACT

We present a scalable mobile multimedia streaming system with device-to-device cooperation that enables common content distribution in dense wireless networking environments. This is particularly applicable to use cases such as delivering real-time multimedia content to fans watching a soccer game in a stadium or to participants attending a major conference in a large auditorium. The key novel characteristics of our system include seamless neighbor discovery and link quality estimation, intelligent clustering and channel allocation algorithms based on constrained minimum spanning trees, robustness against device mobility, and device centric operation with no changes to existing wireless systems. We demonstrate the functionality of the proposed system on Android devices using heterogeneous networks (cellular/WiFi/WiFi-Direct) and show the formation of multiple clusters to allow for scalable operation. The gained insights will help bridge the gap between theoretical and simulation based research conducted in this area and practical operation taking into account the capabilities and limitations of existing wireless technologies and smartphones/tablets.

1. INTRODUCTION

With the advancements in video coding techniques and mobile communications technologies, streaming real time multimedia content to handheld devices is gaining wide popularity [4, 3, 2]. Modern devices with their powerful processors, high definition displays, and multiple wireless interfaces are capable of handling high quality multimedia content. Yet, video quality can be notably impacted in dense wireless network scenarios, due to air interface capacity limitations resulting from competition for available radio resources. To this end, we focus in this work on utilizing

MM '16 October 15-19, 2016, Amsterdam, Netherlands

ACM ISBN 978-1-4503-3603-1/16/10.

DOI: http://dx.doi.org/10.1145/2964284.2973837

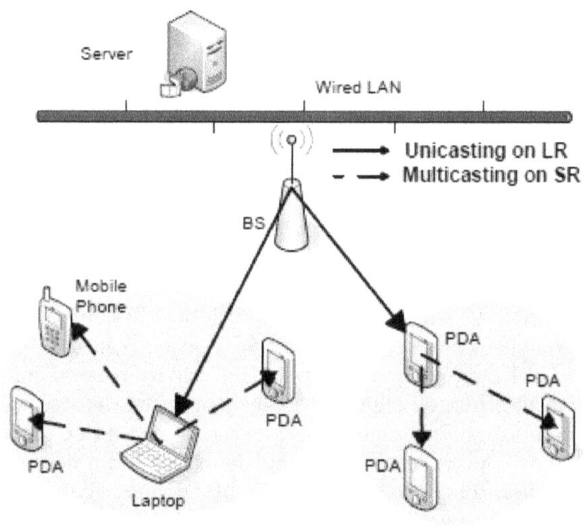

Figure 1: Device-to-device offloading.

device-to-device (D2D) connectivity to offload traffic from the wireless network, whereby mobile devices are divided into cooperative clusters depending on a set of system, geographical, and performance parameters (see Figure 1); in each cluster, a selected master mobile device receives video streams over a long range (LR) interface via WiFi access point (AP) or 3G/4G cellular base station (BS), and forwards them in real time over short range (SR) links to other devices in its cluster. Due to the proximity among cooperating devices and efficiency of short range wireless technologies (e.g. WiFi-Direct), notable performance gains can be achieved in terms of quality of experience and energy consumption[1].

In this demo, we aim at bridging the gap between theoretical/simulation studies in this area of research [2, 6, 7] and practical implementation taking into account the characteristics and constraints of state-of-the-art wireless systems and mobile devices (smartphones, tablets). As part of recent related literature, [5] presents the design and implementation of video streaming system for one group of devices that cooperate among each other to download the same content. In [5], however, the work does not address hierarchical and/or multi-hop transmission to address dense environments with large groups of devices. To this end, we have identified and addressed a wide range of implementation challenges that include seamless device discovery with topology formation, intelligent operation to achieve optimized performance with TCP-based unicasting and UDP-based mutlicasting modes supported over both SR and LR links, dynamic operation that accounts for device mobility and channel variations, and scalable design that is customized to dense environments and that does not require modifications to wireless specifications or deployment of video gateways.

2. DESIGN AND IMPLEMENTATION

In this section, we present the overall design of the mobile cooperative multimedia streaming system. The system architecture is composed of three key components: the management server, the content server and the mobile client application. The content server hosts the video files that the client may gain access to. The management server and clients are agnostic to the content server as long as it provides access to the video files through known URIs. The content server can be, for example, a standard HTTP web server, an FTP file server, or an RTSP streaming server. Client devices access the content server over the Internet through a wireless network infrastructure. The implemented testbed supports 3G/4G cellular and WiFi for LR connectivity and WiFi-Direct for SR connectivity.

The management server is the main component in the system architecture as it features peer devices management, optimized group formation with dynamic adaptation, and content management. The mobile client application does not have to be manually configured with the server parameters; the server implements network discovery protocols to allow client devices to automatically discover and fetch the server parameters. The server and client communications adopt a command-response model. The server issues commands to a subset of connected devices, the clients act upon the commands and send corresponding results back to the server. Moreover, for WiFi networks, the management server has an AP control submodule that is responsible for configuring the network's APs (e.g., channel allocation and power management). For optimized group formation, we developed low-complexity algorithms based on minimum spanning tree algorithm, however, with depth constraint to limit the number of hops to two and bounded-degree to limit the number of peer devices per cluster. The bounded degree is particularly important to system configuration with unicasting on the SR to avoid overloading the master device (cluster head) that disseminates the video content to all peer devices within its cluster.

Upon connection, the management server examines the network topology by requesting the list of WiFi-Direct neighbors from all devices. Each device then sends its list of neighbors in addition to perceived performance metrics such as the received signal strength from each device. Based on this information, the server decides on the role of each device in a way that optimizes offloading gains while maintaining high multimedia streaming quality. Next, the sever informs the device about their respective roles whether *master* devices or *peer* devices. Figure 2 shows sample protocol messages between the devices and the management server. Peer devices establish WiFi-Direct connections to their designated master devices that are supposed to relay to them the video from the content server. Finally, the server sends a *play* command with the URI of the video to launch video streaming be it real-time or stored video transmission. At this stage, all master devices connect to the content server and start receiving the video. While the video data is being received, a master device plays the data and simultaneously forwards the received stream to peer devices within its cluster. For SR communication between master and its peers, our implementation supports both options of TCP-based unicasting and UDP-based multicasting. Multicasting is used for larger clusters within the network in order to relieve master devices from many TCP-based streaming connections and thus allow for scalable operation. In the case of multicasting-based SR, a master creates a multicast group using pre-defined multicast IP and port number and informs each connecting peer about the multicast socket address. Due to the fact that UDP is used in multicasting, the master appends a sequence number to each video-data payload to support packet re-ordering and/or re-transmission for better streaming quality. Retransmitted packets if applicable are unicasted to the requesting device.

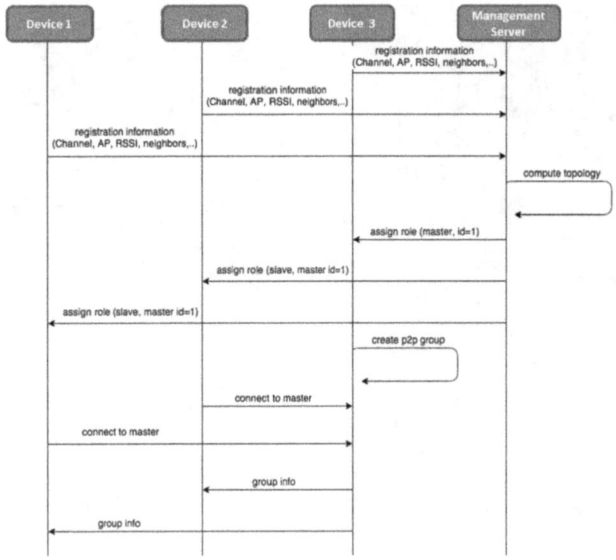

Figure 2: Sample protocol messages.

Moreover, our testbed is extended to support robust operation subject to network dynamics with devices joining, leaving, or moving within a given area. This becomes extremely critical when the moving device is a master and thus its mobility might affect the operation of all peers within its cluster. To address this, our mobile application includes a signaling and discovery intelligence module that monitors and exchanges control information with the management server on a regular basis. The control information includes specifically the signal strength with respect to all mobile devices and APs in the vicinity and is used to adapt multimedia streaming strategies with proper recovery mechanisms. On the algorithmic level, we implement localized modifications to our clustering solution to minimize service interruptions and algorithm complexity.

Our mobile application is Android-based and has a friendly user interface with flexible options that can be set by the users. Figure 3 shows a snapshot of the application showing parameter setting view and video streaming view.

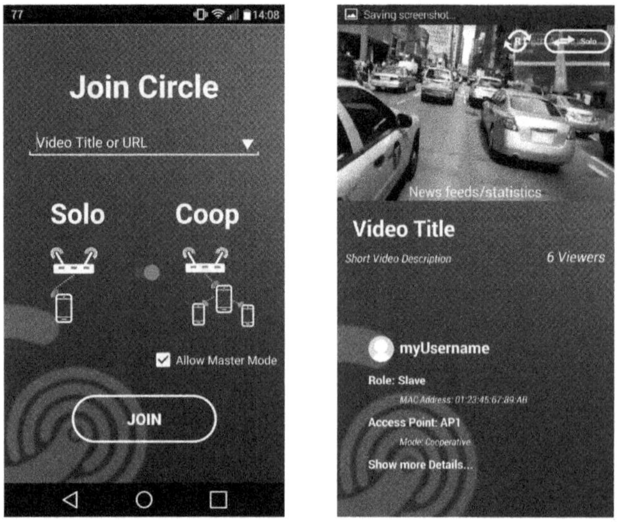

Figure 3: Mobile application interface.

3. CONCLUSIONS

We presented the general design and implementation features of a complete multimedia streaming system that utilizes device-to-device connectivity for traffic offloading in dense wireless networks. Our system implements features that facilitate dynamic, scalable, and robust operation under realistic network conditions and device constraints.

4. ACKNOWLEDGEMENTS

This work was made possible by NPRP grant 7-1529-2-555 from the Qatar National Research Fund (a member of The Qatar Foundation). The statements made herein are solely the responsibility of the authors.

5. REFERENCES

[1] L. Al-Kanj, Z. Dawy, and E. Yaacoub. Energy-aware cooperative content distribution over wireless networks: Design alternatives and implementation aspects. *IEEE Communications Surveys and Tutorials*, 15(4):3828–3847, 2013.

[2] S. Almowuena, M. Rahman, C. Hsu, A. A. Hassan, and M. Hefeeda. Energy-aware and bandwidth-efficient hybrid video streaming over mobile networks. *IEEE Transactions on Multimedia*, 18(1):102–115, January 2016.

[3] A. Detti, B. Ricci, and N. Blefari-Melazzi. Mobile peer-to-peer video streaming over information-centric networks. *Elsevier Computer Networks*, 81:272–288, April 2015.

[4] Z. Khan, A. Vasilakos, B. Barua, S. Shahabuddin, and H. Ahmadi. Cooperative content delivery exploiting multiple wireless interfaces: methods, new technological developments, open research issues and a case study. *Springer Wireless Networks*, published online in September 2015.

[5] A. Le, L. Keller, H. Seferoglu, and B. C. et. al. Microcast: Cooperative video streaming using cellular and local connections. *IEEE/ACM Trans. on Networking*, PP(99), December 2015.

[6] E. Yaacoub, Z. Dawy, S. Sharafeddine, and A. Abu-Dayya. Joint energy-distortion aware algorithms for cooperative video streaming over lte networks. *Elsevier Signal Processing: Image Communication*, 28(9), October 2013.

[7] A. Zahran, J. Quinlan, D. Raca, C. Sreenan, E. Halepovic, R. Sinha, R. Jana, and V. Gopalakrishnan. Oscar: an optimized stall-cautious adaptive bitrate streaming algorithm for mobile networks. *Proceedings of the 8th International Workshop on Mobile Video*, May 2016.

Leveraging ICN for Secure Content Distribution in IP Networks

Syed Obaid Amin, Qingji Zheng*, Ravishankar Ravindran and GQ Wang
Huawei Research Center, Santa Clara, CA, USA
{obaid.amin, ravi.ravindran, gq.wang}@huawei.com, *qingjizheng@gmail.com

ABSTRACT

Recent studies shows that by the end of 2016 more than 60% of Internet traffic would be running on HTTPS. In presence of secure tunnels such as HTTPS, transparent caching solutions become in vain, as the application payload is encrypted by lower level security protocols. This paper addresses this issue and provides an alternate approach, for contents caching without compromising their security. There are three parts to our proposal. First, we propose two new IP layer primitives that allow routers to differentiate between IP and ICN flows. Second, we introduce DCAR (Dual-mode Content Aware Router), which is a traditional IP router enabled to understand the proposed IP primitives. Third, design of DISCS (DCAR based Information centric Secure Content Sharing) framework is proposed that leverages DCAR to allow content object caching along with security services that are comparable to HTTPS. Finally we share details on realizing such system.

Keywords

Secure content sharing, ICN, Caching, TLS

1. INTRODUCTION

Transparent caching helps in content sharing by storing popular contents in strategic network locations, so that multiple requests for similar contents can be served from the local caches. This reduces the amount of transit traffic across operators' networks, the load on the content provider or CDNs, backbone bandwidth requirements and the end-users experience low latency. However, in recent years there is a surge in encrypted traffic. The study in [1] estimates that by the end of 2016 more than 60% of the Internet traffic would be running on HTTPS. In presence of HTTPS the transparent caching renders in vain, as application payload is encrypted by TLS (Transport Layer Security) [2], the protocol that lies under HTTPS.

This paper addresses the loss of cacheability in presence of such encrypted channels and proposes an alternate approach, called DISCS (DCAR based Information centric Secure Content Sharing), that provides security services comparable to HTTPS along with transparent caching of contents. The DISCS architecture operates over two channels: first, an encrypted end-to-end control channel based on HTTPS, that is used for authentication and exchanging meta-data and keys; second, a content distribution channel based on ICN APIs is used for fetching encrypted data objects from a DISCS enabled infrastructure. ICN proposes named-networking as the narrow waist, i.e. internetworking is based on information identifiers instead of host addresses [3, 4]. But, enabling ICN requires new infrastructure, making immediate deployments seems impractical. Our proposal, instead, aims for the incrementally upgrading current IP deployment with minimum changes to current Internet architecture, leveraging ICN benefits of in-network caching and content-based security. This work considers CCN as the ICN protocol, but is equally applicable to other ICN protocols such as MobilityFirst [5] .

There are two main architectural components of our proposal: first, we propose two new IP layer primitives that allow routers to differentiate between IP and ICN flows, then we introduce DCAR (Dual-mode Content Aware Router), which is a traditional IP router operating on the new IP primitives to differentiate IP and ICN flows. In addition, DCAR incorporates caches that can be used to store ICN content objects. In an overlay deployment, DCAR intercepts ICN[1] flows and fulfills an Interest if a matching content object can be found in its cache/content store. Like transparent caches, DCAR provides reduced RTT (Round Trip Time), improved throughput and reduces upstream bandwidth requirements.

Following is the layout of our paper. From Section 2 we begin our discussion by highlighting the fields that can be used in IPv4 and IPv6 header for marking with aforementioned primitives. DCAR design and its related issues are discussed in Section 3. Description about DISCS framework is provided in Section 4. Implementation and demo details are discussed in Section 5 and Section 6, respectively. Finally, we conclude our paper in Section 7.

2. IP PRIMITIVES

The incremental upgrade of IP routers to handle ICN Interest and Content object is achieved by allowing IP layer to differentiate ICN flows from IP flows. For this, we define two new IP primitives, IP-I (IP-Interest) and IP-C (IP-Content).

[1]From here on the terms ICN and CCN will be used interchangeably.

MM '16 October 15-19, 2016, Amsterdam, Netherlands

ACM ISBN 978-1-4503-3603-1/16/10.
DOI: http://dx.doi.org/10.1145/2964284.2973838

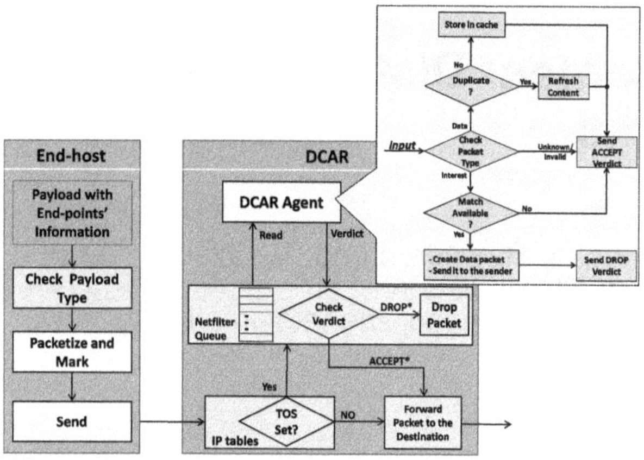

*The **ACCEPT** verdict signals that the packet should be handled according to default forwarding rules, while the **DROP** verdict signals that **DCAR Agent** can handle the packet, there is no need to forward it further.

Figure 1: DCAR Flow Diagram

IP-I indicates that the IP packet encapsulates an ICN Interest, while IP-C indicates that the IP packet encapsulates an ICN Content object. The demo system ensures that single IP packets carries no more than one ICN packet. DSCP that comprises of 6 bits in IPv4 header offers experimental and future standards space that can be used to identify Interest and Content object. In IPv6, Traffic Class bits can be used for the same purpose.

3. DCAR (DUAL-MODE CONTENT AWARE ROUTER)

Figure 1 shows the packet flow in a DCAR router. Upon packet arrival, DCAR checks the ToS byte of the IP packet. If it is set to IP-I or IP-C, the packet is forwarded to the *DCAR agent* for further processing. If the packet is not marked as an ICN packet, it is forwarded to the destination using default IP forwarding rules. The DCAR agent is a process that manages the content store (CS) against which the Interest packet in the IP-I packet is matched. If there is a content object with the exact name it is returned to the consumer using the IP source address from the original IP packet; else the IP-I packet is forwarded to the destination available in the destination address of the received IP packet. Similarly when a DCAR router encounters an IP-C packet, before forwarding it to the destination it can make a decision to cache this ICN content object based on the meta-data attributes in the content object.

4. DISCS FRAMEWORK

To enable secure content sharing, the DISCS framework utilizes two channels for communication between the consumer and producer. Towards this, as shown in Figure 2, both the consumer and producer uses HTTPS and ICN stack. The HTTP stack enables a secure control channel that is used for authentication, exchanging key and other related information in a secure manner between consumer and producer; while the ICN channel is used for content distribution using CCN APIs. The producer side also incorporates a content store or cache, that is used to host contents. In unsecure mode of operation, the DISCS can bypass HTTPS channel. However, if security features are required, the HTTPS stack is used. The API layer provides a clean interface to the applications and handles many functions such as name resolution, setting or tearing up a secure channel and providing ICN encapsulation on application payload.

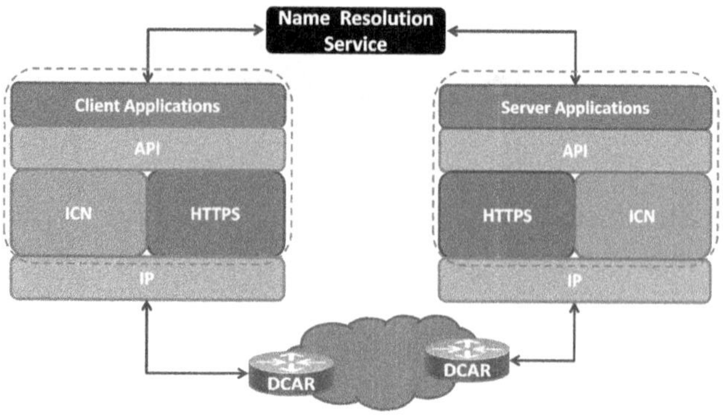

Figure 2: DISCS component diagram.

4.1 Secure content sharing

In following we explain the flow of the secure content sharing using DISCS:

1. The producer creates a manifest as shown in Figure 3 and publishes it with the help of Name Resolution Service on some routeable name.
2. The consumer resolves the content name using the Naming service to the producer's location.
3. The consumer then initiates a secure connection to the producer using HTTPS and authenticates him.
4. Producer upon authentication of the consumer (for e.g. using user-id and password) provides him manifest and keys to decrypt the contents.
5. The consumer then issues the Interests on the hash-ids provided in the manifest. Before sending each Interest out, the ToS field of the IP packet encapsulating that Interest is marked with IP-I primitive.
6. The IP-I packet is then intercepted by DCAR enroute, which checks its CS for the possible content match against the encapsulated Interest and upon failure forwards the IP-I packet to the connection end-point i.e. producer. Otherwise, the matched content is sent back to the consumer encapsulated by IP-C packet.
7. If the content resolution fails at the DCAR, the IP-I packet reaches to the producer, which sends back the encrypted content in IP-C encapsulation.
8. On the way back, DCAR identifies the IP-C packet and stores the encapsulated content in the content store before forwarding IP-C packet to the consumer.
9. Finally, future consumers after authentication and getting manifest file can take advantage of the cached contents.

5. PROTOTYPING DISCS

We prototyped DISCS which involves end-host enhancements and the implementation of DCAR. The host applications uses two sockets, one for ICN communication and one for HTTPS session. The ICN socket talks to a modified version of CCN forwarder. The key change in the CCN forwarder is to mark the ToS bits of the encapsulating IP

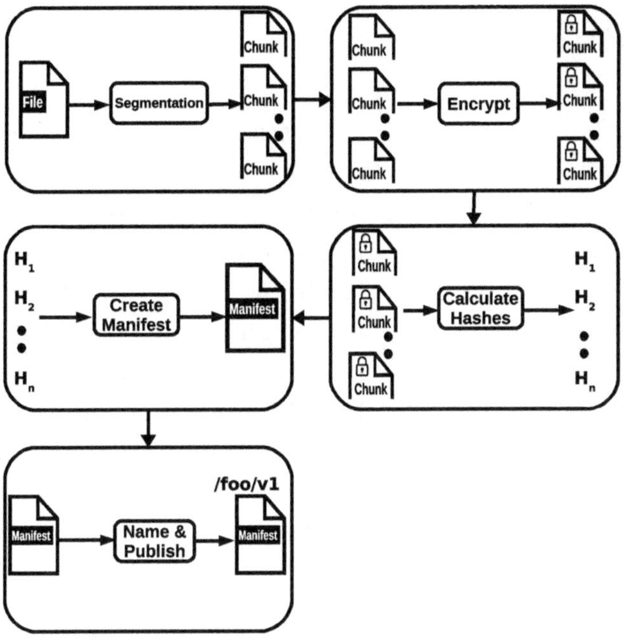

Figure 3: Preparing contents for sharing.

packet with the proposed IP primitives before handing it to the lower layer.

For the proof-of-concept deployment of DCAR, we used *iptables* along with *netfilter-queues*, so that processing of packets and forwarding decision can be done at user space. Figure 1 shows the major components of DCAR. As the packet ingresses the DCAR, the iptables checks the ToS field of the incoming packet. If it is marked as an IP-I or IP-C packet, the packet is handed-over to the netfilter-queue. The DCAR agent then receives the packet and process them as shown in the flowchart of Figure 1. The netfilter-queue provides two primitives to take decision on the enqueued packets – *Accept* and *Drop*. If an incoming packet is an Interest packet, and can be satisfied by DCAR, then DCAR agent notifies netfilter-queue by sending a *Drop* verdict. It means that the Interest has been satisfied by the DCAR and there is no need to forward it further. If a packet, however, cannot be satisfied by the DCAR agent, it sends an *Accept* verdict to the netfilter-queue which in turns forwards the packet to the tunnel end-point, according to default IP forwarding rules. The DCAR agent is a trimmed down version of CCNx-0.8.2 forwarding daemon, 'ccnd.c', without FIB, PIT or any face management logic. Even a very suboptimal code of DCAR agent consists of around 1600 lines of code. To make sure that each IP packet doesn't carry more than one ICN packet, we disabled piggy-backing of Interest and Content object in ICN packets. Finally, the current version of DCAR doesn't support fragmented IP packets; mainly because of the tools used for the user space implementation. Therefore the CCN level Content object chunks should match the IP transport level MTU requirements.

6. DEMO SETUP

This demo shows the performance of DISCS in both secure and insecure modes. In the insecure mode, the consumer is connected to a video producer via DCAR in a line topology as an IP overlay, as shown in Figure 4. To emulate multiple consumers, we disabled CCNx client side caching and spawns multiple video clients requesting the same content, forcing each request to go to the producer through the DCAR. We used ccnseqwriter, a CCN utility, to host the file at producer, while ccncat is used to fetch the file at the consumer, with the default pipeline size of 4. The size of each chunk is 8KB where as the minimum Ethernet layer MTU is set to 9KB.

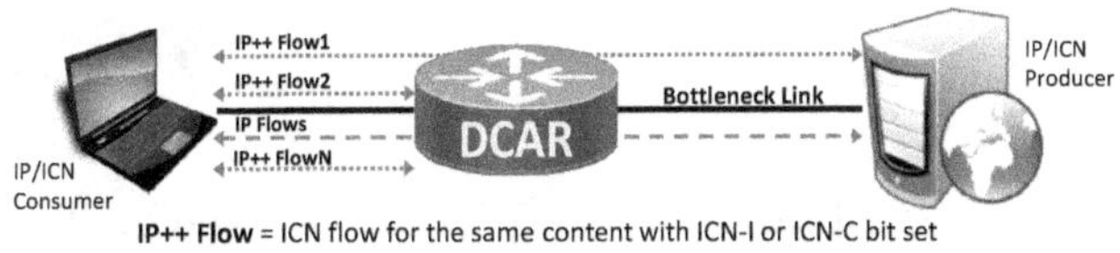

Figure 4: Network Topology

In this setup, the link between DCAR and producer is the bottleneck that is provisioned for one video stream. In the absence of DCAR as we increase the number of the video clients, the video quality of each client suffers as each request is going to the producer and congesting the bottleneck link. However, in presence of DCAR as the number of clients increases, the hit ratio of Interest for a similar content increases, which helps in maintaining the perceived video quality. The second part of the demo shows the advantages of DISCS framework when secure content sharing is enabled. In this case, the data consumers are introduced in a exponential manner at mean of 1s. The goals is to show that the performance of DISCS in terms of throughput is better than *scp* (secure copy), a widely used tool for secure file sharing. Please note that to compare the performance with secure file sharing, we first encrypt the shareable content using RC5 algorithm and the decryption key is shared offline to avoid explicit manifest communication. This scenario highlights the security, trust and privacy features that the DISCS framework enables, while the edge multicast performance in this case is similar to the previous scenario.

7. CONCLUSION

This paper proposes a new architecture called DISCS (DCAR based Information centric Secure Content Sharing) which takes advantage of ICN and incrementally upgraded IP infrastructure in the data plane and HTTPS in the service plane to bootstrap secure content transaction. We are currently investigating DISCS performance in different network scenarios and also various ways to provide robust key management mechanims.

8. REFERENCES

[1] Sandvine - internet traffic encryption. https://www.sandvine.com/trends/encryption.html. Accessed: Nov-03-2015.

[2] Tim Dierks. The Transport Layer Security (TLS) Protocol Version 1.2. RFC 5246, October 2015.

[3] CCNx1.0 protocol specification, http://www.ietf.org/mail-archive/web/icnrg/current/pdfZyEQRE5tFS.pdf.

[4] Named Data Networking. [Project Website]: http://www.named-data.net/.

[5] Arun Venkatramani, et al. Mobilityfirst: A mobility-centric and trustworthy internet architecture. In *ACM Sigcomm CCR, Volume 44, Number 3*, 2014.

Author Index

www.ingramcontent.com/pod-product-compliance
Lightning Source LLC
LaVergne TN
LVHW080103011026
849160LV00013B/1023
9781450346849